Webster's
New American
Crossword Puzzle
Dictionary

Created in Cooperation
with the Editors of
MERRIAM-WEBSTER

SMITHMARK
REFERENCE

This edition published in 1995 by
SMITHMARK Publishers.
a division of U.S. Media Holdings, Inc.
16 East 32nd Street
New York, NY 10016

SMITHMARK books are available for bulk purchase for sales promotion and premium use. For details write or call the manager of special sales, SMITHMARK Publishers 16 East 32nd Street, New York, NY 10016.

Library of Congress Cataloging-in-Publication Data

Webster's new American crossword puzzle dictionary.
p. cm.
"Created in cooperation with the editors of Merriam-Webster Inc."
–Pref.
ISBN 0-8317-9164-0
1. Crossword puzzles—Glossaries, vocabularies, etc. I. Merriam-Webster, Inc.
GV1507.C7W376 1995
793.73'2'03—dc20   *95-2047*
                                                              CIP

Printed in the United States of America

10 9 8 7 6 5 4

Preface

Webster's New American Crossword Puzzle Dictionary has
been edited to meet the specific needs of crossword puzzle
solvers. Based on actual crossword puzzle clues, entries
have been selected from a wide range of Merriam-Webster
reference books and the Encyclopaedia Brittanica, making
this book one of the most comprehensive of its kind. Because
of the wide range of information contained in this book, it can
also be used as a source of much general reference material.

Webster's New American Crossword Puzzle Dictionary was
created in cooperation with the editors of Merriam-Webster
Inc., a company that has been publishing dictionaries for
nearly 150 years.

Introduction

Main Entries

The organization of *Webster's Crossword Puzzle Dictionary* is structured in accordance with the way in which crossword puzzles are constructed and solved. The main entries and their subcategories correspond to the numbered clues given in the puzzle, and the answer words that follow the main entries are possibilities for filling in the blanks provided.

Main entries appear in boldface type and are entered in alphabetical order letter by letter. Those beginning with *Mc-* are alphabetized as if spelled *Mac-*; thus **McTeague author** appears before **mad**. We have endeavored to make the range of entries as comprehensive as possible in a book of this size so as to enable the user to meet the challenges of even the most difficult puzzles.

These entries include names of persons (as biblical, famous, legendary, literary and mythological), places (as countries, islands, mountains, rivers, states, and seas), and miscellaneous things (as chemical elements, coins, drinks, games, and wines). Also included are titles of famous books, operas, and works of art. The bulk of the main entries, however, consists of words that have synonyms or closely related words.

Entries may be a single word, a group of words, or a blank with a word or group of words (as **Damocles'** _____ or _____ **d'Azur**). Parts of speech are not indicated since they are not usually provided in puzzle clues.

Subcategories

When the main entry is a large category (as at **animal, composer,** and **river**), the list of answer words is broken down into alphabetically arranged subcategories for easy access. Each subcategory is introduced by an appropriate boldface italic word or words. If you want to find, for example, the name of a French composer, first look for the entry **composer** and then under it the subcategory **French**. Subcategories may indicate various kinds of relationships to the main entry, for example, personal (father, mother, etc.), political (capital, kingdom, etc.), literary (author, character, etc.), or artistic (painter, sculptor, etc.). They may indicate a nationality, a language or dialect, or a particular example or type. Also included as subcategories are prefixes, suffixes, combining forms, and chemical symbols related to the main entry.

Answer Words

When more than one answer is possible to a clue represented by a main entry, the answer words are grouped together according to the number of letters they contain. The specific number appears in boldface before each numerical grouping, and within each grouping answer words are alphabetized. Even when only a single answer word is given, the boldface number of its letters precedes it. Answer words usually range from two to thirteen letters since longer answers are rarely asked for. However, some answers (as titles and nicknames) may consist of more than one word and may exceed thirteen letters. Some answers are not actual words; these include abbreviations, prefixes, suffixes, combining forms, and chemical symbols, which are commonly called for in crossword puzzles.

In a single list of answer words you may find grouped together words that seem unrelated to one another. This results when the answer words are of various parts of speech or are synonymous with only one meaning of a main entry that has more than one meaning. Thus, answer words, although related to the main entry, may not be synonymous with each other.

Guide Words

In order to facilitate finding a particular entry, the first main entry on each left-hand page is printed at the top of that page in larger boldface type. Likewise, the last main entry on each right-hand page is printed at the top of that page. These two guide words indicate the alphabetical range of main entries on the two pages.

Cross-References

Occasionally a reduced boldface cross-reference to another main entry is given instead of answer words. For example, at **anywise** you are directed to see **anyhow** for answer words because these two main entries are synonymous, and at **Arthur** you are referred to **King Arthur** for the answer words. These cross-references save space and allow a greater number of main entries than would otherwise be possible.

A

Aaron *brother:* 5 Moses *father:* 5 Amram
sister: 6 Miriam *son:* 5 Abiku, Nadab
7 Eleazer, Ithamar
aback 5 short 6 sudden 7 unaware
8 suddenly, unawares 10 unawaredly
12 unexpectedly
abacus *Chinese:* 7 swanpan 8 shwanpan
abaft 3 aft 4 back 5 after 6 astern, back
of, behind
abalienate 4 cede, deed 5 alien 6 assign,
convey, remise 8 make over, sign over,
transfer
abalone 5 ormer
abandon 3 fun 4 cede, drop, ease, junk,
play, quit 5 chuck, leave, scrap, sport,
waive, yield 6 desert, disuse, give up, laxity,
maroon, reject, resign, turn up 7 cast off,
discard, forsake, freedom, laxness, liberty,
license, unguard 8 hand over, renounce,
wildness 9 looseness, repudiate, surrender,
throw over 10 exuberance, relinquish,
unruliness, wantonness 11 naturalness,
spontaneity, unrestraint 12 heedlessness,
incontinence, unconstraint
13 impulsiveness
abandoned 4 lewd, lorn 6 wanton 7 corrupt, debased, riotous, uncouth
8 depraved, derelict, deserted, desolate, forsaken, solitary 9 debauched, dissolute,
lecherous, perverted, reprobate 10 degenerate, lascivious, licentious, profligate
12 incorrigible, unprincipled
abase 4 fawn, sink 5 cower, lower, toady
6 bemean, cringe, debase, demean, demote,
grovel, humble, reduce 7 degrade, truckle
8 cast down, diminish 9 downgrade,
humiliate
abash 4 faze 5 abase 6 demean, humble,
rattle 7 confuse 8 confound 9 discomfit,
embarrass, humiliate 10 disconcert
abashment 6 unease 9 confusion
10 uneasiness 12 discomfiture, discomposure 13 disconcertion, embarrassment
abate 3 ebb 4 fall, lull, wane 5 annul,
close, let up, quash, taper 6 lessen, negate,
recede, reduce, relent, weaken 7 abolish,
die away, die down, dwindle, ease off, nullify, slacken, subside, vitiate 8 abrogate,
decrease, diminish, moderate, taper off
9 drain away, eradicate 10 annihilate, invalidate 11 exterminate

abatement 6 rebate 8 discount 9 deduction, reduction 11 subtraction
abbot *female:* 6 abbess
abbreviate 3 cut 7 abridge, curtail, cut
back, shorten
abbreviation 7 acronym 10 abridgment,
shortening
abdicate 5 demit, leave 6 reject, resign
7 abandon 8 renounce, withdraw 9 surrender, throw away 10 relinquish
abdomen 3 gut, pot 5 belly, tummy
6 middle, paunch, venter 7 midriff, stomach 8 potbelly 9 bay window 10 midsec-
tion 11 breadbasket *combining form:*
6 ventri, ventro *depression:* 5 navel
abduct 5 seize 6 kidnap, snatch 10 spirit
away
abecedarian 4 tyro 7 amateur, dabbler
9 smatterer 10 dilettante
Abel *brother:* 4 Cain, Seth *father:* 4 Adam
mother: 3 Eve *slayer:* 4 Cain
Abelard *son:* 9 Astrolabe *wife:* 7 Heloise
abele 6 poplar
aberrant 3 odd 6 errant, erring 7 deviant,
devious, strange, unusual 8 abnormal, atypical, peculiar 9 anomalous, deviative, different, disparate, divergent, eccentric, untypical 11 exceptional, heteroclite
aberration 4 slip 6 lunacy, oddity, rarity
7 madness, mistake, turning 8 insanity
9 curiosity, departure, deviation, diversion,
unbalance 10 alienation, deflection, divergence, insaneness 11 abnormality,
derangement, distraction, psychopathy
abet 3 aid, egg 4 goad, help, prod, spur,
urge 6 assist, exhort, foment, incite, stir
up 8 advocate 9 encourage, instigate
11 countenance
abettor 9 accessory 10 accomplice
11 confederate, conspirator
13 coconspirator
abeyance 5 break, pause 7 latency,
respite 8 dormancy, interval 10 quiescence, quiescency, suspension 11 cold
storage 12 intermission, interruption
abeyant 6 latent 7 dormant, lurking
8 deferred 9 postponed, quiescent,
repressed 10 suppressed 11 intermitted
abhor 4 hate 5 scorn 6 detest, loathe
7 contemn, despise, disdain 8 execrate
9 abominate

abhorrence 4 hate 6 dismay, hatred, horror 8 aversion, distaste, loathing 9 repulsion, revulsion 10 repellency, repugnance 11 abomination, detestation

abhorrent 6 horrid, odious 7 hatable, hateful 8 hateable 9 invidious, obnoxious, repellent, repugnant, revulsive 10 abominable, detestable 11 uncongenial 12 antipathetic 13 unsympathetic

Abi *father:* 9 Zechariah *husband:* 4 Ahaz *mother:* 8 Hezekiah

abide 4 bear, last, live, stay, take, wait 5 brook, cling, dwell, exist, stand, stick, tarry 6 accede, accept, adhere, cleave, endure, linger, remain, reside, suffer 7 consent, hang out, perdure, persist, receive, stomach, subsist, swallow 8 continue, tolerate 11 stick around

abiding 4 firm, sure 6 steady 7 durable, lasting 8 enduring 9 steadfast 10 perdurable, persistent 11 unfaltering, unqualified 12 never-failing, wholehearted 13 unquestioning

Abiel *grandson:* 4 Saul 5 Abner *son:* 3 Ner 4 Kish

abigail 4 maid

Abigail's husband 5 David, Nabal

ability 5 knack, might, skill 6 talent 7 address, aptness, command, faculty, know-how, mastery, prowess 8 adequacy, aptitude, capacity, deftness, facility 9 dexterity, expertise, expertism, handiness, ingenuity 10 adroitness, capability, cleverness, competence, efficiency, expertness, mastership 11 proficiency 13 qualification, qualifiedness

Abital's husband 5 David

abject 9 underfoot 11 downtrodden

abjure 4 cede 5 unsay 6 desert, disown, recall, recant 7 abandon, disavow, forsake, retract 8 forswear, palinode, renounce, take back, withdraw 9 repudiate, surrender 10 relinquish

ablaze 5 afire, aglow, fiery 6 aflame, alight 7 burning, flaming, flaring, ignited 8 aflicker 11 conflagrant

able 4 good, keen 5 alert, sharp, smart 6 au fait, brainy, clever, expert, proper, wicked 7 capable, go-ahead, skilled 8 skillful 9 brilliant, competent, effective, effectual, efficient, qualified 10 proficient 11 intelligent 12 enterprising

abnegation 6 denial 10 self-denial 12 renouncement, renunciation

Abner *cousin:* 4 Saul *father:* 3 Ner *slayer:* 4 Joab

abnormal 3 odd 5 undue, weird 6 offkey 7 deviant, offtype, unusual 8 aberrant, atypical 9 anomalous, deviative, divergent, irregular, paratypic, unnatural, unregular, untypical 11 heteroclite, uncustomary

13 heteromorphic, preternatural *combining form:* 3 mal 4 anom, poly 5 anomo, pseud 6 pseudo *prefix:* 3 dys, par 4 para

abnormality 5 lusus

abode 4 home 5 house 8 domicile, dwelling 9 residence, residency 10 commorancy, habitation

abolish 4 undo 5 abate, annul, quash 6 cancel, negate, repeal, revoke, vacate 7 blot out, nullify, rescind, vitiate, wipe out 8 abrogate, disallow, disannul 9 eradicate, extirpate 10 annihilate, circumduct, extinguish, invalidate 11 exterminate

abolitionist 4 Mott, Weld 5 Lundy, Smith, Stowe 6 Birney, Lowell, Parker, Tappan 8 Douglass, Garrison, Phillips, Whittier

abominable 6 cursed, horrid, odious 7 hateful 8 accursed, hateable 9 abhorrent, loathsome, offensive, repugnant, revolting 10 detestable

abominable snowman 4 yeti

abominate 4 damn, hate 5 abhor, curse 6 detest, loathe 8 execrate 9 objurgate

abomination 4 hate, pest 5 bogey, scorn, trial 6 hatred, horror, plague 7 bugaboo, bugbear, disdain, dislike, incubus 8 anathema, aversion, contempt, disfavor, distaste, loathing 9 annoyance, bête noire, disrelish, repulsion, revulsion 10 abhorrence, black beast, repugnance, repugnancy 11 detestation

aboriginal 6 native, savage 7 endemic 8 barbaric, primeval 9 barbarian, barbarous, primitive 10 indigenous, primordial 13 autochthonous

aborigine 3 abo 6 native

abortive 4 vain 6 futile, unripe 7 useless 8 bootless, immature, unformed 9 fruitless 10 unavailing 11 ineffective, ineffectual, unavailable 12 unproductive

abound 4 flow, teem 5 crawl, swarm

abound in *suffix:* 5 ulent

abounding 4 full, rife 5 alive 6 jammed, packed 7 replete, stuffed, teeming 8 swarming, thronged 11 overflowing

abounding in *suffix:* 3 ose, ous 4 ious

about 2 on, re 4 as to, back, in re, most, much, near, nigh, over, upon, with 5 again, anent, circa, round 6 all but, almost, anyhow, around, nearby, nearly 7 anywise, apropos, through 8 at random, backward, casually, randomly, to and fro 9 aimlessly, as regards, haphazard, in reverse 10 carelessly, concerning, near-at-hand, respecting, throughout 11 any which way, haphazardly, practically 12 circuitously 13 approximately, helter-skelter

about-face 4 turn 7 reverse 8 reversal 9 reversion, volte-face 11 reversement

above 3 o'er 4 over, past 5 aloft, supra 6 beyond 8 overhead *combining form:*

6 supero *prefix:* **3** sur **4** over **5** hyper, super, supra

above all **7** chiefly

aboveboard **4** open **7** artless **8** straight **9** ingenuous **10** forthright, scrupulous **12** plain dealing

abracadabra **4** cant **5** argot **6** jargon **7** mummery **9** gibberish **10** hocus-pocus, mumbo jumbo **13** mystification

abrade **3** bug, irk, rub **4** burn, fret, gall, rasp, wear **5** annoy, chafe, erode, grate, graze **6** bother, flurry, ruffle, scrape **7** corrade, corrode, eat away, perturb, provoke **8** exercise **9** excoriate

Abraham *birthplace:* **2** Ur *brother:* **5** Haran, Nahor *concubine:* **5** Hagar *father:* **5** Terah *grandfather:* **5** Nahor *grandson:* **4** Esau *nephew:* **3** Lot *son:* **5** Isaac, Medan, Shuah **6** Midian, Zimran **7** Ishmael *well:* **9** Beer-Sheba *wife:* **5** Sarah **7** Keturah

Abraham's bosom **4** Zion **5** bliss **6** Canaan, heaven **7** elysium, nirvana **8** empyrean, paradise **10** Civitas Dei **12** New Jerusalem

abreast **2** up **6** au fait, versed **7** versant **8** familiar, informed, up-to-date **9** au courant **10** acquainted, conversant **12** contemporary

abridge **3** cut **5** limit, slash **6** lessen, minify, narrow, reduce **7** curtail, cut back, shorten **8** condense, diminish, minimize, restrict, retrench **10** abbreviate

abridgment **3** sum **5** brief **6** aperçu, digest, précis, sketch **7** capsule, epitome, outline, summary **8** abstract, boildown, breviary, breviate, syllabus, synopsis **9** summation, summing-up **10** compendium, conspectus **12** condensation

abroad **6** afield **7** oversea **8** overseas

abrogate **4** ruin, undo, void **5** abate, annul, quash, wreck **6** cancel, negate, vacate **7** abolish, blot out, nullify, vitiate **8** dissolve **9** discharge **10** annihilate, extinguish, invalidate, obliterate

abrupt **4** curt **5** bluff, blunt, brief, brisk, crisp, gruff, hasty, quick, ready, sharp, sheer, short, steep **6** casual, crusty, snippy, speedy, sudden **7** arduous, brusque, hurried, rushing **8** headlong, informal **9** impetuous **11** precipitant, precipitate, precipitous, short-spoken, subitaneous **13** unceremonious

abruptly **5** short **6** sudden **7** asudden **8** suddenly **9** forthwith

abruptness **10** brusquerie

Absalom *commander:* **5** Amasa *father:* **5** David *mother:* **7** Maachah *sister:* **5** Tamar *slayer:* **4** Joab

abscess **4** boil, sore **5** botch, ulcer **6** lesion, pimple, trauma **7** pustule **8** furuncle **9** carbuncle

abscond **2** go **3** fly **4** flee, quit **5** break, leave, scape **6** decamp, escape **8** withdraw

absence **4** lack, need, void, want **6** dearth, defect, vacuum **7** default, drought, failure **9** privation **10** deficiency **13** insufficiency

absent **4** away, gone, lost **7** bemused, faraway, lacking, missing, omitted, wanting **8** distrait, heedless **9** forgetful **10** abstracted

absentminded **4** lost **7** bemused, faraway **8** distrait, heedless, unseeing **10** abstracted, unnoticing **11** inattentive, inconscient, preoccupied, unobserving **12** unperceiving

absent without leave **4** AWOL

absolute **4** hard, pure, real, true **5** ideal, sheer, utter **6** actual, simple **7** eternal, factual, genuine, perfect, unmixed **8** complete, despotic, flawless, infinite, outright, positive, ultimate, unflawed **9** arbitrary, autarchic, boundless, downright, fleckless, imperious, masterful, out-and-out, sovereign, tyrannous, unalloyed, undiluted, unlimited **10** autocratic, autonomous, consummate, impeccable, monocratic, tyrannical **11** categorical, dictatorial, domineering, independent, note-perfect, unmitigated, unqualified **12** indefectible, totalitarian, transcendent **13** authoritarian

absolutely **6** easily **9** doubtless **10** definitely, positively **11** doubtlessly **13** unequivocally

absolution **6** pardon **7** amnesty **11** condonation

absolutism **9** Caesarism **12** dictatorship

absolve **4** free **5** clear, spare **6** acquit, excuse, exempt, let off, shrive **7** release, relieve **8** dispense **9** discharge, exculpate, exonerate, vindicate **10** disculpate

absorb **5** imbue **6** embody, engage, imbibe, infuse, sponge **7** consume, engross, immerse, inhaust, involve **8** permeate **9** preoccupy **10** assimilate, impregnate, monopolize **11** incorporate

absorbed **4** deep, rapt **6** intent **7** engaged, wrapped **8** immersed, involved **9** engrossed, wrapped up **11** preoccupied

absorbent cotton **7** pledget

absorbing **9** consuming **10** engrossing **12** monopolizing

abstain **4** curb, deny, keep **5** forgo, spurn **6** eschew, refuse, reject **7** decline, forbear, refrain **8** abnegate, hold back, teetotal, withhold **9** constrain

abstemious **5** sober **7** ascetic, austere, sparing **9** abstinent, continent, temperate **11** self-denying

abstentious see **abstemious**

abstinence 8 sobriety 10 continence, temperance 12 renunciation

abstinent see **abstemious**

abstract 4 lift 5 annex, brief, filch, ideal, pinch, steal, swipe, unfix 6 detach, divide, pilfer 7 epitome, neutral, purloin, utopian 8 academic, boildown, breviary, breviate, detached, notional, separate, synopsis, uncouple 9 colorless, disengage, visionary 10 abridgment, conceptual, conspectus, disconnect, dissociate, impersonal, inconcrete 11 appropriate, impractical, speculative, theoretical, unpassioned 12 condensation, disassociate, hypothetical, transcendent 13 disinterested

abstracted 4 lost, rapt 6 absent, intent 7 bemused, faraway 8 distrait, heedless 9 engrossed, oblivious, unmindful, unminding 11 inattentive, inconscient, preoccupied 12 absentminded

abstruse 4 deep 5 heavy, ideal 6 knotty, occult, orphic, secret 7 complex 8 esoteric, hermetic, profound 9 intricate, recondite 10 acroamatic 11 complicated 12 hypothetical

absurd 5 balmy, comic, crazy, droll, funny, loony, potty, silly, wacky 6 insane 7 asinine, fatuous, foolish 8 farcical 10 irrational 11 harebrained 12 preposterous, unreasonable

absurdity 5 folly 7 inanity 8 insanity, nonsense 9 craziness, dottiness, silliness 11 foolishness, witlessness 13 senselessness

abundance 4 ease 6 enough, galore, plenty 7 lashins 8 adequacy, lashings, thriving 10 lavishness, prosperity 11 prodigality, sufficiency *Scottish:* 5 routh, rowth

abundant 4 lush, rife 5 ample, thick 6 common, lavish, plenty 7 copious, crammed, crowded, liberal, profuse, replete 8 generous, prolific 9 bounteous, bountiful, luxuriant, plenteous, plentiful

abuse 3 mar, mud 4 harm, hurt 5 decry, spoil, wrong 6 damage, debase, impair, injure, mess up, misuse, rating, revile 7 calumny, corrupt, cursing, exploit, obloquy, oppress, outrage, pervert, profane, railing 8 belittle, berating, derogate, discount, illtreat, maltreat, minimize, misapply, mistreat, reviling, swearing 9 contumely, desecrate, disparage, dispraise, invective, manhandle, misemploy, mishandle, persecute, profanity 10 defamation, depreciate, impose upon, malignment, scurrility 12 billingsgate, vilification, vituperation

abusive 5 dirty 6 odious 7 scurril 8 scurrile 9 aspersing, insulting, invective, maligning, offending, offensive, outraging, truculent, vilifying 10 affronting, scurrilous, vitu-

perous 11 opprobrious 12 contumelious, vituperative, vituperatory

abut 4 join, line 5 flank, march, touch, verge 6 adjoin, border 8 neighbor 11 communicate

abutting 4 next 7 joining 8 adjacent, touching 9 adjoining, bordering, impinging 10 approximal, connecting, contiguous, juxtaposed 12 conterminous

abysm 4 gulf 5 chasm

abysmal 4 deep 8 infinite, profound 9 plumbless, soundless 10 bottomless, fathomless 11 illimitable, plummetless 12 unfathomable

abyss 3 pit 4 gulf, hell 5 chasm, depth, hades, Sheol 6 Tophet 7 Gehenna, inferno 8 deepness 9 perdition 10 profundity, underworld 11 netherworld 12 profoundness

academic 5 booky 6 closet 7 bookish, utopian 8 gownsman, pedantic 10 scholastic 11 book-learned, impractical, quodlibetic, speculative, theoretical

academic year part 4 term 7 quarter 8 semester 9 trimester

accede 3 let, yes 5 agree, allow 6 assent, concur, permit 7 consent 9 acquiesce, cooperate, subscribe

accelerate 5 hurry, impel, speed 6 hasten, step up 7 quicken, swiften

acceleration 7 speedup

accent 4 beat, tone 5 meter, pulse, throb 6 rhythm, stress 7 cadence 8 emphasis 9 pulsation 10 inflection, intonation *Irish:* 6 brogue *Scottish:* 4 burr *Southern:* 5 drawl

accent mark 5 acute, grave

accentuation see **accent**

accept 3 bow, buy, see 4 bear, take 5 adopt, agree, catch, favor, go for, grasp, yield 6 admire, endure, esteem, follow, pocket, take in 7 agree to, approve, believe, compass, receive, respect, swallow 8 assent to, bear with, hold with, tolerate, tough out 9 agree with, apprehend, approbate 10 capitulate, comprehend, understand 11 countenance, subscribe to

acceptable 4 good 6 decent 7 average 8 adequate, all right, bearable, ordinary 9 endurable, tolerable 10 sufficient 11 commonplace, supportable 12 satisfactory 13 unexceptional, unimpeachable

acceptably 4 well 5 amply, right 8 properly, suitably 9 fittingly 10 adequately, becomingly 13 appropriately

acceptant 8 suasible, swayable 9 receptive 10 responsive 11 persuadable, persuasible 13 influenceable

acceptation 5 sense 6 import 7 meaning, message, purport 10 intendment 12 significance, significancy **13** signification, understanding

accepted 5 sound, usual **6** proper **7** chronic, correct, routine **8** habitual, orthodox, received **9** customary **10** accustomed, recognized, sanctioned **11** established **12** conventional

access 3 fit, way **4** adit, door, gust, pang, turn **5** burst, entry, onset, route, sally, spell, throe **6** attack, entrée, stitch, taking, twinge **7** flare-up, ingress, passage, seizure **8** entrance, eruption, outburst **9** admission, explosion **10** admittance

accessible 4 open **6** public, usable **9** operative **10** employable **11** practicable **12** approachable, unrestricted

accession 4 rise **5** raise **8** addition, increase **9** accretion, increment **12** augmentation

accessory 7 abettor, adjunct, fitting **8** addition, adjuvant, appendix **9** accretion, ancillary, appendage, auxiliary, increment, secondary, tributary **10** accomplice, coincident, collateral, concurrent, incidental, subsidiary **11** appurtenant, concomitant, confederate, conspirator, subordinate, subservient **12** adventitious, appurtenance, contributory **13** accompaniment, coconspirator

accident 3 hap **4** fate, luck **5** fluke **6** chance, hazard, kismet, mishap **7** destiny, fortune **8** calamity, casualty, fortuity **9** mischance **10** misfortune **12** misadventure

accidental 3 odd **5** fluky **6** casual, chance, random **7** unmeant **9** chromatic, dependent, unplanned, unwitting **10** coincident, contingent, fortuitous, undesigned, unintended, unpurposed **11** conditional, inadvertent **13** unintentional

accidentally 5 haply

acclaim 4 hail **5** cheer, éclat, exalt, glory, honor, roose **6** homage, kudize, praise **7** applaud, commend, glorify, magnify, ovation, root for **8** applause, plaudits **9** recommend, reverence **10** compliment

acclamation 8 applause, plaudits

acclimate 6 harden, season **7** toughen **9** climatize

acclimatize see **acclimate**

accolade 4 bays **5** award, badge, honor, kudos **7** laurels **10** decoration **11** distinction

accommodate 3 fit **4** hold, suit, tune, vary **5** adapt, alter, defer, favor, house, humor, lodge, put up, yield **6** adjust, attune, bestow, billet, change, encase, harbor, modify, oblige, square, submit, tailor **7** cater to, conform, contain, enclose, indulge, quarter **8** domicile **9** entertain, harmonize, integrate, reconcile **10** coordinate, proportion **11** convenience, domiciliate **12** reconciliate

accommodations 4 keep, room **7** housing, lodging, shelter **8** lodgment **12** room and board

accompaniment 4 mate **6** fellow **7** comrade, consort, partner **8** addition **9** accessory, associate, attendant, colleague, companion, corollary **10** assistance, complement, enrichment, equivalent, supplement **11** concomitant, enhancement **12** augmentation

accompany 4 join, lead **5** bring, guide, pilot, steer **6** attend, convoy, escort **7** combine, conduct, consort, esquire **8** chaperon **9** associate **11** consort with

accompanying 8 incident **9** ancillary, attendant, attending, satellite **10** coincident, collateral **11** concomitant

accomplice 5 aider **6** flunky, helper, stooge **7** abettor **9** accessory, assistant **11** confederate, conspirator **13** coconspirator

accomplish 3 win **4** gain **5** reach, score **6** attain, fulfil, rack up **7** achieve, fulfill, realize, succeed

accomplished 4 ripe **5** adept **6** expert **8** finished, masterly **9** all-around, many-sided, perfected, versatile, virtuosic **10** consummate, proficient

accomplishment 3 act, art **4** deed **5** craft, doing, skill, thing **6** action, finish **8** fruition **9** adeptness, expertise **10** attainment, expertness **11** achievement, acquirement, acquisition, proficiency

accord 4 deal, fuse, give, jibe, tune **5** agree, award, blend, chime, fit in, grant, merge, tally, union **6** chorus, concur, confer, square **7** concede, concert, conform, empathy, harmony **8** affinity, coalesce, coincide, dovetail, sympathy **9** agreement, harmonize, vouchsafe **10** attraction, consonance, correspond, solidarity **11** concordance **13** understanding

accordant 9 congruous **10** harmonious

accordingly 2 so **4** ergo, then, thus **5** hence **9** therefore, thereupon **12** consequently

accost 3 dog **4** dare, face, hail **5** annoy, front, greet, hound, worry **6** bother, call to, halloo, pester, salute **7** address, affront, apply to, bespeak, outface, outrage **8** approach, confront **9** challenge **10** buttonhole **11** memorialize

accouchement 7 lying in **8** childbed **11** confinement

account 3 tab, use **4** bill, deem, note, rate, view **5** avail, favor, score, story, value, worth **6** assess, esteem, reason, reckon, regard, report, repute **7** dignity, explain, expound, fitness, history, invoice, justify, recital, respect, service, utility, version **8** appraise, consider, estimate, evaluate

9 advantage, chronicle, elucidate, narrative, rationale, reckoning, relevance, statement, valuation **10** admiration, estimation, reputation, usefulness **11** consequence, distinction, explain away, explanation, rationalize **13** applicability, consideration, justification

accountable 6 liable **8** amenable **10** answerable **11** responsible

account book 6 ledger

accounting *branch of:* **11** bookkeeping

accouter 3 arm, rig **4** deck, gear **5** adorn, dress, equip, fix up, ready **6** attire, fit out, outfit **7** appoint, furnish, prepare, turn out **8** decorate **9** embellish

accouterment 4 gear **6** outfit, tackle **7** bravery, regalia **8** matériel, tackling **9** apparatus, equipment, machinery, trappings **11** furnishings, habiliments **12** appointments **13** paraphernalia

accredit 2 OK **3** lay **4** okay **5** refer **6** assign, attest, charge, enable, impute **7** approve, ascribe, certify, commend, empower, endorse, license **8** sanction, vouch for **9** attribute, authorize, recommend **10** commission

accretion 4 rise **5** raise **7** adjunct **8** addition, increase **9** accession, appendage, increment **10** attachment **11** enlargement **12** augmentation

accumulate 4 heap, hive, mass, pile **5** amass, hoard, lay by, lay in, lay up, stock, uplay **6** garner, gather, roll up **7** backlog, collect, lay down, store up **8** assemble, treasure **9** stockpile

accumulation 4 bank, heap, mass, pile **5** hoard, stock, store, trove **7** buildup, cumulus, reserve **9** amassment **10** collection **11** aggregation **13** agglomeration

accumulative 5 chain **8** additive, additory **9** summative **11** aggregative **12** augmentative

accuracy 9 exactness, precision **10** definition, exactitude **11** correctness, preciseness **12** definiteness

accurate 4 nice **5** exact, right **6** proper **7** certain, correct, precise **8** reliable, rigorous **9** authentic **10** dependable

accursed 6 odious **7** hateful **8** damnable **9** abhorrent, execrable, offensive, repugnant, revolting **10** abominable, detestable

accusation 6 charge **8** delation **10** allegation, indictment *false:* **7** calumny

accuse 3 tax **5** blame **6** charge, delate, indict **7** arraign, censure, impeach **8** denounce **9** criminate, criticize, inculpate, reprobate **11** incriminate

accustom 3 use **4** wont **5** adapt, inure **6** adjust, harden, season **9** habituate **11** acclimatize, familiarize

accustomed 5 usual **7** chronic, routine

8 accepted, everyday, habitual, standard **9** confirmed **10** habituated, regulation **11** commonplace **12** conventional

ace 3 bit, jot **4** atom, hair, iota, mite **5** crumb, minim, speck **7** whisker **8** molecule, particle **11** hairbreadth

ace and face card 7 natural **9** blackjack

acedia 5 sloth

acerb 3 dry **4** acid, sour, tart **7** acetose, caustic **9** acidulous, corrosive, sarcastic **12** archilochian

acerbate 7 envenom **8** embitter

acerbic see **acerb**

acerbity 7 acidity, sarcasm **8** acrimony, asperity, dourness, mordancy, sourness, tartness **9** harshness, roughness, surliness **10** bitterness, causticity **11** crabbedness, saturninity

Achates' companion 6 Aeneas

ache 3 yen **4** hurt, long, lust, pain, pang, pine, pity, rack, sigh **5** crave, throe, yearn **6** hanker, hunger, injury, misery, stitch, suffer, thirst, twinge **7** feel for **8** yearning **10** sorrow over **11** commiserate **13** compassionate *Scottish:* **5** stoun **6** stound

acheronian 5 black, bleak, drear **6** dismal, gloomy **7** joyless **8** desolate, funereal **9** cheerless

achieve 2 do **3** get, win **4** gain **5** reach, score **6** attain, finish, obtain, rack up, secure **7** acquire, execute, perform, realize **8** complete, conclude **9** actualize **10** accomplish

achievement 4 deed, feat **6** finish **7** exploit **10** attainment **11** acquirement, acquisition, tour de force

Achilles *adviser:* **6** Nestor *companion:* **9** Patroclus *father:* **6** Peleus *horse:* **7** Xanthus *lover:* **7** Briseis *mother:* **6** Thetis *slayer:* **5** Paris *victim:* **6** Hector *vulnerable part:* **4** heel

Achilles' heel 8 soft spot

aching 4 sore **7** algetic, hurtful, hurting, painful **10** afflictive

Achsah *father:* **5** Caleb *husband:* **7** Othniel

achy 4 sore

acicular 5 acute, peaky, piked, sharp **6** peaked **7** pointed

acid 3 dry **4** sour, tart **5** acerb **7** acerbic, acetose *bleaching:* **6** oxalic *combining form:* **3** oxy **4** acet **5** aceto *fatty:* **6** capric **7** caproic, stearic **8** caprylic *found in apples:* **5** malic *found in cranberries:* **7** benzoic *found in grapes:* **8** tartaric *found in lemons:* **6** citric *found in rhubarb:* **6** oxalic *found in sour milk:* **6** lactic *indicator:* **6** litmus *kind:* **5** amino, boric, iodic, malic **6** acetic, bromic, formic, nitric, oxalic, tannic **7** chloric, nitrous, silicic **8** carbolic, carbonic, chlorous, muriatic, sulfuric **9** aqua

regia **12** hydrochloric *neutralizer:* **4** base
6 alkali *tanning:* **6** tannic **8** catechin *vinegar:* **6** acetic
acid radical *combining form:* **3** oyl
acidulous **3** dry **4** sour, tart **5** acerb,
sharp **6** biting **7** acerbic, acetose, cutting,
piquant, pungent
Acis *lover:* **7** Galatea *slayer:*
10 Polyphemus
acknowledge **3** own **4** avow, deem, tell,
view **5** admit, agree, allow, grant, let on,
own up **6** accept, fess up, reveal **7** concede, confess, declare, divulge **8** announce,
consider, disclose, proclaim **9** recognize
acknowledgment **6** credit **11** recognition
acme **4** apex, peak **6** apogee, climax, summit, tiptop, vertex, zenith **8** capstone,
meridian, pinnacle **11** culmination
acorn *combining form:* **5** balan **6** balano
sprouter: **3** oak
acoustic **5** aural **6** audile **8** auditory
acquaint **4** clew, clue, post, tell, warn
6 advise, fill in, inform, notify, orient, wise
up **7** apprise, present **8** accustom **9** habituate, introduce
acquaintance **4** mate **5** amigo, crony
6 friend **7** comrade **8** familiar, intimacy, intimate **9** associate, companion, confidant
10 experience **11** familiarity
acquainted **6** au fait, versed **7** abreast,
versant **8** familiar, informed **9** au courant
10 conversant
acquiesce **3** bow, yes **5** agree **6** accede,
assent, concur **7** consent **9** reconcile,
subscribe
acquiescence **9** deference **10** compliance, conformity **11** resignation
12 complaisance
acquiescent **7** passive **8** resigned, yielding **10** submissive **11** unresistant, unresisting **12** nonresistant, nonresisting
acquire **3** add, get, win **4** earn, form, gain,
land, make **5** amass, annex, reach **6** garner, obtain, pick up, secure **7** bring in, collect, develop, procure **8** cumulate **9** knock
down **10** accumulate
acquirement **6** finish **7** advance **8** addition **9** accretion, erudition **10** attainment
11 achievement, acquisition, advancement
acquisition see **acquirement**
acquisitive **5** itchy **6** grabby, greedy
8 covetous, desirous, grasping
10 prehensile
acquit **3** act **4** bear, free **5** carry, clear
6 behave, deport **7** absolve, comport, conduct, release **8** liberate **9** discharge, exculpate, exonerate, vindicate **10** disculpate
acres **4** land **5** manor **6** estate
7 demesne
acrid **4** sour **5** harsh, sharp **6** biting, bitter **7** austere, caustic, cutting **9** amaroidal
10 astringent
acrimonious **3** mad **5** angry, cross, irate,
testy, wroth **6** cranky, ireful, wrathy,
wrothy **8** wrathful, wrothful **9** indignant,
irascible, splenetic **11** belligerent, contentious, quarrelsome
acrimony **5** spite **6** animus, malice, rancor **7** ill will **8** acerbity, asperity, mordancy
9 animosity, antipathy, malignity **10** bitterness **11** malevolence
Acrisius *daughter:* **5** Danae *slayer:*
7 Perseus
across **4** over **6** beyond **7** athwart
12 transversely *prefix:* **2** di **3** dia **4** over
5 trans
act **2** do **3** run **4** bear, deed, fake, feat,
play, sham, work **5** bluff, doing, feign, put
on, serve **6** acquit, affect, assume, behave,
demean, deport **7** comport, conduct,
exploit, operate, perform, portray, pretend
8 function, simulate **9** discourse, officiate,
personate **10** masquerade **11** counterfeit,
impersonate *suffix:* **2** cy, th **3** ade, ate, ice,
ion, ism
acting **6** pro tem **7** interim **9** ad interim,
temporary **10** pro tempore
actinium *symbol:* **2** Ac
action **4** case, deed, fray, suit, work
5 cause, doing **6** affray, battle, combat
7 lawsuit, process, service **8** behavior, conflict, function **9** discharge, execution, operation, procedure **10** engagement, proceeding **11** performance *combining form:* **3** cin,
kin **4** cino, kine, kino **5** cinet, kinet
6 cineto, kineto, praxia, praxis *suffix:* **2** al,
cy **3** ade, ing, sis **4** ance, ence, esis, ment,
osis **5** ation **7** isation, ization *unwise:*
8 impolicy
action painting **7** tachism
activate **4** stir, wake **5** rally, rouse,
waken **6** arouse, awaken **8** energize,
vitalize
activation *combining form:* **7** kinesis
active **4** busy, live, spry, yare **5** agile, alert,
alive, brisk, zippy **6** brisky, lively, nimble
7 driving, dynamic, running, working **8** animated, spirited, vigorous **9** assiduous, energetic, operative, sprightly, vivacious
11 functioning, industrious **12** enterprising
activity **8** exercise, exertion **10** exercising
actor **4** mime **5** mimic, party **6** mummer,
player, sharer **7** trouper **8** partaker, thespian **9** performer **11** participant **12** impersonator, participator *name:* **3** Cox (Wally),
Dix (Richard), Fox (Michael J.), Lom (Herbert), Mix (Tom), Ray (Aldo) **4** Alda (Alan,
Robert), Bean (Orson), Blue (Ben), Bond
(Ward), Cobb (Lee J.), Coco (James), Culp
(Robert), Dean (James), Duff (Howard), Egan
(Richard), Falk (Peter), Ford (Glenn, Harri-

son), Foxx (Redd), Geer (Will), Grey (Joel), Hale (Alan), Hill (Arthur), Hope (Bob), Hurt (William), Ives (Burl), Jory (Victor), Kaye (Danny), Kean (Edmund), Keel (Howard), Ladd (Alan), Lahr (Bert), Lord (Jack), Lunt (Alfred), Marx (Chico, Groucho, Harpo), Muni (Paul), Ngor (Haing S.), Peck (Gregory), Raft (George), Ryan (Robert), Shaw (Robert), Todd (Richard), Tone (Franchot), Torn (Rip), Webb (Clifton, Jack), Wynn (Ed, Keenan), York (Michael) **5** Adler (Luther), Allen (Woody), Arkin (Alan), Asner (Ed), Autry (Gene), Ayres (Lew), Barry (Gene), Bates (Alan), Beery (Noah, Wallace), Berle (Milton), Boone (Richard), Brady (Scott), Brand (Neville), Burns (George), Caine (Michael), Candy (John), Clark (Dane), Conte (Richard), Cooke (Alistair), Corey (Wendell), Cosby (Bill), Davis (Sammy Jr.), Delon (Alain), Donat (Robert), Evans (Maurice), Ewell (Tom), Finch (Peter), Flynn (Errol), Fonda (Henry, Peter), Gabin (Jean), Gable (Clark), Gould (Elliot), Grant (Cary), Gwenn (Edmund), Hardy (Oliver), Hayes (Gabby), Irons (Jeremy), Jaffe (Sam), Jones (Dean), Kazan (Elia), Keach (Stacy), Keith (Brian), Kelly (Gene), Kiley (Richard), Kline (Kevin), Lamas (Fernando, Lorenzo), Lanza (Mario), Lewis (Jerry), Lloyd (Harold), Lorre (Peter), Lukas (Paul), Lynde (Paul), March (Frederic), McCoy (Tim), Mills (John), Mineo (Sal), Moore (Victor), Nimoy (Leonard), Niven (David), Nolan (Lloyd), Nolte (Nick), Oakie (Jack), Oland (Warner), O'Neal (Patrick, Ryan), Payne (John), Pesci (Joe), Power (Tyrone), Price (Vincent), Quale (Anthony), Quinn (Anthony), Rains (Claude), Scott (George C., Randolph), Segal (George), Sheen (Charlie, Martin), Stack (Robert), Stamp (Terence), Tracy (Spencer), Tufts (Sonny), Wayne (John), Wilde (Cornel), Wills (Chill), Young (Gig, Robert) **6** Abbott (Bud), Albert (Eddie), Ameche (Don), Arness (James), Backus (Jim), Balsam (Martin), Barker (Lex), Baxter (Warner), Beatty (Warren), Begley (Ed), Bogart (Humphrey), Bolger (Ray), Bosley (Tom), Brando (Marlon), Brooks (Mel), Burton (Richard), Caesar (Sid), Cagney (James), Callan (Michael), Cantor (Eddie), Carney (Art), Chaney (Lon), Coburn (Charles, James), Colman (Ronald), Conway (Tim, Tom), Coogan (Jackie), Cooper (Gary), Cotten (Joseph), Crabbe (Buster), Cronyn (Hume), Crosby (Bing), Cruise (Tom), Culkin (Macaulay), Curtis (Tony), Dailey (Dan), Danson (Ted), Danton (Ray), Darren (James), De Niro (Robert), De Vito (Danny), Dullea (Keir), Duryea (Dan), Duvall (Robert), Ferrer (Jose, Mel), Fields (W.C.), Finney (Albert), Garner (James), Gibson (Hoot), Gorcey (Leo), Greene (Lorne, Richard), Harris (Richard),

Harvey (Laurence), Hayden (Sterling), Heflin (Van), Heston (Charlton), Hingle (Pat), Holden (Bill), Howard (Trevor), Hudson (Rock), Hunter (Jeffrey, Tab), Huston (John, Walter), Jacobi (Lou), Jagger (Dean), Keaton (Buster, Michael), Knotts (Don), Kruger (Otto), Landau (Martin), Landon (Michael), Laurel (Stan), Lemmon (Jack), Lugosi (Bela), MacRae (Gordon), Malden (Karl), Martin (Dean), Marvin (Lee), Massey (Raymond), Mature (Victor), McCrea (Joel), Meeker (Ralph), Menjou (Adolphe), Morley (Robert), Morris (Wayne), Morrow (Vic), Mostel (Zero), Murphy (Audie, Eddie), Murray (Bill, Don), Nelson (Ozzie), Newley (Anthony), Newman (Paul), O'Brian (Hugh), O'Brien (Edmund, Pat), O'Toole (Peter), Pacino (Al), Parker (Fess), Poston (Tom), Powell (Dick), Reeves (Steve), Reiner (Carl, Rob), Rennie (Michael), Ritter (John, Tex), Rogers (Roy, Wayne, Will), Romero (Cesar), Rooney (Mickey), Schell (Maximilian), Sharif (Omar), Slezak (Walter), Swayze (Patrick), Talbot (Lyle), Taylor (Robert, Rod), Thomas (Danny, Richard), Toomey (Regis), Tucker (Forrest), Turpin (Ben), Vaughn (Robert), Voight (Jon), Wagner (Robert), Walker (Robert), Warden (Jack), Weaver (Dennis, Fritz), Welles (Orson), Werner (Oskar), Wilder (Gene) **7** Abraham (F. Murray), Andrews (Dana), Astaire (Fred), Aykroyd (Dan), Bellamy (Ralph), Bogarde (Dirk), Bridges (Beau, Jeff, Lloyd), Bronson (Charles), Brynner (Yul), Bushman (Francis X.), Buttons (Red), Calhern (Louis), Calhoun (Rory), Cameron (Rod), Carlson (Richard), Carroll (Leo G.), Chaplin (Charlie), Connery (Sean), Connors (Chuck, Mike), Conried (Hans), Costner (Kevin), da Silva (Howard), DeLuise (Dom), Donahue (Troy), Donlevy (Brian), Douglas (Kirk, Melvyn, Michael, Paul), Dreyfus (Richard), Edwards (Vince), Feldman (Marty), Freeman (Morgan), Garrick (David), Gazzara (Ben), Gielgud (John), Gleason (Jackie), Gossett (Louis), Granger (Farley, Stewart), Guiness (Alec), Hackman (Gene), Henreid (Paul), Hoffman (Dustin), Homeier (Skip), Homolka (Oscar), Hopkins (Anthony), Ireland (John), Janssen (David), Johnson (Don, Van), Jourdan (Louis), Jurgens (Curt), Karloff (Boris), Kennedy (Arthur, George), Klugman (Jack), Lawford (Peter), Leonard (Sheldon), MacLane (Barton), Maharis (George), Matthau (Walter), McCarey (Leo), McGavin (Darren), McQueen (Steve), Merrill (Gary), Milland (Ray), Mitchum (Robert), Montand (Yves), Navarro (Ramon), Newhart (Bob), O'Connor (Carroll, Donald), Olivier (Laurence), Palance (Jack), Paulsen (Pat), Peppard (George), Perkins (Anthony), Persoff (Nehemiah), Pickens (Slim), Pidgeon (Walter), Poitier (Sidney),

Preston (Robert), Randall (Tony), Redford (Robert), Robards (Jason), Robeson (Paul), Salvini (Tommaso), Sanders (George), Savalas (Telly), Scourby (Alexander), Selleck (Tom), Sellers (Peter), Silvers (Phil), Sinatra (Frank), Skelton (Red), Skinner (Otis), Steiger (Rod), Stewart (James), Tamblyn (Russ), Ustinov (Peter), Vallone (Raf), Van Dyke (Dick), Wallach (Eli), Widmark (Richard), Wilding (Michael), Winters (Jonathan), Woolley (Monty) **8** Basehart (Richard), Bickford (Charles), Blackmer (Sidney), Borgnine (Ernest), Buchanan (Edgar), Buchholz (Horst), Carrillo (Leo), Chandler (Jeff), Costello (Lou), Cummings (Robert), Day-Lewis (Daniel), Eastwood (Clint), Forsythe (John), Gardiner (Reginald), Garfield (John), Harrison (Noel, Rex), Hemmings (David), Holbrook (Hal), Holloway (Stanley), Jannings (Emil), Kilbride (Percy), Kingsley (Ben), Langella (Frank), Laughton (Charles), Lockhart (Gene), Marshall (E.G., Herbert), McDowell (Malcolm), McLaglen (Victor), Meredith (Burgess), Mitchell (Thomas), O'Connell (Arthur), O'Herlihy (Dan), Rathbone (Basil), Redgrave (Michael), Reynolds (Burt), Ritchard (Cyril), Robinson (Edward G.), Sarrazin (Michael), Scofield (Paul), Stallone (Sylvester), Sullivan (Barry), Von Sydow (Max), Whitmore (James) **9** Amsterdam (Morey), Barrymore (John, Lionel), Carnovsky (Morris), Carradine (David, John, Robert), Courtenay (Tom), Depardieu (Gerard), Fairbanks (Douglas), Franciosa (Anthony), Hardwicke (Cedric), Hyde-White (Wilfrid), Lancaster (Burt), MacMurray (Fred), Montalban (Ricardo), Pleasance (Donald), Robertson (Cliff, Dale), Zimbalist (Efrem) **10** Fitzgerald (Barry), Montgomery (Robert), Richardson (Ralph), Sutherland (Donald, Kiefer), Washington (Denzel) **11** Greenstreet (Sydney), Mastroianni (Marcello) **13** Kristofferson (Kris) **actor's** *quest:* 4 part, role *signal:* 3 cue **actress** 3 Bow (Clara), Day (Doris), Dee (Sandra), Dru (Joanne), Gam (Rita), Loy (Myrna), May (Elaine) **4** Bara (Theda), Barr (Roseanne), Cass (Peggy), Cher, Coca (Imogene), Dahl (Arlene), Duke (Patty), Eden (Barbara), Foch (Nina), Gish (Lillian), Hawn (Goldie), Holm (Celeste), Hunt (Linda, Marsha), Hyer (Martha), Kahn (Madeline), Kerr (Deborah), Lake (Veronica), Lisi (Virna), Main (Marjorie), Mayo (Virginia), Neal (Patricia), Raye (Martha), Rigg (Diana), Ross (Katharine), Rush (Barbara), Ryan (Peggy), Weld (Tuesday), West (Mae), Wood (Natalie, Peggy), Wray (Fay), York (Susannah) **5** Adams (Maude), Arden (Eve), Astor (Mary), Bates (Kathy), Bloom (Clair), Booth (Shirley), Britt (May), Bruce (Virginia), Buzzi (Ruth), Caron (Leslie), Close (Glenn), Crain

(Jeanne), Davis (Bette, Geena, Judy), Dunne (Irene), Eggar (Samantha), Fonda (Jane), Gabor (Eva, Zsa Zsa), Garbo (Greta), Grant (Lee), Hagen (Uta), Hasso (Signe), Hayes (Helen), Henie (Sonja), Howes (Sally Ann), Jones (Jennifer, Shirley), Kelly (Patsy), Lange (Jessica), Leigh (Janet, Vivien), Lenya (Lotte), Loren (Sophia), Mason (Pamela), Miles (Sarah), Miles (Vera), Moore (Mary Tyler, Terry), North (Sheree), Novak (Kim), O'Hara (Maureen), Olson (Nancy), O'Neal (Tatum), Picon (Molly), Pitts (Zasu), Roman (Ruth), Saint (Eva Marie), Scott (Lizbeth, Martha), Smith (Alexis, Maggie), Storm (Gale), Tandy (Jessica), Welch (Raquel), Wiest (Dianne), Wyatt (Jane), Young (Loretta) **6** Angeli (Pier), Bacall (Lauren), Barrie (Wendy), Baxter (Anne), Bergen (Candice, Polly), Blaine (Vivian), Cannon (Dyan), Davies (Marion), Del Rio (Dolores), Dennis (Sandy), Diller (Phyllis), Duncan (Sandy), Fabray (Nanette), Farrow (Mia), Foster (Jodie), Garner (Peggy Ann), Garson (Greer), Gaynor (Mitzi), Gordon (Ruth), Grable (Betty), Grimes (Tammy), Harlow (Jean), Harper (Valerie), Harris (Julie), Hunter (Kim), Hussey (Ruth), Huston (Anjelica), Hutton (Betty), Keaton (Diane), Keeler (Ruby), Lamarr (Hedy), Lamour (Dorothy), Lasser (Louise), Laurie (Piper), Louise (Tina), Lupino (Ida), MacRae (Sheila), Malone (Dorothy), Martin (Mary), Matlin (Marlee), McGraw (Ali), Merkel (Una), Monroe (Marilyn), Moreau (Jeanne), Moreno (Rita), Oberon (Merle), O'Brien (Margaret), Palmer (Lili), Parker (Suzy), Powers (Stephanie), Prowse (Juliet), Remick (Lee), Ritter (Thelma), Rogers (Ginger), Sidney (Sylvia), Spacek (Sissy), Streep (Meryl), Taylor (Elizabeth), Temple (Shirley), Thomas (Marlo), Tiffin (Pamela), Tomlin (Lily), Turner (Kathleen, Lana), Walker (Nancy), Wilson (Marie), Wright (Teresa), Wynter (Dana) **7** Allyson (June), Andress (Ursula), Andrews (Julie), Bergman (Ingrid), Burnett (Carol), Darnell (Linda), DeCarlo (Yvonne), Dukakis (Olympia), Dunaway (Faye), Dunnock (Mildred), Fleming (Rhonda), Fricker (Brenda), Gardner (Ava), Garland (Judy), Goddard (Paulette), Grayson (Kathryn), Hayward (Susan), Hepburn (Audrey, Katharine), Jackson (Glenda), Langtry (Lillie), Learned (Michael), Lombard (Carole), Magnani (Anna), Mangano (Silvana), McGuire (Dorothy), McKenna (Siobhan), Mimieux (Yvette), Miranda (Carmen), Natwick (Mildred), Perrine (Valerie), Podesta (Rosanna), Roberts (Julia), Russell (Jane, Rosalind), Shearer (Norma), Simmons (Jean), Stevens (Stella), Swanson (Gloria), Thaxter (Phyllis), Tierney (Gene), Ullmann (Liv), Winfrey (Oprah), Winters (Shelley), Withers (Jane) **8** Anderson

(Judith), Ashcroft (Peggy), Bancroft (Anne), Bankhead (Tallulah), Basinger (Kim), Blondell (Joan), Byington (Spring), Caldwell (Zoe), Channing (Carol), Christie (Julie), Crawford (Joan), Dewhurst (Colleen), Dietrich (Marlene), Dressler (Marie), Fletcher (Louise), Fontaine (Joan), Fontanne (Lynn), Goldberg (Whoopi), Griffith (Melanie), Hayworth (Rita), Lansbury (Angela), Lawrence (Gertrude), Leachman (Cloris), Leighton (Margaret), Lindfors (Viveca), Lockhart (June), Lovelace (Linda), MacLaine (Shirley), Mercouri (Melina), Minnelli (Liza), Pfeiffer (Michelle), Pickford (Mary), Prentiss (Paula), Redgrave (Lynn, Vanessa), Rowlands (Gena), Signoret (Simone), Stanwyck (Barbara), Sullavan (Margaret), Talmadge (Norma), Thompson (Sada), Williams (Esther), Woodward (Joanne) **9** Barrymore (Ethel), Bernhardt (Sarah), Christian (Linda), Dickinson (Angie), Kellerman (Sally), Mansfield (Jayne), Moorehead (Agnes), O'Sullivan (Maureen), Pleshette (Suzanne), Plowright (Joan), Schneider (Romy), Singleton (Penny), Stapleton (Jean, Maureen), Strasberg (Susan), Streisand (Barbra), Struthers (Sally), Thorndike (Sybil), Vera-Ellen **10** Lanchester (Elsa), Montgomery (Elizabeth), Rutherford (Margaret), Tushingham (Rita) **11** de Havilland (Olivia), McCambridge (Mercedes), Riefenstahl (Leni) **12** Lollabrigida (Gina)

actual 4 hard, real, true **6** extant **7** genuine **8** absolute, bona fide, concrete, existent, material, physical, positive, tangible, unfabled **9** authentic, objective, veridical **10** legitimate, phenomenal, undeniable **12** indisputable

actuality 4 fact **5** being **7** reality **9** existence, substance **10** embodiment **11** incarnation, materiality

actually 4 very **5** truly **6** really **7** de facto **9** genuinely, veritably

actuate 4 move, stir **5** drive, impel, rouse **6** arouse, propel, set off **7** provoke, trigger **8** mobilize, vitalize **9** circulate, galvanize

act up 9 misbehave

acumen 3 wit **8** astuticy, keenness **9** acuteness, sharpness **10** astuteness, shrewdness **11** discernment, penetration, percipience **12** perspicacity

acute 4 dire, high, keen **5** peaky, piked, sharp **6** argute, peaked, piping, shrill, treble, urgent **7** crucial, cutting, exigent, pointed **8** acicular, critical, incisive, piercing, shooting, stabbing **9** aciculate, acuminate, acuminous, cuspidate, desperate, knifelike, observant, sensitive, trenchant **10** perceptive **11** climacteric, penetrating, penetrative, quick-witted, sharp-witted *combining form:* **3** oxy

adage 3 saw **4** word **6** byword, saying, truism **7** proverb **8** aphorism, apothegm

Adah *husband:* **4** Esau **6** Lamech *son:* **5** Jabal, Jubal **7** Eliphaz

Adam *grandson:* **4** Enos **5** Enoch *rib:* **3** Eve *son:* **4** Abel, Cain, Seth *teacher:* **6** Raisel *wife:* **3** Eve **6** Lilith

adamant 5 rigid **8** immobile, obdurate **9** immovable, unbending, unswaying **10** inexorable, inflexible, relentless, unbendable, unyielding **12** unsubmitting

adapt 3 fit **4** suit **5** refit **6** adjust, square, tailor **7** conform **9** acclimate, reconcile **11** acclimatize, accommodate

adaptable 6 mobile, pliant, supple **7** ductile, plastic, pliable **8** moldable **9** all-around, malleable, many-sided, versatile

add 3 sum, tot **4** cast, foot, tote **5** affix, annex, tally, total **6** append, attach, figure, reckon, tack on, take on **7** augment, compute, enlarge, subjoin, summate **8** compound, increase, totalize **9** calculate

added 3 new **4** else, more **5** fresh, other **7** another, farther, further **10** additional

addendum 5 rider **7** allonge **8** addition **10** supplement

ad design 4 logo

addict 3 fan **4** bias, buff **5** hound, lover **6** adjust, junkie, votary, zealot **7** devotee, fanatic, habitué, hophead **9** habituate **10** aficionado, enthusiast, predispose

addition 4 plus, rise **5** extra, raise, rider **7** accrual, adjunct **8** addendum, appanage, increase **9** accession, accessory, accretion, extension, increment **10** accruement, supplement **12** appurtenance, augmentation *number:* **6** addend **7** summand

additional 3 new **4** else, more **5** extra, fresh, other **7** another, farther, further **9** accessory **12** supplemental **13** supplementary

additionally 3 too, yea, yet **4** also, more, then **5** again **6** as well, withal **7** addedly, besides, further **8** likewise, moreover **11** furthermore

additive 5 chain **8** extender **9** summative **10** cumulative **12** accumulative

addle 5 mix up **6** ball up, fuddle **7** confuse, fluster, nonplus, perplex **8** befuddle, bewilder, confound, distract, throw off **9** dumbfound

address 3 aim, air, set, sue, woo **4** hail, mien, port, send, ship, tact, talk **5** apply, court, greet, level, point, poise, remit, route, skill, speak **6** accost, attend, call to, devote, direct, pursue, relate, salute, speech **7** bearing, bespeak, consign, forward, incline, know-how, lecture, prowess, tutoyer **8** appeal to, approach, converse, deftness, demeanor, dispatch, petition, presence, talk with, transmit **9** dexterity, diplomacy, expertise **10** adroitness, allocution, buckle down, competence, deportment, efficiency **11** comportment, memorialize, proficiency, savoir faire, superscribe, tactfulness **12** apostrophize

adduce **3** lay **4** cite **5** offer **6** allege, submit, tender **7** advance, present, proffer, propose, suggest **8** document **9** exemplify **10** illustrate

add up to **4** mean **5** spell **6** denote, import, intend **7** connote, express, signify

adept **4** deft, whiz **5** crack **6** adroit, expert, master, wizard **7** skilled **8** masterly, skillful, virtuoso **9** dexterous, masterful **10** proficient **11** crackerjack **12** professional

adequacy **5** might **6** enough **7** ability **8** capacity **10** capability, competence, sufficient **13** qualification

adequate **6** common, decent, enough **8** all right **9** competent, sufficing **10** acceptable, sufficient **11** comfortable **12** satisfactory **13** unexceptional, unimpeachable

adequately **4** well **5** amply, right **6** enough **8** properly, suitably **9** fittingly **10** becomingly **13** appropriately

adhere **5** cling, stick **6** adsorb, cleave, cohere

adherence **4** bond **5** cling **7** loyalty **8** adhesion, clinging, cohesion, fidelity, stickage, sticking **9** constancy **10** attachment, concretion **11** cementation **12** faithfulness **13** agglutination

adherent **6** cohort **7** sectary **8** disciple, follower, henchman, partisan, sectator, stalwart **9** satellite, supporter **suffix: 3** ite

adhering **8** osculant

adhesion see **adherence**

adhesive **5** gluey, gooey, gummy, tacky **6** clingy, cloggy, sticky **7** stickum **8** mucilage

adieu **2** by **5** congé **6** bye-bye, so long **7** cheerio, good-bye, parting **8** farewell, toodle-oo **11** leave taking

ad interim **6** acting, pro tem, supply **9** temporary **10** pro tempore

adipose **3** fat **5** fatty

adiposity **7** fatness, obesity **10** corpulence, fleshiness

adit **3** way **4** door **5** entry **6** access, entrée **7** ingress **8** entrance **9** admission **10** admittance

adjacent **5** handy **6** nearby **7** close-by **8** abutting, touching **9** adjoining, bordering **10** approximal, contiguous, convenient, juxtaposed, near-at-hand **11** close-at-hand, neighboring **12** conterminous

adjoin **4** abut, line, meet **5** march, touch, verge **6** border, butt on **8** neighbor **11** communicate

adjoining see **abutting**

adjourn **4** rise, stay **5** close, defer, delay **6** hold up, put off, recess, shelve **7** break up, disband, hold off, suspend **8** dissolve, hold over, postpone, prorogue **9** prorogate, terminate

adjudge **6** umpire **7** referee **9** arbitrate **10** adjudicate

adjudicate see **adjudge**

adjunct **5** affix **8** addition, appanage, appendix **9** accessory, accretion, appendage **10** attachment **12** appurtenance

adjust **3** fit, fix, rig **4** suit, tune **5** adapt, order, right **6** accord, attune, orient, square, tailor, tune up **7** arrange, conform, correct, rectify **8** modulate, regulate **9** habituate, harmonize, reconcile **11** accommodate

adjuvant **9** accessory, ancillary, auxiliary **10** collateral, subsidiary **11** appurtenant, subservient **12** contributory

ad-lib **9** improvise **11** extemporize, improvisate

Admetus *father:* **6** Pheres *wife:* **8** Alcestis

administer **3** run **4** deal, give **5** issue **6** direct, govern, manage, render, strike **7** conduct, deal out, deliver, dole out, execute, give out, inflict, mete out **8** carry out, dispense, share out **9** apportion, supervise **10** distribute, portion out

administrate **6** govern, render **7** execute **8** carry out

administration *system of:* **11** bureaucracy

administrator **4** exec **7** manager, officer **8** official **9** executive

admirable **6** august, worthy **8** laudable **9** deserving, estimable, meritable, praisable **11** commendable, meritorious, thankworthy **12** praiseworthy

admiral *American:* **4** Byrd, Sims **5** Dewey, Stark **6** Halsey, Nimitz **7** Zumwalt **8** Farragut, Rickover, Spruance *Confederate:* **6** Semmes *Dutch:* **5** Tromp *English:* **6** Nelson, Rodney, Vernon **7** Hawkins **8** Beaufort, Jellicoe, Villiers **11** Mountbatten *French:* **10** Villeneuve *German:* **4** Spee **8** Donitz, Raeder **7** Tirpitz *Japanese:* **4** Togo **5** Yonai **8** Yamamoto *Spanish:* **8** Menendez

admiration **5** amaze, favor **6** esteem, regard, wonder **7** account, respect **9** amazement, marveling **10** estimation, wonderment **12** appreciation

admire **5** adore, prize, value **6** esteem, regard, relish, revere **7** adulate, cherish, lionize, respect, worship **8** consider, treasure, venerate **9** delight in, reverence **10** appreciate

admirer **3** fan **6** votary **7** amateur, devotee, fancier

admission **3** way **4** adit, door **5** entry

6 access, entrée **7** ingress **8** entrance
10 admittance
admit **3** own **4** avow, take **5** agree, allow,
enter, grant, let on, lodge, own up **6** fess
up, harbor, permit, suffer, take in **7** concede, confess, receive, shelter **9** entertain,
introduce, recognize **11** acknowledge
admittance see **admission**
admix **5** merge **6** mingle **8** comingle,
immingle **9** commingle **11** intermingle
admixture **4** dash **5** alloy, shade, smack,
spice, taint, tinge **7** amalgam **8** compound
9 composite **10** adulterant, denaturant
12 amalgamation
admonish **4** warn **5** chide **6** lesson, monish, rebuke **7** caution, reprove, tick off
8 call down, reproach **9** reprimand
admonishing **7** warning **8** monitory
10 cautionary, cautioning, monitorial
admonition **3** rap, wig **6** caveat, rebuke
7 caution, chiding, reproof, warning **9** reprimand **11** forewarning
ado **4** fuss, stir **5** tizzy, whirl **6** bustle,
flurry, furore, pother, uproar **7** turmoil
9 confusion
adolescence **5** youth **6** spring
7 puberty **9** greenness, youthhood
10 juvenility, pubescence, springtide, springtime **12** youthfulness
adolescent **4** teen **6** teener **8** preadult,
teenager
Adonijah *brother:* **5** Amnon **7** Absalom,
Chileab *father:* **5** David *mother:* **7** Haggith
slayer: **7** Benaiah
Adonis *lover:* **5** Venus **9** Aphrodite
mother: **5** Myrrh **6** Myrrha *slayer:* **4** boar
adopt **4** take **6** affect, assume, take on,
take up **7** embrace, espouse
adoption **8** espousal **9** embracing
11 embracement
adorable **4** lush **7** darling, lovable **8** heavenly, lovesome, luscious **9** ambrosial, delicious **10** delectable, delightful
11 scrumptious
adoration **4** love **7** passion, worship
8 devotion, idolatry **9** affection
11 idolization
adore **4** love **6** admire, dote on, esteem,
revere **7** idolize, worship **8** dote upon,
enshrine, venerate **9** affection, delight in,
reverence
adorn **4** deck, trim **5** prank, primp, prink
6 bedeck, doll up, enrich, pretty, richen
7 bedizen, dress up, enhance, furbish, garnish, smarten **8** beautify, decorate, ornament, prettify, spruce up, titivate
9 embellish
adornment **5** decor **6** finery **7** garnish
8 ornament **9** caparison **10** decoration
11 centerpiece **13** embellishment
ad rem **7** apropos, germane **8** apposite,

material, pointful, relevant **9** pertinent
10 applicable **11** applicative, applicatory
adroit **3** sly **4** deft **5** canny, handy, smart
6 astute, clever, nimble, shrewd **7** cunning
8 dextrous, skillful **9** dexterous, ingenious,
workmanly **11** intelligent, quick-witted,
workmanlike **13** perspicacious
adroitness **3** art **5** craft, skill **7** address,
cunning, know-how, prowess, sleight
8 deftness **9** dexterity, expertise, readiness
adulation **7** acclaim, blarney **8** applause,
flattery, soft soap **12** blandishment
adult **4** aged, ripe **5** grown **6** mature
7 grown-up, matured, ripened **9** full-blown,
full-grown **11** full-fledged
adulterant **5** alloy **9** admixture
10 denaturant
adulterate **4** thin **5** taint **6** debase, defile,
dilute, doctor, dope up, weight **7** pollute
8 denature, impurify **10** tamper with
adumbrate **3** dim, fog **4** bode, call, hint,
mist, murk **5** augur, cloud, draft **6** darken,
shadow, sketch **7** becloud, bespeak, betoken, obscure, outline, portend, predict, presage, suggest **8** block out, chalk out, forebode, forecast, foretell, indicate, prophesy,
rough out, skeleton **9** obfuscate, prefigure
10 foreshadow, vaticinate **11** prefigurate,
skeletonize **12** characterize
adumbration **4** hint, sign **5** shade,
umbra **6** shadow **7** umbrage **8** penumbra
10 intimation, suggestion
advance **3** aid **4** cite, help, lend, loan,
move **5** get on, march, raise, serve
6 adduce, allege, assist, course, foster,
mature, prefer, uplift **7** develop, elevate, forward, further, headway, ongoing, present,
proceed, promote, upgrade **8** anabasis,
approach, encroach, get along, heighten,
increase, overture, progress **9** encourage,
evolution **11** development, furtherance,
improvement, progression **12** breakthrough
advanced **7** forward, liberal, radical **8** tolerant **10** precocious **11** broad-minded,
progressive
advancement **5** march **7** headway
8 progress **9** promotion **10** preference
advantage **3** use **4** boon, edge, good,
lead, odds, sake **5** asset, avail, bulge,
serve **6** better, profit **7** account, benefit, fitness, godsend, mastery, service, welfare
8 blessing, handicap, interest, leverage
9 allowance, head start, relevance, upper
hand, well-being **10** ascendancy, domination, leadership, prosperity, usefulness
11 benediction, superiority **12** running start
advantageous **4** good **6** paying, toward,
useful **7** benefic, gainful, helpful **8** favoring,
remedial, salutary **9** conducive, desirable,
expedient, favorable, lucrative **10** beneficial,

profitable, propitious, well-paying, worthwhile **11** moneymaking **12** remunerative

advent **6** coming **7** arrival, hearing **8** approach

adventitious **6** casual **10** accidental, contingent, fortuitous, incidental **12** supervenient

adventure **4** feat, gest, risk **5** quest, wager **6** chance **7** emprise, exploit **8** escapade **10** enterprise

adventuresome see **adventurous**

adventurous **4** bold, rash **5** brash **6** daring **7** doughty **8** intrepid, reckless **9** audacious, daredevil, foolhardy, impetuous, imprudent **11** temerarious

adversary **3** con **4** anti **5** match **7** opposer **8** opponent **9** oppugnant **10** antagonist

adverse **4** anti **7** counter, harmful, hurtful, opposed **8** contrary, negative, opposing **9** injurious, oppugnant **11** deleterious, detrimental, obstructive, unfavorable **12** antagonistic, antipathetic **13** counteractive

adversity **4** dole **6** misery, mishap **7** tragedy **8** distress **9** mischance, suffering **10** misfortune **11** contretemps

advert **4** note **5** refer **6** allude, notice, remark **7** bring up, observe **8** point out

advertent **6** arrect **7** heedful **9** attentive, intentive, observant, regardful

advertise **4** plug, puff, push **5** boost **6** blazon, report **7** build up, declare, promote, publish **8** announce, ballyhoo, proclaim **9** broadcast, publicize **10** annunciate, bruit about, promulgate

advertisement **2** ad **4** bill, plug, sign **5** blurb, flyer **6** notice, poster **7** affiche **9** billboard, broadcast, promotion, publicity **10** commercial, propaganda **11** declaration, publication **12** announcement, proclamation, promulgation **13** pronouncement

advertising **7** buildup, puffery **9** publicity

advice **4** news, word **7** caution, counsel, tidings, warning **8** guidance, teaching **10** admonition **11** information, instruction **12** intelligence

advisable **4** wise **6** seemly **7** politic, prudent **8** sensible, suitable, tactical **9** expedient

advise **4** clew, clue, post, tell, warn **6** confab, confer, fill in, huddle, inform, notify, parley, powwow, wise up **7** apprise, caution, consult, counsel **8** acquaint, forewarn **9** recommend **11** confabulate

advised **7** studied **8** designed, intended, prepense, studious **10** considered, deliberate, thought-out **11** intentional **12** premeditated

advocacy **7** defense

advocate **4** back **5** favor **6** preach, uphold **7** promote, support **8** backstop,

champion, exponent, side with **9** encourage, expounder, proponent, supporter **11** countenance *combining form:* **4** crat *suffix:* **5** arian

Aeacus *father:* **4** Zeus *mother:* **6** Aegina *son:* **6** Peleus **7** Telamon

Aedon *brother:* **7** Amphion *sister-in-law:* **5** Niobe *son (victim):* **6** Itylus

Aeetes *daughter:* **5** Medea *father:* **6** Helios

Aegaeon see **Briareus**

Aegeon's wife **7** Aemilia

Aegeus'son **7** Theseus

aegis **4** ward **5** armor, guard **6** shield **7** backing, defense **8** armament, auspices, security **9** patronage, safeguard **10** protection **11** sponsorship

Aegisthus *father:* **8** Thyestes *lover:* **12** Clytemnestra *mother:* **7** Pelopia *slayer:* **7** Orestes *victim:* **6** Atreus **9** Agamemnon

Aegyptus *brother:* **6** Danaus *father:* **5** Belus *mother:* **8** Anchinoe *son:* **7** Lynceus

Aeneas *companion:* **7** Achates *father:* **8** Anchises *mother:* **5** Venus **9** Aphrodite *son:* **5** Iulus **8** Ascanius *wife:* **6** Creusa **7** Lavinia

Aeneid *author:* **6** Vergil, Virgil *first words:* **16** arma virumque cano *hero:* **5** Aneas

Aeolus *brother:* **5** Dorus **6** Xuthus *daughter:* **6** Canace **7** Alcyone **8** Halcyone *father:* **6** Hellen **8** Poseidon *mother:* **9** Melanippe *son:* **7** Athamas **9** Salmoneus

aeon **3** age **7** dog's age **8** blue moon, coon's age, eternity

aerate **3** air **6** aerify **9** oxygenate, ventilate

aerial **4** airy **5** lofty **6** towery, vapory **7** soaring, spiring, topless **8** ethereal, towering, vaporous **9** pneumatic **10** impalpable **11** atmospheric

aerie, aery, eyrie **4** nest **5** brood **9** penthouse

aeronaut **4** Fogg **5** pilot **7** aviator **8** Zeppelin **10** balloonist

Aerope *husband:* **6** Atreus *lover:* **8** Thyestes *son:* **8** Menelaus **9** Agamemnon

aery **6** aerial **8** ethereal **9** visionary

Aesculapius *daughter:* **6** Hygeia **7** Panacea *father:* **6** Apollo *mother:* **7** Coronis *slayer:* **4** Zeus **7** Jupiter *son:* **7** Machaon **9** Podalirus *teacher:* **6** Chiron *wife:* **6** Epione

Aeson *brother:* **6** Pelias *son:* **5** Jason

aesthete **10** dilettante **11** cognoscente, connoisseur

Aether's father **6** Erebus

affable **6** genial, gentle, polite **7** amiable,

cordial **8** gracious, sociable **9** congenial, courteous

affair 4 love **5** amour, thing **6** matter **7** concern, liaison, palaver, romance **8** business, intrigue **10** proceeding

affect 3 act, get **4** fake, move, sham, sway **5** bluff, carry, feign, haunt, put on, touch **6** assume, resort, strike **7** actuate, impress, inspire, pretend **8** frequent, simulate **9** influence **11** counterfeit

affectation 4 airs, lugs, pose **9** mannerism, prettyism

affected 5 put-on **6** chichi, la-di-da, tootoo **7** assumed, feigned, genteel, mincing, stilted **8** involved, mannered, overnice, précieux, precious, spurious **9** concerned, conscious **10** artificial, implicated, interested **11** alembicated, overrefined, pretentious **13** self-conscious

affected with/by *combining form:* **6** pathic *suffix:* **2** ic **4** ical

affecting 6 moving **8** poignant, touching **9** troubling **10** disturbing, impressive **11** distressful, distressing

affection 4 bias, love, mark **5** savor, trait **6** doting, malady, virtue, warmth **7** ailment, concern, disease, emotion, feature, feeling, leaning, passion, quality, worship **8** devotion, disorder, fondness, interest, penchant, property, sickness, sympathy, syndrome **9** attention, attribute, character, complaint, condition, infirmity, sentiment **10** attachment, propensity, tenderness **12** predilection

affectionate 4 dear, fond, warm **6** doting, loving, tender **7** devoted **8** lovesome **11** sympathetic

affective 6 moving **7** emotive **9** emotional

affectivity 7 emotion, feeling, passion **9** sentiment

affianced 7 engaged **8** intended, plighted, promised **9** betrothed **10** contracted

affiche 4 bill **6** poster **7** placard **8** handbill

affidavit certificate 5 jurat

affiliated 4 akin **6** agnate, allied **7** cognate, connate, kindred, related **8** incident **10** connatural **11** consanguine

affiliation 5 tie-up **6** hookup **7** cahoots **8** alliance **10** connection **11** association, combination, conjunction, partnership **12** conjointment

affinity 6 simile **7** analogy **8** likeness, sympathy **9** alikeness, semblance **10** attraction, comparison, similarity, similitude **11** resemblance *combining form:* **5** phily, trope **6** philia **7** tropism

affirm 3 say, yes **4** aver, avow **5** state, vouch **6** assert, attest, avouch, depose **7** certify, declare, profess, protest, witness **9** guarantee

affirmative 2 ay **3** aye, yes **8** positive

affix 3 add **5** annex, rivet **6** append, attach, fasten **7** subjoin

afflict 3 try, vex **4** rack **5** annoy, harry, press, smite, worry, wound, wring **6** bother, harass, harrow, martyr, pester, plague, strike **7** agonize, crucify, torment, torture **9** martyrize **10** excruciate

afflicted 6 dolent, rueful, woeful **7** doleful, ruthful **8** dolorous, stricken, wretched **9** miserable, sorrowful

affliction 3 rue, woe **4** care, dole **5** cross, grief, trial **6** mishap, ordeal, regret, sorrow **7** anguish, illness **8** disorder, sickness, unhealth **9** heartache, infirmity, mischance **10** heartbreak **11** tribulation *suffix:* **4** itis

afflictive 4 dire, sore **6** aching, bitter, woeful **7** algetic, galling, hurtful, hurting, painful **8** grievous **10** calamitous, deplorable, lamentable **11** distasteful, distressing, regrettable, unfortunate, unpalatable **13** heartbreaking

affluent 4 rich **7** moneyed, opulent, wealthy

affray 3 row **5** brawl, clash, fight, melee **6** fracas **7** ruction, scuffle **8** skirmish **9** scrimmage **10** donnybrook

affright 3 awe **5** alarm, scare, spook **7** startle, terrify **9** terrorize

affront 4 face, meet, slap **6** insult, offend, slight **7** despite, offense, outrage **8** dishonor **9** aspersion, contumely, criticize, encounter, indignity **10** defamation

aficionado 3 fan **4** buff **5** hound, lover **6** addict, votary **7** devotee, habitué

afield 4 away **5** amiss, badly, wrong **6** astray

afire see **aflame**

aflame 5 afire, aglow, fiery **6** ablaze, alight **7** blazing, burning, flaming, flaring, ignited **8** aflicker **11** conflagrant

afraid 3 shy **4** wary **5** chary, jumpy, loath, scary, timid **6** aghast, averse, scared, trepid **7** afeared, anxious, ascared, fearful, uneager **8** cautious, hesitant, skittish, timorous **9** reluctant, terrified, unwilling **10** frightened **11** disinclined **12** apprehensive

afresh 3 new **4** anew, over **5** again, newly **6** de novo, lately, of late **8** once more, recently

Africa *country:* **4** Chad, Mali, Togo **5** Benin, Congo, Egypt, Gabon, Ghana, Kenya, Libya, Niger, Sudan, Zaire **6** Angola, Gambia, Guinea, Malawi, Rwanda, Uganda, Zambia **7** Algeria, Burundi, Lesotho, Liberia, Morocco, Namibia, Nigeria, Senegal, Somalia, Tunisia **8** Botswana, Cameroon, Djibouti, Ethiopia, Tanzania, Zimbabwe **9** Cape Verde, Mauritius, Swaziland **10** Ivory Coast, Madagascar, Mauritania, Mozambique, Seychelles **11** Burkina Faso,

Sierra Leone, South Africa **12** Guinea Bissau **13** Comoro Islands *ethnic group:*
3 Ibo **4** Akan, Arab, Boer, Copt, Fula, Issa, Moor, Zulu **5** Bantu, Fulah, Galla, Hausa, Kongo, Mande, Negro, Pygmy, Swazi, Wolof **6** Beduin, Berber, Fulani, Hamite, Herero, Kaffir, Kikuyu, Nubian, Somali, Tuareg, Ubangi, Yoruba **7** Ashanti, Bedouin, Bushman, Malinke, Swahili **8** Egyptian, Mandingo **9** Hottentot *language:* **3** Ibo **4** Urdu **5** Bantu, Galla, Hausa **6** Arabic, Berber, Somali, Yoruba **7** Amharic, Bambara, Swahili **8** Malagasy **9** Afrikaans

aft 6 astern

after 3 for **4** back, hind, next, past, rear **5** below, later, since **6** behind, beyond, hinder, retral **7** by and by, ensuing **8** hindmost, latterly **9** following, posterior **10** subsequent **12** postliminary, subsequently

after all 3 yet **4** still **6** though **7** howbeit, however **11** nonetheless **12** nevertheless

aftereffect 5 issue **6** result, upshot **7** outcome **8** causatum **11** consequence, eventuality

afterlife 6 beyond **8** eternity **9** hereafter

aftermath see **aftereffect**

afterward 4 next, to-be **5** later **6** behind, future, offing **7** by-and-by **8** latterly **9** hereafter **12** subsequently

afterword 8 epilogue

Agag *kingdom:* **6** Amalek *slayer:* **6** Samuel

again 4 also, anew, back, over **5** about **6** afresh, around, de novo **7** besides, further **8** once more **12** additionally *combining form:* **2** an **3** ana **4** pali *prefix:* **2** re

again and again 3 oft **4** much **5** often **8** ofttimes **10** frequently, oftentimes, repeatedly

against 4 agin **6** contra, facing, toward, versus **7** apropos, despite, vis-à-vis **8** fronting, touching **9** in spite of **10** concerning, respecting *prefix:* **2** ob **3** ant **4** anti **6** contra **7** counter

Agamemnon *avenger:* **7** Orestes *brother:* **8** Menelaus *daughter:* **7** Electra **9** Iphigenia *father:* **6** Atreus *slayer:* **9** Aegisthus *son:* **7** Orestes *wife:* **12** Clytemnestra

agape 6 aghast **7** shocked **8** dismayed **10** confounded **11** dumbfounded, overwhelmed **12** thunderstruck

agate 3 mib, taw **6** marble **7** shooter

Agave *father:* **6** Cadmus *husband:* **6** Echion *mother:* **8** Harmonia *sister:* **3** Ino **6** Semele **7** Autonoe *son:* **8** Pentheus

age 3 eon, era **4** aeon, grow, ripe, time **5** epoch, ripen **6** grow up, mature, mellow, period **7** develop **8** blue moon, caducity, eternity, maturate

aged 3 old **4** ripe **5** hoary, olden **6** mellow, senior **7** ancient, antique, elderly, matured, ripened **8** Noachian, timeworn **9** senescent, venerable **11** patriarchal **12** antediluvian

ageless 7 eternal **8** dateless, timeless **10** intemporal

agency 4 mean **5** cause, organ **6** medium **7** channel, vehicle **8** ministry **10** instrument

agenda 6 docket **7** program **8** calendar, schedule **9** timetable *entry:* **4** item

Agenor *brother:* **5** Belus *daughter:* **6** Europa *father:* **7** Antenor, Neptune **8** Poseidon *mother:* **5** Libya *son:* **6** Cadmus

agent 3 fed, spy **4** doer, mean, tool **5** actor, organ, proxy, spook **6** deputy, factor, medium **7** channel, proctor, steward, vehicle **8** assignee, attorney, executor, institor, minister, ministry **9** activator, go-between, middleman **10** instrument, procurator *combining form:* **4** stat *suffix:* **3** ant

age-old 7 ancient, antique **8** timeworn **9** venerable **12** antediluvian

agglomerate 4 heap, mass, pile **9** aggregate **11** aggregation

agglomeration 5 hoard, trove **9** aggregate, amassment **10** collection, cumulation **11** aggregation

aggrandize 5 boost, exalt, honor **6** beef up, expand, extend **7** augment, build up, dignify, enlarge, ennoble, glorify, magnify, sublime **8** heighten, increase, multiply **11** distinguish

aggravate 4 gall **5** annoy, grate, mount, peeve, pique, rouse, upset **6** burn up, deepen, nettle, worsen **7** bedevil, disturb, enhance, magnify, perturb, provoke **8** heighten, irritate **9** intensify **10** exasperate

aggravation 6 bother, pother **9** annoyance

aggregate 3 all, sum **4** body, bulk, floc **5** add up, gross, total, whole **6** amount, budget, number **7** quantum **8** entirety, quantity, totality **11** agglomerate **12** conglomerate **13** agglomeration *suffix:* **3** ery

aggregation 4 ruck **5** crowd, group, hoard, trove **6** muster **7** company **8** assembly **9** amassment, congeries, gathering **10** assemblage, collection, cumulation **11** agglomerate **12** accumulation

aggression 4 raid **5** fight, onset **6** attack **7** assault, offense **8** invasion **9** incursion, offensive, onslaught, pugnacity **10** assailment **12** belligerence **13** combativeness

aggressive 5 pushy **6** fierce **7** scrappy, vicious **8** militant **9** assertive, combative,

imperious 11 belligerent, contentious, domineering, hard-hitting

aggressiveness 11 bellicosity **12** belligerence, belligerency

aggrieve 4 hurt, pain **5** annoy, harry, worry, wrong **6** harass, injure, plague **7** afflict, oppress, torment **8** distress **9** constrain, persecute

aghast 4 agog, awed **5** agape **6** afraid, amazed, scared **7** anxious, fearful, shocked **8** appalled, dismayed, startled **9** horrified, terrified **10** astonished, confounded, frightened **11** awestricken, dumbfounded, overwhelmed **12** horror-struck **13** flabbergasted, thunderstruck

agile 4 deft, spry, yare **5** brisk, catty, lithe, zippy **6** active, adroit, limber, lively, nimble, supple, volant **7** lissome **8** dextrous **9** dexterous, sprightly

agitate 4 rile, rock **5** argue, drive, impel, peeve, shake, upset **6** bother, debate, flurry, joggle, ruffle **7** discuss, dispute, disturb, fluster, perturb, provoke, tempest, unhinge **8** convulse, irritate **9** thrash out **10** discompose, exasperate

agitation 4 flap, stew **6** bustle, dither, lather, pother, tumult **7** tempest, turmoil **9** commotion, confusion **10** turbulence

agitator 7 inciter **8** fomenter **10** instigator

Aglaia see **Graces**

Aglauros, Agraulos father: 7 Cecrops **sister: 5** Herse **9** Pandrosos

aglow 5 afire **6** ablaze, aflame, alight, lucent **7** radiant, shining **8** aflicker, gleaming, luminous

agnate 4 akin, like **5** alike **6** allied **7** cognate, connate, kindred, related, similar **9** analogous **10** affiliated **11** consanguine **13** corresponding

agnostic 7 infidel, skeptic **11** disbeliever

ago 2 by **4** gone, past, syne, yore **5** since

agog 4 avid **5** eager **6** ardent, roused **7** excited, popeyed **9** impatient

agonize 4 fret, gall, rack **5** chafe **6** harrow, squirm, suffer, writhe **7** afflict, torment, torture, trouble **8** distress **10** excruciate

agonizing 7 intense, racking, tearing **9** harrowing, torturing, torturous **10** tormenting **12** excruciating

agony 4 pain **5** dolor **6** misery **7** passion **8** distress **9** suffering

agrarian 5 rural **6** rustic **8** agrestal, pastoral **10** campestral **12** agricultural

Agraulos see **Aglauros**

agree 3 yes **4** jibe, suit **5** admit, check, equal, fit in, match, tally **6** accede, accord, assent, concur, square **7** comport, concede, concert, concord, conform, consent **8** check out, coincide, dovetail **9** acquiesce, harmonize, recognize, subscribe **10** correspond **11** acknowledge

agreeable 4 nice **7** affable, welcome **8** amenable, pleasant, pleasing **9** congenial, congruous, consonant, favorable **10** compatible, consistent, gratifying **11** pleasurable, pleasureful, sympathetic

agreed 2 OK **3** aye, yea, yep, yes **4** okay **8** all right, okeydoke

agreement 4 bond, deal, pact **6** accord, treaty, unison **7** bargain, compact, concord, entente, harmony **8** contract, covenant **9** concordat **10** consonance **11** concordance

agree with 3 fit **4** suit **5** befit **6** become **10** go together

agricultural 8 agrarian *combining form:* **4** agro

agriculture 7 farming, tillage **8** agronomy **9** husbandry

Agrippina's son 4 Nero

aground 7 beached **8** stranded

Ahab daughter: 8 Athaliah *father:* **4** Omri *wife:* **7** Jezebel

Ahasuerus kingdom: 6 Persia *wife:* **6** Esther, Vashti

Ahaz kingdom: 5 Judah *son:* **8** Hezekiah *wife:* **3** Abi

Ahaziah father: 4 Ahab **5** Joram **7** Jehoram *kingdom:* **5** Judah **6** Israel *mother:* **7** Jezebel **8** Athaliah *sister:* **9** Jehosheba **11** Jehosobeath

ahead 4 alee, ante, fore **5** forth **6** before, onward **7** onward, onwards **8** forwards, previous **9** in advance **10** beforehand **11** precedently **12** antecedently

Ahinoam father: 7 Ahimaaz *husband:* **4** Saul **5** David *son:* **5** Amnon

aid 4 abet, hand, help, lift **6** assist, helper, relief, succor **7** ancilla, backing, comfort, help out, succour, support **8** benefact, succorer **9** assistant, attendant, coadjutor **10** assistance, benefactor, coadjutant, lieutenant, ministrant, mitigation **11** alleviation, assuagement

Aida composer: 5 Verdi *father:* **8** Amonasro *lover:* **7** Radames *rival:* **7** Amneris

aide 6 deputy, second **7** orderly **9** assistant, coadjutor **10** coadjutant, lieutenant

ail 4 cark **5** upset, worry **7** afflict, trouble **8** distress

ailing 3 ill, low **4** mean, weak **6** donsie, droopy, offish, poorly, sickly, unwell **8** off-color **9** enfeebled **10** indisposed **11** debilitated

ailment 3 ill **6** malady, unrest **7** disease, ferment, turmoil **8** disorder, disquiet, sickness, syndrome **9** affection, complaint, condition, infirmity **10** inquietude **11** disquietude, restiveness **12** restlessness

aim 3 try **4** cast, goal, head, mark, mean, plan, want, wish **5** angle, essay, focus, level, point, slant, train **6** aspire, design, desire, direct, intend, strive, target, zero in **7** address, attempt, propose, purpose **8** ambition, endeavor **9** objective **11** contemplate

aimless 6 random **9** desultory, haphazard, hit-or-miss, irregular, unplanned **10** designless **11** purposeless

air 3 sky **4** aura, feel, mien, mood, port, song, tune, vent **5** state, style **6** aerate, aerify, manner, melody, reveal, strain **7** bearing, declare, divulge, express, feeling, melisma, publish, quality **8** demeanor, presence, proclaim **9** broadcast, character, semblance, ventilate **10** atmosphere, deportment **11** comportment *combining form:* **3** aer, atm **4** aeri, aero, atmo **5** pneum **6** pneumo **7** pneumat **8** pneumato

aircraft 5 blimp, drone, plane **6** glider **7** airship, balloon, chopper **8** aerodyne, aerostat, airplane, jetliner, zeppelin **9** dirigible **10** helicopter *carrier:* **7** flattop **8** birdfarm *designer:* **6** Fokker, Martin **7** Junkers, Tupolev **8** Northrop, Sikorsky, Yakovlev **13** Messerschmitt

airless 5 close, stivy **6** stuffy, sultry **8** stifling **10** breathless **11** suffocating

airman 5 flier, pilot **6** fly-boy **7** aviator

air movement 5 draft **7** updraft **9** downdraft

air navigation system 5 loran, navar, radar

airplane 3 jet, SST **4** STOL, VTOL **5** avion, VSTOL **6** bomber **7** fighter **8** autogiro, autogyro **9** transport *A-bomb-dropper:* **8** Enola Gay *battle:* **8** dogfight *body:* **8** fuselage *commercial:* **5** liner *engine:* **3** jet **6** fanjet **7** propjet **8** turbofan, turbojet **9** turboprop *engine casing:* **7** nacelle *engineless:* **6** glider *instrument:* **5** radar, radio **7** compass **9** altimeter, gyroscope **10** tachometer **11** transponder *maneuver:* **4** buzz, dive, loop, roll **8** nosedive **9** chandelle **10** barrel roll *movement:* **3** yaw **4** bank, spin **5** pitch **8** tailspin *part:* **3** fin **4** flap, nose, prop, tail, wing **5** cabin, wheel **6** engine, rudder **7** aileron **8** airscrew, elevator **9** empennage, propeller **10** stabilizer, stabilator *pilotless:* **5** drone *shelter:* **6** hangar *target:* **6** drogue *vapor:* **8** contrail

airport 5 drome, field **7** helipad **8** airdrome, airfield, heliport **9** aerodrome *building:* **8** terminal *flag:* **8** windsock *name:*

    Amsterdam: **8** Schiphol *Atlanta:* **10** Hartsfield *Boston:* **5** Logan *Chicago:* **5** O'Hare *Copenhagen:* **7** Kastrup *Dublin:* **7** Shannon *London:* **7** Gatwick **8** Heathrow *New York:* **3** JFK **7** Kennedy **9** La Guardia *Paris:*

4 Orly **8** DeGaulle **9** Le Bourget *Rome:* **7** Da Vinci *Washington:* **6** Dulles *part:* **5** apron, tower **6** runway **7** taxiway

airs 4 lugs, pose, show **6** vanity **9** loftiness, mannerism, prettyism, vainglory **11** affectation, ostentation

airship 8 zeppelin **9** dirigible

airtight 8 hermetic

airwaves nuisance 6 static

airy 4 rare, thin **5** blowy, gusty, light, lofty, windy **6** aerial, bouncy, breezy, dainty, towery, vapory **7** buoyant, gaseous, soaring, spiring, tenuous **8** animated, delicate, ethereal, rarefied, spirited, supernal, towering, vaporous, volatile **9** expansive, frivolous, pneumatic, resilient, windswept **10** diaphanous **11** atmospheric, skyscraping **12** effervescent, high-spirited

Ajax's father 6 Oileus **7** Telamon

akin 4 like **5** alike **6** agnate, allied **7** cognate, connate, kindred, related, similar, uniform **8** parallel **9** analogous, consonant **10** affiliated, comparable, connatural **11** consanguine **13** corresponding

Alabama 7 capital **10** Montgomery *college, university:* **5** Miles **6** Auburn, Mobile **8** Tuskegee **9** Talladega **10** Huntingdon *largest city:* **10** Birmingham *nickname:* **11** Cotton State **12** Heart of Dixie *state flower:* **8** camellia

alacrity 8 celerity, dispatch **9** briskness, eagerness, quickness, readiness **10** enthusiasm, expedition, promptness **11** promptitude

alamo 6 poplar **10** cottonwood

a la mode 4 chic, tony **6** modish, tonish, trendy **7** dashing, stylish **9** exclusive **11** fashionable

alarm 3 SOS **4** fear **5** alert, dread, larum, panic, scare, siren, spook, upset **6** dismay, fright, horror, terror, tocsin **7** startle, terrify, warning **8** affright, frighten **9** terrorize **11** forewarning, trepidation **13** consternation

alarmable 4 edgy **8** agitable, skittery, skittish, volatile **9** excitable, startlish **11** combustible

Alaska *capital:* **6** Juneau *largest city:* **9** Anchorage *state flower:* **11** forget-me-not

Albania *capital:* **6** Tirane *monetary unit:* **3** lek

albatross 5 goony **6** gooney, goonie

albeit 5 while **6** much as, though **7** whereas **8** although

Alberta *capital:* **8** Edmonton *university:* **7** Calgary **10** Lethbridge

Albion 7 England

album 3 ana **6** record **7** garland, omnibus **8** register **9** anthology **10** miscellany **11** florilegium

Alcestis *father:* 6 Pelias *husband:*
7 Admetus *rescuer:* 8 Heracles, Hercules
alchemist 10 Paracelsus
Alcina *sister:* 7 Morgana 10 Logistilla *victim:* 6 Rogero 8 Astolpho, Ruggiero
Alcinous *daughter:* 8 Nausicaa *wife:*
5 Arete
Alcmaeon *father:* 10 Amphiaraus
mother: 8 Eriphyle *wife:* 10 Callirrhoe
Alcmene *husband:* 10 Amphitryon *son:*
8 Heracles, Hercules
alcohol 4 grog 5 booze, drink, hooch,
juice 6 liquor, tipple 7 spirits 9 aqua vitae,
firewater *name:* 4 amyl 5 butyl, cetyl,
ethyl 6 glycol, methyl, sterol 7 butanol, eth-
anol, mannite, menthol 8 glycerin, glycerol,
inositol, mannitol, methanol 9 isopropyl
11 cholesterol *used in perfumes:* 5 nerol
7 borneol, linalol 8 farnesol, geraniol,
linalool
alcoholic 4 hard 8 bibulous 9 spiritous
10 spirituous 11 dipsomaniac
12 intoxicating
alcoholic drink see under **beverage**
alcoholized 5 drunk
alcove 6 gazebo, pagoda 9 belvedere
Japanese: 8 tokonoma
Alcyone *father:* 5 Atlas 6 Aeolus *husband:* 4 Ceyx *mother:* 7 Pleione *sisters:*
8 Pleiades
ale 3 nog 4 nogg
Alea 6 Athena
alehouse 3 pub 4 café 6 bistro 7 cabaret 8 beer hall 9 bierstube, brasserie,
honky-tonk, nightclub 10 beer garden
11 rathskellar
Alemanus *father:* 7 Histion *grandfather:*
6 Japhet
alert 3 SOS 4 keen, warn 5 alarm, quick,
ready, sharp, smart 6 brainy, bright, clever,
frisky, lively, tocsin 7 heedful, knowing,
mindful, wakeful 8 animated, open-eyed,
spirited, vigilant, watchful 9 attentive, brilliant, mercurial, sprightly, vivacious, wide-
awake 11 intelligent, quick-witted, ready-
witted *Scottish:* 4 gleg 8 wakerife
Alexander *birthplace:* 5 Pella *conquest:*
4 Tyre 5 Egypt, Issus 6 Arbela, Greece,
Persia 7 Parthia 8 Granicus *father:*
6 Philip *general:* 9 Antipater *horse:*
10 Bucephalus *kingdom:* 9 Macedonia
mother: 8 Olympias *teacher:* 9 Aristotle
wife: 6 Roxana
alfalfa 6 lucern 7 lucerne
alfresco 7 open-air, outdoor, outside
9 out-of-door 10 hypaethral
alga 6 desmid, diatom 7 seaweed *blue-
green:* 6 nostoc *brown:* 4 kelp 5 fucus
8 rockweed *combining form:* 7 phyceae
green: 8 conferva 9 chlorella *red:* 4 nori
7 amanori

algebra term 4 root 6 factor 8 binomial,
equation, monomial, variable 9 quadratic
10 polynomial
Algeria *capital:* 7 Algiers *ethnic group:*
4 Arab 6 Berber *monetary unit:* 5 dinar
port: 4 Oran
algetic 4 sore 6 aching 7 hurtful, hurting,
painful 10 afflictive
Ali *son:* 5 Hasan 6 Husayn *wife:* 6 Fatima
alias 3 AKA 6 anonym 7 pen name
9 pseudonym 10 nom de plume 11 nom de
guerre
alibi 4 plea 6 excuse 7 pretext
alien 6 exotic 7 foreign, inconnu, strange
8 estrange, outcomer, outsider, stranger,
transfer 9 auslander, extrinsic, foreigner,
outlander 10 extraneous, outlandish
alienate 4 part, wean 6 assign, convey,
remise 8 disunify, disunite, estrange, sign
over, transfer 9 disaffect 10 relinquish
alienation 6 lunacy 7 madness 8 insanity 9 unbalance 10 aberration, insaneness
11 derangement, distraction, psychopathy
12 disaffection, estrangement
alight 4 land 5 afire, aglow, fiery, perch,
roost 6 ablaze, aflame, bright, settle
7 blazing, burning, deplane, detrain, flaming,
flaring, glowing, ignited, set down, sit down
8 aflicker, dismount 9 effulgent, refulgent,
touch down 11 conflagrant
align 4 line, true 5 range 6 adjust, line up
8 regulate 9 allineate
alike 4 akin, same 7 similar, uniform 8 parallel 9 analogous, consonant 10 comparable 13 corresponding *combining form:*
2 is 3 hom, iso 4 homo
alikeness 6 simile 7 analogy 8 affinity
9 semblance 10 comparison, similarity,
similitude 11 resemblance
aliment 3 pap 4 food 7 pabulum 9 nutriment 10 sustenance 11 nourishment
alimentary 9 nutritive 11 nutritional
alimentary canal 7 enteron
alimentation 4 keep 5 bread 6 living
7 support 10 livelihood, sustenance
11 maintenance, subsistence
alimony see **alimentation**
alive 4 rife 5 awake, aware, fresh, quick,
vital 6 active, extant, living, zoetic 7 animate, dynamic, knowing, replete, running,
teeming, working 8 animated, existent,
existing, sensible, sentient, swarming,
thronged 9 abounding, au courant, cognizant, conscious, operative, wide-awake
11 functioning, overflowing
alkali metal 6 cesium, sodium 7 lithium
8 francium, rubidium 9 potassium
alkaline substance 3 lye, reh 4 lime,
soda, usar 5 borax 6 potash 7 ammonia,
antacid 8 pearl ash, saltwort 11 caustic
soda

alkali's opposite 4 acid
alkalize 6 basify
alkaloid 4 base *hallucinogenic:* **7** harmine **9** harmaline *medicinal:* **5** ergot
6 heroin **7** cocaine, codeine, emetine, eserine, harmine, quinine **8** atropine, caffeine, ecgonine, lobeline, morphine **9** ephedrine, harmaline, quinidine, reserpine **11** scopolamine *narcotic:* **6** heroin **7** cocaine, codeine **8** morphine *poisonous:* **6** conine
7 tropine **8** atropine, nicotine, solanine, thebaine **9** aconitine **11** scopolamine
all 3 sum **4** each **5** every, gross, quite, total, whole **6** apiece, entire, in toto, purely, wholly **7** exactly, totally, utterly **8** complete, entirety, everyone, outright, totality
9 aggregate, everybody **10** altogether, everything *combining form:* **3** omn, pam, pan **4** omni, pano, pant **5** panta, panto
all-around 7 general, overall **8** complete, sweeping, synoptic **9** adaptable, many-sided, panoramic, versatile **10** consummate **11** wide-ranging **13** comprehensive
allay 4 balm, calm, ease, lull **5** quiet, still
6 settle, soothe, subdue **7** assuage, compose, lighten, mollify, quieten, relieve **8** mitigate **9** alleviate **11** tranquilize
all but 4 most, much, nigh **5** about
6 almost, nearly **8** as good as, as much as, well-nigh **11** essentially, practically
13 approximately
allegation 8 pleading **9** assertion
allege 3 lay **4** cite **5** offer, state **6** adduce, assert **7** advance, declare, present, profess
alleged 7 dubious, would-be **8** doubtful, so-called, specious, supposed **9** pretended, professed, purported, soi-disant **10** ostensible, self-styled
allegiance 5 ardor, piety **6** fealty, homage **7** loyalty **8** devotion, fidelity
12 faithfulness
allegiant 4 true **5** liege, loyal **6** ardent
7 staunch **8** constant, faithful, resolute
9 steadfast
allegory 4 myth **5** fable **7** parable **8** apologue **9** symbolism **10** figuration
12 typification
allergy 5 atopy **8** aversion, dyspathy
9 antipathy, rejection, repulsion
alleviate 4 cure, ease **5** allay **6** remedy
7 assuage, lighten, mollify, relieve
8 mitigate
alleviation 4 ease **6** relief **8** easement
10 mitigation
all-fired 5 utter **6** blamed, dashed, deuced **7** blasted, blessed, doggone, goldarn **8** infernal
alliance 5 tie-up, union **6** hookup, league
7 cahoots **9** anschluss, coalition **10** connection, federation **11** affiliation, association, combination, confederacy, conjunction,

partnership, unification **12** conjointment
13 confederation
allied 4 akin **6** agnate, linked, united
7 cognate, connate, kindred, related **8** incident **10** affiliated, connatural
11 consanguine
all in 5 spent **6** bleary, effete, used up
7 drained, far-gone, worn-out **8** depleted
9 exhausted, washed-out
all in all 5 quite **6** in toto, purely, wholly
7 en masse, totally, utterly **9** generally
10 altogether, by and large, on the whole
allineate 4 line **5** align, range **6** line up
allness 8 entirety, totality
allocate 4 give **5** allot, allow **6** assign
7 earmark, mete out **9** admeasure, apportion, designate
allocution 4 talk **6** speech **7** address, lecture
allot 4 give **5** grant **6** accord, assign
7 deal out, dole out, mete out **8** allocate, dispense **9** admeasure, apportion
10 distribute
allotment 3 cut **4** bite, meed, part
5 quota, share, slice **6** ration **7** measure, partage, portion, quantum **9** allowance
all-out 5 total **9** full-blown, full-scale, unlimited **12** totalitarian
all over 10 everyplace, everywhere, far and near, far and wide, high and low, throughout
allow 3 let, lot, own **4** give **5** admit, allot, brook, grant, leave, let on, stand **6** assign, endure, fess up, permit, suffer **7** concede, confess, mete out **8** allocate, tolerate
9 admeasure, apportion **11** acknowledge
allowance 3 aid, cut, lot **4** bite, edge, help, meed, odds, part, tret **5** grant, leave, quota, share, slice **6** corody, permit, ration
7 consent, corrody, measure, partage, portion, quantum, subsidy, vantage **8** handicap, pittance, sanction **9** advantage, allotment, head start **10** assistance, concession, permission, sufferance
13 accommodation, apportionment, authorization
alloy 5 blend **6** fusion **7** amalgam, mixture **8** compound **9** admixture, composite
10 adulterant, denaturant **11** interfusion
12 amalgamation, intermixture *brass-like:*
6 latten, lattin *copper-sulfur:* **6** niello *copper-tin:* **6** bronze *copper-zinc:* **5** brass
6 tambac, tombac, tombak **8** arsedine
gold-like: **6** oreide, ormolu, oroide *gold-silver:* **8** electrum *iron-carbon:* **5** steel *iron-nickel:* **5** invar **7** elinvar *mercury:* **7** amalgam *pewter-like:* **5** bidri *tin-lead:* **5** calin, terne **6** pewter, solder *tin-zinc:* **6** oreide, oroide *used in jewelry:* **6** oreide, oroide, tombac
all-powerful 8 almighty **10** omnipotent
all right 2 OK **3** aye, yea, yep, yes

4 good, jake, okay **6** agreed, decent **8** adequate, okeydoke **9** tolerable **10** acceptable **12** satisfactory

all round   7 overall **10** everyplace, everywhere, far and near, far and wide, high and low, throughout

all there   4 sane **5** lucid, right **6** normal **12** compos mentis

All the Way Home author   4 Agee

allude   4 hint **5** imply, refer **6** advert **7** bring up, suggest **8** intimate

allure   4 bait, draw, take, tole, toll, wile **5** charm, decoy, tempt **6** appeal, entice, entrap, lead on, seduce **7** attract, bewitch, enchant, glamour **8** charisma, inveigle, witchery **9** captivate, fascinate, magnetism, magnetize **10** witchcraft **11** fascination

allurement   4 bait, call, draw, pull, trap **5** decoy, snare **6** appeal, come-on **9** seduction **10** attraction, enticement, seducement, temptation **12** drawing power, inveiglement

alluring   5 siren **8** charming **9** appealing, beguiling, glamorous, seductive **10** appetizing, attractive, bewitching, enchanting **11** captivating, fascinating

ally   4 join **5** unite **6** friend, helper **7** comrade, partner **8** federate **9** affiliate, associate, bedfellow, colleague, supporter **10** accomplice **11** confederate **12** collaborator

almighty   3 God **7** Creator **10** omnipotent **11** all-powerful

almost   4 nigh **5** about **6** all but, nearly **8** as good as, as much as, well-nigh **9** nearabout, virtually **11** essentially, practically **13** approximately *Scottish:* **6** feckly

alms   7 charity **8** donation, offering **11** benefaction, beneficence **12** contribution

Aloeus   father: 7 Neptune **8** Poseidon *mother:* **6** Canace *son:* **4** Otus **9** Ephialtes *wife:* **9** Iphimedia

aloft   4 high, over **5** above **6** upward **7** skyward **8** overhead *combining form:* **4** hyps **5** hypsi, hypso

Aloha State   6 Hawaii

alone   4 only, sole, solo **5** apart, solus **6** lonely, singly, solely, unique **7** isolate, removed **8** detached, entirely, isolated, lonesome, peerless, singular, solitary **9** matchless, unequaled, unmatched, unrivaled **10** unexampled, unexcelled **11** exclusively, unsurpassed **12** unparalleled, unrepeatable **13** unaccompanied

aloneness   8 solitude **9** isolation

along   3 too, yet **4** also **5** forth **6** as well, onward **7** besides, forward **8** likewise, moreover **11** furthermore **12** additionally

alongside   2 by **6** beside, next to **7** fornent *prefix:* **3** par **4** para

along with   combining form: 3 sym, syn

aloof   4 cold, cool **5** proud **6** casual, chilly, frigid, offish, remote **7** distant, haughty **8** arrogant, detached, reserved, reticent, solitary **9** unbending, uncurious, withdrawn **10** disdainful, restrained, unsociable **11** constrained, indifferent, standoffish, unconcerned **12** uninterested

alp   4 peak **5** mount **8** mountain

alpaca's habitat   4 Peru **5** Andes **7** Bolivia

alpha   4 dawn **5** start **6** outset **7** dawning, genesis, opening **8** outstart **9** beginning **12** commencement

alphabet   4 ABC's **7** grammar, letters **8** elements **9** rudiments **10** principles **12** fundamentals *Arabic:* **2** ba, fa, ha, ra, ta, ya, za **3** ayn, dad, dal, gaf, jim, kaf, kha, lam, mim, nun, sad, sin, tha, waw, zay **4** alif, dhal, shin **5** ghayn *Greek:* **2** mu, nu, pi, xi **3** chi, eta, phi, psi, rho, tau **4** beta, iota, zeta **5** alpha, delta, gamma, kappa, omega, sigma, theta **6** lambda **7** epsilon, omicron, upsilon *Hebrew:* **2** he, pe **3** mem, nun, sin, taf, tav, taw, tet, vav, waw, yod, yud **4** alef, ayin, beth, caph, heth, kaph, koph, qoph, resh, shin, teth **5** aleph, cheth, gimel, lamed, sadhe, tsade, zayin **6** daleth, samekh *Old Irish:* **4** ogam **5** ogham *runic:* **7** futhark, futhorc, futhork

Alphenor's mother   5 Niobe

Alpheus   beloved: 8 Arethusa *father:* **7** Oceanus *form:* **5** river *mother:* **6** Tethys

Alpine   animal: 4 ibex **7** chamois *climber:* **10** alpestrian *dance:* **5** gavot **7** gavotte *dress:* **6** dirndl *goat:* **4** ibex *herdsman:* **4** senn *house:* **6** chalet *lake:* **4** Como, Iseo **5** Garda **6** Geneva, Luzern **8** Maggiore **9** Constance, Neuchatel *pass:* **3** col **5** Cenis **7** Brenner, Simplon **9** St. Bernard *peak:* **5** Blanc, Eiger **7** Bernina **8** Jungfrau **10** Matterhorn *plant:* **9** edelweiss *primrose:* **8** auricula *resort:* **5** Davos **7** Bolzano, Zermatt **8** Chamonix, Grenoble **9** Innsbruck **10** Interlaken **11** Sankt Moritz *river:* **5** Rhine, Rhone *snowfield:* **4** firn, neve *staff:* **10** alpenstock *state:* **5** Tirol, Tyrol **7** Bavaria *tunnel:* **5** Blanc, Cenis **7** Arlberg, Simplon **10** St. Gotthard *wind:* **4** bise, bora **5** foehn

already   4 even, once **6** before **7** earlier **8** formerly **9** erstwhile **10** heretofore, previously

also   3 too, yet **4** more **5** again, along, still **6** as well, withal **7** besides, further **8** likewise, moreover **9** similarly **10** in addition **11** furthermore **12** additionally

also-ran   5 loser

altar   boy: 6 server **7** acolyte *cloth:* **4** pall **5** palla **7** frontal *hanging:* **6** dorsal, dossal, dossel *platform:* **8** predella *screen:* **7** reredos *shelf:* **6** gradin **7** gradine, retable *site:* 4 apse, bema *table:* 5 mensa *vessel:* 5 cruet, paten 7 chalice 8 ciborium 10 monstrance

alter 4 geld, turn, vary 5 adapt 6 adjust, change, jigger, modify, mutate, neuter, temper 8 moderate, modulate 9 refashion

alteration 4 turn 5 shift 6 change 8 mutation 9 variation 10 adaptation, adjustment, changeover, conversion, transition 12 modification 13 metamorphosis

altercate 4 spat, tiff 5 argue, scrap 6 bicker 7 brabble, dispute, quarrel, wrangle 8 squabble 9 caterwaul

altercation 3 row 4 tiff 6 combat, fracas 7 contest, dispute, quarrel, wrangle 8 argument, squabble 9 bickering 10 falling-out 11 controversy, embroilment

alternate 3 sub 5 proxy 6 fill-in, rotate 7 stand-in 8 periodic 9 change off, fluctuate, oscillate, recurrent, recurring, replacing, surrogate 10 equivalent, isochronal, periodical, substitute 11 isochronous, locum tenens, pinch hitter, replacement 12 intermittent

alternately 6 in lieu, rather 7 instead

alternative 5 proxy 6 choice, option 8 druthers, election 9 selection, surrogate 10 preference, substitute 11 contingency, possibility

Althaea *father:* 8 Thestius *husband:* 6 Oeneus *son:* 8 Meleager *victim:* 8 Meleager

although 4 when 5 while 6 albeit, much as 7 howbeit, whereas

altitude 6 height 9 elevation

altitudinous 4 high, tall

altogether 4 well 5 quite 6 in toto, wholly 7 en masse, exactly, totally, utterly 8 all in all, entirely 9 generally, perfectly 10 by and large, completely, on the whole, thoroughly

altruistic 6 humane 7 liberal 8 generous 9 unselfish 10 benevolent, bighearted, charitable, open-handed 11 magnanimous, noble-minded 12 eleemosynary, humanitarian 13 philanthropic

alum 4 grad 6 emetic 7 styptic 8 graduate 10 astringent

aluminum *symbol:* 2 Al

always 4 ever 7 forever 8 evermore 9 eternally 10 constantly, invariably 11 forevermore, in perpetuum, perpetually 12 continuously

amalgam see **amalgamation**

amalgamate 3 mix 4 fuse, meld 5 admix, merge, unify, unite 6 mingle 8 compound, intermix 9 interfuse 11 consolidate, intermingle

amalgamation 5 alloy, blend 6 fusion, merger 7 compost, mixture 8 compound

9 admixture, composite 10 commixture 13 consolidation

Amalthea *form:* 4 goat *horn:* 10 cornucopia *nursling:* 4 Zeus

Amasa *father:* 6 Hadlai, Jether *mother:* 7 Abigail

amass 4 bulk, hive 5 hoard, lay up, uplay 6 garner, gather, roll up 7 store up 8 cumulate 9 stockpile 10 accumulate

amassment 5 hoard, trove 9 colluvies 10 collection, cumulation 11 aggregation 12 accumulation 13 agglomeration

Amata's husband 7 Latinus

amateur 4 tyro 6 novice, tinker, votary 7 admirer, dabbler, devotee 8 beginner, neophyte, putterer 9 greenhorn, smatterer 10 apprentice, enthusiast, uninitiate 11 abecedarian

amateurish 3 raw 5 crude, green 6 clumsy, flawed 7 jackleg 8 dabbling 9 deficient, unskilled, untutored 10 dilettante, unfinished 12 dilettantist

amative 6 erotic 7 amorous 11 aphrodisiac

amaze 6 wonder 7 astound 8 astonish, surprise 9 dumbfound, marveling 10 admiration, wonderment 11 flabbergast 12 confoundment

amazement 6 wonder 8 surprise 9 marveling 10 admiration, wonderment 12 confoundment

amazing 7 strange 8 wondrous 9 marvelous, wonderful 10 astounding, miraculous, prodigious, stupendous, surprising 11 astonishing

amazon 5 harpy, scold, shrew, vixen 6 ogress, virago 8 fishwife 9 termagant, Xanthippe

ambassador 5 agent, envoy 6 legate 8 diplomat, emissary 9 messenger *papal:* 6 nuncio

ambience 6 medium, milieu 7 climate 10 atmosphere 11 environment, mise-enscène 12 surroundings

ambiguity 7 evasion 9 equivoque, obscurity, vagueness 11 amphibology, uncertainty 12 equivocality, equivocation 13 double meaning

ambiguous 5 fishy, vague 6 opaque, unsure 7 dubious, obscure, suspect, unclear 8 doubtful 9 equivocal, tenebrous, uncertain, unsettled 10 inexplicit 11 problematic 12 questionable

ambit 5 limit, orbit, range, reach, scope, sweep 6 extent, radius 7 circuit, compass, purview 8 extension, perimeter, periphery 13 circumference

ambition 3 aim 4 goal, hope, mark, wish 5 dream, drive 6 desire, spirit, target 7 avidity, purpose 9 eagerness, intention, objective **10** aspiration, enterprise, get-up-and-go, initiative

ambitious 4 avid, bold, keen **5** eager **8** aspiring **9** energetic, grandiose, visionary **10** aggressive **11** hard-working **12** enterprising

ambivalent see **equivocal**

amble 4 mope **5** dally, drift, mosey **6** bummel, dawdle, linger, stroll **7** saunter

ambrosial 4 lush **5** balmy, spicy, sweet, yummy **6** aromal, savory **7** darling **8** adorable, aromatic, fragrant, heavenly, luscious, perfumed, redolent **9** delicious **10** delectable, delightful **11** scrumptious

ambulant 6 roving **7** nomadic, vagrant, walking **8** vagabond **9** itinerant **11** peripatetic

ambulate 4 hoof, pace, step, walk **5** tread, troop **6** foot it **7** traipse

ambulatory see **ambulant**

ambuscade 6 ambush **10** ambushment

ambush 4 trap **5** snare **6** assail, attack, entrap, lay for, waylay **7** assault, ensnare, scupper **8** surprise **9** ambuscade

ameliorate 4 help, mend **5** amend **6** better, perk up **7** improve, relieve **8** mitigate **10** convalesce, recuperate

amenable 4 tame **6** docile, liable, pliant **7** plastic, pliable, subdued, willing **8** biddable, obedient **9** adaptable, malleable, receptive, tractable **10** answerable, responsive **11** accountable, responsible

amend 4 help **5** right **6** better, repair **7** correct, improve, rectify **9** meliorate **10** ameliorate

amends 7 redress **8** reprisal **9** indemnity, quittance **10** recompense, reparation **11** restitution **12** compensation

amenities 5 mores **6** manner **8** decorums **9** etiquette **10** civilities **11** proprieties

amenity 5 charm, frill, luxus **6** luxury **7** comfort **8** civility, courtesy, facility **9** attention, gallantry, geniality, pleasance **10** affability, amiability, betterment, cordiality, enrichment, politeness **11** convenience, enhancement, improvement, sociability **12** agreeability, extravagance, graciousness, gratefulness, pleasantness **13** agreeableness, courteousness, enjoyableness

ament 4 fool, zany **5** idiot, moron **6** catkin, cretin **7** half-wit, natural **8** imbecile **9** simpleton

amerce 4 fine **5** mulct **6** punish **8** penalize

amercement 4 fine **5** mulct **7** forfeit, penalty

American *with Japanese-born parents:* **5** nisei

American League *Baltimore:* **7** Orioles *Boston:* **6** Red Sox *California:* **6** Angels *Chicago:* **8** White Sox *Cleveland:* **7** Indi-

ans *Detroit:* **6** Tigers *Kansas City:* **6** Royals *Milwaukee:* **7** Brewers *Minnesota:* **5** Twins *New York:* **7** Yankees *Oakland:* **9** Athletics *Seattle:* **8** Mariners *Texas:* **7** Rangers *Toronto:* **8** Blue Jays

America, the Beautiful *music:* **4** Ward *words:* **5** Bates

americium *symbol:* **2** Am

Amfortas *father:* **7** Titurel *opera:* **8** Parsifal

amiability 7 amenity **9** geniality, pleasance **10** cordiality **12** gratefulness, pleasantness **13** agreeableness, enjoyableness

amiable 4 kind, mild, warm **6** benign, genial, gentle, kindly **7** affable, cordial, lenient **8** gracious, mannerly, obliging **9** courteous **10** responsive **11** complaisant, good-humored, good-natured, warmhearted **12** good-tempered

amicable 7 pacific **8** empathic, friendly, peaceful **9** congenial, peaceable **10** harmonious, like-minded, neighborly **11** sympathetic **13** understanding

amical 8 friendly **9** congenial **10** harmonious

amid 5 among, midst **6** during **10** throughout

amigo 4 mate **6** friend **8** familiar, intimate **9** confidant **12** acquaintance

amino acid 4 dopa **6** leucin, lysine, serine, toluid, valine **7** cystein, cystine, glycine, leucine, proline, toluide **8** cysteine, dopamine, histidin, thyroxin, toluidin, tyrosine

Amis novel 8 Lucky Jim

amiss 3 bad **4** awry, poor **5** badly, wrong **6** afield, astray, faulty, flawed, guilty, rotten, sinful, unholy **7** wrongly **8** blamable, blameful, culpable, faultily **9** defective, imperfect **10** censurable **11** blameworthy, incorrectly, unfavorably **12** inaccurately **13** demeritorious, reprehensible

amity 6 comity **7** concord, harmony **8** goodwill **10** friendship, kindliness **11** benevolence **12** friendliness

Ammonite god 6 Molech

amnesty 6 pardon **10** absolution

Amnon *father:* **5** David *half sister:* **5** Tamar *mother:* **7** Ahinoam

Amon *father:* **8** Manasseh *son:* **6** Josiah

Amonasro's daughter 4 Aida

among 3 mid **4** amid **5** midst **7** between *prefix:* **5** inter

amorist 5 lover, Romeo **7** Don Juan, gallant **8** Casanova, lothario, paramour

amorous 6 erotic **7** amative, amatory, lustful **8** enamored **10** infatuated **11** aphrodisiac

amorousness 4 love **5** amour **7** passion

amorphous 8 formless, inchoate, unformed, unshaped **9** shapeless

amount 4 body, bulk, core, dose **5** add up,

equal, price, reach, run to, sense, total,
touch **6** budget, burden, dosage, embody,
matter, number, thrust, upshot **7** include,
purport, quantum, run into, subsume
8 approach, comprise, quantity **9** aggregate, substance **12** correspond to *owed:*
4 debt *Scottish:* **4** haet **7** bittock *small:*
3 bit, jot **4** atom, drop, iota, mite, whit
5 minim, spark, speck, trace **7** modicum,
smidgen **8** molecule, particle **9** scintilla
amour **4** love **5** lover **6** affair **7** liaison,
passion, romance **8** intimacy, intrigue
10 love affair **12** entanglement, relationship
amour propre **5** pride **6** vanity **7** conceit **8** self-love, vainness **9** vainglory
10 narcissism, self-esteem, self-regard
11 self-conceit, self-respect
13 conceitedness
amphetamines **5** speed **6** dexies, hearts,
uppers **7** bennies, Dexoxyn **8** greenies,
pep pills, Preludin **9** Dexedrine **10** Benze-
drine, Methedrine
amphibian *burrowing:* **9** caecilian
extinct: **7** eryopid *family:* **7** Hylidae, Ranidae **9** Bufonidae, Proteidae, Sirenidae
genus: **4** Bufo, Hyla, Rana **5** Acris, Siren
7 Aneides, Eurycea **8** Ascaphus, Ensatina,
Manculus, Necturus, Trituras **9** Ambys-
toma, Plethodon *legless:* **9** caecilian
order: **5** Anura **7** Caudata **9** Salientia
tailed: **3** eft, olm **4** newt **7** caudate, proteus, uredele **10** salamander *tailless:*
4 frog, hyla, toad **8** bullfrog, tree toad
10 batrachian, salientian *wormlike:* **9** caecilian *young:* **7** tadpole **9** polliwog
Amphion *brother:* **6** Zethus *conquest:*
6 Thebes *father:* **4** Zeus *mother:*
7 Antiope *sister:* **5** Aedon *wife:* **5** Niobe
Amphitrite *father:* **6** Nereus *husband:*
7 Neptune **8** Poseidon *mother:* **5** Doris
son: **6** Triton
Amphitryon's wife **7** Alcmene
ample **5** great, large, roomy **6** lavish,
plenty **7** copious, liberal, profuse **8** abundant, generous, handsome, prodigal, spacious **9** bounteous, bountiful, capacious,
plenteous, plentiful **10** commodious
amplify **5** swell **6** dilate, expand
7 develop, distend, enlarge, inflate
8 increase **9** elaborate
amplitude **4** size **5** scope, space
6 spread **7** bigness, breadth, expanse,
stretch **8** distance, fullness, wideness
9 expansion, greatness, largeness, magnitude, roominess **11** sizableness **12** sizea-
bleness, spaciousness **13** capaciousness
Amram *father:* **4** Bani **6** Dishon, Kohath
wife: **8** Jochebed
amulet **4** juju, luck, zemi **5** charm **6** fetish,
grigri, mascot **7** periapt **8** greegree, gris-

gris, talisman **10** lucky piece, phylactery,
rabbit-foot
Amulius' brother **7** Numitor
amuse **4** wile **5** charm **6** divert **7** animate,
beguile, delight, enchant, enliven **8** distract,
recreate **9** entertain, fascinate
amusement **9** diversion **10** recreation
11 dissipation, distraction **13** entertainment
amusement park **7** funfair
amusement show **8** carnival
amusing **5** droll, funny **7** comical, risible
8 humorous **9** laughable, ludicrous
Amycus *father:* **7** Neptune **8** Poseidon
friend: **8** Heracles, Hercules *mother:*
5 Melia
Amymone *father:* **6** Danaus *son:*
8 Nauplius
ana **5** varia **9** anecdotes **10** collection, miscellany **11** memorabilia
anabasis **5** march **7** advance, headway,
ongoing **8** progress **11** advancement,
proficiency
anadem **5** crown **6** wreath **7** chaplet,
coronal, coronet, garland
anagogic **6** mystic, occult **8** mystical,
telestic **9** symbolical **11** allegorical
analects **4** posy **5** album **7** garland, omnibus **9** anthology **10** miscellany
11 florilegium
analgesic **7** anodyne **10** anesthetic, pain-
killer
analogous **4** akin, like **5** alike **7** kindred,
similar, uniform **8** parallel **9** consonant
10 comparable
analogue **5** match **7** cognate **8** congener,
parallel **9** correlate **11** counterpart, countertype **13** correspondent
analogy **6** simile **8** affinity, likeness, metaphor **9** alikeness, semblance **10** comparison, similarity, similitude **11** resemblance
analysis **4** scan, view **5** audit **6** review,
survey **7** breakup, checkup **8** exegesis,
scrutiny **9** breakdown **10** dissection,
inspection, resolution **11** examination
13 perlustration
analytic **4** keen **5** acute, sharp **6** subtle
7 logical **8** piercing **11** penetrating
13 ratiocinative
analyze **7** dissect, examine, inspect,
resolve **8** classify **9** anatomize, break
down, decompose **10** decompound, scrutinize **11** investigate
analyze grammatically **5** parse
Ananias **4** liar **6** fibber **7** fibster **8** perjurer **9** falsifier **11** storyteller **12** prevaricator *coconspirator:* **8** Sapphira *father:*
9 Nedebaeus *wife:* **8** Sapphira
anarch see **anarchist**
anarchism **4** riot **7** misrule **8** disorder
9 distemper

anarchist 5 rebel 8 frondeur, mutineer, revolter 9 insurgent 10 malcontent

anarchy 4 riot 5 chaos 7 misrule 8 disorder 9 distemper, mobocracy 10 ochlocracy 11 lawlessness

anathema 5 curse 6 pariah 7 bugbear, censure, malison, outcast, reproof 9 bête noire 10 black beast 11 abomination, commination, detestation, imprecation, malediction 12 condemnation, denunciation

anathematize 4 damn 5 curse 8 execrate 9 objurgate

anatomical depression 5 fossa, fovea

anatomical tube 3 vas 4 duct 5 canal

anatomist 5 Wolff 6 Harvey 8 Vesalius

anatomize 7 analyze, dissect, resolve 9 break down, decompose 10 decompound

Anaxarete's lover 5 Iphis

Anaxo *brother:* 10 Amphitryon *daughter:* 7 Alcmene *father:* 7 Alcaeus *husband:* 9 Electryon

ancestor 8 forebear, foregoer 9 ascendant, precursor, prototype 10 antecedent, antecessor, forefather, forerunner, progenitor 11 predecessor 12 primogenitor

ancestral sequence 8 pedigree 9 bloodline, genealogy

ancestry 4 race 5 blood, breed, stock 6 family, origin, source 7 descent, kindred, lineage 8 pedigree 10 derivation, extraction

Anchises' son 6 Aeneas

anchor 3 fix 4 moor 5 catch 6 fasten, secure 7 grapnel, killick, killock *line:* 7 catfall *part:* 4 ring 5 crown, fluke, shank

anchorage 4 port 5 chuck, haven, roads 6 harbor, riding 7 mooring 9 harborage, roadstead

anchors ___ 6 aweigh

ancient 3 old 4 aged 5 elder, hoary, olden 6 age-old, doting, primal, senior 7 antique, elderly, oldster 8 Noachian, oldtimer, primeval, timeworn 9 doddering, venerable 10 primordial 12 antediluvian *combining form:* 4 pale 5 palae, paleo 6 archae, archeo, palaeo 7 archaeo

ancient capital 4 Susa 5 Balkh, Calah, Isker, Kalhu, Ninus, Sibir 6 Bactra, Nimrud 7 Nineveh, Shushan 10 Persepolis

ancient city *Asia Minor:* 4 Nice, Teos 5 Tyana 6 Edessa, Nicaea 7 Antioch 13 Halicarnassus *Babylonia:* 4 Sura 5 Accad, Agade, Akkad, Eridu, Larsa 7 Ellasar *Bengal:* 4 Gaur 9 Lakhnauti *Canaan:* 5 Gezer *Cyprus:* 7 Salamis *Egypt:* 2 On 6 Thebes 7 Memphis 10 Heliopolis *Etruria:* 4 Veii *Euphrates River:* 7 Babylon *Greece:* 5 Crisa 6 Athens, Sparta 7 Calydon 10 Lacedaemon *Ionia:* 4 Myus, Teos 5 Chios, Samos 6 Priene 7 Ephesus, Lebedos, Miletus, Phocaea 8 Colophon, Erythrae 10 Clazomenae *Italy:* 5 Locri 7 Pompeii 11 Herculaneum *Latium:* 5 Gabii 9 Alba Longa *Mayan:* 4 Coba 5 Tikal *Nile River:* 5 Meroe *North Africa:* 5 Utica 8 Carthage *Palestine:* 4 Gaza 5 Ekron, Endor, Sodom 6 Beroea, Bethel, Gilead, Hebron 7 Jericho, Samaria 8 Ashkelon 9 Capernaum, Jerusalem *Peloponnesus:* 5 Tegea 6 Sparta 7 Corinth *Sumeria:* 2 Ur 4 Kish, Uruk 5 Erech, Larsa 6 Lagash *Turkey:* 5 Assos, Assus 9 Byzantium *Yucatan:* 5 Uxmal

ancient country *Adriatic coast:* 7 Illyria *Africa:* 10 Mauretania *Arabian Peninsula:* 5 Sheba *Asia:* 4 Aram 5 Media, Minni, Syria 7 Armenia, Ash Sham, Bactria *Asia Minor:* 5 Lydia, Mysia 6 Aeolis, Pontus 7 Cilicia, Phrygia 8 Bithynia *Balkan:* 7 Macedon 9 Macedonia *Black Sea:* 7 Colchis *Dead Sea:* 4 Edom *Euphrates River:* 9 Babylonia *Europe:* 4 Gaul 5 Dacia 6 Gallia *gold-rich:* 5 Ophir *Italy:* 6 Latium 7 Etruria *Nile valley:* 4 Cush *Peloponnesus:* 4 Elis 7 Arcadia *Syria:* 9 Phoenicia

ancient empire 6 Median 7 Hittite, Persian 8 Assyrian, Athenian, Chaldean, Egyptian, Seleucid 9 Ptolemaic 10 Babylonian

ancient kingdom *Anglo-Saxon:* 6 Wessex *Asia:* 4 Ghor, Ghur *Celtic:* 7 Cumbria *China:* 3 Shu *Euphrates valley:* 4 Hira 7 Al-Hirah *Greece:* 8 Pergamon, Pergamum *North Of Assyria:* 3 Van 6 Ararat, Urartu *Palestine:* 5 Judah 6 Israel *Persian Gulf:* 4 Elam *Portugal:* 7 Algarve *Spain:* 4 Leon 6 Aragon 7 Castile, Galicia, Granada, Navarre *Syria:* 4 Moab *Welsh:* 5 Powys *West Sahara:* 4 Gana 5 Ghana

ancient monument 6 sphinx 7 obelisk, pyramid

ancient royal forest 4 Dean 8 Sherwood

ancient town *Africa:* 4 Zama *Armenia:* 4 Dwin, Tvin *Asia Minor:* 4 Soli 5 Derbe, Issus, Soloi *Attica:* 6 Icaria *Black Sea:* 5 Olbia 9 Apollonia *Greece:* 4 Abae, Opus 8 Marathon *Italy:* 4 Elea, Luna 5 Cumae, Velia *Latium:* 5 Ardea, Cures *Macedonia:* 5 Pydna, Stobi 9 Apollonia *Peloponnesus:* 5 Asine *Persia:* 6 Hormuz 8 Harmozia *Sicily:* 5 Hybla *Spain:* 5 Munda *Tatar:* 5 Isker, Sibir *Wendish:* 5 Julin

ancilla 3 aid 4 help 6 helper 7 striker 9 assistant, attendant

ancillary 8 adjuvant, incident 9 accessory, attendant, attending, auxiliary, satellite 10 coincident, collateral, subsidiary 11 appurtenant, concomitant, subservient 12 accompanying, contributory

andiron 7 firedog

androgynous 8 bisexual
13 hermaphrodite
android 5 robot 9 automaton
Andromache *husband:* 6 Hector
7 Helenus, Pyrrhus 11 Neoptolemus *son:*
8 Astyanax, Molossus
Andromeda *father:* 7 Cepheus *husband:* 7 Perseus *mother:* 10 Cassiopeia
rescuer: 7 Perseus
___ **and warp** 4 woof
anecdote 4 tale, yarn 5 story 7 episode,
recital 8 relation 9 narration, narrative
anemic 4 pale 6 pallid, watery 8 waterish 9 bloodless
anent 2 re 4 in re 5 about, as for 7 apropos 8 touching 9 as regards 10 concerning 13 with respect to
anesthetic 4 dull, hard 5 rocky 7 anodyne 9 analgesic, bloodless, insensate
10 impassible, insensible, pain-killer
11 insensitive *combining form:* 5 caine
medical: 5 ether 6 spinal 7 eucaine
8 morphine, procaine 9 halothane, novocaine 10 benzocaine, chloroform, tetracaine 11 scopolamine
anesthetized 4 dead, numb 6 asleep,
numbed 8 benumbed, deadened 9 senseless, unfeeling 10 insensible 11 insensitive
anew 4 over 5 again 6 afresh, de novo,
lately, of late 8 once more, recently *combining form:* 2 an 3 ana 4 pali *prefix:* 2 re
angel 6 backer, cherub, patron, surety
7 sponsor 8 backer-up 9 celestial, guarantor *biblical:* 5 Uriel 7 Gabriel, Michael,
Raphael *fallen:* 7 Lucifer *hierarchy:*
6 powers 7 thrones, virtues 8 cherubim,
seraphim 9 dominions *of death:* 6 Azrael
angelic 4 holy 5 godly 7 saintly
8 cherubic
Angelica *father:* 9 Galaphron *husband:*
6 Medoro *lover:* 7 Orlando
anger 3 ire, irk, vex 4 bile, boil, burn, fume,
fury, huff, rage, rant, rave, rile 5 annoy,
pique, storm, wrath 6 blow up, choler, dander, enrage, madden, nettle, offend, seethe
7 affront, bristle, dudgeon, flare up, incense,
outrage, provoke, steam up, umbrage 8 boil
over, irritate 9 aggravate, annoyance, infuriate 10 exasperate 11 indignation, infuriation 12 exasperation
angered easily 4 rily 5 riley 9 irascible
angle 3 aim, axil, bend, bias, fish,
hand, hint, skew, turn 5 facet, phase, slant
6 aspect, crotch 7 flexure, outlook, turning
8 flection 9 direction, viewpoint 10 standpoint *combining form:* 3 gon 4 goni
5 gonio 6 anguli, angulo
Anglo-Saxon *army:* 4 fyrd *assembly:*
4 moot 5 gemot 6 gemote *coin:* 3 ora
5 sceat 6 mancus *council:* 9 heptarchy
county: 5 shire *court:* 4 moot 5 gemot

6 gemote *crown tax:* 4 geld *epic:* 7 Beowulf *free servant:* 5 thane, thegn *god:*
3 Ing *goddess of fate:* 4 Wyrd *historian:*
4 Bede *king:* 3 Ine, Ini 4 Edwy 5 Edgar,
Edred 6 Alfred, Edmund, Edward, Egbert
8 Ethelred *kingdom:* 4 Kent 5 Essex
6 Mercia, Sussex, Wessex 10 East Anglia
11 Northumbria *king's council:* 5 witan *letter:* 3 edh, eth, wen, wyn 4 wynn 5 thorn
nobleman: 4 earl *poet:* 4 scop *prince:*
8 atheling *sheriff:* 5 reeve 6 gerefa *slave:*
4 esne *tenant:* 6 geneat *village:* 3 ham
warrior: 5 thane, thegn
angry 3 mad 4 rily, sore, waxy 5 irate,
riley, upset, vexed, wroth 6 heated, ireful,
put out, shirty, wrathy, wrothy 7 enraged,
furious, uptight 8 choleric, incensed, maddened, worked up, wrathful, wrothful
9 indignant, perturbed, wrought up
10 aggravated, infuriated 11 acrimonious,
exasperated
anguish 3 rue, woe 4 ache, care, dole,
pain, pang 5 grief, throe, worry 6 regret,
sorrow 7 anxiety, torment, torture 9 heartache 10 affliction, heartbreak
angular 4 bony, lank, lean 5 crude, gaunt,
lanky, rough, spare 6 skinny 7 scraggy,
scrawny 8 rawboned, unworked 9 roughhewn, undressed 10 unfinished, unpolished 11 unfashioned
anima 4 soul 6 pneuma, psyche, spirit
9 élan vital 10 vital force
animadversion 4 slam, slur 7 censure,
obloquy 9 aspersion, criticism, stricture
10 accusation, imputation, reflection
11 insinuation 12 reprehension
animadvert 5 state, utter 6 remark
7 comment, declare, observe
10 commentate
animal 5 beast, brute, feral 6 brutal, carnal, ferine 7 beastly, bestial, brutish, critter,
fleshly, sensual, swinish, wilding 8 creature,
wildling *antlered:* 3 elk 4 axis, deer
5 moose 7 caribou 8 reindeer *aquatic:*
3 eel 4 fish, frog, seal 5 otter, whale
6 dugong, sea cow, walrus 7 dolphin, manatee, octopus 8 bryozoan, porpoise 9 alligator, crocodile *arboreal:* 2 ai 4 bird,
unau 5 chimp, coati, koala, lemur, sloth
6 gibbon, monkey 7 opossum, tarsier
8 kinkajou, marmoset, squirrel 9 orangutan
burrowing: 4 mole 5 brock, ratel
6 badger, gopher, marmot, rabbit
7 echidna 9 armadillo, groundhog, woodchuck *castrated:* 2 ox 5 capon, spado,
steer 6 barrow, wether 7 gelding *combining form:* 2 zo 3 zoa (plural), zoo 4 zoon
6 theria (plural) 7 therium *draft:* 2 ox
3 yak 4 mule, oxen (plural) 5 horse 6 donkey 8 elephant *exhibit:* 3 zoo *extinct:*
3 moa 4 dodo, urus 6 quagga 7 mam-

moth **8** dinosaur, eohippus, mastodon **9** solitaire, trilobite *female:* **3** cow, dam, doe, ewe, hen, pen, roe, sow **4** mare, puss **5** bitch, goose, jenny, nanny, vixen **6** jennet **7** lioness *four-footed:* **9** quadruped *four-limbed:* **8** tetrapod *free-swimming:* **6** nekton *hibernating:* **4** bear, frog, toad **5** skunk, snake **7** polecat **8** chipmunk **9** groundhog, woodchuck *horned:* **2** ox **3** ram, yak **4** bull, goat, ibex, kudu **5** addax, ariel, badak, bison, eland, rhino **6** cattle, koodoo **7** buffalo, gazelle, giraffe, unicorn **8** antelope *humped:* **2** ox **3** elk, yak **4** zebu **5** bison, camel, moose *imaginary:* **5** snark *insect-eating:* **4** mole, newt **5** gecko, shrew **6** numbat **7** echidna **8** aardvark, anteater, hedgehog, pangolin, tamandua **10** salamander *lover:* **8** zoophile *male:* **3** cob, ram, tom **4** boar, buck, bull, cock, stag, stud **5** billy, steer **6** gander **7** gobbler, rooster **8** bachelor, stallion *many-celled:* **8** metazoan *many-footed:* **9** centipede, millipede *marsupial:* **4** tait **5** koala **6** cuscus, numbat, wombat **7** dasyure, opossum, wallaby **8** kangaroo **9** bandicoot, phalanger *meat-eating:* **9** carnivore *mythical:* **4** yale **5** hodag, Hydra, kylin **6** bunyip, dragon, kraken, sphinx **7** centaur, griffin, mermaid, Pegasus, unicorn **8** basilisk, Cerberus, Minotaur *one-celled:* **9** protozoan *Peruvian:* **5** llama **6** alpaca, vicuna *plant-eating:* **9** herbivore *skin disease:* **5** mange *snouted:* **5** coati, tapir **8** mongoose; (see also **animal**, *insect-eating*) *spotted:* **4** axis, paca **6** calico, jaguar, ocelot **7** cheetah, leopard, piebald **8** skewbald **9** dalmatian *striped:* **4** kudo **5** tiger, zebra **6** koodoo, quagga *suffix:* **4** acea (plural) **5** acean *trail:* **3** pug **4** foil, slot **5** spoor *tusked:* **6** walrus **7** warthog **8** elephant *two-footed:* **5** biped *web-footed:* **4** duck, frog, toad **5** goose, otter **6** beaver **8** duckbill, platypus *young:* **3** cub, kid, kit, pup **4** calf, colt, fawn, foal, joey, lamb **5** bunny, chick, kitty, poult, shoat, stirk, whelp **6** cygnet, farrow, heifer, kitten, piglet **7** bullock, gosling, lambkin **8** suckling, yeanling, yearling **9** fledgling

animal behavior *study of:* **8** ethology

animal fat **4** suet **6** tallow

animalism **7** lechery **9** carnality **10** sensualism, sensuality, unchastity **11** fleshliness, lustfulness **13** lecherousness

animalize **4** warp **6** debase **7** corrupt, deprave, pervert, vitiate **9** brutalize **10** bestialize, demoralize

animal life **5** fauna

animals *suffix:* **3** ata, ida, ini **4** idae, idea

animate **4** fire **5** cheer, drive, exalt, impel, liven, nerve, steel **6** inform, vivify **7** actuate, chirk up, enliven, hearten, inspire, quicken,

refresh **8** activate, embolden, inspirit, motivate, vitalize **9** encourage, enhearten **10** invigorate, vivificate

animated **3** gay **4** cant, keen **5** alert, alive, canty, vital **6** lively, living, zoetic **7** zestful **8** spirited **9** exuberant, sprightly, vitalized, vivacious **12** high-spirited

animation **3** vim **4** brio, dash, élan, life, zing **5** oomph, verve **6** esprit, spirit

animosity **6** enmity, rancor **9** antipathy, hostility **10** antagonism

animus **4** plan, soul **5** design, enmity, intent, pneuma, psyche, rancor, spirit **7** meaning, purpose **9** antipathy, élan vital, hostility, intention **10** antagonism, intendment, vital force

Anius *daughter:* **4** Oeno **5** Elais **6** Spermo *father:* **6** Apollo *mother:* **5** Rhoeo

ankle **6** tarsus *combining form:* **4** tars **5** tarso

annals **7** history **9** chronicle

Anna's sister **4** Dido

annex **3** add, arm, cop, ell, nim, win **4** gain, hook, join, land, take, wing **5** affix, seize, steal, unite **6** append, attach, fasten, obtain, pick up, secure, take on **7** acquire, preempt, procure, purloin, subjoin **8** accroach, addition, arrogate, superadd **9** extension, sequester **10** commandeer, confiscate **11** appropriate, expropriate

Annie Oakley **4** pass

annihilate **4** raze, ruin, undo **5** abate, annul, crush, quash, quell, wrack, wreck **6** murder, negate, quench, squash, uproot **7** abolish, blot out, destroy, expunge, nullify, put down, root out, vitiate, wipe out **8** abrogate, decimate, demolish, massacre, suppress **9** eradicate, extirpate, slaughter **10** extinguish, invalidate, obliterate **11** exterminate

annihilative **7** ruinous **8** wrackful, wreckful **10** shattering **11** destructive

anniversary *hundredth:* **9** centenary **10** centennial *tenth:* **9** decennial *thousandth:* **10** millennial **11** millenniary

annotate **5** gloss **7** comment, explain **9** elucidate **10** commentate

announce **5** augur, sound **6** attest, blazon, herald **7** bespeak, betoken, declare, forerun, presage, present, publish, testify, witness **8** foreshow, foretell, indicate, proclaim **9** advertise, broadcast, harbinger **10** bruit about, promulgate **11** preindicate

announcement **9** broadcast **11** declaration, publication **12** proclamation, promulgation **13** advertisement

annoy **3** bug, irk, vex **4** bait, fret, gall, gnaw, miff **5** chafe, chivy, harry, peeve, tease, upset, worry **6** abrade, badger, bother, harass, heckle, hector, pester, plague, ruffle **7** agitate, bedevil, disturb, hagride, perturb, provoke **8** distress, exercise, irritate **9** beleaguer *Scottish:* **4** fash

annoyance **3** ire **4** pest **5** anger, trial **6** bother, irking, pester, plague, pother, vexing **7** teasing **8** distress, irritant, nuisance, vexation **9** besetment, bothering, pestering, provoking **10** affliction, botherment, harassment **11** aggravation, botheration, indignation, provocation **12** exasperation

annoying **5** pesky

annual **5** plant **6** flower, yearly **7** almanac **8** yearbook

annul **4** undo, void **5** abate, erase, quash **6** cancel, delete, efface, negate, revoke, vacate **7** abolish, blot out, expunge, nullify, redress, rescind, vitiate, wipe out **8** abrogate, dissolve **9** cancel out, discharge, frustrate **10** annihilate, counteract, extinguish, invalidate, neutralize, obliterate **11** countermand

annunciate **5** sound, state **7** declare, publish **8** proclaim **9** advertise, broadcast **10** bruit about, promulgate

anodyne **6** opiate **8** narcotic, nepenthe, sedative **9** analgesic, calmative, soporific **10** anesthetic, depressant, pain-killer **12** tranquilizer

anointing **7** unction

anomalous **6** off-key **7** deviant, foreign, strange **8** aberrant, abnormal, atypical, peculiar **9** deviative, divergent, irregular, unnatural, untypical **11** heteroclite **13** preternatural

anon **4** soon, then, when **5** again **7** by and by, shortly **8** directly **9** presently

anonym **5** alias **11** nom de guerre

anonymous **7** unknown, unnamed **8** nameless **9** incognito **10** innominate **11** unspecified **12** undesignated, unidentified, unrecognized

another **3** new **4** else, more **5** added, fresh **7** farther, further **10** additional

anschluss **5** union **6** league **8** alliance **9** coalition **10** federation **11** confederacy **13** confederation

anserine **5** silly **6** stupid **9** gooselike

answer **4** fill, meet **5** rebut, reply **6** come in, refute, rejoin, result, retort, return **7** fulfill, respond, satisfy **8** antiphon, rebuttal, response, solution **9** rejoinder **10** refutation **11** recriminate **13** countercharge

answerable **5** bound **6** liable **7** obliged **8** amenable **9** compelled, duty-bound, obligated **11** accountable, constrained, responsible

ant **5** emmet **9** carpenter *combining form:* **6** myrmec **7** myrmeco *relating to:* **6** formic *worker:* **6** ergate

Antaean **4** huge **5** giant **6** heroic

7 titanic **8** colossal, gigantic **9** cyclopean, Herculean **10** gargantuan

Antaeus *father:* **7** Neptune **8** Poseidon *mother:* **2** Ge **4** Gaea *slayer:* **8** Heracles, Hercules

antagonism **3** con **6** animus, enmity, rancor **7** discord **8** friction, opposure **9** animosity, antipathy, hostility **10** antithesis, opposition, oppugnancy, resistance **11** contrariety **12** disagreement

antagonist **3** con **4** anti **5** match **7** opposer **8** opponent **9** adversary, oppugnant

antagonistic **4** anti **6** averse, bitter **7** adverse, hostile, opposed **8** clashing, contrary, inimical, opposing **9** oppugnant, rancorous, vitriolic **10** antonymous, discordant **11** conflicting, contrariant, inconsonant **12** antipathetic, incompatible *combining form:* **7** enantio

ante **3** bet, pot **5** stake, wager

anteater see **animal,** *insect-eating*

antecede **7** forerun, precede, predate **8** foredate

antecedence **8** priority **12** previousness

antecedent **4** fore **5** cause, prior **6** former, reason **8** ancestor, anterior, forebear, foregoer, occasion, previous **9** condition, foregoing, precedent, preceding, precursor, prototype **10** forerunner **11** determinant, predecessor

antedate see **antecede**

antediluvian **3** old **4** aged, fogy **5** hoary **6** age-old, fogram, fossil, square **7** ancient, antique **8** mossback, Noachian, timeworn **10** fuddy-duddy **12** old-fashioned **13** stick-in-the-mud

antelope **3** gnu, kob **4** guib, koba, kudu, oryx, poku, puku, suni, tora **5** addax, beira, beisa, bongo, eland, goral, nagor, nyala, oribi, saiga, serow, tiang **6** dik-dik, duiker, grimme, impala, lechwe, lelwel, nilgai **7** blesbok, bubalis, chamois, defassa, dibatag, gazelle, gemsbok, gerenuk, grysbok, sassaby **8** agacella, bontebok, bushbuck, reedbuck, sing-sing, steinbok **9** duikerbok, kleeneboc, sitatunga, springbok, waterbuck **10** hartebeest **12** klipspringer *extinct:* **7** blaubok **9** blaauwbok *family:* **7** Bovidae *female:* **3** doe *four-horned:* **6** chouka **7** chikara **10** chousingha *male:* **4** buck *mythical:* **4** yale *young:* **3** kid

antenna **4** yagi **5** aerial, dipole **8** monopole

Antenor *father:* **8** Aesyetes *son:* **6** Agenor *wife:* **6** Theano

anterior **4** past **5** prior **6** former **8** previous **9** foregoing, precedent, preceding **10** antecedent

Anteros *brother:* **4** Eros *father:* **4** Ares,

Mars *mother:* 5 Venus 9 Aphrodite *opposite:* 4 Eros

anthology 3 ana 4 posy 5 album 7 garland, omnibus 8 analects, delectus, treasury 10 collection, miscellany 11 compilation, florilegium

anthropoid 3 ape 6 monkey 7 gorilla, manlike, primate 8 hominoid, humanoid 10 chimpanzee

anthropologist 4 Boas, Mead 5 Black, Keith, Sapir, Tylor 6 Dubois, Frazer, Hooton, Leakey, Linton, Morgan 7 Kroeber, Wissler 8 Benedict, Washburn 10 Malinowski 11 Weidenreich, Westermarck

anti 3 con 7 adverse, opposed, opposer 8 opponent, opposing 9 adversary, oppugnant 10 antagonist 12 antagonistic, antipathetic

antiaircraft fire 4 flak

antibiotic 7 colicin 8 viomycin 9 polymyxin 10 bacitracin, novobiocin, penicillin 11 bacteriocin, tyrothricin 12 streptomycin, tetracycline

antic 4 dido, lark 5 caper, comic, prank, trick 6 frisky, frolic, lively, pranky, shines 7 bizarre, comical, foolish, playful, roguish 8 farcical, gamesome, prankful, prankish, spirited 9 fantastic, grotesque, laughable, ludicrous, sprightly 10 frolicsome, rollicking, shenanigan, tomfoolery 11 mischievous, monkeyshine

anticipate 3 see 5 await 6 divine, expect 7 foresee, preknow, presage, prevent, previse 8 forecast, forefeel, foreknow, foretell, outguess 9 apprehend, forestall, foretaste, prevision, visualize

anticipation 10 expectancy 11 expectation

anticipatory 7 atiptoe 9 expectant, expecting

Anticlea *father:* 9 Autolycus *husband:* 7 Laertes *son:* 7 Ulysses 8 Odysseus

antidote 4 cure 6 remedy 7 negator 9 nullifier 10 corrective 11 counterstep, neutralizer 12 counteragent 13 counteractant, counteractive

Antigone *brother:* 9 Polynices *father:* 7 Oedipus *mother:* 7 Jocasta *sister:* 6 Ismene *uncle:* 5 Creon

Antilochus *father:* 6 Nestor *friend:* 8 Achilles *slayer:* 6 Memnon

antimony 7 stibium *combining form:* 4 stib 5 stibi, stibo 6 stibio *symbol:* 2 Sb

Antiope *father:* 6 Asopus *husband:* 5 Lycus 7 Theseus *queen of:* 7 Amazons *son:* 6 Zethus 7 Amphion 10 Hippolytus

antipasto 4 whet 7 zakuska 9 appetizer 11 hors d'oeuvre

antipathetic 7 adverse, opposed 8 aversive, clashing, contrary, opposing, opposite, ungenial 9 abhorrent, antipodal, loathsome,

obnoxious, oppugnant, repellent, repugnant, repulsive 10 antonymous, discordant, disgusting 11 conflicting, contrariant, distasteful, uncongenial 12 antagonistic 13 contradictory, unsympathetic

antipathy 6 animus, enmity, rancor 7 allergy, dislike 8 aversion, distaste, dyspathy 9 animosity, hostility 10 abhorrence, antagonism, repellency

antiphon 5 reply 6 answer, retort, return 7 respond 8 response 9 rejoinder

antipodal 5 polar 7 counter, reverse 8 contrary, converse, opposite 9 diametric 11 diametrical 12 antithetical 13 contradictory

antipode 6 contra 7 counter, reverse 8 contrary, converse, opposite 10 antithesis 11 counterpole 13 contradictory

antiquate 7 outdate, outmode 8 obsolete 9 obsolesce 12 superannuate

antiquated 5 dated, fusty, moldy, passé 7 antique, archaic 8 obsolete, old-timey, outmoded 10 oldfangled 12 old-fashioned

antique 3 old 4 aged 5 dated, hoary, passé 6 age-old 7 ancient, archaic 8 Noachian, old-timey, outdated, outmoded, timeworn 9 ancestral, out-of-date, venerable 10 antiquated, oldfangled 12 antediluvian, old-fashioned

antiquity *combining form:* 6 archae, archeo 7 archaeo

antiseptic 6 iodine 7 alcohol 8 peroxide 9 boric acid, carvacrol, germicide, merbromin 10 gramicidin 12 carbolic acid, disinfectant *pioneer:* 6 Lister

antisocial 7 ascetic, austere 8 eremitic, reserved, solitary 9 reclusive, withdrawn 11 introverted, standoffish 12 misanthropic

antithesis 3 con 6 contra 7 counter, reverse 8 antipode, antipole, contrary, converse, opposite, opposure 10 antagonism, opposition 11 contrariety, counterpole 13 contradictory

antithetical 5 polar 7 counter, reverse 8 contrary, converse, opposite 9 antipodal, diametric 10 antipodean 11 diametrical 13 contradictory

antlike 9 myrmecoid

Antony, Mark *defeat:* 6 Actium *friend:* 6 Caesar *lover:* 9 Cleopatra *wife:* 7 Octavia

Anubis' father 6 Osiris

anus *combining form:* 3 ano 5 proct 6 procta, procti, procto

anvil *combining form:* 5 incud 6 incudo

anxiety 4 care 5 doubt, dread, panic, worry 6 unease 7 concern 8 disquiet, distress, mistrust, suspense 9 suffering 10 solicitude, uneasiness 11 concernment, disquietude, uncertainty

anxious 4 agog, avid, keen 5 eager, scary,

upset **6** afraid, aghast, ardent, scared, uneasy **7** alarmed, fearful, jittery, worried **8** agitated, appetent, troubled **9** impatient, perturbed, terrified **10** breathless, disquieted, frightened **12** apprehensive

any 4 some

anyhow 6 random **8** at random, randomly **9** haphazard **11** any which way, haphazardly **13** helter-skelter

anytime 4 ever **5** at all

anyway 4 ever, once **5** at all

anywise see **anyhow**

A1 4 tops **5** prime **6** Grade A **8** five-star, superior **9** excellent, first rate, front-rank, number one, top-drawer **10** blue-ribbon, first-class

apace 4 fast **7** flat-out, hastily, quickly, rapidly, swiftly **8** speedily **9** posthaste **12** lickety-split **13** expeditiously

Apache chief 7 Cochise **8** Geronimo

apart 5 alone, aside **6** singly **7** asunder, isolate, removed, sky-high **8** detached, isolated, one by one **9** severally **10** separately **12** individually **13** independently, unaccompanied *combining form:* **4** dich **5** chori, dicho *prefix:* **3** dis

apart from 3 bar, but **4** save **6** except, saving **7** barring, besides **9** outside of **11** exclusive of

apartheid 10 separation, separatism **11** segregation **12** separateness

apartment 4 flat, room **5** rooms, suite **6** rental, walk-up **7** chamber, flatlet **8** lodgings, tenement

apathetic 3 dry **4** dull, limp **5** inert, stoic **6** stolid, torpid **7** callous, languid, unmoved **8** sluggish **9** impassive, untouched **10** anesthetic, insensible, phlegmatic, spiritless **11** indifferent, insensitive **12** matter-of-fact

apathy 6 acedia, phlegm, torpor **8** coldness, lethargy, obduracy, stoicism **9** disregard, inertness, lassitude, passivity, stolidity, torpidity, unconcern **10** detachment, dispassion **11** callousness, disinterest, impassivity, insouciance **12** heedlessness, indifference, listlessness **13** insensibility, insensitivity, unmindfulness

ape 4 copy, mime, mock **5** magot, mimic **6** baboon, gibbon, monkey, parody, pongid, simian **7** copycat, gorilla, imitate, take off **8** travesty **9** burlesque, orangutan **10** caricature, chimpanzee, orangoutan *combining form:* **6** pithec **7** pitheco **8** pithecus

aperçu 6 digest, précis, sketch, survey **7** pandect, sylloge **8** syllabus **10** compendium

aperitif 4 whet **5** drink **8** cocktail **9** appetizer

aperitive 5 sapid, tasty **6** savory **8** saporous, tasteful **9** palatable, toothsome

10 appetizing, flavorsome **13** mouth-watering

aperture 3 gap **4** gash, hole, slit, vent **5** break, chasm, cleft, slash **6** breach, outlet **7** opening, orifice, pinhole **8** puncture **10** interstice **11** perforation **13** discontinuity

apery 7 mimicry

apex 3 cap, tip, top **4** acme, cusp, noon, peak, roof **5** crest, crown, limit, point **6** apogee, climax, comble, culmen, summit, vertex, zenith **8** capsheaf, capstone, meridian, noontide, pinnacle, ultimate **9** crescendo, fastigium, sublimity **11** culmination, ne plus ultra **12** quintescence *combining form:* **3** ace **4** apic **5** apici, apico

Aphareus' son 4 Idas **7** Lynceus

aphorism 4 rule **5** axiom, gnome, maxim, moral **6** dictum, truism **7** brocard **8** apothegm

aphrodisia 4 itch, lust **6** desire **7** passion **9** eroticism, prurience, pruriency **11** lustfulness **13** concupiscence, lickerishness

aphrodisiac 6 erotic **7** amative, amatory, amorous

Aphrodite 5 Venus *consort:* **4** Ares **6** Vulcan **10** Hephaestus *father:* **4** Zeus **7** Jupiter *goddess of:* **4** love *mother:* **5** Dione *son:* **4** Eros **5** Cupid **6** Aeneas **7** Priapus

apiarist 6 beeman **9** beekeeper, beemaster

apical 3 top **7** highest, topmost **8** loftiest **9** uppermost

apiculture 10 beekeeping

apiece 3 all **4** each **5** aside **6** singly **8** one by one, per caput **9** per capita **12** individually, respectively

apish 7 slavish **9** emulative, imitative

aplomb 4 ease **5** poise **8** coolness, easiness **9** assurance, composure, sangfroid, self-trust **10** confidence, equanimity **11** nonchalance, savoir faire **13** self-assurance

apocalypse 6 oracle, vision **8** prophecy **10** revelation

apocalyptic 4 dire **5** vatic **6** mantic **7** baleful, baneful, direful, fateful, fatidic, ominous, unlucky **8** Delphian, oracular **9** ill-boding, prophetic, sibylline, vaticinal **11** prophetical, threatening **12** inauspicious

apocopate 5 elide

apocryphal 5 false, wrong **6** untrue **7** dubious **8** doubtful, spurious **9** incorrect, ungenuine **11** unauthentic

apogee 4 acme, apex, peak **6** climax, summit, zenith **8** capstone, meridian, pinnacle **11** culmination

Apollo 6 Helios **7** Phoebus *beloved:* **6** Cyrene, Daphne **8** Calliope *birthplace:*

5 Delos *father:* **4** Zeus **7** Jupiter *mother:* **4** Leto **6** Latona *oracle:* **6** Delphi *sister:* **5** Diana **7** Artemis *son:* **3** Ion **7** Orpheus *temple:* **6** Delphi

Apollyon 5 devil, fiend, Satan **6** diablo **7** Lucifer, Old Nick, serpent **9** Beelzebub **10** Old Scratch **13** Old Gooseberry

apologetic 5 sorry **7** defense **8** contrite, penitent **9** regretful, repentant **10** remorseful **11** attritional, penitential **12** compunctious **13** justification

apologia 7 defense **11** elucidation, explanation **13** clarification, justification

apologue 4 myth **5** fable **7** parable **8** allegory

apology 6 excuse **7** defense, redress, regrets, support **8** espousal, mea culpa **9** admission **10** advocating, advocation, concession, confession **11** championing **13** justification

aporetic 6 show-me **9** quizzical, skeptical **11** incredulous, questioning, unbelieving **12** disbelieving

apostasy 7 perfidy **9** defection, desertion, falseness, recreancy

apostate 8 defector, recreant, renegade, runagate, turncoat **9** turnabout **13** tergiversator

apostatize 4 turn **6** defect, desert **8** renounce **9** repudiate **10** tergiverse **12** tergiversate

a posteriori 9 inducible, inductive

apostle 4 John, Jude, Paul **5** James, Judas, Peter, Silas, Simon **6** Andrew, Philip, Thomas **7** Matthew **8** Barnabas, disciple, follower, Matthias, preacher **9** missioner **10** colporteur, evangelist, missionary **11** Bartholomew **12** propagandist *of Germany:* **8** Boniface *of Ireland:* **7** Patrick *of the English:* **9** Augustine *of the French:* **5** Denis *of the Gauls:* **8** Irenaeus *of the Gentiles:* **4** Paul *of the Goths:* **7** Ulfilas *to the Indians:* **9** John Eliot

apothecary 7 chemist **8** druggist **10** pharmacist

apothegm 4 rule **5** axiom, gnome, maxim, moral **6** dictum, truism **7** brocard **8** aphorism

apotheosis 6 height **7** epitome **8** last word, ultimate **9** elevation **10** exaltation **11** deification, ennoblement, idolization, lionization **12** enshrinement, quintessence **13** dignification, glorification

appall 3 awe **4** faze **5** daunt, shake **6** dismay **7** horrify, overawe **11** consternate

appalling 5 awful **7** fearful **8** daunting, dreadful, horrible, horrific, shocking, terrible, terrific **9** dismaying, frightful **10** formidable, horrifying

appanage 5 right **9** privilege **10** birthright, perquisite **11** prerogative

apparatus 4 gear, tool **6** outfit, tackle **7** utensil **8** materiel, tackling **9** equipment, implement, machinery **10** instrument **11** habiliments **13** accouterments, paraphernalia *combining form:* **4** stat

apparel 4 clad, duds, garb, togs **5** array, dress **6** attire, clothe **7** clothes, garment, raiment **8** clothing, enclothe **10** attirement **11** habiliments

apparent 5 clear, plain **6** patent **7** evident, obvious, seeming **8** distinct, illusive, illusory, manifest, palpable, semblant **9** prominent **10** Barmecidal, noticeable, observable, ostensible **11** discernible, perceivable, unambiguous, unequivocal

apparently *combining form:* **5** quasi

apparition 5 bogey, ghost, shade, spook, umbra **6** shadow, spirit, wraith **7** eidolon, phantom, specter **8** illusion, phantasm, revenant, spectrum **13** hallucination

appeal 3 beg **4** call, lure, plea, pray, pull, suit **5** brace, charm, crave, plead **6** allure, excite, invoke, orison, prayer, sue for **7** attract, beseech, entreat, glamour, implore **8** charisma, entreaty, interest, intrigue, petition **9** fascinate, importune, magnetism, seduction **10** allurement, attraction, supplicate **11** application, fascination, imploration **12** drawing power, solicitation, supplication

appealing 5 siren **8** alluring, charming **9** seductive **10** attracting, attractive, bewitching, enchanting **11** captivating, fascinating

appear 4 look, loom, rise, seem, show **5** arise, issue, sound **6** arrive, emerge **7** emanate **11** materialize

appearance 3 air **4** face, look, mien, pose, show **5** front, guise **6** aspect, facade, facies, manner **7** bearing, seeming, showing **8** demeanor **9** semblance **10** simulacrum **11** countenance *combining form:* **5** phane, phany

appease 4 calm **6** pacify, soothe **7** assuage, content, gratify, mollify, placate, relieve, satisfy, sweeten **10** conciliate, propitiate

appellation 4 name **5** nomen, style, title **7** moniker **8** cognomen **11** designation **12** denomination

append 3 add **5** annex **6** take on **7** subjoin **8** superadd

appendage 3 arm, fin, leg, tab, tag **4** barb, flap, horn, limb, seta, tail, wing **5** extra **6** cercus **7** adjunct, antenna, elytron, stipule **8** pedipalp, pendicle, tentacle **9** accessory, auxiliary **10** collateral, incidental, supplement **12** appurtenance, nonessential

appendix 5 rider **7** adjunct, codicil

8 addendum **9** accessory **10** supplement **12** appurtenance

apperception 5 grasp **11** recognition **12** apprehension, assimilation **13** comprehension, understanding

appertain 5 apply **6** bear on, belong, relate **8** bear upon

appetence 5 taste **7** stomach

appetent 4 agog, avid, keen **5** eager **6** ardent **7** anxious, athirst, craving, lusting, thirsty **8** desirous, yearning **9** impatient **10** breathless

appetite 4 bent, bias, itch, lust, urge **5** taste **6** desire, hunger, liking **7** craving, leaning, passion, stomach **8** cupidity, fondness, gluttony, penchant, soft spot, voracity, weakness **10** proclivity, propensity **11** inclination *combining form:* **6** orexia *insatiable:* **7** bulimia

appetizer 4 whet **6** canapé, savory, tidbit **7** zakuska **8** delicacy **9** antipasto **11** hors d'oeuvre

appetizing 5 sapid, tasty **6** savory **8** saporous **9** aperitive, palatable, relishing, toothsome **10** flavorsome **13** mouthwatering

applaud 4 clap, hail, laud, root **5** bravo, cheer, extol **6** kudize, praise, rise to **7** acclaim, commend **9** recommend **10** compliment

applause 4 hand **6** bravos, cheers **7** acclaim, ovation, rooting **8** cheering, clapping, plaudits **11** acclamation

apple 4 crab, pome **6** pippin, russet **7** Baldwin, costard, Duchess, Stayman, Wealthy, Winesap **8** Cortland, greening, Jonathan, McIntosh, pearmain **9** Delicious **10** Rome Beauty **11** Granny Smith, Gravenstein, Northern Spy, Transparent *combining form:* **4** pomi *genus:* **5** Malus *juice:* **5** cider *relating to:* **5** malic

applejack 5 cider **6** brandy

apple knocker 4 hick, jake **5** yokel **6** rustic **7** bucolic, bumpkin, hayseed, hoosier, redneck **10** provincial

apple-polish 4 fawn **5** cower, toady **6** cringe, grovel, kowtow **7** honey up, truckle **8** bootlick **9** brownnose

apple-polisher 5 toady **6** bootlick, clawback, groveler, lickspit **9** brownnose, sycophant **10** bootlicker, brownnoser, footlicker **11** lickspittle

applesauce 5 fudge, hooey **6** bunkum **7** baloney, rubbish, twaddle **8** malarkey, nonsense **9** poppycock **12** blatherskite

appliance 3 use **4** play **6** usance **9** operation **10** employment **11** application *kitchen:* **4** oven **5** mixer, range, stove **7** blender, toaster **9** can opener **10** dishwasher **12** refrigerator

applicability 3 use **5** avail **7** account, fit-

ness, utility **9** advantage, relevance **10** usefulness

applicable 3 apt, fit **4** just, meet **5** ad rem **6** seemly **7** apropos, correct, fitting, germane **8** apposite, material, pointful, relevant, suitable **9** befitting, pertinent **10** felicitous **11** applicative, applicatory, appropriate

applicant 6 seeker **7** hopeful **8** aspirant **9** candidate

application 3 use **4** heed, plea, suit **5** study **6** appeal, debate, orison, prayer, usance **8** entreaty, exercise, exertion, petition **9** appliance, attention, operation **10** employment, exercising **11** imploration, imprecation **12** deliberation, supplication **13** concentration, consideration

applicatory 5 ad rem **7** apropos, germane **8** apposite, material, pointful, relevant **9** pertinent

applied *combining form:* **6** techno

apply 3 use **4** bend, give, turn, urge **5** press **6** accost, appeal, bear on, bestow, devote, direct, employ, handle, relate, resort, take on **7** address, beseech, entreat, implore, pertain, utilize **8** approach, bear upon, exercise, petition, set about **9** appertain, importune, undertake **10** buckle down

appoint 3 arm, rig, tap **4** gear, name **5** equip **6** assign, finger, fit out, outfit **7** dress up, furbish, furnish, turn out **8** accouter, accredit, delegate, nominate **9** authorize, designate, embellish **10** commission

appointment 3 job **4** date, post, spot **5** berth, place, tryst **6** billet, office **8** position **9** situation **10** connection, engagement, rendezvous **11** assignation

apportion 3 lot **4** give **5** allot, allow, divvy, quota, serve, share, split **6** assign, bestow, divide, parcel, ration **7** deal out, dish out, dole out, measure, mete out, prorate **8** allocate, dispense, separate, share out **9** admeasure, partition **10** administer, distribute

apportionment 4 meed, part **5** quota, share **6** ration **7** measure, quantum **9** allotment, allowance

apposite 5 ad rem **6** timely **7** apropos, germane **8** material, pointful, relevant **9** pertinent **10** applicable **11** applicative, applicatory

appositeness 5 order **9** propriety **10** expediency **11** suitability

appraisal 5 stock **8** estimate, judgment **9** valuation **10** assessment, estimation, evaluation

appraise 4 rate **5** assay, audit, judge, set at, value **6** assess, survey **7** adjudge, examine, inspect, valuate **8** estimate, evaluate **10** scrutinize

appreciable 5 clear, plain **7** evident, obvious **8** apparent, concrete, manifest, material, palpable, sensible, tangible **10** detectable, observable **11** discernible, perceptible, substantial

appreciate 4 know, like, love **5** enjoy, grasp, prize, savor, value **6** admire, esteem, fathom, regard, relish **7** apprize, cherish, cognize, respect **8** treasure **9** apprehend, delight in **10** comprehend, understand

appreciation 7 tribute **9** gratitude **11** recognition, testimonial **12** gratefulness

apprehend 3 dig, nab, see **4** bust, fear, know, take, twig **5** catch, grasp, pinch, run in, seize, sense **6** absorb, accept, arrest, detain, digest, divine, fathom, pick up, take in, wise up **7** catch on, cognize, compass, foresee, make out, preknow, previse, realize **8** conceive **9** penetrate, recognize, visualize **10** anticipate, appreciate, understand

apprehensible 5 lucid **8** knowable, luminous **10** fathomable

apprehension 4 care, fear, idea **5** alarm, angst, dread, pinch, worry **6** arrest, notion, pickup, unease **7** anxiety, capture, concern, thought **8** disquiet **9** agitation, detention, misgiving **10** conception, foreboding, perception, solicitude, uneasiness **11** disquietude, premonition

apprehensive 5 alive, awake, aware **6** afraid **7** anxious, fearful, knowing **8** sensible, sentient **9** cognizant, conscious

apprentice 4 colt, tyro **6** novice, rookie **7** learner, trainee **8** beginner, freshman, neophyte, newcomer **9** novitiate **10** tenderfoot

apprenticed 5 bound **8** articled **10** indentured

apprise 4 clue, post, tell, warn **6** advise, fill in, inform, notify, reveal, wise up **8** acquaint, announce **11** communicate

apprize 5 value **6** esteem **7** cherish **8** treasure **10** appreciate

approach 4 near, nigh **5** reach, rival, touch, verge **6** accost, advise, amount, border, trench **7** address, advance, apply to, attempt, bespeak, consult **8** endeavor, overture **11** approximate

approaching 6 coming **7** nearing **8** oncoming, upcoming **11** forthcoming

approbate 5 favor **6** accept **7** approve **11** countenance

approbation 2 OK **4** okay **5** favor **6** esteem **8** approval, blessing, goodwill, sanction **10** admiration **11** benediction

approbatory 9 favorable

appropinquity 9 immediacy, proximity **10** contiguity

appropriate 3 apt, cop, due, fit **4** grab, just, lift, meet, take, true **5** annex, claim, exact, filch, grasp, pinch, right, seize, steal, swipe, usurp **6** assume, pilfer, proper, snatch, snitch, timely, useful, worthy **7** condign, desired, fitting, germane, merited, preempt, purloin **8** accroach, apposite, arrogate, deserved, eligible, entitled, relevant, rightful, suitable **9** befitting, opportune, pertinent, requisite, sequester **10** acceptable, admissible, applicable, commandeer, confiscate, convenient, felicitous, seasonable

appropriately 4 well **5** amply, right **8** properly, suitably **9** fittingly **10** acceptably, adequately, becomingly

appropriateness 3 use **5** order **7** account, aptness, fitness, service, utility **8** meetness **9** advantage, propriety, relevance, rightness **10** expediency, usefulness

appropriation 5 grant **7** stipend, subsidy **9** allotment, allowance **10** subvention

approval 2 OK **4** okay **5** favor **8** applause, blessing, sanction, suffrage **10** acceptance, compliment **11** approbation, benediction, endorsement **12** commendation

approve 2 OK **4** okay **5** clear, favor, go for **6** accept, back up, praise, ratify, uphold **7** applaud, certify, commend, condone, confirm, endorse, initial, stand by, support, sustain **8** accredit, hold with, sanction **9** approbate **10** compliment **11** countenance

approximal 8 abutting, adjacent, touching **9** adjoining, bordering **10** contiguous, juxtaposed **12** conterminous

approximate 4 near, nigh, rude **5** judge, place, rough **6** reckon **8** approach, estimate, relative **11** comparative

approximately 4 most, nigh **5** about **6** all but, almost, nearly **8** well-nigh **9** nearabout **11** practically

appurtenance 7 adjunct **8** appendix **9** accessory, appendage, equipment, furniture **11** furnishings

appurtenant 8 adjuvant **9** accessory, ancillary, auxiliary **10** collateral, subsidiary **11** subservient **12** contributory

a priori 8 dogmatic, reasoned **9** deducible, deductive, derivable

apriorism 5 posit **6** thesis **7** premise **9** postulate **10** assumption **11** postulation, presumption, supposition

apron 5 stage **8** pinafore

apropos 2 re **4** as to, in re, meet **5** about, ad rem, anent, as for **6** proper **7** germane **8** apposite, material, pointful, relevant, touching **9** as regards, pertinent, regarding **10** applicable, as respects, concerning, respecting **11** applicative, applicatory, in respect to **13** with respect to

Apsu *daughter:* **6** Lahamu *son:* **5** Lahmu *wife:* **6** Tiamat

apt 3 fit **4** just, meet **5** alert, given, prone,

quick, ready 6 bright, liable, likely, prompt, proper 7 apropos, fitting 8 apposite, disposed, inclined, relevant, suitable 9 befitting, pertinent 10 felicitous 11 appropriate

aptitude 4 bent, gift 5 flair, knack 6 genius, talent 7 ability, fitness 8 capacity, tendency 10 propensity 11 disposition

aptness 4 bent, gift 5 flair, knack, order 6 genius, talent 7 faculty, fitness 8 meetness 9 propriety, rightness 10 expediency 11 suitability

aquake 5 shaky 7 aquiver, shaking 9 quivering, shivering, trembling, tremorous, tremulant, tremulous

aqua vitae 4 grog 5 booze, drink, hooch 6 liquor, tipple 7 alcohol, spirits 9 firewater

aqueduct 5 canal 6 course 7 channel, conduit 11 watercourse

Aquila star 6 Altair

aquiver see **aquake**

Arab country 4 Iraq, Oman 5 Egypt, Libya, Qatar, Sudan, Syria, Yemen 6 Jordan, Kuwait 7 Algeria, Bahrain, Lebanon, Morocco, Tunisia 11 Saudi Arabia

arable 7 fertile 8 fruitful, tillable 10 cultivable, productive

Arachne *father:* 5 Idmon *form:* 6 spider *mother:* 6 Cyrene *rival:* 6 Athena 7 Minerva

arachnid 4 mite, tick 6 acarus, spider 8 scorpion 9 phalangid, tarantula 10 harvestman

Aran *brother:* 2 Uz *father:* 6 Dishan

arbiter 5 judge 6 umpire 7 referee 9 moderator

arbitrary 4 rash 7 erratic, wayward 8 absolute, arrogant, despotic, freakish, heedless, oracular, whimsied 9 autarchic, impetuous, tyrannous, vagarious, whimsical 10 autocratic, capricious, monocratic, tyrannical 11 dictatorial, magisterial, precipitate 12 unreasonable 13 authoritarian

arbitrate 5 judge 6 umpire 7 adjudge, mediate, referee 9 intervene 10 adjudicate 12 intermediate

arbitrator 5 judge 6 umpire 7 referee 8 mediator 9 moderator

arbor 5 bower 6 casino, gazebo 7 pergola 9 belvedere 11 summerhouse

arc 3 bow, lob 4 arch, bend 5 curve, round 7 rainbow 9 curvation, curvature

arcadia 4 Eden, Zion 6 heaven, utopia 8 paradise 9 Cockaigne, fairyland, Shangri-la 10 lubberland, wonderland 12 promised land

arcane 6 mystic, secret 8 numinous 10 cabalistic, mysterious, unknowable 11 inscrutable 12 impenetrable 13 unaccountable

Arcas *father:* 4 Zeus 7 Jupiter *mother:* 8 Callisto

arch 3 bow, coy 4 bend, hump, pert 5 chief, cocky, curve, first, fresh, roach, round, saucy, vault 6 bantam, camber, cheeky, cocket, impish 7 leading, playful, premier, roguish 8 champion, flippant, foremost, malapert 9 curvation, curvature, principal 10 coquettish 11 mischievous *inner curve:* 8 intrados *kind:* 4 flat, ogee 5 ogive, round, Tudor 6 lancet 7 rampart, trefoil 9 horseshoe, primitive, segmental 10 shouldered 11 equilateral *outer curve:* 8 extrados *part:* 8 keystone, springer, voussoir *pointed:* 4 ogee 5 ogive

archaeological site *Africa:* 8 Zimbabwe *Crete:* 7 Knossos *Egypt:* 6 Naqada 9 Al-Bahnasa 11 Oxyrhynchus *England:* 10 Stonehenge *Greece:* 7 Mycenae, Olympia *Iraq:* 2 Ur 4 Isin, Nuzi 5 Issin 7 Babylon, Nineveh *Israel:* 7 Jericho *Italy:* 7 Pompeii *Turkey:* 4 Troy 9 Hissarlik

archaeologist 5 Evans 6 Carter 7 Thomsen, Woolley, Worsaae 8 Breasted, Goodyear, Piranesi 10 Schliemann 11 Winckelmann

archaic 3 old 5 dated, passé 6 bygone 7 antique 8 outdated 9 out-of-date, primitive, unevolved 10 antiquated 11 undeveloped 12 old-fashioned *combining form:* 4 pale 5 palae, paleo 6 palaeo

arched 4 bent 5 bowed, round 6 curved 7 arrondi, rounded 8 arciform 11 curvilinear *combining form:* 3 tox 4 toxi, toxo

archer 4 Tell 5 Cupid 6 bowman 9 Robin Hood 11 Sagittarius

archery *combining form:* 3 tox 4 toxi, toxo

archetypal 5 ideal, model 7 classic, typical 9 classical, exemplary 12 paradigmatic, prototypical

archetype 5 ideal, model 6 mirror 7 example, pattern 8 exemplar, original, paradigm, standard 9 beau ideal, prototype 10 protoplast

archfiend 5 demon, devil, Satan 8 succubus

Archimedes' cry 6 eureka

archipelago *Asian:* 5 Malay *Canada:* 6 Arctic *Japan:* 4 Goto 9 Gotoretto *Norway:* 11 Spitsbergen *off Scotland:* 7 Orcades, Orkneys 13 Orkney Islands *off South America:* 14 Tierra del Fuego

architect 4 sire 5 maker 6 author, father 7 creator, founder 8 designer, inventor 9 generator, patriarch 10 originator *American:* 3 Pei 5 McKim, Stone, Weese, White 6 Breuer, Rogers, Soleri, Upjohn, Walter, Warren, Wright 7 Johnson, Latrobe, Renwick, Sturgis 8 Bulfinch, Saarinen, Sullivan, Thornton, Yamasaki 10 Richardson *Brazilian:* 8 Niemeyer *English:* 4 Shaw, Wood, Wren 5 Jones, Scott, Wyatt 6 Street, Voysey **8** Vanbrugh *Finnish:* **5** Aalto *French:* **6** Perret **11** Le Corbusier *German:* **8** Schinkel *German-American:* **7** Gropius *Italian:* **6** Romano **7** da Vinci, Orcagna, Peruzzi, Raphael, Vignola **8** Palladio, Sangallo, Terragni **9** Sansovino **12** Michelangelo *Japanese:* **5** Tange *Roman:* **9** Vitruvius

architecture **6** design, makeup **9** formation **11** composition **12** constitution, construction *ornament:* **4** boss, fret **5** gutta **6** finial, pampre, patera, volute **7** cabling, console, crocket, diglyph **8** encarpus, triglyph, vignette **9** arabesque, guilloche, modillion *style:* **5** Doric, Greek, Ionic, Tudor **6** Gothic, Norman, Rococo **7** Baroque **8** Colonial, Georgian **9** Byzantine, Victorian **10** Corinthian, Romanesque **11** Renaissance **13** Mediterranean

archive **6** record **7** library **8** document, monument **9** athenaeum

arch-shaped **8** arciform

arctic **3** icy **4** cold, cool **5** chill, gelid, nippy **6** chilly, frosty, hiemal **7** glacial, numbing **8** freezing, hibernal **11** hyperborean *animal:* **3** auk, fox **4** bear, hare, seal, vole **5** sable, whale **6** ermine, marten **7** caribou, lemming **8** reindeer **9** ptarmigan *base:* **4** Etah (Greenland) *bird:* **3** auk *cetacean:* **7** narwhal *current:* **8** Labrador *dog:* **5** husky **7** Samoyed **8** malamute, malemute *explorer:* **4** Byrd, Cook **5** Bylot, Davis, Peary **6** Baffin, Bennet, Bering, Henson, Hudson, Nansen, Nobile **7** Barents, Wilkins, Wrangel **8** Amundsen **9** Ellsworth, Mackenzie, Macmillan **10** Stefansson *forest:* **5** taiga *jacket:* **5** parka **6** anorak *people:* **4** Lapp **5** Aleut, Yakut **6** Eskimo, Koryak, Tungus, Zyrian **7** Chukchi, Samoyed **9** Kamchadal *sea:* **4** Kara **6** Laptev **7** Barents, Chukchi **8** Beaufort **9** Greenland *transport:* **7** dogsled *treeless plains:* **6** tundra

ardent **3** hot **4** agog, avid, keen, true **5** eager, fiery, loyal **6** fervid, heated, intent, red-hot, strong, torrid **7** anxious, athirst, blazing, burning, earnest, fervent, flaming, intense, staunch **8** appetent, constant, desirous, faithful, powerful, resolute, sizzling, vehement, white-hot **9** allegiant, impatient, impetuous, impulsive, scorching, steadfast **10** breathless, hot-blooded, passionate **11** impassioned **12** enthusiastic

ardor **4** fire, zeal, zest, zing **5** gusto, piety, verve **6** fealty, fervor, spirit, warmth **7** avidity, loyalty, passion **8** devotion, fidelity **9** calenture, eagerness **10** allegiance, enthusiasm **12** faithfulness

arduous **4** hard **5** rough, sheer, steep, tight **6** abrupt, trying, uphill **7** labored, operose, tricksy **8** sideling, toilsome **9** difficult,

laborious, strenuous **11** precipitate, precipitous

area **4** belt, zone **5** field, place, range, realm, scene, space, tract **6** domain, locale, region, sector, sphere **7** expanse **8** district, locality, province, vicinage, vicinity **9** bailiwick, territory **12** neighborhood *combining form:* **3** gea **4** gaea *dark, shaded:* **5** umbra *unit:* **4** acre **7** hectare

arena **5** scene **7** stadium, theater **8** coliseum **10** hippodrome **12** amphitheater

Ares **4** Mars *consort:* **5** Venus **9** Aphrodite *father:* **4** Zeus **7** Jupiter *mother:* **4** Enyo, Hera, Juno *son:* **5** Remus **7** Romulus

arête **5** crest, merit **6** virtue **7** quality **10** excellence, excellency, perfection

Arethusa's pursuer **7** Alpheus

argent **6** silver **7** silvern, silvery

Argentina *capital:* **11** Buenos Aires *monetary unit:* **4** peso

Arges **7** Cyclops *brother:* **7** Brontes **8** Steropes *father:* **6** Uranus *mother:* **4** Gaea

argon *symbol:* **2** Ar

Argonauts' leader **5** Jason

argot **4** cant **5** lingo, slang **6** jargon, patois, patter **7** dialect **10** vernacular

arguable **4** moot **7** dubious **8** doubtful **9** debatable, uncertain **10** disputable **11** problematic **12** questionable

argue **4** moot **5** claim, clash **6** assert, attest, bicker, debate, differ, hassle, object **7** agitate, bespeak, canvass, contend, discept, discuss, dispute, dissent, justify, protest, quarrel, quibble, stickle, testify, witness, wrangle **8** announce, conflict, disagree, indicate, maintain, polemize, squabble **9** thrash out **10** polemicize **11** expostulate, remonstrate

argument **3** row **4** fuss **5** theme, topic **6** debate, dustup, hassle, motive, reason, rumpus **7** dispute, polemic, sorites, subject, wrangle **8** rebuttal **10** contention, dissension, squabbling **11** controversy, disputation, embroilment **12** disagreement

argumentation **6** debate **7** dispute, mooting, oratory **8** forensic, rhetoric **9** dialectic **11** controversy, disputation

argumentative **9** litigious, polemical **11** contentious **12** disputatious **13** controversial

Argus *father:* **4** Zeus **7** Jupiter *mother:* **5** Niobe *slayer:* **6** Hermes **7** Mercury

argute **4** high **5** cagey, heady, savvy, sharp **6** piping, shrewd, shrill, treble **8** piercing **9** sagacious **13** perspicacious

aria **3** lay **4** hymn, lied, song **5** ditty **7** descant

Ariadne *father:* **5** Minos *husband:* **7** Theseus *mother:* **8** Pasiphae

arid 3 dry 4 drab, dull, sere 5 dusty, tepid
6 barren, boring, dreary 7 bone-dry, insipid,
sterile, tedious, thirsty 8 bromidic, droughty,
wearful 9 dryasdust, infertile, unwatered,
waterless, wearisome 10 unfruitful
12 moistureless 13 uninteresting
Ariel's master 8 Prospero
Aries 3 ram
aright 4 well 5 fitly 6 justly, nicely
8 decently, properly 9 correctly, fittingly
10 decorously
arise 4 lift, soar 5 begin, get up, issue,
mount, start 6 ascend, aspire, spring,
uprear 7 emanate, proceed 8 commence
9 originate
Aristaeus *father:* 6 Apollo *mother:*
6 Cyrene *son:* 7 Actaeon *wife:* 7 Autonoe
aristarch 5 momus 6 carper, critic, Zoilus
7 caviler, knocker 10 criticizer
11 faultfinder
aristocracy 5 elite 6 bon ton, gentry, jet
set 7 who's who 8 nobility, noblesse, smart
set 9 beau monde, blue blood, gentility,
haut monde 10 patricians, patriciate, upper
class, upper crust 13 carriage trade
aristocrat 9 blue blood, gentleman, patrician *ancient Greek:* 8 eupatrid *Russian:*
5 boyar 6 boyard
Aristophanes play 6 Plutus 8 The Birds,
The Frogs 9 The Clouds
arithmetic 4 math 8 figuring 9 ciphering,
reckoning 11 calculation, computation,
mathematics
Arizona *capital:* 7 Phoenix *college:*
11 Grand Canyon *motto:* 11 God Enriches
nickname: 16 Grand Canyon State *state
bird:* 10 cactus wren *state flower:*
13 saguaro cactus
Arkansas *capital:* 10 Little Rock *motto:*
13 The People Rule *state bird:* 11 mockingbird *state flower:* 12 apple blossom
arm 3 bay, ell, gun, rig 4 cove, gear, gulf,
wing 5 annex, bayou, equip, firth, force,
inlet, power 6 fit out, harbor, muscle, outfit,
slough, weapon 7 appoint, furnish, turn
out 8 accouter, strength 9 extension
bone: 4 ulna 6 radius 7 humerus *combining form:* 6 brachi 7 brachio *muscle:*
6 biceps 7 triceps
armada 4 navy 5 fleet
armadillo *genus:* 7 Dasypus *giant:*
4 tatu 5 tatou *nine-banded:* 4 peba, peva
relative: 5 sloth 8 anteater *seven-
banded:* 6 mulita *six-banded:* 5 poyou
6 peludo *small:* 5 pichi 10 pichiciago
11 quirquincho *three-banded:* 4 apar
5 apara *twelve-banded:* 5 tatouay
armament 4 ward 5 aegis, armor, guard
6 shield 7 defense 8 security 9 safeguard 10 protection

armamentarium 4 fund 5 stock, store
6 supply 9 inventory
armchair 8 fauteuil
armed *combining form:* 5 hoplo
armed attendant 9 bodyguard
armed forces 4 army, navy 6 troops
8 air force, military 10 servicemen
armistice 5 truce 9 cease-fire
armor 4 mail, ward 5 aegis, cover, guard
6 shield 7 buckler, defense, shelter 8 armament, security 9 safeguard 10 protection
arm: 8 brassart *armpit:* 8 pallette *buttocks:* 5 culet *coat:* 7 hauberk 10 brigan-
dine *combining form:* 5 hoplo *elbow:*
6 couter 9 cubitiere *face:* 5 visor 6 beaver
flexible: 4 mail *foot:* 7 sabaton, soleret
8 sabbaton, solleret *forearm:* 8 vambrace
hand: 8 gauntlet *head:* 6 helmet *horse:*
4 bard 5 barde 6 crinet 7 peytral, peytrel,
poitrel 8 chamfron, chanfron, criniere
knee: 11 genouillere *leg:* 4 jamb 5 jambe
6 greave 7 jambeau *mail:* 4 coif 7 hauberk 8 chausses *neck:* 6 camail *shoulder:* 7 ailette 8 pauldron, pouldron 9 epau-
liere *skirt:* 6 tonlet *suit:* 7 panoply *thigh:*
4 tace 5 cuish, tasse 6 tasset, tuille 8 flan-
card 9 flanchard *throat:* 6 gorget
armory 4 dump 5 depot 7 arsenal
8 magazine
armpit 6 axilla 8 underarm *Scottish:*
5 oxter
arms 7 ensigns, warfare 8 weaponry
army 4 host, rout 5 crowd, flock, horde
6 legion, scores 7 militia 9 multitude *combat arm:* 5 armor 8 infantry 9 artillery
commission: 6 brevet *Fort:* 3 Dix, Lee,
Ord 4 Hood, Knox, Polk, Sill 5 Bliss, Bragg,
Lewis, Meade, Riley 6 Carson, Eustis, Gordon, Monroe, Rucker 7 Belvoir, Benning,
Jackson, Shafter 8 Campbell, Holabird,
Huachuca, Monmouth 9 McClellan,
McPherson 10 Sam Houston 11 Leavenworth *law enforcer:* 2 MP *mascot:* 4 mule
meal: 4 chow, mess *mine layer:* 6 sapper
NCO: 8 corporal, sergeant *officer:*
5 major 7 captain, colonel, general, warrant 10 lieutenant *post:* 4 base, camp, fort
postal abbreviation: 3 APO *relating to:*
7 martial 8 military *school:* 3 OCS, OTS
7 academy 9 West Point *store:* 2 PX
10 commissary 12 post exchange *unit:*
5 corps, squad, troop 7 brigade, cavalry,
company, platoon 8 division, regiment *vehicle:* 4 jeep, tank 9 half-track
Arnold's coconspirator 5 André
aroma 4 balm, odor 5 scent, smell, spice
7 bouquet, incense, perfume 9 fragrance,
redolence
aromatic 5 balmy, spicy, sweet 6 savory
7 perfumy 8 fragrant, perfumed, redolent
9 ambrosial

around 4 back, near, nigh, over 5 about, again, circa 6 anyhow, extant, nearby, random 7 anywise, through 8 at random, existent, existing, randomly 9 haphazard 10 throughout 11 any which way, haphazardly 13 helter-skelter *prefix:* 4 ambi, amph, peri 5 amphi 6 circum

around-the-clock 8 constant 9 continual, incessant, perpetual 10 continuous 11 unremitting 13 uninterrupted

arouse 4 fire, stir, wake, whet 5 alert, pique, rally, waken 6 awaken, bestir, excite, incite, kindle, work up 7 inflame 9 challenge

arraign 3 tax, try 6 accuse, charge, indict 7 impeach 9 criminate, inculpate 11 incriminate

arrange 4 plan, sort 5 array, chart, order, unify 6 assort, codify, design, devise, lay out, map out, scheme, set out 7 dispose, marshal 8 organize, sequence, tabulate 9 blueprint, harmonize, integrate, methodize 10 categorize, symphonize, synthesize 11 choreograph, orchestrate, systematize

arrangement 5 order, setup 6 layout, lineup, series 8 ordering, sequence 9 structure 11 disposition 12 distribution *combining form:* 4 taxy 5 taxis 6 tactic *of five objects:* 8 quincunx *suffix:* 4 osis

arrant 4 rank 5 gross, total, utter 6 brassy, brazen 7 blatant, flat-out 8 absolute, complete, impudent, infernal, overbold 9 barefaced, downright, out-and-out, shameless, unabashed 10 unblushing

arras 7 drapery 8 tapestry

array 3 lot 4 clad, garb, pomp, show 5 batch, bunch, clump, dress, group, order 6 attire, bundle, clothe, parade 7 apparel, arrange, cluster, display, dispose, garment, marshal, panoply, raiment 8 enclothe, organize, spectrum 11 systematize

arrears 3 due 4 debt 9 liability 12 indebtedness

arrect 6 raised 7 heedful, stand-up, upright 9 advertent, attentive, intentive, observant, regardful 10 straight-up, upstanding

arrest 3 nab 4 bust, halt, jail, stay, stem, stop 5 catch, check, pinch, run in, stall 6 collar, detain, lock up, pickup, pull in, retard, stop up 7 capture, contain, seizure 8 imprison, obstruct, restrain 9 apprehend, detention, interrupt 11 incarcerate 12 apprehension

arresting 6 marked, signal 7 salient 9 affective, appealing, prominent 10 attractive, enchanting, impressive, noticeable, remarkable 11 conspicuous, outstanding

arride 6 divert, please 7 beguile, delight, gladden, gratify 8 pleasure 9 delectate, entertain

arrival 6 advent, coming 7 success 8 entrance, incoming 9 emergence 10 appearance

arrive 4 come, show 5 get in, reach 6 show up, thrive, turn up 7 prosper, succeed 8 flourish

arriviste 7 parvenu, upstart 8 roturier 12 nouveau riche

arrogance 5 pride 6 hubris, hybris, morgue 7 disdain, hauteur 9 loftiness, superbity 11 haughtiness

arrogant 5 cocky, proud, puffy, wiggy 6 lordly, snooty, snotty, stuffy 7 bloated, haughty, pompous 8 cavalier, fastuous, insolent, superior 10 disdainful, peremptory, pontifical 11 domineering, highfalutin, magisterial, overbearing 12 supercilious 13 high-and-mighty, self-important *Scottish:* 7 paughty

arrogate 4 grab, take 5 annex, seize, usurp 6 assume 7 preempt 8 accroach, take over 9 sequester 10 commandeer, confiscate 11 appropriate, expropriate

arrondi 4 bent 5 arced, bowed, round 6 arched, curved 7 rounded 8 arciform 11 curvilinear

arrow *combining form:* 3 tox 4 toxi, toxo 7 hastato *poison:* 4 upas 5 urare, urari 6 antiar, curara, curare, curari, oorali 7 woorali, woorari 8 antiarin

arrow-like 6 beloid 7 hastate 8 sagittal 9 sagittate

arrowroot 3 pia 5 araru, tuber 6 ararao 7 coontie, maranta

arroyo 3 gap 4 draw 5 brook, chasm, cleft, clove, creek, gorge, gulch, gully 6 clough, coulee, ravine, stream 7 channel

arsenal 4 dump 5 depot, store 6 armory 8 magazine 10 depository, repository, storehouse

arsenic *symbol:* 2 As

arsonist 5 firer, torch 7 firebug 10 incendiary

art 5 craft, skill, trade 6 métier 7 cunning, finesse, know-how, slyness 8 artifice, foxiness, vocation, wiliness 9 cageyness, canniness, dexterity, expertise 10 adroitness, craftiness, handicraft, profession *combining form:* 4 typy 6 techno *faddish:* 6 kitsch *style:* 2 op 3 pop 6 rococo 7 baroque, Bauhaus, Islamic, optical, surreal 8 abstract, cubistic, romantic 9 arabesque, Byzantine, Christian, classical, dadaistic, realistic 11 Renaissance 12 naturalistic, surrealistic *suffix:* 3 ery 4 ship

Artegal's wife 11 Britomartis

Artemis 5 Diana *birthplace:* 5 Delos *brother:* 6 Apollo *father:* 4 Zeus 7 Jupiter *mother:* 4 Leto 6 Latona *priestess:* 9 Iphigenia

artery 3 way 4 path, road 5 aorta, track

6 avenue, street, vessel **7** carotid, highway **8** coronary **9** boulevard **12** thoroughfare

artful 3 sly **4** foxy, oily, wily **5** suave **6** adroit, astute, crafty, smooth, tricky **7** cunning **8** guileful **9** dexterous, insidious **10** diplomatic

arthropod 3 bee, fly **4** crab, moth **6** beetle, insect, shrimp **7** lobster **8** arachnid, barnacle, chilopod, diplopod, myriapod, myriopod **9** butterfly, centipede, cockroach, millipede **10** crustacean *body segment:* **6** somite, telson **8** metamere *class:* **7** Insecta **8** Symphyla **9** Arachnida, Chilopoda, Crustacea, Diplopoda, Pauropoda *limb segment:* **6** podite **8** podomere

Arthur see **King Arthur**

article 2 an **3** the **4** item **5** essay, paper, point, theme, thing **6** object **7** element **10** particular **11** composition, stipulation

articled 5 bound **10** indentured

articulate 3 say **4** join, oral **5** order, utter, vocal **6** fluent, prolix, relate, sonant, spoken, voiced **7** connect, phonate **8** eloquent **9** enunciate, garrulous, harmonize, integrate, pronounce, talkative **10** coordinate **11** concatenate **12** smooth-spoken

artifice 4 play, ploy, ruse, wile **5** craft, feint, guile, trick **6** deceit, device, gambit **7** cunning, knavery, slyness **8** foxiness, trickery, wiliness **9** adeptness, cageyness, canniness, chicanery, ingenuity, rascality, stratagem **10** adroitness, cleverness, craftiness **11** skulduggery

artificial 4 fake, mock, sham **5** dummy, false, put-on **6** ersatz, forced, unreal **7** assumed, feigned, labored, man-made, pretend **8** affected, spurious **9** contrived, imitation, insincere, simulated, synthetic, unnatural **10** fabricated, factitious, fictitious, substitute

artillery 6 rocket **8** cannonry, howitzer, ordnance, weaponry

artillery plant 11 burning bush

artisan 7 builder, workman **9** carpenter, craftsman

artist 3 ace **4** whiz **5** adept **6** expert, master, wizard, wonder **8** virtuoso **10** firstrater, past master, topnotcher *garb:* **5** smock *knife:* **7** spatula *medium:* **3** oil **5** chalk, paint **6** pastel **7** tempera **8** charcoal **10** watercolor *pigment board:* **7** palette *stand:* **5** easel *workshop:* **6** studio **7** atelier (see also **painter**)

artless 4 free **5** naive **6** simple **7** natural **8** trusting, unartful **9** childlike, ingenuous, unstudied **10** aboveboard, forthright, unaffected, unschooled **12** unartificial, unsuspicious

arty 8 imposing **9** overblown **11** pretentious **12** high-sounding

as 3 for **5** being, since, while **7** because **11** considering

Asa *father:* **6** Abijam **7** Elkanah *grandfather:* **8** Rehoboam *grandmother:* **6** Maacah

___ **as a pin 4** neat

as a rule 7 usually **8** commonly **9** generally **10** frequently, ordinarily

Ascanius 5 Iulus *father:* **6** Aeneas

ascend 4 lift, rise, soar **5** arise, climb, crest, mount, scale **6** aspire, uprear **7** upclimb **8** escalade, escalate, surmount

ascendancy 8 dominion **9** dominance, masterdom, supremacy **10** domination, prepotency **11** preeminence, sovereignty **13** preponderance

ascendant 6 master **7** regnant **8** ancestor, dominant, forebear **9** paramount, precursor, prevalent, sovereign **10** forefather, forerunner, progenitor **11** overbearing, predecessor, predominant, predominate **12** preponderant, primogenitor

ascension 4 rise **6** rising

ascent 4 rise **5** climb **6** rising **7** raising **9** elevation, uplifting

ascertain 5 learn **7** catch on, find out, unearth **8** discover **9** determine

ascetic 3 nun **4** monk **5** stern, stoic **6** hermit, severe **7** austere, eremite, recluse **8** anchoret **9** abstinent, anchorite, mortified **10** abstemious, astringent, forbearing, restrained **11** disciplined, selfabasing, self-denying *ancient Hebrew:* **6** Essene *Buddhist:* **5** bonze **7** bhikshu *early Christian:* **7** stylite *Hindu:* **4** Yogi **5** fakir, Yogin

Asclepius see **Aesculapius**

ascribe 3 lay **4** cite **5** refer **6** assign, charge, credit, impute **8** accredit **9** attribute

Asenath *husband:* **6** Joseph *son:* **7** Ephraim **8** Manasseh

aseptic 8 retiring **9** shrinking, unaffable, withdrawn **10** restrained **11** unexpansive

asexual 6 agamic **7** agamous *combining form:* **4** agam **5** agamo

as for 2 re **4** in re **7** apropos **8** touching **9** regarding **10** concerning, respecting

as good as 4 nigh **5** about **6** all but, almost, nearly **8** well-nigh **9** just about, nearabout **11** essentially, practically **13** approximately

ash 4 soot **7** cinders, residue **8** clinkers

ashake 6 aquake **7** aquiver, ashiver, quaking **9** quivering, shivering, trembling, tremulous

ashamed 6 abased, abject **7** abashed, hangdog, humbled **8** contrite, penitent **9** chagrined, mortified, repentant **10** humiliated **11** discomfited, embarrassed

ashen 4 gray, pale **5** faded, livid, lurid, waxen **6** doughy, pallid **7** ghostly, macabre **8** blanched, bleached **9** cinereous, colorless **10** corpselike

Asher *daughter:* **5** Serah *father:* **5** Jacob *mother:* **6** Zilpah *son:* **4** Isui **6** Beriah, Ishuah, Jimnah

Ashhur *father:* **6** Hezron *mother:* **5** Abiah

ashiver see **ashake**

Asia *country:* **4** Iran, Iraq, Laos, Oman **5** China, India, Japan, Nepal, Qatar, Syria, Yemen **6** Bhutan, Cyprus, Israel, Jordan, Kuwait, Taiwan **7** Bahrain, Lebanon, Myanmar, Vietnam **8** Cambodia, Malaysia, Maldives, Mongolia, Pakistan, Sri Lanka, Thailand **9** Indonesia, Kampuchea, Singapore **10** Bangladesh, North Korea, South Korea **11** Afghanistan, Philippines, Saudi Arabia *ethnic group:* **3** Han, Jew, Lao, Tai **4** Arab, Kurd, Moor, Shan, Thai, Turk **5** Karen, Khmer, Malay, Tajik, Tamil, Uzbek **6** Burman, Indian, Korean, Lepcha, Manchu, Mongol, Sindhi **7** Baluchi, Bengali, Chinese, Iranian, Persian, Punjabi, Tibetan **8** Armenian, Assyrian, Japanese, Javanese, Nepalese **9** Dravidian, Indo-Aryan, Pakistani, Sinhalese **10** Circassian, Montagnard, Singhalese, Vietnamese **13** Khalkha Mongol *language:* **3** Lao **4** Urdu **5** Hindi, Malay, Tamil, Uzbek **6** Arabic, Hebrew, Korean, Nepali **7** Bengali, Burmese, Khalkha, Kurdish, Persian, Tibetan, Turkish, Yiddish **8** Armenian, Japanese, Javanese, Mandarin **9** Cambodian **10** Vietnamese **15** Bahasa Indonesia

aside **4** awry **5** apart, askew **6** askant, aslant, aslope **7** askance, slantly **8** excursus, sideways **9** excursion, obliquely, slantways, slantwise **10** digression, discursion, divagation, slantingly **11** parenthesis

aside from **3** bar **4** save **6** bating, except **7** barring, besides **9** excluding, outside of **11** exclusive of

as if *combining form:* **5** quasi

asinine **5** silly **6** absurd, simple **7** fatuous, foolish, puerile, witless **8** mindless **9** brainless **10** irrational, weak-headed

ask **3** beg, bid **4** quiz, seek **5** crave, exact, query **6** appeal, demand, desire, invite **7** beseech, call for, canvass, consult, enquire, entreat, examine, implore, inquire, request, require, solicit **8** question **9** catechize, importune **11** interrogate *Scottish:* **5** speer, speir

askance **4** awry **5** askew **8** cockeyed **9** cock-a-hoop, crookedly, cynically **10** critically, doubtfully, doubtingly **11** skeptically **12** suspiciously **13** distrustfully, mistrustfully

asker **6** beggar, prayer, suitor **9** suppliant **10** petitioner, supplicant **11** supplicator

askew **4** awry **6** askant **7** askance **8** cockeyed **9** cock-a-hoop, crookedly

aslant **5** aside **6** aslope **8** sideways, sidewise **9** obliquely **11** slaunchways *combining form:* **5** plagi **6** plagio

asleep **4** dead, idle, numb **5** inert **6** dozing, numbed **7** defunct, dormant, napping **8** benumbed, deadened, inactive **9** exanimate, senseless, unfeeling **10** insensible, unanimated **11** unconscious **12** anesthetized

as long as **3** for **5** cause, since **6** seeing **7** because, whereas **11** considering

as much as **6** all but, almost **8** well-nigh **11** essentially, practically

asomatous **8** bodiless **10** discarnate, immaterial, unphysical **11** disembodied, incorporeal **13** insubstantial

aspect **4** look, mien, side **5** angle, facet, phase **7** bearing, seeming **10** appearance

asperity **5** rigor **8** acerbity, acrimony, grimness, hardness, hardship, mordancy, tartness **9** harshness, roughness **10** bitterness, difficulty, inclemency, inequality, unevenness **11** vicissitude **12** irregularity, irritability

asperous **5** harsh, rough **6** craggy, jagged, rugged, uneven **7** scraggy, unlevel **8** scabrous, unsmooth

asperse **4** slur **5** libel **6** defame, insult, malign **7** baptize, immerse, slander, traduce **8** christen, sprinkle **9** denigrate **10** calumniate, scandalize

aspersion **4** muck, slam, slur **5** abuse **7** calumny, obloquy, slander **9** invective, stricture **10** detraction, reflection **12** vituperation **13** animadversion

asphalt **7** bitumen **8** blacktop

asphyxiate **5** choke **6** stifle **7** quackle, smother **9** suffocate

aspirant **6** seeker **7** hopeful **9** applicant, candidate

aspiration **3** aim **4** goal **6** desire **8** ambition **9** objective **10** pretension **13** ambitiousness

aspire **3** aim, try **4** long, pant, rise, soar **5** arise, mount **6** ascend, hunger, thirst, uprear

aspiring **7** emulous, wanting, wishful **8** vaulting, yearning **9** ambitious

as regards **2** re **4** in re **7** apropos **8** touching **10** concerning, respecting

ass **4** donk, fool, jerk, moke **5** burro, idiot **6** donkey **8** imbecile **10** nincompoop *female:* **5** jenny *male:* **4** jack *wild Asian:* **5** kiang **6** onager **8** chigetai

assail **4** beat **5** beset, pound, storm **6** attack, buffet, fall on, oppugn, pummel, strike **7** aggress, assault **8** fall upon

assailment **5** onset **6** attack **7** assault, offense **9** offensive, onslaught **10** aggression

Assam silkworm **4** eria

assassin 3 gun 5 bravo 6 gunman, hit man 7 torpedo 8 murderer 9 cutthroat 10 gunslinger, hatchet man, triggerman *of Caesar:* 6 Brutus 7 Cassius *of Garfield:* 7 Guiteau *of J.F. Kennedy:* 6 Oswald *of Lincoln:* 5 Booth *of Marat:* 6 Corday *of R.F. Kennedy:* 6 Sirhan

assassinate 4 cool, do in, kill 6 finish, murder, rub out 7 bump off, execute, put away 8 knock off 9 liquidate

assault 3 mug, war 4 raid 5 beset, fight, onset, set-to, storm 6 assail, attack, fall on, onfall, strike 7 aggress, mugging, offense 8 fall upon, invasion 9 offensive, onslaught 10 aggression, assailment

assay 3 try 4 rate, seek 5 offer, value 6 assess, strive, survey 7 attempt, valuate, venture 8 appraise, endeavor, estimate, evaluate, struggle 9 undertake

assemblage 4 ruck 5 crowd, group 6 muster 7 company, turnout 9 gathering 10 collection 11 aggregation 12 congregation

assemble 4 call, form, make, mass, mold 5 amass, build, clump, group, shape 6 gather, muster, summon 7 cluster, collect, convene, convoke, fashion, marshal, produce, round up 8 congress, contrive 9 aggregate, forgather 10 accumulate, congregate 11 manufacture, put together

assembly 4 band, bevy, crew, ruck 5 bunch, covey, crowd, group, party, rally 6 muster, troupe 7 cluster, company, meeting 8 conclave 9 congeries, gathering 10 collection 11 association 12 congregation *American Indian:* 6 powwow *ancient Greek:* 8 ecclesia *ancient Roman:* 7 comitia *anglo-Saxon:* 4 moot 5 gemot 6 gemote 8 folkmoot, folkmote *ecclesiastical:* 5 synod 10 consistory *Hawaiian:* 3 hui *Irish:* 4 feis *legislative:* 4 diet 6 senate 8 congress 10 parliament *medieval English:* 7 husting *place:* 4 hall, room 5 agora 10 auditorium *Russian:* 4 duma *witches':* 6 sabbat 7 sabbath

assent 3 yes 5 agree 6 accede 7 consent 9 acquiesce, subscribe

assert 4 aver, avow 5 argue, claim, state, utter, voice 6 adduce, affirm, avouch, defend, depose, submit 7 advance, contend, declare, justify, profess, protest, publish, warrant 8 announce, constate, maintain, proclaim 9 broadcast, predicate, vindicate 10 promulgate 11 disseminate

assertive 4 sure 5 pushy 7 assured, certain, pushing 8 cocksure, emphatic, forceful, positive, sanguine 9 confident, insistent 10 aggressive, resounding 11 affirmative, self-assured 13 self-confident

assertory 5 pushy 7 pushing 8 militant 10 aggressive

assess 4 deem, levy, rate 5 assay, exact, judge, put on, set at, value, weigh 6 impose, reckon, survey 7 account, valuate 8 appraise, consider, estimate, evaluate

assessment 3 tax 4 duty, levy 5 stock 6 impost, tariff 8 estimate, judgment 9 appraisal, valuation 10 estimation, evaluation 12 appraisement

asset 6 credit 8 resource 9 advantage 11 distinction

assets 5 means, money 6 wealth 7 capital 8 bankroll, property 9 resources, valuables

assiduous 4 busy 7 moiling, operose, zealous 8 diligent, sedulous, tireless 9 laborious 11 hard-working, industrious 13 indefatigable

assiduously 4 hard 9 earnestly, intensely 10 thoroughly 11 intensively 12 exhaustively 13 painstakingly, unremittingly

assign 3 fix, set 4 cede, deed, give 5 allot, allow, refer 6 charge, convey, credit, define, impute, remise, settle 7 appoint, ascribe, lay down, mete out, station 8 accredit, allocate, make over, relegate, sign over, transfer 9 admeasure, apportion, attribute, establish, prescribe 10 pigeonhole

assignation 4 date 5 tryst 9 allotment 10 engagement, rendezvous 11 appointment, get-together

assignee 5 agent, proxy 6 deputy, factor 8 attorney

assignment 3 job 4 duty, task 5 chare, chore, stint 6 devoir 10 obligation

assimilate 5 adopt, liken, match 6 absorb, equate, imbibe, insorb 7 compare, inhaust, paragon 8 parallel 11 incorporate

assimilation 9 awareness 11 mindfulness, recognition 12 apperception 13 consciousness

assist 3 aid 4 abet, help, lift 5 do for, stead 6 relief, succor 7 comfort, help out, secours, support 8 benefact 9 cooperate

assistance 3 aid 4 help, lift 6 relief, succor 7 backing, comfort, secours, subsidy, support 9 upholding 10 subvention, supporting

assistant 3 aid 4 aide, help 5 aider 6 flunky, helper, lackey, minion, second, stooge 7 acolyte, ancilla, orderly, striker 8 adjutant, henchman 9 attendant, auxiliary, coadjutor 10 aide-de-camp, coadjutant, lieutenant 12 right-hand man

assistive 6 aidant, aiding 7 helpful 11 serviceable

assize 3 law 4 rule 5 canon, edict 6 decree 7 precept, statute 8 standard 9 ordinance, prescript 10 regulation

associate 3 pal 4 ally, chum, join, link, mate, yoke 5 buddy, crony, match, merge, unite 6 cohort, comate, couple, fellow, friend, hobnob, relate 7 bracket, combine, compeer, comrade, conjoin, connect, consort, partner 8 confrere, familiar, federate, intimate 9 affiliate, bedfellow, colleague, companion, copartner 10 accomplice, amalgamate, compatriot, complement, consociate 11 concomitant, confederate, correlative, counterpart, running mate 12 acquaintance 13 accompaniment, brother-in-arms, comrade-in-arms

associated *combining form:* 3 sym, syn

associated with *suffix:* 2 ic 4 ical

association 4 axis, bloc, club, hint 5 guild, order, tie-up, union 6 hookup, league 7 cahoots, circuit, concert, society 8 alliance, congress, overtone, relation, sodality, teamwork 9 coalition, undertone 10 conference, connection, federation, fellowship, fraternity, suggestion 11 affiliation, brotherhood, combination, conjunction, connotation, cooperation, implication, partnership 12 conjointment, organization, relationship, togetherness 13 collaboration

assort 5 class, group, order 7 arrange 8 classify, stratify 9 methodize 10 categorize, pigeonhole 11 systematize

assorted 5 mixed 6 fitted, motley, suited, varied 7 adapted, matched 8 chowchow 11 conformable, promiscuous 12 conglomerate, multifarious 13 heterogeneous, miscellaneous

assortment 4 olio 6 jumble, medley 7 mélange, variety 8 mishmash, pastiche 9 potpourri 10 hodgepodge, miscellany 11 gallimaufry

assuage 4 calm, ease 5 allay 6 pacify, soothe 7 appease, lighten, mollify, placate, relieve 8 mitigate 9 alleviate 10 conciliate, propitiate

as such 5 per se 13 intrinsically

assumably 6 likely 8 probably 9 doubtless

assume 3 act, don 4 fake, sham, take 5 bluff, feign, get on, posit, put on, seize, usurp 6 affect, draw on, expect, reckon, slip on, strike, take on 7 believe, imagine, preempt, premise, presume, pretend, suppose, suspect 8 accroach, arrogate, shoulder, simulate 9 postulate 10 commandeer, presuppose, understand 11 appropriate, counterfeit

assumed 5 put on 7 feigned 8 affected, delusory, putative, spurious 9 deceptive 10 artificial, factitious

assumption 5 posit 6 thesis 7 premise, surmise 9 apriorism, postulate 10 conjecture 11 supposition

assurance 5 nerve, troth 6 aplomb, parole, pledge, safety, surety 8 audacity, safeness, security, sureness, temerity 9 brashness, certainty, certitude, cockiness, composure, guarantee, hardiness, sangfroid, self-trust 10 brazenness, confidence, conviction, equanimity 11 presumption

assure 5 cinch 6 ensure, insure, secure 7 promise, satisfy 8 convince, persuade

assured 4 cool 6 secure 7 certain, decided 8 clear-cut, composed, definite, sanguine 9 collected, confident, unruffled 10 pronounced, undoubtful 11 unflappable 13 imperturbable, self-confident

assuredness 6 surety 9 certainty, certitude 10 confidence, conviction

Assyria *capital:* 5 Calah 7 Nineveh *city:* 4 Hara, Opis 5 Ashur, Assur, Kalhu 6 Asshur *god:* 3 Sin 4 Asur, Nabu 5 Ashur, Assur, Nusku 6 Asshur, Tammuz 7 Ninurta *goddess:* 6 Ishtar *king:* 3 Pul 6 Sargon 11 Sennacherib, Shalmaneser 12 Ashurbanipal, Assurbanipal *language:* 7 Aramaic *measure:* 4 cane, foot 5 gasab, makuk 6 artaba, gariba 7 mansion *queen:* 9 Semiramis *river:* 6 Tigris *writing:* 9 cuneiform

astatine *symbol:* 2 At

astern 3 aft 4 rear 5 abaft

Asterope *father:* 5 Atlas *mother:* 7 Pleione *sisters:* 8 Pleiades

as to 2 re 4 in re 7 apropos 8 touching 9 regarding 10 concerning, respecting

astonish 5 alarm, amaze 7 astound 8 affright, dumfound, surprise 9 dumbfound 11 flabbergast

astonishing 7 amazing 8 wondrous 9 marvelous, wonderful 10 astounding, miraculous, prodigious, stupendous, surprising 11 spectacular 12 breathtaking

astound 5 amaze 8 astonish, dumfound, surprise 9 dumbfound 11 flabbergast

astounding see **astonishing**

Astraea *father:* 4 Zeus 7 Jupiter *mother:* 6 Themis

astral 6 dreamy, starry 7 exalted, highest, stellar 8 sidereal 9 daydreamy, stellular, top-drawer, unworldly, visionary 10 topranking 11 daydreaming 12 otherworldly

astray 4 awry 5 amiss, badly, wrong 6 afield

astricted 5 bound 7 costive 10 obstipated 11 constipated

astringent 4 keen 5 acrid, harsh, sharp, stern, tonic 6 biting, bitter, severe, strict 7 ascetic, austere, caustic, cutting, styptic 8 incisive, roborant 11 contracting 12 constrictive

astrologer 11 Nostradamus

astrological aspect 5 trine 7 sextile 8 quartile 10 opposition 11 conjunction

astronaut 4 Ride (Sally) 5 Glenn (John),

Young (John) **6** Aldrin (Edwin), Lovell (James), Worden (Alfred) **7** Collins (Michael), Gagarin (Yuri), Schirra (Walter), Shepard (Alan), Yegorov (Boris) **8** Stafford (Thomas) **9** Armstrong (Neil), McAuliffe (Christa) **10** Tereshkova (Valentina)

astronomer *American:* **3** See **6** Lowell **7** Langley, Newcomb **8** Tombaugh **9** Pickering **11** Schlesinger *Austrian:* **13** Schwarzschild *Dutch:* **6** Sitter **7** Huygens *English:* **4** Ryle, Wren **6** Halley, Lovell **7** Lockyer, Parsons **8** Herschel *French:* **6** Picard **7** Laplace, Messier *German:* **4** Wolf **5** Vogel **6** Kepler, Muller, Struve *Greek:* **12** Eratosthenes *Italian:* **7** Galilei **12** Schiaparelli *Persian:* **11** Omar Khayyam *Polish:* **10** Copernicus *Swedish:* **7** Celcius *Swiss:* **6** Zwicky

astute 3 sly **4** deep, foxy, keen, wily **5** cagey, heady, savvy, sharp **6** argute, artful, crafty, shrewd, tricky **7** cunning, knowing **8** guileful **9** astucious, insidious, sagacious **13** perspicacious

astuteness 3 wit **6** acumen **8** keenness **10** shrewdness **11** discernment, penetration, percipience **12** perspicacity

Astyanax *father:* **6** Hector *mother:* **10** Andromache

asunder 5 apart

as usual 8 wontedly **10** habitually **11** customarily **12** consistently

asweat 5 puggy **8** perspiry **10** perspiring

as well 3 too, yet **4** also, even, just, more **7** besides, exactly **8** likewise, moreover **9** expressly, precisely **11** furthermore **12** additionally

as well as 6 beside, beyond **7** besides **12** over and above

as yet 5 so far **7** earlier, thus far **8** hitherto

asylum 4 home, port **5** cover, haven **6** covert, harbor, refuge **7** retreat, shelter **8** bughouse, loony bin, madhouse, nuthouse, security **9** harborage, sanctuary **10** booby hatch, crazy house, sanatorium **11** institution

asymmetric 6 uneven **7** unequal **8** lopsided **9** irregular **10** off-balance, unbalanced **12** overbalanced

Atalanta *husband:* **8** Melanion *suitor:* **10** Hippomenes

at all 4 ever, once **6** anyway, soever **7** anytime, anywise *Scottish:* **3** ava

ataraxy 8 calmness, coolness **9** composure, sangfroid **10** equanimity

atavism 9 reversion, throwback

ataxia 5 chaos, snarl **6** huddle, muddle **7** clutter **8** disarray, disorder **9** confusion

at close hand 4 near, nigh **6** nearby

atelier 6 studio **7** bottega **8** workshop

Athamas *daughter:* **5** Helle *father:* **6** Aeolus *son:* **7** Phrixos, Phrixus **8** Learchus *wife:* **3** Ino **7** Nephele

Athena, Athene 7 Minerva *attribute:* **3** owl **5** Aegis **7** serpent *father:* **4** Zeus *names:* **4** Alea, Nike **5** Areia **6** Ergane, Hippia, Hygeia, Itonia, Pallas, Polias **8** Apaturia **9** Parthenos, Promachos **10** Chalinitis *shield:* **4** Egis **5** Aegis *statue:* **9** Palladium *temple:* **9** Parthenon

athenaeum 7 library **8** archives

Athens *citadel:* **9** Acropolis *founder:* **7** Cecrops *last king:* **6** Codrus *marketplace:* **5** agora *rival:* **6** Sparta *senate:* **5** boule *temple:* **9** Parthenon

athirst 3 dry **4** avid, keen **5** eager **6** ardent **7** anxious, dried-up **8** appetent **9** impatient **10** dehydrated, desiccated

athlete 4 jock **6** player **7** acrobat, gymnast, tumbler

athlete's foot 8 ringworm

athletic 6 active, brawny, sinewy **8** muscular, vigorous **9** energetic, strenuous *contest:* **4** agon, game **5** match *field:* **4** oval, ring, rink **5** arena, court **7** diamond, stadium **8** gridiron *prize:* **3** cup **5** medal **6** trophy

athletics 5 games **6** sports **8** exercise **10** gymnastics, recreation **12** calisthenics

athwart 4 over **5** cross **6** across, beyond **9** crossways, crosswise **12** transversely

atiptoe 9 expectant, expecting **10** anticipant **12** anticipative, anticipatory

Atlas *brother:* **10** Prometheus *daughter:* **5** Hyads **6** Hyades **8** Pleiades **10** Atlantides *father:* **7** Iapetus *mother:* **7** Clymene *race:* **5** Titan *wife:* **7** Pleione

at last 7 finally

Atli *slayer:* **6** Gudrun *wife:* **6** Gudrun

atmosphere 3 air **4** aura, mood **6** aether, medium, milieu **7** ambient, climate, feeling, quality **8** ambiance, ambience **9** semblance **11** environment, mise-en-scène **12** surroundings *stratum:* **9** exosphere **10** ionosphere, mesosphere **11** chemosphere, ozonosphere, troposphere **12** stratosphere, thermosphere *sun's:* **12** chromosphere

atmospheric 4 airy **6** aerial **9** pneumatic

atoll 6 island *equatorial area:* **11** Baker Island *Indian Ocean:* **4** Male *Kiribati:* **4** Beru **5** Abaiang, Abemama, Apamama *Marshall Islands:* **4** Ebon, Mili, Ujae **6** Bikini **8** Eniwetok **9** Kwajalein *Northern Cook Islands:* **8** Manahiki *North of Samoa:* **7** Fakaofo *Pacific:* **5** Makin **8** Johnston **10** Butaritari, Palmerston *Tokelau:* **5** Atafu **10** Duke of York *Tuamotu:* **10** Anaa Island **11** Chain Island *Tuvalu:* **8** Funafuti

atom 3 bit, jot **4** iota, mite **5** minim, touch, trace **6** tittle **7** modicum, smidgen **8** particle *charged:* **3** ion **5** anion *group:* **7** radical

atomic particle 3 ion 4 beta, muon, pion
5 alpha, boson, meson 6 baryon, hadron,
lepton, proton 7 fermion, hyperon, neutron,
nucleon 8 electron, mesotron, neutrino,
positron, thermion *hypothetical:* 5 quark
6 parton

atomize 4 ruin 5 smash, wreck 6 rub out
7 destroy, shatter 8 demolish, destruct,
dynamite, nebulize 9 devastate, pulverize

at once 3 now 4 away 8 directly, first off,
together 9 forthwith, instantly, right away
11 immediately, straightway 12 concurrently, straightaway

atone 3 pay 6 repent 7 expiate, satisfy
10 compensate, recompense

atoner 8 penitent

Atossa *father:* 5 Cyrus *husband:*
6 Darius 7 Smerdes 8 Cambyses *son:*
6 Xerxes

atramentous 3 jet 4 ebon, inky 5 black,
ebony, raven, sable 10 pitch-black

at random 5 about 6 anyhow 7 anywise
9 haphazard 11 any which way, haphazardly 13 helter-skelter

Atreus *brother:* 8 Thyestes *father:*
6 Pelops *mother:* 10 Hippodamia *slayer:*
9 Aegisthus *son:* 8 Menelaus 9 Agamemnon 11 Pleisthenes *victim:* 11 Pleisthenes
wife: 6 Aerope

atrocious 4 foul, vile 6 horrid, odious, savage 7 heinous, noisome, obscene 8 shocking 9 desperate, execrable, loathsome,
monstrous, offensive, repulsive, sickening
10 abominable, despicable, disgusting, outrageous, scandalous 12 contemptible

atrocity 8 enormity, savagery 9 brutality
11 heinousness 13 monstrousness

atrophy 7 decline 8 downfall 9 decadence, downgrade 10 degeneracy, devolution 11 declination 12 degeneration
13 deterioration *combining form:* 4 necr
5 necro

attach 3 add, fix, tie 4 bind 5 affix, annex,
rivet 6 adhere, append, fasten

attached 7 sessile

attachment 4 love 6 fealty 7 loyalty
8 adhesion, devotion, fidelity, fondness
9 adherence, affection, constancy 10 allegiance 12 faithfulness

attack 3 fit 4 raid, rush 5 beset, blitz,
drive, fight, foray, onset, sally, siege, spasm,
spell, storm, throe 6 access, ambush,
assail, banzai, battle, charge, fall on, harass,
have at, invade, irrupt, onfall, savage, sortie,
strike, tackle, turn on 7 aggress, assault,
besiege, bombard, offense, seizure 8 fall
upon, outbreak, paroxysm 9 beleaguer,
incursion, offensive, onslaught, pugnacity
10 aggression, assailment 11 bellicosity
12 belligerence 13 combativeness *combining form:* 5 lepsy 6 lepsia, lepsis

attacker *combining form:* 6 mastix

attain 3 get, win 4 gain 5 reach, score
6 rack up 7 achieve, realize 10 accomplish

attainment 11 achievement, acquirement,
acquisition, realization

attempt 3 try 4 seek, stab 5 assay,
essay, offer, trial 6 strive 7 venture
8 endeavor, striving, struggle 9 undertake
11 undertaking

attend 3 aid 4 hear, heed, help, mind
5 watch 6 assist, convoy, escort, listen
7 care for, conduct, hearken, oversee
8 chaperon 9 accompany, companion,
supervise 11 consort with

attendant 3 aid 4 help 6 helper, lackey
7 ancilla, doorman, orderly, servant, striker
8 incident 9 ancillary, assistant, satellite
10 bridesmaid, coincident, collateral
11 chamberlain, concomitant 12 accompanying *ancient Roman:* 6 lictor *in court:*
7 bailiff 8 tipstaff

attendants 5 suite, train 7 cortege, retinue 9 entourage

attention 4 heed, mark, note 5 study
6 notice, regard, remark 7 amenity 8 courtesy, sedulity 9 assiduity, awareness, diligence, gallantry 10 absorption, cognizance,
observance 11 application, engrossment,
mindfulness, observation, sensibility
12 deliberation, sedulousness 13 concentration, consciousness, consideration

attention getter 4 ahem 5 gavel

attentive 5 alert, aware 6 arrect, intent
7 heedful, mindful 8 open-eyed 9 advertent, observant, open-eared, regardful
10 interested, thoughtful 11 considerate
13 concentrating

attenuate 3 sap 4 rare, slim, thin 5 blunt,
reedy 6 lessen, rarefy, shrink, slight, stalky,
subtle, twiggy, weaken 7 cripple, deflate,
disable, slender, squinny, subtile, tenuous,
unbrace 8 enfeeble, rarefied, wiredraw
9 dissipate, undermine 10 debilitate

attest 5 argue, swear, vouch 6 affirm, verify 7 bespeak, betoken, certify, point to,
testify, witness 8 announce, indicate
10 asseverate

attestation 5 proof 7 witness 8 evidence 9 testament, testimony 11 testimonial 12 confirmation

attic 4 loft 6 garret 8 cockloft

at times 9 sometimes 10 now and then
11 ever and anon, now and again 12 here
and there

attire 4 clad, duds, garb, togs 5 array,
dress 6 clothe, outfit 7 apparel, clothes,
garment, raiment 8 accouter, clothing,
enclothe 11 habiliments

attirement see **clothes**

attitude 4 pose 5 stand 6 stance 7 pos-

ture **8** carriage, demeanor, position, positure **11** point of view
attitudinize 4 pose **7** pass for, pass off,
posture **10** masquerade
attorney 5 agent, proxy **6** deputy, factor,
lawyer **7** counsel **8** assignee **9** barrister,
counselor, solicitor **10** counsellor
attract 4 draw, lure, wile **5** charm, court,
tempt **6** allure, appeal, draw in, entice,
invite, seduce **7** beguile, bewitch, enchant,
solicit **8** interest, intrigue, inveigle **9** captivate, fascinate, magnetize
attraction 4 bait, call, draw, lure, pull
5 charm, mecca **6** appeal, liking **8** affinity,
cynosure, sympathy **9** seduction **10** allurement **12** drawing power
attractive 4 cute, fair, sexy **5** bonny,
dishy, siren **6** comely, lovely, luring, pretty
7 Circean, likable **8** alluring, charming,
engaging, enticing, fetching, handsome,
inviting, magnetic, mesmeric, tempting
9 appealing, beauteous, beautiful, beckon-
ing, glamorous, seductive **10** bewitching,
enchanting **11** captivating, fascinating,
good-looking, tantalizing **13** prepossessing
attractiveness 5 charm **6** appeal, beauty,
glamor
attribute 4 mark **5** refer, trait **6** assign,
charge, credit, emblem, impute, symbol, virtue **7** ascribe, earmark, feature, quality
8 accredit, property **9** character
attrition 3 rue **4** ruth, wear **7** penance,
remorse **8** abrasion, friction **9** penitence,
penitency **10** repentance **12** contriteness
attritional 5 sorry **8** contrite, penitent
9 regretful, repentant **10** apologetic,
remorseful **11** penitential
attune 7 balance, conform **9** harmonize,
integrate, reconcile **10** coordinate, proportion **11** accommodate
atypical 3 odd **5** queer **7** deviant,
strange **8** aberrant, abnormal, peculiar
9 anomalous, deviative, different, irregular,
unnatural **11** exceptional, heteroclite
13 preternatural
auberge 3 inn **5** hotel, lodge **6** hostel, tavern **7** hospice **8** hostelry **9** roadhouse
11 caravansary, public house
Auber opera 10 Fra Diavolo
au courant 5 awake, aware **6** au fait,
versed **7** abreast, knowing, versant, witting **8** familiar, informed, sentient, up-to-
date **9** cognizant, conscious
10 acquainted, conversant **12** contemporary **13** up-to-the-minute
auction *Scottish:* **4** roup
audacious 4 bold, rash **5** brash, brave,
saucy **6** brazen, daring **7** valiant **8** fearless, impudent, insolent, intrepid, reckless,
unafraid, uncurbed, valorous **9** daredevil,
dauntless, foolhardy, shameless,

undaunted, venturous **10** courageous,
ungoverned, unhampered **11** adventurous,
impertinent, temerarious, uninhibited,
untrammeled, venturesome **12** contumelious, unrestrained **13** adventuresome
audacity 4 gall **5** brass, nerve **6** mettle,
spirit **7** courage **8** temerity **9** assurance,
brashness, cockiness, hardihood, hardiness,
impudence **10** brazenness
audible 5 aural **9** auricular
audibly 5 aloud
audience 6 public **7** hearing **8** audition
9 clientage, clientele, following
10 spectators
audile 5 aural **8** acoustic
audit 4 scan **5** check, probe **6** review, survey **7** checkup **8** analysis, scrutiny
10 inspection **11** examination **13** investigation, perlustration
audition 7 hearing **8** audience
auditory 5 aural **8** acoustic
au fait 4 able **5** right **6** decent, proper,
versed **7** abreast, capable, correct, versant **8** becoming, decorous, familiar,
informed **9** au courant, befitting, competent,
qualified **10** acquainted, conforming,
conversant
au fond 8 at bottom **9** basically, in
essence **11** essentially **13** fundamentally
Augean stable 3 sty **4** sink **5** Sodom
7 cesspit **8** cesspool
auger *combining form:* **6** trypan
7 trypano
Auge's son 8 Telephus
aught 4 zero **5** zilch **6** cipher **7** nothing
8 goose egg
augment 3 wax **4** hike, rise **5** boost,
build, exalt, mount, raise **6** beef up, expand,
extend **7** enlarge, magnify, upsurge **8** compound, heighten, increase, manifold, multiply **10** aggrandize
augmentation 4 rise **5** annex, extra,
raise **7** adjunct **8** addition, increase
9 accession, accretion, increment **10** complement, enrichment **11** enhancement
13 accompaniment
augur 4 bode, omen **7** betoken, portend,
predict, presage, promise, prophet, suggest **8** forebode, forecast, foreshow, foretell, indicate, prophesy, soothsay **9** adumbrate, foretoken, predictor, prefigure
10 forecaster, foreshadow, foreteller, prophesier, vaticinate **11** Nostradamus
13 prognosticate
augury 4 omen **6** boding **7** portent, presage **8** bodement **9** foretoken
10 prognostic
august 5 grand, noble **6** lordly **7** stately
8 baronial, imposing, majestic, princely,
splendid **9** grandiose **11** magnificent
___ **au lait 4** café

au naturel 3 raw 4 nude 5 naked
6 unclad 8 buff-bare, stripped 9 unclothed, undressed 10 stark-naked

aura 3 air 4 feel, glow, halo, mood
5 aroma 6 nimbus 7 aureole, feeling
8 mystique, radiance 9 emanation, semblance 10 atmosphere

aural 6 audile 7 audible 8 acoustic, auditory 9 auricular

aureate 7 flowery 8 sonorous 9 bombastic, overblown 10 euphuistic, rhetorical
11 declamatory 13 grandiloquent

auricular 5 aural 7 audible

Auriga star 7 Capella

aurora 4 dawn, morn 7 dawning, morning, sunrise 8 cockcrow, daybreak

Aurora 3 Eos *goddess of:* 4 dawn *husband:* 8 Tithonus *son:* 6 Memnon

auslander 5 alien 7 inconnu 8 outcomer, outsider, stranger 9 foreigner

auspex 5 augur 7 prophet 8 foreseer
10 forecaster, foreteller, prophesier, soothsayer 11 Nostradamus

auspices 5 aegis 7 backing 9 patronage
11 sponsorship

auspicious 6 benign, bright, dexter, timely 7 hopeful, rosy 9 favorable, fortunate, opportune, well-timed 10 prosperous, seasonable

Austen novel 4 Emma 10 Persuasion
17 Pride and Prejudice

Auster see **Notus**

austere 4 bare, dour, grim, hard 5 acrid, bleak, grave, harsh, sharp, stern 6 bitter, severe, simple, somber 7 ascetic, serious 9 stringent, unadorned 10 astringent

Australia *capital:* 8 Canberra *largest city:* 6 Sydney *monetary unit:* 6 dollar

Austria *capital:* 6 Vienna *dynasty:*
8 Habsburg, Hapsburg *monetary unit:*
9 schilling

autarchic 4 free 8 absolute, despotic, dogmatic, separate 9 arbitrary, imperious, sovereign, tyrannous 10 autocratic, autonomous, monocratic, tyrannical 11 independent, self-reliant

authentic 4 real, true 5 pukka, right, solid, sound, valid 6 trusty 7 certain, factual, genuine 8 accurate, bona fide, credible, faithful, reliable 9 simon-pure, undoubted, veritable 10 convincing, dependable, sure-enough 11 indubitable, trustworthy 12 questionless

authenticate 6 verify 7 bear out, confirm, justify, voucher 8 validate 11 corroborate
12 substantiate

author 4 sire 5 maker 6 father, penman, proser, scribe, writer 7 creator, founder 8 inventor, novelist, prosaist 9 architect, generator, patriarch 10 originator *American:* 3 Bly, Nin, Poe 4 Agee, Buck, Dana, Grey, King, Mann, Rand, Roth, Uris, West

5 Aiken, Alger, Barth, Crane, Harte, Oates
5 O'Hara, Paine, Steel, Stein, Stone, Stowe, Turow, Twain, Tyler, Welty, White, Wolfe, Wylie 6 Alcott, Bellow, Cabell, Cather, Clancy, Cooper, Ferber, Harris, Hersey, Holmes, Hudson, Hughes, Irving, Jewett, Kidder, London, Mailer, Miller, Morley, Norris, Parker, Porter, Potter, Runyon, Singer, Styron, Updike, Warren, Wilder, Wilson, Wister, Wright 7 Baldwin, Beattie, Clemens, Cozzens, Farrell, Gardner, Garland, Glasgow, Heyward, Howells, Jarrell, Johnson, Kerouac, Lardner, Malamud, Masters, Mumford, Nabokov, Rexroth, Richter, Roberts, Saroyan, Sheehan, Thoreau, Thurber, Wharton 8 Anderson, Caldwell, Faulkner, Marquand, Melville, Michener, Mitchell, Remarque, Rinehart, Salinger, Sandburg, Sinclair, Spillane, Stockton, Vonnegut
9 Burroughs, Dos Passos, Hawthorne, Hemingway, Isherwood, McCullers, Steinbeck, Wodehouse, Woollcott 10 Fitzgerald, Tarkington *Australian:* 4 West 5 White
10 Richardson *Austrian:* 5 Kafka 7 Suttner 10 Schnitzler *Canadian:* 3 Roy
5 Kirby 6 Atwood, Davies 7 Leacock, Raddall, Richler, Service 8 Woodcock 9 de la Roche, MacLennan *Chinese:* 5 Han Yu
Czech: 5 Capek *Danish:* 4 Rode, Wied
6 Jensen 7 Holberg *Dutch:* 6 Vondel
English: 4 Amis, Ford, Lyly, Saki, Snow, Ward, West 5 Defoe, Doyle, Eliot, Hardy, James, Lewis, Lowry, Milne, Powys, Reade, Spark, Swift, Waugh, Wells, White, Woolf, Young 6 Archer, Austen, Belloc, Brontë, Bunyan, Butler, Conrad, Graves, Greene, Hilton, Huxley, Lytton, Malory, Orwell, Powell, Sayers, Sterne, Storey, Walton 7 Ballard, Burgess, Dickens, Durrell, Fleming, Follett, Forster, Golding, Kipling, Maugham, Sassoon, Shelley, Sitwell, Southey, Surtees, Tolkien, Walpole, Wyndham 8 Christie, Forester, Koestler, Lawrence, Macaulay, Meredith, Sillitoe, Smollett, Strachey, Trollope, Zangwill 9 De Quincey, Du Maurier, Goldsmith, Mansfield, Masefield, Priestley, Radcliffe, Thackeray 10 Chesterton, Galsworthy, Richardson 12 Quiller-Couch *Finnish:*
7 Waltari 9 Sillanpaa *French:* 4 Gide, Hugo, Kock, Sade, Sand, Zola 5 Camus, Dumas, Sagan, Stael, Verne, Vigny 6 Balzac, Daudet, France, Proust, Sartre 7 Cocteau, Gautier, Malraux, Mauriac, Maurois, Merimée, Rolland, Romains, Simenon
8 Beauvoir, Flaubert, Marivaux, Rabelais, Stendhal, Voltaire 9 Giraudoux 10 Maupassant, Saint-Simon 12 Robbe-Grillet *German:* 4 Böll 5 Grass, Hesse, Storm, Tieck, Zweig 6 Toller 7 Fontane, Richter, Wieland 8 Hoffmann, Schlegel 9 Hauptmann, Sudermann 10 Wassermann *Greek:*

6 Lucian **11** Kazantzakis *Hungarian:*
5 Jokai *Icelandic:* **7** Laxness *Irish:*
5 Joyce **6** Stoker **7** Beckett, O'Connor,
Russell **8** O'Faolain, Stephens **9** O'Flaherty
Italian: **5** Verga **6** Silone **7** Manzoni, Mora-
via **8** Boccacio **9** Vittorini **10** Pirandello,
Straparola *Japanese:* **7** Mishima **8** Kawabata, Murasaki **9** Yokomitsu, Yoshikawa
Lebanese: **6** Gibran *Norwegian:* **3** Lie
6 Hamsun, Undset **8** Björnson, Kielland
Norwegian-American: **7** Rolvaag *Polish:*
7 Reymont **8** Zeromski **11** Sienkiewicz
Portuguese: **6** Pessoa *Roman:* **5** Pliny,
Varro *Russian:* **5** Gorki **7** Andreev, Tolstoy **8** Turgenev, Zamyatin **9** Lermontov,
Sholokhov **10** Dostoevsky **11** Dostoyev-
sky, Yevtushenko **12** Solzhenitsyn *Scottish:* **4** Lang **5** Scott **6** Barrie, Buchan
8 Urquhart **9** Stevenson *Spanish:*
6 Baroja **7** Alarcon **9** Cervantes *Swedish:*
7 Johnson, Rydberg **8** Lagerlof **10** Lagerkvist, Strindberg *Swiss:* **4** Wyss **6** Frisch
9 Spitteler *Welsh:* **4** Owen **5** Evans,
Wynne *Yiddish:* **4** Asch
authoritarian 6 strict **8** dogmatic **9** dictative, stringent **10** oppressive, totalistic
11 dictatorial, doctrinaire, magisterial
12 totalitarian
authoritative 4 sure, true **5** sound
8 accepted, attested, dogmatic, official,
orthodox **9** canonical, dictative, ex officio,
trustable **10** dependable, ex cathedra,
sanctioned **11** cathedratic, dictatorial, doctrinaire, irrefutable, magisterial, trustworthy
12 indisputable
authority 4 rule, sway **6** credit, expert,
master, weight **7** command, control, mastery **8** prestige, virtuoso **9** influence
10 domination, governance, government,
past master **12** jurisdiction
authorization 5 leave **6** permit **7** consent, go-ahead, mandate **8** sanction
9 allowance, clearance **10** green light, permission, sufferance
authorize 3 let **4** vest **5** allow **6** enable,
invest, permit **7** approve, empower,
endorse, entitle, license, qualify, warrant
8 accredit, sanction **10** commission
11 countenance
auto see **automobile**
autobiographer 6 memoirist
autobiography 4 life, vita **5** diary
6 memoir **7** journal **11** confessions
autochthonous 6 native **7** endemic
10 aboriginal, indigenous
autocracy 7 tyranny **9** despotism
12 dictatorship
autocratic 7 haughty **8** absolute, arrogant, despotic **9** arbitrary, tyrannous
10 tyrannical

autodidactic 10 self-taught **12** self-
educated
autograph 3 ink **4** sign **9** signature, subscribe **11** John Hancock
autoist 6 driver **8** motorist, operator
Autolycus *daughter:* **8** Anticlea *father:*
6 Hermes **7** Mercury
automate 8 robotize
automatic 8 habitual **9** impulsive, reflexive **10** mechanical, self-acting,
unprompted **11** instinctive, involuntary, perfunctory, spontaneous, unmeditated *combining form:* **4** self
automaton 5 golem, robot **7** android,
machine
automobile 3 bus, car **5** buggy, coupe,
racer, sedan **6** jalopy, tourer **7** flivver, hardtop, machine **8** dragster, motorcar, roadster, runabout *British:* **2** MG **6** Anglia, Austin, Jaguar **7** Bentley, Daimler, Hillman,
Sunbeam, Triumph **8** Vauxhall **10** Rolls-
Royce **11** Austin-Healy *French:* **5** Simca
7 Citroen, Peugeot, Renault *German:*
3 BMW **7** Porsche **10** Volkswagen
12 Mercedes-Benz *Italian:* **4** Fiat **6** Lan-
cia **7** Ferrari **8** Maserati **9** Alfa-Romeo
Japanese: **5** Honda, Mazda **6** Datsun,
Subaru, Toyota *Swedish:* **4** Saab **5** Volvo
automotive pioneer 4 Benz, Ford, King,
Olds **5** Evans, Roper **6** Cugnot, Duryea,
Lenoir, Winton **7** Daimler, Stanley
8 Morrison
Autonoe *father:* **6** Cadmus *husband:*
9 Aristaeus *mother:* **8** Harmonia *sister:*
5 Agave *son:* **7** Actaeon
autonomous 4 free **8** separate
9 autarchic, sovereign **11** independent
12 self-governed, uncontrolled
autopsy 8 necropsy **10** postmortem
auto racer 8 Foyt (A. J.) **4** Hill (Graham)
5 Clark (Jim), Petty (Richard), Unser (Al,
Bobby) **6** Fangio (Juan) **7** Brabham (Jack),
Stewart (Jackie) **8** Andretti (Mario)
autumn casualty 3 DST (Daylight Saving
Time) **6** leaves
auxiliary 4 aide **6** helper **7** reserve
8 adjutant, adjuvant **9** accessory, ancillary,
assistant, coadjutor **10** additional, collateral,
subsidiary **11** appurtenant, subservient
12 contributory **13** complementary, supplementary *verb:* **2** am, do, is **3** are, can, did,
had, has, may, was **4** been, does, have,
must, were, will **5** could, might, ought, shall,
would **6** should
avail 3 use **5** serve **6** profit **7** account,
benefit, fitness, service **9** advantage, relevance **10** usefulness **13** applicability
available 8 gettable **9** securable
10 attainable, obtainable, procurable
11 purchasable

avalanche 5 flood, slide 8 mudslide, rockfall 9 landslide, rockslide, snowslide

avarice 5 greed 7 avidity 8 cupidity, rapacity 10 greediness 12 covetousness, graspingness

avenge 5 repay, right 7 pay back, redress, requite 9 retaliate, retribute, vindicate

avengement 7 revenge 8 reprisal, requital, revanche 9 vengeance 11 counterblow, retaliation, retribution

avenue 3 way 4 path, road 5 track 6 artery, street 7 highway 9 boulevard 12 thoroughfare

aver 4 avow 5 state 6 affirm, assert, avouch, depose 7 declare, profess, protest 8 constate, maintain 9 predicate

average 3 par 4 fair, mean, norm, so-so 6 common, median, medium 8 mediocre, middling, moderate, ordinary 11 indifferent 12 intermediate

averagely 4 so-so 6 enough, fairly, rather 8 passably 9 tolerably 10 moderately

avernal 7 hellish, stygian 8 infernal, plutonic 9 cimmerian, plutonian

averse 5 balky, loath 6 afraid 7 uneager 8 backward, hesitant 9 reluctant, resistant, unwilling 10 indisposed 11 disinclined

aversion 4 fear, hate 5 dread 6 hatred, horror 7 allergy, disgust, dislike 8 disfavor, distaste, dyspathy, loathing 9 antipathy, disliking, disrelish, repulsion, revulsion 10 abhorrence, antagonism, repugnance 11 abomination, detestation, displeasure 13 indisposition

aversive 8 ungenial 9 repellent, repugnant 11 uncongenial 12 antipathetic 13 unsympathetic

avert 4 foil, turn, veer, ward 5 check, deter 6 thwart 7 deflect, forfend, obviate, prevent, rule out 8 preclude, stave off
9 forestall, frustrate

avian 8 ornithic

aviary 4 cage 6 volary 8 dovecote, ornithon 9 birdhouse, columbary, dovehouse

aviator 3 ace 5 flier, pilot 6 airman, flyboy, Wright 7 birdman, Earhart 9 Lindbergh 10 Richthofen 12 Rickenbacker

avid 4 agog, keen 5 eager 6 ardent, greedy 7 anxious, athirst, craving, thirsty, wanting 8 appetent, covetous, desirous 9 impatient 10 breathless

avidity 5 greed 7 avarice 8 cupidity, rapacity

avoid 4 bilk, duck, shun, snub 5 avert, elude, evade, shirk 6 bypass, divert, escape, eschew 7 obviate, prevent 8 preclude

avoidance 6 escape 7 come-off, elusion, evasion 8 escaping, escapism, eschewal, shunning 9 runaround *combining form:* 4 phob 5 phobo

avouch 3 own 4 aver, avow 5 admit 6 affirm, assert, depose 7 confess, confirm, declare, profess, protest 8 constate 9 predicate 11 acknowledge, corroborate

avow 3 own 4 aver 5 admit, allow, grant, let on, own up 6 affirm, assert, avouch, depose, fess up 7 concede, confess, declare, profess, protest 8 constate, maintain 9 predicate 11 acknowledge

await 4 hope 6 expect 7 count on

awake 4 stir 5 alive, aware, rouse 6 roused 7 aroused 8 sensible, sentient 9 au courant, cognizant, conscious, stirred up

awaken 4 stir, whet 5 alert, rally, rouse 6 arouse, bestir, kindle

awanting 4 sans 5 minus 7 lacking, without

award 4 give, kudo 5 badge, endow, grant, honor, kudos, medal, prize 6 accord, bestow, confer 7 concede, laurels, tribute 8 accolade 9 vouchsafe 10 blue ribbon, decoration 11 distinction *motion picture:* 5 Oscar *mystery novel:* 5 Edgar *record:* 6 Grammy *television:* 4 Emmy *theater:* 4 Tony

aware 5 alert, alive, awake 7 heedful, knowing, mindful, witting 8 informed, sensible, sentient 9 au courant, cognizant, conscious 10 conversant 12 apprehensive

awash 4 full 6 jammed, loaded, packed 7 brimful, crammed, crowded, stuffed 8 brimming 9 chock-full

away 3 far, fro, now, off 4 afar, gone, over 5 apart, aside, forth, hence 7 lacking, missing, omitted, wanting 8 directly, first off, right off 9 forthwith, instantly, therefrom 11 immediately

away from *prefix:* 2 ap 3 aph, apo

awe 4 fear 5 alarm, scare 6 fright, wonder 7 startle, terrify 8 affright, frighten 9 reverence, terrorize 10 veneration, wonderment

aweigh 5 atrip

aweless 4 bold 5 brave 7 valiant 8 fearless, intrepid, unafraid, valorous 9 dauntless, undaunted 10 courageous

awesome 4 eery 5 eerie 6 august, dreary, solemn 7 sublime 8 dreadful, imposing, terrific

awful 7 fearful 8 dreadful, horrible, horrific, shocking, terrible, terrific 9 appalling, frightful 10 formidable

awfully 4 much, very 6 hugely 7 greatly 8 whacking, whopping 9 extremely

awhile *Scottish:* 4 awee

awkward 5 gawky, inept, splay 6 clumsy, gauche, wooden 7 gawkish, halting, lumpish, unhandy, unhappy 8 bumbling, bungling, ungainly **9** graceless, ham-handed, ill-chosen, lumbering, maladroit **10** blundering, bunglesome, unskillful **11** heavy-handed, splathering, unfortunate **12** discommoding, embarrassing, incommodious, inconvenient, infelicitous **13** discommodious

awning *ancient Roman:* **8** velarium

awry **5** amiss, askew, badly, wrong **6** afield, askant, astray **7** askance **8** cock-eyed **9** cock-a-hoop, crookedly **11** unfavorably *Scottish:* **5** aglee, agley

ax, axe **3** adz, can **4** adze, fire, sack **5** hache **6** bounce **7** boot out, chopper, cleaver, dismiss, hatchet, kick out **8** tomahawk **9** discharge, terminate *blade:* **3** bit *double-headed:* **6** twibil **7** twibill *handle:* **5** helve *ice:* **6** piolet

axiom **3** law **4** rule **5** gnome, maxim, moral **6** dictum, truism **7** brocard, theorem **8** aphorism, apothegm **9** principle **10** principium **11** fundamental

aye **2** OK **3** yea, yep, yes **4** okay **8** all right

Azariah *brother:* **7** Ahimaaz *father:* **4** Obed **5** Zadok **6** Nathan **7** Ahimaaz, Hilkiah, Jeroham, Johanan **8** Hoshaiah, Maaseiah **11** Jehoshaphat *son:* **7** Seraiah

Aztec *capital:* **12** Tenochtitlan *conqueror:* **6** Cortes, Cortez *emperor:* **9** Montezuma *god:* **4** Xipe **6** Eecatl, Meztli, Tlaloc **9** Xipetotec **11** Xiuhtecutli **12** Quetzalcoatl *hero:* **4** Nata *language:* **7** Nahuatl *temple:* **8** teocalli

B

baa **5** bleat

Babbitt **4** boob **8** boeotian **10** middlebrow, philistine *author:* **5** Lewis

babblative **5** gabby, talky **6** chatty **9** garrulous, talkative **10** loquacious **11** loose-lipped **12** loose-tongued, multiloquent

babble **3** gab, jaw, yak, yap **4** blab, chat **5** clack, prate, run on **6** burble, drivel, gibber, jabber, patter, piffle, rattle, yammer **7** blabber, blather, chatter, maunder, palaver, prattle, twaddle **8** nonsense **9** gibberish **11** jabberwocky

babbler *Scottish:* **7** blellum

babe **6** infant **7** neonate, newborn **8** bantling

babel **3** din **6** clamor, hubbub, jangle, racket, tumult, uproar **10** hullabaloo, tintamarre **11** pandemonium

baboon **6** chacma **8** mandrill **9** hamadryas

babushka **8** bandanna, kerchief

baby **3** tot **5** sissy, spoil **6** cocker, coddle, cosset, dote on, infant, pamper **7** bambino, cater to, indulge, neonate, newborn, papoose, toddler **8** bantling, dote upon, nursling, suckling, weakling, weanling **11** mollycoddle *ailment:* **5** colic, croup *baptismal robe:* **7** chrisom *bed:* **4** crib **6** cradle **8** bassinet *bedroom:* **7** nursery *breechcloth:* **6** diaper *cap:* **6** biggin, bonnet *carriage:* **4** pram **5** buggy **8** stroller **12** perambulator *doctor:* **12** pediatrician *food:* **3** pap **4** milk **6** pablum *garment:* **7** rompers *Italian:* **7** bambino *napkin:* **3** bib *nurse:* **4** nana *outfit:* **7** layette *powder:* **4** talc *shoe:* **6** bootee *Spanish:* **4** bebé, nene *unborn:* **5** fetus

baby grand **5** piano

babyhood **7** infancy

babyish **7** puerile **8** childish, immature **9** infantile, infantine

Babylonian **6** lavish **9** luxurious *abode of the dead:* **5** Aralu *capital:* **7** Babylon *chaos:* **4** Apsu *city:* **2** Ur **5** Accad, Akkad **6** Cunaxa, Cuthah *crown prince:* **10** Belshazzar *division:* **5** Accad, Akkad, Sumer *earth mother:* **6** Ishtar *first ruler:* **6** Nimrod *god:* **2** Ea, Zu **3** Anu, Bel, Hea, Sin **4** Adad, Addu, Apsu, Enzu, Irra, Nabu, Nebo **5** Alala, Alalu, Dagan, Enlil, Kingu, Lahmu, Mummu, Ninib, Siris **6** Anshar, Marduk, Namtar, Nannar, Nergal, Ramman, Tammuz **7** Shamash **8** Ningirsu *goddess:* **4** Gula, Nina **5** Aruru, Belit **6** Allatu, Belili, Beltis, Ishtar, Kishar, Lahamu, Ningal, Tiamat **7** Baalath, Damkina *hero:* **5** Adapa, Etana **9** Gilgamesh *king:* **6** Sargon **9** Hammurabi *priest:* **2** en *priestess:* **5** entum *river:* **6** Tigris **9** Euphrates *ruler of the dead:* **6** Nergal *storm god:* **4** Adad, Adda, Addu *sun god:* **3** Bel **7** Shamash *tower:* **5** Babel **8** ziggurat *waters:* **4** Apsu **6** Tiamat *winged dragon:* **6** Tiamat

baccalaureate **6** degree **8** bachelor

bacchanal 4 orgy 5 party 7 debauch
10 saturnalia 11 bacchanalia
bacchanalian 7 drunken, reveler
9 orgiastic
bacchanal's cry 4 evoe 5 evohe
Bacchus 8 Dionysus *attendant:* 6 maenad
father: 4 Zeus 7 Jupiter *lover:* 5 Venus
9 Aphrodite *mother:* 6 Semele *son:* 7 Priapus *staff:* 7 thyrsus
Bach *birthplace:* 8 Eisenach *composition:* 5 fugue, motet, suite 6 sonata 7 cantata, chorale, partita, prelude, toccata
8 concerto, fantasia, oratorio, sinfonia
deathplace: 7 Leipzig *musical style:*
7 baroque *religion:* 8 Lutheran
back 3 aid 4 abet, fund, help, hind, rear
5 about, again, dorsa (plural), round, spine,
stake 6 around, assist, dorsum, hinder,
rachis, recede, remote, retral, uphold
7 endorse, finance, promote, retract, retreat,
reverse, sponsor, support 8 advocate,
bankroll, champion, frontier, hindmost, rearward, side with 9 in reverse, posterior, retrocede, vertebrae (plural) 10 outlandish, retrograde, round about *ailment:* 7 lumbago
10 rheumatism *combining form:* 2 an
3 ana, not 4 dors, noto 5 dorsi, dorso,
notus 6 opisth 7 opistho *of a book:*
5 spine *of an arthropod:* 6 tergum *of an
insect:* 5 notum *of the neck:* 4 nape
6 scruff *prefix:* 2 re 4 post 5 retro *relating
to:* 6 dorsal
back answer 6 retort 7 riposte 8 comeback, repartee
backbiter 9 slanderer
backbiting 5 abuse 7 calumny, obloquy,
scandal, slander 8 libelous 9 invective,
maligning, traducing, vilifying 10 calumnious, defamation, defamatory, detracting,
detraction, detractive, scandalous, slanderous 12 belittlement, depreciation, vituperation 13 disparagement
backbone 4 grit, guts 5 moxie, nerve,
spine, spunk 6 pillar, rachis 8 mainstay
9 fortitude, vertebrae (plural) 12 spinal
column
backcountry 4 bush 6 sticks 7 boonies
8 frontier 9 boondocks 10 hinterland
backcourtman 5 guard
back down 4 balk 5 demur, welsh 6 beg
off, cry off, recall, recant, renege, resile
7 disavow, retract, stickle 8 withdraw
9 weasel out
backer 5 angel 6 patron, surety 7 sponsor 8 promoter 9 guarantor 10 bankroller,
meal ticket
backfire 6 fizzle 8 kick back, miscarry
9 boomerang 11 fall through
background 7 scenery
backhanded 7 devious 8 indirect
9 sarcastic

backing 4 help 5 aegis 7 support 8 auspices 9 patronage 10 assistance
11 sponsorship
backland see **backcountry**
backlash 5 slack 6 recoil 8 reaction
backlog 5 hoard, stock, store 7 nest egg,
reserve 9 inventory, reservoir, stockpile
back of 5 abaft 6 behind
back off see **back down**
backpack 8 knapsack, packsack, rucksack 9 haversack
backpedal see **back down**
backset 5 check 7 reverse 8 reversal
backside 4 rear, rump, seat 5 fanny,
hiney 6 behind, bottom, heinie 8 buttocks,
derriere 9 posterior
backslide 5 lapse 6 return, revert
7 regress, relapse 9 retrovert 10 recidivate
backstabbing 7 calumny, scandal, slander 10 defamation, detraction 12 belittlement, depreciation 13 disparagement
backstairs 6 secret, sordid 7 furtive
10 scandalous
backstop 6 uphold 7 support 8 advocate,
champion, side with
back talk 3 lip 4 guff, sass 5 mouth,
sauce 9 impudence, insolence
backtrack 7 retrace, retreat, reverse
backward 3 shy 4 dull, slow 5 about,
again, loath, round, timid 6 around, averse,
demure, modest, retral, stupid 7 bashful,
moronic, uneager 8 hesitant, ignorant,
inverted, retarded, retiring, retrorse,
reversed 9 benighted, diffident, dim-witted,
in reverse, reluctant, unwilling 10 behindhand, half-witted, indisposed, retrograde,
round about, slow-witted, uncultured
11 disinclined, thickheaded, undeveloped
12 feebleminded, self-effacing, simpleminded, uncultivated 13 unprogressive
backwoods see **backcountry**
backwoodsman 4 hick, jake 5 yokel
6 rustic 7 bumpkin, hillman 9 hillbilly
10 provincial
bacon *side:* 6 flitch, gammon *slice:*
6 rasher
Bacon work 12 Novum Organum
bacteria 5 cocci 7 bacilli, vibrios 8 spirilla
culture medium: 4 agar *destroyer:*
10 antibiotic
bacterial disease 7 anthrax, leprosy, tetanus 8 syphilis 9 gonorrhea, pneumonia
10 diphtheria
bacteriologist *American:* 6 Enders
7 Noguchi, Theiler *British:* 7 Fleming
French: 5 Widal 7 Nicolle, Pasteur *German:* 4 Cohn, Koch 5 Klebs 7 Behring, Lof-
fler 10 Wassermann *Japanese:* 8 Kitazato
Russian: 11 Metchnikoff *Swiss:* 6 Yersin
bad 3 ill, low 4 down, evil, foul, null, poor,
sour, void 5 amiss, lousy, rough, rowdy,

tough, wrong **6** arrant, nocent, putrid, rancid, rotten, sinful, unruly, wicked **7** decayed, froward, harmful, hateful, hurtful, immoral, invalid, naughty, nocuous, noisome, noxious, peccant, spoiled, tainted, unhappy, unsound, vicious **8** damaging, dejected, downcast, inferior, perverse, wretched **9** abhorrent, defective, deficient, depressed, execrable, injurious, loathsome, miserable, obnoxious, offensive, putrefied, reprobate, repulsive, sickening, woebegone **10** decomposed, disgusting, disorderly, dispirited, ill-behaved, indecorous, iniquitous, unpleasant **11** deleterious, detrimental, displeasing, distasteful, distressing, downhearted, intolerable, misbehaving, mischievous, unfavorable **12** disagreeable, disconsolate, insufferable, unacceptable **13** objectionable *combining form:* **3** cac, mal **4** caco *comparative:* **5** worse *prefix:* **3** dys, mis *superlative:* **5** worst

Badebec *husband:* **9** Gargantua *son:* **10** Pantagruel

Baden, for one **3** spa

badge **3** pin **5** award, honor, kudos **6** button, emblem **7** laurels **8** accolade, insignia **10** decoration **11** distinction

badger **4** bait, ride **5** brock, chivy, hound **6** heckle, hector **8** balisaur, bullyrag *group of:* **4** cete

Badger State **9** Wisconsin

badinage **6** banter **7** joshing, kidding **8** backchat, repartee, snip-snap **9** cross talk **10** persiflage

badland **4** wild **5** waste **6** barren, desert **8** wildness **10** wilderness

badly **4** awry, illy **5** amiss, wrong **6** afield, astray **7** harshly, roughly **8** severely **9** painfully **10** rigorously **11** unfavorably *combining form:* **3** mal

badman **4** hood, thug **6** bandit, outlaw **7** bandido, hoodlum, villain **8** criminal, hooligan **9** desperado

bad mark **3** gig **7** demerit

bad-tempered **6** cranky, crusty, touchy **8** choleric **9** dyspeptic **10** ill-humored, ill-natured, tempersome **12** cantankerous

Baedeker **5** guide **6** manual **8** handbook **9** guidebook, vade mecum **10** compendium **11** enchiridion

baffle **4** balk, bilk, foil, ruin **5** addle, mix up, stump **6** muddle, puzzle, thwart **7** confuse, flummox, mystify, nonplus **8** befuddle, confound **9** dumbfound, frustrate **10** circumvent, disappoint

bafflement **9** confusion **10** perplexity

bag **3** cop, nab, net **4** grip, hook, land, nail, poke, sack **5** biddy, catch, crone, pouch, purse, seize, steal **6** beldam, collar, secure **7** capture, satchel **8** backpack, knapsack, reticule, suitcase **9** apprehend

bagatelle **6** trifle

baggage **4** gear **5** hussy, tramp, trull, wench **6** wanton **7** effects, luggage, trollop **8** slattern, strumpet

Baghdad *founder:* **6** Mansur *river:* **6** Tigris

bagnio **7** brothel **8** bordello, cathouse **10** bawdy house, whorehouse

Bagnold **4** Enid

bagpipe *part:* **5** drone **7** bourdon, chanter *sound:* **5** skirl

Bahamas' capital **6** Nassau

bail **3** dip **4** bond, lade **5** ladle, scoop **6** surety **8** guaranty, security, warranty **9** guarantee

bailiwick **5** field, realm **6** domain, sphere **7** demesne, terrain **8** district, dominion, province **9** champaign, territory **12** jurisdiction

bait **3** nag **4** lure, ride, toll, trap **5** chivy, decoy, harry, hound, leger, snare, tempt **6** allure, badger, come-on, entice, entrap, harass, heckle, hector, lead on, ledger, molest, pester, seduce **7** torment **8** bullyrag, inveigle **9** persecute **10** allurement, enticement, seducement, temptation **12** inveiglement

bake **4** burn, cook, fire, kiln **5** broil, roast **6** saggar, sagger, scorch **7** scallop, scollop, swelter

baked clay **7** ceramic

baker's dozen **8** thirteen

bakers' yeast **6** leaven

baking **3** hot **5** fiery **6** red-hot, torrid **7** burning **8** broiling, scalding, sizzling, white-hot **9** scorching *chamber:* **4** kiln, oven

baksheesh **3** tip **4** alms **5** favor **6** reward **8** gratuity

Balaam *beast:* **3** ass **6** donkey *father:* **4** Beor

balance **4** rest **5** level, poise **6** adjust, attune, make up, offset, redeem, set off, stasis **7** harmony, remains, remanet, remnant, residue **8** atone for, coolness, leavings, outweigh, residual, residuum, symmetry **9** composure, congruity, equipoise, harmonize, remainder, stability **10** compensate, equanimity, proportion, steadiness **11** consistency, countervail, equilibrium, self-control **12** counterpoise *combining form:* **5** stato

bald **4** bare, nude **5** naked, plain **6** shaven, smooth **8** glabrous, hairless **9** unadorned **11** undecorated, ungarnished **12** unornamented **13** unembellished

baldachin **4** silk **6** canopy, fabric

Balder, Baldur *father:* **4** Odin *mother:* **5** Frigg **6** Frigga *slayer:* **4** Hoth, Loke, Loki **5** Hoder, Hothr *son:* **7** Forsete, Forseti *wife:* **5** Nanna

balderdash 3 rot 4 bosh 5 bilge 6 blague, bushwa 7 eyewash, rubbish 8 claptrap, malarkey, nonsense
baldness 8 alopecia
baldpate 7 widgeon 8 skinhead
balefire 6 beacon
baleful 4 dire, evil 6 malign 7 direful, fateful, malefic, ominous 8 sinister 9 ill-boding, ill-omened 10 maleficent, pernicious 11 apocalyptic, threatening 12 unpropitious
balk 3 gag, jib, shy 4 beam, dash, foil, ruin 5 demur 6 baffle, boggle, refuse, thwart, timber 7 scruple, stickle, stumble 8 hang back 9 frustrate 10 circumvent, disappoint
balky 5 loath 6 averse, ornery 7 froward, restive, wayward 8 contrary, hesitant, perverse 9 reluctant 11 wrongheaded 12 cross-grained
ball 3 orb, wad 5 dance, globe, round 6 sphere 7 rondure 8 conglobe, ensphere 10 conglobate *batted high:* 3 fly *batted straight:* 5 liner *combining form:* 5 globo, spher 6 sphaer, sphero 7 sphaera, sphaero *of thread or yarn:* 4 clew *ornamental:* 6 pom-pom, pompon *tiny:* 7 globule
ballad 3 lay 4 lied, poem, song 7 calypso *rhyme:* 4 ABCB *singer:* 8 minstrel 10 troubadour
ballast 5 poise 6 steady 9 stabilify, stabilize 11 stabilitate
ballerina 6 dancer 7 danseur 8 coryphee, danseuse 9 figurante 11 dancing girl
ballet *costume:* 4 tutu 6 tights 7 leotard *dancer:* 7 danseur 8 coryphee, danseuse, figurant 9 ballerina, figurante *for two:* 9 pas de deux *handrail:* 5 barre *jump:* 4 jeté 8 ballonné 9 entrechat *knee bend:* 4 plié *position:* 6 pointe 8 attitude 9 arabesque *step:* 3 pas 8 glissade *turn:* 6 chaîné 9 pirouette
ball game see at **game**
balloon sail 9 spinnaker
ball-shaped 7 globoid, globose 8 globular, spheroid 9 globulous, spherical
ball up 4 clew 5 addle 6 fuddle 7 confuse, fluster 8 befuddle, bewilder, distract, throw off
ballyhoo 4 tout 6 herald, hoopla 7 trumpet 9 publicity
balm 4 lull 5 allay, aroma, cream, quiet, salve, scent, spice, still 6 cerate, chrism, settle, soothe 7 bouquet, compose, incense, perfume, unction, unguent 8 ointment 9 fragrance, redolence 11 tranquilize
balmacaan 8 overcoat
balm of Gilead 6 poplar 9 balsam fir 12 balsam poplar
balmy 4 mild, soft 5 bland, faint, spicy, sweet 6 aromal, easing, gentle, insane, savory, smooth 7 foolish, lenient, perfumy 8 aromatic, fragrant, perfumed, pleasant,

pleasing, redolent, soothing 9 agreeable, ambrosial
baloney 3 rot 4 bosh, bull, bunk 5 hokum 7 hogwash, rubbish 8 nonsense
balsam poplar 9 tacamahac 10 hackmatack 12 balm of Gilead
Balthazar's gift 5 myrrh
Baltic *native:* 4 Lett 7 Latvian 8 Estonian 10 Lithuanian *state:* 6 Latvia 7 Estonia 9 Lithuania
balustrade 4 rail 7 railing 8 banister
Balzac character 6 Goriot 7 Grandet 9 Birotteau
bamboozle 4 bilk, dupe, fool, gull, hoax 5 trick 6 befool 7 chicane, swindle 8 flimflam, hoodwink 11 hornswoggle
ban 4 tabu 5 taboo 6 enjoin, forbid, outlaw 7 prohibit 9 interdict 11 forbiddance, prohibition 12 interdiction, proscription
Ban *ally:* 6 Arthur *son:* 8 Lancelot
banal 4 flat 5 bland, corny, trite, vapid 6 watery 7 insipid, sapless 8 waterish 9 hackneyed 10 namby-pamby, pedestrian, wishy-washy 11 commonplace
banality 6 cliché, truism 7 bromide 8 prosaism 9 platitude 10 prosaicism, shibboleth 11 commonplace
banana oil 5 hokum
banausic 4 blah, dull, poky 6 dreary, earthy, stodgy 7 humdrum, mundane, sensual, worldly 8 temporal 10 monotonous, pedestrian 13 materialistic
band 4 belt, club, crew, gang, gird, tape 5 bunch, corps, covey, group, party, strap, strip, troop, unite 6 concur, fillet, girdle, league, outfit, ribbon, streak, team up, troupe 7 cluster, combine, company, conjoin 8 begirdle, cincture, coadjute, engirdle, symphony 9 cooperate, orchestra 10 encincture 12 philharmonic *combining form:* 3 zon 4 taen, zono 5 taeni 6 taenio *Mexican:* 8 mariachi *neck:* 6 torque *of flowers:* 7 wreathe *small:* 5 combo
bandage 4 bind 5 dress 6 swathe 7 swaddle
bandanna 8 babushka, kerchief
bandeau 5 strip 6 fillet, ribbon, stripe 9 brassiere
banderilla 4 dart
banderole 4 flag, jack 6 banner, burgee, ensign, pennon 7 pennant 8 streamer
bandicoot 3 rat
bandit 6 badman, outlaw, raider, sacker 7 bandido, brigand, cateran, forager, ravager 8 marauder, pillager 9 cutthroat, desperado, holdup man, plunderer 10 freebooter, highwayman 11 bushwhacker *of India:* 6 dacoit
bandleader 7 maestro 8 choragus 9 conductor
bandolier 4 belt

bandwagon 3 fad 4 chic, mode, rage
5 craze, style, vogue 7 fashion
bandy 4 flip, toss 6 banter 8 exchange
11 interchange
bane 4 ruin 5 venom, virus 6 poison
7 bugaboo, bugbear, undoing 8 downfall
9 contagion, destroyer, ruination
11 destruction
baneful 4 dire 6 deadly 7 fateful, noxious,
ominous 9 ill-boding, ill-omened, injurious,
pestilent, unhealthy 10 pernicious 11 apocalyptic, pestiferous, threatening 12 pestilential, unpropitious
bang 3 bat, hit, pep, pop, rap 4 bash, beat,
belt, blow, boom, clap, kick, push, shot,
slam, sock, wham, whop 5 blast, burst,
crash, noise, punch, sharp, smack, smash,
sound, vigor, whack 6 thrill, wallop 7 surpass 8 smack-dab, squarely, vitality
9 explosion
Bangladesh *capital:* 5 Dacca, Dhaka
monetary unit: 4 taka
bang-up 5 dandy 7 capital 8 five-star,
top-notch, whiz-bang 9 excellent, first-rate
10 first-class 11 first-string
banish 4 oust 5 debar, eject, evict, exile,
expel 6 deport, put out, run out 7 cast out,
dismiss, exclude, expulse, shut out, turn
out 8 displace, drive out, relegate 9 discharge, ostracize, rusticate 10 expatriate
13 excommunicate
banishment 5 exile 9 expulsion, ostracism 10 relegation 11 deportation
12 displacement
Bani's son 3 Uel 5 Amram, Rehum
banister 4 rail 7 railing 10 balustrade
bank 4 heap, hill, mass, pile, save 5 beach,
coast, levee, mound, shore, stack, stash
6 invest, margin, rely on, rivage, strand
7 build on, count on, deposit, lay away, pyramid, trust in, trust to 8 depend on, lay
aside, reckon on, rely upon, salt away, set
aside, sock away 10 depend upon, stream-
side 11 calculate on 12 squirrel away
bank deal 4 loan
bankroll 4 back 5 stake 7 finance
9 grubstake 10 capitalize
bankrupt 4 bare, bust, do in, ruin 5 break,
drain, strip, use up, wreck 6 divest, fold up,
pauper 7 deplete, deprive, exhaust 9 pauperize 10 impoverish
bankruptcy 4 ruin 7 failure 9 depletion,
sterility 10 barrenness, exhaustion
banned 7 illegal, illicit, tabooed 8 enjoined,
verboten 9 forbidden 10 prohibited,
proscribed
banner 4 flag, jack 6 bang-up, ensign,
pennon 7 pendant, pennant 8 champion,
five-star, gonfalon, gonfanon, standard,
streamer, top-notch 9 banderole, excellent,
first-rate, front-rank 10 blue-ribbon, first-

class 11 first-string *Roman:* 7 labarum
8 vexillum
bannerol 4 flag, jack 6 ensign, pennon
7 pendant, pennant 8 streamer
banquet 4 feed 5 feast 6 dinner, junket,
regale, repast, spread
banquette 4 seat 5 bench, shelf
8 platform
bantam 4 arch, fowl, grig, pert 5 saucy,
small 6 little, petite 8 malapert, smallish
banter 3 fun, kid, rag, rib 4 fool, jest, jive,
joke, josh, razz 5 chaff, jolly, tease 7 teasing 8 backchat, badinage, chitchat,
exchange, repartee, snip-snap 9 small talk
10 persiflage 11 give-and-take
bantling 4 babe, baby 6 infant 7 neonate,
newborn
baptize 3 dub 4 call, name 5 title
6 purify 7 asperse, cleanse, immerse
8 christen, sprinkle 9 designate
10 denominate
bar 3 ban, dam, pub, rod, tap 4 bate, café,
curb, dive, halt, save, slab, snag, stop
5 block, brake, court, fence, ingot, limit,
stick, strip 6 billet, bistro, except, hinder,
impede, lounge, saloon, tavern 7 barrier,
buvette, cabaret, cantina, confine, delimit,
exclude, gin mill, rule out, rummery, rum-
shop, suspend, taproom 8 alehouse, blockade, count out, drinkery, drunkery, grogshop, lawcourt, obstacle, obstruct,
pothouse, prelimit, restrict, traverse, tribunal 9 aside from, barricade, eliminate,
excluding, honky-tonk, nightclub, outside of,
roadblock, roadhouse 11 exclusive of,
obstruction, rathskeller 12 circumscribe,
watering hole *iron:* 6 rabble
barb 4 dart 5 shaft *combining form:*
3 onc 4 onch, onci, onco 5 oncho
Barbados *capital:* 10 Bridgetown *monetary unit:* 6 dollar
barbarian 3 Hun 4 Goth, rude, wild
5 brute 6 savage, Vandal 8 Visigoth 9 foreigner, Ostrogoth
barbarism 6 misuse 8 malaprop, slangism, solecism 9 neologism, vulgarism
10 corruption 11 impropriety, malapropism
13 vernacularism, vernacularity
barbarity 7 cruelty 8 atrocity
10 inhumanity
barbarous 4 fell, grim, rude, wild 5 cruel
6 brutal, fierce, Gothic, savage, unholy, vulgar, wicked 7 Hunnish, inhuman, lowbrow,
uncivil, ungodly, wolfish 8 backward, fiendish, inhumane, sadistic 9 benighted, ferocious, graceless, heartless, primitive, tasteless, truculent 10 outlandish, outrageous,
philistine, unmerciful 11 unchristian, uncivilized 12 uncultivated
Barbary ape 5 magot

Barbary state 5 Tunis 7 Algiers, Morocco, Tripoli
barbate 7 bearded 9 whiskered 11 bewhiskered
barber 6 shaver 7 clipper, cropper, friseur 8 coiffeur 9 coiffeuse 10 haircutter 11 hairdresser, hair stylist
Barber of Seville *author:* 12 Beaumarchais *character:* 6 Figaro, Rosina, Rosine 7 Bartolo, Basilio 8 Almaviva, Bartholo *composer:* 7 Rossini 9 Paisiello
barber's itch 8 ringworm
bard 4 muse, poet, scop 5 skald 8 jongleur, minstrel 10 Parnassian, troubadour
bardlet 6 rhymer 8 poetling, verseman 9 poetaster, poeticule, rhymester, versifier 10 versesmith 11 versemonger 12 versificator
Bard of Avon 11 Shakespeare
bare 4 bald, mere, nude, open, show, very, void 5 clear, empty, naked, stark, strip 6 barren, denude, divest, expose, peeled, reveal, unclad, unveil, vacant 7 baldish, denuded, deprive, disrobe, emptied, exhibit, exposed, uncover, unrobed, vacuous 8 bankrupt, denudate, disclose, stripped 9 dismantle, unattired, unclothed, uncovered, undressed *combining form:* 4 gymn, nudi, psil 5 gymno, psilo
barefaced 5 blunt 6 arrant, brassy, brazen 7 blatant 8 impudent, overbold 9 shameless, unabashed 10 unblushing 11 temerarious
barefoot 6 unshod 8 shoeless 9 discalced 10 unsandaled 11 discalceate
bareheaded 7 hatless
barely 4 just 6 hardly, scarce 8 scarcely
bargain 3 buy 4 bond, deal, pact, swap 5 steal, trade, truck 6 barter, dicker, haggle, higgle, palter 7 chaffer, compact, traffic 8 closeout, contract, covenant, exchange, giveaway, huckster 9 agreement, negotiate 10 compromise, convention, loss leader, pennyworth 11 transaction
barge 4 scow 5 clump, stump 6 lumber 7 galumph, stumble
baritone *American:* 5 Gorin 6 Milnes, Warren 7 MacNeil, Merrill, Reardon, Tibbett 8 Guarrera, Warfield *English:* 6 Bailey *German:* 4 Prey *Italian:* 5 Gobbi 8 Raimondi
barium *symbol:* 2 Ba
bark 3 arf, yap, yip 4 snap, woof, yelp 5 snarl *combining form:* 6 phello 7 cortico *Scottish:* 4 yaff
barkeeper see **bartender**
barkentine 4 ship
bark remover 4 spud 7 spudder
Barlow epic 9 Columbiad
barman see **bartender**

Barmecidal 8 apparent, illusive, illusory, semblant 10 ostensible
barn 6 stable 10 storehouse *area of:* 4 loft 7 hayloft
barnacle 5 leech 7 sponger 8 hanger-on, parasite 10 freeloader 11 bloodsucker 12 lounge lizard
barnstorm 4 tour 5 pilot 6 travel
Barnum *elephant:* 5 Jumbo *midget:* 8 Tom Thumb *partner:* 6 Bailey
barnyard 4 foul 5 dirty, nasty 6 coarse, filthy, smutty, vulgar 7 obscene, raunchy 8 indecent
baron 4 czar, king 5 mogul 6 tycoon 7 magnate
baronial 5 grand, noble, royal 6 august, lordly 7 stately 8 imposing, majestic 9 grandiose 11 magnificent
baroque 4 gilt, rich 6 florid, ornate, rococo 8 luscious 10 flamboyant, ornamented
Baroque *architect:* 7 Bernini 8 Boromini *composer:* 4 Bach 6 Handel 9 Scarlatti 10 Monteverdi *painter:* 6 Rubens 7 El Greco, Poussin 8 Carracci 9 Velazquez 10 Caravaggio *sculptor:* 7 Bernini, Coustou 8 Coysevox, Girardon
bar pin 9 brochette
barrack 6 billet, casern 7 caserne 8 quarters
barracuda 4 fish, spet 5 barry, senet 6 becuna, becune, picuda, sennet 10 guaguanche, guaguancho
barrage 4 hail 5 burst, salvo, storm, surge 6 shower, stream, volley 8 drumfire 9 broadside, cannonade, fusillade 11 bombardment
barrel 3 keg, run, tun 4 butt, cask, much, peck, pipe, rush, whiz 5 fleet, hurry, speed 6 hasten 7 rundlet 8 hogshead 9 great deal *maker:* 6 cooper *part:* 4 hoop 5 stave *stopper:* 4 bung *support:* 6 gantry
barrelhouse 3 zip 4 dive, rush, whiz 5 hurry, joint 6 hasten, hustle 7 hangout 9 honky-tonk
barren 3 dry 4 arid 5 bleak, stark, waste 6 desert, effete, fallow 7 badland, parched, sterile 8 desertic, heirless, impotent, infecund, wild land 9 childless, infertile, unbearing, unfertile, wasteland 10 unfruitful, untillable, wilderness 12 hardscrabble, unproductive
barricade 3 bar 4 stop, wall 5 block, fence 7 barrier, railing 8 blockade 9 blank wall, roadblock *of trees:* 6 abatis
Barrie character 4 John 5 Peter, Tommy, Wendy 7 Michael 8 Crichton 9 Tiger Lily 10 Tinker Bell 11 Captain Hook
barrier see **barricade**
barring 3 but 4 save 6 bating, except,

saving 9 aside from, excluding, outside of **11** exclusive of

barrister 6 lawyer **7** counsel **8** attorney

barroom 3 pub **6** lounge, saloon, tavern **7** taproom **8** dramshop, drinkery, groggery, grogshop

bar sinister 4 blot, blur, onus, slur, spot **5** brand, odium, stain **6** stigma **8** black eye

bartender 7 tapster **8** boniface **10** mixologist **12** saloonkeeper

barter 4 swap **5** trade, truck **7** bargain, traffic **8** exchange *Scottish:* **6** niffer

Bartered Bride composer 7 Smetana

Baruch father: 6 Neriah, Zabbai *occupation: 6* scribe

basal 5 basic **6** bottom, lowest **7** primary, radical **8** simplest **10** bottommost, elementary, nethermost, pedimental, rudimental, underlying **11** fundamental, rudimentary **12** foundational

base 3 bad, bed, fix, low **4** evil, foot, mean, poor, prop, root, seat, ugly, vile **5** build, cheap, dirty, found, lousy, lowly, nadir, plant, set up, sorry, stand, tatty **6** bottom, common, filthy, ground, humble, paltry, scurvy, shoddy, sleazy, sordid, trashy, wicked **7** bedrock, caitiff, footing, ignoble, lowborn, low-down, servile, squalid, support **8** beggarly, buttress, cowardly, pedestal, plebeian, recreant, unwashed, unworthy, wretched **9** construct, dastardly, degrading, establish, framework, loathsome, low-minded, predicate **10** abominable, despicable, foundation, groundwork, substratum, unennobled **11** disgraceful, humiliating, ignominious **12** contemptible, meanspirited, substructure, underpinning

baseball abbreviation: 2 AB, AL, BA, BB, BI, CF, DH, DP, ER, FA, HR, IP, LF, LP, NL, RF, SB, SO, SS, WP **3** ERA, HSP, LOB, MVP, PCT, RBI *founder: 9* Doubleday *glove: 4* mitt *official: 3* ump **6** umpire *pitch: 4* drop, heat **5** curve, smoke **6** change, heater, sinker, slider, slurve **7** spitter **8** change-up, fadeaway, fastball, fork ball, knuckler, palm ball, spitball **9** brushback, screwball **12** change of pace, knuckle curve *player: 6* batter **7** baseman, catcher, fielder, pitcher **9** infielder, shortstop **10** outfielder **11** left fielder **12** right fielder **13** center fielder *practice fly ball: 5* fungo *term: 3* bag, bat, box, fan, fly, out, run, tag, tap, tip **4** balk, ball, base, bean, bunt, cage, deck, foul, hook, line, mitt, pill, pole, save, walk **5** alley, apple, bench, bloop, clout, count, drive, error, flare, glove, homer, liner, mound, pop-up, slide, swing **6** assist, clutch, double, dugout, groove, ground, inning, inside, pop fly, pop-out, powder, putout, rubber, runner, single, strike, triple, windup **7** battery, blooper, bullpen,

cleanup, diamond, floater, fly ball, home run, infield, manager, outside, pickoff, rhubarb, sidearm, squeeze, stretch **8** baseline, beanball, delivery, foul ball, grounder, keystone, outfield, pinch-hit, rosin bag, southpaw **9** full count, home plate, hot corner, line drive, sacrifice, strikeout, two-bagger **10** double play, frozen rope, ground ball, scratch hit, strike zone **11** knuckleball, pinch hitter, squeeze play, three-bagger **12** Texas leaguer

baseballer 3 Ott (Mel) **4** Cobb (Ty), Dean (Dizzy), Ford (Whitey), Foxx (Jimmy), Mays (Willie), Rose (Pete), Ruth (Babe), Ryan (Nolan) **5** Aaron (Henry), Banks (Ernie), Bench (Johnny), Berra (Yogi), Boggs (Wade), Brock (Lou), Carew (Rod), Clark (Will), Grove (Lefty), Gwynn (Tony), Kiner (Ralph), Maris (Roger), Spahn (Warren), Young (Cy), Yount (Robin) **6** Feller (Bob), Foster (George), Gehrig (Lou), Gibson (Bob), Gooden (Dwight), Herzog (Whitey), Hunter (Catfish), Koufax (Sandy), Mantle (Mickey), Morgan (Joe), Musial (Stan), Palmer (Jim), Seaver (Tom), Wagner (Honus) **4** Canseco (José) **7** Carlton (Steve), Clemens (Roger), Hornsby (Roger), Hubbell (Carl), Jackson (Reggie), Johnson (Walter), Puckett (Kirby), Schmidt (Mike), Speaker (Tris) **8** Anderson (Sparky), Clemente (Roberto), DiMaggio (Joe), Robinson (Jackie), Williams (Ted) **9** Alexander (Grover), Henderson (Rickey), Hershiser (Orel), Killebrew (Harmon), Mattingly (Don) **10** Campanella (Roy), Strawberry (Darryl), Valenzuela (Fernando) **11** Yastrzemski (Carl)

baseball team see **American League; National League**

baseboard 7 molding **8** skirting

baseborn 3 low **4** mean **5** lowly **6** humble **7** bastard, ignoble, natural **8** plebeian, spurious, unwashed **11** misbegotten **12** illegitimate

baseless 4 idle, vain **5** empty, false, wrong **9** pointless, senseless, unfounded, untenable **10** gratuitous, groundless, ungrounded **11** uncalled-for, unnecessary, unsupported, unsustained, unwarranted **12** indefensible **13** unjustifiable

basement 6 bottom, ground **10** foundation, groundwork, substratum **12** substructure

base on balls 4 pass, walk

bash 3 bat **4** belt, blow, slam, whop **5** crack, smack, smash, whack **6** wallop **7** blowout, shindig

Bashan last king: 2 Og *people: 7* Rephaim

Bashemath father: 7 Ishmael *husband: 4* Esau *sister: 8* Nebaioth

bashful 3 coy, shy **5** mousy, timid

6 demure, modest 7 abashed 8 retiring, timorous 9 diffident, recoiling, shrinking, unassured 11 embarrassed, unassertive

basic 4 main 5 basal, chief 6 bottom 7 capital, element, primary, radical 8 rudiment 9 elemental, essential, primitive, principal 10 elementary, substratal, underlying 11 fundamental 12 foundational 13 part and parcel

basically 6 au fond 9 in essence 11 essentially 13 fundamentally

basic point 4 crux, gist 7 essence

basin 3 cwm, dip, sag 4 sink 6 cirque, hollow 7 sinkage 8 sinkhole, washbowl 9 concavity 10 depression *liturgical:* 5 stoup 7 piscina

basis 4 root, seat 5 axiom, heart, right 6 bottom, ground, reason 7 bedrock, essence, footing, grounds, premise, theorem, warrant 9 postulate, principle 10 assumption, foundation, groundwork, substratum 11 fundamental, presumption 12 substructure, underpinning 13 justification

bask 3 sun 4 roll 5 revel 6 wallow, welter 7 indulge, rollick 9 luxuriate

basket 5 frail 6 dosser, gabion 7 pannier

basketball *inventor:* 8 Naismith *official:* 6 umpire 7 referee *player:* 5 cager, guard 6 center 7 forward 8 hoopster, swingman *team:* 4 five 7 quintet *term:* 3 gun, jam, key 4 cage, dunk, pass 5 board, lay-up, press, shoot, tip-in 6 freeze, tap-off, tip-off, travel 7 dribble, keyhole, rebound, throw-in, time-out 8 alley-oop, jump ball, slam dunk 9 backboard, backcourt, field goal, free throw 11 ball control

basketballer 3 Bol (Manute) 4 Bird (Larry), Reed (Willis), West (Jerry) 5 Barry (Rick), Cousy (Bob), Ewing (Patrick), Mikan (George) 6 Baylor (Elgin), Cowens (Dave), Erving (Julius), Jordan (Michael), McAdoo (Bob), McHale (Kevin), Pippin (Scottie), Walton (Bill), Worthy (James) 7 Barkley (Charles), Frazier (Walt), Johnson (Magic), Russell (Bill), Wilkins (Dominique) 8 Auerbach (Red), Havlicek (John), Olajuwon (Akeem) 9 Robertson (Oscar) 11 Abdul-Jabbar (Kareem), Chamberlain (Wilt)

Basmath's father 7 Solomon

Basque *cap:* 5 beret *game:* 6 pelota 7 jai alai *mountains:* 8 Pyrenees *province:* 5 Alava 7 Vizcaya 9 Guipuzcoa

bass 6 singer 7 crappie, jewfish, sunfish 8 cabrilla *American:* 5 Hines, Ramey, Tozzi 6 Morris 7 Plishka, Robeson 8 Flagello *Bulgarian:* 8 Ghiaurov *Italian:* 5 Siepi *Russian:* 9 Chaliapin *Swiss:* 6 Corena

bassinet 4 pram 9 baby buggy 12 baby carriage, perambulator

bastard 5 cross 6 by-blow, hybrid 7 mon-

grel 8 baseborn, spurious, whoreson 10 fatherless, unfathered 11 chance child, misbegotten 12 filius populi, illegitimate, natural child 13 filius nullius *combining form:* 4 noth 5 notho

bastardize 4 warp 6 debase 7 corrupt, debauch, deprave, pervert, vitiate 9 brutalize 10 bestialize, demoralize

bastardly 4 mean 12 contemptible

baste 3 wig 4 beat, drub, lash, mill, pelt, rail, whip 5 paste, scold 6 batter, berate, larrup, pummel, stitch, thrash, wallop 7 bawl out, belabor, chew out, clobber, tell off 8 bless out 10 tongue-lash

bastille 4 jail 6 prison

bastinado 3 bat 4 bash, beat, blow 5 crack, pound, smack, smash, stick, whack 6 cudgel, thwack, wallop 8 bludgeon

bastion 7 bulwark, parapet, rampart 10 breastwork

bat 3 bag, bop, bum, gad, hag, jag 4 belt, biff, blow, bust, club, mace, roam, rove, slam, sock, tear, trot, whop, wink 5 baton, biddy, binge, blink, booze, crack, crone, drunk, mooch, smack, spree, witch 6 beldam, bender, cudgel, ramble, rantan, thwack, wander 7 meander, nictate, traipse, twinkle 8 bludgeon 9 chiropter, flying fox, gallivant, nictitate, reremouse, truncheon 10 knobkerrie, shillelagh *combining form:* 8 nycteris *European:* 7 noctule 8 serotine 9 pipistrel 11 pipistrelle *Malaysian:* 6 kalong

batch 3 lot, set 5 array, bunch, clump, group 6 bundle, clutch, parcel 7 cluster

bate 4 omit 6 deduct, except 7 exclude 8 moderate, restrain

bath 3 spa, tub 4 wash 5 hydro, wells 6 shower 7 springs 13 watering place *combining form:* 5 balne 6 balneo *relating to:* 7 balneal

bathe 3 lap, lip, sop, tub 4 bask, lave, soak, soap, wash 5 douse, flush, souse 6 shower

bathetic 5 mushy, soppy, stale, tired, trite 6 cliché 8 clicheéd 7 maudlin, mawkish 9 hackneyed 11 commonplace, sentimental, stereotyped, tear-jerking 13 stereotypical

bathing suit 6 bikini, trunks 7 maillot

bathroom 2 WC 6 toilet 8 lavatory

Bathsheba *father:* 5 Eliam *husband:* 5 David, Uriah *son:* 7 Solomon

bathtub gin 5 hooch 7 bootleg 9 moonshine 11 mountain dew

bating 3 bar, but 4 save 6 except, saving 7 barring 9 aside from, excluding, outside of 11 exclusive of

baton 4 club, mace, wand 5 billy

6 cudgel **7** war club **8** bludgeon **9** billy club, truncheon **10** nightstick

batrachian 4 frog, toad **9** amphibian **10** salientian

batter 4 beat, drub, lame, maim, maul **5** baste, pound, wreck **6** bruise, buffet, bung up, mangle, pummel, thrash, wallop **7** belabor, clobber, contuse, cripple, disable, lambast, shatter **8** lacerate, lambaste, mutilate **9** disfigure

battery 3 lot **4** body **5** array, batch, bunch, clump, group **6** bundle **7** cluster

battery terminal 5 anode **7** cathode

battle 3 tug, war **5** brush, clash, fight **6** action, assail, attack, combat, oppugn, sortie **7** assault, bombard, contend, contest **8** conflict, skirmish **9** encounter, onslaught, scrimmage **10** engagement **11** hostilities *combining form:* **5** machy

battle-ax 6 twibil **7** twibill

Battle Born State 6 Nevada

battle cry 5 motto **9** catchword *Japanese:* **6** banzai

battlement 7 parapet

battlesome 6 brawly **7** scrappy **8** brawling **9** brawlsome **11** quarrelsome

batty 4 nuts **5** crazy, wacky **6** crazed, insane, maniac, screwy **7** cracked **8** deranged **9** bedlamite

bauble 5 curio **6** gewgaw, trifle **7** bibelot, novelty, trinket, whatnot **8** gimcrack **9** objet d'art **10** knickknack

Baucis' husband 8 Philemon

bavardage 6 by-talk **8** chitchat, trifling **9** small talk

Bavaria 6 Bayern *capital:* **6** Munich *city:* **8** Augsburg, Bayreuth, Wurzburg **9** Nuremburg *king:* **6** Ludwig *patron saint:* **6** Rupert

bawd 4 drab, moll **5** poule, whore **6** harlot, hooker **8** meretrix **10** prostitute **11** nightwalker **12** streetwalker

bawdy house 4 stew **6** bagnio **7** brothel **8** bordello, cathouse, joyhouse **10** whorehouse **11** parlor house **13** sporting house

bawl 3 cry, sob **4** howl, roar, rout, wail, weep, yell, yowl **5** shout **6** bellow, boohoo, clamor, holler, scream, shriek, squall, yammer **7** blubber, bluster, screech

bawl out 3 wig **4** lash **5** scold **6** berate **7** chew out, condemn, tell off, upbraid **8** bless out, denounce **10** tongue-lash

bay 3 arm **4** cove, gulf, howl, wail **5** award, badge, bayou, bight, creek, firth, honor, inlet, kudos, quest **6** harbor, slough **7** laurels, ululate **8** accolade **10** decoration **11** distinction *Aegean Sea:* **5** Anzac *Africa:* **6** Walvis *Alaska:* **7** Glacier *Angola:* **5** Bengo, Tiger **6** Tigres *Antarctica:* **3** Ice **8** Amundsen *Arabian Sea:*

4 Qamr **5** Kamar *Argentina:* **6** Blanca *Australia:* **5** Anson, Shark **6** Botany, Sharks **9** Discovery *Baltic:* **4** Hano, Kiel **6** Danzig, Kieler **9** Pomerania **10** Pomeranian, Pommersche *Barents Sea:* **4** Kola **7** Pechora *Beaufort Sea:* **7** Prudhoe **9** Mackenzie *Bismarck Sea:* **5** Kimbe *Brazil:* **9** Guanabara *Bristol Channel:* **10** Carmarthen *California:* **5** Morro **8** Monterey, San Diego **12** San Francisco *Canada:* **5** Fundy *Cape Breton Island:* **4** Mira *Capetown:* **5** Table *Caribbean Sea:* **5** Limon **8** Chetumal *Central America:* **7** Fonseca *China:* **4** Mirs *Crete:* **4** Suda **5** Canea *Cuba:* **4** Broa, Mora, Nipe **10** Guantanamo *Dominican Republic:* **4** Ocoa *East River:* **8** Flushing *Ecuador:* **5** Manta *Egypt:* **6** Abukir **7** Aboukir *Eire:* **4** Clew **7** Brandon *English Channel:* **3** Tor **4** Lyme **5** Seine *Estonia:* **5** Parnu **6** Pyarnu *Europe:* **6** Biscay **11** Aquitanicus *Florida:* **8** Biscayne *Greenland:* **5** Disko **6** Baffin **8** Melville *Gulf of Alaska:* **3** Icy **5** Woman **12** Resurrection *Gulf of Boothia:* **5** Pelly *Gulf of California:* **5** Adair *Gulf of Guinea:* **5** Benin, Bonny **6** Biafra *Gulf of Mexico:* **5** Tampa **6** Mobile **7** Aransas **8** Campeche, Sarasota **9** Matagorda, Pensacola **10** San Antonio, Terrebonne **11** Atchafalaya, Ponce de Leon **12** Apalachicola **13** Corpus Christi *Gulf of St. Lawrence:* **5** Bonne, Gaspé *Hawaii:* **5** Koloa, Lawai *Hong Kong:* **4** Deep *Honshu:* **3** Ise **5** Mutsu, Osaka, Owari, Tokyo **6** Atsuta, Sagami *Hudson River:* **7** New York *Iceland:* **4** Faxa, Huna **8** Faxafloi *Indian Ocean:* **6** Bengal **15** Great Australian *Indonesia:* **4** Bima, Kayo **5** Saleh **8** Humboldt *Irish Sea:* **4** Luce **7** Dundalk *Jamaica:* **4** Long *Japan:* **4** Tosa *Java:* **4** Lada **5** Peper *Java Sea:* **7** Batavia **8** Djakarta *Kara Sea:* **6** Enisei **7** Yenisei *Lake Erie:* **8** Sandusky *Lake Huron:* **7** Saginaw, Thunder *Lake Michigan:* **5** Green **13** Grand Traverse *Lake Ontario:* **11** Irondequoit *Lake Superior:* **5** Huron **8** Keweenaw **9** Whitefish *landlocked:* **5** Lamon *Long Island Sound:* **6** Oyster *Madagascar:* **8** Antongil *Maine:* **5** Casco **7** Machias **9** Penobscot *Marquesas Islands:* **5** Anaho *Maryland-Virginia:* **10** Chesapeake **12** Chincoteague *Massachusetts:* **6** Boston **7** Cape Cod **8** Buzzards, Plymouth *Mediterranean:* **9** Famagusta *Mozambique:* **5** Memba, Pemba *Nantucket Sound:* **5** Lewis *New Brunswick:* **13** Passamaquoddy *Newfoundland:* **4** Hare **5** White **7** Fortune *New Guinea:* **3** Oro **5** Berau, Hansa, Milne *New Jersey:* **5** Great **6** Newark **7** Raritan **8** Barnegat *New York:* **7** Jamaica *New Zealand:* **5** Hawke **6** Tasman **11** Hauraki Gulf *North*

Carolina: 6 Onslow *North Sea:* 4 Jade 9 Jadebusen *Northwest Territories:* 5 Wager 7 Repulse 8 Franklin 9 Frobisher *Nova Scotia:* 8 Cobequid *Oregon:* 4 Coos *Philippines:* 5 Baler, Pilar, Sogod 6 Butuan *Puerto Rico:* 5 Sucia *Quebec:* 6 Ungava *Red Sea:* 4 Foul *Rhode Island:* 12 Narragansett *Russia:* 4 Amur 5 Aniva, Chaun 6 Ussuri 7 Amurski *Scotland:* 5 Enard *Sea of Japan:* 13 Peter the Great *Solomon Islands:* 4 Deep *South Africa:* 5 Algoa, False *South Carolina:* 4 Bull, Long *South China Sea:* 4 Bias, Datu, Taya 5 Dasol, Subic, Subig 6 Brunei, Paluan 7 Camranh *Spain:* 5 Cadiz 9 Gibraltar *Spitsbergen:* 5 Cross, Kings *Sri Lanka:* 4 Palk *Strait of Gibraltar:* 7 Tangier *Sumatra:* 5 Bajur 10 Koninginne *Sydney:* 6 Botany *Tasmania:* 5 Storm *Texas:* 7 Trinity *Tyrrhenian Sea:* 6 Naples 7 Paestum *Wales:* 9 Carnarvon 10 Caernarvon *Washington:* 5 Dabob 6 Skagit *Western Sahara:* 8 Rio de Oro *West Indies:* 5 Coral *White Sea:* 5 Onega *Yellow Sea:* 5 Korea

baygall 3 bog, fen 4 mire, moss, quag, sump 5 marsh, swamp 6 morass 9 swampland

bayou 3 arm, bay 4 cove, gulf 5 bight, creek, firth, inlet 6 harbor, slough *Louisiana:* 5 Macon 9 Lafourche 10 Terrebonne *Mississippi:* 9 Chickasaw

Bay State 13 Massachusetts

bay window 3 pod, pot 6 paunch 8 potbelly 11 corporation

bazoo 3 boo 4 bird, hiss, hoot, pooh, razz 7 catcall 8 pooh-pooh 9 raspberry 10 Bronx cheer

bazooka's target 4 tank

be 4 go on, hold, live, move 5 abide, exist, stand 6 endure, obtain, remain 7 breathe, persist, prevail, subsist 8 continue

beach 4 bank 5 coast, shore, wreck 6 pile up, strand 8 cast away, lakeside 9 lakeshore, shipwreck 10 oceanfront *Hawaii:* 7 Waikiki *Massachusetts:* 9 Nantasket *New York:* 10 Fire Island

____ **Beach** 5 Dover

beached 7 aground 8 grounded, stranded

beachhead 8 foothold

beachwear see **bathing suit**

beacon 5 flare 6 pharos 7 bonfire 8 balefire 9 watchfire 10 lighthouse

beak 3 neb, nib 4 bill, cape, naze, nose, peck, pick 5 point, snoot, snout 6 beezer, pecker 7 sneezer 8 foreland, headland 9 proboscis, schnozzle 10 promontory *combining form:* 5 rostr 6 rhamph, rostri, rostro 7 rhampho 8 rhynchus

beaklike part 7 rostrum

be-all and end-all 3 sum 4 pith, root, soul, tote 5 stuff, total, whole 6 bottom,

marrow 7 essence 8 entirety, sum total, totality 9 aggregate, substance 10 rock bottom 12 quintessence

beam 3 can, ray 4 balk, burn, grin, rear, seat 5 fanny, gleam, shaft, shine, shoot, smile 6 behind, bottom, lintel, rafter, timber 7 radiate 8 backside, buttocks, crosstie, derriere 9 posterior

beaming 6 bright, lucent 7 fulgent, lambent, radiant 8 luminous 9 brilliant, effulgent, refulgent 12 incandescent

bean 3 dry, wax 4 bush, coco, conk, dome, head, lima, mung, navy, pole, poll, snap 5 baked, brain, broad, horse, jelly, pinto 6 belfry, coffee, frijol, kidney, noddle, noggin, noodle, string 7 frijole, jumping 9 headpiece 10 stringless *of india:* 3 urd

beano 5 bingo

Bean Town 6 Boston

beany 5 fiery 6 spunky 7 gingery, peppery 8 spirited 10 mettlesome 11 highhearted 12 high-spirited

bear 2 go 3 act, bow, jag, jam, lug, try 4 born, buck, form, go on, have, head, hump, lump, make, pack, push, quit, show, take, tote 5 abide, allow, apply, beget, birth, breed, bring, brook, bruin, carry, crowd, crush, defer, ferry, fruit, press, refer, shape, squab, stand, stick, touch, yield 6 accept, acquit, affect, attend, behave, convey, convoy, create, demean, deport, digest, endure, escort, invent, permit, pocket, relate, seller, set out, squash, squish, squush, submit, suffer 7 afflict, comport, concern, condone, conduct, deliver, display, exhibit, fashion, involve, pertain, possess, produce, squeeze, stomach, support, sustain, swallow, take off, torment, torture, turn out 8 chaperon, engender, fructify, generate, light out, multiply, parallel, shoulder, stick out, sweat out, tolerate, tough out 9 accompany, acquiesce, appertain, companion, fabricate, procreate, propagate, reproduce, strike out, transport 10 bring forth, correspond 11 consort with, countenance *Alaskan:* 5 polar 6 kodiak *Australian:* 5 koala *combining form:* 4 arct 5 arcto *family:* 7 Ursidae *genus:* 5 Ursus *kind:* 3 sun 5 black, brown, honey, koala, polar, sloth 6 kodiak 7 grizzly 10 spectacled *relating to:* 6 ursine *young:* 3 cub

bearable 7 livable 9 allowable, endurable, tolerable 10 acceptable, admissible, sufferable 11 supportable, sustainable 12 satisfactory

beard 4 barb, dare, defy, face, fuzz 5 brave, front 6 beaver, goatee 7 galways, outdare, outface, stubble, Vandyke, venture 8 imperial, whiskers 9 burnsides, challenge 11 muttonchops 12 side-whiskers *combining form:* 5 pogon 6 pogono *on* *grain:* **3** awn *pointed:* **6** goatee **7** Vandyke

bearded 5 hairy **7** barbate, goateed, stubbed, stubbly **8** unshaven **9** whiskered **11** bewhiskered

bear down 5 crush **6** defeat, reduce, subdue **7** conquer **8** vanquish **9** overpower, subjugate

bearer 5 envoy **6** coolie, porter, redcap, skycap **7** bellboy, bellhop, bellman, carrier, courier, drogher **8** cargador, emissary **9** messenger **11** internuncio *combining form:* **3** fer **4** pher, phor **5** phora, phore **6** phorae (plural), phorum

bearing 3 air, set **4** brow, look, mien, port, pose **5** birth, front, poise, stand **6** aspect, stance **7** address, conduct, display, posture **8** attitude, behavior, birthing, carriage, delivery, demeanor, presence **10** childbirth, deportment **11** comportment, parturition *combining form:* **6** ferous, gerous, parous **7** igerous, phorous

bearish 5 waspy **6** cranky, ornery **7** dubious, waspish **8** cankered, vinegary **9** crotchety, declining **10** vinegarish **11** pessimistic **12** cantankerous

bearlike 6 ursine, ursoid **8** ursiform

bear out 6 verify **7** confirm, justify **8** validate **11** corroborate **12** authenticate, substantiate

bear up 4 prop **5** brace, carry **6** uphold **7** bolster, shore up, support, sustain **8** buttress

beast 5 brute **6** animal **7** beastie, critter, varmint **8** behemoth, creature **9** quadruped *combining form:* **4** ther **5** thero **6** theria (plural), therio **7** therium

beastly 5 brute, feral **6** animal, brutal, ferine **7** bestial, brutish, swinish

beat 2 do **3** get, gyp, lam, tan, top, wag, win **4** balk, best, bilk, cane, comb, dash, drub, drum, dump, flog, foil, grub, lace, lash, lick, maul, pelt, rake, ruin, trim, wale, wave, welt, whip, whop **5** baste, baton, cheat, cozen, curry, excel, lay on, meter, outdo, paste, pound, pulse, rhyme, scoop, scour, smear, stick, stump, swing, throb, tromp, whisk **6** baffle, batter, better, buffet, chouse, cudgel, diddle, exceed, forage, hammer, larrup, muss up, pummel, rhythm, search, switch, thrash, thwart, waggle, wallop, woggle **7** belabor, buffalo, cadence, cadency, clobber, conquer, defraud, lambast, measure, nonplus, prevail, pulsate, ransack, rough up, rummage, shellac, smother, surpass, triumph, trounce **8** bludgeon, finecomb, flimflam, lambaste, malleate, outshine, outstrip, overcome, rhythmus **9** bastinado, exclusive, frustrate, fustigate, overreach, palpitate, transcend **10** circumvent, disappoint, pistol-whip

beat down 5 crush **6** defeat, reduce, subdue **7** conquer **8** vanquish **9** overpower, subjugate

beating 4 rout **5** lumps **6** defeat, hiding **7** debacle, licking **8** drubbing **9** overthrow, pulsating, thrashing **10** defeasance **11** shellacking **12** vanquishment

beatitude 5 bliss **7** ecstasy, rapture **9** happiness, transport **11** blessedness **12** blissfulness

Beatles 4 John, Paul **5** Ringo **6** George

beau 5 flame, lover, swain **6** steady **7** beloved **8** truelove, young man **9** boyfriend, inamorato **10** sweetheart

Beau Brummel 3 fop **5** dandy **7** coxcomb **8** macaroni **9** exquisite **11** petit-maître **12** lounge lizard

beau ideal 5 model **6** mirror **7** example, pattern **8** ensample, exemplar, paradigm, standard **9** archetype

Beaumarchais' hero 6 Figaro

beauteous 4 fair **5** bonny **6** comely, lovely, pretty **8** handsome **10** attractive **11** good-looking

beautiful 4 fair **5** bonny **6** choice, comely, lovely, pretty, proper, superb **7** elegant, sublime **8** glorious, gorgeous, handsome, pleasing, splendid, stunning **9** exquisite **10** attractive, eye-filling, personable **11** good-looking, resplendent, well-favored **12** eye-appealing *combining form:* **4** cali, calo **5** calli, callo

beautiful people 6 jet set **8** smart set

beautify 4 deck, trim **5** adorn, grace, prank **6** bedeck **7** dress up, garnish **8** decorate, ornament, prettify **9** embellish, glamorize

beauty 5 belle, dream, peach, toast **6** eyeful, looker, lovely **7** charmer, dazzler, stunner **8** knockout **9** eye-opener **10** goodlooker *combining form:* **4** cali, calo **5** calli, callo

beaver 5 beard **6** rodent **8** whiskers *family:* **10** Castoridae *genus:* **6** Castor *home:* **5** lodge *young:* **3** kit, pup

Beaver State 6 Oregon

becalm 4 lull **5** allay, quiet, still **6** settle, soothe **7** compose, quieten **11** tranquilize

because 2 as **3** for, now **5** being, since **6** seeing **7** whereas **8** as long as **10** inasmuch as **11** considering

because of 4 over **5** due to **7** owing to, through

Becher's father 7 Ephraim **8** Benjamin

Beckett work 4 Play, Watt **6** Molloy, Murphy **7** Endgame **9** Happy Days **14** Krapp's Last Tape **15** Waiting for Godot

becloud 3 dim, fog **4** blur **5** bedim, befog, muddy **6** darken, puzzle **7** confuse, eclipse, obscure, perplex **8** befuddle **9** obfuscate

become 2 go 3 fit, get, run, wax 4 come, grow, rise, soar, suit, turn 5 arise, befit, mount 6 go with 7 enhance, flatter 9 agree with 10 go together *suffix:* 3 ize

becoming 4 nice 5 right 6 decent, proper, seemly 7 correct, fitting 8 decorous, suitable, tasteful 9 befitting 10 attractive, conforming, flattering 11 appropriate, comme il faut *suffix:* 6 escent 7 escence

bed 3 cot 4 base, bunk, flop, rest, seat, twin 5 basis 6 bottom, cradle, double, ground, Murphy, pallet, pile in, retire, roll in, tuck in, turn in 7 bedrock, trundle 8 rollaway 10 foundation, substratum *combining form:* 4 clin 5 clino *of India:* 7 charpai, charpoy

Bedad's son 5 Hadad

bedamn 4 cuss 5 curse, swear 8 execrate 9 imprecate

bedaub 3 dab 5 smarm, smear 6 smudge 7 besmear, plaster

bedaze 4 stun 6 bemuse, benumb 7 petrify, stupefy 8 paralyze

bedazzle 4 daze 5 blind

bedbug 5 cimex 6 chinch 7 cimices (plural)

bedcover 5 quilt 6 afghan, spread 8 coverlet, coverlid 11 counterpane

bedeck 4 trim 5 adorn, prank 6 bedaub 7 bedizen, dress up, garnish 8 beautify, decorate, ornament 9 embellish

Bedeiah's father 4 Bani

bedevil 5 annoy, harry, tease, worry 6 harass, pester, plague 7 hagride, wherret 9 tantalize

bedevilment 7 trouble 8 disorder, vexation 9 confusion

bedfellow 4 ally 9 associate

bedim 3 fog 5 befog, cloud, gloom 6 darken 7 becloud, eclipse, obscure 9 obfuscate

bedlamite 3 mad, nut 4 loon, nuts 5 batty, crazy, loony 6 dement, insane, madman, maniac 7 cracked, lunatic, madling 8 demented, deranged 9 non compos

bedog 3 tag 4 tail 5 trail 6 shadow

bedouin 4 Arab 5 nomad

bedraggled 5 faded, seedy 6 shabby, tagrag 7 rundown 8 decrepit, tattered 10 down-at-heel, threadbare 11 dilapidated

bedridden 4 weak 6 feeble, infirm, laid up, sickly 7 bedfast 8 confined 13 incapacitated

bedrock 4 base, root 5 basis 6 ground 7 footing 10 foundation, groundwork, substratum 12 substructure, underpinning

bedroom 7 boudoir

bedspread 8 coverlet, coverlid 11 counterpane

bed-wetting 8 enuresis

bee *combining form:* 3 api *family:* 6 Apidae 8 Bombidae *food:* 6 nectar *genus:* 4 Apis 5 Osmia 6 Bombus 8 Ceratina 9 Megachile *glue:* 8 propolis *group:* 5 swarm 6 colony *house:* 6 apiary *kind:* 5 drone, mason, queen 6 cuckoo, mining, sewing, worker 8 honeybee, quilting, spelling 9 bumblebee, carpenter 10 leafcutter *nest:* 4 hive, skep *product:* 3 wax 5 honey *relating to:* 5 apian 8 apiarian *study of:* 8 apiology *wax cells:* 9 honeycomb

beechnuts 4 mast

beef 3 arm 4 crab, fuss, miff, thew, tiff, yaup, yawp 5 bitch, bleat, boost, brawl, brawn, force, gripe, might, power, sinew, steam, vigor 6 energy, expand, extend, muscle, squawk, yammer 7 augment, blow off, dispute, enlarge, magnify, quarrel, rhubarb 8 heighten, increase, multiply, squabble, strength 9 bellyache, bickering, strong arm 10 aggrandize, falling-out 11 altercation *cut:* 3 rib 4 loin, rump, side 5 chuck, flank, plate, round, shank 7 brisket, sirloin 10 tenderloin *grade:* 4 good 5 prime 6 choice 7 utility 8 standard 10 commercial *order:* 4 rare 6 medium 8 well-done

beefeater 6 warder, yeoman

beefheaded 4 dull 5 dense 6 stupid 10 numskulled

beefy 5 burly, hefty, husky

Beehive State 4 Utah

beekeeper 8 apiarian, apiarist 12 apiculturist

beekeeping 10 apiculture

Beeliada's father 5 David

beeline 3 nip, zip 4 whiz 5 hurry, speed 6 bullet, hustle, rocket 7 hotfoot 8 highball

Beelzebub 5 devil, fiend, Satan 6 diablo 7 Lucifer, Old Nick, serpent 8 Apollyon 10 Old Scratch 13 Old Gooseberry

beer 3 ale 4 bock, brew 5 draft, lager, stout, weiss 6 porter 7 pilsner 8 pilsener *cup:* 3 mug 4 toby 5 stein 6 flagon, seidel 7 tankard 8 schooner 9 blackjack *drinking place:* 3 inn, pub 6 saloon, tavern *ingredient:* 4 hops, malt 5 yeast 6 barley *maker:* 6 brewer *mythical inventor:* 9 Gambrinus *plant:* 7 brewery *Russian:* 5 kvass *Scottish:* 10 barley-bree, barleybroo *slang:* 4 suds *Tibetan:* 5 chang

beer hall 5 stube 8 alehouse, mughouse

Beeri *daughter:* 6 Judith *son:* 5 Hosea

beet 5 chard 6 mangel, wurzel 7 mangold *family:* 9 goosefoot

Beethoven, Ludwig van *birthplace:* 4 Bonn *opera:* 7 Fidelio *overture:* 6 Egmont 7 Leonore 10 Coriolanus, Prometheus *sonata:* 8 Kreutzer, Pastoral 9 Moonlight 10 Pathetique *symphony:* 6 Choral, Eroica 8 Pastoral

beetle 3 jut 4 hang, poke, pout 5 bulge, pouch 7 project 8 bend over, lean over, overhang, protrude, stand out, stick out *click:* 6 cucuyo, elater 7 firefly 8 cucubano, skipjack *dung:* 6 scarab 9 tumblebug *front wing:* 6 elytra (plural) 7 elytron *fruit-eating:* 8 curculio *insect-eating:* 7 ladybug 8 ladybird *kind:* 3 dor 4 bean, dorr, dung, fire, June, stag 5 click, flour, grain, tiger, water 6 carpet, chafer, dor bug, ground, May bug, meloid, museum 7 blister, cadelle, carabid, firefly, goldbug, goliath, June bug, vedalia 8 ambrosia, figeater, Japanese, lampyrid, passalid, pinch bug 9 bombadier, longicorn, potato bug 10 cockchafer, rhinoceros *order:* 10 Coleoptera *ornamental:* 6 scarab *sacred:* 6 scarab *snouted:* 6 weevil 7 billbug 8 curculio 9 wood borer *young:* 4 grub 5 larva 8 wireworm

beetlehead 4 dolt, dope 5 dunce 8 dumbbell

beetleheaded 4 dull 5 dense 6 stupid 10 numskulled

beet soup 6 borsch, borsht 7 borscht

befall 2 go 3 hap 5 break, occur 6 betide, chance, happen 7 come off, develop, fall out

befit 4 suit 6 become, go with 9 agree with 10 go together

befitting 3 apt 4 just, meet, nice 5 happy, right 6 decent, proper, seemly 7 correct 8 becoming, decorous, suitable 10 conforming, felicitous 11 appropriate, comme il faut *suffix:* 2 ly

befog 3 dim 4 blur 5 bedim, cloud, muddy 6 darken, puzzle 7 becloud, confuse, eclipse, obscure, perplex, stumble 8 bewilder, confound 9 obfuscate, overcloud 13 metagrobolize

befool 4 dupe, gull, hoax 5 trick 7 chicane 8 hoodwink 9 bamboozle, victimize 11 hornswoggle

before 2 to 3 ere 4 ante, once, then, till, up to 5 ahead, until 6 facing, sooner, up till 7 ahead of, already, earlier, forward, prior to 8 formerly, previous 9 erstwhile, in advance, preceding 10 heretofore, previously 11 confronting, in advance of, precedently 12 antecedently *combining form:* 4 fore 6 proter 7 protero *prefix:* 2 ob 3 pre, pro 4 ante

befoul 4 slur 5 dirty, smear 6 defame, malign 7 blacken, pollute, slander, spatter, traduce 9 bespatter, denigrate 11 contaminate

befuddle 4 daze 5 addle, mix up 6 ball up 7 confuse, fluster 8 bewilder, distract, throw off 9 bumfuzzle

befuddlement 3 fog 4 daze, haze, maze 5 mix-up 9 confusion 10 muddlement 11 muddledness

beg 3 ask, nag, sue 4 pray 5 brace, cadge, crave, plead, press, worry 6 appeal, call on, demand, invoke, obtest 7 beseech, besiege, conjure, entreat, implore, request, solicit 8 petition 9 importune 10 supplicate

begem 5 beset, jewel 7 bejewel, enjewel

beget 4 bear, sire 5 breed 6 father 7 produce 8 generate, multiply 9 procreate, propagate, reproduce 11 progenerate

begetting *combining form:* 4 gony

beggar 4 hobo 5 asker, tramp 6 bummer, cadger, pauper, prayer, sponge, suitor 7 moocher, sponger 8 deadbeat 9 schnorrer, suppliant 10 down-and-out, freeloader, panhandler, petitioner, supplicant 11 bindle stiff, supplicator

beggared 4 flat, poor 5 broke, needy 8 dirt poor, indigent 9 destitute 11 fortuneless, impecunious 12 impoverished

beggarly 4 mean 5 cheap, sorry 6 cheesy, measly, paltry, scurvy, shabby, trashy 7 pitiful 8 pitiable, wretched 10 despicable, despisable 12 contemptible

Beggar's Opera *music:* 7 Pepusch *painting:* 7 Hogarth *text:* 3 Gay

beggarweed 6 dodder, spurry 9 knotgrass

beggary 4 need, want 6 penury 7 bumming, cadging, poverty 8 mooching 9 indigence, mendicity, neediness, pauperism 10 mendicancy 11 destitution, panhandling

begin 4 open 5 arise, dig in, enter, found, set to, start 6 attack, broach, get off, launch, spring, tackle, take up, tee off 7 break in, jump off, kick off, lead off, prepare, usher in 8 commence, embark on, initiate 9 establish, institute, introduce, originate 10 embark upon, inaugurate

beginner 4 colt, tiro, tyro 6 novice, rookie 8 freshman, neophyte, newcomer 9 novitiate 10 apprentice, tenderfoot

beginning 4 dawn, rise, root 5 alpha, basal, birth, onset, start 6 anlage, origin, outset, primal, setout, source, spring, sprout 7 dawning, genesis, infancy, initial, nascent, opening 8 creation, exordium, outstart, prologue, rudiment, simplest 9 dayspring, elemental, emergence, inception, inceptive, incipient 10 appearance, elementary, incipiency, initiative, initiatory, opening gun, rudimental 11 origination, rudimentary 12 commencement, introductory *combining form:* 3 acr, akr 4 acro, akro, arch *suffix:* 6 escent

begird 3 hem 4 band, belt, ring 5 beset, round 6 circle, girdle 8 cincture, encircle, engirdle, surround 9 encompass 10 encincture

begirdle 4 band, belt 6 engird 8 cincture
10 encincture

begone 4 kite 5 scram 6 decamp, get
out 7 buzz off, skiddoo, take off, vamoose
8 clear out, hightail 9 skedaddle

begrime 4 foul, soil 5 dirty 6 besoil,
smirch, smooch, smudge, smutch 7 tarnish

begrudge 4 envy

beguile 4 lure, play, wile 5 bluff, fleet,
while 6 betray, delude, entice, humbug,
illude, jockey, juggle, seduce, take in
7 deceive, exploit, finesse, mislead
8 maneuver 10 manipulate 11 double-
cross

beguiling 5 false 8 deluding, delusive,
delusory 9 deceiving, deceptive 10 fallacious, misleading

Behan's autobiography 10 Borstal Boy

behave 2 do 3 act 4 bear, go on, move,
quit, take, work 5 carry, react 6 acquit,
demean, deport, direct, manage 7 comport,
conduct, control, disport, operate, perform
8 function

behavior 6 manner 7 bearing, conduct
8 demeanor 10 deportment
11 comportment

behead 4 neck 9 decollate 10 decapitate,
guillotine

beheaded noblewoman 4 Grey (Lady
Jane) 6 Boleyn (Anne) 9 Catherine
10 Antoinette (Marie)

behemoth 5 giant, whale 7 mammoth,
monster 9 leviathan

behemothic 4 huge 7 mammoth, titanic
8 colossal, gigantic 9 Herculean, monstrous 10 gargantuan, mastodonic
11 elephantine

behest 4 word 5 order 6 charge,
demand 7 bidding, command, dictate, mandate, request 9 prompting 10 injunction
12 solicitation

behind 3 can 4 next, rump 5 abaft, after,
below, fanny, hiney, infra, later, since
6 back of, bottom, heinie 7 by and by
8 backside, buttocks, derriere, latterly
9 afterward, following, posterior 10 afterwhile 12 subsequently, subsequent to **combining form:** 7 postero **prefix:** 3 met
4 meta, post 5 retro

behindhand 3 lax 4 late 5 lated, slack,
tardy 6 in debt, remiss 7 belated, overdue
8 backward, careless, derelict 9 in arrears,
negligent 10 delinquent, neglectful, regardless, unpunctual 11 undeveloped 12 disregardful 13 unprogressive

behold 3 see 4 espy, mark, note, view
6 descry, notice 7 discern, observe 11 distinguish **French:** 5 voilà **Latin:** 4 ecce

beholden 7 obliged 8 indebted
9 obligated

beholder 6 viewer 7 watcher, witness

8 by-sitter, looker-on, observer, onlooker
9 bystander, spectator 10 eyewitness

being 2 as 3 for, man 4 body, esse, soul
5 human, since, stuff, thing, wight 6 entity,
matter, mortal, nature, object, person, seeing 7 because, essence, texture, whereas
8 as long as, creature, essentia, existent,
material 9 actuality, character, existence,
personage, something, substance 10 inasmuch as, individual 11 considering, personality 12 essentiality 13 individuality **suffix:**
2 ic 3 ant, ent 4 ical

bejewel 3 gem 5 begem, beset 7 diamond, encrust, spangle 9 bespangle

Bel *father:* 2 Ea *wife:* 5 Belit 6 Beltis

bel ___ 5 canto 6 esprit

Bel ___ 5 Paese

Bela *father:* 4 Beor 8 Benjamin *son:*
3 Ard

belabor 4 beat, drub 5 baste, pound
6 batter, buffet, pummel, thrash, wallop
7 lambast 8 lambaste

Belait 6 Europe

belated 5 dated, passé, tardy 7 antique,
archaic, overdue 8 outdated, outmoded
9 out-of-date 10 antiquated, behindhand,
oldfangled, unpunctual 12 old-fashioned

belch 4 burp, spew 5 eject, erupt, expel
6 irrupt 8 disgorge, eructate

beleaguer 4 gnaw 5 annoy, beset, harry,
siege, storm, tease, worry 6 harass, invest,
pester, plague 7 bedevil, besiege, hagride
8 blockade

belfry 7 clocher 8 carillon 9 bell tower,
campanile *dweller:* 3 bat

Belgium *capital:* 8 Brussels *commercial
center:* 4 Gent 5 Ghent *horse breed:*
9 Brabançon *language:* 6 French 7 Flemish *monetary unit:* 5 franc *people:* 7 Fleming, Flemish, Walloon *province:* 5 Liège,
Namur 7 Antwerp, Brabant, Hainaut, Lim-
burg 8 Flanders 10 Luxembourg *violinist:*
5 Ysaye

belie 4 hide, warp 5 color, twist 6 garble
7 conceal, distort, falsify, pervert 8 disguise, disprove, miscolor, misstate, negative 10 contradict, contravene, controvert
12 misrepresent

belief 3 ism 4 idea, mind, view 5 credo,
creed, dogma, faith, tenet, trust 6 assent,
credit 7 concept, feeling, opinion, precept
8 credence, doctrine, religion, sureness
9 assurance, certainty, certitude, principle,
sentiment 10 conviction, persuasion

believable 5 solid 6 likely 7 tenable
8 credible, possible, probable, rational
9 colorable, plausible 10 convincing, creditable, impressive, meaningful, persuasive,
presumable, reasonable, satisfying, supposable 11 conceivable, substantial

believe 3 buy 4 deem, feel, hold, take

5 admit, sense, think, trust **6** accept, assume, credit, expect, gather, reckon, repute **7** imagine, suppose, suspect, swallow **8** accredit, consider **10** understand

belittle 5 decry **8** derogate, diminish, discount, minimize, write off **9** criticize, discredit, disparage, dispraise, underrate **10** depreciate, undervalue **11** detract from **13** underestimate

belittlement 4 tale **7** calumny, scandal, slander **10** backbiting, defamation, detraction **12** backstabbing, depreciation **13** disparagement

bell 4 bong, peal, ring, toll **5** chime, knell

bell-bottoms 5 pants **8** trousers

bell cow 4 dean, lead **5** doyen, guide, pilot **6** leader

Bellerophon *father:* **7** Glaucus **8** Poseidon *grandfather:* **8** Sisyphus *horse:* **7** Pegasus *victim:* **7** Chimera

belles lettres 10 literature

belletrist 4 poet **6** author, writer

bellflower 9 campanula

___ **belli 5** casus

bellicose 7 scrappy, warlike **8** factious, fighting, militant **9** assertive, combative, truculent **10** aggressive, pugnacious, rebellious **11** belligerent, contentious, quarrelsome **12** gladiatorial

belligerence 5 fight **6** attack **9** pugnacity **10** aggression, truculence **13** combativeness

belligerent 3 hot **6** ardent, fierce **7** hostile, scrappy, warlike, warring **8** battling, fighting, invading, militant, ructious **9** attacking, bellicose, combative, truculent **10** aggressive, pugnacious **11** contentious, hot-tempered, quarrelsome **12** antagonistic, gladiatorial

Bellini *opera:* **5** Norma **8** Il Pirata **9** I Puritani **12** La Sonnambula *sleepwalker:* **5** Amina

bell metal 6 bronze

bellow 3 bay, cry, low, moo **4** bark, bawl, roar, rout, wail, yelp **6** clamor **7** bluster

Bellow character 6 Herzog **7** Sammler **9** Henderson **10** Augie March

bell ringer 3 hit, wow **4** bang **5** smash **6** toller **7** success **12** carillonneur

bell ringing 11 campanology

bell-shaped 11 campanulate

bell sound 4 ding, dong, peal, ring, ting, toll **5** clang, knell **6** tinkle

bell tower 6 belfry **7** clocher **8** carillon **9** campanile

___ **bellum 4** ante, post

bellwether 4 dean, lead **5** doyen, guide, pilot **6** leader

belly 3 gut **5** tummy **6** paunch, venter **7** abdomen, stomach *combining form:*

5 gastr **6** gaster, gastro, ventri, ventro **7** gastero, gastria *Scottish:* **4** wame

bellyache 4 beef, crab, fuss, yaup, yawp **5** bitch, bleat, colic, gripe **6** gripes, squawk, yammer **7** blow off **12** collywobbles

bellyacher 4 crab **5** crank **6** griper, grouch, kicker **7** grouser **8** grumbler **10** complainer, malcontent **11** faultfinder

belly button 5 navel

belong 2 go **3** fit, set **4** suit, vest **5** agree, befit, chime, match, tally **6** accord, become, inhere **7** indwell, pertain **9** appertain, harmonize **10** correspond

belonging *suffix:* **2** an, ar **3** ary, ean, ian, ine

belongings 5 goods **6** estate, things **7** effects **8** chattels, movables **10** possession

beloved 3 pet **4** baby, beau, dear, love **5** flame, honey, lover, sweet **6** steady **7** darling, sweetie **8** blue-eyed, favorite, ladylove, loveling, precious, truelove **9** boyfriend, inamorata, inamorato, sweetling **10** fair-haired, girl friend, heartthrob, sweetheart

below 4 next **5** after, infra, since, under **6** behind, nether **7** beneath **9** following **10** underneath **12** subsequent to *combining form:* **6** infero *prefix:* **3** sub **5** infra

belt 3 bat, bop **4** area, band, bash, biff, blow, gird, loop, ring, sash, slam, slug, sock, whop, zone **5** blast, smack, smash, strap, strip, tie up, tract **6** begird, cestus, circle, engird, girdle, region, wallop **7** baldric, caestus, clobber, stretch **8** begirdle, ceinture, cincture, encircle, engirdle **9** bandoleer, bandolier, territory, waistband **10** cummerbund, encincture *celestial:* **6** zodiac *combining form:* **3** zon **4** zono

belt highway 8 ring road

Belus *brother:* **6** Agenor *daughter:* **4** Dido *father:* **7** Neptune **8** Poseidon *mother:* **5** Libya *son:* **6** Danaus **7** Cepheus, Phineus **8** Aegyptus

belvedere 6 alcove, gazebo, pagoda **11** garden house, summerhouse

bemean 4 sink **5** abase, lower **6** debase, humble **7** degrade **8** cast down **9** humiliate

bemedaled 9 decorated **10** beribboned

bemired 4 miry, oozy **5** muddy **6** claggy, clarty

bemoan 3 rue **4** weep **6** bewail, grieve, lament, regret **7** deplore **8** complain

bemuse 4 daze, stun **5** addle **6** bedaze, benumb, puzzle **7** fluster, perplex, petrify, stupefy **8** paralyze

bemused 4 lost **6** absent **7** faraway **8** distrait **10** abstracted **11** inconscient, preoccupied **12** absentminded

bench 6 settee *church:* **3** pew *outdoor:* **6** exedra *upholstered:* **9** banquette

benchmark 5 gauge **7** measure **8** standard **9** criterion, yardstick **10** touchstone

bend 2 go **3** arc, bow, jut, nod, yaw **4** arch, bias, cave, curl, flex, give, hang, hook, lean, tack, turn **5** angle, apply, break, crook, curve, round, shift, stoop, throw, yield **6** beetle, buckle, devote, direct, double, fold up, inflex **7** address, crumple, dispose, flexure, incline, turning **8** collapse, flection, lean over, overhang **9** curvation, curvature, deviation **10** buckle down, deflection, predispose

bendable 6 pliant, supple **7** elastic, pliable **8** flexible

bender see **binge**

bending *combining form:* **7** sphingo

___ bene 4 nota

beneath 5 below, under *prefix:* **3** hyp, sub **4** hypo **5** infra

___ Benedict 4 eggs

benediction 2 OK **4** boon, good, okay **5** favor, grace **6** thanks **7** benefit, benison, godsend **8** approval, blessing **9** advantage **11** approbation **12** thanksgiving

benefact 3 aid **4** abet, help **5** do for, stead **6** assist **7** help out

benefaction 4 alms **7** charity **8** donation, offering **11** beneficence **12** contribution

beneficence see **benefaction**

beneficial 4 good **5** brave **6** toward, useful **7** helpful **8** favoring, salutary **9** favorable, wholesome **10** propitious **12** advantageous

beneficiary 4 heir **5** donee **6** vassal **7** legatee **9** feudatory *suffix:* **2** ee

beneficiate 5 treat **6** reduce **7** prepare, process

benefit 3 aid **4** boon, gain, good, help, sake **5** avail, build, favor, serve **6** assist, behalf, behoof, better, profit, succor **7** account, advance, further, godsend, improve, promote, relieve, welfare, work for **8** blessing, interest **9** advantage, wellbeing **10** ameliorate, prosperity **11** benediction **12** contribute to

benevolence 4 boon, gift **5** amity, favor **6** comity **7** largess, present **8** goodwill **10** compliment, friendship, kindliness **12** friendliness

benevolent 3 big **4** good, kind **5** lofty **6** do-good, humane, kindly **7** liberal **8** generous **10** altruistic, beneficent, bighearted, charitable, chivalrous, openhanded **11** considerate, freehearted, magnanimous **12** eleemosynary, greathearted, humanitarian, largehearted **13** compassionate, philanthropic, tenderhearted

benighted 8 backward, ignorant, untaught **9** untutored **10** illiterate, uneducated, uninformed, unlettered, unschooled **11** empty-headed, know-nothing **12** unstructed **13** unenlightened, unprogressive

benign 4 kind, mild **6** bright, dexter, gentle, humane, kindly **7** clement **8** gracious, merciful **9** favorable, fortunate **10** auspicious, benevolent, charitable, forbearing, propitious **11** good-hearted

Benin *capital:* **9** Porto Novo *largest city:* **7** Cotonou *monetary unit:* **5** franc

benison 8 blessing **11** benediction

Benjamin *brother:* **6** Joseph *father:* **5** Jacob *mother:* **6** Rachel

bent 3 set **4** bias, head, nose, turn **5** arced, bowed, flair, knack, round **6** arched, curved, genius, intent, talent **7** arrondi, decided, faculty, leaning, rounded, settled, uncinal **8** arciform, decisive, inflexed, penchant, resolute, resolved, tendency, uncinate **9** inclining **10** determined, proclivity, propensity **11** curvilinear, disposition, inclination **12** predilection *combining form:* **4** cyrt **5** ancyl, ankyl, curvi, cyrto **6** anchyl, ancylo, ankylo, campto **7** anchylo

benumb 4 daze, dull, mull, stun **5** blunt **6** bedaze, bemuse, deaden **7** petrify, stupefy **8** paralyze **11** desensitize

benumbed 6 asleep **9** senseless, unfeeling **10** insensible **11** insensitive **12** anesthetized

benzene *combining form:* **4** phen **5** pheno

Beor's son 4 Bela **6** Balaam

bequeath 4 will **5** leave **6** devise, hand on, legate, pass on **8** hand down, transmit

bequest 6 devise, legacy **11** inheritance

berate 3 jaw **4** rail, rate **5** scold **6** revile **7** bawl out, chew out, upbraid **10** tonguelash, vituperate

berceuse 7 lullaby **10** cradlesong

bereave 3 rob **4** lose, oust **6** divest **7** deprive **10** disinherit, dispossess

bereaved 6 bereft **9** sorrowing **10** distressed

Berechiah's son 9 Zechariah

Bergen's dummy 5 Snerd **8** McCarthy

Beriah's father 5 Asher **6** Shimei, Shimhi **7** Ephraim

berkelium *symbol:* **2** Bk

Bermuda grass 4 doob

Bernice *brother:* **7** Agrippa *father:* **5** Herod *husband:* **6** Polemo *lover:* **5** Titus **9** Vespasian

berry 4 wort **5** bacca, fruit, grape, whort **6** banana, tomato **7** bramble, currant, madrona, madrone, madrono, whortle **8** allspice *combining form:* **4** cocc **5** cocci, cocco *Latin:* **6** acinus *medicinal:* **5** cubeb

berry-bearing 7 baccate **11** bacciferous

berrylike 7 baccate, coccoid

berth 3 job **4** dock, pier, post, quay, slip, spot **5** jetty, levee, place, wharf **6** billet,

office **8** position **9** situation **10** connection **11** appointment
Bertha's son 7 Orlando
beryllium *symbol:* **2** Be
beseech see **beg**
beset 3 gem, hem **4** gird, ring **5** begem, jewel, storm **6** assail, attack, circle, fall on, girdle, infest, invest, strike **7** aggress, assault, bejewel, besiege, compass, enjewel, environ, overrun **8** blockade, encircle, fall upon, surround **9** beleaguer, encompass, overswarm **10** overspread
besetment 4 pest **6** bother, pester, plague **8** irritant, nuisance **9** annoyance **10** botherment **11** botheration **12** exasperation
besetting 8 dominant, haunting **9** obsessive, principal **10** persistent
beside 2 by **3** bar, but **4** near, nigh, save **5** round **6** beyond, except, nearby, next to **7** barring **8** as well as, opposite **9** alongside, aside from, excluding, outside of **11** exclusive of **12** over and above *prefix:* **2** ep **3** eph, epi, par **4** para
besides 3 bar, but, new, too, yet **4** also, else, more, save, then **5** added, again, along, other **6** as well, beyond, except **7** barring, farther, further **8** as well as, likewise, moreover **9** aside from, excluding, otherwise, outside of **10** additional, in addition **11** exclusive of, furthermore **12** additionally, over and above
besiege 4 trap **5** beset, hem in **6** assail, attack, invest **7** assault **8** blockade, encircle, surround **9** beleaguer, encompass
besmear 3 dab, tar **4** daub, soil **5** smarm, stain, sully, taint **6** bedaub, defile, smudge **7** plaster, tarnish **8** besmirch, discolor
besmirch see **besmear**
besoil 4 foul **5** dirty, grime **6** smirch, smooch, smudge, smutch **7** begrime, tarnish
besom material 5 twigs
besotted 5 dotty, drunk **8** enamored **9** infatuate **10** infatuated
bespatter 4 slur, spot **5** smear **6** befoul, bespot, defame, malign **7** asperse, blacken, slander, traduce **9** denigrate
bespeak 3 ask **4** book, hire **6** accost, attest, desire **7** address, apply to, betoken, request, reserve, solicit, testify, witness **8** announce, approach, indicate **9** preengage
bespeckle 3 dot **6** pepper **7** freckle, stipple **8** sprinkle
best 3 gem, pip, top **4** beat, down, most, pick **5** cream, elite, excel, model, outdo, pride, prime, prize, worst **6** better, choice, defeat, exceed, flower, master **7** conquer, greater, largest, paragon, pattern, prevail, surpass, triumph **8** exemplar, nonesuch,

outshine, outstrip, overcome, primrose **9** nonpareil, transcend **10** bettermost *combining form:* **6** aristo
bestial 5 brute, feral **6** animal, brutal, ferine **7** beastly, brutish, swinish
bestialize 4 warp **6** debase **7** corrupt, debauch, deprave, pervert, vitiate **9** brutalize **10** bastardize, demoralize
bestir 4 wake, whet **5** rally, rouse, waken **6** arouse, awaken, kindle **9** challenge
bestow 3 use **4** bunk, give, pack **5** apply, board, grant, house, lodge, put up, store **6** billet, confer, devote, donate, employ, handle, harbor, lavish **7** exploit, hand out, present, quarter, utilize **8** domicile, exercise, give away **9** entertain, warehouse *Scottish:* **7** propine
bestower 5 donor, giver **7** donator **9** conferrer, presenter
bestrew 3 sow **5** straw **7** disject, scatter **9** broadcast **11** disseminate
bestride 4 back **5** mount **8** straddle, striddle
bet 3 lay, pot, set **4** ante, game, play, risk **5** banco, put on, stake, wager **6** gamble, parlay *racing:* **6** exacta **8** perfecta, quinella, quiniela *taker:* **6** bookie
Betelgeuse 4 star *constellation:* **5** Orion
betel palm 5 areca
bête noire 4 hate **7** bugbear **8** anathema **10** black beast **11** abomination, detestation
bethink 4 cite, mind **6** recall, remind, retain, revive **8** remember **9** recollect, reminisce **10** retrospect
Bethuel *daughter:* **7** Rebekah *father:* **5** Nahor *mother:* **6** Milcah *son:* **5** Laban *uncle:* **7** Abraham
betide 2 go **3** hap **5** break, occur **6** befall, chance, happen **7** come off, develop, fall out
betimes 4 soon **5** early **6** timely **8** oversoon **10** seasonably **11** prematurely
betoken 4 bode, omen **5** argue, augur **6** attest **7** bespeak, portend, presage, promise, testify, witness **8** announce, forebode, foreshow, indicate **9** foretoken **10** foreshadow
betray 4 sell, show, tell, trap **5** bluff, cross, snare, spill, split **6** delude, desert, entrap, evince, humbug, illude, inform, juggle, reveal, take in, turn in, unveil **7** beguile, betoken, blab out, deceive, divulge, ensnare, mislead, sell out, uncover **8** disclose, discover, evidence, give away, indicate, manifest, renegade **10** apostatize **11** collaborate, demonstrate, double-cross
betrayal 7 treason
betrayer 3 rat **4** fink, nark **6** snitch **7** stoolie, tattler, traitor **8** informer,

squealer, turncoat **10** talebearer, tattletale **11** stool pigeon

betroth 6 pledge **8** affiance

betrothal 8 espousal **10** engagement

betrothed 6 fiancé **7** engaged, fiancée, pledged **8** intended, plighted, promised, wife-to-be **9** affianced, bride-to-be **10** contracted **11** husband-to-be

better 3 top, win **4** beat, best, good, help, more, most **5** amend, elder, excel, outdo **6** choice, exceed, senior **7** greater, improve, largest, success, surpass, triumph, victory **8** brass hat, higher-up, outshine, outstrip, superior, whip hand **9** advantage, desirable, exceeding, excellent, meliorate, transcend, upper hand **10** ameliorate, preferable, surpassing **11** exceptional, superiority

bettor 7 wagerer

between 5 among, twixt **6** atwixt **7** betwixt *prefix:* **5** inter, intra

betweentimes 11 at intervals

bevel 4 bias **6** biased **7** slanted **8** diagonal, slanting

beverage 3 ade, nog, pop, tea **4** mate, milk, soda **5** cider, cocoa, drink, juice, shake **6** coffee, eggnog, frappe, malted, nectar **7** potable **8** lemonade, libation, potation **9** drinkable, milk shake *alcoholic:* **3** ale, gin, rum **4** beer, grog, mead, wine **5** cider, julep, negus, punch, stout, toddy, vodka **6** bishop, brandy, caudle, cooler, liquor, rickey, shandy, sherry, whisky **7** liqueur, martini, sangria, tequila, whiskey **8** cocktail, highball, sillabub, sillibub, syllabub, vermouth *Australasian:* **4** kava *British:* **5** perry, stout **6** stingo *carbonated:* **4** cola, soda **6** rickey **8** root beer **9** ginger ale *central Asian:* **5** kumys **6** koumis, koumys, kumiss, kumyss **7** koumiss, koumyss *Dutch:* **7** schnaps **8** schnapps *from camel's milk:* **5** kumys **6** koumis, koumys, kumiss, kumyss **7** koumiss, koumyss *from cow's milk:* **5** kefir *Greek:* **4** ouzo **7** oenomel, oinomel, retsina, retzina *Irish:* **5** usque **6** poteen **7** potheen, potteen **8** usquabae, usquebae **10** usquebaugh *medicinal:* **6** elixir *Mexican:* **6** pulque **7** tequila *of the gods:* **6** nectar *Oriental:* **4** sake, saki **6** arrack, samshu *Russian:* **5** kefir, kvass, quass, vodka *Scottish:* **4** yill **6** scotch *South American:* **4** maté **5** yerba *Swedish:* **5** glogg *Turkish:* **4** raki *West Indies:* **3** rum **5** tafia

bevy 4 band, crew **5** bunch, covey, group, party **7** cluster **8** assembly

bewail 4 moan, weep **6** bemoan, grieve **7** deplore

beware 4 heed, mind **5** watch **6** attend, notice **7** look out **8** watch out

bewhiskered 7 barbate, bearded

bewilder 3 fog **4** stun **5** addle, befog, mix up **6** baffle, ball up, fuddle, muddle, puzzle **7** confuse, fluster, perplex, stumble **8** befuddle, confound, distract **9** bumfuzzle **13** metagrobolize

bewitch 3 hex **4** draw, snow, take, wile **5** charm, spell, trick **6** allure, dazzle, voodoo **7** attract, bedevil, enchant, possess **8** demonize, ensorcel, overlook **9** beglamour, captivate, ensorcell, fascinate, magnetize, sorcerize

bewitching 8 alluring, charming, magnetic, mesmeric **9** seductive **10** attractive

bewitchment 5 magic **7** sorcery **8** witchery, wizardry **9** conjuring, magicking **10** necromancy, witchcraft **11** incantation

beyond 3 new, yon **4** else, more, over, past **5** above, added, after, other **6** across, beside, yonder **7** athwart, besides, farther, further, outside, without **8** as well as **9** afterlife, hereafter, otherwise **10** additional, afterworld, otherworld **12** over and above, transversely *combining form:* **6** preter **7** praeter *prefix:* **3** met, par **4** meta, over, para **5** extra, hyper, super, trans, ultra

bias 4 bend, bent, skew **5** angle, bevel, slant **7** beveled, dispose, incline, leaning, slanted **8** diagonal, penchant, slanting **9** inclining, influence, prejudice, viewpoint **10** partiality, predispose, prepossess, proclivity, standpoint **11** disposition, inclination **12** one-sidedness, predilection

biased 6 swayed, warped **7** bigoted, colored, partial, slanted **8** disposed, inclined, one-sided, partisan, slanting **9** jaundiced, unneutral **10** influenced, interested, prejudiced **11** opinionated, predisposed, tendentious **12** prepossessed **13** unindifferent

bibelot 5 curio **6** bauble, gewgaw, trifle **7** novelty, trinket, whatnot **8** gimcrack **9** objet d'art **10** knickknack

Bible *abbreviation:* **2** Ex, Is, Jn, Lk, Mk, Mt, Ps **3** Col, Cor, Dan, Eph, Gal, Gen, Hab, Heb, Hos, Jas, Jer, Jon, Lam, Lev, Mal, Mic, Neh, Num, Pet, Rev, Rom, Sam, Tim, Tit **4** Deut, Ezek, Josh, Judg, Obad, Phil, Prov, Zech, Zeph **5** Chron, Thess **6** Eccles, Philem *Apocrypha book:* **5** Tobit **6** Baruch, Esdras, Esther, Judith **7** Susanna **8** Manasseh, Manasses **9** Maccabees *New Testament book:* **4** Acts, John, Jude, Luke, Mark **5** James, Peter, Titus **6** Romans **7** Hebrews, Matthew, Timothy **8** Philemon **9** Ephesians, Galatians **10** Colossians, Revelation **11** Corinthians, Philippians **13** Thessalonians *Old Testament book:* **3** Job **4** Amos, Ezra, Joel, Ruth **5** Hosea, Jonah, Kings, Micah, Nahum **6** Daniel, Esther, Exodus, Haggai, Isaiah, Joshua, Judges, Psalms, Samuel **7** Ezekiel, Genesis, Malachi, Numbers, Obadiah **8** Habakkuk, Jeremiah, Nehemiah,

Proverbs **9** Leviticus, Zechariah, Zephaniah **10** Chronicles **11** Deuteronomy **12** Ecclesiastes, Lamentations **13** Song of Solomon *part:* **4** book **5** verse **7** chapter **9** testament *translator:* **4** Knox **5** Eliot **6** Jerome, Luther **7** Erasmus, Tyndale, Zwingli **8** Wycliffe **9** Coverdale *version:* **4** Geez **5** Douay, Itala **6** Coptic, Gothic, Syriac, Targum **7** Vulgate **8** Peshitta **9** Jerusalem, King James, Masoretic, Serampore **10** New English, Septuagint **Biblical** *animal:* **4** reem **5** daman **8** behemoth *ascetic order:* **6** Essene *battle:* **7** Jericho *battle site:* **10** Armageddon *charioteer:* **4** Jehu *city, town:* **2** Ai, Ur **3** Ain, Dan, Lod, Luz, Nob **4** Bela, Cana, Gath, Gaza, Nain, Nebo, Tyre, Zoar **5** Bezer, Calno, Derbe, Ekron, Endor, Gerar, Golan, Haifa, Haran, Joppa, Lydda, Ramah, Sidon, Sodom, Tekoa, Zorah **6** Ashdod, Asshur, Beroea, Bethel, Calneh, Dothan, Emmaus, Gadara, Gibeah, Gibeon, Gilgal, Hebron, Kadesh, Lystra, Mizpah, Ophrah, Rimmon, Shiloh, Shunem, Siloan, Smyrna, Tarsus **7** Antioch, Askelon, Baalbec, Bethany, Corinth, Ephesus, Ephraim, Iconium, Jericho, Jezreel, Magdala, Nineveh, Samaria, Shechem **8** Caesarea, Chorazin, Damascus, Gomorrah, Michmash, Nazareth, Philippi, Tiberias **9** Beersheba, Beth-horon, Bethlehem, Bethsaida, Capernaum, Jerusalem *coin:* (see at **Hebrew**) *coney:* **5** daman *desert:* **5** Sinai *garden:* **4** Eden **8** Paradise *giant:* **4** Anak, Emim **7** Goliath *giant slayer:* **5** David *hill:* **4** Zion *hunter:* **6** Nimrod *judge:* **3** Eli **4** Ehud, Elon, Jair, Tola **5** Abdon, Ibzan **6** Gideon, Samson, Samuel **7** Deborah, Othniel, Shamgar **8** Jephthah *king:* **2** Og **3** Asa **4** Agag, Ahab, Ahaz, Amon, Bera, Elah, Jehu, Omri, Reba, Saul **5** David, Herod, Hiram, Joash, Joram, Nadab, Pekah, Rezin, Zimri **6** Abijam, Baasha, Birsha, Hoshea, Japhia, Josiah, Jotham, Uzziah **7** Ahaziah, Amaziah, Azariah, Jehoash, Jehoram, Menahem, Shallum, Solomon **8** Hezekiah, Jehoahaz, Jeroboam, Manasseh, Rehoboam, Zedekiah **9** Jehoiakim, Zechariah **10** Jehoiachin **11** Jehoshaphat *land:* **3** Nod, Pul **4** Aram, Elam, Moab, Seba, Seir **5** Judah, Judea, Perea **6** Bashan, Canaan, Goshen, Israel **7** Chaldea, Galilee, Samaria **9** Palestine *land of plenty:* **6** Goshen *measure:* (see at **Hebrew**) *mountain:* **3** Hor **4** Ebal, Nebo, Peor, Seir **5** Horeb, Sinai, Tabor **6** Abarim, Ararat, Carmel, Gilboa, Gilead, Hermon, Moriah, Olivet, Pisgah **7** Gerizim, Lebanon *name:* **2** Er, Ir, Ur **3** Abi, Asa, Bel, Dan, Eli, Eri, Eve, Gad, Ham, Hen, Hod, Hul, Hur, Ira, Iri, Iru, Job, Lot, Ner, Nun, Ram, Reu, Toi, Uel, Uri, Zur **4** Abel, Adah, Adam, Agag,

Ahab, Ahaz, Amon, Aran, Bela, Beor, Boaz, Buzi, Cain, Cush, Dodo, Ebal, Ebed, Eber, Eder, Ehud, Elah, Elam, Elon, Enan, Enos, Eram, Esau, Ezer, Gaal, Gadi, Gera, Guni, Hazo, Heli, Hori, Ibri, Iddo, Igal, Irad, Iram, Ishi, Izri, Jada, Jael, Jair, Jehu, Joab, Joah, Joel, John, Kish, Kore, Lael, Leah, Levi, Lois, Maon, Mark, Mary, Mica, Moab, Moza, Naam, Nebo, Neri, Noah, Obal, Obed, Oded, Ohad, Ohel, Omar, Omri, Onam, Onan, Oreb, Oren, Ozem, Ozni, Paul, Puah, Reba, Rosh, Ruth, Salu, Saph, Sara, Saul, Seth, Shem, Shua, Sodi, Suah, Susi, Tema, Tola, Ucal, Ulam, Uzai, Uzal, Uzzi, Zeeb, Zeri, Ziza, Zuar **5** Aaron, Abiel, Abner, Amasa, Amnon, Amram, Asher, Bedad, Bedan, Beeri, Caleb, Carmi, Chuza, Cozbi, David, Debir, Deuel, Dinah, Eliab, Eliam, Elias, Eliel, Eliud, Emmor, Enoch, Ephah, Ephai, Ephod, Esrom, Ethan, Ezbon, Gaham, Galal, Gazez, Gomer, Hadad, Hagar, Haggi, Haman, Hamul, Hanan, Hanun, Haran, Harum, Heber, Helah, Heleb, Helek, Helon, Hemam, Heman, Herod, Hirah, Hobab, Horam, Hosea, Ibhar, Imlah, Imnah, Isaac, Iscah, Ishui, Ithra, Ittai, Izhar, Jaasu, Jabal, Jacob, Jahdo, Jakeh, Jalam, Jalon, James, Jamin, Janna, Jared, Jarib, Jeiel, Jerah, Jered, Jesse, Jeush, Jezer, Joash, Jobab, Jogli, Jonah, Jonas, Joram, Jubal, Judah, Judas, Korah, Laban, Lahad, Lahmi, Laish, Libni, Lotan, Mahli, Mahol, Mamre, Maoch, Massa, Merab, Mered, Mesha, Micah, Moses, Mushi, Nabal, Nadab, Nahor, Naomi, Nehum, Nogah, Nohah, Ocram, Onias, Ophir, Orpah, Othni, Palal, Pallu, Palti, Pekah, Peleg, Pelet, Perez, Peter, Puvah, Rahab, Raham, Raphu, Regem, Rekem, Reuel, Rezon, Rizia, Rufus, Sacar, Sallu, Sarah, Segub, Seled, Serah, Sered, Serug, Shama, Shaul, Sheal, Sheba, Shema, Shiza, Shobi, Shuah, Shual, Shuni, Simon, Tahan, Tamar, Tarah, Tebah, Terah, Tibni, Tilon, Timna, Tubal, Uriah, Uriel, Uthai, Uzzah, Zabad, Zabdi, Zabud, Zadok, Zaham, Zebah, Zephi, Zepho, Zerah, Zibia, Zimri, Zohar **6** Abital, Achsah, Ashhur, Balaam, Baruch, Becher, Beriah, Bilhah, Binnui, Canaan, Cheran, Chesed, Daniel, Dathan, Dishan, Dishon, Elasah, Eliada, Elijah, Elisha, Elpaal, Eshban, Eshcol, Esther, Eunice, Gesham, Gideon, Gilead, Ginath, Hanani, Hannah, Hanoch, Hareph, Hebron, Hemdam, Hepher, Hezion, Hezron, Hodesh, Hoglah, Hophni, Hoshea, Hotham, Hothir, Huldah, Hupham, Hushim, Isaiah, Ishbak, Ishpah, Ishpan, Ishuah, Israel, Ithiel, Ithran, Izliah, Izziah, Jaalam, Jabesh, Jachin, Jahath, Japhia, Jashub, Jehiel, Jehush, Jemuel, Jesher, Jeshua, Jether, Jethro, Jeziel, Jezoar, Joahaz, Joakim, Joanna, Joelah,

Joiada, Joktan, Joseph, Joshah, Joshua, Josiah, Jotham, Judith, Kareah, Kemuel, Keziah, Kohath, Laadah, Lamech, Maacah, Maadai, Machir, Mahali, Mahlah, Mahlon, Malcam, Manoah, Martha, Matred, Mattan, Melech, Merari, Midian, Milcah, Miriam, Mirmah, Misham, Naamah, Naaman, Naarah, Nahash, Nahath, Nathan, Nemuel, Nepheg, Neriah, Nimrod, Ochran, Ophrah, Pagiel, Paruah, Pasach, Paseah, Peleth, Penuel, Peresh, Philip, Pilate, Pispah, Pithon, Prisca, Putiel, Raamah, Rachel, Raddai, Ramiah, Ramoth, Raphah, Reaiah, Rechab, Reuben, Rimmon, Rinnah, Rizpah, Rohgah, Salmon, Salome, Samson, Samuel, Shaaph, Shamir, Sharai, Sheber, Shelah, Shemer, Shephi, Shepho, Shilem, Shilhi, Shimea, Shimei, Shimri, Shiphi, Shobab, Shobal, Shoham, Shomer, Shuham, Simeon, Tahash, Tahath, Talmai, Thomas, Tikvah, Tirzah, Tobias, Urijah, Uzziah, Uzziel, Vaniah, Vashni, Vashti, Vophsi, Zaavan, Zabbai, Zaccur, Zalaph, Zebiah, Zephon, Zeresh, Zereth, Zeruah, Zetham, Zibiah, Zichri, Zillah, Zilpah, Zimmah, Zimran, Zippor, Zoheth, Zophah, Zuriel *patriarch:* (see at **Hebrew**) *people:* 6 Kenite, Levite 7 Amorite, Edomite, Elamite, Moabite 9 Israelite *plains:* 4 Maab 5 Mamre 7 Jericho *plotter:* 5 Haman *poem:* 5 psalm *pool:* 5 Gihon 6 Shelah, Siloam 8 Bethesda *priest:* 3 Eli 4 Levi 5 Aaron, Annas 8 Caiaphas *Promised Land:* 6 Canaan *pronoun:* 2 ye 3 thy 4 thee, thou 5 thine *prophet:* (see **prophet** entry) *Psalmist:* 5 David *punishment:* 7 stoning *queen:* 5 Sheba 6 Esther, Vashti 7 Candace, Jezebel 8 Athaliah *reproach:* 4 raca *river:* 3 Zab 4 Nile 5 Abana, Arnon 6 Abanah, Jabbok, Jordan, Kishon *sacred object:* 4 urim 7 thummin *scribe:* 6 Baruch *sea:* 3 Red 4 Dead 7 Galilee *sea monster:* 9 Leviathan *spice:* 5 aloes, myrrh 6 cassia, onycha, stacte 7 calamus 8 cinnamon, galbanum 12 frankincense *spy:* 5 Caleb *temptress:* 3 Eve 7 Delilah *thief:* 8 Barabbas *tree:* 5 cedar *valley:* 4 Baca, Elah 6 Hinnon, Kidron, Shaveh, Siddim *verb ending:* 3 eth *weed:* 4 tare *well:* 3 Ain 4 Esek 6 Jacob's *witch's home:* 5 Endor
bibliography 4 list 7 catalog, history
bibliopole 7 bookman 10 bookdealer, bookseller
bicker 3 row, war 4 spat, tiff 5 argue, clack, fight, scrap 6 argufy, battle, hassle, rattle, ruttle 7 brabble, clatter, clitter, contend, dispute, fall out, quarrel, quibble, shatter, wrangle 8 squabble 9 altercate, caterwaul
bickering 3 row 4 spat 5 run-in 6 hassle 7 dispute, quarrel, wrangle 8 squabble 11 altercation, embroilment

bicycle 4 bike 9 high-riser 11 high-wheeler *brake:* 7 caliper, coaster *for two:* 6 tandem *rider:* 6 cycler 7 cyclist *ten-speed:* 10 derailleur
bid 3 ask 4 tell, warn 5 order 6 charge, direct, enjoin, invite, summon 7 command, request 8 instruct
biddable 6 docile 7 amiable, docious 8 amenable, obedient, obliging 9 tractable 11 good-natured
bidding 4 call, word 5 order 6 behest, charge 7 command, dictate, mandate 9 summoning 10 injunction
biddy 3 bag, bat, hag 4 drab, girl, maid, trot 5 crone, witch 6 beldam
bide 4 live, stay, wait 5 dwell, tarry 6 linger, remain, reside 7 hang out 8 continue 11 stick around
bier 10 catafalque
biff 3 bop, hit 4 belt, blow, ding, nail, sock, whop 5 catch, clout, devel, pound, slosh, smack, whack 6 strike, thwack, wallop
bifold see **binary**
bifurcate 4 fork 5 split 6 branch, divide 8 separate 11 dichotomize, dichotomous
bifurcation 4 fork 6 branch 8 division 9 dichotomy 10 separation
big 3 fat 4 arty, bull, full, gone, lion, much, very 5 ample, awash, awful, great, heavy, hefty, husky, large, lofty, major, roomy, sated 6 biggie, bigwig, bumper, clumsy, gravid, hugely, packed, parous 7 awfully, brimful, copious, crammed, crowded, glutted, greatly, hulking, notable, replete, sizable, stuffed, swollen, weighty 8 enceinte, generous, imposing, inflated, material, oversize, pregnant, spacious 9 capacious, chock-full, distended, expectant, expecting, extensive, extremely, important, momentous, overblown, satisfied 10 benevolent, chivalrous, commodious, large-scale, meaningful, voluminous 11 considerate, heavyweight, magnanimous, overflowing, pretentious, significant, substantial 12 considerable, greathearted, high-sounding 13 comprehensive, consequential
Big Bertha's birthplace 5 Essen
Big Dipper *constellation:* 9 Ursa Major *star:* 5 Alcor, Dubhe, Merak, Mizar
bigfoot 4 Omah 9 Sasquatch
biggety 4 bold, wise 5 fresh, nervy, sassy 6 cheeky 7 forward 8 impudent 10 procacious 11 smart-alecky
bighearted 7 liberal 10 openhanded
big house 3 can, jug, pen 4 jail 5 clink 6 lockup, prison 7 slammer 8 hoosegow 11 reformatory 12 penitentiary
bight 3 arm, bay 4 cove, gulf 5 bayou, creek, firth, inlet 6 harbor, slough
bigmouthed 4 loud 10 boisterous

bigness 4 size 9 amplitude, greatness, largeness, magnitude 11 sizableness
bigot 6 maniac, racist, zealot 7 fanatic
bigoted 6 biased, narrow 9 hidebound, illiberal, lily-white 10 brassbound, intolerant, prejudiced, unenlarged 11 small-minded 12 conservative, narrow-minded
big shot 3 VIP 5 celeb, nabob 6 bigwig, fat cat 7 notable 8 big wheel 9 big cheese, celebrity, dignitary 13 high-muck-a-muck
bijouterie 6 jewels 7 jewelry 8 trinkets
bile *combining form:* 4 bili, chol 5 chole, cholo
bilge 4 bunk 5 hooey, trash 6 bushwa 7 hogwash, malarky, rubbish 8 nonsense 10 balderdash
Bilhah's son 3 Dan 8 Naphtali
Bilhah's father 7 Jediael
bilk 3 gyp, shy 4 balk, beat, dash, duck, foil, kite, ruin, shun 5 avoid, cheat, cozen, dodge, elude, evade, shake 6 baffle, chouse, diddle, double, escape, eschew, thwart 7 defraud 8 flimflam 9 frustrate, overreach 10 circumvent, disappoint
bill 3 neb, nib, tab 4 beak, bone, buck, cape, fish, head, naze, oner, peak, skin 5 check, point, score, visor 6 damage, dollar, pecker, poster 7 account, affiche, charges, invoice, ironman, placard, smacker 8 foreland, frogskin, handbill, headland 9 reckoning, smackeroo, statement 10 promontory *five-dollar:* 3 fin *of a bird:* 3 neb, nib 4 beak *one-dollar:* 4 buck *ten-dollar:* 7 sawbuck
billet 3 bar, bed, hut, job, rod 4 post, slab, spot 5 berth, board, house, ingot, lodge, place, put up, stick, strip 6 bestow, canton, harbor, office 7 quarter 8 domicile, position 9 entertain, situation 10 connection 11 appointment
billet-doux 8 mash note 10 love letter
billfold 6 wallet
billiards term 3 cue 4 foot, head, pool, rack, spot 5 break, carom, chalk, masse 6 bridge, cannon, corner, inning, miscue, pocket, string 7 bricole, cue ball, cushion, scratch 8 balkline, cue stick, rotation 9 eight ball 10 object ball
billingsgate 5 abuse 7 obloquy 9 contumely, invective 10 scurrility 12 vituperation
billion *British:* 8 milliard *combining form:* 4 giga
billionth *combining form:* 4 nano
bill of fare 4 menu 7 program 11 carte du jour
bill of lading 7 receipt
billy club 5 baton 6 cudgel 8 bludgeon 9 truncheon 10 knobkerrie, nightstick
bin 3 box 4 crib, vina 5 frame, pungi, stall 6 hamper, trough 9 container 10 receptacle *for coal:* 6 bunker *for fish:* 5 kench

binary 4 dual 5 duple 6 bifold, double, duplex 7 twofold 9 dualistic
bind 3 tie 4 frap, gird, tape 5 chain, dress, tie up 6 cement, enserf, fetter, ligate 7 bandage, confine, enchain, spancel 8 astringe, enfetter, ligature 9 constrict *bird's wings:* 6 pinion *to secrecy:* 4 tile, tyle *with twigs:* 5 withe
binding *combining form:* 5 desis
binge 3 bat, bum, bun, jag 4 bust, orgy, soak, tear, time, toot 5 blast, booze, drunk, fling, souse, spree 6 bender, ran-tan 7 blowoff, blowout, carouse, debauch, rampage, splurge, wassail 8 carousal, rowdydow 9 bacchanal, brannigan 11 bacchanalia, compotation
bingo 5 beano
Binnui *father:* 7 Henadad *son:* 7 Noadiah
biographer 9 memoirist *American:* 5 Weems 6 Parton 7 Freeman 8 Bradford, Sandburg *English:* 6 Aubrey, Morley, Walton 7 Boswell 8 Strachey *French:* 7 Maurois *German:* 6 Ludwig *Greek:* 8 Plutarch *Italian:* 6 Vasari *Roman:* 9 Suetonius
biography 3 bio 4 life, obit 5 diary, story 6 memoir 7 history, journal, letters, profile 8 obituary 11 confessions
biological category 5 class, genus, order 6 family, phylum 7 species, variety 10 subspecies
bionomics 7 ecology
birchbark 5 canoe
bird *African:* 4 coly, fink, taha, tock 5 paauw 6 barbet, bulbul, jabiru, quelea, whidah 7 courser, finfoot, marabou, ostrich, touraco 8 hornbill, oxpecker, parakeet, umbrette 9 beefeater, broadbill, francolin, napecrest, trochilus 10 hammerhead, tambourine *antarctic:* 4 skua 7 penguin 10 sheathbill *aquatic:* 3 auk, cob, ern, mew 4 cobb, coot, duck, erne, gony, gull, loon, skua, swan, teal, tern 5 booby, cahow, goose, grebe, murre, rotch, solan 6 fulmar, gannet, hagdon, petrel, puffin, rotche, scoter, wigeon 7 anhinga, dovekey, dovekie, finfoot, mallard, moorhen, pelican, penguin, skimmer, widgeon 8 alcatras, baldpate, dabchick, murrelet 9 albatross, cormorant, gallinule, guillemot, kittiwake 10 shearwater, sheathbill *arctic:* 3 auk 4 knot, skua, xema 5 murre, rotch 6 fulmar, jaeger, rotche 7 dovekey, dovekie 9 guillemot *Asian:* 4 kora, myna, ruff, smew 5 mynah, pewit, pitta 6 chukar, drongo, dunlin, hoopoe 7 courser, hill tit, lapwing, peacock, sirgang 8 accentor, dotterel, hornbill, parakeet, tragopan, wheatear 9 brambling, francolin *Australian:* 3 emu 4 kahu, koel, koil, lory 5 arara, galah, pitta 6 drongo, leipoa 7 boobook, bustard, figbird, waybung 8 bellbird, bush-

lark, cockatoo, lorikeet, lyrebird, manucode, megapode, morepork, parakeet **9** cassowary, coachwhip, frogmouth, pardalote **blackbird: 3** ani, daw, pie **4** crow, merl, rook **5** amsel, merle, ousel, ouzel, raven **6** chough, magpie, thrush **7** grackle, jackdaw, redwing **carrion-eating: 4** aura **5** urubu **6** condor **7** buzzard, vulture **Central American: 4** guan, ibis **5** booby, macaw **6** barbet, jabiru, toucan **7** bittern, cotinga, jacamar, quetzal, tinamou **8** curassow, troupial **chimney-nesting: 5** swift **class: 4** Aves **colony: 5** roost **7** rookery **combining form: 5** ornis **6** ornith **7** ornitho **8** ornithes (plural) **corvine:** (see **crow family** below) **crocodile: 9** trochilus **crow family: 3** daw, jay, kae **4** rook **5** raven **6** chough, corbie, magpie **7** jackdaw **diving: 3** auk **4** smew **5** grebe, murre **6** dipper, petrel **8** murrelet **9** guillemot, merganser **European: 3** mag, mew, nun **4** clee, darr, gled, mall, merl, pope, rook, ruff, shag, smew, wren **5** amsel, crake, egret, finch, glede, merle, ousel, ouzel, pewit, pipit, terek, whaup **6** cuckoo, dunlin, hoopoe, linnet, martin, merlin, missel, redleg, roller, thrush **7** bustard, jackdaw, kestrel, lapwing, martlet, ortolan, redwing, ruddock, sparrow, wagtail, wryneck **8** accentor, blackcap, brantail, dabchick, dotterel, garganey, nightjar, nuthatch, peesweep, redstart, reedling, starling, throstle, wheatear, whimbrel, whinchat, woodcock **9** brambling, chaffinch, crossbill, fieldfare, stonechat **10** chiffchaff, goatsucker, kingfisher **11** lammergeier **extinct: 3** moa **4** dodo, mamo **8** Diatryma **9** aepyornis, solitaire **fabulous: 3** roc **5** hansa **6** simurg **7** phoenix, simurgh **flightless: 3** emu, moa **4** dodo, kagu, kiwi, rhea, weka **5** kakapo, ratite, takahe **7** apteryx, ostrich, penguin, roatelo **8** Diatryma, notornis **9** cassowary **fruit-eating: 4** coly **6** parrot, toucan **game: 4** duck, guan, rail, sora, teal **5** brant, goose, quail, snipe **6** chukar, grouse, turkey **7** bustard, mallard, pintail, widgeon **8** baldpate, bobwhite, moorfowl, pheasant, shoveler, tragopan, wildfowl, woodcock **9** merganser, partridge, ptarmigan **ground-dwelling: 5** colin, quail **6** grouse, peahen, turkey **7** chicken, peacock, peafowl **8** bobwhite, moorfowl, pheasant **9** partridge, ptarmigan **Hawaiian: 2** io **3** ava, ioa, iwa **4** koae, mamo, moho, omao **Indian: 4** baya, kala, koel, koil **5** sarus, shama **6** argala, bulbul, homrai, luggar **7** peacock **8** adjutant, amadavat, tragopan **Jamaican: 7** vervain **large: 3** emu, moa **4** guan **5** eagle **6** curlew, jabiru, willet **7** bustard, megapod, ostrich, pelican, seriema **8** curassow, megapode, shoebill **largest: 7** ostrich **Madagascar:**

6 drongo **7** anhinga, kirombo, roatelo **marsh: 4** coot, rail, sora **5** crane, snipe, stilt **8** reedling **9** gallinule **Mexican: 6** jacana **mythical: 3** roc **7** phoenix **9** feng-huang, feng-hwang **New Zealand: 3** ihi, kea, poe, tui **4** huia, kaka, kaki, kiwi, koko, ruru, titi, weka **6** kakapo **7** apteryx **8** morepork, notornis **nocturnal: 3** owl **5** cahow, owlet **7** bullbat, dorhawk **8** guacharo, nightjar **9** nighthawk **10** goatsucker **North American: 3** ani, tit **4** coot, pape, sora, stib, wamp, wren **5** booby, colin, crane, egret, junco, murre, robin, swift, veery, vireo **6** chebec, darter, dunlin, fulmar, grouse, hagdon, phoebe, towhee, turkey, verdin, willet **7** anhinga, blue jay, catbird, flicker, grackle, tanager **8** bobolink, bobwhite, cardinal, killdeer, nuthatch, thrasher, titmouse, wheatear **9** chickadee, crossbill, nighthawk, partridge, snakebird **10** bufflehead **12** whippoorwill **of Arabian Nights: 3** roc **of brilliant plumage: 4** lory, toco, tody **5** macaw, pitta **6** oriole, parrot, toucan, trogon **7** jacamar, kirombo, minivet **8** lorikeet, parakeet, pheasant, tragopan **of omen: 7** waybird **of peace: 4** dove **of prey: 3** owl **4** gled, hawk, kite **5** buteo, eagle, glead, glede, harpy **6** condor, elenet, falcon, osprey, raptor **7** buzzard, goshawk, harrier, kestrel, vulture **8** caracara **9** accipiter **11** lammergeier **relating to: 5** avian, avine **6** ornithic **shore: 3** auk **4** gull, ruff, tern **5** reeve, snipe, stilt **6** avocet, avoset, curlew, dunlin, plover, puffin, willet **7** lapwing, skimmer **8** dotterel, killdeer, redshank, whimbrel, woodcock **9** phalarope, sandpiper, turnstone **small: 3** tit **4** tody, wren **5** finch, pewee, pipit, serin, sylph, vireo **6** canary, sappho, tomtit, verdin **7** manakin, sparrow **8** titmouse **9** chickadee **songbird: 3** jay, tit **4** chat, crow, lark, wren **5** finch, mavie, mavis, pipit, robin, shama, veery, vireo **6** bulbul, canary, dipper, linnet, oriole, shrike, thrush **7** catbird, creeper, hill tit, kinglet, redwing, skylark, sparrow, swallow, tanager, titlark, wagtail, warbler, waxwing **8** accentor, amadavat, bobolink, brantail, cardinal, nuthatch, philomel, redstart, starling, thrasher, whinchat, woodlark **9** chickadee, stonechat **10** chiffchaff, flycatcher **11** nightingale **South American: 3** ara, hia **4** anna, guan, jacu, loro, mitu, rhea, soco, toco, yeni **5** chaja, egret, macaw, potoo, sylph **6** chunga, cracid, jabiru, motmot, sappho, toucan **7** cariama, cotinga, hoatzin, jacamar, limpkin, manakin, seriema, tinamou **8** boatbill, caracara, curassow, guacharo, hoactzin, screamer, tapaculo, tapaculo, terutero, troupial **9** campanero, trumpeter **talking: 4** myna **5** mynah **6** parrot **tropical: 3** ani

6 barbet, drongo, motmot, quezal, toucan, trogon 7 cacique, hoatzin, jacamar, manakin, quetzal, sawbill, waxbill 8 guacharo, hoactzin, troupial *turkey-like:* 8 curassow *unfledged:* 4 eyas 5 chick 6 gorlin 8 nestling *wading:* 4 ibis, rail 5 crane, egret, heron, stork 6 godwit, jabiru, jacana 7 bittern, courlan, limpkin, tattler 8 boatbill, flamingo, shoebill, umbrette 9 spoonbill 10 hammerhead *web-footed:* 3 auk 4 duck, loon, swan 5 goose, murre 6 avocet, avoset, darter, fulmar, gannet, petrel, puffin 7 anhinga, pelican, penguin 8 shoveler 9 albatross, cormorant, guillemot, merganser, razorbill, snakebird 10 shearwater *West Indian:* 3 ani 4 tody

birdbrain 5 dummy, dunce, idiot, moron 7 dullard 8 dullhead, dumbbell 9 ignoramus, simpleton 10 rattlehead 11 featherhead

birdcage *large:* 6 aviary, volary, volery

birdlife 5 ornis 8 avifauna

bird pepper 8 capsicum

birds' eggs *study of:* 6 oology

bird's head *top:* 5 pilea (plural) 6 pileum

birr 3 pep 4 tuck 5 moxie, vigor 6 energy 7 potency 9 hardihood

birth 4 dawn, flow, rise, slip, stem 5 arise, issue, onset, start 6 outset, spring 7 bearing, emanate, genesis, opening, proceed 8 geniture, nascence, nascency, nativity, outstart 9 beginning, originate 10 derive from 12 commencement *combining form:* 4 toky

birth-control leader 6 Sanger

birth flower *April:* 5 daisy *August:* 9 gladiolus *December:* 10 poinsettia *February:* 8 primrose *January:* 9 carnation *July:* 8 sweet pea *June:* 4 rose *March:* 6 violet *May:* 15 lily of the valley *November:* 13 chrysanthemum *October:* 6 dahlia *September:* 5 aster

birthmark 4 mole 5 nevus, point, trait 7 feature 9 character

birthright 6 legacy 8 appanage, heritage 9 heritance, patrimony, privilege 10 perquisite 11 inheritance, prerogative

birthroot 8 trillium

birthstone *April:* 7 diamond 8 sapphire *August:* 7 peridot 8 sardonyx *December:* 6 zircon 9 turquoise *February:* 8 amethyst *January:* 6 garnet *July:* 4 ruby *June:* 5 agate, pearl 11 alexandrite *March:* 6 jasper 10 aquamarine, bloodstone *May:* 7 emerald *November:* 5 topaz *October:* 4 opal 10 tourmaline *September:* 8 sapphire 10 chrysolite

biscuit 3 bun 4 roll, rusk, snap 6 bisque, cookie 7 cracker 8 cracknel, hardtack *Scottish:* 4 bake

bishop *district:* 7 diocese *headdress:*

5 miter, mitre *seat of office:* 3 see *skullcap:* 9 zucchetto *staff:* 7 crosier, crozier *throne:* 8 cathedra

bishopric 3 see 7 diocese

bismuth *symbol:* 2 Bi

bison *European:* 6 wisent 7 aurochs *family:* 7 Bovidae *North American:* 7 buffalo

bistered 4 dark 5 brown, dusky, swart 6 brunet, swarth 7 swarthy 11 dark-skinned

bistro 4 café 6 nitery 7 cabaret, hot spot 8 nightery 9 nightclub, night spot 11 discotheque 13 watering place

bit 3 end, jot 4 atom, bite, curb, drop, iota, mite, time, whet 5 check, minim, scrap, space, speck, spell, while 6 bridle, hold in, morsel 7 inhibit, smidgen, stretch 8 fragment, hold back, hold down, molecule, mouthful, particle, restrain, withhold 9 constrain

bit by bit 9 gradually, piecemeal

bitch goddess 7 success

bite 3 cut, eat, lot 4 burn, chaw, chew, gnaw, part, tapa 5 bever, chack, champ, chomp, erode, mug-up, munch, piece, quota, scour, share, slice, smart, snack, stang, sting, tooth 6 crunch, morsel, nibble 7 corrode, eat away, partage, portion, scrunch 8 mouthful 9 allotment, allowance, masticate

Bithiah's husband 5 Mered

biting 5 crisp, nippy 7 cutting, ingoing, mordant 8 clear-cut, incisive 9 sarcastic, trenchant 11 penetrating

bitter 3 bad 4 acid, hard, tart 5 acerb, acrid, harsh, sharp 6 brutal, picric, rugged, severe, woeful 7 austere, divided, galling, hostile, painful 8 grievous, rigorous, virulent 9 alienated, amaroidal, rancorous, vexatious, vitriolic 10 afflictive, disturbing, unpleasant 11 distasteful, distressing, intemperate, unpalatable 12 antagonistic, disagreeable *combining form:* 4 picr 5 picro

bitterness 8 acrimony, asperity

bitterroot 7 dogbane

bitumen 3 tar 5 pitch 7 asphalt, naphtha 8 blacktop

bivalve 4 clam, spat 6 cockle, mussel, oyster, pholas 7 geoduck, goeduck, mollusk, pandora, piddock, scallop 10 brachiopod

bivouac 4 camp 6 encamp, laager, maroon 10 encampment

bizarre 3 odd 5 antic, queer, weird 7 curious, oddball, strange, unusual 8 peculiar, singular 9 fantastic, grotesque 10 outlandish

Bizet opera 6 Carmen

blab 3 gab, yak 4 chat, talk, tell 5 rumor 6 babble, betray, gabble, gossip, jabber, reveal, tattle **7** chatter, divulge, palaver **8** disclose, give away

blabber 3 gab **4** chat **5** clack, drool, prate **6** babble, drivel, gabber, gabble, jabber, magpie, prater **7** blather, chatter, palaver, prattle, twaddle **8** jabberer, prattler **9** chatterer **10** chatterbox

blabbermouth 6 gabber, magpie, prater **7** windbag **8** jabberer, prattler **9** bandarlog **10** chatterbox

black 3 jet **4** ebon, foul, inky, noir, onyx **5** bleak, dirty, ebony, nasty, raven, sable, slate, soily, utter **6** bruise, dismal, dreary, filthy, gloomy, grubby, impure, pitchy, somber **7** contuse, piceous, squalid, unclean **8** absolute, charcoal, complete, funereal, outright **9** downright, out-and-out, pitch-dark **10** depressing, depressive, oppressive **11** atramentous, dispiriting *combining form:* **3** mel **4** atro, mela, melo **5** melam, melan **6** melano

blackball 4 veto **7** boycott, exclude **9** ostracize

black bass 7 sunfish **10** priestfish

black beast 4 hate **7** bugbear **8** anathema **9** bête noire **11** abomination, detestation

blackbird see at **bird**

black cohosh 7 bugbane

black crappie 7 sunfish **10** calico bass

black death 6 plague

black diamond 4 coal **8** hematite **9** carbonado

blacken 4 slur, soot **5** libel, smear **6** defame, malign, vilify **7** asperse, slander, traduce **10** calumniate

black eye 4 blot, onus, slur **5** mouse, odium, stain **6** shiner, stigma **11** bar sinister

blackfish 5 whale **6** bowfin, salmon, tautog **7** galjoen **8** luderick

Black Forest *city:* **10** Baden-Baden *peak:* **8** Feldberg *river:* **5** Rhine **6** Danube

black gold 3 oil **9** maldonite, petroleum

blackguard 4 heel **5** knave, rogue **6** rascal **7** lowlife, villain **9** miscreant, scoundrel

blackhead 4 clam **5** sebum **6** comedo, mussel **9** scaup duck

blackheart 9 sandpiper **12** whortleberry

blackjack 3 oak **6** coerce **7** tankard **9** scaup duck **10** sphalerite

black lead 8 graphite

black letter 6 Gothic **10** Old English

black magic 10 witchcraft

blackmail 6 extort **8** chantage **9** extortion

Black Muslim founder 5 Farad

black out 5 annul, erase, faint, swoon **6** cancel, delete, efface **7** expunge **10** obliterate

blackpoll 7 warbler

Black Prince 6 Edward

Blackshirt 7 fascist

blacksmith 4 fish **6** forger, plover **7** farrier, striker **10** horseshoer

blacktail 6 dassie **11** salmon trout

blackthorn 4 cane, plum **7** pear haw **8** cocktail

black vomit 11 hematemesis, yellow fever

blackwash 5 libel **6** malign, vilify **7** asperse, slander, traduce **9** denigrate **10** calumniate, scandalize, villainize

black widow 6 spider

bladder 3 sac **4** cyst **5** pouch **6** vesica **7** blister, vacuole **7** vesicae (plural), vesicle **8** vesicula **9** vesiculae (plural) *combining form:* **3** asc **4** asci, asco, cyst, phys **5** cysto, physo

blah 4 bosh, dull **5** hooey **6** bunkum, dreary, humbug, stodgy **7** humdrum **8** banausic, nonsense, pishposh, plodding **10** balderdash, monotonous, pedestrian

blamable see **blameworthy**

blame 3 rap **4** onus **5** fault, guilt, knock **6** accuse **7** censure, condemn **8** denounce, reproach **9** criticize, reprehend, reprobate **10** accusation, denunciate, imputation **12** condemnation, denunciation, reprehension *Scottish:* **4** wite, wyte **6** dirdum

blameless 4 good, pure **5** clean **8** innocent, unguilty **9** crimeless, exemplary, faultless, guiltless, lily-white, righteous **10** inculpable

blameworthy 5 amiss **6** guilty, sinful, unholy **8** culpable, faultful **10** censurable, delinquent, illaudable, punishable **13** reprehensible, uncommendable

blanch 4 pale **5** quail, start, white, wince **6** bleach, flinch, recoil, shrink, whiten **7** decolor, squinch

blanched 3 wan **4** ashy, pale **5** ashen, livid, waxen **6** doughy, pallid **9** colorless

Blancheflor's beloved 6 Flores, Floris

bland 4 flat, mild, soft **5** balmy, banal, suave, vapid **6** gentle, smooth, urbane, watery **7** insipid, lenient, sapless **8** waterish **10** namby-pamby, wishy-washy

blandish 3 con **4** coax **6** cajole **7** blarney, flatter, wheedle **8** soft-soap **9** sweet-talk

blandishment 3 oil **7** blarney, incense **8** flattery, soft soap **9** adulation

blank 4 skip **5** chasm, empty, utter **6** vacant **7** deadpan **8** absolute, omission **9** downright, out-and-out, oversight **11** preterition **12** inexpressive, unexpressive

blanket 3 cap **5** cover, crown **6** afghan, stroud **7** overlay **8** overcast **10** overspread *Spanish:* **6** sarape, serape

blankness 7 vacancy, vacuity **9** emptiness **11** vacuousness

blare 5 shout **6** scream, shriek

blaring 4 loud **7** roaring **8** piercing

10 stentorian 11 full-mouthed, stentorious
12 earsplitting

blarney 3 con, oil 4 coax 6 cajole
7 incense, wheedle 8 blandish, flattery, soft
soap 9 adulation, sweet-talk
12 blandishment

blasé 5 jaded 7 knowing, worldly 8 mondaine 9 apathetic 11 indifferent, worldlywise 12 disenchanted, disentranced,
sophisticate 13 disillusioned, sophisticated

blaspheme 5 abuse, curse, swear
6 revile 7 profane

blasphemous 7 profane 12 sacrilegious

blasphemy 5 abuse 7 cursing, cussing,
shaming 8 swearing 9 befouling, profanity,
sacrilege, violation 10 execration 11 desecration, imprecation, profanation

blast 4 bang, beat, belt, boom, clap, dash,
drub, ruin, slam, slug, toot, wham, whip
5 burst, crack, crash, smash, wreck
6 blight, wallop 7 destroy, lambast 8 lambaste 9 overwhelm

blat 6 cry out 7 exclaim 8 blurt out
9 ejaculate

blatant 4 loud 5 gaudy, overt 6 arrant,
brassy, brazen, flashy, garish, patent, tawdry 7 glaring 8 impudent, overbold, strident 9 barefaced, clamorous, shameless,
unabashed 10 boisterous, unblushing,
vociferant, vociferous 11 loudmouthed
12 obstreperous

blather 4 bosh 5 drool, hokum, prate
6 babble, bunkum, drivel, gabble 7 blabber,
prattle, twaddle 8 nonsense 10 balderdash, double-talk, flapdoodle

blaze 4 glow 5 blare, flame, flare, glare,
shine 7 declare 8 announce, proclaim
10 incandesce 11 scintillate *Scottish:*
3 low 4 lowe

blazes 4 hell 5 abyss, hades, Sheol
6 Tophet 7 Gehenna, inferno 9 perdition

blazing 5 afire, fiery 6 aflame, alight,
ardent, fervid, red-hot 7 burning, fervent,
flaming, flaring, ignited 9 perfervid 10 passionate 11 conflagrant, impassioned

blazing star 8 tritonia 9 colicroot

blazon 5 sound 7 declare, publish
8 announce, proclaim 9 advertise, broadcast 10 annunciate, bruit about, promulgate

bleach 5 white 6 blanch, blench, whiten
7 decolor 8 peroxide

bleak 4 dour, grim, hard 5 harsh 6 dismal,
dreary, gloomy, severe, somber 7 austere
8 funereal 9 stringent 10 depressing,
oppressive 13 disheartening

blear 3 dim 4 blur, dull 5 faint, vague
7 obscure, shadowy, unclear 10 ill-defined,
indistinct

bleary 3 dim 5 all in, faint, spent, vague
6 effete, used up 7 drained, far-gone,
obscure, shadowy, unclear, worn-out

8 depleted 9 exhausted, washed-out 10 ill-defined, indistinct

bleat 3 baa 4 crab, fuss, yawp 5 gripe
6 squawk, yammer 7 blow off

bleed 4 ooze, seep, weep 5 exude, mulct,
stick, sweat 6 fleece, strain 8 transude

bleeding heart 8 dicentra
11 sympathizer

blemish 3 mar 4 flaw, harm, hurt, scar,
vice, wart 5 fault, spoil 6 blotch, damage,
defect, impair, injure 7 blister, tarnish, vitiate 8 pockmark 13 disfigurement

blench 5 quail, start, white, wince
6 bleach, flinch, recoil, shrink, whiten
7 decolor, squinch

blend 3 mix 4 fuse, meld 5 alloy, immix,
unify, unite 6 commix, fusion 7 amalgam,
arrange, combine, mixture 8 coalesce, compound, conflate, immingle, intermix 9 commingle, composite, harmonize, integrate,
interfuse 10 amalgamate, commixture,
symphonize, synthesize 11 interfusion,
orchestrate 12 amalgamation, intermixture

bless 4 laud 5 extol 6 hallow, praise
7 glorify 8 eulogize, sanctify 9 celebrate
10 consecrate, panegyrize

blessed 4 holy 6 sacred 7 saintly 8 hallowed 9 unprofane 10 sanctified
11 consecrated

blessedness 5 bliss 9 beatitude, happiness 12 blissfulness

blessing 2 OK 4 boon, good, okay
5 favor, grace 6 thanks 7 benefit, benison,
godsend 8 approval 9 advantage
11 approbation, benediction
12 thanksgiving

blight 3 nip 4 dash, ruin 5 blast 7 disease

blimp 5 fatso, fatty 7 airship 8 zeppelin
9 dirigible

blind 4 daze, dull 5 decoy, drunk, front,
shill 6 capper, dazzle 7 eyeless, muddled,
shutter 8 bedazzle, unseeing 9 pixilated,
shillaber, sightless 10 inebriated, lackluster,
lusterless, visionless 11 intoxicated *combining form:* 5 typhl 6 typhlo

blind alley 6 pocket 7 dead end,
impasse 8 cul-de-sac

blind god 4 Hoth 5 Cupid, Hoder, Hodur,
Hothr

blindworm 6 lizard

blink 3 bat 4 wink 5 flash 7 flicker, nictate, twinkle 9 nictitate

blink at 4 omit 6 forget, ignore, slight
7 connive, neglect 8 discount, overlook
9 disregard

blip 3 box 4 cuff, slap 5 smack, spank
6 buffet, censor, screen 9 expurgate
10 bowdlerize

bliss 4 Zion 6 Canaan, heaven 7 elysium,
nirvana 8 empyrean, paradise 9 beatitude,
happiness 11 blessedness

blissful 5 happy 6 elated 8 beatific, ecstatic, euphoric 9 contented

blissfulness 7 ecstasy 8 euphoria 9 beatitude, happiness 10 exaltation 11 blessedness

blister 4 bleb, flay 5 blain, bulla, slash 6 canker, scathe, scorch 7 lambast, scarify, scourge, vesicle 8 lambaste, vesicate 9 castigate, excoriate *combining form:* 7 vesicul 8 vesiculo

blithe 3 gay 4 boon 5 jolly, merry, sunny 6 cheery, chirpy, jocund, jovial 7 gleeful 8 cheerful, chirrupy, mirthful, sunbeamy 9 lightsome 12 lighthearted

blithering 4 rank 5 gross, utter 7 blasted 8 absolute, outright, positive 9 downright, out-and-out

blithesome see **blithe**

blitz 4 raid 7 bombard 10 mass attack 11 bombardment

bloated 5 puffy 6 stuffy 7 pompous 8 arrogant 10 pontifical 11 magisterial 13 self-important

bloc 4 ring 5 party 7 combine, faction 9 coalition 11 combination

block 3 bar, dam, ell 4 clog, fill, plug, stop, wall, wing 5 annex, brake, choke, close 6 cut off, hinder, impede 7 barrier, congest, occlude, stopper 8 obstruct 9 barricade, extension, intercept

blockade 3 bar 4 stop, wall 5 beset, siege 6 invest 7 barrier, besiege 9 barricade, beleaguer, blank wall, roadblock

blockbuster 4 bomb

blockhead 4 dolt, dope 5 dunce, idiot, ninny 8 clodpate, dumbbell, numskull 9 simpleton 10 thickskull

blockheaded 4 dumb 5 dense, thick 6 stupid 7 doltish 10 numskulled

block out 5 close, draft 6 screen, shroud, sketch 7 outline, shut off 8 obstruct, skeleton 9 adumbrate 12 characterize

block up 4 clog, plug, stop

bloke 3 guy, man 4 chap, gent 6 fellow 9 gentleman

blond 4 fair 5 light, straw 6 flaxen, golden 7 towhead 8 platinum 9 towheaded

blood 4 gore 6 murder, origin 7 descent, lineage 8 ancestry 10 extraction *cancer of:* 8 leukemia *cell:* 3 red 4 poly 5 white 8 hemocyte, monocyte, platelet 9 corpuscle, leukocyte 10 lymphocyte 11 erythrocyte, granulocyte *clot:* 8 thrombus *clotted:* 4 gore *coloring matter:* 10 hemoglobin *combining form:* 3 hem 4 emia, haem, hema, hemi, hemo 5 aemia, haema, haemo, hemat, hemia 6 haemat, haemia, hemato, sangui 7 haemato 8 sanguini, sanguino *disease:* 6 anemia 8 leukemia 10 hemophilia *factor:* 2 RH *feud:*

8 vendetta *fluid part:* 5 serum 6 plasma *of the gods:* 5 ichor *particle in:* 7 embolus *poisoning:* 6 pyemia 7 toxemia 8 copremia, sapremia 10 septicemia *pressure:* 8 systolic 9 diastolic *relating to:* 5 hemal, hemic 7 hematal *serum:* 6 plasma *study of:* 10 hematology *sugar:* 7 glucose

bloodbath 7 carnage 8 butchery, massacre 9 slaughter

bloodless 4 dull, hard, pale 6 anemic, pallid, watery 8 waterish 9 insensate 10 anesthetic, insensible 11 insensitive

bloodletting 10 phlebotomy 11 venesection

bloodlike 8 hematoid

bloodline 6 family, strain

bloodroot 7 puccoon 8 turmeric 10 tetterwort 11 Indian paint

bloodshed *place of:* 8 aceldama

bloodstained 4 gory 7 imbrued 8 sanguine 10 sanguinary 11 ensanguined, sanguineous

bloodstone 10 chalcedony

bloodsucker 4 tick 5 lamia, leech 6 lizard, sponge 7 sponger, vampire 8 barnacle, hanger on, parasite 10 freeloader 12 lounge lizard

bloodthirsty 8 sanguine 9 homicidal, murdering, murderous 10 sanguinary 11 sanguineous

blood vessel 4 vein 5 aorta 6 artery 7 jugular 9 capillary *combining form:* 3 vas 4 angi, vasi, vaso 5 angio *rupture:* 6 rhexis

bloodwort 6 yarrow 8 centaury 10 herb robert 11 salad burnet

bloody 4 gory, grim 6 imbrued 8 sanguine 9 cutthroat, homicidal, murdering, murderous 10 sanguinary 11 ensanguined, sanguineous 12 slaughterous

bloom 4 blow, glow, posy 5 blush 6 flower 7 blossom, burgeon 10 effloresce

blooper 4 slip, trip 5 boner, break, error, fluff, gaffe, lapse 6 boo-boo, bungle 7 blunder, faux pas, mistake 8 solecism 9 indecorum 11 impropriety

blossom 3 bud 4 blow, glow, open, posy 5 bloom, blush, flush 6 flower, unfold 7 burgeon 10 effloresce

blot 4 blur, onus, slur, smut, spot 5 brand, odium, stain 6 stigma 7 bestain, blemish 8 black eye, discolor 11 bar sinister

blotch 6 macula, macule, mottle 7 splodge, splotch *combining form:* 5 macul 6 maculi, maculo

blot out 5 abate, annul, erase 6 cancel, delete, efface 7 abolish, expunge 9 eradicate, extirpate 10 annihilate, extinguish, obliterate 11 exterminate

blouse 5 middy, shirt, smock, tunic 6 basque, guimpe

bloviate 4 rant, rave 5 mouth, orate 7 declaim, soapbox 8 harangue, perorate

blow 3 bop, fan, hit, jar 4 bang, bash, belt, biff, brag, bump, cuff, gasp, gust, huff, jolt, pant, puff, slam, slug, swat, whop, wind 5 bloom, boast, break, crack, pound, prate, punch, shock, slosh, smack, smash, vaunt, waste, whack 6 flower, impact, ruffle, thwack, wallop, winnow 7 blossom, burgeon, consume, fritter, respite 8 breather, knockout, outbloom, squander 9 bastinado, collision, dissipate, gasconade, throw away 10 concussion, effloresce, frivol away, percussion, trifle away 11 rodomontade

blow-by-blow 6 minute 8 detailed, itemized, thorough 9 clocklike 10 particular

blowhard see **boaster**

blow in 4 come 6 arrive, show up, turn up

blowout 4 bash 6 shindy 7 shindig

blowsy 5 dowdy 6 frowsy, sordid 8 slattern 10 slatternly 13 draggletailed

blow up 4 boil, burn, fume, rage 5 anger, burst, go off 6 seethe 7 bristle, explode 8 boil over, detonate, disprove, dynamite 9 discredit

blowy 4 airy 5 gusty, windy 6 breezy

blubber 3 cry, sob 4 pipe, wail, weep 6 boohoo

bludgeon 3 bat 4 club 5 baton, billy, bully 6 cudgel, hector 7 bluster, war club 8 browbeat, bulldoze, bullyrag 9 bastinado, billy club, strong-arm, truncheon 10 intimidate, nightstick *British:* 4 cosh

blue 3 low, sea 4 down, racy 5 ocean, salty, shady, spicy 6 purple, risqué, wicked 7 profane 8 dejected, downcast, off-color 9 depressed, woebegone 10 dispirited, suggestive 11 downhearted 12 disconsolate *combining form:* 3 ind 4 cyan, indi, indo 5 cyano *dark:* 5 perse 6 indigo *grayish:* 5 merle, slate 7 celeste *greenish:* 4 aqua, bice, cyan, teal 5 beryl 6 cobalt 7 azurite 8 calamine 9 turquoise *moderate:* 5 copen *reddish:* 5 smalt 6 marine, purple, violet 7 cyanine, gentian, lobelia 8 mazarine *sky:* 5 azure 8 cerulean

___ **Blue** 3 Ben

blue blood 5 elite 6 aristo, gentry 7 aristoi 9 gentility, gentleman, patrician 10 aristocrat, upper class 11 aristocracy

bluebonnet 4 Scot 6 parrot 10 cornflower

Blue Boy painter 12 Gainsborough

bluecoat 3 cop 5 bobby 6 copper 8 Dogberry 9 constable, policeman

blue-eyed 8 favorite, precious 10 fairhaired

Bluegrass State 8 Kentucky

Blue Grotto site 5 Capri

bluejacket 6 sailor

blue jeans 6 denims

blue moon 3 age, eon 4 aeon 7 dog's age 8 coon's age, eternity 12 donkey's years

bluenose 4 prig 5 prude 7 puritan 8 comstock 9 Mrs. Grundy, nice Nelly 10 goody-goody

bluenosed 4 prig, prim 6 prissy, stuffy 7 prudish 8 priggish 9 Victorian 10 tightlaced 11 puritanical, straitlaced

blue-pencil 4 edit 6 delete, revise

bluepoint 6 oyster

blueprint 4 cast, plan 5 chart 6 design, devise, scheme, sketch 7 arrange, outline, project 8 game plan, strategy

blue-ribbon 3 top 5 prime 6 Grade A 7 capital 8 five-star, top-notch 9 excellent, first-rate, top-drawer 10 first-class 11 firststring

blues 5 dumps, gloom 7 dismals, sadness 9 dejection 10 depression, melancholy 11 unhappiness 12 mournfulness

bluff 3 act 4 curt, fake, fool, sham 5 blunt, feign, frank, gruff, rough, sharp, trick 6 abrupt, affect, assume, betray, candid, crusty, delude, direct, humbug, illude, snippy 7 beguile, brusque, deceive, mislead, pretend 8 snippety 9 outspoken 10 forthright, no-nonsense 11 counterfeit, double-cross, plainspoken, short-spoken

blunder 4 bull, goof, mess, slip, trip 5 boner, botch, error, fluff, gaffe, gum up, lapse 6 bobble, bollix, bumble, bungle, goof up 7 blooper, louse up, mistake, stumble 8 flounder

blunderbuss 3 gun 7 bungler, firearm

blunt 4 bald, curt, dull, mull, numb 5 bluff, brief, gruff, short 6 abrupt, benumb, crusty, deaden, obtund, obtuse, snippy, snubby, weaken 7 brusque, cripple, disable, disedge, stupefy 8 enfeeble, hebetate, snippety 9 attenuate, undermine 10 debilitate 11 desensitize 12 unstrengthen

blur 3 dim, fog 4 blot, dull, mist, onus, slur, spot 5 befog, blear, brand, cloud, muddy, odium, smear, stain, taint 6 smudge, stigma 7 becloud, besmear, confuse, tarnish 8 besmirch, black eye, discolor 11 bar sinister *in printing:* 6 mackle

blurb 2 ad 4 plug, puff 6 notice 7 puffing, write-up 12 commendation

blurt 4 blat, bolt 6 cry out 7 exclaim 9 ejaculate

blush 4 glow, rose 5 bloom, color, flush, rouge 6 mantle, pinken, redden 7 blossom, crimson, roseate

bluster 4 bawl, huff, rage, roar, rout 5 blast, bully, storm 6 bellow, clamor, hector 7 dragoon 8 bludgeon, browbeat, bulldoze, bullyrag 10 intimidate

blustery 4 wild 5 rough 6 raging, stormy

7 furious **8** stormful **9** turbulent
11 tempestuous
boa 5 scarf, snake
board 4 slab **5** get on, house, lodge, put
up, table **6** bestow, billet, embark, harbor
7 emplane, entrain, quarter *artist's:*
7 palette
board game see at **game**
boarding house 7 pension **8** pensione
boardwalk 9 promenade
boast 4 blow, brag, crow, puff **5** exalt,
mouth, prate, preen, vaunt **7** bluster, show
off, swagger **9** gasconade **11** rodomontade
boaster 6 blower, gascon **7** bragger,
vaunter **8** blowhard, braggart, puckfist,
rodomont **11** braggadocio, rodomontade
boastful 6 braggy **8** arrogant, braggart,
vaunting **9** big-headed, conceited **11** pretentious, rodomontade **12** braggadocian,
vainglorious **13** swelled-headed *Scottish:*
6 vaunty
boat 3 ark **4** ship **6** vessel **7** steamer
above-water: **9** hydrofoil *Arab:* **4** dhow
bottom projection: **4** keel *British:* **5** coble
6 wherry **7** coracle *Canadian:* **6** bateau
canoe-like: **7** pirogue *captain:* **7** skipper
cargo: **3** hoy **4** scow **5** barge **6** wherry
7 drogher, gabbard, gabbart, lighter **8** canaller *Chinese:* **4** junk **6** sampan *dock,*
basin: **6** marina *Dutch:* **6** dogger, hooker,
schuit, schuyt **8** bilander *Egyptian:* **6** sandal **8** dahabeah *Eskimo:* **5** kayak, umiak
6 oomiak **7** bidarka **8** bidarkee *fishing:*
4 dory **5** coble, smack **6** dogger, lugger
7 caravel, coracle, tartana, trawler *flat-bot-*
tomed: **4** dory, keel, punt, scow **5** barge,
coble **6** bateau, bugeye **7** lighter, pontoon
French: **7** caravel *front end of:* **3** bow
4 fore, prow *hide-covered:* **7** coracle
Indian: **4** doni **5** dhoni **7** masoola *Indone-*
sian: **4** prao, prau, proa **5** prahu *Irish:*
7 currach, curragh *Italian:* **7** gondola *land-*
ing: **3** LST *Levantine:* **4** saic **5** caique
mail: **6** packet *Mediterranean:* **6** settee
motor: **7** cruiser, inboard **8** outboard, runabout *narrow:* **4** punt **5** canoe, scull, shell
7 gondola **8** canaller *Nile river:* **6** sandal
8 dahabeah *on a ship:* **3** gig **5** jolly
6 launch **7** pinnace *Philippine:* **5** banca,
casco *pole-propelled:* **4** punt **7** gondola
Polynesian: **4** pahi *race:* **7** regatta *rac-*
ing: **3** gig **5** scull, shell, yacht **6** torpid *rear*
end of: **3** aft **5** stern *river:* **4** scow
5 barge, canoe, ferry **6** packet, sampan,
wherry *round:* **4** gufa **5** goofa, guffa
6 goofah *rowing:* **4** dory **5** coble, scull,
shell, skiff **6** caique, dinghy, randan *sail-*
ing: **4** yawl **5** ketch, skiff, sloop, smack,
yacht **6** cutter, lateen, lugger, settee **7** pinnace **8** lateener, schooner *Scandinavian:*
4 pram **5** praam *Scottish:* **5** coble **7** cur-

rach, curragh, gabbard, gabbart *scouting:*
7 vedette, vidette *small:* **3** cog **4** dory
5 coble, skiff **6** bugeye, cockle, dinghy
7 coracle, shallop *song:* **9** barcarole
10 barcarolle *three-hulled:* **8** trimaran
three-oared: **6** randan *towing:* **3** tug *twin-*
hulled: **9** catamaran *two-masted:* **4** yawl
5 ketch **8** schooner
boatman 5 poler **6** Charon **7** oarsman,
paddler **8** deckhand **9** gondolier
boat-shaped 8 scaphoid **9** cymbiform,
navicular *combining form:* **5** scaph **6** sca-
pho *ornament:* **3** nef
boatswain 4 bos'n **5** bosun **6** jaeger
10 tropic bird
Boaz's wife 4 Ruth
bob 3 jig, nod, rap, tap **4** buff, crop, dock
5 bunch, float, gigue **6** weight **7** cluster,
nosegay
bobbery 3 row **4** fray **5** brawl, fight,
melee **6** affray, fracas, hubbub **7** ruction
10 donnybrook **11** disturbance
bobbin 4 pirn **5** quill, spool **7** spindle
bobble 4 mess **5** botch, gum up **6** bollix,
bungle, goof up **7** louse up
bobby 6 copper, peeler **7** officer **9** constable, policeman
bobwhite 5 quail **9** partridge
Boccaccio *beloved:* **9** Fiammetta *tales:*
9 Decameron
bode 4 omen **5** augur **7** betoken, portend,
presage, promise **8** foreshow **9** foretoken
10 foreshadow
bodement 4 omen **6** augury **7** portent,
presage **9** foretoken **10** prognostic
bodiless 9 asomatous, unfleshly **10** discarnate, immaterial, unphysical **11** disembodied, incorporeal **13** insubstantial
bodily 6 carnal **7** fleshly, sensual, somatic
8 corporal, physical **9** corporeal
body 4 bulk, core, mass, mort, pith, soma
5 array, batch, bunch, clump, group, stiff,
stock, torso **6** amount, budget, bundle, burden, corpse, corpus, object, parcel, staple,
upshot, volume **7** cadaver, carcass, cluster,
corpora (plural), purport, quantum, remains
8 physique, quantity **9** aggregate, substance *combining form:* **4** dema, soma,
some, somi (plural) **5** somat, somia, somus
6 somata (plural), somato *suffix:* **2** cy
body cavity 5 cecum, sinus **6** coelom
7 abdomen **8** hemocoel
body check 5 block
bodyguard 9 attendant, protector
body of water 3 bay, sea **4** gulf, lake,
pond, pool **5** bight, brook, creek, fiord, firth,
fjord, inlet, ocean, river **6** lagoon **7** channel,
estuary **9** reservoir
body passage 4 duct, iter, vein **5** canal
6 artery, meatus, vessel **7** trachea
body politic 5 state **6** nation

boeotian 4 boob 7 Babbitt 10 middle-brow, philistine

bog 3 fen 4 mire, quag 5 marsh, swamp 6 morass 8 quagmire 9 swampland *combining form:* 4 helo

Bogart film 6 Sahara 7 Dead End, Sabrina 8 Key Largo 10 Casablanca, High Sierra 11 The Big Sleep

bog down 5 delay 6 detain, hang up, retard, slow up 7 set back, slacken 10 decelerate

bogey 5 ghost, shade, spook 6 spirit, wraith 7 phantom, specter 8 revenant 10 apparition

boggle 3 gag, jib, shy 4 balk, mess 5 botch, demur, gum up, stick 6 bollix, bungle, cobble, goof up, strain 7 louse up, nonplus, scruple, stagger, stickle, stumble 9 dumbfound

bogus 4 fake, sham 5 false, phony, snide 6 forged, pseudo 8 spurious 9 brummagem, imitation, pinchbeck 11 counterfeit

Boheme, La *character:* 4 Mimi 7 Rodolfo *composer:* 7 Puccini *setting:* 5 Paris

Bohemian 7 beatnik, dropout 8 maverick 9 eccentric 10 iconoclast 13 nonconformist

bohunk 3 oaf 4 gawk, lout, lump 5 klutz 6 lubber, lummox 7 palooka

boil 4 bolt, burn, dash, fume, race, rage, rush, stew 5 anger, churn, fling, poach, shoot 6 blow up, bubble, charge, coddle, pimple, seethe, simmer 7 abscess, bristle, ferment, flare up, pustule, smolder 8 furuncle 9 carbuncle

boil down 8 simplify 10 streamline

boiled *combining form:* 5 cocto

boiler suit 8 coverall

boiling 3 hot 5 fiery 6 baking, red-hot 7 burning 8 scalding, sizzling 9 scorching 10 blistering

boil over 4 burn, fume, rage 5 anger 6 blow up, seethe 7 bristle, flare up

boisterous 5 noisy, rowdy 6 unruly 7 blatant, raucous, riotous 8 rowdyish, strident 9 clamorous, termagant, turbulent 10 disorderly, rollicking, rowdydowdy, tumultuous, vociferant, vociferous 11 loudmouthed, openmouthed 12 obstreperous, rambunctious

Boito opera 11 Mefistofele

bold 4 pert, wise 5 bluff, brave, fresh, nervy, sassy, saucy 6 brazen, cheeky 7 doughty, forward, valiant 8 fearless, impudent, insolent, intrepid, unafraid 9 audacious, dauntless, undaunted 10 courageous, procacious 11 impertinent, smart-alecky 12 contumelious

boldhearted 5 brave 7 doughty, valiant 8 fearless, intrepid, unafraid 9 audacious, dauntless, undaunted 10 courageous

boldness 4 gall 5 nerve 7 chutzpa 8 audacity, chutzpah, temerity 9 hardihood, impudence, insolence, insolency 10 brazenness, disrespect 12 impertinence

Bolero composer 5 Ravel

Bolivia *capital:* 5 La Paz, Sucre *monetary unit:* 4 peso

bollix 4 flub, mess 5 botch, gum up 6 bobble, bungle, fumble, goof up 7 louse up

Bolshevik 3 Red 6 commie 7 comrade 9 communist

bolshevism 9 communism

bolster 4 prop 5 brace, carry 6 bear up, buoy up, upbear, uphold 7 shore up, support, sustain 8 backstop, buttress 9 reinforce, underprop 10 strengthen

bolt 3 fly, run 4 cram, dash, flee, gulp, jump, lash, race, rush, tear 5 chase, rivet, scoot, shoot, skirr, slosh, start 6 charge, cry out, englut, gobble, guzzle, spring 7 exclaim, kingpin, make off, scamper, startle 8 blurt out 9 ejaculate, skedaddle 11 ingurgitate 13 thunderstroke

bomb 3 dud 4 bust, flop 5 blitz, lemon, loser, shell 7 failure 9 cannonade

bombard 4 pelt 5 blitz, shell 6 strike 7 assault 9 cannonade

bombardment 4 hail 5 burst, salvo 6 shower, volley 7 barrage 8 drumfire 9 broadside, cannonade, fusillade

bombardon 4 bass 7 helicon 8 bass tuba

bombast 4 rant 7 fustian 8 rhapsody, rhetoric, tumidity 9 turgidity 11 highfalutin, rodomontade

bombastic 7 aureate, flowery, swollen 8 sonorous 9 overblown 10 euphuistic, rhetorical 11 declamatory 12 magniloquent 13 grandiloquent

bombed 5 drunk 11 intoxicated

bombinate 3 hum 4 buzz 5 drone, strum, thrum 6 bumble

bombshell 8 surprise

bomb shelter 4 abri

bona fide 4 real, true 7 genuine 9 authentic, undoubted, veritable 10 sure-enough 11 indubitable

bona fides 9 good faith, sincerity 11 sincereness

bonanza 4 mine 8 eldorado, Golconda, gold mine, treasury 13 treasure trove

bonbon 5 candy 7 fondant 8 confetti (plural), confetto

bond 3 tie 4 bail, knot, link, pact, yoke 5 nexus 6 surety 7 bargain, compact 8 adhesion, clinging, cohesion, contract, covenant, guaranty, ligament, ligature, security, stickage, sticking, vinculum, warranty 9 adherence, agreement, coherence, guarantee 10 connection, connective, convention 11 transaction *combining form:* 4 desm 5 desmo

bondage 4 yoke 6 thrall 7 helotry, peonage, serfage, serfdom, slavery 9 servility, servitude, thralldom, villenage 11 enslavement, subjugation

bondsman 5 slave 7 chattel 9 mancipium

bone *ankle:* 5 talus 6 tarsus *arm:* 4 ulna 6 radius 7 humerus *back:* 5 spine 8 vertebra 9 vertebrae (plural) *breast:* 7 sternum *calf:* 6 fibula *cavity:* 5 fossa *change into:* 6 ossify *cheek:* 5 malar 6 zygoma *chest:* 3 rib *collar:* 8 clavicle *combining form:* 3 ost 4 osse, ossi, oste 5 osseo, osteo 6 osteon, osteus *face:* 5 malar, nasal 7 frontal 8 temporal *finger:* 7 phalanx 8 phalange *foot:* 6 tarsus 9 calcaneum, calcaneus 10 astragalus, metatarsus *hand:* 10 metacarpus *head:* 5 skull, vomer 7 cranium 8 parietal, sphenoid 9 occipital *heel:* 9 calcaneum, calcaneus *hip:* 5 ilium, pubis 6 pelvis 7 ischium *jaw:* 7 maxilla 8 mandible *kneecap:* 7 patella *Latin:* 2 os 5 ossa (plural) *leg:* 5 femur, tibia 6 fibula 7 patella *lower back:* 6 coccyx, sacrum *middle ear:* 5 anvil, incus 6 hammer, stapes 7 malleus, stirrup *relating to:* 6 osteal *shin:* 5 tibia *shoulder blade:* 7 scapula *small:* 7 ossicle *thigh:* 5 femur *toe:* 7 phalanx 8 phalange *U-shaped:* 5 hyoid *wrist:* 6 carpus

bonehead 5 dunce 8 clodpate, numskull 10 thick-skull

bone-like 7 osseous, osteoid

boner see **blooper**

bone up 4 cram 5 study 6 review

bong 4 bell, peal, ring, toll 5 chime, knell

boniface 8 publican, taverner 9 barkeeper, innholder, innkeeper, saloonist 12 saloonkeeper

bonkers 5 crazy 6 insane

bonny 4 fair 6 comely, lovely, pretty 9 beauteous, beautiful 10 attractive 11 good-looking

bon vivant 7 epicure, gourmet 8 gourmand 10 gastronome 11 gastronomer 12 gastronomist, man-about-town

bon voyage 8 farewell, good trip

bony 4 lank, lean 5 gaunt, lanky, spare 6 skinny 7 angular, scraggy, scrawny 8 rawboned

boo 4 hiss, hoot, razz 5 bazoo 7 catcall 8 cannabis 9 marijuana, raspberry

boob 3 oaf 4 dolt, goof, goon 5 chump, dunce 7 Babbitt, fathead 8 boeotian, dolthead, lunkhead 10 middlebrow, philistine

boo-boo see **blooper**

booby hatch 6 asylum 8 loony bin, madhouse, nuthouse 9 funny farm

booby trap 7 pitfall, springe 8 deadfall, trapfall

boodle 4 bilk, loot, mint 5 booty, cheat, cozen, prize, spoil 6 bundle, chisel, chouse, diddle, packet 7 defraud, fortune, plunder 8 flimflam 10 plunderage

boohoo 3 cry, sob 4 blub, wail, weep 7 blubber

book 4 list, tome 5 album, codex, novel, tract 6 enroll, folder, manual, scroll, volume 7 catalog, edition, leaflet, reserve, writing 8 brochure, hardback, inscribe, pamphlet, schedule, softback, treatise 9 monograph, preengage 10 compendium 11 publication *combining form:* 6 biblio *of psalms:* 7 psalter *of public records:* 5 liber

bookdealer 10 bibliopole 11 bouquiniste

bookie see **bookmaker**

bookish 7 learned 8 academic, literary, pedantic 9 scholarly

bookkeeping term 4 loss 5 asset, audit, check, debit, entry 6 budget, credit, income, ledger, profit 7 account, balance, expense, invoice, voucher 8 discount, interest 9 liability 12 depreciation

bookmaker 6 binder, bookie, editor 7 printer 9 publisher

book of account 6 ledger, record 7 journal 8 register

bookplate 5 label 8 ex libris

bookstall 5 kiosk 9 newsstand

boom 4 bang, clap, slam, wham 5 blast, burst, crack, crash, smash 7 thunder 10 prosperity

boomerang 8 backfire, backlash, kick back 10 bounce back

booming 6 robust 7 roaring, thrifty 8 thriving 10 prospering, prosperous 11 flourishing

boon 4 gift, good 5 favor, jolly, merry 6 blithe, jocund, jovial 7 benefit, festive, gleeful, godsend, largess, present 8 blessing, mirthful 9 advantage 10 blithesome 11 benediction, benevolence

boondocks 6 sticks 8 backland, backwash, frontier 9 backwater, backwoods 10 hinterland 11 backcountry

boor 3 oaf 4 lout 5 chuff, churl, clown, yahoo, yokel 6 lummox, mucker, rustic 7 buffoon, bumpkin, grobian, peasant 10 clodhopper

boorish 4 rude 6 coarse, rugged, vulgar 7 ill-bred, loutish, lowbred, lumpish, uncivil 8 churlish, cloddish, clownish, impolite, lubberly, swainish 9 graceless, tasteless, unrefined 10 robustious, uncultured, ungracious, unpolished 11 clodhopping, illmannered, uncivilized

boost 2 up 3 wax 4 hike, jump, plug, push, rise 5 put up, raise 6 beef up, expand, extend, jack up 7 augment, enlarge, magnify, promote, upgrade 8 heighten, increase, multiply 9 advertise 10 aggrandize 12 breakthrough

boot 2 ax 4 bang, fire, kick, sack, tyro
5 chase, chuck, eject, evict 6 bounce, novice, rookie, thrill 7 dismiss, extrude, kick
out 8 beginner, freshman, neophyte, throw
out 9 discharge, terminate 10 apprentice,
tenderfoot *kind:* 5 kamik, wader 6 arctic,
chukka, crakow, gaiter, galosh, golosh,
mucluc, mukluk 7 bottine, cothurn, gambado, jodhpur, shoepac 8 balmoral,
cothurni (plural), muckluck, overshoe, shoe-
pack 9 cothurnus 10 Wellington *Scottish:*
8 gamashes (plural)

Boötes star 8 Arcturus

booth 5 kiosk, stall, stand

boot hill 8 cemetery 9 graveyard 12 burial
ground

bootleg 3 run 5 hooch 7 smuggle
9 moonshine 10 bathtub gin, contraband
11 mountain dew

bootless 4 vain 6 futile 7 useless 8 abortive 9 fruitless 10 profitless, unavailing
11 ineffective, ineffectual 12 unproductive,
unprofitable

bootlick 4 fawn 5 cower, toady 6 cringe,
grovel, kowtow 7 truckle 9 brownnose
11 apple-polish

bootlicker 4 toad 5 toady 7 spaniel
8 lickspit 9 sycophant, toadeater
11 lickspittle

booty 4 loot, swag 5 prize, spoil 6 boodle 7 plunder 10 plunderage

booze 3 jag 4 grog, swig 5 binge, drink,
hooch, sauce, souse, swill 6 bender, guzzle, imbibe, liquor, tipple 7 carouse, spirits,
swizzle 8 liquor up 9 aqua vitae, brannigan,
firewater

boozehound 4 lush, wino 5 drunk
6 sponge 7 guzzler 8 drunkard 9 inebriate

boozer see **boozehound**

bop 3 bat 4 bash, belt, biff, blow, sock,
whop 5 pound, smack

borax 6 tincal

Bordeaux wine *district:* 5 Medoc
6 Graves *grape:* 6 Malbec, Merlot 8 Cabernet *name:* 5 Arsac, Ludon, Macau
6 Moulis 7 Labarde, Margaux, Pomerol
8 Cantenac, Pauillac 9 St. Julien, St.
Emilion, St. Estephe, St. Laurent *red:*
6 claret

bordello see **brothel**

border 3 hem, lip, rim 4 abut, brim, edge,
join, line 5 bound, brink, flank, frame,
march, marge, skirt, touch, verge 6 adjoin,
butt on, define, fringe, limbus, margin,
trench 7 outline, selvage 8 approach, befr-
inge, boundary, frontier, neighbor, sideline,
surround 9 marchland, perimeter, periphery 11 butt against, communicate *embroidered:* 6 orfray 7 orphrey *inlaid:* 8 purfling
raised: 7 coaming

bordereau 4 note 10 memorandum

bordering 8 abutting, adjacent, touching
9 adjoining 10 approximal, contiguous, juxtaposed 12 conterminous

borderland 5 march 8 frontier
9 marchland

borderline 7 unclear 8 doubtful 9 ambiguous, dubitable, equivocal, uncertain, undecided, unsettled 11 problematic

border line 8 boundary 11 demarcation

border state 8 Delaware, Kentucky, Maryland, Missouri, Virginia

bore 4 gape, gawk, gaze, pall, peer, ream,
tire 5 auger, drill, ennui, glare, gloat, prick,
punch, stare, weary 6 goggle, wimble
7 fatigue 8 puncture 9 perforate

boreal 3 icy 4 cold, cool 5 chill, gelid
6 arctic, chilly, frosty 7 glacial 8 freezing

Boreas *beloved:* 8 Orithyia *brother:*
5 Notus 8 Hesperus, Zephyrus *father:*
8 Astraeus *mother:* 3 Eos *son:* 5 Zetes
6 Calais

boredom 4 yawn 5 ennui 6 tedium
7 fatigue 8 doldrums 9 weariness

borer *combining form:* 6 trypan 7 trypano

Borgia 6 Alonso, Cesare 7 Rodrigo
8 Lucrezia

boring 4 dull 6 dreary, stodgy, tiring
7 humdrum, irksome, tedious 8 drudging,
tiresome 10 monotonous

born 3 née 6 inbred 7 built-in 8 inherent
9 intrinsic 10 congenital, deep-seated, ingenerate *combining form:* 3 gen 4 gene
6 genous 7 genetic

borne by the wind 5 eolic 6 aeolic,
eolian 7 aeolian

Borodin opera 10 Prince Igor

borough 4 burg, town 5 burgh 7 village
8 township *Scottish:* 5 brugh

bosh see **bunkum**

bosom 4 soul 5 heart 6 breast

bosomy 5 busty, buxom 6 chesty

boss 4 head 5 chief 6 honcho, leader,
master, survey 7 headman, oversee
8 chaperon, hierarch, overlook, superior
9 chieftain, dominator, supervise 11 quarterback, superintend *African:* 5 bwana

bossy 8 imperial 9 imperious, masterful
10 high-handed, imperative, peremptory
11 domineering, magisterial, overbearing

botanist *American:* 4 Gray (Asa) 5 Sears
(Paul B.) 6 Bailey (Liberty), Bessey
(Charles), Carver (George W.) 7 Bartram
(John), Burbank (Luther) 9 Fairchild (David)
Austrian: 6 Mendel (Gregor) *British:*
6 Sloane (Sir Hans) *Danish:* 7 Warming
(Johannes) *Dutch:* 2 De Vries (Hugo) *Ger-
man:* 4 Cohn (Ferdinand), Mohl (Hugo
Von) 5 Sachs (Julius von) *Irish:* 6 Harvey
(William) *Scottish:* 5 Brown (Robert) *Swed-
ish:* 8 Linnaeus (Carolus) *Swiss:* 6 Nageli
(Karl) 8 Candolle (Augustin)

botany branch 8 algology, bryology, mycology 9 phycology 10 palynology 11 hydroponics, pteridology 12 bacteriology

botch 3 dub 4 blow, flub, mess, muck, muff, mull, muss 5 fluff, gum up, mix-up, spoil 6 bobble, boggle, bollix, bumble, bungle, cobble, foozle, fumble, goof up, mess up, mucker, muddle 7 blunder, louse up 8 bugger up, shambles 9 mishandle, mismanage 10 misconduct

botchy 5 messy 6 sloppy, untidy 8 careless, slapdash, slipshod, slovenly 10 unthorough

both *combining form:* 3 bis *prefix:* 4 ambi, amph 5 amphi

bother 3 bug, irk, vex 4 fret, pest 5 annoy, chafe, upset 6 abrade, flurry, harass, pester, plague, ruffle 7 agitate, disturb, fluster, perturb, provoke, unhinge 8 disquiet, irritant, nuisance 9 annoyance, besetment 10 discompose 11 aggravation 12 exasperation 13 inconvenience

botheration 4 pest 6 pester, plague 8 irritant, nuisance 9 annoyance, besetment 11 aggravation 12 exasperation

Botswana *capital:* 8 Gaborone *monetary unit:* 4 pula

bottle 4 vial 5 ampul, cruet, cruse, flask, phial 6 ampule, carafe, fiasco, flacon, magnum, vessel 8 decanter, jeroboam 9 container *baby's:* 6 nurser

bottle gourd 8 calabash

bottleneck 7 impasse 8 obstruct, paralyze, slowdown, throttle

bottom 3 bed 4 base, foot, seat, sole 5 basal, basic, fanny, found, hiney, nadir 6 behind, breech, heinie, lowest 7 bedrock, essence, footing, primary, rear end 8 backside, buttocks, derriere 9 establish, lowermost, posterior, predicate, underbody, undermost, underside 10 foundation, nethermost, underlying, underneath 11 fundamental 12 foundational, quintessence, substructure, undersurface

bottom dog 4 prey 6 victim 8 casualty

bottomless 4 deep 7 abysmal 8 baseless 9 plumbless, soundless, unfounded 10 fathomless, gratuitous, groundless, ungrounded 11 plummetless, uncalled-for, unwarranted 12 unfathomable

bottommost 6 lowest 9 lowermost, undermost 10 nethermost

bough 4 limb 6 branch

boulevard 3 way 4 path, road 5 track 6 artery, avenue, street 7 highway 12 thoroughfare

boulevardier 7 flaneur, trifler 9 bon vivant 12 man-about-town

bounce 2 ax 3 hop 4 fire, jump, leap, sack 5 bound, vault 6 hurdle, spring

7 boot out, dismiss, kick out, saltate 9 discharge, terminate

bounce back 7 rebound, recover 8 backfire, backlash 9 boomerang

bounce off 5 carom

bouncer 4 goon 7 chucker 8 houseman 9 muscleman, strong arm

bouncy 4 airy 7 buoyant, elastic 8 volatile 9 expansive, resilient 12 effervescent

bound 3 end, hem, hop, rim 4 edge, jump, leap, term 5 limit, skirt, vault, verge 6 border, bounce, define, demark, finite, fringe, hurdle, margin, spring 7 delimit, limited, mark out, measure, saltate 8 articled, confines, surround 9 demarcate, determine 10 delimitate, indentured, limitation 11 apprenticed

boundary 5 ambit 6 limits 7 compass 8 confines, environs, purlieus 9 precincts

bounder 3 cad, cur 6 rotter

boundless 7 endless 8 infinite 9 limitless, unlimited 10 indefinite, unmeasured 11 measureless 12 immeasurable

bounteous 4 free 5 ample 6 plenty 7 copious, liberal 8 abundant, generous, handsome 9 plenteous, plentiful, unsparing 10 freehanded, munificent, openhanded

bountiful see bounteous

Bounty captain 5 Bligh

bouquet 4 balm, kudo, posy 5 aroma, scent, spice 7 corsage, garland, incense, nosegay, orchids, perfume 9 fragrance, redolence 10 compliment 11 arrangement, boutonniere

bourgeois 10 philistine 11 middle-class 12 capitalistic

bourgeoisie 11 middle class

bout 4 tour, turn 5 shift, siege, spell, stint, trick

bovine 2 ox 3 cow, yak 4 anoa, bull, calf, gaur, neat, zebu 5 bison, gayal, steer, stirk 6 catalo, cattle, wisent 7 aurochs, banteng, buffalo, bullock, cattalo 8 longhorn *genus:* 3 Bos *sound:* 3 low, moo

bow 3 arc 4 arch, bend, lout, turn 5 angle, crook, curve, defer, round, yield 6 congee, curtsy, salaam, submit 7 flexure, succumb, turning 8 flection 9 curvation, curvature 10 capitulate 11 buckle under 12 knuckle under

bowdlerize 4 blip 6 censor, screen 9 expurgate

bowed 4 bent 5 arced, bandy, round 6 arched, curved 7 arrondi, rounded 8 arciform 9 bowlegged 11 bandy-legged, curvilinear *combining form:* 3 tox 4 toxi, toxo

bowel 3 gut 4 draw 6 paunch 10 eviscerate, exenterate

bower 5 arbor 7 pergola

bowery 7 skid row 8 skid road

bowfin 7 mudfish

bowl 5 arena, basin, jorum, mazer, stade
6 tureen, vessel 7 stadium 8 coliseum
ornamental: 5 tazza
bowlegged 5 bandy
bowler 3 hat 5 derby 6 kegler 7 kegeler
Bowl game 3 Sun (El Paso) 4 Rose (Pasadena) 5 Aloha (Honolulu), Gator (Jacksonville), Peach (Atlanta), Pecan (Abilene), Sugar
(New Orleans), Super 6 Cotton (Dallas),
Fiesta (Tempe), Orange (Miami), Senior
(Mobile) 7 Holiday (San Diego), Liberty
(Memphis) 10 Bluebonnet (Houston), California (Fresno) 12 Independence (Shreveport) 7 Florida Citrus (Orlando)
bowling 7 kegling 8 kegeling *British:*
8 skittles *Italian:* 5 bocce, bocci 6 boccia,
boccie *term:* 3 pin 4 hook, lane, spot
5 curve, frame, spare, split 6 gutter, strike,
string, turkey 7 duckpin 9 candlepin
bowl over 3 wow 4 stun 5 floor 6 dismay 8 surprise 9 overwhelm 10 disconcert
box 3 bin 4 case, cell, chop, cuff, kist, loge,
slap, sock 5 booth, chest, clout, crate, fight,
punch, smack, spank, stall, trunk 6 buffet,
carton, casket, coffin, hopper, packet,
square 7 confine, enclose, package 8 canister 9 container, enclosure, rectangle
10 pigeonhole, receptacle 11 compartment
ancient: 4 arca *for a document:* 7 hanaper
for ammunition: 7 caisson *for an official
seal:* 7 skippet
boxer 7 fighter, palooka, puncher, slugger
8 pugilist 9 flyweight 11 heavyweight, lightweight 12 bantamweight, middleweight,
welterweight 13 featherweight *champ:*
3 Ali (Muhammad) 5 Louis (Joe), Moore
(Archie), Tyson (Mike) 6 Hearns (Thomas),
Holmes (Larry), Spinks (Leon, Michael), Tun-
ney (Gene), Walker (Mickey) 7 Charles (Ezz-
ard), Corbett (James), Dempsey (Jack),
Foreman (George), Frazier (Joe), Johnson
(Jack), Leonard (Sugar Ray), Sharkey (Jack),
Walcott (Joe) 8 Marciano (Rocky), Robinson
(Sugar Ray), Sullivan (John L.) 9 Armstrong
(Henry), Holyfield (Evander), Patterson
(Floyd), Schmeling (Max)
boxing 8 pugilism 10 fisticuffs 13 prizefighting *term:* 2 KO 3 jab, TKO 4 bell,
blow, bout, duck, foul, hook, ring, rope,
spar 5 break, count, feint, glove, judge,
match, parry, punch, round, swing, towel
6 bucket, canvas, corner, sponge 7 low
blow, referee 8 heavy bag, knockout, pugilism, sped bag, uppercut 9 knockdown
11 punching bag
boy 3 lad, son 5 gamin, sonny 6 laddie,
nipper, shaver 7 gossoon 9 shaveling,
stripling, youngster *combining form:*
3 ped 4 paed, paid, pedo 5 paedo, paido
country: 5 swain *errand:* 5 gofer 8 lobby-
gow *French:* 6 garçon *Latin:* 4 puer *mis-*

chievous: 6 urchin *small:* 3 tad *Spanish:*
4 niño
boyfriend 4 beau 5 beaux (plural), flame,
lover, swain 6 fiancé, steady 7 beloved
8 paramour, truelove 9 inamorato
10 heartthrob, sweetheart
Boy Scout *founder:* 11 Baden-Powell
gathering: 8 jamboree *motto:* 10 be prepared *rank:* 9 Life Scout, Star Scout
10 Eagle Scout, Tenderfoot *unit:* 5 troop
6 patrol
Boys Town *founder:* 8 Flanagan *state:*
8 Nebraska
B.P.O.E. member 3 Elk
Brabantio's daughter 9 Desdemona
brabble 3 gab, row 4 chat, spat, tiff
5 clack, scrap 6 bicker, cackle, hassle, jabber 7 chatter, dispute, fall out, palaver, prattle, quarrel, wrangle 8 squabble 9 bickering, brannigan, caterwaul 10 falling-out
11 altercation 12 tittle-tattle
brace 3 beg, duo 4 dyad, gird, pair, pray,
prop, stay 5 plead, ready, shore, steel
6 appeal, bear up, column, couple, splent,
splint, upbear, uphold 7 beseech, bolster,
doublet, entreat, fortify, implore, prepare,
refresh, shore up, support, sustain, twosome 8 buttress 9 importune
10 strengthen, supplicate 11 underpinner
12 underpinning 13 underpropping
bracelet 6 bangle 8 wristlet
bracing 5 tonic 9 animating 10 quickening, vitalizing 11 stimulating, stimulative
12 exhilarating, exhilarative, invigorating
bracket 3 wed 4 join, link 5 unite 6 couple, relate 7 collate, combine, compare,
conjoin, connect 8 contrast 9 associate
bract 4 leaf 5 glume, palea, palet 6 paleae
(plural), spathe 8 phyllary
brad 4 nail
Bradamant *brother:* 7 Rinaldo *husband:*
6 Rogero 8 Ruggiero
Bradbury's forte 5 sci-fi
brag 4 blow, crow, puff 5 boast, mouth,
prate, vaunt 9 gasconade 11 rodomontade
braggadocian 8 boastful, braggart,
vaunting 11 rodomontade
braggadocio 7 boaster 8 boasting, braggart, bragging 9 cockiness 10 cockalorum
braggart 6 blower 7 boaster, vaunter,
windbag 8 blowhard, boastful, fanfaron,
puckfist, rodomont, vaunting 11 braggadocio, rodomontade 12 braggadocian
Brahmin 7 egghead 8 highbrow 10 double-dome 12 intellectual
braid 4 plat 5 plait, queue 7 galloon, pigtail 8 soutache 10 intertwine, interweave
gold or silver: 5 orris *hemp:* 5 tagal
brain 3 wit 4 bean, conk, head, mind
7 concuss 9 intellect 10 gray matter
12 intelligence *bone:* 5 skull 7 cranium

clot: 10 thrombosis **combining form:**
6 cerebr, enceph 7 cerebri, cerebro 8 cerebell 9 cerebelli, cerebello, encephalo, encephaly 10 encephalia, encephalus **gland:**
6 pineal 9 pituitary **layer:** 4 obex 6 cortex **lobe:** 6 limbic, vermis 7 frontal 8 parietal, temporal 9 occipital **membrane:** 3 pia 4 dura, tela 6 meninx 8 pia mater 9 arachnoid, dura mater **part:** 4 aula, lobe 7 medulla 8 cerebrum, thalamus 9 sensorium, ventricle 10 cerebellum, hemisphere 12 diencephalon **relating to:** 8 cerebral 10 encephalic **ridge:** 4 gyri (plural) 5 gyrus **vertebrate:** 10 encephalon **wave record:** 3 EEG **white matter:** 4 alba

brainchild 7 coinage 9 invention 11 contrivance

brainless 6 simple 7 asinine, foolish, unwitty, witless 8 mindless 9 nitwitted, senseless 10 weak-minded

brainless one 5 ament

brainpower 3 wit 5 sense 9 mentality, mother wit 12 intelligence

brainsick 4 daft 5 batty, crazy 6 crazed, insane 7 cracked, lunatic 8 demented, deranged 9 bedlamite

brainstorm 4 idea 11 inspiration

brainteaser 6 puzzle

brainwashing 10 persuasion

brainwork 7 thought 10 cogitation, reflection 11 cerebration, speculation 12 deliberation

brainy 5 alert, sharp, smart 6 bright, clever 7 knowing 9 brilliant 11 intelligent, quick-witted, ready-witted

brake 3 bar, dam 4 slow, stop 5 block 6 hinder, impede 8 obstruct 10 overslaugh

branch 4 gill, limb, rami (plural) 5 bough, brook, creek, ramus 6 ramify, runnel, stream 7 rivulet **relating to:** 5 ramal 7 ramular

branched 6 ramate, ramose, ramous 8 ramulose, ramulous **combining form:** 7 cladous

brand 4 blot, blur, logo, mark, onus, slur, spot 5 odium, stain 6 stigma 8 black eye, logotype 9 trademark 11 bar sinister

brandish 4 show 5 flash 6 expose, flaunt, parade 7 display, disport, exhibit, show off, trot out

brand-new 4 mint 5 clean, fresh 6 unused 8 pristine 9 untouched 12 spick-and-span

brandy 4 marc 5 pisco, rakia 6 cognac, grappa, kirsch, rakija 7 quetsch 8 armagnac, calvados, slivovic 9 applejack, framboise, mirabelle, slivovitz 11 aquardiente

brannigan 3 row 4 bust 5 binge, fight, spree 6 bender, hassle, ruckus 7 brabble, carouse, dispute, quarrel, wassail, wrangle 10 falling out 11 altercation

brash 4 bold 5 hasty 6 brazen, madcap, uppish, uppity 7 forward, pushful, pushing 8 reckless, tactless 9 ebullient, exuberant, hot-headed, impetuous, impolitic, maladroit, presuming, unpolitic, untactful, vivacious 10 ill-advised, incautious 11 overweening, thoughtless 12 effervescent, high-spirited, presumptuous, undiplomatic 13 inconsiderate, self-asserting, self-assertive

brashness 4 gall 5 brass, cheek, crust, nerve 8 audacity, temerity 9 assurance, hardihood, hardiness 10 confidence, effrontery 11 presumption

brass 4 gall 5 cheek, crust, nerve 9 brashness 10 confidence, effrontery 11 presumption **combining form:** 5 chalc, chalk 6 chalco, chalko

brassbound 5 brash, rigid 6 narrow, uppish, uppity 7 adamant, bigoted, forward, pushful 8 obdurate 9 illiberal, presuming, unbending 10 inexorable, inflexible, intolerant, relentless, unyielding 11 overweening, small-minded 12 narrow-minded, presumptuous, single-minded 13 self-asserting, self-assertive

brass hat 5 elder 6 better, senior 8 higher-up, superior

brass tacks 7 details

brass worker 7 brasier, brazier

brassy see **brazen**

brave 4 bold, dare, defy, face, game, good 5 gutsy, hardy, manly, noble, stout, vivid 6 daring, gritty, heroic, manful, plucky, spunky, useful 7 aweless, benefic, defiant, doughty, gallant, helpful, outdare, outface, valiant, venture 8 colorful, fearless, intrepid, resolute, spirited, stalwart, unafraid, valorous 9 audacious, challenge, dauntless, favorable, soldierly, steadfast, undaunted, unfearful, unfearing 10 beneficial, courageous, propitious, unblenched 11 boldhearted, lionhearted, unblenching, undauntable, unflinching, venturesome 12 advantageous, greathearted, stouthearted, unfrightened

Brave New World author 6 Huxley

bravery 4 grit 5 pluck 6 daring, spirit 7 courage, heroism 8 audacity, boldness 9 fortitude, gallantry 11 intrepidity 12 intrepidness **false:** 7 bravado

brawl 3 row 4 feud, fray, maul, riot, spat, tiff 5 broil, fight, melee, scrap, set-to 6 affray, bicker, dustup, fracas, hassle, mellay, rumble, tussle 7 bobbery, brabble, dispute, quarrel, ruction, scuffle, wrangle 8 dogfight, eruption, rowdydow, slugfest, squabble, struggle, upheaval 9 bickering, caterwaul, commotion, fistfight, imbroglio, scrimmage 10 donnybrook, fisticuffs, free-for-all 11 altercation, disturbance

brawn 4 beef, thew 5 might 6 muscle

brawny 5 beefy, lusty, tough 6 sinewy 8 athletic, muscular, vigorous

bray 4 buck 5 crush 6 powder 9 comminute, pulverize, triturate 12 contriturate

brazen 4 bold, loud 5 gaudy, saucy 6 arrant, brassy, flashy, garish, tawdry, tinsel 7 aeneous, blatant, chintzy, glaring 8 impudent, insolent, overbold 9 audacious, barefaced, shameless, unabashed 10 procacious, unblushing 11 impertinent 12 contumelious, meretricious

Brazil *explorer:* 6 Cabral *largest city:* 8 Sao Paulo *monetary unit:* 8 cruzeiro

breach 3 gap 4 hole, open, rent, rift 5 break, split 6 hiatus, lacuna, offend, schism 7 discord, disrupt, fissure, infract, interim, opening, rupture, violate 8 disunity, division, fracture, infringe, interval, trespass 9 severance, violation 10 alienation, contravene, infraction, separation, transgress 12 estrangement, infringement, interruption 13 contravention, discontinuity, transgression

bread 3 bun 4 feed, food, grub 5 money 6 cocket, living, simnel, viands 7 biscuit, edibles, nurture, support 8 victuals 9 provender 10 livelihood, provisions, sustenance 11 comestibles, maintenance, subsistence *blessed:* 7 eulogia 9 antidoron *boiled:* 4 cush 6 panada *browned:* 5 toast 6 sippet 7 crouton 8 zwieback *combining form:* 4 arto *communion:* 4 azym, host 5 azyme, wafer 9 eucharist *consecrated:* 9 eucharist *cube:* 7 crouton *from heaven:* 5 manna *hard and crisp:* 4 rusk 8 zwieback *ingredient:* 4 meal 5 flour, yeast 6 leaven *Jewish:* 5 matzo 6 hallah, matzoh 7 challah *maker:* 5 baker *relating to:* 6 panary *roll:* 5 bagel *Scottish:* 7 bannock *small piece:* 6 sippet *soup:* 6 panada *spread:* 3 jam 4 oleo 5 jelly 6 butter *unleavened:* 4 azym 5 azyme, matzo 6 matzoh *with fruit and nuts:* 7 stollen

bread and butter 4 keep 6 living 7 support 10 livelihood, sustenance 11 maintenance, subsistence 12 alimentation

breadbasket 7 stomach

breadth 5 range, reach, scope, space, sweep 6 spread 7 compass, expanse, stretch 8 distance, fullness, wideness 9 amplitude, expansion

break 3 gap 4 bust, cave, fail, flee, fold, hole, leak, plow, rent, rift, ruin 5 boner, burst, crack, crash, gaffe, rebut, scape, solve, spell, split, yield 6 befall, betide, breach, chance, convey, decode, demote, escape, fold up, get out, happen, hiatus, lacuna, offend, plow up, reduce, refute, schism, sunder 7 abscond, blooper, come off, come out, confute, crumble, crumple,

declass, degrade, demerit, fall out, faux pas, fissure, infract, interim, opening, respite, rupture, shatter, time-out, violate 8 bankrupt, breather, collapse, confound, decipher, disprove, dissolve, fracture, fragment, interval 9 downgrade, interlude, pauperize 10 contravene, controvert, impoverish, transgress 11 communicate, impropriety, interregnum, opportunity, parenthesis 12 intermission, interruption 13 discontinuity

breakable 5 frail 7 fragile 8 delicate, shattery 9 frangible 11 fracturable, shatterable

breakaway 4 prop 10 escarpment, scrummager

breakdown 5 crash, smash, wreck 7 crack-up, debacle, smashup 8 analysis, collapse 10 dissection, resolution

break down 3 rot 4 wilt 5 decay, spoil, taint 6 cave in, digest, molder 7 analyze, crumble, dissect, give out, putrefy, resolve, succumb 9 anatomize, decompose 10 decompound 12 disintegrate

breaker *combining form:* 5 clast 7 clastic

breakfront 7 cabinet 8 bookcase

break in 5 train 8 initiate 9 interrupt

breaking up *combining form:* 7 schises (plural), schisis *suffix:* 4 lyse, lyze

breakneck 4 fast 5 fleet, hasty, quick, rapid, swift 6 speedy 10 expeditive, harefooted 11 expeditious

break out 5 erupt 6 escape 7 explode 10 burst forth

breakthrough 4 hike, rise 5 boost 7 advance, upgrade 8 increase

break through 5 burst 6 breach 7 rupture

breakup 8 analysis 10 dissection

break up 4 part 6 divide, sunder 7 disband, disjoin, disrupt, rupture 8 disjoint, disperse, dissever, dissolve, disunite, separate

breast 5 bosom, chest, heart *animal:* 7 brisket *combining form:* 3 maz 4 mast, mazo 5 masto, stern, steth 6 mastia (plural), sterno, stetho

breastbone 7 sternum

breast-feed 5 nurse 6 suckle 7 nourish

breast-shaped 9 mammiform

breastwork 7 bastion, bulwark, parapet, rampart

breath 4 blow, dash, hint 5 break, spell, trace, whiff 6 streak 7 respite, soupçon 9 suspicion 10 suggestion *combining form:* 4 pnea 5 pneum, pnoea 6 pneumo 7 pneumat 8 pneumato

breathe 2 be 4 live, rest, sigh 5 exist 6 exhale, expire, inhale 7 confide, inspire, respire, subsist, whisper

breather 5 break, spell 7 respite

breathing *labored:* 7 dyspnea

8 dyspnoea *normal:* **6** eupnea **7** eupnoea
rapid: **8** polypnea **9** polypnoea
breathing apparatus 10 respirator
underwater: **5** scuba
breathing orifice 8 blowhole, spiracle
breathless 4 agog, avid, keen **5** close,
eager, stivy **6** ardent, stuffy, sultry **7** airless, anxious, athirst, thirsty **8** appetent, stifling **9** impatient **11** suffocating
breathtaking 8 exciting **9** thrilling
11 astonishing
Brecht play 4 Baal **7** Galileo **13** Mother
Courage
breech 4 rear, rump **5** fanny **6** behind,
bottom **8** backside, buttocks, derriere
9 fundament, posterior
breechclout 9 loincloth
breed 3 ilk **4** bear, grow, kind, sire, type
5 beget, cause, class, hatch, raise **6** father,
induce, nature **7** produce, species, variety
8 engender, generate, multiply, muster up
9 character, cultivate, procreate, propagate,
reproduce **11** progenerate
breeding 5 grace **6** polish **7** culture
9 gentility **10** refinement **11** cultivation
breeding ground 6 hotbed **8** hothouse
10 forcing bed **12** forcing house
breeze 3 zip **4** snap **5** cinch, waltz
6 zephyr **8** duck soup, kid stuff, pushover
10 child's play
breezy 4 airy **5** blowy, gusty, windy
6 casual, dégagé **7** relaxed, unfussy
8 informal **9** easygoing **11** low-pressure
13 unconstrained
breviary 5 brief **7** epitome **8** abstract,
boildown, synopsis **10** conspectus
11 abridgement **12** condensation
breviloquent 4 curt **5** bluff, blunt, brief,
gruff, rough, short, terse **6** abrupt, crusty
7 brusque, concise, laconic, summary
8 succinct **11** compendious **13** short and
sweet
brevity 8 laconism **9** briefness, shortness,
terseness **11** conciseness **12** succinctness
brew 4 loom **6** foment, gather, impend
9 forthcome, potpourri **10** miscellany
Briareus 7 Aegaeon *father:* **6** Uranus
mother: **2** Ge **4** Gaea
bribe 3 buy, fix, sop **6** buy off, square, suborn **7** corrupt **10** tamper with
bric-a-brac 6 curios
brick 5 block *handler:* **6** hacker *layer:*
5 mason *laying:* **7** masonry *material:*
4 clay, marl *oven:* **4** kiln *pile:* **4** hack *row:*
6 course *sun-dried:* **3** bat **5** adobe *trough*
for carrying: **3** hod *wooden:* **3** nog
bridal 7 spousal, wedding **8** marriage, nuptials **9** espousals
bridal wreath 6 spirea
bridge 4 span *kind:* **4** arch, draw, rope
5 swing, truss **7** bascule, covered, natural,

pontoon, trestle, viaduct **10** cantilever, suspension *term:* **3** bid **4** book, east, pass,
ruff, slam, suit, void, west **5** bonus, dummy,
north, raise, south, trick, trump **6** double,
renege, rubber **7** auction, finesse, no-trump,
overbid **8** contract, jump call, redouble
9 grand slam, overtrick, singleton **10** little
slam, undertrick, vulnerable
bridge-like game 5 whist **6** hearts
bridle 3 bit **4** curb, rein **5** check **6** hold in,
manage **7** control, inhibit, repress **8** hold
back, hold down, restrain, suppress, withhold **9** constrain
brief 4 curt **5** bluff, blunt, gruff, short,
terse **6** abrupt, crusty, snippy **7** brusque,
concise, epitome, laconic, passing
8 abstract, boildown, breviary, breviate,
fleeting, snippety, succinct, synopsis
9 momentary, transient **10** conspectus
11 abridgement, compendiary, compendious **12** breviloquent, condensation
13 short and sweet *combining form:*
5 brevi
brig 4 jail **6** cooler, lockup, prison **7** slammer **8** stockade **9** guardroom
brigand 6 bandit, bummer, looter **7** cateran, forager **8** marauder, pillager **9** plunderer **10** depredator, freebooter
brigandage 7 pillage **11** depredation
bright 4 glad, keen **5** alert, brave, clear,
light, lucid, nitid, sharp, shiny, smart, vivid
6 benign, brainy, cheery, clever, colory, dexter, lively, lucent **7** animate, beaming, blazing, flaming, fulgent, glowing, knowing, lambent, lighted, radiant **8** animated, cheerful,
colorful, gleaming, luminous, lustrous, spirited, sunshiny **9** brilliant, effulgent, favorable, fortunate, refulgent, sparkling, sprightly,
vivacious **10** auspicious, glistening, glittering, precocious, propitious, shimmering
11 illuminated, intelligent, quick-witted,
ready-witted **12** incandescent **13** scintillating *combining form:* **6** lampro
brighten 5 cheer, shine **6** polish **7** burnish, enliven, furbish, gladden **8** illumine
10 illuminate
brightness 5 éclat **6** luster, reflet **8** radiance, radiancy, splendor **9** luminance
10 brilliance, luminosity *measure of:* **3** lux
4 phot **5** lumen **6** candle **7** candela
10 footcandle
brilliance see **brightness**
brilliant 4 sage, wise **5** sharp, smart
6 brainy, bright, clever, lucent **7** beaming,
fulgent, knowing, lambent, radiant **8** luminous **9** effulgent, refulgent **11** intelligent,
quick-witted, ready-witted **12** incandescent **13** knowledgeable
brilliantine 6 pomade
brim 3 hem **4** edge **5** brink, skirt, verge,

visor **6** border, fringe, margin **9** perimeter, periphery

brimful see **brimming**

brimming 3 big **4** full **5** awash **6** filled, jammed, loaded, packed **7** crammed, crowded, replete, stuffed, teeming, welling **8** swelling **9** chock-full

brimstone 6 sulfur *combining form:* **3** thi **4** thio

brine 3 sea **4** deep, main **5** ocean

bring 4 lead, sell **5** fetch **7** convert **8** persuade

bring about 4 make **5** cause **6** draw on, effect, secure **7** produce

bring around 6 induce, prompt **7** win over **8** convince, persuade, talk into **9** argue into **11** prevail upon

bring back 6 recall, return, revive **7** restore **8** retrieve, revivify

bring down 4 drop, fell **5** floor, level **6** ground, tumble **9** prostrate

bring forth 4 bear **7** deliver

bring forward 6 adduce **7** present, produce **9** introduce

bring in 3 get, pay, win **4** earn, gain, make, sell **5** fetch, yield **6** return **7** acquire

bringing *suffix:* **3** fic

bring off 6 effect **8** carry out **10** effectuate **12** carry through

bring out 3 say **4** tell **5** educe, state, utter **7** chime in, declare, deliver

bring together 4 join **5** batch, blend, merge, unify, unite **7** collect, compact, compile **9** integrate **10** synthesize **11** consolidate

bring up 4 halt, moot, rear, stop **5** breed, raise, refer, train **6** advert, allude, broach, draw up, foster, haul up, pull up **7** educate, mention, nourish, nurture **8** point out **9** cultivate, introduce **10** provide for

brink 3 hem **4** brim, edge **5** point, skirt, verge **6** border, fringe, margin **9** perimeter, periphery, threshold

briny 5 salty

brio 3 vim **4** dash, élan, zing **5** oomph, verve **6** esprit, spirit **9** animation

briolette 7 diamond

Briseis' lover 8 Achilles

brisk 4 spry, yare **5** agile, quick, zippy **6** active, adroit, lively, nimble, volant **9** sprightly

bristle 4 boil, burn, fume, rage, seta **5** anger, setae (plural) **6** blow up, chaeta, seethe **7** chaetae (plural), flare up **8** boil over *combining form:* **4** seti **5** chaet **6** chaeta, chaeto **7** chaetae (plural), chaetes, chaetus *Scottish:* **5** birse

British *air force:* **3** RAF *airplane:* **8** Spitfire *bailiff:* **5** reeve *bar:* **3** pub **5** local *bard:* **4** scop *barge:* **6** wherry *bed:* **4** doss *beer:* **6** swipes *boat, ancient:* **7** coracle

boat, fishing: **5** coble **6** hooker *boy:* **6** nipper *cathedral city:* **3** Ely **4** York **5** Truro **6** Durham, Exeter **7** Lincoln **8** Coventry, Hereford, St. David's **9** Salisbury, Worcester **10** Canterbury, Gloucester *Channel Island:* **4** Sark **6** Jersey **8** Alderney, Guernsey *china:* **5** Spode *coal carrier:* **4** corf *coin, current:* **5** pence (plural), penny **9** halfpenny *coin, old:* **3** bob, ora **5** ackey, angel, crown, groat, noble **6** bawbee, florin, George, guinea, seskin, sovran, tanner, teston **7** angelot, carolus **8** farthing, shilling **9** dandiprat, halfcrown, sovereign **10** threepence *colony, former:* **4** Aden, Cape **5** Adana, Kenya, Malta, Natal **6** Ceylon, Cyprus, Gambia **7** Jamaica, Sarawak **9** Gold Coast, Singapore, Transvaal **10** Basutoland, New Zealand **11** Orange River, Sierra Leone **12** Bechuanaland *conservative party:* **4** Tory *country gentleman:* **6** squire *county:* **4** Kent, York **5** Derby, Devon, Essex, Hants, Salop **6** Dorset, Durham, Oxford, Surrey, Sussex **7** Bedford, Rutland, Suffolk, Warwick **8** Cheshire, Cornwall, Hereford, Hertford, Somerset, Stafford **9** Berkshire, Hampshire, Lancaster, Leicester, Wiltshire, Worcester **10** Cumberland, Gloucester, Shropshire **11** Westmorland *court, local:* **8** hustings *court, medieval:* **4** eyre *cow barn:* **4** byre *dance, ancient:* **6** morris *dandy:* **4** toff *elevator:* **4** lift *farm, small:* **5** croft *field:* **5** croft *flashlight:* **5** torch *football:* **5** rugby *forest:* **5** Arden, weald **8** Sherwood *freeman:* **5** ceorl, churl, thane *game:* **5** darts, rugby **6** soccer **7** cricket *gasoline:* **6** petrol *gun:* **4** Bren, Sten *hat:* **6** bowler *hat, military:* **5** busby *headmaster:* **4** beak *horse:* **5** screw **6** garron *horse dealer:* **5** coper *hunt:* **5** chevy, chivy *hut:* **6** Nissen *idler:* **4** spiv *innkeeper:* **8** publican *jail:* **4** gaol *king, legendary:* **3** Lud **4** Beli, Bran **6** Arthur **7** Artegal, Belinus, Elidure **8** Brannius *laborer:* **5** navvy, prole *landowner:* **6** squire *language, ancient:* **6** Celtic, Cymric **9** Brythonic *lawyer:* **9** barrister, solicitor *legislature:* **10** parliament *letter, old:* **3** wen **5** thorn *liberal party:* **4** Whig *magistrate:* **4** beak *malt liquor:* **6** porter *measure:* **3** ell, pin **4** boll, comb, coom, cran, goad, hand, hide, last, pool, rood, trug, yoke **5** bodge, coomb, digit, float, floor, hutch, jugum, stack, truss **6** bovate, cranne, firkin, oxgang, pottle, runlet, strike, sulung, tierce **7** rundlet, tertian, virgate **8** carucate, chaldron, puncheon **9** kilderkin, shaftment, shathmont **10** barleycorn *molasses:* **7** treacle *news agency:* **7** Reuters *nobleman:* **4** duke, earl, lord, peer **5** baron **6** prince **8** marquess, viscount *nurse:* **6** sister *order:*

6 Garter *ore carrier:* 4 corf *peasant:*
5 churl *peddler:* 7 chapman *people,
early:* 4 Celt, Jute, Pict 5 Angle, Iceni,
Saxon *poet:* 4 scop *policeman:* 5 bobby
6 copper, peeler *political party:* 4 Tory,
Whig 6 Labour *pope:* 8 Adrian IV *pottery:*
5 Spode *prince:* 6 Andrew 7 Charles *princess:* 4 Anne 8 Margaret *printer:* 6 Caxton *prison:* 7 Newgate 8 Dartmoor
13 Tower of London *queen, ancient:*
8 Boadicea *racetrack:* 5 Ascot 10 Epsom
Downs *resort:* 4 Bath 7 Margate 8 Brighton 9 Blackpool *rifle:* 7 Enfield *royal
house:* 4 York 5 Tudor 6 Stuart 7 Hanover, Windsor 9 Lancaster 11 Plantagenet
royal residence: 7 Windsor *school:*
4 Eton 5 Rugby 6 Harrow *school, military:* 9 Sandhurst *seaman:* 6 rating *serf:*
4 esne 6 thrall *solitaire:* 8 patience *spa:*
4 Bath 5 Epsom 6 Buxton 7 Matlock
8 Brighton 10 Cheltenham *stables:*
4 mews *stool pigeon:* 4 nark *streetcar:*
4 tram *tavern:* 3 pub *tax:* 3 VAT 4 geld
6 excise *thicket:* 7 spinney *tinworks:*
8 stannary *tobacco packet:* 5 screw *tourist:* 7 tripper *truck:* 5 lorry *tutor:* 3 don
valley: 4 dene *wage earner:* 5 prole
weight: 4 keel 5 stone *woman in the
navy:* 4 Wren *wrench:* 7 spanner
British Columbia *capital:* 8 Victoria *largest city:* 9 Vancouver
Britomartis 7 Artemis 8 Dictynna
brittle 5 crisp, short 7 crackly, crumbly,
crunchy, friable
broach 3 pin 4 clip, moot 7 bring up, mention 9 introduce, ventilate 10 speak about
broad 4 wide 6 risqué, scopic 7 liberal,
radical 8 advanced, extended, off-color,
scopious, tolerant 9 expansive, extensive
10 suggestive 11 broad-minded, progressive *combining form:* 4 eury, lati, plat
5 platy
broadcast 3 sow 5 straw, strew 6 blazon 7 bestrew, declare, disject, publish,
scatter 8 announce, proclaim, televise,
transmit 9 advertise 10 annunciate, bruit
about, promulgate 11 blaze abroad, declaration, disseminate, publication
12 announcement, proclamation, promulgation 13 advertisement, pronouncement
broaden 4 open 5 widen 6 expand
9 breadthen, spread out
broadloom 6 carpet
broad-minded 4 wide 7 liberal, radical
8 advanced, tolerant 11 progressive
broadside 4 hail 5 burst, salvo, storm
6 shower, volley 7 barrage 9 cannonade,
fusillade 11 bombardment
broadtail 5 sheep 6 parrot 7 karakul,
rosella 8 lambskin
Brobdingnagian 4 huge 5 giant

7 Antaean, mammoth, titanic 8 colossal,
gigantic 9 cyclopean, monstrous
10 gargantuan
brocaded 6 broché
brocard 4 rule 5 axiom, gnome, maxim,
moral 6 dictum, truism 8 aphorism,
apothegm
brochette 4 spit 6 skewer
broil 4 bake, burn, cook, fray 5 brawl, fight,
grill, roast 6 affray, fracas, scorch 7 bobbery, ruction, swelter 10 donnybrook, free-for-all
broiling 3 hot 5 fiery 6 baking, red-hot,
torrid 7 burning 8 scalding, sizzling
9 scorching 10 sweltering
broke 4 flat, poor 5 needy, stony 8 beggared, dirt poor, indigent, strapped
9 destitute
broken-down 5 dingy, seedy, tacky
6 shabby, tagrag 8 decrepit, tattered
10 threadbare 11 dilapidated
brokenhearted 7 crushed 8 dejected
9 depressed
broker 8 mediator 9 go-between, middleman 10 interagent, interceder 11 intercessor 12 entrepreneur, intermediary, intermediate 13 intermediator
bromide 6 cliché, truism 8 banality, prosaism 9 platitude 10 prosaicism, shibboleth
11 commonplace, rubber stamp
bromidic 3 dry 4 arid, dull 5 dusty
7 insipid, tedious 8 wearial 9 dryasdust,
wearisome 13 uninteresting
bromine *symbol:* 2 Br
bronco 5 horse 6 cayuse 7 mustang *Australian:* 6 brumby
Brontë *character:* 9 Catherine, Rochester 10 Heathcliff *novel:* 8 Jane Eyre
16 Wuthering Heights *sisters:* 4 Anne
5 Emily 9 Charlotte
Bronx cheer 3 boo 4 hiss, razz 5 bazoo
7 catcall 9 raspberry
brooch 3 pin 4 clip
brood 3 set, sit 4 mope, seed 5 cover
6 scions 7 despond, progeny 8 children
9 offspring 11 descendants, progeniture
brook 4 bear, gill, race, rill, take 5 abide,
creek, stand 6 arroyo, endure, rillet, runnel,
stream, suffer 7 rivulet, stomach, swallow
8 tolerate *Scottish:* 6 burnie
broom 5 besom, brush, shrub, sweep,
whisk 7 heather *combining form:* 5 scopi
broth 5 stock 6 brewis 8 bouillon, consomme *Scottish:* 4 bree, broo
brothel 6 bagnio 7 lupanar 8 bordello, cathouse, seraglio 9 call house 10 bawdy
house, fancy house 11 parlor house
13 sporting house
brother 3 bub, kin 4 monk 5 friar 7 comrade *French:* 5 frère *Italian:* 3 fra 5 frate

8 fratello *Latin:* **6** frater *relating to:* **9** fraternal *Spanish:* **7** hermano

brotherhood 4 club **5** guild, order, union **6** league **7** society **8** sodality **10** fellowship, fraternity **11** association

brotherly 4 kind **10** cherishing **12** affectionate

Brothers Karamazov 4 Ivan **6** Alexei, Dmitri **10** Smerdyakov

brouhaha 3 din **4** coil, fuss **5** babel **6** clamor, furore, hubbub, hurrah, jangle, racket, ruckus, rumpus, shindy, tumult, uproar **8** foofaraw **9** commotion **10** hullabaloo **11** pandemonium

brow 5 frons, front **8** forehead

browbeat 3 cow **5** bully **6** harass, hector **7** bluster, dragoon **8** bludgeon, bulldoze, bullyrag **10** intimidate

brown 4 dark, sear **5** dusky, toast **6** gloomy, scorch, tanned **7** swarthy *dark:* **5** sepia, umber **9** chocolate *grayish:* **3** dun **6** bister, bistre *light:* **3** tan **4** ecru, fawn **5** beige, hazel, khaki, tawny *moderate:* **4** teak **6** sahara, sienna *reddish:* **3** bay **4** roan **5** henna **6** auburn, russet, sorrel, titian **8** chestnut *yellowish:* **6** bronze **12** butterscotch

Brown Bomber 5 Louis (Joe)

brown coal 7 lignite

brownie 3 elf, fay **5** fairy, nisse, pixie **6** sprite

Browning poem 8 Prospice **11** Pippa Passes **12** Rabbi Ben Ezra **13** Fra Lippo Lippi, My Last Duchess

brown recluse 6 spider

brownshirt 4 Nazi **12** storm trooper

browse 4 scan, skim **6** go over, peruse **7** dip into, run over **8** glance at, look over **10** glance over, run through **11** flip through, leaf through, riff through, skim through **12** thumb through **13** riffle through

bruise 4 mash, pulp **5** black, crush **6** batter, squash **7** becrush, contuse **8** abrasion, black eye **9** contusion

bruit about 6 blazon **7** declare, publish **8** announce, proclaim **9** advertise, broadcast **10** annunciate, promulgate **11** blaze abroad

bruja 3 hag, hex **5** lamia, witch **9** sorceress **10** witchwoman **11** enchantress

brume 4 film, haze, mist **5** smaze

brummagem 4 fake, sham **5** bogus, false, phony, snide **6** pseudo, tinsel **8** spurious **9** pinchbeck **11** counterfeit

brunet 4 dark **5** dusky, swart **6** swarth **7** swarthy **8** bistered

Brunhild's husband 6 Gunnar **7** Gunther

brush 4 clip, fray, kiss, skim **5** clash, graze, melee, run-in, set-to, shave, sweep **6** affray, glance, mellay, scrape **7** contact **8** skirmish **9** encounter, scrimmage, sideswipe **10** velitation *combining form:* **5** scopi

brusque 4 curt **5** bluff, blunt, brief, gruff, short **6** abrupt, crusty, snippy **8** snippety

brutal 4 hard **5** feral, harsh **6** animal, bitter, ferine, rugged, severe **7** beastly, bestial, swinish **8** rigorous **9** inclement **11** intemperate

brutalize 4 warp **6** debase **7** corrupt, debauch, deprave, pervert, vitiate **10** bastardize, bestialize, demoralize

brute 5 beast, feral **6** animal, ferine **7** beastly, bestial, swinish **8** creature

brutish 3 low **4** base, mean, vile **5** crude, feral **6** animal, coarse, ferine, scurvy **7** beastly, bestial, swinish **11** animalistic

bryophyte 4 moss **9** liverwort

Brythonic see Cymric

bubble 3 lap **4** boil, stir, wash **5** churn, dream, slosh, swash **6** burble, gurgle, seethe, simmer **7** chimera, fantasy, ferment, smolder **8** illusion **9** pipe dream

bubbly 8 effusive **9** champagne, exuberant, sparkling

buccaneer 5 rover **6** pirate, sea dog **7** corsair, sea wolf **8** picaroon, sea rover **9** sea robber **10** freebooter

buck 3 fop, guy, lug, man **4** bear, bill, bray, chap, dude, duel, gent, pack, tote **5** carry, crush, dandy, ferry, fight, horse, pitch, repel, throw **6** combat, convey, dollar, fellow, oppose, powder, resist, unseat **7** contest, coxcomb, dispute, sawbuck, trestle, unhorse **8** sawhorse, traverse **9** comminute, exquisite, gentleman, pulverize, transport, triturate, withstand, workhorse **11** Beau Brummel **12** contriturate

bucket 3 fly, run **4** pail, rush, whiz **5** hurry, speed **6** barrel, hasten, hustle **7** grapple **9** clamshell

Buckeye State 4 Ohio

buckle down 5 apply, set to **6** devote, direct, fall to, jump in, wade in **7** address, pitch in **8** jump into, wade into

buckle under 3 bow **4** cave, give **5** defer, yield **6** submit **7** knuckle, succumb **10** capitulate

Buck novel 12 The Good Earth

buckram 5 stiff **6** wooden **7** stilted **9** cardboard **11** muscle-bound

buck up 5 cheer **6** solace **7** comfort, console, upraise

bucolic 4 hick, jake **5** rural, yokel **6** rustic **7** bumpkin, country, hayseed, hillman, hoosier, outland **8** agrestic, pastoral **9** chawbacon **10** campestral, out-country, provincial **11** countrified

bud 4 germ, seed **5** chick, child, spark **6** embryo **8** juvenile, young one **9** youngling, youngster *combining form:* **5** blast **6** blasto

Buddha 7 Gautama 10 Siddhartha *Chinese:* 2 Fo *dialogues:* 5 sutra *disciple:* 6 Ananda *Japanese:* 5 Amida, Amita *mother:* 4 Maya *son:* 6 Rahula *teachings:* 6 dharma *wife:* 9 Yasodhara

Buddhism 5 Daijo, Foism, Kegon 7 Lamaism 8 Hinayana, Mahayana

Buddhist *bronze image:* 8 Daibutsu *chant:* 6 mantra *column:* 3 lat *dialogues:* 5 sutra *doctrine:* 7 trikaya *enlightenment:* 6 satori *evil spirit:* 4 Mara *fate:* 5 karma *fertility spirit:* 6 yaksha, yakshi *gateway:* 5 toran 6 torana *god:* 4 deva *hatred:* 4 dosa *hell:* 6 Naraka *language:* 4 Pali *mendicant:* 7 bhikshu *monastery:* 4 tera *monk:* 2 bo 4 lama 5 arhat, bonze, yahan 7 bhikshu, poongee 8 poonghee, poonghie, talapoin *monument, mound:* 5 stupa *novice:* 5 goyin *paradise:* 4 Jodo *religious community:* 6 sangha *sacred city:* 5 Lhasa *saint:* 5 arhat *school:* 5 ritsu *scripture:* 9 Tripitika *sect:* 3 Zen 6 tendai *shrine:* 4 tope 5 stupa 6 dagaba, dagoba 7 chorten *spell:* 6 mantra *spiritual leader:* 4 guru 9 Dalai Lama *state of happiness:* 7 nirvana *temple:* 6 pagoda, vihara *throne:* 5 asana *title:* 7 mahatma *tree of enlightenment:* 2 bo 5 bodhi, pipal *tutelary spirit:* 6 yaksha, yakshi *will to live:* 5 tanha

buddy 3 pal 4 chum 5 crony 6 comate, friend 7 comrade 9 associate, companion 11 running mate

buddy-buddy 4 cozy 5 pally 6 chummy 8 intimate

budgerigar 6 parrot 8 lovebird, parakeet 9 parrakeet

budget 4 body, bulk 5 total 6 amount 7 quantum 8 quantity 9 aggregate

budtime 6 spring 10 springtide

Buenos ___ 5 Aires

buff 3 fan, rub 5 glaze, gloss, shine 6 addict, glance, polish, votary 7 burnish, devotee, furbish, habitué 10 aficionado

buffalo 4 anoa, balk, beat, bilk, dash, foil, ruin 5 bison, stump 6 baffle 7 carabao, nonplus 9 frustrate 10 circumvent, disappoint *Philippines:* 7 tamarao, tamarau, timarou

buffalo grass 5 grama 6 gramma

buffet 3 box 4 beat, blip, chop, cuff, drub, poke, slap, sock 5 clout, pound, punch, smack, spank 6 batter, pummel, thrash, wallop 7 belabor, lambast 8 lambaste

buffoon 4 zany 5 clown 9 harlequin 11 merry-andrew

bug 3 irk, nut, vex 4 fret, gall 5 annoy 6 bother, insect, zealot 7 fanatic, provoke, wiretap 10 enthusiast

bugaboo see **bugbear**

bugbear 4 bogy, fear, ogre 5 bogey 6 goblin 7 problem, specter, spectre 8 anathema, bogeyman 9 bête noire, boogeyman, hobgoblin 10 black beast 11 abomination, detestation

bugle *blare:* 7 tantara *call:* 4 mess, taps 6 sennet, tattoo 7 retreat 8 assembly, reveille

Bugs ___ 4 Baer 5 Bunny

build 3 wax 4 form, make, mold, rise 5 boost, erect, forge, frame, mount, put up, raise, run up, shape 6 expand, uprear 7 augment, enlarge, fashion, habitus, magnify, produce, throw up, upsurge 8 assemble, compound, heighten, increase, multiply, physique 9 construct, fabricate 10 aggrandize 11 manufacture 12 constitution

builder 10 contractor

builder's knot 10 clove hitch

building 3 hut 6 fabric 7 edifice 9 structure *addition:* 3 ell 4 wing 5 annex *compartment:* 3 bay 4 room 6 office *connector:* 9 breezeway *farm:* 4 barn, crib, shed, silo *for apartments:* 8 tenement *for arms:* 7 arsenal *for fodder:* 4 silo *for gambling:* 6 casino *for grain:* 4 silo 7 granary 8 elevator *for horses:* 6 stable *for manufacture:* 4 shop 5 plant 7 factory *for music:* 4 hall 10 auditorium, opera house *for sports:* 3 gym 4 bowl 5 arena 7 stadium 8 coliseum 9 gymnasium 10 hippodrome *material:* 4 iron, wood 5 adobe, brick, glass, steel, stone 6 cement 8 concrete *medieval:* 6 castle *projection:* 3 bay, ell 4 wing 5 annex 6 dormer 7 cornice *round:* 7 rotunda

build up 4 puff 5 erect 9 advertise, construct, establish, publicize 10 press-agent

built-in 6 inborn, inbred, innate 8 inherent 9 essential, ingrained 10 congenital, deep-seated, indwelling

bulb 3 bud 4 leek, lily, sego 5 onion, tulip 6 garlic, squill 8 daffodil, hyacinth 9 amaryllis, narcissus *segment:* 5 clove

bulb-like bud 4 corm 5 tuber 7 rhizome

Bulgaria *capital:* 5 Sofia *monetary unit:* 3 lev

bulge 3 jut 4 bump, edge, lump, poke, pout 5 pouch, swell 6 beetle, dilate, expand 7 distend, project 8 handicap, overhang, protrude, stand out, stick out, swelling 9 advantage, allowance, head start, outthrust 10 projection, protrusion 11 protuberate 12 protuberance

bulk 4 body, core, loom, mass 5 total 6 amount, budget, corpus, object, staple, volume 7 bigness, quantum 8 quantity, stand out 9 aggregate, greatness, largeness, magnitude, substance *combining form:* 4 onco 5 oncho

bull 3 big, fat 4 slip, toro, trip 5 boner, buyer, error, fluff, husky, lapse, large 6 bungle **7** blooper, blunder, mistake **8** oversize *combining form:* **4** taur **5** tauri, tauro

bulldoze 3 cow **4** push **5** bully, press, shove **6** hector, hustle, jostle **7** bluster, dragoon **8** bludgeon, browbeat, bullyrag, shoulder **10** intimidate

bullet 3 fly, zip **4** whiz **5** hurry **6** barrel, dumdum, tracer *size:* **7** caliber, calibre

bull fiddle 10 contrabass, double bass

bullfighter 6 torero **7** matador, picador **8** toreador **9** cuadrilla **11** cuadrillero **12** banderillero *famous:* **6** Arruza **8** Belmonte, Joselito, Manolete **10** El Cordobes

bullfighting *arena:* **5** plaza *cheer:* **3** olé *hero:* **6** torero **7** matador **8** toreador *lancer:* **7** picador *red cloth:* **6** muleta *Spanish:* **7** corrida *team:* **9** cuadrilla

bullheaded 6 mulish **8** perverse **9** obstinate, pigheaded **10** headstrong, refractory, self-willed **11** intractable, stiff-necked **12** pertinacious

bullwork 4 moil, toil **5** grind, labor, sweat **6** drudge **7** travail **8** drudgery

bully 3 cow **4** fine, punk **5** meany **6** hector, meanie, menace, pander **7** bluster, dragoon, harrier, torment **8** ballyrag, bludgeon, browbeat, bulldoze, bullyrag, harasser, threaten **9** bulldozer, excellent, first-rate, front-rank, tormenter **10** browbeater, intimidate, macquereau, persecutor **11** antagonizer, intimidator

bullyrag see **bulldoze**

bulwark 4 fend **5** cover, guard **6** defend, screen, secure, shield **7** bastion, parapet, protect, rampart **8** fortress **9** safeguard **10** breastwork, stronghold

bum 3 beg, jag, vag **4** bust, hobo, idle, laze, lazy, loaf, loll, slug **5** binge, cadge, drunk, idler, mooch, tramp **6** bender, dawdle, loafer, loiter, lounge, slouch **7** carouse, drifter, floater, goof off, vagrant, wassail **8** derelict, dolittle, faineant, slugabed, sluggard, vagabond **9** brannigan, do-nothing, goldbrick, lazybones, panhandle **10** street arab

bumbershoot 8 umbrella

bumble 3 hum **4** buzz, muff **5** botch, drone, lurch, strum, thrum **6** bobble, bollix, bungle, fumble, mucker **7** blunder, stumble **9** bombinate

bumbling 5 inept **6** gauche, wooden **7** awkward, halting, unhandy, unhappy **9** ham-handed, maladroit **11** heavy-handed

bummer 6 bandit, beggar, cadger, looter **7** brigand, cateran, forager, moocher **8** marauder, pillager **9** plunderer **10** depredator, freebooter, panhandler

bump 3 hit, jar **4** bang, bust, jolt, knot, knur, lump, slam **5** break, bunch, carom, clash, crash, gnarl, knock, shock **6** demote, impact, jostle, reduce, strike, wallop **7** col-

lide, declass, degrade, demerit, disrate, mudhole, pothole **8** disgrade, pumpknot, swelling **9** chuckhole, collision, downgrade **10** concussion, percussion **12** protuberance

bumpkin 4 hick, jake, rube **6** joskin, rustic **7** bucolic, hayseed, hoosier **9** chawbacon **10** clodhopper, provincial

bump off 4 do in, kill **6** finish, murder **7** execute, put away **9** liquidate **11** assassinate

Bumppo, Natty *alias:* **7** Hawkeye **10** Deerslayer, Pathfinder *creator:* **6** Cooper

bumptious 8 arrogant **9** conceited, obtrusive

bumpy 5 jerky, nubby, ridgy, rough **6** bouncy, jouncy **7** jolting

bunch 3 lot, set **4** band, bevy, body, bump, crew, knot, lump, push **5** batch, clump, covey, crowd, group, party **6** bundle, circle, clutch, parcel **7** cluster **8** assembly

bunco steerer 3 gyp **6** con man **7** diddler, sharper **8** swindler **9** defrauder, trickster **12** double-dealer **13** confidence man

bundle 3 lot, pot, set, wad **4** bale, body, mint, pile **5** array, batch, bunch, clump, group, sheaf **6** bindle, boodle, fardel, packet, parcel **7** cluster, fortune *of grain:* **5** sheaf, shock, stook *of hay:* **4** bale, wase *of sticks:* **5** fagot **6** faggot **7** fascine *small:* **8** fascicle

bungle 4 bull, flub, muff, slip, trip **5** boner, botch, error, fluff, gum up, lapse **6** bollix, foozle, goof up **7** blooper, blunder, louse up, mistake

bungler 5 klutz **8** shlemiel **9** blunderer, schlemiel **10** stumblebum **11** blunderbuss

bunglesome 6 clumsy **7** awkward

bunk 3 hut **5** board, hokum, house, lodge, put up **6** bestow, billet, harbor, humbug **7** baloney, quarter **8** domicile, nonsense **9** poppycock

bunkum 4 jazz **5** hokum **7** baloney **8** flimflam, nonsense **9** poppycock **10** balderdash

Bunyanesque 4 huge **7** mammoth, titanic **8** colossal, gigantic **9** Herculean, monstrous **10** behemothic, gargantuan, prodigious

buoy 4 prop **6** uphold **7** bolster, support, sustain **9** underprop

buoyancy 10 ebullience, exuberance, exuberancy **13** effervescence

buoyant 4 airy **6** bouncy **7** elastic **8** volatile **9** expansive, resilient **12** effervescent

burble 3 yak **4** chat, wash **5** clack, run on, slosh, swash **6** babble, bubble, gabble, gurgle, rattle, yammer **7** chatter, prattle

burden 3 tax **4** clog, duty, gist, haul, lade, load, onus, task **5** cargo, weigh **6** amount, charge, cumber, lading, lumber, saddle, upshot, weight **7** afflict, freight, oppress, payload, purport **8** encumber, handicap, overload **9** millstone, substance **10** deadweight

burdensome 5 tough **6** taxing **7** exigent, onerous, weighty **8** exacting, grievous **9** demanding **10** oppressive

bureau 5 chest **7** dresser **10** chiffonier

bureaucrat 8 mandarin, official **11** functionary **12** civil servant

burg 6 hamlet, Podunk **7** cowtown, mudhole, village **8** hick town, tank town **11** whistle-stop **12** one-horse town **13** jerkwater town

burgee 4 flag, jack **6** banner, ensign, pennon **7** pendant, pennant **8** standard, streamer

burgeon 4 blow **5** bloom, build, mount, run up **6** expand, flower, sprout **7** augment, blossom, enlarge **8** heighten, increase, multiply, outbloom, snowball **10** effloresce

burghal 4 city **5** urban **9** municipal

burgher 3 cit **5** towny **6** towner **7** citizen, townman **8** townsman

burglar 4 yegg **5** thief **6** robber **7** yeggman *loot:* **4** swag

burglarize 3 rob **6** burgle **7** ransack **10** housebreak

burgomaster 5 mayor **10** magistrate

Burgundy wine *grape:* **5** Gamay, Pinot *red:* **8** Mercurey **10** Beaujolais *white:* **5** Rully **6** Chagny **7** Chablis **10** Montrachet **13** Pouilly-Fuissé

burial 4 tomb **5** grave **7** funeral **8** exequies **9** interment, obsequies, sepulcher, sepulture **10** entombment, inhumation *box:* **6** casket, coffin *ceremony:* **7** funeral *coffin stand:* **4** bier *mound:* **3** low **6** barrow **7** tumulus *tomb:* **9** mausoleum, sepulcher, sepulchre

burial ground 8 boot hill, cemetery **8** God's acre **9** graveyard **10** necropolis **11** polyandrium **12** memorial park, potter's field *early Christian:* **8** catacomb

burlap 5 gunny **6** fabric **7** bagging, sacking **10** wrapping *fiber:* **4** hemp, jute

burlesque 3 ape **4** mock, sham **5** farce, mimic **6** parody **7** imitate, mockery, takeoff **8** travesty **10** caricature

burly 5 beefy, hefty, husky

Burma 7 Myanmar *capital:* **7** Rangoon

burn 4 bake, beam, bite, boil, char, cook, fire, fume, kiln, melt, rage, sere **5** anger, blaze, broil, chark, creek, flame, flare, gleam, light, parch, roast, scald, shine, singe, smart, smoke, sting, toast **6** blow up, ignite, kindle, scorch, seethe, stream **7** bristle, combust, consume, cremate, flare up, inflame, radiate, smolder, sputter, swelter **8** boil over, smoulder **9** carbonize, cauterize **10** incinerate *Scottish:* **7** scowder **8** scouther

burnable 9 flammable, ignitable **11** combustible, inflammable

burned-out 7 worn-out **8** fatigued **9** destroyed, exhausted **10** broken-down **11** debilitated

burning 3 hot **4** dire **5** afire, aglow, fiery **6** ablaze, aflame, alight, ardent, fervid, heated, hectic, red-hot, torrid, urgent **7** blazing, clamant, exigent, fervent, fevered, flaming, flaring, glowing, ignited, instant, lighted **8** broiling, feverish, pressing, sizzling, white-hot **9** clamorous, scorching **10** imperative, passionate **11** conflagrant, impassioned, importunate **12** incandescent *combining form:* **4** igni *malicious:* **5** arson *relating to:* **5** pyric

burnish 3 rub **4** buff **5** glaze, gloss, shine **6** glance, polish **7** furbish

burnished 5 shiny **6** glossy, sheeny **7** shining **8** gleaming, lustrous, polished **10** glistening

burnsides 5 beard **8** whiskers **10** sideboards **11** dundrearies, muttonchops **12** side-whiskers

burp 5 belch, eruct **8** eructate

burro 3 ass **4** donk **6** donkey **7** jackass

Burroughs' hero 6 Tarzan

burrow 3 den **4** hole, lair, snug **5** couch, hovel, lodge **6** cuddle, nestle, nuzzle **7** snuggle

burst 4 bang, boom, clap, gust, rive, slam, wham **5** blast, crack, crash, erupt, flare, go off, lunge, sally, salvo, smash, storm **6** access, blow up, plunge, shiver, shower, volley **7** barrage, explode, flare-up, rupture, shatter **8** break out, detonate, drumfire, eruption, fragment, mushroom, outbreak, splinter, splitter **9** broadside, cannonade, explosion, fusillade **11** bombardment

bursting 8 erumpent *combining form:* **7** rrhexis, rrhexes (plural)

bury 4 hide, tomb **5** cache, cover, inter, plant, stash **6** coffin, entomb, inhume, screen **7** conceal, lay away, put away, secrete **8** ensconce **9** sepulcher, sepulture

bush 4 rose **5** lilac, shrub, wahoo **6** azalea, cassis, privet **7** currant, weigela **8** backland, backwash, barberry, frontier, hazelnut **9** backwater, backwoods, forsythia, manzanita, out-country **10** gooseberry, hinterland **11** pussy willow **12** rhododendron *combining form:* **5** thamn **6** thamno

bush-league 5 minor **8** mediocre **10** inadequate, second-rate

bushranger 8 woodsman **12** frontiersman

bushwa 4 bosh **5** hooey **6** bunkum **7** baloney, eyewash **8** malarkey, nonsense **9** poppycock **10** balderdash, flapdoodle

bushwhacker 6 bandit, outlaw, raider, sniper **8** woodsman **9** guerrilla

bushy 5 bosky

business 3 job 4 duty, firm, line, role, work 5 trade 6 affair, custom, matter, office, outfit, racket 7 calling, company, concern, lookout, palaver, pursuit, traffic 8 commerce, function, industry, province 9 patronage 10 employment, enterprise, occupation 13 establishment *expense:* 8 overhead *syndicate:* 6 cartel

businesslike 7 serious 9 efficient, practical 10 purposeful, systematic

businessman 6 dealer, trader, tycoon 7 magnate 8 merchant, tradesman 10 trafficker 12 merchandiser

buss 4 kiss, peck 5 smack 6 smooch 8 osculate

bust 3 dud, jag, nab 4 bomb, bump, fail, flop, fold, raid, ruin 5 binge, break, crash, lemon, loser, spree 6 arrest, bender, demote, fold up, pauper, reduce 7 carouse, declass, degrade, demerit, disrate, failure 8 bankrupt, disgrade 9 downgrade, pauperize 10 impoverish

bustard *African:* 7 korhaan 8 knorhaan *genus:* 4 Otis *relating to:* 7 otidine

bustle 3 ado, fly, run 4 flit, fuss, rush, stir, to-do 5 hurry, whirl, whisk 6 clamor, flurry, furore, hassle, hasten, hubbub, hustle, pother, tumult, uproar 7 turmoil 9 commotion, whirlpool, whirlwind 10 hurly-burly

bustling 4 busy 5 brisk, fussy 6 active, lively 7 hopping, humming, popping 9 energetic

busty 5 buxom 6 bosomy, chesty 11 full-bosomed

busy 5 fussy 6 engage, lively, occupy 7 engaged, engross, hopping, humming, immerse, popping, working 8 bustling, employed, hustling, occupied 9 assiduous, intrusive, obtrusive, officious 10 meddlesome 11 impertinent

busybody 5 prier, pryer, snook, snoop 6 butt-in, gossip, rubber 7 meddler, Paul Pry 8 informer, kibitzer, quidnunc 9 pragmatic 10 newsmonger, pragmatist, rubberneck 11 nosey Parker, rumormonger 12 gossipmonger, intermeddler

but 3 bar, yet 4 just, only, save 5 alone 6 bating, except, merely, saving, simply, solely, unless 7 barring, besides, however 8 entirely 9 aside from, excluding, outside of 11 exclusively

butcher 4 slay 9 slaughter

butcher-bird 6 shrike

butcherly 6 bloody, clumsy, savage 10 unskillful

butchery 7 carnage 8 massacre 9 bloodbath, bloodshed, slaughter

Butler, Samuel *novel:* 7 Erewhon 16 The Way of All Flesh *poem:* 8 Hudibras

butt 3 keg, tun 4 abut, cask, dupe, fool, gull, jest, join, joke, line, mark, mock, pipe 5 chump, touch, verge 6 adjoin, barrel, border, jestee, pigeon, sucker, target, victim 7 fall guy, gudgeon, mockery 8 derision, hogshead, neighbor 9 cigarette, pilgarlic 11 communicate, sitting duck 13 laughingstock

butter *artificial:* 4 oleo 9 margarine 13 oleomargarine *Indian:* 3 ghi 4 ghee *piece:* 3 pat *semifluid:* 3 ghi 4 ghee *tree:* 4 shea *tub:* 6 firkin

butterball 5 blimp, fatty 8 dumpling

butterfish 5 coney 6 gunnel

butterfly 5 diana, satyr, zebra 6 copper, morpho 7 admiral, buckeye, kallima, monarch, satyrid, skipper, sulphur, troilus, vanessa, viceroy 8 crescent, grayling, milkweed, victoria 9 aphrodite, metalmark, nymphalid, wood nymph 10 fritillary, hairstreak, parnassius 11 checkerspot, swallowtail *bush:* 8 buddleia *fish:* 6 blenny, chiton 7 gurnard *larva:* 11 caterpillar *lily:* 8 mariposa *order:* 11 Lepidoptera *plant:* 8 oncidium *pupa:* 9 chrysalis *scientist:* 13 lepidopterist

butterlike 8 butyrous 11 butyraceous

butt-in 7 meddler 8 busybody, kibitzer, quidnunc

butt in 6 horn in, meddle 7 intrude, obtrude 8 busybody, chisel in 9 interfere, interlope 10 intertrude, monkey with, tamper with 11 intermeddle

buttinsky see **butt-in**

buttocks 4 prat, rear, rump, seat, tail 5 fanny, hiney, nates, podex 6 behind, bottom, breech, heinie 7 hind end, hunkers, keester, keister, rear end, tail end 8 backside, derriere, haunches 9 fundament, posterior *combining form:* 3 pyg 4 pyga, pygo 5 pygia 6 procta

button *Japanese:* 7 netsuke

buttonball 8 sycamore

button-down 6 square 8 orthodox, straight 12 conventional

buttonwood 8 sycamore 13 white mangrove

buttress 4 prop, stay 5 brace, shore 6 bear up, column, upbear, uphold 7 bolster, shore up, support, sustain 11 underpinner 12 underpinning 13 underpropping

buxom 5 busty 6 bosomy, chesty 7 shapely, stacked 10 curvaceous 11 full-bosomed, full-figured

buy 3 get 5 bribe 6 obtain, ransom, redeem 7 acquire, bargain, believe 8 closeout, purchase 10 pennyworth, tamper with *Scottish:* 4 coff

buy back 6 redeem

buyer 6 emptor, vendee 8 customer 9 purchaser

buy off 3 fix, sop 5 bribe 10 tamper with

Buzi's son 7 Ezekiel
buzz 3 hum 4 fizz, hiss, whir, whiz
  5 drone, rumor, strum, thrum, whirr, whish
  6 bumble, fizzle, gossip, report, rumble, sizzle, wheeze, whoosh 7 whisper 8 sibilate
  9 bombinate 11 scuttlebutt
by 3 per, via 4 as to, near, nigh, over, with
  5 adieu, round 6 beside, nearby, next to, so
  long 7 good-bye, through 8 farewell
  9 alongside 11 according to
by and by 4 anon, next, soon 5 after,
  infra, later 7 shortly 8 directly, latterly
  9 afterward, presently 10 afterwhile
  12 subsequently
by and large 7 en masse 8 all in all
  9 generally 10 altogether, on the whole
by dint of see **by means of**
bye-bye 5 adieu 6 so long 7 cheerio
  8 farewell, toodle-oo
bygone 3 old 4 dead, late, lost, once,
  past 5 dated, olden 6 former, whilom
  7 antique, archaic, belated, defunct, extinct,
  old-time, onetime, quondam 8 departed,
  sometime, vanished 9 erstwhile, out-of-
  date 10 antiquated, oldfangled 12 old-
  fashioned
by means of 3 per, via 4 with 7 through

byname 7 moniker 8 nickname 9 sobriquet 10 hypocorism
bypass 5 burke, skirt 6 detour 8 sidestep 10 circumvent
byplace 4 nook 5 niche 6 cranny
by-product 7 spin-off 8 offshoot 9 outgrowth 10 derivative, descendant
Byron work 4 Cain, Lara 5 Beppo 6 Werner 7 Don Juan, Manfred 9 The Giaour
  10 The Corsair 12 Childe Harold
bystander 6 viewer 7 watcher, witness
  8 beholder, looker-on, observer, onlooker
  9 spectator 10 eyewitness
by stealth 7 sub rosa 8 covertly, secretly
  9 furtively, privately 13 clandestinely
by virtue of   see **by means of**
by way of   see **by means of**
byword 3 saw 5 adage 6 phrase, saying,
  slogan 7 proverb 8 nickname 9 sobriquet
  10 hypocorism, shibboleth 11 catchphrase
Byzantine 6 daedal, knotty 7 complex,
  gordian 8 involved 9 elaborate, intricate
  11 complicated 12 labyrinthine 13 sophisticated *emperor:* 3 Leo 4 Zeno 5 Basil
  6 Bardas, Justin, Phocas 7 Michael,
  Romanus 9 Heraclius, Justinian 10 Nice-
  phorus, Theodosius *empress:* 3 Zoe
  5 Irene 8 Theodora

C

cab 4 hack, taxi
cabal 3 mob 4 camp, clan, plot, ring
  5 covin 6 circle, clique, scheme 7 coterie,
  ingroup 8 intrigue, practice 9 camarilla
  10 conspiracy 11 machination
cabaletta 4 aria, song
cabalistic 6 arcane, mystic 8 numinous
  9 mysterial, unguessed 10 mysterious,
  unknowable 11 inscrutable 12 impenetrable 13 unaccountable
caballero 6 knight 8 cavalier, horseman
  9 chevalier
cabaret 4 café 6 nitery 7 hot spot 8 nightery 9 nightclub, night spot 10 supper
  club 11 discotheque 12 watering hole
cabbage 3 nab, nip 4 hook, lift 5 kraut,
  money, pinch, steal 6 collar 7 purloin
  10 greenbacks, sauerkraut 11 appropriate
  disease of: 6 mildew, mosaic 7 root rot,
  yellows 8 blackleg, club root *family:* 4 cole,
  kail, kale, rape 5 colza, savoy 6 turnip

  7 collard, mustard 8 broccoli, coleseed,
  colewort, kohlrabi, rutabaga 11 cauliflower
cabbagehead   see **dunce**
cabdriver 4 hack 5 cabby 6 cabbie
cabin 3 cot, hut 4 camp 5 lodge, shack
  6 cabana, shanty 7 cottage 9 stateroom
cabin cruiser 4 boat 9 motorboat
cabinet 7 armoire, commode 8 cupboard
cabinetmaker *American:* 5 Phyfe 6 Bel-
  ter, Wright 7 Goddard 8 McIntire, Townsend *English:* 4 Adam, Hope, Kent
  5 Smith 8 Sheraton 11 Hepplewhite
  French: 6 Boulle 8 Caffieri, Cressent *German:* 10 Weisweiler
cable 4 rope, wire 6 stitch
cabriolet 8 carriage
cache 4 bury, hide 5 cover, plant, stash,
  store 7 conceal, secrete 8 ensconce
cachet 4 rank 5 state 6 status 7 dignity,
  stature 8 position, prestige, standing
  11 consequence

cachinnate 5 laugh

cackle 3 gab, jaw 4 blab, chat 5 clack, run on 6 babble, burble, gabble, gaggle 7 blabber, blatter, chatter, prattle

cacoëthes 5 mania

cacophonic 9 dissonant, immusical, unmusical 10 discordant, inharmonic 11 disharmonic 12 inharmonious, unharmonious 13 disharmonious

cacophonous see **cacophonic**

cacophony 10 dissonance

cactus 5 dildo, nopal 6 cereus, cholla, mescal, peyote 7 airampo, bisnaga, biznaga, opuntia, saguaro, sahuaro 8 chichipe 11 prickly pear *fruit:* 6 cochal

cad 3 cur 4 heel, lout 5 creep, louse 6 rotter 7 bounder 9 yellow dog

cadaver 4 body, mort 5 stiff 6 corpse 7 carcass, remains

cadaverous 5 gaunt 6 wasted 7 ghastly, ghostly, shadowy 8 skeletal, spectral 9 deathlike, emaciated, ghostlike 10 corpselike

cadence 4 beat 5 meter, pulse, rhyme, swing, throb 6 rhythm 7 measure 8 rhythmus 9 pulsation

cadency see **cadence**

cadet 4 pimp 5 bully, plebe 6 pander 8 fancy man 10 macquereau

cadge 3 beg, bum 5 mooch 6 sponge 9 panhandle

cadmium *symbol:* 2 Cd

Cadmus *daughter:* 3 Ino 5 Agave 6 Semele 7 Autonoe *father:* 6 Agenor *sister:* 6 Europa *victim:* 6 dragon *wife:* 8 Harmonia

caducity 3 age 6 old age 7 dotardy 10 dotingness, senescence 11 elderliness, senectitude

Caesar *assassin:* 6 Brutus 7 Cassius *battle:* 4 Zela 9 Pharsalus *conquest:* 4 Gaul *eulogist:* 6 Antony *message:* 12 veni, vidi, vici *river:* 7 Rubicon *utterance:* 9 et tu Brute *wife:* 7 Pompeia 8 Cornelia 9 Calpurnia

Caesarism 10 absolutism 12 dictatorship

café 5 diner 6 nitery 7 beanery, cabaret, hot spot 8 cookshop, nightery 9 lunchroom, nightclub, night spot 10 coffee shop, supper club 11 discotheque, eating house 12 luncheonette, watering hole 13 watering place

café ____ 6 au lait, filtre

cage 3 hem, mew, pen 4 coop, jail 6 immure, shut in 7 close in, enclose, envelop 8 imprison 11 incarcerate

cagey 3 sly 5 heady 6 argute, astute, shrewd 9 astucious, sagacious 13 perspicacious

cageyness 3 art 5 craft 7 cunning, sly-

ness 8 artifice, foxiness, wiliness 9 canniness 10 artfulness, craftiness

cahoots 5 tie-up 6 hookup 8 alliance 10 connection 11 affiliation, association, combination, conjunction, partnership 12 togetherness

caiman 6 jacare 9 crocodile

Cain *brother:* 4 Abel, Seth *father:* 4 Adam *land:* 3 Nod *mother:* 3 Eve *nephew:* 4 Enos *son:* 5 Enoch *victim:* 4 Abel

Caine Mutiny author 4 Wouk

cajole 3 con 4 coax 7 beguile, blarney, wheedle 8 blandish, soft-soap 9 sweet-talk

cake 3 dry, set 4 coat, rime 5 cover, crust 6 harden 7 congeal, encrust, incrust 8 indurate, solidify 10 incrustate *almond:* 8 macaroon *chocolate:* 7 brownie *coffee:* 5 babka 6 kuchen *cornmeal:* 4 pone 8 tortilla *crisp, thin:* 5 wafer *flat:* 5 cooky 6 cookie *oatmeal:* 4 farl 5 farle, scone 7 bannock *of food:* 5 patty 6 pattie *ring-shaped:* 5 donut 6 jumbal, jumble 8 doughnut *rum-soaked:* 4 baba *Scottish:* 4 farl 5 farle, scone *shell-shaped:* 9 madeleine *toasted:* 7 crumpet *topping:* 5 icing 8 frosting, streusel *twisted:* 7 cruller *unleavened:* 8 tortilla *wheat:* 4 puri *without flour:* 5 torte *without shortening:* 6 sponge

Cakes and Ale author 7 Maugham

cakewalk 4 romp, rout 5 dance, strut 6 prance 7 runaway

calaboose 4 jail 5 clink, pokey 6 cooler, lockup, prison 8 hoosegow

Calais *brother:* 5 Zetes *father:* 6 Boreas *mother:* 8 Orithyia

calamitous 4 dire 5 fatal 6 woeful 7 fateful, ruinous 8 grievous 10 afflictive, deplorable, disastrous, lamentable 11 cataclysmic, distressing, regrettable, unfortunate 12 catastrophic 13 heartbreaking

calamity 4 ruin, woes 5 wreck 7 tragedy 8 disaster 9 cataclysm 10 affliction 11 catastrophe, tribulation 12 misadventure

Calamity ____ 4 Jane

calamity howler 9 Cassandra, pessimist, worrywart

calcar 4 oven

calcium *symbol:* 2 Ca

calculate 5 count, value 6 assess, cipher, figure, reckon 7 compute 8 appraise, estimate, evaluate 9 ascertain, determine

calculated 7 planned

calculating 3 sly 4 wary, wily 5 chary 6 artful, crafty 7 careful, cunning, guarded 8 cautious, discreet, gingerly, guileful 11 circumspect, considerate

calculating device 6 abacus *ancient Peruvian:* 5 quipo, quipu

calculation 8 figuring 9 ciphering, reckoning **10** arithmetic, estimation **11** computation

calculus *combining form:* **4** lith **5** litho

Caleb *daughter:* **6** Achsah *father:* **6** Hezron **9** Jephunneh *son:* **3** Hur, Iru

Caledonia **8** Scotland

calembour **3** pun **11** paronomasia

calendar **4** card, sked **6** agenda, docket **7** program **8** schedule **9** programma, time-table *abbreviation:* **3** Apr, Aug, Dec, Feb, Fri, Jan, Mar, Mon, Nov, Oct, Sat, Sep, Sun, Tue, Wed **4** Sept **5** Thurs *ecclesiastical:* **4** ordo **8** menology

calenture **4** fire, zeal **5** ardor **6** fervor, hurrah **7** passion **10** enthusiasm

calf *hide:* **3** kip *leather:* **3** elk *meat:* **4** veal *stray:* **4** dogy **5** dogie *unbranded:* **8** maverick

Caliban **5** slave *master:* **8** Prospero *witch-mother:* **7** Sycorax

caliber **5** class, grade, merit, value, worth **6** virtue **7** quality, stature

calibrate **7** measure **9** systemize **11** standardize

California *capital:* **10** Sacramento *college, university:* **3** USC **4** UCLA **5** Biola **8** Stanford **10** Pepperdine **12** San Francisco *colonizer:* **6** Sutter *fault zone:* **10** San Andreas *largest city:* **10** Los Angeles *motto:* **6** Eureka *nickname:* **11** Golden State *state flower:* **11** golden poppy

californium *symbol:* **2** Cf

caliginous **3** dim **4** dark, dusk **5** dusky, murky **6** gloomy **7** obscure **9** lightless, tenebrous **13** unilluminated

Caligula's mother **9** Agrippina

caliology topic **4** nest

caliph's name **3** Ali **7** Abu Bakr

Calista's seducer **8** Lothario

calisthenics **9** exercises

call **3** bid, cry, dub **4** bawl, draw, hail, hoot, howl, lure, name, note, page, pull, roar, song, term, yell, yowl **5** augur, cause, claim, exact, greet, hallo, hollo, phone, pop in, shout, title, visit **6** accost, appeal, bellow, come by, drop by, drop in, holler, invite, look in, look up, reckon, salute, stop by, stop in, summon **7** address, baptize, convene, convoke, entitle, portend, predict, presage, round up, solicit, summons **8** assemble, christen, estimate, forecast, foretell, occasion, prophesy **9** adumbrate, challenge, designate, necessity, postulate, seduction, telephone **10** allurement, attraction, denominate, vaticinate, visitation, vociferate **11** approximate, requisition **12** drawing power **13** prognosticate

calla **4** lily

call down **5** chide **6** lesson, monish, rebuke **7** reprove, tick off **8** admonish, reproach **9** reprimand

called **6** yclept **7** ycleped

caller **5** guest **7** visitor **8** visitant

call for **3** ask **5** crave **6** demand **7** require **11** necessitate

call forth **5** evoke **6** elicit **7** conjure

calligrapher **6** penman **7** copyist **9** engrosser

calligraphist see **calligrapher**

calligraphy **4** hand **6** ductus, script **10** penmanship **11** handwriting

call in **6** summon **7** convene

calling **3** art, job **4** work **5** craft, trade **6** métier **7** mission, pursuit **8** business, life-work, vocation **10** employment, handicraft, occupation, profession

Calliope **4** Muse *father:* **4** Zeus **7** Jupiter *mother:* **9** Mnemosyne *son:* **7** Orpheus

Callisto *lover:* **4** Zeus **7** Jupiter *son:* **5** Arcas

call off **5** scrub **6** cancel

Call of the Wild *author:* **6** London *dog:* **4** Buck

call on **5** visit **7** require

callosity **8** hardness **9** thickness

callous **5** stony **8** obdurate **9** heartless, indurated, unfeeling **11** coldhearted, hard-hearted, unemotional **12** case-hardened, stonyhearted **13** unsympathetic

callow **3** raw **5** fresh, green, young **6** infant, unripe **7** untried **8** immature, juvenile, unversed, youthful **9** unfledged **10** unseasoned **11** unpracticed **13** inexperienced, unexperienced

call's partner **4** beck

call up **5** draft, evoke **6** summon **8** mobilize

calm **4** cool, easy, hush, lull **5** allay, peace, quiet, relax, salve, still **6** hushed, pacify, placid, poised, sedate, serene, settle, smooth, soothe, stable, steady, stilly **7** appease, assuage, compose, halcyon, mollify, pacific, placate, resting, staunch **8** composed, inactive, peaceful, reposing, tranquil **9** collected, easygoing, impassive, possessed, quiescent, unruffled **10** nonchalant, phlegmatic, untroubled **11** tranquilize, unflappable **12** even-tempered, self-composed **13** imperturbable, self-possessed

calmant **8** quietive, sedative

calmative see **calmant**

calmness **6** phlegm **7** ataraxy **8** coolness **9** composure, sangfroid **10** equanimity

calumniate **5** libel **6** defame, malign, vilify **7** asperse, slander, traduce **9** denigrate **10** scandalize, villainize

calumnious **8** libelous **9** maligning, traducing, vilifying **10** backbiting, defamatory, detracting, detractive, scandalous, slanderous

calumny **7** scandal, slander **10** backbiting,

defamation, detraction, reflection **12** back-stabbing, belittlement, depreciation **13** disparagement

Calvados 6 brandy

calvary 5 cross, trial **6** ordeal **10** affliction, visitation **11** tribulation

Calypso *beloved:* **7** Ulysses **8** Odysseus *island:* **6** Ogygia

calyx part 5 sepal

camaraderie 5 cheer **7** jollity **10** affability **11** sociability **12** conviviality, friendliness

camarilla 3 mob **4** camp, clan, ring **5** cabal **6** circle, clique **7** coterie, ingroup

Cambodia 9 Kampuchea *capital:* **8** Pnom penh *monetary unit:* **4** riel

camel *driver:* **6** sarwan *one-humped:* **9** dromedary *two-humped:* **8** Bactrian

camel hair fabric 3 aba

camelopard 7 giraffe

Camelot 6 palace *lord:* **6** Arthur

Camembert 6 cheese

cameraman 6 photog **7** lensman **8** photoist **12** photographer

Cameroon *capital:* **7** Yaounde *largest city:* **6** Douala *monetary unit:* **5** franc

Camilla *father:* **7** Metabus *slayer:* **5** Aruns

Camille's creator 5 Dumas

camouflage 4 mask **5** cloak **8** disguise **9** dissemble **11** dissimulate

camp 3 cot, hut, mob **4** clan, ring, tent **5** cabal, cabin, lodge, shack **6** circle, clique, shanty **7** bivouac, caboose, coterie, cottage, ingroup **9** camarilla

campaigner 9 candidate

campanile 6 belfry **8** carillon **9** bell tower

campestral 5 rural **6** rustic **7** bucolic, country, outland **8** agrestic, pastoral **10** out-country, provincial **11** countrified

campus see **college**

Camus work 5 Rebel **6** Plague **8** Caligula, Stranger

can 4 fire **7** dismiss **9** container, discharge **10** receptacle *combining form:* **5** scyph **6** scyphi, scypho

Canaan 4 Zion **5** bliss **6** heaven **7** elysium, nirvana **8** empyrean, paradise *father:* **3** Ham *grandfather:* **4** Noah

Canaanite god 3 Mot **4** Baal **6** Molech, Moloch

Canace *brother:* **8** Macareus *father:* **6** Aeolus

Canada *capital:* **6** Ottawa *college, university:* **6** McGill **8** McMaster **9** Concordia *largest city:* **8** Montreal *monetary unit:* **6** dollar *province:* **6** Quebec **7** Alberta, Ontario **8** Manitoba **10** Nova Scotia **12** New Brunswick, Newfoundland, Saskatchewan *provincial park:* **5** Gaspé **7** Rondeau **9** Garibaldi

Canadian insurgent 4 Riel

canaille 3 mob **6** masses, rabble **8** riffraff, unwashed **11** proletariat

canal 4 duct **6** course **7** channel, conduit **8** aqueduct **11** watercourse *Africa:* **4** Suez **8** Ismailia *Belgium:* **6** Albert *Canada:* **7** Welland *Central America:* **6** Panama *China:* **5** Grand **7** Da Yunhe *combining form:* **4** meat **5** meato *Florida:* **10** Saint Lucie *Germany:* **4** Kiel *Greece:* **7** Corinth *Massachusetts:* **7** Cape Cod *Michigan:* **3** Soo *Netherlands:* **8** Noord Zee, North Sea **13** Amsterdam Ship *New York:* **4** Erie **6** Oswego **9** Champlain *Ontario:* **6** Rideau *Thailand:* **6** khlong *Venice:* **5** Grand

canapé spread 4 paté

canard 3 fib, lie **4** tale **5** spoof **7** falsity, untruth **8** untruism **9** falsehood **13** prevarication

canary 4 fink **6** snitch **7** stoolie **8** informer, squealer

Canary Islands 5 Ferro, Lobos, Palma **6** Gomera, Hierro **7** Inferno **8** Graciosa, Tenerife **9** Alegranza, Lanzarote

canary yellow 6 meline

cancel 3 end **4** drop, x out **5** annul, erase, scrub **6** delete, efface, negate, revoke **7** blot out, call off, expunge, redress, rescind, sublate, wipe out **8** black out **9** frustrate, terminate **10** counteract, invalidate, neutralize, obliterate **12** countercheck

cancer 5 tumor **9** carcinoma *combining form:* **6** carcin **7** carcino *treatment:* **5** X rays **7** surgery **9** radiation **12** chemotherapy

cancer-causing 12 carcinogenic *substance:* **10** carcinogen

cancer-like 8 cancroid

candescent 7 glowing **8** dazzling

Candia 5 Crete

candid 4 fair, just, open **5** frank, plain **6** honest **8** unbiased **9** equitable, impartial, objective, uncolored **10** aboveboard, forthright, scrupulous, unreserved **11** openhearted, unconcealed, undisguised **12** undissembled, unprejudiced **13** dispassionate, undissembling

candidate 6 seeker **7** hopeful, nominee, stumper **8** aspirant **9** applicant, dark horse **10** campaigner

Candide *author:* **8** Voltaire *lover:* **9** Cunegonde *tutor:* **8** Pangloss *valet:* **7** Cacambo

candle 6 bougie **8** bayberry *holder:* **6** lampad, sconce **7** menorah, pricket **9** girandole **10** candelabra **11** candelabrum *material:* **3** wax **4** wick **6** tallow **7** stearin **8** paraffin *religious:* **6** votive **7** paschal *slender:* **5** taper

candlefish 8 eulachon *relative:* **5** smelt

candlepins 7 bowling

candy 5 honey 7 sweeten 9 sugarcoat, sugar over *kind:* 4 rock 5 fudge, gundy, lolly, sweet, taffy, toffy 6 bonbon, comfit, dragée, jujube, nougat, toffee 7 brittle, caramel, fondant, gumdrop, penuche, praline 8 licorice, lollipop, lollypop, marzipan, sourball, taiglach, teiglach 9 chocolate, jelly bean, nonpareil, sweetmeat 10 confection 12 butterscotch *medicated:* 7 lozenge 9 cough drop

Canea's land 5 Crete

canine 3 dog 4 tyke 5 hound, pooch

Canis Major star 6 Sirius

Canis Minor star 7 Procyon

canker 5 stain 6 debase 7 corrupt, debauch, deprave, pervert, vitiate 9 animalize 10 bestialize, demoralize

cankered 5 waspy 6 cranky, ornery 7 bearish, waspish 8 vinegary 9 crotchety 10 vinegarish 12 cantankerous, crossgrained

canker sore 5 ulcer 6 lesion 10 ulceration

cannabis 3 pot 4 hemp 5 bhang, ganja, grass 7 hashish 9 marijuana

canned 6 pocket, potted 7 capsule 9 condensed 10 epitomized

Cannery Row author 9 Steinbeck

cannibalic 4 grim 5 cruel 6 fierce, savage 7 inhuman, wolfish 8 inhumane 9 barbarous, ferocious, truculent

canniness 3 art 5 craft 7 caution, cunning, slyness 8 artifice, foxiness, prudence, wiliness 9 cageyness, foresight 10 artfulness, craftiness, discretion, precaution, providence 11 forethought 12 discreetness

cannon 6 pom-pom 8 howitzer, ordnance 9 artillery *part:* 5 chase 6 breech 8 cascabel, trunnion *slang:* 6 pistol 10 pickpocket

cannonade 4 bomb, hail 5 blitz, burst, salvo, shell 6 shower, volley 7 barrage, bombard 8 drumfire 9 broadside, fusillade 11 bombardment

cannonball 4 dive 5 speed 7 missile

cannoneer 6 gunner

cannon fodder 8 infantry, soldiers

canny 3 sly 4 wise 5 chary, quick, sharp, slick, smart 6 adroit, clever, frugal, saving 7 cunning, knowing, sparing, thrifty 9 dexterous, ingenious, provident, stewardly 10 economical, unwasteful 11 quick-witted, sharp-witted 12 nimble-witted

canoe 6 dugout 7 pirogue, piroque *ancient:* 7 coracle *Central American:* 6 pitpan *Eskimo:* 5 kayak, umiak 6 oomiak 7 bidarka *Guianan:* 6 corial *Latin American:* 5 bungo *Malabar Coast:* 6 ballam *Maori:* 4 waka *Philippine:* 5 banca 6 baroto *Polynesian:* 4 pahi

canon 3 law 4 rule 5 dogma, edict, tenet 6 assize, decree 7 precept, statute

8 decretum, doctrine 9 ordinance 10 regulation

canonical 5 sound 8 accepted, orthodox, received 10 sanctioned 13 authoritative

canonical hour 4 none, sext 5 lauds, prime, terce 6 matins, tierce 7 vespers 8 compline

canonicals 9 vestments

can opener 9 church key

canopy 3 sky 5 cover 6 awning 7 marquee, shelter 8 covering 9 baldachin 10 baldachino 11 baldacchino *canvas:* 4 tilt

cant 3 tip 4 heel, lean, list, tilt 5 argot, idiom, lingo, slang, slant, slope 6 jargon, patois, patter, speech 7 dialect, diction, incline, lexicon, palaver, recline 8 language 9 hypocrisy 10 dictionary, pharisaism, sanctimony, Tartuffery, Tartuffism, vernacular, vocabulary 11 phraseology, terminology 12 pecksniffery

cantaloupe 5 melon 9 muskmelon

cantankerous 4 dour, sour 5 cross, huffy, waspy 6 cranky, crusty, morose, ornery 7 bearish, crabbed, prickly, waspish 8 cankered, liverish, petulant, snappish, vinegary 9 crotchety, dyspeptic, irascible, irritable 10 ill-natured, vinegarish 12 crossgrained

canter 3 bum, vag 4 gait, hobo 5 tramp 7 drifter, vagrant 8 derelict, vagabond 10 street arab 11 bindle stiff

Canterbury *archbishop:* 3 Odo 6 Anselm, Becket, Parker 7 Cranmer, Dunstan 9 Augustine

Canterbury Tales *author:* 7 Chaucer *inn:* 6 Tabard

canticle 3 ode 4 hymn, song 10 Benedicite, Benedictus, Magnificat 12 Nunc Dimittis

canticles 11 Song of Songs 13 Song of Solomon

cantilever 6 bridge 7 support

cantillate 4 sing 5 chant 6 recite

cantina 3 bar, pub 6 saloon, tavern 7 barroom, gin mill, rum hole 8 drinkery, groggery, pothouse

canton 6 billet 7 quarter 8 district, division

cantor 5 hazan 6 chazan, hazzan 7 chazzan 9 precentor

canvas 4 duck, sail, tarp, tent 6 awning 8 painting 9 tarpaulin

canvasback 4 duck

canvass 3 con, vet 4 case, drum, moot 5 argue, study 6 debate, drum up, survey 7 agitate, check up, discept, discuss, dispute, examine, inspect, solicit 9 check over, thrash out 10 scrutinize

canyon 5 cajon, chasm, gorge, gulch 6 ravine, valley 10 depression *Colorado*

River: 5 Grand **mouth:** 4 abra **Snake river:** 5 Hells
cap 3 cob, top 4 best, pass 5 beret, cover, crest, crown, trump 6 barret, beanie, climax, exceed, top off 7 blanket, overlay, surpass 8 outshine, outstrip, overcast, round off, surmount 9 culminate, finish off, transcend 10 overspread **academic:** 11 mortarboard **brimless:** 3 tam 5 beret, calot 7 calotte **clergyman's:** 5 miter, mitre 7 biretta 9 zucchetto **combining form:** 8 calyptri, calyptro **cone-shaped:** 3 taj **hoodlike:** 4 coif **hunter's:** 7 montero **jester's:** 7 coxcomb 9 cockscomb **Jewish:** 8 yarmulke **knitted:** 5 toque, tuque **military:** 4 kepi **mushroom:** 6 pileus **Muslim:** 3 taj **part:** 4 bill, brim, flap, peak 5 visor 7 earflap **Roman:** 6 pileus **Scottish:** 3 tam 5 mutch 6 bonnet 8 balmoral 9 glengarry 11 tam-o'-shanter **sheepskin:** 6 calpac, kalpak 7 calpack **Turkish:** 6 calpac, kalpak 7 calpack
capability 3 art 5 craft, might, skill 7 ability, cunning, potency 8 adequacy, capacity, efficacy 10 competence, efficiency 13 effectiveness, qualification, qualifiedness
capable 4 able, good 6 au fait, proper, wicked 9 competent, qualified **suffix:** 3 ile 4 able, ible
capacious 4 wide 5 ample, roomy 7 copious 8 abundant, spacious 10 commodious
capacitance **unit of:** 5 farad
capacity 4 bent, gift, rank 5 knack, might, place, state 6 status, talent 7 ability, caliber, faculty, footing, station, stature 8 adequacy, position, standing 9 character, situation 10 capability, competence 13 qualification, qualifiedness **unit of:** 4 gill, peck, pint 5 liter, minim, quart 6 bushel, gallon 8 fluidram 10 fluidounce, milliliter
Capaneus **slayer:** 4 Zeus **wife:** 6 Evadne
caparison 8 clothing 9 adornment
cape 4 beak, bill, head, naze, ness 5 point 8 foreland, headland, pelerine 10 promontory **clergyman's:** 7 mozzetta 8 mozzetta **papal:** 5 fanon, orale
Cape **Africa:** 4 Juby, Yubi 5 Blanc 6 Blanco 7 Agulhas **Alaska:** 3 Icy 4 Nome 5 Ocean 11 Krusenstern **Algeria:** 3 Fer **Antarctica:** 3 Ann 4 Dart 5 Adare **Arctic:** 5 North 8 Nordkaap **Asia:** 5 Aniva **Australia:** 5 Byron, Otway, Sandy, Smoky 6 Arnhem 9 Van Diemen **Baffin Island:** 4 Dyer **Black Sea:** 5 Yasun **Borneo:** 4 Datu 6 Datoek **Brazil:** 4 Frio, Raso 5 Norte **California:** 9 Mendocino **Canada:** 5 North **Caribbean:** 8 Honduras **Colombia:** 5 Aguja **Costa Rica:** 5 Velas **Crete:** 5 Plaka **Croatia:** 5 Ploca 6 Planka **Cuba:** 4 Cruz 5 Maisi **Denmark:** 4 Skaw 6 Skagen **Desolación island:** 5 Pilar 6 Pillar **Dji-**

bouti: 3 Bir **Egypt:** 5 Banas **England:** 8 Bolerium, Lands End **Florida:** 5 Sable 7 Kennedy 9 Canaveral **Greece:** 4 Busa 5 Gallo, Malea, Papas, Vouxa 6 Araxos, Maleas 7 Akritas **Guadalcanal:** 4 West **Guinea:** 5 Verga **Gulf of California:** 5 Lobos **Gulf of Guinea:** 5 Lopez **Gulf of Mexico:** 4 Rojo **Hawaii:** 5 Ka Lae, South 10 South Point 11 Diamond Head **Hispaniola:** 5 Beata **Honshu:** 3 Iro, Oma 5 Inubo, Kyoga, Nyudo **Iceland:** 4 Horn 5 North **Indonesia:** 4 Vals 5 False **Japan:** 4 Esan, Nomo, Sata, Soya 5 Erimo, Kamui **Liberia:** 5 Mount **Libya:** 3 Tin 4 Milh **Long Island Sound:** 10 Throgs Neck **Malay Peninsula:** 5 Bulat 7 Romania **Malaysia:** 4 Piai 5 Sirik **Massachusetts:** 3 Ann, Cod **Mediterranean:** 5 Ajdir **Mexico:** 4 Buey **Morocco:** 3 Sim 4 Guir, Rhir **Namibia:** 4 Fria 5 Cross **Newfoundland:** 4 Pine 5 Bauld **New Jersey:** 3 May **New Zealand:** 4 East 5 Brett, North, South, Table **North Carolina:** 4 Fear 7 Lookout 8 Hatteras **Northwest Territories:** 8 Bathurst **Nova Scotia:** 5 Canso 6 Breton **Oman:** 3 Nus 4 Hadd **Ontario:** 4 Hurd, Rich **Pakistan:** 5 Monze, Muari **Portugal:** 4 Roca **Puerto Rico:** 4 Rojo **Quebec:** 5 Gaspé **Red Sea:** 5 Kasar **Sicily:** 4 Boeo, Faro 7 Lilibeo, Passero, Pelorus **Solomon Islands:** 5 Zelee **Somalia:** 4 Asir 5 Assir, Hafun **South Africa:** 4 Seal 8 Good Hope **South America:** 4 Horn **Spain:** 3 Nao 4 Gata 5 Creus, Penas 9 Trafalgar **Syria:** 5 Basit **Taiwan:** 5 O-luan 7 Garam Bi **Tasmania:** 5 Table **Tierra del Fuego:** 5 Penas **Tunisia:** 5 Blanc **Turkey:** 3 Boz 4 Baba, Ince, Kara, Krio 6 Lectum 8 Bozburun 9 Inceburun, Karaburun **Vancouver Island:** 5 Scott **Virginia:** 5 Henry **Washington:** 5 Alava
Čapek **coinage:** 5 robot **play:** 3 R.U.R.
caper 4 dido, lark, romp 5 antic, frisk, prank, shine, trick 6 cavort, frolic, gambol 7 roguery, rollick 8 escapade, mischief 9 capriccio, devilment 10 impishness, shenanigan, tomfoolery 11 monkeyshine, waggishness
Capetown's famous son 5 Smuts
capillary 4 tube 6 vessel 8 hairlike 11 blood vessel
capital 3 top 4 cock, fine, main, rank 5 basic, chief, dandy, gross, major, prime, vital 6 assets, famous, wealth 7 glaring 8 cardinal, dominant, five-star, flagrant, topnotch 9 egregious, essential, excellent, first-rate, number one, principal, resources 10 first-class, preeminent, underlying 11 fundamental, outstanding, predominant **Admiralty Islands:** 8 Lorengau **Afghanistan:** 5 Kabul **Alberta:** 8 Edmonton **Angola:** 6 Luanda **Antigua:** 7 St. Johns

Armenia: 6 Erevan, Erivan 7 Yerevan
Assam: 6 Dispur *Azerbaijan:* 4 Baku
Belize: 8 Belmopan *Belarus:* 5 Minsk *Bhutan:* 6 Thimbu *Bophuthatswana:* 8 Mmabatho *Botswana:* 8 Gaborone *Dominica:*
6 Roseau *Equatorial Guinea:* 6 Malabo
Estonia: 7 Tallinn *Ethiopia:* 10 Addis
Ababa *Faeroe Islands:* 9 Thorshavn *Falkland Islands:* 7 Stanley *French Guiana:*
7 Cayenne *Galapagos Islands:* 12 San
Cristobal *Georgia, Republic of:* 7 Tbilisi
Ghana: 5 Accra *Greenland:* 7 Godthab
Guam: 5 Agana *Guinea:* 7 Conakry
Kazakhstan: 7 Alma Ata *Kirghizia:* 7 Bishkek *Kiribata:* 6 Tarawa *Latvia:* 4 Riga *Lithuania:* 7 Vilnius *Malaysia:* 11 Kuala Lumpur *Manitoba:* 8 Winnipeg *Mauritania:*
10 Nouakchott *Moldova:* 8 Kishinev *Mongolia:* 9 Ulan Bator *Montserrat:* 8 Plymouth *Mozambique:* 6 Maputo *Myanmar:*
6 Yangon *Namibia:* 8 Windhoek *Newfoundland:* 10 Saint Johns *Northern Ireland:* 7 Belfast *Northern Territory:* 6 Darwin *North-West Frontier Province:*
8 Peshawar *Northwest Territories:* 11 Yellowknife *Nova Scotia:* 7 Halifax *Orange Free State:* 12 Bloemfontein *Papua New Guinea:* 11 Port Moresby *Prince Edward Island:* 13 Charlottetown *Puerto Rico:*
7 San Juan *Queensland:* 8 Brisbane
Réunion: 10 Saint Denis *Saint Helena:*
9 Jamestown *Saint Lucia:* 8 Castries *Saskatchewan:* 6 Regina *Scotland:* 9 Edinburgh *Seychelles:* 8 Victoria *Shetland:*
7 Lerwick *Sicily:* 7 Palermo *Sierra Leone:*
8 Freetown *Sikkim:* 7 Gangtok *Sind:*
7 Karachi *Slovenia:* 9 Ljubljana *Solomon Islands:* 7 Honiara *South Australia:*
8 Adelaide *South-West Africa:* 8 Windhoek *Suriname:* 10 Paramaribo *Swaziland:*
7 Mbabane *Tadzhikistan:* 8 Dushanbe
Tahiti: 7 Papeete *Tasmania:* 6 Hobart
Tibet: 5 Lhasa *Tirol:* 9 Innsbruck *Tonga:*
9 Nukualofa *Transkei:* 6 Umtata *Turkmenistan:* 9 Ashkhabad *Ukraine:* 4 Kiev *Uruguay:* 10 Montevideo *Uttar Pradesh:*
7 Lucknow *Uzbekistan:* 8 Tashkent
Venda: 11 Thohoyandou *Victoria:* 9 Melbourne *Vietnam:* 5 Hanoi *Wales:* 7 Cardiff
Western Australia: 5 Perth *Yukon:*
10 Whitehorse (see also names of individual countries and states)
capitalist 8 investor 9 bourgeois, financier, plutocrat
capitalistic 9 bourgeois
capitalize 3 aid 4 back, fund, help
5 stake 6 assist 7 finance, promote, sponsor, support 8 bankroll 9 grubstake, subsidize
capital sin see **deadly sin**
Capitol Hill sound 3 aye, nay

capitulate 3 bow 4 cave 5 defer, yield
6 submit 7 knuckle, succumb 11 buckle under 12 knuckle under
capitulation 8 dedition 9 surrender
10 submission
capper 5 blind, decoy, shill, stick
9 shillaber
capriccio 5 caper, fancy, prank 6 whimsy
caprice 3 bee 4 mood, vein, whim
5 crank, fancy, freak, habit, humor, trait, trick 6 foible, maggot, megrim, notion, temper, vagary, whimsy 7 boutade, conceit
8 crotchet 9 mannerism 11 peculiarity
12 whigmaleerie 13 inconsistency
capricious 4 iffy 5 moody 6 chancy, fickle 7 erratic, wayward 8 freakish, ticklish, unstable, variable, volatile, whimsied
9 arbitrary, fluctuant, humorsome, mercurial, uncertain, vagarious, whimsical 10 changeable, inconstant, lubricious 12 effervescent, incalculable 13 temperamental, unpredictable
capsheaf see **capstone**
capsize 4 keel 5 upset 8 collapse, overturn
capstone 4 acme, apex, peak 6 apogee, climax, summit 8 capsheaf, meridian, pinnacle 11 culmination
capsule 6 canned, pocket, potted 9 condensed 10 epitomized *combining form:*
4 thec 5 theci, theco
capsulize 7 enclose 8 condense
captain 7 skipper 11 four-striper *fictional:* 4 Ahab, Nemo 5 Bligh, Queeg
pirate: 4 Kidd
Captains Courageous author 7 Kipling
caption 6 legend 7 cutline 8 overline
9 underline
captious 5 testy 6 critic, snappy 7 carping, finicky, peevish 8 caviling, contrary, critical, exacting, perverse, petulant, snappish 9 cavillous, demanding, irritable
10 censorious 12 faultfinding, overcritical
13 hypercritical
captivate 4 draw, grip, hold, take, wile
5 charm 6 allure, please 7 attract, bewitch, delight, enchant, gratify 8 enthrall 9 fascinate, magnetize, mesmerize, spellbind
captivating 8 magnetic 9 appealing, glamorous, seductive
captive 7 hostage 8 prisoner
captivity 11 confinement 12 imprisonment
capture 3 bag, get, nab 4 nail, take
5 catch, cotch 6 collar, secure 7 prehend
Capuan 4 lush 5 plush 6 deluxe 7 opulent 8 luscious, palatial 9 luxuriant, luxurious, sumptuous 11 upholstered
car 4 auto, heap 5 buggy, coach, coupe, crate, motor, sedan, wreck 6 hotrod, jalopy, junker 7 clunker, flivver, hardtop, machine, phaeton 8 dragster, motorcar, roadster,

runabout **9** limousine **10** automobile, touring car **11** convertible **12** station wagon (see also **automobile**)

caramel-like 5 chewy

caravansary 3 inn **5** hotel, lodge **6** hostel, tavern **7** auberge, hospice **8** hostelry **9** roadhouse **11** public house

carbohydrate 5 sugar **6** starch **7** glucose, lactose, sucrose **8** fructose, glycogen **9** cellulose, galactose *suffix:* **3** ose

carbon 4 coal, coke, soot **8** graphite, plumbago **9** lampblack *combining form:* **7** anthrac **8** anthraco

carbonate 6 aerate

carbon compound *suffix:* **2** an **3** ane, ene, yne **5** ylene

carbon copy 5 ditto **7** replica **9** duplicate, facsimile **11** replication **12** reproduction **13** reduplication

carbonize 4 burn, char

carboxyl *suffix:* **3** oic **4** onic

carbuncle 4 boil **6** pimple **7** abscess, pustule *combining form:* **7** anthrac **8** anthraco

carcass 4 body, mort **5** stiff **6** corpse, deader **7** cadaver, remains

carcinoid 5 tumor

carcinoma 5 tumor **6** cancer

card 3 wag **4** menu, sked, zany **5** joker, trump **6** agenda, docket **7** program **8** calendar, comedian, humorist, schedule **9** programma, timetable **11** carte du jour *fortune-telling:* **5** tarot *spot:* **3** pip

cardboard 5 stiff **6** unreal, wooden **7** bristol, buckram, stilted **10** unlifelike **11** muscle-bound, stereotyped, unrealistic

card-carrying 7 genuine **11** full-fledged

card game see at **game**

cardiac stimulant 7 ouabain **9** digitalis

cardialgia 9 heartburn

cardinal 5 vital **6** ruling **7** central, pivotal **9** essential **10** overriding, overruling **11** fundamental **12** constitutive

cardinal point 4 east, west **5** north, south

cardinal suffix 2 ty **4** teen

Cardinal Virtue 7 justice **8** prudence **9** fortitude **10** temperance

care 3 rue, woe **4** dole, fear, heed, mind, reck, tend, ward **5** alarm, grief, nurse, pains, serve, trial, trust, watch, worry **6** attend, charge, dismay, effort, mother, regard, regret, sorrow, strain, stress, unease, wait on **7** anguish, anxiety, concern, conduct, custody, keeping, running, tension, trouble **8** disquiet, exertion, handling, interest, suspense, tendance **9** agitation, alertness, attention, curiosity, heartache, misgiving, oversight, vigilance **10** affliction, enthusiasm, foreboding, heartbreak, intendance, management, minister to, solicitude, uneasiness **11** concernment, dis-

quietude, disturbance, heedfulness, safekeeping, supervision **12** apprehension, guardianship, perturbation, watchfulness **13** consciousness, consideration, consternation

careen 4 sway **5** lurch, swing, weave **6** wobble **7** stagger

career 4 race, rush, rush **5** chase, speed **6** course **7** calling **8** vocation

care for 4 like, mind, tend **5** nurse **6** foster

carefree 4 wild **6** breezy **8** feckless, reckless **9** lightsome **10** free-minded, incautious, insouciant **12** happy-go-lucky, lighthearted **13** irresponsible

careful 4 safe, wary **5** chary, exact, fussy **6** intent **7** duteous, dutiful, finical, finicky, guarded, heedful, precise, prudent, studied **8** accurate, cautious, critical, discreet, gingerly, punctual **9** attentive, observant, provident, religious **10** deliberate, meticulous, particular, scrupulous **11** calculating, circumspect, considerate, foresighted, painstaking, punctilious **12** conscionable **13** conscientious

carefully 8 gingerly

careless 3 lax **4** rash, wild **5** messy, slack, unfit **6** botchy, remiss, sloppy, unneat, untidy **7** raunchy, unkempt **8** derelict, feckless, heedless, reckless, slapdash, slipshod, slovenly, uncaring **9** forgetful, incapable, negligent, oblivious, unheeding, unmindful, unrecking **10** behindhand, delinquent, disheveled, inadequate, incautious, neglectful, regardless, unthinking, unthorough **11** inadvertent, inattentive, thoughtless, unconcerned, unqualified **12** disregardful, irreflective, unfastidious, uninterested, unreflective **13** irresponsible

caress 3 pat, pet, toy **4** love, neck **5** dally, flirt **6** cocker, coddle, coquet, cosset, cuddle, dandle, fondle, nuzzle, pamper, stroke, trifle **7** indulge

caressive 7 calming **8** soothing

caretaker 9 custodian

careworn 5 drawn, jaded **6** fagged **7** haggard, pinched **8** troubled, tuckered **9** exhausted **10** distressed

cargo 4 haul, load **6** burden, lading **7** freight, payload

caricature 4 fake, mock, sham **5** farce, phony **6** parody **7** cartoon, lampoon, mockery, takeoff **8** travesty **9** burlesque, clinquant, imitation **10** pasquinade **13** laughingstock

carillon 6 belfry **9** bell tower, campanile

caritas 5 grace, mercy **6** lenity **7** charity **8** clemency

cark 3 ail **4** fret, fuss, stew **5** upset, worry **6** pother **7** trouble **8** distress

Carmen *author:* **7** Mérimée *composer:*

5 Bizet *lover:* **7** Don José *toreador:*
9 Escamillo

Carmi *father:* **6** Reuben *son:* **5** Achan

carnage 8 butchery, massacre **9** bloodbath, bloodshed, slaughter

carnal 4 lewd **5** gross **6** animal, bodily,
coarse, earthy, vulgar, wanton **7** earthly,
fleshly, lustful, mundane, obscene, sensual,
somatic, worldly **8** corporal, material, physical, sensuous **9** corporeal **10** lascivious

carnation 4 pink **5** color **6** flower

carnival *attraction:* **4** ride **6** midway
8 sideshow **10** concession *character:*
5 shill **6** barker, hawker **7** grifter, spieler
New Orleans: **9** Mardi Gras *performer:*
4 geek

carol 4 song **6** ballad *Christmas:* **4** noel

carom 3 dap **4** skim, skip **5** graze
6 glance **8** ricochet

carotid's relative 5 aorta

carousal 3 bat, jag **4** tear **5** binge, booze,
drunk, spree **6** bender **7** blowoff **9** brannigan *Scottish:* **6** splore

carouse 4 hell, riot **5** revel **6** frolic **7** roister, wassail *Scottish:* **4** birl **5** birle

carp 3 nag **4** fuss **5** cavil **6** peck at
7 henpeck

carpe ___ 4 diem

carpenter 3 ant, bee **6** joiner, wright
7 artisan, builder, workman **9** craftsman

carpentry 7 joinery

carper 5 momus **6** critic, Zoilus **7** caviler,
knocker **9** aristarch **10** criticizer **11** faultfinder, smellfungus

carpet 3 mat, rug **5** tapis **6** velvet, Wilton
8 Brussels, moquette, Venetian **9** Axmin-
ster, broadloom *Afghan:* **5** Herat *Persian:*
Indian: **4** Agra *Persian:* **4** kali **6** Kerman,
Keshan, Kirman, Sarouk *Turkish:* **5** Koula,
Ladik **8** Ghiordes

carpet beetle 10 buffalo bug

carpet knight 8 hedonist, sybarite

carping 6 critic, jawing **7** blaming, railing
8 blameful, captious, caviling, critical **9** cavillous, damnatory **10** censorious, upbraid-
ing **11** criticizing, objurgatory, reproachful,
reprobating, reprobatory **12** condemnatory,
faultfinding, overcritical, reprehending
13 hypercritical

carrageen 7 seaweed **9** Irish moss

carrefour 5 plaza **6** square **10** crossroads

carriage 3 rig **4** pose **5** stance **7** posture,
transit, voiture **8** attitude, carrying, positure **9** transport **10** conveyance **12** transporting *American:* **5** buggy **8** dearborn,
rockaway **9** buckboard *attendant:*
6 flunky **7** flunkey, footman *baby:* **4** pram
5 buggy **8** stroller **12** perambulator
driver: **4** hack **5** cabby **8** coachman *folding top:* **6** calash *four-wheeled:* **4** sado,
trap **5** buggy, coupe **6** berlin, calash, fiacre,

landau, surrey **7** britska, cariole, dos-a-dos,
hackney, phaeton **8** barouche, britzska,
brougham, carriole, carryall, clarence, dearborn, rockaway, sociable, stanhope, taran-
tas, victoria **9** buckboard *Indian:* **6** gharri,
gharry *Javanese:* **4** sado *man-drawn:*
6 riksha **7** rikisha, rikshaw **10** jinrikisha
Philippine: **6** calesa **7** calesin **9** carromata
Russian: **6** drosky, troika **7** droshky **8** tar-
antas **9** tarantass *stately:* **7** caroche *three-
horse:* **6** troika *two-wheeled:* **3** gig
4 shay, trap **5** buggy, sulky **6** calesa,
chaise, dennet, hansom, herdic, whisky
7 caleche, calesin, dogcart, tilbury, whiskey
8 curricle **9** cabriolet, carromata *with attendants:* **8** equipage

carriage trade 5 elite **6** flower, gentry
7 quality **9** blue blood, gentility **10** upper
class, upper crust **11** aristocracy

carrick bend 4 knot

carrier 5 envoy **6** bearer, porter, vector
7 airline, courier, drogher, vehicle **8** emissary **9** messenger **11** internuncio *combining form:* **4** pher, phor **5** phora, phore
6 phorae (plural), phorum

Carroll character 5 Alice **6** Hatter
8 Dormouse **9** March Hare **10** Mock
Turtle **11** White Rabbit **12** Humpty Dumpty

carrot 4 meed, plum **5** prize **6** reward
7 guerdon, premium **8** dividend

carry 3 act, get, jag, lug **4** bear, buck,
have, hump, keep, move, pack, pipe, prop,
quit, send, sway, take, tote, waft **5** brace,
bring, ferry, fetch, shift, stock, touch
6 acquit, affect, bear up, behave, convey,
demean, deport, funnel, remove, siphon,
strike, upbear, uphold **7** bolster, channel,
comport, conduct, disport, impress, inspire,
possess, shore up, support, sustain, traject
8 buttress, transfer, transmit **9** influence,
transport

carrying *combining form:* **7** phorous

carrying case 7 holdall

carry off 4 down, kill, slay **6** cut off, finish,
lay low, spirit **7** destroy, put away, take off
8 dispatch

carry on 3 run **4** go on, keep, rant, rave
5 act up, cut up, horse **6** direct, hang on,
manage, ordain **7** conduct, operate, persist **9** horseplay, persevere

carry out 6 effect, govern, render **7** execute, fulfill **8** bring off, complete, finalize,
transact **9** discharge, prosecute **10** administer, effectuate **12** administrate

carry over 8 postpone, transfer

carrytale 5 clack, tabby **6** gossip **8** gossiper, quidnunc **10** newsmonger **12** gossipmonger **13** scandalmonger

carry through 4 last **5** abide **6** effect,
endure **7** perdure, persist **8** bring off, continue **10** effectuate

cart 4 dray, haul 5 carry 6 barrow, convey 7 tumbrel, tumbril 8 carriage 9 transport *Indian:* 5 tonga *racing:* 5 sulky
___ **carte** 3 a la
___ **Carte** 5 D'Oyly
carte blanche 3 say 5 power, right, sayso 7 license 8 free hand 9 authority 10 blank check 11 prerogative
carte d'entrée 6 ticket
carte du jour 4 menu
cartel 4 bloc, dare, defy, pool 5 chain, group, stump, trust 7 combine 8 defiance 9 challenge, syndicate 10 consortium
Carthaginian *goddess of the moon:* 5 Tanit 6 Tanith *queen:* 4 Dido 6 Elissa
cartilage 6 tissue 7 gristle *combining form:* 6 chondr 7 chondri, chondro
cartogram 3 map
cartographer *English:* 5 Smith *Flemish:* 6 Kremer 8 Mercator, Ortelius *German:* 13 Waldseemuller *Greek:* 7 Ptolemy
cartography 9 mapmaking
cartoonist 4 Capp (Al), Nast (Thomas), Szep 5 Davis (Jim), Gould (Chester), Kelly (Walt), Young (Chic) 6 Disney (Walt), Larson (Gary), Schulz (Charles) 7 Mauldin (Bill), Trudeau (Garry) 8 Goldberg (Rube), Groening (Matt)
cartouche 5 brown, frame 6 shield
cartridge 4 case, tube 5 shell 8 cylinder
cartwheel 4 coin 6 tumble 10 handspring
carve 3 cut 5 sculp, sever, slice, split 6 chisel, cleave, sculpt, sunder 7 dissect 8 dissever 9 sculpture
Casanova 4 wolf 5 Romeo 6 chaser, masher 7 amorist, Don Juan, gallant 8 lothario, paramour 9 ladies' man, philander, womanizer 10 lady-killer 11 philanderer
cascade 5 chute, falls, sault, spout 8 cataract 9 waterfall
case 3 con, pod, vet 4 etui, hull, husk, skin, suit, view 5 cause, event, order, shape, shell, shuck, spook, state, study 6 action, estate, oddity, repair, sample 7 canvass, check up, episode, examine, example, inspect, lawsuit, oddball 8 incident, instance, original, sampling, specimen 9 character, check over, condition, eccentric, situation 10 occurrence, scrutinize 11 eventuality 12 circumstance, illustration *combining form:* 4 thec 5 theca, theci, theco 6 thecae (plural), thecia (plural) 7 thecium *grammatical:* 6 dative 8 ablative, genitive, vocative 9 objective 10 accusative, nominative, possessive
casebearer 5 larva 11 caterpillar
case-hardened 7 callous 10 insensible
case history 6 sample 7 example 8 instance, sampling, specimen 12 illustration

casement 6 window
Casey at the Bat poet 6 Thayer
cash 4 coin, jack 5 bread, dough, money 6 mazuma, wampum 7 scratch, shekels 11 legal tender
cashier 2 ax 3 bar, can 4 cast, fire, oust, sack, shed 5 eject, expel, scrap 6 bounce, reject, shelve, slough 7 boot out, discard, dismiss, exclude, kick out 8 abdicate, jettison, pass over, throw out 9 discharge, eliminate, terminate, throw away
cash in 3 die 4 conk, drop 5 croak 6 pop off 7 kick off, succumb 8 check out, pass away
casino attendant 8 croupier
cask 3 keg, tun 4 butt, pipe 6 barrel 8 hogshead
casket 3 box 5 chest 6 coffin
Cassandra 7 seeress 9 doomsayer, pessimist, worrywart 10 prophetess 11 crepehanger *brother:* 7 Helenus *father:* 5 Priam *lover:* 9 Agamemnon *mother:* 6 Hecuba *slayer:* 12 Clytemnestra
casserole 4 dish
Cassiopeia *daughter:* 9 Andromeda *husband:* 7 Cepheus *kingdom:* 8 Ethiopia
Cassio's mistress 6 Bianca
cassock 7 soutane
cast 3 add, aim, hue, lay, sum, tot, way 4 dash, drop, face, fire, foot, form, hint, hurl, junk, kind, look, mold, plan, shed, sort, tint, tone, toss, tote, turn, type 5 chart, class, color, fling, heave, leave, level, pitch, point, scrap, shade, shape, sling, smack, throw, tinge, total, touch, trace, train, weird, yield 6 design, devise, direct, figure, launch, nature, reject, slough, stripe, visage, zero in 7 address, arrange, cashier, discard, dope out, incline, moulage, project, scatter, soupçon, summate, variety 8 abdicate, disperse, forecast, jettison, prophecy, totalize 9 blueprint, broadcast, character, prevision, prognosis, suspicion, throw away 10 distribute, expression, intimation, prediction, suggestion 11 countenance, description, foretelling 12 conformation 13 configuration
cast about 4 hunt, seek 5 quest 9 ferret out, search for, search out
cast a spell 3 hex
cast away 4 blow 5 beach, waste, wreck 6 pile up, strand 7 consume, fritter 8 squander 9 dissipate, shipwreck
castaway 5 leper 6 pariah 7 Ishmael, outcast 8 derelict 10 Ishmaelite 11 offscouring, untouchable
cast down 3 bad, low 4 down, sink 5 abase, lower 6 bemean, debase, demean, humble 7 degrade 8 dejected, downcast 9 depressed, humiliate, woebegone 10 dispirited 11 crestfallen 12 disconsolate

castigate 3 wig 4 beat, drub, flay, rail, rate 5 baste, slash 6 berate, pummel, punish, scathe, scorch, thrash 7 belabor, blister, chasten, correct, lambast, scarify, scourge, upbraid 8 chastise, lambaste, lash into, penalize 9 excoriate 10 discipline, tongue-lash

castigation 3 rod 8 punition 10 correction, discipline, punishment 12 chastisement

cast iron 7 spiegel

castle 5 manor, villa 7 chateau, mansion *adjunct:* 4 moat *gate:* 10 portcullis *ledge:* 7 rampart *structure:* 6 turret *tower:* 4 keep 6 donjon *wall:* 6 bailey 10 battlement

castle-builder 7 dreamer, utopian 8 idealist 9 ideologue, visionary

cast off 5 fling, let go, loose, untie 6 slough, unmoor 7 unhitch 8 unfasten

Castor *brother:* 6 Pollux 10 Polydeuces *constellation:* 6 Gemini *father:* 4 Zeus 9 Tyndareus *mother:* 4 Leda *sister:* 5 Helen *slayer:* 4 Idas

castor oil 9 cathartic, lubricant

cast out 4 oust 5 exile, expel 6 banish, deport 7 expulse 8 displace 9 ostracize, transport 10 expatriate

cast overboard 8 jettison

castrate 3 fix 4 geld 5 alter, unman, unsex 6 neuter 7 unnerve 8 enervate, mutilate, unstring 9 sterilize 10 emasculate 11 desexualize

castrato singer 9 Farinelli

casual 5 aloof, fluky, light, minor, petty 6 breezy, chance, degage, little, remote 7 offhand, relaxed, trivial, unfussy 8 detached, informal 9 easygoing, extempore, impromptu, impulsive, incurious, small-beer, uncurious, unplanned, withdrawn 10 accidental, contingent, fortuitous, improvised, incidental, shoestring 11 indifferent, low-pressure, spontaneous, unconcerned, unimportant 12 uninterested 13 disinterested, insignificant, unconstrained

casualty 4 prey 5 death, fatal 6 mishap, victim 8 accident, fatality, underdog 9 bottom dog, mischance 12 misadventure

casuistry 7 fallacy, sophism 8 delusion 9 deception, sophistry 12 equivocation, speciousness, spuriousness 13 deceptiveness

casus ____ 5 belli

cat 4 eyra, lion, lynx, puma, puss 5 felid, kitty, ounce, pussy 6 bobcat, cougar, feline, kaffir 7 caracal 12 mountain lion *catlike animal:* 5 civet, genet, zibet 6 zibeth 7 linsang *combining form:* 5 aelur, ailur 6 aeluro, ailuro *disease:* 9 distemper *domestic:* 3 Rex 4 Manx 5 tabby 6 calico 7 Burmese, Persian, Siamese 8 long-hair 9 Himalayan, shorthair 10 Abyssinian *extinct:* 10 saber-tooth *fastest:* 7 cheetah *female:* 5 queen 7 lioness, tigress 9 grimalkin *genus:* 5 Felis *grinning:* 8 Cheshire *group:* 7 clowder *male:* 3 tom *relating to:* 6 feline *ring-tailed:* 6 serval *Scottish:* 8 baudrons *sound:* 3 mew 4 hiss, meow, purr, roar 5 miaou, miaow, miaul 9 caterwaul *spotted:* 4 pard 6 jaguar, margay, ocelot, serval 7 cheetah, leopard, panther *striped:* 5 tiger *tailless:* 4 Manx *young:* 6 kitten

cataclysm 4 pour, woes 5 flood, spate 6 deluge 7 niagara, torrent, tragedy 8 calamity, cataract, disaster, flooding, overflow 10 inundation 11 catastrophe 12 misadventure

cataclysmic 5 fatal 7 fateful, ruinous 10 calamitous, disastrous 12 catastrophic

catacomb 5 crypt, vault 10 undercroft

catafalque 4 bier

catalog 4 book, list, roll 5 admit, count, enter, tally 6 enroll, number, roster 7 itemize, program 8 inscribe, register, roll call, schedule, syllabus 9 enumerate, introduce, inventory 10 prospectus *of books:* 11 bibliotheca *of goods:* 9 inventory *of saints:* 9 hagiology

catalyst 4 goad, spur 7 impetus, impulse 8 stimulus 9 incentive, stimulant 10 incitation, incitement, motivation

catamaran 4 boat, raft

catamount 4 lynx 6 cougar

cataract 5 chute, falls, flood, sault, spate, spout 6 deluge 7 cascade, niagara, torrent 8 flooding, overflow 9 cataclysm, waterfall 10 inundation

catastrophe 3 woe 7 tragedy 8 calamity, disaster 9 cataclysm 12 misadventure

catastrophic 5 fatal 7 fateful, ruinous 10 calamitous, disastrous 11 cataclysmic

Catawba 4 wine 5 river

catcall 3 boo 4 bird, hiss, hoot, pooh, razz 5 bazoo 8 pooh-pooh 9 raspberry 10 Bronx cheer

catch 3 bag, con, fix, get, hit, nab, net, see, wed 4 ding, dupe, espy, find, fool, grab, grip, gull, hoax, moor, nail, snag, sock, spot, take, trap 5 abash, benet, block, clasp, clout, grasp, hit on, marry, reach, seize, smite, snare, stick, stump, trick, whack 6 accept, anchor, arrest, baffle, clutch, collar, cut off, descry, detect, entrap, fasten, flurry, follow, put out, rattle, secure, snatch, strike, take in, tangle, turn up 7 capture, chicane, confuse, disturb, ensnare, espouse, fluster, grapple, hit upon, nonplus, perplex, prehend 8 confound, contract, entangle, flimflam, hoodwink, meet with, overhaul, overtake 9 apprehend, bamboozle, embarrass, encounter, intercept

10 comprehend, understand **12** come down with

catchall term **3** etc.

Catcher in the Rye *author:* **8** Salinger *character:* **9** Caulfield (Holden)

catcher's glove **4** mitt

catching **6** taking **10** contagious, infectious **12** communicable

catch on **3** see **4** hear **5** learn **6** tumble **7** find out, unearth **8** discover **9** ascertain, determine

catchphrase see **catchword**

Catch-22 author **6** Heller

catch up **4** hold **8** enthrall **9** fascinate, mesmerize, spellbind

catchword **5** maxim, motto **6** byword, phrase, slogan **9** battle cry, watchword **10** shibboleth

catchy **6** fitful, spotty, tricky **8** sporadic **9** appealing, desultory, irregular, spasmodic

catechist **7** teacher

catechize **3** ask **4** quiz **5** query **7** examine, inquire **8** question **11** interrogate

catechumen **7** convert, student

categorical **4** sure **6** direct **7** certain, decided, express **8** absolute, clean-cut, clear-cut, definite, explicit, positive, specific, ultimate **9** downright **10** definitive, forthright **11** unambiguous, unequivocal

categorize **3** peg **4** sort **5** class, group **6** assort **7** put down **8** classify, identify, nail down **10** pigeonhole

category **4** tier **5** class, genre, grade, group **6** league **8** grouping **10** pigeonhole

catenation **6** series **10** connection

catercorner **9** slantways, slantwise **10** cornerwise, diagonally **12** slantingways

caterpillar **5** larva **7** cutworm, webworm **8** armyworm, silkworm **10** casebearer *combining form:* **5** campa, eruci

cater to **4** baby **5** humor, spoil **6** cocker, coddle, cosset, cotton, pamper **7** gratify, indulge **11** mollycoddle

caterwaul **3** row **4** howl, meow, spat, tiff **5** miaou, miaow, miaul, scrap **6** bicker **7** brabble, fall out, quarrel, wrangle **8** squabble

catharsis **9** cleansing, purgation **10** lustration **11** expurgation **12** purification

cathartic **9** castor oil, purgative

Cathay **5** China

cathedral **5** duomo **6** church *passage:* **5** slype

catholic **6** cosmic, global **7** general, generic **8** eclectic **9** extensive, inclusive, planetary, universal, worldwide **10** ecumenical, large-scale **12** cosmopolitan **13** comprehensive

catholicity **10** liberality **12** universality

catholicon **6** elixir **7** cure-all, nostrum, panacea

catkin **5** ament

catlike **5** catty **6** feline **7** furtive **8** stealthy

catnap **6** siesta, snooze **10** forty winks

Cat on a Hot ___ **7** Tin Roof

cat's-paw **4** pawn, tool **6** puppet, stooge

cattail **4** rush

cattle **4** kine, neat, oxen **5** bovid **6** bovine *breed:* **5** Angus, Devon, Kerry **6** Durham, Jersey, Sussex **7** Brahman, Hariana, Red Poll, Sahiwal **8** Ayrshire, Charbray, Galloway, Guernsey, Hereford, Highland, Holstein, Limousin, Longhorn **9** Charolais, Red Polled, Shorthorn, Simmental **10** Brown Swiss, Charollais **11** Dutch Belted *call:* **4** sook **6** sookie *castrated:* **5** steer *catching rope:* **5** lasso **6** lariat *combining form:* **4** bovi *cry:* **3** low, moo *dehorn:* **4** poll *disease:* **4** loco **5** bloat **6** garget, nagana **7** anthrax, locoism, measles, murrain **8** blackleg, lumpy jaw, mastitis, staggers **10** rinderpest, Texas fever **11** brucellosis *extinct breed:* **9** Teeswater *family:* **7** Bovidae *feed:* **6** fodder **7** farrago *female:* **3** cow *foot:* **4** hoof *genus:* **3** Bos *goddess:* **6** Bubona *grazing land:* **5** range **7** pasture *group:* **4** herd **5** drove *herdsman:* **6** cowboy, drover, gaucho **7** vaquero **8** wrangler **10** cowpuncher *hornless:* **5** muley **6** mulley *hybrid:* **7** cattalo *identification:* **5** brand *Indian:* **4** dhan *jowl:* **6** dewlap *male:* **4** bull *pen:* **6** corral *round up:* **7** wrangle *stable:* **4** barn, byre *steal:* **6** rustle *unbranded:* **8** maverick *wild flight:* **8** stampede *young:* **4** calf *young, motherless:* **5** dogie

catty **4** evil, spry, yare **5** agile, brisk, zippy **6** active, bitchy, feline, lively, nimble, volant, wicked **7** catlike, furtive, hateful, vicious **8** spiteful, stealthy **9** malicious, rancorous, sprightly **10** despiteful, malevolent

Caucasian *capital:* **4** Baku **7** Tbilisi, Yerevan *republic:* **7** Armenia, Georgia **10** Azerbaijan

Caucasus *peak:* **6** Elbrus *people:* **5** Osset

caucho **3** ule **4** hule **6** rubber

caudal *appendage:* **4** tail *combining form:* **2** ur **3** uro

cause **4** call, case, goad, make, root, suit **5** breed, evoke, get up, hatch **6** action, author, draw on, effect, elicit, induce, motive, origin, reason, secure, source, spring, work up **7** creator, impulse, lawsuit, produce, provoke **8** engender, generate, muster up, occasion **9** generator, incentive, necessity **10** antecedent, bring about, inducement, obligation, originator, prime mover **11** determinant **13** consideration *combining form:* **4** etio **5** aetio, aitio

cause ___ **7** célèbre

caused by *suffix:* **2** ic **4** ical

causerie 3 rap 4 chat, chin, talk, yarn 5 prose

causing *combining form:* 7 facient, factive *suffix:* 3 fic 4 able, ible

caustic 4 keen, tart 5 acerb, acrid, acute, crisp, harsh, rough, salty, sharp, terse 6 biting, bitter, ironic, severe 7 acerbic, cutting, mordant, pungent, satiric 8 incisive, scathing, stinging, succinct 9 corrosive, sarcastic, stringent, trenchant 10 mordacious 12 archilochian *solution:* 3 lye

cauterize 4 burn, sear

caution 4 warn 6 caveat 7 warning 8 forewarn, monition, prudence 9 canniness, chariness, foresight 10 admonition, discretion, precaution, providence 11 commonition, forethought, forewarning 12 discreetness

cautionary 4 wary 6 surety 8 cautious, monitive, monitory, security 10 admonitory

cautious 4 cozy, safe, wary 5 alert, cagey, canny, chary 6 shrewd 7 careful, guarded, politic, prudent 8 discreet, gingerly, scheming, vigilant, watchful 9 judicious, provident 11 calculating, circumspect, considerate, foresighted 13 prethoughtful

cavalcade 6 parade, series 8 sequence 10 procession

cavalier 5 lofty, proud 6 knight 7 haughty 8 arrogant, horseman, insolent, superior 9 caballero 10 disdainful 11 overbearing 12 supercilious 13 high-and-mighty

cavalryman 6 lancer 7 dragoon, trooper *Algerian:* 5 spahi 6 spahee *horse:* 5 waler *Prussian:* 4 ulan 5 uhlan *Russian:* 7 cossack *Turkish:* 5 spahi 6 spahee *weapon:* 5 lance, saber 7 carbine

cave 3 bow, den 4 bend, drop, give, grot, lair 5 antre, break, defer, yield 6 fold up, grotto, hollow, submit 7 crumple, knuckle, succumb 8 collapse 9 break down 10 capitulate, subterrane 11 buckle under 12 knuckle under, subterranean *combining form:* 6 speleo *dweller:* 3 bat 4 bear, lion 6 hermit 9 Cro-Magnon 10 troglodite 11 Neanderthal *explorer:* 9 spelunker *formation:* 10 stalactite, stalagmite *France:* 7 Lascaux 10 Rouffignac 13 Gouffre Berger *Iceland:* 7 Singing *Indiana:* 9 Wyandotte *Iraq:* 8 Shanidar *Kentucky:* 7 Mammoth *New Zealand:* 7 Waitomo *rock:* 8 dolomite 9 limestone *South Africa:* 5 Cango *Spain:* 8 Altamira *study of:* 10 speleology

caveat 6 notice 7 caution, warning 8 monition 10 admonition 11 commonition, forewarning

caveat ___ 6 emptor

cave-dwelling *combining form:* 6 troglo

cavern 6 grotto 10 subterrane 12 subterranean *Capri:* 10 Blue Grotto *combining*

form: 4 antr 5 antro *Montana:* 13 Lewis and Clark *New Mexico:* 8 Carlsbad *Tennessee:* 10 Cumberland *Virginia:* 5 Luray

cavernous 4 vast 6 gaping, hollow 7 chasmal, yawning 10 commodious, sepulchral 11 reverberant

caviar 3 roe 4 eggs 6 relish *source:* 6 beluga 7 sterlet 8 sturgeon

cavil 4 carp, momi (plural) 7 chicane, quibble

caviler 5 momus 6 carper, critic, Zoilus 7 knocker 9 aristarch 10 criticizer 11 faultfinder, smellfungus

caviling 4 mean 5 fussy, petty, small 6 critic, pickly 7 carping, finicky 8 captious, contrary, critical, exacting, niggling 9 demanding 10 censorious, nitpicking 12 faultfinding, overcritical 13 hairsplitting, hypercritical

cavity 3 pit 4 bore, hole, void 6 boring, hollow 7 vacuity *body:* 5 antra (plural), sinus 6 antrum 8 follicle, hemocoei *combining form:* 3 cel 4 antr, caec, ceci, ceco, cele, celo, coel 5 antro, caeci, caeco, coele, coelo *in a glacier:* 6 moulin

cavort 4 romp 5 caper, cut up, frisk 6 frolic, gambol 7 carry on, rollick 9 horseplay 10 roughhouse 11 horse around

caw 4 yaup, yawp 6 squall, squark, squawk

cay 3 key 4 isle, reef

cayenne 6 pepper *genus:* 8 Capsicum

cayman see **caiman**

Cayuga chief 5 Logan

cease 3 erd 4 halt, quit, stop 5 close 6 desist, ending, finish, period 8 conclude, give over, intermit, knock off, leave off, surcease 9 cessation, terminate 10 conclusion, desistance 11 discontinue, termination

cease-fire 5 truce 9 armistice

ceaseless 7 endless, eternal 8 constant, immortal, unending 9 continual, perpetual, unceasing 10 continuous 11 amaranthine, everlasting, never-ending, unremitting 12 interminable 13 uninterrupted

Cecrops' daughter 5 Herse 8 Aglauros 9 Pandrosos

cecum *combining form:* 5 typhl 6 typhlo

cede 4 deed 5 alien, grant, leave, waive, yield 6 accord, assign, convey, give up, remise, resign 7 abandon, concede 8 alienate, hand over, make over, sign over, transfer 9 surrender, vouchsafe 10 abalienate, relinquish

ceiling *elaborate:* 7 plafond

ceinture 4 belt, sash 6 girdle 8 cincture 9 waistband

Celaeno *father:* 5 Atlas *mother:* 7 Pleione *sisters:* 8 Pleiades

celebrate 4 fete, hymn, keep, laud 5 bless, cry up, extol 6 praise 7 glorify,

maffick, magnify, observe **8** eulogize **9** solemnize **10** panegyrize **11** commemorate
celebrated 5 famed, great, noted **6** famous **7** eminent, notable **8** renowned **9** prominent **11** illustrious **13** distinguished
celebration 4 fete, gala **6** fiesta **7** jubilee **8** festival, jamboree
célèbre 5 cause
celebrity 3 VIP **4** fame, hero, lion, name, star **5** éclat **6** renown, repute, worthy **7** big name, mahatma, notable **8** cynosure, immortal, luminary, somebody **9** notoriety, personage, superstar **10** notability, reputation
celerity 4 gait, pace **5** haste, hurry, speed **6** hustle, rustle **8** alacrity, dispatch, legerity, rapidity, velocity **9** briskness, quickness, swiftness **10** expedition, speediness
celery *genus:* **5** Apium *green:* **6** pascal *relative:* **6** carrot **7** parsley, parsnip *white:* **8** blanched *wild:* **8** smallage
celestial 7 blessed, elysian **8** beatific, empyreal, empyrean, ethereal, heavenly, Olympian, supernal **9** unearthly **12** otherworldly, transmundane
celestial body 3 sun **4** moon, star **5** comet **6** meteor, nebula, planet **8** asteroid **9** satellite *hypothetical:* **9** black hole
Celestial Empire 5 China
cell 4 room, zoid **5** cubby, zooid **7** cubicle **11** compartment *blood:* **8** hemocyte *combining form:* **3** cyt **4** cyte, cyto, phag **5** blast, gamet, phage **6** gameto, gonidi **7** gonidio *disease:* **6** cancer *division:* **7** meiosis, mitosis *fertilized egg:* **6** zygote *material:* **3** DNA, RNA **7** protein **9** chromatin, cytoplasm **10** protoplasm *nerve:* **6** neuron *part:* **4** gene **7** nucleus, vacuole **8** ribosome **10** chromosome *reproductive:* **3** egg **4** germ, ovum **5** sperm **6** gamete **8** gonidium
cellist *American:* **4** Rose **6** Lesser, Parnas **7** Nelsova, Parisot, Starker **8** Schuster *English:* **5** du Pré *Russian:* **11** Piatigorsky **12** Rostropovich *Spanish:* **6** Casals
cellophane 4 wrap **7** wrapper **8** wrapping **9** packaging
celluloid 4 film **7** plastic
cement 4 bind, join **5** unify, unite **6** mortar **8** concrete *combining form:* **4** lith *ingredient:* **4** lime **6** silica **7** alumina **8** magnesia, pozzolan **9** iron oxide, pozzolana
cemetery 8 boneyard, boot hill, catacomb **8** God's acre **9** graveyard **10** churchyard, necropolis **11** polyandrium **12** burial ground, memorial park, potter's field *underground:* **8** catacomb
cense 7 thurify
censer 8 thurible *carrier:* **8** thurifer

censor 4 blip, edit **5** purge **6** cut out, delete, excise, narrow, purify, screen **7** clean up, exscind **8** restrain, restrict **9** expurgate, red-pencil **10** blue-pencil, bowdlerize
censorious 6 critic **7** carping, chiding **8** captious, caviling, critical **9** cavillous, culpatory **10** accusatory, condemning, denouncing **11** reproachful **12** condemnatory, denunciatory, faultfinding, overcritical, reprehending **13** hypercritical
censurable 5 amiss, wrong **6** guilty, sinful, unholy **8** blamable, blameful, culpable, doubtful, improper, wrongful **9** incorrect **11** blameworthy **12** inadmissible, questionable, unacceptable **13** demeritorious, discreditable, objectionable, reprehensible
censure 3 rap **4** skin **5** blame, knock, scorn, scout **6** oppose, rebuke, reject, strafe **7** condemn, contemn, disdain, reprove **8** denounce, disallow, reproach **9** criticize, reprehend, reprimand, reprobate **10** denunciate, disapprove, stigmatize
centaur 6 Chiron, Nessus
Centaurus star 4 Beta **5** Alpha
Centennial State 8 Colorado
center 3 hub, mid **4** core, mean, pith, root, seat **5** focus, heart, midst, quick **6** dynamo, inside, medial, median, middle **7** central, essence, halfway, midmost **8** interior, midpoint, omphalos, polestar **9** activator, energizer, stimulant **10** focal point, middlemost **11** equidistant **12** intermediary, intermediate
centerboard 4 keel
centerfold 7 foldout **8** gatefold
centipede 9 arthropod *class:* **9** Chilopoda
central 3 key, mid **4** main, mean **5** basic, chief, focal **6** master, medial, median, middle, ruling, signal **7** leading, pivotal, primary, radical, salient **8** cardinal, dominant, foremost **9** essential, important, paramount **10** overriding, overruling **11** controlling, fundamental, outstanding, predominant, significant **12** all-absorbing, intermediary, intermediate, preponderant
Central African Republic *capital:* **6** Bangui *monetary unit:* **5** franc
Central America *country:* **6** Panama **8** Honduras **9** Costa Rica, Guatemala, Nicaragua **10** El Salvador *ethnic group:* **6** Indian **7** Mestizo, Spanish *language:* **7** Nahuatl, Spanish
centripetal 8 unifying **10** compacting **11** integrative **12** centralizing **13** concentrating, consolidating
centurion 7 officer, soldier **9** commander
century plant *genus:* **5** Agave
cephalalgia 8 headache
cephalopod 5 squid **7** mollusk, octopus **10** cuttlefish

Cepheus *daughter:* 9 Andromeda *kingdom:* 8 Ethiopia *wife:* 10 Cassiopeia

cerate 4 balm 5 cream, salve 6 chrism 7 unction, unguent 8 ointment

cerberus 6 custos, keeper, warden 8 claviger, guardian, watchdog 9 custodian

Cerberus *father:* 6 Typhon *form:* 3 dog *mother:* 7 Echidna

cereal 4 meal, mush 5 gruel 6 farina 7 oatmeal 8 cornmeal, porridge *grass:* 3 rye 4 corn, oats, ragi, rice 5 emmer, maize, spelt, wheat 6 barley, millet 7 sorghum 9 buckwheat *North African:* 8 couscous *Russian:* 5 kasha

cerebral 6 mental 7 psychic 8 highbrow 9 psychical 10 highbrowed 12 intellective, intellectual 13 psychological *combining form:* 5 psych 6 psycho

cerebrate 5 think 6 reason 7 reflect 8 cogitate 9 speculate 10 deliberate

cerebration 7 thought 9 brainwork 10 cogitation, reflection 11 speculation 12 deliberation

ceremonial 3 set 5 fixed, lofty, rigid, stiff 6 august, formal, ritual, solemn 7 courtly, starchy, stately, studied 8 mannered, stylized 10 liturgical 11 ritualistic

ceremonious 6 formal, moving, proper, seemly, solemn 7 stately 8 decorous, imposing, majestic, striking 9 grandiose 10 impressive 12 conventional

ceremony 4 form, rite 6 ritual 7 liturgy, service 9 formality 10 observance *Jewish:* 8 habdalah, havdalah 10 bar mitzvah, bas mitzvah 11 bath mitzvah *university:* 8 encaenia

Ceres 7 Demeter *daughter:* 10 Persephone, Proserpina, Proserpine *father:* 6 Cronus, Saturn *mother:* 3 Ops 4 Rhea

cerium *symbol:* 2 Ce

certain 3 one, set 4 firm, many, some, sure, true 5 fated, fixed 6 divers, stated, sundry 7 assured, ensured, insured, settled, several, various 8 accurate, cocksure, credible, definite, numerous, positive, provable, reliable, sanguine, surefire, unerring 9 authentic, certified, confident, doubtless, necessary, plausible, unfailing, warranted 10 dependable, guaranteed, inarguable, ineludible, inevasible, inevitable, infallible, returnless, stipulated, undeniable, unevadable, verifiable 11 confirmable, indubitable, ineluctable, inescapable, irrevocable, trustworthy, unalterable, unavoidable, undoubtable, unescapable 12 demonstrable, indefeasible, indisputable, well-grounded 13 establishable, incontestable, predestinated, predetermined, uncontestable

certainty 6 surety 8 firmness, sureness 9 assurance, certitude, dogmatism 10 confidence, conviction, positivism, steadiness 11 assuredness, staunchness 12 absoluteness, definiteness, positiveness

certificate 3 IOU 4 bond, note 6 coupon, notice, ticket 7 diploma, license, receipt, voucher 8 contract, document 9 testimony 10 credential

certifier 6 notary

certify 2 OK 4 aver, avow, okay 5 vouch 6 assert, attest, avouch 7 approve, endorse, license, profess, warrant, witness 8 accredit, guaranty, notarize, sanction 9 authorize, guarantee 10 commission

Cervantes' hero 10 Don Quixote

cesium *symbol:* 2 Cs

cessation 3 end 4 stop 5 cease, close 6 ending, finish, period 10 conclusion, desistance 11 termination

cesspool 3 den, sty 4 sink 5 Sodom 11 pandemonium 12 Augean stable

Cetus star 4 Mira

cgs unit 3 erg 4 dyne, gram, phot 5 gauss, poise, stilb 6 second, stokes 7 lambert, maxwell, oersted 10 centimeter

Chablis 4 wine 8 Burgundy

Chad *capital:* 8 N'Djamena *monetary unit:* 5 franc

chafe 3 irk, rub, vex 4 flay, fret, gall, hurt, peel, skin, wear 5 annoy, erode, graze 6 abrade, bother, damage, impair, injure, ruffle, scrape 7 corrode, inflame, provoke, scratch 8 exercise, irritate 9 excoriate

chaff 3 fun, kid, rag, rib 4 jest, joke, josh, razz 5 jolly 6 banter

chaffer 3 beg 4 coax 5 plead 6 dicker, haggle, higgle, palter 7 bargain 8 huckster

chafing 7 fretful 9 impatient, unpatient

chagrined 5 upset 6 shamed 7 ashamed, crushed 8 mortified, perturbed 11 discomposed 12 disconcerted

chain 3 row 4 bond, gyve, iron 5 group, train, trust 6 cartel, catena, fetter, hobble, series, string, tether 7 combine, manacle, shackle 8 additive, additory, handcuff, sequence 9 summative, syndicate 10 cumulative, succession 11 alternation, concatenate, consecution, progression, stereotyped 12 accumulative, conglomerate 13 concatenation, stereotypical *adjunct:* 8 sprocket *collar:* 6 torque *combining form:* 6 strept 7 strepto *gang:* 6 coffle *ornamental:* 10 chatelaine *ship's:* 3 tye *sound:* 5 clank

chain ___ 3 saw 4 gang, mail 5 smoke, store 6 letter 8 reaction

Chained Lady 9 Andromeda

chainlike 8 catenate

chain-shaped 10 catenulate

chair 4 seat 5 stool 6 rocker 7 preside *back:* 5 splat *bishop's:* 8 cathedra *portable:* 5 sedan *reclining:* 12 chaise longue, chaise lounge *royal:* 6 throne *type:* 4 club,

easy **6** morris **7** rocking **8** captain's, cog-
swell **9** reclining **10** ladder-back

chalcedony **4** onyx, sard **5** agate **6** jasper, quartz **9** carnelian **10** bloodstone
11 chrysoprase

chalice **3** ama, cup **5** amula, grail

chalk *combining form:* **4** calc **5** calci,
calco **8** calcareo

chalk out **5** draft **6** sketch **7** outline
8 block out, rough out, skeleton **9** adumbrate **11** skeletonize **12** characterize

chalk up **3** get, win **4** gain, have **5** annex
6 obtain, pick up, secure **7** acquire, procure

challenge **3** try **4** call, dare, defi, defy,
face, stir, wake, whet **5** beard, brave, claim,
demur, doubt, exact, front, rally, rouse,
stump, waken **6** arouse, awaken, banter,
bestir, cartel, demand, kindle, strive **7** calling, dispute, outdare, protest, require,
solicit, venture **8** claiming, defiance, demurral, demurrer, exacting, mistrust, question,
struggle **9** demanding, objection, postulate
10 difficulty, insistence **11** importuning, requisition **12** remonstrance **13** remonstration

challenger **5** rival **8** opponent **9** adversary, contender **10** competitor, contestant

chamber **4** cell, room **5** haven, house
6 harbor, shield **7** cubicle, shelter **9** apartment *combining form:* **6** thalam **7** thalamo
in Egyptian tomb: **6** serdab *underground:*
8 hypogeum

chambered **10** cancellate, cancellous

chamberlain **6** priest **7** officer, servant
9 attendant, treasurer

chameleon **6** lizard

chameleonic **6** fickle **10** changeable,
inconstant

chamois **4** gems **5** gemse **6** shammy
7 leather **8** antelope, ruminant *habitat:*
4 Alps *Old Testament:* **6** aoudad

chamois-like animal **4** ibex **5** goral
6 gooral **7** klipbok **12** klipspringer

champ **3** gum, nip **4** bite, chew, mash,
peck, pick **5** chomp, crush, mouth, munch
6 crunch, mumble, nibble **7** chumble,
scrunch **8** macerate, ruminate **9** masticate

champagne **4** wine **5** color **6** bubbly
bucket: **4** icer *center:* **5** Reims

Champagne *capital:* **6** Troyes

champaign **5** field **6** domain, sphere
7 demesne, terrain **8** dominion, province
9 bailiwick, territory

champignon **6** fungus **8** mushroom

champion **4** arch, back, boss, head
5 chief, dandy, first, prime **6** uphold **7** capital, contend, leading, premier, support, titl-
ist **8** advocate, backstop, exponent, fight
for, foremost, side with, splendid, superior,
top-notch, whiz-bang **9** excellent,
expounder, principal, proponent, supporter
10 blue-ribbon **11** illustrious, outstanding,

titleholder **13** distinguished *medieval:*
7 paladin

championing *prefix:* **3** pro

championship **5** crown, title **7** defense,
pennant **8** advocacy

chance **2** go **3** hap, hit, lot, odd **4** bump,
fate, luck, meet, risk, shot, show, time
5 break, fluke, fluky, light, occur, wager
6 befall, betide, casual, gamble, happen,
hazard **7** come off, fall out, fortune, offhand,
opening, outlook, stumble, venture **8** accident, careless, fortuity, heedless, occasion,
prospect **9** advantage, adventure, transpire **10** accidental, fortuitous, incidental,
likelihood **11** opportunity, possibility, probability *even:* **6** toss-up

chancellor **5** judge **6** priest **7** adviser,
officer **8** minister **9** secretary *German:*
6 Brandt, Erhard, Hitler **7** Schmidt **8** Aden-
auer, Bismarck

chancy **4** iffy **5** dicey, fluky, hairy, risky
6 touchy, tricky **7** erratic, unsound **8** perilous, ticklish **9** dangerous, fluctuant, hazardous, uncertain, whimsical **10** capricious,
jeopardous, precarious **11** speculative,
treacherous **12** incalculable
13 unpredictable

change **3** fix **4** geld, swap, turn, vary
5 alter, shift, sport, trade, unsex **6** avatar,
invert, modify, mutate, neuter, reform,
revamp, revert, revise, switch **7** commute,
convert, inverse, novelty, replace, reverse
8 castrate, exchange, mutation, mutilate,
revision, transfer **9** deviation, diversify, per-
mutate, refashion, sterilize, transform, transmute, transpose, variation, variegate
10 aberration, alteration, conversion, divergence, innovation, substitute, transplace
11 desexualize, interchange, permutation,
transfigure, vicissitude **12** metamorphose,
modification, transmogrify **13** metamorphosis, transmutation *sudden:* **8** peripety
10 peripeteia

changeable **5** fluid **6** fickle, labile, mobile,
pliant, shifty **7** movable, mutable, plastic,
protean, unfixed **8** moveable, restless, slippery, ticklish, unstable, unsteady, variable,
volatile, weathery **9** adaptable, mercurial,
uncertain, unsettled **10** capricious, inconstant, lubricious **13** kaleidoscopic,
temperamental

change decor **4** redo

changeless **5** fixed **6** steady **7** regular,
uniform **8** constant, resolute **9** steadfast
10 invariable

change off **9** alternate

change of heart **8** reversal

change of life **9** menopause
11 climacteric

change of pace **5** pitch, shift

changeover 5 shift 10 alteration, conversion

channel 3 way 4 duct, mean, pass, pipe 5 agent, canal, carry, organ 6 agency, convey, course, funnel, groove, medium, siphon, strait 7 conduct, conduit, passage, vehicle 8 aqueduct, ministry, pipeline, transmit 10 instrument 11 watercourse *Africa-Madagascar:* 10 Mozambique *Atlantic-Nantucket Sound:* 8 Muskeget *Atlantic-North Sea:* 7 English *California:* 12 Santa Barbara *Caribbean-Gulf of Mexico:* 6 Yucatń *combining form:* 3 vas 4 vasi, vaso 5 solen 6 soleno *Ellesmere-Greenland:* 7 Robeson 10 Smith Sound *Ganges:* 5 Hugli 7 Hooghly *Hawaii:* 5 Kaiwi, Kauai *Japan:* 5 Bungo *Long Island:* 13 Rockaway Inlet *Mediterranean:* 5 Malta *Northwest Territories:* 9 M'Clintock *Pakistan:* 4 Nara *Scotland:* 5 Minch *Tierra del Fuego:* 6 Beagle *Tigris-Euphrates:* 11 Shatt-al-Arab *Virginia:* 12 Hampton Roads *West Indies:* 9 Old Bahama 10 Saint Lucia

channel bass 4 drum 7 redfish

"Chanson ___" 6 Triste

chanson de 5 geste

chant 4 sing, tune 8 vocalize 10 cantillate *Gregorian:* 9 plainsong 12 cantus firmus *Jewish:* 6 Hallel

chanteuse 6 singer 10 cantatrice

chanticleer 4 cock 7 rooster

chaos 4 void 5 snarl 6 ataxia, huddle, muddle 7 anarchy, clutter, misrule 8 disarray, disorder 9 confusion, mobocracy 10 ochlocracy, unruliness 11 lawlessness

Chaos *daughter:* 3 Nox, Nyx 4 Gaea *son:* 6 Erebus

chap 3 guy, man 4 gent 6 fellow 9 gentleman *British:* 5 bloke

chaparral 7 thicket

chaparral bird 10 roadrunner

chaperon 4 boss 5 guide 6 attend, convoy, escort, survey 7 conduct, oversee 9 accompany, companion, supervise 11 consort with, quarterback, superintend

chapfallen see **crestfallen**

chaplain 5 padre 8 sky pilot

chaplet 5 crown 6 anadem, rosary, wreath 7 coronal, coronet, garland

char 4 burn 9 carbonize

character 3 ilk, rep, VIP 4 case, fame, kind, mark, mind, name, quiz, rank, role, sign, sort, soul, type 5 chief, humor, nabob, place, point, savor, state, trait 6 bigwig, cipher, device, kidney, letter, makeup, mettle, nature, oddity, report, repute, spirit, status, stripe, symbol, temper, virtue, zombie 7 big shot, courage, feature, footing, notable, oddball, persona, quality, station, variety 8 big-timer, capacity, eminence, identity, monogram, original, position, property, standing, uniquity 9 affection, attribute, birthmark, dignitary, eccentric, intellect, reference, situation 10 complexion, notability, reputation, resolution, uniqueness 11 credentials, description, disposition, distinction, personality, temperament, testimonial 13 individualism, individuality *chief:* 4 hero 11 protagonist *defect:* 8 hamartia *suffix:* 3 ery

character assassination 7 calumny, scandal, slander 10 backbiting, defamation, detraction 12 backstabbing, belittlement, depreciation 13 disparagement

characteristic 4 mark, odor, sign, tang 5 badge, point, savor, smack, token, trait 6 flavor, normal, proper, virtue 7 feature, natural, quality, regular, special, typical 8 especial, peculiar, property, specific 9 affection, attribute, birthmark, character, diacritic 10 diagnostic, individual, particular 11 differentia, distinctive, singularity 13 idiosyncratic

characteristic of *suffix:* 2 ic, ly 3 ish, ist 4 ical 5 istic 7 istical

characterize 4 mark 5 draft 6 define, sketch 7 outline, qualify 8 block out, chalk out, describe, identify, rough out, skeleton 9 adumbrate, signalize 11 distinguish, individuate, peculiarize, personalize, singularize, skeletonize 13 differentiate, individualize

characterized by *suffix:* 2 al, ic 3 ful, ial, ous 4 ical

characterless 4 weak 5 sissy 6 futile 7 unmanly 8 childish, impotent 9 infantile, powerless, sissified 10 namby-pamby, panty-waist, wishy-washy

charade 7 pageant 8 disguise, pretense 10 pretension 11 make-believe

chare 3 job 4 duty, task 5 chore, stint 6 devoir 10 assignment

charge 3 ask, bid, fee, lay, tab, tax 4 bill, boil, bolt, care, clog, cost, dash, duty, fill, heap, lade, lash, load, must, need, onus, pack, pile, race, rate, rush, task, tear, tell, toll, warn, word 5 chase, choke, fling, order, ought, place, price, refer, right, shoot, trust, weigh 6 accuse, adjure, assign, behest, burden, credit, cumber, devoir, direct, enjoin, impugn, impute, indict, saddle, tariff, weight 7 arraign, ascribe, bidding, command, conduct, dictate, entrust, expense, impeach, mandate, pervade, request, running, solicit 8 accredit, business, encumber, handling, instruct, permeate, price tag, reproach, saturate 9 attribute, committal, criminate, inculpate, millstone, oversight, penetrate, percolate, reprehend, transfuse 10 commitment, deadweight, impregnate, injunction, intendance, management, obligation 11 impenetrate, incriminate, supervision

chargeable 6 liable 11 responsible
chargeless 4 free 6 gratis 8 costless
10 gratuitous 13 complimentary
charger 5 horse, mount, steed 7 courser
8 war-horse
chariness 7 caution 8 prudence
chariot 5 essed 6 esseda, essede *four-horse:* 8 quadriga *two-horse:* 4 biga
charioteer 5 drive, pilot 6 Auriga, driver
charisma 5 charm 6 allure, appeal,
duende, glamor 7 glamour 8 witchery
9 magnetism 10 witchcraft 11 fascination
charitable 4 easy, good 6 benign,
humane, kindly 7 clement, helpful, lenient
8 merciful, obliging, tolerant 9 indulgent
10 altruistic, benevolent, forbearing,
thoughtful 11 considerate, kindhearted,
sympathetic 12 eleemosynary, humanitarian 13 accommodating, philanthropic
charity 4 alms, love 5 amity, grace,
mercy 6 lenity 7 caritas 8 altruism, clemency, donation, goodwill, offering 9 affection 10 attachment, humaneness, kindliness 11 benefaction, beneficence,
benevolence 12 contribution, friendliness
charivari 5 babel 6 medley 8 serenade,
shivaree 10 hodgepodge 11 celebration
charlatan 4 sham 5 bluff, quack 8 imposter 9 quackster 10 mountebank 11 fourflusher, quacksalver 12 saltimbanque
Charlemagne *brother:* 8 Carloman
father: 5 Pepin *knight:* 4 Ivon, Oton
5 Gerin, Ivory 6 Anseis, Gerard, Gerier, Oliver, Roland, Samson 7 Olivier, paladin
8 douzeper, Engelier 9 Berengier *nephew:*
6 Roland 7 Orlando *sword:* 7 Joyeuse *traitor:* 4 Gano 7 Ganelon
Charles's Wain 9 Big Dipper
charleston 5 dance
Charley's Aunt author 6 Thomas
Charlie Brown creator 6 Schulz
Charlie McCarthy 5 dummy 6 stooge
friend: 5 Snerd *voice:* 6 Bergen
charm 3 hex 4 draw, juju, luck, lure, rune,
take, wile, zemi 5 spell, witch 6 allure, amulet, appeal, enamor, fetish, glamor, mascot,
voodoo 7 attract, bewitch, enchant
8 enthrall, talisman, witchery 9 captivate,
ensorcell, fascinate, magnetism, magnetize
10 allurement, attraction, phylactery, witchcraft 11 conjuration, fascination, incantation 12 gratefulness 13 agreeableness
charmed 8 enamored 9 bewitched,
enchanted, entranced 10 captivated,
fascinated
charmer 4 mage 5 magus 6 magian, wizard 7 warlock 8 conjurer, magician, sorcerer 9 enchanter 11 necromancer
charming 5 siren 7 drawing, winsome
8 adorable, alluring, magnetic 9 glamorous,

seductive 10 attracting, attractive, enchanting 11 captivating
Charon 7 boatman 8 ferryman *father:*
6 Erebus *mother:* 3 Nox *river:* 4 Styx
Charpentier opera 6 Louise
charpoy 3 bed, cot
chart 3 map 4 cast, plan, plat, plot
5 graph, table 6 design, devise, scheme
7 arrange, dope out, project 9 blueprint
10 tabulation
charter 3 let 4 deed, hire, rent 5 lease
10 conveyance
Chartreuse 7 liqueur
chary 4 safe, wary 5 canny, loath 6 frugal,
saving 7 careful, guarded, sparing, thrifty
8 cautious, discreet, gingerly, hesitant
9 inhibited, provident, reluctant, stewardly
10 economical, restrained, unwasteful
11 calculating, circumspect, considerate,
constrained, disinclined
Charybdis 9 whirlpool *rock associated
with:* 6 Scylla
chase 3 out, run 4 boil, bolt, dash, game,
hunt, lash, prey, race, rush, tear 5 chivy,
chuck, eject, evict, fling, shoot, speed, trail
6 career, charge, course, follow, pursue,
quarry, venery 7 boot out, dismiss, extrude,
hunting, kick out, pursuit 8 throw out
chase away 4 shoo
chaser 4 wolf 6 masher 7 Don Juan
8 Casanova 9 ladies' man, philander, womanizer 10 lady-killer 11 philanderer
chasm 3 gap 4 gulf, skip 5 abysm, abyss,
blank, cleft, clove, gorge, gulch, split
6 arroyo, clough, ravine, schism 8 cleavage,
omission, overlook 9 oversight 11 preterition 13 pretermission
chasmal 7 yawning 9 cavernous
chassepot 5 rifle
chaste 4 pure 5 clean, moral 6 decent,
modest, proper, seemly, vestal, virgin 7 ethical 8 becoming, decorous, maidenly, spotless, virginal, virtuous 9 abstinent, continent, righteous, stainless, undefiled,
unsullied 10 immaculate 11 unblemished
chasten 3 try 5 abase 6 humble, punish
7 afflict, correct 8 chastise 9 castigate,
humiliate 10 discipline
chastise 4 beat 5 baste 6 pummel, punish, thrash 7 belabor, chasten, correct
9 castigate 10 discipline
chastisement 3 rod 8 punition 10 correction, discipline, punishment
11 castigation
chat 3 gab, jaw, rap, yak, yap 4 blab, chin,
gush, talk, yarn 5 clack, prate, prose, run
on, visit 6 babble, burble, cackle, confab,
dither, gabble, gossip, jabber, parley, patter,
rattle, yak-yak, yammer, yatter 7 chatter,
clatter, palaver, prattle, smatter, twaddle,
twitter 8 causerie, chin-chin, colloque, collo-

quy, converse, dialogue, lallygag **9** tête-à-tête, yakety-yak **11** confabulate **12** bibble-babble, conversation, tittle-tattle **13** confabulation

chateau 5 manor, villa **6** castle **7** mansion

chateaubriand 5 steak **10** tenderloin

Chateaubriand novel 4 René **5** Atala **10** Les Natchez

chatelain 6 warden **8** governor **9** castellan

chatelaine 4 hook, wife **5** clasp **8** mistress

chattel 5 slave **7** bondman **8** bondsman **9** bondslave, mancipium

chatter 3 gab, jaw, yak **4** blab, bull, chat **5** clack, prate **6** babble, burble, cackle, gabble, gibber, gossip, jabber, natter, patter, yak-yak, yammer, yatter **7** blabber, blather, blatter, blither, brabble, palaver, prattle **8** chin-chin, chitchat **9** small talk, yakety-yak **12** bibble-babble, gibble-gabble, talkee-talkee, tittle tattle

chatterbox 5 tabby **6** chewet, gabber, gossip, magpie, prater **7** blabber **8** busybody, jabberer, prattler, quidnunc **9** bandar-log, blabmouth, chatterer **10** newsmonger, tattletale **13** scandalmonger

chatty 5 gabby, talky, wordy **9** garrulous, talkative **10** babblative, loquacious **11** loose-lipped **12** loose-tongued, multiloquent **13** multiloquious

chauffeur 5 drive **6** driver **9** transport

chauvinism 8 jingoism **10** partiality, patriotism **11** nationalism

cheap 3 bad, low **4** base, fake, mean, poor, sham, vile **5** petty, phony, sorry, tatty, wrong **6** cheesy, common, flashy, garish, measly, paltry, rotten, scurvy, shabby, shoddy, sleazy, tawdry, trashy, undear **7** chintzy, cut-rate, low-cost, pitiful, popular, reduced **8** beggarly, inferior, pitiable, rubbishy, terrible, trifling, trumpery, uncostly **9** brummagem, low-priced, rubbishly, valueless, worthless **10** despicable, despisable, reasonable, rubbishing **11** inexpensive **12** contemptible, meretricious

cheapen 5 decry, lower **7** devalue **8** mark down, write off **9** devaluate, downgrade, write down **10** depreciate, undervalue

cheap-jack 6 hawker, monger, vendor **7** higgler, packman, peddler **8** huckster, inferior, outcrier **9** worthless

cheapskate 4 skin **5** chuff, miser, stiff **7** niggard **8** muckworm, tightwad **9** skinflint **11** cheeseparer

cheat 3 con, gyp **4** beat, bilk, burn, dupe, fool, gull, hoax, ream, sell, take **5** bunco, cozen, crook, fraud, fudge, hocus, put-on, screw, short, slick **6** befool, boodle, chisel, chouse, con man, deceit, delude, diddle,

extort, fleece, humbug, sucker **7** beguile, chicane, deceive, defraud, diddler, hoaxing, mislead, sharper, swindle **8** cozening, flimflam, swindler, trickery **9** chicanery, deception, defrauder, fourberie, imposture, overreach, trickster **10** dishonesty, hankypanky **11** double-cross, highbinding **12** double-dealer **13** bamboozlement, confidence man, double-dealing *on a check:* **4** kite

check 2 go **3** bit, tab, try **4** balk, bill, curb, foil, halt, jibe, rein, stay, stem, stop, test, tick **5** agree, cease, prove, score, stall, tally **6** accord, arrest, baffle, bridle, damage, desist, hold in, square, thwart **7** backset, conform, examine, inhibit, obviate, prevent, repress, reverse, setback **8** dovetail, hold back, hold down, preclude, restrain, reversal, suppress, withhold **9** constrain, frustrate, interrupt **10** circumvent, correspond **11** discontinue

checklist 7 catalog **9** catalogue, inventory

checkmate 6 arrest, corner, defeat, thwart **7** counter

check over 3 con, vet **4** view **5** study **6** survey **7** canvass, check up, examine, inspect **10** scrutinize

checkup 7 medical **8** physical **10** inspection **11** examination

cheek 4 face, gall **5** brass, crust, nerve **9** brashness **10** confidence, effrontery **11** presumption *combining form:* **3** mel **4** melo **5** bucco

cheekbone 5 malar

cheeky 4 bold, pert, wise **5** fresh, nervy, sassy, smart **7** forward **8** impudent **11** smart-alecky

cheep 4 chip, peep **5** chirp, tweet **7** chipper, chirrup, chitter, tweedle, twitter

cheer 3 rah **4** root **5** bravo, huzza, nerve, steel **6** buck up, hoorah, hooray, hurrah, hurray, huzzah, solace **7** animate, applaud, comfort, console, hearten, upraise **8** embolden, inspirit **9** encourage, enhearten **10** strengthen *corrida:* **3** olé

cheerful 3 gay **4** airy, glad, rosy **5** chirk, corky, jolly, merry, riant, sunny **6** blithe, bright, chirpy, jaunty, jocund, lively **7** beamish, buoyant, radiant **8** animated, carefree, chirrupy, debonair, sunbeamy **9** lightsome, vivacious **12** lighthearted *Scottish:* **5** cadgy

cheerio 2 by **5** adieu **6** bye-bye, so long **7** good-bye **8** farewell, toodle-oo

cheerless 4 drab **5** bleak **6** dismal, dreary, gloomy, somber **8** funereal **9** dejecting **10** depressing, oppressive, tenebrific **11** dispiriting

cheese 3 pot **4** blue, jack **5** brick, cream, store **6** farmer **7** cottage, process **9** pineapple, smearcase *American:* **8** Longhorn

11 Liederkranz **12** Monterey Jack *Belgian:* **9** Limburger **brown:** **6** mysost **7** gjetost *Canadian:* **3** Oka **combining form:** **3** tyr **4** case, tyro **5** caseo **curdling agent:** **6** rennet, rennin *Danish:* **4** Tybo **5** Esrom **6** Samsoe **7** Havarti *dish:* **6** fondue **7** rarebit, soufflé *Dutch:* **4** Edam **5** Gouda **6** Leyden *English:* **7** cheddar, Stilton **8** Cheshire **10** Lancashire *French:* **4** Brie **7** fromage, Livarot **9** Camembert, reblochon, Roquefort **10** Neufchâtel **11** Pont l'Évêque, Port du Salut *German:* **4** kase **6** Tilsit **7** Muenster, Tilsiter *Greek:* **4** feta **7** kasseri *green:* **7** sapsago *Italian:* **6** Romano **7** fontina, ricotta **8** Bel Paese, Parmesan, pecorino **9** provolone **10** Gorgonzola, mozzarella **12** caciocavallo *lover:* **9** turophile **main ingredient:** **6** casein *Norwegian:* **6** mysost **7** gjetost, primost **9** gammelost, Jarlsberg, taffelost **10** Noekkelost *Oriental:* **4** tofu *protein:* **6** casein *Scottish:* **6** Dunlop, Orkney **7** kebbock, kebbuck *Swedish:* **8** graddost *Swiss:* **6** Saanen **7** Gruyère, sapsago **8** Vacherin **10** Emmentaler **11** Emmenthaler *uncured:* **7** cottage *Welsh:* **10** Caerphilly *whey:* **5** ziger **6** zieger
cheesecloth **5** gauze
cheeselike **6** caseic **7** caseous
cheeseparer **4** skin **5** chuff, miser, stiff **7** niggard **8** muckworm, tightwad **9** skinflint **10** cheapskate
cheeseparing **4** mean **5** cheap, close, tight **6** shabby, stingy **7** miserly **8** grudging **9** illiberal, niggardly, penurious **11** closefisted, tightfisted **12** parsimonious **13** penny-pinching
cheesy **4** mean, poor **5** cheap, tatty **6** common, shoddy, sleazy, trashy **7** caseous **8** rubbishy
chef d'oeuvre **7** classic **9** showpiece **10** magnum opus, masterwork **11** masterpiece, tour de force
Chekhov, Anton *play:* **6** Ivanov **7** Sea Gull **10** Uncle Vanya **12** Three Sisters **13** Cherry Orchard
chelonian **6** turtle **8** tortoise
chemical *agent:* **8** catalyst *combining form:* **2** is, ol, ox, yl **3** aci, hex, iod, iso, mer, ole, oxa, oxo, oyl, pyr, thi, tri, ure **4** acet, amid, amin, hept, hexa, hydr, iodo, orth, poly, pyro, quin, tetr, thio **5** aceto, amido, amino, hepta, hydro, ortho, quino, tetra, xanth **6** ammino, xantho *combining power:* **7** valence *compound:* **4** acid, base, diol, enol, imid, oxim, salt, tepa, urea **5** amide, amine, diene, ester, imide, imine, indol, orcin, oxime, purin, pyran, salol, tolan, triol **6** alkali, benzin, benzol, diamin, emodin, guanin, halide, hydrid, indole, inulin, ionone, isatin, isolog, isomer, ketone, lactam, maltol,

metepa, natron, nitril, pterin, purine, pyrone, pyrrol, quinol, retene, silane, skatol, tannin, tetryl, thiram, thymol, tolane, triene, trimer, uracil, ureide, yttria, zeatin **7** barilla, benzene, benzole, cumarin, diamide, diamine, diazine, diazole, diester, flavone, guanine, heptose, hydride, indamin, indican, indoxyl, isatine, levulin, metamer, monomer, naphtol, nitrile, orcinol, oxazine, phytane, picolin, polyene, polymer, pyrrole, quinoid, quinone, salicin, skatole, steroid, taurine, terpene, thiazin, thiazol, thymine, tolidin, triazin, urethan, uridine, vitamer, xylidin **8** cephalin, cyanamid, disulfid, elaterin, fluorene, furfural, guaiacol, hematein, hexamine, indamine, isologue, kephalin, lichenin, limonene, melamine, naloxone, naphthol, palmitin, phenazin, phosphid, phthalin, picoline, piperine, pristane, quinolin, resorcin, salicine, santonin, siloxane, sodamide, sorbitol, spermine, squalene, stilbene, strontia, tautomer, thiazine, thiazole, thiophen, thiotepa, thiourea, tolidine, triazine, triazole, triptane, tyramine, urethane, vanillin, warfarin, xanthene, xanthine, xanthone, xylidine, ytterbia, zaratite, zirconia *element:* (see at **element**) *prefix:* **2** di **3** dia, met **4** meta *quantity:* **4** mole *radical:* **4** acyl, amyl, cyan **5** allyl, butyl, ethyl, tolyl **6** acetyl, formyl, methyl, oxalic, phenyl, propyl, toluyl **7** benzoyl *reaction:* **5** redox *salt:* **5** niter, nitre, urate, ziram **6** haloid, humate, malate, oleate, phytin **7** ferrate, formate, gallate, maleate, pectate, persalt, picrate, tannate, toluate, zincate **8** fumarate, pyruvate, racemate, selenate, silicate, stearate, tartrate, thionate, titanate, valerate, vanadate, xanthate *suffix:* **2** id, il, in, ol, on **3** ane, ase, ate, ein, ene, ide, ile, ine, ite, ium, oic, oin, one, ose, ous, yne **4** eine, idin, itol, oate, olic, onic **5** idine, onium, oside, ylene *warfare agent:* **7** tear gas **8** vesicant **10** mustard gas
chemist **7** analyst **8** druggist **10** apothecary, pharmacist *American:* **4** Urey **6** Remsen, Sumner **7** Onsager, Pauling, Seaborg **8** Hoffmann, Langmuir, Mulliken, Richards, Woodward *Austrian:* **4** Kuhn **5** Pregl *British:* **6** Ramsay **8** Smithson *Dutch:* **8** van't Hoff *English:* **4** Abel, Davy **5** Soddy **6** Dalton **7** Faraday **9** Priestley, Wollaston **10** Williamson *French:* **5** Curie **7** Moissan, Pasteur **8** Sabatier **9** Lavoisier *German:* **5** Haber **6** Bunsen, Liebig, Nernst, Wittig, Wohler **7** Fischer, Hofmann, Ostwald, Wallach, Wieland, Windaus, Ziegler **9** Zsigmondy **10** Erlenmeyer, Staudinger **11** Willstatter *Italian:* **5** Natta **8** Avogadro *Russian:* **7** Semenov **8** Zelinsky **9** Mendeleev *Scottish:* **4** Todd *Swedish:* **8** Svedberg *Swiss:* **6** Karrer, Werner (see also under **Nobel Prize Winner**)

chemist's vessel 4 vial 5 ampul, flask, phial 6 aludel, ampule, beaker, mortar, retort 7 ampoule, matrass 8 bolt head, crucible, cylinder, test tube

chemoreceptor 8 taste bud

cheongsam 5 dress

Cheops 5 Khufu 7 pyramid

Cheran's father 6 Dishon

cherish 4 keep, save 5 guard, nurse, prize, value 6 admire, defend, esteem, foster, harbor, nursle, relish, revere, shield 7 apprize, nourish, nurture, shelter 8 conserve, preserve, treasure, venerate 9 cultivate, delight in, entertain, reverence, safeguard 10 appreciate

Cherokee *chief:* 4 Ross *historian:* 7 Sequoya

cherry *dark:* 4 Bing *family:* 4 rose 8 Rosaceae *genus:* 6 Prunus *hybrid:* 4 Duke *sour:* 7 morello 8 amarelle *sweet:* 4 Bing, gean 7 mazzard, oxheart 9 Bigarreau *wild:* 7 marasca, mazzard 10 maraschino

cherry bomb 11 firecracker

Cherry Orchard author 7 Chekhov

cherrystone 4 clam 6 quahog

chersonese 9 peninsula

Chesed *father:* 5 Nahor *wife:* 6 Milcah

chess *champion:* 3 Tal 4 Euwe 6 Karpov, Lasker 7 Fischer, Smysolv, Spassky 8 Alekhine, Kasparov, Steinitz 9 Botvinnik, Petrosian 10 Capablanca *draw game:* 9 stalemate *goal:* 4 mate 9 checkmate *move:* 6 castle, gambit 10 fianchetto *opening:* 6 gambit *piece:* 4 king, pawn, rook 5 queen 6 bishop, knight *risk:* 6 gambit *term:* 3 net, pin 4 biff, draw, file, fork, mate, rank 5 check 6 attack, castle, gambit, skewer 7 capture, develop, end game 9 checkmate, en passant 10 fianchetto, middle game 11 combination

chest 4 kist 6 breast, bureau, coffer, lowboy, thorax, wangan, wangun 7 dresser, highboy, wanigan 8 treasury, wannigan 9 exchequer 10 chiffonier *combining form:* 5 stern 6 sterno, stetho, thorac 7 thoraci, thoraco

chesterfield 4 sofa 8 overcoat 9 davenport

chestnut 4 tree 5 color, horse 6 cliché, marron 10 brownstone, chinquapin *extract:* 6 tannin *Polynesian:* 4 rata *water:* 4 ling

cheval glass 6 mirror

chevalier 5 noble 6 knight 8 horseman 9 caballero, gentleman

chevron 6 stripe

chew 3 eat, gum 4 bite, chaw, gnaw 5 champ, chomp, chump, crump, munch 6 crunch, devour, mumble, nibble 7 chumble, consume, scrunch 8 ruminate 9 masticate

chewing gum 6 chicle

chew out 3 jaw, wig 5 scold 6 revile 7 bawl out, tell off 10 tongue-lash, vituperate

Chiang ___ 7 Kai-shek

chic 3 cry, fad 4 mode, rage 5 craze, smart, style, swank, swish, vogue 6 furore, modish, trendy, with-it 7 dashing, fashion, stylish 9 exclusive 10 dernier cri 11 fashionable

chicane 4 dupe, fool, gull, hoax, ploy, ruse, wile 5 cavil, feint, fraud, trick 6 befool, gambit 7 quibble 8 artifice, flimflam, hoodwink, maneuver, trickery 9 bamboozle, deception, stratagem, victimize 10 dishonesty, hanky-panky 11 furtiveness, highbinding 13 double-dealing

chicanery 4 plot 5 fraud 8 intrigue, trickery 11 machination

chichi 5 showy, swank 6 dressy, la-di-da 7 splashy 8 affected, overnice, peacocky, précieux, precious 10 flamboyant, peacockish 11 alembicated, overrefined, pretentious 12 orchidaceous, ostentatious

chick 3 kid 5 child 6 moppet, nipper 8 juvenile, young one 9 youngling, youngster

chickadee 8 titmouse *family:* 7 Paridae

Chickasaw chief 5 mingo

chicken 4 fowl, funk 5 sissy 6 coward, craven, funker 7 dastard, gutless, quitter, unmanly 8 cowardly, poltroon 9 spunkless 11 lily-livered, poltroonish, yellowbelly 12 poor-spirited 13 pusillanimous *breed:* 4 Java 6 Ancona, Brahma, Cochin, Lamona, Redcap, Sussex 7 Buckeye, Cornish, Dorking, Holland, Leghorn, Minorca 8 Delaware, Dominick, Langshan 9 Buttercup, Dominique, Orpington, Wyandotte 10 Australorp 11 Jersey Giant, Rock Cornish *castrated:* 5 capon *cooking:* 5 fryer 7 broiler, roaster *disease:* 5 gapes 8 pullorum 11 coccidiosis *female:* 3 hen 6 pullet *genus:* 6 Gallus *male:* 4 cock 7 rooster 8 cockerel *pen:* 4 coop *small:* 6 bantam *sound:* 6 cackle

chicken feed 7 peanuts 8 pittance

chicken pox 9 varicella

chickpea 8 garbanzo

chickweed 4 pink 7 potherb

chicle 3 gum 10 chewing gum

chicory 7 witloof

chide 4 rate 5 scold, sneap 6 berate, lesson, monish, rebuke 7 reprove, tick off, upbraid 8 admonish, call down, reproach 9 reprimand

chiding 3 rap, wig 6 rebuke 7 reproof 8 reproach 9 reprimand 10 admonition 12 admonishment

chief 4 arch, boss, cock, duce, head, jefe, lion, main, star 5 first, major, prime 6 bigwig, führer, honcho, leader, master, potent, primal, ruling, sachem 7 capital, headman, leading, notable, premier, primary, stellar, telling, weighty 8 bigtimer, big wheel, champion, dictator, dominant, eminence, foremost, hierarch, luminary 9 dignitary, dominator, effective, important, momentous, number one, principal, prominent 10 notability, preeminent 11 controlling, outstanding, predominant, significant 13 consequential *combining form:* 4 prot 5 proto *commander:* 4 CINC *prefix:* 4 arch 5 archi *Spanish:* 4 jefe

Chief Justice 3 Jay 4 Taft 5 Chase, Stone, Taney, Waite, White 6 Burger, Fuller, Holmes, Hughes, Vinson, Warren 8 Marshall 9 Ellsworth

chiefly 6 mainly, mostly 7 largely, overall 9 generally, primarily 11 principally 13 predominantly

chiffchaff 4 bird 7 warbler

chiffonier 5 chest 6 bureau 7 dresser

chigger 4 mite 6 chigoe, red bug

chignon 3 bun 4 knot

chilblain 4 sore 8 swelling 12 inflammation

child 3 kid 5 minor, youth 6 cherub, moppet, nipper, teener 7 dickens 8 innocent, juvenile, runabout, teenager, young one 9 sweetling, youngling, youngster 10 adolescent 11 teenybopper *combining form:* 3 ped 4 paed, paid, pedo 5 paedo, paido, tecno *gifted:* 7 prodigy *homeless:* 4 waif *parentless:* 6 orphan *Scottish:* 5 bairn *spoiled:* 4 brat *young:* 3 tot 4 baby, tike, tyke 6 infant, kiddie 8 bantling, weanling

childish 4 slow 5 naive, silly 6 simple 7 asinine, babyish, fatuous, foolish, kiddish, moronic, puerile 8 arrested, backward, immature, retarded 9 infantile, infantine *Scottish:* 7 bairnly 8 bairnish

childless 6 barren 7 sterile

childlike 6 docile, filial 7 natural 8 innocent, trustful, trusting 9 ingenuous

child's play 4 snap 5 cinch, setup 6 breeze, picnic 8 duck soup, kid stuff, pushover

Chile *capital:* 8 Santiago *chief export:* 6 copper *conqueror:* 8 Valdivia *monetary unit:* 4 peso

Chileab *father:* 5 David *mother:* 7 Abigail

chili con ___ 5 carne

Chilion *father:* 9 Elimelech *mother:* 5 Naomi

chill 3 icy 4 ague, cold, cool 5 gelid, nippy 6 arctic, chilly, deject, formal, frigid, frosty 7 distant, glacial 8 dispirit, freezing, reserved, solitary 9 disparage, withdrawn 10 abstracted, demoralize, discourage, dis-

hearten 11 emotionless, indifferent, standoffish, unemotional 12 uninterested 13 disinterested

chiller 7 shocker 8 thriller

chilly 3 raw 4 cold 5 algid 7 coldish

chilopod 9 centipede

chime 4 bell, bong, peal, ring, toll, tune 5 knell 6 accord 7 concord, harmony 9 agreement 10 consonance 11 concordance

chime in 3 say 4 tell 5 state, utter 6 chip in 7 break in, declare, deliver 8 bring out, throw out 9 interrupt

chimera 5 dream 6 bubble 7 fantasy, rainbow 8 illusion, phantasy 9 pipe dream

Chimera *father:* 6 Typhon *mother:* 7 Echidna *slayer:* 11 Bellerophon

chimerical 6 absurd, unreal 7 fictive, utopian 8 delusive, delusory, fabulous, fanciful, illusory, mythical 9 ambitious, deceptive, fantastic, fictional, imaginary 10 fictitious 11 pretentious 12 preposterous, supposititious

chiming 7 musical 8 blending, harmonic 9 consonant, symphonic 10 harmonious 11 symphonious

chimney 3 lum 4 flue, tube 5 stack 10 smokestack *corner:* 8 fireside 9 inglenook *output:* 3 gas 4 fume, soot 5 smoke

chimpanzee 3 ape 6 monkey 7 primate 10 anthropoid *kin:* 7 gorilla

chin 3 rap 4 chat, talk, yarn 5 prose, visit 6 mentum 8 causerie, colloque, converse *combining form:* 5 genio, mento

china 6 dishes 7 ceramic 8 crockery 9 porcelain 11 earthenware *maker:* 3 Bow 5 Hizen, Imari, Spode 6 Doccia, Sèvres 7 Bristol, Chelsea, Dresden, Limoges, Meissen 8 Caughley, Haviland, Wedgwood

China *capital:* 6 Peking 7 Beijing *largest city:* 8 Shanghai *monetary unit:* 4 yuan *old name:* 6 Cathay *province:* 5 Anhui, Gansu, Hebei, Henan, Hubei, Hunan, Jilin 6 Fujian, Shanxi, Yunnan 7 Guizhou, Jiangsu, Jiangxi, Qinghai, Shaanxi, Sichuan 8 Liaoning, Shandong, Szechwan, Zhejiang 9 Guangdong 12 Heilongjiang *region:* 5 Tibet 6 Xizang 10 Nei Monggol 12 Ningxia Huizu 13 Inner Mongolia, Xinjiang Uygur

china clay 6 kaolin

chinchilla 3 fur 6 rodent

chine 5 crest, ridge 7 hogback

Chinese *administrative unit:* 2 fu 5 hsien *archway:* 6 pai-lou *aromatic root:* 7 ginseng *artichoke:* 6 crosne 7 chorogi, crosnes 8 knotroot *assembly:* 3 hui *bamboo:* 7 whangee *boat:* 4 junk 6 sampan *boat-dweller:* 3 Tan 5 Tanka *bow:* 6 kowtow *Buddha:* 2 Fo *Buddhism:* 5 Foism *cabbage:* 6 pechay 7 pakchoi *card game:* 6 fan tan *cauterizing agent:* 4 moxa *civet:* 5 rasse *combining form:* 4 Sino 5 Chino 6 Sinico *conveyance:* 7 pedicab, ricksha 10 jinrikisha *date:* 6 jujube *deer:* 8 elaphure *dialect:* 2 Wu 4 Amoy 5 Hakka 6 Swatow 7 Foochow 8 Mandarin 9 Cantonese, Pekingese *dictator:* 10 Mao Tse-tung *distance unit:* 2 li *dog:* 4 chow, Peke 9 Pekingese *dulcimer:* 7 yang-kin 8 yang ch'in *dynasty:* 2 Wu 3 Ch'i, Han, Sui, Wei, Yin 4 Ch'en, Ch'in, Chou, Hsia (first), Ming, Sung, T'ang, Tsin, Yuan 5 Ch'ing, Liang, Shang 6 Manchu, Mongol, Shu Han *fabric:* 5 pekin 6 pongee, tussah 7 tsatlee 8 shantung *feminine principle:* 3 yin *festival:* 8 Ch'in Ming *feudal state:* 3 Wei *figurine:* 5 magot *food:* 6 subgum, won ton 7 foo yong *fruit:* 6 lichee, litchi, loquat 7 kumquat 8 mandarin *gambling game:* 6 fan tan *gazelle:* 6 dzeren, dzeron *god:* 4 joss, Shen 7 Shang-ti, Tien Chu *gong:* 6 tamtam *grass:* 3 bon *gruel:* 6 congee *herb:* 5 ramee, ramie 7 ginseng *idol:* 4 joss *jute:* 7 chingma *laborer:* 6 coolie *legendary emperor:* 7 Huang Ti *liquid measure:* 5 cheng, sheng *liquor:* 6 samshu *magnolia:* 5 yulan *mandarin's residence:* 5 yamen *masculine principle:* 4 yang *military leader:* 7 warlord *money, silver:* 5 sycee *moon guitar:* 6 yue-kin 8 yueh-ch'in *musical instrument:* 3 kin 4 ch'in, pipa 5 cheng, hsiao 6 yue-kin 8 yang ch'in, yueh ch'in *nurse:* 4 amah *official:* 4 kuan 8 mandarin *official seal:* 4 chop *oil:* 4 tung *omelet:* 7 foo yong *ox:* 4 zebu *pagoda:* 2 ta 3 taa *peony:* 6 moutan *permit:* 4 chop *porcelain:* 4 chin, Ming 7 celadon, Nankeen 8 mandarin *pottery:* 4 Kuan, Ming 5 Chien 7 boccaro, tz'u-chou *prefecture:* 2 fu *puzzle:* 7 tangram *race:* 9 Mongoloid *religion:* 5 Foism 6 Taoism 8 Buddhism 12 Confucianism *rice song:* 6 yang ko *sauce:* 3 soy *secret society:* 4 tong *sheep:* 3 sha 5 urial 6 oorial *silkworm:* 6 tussah 7 tussore 8 ailanthus *string money:* 4 tiao *tea:* 5 bohea, congo, hyson 6 congou, oolong 8 souchong *temple:* 2 ta 3 taa 6 pagoda *tree:* 4 tung 6 gingko, ginkgo, loquat, wampee 7 kumquat 8 mandarin *unicorn:* 3 lin *vine:* 5 kudzu 7 yangtao *weight:* 3 fan, fen, tan 4 mace, tael 5 catty, liang, picol, picul

chink 4 rift, rima, rime 5 cleft, clink, crack, split 6 jingle, tingle, tinkle 7 fissure 8 rimation

chinquapin 3 nut 8 chestnut

chintzy 4 loud 5 cheap, gaudy 6 brazen, flashy, garish, tawdry, tinsel 7 blatant, glaring 12 meretricious

chip in 6 kick in 7 break in, chime in, pitch in 9 interrupt, subscribe 10 contribute 11 come through

chipmunk 6 hackee, rodent *family:* 8 squirrel 9 Sciuridae

chipper 3 gay 4 keen, neat, peep, snug, tidy, trig, trim 5 alert, cheep, chirm, chirp, tweet 6 bright, lively 7 animate, chirrup, chitter, orderly, tweedle, twitter 8 animated, spirited 9 shipshape, sprightly, vivacious 11 uncluttered, well-groomed 12 spick-and-span

chirk 3 gay 5 cheer 6 blithe, bright, cheery, chirpy, lively 7 animate, chipper, hearten 8 animated, cheerful, chirrupy, embolden, inspirit, sunbeamy 9 encourage, enhearten, lightsome, sprightly, vivacious 10 strengthen

chirography 4 fist, hand 6 ductus, script 10 penmanship 11 calligraphy, handwriting

chiromancy 9 palmistry

Chiron 7 centaur *father:* 6 Cronus *mother:* 7 Philyra *pupil:* 5 Jason 8 Achilles, Heracles, Hercules 9 Asclepius 11 Aesculapius

chiropody 8 podiatry

chiropractic *founder:* 6 Palmer

chiropter 3 bat

chirp 4 chip, peep 5 cheep, chirm, tweet 7 chipper, chirrup, clutter, tweedle, twitter

chirpy 5 chirk, sunny 6 blithe, cheery 8 cheerful, chirrupy, sunbeamy 9 lightsome

chirrup 4 chip, peep 5 cheep, chirm, chirp, tweet 7 chipper, chitter, tweedle, twitter

chisel 3 gyp 4 beat, bilk 5 carve, cheat, cozen, cut in, sculp 6 butt in, diddle, horn in, sculpt 7 defraud, intrude, obtrude 9 sculpture 10 intertrude

chiselly 3 bad 4 sour 6 rotten 7 unhappy 10 unpleasant 11 displeasing 12 disagreeable

chit 3 kid 4 memo, note 5 chick, child 6 moppet 8 juvenile, notandum, notation, young one 9 youngster 10 memorandum

chitchat 5 clack 6 babble, by-talk, cackle, gabble 7 chatter, prattle 8 trifling 9 bavardage, small talk 12 talkee-talkee, tittle-tattle

chitter 4 chip, peep 5 cheep, chirp, tweet 7 chipper, chirrup, tweedle, twitter

chivalric see **chivalrous**

chivalrous 3 big 5 lofty, manly, noble 8 generous, knightly 10 benevolent 11 considerate, magnanimous 12 greathearted

chivy, chivvy 3 try 4 bait, ride 5 chase, hound, trail 6 badger, follow, heckle, hector, pursue 7 afflict, torment 8 bullyrag

Chloe 11 shepherdess *beloved:* 7 Daphnis

chlordane 11 insecticide

chloride 4 salt 5 ester 7 muriate

chlorine *symbol:* 2 Cl

Chloris *father:* **7** Amphion *husband:* **6** Neleus **8** Zephyrus *mother:* **5** Niobe *son:* **6** Nestor

chloroform **7** anodyne, solvent **10** anesthetic

choate **4** full **5** whole **6** entire **7** perfect **8** complete, integral

chockablock **4** full **6** jammed, packed **7** brimful, crammed, crowded, jam-full, stuffed **8** bung-full **9** jam-packed

chocolate **3** bar **5** candy, cocoa, color, drink **8** beverage

Chocolate Soldier composer **6** Straus

chocolate tree **5** cacao

choice **3** fat, top **4** best, pick, rare **5** cream, elite, pride, prime, prize **6** chosen, culled, dainty, flower, option, picked, rating, select **7** elegant, finding, supreme, verdict **8** decision, delicate, druthers, election, judgment, peerless, selected, superior, volition **9** appraisal, exquisite **8** recherché **9** selection **10** evaluation, preeminent, preference, surpassing **11** alternative, superlative, unsurpassed **12** incomparable, transcendent **13** determination *even:* **6** toss-up

choicy **4** nice **5** fussy, picky **6** choosy **7** finical, finicky **9** finicking **10** fastidious, particular **11** persnickety

choir **6** chorus *area:* **4** loft **7** chancel, gallery *assistant:* **9** succentor *leader:* **6** cantor **8** choragus **9** precentor *member:* **9** chorister *section:* **4** alto, bass **5** tenor **7** soprano *vestment:* **4** gown, robe **5** cotta **8** surplice

choke **4** clog, fill, heap, hush, load, pack, pile, plug, stop **5** block, close, quiet, shush, still **6** charge, shut up, stifle **7** congest, occlude, quieten, silence, smother, stopper **8** obstruct, strangle, throttle **9** suffocate **10** asphyxiate

choking **8** quashing, stifling **9** quenching, squashing **10** repression, smothering, squelching, strangling **11** suppression

choleric **3** mad **4** waxy **5** angry, fiery, irate, ratty, testy, wroth **6** cranky, heated, ireful, spunky, tetchy, touchy, wrathy **7** carping **8** captious, wrathful **9** indignant, irascible, temperish **11** acrimonious, hot-tempered **12** fault-finding **13** quick-tempered

cholla **6** cactus

chomp **4** bite, chew **5** champ, chump, munch **6** crunch **7** scrunch **8** ruminate **9** masticate

choose **3** opt **4** cull, like, love, mark, pick, take, want, will, wish **5** adopt, elect, favor **6** desire, optate, opt for, please, prefer, select **7** embrace, espouse, pick out **8** handpick **9** single out

choosy **4** nice **5** fussy **7** finical, finicky

8 delicate **9** finicking **10** fastidious, particular, pernickety **11** persnickety

chop **3** box, cut, hew **4** cuff, dice, fell, hack, hash, poke, slap **5** clout, cut up, mince, smack, spank **6** buffet, hackle **8** fragment

chop-chop **4** fast **7** flat-out, hastily, quickly, rapidly **8** full tilt, promptly, speedily **9** posthaste **12** lickety-split

chophouse **10** restaurant

Chopin *birthplace:* **6** Poland *instrument:* **5** piano *lover:* **4** Sand (George)

chord **4** line **5** triad **6** tetrad **9** harmonize *sequence:* **7** cadence

chore **3** job **4** duty, task **5** stint, trial **6** devoir, effort **8** taskwork **10** assignment **11** tribulation

choreograph **6** direct **7** arrange, compose

choreographer *American:* **4** Feld, Lang **5** Ailey, Fosse, Shawn, Tharp **6** Fokine, Graham, Taylor, Tetley **7** de Mille, Massine, Robbins, Tamiris, Weidman **8** Humphrey **10** Balanchine, Cunningham *English:* **5** Tudor **6** Ashton, Weaver **9** MacMillan *French:* **6** Béjart, Perrot, Petipa **7** Noverre *German:* **5** Jooss *Mexican:* **5** Limon *Russian:* **8** Nijinska

chorography **3** map **9** mapmaking

chortle **5** laugh, tehee **6** giggle, guffaw, hee-haw, titter **7** chuckle, snicker, sniggle

chorus **4** tune **6** accord **7** concert, concord, harmony **10** consonance

chorus girl **7** chorine

chosen **4** pick **5** elect **6** picked, select **8** selected **9** exclusive

Chou ___ **5** En-Lai

chouse **3** gyp, jig **4** beat, bilk, play, ploy, ruse **5** cheat, cozen, feint, trick **6** diddle, gambit **7** defraud, gimmick, whizzer **8** artifice, flimflam

chow **4** feed, food, grub, meal **6** repast, viands **7** edibles, nurture **8** victuals **9** provender, refection **10** provisions **11** comestibles

chowchow **4** brew, hash, stew **5** mixed **6** jumble, medley, motley, relish, varied **7** mélange **8** assorted, mishmash, preserve **9** potpourri **10** hodgepodge, miscellany **11** promiscuous **12** conglomerate, multifarious **13** heterogeneous, miscellaneous

chowderhead **4** dope **5** dunce, noddy **6** noodle **7** schnook **9** lame-brain

chowhound **7** glutton **8** gourmand

chrism **3** oil **4** balm **5** cream, salve **6** cerate **7** unction, unguent **8** ointment

christen **3** dub **4** call, name, term **5** style, title **7** asperse, baptize, entitle, immerse **8** sprinkle **9** designate **10** denominate

christening **7** baptism

Christian 5 right 6 decent, proper, seemly 8 becoming, decorous 9 befitting, civilized *denomination:* 6 Mormon, Quaker 7 Baptist 8 Anglican, Catholic, Lutheran 9 Calvinist, Methodist 12 Episcopalian *Eastern rite:* 5 Uniat 6 Uniate *Egyptian:* 4 Copt *love feast:* 5 agape *martyr, first:* 7 Stephen *symbol:* 3 IHS 4 rood 5 cross 7 ichthus, ichthys

Christian Science founder 4 Eddy (Mary Baker)

____ **Christie** 6 Agatha

Christina's World painter 5 Wyeth

Christmas 4 Noel, Xmas, yule 8 Nativity, yuletide *symbol:* 7 Yule log

Christmas Carol, A *author:* 7 Dickens *character:* 7 Scrooge, Tiny Tim 8 Cratchit

Christogram 6 Chi-Rho

Christopher Robin creator 5 Milne

chromatic 8 colorful 10 accidental

chromium *symbol:* 2 Cr

chromosome component 3 DNA 4 gene 8 telomere 10 centromere, chromomere

chronic 5 usual 6 wonted 7 routine 8 accepted, habitual 9 confirmed, customary 10 accustomed, habituated

chronicle 4 list 5 story 6 annals, record, relate, report 7 account, history, recital, version 8 describe 9 narration, narrative, recountal

chronograph 5 watch 9 timepiece

chronometer 5 clock, watch 9 timepiece

chrysalis 4 pupa 8 covering

Chryseis *captor:* 9 Agamemnon *father:* 7 Chryses

Chrysippus *father:* 6 Pelops *slayer:* 6 Atreus 8 Thyestes

chthonian 6 Hadean 8 infernal, plutonic 9 plutonian, Tartarean 10 sulphurous

chubby 5 plump, podgy, pudgy, round, tubby 6 plumpy, rotund 8 plumpish, roly-poly 10 roundabout

chuck 4 cast, junk, quit, shed 5 chase, ditch, eject, evict, scrap 6 desert, reject, slough 7 abandon, boot out, discard, dismiss, extrude, forsake, kick out 8 jettison, renounce, throw out 9 throw away, throw over

chucker 7 bouncer 8 houseman

chuckle 5 laugh, tehee 6 giggle, guffaw, hee-haw, titter 7 chortle, snicker, sniggle

chucklehead 4 dope 5 dunce, noddy 6 noodle 7 schnook 9 lame-brain

chuff 4 boor, glum, ugly 5 churl, clown, hunks, miser, nabal, stiff, sulky, surly 6 gloomy, morose, mucker, sullen 7 crabbed, grobian, niggard, scrooge 8 muckworm 9 skinflint 10 clodhopper 12 moneygrubber

chum 3 pal 5 buddy, crony, cully 6 comate, friend 7 comrade 9 associate, companion 11 running mate

chumble 4 chew 5 champ, chomp, munch 6 crunch 7 scrunch 8 ruminate 9 masticate

chummy 4 cozy 5 close, pally, thick 8 familiar, intimate 10 buddy-buddy, palsy-walsy 12 confidential

chump 3 oaf, sap 4 boob, butt, chaw, chew, dolt, dupe, fool, goof, goon, gull, mark 5 booby, dunce, munch 6 crunch, pigeon, sucker 7 fall guy, fathead, gudgeon, scrunch 8 dolthead, lunkhead, ruminate 9 masticate

chunk 3 gob, wad 4 clod, hunk, lump 5 clump, hunch 6 nugget

chunky 5 dumpy, squat 6 chubby, rotund, stocky, stubby, stumpy 8 heavyset, thickset 11 thick-bodied

church 4 cult, fane, kirk, sect 5 creed, faith 6 temple 7 minster 8 basilica, religion 9 cathedral, communion, spiritual 10 connection, house of God, persuasion, tabernacle 12 denomination 13 house of prayer *adjunct:* 6 belfry 7 steeple 9 bell tower *basin:* 4 font 5 stoup *bench:* 3 pew *bishop's:* 9 cathedral *Buddhist:* 2 ta 3 taa 6 pagoda *calendar:* 4 ordo *caretaker:* 6 sexton *chapel:* 7 oratory *combining form:* 7 ecclesi 8 ecclesio *council:* 5 synod *court:* 4 Rota 10 consistory *creed:* 6 Nicene 8 Apostles' *district:* 6 parish 7 diocese *father:* 5 Basil 6 Jerome, Justin, Origen 7 Clement 8 Ignatius 9 Augustine 10 Chrysostom, Tertullian, theologian *fund-raiser:* 6 bazaar *governing body:* 5 curia 7 classis 10 consistory *head:* 4 pope 7 pontiff *land:* 5 grebe *law:* 5 canon *member:* 11 communicant *Muslim:* 6 mosque *of a monastery:* 7 minster *officer:* 5 elder, vicar 6 beadle, deacon, sexton, verger, warden 9 presbyter, sacristan *part:* 4 apse, bema, loft, nave 5 aisle, altar, choir 6 vestry 7 chancel, gallery, narthex, steeple 8 sacristy, transept 9 baptistry, sanctuary 10 baptistery, clerestory *porch:* 6 parvis 7 galilee *pulpit:* 4 ambo *reader:* 6 lector *recess:* 4 apse *revenue:* 5 tithe *room:* 6 vestry 8 sacristy *Scottish:* 4 kirk *seat for clergy:* 7 sedilia *service:* 4 mass 6 matins 7 vespers 8 evensong 9 communion *small:* 6 chapel *tribunal:* 4 Rota *vault:* 5 crypt

Churchill, Winston *daughter:* 4 Mary 5 Diana, Sarah *father:* 8 Randolph *mother:* 6 Jennie *Order:* 6 Garter *phrase:* 11 Iron Curtain *son:* 8 Randolph *trademark:* 5 cigar *wife:* 10 Clementine

church key 9 can opener

churchman 6 cleric, divine, parson, priest

8 clerical, minister, preacher, reverend
9 clergyman **12** ecclesiastic

churl 4 boor, clod **5** chuff, clown
6 mucker **7** grobian **10** clodhopper

churlish 4 curt, dour **5** blunt, crude, gruff,
naive, surly **6** coarse, crusty **7** boorish,
brusque, loutish, lowbred **8** cloddish, clownish **10** uncultured, unpolished, unschooled
11 clodhopping, uncivilized **12** discourteous

churn 4 boil, stir **6** bubble, seethe, simmer **7** ferment, smolder *Scottish:* **4** kirn

chute 5 falls, sault, spout **7** cascade
8 cataract **9** waterfall

Chuza's wife 6 Joanna

cicatrix 4 scar **13** scarification

Cicero *forte:* 7 oratory *target:* **8** Catiline
10 Mark Antony

Cid 4 epic, hero, play, poem **5** opera *composer:* **8** Massenet *meaning:* **4** lord
name: **4** Diaz (Rodrigo, Ruy) **5** Bivar *playwright:* **9** Corneille *sword:* **6** Colada,
Tizona *wife:* **6** Jimena, Ximena

cigar 4 toby **5** breva, stogy **6** concha,
corona, Havana, Manila, stogie **7** bouquet,
cheroot, culebra, Londres, regalia, trabuco
8 panatela, perfecto, pickwick, puritano
9 belvedere *case:* **7** humidor *color:*
5 claro **6** maduro **8** colorado

cigarette 3 cig, fag **4** butt **5** smoke
6 gasper **10** coffin nail

cigarfish 4 scad

cilium 4 hair, lash **7** eyelash **8** barbicel
combining form: **7** blephar **8** blepharo

cimmerian 7 avernal, hellish, stygian
8 infernal, plutonic **9** plutonian
11 pandemoniac

cinch 4 snap **5** setup **6** assure, breeze,
ensure, insure, picnic, secure **8** duck soup,
kid stuff, pushover **10** child's play

cinchona bark extract 7 quinine

cincture 4 band, belt, gird, sash **6** begird,
engird, girdle **8** begirdle, engirdle
9 waistband

cinders 3 ash **5** ashes **8** clinkers

cinema 4 film, show **5** flick, movie **7** picture **9** photoplay **11** picture show
13 motion picture, moving picture

cinereous 4 gray **5** ashen

cinnabar 3 ore **7** mineral **9** vermilion
color: **3** red

cinnamon bark 6 cassia

cinnamon stone 6 garnet **8** essonite

cipher 3 zip **4** zero **5** aught, digit, ought,
zilch **6** figure, naught, nobody, nought,
number, reckon **7** chiffer, compute, integer,
nothing, nullity, numeral, whiffet **8** estimate,
goose egg, monogram, whipster **9** calculate, nonentity **11** whole number

ciphering 10 arithmetic **11** calculation,
computation

circa 4 near, nigh **5** about **6** around,
nearby **7** close on

circadian 5 daily **7** diurnal **9** quotidian

Circe 5 siren **9** sorceress *brother:*
6 Aeetes *father:* **3** Sol **6** Helios *home:*
5 Aeaea *lover:* **7** Ulysses **8** Odysseus
niece: **5** Medea *son:* **5** Comus
9 Telegonus

Circean 6 luring **8** enticing, fetching,
tempting

circinate 6 coiled

circle 3 hem, lot, mob, set **4** camp, clan,
gird, gyre, halo, loop, push, ring, roll, turn
5 bunch, cabal, crowd, cycle, group, orbit,
range, round, scope, wheel, whorl **6** begird,
clique, corona, extent, girdle, gyrate, length,
radius, rotary, rotate **7** compass, coterie,
cronies, environ, friends, ingroup, revolve,
rondure **8** comrades, encircle, surround
9 camarilla, dimension, encompass, extension, extensity, intimates **10** associates, circumduct, companions **12** acquaintance
bisector: **8** diameter *colored:* **6** areola,
areole *combining form:* **3** gyr **4** cycl, gyro
5 cyclo *graph:* **8** pie chart *luminous:*
4 aura, halo **6** corona, nimbus **7** aureola,
aureole *part:* **3** arc **6** sector **8** quadrant
small: **4** disk **7** annulet **8** roundlet

circlet 4 band, ring **8** bracelet, headband
for head or helmet: **7** coronal, coronel

circuit 3 way **4** gyre, loop, tour, trip, turn
5 ambit, round, route, wheel, whirl
6 course, league **7** compass, journey, travels **8** gyration, rotation **9** perimeter, periphery, round trip **10** conference, revolution,
roundabout **11** association, circulation
13 circumference

circuitous 7 oblique **8** circular, indirect
10 collateral, roundabout

circuit rider 9 clergyman

circular 4 bill **5** flier, flyer, gyral, round
7 annular, cycloid, discoid **8** handbill **10** circuitous *file:* **11** wastebasket *motion:*
4 eddy, gyre, spin **5** whirl **8** gyration, rotation **10** revolution *plate:* **4** disc, dish, disk

circularize 4 poll **9** publicize

circulate 4 flow **5** strew **6** rotate, set off,
spread **7** actuate, diffuse, radiate, revolve
8 disperse, exchange, mobilize **9** propagate **10** distribute **11** disseminate,
interchange

circulation 4 gyre, turn **5** round, wheel,
whirl **7** circuit **8** gyration, rotation
10 revolution

circulator 6 gossip **8** gossiper, quidnunc
9 carrytale **10** newsmonger **11** rumormonger **12** gossipmonger

circumambulate 4 roam, rove **5** drift,
mooch, range, stray **6** ramble, wander
7 meander **8** straggle

circumciser 5 mohel

circumcision *Jewish:* 5 Berit, Brith
10 Brith Milah

circumference 3 rim 5 ambit 6 border,
bounds, limits, margin 7 circuit, compass
8 boundary, confines 9 perimeter, periphery

circumflex 9 diacritic

circumfuse 7 envelop 8 surround

circumjacent 11 surrounding

circumlocution 8 pleonasm, verbiage
9 tautology, verbality 10 periphrase, redundancy, roundabout 11 periphrasis
13 circumambages

circumnavigate 5 skirt 6 bypass,
detour 10 circumvert

circumnavigator 4 Cook 5 Drake
8 Magellan, van Noort 9 Cavendish

circumscribe 3 bar 5 limit 6 fetter, hamper 7 confine, delimit, trammel 8 prelimit,
restrict 10 delimitate

circumscribed 5 bound, fixed 6 finite,
narrow, strait 7 bounded, cramped, precise 8 definite 11 determinate

circumscription 5 cramp, stint
9 restraint, stricture 10 constraint, limitation 11 confinement, restriction 12 ball and
chain 13 constrainment

circumspect 4 safe, wary 5 chary
7 careful, guarded 8 cautious, discreet, gingerly 10 meticulous, scrupulous 11 calculating, considerate, punctilious

circumstance 4 fate, item 5 event, moira,
thing 6 detail, factor, kismet 7 destiny, element, episode, portion 8 incident, occasion 9 component, happening 10 occurrence, particular 11 constituent

circumstantial 4 full, nice 5 close, exact
6 minute, strict 7 precise, replete 8 accurate, complete, detailed, itemized, thorough
9 clocklike 10 blow-by-blow, particular

circumvent 4 balk, beat, bilk, dash, dupe,
foil, ruin 5 avoid, burke, elude, evade, skirt,
trick 6 baffle, befool, bypass, detour,
escape, thwart 8 hoodwink, outflank, sidestep 9 frustrate 10 disappoint

circumvolution 4 gyre, turn 5 round,
wheel, whirl 7 circuit 8 gyration, rotation
10 revolution 11 circulation

circus 4 ring 5 arena 6 big top, cirque
9 spectacle 12 amphitheater *animal:*
4 bear, flea, lion, seal 5 horse, tiger 8 elephant *attraction:* 5 freak 8 sideshow
owner: 6 Bailey, Barnum 8 Ringling *performer:* 5 clown, tamer 7 acrobat, athlete,
juggler, tumbler 9 aerialist, fire eater
worker: 7 rouster 10 roustabout

citadel 4 fort 7 redoubt 8 fastness, fortress 10 stronghold *of Carthage:* 5 Bursa,
Byrsa *Russian:* 7 kremlin

citation 5 award 6 eulogy, reward 7 guerdon, tribute 8 encomium 9 panegyric
10 salutation

cite 4 name, tell 5 count, offer, quote
6 adduce, allege, number, recall, remind,
retain, revive 7 advance, bethink, mention,
present, specify 8 instance, remember
9 enumerate, recollect, reminisce
10 retrospect

citizen 5 towny 6 towner 7 burgess,
burgher, subject, townman 8 national,
townsman

Citizen Kane *director* 6 Welles

citron 4 tree 5 melon 6 yellow

citrus *family:* 3 rue 8 Rutaceae *fruit:*
4 lime 5 lemon 6 citron, orange 7 kumquat, tangelo 8 bergamot, mandarin, shaddock 9 tangerine 10 grapefruit

city 4 burg 5 urban 7 burghal 9 municipal
Alamo: 10 San Antonio *combining form:*
5 polis *Eternal:* 4 Rome *French:* 5 ville
heavenly: 4 Sion, Zion *Latin:* 4 urbs
Motor: 7 Detroit *of Bells:* 10 Strasbourg *of
Bridges:* 6 Bruges *of Brotherly Love:*
12 Philadelphia *of David:* 9 Jerusalem *official:* 5 mayor 7 manager 8 alderman
10 councilman *of God:* 6 heaven 8 paradise *of Gold:* 8 Eldorado *of Kings:* 4 Lima
of Lights: 5 Paris *of Lilies:* 8 Florence *of
Masts:* 6 London *of Rams:* 6 Canton *of
Refuge:* 6 Medina *of Saints:* 8 Montreal *of
Seven Hills:* 4 Rome *of the dead:*
10 Necropolis *of Victory:* 5 Cairo *planner:*
8 urbanist *section:* 4 slum, ward 5 block,
plaza 6 barrio, ghetto, square, uptown
8 business, downtown, red-light 11 residential *slicker:* 4 dude *windy:* 7 Chicago

city-state *Greek:* 5 polis 6 poleis (plural)

city, town, village (see also **capital**)
Afghanistan: 5 Balkh, Farah, Herat, Kushk
Alabama: 3 Opp 4 Arab, Boaz, Elba
5 Eutaw, Selma 6 Dothan, Mobile 7 Decatur,
Florala 8 Prichard 10 Birmingham, Hunts-
ville, Tuscaloosa *Alaska:* 5 Kenai, Sitka
6 Bethel, Kodiak, Valdez 9 Anchorage, Fair-
banks, Ketchikan *Albania:* 4 Fier 5 Berat,
Korce, Kukes, Vlore *Alberta:* 4 Olds
5 Hanna, Leduc, Taber 7 Calgary 10 Lethbridge *Algeria:* 4 Oran 5 Batna, Blida,
Medea, Saida, Setif 6 Annaba, Bechar
Argentina: 4 Azul, Goya 5 Junin, Lanus,
Lujan, Merlo, Salta, Tigre 6 Parana 7 Cordoba, La Plata, Mendoza, Rosario, San
Juan, Santa Fe 11 Bahia Blanca *Arizona:*
3 Ajo 4 Eloy, Mesa, Yuma 5 Globe,
Tempe 6 Tucson 7 Sun City, Winslow
8 Glendale, Prescott 9 Flagstaff 10 Casa
Grande, Scottsdale *Arkansas:* 4 Mena
5 Beebe, Cabot, Earle, Ozark, Wynne
9 Fort Smith, Pine Bluff, Texarkana *Australia:* 3 Ayr 5 Dalby, Dubbo, Unley 8 Rand-
wick 9 Bankstown, Blacktown, Newcastle
10 Kalgoorlie, Parramatta, Sutherland, Wollongong 12 Alice Springs *Austria:* 4 Enns,

Graz, Linz, Wels **5** Lienz, Steyr, Traun
8 Salzburg **9** Innsbruck **10** Klagenfurt
Azerbaijan: **9** Kirovabad *Bangladesh:*
5 Bogra, Pabna **6** Khulna **10** Chittagong
Belarus: **5** Brest, Gomel, Mozyr, Pinsk
6 Grodno **7** Mogilev, Vitebsk *Belgium:*
3 Ath, Hal, Huy, Mol **4** Amay, Dour, Geel,
Genk, Gent, Hoei, Luik, Mons, Vise **5** Aalst,
Arlon, Diest, Dison, Eupen, Evere, Ghent,
Gilly, Halle, Hamme, Hornu, Ieper, Jette,
Jumet, Leuze, Liege, Menen, Namen,
Namur, Ronse, Theux, Thuin, Uccle, Ukkel,
Wavre, Ypres **6** Bruges **7** Antwerp
Bolivia: **5** Oruro, Uyuni **9** Santa Cruz
10 Cochabamba *Bosnia and Herzego-*
vina: **5** Bihac, Brcko, Jajce, Tuzla **8** Sara-
jevo *Botswana:* **4** Maun **5** Kanye *Brazil:*
4 Codo, Para **5** Bahia, Bauru, Belem,
Ceara, Natal **6** Campos, Canoas, Caxias,
Ilheus, Maceio, Manaus, Olinda, Recife,
Santos **7** Aracaju, Caruaru, Goiania, Jun-
diai, Marilia, Niteroi, Pelotas, Sao Luis, Uber-
aba, Vitoria **8** Campinas, Colatina, Curitiba,
Londrina, Salvador, Santarem, Sao Paulo,
Sorocaba, Teresina **9** Caratinga, Fortaleza,
Guarulhos, Rio Grande **10** Guarapuava,
Joao Pessoa, Juiz de Fora, Nova Iguacu,
Pernambuco, Petropolis, Piracicaba, Santa
Maria, Santo Andre, Uberlandia **11** Campo
Grande, Caxias do Sul, Ponta Grossa, Porto
Alegre **12** Montes Claros, Rio de Janeiro,
Teofilo Otoni, Volta Redonda **13** Belo Hori-
zonte, Campina Grande, Duque de Caxias,
Florianopolis, Mogi das Cruzes, Riberiao
Preto *British Columbia:* **5** Comox **9** Van-
couver *Bulgaria:* **3** Lom **4** Ruse **5** Varna,
Vidin **6** Burgas **7** Plovdiv **11** Stara Zagora
Burkina Faso: **13** Bobo Dioulasso *Califor-*
nia: **4** Brea, Galt, Lodi, Ojai **5** Arvin, Azusa,
Ceres, Chico, Chino, Dixon, Hemet, Indio,
Norco, Ripon, Ukiah, Wasco, Yreka **6** Dow-
ney, Encino, Fresno, Oxnard, Pomona, Son-
oma **7** Anaheim, Burbank, Compton, Fre-
mont, Hayward, Modesto, Oakland, San
Jose, Seaside, Soledad, Van Nuys **8** Berke-
ley, Glendale, Palo Alto, Pasadena, San
Diego, Santa Ana, Stockton, Torrance, Yuba
City **9** El Segundo, Hollywood, Long Beach,
Menlo Park, Riverside, Sausalito **10** Carmi-
chael, Chowchilla, Chula Vista, Culver City,
Los Angeles, Pismo Beach, San Leandro,
Santa Clara **11** Bakersfield, Laguna Beach,
Pebble Beach, Redwood City, San Cle-
mente, Santa Monica **12** Beverly Hills, Mis-
sion Viejo, Redondo Beach, San Francisco,
Santa Barbara **13** San Bernardino, San Luis
Obispo *Cameroon:* **4** Buea, Edea **5** Kribi,
Lomie **6** Douala *Canada:* **5** Banff, Edson,
Hanna, Leduc, Rouyn **6** Regina **7** Calgary,
Halifax, Toronto, Windsor **8** Hamilton, Mon-
treal, Moose Jaw, Victoria, Winnipeg

9 Saint John, Saskatoon, Vancouver
10 Lethbridge, Saint Johns, Sherbrooke,
Thunder Bay, Whitehorse **11** Fredericton,
Yellowknife **12** Peterborough **13** Charlotte-
town, Trois Rivieres *Central African Repub-*
lic: **5** Bouar *Chad:* **4** Sarh *Chile:* **4** Lebu,
Lota, Tome **5** Ancud, Angol, Arica, Maipu,
Penco, Rengo, Talca **10** Concepcion, Talca-
huano, Valparaiso **11** Antofagasta *China:*
4 Amoy, Jian, Luan, Yaan **5** Hefei, Jilin,
Jinan, Lhasa, Qinan, Ssuan, Wuhan, Yibin,
Yumen **6** Andong, Anqing, Anshan,
Anshun, Anyang, Beihai, Canton, Datong,
Foshan, Fushun, Guilin, Haikou, Handan,
Harbin, Hoihao, Jilong, Luzhou, Mukden,
Ningbo, Pengbu, Suzhou, Urumqi, Xiamen,
Xuzhou, Yanggu, Yichun, Yining, Zhangi,
Zhaoan **7** Baoding, Changan, Chengdu,
Dandong, Guiyang, Huainan, Jiamusi, Jia-
xing, Kaifeng, Kunming, Luoshan, Luoyang,
Nanking, Nanning, Shantou, Taiyuan, Wan-
xian, Weifang, Yizhang **8** Changchi, Chang-
sha, Dangshan, Hangzhou, Hanzhong,
Hengyang, Huangshi, Jiangmen, Jiujiang,
Kueiyang, Liaoyang, Nanchang, Shanghai,
Shangrao, Shaoyang, Tianshui, Zhenjing
9 Changchun, Chenjiang, Chongqing,
Chungking, Huangshih, Zhenjiang **10** Jing-
dezhen, Laojunmiao **11** Qinhuangdao,
Zhangjiakou *Colombia:* **4** Buga, Cali
5 Bello, Mocoa, Neiva, Ocana, Pasto, Tulua,
Tunja **6** Cucuta, Ibague **7** Cienaga, Pal-
mira, Pereira **8** Medellin, Monteria **9** Cartagena, Manizales **10** Santa Marta **11** Buca-
ramanga **12** Barranquilla *Colorado:*
5 Craig **6** Arvada, Salida **7** Alamosa,
Durango, Greeley, La Junta **8** Brighton,
Gunnison, Lakewood, Longmont, Loveland,
Montrose, Thornton **9** Englewood, Estes
Park, Leadville, Littleton, Rocky Ford
10 Broomfield, Castle Rock, Fort Lupton,
Fort Morgan, Monte Vista, Northglenn, Wal-
senburg, Wheat Ridge **11** Fort Collins
13 Grand Junction *Connecticut:* **5** Byram
6 Bethel, Bolton, Darien, Easton, Granby,
Groton, Haddam, Hamden, Moosup, Som-
ers, Weston **7** Ansonia, Bethany, Danbury,
Enfield, Ledyard, Meriden, Milford, New-
town, Niantic, Norwalk, Norwich, Old Lyme,
Pomfret, Seymour, Tolland, Windham,
Winsted, Wolcott **8** Branford, Cromwell,
East Lyme, Guilford, New Haven, Simsbury,
Stamford, Suffield, Westport **9** Danielson,
Deep River, East Haven, Ellington, Green-
wich, Harwinton, Killingly, Montville, New
Canaan, Newington, New London, Pawca-
tuck, Rocky Hill, Southbury, Thomaston,
Waterbury, Waterford, West Haven
10 Bridgeport, Brookfield, East Granby,
East Haddam, Farmington, Gales Ferry,
Kensington, Litchfield, New Britain, New Mil-

ford, North Haven, Plainville, Ridgefield, Stonington, Terryville, Torrington **11** Beacon Falls, East Norwalk, East Windsor, Forestville, Glastonbury, Marlborough, Middlefield, Old Saybrook, Southington, Wallingford, Willimantic **12** Collinsville, East Hartford, New Fairfield, South Norwalk, South Windsor, West Hartford, Wethersfield, Windsor Locks **13** North Branford, Thompsonville *Croatia:* **4** Pula **5** Sisak, Zadar **6** Rijeka, Zagreb **9** Dubrovnik *Cuba:* **5** Banes, Bauta **7** Holguin **8** Camaguey, Marianao, Matanzas **10** Cienfuegos *Cyprus:* **7** Kyrenia, Larnaca **8** Limassol **9** Famagusta *Czechoslovakia:* **4** Brno, Cheb **5** Decin, Nitra, Opava, Pisek, Plzen, Tabor **6** Kosice **7** Ostrava **10** Bratislava *Delaware:* **5** Lewes **7** Seaford **10** Harrington, Wilmington *Denmark:* **5** Arhus, Skive, Vejle **6** Alborg, Odense, Viborg **13** Frederiksberg *Dominican Republic:* **4** Azua, Bani, Moca **5** Cotui, Nagua, Neiba *Ecuador:* **4** Loja **5** Canar, Daule, Manta, Pinas **9** Guayaquil *Egypt:* **4** Giza, Idfu, Isna, Qena **5** Asyut, Benha, Disuq, Girga, Luxor, Minuf, Tahta, Tanta **6** Helwan **7** El Arish, Zagazig **8** Damanhur, Damietta, El Faiyum, Ismailia, Port Said *Eire:* **4** Athy, Birr, Cobh, Naas, Tuam **5** Ennis, Sligo **6** Carlow, Galway, Tralee **7** Dundalk, Kildare, Wexford, Wicklow **8** Kilkenny, Monaghan **9** Castlebar, Killarney, Tipperary, Waterford **10** Balbriggan *England:* **4** Bath, Eton, Hove, Ryde, York **5** Bacup, Brent, Brigg, Colne, Corby, Cowes, Egham, Eling, Esher, Eston, Goole, Leeds, Leigh, Lewes, Luton, Oadby, Poole, Ryton, Wigan **6** Bexley, Bolton, Dudley, Merton, Oldham, Torbay, Warley, Welwyn **7** Bristol, Bromley, Croydon, Hackney, Ipswich, Malvern, Norwich, Salford, Seaford, Walsall **8** Abingdon, Basildon, Brighton, Coventry, Hastings, Hatfield, Havering, Hertford, Lewisham, Plymouth, Wallsend **9** Aylesbury, Blackpool, Islington, Leicester, Liverpool, Sheffield **10** Birkenhead, Canterbury, Colchester, Manchester, Nottingham, Portsmouth, Sunderland **11** Bournemouth, Northampton, Southampton **12** Peterborough, Stoke-on-Trent, West Bromwich **13** Melton Mowbray, Middlesbrough, Southend-on-Sea, Wolverhampton *Estonia:* **5** Parnu, Tartu *Ethiopia:* **5** Aksum, Harar **6** Asmara **8** Dire Dawa *Finland:* **4** Kemi, Oulu, Pori **5** Espoo, Hango, Kotka, Lahti, Rauma, Turku, Vaasa **7** Tampere *Florida:* **4** Leto, Mims, Ojus, Tice **5** Dania, Davie, Largo, Miami, Ocala, Ocoee, Oneco, Tampa **6** DeLand **7** Hialeah, Key West, Orlando **8** Gulfport, Key Largo, Lakeland, Sarasota **9** Boca Raton, Bradenton, Fort Myers, Hollywood, Kissimmee, Palm Beach,

Pensacola, Vero Beach **10** Clearwater, Cocoa Beach, Fort Pierce, Miami Beach, Titusville **11** Coral Gables, Gainesville, Key Biscayne, St. Augustine, Winter Haven **12** Apalachicola, Daytona Beach, Ft. Lauderdale, Jacksonville, Pompano Beach, St. Petersburg **13** Chattahoochee *France:* **3** Dax, Pau **4** Agde, Agen, Albi, Ales, Auch, Caen, Gien, Laon, Lyon, Metz, Orly, Reze, Sens, Sete, Vire **5** Arles, Arras, Auray, Auton, Avion, Berck, Blois, Bondy, Brest, Creil, Digne, Dijon, Douai, Dreux, Flers, Gagny, Laval, LePuy, Lille, Lunel, Meaux, Melun, Muret, Nimes, Niort, Noyon, Reims, Revin, Rodez, Rouen, Royan, Tours, Tulle, Vichy, Vitre **6** Amiens, Angers, Calais, Cannes, Evreux, LeMans, Nantes, Nevers, Rennes, Thiers, Toulon **7** Ajaccio, Avignon, Bethune, Bourges, LeHavre, Limoges, Lorient, Lourdes, Orleans, Roubaix **8** Bordeaux, Gentilly, Grenoble, Toulouse **9** Cherbourg, Le Creusot, Marseille, Montreuil **10** Draguignan, Strasbourg, Versailles **11** Montpellier **12** Saint Etienne **13** Aix en Provence *Georgia:* **4** Adel, Alma, Arco **5** Jesup, Macon, McRae **7** Calhoun **8** Americus, Marietta, Savannah, Valdosta **9** Brunswick *Georgia, Republic of:* **6** Batumi **7** Kutaisi, Sukhumi, Tbilisi *Germany:* **3** Aue, Hof, Ulm **4** Gera, Goch, Hamm, Jena, Kehl, Kiel, Koln, Marl, Suhl **5** Aalen, Ahlen, Borna, Bruhl, Calbe, Celle, Duren, Emden, Essen, Forst, Fulda, Furth, Gotha, Greiz, Hagen, Halle, Hanau, Herne, Hurth, Kleve, Lemgo, Lobau, Mainz, Neuss, Peine, Pirna, Riesa, Stade, Thale, Trier, Wesel, Zeitz **6** Aachen, Bremen, Coburg, Dachau, Dessau, Erfurt, Kassel, Lubeck, Munich, Rheydt **7** Cologne, Dresden, Koblenz, Krefeld, Leipzig, Munchen, Munster, Potsdam, Rostock, Zwickau **8** Augsburg, Bayreuth, Chemnitz, Cuxhaven, Dortmund, Duisburg, Hannover, Mannheim, Nurnburg, Wurzburg **9** Bielefeld, Brunswick, Darmstadt, Karlsruhe, Magdeburg, Nuremburg, Oldenburg, Osnabruck, Remscheid, Stuttgart, Wiesbaden, Wuppertal **10** Baden Baden, Dusseldorf, Heidelberg, Oberhausen, Regensburg, Salzgitter **11** Brandenburg, Bremerhaven, Saarbrucken **12** Braunschweig **13** Gelsenkirchen *Ghana:* **2** Wa **4** Axim, Keta, Tema **5** Lawra, Yendi **6** Kumasi *Greece:* **3** Kos **4** Arta **5** Argos, Lamia, Nemea, Volos **6** Sparta **7** Corinth **12** Thessaloniki *Guatemala:* **5** Coban *Guinea:* **4** Labe *Hawaii:* **4** Aiea, Hilo, Laie **5** Kapaa, Lihue, Maili **6** Kailua **7** Kaneohe, Wailuku *Honduras:* **5** Danli *Hong Kong:* **7** Kowloon *Hungary:* **3** Ozd **4** Eger, Gyor, Pecs **5** Abony, Bekes **6** Szeged **7** Miskolc **8** Debrecen

Idaho: 4 Buhl 5 Nampa 6 Driggs, Dubois, Weiser 7 Gooding, Orofino, Payette, Rexburg 8 Caldwell 9 Blackfoot, Pocatello, Sandpoint, Twin Falls 11 Coeur d' Alene, Grangeville, Saint Maries, Soda Springs 12 Bonners Ferry, Mountain Home, Saint Anthony 13 American Falls *Illinois:* 4 Dupo, Pana 5 Aledo, Alsip, Alton, Carmi, Elgin, Galva, Lacon, Niles, Olney, Pekin, Plano, Posen 6 Albion, DeKalb, Galena, Hardin, Joliet, Macomb, Moline, Paxton, Peoria, Skokie, Toulon, Urbana 7 Chicago, Decatur, Glencoe, Oak Lawn, Oquawka, Tuscola, Watseka, Wheaton 8 Carthage, Evanston, Golconda, Hennepin, Kankakee, La Grange, Monmouth, Rockford, Vandalia, Waukegan 9 Belvidere, Effingham, Galesburg, Park Ridge, Rushville, Yorkville 10 Belleville, Carbondale, Carrollton, Des Plaines, Metropolis, Northbrook, Rock Island 11 Carlinville, Jerseyville, Lindenhurst, McLeansboro, Murphysboro, Shawneetown, Taylorville 12 Edwardsville, Highland Park, Mount Carroll 13 Lawrenceville, Mount Sterling, Pinckneyville *India:* 3 Mau 4 Agra, Ahwa, Bhuj, Durg, Gaya, Kota, Mhow, Puri, Rewa, Tonk, Ziro 5 Adoni, Aimer, Akola, Alwar, Arcot, Arrah, Banda, Barsi, Bidar, Bihar, Churu, Damoh, Delhi, Dewas, Eluru, Gonda, Jalna, Jammu, Karur, Miraj, Morvi, Nasik, Patan, Patna, Poona, Sagar, Satna, Sikar, Simla, Surat, Thana 6 Baroda, Bhopal, Bombay, Guntur, Howrah, Jaipur, Jhansi, Kanpur, Meerut, Mysore, Nagpur, Raipur, Rajkot, Ranchi, Ujjain 7 Aligarh, Asansol, Belgaum, Bikaner, Burdwan, Cuttack, Gauhati, Gwalior, Jodhpur, Kurnool, Lucknow, Madurai, Mathura, Nellore, Patiala, Vellore 8 Alleppey, Amravati, Amritsar, Bareilly, Bhatpara, Calcutta, Dehra Dun, Jabalpur, Jamnagar, Kakinada, Kolhapur, Ludhiana, Malegaon, Sholapur, Srinagar, Varanasi 9 Ahmadabad, Allahabad, Bangalore, Bhagalpur, Bhavnagar, Darbhanga, Gorakhpur, Hyderabad, Jullundur, Kamarhati, Mangalore, Moradabad, Nagercoil, Thanjavur, Tuticorin 10 Ahmadnagar, Chandigarh, Coimbatore, Jamshedpur, Saharanpur, Trivandrum, Ulhashagar, Vijayawada 11 Garden Reach, Muzaffarpur, Rajahmundry 12 Hubli Dharwar, Secunderabad, Shahjahanpur 13 Machilipatnam *Indiana:* 5 Berne, Paoli, Vevay 6 Delphi, Kokomo, Marlon, Muncie, Tipton 7 Bedford, Corydon, Elkhart, La Porte, Winamac 8 Bluffton, Kentland 9 Boonville, Cannelton, Fort Wayne, New Albany, Rushville, South Bend, Vincennes 10 Brookville, Brownstown, Crown Point, Evansville, Logansport, Scottsburg, Terre Haute, Valparaiso 11 Greencastle, Noblesville, Shelbyville 12 Connersville, Lawrenceburg, Martinsville *Indonesia:* 4 Pati 5 Bogor, Garut, Kudus, Medan, Tegal, Turen 6 Batang, Kediri, Madiun, Malang, Manado, Padang 7 Bandung 8 Semarang, Surabaja, Tjirebon 9 Palembang, Pontianak, Surakarta 10 Pekalongan 11 Tasikmalaja 12 Bandjarmasin *Iowa:* 4 Adel, Tama 5 Albia, Clive, Onawa, Pella 6 Algona, Cresco, Eldora, Harlan, Keokuk, Le Mars, Red Oak, Sibley, Waukon 7 Allison, Anamosa, Carroll, Clinton, Corydon, Creston, Decorah, Denison, Dubuque, Elkader, Marengo, Osceola, Ottumwa, Wapello, Waverly 8 Camanche, Chariton, Clarinda, Ida Grove, Mount Ayr, Primghar 9 Davenport, Fort Dodge, Indianola, Keosauqua, Maquoketa, Muscatine, Oskaloosa, Storm Lake, West Union, Winterset 10 Emmetsburg, New Hampton, Rock Rapids, Spirit Lake 11 Cedar Rapids, Estherville, Fort Madison 12 Grundy Center 13 Council Bluffs, Guthrie Center *Iran:* 3 Qum 4 Amul, Arak, Khoi, Sari, Yazd, Yezd 5 Ahwaz, Babol, Rasht 6 Abadan, Meshed, Shiraz, Tabriz 7 Esfahan, Hamadan, Isfahan, Mashhad *Iraq:* 3 Ana, Kut 5 Amara, Basra, Erbil, Hilla, Mosul, Rutba 6 Kirkuk 7 An Najaf *Ireland:* (see *Eire,* above) *Israel:* 5 Afula, Haifa, Holon 8 Nazareth, Ramat Gan 9 Beersheba *Italy:* 4 Acri, Alba, Asti, Bari, Enna, Este, Fano, Gela, Iesi, Lodi, Lugo, Pisa 5 Adria, Agira, Anzio, Aosta, Arola, Cantu, Capua, Carpi, Crema, Cuneo, Eboli, Fermo, Fondi, Forli, Gaeta, Imola, Ivrea, Lecce, Lecco, Lucca, Massa, Melfi, Menfi, Monza, Padua, Parma, Prato, Turin 6 Assisi, Foggia, Modena, Naples, Rimini, Venice, Verona 7 Bergamo, Bolzano, Brescia, Catania, Leghorn, Palermo, Pescara, Salerno, Taranto, Trieste 8 Cagliari, La Spezia, Piacenza *Ivory Coast:* 6 Bouake *Jamaica:* 6 May Pen 10 Montego Bay *Japan:* 3 Ina, Ise, Ito, Ota, Tsu, Ube, Uji, Yao 4 Ageo, Anan, Gifu, Hagi, Himi, Hofu, Iida, Joyo, Kaga, Kobe, Kofu, Kure, Miki, Mito, Naha, Nara, Noda, Oita, Otsu, Saga, Saku, Soka, Tosu, Ueda, Yono 5 Akita, Atami, Beppu, Chiba, Chofu, Daito, Fukui, Hanno, Hyuga, Imari, Itami, Iwaki, Iwata, Izumi, Izumo, Kiryu, Kochi, Kyoto, Minoo, Odate, Ogaki, Okawa, Okaya, Omiya, Omuta, Osaka, Otaru, Oyama, Sabae, Saiki, Sanjo, Suita, Tenri, Urawa, Yaizu, Zushi 6 Akashi, Aomori, Himeji, Kadoma, Kurume, Matsue, Mitaka, Nagano, Nagoya, Numazu, Sasebo, Suzuka, Toyama, Yonago 7 Fukuoka, Hitachi, Ibaraki, Imabari, Iwakuni, Kawagoe, Kodaira, Kushiro, Machida, Matsudo, Morioka, Muroran, Niigata, Niihama, Nobeoka, Obihiro, Odawara, Okayama, Okazaki, Sapporo, Shimizu, Takaoka, Tottori **8** Ashikaga, Fujisawa, Fukuyama, Hachioji, Hakodate, Hirakata, Hirosaki, Ichihara, Ichikawa, Kakogawa, Kamakura, Kanazawa, Kawasaki, Koriyama, Kumagaya, Kumamoto, Maebashi, Miyazaki, Nagasaki, Neyagawa, Onomichi, Shizuoka, Takasaki, Toyonaka, Wakayama, Yamagata, Yokohama, Yokosuka **9** Amagasaki, Asahikawa, Chigasaki, Fukushima, Funabashi, Hachinohe, Hamamatsu, Hiratsuka, Hiroshima, Kagoshima, Kawaguchi, Kishiwada, Koshigaya, Kurashiki, Matsubara, Matsumoto, Matsusaka, Matsuyama, Moriguchi, Musashino, Tachikawa, Takamatsu, Takatsuki, Tokushima, Tomakomai, Toyohashi, Yamaguchi, Yokkaichi **10** Ichinomiya, Ishinomaki, Kitakyushu, Miyakonojo, Takarazuka, Utsunomiya, Yatsushiro **11** Nishinomiya, Shimonoseki **12** Higashiosaka **13** Aizuwakamatsu *Jordan:* **5** Irbid **6** Nablus *Kansas:* **4** Gove, Iola **5** Colby, Hoxie, Lakin, Leoti, Paola, Pratt **6** Atwood, Beloit, Girard, Holton, Larned, Olathe, Salina **7** Abilene, Dighton, Emporia, Garnett, Hugoton, Jetmore, Kinsley, Mankato, Oberlin, Osborne, Wichita **8** Cimarron, Goodland, La Crosse, Sublette, Wakeeney **9** Coldwater, Fort Scott, Great Bend, Oskaloosa **10** Clay Center, Hutchinson **11** Leavenworth, Smith Center, Yates Center **12** Council Grove, Overland Park **13** Medicine Lodge, Sharon Springs *Kazakhstan:* **6** Guryev, Uralsk **8** Balkhash, Chimkent, Dzhambul, Kyzl Orda, Pavlodar **9** Karaganda **10** Aktyubinsk **11** Tselinograd **13** Petropavlovsk, Semipalatinsk *Kentucky:* **4** Inez **5** Cadiz, Hyden, McKee **6** Elkton, Harlan **7** Ashland, Campton, Greenup, Hickman, Hindman, Owenton, Paducah, Stanton **8** Bardwell, Carlisle, Fort Knox, La Grange, Mayfield **9** Bardstown, Covington, Cynthiana, Eddyville, Lexington, Maysville, Owensboro, Pikeville, Pineville, Smithland, Southgate, Vanceburg, Wickliffe **10** Booneville, Frenchburg, Hawesville, Louisville, Whitesburg **11** Beattyville, Brooksville, Burkesville, Hardinsburg, Harrodsburg, Hodgenville, Leitchfield, Morganfield, Mount Olivet, Owingsville, Paintsville, Scottsville, West Liberty **12** Barbourville, Bowling Green, Catlettsburg, Flemingsburg, Hopkinsville, Madisonville, Munfordville, Prestonsburg, Russellville, Salyersville, Taylorsville **13** Elizabethtown, Mount Sterling, Nicholasville, Tompkinsville *Kenya:* **4** Embu **5** Nyeri **6** Kisumu, Nakuru **7** Mombasa *Kirghizia:* **3** Osh **5** Naryn *Laos:* **5** Pakse **11** Savannakhet **12** Luang Prabang *Latvia:* **9** Ventspils **10** Daugavpils *Lebanon:* **5** Sidon, Zahle *Libya:* **4** Homs **5** Derna, Zawia **6** Tobruk **8** Benghazi *Lith-*

uania: **6** Kaunas **8** Klaipeda *Louisiana:* **4** Jena **5** Amite, Arabi, Houma, Mamou, Norco, Rayne **6** Colfax, Edgard, Gretna, Minden, Ruston **7** Arcadia, Bastrop, Marrero, Oberlin **8** Bogalusa, De Ridder, Metairie, New Roads, Oak Grove, Westwego **9** Abbeville, Chalmette, Coushatta, Hahnville, Leesville, New Iberia, Opelousas, Port Allen, Thibodaux, Winnfield, Winnsboro **10** Marksville, New Orleans, Plaquemine, Shreveport **11** Farmerville, Franklinton, Lake Charles, Ponchatoula, Ville Platte **12** Natchitoches **13** Napoleonville *Macedonia:* **4** Stip **5** Debar, Ohrid **6** Skopje *Madagascar:* **8** Tamatave **9** Antsirane, Mahajanga **11** Antsiranana **12** Fianarantsoa *Maine:* **4** Milo, Saco **5** Eliot, Orono **6** Auburn, Bangor, Gorham **7** Berwick, Houlton, Kittery, Machias, Rumford **8** Lewiston, Portland, Rockland **9** Bar Harbor, Biddeford, Brunswick, Ellsworth, Kennebunk, Skowhegan, Wiscasset **10** South Paris **11** Millinocket, Presque Isle **13** South Portland *Malawi:* **5** Zomba **8** Blantyre *Malaysia:* **4** Ipoh **5** Gemas, Klang **6** Kelang, Penang, Pinang **11** Johore Bahru *Mali:* **5** Kayes, Mopti, Segou **7** Sikasso *Maryland:* **5** Bowie **6** Denton, Elkton, Towson **8** Bethesda, Landover, Snow Hill **9** Baltimore, Rockville **10** Beltsville, Hagerstown **11** Chestertown, College Park, Leonardtown **12** Havre de Grace, Silver Spring **13** Upper Marlboro *Massachusetts:* **4** Ayer **5** Acton, Athol, Lenox, Salem **6** Agawam, Boston, Dedham, Hadley, Ludlow, Malden, Monson, Natick, Saugus, Woburn **7** Danvers, Duxbury, Holyoke, Hyannis, Medford, Methuen, Needham, Raynham, Seekonk, Swansea, Taunton, Walpole, Waltham, Wareham **8** Brockton, Chicopee, Falmouth, Plymouth, Rockport, Scituate, Somerset, Uxbridge, Yarmouth **9** Attleboro, Braintree, Brookline, Deerfield, Edgartown, Fall River, Fitchburg, Haverhill, Lexington, Southwick, Tewksbury, Westfield, Wilbraham, Worcester **10** Barnstable, Framingham, Gloucester, Greenfield, Leominster, Longmeadow, New Bedford, North Adams, Swampscott, Winchendon **11** Belchertown, Easthampton, Northampton, South Hadley, Springfield **12** Mattapoisett, Provincetown, Turners Falls, West Yarmouth, Williamstown *Mauritania:* **4** Atar **5** Kaedi **6** Dakhla *Mexico:* **4** Leon **5** Ameca, Choix, Tepic **6** Celaya, Colima, Merida, Oaxaca, Puebla, Toluca **7** Durango, Guasave, Morelia, Reynosa, Tampico, Tijuana, Tlalpan, Torreon, Uruapan **8** Chetumal, Coyoacan, Culiacan, Ensenada, Mazatlan, Saltillo, Tuxtepec **9** Fresnillo, Ixtacalco, Monterrey, Queretaro, Salamanca, Tapachula **10** Cuernavaca, Hermosillo, Ixtapalapa, Xochimilco **11** Guadalajara, Nueva Laredo **12** Azcapotzalco **13** Ciudad Obregon, Coatzacoalcos, San Luis Potosi, Veracruz Llave **Michigan:** **3** Mio **4** Alma, Caro, Holt, Novi **5** Ionia, L'Anse, Niles **6** Adrian, Alpena, Bad Axe, Lapeer, Otsego, Paw Paw **7** Allegan, Corunna, Detroit, Gladwin, Livonia, Midland, Saginaw **8** Ann Arbor, Bessemer, Dearborn, Escabana, Grayling, Hastings, Houghton, Kalkaska, Manistee, Munising, Muskegon, Newberry, Petoskey, Sandusky **9** Big Rapids, Cheboygan, Coldwater, Hillsdale, Kalamazoo, Ludington, Menominee, Ontonagon, Port Huron, Roscommon, Ypsilanti **10** Cassopolis, Charlevoix, Eagle River, Grand Haven, Manistique, West Branch, White Cloud **11** Battle Creek, East Lansing, Grand Rapids, Harrisville, Saint Ignace **12** Crystal Falls, Highland Park, Iron Mountain, Mount Clemens **13** Mount Pleasant **Minnesota:** **3** Ely **4** Mora **5** Anoka, Edina, Osseo **6** Aitkin, Bagley, Benson, Chaska, Duluth, Milaca, New Ulm, Wadena, Waseca, Windom, Winona **7** Bemidji, Glencoe, Hallock, Hibbing, Luverne, Mankato, Red Wing, Slayton, Wabasha, Wheaton **8** Baudette, Brainerd, Elk River, Le Center, Mahnomen, Moorhead, Owatonna, Shakopee **9** Albert Lea, Blue Earth, Caledonia, Crookston, Elbow Lake, Fairbault, Pipestone, Saint Paul, Silver Bay **10** Ortonville, Park Rapids, Saint Cloud, Saint James, Saint Peter, Stillwater, Two Harbors **11** Bloomington, Fergus Falls, Grand Marais, Little Falls, Long Prairie, Mantorville, Minneapolis, Worthington **12** Breckenridge, Detroit Lakes, Granite Falls, Red Lake Falls, Redwood Falls **Mississippi:** **4** Iuka **5** Amory **6** Biloxi, Leland, McComb, Purvis, Sardis, Sumner, Tunica, Tupelo, Vaiden, Winona **7** Belzoni, Brandon, Fayette, Okolona, Quitman, Wiggins **8** Ackerman, Gulfport, Hernando, Lucedale, Meridian, Paulding, Pontotoc, Rosedale, Walthall **9** Greenwood, Indianola, Meadville, New Albany, Pittsboro, Senatobia, Vicksburg, Woodville **10** Batesville, Bay Springs, Booneville, Brookhaven, Clarksdale, Ellisville, Hazlehurst, New Auguste, Pascagoula, Port Gibson, Starkville, Waynesboro **11** Coffeeville, Hattiesburg, Leakesville, Mayersville, Poplarville, Rolling Fork, Water Valley **12** Holly Springs **13** Bay Saint Louis **Missouri:** **3** Ava **4** Linn **5** Eldon, Hayti, Ladue, Rolla **6** Galena, Kahoka, Neosho, Potosi **7** Hermann, Ironton, Kennett, Linneus, Osceola, Palmyra, Sedalia **8** Doniphan, Gallatin, Hannibal **9** Boonville, Camdenton, Cassville, Hartville, Hillsboro, Maryville, Maysville, New Madrid, Pineville, Tuscum-

bia, Warrenton **10** Kirksville, Marble Hill, Marshfield, Perryville, Saint Louis, Steelville, Unionville, West Plains **11** Keytesville, Poplar Bluff, Saint Joseph, Warrensburg **12** Saint Charles **13** Harrisonville **Mongolia:** **5** Kobdo **6** Darhan **10** Choybalsan **Montana:** **5** Havre, Libby **6** Hardin, Hysham, Polson, Scobey, Wibaux **7** Bozeman, Broadus, Choteau, Cut Bank, Ekalaka, Ryegate, Winnett **8** Billings, Glendive, Missoula, Red Lodge **9** Big Timber, Deer Lodge, Harlowton, Kalispell, Wolf Point **10** Fort Benton, Great Falls, Plentywood **13** Thompson Falls **Montenegro:** **8** Titograd **Morocco:** **4** Safi, Taza **5** Nador, Oujda **6** Agadir, Meknes **7** Kenitra **9** Marrakesh **10** Casablanca **Mozambique:** **5** Beira **7** Nampula **9** Quelimane, Quilimane **Myanmar:** **3** Pyu **4** Paan **5** Akyab, Bhamo, Chauk, Katha, Magwe, Minbu, Mogok, Tavoy **7** Bassein **8** Mandalay **Namibia:** **5** Outjo **6** Tsumeb **12** Keetmanshoop **Nebraska:** **3** Ord **5** Cozad, Omaha, Ponca, Tryon, Wahoo **6** Elwood, Gering, McCook, Minden, Muilen, Neligh, Pender, Sidney, Wilber **7** Burwell, Chadron, Fremont, Kearney, Kimball, Osceola, Tekamah **8** Beatrice, Chappell, Fairbury, Hastings, Holdrege, Ogallala, Red Cloud, Schuyler, Tecumseh, Thedford **9** Ainsworth, Benkelman, Broken Bow, Fullerton, Papillion **10** Clay Center, Hartington, Springview, Stockville **11** Grand Island, Hayes Center, North Platte, Plattsmouth **Netherlands:** **3** Ede, Epe, Oss **4** Echt, Tiel, Uden **5** Aalst, Assen, Delft, Emmen, Soest, Vaals, Venlo, Vught, Weert, Weesp, Zeist **6** Arnhem **7** Haarlem, Tilburg, Utrecht **8** Enschede, Nijmegen **9** Apeldoorn, Eindhoven, Groningen, Rotterdam, Zandvoort **Nevada:** **3** Ely **4** Elko, Reno **6** Fallon, Minden, Pioche **7** Tonopah **8** Las Vegas, Lovelock **9** Goldfield, Yerington **10** Winnemucca **New Brunswick:** **5** Minto **9** Dalhousie **10** Edmundston, Richibucto **12** Hopewell Cape, Perth Andover, Saint Andrews **Newfoundland:** **5** Burin **6** Wabana **New Hampshire:** **5** Derry, Keene **6** Exeter, Gorham, Nashua **7** Hanover, Laconia, Ossipee **8** Hinsdale, Seabrook **9** Littleton, Merrimack **10** Portsmouth, Woodsville **New Jersey:** **4** Atco, Lodi **6** Camden, Newark, Nutley, Rahway **7** Bayonne, Clifton, Hoboken, Hohokus, Paramus, Passaic, Raritan, Teaneck **8** Freehold, Metuchen, Paterson, Vauxhall, Woodbury **9** Belvidere, Bridgeton, Glassboro, Lakehurst, Maplewood, Menlo Park, Montclair, Riverside, Toms River **10** Asbury Park, Bloomfield, Cherry Hill, East Orange, Flemington, Hackensack, Mount Holly, Perth Amboy, Piscataway, Plainfield, Somerville,

West Orange **11** Mays Landing, South Orange **13** Palisades Park *New Mexico:* **4** Mora, Taos **5** Belen, Hobbs, Raton **6** Clovis, Deming, Grants **7** Roswell, Socorro **8** Estancia, Los Lunas, Mosquero, Portales **9** Carrizozo, Las Cruces, Lordsburg, Los Alamos, Lovington, Santa Rosa, Tucumcari **10** Alamogordo, Bernalillo, Fort Sumner **11** Albuquerque *New York:* **4** Elma, Ovid **5** Depew, Ilion, Islip, Le Roy, Nyack, Olean, Owego, Utica **6** Attica, Cohoes, Delmar, Elmira, Ithaca, Oneida **7** Batavia, Corning, Geneseo, Katonah, Mineola, Penn Yan, Suffern, Yonkers **8** Bay Shore, Cortland, Herkimer, Hyde Park, Lockport, Mayville, Ossining, Syracuse, Valhalla **9** Greenport, Hempstead, Patchogue, Riverhead, Rochester, Scarsdale, Schoharie **10** Binghamton, Glens Falls, Haverstraw, Huntington, Lackawanna, Lake George, Lake Placid, Mamaroneck, Massapequa, Mount Kisco, Rensselaer, Wampsville, Watervliet **11** Ballston Spa, Canajoharie, Canandaigua, Cheektowaga, Cooperstown, Farmingdale, Hudson Falls, Irondequoit, Plattsburgh, Port Chester, Saint George, Schenectady, Southampton, Watkins Glen, White Plains **12** Lake Pleasant, Little Valley, Poughkeepsie **13** Mechanicville, Port Jefferson *New Zealand:* **4** Hutt, Tawa **5** Levin, Taupo, Waihi **7** Dunedin **8** Auckland **12** Christchurch *Nicaragua:* **4** Leon **5** Boaco, Rivas *Nigeria:* **3** Aba, Ado, Ede, Ife, Iwo, Jos, Owo, Oyo **4** Kano, Ondo **5** Akure, Enugu, Gusau, Okene, Zaria **6** Ibadan, Ilesha, Ilorin, Kaduna, Mushin, Sokoto **7** Onitsha, Oshogbo **8** Abeokuta **9** Maiduguri, Ogbomosho **12** Port Harcourt *North Carolina:* **4** Dunn **5** Ayden, Elkin, Erwin, Oteen, Sylva **6** Burgaw, Dobson, Durham, Lenoir, Manteo, Marlon, Shelby, Sparta, Winton **7** Bayboro, Brevard, Edenton, Kinston, New Bern, Newland, Raeford, Roxboro, Sanford, Tarboro **8** Asheboro, Beaufort, Gastonia, Snow Hill **9** Albemarle, Asheville, Charlotte, Currituck, High Point, Louisburg, Lumberton, Morganton, Pittsboro, Southport, Wadesboro, Warrenton, Wentworth **10** Burnsville, Chapel Hill, Gatesville, Greensboro, Hayseville, Laurinburg, Lillington, Lincolnton, Mocksville, Reidsville, Rockingham, Smithfield, Whiteville, Wilkesboro **11** Bakersville, Kenansville, Statesville, Swanquarter, Waynesville, Williamston, Yadkinville, Yanceyville **12** Fayetteville, Hillsborough, Murfreesboro, Robbinsville, Taylorsville, Winston Salem **13** Rutherfordton *North Dakota:* **4** Mott **5** Cando, Fargo, Minot, Rolla **6** Amidon, Ashley, Bowman, Formon, Lakota, Linton, Medora, Mohall **7** La Moure, Langdon

8 Bowbells, McClusky, Wahpeton, Washburn **9** Bottineau, Dickinson, Ellendale, Fessenden, Fort Yates, Hettinger, Williston **10** Carrington, Devils Lake, Grand Forks **11** Minnewaukan, New Rockford *Northern Ireland:* **5** Derry, Larne, Newry, Omagh **6** Antrim, Armagh **8** Limavady **9** Ballymena, Banbridge, Coleraine, Craigavon, Dungannon, Newcastle **10** Ballymoney **11** Ballycastle, Downpatrick, Enniskillen, Londonderry, Magherafelt **13** Carrickfergus *North Korea:* **5** Haeju, Nampo **6** Wonsan **7** Hamhung, Kaesong, Sinuiju **8** Ch'ongjin, Kimchaek **9** P'yongyang *Norway:* **4** Bodo **5** Hamar, Skien **6** Tromso **9** Stavanger, Trondheim *Nova Scotia:* **5** Digby **6** Pictou **7** Arichat, Baddeck **8** Port Hood **9** Kentville, Lunenburg, Shelburne, Westville **10** Antigonish **11** Guysborough *Ohio:* **4** Kent **5** Akron, Berea, Bryan, Cadiz, Carey, Eaton, Heath, Logan, Niles, Parma, Piqua, Solon, Xenia **6** Canton, Celina, Dayton, Elyria, Euclid, Kenton, Lorain, Marion, Medina, Sidney, Tiffin, Toledo **7** Ashland, Batavia, Bucyrus, Chardon, Findlay, Ironton, Oakwood, Pomeroy, Ravenna, Van Wert, Wauseon, Waverly, Wooster **8** Caldwell, Conneaut, Marietta, Paulding, Sandusky **9** Ashtabula, Cleveland, Coshocton, Mansfield, West Union **10** Cincinnati, Gallipolis, Wapakoneta, Woodsfield, Zanesville **11** Chillicothe, Circleville, Millersburg, Mount Gilead, Painesville, Port Clinton **12** New Lexington, Steubenville **13** Bellefontaine, Cuyahoga Falls, Upper Sandusky *Oklahoma:* **3** Ada **4** Alva, Enid **5** Altus, Atoka, Sayre, Tulsa **6** Arnett, Durant, El Reno, Guymon, Hollis, Idabel, Lawton, Madill, Mangum, Nowata, Okemah, Poteau, Taloga, Vinita, Wewoka **7** Antlers, Ardmore, Cordell, Eufaula, Newkirk, Purcell, Sapulpa, Stigler, Watonga, Waurika **8** Anadarko, Coalgate, Okmulgee, Pawhuska, Sallisaw, Stilwell **9** Chickasha, Claremore, Frederick, McAlester, Tahlequah, Wilburton **10** New Cordell, Stillwater, Tishomingo **11** Holdenville, Pauls Valley **12** Bartlesville *Oman:* **3** Sur **6** Matrah **7** Salalah *Ontario:* **4** Ajax, Wawa, York **6** Barrie, Guelph, Kenora, Minden, Picton, Sarnia, Simcoe **7** Cobourg, Gore Bay, Napanee, Sudbury, Windsor **8** Brampton, Cochrane, Goderich, North Bay, Pembroke, Prescott **9** Brantford, Kitchener, L'Original, Newmarket, Owen Sound, Walkerton **10** Belleville, Brockville, Haileybury, Parry Sound, Thunder Bay **11** Bracebridge, Fort Frances, Mississauga, Orangeville **12** Peterborough, St. Catharines *Oregon:* **4** Moro **5** Canby, Nyssa **6** Condon, Eugene **7** Heppner **8** Coquille, La Grande, Lakeview, Portland, Roseburg

9 Clackamas, Corvallis, Gold Beach, Hood River, Pendleton, The Dalles, Tillamook 10 Grants Pass, Prineville 11 McMinnville 12 Klamath Falls *Pakistan:* 5 Bannu, Bhera, Kasur, Kohat 6 Gujrat, Lahore, Mardan, Multan, Quetta, Sukkur 7 Karachi, Sialkot 8 Lyallpur, Peshawar, Sargodha 9 Hyderabad 10 Bahawalpur, Gujranwala, Rawalpindi *Paraguay:* 3 Ita 4 Yuty 5 Belen, Luque, Pilar *Pennsylvania:* 4 York 5 Avoca, Darby, Muncy, Paoli 6 Easton 7 Altoona, Bedford, Clarion, Hanover, Hershey, Laporte, Latrobe, Reading, Ridgway, Sunbury 8 Carlisle, Edinboro, Hazleton, Montrose, Scranton, Somerset, Tionesta 9 Allentown, Ebensburg, Honesdale, Jim Thorpe, Lancaster, Lewisburg, Lock Haven, Meadville, New Castle, Smethport, Wellsboro 10 Bellefonte, Bloomsburg, Brookville, Carbondale, Clearfield, Gettysburg, Greensburg, Huntingdon, Kittanning, McKeesport, Middleburg, Pittsburgh, Pottsville, Waynesburg 11 Coudersport, Stroudsburg, Tunkhannock, Valley Forge, West Chester, Wilkes Barre 12 Chambersburg, Conshohocken, Philadelphia, State College, Williamsport 13 Hollidaysburg, Kennett Square, New Bloomfield *Peru:* 3 Ica, Ilo 5 Ancon, Cuzco, Jauja, Junin, Lamas, Pisco, Piura, Tacna 6 Callao 8 Arequipa, Chiclayo, Trujillo *Philippines:* 3 Iba 4 Bago, Bais, Boac, Bogo, Cebu, Daet, Jolo, Lipa, Mati 5 Basco, Bulan, Cadiz, Danao, Davao, Digos, Gapan, Gubat, Iriga, Laoag, Ormoc, Silay, Tagum, Vigan 6 Butuan, Iloilo 7 Angeles, Bacolod, Basilan 8 Batangas, Calbayog 9 Zamboanga 13 General Santos *Poland:* 4 Lodz, Nysa, Pila, Zary 5 Brzeg, Bytom, Bytow, Chelm, Gubin, Ilawa, Jaslo, Konin, Kutno, Lomza, Luban, Lubin, Mlawa, Olawa, Opole, Plock, Radom, Rumia, Sanok, Sopot, Tczew, Torun, Tychy, Ursus, Zagan 6 Gdansk, Gdynia, Kielce, Lublin, Poznan, Zabrze 7 Chorzow, Gliwice, Wroclaw 8 Katowice, Szczecin 9 Bialystok, Bydgoszcz, Sosnowiec, Walbrzych 10 Ruda Slaska 11 Czestochowa 12 Bielsko Biala *Portugal:* 4 Faro 5 Braga, Evora 6 Oporto *Prince Edward Island:* 10 Summerside *Puerto Rico:* 5 Ponce 7 Bayamon *Quebec:* 4 Alma 5 Amqui, Anjou, Granb, Laval, Levis, Magog, Percé, Rouyn 6 Ham Sud, Matane, Val d'Or 7 Bedford, Lachute 8 Cap Santé, Joliette, LacBrome, Maniwaki, Montreal, Rimouski, Roberval, Sept Iles, Waterloo 9 Becancour, Cookshire, Iberville, Inverness, La Malbaie, La Prairie, Longueuil, Montmagny, Saint Jean, Tadoussac, Vaudreuil, Vercheres 10 Ayers Cliff, Baie Comeau, Chicoutimi, Huntingdon, Marieville, St. Henedine, St. Julienne, Ville Marie,

Yamachiche 11 Beauharnois, Lac Megantic, L'Assomption, Louiseville, Mont Laurier, Napierville, New Carlisle, Sainte Croix, Saint Pascal 12 Loretteville, Saint Liboire, Saint Raphael 13 Baie Saint Paul, Berthierville, Chateau Richer, Coteau Landing, Drummondville, Papineauville, Riviere du Loup, Sainte Martine, Thetford Mines, Trois Rivieres *Rhode Island:* 7 Newport, Rumford, Warwick 8 Apponaug, Coventry, Cranston, Tiverton, Westerly 9 Hopkinton, Pawtucket 10 Woonsocket 11 West Warwick 12 Narragansett, West Kingston 13 East Greenwich *Romania:* 3 Dej 4 Aiud, Arad, Cluj, Deva, Husi, Iasi 5 Anina, Bacau, Buzau, Carei, Lugoj, Sibiu, Turda 6 Braila, Brasov, Galati, Oradea 7 Craiova 8 Ploiesti 9 Constanta, Timisoara *Russia:* 3 Kem, Ufa 4 Inta, Luga, Okha, Omsk, Orel, Orsk, Perm, Tula, Tura, Zima 5 Aldan, Artem, Chita, Ishim, Kansk, Lysva, Onega, Penza, Pskov, Rzhev, Salsk, Serov, Sochi, Sokol, Tomsk, Tulun, Volsk, Yurga 6 Bratsk, Kaluga, Kovrov, Kurgan, Rostov, Ryazan, Samara, Syzran, Tambov, Tyumen, Vyborg, Yelets 7 Angarsk, Armavir, Barnaul, Bryansk, Irkutsk, Ivanovo, Izhevsk, Kalinin, Kolomna, Lipetsk, Magadán, Nalchik, Norilsk, Rybinsk, Saransk, Saratov, Shakhty, Ulan Ude, Vologda, Yakutsk, Zhdanov 8 Belgorod, Kemerovo, Kostroma, Murmansk, Nakhodka 7 Novorod 8 Orenburg, Smolensk, Taganrog, Vladimir, Voronezh 9 Archangel, Astrakhan, Berezniki, Kiselevsk, Krasnodar, Rubtsovsk, Serpukhov, Stavropol, Syktyvkar, Ulyanovsk, Volgograd, Yaroslavl 10 Cheboksary, Dzerzhinsk, Khabarovsk, Yoshkar Ola 11 Chelyabinsk, Cheremkhovo, Cherepovets, Krasnoyarsk, Makhachkala, Novosibirsk, Prokopyevsk, Sterlitamak, Verkhoyansk, Vladikavkaz, Vladivostok 12 Magnitogorsk, Novokuznetsk, Novomoskovsk, Severodvinsk 13 Yekaterinburg *Saskatchewan:* 8 Moose Jaw 10 Assiniboia *Saudi Arabia:* 4 Jauf, Taif 5 Jidda 6 Medina *Scotland:* 3 Ayr 4 Alva, Caol, Dyce, Oban 5 Alloa, Annan, Beith, Cowie, Cupar, Dalry, Ellon, Kelso, Kelty, Largs, Leven, Nairn, Patna, Troon 6 Dundee 7 Glasgow 8 Aberdeen 9 Inverness *Senegal:* 5 Thies 6 Kaolak 7 Kaolack *Serbia:* 3 Bor, Nis, Pec 4 Ruma 5 Becej, Cacak, Pirot, Sabac, Senta, Vrbas, Vrsac 7 Novi Sad 8 Subotica *Slovenia:* 4 Bled 5 Celje, Koper, Kranj 9 Ljubljana *Somalia:* 3 Eil 5 Afgoi, Alula, Brava, Burao, Obbia 7 Berbera, Kismayu *South Africa:* 5 Brits, Ceres, De Aar, Nigel, Paarl 6 Benoni, Durban 7 Springs 8 Boksburg, Mafeking 9 Germiston, Kimberley, Uitenhage 10 East London

11 Krugersdorp, Vereeniging 12 Johannesburg 13 Port Elizabeth *South Carolina:* 5 Aiken, Cayce, Saxon 6 Saluda, Sumter 7 Bamberg, Gaffney, Laurens, Manning, Pickens 8 Barnwell, Beaufort, Newberry, Rock Hill, Walhalla 9 Abbeville, Allendale, Edgefield, Greenwood, Kingstree, McCormick, Ridgeland, Winnsboro 10 Charleston, Darlington, Greenville, Orangeburg, Walterboro 11 Bishopville, Myrtle Beach, Spartanburg 12 Moncks Corner 13 Bennettsville, Saint Matthews *South Dakota:* 5 Burke, Hayti, Leola, Murdo, Onida, Selby 6 Armour, De Smet, Dupree, Kadoka, Olivet 7 Milbank, Sturgis, Tyndall, Yankton 8 Deadwood, Elk Point, Faulkton, Highmore, Kennebec, Redfield 9 Brookings, Clear Lake, Flandreau, Lake Andes 10 Fort Pierre, Gannvalley, Plankinton, Sioux Falls, Timber Lake 12 Belle Fourche *South Korea:* 3 Iri 4 Yosu 5 Cheju, Masan, Mokpo, Pusan, Suwon, Taegu, Ulson, Wonju 6 Chinju, Chonju, Inchon, Kunsan, Taejon 7 Kwangju *Spain:* 4 Adra, Baza, Elda, Jaca, Jaen, Leon, Loja, Lugo, Olot, Reus, Vich, Vigo 5 Albox, Alcoy, Alora, Baena, Cadiz, Ceuta, Cieza, Ecija, Eibar, Elche, Gijon, Ibiza, Jodar, Lorca, Mahon, Oliva, Osuna, Palma, Ronda, Soria, Ubeda 6 Bilboa, Burgos, Cuenca, Malaga, Murcia, Oviedo 7 Almaden, Almeria, Cordoba, Durango, Granada, Seville, Tarrasa, Vitoria 8 Alicante, La Coruna, Pamplona, Sabadell, Valencia 9 Barcelona, Salamanca, Santander, Saragossa 10 Hospitalet, Valladolid 12 San Sebastion *Sri Lanka:* 5 Galle, Kandy 6 Jaffna 10 Batticaloa *Sudan:* 4 Juba 5 Kodok, Kosti 8 Omdurman *Sweden:* 4 Lund, Umea 5 Boden, Boras, Falun, Gavle, Lulea, Malmo, Nacka, Pitea, Solno, Vaxjo, Visby, Ystad 7 Uppsala 8 Goteborg 9 Jonkoping *Switzerland:* 3 Zug 4 Biel, Chur, Thun 5 Aarau, Arbon, Baden, Basel, Koniz 6 Lugano, Zurich 7 Lucerne 8 Lausanne *Syria:* 4 Hama, Homs 5 Idlib 6 Aleppo 7 Latakia *Tanzania:* 5 Lindi, Mbeya, Tanga 6 Dodoma 8 Zanzibar *Tennessee:* 5 Alcoa, Erwin, Rives 6 Celina, Dunlap, Loudon, Ripley, Selmer 7 Memphis, Waverly 8 Gallatin, Oak Ridge, Rutledge, Tazewell, Wartburg 9 Dandridge, Dyersburg, Hohenwald, Jacksboro, Jonesboro, Knoxville, Lewisburg, Maryville, Pikeville 10 Cookeville, Crossville, Gainesboro, Hartsville, Smithville, Sneedville, Somerville, Waynesboro 11 Blountville, Chattanooga, Clarksville, Greeneville, McMinnville, Rogersville, Sevierville, Shelbyville, Tiptonville 12 Decaturville, Elizabethton, Lawrenceburg, Madisonville, Maynardville, Murfreesboro *Texas:* 4 Azle, Roby, Vega, Waco 5 Alvin, Anson, Baird, Bowie, Bryan, Clute, Cuero, Emory, Ennis, Freer, Hondo, Marfa, Mexia, Olney, Ozona, Pampa, Pecos, Pharr, Plano, Sealy, Tulia, Vidor, Wylie 6 Belton, Boerne, Bonham, Burnet, Conroe, Dallas, Del Rio, Denton, El Paso, Gilmer, Goliad, Jayton, Lamesa, Laredo, Linden, Lufkin, Menard, Morton, Odessa, Quanah, Sarita, Seguin, Sinton, Tahoka, Tilden, Uvalde 7 Abilene, Anahuac, Bandera, Bastrop, Big Lake, Brenham, Cotulla, Crowell, Dalhart, Denison, Dimmitt, Farwell, Houston, Kaufman, Kountze, Lubbock, Mentone, Mertzon, Midland, Refugio, San Saba, Stanton, Van Horn, Wharton 8 Amarillo, Angleton, Beaumont, Beeville, Cleburne, Eastland, Eldorado, Floydada, Giddings, Glen Rose, Gonzales, Granbury, Groveton, Hemphill, La Grange, Lampasas, Lipscomb, Longview, McKinney, Monahans, Montague, Muleshoe, Pearsall, Perryton, Rockwall, Spearman, Stinnett 9 Arlington, Aspermont, Ballinger, Bellville, Big Spring, Brownwood, Childress, Clarendon, Corsicana, Crosbyton, Eagle Pass, Fort Davis, Fort Worth, Galveston, Groesbeck, Henrietta, Hillsboro, Jacksboro, Kerrville, Levelland, Paint Rock, Palo Pinto, Plainview, San Angelo, Sanderson, San Marcos, Silverton, Woodville 10 Brownfield, Coldspring, Falfurrias, Gatesville, George West, Jourdanton, Kingsville, Port Arthur, Port Lavaca, San Antonio, Sweetwater, Waxahachie 11 Brownsville, Floresville, Goldthwaite, Littlefield, Nacogdoches, Rocksprings, Weatherford 12 Breckenridge, Daingerfield, Fort Stockton, Hebbronville, New Braunfels, Raymondville, San Augustine, Sierra Blanca, Stephenville, Throckmorton, Wichita Falls 13 Brackettville, Corpus Christi, Hallettsville *Thailand:* 3 Nan, Tak 5 Phrae, Roi Et, Surin 8 Songkhla *Tunisia:* 4 Beja, Sfax 5 Gabes, Gafsa 7 Bizerte *Turkey:* 5 Adana, Bursa, Izmir, Konya, Sivas 6 Erzurm, Samsun 7 Kayseri, Malatya 8 Istanbul 9 Eskisehir, Gaziantep 10 Diyarbakir *Turkmenistan:* 8 Nebit Dag *Uganda:* 5 Jinja, Mbale 7 Entebbe *Ukraine:* 4 Lvov, Sumy 5 Lutsk, Rovno 6 Odessa 7 Donetsk, Kharkov, Kherson, Poltava 8 Vinnitsa, Zhitomir 9 Chernigov, Krivoy Rog, Nikolayev 10 Chernovtsy, Kirovograd, Kremenchug, Sevastopol, Simferopol, Zaporozhye *United Arab Emirates:* 5 Ajman, Dubai 7 Sharjah 8 Fujairah 12 Ras al Khaimah *Uruguay:* 4 Melo 5 Minas, Pando, Rocha, Salto *Utah:* 3 Loa 4 Lehi, Moab, Orem 5 Konab, Manti, Nephi, Ogden, Provo 6 Tooele 7 Parowan 8 Duchesne 9 Coalville, Panguitch 10 Castle Dale 11 Saint George *Uzbekistan:* 5 Nukus 6 Kokand

7 Bukhara, Fergana 8 Andizhan, Chirchik, Namangan 9 Samarkand *Venezuela:* 4 Coro 5 Anaco, Cagua 6 Merida 7 Cabimas, Maracay 8 Valencia 9 Maracaibo 12 Barquisimeto, San Cristobal *Vermont:* 5 Barre 7 Chelsea, Newfane, Rutland 8 Winooski 9 Guildhall, North Hero 10 Bennington, Burlington, Middlebury 11 Brattleboro, Saint Albans, St. Johnsbury 12 Bellows Falls *Vietnam:* 3 Hue 4 Vinh 5 Da Lat, Hoi An, My Tho 6 Da Nang 7 Nam Dinh, Qui Nhon 8 Haiphong, Nha Trang *Virginia:* 4 Tabb 5 Luray, Surry 6 Grundy, Saluda 7 Accomac, Boydton, Mathews, New Kent, Norfolk 8 Abingdon, Culpeper, Leesburg, Manassas, Montross, Nottoway, Poquoson, Powhatan, Rustburg, Tazewell 9 Arlington, Clintwood, Courtland, Dinwiddie, Eastville, Farmville, Fincastle, Goochland, Lunenburg, Lynchburg 10 Appomattox, Berryville, Front Royal, Hillsville, Jonesville, King George, Lovingston, Pearisburg, Portsmouth, Rocky Mount, Wytheville 11 Heathsville, King William, Newport News, Warm Springs 12 Prince George, Spotsylvania, Tappahannock 13 Stanardsville *Wales:* 4 Rhyl 5 Neath, Risca, Tenby, Tywyn 7 Cardiff, Cwmbran, Denbigh, Swansea 8 Aberdare, Bridgend 10 Llangollen *Washington:* 4 Omak 5 Brier, Camas, Kelso, Lacey, Pasco, Selah 6 Asotin, Colfax, Tacoma, Yakima 7 Ephrata, Everett, Pomeroy, Prosser, Seattle, Spokane 8 Bellevue, Chehalis, Colville, Okanogan 9 Cathlamet, Montesano, Ritzville, Snohomish, Wenatchee 10 Bellingham, Coupeville, Ellensburg, Goldendale, Walla Walla, Waterville 11 Port Angeles, Port Orchard 12 Friday Harbor, Port Townsend *West Virginia:* 5 Nitro, Welch 6 Elkins, Hamlin, Hinton, Keyser, Ripley 7 Beckley, Parsons, Weirton 8 Kingwood, Philippi, Wheeling 9 Glenville, Marlinton, Pineville, Wellsburg 10 Buckhannon, Clarksburg, Huntington, Moorefield, Morgantown, Petersburg, Saint Marys, Williamson 11 Grantsville, Harrisville, Martinsburg, Moundsville, Parkersburg 12 Middlebourne, Summersville 13 New Cumberland, Point Pleasant *Wisconsin:* 4 Kiel 5 Ripon, Tomah 6 Antigo, Barron, Durand, Hurley, Oconto, Racine, Wausau 7 Baraboo, Chilton, Crandon, Elkhorn, Hayward, Kenosha, Keshena, Mauston, Merrill, Oshkosh, Shawano, Viraqua, Waupaca, Wautoma 8 Appleton, Green Bay, Kewaunee, La Crosse, Montello, Phillips, Washburn, Waukesha, West Bend 9 Eau Claire, Ellsworth, Fond du Lac, Green Lake, Ladysmith, Manitowoc, Marinette, Menomonie, Milwaukee, Sheboygan, Shell Lake, Wauwatosa, West Allis, Whitehall 10 Balsam Lake, Darlington, Dodgeville, Eagle River, Grantsburg, Janesville 11 Neillsville, Sturgeon Bay 12 Stevens Point, Whitefish Bay 13 Chippewa Falls *Wyoming:* 4 Lusk 5 Casper, Lander 7 Laramie, Rawlins, Worland 8 Gillette, Kemmerer, Pinedale, Sheridan, Sundance 9 Wheatland 10 Green River 11 Rock Springs, Thermopolis *Yemen:* 5 Taizz 7 Hodeida, Mukalla *Zaire:* 4 Boma 6 Bukavu, Likasi 7 Kananga 9 Kisangani, Mbuji Mayi 10 Lubumbashi *Zambia:* 5 Kabwe, Kitwe, Mansa, Mbala, Mongu, Ndola *Zimbabwe:* 5 Gwelo 6 Umtali 8 Bulawayo

civet 3 cat *African:* 7 nandine *Asian:* 5 zibet 6 zibeth *Chinese:* 5 rasse *East Indian:* 6 musang 9 tangalung *Indian:* 6 bondar *Madagascar:* 5 fossa 8 fanaloka *Malaysian:* 8 mampalon *relative:* 5 genet

civic 6 public 8 national

civil 5 bland, suave 6 polite, public, urbane 7 affable, cordial, courtly, genteel, politic, refined 8 gracious, mannerly, national, obliging, well-bred 9 courteous 10 cultivated, diplomatic 12 well-mannered 13 accommodating

civility 6 comity 7 amenity, decorum 9 etiquette, propriety 10 politeness

civilization 7 culture

civilized 5 bland, suave 6 decent, polite, proper, smooth, urbane 7 refined 8 decorous 9 befitting, Christian 10 conforming 11 comme il faut 13 sophisticated

civil rights *leader:* 4 King *organization:* 4 ACLU, CORE 5 NAACP

Civil War *admiral:* 8 Buchanan, Farragut *battle:* 6 Shiloh 7 Bull Run 8 Antietam, Manassas 9 Mobile Bay, Nashville, Vicksburg 10 Cold Harbor, Gettysburg 11 Chattanooga, Chickamauga *general:* 3 Lee 4 Hood, Pope 5 Bragg, Buell, Ewell, Grant, Meade, Sykes 6 Hooker 7 Forrest, Jackson, Sherman 8 Burnside, Johnston, Sheridan 9 McClellan, Rosecrans, Schofield 10 Beauregard *ship:* 7 Monitor 9 Merrimack

civil wrong 4 tort

Civitas Dei 4 Zion 5 bliss 6 Canaan, heaven 7 elysium, nirvana 8 empyrean, paradise 12 New Jerusalem 13 Abraham's bosom

clabber 5 curds

clack 3 gab, jaw, yak 4 blab, chat 5 prate, sieve, tabby 6 babble, bicker, gabble, gossip, jabber, rattle 7 blabber, chatter, clatter, clitter, palaver, prattle, shatter 8 quidnunc, telltale 9 carrytale, yakety-yak 10 talebearer 11 rumormonger 13 scandalmonger

clad 4 face, garb, side, skin 5 array, dress

6 attire, clothe **7** apparel, garment, raiment, sheathe **8** enclothe

claim 4 call, dibs **5** argue, exact, right, share, stake, title **6** adduce, allege, assert, defend, demand **7** advance, contend, justify, purport, require, solicit, warrant **8** interest, maintain, pretense **9** assertion, challenge, postulate, privilege, vindicate **10** birthright, pretension **11** affirmation, declaration, prerogative, requisition **12** protestation

clairvoyance 3 ESP

clairvoyant 4 seer

clam 5 razor **6** gweduc, quahog **7** bivalve, coquina, geoduck, goeduck, gweduck, mollusk, quahaug, steamer **11** cherrystone *genus:* **3** Mya

clamant 4 dire **6** crying, urgent **7** burning, exigent, instant **8** pressing **9** clamorous **10** imperative **11** importunate

clamber 5 climb, crawl, scale **8** scrabble, scramble, struggle

clamor 3 din **4** bawl, roar, rout, to-do **5** babel, claim, whirl **6** bellow, bustle, debate, demand, hassle, hubbub, jangle, outcry, racket, tumult, uproar, upturn **7** agitate, bluster, dispute, ferment, turmoil **8** upheaval **9** commotion **10** convulsion, hullabaloo, hurly-burly, tintamarre **11** pandemonium

clamorous 4 dire **5** vocal **6** crying, urgent **7** begging, blatant, burning, clamant, exigent, instant, voluble **8** adjuring, eloquent, pressing, strident **9** imploring **10** articulate, boisterous, imperative, multivocal, vociferant, vociferous **11** importunate, loudmouthed, openmouthed **12** obstreperous

clamp 4 grip, hold, vise **5** clasp, grasp, gripe **6** clench, clinch, clutch, tenure **7** grapple

clamshell 6 bucket **7** grapple

clan 3 mob **4** camp, folk, race, ring **5** cabal, house, stock, tribe **6** circle, clique, family **7** coterie, ingroup, kindred, lineage **9** camarilla *emblem:* **5** totem

clandestine 3 sly **4** foxy **6** artful, covert, secret **7** furtive, illicit **8** hush-hush, stealthy **10** undercover **12** hugger-mugger, illegitimate **13** surreptitious, under-the-table

clang 3 din **4** ding, peal **5** noise **6** jangle

clangorous 5 noisy **7** rackety **8** clattery, noiseful, sonorous **10** uproarious

clap 4 bang, boom, slam, wham **5** blast, burst, crack, crash, smash **7** applaud

claptrap 4 bull **5** hokum **6** bunkum, drivel, humbug **7** baloney, twaddle **8** malarkey, nonsense **10** flapdoodle

Clare Boothe _____ 4 Luce

claret 3 red **4** wine **8** Bordeaux

clarify 5 clean, clear **6** define, purify, settle **7** analyze, cleanse, clear up, explain

8 depurate, simplify **9** break down, delineate, elucidate, formulate **10** illuminate, illustrate **13** straighten out

clarion 4 fair, fine **5** clear, sunny **8** pleasant, rainless, sunshiny **9** cloudless, unclouded **10** undarkened

clarity 4 care **6** nicety **8** accuracy, lucidity **9** clearness, fussiness, limpidity, plainness, precision, propriety **10** exactitude **11** perspicuity **12** articulation, correctitude

clash 3 jar, row, try **4** bump, fray, fret, gall, jolt, riot **5** brawl, broil, brush, crash, grate, melee, scrap, set to, shock, smash **6** action, affray, battle, fracas, impact, jangle, mellay, rumpus, wallop **7** collide, discord **8** conflict, mismatch, skirmish **9** collision, disaccord, encounter, scrimmage **10** concussion, engagement **11** embroilment **12** disharmonize

clasp 3 hug **4** clip, coil, grip, hold, take **5** clamp, grasp, gripe, press, tache **6** clench, clinch, clutch, enfold, tenure **7** embrace, grapple, squeeze **10** chatelaine

class 3 ilk **4** head, hold, kind, mark, part, rank, rate, sort, tier, type **5** allot, brand, caste, color, gauge, genre, genus, grade, grain, group, judge, order, score, stamp, style **6** assess, assign, assort, branch, divide, kidney, league, nature, reckon, regard, stripe **7** account, bracket, caliber, feather, quality, section, species, variety **8** appraise, category, consider, division, evaluate, grouping, separate **10** categorize, pigeonhole **11** description **12** denomination *Hindu:* **5** caste, varna *middle:* **11** bourgeoisie *school:* **6** junior, senior **8** freshman **9** sophomore *scientific:* **5** genus **6** genera (plural) *suffix:* **2** cy *working:* **11** proletariat

classic 3 top **4** fine **5** ideal, model, prime **6** famous **7** capital, typical, vintage **8** champion, superior, top-notch **9** classical, excellent, exemplary **10** magnum opus, masterwork, prototypal **11** chef d'oeuvre, masterpiece, tour de force **12** paradigmatic, prototypical

classification 4 sort, type **5** genre, genus, grade, order **6** family, genera (plural), phylum, rating **7** species **8** category, division, grouping, taxonomy, typology **11** arrangement

classified 6 secret **9** top secret **12** confidential

classify 4 rank, rate, sort **5** grade, group **6** assort **8** evaluate **10** categorize, pigeonhole

classy 2 in **4** tony **5** sharp, swank, swish **6** modish, tonish **7** dashing, stylish **11** fashionable

clatter 3 gab, jaw **4** chat, to-do **5** clack, run on **6** babble, bicker, clamor, dither, hassle, hubbub, pother, rattle, tumult, uproar

7 chatter, clitter, shatter, turmoil **9** commotion **10** hurly-burly *Scottish:* **7** brattle
clattery **5** noisy **7** rackety **8** noiseful, sonorous **10** clangorous, uproarious
Claudia's husband **6** Pilate
Claudio's beloved **4** Hero
Claudius *nephew:* **6** Hamlet *slayer:* **6** Hamlet **9** Agrippina *successor:* **4** Nero
claviger **6** custos, keeper, warden **8** cerberus, guardian, watchdog **9** custodian
claw **3** dig **4** nail, tear **5** chela, grasp, grope, seize, talon, uncus **6** clutch, scrape, ungual, unguis, ungula **7** scratch *combining form:* **4** chel **5** cheli, onych, ungui **6** onycho **8** onychium
clay **3** cob, pug **4** galt, leck, loam, lute, marl **5** argil, brick, earth, gault, loess, ocher, ochre, rabat **6** clunch **8** camstone *baked:* **4** bole, tile **5** adobe, brick *box:* **6** saggar, sagger *brick:* **3** bat *building:* **5** adobe *ceramic:* **10** terra-cotta *combining form:* **3** pel **4** pelo **6** argill **7** argilli, argillo **10** argillaceo *constituent:* **6** silica **7** dickite, nacrite **8** feldspar, silicate **9** kaolinite *friable:* **4** bole *in glass:* **4** tear *made of:* **7** fictile *mold:* **3** dod *porcelain:* **6** kaolin **7** kaoline *red:* **4** bole **8** laterite, sinopite *rock:* **5** shale *slab:* **3** bat *sticky:* **8** gumbotil *tobacco pipe:* **6** dudeen *watery mixture:* **4** slip *white:* **6** kaolin **7** kaoline
clay pigeon **6** target
clean **3** gut **4** dust, fair, pure, swab, tidy, trim, wash, wipe **5** dress, fresh, groom, order, purge, renew, scour, scrub, sweep **6** bright, chaste, decent, modest, neaten, police, purify, spruce, vacuum **7** clarify, freshen, furbish, shining, sinless **8** brighten, depurate, innocent, renovate, spotless, unguilty, unsoiled **9** blameless, crimeless, faultless, guiltless, sparkling, stainless, taintless, undefiled, unsullied, untainted, wholesome **10** immaculate, inculpable **11** recondition, sportsmanly, unblemished **12** spick-and-span, straighten up **13** sportsmanlike *ship's bottom:* **5** bream
clean-cut **7** express **8** definite, explicit, specific **10** definitive **11** categorical, unambiguous
cleaner see **cleanser**
cleanhanded **8** innocent
clean-limbed **4** trim **7** shapely **8** shapeful **10** statuesque, well-turned
cleanse **5** purge, rinse **6** purify, refine **7** clarify, deterge **8** depurate, lustrate, sanitize **9** disinfect, expurgate, sterilize
cleanser **3** lye **4** soap **6** bleach **9** detergent
cleansing **9** catharsis, purgation **10** lustration **11** expurgation **12** purification
Cleante *father:* **8** Harpagon *lover:* **9** Angelique

clear **3** get, net, pay, rid, win **4** bare, earn, fade, fair, fine, gain, leap, lose, make, over, pure, quit, sink, void, well **5** à fond, close, empty, exact, fully, glean, lucid, milky, overt, pay up, plain, quite, repay, solve, stark, sunny, untie, vault **6** acquit, better, gather, hurdle, limpid, lucent, obtain, patent, pay off, pick up, public, secure, settle, simple, square, vacant, vacate, vanish **7** absolve, acquire, clarify, clarion, cleanse, clean up, crystal, defined, evanish, evident, explain, improve, obvious, precise, rule out, satisfy, untwine, utterly, vacuous **8** apparent, definite, distinct, entirely, evanesce, explicit, knowable, luculent, luminous, manifest, overleap, palpable, pellucid, pleasant, rainless, scot-free, sensible, shake off, sunshiny, surmount, tangible, throw-off, unburden, unhidden, univocal, untangle **9** cloudless, disappear, discharge, eliminate, elucidate, evaporate, exculpate, exonerate, extricate, graspable, liquidate, meliorate, negotiate, perfectly, published, stabilize, tralucent, unblurred, unclouded, vindicate **10** accumulate, altogether, ameliorate, completely, disculpate, disentwine, illuminate, illustrate, opalescent, openhanded, seethrough, translucid, undarkened, unentangle, unobscured, unscramble **11** appreciable, conspicuous, disencumber, disentangle, open-and-shut, perceptible, perspicuous, translucent, transparent, unambiguous, unequivocal, unperplexed **12** recognizable, transpicuous, unmistakable **13** apprehensible, uncomplicated
clearance **7** go-ahead **10** green light **13** authorization
clear away **6** remove **7** take out **9** discumber **10** disembroil **12** disembarrass
clear-cut **4** nice **5** crisp, exact, lucid, plain **6** biting, lucent **7** assured, crystal, cutting, decided, express, ingoing, precise **8** definite, distinct, explicit, incisive, luminous, manifest, pellucid, specific **9** trenchant, unblurred, undoubted **10** definitive, pronounced, undisputed **11** categorical, indubitable, penetrating, translucent, transparent, unambiguous **12** transpicuous, unquestioned
clear-eyed **10** discerning
clearheaded **10** perceptive
clear out **4** kite **5** scram **6** begone, decamp, get out **7** skiddoo, take off, vamoose **8** hightail **9** skedaddle
clear-sightedness **3** wit **6** acumen **8** astucity, keenness **10** astuteness, shrewdness **11** discernment, penetration, percipience
clear up **5** solve **6** cipher, unfold **7** clarify, dope out, explain, resolve, unravel **8** deci-

pher, dissolve **9** elucidate, figure out, puzzle out **10** illuminate, illustrate

clearwing 4 moth

cleat 4 bitt **5** cavel, chock, kevel **6** batten **7** bollard, coxcomb, dolphin

cleavage 5 chasm, cleft, split **6** schism

cleave 3 cut, hew, rip **4** chop, join, link, rend, rive, tear **5** carve, cling, sever, slice, split, stick, unite **6** adhere, cohere, divide, sunder **7** combine, conjoin, dissect, divorce **8** dissever, separate **9** associate

cleft 3 gap **4** rift, rima, rime, slit **5** chasm, chink, clove, crack, gorge, gulch, split **6** arroyo, clough, ravine, schism **7** crevice, fissure **8** cleavage, rimation *combining form:* **5** fissi, schiz **6** schizo **7** schisto

clemency 5 grace, mercy **6** lenity **7** caritas, charity **8** fairness, justness, lenience, leniency, mildness **9** endurance, tolerance **10** gentleness, indulgence, sufferance, toleration **11** forbearance **12** mercifulness **13** equitableness

clement 4 easy, kind, mild **6** benign, humane, kindly, tender **7** lenient **8** merciful, tolerant **9** benignant, indulgent **10** benevolent, charitable, forbearing **11** sympathetic **13** compassionate

clench 4 grip, grit, hold **5** clamp, clasp, grasp, gripe **6** clinch, clutch, tenure **7** grapple

Cleopatra *attendant:* **4** Iras **8** Charmian *brother:* **7** Ptolemy *husband:* **7** Ptolemy *killer:* **3** asp *lover:* **6** Antony, Caesar *river:* **4** Nile

Cleopatra's Needle 7 obelisk

clepsydra 9 timepiece **10** water clock

clerestory 7 gallery

clergyman 5 clerk, padre, vicar **6** bishop, cleric, curate, divine, father, parson, pastor, priest, rector **7** dominie, pontiff, prelate **8** chaplain, clerical, minister, ordinary, preacher, pulpiter, reverend, shepherd, sky pilot **9** churchman, predicant, pulpiteer **10** ecclesiast, evangelist, missionary, sermonizer **11** pulpitarian **12** ecclesiastic *American:* **4** Hale, King **5** Eliot, Stone, Weems **6** Dwight, Holmes, Hooker, Mather, Merton, Parker, Powell, Taylor **7** Beecher, Harvard, Russell **10** Muhlenberg *English:* **4** Ward **5** Donne, Paley, Smith **6** Cotton, Fuller, Taylor **7** Cranmer, Parsons **8** Kingsley *French:* **8** Teilhard **10** Schweitzer *home:* **5** manse **6** priory **7** rectory **8** vicarage **9** monastery, parsonage *traveling:* **12** circuit rider

cleric see **clergyman**

clerisy 8 literati **10** illuminati **13** intellectuals

clerk 3 nun **4** monk **5** steno **6** cleric, scribe **7** scholar **8** minister **9** clergyman, secretary **11** salesperson **12** stenographer

clerkish 4 nice **5** fussy, picky **6** choosy **7** finical, finicky **9** finicking, squeamish **10** fastidious, particular

clever 3 apt, sly **4** able, deft, good, racy, slim **5** adept, alert, canny, funny, handy, quick, ready, salty, sharp, slick, smart, witty **6** adroit, brainy, bright, crafty, expert, nimble, pretty, prompt, tricky, wicked **7** amusing, capable, cunning, knowing, piquant, risible, skilled **8** dazzling, fanciful, humorous, masterly, pleasing, skillful **9** all-around, brilliant, competent, deceitful, dexterous, facetious, ingenious, laughable, many-sided, qualified, sparkling, sprightly, versatile, whimsical, workmanly **10** neat-handed, proficient **11** coruscating, intelligent, quick-witted, ready-witted, workmanlike **12** entertaining **13** scintillating

cliché 5 stale, trite **6** truism **7** bromide **8** banality, bathetic, prosaism, timeworn **9** hackneyed, platitude **10** prosaicism **11** commonplace, stereotyped **13** stereotypical

click 2 go **4** tick **6** go over, pan out **7** come off, succeed **8** prove out

click beetle 6 elater **8** elaterid

client 6 patron **8** customer

cliff 4 crag **5** bluff, cleve, scarp **7** clogwyn **8** headland, palisade **9** precipice *Scottish:* **5** heuch, heugh

climacteric 4 dire **5** acute **7** crucial **8** critical **9** desperate, menopause **12** change of life

climate 6 medium, milieu **7** ambient **8** ambience **10** atmosphere **11** environment, mise-en-scène **12** surroundings *combining form:* **6** meteor **7** meteoro

climatize 6 harden, season **7** toughen **9** acclimate

climax 3 cap, end **4** acme, apex, peak **5** crown **6** apogee, finish, summit, top off **8** capsheaf, capstone, conclude, meridian, pinnacle, round off **9** culminate, finish off, terminate **11** culmination *in drama:* **10** catastasis

climb 4 shin, upgo **5** mount, scale, speel **6** ascend **7** clamber **8** escalade, escalate

climbing 8 scandent

climbing iron 7 crampon

clinch 3 hug **4** grip, hold **5** clamp, clasp, grasp, gripe, press **6** clutch, enfold, tenure **7** embrace, grapple, squeeze

cling 4 bond **5** stick **6** adhere, cleave, cohere **8** adhesion, cohesion, stickage, sticking **9** adherence, coherence

clingfish 6 remora

clingstone 5 peach

clink 3 can, jug **4** jail, stir **5** pokey **6** cooler, jingle, lockup, tingle, tinkle **7** chinkle, slammer **8** hoosegow **9** calaboose

clinkers 3 ash **5** ashes **7** cinders

clinquant 6 tinsel 10 glittering

Clio see **Muse**

clip 3 cut, mow, pin 4 crop, pare, skin, soak, trim 5 lower, prune, shave, shear, skive, slash, stick 6 broach, brooch, fleece, reduce 7 cut back, cut down 8 mark down 10 overcharge

clique 3 mob, set 4 camp, clan, ring 5 cabal 6 circle 7 coterie, faction, in-group 9 camarilla

cloak 4 cape, face, mask, robe, show, veil, wrap 5 cover, guise 6 facade, joseph, mantle, poncho, screen, shroud, veneer 7 blanket, curtain, manteau 8 disguise 9 dissemble, semblance 10 camouflage 11 dissimulate *ancient Greek:* 7 chlamys *ancient Roman:* 5 palla, sagum 6 abolla 7 paenula, pallium *Arab:* 3 aba *combining form:* 6 pallio *fur:* 7 pelisse *hooded:* 5 capot 6 capote 7 burnous 8 burnoose, cardinal *Indian:* 5 choga *Jewish:* 6 kittel *liturgical:* 4 cope *monk's:* 8 analabos *Moroccan:* 5 jelab 7 jellaba 8 djellaba *over armor:* 6 tabard 7 surcoat *Spanish:* 4 capa 5 manta *Turkish:* 6 dolman *waterproof:* 6 poncho

clobber 4 belt, slam, slug 5 blast, brain, clout, smash 6 wallop

clochard 3 vag 4 hobo 5 tramp 6 canter 7 drifter, floater, vagrant 8 roadster, vagabond 11 bindle stiff

clock 4 time 9 timepiece 11 chronometer *ship-shaped:* 3 nef *water:* 9 clepsydra

clocklike 4 full 6 minute 7 precise, regular 8 detailed, itemized, thorough 10 blow-by-blow, particular

clockmaker 10 horologist

clockwise 6 deasil 8 positive 11 right-handed

clod 3 gob, wad 4 boob, dolt, dope, hunk, lump 5 chump, chunk, clump, dummy, dunce, hunch 6 dimwit, nugget 8 dumbbell 9 blockhead, lamebrain

cloddish 7 boorish, ill-bred, loutish 8 churlish, clownish 9 unrefined 10 uncultured, unpolished 11 uncivilized

clodhopper 4 boor, hick, lout, shoe 5 chuff, churl, clown, yokel 6 mucker, rustic 7 bumpkin, grobian, hayseed, hoosier, redneck 9 chawbacon

clog 3 gum, tax, tie 4 curb, fill, lade, load, plug, stop 5 block, choke, close, leash, weigh 6 burden, charge, cumber, fetter, hamper, hobble, hog-tie, lumber, saddle 7 congest, occlude, shackle, stopper, trammel 8 encumber, obstruct 9 cumbrance, entrammel, hindrance, impedance 10 impediment 11 encumbrance

cloister 7 seclude 9 sequester

Cloister and the Hearth
  author

5 Reade

cloistered 7 recluse, secluse 8 hermetic, secluded 9 seclusive 11 sequestered

cloistered one 3 nun 4 monk

Clorinda *beloved:* 7 Tancred *father:* 6 Senapo *guardian:* 6 Arsete *slayer:* 7 Tancred

close 3 end 4 bang, clap, clog, face, fill, firm, halt, hard, meet, near, next, nigh, plug, quit, seal, shut, slam, stop, taut 5 abate, block, cease, choke, debar, dense, front, handy, humid, muggy, solid, stivy, taper, tense, thick, tight 6 almost, chummy, desist, ending, finale, finish, lessen, narrow, nearby, nearly, period, reduce, screen, shroud, silent, sticky, stingy, stuffy, sultry, windup, wrap up 7 airless, compact, congest, crowded, dwindle, exclude, miserly, nearest, occlude, shut off, shut out, stopper 8 abutting, adjacent, block out, complete, conclude, decrease, diminish, familiar, finalize, intimate, nearmost, obstruct, obturate, reserved, reticent, stifling, taciturn, taper off, ultimate, write off 9 adjoining, cessation, compacted, condensed, determine, drain away, encounter, immediate, nearabout, niggardly, penurious, proximate, terminate 10 breathless, compressed, conclusion, consummate, contiguous, contracted, convenient, desistance, near-at-hand 11 constricted, impermeable, neighboring, substantial, suffocating, termination, tight-lipped 12 cheeseparing, confidential, consolidated, impenetrable, parsimonious, tight-mouthed 13 pennypinching *combining form:* 4 pync, sten 5 plesi, pynco, steno 6 plesio

closed *combining form:* 5 clist 6 cleist, clisto, occlus 7 cleisto, occluso

closed-minded 4 deaf 8 unpliant 9 obstinate, pigheaded, unpliable 10 bullheaded, hardheaded, self-willed, unyielding 11 intractable

closefisted 6 stingy 7 miserly 8 clinging, grasping 9 clutching, niggardly, tenacious 13 penny-pinching

close in 3 hem, mew 4 cage, coop 5 fence, hedge 6 corral, immure 7 enclose, envelop

close-knit 8 intimate

close-lipped 6 silent 8 reserved, reticent, taciturn 12 tight-mouthed

closely 4 hard 7 sharply 8 intently, minutely 9 carefully, heedfully, mindfully 11 searchingly 12 meticulously, scrupulously, thoughtfully 13 punctiliously

close match 6 tossup

closemouthed see **close-lipped**

closeness 8 intimacy

close off 6 cut off, enisle, island 7 isolate 8 insulate, separate 9 segregate, sequester

closet 6 hushed, inside, office 7 private
8 academic 11 speculative, theoretical
12 confidential

closing 3 end, lag 4 last, stop 5 final
6 ending, finish, latest, latter, period 8 eventual, hindmost, terminal, ultimate 9 cessation 10 concluding, desistance
11 termination

closure 3 cap, lid 8 fastener 9 cessation
combining form: 6 clisis 7 cleisis

clot 3 gel, set 4 body, jell 5 array, batch,
bunch, clump, group, jelly 6 bundle, gelate
7 battery, cluster, congeal, jellify 8 coagulum, thrombus 10 coagulate 10 gelatinize
combining form: 6 thromb 7 thrombo

cloth see **fabric**

clothe 3 tog 4 clad, deck, do up, garb,
robe 5 array, cloak, drape, dress, endue,
equip, tog up 6 attire, bedeck, invest, mantle, outfit, rig out, swathe, tog out 7 apparel,
bedrape, costume, dress up, garment, raiment, vesture 8 accouter, enclothe

clothes 3 rig 4 duds, garb, rags, togs
5 array, dress, getup 6 attire, outfit, things
7 apparel, costume, raiment, rigging, toggery, vesture 8 clothing 9 vestments
10 attirement 11 habiliments *basket:*
6 hamper *civilian:* 5 mufti *relating to:*
8 vestiary

clothes moth genus 5 Tinea

clothespress 3 kas 7 armoire
8 wardrobe

clothes tree 8 costumer

cloud 3 dim, fog, tar 4 army, blur, host,
rout 5 addle, befog, crowd, flock, gloom,
muddy, smear, sully, taint 6 legion, muddle,
puzzle, scores, shadow, smudge
7 becloud, besmear, confuse, obscure, perplex, tarnish 8 befuddle, besmirch, discolor,
distract, overcast 9 adumbrate, multitude
combining form: 4 cirr 5 cirrh, cirri, cirro,
nepho, nimbo 6 cirrhi, cirrho, nephel
7 nephelo *type:* 6 cirrus, nimbus 7 cumulus, stratus 11 altocumulus, altostratus
12 cirrocumulus, cirrostratus, cumulonimbus, nimbostratus 13 stratocumulus

cloudburst 6 deluge, shower 8 downpour,
rainfall

clouded 4 open 5 shady 7 dubious,
unclear 8 doubtful 9 ambiguous, equivocal,
uncertain, unsettled 11 problematic

cloudless 4 fair, fine 5 clear, sunny
7 clarion 8 pleasant, rainless, sunshiny
10 undarkened

cloud-like mass 6 nebula

cloudy 4 dull, hazy 5 foggy, heavy, misty,
mucky, murky, mushy, vague 6 vapory
7 louring 8 lowering, nubilous, overcast,
vaporous

clough 3 gap 5 chasm, cleft, clove, gorge,
gulch 6 arroyo, ravine

clout 2 in 3 box, hit 4 biff, chop, cuff, ding,
drag, nail, poke, pull, slam, slap, slog, slug,
sock 5 paste, punch, smack, smite, whack
6 buffet, strike 9 influence

clove 3 gap 5 chasm, cleft, gorge, gulch
6 arroyo, clough, ravine

clove hitch 4 knot

cloven-footed 8 fissiped

clover 5 lotus 6 alsike, ladino, lucern
7 alfalfa, berseem, lucerne, melilot, trefoil
8 four-leaf, shamrock 9 lespedeza *family:*
3 pea *genus:* 9 Trifolium

clown 3 wag 4 boor, fool, hick, jake, mime,
rube, zany 5 chuff, churl, cutup, joker
6 jester, mucker, mummer, rustic 7 bucolic,
buffoon, bumpkin, farceur, grobian, hayseed, hoosier 8 comedian, jokester 9 harlequin 10 mountebank 11 merry-andrew
French: 7 pierrot *operatic:* 5 buffo *Spanish:* 8 gracioso

clownish 3 row 4 rude, zany 6 clumsy,
gauche 7 awkward, boorish, ill-bred, loutish, lumpish, uncouth 8 churlish, cloddish
9 unrefined 10 uncultured, unpolished
11 uncivilized

cloy 4 fill, glut, jade, pall, sate 5 gorge
6 stodge 7 satiate, surfeit

club 3 bat 4 mace 5 baton, billy, guild,
order, union 6 bistro, cudgel, league
7 society 8 bludgeon, sodality, sorority
9 truncheon 10 fellowship, fraternity, knobkerrie, nightstick 11 association, brotherhood *Australian:* 5 waddy *college:*
8 sorority 10 fraternity *combining form:*
5 clavi 6 rhopal 7 rhopalo *Irish:* 8 shillala
10 shillelagh *women's:* 7 sorosis

clubfoot 7 talipes

cluck 4 fowl, simp 5 dunce 6 dimwit, nitwit 7 lackwit, pinhead, wantwit 9 dumb
bunny 13 featherweight

clue 3 cue 4 hint, post, tell, warn, wind
6 advise, fill in, inform, notify, notion, wise
up 7 apprise, inkling 8 acquaint, telltale
10 indication, intimation, suggestion

clump 3 gob, lot, set, wad 4 body, clod,
hunk, lump 5 array, barge, batch, bunch,
chunk, group, hunch, stump 6 bundle, jumble, lumber, nugget, parcel 7 cluster, clutter, galumph, stumble 10 hodgepodge

clump of grass 4 tuft 6 tuffet

clumsy 5 bulky, gawky, inept, splay
6 gauche, klutzy, wooden 7 awkward, hulking, lumpish, uncouth, unhandy, unhappy
8 bumbling, ungainly, unwieldy 9 graceless,
ham-handed, inelegant, lumbering, maladroit 10 bunglesome 11 heavy-handed

clumsy one 3 oaf 4 lout 5 klutz 6 lummox 7 bungler

clunk 4 thud 5 clonk, thump

clunker 4 heap 5 crate, wreck 6 jalopy,
junker

cluster 3 lot, set 4 band, bevy, body, crew 5 array, batch, bunch, clump, covey, group, party 6 bundle, clutch, gather, parcel 7 collect, package, round up 8 assemble, assembly, cumulate 9 aggregate, associate 10 accumulate *combining form:* 3 cym, kym 4 cymo, kymo

cluster bean 4 guar

clutch 3 nab, set 4 body, grab, grip, hold, keep, take 5 array, batch, bunch, catch, clamp, clasp, clump, grasp, gripe, group, seize 6 bundle, clench, clinch, harbor, parcel, snatch, tenure 7 cherish, cluster, grapple *Scottish:* 5 cleek 7 claucht, claught

clutter 4 hash, mash, mess, muss, ruck 5 chaos, snarl 6 ataxia, huddle, jumble, jungle, litter, medley, muddle, tumble 7 mélange, rummage, shuffle 8 disarray, disorder, mishmash, scramble 9 confusion, macedoine 10 hodgepodge 12 huggermugger

Clydesdale 5 horse

Clymene *father:* 7 Oceanus *husband:* 7 Iapetus *mother:* 6 Tethys *son:* 5 Atlas 10 Epimetheus, Prometheus

Clytemnestra *brother:* 6 Castor, Pollux 10 Polydeuces *daughter:* 7 Electra 9 Iphigenia *father:* 9 Tyndareus *husband:* 9 Agamemnon *lover:* 9 Aegisthus *mother:* 4 Leda *slayer:* 7 Orestes *son:* 7 Orestes *victim:* 9 Agamemnon, Cassandra

Clytie *beloved:* 6 Apollo *form:* 9 sunflower 10 heliotrope

coach 5 stage, train, tutor 8 carriage 10 instructor

coadjutant 3 aid 4 aide 9 assistant 10 aide-decamp, lieutenant

coadjute 4 band 5 unite 6 concur, league 7 combine, conjoin 9 cooperate

coadjutor see **coadjutant**

coadunation 5 union 6 merger 7 melding, merging 8 mergence 9 coalition 11 combination, unification 13 consolidation

coagulate 3 dry, gel, set 4 clot, jell 5 jelly 6 curdle, freeze, gelate, harden 7 compact, congeal, jellify, thicken 8 coalesce, concrete, condense, solidify 9 dehydrate 10 gelatinize, inspissate 11 concentrate, consolidate

coal *combining form:* 7 anthrac, carboni 8 anthraco *distillate:* 3 tar *dust:* 4 coom, smut, soot 5 coomb, slack *element:* 6 carbon *fused leavings:* 4 slag 7 clinker *glowing:* 5 ember, gleed *hard:* 10 anthracite *lump:* 3 cob *miner:* 7 collier *region:* 4 Saar *residue:* 4 coke *shaly:* 9 tasmanite *soft:* 6 cannel 10 bituminous

coalesce 3 mix, wed 4 fuse, join, link 5 blend, cling, merge, stick, unite 6 adhere, cleave, mingle, relate 7 bracket, combine, conjoin, connect 9 associate

coalition 4 bloc, ring 5 party, union 6 league, merger 7 combine, faction, melding, merging 8 alliance, mergence 9 anschluss 10 federation 11 coadunation, combination, confederacy, unification 13 confederation, consolidation

coarse 3 low, raw 4 foul, rude 5 caked, cakey, crass, crude, dirty, gross, lumpy, nasty, rough, rowdy, tacky 6 common, filthy, grainy, incult, smutty, vulgar 7 boorish, obscene, raffish, raunchy, uncouth 8 granular, indecent, inexpert, prentice 9 inelegant, roughneck, unrefined, vulgarian 10 uncultured 11 particulate 12 scatological, uncultivated *food:* 6 fodder

coast 4 bank 5 beach, drift, shore, slide 6 strand 8 littoral *of Antarctica:* 4 Knox *of west Africa:* 5 Ivory *swampy:* 7 maremma

coastal 8 littoral

coaster 4 sled

coat 5 layer, plate, tunic 6 blazer, duster, jacket, patina, raglan, reefer, ulster, veneer 7 cutaway, paletot 8 covering, mackinaw, tegument 9 newmarket, redingote 10 integument *animal:* 3 fur 4 hide, pelt, wool 6 pelage *arctic:* 5 parka *fur-lined:* 7 pelisse *glossy:* 5 glacé *kind:* 3 car, pea, top 5 frock 6 trench *Levantine:* 6 caftan *medieval:* 8 gambeson *of arms:* 5 crest 6 blazon, emblem, shield, tabard 7 surcoat 8 blazonry 9 escucheon 10 escutcheon *of egg white:* 5 glair 6 glaire *of gold:* 4 gild, gilt *of mail:* 6 byrnie 7 hauberk *Scottish:* 4 jupe *seaman's:* 5 grego *soldier's:* 5 frock, tunic 6 capote *waterproof:* 7 slicker 10 mackintosh

coating 4 film 5 layer 6 finish, patina, veneer 7 lacquer 8 covering

coax 3 con, get 4 lure, urge 5 press, tease, tempt 6 cajole, entice, fleech, induce, pester, plague 7 blarney, prevail, wheedle 8 blandish, butter up, inveigle, persuade, soft-soap 9 importune, sweet talk *Scottish:* 7 cuittle

cob 3 cap 4 ding, swan 5 excel, horse, outdo 6 exceed 7 surpass 8 outmatch, outshine, outstrip

cobalt *symbol:* 2 Co

cobble 4 make, mend, mess 5 botch, patch, snafu, stone 6 bollix, bungle, foul up, goof up, mucker, repair 7 confuse, louse up, screw up, snarl up

cobbler 3 pie 4 fish 5 drink 7 catfish, pompano 9 shoemaker 10 threadfish

cobbler's form 4 last

cobelligerent 4 ally

cobweb 3 net 4 mesh, toil, trap 8 gossamer 12 entanglement

coccyx 8 tailbone

cochineal 3 dye 6 insect

cochleate 6 spiral 11 shell-shaped

cock 3 tap 4 bank, boss, gate, head, heap, hill, lord, mass, pile, rick 5 chief, drift, mound, stack, swank, swell, valve 6 faucet, honcho, leader, master, spigot 7 headman, hydrant, pyramid, rooster, swagger 8 hierarch, mountain 9 chieftain, dominator, number one, principal 10 preeminent 11 chanticleer, pontificate

cock-a-doodle-doo 4 blow, brag, crow, puff 5 boast, mouth, prate, vaunt 9 gasconade 11 rodomontade

cock-a-hoop 4 awry 5 askew 6 askant 7 askance 8 exultant, exulting, jubilant 9 crookedly, triumphal 10 triumphant

Cockaigne 4 Zion 6 heaven, utopia 7 arcadia 8 paradise 9 fairyland, Shangri-la 10 lubberland, wonderland 12 promised land

cockalorum 8 leapfrog 11 braggadocio

cockamamy 10 incredible, ridiculous

cock-and-bull story 3 fib, lie 6 canard 7 falsity, untruth 9 falsehood 13 prevarication

cockatoo bush 9 blueberry

cockcrow 4 dawn, morn 5 light, sunup 6 aurora 7 dawning, morning, sunrise 8 daybreak, daylight

cocker 4 baby 5 humor, spoil 6 coddle, cosset, pamper 7 cater to, indulge 11 mollycoddle

cockeyed 4 awry 5 askew, boozy, drunk 6 askant 7 askance, muddled 9 crookedly, disguised, pixilated, plastered 10 inebriated 11 intoxicated

cockle 4 fret 6 dimple, riffle, ripple

cockleshell 4 boat

cockscomb see **coxcomb**

cocksure 7 certain 8 positive 9 confident

cocktail 5 Bronx, drink, zombi 6 zombie 7 martini, Sazerac, sidecar 8 aperitif, daiquiri, pink lady, salty dog, sangrita, sombrero 9 aperitive, appetizer, Manhattan 10 Bloody Mary, Margarita *fruit:* 9 macedoine *gasoline:* 7 Molotov

cocktail lounge 3 bar, pub 6 saloon, tavern 7 barroom, gin mill, taproom 8 groggery, pothouse

Cocktail Party author 5 Eliot

coconspirator 7 abettor 9 accessory 10 accomplice 11 confederate

coconut meat 5 copra

coddle 4 baby 5 humor, spoil 6 cosset, cotton, pamper 7 cater to, indulge 11 mollycoddle

code 6 cipher 7 encrypt 8 encipher *kind:* 3 zip 4 area 5 Morse, penal *message in:* 10 cryptogram

code word see **communications code word**

codicil 5 rider 8 addendum, appendix 10 supplement

codswallop 8 nonsense

coefficient 8 coacting, coactive, conjoint, synergic 10 synergetic 11 cooperative

coelenterate 5 coral 7 hydroid 9 jellyfish 10 sea anemone

coerce 3 cow 4 make, push, urge 5 beset, bully, force 6 compel, menace, oblige 8 browbeat, bulldoze, threaten 9 blackjack, constrain, terrorize 10 intimidate

coercion 5 force 6 duress, menace, threat 8 menacing 10 compulsion, constraint 11 threatening

coeval see **contemporary**

coexistent see **contemporary**

coffee *alkaloid:* 7 caffein 8 caffeine *bean:* 3 nib *cake:* 6 kuchen *cup:* 9 demitasse *cup holder:* 4 zarf *French:* 4 café *grinder:* 4 mill *kind:* 4 drip, java 5 mocha 7 arabica, instant 8 espresso *maker:* 6 biggin 10 percolator *pot:* 3 urn

coffee shop 4 café 5 diner 8 snack bar 9 hash house, lunchroom 11 eating house, greasy spoon 12 luncheonette

coffer 5 chest 8 treasury, war chest 9 exchequer

coffin 3 box 4 kist 6 casket *carrier:* 6 hearse 10 pallbearer *nail:* 9 cigarette *stand:* 4 bier 10 catafalque

cogency 5 force, point, punch 7 bearing, concern 8 validity 9 relevance, validness 10 connection, pertinence 13 effectiveness

cogent 5 solid, sound, valid 6 potent 7 telling, weighty 8 forceful, forcible, powerful, puissant 9 justified 10 compelling, convincing, meaningful, persuasive, satisfying 11 influential, significant, well-founded 12 constraining, satisfactory, well-grounded 13 consequential

cogitate 4 plot 5 think 6 devise, reason 7 collude, connive, imagine, reflect 8 conceive, conspire, contrive, envisage, envision, intrigue 9 cerebrate, machinate, scheme out, speculate 10 deliberate

cogitation 7 thought 9 brainwork 10 reflection 11 cerebration, speculation 12 deliberation

cogitative 7 pensive 8 thinking 9 pondering 10 meditative, reflecting, reflective, ruminative, thoughtful 11 speculative 13 contemplative

cognate 4 akin 6 agnate, allied, common 7 connate, general, generic, kindred, related 8 incident 9 universal 10 affiliated, connatural 11 consanguine

cognition 9 knowledge 10 perception *combining form:* 5 gnosy 6 gnosia, gnosis

cognizance 4 heed, mark, note 6 notice, regard, remark 9 attention 10 observance 11 observation

cognizant 5 alive, awake, aware 7 know-

ing, witting **8** sensible, sentient **9** au courant, conscious **12** apprehensive
cognize 4 know **5** grasp **6** fathom
9 apprehend **10** appreciate, comprehend,
understand
cognomen 4 name **5** style, title **7** epithet,
moniker **11** appellation, appellative, designation **12** compellation, denomination
cognoscente 5 judge **6** critic, expert
8 aesthete **9** authority **10** dilettante, proficient, specialist **11** connoisseur
cognoscible 8 knowable
cohere 2 go **4** fuse, join **5** agree, blend,
check, cling, fit in, merge, stick, unite
6 accord, cleave **7** combine, comport, conform, connect **8** check out, coalesce, dovetail **9** associate **10** correspond
coherence 4 bond **5** cling, union, unity
8 adhesion, clinging, cohesion, stickage,
sticking **9** congruity, integrity **10** conformity, solidarity **11** consistency
coherent 7 unified **9** connected
10 consistent
cohesion see **coherence**
cohort 4 mate **6** fellow **7** partner, sectary
8 adherent, confrere, disciple, follower,
henchman, partisan, sectator **9** associate,
copartner, satellite, supporter
10 consociate
coif 3 cap **4** hood **6** hairdo **8** skullcap
coiffure 6 hairdo **9** headdress *aid:* **3** net,
rat **5** snood
coil 4 curl, fuss, loop, ring, turn, wind
5 helix, twine, twist **6** furore, rotate, ruckus,
rumpus, shindy, spiral, tumult, uproar
7 entwine, revolve, shindig, turmoil,
wreathe **8** brouhaha, foofaraw **9** commotion, corkscrew *combining form:* **4** spir
5 spiri, spiro
coiled 7 tortile **9** circinate
coin 4 mint *Afghanistan:* **3** pul *Albania:*
3 lek *Algeria:* **5** dinar **7** centime *ancient
Greek:* **4** obol *ancient Muslim:* **5** dinar
ancient Roman: **6** follis **8** denarius *Argentina:* **4** peso **7** centavo *Australia:* **4** cent
6 dollar *Austria:* **8** groschen **9** schilling
Bahamas: **4** cent **6** dollar *Bahrain:* **4** fils
5 dinar *Barbados:* **4** cent **6** dollar *Belgium:* **5** franc **7** centime *Benin:* **5** franc
Bhutan: **7** chetrum **8** ngultrum *Bolivia:*
7 centavo *Botswana:* **4** pula **5** thebe *Brazil:* **7** centavo **8** cruzeiro *Bulgaria:* **3** lev
8 stotinka *Burundi:* **5** franc *Cameroon:*
5 franc *Canada:* **4** cent **6** dollar *Cape
Verde Islands:* **6** escudo *Chile:* **4** peso
7 centavo *China:* **3** fen **4** jiao, yuan
5 chiao *Columbia:* **4** peso **7** centavo *Costa
Rica:* **5** colon *Cuba:* **4** peso **7** centavo
Cyprus: **4** cent **5** pound *Czechoslovakia:*
5 haler **6** koruna *defective:* **4** fido *Denmark:* **3** ore **5** krone *Dominican Repub-

lic: **4** peso **7** centavo *Ecuador:* **5** sucre
7 centavo *edge:* **7** milling *Egypt:* **7** piastre
8 millieme *Ethiopia:* **4** cent *European
gold:* **5** ducat *Fiji:* **4** cent **6** dollar *Finland:* **5** penni **6** markka *former:* **3** lek, mil,
pie **4** anna, besa, cash, doit, duit, kran,
para, pice **5** crown, fanam, litas, mohur,
paisa, rupia, shahi, toman **6** centas, heller,
kopeck, macuta, pagoda, tangka **7** santims,
sapeque **8** farthing, maravedi, sixpence,
skilling **9** half penny, rigsdaler **10** Indian
head, reichsmark, threepence **13** rei-
chspfennig *France:* **5** franc **7** centime
Gambia: **5** butut **6** dalasi *Germany:*
4 mark **7** pfennig *Ghana:* **4** cedi **6** pesewa
Great Britain: **6** guinea **8** new penny
9 sovereign *Greece:* **6** lepton **7** drachma
Guatemala: **7** centavo, quetzal *Guinea-
Bissau:* **4** peso *Guyana:* **4** cent **6** dollar
Haiti: **6** gourde **7** centime *Honduras:*
7 centavo, lempira *Hungary:* **6** forint *Ice-
land:* **5** eyrir, krona *India:* **5** paisa, rupee
Indonesia: **3** sen **6** rupiah *Iran:* **4** rial
Iraq: **5** dinar *Ireland:* **5** penny **8** far-
thing *Israel:* **5** agora **6** shekel *Italy:* **4** lira
Jamaica: **4** cent **6** dollar *Japan:* **3** rin, sen,
yen *Jordan:* **3** fil **5** dinar *Kenya:* **8** shilling
Korea, North: **3** won **4** chon *Korea,
South:* **3** won *Kuwait:* **4** fils *large:* **9** cartwheel *Lebanon:* **5** livre **7** piaster, piastre
Lesotho: **4** loti *Liberia:* **4** cent **6** dollar
Libya: **6** dirham *Luxembourg:* **5** franc
Madagascar: **5** franc *Malawi:* **6** kwacha
7 tambala *Malta:* **4** cent **6** pound *Mauritania:* **7** ouguiya *Mauritius:* **4** cent **5** rupee
Mexico: **4** peso **7** centavo *Monaco:*
5 franc *Morocco:* **6** dirham *Mozambique:*
7 metical *Nepal:* **5** paisa, rupee *Netherlands:* **4** cent **6** florin, gulden *New Zealand:* **4** cent **6** dollar *Nicaragua:* **7** centavo, cordoba *Nigeria:* **4** kobo *Norway:*
3 ore **5** krone *old Hungarian:* **5** pengo *old
Italian:* **5** scudo *old Swedish:* **8** skilling
Oman: **4** rial *Pakistan:* **4** pice **5** paisa *Panama:* **6** balboa **9** centesimo *Papua-New
Guinea:* **4** kina, toea *Paraguay:* **7** centimo,
guarani *Peru:* **4** inti **7** centimo *Philippines:* **4** piso **7** sentimo *Poland:* **5** grosz,
zloty *Portugal:* **6** escudo **7** centavo
Qatar: **6** dirhem *Roman:* **6** aureus, bezant
7 solidus *Romania:* **3** leu *Russia:*
5 kopek **6** rouble *Rwanda:* **5** franc *San
Marino:* **4** lira *Saudi Arabia:* **5** halala *Seychelles:* **4** cent **5** rupee *side of a:*
7 obverse *Sierra Leone:* **4** cent *Singapore:* **4** cent **6** dollar *South Africa:* **4** cent,
rand **10** krugerrand *Spain:* **6** peseta
7 centimo *Sri Lanka:* **4** cent **5** rupee
stamping metal: **8** planchet *Suriname:*
4 cent **6** gulden *Swaziland:* **4** cent **9** lilan-
geni *Sweden:* **3** ore **5** krona *Switzerland:*

5 franc **6** rappen *Syria:* 5 pound *Tanzania:* 8 shilingi *Thailand:* 3 att 4 baht *thick:* 7 piefort 8 piedfort *Tonga:* 6 pa'anga, seniti *Trinidad and Tobago:* 4 cent 6 dollar *Tunisia:* 5 dinar *Turkey:* 4 lira 5 kurus *Uganda:* 8 shilling *United Arab Emirates:* 6 dirham *United States:* 4 dime 5 penny 6 dollar, nickel 7 quarter 10 half dollar *Uruguay:* 4 peso 9 centesimo *Vatican City:* 4 lira *Venezuela:* 7 bolivar *Western Samoa:* 4 sene, tala *Zambia:* 5 ngwee 6 kwacha *Zimbabwe:* 4 cent 6 dollar

coinage 9 invention, neologism 10 brainchild 11 contrivance

coincide 4 jibe 5 agree, equal, match, tally 6 accord, concur 7 concert, concord 9 harmonize 10 correspond

coincident 9 ancillary, attendant, attending, satellite 10 collateral 11 concomitant 12 accompanying

coincidentally 6 at once 8 together 12 concurrently

coin-shaped 8 nummular

colander's cousin 5 sieve 6 sifter 8 strainer

cold 3 icy, raw 4 cool, dead, iced 5 algid, bleak, brisk, chill, crisp, drear, frore, gelid, nippy, polar 6 arctic, biting, chilly, dismal, frigid, frosty, frozen, gloomy, somber, wintry 7 bracing, cutting, defunct, extinct, glacial, joyless, nipping, shivery 8 chilling, comatose, deceased, departed, freezing, heatless, lifeless 9 cheerless, chillsome, exanimate, inanimate, inhibited, senseless 10 impersonal, insensible, oppressive, undersexed 11 dispiriting, emotionless, inconscious, indifferent, passionless, unconscious, unemotional 12 matter-of-fact, unresponsive 13 unimpassioned, unsympathetic *combining form:* 3 cry, kry 4 cryo, kryo 5 frigo 7 psychro *common:* 6 coryza *symptom:* 5 cough, fever 6 sneeze 7 catarrh

cold ____ 3 war 4 cash, cuts, feet, fish, pack, room, sore, wave 5 cream, frame, front, patch, steel, sweat, water 6 turkey 7 storage 8 shoulder

cold-blooded 7 callous 8 hardened, obdurate 9 heartless, unfeeling 10 hardboiled, impersonal 11 emotionless, hardhearted 12 matter-of-fact, stonyhearted 13 unimpassioned

cold box 4 icer

cold feet 4 fear 5 alarm, dread, panic 6 dismay, fright, horror, terror 11 trepidation 13 consternation

coldhearted see **cold-blooded**

cold-shoulder 3 cut 4 snob, snub 9 ostracize

cold storage 7 latency 8 abeyance, abey-

ancy, doldrums, dormancy 10 quiescence, quiescency, suspension 12 intermission, interruption

cole 4 rape 7 cabbage 8 broccoli, kohlrabi 11 cauliflower

Coleridge poem 9 Kubla Khan 10 Christabel

Colette character 4 Gigi 5 Cheri 8 Claudine

colewort 4 kale 7 cabbage

colic 5 gripe 9 bellyache 11 stomachache 12 collywobbles

coliseum 4 bowl 5 stade 7 stadium

collapse 2 go 4 bend, cave, drop, fail, flag, give, tire, wilt 5 break, crash, droop, smash, weary, wreck, yield 6 cave in, fold up, peg out, weaken 7 breakup, crack-up, crumple, debacle, deflate, exhaust, failure, founder, give out, play out, ruining, shatter, smashup, succumb, undoing 8 flake out, languish 9 break-down, cataclysm, ruination 10 disruption 11 catastrophe, destruction 12 disintegrate

collar 3 bag, cop, get, nab, nip 4 hook, lift, nail, take 5 catch, steal 6 corner, secure 7 capture, prehend 8 bottle up 11 appropriate *armor:* 6 gorget *boy's:* 4 Eton *chain:* 4 torc 6 torque *horse:* 7 bargham *jeweled:* 6 carcan 8 carcanet *laceedged:* 6 rabato, rebato *medieval:* 10 chevesaile *metal:* 4 torc 6 torque *Philippine:* 7 panuelo *pleated:* 4 ruff *wooden:* 4 cang 6 cangue

collarbone 8 clavicle

collate 7 arrange, bracket, compare 8 contrast 9 integrate

collateral 3 sub 5 under 6 allied 7 cognate, kindred, oblique, related, subject 8 adjuvant, circular, incident, indirect 9 accessory, ancillary, attendant, attending, auxiliary, dependent, satellite, secondary, tributary 10 circuitous, coincident, reciprocal, roundabout, subsidiary 11 adminicular, appurtenant, concomitant, subordinate, subservient 12 accompanying, confirmative, confirmatory, contributory, verificatory 13 complementary, corresponding, corroborative, corroboratory

colleague 3 pal 4 aide, chum 5 buddy, crony 6 fellow, helper 7 compeer, partner 8 confrere, co-worker 9 assistant, associate, companion, copartner 10 compatriot, consociate, workfellow

collect 4 draw, make, rank, rein 5 array, group, infer, judge, order, raise 6 deduce, deduct, derive, gather, muster 7 cluster, compile, compose, control, dispose, make out, marshal, round up 8 assemble, conclude, congress, restrain 10 congregate, rendezvous, simmer down

collected 4 calm, cool, easy, smug, sure

5 quiet, still 6 placid, poised, serene
7 assured 8 composed, peaceful, sanguine,
tranquil 9 confident, easygoing, possessed,
unruffled 10 complacent, nonchalant
11 unflappable 13 imperturbable, self-possessed, self-satisfied

collection 3 ana, kit, lot 4 band, bevy,
clan, crew, olio, ruck 5 bunch, clump,
crowd, group, hoard, party, trove 6 medley,
muster, outfit 7 cluster, company, variety
8 assembly, caboodle 9 aggregate, amassment, colluvies, congeries, gathering
10 assemblage, assortment, cumulation,
miscellany 11 aggregation 12 accumulation, congregation 13 agglomeration, armamentarium *miscellaneous:* 4 hash, olio
6 jumble, medley 7 mélange, mixture
8 mishmash, pastiche 9 bric-a-brac, potpourri 10 hodgepodge, salmagundi 11 olla
podrida *of anecdotes:* 3 ana *of animals:*
3 zoo 9 menagerie *of artistic works:*
6 museum 7 gallery *of clothes:* 8 wardrobe *of dried plants:* 9 herbarium *of
facts:* 4 data *of literary pieces:* 5 sylva
8 analecta, analects 9 anthology *of proper
names:* 11 onomasticon *of reports:* 4 file
7 dossier *of trinkets:* 10 bijouterie *suffix:*
3 ery

collective *association, Russian:* 5 artel
farm, Israeli: 7 kibbutz *farm, Russian:*
7 kolkhoz

collector *of bird's eggs:* 8 oologist *of
books:* 11 bibliophile *of coins:* 11 numis-
matist *of fares:* 9 conductor *of phonograph records:* 10 discophile *of stamps:*
11 philatelist

colleen 4 girl, lass *country:* 4 Eire, Erin
7 Ireland

college *building:* 3 gym, lab 4 dorm, hall
campus area: 4 quad 10 quadrangle *class
meeting:* 3 lab 7 lecture, seminar 8 tuto-
rial, workshop *degree:* 2 AA, AB, BA, BD,
BS, CE, DD, MA, MD, MM, MS 3 BLS,
DST, LLB, LLD, MBA, MEd, MFA, MLS,
PhD 5 LittD *graduate:* 6 alumna, alumni
(plural) 7 alumnae (plural), alumnus *official:* 4 dean 5 prexy 6 bursar, regent
7 proctor, provost, trustee 8 chairman,
chaplain, director 9 counselor, librarian,
president, registrar *oldest in U.S.:* 7 Harvard *oldest women's in U.S.:* 12 Mount
Holyoke *permit for absence:* 5 exeat *relating to:* 8 academic 10 collegiate *social
group:* 4 frat 8 sorority 10 fraternity
song: 9 alma mater *student class:*
4 soph 5 frosh 6 junior, senior 8 freshman 9 sophomore *teacher:* 3 don 4 prof
5 tutor 8 academic 9 professor 10 instructor *term:* 7 quarter, session 8 semester
9 trimester *VIP:* 4 BMOC *woman:* 4 coed

college athletic team *Air Force:* 7 Falcons *Alabama:* 11 Crimson Tide *Arizona:*
8 Wildcats *Arizona State:* 9 Sun Devils
Arkansas: 10 Razorbacks *Arkansas
State:* 7 Indians *Army:* 6 Cadets *Auburn:*
6 Tigers *Baylor:* 5 Bears *Boston College:*
6 Eagles *Boston University:* 8 Terriers
Brigham Young: 7 Cougars *Brown:* 6 Bru-
ins *California:* 11 Golden Bears *Central
Michigan:* 9 Chippewas *Cincinnati:*
8 Bearcats *Citadel:* 8 Bulldogs *Clemson:*
6 Tigers *Colgate:* 10 Red Raiders *Colorado:* 9 Buffaloes *Colorado State:* 4 Rams
Columbia: 5 Lions *Connecticut:* 7 Huskies
Cornell: 6 Big Red *Dartmouth:* 8 Big
Green *Davidson:* 8 Wildcats *Delaware
State:* 7 Hornets *Drake:* 8 Bulldogs
Duke: 10 Blue Devils *Eastern Kentucky:*
8 Colonels *Eastern Michigan:* 6 Hurons
Florida: 6 Gators *Florida State:* 9 Semi-
noles *Fresno State:* 8 Bulldogs *Furman:*
8 Palidans *Georgia:* 8 Bulldogs *Georgia
Tech:* 13 Yellow Jackets *Harvard:* 7 Crim-
son *Hawaii:* 15 Rainbow Warriors *Holy
Cross:* 9 Crusaders *Houston:* 7 Cougars
Howard: 6 Bisons *Idaho:* 7 Vandals *Idaho
State:* 7 Bengals *Illinois:* 6 Illini *Illinois
State:* 8 Redbirds *Indiana:* 8 Hoosiers
Indiana State: 9 Sycamores *Iowa:*
8 Hawkeyes *Iowa State:* 8 Cyclones *Kansas:* 8 Jayhawks *Kansas State:* 8 Wildcats *Kent State:* 13 Golden Flashes *Kentucky:* 8 Wildcats *Lehigh:* 9 Engineers
Louisiana State: 6 Tigers *Louisiana
Tech:* 8 Bulldogs *Maine:* 10 Black Bears
Maryland: 5 Terps 9 Terrapins *Massachusetts:* 9 Minutemen *Miami (Florida):*
10 Hurricanes *Miami (Ohio):* 8 Redskins
Michigan: 10 Wolverines *Michigan State:*
8 Spartans *Minnesota:* 7 Gophers *Mississippi:* 6 Rebels *Mississippi State:* 8 Bulldogs *Missouri:* 6 Tigers *Montana:* 9 Griz-
zlies *Montana State:* 7 Bobcats *Navy:*
10 Midshipmen *Nebraska:* 11 Cornhuskers
Nevada: 6 Rebels 8 Wolfpack *New Hampshire:* 8 Wildcats *New Mexico:* 5 Lobos
New Mexico State: 6 Aggies *North Carolina:* 8 Tar Heels *North Carolina State:*
8 Wolfpack *Northeastern:* 7 Huskies
Northwestern: 8 Wildcats *Notre Dame:*
13 Fighting Irish *Ohio State:* 8 Buckeyes
Ohio University: 7 Bobcats *Oklahoma:*
7 Sooners *Oklahoma State:* 7 Cowboys
Oregon: 5 Ducks *Oregon State:*
7 Beavers *Pennsylvania:* 7 Quakers *Pennsylvania State:* 12 Nittany Lions *Pittsburgh:* 8 Panthers *Princeton:* 6 Tigers *Purdue:* 12 Boilermakers *Rhode Island:*
4 Rams *Rice:* 4 Owls *Rutgers:* 14 Scarlet
Knights *San Diego State:* 6 Aztecs *San
Jose State:* 8 Spartans *South Carolina:*
9 Gamecocks *South Carolina State:* 8 Bull-

dogs *Southern California:* **7** Trojans
Southern Illinois: **7** Salukis *Southern
Methodist:* **8** Mustangs *Stanford:*
9 Cardinals *Syracuse:* **9** Orangemen *Temple:* **4** Owls *Tennessee:* **10** Volunteers
Tennessee State: **6** Tigers *Tennessee
Tech:* **12** Golden Eagles *Texas:* **9** Longhorns *Texas A&M:* **6** Aggies *Texas Christian:* **11** Horned Frogs *Texas Southern:*
6 Tigers *Texas Tech:* **10** Red Raiders
Toledo: **7** Rockets *Tulane:* **9** Green Wave
UCLA: **6** Bruins *UNLV:* **12** Runnin' Rebels
Utah: **4** Utes *Utah State:* **6** Aggies *Vanderbilt:* **10** Commodores *Villanova:* **8** Wildcats *Virginia:* **9** Cavaliers *VMI:* **7** Keydets
VPI: **8** Gobblers *Wake Forest:* **12** Demon
Deacons *Washington:* **7** Huskies *Washington State:* **7** Cougars *West Virginia:*
12 Mountaineers *William & Mary:* **7** Indians
Wisconsin: **7** Badgers *Wyoming:* **7** Cowboys *Yale:* **4** Elis **8** Bulldogs

collide **3** hit, ram **4** bump **5** carom, clash,
crash, smash **6** strike **7** impinge **8** conflict

collision **4** bump, jolt **5** clash, crash,
shock, smash, wreck **6** impact, pileup
7 crack-up, smashup **10** concussion, percussion **11** destruction **12** demolishment

collocate **3** set **5** place **7** arrange
8 position

collogue **5** treat **6** advise, confab, confer,
huddle, parley, powwow **7** consult
11 confabulate

colloid **3** gel, sol **4** agar **8** hydrogel,
hydrosol

colloque **4** chat, chin, talk, yarn **5** visit
8 converse

colloquial **6** patois, vulgar **7** vulgate
8 familiar, informal **10** vernacular

colloquium **7** palaver, seminar **10** conference, rap session

colloquy **4** chat, talk **6** parley **7** palaver,
seminar **8** converse, dialogue **10** conference, rap session **12** conversation
13 confabulation

collude **4** plot **6** devise **7** connive **8** cogitate, conspire, contrive, intrigue **9** machinate, scheme out

collusion **10** complicity, connivance

colluvies **4** hash **5** hoard, trove **6** jumble,
medley **7** mélange **8** mishmash, pastiche
9 amassment, potpourri **10** assortment, collection, cumulation, hodgepodge, miscellany **11** aggregation **12** accumulation
13 agglomeration

collywobbles **5** colic, gripe **9** bellyache
11 stomachache

Colombia *capital:* **6** Bogota *highest
peak:* **9** Cristobal *monetary unit:* **4** peso

Colonel Blimp **10** fuddy-duddy **12** stuffed
shirt

colonnade **4** stoa

color **3** dye, hue **4** cast, flag, glow, jack,
pink, rose, show, tint, tone **5** belie, blush,
flush, paint, rouge, shade, stain, tinct, tinge,
twist **6** banner, ensign, mantle, pennon, pinken, redden, stance **7** crimson, distort, falsify, pennant, pigment **8** attitude, disguise,
dyestuff, gonfalon, misstate, overdraw, position, standard, streamer, tincture **9** embellish, embroider, oriflamme, overpaint, overstate, semblance **10** exaggerate
12 chromaticity, misrepresent *band:*
5 facia, vitta **6** fascia *combining form:*
5 chrom **6** chromo **7** chromat **8** chromato
9 chromasia *primary:* **3** red **4** blue **6** yellow *relating to:* **9** chromatic *secondary:*
5 green **6** orange, purple *soft:* **6** pastel

Colorado *academy, college:* **5** Regis
10 U.S. Air Force *capital:* **6** Denver *nickname:* **15** Centennial State *park:* **5** Estes
state bird: **11** lark bunting *state flower:*
9 columbine

colorant **3** dye **5** stain **7** pigment **8** dyestuff, tincture

coloration *combining form:* **6** chroia,
chromy **7** chromia

colored **6** biased, warped **7** bigoted, partial **8** one-sided, partisan **9** jaundiced
10 prejudiced **11** tendentious **12** prepossessed *combining form:* **6** chroic, chrome
7 chromat, chroous **8** chromato

colorful **3** gay **5** gaudy, showy, vivid
6 bright, flashy, florid, garish **7** splashy

coloring **4** face, mask, show **5** front,
guise, put-on **6** facade **8** disguise **9** hyperbole, semblance **12** embroidering, exaggeration **13** embellishment, overstatement

coloring matter *combining form:* **5** phyll

colorist **6** tinter

colorless **3** wan **4** ashy, drab, dull, flat,
pale **5** ashen, livid, lurid, prosy, waxen,
white **6** albino, doughy, pallid **7** insipid,
neutral, prosaic **8** abstract, blanched,
detached, lifeless, tintless **10** achromatic,
impersonal, lackluster, lusterless, pokerfaced **11** unpassioned **13** disinterested,
dispassionate, unimaginative *combining
form:* **4** leuc, leuk **5** leuco, leuko

colossal **4** huge, vast **7** mammoth, titanic
8 gigantic **9** cyclopean, monstrous
10 behemothic, gargantuan **11** elephantine

Colossus of **6** Rhodes

colporteur **7** apostle **9** missioner
10 evangelist, missionary **12** propagandist

colt **4** tyro **6** novice, rookie **8** beginner,
freshman, neophyte, newcomer **9** fledgling,
novitiate

coltish **6** elvish, frisky, impish **7** larkish,
playful, puckish, waggish **10** frolicsome
11 mischievous

columbary **8** dovecote, pigeonry **9** dovehouse **11** culverhouse, pigeon house

Columbine *beloved:* 9 Harlequin *father:* 9 Pantaloon

columbium *symbol:* 2 Cb

Columbus *birthplace:* 5 Genoa *patron:* 8 Isabella 9 Ferdinand *ship:* 4 Nina 5 Pinta 10 Santa Maria *son:* 5 Diego *starting point:* 5 Palos

column 3 row 4 pier, prop 5 brace, shore 6 pillar 7 support 8 buttress, pilaster 11 underpinner 12 underpinning 13 underpropping *base:* 4 ordo 5 socle 6 plinth 9 stylobate *bulge:* 7 entasis *female figure:* 8 caryatid *male figure:* 5 atlas 7 telamon 8 atlantes (plural) *style:* 5 Doric, Ionic 10 Corinthian *top:* 7 capital 8 chapiter

coma 5 faint, sleep, swoon 6 stupor, torpor 7 languor, slumber, syncope 8 blackout, dullness, hebetude, lethargy 9 lassitude, torpidity

comate 3 pal 4 chum 5 buddy, crony 7 comrade 9 associate, companion 11 running mate

comatose 5 dopey, heavy 6 stupid, torpid 8 sluggish 9 lethargic, senseless 10 insensible, slumberous 11 inconscious, unconscious 12 hebetudinous

comb 4 grub, rake, sift, sort 5 probe, scour 6 forage, search, winnow 7 ransack, rummage 8 finecomb, separate 11 investigate *combining form:* 4 loph 5 lopho 6 pectin 7 pectini

combat 3 war 4 buck, duel 5 fight, repel 6 action, battle, oppose, resist, strife 7 contend, contest, dispute, service 8 traverse 9 withstand

combating *prefix:* 4 anti

combative 7 warlike 8 militant, vigorous 9 agonistic, bellicose, truculent 10 pugnacious 11 belligerent, contentious, quarrelsome 12 gladiatorial

combativeness 5 fight 6 attack 9 pugnacity 10 aggression 11 bellicosity 12 belligerence

combe 4 dale, glen, vale 6 valley

combination 4 bloc, pool, ring 5 party, tie-up, union 6 hookup, merger 7 cahoots, faction, melding, merging 8 alliance, mergence 9 aggregate, coalition 10 connection 11 affiliation, association, coadunation, conjunction, partnership; unification 13 consolidation *combining form:* 4 hapt 5 hapto

combine 3 add, mix, wed 4 band, bloc, fuse, join, link, pool, ring 5 blend, chain, group, merge, party, trust, unify, union, unite 6 cartel, concur, embody, league, mingle, relate 7 bracket, conjoin, connect, faction 8 coadjute, coalesce 9 associate, coalition, commingle, cooperate, integrate, syndicate 10 amalgamate 11 consolidate,

incorporate 12 conglomerate *Japanese:* 8 zaibatsu

combined action 7 synergy 8 synergia

combust 4 burn 10 incinerate

combustible 4 edgy, fuel 8 agitable, burnable, skittery, skittish, volatile 9 alarmable, excitable, flammable, ignitable, startlish 11 inflammable *material:* 3 gas, oil 4 coal, peat, wood 6 tinder

come 4 flow, grow, near, show, stem 5 add up, arise, get in, issue, occur, reach, run to, sum to, total 6 amount, arrive, befall, betide, happen, number, show up, spring, turn up 7 advance, develop, emanate, proceed 8 approach, hail from 9 aggregate, originate, transpire 10 derive from *a cropper:* 4 fail, fall *across:* 4 find, meet 8 discover 9 encounter *apart:* 12 disintegrate *at:* 6 attack, attain *away:* 5 leave 6 depart *before:* 7 precede *between:* 9 interfere, interpose *clean:* 7 confess *down from:* 6 alight *forth:* 5 issue 6 appear, emerge *forward:* 9 volunteer *from:* 6 derive, result *into:* 5 enter 7 acquire *near:* 5 verge 8 approach *round:* 5 rally 7 get well, recover *to pass:* 5 occur 6 happen *up:* 5 arise *upon:* 4 find, meet 6 affect, attack 7 afflict 8 discover 9 encounter

comeback 6 retort 7 riposte 8 repartee

come by 3 see 4 call, gain 5 pop in, run in, visit 6 attain, drop in, look in, look up, step in 7 acquire, inherit

comedian 3 wag, wit 4 card, zany 5 comic, droll, joker 6 jester 8 funnyman, humorist, jokester, quipster

comedo 9 blackhead

comedown 4 fall, ruin 5 crash 7 descent, setback 8 collapse

come down with 3 get 5 catch 8 contract

comedy 5 humor 8 drollery 9 drollness, funniness, wittiness 10 comicality 12 humorousness

come in 5 enter, reply 6 answer, rejoin, retort, return 7 ingress, respond 9 penetrate

comely 4 fair, nice 5 bonny, sonsy 6 lovely, pretty, proper, seemly, sonsie 7 correct 8 becoming, decorous, handsome 9 beauteous, beautiful, befitting, civilized 10 attractive 11 good-looking

come off 3 hap 5 break, click, occur 6 befall, betide, go over, happen, pan out 7 develop, succeed 8 prove out

come-off 6 escape 7 elusion, evasion 8 escaping, eschewal, shunning 9 avoidance, runaround

come-on 4 bait, lure, trap 5 cheat, decoy, rogue, snare 6 con man, gypper 8 swindler 9 trickster 10 allurement, enticement, seducement, temptation 11 flimflammer

12 bunco steerer, double-dealer, inveiglement **13** confidence man

come out **4** leak **5** break, debut **6** emerge **9** transpire

come out with **3** say **4** tell **5** state, utter **7** declare, deliver

comestible **6** edible **7** eatable **8** esculent

comestibles **4** feed, food, grub **6** viands **7** edibles **8** victuals **9** provender **10** provisions

come through **6** chip in, kick in **7** pitch in, ride out, survive **9** subscribe **10** contribute

come together **4** meet **7** synapse **8** converge

comeuppance **3** due **5** lumps, merit **6** rights **7** deserts **9** deserving

comfort **3** aid **4** help, lift **5** cheer **6** assist, buck up, relief, solace, succor **7** amenity, condole, console, relieve, secours, support, upraise **8** facility, reassure **10** assistance, sympathize **11** commiserate, convenience

comfortable **4** cozy, easy, homy, snug, soft **5** comfy, cushy, homey **6** loungy **7** content, easeful, pleased, restful, welcome, well-off **8** adequate, homelike, pleasant, pleasing, well-to-do **9** agreeable, competent, satisfied, sufficing, well-fixed **10** gratifying, prosperous, sufficient, well-heeled **11** substantial **12** satisfactory

comforter **4** pouf, puff **5** quilt **9** eiderdown

comfortless **5** harsh **7** uncomfy **12** inconsolable **13** discomforting

comfy **4** cozy, easy, homy, snug, soft **5** cushy, home **7** easeful **8** homelike **11** comfortable

comic **3** wag, wit **5** antic, droll, funny, joker **6** jester **7** risible **8** comedian, farcical, funnyman, gelastic, humorist, jokester, quipster **9** laughable, ludicrous **10** ridiculing, ridiculous **strip:** **7** funnies

comical **4** zany **5** droll, funny, silly **6** absurd, impish **7** foolish, risible, roguish, waggish **8** farcical, gelastic, sportive **9** laughable, ludicrous **10** ridiculous

coming **4** next **6** advent **7** arrival, ensuing, nearing **9** following **11** approaching **forth:** **7** issuant

comity **5** amity **7** concord, harmony **8** goodwill **10** friendship, kindliness **11** benevolence, camaraderie, comradeship **12** friendliness

comma **4** lull **5** pause **8** interval **9** pausation

command **3** bid, law **4** rule, sway, tell, warn, word **5** canon, might, order, power, skill **6** adjure, behest, charge, compel, direct, enjoin, manage **7** ability, bidding, captain, conduct, control, dictate, know-how, mandate, mastery, precept, statute **9** authority, constrain, direction, directive,

expertise, expertism, ordinance **10** domination, expertness, injunction, mastership **11** instruction **12** jurisdiction **to go:** **4** mush **6** avaunt, begone, giddap **to stop:** **4** whoa **5** avast

commandeer **4** take **5** annex, seize, usurp **6** assume **7** preempt **8** accroach, arrogate **9** sequester **10** confiscate **11** appropriate, expropriate

commander **4** boss, head **6** honcho, leader, master **7** captain, general, headman, officer **8** decurion, hierarch **9** dominator

commandment **3** law **4** rule **5** edict, order **6** decree **7** mitsvah, mitzvah, precept, statute

Commedia dell' ___ **4** Arte

comme il faut **4** nice **5** right **6** decent, proper, seemly **7** correct **8** becoming, decorous **9** befitting **10** conforming

commemorate **4** keep **7** observe **8** monument **9** celebrate, solemnize **11** memorialize **13** monumentalize

commemorative **8** memorial

commence **4** open **5** arise, begin, enter, start **6** launch, take up **7** kick off, lead off **8** embark on **9** originate **10** embark upon, inaugurate

commencement **4** dawn **5** alpha, birth, onset, start **6** outset **7** dawning, genesis, opening **8** outstart **9** beginning

commend **4** hail, laud **5** extol **6** commit, kudize, praise, tender **7** acclaim, applaud, approve, confide, consign, entrust, proffer **8** hand over, relegate, turn over **10** compliment

commendable **6** worthy **8** laudable **9** admirable, deserving, estimable, meritable, praisable **11** meritorious, thankworthy **12** praiseworthy

commensurable see **commensurate**

commensurate **4** even **5** equal **11** symmetrical **12** proportional

comment **4** note **6** notice, remark, review **7** observe **8** critique, reviewal **9** criticism **10** animadvert **11** observation **12** obiter dictum

commerce **5** trade, truck **7** contact, traffic **8** business, congress, dealings, exchange, industry **9** communion **11** interchange, intercourse **13** communication

commercial **2** ad **8** business **10** mercantile **13** advertisement

commie **3** Red **9** Bolshevik, communist

commination **5** curse **7** malison **8** anathema **11** imprecation, malediction

commingle **3** mix **5** immix, merge, unify **8** compound, intermix **9** integrate **10** amalgamate

comminute **4** bray, buck **5** crush **6** powder **9** pulverize, triturate **12** contriturate

commiserable 4 poor 6 rueful 7 piteous, pitiful 8 pathetic, pitiable

commiserate 4 ache, pity 7 feel for 10 sympathize 13 compassionate

commiseration 3 rue 4 pity, ruth 8 sympathy 10 compassion

commission 3 bid 4 name 5 board, order 6 charge, depute, enable, enjoin 7 appoint, command, council, empower, license 8 accredit, delegate, deputize, instruct, nominate 9 authorize, designate

commit 2 do 5 allot 6 assign, invest, ordain 7 commend, confide, consign, entrust, execute, perform, pull off, trustee 8 hand over, relegate, turn over 10 perpetuate

commitment 4 duty, must, need 5 ought 6 charge, devoir 10 obligation

committal see **commitment**

commixture 6 fusion 7 compost 9 composite 11 interfusion

commodious 4 wide 5 ample, roomy 8 spacious 9 capacious

commodities 5 goods, items, wares 6 things 8 articles 9 vendibles 11 merchandise

common 4 flat, park, poor 5 cheap, joint, plaza, prosy, stale, tatty, trite, typic, usual 6 decent, garden, impure, mutual, normal, paltry, shared, shoddy, sleazy, square, trashy 7 defiled, general, generic, natural, prosaic, regular, routine, typical 8 adequate, all right, communal, conjoint, conjunct, déclassé, everyday, familiar, frequent, inferior, low-grade, ordinary 9 customary, pleasance, prevalent, tolerable, universal 10 desecrated, second-rate, sufficient, uneventful, unexciting 11 intermutual, second-class 12 matter-of-fact, satisfactory, second-drawer, unnoteworthy 13 unexceptional, unimpeachable, uninteresting **combining form:** 3 cen 4 caen, ceno, coen 5 caeno, coeno

commonalty 3 mob 5 plebs 6 masses, people, plebes, public, rabble 7 commune 8 populace 9 hoi polloi, multitude, plebeians 11 proletariat, rank and file, third estate

commoners see **commonalty**

commonition 6 caveat 7 caution, warning 11 forewarning

commonplace 5 lowly, tired, trite, usual 6 cliché, normal, truism 7 bromide, clichéd, general, inanity, mundane, natural, prosaic, regular, typical, workday 8 banality, bromidic, chestnut, everyday, ordinary, prosaism, shopworn, timeworn, well-worn, workaday 9 platitude, prevalent, triteness 10 prosaicism, shibboleth, stereotype, threadbare, uneventful 11 stereotyped 12 unnoteworthy 13 stereotypical, unexceptional

common sense 6 wisdom 8 gumption, judgment

Common Sense author 5 Paine

commorancy 4 home 5 abode, house 8 domicile, dwelling 9 residence, residency 10 habitation

commotion 3 din, row 4 coil, flap, fuss, moil, riot, stew, stir, to-do 5 hurly, storm, upset, whirl 6 bustle, clamor, dither, flurry, fracas, furore, hassle, hoopla, hubbub, hurrah, lather, outcry, pother, racket, ruckus, rumpus, shindy, tow-row, tumult, uproar, upturn 7 clatter, ferment, fluster, ruction, shindig, turmoil, whoopla 8 brouhaha, disquiet, foofaraw, rowdydow, upheaval, uprising 9 agitation, confusion 10 convulsion, hullabaloo, hurly-burly, turbulence 11 pandemonium 12 perturbation

commove 5 elate 6 excite 7 inspire 9 stimulate 10 exhilarate

communal 5 joint 6 common, mutual, public, shared 8 conjoint, conjunct 11 intermutual

commune 6 confer 8 commerce, converse, district 10 collective 12 conversation *Israeli:* 7 kibbutz *Russian:* 3 mir 7 kolkhoz

communicable 8 catching 9 expansive, garrulous, talkative 10 contagious, infectious

communicate 4 abut, join, tell 5 touch, verge 6 adjoin, border, butt on, convey, impart, pass on, reveal, signal 7 contact, divulge 8 disclose, neighbor, transmit

communication 4 talk, word 7 contact, message, missive, talking 8 commerce, converse, exchange 9 directive 10 conversing, discussing, discussion 11 interchange, intercourse 12 conversation *means:* 2 TV 4 drum, note 5 media, phone, radio 6 letter, medium, pigeon, speech 9 telegraph, telephone 10 television *system:* 8 language

communications code word 4 Alfa, Echo, Golf, Kilo, Lima, Mike, Papa, Xray, Zulu 5 Bravo, Delta, Hotel, India, Oscar, Romeo, Tango 6 Quebec, Sierra, Victor, Yankee 7 Charlie, Foxtrot, Juliett, Uniform, Whiskey 8 November

communicative 7 voluble 9 expansive, garrulous, talkative 10 loquacious

communion 4 cult, sect 5 creed, faith, truck 6 church 7 contact, traffic 8 commerce, converse, dealings, religion 10 connection, persuasion 11 intercourse 12 denomination *cloth:* 8 corporal *cup:* 3 ama 7 chalice *plate:* 5 paten

communism 8 Leninism 10 bolshevism

Communist 3 red 5 pinko 6 commie 7 comrade, Marxist 8 Leninist 9 Bolshevik, Stalinist 10 Trotskyist

Communist leader *Chinese:* **10** Mao Tse-tung *Russian:* **5** Lenin **6** Stalin **7** Trotsky **10** Khrushchev

community 4 city, town **6** people, public **7** enclave, society **12** neighborhood *ecological:* **10** biocenosis

commute 5 alter **6** change, travel **7** convert **8** exchange, transfer **9** transform, translate, transmute, transpose **10** compensate, substitute **11** interchange, transfigure **12** metamorphose, transmogrify

compact 4 bond, firm, hard **5** close, dense, pithy, thick, tight, unify **6** packed **7** bargain, bunched, crowded **8** compress, condense, contract, covenant **9** agreement, integrate **10** convention **11** concentrate, consolidate, transaction **12** epigrammatic *combining form:* **4** pycn **5** pycno

companion 3 pal **4** chum, fere, mate, twin **5** buddy, crony, match **6** attend, cohort, comate, double, escort, fellow **7** comrade, conduct, consort, partner **8** chaperon, helpmate, helpmeet **9** accompany, associate, colleague, duplicate **10** coordinate, reciprocal **11** concomitant, consort with, running mate **13** accompaniment

companionable 6 social **7** amiable **8** sociable **9** convivial **11** good-natured

companionship 7 company, society **10** fellowship

company 3 mob **4** band, club, crew, firm, gang, pack, ruck, team **5** corps, group, house, party, troop **6** attend, clique, convoy, guests, muster, outfit, troupe **7** concern, conduct, coterie, society, visitor **8** assembly, business, chaperon, visitors **9** companion, gathering **10** assemblage, collection, enterprise, fellowship **11** aggregation, association, camaraderie, comradeship **12** congregation, consociation **13** companionship, establishment

comparable 4 akin, like **5** alike **6** agnate **7** similar, uniform **8** parallel **9** consonant **13** corresponding, undifferenced

comparative 4 near **8** relative **11** approximate *suffix:* **2** er

compare 5 liken, match **6** equate **7** bracket, collate, paragon **8** contrast, parallel **9** correlate **10** assimilate

comparison 6 simile **7** analogy **8** affinity, likeness **9** alikeness, semblance **10** similarity, similitude **11** resemblance

compass 3 get, hem, see, win **4** gain, gird, ring **5** ambit, annex, catch, field, grasp, orbit, range, reach, round, scope, sweep **6** bounds, circle, domain, extent, girdle, limits, obtain, radius, secure, sphere, take in **7** acquire, circuit, environ, procure, purview **8** boundary, confines, encircle, environs, purlieus, surround **9** apprehend, enclosure, extension, perimeter, periphery, precincts **10** comprehend, understand **13** circumference *kind:* **4** gyro **5** solar **8** lensatic, magnetic *stand:* **8** binnacle

compassion 3 rue **4** pity, ruth **5** mercy **7** charity, empathy **8** clemency, humanity, sympathy **10** humaneness **11** benevolence **13** commiseration, fellow feeling

compassionate 4 pity, warm **6** humane, tender **7** clement, feel for **10** responsive **11** commiserate, kindhearted, softhearted, sympathetic, warmhearted

compassionless 5 stony **7** callous **8** obdurate **9** heartless, unfeeling **11** cold-blooded, hardhearted, ironhearted **12** stony-hearted

compass point 2 NE, NW, SE, SW **3** ENE, ESE, NNE, NNW, SSE, SSW, WNW, WSW **4** east, west **5** north, rhumb, south *Scottish:* **4** airt

compatible 6 proper **8** suitable **9** agreeable, congenial, congruous, consonant **10** consistent **11** sympathetic

compatriot 7 compeer **8** confrere **9** associate, colleague

compeer see **compatriot**

compel 4 hale, make, urge **5** drive, force **6** coerce, impose, oblige **7** concuss, enforce **9** constrain *Scottish:* **3** gar

compellation 4 name **5** nomen, style, title **7** moniker **8** cognomen **11** appellative, designation **12** denomination

compendious 4 curt **5** brief, short **7** compact, concise, laconic, summary **8** succinct **12** breviloquent **13** short and sweet

compendium 5 brief, guide **6** aperçu, digest, manual, précis, sketch, survey **7** pandect, sylloge **8** Baedeker, handbook, overview, syllabus **9** guidebook, vade mecum **10** abridgment, conspectus **11** enchiridion

compensate 3 pay **5** repay **6** make up, offset, redeem, set off **7** balance, guerdon, requite **8** atone for, outweigh **9** indemnify, reimburse **10** counteract, neutralize, recompense, remunerate **11** countervail **12** counterpoise

compensation 6 amends, reward, salary **7** payment, redress **8** reprisal, requital, solatium **9** indemnity, quittance **10** recompense, reparation **11** restitution

compete 3 vie **5** fight, match, rival **6** battle, strive **7** contend, contest, dispute, emulate, tourney **8** rivalize, struggle

competence 5 might **6** enough **7** ability **8** adequacy, capacity **10** capability **11** sufficiency **13** qualification, qualifiedness

competent 4 able **5** adept **6** au fait, decent, enough, proper **7** capable, skilled **8** adequate, masterly **9** qualified, sufficing

10 sufficient 11 comfortable
12 satisfactory

competition 4 game, meet 5 match, rival
6 strife 7 contest, rivalry, warfare 8 concours, conflict, corrival, striving, struggle,
tug-of-war 9 emulation, rencontre

competitor 5 rival 8 corrival, opponent
9 adversary 10 antagonist, contestant

compile 4 edit 6 gather, muster, select
7 collect 8 assemble

complacence see **complacency**

complacency 5 pride 6 egoism 7 conceit, egotism 9 vainglory 10 narcissism
11 amour propre, consequence
13 conceitedness

complacent 4 smug 7 assured 8 egotistic, priggish 9 conceited, confident, egotistic 11 self-assured, self-pleased 13 selfconfident, self-contented, self-possessed,
self-satisfied

complain 3 nag 4 crab, fuss, kick, wail
5 gripe, grump, whine 6 grouch, grouse,
murmur, pester, repine, yammer 7 grizzle,
grumble, protest 9 bellyache

complainer 4 crab 5 crank 6 griper,
grouch, kicker 7 grouser 8 grumbler, sourpuss 10 malcontent 11 faultfinder

complaint 3 ill 5 gripe 6 malady 7 ailment, disease, protest 8 disorder, sickness,
syndrome 9 affection, condition, infirmity

complaisant 4 easy, mild 7 amiable,
lenient 8 generous, obliging 9 agreeable,
indulgent 11 good-humored, good-natured
12 good-tempered

complement 4 crew 7 pendant 9 correlate 10 enrichment, supplement 11 counterpart, enhancement 12 augmentation
13 accompaniment

complementary *prefix:* 7 counter

complete 3 end 4 done, full, halt 5 close,
ended, gross, total, uncut, utter, whole
6 choate, entire, finish, wind up, wrap up
7 achieve, fulfill, perfect, perform, plenary,
through 8 absolute, conclude, finished, integral, outright, realized, thorough, totalize,
ultimate, undocked, whole-hog 9 concluded, determine, discharge, downright,
full-dress, implement, out-and-out, terminate 10 accomplish, consummate, exhaustive, terminated, unabridged 11 uncondensed, unmitigated 13 thoroughgoing,
unabbreviated *combining form:* 3 hol, tel
4 holo, tele, telo 5 teleo

completed 4 done, over 5 ended
7 through 8 finished 9 concluded
10 terminated

completion 3 end 6 finish *combining
form:* 6 teleut 7 teleuto

complex 5 vague 6 daedal, knotty, system, varied 7 gordian, mixed-up, network,
obscure 8 baffling, compound, confused,

involved, puzzling 9 Byzantine, composite,
confusing, elaborate, intricate 10 mysterious, mystifying, perplexing 11 bewildering,
complicated, confounding 12 labyrinthine
13 heterogeneous, sophisticated

complexion 3 hue 4 tint 5 color, humor,
tinge 6 makeup, nature, temper 8 tincture
9 character 11 disposition, personality, temperament 13 individualism, individuality

complexionless 4 ashy, pale 5 ashen,
livid, lurid, waxen 6 doughy, pallid
8 blanched 9 colorless

compliance 8 docility 9 obedience
10 conformity 11 amenability, resignation
12 acquiescence, tractability

complicate 5 mix up, ravel, snarl, upset
6 jumble, muddle, tangle 7 perplex 8 disorder, entangle 10 disarrange

complicated 4 hard 5 fancy 6 daedal,
knotty 7 complex, gordian 8 abstruse,
involved 9 Byzantine, elaborate, intricate,
recondite 12 labyrinthine 13 sophisticated

complicity 9 collusion 10 connivance
11 involvement

compliment 4 hail, kudo, laud 6 kudize,
praise 7 acclaim, applaud, bouquet, commend, orchids, tribute 8 accolade, encomium 9 laudation, recommend
12 commendation

complimentary 4 free 6 gratis 8 costless 10 chargeless, gratuitous

comply 4 keep, mind, obey 6 follow, submit 7 conform, observe 9 acquiesce

component 4 part 6 factor 7 element
10 ingredient 11 constituent

comport 3 act 4 bear, go on, quit 5 agree,
carry, check, fit in, tally 6 accord, acquit,
behave, demean, square 7 conduct
8 dovetail 9 harmonize 10 correspond

comportment 3 air, set 4 mien 5 tenue
7 address, bearing, conduct 8 behavior,
demeanor, presence

compose 4 balm, calm, cool, form, lull,
make, rein 5 allay, quiet, relax, still, verse,
write 6 becalm, create, devise, indite,
invent, make up, settle, solace, soothe
7 collect, comfort, console, contain, control,
dream up, repress, versify 8 comprise, melodize, mitigate, moderate, modulate,
restrain, suppress, tune down 9 originate,
re-collect 10 constitute, simmer down
11 tranquilize *type:* 3 set

composed 4 calm, cool, easy 5 quiet,
staid, still 6 placid, poised, sedate, serene
8 tranquil 9 collected, easygoing, possessed, repressed, unruffled 10 nonchalant,
suppressed 11 unflappable 13 imperturbable, self-possessed

composer 4 bard, poet 5 odist 6 author,
lyrist, penman, scorer, writer 7 elegist,
hymnist 8 compiler, essayist, lyricist, melo-

dist, monodist, novelist **9** balladist, dramatist, harmonist, scenarist, songsmith, tunesmith, wordsmith **10** compositor, typesetter *American:* **3** Kay **4** Cage, Cash, Hill, Ives, Kern, Work **5** Arlen, Bland, Bloch, Cohan, Dylan, Friml, Glass, Gould, Grofé, Handy, Mason, Moore, Sousa, Still **6** Barber, Berlin, Cowell, Emmett, Foster, Hanson, Harris, Joplin, McKuen, Morton, Oliver, Parker, Piston, Porter, Seeger, Taylor, Varese **7** Babbitt, Brubeck, Copland, Gilbert, Gilmore, Goldman, Guthrie, Herbert, Loesser, Maxwell, Menotti, Rodgers, Romberg, Schuman, Thomson, Tiomkin **8** Billings, Burleigh, Damrosch, Gershwin, Kreisler, Sessions, Sondheim, Spalding, Williams **9** Bacharach, Bernstein, Ellington, Ledbetter, MacDowell **10** Blitzstein, Gottschalk *Argentinian:* **9** Ginastera *Australian:* **8** Grainger *Austrian:* **4** Berg, Wolf **5** Haydn **6** Czerny, Mahler, Mozart, Straus, Sulzer, Webern **7** Strauss **8** Bruckner, Schubert **9** Schönberg *Belgian:* **5** Ysaye *Brazilian:* **10** Villa-Lobos *Czech:* **3** Suk **6** Dvořák **7** Janáček, Kubelik, Smetana *Danish:* **7** Nielsen *Dutch:* **9** Sweelinck *English:* **4** Arne, Byrd **5** Elgar **6** Delius, Morley, Tallis, Walton, Wesley **7** Britten, Dowland, Gibbons, Purcell, Weelkes **8** Sullivan **11** Lloyd Webber *Finnish:* **8** Palmgren, Sibelius *Flemish:* **5** Dufay, Lasso **6** Lassus **8** Willaert *French:* **4** Indy, Lalo **5** Auber, Bizet, Dukas, Fauré, Ibert, Jarre, Lully, Ravel, Satie, Widor **6** Boulez, Campra, Franck, Gounod, Rameau, Thomas **7** Berlioz, Debussy, Delibes, Milhaud, Poulenc **9** Chabrier, Couperin, Honegger, Massenet, Messiaen **9** Offenbach *German:* **4** Bach, Orff **5** Bruch, Gluck, Reger, Spohr, Weber, Weill **6** Brahms, Handel, Schutz, Vogler, Wagner **7** Hassler, Richter, Silcher, Strauss **8** Schumann, Telemann **9** Beethoven, Buxtehude, Hindemith, Meyerbeer **10** Praetorius **11** Humperdinck, Mendelssohn, Stockhausen *Hungarian:* **5** Lehar, Liszt **6** Bartok, Kodaly, Ligeti **8** Dohnanyi *Italian:* **4** Peri **5** Boito, Verdi, Vinci **6** Busoni, Viotti, Vitali **7** Bellini, Corelli, Martini, Puccini, Rossini, Tartini, Vivaldi **8** Clementi, Gabrieli, Mascagni, Paganini, Respighi **9** Cherubini, Donizetti, Pergolesi, Scarlatti, Tommasini **10** Boccherini, Monteverdi, Palestrina, Ponchielli, Zingarelli **11** Frescobaldi, Leoncavallo **12** Dallapiccola *Mexican:* **6** Chavez *Norwegian:* **5** Grieg *Polish:* **6** Chopin **10** Paderewski, Penderecki, Wieniawski *Romanian:* **7** Xenakis *Russian:* **6** Glinka **7** Borodin **8** Glazunov, Scriabin **9** Prokofiev **10** Mussorgsky, Rubinstein, Stravinsky, Tcherepnin **11** Tchaikovsky **12** Rachmani-

noff, Shostakovich *Spanish:* **5** Falla, Vives **6** Garcia **7** Albéniz **8** Granados, Victoria

composite **3** mix **6** hybrid **7** amalgam, complex, compost, mixture, montage **8** compound **9** immixture **10** commixture **11** combination **12** amalgamation, intermixture

composition **5** essay, paper, theme **6** design, makeup **7** article, morceau, writing **8** fantasia **9** formation **10** compromise **12** architecture, constitution, construction *choral:* **5** motet *for eight:* **5** octet *for five:* **7** quintet *for four:* **7** quartet *for nine:* **5** nonet *for one:* **4** solo **5** scena *for seven:* **6** septet *for six:* **6** sextet *for three:* **4** trio *for two:* **4** duet **6** duetto *instrumental:* **3** jig **4** reel **5** étude, fugue, gigue, march, rondo, suite **6** sonata **7** caprice, partita, prelude, scherzo **8** allemand, concerto, fantasia, overture, rhapsody, saraband, sinfonia, symphony, tone poem **9** capriccio, sarabande **10** intermezzo *vocal:* **4** aria, lied, mass, song **5** canon, carol, chant, motet, opera, round **6** arioso, ballad, chorus **7** cantata, chanson, chantey, chorale, lullaby, requiem **8** berceuse, madrigal, oratorio **9** barcarole, plainsong, spiritual **12** cantus firmus

compos mentis **4** sane **5** lucid **6** normal

composure **6** phlegm **7** ataraxy **8** calmness, coolness **9** sangfroid **10** equanimity

compound **3** mix **4** join, link **5** admix, alloy, blend, boost, immix, unite **6** commix, couple, expand, extend, fusion, make up, mingle **7** amalgam, augment, bracket, complex, compost, connect, enlarge, magnify, mixture **8** coagment, coalesce, comingle, heighten, increase, intermix, multiply **9** admixture, associate, coadunate, commingle, composite **10** aggrandize, commixture **11** intermingle **12** amalgamation *aromatic:* **7** depside *chemical:* (see at **chemical**) *combining form:* **5** genin *medicinal:* **7** quassin **8** magnesia *protein:* **7** peptone *sulfur:* **5** thiol **6** sulfid **7** sulfide, sulfone **8** sulfonal, sulfuryl, sulphide, sulphone *volatile:* **8** cymogene

comprehend **3** dig, get, see **4** know **5** catch, grasp **6** accept, embody, fathom, take in **7** cognize, compass, contain, embrace, include, involve, subsume **8** perceive **9** encompass **10** appreciate, understand

comprehendible **5** lucid **8** knowable, luminous **9** graspable **10** fathomable **12** intelligible **13** apprehensible

comprehensible see **comprehendible**

comprehensive **4** full, wide **5** broad **6** global **7** general, overall **8** sweeping **9** all-around, inclusive **12** encyclopedic

comprehensiveness 5 scope
7 breadth 8 fullness, wideness 9 amplitude
compress 3 jam 4 bear, cram, push
5 crowd, crush, press, stupe 6 shrink,
squash, squish 7 bandage, compact, pledget, squeeze 8 condense, contract, laminate 9 constrict 11 concentrate
comprise 4 form, make 6 make up
7 compose, contain, include 10 constitute
compromise 4 mean, pact, risk 5 peril
6 hazard, menace 7 bargain, compact,
imperil, jeopard 8 contract, endanger, jeopardy 9 agreement, middle way 10 golden
mean, jeopardize 11 composition 12 middle ground
compulsion 4 itch, need, urge 5 drive,
force 6 duress 8 coercion, exigency, violence 9 necessity 10 constraint
compulsory 8 required 9 imperious, mandatory 10 imperative, obligatory
compunction 3 rue 4 ruth 5 demur,
qualm 6 squeam 7 penance, remorse,
scruple 9 attrition, hesitancy, penitence,
penitency 10 conscience, contrition, hesitation, repentance 12 contriteness
compunctious 5 sorry 8 contrite, penitent 9 regretful, repentant 10 apologetic,
remorseful 11 attritional, penitential
computation 8 figuring 9 ciphering, reckoning 10 arithmetic, estimation
11 calculation
compute 5 total 6 cipher, figure, reckon
8 estimate 9 calculate
computer 6 abacus 7 machine 10 calculator 13 adding machine *data:* 7 readout
8 printout, software *information:* 4 data
instruction: 5 macro *inventor:* 7 Babbage
language: 5 ALGOL, BASIC, COBOL
7 FORTRAN *operator:* 9 programer
10 programmer *type:* 6 analog 7 digital
comrade 3 pal 4 ally, chum, mate
5 buddy, crony 6 comate, fellow, frater
7 brother, consort 8 tovarich, tovarish
9 associate, communist, companion
comstock 4 prig 5 prude 6 Grundy
7 puritan 8 bluenose 9 Mrs. Grundy, nice
Nelly 10 goody-goody
con 4 anti, bilk, coax, dupe, fool, hoax,
scam, view 5 learn, study, trick 6 befool,
cajole, gammon, inmate, survey 7 blarney,
canvass, chicane, convict, deceive, examine, inspect, opposer, swindle, wheedle
8 blandish, flimflam, hoodwink, jailbird,
memorize, opponent, opposure, prisoner,
soft soap 9 adversary, bamboozle, check
over, oppugnant, sweet-talk 10 antagonism, antagonist, antithesis, opposition,
scrutinize 11 contrariety, hornswoggle
concatenate 4 join, link 5 unite 7 connect 9 integrate 10 articulate

concave 6 arched 7 vaulted 8 bowllike
9 depressed *combining form:* 7 coelous
concavity 3 dip, sag 4 bowl, dent, sink
5 basin 6 hollow 7 sinkage 8 sinkhole
10 depression
conceal 4 bury, hide, veil 5 cache, cloak,
cover, stash 6 occult, screen 7 secrete
8 ensconce, enshroud, palliate
10 camouflage
concealed 5 privy 6 buried, covert, hidden, secret 7 guarded 8 obscured,
shrouded, ulterior 11 clandestine *combining form:* 4 adel 5 adelo
concede 3 own 4 avow 5 admit, allow,
award, grant, let on, own up 6 accord, fess
up 7 confess 9 vouchsafe
11 acknowledge
conceit 4 idea, whim 5 fancy, freak,
humor, image, pride 6 egoism, megrim,
notion, vagary, vanity 7 boutade, caprice,
concept, egotism, thought 8 crotchet, self-
love, smugness, snobbery, vainness 9 self-
glory, self-pride, vainglory 10 conception,
impression, narcissism, perception, self-
esteem 11 amour propre, complacence,
complacency, consequence, self-opinion,
swelled head 12 apprehension, intellection
13 outrecuidance
conceited 4 vain 6 snobby, snooty
7 pompous, stuck-up 8 snobbish 12 narcissistic, vainglorious
conceitedness 6 vanity 8 self-love, vainness 9 vainglory 10 narcissism, self-
esteem 11 amour propre
conceivable 6 likely, mortal 7 earthly
8 possible, probable 9 thinkable 10 imaginable, supposable
conceive 4 form, make 5 beget, fancy,
grasp, think 6 accept, assume, expect, follow, gather, ponder, vision 7 believe, compass, feature, imagine, realize, suppose,
suspect 8 cogitate, envisage, envision,
meditate, ruminate 9 apprehend, speculate,
visualize 10 comprehend, excogitate,
understand
concentrate 3 fix 4 heap, mass, meet,
pile 5 focus, rivet, unify 6 fasten, fixate,
gather, shrink 7 collect, compact 8 assemble, compress, condense, contract, converge 9 constrict, integrate 11 consolidate
concentrated 5 fixed, lusty, whole
6 fierce, potent, robust, strong 7 furious,
intense 8 vehement 9 exclusive, exquisite,
undivided 10 full-bodied, unswerving
12 undistracted
concentrating 8 unifying 10 compacting
11 centripetal, integrative 12 centralizing
13 consolidating
concentration 4 heed 5 study 6 debate
9 attention 11 application 12 deliberation
13 consideration

concept 4 idea 5 image 6 notion 7 conceit, thought 10 impression, perception 12 apprehension, intellection

conception 4 idea 5 image, start 6 notion 7 conceit, thought 9 beginning 10 impression, perception 12 apprehension, intellection

conceptual 5 ideal 8 abstract, notional 9 imaginary, visionary 10 ideational 12 transcendent

concern 4 care, firm, heed 5 doubt, worry 6 affair, gadget, matter, outfit, regard, unease, wonder 7 anxiety, company, dubiety, lookout, palaver 8 business, disquiet, interest, mistrust 9 attention, curiosity, dubiosity, misgiving, occasions, suspicion 10 enterprise, inquietude, skepticism, solicitude, uneasiness 11 carefulness, disquietude, heedfulness, incertitude, uncertainty, uncertitude 12 apprehension 13 consciousness, consideration, establishment

concerned 8 affected, involved 10 implicated, interested

concerning 2 re 4 as to, in re 5 about, anent, as for 7 against, apropos 9 as regards, regarding 10 respecting

concert 4 tune 5 agree 6 accord, chorus, concur, settle 7 arrange, benefit, concord, harmony, recital 8 coincide 9 cooperate, harmonize, negotiate 10 consonance 11 performance

concert hall 5 odeon, odeum 10 auditorium

concession 5 favor 6 gambit 9 allowance, privilege 10 compromise 12 acquiescence

conch 5 shell 6 mussel 7 mollusk

concierge 6 porter, warden 7 doorman, janitor 9 custodian 10 doorkeeper

conciliate 4 calm, ease 5 quiet 6 pacify, soothe 7 appease, assuage, mollify, placate, sweeten 10 propitiate 11 tranquilize

concise 4 curt 5 brief, pithy, short, terse 7 compact, laconic, summary 8 abridged, succinct 9 condensed 10 compressed, contracted 11 compendary, compendious 12 breviloquent 13 short and sweet

conclude 3 end 4 draw, halt, rule, stop 5 close, infer, judge 6 decide, deduce, deduct, derive, figure, finish, gather, reason, settle, wind up, wrap up 7 collect, resolve 8 complete, ultimate 9 determine, terminate

concluding 4 last 5 final 6 latest, latter 7 closing 8 eventual, hindmost, terminal, ultimate

conclusion 3 end 4 stop 5 cease, close, finis 6 ending, epilog, finale, finish, period, windup 7 closing, closure 8 decision, epilogue, illation, judgment, sequitur 9 cessation, deduction, inference 10 desistance,

resolution, settlement 11 termination 13 determination, ratiocination

conclusive 4 last 5 final 6 cogent 7 telling 8 deciding, decisive 10 compelling, convincing, definitive 11 determinant, determinate, irrefutable 12 irrefragable, unanswerable

concoct 3 mix 4 brew, cook 5 frame, hatch 6 cook up, create, devise, invent, make up, vamp up 7 dream up, hatch up 8 conceive, contrive 9 formulate, originate

concomitant 4 mate 6 fellow 7 consort 8 adjuvant, incident 9 accessory, ancillary, associate, attendant, attending, companion, satellite 10 coincident, collateral 12 accompanying 13 accompaniment, supplementary

concord 4 pact, tune 5 agree, chime, unity 6 accord, chorus, concur, treaty 7 concert, harmony, rapport 8 coincide 9 agreement, harmonize 10 consonance, convention

concordance 4 tune 5 chime 6 accord 7 harmony 9 agreement 10 consonance

concordant 8 agreeing 9 congruous 10 harmonious

concourse 6 throng 7 joining, meeting 8 junction 9 gathering 10 concursion, confluence

concrete 3 set 4 join, link 5 beton, solid, unite 6 couple, harden 7 bracket, combine, congeal, connect 8 coalesce, compound, indurate, solidify 9 associate **component:** 4 sand 5 water 6 gravel

concubine 7 hetaera, hetaira, odalisk 8 mistress 9 odalisque

concupiscence 4 lust 6 desire 7 passion 9 eroticism, prurience, pruriency 10 aphrodisia 11 lustfulness 13 lickerishness

concupiscent 3 hot 7 goatish, lustful, satyric 8 prurient 9 lickerish 10 lascivious, libidinous, passionate

concur 4 band, jibe 5 agree, unite 6 accord, league 7 combine, concert, concord, conjoin, go along 8 coadjute, coincide 9 cooperate, harmonize

concurrent 6 coeval 10 coetaneous, coexistent, coexisting, synchronal, synchronic 11 synchronous 12 contemporary, simultaneous

concurrently 6 at once 8 together 12 coincidently

concuss 3 jar 4 rock 5 force, shake, shock 6 coerce, compel, oblige 7 agitate, shotgun 8 convulse 9 constrain

concussion 3 jar 4 bump, jolt 5 clash, clout, crash, shock, smack 6 impact 7 beating, jarring, jolting, shaking 8 pounding 9 buffeting, collision

condemn 3 rap 4 damn, doom 5 blame, decry, knock 7 censure, convict

8 denounce, sentence **9** criticize, proscribe, reprehend, reprobate **10** denunciate

condensation 3 dew **5** brief **7** epitome, summary **8** abstract, boildown, breviary, breviate, synopsis **10** abridgment, conspectus

condense 3 sum **5** sum up **6** digest, reduce, shrink **7** abridge, capsule, compact, shorten, summate **8** boil down, compress, contract **9** capsulize, constrict, epitomize, inventory, summarize, synopsize **10** abbreviate **11** concentrate, consolidate

condescend 5 deign, stoop **6** unbend

condign 3 due, fit **4** fair, just **5** right **7** merited **8** deserved, rightful, suitable **9** requisite **11** appropriate **13** rhadamanthine

condiment 3 soy **4** salt **5** caper, curry, sauce, spice **6** catsup, pepper, relish **7** chutney, ketchup, mustard, paprika, vinegar **8** dressing, turmeric **9** seasoning **10** mayonnaise

condition 2 if **3** ill **4** case, mode **5** order, shape, state, terms **6** estate, fettle, kilter, malady, repair, status **7** ailment, disease, fitness, posture, proviso, strings **8** disorder, sickness, syndrome **9** affection, complaint, essential, exception, infirmity, necessity, provision, requisite, situation **10** limitation, sine qua non **11** requirement, reservation, stipulation **12** prerequisite **13** qualification *suffix:* **2** or, th, ty **3** dom, ery, ice, ile, ion, ism **4** ance, ancy, ence, ency, ment, ness, oses (plural), osis, ship **5** ation

conditional 4 iffy **7** reliant **8** relative **9** dependent, provisory, qualified, tentative, uncertain **10** contingent, restricted **11** provisional **12** provisionary

condolence 3 rue **4** pity, ruth **8** sympathy **10** compassion **13** commiseration

condonable 7 tenable **9** excusable, tolerable **10** acceptable, defensible, vindicable **11** justifiable, warrantable

condone 5 remit **6** excuse, pardon **7** forgive **8** overlook

conduce 4 lead, tend **7** redound **10** contribute

conduct 3 act, run **4** bear, care, head, lead, quit, show **5** guide, pilot, route, steer, tenue, usher **6** acquit, attend, behave, charge, convey, convoy, demean, deport, direct, escort, funnel, handle, keep up, manage, ordain **7** arrange, carry on, channel, company, comport, control, operate, oversee, running, traject **8** behavior, chaperon, handling, shepherd, transmit **9** accompany, companion, oversight, supervise **10** administer, deportment, intendance, management **11** comportment, supervision

conductor 5 guide **6** copper, escort, leader **7** maestro **8** conveyor, director, motorman **10** bandleader **11** impressario *American:* **4** Shaw **5** Grofé, Stock, Szell **6** Levine, Maazel, Previn, Reiner, Thomas, Walter **7** Fiedler, Monteux, Ormandy **8** Damrosch, Williams **9** Bernstein, Leinsdorf, Rodzinski, Steinberg, Stokowski **11** Kostelanetz, Mitropoulos *Australian:* **7** Bonynge *Austrian:* **4** Bohm **6** Mahler **10** von Karajan *Belgian:* **5** Ysaye *British:* **5** Solti *Canadian:* **9** MacMillan *Czech:* **7** Kubelik *English:* **4** Wood **5** Boult **7** Beecham, Malcolm, Sargent **8** Goossens **10** Barbirolli *French:* **5** Munch **6** Boulez, Pretre *German:* **4** Muck **5** Spohr, Weber **9** Klemperer, Scherchen **11** Furtwangler, Mendelssohn *Hungarian:* **5** Seidl **7** Nikisch, Richter *Indian:* **5** Mehta *Italian:* **6** Abbado **9** Toscanini *Japanese:* **5** Ozawa *Mexican:* **6** Chavez *Russian:* **12** Koussevitzky *Spanish:* **6** Iturbi *stick:* **5** baton *suffix:* **3** eer *Swiss:* **8** Ansermet

conduit 4 duct, main, pipe **5** canal **6** course **7** channel **8** aqueduct, penstock, pipeline **11** watercourse

coney 4 pika **5** hyrax **6** rabbit **10** butterfish

confab 4 chat **5** treat **6** advise, confer, huddle, parley, powwow **7** consult **8** collogue

confabulate see **confab**

confabulation 3 rap **4** chat, talk **6** parley **8** colloquy, converse, dialogue **10** conference, discussion **12** conversation, deliberation

confection see **candy**

confederacy 5 union **6** league **8** alliance **9** anschluss, coalition **10** federation

confederate 3 reb **4** ally **5** rebel, unite **6** fellow **7** abettor, partner **8** conspire **9** accessory, associate, colleague **10** accomplice **11** conspirator **12** collaborator **13** coconspirator *admiral:* **6** Semmes *capital:* **8** Richmond *color:* **4** gray *general:* **3** Lee **4** Hill, Hood **5** Bragg, Ewell, Price, Smith **6** Morgan, Stuart **7** Forrest, Hampden, Jackson, Pickett **8** Johnston **9** Pemberton **10** Beauregard, Longstreet *president:* **5** Davis *soldier:* **9** butternut *spy:* **4** Boyd (Belle) *vice-president:* **8** Stephens

confederation see **confederacy**

confer 4 give, meet, talk **5** allot, award, grant, speak, treat **6** accord, advise, bestow, confab, huddle, parley, powwow **7** consult, discuss, present **8** collogue, colloque, converse **10** deliberate **11** confabulate

conference 3 rap **4** loop, talk **5** synod, wheel **6** league, parley, powwow **7** circuit, meeting, palaver, seminar **8** colloquy **9** symposium **10** colloquium, discussion,

rap session, round robin, round table
11 association 12 deliberation
13 confabulation

confess 3 own 4 avow, sing 5 admit, allow, grant, let on, own up 6 reveal 7 concede, divulge 8 disclose 11 acknowledge

confession 5 creed 6 avowal 7 peccavi 9 admission, statement 10 disclosure

confidant 4 mate 5 amigo 6 friend 8 familiar, intimate 11 cater-cousin 12 acquaintance

confide 4 tell 6 bestow, commit 7 breathe, commend, consign, entrust, present, whisper 8 hand over, relegate, turn over

confidence 4 gall, hope 5 brass, cheek, faith, nerve, stock, trust 6 aplomb, surety 7 courage 8 reliance, sureness 9 assurance, brashness, certainty, certitude, self-trust 10 conviction, dependence, effrontery, equanimity 11 assuredness *game:* 4 scam 5 bunco, bunko, grift, sting 7 swindle

confidence man 3 gyp 7 diddler, grifter, sharper, sharpie 8 swindler 9 defrauder, trickster 11 bunco artist 12 bunco steerer

confident 4 bold, sure 5 brash, brave, cocky, perky, pushy 6 secure, uppity 7 assured, certain, pushful 8 cocksure, fearless, intrepid, positive, sanguine, trustful, unafraid 9 dauntless, presuming, undaunted 10 brassbound, courageous, undoubtful 11 overweening, self-assured, self-reliant 12 presumptuous 13 self-assertive, self-possessed

confidential 5 close, privy, thick 6 chummy, closet, hushed, inside, secret 7 private 8 familiar, intimate 9 auricular

configuration 4 cast, form 5 shape 6 figure 7 contour, outline, pattern 12 conformation

confine 3 bar, box, end, mew, pen 4 cage, coop, crib, jail, term 5 bound, cramp, limit, orbit, range, reach, scope, sweep 6 embank, encage, extent, immure, intern, radius 7 delimit, enclose, pinfold, purview 8 bastille, boundary, imprison, localize, prelimit, restrict 9 constrain, periphery 10 delimitate, limitation 11 incarcerate 12 circumscribe 13 circumference

confinement 5 cramp 7 lying-in 8 childbed 9 captivity, restraint 10 constraint 11 restriction 12 accouchement, imprisonment 13 constrainment

confines 6 bounds, limits 7 compass 8 boundary, environs, purlieus 9 precincts

confirm 3 fix, set 4 back 5 check, prove, vouch 6 attest, ratify, uphold, verify 7 bear out, certify, justify, support 8 check out, validate 11 corroborate 12 authenticate, substantiate

confirmation 5 proof 7 witness 8 evidence 9 testament, testimony 11 attestation, testimonial

confirmed 3 set 5 fixed, sworn 7 chronic, settled 8 deep-dyed, definite, habitual, ratified 9 hard-shell 10 accustomed, deep-rooted, deep-seated, entrenched, habituated, inveterate 13 bred-in-the-bone, dyed-in-the-wool

confiscate 4 take 5 annex, seize, usurp 7 escheat, preempt 8 accroach, arrogate 9 sequester 10 commandeer 11 appropriate, expropriate

confiture 3 jam 8 conserve, preserve

conflagrant 5 afire, fiery 6 ablaze, aflame, alight 7 blazing, burning, flaming, flaring, ignited

conflagration 4 fire 5 blaze 7 inferno 9 holocaust

conflict 3 jar, war 4 bout, duel, meet, rift, vary 5 clash, fight 6 battle, combat, differ, jangle, oppose, strife 7 contest, discord, dispute, dissent, meeting, rivalry, warfare 8 argument, concours, disagree, disunity, mismatch, striving, struggle, tug-of-war, variance 9 disaccord, emulation, encounter, rencontre 10 contention, difference, dissension, dissidence 11 competition, controversy 12 disharmonize

conflicting 7 warring 8 clashing, contrary 9 dissonant 10 contending, discordant, discrepant 11 contrariant, incongruent, incongruous, inconsonant 12 antagonistic, antipathetic, disconsonant, incompatible, inconsistent, inharmonious

confluence 7 meeting 8 junction 9 concourse, gathering 10 concursion

conform 3 fit 4 jibe, mind, obey, suit, tune 5 adapt, agree, fit in, yield 6 accord, adjust, attune, comply, follow, square, submit, tailor 7 observe 8 dovetail, quadrate 9 acquiesce, harmonize, integrate, reconcile 10 coordinate, correspond, proportion, tailor-make 11 accommodate 12 reconciliate

conformable 6 fitted, suited 7 adapted, matched 8 assorted, suitable

conformation 4 cast, form 5 shape 6 figure 13 configuration

conforming 4 nice, typy 5 typey 6 decent, proper, seemly 7 uniform 8 becoming, decorous 9 befitting, civilized 11 comme il faut

conformity 7 decorum, harmony 8 affinity, legalism, normalcy 9 coherence, congruity, obedience 10 compliance, submission 11 consistency, resignation 12 acquiescence

confound 3 mix 4 faze, pose, stun 5 abash, befog, evert, mix up, rebut 6 baffle, puzzle, rattle, refute 7 confuse, confute,

misdeem, mistake, perplex, stumble, stupefy **8** bewilder, disprove **9** discomfit, dumbfound, embarrass **10** controvert, disconcert, disconfirm **11** misidentify **13** metagrobolize
confounded 4 rank **5** agape, gross, utter **6** aghast, blamed, cursed, cussed, damned **7** blasted, blessed, shocked **8** absolute, dismayed, infernal, outright **9** consarned, dad-burned, execrable, out-and-out **11** dumbfounded, overwhelmed, straight-out, unmitigated **13** thunderstruck
confrere see **colleague**
confront 4 defy, face, meet **5** brave **6** accost, breast, oppose **9** challenge, encounter
confuse 3 fog, mix **4** blur, faze, mull, pose, warp **5** abash, addle, befog, cloud, dizzy, mix up, muddy, twist, upset, wrest **6** baffle, ball up, bemuse, flurry, foul up, fuddle, garble, jumble, mess up, muddle, puzzle, rattle, wrench **7** agitate, becloud, derange, disrupt, flummox, fluster, misdeem, mislead, mistake, nonplus, perplex, perturb, pervert, snarl up **8** bedazzle, befuddle, bewilder, confound, disorder, disquiet, distract, throw off, unsettle **9** discomfit, embarrass **10** disarrange, discompose, disconcert **11** disorganize, misidentify **12** misrepresent **13** metagrobolize
confused 4 lost **5** muddy, muzzy, vague **7** at a loss, mixed up **9** perplexed **10** bewildered, topsy-turvy **12** disconcerted
confusion 3 din **4** flap, loss, mess, muck, ruin, stew **5** babel, chaos, havoc, mix-up, snafu, snarl **6** ataxia, bedlam, dither, foul-up, hubbub, huddle, jumble, lather, muddle, pother, tumult, unease **7** clutter, turmoil **8** disarray, disorder, misorder, pell-mell **9** abashment, agitation, commotion, ruination **10** hullabaloo, turbulence, uneasiness **11** bedevilment, derangement, destruction, devastation, disturbance, pandemonium **12** discomfiture, discomposure, razzle-dazzle **13** disconcertion, embarrassment
confute 4 deny **5** break, evert, rebut **8** confound, disprove **10** controvert, disconfirm
congé 3 bow **5** adieu **7** good-bye, parting **8** farewell **9** dismissal **11** leave-taking
congeal 3 dry, gel, set **4** cake, clot, curd, jell **5** jelly **6** curdle, gelate, harden **7** jellify, stiffen, thicken **8** concrete, indurate, solidify **9** coagulate **10** gelatinize
congener 3 ilk **4** kind, sort, type **5** class, genus
congenial 4 good, nice **6** amical, social **7** affable, cordial, kindred, welcome **8** amicable, friendly, gracious, pleasant, pleasing, sociable **9** agreeable, congruous, consonant, favorable **10** compatible, consistent,

gratifying, harmonious **11** cooperative, pleasurable, sympathetic **13** companionable
congenital 6 inborn, inbred, innate, native **7** connate, natural **8** inherent **9** essential, ingrained, inherited, intrinsic **10** connatural, deep-seated, indigenous, indwelling, unacquired
conger 3 eel **4** pike
congeries 4 ruck **5** group **6** muster **7** company **8** assembly **9** gathering **10** assemblage, collection **11** aggregation **12** congregation
congest 3 jam **4** clog, fill, plug, stop **5** block, choke, close, crowd **7** occlude **8** obstruct
conglobate 4 ball **5** round **6** sphere **8** ensphere
conglomerate 4 heap, mass, pool **5** chain, group, mixed, trust **6** cartel, motley, varied **7** combine **8** assorted, chowchow **9** aggregate, syndicate **11** aggregation, promiscuous **12** multifarious **13** agglomeration, heterogeneous, miscellaneous
conglomeration 5 hoard, trove **9** aggregate, amassment, colluvies **10** collection, cumulation **11** agglomerate, aggregation **12** accumulation
Congo *capital:* **11** Brazzaville *monetary unit:* **5** franc
congratulate 4 laud **6** salute **10** compliment, felicitate
congregate 4 meet, teem **5** raise, swarm **6** gather, muster **7** collect, convene **8** assemble, congress **9** forgather **10** rendezvous
congregation 4 host, mass, ruck **5** crowd, group **6** muster **7** company, meeting **8** assembly, audience **9** gathering **10** assemblage, collection
congress 4 club, diet **5** guild, synod, union **6** gather, league, muster **7** collect, society **8** assemble, assembly **9** forgather **10** congregate, fellowship, fraternity, parliament, rendezvous **11** association, brotherhood, Capitol Hill, legislature
congressman 7 senator **8** delegate **10** legislator **14** representative
congruity 9 agreement, coherence **10** conformity **11** consistency
congruous 3 apt, fit **7** fitting **9** accordant, agreeable, congenial, consonant **10** compatible, concordant, consistent, harmonious **11** appropriate, sympathetic
conjectural 7 reputed **8** putative, supposed **11** suppositive, suppository **12** hypothetical, supposititious **13** suppositional
conjecture 5 fancy, guess, infer **6** assume, theory **7** presume, pretend, sup-

pose, surmise, suspect **9** inference, speculate **11** speculation, supposition

conjoin 3 wed **4** band, knit, link, yoke
5 unite **6** concur, couple, league, relate
7 combine, connect **8** coadjute **9** associate, cooperate

conjoint 6 common, mutual, public,
shared **8** coacting, coactive, communal,
conjunct, synergic **10** synergetic **11** coefficient, cooperative, intermutual

conjointly 8 mutually, together

conjointment 5 tie-up, union **6** hookup
7 cahoots, wedding **8** alliance **9** coalition
10 connection **11** affiliation, association,
combination, conjunction, partnership

conjugal 6 wedded **7** marital, married,
nuptial, spousal **8** hymeneal **9** connubial
11 matrimonial

conjugality 7 wedlock **8** marriage **9** matrimony **12** connubiality

conjugate 4 join, link, yoke **5** yoked
6 couple, joined, linked **7** bracket, combine,
conjoin, connect, coupled **8** coalesce
9 associate, connected

conjunct 5 joint **6** common, mutual, public,
shared **8** communal **11** intermutual

conjunction 2 as, if, or, so **3** and, but, for,
nor, tho, yet **4** as if, lest, than, then, when
5 since, tie-up, union, until, while **6** either,
hookup, though, unless, whenas, whilst
7 because, neither, wedding, whereas,
whether **8** alliance, although, moreover
9 coalition, therefore **10** connection
11 affiliation, association, combination, partnership **12** conjointment

conjuration 4 rune **5** charm, spell, trick
11 incantation, legerdemain

conjure 3 beg **4** pray **5** brace, crave
6 appeal, invoke **7** beseech, entreat,
implore **9** importune **10** supplicate

conjurer 4 mage, seer **5** magus **6** magian,
shaman, wizard **7** warlock **8** magician, sorcerer **9** enchanter, trickster, voodooist
11 illusionist, necromancer

conjuring 5 magic **7** sorcery **8** witchery,
wizardry **10** necromancy, witchcraft
11 bewitchment, enchantment, legerdemain,
thaumaturgy

conk 3 die, hit, rap **4** swat **5** knock
7 decease **8** pass away

con man see **confidence man**

connate 4 akin **6** allied, inborn, native
7 kindred, natural, related **8** incident, inherent **9** elemental, essential, inherited, intrinsic **10** affiliated, congenital, deep-seated,
indigenous, indwelling, unacquired
11 consanguine

connatural see **connate**

connect 3 tie, wed **4** bind, join, link, yoke
5 marry, unite **6** attach, bridge, couple, fas-

ten, relate **7** combine, conjoin **9** affiliate,
associate, interlock

connected with suffix: 3 ast **4** aria
5 arium, orial

**Connecticut academy, college, univer-
sity: 4** Yale **7** Trinity **8** Hartford, New
Haven, Wesleyan **9** Fairfield **10** Bridgeport,
Quinnipiac **11** Sacred Heart, Saint Joseph
12 U.S. Coast Guard **capital: 8** Hartford
nickname: 11 Nutmeg State **12** Blue Law
State **state bird: 13** American robin **state
flower: 14** mountain laurel

connection 3 job **4** cult, post, seam, sect,
spot **5** creed, joint, nexus, tie-in, tie-up,
union **6** billet, hookup **7** joining **8** alliance,
coupling, junction, juncture, position, religion **9** communion, situation **10** catenation **11** affiliation, appointment, association,
combination, conjunction, partnership
12 conjointment, denomination,
togetherness

connective 2 or **3** and, nor **6** either
7 neither **8** syndetic **11** conjunction,
conjunctive

connivance 9 collusion **10** complicity

connive 4 plot, wink **5** blink **6** devise,
wink at **7** blink at, collude **8** cogitate, conspire, contrive, intrigue **9** machinate,
scheme out

connoisseur 6 expert **7** epicure, gourmet **8** aesthete, gourmand, highbrow
9 bon vivant **10** dilettante **11** cognoscente

connotation 4 hint **7** meaning **8** overtone **9** undertone **10** suggestion **11** association, implication

connote 4 hint, mean **5** imply, spell
6 import, intend **7** add up to, express, signify, suggest **8** intimate **9** insinuate

connubial 6 wedded **7** marital, married,
nuptial, spousal **8** conjugal, hymeneal
11 matrimonial

connubiality 7 wedlock **8** marriage
9 matrimony **11** conjugality

conquer 3 win **4** beat, best, foil, lick, tame,
whip **5** crush **6** defeat, hurdle, master, outwit, reduce, subdue, thwart **7** prevail, triumph **8** bear down, beat down, overcome,
override, surmount, vanquish **9** checkmate,
overpower, overthrow, overwhelm, subjugate **10** overmaster

conquest 3 win **4** rout **7** routing, subdual,
triumph, victory **9** overthrow

Conrad character: 3 Jim **4** Axel, Lena
5 Flora, Kurtz **6** Marlow **7** Almayer
8 MacWhirr, Nostromo **work: 5** Youth
6 Chance **7** Lord Jim, Typhoon, Victory
8 Nostromo **11** Secret Agent **14** Almayer's
Folly

consanguine 4 akin **6** agnate, allied
7 cognate, connate, kindred, related **8** incident **10** affiliated, connatural

conscience 5 demur, qualm, sense
6 psyche, squeam **7** scruple
11 compunction
conscienceless 6 amoral, shifty, tricky,
unfair **7** devious **12** unprincipled
conscientious 4 fair, just, true **5** exact,
fussy, right **6** honest **7** careful, dutiful,
heedful, upright **8** punctual, studious
9 honorable **10** meticulous, scrupulous
11 painstaking, punctilious **12** conscionable
conscionable see **conscientious**
conscious 5 alive, awake, aware **7** knowing, mindful, witting **8** affected, mannered,
sensible, sentient, vigilant, watchful **9** attentive, au courant, cognizant **10** conversant,
perceptive
consciousness 4 care, heed **6** regard
7 concern **9** awareness **11** carefulness,
needfulness
conscribe, conscript 5 draft **6** enlist,
enroll, muster
consecrate 5 bless **6** anoint, devote, hallow **8** dedicate, sanctify
consecrated 4 holy **6** sacred **7** blessed
8 hallowed **9** unprofane **10** sanctified *oil:*
6 chrism *thing:* **6** sacrum
consecution 3 row **5** chain, order, train
6 sequel, series **8** sequence **10** procession, succession **11** progression
consecutive 4 next **5** after, later
6 serial **7** ensuing, sequent **9** enlarging, following, succedent **10** increasing, sequential, subsequent, succeeding, successive
11 progressive **12** successional
13 subsequential
consent 3 let, yes **5** agree, allow, leave,
yield **6** accede, accord, assent, comply,
concur, permit **7** approve **8** sanction
9 acquiesce, agreement, allowance, subscribe **10** permission, sufferance
13 authorization, understanding
consentaneous 5 solid **9** unanimous
11 consentient
consequence 3 end **4** fame, pith, rank
5 event, honor, issue, pride, state **6** cachet,
effect, egoism, import, moment, renown,
repute, result, sequel, status, upshot,
weight **7** conceit, dignity, egotism, outcome, stature **8** position, prestige,
sequence, standing **9** aftermath, magnitude, vainglory **10** importance, narcissism,
reputation **11** aftereffect, amour propre,
complacence, complacency, weightiness
12 significance **13** conceitedness,
momentousness
consequent 5 sound **7** logical **8** rational,
sensible **9** following, resulting **10** reasonable **11** intelligent
consequential 3 big **7** weighty **8** material **9** important, momentous **10** meaning-

ful **11** significant, substantial
12 considerable
consequently 2 so **4** ergo, then, thus
5 hence **9** therefore, thereupon
11 accordingly
conservation 4 care **6** saving **7** control,
keeping **8** managing **9** attention, directing,
governing, preserval, salvation **10** cherishing, husbanding, management, protection
11 safekeeping **12** preservation,
sustentation
conservative 4 tory, wary **5** chary, right
6 proper **7** diehard, puritan **8** cautious, discreet, moderate, old liner, orthodox, rightist,
standpat **9** temperate, unextreme **10** controlled, reasonable, restrained **11** bitter-
ender, circumspect, reactionary, right-winger, standpatter, unexcessive
conserve 3 can, jam **4** save **6** keep up
7 support, sustain **8** maintain, preserve
9 confiture
consider 3 eye, see **4** deem, feel, hold,
mind, muse, rate, rule, scan, view **5** fancy,
infer, judge, sense, study, think, weigh
6 admire, credit, esteem, gather, look at,
ponder, reason, reckon, regard **7** account,
believe, bethink, examine, imagine, inspect,
perpend, reflect, respect **8** cogitate, conceive, conclude, gaze upon, look upon, meditate, prescind, ruminate, think out **9** speculate, think over **10** excogitate, scrutinize
11 contemplate
considerable 3 big **4** good, tidy **5** hefty,
large, major **6** active, goodly, pretty **7** notable, sizable, weighty **8** material, sensible
9 effective, extensive, important, momentous **10** large-scale, meaningful **11** efficacious, respectable, significant, substantial
13 consequential
considerably 3 far **4** well **5** quite
6 rather **8** somewhat **13** significantly
considerate 3 big **4** kind, safe, wary
5 chary, lofty **6** kindly, polite, tender **7** amiable, careful, guarded **8** cautious, discreet,
generous, gingerly, obliging **9** attentive
10 benevolent, chivalrous, thoughtful
11 calculating, circumspect, complaisant,
magnanimous, sympathetic, warm-hearted
12 greathearted **13** compassionate
consideration 4 heed **5** cause, favor,
mercy, study **6** debate, esteem, motive,
reason, regard, spring **7** account, concern,
respect **9** attention, awareness **10** admiration, estimation, solicitude **11** application,
forbearance, heedfulness, mindfulness
12 deliberation **13** concentration
considered 7 advised, studied, willful
8 designed, prepense, studious **9** voluntary **10** deliberate, thought-out **11** intentional **12** aforethought, premeditated
consign 4 give, send, ship **5** allot, award,

remit, route, yield **6** commit, devote
7 address, commend, confide, entrust, forward **8** dispatch, hand over, relegate, transmit, turn over **9** surrender

consist 2 be, go **3** lie **4** rest **5** abide, agree, dwell, exist, fit in **6** accord, inhere, repose, reside **7** comport, conform, consort, subsist **8** dovetail **10** correspond

consistency 7 aptness, concord, fitness, harmony **8** evenness, felicity, firmness, likeness **9** agreement, coherence, congruity **10** apposition, conformity, consonance, similarity **11** suitability

consistent 4 same, true **8** constant **9** agreeable, congenial, congruous, consonant, unfailing, unvarying **10** compatible, invariable, unchanging **11** sympathetic

consistently 7 as usual, usually **8** wontedly **10** habitually **11** customarily

console 4 calm **5** cheer, table **6** buck up, solace **7** animate, cabinet, comfort, hearten, relieve, upraise **8** inspirit **11** tranquilize

consolidate 3 mix, set **4** fuse **5** blend, merge, unify, unite **7** compact **8** compress, condense, solidify **9** integrate **10** amalgamate, strengthen **11** concentrate

consolidation 5 union **6** merger **7** melding, merging **8** mergence **9** coalition **11** coadunation, combination, unification **12** amalgamation

consonance 4 tune **5** chime **6** accord, chorus **7** concert, concord, harmony **9** agreement **11** concordance

consonant 4 akin, like **5** alike, round **6** agnate, fortis, rotund **7** chiming, musical, orotund, ringing, similar, uniform, vibrant **8** blending, harmonic, parallel, plangent, resonant, sonorant, sonorous **9** accordant, agreeable, analogous, congenial, congruous **10** coincident, comparable, compatible, consistent, harmonious, resounding **11** conformable, sympathetic, symphonious **13** corresponding *kind:* **4** stop, surd **5** nasal, velar **6** atonic, voiced **7** lateral, palatal, spirant **8** alveolar, bilabial, unvoiced **9** fricative, voiceless

consort 4 bear, mate, wife **5** agree, group, tally **6** accord, attend, convoy, fellow, spouse, square **7** company, comport, conduct, conform, husband **8** assembly, chaperon, dovetail **9** accompany, associate, companion, harmonize **10** correspond **11** concomitant **13** accompaniment

consortium 4 club **5** guild, order, union **6** league **7** society **8** congress **10** fellowship, fraternity **11** association

conspectus 5 brief **7** epitome **8** abstract, boildown, breviary, breviate, synopsis **10** abridgment **12** condensation

conspicuous 5 clear, plain, showy **6** marked, patent, signal **7** blatant, eminent,

evident, obvious, pointed, salient **8** apparent, distinct, flagrant, manifest, striking **9** arresting, arrestive, egregious, prominent **10** celebrated, noticeable, openhanded, remarkable **11** illustrious, outstanding

conspiracy 4 plan, plot **5** cabal, covin **6** scheme **8** intrigue, sedition **9** treachery **11** machination

conspirator 7 abettor **9** accessory **10** accomplice **11** confederate

conspire 4 plot **5** cabal **6** devise **7** collude, complot, connive **8** cogitate, contrive, intrigue **9** machinate, scheme out

constancy 6 fealty **7** loyalty **8** adhesion, fidelity **9** adherence, diligence **10** attachment **12** faithfulness

constant 4 even, fast, same, true **5** fixed, liege, loyal **6** ardent, dogged, stable, steady **7** abiding, chronic, endless, equable, lasting, stabile, staunch, uniform **8** clinging, enduring, faithful, unending **9** allegiant, ceaseless, confirmed, continual, immovable, immutable, obstinate, perpetual, steadfast, unceasing, unfailing, unmovable, unvarying **10** changeless, consistent, continuous, inflexible, invariable, inveterate, persistent, persisting, unchanging, unwavering **11** everlasting, inalterable, persevering, unalterable, unremitting **12** interminable, pertinacious, unchangeable, unmodifiable **13** unfluctuating

Constantine *birthplace:* **4** Nish *mother:* **6** Helena *son:* **7** Crispus *victim:* **6** Fausta **7** Crispus *wife:* **6** Fausta

constantly 4 ever **6** always **10** invariably **11** perpetually **12** continuously

constellation 5 group **7** pattern **10** assemblage, collection **11** arrangement *Altar:* **3** Ara *Archer:* **11** Sagittarius *Arrow:* **7** Sagitta *Balance:* **5** Libra *Big Dipper:* **9** Ursa Major *Bird of Paradise:* **4** Apus *Bull:* **6** Taurus *Centaur:* **9** Centaurus *Chained Lady:* **9** Andromeda *Chameleon:* **10** Chamaeleon *Champion:* **7** Perseus *Charioteer:* **6** Auriga *Clock:* **10** Horologium *Colt:* **8** Equuleus *Crab:* **6** Cancer *Crane:* **4** Grus *Cross:* **4** Crux *Crow:* **6** Corvus *Crown:* **6** Corona *Cup:* **6** Crater *Dolphin:* **9** Delphinus *Dove:* **7** Columba *Dragon:* **5** Draco *Eagle:* **6** Aquila *Fishes:* **6** Pisces *Fly:* **5** Musca *Flying Fish:* **6** Volans *Furnace:* **6** Fornax *Graving Tool:* **6** Caelum *Greater Dog:* **10** Canis Major *Hare:* **5** Lepus *Herdsman:* **6** Boötes *Horned Goat:* **11** Capricornus *Hunter:* **5** Orion *Indian:* **5** Indus *Keel:* **6** Carina *Lady in the Chair:* **10** Cassiopeia *Larger Bear:* **9** Ursa Major *Larger Dog:* **10** Canis Major *Lesser Dog:* **10** Canis Minor *Lion:* **3** Leo *Little Dipper:* **9** Ursa Minor *Little Fox:* **9** Vulpecula *Lizard:*

7 Lacerta *Lyre:* 4 Lyra *Mariner's Compass:* 5 Pyxis *Monarch:* 7 Cepheus *Net:* 9 Reticulum *Painter's Easel:* 6 Pictor *Pair of Compasses:* 8 Circinus *Peacock:* 4 Pavo *Pump:* 6 Antlia *Ram:* 5 Aries *Rescuer:* 7 Perseus *River Po:* 8 Eridanus *Sails:* 4 Vela *Scorpion:* 8 Scorpius *Serpent:* 7 Serpens *Serpent Holder:* 9 Ophiuchus *Sextant:* 7 Sextans *Shield:* 6 Scutum *Smaller Bear:* 9 Ursa Minor *Square:* 5 Norma *Stern:* 6 Puppis *Swan:* 6 Cygnus *Table:* 5 Mensa *Toucan:* 6 Tucana *Triangle:* 10 Triangulum *Twins:* 6 Gemini *Unicorn:* 9 Monoceros *Virgin:* 5 Virgo *Water Carrier:* 8 Aquarius *Water Monster:* 5 Hydra *Water Snake:* 6 Hydrus *Whale:* 5 Cetus *Winged Horse:* 7 Pegasus *Wolf:* 5 Lupus

consternate 5 daunt, shake 6 appall, dismay 7 horrify

consternation 4 fear 5 alarm, dread, panic 6 dismay, fright, horror, muddle, terror 9 confusion, trepidity 10 muddlement, perplexity 11 distraction, trepidation 12 bewilderment

constipate 6 stifle 7 trammel 8 stagnate, stultify

constituent 4 part 5 piece, voter 6 factor, member 7 element, portion 8 division, fraction 9 component, principal 10 ingredient

constitute 4 form, make 5 enact, found, set up, start 6 create, embody, make up 7 compose 8 complete, comprise, organize 9 establish, institute

constitution 3 law 4 code 5 build, canon, habit 6 design, makeup, nature 7 habitus 8 physique 9 formation, ordinance, structure 11 composition 12 architecture, construction

Constitution 12 Old Ironsides

constitutional 4 turn, walk 6 inborn, inbred, innate, ramble, stroll 7 built-in, saunter 8 inherent 9 essential, ingrained, intrinsic 10 congenital, deep-seated

Constitution State 11 Connecticut

constitutive 5 vital 8 cardinal 9 essential 11 fundamental

constrain 3 ban, bar, jam, jug 4 bear, curb, deny, hurt, jail, make, pain, push 5 check, crowd, crush, force, press 6 bridle, coerce, compel, enjoin, grieve, hold in, immure, injure, intern, oblige, squash, squish 7 abstain, concuss, confine, deprive, inhibit, refrain, shotgun, squeeze 8 aggrieve, bastille, disallow, distress, hold back, hold down, imprison, restrain, restrict, withhold 11 incarcerate

constraint 4 bond 5 check, cramp, force 6 duress 8 coercion, violence 9 restraint 10 compulsion, repression 11 confinement, restriction, suppression

constrict 4 curb, stop 5 choke, limit, strap 6 hamper, narrow, pucker, shrink 7 confine, inhibit, squeeze, tighten 8 astringe, compress, condense, contract, restrain, strangle, stultify 9 constrain 10 constipate, constringe 11 concentrate 12 circumscribe

constrictor 3 boa 5 snake 6 muscle 8 anaconda 9 sphincter, strangler

construct 4 form, make, rear 5 build, erect, forge, frame, put up, raise, set up 6 devise, uprear 7 build up, fashion, produce 8 assemble 9 establish, fabricate, hammer out 11 put together

construction 6 design, expose, makeup 8 building, exegesis 9 construal, formation 10 exposition 11 composition, explanation, explication 12 architecture, constitution

constructive 7 helpful, virtual 8 implicit 9 practical

construe 7 analyze, explain, expound 8 spell out 9 explicate, interpret, translate

consuetude 3 use 4 wont 5 habit, trick, usage 6 custom, manner, praxis 8 habitude, practice

consult 3 ask 5 refer, treat 6 advise, confab, confer, huddle, parley, powwow 7 counsel, examine 8 collogue, consider 11 confabulate

consume 2 go 3 eat, use 4 down, gulp, meal, raze, ruin, take, wolf 5 crush, drink, eat up, gorge, sew up, shift, spend, swill, use up, waste, wreck 6 absorb, devour, expend, feed on, finish, guzzle, ingest 7 destroy, engross, exhaust, fritter, put away, put down, swallow 8 gobble up, squander 9 dissipate, overwhelm, partake of, polish off, throw away 10 annihilate, extinguish, frivol away, monopolize, run through, trifle away

consumer advocate 5 Nader

consuming 9 absorbing 10 engrossing 12 monopolizing

consummate 3 end 4 able, halt, ripe 5 close, utter 6 finish, gifted, superb, wind up, wrap up 7 perfect, skilled, supreme, trained 8 absolute, complete, conclude, finished, flawless, outright, peerless, positive, talented, ultimate 9 downright, faultless, out-and-out, perfected, practiced, terminate, virtuosic 10 impeccable, inimitable 11 superlative, unmitigated 12 accomplished 13 thoroughgoing, unsurpassable

consumption 2 TB 3 use 5 decay, waste 8 phthisis 11 white plague 12 tuberculosis

contact 3 get 4 abut, meet 5 reach, touch, union 6 accord 7 harmony, oneness, rapport, taction 8 commerce, nearness, relation, tangency, touching 9 closeness, communion, proximity 10 connection, contiguity, fellowship **11** association, contingence, impingement, intercourse, propinquity **13** communication, companionship *combining form:* **4** hapt **5** hapto

contagion 3 pox **4** bane **5** taint, venom, virus **6** miasma, poison **7** disease **9** pollution **10** corruption **13** contamination

contagious 6 catchy, taking **8** catching **10** infectious **12** communicable

contain 4 have, hold, keep, take **5** admit, house, lodge **6** embody, take in **7** collect, compose, control, embrace, include, involve, receive, repress, smother, subsume **8** comprise, restrain **9** encompass **10** comprehend, simmer down **11** accommodate

container 3 bag, bin, box, can, cup, jar, keg, mug, pod, pot, tin, tub, urn, vat **4** cage, case, cask, drum, etui, ewer, pail, sack, silo, tank, vase, vial, well **5** chest, crate, cruet, flask, glass, gourd, phial, pouch **6** basket, bottle, carafe, carton, casket, coffin, cooler, goblet, hamper, hatbox, holder, inkpot, shaker **7** bandbox, capsule, chalice, inkwell, package, pitcher, thermos **8** canister, catchall, decanter, envelope, hogshead, jerrican, puncheon **10** receptacle *liturgical:* **3** pix, pyx **7** chalice **8** ciborium

containing *suffix:* **2** ic **4** ical

contaminate 4 foul, harm, soil **5** dirty, spoil, stain, taint **6** befoul, debase, defile, infect, injure, poison **7** corrupt, deprave, pervert, pollute, tarnish, vitiate **9** desecrate **10** adulterate

conte 4 tale **5** story **9** narrative

contemn 4 hate **5** abhor, scorn, scout, spurn **7** despise, disdain **8** look down

contemplate 3 aim, eye **4** mean, mull, muse, plan, scan, view **5** study, think, weigh **6** design, intend, look at, ponder **7** examine, inspect, perpend, propose, purpose, reflect **8** consider, gaze upon, look upon, meditate, think out **9** think over **10** excogitate, scrutinize

contemplation 5 study **6** musing **7** thought **8** thinking **9** brainwork, pondering **10** cogitation, meditation, reflection, rumination **11** cerebration, speculation **12** deliberation

contemplative 6 musing **7** pensive **8** thinking, weighing **9** pondering, reasoning **10** cogitative, meditative, reflecting, reflective, ruminative, thoughtful **11** speculative

contemporary 2 up **6** coeval, extant **7** abreast, current, instant, present **8** existent, existing, todayish, up-to-date **9** au courant **10** coetaneous, coexistent, coexisting, coincident, concurrent, present-day, synchronal, synchronic **11** concomitant, synchronous **12** simultaneous **13** up-to-the-minute

contempt 5 scorn, shame **6** hatred, infamy **7** despite, disdain, mockery, sarcasm **8** aversion, defiance, despisal, disfavor, disgrace, dishonor, distaste, ignominy **9** antipathy, contumacy, discredit, disesteem, disrepute **10** opprobrium, repugnance **11** despisement **12** stubbornness **13** disparagement, recalcitrance

contemptible 3 bad, low **4** base, evil, mean, poor, vile **5** cheap, sorry **6** abject, odious, scummy, scurvy, shabby, sordid **7** hateful, ignoble, pitiful **8** beggarly, infamous, inferior, pitiable, shameful **9** abhorrent **10** abominable, despicable, despisable, detestable, disgusting **11** ignominious

contemptible one *suffix:* **3** een, eer

contemptuous 7 haughty **8** arrogant, scornful **10** disdainful **12** supercilious

contend 3 say, tug, vie, war **4** cope, face, meet, tell, urge **5** argue, brawl, claim, fight, rival **6** assert, battle, charge, combat, defend, enjoin, oppose, oppugn, report, resist **7** compete, contest, justify, warrant **8** confront, cope with, maintain **9** encounter, vindicate, withstand

___ contendere 4 nolo

content 4 cozy, gist **5** happy **6** at ease **7** appease, gratify, satisfy **9** satisfied, substance **12** significance

contention 3 war **4** feud **6** hurrah, rumpus, strife, thesis **7** discord, dispute, dissent, quarrel, rivalry, wrangle **8** argument, conflict, disunity, squabble, variance **9** disaccord **10** difference, dissension, dissidence **11** altercation, competition, controversy **12** contestation *Scottish:* **5** sturt

contentious 5 fiery **7** carping, froward, peppery, scrappy, warlike **8** captious, caviling, contrary, militant, perverse **9** bellicose, combative, hotheaded, impetuous, litigious, polemical, truculent **10** pugnacious **11** belligerent, quarrelsome **12** disputatious, faultfinding, gladiatorial **13** argumentative, controversial

conterminous 8 abutting, adjacent, touching **9** adjoining, bordering **10** approximal, contiguous, juxtaposed

contest 3 sue, vie **4** bout, buck, duel, feud, fray, game, meet, race, tilt **5** clash, fight, match, repel, rival, trial **6** battle, combat, debate, oppose, resist, strife, trying **7** compete, contend, dispute, rivalry, testing, warfare **8** argument, concours, conflict, endeavor, skirmish, striving, struggle, tug-of-war **9** emulation, encounter, rencontre, withstand **10** engagement, tournament **11** competition *combining form:* **5** machy

contiguity 9 adjacency, confinity, immediacy, proximity **11** propinquity **13** appropinquity

contiguous 4 near, next, nigh 5 close 6 nearby 7 close-by 8 abutting, adjacent, touching 9 adjoining, bordering 10 approximal, juxtaposed, near-at-hand 11 close-at-hand, neighboring 12 conterminous

continence 6 purity, virtue 8 chastity, sobriety 10 abstinence, chasteness, moderation, temperance 13 self-restraint, temperateness

continent 4 Asia, mass, pure 5 sober 6 Africa, chaste, curbed, Europe 7 America, bridled 8 mainland 9 abstinent, Australia, inhibited, temperate 10 abstemious, Antarctica, restrained 11 abstentious 12 North America, South America *lost:* 8 Atlantis

continental pool 3 EEC 12 Common Market

contingence 5 touch 7 contact

contingency 4 pass 5 break, event, pinch 6 chance, crisis, strait 8 exigency, juncture, occasion, zero hour 9 emergency 10 crossroads 11 opportunity, possibility 12 turning point

contingent 3 odd 5 fluky 6 casual, chance, likely 7 reliant 8 possible, probable, relative 9 dependent 10 accidental, fortuitous, incidental, unforeseen 11 conditional 13 unanticipated, unforeseeable

continual 6 steady 7 abiding, endless, running, staying 8 constant, enduring, minutely, timeless, unending, unwaning 9 ceaseless, incessant, perpetual, unceasing, unfailing, unvarying 10 continuous, persistent, persisting, relentless, unchanging, unflagging 11 everlasting, unremitting 12 interminable 13 unintermitted, uninterrupted

continually 4 ever 6 always 7 forever, running 8 together 10 constantly 11 incessantly, night and day 12 successively 13 consecutively

continuance 3 run 4 stay 5 delay 6 sequel 8 duration, survival 9 constancy, longevity 10 permanence 11 persistence 12 postponement, prolongation

continuation 3 run 8 duration 9 endurance, extension 11 persistence, protraction 12 prolongation

continue 4 go on, last, ride, stay 5 abide, renew, run on 6 endure, pick up, remain, reopen, resume, retain, take up 7 carry on, outlast, outlive, perdure, persist, prolong, restart, survive 8 maintain, postpone 9 carry over, persevere 10 recommence 12 carry through

continuing 3 old 7 ongoing 8 constant, enduring, lifelong 9 long-lived, perennial 10 inveterate 11 long-lasting

continuity 6 script 8 duration, scenario 9 endurance 11 persistence

continuous see **continual**

continuously see **continually**

contort 3 wry 4 bend, warp, wind 5 curve, gnarl, twist, wring 6 deform, writhe 7 distort, grimace, torture 8 misshape

contortionist 7 acrobat

contour 4 form, line 5 curve, shape 7 outline, profile 9 lineament, lineation 10 figuration, silhouette 11 delineation

contra 5 again 6 facing, toward 7 against, counter, reverse, vis-à-vis 8 antipode, antipole, converse, fronting, opposite 9 vice versa 10 antithesis, conversely, oppositely

contraband 3 hot 5 taboo 6 banned 7 bootleg, illegal, illicit, shut out, smuggle 8 excluded 9 forbidden 10 prohibited, proscribed 11 disapproved

contract 3 get 4 bond, fail, knit, pact, sink, take 5 catch, cause, incur, lease, limit, upset 6 engage, induce, lessen, obtain, reduce, shrink, treaty, weaken 7 abridge, acquire, afflict, bargain, betroth, bring on, compact, decline, derange, dwindle, wrinkle 8 affiance, compress, condense, covenant, decrease, diminish, disorder, restrict, sicken of 9 agreement, betrothal, constrict, indispose, succumb to 10 convention, sicken with 11 concentrate, transaction 12 come down with *maritime:* 8 bottomry *part:* 6 clause 7 article, proviso

contraction 3 it's, tic 4 ain't, can't, don't, flex, isn't, won't 5 aren't, cramp, didn't, spasm 7 elision 9 reduction, shrinkage 10 abridgment 12 abbreviation *heart's:* 7 systole *poetic:* 3 e'en, e'er, o'er, 'tis 4 ne'er, 'twas 5 'twere, 'twill

contradict 4 deny 5 belie, cross, rebut 6 impugn, negate 7 dispute, gainsay 8 negative, traverse 9 disaffirm 10 contravene

contradiction 6 denial 7 paradox 8 antinomy, negation 10 gainsaying

contradictory 7 counter, reverse 8 antipode, antipole, contrary, converse, negating, opposite 9 antipodal 10 antipodean, antithesis, nullifying 11 counterpole 12 antagonistic, antithetical 13 counteractive

contraption 3 rig 6 device, gadget 7 machine 11 contrivance

contrariety 3 con 8 opposure 10 antagonism, antithesis, opposition

contrariwise 5 again 9 vice versa 10 conversely, oppositely

contrary 5 balky, polar 6 averse, ornery, unruly 7 counter, froward, restive, reverse, wayward 8 antipode, antipole, clashing, converse, opposite, perverse, recusant, stubborn 9 antipodal, diametric, dissident, obstinate, vice versa 10 antipodean, antithesis, conversely, discordant, headstrong, oppositely, rebellious, refractory 11 conflicting, counterpole, dissentient, intractable, wrongheaded **12** antagonistic, antipathetic, antithetical, contumacious, cross-grained, recalcitrant **13** contradictory, insubordinate, nonconforming, nonconformist *prefix:* **3** dis **5** retro **6** contra **7** counter

contrast 7 compare **9** diversity **10** comparison, difference, divergence

contravene 4 defy, deny **5** break, cross, fight, spurn **6** abjure, breach, combat, disown, impugn, negate, offend, oppose, reject, resist **7** exclude, gainsay, infract, violate **8** disclaim, infringe, negative, traverse **9** disaffirm, repudiate **10** contradict, transgress

contravention 3 sin **4** vice **5** crime **6** breach **7** offense **8** trespass **9** violation **10** infraction **12** infringement **13** transgression

contretemps 4 slip **6** mishap **7** tragedy **9** adversity, mischance **10** misfortune

contribute 3 aid **4** give, help, tend **5** add to **6** assist, chip in, donate, kick in, submit, supply **7** augment, conduce, fortify, pitch in, recruit, redound **9** reinforce, subscribe **10** strengthen, supplement **11** come through

contribution 4 alms, gift **5** share **7** charity, present **8** donation, offering **11** benefaction, beneficence

contributory 8 adjuvant **9** accessory, ancillary, auxiliary **10** collateral, subsidiary **11** appurtenant, subservient

contrite 5 sorry **8** penitent **9** regretful, repentant **10** apologetic, remorseful **11** attritional, penitential **12** compunctious

contriteness see **contrition**

contrition 3 rue **4** ruth **7** penance, remorse **9** attrition, penitence, penitency **10** repentance **11** compunction

contrivance 3 art **6** device **7** coinage, machine **8** artifice **9** apparatus, invention **10** brainchild **11** contraption

contrive 3 rig **4** fake, make, move, plan, plot **5** fix up, frame **6** cook up, devise, handle, invent, make up, scheme, vamp up, wangle **7** collude, concoct, connive, develop, dream up, fashion, hatch up, project, work out **8** cogitate, conspire, intrigue **9** elaborate, fabricate, formulate, machinate, scheme out

contrived 5 hokey **6** forced **7** labored **10** artificial

control 4 curb, rein, rule, sway **5** might, power, quell **6** adjust, bridle, corner, direct, govern, handle, manage, master, subdue **7** command, compose, contain, mastery, repress, smother, strings **8** dominate, monopoly, regulate, restrain **9** authority, supervise **10** discipline, domination **12** jurisdiction

controlled 4 tame **8** discreet, moderate

9 temperate, unextreme **10** reasonable, restrained **11** unexcessive **12** conservative

controversial 7 eristic **9** litigious, polemical **11** contentious **12** disputatious **13** argumentative

controversy 3 row **4** miff, tiff **6** debate, rumpus, strife **7** dispute, quarrel, wrangle **8** argument, squabble **9** bickering **10** contention, falling-out **11** altercation, embroilment

controvert 4 deny **5** break, rebut **6** oppugn, refute **7** confute **8** confound, disprove, question **9** challenge **10** disconfirm

contumacious 6 unruly **7** froward **8** contrary, factious, insolent, mutinous, perverse **9** insurgent, seditious **10** rebellious **13** insubordinate

contumacy 7 despite **8** contempt, defiance **12** stubbornness **13** recalcitrance

contumelious 4 bold **5** saucy **6** brazen **7** abusive, scurril **8** impudent, insolent, scurrile **9** audacious, invective, truculent **10** scurrilous, vituperous **11** impertinent, opprobrious **12** vituperative, vituperatory

contumely 4 slap **5** abuse **6** insult **7** affront, despite, obloquy **9** aspersion, indignity, invective, stricture **10** scurrility **12** billingsgate, vituperation **13** animadversion

contuse 5 black **6** bruise, injure

conundrum 3 why **6** enigma, puzzle, riddle **7** mystery, problem **10** puzzlement **13** Chinese puzzle, mystification

convalesce 4 mend **7** improve, recover **10** recuperate

convene 3 sit **4** call, meet, open **6** call in, gather, muster, summon **7** convoke, summons **8** assemble **10** congregate

convenience 4 ease **6** toilet **7** amenity, benefit, comfort

convenient 3 fit **4** good, meet, near, next, nigh **5** close, handy **6** nearby, proper, useful **7** close-by **8** adjacent, suitable **9** immediate **10** accessible, near-at-hand **11** appropriate, close-at-hand

convent 4 abbey **6** friary, priory **7** nunnery **9** monastery, sanctuary

convention 3 law **4** bond, form, pact, rule **5** canon, usage **6** accord, custom, treaty **7** bargain, compact, concord, meeting, precept **8** assembly, contract, covenant, practice **9** agreement, gathering, tradition **10** convenance **11** transaction **13** understanding

conventional 5 trite, usual **6** decent, formal, normal, proper, seemly, solemn, square **7** correct, stately **8** decorous, moderate, ordinary, orthodox, priggish, reliable, straight **9** temperate **10** button-down, ceremonial, dependable, fastidious, restrained, scrupulous **11** ceremonious, commonplace, constrained, responsible, traditional **12** conservative **13** conscientious

conventionalize 5 adapt **7** conform, stylize

converge 4 join, meet **5** focus **8** approach **9** concenter **11** concentrate

conversant 5 awake, aware **6** au fait, versed **7** abreast, knowing, witting **8** familiar, informed, sensible, sentient, up-to-date **9** au courant, cognizant, conscious **10** acquainted, perceptive, percipient **12** apprehending, apprehensive **13** comprehending

conversation 4 chat, talk **6** confab, debate, parley, speech **7** comment, talking **8** causerie, colloquy, dialogue, duologue, repartee, shoptalk **9** cross talk, discourse, tête-à-tête **10** discussion **13** confabulation

conversation piece 6 oddity **9** curiosity

converse 4 chat, chin, talk, yarn **5** polar, speak, visit **6** contra, parley **7** commune, counter, reverse **8** antipode, antipole, colloque, colloquy, contrary, dialogue, opposite **9** antipodal, communion, diametric, discourse **10** antipodean, antithesis **11** counterpole **12** antithetical **13** communication, confabulation, contradictory

conversely 6 contra **8** contrary **9** vice versa **10** contrawise, oppositely **12** contrariwise

conversion 5 shift **6** change **7** novelty, rebirth, turning **8** metanoia, mutation, reversal **9** about-face **10** alteration, changeover, innovation **11** permutation, reclamation **12** modification, regeneration **13** metamorphosis, qualification, transmutation

convert 4 lead, make, move, save, sway **5** alter, bring, forge **6** change, redeem, reform **7** commute, incline **8** persuade **9** proselyte, transform, translate, transmute, transpose **11** proselytize, transfigure **12** metamorphose, transmogrify *Christian:* **10** catechumen

convex 5 bowed, toric **6** arched, curved **7** bulging, gibbous, rounded

convey 3 lug **4** bear, buck, cart, cede, deed, pack, pipe, send, tote **5** bring, carry, ferry **6** assign, funnel, impart, pass on, remise, siphon **7** channel, conduct, consign, project, traject **8** make over, sign over, transfer, transmit **9** put across, transport **11** communicate

conveyance 3 car **4** auto, cart, deed, sled **5** coach, coupe, sedan, stage, wagon **7** charter, trailer, transit, vehicle **8** carriage, carrying **9** transport **10** automobile **12** transporting *public:* **2** el **3** bus, cab **4** taxi, tram **5** plane, train **7** ricksha, trolley **8** airplane, monorail, railroad, rickshaw **9** streetcar **10** jinricksha, jinrikisha

convict 4 find **5** felon, lifer **6** inmate, trusty **7** captive **8** criminal, jailbird, prisoner, sentence **10** malefactor

conviction 4 mind, view **5** creed, faith **6** belief, surety **7** feeling, opinion **8** doctrine, sureness **9** assurance, certainty, certitude, sentiment **10** confidence, persuasion **11** assuredness

convince 3 get **4** draw **6** assure, induce, prompt **7** satisfy, win over **8** persuade, talk into **9** argue into, prevail on **11** bring around, prevail upon

convincing 5 solid, sound, valid **6** cogent, trusty **7** telling **8** credible, faithful **9** authentic **10** persuasive, satisfying **11** trustworthy **12** satisfactory

convivial 3 gay **5** jolly, merry **6** jocund, jovial, lively, social **7** festive **8** sociable **9** vivacious **13** companionable

convocation 5 synod **7** council, meeting **8** assembly **9** gathering **10** assemblage **12** congregation

convoke 3 ask, bid, sit **4** call, meet **6** gather, invite, summon **7** collect, convene, request **8** assemble **10** congregate

convoluted 5 snaky **6** coiled **7** complex, sinuous, winding **8** flexuous, tortuous **9** meandrous **10** meandering, serpentine **11** anfractuous

convoy 4 bear **5** guard, guide, train **6** attend, defend, escort, shield **7** company, conduct, protect **9** accompany, companion, safeguard **11** consort with

convulse 4 rock **5** shake **7** agitate, concuss **8** tetanize

convulsion 3 fit **5** spasm **6** attack, clamor, outcry, tumult, uproar, upturn **7** ferment, quaking, rocking, shaking **8** disaster, laughter, upheaval **9** commotion, trembling

cook 3 fix, fry **4** bake, boil, burn, chef, melt, stew **5** broil, frame, grill, poach, roast, sauté, steam **6** braise, devise, invent, make up, scorch, simmer **7** concoct, dream up, griddle, hatch up, parboil, prepare, swelter **8** barbecue, cocinero, contrive **9** formulate

cooked 4 done *combining form:* **5** cocto *with tomatoes:* **10** cacciatore

cookery 7 cuisine **8** magirics *expert:* **5** Bates, Beard, Child **6** Farmer **7** Crocker **9** Claiborne

cookie 4 cake, snap **7** biscuit, brownie **8** macaroon **10** gingersnap

cooking *appliance:* **4** oven **5** mixer, range, stove **7** blender, toaster **10** rotisserie *implement:* **3** cup, pan, pot, wok **4** olla **5** ladle, sieve, spoon, whisk **6** frypan, grater, masher, sifter, tureen **7** griddle, skillet, spatula **8** colander **9** eggbeater **10** rolling pin **12** measuring cup *room:* **6** galley **7** kitchen

cool 3 fan, ice **4** calm, cold **5** allay, aloof,

chill, frore, gelid, nippy, sober **6** arctic, chilly, frigid, frosty, offish, placid, serene, stolid **7** assured, collect, compose, control, distant, repress **8** composed, detached, freezing, reserved, restrain, solitary, suppress, tranquil **9** collected, confident, impassive, unruffled, withdrawn **10** nonchalant, phlegmatic, simmer down, unsociable **11** indifferent, standoffish, unflappable **12** happy-go-lucky **13** imperturbable, self-possessed

cooler 3 fan **4** coop, icer, jail **6** lockup, prison **11** refrigerant **12** refrigerator

cooling device 3 fan **4** icer **6** icebox **7** freezer **12** refrigerator

coolness 6 aplomb, phlegm **7** ataraxy **8** calmness **9** composure, sangfroid **10** equanimity

coop 3 hem, mew, pen **4** cage, jail **5** cramp, fence **6** corral, shut in **7** close in, confine, enclose, envelop **9** enclosure

cooperate 5 agree, unite **6** concur, league **7** combine, conjoin, connive **8** coadjute, coincide **11** collaborate

cooperation 8 teamwork

cooperative 8 coacting, coactive, conjoint, synergic **9** concerted **10** synergetic **11** coefficient **13** collaborative, uncompetitive

coordinate 4 mate, tune **5** adapt, atune, match **6** fellow **7** conform, vis-à-vis **9** companion, harmonize, integrate, reconcile **10** proportion, reciprocal **11** accommodate **12** reconciliate

cop 3 nab **4** lift, take **5** filch, pinch, steal, swipe **7** gumshoe, officer, purloin **8** bluecoat **9** patrolman, policeman **11** appropriate

copacetic 4 fine, okay **5** dandy **12** satisfactory

cope 4 arch, bend, face **5** cover, dress, get by, match, notch, vault **6** canopy, handle, make do, manage, mantel, muzzle **8** deal with **9** encounter

copestone 5 crown

copious 4 full, lush, rich **5** ample **6** lavish, plenty **7** liberal, profuse, replete **8** abundant, generous **9** abounding, bounteous, bountiful, exuberant, luxuriant, plenteous, plentiful

cop-out 6 excuse **7** pretext, retreat

copper 4 cent, coin **5** metal, penny, token **6** cuprum **9** butterfly, policeman **combining form: 4** cupr **5** chalc, chalk, cupri, cupro **6** chalko **item: 4** cent **5** penny **6** kettle **sulfate: 7** vitriol **9** bluestone **11** blue vitriol **symbol: 2** Cu

copperhead 5 snake, viper **8** squirrel

coppice 4 bosk, wood **5** copse, grove **6** bosque, forest, growth **7** thicket **9** brushwood, underwood

copse see **coppice**

Copt 8 Egyptian

copula 4 link **5** union **7** coupler

copy 3 ape **4** echo, fake, mock, sham **5** ditto, mimic **6** carbon, ectype, effigy, ersatz, parody, repeat **7** emulate, imitate, replica, takeoff **8** knockoff, likeness, simulate, travesty **9** burlesque, duplicate, facsimile, imitation, replicate, reproduce **10** carbon copy, impression, simulacrum, transcribe **11** counterfeit, counterpart, reduplicate, replication **12** reproduction **13** reduplication

copyist 6 scribe **9** engrosser **10** plagiarist **12** calligrapher **13** calligraphist

copyread 4 edit

coquet 3 toy **4** fool **5** dally, flirt **6** lead on, trifle **11** string along

coquette 4 vamp **5** flirt **11** hummingbird

coquettish 3 coy **4** arch **7** roguish

coral 3 red **4** pink **5** palus, polyp **6** palule **8** skeleton **9** limestone

coral reef 5 atoll **off Australia: 5** Wreck **world's largest: 12** Great Barrier

cord 3 tie **4** band, lace, pile, rope, whip, wire, yarn **5** cable, nerve, stack **6** strand, string, tendon, thread **7** amentum **twisted: 7** torsade

cordage 4 rope **5** ropes **7** rigging **fiber: 4** bast, eruc, hemp, imbe, jute, pita **5** sisal

Corday's victim 5 Marat

Cordelia father: 4 Lear **sister: 5** Regan **7** Goneril

cordial 4 warm **5** drink, sonsy **6** genial, hearty, tender **7** affable, liqueur, sincere **8** friendly, gracious, sociable **9** congenial, courteous, heartfelt **10** hospitable, responsive **11** sympathetic, warmhearted **12** wholehearted

cordiality 5 ardor, favor **6** warmth **7** amenity **8** approval, sympathy **9** geniality, mutuality, pleasance **10** amiability **12** agreeability, friendliness, pleasantness **13** agreeableness, enjoyableness

cordon 4 lace **5** braid **6** circle, ribbon **7** barrier **blue: 4** chef, cook **6** ribbon **10** decoration

core 3 hub, nub **4** base, body, bulk, gist, mass, meat, pith, root **5** basis, cadre, focus, heart, midst, quick **6** amount, burden, center, corpus, middle, origin, staple, thrust, upshot **7** purport **8** midpoint **9** substance **10** foundation

corf 3 tub **4** cage **5** truck **6** basket

corium 4 skin **5** cutis, layer **6** dermis

cork 4 bark, plug, seal, stop **5** float **6** bobber **7** stopper, stopple **combining form: 6** phello

corker 4 lulu **5** dandy, dilly **8** jim-dandy, knockout **9** humdinger **11** crackerjack, lalapalooza

corkscrew 4 coil, curl, wind 5 twine, twist 6 spiral 7 entwine, wreathe

cormorant 4 bird, shag 7 glutton 8 Scottish *norie:* 5 scart

corn 3 zea 4 meal, salt, samp 5 grain, maize 6 clavus, hominy 9 granulate *bread:* 4 pone 7 bannock *Indian:* 3 zea 5 maize 6 mealie *kind:* 3 pop 4 dent 5 flint, flour, sweet 6 Indian *pest:* 5 borer *piece:* 3 cob, ear 5 spike 6 kernel, nubbin

Corncracker State 8 Kentucky

corner 3 box, fix, jam, nab 4 hole, nook, trap, tree 5 angle, catch, coign, niche, seize 6 collar, cranny, dogleg, pickle, plight, recess, scrape 7 capture, dilemma, impasse, trouble 8 bottle up, monopoly 10 bring to bay 11 predicament *combining form:* 4 goni 5 gonio 6 anguli, angulo *of eye:* 7 canthus

cornerstone 4 base 5 basis 7 support 10 foundation, groundwork

cornet 4 cone, horn 5 zinke 8 woodwind 9 cornopean 10 instrument

cornflower 10 bluebonnet, bluebottle

Cornhusker State 8 Nebraska

cornice 3 cap 4 band, eave 5 crown 6 geison 7 molding 8 swanneck *combining form:* 6 geisso

cornmeal 4 masa, samp 5 atole 7 hoecake *mush:* 7 polenta

cornucopia 4 cone, horn 9 abundance 12 horn of plenty

Cornwallis *adversary:* 6 Greene *surrender site:* 8 Yorktown

corny 5 banal, stale, tired, trite 6 old hat 7 clichéd 8 shopworn 9 hackneyed 10 warmed over 11 commonplace, sentimental, stereotyped

corollary 6 effect, result, sequel, upshot 8 sequence 9 resulting 10 associated, end product, equivalent 11 aftereffect, consequence, precipitate

corona 4 halo 5 cigar, crown, glory 6 circle, rosary, wreath 7 aureola, aureole, circlet, fermata, garland

coronal see **coronet**

coroner 7 crowner, officer 8 examiner

coronet 4 band 5 crown 6 anadem, circle, wreath 7 chaplet, circlet, garland

Coronis *form:* 4 crow *son:* 9 Asclepius 11 Aesculapius

corporal 3 NCO 5 fanon 6 bodily, carnal 7 fleshly, somatic 8 physical

corporate 6 united 7 unified 8 combined 9 aggregate

corporeal 5 hylic, somal 6 bodily, carnal 7 fleshly, somatic 8 material, physical, sensible, tangible 9 objective 10 phenomenal 11 substantial

corps 4 band 5 party, troop 6 outfit, troupe 7 company

corpse 4 body, mort 5 bones, stiff 7 cadaver, carcass, carrion, remains *combining form:* 4 necr 5 necro

corpselike 4 dead 6 deadly 7 deathly, ghastly, ghostly, shadowy 8 deadened, deathful, spectral 10 cadaverous

corpulence 7 fatness, obesity 9 adiposity 10 fleshiness

corpulent 3 fat 5 bulky, gross, heavy, obese, plump, stout 6 fleshy, portly 7 weighty 9 overblown 10 overweight

corpus 4 body, bulk, core, mass 6 oeuvre, staple 9 substance

corpuscle 4 cell 7 hematid 8 hemocyte, monocyte 9 leukocyte 10 lymphocyte 11 erythrocyte, granulocyte

corral 3 hem, mew, pen 4 cage, coop 5 fence, hedge 6 shut in 7 close in, confine, enclose 8 surround 9 enclosure

correct 3 fit, fix 4 done, edit, mend, true 5 amend, emend, exact, right 6 adjust, better, decent, proper, punish, reform, remedy, revise, seemly 7 chasten, improve, perfect, precise, rectify, redress 8 accurate, becoming, chastise, decorous, emendate, flawless, make over, regulate 9 castigate, faultless, veracious, veridical 10 conforming, discipline, impeccable, meticulous, scrupulous 11 comme il faut, punctilious, undistorted 12 conventional *combining form:* 4 orth 5 ortho

correction 3 rod 8 punition 10 discipline, punishment 11 castigation 12 chastisement

corrective 4 cure 6 remedy 8 antidote, remedial 11 counterstep 12 counteragent 13 counteractant, counteractive

correctness 5 order 7 decorum 8 accuracy 9 coherence, congruity, exactness, precision, propriety 10 definitude, exactitude, properness, seemliness 11 orderliness, preciseness 12 decorousness, definiteness

correlate 5 match 6 analog 7 pendant 8 analogue, parallel 10 complement 11 counterpart, countertype 13 correspondent

correlative 2 if, or 3 nor 4 then 6 either 7 neither, related 10 reciprocal 13 corresponding

correspond 4 jibe, suit 5 agree, equal, match, write 6 accord, concur 7 conform, consort 9 dovetail 9 harmonize 11 communicate

correspondence 4 mail 7 letters 8 homogeny, symmetry 9 agreement, congruity 10 conformity 11 consistency *mathematical:* 7 mapping 8 function

correspondent 5 match 6 analog, pen pal, writer 7 fitting 8 analogue, parallel, suitable **9** correlate **11** counterpart, countertype

corresponding 4 akin, like **5** alike **6** agnate **7** similar **8** parallel **9** analogous, consonant **10** comparable *prefix:* **7** counter

correspondingly 2 so **4** also **8** likewise **9** similarly

corrida 9 bullfight *shout:* **3** olé

corridor 4 hall **7** couloir, hallway, passage **10** passageway

corroborate 6 verify **7** bear out, confirm, justify **8** validate **12** authenticate, substantiate

corroborative 7 helping **9** ancillary, assisting, auxiliary **10** collateral, supportive **11** adminicular **12** confirmative, confirmatory, verificatory

corroboratory see **corroborative**

corrode 3 eat **4** bite, gnaw, rust **5** erode, scour **7** eat away **8** wear away

corrosive 5 acerb **7** acerbic, caustic **9** sarcastic **12** archilochian

corrosiveness 7 sarcasm **8** acerbity **10** causticity

corrugation 4 fold, ruck **5** plica, ridge, rivel **6** crease, furrow, rimple **7** crinkle, wrinkle

corrupt 3 low, rot **4** foul, ruin, turn, warp **5** abase, decay, snide, spoil, stain, taint, venal, wreck **6** abased, befoul, debase, defile, molder, rotten, smirch **7** baneful, crooked, crumble, debauch, degrade, deprave, devious, knavish, noxious, oblique, pervert, putrefy, tarnish, vicious, vitiate **8** bribable, degraded, depraved, infamous, perverse, two-faced **9** animalize, break down, decompose, dishonest, faithless, mercenary, miscreant, nefarious, reprobate, unethical **10** bastardize, degenerate, demoralize, flagitious, inconstant, perfidious, pernicious, unfaithful, unreliable, villainous **11** deleterious, detrimental, treacherous **12** blackguardly, disintegrate, undependable, unprincipled, unscrupulous **13** double-dealing, untrustworthy

corruptible 5 venal **7** buyable **8** bribable **11** purchasable

corruption 4 vice **7** jobbery **8** slangism, solecism **9** barbarism, depravity, vulgarism **10** immorality, wickedness **11** impropriety **13** vernacularism, vernacularity

corsair 5 rover **6** pirate, sea dog **7** sea wolf **8** picaroon, sea rover **9** buccaneer, sea robber **10** freebooter

corset 6 bodice, girdle **7** support

cortex 4 bark, peel, rind **8** peridium *combining form:* **7** cortico

Cortland 5 apple

corundum 4 ruby **5** emery, topaz **7** emerald **8** abrasive, amethyst, sapphire

coruscate 5 flash, gleam, glint **7** glisten, glitter, sparkle **11** scintillate

Corvino's wife 5 Celia

corybantic 3 mad **4** wild **5** rabid **7** frantic, furious **8** frenetic, frenzied **9** delirious

coryphée 6 dancer, hoofer **7** danseur **8** danseuse, figurant **9** ballerina, figurante **10** ballet girl **11** dancing girl

Cosi fan tutte composer 6 Mozart

cosmetic 4 kohl **5** henna, rouge **6** ceruse, makeup, powder **7** blusher, bronzer, mascara **8** lipgloss, lipstick **9** eye shadow **10** nail polish **11** beautifying, superficial

cosmetologist 10 beautician

cosmic 6 global **8** catholic **9** planetary, universal, worldwide **10** ecumenical **12** cosmopolitan

cosmopolitan 6 cosmic, global, smooth, urbane **8** catholic, cultured, polished **9** civilized, planetary, universal, worldwide **10** cultivated, ecumenical **11** worldly-wise **12** metropolitan **13** sophisticated

cosmos 5 world **6** nature **8** creation, universe

Cossack *army:* **3** Don **4** Ural **5** Kuban **6** voisko *district:* **6** okrugi *land:* **7** Ukraine *leader:* **5** Razin **6** ataman, hetman, Mazepa **7** Bulavin **8** Pugachev *novel:* **10** Taras Bulba *village:* **8** stanitsa, stanitza

cosset 3 pet **4** baby, love **5** humor, spoil **6** caress, cocker, coddle, cuddle, dandle, fondle, pamper **7** cater to, indulge **11** mollycoddle

cost 3 tab **4** rate, toll **5** price **6** charge, outlay, tariff **7** expense **8** price tag **11** expenditure **12** disbursement *business:* **8** overhead

Costa Rica *capital:* **7** San José *monetary unit:* **5** colon

costermonger 6 hawker **7** peddler **9** barrow boy, barrowman

costive 4 mean **5** bound, close, tight **6** stingy **7** miserly **9** astricted, penurious **10** hardfisted, obstipated **12** cheeseparing, parsimonious

costless 4 free **6** gratis **10** chargeless, gratuitous **13** complimentary

costly 4 dear, high **5** fancy, pricy, steep, stiff **6** pricey **7** premium **8** precious, valuable **9** excessive, expensive, priceless **10** exorbitant, inordinate, invaluable **11** extravagant, inestimable

costume 3 rig **4** garb, mode **5** dress, getup, guise, style **6** outfit, setout **7** fashion, turnout

cot 3 hut **4** camp **5** cabin, lodge, shack **6** shanty **7** cottage *hanging:* **7** hammock *wheeled:* **6** gurney

coterie 3 mob **4** camp, clan, ring **5** cabal **6** circle, clique **7** ingroup **9** camarilla

cottage 3 hut **4** camp **5** cabin, lodge,

shack **6** shanty **8** bungalow *Russian:*
5 dacha *Swiss:* **6** chalet
cotton 4 take **5** agree, grasp, toady
6 accept, coddle, kowtow **7** cater to, honey
up **8** bootlick, perceive **9** apprehend, harmonize **10** comprehend, fraternize, understand *cleaner:* **3** gin **5** willy **6** linter, willow
cloth: **4** jean, pima **5** khaki **6** canvas
7 galatea, jaconet, percale, silesia *cloth,
Indian:* **5** Surat **6** humhum **7** dhurrie
comb: **4** card *Egyptian:* **4** maco *fabric:*
3 rep **4** duck, lawn, leno, mull, repp
5 chino, crash, denim, doria, drill, manta,
scrim, terry, wigan **6** calico, chintz, dimity,
madras, muslin, nankin, sateen, satine
7 batiste, etamine, fustian, nankeen, nanking, organdy **8** drilling, nainsook **9** grenadine **10** seersucker *fabric, lustrous:*
6 sateen, satine *fabric, sheer:* **5** voile *fiber,
short:* **4** noil *fuzz remover:* **6** linter *knot:*
3 nep **4** slub *measure:* **3** lea **4** hank, pick,
yard **5** count, skein *pad:* **7** pledget *pod:*
4 boll *refuse:* **5** flock **8** grabbots *seed
separator:* **3** gin *sheet:* **3** bat **4** batt
thread: **5** lisle
Cotton State 7 Alabama
cottonwood 5 alamo **6** poplar
cottony 4 soft **5** silky **6** satiny, silken
7 velvety
Coty or Descartes 4 René
couch 3 den, put **4** lair, sink, sofa, word
5 divan, droop, lodge, lower **6** burrow,
daybed, phrase **7** depress, express, let
down **9** davenport, formulate
12 chesterfield
cougar 3 cat **4** puma **7** panther
9 catamount
cough 6 tussis *drop:* **6** troche **7** lozenge
couloir 4 hall **5** gorge **7** hallway, passage
8 corridor **10** passageway
council 4 diet **5** junta **6** senate **7** cabinet,
meeting **8** assembly, conclave, congress,
ministry **10** conference, federation **12** con-
sultation *ancient Greek:* **5** boule *church:*
5 synod **10** consistory *medieval English:*
4 moot **5** gemot **6** gemote **7** husting
8 hustings *Muslim:* **5** divan, diwan *Russian:* **4** duma **5** douma **6** soviet *secret:*
5 cabal, junto *Spanish:* **7** cabildo
counsel 4 urge, warn **5** order **6** advice,
advise, charge, direct, enjoin, lawyer,
prompt **7** suggest **8** admonish, advocate,
attorney **9** prescribe, recommend, reprehend **10** advisement *British:* **9** barrister,
solicitor
count 3 add, sum, tot **4** hope, look, mean
5 tally, total, weigh **6** bank on, census,
expect, figure, import, matter, number,
reckon, rely on **7** build on, compute, signify,
trust in, trust to **8** bank upon, depend on,
estimate, militate, numerate, quantify,

reckon on, rely upon **9** calculate, enumerate **10** depend upon **11** calculate on
countenance 3 mug **4** back, cast, face,
look, phiz **5** favor, go for **6** accept, visage
7 approve, commend, support **8** advocate,
features, hold with **9** approbate, encourage **10** expression *combining form:* **6** prosop **7** prosopo
counter 3 pit, vie **4** anti **5** match, polar
6 oppose **7** adverse, hostile, reverse
8 antipode, antipole, contrary, converse,
impeding, opposite **9** antipodal, diametric,
hindering, oppugnant **10** antipodean, antithesis **11** obstructive **12** antagonistic, antithetical **13** contradictory
counteract 3 fix **5** annul **6** negate **7** correct, rectify, redress **8** negative **9** cancel
out, frustrate **10** neutralize
counteractant 4 cure **6** remedy **8** antidote **10** corrective
counteragent see **counteractant**
counterbalance 6 make up, offset,
redeem, set off **7** correct, rectify **8** atone
for, outweigh **10** compensate
counterblow 7 revenge **8** avenging, reprisal, requital, revanche **9** vengeance
10 avengement **11** retaliation, retribution
countercheck 5 annul **6** negate
7 redress **8** negative **9** cancel out, frustrate **10** neutralize
counterfeit 3 act, ape, gyp **4** copy, fake,
hoax, sham **5** bluff, bogus, dummy, false,
feign, fraud, mimic, phony **6** affect, assume,
deceit, pseudo **7** feigned, imitate, pretend
8 delusive, delusory, simulate, spurious
9 brummagem, deception, deceptive, imposture, pinchbeck, pretended, simulated
10 fraudulent, misleading, simulacrum *combining form:* **5** pseud **6** pseudo
counterpane 6 spread **8** bedcover, coverlet **9** bedspread
counterpart 4 like **5** equal, match **6** analog **7** vis-à-vis **8** analogue, parallel **9** correlate **10** complement, coordinate, equivalent **13** correspondent
counterpoise 4 trim **6** make up, offset,
redeem, set off, stasis, steady **7** balance,
ballast **8** atone for, outweigh **9** stabilize
10 compensate **11** equilibrium
counterpole see **opposite**
countersign 4 word **8** password
9 watchword
countertype 5 match **6** analog **8** analogue, parallel **9** correlate
13 correspondent
countervail 4 foil **6** offset, redeem, set off,
thwart **7** balance, correct, rectify **8** atone
for, outweigh, overcome, surmount **9** frustrate **10** compensate
countless 6 untold **10** innumerous, numberless, unnumbered **11** innumerable

12 unnumberable *combining form:* **4** myri **5** myria, myrio

Count of Monte Cristo 6 Dantes
author: **5** Dumas

count out 3 bar **4** bate **5** debar **6** except **7** exclude, rule out, suspend **9** eliminate

countrified 5 rural **6** rustic **7** bucolic **8** agrestic, pastoral **10** campestral, provincial

country 4 home, land, soil **5** rural **6** nation, rustic **7** bucolic, outland **8** agrestic, homeland, pastoral **10** campestral, fatherland, motherland, provincial *dance:* **4** reel *home:* **5** manor, ranch, villa **8** hacienda *music:* **9** bluegrass *road:* **4** lane, path **5** byway

country jake 4 hick, rube **5** clown **6** rustic **7** bumpkin, hayseed **9** hillbilly **10** clodhopper **12** backwoodsman

coup 4 blow, plan **5** d'etat, upset **6** putsch, stroke **8** takeover **9** stratagem

couple 3 duo **4** dyad, join, link, mate, pair, span, team, yoke **5** brace, hitch, marry, unite **6** hook up **7** bracket, combine, conjoin, connect, doublet, harness, twosome **8** coalesce

coupler 4 link, ring **7** shackle *in an organ:* **7** tirasse *railroad:* **7** drawbar

couplet 4 pair **5** twins **7** distich

coupling 4 seam **5** joint, union **7** joining **8** junction, juncture **10** connection

courage 4 grit, guts **5** heart, moxie, pluck, spunk, valor **6** mettle, spirit **7** bravery, heroism **8** audacity, backbone, boldness, firmness, tenacity, valiance, valiancy **9** assurance, fortitude, gallantry **10** resolution **11** doughtiness, intrepidity, persistence **12** fearlessness **13** dauntlessness, determination

courageous 4 bold **5** brave, fiery, stout **6** manful, plucky, spunky, strong **7** doughty, valiant **8** fearless, intrepid, unafraid, valorous **9** audacious, dauntless, tenacious, undaunted **12** high-spirited

courier 5 envoy **6** bearer, legate, nuncio **7** carrier, emissary **9** go-between, messenger **11** internuncio

course 3 row, run, way **4** dart, dash, duct, line, path, plan, race, road, rush, tear **5** canal, chain, chase, hurry, orbit, order, range, route, scoot, scope, speed, trend **6** career, design, hasten, hustle, manner, policy, polity, scheme, scurry, sequel, series, sprint, string, system **7** advance, channel, circuit, conduit, passage, pattern, program, regimen, routine, scamper **9** aqueduct, progress, sequence **9** procedure **10** succession **11** progression *combining form:* **4** drom **5** dromo *dinner:* **5** salad **6** entrée

7 dessert **9** blue plate *of study:* **8** syllabus **10** curriculum

courser 4 bird **7** charger **8** huntsman, war-horse

court 3 bar, woo **4** quad, yard **5** charm, judge, spark **6** allure, pursue **7** address, justice, romance **8** tribunal **9** captivate, curtilage, enclosure **10** magistrate, quadrangle, sweetheart *action:* **4** suit **5** trial **6** appeal, assize **7** hearing, inquest, lawsuit **10** proceeding *calendar:* **6** docket *call to:* **7** summons **8** subpoena **11** arraignment *circuit:* **4** eyre *crier's call:* **4** oyes, oyez *decision:* **6** assize **7** finding, verdict **8** judgment *ecclesiastical:* **4** Rota **5** Curia **10** consistory *former English:* **4** leet *Indian:* **6** durbar *kind:* **4** moot **5** civil **6** county, family **7** circuit, customs, federal, supreme **8** chancery, criminal, district, juvenile, kangaroo, superior **9** appellate, municipal **11** territorial *medieval English:* **4** eyre, moot **5** gemot **6** gemote **7** husting **8** hustings *minutes:* **4** acta *of equity:* **8** chancery *officer:* **2** DA **5** clerk, crier, judge **6** puisne **7** bailiff, justice, marshal, sheriff **10** prosecutor *order:* **4** writ **5** arret, edict **6** decree **7** summons **8** mandamus, subpoena *panel:* **4** jury *relating to:* **5** aulic **8** judicial *session:* **6** assize **7** sitting **8** sederunt

courteous 5 civil **6** polite **7** genteel **8** mannerly **9** attentive **10** thoughtful **11** considerate **12** well-mannered

courter 5 wooer **6** suitor

courtesy 5 favor **6** comity **7** amenity, service **8** chivalry, civility, kindness **9** attention, gallantry, geniality **10** affability, cordiality, indulgence **11** courtliness **12** complaisance, dispensation, graciousness **13** attentiveness, consideration

court game see under **game**

courtly 4 prim **5** civil, lofty, preux, stiff **6** august, formal **7** gallant, starchy, stately, stilted, studied **8** gracious, imposing **9** civilized, dignified **11** ceremonious **12** conventional

courtship 4 suit **6** wooing **7** romance *former custom of:* **8** bundling

courtyard 4 quad **5** garth, patio **6** atrium **7** cortile **9** curtilage **10** quadrangle

Cousteau, Jacques *ship:* **7** Calypso *vehicle:* **11** bathysphere

cove 3 arm, bay **4** gulf **5** bayou, bight, creek, firth, inlet **6** harbor, slough

covenant 3 vow **4** bond, pact **5** agree, swear **6** concur, pledge, plight **7** bargain, compact **8** contract **9** agreement **10** convention **11** transaction

cover 3 cap, lid **4** bury, fend, hide, hood, mask, wrap **5** brood, cache, cloak, crown, guard, guise, haven, put-on, stash, track **6** asylum, bush up, canopy, defend, enfold, enwrap, facade, harbor, hiding, refuge, safety, screen, secure, shield, shroud, travel 7 blanket, bulwark, conceal, enclose, envelop, overlay, protect, retreat, secrete, shelter 8 disguise, ensconce, overcast, pass over, security, traverse 9 harborage, safeguard, sanctuary, semblance, superpose 10 false front, masquerade, overspread 11 concealment, superimpose *combining form:* 8 operculi *rooflike:* 6 awning, canopy *the eyes:* 9 blindfold *the face:* 4 mask, veil *the mouth:* 6 muzzle *with asphalt:* 4 pave *with cloth:* 5 drape *with dirt:* 6 bemire, besoil 8 besmirch *with jewels:* 5 begem *with straw:* 6 thatch

coverall 10 boiler suit

covered *combining form:* 5 crypt, krypt 6 crypto, krypto

covered wagon 9 Conestoga

covering *anatomical:* 5 theca, velum 6 tegmen 7 velamen 8 tegument 10 integument *close-fitting:* 6 sheath 9 sheathing *cloth:* 5 sheet *combining form:* 4 cole, derm, steg 5 coleo, derma, stego *flap:* 9 operculum *for a book:* 6 jacket *for a cigar:* 7 wrapper *for a coffin:* 4 pall *for a corpse:* 6 shroud 8 cerement *for a package:* 7 wrapper *for concealment:* 10 camouflage *for food:* 4 cosy, cozy *for soil:* 5 mulch *metal:* 4 mail 5 armor *of a diatom:* 6 lorica *of a plant ovary:* 8 pericarp *of a seed:* 4 aril, case 5 testa *of fruits:* 4 peel, rind *of gloom:* 4 pall *of grain:* 4 hull, husk 5 chaff *shell-like:* 8 carapace *thin:* 4 film 6 patina, veneer *waterproof:* 4 tarp 9 tarpaulin

coverlet 6 spread 8 bedcover 9 bedspread 11 counterpane

covert 5 haven, privy 6 asylum, buried, harbor, hidden, masked, refuge, secret 7 cloaked, furtive, guarded, retreat, shelter, sub-rosa 8 hush-hush, obscured, shrouded, stealthy, ulterior 9 concealed, disguised, harborage, sanctuary 10 dissembled, undercover 11 camouflaged, clandestine 12 hugger-mugger 13 surreptitious, under-the-table

covertly 7 sub rosa 8 in camera, secretly 9 by stealth, furtively, privately 10 stealthily 12 hugger-mugger 13 clandestinely

covet 4 want, wish 5 crave 6 desire 10 desiderate

covetous 4 avid, keen 5 eager, itchy 6 grabby, greedy 7 envious, hoggish, jealous, piggish, selfish, swinish 8 desirous, esurient, grasping, grudging, ravenous 9 rapacious, voracious 10 gluttonous 11 acquisitive

covey 4 band, bevy, crew 5 bunch, group, party 7 cluster 8 assembly

covin 4 plot 5 cabal 6 scheme 8 intrigue 10 conspiracy 11 machination

cow (see also **cattle**) 4 faze, kine (plural), neat 5 abash, bossy, bully, daunt 6 appall, bovine, dismay, hector, rattle 7 bluster, dragoon 8 bludgeon, browbeat, bulldoze, bullyrag 9 discomfit, embarrass, strong-arm 10 disconcert, intimidate *cud:* 5 rumen *French:* 5 vache *hornless:* 5 doddy, muley 6 doddie, mulley 7 pollard *mammary gland:* 5 udder *pasture:* 7 vaccary *pen:* 6 corral *shed:* 4 barn, byre 7 shippen, shippon *Spanish:* 4 vaca *young:* 4 calf 5 stirk 6 heifer

coward 4 baby 6 craven 7 caitiff, chicken, dastard, gutless, milksop, quitter, unmanly 8 poltroon, recreant, weakling 9 fraidy-cat, jellyfish, spunkless 10 scaredy-cat 11 lily-livered, poltroonish, yellowbelly 12 invertebrate, poor-spirited 13 pusillanimous

___ Coward 4 Noel

cowardly 4 vile 6 afraid, craven, yellow 7 caitiff, chicken, fearful, gutless, panicky, unmanly 8 cravenly, poltroon, recreant, timorous 9 dastardly, spunkless, worthless 11 lily-livered, milk-livered, poltroonish 12 fainthearted, poor-spirited, white-livered 13 pusillanimous

cowboy 4 waddy 6 drover, herder, waddie 7 puncher, rancher 8 buckaroo, buckeroo, herdsman, wrangler 9 cattleman 10 cowpuncher 12 broncobuster *contest:* 5 rodeo *legendary:* 9 Pecos Bill *leggings:* 5 chaps *movie:* 6 Tom Mix 8 Cisco Kid 9 Gene Autry, Roy Rogers 15 Hopalong Cassidy *rope:* 5 lasso, reata, riata 6 lariat *Spanish-American:* 6 charro, gaucho 7 llanero, vaquero

cower 4 fawn 5 quail, toady, wince 6 blench, cringe, flinch, grovel, kowtow, recoil, shrink 7 honey up, truckle 8 bootlick 9 brownnose 11 apple-polish

cowfish 6 dugong, sea cow 7 grampus, manatee 8 sirenian

cowl 3 cop 4 hood, monk 5 amice 6 almuce 7 capuche

cowpox 8 vaccinia

cowpuncher see **cowboy**

coxcomb 3 fop 4 buck, dude 5 blood, dandy 8 macaroni 9 exquisite 11 Beau Brummel 12 lounge lizard

coy 3 shy 4 arch 5 timid 6 decent, demure, proper, seemly 7 bashful, playful 8 decorous, retiring, skittish 9 diffident, kittenish, unassured 10 capricious, coquettish 11 mischievous, unassertive 12 self-effacing

Coyote State 11 South Dakota

coypu 6 rodent *fur:* 6 nutria

Cozbi's father 3 Zur

cozen 3 gyp 4 beat, bilk 5 cheat 6 betray,

delude, diddle, humbug, illude, take in
7 beguile, deceive, defraud, mislead, sell
out, swindle **8** flimflam **11** double-cross

cozy 4 easy, safe, snug, soft **5** comfy,
cushy, pally **6** chummy, secure **7** easeful
8 covering, intimate **10** buddy-buddy, palsy-
walsy **11** comfortable

crab 4 beef, fuss, yaup, yawp **5** bleat,
gripe **6** griper, grouch, kicker, squawk,
yammer **7** decapod, grouser, growler
8 arthopod, grumbler **9** bellyache, shellfish
10 bellyacher, complainer, crosspatch, crustacean **11** faultfinder *claw:* **5** chela **6** nipper *combining form:* **6** carcin **7** carcino
constellation: **6** Cancer *genus:* **3** Uca
6 Birgus **7** Limulus, Pagurus *hermit:*
8 pagurian *kind:* **3** pea **4** blue, king, pine,
rock **5** ghost, purse **6** hermit, partan, spider **7** fiddler **9** Dungeness, horseshoe
king, horseshoe: **7** limulus **8** limuloid *relating to:* **7** cancrid *resembiing:* **8** cancroid

crabbed 4 dour, glum **5** blunt, gruff, huffy,
sulky, surly, testy **6** cranky, crusty, gloomy,
morose, sullen **7** brusque **8** choleric, snappish **9** irascible, irritable, saturnine,
splenetic

crabby see **crabbed**

crab-like 8 cancroid

crabwise 8 sidelong, sideward, sideways
9 laterally

crack 2 go **3** gag, try **4** bang, bash, belt,
blow, boom, chap, clap, jape, jest, joke,
quip, rent, rift, rima, rime, shot, slam, slap,
slit, snap, stab, wham, whop **5** adept, blast,
break, burst, chink, cleft, crash, flash, fling,
jiffy, smack, smash, split, whack, whirl
6 cranny, decode, expert, master, moment
7 crevice, decrypt, fissure, instant, skilled
8 crevasse, decipher, drollery, interval, masterly, rimation, skillful, superior **9** bastinado,
excellent, masterful, witticism **10** interstice,
percussion, proficient **11** split second
12 cryptanalyze **13** discontinuity

crackbrain 3 nut **4** kook **5** crank
6 cuckoo **7** lunatic **8** crackpot **9** ding-a-
ling, screwball

crackdown 8 quashing **10** repression
11 suppression

cracked 3 mad **4** daft, nuts **5** batty,
crazy, daffy **6** crazed, cuckoo, insane,
maniac, rimose, rimous, screwy **7** lunatic
8 demented

cracker 5 wafer **7** biscuit, saltine **8** Georgian **9** Floridian

crackerjack 4 lulu **5** adept, dandy, dilly,
nifty **6** corker, expert, master **7** skilled
8 jim-dandy, knockout, masterly, skillful
9 humdinger, masterful **10** proficient
11 lalapalooza

crackle 4 snap **7** sparkle **9** crepitate

crackpot 3 nut **4** case, kook, loon

5 crank, loony **6** cuckoo, madman, maniac,
oddity **7** dingbat, lunatic, oddball **9** character, ding-a-ling, eccentric, harebrain,
screwball

crack-up 5 crash, smash, wreck **6** pileup
7 debacle, decline, smashup **8** collapse
9 breakdown **13** deterioration

cradlesong 7 lullaby **8** berceuse

craft 3 art, job **5** skill, trade **6** métier
7 calling, cunning, know-how, slyness
8 artifice, foxiness, vocation, wiliness
9 cageyness, canniness, dexterity, expertise **10** adroitness, artfulness, profession
combining form: **6** techno, techny

craftiness 3 art **7** cunning, slyness **8** artifice, foxiness, wiliness **9** cageyness, canniness **10** artfulness

craftsman 5 smith **6** carver, potter,
weaver, wright **7** artisan, builder, jeweler
9 carpenter

crafty 3 sly **4** foxy, keen, wily **5** acute,
sharp **6** adroit, artful, astute, clever, tricky
7 cunning, fawning **8** guileful **9** deceitful,
insidious *Scottish:* **6** sleeky **7** sleekit

cragged 5 harsh, rough **6** jagged, rugged,
uneven **7** scraggy **8** asperous, scabrous,
unsmooth

craggy see **cragged**

cram 3 jam, ram **4** bolt, fill, gulp, heap,
load, pack, tamp, wolf **5** chock, crowd,
crush, drive, force, press, shove, study,
stuff, wedge **6** bone up, englut, gobble,
guzzle, review, squash, thrust **7** jam-pack,
overeat, squeeze **11** ingurgitate

crammed 4 full **5** awash **6** jammed,
loaded, packed **7** brimful, crowded,
stuffed **8** brimming **9** chock-full

cramp 5 stint **7** shackle **8** confined
9 restraint, stricture **10** constraint, limitation **11** confinement, restriction **12** incommodious **13** constrainment

cramped 4 tiny **5** close, small, tight **6** little, minute, narrow **8** confined **9** two-by-
four **12** incommodious

cranberry 9 vaccinium *tree:* **7** pembina

crane 4 bird, boom **7** derrick **9** cormorant **10** demoiselle *arm:* **3** jib *genus:*
4 Grus *Indian:* **5** sarus *resembling:*
6 gruine *ship's:* **5** davit *traveling:* **5** jenny,
titan **7** goliath

Crane's hero 12 Henry Fleming

cranium 5 skull

crank 3 bee, nut **4** crab, kook **5** fancy
6 cuckoo, griper, grouch, notion, vagary
7 boutade, caprice, conceit, grouser,
growler, lunatic **8** crackpot, crotchet, grumbler, sourpuss **9** ding-a-ling, harebrain,
screwball **10** bellyacher, crackbrain, crosspatch **11** faultfinder

cranky 4 daft **5** crazy, cross, daffy, ratty,
testy, waspy **6** crazed, cuckoo, insane,

ornery, tetchy, touchy **7** bearish, cracked, froward, waspish **8** cankered, choleric, contrary, vinegary **9** crotchety, irascible, temperish **10** bad-humored, ill-humored, vinegarish **11** hot-tempered **12** cantankerous, crackbrained, cross-grained, disagreeable **13** quick-tempered

cranny 4 nook **5** niche **7** byplace

crash 3 din, jar, ram **4** bang, boom, bump, bust, clap, fail, fold, jolt, slam, wham **5** blast, break, burst, crack, shock, smash, wreck **6** impact, pileup **7** collide, crack-up, debacle, smashup **8** accident, collapse **9** breakdown, collision **10** concussion, percussion

crashing 5 gross, utter **7** blasted **8** absolute, infernal, positive **9** downright **10** confounded, consummate

crass 3 raw **4** rude **5** crude, gross, rough **6** coarse, vulgar **7** loutish, uncouth **8** churlish **9** inelegant, unrefined

crate 4 heap **5** wreck **6** jalopy, junker **7** clunker

crater 3 pit **4** hole, pock **6** cavity **7** caldera **10** depression *Hawaiian:* **7** Kilauea

cravat 3 tie **4** band **5** scarf **7** bandage, necktie

crave 3 ask, beg **4** ache, long, lust, pine, pray, sigh, want, wish **5** brace, covet, plead **6** appeal, demand, desire, hanker, hunger, thirst **7** beseech, call for, entreat, implore, require, suspire **9** importune **10** desiderate, supplicate **11** necessitate

craven 4 funk **6** coward, funker **7** chicken, dastard, gutless, quitter, unmanly **8** cowardly, poltroon **9** spunkless **11** lily-livered, plotroonish, yellowbelly **12** poor-spirited **13** pusillanimous

craving 4 itch, lust, urge **6** desire **7** passion **8** appetite **10** appetition

crawl 4 flow, inch, teem **5** creep, slide, snail, snake, swarm **6** abound, grovel **9** pullulate

crawling 6 repent **7** reptant

craze 3 fad **4** chic, rage **5** crack, fever, furor, mania, style, vogue **6** frenzy, furore, madden **7** derange, fashion, unhinge **8** distract **9** unbalance **10** dernier cri, enthusiasm

craziness 5 folly **7** inanity **8** insanity **9** absurdity, dottiness, silliness **11** foolishness, witlessness **13** senselessness

crazy 3 fey, mad **4** daft, gaga, loco, luny, nuts, wack **5** balmy, batty, daffy, dotty, goofy, loony, nutty, silly, wacky, whack **6** absurd, cuckoo, insane, looney, madman, maniac, screwy, teched, whacky **7** bonkers, cracked, foolish, lunatic, tetched, touched, unsound **8** crackpot, demented, deranged **9** bedlamite, possessed, senseless **10** crackbrain, moonstruck, unbalanced

11 harebrained **12** preposterous *British:* **5** potty **6** scatty *Scottish:* **3** wud

crazy house 6 asylum **8** loony bin **9** funny farm **10** booby hatch

cream 3 top **4** balm, beat, best, pick, whip **5** blast, elite, pride, prime, prize, salve **6** cerate, choice, chrism **7** clobber, unction, unguent **8** lambaste, ointment

crease 4 fold, ruck **5** plica, ridge, rivel **6** furrow, rimple **7** crinkle, wrinkle **11** corrugation

create 4 make, sire **5** found, hatch, set up, spawn, start **6** father, parent **7** compose, produce **8** conceive, engender, generate **9** establish, formulate, institute, originate, procreate **10** constitute

creation 5 world **6** cosmos, kosmos, nature **8** megacosm, universe **9** macrocosm **11** macrocosmos

creative 8 original **9** demiurgic, deviceful, ingenious, inventive **10** innovative, innovatory **11** originative **12** innovational

creator 4 sire **5** maker **6** author, father **7** founder **8** inventor **9** architect, generator, patriarch **10** originator

creature 3 man **5** beast, being, brute, human, toady **6** animal, minion, mortal, person **7** critter **8** truckler **9** personage, sycophant *fabled:* **3** elf, imp **4** ogre, puck **5** dwarf, fairy, giant, gnome, troll **6** dragon, goblin, merman, sprite **7** brownie, gremlin, mermaid, monster, unicorn **9** hobgoblin **10** leprechaun; (see also **monster**) *winged:* **4** bird, fowl **8** volatile

credence 5 faith, trust **6** belief, credit **8** reliance **10** confidence

credentials 6 papers **9** character, documents, reference **11** testimonial **13** documentation

credible 5 solid, sound, valid **6** trusty **8** faithful, rational **9** authentic, colorable, plausible **10** believable, convincing, reasonable, satisfying **11** trustworthy **12** satisfactory

credit 3 lay **4** deem, feel **5** asset, faith, honor, refer, sense, think, trust **6** assign, belief, charge, impute, notice, weight **7** ascribe, believe **8** consider, credence, prestige, reliance **9** attribute, authority, influence **10** confidence **11** recognition

creditable 7 reputed **9** colorable, estimable, plausible, reputable **10** believable **11** respectable **13** well-thought-of

credo 5 creed **6** belief **8** ideology

credulous 5 naive **6** unwary **7** dupable **8** gullible, trustful, trusting **9** accepting, believing **12** unsuspecting, unsuspicious **13** unquestioning

creed 4 cult, sect **5** credo, faith **6** belief, church **8** ideology, religion **9** communion **10** connection, persuasion **12** denomination

creek 3 ria 4 gill, race, rill 5 brook
6 arroyo, rillet, runlet, runnel, stream
7 freshet, rivulet 8 brooklet 9 streamlet

creep 4 edge, inch, lurk, slip 5 crawl, glide,
shirk, skulk, slide, slink, snake, sneak, steal
6 tiptoe 7 gumshoe, slither, sniggle, wriggle 9 pussyfoot

creeping 6 repent 7 reptant *combining
form:* 6 herpet 7 herpeto

crème de la crème 4 best 5 elite 6 gentry 7 aristoi 8 optimacy 9 blue blood, haut
monde 10 upper crust 11 aristocracy

Cremona family 6 Amatis

Creon *daughter:* 6 Creusa, Glauce,
Glauke *sister:* 7 Jocasta *son:* 6 Haemon
victim: 8 Antigone

crepehanger 9 Cassandra, pessimist,
worrywart

crescendo 4 acme, apex, peak 5 crest
6 apogee, climax, culmen 8 capstone,
meridian 11 culmination

crescent-shaped 6 lunate 7 lunated
body or surface: 8 meniscus *combining
form:* 5 selen 6 seleni, seleno

crest 3 cap, top 4 acme, apex, noon, peak,
roof 5 arête, chine, crown, ridge 6 apogee,
climax, summit, vertex 7 hogback 8 pinnacle, surmount 9 crescendo, fastigium
11 culmination *combining form:* 4 loph
5 lophi, lopho 6 lophio *of a wave:*
8 whitecap

crestfallen 3 low 4 blue, down 8 cast
down, dejected, downcast 9 depressed
10 dispirited 11 downhearted
12 disconsolate

Crete *ancient city:* 7 Cnossus, Knossos
8 Phaistos *ancient name:* 6 Candia *capital:* 5 Canea *goddess:* 8 Dictynna 11 Britomartis *guard:* 5 Talos *king:* 5 Minos
9 Idomeneus *maze:* 9 labyrinth *monster:*
8 Minotaur *mountain:* 3 Ida *princess:*
7 Ariadne

cretin 4 fool, zany 5 ament, idiot, moron
6 zombie 7 half-wit 8 imbecile 9 simpleton

Creusa *father:* 5 Priam *husband:*
6 Aeneas *mother:* 6 Hecuba *son:* 3 Ion
8 Ascanius

crevice 4 seam, slit 5 chink, cleft, crack,
grike 6 cranny 7 fissure 8 cleavage, crevasse 10 interstice

crew 4 band, bevy, gang, team 5 bunch,
covey, group, party 7 cluster, retinue
8 assembly

crib 3 bed, bin, box, hut, key 4 pony, trot,
weir 5 cheat, crate, hovel, stall, steal 6 cradle, crèche, manger, pilfer 7 barrier, brothel,
purloin 8 bassinet, bedstead, bordello
9 enclosure 10 plagiarism, plagiarize

cricket *period of play:* 7 innings *team:*
6 eleven *term:* 2 on 3 leg, off, rot 4 bowl

5 pitch 6 bowler, wicket, yorker 7 bats-
man, striker 9 fieldsman *turn at bat:* 4 over

crime 3 sin 4 evil, tort 6 breach, delict, felony 7 misdeed, offense 8 delictum, iniquity 9 diablerie, violation 10 illegality,
wrongdoing 11 misdemeanor 13 transgression *instructor:* 5 Fagin

Crimea *capital:* 10 Simferopol *city:*
5 Kerch, Yalta 11 Sevastopol *river:* 4 Alma
sea: 4 Azov *strait:* 5 Kerch

criminal 4 hood, thug 5 crook, felon
6 outlaw 7 convict, illegal, illicit, lawless,
mobster 8 fugitive, gangster, jailbird,
offender, unlawful, wrongful 9 racketeer,
wrongdoer 10 lawbreaker, malefactor, tres-
passer 12 illegitimate, transgressor *habitual:* 8 repeater 10 recidivist

criminate 3 tax 6 accuse, charge, indict
7 arraign, impeach 9 inculpate

crimp 3 bar, bit, rub 4 friz, snag 5 check,
frizz, screw 6 bridle, hamper, hold in, hurdle, rimple, ruck up, rumple 7 crinkle, crumple, inhibit, scrunch, wrinkle 8 hold back,
hold down, mountain, obstacle, restrain,
withhold 9 constrain 10 impediment
11 Chinese wall, obstruction

crimple 5 screw 6 ruck up, rumble 7 crinkle, crumple, scrunch, wrinkle

crimson 3 red 4 glow, pink, rose 5 blush,
color, flush, rouge 6 mantle, pinken, redden

cringe 4 fawn 5 cower, quail, toady,
wince 6 blench, flinch, grovel, kowtow,
recoil, shrink, slaver 7 truckle 8 bootlick
11 apple-polish

crinkle 4 fold, ruck 5 crimp, plica, ridge,
rivel, screw 6 crease, furrow, rimple, ruck
up, rumple 7 crimple, crumple, scrunch
11 corrugation

crinkly 5 crepy 6 crepey

cripple 3 sap 4 lame, maim 5 blunt,
palsy 6 disarm, mayhem, weaken 7 disable, dislimb, unbrace 8 enfeeble, mutilate,
paralyze 9 attenuate, dismember, prostrate,
undermine 10 debilitate, immobilize
12 incapacitate, unstrengthen

cripples' patron saint 5 Giles

crisis 4 pass 5 pinch 6 strait 8 exigency,
juncture, zero hour 9 emergency 10 crossroads 11 contingency 12 turning point

crisp 5 short 6 biting 7 brittle, crumbly,
crunchy, cutting, friable, ingoing 8 clear-cut,
incisive 9 trenchant 11 penetrating

crisscross 9 decussate, intersect

criterion 5 gauge 7 measure 8 standard
9 benchmark, yardstick 10 touchstone

critic 5 momus 6 carper, Zoilus 7 carping,
caviler, knocker 8 captious, caviling, cen-
surer, quibbler 9 aristarch, belittler, cavillous, muckraker, nitpicker 10 censorious,
disparager, mudslinger 11 faultfinder,
smellfungus

critical 4 dire 5 acute, fussy 7 carping, crucial, finicky, pivotal, weighty 8 captious, caviling, decisive 9 cavillous, demeaning, desperate, important, momentous 10 belittling, censorious, conclusive, particular 11 climacteric, disparaging, significant 12 faultfinding 13 consequential, determinative *study:* 6 examen 8 exegesis

criticism 5 blame 6 notice, rebuke, review 7 censure, comment, opinion, reproof 8 analysis, critique, diatribe, judgment, reproval, reviewal 9 appraisal 10 assessment, commentary 11 examination, observation

criticize 3 pan, rap 4 carp 5 blame, blast, cavil, cut up, fault, knock, roast, scold 6 rebuke, scathe 7 censure, condemn, reprove 8 badmouth, denounce, lambaste 9 castigate, fustigate, reprehend, reprobate 10 denunciate

criticizer 5 momus 6 carper, Zoilus 7 caviler, knocker 9 aristarch 11 faultfinder

critique see **criticism**

critter 5 beast, brute 6 animal 8 creature

Crius *father:* 6 Uranus *mother:* 4 Gaea *son:* 8 Astraeus

croak 3 die 5 scold 6 grouch, grouse, murmur, mutter 7 grumble, quarrel 8 complain

croaking 5 gruff, husky 6 hoarse

croaky see **croaking**

Croatia *capital:* 6 Zagreb *city:* 5 Split 6 Osijek, Rijeka

crock 3 jar, pot 4 smut, soot 7 disable 8 potsherd 11 earthenware

crocodile 7 reptile *bird:* 6 plover 9 trochilus *Indian:* 6 gavial *relative:* 9 alligator *South American:* 6 caiman, cayman, jacare *Southeast Asian:* 6 muggar, mugger, muggur

Croesus' kingdom 5 Lydia

Cromwell, Oliver *regiment:* 9 Ironsides *son:* 7 Richard *victory site:* 6 Naseby

crone 3 hag 4 drab, trot 5 biddy, witch 6 beldam

Cronus 5 Titan 6 Saturn *daughter:* 4 Hera 6 Hestia 7 Demeter *father:* 6 Uranus *mother:* 4 Gaea *sister:* 4 Rhea 6 Cybele, Tethys *son:* 4 Zeus 5 Hades 7 Jupiter, Neptune 8 Poseidon *wife:* 4 Rhea 6 Cybele

crony 3 pal 4 chum 5 buddy 6 comate 7 comrade 9 associate, companion 11 running mate

crook 3 bow 4 bend 5 curve, round, thief 6 bandit, robber

crooked 5 lying, snaky, snide, venal 6 curved, errant, shifty, zigzag 7 bending, corrupt, curving, devious, winding 8 rambling, ruthless, tortuous, twisting 9 deceitful, dishonest, underhand 10 fraudulent,

meandering, serpentine, untruthful 12 unscrupulous 13 double-dealing *combining form:* 5 ancyl, ankyl 6 anchyl, ancylo, ankylo 7 anchylo

crookedly 4 awry 5 askew 6 askant 7 askance 8 cockeyed 9 cock-a-hoop

croon 3 hum, low 4 lull, moan, sing, wail 6 lament, murmur

crop 3 cut, hew, mow, top 4 chop, clip, pare, snip, trim 5 prune, shave, shear, skive 7 harvest, pollard 8 fruitage, truncate 10 detruncate

cropping 7 harvest, reaping 9 gathering 10 harvesting 11 ingathering

croquet 5 roque

crosier 5 staff

cross 4 deny, mule, over, rood 5 ratty, testy, trial 6 betray, cranky, hybrid, impugn, negate, ordeal, tetchy, touchy 7 athwart, calvary, carping, gainsay, mongrel, sell out 8 captious, choleric, traverse 9 decussate, disaffirm, half blood, half-breed, hybridize, intersect, irascible, temperish 10 affliction, contradict, contravene, interbreed, transverse, visitation 11 tribulation 13 quick-tempered *a river:* 4 ford *bearer:* 8 crucifer *combining form:* 6 stauro *decoration:* 4 Iron 8 Victoria *Egyptian:* 4 ankh *kind:* 3 tau 5 Greek, Latin, papal 6 Celtic, fleury, formée, moline, pommée, potent 7 avellan, botonée, Calvary, Maltese 8 crucifix, fourchée, Lorraine, quadrate 11 patriarchal 12 Saint Andrew's 13 Saint Anthony's *section:* 5 slice *stroke of a letter:* 5 serif

crossbow 8 arbalest, arbalist

crossbreed 4 mule 6 hybrid 7 bastard, mongrel 9 half blood, half-breed, hybridize 10 interbreed

crosscut 9 decussate, intersect

cross-examination 5 grill 8 grilling 11 questioning, third degree 13 interrogation

cross-eye 6 squint 9 esotropia 10 strabismus

crossing 6 thwart 8 traverse 10 transverse 11 transversal

cross out 6 cancel, delete

crosspatch 4 crab 5 crank 6 griper, grouch 7 grouser, growler 8 grumbler, sorehead, sourpuss 10 complainer

crossroads 4 pass 5 pinch 6 crisis, strait 8 exigency, juncture, zero hour 9 carrefour, emergency 11 contingency 12 intersection, turning point *goddess:* 6 Hecate, Hekate, Trivia

cross-shaped 8 cruciate 9 cruciform

crossways 6 across 7 athwart 10 diagonally 12 transversely

crosswise see **crossways**

crotchet 4 whim 5 fancy, freak, quirk

6 megrim, vagary **7** boutade, caprice, conceit **12** eccentricity

crotchety 5 waspy **6** cranky, ornery **7** bearish, waspish **8** cankered, contrary, vinegary **10** vinegarish **12** cantankerous, cross-grained

crouch 4 bend, duck **5** cower, hunch, squat, stoop **6** huddle **10** hunker down **11** scrooch down

crow 4 blow, brag, puff **5** boast, exult, mouth, prate, vaunt **9** gasconade **11** rodomontade *colony:* **7** rookery *combining form:* **5** corax *cry:* **3** caw *family:* **3** daw, jay **4** rook **5** raven **6** chough, corvid, hoodie, magpie **7** jackdaw **8** Corvidae *genus:* **6** Corvus *Hawaiian:* **5** alala *relating to:* **7** corvine

crowbar 3 pry **5** jimmy, lever **7** gablock **8** gavelock

crowd 3 jam, lot, mob, set **4** army, bear, cram, herd, host, push, rout, ruck **5** bunch, cloud, crush, drove, flock, group, horde, press, serry, shove, swarm, troop **6** circle, gaggle, huddle, legion, rabble, scores, squash, squish, squush, throng **7** cluster, company, squeeze **8** assembly **9** congeries, gathering, multitude **10** assemblage, collection **11** aggregation **12** congregation

crowded 4 full **5** awash, close, dense, thick, tight **6** jammed, loaded, packed **7** brimful, compact, crammed, stuffed **8** brimming, populous **9** chock-full

crow-like 7 corvoid

crown 3 cap, top **4** acme, apex, peak, roof **5** cover, crest, tiara **6** anadem, climax, diadem, laurel, summit, top off, vertex, wreath, zenith **7** chaplet, coronal, coronet, garland, overlay **8** meridian, overcast, pinnacle, round off, surmount **9** culminate, fastigium, finish off **10** overspread **11** culmination *combining form:* **6** corono **7** stephan **8** stephano *Egyptian:* **7** pschent

crucial 4 dire **5** acute, vital **8** critical, decisive **9** desperate, important, necessary **10** imperative **11** climacteric

crucible 4 test **5** trial **6** ordeal **10** affliction **11** tribulation

crucifix 4 rood **5** cross

crucifixion site 7 Calvary **8** Golgotha

crucify 4 kill **5** smite **6** harrow, martyr **7** afflict, agonize, mortify, torment, torture **10** excruciate

crud 3 goo **4** gook, gunk, junk, muck **5** filth, slime, trash **6** debris, sludge **7** rubbish

crude 3 raw **4** foul, poor **5** crass, dirty, gross, rough **6** coarse, filthy, gauche, impure, native, ribald, risqué, smutty, unhewn, vulgar **7** boorish, ill-bred, loutish, lowbred, obscene, raunchy, uncouth **8** backward, barnyard, cloddish, ignorant,

immature, indecent, inexpert, inferior, prentice, unformed, ungraded, unsorted, unworked **9** graceless, inelegant, roughhewn, run-of-mine, unrefined, unskilled, untrained **10** amateurish, unfinished, unpolished **11** clodhopping, ineffective **12** unproficient **13** unenlightened

cruel 4 fell, grim, mean **6** brutal, fierce, savage **7** bestial, brutish, heinous, inhuman, wolfish **8** inhumane, ruthless **9** atrocious, barbarous, ferocious, heartless, monstrous, truculent, unpitying **10** relentless **12** bloodthirsty

cruise 4 sail **6** voyage

cruiser 4 boat **7** warship **9** patrol car, powerboat

crumb 3 bit, jot **4** iota **5** ounce, scrap, shred **7** smidgen **8** particle

crumble 3 rot **5** decay, spoil, taint **6** molder **7** putrefy **8** collapse **9** break down, decompose **12** disintegrate

crumbly 5 crisp, short **7** brittle, crunchy, friable

crumple 3 wad **4** bend, cave, give **5** break, crimp, screw, yield **6** fold up, rimple, ruck up **7** crinkle, scrunch, wrinkle **8** collapse

crunch 4 chew **5** champ, chomp, chump, munch **7** chumble **8** ruminate **9** masticate

Crusader *English:* **7** Richard *French:* **6** Philip, Robert **7** Godfrey, Raymond **8** Montfort *German:* **9** Frederick *Norman:* **7** Tancred **8** Bohemund *Preacher:* **7** Bernard **14** Peter the Hermit

crusading 11 evangelical **12** evangelistic

crush 3 jam **4** bear, beat, bray, buck, cram, dash, mash, pulp, push, ruin **5** crowd, drove, horde, press, quash, quell, smash, wreck **6** béguin, bruise, defeat, pestle, powder, quench, reduce, squash, squish, squush, subdue, throng **7** abolish, blot out, conquer, contuse, destroy, passion, put down, repress, scrunch, squeeze, squelch **8** bear down, beat down, demolish, suppress, vanquish **9** comminute, multitude, overpower, pulverize, puppy love, subjugate, triturate **10** annihilate, extinguish, obliterate **11** infatuation **12** contriturate

crust 4 cake, rime

crustacean 4 crab, flea, scud **5** louse, prawn **6** isopod, shrimp, slater, sow bug **7** copepod, daphnia, decapod, lobster, pill bug **8** amphipod, anomuran, barnacle, crawfish, crayfish, macruran, ostracod, sand flea **9** arthropod, beach flea, schizopod, shellfish, water flea, wood louse **10** brachyuran, stomatopod, whale louse **11** branchiopod *aggregate of:* **5** krill *appendage:* **5** exite **6** endite **7** pleopod *body segment:* **6** somite, telson **8** metamere *claw:* **5** chela **6** pincer *covering substance:*

6 chitin *larva:* 5 alima 8 nauplius *limb segment:* 6 podite 8 podomere

crusty 4 curt, foul, rank 5 bluff, blunt, brief, dirty, gross, gruff, short, testy 6 abrupt, coarse, cranky, filthy, snippy 7 brusque, crabbed, obscene, raunchy, waspish 8 choleric, snippety 9 irascible, irritable, saturnine, splenetic 10 fescennine

crux 3 nub 4 core, gist, meat, pith 6 kernel, thrust 7 purport 9 substance

cry (see also **exclamation**) 3 sob 4 bawl, blub, call, howl, moan, pule, rage, song, wail, weep, yaup, yawp, yell, yowl 5 bleat, craze, groan, hallo, hollo, motto, mourn, on-dit, rumor, shout, sniff, trend, vogue, whine, whoop 6 boohoo, furore, gossip, holler, lament, report, rumble, scream, snivel, squawk, squeak, squeal 7 blubber, fashion, hearsay, screech, ululate, whimper 9 advertise, publicize 10 vociferate 11 scuttlebutt *bacchanals':* 4 evoe *calf:* 5 bleat *cat:* 3 mew 4 meow 5 miaou *cattle:* 3 low, moo *chick:* 4 peep 5 cheep *court:* 4 oyes, oyez *crane:* 5 clang *crow:* 3 caw *dog:* 3 arf 4 bark, woof *donkey:* 4 bray 6 heehaw *duck:* 5 quack *frog:* 5 croak *goat:* 5 bleat *goose:* 4 honk 5 clang, cronk *hen:* 6 cackle *horse:* 5 neigh 6 nicker, whinny 7 whicker *lion:* 4 roar *owl:* 4 hoot *pig:* 4 oink 5 grunt *raven:* 5 croak, cronk *sheep:* 5 bleat *songbird:* 5 chirp, tweet *turkey:* 6 gobble

cry down 5 decry 8 belittle, derogate, diminish 9 disparage 10 depreciate 11 detract from, opprobriate

crying 4 dire 6 urgent 7 burning, clamant, exigent, heinous 8 pressing, shocking 9 atrocious, clamorous, desperate, monstrous 10 imperative, outrageous, scandalous 11 importunate

cry off 5 welsh 6 renege, resile 7 back out 8 back down 9 backpedal, backwater

cry out 4 blat, blat 7 exclaim 9 ejaculate

crypt 4 cave, cell 5 vault 7 chamber 8 catacomb 10 undercroft 11 compartment

cryptanalyze 5 break, crack 6 decode 7 decrypt 8 decipher

cryptic 4 dark 5 murky, vague 6 opaque 7 obscure, unclear 8 abstruse, Delphian 9 enigmatic, tenebrous 10 mysterious, mystifying 12 unfathomable

crystal 5 clear, lucid 6 lucent 8 clear-cut, luminous, pellucid 9 unblurred 11 translucent, transparent 12 transpicuous *combining form:* 5 blast 6 hedron

Cry, the Beloved Country
author
5 Paton

cry up 4 laud 5 bless, extol 6 praise 7 glorify, magnify 8 eulogize 9 celebrate 10 panegyrize

Cuba *capital:* 6 Havana *chief export:* 5 sugar *monetary unit:* 4 peso *premier:* 6 Castro (Fidel)

cubbyhole 5 niche 6 recess 7 cubicle

cube 3 die 4 dice (plural)

cubic meter 5 stere

Cub Scout *rank:* 4 Bear, Wolf 6 Bobcat 7 Webelos *unit:* 3 den 4 pack

Cuchulainn *father:* 3 Lug 4 Lugh *foe:* 4 Medb 5 Maeve *kingdom:* 6 Ulster *mother:* 8 Dechtire *son:* 8 Conlaoch *victim:* 8 Conlaoch *wife:* 4 Emer

cuckoo 3 nut 4 daft, kook 5 crank, crazy, daffy, nutty 6 crazed, insane 7 cracked, lunatic 8 crackpot 9 ding-a-ling, harebrain, screwball 12 crackbrained *bird:* 3 ani

cucumber 4 pepo 6 gerkin 7 gherkin

cuddle 3 pet 4 snug 6 burrow, caress, cosset, dandle, fondle, nestle, nuzzle 7 embrace, snuggle

cuddlesome 8 huggable

cudgel 3 bat 4 cane, club, mace 5 baton, billy 6 paddle 7 war club 8 bludgeon, spontoon 9 billy club, blackjack, truncheon 10 knobkerrie, nightstick

cue 4 clue, hint 6 notion 7 inkling 8 telltale 10 indication, intimation, suggestion

cuff 3 box, hit 4 blip, chop, clip, poke, slap, sock 5 clout, punch, smack, spank 6 buffet, wallop 8 haymaker

cul-de-sac 6 pocket 7 dead end, impasse 10 blind alley

cull 4 pick 5 elect, glean 6 choose, garner, gather, optate, opt for, pick up, prefer, select 7 extract 9 single out

culminate 3 cap 5 crown 6 climax, top off 8 round off 9 finish off

culmination 4 acme, apex, noon, peak 6 apogee, climax, summit 8 meridian, pinnacle 11 ne plus ultra

culpability 4 onus 5 blame, fault, guilt

culpable 5 amiss 6 guilty, sinful, unholy 8 blamable, blameful 10 censurable 11 blameworthy, impeachable 13 demeritorious, reprehensible

cult 4 sect 5 creed, faith 6 church 8 religion 9 communion 10 connection, persuasion 12 denomination *suffix:* 3 ism

cultivable 6 arable 8 tillable

cultivatable see **cultivable**

cultivate 4 farm, grow, tend, till, work 5 breed, dress, nurse, raise 6 foster, nursle, refine 7 cherish, nourish, nurture, produce 9 propagate

cultivated 6 urbane 7 genteel, refined 8 cultured, polished, well-bred 9 courteous, distingué

cultivation 6 polish 7 culture 8 breeding 10 refinement

culture 5 class 6 polish 8 breeding, elegance, learning, urbanity 9 education, erudition, gentility **10** refinement **11** cultivation, savoir faire **12** civilization **13** enlightenment

cultured **6** urbane **7** erudite, genteel, learned, refined **8** educated, literate, polished, well-bred **9** civilized, distingué **10** cultivated **11** enlightened

culture medium **4** agar

culverhouse **8** dovecote, pigeonry **9** columbary

cumber **3** tax **4** clog, lade, load, task **6** burden, charge, saddle

cumbersome **7** awkward, unhandy **8** cumbrous, unwieldy **9** ponderous

cumbrance **4** clog **6** burden **7** trouble **9** hindrance, impedance **10** impediment

cumbrous see **cumbersome**

cum ___ salis **5** grano

cumshaw **3** tip **7** largess **8** gratuity **9** lagniappe, pourboire **10** perquisite

cumulate **4** hive **5** amass, lay up, uplay **6** garner, roll up **7** store up **9** stockpile

cumulation **5** hoard, trove **9** amassment, colluvies, stockpile **10** collection **11** aggregation **13** agglomeration

cumulative **5** chain **8** additive, additory **9** summative **10** increasing **11** multiplying

cunning **3** art, sly **4** deep, foxy, keen, wary, wily **5** acute, canny, craft, guile, savvy, sharp, skill, smart **6** adroit, artful, astute, clever, crafty, deceit, tricky **7** finesse, know-how, knowing, slyness **8** artifice, deftness, facility, foxiness, guileful, subtlety, wiliness **9** adeptness, cageyness, canniness, dexterity, dexterous, duplicity, expertise, ingenious, ingenuity, insidious, masterful, sharpness, slickness **10** adroitness, artfulness, cleverness, craftiness, shiftiness, shrewdness, trickiness **12** dissemblance **13** dexterousness, dissimulation, ingeniousness

cup **3** mug **4** toby **5** grail, jorum, stein **6** beaker, seidel **7** chalice, tankard **8** schooner *assayer's:* **5** cupel *combining form:* **5** cotyl, cyath, scyph **6** cotyli, cotylo, cyatho, scyphi, scypho *diamond cutter's:* **3** dop *handle:* **3** ear, lug *holder:* **4** zarf *liturgical:* **3** ama **5** amula, calix **7** chalice *Scottish:* **4** tass *small:* **6** noggin **7** canakin, canikin **8** cannikin **9** demitasse *sports:* **5** Davis, Ryder **6** Curtis **7** Stanley **8** America's, Wightman *two-handled:* **3** tyg

cupbearer of the gods **4** Hebe **8** Ganymede

cupboard **3** kas **5** ambry, cubby, cuddy **6** buffet, closet, larder, pantry **7** armoire, cabinet **8** credence, credenza **9** sideboard

Cupid **4** Amor, Eros **6** cherub **7** amorino **8** amoretto *beloved:* **6** Psyche *brother:* **7** Anteros *father:* **6** Hermes **7** Mercury *mother:* **5** Venus **9** Aphrodite *title:* **3** Dan

cupidity **4** lust **5** greed **6** desire **7** avarice, avidity, craving, passion **8** rapacity, voracity **9** eagerness **10** greediness **11** infatuation **13** rapaciousness

cupola **4** dome **5** vault **6** turret **7** furnace, lantern, lookout

cup-shaped **8** scyphate

cur **3** cad, dog **4** scum, toad **5** skunk, snake **6** rotter **7** bounder, stinker **8** riffraff, stinkard **9** yellow dog

curative **5** tonic **7** healing **8** remedial, salutary, sanative, sanatory **9** medicinal, remedying, vulnerary, wholesome **10** beneficial, corrective, medicative **11** restorative, therapeutic **12** invigorating

curb **3** bit, tie **4** clog, deny **5** check, leash, tie up **6** bridle, fetter, hamper, hobble, hogtie, hold in **7** abstain, inhibit, refrain, repress, shackle **8** hold back, hold down, restrain, suppress, withhold **9** constrain, entrammel *British:* **4** kerb

curd see **curdle**

curdle **4** clot, sour **5** spoil **7** clabber, thicken **9** coagulate *Scottish:* **6** lapper, lopper

cure **3** age **4** heal **6** physic, remedy **7** restore **8** antidote, medicant, medicine **9** pharmacon **10** corrective, medicament, medication **11** counterstep **12** counteragent **13** counteractant, counteractive *fish:* **6** kipper

cure-all **6** elixir **7** nostrum, panacea **10** catholicon

cureless **8** hopeless **9** incurable, insanable, uncurable **10** impossible **11** immedicable, irreparable **12** irremediable **13** uncorrectable

curio **3** toy **6** bauble, gewgaw, trifle **7** bibelot, trinket, whatnot **9** bric-a-brac, objet d'art, **10** knickknack

curiosity **6** marvel, oddity, rarity, regard, wonder **7** anomaly, concern **8** interest, nonesuch

curious **3** odd **4** nosy **5** nosey, peery, queer, weird **6** prying, quaint, snoopy **7** bizarre, oddball, strange, unusual **8** peculiar, singular **9** inquiring **11** inquisitive, inquisitory, questioning **12** disquisitive **13** inquisitorial, investigative

curium *symbol:* **2** Cm

curl **4** coil, friz, kink, wind **5** frizz, twine, twist **6** spiral **7** entwine, frizzle, ringlet, wreathe **9** corkscrew

curling *match:* **8** bonspiel *period of play:* **3** end *team:* **4** four *term:* **3** tee **4** hack, rink **5** house, stone

curly **5** kinky **6** frizzy

currency **4** cash **5** dough, lucre, money, scrip **11** legal tender *premium:* **4** agio *unit:* (see individual country)

current 3 run 4 eddy, flow, flux, rife, rush, tide 5 drift, flood, spate, tenor, trend 6 extant, modern, stream 7 instant, popular, present, rampant, regnant, topical 8 existent, tendency, up-to-date 9 prevalent 10 present-day, prevailing, widespread 11 fashionable 12 contemporary *air:* 4 gale, gust, wind 5 blast, draft 6 breeze, squall, vortex, zephyr 7 cyclone, indraft, tornado, twister, typhoon, updraft 8 outdraft 9 downdraft, hurricane, whirlwind 10 slipstream *combining form:* 4 rheo *ocean:* 7 riptide 8 undertow 9 maelstrom, whirlpool *unit:* 6 ampere 8 abampere 10 statampere

Currier's partner 4 Ives

curry 4 drug, whip 6 thrash 9 overwhelm

curse 4 cuss, damn, oath 5 swear 6 bedamn, plague 7 damning, malison, scourge 8 anathema, cussword, execrate 9 blaspheme, blasphemy, expletive, imprecate, objurgate, profanity, sacrilege, swearword 10 execration, pestilence 11 commination, imprecation, malediction, objurgation, profanation 12 anathematize, denunciation

cursed 6 damned, odious 7 blasted, blessed, doggone, dratted 8 damnable, infernal 9 execrable 10 confounded 13 blankety-blank

cursive 4 easy 6 fluent, smooth 7 flowing, running 10 effortless

cursory 5 brief, hasty, quick, rapid, short 7 hurried, shallow, sketchy 9 depthless 10 uncritical 11 superficial

curt 5 bluff, blunt, brief, gruff, short 6 abrupt, crusty, snippy 7 brusque, concise, laconic, summary 8 snippety, succinct 11 compendiary, compendious 12 breviloquent 13 short and sweet

curtail 3 cut 5 slash 6 lessen, minify 7 abridge, cut back, shorten 8 diminish, retrench 10 abbreviate

curtain 4 drop, veil 5 drape 6 screen 7 barrier *doorway:* 8 portiere *holder:* 3 rod *Indian:* 6 pardah, purdah *rod concealer:* 7 valance *sash:* 7 tieback *stage:* 4 drop 8 backdrop

curtains 3 end 5 death 6 demise 7 decease, drapery

curtilage 4 quad, yard 5 court 9 enclosure 10 courthouse, quadrangle

curvaceous 5 buxom 7 rounded, shapely, stacked 9 Junoesque 13 well-developed

curvation 3 arc, bow 4 arch, bend 5 round

curvature (see **curvation**) *of the spine:* 8 kyphosis, lordosis 9 scoliosis

curve 3 arc, bow 4 arch, bend, coil, curl, turn, veer, wind 5 crook, round, twist 6 convex, spiral, swerve 7 concave, flexure, rondure, sinuate *of an arch:* 8 extrados, intrados *pitcher's:* 4 hook *plane:* 7 cissoid, cycloid, limaçon 8 parabola, sinusoid, trochoid 9 hyperbola *S-shaped:* 3 ess 4 ogee 7 sigmoid

curved 4 bent 5 arced, bowed, round 6 arched 7 arcuate, arrondi, bending, crooked, embowed, falcate, rounded, twisted 8 arciform, twisting 9 declinate *combining form:* 4 cyrt 5 ancyl, ankyl, curvi, cyrto 6 anchyl, ancylo, ankylo, campto 7 anchylo, clastic *implement:* 6 sickle *molding:* 4 ogee *sword:* 8 scimitar

curvilinear see **curved**

curvy see **curvaceous; curved**

Cush *father:* 3 Ham *son:* 6 Nimrod

cushion 3 mat, pad 5 squab 6 absorb, buffer, pillow 7 bolster, hassock, pillion 8 palliate *Indian:* 4 gadi 5 gaddi

cushy 4 cozy, easy, snug, soft 5 comfy 7 easeful 11 comfortable

cusp 3 tip 4 apex, peak 5 point

cuspid 6 canine 8 eyetooth

cuspidate 5 acute, piked, sharp 6 peaked 7 pointed 8 acicular 9 aciculate, acuminate, acuminous

cuss 3 guy, man 4 chap, damn, oath 5 curse, swear 6 bedamn, fellow 8 execrate 9 expletive, imprecate, swearword

cussword 4 oath 5 curse, swear 9 expletive, swearword

custard 4 flan 5 apple, papaw 8 sweetsop

custodian 6 keeper, warden 7 curator, steward 8 cerberus, claviger, guardian, overseer, watchdog 9 caretaker 10 supervisor

custody 4 care, ward 5 trust 6 charge 7 keeping 10 caretaking, management, protection 11 safekeeping, supervision 12 guardianship

custom 3 use 4 want 5 habit, mores (plural), trade, trick, usage 6 manner, praxis, ritual 7 folkway, precept, traffic 8 business, habitude, practice 9 patronage 10 consuetude, tailor-made 11 made-to-order *Latin:* 3 mos

customary 5 usual 6 common, wonted 7 chronic, general, routine 8 accepted, everyday, familiar, frequent, habitual, orthodox, standard 10 accustomed 11 traditional 12 conventional

custom-built 10 tailor-made 11 made-to-order

customer 5 buyer 6 client, patron 7 shopper 8 consumer 9 purchaser *aggregate of:* 9 clientele *frequent:* 7 habitué

customized see **custom-built**

custom-made see **custom-built**
cut 3 hew, ilk, lop, mow, saw 4 bite, chop, clip, crop, dice, dock, fell, gash, hack, kind, nick, pare, part, reap, slit, snip, snob, snub, sort, tear, thin, trim, type 5 bevel, carve, ditch, drunk, filet, knife, lathe, lower, mince, notch, piece, prune, quota, sever, share, shave, shear, skive, slash, slice, split, stamp, wound 6 cleave, dilute, divide, fillet, hackle, incise, member, moiety, open up, parcel, pierce, reduce, scythe, sickle, sunder, trench, weaken 7 abridge, curtail, dissect, operate, partage, portion, scissor, section, segment, shorten 8 amputate, dissever, division, lacerate, mark down, retrench, separate 9 allotment, allowance, ostracize 10 abbreviate 11 description, intoxicated 12 cold-shoulder *combining form:* 4 sect, tomy 6 tomous *of beef:* 3 rib 4 loin, rump 5 baron, chine, chuck, flank, plate, roast, round, shank, steak 6 cutlet, saddle 7 brisket, sirloin 8 shoulder 9 aitchbone
cut across 8 transect 9 transcend
cut-and-dried 7 routine
cutaneous 6 dermal
cutaway 4 coat, dive
cut back 4 clip, pare 5 lower, shave, slash 6 reduce 7 abridge, curtail, shorten 8 mark down, retrench 10 abbreviate
cut down 4 clip, pare 5 lower, shave, slash 6 reduce
cute 3 sly 5 sharp 6 clever, dainty, pretty, quaint, shrewd 7 cunning 8 affected 9 ingenious 10 attractive
cut in 6 horn in 7 intrude, obtrude 8 chisel in 10 intertrude
cutlass 5 sword 7 machete
cut off 2 ax 3 axe, lop 4 kill, slay 5 block, catch, scrag 6 enisle, finish, lay low 7 destroy, isolate 8 amputate, dispatch, insulate, separate 9 intercept, segregate, sequester 10 disinherit
cut out 5 usurp 6 delete, excise, exsect, resect 7 exscind 8 displace, supplant 9 eliminate, extirpate
cutpurse 5 thief 10 pickpocket
cut short 3 bob 4 clip, crop, dock, poll 5 abort, check, shear 7 curtail
cuttable 7 sectile 8 scissile
cutter 4 boat, sled 6 editor, sleigh 7 incisor 9 cutthroat
cutthroat 3 gun 5 bravo 6 gunman, hit man 7 torpedo 8 assassin 10 gunslinger, hatchet man, triggerman
cutting 4 crisp 6 biting 7 ingoing 8 clearcut, incisive, piercing 9 trenchant 11 penetrating *combining form:* 5 cidal *edge:* 5 blade *remark:* 3 dig *tool:* 2 ax 3 adz, axe, hob, saw 4 adze 5 knife, lathe, mower, plane, razor 6 reaper, scythe,

shears, sickle 7 hatchet 8 scissors, tomahawk
cutting out *combining form:* 6 ectomy
cuttlefish 7 mollusk 10 cephalopod *ink:* 5 sepia *relative:* 5 squid 7 octopus
cut up 3 pan, rap 4 dice, hash, romp 5 caper, clown, horse, knock, mince 6 cavort, sliver 7 carry on, censure, condemn, show off 8 denounce 9 criticize, horse-play, misbehave, reprehend, reprobate 10 roughhouse
cutup 3 wag 4 zany 5 clown, joker 7 farceur 8 jokester
Cybele 4 Rhea *beloved:* 5 Attis *brother:* 6 Cronus *father:* 6 Uranus *husband:* 6 Cronus *mother:* 2 Ge 4 Gaea *son:* 4 Zeus 7 Jupiter, Neptune 8 Poseidon
cybernetics founder 6 Wiener
cycle 4 bike, loop, ring 5 chain, round, wheel 6 circle, course, series 7 circuit 8 sequence 10 succession, two-wheeler, velocipede
cyclone 7 tornado, twister
cyclopean 4 huge 7 Antaean, mammoth, titanic 8 colossal, gigantic 9 Herculean, monstrous 10 gargantuan 11 elephantine
Cyclops 5 Arges 7 Brontes 8 Steropes 10 Polyphemus
Cycnus *father:* 4 Ares, Mars *slayer:* 8 Hercules
Cygnus *form:* 4 swan *friend:* 7 Phaeton *star:* 5 Deneb
cylinder 4 drum, lock, pipe, tube 5 spool 6 barrel, bobbin, platen, roller
cylindrical 5 tubal 6 terete, tubate 7 tubular 8 tubelike, tuberoid, tubiform, tubulose, tubulous
cyma recta 4 ogee
cymbals *dancer's:* 3 tal 7 crotala
Cymbeline *daughter:* 6 Imogen *son:* 9 Arviragus, Guiderius
Cymric 5 Welsh 6 Celtic 9 Brythonic *bard:* 8 Taliesin *Elysium:* 6 Annwfn *god:* 5 Lludd *of Elysium:* 5 Arawn *of the dead:* 5 Pwyll *of the seas:* 3 Ler 4 Llyr 5 Dylan *of the sky:* 7 Gwydion *of the sun:* 4 Lleu, Llew *of the underworld:* 4 Gwyn *goddess:* 3 Don 9 Arianrhod *magician:* 6 Merlin
Cymry land 5 Wales
cynical 3 wry 6 ironic 8 sardonic
Cynthia 4 Luna, moon 5 Diana 7 Artemis
cyprian 4 jade, slut 5 hussy, tramp 6 wanton 7 jezebel, trollop 8 slattern, strumpet
Cyprus *capital:* 7 Nicosia *language:* 5 Greek 7 Turkish
Cyrano 4 poet 7 duelist *author:* 7 Rostand *feature:* 4 nose

Cyrus *conquest:* 5 Lydia, Media 7 Babylon *daughter:* 6 Atossa *empire:* 7 Persian *father:* 8 Cambyses *son:* 8 Cambyses
Cytherea 5 Venus 9 Aphrodite
czar 4 king 5 baron, mogul 6 prince, tycoon 7 magnate *Russian:* 4 Ivan 5 Basil,

Peter 6 Alexis, Feodor, Fyodor 7 Michael, Romanov 8 Nicholas, Romanoff, Theodore 9 Alexander 12 Boris Godunov
czar's wife 7 czarina 8 czaritza
Czechoslovakia *capital:* 6 Prague *monetary unit:* 6 koruna

D

D.A., e.g. 4 atty
dab 3 hit, pat 4 blow, chit, lump, peck, spot 5 clout, smear 6 bedaub, blotch, smudge 7 besmear, plaster, portion, splotch
dabbler 4 tyro 7 amateur 9 smatterer 10 dilettante, uninitiate 11 abecedarian
dabbling 7 jackleg, shallow 8 ungifted 9 unskilled 10 amateurish, dilettante, unfinished 11 superficial 12 dilettantish, dilettantist
dabchick 5 grebe 9 hell-diver
Dadaist 3 Arp, Ray 4 Ball 5 Grosz, Tzara 7 Duchamp, Picabia 10 Schwitters
daedal 6 knotty 7 complex, gordian 8 involved 9 Byzantine, elaborate, intricate 11 complicated 12 labyrinthine 13 sophisticated
Daedalus 9 architect, artificer *construction:* 9 Labyrinth *father:* 6 Metion *son:* 6 Icarus *victim:* 5 Talos 6 Perdix
daffy see **daft**
daft 3 mad 4 loco, luny, wild 5 balmy, crazy, giddy, potty, silly 6 crazed, cuckoo, insane, maniac 7 cracked, foolish, idiotic, lunatic, unsound 8 demented, deranged, imbecile 9 bedlamite 10 unbalanced
Dag *father:* 7 Delling *horse:* 9 Skinfaksi *mother:* 4 Nott
Dagda *chief god of the:* 5 Gaels, Irish *daughter:* 6 Brigit *instrument:* 4 harp *son:* 6 Aengus *wife:* 5 Boann
dagger 4 dirk 5 skean, skeen, skene 6 bodkin 8 stiletto *handle:* 4 hilt *medieval:* 6 anlace
daily 7 diurnal 9 circadian, quotidian
dainty 4 airy, nice, rare 5 fussy, goody, light, treat 6 choice, morsel, select, tidbit, titbit 7 elegant, finical, finicky 8 delicacy, delicate, ethereal, kickshaw, superior 9 exquisite, finicking, recherché 10 delightful, diaphanous, fastidious, particular, pernickety 11 persnickety

dairy 8 creamery
dais 7 rostrum, terrace 8 platform
daisy 5 oxeye *British:* 10 moonflower *Scottish:* 5 gowan
Daisy Miller author 5 James
Daksha's father 6 Brahma
dale 4 glen 6 valley
dally 3 lag, toy 4 drag, fool, idle, play, poke 5 delay, flirt, tarry, trail 6 coquet, dawdle, frolic, lead on, linger, loiter, put off, trifle, wanton 11 string along 13 procrastinate
Dalphon's father 5 Haman
dam 3 bar 4 stay, stem, stop, weir 5 block, brake, check, choke 6 hinder, impede 7 barrier, repress 8 blockade, obstacle, obstruct, suppress 10 overslaugh
damage 3 mar 4 blot, harm, hurt, loss, ruin 5 abuse, burst, cloud, spoil, wound 6 deface, impair, injure, injury, scathe 7 blemish, destroy, marring, tarnish, vitiate 8 destruct, ill-treat, maltreat, mischief, mistreat, mutilate, sabotage 9 prejudice, vandalism 10 dilapidate, impairment *relating to:* 5 noxal
damaging 3 bad 4 evil 6 nocent 7 harmful, hurtful, nocuous 9 injurious 11 deleterious, detrimental, mischievous
dame 4 lady 5 woman 6 beldam, gammer, matron 7 dowager, grandam 9 matriarch
Damien's island 7 Molokai
Damkina *husband:* 2 Ea *son:* 6 Marduk
damn 4 cuss, doom, drat, durn 5 curse, swear, whoop 7 condemn, doggone 8 execrate, sentence 9 abominate, imprecate, objurgate, proscribe 10 vituperate 12 anathematize
damnable 4 dang, darn 5 gross, utter 6 blamed, cursed, cussed, odious 7 blasted, dratted, hateful 8 accursed, infernal, outright 9 abhorrent, dad-burned, downright, execrable, out-and-out 11 unmitigated

damned 4 dang, darn, durn, lost, rank, very 5 gross, utter 6 blamed, cursed, cussed, dashed, doomed 7 awfully, blasted, doggone, dratted, goldarn 8 absolute, accursed, blighted, blinding, complete, infernal, outright, whopping 9 dad-blamed, downright, execrable, extremely, out-and-out, perishing, reprobate 10 confounded, dad-blasted 11 straight-out, unmitigated 13 anathematized, blankety-blank

Damocles' ___ 5 sword

Damon's friend 7 Pythias

damp 3 wet 4 dank, dewy, mist 5 humid, juicy, moist, muggy, musty, rainy, soggy 6 clammy, moisty 7 bedewed, moisten, wettish 8 humidify, humidity, moisture

dampen 4 mute 6 deaden, muffle, sponge, stifle

damsel 3 gal 4 girl, lass, maid, miss 5 missy, wench 6 lassie, maiden, moppet 8 donzella, princess 10 demoiselle

Dan *father:* 5 Jacob *mother:* 6 Bilhah *son:* 6 Hushim

Danaë *father:* 8 Acrisius *lover:* 4 Zeus *son:* 7 Perseus

Danaus *brother:* 8 Aegyptus *daughters:* 8 Danaides *father:* 5 Belus *founder of:* 5 Argos *grandfather:* 7 Neptune 8 Poseidon

dance 3 hop, jig, tap 4 ball, duet, flit, foot, giga, heel, hoof, juba, leap, lope, move, reel, skit, step 5 bamba, brawl, cooch, galop, gigue, hover, lindy, mambo, mixer, polka, rumba, sally, stomp, swing, tread, valse 6 adagio, ballet, bolero, boogie, Boston, cancan, chassé, chi-chi, foot it, formal, frolic, german, hoof it, redowa, rhumba, shimmy 7 beguine, coranto, courant, flicker, flitter, flutter, hoedown, onestep, shuffle 8 Alley Cat, cakewalk, chaconne, cotillon, courante, couranto, fandango, flamenco, galliard, galopade, glissade, hula-hula, rigadoon, rigandon 9 allemande, jitterbug *art of:* 11 terpsichore 12 choreography *Austrian:* 7 ländler *ballroom:* 5 congo, rumba, tango 6 chacha 7 fox-trot, mazurka, twostep 8 merengue 9 cotillion 10 Charleston *Bohemian:* 5 polka *Brazilian:* 5 samba 6 maxixe 9 bossa nova *chorus:* 5 strut *combining form:* 5 chore 6 choreo, chorio *country:* 3 hay 8 anglaise, hornpipe *couple:* 5 polka *court:* 6 pavane 8 saraband 9 allemande, sarabande *Cuban:* 5 conga 8 habanera *designer:* 13 choreographer *East Indian:* 5 mudra *English:* 6 morris *folk:* 4 hora, kolo 8 hornpipe 10 tarantella, tarantelle *formal:* 4 prom *French:* 5 gavot 7 bourrée, gavotte 8 lanciers 10 carmagnole *garment:* 4 tutu 7 leotard *graceful:* 6 minuet *Haitian:* 4 juba *Hungarian:* 7 Csardas, Czardas *Indian:* 6 nautch

instrument: 8 castanet *Irish:* 6 fading *Israeli:* 5 horah *Italian:* 9 rigoletto *lively:* 4 reel, trot 6 rhumba 7 bourrée 9 shakedown *modern:* 3 toe *movement:* 4 step 6 minuet 8 glissade 9 allemande, pirouette *1920's:* 10 Charleston *old-time:* 7 hoedown 8 chaconne *Polish:* 5 polka 7 mazurka 8 mazurka *Polynesian:* 4 hula *round:* 5 carol, waltz 6 carole *shoes:* 5 pumps 8 slippers *slipper:* 7 toeshoe *slow:* 5 pavan, pavin 6 adagio, pavane *South American:* 7 carioca *Spanish:* 4 jota 6 bolero 7 zapateo 8 cachucha, saraband *springy:* 3 jig *square:* 7 lancers 9 quadrille *stately:* 5 pavan 8 saraband 9 sarabande *step:* 3 pas 4 riff, shag 6 pickup *voluptuous:* 5 belly *woman's:* 6 cancan

dancer 6 hoofer, hopper 7 chorine, clogger, danseur, prancer, stepper 8 coryphée, danseuse, figurant 9 ballerina, chorus boy, chorus man, figurante 10 ballet girl, cakewalker, chorus girl *American:* 4 Feld, Lang, Tune 5 Kelly 6 Duncan, Graham, Taylor 7 Astaire, Bujones, de Mille, Gregory, Martins, Massine, McBride, St. Denis, Tamiris 8 Kirkland, Villella 9 Tallchief *ballet:* 6 étoile 7 soliste *Danish:* 8 Tomasson *English:* 5 Somes, Tudor 7 Markova 8 Fonteyne *female:* 8 devadasi *French:* 6 Bejart, Perrot, Petipa *German:* 5 Jooss *Italian:* 5 Grisi *Javanese:* 7 serimpi *Mexican:* 5 Limon *Russian:* 5 Lifar 7 Nureyev, Pavlova, Ulanova 8 Danilova, Makarova, Nijinsky, Semenova, Vaganova 10 Karasavina 11 Baryshnikov *Scottish:* 7 Shearer *sword:* 7 bouffon 8 matachin *Zuni:* 7 shalako

dancing 6 ballet 7 saltant 11 choreography, terpsichore 12 choreography *mania:* 9 tarantism

dandle 3 pet 4 love 6 caress, cosset, cuddle, pamper

dandruff 5 scurf 6 furfur

dandy 3 fop 4 beau, buck, dude, fine, lulu, toff 5 dilly, nifty, peach, swell 6 peachy 7 coxcomb 8 popinjay, terrific 9 excellent, first-rate, humdinger, hunky-dory, marvelous 11 Beau Brummel, crackerjack 12 lounge lizard

dang 4 darn, durn 5 utter 6 cursed, cussed, damned 7 blasted, blessed, dratted, goldarn, regular 8 absolute, outright 9 downright 10 confounded, consummate 11 unmitigated

danger 4 risk 5 peril 6 hazard, menace, plight, threat 7 pitfall 8 distress, jeopardy *signal:* 4 bell 5 alarm, siren 6 redeye, tocsin

dangerous 4 fell 5 dicey, grave, hairy, nasty, risky 6 chancy, scathy, unsafe, unsure, wicked **7** parlous, serious, unsound, vicious **8** grievous, insecure, menacing, perilous **9** hazardous, unhealthy **10** jeopardous, precarious **11** threatening

dangle **4** hang **5** droop, sling, swing **6** depend **7** suspend

Daniel *American pioneer:* **5** Boone *father:* **5** David *mother:* **7** Abigail *statesman:* **7** Webster

Danish *hero:* **5** Ogier *king:* **9** Christian, Frederick *queen:* **9** Margrethe

dank **3** wet **4** damp **5** humid, moist **6** clammy, dampen, moisty **7** dampish, wetness, wettish **8** moisture

Dante *beloved:* **8** Beatrice *birthplace:* **8** Florence *daughter:* **7** Antonia *deathplace:* **7** Ravenna *party:* **6** Guelph **7** Bianchi *patron:* **5** Scala *teacher:* **6** Latini *wife:* **5** Gemma *work:* **7** Inferno **8** Commedia, Convivio **9** Vita Nuova

Dantean division **5** canto

Danton's colleague **5** Marat

Danzig **6** Gdańsk

dap **4** skim, skip **5** carom, graze **6** glance **8** ricochet

Daphne *father:* **5** Ladon **6** Peneus *form:* **10** laurel tree *pursuer:* **6** Apollo **9** Leucippus

Daphnis' lover **5** Chloe

dapper **4** neat, trim **5** natty, sassy **6** jaunty, rakish, spiffy, spruce, sprucy **7** bandbox, doggish, foppish, stylish **8** sparkish **11** well-groomed

dapple **4** spot **5** fleck, patch

dappled **6** dotted, motley **7** flecked, mottled, spotted **8** freckled **9** multihued **10** discolored, multicolor, variegated, versicolor **11** varicolored **12** multicolored, particolored, versicolored

Dardanelles **10** Hellespont

Dardanus *descendants:* **7** Trojans *father:* **4** Zeus **7** Jupiter *mother:* **7** Electra

dare **4** defi, defy, face, risk **5** beard, brave, front, stump **6** brazen, cartel, hazard **7** attempt, outface, venture **8** confront, defiance **9** challenge

daredevil see **daring**

darer **4** hero **6** risker

daring **4** bold, pert, rash, wild **5** brave, nerve **6** heroic **7** courage, heroism **8** boldness, devilish, fearless, reckless, temerity **9** audacious, daredevil, foolhardy, venturous **10** courageous, jeopardous **11** adventurous, temerarious, venturesome **13** adventuresome

Darius *father:* **9** Hystaspes *son:* **6** Xerxes *wife:* **6** Atossa

Darjeeling **3** tea

dark **3** dim, dun, sad, wan **4** dusk, murk **5** black, blind, brown, cloud, dingy, dusky, mirky, murky, night, shady, sooty, swart, umber, unlit, vague **6** brunet, cloudy, dismal, gloomy, opaque, somber, sombre, swarth, swarty, wicked **7** aphotic, cryptic, duskish, obscure, rayless, shadowy, stygian, subfusc, sunless, swarthy, unclear **8** abstruse, bistered, Delphian, gloomful, ignorant, mystical, sinister **9** ambiguous, enigmatic, lightless, secretive, tenebrous, unlighted **10** caliginous, indistinct, mysterious, mystifying, pitch-black **11** black-a-vised **13** unilluminated *combining form:* **3** mel **4** mela, melo **5** melam, melan **6** melano *poetic:* **4** ebon

darken **3** dim, fog **4** dull, dusk, haze, murk **5** bedim, blind, cloud, gloom, lower, shade, sully, umber **6** shadow **7** becloud, benight, blacken, eclipse, embrown, obscure, opacate, tarnish **8** melanize, overcast **9** obfuscate, overcloud **10** overshadow *Scottish:* **5** gloam

dark-haired *female:* **8** brunette *male:* **6** brunet

darkness **4** dusk, mirk, murk **5** black, gloom, night, shade, umbra **6** shadow **7** privacy, secrecy **8** midnight, twilight

dark-skinned **5** dusky, swart **6** brunet, swarth **7** swarthy **8** bistered, melanous **11** black-a-vised

darling **3** pet **4** chou, dear, duck, love, lush **5** deary, ducky, flame, honey, loved, sweet **7** beloved, pigsney, sweetie **8** adorable, favorite, heavenly, precious **9** ambrosial **10** delectable, delightful, fair-haired, honeybunch, sweetheart

darn **4** mend **5** patch, utter **6** blamed, cursed, cussed, damned, repair **7** blasted, doggone **8** infernal, outright **9** downright **10** confounded **11** straight-out **13** blankety-blank

darn it *French:* **3** zut

dart **3** fly, jet, run, shy **4** barb, bolt, buzz, flit, leap, sail, scud, skim **5** arrow, bound, fling, hurry, lance, scamp, scoot, shaft, shoot, skirr, spear, speed, spurt **6** glance, hasten, scurry, spring, sprint, squirt **7** javelin, missile, scamper **8** jaculate *barbed:* **10** banderilla

D'Artagnan's friends **5** Athos **6** Aramis **7** Porthos

Dartmouth location **7** Hanover

darts terms **3** leg **4** bust **5** split **6** dosser, double, flight, hockey, treble **8** bull's-eye **10** clock board

Darwin **7** Charles *ship:* **6** Beagle *theory:* **9** evolution

dash **3** nip, pep, run, vim, zip **4** balk, bang, beat, bilk, boil, bolt, brio, élan, foil, hint, hurl, life, pelt, race, ruin, rush, slam, tear, tick, zing **5** ardor, blast, break, chase, crush, drive, fling, oomph, scoot, shoot, smack, speed, spice, style, throw, trace, verve

6 baffle, blight, charge, energy, esprit, hurtle, hyphen, scurry, spirit, sprint, streak, thrust, thwart, trifle 7 bravura, collide, scamper, shatter, soupçon, spatter, splotch 8 confound, tincture 9 animation, bespatter, frustrate 10 circumvent, disappoint, sprinkling, suggestion

dashboard reading 4 fuel 5 speed 7 mileage

dashing 3 gay 4 bold, chic, keen 5 alert, showy, smart, swank, swish 6 bright, dapper, jaunty, lively, modish, swanky, with-it 7 animate, rousing, stylish 8 animated, spirited 9 vivacious 11 fashionable

Das Kapital author 4 Marx

dassie 9 blacktail

dastard 4 funk 6 coward, craven, funker 7 chicken, quitter 8 poltroon 11 yellowbelly

dastardly 4 base, mean

data 5 facts, input 8 material 11 information

date 3 age, era, woo 5 court, epoch, tryst 6 cutoff, escort 7 take out 8 deadline 9 accompany 10 engagement, rendezvous 11 anniversary, appointment, assignation *abbreviation:* 4 appt

dated 3 old 5 passé 6 démodé, old hat 7 archaic 8 obsolete, outmoded 10 antiquated 12 old-fashioned 13 unfashionable

Dathan's father 5 Eliab

datum 4 fact

daub 4 blob, blot, spot 5 fleck, paint, smear 6 dapple, smudge, splash 7 besmear, dribble, plaster, spatter, speckle, splotch 9 variegate

daughter *Carter's:* 3 Amy *Cher's:* 8 Chastity *Cole's:* 7 Natalie *Elizabeth II's:* 4 Anne *Fonda's:* 4 Jane *Ford's (Gerald):* 5 Susan *Garland's:* 11 Liza Minelli *Johnson's (Lyndon):* 4 Lucy 5 Linda *Kennedy's (John F.):* 8 Caroline *Nixon's:* 5 Julie 6 Tricia *Sinatra's:* 5 Nancy

Daughter of the Moon 7 Nokomis

daunt 3 cow 6 dismay, subdue 7 conquer, horrify, terrify 8 frighten 10 disconcert, discourage, dishearten, intimidate

dauntless 4 bold, game 5 brave 8 fearless, unafraid 9 unfearful, unfearing 10 courageous, invincible 11 indomitable, lionhearted

dauntlessness 4 guts 5 heart, pluck, spunk 6 mettle, spirit 7 cojones, courage 10 resolution

davenport 4 desk, sofa 12 chesterfield

David *commander:* 4 Joab 5 Amasa *companion:* 8 Jonathan *daughter:* 5 Tamar *father:* 5 Jesse *rebuker:* 6 Nathan *scribe:* 7 Seraiah *singer:* 5 Heman *son:* 5 Amnon 7 Absalom, Solomon *wife:* 7 Abigail, Ahinoam 9 Bathsheba

David, for one 4 camp

David Copperfield *author:* 7 Dickens *character:* 4 Dora, Heep 5 Agnes, Uriah 6 Barkis, Betsey 7 Creakle 8 Micawber 9 Murdstone, Wickfield 10 Steerforth *nurse:* 8 Peggotty (Clara)

dawdle 3 lag 4 drag, idle, jauk, laze, lazy, loaf, loll, poke 5 dally, delay, tarry, trail 6 linger, loiter, lounge, put off, putter, trifle 7 fritter 8 lallygag, lollygag 13 procrastinate

dawn 4 morn 5 alpha, light, onset, start, sunup 6 aurora, outset 7 genesis, morning, opening, sunrise 8 cockcrow, daybreak, daylight, outstart 9 beginning 11 cockcrowing 12 commencement

day 3 era, sun 4 time 8 lifetime *abbreviation:* 3 Fri, Mon, Sat, Sun, Thu, Tue, Wed 4 Thur, Tues 5 Thurs *before:* 3 eve *church calendar:* 5 feria *French:* 4 jour *German:* 3 Tag *holy:* 5 feast *hot:* 8 scorcher *hour:* 4 noon *Latin:* 4 dies *Spanish:* 3 dia

day blindness 11 hemeralopia

daybreak 4 dawn, morn 5 sunup 6 aurora 7 dawning, morning, sunrise 8 cockcrow 11 cockcrowing

daydream 4 muse 5 fancy 6 revery, vision 7 fantasy, reverie 8 phantasm, phantasy

days *fourteen:* 9 fortnight *of yore:* 3 eld

daystar 3 Sol, sun 7 phoebus

daze 3 fog 4 haze, stun 5 blind, dizzy 6 bemuse, benumb, dazzle, fuddle, muddle, trance 7 confuse, mystify, petrify, stupefy 8 astonish, bedazzle, befuddle, bewilder, confound, disorder, distract, paralyze 9 dumbfound, overwhelm 10 muddlement 11 muddledness 12 befuddlement

dazed 5 woozy 6 doiled, groggy, punchy 7 witless 8 dithered

___ d'Azur 4 Cote

dazzle 5 blind, shine 8 bewilder, outshine

dazzling 6 flashy, garish 7 fulgent, glowing, radiant 9 brilliant 10 candescent

deacon 4 calf 6 cleric, doctor, layman 7 officer 10 adulterate

dead 3 dim 4 cold, dull, flat, gone, late, lost, numb 5 bleak, blind, inert, muted, passé, quiet, slain, utter 6 asleep, buried, bygone, dismal, fallen, lapsed, numbed 7 defunct, disused, exactly, expired, extinct, outworn, tedious 8 benumbed, deceased, departed, inactive, lifeless, obsolete, outmoded 9 apathetic, deathlike, exanimate, inanimate, senseless, unfeeling 10 breathless, corpselike, insensible, insentient, lackluster, lusterless, monotonous, motionless, spiritless, unanimated, unexciting 11 inoperative, insensitive, unconscious 12 anesthetized, extinguished, unresponsive *Australian:* 4 bung *British:* 5 napoo 6 napooh *combining form:* 4 necr 5 necro

dead duck 5 goner

deaden 4 dull, kill, mull, mute, numb, stun 5 blunt 6 benumb, dampen, muffle, obtund, opiate, stifle 7 mortify, petrify, smother, stupefy 8 paralyze 10 devitalize 11 anesthetize, desensitize

dead end 4 halt 6 pocket 7 impasse 8 cul-de-sac 10 blind alley, bottleneck, standstill

deadened 4 numb 6 asleep, corpsy, numbed 7 deathly 8 benumbed, deathful 9 deathlike, senseless, unfeeling 10 corpselike, insensible 11 insensitive 12 anesthetized

deadfall 4 trap 7 springe 9 booby trap, mousetrap

deadliness 8 fatality 9 lethality, mortality

deadlock 3 tie 4 draw 6 logjam 7 dogfall, impasse 8 standoff, stoppage 9 stalemate 10 standstill

deadly 4 dire 5 fatal, toxic 6 corpsy, lethal, mortal 7 baneful, capital, killing, noxious, ruinous, slaying 8 deathful, lethally, venomous, virulent 9 deathlike, pestilent, poisonous 10 corpselike, pernicious 11 destructive, mortiferous, pestiferous 12 pestilential

deadpan 5 blank, empty 6 vacant 12 inexpressive, unexpressive

dead shot 8 marksman

Dead Souls author 5 Gogol

dead to rights 9 red-handed

deadweight 3 tax 4 duty, load, onus, task 6 burden, charge 9 millstone

deafen 3 din

deal 4 dole, give, sale 5 allot, serve, shake, share, trade, treat 6 accord, bestow, divide, impart, lot out, parcel, strike 7 bargain, deliver, dish out, dole out, inflict, mete out, portion, scatter, wrestle 8 disburse, dispense, disperse, separate, share out 9 agreement, apportion, negotiate, partition 10 administer, distribute, measure out, portion out 11 transaction 13 understanding *great:* 4 lots 5 loads *out:* 8 dispense 9 apportion 10 administer, distribute *secretly:* 7 trinket *with:* 4 play 5 serve, treat 6 handle

dealer 4 bank 5 agent 6 banker, broker, seller, trader 8 chandler, merchant, operator 9 tradesman 10 negotiator, trafficker 11 businessman, distributer, distributor 12 merchandiser *British:* 6 draper, jobber, mercer 7 chapman *card:* 6 farmer *horse:* 5 coper *women's clothing:* 7 modiste

dealings 5 truck 7 affairs, matters, traffic 8 business, commerce, concerns 11 intercourse

dealing with *suffix:* 2 ic 4 ical

dean 4 head 5 doyen, guide, pilot 6 leader, priest, senior 7 officer 10 bellwether

dear 3 hon, pet 4 fond, high, lamb, love 5 honey, loved, sweet 6 costly, doting, loving, scarce 7 beloved, darling, devoted, lovable, machree, querida, special, tootsie 8 especial, favorite, loveling, lovesome, precious, valuable 9 cherished, expensive, heartfelt, sweetling 10 fair-haired, heartthrob, honeybunch, sweetheart 12 affectionate *French:* 4 cher 5 chère *Irish:* 4 agra *Scottish:* 2 jo

dear one *suffix:* 3 een

dearth 4 lack, want 6 defect, famine 7 absence, default, paucity, poverty 8 scarcity 9 privation, scantness 10 deficiency, meagerness, scantiness *combining form:* 5 penia

death 3 end 4 bane, exit 5 decay, night, sleep 6 demise, ending, expiry 7 decease, parting, passage, passing, quietus, silence 8 biolysis, casualty, curtains, fatality, necrosis, thanatos 9 bloodshed, departure 10 defunction, expiration, extinction, grim reaper 11 dissolution, termination 12 annihilation *after:* 10 posthumous *combining form:* 6 thanat 7 thanato *easy:* 10 euthanasia *music:* 5 dirge, elegy 8 threnody *notice:* 4 obit 8 obituary 9 necrology *of tissue:* 8 gangrene *portending:* 6 funest *put to:* 3 gas 4 hang, kill, slay 5 choke, lynch 6 murder, stifle 8 strangle, throttle 9 suffocate 11 assassinate, electrocute *rate:* 9 mortality *rites:* 7 funeral

deathless 7 abiding, eternal, lasting, undying 8 immortal 10 persisting 12 imperishable

deathlike see **deathly**

deathly 5 fatal 6 grisly, lethal, mortal 7 ghastly, haggard, macabre, stygian 8 deadened, gruesome, mortally 9 pestilent 10 cadaverous, corpselike 11 mortiferous 12 pestilential

debacle 4 rout 5 crash, smash, wreck 6 defeat 7 beating, crack-up, failure, licking, smashup 8 collapse, drubbing 9 breakdown, cataclysm, overthrow, trouncing 10 defeasance 11 shellacking 12 vanquishment

debar 4 bate 6 except, forbid, refuse 7 deprive, exclude, prevent, rule out, suspend 8 count out, preclude, prohibit 9 eliminate

debark 4 land

debase 3 mar, rot 4 harm, sink, warp 5 alloy, lower, spoil, stain, stoop, taint 6 bemean, canker, damage, defile, demean, dilute, dope up, humble, impair, injure, poison, reduce, vilify, weaken, worsen 7 corrupt, degrade, deprave, devalue, pervert, pollute, traduce, vitiate 8 cast down, dishonor 9 animalize, brutalize, humiliate, undermine 10 adulterate, bastardize, bes-

tialize, degenerate, demoralize
11 contaminate

debatable 4 moot 7 dubious 8 arguable, doubtful, mootable 9 uncertain 11 problematic 12 questionable

debate 4 fray, heed, moot 5 argue, fight, plead, rebut, study 6 hassle 7 agitate, canvass, contend, contest, discept, discuss, dispute, mooting, quarrel, wrangle 8 argument, consider, forensic, question 9 altercate, attention, dialectic, thrash out 10 toss around 11 application, controversy, disputation 12 deliberation 13 argumentation, concentration, consideration *art of:* 9 forensics *expert:* 7 eristic *place for:* 5 forum

debauch 4 orgy, undo, warp 5 party 6 seduce 7 corrupt, deprave, pervert, vitiate 9 bacchanal, brutalize 10 bastardize, bestialize, demoralize, saturnalia 11 bacchanalia

debauched 4 lewd 6 wanton 7 vitiate 8 depraved, vitiated 9 corrupted, dissolute, lecherous, libertine, perverted 10 lascivious, libidinous, licentious

debilitate 3 sap 5 blunt 6 weaken 7 cripple, disable, unbrace 8 enfeeble 9 attenuate, extenuate, undermine 10 devitalize 12 unstrengthen

debilitated 4 weak 6 feeble, infirm, sapped 8 burnt-out, decrepit 9 burned-out

debility 7 astheny, disease, malaise 8 asthenia, weakness 9 infirmity 10 feebleness, infirmness, sickliness 11 decrepitude 13 unhealthiness *combining form:* 6 asthen 7 astheno

Debir *kingdom:* 5 Eglon *slayer:* 6 Joshua

debonair 6 urbane 8 carefree, charming, graceful 10 nonchalant 11 lighthearted

Deborah's husband 9 Lappidoth

debris 4 junk, slag 5 offal, trash, waste 6 litter, refuse, rubble, spilth 7 garbage, rubbish 8 detritus, riffraff *rock:* 5 talus 7 eluvium 8 colluvia

debt 3 due, sin 4 evil 5 wrong 6 arrear 7 arrears, default, deficit 9 arrearage, demurrage, liability 10 obligation, wickedness 11 delinquency *acknowledgment:* 3 IOU 4 bill 5 check

debtless 7 solvent

debunk 6 expose, show up, unmask 7 uncloak, undress 8 discover, unshroud

Debussy's La ___ 3 Mer

debut 7 come out, opening 8 entrance, premiere 9 beginning 12 introduction

decadence 7 decline 8 downfall 9 downgrade 10 declension, degeneracy, devolution 11 declination, degradation 12 degeneration, dégringolade 13 deterioration

decadent 6 effete 8 overripe 10 degenerate

decalogue verb 5 shalt

Decameron, The *author:* 9 Boccaccio *heroine:* 8 Griselda

decamp 2 go 3 fly 4 exit, flee 5 break, leave, scape, scram 6 begone, escape, get out, retire 7 abscond, run away, skiddoo, slip off, take off 8 clear out, hightail, withdraw 9 skedaddle

decanter 6 bottle, carafe

decapitate 4 head, raze, ruin, undo 5 wrack, wreck 6 behead, unmake 7 destroy, unbuild 8 decimate, demolish 9 decollate 10 guillotine

decapod 6 shrimp 7 mollusk 10 crustacean

decathlon champ 6 Jenner (Bruce), Toomey (Bill) 7 Johnson (Rafer), Mathias (Bob) 8 Campbell (Milton), Thompson (Daley)

decay 3 ebb, rot 4 fade, sour, turn, wane 5 spoil, taint, waste 6 blight, curdle, fading, molder, wither 7 corrupt, crumble, failure, ferment, moulder, putrefy 8 putresce 9 break down, decompose 11 deteriorate 12 dilapidation, disintegrate, putrefaction 13 deterioration

decayed 3 bad 6 effete, putrid, rotten 7 carious, spoiled 8 decadent, overripe 10 degenerate

decease 3 die 4 fail, pass 5 death, sleep 6 cash in, demise, depart, expire, perish 7 passing, quietus, succumb 8 pass away 9 departure 10 defunction 11 dissolution

deceit 3 gyp 4 hoax, sham 5 fraud, guile 6 humbug 7 chicane, cunning, swindle 8 artifice, flimflam, spoofery, trickery 9 chicanery, duplicity, imposture 12 dissemblance 13 dissimulation, double-dealing

deceitful 3 sly 4 foxy, wily 5 false, lying 6 artful, crafty, fickle, hollow, shifty, sneaky, tricky 7 cunning, knavish, roguish 8 delusive, delusory, guileful, unhonest 9 dishonest, insidious, insincere, underhand 10 fallacious, mendacious, misleading, untruthful 11 treacherous, underhanded

deceivable 7 dupable 8 gullible

deceive 3 con, fob, fop, fub, lie 4 bilk, dupe, flam, fool, gaff, gull, hoax, jilt, mock, wyle 5 blind, bluff, cheat, cozen, dodge, hocus, spoof, trick 6 baffle, befool, betray, delude, humbug, illude, juggle, palter, take in 7 beguile, defraud, mislead, sell out, two-time 8 flimflam, hoodwink 9 bamboozle, four-flush 11 double-cross 12 misrepresent

deceiving 5 false 8 deluding, delusive, delusory 9 beguiling 10 fallacious, misleading

decelerate 5 delay 6 retard, slow up 7 slacken 8 slow down

decency 7 decorum, dignity, fitness 9 etiquette, propriety 10 seemliness

decent 4 fair, good, just, nice, pure

5 clean, right **6** chaste, common, enough, honest, modest, proper, seemly **7** average, correct, fitting **8** adequate, all right, becoming, decorous, spotless **9** befitting, competent, stainless, sufficing, tolerable, undefiled, unsullied **10** acceptable, conforming, immaculate, sufficient **11** comfortable, comme il faut, presentable, respectable, unblemished **12** satisfactory **13** unexceptional, unimpeachable

deception 3 gyp **4** flam, gaff, gull, hoax, hype, ruse, sham, wile **5** cheat, craft, fraud, guile, magic, put-on, spoof, trick **6** dupery, humbug, mirage **7** chicane, cunning, fallacy, fantasm, knavery, sophism **8** cheating, cozening, flimflam, illusion, intrigue, phantasm, subtlety, trickery, trumpery, wiliness **9** casuistry, chicanery, duplicity, fourberie, imposture, sophistry, treachery **10** artfulness, camouflage, defrauding, dishonesty, hanky-panky, subterfuge **11** dipsy-doodle, highbinding, indirection **12** speciousness, spuriousness **13** double-dealing *Scottish:* **7** blaflum

deceptive 5 false **6** artful, crafty, tricky **7** seeming, trickie **8** deluding, delusory, illusory, specious, trickish **9** beguiling **10** fallacious, misleading

deceptiveness 7 fallacy, sophism **8** delusion **9** casuistry, sophistry **12** equivocation, speciousness, spuriousness

decide 3 opt **4** rule, will **5** judge **6** figure, settle **7** adjudge, resolve **8** conclude **9** determine **10** adjudicate

decided 3 set **4** firm, flat, sure **5** fixed **6** intent **7** assured, certain, obvious, settled **8** clear-cut, cocksure, definite, explicit, positive, resolute, resolved **10** determined, pronounced **11** categorical, established, unequivocal **12** unmistakable

decimate 4 raze, ruin, undo **5** wrack, wreck **6** unmake **7** destroy, unbuild, unframe, wipe out **8** demolish, massacre **9** slaughter **10** annihilate **11** exterminate

decipher 5 break, crack, solve **6** decode, reveal, unfold **7** analyze, decrypt, resolve, unravel **8** unriddle **9** figure out, puzzle out, translate **12** cryptanalyze

decision 4 fiat **6** choice, ruling **7** resolve, verdict **8** firmness, judgment, sentence, umpirage **9** selection **10** conclusion, resolution, settlement **12** resoluteness **13** determination, purposiveness *rabbinical:* **9** responsum

decisive 3 set **4** bent **6** intent **7** assured, crucial, settled **8** critical, resolute, resolved **9** imperious, masterful **10** determined, imperative, peremptory **11** self-assured **13** self-confident

deck 4 trim **5** adorn, array, dress, equip, floor, prank **6** attire, blazon, clothe

7 apparel, appoint, furnish, garland, garnish **8** accouter, accoutre, beautify, decorate, emblazon, ornament, platform **9** embellish *chief:* **4** bos'n **9** boatswain *high:* **4** poop *lowest:* **5** orlop *out:* **5** fix up, primp, slick, spiff, tog up **6** doll up **7** dress up, gussy up **8** spruce up *part:* **7** scupper

deckhand 3 gob **6** sailor **7** rouster, swabbie

declaim 4 rant, rave **5** mouth, orate, speak, utter **6** recite **7** elocute, inveigh, soapbox **8** bloviate, harangue, perorate

declamatory 7 aureate, flowery **8** sonorous **9** bombastic, high-flown **10** euphuistic, oratorical, rhetorical **12** magniloquent **13** grandiloquent

declaration 4 word **6** avowal, oracle, report **9** broadcast, statement **10** disclosure **12** announcement **13** advertisement, pronouncement

declare 3 say, vow **4** aver, avow, deny, tell, toot, vend, vent **5** sound, state, utter, voice **6** affirm, allege, assert, assure, avouch, blazon, depone, depose, herald, report, reveal **7** chime in, deliver, divulge, express, profess, protest, publish, signify, testify **8** announce, bring out, constate, disclose, indicate, proclaim, throw out **9** advertise, broadcast, predicate, pronounce **10** annunciate, bruit about, promulgate **11** blaze abroad, come out with, disseminate *a saint:* **8** canonize *in cards:* **3** bid **4** meld *invalid:* **5** annul

declare off 5 welsh **6** renege, resile **7** back out **8** back down **9** backpedal, backwater

declass 4 bump, bust **5** break **6** demote, reduce **7** degrade, demerit, disrate **8** disgrade **9** downgrade

déclassé 4 hack, mean, poor **6** common **8** inferior, low-grade **10** second-rate **11** second-class **12** second-drawer

declension 8 downfall **9** decadence, downgrade **10** degeneracy **12** dégringolade

declination 6 ebbing, waning **7** failure **8** downfall **9** decadence, downgrade **10** degeneracy **12** dégringolade

decline 3 dip, ebb, jib, rot, sag, set **4** balk, dive, drop, fade, fail, fall, flag, loss, sink, slip, wane **5** abate, demur, droop, lapse, lower, slide, slope, slump, spurn **6** ebbing, go down, recede, refuse, reject, renege, waning, weaken, worsen **7** abstain, atrophy, descend, descent, dismiss, drop-off, dwindle, failure, falloff, forbear, refrain, relapse, sell-off, sinkage, subside **8** comedown, decrease, downfall, downturn, languish, lowering, toboggan, turn down **9** backslide, decadence, downgrade, downslide, downswing, downtrend, reprobate, repudiate, weakening **10** degeneracy, degenerate, depression, devolution, disapprove, disimprove, falling off, retrograde **11** backsliding, deteriorate **12** degeneration, dégringolade, disintegrate **13** deterioration *combining form:* **4** clin **5** clino

declivitous 6 sloped, tilted, tipped **7** leaning, oblique, pitched, sloping **8** inclined **9** inclining

declivity 3 dip **4** drop, fall **5** slope **7** descent **8** gradient **11** inclination

decode see **decipher**

decollate 4 head **6** behead **10** guillotine

decolor 5 white **6** blanch, bleach, blench, whiten **7** wash out **11** achromatize

decompose 3 rot **4** turn **5** decay, spoil, taint **6** molder **7** analyze, break up, crumble, dissect, putrefy, resolve **8** dissolve **9** anatomize, break down **12** disintegrate

decomposition *combining form:* **4** lyses (plural) **5** lysis

decorate 4 pink, trim **5** adorn, dress, frill, prank **6** bedeck, emboss **7** cornice, dress up, festoon, furnish, garnish, miniate, appliqué **8** beautify, emblazon, ornament **9** embellish *a border:* **6** purfle

decorated 6 ornate **7** adorned, wrought **9** bemedaled **10** beribboned

decoration 2 PH **3** DSC, DSM **4** bays **5** award, badge, honor, kudos, medal **6** boulle, doodad, plaque **7** laurels **8** accolade, fretting, fretwork, ornament, vignette *cutout:* **8** appliqué *furniture:* **4** buhl **8** buhlwork

decorous 3 fit **4** done, good, nice, prim **5** right **6** au fait, comely, decent, proper, seemly **7** correct, elegant, fitting **8** becoming, suitable **9** befitting, civilized, de rigueur **10** conforming **11** appropriate, respectable, well-behaved

decorously 4 well **5** fitly **6** justly, nicely **7** rightly **8** properly **9** correctly, fittingly **11** befittingly

decorousness 5 order **9** propriety **11** orderliness **12** correctitude

decorticate 4 flay, hull, peel, skin **5** scale, scalp, strip **6** denude

decorum 5 order **7** decency, dignity, modesty **9** etiquette, propriety **10** properness, seemliness **11** correctness, orderliness **12** correctitude, decorousness

decoy 4 bait, lure, toll, trap **5** blind, plant, shill, snare, stick, tempt **6** allure, capper, delude, entice, entrap, lead on, pigeon, seduce **7** deceive, mislead **8** inveigle, trickery **9** deception, shillaber **10** allurement, enticement, seducement, temptation **12** inveiglement

decrease 3 cut, ebb **4** bate, clip, drop, ease, fall, loss, sink, trim, wane **5** abate, allay, close, lower, taper, waste **6** deduct,

lessen, rebate, recede, reduce, shrink **7** abridge, atrophy, curtail, cut back, cut down, dwindle, letdown, lighten, peak out, shorten, slacken, subside **8** contract, diminish, downturn, moderate, peter out, retrench, rollback, subtract, taper off **9** alleviate, drain away **10** abbreviate, diminution

decree 3 act, law, set **4** fiat, rule **5** canon, edict, enact, judge, order, tenet, ukase **6** assize, behest, charge, dictum, firman, impose, ordain, ruling **7** adjudge, appoint, bidding, command, dictate, lay down, mandate, precept, statute **8** judgment, sentence **9** directive, enactment, judgement, ordinance, prescribe, prescript **10** adjudicate, injunction, plebiscite, regulation **11** declaration **12** adjudication, announcement, proclamation, promulgation **13** pronouncement *Muslim:* **5** irade

decrepit 3 old **4** aged, lame, weak, worn **5** frail, seedy, tacky, tired **6** creaky, feeble, flimsy, infirm, senile, shabby, sloppy, tagrag, wasted, weakly **7** cast-off, failing, fragile, haggard, run-down, unkempt, unsound **8** slipshod **10** bedraggled, broken-down, down-at-heel, threadbare **13** insubstantial, unsubstantial

decrepitude 7 disease, malaise **8** debility **9** infirmity **10** infirmness, sickliness **13** unhealthiness

decretum 3 law **4** rule **5** canon, edict **6** assize **7** precept, statute **9** ordinance **10** regulation

decry 3 boo **4** slur **5** abuse, lower **6** lessen **7** asperse, censure, condemn, degrade, detract, devalue, run down **8** belittle, denounce, derogate, diminish, discount, mark down, minimize, take away, take from, write off **9** criticize, deprecate, devaluate, disparage, dispraise, downgrade, reprehend, reprobate, underrate, write down **10** depreciate, disapprove, undervalue **11** detract from, opprobriate

decrypt see **decipher**

decumbent 4 flat **5** prone **9** prostrate, reclining

decussate 5 cross **8** crosscut **9** intersect **10** criss-cross, intercross

dedicate 3 vow **6** devote, hallow **10** consecrate

deduce 4 draw, lead **5** infer, judge, trace **6** derive, evolve, gather **7** collect, explain, extract, make out **8** cogitate, conclude

deduct 4 bate, dock, draw, take **5** abate, allow, infer, judge **6** derive, gather, remove **7** collect, make out, take off, take out **8** abstract, conclude, discount, knock off, roll back, subtract, take away

deduction 3 cut **6** rebate **7** dockage **8** decrease, discount, illation, judgment, sequitur, write-off **9** abatement, decrement, inference **10** conclusion **13** ratiocination

deductive 7 a priori **8** dogmatic, illative, reasoned **9** derivable **11** inferential **13** ratiocinative

deed 3 act **4** cede, fact, fait, feat, pact **5** doing, quest, thing, title **6** action, assign, convey, escrow, remise **7** charter, compact, exploit **8** alienate, contract, covenant, make over, practice, sign over, transfer **9** adventure **10** abalienate, conveyance, enterprise **11** achievement, performance, tour de force *brutal:* **8** atrocity *evil:* **3** sin **11** malefaction

deem 3 say **4** feel, hold, hope, know, tell, view **5** judge, opine, sense, think **6** credit, divine, reckon, regard **7** account, adjudge, believe **8** consider, proclaim **10** conjecture

de-emphasize 8 downplay, play down **9** soft-pedal

deep 3 low, sly **4** foxy, hard, late, rapt, wily, wise **5** abyss, acute, grave, heavy, ocean **6** artful, astute, crafty, growly, intent, middle, occult, orphic, remote, secret, shrewd, tricky **7** abysmal, complex, cunning, devious, engaged, extreme, intense, obscure, serious, unmixed **8** absorbed, abstruse, esoteric, grievous, guileful, hermetic, immersed, involved, profound **9** developed, engrossed, firmament, insidious, intensive, recondite, sagacious, unalloyed, wrapped up **10** acroamatic, bottomless, mysterious, profoundly **11** complicated, preoccupied *combining form:* **5** bathy *pink:* **5** coral

deep-dyed 5 sworn **7** settled **9** confirmed, hard-shell **10** entrenched, inverate **13** bred-in-the-bone

deepen 4 rise **5** mount, rouse **6** darken **7** enhance, magnify, thicken **8** heighten, redouble **9** aggravate, intensate, intensify **10** strengthen

deepness 4 drop **5** abyss, depth **10** profundity

deep-rooted see **deep-dyed**

deep-sea *combining form:* **5** bathy

deep-seated 5 sworn **6** inborn, inbred, innate **7** connate, settled **8** inherent, profound **9** confirmed, hard-shell, ingrained, intrinsic **10** congenital, entrenched, indwelling, inveterate **13** bred-in-the-bone, dyed-in-the-wool

deep water 6 plight **7** dilemma **11** predicament

deer 3 elk, roe **4** buck, musk, stag **5** brown, moose **6** wapiti **7** caribou, venison **8** bobolink **10** camel's hair *Asian:* **4** axis **6** chital, sambar, sambur **7** muntjac, sambhar, sambhur **8** muntijak *British:* **4** hart *combining form:* **5** cervi *female:* **3** doe *female red:* **4** hind *male:* **4** hart **7** roebuck *male red:* **4** stag **8** staggard,

staggart *meat:* **5** jerky **7** venison *path:* **3** run **5** trail *red:* **7** brocket *relating to:* **6** damine **7** cervine *track:* **4** slot **5** spoor *young:* **3** kid **4** fawn

Deerslayer *author:* **6** Cooper *character:* **11** Natty Bumppo **12** Chingachgook

deface 3 mar **4** foul, harm, ruin, scar **5** spoil **6** batter, damage, deform, injure, mangle **7** blemish, distort **8** misshape, mutilate **9** disfigure, vandalize **10** disfashion, disfeature

de facto 6 really **8** actually **9** genuinely, veritably

defalcation 4 lack **7** deficit, failing, failure **8** shortage, underage **10** deficiency, inadequacy, negligence, scantiness **13** insufficience, insufficiency

defamation 4 tale **7** calumny, scandal, slander **10** backbiting **12** backstabbing, belittlement **13** disparagement

defamatory 8 libelous **9** maligning, traducing, vilifying **10** backbiting, calumnious, detracting, detractive, scandalous, slanderous

defame 4 foul **5** abase, cloud, libel, smear **6** injure, malign, vilify **7** asperse, blemish, scandal, slander, traduce **8** dishonor, vilipend **9** blackwash, denigrate **10** calumniate, scandalize, villainize

default 4 fail, lack, omit, want **6** dearth, defect **7** absence, failure, neglect **9** oversight, privation **10** negligence **11** delinquency, dereliction **12** imperfection

defeasance 4 rout **7** beating, debacle, licking **8** drubbing **9** overthrow **11** shellacking **12** discomfiture, vanquishment

defeat 4 best, down, drub, foil, lick, loss, rout, ruin, sink, stop, undo, whip **5** check, crush, outdo, skunk, swamp, waste, whomp, worst **6** outgun, reduce, subdue **7** beating, conquer, debacle, destroy, failure, licking, nose out, outplay, outvote, repress, setback, shellac, trounce **8** outfight, outtrump, overcome, overvote, vanquish, waterloo **9** downthrow, frustrate, insuccess, overpower, overthrow, subjugate, thrashing, trouncing, unsuccess **10** nonsuccess **11** shellacking **12** discomfiture, vanquishment

defecate 5 purge, stool **6** purify, refine **7** clarify **9** discharge

defect 3 bug **4** flaw, lack, vice, want **5** botch, error, fault **6** damage, dearth, desert, foible, injury, malady **7** absence, blemish, default, failing, frailty **8** drawback, renounce, weakness **9** infirmity, privation, repudiate **10** apostatize, deficiency, tergiverse **11** shortcoming, imperfection, tergiversate *timber:* **4** knot *visual:* **6** myopia, squint **9** amblyopia, hyperopia **10** presbyopia, strabismus **11** hemeralopia

defection 8 apostasy 9 falseness, forsaking, recreancy 10 disloyalty
11 abandonment

defective 3 bad, ill 4 poor, sick 5 amiss, flawy 6 broken, faulty, flawed 7 damaged, lacking, unsound, wanting 8 deranged, impaired 9 corrupted, deficient, imperfect, unhealthy 10 disordered, inaccurate, inadequate, incomplete, uncomplete 12 insufficient *combining form:* 4 atel 5 atelo

defector 3 rat 7 traitor 8 apostate, recreant, renegade, runagate, turncoat 9 turnabout 13 tergiversator

defend 4 back, hold, save 5 argue, claim, cover, fight, guard 6 assert, screen, secure, shield, uphold 7 bulwark, contend, justify, protect, support, warrant 8 advocate, champion, conserve, garrison, maintain, preserve 9 safeguard, vindicate 11 rationalize

defendable see **defensible**

defendant 7 accused, libelee 8 libellee

defender 8 advocate, champion, guardian 9 protector *of people's rights:*
7 tribune

defense 4 egis, fort, ward 5 aegis, alibi, armor, guard 6 answer, excuse, sconce, shield 7 apology, bulwark, rampart, shelter 8 apologia, armament, fastness, fortress, muniment, security 9 safeguard 10 apologetic, protection, stronghold 11 exculpation, explanation 13 justification *organization:* 4 NATO 5 NORAD, SEATO *outer:*
6 tenail 8 tenaille

defenseless 8 helpless 11 unprotected

defensible 7 tenable 9 excusable
10 condonable

defer 3 bow 4 cave, stay, wait 5 adapt, delay, remit, stall, waive, yield 6 accede, adjust, hold up, put off, shelve, submit 7 adjourn, conform, hold off, knuckle, lay over, put over, succumb, suspend 8 hold over, intermit, postpone, prorogue 9 acquiesce 10 capitulate 11 accommodate, buckle under 12 knuckle under
13 procrastinate

deference 5 honor 6 homage 9 obeisance 10 compliance, submission

deferential 5 silky 6 silken 7 duteous, dutiful 9 disarming, regardful 10 respectful, saccharine 11 insinuating, insinuative 12 ingratiating, ingratiatory

defiance 4 dare 5 stump 6 cartel 7 bravado, despite 8 audacity, boldness, contempt, temerity 9 challenge, contumacy, enjoinder, hardihood, impudence, insolence 10 brazenness, effrontery, insurgency, unruliness 12 contrariness, factiousness, stubbornness

deficiency 3 sin 4 lack, want 5 fault, minus 6 dearth 7 absence, blemish, demerit, failing, failure 8 scarcity, shortage,

underage 9 privation 10 inadequacy, scantiness 11 defalcation, shortcoming
12 imperfection *combining form:* 5 penia *mental:* 6 idiocy 7 amentia *oxygen:*
8 asphyxia

deficient 3 shy 5 minus, scant, short 6 faulty, flawed, meager, meagre, measly, scanty, scarce 7 bobtail, failing, lacking, unsound, wanting 8 impaired 9 defective, imperfect 10 inadequate, incomplete, uncomplete *combining form:* 6 privic

deficit 4 lack 7 failure 8 shortage, underage 10 inadequacy, scantiness 11 defalcation 13 insufficience, insufficiency

defile 3 tar 4 foul, pass, rape, soil 5 dirty, shame, smear, spoil, stain, sully, taint 6 befoul, debase, ravish 7 besmear, corrupt, outrage, pollute, profane, tarnish, violate 8 besmirch, deflower, discolor, dishonor 9 deflorate, desecrate
11 contaminate

defiled 6 impure 7 unclean 8 profaned
10 desecrated

define 3 fix, hem, rim, set 4 edge, etch, term 5 bound, limit, skirt, verge 6 assign, border 7 clarify, delimit, lay down, mark off, mark out, outline 8 surround 9 delineate, demarcate, prescribe 12 characterize

definite 3 set 4 sure 5 clear, final, fixed, sharp, solid 6 narrow 7 assured, certain, decided, express, limited, precise, settled 8 clean-cut, clear-cut, distinct, explicit, limiting, positive, specific 10 conclusive, determined, forthright, pronounced, restricted
11 categorical, determinate, established, unambiguous, unequivocal 12 unmistakable 13 circumscribed

definiteness 8 accuracy 9 exactness
10 exactitude

definitive 4 last 5 final 7 express 8 absolute, clean-cut, clear-cut, explicit, settling, specific, terminal, ultimate 10 concluding, conclusive 11 categorical, determining, unambiguous

definitiveness see **definiteness**

definitude see **definiteness**

deflect 4 bend, warp 5 avert, parry, pivot, sheer, wheel, whirl 6 detour, divert, swerve 7 deviate, diverge, hold off, keep off, refract 9 volte-face

deflection 3 yaw 4 bend, tack, turn, veer 5 curve, shift 6 double, swerve 7 bending, turning, veering 8 swerving 9 departure, diversion 10 divergence *combining form:*
7 sphingo

deflorate see **deflower**

deflower 4 rape 5 force, harry, havoc, spoil 6 defile, devast, devour, ravage, ravish 7 despoil, outrage, violate 8 desolate 9 depredate, desecrate, devastate

Defoe *character:* 6 Crusoe, Friday, Roxana 12 Moll Flanders *heroine:* 4 Moll

deform 3 mar 4 flaw, maim, warp, wind 5 spoil 6 batter, damage, deface, impair, injure, mangle 7 blemish, contort, cripple, distort, torture 8 misshape, mutilate 9 disfigure 10 disarrange

deformity 4 flaw 7 blemish, harelip 8 misshape, ugliness 10 aberration, corruption, impairment 11 abnormality, impropriety 12 irregularity, malformation

___ **de France** 3 Île

defraud 3 gyp 4 beat, bilk, hoax, take 5 cheat, cozen, mulct, rogue, trick 6 chouse, fleece 7 swindle 8 flimflam 9 bamboozle

deft 4 neat 5 adept, agile, handy, quick 6 adroit, clever, expert, nimble 8 dextrous, skillful 9 dexterous, ingenious 10 neat-handed

deftness 7 address, prowess, sleight 9 dexterity, readiness

defunct 4 cold, dead, gone, late, lost 5 inert 6 asleep, bygone 7 extinct 8 deceased, departed, finished, inactive, lifeless, vanished 9 exanimate, inanimate

defy 4 dare, face, gibe, mock 5 beard, brave, flout, front, scorn, spurn, stump 6 cartel, ignore 7 affront, outdare, outface, venture 9 challenge

dégagé 6 breezy, casual 7 relaxed, unfussy 8 informal 9 easygoing 10 unreserved 11 low-pressure 13 unconstrained

degeneracy see **degeneration**

degenerate 3 rot 4 sink 5 lapse 6 effete, rotten, worsen 7 corrupt, decayed, decline, descend, vicious, vitiate 8 decadent, depraved, infamous, overripe 9 backslide, miscreant, nefarious, unhealthy 10 disimprove, flagitious, villainous

degeneration 7 atrophy, decline 8 downfall, lowering 9 decadence, depravity, downgrade 10 perversion, regression 12 dégringolade, depravedness

degradation 4 fall 7 decline, descent 11 downgrading

degrade 4 bump, bust, sink 5 abase, break, decry, lower 6 bemean, damage, debase, demean, demote, depose, expose, humble, lessen, reduce 7 corrupt, declass, demerit, deprive, detract, disrate, pervert, put down 8 belittle, cast down, derogate, diminish 9 decompose, disparage, humiliate, reduction 12 depolymerize

degree 3 peg 4 heat, rank, rate, rung, step, term, tier 5 grade, honor, notch, order, pitch, point, ratio, scale, shade, stage, stair 6 extent 7 measure, station 8 standing 9 dimension, magnitude 10 proportion *academic:* 2 BA, BS, MA, MD, MS 3 DDS, LLB, LLD, MBA, MFA, PhD *highest:* 8 cum laude 13 magna cum laude, summa cum laude *of combining power:* 7 valence *of height:* 5 grade *of importance:* 7 caliber, calibre *of outward slope:* 5 splay *seeker:* 9 candidate *slight:* 4 hair *suffix:* 2 ty 3 ity 4 ance, ness *utmost:* 4 acme

dégringolade see **degeneration**

___ **de guerre** 3 nom

dehydrate 3 dry 4 sear 5 parch 9 desiccate, exsiccate

Deianira *brother:* 8 Meleager *father:* 6 Oeneus *husband:* 8 Heracles, Hercules *mother:* 7 Althaea *victim:* 8 Heracles, Hercules

Deidamia *father:* 9 Lycomedes *husband:* 9 Pirithous *son:* 11 Neoptolemus

deific 5 godly 6 divine 7 godlike

deification 10 apotheosis

deign 5 stoop 10 condescend

Deiphobus *brother:* 5 Paris 6 Hector *father:* 5 Priam *mother:* 6 Hecuba *wife:* 5 Helen

Deirdre *beloved:* 5 Noisi *father:* 5 Felim

deity 3 god 4 deva 5 numen 6 numina (plural) 7 goddess, godhead, godhood, godling, godship 8 Almighty, divinity 12 supreme being (see also at **Greek; Hindu; Norse; Roman**)

deject 5 chill 8 dispirit 9 disparage 10 demoralize, discourage, dishearten

dejected 3 low, sad 4 blue, down, glum, sunk 6 gloomy, somber, sombre 7 hangdog, humbled, unhappy 8 downcast, wretched 9 cheerless, depressed, woebegone 10 despondent, spiritless 11 crestfallen, downhearted 12 disconsolate

dejection 5 dumps 7 despair 10 melancholy 12 mournfulness

Delaware *capital:* 5 Dover *largest city:* 10 Wilmington *nickname:* 10 First State 12 Blue Hen State, Diamond State *state flower:* 12 peach blossom

delay 3 lag 4 drag, hold, mire, mull, poke, slow 5 check, defer, deter, embog, stall, tarry, trail 6 dawdle, detain, hang up, hinder, hold up, impede, linger, loiter, put off, retard, shelve, slow up 7 adjourn, bog down, hold off, prolong, respite, set back, slacken, suspend 8 hangfire, hesitate, hold over, intermit, obstruct, postpone, prorogue, reprieve, slow down 9 detention, hindrance, lingering 10 decelerate, dillydally, moratorium, suspension 13 procrastinate

delaying 8 dilatory, moratory

delectable 4 lush 5 sapid, tasty, yummy 6 choice, savory 7 darling 8 heavenly, luscious, pleasing 9 ambrosial, delicious, exquisite, toothsome 10 delightful 11 scrumptious

delectation 3 joy 6 relish 7 delight, joyance **8** fruition, pleasure **9** diversion, enjoyment

delegate 4 name, send **5** agent, envoy, proxy **6** assign, charge, commit, depute, deputy **7** appoint, ascribe, consign, empower, entrust **8** deputize, emissary, transfer **9** authorize, catchpole, spokesman **10** commission, mouthpiece **12** representant

delete 4 omit, x out **5** annul, blank, erase, purge **6** cancel, censor, efface, remove **7** blot out, destroy, expunge, wipe out **8** black out, cross out **9** eliminate, eradicate **10** blue-pencil, obliterate

deleterious 3 bad **6** nocent **7** harmful, hurtful, nocuous, ruinous **8** damaging **11** destructive, detrimental, mischievous, prejudicial

deletion 7 erasure **8** omission **10** deficiency

deliberate 4 cool, muse, pore, slow **5** chary, meant, study, think, weigh **6** ponder, reason, regard **7** advised, careful, heedful, laggard, planned, reflect, schemed, studied, unhasty, willful, willing, witting **8** cautious, cogitate, consider, designed, dilatory, intended, measured, meditate, mull over, prepense, ruminate, studious, talk over, turn over, unforced **9** leisurely, meditated, projected, speculate, unhurried, voluntary **10** calculated, considered, purposeful, thought-out **11** circumspect, intentional **12** aforethought, premeditated, unprescribed

deliberately 9 on purpose, purposely **10** purposedly **11** purposively

deliberation 3 rap **4** heed **5** study **6** debate **7** thought **9** brainwork **10** conference, discussion

Delibes *ballet:* **6** Sylvia **8** Coppelia, La Source *opera:* **5** Lakmé

delicacy 4 cate **5** goody, treat **6** caviar, dainty, luxury, morsel, nicety, tidbit, titbit **7** caviare **8** kickshaw **10** daintiness **11** bonne bouche

delicate 4 airy, fine, lacy, mild, nice, rare, soft, weak **5** balmy, frail, fussy, light **6** aerial, choice, dainty, flimsy, gentle, pastel, petite, queasy, select, slight, subtle, tender, touchy, tricky **7** elegant, finical, finicky, fragile, lenient, politic, refined, tactful, tenuous **8** ethereal, feathery, finespun, gossamer, graceful, hairline, shattery, superior, tactical, ticklish **9** breakable, exquisite, finicking, frangible, recherché, sensitive, squeamish **10** diplomatic, fastidious, particular, precarious **11** fracturable, persnickety, shatterable **13** hair-splitting

delicatesse 4 tact **5** poise **7** address **9** diplomacy **11** savoir faire, tactfulness

delicatessen 11 charcuterie

delicious 4 lush **5** sapid, yummy **6** choice, savory **7** darling **8** adorable, heavenly **9** ambrosial, exquisite, palatable, toothsome **10** appetizing, delectable

delight 3 joy **4** glee **5** amuse, bliss, charm, enjoy, exult, glory, mirth, revel **6** arride, divert, please, regale, relish **7** enchant, gladden, gratify, happify, jollity, joyance, rapture, rejoice, triumph **8** enravish, entrance, fruition, hilarity, jubilate, pleasure, savoring **9** delectate, enjoyment, enrapture, entertain **11** contentment, delectation **12** satisfaction *in:* **4** like, love **5** adore, enjoy, savor **6** admire **7** cherish **10** appreciate

delightful 4 lush **5** yummy **6** dreamy, savory **7** darling, elysian **8** adorable, alluring, charming, heavenly, luscious, pleasant, pleasing **9** agreeable, ambrosial **10** attractive, delectable, enchanting, gratifying **11** fascinating, scrumptious

Delilah's victim 6 Samson

delimit 3 bar **5** bound **6** demark **7** confine, mark out, measure **8** restrict **9** demarcate, determine **12** circumscribe

delineate 3 map **4** etch, limn **5** chart, image, trace **6** define, depict, render, survey **7** outline, picture, portray **8** describe **9** interpret, represent

delineation 5 story **7** account, contour, drawing, outline, picture, profile **10** silhouette **11** portraiture, presentment

delinquency 5 lapse **7** default, failure, misdeed, neglect **8** omission **9** oversight **10** misconduct **11** dereliction

delinquent 3 lax **5** slack **6** remiss **8** careless **9** negligent **10** behindhand, regardless **12** disregardful, transgressor

deliquesce 3 run **4** flux, fuse, melt, thaw **5** decay **7** liquefy **8** dissolve **9** decompose, disappear **12** disintegrate

delirious 3 mad **4** wild **5** crazy, manic, rabid **6** crazed, insane, maniac, raving **7** frantic, lunatic **8** confused, demented, deranged, ecstatic, frenetic, frenzied, rambling **9** rapturous, wandering **10** bewildered, corybantic, distracted, irrational **11** overexcited, overwrought **12** unreasonable *Scottish:* **8** brainish

delirium 5 furor **6** fervor, frenzy, ravery **7** ecstasy, jimjams, rapture

delirium _____ 7 tremens

deliver 3 say **4** bail, bear, deal, feed, find, give, hand, save, take, tell, yean **5** bring, pitch, serve, speak, state, throw, utter, whelp **6** convey, redeem, rescue, strike, supply, unbind **7** chime in, consign, declare, inflict, present, provide, release **8** bring out, dispatch, dispense, hand over, liberate, transfer, transmit, turn over **9** surrender

10 administer, bring forth, emancipate **11** come out with

deliverance 6 rescue **7** opinion, release **8** decision **10** liberation **12** disburdening

delivery 5 birth **6** rescue **7** address, bearing **8** shipment **9** rendition **10** childbirth **11** parturition **12** childbearing *combining form:* **4** toky

dell 4 dale **6** dingle, hollow, valley

Delphian 4 dark **5** vatic **6** mantic **7** cryptic, fatidic **8** oracular **9** enigmatic, prophetic, sibylline, vaticinal **10** mystifying **11** apocalyptic, prophetical

delude 5 bluff, trick **6** betray, humbug, juggle, take in **7** beguile, deceive, mislead **8** impose on **11** double-cross

deluge 3 sea, sop, wet **4** gush, pour, soak **5** douse, drown, flood, souse, spate, swamp, whelm **6** drench, engulf **7** niagara, torrent **8** cataract, downpour, flooding, inundate, overcome, overflow, submerge **9** cataclysm, overwhelm **10** cloudburst, inundation

delusion 5 dream, fancy **6** mirage **7** eidolon, fallacy, fantasy, figment, phantom, sophism **8** daydream, phantasm **9** casuistry, deception, sophistry **10** apparition, misleading **11** ignis fatuus **12** equivocation, speciousness, spuriousness **13** deceptiveness, hallucination

delusive 5 false **8** fanciful, illusory, quixotic **9** beguiling, deceiving, deceptive, fantastic, imaginary, visionary **10** chimerical, fallacious, misleading

delusory see **delusive**

deluxe 4 lush **5** plush **6** Capuan, choice **7** elegant, opulent **8** luscious, palatial **9** exquisite, luxuriant, luxurious, recherché, sumptuous **11** upholstered

delve 3 dig, dip **4** hole, mine, void **6** cavity, fathom, hollow, pocket, quarry, vacuum **7** vacancy, vacuity *into:* **4** sift **5** probe **7** explore **8** prospect **11** investigate

delving 5 probe, quest **7** inquest, inquiry, probing **8** research **11** inquisition **13** investigation

demagnetize 6 deperm **7** degauss

demagogue 6 leader **7** inciter **8** agitator, fomenter **9** firebrand **10** instigator **12** rabble-rouser

demand 3 ask, use **4** call, need, take, want **5** claim, crave, exact, force, order **6** compel, direct, elicit, enjoin, expect, oblige **7** call for, request, require, solicit **8** occasion **9** challenge, constrain, postulate **11** requirement, requisition

demanding 5 rigid, stern, tough **6** severe, strict, taxing, trying **7** exigent, onerous, weighty **8** grievous, rigorous **9** stringent **10** burdensome, oppressive

demarcate 5 bound, limit **6** define, set

off **7** delimit, mark out, measure **8** separate, set apart **9** determine, segregate **10** delimitate **11** distinguish **12** circumscribe, discriminate **13** differentiate

demarcation 10 border line, separation **11** distinction

demean 3 act **4** bear, go on, mien, quit, sink **5** abase, carry, decry, lower **6** acquit, behave, debase, deport, humble **7** comport, conduct, degrade, detract **8** behavior, belittle, cast down, derogate **9** disparage, humiliate

demeanor 3 air, set **4** mien, port **7** address, bearing, conduct **8** behavior, carriage, portance, presence **10** deportment **11** comportment

demented 3 mad **4** luny **5** crazy, nutty **6** crazed, insane, maniac **7** lunatic, unsound **8** deranged, frenzied **9** delirious **10** hysterical, unbalanced

___ **de mer 3** mal

demerit 3 sin **4** bump, bust, mark **5** break, fault **6** demote, reduce **7** declass, degrade, disrate **8** disgrade **9** downgrade **10** deficiency **11** shortcoming **12** imperfection

demesne 5 field **6** domain, estate, sphere **7** terrain **8** dominion, province **9** bailiwick, champaign, territory *house:* **5** manor

Demeter see **Ceres**

demigod 8 superman **10** superhuman

demise 3 die **4** drop, pass **5** death, sleep **6** cash in, depart, ending, expire **7** decease, passing, quietus, silence, succumb **8** curtains, pass away **10** defunction, expiration, extinction **11** dissolution **12** annihilation

demit 4 sink **5** couch, droop, lower **6** resign **7** depress, let down **8** abdicate, renounce, withdraw

demiurgic 8 creative, original **9** deviceful, formative, ingenious, inventive **10** innovative, innovatory **11** originative **12** innovational

demobilize 6 dispel **7** break up, disband, scatter **8** disperse, separate **9** discharge, muster out

democratic 7 popular **10** self-ruling **13** self-governing

Democratic party symbol 6 donkey

démodé 5 dated, passé **7** antique, archaic, belated **8** old-timey, outdated **9** out-of-date **12** old-fashioned

demoiselle 5 crane **6** damsel **9** damselfly **10** damselfish **11** earth pillar

demolish 4 raze, ruin, undo **5** crush, level, smash, total, wrack, wreck **6** unmake **7** destroy, unbuild, unframe **8** decimate

demolition bomb 11 blockbuster

demon 3 hag, imp **4** ogre **5** devil, fiend,

genie, ghoul, Satan, witch **7** incubus, villain, warlock **9** archfiend *Arabic:* **5** afrit **6** afreet *female:* **5** lamia **7** succuba, succubi (plural) **8** succubae (plural), succubus *Samoan:* **4** aitu *small:* **8** devilkin

demoniac see **demonic**

demonian see **demonic**

demonic 7 satanic **8** devilish, diabolic, fiendish **10** serpentine, unhallowed **11** diabolonian

demonstrate 3 try **4** mark, show, test **5** prove **6** evince, expose, ostend **7** display, exhibit, make out **8** evidence, manifest, proclaim **9** determine, establish

demonstration 4 show **5** proof **7** display **9** spectacle

demonstrative 4 here, open, that, this **7** profuse **8** effusive, outgoing **9** expansive, exuberant, outspoken **10** epideictic, outpouring, unreserved **12** unrestrained **13** unconstrained

demoralize 4 warp **5** chill, unman **6** debase, deject, weaken **7** corrupt, debauch, deprave, pervert, unnerve, vitiate **8** dispirit **9** disparage, undermine **10** bastardize, debilitate, discourage, dishearten

Demosthenes *for one:* **6** orator *oration:* **9** Olynthiac, Philippic

demote 4 bump, bust **5** break, lower **6** reduce **7** declass, degrade, demerit, disrate **8** disgrade **9** downgrade

demulcent 8 soothing **9** softening

demur 3 gag, jib, shy **4** balk **5** qualm, stick, waver **6** boggle, falter, object, oppose, squeam, strain **7** protest, scruple, stickle, stumble **8** aversion, hesitate, question **9** challenge, hesitancy, objection, vacillate **10** conscience, difficulty, hesitation, indecision, reluctance **11** compunction, deprecation, disapproval, remonstrate, uncertainty **12** protestation, remonstrance **13** remonstration, unwillingness

demure 3 coy, mim, shy **4** prim **5** timid **6** modest, silent **7** bashful **8** backward, reserved, reticent, retiring **9** diffident, unassured **11** unassertive

demurral 7 protest **8** question **9** challenge, objection **10** difficulty **12** remonstrance **13** remonstration

demurrer see **demurral**

den 3 sty **4** base, cave, goal, home, lair, room, sink **5** couch, lodge, Sodom **6** burrow, cavern, hollow **7** cesspit, dayroom, hideout **8** cesspool, hideaway, playroom, workroom **11** pandemonium **12** Augean stable *rabbit:* **6** warren

denial 2 no **3** nay **7** refusal, refutal **8** disproof, negation, rebuttal **9** rejection **10** abnegation, gainsaying, refutation **11** declination, repudiation **12** disallowance,

renouncement, renunciation **13** contradiction, controversion

denigrate 5 libel, sully **6** darken, defame, malign, vilify **7** asperse, slander, traduce **8** belittle, tear down **10** calumniate, scandalize

denims 9 blue jeans

denizen 5 liver **6** native **7** dweller, habitué, haunter, resider **8** habitant, occupant, resident **9** indweller **10** frequenter, inhabitant

Denmark *capital:* **10** Copenhagen *monetary unit:* **5** krone

denominate 3 dub **4** call, name, term **5** style, title **7** baptize, entitle **8** christen

denomination 4 cult, name, sect **5** creed, faith, nomen, style, title **6** church **8** category, cognomen, religion **9** communion **10** persuasion **11** appellative *religious:* **6** Jewish, Muslim **7** Baptist **8** Lutheran **9** Adventist, Episcopal, Mennonite, Methodist **12** Presbyterian **13** Roman Catholic

denotation 4 name, sign **7** meaning **10** signifying

denote 4 mark, name, show **5** spell **6** import, intend **7** add up to, express **8** indicate **9** designate, insinuate, represent

denouement 6 result **7** outcome

denounce 3 rap **4** skin **5** blame, blast, decry, knock **6** accuse, scathe **7** arraign, censure, condemn, redbait, upbraid **9** criticize, reprehend, reprobate **10** denunciate, vituperate **11** incriminate **12** anathematize

de novo 4 anew, over **5** again **6** afresh **8** once more **9** over again

dense 4 dull, dumb **5** close, heavy, massy, solid, thick, tight **6** obtuse, opaque, stupid **7** compact, crammed, crowded, doltish, serried **8** blockish, imporous **9** fatheaded, jampacked **10** numskulled **11** block-headed, thickheaded **12** impenetrable *combining form:* **4** pycn, pykn **5** pachy, pycno, pykno

dent 4 bash, nick **5** dinge, notch, tooth **6** dimple

dental structures 5 brace **6** bridge **10** bridgework

denticulate 7 serrate, serried **8** sawedged, saw-tooth, serrated **10** saw-toothed

dentin 6 enamel

denude 4 bare **5** strip **6** divest **7** deprive, disrobe **8** bankrupt, unclothe **9** dismantle

denunciate see **denounce**

deny 4 curb **5** cross, forgo, rebut **6** disown, eschew, forbid, impugn, negate, refuse, refute, reject, renege **7** abstain, confute, deprive, disavow, forbear, forsake, gainsay, refrain **8** abnegate, disallow, disclaim, forswear, hold back, keep back, negative, renounce, traverse, withhold **9** constrain, disaffirm **10** contradict, contravene, controvert

depart 2 go 3 die 4 exit, flee, pass, quit 5 leave, stray 6 begone, decamp, demise, desert, differ, expire, get off, perish, ramble, recede, retire, set out, skidoo, swerve, wander 7 abandon, abscond, decease, deviate, digress, diverge, excurse, forsake, get away, pull out, skiddoo, succumb 8 divagate, pass away, withdraw

departing 7 good-bye 8 farewell 11 valedictory

department 6 branch, sphere 8 division, province 11 subdivision

departure 4 exit 5 break, death, going 6 egress, exodus, flight 7 exiting, leaving, retreat, turning 8 farewell, offgoing, outgoing, quitting 9 deviation, diversion, egression 10 aberration, decampment, deflection, divergence, setting-out, withdrawal 11 leave-taking *of a ship:* 6 sortie *point:* 7 outport

depend 4 bank, hang, lean, rely, rest, turn 5 count, hinge, sling 6 bank on, dangle, hang on, rely on, turn on 7 build on, count on, hinge on, stand on 8 reckon on 11 calculate on

dependable 4 sure, true 5 loyal, solid, tried 6 secure, steady, trusty 7 certain, staunch 8 accurate, constant, faithful, reliable, surefire 9 authentic, steadfast 11 responsible, trustworthy 12 tried and true 13 authoritative *Scottish:* 6 sicker

dependence 4 hope 5 faith, stock, trust 8 reliance

dependent 3 sub 4 iffy 5 child, under 6 minion, sponge, vassal 7 limited, reliant, relying, sponger 8 clinging, relative 9 accessory, ancillary, provisory, secondary, tributary, uncertain 10 collateral, contingent, restricted 11 appurtenant, conditional, provisional, subordinate

depict 4 draw, limn 5 image, paint 6 recite, relate, render, report, sketch 7 depaint, express, impaint, narrate, outline, picture, portray, recount 8 describe, emblazon 9 delineate, interpret, represent 12 characterize

depiction 7 picture 9 portrayal 11 portraiture, presentment

deplete 3 sap 4 draw 5 bleed, drain, empty, use up 6 expend, lessen, reduce, weaken 7 consume, disable, draw off, exhaust 8 bankrupt, decrease, diminish, draw down, enfeeble 9 undermine 10 impoverish

depleted 5 all in, spent 6 bleary, effete, used up 7 far-gone, worn-out 8 bankrupt 9 washed-out

deplorable 4 dire 5 awful 6 woeful 8 dolorous, dreadful, grievous, mournful, terrible, wretched 9 sickening 10 afflictive, calamitous, disastrous, horrifying 11 distressing, unfortunate 12 heartrending 13 heartbreaking

deplore 3 rue 4 moan, weep 5 mourn 6 bemoan, bewail, grieve, lament, regret, repent, sorrow 9 deprecate 10 disapprove, sorrow over

___ **de plume** 3 nom

depone 5 swear 6 assert 7 testify

___ **-de-pont** 4 tête

deport 3 act 4 bear, go on, oust, quit 5 carry, exile, expel 6 acquit, banish, behave, demean 7 conduct, expulse 8 displace, relegate 10 expatriate

deportee 2 DP 5 exile 8 expellee

deportment 3 air, set 4 mien, port 5 tenue 7 address, bearing, conduct 8 behavior, carriage, demeanor, presence

depose 4 aver, avow, oust 5 swear 6 affirm, assert, avouch, devest, divest, remove, unmake 7 declare, decrown, profess, protest, testify, uncrown 8 constate, dethrone, discrown, displace, throw out, unthrone 9 disthrone, overthrow, predicate 11 disenthrone

deposit 3 lay, set 4 bank, drop, dump, fund, lees, pawn, stow 5 chest, dregs, lodge, place, put by, store 6 entomb, settle 7 consign, grounds 8 sediment 9 settlings 11 precipitate 13 precipitation *alluvial:* 5 delta *black:* 4 soot *calcium carbonate:* 10 stalactite, stalagmite *containing gold:* 6 placer *eggs:* 5 spawn *geologic:* 7 horizon *glacial:* 4 till 5 drift, esker 7 moraine *loam:* 5 loess *mineral:* 4 lode 10 concretion *muddy:* 6 sludge *sand:* 4 bank 5 beach *sedimentary:* 4 silt *skeletal:* 5 coral *stolen goods:* 5 fence *stream:* 8 alluvium, sediment *tooth:* 6 tartar

deposition 6 burial 7 placing 8 sediment 9 testimony 10 testifying

depository 4 bank, safe 5 attic, store, vault 7 arsenal 8 magazine 10 storehouse *for bones:* 7 ossuary

depot 4 bank, base, dump 5 store 6 armory 7 arsenal, station 8 magazine, terminal, terminus 9 warehouse 10 repository, storehouse 12 station house

deprave 4 warp 6 debase, malign 7 corrupt, debauch, pervert, vitiate 9 brutalize 10 bastardize, bestialize, demoralize

depraved 3 bad 4 evil, ugly, vile 6 putrid, rotten, warped, wicked 7 bestial, corrupt, debased, immoral, twisted, vicious, vitiate 8 degraded, perverse, vitiated 9 corrupted, debauched, miscreant, nefarious, perverted, unhealthy 10 degenerate, flagitious, villainous

depravity 4 vice 8 villainy 10 corruption, immorality, wickedness

deprecate 5 frown 6 object 7 detract

8 derogate, disfavor **9** disesteem **10** disapprove, discommend **12** disapprove of

depreciate **5** abate, abuse, decry, erode, lower **6** lessen, reduce, soften **7** cheapen, devalue, dwindle **8** belittle, decrease, derogate, diminish, discount, mark down, minimize, write off **9** devaluate, disparage, dispraise, downgrade, underrate, write down **10** devalorize, undervalue **11** detract from

depreciation **7** calumny, scandal, slander **8** discount **10** backbiting **12** backstabbing, belittlement **13** disparagement

depreciative **8** slighting **10** derogatory, detracting **11** disparaging, dyslogistic, underrating **12** undervaluing

depreciatory see **depreciative**

depredate **4** sack **5** waste **6** devour, ravage **7** despoil, pillage, plunder **8** desolate, lay waste, prey upon, spoliate **9** desecrate, devastate

depredator **6** looter, raider **7** forager, spoiler **8** marauder **10** freebooter

depress **4** damp, dash, dent, fall, sink **5** chill, couch, demit, droop, lower, slump **6** dampen, deject, dismay, indent, sadden **7** decline, let down, oppress, trouble **8** contrist, dispirit, enfeeble **9** disparage, weigh down **10** discourage, dishearten

depressant **5** black, bleak **6** dismal, dreary, gloomy **9** cheerless **10** oppressive **11** dispiriting

depressed **3** bad, low, sad **4** blue, down, glum, sunk **6** broody, gloomy, glumpy, hollow, lonely, somber **7** hippish, letdown **8** dejected, downcast **9** woebegone **10** dispirited, lugubrious, melancholy, spiritless **11** downhearted, melancholic **12** disconsolate **13** disadvantaged

depressing **3** sad **4** blue **5** black, bleak, chill **6** dismal, dreary, gloomy, somber, triste **7** joyless **8** funereal, mournful **9** saddening **10** melancholy, oppressive **11** melancholic **13** disheartening

depression **3** dip, low, pit, sag **4** drop, hole, sink, vale **5** basin, blues, crash, dumps, gloom, notch, scoop, slump **6** cavity, crater, hollow, pocket, valley **7** cyclone, decline, sadness, sinkage, sinking **8** sinkhole **9** concavity **10** melancholy, stagnation **11** unhappiness **12** mournfulness *anatomical:* **5** fossa, fovea **6** foveae (plural) **7** foveola, foveole **8** foveolae (plural), foveolet *between breasts:* **8** cleavage *geographic:* **7** Qattara *in ridge:* **3** col *in snow:* **8** sitzmark *small:* **4** dent **6** dimple

depressive see **depressant**

deprivation **4** loss **11** bereavement, deprivement, divestiture **13** dispossession

deprive **3** rob **4** bare, lose, oust **5** strip **6** denude, divest **7** bereave, disrobe **8** bankrupt, denudate, disseize **9** disman-

tle **10** disinherit, dispossess *of brilliancy:* **4** dull **6** deaden *of courage:* **7** unnerve *of sensation:* **6** benumb *of sense and judgment:* **9** inebriate *of virginity:* **8** deflower

deprive of *prefix:* **2** de **3** dis

depth **4** drop **5** abyss **7** lowness **8** deepness **9** acuteness **10** profundity **11** penetration **12** profoundness *combining form:* **4** bath **5** batho, bathy *measure:* **6** fathom *measuring instrument:* **4** gage **5** gauge *of water:* **5** draft **7** draught

depthless **7** cursory, shallow, sketchy **10** uncritical **11** superficial

dept. of ___ **2** ed **3** agr, com, def, int **4** comm **5** labor, state, trans **7** justice

depurate **5** clean **6** purify **7** clarify, cleanse

deputize **8** delegate **10** commission

deputy **5** agent, proxy **6** factor **8** assignee, attorney, delegate **9** catchpole **12** representant *prefix:* **2** co

derange **5** craze, upset **6** frenzy, madden, mess up, sicken **7** disturb, perturb, rummage, unhinge **8** disarray, disorder, distract, unsettle **9** interrupt, unbalance **10** discompose **11** disorganize

deranged **3** mad **5** crazy **6** crazed, insane, maniac **7** cracked, lunatic, unsound **8** demented **9** disturbed **10** disordered, unbalanced

derangement **6** lunacy **7** madness **8** disorder, insanity **9** confusion, unbalance **10** aberration, alienation, insaneness **11** distraction, disturbance, psychopathy, unsoundness

derby **3** hat **4** race, shoe **6** cheese **7** contest **9** horse race **10** field trial

derelict **3** bum, lax, vag **4** hobo, lorn **5** dingy, faded, leper, seedy, slack, tramp **6** pariah, remiss, shabby, unused **7** drifter, floater, Ishmael, outcast, run-down, uncouth, vagrant **8** careless, castaway, deserted, desolate, forsaken, solitary, vagabond **9** abandoned, forgotten, negligent **10** behindhand, delinquent, Ishmaelite, neglectful, regardless, street arab, threadbare, unreliable **11** dilapidated, offscouring, untouchable **12** disregardful, undependable **13** irresponsible, untrustworthy

dereliction **5** fault **7** default, failure, neglect **9** deviation, oversight **11** abandonment, delinquency, shortcoming

deride **4** lout, mock, quiz, razz, twit **5** fleer, rally, scoff, scout, taunt **7** catcall **8** ridicule

de rigueur **4** nice **5** right **6** au fait, decent, proper **7** correct **8** becoming, decorous **11** comme il faut

derision **4** butt, jest, joke, mock **5** sport **6** jestee **7** mockery **9** pilgarlic **13** laughingstock

derisive sound **3** boo **4** hiss

derivable 7 a priori 8 dogmatic, reasoned 9 deducible, deductive

derivation 4 root, well 6 origin, source, whence 7 descent 8 fountain 9 etymology 10 provenance, wellspring 11 provenience

derivative 7 spin-off 8 offshoot 9 by-product, outgrowth, secondary 10 descendant

derive 3 get 4 draw, stem, take 5 adapt, educe, infer, judge 6 deduce, deduct, evolve, gather 7 acquire, collect, emanate, make out, work out 8 arrive at, conclude 9 formulate, originate 10 excogitate

derive from 4 flow, head, rise, stem 5 arise, issue 6 spring 7 emanate, proceed 9 originate

dernier cri 3 cry, fad 4 chic, mode, rage 5 craze, style, vogue 6 furore 7 fashion 8 last word

derogate 5 decry 8 belittle, diminish, minimize, write off 9 disparage, dispraise 10 depreciate 11 detract from, opprobriate

derogatory 5 snide 8 decrying, scornful, spiteful 9 degrading, demeaning, malicious, maligning, slighting, vilifying 10 belittling, calumnious, detracting, disdainful, malevolent, pejorative 11 disparaging, dyslogistic 12 contumelious, depreciative

derout 8 stampede

derrick 5 hoist

derriere 4 beam, rear, seat 5 fanny 6 behind, bottom 7 rear end 8 backside, buttocks 9 posterior

derring-do 5 nerve 7 bravado, bravery, courage

dervish 4 monk 9 mendicant *cap:* 3 taj *in Arabian Nights:* 4 Agib *practice:* 7 dancing, howling 8 whirling *wandering:* 8 calender

descant 3 air, lay 4 aria, hymn, lied, sing, song, tune 5 ditty 6 melody, remark, strain, warble 7 discuss, dissert, measure, melisma, melodia 8 diapason, dilate on 9 discourse, expatiate, sermonize 10 dilate upon, dissertate 11 observation 12 counterpoint

Descartes' axiom 13 cogito ergo sum

descend 3 rot 4 drop, fall, pass, sink 5 lower, stoop, swoop 6 alight, derive, go down, worsen 7 decline 8 come down 9 originate 10 degenerate, disimprove, retrograde, spring from 11 deteriorate 12 disintegrate *by rope:* 6 rappel

descendant 3 son 5 scion 7 progeny, spin-off 8 offshoot, relative 9 by-product, outgrowth 10 derivative *suffix:* 3 ite

descendants 4 seed 5 brood, issue 7 progeny 8 children 9 offspring, posterity 11 progeniture

descent 3 dip 4 drop, fall 5 birth, blood,

slope 6 origin 7 decline, drop-off, incline, lineage, sinking 8 ancestry, comedown, gradient, pedigree, plunging, stooping 9 declivity, downgrade 10 derivation, extraction, plummeting 11 origination 12 discomfiture *airplane:* 8 approach *parachute:* 4 jump 7 bailout

describe 4 limn 5 image, label, state 6 denote, depict, recite, relate, render, report 7 explain, express, mark out, narrate, outline, picture, portray, recount, signify 8 rehearse, vignette 9 chronicle, delineate, interpret, represent 10 illustrate 11 distinguish 12 characterize *grammatically:* 5 parse

description 3 ilk 4 kind, sort, tale, type, yarn 5 story 6 nature 7 account, picture, recital, variety, version 8 anecdote 9 character, chronicle, narrative, portrayal, recountal 10 recounting 11 portraiture, presentment

descry 3 see 4 espy, find, mark, note, spot, view 5 catch, hit on 6 behold, detect, spy out, turn up 7 discern, hit upon, observe 8 discover, meet with, perceive 9 encounter 11 distinguish

Desdemona *father:* 9 Brabantio *husband:* 7 Othello *slanderer:* 4 Iago *slayer:* 7 Othello

desecrate 4 sack 5 waste 6 defile, devour, ravage 7 despoil, pillage, profane 8 spoliate 9 depredate, devastate

desecration 9 blasphemy, sacrilege

desensitize 4 dull, mull, numb 5 blunt 6 benumb, deaden

desert 2 go 3 fly, rat 4 flee, quit, turn, wild 5 chuck, leave, waste 6 barren, betray, decamp, defect, depart, escape, maroon, strand, Tanami 7 abandon, abscond, badland, forsake 8 Karakumy, renounce, wild land, wildness 9 repudiate, throw over, wasteland 10 apostatize, tergiverse, wilderness 12 tergiversate *African:* 6 Libyan, Sahara 7 Arabian 8 Kalahari *Arizona:* 7 Painted *Asian:* 4 Gobi, Thar 6 Syrian 7 Kara Kum, Qara Qum 8 Kyzyl Kum 10 Great Sandy *basin bottom:* 5 playa *beast:* 5 camel 9 dromedary *California:* 6 Mohave, Mojave *clay:* 5 adobe *combining form:* 4 erem 5 eremo *dweller:* 4 Arab 5 nomad 6 Berber, Libyan, Malian, Nubian 8 Algerian, Egyptian, Maghrebi, Maghribi, Sudanese 11 Mauritanian *fertile area:* 5 oases (plural), oasis *garb:* 3 aba *hallucination:* 6 mirage *region:* 3 erg *Saudi Arabia:* 7 An Nafud *Sudan:* 6 Nubian *travel group:* 7 caravan *valley:* 6 bolson *wind:* 7 sirocco

deserted 4 bare, lorn 5 empty 6 barren, vacant 7 uncouth 8 derelict, desolate, forsaken, solitary 9 abandoned 10 unoccupied 11 uninhabited

deserter 3 rat 4 AWOL 6 bolter 7 runaway 8 apostate, fugitive, renegade, runagate, turncoat

desertion 7 perfidy 8 apostasy 9 falseness, recreancy, treachery 11 abandonment

deserts 3 due 11 comeuppance

deserve 3 get, win 4 earn, gain, rate 5 merit 6 demand

deserved 3 due 4 just 5 right 7 condign, merited 8 rightful, suitable 9 requisite 11 appropriate 13 rhadamanthine

deserving 3 due 5 lumps, merit 6 rights, worthy 8 laudable 9 admirable, estimable, meritable, praisable 11 comeuppance, commendable, meritorious, thankworthy 12 praiseworthy

desexualize 3 fix 4 geld 5 alter, unsex 6 change, neuter 8 castrate, mutilate

desiccate 3 dry 4 fade, sear 5 decay, drain, dry up, parch, wizen 6 divest, wither 7 deplete, exhaust, shrivel 9 dehydrate 10 devitalize

desiderate 4 want, wish 5 covet, crave 6 choose, desire

design 3 aim 4 cast, draw, form, mean, mind, plan, plot, will 5 chart, decal, draft, frame, model, motif 6 animus, create, device, devise, devote, figure, intend, intent, invent, lay out, makeup, map out, motive, scheme, set out, sketch 7 arrange, diagram, dope out, drawing, execute, fashion, meaning, outline, pattern, prepare, produce, project, propose, purpose, thought, tracing 8 conation, contrive, creation, game plan, intrigue, strategy, thinking, volition 9 blueprint, construct, delineate, direction, formation, intention, invention 10 decoration, figuration, intendment, reflection 11 arrangement, composition, contemplate, delineation, disposition, machination 12 architecture, constitution, construction, deliberation *book:* 6 fillet 8 vignette *carpet:* 3 gul 9 medallion *incised:* 8 intaglio *Indonesian:* 5 batik *inlaid:* 6 mosaic *of squares:* 5 check *openwork:* 8 filigree *perforated:* 7 stencil *raised:* 8 repoussé *skin:* 6 tattoo *textile:* 8 polka dot *velvety:* 8 flocking

designate 3 dub, opt, tap 4 call, make, name, pick, term 5 allot, elect, label, style, title 6 assign, choose, denote, depute, finger, induct, select, single 7 appoint, baptize, declare, dictate, earmark, entitle, mete out, reserve, signify, specify 8 allocate, christen, identify, stand for 9 apportion, stipulate 10 decide upon 11 appropriate 12 characterize

designation 4 name 5 nomen, style, title 6 naming 8 cognomen, monicker 9 allotment 10 indicating, pigeonhole 11 appellative, identifying 12 pigeonholing

designed 7 advised, decided, studied 8 prepense, resolved, studious 10 considered, deliberate, determined, thought-out 12 aforethought, premeditated

designedly 9 on purpose, purposely 10 prepensely 11 purposively 12 deliberately 13 intentionally

designless 4 spot 6 random 9 desultory, haphazard, hit-or-miss, unplanned 12 unconsidered

desirable 6 suited 7 optimal 9 excellent, expedient

desire 3 aim, ask, yen 4 envy, eros, hope, itch, like, long, lust, pant, pine, urge, want, wish 5 covet, crave, enjoy, fancy, greed, yearn 6 asking, aspire, choice, choose, hanker, hunger, pining, thirst 7 avarice, bespeak, craving, entreat, impulse, longing, passion, request, solicit 8 appetite, cupidity, petition, rapacity, striving, yearning 9 appetency, eroticism, hankering, hungering, prurience, pruriency, thirsting 10 aphrodisia, appetition, attraction, preference 11 inclination, lustfulness 13 concupiscence, lickerishness *combining form:* 6 orexia *for liquids:* 6 thirst *restless:* 4 itch

desired 4 true 5 right 6 proper 7 fitting 11 appropriate

desirous 5 itchy 6 grabby, greedy 7 athirst, envious, wishful 8 appetent, covetous, grasping 10 prehensile, solicitous 11 acquisitive

desist 4 halt, quit, stop 5 cease, deval, yield 6 resign 7 abandon, abstain, forbear, hold off 8 give over, knock off, leave off, surcease 10 relinquish 11 discontinue, refrain from

desistance 3 end 4 stop 5 cease, close 6 ending, finish, period 9 cessation 10 conclusion 11 termination

desk 5 booth, stand, table 7 counter, lectern, roll top 8 lapboard 9 secretary 10 escritoire, secretaire *adjunct:* 8 inkstand, standish *item:* 3 pad 7 blotter, inkwell *library:* 6 carrel 7 carrell *Scottish:* 3 pew

desman 3 fur 4 pelt 6 mammal

___ **de soie, French silk** 4 peau

desolate 4 bare, dark, lorn, poor, sack 5 black, bleak, drear, empty, murky, stark, waste 6 barren, devoid, devour, dismal, gloomy, ravage, ruined, somber, vacant 7 despoil, joyless, pillage, uncouth 8 bereaved, derelict, deserted, forsaken, funereal, lay waste, lifeless, solitary, spoliate 9 abandoned, cheerless, depredate, desecrate, destitute, devastate, sorrowful 10 acheronian, unoccupied 11 dilapidated, uninhabited **12** inconsolable, unconsolable **13** disheartening

desolation 6 sorrow **7** sadness **9** wasteland **11** abandonment

despair 4 drop **5** yield **6** give up, resign **7** abandon **8** renounce **9** surrender **10** relinquish

despairing 7 cynical, forlorn **8** hopeless **9** depressed, oppressed **10** melancholy **11** atrabilious, melancholic, pessimistic, weighed down **12** misanthropic **13** brokenhearted

desperado 6 badman, bandit, outlaw **7** bandido, convict **8** criminal **10** lawbreaker

desperate 4 dire, rash **5** acute **6** balked, crying, fierce, foiled **7** baffled, crucial, forlorn, furious, heinous, intense, vicious, violent **8** critical, headlong, hopeless, reckless, shocking, terrible, thwarted, vehement **9** atrocious, exquisite, foolhardy, monstrous, outwitted **10** frustrated, outrageous, scandalous **11** climacteric, precipitate, venturesome **12** circumvented, concentrated, overpowering **13** irretrievable, overmastering, uncollectable

despicable 3 low **4** base, mean, ugly, vile **5** cheap, sorry **6** abject, scummy, scurvy, shabby, sordid **7** ignoble **8** beggarly, infamous, wretched **9** loathsome **11** disgraceful, ignominious **12** contemptible

despisable see **despicable**

despise 4 hate, shun, snub **5** abhor, avoid, scorn, scout, spurn **6** detest, eschew, ignore, loathe, reject, slight **7** contemn, disdain **8** execrate, look down, misprize, overlook, renounce **9** abominate, disregard, repudiate

despised one 6 pariah

despisement 4 hate **5** scorn **6** hatred, malice **7** disdain, ill will **8** aversion, contempt, loathing **10** abhorrence **11** detestation, malevolence

despite 3 cut **4** harm, hate, hurt, slap, snub **5** altho, scorn **6** grudge, hatred, injury, insult, malice, rebuff, slight, spleen **7** affront, against, disdain, disgust, dislike, ill will **8** although, aversion, contempt, defiance, disfavor, distaste, loathing, spurning **9** contumacy, contumely, indignity, insolence, in spite of, malignity, rejection **10** abhorrence, incivility, malignancy **11** abomination, detestation, discourtesy, indignation, in the face of, malevolence, repudiation **12** cold shoulder, regardless of, spitefulness, stubbornness **13** disparagement, maliciousness, recalcitrance

despiteful 4 evil **5** catty **6** bitchy, wicked **7** vicious **9** malicious, rancorous **10** malevolent

despoil 4 sack **5** blast, strip, waste, wreck **6** denude, devour, ravage **7** pillage, plunder **8** desolate, spoliate **9** depredate, desecrate, devastate, strip away, wrest away

despoiler 6 looter, ruiner, sacker, vandal **7** defacer, forager, wrecker **8** marauder, pillager, ruinator **9** destroyer, plunderer, spoliator **10** depredator, freebooter

Despoina 8 mistress **10** Persephone *husband:* **5** Hades *realm:* **10** underworld

despond 3 sag **4** mope **5** brood, droop **6** give up **8** languish

despondency 5 blues, dumps, gloom **6** misery, sorrow **7** despair **9** dejection **10** blue devils, depression, melancholy

despondent 3 sad **7** forlorn **8** dejected, downcast, grieving, hopeless, mourning **9** depressed, sorrowful, woebegone **10** dispirited, melancholy **11** discouraged **12** disconsolate, disheartened

despot 4 duce **5** ruler **6** tyrant **7** autarch, emperor **8** autocrat, dictator **9** oppressor, strong man

despotic 8 absolute, tyrannic **9** arbitrary, autarchic, tyrannous **10** autocratic, monocratic, tyrannical

despotism 7 tsarism, tyranny, tzarism **8** autarchy **9** autocracy **10** domination **12** dictatorship

despotize 7 dictate, oppress **8** dominate, domineer, overlord **9** tyrannize

desquamate 4 peel **5** scale **7** peel off **8** flake off, scale off **9** exfoliate

dessert 3 ice, pie **4** cake, flan, fool, tart **5** Betty, bombe, coupe, fruit, grunt, halva, melba, slump, torte **6** afters, cheese, Danish, éclair, frappe, gateau, halvah, hermit, junket, kuchen, mousse, pastry, sorbet, sundae, trifle **7** cassata, cobbler, custard, gelatin, mazarin, parfait, pudding, sabayon, sherbet, spumone, spumoni, strudel **8** Bismarck, flummery, ice cream, marquise, napoleon, pandowdy, streusel, taiglach, teiglach, turnover **9** charlotte, cream puff, petit four, shortcake **10** blancmange, brown Betty, cheesecake, frangipane, marguerite, zabaglione **11** baked Alaska, banana split, gingerbread **12** hasty pudding, zuppa inglese *chilled:* **6** mousse *custard:* **8** zabaione, zabajone *French:* **5** bombe **6** éclair, frappe, gateau, mousse **7** mazarin, parfait, sabayon **8** marquise **9** petit four **10** blancmange, frangipane *frozen:* **5** bombe **7** parfait, sherbet **8** sherbert *German:* **6** kuchen **7** strudel *Italian:* **7** cannoli, cassata, spumone, spumoni **10** zabaglione **12** zuppe inglese *Jewish:* **8** taiglach, teiglach *pastry:* **6** quiche *soft:* **3** pud **7** pudding *Turkish:* **5** halva **6** halvah

destination 3 end, use 6 object 7 purpose 10 appointing

destine 3 fix 4 fate 6 assign, decree, devise, direct, doom to, intend 7 preform 8 dedicate, set aside 9 determine, preordain 10 foreordain 12 predetermine

destiny 3 lot 4 doom, fate, goal 5 moira, weird 6 design, future, intent, kismat, kismet 7 fortune, portion 9 intention, objective 12 circumstance

destitute 4 bare, poor, void 5 empty, needy 6 bereft, devoid 7 drained 8 bankrupt, depleted, dirt poor, divested, indigent, innocent, stripped 9 deficient, exhausted, penurious 10 bankrupted, stone-broke 11 impecunious, necessitous 12 impoverished *of water:* 9 anhydrous

destitute of *prefix:* 2 an *suffix:* 4 less

destitution 4 lack, need, want 6 dearth, penury 7 absence, poverty 9 adversity, indigence, neediness 10 misfortune

destroy 3 zap 4 doom, down, kill, raze, ruin, sack, slay, undo, wipe 5 fordo, havoc, shoot, smash, total, waste, wrack, wreck 6 cut off, finish, foredo, injure, lay low, mangle, quench, ravage, rubble, rub out, unmake 7 abolish, atomize, nullify, pillage, put away, ruinate, shatter, subvert, take off, unbuild, unframe, wipe out 8 carry off, decimate, demolish, dispatch, dissolve, dynamite, fumigate, mutilate, pull down, sabotage, tear down 9 devastate, discreate, dismantle, eradicate, extirpate, pulverize 10 annihilate, counteract, decapitate, extinguish, neutralize 11 exterminate *suffix:* 4 lyse, lyze

destroyer 4 bane, ruin 6 ruiner, tin can, vandal 7 defacer, undoing, warship, wrecker 8 downfall, ruinator 9 despoiler, ruination *combining form:* 4 cide 5 clast 7 clastic, phthora

destroying *combining form:* 5 cidal 7 clastic *prefix:* 3 ant 4 anth, anti

destruction 4 bane, loss, ruin 5 havoc 7 killing, undoing 8 downfall 9 confusion 10 impairment *combining form:* 4 lyses (plural) 5 lysis 6 clasia, clasis

destructive 5 fatal 6 deadly, lethal, mortal 7 baneful, ruinous 8 wrackful, wreckful 9 injurious 10 calamitous, disastrous, shattering 11 deleterious, detrimental

desuetude 3 end 5 cease, close 6 disuse, ending 7 closing, closure, neglect 8 disusage 9 cessation 10 conclusion, suspension 11 abandonment

desultory 6 casual, catchy, fickle, fitful, random, spotty 7 aimless, erratic, vagrant 8 shifting, sporadic, wavering 9 haphazard, hit-or-miss, mercurial, spasmodic, unplanned 10 capricious, designless, digressive, disorderly, inconstant 11 purposeless 12 unconsidered, unmethodical, unsystematic

detach 4 part, wean 5 sever, unfix 6 cut off, sunder, unhang 7 disjoin, divorce 8 abstract, dismount, disunite, separate, uncouple, withdraw 9 disengage, dismantle, dismember 10 disconnect, dissociate 11 disassemble 12 disaffiliate, disassociate

detached 5 alone, aloof, apart 6 casual, remote 7 distant, isolate, neutral, removed 8 abstract, isolated, separate, unbiased 9 colorless, incurious, uncurious, withdrawn 10 impersonal, poker-faced 11 indifferent, unconcerned, unconnected, unpassioned 12 uninterested 13 disinterested, dispassionate, unaccompanied *combining form:* 2 ap 3 aph, apo

detachment 7 divorce, rupture, split up 8 disunion, division 9 partition 10 neutrality, separation 11 dissolution, divorcement 12 unworldliness *combining form:* 5 lyses (plural), lysis

detail 4 item, list, part 5 point, thing 6 assign, relate, report 7 article, element, listing, minutia, program, specify 8 elements, minutiae (plural) 9 enumerate, stipulate 10 brass tacks (plural), particular 11 specificate, specificize 12 circumstance 13 particularize

detailed 4 full 6 minute 7 copious 8 abundant, itemized, thorough 9 clocklike 10 blow-by-blow, exhausting, exhaustive, particular 13 thoroughgoing

detain 3 nab 4 bust, curb, hold, keep, mire 5 check, delay, embog, pinch, run in 6 arrest, hang up, pick up, pull in, retard, slow up 7 bog down, inhibit, keep out, reserve, set back, slacken 8 hold back, keep back, restrain, slow down, withhold 9 apprehend 10 buttonhole, decelerate *in conversation:* 10 buttonhole

detect 4 espy, find, spot 5 catch, hit on 6 descry, turn up 7 discern, hit upon, rectify 8 discover, meet with 9 ascertain, encounter 10 demodulate

detectable 8 sensible, tangible 11 perceptible

detecting device 5 radar, sonar 6 solion 7 antenna, sferics 8 spherics 13 Geiger counter

detection 4 find 6 espial, strike 9 discovery 10 laying open, unearthing *system:* 5 radar, sofar

detective 3 tec 4 dick, G-man 5 roper 6 shamus, sleuth 7 gumshoe, shoofly 8 hawkshaw, informer, Sherlock 9 inspector 12 investigator 13 police officer *fictional:* 4 Chan (Charlie), Moto (Mr.) 5 Dupin (Auguste), Lecoq, Spade (Sam), Trent (Philip) 6 Carter (Nick), Holmes (Sherlock),

Poirot (Hercule), Wimsey (Peter) **7** Charles (Nick) **11** Father Brown

detective story writer 3 Poe (Edgar Allan) **5** Doyle (Arthur Conan), James (P.D.), Queen (Ellery), Stout (Rex) **6** Parker (Robert), Sayers (Dorothy) **7** Bentley (E.C.), Biggers (Earl), Collins (Wilkie), Fleming (Ian), Gardner (Erle Stanley), Hammett (Dashiell) **8** Chandler (Raymond), Christie (Agatha), Gaboriau (Emile), Marquand (John) **10** Chesterton (G.K.)

detent 3 dog **4** pawl **5** catch, click

detention 3 nab **5** delay, pinch **6** arrest, pickup **10** arrestment, internment **12** apprehension, imprisonment

deter 5 avert, block, debar, scare **6** divert, hinder, impede **7** forfend, inhibit, obviate, prevent, rule out, shut out, ward off **8** dissuade, frighten, obstruct, preclude, restrain, stave off **9** disadvise, forestall, turn aside **10** discourage

deterge 7 cleanse, wash off

detergent 4 soap **6** alkali **8** cleanser **9** cleansing

deteriorate 3 mar, rot **4** fade, fail, flag, sink **5** decay, dwine, spoil **6** impair, lessen, weaken, worsen **7** crumble, decline, descend **8** languish **9** decompose, undermine **10** debilitate, depreciate, disimprove, retrograde

deterioration 4 ruin **5** decay **6** dry rot, ebbing, waning **7** atrophy, decline, failure, rotting **8** decaying, downfall, spoiling **9** crumbling, decadence, downgrade, lessening **10** debasement, declension, degeneracy, impairment **12** dégringolade

determinant 4 gene, mark **5** agent, cause, trait **6** factor, reason, weight **7** radical **8** occasion **9** attribute, authority, influence **10** antecedent **11** differentia

determinate 4 spot **5** fixed, place **6** cymose, finger, narrow **7** limited, precise, settled **8** constant, definite, diagnose, identify, pinpoint **9** arbitrary, ascertain, immovable, immutable, recognize **10** definitive, inflexible, invariable, restricted **11** distinguish, established, inalterable, unalterable **12** unchangeable, unmodifiable **13** circumscribed, diagnosticate

determination 6 fixing **7** purpose, resolve **8** decision, firmness **9** resolving **10** conclusion, settlement **11** decidedness **12** resoluteness **13** purposiveness

determine 3 end, fix, see, set **4** bias, fate, halt, hear, move, rule, show **5** bound, close, drive, impel, learn, limit, prove **6** decide, direct, doom to, figure, finish, induce, ordain, settle, tumble, wind up, wrap up **7** actuate, catch on, control, delimit, destine, dispose, find out, incline, make out, mark out, measure, preform, purpose, resolve, unearth

8 complete, conclude, discover, persuade, regulate, ultimate **9** ascertain, demarcate, establish, preordain, resolve on, terminate **10** delimitate, foreordain, predestine, predispose **11** demonstrate

determined 3 set **4** bent **6** intent **7** decided, earnest, serious, settled **8** decisive, hellbent, resolute, resolved **10** purposeful, unwavering **11** unfaltering **12** unhesitating

detest 4 hate **5** abhor, spurn **6** loathe, reject **7** despise, dislike **8** execrate **9** abominate, repudiate

detestable 4 foul, vile **5** sorry **6** damned, horrid, odious **7** hateful, heinous **9** abhorrent, execrable, loathsome **10** abominable, despicable **12** contemptible

detestation 4 hate **6** hatred, horror **7** bugbear, disgust, dislike **8** anathema, aversion, loathing **9** antipathy, bête noire, repulsion, revulsion **10** abhorrence, black beast, repugnance

dethrone 6 depose, divest, unmake **7** uncrown **8** discrown, displace

detonate 5 burst, go off **6** blow up **7** explode **8** mushroom

detonator 3 cap **4** fuse, fuze **9** explosive **11** blasting cap

detour 5 avoid, skirt **6** bypass **7** deflect **9** deviation, runaround **10** circumvent, roundabout

detract 4 draw **5** decry, libel **6** divert, lessen, reduce **7** slander **8** belittle, decrease, derogate, diminish, discount, minimize, write off **9** disparage, dispraise **10** depreciate

detracting 8 libelous **9** maligning, traducing, vilifying **10** calumnious, defamatory, derogatory, pejorative, scandalous, slanderous **11** disparaging, dyslogistic **12** depreciative, depreciatory

detraction 4 harm, hurt, tale **5** libel, wrong **6** damage, injury **7** calumny, scandal, slander **8** libeling **9** aspersion, injustice, maligning, traducing **10** backbiting, slandering, sycophancy **12** backstabbing, belittlement **13** disparagement

detriment 4 harm, hurt **6** damage, injury **7** marring **8** drawback, handicap, mischief, spoiling **10** disability **12** disadvantage

detrimental 3 bad, ill **4** evil **7** adverse, harmful, hurtful, nocuous **8** damaging, negative **9** injurious **11** deleterious, mischievous, unfavorable

detritus 4 tufa, tuff **5** scree, talus **6** debris

Detroit *county:* **5** Wayne *founder:* **8** Cadillac *lake:* **4** Erie **10** Saint Clair *sobriquet:* **6** Motown **9** Motor City

de trop 5 extra, spare **6** excess **7** surplus **11** superfluent, superfluous **13** supernumerary

detruncate 3 top 4 crop 7 pollard

Deucalion *father:* 10 Prometheus *kingdom:* 6 Phthia *mother:* 7 Clymene *son:* 6 Hellen *wife:* 6 Pyrrha

Deuel's son 8 Eliasaph

dev, deva 3 god

Devaki's son 7 Krishna

deval 4 halt, quit, stop 5 cease 6 desist 8 give over, knock off, leave off, surcease 11 discontinue

De Valera 5 Eamon

devaluate 5 decry, lower 8 mark down, write off 9 underrate, write down 10 depreciate, undervalue

devaluation 7 atrophy, decline 8 downfall 9 decadence 10 declension, degeneracy

devalue see **depreciate**

devastate 4 sack 6 devour, ravage 7 despoil, pillage 8 desolate, lay waste, overcome, spoliate 9 depredate, desecrate, overpower, overwhelm

devastation 4 loss, ruin 5 havoc 9 confusion

devel 3 hit 4 biff, ding, nail, sock 5 clout, slosh, smite, whack 6 strike

develop 2 go 3 age, get 4 form, gain, grow, ripe 5 break, occur, phase, reach, ripen 6 attain, befall, betide, chance, dilate, enroot, evolve, expand, grow up, happen, lay out, mature, mellow, obtain, open up, thrive, unfold, unfurl 7 achieve, acquire, advance, amplify, burgeon, come off, convert, enlarge, expound, fall out, prepare, promote, prosper, realize 8 flourish, maturate 9 actualize, elaborate, establish, transpire 11 come to light, materialize 13 differentiate *rapidly:* 7 burgeon 8 bourgeon

development 5 phase 6 growth, phasis 7 advance, ongoing 8 ontogeny, progress, upgrowth 9 evolution, expansion, flowering, phylogeny, unfolding 11 elaboration, progression *combining form:* 5 plasy 6 plasia, plasto *of life:* 10 biogenesis

Devi 7 goddess *consort:* 4 Siva *father:* 7 Himavat *name:* 3 Uma 4 Kali 5 Durga, Gauri 6 Chandi 7 Parvati

deviant 6 off-key 8 aberrant, abnormal, atypical 9 anomalous, divergent, irregular, unnatural, unregular, untypical 11 heteroclite 13 preternatural

deviate 3 err, yaw 4 veer 5 sheer, stray 6 depart, swerve, wander 7 digress, diverge, pervert 9 turn aside 13 sexual pervert

deviation 3 yaw 4 bend, tack, turn 5 error, fault, lapse, shift 6 breach, change, double 7 anomaly, blunder, failing, turning, veering 9 departure, diversion 10 divergence 13 transgression

device 4 play, ploy, tool, type, wile, will 5 feint, motif, motto, shift, trick 6 design, desire, dingus, emblem, figure, gadget, gambit, hickey, motive, resort, scheme, symbol 7 gimmick, machine, pattern, project, utensil 8 artifice, creation, insignia, maneuver, resource 9 apparatus, appliance, attribute, doohickey, expedient, implement, invention, makeshift, mechanism, stratagem 10 instrument, thingumbob 11 contraption, contrivance, inclination *automatic:* 5 servo *baseball:* 11 batting cage *binding:* 5 clamp *combining form:* 4 stat *cooking:* 7 hibachi *electrical:* 8 inverter *electronic:* 7 vocoder *energy changing:* 9 converter, convertor *fastening:* 6 zipper *grasping:* 4 tong *heating:* 8 radiator *hoisting:* 5 lewis 8 lewisson *holding:* 4 vise 5 clamp *in an airplane:* 7 gosport *irrigation:* 6 shaduf 7 shadoof *light-generating:* 7 lampion *literary:* 5 irony *mechanical:* 6 gadget *oil lamp:* 8 pickwick *remote-control:* 6 selsyn 7 synchro *respiratory:* 8 pulmotor *restraining:* 8 holdback *seed-sewing:* 11 broadcaster *ship's:* 7 euphroe *speed of rotation:* 4 tach *stabilizing:* 8 gyrostat *temperature measurement:* 7 thermal *warning:* 5 siren *weighing:* 5 scale, trone *wiretapping:* 3 bug

devil 4 deil, haze, limb 5 annoy, beast, brute, demon, error, fiend, knave, rogue, Satan, scamp, tease 6 Belial, Cloots, diablo, dybbuk, pester, rascal, spirit 7 caitiff, Clootie, dickens, Lucifer, Old Nick, serpent, tempter, torment, villain 8 Apollyon, Mephisto, mischief, scalawag, Succubus 9 Archfiend, Beelzebub, cacodemon, scoundrel, skeezicks 10 blackguard, Old Scratch 11 firecracker, rapscallion 13 Old Gooseberry *combining form:* 6 diabol 7 diabolo

devil-devil 4 rune 5 charm, spell 11 conjuration, incantation

devilfish 3 ray 7 octopus 10 cephalopod

devilish 3 bad 4 evil 6 cursed, wicked 7 demonic, extreme, satanic 8 accursed, damnable, demoniac, demonian, diabolic, fiendish 9 excessive, execrable, nefarious 10 diabolical, iniquitous, serpentine, unhallowed, villainous 11 diabolonian, excessively

devilkin 3 imp

devil-may-care 3 gay 4 fast, rash, wild 6 rakish, sporty 7 raffish 8 rakehell, reckless

devilment see **deviltry**

devilry see **deviltry**

devil's-bones 4 dice, tats 5 cubes, ivory

deviltry 7 roguery, waggery 8 mischief 9 diablerie 11 roguishness, waggishness 12 sportiveness

devious 3 sly 4 foxy 5 stray 6 artful,

astray, crafty, errant, erring, remote, roving, secret, shifty, sneaky, tricky, unfair **7** bending, crooked, cunning, curving, erratic, obscure, removed, retired, winding **8** aberrant, guileful, indirect, lonesome, sneaking, twisting **9** diverting, underhand, wandering **10** digressing, roundabout

devise 4 cast, form, plan, plot, will **5** chart, forge, frame, leave, shape **6** cook up, create, design, invent, legacy, legate, make up, scheme, vamp up **7** arrange, bequest, collude, concoct, connive, dope out, dream up, hatch up, project **8** bequeath, cogitate, collogue, conspire, contrive, discover, intrigue, property **9** blueprint, determine, formulate, machinate, scheme for, scheme out **11** inheritance

devitalize 5 dry up **6** weaken **7** deprive, destroy **9** desiccate **10** eviscerate

devoid 4 bare **5** empty **6** barren **7** lacking, wanting **8** free from, innocent **9** deficient, destitute

devoir 3 job **4** duty, must, need, task **5** chare, chore, ought, right, stint **6** charge **9** committal **10** assignment, commitment, obligation

devolution 7 atrophy, decline, passing **8** downfall, receding, transfer **9** conferral, decadence, recession **10** declension, degeneracy, regression **12** dégringolade, retrograding, transference **13** retrogression

devolve 4 pass **8** hand down, transfer

devote 3 try, use, vow **4** bend, damn, doom, give, turn **5** apply, throw **6** addict, adjust, attach, bestow, commit, direct, donate, employ, give up, hallow, strive, take to, wrap up **7** address, attempt, confide, consign, entrust, hand out, present, provide, utilize **8** dedicate, endeavor, give away, sanctify, struggle **9** confirm in, habituate **10** buckle down, consecrate

devoted 4 dear, fond, true **5** loyal **6** ardent, doting, fervid, loving **7** zealous **8** constant, faithful, lovesome **10** thoughtful **12** affectionate *religiously:* **6** oblate

devotee 3 fan **4** buff **5** hound, lover **6** addict, votary **7** admirer, amateur, fancier, habitué **8** follower **9** supporter **10** aficionado, enthusiast *suffix:* **3** ite

devotion 4 love, zeal **5** ardor, piety **6** fealty, fervor, prayer **7** loyalty, passion **8** fidelity, fondness **9** reverence **10** allegiance, attachment, enthusiasm **12** faithfulness *combining form:* **5** latry *religious:* **6** novena

devour 3 eat **4** meal, ruin, sack, take, wolf **5** eat up, enjoy, use up, waste, wreck **6** absorb, engulf, feed on, ingest, ravage, relish **7** consume, despoil, destroy, exhaust, feast on, gloat on, pillage, revel in **8** demolish, desolate, dispatch, prey upon, spoliate, squander **9** delight in, depredate, desecrate, devastate, dissipate, feast upon, gloat over, partake of, polish off, rejoice in, swallow up **10** annihilate

devouring 4 avid **6** greedy **9** voracious *combining form:* **6** vorous

devout 4 holy **5** godly, pious **6** ardent, fervid, hearty **7** adoring, fervent, sincere, zealous **8** reverent, revering **9** pietistic, prayerful, religious **10** venerating, worshiping

devoutness 5 piety

dew 3 wet **5** sweat, tears **8** moisture **12** perspiration

dexter 5 right, white **6** benign, bright **9** favorable, fortunate **10** auspicious, propitious

dexterity 3 art **5** craft, skill **7** address, cunning, know-how, prowess, sleight **8** deftness **9** adeptness, expertise, readiness **10** adroitness, smoothness **12** skillfulness

dexterous 3 sly **4** deft, easy, slim **5** adept, agile, canny, coony, handy **6** adroit, artful, clever, expert, facile, nimble, smooth **7** cunning, skilled **8** masterly, skillful, sleighty **9** ingenious **10** effortless, neat-handed, proficient

diablerie 3 sin **4** evil, tort **5** crime, wrong **7** devilry, roguery, sorcery, waggery **8** deviltry, iniquity, mischief, satanism **9** devilment **10** black magic, wickedness, witchcraft, wrongdoing **11** roguishness, waggishness **12** sportiveness

diablo 5 devil, fiend, Satan **7** Lucifer, Old Nick, serpent **8** Apollyon **9** Beelzebub **10** Old Scratch **13** Old Gooseberry

diabolic 4 evil **6** wicked **7** demonic, satanic **8** demoniac, demonian, devilish, fiendish **10** serpentine, unhallowed **11** diabolonian

diabolism see **diablerie**

diacritic 5 breve, haček, tilde **6** macron, proper **7** cedilla **8** dieresis, peculiar **9** diaeresis **10** circumflex, individual **11** distinctive **13** idiosyncratic *Arabic:* **5** hamza **6** hamzah

diadem 5 crown **6** empire **8** headband **11** sovereignty

diagnose 4 spot **5** place **6** finger **8** identify, pinpoint **9** recognize **11** determinate, distinguish

diagnostic 6 proper **8** peculiar **9** diacritic **10** indicating, indicative, individual **11** distinctive **13** idiosyncratic

diagonal 4 bias **5** bevel **6** biased **7** beveled, slanted **8** inclined, slanting **9** slantways

diagonally 8 bendwise **9** slantwise **10** cornerwise **11** catercorner, catty-corner, kitty-corner, slaunchways **12** slantingways

diagram 5 chart, graph 7 isotype
9 represent

dial 3 map, mug, pan 4 face, phiz, puss,
tune 6 kisser, visage 7 control 8 features
10 manipulate 11 countenance

dialect 4 cant 5 argot, idiom, koine, lingo,
slang 6 jargon, patois, patter, speech,
tongue 8 language, localism 10 vernacular 11 regionalism, terminology 13 provin-
cialism *Georgia:* 6 Gullah *London:*
7 cockney

dialectic 5 logic 6 debate 7 mooting
8 forensic 11 disputation 13 argumentation

dialogue 4 chat, talk 6 parley 8 colloquy,
converse 12 conversation 13 confabulation

diameter 5 chord 8 bisector 9 thickness

diametric 5 polar 7 counter, opposed,
reverse 8 contrary, converse, opposite
9 antipodal 10 antipodean 12 antithetical
13 contradictory

diamond 3 gem 5 stone 6 bright 9 brilliant, sparkling *baseball:* 7 infield *element:* 6 carbon *famous:* 4 Hope, Pitt
5 Sancy 6 Orloff, Regent 8 Braganza, Culli-
nan, Kohinoor 9 Excelsior 10 Great Mogul
holder: 3 dop 4 dopp *inferior:* 4 bort
5 boart, bortz *oval:* 9 briolette *playing
card:* 7 lozenge *state:* 8 Delaware *surface:* 5 facet

Diana see **Artemis**

Diana monkey 7 roloway

diapason 3 air, lay 4 tune 5 range,
scope 6 melody, strain, warble 7 compass,
descant, measure, melisma, melodia
10 tuning fork

diaper 4 didy 5 didie, nappy 6 nappie

diaphanous 5 filmy, gauzy, sheer, vague
6 flimsy 7 tiffany 8 ethereal, gossamer
11 transparent 13 insubstantial

diaphragm 4 stop 9 partition *combining
form:* 5 phren 8 phreni, phreno

diarist 1 Gide (André) 5 Frank (Anne),
Pepys (Samuel), Scott (Walter) 6 Burney
(Fanny) 7 Boswell (James) 8 Robinson
(Henry) 10 chronicler, journalist

diary 6 record 7 daybook, diurnal, journal,
logbook 8 register 9 chronicle

diaskeuast 6 editor

diastase 6 enzyme

diatribe 6 tirade 7 polemic 8 harangue,
jeremiad 9 criticism, philippic

dibs 4 gelt 5 blunt, brass, bread, chips,
claim, dough, money, syrup, title 6 dinero,
do-re-mi, rights 7 cabbage 8 pretense
10 pretension 11 reservation

dice 4 cast, shed, tats 5 bones, cubes,
ivory, scrap 6 reject, slough 7 cashier,
checker, discard 8 jettison, throw out
9 throw away 11 devil's-bones *combining
form:* 8 astragal 9 astragalo *game:*

5 craps *losing throw:* 7 missout *singular:*
3 die *throw:* 7 boxcars 9 snake eyes

dicer 7 gambler

dichotomize 4 part 5 sever 6 divide, sunder 7 break up, disjoin, dissect 8 disjoint,
disunite, separate

dichotomous 9 bifurcate

dichotomy 7 forking 9 bisection, branching, splitting 11 bifurcation

Dickens *birthplace:* 10 Portsmouth *captain:* 6 Cuttle *character:* 3 Pip, Tim
4 Dora, Gamp, Nell 5 Fagin 6 Bumble, Carton, Cuttle, Darnay, Dombey, Oliver 7 Barnaby, Defarge, Manette, Scrooge, Tiny Tim
8 Micawber, Pickwick 9 Bill Sikes, Peck-
sniff, Uriah Heep 10 Chuzzlewit *hero:*
6 Carton (Sidney) *nationality:* 7 English *pen
name:* 3 Boz *villain:* 5 Fagin *work:* 9 Hard
Times 10 Bleak House 11 Oliver Twist
12 Barnaby Rudge 15 Tale of Two Cities
16 David Copperfield 17 Great
Expectations

dicker 4 deal, swap 6 barter, haggle, higgle, palter 7 bargain, chaffer 8 huckster
11 negotiation

dickey 4 weak 5 gilet, shaky 6 unsure,
wobbly 8 insecure, rootless, unstable,
wavering 9 fluctuant 10 shirtfront
11 vacillating

dictate 3 bid, say, set 4 lead, rule, tell,
word 5 guide, order, speak, utter 6 behest,
charge, decree, diktat, direct, enjoin, govern,
impose, manage, ordain, recite 7 bidding,
command, control, lay down, mandate, read
off 8 instruct 9 directive, prescribe
10 injunction 12 prescription

dictative 8 dogmatic 11 doctrinaire, magisterial 13 authoritarian

dictator 4 duce 6 despot, tyrant 7 arbiter
8 martinet 9 oppressor, strong man
10 magistrate *German:* 6 Hitler (Adolf) *Italian:* 9 Mussolini (Benito) *military:* 8 caudillo
Spanish: 6 Franco (Francisco)

dictatorial 4 firm 5 bossy, proud, stern
7 haughty 8 absolute, arrogant, despotic,
dogmatic 9 arbitrary, imperious, masterful
10 autocratic, imperative, peremptory, tyrannical 11 doctrinaire, domineering, overbearing 12 totalitarian 13 authoritarian,
authoritative

dictatorship 7 tyranny 9 autocracy, Caesarism, despotism 10 absolutism

diction 6 phrase 7 wordage, wording
8 parlance, phrasing, verbiage 9 verbalism
11 phraseology *suffix:* 3 ese

dictionary 4 cant 6 jargon 7 lexicon,
palaver 8 language, wordbook 10 repository, vocabulary 11 terminology 13 reference book *compiler:* 7 Johnson (Samuel),
Webster (Noah) 13 lexicographer *geo-
graphical:* 9 gazetteer *of prosody:* 6 gra-

dus *of synonyms:* **8** thesauri (plural)
9 thesaurus

dictum 4 rule **5** axiom, gnome, maxim,
moral **6** saying, truism **7** brocard, opinion
8 aphorism, apothegm **9** statement
13 pronouncement

didactic 3 dry **5** moral **6** teachy
7 preachy **8** advisory, sermonic **9** horta-
tive **10** moralizing, preceptive **11** exhorta-
tive, sermonizing

diddle 3 gyp **4** beat, bilk, hoax, idle, laze,
loaf, loll, take **5** cheat, cozen, drone
6 chouse, dawdle, delude, loiter, lounge
7 defraud **8** lallygag **9** overreach, waste
time

diddler 3 gyp **5** cheat **6** con man
7 grifter, sharper **9** defrauder, trickster
12 double-dealer **13** confidence man

dido 3 toy **5** curio, frill **6** bauble, gewgaw,
trifle **7** bibelot, trinket, whatnot **8** furbelow,
gimcrack **10** knickknack

Dido 6 Elissa *brother:* **9** Pygmalion *city
founded by:* **8** Carthage *father:* **5** Belus
6 Mutton *husband:* **7** Acerbas **8** Sichaeus
lover: **6** Aeneas

Dido and Aeneas composer 7 Purcell

die 3 ebb, pip **4** bate, conk, dado, drop, fall,
fate, long, mold, pass, stop, wane **5** abate,
block, cease, croak, let up, swelt **6** cash in,
chance, cop out, demise, depart, expire,
kick in, matrix, peg out, perish, pop off,
recede **7** decease, ease off, fortune, kick
off, pass out, slacken, subside, succumb
8 check out, languish, moderate, pass away,
snuff out **9** disappear, grow faint *from hunger:* **6** starve *loaded:* **6** fulham, fullam

____ **die 4** sine **3** bis in (twice a day), ter in
(thrice a day) **6** quater in (four times a day)

die-away 4 limp **7** languid **8** listless
9 enervated **10** languorous, spiritless
11 languishing **13** lackadaisical

diehard 4 tory **5** blimp, fixed, right, white
7 Bourbon, old fogy **8** mossback, old liner,
pullback, rightist, royalist, standpat, true
blue **9** right wing **10** praetorian **11** bitter-
ender, reactionary, reactionist, right-center,
right-winger, standpatter **12** conservative,
intransigent **13** reactionarist, stick-in-the-
mud

____ **diem 5** carpe

Dies ____ **4** Irae **7** faustus

diet 4 fast, feed **8** assembly **10** parliament

Diet of ____ **5** Worms **6** Speyer, Spires
8 Augsburg

____ **-dieu 4** prie

Dieu ____**, British motto 10** et mon droit

differ 3 jar **4** vary **5** argue, clash **6** bicker,
debate, depart, divide, oppose **7** deviate,
discord, dispute, dissent, diverge, quarrel
8 conflict, disagree, squabble **9** disaccord

difference 4 know **5** clash, sever

6 change, effect, strife **7** discern, discord,
dissent **8** alterity, conflict, disunity, separate, variance **9** disaccord, extricate, otherness, variation **10** contention, discrepate,
dissension, divergency, severalize, unlikeness **11** controversy, discrepancy, distinction, distinguish **12** disagreement, discriminate, dissemblance, modification
13 dissimilarity, dissimilitude *slight:*
5 shade **8** hairline

different 5 other **6** divers, single, sundry,
unlike **7** another, distant, diverse, several,
special, unalike, unequal, unusual, various
8 discrete, distinct, opposite, peculiar, separate **9** disparate, divergent, otherwise, unsimilar **10** dissimilar, individual, particular
11 distinctive *combining form:* **3** all **4** allo
5 heter **6** hetero **7** diversi

differentiate 4 know **5** sever **7** discern
8 separate **9** extricate **10** comprehend, discrepate, severalize, understand **11** distinguish **12** discriminate

difficult 4 hard **6** uphill **7** arduous, awkward, labored, obscure, operose, problem
8 perverse, puzzling, stubborn, toilsome
9 effortful, hampering, laborious, strenuous
11 problematic *combining form:* **4** mogi
prefix: **3** dys

difficulty 3 fix, jam **4** beef, nodi (plural)
4 pass, snag **5** cavil, demur, fight, nodus,
pinch, rigor **6** bother, hassle, pickle, plight,
scrape, strait **7** dilemma, dispute, pitfall,
problem, protest, quarrel, trouble **8** asperity, demurral, demurrer, exigency, hardness,
hardship, obstacle, quandary, question,
squabble **9** bickering, challenge, emergency, objection **10** falling-out, impediment **11** altercation, arduousness, controversy, obstruction, predicament, vicissitude
12 disagreement, remonstrance **13** embarrassment, inconvenience, remonstration

diffidence 7 modesty, reserve **8** distrust
11 bashfulness

diffident 3 coy, shy **5** timid **6** demure,
modest **7** bashful **8** hesitant, retiring
9 blenching, flinching, reluctant, shrinking,
unassured **11** distrustful, unassertive
12 self-effacing

difform 6 uneven **7** unequal **8** lopsided
10 asymmetric **13** unsymmetrical

diffuse 3 lax **4** full, long **5** loose, slack,
strew, windy, wordy **6** casual, expand,
extend, lavish, prolix, random, spread
7 copious, lengthy, osmolar, osmotic, perfuse, radiate, scatter, send out, verbose
8 disperse, intersow, permeate **9** broadcast, circulate, desultory, exuberant, interlard, propagate, redundant, scattered,
spreading, spread out **10** distribute, long-
winded, palaverous, widespread **11** disseminate, intersperse **13** intersprinkle

diffusion   7 osmoses (plural), osmosis
9 broadcast, prolixity, spreading
10 scattering
dig   3 jab, jog, ram, run **4** grub, hole, holk, howk, like, mind, mine, poke, prod, root, sift, sink, site, spud, stab **5** delve, ditch, drive, enjoy, enter, grind, nudge, probe, punch, scoop, spade, stick **6** burrow, drudge, go into, pierce, plunge, quarry, relish, rootle, shovel, thrust, trench, tunnel **7** explore, root out, unearth **8** excavate, look into, prospect **9** delve into, hollow out, penetrate **10** excavation **11** inquire into, investigate *out:* **6** exhume *up:* **7** unearth
digest   2 go **3** sum **4** bear, cook, take **5** abide, brook, stand, sum up **6** aperçu, codify, endure, précis, sketch, survey **7** pandect, stomach, summate, swallow, sylloge **8** compress, condense, nutshell, syllabus, synopsis, tolerate **9** epitomize, inventory, summarize, synopsize **10** abridgment, compendium, comprehend, periodical **11** compilation
digestion   combining form: 6 pepsia, peptic *good:* **7** eupepsy **8** eupepsia *poor:* **9** dyspepsia
digger   4 plow **5** miner
digit   3 toe **5** thumb **6** cipher, figure, finger, number, pinkie **7** chiffer, integer, numeral **11** whole number *abbreviation:* **2** no. *combining form:* **6** dactyl, digiti **7** dactylo, dactyly **8** dactylia **9** dactylism, dactylous
dignified   4 prim **6** proper **7** stately **8** decorous
dignify   5 erect, exalt, honor **6** uprear **7** ennoble, glorify, sublime **10** aggrandize **11** distinguish
dignitary   3 VIP **4** lion **5** chief, nabob **6** leader **7** notable **8** eminence, luminary **10** notability **13** high-muck-a-muck
dignity   4 rank **5** grace, honor, merit, poise, state, worth **6** cachet, ethics, status, virtue **7** address, decency, decorum, majesty, stature **8** elegance, grandeur, morality, nobility, position, prestige, standing **9** etiquette, grandness, nobleness, propriety **10** augustness, excellence, perfection, seemliness **11** consequence, ethicalness **12** magnificence *suffix:* **3** dom **4** ship
digress   4 roam **5** drift, stray **6** depart, ramble, swerve, wander **7** deviate, diverge, excurse **8** divagate
digression   5 aside **7** episode, excurse **8** drifting, excursus, incident, rambling, straying **9** departure, deviation, wandering **10** deflection, divagation, divergence **11** parenthesis, underaction
dike   4 bank, pond, pool **5** drain, fix up, levee, slick, spiff **6** doll up, dude up **7** barrier, deck out, doll out, dress up, gussy up

8 aboideau, causeway, spruce up
11 watercourse
dilapidate   4 do in, ruin **5** decay, wreck **6** forget, ignore, slight **7** crumble, neglect **8** bankrupt, overlook **9** decompose, disregard, shipwreck **12** disintegrate
dilapidated   5 dingy, faded, seedy, tacky **6** beat-up, marred, shabby, tagrag **7** damaged, decayed, injured, run-down **8** crumbled, impaired **10** broken-down, down-at-heel, threadbare
dilapidation   5 decay, waste **6** debris
dilate   5 swell, widen **6** expand, extend, recite **7** amplify, augment, broaden, descant, discuss, dissert, distend, enlarge, narrate, prolong, recount **8** describe, expanded, increase, lengthen, protract, rehearse **9** discourse, expatiate, sermonize **10** dissertate
dilatory   3 lax **4** slow **5** slack, tardy **6** remiss **7** laggard, unhasty **9** leisurely, negligent, unhurried **10** deliberate, neglectful
dilemma   3 box, fix, jam **4** hole, spot **6** choice, corner, pickle, plight, scrape **7** problem **8** argument, quandary **10** perplexity **11** predicament **12** bewilderment **13** mystification
dilettante   4 tyro **7** amateur, dabbler, jackleg **8** aesthete, dabbling, ungifted **9** smatterer, unskilled **10** amateurish, unfinished, uninitiate **11** abecedarian, cognoscente, connoisseur
dilettantish   see amateurish
diligence   8 industry **9** assiduity **11** persistence **12** perseverance
diligent   7 operose **8** sedulous **9** assiduous **10** persistent, persisting, unflagging **11** industrious, persevering
dill plant   4 anet
dilly   3 pip **4** lulu **5** dandy, nifty, peach **6** corker, dinger, doozer, pippin, ripper, rouser **8** jim-dandy, knockout **9** humdinger **10** ripsnorter **11** crackerjack, lalapalooza
dillydally   see delay
dilute   3 cut **4** thin, weak **5** alter, washy **6** debase, modify, temper, watery, weaken **7** liquefy, qualify, reduced **8** deprived, diminish, impaired, moderate, waterish, weakened **9** enfeebled, water down **10** deliquesce **11** adulterated, watered-down **12** impoverished **13** sophisticated
dim   3 fog, mat **4** blur, dark, dead, dull, dusk, fade, flat, haze, hazy, pale **5** befog, blear, blind, cloud, dusky, faint, muddy, murky, muted, vague **6** bleary, darken, gloomy **7** becloud, dislimn, eclipse, low beam, obscure, shadowy, subdued, tarnish, unclear **9** lightless, obfuscate, tenebrous **10** caliginous, ill-defined, indistinct, lacklus-

ter, lusterless **12** parking light, undetermined **13** unilluminated

dime novel 4 pulp **7** chiller, shocker **8** dreadful, thriller **10** yellowback **12** blood-curdler, killer-diller **13** penny dreadful

dimension 4 size **5** scope, trait, width **6** aspect, extent **7** measure, quality **8** lifelike **9** magnitude **10** yard lumber **11** proportions

diminish 3 ebb **4** bate, wane **5** abate, abuse, close, decry, peter, taper **6** lessen, minify, reduce, temper **7** abridge, curtail, dwindle, subside **8** belittle, decrease, derogate, minimize, moderate, taper off, write off **9** attenuate, disparage, dispraise, drain away, extenuate **10** depreciate **11** detract from

diminishing 7 calando

diminutive 3 wee **4** tiny **5** small, teeny, weeny **6** minute, teensy **9** miniature **10** teeny-weeny **11** lilliputian **12** teensy-weensy

diminutive one *suffix:* **2** el, et, ey, ia (plural), ie **3** cle, ium, kin, ock, ula, ule, uli (plural) **4** ella, ette, illa, ling, ulae (plural), ulum, ulus **5** ellae (plural), illae (plural)

dimmet 4 dusk **7** evening **8** eventide, gloaming, owl-light, twilight **9** nightfall

dimple 4 fret **5** mound **6** cockle, hollow, riffle, ripple **10** depression

dim-sighted 8 purblind **9** half-blind

dimwit 4 simp **5** cluck, dunce **7** pinhead **9** dumb bunny, dumb cluck **13** featherweight

dim-witted 4 dull, slow **7** moronic **8** backward, imbecile, retarded **12** feebleminded, simpleminded

din 3 row **5** babel, chirm, clash, music, noise, sound **6** bedlam, clamor, deafen, hubbub, jangle, racket, rattle, tumult, uproar **7** clangor, clatter, resound **8** blatancy, brouhaha, racketry **9** commotion, stridency **10** hullabaloo, percussion, tintamarre **11** pandemonium **13** clamorousness

Dinah 5 Shore *brother:* **4** Levi **6** Simeon *father:* **5** Jacob *mother:* **4** Leah

dine 3 eat, sup **4** feed

diner 3 bar **4** café **6** eatery **7** counter, hashery **8** snack bar **9** hash house **10** coffee shop, quick-lunch, restaurant **11** eating house, greasy spoon **12** lunch counter, sandwich shop

dinette *ancient Roman:* **5** oecus

ding 3 hit **4** beat, best, damn, sock **5** catch, clang, clout, outdo, outgo, whack **6** better, exceed, strike **7** surpass **8** outmatch, outshine

ding-a-ling 3 nut **4** kook **5** crank **6** cuckoo **7** lunatic **8** crackpot **9** harebrain, screwball **10** crackbrain

dinge 4 dent **5** blues, dumps, gloom

6 batter **7** sadness **9** dejection **10** depression, melancholy **11** unhappiness **12** mournfulness

dinghy 5 yacht **7** rowboat **8** life raft, sailboat

dingle 4 dale, dell **6** ravine, valley **9** storm door **10** passageway

dingus 5 gizmo **6** doodad, gadget, jigger **7** do-funny, thingum **9** doohickey **10** thingumbob **11** thingumajig

dingy 4 dark, drab, dull, mean **5** dirty, dusky, faded, murky, seedy, tacky, tired **6** gloomy, grimed, shabby, smutty, soiled **7** run-down, squalid, sullied **8** smirched **9** tarnished **10** broken-down, discolored, down-at-heel, threadbare **11** dilapidated

dinky 5 minor, small **6** lesser **8** small-fry **9** secondary, small-time **11** minor league **13** insignificant

dinner 4 fete, meal **5** feast **6** entrée, junket, regale, spread **7** banquet **8** festival, luncheon **9** breakfast, collation **10** table d'hôte *coat:* **3** tux **6** tuxedo *course:* **4** meat, soup **6** entrée **7** dessert **9** appetizer *Jewish:* **5** seder **7** sedarim (plural)

"Dinner ___" 7 at Eight

dinosaur 8 theropod **10** allosaurus **11** stegosaurus, triceratops **12** brontosaurus **13** tyrannosaurus

dinosauric 4 huge **7** mammoth **8** colossal, enormous **9** cyclopean, leviathan **10** behemothic, gargantuan, mastodonic **11** elephantine

dint 5 force, might, notch, power, sinew, vigor **6** energy, hollow, virtue **7** drive in, impress, imprint, potency **8** strength **9** puissance **10** impression **11** indentation

diocese 3 see **9** bishopric *Eastern Orthodox:* **7** eparchy *subdivision:* **6** parish

diode 9 rectifier **12** electron tube *type of:* **8** kenotron

Diomedes *city founded by:* **4** Arpi *father:* **4** Ares, Mars **6** Tydeus *foe:* **6** Aeneas, Hector *slayer:* **8** Hercules *victim:* **6** Rhesus

Dione 5 Titan *cult partner:* **4** Zeus *daughter:* **5** Venus **9** Aphrodite *father:* **7** Oceanus *lover:* **4** Zeus *mother:* **6** Tethys

Dionysus see **Bacchus**

Dionyza's husband 5 Cleon

Dioscuri 5 twins **6** Anaces, Anakes, Castor, Gemini, Pollux *father:* **4** Zeus **9** Tyndareus *mother:* **4** Leda *sister:* **5** Helen

dip 3 sag, set **4** bail, dish, draw, drop, duck, dunk, fall, lade, sink, skew, skid, slip, slue, tilt, veer **5** basin, depth, douse, ladle, lower, pitch, reach, sauce, scoop, sheer, slope, slump, souse, spoon, stoop **6** candle, go down, hollow, plunge, swerve, thrust, tumble **7** decline, delving, descend, descent, explore, falloff, immerse, plummet, sinkage **8** bucket up, decrease, downturn, lowering, nose-dive, sinkhole, submerge, submerse, train off **9** concavity, declivity, downslide, downswing, downtrend, immersion **10** depression, divergence, plunge into **11** inclination *kind:* **4** clam **5** onion **10** blue cheese

diphthong 2 ae, ai, ea, ei, oe, oi, ou, oy **7** digraph **8** ligature

diploma 6 letter **7** charter, writing **8** document

diplomacy 4 tact **5** poise **7** address **10** adroitness, artfulness, settlement **11** delicatesse, savoir faire, tactfulness

diplomatic 4 wily **5** bland **6** artful, astute, crafty, polite, shrewd, smooth **7** politic, tactful **8** delicate, guileful, tactical **9** courteous **12** paleographic

diplomat's office 7 embassy

diplopod 9 millipede

dipper 3 cup **4** bird, grab **5** ladle, scoop **6** bucket, holder **10** bufflehead, water ouzel

dippy 5 crazy, silly, wacky **6** absurd, insane **7** foolish **9** fantastic **11** harebrained **12** preposterous

dipsomania 10 alcoholism

dire 5 acute, awful **6** crying, dismal, urgent, woeful **7** baleful, baneful, burning, clamant, crucial, exigent, extreme, fateful, fearful, instant, ominous, painful **8** critical, dreadful, grievous, horrible, pressing, shocking, sinister, terrible, terrific **9** appalling, cheerless, clamorous, desperate, frightful, ill-boding **10** afflictive, calamitous, deplorable, depressing, imperative, lamentable, oppressing, oppressive **11** apocalyptic, climacteric, distressing, importunate, regrettable, threatening, unfortunate **12** inauspicious, unpropitious **13** heartbreaking

direct 3 aim, bid, due, fix, lay, run, see, set **4** beam, bend, cast, dead, give, head, keep, lead, mark, next, open, show, tell, turn, warn **5** allot, apply, focus, frank, guide, issue, label, level, order, pilot, plain, point, refer, right, route, steer, throw, train **6** assign, candid, charge, custos, define, devote, divert, enjoin, escort, extend, fasten, govern, handle, lineal, linear, manage, ordain, settle, zero in **7** address, carry on, command, conduct, control, genuine, incline, nonstop, operate, oversee, present, preside, primary, project, request, through **8** dispatch, dominate, instruct, man-to-man, point out, regulate, shepherd, straight, unbroken, verbatim **9** determine, effective, firsthand, immediate, literally, literatim, out-and-out, prescribe, proximate **10** administer, buckle down, channelize, contiguous, continuous, explicitly, inevitable, proceeding, straightly, unhampered, unreserved, unswerving **11** categorical, substantive, superscribe,

unconcealed, undeviating, undisguised, unequivocal, word for word **12** undissembled **13** undeviatingly, uninterrupted *a helmsman:* **4** conn *proceedings:* **7** preside

direction (see also **compass point**) **3** way **4** east, line, path, role, side, west **5** angle, north, order, point, slant, south, tenor **6** charge, course, design, sphere **7** bearing, channel, command, guiding, outlook, respect **8** guidance, pointing **9** clockwise, viewpoint **10** standpoint *blowing:* **7** leeward **8** windward *combining form:* **5** phoro *court:* **5** order *for Muslims praying:* **5** kibla **6** keblah, kildah *horizontal:* **7** azimuth *main line of:* **4** axis *musical:* (see **musical direction**) *of a linear arrangement:* **5** grain *square dance:* **4** call *without fixed:* **7** astatic

directive 4 memo, word **5** edict, ukase **6** decree, notice, ruling **7** bidding, message **8** exemplar **10** assignment, injunction, memorandum **11** instruction **13** communication, pronouncement

directly 3 due **4** anon, away, dead, soon **5** right, spang **6** at once **7** by and by, shortly **8** first off, in person, squarely, straight, verbatim **9** forthwith, instanter, instantly, literally, literatim, presently, right away **10** face-to-face, straightly **11** immediately, straight off, straightway, word for word **12** contiguously **13** undeviatingly, unqualifiedly

director 4 head **5** chief **6** leader **7** manager **9** conductor **10** supervisor

directory 4 list, ordo **5** guide, index **8** treatise **11** compilation

direful see **fearful; ominous**

dirge 4 hymn, song **6** lament **7** epicede, requiem **8** threnody **9** epicedium **11** lamentation *Gaelic:* **8** coronach

dirigible 7 airship **8** zeppelin **9** steerable

dirk 4 stab **5** sword **6** dagger

dirt 4 land, sand, soil, spot **5** earth, filth, fraud, grime, stain **6** gossip, gravel, ground **7** chicane, dry land, squalor **9** chicanery, deception, excrement, fourberie **10** corruption, dishonesty, hanky-panky, terra firma **11** highbinding, uncleanness **13** double-dealing, sharp practice

dirt poor 4 flat **5** broke **8** beggared, indigent **9** destitute, penurious **10** stonebroke **12** impoverished

dirty 3 low, tar **4** foul, smut, soil, wild **5** bawdy, black, dungy, grime, grimy, messy, mucky, muddy, murky, nasty, rough, smear, soily, sooty, stain, sully, taint **6** basely, befoul, begrim, besoil, coarse, dreggy, filthy, grubby, impure, raging, smirch, smooch, smudge, smudgy, smutch, smutty, soiled, sordid, stormy, vulgar **7** abusive, begrime, besmear, clouded, defiled, draggly, dullish, furious, hateful, immoral, obscene, piggish, raunchy, smoochy, smutchy, squalid, sullied, tainted, tarnish, unclean **8** begrimed, besmirch, blustery, discolor, draggled, grievous, indecent, polluted, scroungy, stormful, unchaste **9** uncleanly **10** blustering, scurrilous **11** distressing, regrettable, tempestuous **12** contaminated, contemptible, scatological **13** draggletailed

Dis see **Pluto**

disability 8 drawback, handicap **9** detriment

disable 3 mar, sap **4** harm, hurt, maim, ruin **5** blunt, spoil, wreck **6** batter, disarm, mangle, weaken **7** cripple, deprive, invalid, unbrace **8** enfeeble, mutilate, paralyze **9** attenuate, prostrate, undermine **10** debilitate, disqualify, immobilize **12** incapacitate, unstrengthen *a racehorse:* **6** nobble

disabuse 4 free **5** amend, emend, purge **7** correct, rectify, redress, release, unblind **8** liberate, undelude **9** disillude, enlighten, undeceive **10** illuminate **11** disillusion

disaccharide 7 lactose, maltose, sucrose

disaccord 3 jar **4** vary **5** clash **6** differ, divide, jangle, strife **7** dissent **8** conflict, disunity, mismatch, variance **10** contention, difference, dissension, dissidence **12** disharmonize

disadvantage 3 bar **4** harm, loss **6** hamper **8** blocking, drawback, handicap, obstacle **9** detriment, hindrance, prejudice **10** impediment, imposition **11** obstruction

disadvantaged 7 lacking **8** deprived **9** depressed

disadvise 5 deter **6** divert **8** dissuade **10** discourage

disaffect 4 wean **5** alien, upset **7** agitate, disturb **8** alienate, diminish, disquiet, disunify, disunite, estrange **10** discompose

disaffection 9 hostility **12** estrangement

disaffirm 4 deny **5** annul, cross **6** impugn, negate **7** gainsay, reverse **8** negative, traverse **9** repudiate **10** contradict, contravene

disagree 4 vary **5** clash **6** differ, divide **7** discord, dissent

disagreeable 3 bad **4** sour **5** waspy, whiny **6** rotten, snappy, twitty, woeful **7** helluva, peevish, pettish, unhappy, waspish **8** annoying, petulant **9** offensive, querulous **10** disturbing, unpleasant **11** displeasing, distressing

disagreement 3 row **4** spat **5** clash **7** discord, dispute, quarrel **8** variance **10** contention, difference, dissension, divergence, unlikeness **11** controversy, discrepancy, incongruity

disallow 4 deny, veto **5** debar **6** disown,

refuse, reject **7** disavow, exclude, shut out **8** disclaim, keep back, withhold **9** repudiate

disallowance 6 denial **7** refusal **9** rejection

___ **-disant 3** soi

disappear 2 go **4** fade **5** clear, leave **6** vanish **7** evanish **8** evanesce **9** evaporate

disappoint 4 balk, beat, bilk, dash, foil, ruin **6** baffle, defeat, thwart **9** frustrate **10** circumvent

disappointment 7 failure **9** bringdown **11** frustration

disapproval 4 veto **7** censure, dislike **9** rejection *expression of:* **3** boo **4** hiss, hoot, jeer **7** catcall **9** raspberry **10** Bronx cheer

disapprove 5 blame, decry, frown, pshaw, spurn **6** object, refuse, reject **7** censure, condemn, decline, detract, dislike, dismiss **8** denounce, disfavor, turn down **9** criticize, deprecate, disesteem, disparage, dispraise, reprehend, reprobate, repudiate **10** depreciate, discommend **11** expostulate, remonstrate

disarm 5 charm **6** allure **7** attract, bewitch, cripple, enchant, unsteel, win over **8** paralyze **9** captivate, deprive of, fascinate, prostrate **10** immobilize **12** incapacitate

disarming 5 silky **6** silken **10** saccharine **11** deferential, insinuating, insinuative **12** ingratiating, ingratiatory

disarrange 4 mess **6** jumble, mess up, mislay **7** disturb, replace, rummage **8** disorder, displace, misplace, overturn, unsettle **10** discompose **11** disorganize

disarray 5 chaos, snarl **6** ataxia, huddle, jumble, mess up, muddle, unrobe **7** clutter, derange, disturb, rummage **8** disorder, unsettle **9** confusion **10** discompose **11** disorganize

disassemble 8 dismount, separate, take down, tear down **9** dismantle, dismember, take apart

disassociate 5 unfix **6** detach **8** abstract, uncouple **9** disengage **10** disconnect

disaster 3 woe **4** rock, ruin **6** fiasco, injure, mishap **7** failure, tragedy **8** accident, calamity, casualty, distress, fatality **9** adversity, cataclysm, mischance **10** misfortune **11** catastrophe **12** misadventure

disastrous 4 dire **5** fatal **7** fateful, hapless, ruinous **8** luckless **10** calamitous **11** cataclysmic, destructive, unfortunate **12** catastrophic

disavow 4 deny **6** disown, impugn, negate, recant **8** disclaim, negative **9** repudiate

disband 4 part **5** sever **6** dispel, divide,

sunder **7** break up, disjoin, dissect, divorce, scatter **8** disjoint, disperse, dissever, dissolve, disunite, separate **9** dissipate **11** dichotomize

disbelieve **5** doubt, scorn, scout **6** eschew, reject **7** suspect **8** distrust, mistrust, question **9** discredit

disbeliever **5** cynic **7** doubter, sceptic, skeptic

disbelieving **6** show-me **8** aporetic **9** quizzical, skeptical **11** incredulous, questioning

disburden **6** unlade, unload, unship, unstow **7** discard, off-load **8** get rid of, jettison **9** discharge

disburse **3** pay **4** deal, give **5** divvy, spend **6** defray, divide, expend, lay out, lot out, outlay, pay out **7** dole out, fork out **8** dispense, disperse, shell out **9** partition **10** distribute, measure out

disbursement **4** cost **6** outlay **7** expense **11** expenditure

discard **4** cast, drop, dump, junk, oust, shed, waif **5** chuck, ditch, eject, let go, scrap, sluff, spurn **6** desert, reject, slough **7** abandon, cashier, cast off, deep-six, dismiss, forsake, wash out **8** abdicate, get rid of, jettison, lay aside, shuck off, throw out **9** repudiate, throw away

discarnate **8** bodiless **9** asomatous, unfleshly **10** immaterial, unembodied, unphysical **11** disembodied, incorporeal, nonphysical **13** insubstantial

discept **4** moot **5** argue **6** debate **7** agitate, canvass, dispute **9** thrash out **10** toss around

discern **3** see **4** know, note, view **5** sever **6** behold, descry, detect, divine, notice, remark **7** foresee, observe **8** perceive, separate **9** apprehend, ascertain, extricate **10** anticipate, difference, severalize **11** distinguish **13** differentiate

discernible **8** palpable **10** detectable, observable **11** appreciable

discerning **4** sage, wise **7** gnostic, knowing **9** clear-eyed, insighted, sagacious **10** insightful, perceptive **11** wisehearted **13** knowledgeable

discernment **3** wit **6** acumen, reason **8** keenness, sagacity **9** intuition **10** astuteness, shrewdness **11** penetration, percipience **12** perspicacity **13** sagaciousness

discharge **2** ax **3** can, pay, run **4** drop, emit, fire, flow, free, oust, pour, quit, sack, vent, void **5** annul, clear, eject, empty, expel, exude, let go, loose, pay up, quash, rheum, shoot, spare, utter **6** bounce, excuse, exempt, let fly, let off, loosen, outlet, remove, settle, square, unbind, unlade, unload, unship, unstow, vacate **7** absolve, boot out, cashier, deliver, dismiss, exclude,

execute, fulfill, give off, kick out, manumit, off-load, release, relieve, removal, replace, satisfy, unchain **8** abrogate, clear off, clear out, dispense, displace, dissolve, emission, get rid of, liberate, separate, set aside, supplant, throw off **9** acquittal, bleach out, disburden, disenroll, eliminate, explosion, expulsion, liquidate, muster out, pour forth, pronounce, send forth, supersede, terminate, unloading, unshackle **10** deactivate, demobilize, disembogue, emancipate, give vent to, inactivate, liberation, separation **11** acquittance, exoneration, fulfillment **13** privilege from *combining form:* **5** rrhea **6** rrhoea **7** rrhagia *concentrated:* **7** barrage *electrical:* **5** spark **6** leader **8** streamer **9** lightning **12** leader stroke *from the body:* **5** egest **7** excrete *simultaneous:* **5** salvo

discinct **3** lax **5** slack **6** remiss **8** careless, derelict **9** negligent **10** behindhand, delinquent, neglectful **12** disregardful

disciple **6** cohort, zealot **7** apostle, fanatic, sectary **8** adherent, follower, henchman, partisan, sectator **9** satellite, supporter **10** enthusiast

disciplinarian **6** ramrod **8** martinet

disciplinary **7** ordered **8** punitive, punitory **9** punishing **11** castigatory

discipline **3** rod **4** curb, lead, whip, will **5** check, drill, guide, spank, teach, train **6** bridle, direct, manage, method, punish, reduce, school, subdue **7** chasten, conduct, control, correct, educate, inhibit, scourge **8** approach, chastise, instruct, overcome, penalize, punition, restrain, training **9** castigate, obedience, subjugate, will-power **10** correction, experience, punishment **11** castigation, self-command, self-control, self-mastery **12** chastisement **13** self-restraint

disclaim **4** deny **5** spurn **6** abjure, disown, recant, refuse, reject **7** disavow, gainsay, retract **8** belittle, disallow, forswear, minimize, renounce, traverse **9** challenge, criticize, deprecate, disparage, repudiate **10** contradict, contravene

disclose **3** own **4** avow, open, tell **5** admit, mouth, spill **6** betray, expose, reveal, unveil **7** blab out, confess, display, divulge, unclose, uncover **8** discover, give away, unclothe **9** make known **11** acknowledge

disclosure **6** exposé **10** confession, revelation **11** divulgation

discolor **3** tar **4** blot, dull, fade, smut, soil **5** smear, stain, sully, taint, tinge **6** defile, motley, streak **7** besmear, bestain, dappled, tarnish **8** besmirch **9** multihued **10** variegated

discoloration 5 stain *combining form:* 6 chroia

discomfit 3 irk, vex 4 faze, foil, rout 5 abash, annoy, upset 6 bother, defeat, rattle, thwart 7 confuse, disturb, perturb 8 confound 9 embarrass

discomfiture 4 rout 5 upset 6 damage, defeat, injury, unease 7 beating, debacle, descent, licking 8 comedown, disquiet, drubbing, prickles 9 abashment, agitation, commotion, confusion, overthrow 10 defeasance, uneasiness 11 frustration, shellacking 12 perturbation, vanquishment 13 embarrassment, inconvenience

discomfort 6 unease 7 malaise, misease 9 annoyance 10 uneasiness 13 embarrassment

discomforting see **uncomfortable**

discommend 5 frown 6 object 7 censure 8 admonish, disfavor 9 criticize, deprecate, disesteem, reprehend 10 disapprove

discommode 3 irk, vex 5 upset 6 bother, flurry, put out 7 fluster, perturb, trouble 8 put about 9 disoblige 13 inconvenience

discompose 3 irk, vex 5 annoy, harry, upset, worry 6 bother, dismay, flurry, harass, mess up, pester, plague, untune 7 agitate, derange, disturb, fluster, perturb, rummage, unhinge 8 disagree, disarray, disorder, disquiet, unsettle 9 embarrass 10 disarrange 11 disorganize

discomposure 6 unease 9 abashment, agitation, confusion 10 uneasiness 12 perturbation 13 embarrassment

disconcert 4 faze 5 abash, upset 6 puzzle, rattle, ruffle 7 break up, confuse, nonplus, perplex 8 bewilder, confound 9 embarrass, frustrate

disconfirm 5 break, evert, rebut 6 refute 7 confute 8 confound, disprove 10 controvert

disconnect 5 sever, unfix 6 detach 8 abstract, separate, uncouple

disconnected 7 muddled 8 inchoate 10 incoherent, incohesive 11 unorganized 12 uncontinuous

disconsolate 3 bad, low, sad 4 cold, down 5 bleak, drear 6 gloomy, somber, woeful 7 doleful, joyless, unhappy 8 dejected, downcast 9 cheerless, depressed, saddening, sorrowful, woebegone 10 depressing, melancholy 11 comfortless, crestfallen, downhearted

discontent 9 dysphoria 10 inquietude, uneasiness

discontented 5 upset 6 uneasy 7 unhappy 8 restless 9 perturbed 11 ungratified, unsatisfied

discontented one see **complainer**

discontinuance see **discontinuation**

discontinuation 3 end 5 cease, close 6 ending, finish 7 closing 9 desuetude 10 conclusion, desistance

discontinue 3 end 4 halt, quit, stop 5 cease, sever 6 desist, give up 8 break off, give over, knock off, leave off, surcease 9 terminate

discontinuity 3 gap 4 hole 5 break 6 breach, lacuna 7 opening

discontinuous 7 muddled 8 inchoate, separate 10 incoherent, incohesive 11 unconnected, unorganized

discord 3 jar 4 vary 5 clash 6 differ, divide, enmity, jangle, rancor, strife 7 unpeace 8 conflict, contrast, division, mischief, mismatch, variance 9 animosity, antipathy, collision, hostility, inharmony 10 antagonism, contention, difference, opposition 11 incongruity 12 inconsonance, polarization 13 inconsistency *goddess:* 3 Ate 4 Eris

discordant 5 harsh 7 jarring 8 clashing, contrary 9 immusical, unmixable, unmusical 10 cacophonic, inharmonic 11 cacophonous, conflicting, contrariant, incongruent, incongruous, inconsonant, quarrelsome, uncongenial 12 antagonistic, antipathetic, incompatible, inconsistent, inharmonious, unharmonious

discotheque 4 café, gogo 6 nitery 7 cabaret, hot spot 8 nightery 9 nightclub, night spot 10 supper club 12 watering hole 13 watering place

discount 4 fail, omit, take 5 abuse, decry 6 deduct, forget, ignore, lessen, rebate, slight 7 neglect, take off, take out 8 belittle, derogate, diminish, draw back, knock off, minimize, overlook, overpass, subtract, take away 9 abatement, deduction, reduction, substract, underrate 10 anticipate, depreciate 11 detract from, subtraction

discountenance 4 faze 5 abash, frown 6 object, rattle 7 confuse, reprove 8 confound, reproach 9 deprecate, embarrass 10 put to shame

discourage 3 irk, try, vex 4 damp 5 check, chill, deter, droop, scare, weigh 6 bother, dampen, deject, divert, hinder, lessen 7 afflict, depress, inhibit, prevent, trouble 8 frighten, restrain 10 demoralize

discouraging 5 black, bleak 6 dreary, gloomy 9 deterring, hindering 10 depressing, depressive, oppressive

discourse 3 act 4 play, talk 5 argue, enact, essay, orate, paper, speak, voice 6 expand, memoir, remark, sermon, speech, thesis 7 amplify, article, comment, descant, develop, enlarge, explain, expound, lecture, perform, playact 8 converse, harangue, perorate, rhetoric, speaking, tractate, treatise 9 elaborate, expatiate, monograph, personate, sermonize, utterance **10** commentate, expression, monography **11** impersonate, interchange **12** conversation **13** verbaliza-tion *art of:* **8** rhetoric *combining form:* **3** log **4** logo, logy **5** logia, logue *religious:* **6** homily, sermon

discourteous 4 rude **7** ill-bred, incivil, uncivil **8** impolite **10** ungracious, unman-nerly **11** ill-mannered, impertinent

discover 3 see **4** espy, find, hear, note, spot, tell **5** learn, mouth, spill **6** betray, debunk, descry, detect, expose, reveal, show up, tumble, unmask **7** catch on, divulge, find out, observe, publish, uncloak, unclose, undress, unearth **8** give away, per-ceive, proclaim, unshroud **9** advertise, ascertain, determine, encounter, make known

discovery 4 find **5** trove **6** espial, strike **7** finding **8** exposure **9** detection **10** expo-sition, revelation, unearthing **11** recognition

discredit 4 ruin **5** doubt, odium, shame, shoot **6** blow up, expose, infamy, show up **7** asperse, destroy, explode, obloquy **8** ignominy, puncture, reproach **9** unbe-lieve **10** opprobrium

discreditable 5 shady **6** shabby, shoddy **8** shameful **10** inglorious **11** ignominious

discreet 4 safe, wary **5** chary, muted, plain **6** modest, simple **7** careful, guarded, prudent, tactful **8** cautious, gingerly, moder-ate **9** temperate, unadorned, unextreme **10** controlled, reasonable, restrained **11** calculating, circumspect, considerate, inelaborate, unelaborate, unexcessive, unobtrusive **12** conservative, unbeautified **13** unpretentious

discrepancy 8 alterity **9** otherness, varia-tion **10** difference, divergence, divergency, unlikeness

discrepant 7 diverse, varying **8** contrary **9** different, divergent, unmixable **11** conflict-ing, incongruent, incongruous, inconsonant **12** incompatible, inconsistent

discrete 8 detached, separate **9** counta-ble **13** noncontinuous

discretion 4 tact **5** sense **6** wisdom **7** caution, secrecy **8** delicacy, judgment, prudence, wariness **9** canniness, foresight, restraint **10** providence **11** forethought

discriminate 4 know, note **5** sever **6** remark **7** analyze, compare, make out **8** contrast, perceive, separate **9** extricate **10** difference, severalize **13** differentiate

discriminating 4 wise **6** select **7** careful, prudent **8** eclectic **9** judicious, selective **10** analytical

discrimination 3 wit **5** sense **6** acumen **8** astucity, judgment, keenness **10** astute-ness, shrewdness **11** percipience **12** perspicacity

discriminatory 6 biased, unfair, unjust **7** partial **8** partisan **10** prejudiced **11** ineq-uitable **12** prepossessed

disculpate 5 clear **6** acquit **7** absolve **9** exonerate, vindicate

discursion 5 aside **8** excursus **10** divaga-tion **11** parenthesis

discursive 6 chatty, roving **7** roaming **8** rambling **9** desultory *group discussion:* **11** bull session

discuss 4 moot **5** argue, parle, weigh **6** caucus, debate, parley **7** agitate, can-vass, descant, expound **8** consider, con-verse, hash over, talk over **9** elucidate, expatiate, explicate, interpret, talk about, thrash out **10** deliberate, toss around **11** investigate *business:* **8** talk shop *lightly:* **5** bandy *thoroughly:* **7** exhaust

discussion 3 rap **6** confab **8** argument **10** conference **11** ventilation **12** delibera-tion **13** confabulation

discus thrower 6 Oerter (Al) **10** disco-bolus **11** Rashchupkin (Viktor)

disdain 5 abhor, pride, scorn, scout **6** morgue **7** contemn, despise, despite, hauteur **8** aversion, contempt, despisal, dis-prize, look down **9** antipathy, arrogance, insolence, loftiness, superbity **11** despise-ment, haughtiness

disdainful 5 proud **6** averse, lordly **7** haughty **8** arrogant, cavalier, insolent, scorning, scouting, spurning, superior **9** despising, rejecting **10** contemning **11** overbearing, repudiating **12** antipathic, contemptuous, supercilious **13** high and mighty, unsympathetic

disease 3 bug, ill **5** virus **6** blight, malady, scurvy **7** ailment, anthrax, cholera, derange, endemic, illness, malaise, mycosis, purpura, rickets **8** debility, epidemic, leukemia, myx-edema, paludism, pandemic, pellagra, rachi-tis, sickness, syndrome, zoonoses (plural), zoonosis **9** affection, black lung, complaint, condition, infirmity, sclerosis **10** alteration, blackwater, bronchitis, feebleness, impair-ment, infirmness, rachitides (plural), sickli-ness **11** decrepitude, derangement **13** unhealthiness *animal:* **5** mange, surra **8** enzootic, epizooty *blood:* **8** leucemia, leu-kemia, leukoses (plural), leukosis *cabbage:* **8** clubroot *cattle:* **6** cowpox **7** murrain, vaccina **8** blackleg, vaccinia *caused by bacteria:* **11** brucellosis *cereal grass:* **4** smut *children's:* **7** rubella **10** chicken pox *citrus tree:* **8** tristeza *classification:* **8** nosology *combining form:* **3** nos **4** noso, path **5** patho *communicable:* **12** tubercu-losis *disseminator:* **7** carrier *eye:* **8** glau-coma, trachoma *fish:* **3** ich *foretelling of:*

9 prognosis *hair follicle:* 7 sycoses (plural), sycosis *heart:* 11 cardiopathy *horse:* 4 clap 5 faroy 6 nagana, spavie, spavin 7 dourine, sarcoid 8 glanders *identification of:* 9 diagnosis *industrial:* 10 byssinosis *infectious:* 4 mono 6 typhus 7 malaria, tetanus, typhoid *liver:* 9 cirrhosis, hepatitis *livestock:* 7 locoism *lung:* 8 phthisic, phthisis 9 pneumonia *lymph glands:* 6 struma 8 scrofula *metabolic:* 4 gout *nervous system:* 4 kuru *of beets:* 8 heartrot *of mammals:* 10 babesiasis *parasitic:* 3 rot *plant:* 4 wilt 5 edema, scurf 6 blotch 7 frogeye 8 gummosis *poultry:* 7 fowlpox *respiratory:* 6 asthma *sheep:* 3 gid 7 scrapie 10 bluetongue *skin:* 4 acne 5 favus, hives, lupus, mange, pinta, tinea 6 eczema, tetter 7 leprosy, pemphix, prurigo, scabies 8 impetigo, keratoma, miliaria, pyoderma, ringworm, vitiligo, xanthoma 9 keratomas (plural), psoriasis, xanthomas (plural) 10 keratomata (plural), xanthomata (plural) *suffix:* 3 ses (plural), sis 4 itis, oses (plural), osis 5 iases (plural), iasis *swine:* 8 bullnose *syphilitic:* 5 tabes *throat:* 5 croup *tropical:* 4 pian 5 sprue 6 carate, dengue 8 psiloses (plural), psilosis *venereal:* 8 syphilis 9 chancroid, gonorrhea *viral:* 3 flu 4 noma 5 mumps, polio 6 grippe, rabies, zoster 7 ecthyma, measles, rubella, rubeola, variola 8 morbilli, psorosis, smallpox 13 poliomyelitis

diseased 6 sickly 7 fevered *combining form:* 3 cac 4 cace, caco *prefix:* 3 dys

disembark 4 land 6 alight 8 go ashore

disembarrass 3 rid 5 clear, untie 7 relieve, untwine 8 unburden, untangle 9 extricate 10 unentangle

disembodied 9 asomatous, unfleshly 10 immaterial, unphysical 11 incorporeal, nonphysical 13 insubstantial

disembogue 4 emit, flow, pour, void 6 emerge 7 give off, pour out 9 discharge

disembowel 3 gut 6 paunch, remove 7 exhaust 10 eviscerate, exenterate

disembroil 7 untwine 8 untangle 9 extricate 10 unentangle, unscramble

disemploy 2 ax 3 can 4 drop, fire, sack 5 let go 6 bounce, let out 7 boot out 9 terminate

disenchanted 5 blasé 7 knowing, worldly 8 mondaine 9 world-wise 11 worldly-wise 12 sophisticate 13 sophisticated

disencumber 5 untie 7 lighten, relieve, untwine 8 free from, untangle 9 alleviate, extricate 10 unentangle, unscramble

disengage 4 free, undo 5 loose, unfix 6 detach, unbind 7 release, unloose 8 abstract, liberate, uncouple, unfasten, unloosen 9 extricate

disentangle 4 part 5 sever, untie 6 detach, sunder 7 unravel, untwine 8 separate 9 extricate 10 unscramble 13 straighten out

disenthrall 4 free 5 loose 6 loosen, unbind 7 manumit, release, unchain 8 liberate 10 emancipate

disenthrone 6 depose, unmake 7 uncrown

disentranced see **disenchanted**

disentwine 5 untie 8 untangle 9 extricate 10 unentangle, unscramble

disesteem see **disfavor**

disfavor 5 frown, odium 6 infamy, object 7 obloquy 8 aversion, bad books, disgrace, ignominy, mistrust 9 deprecate, detriment 10 opprobrium 13 indisposition

disfigure 3 mar 4 foul 5 spoil 6 deface, deform, injure, mangle 8 mutilate

disfranchise 7 deprive 8 take away

disgorge 4 barf, spew 5 belch, eject, empty, eruct, erupt, expel, vomit 6 irrupt, spit up 7 bring up, throw up, upchuck

disgrace 4 blot, spot 5 brand, odium, shame, shend, stain 6 infamy, stigma 7 attaint, ill luck, obloquy, stigmas (plural) 8 black eye, contempt, debasing, humbling, ignominy, stigmata (plural) 9 abasement 10 debasement, misfortune, opprobrium 11 degradation, humiliation

disgraceful 5 shady 6 indign, shabby, shoddy 10 inglorious, unbecoming 11 ignominious 13 unrespectable

disgruntled 4 sore 9 uncontent 10 malcontent 11 uncontented, ungratified 12 malcontented

disguise 4 face, hide, mask, sham, show 5 belie, cloak, color, feign, front, put on 6 affect, assume, facade, garble, veneer 7 charade, conceal, dress up, falsify, obscure, pageant, pretend 8 artifice, coloring, delusion, pretense, simulate 9 deception, obfuscate 10 camouflage, false front, pretension 11 counterfeit, insincerity, make-believe 12 misrepresent, speciousness

disguisement 4 face, mask 5 cloak, color, cover, front 6 facade 8 coloring 10 false front

disgust 5 repel, shock 6 nausea, offend, reluct, revolt, sicken 7 outrage, repulse 8 aversion, nauseate 10 repugnance 13 squeamishness

disgusted 4 sick 5 fed up, tired, weary

disgusting 4 foul, vile 5 nasty 7 noisome 9 loathsome, offensive, repellent, repugnant, repulsive, revolting, sickening *behavior:* 11 beastliness

dish 4 food, stew, tray 5 salmi 6 shelve, tureen 7 platter 8 cup of tea, get rid of, scrapple, set aside *baked:* 7 soufflé *baking:* 7 scallop 12 scallop shell *cheese:*

7 ramekin, rarebit **8** raclette, ramequin *Chinese:* **6** won ton *deep:* **9** casserole *Hungarian:* **7** goulash *Italian:* **7** lasagna, lasagne, ravioli *Japanese:* **7** sashimi, tempura **8** sukiyaki *Mexican:* **5** tamal **6** tamale *Middle Eastern:* **8** moussaka *ornamental:* **7** epergne *principal:* **6** entrée *rice:* **7** risotto *rice and meat:* **5** pilaf, pilau, pilaw **6** pilaff *Scottish:* **6** haggis *shallow:* **6** saucer

Dishan's son **2** Uz **4** Aran

disharmonic see **discordant**

disharmonious see **discordant**

disharmonize **3** jar **5** clash **6** jangle **8** conflict, mismatch

disharmony **6** strife **7** discord, unpeace **8** conflict, variance **10** contention, difference, dissension, dissention

dishearten **5** chill **6** deject **7** depress **10** demoralize

disheartening **5** black, bleak **6** dreary, gloomy, somber **8** funereal **10** depressing, depressive, despondent, oppressive **11** pessimistic

dishes **4** ware *clay:* **7** pottery *porcelain:* **5** china

dishevel **5** touse, towse **6** tousel, tousle, touzle

disheveled **5** messy **6** sloppy, untidy **7** raunchy, ruffled, unkempt **8** ill-kempt, slipshod, slovenly, straggly, uncombed **12** unfastidious

dishonest **5** false, lying, snide **6** shifty, tricky **7** corrupt, crooked, devious, furtive, knavish, oblique, roguish **8** cheating, cozening, two-faced **9** deceitful, faithless, insidious, swindling **10** defrauding, fraudulent, mendacious, perfidious, untruthful **13** double-dealing, untrustworthy

dishonesty **5** fraud **7** chicane, roguery **8** trickery **9** chicanery, deception, fourberie **10** hanky-panky **11** highbinding **13** double-dealing, faithlessness

dishonor see **disgrace**

dishonorable see **disgraceful**

Dishon's father **4** Anah

dish out **4** dole, give, hand **6** supply **7** deliver, furnish, provide **8** dispense, hand over, transfer, turn over

disillusioned see **disenchanted**

disimprison **4** free **5** loose **6** unbind **7** manumit, release, unchain **8** liberate **9** unshackle **10** emancipate

disinclination **7** dislike **8** aversion **13** indisposition, unwillingness

disinclined **3** shy **5** loath **6** afraid, averse, shying **7** balking, dubious, uneager **8** backward, boggling, doubtful, hesitant, opposing, sticking **9** objecting, reluctant, resisting, stickling, unwilling, unwishful **10** indisposed,

protesting **12** antipathetic **13** unsympathetic

disinfect **7** cleanse **9** sterilize

disingenuous **3** sly **4** foxy, wily **5** false **6** artful, crafty, tricky **7** cunning, devious, feigned, oblique, unfrank **8** guileful, indirect, uncandid **9** insidious, insincere

disinherit **3** rob **4** lose, oust **6** cut off **7** bereave, deprive **9** deprive of, repudiate

disintegrate **3** rot **4** sink, turn **5** break, decay, spoil, taint **6** molder, worsen **7** crumble, decline, descend, putrefy, scatter, shatter **8** separate **9** break down, decompose **10** deliquesce, retrograde *suffix:* **4** lyse, lyze

disintegrating *combining form:* **7** clastic

disintegration *combining form:* **5** lyses (plural), lysis

disinter **5** dig up **6** exhume, unbury **7** unearth **8** exhumate **9** uncharnel

disinterest **6** apathy **8** lethargy **9** lassitude, unconcern **11** insouciance **12** heedlessness, indifference, listlessness **13** unmindfulness

disinterested **4** fair, just **5** aloof **6** casual, remote **7** neutral **8** abstract, detached, negative, unbiased **9** apathetic, colorless, impartial, incurious, withdrawn **10** impersonal, poker-faced **11** indifferent, unconcerned, unpassioned

disjoin **4** part **5** sever **6** divide, sunder, unglue, unlink **7** break up, divorce, unstick **8** separate

disjoint **4** part **5** sever, upset **6** divide, luxate, mess up, muddle, sunder **7** break up, rummage **8** disorder, separate **9** uncombine

disjointed **7** muddled **8** inchoate **10** incoherent, incohesive **11** unconnected, unorganized **12** uncontinuous

disk **4** chip, puck **5** wafer **6** record *metal:* **4** slug *ornamental:* **6** bangle, sequin

dislike **4** hate **6** detest, hatred, resent **8** aversion, distaste **9** prejudice **10** repugnance **11** deprecation, detestation **13** indisposition *object of:* **8** anathema

disliking **8** aversion **13** indisposition

dislimb **4** maim **6** mayhem **7** cripple **8** mutilate

dislimn **3** dim **5** bedim, cloud, gloom **6** darken **7** becloud, obscure **8** overcast **9** adumbrate, obfuscate

dislocate **4** move, ship **5** mix up, shift **6** jumble, remove **7** rummage **8** disorder, transfer

dislodge **5** expel **6** remove **8** drive out

disloyal **5** false **6** untrue **8** recreant **9** alienated, estranged, faithless **10** perfidious, traitorous, unfaithful **11** treacherous

disloyalty **7** falsity, perfidy, treason

9 falseness, treachery 10 infidelity
13 faithlessness

dismal 5 black, bleak 6 dreary, gloomy,
somber 8 funereal 10 depressing, depressive, oppressive 13 disheartening

dismantle 4 bare, lift, raze, ruin, undo
5 annul, strip, wrack, wreck 6 denude,
divest, recall, repeal, revoke 7 deprive,
destroy, rescind, reverse, strip of, unbuild,
uncloak 8 bankrupt, decimate, demolish,
denudate, dismount, take down, wear
down 10 annihilate, do away with

dismay 4 faze, fear 5 abash, alarm, appal,
daunt, dread, panic, scare, shake, upset
6 appall, bother, flurry, fright, horror, puzzle,
rattle, subdue, terror 7 agitate, fluster, horrify, mystify, nonplus, perplex, perturb, terrify, unhinge 8 affright, bewilder, confound,
frighten 9 dumbfound, embarrass 10 discompose 11 consternate, trepidation
12 perturbation 13 consternation

dismayed 5 agape, fazed 6 aghast 7 rat-
tled, shocked 10 confounded 11 dumbfounded, overwhelmed 13 thunderstruck

dismember 4 maim, part 5 sever 6 mangle, mayhem, sunder 7 cripple 8 dismount,
mutilate, separate, take down

dismiss 2 ax 3 can, out 4 cast, drop, fire,
sack, shed 5 chase, chuck, eject, evict, let
go, scoff, scorn, spurn 6 bounce, depose,
lay off, let out, refuse, reject, remove, retire,
slough, unseat 7 boot out, cashier, contemn, decline, divorce, extrude, kick out,
kiss off, put away, suspend, turn off 8 furlough, pooh-pooh, ridicule, throw out, turn
away, turn down 9 reprobate, repudiate,
terminate

dismissal 5 congé 6 layoff, ouster
7 removal 8 brushoff

dismount 6 alight, detach, get off
7 unhorse 8 separate, take down 10 alight
from

Disney 4 Walt 10 cartoonist *character:*
4 Huey 5 Daisy, Dewey, Dumbo, Goofy,
Louie, Pluto 6 Donald, Mickey, Minnie *classic:* 8 Fantasia

disobedient 6 unruly 7 naughty, willful
8 contrary 10 headstrong, rebellious
12 contumacious, obstreperous, recalcitrant 13 insubordinate

disoblige 6 offend, put out 7 affront, trouble 8 put about 9 incommode
13 inconvenience

disorder 3 ill 4 riot, turn 5 chaos, mix up,
snarl, upset 6 anomie, ataxia, huddle, jumble, malady, mess up, muddle, muss up,
rumple, sicken, tumble, tumult 7 ailment,
anarchy, clutter, confuse, derange, disease,
embroil, illness, misdeed, misrule, rummage,
shuffle, turmoil, unhinge 8 disjoint, sickness, syndrome, unhealth, unsettle,

upheaval 9 affection, agitation, anarchism,
commotion, complaint, condition, confusion,
infirmity 10 affliction, convulsion, misconduct, turbulence 11 bedevilment, misdemeanor 13 indisposition *mental:*
8 paranoia

disordered 4 daft 5 crazy 6 crazed,
insane 7 cracked, lunatic, muddled
8 demented, deranged, inchoate 9 bedlamite 10 incoherent, incohesive 11 unconnected, unorganized 12 uncontinuous

disorderly 5 rowdy 6 unruly 7 raucous
8 rowdyish 9 termagant, turbulent 10 boisterous, rowdydowdy, tumultuous
11 rumbustious

disorderly house 6 bagnio 7 brothel
8 bordello

disorganize 5 upset 6 jumble, mess up
7 derange 8 unsettle

disoriented 4 lost

disown 4 deny 8 disclaim, renounce
9 repudiate

disparage 5 abuse, chill, decry 6 deject,
slight 7 downcry, run down 8 bad mouth,
belittle, derogate, minimize, write off
10 demoralize, depreciate 11 detract from

disparagement 4 tale 5 scorn 7 calumny, despite, scandal, slander 8 contempt, despisal 9 aspersion, indignity, stricture 10 backbiting, defamation, detraction,
diminution, reflection 11 despisement
12 backstabbing, belittlement, depreciation
13 animadversion

disparate 6 unlike 7 diverse, unalike,
unequal, various 9 different, divergent, unsimilar 11 inconsonant 12 incompatible,
inconsistent

disparity 8 alterity 9 otherness 10 difference, divergence, divergency, inequality,
unevenness, unlikeness

dispassionate 4 calm, cool, fair, just,
open 5 aloof, equal, frank 7 neutral
8 abstract, composed, detached, judicial,
unbiased 9 colorless, equitable, impartial,
uncolored, unruffled 10 aboveboard, impersonal, poker-faced 11 indifferent, unflappable 12 uninfluenced, unprejudiced
13 imperturbable

dispatch 4 kill, send, ship, slay 5 eat up,
haste, hurry, remit, route, scrag, speed
6 cut off, devour, finish, hasten, hustle, lay
low, rustle 7 address, consign, destroy, forward, killing, message, put away, quicken,
take off 8 alacrity, carry off, celerity, get rid
of, goodwill, riddance, shipment, transmit
9 diligence, polish off, readiness, swiftness
10 expedition, put to death, speediness
11 promptitude

dispatch boat 5 aviso 6 packet

dispel 4 oust 5 eject 7 crumble, scatter
9 clear away, drive away

dispensable 5 minor **7** trivial **8** needless, unneeded **9** redundant **10** unrequired **11** superfluous, unessential, unimportant, unnecessary **12** nonessential

dispensary 6 clinic

dispensation 5 favor **7** service **8** courtesy, kindness, ordering **9** remission **10** indulgence, management

dispense 3 ply **4** deal, give, hand **5** spare, swing, wield **6** divide, excuse, exempt, handle, let off, let out, supply **7** absolve, deal out, deliver, dish out, dole out, furnish, mete out, portion, prorate, provide, release, relieve **8** deal with, hand over, maneuver, share out, transfer, turn over **9** apportion, discharge, partition **10** administer, distribute, manipulate, measure out, portion out

disperse 3 sow **4** deal **5** spray, strew **6** divide, lot out, spread **7** break up, diffuse, disband, disject, dole out, radiate, scatter **9** circulate, partition, propagate **10** distribute, measure out

dispersion 7 colloid **9** spreading **10** scattering *combining form:* **3** lyo

dispirit 5 chill **6** deject **7** depress **10** demoralize, discourage

dispirited 3 low, sad **4** blue, flat **8** cast down, dejected, downcast, lifeless **9** depressed, woebegone **10** melancholy **11** downhearted

dispiriting 5 black, bleak **6** dreary, gloomy **8** funereal **9** cheerless **10** depressing, depressive, oppressing

displace 4 oust **5** exile, expel, shift, usurp **6** banish, cut out, deport, depose, unmake, winkle **7** expulse, uncrown **8** crowd out, dethrone, redirect, relegate, supplant **9** transport **10** expatriate, substitute

displaced person 2 DP **6** émigré **7** evacuee, refugee **8** fugitive

display 4 open, pomp, show **5** array, flash, offer, shine **6** evince, expose, flaunt, lay out, parade, reveal, setout, spread, unfold, unveil **7** exhibit, fanfare, panoply, showing, show off, trot out, uncover **8** blazonry, brandish, describe, evidence, manifest, unclothe **9** showiness, spectacle **10** exhibiting, exhibition, pretension **11** demonstrate, ostentation **13** demonstration, manifestation

displeasing 3 bad **4** sour **6** rotten, vexing **7** irksome, unhappy **8** annoying **10** bothersome, unpleasant

displeasure 4 pain **5** anger **6** sorrow **8** aversion, vexation **10** uneasiness **11** indignation, unhappiness **13** indisposition

disport 3 act, fun **4** bear, game, go on, play, show **5** amuse, carry, flash **6** acquit,

behave, demean, divert, expose, flaunt, parade **7** conduct, exhibit, jollity, pastime, show off, trot out **8** brandish, recreate **9** diversion, entertain, merriment **10** recreation

disposal 5 order **7** dumping, junking **8** bestowal, chucking, jettison, ordering, riddance, sequence **9** clearance, scrapping **10** demolition, destroying, relegation **11** arrangement, demolishing, destruction **12** throwing away, transference

dispose 4 bend, bias **5** array, order **7** arrange, incline, marshal, prepare **8** organize **9** make ready, methodize **11** systematize *of:* **4** sell **5** scrap **6** finish, handle **7** destroy, discard

disposed 4 fain **5** prone, ready **6** minded **7** willing **8** inclined

disposition 4 bent, cast, mood, tone, type, vein **5** being, humor, order, stamp, tenor **6** makeup, nature, temper **7** control, dumping, junking, leaning **8** jettison, ordering, penchant, riddance, sequence, tendency **9** character, direction, inclining, scrapping **10** complexion, management, proclivity, propensity **11** arrangement, controlling, inclination, personality, temperament **12** predilection, throwing away **13** individualism, individuality *favorable:* **8** optimism *unfavorable:* **9** pessimism

dispossess 3 rob **4** lose, oust **5** eject **6** banish, divest **7** bereave, deprive

dispossession 4 loss **6** ouster **9** privation **11** deprivation, deprivement, divestiture

dispraise 5 decry **8** belittle, derogate, diminish, minimize **10** depreciate **11** detract from, opprobriate **12** depreciation

disproportion 8 imparity, mismatch **10** inequality, unevenness

disproportionate 6 uneven **7** unequal **8** lopsided **9** irregular **10** asymmetric, off-balance, unbalanced **12** overbalanced **13** unsymmetrical

disprove 5 break, evert, rebut, shoot **6** blow up, impugn, refute **7** confute, explode **8** confound, negative, overturn, puncture, traverse **9** discredit, overthrow **10** contravene, controvert

disputable 4 moot **7** dubious **8** doubtful **9** uncertain **11** problematic

disputation 6 debate **7** mooting **8** forensic **9** dialectic **11** controversy

dispute 4 buck, duel, miff, moot, tiff **5** argue, doubt, fight, rebut, repel **6** argufy, bicker, combat, debate, hassle, oppose, refute, resist, rumpus, strife **7** agitate, canvass, confute, contend, contest, discuss, quarrel, quibble, wrangle **8** argument, conflict, mistrust, question, squabble, traverse **9** bickering, challenge, thrash out, withstand **10** contention, controvert, falling-out, toss around **11** altercation, controversy, embroilment *Scottish:* **6** threap, threep

disqualified 5 unfit **8** unfitted **9** incapable **10** ineligible, unequipped **11** incompetent

disqualify 3 bar **5** debar **6** except **7** exclude, rule out, suspend **9** deprive of, eliminate, make unfit **12** incapacitate *as judge:* **6** recuse

disquiet 4 care **5** upset, worry **6** bother, flurry, unease, unrest, untune **7** agitate, ailment, anxiety, concern, ferment, fluster, perturb, trouble, turmoil, unhinge **10** discompose, solicitude, uneasiness **11** concernment, restiveness **12** restlessness **13** Sturm und Drang

disquietude 4 care **5** worry **6** unease, unrest **7** ailment, anxiety, concern, ferment, turmoil **9** agitation **10** uneasiness **11** concernment, restiveness **12** restlessness **13** Sturm und Drang

Disraeli, Benjamin *novel:* **7** Tancred

disregard 4 fail, omit **6** apathy, forget, ignore, slight **7** blink at, neglect **8** ignoring, lethargy, omission, omitting, overlook, overpass **9** blink away, lassitude, slighting, unconcern **10** forgetting, neglecting **11** insouciance, overlooking **12** heedlessness, indifference, listlessness **13** unmindfulness

disregardful 3 lax **5** slack **6** remiss **8** careless, derelict, heedless **9** negligent **10** behindhand, delinquent, neglectful, regardless

disremember 6 forget

disreputable 4 mean **5** cheap, dingy, faded, seedy, shady, sorry **6** abject, scurvy, shabby, shoddy, sordid **7** run-down **8** beggarly, decrepit, pitiable, shameful **10** bedraggled, down-at-heel, inglorious, threadbare **11** dilapidated, ignominious **12** contemptible

disrepute 5 odium, shame **6** infamy **7** obloquy **8** disgrace, ignominy **10** opprobrium

disrespect 8 boldness **9** hardihood, impudence, insolence, insolency **10** incivility **12** impertinence, insolentness

disrespectful 4 rude **7** ill-bred, incivil, uncivil **8** impolite, impudent **10** ungracious **11** ill-mannered, impertinent

disrobe 4 bare **5** strip **6** denude, divest **7** deprive, strip of, undress **8** bankrupt, denudate, unclothe

disrupt 4 hole, open **5** upset **6** breach, mess up, muddle **7** rummage, rupture **8** disorder, unsettle **10** break apart

dissatisfaction 7 dislike **8** aversion **10** uneasiness

dissatisfactory 3 bad **4** poor **5** amiss, wrong **6** rotten

dissatisfied 5 irked, vexed **7** annoyed **8** bothered **9** uncontent **10** malcontent **11** uncontented **12** discontented, malcontented

dissect 3 cut **4** part **5** carve, probe, sever, slice, split **6** cleave, divide, pierce, sunder **7** analyze, break up, resolve **8** separate **9** anatomize, break down, decompose, penetrate **10** decompound **11** dichotomize

dissection *of animals:* **7** zootomy

dissemblance 5 guile **6** deceit **7** cunning **8** alterity **9** duplicity, otherness **10** difference, divergence, divergency, unlikeness

dissemble 4 mask **5** cloak, feign **7** conceal, dress up **8** disguise **10** camouflage

dissembler 8 pharisee, Tartuffe **9** hypocrite, lip server

disseminate 3 sow **5** straw, strew **6** blazon, spread **7** bestrew, declare, diffuse, publish, radiate, scatter, send out **8** announce, permeate, proclaim **9** advertise, broadcast, circulate, propagate, publicize, spread out **9** annunciate, promulgate **11** blaze abroad

dissension 6 strife **7** discord, quarrel, wrangle **8** argument, conflict, variance **9** bickering **10** contention, difference, quarreling **11** altercation, controversy

dissent 3 shy **4** balk, vary **5** demur **6** boggle, differ, divide, heresy, object, schism, strife **7** stickle **8** conflict, variance **9** misbelief **10** contention, difference, heterodoxy **11** unorthodoxy **12** nonagreement **13** nonconformism, nonconformity

dissenter 7 heretic, sectary **10** schismatic, separatist **11** misbeliever, schismatist **13** nonconformist

dissertation 6 memoir, thesis **8** tractate, treatise **9** discourse, monograph, treatment **10** monography

disservice 6 injury **8** mischief

dissever 3 cut **4** part **5** carve, slice, split **6** cleave, divide, sunder **7** divorce **8** separate **11** dichotomize

dissidence 6 heresy, schism, strife **7** discord **9** misbelief **10** contention, heterodoxy **11** unorthodoxy **13** nonconformism, nonconformity

dissident 7 heretic, sectary **9** differing, heretical, heterodox, sectarian **10** schismatic, separatist, unorthodox **11** contentious, misbeliever, quarrelsome, schismatist **12** unharmonious **13** nonconformist

dissimilar 6 unlike **7** diverse, unalike, unequal, various **8** contrary, opposite **9** different, divergent **10** antonymous **12** antithetical **13** contradictory

dissimilarity 8 variance **9** diversity, otherness, severance **10** difference, divergence,

divergency, unlikeness **11** incongruity
12 divarication, inconsonance **13** heterogeneity, inconsistency

dissimulate see **dissemble**

dissimulation 5 guile **6** deceit, hiding
7 cunning, masking **8** cloaking, feigning,
pretense, shamming **9** duplicity, hypocrisy,
secreting **10** catabolism, concealing, pharisaism, pretending, sanctimony
12 camouflaging

dissimulator see **dissembler**

dissipate 4 blow **5** waste **6** vanish
7 consume, crumble, fritter, scatter **8** evanesce, fool away, squander **9** evaporate,
throw away **10** frivol away, trifle away
11 blunder away

dissociate 5 unfix **6** cut off, detach
8 abstract, alienate, estrange, uncouple

dissolute 3 lax **4** fast, wild **5** light, loose,
slack **6** rakish, wanton **7** lawless, raffish,
wayward **9** abandoned, reprobate **10** licentious, profligate **12** unprincipled, unrestrained **13** self-abandoned

dissolution 5 death, decay, sleep
6 demise **7** decease, divorce, passing, quietus, rupture, silence, split-up **8** curtains,
division **10** detachment, profligacy
11 divorcement **combining form: 3** lys
4 lysi, lyso **5** lyses (plural), lysis

dissolvable 7 soluble

dissolve 3 end **4** flux, fuse, melt, ruin,
thaw, undo, void **5** annul, quash, wrack,
wreck **6** recess, unfold, vacate, vanish
7 adjourn, break up, clear up, destroy, disband, immerse, liquefy, resolve, shatter,
unravel **8** abrogate, decimate, decipher,
demolish, destruct, fade away, get rid of,
liquesce, prorogue, separate **9** decompose,
figure out, lose power, prorogate, puzzle
out, terminate, waste away **10** annihilate,
deliquesce, do away with **13** superimposing
suffix: 4 lyse, lyze

dissonance 6 strife **7** discord **8** conflict
9 cacophony **10** contention, difference
11 incongruity

dissonant 4 rude **5** harsh **6** hoarse, rugged **7** grating, jarring, raucous **8** strident
9 immusical, unmixable, unmusical
10 cacophonic, inharmonic **11** cacophonous, conflicting, incongruent, incongruous
12 incompatible, inconsistent, inharmonious

dissuade 5 deter **6** dehort, divert **10** discourage, disincline

distaff 6 female

distance 3 way **4** area, size, ways
5 ambit, orbit, piece, range, reach, route,
scope, space, spell, sweep **6** course,
degree, extent, length, milage, outrun,
radius, spread **7** breadth, compass,
expanse, mileage, outpace, purview,
reserve, spacing, stretch **8** alterity, cold-

ness, interval, outspeed, outstrip **9** amplitude, expansion, extension, otherness
10 difference, divergence, divergency,
remoteness, separation, unlikeness **11** distinction, perspective **12** dissemblance
13 dissimilarity, dissimilitude **angular: 8** latitude **9** longitude **between levels: 4** drop
between rails: 4 gage **between supports:**
4 span **from bottom to top: 6** height **geometric: 8** altitude **greatest perpendicular:**
6 camber **measuring instrument: 8** odograph, odometer **9** pedometer, telemeter
11 range finder **minute: 4** hair **perpendicular: 5** depth **shortest: 7** beeline **12** straight
line **the wind blows: 5** fetch

distant 3 far, shy **4** afar, cold, cool
5 aloof, apart **6** far-off, remote **7** diverse,
faraway, haughty, obscure, removed, spacial, spatial, unalike, unequal, various **8** farflung, isolated, off-lying, outlying, reserved,
retiring, secluded, solitary **9** different, divergent, separated, unsimilar, withdrawn
10 unsociable **11** out-of-the-way, sequestered, standoffish **combining form: 3** tel
4 tele, telo

distaste 7 dislike **8** aversion **9** antipathy,
hostility, revulsion **10** abhorrence, repugnance **13** indisposition

distasteful 4 flat **6** bitter, odious **7** galling, insipid, painful **8** grievous, unsavory
9 loathsome, obnoxious, repellent, repugnant, repulsive, savorless, tasteless
10 abominable, afflictive, detestable, flavorless **11** ill-flavored, unpalatable
12 unappetizing

distemper 4 riot **5** mix up, paint **6** choler,
muddle **7** anarchy, derange, disease, misrule, rummage **8** disorder **9** anarchism,
strangles **10** affliction **11** derangement
13 panleucopenia

distend 5 bloat, swell **6** dilate, expand,
extend **7** amplify, augment, enlarge, inflate
8 increase, lengthen **10** stretch out

distill 4 drib, drip, drop, weep **6** infuse,
purify **7** dribble, trickle **11** concentrate

distillation apparatus 5 still **7** alembic,
limbeck

distinct 4 sole **5** clear, lucid, plain **6** patent, single **7** defined, diverse, evident,
express, notable, obvious, special, unusual,
various **8** apparent, clear-cut, definite,
especial, explicit, manifest, palpable, peculiar, separate, specific **9** different, divergent **10** individual, particular, prescribed
11 categorical, perspicuous, unambiguous,
unequivocal **combining form: 4** idio
5 chori **7** chorist **8** choristo

distinction 4 bays, rank **5** award, badge,
class, grade, honor, kudos **6** nicety,
renown **7** laurels **8** accolade, alterity, eminence, prestige **9** otherness **10** difference,

divergence, divergency, prominence, prominency, unlikeness **11** differentia, preeminence **12** significance **13** dissimilarity

distinctive 6 proper, single, unique **8** peculiar, separate **9** diacritic **10** diagnostic, individual **11** outstanding **13** idiosyncratic

distingué 6 urbane **7** genteel, refined **8** cultured, polished, well-bred **10** cultivated

distinguish 3 see **4** know, mark, note, part, spot, view **5** erect, exalt, honor, place **6** descry, finger, notice, remark, set off **7** dignify, ennoble, glorify, magnify, mark off, observe, pick out, qualify, sublime **8** diagnose, identify, perceive, pinpoint, separate **9** demarcate, extricate, recognize, signalize, single out **10** aggrandize, difference **11** determinate, individuate, singularize **12** characterize **13** diagnosticate, differentiate, individualize

distinguished 5 famed, grand, great **6** famous **7** courtly, eminent, notable, stately **8** imposing, renowned **9** dignified, prominent **10** celebrated, celebrious **11** illustrious

distort 4 bend, warp, wind **5** alter, belie, color, curve, twist, wrest **6** change, deform, garble **7** falsify, pervert, torture **8** miscolor, misshape, misstate **11** misconstrue **12** misinterpret, misrepresent

distortion 8 misshape **9** deformity

distract 5 addle, craze, mix up **6** ball up, frenzy, fuddle, harass, madden **7** confuse, derange, fluster, unhinge **8** befuddle, bewilder, confound, throw off **9** unbalance

distraction 6 lunacy **7** madness **8** insanity **9** amusement, diversion, unbalance **10** insaneness, perplexity **11** derangement, psychopathy **13** entertainment

distrait 4 lost **5** upset **6** absent **7** bemused, faraway, worried **8** harassed, troubled **9** tormented **10** abstracted **11** inattentive, inconscient, preoccupied **12** absentminded

distraught 3 mad **4** daft, nuts **5** crazy, upset **6** addled, crazed, insane **7** cracked, frantic, muddled, worried **8** agitated, confused, demented, deranged, harassed, troubled **9** flustered, perturbed, tormented **10** bewildered, nonplussed

distress 3 ail, irk, try, woe **4** ache, cark, hurt, need, pain, pang, pass, rack **5** agony, annoy, cross, dolor, grief, harry, pinch, rigor, throe, trial, upset, weigh, worry **6** bother, grieve, harass, injure, misery, pester, plague, sorrow, strain, strait, stress, twinge **7** afflict, anguish, exhaust, passion, torment, torture, trouble **8** aggrieve, calamity, exigency, hardship **9** adversity, constrain, suffering **10** affliction, difficulty, heartbreak, misfortune, visitation **11** tribulation, vicissi-

tude *call:* **6** Mayday *signal:* **3** SOS **5** alarm

distressing 4 dire **6** woeful **8** grievous, poignant **10** afflictive, calamitous, deplorable, lamentable **11** regrettable, unfortunate **13** heartbreaking

distribute 3 lot **4** deal, give, mete **5** allot, place, strew **6** assign, assort, bestow, divide, donate, lot out, parcel, ration, spread **7** deal out, deliver, diffuse, dole out, dribble, give out, mete out, portion, present, prorate, radiate, scatter **8** allocate, classify, dispense, position, separate **9** apportion, circulate, partition, propagate, spread out **10** administer, measure out *in a tournament:* **4** seed

distribution 5 order **7** density **8** ordering, sequence **9** allotment, placement **10** scattering **11** arrangement, probability **12** spreading out **13** apportionment

distributor 6 jobber **7** carrier **10** wholesaler

district 4 area **5** tract **6** barrio, parcel, region, sector **7** quarter, section **8** division, locality, precinct, vicinage, vicinity **11** subdivision **12** neighborhood *ecclesiastical:* **5** synod **6** parish **7** diocese *Greek:* **4** deme *Indian:* **6** tahsil *judicial:* **7** circuit *London:* **4** Soho *theater:* **6** rialto *Turkish administrative:* **6** sanjak

distrust 5 doubt **7** suspect **8** wariness **9** suspicion **10** disbelieve

distrustful 4 wary **7** jealous **10** suspicious

distrusting 7 cynical **9** sceptical, skeptical **10** suspicious

disturb 4 faze, move, ship **5** alarm, fease, feaze, feeze, rouse, scare, shift, unset, upset **6** bother, damage, flurry, jumble, meddle, mess up, puzzle, remove, stir up, tamper **7** agitate, break up, derange, destroy, fluster, inquiet, perplex, replace, terrify, trouble, unhinge **8** bewilder, disorder, frighten, transfer, unsettle **9** incommode, interfere **11** intermeddle **13** inconvenience, interfere with

disturbance 6 rumpus, unrest **7** bobbery, cyclone, tornado, unquiet **9** agitating, agitation, commotion, variation **10** alteration **11** derangement **12** diastrophism, interruption *atmospheric:* **5** storm *emotional:* **8** neuroses (plural), neurosis *mental:* **6** frenzy **7** phrensy **8** delirium *oceanic:* **7** tsunami

disunify see **disunite**

disunion 6 strife **7** divorce, rupture, split-up **8** conflict, division, variance **9** partition **10** contention, detachment, difference, separation **11** divorcement

disunite 4 part, wean **5** alien **6** divide, sunder **7** break up, divorce, split up **8** alienate, estrange, separate **9** fall apart, uncombine **11** dichotomize

disunity 6 strife **7** discord **8** conflict, variance **10** alienation, contention, difference

ditch 3 cut, dig, pit **4** cast, foss, junk **5** chuck, fosse, scrap **6** reject, sheuch, sheugh, trench, trough **7** abandon, cashier, discard, dismiss, foxhole **8** jettison, throw out **9** throw away **10** excavation

dither 3 gab, jaw, yak **4** chat, flap, halt, stew **5** clack, jumps, quake, run on, shake, waver **6** babble, cackle, falter, quaver, shakes, shiver, tremor, tumult **7** jitters, shivers, shudder, stagger, tremble, turmoil, twitter, whiffle, willies **8** hesitate **9** agitation, commotion, confusion, vacillate, whimwhams **10** turbulence **12** shilly-shally, wiggle-waggle **13** heebie-jeebies

dithyramb 4 hymn, poem **5** chant

dithyrambic 4 wild **5** fiery **6** ardent, fervid, torrid **7** burning, fervent, flaming **9** perfervid, rhapsodic **10** boisterous, passionate **11** impassioned

ditto 4 copy **6** carbon, repeat **7** replica **9** duplicate, facsimile **10** carbon copy **11** replication **12** reproduction **13** reduplication

ditty 3 lay **4** aria, hymn, lied, song **7** descant

diurnal 5 daily **9** circadian, ephemeral, quotidian

divagate 5 stray **6** depart, ramble, wander **7** digress, diverge, excurse

divan 4 sofa **5** couch **7** council **9** davenport **11** smoking room

diva's solo 4 aria

dive 3 bar, pub **4** dash, dump, hole, jump, leap **5** joint, lunge, pitch **6** gainer, lounge, plunge, saloon, tavern **7** barroom, decline, descend, descent, hangout, taproom **8** submerge **9** belly-flop, honky-tonk, jackknife, roadhouse **10** cannonball, submerging **position: 4** pike, tuck **8** straight

diver 4 loon **combining form: 4** dyta **5** dytes

diverge 4 part, vary **5** stray **6** depart, differ, ramble, swerve, wander **7** deflect, deviate, digress, excurse **8** disagree, separate **9** draw apart

divergence 7 parting, turning, variety, varying **8** alterity **9** departure, deviation, differing, otherness **10** aberration, deflection, difference, digression, separation, unlikeness **11** disagreeing, discrepancy, distinction **12** disagreement, dissemblance **13** dissimilarity, dissimilitude

divergent 6 off-key, radial, unlike **7** deviant, distant, unalike, unequal, various **8** aberrant, abnormal, atypical, contrary, opposite **9** anomalous, different, differing, disparate, irregular, radiating, spreading, unnatural, unregular, unsimilar **10** dissimilar **12** antithetical **13** contradictory

divers 4 many, some **6** sundry **7** several, various **combining form: 4** poly, vari **5** parti, party, vario

diver's disease 5 bends **12** aeroembolism

diverse 6 unlike **7** distant, several, unalike, unequal, various **8** contrary, discrete, distinct, manifold, opposite, separate **9** different, differing, disparate, multifold, multiform, multiplex, unsimilar **10** contrasted, dissimilar **11** contrasting, contrastive **12** multifarious **13** contradictory **meanings: 8** polysemy

diversion 3 fun **4** play **5** sport **6** levity, relish **7** disport, turning **8** pleasure, sideshow **9** amusement, departure, deviation, enjoyment, frivolity **10** aberration, deflection, recreation **11** delectation, distraction **13** entertainment

diversity 7 variety **8** multeity **10** difference, unlikeness **11** distinction, variousness **12** multiformity, multiplicity **13** dissimilarity

divert 4 turn, veer **5** alter, amuse, deter **6** swerve **7** deflect, deviate, digress **8** dissuade, distract **9** disadvise, disengage, entertain, turn aside **10** discourage **water: 5** flume

divest 3 rob **4** bare, lose, oust **5** spoil, strip **6** denude **7** bereave, deprive, disrobe, undress **8** bankrupt, denudate, take away **9** dismantle **10** disinherit, dispossess

divide 3 cut **4** chop, deal, fork, part, vary **5** allot, carve, halve, quota, sever, share **6** assign, cleave, differ, lot out, parcel, ration, sector, sunder **7** break up, comport, discord, disjoin, dissect, dissent, divorce, dole out, furcate, portion, prorate, quarter, section, segment, share in, split up **8** allocate, classify, disagree, disburse, disjoint, dispense, disperse, disunite, fraction, graduate, separate **9** apportion, branch out, disaccord, partition, watershed **10** distribute, measure out **11** dichotomize, distinguish **into four parts: 7** quarter **into three parts: 7** trisect **into two parts: 5** halve **6** bisect **9** bifurcate

divided 6 cloven **7** partite **8** multifid **9** disunited, separated **combining form: 3** fid **4** sect **5** fissi, schiz **6** fidate, schizo, tomous **7** chorist **8** choristo

dividend 4 meed, plum **5** bonus, prize **6** carrot, return, reward **7** guerdon, premium

divider 6 bunton **7** compass **9** partition

divination 6 augury **7** insight **8** prophecy **by communication with the dead: 10** necromancy **by dreams: 11** oneiromancy **by figures: 8** geomancy **by lots: 9** sortilege

by numbers: 10 numerology **by rods:** 7 dowsing 11 rhabdomancy **by stars:** 9 astrology **combining form:** 5 mancy

divine 4 holy 5 clerk, godly, infer 6 cleric, deific, parson, priest, sacred 7 foresee, godlike, preknow, previse, suppose 8 clerical, discover, forefeel, foreknow, minister, preacher, prophesy, reverend 9 apprehend, chthonian, churchman, clergyman, marvelous, prevision, religious, visualize 10 anticipate, conjecture, superhuman, theologian 12 ecclesiastic, extramundane, transmundane 13 superphysical

Divine Comedy author 5 Dante

divining ability, for short 3 ESP

divinity 3 god 5 deity 7 godhead 8 theology **female:** 5 nymph 7 goddess

division 3 cut 4 part, unit 5 class, piece 6 member, moiety, parcel, schism 7 discord, dissent, divorce, parting, portion, rupture, section, segment, split-up 8 category, conflict, district, disunion, disunity, variance 9 disaccord, partition 10 detachment, difference, disharmony, dissidence, dissonance, separation 11 dissolution, divorcement 12 disagreement 13 apportionment **Bible:** 5 verse **book:** 7 chapter **British territorial:** 5 shire **building:** 4 wing **cell:** 7 meiosis, mitosis **city:** 4 ward 7 borough 8 precinct **combining form:** 7 kineses (plural), kinesis **contest:** 4 heat 6 inning, period **corolla:** 5 petal **country:** 5 state 6 canton 8 province 10 department, prefecture **family:** 4 side 6 branch **geologic time:** 5 epoch 6 period **hospital:** 4 ward, wing **into two:** 9 bisection 11 bifurcation, bipartition **mankind:** 4 race **meal:** 6 course **music:** 3 bar 4 line 7 measure 8 movement **opera, play:** 3 act 5 scene **poem:** 5 canto, verse 6 stanza **population:** 7 segment, stratum **race:** 3 lap 4 heat **social:** 5 caste, class, tribe **Soviet territorial:** 6 oblast 8 republic **state:** 6 county, parish **term:** 7 quotient **time:** 3 day, eon 4 week, year 5 month 6 decade, minute, moment, second 7 weekend 9 fortnight **tribal:** 4 clan **word:** 8 syllable **zodiac:** 4 sign

divisive 8 factious

divorce 4 part 5 annul, sever, split 6 cancel, sunder 7 break up, disjoin, dismiss, put away, rupture, split-up, unmarry 8 disjoint, dissever, disunion, disunite, separate 9 disaffect, partition 10 detachment, separation 11 dissolution

divot 4 turf

divulge 4 tell 5 mouth, spill 6 betray, gossip, reveal, tattle 7 blab out 8 disclose, discover, give away, proclaim 13 spill the beans

"Dixie" composer 6 Emmett

____ dixit 4 ipse

dizziness 7 vertigo

dizzy 4 daze 5 addle, dazed, giddy, inane, light, mix up, silly, undue 6 addled, ball up, fuddle, muddle, swimmy 7 asinine, confuse, dazzled, extreme, fatuous, flighty, fluster, foolish, fuddled, muddled, puzzled, reeling, stupefy 8 befuddle, bewilder, confused, heedless, skittish, swimming, throw off, towering, whirling 9 befuddled, confusing, excessive, frivolous 10 bewildered, bird-witted, confounded, distracted, exorbitant, immoderate, inordinate 11 empty-headed, extravagant, harebrained, light-headed, vertiginous 12 unmeasurable

DNA **component:** 7 adenine, guanine, thymine 8 cytosine 10 nucleotide 11 deoxyribose **segment:** 7 cistron

do 3 act, end, gyp, pay, put, set 4 bear, beat, bilk, cook, fare, feel, go on, halt, play, quit, show, suit, tire, tour, wash, work 5 break, cheat, clean, close, cover, cozen, enact, exert, get by, get on, occur, serve, shift, tonic, track 6 acquit, befall, behave, betide, chance, chouse, commit, demean, deport, diddle, effect, finish, happen, manage, render, travel, wind up, work at, wrap up 7 achieve, approve, arrange, come off, comport, conduct, defraud, develop, execute, exhaust, fall out, furbish, perform, playact, suffice, undergo, wear out 8 carry out, complete, conclude, decorate, flimflam, get along, pass over, traverse 9 determine, discourse, overreach, personate, stagger on, terminate, transpire 11 impersonate 12 stagger along 13 muddle through **away with:** 5 abate 6 banish 7 abolish 8 demolish, dissolve **without:** 5 forgo 6 forego **wrong:** 3 err

doable 8 feasible, possible

docent 7 teacher 8 lecturer, teaching 10 instructor 11 instructive

docile 4 tame 5 tawie 6 pliant 7 pliable 8 amenable, biddable, obedient 9 adaptable, teachable, tractable 10 submissive

dock 4 pier, quay, rump, slip 5 berth, jetty, levee, wharf 6 hangar, lessen, marina, reduce 7 abridge 8 platform **worker:** 6 lumper 9 stevedore 12 longshoreman

docket 4 card, sked 6 agenda 7 program 8 calendar, schedule 9 timetable

doctor 2 MD 3 fix, vet 4 load, mend 5 medic, patch, treat 6 breeze, debase, dope up, medico, repair, revamp 7 dentist, medical, rebuild, scholar, surgeon 8 overhaul 9 clinician, internist, mediciner, physician 10 adulterate, specialist 11 medicine man, recondition, reconstruct **animal:** 3 vet 12 veterinarian **children's:** 12 pediatrician **famous baby care:** 5 Spock **foot:** 10 podiatrist 11 chiropodist **heart:** 12 cardiologist *slang:* 8 sawbones *teeth:* 7 dentist *women's:* 12 gynecologist

Doctor of the Church 5 Basil 6 Jerome 7 Ambrose, Gregory 9 Augustine 10 Athanasius

doctrinaire 6 dogged, mulish 8 dogmatic, stubborn 9 dictative, obstinate, pigheaded 10 bullheaded 11 dictatorial, magisterial, stiff-necked 12 pertinacious 13 authoritarian, authoritative

doctrine 3 ism 4 doxy 5 axiom, basic, canon, dogma, doxie, tenet 7 plenism 8 teaching 9 principle 11 fundamental, instruction *combining form:* 4 logy 5 logia *legal:* 6 cypres *occult:* 6 cabala, kabala 7 cabbala, kabbala 8 cabbalah, kabbalah *philosophical:* 8 monadism, vitalism *religious:* 8 chiliasm *suffix:* 3 ism

document 5 paper 6 record 8 evidence, monument 9 testimony 11 certificate *travel:* 8 passport

Dodavah's son 7 Eliezer

dodder 8 love vine

doddering 6 doting, senile

dodge 4 duck, jouk, slip 5 avoid, elude, evade, fence, parry, shirk, skirt, slide 6 escape, scheme, weasel 7 evasion, shuffle 8 malinger, sidestep 9 avoidance, expedient, pussyfoot 10 equivocate, tergiverse 12 short circuit, tergiversate

dodger 7 haggler 8 circular, handbill 9 throwaway

Dodger 5 Davis (Tommy) 6 Garvey (Steve), Koufax (Sandy), Snider (Duke), Sutton (Don) 8 Newcombe (Don), Robinson (Jackie) 10 Campanella (Roy) *field:* 7 Ebbetts *manager:* 6 Alston (Walter)

dodo 4 boob, dolt 5 dummy, dunce, idiot, moron 6 dimwit, nitwit 8 numskull 9 simpleton

Dodo's son 7 Eleazar, Elhanan

doe 4 deer 6 almond *young:* 3 teg

doer *suffix:* 2 er, or 3 ast, eer, ier, ist 4 ater, ster

doff 5 douse, uncap, unhat 6 remove, unhelm 7 take off

dog 3 cur, pug, pup, tag 4 bird, chap, chow, fice, mutt, peke, puli, stop, tail, tyke 5 boxer, click, feist, frank, hound, lemon, pooch, puppy, spitz, trail 6 Afghan, bawtie, bowwow, briard, canine, collie, detent, poodle, rascal, saluki, shadow, wiener, wretch 7 andiron, Maltese, mastiff, mongrel, pointer, Samoyed, spaniel, terrier, whippet 8 Airedale, inferior, keeshond, papillon, Pekinese, pinscher, spurious, wirehair 9 Chihuahua, dachshund, Dalmation, Great Dane, greyhound, Pekingese, retriever, schnauzer 10 bloodhound, Pomeranian, Weimaraner 11 frankfurter, wienerwurst 12 Newfoundland, Saint Bernard 13 cocker

spaniel *Alaskan:* 8 malamute, malemiut, malemute *Australian:* 5 dingo 8 warragal, warrigal *barkless:* 7 basenji *combining form:* 3 cyn 4 cyno *Eskimo:* 5 husky *family:* 7 Canidae *FDR's:* 4 Fala *fictional:* 4 Lady 5 Astro, Pluto 6 Big Red 8 McBarker *genus:* 5 Canis *Hungarian:* 6 vizsla *hunting:* 4 alan 5 alant, hound 6 alaunt, beagle, borzoi, saluki, setter 7 harrier, pointer, redbone 8 elkhound, foxhound 9 wolfhound 10 bloodhound 11 basset hound *Indian:* 5 dhole *long-bodied:* 9 dachshund *movie:* 4 Asta, Toto 5 Benji 9 Old Yeller, Rin Tin Tin *name:* 4 Fido, Spot 5 Rover 6 Bowser *of Hades:* 8 Cerberus *Orphan Annie's:* 5 Sandy *powerful:* 11 bull mastiff *Russian:* 6 borzoi 7 Samoyed *shaggy-coated:* 8 komondor *short-legged:* 5 corgi *small:* 3 pom, pug, pup 4 alco, peke 7 whiffet 8 Pekinese 9 Chihuahua, Pekingese 10 Pomeranian *space traveler:* 5 Laika *television:* 5 Tramp 9 Lassie 9 Rin Tin Tin *terrier:* 7 scottie *three-headed:* 8 Cerberus *tiny:* 9 Chihuahua *tooth:* 4 fang *tracking:* 10 bloodhound *two-headed:* 6 Orthos *Welsh:* 5 corgi *young:* 3 pup 5 puppy, whelp

dogbane 10 bitterroot

dog days 8 canicule

dogfall 3 tie 4 draw 8 deadlock, standoff 9 stalemate

dogfight 3 row 4 fray 5 brawl, broil, melee, set-to 6 fracas 7 ruction 10 donnybrook, free-for-all

dogfish 6 bowfin, burbot 8 mud puppy *genus:* 7 Squalus

dogged 5 rigid 7 adamant 8 obdurate 9 insistent, steadfast, unbending 10 brassbound, inexorable, inflexible, persistent, persisting, persistive, relentless, unshakable 11 perseverant, persevering, unremitting 12 single-minded 13 perseverative

doggone 4 damn, darn, rank 5 utter 6 damned 7 blasted, blessed, dratted 8 absolute, infernal, outright 9 dad-burned, out-and-out 10 confounded 11 unmitigated 13 blankety-blank

dogma 5 canon, credo, creed, tenet 6 belief 8 doctrine 10 conviction, persuasion

dogmatic 7 a priori 8 reasoned 9 deducible, deductive, derivable, dictative, doctrinal 11 dictatorial, doctrinaire, magisterial 13 authoritarian, authoritative

dog-paddle 4 swim

dog's age 3 eon 4 aeon, long 8 blue moon, eternity 12 donkey's years

Dog Star 6 Sirius

dogwood 5 sumac 6 cornel 8 red osier 9 boobyalla 11 native broom

do in 4 ruin, slay **5** wreck **6** finish, murder **7** execute, exhaust, frazzle, outtire, outwear, put away, wear out **8** bankrupt, knock off, knock out **9** liquidate, prostrate, shipwreck **10** dilapidate **11** assassinate

doing 3 act **6** action *combining form:* **6** praxes (plural), praxia, praxis *good:* **10** beneficent *suffix:* **3** ant, ent

doit 3 bit, jot **4** damn, dram, drop, hoot, iota, whit **5** whoop **6** trifle **8** particle

doldrums 4 yawn **5** blues, dumps, ennui, gloom, slump **6** apathy, tedium **7** boredom, latency **8** abeyance, abeyancy, dormancy **9** dejection **10** depression, inactivity, quiescence, quiescency, stagnation **12** indifference, listlessness

doleful 4 down **7** piteous, pitiful, ruthful **8** cast down, dejected, downcast, grieving, mournful, mourning, wretched **9** afflicted, cheerless, depressed, miserable, plaintive, sorrowful, sorrowing, woebegone **10** dispirited, lamentable, lugubrious, melancholy **11** crestfallen, downhearted **12** disconsolate

dole out 4 deal, mete **6** divide, parcel, ration **7** mete out **8** disburse, dispense, disperse, share out **9** apportion, partition **10** administer, distribute

doll 3 Ken **6** Barbie, figure, Kewpie, puppet **10** Betsy Wetsy, Raggedy Ann **11** Raggedy Andy *grotesque:* **8** golliwog

dollar 4 bill, buck, oner **8** simoleon

dollop 3 nip, tot **4** dram, drop, jolt, shot, slug **5** snort **7** snifter **8** toothful

Doll's House, A *author:* **5** Ibsen *heroine:* **4** Nora

dolly 4 cart **5** truck **7** stirrer

dolomite 6 marble **9** limestone **10** bitter spar

dolor 5 agony **6** misery, sorrow **7** anguish, passion **8** distress **9** suffering

dolorous 4 dire **6** rueful, woeful **7** ruthful **8** grievous, mournful, wretched **9** afflicted, miserable, plaintive, sorrowful **10** afflictive, calamitous, deplorable, lamentable, lugubrious, melancholy **11** distressing, regrettable **13** heartbreaking

dolphin 5 whale **7** bollard **8** porpoise **9** butterfly *combining form:* **7** delphis

dolt 3 ass, oaf **4** boob, clod, goof **5** booby, chump, dunce **7** dullard, fathead, jughead, saphead, schnook **8** dumnkopf, lunkhead, meathead, numskull **9** blockhead *Scottish:* **4** coof

doltish 4 dull, dumb **5** dense, thick **6** stupid **8** blockish, duncical **9** fatheaded **11** blockheaded **12** beetleheaded

domain 4 walk **5** field, realm **6** sphere **7** demesne, terrain **8** dominion, province **9** bailiwick, champaign, territory *nether:*

4 hell *transcendent:* **6** heaven *Turkish:* **6** beylic, beylik

dome 4 roof **7** ceiling **12** snap fastener

domed hut 5 igloo

Domesday Book money 4 oras

domestic 4 home, tame **6** family, native **7** subdued **8** internal, national **9** household, municipal **10** indigenous, submissive

domesticate 4 tame **5** adopt, train **6** master, subdue **10** housebreak, naturalize **11** familiarize

domicile 3 hut **4** home **5** abode, board, house, lodge, put up **6** bestow, billet, harbor **7** quarter **8** dwelling **9** entertain, residence, residency **10** commorancy, habitation

domiciliate 3 hut **4** bunk, tame **5** board, house, lodge, put up **6** billet, harbor, master, reside **7** quarter

dominance 9 masterdom, supremacy **10** ascendancy, prepotence, prepotency **11** preeminence, sovereignty

dominant 4 main **5** chief, first, major **6** master, ruling **7** capital, leading, regnant, stellar, supreme **8** foremost **9** ascendant, governing, number one, paramount, prevalent, principal, sovereign **10** preeminent, prevailing, surpassing **11** outweighing, overbearing **12** overweighing, preponderant, transcendent **13** overbalancing

dominate 4 rule **5** reign **6** direct, govern, handle, manage, obsess **7** control, overtop, prevail, repress **8** domineer, look down, overarch, overlook, override **9** tower over **10** tower above *at home:* **12** wear the pants

domination 4 sway **5** might, power **7** command, control, mastery, strings **9** authority, masterdom, supremacy **10** ascendancy, prepotence, prepotency, suzerainty **11** preeminence, sovereignty **13** preponderancy

dominator 4 boss, cock, head **5** chief, ruler **6** honcho, leader, master **7** headman **8** hierarch **9** chieftain

domineer 4 rule **5** reign **7** prevail **11** predominate **12** preponderate

domineering 5 bossy **6** lordly **8** arrogant, imperial, insolent **9** imperious, masterful **10** highhanded, imperative, peremptory, tyrannical **11** magisterial

Dominican Republic *capital:* **12** Santo Domingo *island:* **10** Hispaniola *monetary unit:* **4** peso *product:* **5** cocoa, sugar **6** coffee **7** bauxite, tobacco

dominion 3 raj **4** rule, sway **5** field, realm, regna (plural) **6** domain, empery, regnum, sphere **7** demesne, terrain **8** property, province **9** ascendant, bailiwick, champaign, masterdom, ownership, supremacy, territory **10** ascendancy, possession, prepot-

ence, prepotency **11** preeminence, proprietary, sovereignty **13** possessorship
domino 4 mask **5** amice, visor **6** vizard
9 doughface, false face *spot:* **3** pip
don 3 sir **4** lord, pull **5** get on, put on
6 assume, draw on, slip on, strike, take on
7 throw on **8** huddle on
Donalbain *brother:* **7** Malcolm *father:*
6 Duncan
Donar see **Thor**
donate 4 emit, give, loan **6** bestow,
devote, hansel, supply **7** hand out, handsel,
present **8** give away, transfer **10** contribute
donation 3 aid **4** alms, gift, help **5** grant
7 bequest, charity, handsel, subsidy **8** offering **9** endowment **10** assistance **11** beneficence **12** contribution
donator see **donor**
Don Camillo 6 priest
Don Carlos *author:* **8** Schiller *composer:* **5** Verdi *father:* **6** Philip
done 8 all in, ended, right, spent **6** decent,
doomed, effete, gone by, proper, used up
7 correct, drained, dressed, far-gone,
through, worn-out **8** becoming, complete,
decorous, depleted, finished, washed-up
9 befitting, completed, concluded,
exhausted, fitted out **10** conforming, terminated *for:* **4** gone, sunk **5** kaput **8** finished
poetic: **3** o'er
donee 7 grantee **8** receiver **9** appointor,
recipient
done in 5 spent **6** effete, used up **7** far-
gone, worn-out **8** depleted **9** exhausted,
washed-out
Don Giovanni composer 6 Mozart
Donizetti *hero:* **7** Roberto *opera:*
5 Lucia **10** Anna Bolena, La Favorita
11 Don Pasquale **12** Maria Stuarda
Don Juan 4 rake, wolf **5** Romeo **6** chaser,
masher **7** amorist, gallant **8** Casanova,
lothario, paramour **9** ladies' man, libertine,
philander, womanizer **10** lady-killer, profligate **11** philanderer *drama:* **13** The Stone
Guest *home:* **7** Seville *mother:* **4** Inez
poet: **5** Byron
donkey 3 ass **4** fool, jerk **5** burro, idiot
7 jackass **8** imbecile **10** nincompoop
female: **5** jenny
donkey's years 3 age **4** aeon **7** dog's
age **8** blue moon, coon's age, eternity
donkeywork 4 moil, toil **5** grind, labor
6 drudge **7** slavery **8** drudgery, plugging
Donner see **Thor**
donnybrook 4 fray **5** brawl, fight, melee,
set-to **6** affray, fracas **7** bobbery, ruction
10 free-for-all
donor 5 giver **7** donator, granter, grantor
8 bestower **9** conferrer, presenter
11 contributor
do-nothing 3 bum **4** slug **5** idler **6** loafer,

slouch **8** dolittle, fainéant, slugabed, sluggard **9** lazybones
Don Quixote *author:* **9** Cervantes
beloved: **8** Dulcinea *companion:* **11** Sancho Panza *giant:* **8** windmill *home:* **8** La
Mancha *horse:* **9** Rocinante, Rosinante,
Rozinante *squire:* **11** Sancho Panza
doodad 5 gizmo **6** dingus, gadget, jigger
7 do-funny, thingum, trinket **9** doohickey,
rigamajig, thingummy **10** thingumbob
11 thingumajig
doodle 3 ass, toy **4** fool, jerk, mess
5 cheat, idiot, ninny **6** donkey, fiddle, potter,
puddle, putter, tinker, trifle **7** jackass
8 imbecile, scribble **10** mess around,
nincompoop
doohickey see **doodad**
doom 3 lot **4** damn, fate **5** moira, weird
6 decree, kismet **7** condemn, destine, destiny, portion, preform, tragedy **8** calamity,
disaster, sentence **9** cataclysm, determine,
ordinance, preordain, proscribe **10** foreordain, predestine **11** catastrophe **12** circumstance, last judgment, predetermine
doomful 4 dire **7** baleful, baneful, direful,
ominous, unlucky **9** ill-boding **10** portentous **11** apocalyptic **12** inauspicious,
unpropitious
doomsayer 7 killjoy **9** Cassandra, pessimist **11** crepehanger
door 3 way **4** adit **5** entry **6** access,
entrée, portal **7** gateway, ingress, opening
8 entrance, entryway **9** admission
10 admittance **11** entranceway *rear:*
7 postern
doorkeeper 6 porter **7** gateman, ostiary
doormat 7 milksop **8** sufferer, weakling
9 jellyfish **10** namby-pamby, pantywaist
11 Milquetoast, mollycoddle
doorway 5 entry **6** portal **8** entrance,
entryway **11** entranceway *column:* **7** tru-
meau **8** trumeaux (plural)
dope 4 drug **5** dunce, noddy **6** doctor,
heroin, nitwit, noddle, opiate **7** cocaine
8 narcotic **9** lamebrain, marijuana **10** dunderhead **11** chowderhead, chucklehead,
preparation **12** spinning bath
doped 4 high **6** stoned, zonked
7 drugged **8** hopped-up, turned on
9 spaced-out **10** tripped out
dope up 4 load **6** debase, doctor, weight
10 adulterate **12** sophisticate
dopey 5 heavy **6** stupid, torpid
7 bemused, fuddled **8** comatose, sluggish
9 lethargic **10** slumberous
12 hebetudinous
dor 6 beetle
Doric Zeus 3 Zan
Doris *brother:* **6** Nereus *daughters:*
7 Nereids *father:* **7** Oceanus *husband:*
6 Nereus

dormancy 7 latency 8 abeyance, diapause, doldrums 10 quiescence, quiescency, suspension 11 cold storage 12 intermission, interruption

dormant 6 drowsy, latent 7 abeyant, lurking, relaxed 8 immobile, inactive, sluggish 9 lethargic, potential, prepatent, quiescent 10 slow-moving 13 unprogressive

dormer 6 window

dorry 4 boat

dorsal 6 aboral 7 abaxial *combining form:* 6 opisth 7 opistho

___ **d'Orsay** 4 Quai

dorsum 4 back

Dorus *brother:* 6 Aeolus *father:* 6 Hellen

dose 7 measure, portion 8 quantity 10 proportion

Dos Passos trilogy 3 U.S.A.

dot 4 mark, mote, stud 5 dower, dowry, point, speck 6 bestud, pepper, period, pimple 7 freckle, speckle, stipple 8 fly-speck, sprinkle 9 bespeckle 11 intersperse 12 decimal point

dotage 8 senility 11 elderliness, senectitude

dote on 4 like 5 adore, enjoy, fancy 7 idolize, worship

doting 4 dear, fond 5 silly 6 loving, senile 7 asinine, devoted, doddery, fatuous, foolish 8 imbecile, lovesome, overfond 9 doddering 12 affectionate 13 over-indulgent

dotted 6 spotty 8 cribbled, punctate, stippled *with stars:* 4 semé

dotty 5 crazy, loony, wacky 6 absurd, insane 7 foolish 8 besotted, enamored 9 eccentric, fantastic, infatuate 10 infatuated, ridiculous 12 feebleminded, preposterous

double 3 dub, shy, yaw 4 bend, bilk, copy, dual, duck, dupe, fold, mate, shun, tack, turn, twin 5 avoid, duple, elude, evade, image, match, shift 6 bifold, binary, clench, duplex, escape, eschew, paired, ringer, wraith 7 dualize, enlarge, magnify, twofold 8 increase 9 companion, deceitful, deviation, dualistic, duplicate, insincere, replicate 10 coordinate, deflection, reciprocal, simulacrum, understudy 12 ambidextrous, hypocritical 13 spitting image *combining form:* 2 di 3 bin 4 dipl, diss 5 diphy, diplo, disso *prefix:* 2 bi 3 dis

double agent 3 spy

double-barreled 4 dual 5 duple 6 bifold, binary, duplex 7 twofold 9 dualistic

double bass 10 bull fiddle

double-cross 4 sell 5 bluff 6 betray, humbug, illude, juggle, take in 7 beguile, deceive, mislead, sell out 8 betrayal 9 fourflush

doubled *combining form:* 3 bis

double dagger 6 diesis

double-dealer 3 gyp 5 cheat 6 con man 7 diddler, sharper 8 swindler 9 defrauder 10 mountebank 11 flimflammer 13 confidence man

double-dealing 5 fraud 7 chicane 8 mala fide, trickery 9 chicanery, deception, duplicity, fourberie, insincere 10 hankypanky, left-handed 11 highbinding 12 ambidextrous, hypocritical 13 sharp practice

double-dome 7 Brahmin, egghead 8 highbrow 12 intellectual

double-edged 5 vague 7 obscure, unclear 9 ambiguous, ancipital, equivocal, tenebrous, uncertain

double entendre 9 ambiguity, equivoque 11 amphibology 12 equivocality, equivocation

double-faced 5 vague 7 obscure, unclear 8 mala fide 9 ambiguous, equivocal, insincere, tenebrous, uncertain 10 left-handed 12 ambidextrous, hypocritical

double meaning see **double entendre**

double-minded 7 halting 8 hesitant, wavering 10 hesitating, indecisive, irresolute, undecisive 11 vacillating 12 ambidextrous, hypocritical

doublet 3 duo 4 dyad, pair 5 brace 6 couple, jacket 7 twosome

double-talk 4 jazz 5 hokum 6 bunkum, drivel 7 twaddle 8 flimflam, newspeak, nonsense 9 gibberish 10 balderdash 12 gobbledygook

double vision 8 diplopia

doubly *prefix:* 2 bi

doubt 5 qualm 6 wonder 7 concern, dispute, dubiety, misgive, perhaps, suspect, swither 8 distrust, mistrust, question, unbelief 9 challenge, disbelief, dubiosity, suspicion 10 skepticism 11 dubiousness, incertitude, incredulity, uncertainty, uncertitude

doubtable 4 open 7 dubious, suspect 9 ambiguous, equivocal, undecided 10 borderline 11 problematic

doubter 7 skeptic, zetetic 10 headshaker, Pyrrhonian, Pyrrhonist, unbeliever

doubtful 4 hazy, iffy, moot, open 5 fishy, shady, shaky 6 chancy, queasy, uneasy, unsure 7 clouded, dubious, obscure, suspect, unclear 8 arguable, insecure, mootable, unlikely, unstable, wavering 9 ambiguous, debatable, dubitable, equivocal, uncertain, undecided, unsettled 10 borderline, contingent, disputable, hesitating, improbable, impugnable, indecisive, precarious, suspicious, touch-and-go 11 problematic, speculative 12 questionable

doubtfulness 7 concern, dubiety 8 mistrust 9 dubiosity, dubitancy, suspicion 10 skepticism 11 uncertainty, uncertitude

doubting Thomas see **doubter**

doubtless 4 sure 6 easily, likely 7 certain 8 probably 9 assumably 10 absolutely, definitely, positively, presumably 13 presumptively, unequivocally

doubtlessly 4 well 5 truly 6 easily, indeed, really 8 provenly 10 absolutely, definitely, positively 11 undoubtedly 13 unequivocally

douceur 4 gift 7 present 8 gratuity

dough 4 cash 5 bread, money 8 currency 11 legal tender *cooked in honey:* 8 taiglach, teiglach

doughboy 11 infantryman

doughty 4 able, bold 5 brave, manly 6 plucky, spunky, strong 7 valiant 8 fearless, unafraid 9 dauntless, undaunted

doughy 4 ashy, pale 5 ashen, livid, lurid, waxen 6 pallid 8 blanched 9 colorless

do up 3 fix 4 mend, wrap 5 patch 6 doctor, repair, revamp 7 rebuild 8 overhaul 11 recondition, reconstruct

dour 4 glum, grim, hard, ugly 5 bleak, harsh, rigid, sulky, surly 6 dogged, gloomy, morose, severe, strict, sullen 7 austere, crabbed 8 rigorous 9 saturnine, stringent 10 forbidding, implacable, unyielding

douse 3 bat, bop, dip, out, sop, wet 4 doff, duck, dunk, slop, soak 5 bathe, drown, lower, plash, slosh, swash, throw 6 deluge, drench, put off, put out, quench, remove, splash, splosh 7 immerse, slacken, spatter, splurge, spurtle, take off 8 downpour, splatter, submerge, submerse 9 drenching 10 extinguish

douzeper 4 Ivon, Oton 5 Gerin, Ivory, peers 6 Anseis, Gerard, Gerier, Oliver, Roland, Samson 7 Olivier, paladin 8 Engelier 9 Berengier

dove 6 culver, pigeon 8 pacifist 10 pacificist *call:* 3 coo *genus:* 7 Columba

dovecote 6 aviary 8 pigeonry 9 birdhouse, columbary 11 culver house, pigeon house

dovehouse see **dovecote**

dovelike 4 mild, pure 6 gentle 7 lovable 9 columbine

dovetail 4 jibe 5 agree, fit in, tally 6 accord, square 8 check out 9 harmonize 10 correspond 13 interlock with

dovish 7 antiwar 8 pacifist 10 pacifistic

dowager 4 dame 6 matron 9 matriarch 10 grande dame

dowdy 4 drab, slut 5 dated, passé, tacky 6 blowsy, bygone, démodé, frowsy, frumpy, old hat, sordid, stodgy 7 archaic, traipse, vintage 8 frumpish, outdated, outmoded, slattern, slovenly 9 out-of-date, unstylish 10 antiquated, slatternly 11 draggle-tail 12 old-fashioned 13 draggletailed *woman:* 5 frump

dowel 3 pin, rod 5 stick

dower 3 dot 5 endow, endue 6 talent 9 crown with, endowment

dowitcher 5 snipe 8 grayback 9 brownback

down 3 bad, fur, ill, low, off, out 4 best, blue, done, drop, fell, flue, fuzz, kill, lick, lint, pile, sick, slow 5 below, ended, floor, floss, fluff, fully, level, lower, outdo, scrag, slack, throw, under, worst 6 cut off, defeat, fallen, finish, hipped, hurdle, lay low, master, nether 7 conquer, descent, destroy, flatten, for real, handout, swallow, through 8 actively, at hazard, bowl over, carry off, complete, consumed, defeated, dejected, dispatch, feathers, finished, inferior, lay aside, overcome, sluggish, suppress, surmount 9 completed, concluded, depressed, earnestly, earthward, liquidate, processed, seriously, subjacent 10 completely, dispirited, groundward, terminated, vigorously 11 netherwards 12 discomfiture *combining form:* 4 ptil 5 ptilo *prefix:* 2 de 3 cat, hyp, kat 4 cata, cath, cato, hypo, kata

down-and-outer 6 beggar, pauper, wretch

down-at-heel 5 seedy, tacky 6 shabby, tagrag 7 rundown 8 tattered 10 bedraggled, broken down, threadbare 11 dilapidated

downcast 3 bad, low, sad 4 blue, dull, glum, rout, sunk 5 moody, mopey, shaft 6 defeat, droopy, gloomy, hipped, morose 7 beating, debacle, doleful, forlorn, licking 8 dejected, drubbing, listless, soul-sick, troubled 9 depressed, heartsick, heartsore, oppressed, overthrow, woebegone 10 chapfallen, defeasance, despondent, dispirited, distressed, spiritless 11 crestfallen, discouraged, low-spirited 12 disconsolate, disheartened

downcry 5 abuse 8 belittle, derogate, diminish, discount 9 disparage, dispraise 10 depreciate 11 detract from

downfall 4 bane, ruin 7 atrophy, decline, descent, undoing 9 decadence, destroyer, ruination 10 declension, degeneracy, devolution 11 declination, destruction 12 degeneration, dégringolade 13 deterioration

downgrade 4 bump, bust 5 break, decry, lower 6 demote, reduce 7 atrophy, declass, decline, demerit, devalue, disrate 8 mark down, write off 9 decadence, devaluate, write down 10 declension, degeneracy, depreciate, devalorize, devolution, undervalue 12 degeneration, dégringolade 13 deterioration

downhearted see **downcast**

down-in-the-mouth see **downcast**

down payment 7 deposit, earnest

downpour 4 rain 6 deluge 8 rainfall
9 drenching 10 cloudburst
down quilt 5 duvet
downright 4 flat, very 5 gross, plain,
utter 8 absolute, complete, positive 9 out-
and-out, up-and-down 10 sure-enough
11 indubitable, unmitigated
13 thoroughgoing
downslide 3 dip, sag 4 drop, slip
5 slump 7 decline, falloff
downstage area 5 apron
downstairs 5 below 8 servants
downswing see **downslide**
down-to-earth 4 hard 5 sober 9 practical, pragmatic, realistic 10 hard-boiled,
hardheaded 11 unfantastic 12 matter-of-
fact, unidealistic
downtown sign 6 Main St.
downtrend see **downslide**
downtrodden 6 abject, abused
9 oppressed, underfoot 10 maltreated, mis-
treated, persecuted
downturn see **downslide**
downward 8 debasing 9 declining
10 descending, netherward *combining
form:* 4 bath 5 batho
downwardly, downwards see
downward
downy 4 soft 6 fluffy 8 feathery, soothing
combining form: 4 hebe *filler:* 5 eider
doxy 3 ism 4 tart 5 creed, wench 6 harlot 7 opinion, trollop 8 doctrine
doyen 4 dean, lead 5 guide, maven, pilot
6 artist, expert, leader, master 8 virtuoso
9 authority 10 bellwether, master-hand,
past master, proficient 12 passed master
Doyle's detective 6 Holmes
doze 3 nap 5 sleep 6 catnap, drowse
7 drop off, slumber 9 drowse off
dozy see **drowsy**
DP 6 émigré 7 evacuee, refugee 8 fugitive
drab 3 hag 4 bawd, dowd, dull, flat, slut,
trot 5 biddy, bleak, crone, dingy, dowdy,
faded, mousy, muddy, murky, prosy, wench,
whore, witch 6 beldam, dismal, dreary, harlot, mousey 7 hustler, prosaic, subfusc,
traipse 8 desolate, dullness, lifeless, slattern 9 cheerless, colorless 10 lackluster,
lusterless, prostitute 11 dispiriting, draggle-
tail, fille de joie, nightwalker 12 streetwalker
draconian 5 harsh, rigid 6 strict 8 rigorist,
rigorous 9 stringent 10 ironhanded
12 unpermissive
Dracula author 6 Stoker (Bram)
draffy 6 drossy, no-good 7 inutile, nothing
8 unworthy 9 valueless, worthless
draft 3 tap 4 dose, plan, plot, pull, pump,
swig 5 check, claim, drink, frame, press,
swill, taper 6 call up, demand, design,
devise, drench, enroll, induct, potion,
scheme, siphon, sketch 7 compose, con-

coct, current, draught, harness, impress,
outline, portion, prepare, project 8 block
out, chalk out, contrive, muster in, rough
out, skeleton, traction 9 adumbrate, allowance, conscribe, conscript, fabricate, formulate, muster out 11 delineation, skeletonize 12 characterize *avoider:* 6 dodger *of a
law:* 4 bill
drag 3 lug, peg, tow, tug 4 hang, haul,
poke, puff, pull, swig 5 dally, delay, draft,
drain, drink, float, swill, tarry, trail 6 burden,
daggle, dawdle, drench, harrow, loiter, put
off, schlep, search, strain 7 ransack, sagging, schlepp, skidpan, traipse 8 drooping,
friction 9 lag behind, sea anchor 10 conveyance 11 inclination 13 procrastinate
off: 4 cart
dragging 4 long 7 lengthy, tedious
8 drawn-out, longsome, overlong 9 prolonged 10 protracted 12 long-drawn-out
draggle 5 trail 7 shuffle, traipse
8 besmirch
draggle-tail 4 dowd, drab, slut 5 dowdy
7 traipse 8 slattern
draggletailed 5 dowdy 6 blowsy, frowsy,
sordid, untidy 8 slattern, sluttish
10 slatternly
dragnet 5 trawl
dragon 5 beast, Satan 6 wivern 8 basilisk 9 water arum 10 cockatrice *Babylonian:* 6 Tiamat *biblical:* 5 Rahab *Canaanite:* 3 Yam 4 Yamm 5 Lotan *Chinese:*
4 lung *French:* 8 Tarasque *genus:* 5 Draco
Greek: 5 Ladon 9 Eurython *horse:* 6 Fafner, Fafnir *slayer:* 4 Baal, Enki, Zeus
5 Indra 6 Cadmus, Marduk, Sigurd, Yahweh 7 Beowulf, Jupiter, Ninurta, Perseus
8 St. George 9 St. Michael 10 St. Margaret
Sumerian: 3 Kur *two-legged:* 5 wiver
6 wivern, wyvern *Vadic:* 3 Ahi 6 Vritra
dragoon 3 cow 5 bully 6 harass, hector
8 browbeat, bulldoze, bullyrag 9 persecute,
strong-arm, terrorize 10 cavalryman,
intimidate
drag race entry 6 hot rod
drain 3 tap 4 jade, pump, sink, sump, swig,
tire, vent, wear 5 bleed, draft, drink, empty,
leech, sewer, swill, use up, weary 6 burden,
drench, gutter, siphon, trench 7 conduit,
deplete, draw off, exhaust, fatigue 8 bankrupt, draw down, wear down 9 discharge
10 impoverish 11 watercourse *transverse:* 7 culvert
drain away 5 abate, close, taper 6 lessen,
reduce 7 dwindle 8 decrease, diminish,
taper off
drained 5 all-in, spent 6 bleary, effete,
used up 7 far-gone, worn-out 8 depleted
9 exhausted, washed-out
drainpipe 5 spout 9 downspout

drain pit 4 sump

dram 3 bit, nip, tot 4 dash, drop, hoot, iota, jolt, mite, shot, slug, spot, swig 5 crumb, draft, drink, ounce, shred, snort, swill 6 dollop 7 modicum, smidgen, snifter, snorter 8 particle, potation, toothful

drama 4 play 6 boards 7 theater, theatre 8 the stage 10 footlights *former English:* 6 masque *Japanese:* 3 Noh *main part:* 8 epitasis *musical:* 5 opera 8 operetta *suspenseful:* 11 cliff-hanger

dramatic 8 striking, theatral, theatric, thespian 10 histrionic, theatrical *conflict:* 4 agon *scene:* 4 skit

dramatis personae 4 cast

dramatist 10 playwright *American:* 4 Hart, Inge, Rice, Uhry 5 Albee, Mamet, Odets, Payne, Simon 6 Miller, O'Neill, Thomas, Wilson (August, Lanford) 7 Hellman, Kaufman 8 Anderson, Sherwood, Williams 11 Hammerstein, Wasserstein *Austrian:* 10 Schnitzler *Belgian:* 11 Maeterlinck *English:* 3 Fry, Gay 4 Rowe, Tate 5 Milne, Peele, Wilde 6 Coward, Jonson, Pinero, Pinter, Steele, Storey 7 Marlowe, Marston, Osborne, Shaffer, Webster 8 Congreve, Shadwell, Stoppard, Tourneur, Vanbrugh, Zangwill 9 Middleton, Wycherley 11 Shakespeare *French:* 5 Camus, Genet 6 Musset, Racine, Sardou, Sartre, Scribe 7 Anouilh, Ionesco, Labiche, Moliere, Rostand 8 Marivaux 9 Corneille, Giraudoux 12 Beaumarchais *German:* 5 Weiss 6 Brecht, Goethe, Kleist 8 Schiller 9 Hauptmann, Zuckmayer *Greek:* 8 Menander 9 Aeschylus, Euripides, Sophocles 12 Aristophanes *Hindu:* 8 Kalidasa *Irish:* 4 Shaw 5 Behan, Yeats 6 O'Casey 8 Sheridan *Italian:* 7 Alfieri, Giacosa, Goldoni 8 Trissino *Japanese:* 5 Zeami *Norwegian:* 5 Ibsen 8 Bjornson *Roman:* 7 Plautus, Terence *Russian:* 7 Chekhov 8 Zamyatin *Spanish:* 4 Vega 8 Quintero 11 Garcia Lorca *Swedish:* 5 Sachs 10 Strindberg *Swiss:* 6 Frisch

dramaturge see **dramatist**

dramaturgic see **dramatic**

drape 4 roll 5 adorn, cover 6 enfold, enwrap, sprawl, swathe, wrap up 7 curtain, swaddle 8 enswathe, envelope, spraddle, swathe in 11 spread-eagle

drapery 7 curtain 8 hangings

drastic 6 severe 7 extreme, radical 8 rigorous, vigorous 9 purgative

Dravidian language 5 Gondi, Khond, Malto, Tamil 6 Brahui, Kurukh, Telugu 8 Kanarese 9 Malayalam

draw 3 gut, lug, pen, tap, tie, tow, tug, win 4 call, edge, gain, haul, limn, lure, make, move, odds, puff, pull, pump, rise, sink, take, wile 5 alter, angle, bowel, bulge, charm, draft, drain, educe, evoke, infer, judge, paint, start, steep, taper, use up 6 allure, appeal, coulee, crayon, deduce, derive, elicit, entice, extend, gather, indite, induce, infuse, inhale, paunch, pencil, prompt, pucker, seduce, siphon, sketch 7 attract, bewitch, collect, deplete, dogfall, enchant, exhaust, extract, make out, prolong, spin out, stencil, stipple, stretch, vantage, win over 8 bankrupt, conclude, contract, convince, dead heat, deadlock, elongate, handicap, lengthen, persuade, protract, standoff 9 advantage, allowance, argue into, captivate, delineate, drain away, fascinate, formulate, head start, magnetize, represent, seduction, stalemate 10 allurement, attraction, disembowel, eviscerate, exenterate, impoverish, prolongate 11 bring around *forth:* 5 educe 6 elicit 7 extract *from:* 4 milk, pump 5 bleed *the main features of:* 4 etch 6 sketch 7 outline *together:* 3 tie 4 join, lace

draw back 5 wince 6 deduct, recede, recoil, retire 7 retreat, take off, take out 8 discount, knock off, subtract, take away 9 substract

drawback 6 defect, refund 7 trouble 8 handicap 9 detriment, hindrance 10 disability 12 disadvantage 13 inconvenience

draw down 3 get, win 4 earn, gain, make 5 drain, use up 7 acquire, bring in, deplete, exhaust 8 bankrupt 10 impoverish

drawer 9 draftsman *for money:* 4 till

draw in 3 get 6 induce, prompt 7 win over 8 convince, persuade, talk into 9 argue into, prevail on 11 bring around, prevail upon

drawing 4 plan 6 sketch 8 alluring, charming, magnetic 9 appealing 10 attracting, attractive, bewitching, enchanting 11 captivating, fascinating *combining form:* 4 gram *humorous:* 7 cartoon

drawing power 4 call, lure, pull 6 appeal 9 seduction 10 allurement, attraction

drawing room 5 salon 6 saloon 9 reception

drawn 4 worn 7 haggard, pinched 8 careworn

drawn-out 4 long 7 lengthy 8 dragging, extended, longsome, overlong 9 prolonged 10 protracted

draw off 3 tap 4 pump 5 bleed, draft, drain 6 remove, siphon, syphon 8 withdraw

draw on 3 don 5 cause 6 assume, effect, induce, prompt, secure 7 produce, win over 8 convince, persuade, talk into 9 argue into 10 bring about 11 bring around, prevail upon

draw out 6 extend, remove 7 extract, prolong, stretch 8 elongate, lengthen, protract 10 prolongate

draw up 4 halt, make, stop 5 draft, frame 7 prepare 9 formulate

dray 4 cart 7 travois 9 stoneboat

dray horse 4 peon 5 slave 6 drudge, slavey, toiler 11 galley slave

dread 4 fear 5 alarm, panic 6 dismay, fright, horror, terror 7 anxiety 9 trepidity 11 frightening, trepidation 13 consternation *combining form:* 5 phobe 6 phobia, phobic 7 phobous

dreadful 5 awful 6 tragic 7 direful, extreme, fearful, shocker 8 horrible, horrific, shocking, terrible, terrific 9 appalling, dime novel, frightful, revolting, unrefined 10 formidable, unpleasant, yellowback 11 frightening

dreadfully 4 very 6 damned 8 horribly 9 extremely 10 strikingly 11 exceedingly 12 surpassingly 13 frighteningly

dreadnought 10 battleship

dream 4 ache, long, lust, moon, pine, sigh 5 crave, fancy, ideal 6 bubble, hanker, hunger, thirst, vision 7 chimera, fantasy, imagine, rainbow, reverie, suspire 8 illusion, phantasm, phantasy 9 nightmare 10 conceive of *combining form:* 4 onir 5 oneir, oniro 6 oneiro *god:* 8 Morpheus

dreamer 6 mystic 7 utopian 8 idealist, theorist 9 ideologue, visionary 10 Don Quixote, lotus-eater 11 illusionist 13 castle-builder

dreamlike 5 vague 7 shadowy, surreal 8 nebulous

dream up 5 frame, hatch 6 devise, invent 7 concoct 8 contrive 9 formulate

dreamy 4 hazy, idle 5 ideal, nifty, super, vague 6 astral, divine, groovy, peachy 8 fanciful, glorious, pleasing, romantic 9 marvelous, unworldly, visionary, whimsical 10 delightful, idealistic, indistinct 12 otherworldly

dreary 4 blah, dull, poky 5 black, bleak 6 dismal, gloomy, somber, stodgy 7 forlorn, humdrum 8 banausic, funereal, monotone 10 depressing, depressive, enervating, monotonous, oppressive, pedestrian 11 dispiriting 12 discouraging *Scottish:* 5 dowie

dreck 4 junk 5 offal, swill 6 litter, refuse 7 garbage, rubbish 12 outsweepings

dredge 3 dig 5 scoop 6 deepen, search 8 excavate

dregs 3 mob 4 lees, scum 5 trash 6 masses, rabble 7 deposit, grounds 8 canaille, riffraff, sediment, unwashed 9 settlings 11 precipitate, proletariat 13 precipitation

Dreiser *character:* 5 Clyde 6 Carrie, Sondra 7 Roberta 10 Cowperwood *novel:* 8 The Stoic, The Titan 9 The Genius 12 The Financier 17 An American Tragedy

drench 3 sop, wet 4 drag, dunk, lash, pour, soak, swig, teem, wash 5 douse, draft, drain, drink, drouk, drown, souse, steep, swill 6 deluge, seethe, sodden 7 immerse, overwet, pervade 8 oversoak, saturate, submerge, waterlog 10 impregnate

dress 3 gut, rig, tan 4 bind, clad, deck, doll, duds, garb, gown, sack, tend, till, togs, trim, work 5 adorn, align, array, clean, frock, getup, guise, habit, prank, smock 6 attire, bedeck, clothe, dirndl, enrobe, outfit, sacque, setout, tailor 7 apparel, bandage, bedizen, chemise, clothes, costume, garment, garnish, raiment, turnout 8 beautify, beclothe, clothing, covering, decorate, enclothe, ornament 9 cultivate, embellish, make ready 10 attirement 11 habiliments *a wound:* 7 bandage *designer:* 4 Dior 12 Saint-Laurent *extravagantly:* 8 overdeck *finically:* 5 primp *hair:* 6 barber *Hawaiian:* 6 muumuu *leather:* 3 taw *line:* 3 hem *mode of:* 5 habit *of the clergy:* 5 cloth *oriental:* 9 cheongsam *South Seas:* 6 sarong *with the beak:* 5 preen *with vulgarity:* 7 bedizen

dress down 4 lash, rail 5 scold 6 berate 7 bawl out, tell off 10 tongue-lash

dresser 5 chest 6 bureau 10 chiffonier 11 flour bolter *gaudy:* 9 butterfly

dressing 5 sauce 6 catsup 7 bandage, catchup, ketchup 8 stuffing *salad:* 6 French 7 Italian, Russian 10 blue cheese

dressing room 8 vestiary *church:* 6 vestry

dressmaker 6 tailor 7 modiste 9 couturier 10 seamstress

dress up 3 tog 4 clad, mask, smug, tart 5 array, cloak, prank, preen, primp, slick, spiff 6 attire, clothe, tog out 7 apparel, deck out, doll out, smarten 8 disguise, enclothe, prettify, trick off, trick out 9 dissemble 10 camouflage 11 dissimulate

dressy 4 chic 6 formal, frilly, ornate 7 elegant, stylish 9 elaborate

Dreyfus' defender 4 Zola

drib 4 drop, weep 5 trill 6 gobbet 7 distill, droplet, globule, trickle

dribble 4 blow, drip, drop, weep 5 drool, trill, waste 6 drivel, slaver 7 consume, distill, fritter, slabber, slobber, trickle 8 pittance, salivate, squander 9 throw away 10 frivol away, trifle away 11 blunder away

driblet 4 drop 6 gobbet 7 globule 8 pittance

dried acorns 6 camata 8 camatina

dried brick 5 adobe

dried coconut meat 5 copra

dried grape 6 raisin

dried grass 3 hay

dried meat 5 jerky 7 charqui 8 pemmican

dried orchid tubers 5 salep
dried plum 5 prune
drift 3 bat, gad, run 4 bank, bent, cock,
flow, flux, heap, hill, mass, mope, pile, ride,
roam, rush, sail, skid, skim, tide, wash
5 amble, coast, creep, dance, float, flood,
mosey, mound, range, shock, shoot, slant,
slide, spate, stack, stray, tenor, trend
6 bummel, linger, motion, ramble, stream,
stroll, upwaft, wander 7 current, leaning,
maunder, meander, meaning, purport, pyramid, saunter 8 mountain, movement, penchant, sideslip, tendency 9 deviation, gallivant, inclining, substance 10 partiality,
propensity 11 disposition, inclination, progression 12 predilection *languidly:*
5 swoon *of a ship:* 6 leeway *unstratified:*
4 till
drifter 3 bum, vag 4 hobo 5 rover, tramp
6 roamer 7 floater, rambler, vagrant
8 derelict, vagabond, wanderer 9 meanderer 10 street arab, temporizer 12 rolling
stone
driftwood 6 jetsam 7 flotsam 8 wreckage
drill 4 bore, skid 5 prick, punch, snail
6 pierce 7 wildcat 8 exercise, practice,
practise, puncture, rehearse, sideslip 9 penetrate, perforate 10 discipline *command:*
6 at ease 8 left face 9 about face, attention, right face
drink 3 ade, nip, sea, sip, tea 4 brew, deep,
drag, grog, gulp, soak, swig, tope, toss
5 booze, draft, drain, julep, ocean, quaff,
slosh, slurp, sup up, swill, toast 6 absorb,
drench, guzzle, imbibe, jigger, liquid, liquor,
pledge, potion, sup off, tank up, tipple
7 potable, spirits, swallow, swizzle 8 aperitif, beverage, libation, liquor up 9 aqua vitae
after-dinner: 6 frappe *British:* 5 spree
drugged: 6 mickey *honey:* 4 mead *hot:*
5 toddy 6 saloop *liquor:* 5 booze *mixed:*
3 nog 5 zombi 6 zombie *mixer:* 7 swirler
noisily: 5 slurp *of liquor:* 4 dram, shot
5 snort 8 highball *of the gods:* 6 nectar
Scottish: 6 waught *soft:* 7 soda pop *tall:*
4 fizz; (see also **beverage**)
drinkable 6 liquor 7 potable 8 beverage
drinkery 3 bar, pub 4 café 6 lounge,
saloon, tavern 7 barroom, taproom
drinking 8 potation *fountain:* 7 bubbler
horn: 6 rhyton *spree:* 5 binge 6 bender
8 carousal
drip 4 weep 5 trill 7 distill, dribble, spatter,
spurtle, trickle 8 sprinkle
dripping 3 wet 5 runny, soppy 6 soaked,
sodden, soused 7 soaking 8 drenched
9 saturated 11 wringing-wet
drippy 5 mushy, rainy, sappy, sobby,
soupy 6 slushy, sobful 7 drizzly, maudlin,
mawkish 11 sentimental
drive 2 go 3 dig, pep, ram, run, sic, tug

4 auto, bang, dash, élan, goad, herd, moil,
move, prod, push, ride, road, roll, sink, snap,
spin, spur, stab, taxi, toil, tool, trip, turn,
urge 5 burst, chase, defer, force, getup,
grave, guide, impel, labor, lunge, motor,
pilot, pitch, pound, punch, shove, stamp,
steer, stick, surge, tract, vigor, wheel, whirl
6 attack, coerce, compel, convey, exhort,
hammer, plunge, propel, strain, strike, strive,
thrust 7 actuate, impetus, impress, joyride,
operate, produce 8 ambition, mobilize,
momentum, navigate, protract, shepherd,
vitality 9 chauffeur, excursion, impelling,
urge along 10 charioteer, enterprise, get-
up-and-go, initiative *air:* 4 blow *away:*
4 shoo 5 exile, stave 6 aroint *back:*
5 repel 6 defend 7 repulse *close:* 8 tail-
gate *off:* 6 dispel *out:* 8 exorcise
drivel 4 blow, bosh 5 drool, Greek, hooey,
prate, waste 6 babble, gabble, jabber,
slaver 7 blabber, blather, consume, dribble,
fritter, prattle, rubbish, slabber, slobber,
twaddle 8 cast away, claptrap, nonsense,
pishposh, salivate, squander 9 gibberish,
throw away 10 double-talk, flapdoodle, frivol away, trifle away 11 blunder away, jabberwocky 12 blatherskite
driveling 4 flat 5 inane, vapid 6 jejune
7 insipid, sapless 9 innocuous 10 namby-
pamby, wishy-washy 12 milk-and-water
driver 5 cabby 6 cabbie, cabman, hackie,
jarvey, mallet, vanman 7 autoist, hackman,
spanker 8 motorist, muleteer, operator
9 chauffeur, dowitcher 10 taskmaster
11 tamping iron 12 automobilist *fast:*
4 jehu *of an elephant:* 6 mahout *Roman:*
10 charioteer *truck:* 8 teamster
driver's light 8 headlamp
driving 6 active, lively 7 dynamic 9 energetic 12 enterprising
drizzle 8 sprinkle
Dr. Jekyll and Mr. ____ 4 Hyde
drogher 6 bearer, porter 7 carrier
drolerie see **drollery**
6 jester 7 comical, risible 8 comedian, farcical, funnyman, gelastic, humorist, humorous, jokester, quipster 9 burlesque, laughable, ludicrous, whimsical 10 puppet show,
ridiculous
drollery 3 gag, yak 4 jape, jest, joke, quip
5 crack, humor 6 comedy 7 waggery
9 funniness, wisecrack, witticism, wittiness
10 comicality 11 comicalness
12 humorousness
drollness see **drollery**
dromedary 5 camel
drone 3 hum 4 buzz, idle, laze, loaf, loll
5 idler, strum, thrum 6 bumble, dawdle, loiter, lounge 7 bagpipe, male bee 8 parasite 9 bombinate 10 pedal point 12 diddle-
daddle

dronish see **drony**

drony 4 lazy 7 work-shy 8 fainéant, indolent, slothful 9 easygoing, slowgoing

drool 4 guff, rave 5 prate, water 6 babble, bushwa, drivel, gabble, hot air, saliva, slaver 7 blabber, blather, dribble, enthuse, prattle, slabber, slobber, twaddle 8 claptrap, nonsense, rhapsody, salivate 10 balderdash, rhapsodize

droop 3 sag 4 fall, flag, hang, loll, sink, swag, wilt 5 couch, demit, lower, slump 6 dangle, go down, slouch, weaken 7 decline, depress, let down, subside, trollop 8 languish, pine away 11 deteriorate

droopy 3 bad 4 blue, down 6 gloomy 7 doleful 8 cast down, dejected, downcast 9 depressed 10 dispirited 11 downhearted

drop 3 die, dip, nip, sag, tot 4 down, dram, drib, dump, fall, fell, fire, iota, jolt, lose, pass, plop, quit, shot, skid, slip, slot, slug, thud, weep, wilt 5 cease, crumb, depth, floor, gutta, lapse, leave, lower, ounce, pitch, plonk, plump, plunk, scrub, shred, slide, snort, speck, spend, trill 6 bounce, cancel, cave in, crouch, curtsy, demise, depart, expire, fumble, give up, gobbet, go down, goutte, ground, lay low, peg out, plunge, pop off, reduce, resign, smitch, topple, tumble, unload, vanish 7 abandon, boot out, call off, decease, decline, deposit, descend, descent, dismiss, distill, dribble, driblet, fall off, forfeit, give out, globule, lose out, pendant, plummet, relapse, smidgen, snifter, spatter, succumb, trickle 8 bowl down, bowl over, break off, collapse, comedown, deepness, defecate, downturn, fall away, keel over, molecule, nose-dive, particle, pass away, toothful 9 backslide, break down, bring down, declivity, disappear, discharge, downslide, downswing, downtrend, knock down, prostrate, reduction, sacrifice, terminate, throw down 10 depository *of liquid:* 5 gutta *saline:* 4 tear

drop in 3 see 4 call 5 visit 6 come by, look up, stop by 8 come over

droplet 4 drib 6 gobbet 7 globule

drop off 3 sag 4 fall, slip 5 slide, slump 8 fall away

dropout's loss 7 diploma

dropsical 5 puffy, tumid, windy 6 turgid 7 swollen 8 inflated 9 flatulent, overblown, tumescent

dropsied see **dropsical**

dropsy 5 edema 7 hydrops 8 anasarca

dross 4 scum, slag 7 schlock 8 impurity

drossy 6 draffy, no-good 7 inutile, nothing 8 unworthy 9 worthless

drought 4 lack 6 dearth 8 scarcity, shortage

droughty 3 dry 4 arid, sere 7 bone-dry,

thirsty 9 unwatered, waterless 12 moistureless

drove 4 herd, push 5 crowd, crush, flock, horde, press 6 chisel, squash, throng 9 multitude

drown 3 sop, wet 4 sink, soak, stun 5 douse, flood, souse, swamp, whelm 6 dazzle, deluge, drench, engulf 7 immerse, repress 8 inundate, overcome, overflow, submerge 9 knock over, overpower, overwhelm, prostrate, suffocate, tower over 10 extinguish

drowse 3 nod 4 doze 7 doze off, drop off, slumber

drowsy 4 dozy 6 sleepy, snoozy 7 languid, nodding 8 indolent, slumbery 9 lethargic, somnolent, soporific 10 languorous, slumberous 13 lackadaisical

drub 3 tap 4 beat, flay, lick, trim, whip 5 baste, paste, pound, score, slash, smear, stamp 6 batter, berate, buffet, pummel, scorch, thrash, wallop 7 belabor, blister, censure, scourge, shellac 8 lambaste, lash into 9 castigate, excoriate, overwhelm

drubbing 4 rout 6 defeat 7 beating, debacle, licking 9 overthrow, trouncing 10 defeasance 11 shellacking 12 vanquishment

drudge 4 grub, hack, moil, peon, plod, slog, toil, work 5 grind, labor, slave 6 slavey, toiler 7 grubber, slavery 8 bullwork, hireling, plugging 9 dray horse, mercenary, workhorse 10 donkeywork 11 galley slave

drudgery 4 moil, toil, work 5 grind, labor, sweat 7 travail 8 bullwork, plugging, taskwork 10 donkeywork

drudging 6 boring, tiring 7 irksome, tedious 8 boresome, tiresome 10 monotonous

drug 4 dope, lull 5 sulfa 6 downer, opiate, physic, poison, sulpha 7 generic, stupefy, tetanic 8 biologic, medicine, narcotic, nepenthe, pemoline, relaxant, roborant, sedative, thiazide 9 medicinal 10 medicament, medication 12 pharmaceutic *addict:* 6 junkie *agent:* 4 narc *antibiotic:* 8 neomycin *calming:* 8 sedative *combining form:* 8 pharmaco *experience:* 4 trip *seller:* 10 pharmacist *sleep-inducing:* 8 hypnotic 9 soporific

drugged 4 high 5 doped 6 stoned, zonked 8 hopped-up, turned on 9 spaced-out 10 tripped out

druggist 7 chemist 10 apothecary, pharmacist

drugstore 8 pharmacy 10 apothecary

druid 4 bard 6 priest 7 prophet 8 sorcerer *sacred object:* 3 oak 9 mistletoe

drum 4 cask 5 taber, tabla, tabor 6 atabal, barrel, enlist, gather, summon, tabour, tom-

tom, tymbal, tympan **7** canvass, solicit, taboret, taborin, tympani **8** cylinder, taborine, tabourer, tabouret, tympanum *Arab:* **6** atabal *Indian:* **8** mridanga *large:* **4** bass **6** timbal *small:* **5** bongo, tabor **6** tabret **7** taborin, timbrel *string:* **5** snare

drumfire 4 hail **5** salvo, storm **6** shower, volley **7** barrage **9** broadside, cannonade, fusillade **11** bombardment

drumhead 4 skin **7** summary

drummer 4 Rich (Buddy) **5** Krupa (Gene) **7** swagman **8** weakfish

drum up 6 invent **7** canvass, solicit **9** originate *interest:* **8** ballyhoo

drunk 3 fou, jag, sot **4** bust, lush, soak, tear, wino **5** binge, booze, souse, spree, tight, tipsy **6** bender, blotto, boozer, stinko, tiddly, zonked **7** guzzler, pie-eyed, squiffy, stewbum, tippler **8** squiffed **9** brannigan, inebriate **10** boozehound, inebriated **11** intoxicated

drunkard 3 sot **4** lush, soak, wino **5** rummy, stiff, toper **6** bibber, boozer, rumdum, soaker, sponge **7** drammer, fuddler, guzzler, swiller, tippler, tosspot **9** alcoholic, inebriate, swillbowl **10** boozehound **11** dipsomaniac

drunken 5 boozy, tight, tipsy **6** wobbly **7** pie-eyed **8** lurching, unsteady **10** inebriated **11** intoxicated

drupaceous fruit 4 plum **5** peach **6** almond, cherry

Drusilla *brother:* **8** Caligula *father:* **5** Herod **10** Germanicus *husband:* **5** Felix *mother:* **9** Agrippina *sister:* **8** Berenice **9** Agrippina

dry 3 set **4** acid, arid, bare, blot, brut, cake, dull, sear, sour, tart **5** acerb, baked, dusty, empty, harsh, parch, plain, rough, slack, stoic, wizen **6** barren, harden, hoarse, modest, stingy, stolid, thirst, wither **7** acerbic, acetose, athirst, congeal, grating, insipid, jarring, parched, rasping, sapless, shrivel, sterile, tedious, thirsty **8** bromidic, discreet, droughty, indurate, rainless, scariose, scarious, solidify, strident, tearless, teetotal, weariful, withered **9** acidulous, anhydrate, anhydrous, apathetic, dehydrate, desiccate, exsiccate, impassive, juiceless, sugarless, thirsting, unadorned, unwatered, waterless, wearisome **10** dehydrated, desiccated, phlegmatic, stridulous **11** inelaborate, unemotional, ungarnished **12** matter-of-fact, moistureless, unproductive **13** unembellished, unembroidered, uninteresting, unpretentious *biscuit:* **7** cracker **8** hardtack *combining form:* **3** xer **4** xero **5** scler **6** dehydr, sclero **7** dehydro *goods:* **4** wear **6** linens, napery **8** clothing, textiles *out:* **5** sober **8** soberize *period:* **4** sere **6** drouth **7** drought *wine:* **3** sec **4** brut

dryasdust 4 arid, dull **5** dusty **6** pedant **7** insipid, prosaic, tedious **8** bromidic, pedantic, weariful **9** wearisome **10** uninspired **12** uninteresting

dry measure 4 peck, pint **5** quart **6** bushel

Dryope *form:* **5** lotus *husband:* **9** Andraemon *sister:* **4** Iole

dry up 4 wilt **5** mummy, wizen **6** welter, wither **7** mummify, shrivel **8** pipe down **9** desiccate, disappear **10** devitalize

dual 4 twin **5** duple **6** bifold, binary, double, duplex, paired **7** twofold

dualistic 5 duple **6** bifold, binary, double, duplex **7** twofold

dualize 4 dupe **6** double **9** duplicate

dub 4 call, flub, muff, name, term, trim **5** botch, fluff, style, title **6** bobble, boggle, bollix, double, duffer, goof up, thrust **7** baptize, blunder, entitle **8** christen, nickname, rerecord **9** designate **10** denominate

dubiety see **dubiosity**

dubiosity 5 doubt **6** wonder **7** concern **8** mistrust **9** addlement, confusion, suspicion **10** muddlement, skepticism **11** incertitude, uncertainty, uncertitude

dubious 4 moot, open **5** fishy **6** unsure **7** suspect, unclear **8** arguable, doubtful, hesitant, mootable, unlikely, untrusty **9** debatable, dubitable, equivocal, skeptical, trustless, uncertain, undecided **10** disputable, fly-by-night, improbable, unreliable **11** mistrustful, problematic, questioning, unpromising **12** questionable, undependable, undetermined **13** untrustworthy

dubitable 4 open **5** fishy **7** suspect **8** doubtful **9** ambiguous, uncertain, unsettled **10** borderline

duce 6 despot, tyrant **8** dictator **9** Mussolini, oppressor

duck 3 bob, bow, dip, shy **4** bend, bilk, dive, dunk, shun **5** avoid, dodge, douse, elude, evade, fence, parry, shirk, souse, stoop **6** double, escape, eschew, plunge **7** back out, immerse **8** sidestep, submerge, submerse **10** canvasback *Asian:* **5** Pekin **8** mandarin *dabbling:* **7** gadwall, mallard *diving:* **4** smew **7** pochard **9** merganser **10** bufflehead *eggs:* **5** pidan *Eurasian:* **4** smew *European:* **8** garganey, shelduck *genus:* **4** Anas *group:* **4** sord, team **5** brace, flock, skein **6** flight *Hawaiian:* **5** koloa *hunter's screen:* **5** blind *male:* **5** drake *red-wattled:* **7** Muscovy *relating to:* **7** anatine *river:* **4** teal **6** wigeon **7** pintail, widgeon *scaup:* **8** bluebill *sea:* **5** eider, scaup **6** scoter

duckbill 8 platypus **9** monotreme **10** mallangong

duck soup 3 pie **4** snap **5** cinch, setup

6 breeze, picnic **8** kid stuff, pushover
10 child's play

duckweed 6 lemnad

ducky 4 cute, fine **7** darling **8** pleasant,
splendid **9** excellent

duct 4 pipe, tube **5** canal **6** course
7 channel, conduit **11** ink fountain, watercourse *anatomical:* **3** vas **4** vasa (plural)
combining form: **3** vas **4** vasi, vaso

ductile 6 pliant, supple **7** plastic, pliable
8 flexible, moldable **9** adaptable, compliant,
malleable, tractable *metal:* **4** wire

ductless gland see **endocrine gland**

ductus 4 fist, hand **6** script **10** penmanship **11** calligraphy, chirography,
handwriting

dud 3 bad **4** bomb, bust, fake, flop
5 lemon, loser **7** failure **11** ineffective

dude 3 fop **4** buck **5** blood, dandy **7** coxcomb **8** macaroni **9** exquisite **10** tenderfoot **11** Beau Brummel, petit-maître
12 lounge lizard

dudgeon 4 fury, huff, miff, rage **5** pique,
wrath **7** offense, umbrage **10** resentment

duds 4 togs **5** dress **6** attire, things
7 apparel, clothes, raiment **8** clothing
10 attirement **11** habiliments

due 4 debt, fair, good, just, owed **5** lumps,
merit, owing, right **6** direct, earned, lawful,
mature, reward, rights, unpaid **7** arrears,
condign, deserts, exactly, merited, payable,
payment, regular **8** adequate, deserved,
directly, rightful, straight, suitable **9** arrearage, deserving, equitable, liability, requisite,
scheduled, unsettled **10** recompense, satisfying, straightly, sufficient **11** appropriate,
comeuppance, outstanding **12** compensation, indebtedness, satisfaction **13** rhadamanthine, undeviatingly

duel 4 buck **5** fight, repel **6** combat,
oppose, resist **7** contest, dispute **8** conflict,
traverse **9** withstand

duenna 8 chaperon **9** chaperone,
governess

duet *dancer's:* **9** pas de deux

due to 4 over **7** through **9** because of

duff 5 slack **7** pudding **8** coal dust, fine
coal

duffer 4 dolt, dope **5** dunce, idiot **6** dimwit **8** dumbbell, numskull **9** blockhead,
ignoramus

dugout 4 abri **5** banca, canoe **7** piragua,
pirogue

dukedom 5 duchy

dulcet 5 sweet **7** melodic, tuneful, winning,
winsome **8** engaging, euphonic, luscious,
pleasant, soothing **9** melodious **10** euphonious **11** mellisonant

dulcimer *Chinese:* **7** yang-kin *Hungarian:* **8** cimbalom *Persian:* **6** santir
7 santour

dull 3 bad, dim, dry, dun, mat **4** arid, blah,
blue, blur, dead, down, drab, dumb, fade,
flat, hard, hazy, numb, pale, poky, slow
5 befog, blear, blind, blunt, cloud, dense,
dingy, dusty, heavy, inert, matte, muddy,
murky, muted, prosy, thick **6** benumb,
blurry, boring, cloudy, deaden, dreary,
gloomy, leaden, obtund, obtuse, retard, simple, somber, stodgy, stupid, tiring, weaken
7 becloud, blunted, disedge, doltish, humdrum, insipid, irksome, louring, moronic, muffled, prosaic, stupefy, subfusc, tarnish,
tedious, wash out **8** backward, banausic,
bromidic, cast down, deadened, dejected,
deluster, discolor, downcast, duncical,
enfeeble, hebetate, hopeless, imbecile, lifeless, listless, lowering, monotone, nubilous,
overcast, plodding, retarded, sluggish, weariful **9** bloodless, brainless, colorless,
depressed, dim-witted, dryasdust, insensate, ponderous, unfeeling, wearisome
10 anesthetic, beef-witted, devitalize, dispirited, half-witted, impassible, indistinct, insensible, lackluster, lusterless, monotonous,
numskulled, pedestrian, spiritless **11** blear-
witted, desensitize, downhearted, insensitive, overclouded, thickheaded, thick-witted,
unsharpened **12** disheartened, feebleminded, simpleminded **13** uninteresting
combining form: **5** brady

dullard 5 dummy, dunce, idiot, moron
6 stupid **8** dumbbell **9** ignoramus,
simpleton

dulled *combining form:* **5** ambly **6** amblyo

dullness 4 coma **5** sleep **6** apathy, stupor, torpor **7** languor, slumber **8** hebetude,
lethargy, monotony **9** bluntness, dense-
ness, lassitude, stupidity, torpidity
10 drowsiness

duly 8 properly **9** regularly **12** sufficiently

Dumas character 5 Athos **6** Aramis,
Dantes **7** Camille, Porthos **9** D'Artagnan

dumb 3 mum **4** dull, mute **5** dense, quiet,
thick **6** deaden, silent, stupid **7** doltish,
foolish **8** duncical, reticent, taciturn, wordless **9** fatheaded, voiceless **10** numskulled,
speechless, tongue-tied **11** blockheaded,
thick-witted, tight-lipped **12** close-mouthed,
close-tongued, inarticulate, inexpressive,
tight-mouthed, unarticulate, unresponsive

dumbbell see **dullard**

dumbfound 5 amaze **6** boggle
7 astound, nonplus, stagger **8** astonish,
surprise **11** flabbergast

dumbfounded 5 agape **6** aghast,
amazed **7** shocked **8** confused, dismayed
10 bewildered **11** overwhelmed
13 thunderstruck

dummy 4 dolt, mock, sham **5** dunce, false,
idiot, moron **6** effigy, ersatz, layout, stooge,
stupid, yes-man **7** dullard **8** dullhead,

dumbbell, spurious 9 ignoramus, imitation, simpleton, simulated **10** artificial, fictitious, substitute

dump 3 sty **4** cast, drop, junk **5** chuck, depot, ditch, scrap **6** armory, pigpen, pigsty, plunge **7** arsenal, discard, eyesore **8** jettison, magazine, throw out **9** throw away

dumpling 5 blimp, fatty **8** quenelle **10** butterball

dumps 5 blues, gloom **7** sadness **9** dejection **10** depression, melancholy, the dismals **11** unhappiness **12** mournfulness

dumpy 5 squat, thick **6** chunky, slummy, squdgy, stocky, stubby **8** heavyset, thickset **9** shapeless **11** thick-bodied

dun 3 dim **4** dark, dusk, gnaw **5** annoy, brown, dusky, murky, worry **6** darken, gloomy, harass, needle, pester, plague, somber **7** bedevil, hagride, obscure **9** beleaguer, caddis fly, lightless **10** caliginous **12** grayish brown

Duncan's slayer 7 Macbeth

dunce 3 mug, oaf **4** boob, clod, dodo, dolt, dope, fool, goof, jerk, lunk, mutt, poke, simp **5** booby, chump, dummy, idiot, moron, ninny, noddy, prune **6** dimwit, donkey, duffer, nitwit, noodle, stupid, turnip, zombie **7** dullard, fathead, jackass, lackwit, muggins, pinhead, wantwit **8** bonehead, clodpate, clodpoll, dolthead, dullhead, dumbbell, imbecile, ironhead, knothead, lunkhead, numskull **9** birdbrain, blockhead, ignoramus, lamebrain, simpleton, thickhead **10** beetlehead, dunderhead, dunderpate, hammerhead, muddlehead, muttonhead, nincompoop, squarehead, thickskull, woodenhead **11** cabbagehead, chowderhead, chucklehead, knucklehead, pumpkin head **12** featherbrain, scatterbrain **13** featherweight

Dunciad author 4 Pope

duncical 4 dull, dumb **5** dense **6** stupid **7** doltish **8** blockish **9** pinheaded **10** numskulled **11** blockheaded, thickheaded

dunderhead see **dunce**

dunderpate see **dunce**

dundrearies 9 burnsides, sideburns **10** sideboards **11** muttonchops **12** sidewhiskers

dune 5 twine **8** sandbank **area: 3** erg

dung 4 muck **6** manure, ordure **9** excrement **beetle: 3** dor **6** scarab **9** tumblebug **combining form: 4** copr, scat **5** copro, scato

dungaree fabric 5 denim

dungeon 4 cell, jail **5** vault **6** donjon, prison **9** black hole, oubliette

dunghill 6 midden

dungy 4 foul **5** black, dirty, nasty, soily **6** filthy, grubby, sordid **7** squalid, unclean

dunk 3 dip, sop **4** soak **5** douse, souse **7** immerse **8** saturate, submerge, submerse

dunlin 4 stib **9** sandpiper

duo 4 dyad, pair **5** brace **6** couple **7** doublet, twosome

dupe 3 con, job, kid, sap **4** butt, dust, fool, gull, hoax, mark, tool **5** catch, cheat, chump, cozen, patsy, slave, spoof, trick **6** befool, delude, double, outwit, pigeon, puppet, sucker **7** chicane, deceive, defraud, dualize, fall guy, gudgeon, mislead **8** flimflam, hoodwink **9** bamboozle, duplicate, victimize **11** double-cross, hornswoggle

dupery 5 cheat, fraud **7** chicane **9** chicanery, deception **10** dishonesty, hankypanky **13** double-dealing, sharp practice

duple 4 dual **6** bifold, binary, double, duplex **7** twofold **9** dualistic

duplex see **duple**

duplicate 4 copy, mate, same, twin **5** ditto, equal, match **6** carbon, double, fellow **7** dualize, identic, imitate, replica **9** companion, facsimile, identical, reproduce **10** carbon copy, coordinate, equivalent, reciprocal, tantamount **11** counterpart, replication **12** reproduction **prefix: 7** counter

duplicitous 6 shifty, sneaky **7** devious **8** guileful, indirect, sneaking **9** underhand **11** underhanded

duplicity 5 guile **6** deceit **7** cunning, perfidy **9** treachery **10** doubleness **12** dissemblance **13** dissimulation, double-dealing, faithlessness

durability 4 wear **11** lastingness

durable 5 stout **6** strong, sturdy **7** lasting **8** enduring **9** diuturnal, perduring, permanent, tenacious

duramen 9 heartwood

durance 9 restraint **11** confinement **12** imprisonment

duration 3 run **4** span, term, time **6** period **9** endurance **10** continuity **11** continuance, lastingness, persistence

duress 5 force **8** coercion, violence **10** compulsion, constraint

Durga see **Devi**

during 3 mid **4** amid, over **5** midst **10** throughout **prefix: 2** di **3** dia **5** intra

durra 7 sorghum **10** guinea corn **12** Indian millet

durum 5 wheat

dusk 3 dim **4** dark **5** murky **6** darken, gloomy **7** evening, obscure **8** darkness, eventide, glooming, owl-light, twilight **9** lightless, nightfall, tenebrous **10** caliginous **12** semidarkness **13** unilluminated

dusky 3 dim 4 dark 5 black, bleak, drear, murky, swart 6 brunet, dismal, gloomy, opaque, swarth 7 joyless, obscure, swarthy 8 bistered, blackish, desolate, funereal, nubilous 9 ambiguous, cheerless, equivocal, lightless, sibylline, tenebrous 10 acheronion, caliginous, depressing 11 black-a-vised, dark-skinned, double-edged, double-faced 13 unilluminated *combining form:* 4 pheo 5 phaeo

dust 3 row 4 beat, drub, dupe, fool, gull, hoax, lick, sift, whip 5 run-in, trick 6 fracas, hassle, powder, thrash 7 chicane, confuse, dispute, quarrel, shellac 8 flimflam, hoodwink, lambaste, levigate, sprinkle 9 bamboozle, bickering, confusion, overwhelm, powdering 10 besprinkle, falling-out, sprinkling 11 altercation, disturbance, hornswoggle *combining form:* 4 coni 5 conio *Scottish:* 5 stour

dustbowl victim 4 Okie

dustup 3 row 5 run-in 6 fracas, hassle 7 dispute, quarrel 8 argument 9 bickering 10 falling-out 11 altercation

dusty 3 dim, dry 4 arid, dull 5 blowy, stale 6 barren, sordid, stormy 7 clouded, insipid, powdery, tedious 8 bromidic, weariful 9 dryasdust, miserable, wearisome, worthless 12 contemptible, unproductive, unsatisfying 13 uninteresting *Scottish:* 6 stoury

Dutch 7 trouble 8 hot water 9 Afrikaans *commune:* 3 Ede *housewife:* 4 frow *scholar:* 7 Erasmus *uncle:* 3 oom

dutiful 7 duteous 9 regardful 10 respectful 11 deferential

duty 3 job, tax, use 4 goal, levy, load, mark, must, need, onus, role, task 5 chare, chore, ought, stint 6 burden, charge, devoir, impost, object, office, target, tariff, weight 7 purpose, respect, service 8 business, function, province 9 committal, millstone, objective 10 assessment, assignment, commitment, deadweight, obligation

Duvalier's land 5 Haiti

dwarf 3 wee 4 runt, tiny 5 gnome, midge, pygmy, stunt, troll 6 midget, minify, peewee, teensy 7 manikin, minikin 8 suppress, Tom Thumb 9 miniature 10 diminutive, homunculus 11 hop-o'-my-thumb, lilliputian *combining form:* 3 nan 4 nann, nano 5 nanno *in Snow White:* 3 Doc 5 Dopey, Happy 6 Grumpy, Sleepy, Sneezy 7 Bashful *Scottish:* 7 blastie

dwarf elder 8 danewort, goutweed

dwarfish 4 tiny 6 midget 7 minikin 9 itsy-bitsy, itty-bitty, miniature 10 diminutive 11 lilliputian

dwell 3 lie, won 4 bide, live 5 abide, exist 6 inhere, reside 7 consist, hang out

dweller 5 liver 7 denizen, resider 8 habitant, occupant, resident 10 inhabitant *monastic:* 4 monk 5 friar 6 oblate *suffix:* 3 ite

dwelling 4 casa, home 5 abode, house 8 domicile 9 residence, residency 10 brownstone, commoracy, habitation *American Indian:* 4 tipi 5 hogan, tepee 6 pueblo, teepee, wigwam *clergyman's:* 5 manse 7 rectory 9 parsonage *crude:* 5 shack 6 shanty *Eskimo:* 4 iglu 5 igloo *Hindu:* 6 ashram, asrama 7 ashrama *Navaho:* 5 hogan

dwindle 3 ebb 4 fail, wane 5 abate, close, taper 6 lessen, reduce, shrink, weaken 7 decline, subside 8 decrease, diminish, taper off 9 attenuate, drain away, extenuate, fall short, waste away

dyad 3 duo 4 pair 5 brace 6 couple 7 doublet, twosome

dye 5 color, stain 6 reddle, ruddle 7 pigment 8 colorant, nigrosin, pyronine, tincture *blue:* 4 woad 6 cyanin, indigo 7 cyanine, indulin 8 indigoid, induline *for hair:* 5 henna *green:* 7 gallein *plant:* 4 chay, woad 5 chaya, sumac 6 madder *purple:* 6 orchil *red:* 5 eosin 6 eosine, kermes 7 crocein, cudbear, fuchsin, kermess, magenta 8 alizarin, anchusin, croceine, fuchsine, rhodamin, safranin 9 cochineal *reddish:* 5 henna 8 purpurin *reddish brown:* 6 orcein *violet:* 7 thionin 8 thionine *yellow:* 8 orpiment *yellowish red:* 7 achiote, annatto

dyed-in-the-wool 5 sworn 7 devoted, settled 9 confirmed, hard-shell 10 deep-rooted, deep-seated, entrenched, inveterate 13 bred-in-the-bone

dyeing process 5 batik

dyeleaves 8 inkberry 9 sweetleaf

dye red 6 ruddle

dyer's grape 8 pokeweed

dyer's mulberry 6 fustic

dyestuff see dye

dyewood 6 brasil, brazil, fustet, fustic

dying 8 expiring, moribund

dynamic 4 live 5 alive, lusty, vital 6 active 7 intense, running, working 8 forceful, forcible, vigorous 9 energetic, operative, strenuous 10 functional, red-blooded 11 functioning

dynamite 4 raze, ruin 7 destroy, shatter 8 decimate, demolish, destruct, dissolve 9 dismantle, explosive 10 annihilate *inventor:* 5 Nobel

dynamo 6 peeler 7 hustler, rustler 8 go-getter, live wire 9 generator 11 self-starter

dysentery 4 flux 6 scours 8 diarrhea

dyslogistic 9 slighting 10 derogatory, detracting, pejorative 11 disparaging 12 depreciative, depreciatory

dyspathy 7 allergy 8 aversion

dyspepsia 7 pyrosis 9 gastritis, heart-burn 11 indigestion

dyspeptic 6 morose 10 ill-humored, ill-natured, tempersome 11 bad-tempered, hot-tempered, ill-tempered

dysphoria 5 gloom, mopes 7 sadness 9 dejection 10 depression, melancholy 11 unhappiness 12 mournfulness, wretchedness

dysprosium *symbol:* 2 Dy

Dzhugashvili 6 Stalin

E

each 3 all, per 5 every 6 apiece 8 every-one, per caput 9 per capita

eager 3 hot 4 agog, avid, keen 5 itchy, ready 6 ardent, gung ho, heated, hungry, intent, pining, raring 7 anxious, athirst, crav-ing, longing, restive, thirsty, wishful 8 appe-tent, covetous, desirous, on tiptoe, restless, yearning 9 ambitious, hankering, impatient 10 breathless, solicitous 11 acquisitive 12 enthusiastic

eagerness 4 zeal, zest, zing 5 ardor, gusto 6 fervor 7 avidity 8 alacrity, ambi-tion, fervency, keenness 9 quickness 10 enthusiasm

eagle 4 hawk 9 accipiter *combining form:* 4 aeto 5 aetus *nest:* 4 aery 5 aerie, eyrie *North American:* 4 bald 6 golden 10 bald-headed *sea:* 3 ern 4 erne 6 osprey

eagle-eyed 7 lyncean 12 sharp-sighted

eagre 4 bore, flow, wave 5 flood

ear 4 heed, mark, note 6 notice, regard, remark 7 auricle 8 auricula 9 attention 10 observance 11 observation *bone:* 5 anvil, incus 6 hammer, stapes 7 malleus, stirrup *canal:* 5 scala *combining form:* 2 ot 3 aur, oto 4 auri, otic *doctor:* 9 otolo-gist *inner:* 9 labyrinth *middle:* 8 tympanum *outer:* 5 pinna *part:* 4 drum, lobe 5 canal 6 tragus 7 cochlea *relating to:* 4 otic 5 aural 9 auricular *science:* 7 otology

earache 7 otalgia

eardrum 8 tympanum *combining form:* 6 tympan 7 tympano

____ **Earhart** 6 Amelia

earl 4 lord, peer 5 noble 8 nobleman 10 aristocrat

earlier 3 ere, yet 4 once 5 as yet, so far 6 before, sooner 7 already, thus far 8 for-merly, hitherto, previous 9 erstwhile, pre-ceding 10 beforehand, heretofore, previ-ously *combining form:* 4 fore 6 proter 7 protero

earlier than *prefix:* 3 pre, pro

earliest 5 first, prime 6 maiden 7 initial, pioneer, primary 8 original, primeval, pris-tine *combining form:* 2 eo

earlike projection 3 lug

Earl of Avon 4 Eden

early 3 old 5 first, prior 6 primal, timely 7 ancient, betimes 8 germinal, original, oversoon, previous, primeval, pristine, untimely 9 preceding, premature, prima-tive 10 antecedent, antiquated, beforehand, precocious, prevenient, primordial, seasona-bly 11 precipitant, prematurely *combining form:* 4 pale 5 palae, paleo 6 palaeo, palaio

earn 3 bag, get, net, win 4 gain, make, rate, reap 5 gross, merit, score 6 attain, come by, effect, obtain, secure 7 acquire, bring in, deserve, harvest, procure, realize, receive 8 draw down 9 knock down

earnest 4 busy, pawn, warm, zeal 5 grave, sober, staid, token 6 ardent, pledge, sedate, solemn, somber, warmth 7 serious, sincere, warrant, weighty, zeal-ous 8 diligent, interest, pressing, security, sedulous 9 assiduous, attention, heartfelt 10 enthusiasm, intentness, no-nonsense, passionate, sobersided 11 industrious, per-severant, seriousness 12 enthusiastic, wholehearted

earnestly 4 down, hard 7 for real, soberly 8 actively, dingdong, solemnly 9 intensely, seriously, zealously 10 thor-oughly 11 assiduously, intensively 12 exhaustively, thoughtfully 13 painstakingly

earnestness 7 gravity, resolve 8 deci-sion, firmness, sobriety 10 absorption, intentness 11 engrossment, persistence, seriousness 12 deliberation, perseverance 13 concentration, determination

earnings 4 gain 5 lucre 6 income, living, profit, return 8 proceeds

ear shell 7 abalone
earshot 5 sound 7 hearing
earsplitting 4 loud 6 shrill 7 blaring, roaring 8 piercing 10 stentorian 11 full-mouthed, stentorious
earth 3 mud, orb 4 clay, clod, dirt, fill, land, loom, sand, soil, turf, vale 5 glebe, globe, humus, terra, world 6 cosmos, gravel, ground, planet, sphere 7 dry land, subsoil, terrain 8 creation, universe 9 macrocosm 10 terra firma *combining form:* 2 ge 3 geo 6 tellur 7 telluri, telluro *core:* 12 centrosphere *god:* 3 Geb, Keb, Seb 5 Dagan *goddess:* 2 Ge, Ki 4 Erda, Gaea 5 Ceres, Nintu 6 Kishar 7 Demeter, Nerthus *relating to:* 8 telluric 9 planetary, tellurian 11 terrestrial *satellite:* 4 moon *science:* 7 geology 9 geography *Scottish:* 4 yird 5 yirth
earthenware 4 delf 5 delft 7 biscuit, faience, pottery 8 crockery, majolica 9 stoneware 10 terra-cotta
earthlike 7 terrene 11 terrestrial
earthly 6 carnal, likely, mortal 7 mundane, terrene, worldly 8 material, physical, possible, probable, telluric, temporal 9 corporeal, potential, sublunary, tellurian 10 imaginable 11 conceivable, terrestrial, uncelestial, unspiritual
earthquake 5 seism, shake, shock 6 tremor 7 temblor 8 trembler, tremblor *combining form:* 5 seism 6 seismo *measuring device:* 11 seismograph, seismometer *relating to:* 7 seismic *science:* 10 seismology 11 seismometry
earthwork 4 bank, wall 7 bulwark, rampart 10 embankment 13 fortification
earthworm 7 annelid 9 brandling
earthy 3 low 5 dusty, gross, muddy, sandy 6 clayey 7 mundane, sensual, terrene, worldly 8 banausic, telluric, temporal 9 practical, pragmatic, realistic, sublunary, tellurian 10 hard-boiled, hardheaded 11 terrestrial, uncelestial, unfantastic 12 matter-of-fact 13 materialistic, unsentimental
earwax 7 cerumen
ease 3 aid, lax 4 bate, calm, dull, free, help, rest 5 allay, knock, loose, poise, relax, slack, speed 6 assist, better, deaden, loosen, relief, repose 7 abandon, assuage, calming, fluency, forward, further, improve, inertia, leisure, lighten, mollify, promote, relieve, slacken 8 calmness, deftness, diminish, dispatch, facility, idleness, mitigate, moderate, security, soothing, supinity, thriving 9 abundance, alleviate, disengage, expertise, inertness, passivity, readiness, reduction, untighten, well-being 10 adroitness, ameliorate, artfulness, cleverness, efficiency, expertness, facilitate, inactivity, mitigation, moderation, prosperity, relaxation,

smoothness 11 alleviation, naturalness, spontaneity, tranquility 12 skillfulness, tranquillity
easel 5 frame, stand 7 support
easement 6 relief 9 allayment 10 mitigation 11 alleviation 13 mollification
ease off 3 ebb, lax 4 fall, wane 5 abate, let up, loose, relax, slack, unlax 6 loosen, relent, unbend, unwind 7 die away, die down, slacken, subside 8 loosen up, moderate 9 untighten
easily 4 well 6 freely, indeed, simply 7 handily, lightly, readily 8 facilely, smoothly 9 assuredly, certainly, decidedly, doubtless 10 absolutely, definitely, positively 11 competently, dexterously, doubtlessly, efficiently, undoubtedly 12 effortlessly 13 unequivocally *combining form:* 2 eu
east 4 Asia 6 Levant, Orient *German:* 3 ost
Easter 5 Pasch *relating to:* 7 paschal *symbol:* 3 egg 4 lamb 5 bunny 6 rabbit
eastern 8 oriental 9 Levantine *countries:* 6 Orient *name:* 3 Ali 4 Abou *title:* 3 sri
East Germany *monetary unit:* 7 ostmark
East Indies 9 Indonesia *animal:* 7 tarsier *bark:* 5 niepa *bird:* 4 baya 5 argus *boatman:* 6 serang *civet:* 6 musang *fish:* 5 dorab *fruit:* 6 durian, durion *grass:* 4 kans 5 glaga 6 raggee *herb:* 3 pia 4 chay, sola 6 sesame 7 roselle *monkey:* 7 hanuman 8 entelles *musical instrument:* 4 bina, vina *plant:* 2 da 4 bene, jute, sola, sunn 5 benne, kenaf 6 ambary, sesame 9 patchouli *ship:* 7 patamar 8 pattamar *tree:* 3 nim 4 dhak, neem, poon, toon 5 mahua, niepa, salai, simal, siris 6 banyan, deodar, illupi, sissoo 7 champac, hollong 8 mastwood 10 hursinghar *warrior:* 5 singh *wood:* 3 eng
easy 3 lax 4 calm, cozy, fast, glib, mild, soft, well 5 clear, comfy, cushy, light, loose, naive, plain, royal, suave 6 benign, facile, fluent, kindly, placid, poised, polite, secure, serene, simple, smooth, urbane, wanton 7 amiable, clement, courtly, cursive, evident, flowing, lenient, obvious, relaxed, well-off, whorish 8 apparent, clear-cut, composed, distinct, familiar, graceful, gullible, informal, manifest, merciful, obliging, pleasant, sociable, tolerant, tranquil, trusting, unchaste, well-to-do 9 collected, credulous, forgiving, indulgent, lethargic, possessed, well-fixed 10 charitable, diplomatic, effortless, fleeceable, forbearing, prosperous, successful, uninvolved, well-heeled 11 comfortable, complaisant, good-humored, good-natured, susceptible, sympathetic, unambitious 12 good-tempered 13 compassionate, mol-

lycoddling, self-possessed, uncomplicated, untroublesome

easygoing 3 lax 4 calm, lazy 5 drony 6 breezy, casual, dégagé, folksy, placid, poised, serene 7 affable, offhand, relaxed, unfussy, work-shy 8 carefree, careless, composed, fainéant, flexible, indolent, informal, moderate, slothful, tranquil 9 apathetic, collected, off-handed 10 unaffected, unreserved 11 indifferent, low-pressure, unambitious, unconcerned, uninhibited 12 devil-may-care, happy-go-lucky, self-composed 13 self-possessed, unconstrained

easy mark 3 sap 4 butt, dupe, fool, gull 5 chump 6 pigeon, sucker 7 fall guy 9 soft touch

easy street 8 thriving 9 abundance, well-being 10 prosperity

eat 3 sup 4 bite, chow, dine, gnaw, meal, pick, take, wolf 5 erode, feast, gorge, lunch, mouth, scoff, scour, snack, use up 6 devour, feed on, gobble, ingest, nibble 7 banquet, consume, corrode, exhaust, gorge on, swallow 8 dissolve, wear away 9 breakfast, decompose, partake of, polish off 10 gormandize, nibble away

eatable 6 edible 8 esculent 10 comestible

eater 8 consumer *combining form:* 4 phag, vora, vore 5 estes, phaga, phage 6 phagus

eating *combining form:* 4 phag 5 phago, phagy 6 phagia, vorous 7 phagous

eating place 4 café, mess 5 diner, grill 7 automat, beanery, dinette, tearoom 8 cookshop, messroom, snack bar 9 cafeteria, chophouse, lunchroom 10 coffee shop, restaurant 12 luncheonette

Ebal's father 6 Shobal

ebb 4 fade, fall, tide, wane 5 abate, let up 6 recede, relent 7 decline, die away, die down, ease off, retreat, slacken, subside 8 decrease, diminish, moderate 10 retrograde

Ebed's son 4 Gaal

Eber *father:* 6 Elpaal 7 Shashak *son:* 6 Joktan

Eblis 5 Satan *son:* 3 Tir 4 Awar 5 Dasim 8 Zalambur

ebon, ebony 3 jet 4 inky 5 black, jetty, raven, sable 9 pitch-dark 10 pitch-black 11 atramentous

éboulement 9 avalanche, landslide

ebullience 6 gaiety 7 ferment 8 buoyancy, vitality 9 agitation, animation 10 enthusiasm, excitement, exuberance, exuberancy, liveliness 12 exhilaration 13 effervescence

ebullient 5 brash 7 boiling 8 agitated 9 exuberant, vivacious 12 effervescent, high-spirited

eccentric 3 odd 4 case, coot, kook, quiz 5 crank, freak, kooky, queer, wacky, weird 6 oddity, quirky, zombie 7 bizarre, caution, curious, erratic, heretic, oddball, strange 8 bohemian, crackpot, maverick, original, peculiar, singular 9 anomalous, beeheaded, character, dissenter, fantastic, grotesque, irregular, off-center, quizzical, screwball, unnatural 10 off-balance, unbalanced, uncentered 11 exceptional 12 unconformist 13 exceptionable, idiosyncratic, nonconformist

eccentricity 5 quirk 6 oddity 10 aberration 11 peculiarity, strangeness 12 idiosyncrasy

ecclesiastic 5 clerk 6 cleric, divine, parson 8 clerical, minister, preacher, reverend 9 churchman, clergyman

ecclesiastical 5 papal 6 church 8 churchly, clerical, pastoral, priestly 9 apostolic, canonical, episcopal, prelatial, spiritual, synagogal 10 churchlike, pantheonic, pontifical, rabbinical, sacerdotal, templelike 11 churchmanly, ministerial, patriarchal, synagogical, theological 12 episcopalian, evangelistic, tabernacular

ecdysiast 6 peeler, teaser 8 stripper 10 striptease 11 stripteaser

echelon 3 row 4 file, line, rank, tier 5 queue 6 string 9 formation

echidna 5 bitis, snake, viper 8 anteater

Echidna *father:* 7 Phorcys 8 Chrysaor *mother:* 4 Ceto 10 Callirrhoe *offspring:* 5 Hydra 6 dragon, Orthus, Sphinx 7 Chimera 8 Cerberus, Chimaera

echinoderm 6 urchin 8 starfish

echo 4 ring 5 oread 6 repeat, reverb, second 7 imitate, iterate, reflect, resound, revoice 8 resonate, response 9 reiterate 10 reflection, repetition 11 reverberate 12 repercussion 13 reverberation

echoic 9 imitative 12 onomatopoeic 13 onomatopoetic

Echo's beloved 9 Narcissus

éclat 4 bang, dash, fame, pomp 5 kudos 6 luster, renown, repute 7 acclaim, display 8 applause, standing 9 celebrity, notoriety 10 brilliance, brilliancy, prominence, reputation 11 distinction, ostentation

eclectic 5 broad, fussy, mixed, picky 6 choosy, select, varied 7 derived, diverse, finicky, mingled 8 assorted, catholic, elective 9 inclusive, multiform, selective 10 discerning, fastidious, particular 11 diversified 12 multifarious 13 comprehensive, heterogeneous

eclipse 3 dim 4 murk 5 bedim, cloud, cover, excel, shade 6 darken, exceed, shadow 7 becloud, decline, obscure, surpass 8 downfall 9 adumbrate, overcloud 10 overshadow

eclogue 4 idyl, poem 5 idyll 7 bucolic

ecological 8 bionomic *community:* 5 biome *succession:* 7 subsere

ecology 7 bionomy 9 bionomics

economic 8 material 10 profitable *doctrine:* 12 laissez-faire *system:* 7 fascism 9 communism, socialism 10 capitalism 11 syndicalism 12 mercantilism

economical 4 mean 5 canny, chary, close, spare 6 frugal, saving, stingy 7 careful, miserly, prudent, sparing, thrifty 8 skimping 9 niggardly, penny-wise, penurious, provident, scrimping, stewardly 10 forehanded, unwasteful 12 cheeseparing 13 penny-pinching

economist *American:* 6 George, Veblen, Walker, Weaver 8 Friedman 9 Galbraith, Samuelson *Canadian:* 7 Leacock *Dutch:* 9 Tinbergen *English:* 4 Mill 5 Pigou 6 Keynes 7 Malthus, Ricardo *French:* 6 Turgot, Walras 7 Quesnay *German:* 5 Weber *Scottish:* 5 Smith *Swedish:* 6 Myrdal *Swiss:* 8 Sismondi

economize 4 save 5 skimp 6 scrimp 7 husband 8 conserve

economy 6 thrift 7 parcity 8 meanness, prudence, skimping 9 frugality, husbandry, parsimony, scrimping 10 discretion, providence, stinginess 11 carefulness, miserliness, thriftiness 13 niggardliness

ecru 5 beige

ecstasy 3 joy 5 bliss 6 frenzy, heaven 7 delight, elation, madness, rapture 8 euphoria, felicity, gladness, paradise, pleasure, rhapsody 9 beatitude, happiness, transport 10 exaltation, joyfulness 11 blessedness, delectation, enchantment, inspiration 12 blissfulness, exhilaration, intoxication 13 seventh heaven

Ecuador *capital:* 5 Quito *monetary unit:* 5 sucre

ecumenical 6 cosmic, global 7 general 8 catholic 9 inclusive, planetary, universal, worldwide 10 heaven-wide 11 all-covering 12 all-including, all-pervading, cosmopolitan 13 comprehensive

ecumenical council 4 Lyon 5 Trent 6 Nicene, Vienne 7 Ephesus, Lateran, Vatican 9 Chalcedon, Constance

eczema 6 tetter 9 malanders 10 mallenders

edacious 8 ravening, ravenous 9 voracious 10 gluttonous

eddo 4 root, taro

eddy 4 purl 5 gurge, surge, swirl, twirl, whirl, whorl 6 swoosh, vortex 8 backwash 9 backwater, maelstrom, whirlpool 10 back stream 11 back current, counterflow, counterflux *combining form:* 4 dino

edema 5 tumor 6 dropsy 8 anasarca, swelling

Eden 6 heaven, utopia 7 arcadia, elysium 8 paradise *river:* 5 Gihon 6 Pishon 8 Hiddekel 9 Euphrates

edentate 5 sloth 8 anteater 9 armadillo, toothless

Ederyn's father 4 Nudd

Edessa's king 5 Abgar

edge 3 cut, end, hem, lip, rim 4 bank, bite, brim, draw, hone, side, whet 5 bound, brink, bulge, ledge, picot, point, ridge, sidle, skirt, start, sting, verge 6 border, fringe, margin, nosing 7 acidity, outline, serrate, sharpen, vantage 8 acerbity, acridity, boundary, emborder, handicap, keenness, surround, thinness 9 acuteness, advantage, allowance, extremity, head start, knife-edge, perimeter, periphery, sharpness, threshold 10 causticity, shrillness, stringency 11 astringency, penetration 12 incisiveness

edged 5 sharp 7 crenate, cutting, vallate

edge in 4 worm 5 foist 9 insinuate 10 infiltrate

edging 3 hem 4 lace 5 braid 6 border, fringe, lacing

edgy 5 nervy, tense 6 touchy, uneasy 7 excited, restive, uptight 8 agitable, restless, skittery, skittish, volatile 9 alarmable, excitable, impatient, irritable, startlish 10 high-strung

edible 7 eatable 8 esculent 9 palatable 10 comestible *root:* 3 yam 4 beet, taro 6 carrot, radish, turnip 7 parsnip 8 rutabaga 11 sweet potato *seed:* 3 nut, pea 4 bean 6 peanut

edibles 4 food, grub 6 viands 7 nurture 8 victuals 9 provender 10 provisions 11 comestibles

edict 3 law 4 bull, fiat, rule 5 canon, order, ukase 6 decree, dictum, ruling 7 command, precept, statute 8 decretum 9 directive, manifesto, ordinance, prescript 10 instrument, regulation 12 proclamation 13 pronouncement *papal:* 4 bull 8 decretal

Edict of ____ 5 Milan 6 Nantes

edifice 4 pile 6 church 8 building, erection 9 structure

edify 5 teach 6 better, illume, uplift 7 educate, elevate, enhance, improve 8 illumine, instruct 9 elucidate, enlighten, irradiate 10 illuminate

edit 3 cut 4 omit 5 adapt, alter, amend, emend 6 delete, redact, refine, review, revise, reword, select 7 compile, correct, rewrite 8 assemble, copyread 9 rearrange

edition 4 copy 5 issue, print 7 reissue, version 8 printing, variorum 10 impression, reprinting 12 reproduction

editor 8 redactor 10 copyreader 11 proofreader

Edomite's ancestor 4 Esau

educate 4 rear 5 brief, teach, train

6 inform, school 7 explain, nurture
8 instruct 9 enlighten 10 discipline
12 indoctrinate

education 7 culture, science, tuition
8 breeding, coaching, guidance, learning, literacy, pedagogy, teaching, training, tutelage, tutorage, tutoring 9 erudition, knowledge, schooling, tutorship 11 instruction,
learnedness, scholarship 13 enlightenment

educational 11 informative, informatory,
instructive 13 informational, instructional
institution: 6 school 7 academy, college
9 institute 10 university 12 conservatory

educator 5 tutor 7 teacher 9 professor
10 instructor *American:* 4 Mann
6 Conant 8 McGuffey *Italian:* 10 Montes-
sori *Swiss:* 10 Pestalozzi

educe 4 drag, draw, gain, milk, pull
5 evoke, wrest, wring 6 derive, elicit,
evince, evolve, extort, obtain, secure 7 distill, draw out, extract, procure 10 excogitate

eel 4 worm 5 moray, siren, snake 6 conger, murena 7 hagfish, lamprey, muraena,
sniggle 8 wriggler 9 muraenoid *young:*
5 elver

eelboat 5 shuyt

eelpout 6 blenny, burbot 10 muttonfish

eely 6 slippy, wiggly 7 elusive, wriggly
8 slippery, slithery 9 wriggling

eerie 5 scary, weird 6 arcane, crawly,
creepy, spooky 7 bizarre, strange,
uncanny 9 fantastic, grotesque, unearthly
10 mysterious 11 frightening

efface 4 dele, x out 5 annul, erase 6 cancel, delete 7 blot out, destroy, exclude,
expunge, rule out, wipe out 8 black out
9 eliminate, eradicate, extirpate
10 obliterate

effect 3 end 4 make 5 cause, enact,
event, fruit, issue, yield 6 create, draw on,
induce, invoke, render, result, secure,
sequel, upshot 7 achieve, bring on, enforce,
fulfill, outcome, perform, procure, produce,
realize, turn out 8 bring off, carry out, causatum, conceive, generate, sequence
9 actualize, aftermath, corollary, implement,
outgrowth, pursuance 10 accomplish, bring
about, conclusion, denouement, end product 11 consequence, development, eventuality, precipitate 12 carry through, ramification, repercussion

effective 4 able 5 sound, valid 6 causal,
cogent, direct, potent, useful 7 capable,
dynamic, telling, virtual 8 adequate, virtuous 9 competent, efficient, operative
10 compelling, convincing 11 efficacious

effectiveness 5 force, point, power,
punch, verve, vigor 7 cogency, potency
8 efficacy, strength, validity 9 validness
10 capability, efficiency 11 performance

effects 5 goods 6 things 8 chattels, movables 10 belongings 11 possessions

effectual 5 sound, valid 6 potent, strong,
toothy, useful 8 decisive, powerful, virtuous, workable 9 achieving, efficient
10 conclusive, fulfilling 11 efficacious, influential, practicable 13 accomplishing, authoritative, determinative

effectuate 7 execute, fulfill 8 bring off,
carry out 10 accomplish 12 carry through

effeminate 5 sappy, sissy 6 chichi,
female, prissy, silken 7 epicene, foppish,
unmanly 8 overnice, precious, womanish
9 pansified, sissified 10 old-maidish
12 Miss-Nancyish

effervescence 7 fizzing, foaming 8 bub-
bling, buoyancy 10 ebullience, ebullition,
exuberance, exuberancy

effervescent 3 gay 4 airy 5 brash, jolly
6 bouncy, bubbly, lively 7 boiling, buoyant,
elastic, excited, gleeful 8 animated, mirthful,
volatile 9 ebullient, expansive, exuberant,
hilarious, resilient, sparkling, sprightly, vivacious 12 high-spirited

effete 4 done, sere, soft, weak 5 all in,
spent 6 barren, bleary, done in, used up
7 decayed, drained, far-gone, immoral, sterile, worn-out 8 consumed, decadent, decaying, depleted, fatigued, impotent, infecund,
overripe 9 declining, dissolute, enfeebled,
exhausted, infertile, washed-out 10 degenerate, unfruitful 11 debilitated

efficacious 6 active, potent, strong
8 forceful, forcible, powerful, puissant, virtuous 9 effective, effectual, efficient, operative 10 productive 11 influential

efficacy see **effectiveness**

efficiency see **effectiveness**

efficient 4 able 5 adept 6 expert, fitted
7 capable, skilled 8 masterly, skillful, virtuous 9 competent, effective, effectual, qualified 11 efficacious 12 businesslike

effigy 5 dummy, image 7 waxwork 8 likeness, portrait

effloresce 4 blow 5 bloom 6 flower
7 blossom, burgeon 8 outbloom

effluvium 4 odor 5 smell 6 efflux
7 exhaust 9 emanation 10 exhalation

efflux 4 flow 7 outflow 8 effusion
9 emanation

effort 3 job, try 4 task, toil, work 5 chore,
essay, force, labor, might, nisus, pains,
power, while 6 energy, strain 7 attempt,
travail, trouble 8 endeavor, exertion, struggle, taskwork 9 puissance 11 application,
elbow grease

effortful 4 hard 5 rough 6 uphill 7 arduous, labored, operose 8 toilsome 9 difficult,
laborious, strenuous

effortless 4 easy 5 adept, light, ready,
royal 6 expert, facile, fluent, simple,

smooth **7** cursive, flowing, running, skilled **8** masterly, skillful **10** proficient **13** untroublesome

effrontery 4 face, gall **5** brass, cheek, nerve **8** audacity, boldness, temerity **9** assurance, brashness, hardihood, impudence, insolence **10** brazenness, confidence **11** presumption **12** impertinence **13** self-assurance

effulgence 4 glow **5** blaze **8** radiance, splendor **10** brightness, brilliance, luminosity

effulgent 5 vivid **6** bright, lucent **7** beaming, lambent, radiant **8** glorious, luminous, splendid **9** brilliant **11** resplendent **12** incandescent

effuse 4 flow, gush, pour, shed **7** emanate, radiate

effusive 5 gushy **6** sloppy, slushy, smarmy **7** cloying, fulsome, gushing, profuse **8** slobbery **9** expansive, exuberant **10** outpouring, slobbering, unreserved **12** unrestrained **13** demonstrative, unconstrained

eft 4 newt **6** triton **10** salamander

egest 4 void **7** excrete **9** discharge

egg 3 ova (plural), sic **4** goad, ovum, prod, seed, spur, urge **5** drive, ovule, pique, prick, rally **6** arouse, excite, exhort, prompt, stir up **7** agitate **9** instigate, stimulate *before maturation:* **6** oocyte *case:* **5** shell **6** ovisac **7** ootheca *combining form:* **2** oo, ov **3** ovi, ovo *dish:* **6** omelet **8** omelette *fertilized:* **6** zygote **7** oosperm, oospore *fish:* **3** roe **6** caviar *French:* **4** oeuf *part:* **4** yelk, yolk **5** glair, shell, white **7** albumen, latebra **10** blastodisc *product:* **3** zoa (plural) **4** zoon *white:* **5** glair **7** albumen *yolk:* **6** yellow **8** vitellus

egghead 7 Brahmin **8** highbrow **10** double-dome **12** intellectual

eggplant 7 brinjal **8** brinjaul **9** aubergine

egg-shaped 4 ooid, oval **5** ovate, ovoid **6** ooidal **7** oviform

eggshell 8 cascaron

Egil's brother 6 Volund

Eglah *husband:* **5** David *son:* **7** Ithream

eglantine 7 dog rose **10** sweetbrier

Eglantine *father:* **5** Pepin *husband:* **9** Valentine

Eglon *king:* **5** Debir *slayer:* **4** Ehud

ego 4 self **6** vanity **7** conceit **10** self-esteem

egocentric 7 pompous, selfish, stuck-up **9** conceited **10** self-loving **11** self-seeking, self-serving **12** megalomaniac, narcissistic, self-absorbed, self-affected, self-centered, self-involved, vainglorious **13** individualist, self-conceited, self-concerned, self-indulgent

egoism 5 pride **6** vanity **7** conceit **9** self-

glory, self-pride, vainglory **11** self-opinion **13** self-assurance

egomaniacal 7 selfish **11** self-serving **12** self-absorbed, self-centered, self-exalting, self-involved, vainglorious **13** self-concerned

egotism 5 pride **6** vanity **7** conceit **8** boasting, bragging, self-love, vainness, vaunting **9** arrogance, gasconade, gasconism, self-glory, self-pride, vainglory **10** narcissism, self-esteem **11** megalomania, self-opinion, superiority **12** boastfulness **13** conceitedness

egotistic 5 cocky, proud **7** selfish, stuck-up **8** boastful, inflated, puffed up **9** conceited **11** pretentious, self-serving **12** self-absorbed, self-centered, self-involved **13** self-concerned, self-satisfied

egregious 4 rank **5** gross, stark **6** arrant **7** blatant, capital, glaring, heinous **8** flagrant, infamous, outright, shocking **9** atrocious **10** deplorable, outrageous

egress 4 door, exit **5** issue **6** escape, exodus, outlet **7** doorway, exiting, opening, passage **8** emerging, offgoing **9** departure, emergence **10** setting-out, withdrawal

egression 4 exit **6** exodus **7** exiting **8** offgoing **9** departure **10** setting-out, withdrawal

Egypt *capital:* **5** Cairo *monetary unit:* **5** pound

Egyptian 4 Arab, Copt **6** Coptic **7** African, Arabian *burial jar:* **7** canopic *Christian:* **4** Copt *cross:* **4** ankh *dam:* **4** sudd **5** Aswan *dancing girl:* **4** alme **7** ghawazi (plural) **8** ghawazee (plural) *dynasty:* **5** Saite, Xoite **5** Hyksos, Tanite, Theban **7** Persian, Thinite **8** Memphite **9** Bubastite, Ethiopian **10** Diospolite
god:
    chief: **6** Amen-Ra *crocodile-headed:* **5** Sebek *falcon-headed:* **4** Ment **5** Horus, Mentu **6** Sokari **7** Sokaris *ibis-headed:* **5** Thoth **6** Dhouti *jackal-headed:* **6** Anubis *of chaos:* **2** Nu *of creation:* **4** Ptah **5** Phtha *of day:* **5** Horus *of earth:* **3** Geb, Keb, Seb *of evil:* **3** Set **4** Seth **5** Sebek *of life:* **4** Amen, Amon **5** Ammon *of magic:* **5** Thoth **6** Dhouti *of Memphis:* **4** Ptah **5** Phtha **6** Sokari **7** Sokaris *of pleasure:* **3** Bes *of procreation:* **3** Min *of the air:* **3** Shu *of the heavens:* **5** Horus *of the morning sun:* **5** Horus **7** Khepera *of the primeval flood:* **2** Nu *of the setting sun:* **3** Tem, Tum **4** Atmu *of the sun:* **2** Ra, Re **6** Amen-Ra *of Thebes:* **4** Amen **6** Khensu, Khonsu *of the underworld:* **6** Osiris *of war:* **4** Ment **5** Mentu *of wisdom:* **5** Thoth **6** Dhouti *ram-headed:* **4** Amen, Amon **5** Ammon,

Khnum **6** Khnemu *snake:* **4** Apep
5 Apepi
goddess:
  cat-headed: **4** Bast **5** Pakht *cow-
  headed:* **5** Athor **6** Hathor *lioness-
  headed:* **4** Bast **5** Pakht **6** Sekhet *of
  arms:* **4** Anta *of fertility:* **4** Isis *of love
  and mirth:* **5** Athor **6** Hathor *of moisture:* **6** Tefnut *of motherhood:* **4** Apet,
  Isis *of Thebes:* **3** Mut *of the dead:*
  8 Nephthys *of the heavens:* **3** Nut *of
  truth and justice:* **4** Maat *queen of the
  gods:* **4** Sati *vulture-headed:* **3** Mut
  7 Nekhebt **8** Nekhebet
king: (see *king* entry)
language: **6** Arabic, Coptic *measure:*
3 apt, dra, hen, pik, rob **4** draa, roub
5 ardab, ardeb, cubit, farde, keleh, kilah,
sahme **6** artaba, aurure, feddan, keddah,
robbah **7** choryos, daribah, malouah, rou-
bouh, toumnah **8** kassabah, kharouba
10 dira baladi *month:* **4** Apap, Tybi **5** Payni,
Thoth **6** Choiak, Hathor, Mechir, Mesore,
Paophi **7** Pachons **9** Phamenoth, Pharmu-
thi *native:* **4** Arab, Copt **5** Nilot *president:*
5 Sadat **6** Nasser **7** Mubarak *queen:*
9 Cleopatra, Nefertiti *sacred bird:* **4** ibis
season: **4** Ahet, Pert **5** Shemu *skink:*
4 adda *snake symbol:* **6** uraeus *solar
disk:* **4** Aten *soul:* **2** ba, ka **3** akh *sultan:*
7 Saladin *talisman:* **6** scarab *underworld:*
4 Aaru, Duat **6** Amenti *weight:* **3** kat, oka,
oke **4** heml, okia, rotl **5** artal, artel, deben,
kerat, okieh, uckia **6** hamlah, kantar **7** quintal *wind:* **7** chamsin, khamsin, sirocco
8 khamseen
Ehud's victim 5 Eglon
eider 4 down, duck **8** shoreyer
eidetic 5 vivid **8** lifelike
eidolon 4 icon **5** ghost, ideal, image
7 phantom, specter **8** exemplar, phantasm
eight *combining form:* **3** oct **4** octa, octo
  group of: **5** octad, octet **6** octave,
  ogdoad **7** octette **8** octuplet
eighth note 6 quaver
Einstein 6 genius *birthplace:* **3** Ulm
einsteinium *symbol:* **2** Es
Eire 4 Erin **5** Ierne **7** Ireland **8** Hibernia
9 Innisfail *capital:* **6** Dublin *monetary unit:*
5 pound
ejaculate 4 blat, bolt, yell **5** eject, shout
6 cry out **7** exclaim **8** blurt out **10** vociferate
ejaculation see **exclamation**
eject 3 out **4** boot, bump, fire, oust, rout,
sack, shed, spew **5** belch, chase, chuck,
debar, eruct, erupt, evict, expel, spout,
spurn **6** banish, disbar, irrupt, run off,
squirt **7** boot out, discard, dismiss, exclude,
extrude, kick out, rule out, shut out, sputter **8** disgorge, displace, drive off, throw

out **9** discharge, ejaculate, eliminate, repudiate **10** dispossess
eke 4 fill **7** squeeze, stretch
10 supplement
elaborate 4 busy **5** fancy **6** daedal,
dressy, evolve, expand, knotty, ornate,
unfold **7** amplify, clarify, comment, complex, develop, discuss, elegant, enlarge,
explain, expound, gordian **8** detailed,
involved, overdone **9** Byzantine, decorated,
interpret, intricate **10** overworked **11** complicated, embellished, overwrought, painstaking **12** labyrinthine
Elah *father:* **4** Uzzi **5** Caleb **6** Baasha
slayer: **5** Zimri *son:* **6** Hoshea
Elaine *father:* **6** Pelles *lover:* **8** Lancelot
9 Launcelot *son:* **7** Galahad
Elam *capital:* **4** Susa **7** Shushan *father:*
4 Shem *king:* **12** Chedorlaomer
élan 3 vim **4** brio, dash, life, zeal, zest,
zing **5** ardor, gusto, oomph, verve, vigor
6 esprit, spirit **7** impetus, potency **9** animation, eagerness **10** enthusiasm
élan vital 4 soul **5** anima **6** animus,
pneuma, psyche, spirit
elapse 2 go **4** flow, pass, slip **5** glide,
slide **6** expire, run out **8** pass away
Elasah's father 6 Pashur **7** Shaphan
elastic 4 airy **5** lithe **6** bouncy, garter, limber, lively, pliant, rubber, supple, whippy
7 buoyant, ductile, pliable, rubbery, soaring,
springy, stretch **8** animated, flexible, moldable, spirited, stretchy, volatile **9** adaptable,
ebullient, expansive, malleable, resilient,
sprightly, vivacious **10** mettlesome, rubber-
like **11** stretchable
elate 4 buoy **5** cheer, exalt, flush, set up
6 excite, uplift **7** cheer up, commove,
delight, gladden, gratify, inspire, overjoy
8 brighten, inspirit, spirit up **9** encourage
elated 4 glad **5** happy **6** jovial **7** excited,
exulted **8** ecstatic, euphoric, exultant, glad-
some, jubilant, turned-on **9** overjoyed
10 enraptured **11** exhilarated, intoxicated
elater 6 beetle **8** skipjack **11** click beetle
Elatha's son 4 Bres
elation 3 joy **4** glee **7** rapture **8** buoyancy, euphoria **9** happiness, transport
10 exaltation, excitement **12** exhilaration,
intoxication
Elbe tributary 4 Eger, Iser
elbow 4 push **5** ancon, joint, nudge, press,
shove **6** hustle, jostle **8** bulldoze *relating
to:* **7** anconal
El Camino ____ 4 Real
elder 5 prior **6** senior **7** ancient, oldster
8 brass hat, higher-up, old-timer, superior
9 presbyter **10** golden-ager **13** senior citizen *French:* **4** aîné **5** aînée
elderliness 3 age **5** years **6** old age
8 caducity **10** senescence **11** senectitude

elderly 3 old 4 aged, gray 5 aging, olden
6 senile 7 ancient 9 declining

eldorado 4 mine 7 bonanza 8 Golconda,
gold mine, treasury 13 treasure-house,
treasure trove

eldritch 5 eerie, weird 7 uncanny

Eleanor's husband 7 Henry II

Eleazar *brother:* 5 Abihu, Nadab *father:*
4 Dodo 5 Aaron 6 Parosh 8 Abinadab,
Phinehas *son:* 8 Phinehas

elect 3 opt 4 cull, like, mark, name, pick,
rare, take, vote, will, wish 5 admit, co-opt,
judge, saved 6 accept, ballot, choice,
choose, chosen, decide, optate, opt for,
picked, please, prefer, settle, single, vote in
7 appoint, receive, resolve 8 conclude, destined, nominate, ordained, redeemed
9 delivered, designate, determine, exclusive,
single out 10 designated, handpicked, sin-
gled out

election 6 choice 7 primary 9 balloting
10 preference 11 alternative

electioneer 5 stump 8 campaign, politick

elective 6 chosen 8 optional 9 voluntary
13 discretionary, nonobligatory

Electra *brother:* 7 Orestes *father:*
5 Atlas 7 Oceanus 9 Agamemnon *husband:* 7 Pylades, Thaumas *mother:*
6 Tethys 7 Pleione 12 Clytemnestra *sister:* 4 Styx 9 Iphigenia *son:* 6 Iasion
8 Dardanus

electric *appliance:* 3 fan 4 iron, oven
5 clock, drier, mixer, range, stove
6 washer 7 blender, freezer, toaster
12 refrigerator *coil:* 5 tesla 8 solenoid
device: 4 coil, fuse, plug 6 dynamo, magnet, switch 7 battery 8 resistor, rheostat,
varistor 9 amplifier, capacitor, condenser,
generator, rheotrope 11 transformer *generator:* 6 dynamo *particle:* 3 ion 8 thermion
resistance: 6 ohmage *unit:* 3 amp, ohm,
rel 4 volt, watt 5 farad, henry, joule
6 abvolt, ampere 7 coulomb, faraday 8 kil-
ovolt, kilowatt

electric current 2 AC, DC *combining
form:* 5 potam 6 potamo *kind:* 6 direct
11 alternating *power:* 7 wattage *strength:*
8 amperage

electricity 5 juice, spark 7 current 8 vol-
taism 9 galvanism, lightning 10 enthusiasm, excitement *kind:* 6 static 7 current

electrify 3 jar 4 send, stun 6 excite, thrill
7 enthuse, provoke, stagger, startle

electrode 6 dynode *negative:* 7 cathode
positive: 5 anode

electron 3 ion 7 polaron 8 negatron
stream: 10 cathode ray *tube:* 6 triode
7 tetrode 8 dynatron, klystron

Electryon *brother:* 6 Mestor *daughter:*
7 Alcmene *father:* 7 Perseus *mother:*
9 Andromeda *wife:* 5 Anaxo

eleemosynary 6 humane 7 liberal 8 generous 10 altruistic, beneficent, benevolent,
charitable, munificent, openhanded
12 humanitarian 13 philanthropic

elegance 4 chic, pomp, tone 5 charm,
grace, style, taste 6 beauty, luxury, polish
7 culture, dignity 8 chicness, lushness,
poshness, richness, splendor 10 ornate-
ness, refinement 11 cultivation 12 magnificence, tastefulness 13 sumptuousness

elegant 4 chic, fine, posh, rare 5 grand,
noble, swank 6 august, choice, classy,
dainty, lovely, select, swanky, urbane
7 courtly, genteel, opulent, refined, stately
8 cultured, delicate, finished, graceful, handsome, majestic, polished, superior, tasteful
9 beautiful, exquisite, luxurious, recherché,
sumptuous 10 cultivated

elegy 4 poem, song 5 dirge 6 lament,
monody 7 epicede 9 epicedium *Hebrew:*
5 kinah

Elektra composer 7 Strauss

element 4 item, part 5 basic, facet, metal,
piece, point, thing 6 aspect, detail, factor,
member, sector 7 article, feature, portion,
section 8 division, particle, rudiment
9 component, essential, principle 10 ingredient, particular 11 constituent, fundamental 13 part and parcel *chemical:* 3 tin
4 gold, iron, lead, neon, zinc 5 argon,
boron, radon, xenon 6 barium, carbon,
cerium, cesium, cobalt, copper, curium,
erbium, helium, indium, iodine, nickel,
osmium, oxygen, radium, silver, sodium
7 arsenic, bismuth, bromine, cadmium, calcium, fermium, gallium, hafnium, holmium,
iridium, krypton, lithium, mercury, niobium,
rhenium, rhodium, silicon, sulphur, terbium,
thorium, thulium, uranium, yttrium 8 actinium, aluminum, antimony, astatine, chlorine,
chromium, europium, fluorine, hydrogen,
illinium, lutecium, masurium, nitrogen, nobel-
ium, platinum, polonium, rubidium, samar-
ium, scandium, selenium, tantalum, thallium,
titanium, tungsten, vanadium 9 americium,
berkelium, beryllium, columbium, germa-
nium, lanthanum, magnesium, manganese,
neodymium, neptunium, palladium, plutonium, potassium, ruthenium, strontium, tellurium, virginium, ytterbium, zirconium
10 dysprosium, gadolinium, lawrencium,
molybdenum 11 californium, einsteinium,
mendelevium, phosphorous 12 praseodym-
ium 13 protoactinium *hypothetical:*
8 coronium

elemental 4 pure 5 basal, basic, crude,
prime 6 inborn, innate, primal, simple
7 connate, primary, radical 8 inherent, intimate, simplest 9 beginning, essential,
ingrained, intrinsic, primitive 10 deep-

seated, primordial, substratal, underlying **14** constitutional

elementary 4 easy **5** basal, basic **6** simple **8** simplest, unsubtle **9** beginning, essential, prefatory, primitive **10** rudimental, substratal, underlying **11** fundamental, preliminary **12** introductory

elemi 5 animé, resin **9** oleoresin

elephant 5 hathi **6** muckna, tusker **9** pachyderm *boy:* **4** Sabu *driver:* **6** mahout *enclosure:* **5** kraal **6** keddah *extinct:* **7** mammoth **8** mastodon *female:* **3** cow *goad:* **5** ankus **7** ankusha *group:* **4** herd *keeper:* **6** mahout *male:* **4** bull *maverick:* **5** rogue *nose:* **5** trunk **9** proboscis *seat:* **6** howdah *sound:* **4** barr **6** bellow **7** trumpet *tooth:* **4** tusk *tusk:* **5** ivory *young:* **4** calf

elephant-headed god 6 Ganesa **7** Ganesha

elephantine 4 huge **6** clumsy **7** awkward, mammoth **8** colossal, enormous, gigantic **9** graceless, maladroit, monstrous, ponderous **10** behemothic, gargantuan, mastodonic, prodigious, ungraceful, uninspired **11** heavy-footed, heavy-handed

elevate 4 lift, rear, rise **5** boost, elate, ensky, erect, exalt, hoist, raise **6** pick up, prefer, take up, uphold, uplift, uprear **7** advance, enhance, glorify, promote, upgrade, upraise **8** heighten **10** exhilarate

elevated 4 high **5** grand, great, lofty, moral, noble **6** aerial, formal, lifted, raised, superb **7** ethical, exalted, stately, sublime, upright, uprisen **8** eloquent, majestic, towering, upheaved, uplifted, upraised, virtuous **9** dignified, grandiose, high-flown, honorable, righteous **10** high-minded, upstanding **13** grandiloquent

elevation 4 hill, rise **5** boost, mount, raise **6** ascent, height **7** advance, raising **8** altitude, highness, mountain **9** acclivity, promotion, upgrading **10** apotheosis, preference, preferment **11** advancement, ennoblement *indication:* **9** bench mark

elevator 4 cage, lift, silo **5** hoist **6** lifter, raiser **7** hoister *maker:* **4** Otis

eleven *combining form:* **5** undec **6** hendec **7** hendeca

elf 3 fay **4** ouph, peri, pixy **5** fairy, nisse, ouphe, pixie **6** goblin, sprite **7** brownie, gremlin **10** leprechaun

elfin 5 child **6** urchin

elfish see **elvish**

Elgin ____ 7 marbles

Eli 4 Yale *son:* **6** Hophni **8** Phinehas *successor:* **6** Ahitub

Eli ____ 7 Whitney

Eliab *brother:* **5** David *daughter:* **7** Abihail *father:* **5** Helon, Pallu *son:* **6** Abiram, Dathan

Eliada *father:* **5** David *son:* **5** Rezon

Eliakim's father 6 Josiah **7** Hilkiah

Eliam's daughter 9 Bathsheba

Eliashib's father 4 Bani **5** Zattu **8** Elioenai

Eliathah's father 5 Heman

elicit 4 draw, milk **5** bring, cause, educe, evoke, fetch **6** derive, evince, extort **7** extract, provoke **8** bring out **9** call forth

elide 4 fail, omit, pass, skip **6** forget, ignore, slight **7** neglect **8** discount, overlook, suppress **9** disregard

Eliel's father 6 Hebron, Shimhi **7** Shashak

Eliezer's father 5 Harim, Moses **6** Zichri **7** Dodovah

eligible 3 fit **6** fitted, likely, nubile, seemly, suited, worthy **7** capable **8** suitable **9** desirable, qualified, visitable **10** acceptable, preferable **12** marriageable

Elihu ____ 4 Root, Yale

Elijah 5 Elias **7** prophet **8** Tishbite *father:* **5** Harim **7** Jeroham

Elimelech's wife 5 Naomi

eliminate 3 bar **4** bate, oust **5** debar, eject, erase, evict, expel, purge **6** delete, except, remove **7** dismiss, exclude, expunge, obviate, rule out, shut out, suspend, take out **8** count out **9** clear away, freeze out, liquidate

Eliot novel 6 Romola **8** Adam Bede **11** Middlemarch, Silas Marner **14** Mill on the Floss

Eliphal's father 2 Ur

Eliphaz *father:* **4** Esau *mother:* **4** Adah *son:* **5** Teman

Eliphelet's father 5 David **6** Hashum **7** Ahasbai **8** Adonikam

eliquate 4 melt **5** smelt

Elisabeth *husband:* **9** Zacharias *son:* **4** John (the Baptist)

Elisha *father:* **7** Shaphat *servant:* **6** Gehazi

Elishah's father 5 Javan

Elishama's father 5 David **7** Ammihud

Elisheba *brother:* **7** Nahshon *father:* **9** Amminadab *husband:* **5** Aaron *son:* **5** Abihu, Nadab **7** Eleazar, Ithamar

Elishua's father 5 David

Elissa see **Dido**

elite 3 top **4** best, pick **5** cream, elect, pride, prime, prize **6** choice, flower, gentry, jet set, select **7** aristoi, quality, society **8** optimacy, smart set **9** gentility **10** upper class, upper crust **11** aristocracy

Eliud *father:* **5** Achim *son:* **7** Eleazar

elixir 4 balm, cure **6** potion **7** arcanum, cure-all, nostrum, panacea, therapy **10** catholicon **11** therapeutic

Elizaphan see **Elzaphan**

elk 4 deer, losh 5 moose 6 sambar, sambur, wapiti

Elkanah *brother:* 5 Assir 8 Abiasaph *father:* 4 Joel 5 Korah 6 Mahath 7 Jeroham *son:* 6 Samuel *wife:* 6 Hannah 8 Peninnah

ell 3 arm 4 wing 5 annex, block 8 addition 9 extension

ellipse 4 oval 5 curve

elliptical 5 brief, ovate, short 7 concise, cryptic, summary 9 condensed, enigmatic

Elmire's husband 5 Orgon

elocution 7 oratory 8 rhetoric 11 speechcraft

elongate 4 draw 6 extend, string 7 draw out, lengthy, spin out, stretch 8 extended, lengthen, protract, wiredraw 10 lengthened

elongation 9 extension 10 production 11 lengthening, protraction

Elon's father 7 Zebulun

elope 4 flee 6 escape 7 run away

eloquence 5 force, power, vigor 6 fervor, spirit 7 passion 9 facundity 10 expression 12 expressivity, forcefulness

eloquent 4 glib, high, rich 5 lofty, vocal 6 ardent, facund, fervid, fluent, moving, potent 7 fervent, graphic, telling, voluble 8 elevated, forceful, poignant, powerful, pregnant, touching 9 affecting, revealing 10 articulate, expressive, impressive, indicative, meaningful, passionate, persuasive, suggestive 11 impassioned, sententious, significant 12 smooth-spoken 13 silver-tongued

Elpaal's father 9 Shaharaim

Elpalet's father 5 David

else 2 or 3 new 4 more 5 added, fresh, other 7 another, besides, farther, further 9 otherwise 10 additional

elucidate 5 clear, prove 7 clarify, clear up, explain 8 annotate, spell out 9 enlighten, exemplify, interpret 10 illuminate, illustrate

elude 3 fly, shy 4 bilk, duck, flee, foil, shun 5 avoid, dodge, evade 6 baffle, double, escape, eschew, outwit, thwart 9 frustrate 10 circumvate

elusion 6 escape 8 escaping, eschewal, shunning 9 avoidance, runaround

elusive 6 subtle, tricky 7 evasive, phantom 8 baffling, fleeting, fugitive, slippery 10 evanescent, intangible, mysterious 12 imponderable 13 insubstantial

elusory 5 vague 7 evasive 8 nebulous 10 intangible

elvish 5 antic 6 frisky, impish 7 coltish, larkish, playful, puckish, roguish 8 prankish, spiteful 9 kittenish 11 mischievous

elysium 4 Eden, Zion 5 bliss 6 Canaan, heaven 7 nirvana 8 empyrean, paradise 10 Civitas Dei 12 New Jerusalem

elytron 4 wing 5 scale, shard

Elzaphan's father 6 Uzziel 7 Parnach

emaciated 4 bony, lean 5 gaunt 6 skinny, wasted 7 scrawny, starved, wizened 8 skeletal, underfed 10 cadaverous

emaciation 5 tabes 7 atrophy 8 marasmus 10 starvation 11 attenuation

emanate 4 emit, flow, rise, stem 5 arise, birth, exude, issue 6 spring 7 proceed 9 originate 10 derive from

emanation 4 aura, flow 6 efflux 7 outcome 9 effluence 11 consequence

emancipate 4 free 5 loose 6 loosen, unbind 7 manumit, release, unchain 8 liberate, unfetter 9 discharge, unshackle 11 enfranchise

emancipation 7 freedom, release 10 liberation 11 deliverance

emancipator 5 Moses 7 Lincoln 9 deliverer

emasculate 3 wan 4 geld, weak 5 unman 6 soften, weaken 7 unnerve 8 boneless, castrate, enervate, impotent, unstring 9 forceless, spineless 10 devitalize, inadequate 11 ineffective, ineffectual

embalm 5 mummy 7 mummify, perfume 8 preserve

embankment 4 bund, dike, quay 5 levee, mound 7 parados 9 banquette

embargo 5 edict, order 8 blockade, stoppage 10 impediment 11 prohibition

embark 4 open 5 begin, board, enter, set to, start 6 engage, enlist, get off, take up, tee off 7 jump off 8 commence

embarrass 3 vex 4 faze 5 abash, queer, upset 6 bother, flurry, hamper, impede, rattle 7 agitate, chagrin, confuse, flummox, fluster, nonplus, perturb 8 confound, distress 9 discomfit 10 discompose, disconcert

embarrassing 7 awkward 12 discommoding, incommodious, inconvenient 13 discommodious

embarrassment 5 shame 6 strain, unease 7 chagrin 8 distress, vexation 9 abashment, agitation, confusion 10 constraint, difficulty, discomfort, uneasiness 11 humiliation 12 discomfiture, discomposure, perturbation 13 disconcertion, mortification

embassy 5 envoy 8 legation 10 ambassador

embattle 7 fortify, prepare 9 crenelate 10 crenellate

embay 6 shut in 7 shelter 8 encircle, surround

embed 3 fix, set 4 root 5 infix, lodge 7 ingrain 8 entrench

embellish 3 pad 4 deck, gild, trim 5 adorn, array, color, dress, fudge, prank 6 bedeck, blazon, emboss, enrich 7 apparel, dress up, garnish, magnify

8 beautify, decorate, ornament　**9** embroider　**10** exaggerate

embellishment　7 garnish, melisma, mordent　**8** coloring, ornament　**9** fioritura, floridity, hyperbole　**11** ostentation　**12** embroidering, exaggeration　**13** ornamentation

ember　3 ash　**4** coal　**6** cinder

embezzle　4 loot　**5** steal　**6** pilfer, thieve　**8** peculate

embitter　4 sour　**7** envenom　**8** acerbate　**9** acidulate　**10** exacerbate

emblaze　5 adorn　**6** kindle　**9** embellish　**10** illuminate

emblazon　4 deck, laud　**5** adorn, extol　**7** display, glorify　**8** inscribe　**9** celebrate

emblem　3 bar　**4** mace, sign　**5** badge, crest, image, token　**6** device, symbol　**8** insignia, monogram　**9** attribute　**10** coat of arms　**11** adumbration *of mercy:* **8** red cross

embodiment　6 avatar　**7** epitome　**9** archetype　**11** incarnation　**13** manifestation

embody　4 fuse, have　**5** blend, merge, reify, unify, unite　**6** absorb, evince, mirror, take in, typify　**7** combine, compose, contain, embrace, exhibit, include, involve, realize, subsume　**8** manifest　**9** actualize, encompass, epitomize, exemplify, incarnate, integrate, objectify, personify, personize, represent, symbolize　**10** amalgamate, assimilate, comprehend, constitute, illustrate　**11** consolidate, demonstrate, emblematize, exteriorize, externalize, hypostatize, incorporate, materialize, personalize　**12** substantiate

embog　4 mine　**5** delay　**6** detain, hang up, retard, slow up　**7** set back, slacken　**8** slow down　**10** decelerate

embolden　5 cheer, impel, nerve, steel　**6** chance, hazard　**7** animate, chirk up, hearten, inspire, venture　**8** inspirit　**9** encourage, enhearten　**10** strengthen

embolus　4 clog, clot

embosom　7 enclose　**8** surround

emboss　5 adorn, raise　**8** ornament　**9** embellish, embroider

embouchure　5 mouth　**10** mouthpiece

embowel　3 gut　**4** draw　**6** paunch　**10** eviscerate, exenterate

embrace　3 hug　**4** clip, fold, grip, have, hold, lock, wrap　**5** admit, adopt, bosom, clasp, cling, cover, press, twine　**6** accept, cradle, cuddle, embody, enfold, enwind, fondle, nuzzle, take in, take on, take up　**7** cherish, compose, contain, embosom, enclose, entwine, envelop, espouse, include, involve, receive, snuggle, squeeze, subsume, welcome　**8** comprise, encircle　**9** encompass　**10** comprehend　**11** accommodate, incorporate

embrangle　7 confuse

embrocation　8 liniment

embroider　3 pad, sew, tat　**5** color, couch, fudge　**6** emboss, expand, overdo, stitch　**7** amplify, build up, distend, enhance, magnify, stretch, tambour　**8** decorate, ornament　**9** dramatize, elaborate, embellish, overstate　**10** aggrandize, exaggerate　**11** hyperbolize

embroidery　4 lace　**6** edging　**7** cutwork, orphery, pinwork　**8** couching, smocking, tapestry　**10** needlework

embroil　4 mire　**6** tangle　**7** confuse, involve　**8** disorder, distract, entangle　**9** implicate

embroilment　4 tiff　**6** fracas　**7** dispute, quarrel, wrangle　**8** squabble　**9** bickering　**10** falling-out　**11** altercation, controversy, involvement　**12** entanglement

embryo　3 bud　**4** germ, seed　**5** fetus, spark　**7** nucleus　**8** blastula, gastrula *combining form:* **5** blast　**6** blasto

emend　4 edit　**5** alter, right　**6** polish, revise　**7** correct, improve, rectify, retouch

emerald　3 gem　**5** beryl, green, stone

Emerald Isle　4 Eire, Erin　**7** Ireland

emerge　4 flow, loom, rise, show, stem　**5** arise, issue　**6** appear, derive, spring　**7** come out, proceed　**9** originate　**11** materialize

emergency　3 fix　**4** hole, pass, push　**5** pinch　**6** climax, clutch, crisis, strait　**7** squeeze　**8** juncture *money:* **5** scrip

Emerson　*forte:* 5 essay *friend:* **7** Thoreau

emery　5 board　**6** powder　**8** abrasive, corundum

Emesh　*brother:* 5 Enten *father:* **5** Enlil

émeute　4 riot　**6** tumult　**8** outbreak, uprising

emigrant　7 pioneer, settler　**8** colonist

emigré　2 DP　**5** alien, exile　**7** evacuee, refugee　**8** expellee, fugitive　**9** immigrant　**10** expatriate

Emilia　*husband:* 4 Iago　**7** Palamon　*slayer:* **4** Iago

eminence　3 VIP　**4** fame, note, peak, rise　**5** chief, glory, honor, kudos, power, raise　**6** bigwig, credit, height, leader, renown, repute, uprise, weight　**7** dignity, notable　**8** altitude, big-timer, highness, luminary, prestige　**9** authority, dignitary, elevation, greatness, influence, loftiness　**10** famousness, importance, notability, prepotency, projection, prominency, reputation　**11** distinction, superiority

eminent　3 big　**4** high　**5** famed, great, large, lofty, noble, noted　**6** august, famous　**7** big-name, big-time, exalted, notable　**8** dominant, renowned, towering　**9** big league, important, well-known　**10** celebrated, celebrious **11** conspicuous, illustrious, outstanding **13** distinguished

eminently 4 very **6** highly **7** notably **9** extremely **10** remarkably, strikingly **11** exceedingly **12** surpassingly **13** exceptionally

emir 5 chief, noble, ruler, title **8** nobleman **9** chieftain

emissary see **envoy**

emission 4 flow **9** discharge, effluvium, emanation

emit 4 beam, drip, flow, glow, ooze, pour, reek, vent, void **5** expel, exude, issue, loose, utter **6** exhale, expire, let out **7** emanate, excrete, extrude, give off, give out, radiate, release, secrete **8** evacuate, throw off **9** discharge **10** disembogue

emmer 5 grain, spelt, wheat **6** speltz

emmet 3 ant **7** pismire

Emmor's son 7 Shechem

emolliate 6 soften, weaken

emollient 7 lenient **8** lenitive, sedative, soothing

emolument 3 fee, pay **4** hire, wage **6** salary **7** guerdon, stipend **11** pay envelope **12** compensation

emote 3 act **4** gush, rage, rant **5** storm **6** take on **7** carry on, overact

emotion 3 ire, joy **4** fear, glee, hate, love **5** agony, ardor, grief, shame **6** relief, sorrow **7** ardency, despair, disgust, ecstasy, feeling, passion, sadness **8** jealousy, movement, surprise **9** affection, agitation, happiness, sentiment **11** affectivity, sensibility, sensitivity **12** excitability **13** sensitiveness *combining form:* **4** thym **5** thymo **6** thymia

emotional 6 ardent, moving **7** feeling, fervent, soulful **8** sentient, stirring, touching **9** affecting, affective, rhapsodic, sensitive **10** hysterical, passionate, responsive, susceptive **11** rhapsodical, softhearted, susceptible, sympathetic

emotionless 3 icy **4** cold, cool **5** chill, staid **6** frigid, torpid **7** deadpan, distant, glacial **8** reserved **9** apathetic, immovable, impassive, unfeeling **10** impersonal **11** cold-blooded, indifferent **12** matter-of-fact **13** dispassionate, unimpassioned

empathy 4 pity **6** accord, warmth **7** concord, rapport **8** affinity, sympathy **9** communion **10** compassion **12** appreciation, congeniality **13** compatibility, comprehension, fellow feeling, understanding

emperor 4 czar, king, shah, tsar, tzar **5** ruler **6** caesar, kaiser, sultan **7** monarch **8** autocrat, dictator, imperial, padishah **9** sovereign *Japanese:* **6** mikado **8** Hirohito

emphasis 5 focus, force **6** accent, stress, weight **9** attention **10** insistence **12** accentuation

emphasize 4 mark **5** press **6** accent, assert, charge, play up, stress **7** feature **8** pinpoint **9** highlight, italicize, punctuate, spotlight, underline **10** accentuate, underscore

emphatic 6 marked **7** decided, earnest, pointed **8** accented, forceful, positive, stressed, vigorous **9** assertive, energetic, insistent, insistive **10** aggressive, emphasized, resounding, underlined **11** accentuated, assertative

empire 4 rule, sway **5** power, realm, state **6** domain **7** demesne, kingdom, tsardom, tzardom **8** dominion, province **9** territory *ancient:* (see **ancient empire**)

Empire State 7 New York

empirical 7 factual **9** experient **12** experiential, experimental **13** observational

emplacement 7 battery, gallery **8** position

employ 3 add, use **4** busy, hire, work **5** apply, avail, exert, put on **6** bestow, devote, engage, handle, obtain, occupy, retain, secure, take on **7** engross, exploit, procure, utilize **8** exercise, practice

employee 4 hand, help **6** worker **7** servant **8** factotum **9** underling *bank:* **5** clerk, guard **6** teller *hotel:* **4** maid **5** clerk **7** bellboy, bellhop, doorman **9** concierge

employer 4 boss, user

employment 3 job, use **4** line, play, post, task, toil, work **5** trade, usage **6** hiring, office, usance **7** calling, mission, purpose, pursuit **8** business, engaging, exercise, exertion, function, handling, position, vocation **9** appliance, operation, situation **10** engagement, exercising, occupation **11** application, disposition, recruitment, utilization **12** exploitation

emporium 4 mall, mart, shop **5** store **6** bazaar, market **11** marketplace

empower 4 vest **5** endow **6** charge, enable, invest **7** entitle, entrust, license **8** accredit, deputize, sanction **9** authorize, privilege **10** commission

empress 5 queen *French:* **7** Eugenie **9** Josephine *Japanese:* **5** Suiko *of India:* **8** Victoria *Russian:* **4** Anna **7** czarina, tsarina, tzarina **9** Catherine, Elizabeth

empressement 6 fervor, warmth **10** cordiality

emprise 4 feat, gest **7** exploit, venture **9** adventure **11** undertaking

emptiness 4 void **6** hunger, vacuum **7** inanity, vacancy, vacuity

emptor 5 buyer **6** vendee **9** purchaser

___ emptor 6 caveat

empty 3 rid **4** bare, dumb, dump, flat, idle, pour, vain, void **5** banal, blank, clear, drain, inane, petty, silly, stark, vapid **6** barren, devoid, hollow, jejune, otiose, paltry, unload, vacant, vacate **7** deadpan, deplete, drained, exhaust, fatuous, foolish, insipid, trivial, vacated, vacuous **8** depleted, deserted, evacuate, forsaken, ignorant, innocent, nugatory, trifling, unfilled **9** abandoned, destitute, exhausted **10** unoccupied, untenanted **11** godforsaken, ineffectual **12** inexpressive, unexpressive **14** expressionless *combining form:* **3** ken **4** keno *Scottish:* **4** toom

empty-headed 4 rude **5** dizzy, giddy, silly **6** simple, vacant **7** flighty, vacuous **8** ignorant, skittish, untaught **9** benighted, brainless, frivolous **10** illiterate, uneducated, unlettered, unschooled **11** harebrained, know-nothing **12** uninstructed **13** rattlebrained

empyreal 4 airy, holy **6** aerial, divine **7** sublime **8** heavenly **9** celestial, spiritual

empyrean 3 sky **4** Zion **5** bliss, ether **6** heaven, welkin **7** elysium, heavens, nirvana **8** heavenly, paradise **9** celestial, firmament **10** civitas Dei **12** New Jerusalem

emu 4 bird, rhea **6** ratite **9** cassowary

emulate 3 ape **4** copy **5** equal, rival **6** outvie **7** compete, imitate **8** rivalize **9** challenge

emulation 6 strife **7** contest, rivalry, warfare **8** conflict, striving, tug-of-war **9** imitation **10** contention **11** competition

emulous 5 vying **6** aiming **7** athirst **8** aspiring, striving, vaulting **9** ambitious **11** competitive

emulsifier 4 soap

enable 3 fit, let **5** allow, ready **6** permit **7** empower, entitle, license, prepare, qualify **8** accredit, sanction **9** authorize, condition **10** commission

enact 2 do **4** make, pass, play **6** decree, depict, effect, ordain, ratify **7** execute, perform, portray **8** proclaim **9** authorize, discourse, establish, institute, legislate, personate, represent **10** accomplish, bring about, constitute, effectuate **11** impersonate

enactment 3 law **6** action, assize, decree **7** statute **9** ordinance

enamel 5 glaze, gloss, paint

enamored 4 fond **5** dotty **6** loving, mashed, soft on **7** charmed, devoted, smitten **8** besotted, spoony on **9** bewitched, enchanted, entranced, infatuate **10** captivated, fascinated, infatuated, spoony over

Enan's son 5 Ahira

encamp 4 tent **6** settle **7** bivouac

encampment 6 laager **7** bivouac, hutment

encase 7 enclose, envelop, sheathe

enceinte 8 pregnant **9** expectant, expecting **10** parturient

enchain 4 bind **6** fetter

enchant 3 hex **4** draw, send, take, wile

5 charm, spell, witch **6** allure, delude, please, thrill, voodoo **7** attract, bewitch, delight **9** captivate, ensorcell, fascinate, magnetize, mesmerize, spellbind

enchanter 4 mage **5** magus **6** wizard **7** charmer, warlock **8** conjurer, magician, sorcerer **9** voodooist **11** necromancer

enchanting 5 siren **7** sirenic **8** alluring, charming **9** appealing, glamorous, seductive **10** attractive, bewitching, delectable, delightful, intriguing **11** captivating, fascinating

enchantment 3 hex **5** charm, magic, spell **7** sorcery **8** gramarye, witchery, wizardry **9** conjuring, magicking **10** necromancy, witchcraft **11** incantation

enchantress 3 hag, hex **5** bruja, Circe, lamia, Medea, witch **9** sorceress **10** witchwoman

enchiridion 4 book, text **5** guide **6** manual **8** Baedeker, handbook **9** guidebook, vade mecum **10** compendium

encincture 4 band, belt, gird **6** begird, engird, girdle **8** begirdle, engirdle

encipher 4 code

encircle 3 hem **4** band, belt, gird, halo, hoop, ring **5** girth **6** begird, engird, enlace, girdle **7** compass, embrace, enclose, environ, wreathe **8** cincture, surround **9** encompass **12** circumscribe

enclose 3 box, hem, mew, pen, rim **4** cage, coop, mure, veil, wall, wrap **5** bound, fence, hedge, limit **6** circle, closet, corral, encase, enfold, enlock, enwrap, immure, invest, shroud, shut in **7** compass, confine, contain, embosom, envelop, environ, harness **8** encircle, enshroud, ensphere, imprison, insheath, restrict, surround **9** capsulize, encompass **12** circumscribe

enclosure 3 box, haw, mew, pen, sty **4** bawn, cage, cell, coop, cote, fold, quad, tank, trap, wall, weir, yard **5** booly, booth, court, crawl, fence, kench, pound, stall **6** aviary, cancha, corral, cowpen, garden, kennel, paling, prison **7** barrier, cockpit, paddock **8** cincture, cloister, sepiment, stockade **9** cofferdam, courtyard, curtilage **10** quadrangle, sheephouse *African:* **4** boma **5** kraal *elephant:* **6** keddah

encomiast 7 praiser **8** eulogist **10** panegyrist

encomiastic 9 laudative, laudatory, praiseful **11** panegyrical

encomium 4 laud **5** kudos **6** eulogy, praise **7** acclaim, tribute **8** accolade, applause, approval, citation, plaudits **9** laudation, panegyric **10** compliment, salutation **11** acclamation **12** commendation

encompass 3 hem **4** belt, gird, have, ring **5** beset, bound **6** begird, circle, embody, engird, girdle, take in **7** contain, delimit, embrace, enclose, environ, include, involve, subsume **8** encircle, surround **10** comprehend

encore **6** recall, repeat **8** call back **10** repetition

encounter **4** espy, face, find, fray, meet, spot **5** brush, catch, clash, close, fight, front, hit on, run-in, scrap, set-to **6** battle, descry, detect, engage, take on, turn up **7** affront, collide, contest, hit upon, meeting, quarrel **8** argument, conflict, confront, meet with, skirmish **10** contention, velitation

encourage **4** abet, back, push, stir **5** boost, cheer, favor, nerve, pique, rally, serve, steel **6** assist, assure, buck up, excite, foster, incite, induce **7** advance, animate, approve, chirk up, develop, endorse, fortify, forward, further, hearten, improve, prevail, promote, provoke, quicken, support, sustain **8** advocate, embolden, energize, inspirit, reassure, sanction **9** enhearten, galvanize, instigate, patronize, reinforce, stimulate, subsidize **10** invigorate, strengthen **11** countenance

encouragement **4** lift, push **5** boost **7** backing, support

encouraging **4** rosy **6** likely **7** hopeful, roseate **9** promising **10** promiseful **11** rose-colored

encroach **5** poach **6** invade, meddle, trench **7** impinge, intrude **8** entrench, infringe, overstep, trespass **9** interfere, interpose, intervene

encumber **3** tax **4** clog, lade, load **5** beset, block, weigh **6** burden, charge, fetter, hamper, hinder, impede, retard, saddle, weight **7** freight, oppress **8** handicap, obstruct, overload **9** incommode **10** discommode, overburden **13** inconvenience

encumbrance **4** clog, load **6** burden **8** handicap, hardship, mortgage **9** albatross **10** difficulty, impediment **12** disadvantage **13** inconvenience

encyclical **6** letter **7** general **8** circular

encyclopedic **5** broad **7** general **8** complete **9** extensive, inclusive **10** discursive **12** all-embracing, all-inclusive **13** comprehensive

encyclopedist **7** Diderot

end **3** aim, bit, tip **4** coda, goal, halt, part, quit, stop, tail, term **5** bound, cease, close, death, finis, limit, piece, scrap **5** teloi (plural), telos **6** expire, finale, finish, object, period, scotch, windup, wrap up **7** abolish, closing, closure, extreme, leaving, lineman, purpose, remnant, residue **8** boundary, complete, conclude, confines, curtains, finality, fragment, particle, surcease, terminal, terminus, ultimate **9** cessation, desuetude, determine, extremity, objective, remainder,

terminate **10** borderline, completion, conclusion, desistance, expiration, limitation **11** culmination, discontinue, termination **12** consummation **combining form:** **3** acr, akr, tel **4** acro, akro, tele, telo

endanger **4** risk **5** peril **6** chance, expose, hazard, menace **7** imperil, jeopard, venture **8** jeopardy **10** compromise, jeopardize

endeavor **3** aim, try **4** push, seek, toil, work **5** apply, assay, essay, labor, offer, trial **6** hassle, intend, strain, strive **7** address, attempt, purpose, travail **8** exertion, striving, struggle **9** determine, undertake **11** undertaking

ended **4** done, down, over, past **7** through **8** complete, finished **9** completed **10** terminated

endemic **5** local **6** native **8** home-bred **10** aboriginal, indigenous, native-born

ending **4** stop **5** close **6** finale, finish, period, windup **7** closing **9** cessation **10** conclusion, desistance **11** termination

endive **4** herb **7** witloof **8** escarole

endless **7** eternal, forever, undying **8** constant, immortal, infinite, overlong, unending **9** ceaseless, continual, limitless, perpetual, unbounded, unceasing, unlimited **10** continuous, indefinite, unmeasured **11** amaranthine, everlasting, measureless **12** immeasurable, interminable

endmost **8** farthest, furthest

endocrine gland **5** gonad, ovary **6** pineal, testis, thymus **7** adrenal, thyroid **8** pancreas **9** pituitary **11** parathyroid **12** hypothalamus

endomorphic **6** pyknic

endorse **2** OK **4** okay, sign, visa, visé **5** vouch **6** attest, ratify, second, uphold **7** approve, certify, command, stand by, support, witness **8** accredit, advocate, champion, sanction **9** recommend **12** authenticate

endorsement **2** OK **4** fiat, visa **7** support **8** approval, sanction **9** signature

endow **4** back, fund **5** award, dower, found, grant **6** accord, bestow, confer, donate, enable, enrich, supply **7** empower, enhance, finance, promote, provide, sponsor, support **8** bequeath, heighten, organize **9** crown with, subscribe, subsidize **10** contribute

endowment **4** fund, gift **5** dower, dowry, grant, power, skill **6** talent **7** ability, chantry **8** appanage, dotation

end product **5** issue **6** effect, result, sequel, upshot **7** outcome **8** sequence **9** aftermath **11** aftereffect, consequence

endue **4** vest **5** dower, equip **6** clothe, invest, outfit **7** furnish **8** accouter **9** crown with

endurance **4** wind **5** pluck **7** stamina

8 duration, patience, strength 9 tolerance
10 continuity, toleration 11 persistence
12 continuation, perseverance

endure 2 go 4 bear, bide, last, take, wear
5 abide, allow, brook, stand 6 accept, linger, pocket, suffer 7 outlast, outlive, persist, stomach, sustain, swallow, undergo
8 bear with, continue, tolerate, tough out
9 withstand 12 carry through

enduring 3 old 4 fast, firm, sure 5 solid,
sound 6 stable, steady, sturdy 7 abiding,
durable, eternal, lasting, staunch 8 lifelong,
resolute 9 diuturnal, long-lived, perennial,
permanent, steadfast 10 continuing, inveterate, perdurable 11 long-lasting, substantial, unfaltering, unqualified 12 never-failing

Endymion *father:* 8 Aethlius *lover:*
5 Diana 6 Selene

enemy 3 foe 5 rival 7 hostile, invader
8 attacker, emulator, opponent 9 adversary, assailant, combatant, contender
10 antagonist, competitor

energetic 4 spry 5 brisk, fresh, lusty,
peppy, vital, zippy 6 active, breezy, lively
7 driving, dynamic, vibrant 8 animated, spirited, tireless, vigorous 9 sprightly, strenuous, vivacious 10 aggressive, red-blooded
12 enterprising 13 indefatigable

energize 3 arm, pep 4 fuel 5 liven
6 actify, enable 7 empower, fortify, sustain
8 activate, activize, vitalize 9 reinforce
10 invigorate, strengthen

energy 2 go 3 pep, vim, zip 4 beef, birr,
life, tuck 5 force, might, power, sinew,
steam, vigor 6 effort, muscle, spirit
7 potency 8 activity, efficacy, strength
9 hardihood, puissance, toughness
10 mightiness 11 application 12 forcefulness, powerfulness 13 effectiveness, operativeness *excessive:* 7 sthenia *unit:*
3 erg 4 dyne, volt 5 joule 7 quantum
10 horsepower

enervate 3 sap 4 jade, tire 5 unman,
weary 6 soften, weaken 7 disable,
exhaust, fatigue, unnerve 8 enfeeble,
unstring 10 devitalize

enfant terrible 4 limb 5 devil, rogue,
scamp 6 rascal 7 villain 8 mischief, scalawag 9 skeezicks 11 rapscallion

enfeeble 3 sap 5 blunt 6 soften,
weaken 7 cripple, disable, exhaust,
unbrace 8 enervate 9 attenuate, undermine 10 debilitate, devitalize
12 unstrengthen

enfold 3 hug 4 gird, veil, wrap 5 clasp,
cover, drape, press 6 encase, enwrap, girdle, invest, shroud, swathe 7 embrace,
enclose, envelop, environ, squeeze 8 encircle, enshroud, surround 9 encompass,
ensheathe

enforce 5 exact 6 compel, effect, invoke,

oblige 7 execute, fulfill 9 discharge, implement, prosecute 10 accomplish, administer

enfranchise 4 free 6 rescue 7 deliver,
manumit, release 8 liberate 9 extricate
10 emancipate

engage 3 tie 4 bind, busy, face, grip, hire,
meet, mesh, pass, soak 5 fight, imbue, put
on, troth 6 absorb, arrest, attack, battle,
commit, employ, enlist, occupy, pledge,
strike, take on 7 assault, betroth, engross,
immerse, involve, promise 8 affiance,
enthrall, interact 9 captivate, encounter,
fascinate, interlace, interlock, intermesh,
interplay, preoccupy, undertake *passage:*
4 book

engaged 4 busy, deep, rapt 6 intent
7 working, wrapped 8 absorbed, employed,
immersed, intended, occupied, plighted
9 affianced, betrothed, committed,
engrossed, wrapped up 10 contracted
11 preoccupied *person:* 6 fiancé 7 fiancée

engage in 4 wage 5 enter *suffix:* 3 ize

engagement 4 date, word 5 troth, tryst,
visit 6 action, battle, hiring, pledge, plight
7 booking, meeting, promise 8 espousal
9 betrothal, interview 10 betrothing,
employment, invitation, rendezvous
11 assignation

engaging 5 siren, sweet 6 dulcet 7 winning, winsome 8 magnetic, mesmeric
9 glamorous 10 attractive, bewitching,
employment, intriguing 11 fascinating
13 prepossessing

engender 4 stir 5 beget, breed, cause,
hatch, rouse 6 arouse, excite, induce, work
up 7 develop, produce, provoke, quicken
8 generate, muster up, occasion 9 stimulate

engine 5 motor, turbo 7 turbine 10 locomotive *kind:* 3 gas, jet 5 steam 6 diesel
7 turbine 8 gasoline 9 hydraulic *jet:* 8 turbofan, turbojet *part:* 3 cam, rod 4 gear,
plug, pump 5 choke 6 filter, piston 8 cylinder, manifold, throttle 9 condenser, crankcase 10 carburetor 12 transmission
siege: 3 ram 12 battering ram *sound:*
4 chug

engineer 4 plan, plot 5 set up, swing
6 devise, driver, manage, scheme, wangle
7 arrange, finagle 8 contrive, intrigue,
maneuver 9 machinate, negotiate
10 manipulate, mastermind *kind:* 5 civil
6 mining 8 chemical, sanitary 10 electrical,
mechanical 12 aeronautical *military:*
6 sapper

engineers' group *abbreviation:* 4 IEEE

England 6 Albion 7 Britain 9 Britannia
12 Great Britain *capital:* 6 London *monetary unit:* 5 pound

English 7 British *coin:* 5 angel, crown,
groat, pence 6 florin, guinea, seskin
7 angelet 8 farthing, shilling, sixpence, two-

pence **9** fourpence, half crown, halfpenny, sovereign **10** threepence *combining form:* **5** Anglo *farm:* **5** croft *forest:* **5** Arden **8** Sherwood *letter:* **3** zed *measure:* **3** ell, pin, rod, tun **4** comb, coom, gill, hand, hide, line, peck, pint, pipe, pole, pool, span, yard, yoke **5** chain, coomb, crane, digit, hutch, jugum, perch, point, truss **6** barrel, bovate, bushel, fathom, firkin, runlet, strike, sulung **7** furlong, quarter, rundlet, virgate **8** carucate, chaldron, hogshead, puncheon, quartern, standard **9** kilderkin **10** barleycorn *military college:* **9** Sandhurst *patron saint:* **6** George *person:* **4** chap **5** bloke **6** Briton *pirate:* **4** Kidd *princess:* **4** Anne *professor:* **3** don *royal family:* **7** Windsor *saint:* **7** Dunstan **8** Cuthbert *spa:* **4** Bath *sport:* **5** rugby **7** cricket *tavern:* **3** pub *university:* **5** Leeds **6** Oxford **9** Cambridge *weight:* **3** kip, tod **4** keel **5** barge, fagot, stand, stone, tross **6** firkin, fother, fotmal, pocket **7** quintal **8** quartern

English Channel swimmer 6 Ederle (Gertrude)

englut 4 bolt, cram, gulp, slop, wolf **5** slosh **6** gobble, guzzle **11** ingurgitate

engrave 3 cut, fix **4** etch, root **5** carve, chase, embed, infix, print **6** incise, scrive **7** enchase, impress, imprint, ingrain, insculp, instill **8** entrench, inscribe

engraver 6 chaser, etcher *German:* **5** Dürer **10** Schongauer *Italian:* **8** Raimondi

engraving 7 etching, woodcut **8** drypoint, intaglio **9** xylograph *combining form:* **5** glypt **6** glypto

engross 4 bury, busy, fill, grip, hold, soak **5** apply, sew up, write **6** absorb, arrest, engage, indite, occupy, scribe, scroll, take up **7** attract, consume, immerse, involve **8** enscroll, enthrall, inscribe **9** captivate, preoccupy **10** assimilate, monopolize **11** superscribe

engrosser 7 copyist **12** calligrapher **13** calligraphist

engulf 5 drown, flood, swamp, whelm **6** deluge, devour **7** swallow **8** inundate, overflow, submerge **9** overwhelm

enhance 4 lift, rise, suit **5** adorn, exalt, mount, raise, rouse **6** become, deepen **7** augment, elevate, flatter, magnify **8** beautify, heighten, increase, redouble **9** aggravate, embellish, embroider, intensate, intensify **10** exaggerate, strengthen

enhearten 5 cheer, nerve, steel **7** animate, chirk up **8** embolden, inspirit **9** encourage

enigma 3 why **4** crux, knot **5** rebus **6** puzzle, riddle **7** mystery, problem, puzzler, sticker **8** question **9** conundrum **10** closed book, perplexity, puzzlement

12 bewilderment, question mark **13** Chinese puzzle, mystification

enigmatic 4 dark **6** mystic **7** cryptic, obscure **8** Delphian, puzzling **10** mystifying

enisle 6 cut off **7** isolate **8** close off, insulate, separate **9** segregate, sequester

enjoin 3 ban, bid **4** deny, rule, tell, warn **5** order, taboo **6** adjure, advise, charge, decree, direct, forbid, impose, outlaw **7** caution, command, counsel, dictate, inhibit **8** admonish, disallow, forewarn, instruct, prohibit **9** interdict, prescribe

enjoy 3 own **4** fill, have, hold, like, love **5** boast, eat up, fancy, savor **6** occupy, relish, retain **7** command, possess **8** maintain **10** appreciate *a break:* **8** take five

enjoyableness 7 amenity **8** pleasure **9** geniality, pleasance **10** amiability, cordiality **12** agreeability

enjoyment 4 ease, zest **5** gusto, savor **6** relish **7** delight **8** felicity, fruition, pleasure **9** diversion **10** indulgence, recreation, relaxation **11** delectation **12** satisfaction **13** gratification

Enki *consort:* **5** Nintu *son:* **6** Ninsar

enkindle 4 fire **5** light **6** ignite **7** inflame

enlarge 3 wax **4** grow, rise **5** add to, boost, build, mount, widen **6** beef up, expand, extend **7** amplify, augment, develop, greaten, magnify, stretch, upsurge **8** heighten, increase, multiply **9** elaborate, embroider **10** aggrandize, exaggerate

enlargement 4 node **5** tumor **6** growth, nodule **8** addition, increase, swelling **9** accretion, expansion, extension *combining form:* **4** auxe **5** auxae (plural) **6** megaly **7** megalia

enlarging *combining form:* **4** micr **5** micro

enlighten 5 edify, guide, teach, train **6** advise, direct, illume, inform, school, uplift **7** apprise, educate, improve **8** acquaint, illumine, instruct **9** irradiate **10** illuminate

Enlil *father:* **2** An *mother:* **2** Ki *son:* **5** Nanna **6** Nergal, Ninazu *wife:* **6** Ninlil

enlist 4 join **5** enter **6** enroll, join up, muster, sign on, sign up **8** register **9** volunteer

enlistment 5 hitch

enliven 3 pep **4** fire, warm **5** amuse, cheer, pep up, renew, rouse **6** excite, jazz up, vivify **7** animate, inspire, quicken, refresh, restore **8** enspirit, recreate **9** entertain, galvanize, stimulate **10** exhilarate, invigorate, rejuvenate, vivificate

enmesh 4 hook, trap **5** catch **6** draw in, tangle **7** ensnarl, trammel **8** drag into, entangle **9** embrangle, implicate

enmity 4 feud, gall, hate **5** spite **6** animus, hatred, malice, rancor, spleen **7** dislike, ill will **8** aversion, bad blood, loathing **9** animosity, antipathy, hostility, malignity **10** abhorrence, alienation, antagonism, bitterness, malignancy **11** detestation, malevolence **12** disaffection, estrangement, uncordiality

ennoble 5 exalt, honor, raise **6** uplift, uprear **7** dignify, glorify, magnify, sublime **10** aggrandize **11** distinguish

ennui 4 bore, pall, tire, yawn **5** blues, dumps, weary **6** apathy, tedium **7** boredom, fatigue, languor, sadness, satiety, surfeit **8** doldrums **9** dejection, tiredness, weariness **10** depression, melancholy **11** languidness **12** listlessness

Enoch *father:* **4** Cain *son:* **10** Methuselah

Enoch Arden author 8 Tennyson

enormity 7 bigness, outrage **8** atrocity, hugeness, rankness, vastness **9** depravity, flagrancy, graveness, greatness, grossness, immensity, magnitude **11** heinousness, massiveness, seriousness, weightiness **13** atrociousness, monstrousness

enormous 3 big **4** huge, vast **5** great, large **7** immense, mammoth, titanic **8** colossal, gigantic **9** monstrous **10** gargantuan, prodigious, stupendous, tremendous

Enos *father:* **4** Seth *grandfather:* **4** Adam *grandmother:* **3** Eve *uncle:* **4** Abel, Cain

enough 6 fairly, plenty **8** adequacy, adequate, decently, passably **9** abundance, ampleness, averagely, competent, sufficing, tolerably **10** abundantly, acceptably, adequately, admissibly, competence, moderately, sufficient **11** comfortable, sufficiency **12** satisfactory, sufficiently *poetic:* **4** enow

enounce 3 say **5** state, utter **8** proclaim

enrage 3 ire, mad **5** anger **6** madden **7** incense, inflame, steam up, umbrage **9** infuriate

enrapture 5 charm, elate **6** allure, please, ravish, trance **7** attract, enchant, gladden, gratify, rejoice **8** enravish, enthrall, entrance **9** captivate, fascinate, transport

enrich 5 adorn, endow **6** fatten, richen **9** embellish

enroll 4 book, join, list **5** enter **6** enlist, induct, insert, join up, line up, muster, record, sign on, sign up **7** catalog, recruit **8** inscribe, register **11** matriculate

ensconce 4 bury, hide **5** cache, cover, place, plant, stash **6** locate, settle **7** conceal, install, secrete, situate **9** establish

ensemble 5 decor, group, suite, whole **6** outfit **7** costume **9** aggregate

enshroud 4 hide, veil, wrap **5** cloak **6** enfold, enwrap, invest **7** conceal, curtain, enclose, envelop

ensign 4 flag, jack **5** color **6** banner, pennon **7** pennant **8** gonfalon, standard, streamer **9** oriflamme

enslave 4 yoke **5** chain **6** thrall **7** oppress, shackle, subject **8** enthrall **9** subjugate **12** disfranchise

enslavement 4 yoke **6** thrall **7** bondage, helotry, peonage, serfdom, slavery **9** servitude, thralldom, villenage

ensnare 3 bag, net **4** hook, lure, mesh, snag, trap **5** benet, catch, decoy **6** enmesh, entice, entrap, tangle **7** capture, catch up **8** entangle, inveigle

ensnarl 6 enmesh, tangle **7** perplex, trammel **8** entangle **9** embrangle **11** intertangle

ensorcell 3 hex **5** charm, spell, witch **6** voodoo **7** bewitch, enchant

ensorcellment 5 magic **7** sorcery **8** witchery, wizardry **9** conjuring **10** necromancy, witchcraft **11** bewitchment, enchantment, incantation

ensphere 4 ball **5** round **8** conglobe **10** conglobate

ensue 4 stem **5** issue **6** attend, derive, follow, result **7** emanate, proceed, succeed **9** supervene

ensuing 4 next **5** after, later **6** coming **9** following, posterior **10** subsequent **12** postliminary **13** subsequential

ensure 5 cinch **6** secure **7** certify, warrant **9** establish, guarantee

enswathe 4 roll **5** drape **6** enwrap, wrap up **7** envelop, swaddle

entail 6 assign, confer, impose **7** require **8** transmit **11** necessitate

entangle 3 bag **4** clog, mesh, mire, trap **5** benet, catch, ravel, snare, snarl, tie up, twist **6** ball up, burden, enmesh, entrap, fetter, hamper, impede, muddle **7** capture, catch up, embroil, ensnare, ensnarl, involve, perplex, trammel **10** complicate, intertwine, interweave

entanglement 3 web **4** knot, mesh, toil **6** affair, cobweb **7** contact, liaison **8** intrigue **10** enmeshment **11** association, embroilment, ensnarement, involvement

Enten *brother:* **5** Emesh *father:* **5** Enlil

entente 6 treaty **8** alliance **9** agreement, coalition

enter 4 go in, join, list, open, post **5** admit, begin, probe, put in, set to, start **6** come in, docket, enlist, enroll, go into, inject, insert, join up, muster, pierce, record, sign on, sign up, take up **7** ingress, lead off **8** come into, commence, embark on, inscribe, register **9** introduce, penetrate **10** embark upon, inaugurate

enterprise 4 deed, feat, firm, gest, push, task **5** cause, drive, house, vigor **6** action, daring, effort, energy, hustle, outfit **7** attempt, company, concern, courage, exploit, project, pursuit, venture **8** ambition, boldness, business, campaign, endeavor, industry, interest, striving, struggle 9 adventure, eagerness 10 enthusiasm, get-up-and-go, initiative 11 corporation, speculation, undertaking 12 organization, self-reliance 13 ambitiousness, establishment, inventiveness

enterprising 4 bold, busy 5 eager 6 active, daring, hungry, lively 7 craving, dashing, driving, go-ahead, itching, lusting, pushing, zealous 8 aspiring, diligent, hustling, yearning 9 ambitious, audacious, energetic, gumptious 10 aggressive 11 adventurous, hard-working, industrious, up-and-coming, venturesome

entertain 4 host 5 amuse, board, house, lodge, put up 6 bestow, billet, divert, foster, harbor, invite, please, regale 7 cherish, delight, enliven, gladden, gratify, nourish, receive, rejoice 8 domicile, recreate

entertainer 4 host, mime 5 actor, comic 6 amuser, busker, dancer, singer 7 actress, trouper 8 comedian, minstrel *female:* 7 actress, diseuse, hostess 10 comedienne

entertainment 4 fete, play, show, skit 5 cheer, revue, sport 6 circus, gaiety, relief 7 banquet, concert, disport, ridotto 8 pleasure 9 amusement, diversion, enjoyment 10 recreation, relaxation 11 dissipation, distraction

enthrall 4 grip, hold 5 charm 6 absorb, engage, master, subdue 7 catch up, enchant, engross, enslave 8 intrigue 9 fascinate, mesmerize, preoccupy, spellbind, subjugate

enthuse 4 rave, send 5 drool 6 thrill 8 rhapsody 9 electrify 10 rhapsodize

enthusiasm 4 élan, fire, zeal, zest, zing 5 ardor, craze, mania, verve 6 fervor, hurrah, spirit 7 ardency, earnest, passion 8 interest 9 eagerness 10 ebullience

enthusiast 3 bug, fan, nut 4 bear, buff 5 fiend, freak, lover 6 addict, maniac, votary, zealot 7 devotee, fanatic, habitué 8 partisan 9 extremist, supporter 10 aficionado

enthusiastic 4 gaga, keen 5 eager, nutty, rabid 6 ardent, gung ho, hearty, hipped, raring 7 devoted, fervent, zealous 8 hopped-up, obsessed, spirited, vascular 10 passionate

entice 4 bait, coax, lure, toll, wile 5 charm, decoy, tempt 6 allure, cajole, entrap, lead on, seduce 8 inveigle, persuade

enticement 4 bait, lure, trap 5 decoy, snare 6 come-on 10 allurement, seducement, temptation 12 inveiglement

enticer 4 bait, vamp 5 Circe, decoy, siren 7 Lorelei, seducer, taunter, tempter 9 attractor, enchanter, temptress 10 attrac-

tion, seductress 11 enchantress, femme fatale

enticing 5 siren 6 luring 7 circean, likable 8 fetching, inviting, pleasant, pleasing, tempting, witching 9 beguiling 10 attractive, bewitching, enchanting, intriguing 11 captivating, fascinating

entire 3 all 4 full 5 gross, sound, total, whole 6 choate, intact, unhurt 7 perfect, plenary, unified 8 complete, integral, outright, unbroken, unmarred 9 compacted, undamaged, uninjured 10 integrated, unimpaired 12 concatenated, consolidated *combining form:* 3 hol 4 holo 7 integri

entirely 3 but 4 only, well 5 alone, fully, quite 6 solely, wholly 7 utterly 9 perfectly 10 altogether, completely, thoroughly 11 exclusively *combining form:* 3 pam, pan 4 pano

entirety 3 all, sum 5 gross, total, unity, whole 7 allness, complex, omneity, oneness 8 sum total, totality 9 aggregate, integrity, plenitude, wholeness 10 everything 12 collectivity, completeness, universality

entitle 3 dub, let 4 call, name, term 5 allow, style 6 enable, permit 7 baptize, empower, license, qualify 8 christen, headline, nominate 9 authorize, designate 10 denominate

entity 3 ens, sum 4 body, unit 5 being, stuff, thing, whole 6 matter, object, system 8 existent, integral, material, totality 9 existence, integrate, something, substance 10 individual

entomb 4 bury 5 inter, inurn 6 inhume, shrine 8 enshrine 9 sepulcher, sepulture 11 ensepulcher

entombment 6 burial 9 interment, sepulture 10 inhumation

entourage 5 suite, train 7 retinue, toadies 9 courtiers, followers, following, hangers-on, retainers 10 associates, attendants, sycophants

entr'acte 8 interval 9 interlude 12 intermission

entrails 4 guts 5 pluck 6 bowels, tripes, vitals 7 giblets, innards, insides, inwards, viscera 8 stuffing 9 internals 10 intestines *combining form:* 9 splanchno

entrammel 3 tie 4 clog, curb 5 leash 6 fetter, hamper, hobble, hog-tie 7 shackle

entrance 3 way 4 adit, door, gate 5 charm, entry, foyer, mouth 6 access, coming, entrée, please, portal, ravish 7 arrival, attract, bewitch, doorway, enchant, gladden, ingoing, ingress, opening, rejoice 8 aperture, enravish, enthrall, entryway, incoming, open door 9 admission, captivate, enrapture, fascinate, hypnotize, spellbind, threshold, transport **10** admittance, ingression **11** penetration

entrant 7 starter **10** competitor, contestant **11** participant

entrap 3 bag, net **4** bait, lure, toll **5** benet, catch, decoy, snare, tempt **6** allure, entice, entoil, lead on, seduce, tangle **7** catch up, ensnare **8** entangle, inveigle

entreat 3 ask, beg, bid **4** coax, pray, urge **5** crave, plead, press **6** appeal, invoke, pester, plague **7** beseech, implore, wheedle **8** blandish **9** importune **10** supplicate

entreaty 4 plea, suit **6** appeal, orison, prayer **8** petition **11** application, imploration, imprecation **12** supplication

entrée 3 way **4** adit, door **6** access **7** ingress **8** entrance, main dish **9** admission **10** admittance, main course

entrench 3 fix **4** root **5** embed, found, infix, lodge **6** define, ground, invade, settle **7** confirm, implant, ingrain **8** encroach, infringe, trespass **9** establish, interfere, intervene **10** strengthen

entrenched 5 sworn **7** settled **8** deep-dyed **9** confirmed, hard-shell **10** deep-rooted, deep-seated, inveterate **13** bred-in-the-bone, dyed-in-the-wool

entrepôt 9 warehouse **10** storehouse

entrepreneur 6 backer, broker **7** manager **8** mediator, producer, promoter **9** go-between, middleman, organizer **10** contractor, impresario, interagent, interceder, undertaker **11** intercessor **12** intermediary, intermediate **13** administrator, intermediator

entresol 9 mezzanine

entrust 4 bank, give, rely **5** allot, count, leave **6** assign, charge, commit, confer, depend, impose, reckon **7** commend, confide, consign, deliver, deposit **8** allocate, delegate, hand over, relegate, turn over

entry 3 way **4** adit, door **5** debit **6** access, credit, portal **7** doorway, ingress, opening **9** admission, threshold **10** admittance, enlistment, enrollment, ingression

entwine 4 coil, curl, lace, wind **5** braid, twist **6** enmesh, spiral **7** entwist, wreathe **8** entangle **9** corkscrew, interlace **10** interplait, intertwine, interweave

enumerate 4 list, tell **5** count, tally **6** detail, number, recite, relate **7** itemize, mention, recount, specify, tick off **8** identify **9** inventory **10** specialize **13** particularize

enunciate 3 say **4** show **5** state, utter, voice **6** affirm, intone, submit **7** advance, declare, develop, enounce, express, lay down, outline, phonate **8** announce, modulate, proclaim, vocalize **9** formulate, postulate, pronounce **10** articulate

envelop 3 hem, pen **4** cage, coop, hide, mask, roll, veil, wrap **5** cloak, drape, fence,

guard, hedge **6** cocoon, corral, enfold, enwrap, immure, invest, sheath, shield, shroud, shut in, swathe, wrap up **7** enclose, protect, swaddle **8** enshroud, enswathe, surround **10** circumfuse

envenom 6 poison **7** corrupt **8** acerbate, embitter **10** exacerbate

envious 6 greedy **7** jealous, longing **8** appetent, coveting, covetous, desirous, grasping, grudging, yearning **9** green-eyed, invidious, resentful **10** begrudging, umbrageous

environ 3 hem **4** gird, ring **5** beset, fence, limit, round **6** circle, suburb **7** compass, enclose, envelop **8** encircle, go around, surround **9** encompass

environment 6 medium, milieu **7** ambient, climate, context, element, habitat, setting **8** ambience, backdrop **9** situation **10** atmosphere, background, mise-en-scène **12** surroundings *combining form:* **2** ec **3** eco, oec **4** oeco, oiko *science:* **7** ecology

environmentalist 6 Carson (Rachel) **9** ecologist

environs 6 bounds, limits **7** compass, fringes, suburbs **8** boundary, confines, locality, purlieus, vicinity **9** outskirts, precincts **12** neighborhood, surroundings

envisage 4 view **5** fancy, grasp, image, think **6** behold, regard, survey, vision **7** feature, foresee, imagine, picture, realize **8** conceive, envision, look upon **9** objectify, visualize

envision 4 view **5** dream, fancy, image, think **7** feature, foresee, imagine, picture, realize **8** conceive, summon up **9** conjure up, visualize

envoy 6 bearer, consul, deputy, legate, nuncio **7** attaché, carrier, courier **8** diplomat, emissary, minister **9** messenger **10** ambassador, councillor **11** internuncio

envy 4 long, want **5** covet, crave, yearn **6** desire, grudge, hanker **8** begrudge, grudging, jealousy **10** resentment **12** covetousness **13** invidiousness

enwrap 4 roll, veil **5** clasp, drape **6** enfold, invest, shroud, swathe **7** enclose, envelop, sheathe, swaddle **8** enshroud, enswathe

enzyme 5 ficin, lyase, renin, urase **6** kinase, ligase, lipase, mutase, papain, pepsin, rennin, urease, zymase **7** amidase, amylase, cyclase, enolase, guanase, hydrase, inulase, isozyme, lactase, maltase, oxidase, pectase, pepsine, plasmin, ptyalin, rennase, sucrase, trypsin, zymogen **8** aldolase, diastase, elastase, esterase, fumarase, lyzozyme, nuclease, protease, steapsin, thrombin, zymogene **9** biogenase, cellulase, invertase **10** amygdalase *combining form:* **3** zym **4** zyme, zymo *suffix:* **2** in **3** ase

eon see **aeon**

Eos see **Aurora**

épée 5 sword

epergne 5 stand 11 centerpiece

Ephah *father:* 6 Jahdai *lover:* 5 Caleb

ephelis 7 freckle

ephemeral 5 brief, short 7 passing 8 episodic, fleeting, fugitive, volatile 9 fugacious, momentary, temporary, transient 10 evanescent, short-lived, transitory, unenduring 11 impermanent

Ephialtes 5 giant *brother:* 4 Otus *father:* 6 Aloeus 8 Poseidon *mother:* 9 Iphimedia *slayer:* 6 Apollo

Ephod's son 7 Hanniel

Ephraim *brother:* 8 Manasseh *father:* 6 Joseph *grandfather:* 5 Jacob *mother:* 7 Asenath

Ephratah *husband:* 5 Caleb *son:* 3 Hur

epic 4 epos, poem, saga 5 grand, Iliad 6 Aeneid, heroic 7 Beowulf, Odyssey 8 imposing 9 narrative *suffix:* 2 ad

epicene 5 sissy 6 prissy 7 unmanly 9 pansified, sissified 10 effeminate

epicure 7 glutton, gourmet, ravener 8 gourmand, sybarite 9 bon vivant, high liver 10 gastronome 11 connoisseur, gastronomer 12 gastronomist

epicurean 4 lush 7 sensual 8 luscious, sensuous 9 luxurious 10 voluptuous 12 sensualistic

epidemic 3 flu 4 rash 6 plague 8 outbreak 10 pestilence

epidermis 4 skin 7 cuticle

epigram 4 poem 6 saying

epigrammatic 5 meaty, pithy 7 compact, concise, marrowy, piquant

epigraph 5 motto 11 inscription

epilogue 6 ending, sequel 8 follow-up, postlude 9 afterword 10 conclusion, postscript

Epimetheus *brother:* 10 Prometheus *father:* 7 Iapetus *wife:* 7 Pandora

epinard 7 spinach

episode 5 event 8 incident, occasion 9 happening 10 occurrence 12 circumstance

epistaxis 9 nosebleed

epistle 4 note 6 letter 7 missive 13 communication

epitaph 3 R.I.P. 8 hic jacet 11 inscription

epithet 4 name, term 5 title 7 agnomen, moniker 8 cognomen, monicker, nickname 9 sobriquet 11 appellation

epitome 3 sum 5 brief 6 resumé 7 summary 8 abstract, boildown, breviary, breviate, last word, synopsis, ultimate 9 summation, summing-up 10 abridgment, apotheosis, conspectus 12 condensation, quintessence

epitomize 5 sum up 6 digest, embody, mirror, typify 7 outline, summate 8 boil down, condense, nutshell, tabulate 9 capsulize, exemplify, incarnate, inventory, personify, represent, summarize, symbolize, synopsize 10 illustrate 11 emblematize, incorporate

epoch 3 age, day, era 4 date, term, time 6 period 8 interval

equable 4 even, just, same 6 stable, steady 7 orderly, regular, stabile, uniform 8 constant 9 immutable, unvarying 10 equivalent, invariable, methodical, systematic, unchanging 12 unchangeable 13 unfluctuating

equal 3 tie 4 even, fair, just, like, mate, meet, peer, same, twin 5 agree, alike, match, reach, rival 6 accord, amount, equate, even-up 7 emulate, identic, similar, uniform 8 alter ego, parallel 9 duplicate, identical, impartial, measure up, objective 10 competitor, fifty-fifty, tantamount 11 counterpart, symmetrical 12 commensurate, correspond to, proportional, unprejudiced 13 commensurable, corresponding, dispassionate, proportionate *combining form:* 2 is 3 iso 4 equi, pari 5 aequi *French:* 4 égal

equality 3 par 6 equity, parity 7 balance, égalité 8 sameness 10 adequation

Equality State 7 Wyoming

equalize 4 even 5 level 6 square 7 balance

equalizer 6 pistol 8 handicap 10 tying score

equally 6 evenly 8 squarely 10 fifty-fifty 11 impartially

equanimity 5 poise 6 aplomb, phlegm 7 ataraxy, balance 8 calmness, coolness, evenness, serenity 9 assurance, composure, equipoise, placidity, sangfroid 10 confidence, detachment 11 equilibrium, tranquility 12 tranquillity 13 self-assurance

equate 4 even 5 liken, match, treat 6 regard, relate 7 compare, paragon 8 consider, equalize, parallel, similize 9 associate, represent 10 assimilate

equestrian 5 rider 8 horseman

equidistant 3 mid 6 center, medial, median, middle 7 central, halfway, midmost 10 centermost, middlemost

equilibrium 5 poise 6 stasis 7 balance 9 equipoise, steadying 10 steadiness 12 counterpoise 13 stabilization *combining form:* 5 stato

equine 4 colt, mare 5 horse, steed

equip 3 arm, rig 4 gear 5 dress, endow, rig up 6 attire, fit out, outfit, rig out, supply 7 appoint, furnish, prepare, provide, qualify, turn out 8 accouter, accoutre

equipment 3 rig 4 gear 5 traps 6 attire, outfit, tackle, things 7 baggage, fitment 8 fittings, material, materiel, tackling

9 apparatus, machinery, trappings **10** provisions **11** accessories, attachments, habiliments, impedimenta **12** accouterment, accoutrement, provisioning **13** appurtenances, paraphernalia

equitable 4 even, fair, just, same **5** level **6** stable **8** unbiased **9** identical, impartial, objective, uncolored **10** impersonal **12** unprejudiced **13** dispassionate

equity 3 law **7** justice **8** equality, justness

equivalence 3 par **6** parity **8** equality, likeness, sameness **10** adequation **11** correlation

equivalent 4 akin, like, same **5** alike, match **6** agnate **7** identic, obverse, similar **8** parallel **9** analogous, duplicate, identical **10** comparable, reciprocal, substitute, tantamount **11** convertible, correlative, counterpart **12** commensurate **13** corresponding, proportionate

equivocal 4 hazy **5** fishy, vague **7** clouded, dubious, obscure, suspect, unclear **8** doubtful **9** ambiguous, tenebrous, uncertain, undecided **10** ambivalent, borderline, indecisive, indistinct, multivocal, unexplicit **11** problematic **12** disreputable, questionable **13** indeterminate

equivocate 3 fib, lie **5** avoid, cavil, dodge, elude, evade, fence, hedge, parry, skirt **6** escape, eschew, palter, weasel **7** falsify, quibble, shuffle **8** sidestep **9** pussyfoot **10** tergiverse **11** prevaricate **12** tergiversate

equivocation 3 fib, lie **5** lying **6** deceit **7** fallacy, fibbing, hedging, sophism **8** coloring, delusion, haggling **9** ambiguity, casuistry, deception, duplicity, quibbling, sophistry **10** distortion **11** amphibology **12** speciousness, spuriousness **13** deceptiveness, dissimulation, double meaning

equivoque 3 pun **4** quip

era 3 age, day **4** date, term, time **5** epoch, stage **6** period

eradicate 4 dele, raze **5** abate, erase, purge **6** delete, uproot **7** abolish, blot out, destroy, root out, wipe out **8** demolish **9** extirpate, liquidate **10** annihilate, extinguish **11** exterminate

Eran *father:* **9** Shuthelah *grandfather:* **7** Ephraim

erase 4 dele, x out **5** annul, blank **6** cancel, cut out, delete, efface, excise, negate, remove, rub out, scrape **7** abolish, blot out, expunge, nullify, scratch, take out, wipe out **8** black out, blank out, cross off, cross out, disannul, withdraw **9** eliminate, extirpate, sponge out, strike out **10** neutralize, obliterate

Erato see **Muse**

Erbin *father:* **9** Custennin *nephew:* **6** Arthur *son:* **7** Geraint

erbium *symbol:* **2** Er

ere 6 before

Erebus *daughter:* **3** Day **6** Hemera *father:* **5** Chaos *home:* **5** Hades *sister, wife:* **3** Nox, Nyx *son:* **6** Aether, Charon

Erec et ___ 5 Enide

Erechteus *daughter:* **8** Chthonia *father:* **6** Vulcan **10** Hephaestus *mother:* **2** Ge **4** Gaea *slayer:* **4** Zeus **7** Jupiter

erect 4 form, lift, make, rear **5** build, exalt, forge, frame, hoist, honor, put up, raise, run up, set up, shape, upend **6** create, effect, lifted, make up, raised, uprear **7** build up, compose, dignify, elevate, ennoble, fashion, glorify, magnify, produce, stand-up, sublime, upraise, upright **8** elevated, heighten, standing, upraised, vertical **9** construct, establish, fabricate, hammer out **10** aggrandize, bring about, straight-up, upstanding **11** distinguish, manufacture **13** perpendicular

erection 4 pile **7** edifice **8** building **9** structure

eremite 6 hermit **7** ascetic, recluse

Erewhon 6 utopia *author:* **6** Butler

ergo 2 so **4** then, thus **5** hence **9** therefore, thereupon **11** accordingly **12** consequently

Erichthonius *father:* **8** Dardanus *son:* **4** Tros

Eridanus star 8 Achernar

Erigone *dog:* **5** Maera *father:* **7** Icarius *festival:* **5** Aeora

Erin see **Eire**

Erinyes 6 Alecto, Furies **7** Megaera **9** Eumenides, Tisiphone

Eriphyle *brother:* **8** Adrastus *husband:* **10** Amphiaraus *slayer, son:* **8** Alcmaeon

Eris *brother:* **4** Ares, Mars *daughter:* **3** Ate *fruit:* **5** apple *mother:* **3** Nox, Nyx

Eri's father 3 Gad

ermine 3 fur **5** stoat **6** weasel

erode 3 eat, rub **4** bite, gall, gnaw, rust, wear **5** chafe, decay, grate, graze, scour **6** abrade, rub off, ruffle **7** consume, corrade, corrode, crumble, eat away, rub away **8** wear away **9** scrape off **10** scrape away **11** deteriorate **12** disintegrate

Eroica composer 9 Beethoven

Eros see **Cupid**

erotic 4 lewd, sexy **5** bawdy, spicy **6** ardent, carnal, earthy, fervid **7** amative, amatory, amorous, fervent, fleshly, sensual **8** lovesome, prurient, sensuous **9** epicurean, lecherous, lickerish, salacious **10** lascivious, passionate, voluptuous **11** aphrodisiac, impassioned **12** concupiscent

err 3 sin **4** slip, trip **5** lapse, misdo, stray **6** bungle, offend, slip up, wander **7** blunder, deviate, misplay, stumble **8** trespass **10** transgress **12** miscalculate

errand 3 job 4 task 5 chore 7 mission

errand boy 4 page 5 gofer 7 bellboy, bellhop, courier

errant 5 stray 6 roving 7 devious, erratic, naughty, ranging, roaming 8 drifting, fallible, rambling, shifting, straying 9 deviating, itinerant, wandering 10 meandering, unreliable 11 misbehaving, mischievous

erratic 4 iffy, wild 5 queer, stray, wacky, weird 6 chancy 7 bizarre, curving, devious, dubious, oddball, strange, unusual, wayward, winding 8 doubtful, freakish, peculiar, shifting, singular, unstable, variable, volatile, whimsied 9 anomalous, arbitrary, eccentric, fluctuant, irregular, mercurial, uncertain, unnatural, vagarious, wandering, whimsical 10 capricious, changeable, inconstant, meandering, roundabout, undirected 12 incalculable, inconsistent 13 idiosyncratic, unpredictable

erring see **errant**

erroneous 3 off 4 awry 5 amiss, askew, false, wrong 6 untrue 7 unsound 8 mistaken, specious 9 defective, incorrect, misguided 10 inaccurate

error 3 sin 4 bull, flub, muff, slip, trip 5 boner, botch, fault, fluff, lapse 6 boo-boo, bungle, fumble, howler, miscue, slipup 7 blooper, blunder, fallacy, falsity, faux pas, misplay, misstep, mistake, stumble, untruth 8 delusion, illusion, misdoing, screamer 9 falsehood, falseness, indecorum, oversight 10 inaccuracy, misreading 11 impropriety, misjudgment *printing:* 4 typo 6 errata (plural) 7 erratum

ersatz 4 copy, fake, mock, sham 5 dummy, false 8 spurious 9 imitation, simulated, synthetic 10 artificial, factitious, simulacrum, substitute

Erse 5 Irish 6 Celtic, Gaelic 8 Scottish

Er's father 5 Judah

erstwhile 3 old 4 late, once, past 6 before, bygone, former, whilom 7 already, earlier, onetime, quondam 8 formerly, sometime 10 heretofore, previously

eruct 4 burp, emit, spew 5 belch, eject, expel 6 irrupt 8 disgorge

erudite 7 learned 8 lettered, studious, well-read 9 scholarly 10 scholastic

erudition 4 lore 7 culture, letters, science 8 learning, literacy, pedantry 9 education, knowledge 11 bookishness, cultivation, learnedness, scholarship 12 studiousness 13 scholarliness

erupt 3 jet 4 boil, emit, hurl, spew 5 belch, burst, eject, expel, go off, spout, spurt 6 cast up, irrupt 7 cast out, explode 8 break out, detonate, disgorge, throw off, touch off 9 discharge 10 burst forth 11 extravasate

eruption 4 gust, rush 5 burst, flare, sally

6 access 7 flare-up 8 outbreak, outburst 9 commotion, explosion *skin:* 3 zit 4 rash 6 pimple 7 serpigo 8 exanthem

Esau *brother:* 5 Jacob *country:* 4 Edom *descendant:* 7 Edomite *father:* 5 Isaac *father-in-law:* 4 Elon *grandson:* 6 Amalek *mother:* 7 Rebekah *new name:* 4 Edom *son:* 5 Korha, Reuel 7 Eliphaz *wife:* 4 Adah 10 Aholibamah

escalade 5 climb, mount, scale 6 ascend

escalate 4 grow, upgo 5 climb, mount, scale, widen 6 ascend, expand, spread 7 broaden, enlarge, upclimb 8 heighten, increase 9 intensify

escapade 4 lark 5 antic, caper, fling, prank, spree 6 frolic, vagary 7 roguery, rollick 8 mischief

escape 3 fly, lam, shy 4 bilk, duck, flee, flit, jump, miss, shun, skip, skit, slip 5 avoid, break, burke, dodge, elude, evade, shake, skirt 6 bypass, decamp, depart, eschew, flight, outlet, vanish 7 abscond, bail out, come-off, dodging, ducking, duck out, elusion, evasion, get away, make off, release, run away 8 breakout, eschewal, shunning 9 avoidance, bypassing, departure, disappear, runaround 10 circumvent, liberation 11 deliverance, elusiveness, evasiveness 12 sidestepping 13 circumvention *narrow:* 9 close call 10 close shave

escargot 5 snail

escarole 6 endive

escarpment 5 cliff, slope

eschar 4 scab 5 crust 6 lesion

eschew 3 shy 4 bilk, duck, shun 5 avoid, elude, evade, forgo 6 double, escape, forego 7 abstain, forbear, refrain 8 forebear 9 sacrifice

eschewal 6 escape, shying 7 come-off, elusion, evasion 8 escaping, shirking, shunning 9 avoidance, runaround

escort 3 see 4 bear, beau, date, lead, show 5 bring, guard, guide, pilot, route, steer 6 attend, convoy, direct, fellow, squire 7 company, conduct, gallant, vis-à-vis 8 cavalier, chaperon, shepherd 9 accompany, attendant, boyfriend, companion 11 consort with

escritoire 4 desk 9 secretary 10 secretaire 11 writing desk

escrow 4 bond, deed, fund 7 deposit

esculent 6 edible 7 eatable 10 comestible

escutcheon 6 shield

Eshban's father 6 Dishon

Eshcol *ally:* 7 Abraham *brother:* 4 Aner 5 Mamre

esker 2 os 3 ose 4 kame 5 mound, ridge

Eskimo 3 Ita 4 Yuit 5 Aleut 6 Innuit *boat:* 5 bidar, kayak, umiak 7 bidarka *boot:* 5 kamik 6 mukluk *dog:* 5 husky

8 malamute *dwelling:* **5** igloo **9** barrabora **outer garment:** **5** parka *sledge:* **7** komatik

esophagus **4** tube **6** gullet, throat **7** pharynx

esoteric **5** inner **6** mystic, occult, orphic, secret **7** private **8** abstruse, hermetic, profound **9** recondite **10** acroamatic **12** confidential

ESP **9** intuition **12** clairvoyance

espadrille **4** shoe **6** sandal

espalier **7** lattice, railing, trellis

esparto **4** alfa **5** grass

especial **4** main **5** chief **7** express, notable, supreme, unusual **8** dominant, singular, specific, uncommon **9** paramount **10** individual, particular, preeminent, surpassing **11** exceptional, predominant **12** preponderant

especially **7** notably **8** in specie, markedly, uniquely **9** eminently, expressly, supremely, unusually **10** peculiarly, remarkably, singularly **12** particularly, preeminently, specifically **13** distinctively, exceptionally

espial **4** find **6** notice, strike **9** detection, discovery **10** unearthing

espionage **6** spying **8** watching **9** sleuthing **11** observation **12** surveillance

espousal **3** aid **5** troth, union **6** mating **7** support **8** adoption, advocacy, approval, ceremony, marriage **9** betrothal, embracing, promotion **10** acceptance, betrothing, engagement **11** betrothment

espouse **3** wed **4** back, mate **5** adopt, catch, marry **6** accept, take on, take up, uphold **7** approve, embrace, support **8** advocate, champion, maintain

esprit **3** vim, wit **4** brio, dash, élan, life, mind, zing **5** humor, oomph, verve **6** acumen, brains, fervor, mettle, morale, spirit **7** courage, loyalty, passion **8** devotion, tenacity **9** acuteness, animation, sharpness **10** brightness, cleverness, enthusiasm, fellowship **11** camaraderie

esprit de corps see **morale**

espy **3** see **4** find, mark, note, spot, view **5** catch, hit on, sight, watch **6** behold, descry, detect, notice, remark, take in, turn up **7** discern, hit upon, make out, observe, witness **8** meet with **9** encounter, recognize **11** distinguish

____ es Salaam **3** Dar

essay **3** try **4** seek, toil, work **5** assay, labor, offer, paper, piece, study, theme, tract, trial **6** hassle, strive, thesis **7** article, attempt, travail, venture **8** endeavor, exertion, striving, struggle, treatise **9** discourse, undertake **10** discussion, exposition **11** composition, explication, undertaking **12** dissertation

essayist *American:* **5** Cooke **6** Brooks **7** Cousins, Emerson **8** Repplier **10** Crevecoeur *English:* **4** Lamb **5** Pater, Smith **6** Ruskin, Steele **7** Addison, Hazlitt *French:* **9** Montaigne *Greek:* **8** Xenophon *Scottish:* **7** Carlyle

esse **5** being **9** existence

essence **3** ens, nub **4** body, crux, form, gist, pith, root, soul **5** being, fiber, fibre, stuff **6** aspect, bottom, center, entity, kernel, marrow, nature, nubbin, spirit, timber **7** element, quality, texture **8** property **9** attribute, substance **10** distillate, inwardness, rock bottom, virtuality **12** distillation, significance

essential **4** main, must **5** basal, basic, chief, prime, vital **6** inborn, inbred, innate, needed, primal, wanted **7** capital, connate, element, leading, needful, primary **8** cardinal, foremost, inherent, required, rudiment **9** condition, elemental, intrinsic, necessary, necessity, primitive, principal, requisite, right hand, substance **10** congenital, deepseated, elementary, imperative, sine qua non, substratal, underlying **11** fundamental, necessitous, requirement **12** constitutive, precondition, prerequisite **13** indispensable, part and parcel

essentially **6** almost, au fond, really **8** actually, as good as, as much as, wellnigh **9** basically, virtually **11** practically **13** fundamentally, substantially

essonite **6** garnet **13** cinnamon stone

establish **3** fix, lay, put, set **4** base, make, moor, rest, root, show, stay **5** build, enact, endow, erect, found, infix, place, prove, rivet, set up, start, stick **6** attest, bottom, create, decree, enroot, ground, impose, secure, settle, verify **7** build up, clarify, confirm, implant, instill, make out, provide, set down **8** document, entrench, organize **9** authorize, construct, determine, formulate, hammer out, inculcate, institute, legislate, originate, predicate, prescribe **10** constitute **11** corroborate, demonstrate **12** authenticate, substantiate

establishment **4** firm **5** house **6** outfit **7** company, concern, diehard **8** business, Old Guard **9** institute, workplace **10** enterprise, foundation **11** institution **12** conservative

estate **4** case, farm, form, land, rank **5** acres, caste, class, grade, level, manor, order, place, ranch, shape, state, villa **6** quinta, repair **7** station **8** category, hacienda, mesnalty, position, property, standing **9** condition **10** plantation *feudal:* **4** fief **7** fiefdom *first:* **6** clergy *fourth:* **5** press *Indian:* **5** taluk **6** taluka *manager:* **7** steward **8** executor, guardian *second:* **6** nobles **8** nobility *third:* **7** commons

esteem **5** favor, honor, prize, value

6 admire, credit, liking, regard, revere
7 account, apprize, cherish, idolize, respect,
worship **8** approval, consider, treasure,
venerate **9** valuation **10** admiration, appreciate, estimation **12** appreciation
13 consideration

ester 6 oleate **7** acetate **8** compound
9 phosphate *suffix:* **4** oate

Esther *cousin:* **8** Mordecai *father:* **7** Abihail *festival:* **5** Purim *Hebrew name:*
8 Hadassah *husband:* **9** Ahasuerus

estimable 4 good **5** noble **6** worthy
7 admired, reputed **8** esteemed, laudable,
sterling **9** admirable, deserving, honorable,
meritable, praisable, reputable, respected
10 creditable **11** commendable, meritorious, respectable, thankworthy
12 praiseworthy

estimate 3 put, set, sum **4** call, cast, rank,
rate **5** assay, count, fancy, guess, infer,
judge, place, price, prize, round, set at,
stock, value **6** assess, cipher, decide,
deduce, figure, rating, reckon, settle, survey **7** adjudge, compute, imagine, suppose,
surmise, valuate **8** appraise, discover, evaluate, forecast, judgment, round off, sizing
up **9** appraisal, ascertain, calculate, determine, enumerate, reckoning, valuation
10 adjudicate, assessment, conjecture, evaluation, projection **11** approximate, calculation, measurement **12** appraisement

estimation 4 fame **5** favor, honor, stock
6 esteem, regard **7** account, opinion,
respect **8** figuring, judgment **9** appraisal,
ciphering, reckoning, valuation **10** admiration, arithmetic, assessment, evaluation,
impression **11** calculation, computation
12 appraisement **13** consideration

estop 3 bar **7** prevent **8** preclude, prohibit

estrange 4 part, wean **5** alien, sever,
split **6** divide, sunder **7** break up, divorce
8 alienate, disunify, disunite, separate
9 disaffect

estrangement 6 schism **7** divorce **8** division **10** alienation, withdrawal
12 disaffection

estreat 4 copy **5** exact **6** record
7 extract **9** duplicate

estuary 5 firth, frith, inlet, mouth **6** estero
10 tidal river

esurient 6 greedy, hungry **9** voracious

étagère 7 cabinet, whatnot

Etats ____ 4 Unis

etch 5 grave **6** define, depict, incise
7 engrave, impress, imprint, outline, picture,
portray **8** describe, inscribe, set forth
9 delineate, represent

etcher *American:* **7** Pennell **8** Whistler
French: **5** Redon **6** Villon *Italian:* **8** Piranesi *Spanish:* **6** Ribera *Swiss:* **4** Zorn

Eteocles *brother:* **9** Polynices *father:*
7 Oedipus *mother:* **7** Jocasta *slayer:*
9 Polynices

eternal 7 ageless, endless, lasting, undying **8** constant, dateless, immortal, infinite,
timeless, unending **9** ceaseless, continual,
deathless, immutable, permanent, perpetual,
unceasing **10** immemorial, intemporal, perdurable, unchanging **11** amaranthine, everlasting, illimitable, inalterable, never-ending,
sempiternal, unalterable, unremitting
12 interminable

Eternal City 4 Rome

eternally 4 ever **6** always **7** forever
8 evermore **11** forevermore, in perpetuum

eternity 3 age, eon **4** aeon, long **7** dog's
age **8** blue moon, coon's age, infinity
9 afterlife **10** eviternity, infinitude, perpetu-
ity **11** endlessness, immortality **12** infinite-
ness, sempiternity, timelessness

etesian 4 wind **6** annual

Ethan ____ 5 Allen, Brand, Frome

Ethan's father 5 Kishi

Ethbaal's daughter 7 Jezebel

ether 3 air, gas, sky **6** heaven **8** empyrean **10** anesthetic, atmosphere

ethereal 4 aery, airy **5** filmy, light **6** aerial,
vapory **7** fragile **8** delicate, empyreal,
empyrean, gossamer, heavenly, vaporish,
vaporous **9** celestial, vaporlike
13 unsubstantial

ethic 5 ideal, mores, value **6** belief, morals
8 criteria, morality, standard **9** standards
10 moralities, principles

ethical 5 moral, noble **7** upright **8** elevated, virtuous **9** righteous **10** moralistic,
principled, upstanding **11** right-minded

Ethiopia 9 Abyssinia *capital:* **10** Addis
Ababa *emperor:* **7** Menalik **8** Selassie
9 Ras Tafari **13** Haile Selassie *language:*
7 Amharic *measure:* **3** tat **4** cubi, kuba
5 derah, messe **6** cabaho, sinjer, sinzer,
tanica **7** farsakh, farsang *monetary unit:*
4 birr *region:* **4** Bale, Kefa, Welo **5** Arusi,
Gojam, Harer, Shewa, Tigre **6** Gonder,
Sidamo, Welega **7** Eritrea **4** Gemu, Gefa
8 Ilubabor

ethnic 5 pagan **6** racial, tribal **7** gentile,
heathen, infidel, profane **8** national **9** infidelic **11** unchristian **12** non-Christian

etiolate 4 pale **6** bleach, weaken
9 colorless

etiquette 4 form **5** mores **7** conduct,
decency, decorum, dignity, manners
8 behavior, protocol **9** amenities, propriety
10 civilities, convention, deportment, seemliness **11** formalities, proprieties

etna 4 lamp **7** volcano

Etruscan *city, town:* **4** Roma, Veii
5 Caere, Vulci **6** Arezzo **7** Clusium, Felsina,
Perugia **8** Volsinii **9** Florentia, Tarquinia,
Vetulonia *deity:* **3** Tiv, Uni **4** Turm, Usil

5 Tinia 6 Menfra, Nethun, Trithn 7 Velchan 8 Voltumna *king:* 7 Porsena, Tarquin *kingdom:* 7 Etruria

etui 4 case

etymology 6 origin 7 history, origins

etymon 4 root 5 radix

eucalypt 4 yate

eucalyptus eater 5 koala

Eucharist *container:* 3 pyx *plate:* 5 paten *service:* 4 Mass 9 Communion 11 Lord's Supper *vessel:* 8 ciborium *wafer:* 4 host 8 viaticum

___ **Eulenspiegel** 4 Till, Tyll

eulogistic 9 approving, laudative, laudatory, praiseful 11 approbatory, encomiastic, panegyrical 12 commendatory 13 complimentary

eulogize 4 hymn, laud 5 bless, cry up, extol 6 belaud, praise 7 applaud, glorify, magnify 8 bepraise 9 celebrate 10 panegyrize

eulogy 5 eloge 6 praise 7 oration, tribute 8 citation, encomium 9 adulation, panegyric 10 salutation 13 glorification

Eumenides see **Erinyes**

Eunice's son 7 Timothy

eunuch 7 gelding 8 castrate, castrato

euphonic 5 sweet 6 dulcet 7 melodic, tuneful 9 melodious 11 mellisonant

euphony 7 harmony

euphoria 4 glee 6 frenzy 7 ecstasy, elation, madness 10 exaltation 12 exhilaration, intoxication

Euphrosyne see **Graces**

euphuistic 7 aureate, flowery, swollen, verbose 8 colorful, elevated, sonorous 9 bombastic, elaborate, overblown 10 rhetorical 11 declamatory 12 magniloquent 13 grandiloquent

eureka 3 aha

Euridice's husband 7 Orpheus

Euripides play 3 Ion 5 Helen, Medea 6 Hecuba 7 Electra, Orestes 8 Alcestis 10 Andromache, Hippolytus 11 Trojan Women

Europa *brother:* 6 Cadmus *father:* 6 Agenor 7 Phoenix *husband:* 8 Asterius *son:* 5 Minos 8 Sarpedon

Europe 9 continent *country:* 4 Eire 5 Italy, Malta, Spain 6 France, Greece, Latvia, Monaco, Norway, Poland, Sweden 7 Albania, Andorra, Armenia, Austria, Belarus, Belgium, Denmark, Estonia, Finland, Georgia, Germany, Hungary, Iceland, Ireland, Moldova, Romania, Rumania, Ukraine 8 Bulgaria, Portugal 9 Lithuania, San Marino 10 Azerbaijan, Luxembourg 11 Netherlands, Switzerland, Vatican City 13 Liechtenstein, United Kingdom *ethnic group:* 4 Finn, Lapp, Pole, Serb, Turk, Wend 5 Croat, Czech, Dutch, Greek, Gypsy, Irish, Latin, Swede, Swiss, Welsh 6 Basque, French, German, Magyar, Polish, Scotch, Slovak 7 Catalan, English, Finnish, Fleming, Italian, Slovene, Spanish, Swedish, Walloon 8 Albanian, Andorran, Armenian, Croatian, Romanian 9 Bulgarian, Hungarian, Ukrainian 10 Macedonian, Monegasque, Phoenician 12 Byelorussian, Scandinavian *language:* 4 Lapp 5 Czech, Dutch, Greek, Irish, Latin, Welsh 6 Basque, Breton, Danish, French, Gaelic, German, Polish, Slovak 7 Catalan, English, Finnish, Flemish, Italian, Maltese, Romansh, Slovene, Spanish, Swedish, Turkish 8 Albanian, Romanian, Rumanian 9 Bulgarian, Hungarian, Icelandic, Norwegian 10 Macedonian, Portuguese 13 Serbo Croatian *mountain:* 3 Alp 8 Dolomite

europium *symbol:* 2 Eu

Euryale see **Gorgon**

Eurytus *daughter:* 4 Iole *slayer:* 8 Hercules

Euterpe see **Muse**

evacuant 6 emetic 8 diuretic, emptying 9 cathartic, purgative

evacuate 4 void 5 clear, empty, expel 6 remove 7 excrete, exhaust 8 withdraw

evacuee 2 DP 6 émigré 7 refugee 8 fugitive

evade 3 fly, shy 4 bilk, duck, flee, foil, shun 5 avoid, dodge, elude, hedge, parry, shirk 6 bypass, double, escape, eschew, outwit, thwart, weasel 7 shuffle 8 sideslip, sidestep, slip away 9 pussyfoot, turn aside 10 circumvent, equivocate, tergiverse 12 tergiversate

Evadne *father:* 5 Iphis *husband:* 8 Capaneus

evaluate 4 rank, rate 5 assay, class, gauge, grade, set at, value 6 assess, ponder, survey 8 appraise, classify, estimate 9 criticize

evaluation 5 stock 6 rating 7 judging 8 decision, estimate, judgment 9 appraisal 10 assessment, estimation 12 appraisement, appreciation, interpreting

Evander *father:* 6 Hermes 7 Mercury *mother:* 8 Carmenta 9 Carmentis *son:* 6 Pallas

evanesce 4 fade 5 clear, empty 6 dispel, vanish 7 scatter 8 disperse, dissolve 9 disappear, dissipate, evaporate 12 disintegrate

evanescent 6 fading, flying 7 cursory, melting, passing 8 fleeting, fugitive, volatile 9 ephemeral, fugacious, momentary, temporary, transient, vanishing 10 dissolving, short-lived, transitory 12 disappearing

evangelical 6 ardent, fervid 7 zealous 8 militant 9 crusading 10 missionary 11 impassioned 13 proselytizing

Evangeline *author:* 10 Longfellow
  beloved: 7 Gabriel *home:* 6 Acadia
evangelist 4 John, Luke, Mark 5 Moody
  6 Graham, Sunday, Wesley 7 apostle,
  Edwards, Matthew 9 McPherson, missioner 10 colporteur, missionary, revivalist
evangelistic 9 crusading, reforming
  10 missionary
evangelize 6 preach 8 homilize
  9 sermonize
evaporate 4 fade 5 clear 6 vanish
  7 evanish 8 evanesce, vaporize
  9 disappear
evasion 5 dodge 6 escape, excuse
  7 come-off, dodgery, dodging, elusion
  8 escaping, escapism, eschewal, haggling,
  shunning 9 avoidance, quibbling, runaround
evasive 3 sly 4 eely 5 dodgy, vague
  6 shifty 7 elusive, elusory, sliding, unclear
  8 slippery 9 ambiguous, equivocal, shuffling 10 intangible 12 equivocating
eve 4 dusk 5 night 7 sundown
Eve *husband:* 4 Adam *son:* 4 Abel, Cain,
  Seth
even 3 tie, yet 4 fair, flat, just, same
  5 align, equal, exact, flush, grade, level,
  plane, quite, still, truly 6 as well, equate,
  honest, indeed, really, smooth, square, stable, steady, verily 7 already, balance, equable, exactly, flatten, pancake, planate, stabile, uniform 8 balanced, constant, equalize,
  smoothen, so much as, straight, unvaried
  9 continual, equitable, expressly, identical,
  precisely, unvarying 10 absolutely, comparable, consistent, continuous, fifty-fifty, positively, symmetrize, unchanging 11 undeviating 12 unprejudiced 13 fair and square,
  proportionate, unfluctuating *combining
  form:* 5 homal 6 homalo
evening 4 dusk 6 soiree, sunset 7 sundown 8 duskness, eventide, gloaming, twilight 9 afternoon, duskiness, nightfall
  French: 4 soir *Italian:* 4 sera *service:*
  7 vespers *star:* 5 Venus 6 Hesper, Vesper 8 Hesperus
evenness 7 balance 8 equality, fairness,
  flatness 10 equanimity, uniformity
  11 consistency
event 3 act, hap 4 case, deed, fact, feat,
  meet 5 issue, match, treat 6 action, affair,
  chance, effect, result, sequel, upshot 7 contest, delight, episode, exploit, fortune, outcome, product, sequent 8 accident, causatum, fortuity, incident, landmark, milepost,
  occasion, offshoot 9 aftermath, happening,
  milestone, outgrowth, resultant 10 occurrence, phenomenon 11 achievement, aftereffect, competition, consequence, eventuality 12 circumstance, happenstance
eventful 4 busy 9 important, momentous
eventual 3 lag 4 last 5 final 6 ending, lat-

est, latter 7 closing, endmost, ensuing
  8 hindmost, terminal, ultimate 10 concluding, consequent, inevitable, succeeding
eventuality 4 case 5 issue 6 effect,
  result, sequel, upshot 7 outcome 9 aftermath 11 aftereffect, consequence, contingency, possibility
eventually 3 yet 7 finally, someday
  8 sometime 10 ultimately 13 sooner or
  later
eventuate 5 occur 6 happen, result
ever 3 too 4 once, over 5 at all, super
  6 always, anyway, overly, unduly 7 anytime,
  anywise, forever, plaguey, usually 8 mortally, overfull, overmuch 9 eternally,
  extremely, immensely, regularly 10 annoy-
  ingly, constantly, consumedly, grievously,
  invariably 11 excessively, in perpetuum,
  perpetually 12 consistently, continuously
evergreen 3 fir, ivy, yew 4 ilex, pine, tree
  5 cedar, holly, savin 6 laurel, myrtle,
  spruce 7 conifer, cypress, hemlock, juniper,
  redwood, sequoia 8 magnolia 9 mistletoe
  12 rhododendron
Evergreen State 10 Washington
everlasting 7 endless, eternal, forever,
  lasting 8 constant, immortal, infinite, termless, unending 9 boundless, ceaseless,
  continual, limitless, permanent, perpetual,
  unceasing 10 continuous, perdurable
  11 amaranthine, never-ending, unremitting
  13 uninterrupted
evermore 6 always 9 eternally 11 in
  perpetuum
evert 5 upset 9 overthrow
every 3 all 4 each *combining form:*
  3 pam, pan 4 pano *suffix:* 2 ly
everybody 3 all 4 each 8 everyone
everyday 5 banal, lowly, plain, usual
  6 common 7 mundane, prosaic, routine,
  workday 8 familiar, frequent, ordinary,
  workaday 9 customary, plain Jane, quotidian 11 commonplace 12 unremarkable
everyplace see **everywhere**
everything 3 all *French:* 4 tout *German:*
  5 alles
everywhere 7 all over, overall 8 all round,
  wherever 9 all around 10 far and near, far
  and wide, high and low, throughout
evict 3 out 4 oust 5 chase, chuck, eject,
  expel 6 put out 7 boot out, dismiss,
  extrude, kick out, shut out, turn out 8 dislodge, force out, throw out 10 dispossess
evidence 4 clue, mark, show, sign
  5 index, proof, prove, token, trace 6 attest,
  evince, expose, ostend 7 bespeak, betoken, confirm, display, exhibit, indicia, symptom, testify, witness 8 indicate, manifest,
  proclaim 9 testament, testimony 10 illustrate, indication 11 attestation, demon-

strate, significant, testimonial
12 confirmation

evident 5 clear, overt, plain **6** patent
7 glaring, obvious, visible **8** apparent, distinct, manifest, palpable **9** prominent
10 noticeable, pronounced
11 unambiguous

evidently 9 outwardly, seemingly
10 apparently, officially, ostensibly
11 professedly

evil 3 bad, ill, low, sin **4** base, debt, foul,
hard, tort, ugly, vice, vile **5** angry, black,
catty, crime, fetid, wrong **6** malice, nocent,
putrid, sinful, trying, wicked **7** badness,
baleful, baneful, corrupt, devilry, harmful,
hateful, hideous, hurtful, immoral, malefic,
misdeed, nocuous, obscene, offense, ominous, satanic, unlucky, vicious **8** damaging,
damnable, iniquity, satanism, satanity, spiteful, stinking, wrathful **9** atrocious, diablerie,
diabolism, difficult, evildoing, execrable, ill-boding, ill-omened, injurious, loathsome,
malicious, nefarious, offensive, rancorous,
repellent, reprobate, repugnant, repulsive,
revolting **10** calamitous, despiteful, disastrous, flagitious, iniquitous, malevolent, misconduct, pernicious, sinfulness, unpleasant,
wickedness, wrongdoing **11** deleterious,
destructive, detrimental, distasteful, maleficence, mischievous, unfavorable, unfortunate **12** disagreeable, inauspicious ***combining form:* 3** mal

evildoer 3 cur **5** crook, felon **6** bad lot,
sinner **7** culprit, villain **8** criminal
9 miscreant

evil spirit 3 imp **5** demon, devil, fiend
6 daemon

evince 4 mark, milk, show **5** argue, cause,
educe, evoke, prove **6** attest, elicit, expose,
extort, ostend **7** bespeak, betoken, confirm,
display, exhibit, extract, provoke, signify
8 evidence, indicate, manifest, proclaim
9 stimulate **10** bring about, illustrate
11 demonstrate

evirate 4 geld **8** castrate **10** emasculate

eviscerate 3 gut **4** draw **5** bowel
6 paunch **7** embowel **10** disembowel,
exenterate

evocative 6 moving **7** causing, weighty
8 arousing, inducing, pregnant, stirring
9 effecting, producing **10** meaningful, suggestive **11** stimulating

evoke 4 milk, stir **5** educe, raise, rally,
rouse, waken **6** arouse, awaken, call up,
elicit, evince, excite, extort **7** extract
8 summon up **9** call forth, conjure up, stimulate **11** summon forth

evolution 6 change, growth **8** progress,
upgrowth **9** flowering, unfolding **10** biogenesis **11** development, progression

evolve 4 grow **5** educe, get at, ripen

6 change, derive, mature, obtain, open up,
unfold **7** advance, develop **8** progress
9 elaborate **10** excogitate

evulse 4 pull, tear, yank **7** extract

ewe 5 sheep *young:* **6** theave

ewer 3 jug **4** vase **5** basin **7** pitcher

ex 6 former **7** without

exacerbate 5 annoy **6** worsen
7 envenom, inflame, provoke **8** embitter,
heighten, irritate **9** aggravate, intensify
10 exasperate

exact 4 call, even, levy, nice, same, true,
very **5** claim, force, fussy, gouge, pinch, put
on, right, screw, wrest, wring **6** assess,
coerce, compel, demand, extort, impose,
oblige, proper, square, wrench **7** careful,
correct, extract, precise, require, solicit,
squeeze **8** accurate, punctual, rigorous,
selfsame **9** challenge, constrain, identical,
postulate, shake down **10** meticulous, scrupulous **11** painstaking, punctilious, requisition **12** conscionable **13** conscientious
***combining form:* 4** orth **5** ortho

exacting 5 fussy, rigid, stern, tough
6 severe, strict, taxing, trying **7** exigent, finicky, onerous, weighty **8** critical, grievous,
rigorous **9** demanding, stringent **10** burdensome, oppressive, particular

exactitude 8 accuracy **9** precision
10 definitude **11** correctness, preciseness
12 definiteness

exactly 3 all **4** bang, even, just **5** quite,
right, sharp, spang, stick **6** as well, in toto,
square, wholly **7** totally, utterly **8** all in all,
smack-dab, squarely **9** expressly, on the
nose, precisely **10** absolutely, accurately,
altogether, completely, positively
12 specifically

exaggerate 3 pad **5** color, fudge
6 overdo **7** amplify, magnify, overact,
romance **8** overdraw, overrate **9** embellish,
embroider, overstate **10** overcharge
11 hyperbolize, romanticize

exaggeration 7 romance **8** coloring
9 hyperbole **10** caricature, stretching
11 enlargement, overdrawing **12** embroidering, overcoloring **13** amplification,
embellishment, overstatement

exalt 4 fire, laud, lift **5** boost, elate, erect,
extol, honor, pique, raise **6** deepen, enhalo,
inform, praise, uplift, uprear **7** acclaim, animate, build up, dignify, elevate, enhance,
ennoble, glorify, inspire, magnify, promote,
quicken, sublime, upgrade **8** heighten,
inspirit, pedestal, spirit up, stellify **9** encourage, intensify, stimulate **10** aggrandize
11 apotheosize, distinguish

exaltation 3 joy **5** bliss **6** praise
7 delight, ecstasy, elation, rapture **8** euphoria, rhapsody **9** extolment, laudation,
upgrading, uplifting **10** apotheosis **11** deifi-

cation, delectation **12** exhilaration, intoxication **13** dignification, glorification

exalted 4 high **5** first, grand, lofty, noble **6** astral, august, superb **7** eminent, highest, leading, sublime **8** elevated, foremost **9** number one, prominent, top-drawer **10** top-ranking **11** high-ranking, illustrious, outstanding

examination 4 oral, quiz, scan, test, view **5** assay, audit, trial **6** review, survey **7** autopsy, canvass, checkup, hearing, inquest, inquiry, sifting, testing **8** analysis, quizzing, scanning, scrutiny **9** breakdown, check-over, diagnosis, winnowing **10** dissection, inspection **11** questioning **13** catechization, investigation, perlustration **kind: 4** oral **5** final **7** medical, midterm **8** physical **of accounts: 5** audit **of a corpse: 7** autopsy

examine 3 ask, con, try, vet **4** pump, quiz, scan, sift, test, view **5** audit, check, grill, probe, prove, query, study **6** go over, look at, peruse, survey **7** canvass, check up, inquire, inspect, observe **8** check out, look into, look over, overhaul, question **9** catechize, check over **10** scrutinize **11** contemplate, interrogate, investigate **eggs: 6** candle

examiner 6 censor, critic, tester **7** auditor, coroner **9** inspector

examining tool *combining form:* **5** scope

example 4 case **5** ideal, model **6** mirror, sample **7** pattern, problem **8** ensample, exemplar, instance, paradigm, sampling, specimen, standard **9** archetype **11** case history **12** illustration

exanimate 4 dead **8** lifeless **10** spiritless

exasperate 3 get, irk **4** gall, huff, rile, roil **5** peeve, pique **6** nettle, work up **7** agitate **8** irritate **9** aggravate

exasperation 4 pest **6** bother, pester, plague, pother **8** irritant, nuisance, vexation **9** annoyance, besetment **10** botherment, irritation, resentment **11** aggravation, botheration, displeasure

ex cathedra 8 official **9** ex officio **13** authoritative

excavate 3 dig **4** grub **5** scoop, spade **6** dig out, shovel **7** unearth **8** gouge out, scoop out **9** hollow out, quarry out, scrape out

excavation 3 dig, pit **4** hole, mine **5** stope **6** trench

exceed 3 top **4** beat, best, dare, pass **5** break, excel, outdo **6** better, overdo **7** outstep, overrun, presume, surpass, venture **8** outreach, outshine, outstrip, outweigh, overstep **9** overreach, transcend

exceedingly 4 very **6** hugely **7** notably, parlous, vitally **9** extremely **10** remarkably,

strikingly **12** surpassingly **13** exceptionally **prefix: 3** pre **5** ultra

excel 3 top **4** beat, best **5** outdo, shine **6** better, exceed **7** surpass **8** outclass, outshine, outstrip **9** transcend

excellence 5 arête, class, merit, value, worth **6** virtue **7** quality **8** fineness, goodness, niceness **10** perfection, superbness **11** distinction, superiority

excellent 3 top **4** brag, fine, good **5** bully, dandy, nobby, noble, prime, royal, smart **6** bang-up, banner, famous, Grade A, proper, superb, tip-top **7** capital, classic, premium, quality, supreme **8** champion, five-star, splendid, stunning, superior, terrific, top-notch, whiz-bang **9** classical, first-rate, front-rank, high-class, high-grade, marvelous, number one, sovereign **10** blue-ribbon, first-class **11** exceptional, first-string, magnificent, sensational, superlative, unsurpassed **12** incomparable

except 3 bar, but, yet **4** bate, kick, omit, only, save **5** debar **6** bating, beside, exempt, object, reject, saving, unless **7** barring, besides, exclude, however, outside, protest, rule out, suspend **8** count out, pass over **9** apart from, aside from, eliminate, excluding, outside of **11** exclusive of, expostulate, remonstrate

exception 5 demur **7** dissent **9** exclusion, objection

exceptionable 8 unwanted **9** unwelcome **10** ill-favored **11** undesirable **12** inadmissible, unacceptable **13** objectionable

exceptional 4 rare **6** scarce, unique **7** notable, premium, special, strange, unusual **8** distinct, singular, superior, uncommon, unwonted **9** excellent, marvelous, wonderful **10** infrequent, noteworthy, phenomenal, remarkable, unordinary **11** outstanding, uncustomary, unthinkable **12** unimaginable **13** extraordinary

exceptionally 4 very **6** hugely **7** notably, parlous, vitally **9** extremely, unusually **10** especially, remarkably, strikingly **11** exceedingly, marvelously, wonderfully **12** particularly, phenomenally, stupendously, surpassingly

excerpt 4 cite, cull, pick **5** glean, quote **6** choose, select, single **7** extract, pick out

excess 3 fat **4** plus **5** extra, flood, spare **6** de trop **7** overage, surfeit, surplus **8** overflow, overkill, overmuch, overplus, plethora **9** boundless, indulgent, limitless, overboard, overdoing, overspill, overstock, profusion, redundant, unbounded **10** immoderacy, indulgence, oversupply, Saturnalia, surplusage **11** dissipation, overbalance, overmeasure, prodigality, superfluent, superfluity, superfluous, unessential

12 extravagance, immoderation, intemperance 13 overabundance, supernumerary

excessive 4 over 5 dizzy, steep, stiff, super, undue 6 too-too 7 extreme, sky-high 8 overmuch, prodigal, towering 10 dissipated, exorbitant, immoderate, inordinate, untempered 11 extravagant, intemperate, overweening 12 supernatural, unmeasurable, unrestrained 13 overindulgent *combining form:* 4 poly *prefix:* 3 sur

excessively 3 too 4 ever, over 6 overly, unduly 7 parlous 8 overfull, overmuch 9 extremely, immensely 12 inordinately *prefix:* 5 hyper

exchange 4 swap 5 bandy, trade, truck 6 barter, change, market, switch 7 bargain, commute, pay back, replace, traffic 8 displace 10 substitute 11 reciprocate *premium:* 4 agio

exchequer 5 chest 6 coffer 8 treasury, war chest

excise 3 tax 4 toll 5 elide, slash 6 cut off, cut out, delete, exsect, remove, resect 7 exscind, root out 8 amputate 9 eradicate, expurgate, extirpate, strike out

excision 3 cut 7 erasure, removal, surgery 9 resection 11 destruction, extirpation

excitable 4 edgy 6 touchy 8 agitable, skittery, skittish, unstable, volatile 9 alarmable, mercurial, startlish 10 high-strung 11 combustible 13 temperamental

excite 4 fire, move, spur, stir 5 elate, pique, prime, rouse, set up, waken 6 appeal, arouse, stir up, thrill, turn on 7 agitate, attract, commove, disturb, innerve, inspire, perturb, provoke, quicken 8 charge up, disquiet, energize, interest, intrigue, motivate, spirit up, touch off 9 fascinate, galvanize, impassion, innervate, stimulate 10 discompose, exhilarate

excited 3 hot 4 avid 5 eager 6 hectic 7 fevered, frantic 8 aflutter

excitement 3 ado 4 stir 6 furore, warmth 8 delirium, hysteria 9 commotion 11 disturbance, pandemonium

exclaim 4 blat, bolt, roar 5 snort 6 cry out 8 blurt out, burst out 9 ejaculate

exclamation 2 ah, ai, ay, ha, hi, ho, lo, oh, ow, so 3 aah, aha, bah, boo, cry, eek, feh, fie, gee, hah, hey, hic, huh, och, oho, ooh, pah, tsk, tut, ugh, wow, yeh 4 ahem, alas, damn, dang, darn, drat, egad, gosh, heck, hell, oops, ouch, phew, pish, posh, rats, whew, yell, yipe 5 alack, bravo, faugh, golly, humph, pshaw, shout 6 clamor, hurrah, indeed, phooey, shucks 7 doggone, gee whiz, hosanna, jeepers, whoopee 9 expletive 12 interjection *of disgust:* 3 bah, feh, ugh 5 yecch 6 phooey *of dismay:* 4 oh no *of pain:* 2 ow 4 ouch *of relief:* 4 phew *of*

sorrow: 4 alas 5 alack *of surprise:* 2 ah, oh 3 aha, oho, wow *of triumph:* 3 hah

exclude 3 ban, bar 4 bate 5 block, debar, estop 6 banish, disbar, except, put out 7 keep out, lock out, obviate, prevent, rule out, shut out, suspend, ward off 8 close out, count out, preclude, prohibit 9 blackball, blacklist, eliminate, ostracize *prefix:* 3 dis

excluding 3 bar, but 4 less, save 6 bating, except, saving 7 barring, besides 9 outside of 11 exclusive of

exclusive 4 chic, lone, only, pick, sole, tony 5 aloof, elect, elite, scoop, smart, swank, swish, whole 6 chosen, cliquy, picked, select, single, with-it 7 barring, dashing, high-hat, stylish 8 clannish, cliquish, limiting, selected, snobbish, unshared 9 debarring, excluding, preferred, undivided 10 individual, limitative, privileged, unswerving 11 fashionable, prohibitive, restrictive, standoffish 12 aristocratic, concentrated, undistracted

exclusively 3 but 4 only 5 alone 6 solely, wholly 8 entirely 10 completely 12 particularly

excogitate 4 mind 5 educe, study, weigh 6 derive, evolve, invent, ponder 7 develop, perpend, think up 8 consider, contrive, think out 9 think over 11 contemplate

excommunicate 8 unchurch

excoriate 3 rub 4 flay, fret, gall 5 chafe, slash 6 abrade, scathe, scorch 7 blister, scarify, scourge 8 lambaste, lash into 9 castigate

excorticate 4 peel, skin 5 scale, strip

excrement 4 dirt 5 feces 6 ordure, refuse *combining form:* 4 copr, scat 5 copro, scato *of animals:* 4 dung, muck 6 manure *of sea birds:* 5 guano

excrescence 4 wart 6 pimple 7 process 9 outgrowth, processus

excruciate 3 try 4 hurt, pain, rack 5 wound, wring 6 harrow, martyr 7 afflict, agonize, crucify, inflame, torment, torture 8 convulse, irritate

excruciating 5 acute, sharp 7 extreme, racking, rending, tearing 8 piercing, shooting, stabbing 9 agonizing, consuming, harrowing, torturing, torturous 10 tormenting

exculpate 4 free 5 clear, remit 6 acquit, excuse, let off, pardon 7 absolve, amnesty, condone, explain, forgive, justify 9 exonerate, vindicate 11 rationalize

excurse 5 stray 6 depart, ramble, wander 7 digress, diverge 8 divagate

excursion 4 ride, tour, trek, trip, walk 5 aside, jaunt, paseo, sally, tramp 6 cruise, junket, outing, safari 7 circuit, journey 9 round trip 10 digression, divagation,

exhibit 255

expedition, one-way trip, roundabout
11 parenthesis 12 pleasure trip

excusable 6 venial 7 tenable 10 condonable, defensible, forgivable, pardonable, remittable, vindicable 11 justifiable

excuse 4 plea 5 alibi, clear, remit, shift, spare 6 acquit, cop-out, exempt, let off, pardon, reason, wink at 7 absolve, apology, condone, defense, explain, forgive, justify, pretext, regrets, relieve, stopgap 8 dispense, overlook, palliate, pass over, shrug off 9 discharge, exculpate, exonerate, extenuate, gloss over, makeshift, vindicate, whitewash 10 substitute 11 explanation, rationalize 13 justification

execrable 3 bad, low 4 base, foul, vile 6 cursed, cussed, damned 7 blasted, heinous 8 accursed, damnable, horrific, infernal 9 atrocious, loathsome, monstrous, repulsive, revolting 10 confounded, despicable, detestable, horrifying, nauseating

execrate 3 ban 4 cuss, damn, hate 5 abhor, curse, swear 6 bedamn, detest, loathe, revile 7 accurse, censure, condemn, reprove 8 denounce 9 abominate, imprecate, objurgate, reprehend, reprobate 12 anathematize

execute 2 do 3 act 4 do in, hang, kill, slay 5 cause, lynch, purge 6 finish, gibbet, govern, handle, murder, render 7 achieve, bump off, conduct, fulfill, perform, put away 8 carry out, complete, dispatch, knock off, transact 9 discharge, eliminate, implement, liquidate 10 administer, bring about, put through 11 assassinate 12 administrate

execution 6 murder 7 facture, garrote, hanging 8 garrotte 9 beheading 11 performance

executioner 6 hanger 7 hangman, headman 8 headsman

executive 4 dean 6 leader 7 manager, officer 8 director, governor, higher-up, official 9 president 11 supervisor 11 businessman 12 entrepreneur 13 administrator, businesswoman

executor 4 doer 5 agent 9 performer

exegesis 6 exposé 9 construal 10 exposition 11 explanation, explication 12 construction

exemplar 4 soul 5 ideal, model 6 mirror 7 example, pattern 8 ensample, exponent, paradigm, standard 9 archetype, prototype 12 illustration

exemplary 4 good, pure 5 ideal, model 6 worthy 7 classic, typical 8 innocent, laudable, virtuous 9 admirable, blameless, classical, guiltless, righteous 10 inculpable, prototypal, unblamable 11 commendable 12 paradigmatic, praiseworthy, prototypical

exemplify 4 cite 5 quote 6 embody, mir-

ror, typify 7 clarify, clear up 8 spell out 9 enlighten, epitomize, personify, represent, symbolize 10 illuminate, illustrate 11 demonstrate, emblematize

exempt 4 free 5 spare 6 except, excuse, let off 7 absolve, relieve 8 dispense 9 discharge *combining form:* 6 immuno

exemption 7 freedom, release 8 immunity, impunity 9 discharge, exception

exenterate 3 gut 4 draw 5 bowel 6 paunch 7 embowel 10 disembowel, eviscerate

exercise 3 irk, ply, use, vex 4 fret, gall 5 annoy, apply, chafe, drill, exert, sit-up, sport, study, throw, train, wield 6 abrade, action, bestow, bother, employ, foster, handle, lesson, pushup, put out 7 develop, exploit, improve, prepare, problem, provoke, utilize, workout 8 activity, drilling, exertion, movement, practice, rehearse 9 athletics, condition, cultivate, operation 10 employment 11 application 12 calisthenics

exert 3 ply, use 5 apply, throw, wield 6 employ, put out, strain 8 exercise

exertion 3 use 4 toil, work 5 labor, pains, trial, while 6 effort, strain 7 trouble 8 activity, exercise, striving, struggle 9 operation 10 employment, exercising 11 application, elbow grease

exfoliate 4 peel 5 scale 8 flake off 10 desquamate

exhalation 6 breath 7 halitus 9 breathing, effluvium, emanation 10 expiration

exhale 4 blow, emit 6 expire, let out 7 breathe 10 breathe out, outbreathe

exhaust 3 fag, sap 4 do in, draw, tire 5 drain, eat up, spend, use up 6 devour, dispel, expend, finish, overdo, run out, tucker, wash up, weaken 7 consume, deplete, frazzle, outtire, outwear, overply, scatter, wear out 8 bankrupt, disperse, draw down, enfeeble, knock out, overwork 9 dissipate, overdrive, overexert, prostrate 10 debilitate, impoverish, overextend, run through

exhausted 4 beat, dead, done, limp, weak 5 all in, spent, tired 6 bleary, effete, used up 7 drained, far-gone, run-down, worn-out 8 consumed, depleted, dog-tired 9 washed-out

exhaustion 7 fatigue 8 collapse 9 lassitude, tiredness, weariness 11 prostration

exhaustive 5 total 6 all-out 7 radical 8 complete, profound, sweeping, thorough, whole-hog 9 full-blown, full-dress, full-scale, intensive, out-and-out 13 comprehensive, thoroughgoing

exhibit 3 air 4 fair, look, mark, show 5 flash, sight 6 evince, expose, flaunt, ostend, parade 7 display, disport, show off, trot out 8 brandish, evidence, manifest, proclaim, showcase **10** exposition, illustrate **11** demonstrate

exhibition 4 fair, show **5** sight **7** display, pageant, showing **8** offering **9** spectacle **10** exposition **12** presentation **13** demonstration, manifestation

exhilarate 4 buoy, lift **5** boost, cheer, elate, exalt, pep up, set up **6** excite, thrill, uplift **7** animate, commove, delight, enliven, gladden, inspire **8** inspirit, spirit up, vitalize **9** stimulate **10** invigorate

exhilaration 6 firing, gaiety, uplift **7** ecstasy, elation **8** euphoria, gladness **9** animation, elevation **10** exaltation, excitation, excitement, quickening **11** enlivenment, inspiration, stimulation **12** invigoration, vitalization, vivification **13** galvanization

exhort 3 sic **4** goad, prod, spur, urge **5** egg on, plead, prick **6** insist, prompt, propel **8** admonish, call upon **9** stimulate

exhume 3 dig **5** dig up **6** unbury **7** unearth **8** disinter **9** disembalm, disentomb, disinhume, uncharnel

exigency 3 fix, jam **4** need, pass, want **5** pinch, rigor **6** crisis, demand, duress, pickle, scrape, strait **7** dilemma **8** coercion, hardship, juncture, pressure, zero hour **9** necessity **10** compulsion, constraint, crossroads, difficulty, insistence **11** requirement, vicissitude **12** turning point

exigent 5 acute, tough, vital **6** crying, taxing **7** burning, clamant, instant, onerous, weighty **8** exacting, grievous, menacing, pressing **9** clamorous, demanding, insistent, necessary **10** burdensome, imperative, oppressive **11** importunate, threatening

exiguous 4 poor, thin, tiny **5** scant, skimp, small, spare **6** little, meager, narrow, scanty, scrimp, skimpy, slight, sparse **7** limited, scrimpy, slender, tenuous **8** confined **10** diminutive, restricted, straitened

exile 4 oust **5** expel **6** banish, deport, emigré **7** cast out, expulse, outcast, refugee **8** diaspora, displace, drive out, evacuate, expellee, unperson **9** exclusion, expulsion, extradite, migration, nonperson, ostracism, ostracize, transport **10** banishment, dispersion, dispossess, expatriate, relegation, scattering **11** deportation, extradition **12** displacement, expatriation *place of:* **7** Siberia

exist 2 am, be, is **3** are, lie **4** live, move **5** dwell **6** inhere, reside **7** breathe, consist, subsist

existence 3 ens **4** esse, life **5** being, thing **6** entity **7** reality **8** perseity **9** actuality, something **13** individuality *combining form:* **3** ont **4** onto

existent 4 real **5** alive, being, thing

6 actual, around, entity, living **7** instant, present **8** todayish **10** present-day **12** contemporary

existentialist writer 5 Buber, Camus **6** Marcel, Sartre **7** Jaspers **9** Heidegger **11** Kierkegaard

existing 5 alive, being, ontic **6** around, extant, living *Latin:* **6** in esse

exit 2 go **4** door, gate, move, quit **5** going, leave **6** depart, egress, exodus, get off, outlet, portal, retire **7** doorway, get away **8** offgoing, withdraw **9** departure, egression **10** setting-out, withdrawal

exode 5 farce **8** travesty

exodus 4 exit **6** egress, flight **7** exiting **8** offgoing **9** departure, egression, migration **10** emigration, setting-out, withdrawal

Exodus author 4 Uris (Leon)

exonerate 4 free **5** clear **6** acquit, excuse **7** absolve **9** disburden, exculpate, vindicate **10** disculpate

exorbitant 5 dizzy, undue **7** extreme **8** exacting, overmuch, towering **9** excessive, overboard **10** immoderate, inordinate, outrageous **11** extravagant, unwarranted **12** preposterous, unmeasurable

exordium 5 proem **7** preface, prelude **8** foreword, overture, preamble, prologue **9** prelusion **11** preliminary **12** introduction, prolegomenon

exotic 5 alien **7** foreign, strange, unusual **8** alluring, enticing, imported, romantic **9** different, glamorous **10** introduced, mysterious, romanesque **11** fascinating

expand 3 wax **4** grow, open, rise **5** boost, built, mount, swell, widen **6** beef up, detail, dilate, fan out, spread, unfold **7** amplify, augment, bolster, develop, distend, enlarge, inflate, magnify, prolong, stretch, upsurge **8** escalate, heighten, increase, multiply, mushroom, protract **9** discourse, elaborate, expatiate, explicate, outspread **10** aggrandize, outstretch

expanse 4 area, room **5** field, ocean, orbit, range, reach, scope, space, sweep, tract **6** domain, extent, sphere, spread **7** breadth, compass, stretch **8** distance **9** amplitude, immensity, magnitude, territory

expansion 5 space **6** growth, spread **7** breadth, stretch **8** distance, increase **9** amplitude **11** enlargement

expansive 3 big **4** airy, free, wide **5** ample, broad, great, gushy, large **6** bouncy, lavish, scopic **7** buoyant, elastic, liberal **8** effusive, extended, generous, outgoing, scopious, volatile **9** resilient **10** gregarious, openhanded, unreserved **11** extroverted **12** communicable, effervescent, unrestrained **13** communicative, demonstrative, unconstrained

expatiate 6 ramble, recite, relate, wander

7 descant, discuss, dissert, recount 8 dilate on, rehearse 9 discourse, sermonize 10 dilate upon, dissertate

expatriate 4 oust 6 banish, deport, emigré 8 displace, expellee, relegate 9 transport

expect 4 feel, hope, look, take 5 await, sense, think 6 assume, divine, gather 7 believe, count on, foresee, imagine, presume, suppose 8 foreknow 9 apprehend, count upon 10 anticipate, presuppose

expectant 3 big 5 alert, eager, heavy 6 gravid, parous 7 atiptoe, hopeful 8 childing, enceinte, open-eyed, pregnant, watchful 10 parturient 11 openmouthed 12 anticipative, anticipatory

expectation 4 hope 6 design, motive 8 prospect

expectorate 4 spit

expediency 4 step 5 order, shift 6 design, resort, tactic 7 aptness, fitness, measure, stopgap 8 meetness, recourse, resource, strategy 9 makeshift, propriety, rightness, surrogate 10 substitute 11 suitability 12 appositeness, suitableness

expedient 3 fit 4 wise 5 dodge, means, shift 6 agency, medium, refuge, resort, timely, useful 7 fitting, politic, prudent, stopgap 8 feasible, possible, recourse, resource, suitable, tactical 9 advisable, judicious, makeshift, opportune, practical, welltimed 10 beneficial, convenient, instrument, profitable, seasonable, substitute 11 appropriate, practicable, utilitarian 12 advantageous

expedite 3 hie 4 send 5 hurry, issue, speed 6 hasten 7 quicken 8 dispatch 10 accelerate, facilitate

expedition 4 trek, trip 5 haste, hurry, speed 6 hustle, rustle 7 entrada, journey, travels 8 alacrity, campaign, celerity, dispatch, goodwill 9 excursion, readiness, swiftness 10 speediness 11 promptitude, punctuality

expeditious 4 fast 5 fleet, hasty, quick, rapid, ready, swift 6 prompt, speedy 9 breakneck, effective, effectual, efficient 10 harefooted 11 efficacious

expeditiousness 5 haste, hurry, speed 6 hustle, rustle 8 celerity, dispatch 9 swiftness

expel 4 oust, spew 5 belch, eject, eruct, erupt, evict, exile 6 banish, deport, disbar, irrupt 7 blow off, blow out, cast out, drum out, exhaust, expulse, kick out, read out, turn out 8 disgorge, displace 9 ejaculate, eliminate, transport 10 expatriate *prefix:* 3 dis

expellee 6 emigré

expend 2 go 3 pay 4 blow, give 5 spend, use up, waste 6 finish, lay out, outlay, wash up 7 consume, exhaust, fork out 8 disburse, dispense, shell out 10 distribute, run through

expenditure 4 cost 6 outlay 12 disbursement

expense 4 cost, loss, toll 5 price 6 charge, outlay 7 forfeit 8 overhead 9 decrement, sacrifice 10 forfeiture 11 deprivation 12 disbursement

expensive 4 dear, high 6 costly 9 bigticket 10 high-priced, immoderate 12 uneconomical

experience 3 see 4 feel, have, know, live, meet, view 5 savor, skill, taste, trial 6 accept, behold, ordeal, suffer, survey, wisdom 7 know-how, receive, sustain, undergo 8 intimacy, practice 9 encounter, go through 10 background, inwardness 11 familiarity, observation, savoir faire 12 acquaintance *anew:* 6 relive *combining form:* 7 empirio 8 empirico

experienced 3 old, vet 4 wise 6 versed 7 old-line, old-time, skilled, veteran, worldly 8 broken in, seasoned, skillful 9 practical, practiced, qualified, underwent 10 proficient 12 accomplished

experiential see **empirical**

experiment 3 try 4 test 5 probe, study, trial, try on, weigh 6 search, try out 7 analyze, test out 8 analysis, research, trial run 10 scrutinize 11 examination, investigate 13 investigation, trial and error *combining form:* 7 empirio 8 empirico

experimental 4 test 5 trial 9 empirical, temporary, tentative 11 preliminary, preparatory, provisional 13 developmental

experimentation 4 test 5 trial 8 trial run 13 trial and error

expert 3 ace, pro, wiz 4 deft, whiz 5 adept, crack, doyen, maven, mavin, swell 6 adroit, artist, master, mayvin, wizard 7 artiste, skilled, trained 8 masterly, schooled, skillful, virtuoso 9 authority, dexterous, masterful 10 master-hand, past master, proficient, specialist 11 crackerjack 12 passed master, professional *suffix:* 5 ician

expertise 3 art 5 craft, knack, savvy, skill 7 ability, command, cunning, finesse, know-how, mastery 9 dexterity, quickness, readiness 10 adroitness, cleverness, competence, mastership 12 skillfulness 13 ingeniousness

expertness 5 knack, skill 7 ability, command, know-how, mastery 8 facility 10 mastership

expiate 3 pay 5 amend, atone, avert 6 remedy 7 correct, rectify, redress

expiation 9 atonement

expiatory 7 atoning, lustral 9 purgative

10 lustratory **11** purgatorial **12** propitiatory **13** expurgatorial

expiration 3 end **5** death **10** exhalation **11** termination

expire 2 go **3** die **4** conk, pass **5** lapse **6** demise, depart, elapse, exhale, perish, run out **7** decease **8** pass away **10** breathe out, outbreathe

explain 4 undo **5** clear, gloss, gloze, solve **6** acquit, define **7** absolve, account, analyze, clarify, clear up, condone, justify, resolve, unravel **8** annotate, construe, decipher, footnote, spell out, unriddle, untangle **9** break down, elucidate, exculpate, exonerate, interpret, vindicate **10** illuminate, illustrate, unscramble **11** disentangle, rationalize

explain away 7 account, justify **11** rationalize

explanation 3 key **6** excuse, motive, reason **7** account, example, grounds, meaning **8** exegesis **9** construal, rationale **12** unscrambling **13** enlightenment

explanatory 8 exegetic **10** discursive **12** enlightening, illuminating, illustrative, interpretive **13** demonstrative

expletive 4 cuss, oath **5** curse, swear **8** cussword **9** swearword; (see also **exclamation**)

explicate 6 unfold **7** amplify, develop, explain, expound **8** construe, spell out **9** interpret

explication 8 exegesis **9** construal **11** development, enlargement

explicative 8 exegetic **10** scholastic **12** interpretive

explicit 4 open, sure **5** clear, exact, lucid, overt, plain **7** certain, correct, obvious, precise **8** accurate, clean-cut, clear-cut, definite, distinct, specific **10** definitive **11** categorical, perspicuous, unambiguous, unequivocal

explode 3 pop **4** fire **5** blast, burst, erupt, go off, shoot **6** blow up **7** deflate **8** break out, detonate, disprove, dynamite, mushroom, puncture **9** discharge, discredit **10** burst forth

exploit 3 act, job, use **4** blow, coup, deed, feat, gest, play, skin, soak, work **5** abuse, apply, bleed, stick, stunt **6** bestow, effort, employ, fleece, handle, jockey, parlay, stroke **7** beguile, emprise, finesse, utilize, venture **8** exercise, impose on; maneuver **9** adventure, cultivate **10** enterprise, impose upon, manipulate **11** achievement, performance, tour de force

explore 3 try **4** feel, sift, test **5** probe **6** burrow, go into, quarry, search **7** dig into, examine **8** look into, prospect, question **9** delve into, inquisite **11** inquire into, investigate

explorer *African:* **3** Cam, Cao **4** Park **5** Grant, Laird, Speke **6** Akeley, Burton, Lander **7** Covilha, Stanley **8** Covilhao **10** Clapperton **11** Livingstone *American:* **4** Byrd, Hall, Kane, Pike **5** Clark, Lewis, Peary **6** Powell, Wilkes **7** Fremont *Antarctic:* **4** Byrd, Cook, Ross **5** Fuchs, Ronne, Scott **6** Palmer, Rymill, Wilkes **7** Weddell, Wilkins **8** Amundsen, d'Urville **9** Ellsworth **10** Kristensen, Shackleton *Arctic:* **3** Rae **4** Byrd, Cook **5** Davis, Peary **6** Baffin, Bering, Henson, Hudson, Nansen, Nobile **7** Barents, Bennett, Wilkins, Wrangel **8** Amundsen **9** Mackenzie, Macmillan **10** Stefansson *Australian:* **7** Wilkins *Austrian:* **9** Weyprecht *British:* **12** Younghusband *Canadian:* **9** Mackenzie **10** Stefansson *Danish:* **9** Rasmussen *Dutch:* **6** Tasman *English:* **4** Cook **5** Drake, Scott, Smith **6** Baffin, Burton, Hudson **7** Raleigh, Stanley **9** Vancouver **10** Shackleton *French:* **7** Cartier, La Salle, Nicolet **8** Cousteau **9** Champlain, La Perouse, Marquette *French Canadian:* **6** Joliet **7** Jolliet **9** Iberville *German:* **6** Peters **7** Humbolt *Italian:* **5** Cabot **6** Nobile *New Zealand:* **7** Hillary *Norwegian:* **6** Nansen **8** Amundsen, Sverdrup **9** Heyerdahl *Portuguese:* **6** Cabral **8** Magellan *Scottish:* **3** Rae **4** Park, Ross **7** Thomson **11** Livingstone *Spanish:* **6** Balboa, Cortes, de Soto, Pinzon **7** Mendoza, Pizarro **8** Bastidas, Coronado **11** Ponce de Leon

explosion 3 pop, pow **4** bang, gust **5** blast, burst, sally **6** access **7** flare-up **8** outburst **10** detonation

explosive 3 TNT **4** bomb, mine **5** nitro, troty **6** amatol, petard, powder **7** ammonal, cordite, dunnite, grenade, lyddite **8** cheddite, dynamite, fulminic, melinite **9** fulminate **10** detonative **13** nitroglycerin *device:* **3** cap **4** bomb, mine **5** shell **6** petard **7** grenade **8** firework *display:* **9** fireworks *expert:* **5** Maxim *sound:* **3** pop, pow **4** bang, boom

exponent 6 backer **7** booster **8** advocate, champion, defender, partisan, promoter, upholder **9** supporter

expose 3 air **4** bare, open, risk, show **5** flash, peril, strip **6** debunk, flaunt, hazard, parade, reveal, show up, unfold, unmask, unveil **7** display, disport, exhibit, imperil, jeopard, lay open, publish, show off, subject, trot out, uncloak, uncover, undress **8** brandish, disclose, discover, endanger, jeopardy, muckrake, unclothe, unshroud **9** advertise, broadcast

exposé 10 revelation

exposed 4 bare, open **5** naked, prone **6** liable, likely, peeled **7** denuded, evident, menaced, subject, visible **8** apparent, manifest, revealed, stripped, unhidden **9** obnoxious, sensitive, uncovered **10** threatened **11** susceptible, unconcealed

exposition 4 fair, show **7** display, exhibit **8** analysis, exegesis **9** construal, discourse, statement **10** discussion, exhibition **11** delineation

expository 8 critical, exegetic **11** explanative, explanatory **12** interpretive

expostulate 4 kick **5** argue, fight **6** combat, debate, except, object, oppose, resist **7** discuss, dispute, protest **11** remonstrate

exposure 4 risk **5** peril **6** danger **8** jeopardy, openness **9** liability **12** helplessness, susceptivity **13** vulnerability

expound 5 state, teach **7** clarify, comment, explain, express, lecture, present **8** construe, describe, spell out **9** delineate, discourse, exemplify, explicate, interpret **10** illustrate

expounder 7 teacher **8** advocate, champion **9** proponent, supporter

express 3 air, put, say, set **4** give, mean, tell, vent, word **5** couch, crush, frame, spell, state **6** broach, convey, denote, impart, import, intend, phrase, voiced **7** add up to, connote, declare, signify, special, uttered **8** announce, clean-cut, clear-cut, definite, disclose, especial, explicit, intended, proclaim, put about, specific **9** circulate, enunciate, formulate, out-and-out, pronounce, ventilate **10** definitive, individual, particular **11** categorical, communicate, intentional, unambiguous, unqualified *gratitude:* **5** thank *regret:* **9** apologize

expression 4 cast, face, form, look, mien, show, sign, vent, word **5** idiom, issue, motto, token, voice **6** clause, phrase, symbol, visage **7** gesture **8** locution, reminder **9** eloquence, facundity, statement, utterance, verbalism, vividness **10** embodiment, indication, reflection **11** countenance, graphicness, observation **13** demonstration, manifestation *combining form:* **4** logy **5** logia *facial:* **4** grin, phiz **5** frown, scowl, smile, wince **7** grimace *of assent:* **3** aye, nod, yea, yes **4** okay **6** placet **9** exequator *of sorrow:* **4** alas, tear *trite:* **6** cliché **7** bromide **8** banality *witty:* **4** quip **8** atticism

expressionless 4 dead, dull **5** blank, empty, stony **6** stolid, vacant, wooden **7** deadpan, vacuous **9** impassive **10** lackluster **11** inscrutable

expressive 4 rich **5** vivid **6** facund, lively, poetic **7** graphic **8** eloquent, emphatic, pregnant, senseful, spirited **9** pictorial, revealing **10** meaningful, revelatory **11** sententious, significant

expressly 4 even, just **6** as well, namely **8** in specie

expressway 4 road **7** freeway, highway, parkway **8** turnpike

expropriate 4 take **5** annex, seize **7** preempt **8** accroach **9** sequester **10** commandeer, confiscate, dispossess

expulse 4 oust **5** eject **6** banish, deport **7** cast out **8** displace, relegate **9** transport

expulsion 5 exile **7** ousting, removal **8** ejection **9** ostracism **10** banishment, driving out, forcing out, relegation **11** deportation **12** displacement

expunge 4 dele, drop, omit, x out **5** annul, erase **6** cancel, delete, efface **7** blot out, destroy, discard, exclude, wipe out **8** black out **9** eradicate **10** annihilate, obliterate

expurgate 4 blip **5** purge **6** censor, purify, screen **7** cleanse **10** bowdlerize

expurgation 9 catharsis, cleansing

exquisite 3 fop **4** buck, dude, nice, rare **5** acute, blood, dandy **6** choice, dainty, fierce, select, superb **7** coxcomb, elegant, extreme, furious, intense, vicious, violent **8** delicate, finished, flawless, macaroni, superior, terrible, vehement **9** desperate, errorless, faultless, recherché **10** consummate, immaculate, impeccable

exsanguine 6 anemic **9** bloodless

exsect 6 cut out, excise

exsiccate 3 dry **4** sear **5** parch

exsuccous 3 dry **4** sere **7** sapless **8** withered

extant 5 alive, being **6** actual, around, living **7** current, present **8** todayish **9** immediate **10** present-day **12** contemporary

extemporaneous 4 snap **6** casual **7** offhand **8** informal **9** impromptu, impulsive, unstudied **10** improvised, unprepared **11** unrehearsed **12** unthought-out

extempore see **extemporaneous**

extemporize 3 act **5** ad-lib **7** dash off, toss off **8** knock off **9** improvise **11** improvisate

extend 2 go **3** eke, run **4** draw, give, grow, make, open, pose, span, vary **5** allot, award, boost, grant, offer, range, reach **6** accord, attain, beef up, bestow, confer, donate, fan out, spread, tender, unfold **7** advance, amplify, augment, draw out, enlarge, hold out, magnify, present, proceed, proffer, project, prolong, spin out, stretch **8** allocate, continue, elongate, heighten, increase, lengthen, multiply, protract **9** outspread **10** aggrandize, outstretch, prolongate

extended *combining form:* **3** meg **4** mego **5** megal **6** megalo

extension 3 arm, ell **4** area, size, wing **5** ambit, annex, block, orbit, range, reach, scope, sweep **6** radius, spread **7** compass, purview, stretch **8** increase **9** magnitude **10** continuing, drawing out, elongation, production, stretch-out **11** enlargement, lengthening, prolongment, protraction **12** augmentation, continuation, prolongation, spreading out

extensity **5** ambit, orbit, range, reach, scope, sweep **6** radius **7** compass, purview

extensive **3** big **4** vast, wide **5** broad, hefty, large, major **6** scopic **7** blanket, general, immense, sizable **8** scopious, spacious **9** boundless, wholesale **10** large-scale **11** far-reaching, wide-ranging **12** considerable, far-spreading

extent **4** size, tune, writ **5** ambit, field, orbit, order, range, reach, scope, sweep, width **6** amount, degree, domain, matter, radius, sphere **7** breadth, compass, measure, purview **8** province, vicinity **9** magnitude **10** dimensions, proportion

extenuate **4** thin **5** white **6** temper, veneer, whiten **7** explain, justify, qualify, varnish **8** palliate, wiredraw **9** apologize, gloss over, gloze over, sugarcoat, whitewash **10** blanch over **11** rationalize

exterior **4** over **5** ectal, outer **6** facade **7** outmost, outside, outward, surface **8** external **9** outermost

exterminate **4** kill **5** abate **6** uproot **7** abolish, blot out, root out, wipe out **8** massacre **9** finish off, slaughter **10** annihilate, extinguish

external **3** out **4** over **5** ectal, outer **7** outmost, outside, outward **9** outermost **10** peripheral **11** superficial *combining form:* **3** ect **4** ecto

externalize **6** embody **8** manifest **9** incarnate, objectify, personify **12** substantiate

extinct **4** cold, dead, gone, late, lost **5** passé **6** asleep, bygone, fallen **7** archaic, defunct, disused, outworn **8** deceased, departed, lifeless, obsolete, outmoded, perished, vanished **9** collapsed **10** antiquated, overthrown, superseded, unanimated **11** disappeared, nonexistent **12** old-fashioned *combining form:* **4** necr **5** necro

extinction **5** death **11** destruction **12** annihilation, obliteration

extinguish **3** out **5** abate, check, crush, douse, erase, quash, quell **6** put out, quench, squash, stifle, uproot **7** abolish, blot out, blow out, destroy, expunge, put down, root out, smother, wipe out **8** suppress **9** eradicate **10** annihilate, obliterate

extirpate **4** raze **5** erase **6** cut out, efface, excise, resect, uproot **7** abolish, blot out, destroy, expunge, kill off, root out, wipe out **8** demolish **10** annihilate

extol **4** hymn, laud **5** bless, cry up, exalt **6** praise **7** applaud, commend, elevate, glo-rify, magnify **8** eulogize **9** celebrate **10** panegyrize

extort **3** get **4** milk, skin **5** bleed, cheat, educe, evoke, exact, force, gouge, pinch, screw, wrest, wring **6** coerce, compel, demand, elicit, evince, fleece, obtain, secure, wrench **7** squeeze **9** blackmail, shake down

extortion **8** chantage, exaction **9** blackmail

extra **3** odd **4** more, over **5** added, spare **6** de trop, rarely **7** surplus **8** markedly **9** lagniappe, unusually **10** additional, especially, noticeably, uncommonly **11** superfluent, superfluous **12** considerably, particularly, supplemental **13** supernumerary, supplementary *prefix:* **5** hyper, super

extract **3** dig, pry **4** cull, draw, milk, pull, tear, yank **5** educe, evoke, glean, wring **6** avulse, eke out, elicit, evince, evulse, garner, gather, pick up **7** abridge, distill, excerpt, scratch, shorten, squeeze **8** condense

extraction **5** birth, blood **6** origin **7** descent, essence, lineage **8** ancestry, pedigree **9** parentage

extraneous **5** alien, outer **6** exotic **7** foreign **9** pointless, unrelated **10** accidental, immaterial, inapposite, incidental, irrelative, irrelevant **11** impertinent, unessential **12** adventitious, inapplicable **13** inappropriate

extraordinary **3** odd **4** rare **6** unique **7** amazing, notable, unusual **8** singular, terrific, uncommon, unwonted **9** wonderful **10** noteworthy, remarkable, stupendous, tremendous **11** exceptional, unthinkable

extravagance **5** frill, luxus, waste **6** luxury **7** amenity **8** squander, unthrift **9** overdoing **10** lavishness **11** prodigality, superfluity **12** wastefulness

extravagant **4** wild **5** crazy, dizzy, outré, silly, undue **6** absurd, lavish **7** bizarre, foolish, profuse **8** prodigal, towering, wasteful **9** fantastic, ludicrous **10** immoderate, inordinate, profligate, ridiculous, unbalanced **11** exaggerated, implausible, nonsensical **12** preposterous, unmeasurable, unrestrained

extreme **3** top **4** deep, last, peak, wild **5** crest, crown, dizzy, final, limit, rabid, ultra, undue **6** ardent, climax, excess, height, moving, summit, utmost **7** ceiling, drastic, fanatic, intense, maximum, outmost, radical, violent **8** farthest, furthest, pinnacle, remotest, towering, ultraist **9** desperate, excessive, outermost, uttermost **10** immoderate, inordinate, outlandish **11** culmination, furthermost, inordinancy, intolerable, unwarranted **12** consummation, revolutional, unmeasurable, unreasonable **13** revolutionary *degree:* **3** nth

extremely 3 too 4 ever, over, very
6 mighty 7 parlous 8 overfull, overmuch
11 exceedingly

extremist 5 rabid, ultra 7 fanatic, radical
12 revolutionary 13 revolutionary

extremity 3 arm, end, leg, tip 4 acme,
apex, foot, hand, tail 5 limit, verge 6 apogee, vertex, zenith 8 terminal, terminus
combining form: 3 acr, akr 4 acro, akro

extricate 4 free 5 clear, loose, sever,
untie 6 detach, rescue 7 deliver, discern,
release, resolve, unravel, untwine
8 abstract, untangle 9 clear away, disburden, discumber, disengage 10 discrepate,
disembroil, disentwine, disinvolve, severalize, unentangle, unscramble 11 disemburden, disencumber, disentangle, distinguish
12 disembarrass

extrinsic 5 alien, outer 6 gained 7 foreign,
outside, outward 8 acquired, external
10 accidental, extraneous

extrude 3 out 4 spew 5 chase, chuck,
eject, evict 7 boot out, dismiss, kick out,
project 8 throw out

exuberance 4 life, zest 5 ardor 6 spirit
7 abandon, gayness 8 buoyancy 10 friskiness, liveliness 11 zestfulness
13 sprightliness

exuberant 3 gay 4 glad, lush, rank
5 brash, happy 6 ardent, fecund, lavish,
lively 7 diffuse, fertile, opulent, profuse, riotous, zestful 8 fruitful, prodigal, prolific, spirited 9 ebullient, profusive, sprightly, vivacious 10 frolicsome, passionate
12 effervescent, high-spirited

exude 4 emit, ooze, seep, weep 5 bleed,
sweat 6 strain 7 emanate, secrete, trickle
8 perspire 9 discharge, percolate

exult 4 brag, crow 5 boast, gloat, glory
7 delight, rejoice, show off, triumph 8 jubilate 9 celebrate

exultant 4 glad 5 happy 6 elated, joyous
7 flushed 8 jubilant 9 cock-a-hoop, overjoyed, rejoicing, triumphal 10 cock-a-whoop, delighting

exultation 3 joy 7 delight, rapture, triumph 8 gloating 9 jubilance, rejoicing
10 jubilation

exuviate 4 molt, shed, slip 5 moult
6 slough

eye 3 orb, tab 4 gape, gaze, lamp, look,
loop, mind, ring, tail, view 5 grasp, optic,
sight, stare, watch 6 behold, belief, goggle,
look at, ocular, oculus, peeper, regard, seeing, size up, staple, vision, winker 7 blinker,
feeling, opinion 8 attitude, consider, gaze
upon, judgment, look upon, position, scrutiny, thinking 9 sentiment, viewpoint
10 conception, conclusion, conviction, persuasion, rubberneck, scrutinize 11 contemplate 12 surveillance *combining form:*
3 ope, opy 4 ocul, opia, opto 5 oculo
8 ophthalm 9 ophthalma, ophthalmo
10 ophthalmia, ophthalmus *defect:* 6 myopia 9 hyperopia 10 emmetropia, presbyopia 11 astigmatism *disease:* 8 cataract,
glaucoma, trachoma *doctor:* 7 oculist
11 optometrist *opening:* 5 pupil *part:* 4 iris,
lens, uvea 5 pupil 6 cornea, retina, sclera
relating to: 5 optic 7 optical *socket:*
5 orbit *Spanish:* 3 ojo

eye-catching 6 marked, signal 7 pointed,
salient 9 prominent 10 noticeable, remarkable 11 conspicuous

eyedropper 7 pipette

eyeful 6 beauty, looker, lovely 7 stunner
8 knockout

eyeglass 4 lens 5 lense 7 monocle

eyeglasses 5 specs 6 lenses 7 lorgnon
8 pince-nez 9 lorgnette

eyelash 6 cilium

eyelid 8 palpebra 9 palpebrae (plural) *combining form:* 7 blephar 8 blepharo

eyepiece 4 lens 6 ocular

eye-popping 8 exciting, stirring 9 thrilling 10 exhilarant 11 astonishing
12 exhilarative

eyesore 4 mess 5 sight 6 defect, fright
7 blemish, desight 11 monstrosity

eyespot 7 disease, ocellus

eyetooth 6 canine

eyewash 3 rot 5 bilge, hooey 6 bunkum
7 twaddle 8 malarkey, nonsense

eyewitness 6 viewer 7 watcher
8 beholder, by-sitter, looker-on, observer,
onlooker 9 bystander, spectator

eye worm 3 loa

eyrie see **aerie**

Ezbon's father 3 Gad

Ezekiel's father 4 Buzi

Ezer's father 6 Jeshua 7 Ephraim

F

Fabian 4 Shaw 8 cautious 9 socialist

fable 4 myth, tale 5 story 6 legend 7 fiction, figment 8 allegory, apologue *animal:* 8 bestiary

fabric 3 rep, web 4 repp 5 cloth, fiber, grain 7 texture 8 building, material, shirting 9 structure *coarse:* 5 crash, gunny 6 burlap, linsey, ratiné 7 cheviot, hopsack 8 homespun, osnaburg *corded:* 3 rep 4 repp 5 piqué 6 calico, moreen, poplin 7 pinwale 8 corduroy, paduasoy 9 bengaline *cotton:* 4 jean, leno 5 baize, chino, drill, scrim, swiss, wigan 6 chintz, dimity, faille, madras, muslin 7 etamine, galatea, gingham, nankeen, percale, silesia, ticking 8 chambray, dungaree, nainsook, osnaburg, tarlatan *cotton and linen:* 4 huck 7 fustian 9 huckaback *crepe:* 8 marocain *dealer:* 6 draper, mercer *durable:* 4 huck, jean 5 chino, denim, drill 6 frieze, moreen 7 lasting, ticking 8 cretonne, dungaree, osnaburg *embroidered:* 9 baldachin, baldaquin 10 baldachino 11 baldacchino *finishing process:* 8 lustring 9 mercerize 10 causterize *flag material:* 7 bunting *glazed:* 6 chintz 7 cambric, holland *knitted:* 6 tricot 10 balbriggan *linen:* 7 cambric, lockram *looped:* 6 bouclé *lustrous:* 4 silk 5 moiré, satin, surah 7 silesia, taffeta 12 brilliantine *metallic:* 4 lamé *net:* 5 tulle 8 bobbinet, illusion *openwork:* 4 lace 8 filigree *ornamental:* 4 lace 5 braid 6 ribbon 7 bunting *pebbly-surface:* 6 armure 8 baratea *pile-surface:* 5 panne, plush, terry 6 velour, velvet 7 bolivia, duvetyn, velours 8 chenille, moleskin, velveret 9 velveteen *plaid:* 6 tartan *printed:* 5 batik, toile 6 calico, chintz, damask 7 allover, challis, dornick, pintado 8 cretonne, jacquard 11 toile de jouy *raised pattern:* 7 brocade 10 brocatelle *satin weave:* 5 panne *sheer:* 4 lawn 5 gauze, ninon, swiss, voile 6 barege, dimity, tissue 7 batiste, chiffon, cypress, organdy, organza, tiffany 8 tarlatan *silk:* 4 fuji 5 pekin 6 cendal, chappe, pongee, samite, sendal 7 alamode, foulard, grogram, schappe 8 paduasoy, sarcenet, sarsenet, shantung 9 bombazine *striped:* 3 aba 4 abba 5 abaya, pekin 7 galatea, ticking 8 algerine 10 algerienne *synthetic:*

5 ninon, nylon, Orlon, rayon 6 Dacron *twill:* 4 jean 5 chino, drill, serge 7 foulard, galatea, nankeen, silesia, ticking 8 dungaree, shalloon 9 bombazine 10 broadcloth *unfinished:* 6 greige *waterproof:* 7 oilskin *wool:* 5 baize, loden, tweed 6 caddis, camlet, duffel, duffle, melton, merino, wadmad, wadmel, wadmol, witney, woolen 7 caddice, delaine, whitney, woollen 8 algerine, mackinaw, prunella 9 cassimera 10 algerienne *wool, poor quality:* 5 mungo 6 shoddy *wool mixture:* 5 tammy 6 saxony, wincey, winsey 7 drugget, ratteen 8 moquette, shalloon, zibeline *woven:* 4 weft 7 textile

fabricate 4 form, make 5 build, frame, shape 6 devise, invent, make up 7 concoct, fashion, produce, turn out 8 assemble, contrive 9 construct 11 manufacture

fabrication 3 fib, lie 4 opus, work 6 deceit 7 fiction, figment, product, untruth 9 falsehood

fabulist *French:* 10 La Fontaine *Greek:* 4 Esop 5 Aesop *Indian:* 6 Bidpai, Pilpai, Pilpay *Roman:* 8 Phaedrus *Russian:* 6 Krylov

fabulous 7 amazing 8 mythical 9 legendary, wonderful 10 astounding, exorbitant, fictitious, incredible, inordinate, outrageous, prodigious, stupendous 11 astonishing, extravagant 12 mythological *animal:* 6 dragon 7 centaur, unicorn *bird:* 3 roc 6 simurg 7 simurgh *serpent:* 8 basilisk 10 cockatrice

facade 4 face, mask, show 5 color, front, guise, put-on 6 veneer 8 disguise, pretense

face 3 mow, mug, top 4 cast, clad, dare, defy, gall, gaze, look, mask, meet, moue, phiz, pout, show, side, skin, veil 5 await, beard, brass, brave, cheek, cloak, close, cover, fight, front, frown, glare, guise, lower, mouth, nerve, paint, scowl, stare, watch 6 accost, border, brazen, breast, engage, expect, glower, makeup, mazard, muzzle, oppose, resist, take on, visage 7 affront, contend, grimace, outdare, seeming, sheathe, showing, venture 8 confront, disguise, features, mouthing, war paint 9 brashness, challenge, encounter, semblance, withstand 10 appearance, confidence, effrontery, expression, false front, lineaments, maquillage, masquerade, simulacrum **11** countenance, physiognomy

facet **4** hand, side **5** angle, bezel, front, phase **6** aspect

facetious **5** comic, droll, funny, jolly, merry, witty **6** blithe, jocose, jocund, joking, jovial **7** comical, jesting, jocular **8** humorous **9** laughable, ludicrous **12** wisecracking

face-to-face **7** vis-à-vis

facile **4** able, deft, easy, glib **5** light, quick, royal **6** adroit, expert, fluent, simple, smooth **7** cursory, shallow, voluble **9** dexterous **10** effortless, uncritical

facilitate **3** aid **4** ease, help **6** assist **8** expedite

facility **3** aid, wit **4** bent, ease, tact, turn **5** poise, skill **7** abandon, address, amenity, comfort, fitting, leaning **8** aptitude **9** advantage, dexterity, lightness, readiness **10** smoothness **11** convenience, spontaneity **13** accommodation

facing **5** front, panel **6** before, contra, toward, veneer **7** against, vis-à-vis **8** covering, opposite, paneling **11** over against *down:* **5** prone *up:* **6** supine

facsimile **4** copy **5** ditto **6** carbon **7** replica **9** duplicate, imitation **10** carbon copy **11** replication **12** reproduction

fact **5** datum, event, truth **6** detail **7** episode, reality **8** incident **9** actuality, happening **10** observable, occurrence, particular, phenomenon **11** genuineness **12** authenticity, circumstance

faction **4** bloc, camp, part, ring, sect, side, wing **5** junto, party **7** combine **8** offshoot **11** combination

factious **7** warring **8** fighting **9** alienated, estranged, insurgent, seditious **10** contending **11** belligerent, contentious, disaffected, quarrelsome **13** insubordinate

factitious **4** sham **5** false **6** forced **7** assumed, feigned, man-made, shammed **8** affected **9** pretended, simulated, synthetic **10** artificial **13** counterfeited

factor **3** aid **4** doer, gene **5** agent, cause, maker, means, proxy **6** agency, deputy, helper **7** bailiff, element, steward **8** adjutant, assignee, attorney **9** assistant, coadjutor, component, consignee, majordomo, seneschal **10** antecedent, ingredient, instrument **11** determinant

factory **4** mill, shop **5** plant, works

factual **4** hard, true **5** valid **7** certain, genuine **8** absolute, positive **9** authentic, undoubted, veritable

faculty **4** bent, bump, gift, nose, turn **5** flair, knack, power **6** genius, talent **7** aptness, leaning **8** aptitude, capacity, function, instinct, penchant, property **12** predilection

facund **4** rich **8** eloquent, pregnant

10 expressive, meaningful **11** sententious, significant

fad **3** cry **4** chic, mode, rage, whim **5** craze, fancy, style, trend, vogue **6** furore, vagary, whimsy **7** caprice, conceit, fashion **10** dernier cri

fade **3** die, dim, ebb **4** dull, flag, melt, pale, thin **5** abate, clear, muddy **6** lessen, rarefy, vanish, weaken, wither **7** decline, dwindle, evanish, tarnish **8** diminish, dissolve, evanesce, languish, moderate **9** attenuate, disappear, evaporate **10** deliquesce **11** deteriorate

Faerie Queen, The *author:* **7** Spenser *character:* **3** Ate, Una **4** Alma **5** Guyon, Talus **6** Abessa, Amavia, Amoret, Arthur, Cambel, Duessa, Palmer **7** Artegal, Corceca, Fidessa, Maleger, Sansloy **8** Calidore, Florimel, Fradubio, Gloriana, Lucifera, Orgoglio, Satyrane **9** Archimago, Britomart **11** Britomartis

Fafner, Fafnir *brother:* **5** Regin **6** Fasolt, Reginn *father:* **8** Hreidmar *form:* **6** dragon *slayer:* **6** Sigurd **9** Siegfried *victim:* **6** Fasolt **8** Hreidman

fag **4** flag, tire **5** smoke, weary **6** drudge, tucker **7** exhaust, frazzle, outtire, outwear, servant, wear out **8** knock out **9** cigarette, prostrate

fag end **4** butt **7** remnant **8** last part

fail **3** ebb, end **4** bomb, bust, flag, fold, jade, lose, miss, omit, sink, slip, wane **5** break, close, crash, drain, flunk, short **6** falter, finish, forget, ignore, lessen, run out, shrink, slight, weaken, worsen **7** blink at, bust out, decline, default, deplete, dwindle, exhaust, flummox, founder, gazette, give out, neglect, wash out **8** bankrupt, decrease, diminish, discount, languish, miscarry, overlook, overpass **9** blink away, disregard, terminate **10** impoverish **11** deteriorate

failing **3** shy **4** vice **5** fault, scant, short **6** foible, scanty, scarce **7** frailty **8** weakness **9** deficient **10** deficiency, inadequate **12** imperfection, insufficient, unsufficient

failure **3** dud **4** bomb, bust, flop, hash, lack, miss **5** botch, fault, lemon, loser **6** dearth, defeat, ebbing, fiasco, fizzle, laxity, muddle, outage, waning **7** absence, debacle, decline, default, deficit, neglect, paucity, washout **8** collapse, flagging, poorness, scarcity, shortage, underage, weakness **9** insuccess, oversight, slackness, unconcern, unsuccess **10** bankruptcy, deficiency, exhaustion, inadequacy, meagerness, negligence, nonsuccess, remissness, scantiness, skimpiness **11** declination, defalcation, delinquency, dereliction, inferiority, miscarriage, shortcoming **12** debilitation, enfeeblement, imperfection, indifference **13** deterioration, insufficience, insufficiency, might-have-been

fain 4 glad 5 eager, prone, ready
6 minded 7 willing 8 desirous, disposed, inclined 11 predisposed

faint 3 dim, low, wan 4 coma, mild, pale, soft, swim, thin, weak 5 balmy, bland, blear, dusty, fuzzy, small, swoon, vague 6 bleary, feeble, gentle, hushed, smooth 7 blurred, grayout, languid, lenient, muffled, obscure, pass out, shadowy, stifled, syncope, unclear, vertigo 8 black out, listless 9 dizziness, inaudible, undefined 10 ill-defined, indistinct, undistinct

fair 4 calm, even, fine, just, mean, mild, pure, sane, show, so-so 5 balmy, blond, clean, clear, equal, light, right, ruddy, sunny, tawny 6 bazaar, blonde, candid, chaste, comely, common, dainty, decent, honest, lawful, lovely, medium, placid, pretty, square 7 average, clarion, clement, exhibit 8 balanced, carnival, charming, delicate, detached, festival, handsome, mediocre, middling, moderate, ordinary, pleasant, rainless, rational, straight, sunshine, sunshiny, tranquil, unbiased 9 beauteous, beautiful, cloudless, equitable, exquisite, impartial, objective, unclouded, uncolored 10 attractive, enchanting, exhibition, exposition, impersonal, open-minded, reasonable, sunshining, undarkened 11 good-looking, indifferent, nonpartisan, sportsmanly 12 intermediate, unprejudiced 13 disinterested, dispassionate, sportsmanlike, undistinctive, unthreatening

fair-haired 3 pet 4 dear 5 blond, loved 6 blonde 7 beloved, darling 8 blue-eyed, favorite, precious

fairness 6 equity 12 impartiality

fairy 3 elf, imp 4 pixy, puck 5 dwarf, elfin, gnome, nisse, pixie 6 goblin, kobold, sprite 7 banshee, brownie, gremlin 10 leprechaun *king:* 6 Oberon *palace:* 4 shee 5 sidhe *queen:* 3 Mab 7 Titania *shoemaker:* 10 leprechaun

fairy tale *author:* 5 Grimm, Wilde 8 Andersen, Perrault *character:* 6 Gretel, Hansel 8 Rapunzel 9 Snow White 10 Cinderella, Goldilocks

faith 4 cult, hope, sect 5 creed, stock, troth, trust 6 belief, church, credit, dogmas, tenets 8 credence, reliance, religion 9 communion, doctrines 10 confidence, connection, dependence, persuasion 12 denomination *article of:* 5 tenet 9 credendum

faithful 4 fast, firm, just, true 5 exact, liege, loyal, pious, right, tried 6 ardent, loving, steady, strict, trusty 7 binding, devoted, staunch 8 constant, credible, reliable, resolute, trueblue 9 allegiant, authentic, steadfast, veracious, veridical 10 convincing,

dependable 11 trustworthy, undistorted 12 affectionate 13 conscientious, dyed-in-the-wool

faithfulness 5 ardor, piety 6 fealty 7 loyalty 8 adhesion, devotion, fidelity 9 adherence, constancy 10 allegiance, attachment

faithless 5 false 6 fickle, untrue 7 erratic, unloyal 8 disloyal, recreant, unstable, wavering 9 changeful 10 capricious, changeable, inconstant, perfidious, traitorous 11 fluctuating, treacherous

faithlessness 7 falsity, perfidy, treason 8 betrayal 9 treachery 10 disloyalty, infidelity

fake 3 act, gyp 4 hoax, mock, sell, sham 5 bluff, bogus, false, feign, fraud, phony, put on, snide, spoof 6 affect, assume, doctor, forged, framed, humbug, pseudo 7 falsify, pretend 8 impostor, invented, simulate, spurious 9 brummagem, charlatan, concocted, fabricate, imitation, imposture, pinchbeck, pretended, pretender, simulated 10 fabricated, fictitious, fraudulent, simulation 11 counterfeit *combining form:* 5 pseud 6 pseudo

fakir 7 ascetic 9 mendicant

falcon 4 hawk 5 hobby, saker 6 lanner, luggar, merlin 7 kestrel 9 peregrine *male:* 4 jack 6 musket, tassel, tercel 7 sakeret, tiercel 8 lanneret *mature:* 7 haggard, passage *young:* 4 eyas 5 eyess 8 brancher

falcon-headed god see at **Egyptian**

falconry 7 hawking *equipment:* 4 bell, hood, jess, lure 5 bewet, bewit 7 creance *procedure:* 3 imp 4 cope, seel

fall 3 dip, ebb, sag 4 drag, drip, drop, flop, plop, sink, skid, slip, trip, wane 5 abate, beset, crash, droop, lapse, let up, lower, pitch, plonk, plunk, slide, slump, storm, trail, yield 6 assail, attack, dangle, give up, go down, lessen, plunge, relent, sprawl, strike, submit, topple, tumble 7 aggress, assault, cascade, decline, descend, descent, die away, die down, drop off, ease off, go under, plummet, relapse, slacken, stumble, subside, succumb, wipeout 8 decrease, diminish, downcome, downfall, keel over, moderate, nose-dive 9 declivity, surrender

fallacious 3 mad 6 untrue 7 invalid 8 deluding, delusive, delusory 9 beguiling, deceiving, deceptive, illogical, sophistic 10 irrational, misleading, reasonless, unreasoned 11 nonrational 12 unreasonable

fallacy 4 idol 5 error 6 idolum 7 elusion, evasion, falsity, quibble, sophism, untruth 8 delusion 9 casuistry, deception, falsehood, falseness, quibbling, sophistry 12 equivocation, misconstrual, speciousness, spuriousness 13 deceptiveness, erroneousness, misconception

fall back 6 recede, retire 7 relapse,

retract, retreat **8** withdraw **9** retrocede
10 retrograde
fall behind 3 lag
fall flat 4 fail **5** flunk **7** bust out, flummox,
wash out
fall guy 3 sap **4** butt, dupe, fish, fool, goat,
gull **5** chump, patsy **6** pigeon, sucker
7 gudgeon **9** scapegoat **11** whipping boy
falling-out 3 row **4** beef, feud **5** run-in
6 hassle **7** dispute, quarrel **9** bickering
11 altercation, controversy
falloff 3 dip, sag **4** drop, slip **5** slump
7 decline **8** downturn **9** downslide, downswing, downtrend
fall out 2 go **3** row **4** spat, tiff **5** break,
occur, scrap **6** betide, bicker, chance, happen, result **7** brabble, come off, develop,
quarrel, wrangle **8** disagree, squabble
false 4 fake, mock, sham **5** bogus,
dummy, hokey, lying, phony, snide, wrong
6 ersatz, hollow, pseudo, untrue **7** crooked,
devious, seeming, unloyal, unsound **8** apostate, apparent, deluding, delusive, delusory,
disloyal, recreant, renegade, specious, spurious **9** beguiling, brummagem, deceitful,
deceiving, deceptive, dishonest, distorted,
erroneous, faithless, illogical, imitation,
incorrect, pinchbeck, simulated **10** artificial,
fictitious, fraudulent, inaccurate, mendacious, misleading, ostensible, perfidious,
substitute, traitorous, unfaithful, untruthful
11 backsliding, counterfeit, treacherous
combining form: **5** pseud **6** pseudo
false face 4 mask **5** visor **6** domino,
vizard
false front 4 face, mask, show, veil
5 cloak, cover **6** facade **8** disguise
10 masquerade
falsehood 3 fib, lie **4** sham, tale **5** error,
fraud, story **6** canard, deceit, fakery **7** fallacy, falsity, fibbery, untruth **8** feigning, pretense, untruism **9** mendacity **10** unveracity **11** fabrication **13** dissimulation,
erroneousness, prevarication, truthlessness
falseness 5 error **7** fallacy, perfidy,
untruth **8** apostasy **9** defection, desertion,
recreancy **10** disloyalty, infidelity
false teeth 7 denture **8** dentures
falsify 3 fib, lie **4** cook, deny, fake, warp
5 alter, belie, color, fudge, twist **6** change,
doctor, garble, palter **7** contort, distort, pervert **8** miscolor, misstate, traverse **10** contradict, contravene, equivocate **11** prevaricate **12** misrepresent
falsity 3 fib, lie **4** sham, tale **5** bluff, error,
story **6** canard **7** perfidy, untruth **8** untruism **9** falsehood, hypocrisy **10** disloyalty,
infidelity **11** fabrication, insincerity
12 uncandidness **13** erroneousness, faithlessness, prevarication
Falstaff *companion:* **3** Nym **4** Peto **6** Pis-

tol **8** Bardolph *composer:* **5** Verdi *creator:* **11** Shakespeare *play:* **7** Henry IV
prince: **3** Hal *tavern:* **9** Boar's Head
Falstaffian 3 fat **6** coarse, jovial **8** boastful, humorous **9** dissolute
falter 4 halt, limp **5** lurch, quail, quake,
shake, waver **6** blench, dither, flinch, quaver, recoil, shrink, topple, wobble **7** shudder, stagger, stumble, tremble, whiffle
8 hesitate, tick over **9** vacillate **12** shilly-
shally
fame 4 note **5** éclat, glory, honor
6 renown, report, repute **7** acclaim
8 applause, eminence **9** celebrity, character, greatness, notoriety **10** prominence,
reputation **11** acclamation, distinction, preeminence, recognition
famed 5 great, noted **7** eminent, notable
8 renowned **9** prominent **10** celebrated,
celebrious **11** illustrious **13** distinguished
familiar 2 up **4** boon, cozy, easy, mate,
snug **5** amigo, aware, close, fresh, thick
6 au fait, chummy, common, friend, genial,
versed, wonted **7** abreast, affable, cordial,
forward, mindful, prosaic, versant **8** amicable, everyday, frequent, friendly, gracious,
habitual, informed, intimate, sociable **9** au
courant, cognizant, confidant, conscious,
customary, intrusive, obtrusive, officious
10 accustomed, acquainted, conversant,
neighborly **11** cater-cousin, comfortable,
commonplace, impertinent
familiarity 8 intimacy **9** awareness, cognition, knowledge **10** experience, inwardness **12** acquaintance **13** comprehension,
understanding
familiarize 3 use **4** wont **5** adapt, inure
6 adjust, season **8** accustom, acquaint
9 condition, habituate
family 3 kin **4** clan, folk, home, line, race
5 brood, folks, house, issue, stirp, stock,
tribe **6** ménage, strain **7** dynasty, kindred,
lineage, progeny **8** domestic **9** bloodline,
household, offspring *branch:* **6** stirps *lineage:* **4** tree **6** stemma **8** pedigree
9 genealogy
famished 6 hungry **7** starved **8** ravenous,
starving
famous 3 top **5** great, noted **7** capital,
eminent, leading, notable, popular **8** five-
star, renowned, superior, top-notch **9** estimable, excellent, first-rate, honorable, notorious, prominent, reputable, well-known
10 celebrated, celebrious, first-class
11 first-string, illustrious, prestigious,
redoubtable, respectable **13** distinguished,
well-thought-of
fan 4 blow, buff, open, wind **5** hound,
lover **6** addict, expand, extend, rooter, ruffle, spread, unfold, votary, winnow
7 admirer, amateur, devotee, habitué **8** fol-

lower **9** outspread **10** aficionado, enthusiast, outstretch *combining form:* **5** rhipi **6** rhipid **7** rhipido **8** flabelli *horseracing:* **7** turfman *India:* **5** punka **6** punkah *movie:* **7** cineast

fanatic 3 bug, nut **5** bigot, fiend, freak, rabid, ultra **6** maniac, zealot **7** extreme, radical **8** ultraist **9** extremist **10** monomaniac **12** revolutional **13** revolutionary, revolutionist

fancier 6 votary **7** admirer, amateur, devotee

fanciful 5 false, wrong **6** absurd, unreal **7** bizarre, fictive, shadowy, strange **8** fabulous, illusory, imagined, mythical, notional, romantic **9** fantastic, fictional, grotesque, imaginary, legendary **10** apocryphal, chimerical, fictitious **11** unrealistic **12** preposterous

fancy 3 bee, fad **4** idea, like, mind, whim, will **5** dream, fable, freak, humor, image, think **6** liking, megrim, mirage, notion, vagary, vision, whimsy **7** approve, boutade, caprice, chimera, conceit, concept, endorse, feature, fiction, figment, imagine, realize, whimsey **8** conceive, crotchet, daydream, delusion, envisage, envision, illusion, phantasm, phantasy, pleasure, sanction, velleity **9** capriccio, elaborate, intricate, invention, nightmare, visualize **10** conception **11** complicated, envisioning, fabrication, fata morgana, imagination, inclination **12** contrariness, envisagement, perverseness **13** hallucination, irrationality

fan dancer 4 Rand

fandango 4 ball **5** dance

fanfare 4 pomp, show **5** array, shine **6** parade **7** display, panoply **8** flourish *trumpet:* **6** tucket

fanlike 7 plaited, plicate

fanny 4 seat **5** hiney **6** behind, bottom, heinie **7** hind end **8** backside, buttocks, derriere **9** posterior

fanon 5 cloth, orale **7** maniple **8** corporal

fan palm 5 talipot **8** palmetto

fantasize 7 imagine **8** daydream

fantastic 3 odd **4** wild **5** crazy, loony, queer, silly, wacky **6** absurd, adroit, clever, insane, mortal, unreal **7** bizarre, fictive, foolish, massive, strange **8** cracking, delusive, delusory, fanciful, illusory, romantic, singular, towering **9** deceptive, eccentric, fictional, grotesque, imaginary, ingenious, monstrous, unearthly, whimsical **10** capricious, chimerical, fictitious, incredible, irrational, misleading, monumental, prodigious, ridiculous, stupendous, tremendous **11** extravagant, implausible, nonsensical **12** preposterous, suppositious, unbelievable, unreasonable

fantasy 4 whim **5** dream, freak **6** bubble,

vagary, vision, whimsy **7** caprice, chimera, rainbow, whimsey **8** daydream, illusion, phantasm **9** imagining, nightmare, pipe dream **10** bizarrerie, conceiving **11** envisioning, imagination **12** grotesquerie

Fantine's daughter 7 Cosette

far 4 deep, long, well **5** quite **6** rather, remote **7** distant, removed **8** off-lying, outlying, somewhat **12** considerably *combining form:* **3** tel **4** tele, telo

far and away 4 just, very **5** quite **6** by odds **9** by all odds, decidedly, doubtless **10** absolutely, by long odds, definitely, positively **11** by a long shot, undoubtedly

far and near 7 all over, overall **8** all round **9** all around **10** everyplace, everywhere, throughout

far and wide see **far and near**

faraway 4 lost **6** absent, dreamy, remote **7** bemused, distant, removed **8** distrait, heedless, off-lying, outlying **9** oblivious, unheeding, unmindful **10** abstracted, stargazing **11** inconscient, preoccupied **12** absentminded, disregardful

farce 4 mock, sham **7** mockery **8** travesty **9** burlesque **10** caricature

farceur 3 wag **4** zany **5** clown, cutup, joker **8** jokester

farcical 5 comic, droll, funny **6** absurd **7** risible **8** gelastic **9** laughable, ludicrous **10** outrageous, ridiculous **11** extravagant **12** preposterous

fare 2 do, go **3** hie, way **4** diet, food, pass, path, rate, wend **5** get by, get on, shift, track **6** manage, push on, repair, travel **7** advance, journey, proceed **8** get along, progress **12** stagger along

farewell 2 by **3** ave, bye **5** adieu, adios, aloha, congé **6** bye-bye, so long **7** goodbye, parting **9** bon voyage, departing **11** leave-taking, valedictory

farfetched 5 queer **6** forced **7** bizarre, erratic, labored, strange **8** strained **9** eccentric, fantastic, grotesque, recherché

far-flung 6 remote **7** distant, removed **8** off-lying, outlying

farinaceous 5 mealy **7** starchy *food:* **4** meal **5** flour, salep **6** cereal **7** pudding, tapioca

farm 4 till **5** croft, ranch **6** grange, rancho **7** hennery **8** estancia, hacienda, hatchery, steading **9** cultivate, farmstead *building:* **4** barn, shed, silo *Dutch:* **6** bowery *Israeli collective:* **7** kibbutz *Russian:* **7** kolkhoz, sovkhoz

farmer 6 grower, tiller, yeoman **7** granger, planter, rancher **8** ranchero, ranchman **13** agriculturist *Israeli:* **6** halutz *Russian:* **5** kulak *South African:* **4** Boer *tenant:* **6** cotter **7** cottier, crofter **12** sharecropper

farming 7 tillage **8** agronomy **9** geoponics, husbandry **11** agriculture, cultivation, hydroponics

faro **5** monte *bet:* **7** sleeper *card:* **4** case, hock, soda

Faroes whirlwind **2** oe

far-off **6** remote **7** distant, removed **8** outlying

farrier **5** smith **10** blacksmith

farsighted **9** hyperopic, sagacious **10** presbyopic

farther **3** now **4** else, more **5** added, fresh **6** beyond, longer, yonder **10** additional

farthest **6** utmost **7** endmost, extreme, outmost **9** outermost, uttermost

fascinate **4** draw, grip, hold, sway, take, wile **5** charm, touch **6** absorb, affect, allure, appeal, engage, excite, occupy, please, strike **7** attract, bewitch, catch up, delight, enchant, engross, gladden, impress, rejoice **8** enthrall, entrance, interest, intrigue **9** captivate, enrapture, influence, magnetize, mesmerize, preoccupy, spellbind

fascination **5** charm **6** allure, appeal, glamor **7** glamour **8** charisma, witchery **9** magnetism **10** witchcraft **11** enchantment

Fascist **4** Nazi **6** Hitler **9** Mussolini

fashion **3** cry, fad, ton, way **4** chic, form, make, mode, mold, plan, plot, rage, tone, vein, wise, wont **5** build, craft, craze, drift, erect, forge, frame, habit, modus, sculp, shape, style, thing, trend, usage, vogue **6** create, custom, design, devise, furore, manner, method, sculpt, system **7** produce, turn out **8** contrive, practice, tendency **9** bandwagon, construct, fabricate, technique **10** convention, dernier cri

fashionable **4** chic **5** smart, swank, swish **6** modish, with-it **7** a la mode, current, dashing, popular, stylish **9** exclusive, prevalent **13** up-to-the-minute

fashion designer *American:* **9** Gernreich (Rudi) *Anglo-French:* **5** Worth (Charles) *French:* **4** Dior **8** Givenchy (Hubert) **12** Saint-Laurent (Yves) *Italian:* **5** Pucci (Emilio) **7** Cassini (Oleg)

fast **3** gay, lax, set **4** diet, easy, firm, hard, held, keen, lewd, soon, sure, true, wild **5** alert, apace, bawdy, brisk, fixed, fleet, hasty, liege, light, loose, loyal, quick, rapid, slack, stuck, swift, tight, wingy **6** active, ardent, firmly, lively, presto, pronto, raking, rakish, secure, snappy, speedy, sporty, stable, starve, strong, wanton, wedged **7** fixedly, flat-out, fleetly, hastily, lustful, quickly, raffish, rapidly, riotous, satyric, solidly, staunch, swiftly, tightly, whorish **8** careless, chop-chop, constant, faithful, full tilt, heedless, indecent, promptly, rakehell, resolute, speedily, unchaste **9** breakneck, immov-

able, lecherous, libertine, lickerish, posthaste, salacious, tenacious **10** expeditive, harefooted, lascivious, libidinous, licentious, stationary **11** expeditious, incontinent **12** devil-may-care, inextricable, lickety-split **13** expeditiously

fasten **3** bar, bed, fix, gib, peg, pin, put, set, tie **4** bind, hank, hasp, hook, join, lash, link, lock, moor, seal, turn, weld **5** affix, apply, catch, clamp, clasp, cling, embed, focus, hitch, infix, latch, lodge, reeve, rivet, screw, stake, stick, strap, train, unite, wedge **6** adhere, anchor, attach, bundle, button, cleave, cohere, devote, direct, fixate, secure, settle, staple, zipper **7** address, connect, implant, mortise **9** concenter, establish **11** concentrate

fastener **3** pin **4** frog, snap, tack **5** catch **6** button, needle, staple, toggle **10** clothespin

fastidious **4** nice **5** fussy **6** choosy, dainty **7** choosey, finical, finicky **8** critical, exacting **9** demanding, finicking, squeamish **10** particular, pernickety **11** persnickety **13** hypercritical

fastness **4** fort **5** guard **6** adytum, castle **7** citadel, defense, redoubt, retreat, sanctum, shelter **10** protection, stronghold

fat **3** big, oil, top **4** best, bull, deep, flab, lard, pick, rich, suet, wide **5** beefy, broad, bulky, burly, cream, dumpy, elite, great, gross, heavy, husky, large, lipid, obese, pride, prime, pudgy, pursy, round, squat, stout, thick, tubby **6** brawny, choice, chunky, excess, fleshy, flower, grease, portly, rotund, stocky, stubby, tallow **7** adipose, blubber, fertile, orotund, paunchy, porcine, ringing, surfeit, surplus, vibrant, wealthy, weighty **8** blubbery, heavyset, overflow, overkill, overmuch, overplus, oversize, plethora, resonant, sonorant, sonorous, thickset **9** consonant, corpulent, overblown **10** full-bodied, overweight, potbellied, productive, prosperous, resounding **11** superfluity, upholstered **13** overabundance *combining form:* **3** lip **4** adip, lipo, sebi, sebo **5** adipo, lipar, steat **6** liparo, steato

fatal **5** death **6** deadly, doomed, lethal, malign, mortal **7** baleful, baneful, deathly, malefic, ruinous, unlucky **8** casualty, sinister **9** pestilent **10** calamitous, disastrous, ill-starred, maleficent, pernicious **11** cataclysmic, mortiferous **12** catastrophic, pestilential

fatality **5** death **9** virulence **10** deadliness, malignancy **11** noxiousness

fata morgana **6** mirage

fate **3** end, lot **4** doom **5** issue, karma, moira, weird **6** chance, doom to, effect, ending, kismet, result, upshot **7** destine, destiny, fortune, outcome, portion, preform **9** determine, preordain **10** foreordain, predestine **12** circumstance, predetermine **13** inevitability

fateful 5 acute **7** crucial, ominous, ruinous **8** critical, decisive **9** ill-boding, important, momentous **10** calamitous, conclusive, disastrous **11** apocalyptic, cataclysmic, significant, threatening **12** catastrophic, inauspicious, unpropitious **13** determinative

Fates see at **Greek; Norse; Roman**

fathead 3 oaf **4** boob, dolt, goof **5** booby, chump, dunce

fatheaded 5 dense, thick **6** stupid **10** numskulled

father 2 pa **3** dad, get, pop **4** dada, make, papa, père, sire **5** beget, breed, daddy, hatch, maker, motor, mover, padre, pappy, pater, poppa, spawn **6** author, create, parent, priest **7** builder, creator, founder, produce **8** engender, generate, inventor, producer, promoter **9** architect, generator, initiator, organizer, originate, patriarch, procreate, supporter **10** encourager, ingenerate, introducer, originator, prime mover **11** inaugurator, progenerate, promulgator *combining form:* **4** patr **5** patri, patro *of his country:* **6** Cicero **10** Washington *of history:* **9** Herodotus *of medicine:* **11** Hippocrates *of modern surgery:* **4** Paré *of the symphony:* **5** Haydn *of waters:* **11** Mississippi

Father Brown creator 10 Chesterton

fatherland 4 home, soil **7** country

fatherless 7 bastard, natural **8** baseborn, spurious **11** misbegotten **12** illegitimate

Father Time's implement 6 scythe

fathom 4 have, know **5** grasp, plumb, probe, savvy, sound **6** pierce **7** cognize **8** apprehend, penetrate, plumbline, recognize **10** appreciate, comprehend, understand

fathomless 7 abysmal

fatidic 8 Delphian, oracular **9** prophetic, sibylline, vatical **11** prophetical

fatigue 3 irk, vex **4** jade, tire, wear **5** annoy, drain, ennui, spend, weary **6** bother, tucker, weaken **7** deplete, disable, exhaust, languor, wear out **8** weakness, wear down **9** faintness, lassitude, tiredness, weariness **10** debilitate, enervation, exhaustion, feebleness **12** debilitation, listlessness

Fatima *father:* **8** Mohammed, Muhammad *husband:* **9** Bluebeard *step-brother:* **3** Ali

fatness 7 obesity **9** adiposity **10** corpulence

fatten 5 plump **6** batten, enrich **7** plumpen, stouten, thicken

fatty 4 oily **5** blimp, lardy, pudge, suety

6 greasy **7** adipose **8** blubbery, dumpling, potbelly, roly-poly, strapper, unctuous **10** butterball, oleaginous, overweight *combining form:* **3** lip **4** adip, lipo **5** adipo, lipar **6** liparo

fatuous 4 dumb, fond **5** inane, silly **6** absurd, simple, stupid **7** asinine, foolish, idiotic, moronic, unwitty, witless **8** besotted, imbecile **9** brainless, insensate **10** infatuated, weak-headed, weak-minded **11** sheepheaded

faucet 3 tap **4** bung, cock, gate **5** spile, valve **6** spigot **7** bibcock, hydrant, petcock **8** stopcock

Faulkner *character:* **5** Caddy, Jason **7** Candace, Quentin **8** Benjamin *family:* **7** Compson *novel:* **8** Sartoris **9** Sanctuary, The Hamlet **11** As I Lay Dying **13** Light in August

fault 3 nag, sin **4** carp, flaw, flub, lack, onus, slip, vice **5** blame, crime, error **6** defect, foible **7** blemish, blunder, demerit, failing, frailty, mistake, offense **8** weakness **9** infirmity, liability **10** deficiency **11** culpability, shortcoming **12** imperfection **13** answerability, transgression

faultfinder 4 crab **5** grump, momus **6** critic, grouch, Zoilus

faultfinding 6 critic **8** captious, critical **9** cavillous **10** censorious, particular, pernickety **12** overcritical **13** hypercritical

faultless 4 pure **5** clean, whole **6** entire, intact **7** correct, perfect **8** flawless, innocent, unguilty **9** blameless, exquisite **10** immaculate, impeccable, inculpable **13** unimpeachable

faulty 4 sick **5** amiss, wrong **6** flawed, marred **7** damaged, defaced, inexact **8** fallible, specious **9** blemished, defective, deficient, erroneous, imperfect, imprecise, incorrect, uncorrect **10** disfigured, fallacious, inaccurate, inadequate, incomplete *prefix:* **3** dys

Faunus *grandfather:* **6** Saturn *son:* **4** Acis **7** Latinus

Faust *author:* **6** Goethe **7** Marlowe *beloved:* **8** Gretchen *composer:* **6** Gounod

faux pas 4 slip **5** boner, break, error, gaffe **6** boo-boo, bungle, howler **7** blooper, blunder, misstep, mistake, stumble **8** pratfall, screamer, solecism **9** indecorum, oversight **11** impropriety, misjudgment **12** indiscretion

favor 2 OK **3** aid, for, pro **4** back, boon, gift, help, okay **5** prize, value **6** accept, esteem, oblige, pamper, regard **7** account, approve, backing, endorse, forward, indulge, largess, present, respect, service, support **8** advocate, approval, blessing, courtesy, goodwill, hold with, kindness, resemble, sanction, simulate **9** approbate, encourage, patronage **10** admiration, appreciate, assistance, estimation, indulgence **11** accommodate, approbation, benediction, benevolence, convenience, cooperation, countenance **12** dispensation **13** consideration, encouragement

favorable 4 good, kind, nice **5** brave, happy, lucky, white **6** benign, bright, dexter, kindly, timely, toward, useful **7** benefic, helpful, timeous, welcome **8** cheering, grateful, pleasant, pleasing, salutary **9** approving, benignant, fortunate, healthful, laudatory, opportune, praiseful, promising, well-timed, wholesome **10** auspicious, beneficial, gratifying, propitious, prosperous, reassuring **11** approbative, approbatory, encouraging, pleasureful **12** advantageous, commendatory, providential, well-disposed **13** complimentary

favoring 4 good **5** brave **6** toward, useful **7** benefic, helpful **10** beneficial, propitious **12** advantageous **prefix: 3** pro

favorite 3 pet **4** dear **5** loved **6** adored, prized **7** admired, beloved, darling, popular, revered **8** blue-eyed, esteemed, laudable, pleasant, precious **9** cherished, preferred, treasured, well-liked **10** fair-haired

favoritism 4 bias **8** cronyism, nepotism **9** prejudice

fawn 3 bow, woo **4** cave, coax, deer **5** abase, court, cower, crawl, defer, toady, yield **6** cajole, cotton, cringe, debase, demean, grovel, invite, kowtow, slaver, submit **7** flatter, honey up, truckle, wheedle **8** blandish, bootlick **10** ingratiate **11** apple-polish

fawning 4 mean **6** abject, humble, smarmy **7** ignoble, servile, slavish **8** toadyish, toadyism **9** adulatory, compliant, flunkyish, groveling, kowtowing, parasitic, spineless, sycophant, truckling **10** flattering, obsequious, submissive **11** bootlicking, deferential, subservient, sycophantic **12** mealy-mouthed, sycophantish

fay 3 elf **5** fairy, nisse, pixie **6** sprite **7** brownie

faze 3 vex **5** abash, annoy, daunt, worry **6** appall, bother, dismay, muddle, puzzle, rattle **7** confuse, horrify, mystify, nonplus, perplex **8** confound, irritate **9** discomfit, dumbfound, embarrass **10** disconcert

FBI director 6 Hoover

fealty 5 ardor, faith, truth **7** loyalty, support **8** devotion, fidelity, trueness **10** allegiance **11** devotedness **12** faithfulness

fear 3 awe **4** funk **5** alarm, angst, dread, panic, scare, worry **6** dismay, esteem, fright, horror, phobia, terror **7** anxiety, concern, respect **8** cold feet, disquiet, timidity **9** agitation, cowardice, misgiving, reverence, trepidity **10** foreboding **11** disquietude,

trepidation **12** apprehension, cowardliness, discomposure, perturbation, presentiment, timorousness **combining form: 4** phob **5** phobe, phobo **6** phobia, phobic **7** phobous **of animals: 9** zoophobia **of being buried alive: 11** taphephobia **of cats: 12** aelurophobia, ailurophobia **of crowds: 11** ochlophobia **of darkness: 11** nyctophobia **of dirt: 10** mysophobia **of fire: 10** pyrophobia **of heights: 10** acrophobia **of men: 11** androphobia **of new things: 9** neophobia **of open areas: 11** agoraphobia **of pain: 10** algophobia **of strangers: 10** xenophobia **of thunder: 12** brontophobia **of water: 11** hydrophobia **of women: 10** gynophobia

fearful 4 dire, grim **5** awful, lurid, scary, timid **6** afraid, aghast, grisly, malign, scared, uneasy **7** alarmed, anxious, ghastly, jittery, macabre, nervous, panicky, sublime, worried **8** aflutter, agitated, alarming, dreadful, gruesome, horrible, horrific, shocking, sinister, terrible, terrific, timorous **9** appalling, concerned, disturbed, frightful, perturbed, terrified **10** disquieted, formidable, frightened, horrendous, solicitous, terrifying, tremendous **11** discomposed, frightening, redoubtable **12** apprehensive

fearless 4 bold, game, sure **5** brave **6** daring **7** assured **8** intrepid, sanguine, unafraid **9** audacious, confident, dauntless **10** courageous **11** lionhearted

feasible 6 doable, likely, viable **8** possible, workable **9** practical **11** practicable

feast 3 eat **4** dine, meal **6** dinner, regale, repast, spread **7** banquet **8** potlatch **Hawaiian: 4** luau **Scottish: 3** foy

Feast of Lights 8 Hanukkah

Feast of Lots 5 Purim

Feast of Tabernacles 7 Sukkoth

Feast of Weeks 8 Shabuoth

feat 3 act **4** deed, gest **5** geste, stunt, trick **6** action **7** emprise, exploit, venture **9** adventure **10** enterprise **11** achievement, tour de force

feather 3 ilk **4** down, kind, sort, type **5** breed, order, pinna, plume, quill **6** fledge, fletch, pinion **7** species, variety **combining form: 4** pinn, pter, ptil **5** penni, penno, pinni, ptero, ptile, ptilo **kind: 4** down **5** penna, remex **6** covert **7** contour, plumule, rectrix, tectrix, tertial **8** scapular, tertiary **part: 3** web **4** barb, vane **5** shaft **7** barbule **8** barbicel

featherbrained 5 dizzy, giddy, silly **7** flighty **8** skittish **9** frivolous **11** empty-headed, hare-brained **13** rattlebrained

feathered 7 pennate, plumose **8** pennated

feather-like 7 pinnate, plumate **8** pinnated

feathers 7 plumage

featherweight 4 simp 5 dunce, light 6 dimwit, nitwit 7 lackwit, pinhead, unheavy, wantwit

feature 4 item, mark 5 fancy, image, point, savor, think, trait 6 aspect, detail, factor, play up, stress, virtue, vision 7 article, element, imagine, quality, realize 8 conceive, envisage, envision, property 9 affection, attribute, birthmark, character, component, emphasize, italicize, underline, visualize 10 ingredient, particular, underscore 11 constituent

febrile 5 fiery 7 fevered, pyretic 8 feverish

feces 4 dung 5 waste 7 excreta 9 excrement *combining form:* 4 copr, scat 5 copro, scato

feckless 4 wild 6 remiss 7 fustian, useless 8 careless, heedless, uncaring 9 shiftless, uncareful, unheeding, unrecking, worthless 10 incautious, unpurposed, unreliable, unthinking 11 inadvertent, meaningless, purposeless, thoughtless 12 irreflective, undependable, unreflective 13 irresponsible, lackadaisical, untrustworthy

fecund 4 rich 7 fertile 8 childing, fruitful, prolific, spawning 10 productive 11 proliferant

fecundity 9 eloquence, fertility 10 expression 11 prodigality, profuseness, prolificacy 12 expressivity, fruitfulness, productivity

Federalist writer 3 Jay 7 Madison 8 Hamilton

federation 5 union 6 league 8 alliance 9 coalition 11 association, confederacy

fed up 4 sick 5 bored, tired, weary 9 disgusted

fee 3 pay, tax 4 cost, dues, hire, wage 5 price 6 charge, salary 7 expense, payment, stipend, tuition 8 retainer 9 emolument 10 recompense *minting:* 8 brassage 10 seignorage 11 seigniorage *wharf:* 7 quayage

feeble 4 puny, weak 5 frail 6 ailing, flimsy, infirm, senile, sickly, weakly 7 doddery, fragile, sapless, tenuous 8 decrepit 9 doddering 13 insubstantial

feebleminded 4 dull, slow 7 moronic 8 backward, imbecile, retarded 9 dim-witted 10 half-witted, slow-witted 12 simpleminded

feebleness 7 disease, malaise 8 debility 9 infirmity 10 infirmness, sickliness 11 decrepitude

feed 3 eat 4 find, food, give, grub, hand, meal 5 feast, graze 6 devour, fatten, fodder, ingest, repast, supply, viands 7 banquet, consume, deliver, dish out, edibles, furnish, nourish, nurture, provide, sustain 8 dispense, hand over, victuals 9 partake

of, provender, refection 10 provisions *combining form:* 4 phag 5 phago

feed the kitty 4 ante

feel 3 air, paw 4 aura, deem, hold, know, mood 5 grope, guess, savor, sense, sound, taste, think, touch 6 assume, credit, endure, finger, fumble, handle, notice, suffer 7 believe, explore, grabble, observe, palpate, presume, suppose, surmise, suspect, undergo 8 consider, perceive 9 semblance, tactility

feeler 4 palp, test 5 probe, query 6 palpus 7 antenna, inquiry 10 intimation, prospectus 12 trial balloon

feeling 3 air 4 aura, mind, mood, vein, view 5 humor, sense, touch 6 belief, morale, notion, temper 7 emotion, opinion, outlook, passion, sensate 8 attitude, passible, reaction, sentient 9 affection, emotional, semblance, sensation, sensitive, sentiment 10 atmosphere, conviction, persuasion 11 affectivity, emotionable, palpability, sensibility, sensitivity, tangibility *combining form:* 5 pathy 6 pathic

feign 3 act 4 fake, sham 5 bluff, put on 6 affect, assume 7 connive, pretend 8 simulate 11 counterfeit

feint 3 jig 4 fake, hoax, play, ploy, ruse, sham, wile 5 trick 6 gambit 7 whizzer 8 maneuver 9 stratagem *fencing:* 5 appel *hockey:* 4 deke

feldspar 6 albite 8 andesine, sanidine 9 anorthite, moonstone 10 microcline, orthoclase 11 labradorite, plagioclase *clay:* 6 kaolin

felicitate 6 salute 7 commend 10 compliment 12 congratulate

felicitous 3 apt, fit 4 just, meet 5 happy 6 proper, timely 7 apropos, fitting 8 apposite, suitable 9 well-timed 10 applicable, seasonable 11 appropriate

feline 3 cat, tom 4 lion, lynx, pard, puma, puss 5 catty, felid, pussy, tiger 6 bobcat, cougar, jaguar, margay, ocelot, tomcat 7 catlike, cheetah, furtive, leonine, leopard, lioness, panther, tigress, wildcat 8 pussycat, stealthy *hybrid:* 5 liger, tigon 6 tiglon

fell 3 cut, fur, hew 4 chop, down, drop, grim, hide, kill, pelt, raze, skin, ugly 5 cruel, floor, grave, level, major 6 deadly, fierce, ground, jacket, lay low, savage, tumble 7 fearful, flatten, inhuman, mow down, serious, wolfish 8 bowl down, bowl over, grievous, horrible, horrific, inhumane 9 barbarous, bring down, dangerous, ferocious, knock down, knock over, prostrate, shoot down, throw down, truculent

Fellini film 8 Amarcord, Casanova, La Strada 9 Satyricon 11 La Dolce Vita

fellow 2 he 3 boy, bub, guy, joe, lad, man 4 bozo, buck, chap, gent, mate, peer, twin

5 bloke, match 6 codger, cohort, double, hombre, person 7 consort, partner 8 confrere 9 associate, companion, copartner, duplicate, gentleman 10 consociate, coordinate, reciprocal 11 concomitant 12 contemporary *prefix:* 2 co

fellowship 4 club 5 guild, order, union 6 league 7 company, society 8 alliance, sodality 10 fraternity 11 association, brotherhood, camaraderie 13 companionship

felon 8 criminal, offender 10 lawbreaker, malefactor

felt hat 6 fedora

female 4 girl 5 woman 7 womanly 8 feminine, womanish *combining form:* 3 gyn 4 gyne, gyno, gyny 5 gynec, gyneo, thely 6 gynaec, gynaeo, gyneco, gynous 7 gynaeco *suffix:* 3 ess, ine 4 ette, trix

femme fatale 5 siren 7 Lorelei 9 temptress 10 seductress

fen 3 bog 4 mire, quag 5 marsh, swamp 6 morass, slough 7 baygall 8 quagmire

fence 3 bar, hem, mew, pen 4 cage, duck, mure, stop, wall, weir 5 block, dodge, hedge, parry, shirk 6 corral, immure, paling 7 barrier, enclose, railing 8 blockade, palisade, sidestep, stockade 9 barricade, roadblock 12 circumscribe

fencer 7 duelist, épéeist 8 foilsman 9 swordsman

fencing 9 swordplay *attack:* 5 lunge 6 thrust 7 reprise, riposte *defense:* 5 parry *movement:* 4 volt *ploy:* 5 appel *position:* 5 prime, sixte, terce 6 octave, quarte, quinte, tierce 7 seconde, septime *term:* 4 jury 5 forte, lunge, piste 6 flèche, foible, pointe, touché 7 sabreur, stop cut, stop-hit 11 corps-à-corps *touch:* 3 cut, hit 5 punto *weapon:* 4 épée, foil 5 blade, guard, saber, sabre 6 pommel

fend 4 ward 5 avert, avoid, cover, guard, parry, rebut, repel 6 defend, rebuff, resist, screen, secure, shield 7 bulwark, deflect, hold off, keep off, protect, repulse, ward off 8 stave off 9 safeguard

fender 5 guard 6 buffer, shield 8 mudguard

Fenrir *chain:* 8 Gleipnir *father:* 4 Loki *form:* 4 wolf *mother:* 9 Angerboda 10 Angerbotha *slayer:* 5 Vidar 6 Vithar *victim:* 4 Odin

feral 4 wild 5 brute 6 animal, brutal, ferine, fierce, savage 7 beastly, bestial, brutish, inhuman, swinish, untamed, vicious 8 barbaric 9 barbarous, ferocious

Ferber novel 5 Giant, So Big 8 Cimarron, Show Boat, The Girls 9 Ice Palace

Ferber or Millay 4 Edna

Ferdinand *beloved:* 7 Miranda *father:* 6 Alonso

Ferdinand, King *conquest:* 7 Granada

daughter: 6 Joanna *wife:* 8 Germaine, Isabella

ferment 4 boil, stir 5 churn 6 bubble, clamor, foment, leaven, outcry, seethe, simmer, tumult, unrest, upturn 7 agitate, ailment, smolder, turmoil 8 disquiet, upheaval 9 commotion 10 convulsion, inquietude 11 disquietude, restiveness 12 restlessness

fermentation 7 zymosis

fern 4 tree 5 brake, holly, royal 6 Boston 7 bracken, woodsia 8 polypody 10 maidenhair, spleenwort *combining form:* 6 pterid, pteris 7 pterido *leaf:* 5 frond

ferocious 4 fell, grim 5 brute, cruel, feral 6 brutal, fierce, savage 7 bestial, inhuman, vicious, violent, wolfish 8 inhumane, ravening, ravenous 9 barbarous, rapacious, truculent 10 implacable, relentless 12 bloodthirsty

ferret out 4 hunt, seek 5 learn, probe, quest 6 elicit 7 extract 8 discover 9 ascertain, cast about, determine, search for, search out

Ferrex's brother 6 Porrex

ferrule 3 cap, tip 4 band, knob

ferry 3 lug 4 bear, buck, pack, tote 5 carry 6 convey 9 transport

ferryman of Hades 6 Charon

fertile 4 lush, rich 6 fecund 7 bearing, copious 8 abundant, childing, creative, fruitful, pregnant, prolific, spawning, yielding 9 bountiful, ingenious, inventive, luxuriant, plenteous, producing 10 productive 11 proliferant

fertilize 6 enrich 9 pollenate, pollinate 10 impregnate, inseminate

fertilizer 4 dung, marl 5 guano 6 manure 7 compost

ferule 3 rod 5 ruler, stick 6 switch

fervent 3 hot 4 keen 5 eager, fiery 6 ardent, devout, hearty 7 blazing, burning, earnest, glowing, intense, sincere 8 vehement 9 heartfelt, perfervid 10 hot-blooded, passionate 11 impassioned 12 enthusiastic, wholehearted

fervor 4 fire, zeal 5 ardor 6 hurrah, warmth 7 passion 9 calenture, sincerity, vehemence 10 devoutness, enthusiasm, heartiness 11 earnestness

fess up 3 own 4 avow 5 admit, allow, grant, let on, own up 7 concede, confess 11 acknowledge

fester 3 rot 5 ulcer 6 rankle 7 influme, putrefy 8 ulcerate

festina ____ 5 lente

festival 4 fair, fete, gala 5 feast, gaudy 6 fiesta 8 carnival 9 festivity 11 celebration

festive 3 gay 4 gala 5 jolly, merry

6 blithe, jocund, jovial, joyous **7** gleeful **8** mirthful **10** blithesome **12** lighthearted

festivity 5 revel **6** gaiety **7** jollity, revelry, whoopee **8** reveling **9** merriment, revelment **11** celebration, merrymaking

fetch 4 sell **5** bring **7** bring in

fetching 6 luring **7** Circean **8** alluring, enticing, tempting

fete 4 fair **5** party **6** bazaar **8** festival **9** entertain **11** celebration

fetid 4 foul, rank **6** putrid, rancid, smelly **7** rankish, reeking **8** mephitic, stinking **10** malodorous

fetish 4 idol, juju, luck, zemi **5** charm, mania, thing **6** amulet, mascot **7** periapt **8** fixation, gris-gris, penchant, talisman **9** obsession **10** phylactery

fetter 3 tie **4** clog, curb **5** leash **6** hamper, hobble, hog-tie **7** manacle, shackle, trammel **8** handcuff, restrain **9** entrammel

fettle 4 trim **5** order, shape **6** kilter, repair **7** fitness **9** condition

feud 3 row **5** run-in **6** combat, fracas **7** contest, dispute, quarrel **8** argument, squabble, vendetta **9** bickering **10** falling-out **11** altercation, controversy

feudal *estate:* **4** feod, feud, fief *jurisdiction:* **3** soc **4** soke *laborer:* **4** serf *lord:* **5** liege **8** suzerain *service:* **5** avera *tax:* **7** tallage *tenant:* **6** vassal **7** homager, socager, sokeman, vavasor **8** vavasour *tenure of land:* **6** socage *tribute:* **6** heriot

fever 4 ague, fire **6** dengue **7** ferment, pyrexia **9** calenture *combining form:* **5** febri, pyret **6** pyreto *recurrent:* **6** sextan **7** malaria, quartan, quintan, tertian

feverish 3 hot **5** fiery **6** fervid, heated, hectic **7** burning, excited, febrile, flushed, furious, pyretic **8** febrific, frenzied, inflamed **10** passionate **11** overwrought

fever tree 7 blue gum

few 4 rare **6** scarce, seldom, smatch **7** handful, smatter, spatter **8** sporadic, uncommon **10** infrequent, occasional, scattering, smattering, spattering, sprinkling, unfrequent *combining form:* **4** olig **5** oligo, pauci

___-fi 2 hi **3** sci

fiat 5 edict, order **6** decree **7** command **8** sanction **11** endorsement **12** proclamation

fib 3 lie **4** tale **5** story **6** canard, palter **7** falsify, falsity, untruth **9** falsehood, mendacity **10** equivocate **11** evasiveness, prevaricate **13** prevarication

fiber 3 web **4** noil, pita **5** grain, istle **6** fabric, strand, thread **7** texture *brain:* **4** pons *coarse:* **4** adad, jute **8** piassava *coconut husk:* **4** coir, kyar *combining form:* **2** in **3** ino **4** fibr **5** fibro *knot:* **3** nep *rope:* **5** sisal **8** henequen *silky:* **5** kapok *small:*

6 fibril *substructure:* **7** micelle, spongin *synthetic:* **5** nylon, rayon, saran, vinal *woody:* **4** bast *woollike:* **7** lanital

fibrous 4 ropy, wiry **6** sinewy **7** stringy **8** muscular

fibula 5 clasp **7** leg bone

fickle 7 flighty, moonish **8** ticklish, unstable, variable, volatile **9** mercurial **10** capricious, changeable, inconstant, lubricious, unfaithful, unreliable **12** undependable **13** temperamental

fiction 4 tale, yarn **5** fable, story **6** deceit **7** fantasy, figment **9** fish story, invention, narrative **10** concoction **11** fabrication

fictional 5 false, phony **6** unreal **7** fictive **8** fanciful, illusory **9** fantastic, imaginary **10** chimerical, fictitious **12** suppositious

fictitious 4 fake, mock, sham **5** false **6** ersatz, made-up, unreal, untrue **7** assumed, created, fictive **8** cooked-up, fanciful, illusory, invented **9** concocted, fantastic, fashioned, fictional, imaginary, simulated, trumped-up **10** artificial, chimerical, fabricated **12** suppositious *combining form:* **5** pseud **6** pseudo

fiddle 4 fool, mess, play **6** dabble, doodle, fidget, handle, monkey, potter, puddle, putter, tinker, trifle, violin **10** mess around

fiddle-faddle 4 bosh **5** fudge, hooey **6** bunkum, piffle **8** nonsense, pishposh **10** flapdoodle

Fidelio *composer:* **9** Beethoven *hero:* **9** Florestan *heroine:* **7** Leonora

___ fidelis 6 semper

fidelity 5 ardor, piety **6** fealty **7** loyalty **8** adhesion, devotion **9** adherence, constancy **10** allegiance, attachment **11** reliability, staunchness **12** faithfulness **13** dependability, steadfastness

fidget 4 play **6** fiddle, jitter, trifle **7** twiddle

fidgety 5 fussy, jumpy, nervy **6** goosey, spooky **7** jittery, nervous, restive, twitchy **8** restless, twittery **9** unrestful **10** highstrung

field 4 area, walk **5** milpa **6** domain, meadow, region, sphere **7** demesne, terrain **8** dominion, precinct, province **9** bailiwick, champaign, territory **10** department *combining form:* **4** agro

fieldbird 6 plover

field crop 3 hay **5** grain **6** cotton

field deity 3 Pan **4** Faun **5** Fauna

field glasses 10 binoculars

field hand 4 hoer **5** sower **6** picker **7** laborer, planter

Fielding novel 6 Amelia **8** Tom Jones **13** Joseph Andrews

field marshal *Austrian:* **8** Radetzky *British:* **6** Napier, Raglan, Wavell, Wilson **7** Roberts **8** Wolseley **9** Kitchener **10** Montgomery *French:* **4** Foch **6** Joffre,

Pétain *German:* 6 Keitel, Paulus, Rommel, Rupert 9 Mackensen, Rundstedt, Waldersee 10 Kesselring *Japanese:* 8 Sugiyama *Prussian:* 6 Moltke *Russian:* 7 Kutuzov, Suvorov 8 Potemkin

field mouse 4 vole

Field of Blood 8 Aceldama

field officer 5 major 7 colonel

field rat 5 metad

fiend 3 bug, nut 5 bigot, demon, devil, freak, Satan 6 diablo, maniac, zealot 7 fanatic, Lucifer, Old Nick, serpent 8 Apollyon, succubus 9 Beelzebub 10 enthusiast, Old Scratch 13 Old Gooseberry

fiendish 5 cruel 6 malign, savage, wicked 7 baleful, demonic, hellish, inhuman, malefic, satanic, vicious 8 demoniac, demonian, devilish, diabolic, infernal, sinister 9 barbarous, ferocious, malicious, malignant

fierce 4 fell, grim, wild 5 cruel 6 brutal, savage 7 brutish, enraged, furious, inhuman, intense, vicious, violent, wolfish 8 inhumane, maddened, pitiless, ruthless, terrible, tigerish, vehement 9 barbarous, bellicose, desperate, ferocious, merciless, truculent 10 aggressive, cannibalic, infuriated, pugnacious 11 belligerent

fiery 3 hot 5 afire 6 ablaze, aflame, ardent, fervid, fierce, heated, red-hot, spunky, torrid 7 blaring, blazing, burning, febrile, fervent, fevered, flaming, flaring, gingery, igneous, ignited, intense, peppery 8 broiling, feverish, inflamed, scalding, sizzling, spirited, vehement, white-hot 9 hot-headed, perfervid, scorching 10 mettlesome, passionate 11 conflagrant, impassioned 12 high-spirited

fifteen *combining form:* 8 pentadec 9 pentadeca

fifth *combining form:* 5 quint 6 quinti

fig *genus:* 5 Ficus *sacred:* 5 pipal *variety:* 5 eleme, elemi 6 Smyrna

fight 3 row, tug, war 4 beef, bout, buck, duel, feud, fray, spat, tiff 5 brawl, broil, clash, joust, melee, repel, scrap, words 6 affray, attack, battle, bicker, combat, debate, fracas, hassle, oppose, oppugn, resist, strive, tussle 7 contend, contest, crusade, dispute, quarrel, scuffle, wrangle, wrestle 8 skirmish, slugfest, squabble, struggle, traverse 9 bickering, pugnacity, withstand 10 aggression, donnybrook 11 altercation 12 belligerence, disagreement 13 combativeness *combining form:* 5 machy

fighter 2 GI 4 swad 5 boxer 7 soldier, warrior 8 pugilist, scrapper 9 man-at-arms

fighter plane 3 MiG, Roc 4 Zero 5 Sabre 6 Fokker, Hawker, Mirage, Voodoo 7 Corsair, Harrier 8 Spitfire

fighting fish 5 betta

figment 5 dream, fable, fancy 6 bubble 7 chimera, fiction 8 daydream, illusion 9 invention 11 fabrication

figurant 6 dancer, hoofer 7 danseur 8 coryphée

figuration 4 line 5 shape 7 contour, outline, profile 8 allegory 9 lineament, lineation, symbolism 10 silhouette 11 delineation

figure 3 add, sum, tot 4 cast, foot, form, rule, tote 5 build, count, digit, frame, motif, shape, total 6 cipher, decide, design, device, motive, number, reckon, settle, symbol 7 chiffer, compute, integer, numeral, outline, pattern, resolve, summate 8 conclude, estimate, physique, totalize 9 calculate, character, determine, enumerate 11 whole number 12 conformation 13 configuration *geometric:* 4 cone, cube 5 rhomb 6 circle, isogon, square 7 decagon, ellipse, hexagon, nonagon, octagon, polygon, rhombus 8 pentacle, pentagon, rhomboid, tetragon, triangle 9 rectangle 10 hexahedron, octahedron 11 icosahedron 12 dodecahedron, rhombohedron 13 quadrilateral *human:* 4 nude 5 atlas 7 telamon 8 caryatid *ornamental:* 6 statue 8 gargoyle

figure of speech 5 trope 6 aporia, simile 7 imagery, litotes 8 metaphor, metonymy 10 synecdoche

figure out 4 dope 5 crack, solve 6 decode, unfold 7 clear up, resolve, unravel 8 decipher, unriddle, untangle 9 puzzle out 10 unscramble 11 disentangle

figure skating *jump:* 4 axel, loop, lutz 5 split 6 rocker 7 bracket, counter, salchow 11 spreadeagle *spin:* 3 sit 5 camel

Fiji *capital:* 4 Suva *monetary unit:* 6 dollar

filch 3 nim, nip, rob 4 lift 5 pinch, steal, swipe 6 pilfer, snitch 7 purloin

file 3 row 4 line, rank, rasp, tier 5 queue 6 string 7 dossier, echelon

fill 3 gob, jam, jug 4 brim, clog, cloy, cram, glut, heap, jade, load, meet, pack, pall, pile, plug, sate, stop 5 block, choke, close, gorge 6 answer, bumper, charge, stodge 7 congest, engorge, occlude, satiate, satisfy, stopper, surfeit *interstices:* 3 pug 4 calk 5 chink, putty

filled 4 full 5 sated 7 replete 9 saturated

fillet 4 band, orle, tape 5 snood, strip 6 ribbon, stripe 7 bandeau, banding 8 headband *anatomical:* 9 lemniscus *architectural:* 6 cimbia, listel, reglet, taenia *combining form:* 4 taen 5 taeni 6 taenio *meat:* 10 tenderloin

fill-in 3 sub 7 stand-in 9 alternate, surrogate 10 substitute 11 locum tenens, pinch hitter, replacement, succedaneum

fill in 4 clew, clue, post, tell, warn 6 advise,

inform, insert, notify, wise up **7** apprise, throw in **8** acquaint **9** insinuate, interject, interpose, introduce **11** intercalate, interpolate

film 4 cine, haze, mist, show, skin, veil **5** brume, flick, layer, movie, smaze **6** patina **7** picture **8** pellicle **9** celluloid, photoplay **10** cinematize **11** picture show **13** motion picture, moving picture

filmy 4 fine, hazy **5** gauzy, misty, sheer, wispy **6** cloudy, dainty, flimsy **7** tiffany **8** delicate, gossamer **10** diaphanous **11** transparent

filter 4 sift **5** leach, sieve **6** purify, refine, screen, strain **8** filtrate **9** percolate

filth 4 dirt, dung, gore **6** ordure **7** squalor **9** obscenity *combining form:* **4** copr **5** copro

filthy 4 foul, vile **5** black, dirty, dungy, gross, mucky, nasty, soily **6** coarse, grubby, impure, ribald, sloppy, smutty, sordid, vulgar **7** obscene, raunchy, squalid, unclean **8** indecent **9** loathsome, offensive, repulsive, revolting, uncleanly, verminous **12** scatological

filthy lucre 4 cash, loot, pelf **5** dough, money **8** currency **11** legal tender

fin 4 anal **5** pinna **6** caudal, dorsal, pelvic **7** acantha, flipper, ventral **8** pectoral

finagle 5 cheat, trick **6** wangle **7** deceive, snaffle, swindle **8** engineer, maneuver **9** machinate

final 3 lag **4** last **6** ending, latest, latter **7** closing **8** crowning, decisive, eventual, hindmost, terminal, ultimate **9** finishing **10** concluding, conclusive, definitive **11** terminating

finale 3 end **5** close, finis **6** climax, ending, finish, payoff, windup **7** closing **9** cessation **10** conclusion, denouement **11** culmination, termination

finalize 3 end **5** close **6** finish, wind up **8** conclude, solidify **9** terminate **10** consummate

finance 4 back, bank, fund **5** endow, stake **7** promote, revenue, sponsor, support **8** bankroll **9** grubstake, patronize, subsidize **10** capitalize, underwrite

financial 6 fiscal, pocket **8** business, economic, monetary **9** pecuniary **10** commercial *statement:* **12** balance sheet

financier *American:* **4** Hill, Ryan, Sage **5** Baker, Eaton, Field, Gould, Grace, Green **6** Girard, Mellon, Morgan, Morris, Rogers, Yerkes **7** Peabody **10** Vanderbilt *British:* **6** Rhodes **7** Gresham *French:* **6** Necker *German:* **7** Schacht **10** Rothschild

finch 4 pape **5** junco, serin, zebra **6** linnet, siskin, towhee **7** bunting, chewink, redpoll **8** grosbeak, longspur

find 4 espy, give, hand, note, spot **5** catch,

dig up, hit on, sight, solve **6** descry, detect, espial, locate, strike, supply, turn up **7** discern, dish out, furnish, hit upon, provide, scare up **8** discover, dispense, hand over, meet with, transfer, treasure, turn over **9** detection, discovery, encounter **10** unearthing **13** treasure trove

find out 3 see **4** hear **5** learn **6** tumble **7** catch on, unearth **8** discover **9** ascertain, determine

fine 3 tax, top **4** fair, levy, nice **5** bonny, clear, dandy, mulct, sheer, sunny **6** amerce, choice, minute, sconce, subtle **7** capital, clarion, damages, elegant, forfeit, penalty, powdery, refined **8** delicate, five-star, hairline, penalize, pleasant, rainless, splendid, sunshiny, superior, top-notch **9** beautiful, cloudless, enjoyable, excellent, first-rate, unclouded **10** amercement, assessment, first-class, impalpable, pulverized, reparation, undarkened **11** first-string **13** hairsplitting

finery 5 frill **6** gewgaw, tawdry **7** apparel, bravery, clothes, gaudery, regalia **8** foofaraw, frippery, ornament, trimming, war paint **9** full dress **10** Sunday best

finesse 3 art **4** play **5** skill **6** jockey **7** beguile, cunning, exploit **8** maneuver, subtlety **9** dexterity **10** manipulate

Fingal's Cave island 6 Staffa

finger 3 paw, tap, toy **4** feel, make, name, spot **5** digit, index, pinky, place, strum, touch **6** handle, medius, pilfer, pinkie **7** appoint, palpate **8** diagnose, identify, nominate, pinpoint **9** designate, determine, recognize **11** distinguish **13** diagnosticate *bone:* **7** phalanx **9** phalanges (plural) *combining form:* **6** dactyl, digiti **7** dactylo, dactyly **8** dactylia **9** dactylism, dactylous *cymbal:* **8** castanet

fingernail *combining form:* **4** onyx **7** onychia **8** onychium *crescent:* **6** lunule

fingerprint 4 arch, loop **5** whorl

finicky 4 nice **5** fussy **6** choosy, dainty, prissy **7** choosey **9** squeamish **10** fastidious, particular, pernickety **11** persnickety

finish 3 die, end **4** cool, do in, down, halt, kill, slay, stop **5** cease, close, glaze, scrag, spend, use up **6** cut off, ending, expend, finale, murder, polish, wash up, windup, wrap up **7** closing, consume, destroy, execute, exhaust, put away, surface, take off **8** carry off, complete, conclude, dispatch, finalize, knock off, terminus, ultimate **9** cessation, determine, liquidate, terminate **10** attainment, conclusion, desistance, run through **11** achievement, acquirement, acquisition, assassinate, termination *dull:* **3** mat **4** matt **5** matte *second:* **5** place *third:* **4** show

finished 4 done, down, over, ripe **5** ended,

suave **6** closed, smooth, urbane **7** done for, refined, through **8** complete, washed-up **9** completed, concluded, perfected, virtuosic **10** consummate, terminated **12** accomplished

finish off 3 cap **5** crown **6** climax, top off **8** round off **9** culminate

finite 5 bound **7** bounded, defined, limited **9** definable **10** restricted

Finland *capital:* **8** Helsinki *monetary unit:* **6** markka

Finlandia composer 8 Sibelius

Finnish *bath:* **5** sauna *combining form:* **5** Fenno *epic:* **8** Kalevala *god:* **6** Jumala

fin's double 7 tenspot

fir 7 conifer **9** evergreen *genus:* **5** Abies

fire 2 ax **3** can, pep, vim, zip **4** bake, burn, cast, dash, drop, hurl, kiln, sack, stir, toss, zeal, zest, zing **5** ardor, blaze, drive, exalt, flame, flare, fling, glare, gusto, heave, ingle, light, loose, pitch, rouse, salvo, shoot, sling, spark, throw, torch, verve, vigor **6** arouse, bounce, energy, excite, fervor, hurrah, ignite, inform, kindle, launch, spirit, thrill **7** animate, boot out, burnout, dismiss, enliven, enthuse, inferno, inflame, inspire, kick out, passion, provoke **8** enkindle, heighten **9** calenture, discharge, holocaust, intensify, terminate **10** enthusiasm, heartiness, liveliness **13** conflagration *combining form:* **3** pyr **4** igni, pyro *god:* **4** Agni, Loki **6** Vulcan **10** Hephaestus

firearm see **gun**

firebrand 7 hothead, hotspur **8** agitator

firebug 5 torch **8** arsonist **10** incendiary, pyromaniac

firecracker 5 squib **9** explosive **10** cherry bomb, noisemaker

firedog 7 andiron

firedrake 6 dragon

firefly 7 glowfly **12** lightning bug

fire opal 7 girasol

fireplace 5 ingle *equipment:* **6** fender, screen **7** andiron, fireset *part:* **3** hob **6** hearth, mantel

fireplug 7 hydrant

fire up 5 rouse **6** excite, ignite, incite, kindle **7** enflame, enliven, inflame, inspire, provoke **8** enkindle **9** intensify

firework 4 gerb **5** gerbe **6** fizgig, petard, rocket **8** sparkler **10** tourbillon **11** pyrotechnic, tourbillion *cluster:* **9** girandole

firm 3 set **4** fast, hard, sure **5** exact, fixed, house, rigid, solid, sound, stiff, tight, tough **6** outfit, secure, stable, stated, steady, stolid, strong, sturdy **7** abiding, adamant, certain, company, concern, confirm, fixedly, settled, solidly, staunch, tightly, unmoved **8** business, constant, definite, enduring, faithful, resolute, specific **9** inelastic, steadfast, tenacious **10** determined, enterprise,

inflexible, stipulated, unwavering, unyielding **11** established, steadfastly, substantial, unfaltering, unqualified **12** never-failing **13** establishment

firmament 3 sky **6** welkin **7** heavens **8** empyrean

firmness 7 resolve **8** decision, security, solidity, strength, tenacity **9** constancy, soundness, stability **10** resolution, stableness, steadiness **11** decidedness **12** resoluteness **13** determination, purposiveness

first 4 arch, head **5** alpha, chief, least, prime **6** maiden, primal **7** eminent, highest, initial, leading, pioneer, premier, primary, supreme **8** champion, dominant, earliest, foremost, headmost, original, smallest **9** inaugural, initially, paramount, principal, slightest, sovereign **10** aboriginal, preeminent, primordial *combining form:* **4** prot **5** proto

firstborn 4 heir **5** eigne **6** eldest

first-class 3 top **4** A-one, fine **5** prime **6** tip-top **7** capital **8** five-star, superior, top-notch **9** excellent, top-drawer

first fruits 7 annates

firsthand 6 direct **7** primary **9** immediate

first man in space 7 Gagarin

first-rate see **first-class**

first showing 8 premiere

First State 8 Delaware

first-string see **first-class**

firth 3 arm, bay **4** cove, gulf **5** inlet **6** harbor, slough **7** estuary

fiscal 6 pocket **8** monetary **9** financial

fish 3 net, sap **4** butt, cast, dupe, fool, gill, hint **5** angle, chump, seine, trawl, troll **6** sucker **7** fall guy, gillnet, gudgeon, sniggle *angler:* **7** lophiid **9** goosefish *aquarium:* **4** barb **5** betta, danio, guppy, limia, platy, tetra **6** mollie **7** cichlid, gourami, rasbora **8** goldfish **9** angelfish *basket:* **5** creel *catfish:* **6** madtom **8** bullhead, bullpout, hornpout, stonecat *cod:* **4** cusk, hake, ling **5** torsk, burbot, tomcod **7** pollack, pollock *combining form:* **6** ichthy **7** ichthyo, ichthys *croaker:* **4** drum **7** corbina **8** kingfish, seatrout, weakfish **10** squeteague, squiteague *eellike:* **5** moray **6** conger **7** hagfish, lamprey *eggs:* **3** roe **5** spawn *electric:* **4** raad **7** torpedo **9** stargazer *extinct:* **10** coelacanth *flatfish:* **3** dab **4** butt, dace, sole **5** bream, brill, fluke **6** plaice, turbot **7** halibut **8** flounder *food:* **3** cod, eel, ide **4** bass, carp, cero, hake, ling, scup, shad, sole, tuna **5** jurel, perch, scrod, skate, smelt, trout **6** bonito, caviar, kipper, mullet, plaice, pompon, salmon, tautog, weever, wrasse **7** alewife, catfish, cavalla, escolar, grouper, haddock, halibut, herring, pollack, pollock, pompano, pompoon, sardine, snapper, tautaug **8** brisling, crevalle,

flounder, mackerel **9** barracuda *game:*
4 bass, pike, tuna **5** perch, trout **6** grilse,
marlin, salmon, tarpon **8** pickerel **9** swordfish *grunt:* **5** sargo **7** pigfish, tomtate
8 porkfish **10** bluestripe *herring:* **4** shad,
sild **5** sprat **7** alewife, sardine **8** brisling,
pilchard *kind:* **3** ray **4** bass, cero, chub,
dory, goby, jack, pike, rudd, scup, tuna
5 balao, bream, cisco, loach, perch, porgy,
sargo, shark, skate, smelt, snook, tench,
tunny, wahoo **6** anabas, blenny, bonito,
dorado, marlin, minnow, mullet, permit,
puffer, remora, sauger, splake, sucker, tarpon, tautog, warsaw, wrasse **7** anchovy,
boxfish, buffalo, cabezon, capelin, cavalla,
chimera, cowfish, crappie, dolphin, grunion,
haddock, hogfish, jewfish, mojarra, muddler,
mudfish, oarfish, opaleye, piranha, pupfish,
sardine, sawfish, sculpin, snapper, sunfish,
tilapia, vendace, whiting **8** albacore, blowfish, bluefish, bluegill, bonefish, burrfish, chimaera, filefish, gambusia, grayling, halfbeak,
ladyfish, lookdown, lumpfish, lungfish,
mackerel, menhaden, moonfish, pickerel,
pipefish, rockfish, sailfish, seahorse, skipjack, stingray, sturgeon, tilefish, topsmelt,
warmouth, wolffish **9** amberjack, barracuda,
greenling, jacksmelt, killifish, mummichog,
pilotfish, spadefish, swordfish, topminnow,
trunkfish, whitebait, whitefish **10** butterfish,
flying fish, lizardfish, needlefish, parrotfish,
silverside, tripletail, yellowtail **11** harvest-
fish, muskellunge, pumpkinseed, stickle-
back, triggerfish **12** schoolmaster *lumines-
cent:* **9** viperfish **10** midshipman
11 hatchetfish, lanternfish *minnow:* **4** carp,
chub, dace **6** shiner *pan:* **5** bream, perch,
trout **7** crappie, sunfish **8** bluegill, rock
bass **11** pumpkinseed *porgy:* **4** scup
7 pinfish **8** jolthead **10** sheepshead *relating to:* **7** piscine **8** ichthyic *rockfish:*
8 bocaccio, lionfish, rosefish **11** chilipepper
salmon: **3** dog **4** chum, coho **6** sebago
7 chinook, sockeye *spear:* **3** gig **7** harpoon, trident *stew:* **8** cioppino, matelote
13 bouillabaisse *trap:* **3** dam **4** weir **6** eel-
pot **9** fishgarth *trout:* **5** charr **7** oquassa,
rainbow **9** cutthroat **11** Dolly Varden
young: **3** fry **4** parr **5** larva, smolt **6** alevin,
grilse
fisherman 6 angler **8** piscator
fish hawk 6 osprey
fishhook 5 drail *adjunct:* **5** snell *part:*
4 barb **5** shank
fishing area 7 piscary
fishing line 4 trot **7** boulter, setline
8 longline, trotline *float:* **3** bob **5** quill
6 dobber *leader:* **5** snell
fishing lure 3 fly **4** herl
fishing net 5 seine, trawl

fishlike mammal 3 orc **5** whale **7** dolphin **8** porpoise
fish owl 6 ketupa
fishwife 5 harpy, scold, shrew, vixen
6 amazon, ogress, virago **9** termagant,
Xanthippe
fishy 4 cold, dull **7** dubious, suspect
8 doubtful **9** ambiguous, doubtable, dubitable, equivocal, uncertain **10** suspicious
fission element 7 uranium **9** plutonium
fissure 3 gap **4** gash, hole, rent, rift, rima,
rime **5** break, chasm, chink, cleft, crack,
split **6** breach, schism **7** crevice, opening,
rupture **8** crevasse, fracture, rimation
fist 3 job **4** grip, hand **5** grasp, index
6 clench, clutch, ductus, effort, handle,
script **7** attempt **10** penmanship **11** calligb-
raphy, chirography, handwriting
fisticuffs 4 ring **6** boxing **8** pugilism
13 prizefighting
fit 2 go **3** apt, set **4** good, hale, jibe, just,
meet, sane, suit, turn, well **5** adapt, agree,
frame, happy, joint, ready, right, sound,
spasm, spell, tally, throe **6** access, accord,
adjust, attack, become, belong, decent, go
with, make up, proper, seemly, square, tailor, useful **7** capable, conform, healthy, prepare, qualify, seizure, tantrum **8** apoplexy,
assemble, decorous, dovetail, eligible, paroxysm, quadrate, rightful, suitable **9** agree
with, befitting, congruous, consonant, harmonize, reconcile, wholesome **10** applicable, convenient, correspond, felicitous, go
together, tailor-make, well-liking **11** accommodate, appropriate *suffix:* **4** able, ible
fitful 6 catchy, random, spotty **8** periodic,
sporadic, unstable, variable **9** desultory,
haphazard, hit-or-miss, irregular, recurrent,
spasmodic **10** capricious, changeable,
inconstant **11** interrupted
fitness 3 use **4** trim **5** order, shape **6** fettle, kilter, repair **7** account, aptness, service, utility **8** capacity, justness, meetness
9 advantage, condition, propriety, relevance,
rightness, soundness **10** expediency, usefulness **11** eligibility, suitability **12** appositeness, suitableness **13** applicability
fit out 3 arm, rig **4** gear **5** equip **6** outfit
7 appoint, furnish, turn out **8** accouter,
accoutre
fitting 3 apt **4** just, meet, true **5** happy
6 proper, seemly **7** adjunct, apropos,
desired, germane **8** apposite, relevant, suitable **9** accessory, accordant, befitting, pertinent **10** applicable, attachment, concordant,
felicitous, harmonious **11** appropriate
Fitzgerald novel 13 The Last Tycoon
14 The Great Gatsby
five *combining form:* **3** pen **4** pent
5 penta **6** quinqu **7** quinque *group of:*
6 pentad **7** quintet *of trumps:* **5** pedro

five-dollar bill 3 fin
fivefold 7 quinary 9 quintuple
Five Nations 8 Iroquois *member:*
7 Cayugas, Mohawks, Oneidas, Senecas
9 Onondagas
five-sided figure 8 pentagon
five-year period 6 luster, lustre
7 lustrum
fix 3 buy, jam, lay, put, set, sop 4 do up,
geld, make, mend, moor, root, spot, work
5 alter, bribe, catch, embed, focus, lodge,
patch, place, ready, rivet, solve, stick,
unsex 6 adjust, anchor, attach, buy off,
change, corner, doctor, fasten, make up,
neuter, pickle, plight, repair, revamp, scrape,
secure, settle, square, steady, tune up
7 appoint, arrange, dilemma, ingrain, instill,
prepare, rebuild, resolve, specify, work out
8 castrate, entrench, mutilate, overhaul, regulate, renovate 9 concenter, establish, stabilize, sterilize 10 tamper with 11 concentrate, desexualize, predicament, recondition,
reconstruct
fixation 5 craze, mania, thing 9 obsession 11 fascination, infatuation
____ **fixe** 4 idée
fixed 3 pat, set 4 fast, firm, sure 5 tight,
whole 6 frozen, narrow, secure, stable,
stated, steady 7 abiding, certain, limited,
precise, settled 8 constant, definite, enduring, immobile, immotile, immotive, resolute
9 exclusive, immovable, immutable, permanent, steadfast, tenacious, undivided,
unmovable 10 inflexible, invariable,
restricted, stationary, stipulated, unswerving, unwavering 11 determinate, inalterable,
irremovable, unalterable, unfaltering, unqualified 12 concentrated, never-failing,
unchangeable, undistracted, unmodifiable
13 circumscribed *combining form:*
6 aplano
fix up 5 equip, primp, slick, spiff 6 devise,
doll up, supply 7 deck out, doll out, dress
up, furnish, gussy up 8 contrive, spruce up
9 smarten up 11 accommodate
fizzle 4 fail, hiss 6 fiasco 7 failure, sputter
fjord *Baffin Island:* 9 Admiralty *Denmark:*
3 Ise, Lim 5 Lamme *Iceland:* 4 Axar, Eyja
5 Horna, Skaga, Vopna *Norway:* 3 Tys
4 Bokn, Nord, Salt, Stor, Tana, Vest
5 Lakse, Ranen, Sogne 9 Stavanger,
Trondheim *Spitsbergen:* 3 Ice *Svalbard:*
4 Stor
flabbergast 5 amaze, shock 7 astound
8 astonish, surprise 9 dumbfound,
overwhelm
flabby see **flaccid**
flaccid 4 limp, soft, weak 6 feeble, flabby,
flimsy, floppy, sleazy 8 weakened, yielding
flag 3 ebb, sag 4 fade, fail, jack, sign,
swag, wane, wilt 5 abate, color, droop

6 banner, burgee, colors, ensign, fanion, gui-
don, motion, pencel, pennon, signal,
weaken 7 decline, gesture, pendant, pennant 8 bannerol, gonfalon, gonfanon, languish, penoncel, standard, streamer, tri-
color 9 banderole, oriflamme, pennoncel,
signalize 10 Jolly Roger 11 deteriorate
flagellate 4 flog, hide, lash, whip 5 whale
6 stripe, switch, thrash 7 scourge
flagellum 4 whip 5 shoot 6 runner, stolon 7 scourge
flagitious 6 rotten, sinful, wicked 7 corrupt, vicious 8 criminal, depraved, infamous, perverse, shameful 9 miscreant,
nefarious 10 degenerate, scandalous, villainous 11 disgraceful
flagon 3 cup, mug 5 stoup 7 tankard
flagpole 4 mast 5 staff
flagrant 3 bad 4 bold, rank 5 gross
6 wanton 7 capital, glaring, heinous, obvious 8 striking 9 atrocious, egregious, monstrous 10 outrageous 11 conspicuous
flagstone 5 shale, slate
flag-waver 7 patriot 10 patrioteer
12 superpatriot
flail 4 beat, flog, skin, whip 6 strike, thrash,
thresh 7 scourge
flair 4 bent, bump, gift, head, turn 5 knack
6 genius, talent 7 aptness, faculty
8 aptitude
flake 3 bit 4 chip, peel, rack, snow, tray
5 fleck, scale 6 lamina 8 fragment
flake off 4 peel 5 scale 9 exfoliate
10 desquamate
flamboyant 4 rich 5 showy, swank 6 chichi, florid, ornate, rococo 7 baroque,
splashy 8 luscious, peacocky 10 peacockish 11 pretentious 12 orchidaceous,
ostentatious
flame 4 beau, dear, fire, glow, love 5 ardor,
blare, blaze, flare, flash, glare, honey, light,
lover 7 beloved, darling, sweetie 8 ladylove, loveling, truelove 9 boyfriend, inamorata, inamorato 10 girlfriend
flamen 6 priest
flamenco 5 dance, gypsy, music
flaming 5 afire, fiery, flamy 6 ablaze,
aflame, alight, ardent, flambé, red-hot
7 blazing, burning, fervent, flaring, ignited
8 white-hot 10 hot-blooded, passionate
11 conflagrant, impassioned
flammable 8 burnable 9 ignitable
11 combustible
flammable liquid 3 oil 6 acetyl 7 acetone, alcohol 8 gasoline, kerosene
10 turpentine
Flanders *capital:* 5 Lille *language:*
7 Flemish
flannelflower 7 mullein
flap 3 tab 4 clap, fold, leaf, stew 6 crisis,
dither, lather, pother, tongue, tumult 7 aile-

ron, flutter, turmoil **9** agitation, commotion, confusion

flapdoodle 4 bosh **5** fudge **6** bunkum **7** rubbish **8** malarkey, nonsense **9** poppycock **12** blatherskite, fiddle-faddle

flapjack 7 hotcake, pancake **11** griddle cake

flare 4 glow **5** blaze, burst, flame, flash, torch **6** signal **7** flicker **8** eruption, outbreak, outburst

flare-up 4 gust **5** burst, sally **6** access **8** eruption, outburst **9** explosion

flaring 5 afire, fiery **6** ablaze, aflame, alight **7** blazing, burning, flaming, ignited **11** conflagrant

flash 3 ray **4** beam, burn, glow, show **5** blare, blaze, blink, crack, flame, flare, glare, gleam, glint, jiffy, shake, shine, spark **6** dazzle, expose, flaunt, glance, minute, moment, parade, quiver, second **7** display, disport, exhibit, flicker, glimmer, glisten, glitter, instant, radiate, shimmer, show off, spangle, sparkle, trot out, twinkle **8** brandish **9** breathing, coruscate **10** incandesce **11** coruscation, scintillate, split second **13** scintillation

flashy 4 loud **5** gaudy, showy **6** brazen, florid, garish, ornate, tawdry, tinsel **7** blatant, chintzy, glaring **9** sparkling **10** flamboyant, glittering **12** meretricious

flask 5 frame **6** bottle, fiasco, flacon **7** ampulla, canteen, costrel

flat 3 dim, mat **4** dead, drab, dull, even, poor **5** banal, bland, blind, broke, flush, inane, level, muted, needy, plane, prone, prosy, rooms, stale, stony, suite, vapid **6** jejune, planar, rental, smooth **7** insipid, planate, prosaic, sapless **8** dirt poor, lifeless, lodgings, strapped, tenement, unsavory **9** apartment, colorless, decumbent, destitute, downright, innocuous, penurious, prostrate, reclining, recumbent, savorless, tasteless **10** flavorless, lackluster, lusterless, monotonous, namby-pamby, procumbent, stone-broke

flatfish see at **fish**

flatland 4 mesa, moor **5** plain **6** steppe, tundra **7** plateau **9** tableland

flat-out 4 fast, rank **5** apace, utter **6** damned **7** blasted, goldarn, hastily, quickly, rapidly, swiftly **8** absolute, outright, speedily **9** out-and-out, posthaste **11** straight-out, unmitigated **12** lickety-split **13** expeditiously

flatten 3 lay **4** down, even, fell, flat **5** floor, flush, level, plane **6** deject, ground, lay low, smooth **7** depress, mow down **8** smoothen **9** bring down, knock down, prostrate

flattened at the poles 6 oblate

flatter 4 coax, suit **5** toady **6** become,

cajole, praise **7** blarney, enhance, gratify, wheedle **8** blandish, bootlick, inveigle

flattery 3 oil **4** laud **6** praise **7** blarney, fawning, incense **8** cajolery, soft soap, toadying **9** adulation, laudation, truckling **10** sycophancy **11** bootlicking, compliments **12** blandishment, ingratiation

flatulent 4 vain **5** empty, gassy, tumid, windy **6** hollow, turgid **8** dropsied, inflated **9** dropsical, overblown, tumescent

Flaubert *heroine:* **4** Emma *novel:* **8** Salammbo **12** Madame Bovary

flaunt 4 show, wave **5** flash, flout, vaunt **6** expose, parade **7** display, disport, exhibit, flutter, show off, trot out **8** brandish, flourish

flavor 4 tang, zest **5** sapor, savor, smack, taste, tinge **6** relish, season **8** sapidity

flavorless 4 drab, flat **5** stale **7** insipid **8** unsavory **9** tasteless **11** distasteful, unpalatable

flavorsome 5 sapid, tasty **6** savory **9** aperitive, flavorful, palatable, relishing, toothsome **10** appetizing **11** good-tasting

flaw 3 gap, rip **4** rent, tear, vice **5** crack, fault **6** breach, defect **7** blemish, fissure **12** imperfection

flawed 4 sick **5** amiss **6** faulty, marred **7** damaged, spoiled **8** impaired **9** defective, imperfect

flawless 5 ideal, model, sound, whole **6** entire, intact **7** perfect **8** absolute, unbroken, unmarred **9** errorless, exquisite, faultless, fleckless, undamaged **10** immaculate, impeccable, unimpaired **11** note-perfect, unblemished **12** indefectible

flax 5 linen *fiber:* **3** tow **4** harl **5** harle **6** strick *prepare:* **3** ret **4** card **5** dress **6** hackle, scutch *refuse:* **5** hards, hurds

flaxen 5 blond, straw **6** blonde, golden

flay 4 skin **5** slash **6** assail, attack, berate, scathe, scorch **7** blister, censure, scarify, scourge **8** lambaste, lash into **9** castigate, excoriate **10** tongue-lash

flea 5 pulex **6** chigoe, jigger **7** chigger *water:* **7** daphnid

Fleance's father 6 Banquo

fleckless 7 perfect **8** absolute, flawless, unflawed **10** impeccable **11** note-perfect

flection 3 bow **4** bend, turn **5** angle **7** flexure, turning

Fledermaus, Die 3 bat *character:* **5** Adele, Falke, Frank **6** Alfred **9** Rosalinde **10** Eisenstein *composer:* **7** Strauss

fledgling 4 boot, colt, tyro **6** novice, rookie **8** beginner, freshman, neophyte, newcomer **10** apprentice

flee 3 fly, lam, run **4** bolt, scat, shun, skip **5** break, elude, scape, scoot, scram, skirr **6** decamp, escape **7** abscond, make off, scamper, scarper **9** skedaddle

fleece 3 web **4** bilk, clip, milk, rook, skin,

soak, wool **5** bleed, cheat, cozen, mulct, shear, stick, sweat **6** extort, hustle **7** defraud, despoil, plunder, swindle **10** overcharge

fleeceable 4 easy **5** naive **8** gullible **11** susceptible

fleecy 5 hairy **6** pilose, woolly **7** hirsute, pileous **9** whiskered

fleer 4 gibe, gird, jeer, jest, mock **5** flout, laugh, scoff, sneer, taunt **6** quip at **7** scout at **8** fugitive

fleet 3 fly, run **4** fast, flit, navy, sail, spry, wile, wing **5** agile, brisk, hasty, hurry, quick, rapid, speed, sweep, swift, while **6** armada, hasten, hustle, nimble, rocket, speedy **7** beguile **8** flotilla **9** breakneck **10** evanescent, expeditive, harefooted **11** expeditious

fleeting 5 brief **7** passing **8** fugitive, volatile **9** ephemeral, fugacious, momentary, transient **10** evanescent, short-lived, transitory

Fleming, Ian *hero:* **9** James Bond *novel:* **4** Dr. No **10** Goldfinger **11** Thunderball **12** Casino Royale

fleshly 3 lay **6** animal, bodily, carnal **7** profane, secular, sensual, somatic **8** corporal, physical, sensuous, temporal **9** corporeal, epicurean, luxurious, sybaritic **10** voluptuous **3** fat **5** beefy, gross, heavy, obese, plump, stout **6** portly **7** porcine, sarcous, weighty **9** corpulent **10** overweight *fruit:* **4** pome **5** bacca, berry, drupe

Fletcher's partner 8 Beaumont

flex 4 bend **5** tense **7** pliancy, tension

flexible 5 withy **6** docile, floppy, limber, pliant, supple, whippy **7** elastic, pliable, springy, stretch, willowy **8** amenable, stretchy, yielding **9** resilient, tractable **10** manageable

flexuous 5 snaky **7** sinuous, winding **8** tortuous **9** meandrous **10** circuitous, convoluted, meandering, serpentine **11** anfractuous

flick 3 hit **4** blow, cine, film, show **5** movie **6** strike **7** picture **9** photoplay **11** picture show **13** motion picture, moving picture

flicker 4 flit **5** blink, dance, flash, gleam, glint, hover, waver **7** flitter, flutter, glitter, sparkle, twinkle

flickering 7 lambent **8** unsteady

flier 3 ace **5** pilot **6** airman, fly-boy **7** aviator, birdman **8** aviatrix

flight 3 lam **4** rout, slip **5** floor, story **6** escape **7** getaway **8** breakout, escaping **10** escapement

flighty 5 dizzy, giddy, silly, swift **7** foolish **8** freakish, skittish, unstable, volatile **9** frivolous, mercurial, transient **10** capricious, changeable, inconstant **11** empty-headed, harebrained **13** irresponsible, rattlebrained

flimflam 3 gyp **4** beat, bilk, dupe, fake, fool, gull, hoax, jazz, sell, sham **5** cheat, cozen, fraud, freak, hokum, trick **6** befool, chouse, deceit, diddle, drivel, hot air, humbug, pigeon, trifle **7** chicane, deceive, defraud, eyewash, swindle **8** hoodwink, nonsense **9** bamboozle, deception, imposture, moonshine, overreach **10** balderdash, double-talk **11** hornswoggle

flimflammer 3 gyp **4** skin **5** cheat **6** con man **7** diddler, sharper **8** swindler **9** defrauder **12** double-dealer

flimsy 4 limp, thin, weak **5** filmy, frail, gauzy, sheer **6** feeble, flabby, floppy, infirm, sleazy, slight, slimsy, weakly **7** flaccid, fragile, rickety, slimpsy, tiffany, unsound **8** decrepit, delicate, gossamer **10** diaphanous, improbable, incredible **11** implausible, transparent **12** unbelievable, unconvincing

flinch 5 quail, start, wince **6** blanch, blench, recede, recoil, shrink **7** retreat, squinch **8** withdraw

fling 2 go **3** pop, try **4** boil, bolt, cast, dash, emit, fire, gibe, hurl, lash, orgy, race, rush, shot, slap, stab, tear, toss **5** binge, chase, crack, dance, heave, pitch, shoot, sling, spree, throw, whack, whirl **6** charge, launch **7** discard, rampage, sarcasm, splurge **9** disregard, overthrow

flip 3 tap **4** blow, flap, glib, pert, riff **5** drink, flick **6** riffle **8** flippant **10** somersault **11** smart-alecky

flippancy 6 levity **8** archness, pertness **9** cockiness, freshness, frivolity, lightness, sauciness **10** cheekiness, impishness, volatility **11** flightiness, playfulness, roguishness

flippant 4 flip, glib, pert

flip through 4 scan **6** browse **7** dip into, run over **8** glance at **10** glance over

flirt 3 toy **4** dart, flip, flit, fool, minx, play, toss, vamp **5** dally, flick **6** coquet, lead on, trifle, wanton **8** coquette

flit 3 fly, run, zip **4** dart, pass, rush, sail, scud, whiz, wing **5** dance, fleet, flick, float, hover, hurry, scoot, speed, sweep **6** dartle, hasten **7** flicker, flutter

flitter 3 bit **5** dance, flake, hover **7** flicker, flutter, skitter

float 3 bob, fly **4** buoy, cork, dart, hang, raft, ride, sail, scud, skim, waft, wash **5** drift, drink, flood, hover, poise, shoot, skirr **8** levitate **9** negotiate

floater 3 bum, vag **4** hobo **5** tramp **6** boomer **7** drifter, vagrant **8** derelict, vagabond

floating 5 loose **6** adrift, afloat, natant **7** buoyant, movable **8** moveable, shifting

flocculent 6 woolly

flock 3 mob **4** army, bevy, herd, host, pack, rout **5** bunch, cloud, covey, crowd, drove, group 6 flight, legion, scores, volary 9 multitude 11 aggregation

flog 3 tan 4 beat, cane, hide, lash, whip 5 birch, flail, knout, tawse, whale 6 larrup, stripe, switch, thrash 7 exhaust, scourge 10 flagellate

flood 4 bore, flow, flux, pour, rush, tide 5 drift, drown, eager, eagre, spate, swamp, whelm 6 deluge, engulf, stream 7 current, freshet, niagara, torrent 8 cataract, flooding, inundate, overflow, submerge 9 cataclysm, overwhelm 10 inundation, outgushing, outpouring

floor 4 down, drop, fell 5 level, story 6 defeat, ground, lay low 7 flatten, silence 8 audience, bowl down, bowl over 9 bring down, knock down

flop 3 dud 4 bomb, bust, fail, fall, flap 5 lemon, loser 6 fizzle 7 failure

floppy 4 limp 5 loose 6 flabby, flimsy, sleazy 7 flaccid 8 flexible

flora 6 plants 10 vegetation

flora and fauna 5 biota

Florence *bridge:* 12 Ponte Vecchio *cathedral:* 5 Duomo *family:* 6 Medici *gallery:* 6 Uffizi *museum:* 8 Bargello *palace:* 5 Pitti *river:* 4 Arno

florid 4 rich 5 flush, gaudy, ruddy, showy 6 ornate, rococo 7 aureate, baroque, flowery, flushed, glowing 8 figurate, luscious, rubicund, sanguine, sonorous 9 bombastic, overblown 10 euphuistic, flamboyant, rhetorical 11 declamatory, full-blooded 12 magniloquent 13 grandiloquent

Florida *capital:* 11 Tallahassee *college, university:* 4 Nova 5 Barry 6 Eckerd 7 Stetson *discoverer:* 11 Ponce de Leon *Key:* 4 Long, Vaca, West 5 Largo 7 Big Pine 9 Sugarloaf *largest city:* 12 Jacksonville *motto:* 12 In God We Trust *nickname:* 13 Sunshine State *state bird:* 11 mockingbird *state flower:* 13 orange blossom

florilegium 3 ana 4 posy 5 album 7 garland, omnibus 8 analects 9 anthology 10 miscellany

Florimel's husband 7 Marinel

florist's milieu 10 greenhouse

floss 3 fur 4 down, flue, fuzz, lint, pile 5 fluff

flotsam 6 jetsam 8 wreckage 9 driftwood

flounce 5 fling, frill, mince, strut 6 prance, ruffle, sashay 8 flounder, struggle

flounder 5 fling, labor, lurch 6 muddle, wallow 7 blunder, stumble 8 flatfish, struggle

flour 4 atta, bolt, meal, mill 5 grind 6 pinole, powder 9 pulverize *beetle:* 6 weevil

flourish 3 wax 4 brag, grow, wave 5 adorn, bloom, boast, score, swing

6 arrive, flower, stroke, thrive 7 blossom, develop, fanfare, make out, prosper, succeed 8 brandish, curlicue, decorate, ornament 9 grace note

flout 4 gibe, gird, jeer, jest, mock 5 fleer, scoff, scorn, sneer, taunt 6 deride, insult, quip at 7 jeering, mockery 9 disregard

flow 3 run 4 emit, flux, gush, hang, head, pour, rill, rise, roll, rush, stem, teem, tide, void, well 5 arise, crawl, drift, flood, issue, spate, surge, swarm 6 abound, course, gurgle, onrush, ripple, series, sluice, spring, stream 7 cascade, current, emanate, give off, indraft, outflow, proceed 8 fountain, inundate, sequence 9 discharge, originate, pullulate 10 continuity, derive from, disembogue, inundation, menstruate, succession 11 continuance, progression 12 continuation, menstruation *combining form:* 4 rheo 5 rrhea 6 rrhoea 7 rrhagia

flower 3 top 4 best, blow, pick, posy 5 bloom, cream, elite, pride, prime, prize 6 choice, gentry 7 aristoi, blossom, burgeon, develop, fleuron, quality, society 8 optimacy, outbloom 9 gentility 10 effloresce, upper class, upper crust 11 aristocracy 13 inflorescence *buttonhole:* 11 boutonniere *cluster:* 4 cyme 5 spike, umbel 6 corymb, floret, raceme, spadix, thyrse 7 panicle 8 spikelet 9 capitulum, dichasium, glomerule 11 monochasium, polychasium 13 inflorescence *combining form:* 4 anth 5 antho, anthy, flori 6 anthes, anthus 7 anthous, florous *cup:* 5 calyx *garden:* 4 iris, lily, pink, rose 5 aster, canna, daisy, pansy, peony, phlox, poppy, tulip 6 azalia, cosmos, crocus, dahlia, orchid, violet 7 jonquil, petunia 8 camellia, daffodil, gardenia, geranium, gloxinia, hyacinth, larkspur, marigold, primrose 9 carnation, gladiolus, narcissus 10 delphinium, heliotrope 13 chrysanthemum *opening:* 8 anthesis *part:* 5 bract, calyx, ovary, ovule, petal, sepal, style 6 anther, pistil, spathe, stamen, stigma 7 corolla, nectary, pedicel, petiole 8 calyptra, filament, gynecium, peduncle, perianth *spike:* 5 ament 6 catkin, spadix *stalk:* 7 pedicel 8 peduncle *type:* 3 ray 4 disk 6 annual, simple 9 composite, perennial *wild:* 4 flag 5 bluet, daisy, gilia, vetch 6 lupine 7 anemone, arbutus, cowslip, gentian, vervain 8 bluebell, hepatica, trillium 9 buttercup, columbine, dandelion, saxifrage 10 cinquefoil 11 lady slipper 12 lady's slipper

flower arranging 7 ikebana

flowering 6 growth 8 progress, upgrowth 9 evolution, unfolding 10 evolvement 11 development, florescence, progression

flowerless plant 4 fern, moss 6 fungus, lichen 9 liverwort

flower-shaped ornament 7 fleuron

flowery 5 wordy 6 florid, ornate 7 aureate, swollen, verbose 8 sonorous 9 bombastic, overblown 10 euphuistic, rhetorical 11 declamatory 12 magniloquent 13 grandiloquent

Flowery Kingdom 5 China

flowing 4 easy 5 fluid 6 afflux, fluent, smooth 7 copious, cursive, running, streamy 8 freeform 10 effortless *back:* 6 reflux 8 refluent *in:* 6 influx 8 influent *together:* 7 conflux 9 confluent

flow regulator 5 valve

flub 4 mess, muff 5 boner, botch, error, fluff 6 bollix, bungle, goof up 7 blunder, louse up

fluctuate 4 sway, wave 5 swing, waver 8 undulate 9 oscillate, vacillate 10 irresolute

flue 3 fur 4 down, fuzz, lint, pile 5 floss, fluff 7 channel, dragnet, feather, fishnet, passage

fluent 4 easy, free, glib 5 fluid, vocal 6 facile, liquid, smooth 7 cursive, flowing, running, voluble 8 eloquent 9 talkative 10 articulate, effortless, loquacious 12 smooth-spoken

fluff 3 fur 4 bull, down, flub, flue, fuzz, lint, mess, muff, pile, slip, trip 5 boner, botch, error, floss, lapse 6 bollix, bungle, goof up 7 blooper, blunder, louse up, mistake

fluid 4 free 5 water 6 liquid, mobile 7 mutable, protean 8 unstable, unsteady, variable, weathery 9 changeful, unsettled 10 changeable *combining form:* 4 sero *excessive:* 5 edema

fluid pressure record 8 kymogram

fluky 3 odd 6 casual, chance 8 unsteady 9 uncertain 10 accidental, capricious, contingent, fortuitous, incidental

flume 5 chute 6 sluice, stream 7 channel

flummox 4 fail 7 confuse, perplex 8 confound 9 embarrass 10 disconcert

flunky 5 toady 7 footman, servant, steward

flurry 3 ado 4 fuss, gust, stir 5 haste, upset, whirl 6 bother, bustle, furore, pother, scurry 7 agitate, confuse, disturb, fluster, perturb, turmoil, unhinge 8 disquiet 9 agitation, confusion, whirlpool, whirlwind 10 discompose, excitement, turbulence

flush 3 lay 4 even, flat, glow, pink, rich, rose 5 bloom, blush, color, level, plane, rouge, ruddy 6 florid, mantle, pinken, redden, smooth 7 blossom, crimson, flatten, flushed, glowing, moneyed, opulent, planate, wealthy 8 abundant, affluent, rubicund, sanguine, smoothen 11 full-blooded

fluster 5 addle, dizzy, shake, upset 6 ball

up, bother, flurry, fuddle, muddle, puzzle, rattle, ruffle 7 agitate, confuse, disturb, mystify, nonplus, perplex, perturb, unhinge 8 befuddle, bewilder, confound, disquiet, distract 10 discompose

flute 4 fife, roll 5 pleat 6 goffer, groove 7 chamfer, channel, flutist, piccolo, shuttle 8 recorder 9 wineglass *combining form:* 3 aul 4 aulo *player:* 5 piper 7 flutist 8 flautist

flutist *American:* 5 Baker, Baron 7 Robison *British:* 6 Galway *French:* 6 Rampal

flutter 4 beat, flap, flit 5 dance, hover, quake, shake, throb 6 flurry, quaver, quiver, wobble 7 flicker, flitter, pulsate, tremble, vibrate 8 disorder 9 agitation, confusion, palpitate, vibration 11 fluctuation, oscillation

flux 3 run 4 flow, fuse, melt, rush, thaw, tide 5 drift, flood, spate 6 scours, stream 7 current, flowing, liquefy, outflow 8 diarrhea, dissolve, liquesce 9 dysentery 10 deliquesce

fly 3 run, zip 4 bolt, dart, dash, flee, flit, lure, rush, sail, scud, skip, soar, whiz, wing 5 break, fleet, float, glide, hover, hurry, pilot, scape, scoot, shoot, skirr, speed, sweep, whish, whisk 6 aviate, decamp, escape, flight, hasten, hustle 7 abscond, airlift, flutter, hotfoot, make off, scamper 8 highball 9 skedaddle *combining form:* 3 myi 4 myia, myio 5 musci *insect:* 4 gnat, zimb 5 fruit, midge 6 botfly, gadfly, mayfly, tsetse 7 deerfly, sandfly, tachina 8 blackfly, dipteron, horsefly, housefly, mosquito, tachinid 10 bluebottle *larva:* 3 bot 4 bott 6 maggot

fly-by-night 6 unsure 7 dubious 8 untrusty 9 trustless 10 unreliable 12 questionable, undependable 13 untrustworthy

flycatcher 4 tody

flying 5 aloft, brief 6 volant 7 soaring 8 airborne, volitant

Flying Dutchman *composer:* 6 Wagner *heroine:* 5 Senta

flying fish 7 gurnard

flying fox 3 bat 6 kalong 8 fruit bat

flying horse 7 Pegasus 10 hippogriff

flying island 6 Laputa

flying lemur 6 colugo

flying mammal 3 bat

flying saucer 3 UFO

fly in the ointment 5 catch

foam 4 head, scud, scum, suds 5 froth, spume, yeast 6 lather

fob 4 seal 5 chain 6 pocket, ribbon 8 ornament

fob off 5 foist 6 palm on, put off 7 palm off

focus 3 fix, hub, put 4 meet, seat 5 heart, rivet 6 center, fasten, fixate 8 converge,

polestar **9** concenter **11** concentrate, nerve
center

fodder 4 feed, food **6** forage, silage
9 provender *crop:* **3** hay, oat, rye **4** corn
5 maize, vetch, wheat **6** barley, clover, millet **7** alfalfa, sorghum **9** broad bean *storage structure:* **4** silo *store:* **6** ensile

foe 5 enemy, rival **8** opponent **9** adversary **10** antagonist

fog 3 dim **4** blur, daze, haze, mist, murk
5 addle, bedim, brume, cloud, muddy,
vapor **6** darken, muddle, puzzle **7** becloud,
confuse, eclipse, mystify, obscure, perplex,
pogonip **8** bewilder, distract **9** obfuscate,
overcloud **10** muddlement **11** muddledness **12** befuddlement, bewilderment

foggy 4 hazy **5** misty, murky, soupy,
vague **7** brumous, muddled, obscure, tenuous **8** confused, vaporous

foghorn 8 diaphone

fogy 6 square **7** diehard **8** mossback,
standpat **10** back number, fuddy-duddy
12 antediluvian, conservative, mid-Victorian **13** stick-in-the-mud

fogyish 4 tory **5** right **7** die-hard, old-line
8 orthodox **9** out-of-date **10** antiquated
11 reactionary **12** conservative, old-
fashioned

foible 5 fault **7** failing, frailty **8** weakness
11 shortcoming **12** imperfection

foil 4 balk, beat, bilk, curb, dash, faze
5 sword **6** baffle, defeat, rattle, thwart, tissue **7** buffalo, repulse **8** restrain **9** discomfit, embarrass, frustrate **10** circumvent, disappoint, disconcert

foist 3 fob **4** dupe, gull, hoax, wish, worm
5 cheat, trick **6** delude, edge in, fob off,
impose, palm on, work in **7** beguile,
deceive, defraud, inflict, mislead, palm off,
pass off, swindle, work off **8** hoodwink
9 bamboozle, insinuate, overreach
10 infiltrate

fold 3 lap, pen, ply **4** bend, bust, coat, fail,
leaf, ruck, tuck **5** break, crash, drape, flock,
layer, plait, pleat, plica, purse, ridge, rivel
6 crease, cuttle, double, furrow, pucker, rimple **7** confine, crinkle, crumple, embrace,
entwine, envelop, flexure, overlap, plicate,
wrinkle **8** surround **9** plication **11** corrugation *combining form:* **5** ptych **6** ptycho,
valvul **7** valvulo *skin:* **4** ruga **5** plica, rugae
(plural) **6** dewlap, plicae (plural)

folder 4 file **5** cover **6** binder **8** circular

foliage 6 growth, leaves **7** leafage, verdure **9** greenness **10** vegetation

folk 4 clan, race **5** house, laity, stock, tribe
6 family, people **7** kindred, lineage
9 relatives

folklore 4 myth **6** belief, custom, legend,
mythos **9** mythology, tradition
12 superstition

folksinger 4 Baez (Joan), Ives (Burl)
5 Niles (John Jacob), White (Josh) **6** Seeger
(Pete) **7** Chapman (Tracy), Guthrie (Arlo,
Woody) **9** Ledbetter (Huddie)

folktale 7 märchen

follow 3 ape, dog, see, spy, tag **4** copy,
hunt, keep, mind, obey, seek, tail, take
5 after, catch, chase, chivy, ensue, grasp,
hound, trace, track, trail **6** accept, attend,
comply, convoy, pursue, search, shadow,
take in **7** conform, imitate, observe, replace,
succeed **8** displace, exercise, postdate,
practice, supplant **9** accompany, apprehend, supersede, supervene **10** comprehend, understand

follower 3 fan **5** freak, toady **6** addict,
cohort, patron, sequel, votary **7** devotee,
groupie, habitué, sectary, sequent, trailer
8 adherent, advocate, disciple, faithful,
hanger-on, henchman, myrmidon, parasite,
partisan, sectator, tagalong **9** dependent,
satellite, supporter, sycophant **10** aficionado **11** lickspittle *of Theodore Roosevelt:* **9** Bull Moose *suffix:* **3** ite

following 4 next **5** after, below, since,
suite, train **6** behind, public **7** ensuing, retinue, sequent **8** audience **9** clientage, clientele, entourage **10** sequential, subsequent,
succeeding, successive **12** subsequent to

follow-up 6 sequel

folly 4 whim **6** lunacy, vanity **7** fatuity,
foolery, inanity, madness **8** insanity, nonsense **9** absurdity, craziness, dottiness, silliness, stupidity **10** imprudence, indulgence
11 foolishness, witlessness

foment 3 set **4** abet, brew, goad, spur
5 nurse, raise, rouse, set on **6** arouse,
excite, foster, incite, stir up, whip up **7** agitate, ferment, nurture, provoke **9** cultivate,
encourage, instigate

Fomorian one-eyed giant 5 Balor

fond 4 dear, warm **5** basis, silly **6** doting,
loving, tender, upbeat **7** devoted, foolish
8 enamored, lonesome, romantic, sanguine
9 indulgent **10** groundwork, infatuated,
optimistic, responsive **11** sentimental, sympathetic **12** affectionate

fondle 3 hug, pet **4** love **5** clasp **6** caress,
cosset, dandle **7** embrace

fondness 4 love **5** taste **6** liking, relish
8 appetite, devotion, soft spot **9** affection
10 attachment, partiality, propensity
11 inclination **12** predilection

fondness for *combining form:* **5** phily
6 philia *suffix:* **4** itis

fond of *combining form:* **4** phil **5** phile,
philo **6** philic **7** philous

food 3 pap **4** bite, chow, diet, fare, grub,
meal, meat **5** bread, manna, scoff **6** fodder,
viands, vivres **7** aliment, edibles, nurture,
pabulum **8** delicacy, victuals **9** nutriment,

provender **10** provisions, sustenance **11** comestibles, nourishment *combining form:* **4** sito **6** phagia *craving for:* **7** bulimia *divine:* **8** ambrosia *element:* **5** sugar **6** starch **7** mineral, protein, vitamin **12** carbohydrate *from heaven:* **5** manna *lover:* **7** epicure, gourmet **8** gourmand *provision:* **4** mess **6** ration **7** serving *scarcity:* **6** famine *waste:* **4** orts **7** garbage

foofaraw 4 coil, fuss **6** furore, hurrah, ruckus, rumpus, shindy **8** brouhaha **9** commotion

fool 3 ass, fun, kid, rag, rib, sap, toy **4** blow, butt, dolt, dope, dupe, fish, gull, hoax, jerk, jest, joke, josh, mark, poop, razz, simp, wolf, zany **5** amble, ament, chump, clown, comic, dally, dummy, dunce, flirt, goose, idiot, jolly, loser, moron, ninny, noddy, patsy, schmo, silly, trick, waste **6** banter, befool, butt in, coquet, cretin, cuckoo, dimwit, donkey, doodle, horn in, jester, lead on, loiter, madman, meddle, monkey, motley, nincom, nitwit, pigeon, schmoe, simple, stooge, stupid, sucker, trifle, victim, wanton **7** asshead, buffoon, chicane, consume, deceive, fall guy, foolish, fritter, gudgeon, half-wit, jackass, natural, pinhead, saphead, schmuck, tomfool **8** busybody, comedian, dumbbell, easy mark, flimflam, hoodwink, imbecile, lunkhead, mooncalf, numskull, pushover, softhead, squander, underwit, womanize **9** bamboozle, birdbrain, blockhead, dissipate, interfere, interlope, philander, simpleton, throw away **10** frivol away, instrument, mess around, monkey with, nincompoop, play around, tamper with, trifle away **11** featherhead, hornswoggle, merry-andrew, ninnyhammer, rattlebrain, string along **12** featherbrain, scatterbrain **13** laughingstock

foolhardy 4 rash **6** daring **8** headlong, reckless **9** audacious, daredevil, impetuous, venturous **11** adventurous, precipitate, temerarious, venturesome **13** adventuresome

foolish 3 mad **4** daft, fond, rash, zany **5** batty, crazy, dippy, dizzy, dotty, goofy, inane, jerky, loony, loopy, sappy, silly, wacky **6** absurd, insane, simple, stupid, unwise **7** asinine, doltish, fatuous, idiotic, lunatic, moronic, offbeat, unwitty, witless **8** headless, reckless **9** brainless, fantastic, half-baked, imbecilic, laughable, ludicrous, senseless, unearthly **10** half-cocked, half-witted, idleheaded, irrational, ridiculous, unorthodox, weak-headed, weak-minded **11** harebrained, nonsensical

foolishness 4 bull, bunk **5** folly **6** lunacy **7** fatuity, inanity, waggery **8** drollery, insanity, nonsense, unwisdom **9** absurdity

10 imprudence **12** indiscretion **13** senselessness

fool's gold 6 pyrite

foot 3 add, sum, tot **4** base, cast, pace, step, tote, walk **5** dance, nadir, total, tread, troop **6** bottom, figure, hoof it, prance, tootsy **7** summate, tootsie, traipse **8** ambulate, totalize *ailment:* **4** corn **6** bunion, callus *animal:* **3** pad, paw **4** hoof **7** fetlock, flipper, pastern, trotter *bones of:* **5** talus, tarsi (plural) **6** cuboid, tarsal, tarsus **7** phalanx **9** calcaneus, cuneiform, navicular, phalanges (plural) **10** metatarsal *combining form:* **3** ped, pod, pus **4** pede, pedi, pedo, poda, pode, podo **5** podia **6** podium *doctor:* **10** podiatrist **11** chiropodist *metric:* **4** iamb **5** arsis **6** dactyl, thesis **7** anapest, pyrrhic, spondee, trochee *part:* **3** toe **4** arch, ball, claw, nail **5** ankle, digit, talon **6** hallux, instep

football 5 rugby **6** rugger, soccer **7** pigskin *field:* **8** gridiron *foul:* **7** holding, offside **8** clipping **12** interference *official:* **6** umpire **7** referee **8** linesman **9** back judge, line judge **10** field judge *play:* **4** dive, trap **5** sneak, sweep **6** option, screen **7** audible, counter, handoff, rollout, runback **8** dropback **9** crossbuck, off-tackle **10** buttonhook *player position:* **3** end **4** back **5** guard **6** center, safety, tackle **7** flanker, lineman, wideout **8** fullback, halfback, slotback, split end, tailback, tight end, wingback **9** noseguard **10** cornerback, linebacker, nose tackle **11** quarterback **12** defensive end, wide receiver *scoring:* **6** safety **9** field goal, touchdown **10** conversion *starting play:* **7** kickoff *team:* **6** eleven *term:* **4** down, kick, pass, punt, rush, snap **5** blitz, block, squad **6** fumble, huddle, onside, option, safety, spiral **7** end zone, handoff, kickoff, offside, pigskin, quarter, spinner, yardage **8** clipping, crossbar, goal line, goalpost, gridiron, halftime **9** backfield, defensive, field goal, intercept, offensive, placekick, scrimmage, touchback, touchdown **11** broken field **12** interception

footballer 4 Moon (Warren), Rice (Jerry) **5** Baugh (Sammy), Berry (Raymond), Brown (Jim), Ditka (Mike), Elway (John), Jones (Bert, Deacon), Kelly (Jim), Kosar (Bernie), Shula (Don), Starr (Bart) **6** Blanda (George), Butkus (Dick), Graham (Otto), Grange (Red), Greene (Joe), Marino (Dan), Namath (Joe), Payton (Walter), Sayers (Gale), Thorpe (Jim), Tittle (Y. A.), Unitas (Johnny) **7** Dorsett (Tony), Esiason (Boomer), Gifford (Frank), Hornung (Paul), Luckman (Sid), Montana (Joe), Simpson (O. J.) **8** Bradshaw (Terry), Nagurski (Bronko), Staubach (Roger) **9** Dickerson (Eric), Jurgensen (Sonny), Tarkenton (Fran)

footed *combining form:* **3** ped, pod
6 podous

footfall **4** step **5** tread

footing **4** base, rank, seat, term **5** basis,
place, state **6** bottom, ground, status
7 bedrock, seating, station, warrant **8** basement, capacity, position **9** character, situation **10** foundation, groundwork,
substratum

footless **6** apodal

foot lever **5** pedal **7** treadle

footlike **6** pedate **8** pediform

footpad **6** robber **10** highwayman

footprint **3** pug **4** sign, step **5** spoor,
trace, track, tract **7** pugmark, vestige *fossil:* **7** ichnite **9** ichnolite

footslog **4** plod, slop, toil **6** stodge,
trudge **8** plunther

footstep **5** spoor, track, tract **7** vestige

footstone **6** ledger **8** monument **11** grave
marker

footstool **7** hassock, ottoman

fop **4** buck, dude **5** blade, blood, dandy,
spark, sport, swell **6** masher **7** coxcomb,
gallant **8** cavalier, macaroni, popinjay
9 exquisite **10** ladies' man, lady-killer
11 Beau Brummel, petit-maître **12** fashion
plate, lounge lizard, man-about-town

for *prefix:* **3** pro

forage **4** beat, comb, grub, raid, rake
5 scour **6** browse, fodder, ravage, search
7 ransack, rummage **8** finecomb,
scrounge **9** pasturage; (see also **fodder**)

forager **6** raider, sacker **8** marauder,
ravisher

foray **4** raid **5** harry **6** attack, harass,
inroad, invade, maraud, sortie **7** overrun,
pillage **8** invasion **9** incursion, irruption

forbear **4** curb, keep, shun **5** avoid, cease,
evade, forgo, spare **6** bridle, desist, endure,
escape, eschew, forego, suffer **7** abstain,
decline, inhibit, refrain **8** restrain, tolerate,
withhold **9** sacrifice

forbearance **5** grace, mercy **6** lenity
7 charity **8** clemency, lenience, leniency,
mildness, patience **9** restraint, tolerance
10 abstinence, toleration

forbearing **4** easy, mild **6** gentle **7** clement, lenient, patient **8** merciful, tolerant
9 indulgent **10** charitable, thoughtful
11 considerate

Forbes hero **8** Tremaine (Johnny)

forbid **3** ban, bar **4** curb, deny, halt, stop,
veto **5** block, check, debar, estop, taboo
6 enjoin, hinder, impede, outlaw, refuse
7 exclude, inhibit, obviate, prevent, rule out,
shut out **8** obstruct, preclude, prohibit,
restrain **9** interdict, proscribe

forbidden **5** taboo **6** banned **8** verboten
10 prohibited

Forbidden City **5** Lhasa

force **2** od **3** arm, jam, vim, vis **4** beef,
cram, make, move, odyl, push, rape
5 cause, drive, exact, foist, impel, karma,
might, odyle, order, pains, point, power,
press, punch, sinew, speed, spoil, vigor,
visit, wreak, wreck, wrest **6** coerce, compel,
defile, demand, duress, effort, energy,
enjoin, extort, impose, inject, legion, muscle,
oblige, ravish, strain, stress **7** cogency,
command, concuss, headway, impetus,
inflict, outrage, potency, require, sandbag,
shotgun, tension, trouble, violate **8** coercion, deflower, manpower, momentum, obli-
gate, occasion, pressure, shoehorn,
strength, validity, velocity, violence **9** constrain, deflorate, exertions, intensity, puissance, strong arm, validness, vehemence
10 compulsion, constraint *apart:* **5** wedge
unit: **4** dyne

forced **5** rigid, stiff **6** wooden **7** labored
9 contrived, fatiguing, unnatural **10** artificial,
compulsory, exhausting, factitious, farfetched, inflexible **11** involuntary

forceful **6** cogent, mighty, potent, virile
7 dynamic, telling **8** emphatic, forcible, powerful, puissant, vigorous **9** assertive, effective, energetic, insistent **10** compelling,
resounding **12** constraining

forceless **4** weak **5** wimpy **6** feeble
8 impotent **10** emasculate, inadequate
11 ineffective, ineffectual, slack-spined
12 invertebrate

force out see **expel**

forcible **6** mighty, potent **7** intense, violent **8** coercive, emphatic, militant, powerful,
puissant, vehement **9** assertive
10 aggressive

Ford's folly **5** Edsel

for each **3** per

forearm bone **4** ulna **6** radius

forebear **8** ancestor **9** ascendant **10** progenitor **11** antecedents **12** primogenitor

forebode **4** omen **5** augur **7** betoken,
portend, predict, presage, promise **8** foretell

foreboding **4** omen **5** dread **6** augury
7 anxiety, portent, presage, warning
9 prenotion **10** prediction, prognostic
11 premonition, presagement
12 presentiment

forecast **5** augur, guess, infer, weird
6 gather **7** foresee, portend, predict, presage, surmise **8** conclude, foreshow, foretell,
prophecy, soothsay **9** adumbrate, prevision, prognosis **10** conjecture, prediction,
vaticinate **13** prognosticate

forecaster **4** seer **5** augur **6** auspex, oracle **7** prophet **8** haruspex **9** predictor
10 prophesier **11** Nostradamus
13 meteorologist

foreclose **3** bar **5** debar **6** cut off, hinder
7 prevent **8** preclude

forefather see **forebear**
forefeel 6 divine 7 preknow, previse
  9 apprehend, prevision, visualize
forefinger 5 index
forefront 8 vanguard
foregoer 7 example 8 ancestor 9 precursor, prototype 10 antecedent, antecessor
  11 predecessor
foregoing 4 past 5 prior 8 anterior, previous 9 precedent, preceding 10 antecedent
forehanded 7 prudent, thrifty
forehead 4 brow 5 frons, front 8 sinciput 9 sincipita (plural) *combining form:*
  6 fronto *ornamental spot:* 5 tilak
foreign 5 alien 6 exotic 7 strange
  9 extrinsic, obnoxious, repellent, repugnant
  10 accidental, extraneous, immaterial, inapposite, irrelative, irrelevant 11 distasteful,
  impertinent, incongruous, inconsonant
  12 adventitious, inapplicable, incompatible,
  inconsistent 13 inappropriate *combining
  form:* 3 xen 4 xeno
foreigner 5 alien 7 inconnu 8 outsider,
  stranger
foreknow 6 divine 7 previse 8 conclude
  9 apprehend, prevision, visualize
  10 anticipate
foreland 4 beak, bill, cape, head, naze
  5 point 8 headland 10 promontory
forelock 5 bangs, quiff 8 linchpin, split
  pin 9 cotter pin
foreman 4 boss 5 chief 6 gaffer, ganger,
  honcho, leader 7 captain, headman, manager, overman, steward 8 overseer
  10 supervisor
foremost 4 arch, head, main 5 chief, first,
  front 7 initial, leading, premier, supreme
  8 champion, headmost 9 inaugural, principal 10 preeminent
forenoon 4 morn 7 morning
forensics 6 debate 7 mooting 11 disputation 13 argumentation
foreordain 4 fate 6 doom to 7 destine,
  preform 9 determine 10 predestine
  12 predestinate, predetermine
forerun 4 pace 6 herald 7 precede, predate, presage 8 announce, antecede, antedate 9 harbinger 10 anticipate, foreshadow
forerunner 4 mark, omen, sign 5 model,
  token 6 augury, author, herald 7 example,
  pattern, pioneer, portent, presage, symptom, warning 8 ancestor, exemplar
  9 announcer, harbinger, initiator, messenger, precursor, prototype 10 antecedent,
  antecessor, originator, prognostic 11 anticipator, predecessor 12 announcement
foresee 4 espy 6 descry, divine 7 discern,
  predict, preknow, presage, previse 8 perceive, prophesy 9 apprehend, prevision,
  visualize 10 anticipate 13 prognosticate
foreseer 5 augur 6 auspex, oracle

7 diviner, prophet 8 haruspex 9 predictor
  10 prophesier, soothsayer 11 Nostradamus
foreshadow 4 bode, hint, omen 5 augur
  7 betoken, portend, presage, promise
  9 adumbrate, prefigure 11 prefigurate
foresight 6 vision 7 caution 8 prudence,
  sagacity 9 canniness 10 discretion, perception, precaution, prescience, providence 11 discernment 12 clairvoyance
forest 4 bosk, wood 5 copse, grove,
  weald, woods 6 timber 7 coppice, thicket,
  woodlot 8 wildwood, woodland 10 timberland, wilderness *combining form:* 3 hyl
  4 hylo *deity:* 5 dryad 6 sylvan 8 Sylvanus
  English: 5 Arden 8 Sherwood *opening:*
  5 glade *relating to:* 6 sylvan *subarctic:*
  5 taiga *tropical:* 5 selva 6 jungle
forestall 4 ward 5 avert, deter 7 obviate,
  prevent, rule out 8 preclude, stave off
  10 anticipate
Forester *hero:* 10 Hornblower (Horatio)
  novel: 12 African Queen
foretell 4 bode, call, warn 5 augur
  6 divine, reveal 7 declare, divulge, portend,
  predict, presage, promise 8 announce, disclose, proclaim, prophesy, soothsay
  9 adumbrate, apprehend, prefigure
  10 anticipate, vaticinate 13 prognosticate
foreteller see **foreseer**
forethought 5 sense 7 caution 8 gumption, judgment, prudence 9 canniness, foresight 10 discretion, precaution, providence
  12 deliberation, discreetness
  13 premeditation
foretime 4 past, yore 9 yesterday
  10 yesteryear
foretoken 4 bode, hint, mark, note, omen,
  sign 5 augur, badge 6 augury, boding, herald, ostent, shadow 7 inkling, portend, portent, presage, promise, symptom, warning
  8 bodement, forecast 9 harbinger, precursor 10 indication, intimation
forever 3 aye 4 ever 6 always 7 endless,
  eternal 8 eternity, evermore 9 endlessly,
  eternally 11 ceaselessly, continually, everlasting, incessantly, in perpetuum, perpetually, unceasingly 13 everlastingly
forewarning 6 caveat 7 caution 8 monition 10 admonition 11 commonition
foreword 5 proem 7 preface, prelude
  8 exordium, overture, preamble, prologue
  9 prelusion 12 introduction, prolegomenon
for example 2 as, e.g. 6 such as
for fear that 4 lest
forfeit 4 drop, fine, lose 5 mulct 7 penalty 9 sacrifice 10 amercement
forfend 4 ward 5 avert, deter 6 secure
  7 obviate, prevent, protect, rule out, ward
  off 8 preclude, preserve, stave off
forge 4 beat, copy, make, mold 5 build,
  pound, shape 6 smithy 7 advance, fashion,

imitate, produce, turn out **8** bloomery, progress **9** construct, fabricate **11** counterfeit, manufacture, put together

forget 4 fail, omit **5** fluff **6** blow up, ignore, slight, unknow **7** blink at, neglect, unlearn **8** discount, overlook **9** blink away, disregard **11** disremember **12** misrecollect

forgetful 3 lax **5** slack **6** absent, remiss **7** bemused **8** careless, heedless **9** negligent, oblivious, unwitting **10** abstracted, neglectful **11** inattentive, thoughtless **12** absentminded

forgetfulness 5 lethe **7** amnesia **8** oblivion

forgivable 6 venial **10** pardonable

forgive 5 remit **6** excuse, pardon, slight **7** absolve, condone, neglect **8** overlook

forgo 5 leave, waive **6** eschew, give up, resign **7** abandon, forbear **8** abdicate, abnegate, renounce **9** sacrifice, surrender **10** relinquish

fork 6 bisect, branch, crotch **7** utensil *prong:* **4** tine

forlorn 4 vain **5** alone **6** bereft, futile, lonely **7** cynical **8** deserted, desolate, forsaken, helpless, homeless, hopeless, lonesome, solitary, wretched **9** abandoned, depressed, desperate, destitute, fruitless, miserable, oppressed **10** bedraggled, despairing, despondent, desponding, disordered, friendless **11** defenseless, pessimistic **12** disconsolate

form 3 law, way **4** body, cast, make, mode, mold, plan, plot, rite, rule **5** build, canon, forge, found, frame, habit, image, model, shape, style, usage **6** create, custom, design, devise, figure, invent, make up, manner, method, ritual, scheme, system **7** acquire, anatomy, compose, contour, decorum, develop, economy, fashion, liturgy, outline, precept, process, produce, profile, project, turn out **8** ceremony, comprise, organism, organize, practice, skeleton **9** construct, establish, etiquette, fabricate, formality, framework, procedure, propriety, structure **10** ceremonial, constitute, convenance, convention, proceeding, regulation, silhouette **11** manufacture **13** configuration *combining form:* **3** gen **4** gene **5** morph, plasm, plast **6** morpha, morphi (plural) **6** morpho, plasma **7** morphae (plural), morphic **8** morphism **9** morphosis *suffix:* **2** fy **3** ify

formal 3 set **4** prim **5** exact, rigid, stiff **6** dressy, proper, seemly, solemn **7** distant, nominal, orderly, precise, regular, stately, titular **8** decorous, reserved, so-called **9** essential, unbending **10** ceremonial, methodical, systematic **11** ceremonious, syntactical **12** constitutive, conventional

formality 4 form, rite **6** ritual **7** liturgy, service **8** ceremony, insignia **10** ceremonial, convenance, convention, observance

format 4 plan, size **5** shape, style **6** makeup

formation 4 form, rank **6** design, makeup **9** structure **10** production **11** arrangement, composition, development **12** architecture, construction

formative material *combining form:* **5** plasm **6** plasma

former 3 old **4** late, once, past **5** maker, prior **6** bygone, shaper, whilom **7** creator, earlier, onetime, quondam **8** anterior, previous, sometime **9** erstwhile, precedent, preceding **10** antecedent *combining form:* **6** proter **7** protero

formerly 4 erst, once **6** before, whilom **7** already, earlier **9** erstwhile **10** heretofore, previously

formidable 4 hard **5** awful, tough **6** uphill **7** arduous, fearful, labored **8** alarming, dreadful, horrific, shocking, terrible, terrific, toilsome **9** appalling, difficult, effortful, frightful, laborious, strenuous

formless 3 raw **4** rude **5** crude, rough, vague **7** chaotic, obscure, unclear **8** inchoate, unshaped **9** amorphous, shapeless, undefined, unordered **10** immaterial, indefinite, indistinct **11** unorganized

Formosa 6 Taiwan *capital:* **6** Taipei

formulate 3 put **4** make, word **5** couch, draft, frame, hatch **6** cook up, devise, draw up, invent, make up, phrase, vamp up **7** concoct, dream up, express, hatch up, prepare **8** contrive

forsake 4 quit **5** avoid, chuck, leave, spurn **6** defect, depart, desert, reject, resign **7** abandon **8** abdicate, renounce **9** throw over

forsaken 4 lorn **7** uncouth **8** derelict, deserted, desolate, solitary **9** abandoned

forsaker 8 apostate

Forseti *father:* **6** Balder *palace:* **7** Glitnir

forswear 4 deny **5** unsay **6** abjure, recall, recant, reject **7** perjure, retract **8** palinode, renounce, take back, withdraw

fort 6 castle **7** bastion, bulwark, citadel, redoubt **8** fastness, fortress, martello **10** stronghold *Baltimore:* **7** McHenry *New York:* **7** Niagara, Stanwix **8** Schuyler *Ontario:* **9** Frontenac *San Antonio:* **8** The Alamo *South Carolina:* **6** Sumter *Spanish:* **7** alcazar **8** presidio

forte 3 bag **5** thing **6** medium, métier, oyster **7** ability **8** ableness, eminency, long suit, strength **10** competence, efficiency, strong suit **11** strong point

forth 2 on **3** out **4** alee **5** ahead, along **6** onward **7** forward

forthcoming 6 future **7** affable, awaited **8** approach, expected, imminent, sociable

11 anticipated, approaching
12 approachable

for the most part 9 generally 10 on the whole

for the time being 6 pro tem 10 pro tempore

forthright 4 open 5 frank, plain 6 candid, direct, single 7 frankly 10 aboveboard 11 openhearted, undisguised, unvarnished

forthwith 3 now 4 away 5 short 6 at once, sudden 7 asudden 8 abruptly, directly, suddenly 9 instanter, instantly, right away, thereupon 11 immediately, straightway 12 straightaway

fortification 4 boma, moat, wall 5 agger, redan 6 abatis, glacis, sangar, sungar 7 barrier, parapet, rampart, ravelin, redoubt 8 barbican, enceinte, palisade 9 barricade, earthwork 10 breastwork *part:* 7 salient

fortify 3 arm 4 gird, stir 5 brace, rally, ready, renew, rouse, steel 6 arouse 7 bulwark, prepare, protect, rampart, refresh, restore 8 energize, palisade 9 encourage 10 invigorate, strengthen

fortitude 4 grit, guts, pith, sand 5 nerve, pluck, spunk, valor 6 bottom, mettle, spirit 7 bravery, courage, stamina 8 backbone, boldness, strength, tenacity, valiancy 9 constancy, endurance 10 resolution 11 intrepidity 12 fearlessness, perseverance, resoluteness, valorousness 13 dauntlessness, determination

fortress see **fort**

fortuitous 3 odd 5 fluky 6 casual, chance 10 accidental, contingent, incidental

fortuity 3 hap 4 luck 6 chance 8 accident

Fortuna 5 Tyche *symbol:* 5 wheel 6 rudder

fortunate 4 good, well 5 happy, lucky, white 6 benign, bright, dexter 9 favorable 10 auspicious, propitious 12 providential

Fortunate Islands 8 Canaries

fortune 3 lot, pot, wad 4 doom, fate, luck, mint, pile 5 worth 6 boodle, bundle, chance, hazard, packet, riches, wealth 7 destiny, portion, success 8 property 9 luckiness, resources, substance

fortune-teller 4 seer 7 palmist; (see also **foreteller**)

fortune-telling see **divination**

forty winks 3 nap 6 catnap, dog nap, siesta, snooze

forward 2 on, to 3 aid 4 abet, alee, ante, back, bold, help, pert, send, ship, wise 5 ahead, along, brash, eager, fresh, nervy, ready, relay, remit, route, sassy, saucy, serve, smart, ultra 6 cheeky, foster, hasten, onward, uphold, uppish, uppity 7 address, advance, anxious, consign, extreme, further, promote, pushful, pushing, radical, support 8 advanced, champion, dispatch, impudent,

previous, transmit 9 encourage, in advance, presuming 11 overweening, precedently, smart-alecky 12 antecedently, presumptuous 13 self-asserting, self-assertive *prefix:* 4 ante

For Whom the Bell Tolls *author:* 9 Hemingway *character:* 5 Maria, Pablo, Pilar 6 Jordan

foss, fosse 4 moat 5 canal, ditch 6 trench

fossa 3 pit 6 cavity 10 depression

fossil 4 fogy 5 amber 6 square 7 antique 8 calamite, conodont, mossback 10 antiquated, fuddy-duddy 12 antediluvian, mid-Victorian 13 stick-in-the-mud *combining form:* 4 lite, lith, lyte, necr 5 necro, oryct 6 orycto *fuel:* 3 oil 4 coal, peat 9 petroleum

foster 4 back, help, rear, warm 5 favor, house, lodge, nurse, serve 6 assist, harbor, nursle, oblige, uphold 7 advance, cherish, forward, further, nourish, nurture, promote, shelter, support, sustain 8 champion 9 cultivate, encourage, entertain

foul 4 base, soil, vile 5 black, block, dirty, fetid, grime, muddy, nasty, soily 6 besoil, coarse, defile, filthy, grubby, horrid, impure, odious, putrid, rotten, smirch, smooch, smudge, smutch, smutty, vulgar, wicked 7 abusive, begrime, noisome, obscene, pollute, profane, raunchy, squalid, tarnish, unclean 8 dishonor, feculent, indecent, obstruct, polluted, stinking 9 dangerous, desecrate, entangled, loathsome, obnoxious, offensive, repellent, repugnant, repulsive, revolting, uncleanly 10 detestable, disgusting, malodorous 11 contaminate 12 scatological

foul play 5 blood 6 murder 7 killing 8 homicide, violence 12 manslaughter

found 4 base, cast, rear, rest, stay 5 begin, erect, raise, set up, start 6 bottom, create 7 fashion, support, sustain 8 commence, initiate, organize 9 establish, institute, originate, predicate

foundation 3 bed 4 base, rest 5 basis 6 bottom 7 bedrock, footing, roadbed, support, warrant 9 endowment 10 substratum 11 institution 12 organization, substructure, underpinning

foundational 5 basic 6 bottom 7 primary 10 underlying 11 fundamental

founder 4 fail, sink, sire 5 wreck 6 author, damage, go down 7 creator 8 collapse, inventor, submerge, submerse 9 architect, generator, patriarch 10 originator

fountain 3 jet 4 head, root 6 origin, source, spring, whence 8 wellhead 9 inception, reservoir 10 wellspring *nymph:* 6 Egeria

four 6 tetrad 7 quartet 10 quaternion *bag-*

ger: 5 homer 7 homerun *combining form:* 4 tetr 5 quadr, tetra 6 quadri, quadru, quater, tessar 7 tessara, tessera **gills:** 4 pint *hundred:* 5 elite 10 upper crust *inches:* 4 hand *pecks:* 6 bushel **quarts:** 6 gallon

fourberie 5 fraud 7 chicane 8 trickery 9 chicanery, deception 10 dishonesty, hanky-panky

four-flush 5 bluff 6 betray, delude, humbug, juggle, take in 7 beguile, deceive 11 double cross

four-footed animal 8 tetrapod 9 quadruped

Four Horsemen 3 War 5 Death 6 Famine 10 Pestilence

four-in-hand 3 tie 7 necktie

fourpence 5 groat

four-poster 3 bed

fourscore 6 eighty

four-sided figure 6 square 7 rhombus 9 rectangle

foursquare 7 solidly 8 quadrate 9 quadratic 10 forthright 11 quadratical 12 forthrightly

fourteen pounds 5 stone

fourth 7 quarter 8 quadrant, quartern *combining form:* 5 quadr, quart 6 quadri, quadru 7 tetarto

fowl 3 hen 4 bird, cock 5 chick, poult 6 Bantam, pullet 7 chicken, rooster; (see also **chicken; poultry**)

fox 4 fool 5 trick 6 baffle, outwit 7 confuse, Reynard 8 bewilder 9 dissemble *female:* 5 vixen *kind:* 6 corsac, corsak, fennec *Scottish:* 3 tod *young:* 3 cub

foxglove 7 mullein 8 pokeweed 9 fairy bell 10 fingerroot

fox grape 9 muscadine

foxiness 3 art 5 craft 7 cunning 8 artifice 10 cleverness

foxlike 7 vulpine

foxy 3 sly 4 deep, wily 6 artful, astute, clever, crafty, shrewd, tricky 7 cunning 8 guileful 9 deceitful, dishonest, insidious

foyer 5 lobby 8 anteroom, entrance 9 vestibule

fracas 3 row 4 feud 5 brawl, broil, fight, melee, run-in, set-to 6 affray, hassle 7 dispute, quarrel, ruction 8 squabble 9 bickering 10 donnybrook 11 altercation

fraction 3 bit, cut 4 part 5 piece, scrap 6 divide, little 7 portion, section 8 fragment

fractious 4 wild 5 cross, huffy, waspy 6 unruly 7 fretful, peevish, pettish, waspish 8 contrary, indocile, petulant, snappish 9 irritable 10 refractory 11 indomitable, intractable, quarrelsome 12 recalcitrant, ungovernable, unmanageable

fracturable 7 fragile 8 delicate, shattery 9 breakable

fracture 4 rent, rift, tear 5 break, cleft, crack, split 6 breach, schism 7 rupture, violate *combining form:* 7 rrhexis

Fra Diavolo composer 5 Auber

fragile 4 fine, thin, weak 5 crisp, frail, short 6 feeble, flimsy, infirm, slight, weakly 7 brittle, crumbly, crunchy, friable, slender, tenuous, unsound 8 decrepit, delicate, shattery

fragment 3 ace, bit, end, jot 4 atom, chip, iota, part, rive 5 burst, crumb, flake, grain, minim, piece, scrap, shard, sherd, shive, shred, smash, spall 6 morsel, shiver, sliver 7 flinder, shatter 8 particle, splinter, splitter 11 splinterize

fragmentary 4 part 6 broken 7 partial 10 fractional, incomplete 12 disorganized

fragrance 4 balm, odor 5 aroma, scent, smell, spice 7 bouquet, incense, perfume 9 redolence

fragrant 5 balmy, spicy, sweet 6 aromal, savory 7 perfumy 8 aromatic, perfumed, redolent 9 ambrosial, delicious

frail 4 puny, slim, thin, weak 5 petty 6 feeble, flimsy, infirm, sickly, slight, weakly 7 fragile, slender, tenuous, unsound 8 decrepit, delicate, shattery 9 breakable, frangible 11 fracturable, shatterable

frailty 3 sin 4 vice 5 fault 6 foible 7 failing 8 weakness 9 infirmity 11 tenuousness 12 imperfection

frame 4 body, form, make, mold, plan, sash 5 build, cause, draft, easel, erect, forge, shape, state, utter 6 cook up, deckle, devise, draw up, figure, invent, make up, system, vamp up 7 arrange, chassis, concoct, dream up, fashion, hatch up, imagine, prepare, produce 8 casement, conceive, contrive, regulate 9 cartouche, construct, fabricate, formulate *part:* 4 sill, stud 5 joist, plate

framework 4 rack 7 trestle 8 cribbing, cribwork, scaffold, skeleton, studding, studwork, trussing 9 structure *of crossed strips:* 7 lattice, trellis

France *ancient name:* 4 Gaul 6 Gallia *capital:* 5 Paris *combining form:* 5 Gallo *historic province:* 4 Foix 5 Anjou, Aunis, Bearn, Berry, Maine 6 Alsace, Artois, Marche, Poitou 7 Gascony, Guyenne, Picardy 8 Auvergne, Brittany, Burgundy, Dauphine, Flanders, Limousin, Lorraine, Lyonnais, Normandy, Provence, Touraine 9 Angoumois, Champagne, Languedoc, Nivernais, Orleanais, Saintonge, Venaissin 10 Roussillon 11 Bourbonnais, Ile de France 12 Franche Comte *monetary unit:* 5 franc

Francesca's lover 5 Paolo

franchise 4 vote 6 ballot 8 suffrage 9 exemption

frangible 7 brittle, fragile 8 delicate, shattery 9 breakable

frank 3 dog 4 fair, free, just, open 5 bluff, blunt, naive, plain 6 brazen, candid, direct, honest, hot dog, simple, single, wiener 7 natural, sincere, upright 8 man-to-man, unbiased 9 barefaced, impartial, ingenuous, outspoken 10 forthright, scrupulous, single-eyed, unmannered, unreserved 11 open-hearted, plainspoken, unconcealed, undisguised, uninhibited, unvarnished, wienerwurst

Frankenstein author 7 Shelley (Mary)

frankfurter 3 dog 6 hot dog, wiener 11 wienerwurst

Frankie's lover 6 Johnny

Frankish hero 6 Roland

Franklin *birthplace:* 6 Boston *invention:* 5 stove 8 bifocals *pen name:* 11 Poor Richard

frankness 6 candor 8 openness

frantic 3 mad 4 wild 5 rabid 6 insane 7 extreme, furious, violent 8 deranged, feverish, frenetic, frenzied 9 delirious, desperate 10 distraught

fraternal society 4 Elks 5 Moose 6 Eagles, Masons 10 Hibernians, Odd Fellows

fraternity 4 club 5 guild, order, union 6 league 7 company 10 fellowship 11 association, brotherhood 13 brotherliness

fraud 4 fake, hoax, sell, sham 5 cheat, faker, phony, trick 6 deceit, dupery, duping, humbug 7 chicane, defraud, swindle 8 impostor, trickery 9 chicanery, deception, fourberie, imposture, pretender 10 hanky-panky 11 bamboozling, highbinding, hoodwinking 13 bamboozlement, double-dealing, sharp practice

fraudulence 6 deceit 8 quackery, trickery 9 chicanery, deception, fourberie, phoniness 10 dishonesty

fraudulent 4 fake 5 false 7 crooked 8 cheating, guileful, quackish 9 deceitful, deceiving, deceptive, dishonest 10 fallacious

fray 3 row 4 fret 5 brawl, broil, brush, clash, fight, melee 6 combat, debate, strife, tumult 7 discord, dispute, quarrel, ruction, scuffle 8 skirmish 9 commotion, scrimmage 10 contention, dissension, donnybrook

frayed 4 worn 6 ragged 7 shreddy 10 threadbare

frazzle 4 fray, wear 5 upset 6 tucker 7 exhaust, outtire, outwear, wear out 8 knock out 9 prostrate

freak 3 bug, nut 4 whim 5 fancy, fiend, lusus 6 maniac, megrim, oddity, rarity, vagary, whimsy, zealot 7 anomaly, bou-tade, caprice, chimera, conceit, fanatic, monster, whimsey 8 crotchet, misshape, mutation, rara avis 9 androgyne, curiosity 10 aberration, enthusiast 11 abnormality, miscreation, monstrosity 12 malformation, whimsicality

freckle 3 dot 4 spot 7 ephelis, lentigo, speckle, stipple

free 3 lax, rid 4 open 5 clear, loose, round, unmew, unpen, untie, vocal 6 acquit, detach, exempt, gratis, loosen, ransom, redeem, rescue, unbind, uncurb, unpaid, untied, vagile 7 absolve, deliver, liberal, manumit, release, unbound, unchain, unclasp, unleash, unloose 8 autarkic, costless, detached, generous, handsome, liberate, released, separate, sui juris, unburden, unfasten, unloosen, untether 9 autarchic, bounteous, bountiful, delivered, discharge, disengage, exculpate, exonerate, extricate, liberated, outspoken, sovereign, unchained, unchecked, unshackle, unsparing 10 autonomous, chargeless, democratic, emancipate, gratuitous, heart-whole, munificent, openhanded, self-ruling, unconfined, unenslaved, unfettered, unshackled 11 affranchise, disencumber, disentangle, disenthrall, disimprison, emancipated, enfranchise, independent, untrammeled 12 enfranchised, unregimented, unrestrained, unrestricted 13 complimentary, self-directing, self-governing, unconstrained, unrecompensed, unremunerated

freebie 4 gift, pass 7 present 8 giveaway

freebooter 5 rover 6 bandit, bummer, pirate, raider, sea dog 7 brigand, cateran, corsair, forager, sea wolf 8 marauder, picaroon, pillager

freedom 4 ease 5 right, scope, sweep 7 compass, liberty, license, release 8 facility, immunity, latitude, vagility 9 exemption, privilege 10 generosity 11 magnanimity, prerogative 12 emancipation, independence

free-for-all 4 fray 5 brawl, broil, fight, melee, spree 6 affray, fracas 7 ruction 10 donnybrook

freehanded 7 liberal 8 generous 9 bounteous, bountiful, unsparing 10 munificent, openhanded

freeloader 5 leech 6 sponge 8 barnacle, hanger-on, parasite 12 lounge lizard

freeman 4 carl 5 carle, churl, thane, thegn 6 yeoman 7 burgess, burgher, citizen

Free State 8 Maryland

free ticket 4 pass 11 Annie Oakley

freezing 3 icy 4 cold 5 chill, gelid, nippy 6 arctic, chilly, frigid, frosty 7 glacial, shivery *combining form:* 3 cry 4 cryo, kryo

freight 4 haul, load 5 cargo 6 burden, charge, lading 7 payload 9 transport

French *article:* 2 la, le, un 3 les, une *attendant:* 9 concierge *back:* 3 dos *bed:* 3 lit 6 couche *boy:* 6 garçon *brother:* 5 frère *cap:* 5 beret *cardinal:* 7 Mazarin 9 Richelieu *castle:* 7 château *cathedral city:* 5 Paris, Reims, Rouen 6 Amiens, Nantes, Rheims 8 Chartres *clergyman:* 4 abbé, curé, père *combining form:* 5 Gallo 6 Franco *conjunction:* 2 et, ou 4 mais *couturier:* 4 Dior 5 Patou 6 Chanel 7 Balmain 8 Givenchy 9 Courrèges, St. Laurent *daughter:* 5 fille *day:* 5 jeudi, lundi, mardi 6 samedi 8 dimanche, mercredi, vendredi *dear:* 4 cher *department head:* 7 prefect *dream:* 4 rêve *dynasty:* 5 Capet 6 Valois 7 Bourbon *egg:* 4 oeuf *emblem:* 10 fleur-de-lis *empress:* 7 Eugénie 9 Joséphine *exclamation:* 3 zut 4 eheu, hein 9 sacrebleu *farewell:* 5 adieu 8 au revoir *father:* 4 père *forest:* 7 Argonne, Belleau *friend:* 3 ami 4 amie *game:* 3 jeu 4 jeux (plural) *God:* 4 dieu *good:* 3 bon *hat:* 7 chapeau *here:* 3 ici *income:* 5 rente *king:* 3 roi *language:* 9 Provençal *month:* 3 mai 4 août, juin, mars, mois 5 avril 7 février, janvier, juillet *mother:* 4 mère *national anthem:* 12 Marseillaise *opera:* 5 Faust, Lakmé, Manon, Thaïs 6 Carmen, Mignon 7 Werther *pancake:* 5 crêpe *pastry:* 6 éclair 8 napoleon *patron saint:* 4 Denis *policeman:* 4 flic 8 gendarme *porcelain:* 6 Sèvres 7 Limoges *preposition:* 2 de 3 par, sur 4 avec, dans, pour, sans, sous *pretty:* 4 joli 5 jolie *prison:* 8 Bastille *pronoun:* 2 il, je, te, tu, un 3 eux, ils, mes, moi, toi, une 4 elle, nous, vous *Protestant:* 6 Calvin 8 Huguenot *pupil:* 5 élève *queen:* 5 reine *rabbit:* 5 lapin *railroad station:* 4 gare *resort:* 3 Pau 4 Nice 5 Vichy 6 Cannes, Menton 7 Antibes 8 Biarritz *resort area:* 7 Riviera *restaurant:* 6 bistro *revolutionist:* 5 Marat 6 Danton *Revolution party:* 7 Gironde, Jacobin 8 Mountain *Revolution song:* 5 Caira *saint:* 4 Joan 6 Martin *school:* 5 école, lycée *sea:* 3 mer *season:* 3 été 5 hiver 7 automne 9 printemps *servant:* 5 valet *shop:* 8 boutique *shrine:* 7 Lourdes *singer:* 4 Piaf 8 chanteur 9 chanteuse *sister:* 5 soeur *small:* 5 petit 6 petite *soldier:* 5 poilu 6 soldat, Zouave 8 chasseur *son:* 4 fils *star:* 6 étoile *state:* 4 état *stock exchange:* 6 bourse *street:* 3 rue *subway:* 5 metro *there!:* 5 voilà *too much:* 4 trop *very:* 4 très *waiter:* 6 garçon *wartime capital:* 5 Vichy *water:* 3 eau *well:* 4 bien *wineshop:* 6 bistro *wood:* 4 bois *yesterday:* 4 hier

frenetic 3 mad 4 wild 5 crazy, rabid 6 hectic 7 frantic, furious, violent 8 frenzied 9 delirious

frenzied see **frenetic**

frenzy 3 mad 4 amok, fury, rage 5 amuck, craze, furor, mania 6 madden 7 derange, madness, unhinge 8 delirium, distract, insanity 9 unbalance *of a bull elephant:* 4 must 5 musth

frequency unit 5 hertz 7 fresnel

frequent 5 haunt, often, usual, visit 6 affect, attend, common, infest, resort 7 hang out, overrun 8 everyday, familiar, habitual 9 customary 10 hang around

frequenter 6 denizen, habitué, haunter

fresh 3 new, raw 4 anew, bold, else, more, pert, pure, rude, wise 5 added, alive, brisk, crude, green, naive, nervy, novel, other, renew, sassy, saucy, smart, sweet, vital, vivid, young 6 bright, callow, cheeky, lively, modern, recent, unused 7 another, artless, farther, forward, further, natural, uncouth, untried 8 gleaming, impudent, neoteric, original, striking, unversed, virginal, youthful 9 new-sprung, sparkling, unspoiled 10 additional, glistening, newfangled, unseasoned 11 impertinent, modernistic, smart-alecky, unpracticed 12 invigorating, new-fashioned 13 inexperienced

freshet 5 flood, spate

freshman 4 colt, tyro 5 frosh, plebe 6 novice, rookie 8 beginner, neophyte, newcomer 9 novitiate 10 apprentice, tenderfoot

fret 3 irk, nag, rub, vex 4 cark, fray, fume, fuss, gall, gnaw, mope, stew, wear 5 annoy, brood, chafe, grate, ravel, worry 6 abrade, bother, cockle, dimple, dither, harass, nettle, plague, pother, rankle, riffle, ruffle 7 agitate, corrode, disturb, provoke, roughen, torment 8 exercise, irritate 9 excoriate 10 irritation

fretful 5 angry, cross, huffy, waspy 7 carping, chafing, peevish, pettish, waspish 8 captious, caviling, contrary, critical, perverse, petulant, restless, snappish 9 fractious, impatient, irascible, irritable, querulous, unpatient 12 faultfinding

Frey *father:* 5 Njord 6 Njorth *sister:* 5 Freya *wife:* 4 Gerd 5 Gerda, Gerth

Freya *brother:* 4 Frey *father:* 5 Njord 6 Njorth *husband:* 4 Odin

friable 5 crisp, mealy, short 7 crumbly, crunchy

fribble 5 dizzy, giddy, light 7 flighty, trifler 8 trifling 9 frivolous 11 harebrained, lightheaded

friction 7 discord, rubbing 8 abrasion 9 attrition 10 disharmony, dissension, resistance 12 disagreement

friction match 5 vesta 7 lucifer 8 locofoco

Friday's rescuer 6 Crusoe
friend 3 aid, pal 4 ally, chum, mate
5 buddy, crony, matey, serve 7 comrade,
partner 8 alter ego, compadre, familiar, intimate, playmate, sidekick 9 associate, colleague, companion, confidant 10 confi-
dante 11 cater-cousin 12 acquaintance
French: 3 ami 4 amie *Scottish:* 3 eme
Spanish: 5 amiga, amigo
Friend 6 Quaker *founder:* 3 Fox
friendly 5 close, pally 6 amical, chummy,
loving 7 affable, amiable, cordial, devoted
8 amicable, amicably, familiar, intimate,
sociable 9 congenial, favorable, receptive
10 harmonious, hospitable 11 sympathetic
12 affectionate, well-disposed
Friendly Islands 5 Tonga
friends 4 kith
friendship 5 amity 6 accord, comity,
fusion, league 7 concord, empathy, harmony 8 affinity, alliance, goodwill 9 coalition 10 attraction, consonance, federation,
kindliness 11 benevolence
frigate bird 3 ioa, iwa 8 alcatras *genus:*
7 Fregata
Frigga, Frigg *husband:* 4 Odin *son:*
6 Balder
fright 3 awe 4 fear, mess 5 alarm, dread,
panic, scare, shock 6 dismay, horror, terror 7 eyesore, startle, terrify 9 terrorize,
trepidity 11 trepidation
frighten 3 awe, cow 4 faze 5 alarm,
daunt, scare, shock, unman, upset 6 affray,
appall, dismay 7 agitate, astound, horrify,
perturb, startle, terrify, unnerve 8 affright,
browbeat, bulldoze, disquiet 9 terrorize
10 demoralize, discompose, disconcert,
intimidate
frightful 4 grim 5 awful, scary 6 horrid
7 fearful, ghastly, hideous 8 alarming,
dreadful, fearsome, horrible, horrific, shocking, terrible, terrific 9 appalling 10 formidable, horrendous
frigid 3 icy 4 cold, cool, dull 5 bleak, chill
6 arctic, chilly, frosty 7 glacial, hostile,
insipid 8 freezing 9 inhibited 10 undersexed 11 emotionless, indifferent, passionless, unemotional 12 unresponsive
frill 3 air 5 jabot, luxus, ruche 6 luxury, ruffle 7 amenity, flounce, ruching 8 furbelow
11 affectation, superfluity 12 extravagance
fringe 3 hem, rim 4 brim 5 bound, brink,
skirt, verge 6 border, define, edging, margin 7 fimbria 8 surround, trimming
9 perimeter, periphery
frippery 6 finery 7 bravery, regalia
8 trumpery 9 full dress 10 Sunday best
11 ostentation
frisk 4 leap, romp, skip 5 caper, dance
6 cavort, curvet, frolic, gambol, search
7 disport, rollick 9 shake down

frisky 3 gay 5 antic 6 feisty, lively 7 larkish, playful, waggish 8 gamesome, prankish, sportive 9 kittenish 10 frolicsome
fritter 4 blow 5 shred, spend, waste
7 consume 8 cast away, diminish, disperse,
fool away, fragment, squander 9 dissipate,
throw away 10 trifle away
frivolity 3 fun 4 game, jest, play 5 sport
6 levity, toying 8 dallying, flirting, nonsense,
trifling 9 flippancy, lightness 10 coquet-
ting 11 flightiness
frivolous 3 gay 5 dizzy, giddy, light, silly
6 toyish 7 flighty, playful, shallow, trivial
8 carefree, careless, heedless 10 bird-witted, unprofound 11 empty-headed, harebrained, superficial 13 rattlebrained
frog 4 toad 5 ranid 6 anuran 9 amphibian 10 batrachian *combining form:* 4 rani
7 batrach 8 batracho 9 batrachus *family:*
7 Ranidae *genus:* 4 Rana *kind:* 4 hyla
6 peeper 8 bullfrog, tree toad *larva:* 7 tadpole *relating to:* 6 ranine
frogmouth 8 morepork
frolic 3 fun, gay 4 hell, lark, riot, romp
5 caper, dance, frisk, merry, party, prank,
revel, sport, spree, trick 6 cavort, didoes,
gaiety, gambol, prance, shines 7 carouse,
disport, roister, rollick, wassail 9 merriment 10 shenanigan, tomfoolery
frolicsome 3 gay 5 antic 6 frisky, impish
7 coltish, playful, roguish, waggish 8 sportive 9 sprightly 10 rollicking
11 mischievous
from *French, Portuguese, Spanish:* 2 de
German: 3 von *Italian:* 2 da *Scottish:*
4 frae
frondeur 5 rebel 6 anarch 8 mutineer,
revolter 9 anarchist, dissident, insurgent
10 malcontent
front 3 bow, van 4 brow, dare, defy, face,
fore, look, mask, meet, prow, show, veil
5 beard, blind, brave, close, color, put-on
6 accost, before, facade, facing 7 forward,
outdare, outface, venture 8 anterior, coloring, disguise, forehead 9 challenge, encounter 10 appearance, figurehead 11 countenance *combining form:* 6 antero *prefix:*
3 pro
frontier 4 back, bush 5 march 6 border,
remote, sticks 8 backland, backwash,
boundary 9 backwater, backwoods, bordering, marchland, unsettled, up-country
10 borderland, hinterland, outlandish
11 backcountry, exploratory
12 conterminous
frontiersman 5 Boone, Clark 6 Carson
7 pioneer, settler 8 Crockett
10 bushranger
fronton game 7 jai alai
front-rank 5 prime 6 Grade A 8 five-star,
superior, top-notch 9 excellent, first-rate,

top-drawer **10** blue-ribbon, first-class **11** first-string

frontward 8 anterior

frost 4 hoar **6** freeze *combining form:* **4** crym **5** crymo

frostfish 5 smelt **6** tomcod

frost heave 5 pingo

frosting 5 icing **7** topping

frosty 3 icy **4** cold, cool, rimy **5** chill, gelid, hoary, nippy **6** chilly, frigid **7** glacial, shivery **8** freezing, reserved **10** unfriendly

froth 4 barm, foam, scum, suds, vent **5** spume, yeast **6** lather, levity **9** flippancy, frivolity, lightness

froward 5 balky, cross **6** ornery **7** peevish, restive **8** contrary, perverse, petulant **10** refractory **11** disobedient

frown 4 pout, sulk **5** glare, gloom, lower, scowl **6** glower, object **7** grimace **8** disfavor **9** deprecate, disesteem **10** disapprove

frowsy 3 lax **4** mean, rank **5** dowdy, funky, fusty, musty, slack, stale **6** blowsy, remiss, shabby, smelly, sordid **7** noisome, reeking, squalid, unkempt **8** slattern, slovenly, stinking **9** negligent **10** disheveled, disordered, malodorous, neglectful, slatternly **13** draggletailed

frozen 4 hard **5** fixed, frore, gelid, rigid, stiff **6** chilly, frigid **7** chilled **8** benumbed, immobile **9** congealed, impassive, petrified **10** mechanical, unyielding **12** refrigerated

frugal 4 mean, wary **5** canny, chary, spare **6** saving, scanty, Scotch **7** careful, prudent, sparing, thrifty **8** discreet, stinting **9** scrimping, stewardly **10** conserving, economical, meticulous, preserving, unwasteful **12** cheeseparing, parsimonious **13** penny-pinching

frugality 6 thrift **7** economy **8** prudence **9** husbandry **10** providence **11** thriftiness

fruit 5 issue, young **6** result **7** progeny **9** offspring *citrus:* **4** lime **5** lemon **6** citron, orange, pomelo **7** kumquat, tangelo **8** bergamot, mandarin, shaddock **9** tangerine **10** calamondin, grapefruit *combining form:* **4** carp **5** carpo **6** carpia (plural), carpic, carpus, fructi **7** carpium, carpous *decay:* **4** blet *dried:* **5** prune **6** raisin *drink:.* **3** ade **5** juice, punch **7** syconia (plural) **8** syconium *hard-shelled:* **3** nut **4** seed **5** gourd **7** coconut *residue:* **4** marc **6** pomace *seed:* **3** pip *study of:* **8** pomology **9** carpology *subtropical:* **3** fig **4** date, lime **5** lemon, olive **6** citron, orange **7** avocado, kumquat **9** tangerine **10** grapefruit *sugar:* **7** glucose **8** fructose, levulose *temperate zone:* **4** pear, plum, sloe **5** apple, grape, melon, peach, prune **6** casaba, cherry, loquat, quince **7** apricot, azarole, currant **8** dewberry **9** blueberry, cranberry, muskmelon, nectarine, raspberry **10** black-

berry, gooseberry, loganberry, strawberry **11** boysenberry, huckleberry, pomegranate *tropical:* **5** guava, mango **6** ajowan, banana, papaya **7** acerola **8** breadnut, rambutan, tamarind **9** cherimoya, persimmon, pineapple **10** calamondin, mangosteen *type:* **3** nut **4** pepo, pome **5** berry, drupe **6** achene, legume, loment, samara **7** capsule, cypsela, silicle, silique, utricle **11** hesperidium *undeveloped:* **6** nubbin *woody:* **8** xylocarp

fruit basket 8 calathos, calathus

fruitful 4 rich **6** fecund **7** fertile **8** abundant, breeding, childing, prolific, spawning **9** abounding, plenteous, plentiful **10** productive **11** proliferant, propagating, reproducing

fruition 3 joy **7** delight, joyance **8** pleasure **9** enjoyment **10** attainment, conclusion **11** achievement, delectation, fulfillment, realization

fruitless 4 vain **6** barren, foiled, futile **7** sterile, useless **8** abortive, thwarted **9** infertile **10** unavailing **11** ineffective, ineffectual, infructuous, unavailable **12** unproductive, unprofitable

frumpy 4 drab, dull **5** dowdy, tacky **6** stodgy **8** outmoded **9** out-of-date, unstylish

frustrate 3 bar **4** balk, beat, bilk, dash, foil, halt, lick, null, ruin, vain **5** annul, block, check, cross, elude **6** arrest, baffle, blight, cancel, defeat, forbid, hinder, impede, outwit, thwart **7** buffalo, conquer, inhibit, nullify, prevent, redress **8** confound, negative, obstruct, overcome, preclude, prohibit **9** cancel out, checkmate, forestall, interrupt **10** circumvent, counteract, disappoint, neutralize

fry 5 sauté **6** sizzle

frying pan 6 spider **7** griddle, skillet

fuddle 5 mix up **6** ball up, jumble, muddle, tipple **7** confuse, fluster, stupefy **8** bewilder, distract, throw off **10** intoxicate

fuddy-duddy 4 fogy **5** Blimp, fussy **6** fogram, fossil, square **7** fusspot **8** mossback, outdated **10** fuss-budget **12** antediluvian, Colonel Blimp, mid-Victorian, stuffed shirt **13** stick-in-the-mud

fudge 3 pad **4** blur, bosh, fake **5** cheat, color, dodge, hedge, hooey, welsh **6** bunkum **7** distort, hogwash, magnify, traddle **8** contrive, nonsense, overdraw **9** embellish, embroider, overpaint, overstate, poppycock **10** exaggerate, overcharge

fuel 3 gas, oil **4** coal, coke, food, peat, wood **5** stoke **6** petrol **7** support **8** charcoal, gasoline, hypergol, kerosene **9** petroleum, stimulate **13** reinforcement

fugacious 6 flying **7** passing **8** fleeting,

volatile **9** ephemeral, momentary, transient **10** evanescent, short-lived, transitory

fugitive 2 DP **5** exile **6** emigré, outlaw **7** evacuee, lamster, passing, refugee, runaway **8** deserter, fleeting, vagabond, volatile **9** ephemeral, momentary, transient **10** evanescent, perishable, short-lived, transitory

fugue master 4 Bach

Führer, der 6 Hitler

fulfill 4 fill, meet **6** answer, effect, finish **7** achieve, execute, perform, satisfy **8** complete **9** discharge, implement **10** accomplish, effectuate

fulgent 6 bright **7** beaming, radiant, shining **8** luminous **9** brilliant

full 3 big **5** awash, jaded, plumb, round, sated, total, whole **6** choate, entire, gorged, jammed, loaded, minute, packed **7** brimful, copious, crammed, crowded, glutted, orotund, perfect, replete, satiate, stuffed, teeming **8** brimming, complete, detailed, integral, itemized, satiated, thorough **9** abounding, clocklike, jam-packed, plentiful, surfeited

full-blooded 4 rich **5** flush, ruddy **6** ardent, florid **7** flushed, genuine, glowing **8** forceful, pedigree, purebred, rubicund, sanguine **9** impelling, pedigreed, pureblood **12** thoroughbred

full bloom 8 anthesis

full-blown 4 lush, ripe **5** adult, total **6** allout, mature **7** grown-up, matured, ripened **9** unlimited **12** totalitarian

full-bodied 5 lusty, stout **6** potent, robust, strong **9** corpulent **11** substantial

full-bosomed 5 busty, buxom **6** chesty

full dress 6 finery **7** bravery, regalia **8** frippery **10** Sunday best

full-figured 6 zaftig, zoftig

full-fledged 4 ripe **5** adult, grown **6** mature **7** genuine, grown-up, matured, ripened **12** card-carrying

full-grown 4 ripe **5** adult **6** mature **7** matured, ripened

fullness 5 scope **6** plenty **7** breadth, satiety **9** abundance, amplitude, repletion **10** perfection **12** completeness

full of suffix: 3 ose, ous **4** ious

full-scale 5 total **6** all-out **8** complete **9** unlimited **12** totalitarian

full tilt 4 fast **7** flat-out, hastily, quickly, rapidly, swiftly **8** speedily **9** posthaste **12** lickety-split **13** expeditiously

fulsome 3 fat **4** full, glib, oily **5** bland, plump, slick, soapy, suave **6** lavish, sating, smarmy, smooth **7** buttery, canting, cloying, copious, profuse **8** abundant, unctious, unctuous **9** bombastic, excessive, exuberant, repulsive, satiating, sickening, wheedling **10** disgusting, flattering, nauseating, oleaginous **11** extravagant, oily-tongued,

pharisaical **12** honey-mouthed, honeytongued, hypocritical, ingratiating, magniloquent, mealy-mouthed, pecksniffian

Fulton's steamboat 8 Clermont

fumble 3 paw **4** feel, flub, mess, muff **5** botch, error, grope **6** bobble, bollix, bungle, goof up, muddle, mumble, murmur, mutter **7** blunder, louse up, misplay, swallow **8** flounder

fume 4 boil, burn, odor, rage, reek, snit, stew **5** anger, smoke, sweat, tizzy, vapor **6** blow up, seethe, swivet **7** bristle, flare up **8** boil over **10** exhalation

fun 3 gag, kid, rag, rib **4** fool, game, glee, jest, joke, josh, play, razz **5** jolly, mirth, sport **6** banter, gaiety **7** disport, jollity, teasing, whoopee **8** hilarity, mischief, ridicule **9** amusement, diversion, high jinks, horseplay, jocundity, joviality, merriment **10** blitheness, pleasantry, recreation **13** entertainment

function 2 do, go **3** act, job, run, use **4** duty, goal, mark, role, take, task, work **5** power, react, serve **6** affair, behave, object, office, target **7** concern, faculty, operate, perform, purpose, service **8** activity, behavior, business, ceremony, occasion, province **9** objective, officiate, operation **suffix: 2** cy **3** ure **trigonometric: 4** sine **6** cosine, secant **7** tangent **8** cosecant **9** cotangent

functional 5 handy, utile **6** useful **7** working **9** practical **11** practicable, serviceable, utilitarian **12** occupational

functioning 4 live **5** alive **6** active **7** dynamic **9** operative

fund 4 pool **5** endow, stock, store **6** supply **7** capital, finance, reserve **9** inventory, subsidize **10** accumulate

fundament 4 beam, rear, rump, seat **6** behind, bottom **8** backside, buttocks, derriere **9** posterior **10** foundation

fundamental 3 law **4** pure **5** axiom, basal, basic, prime, vital **6** bottom, factor, primal **7** needful, primary, radical, theorem **8** cardinal, dominant **9** component, essential, formative, important, necessary, paramount, primitive, principal, principle, requisite **10** elementary, primordial, principium, substratal, underlying **11** constituent, irreducible **12** constitutive, foundational

fundamentalist 4 tory **5** right **7** diehard **8** old liner, standpat **11** bitter-ender, rightwinger, standpatter **12** conservative

fundamental nature 7 essence

fund-raiser 6 dinner **8** telethon

funeral 6 burial **car: 6** hearse **director: 9** mortician **10** undertaker **oration: 6** eulogy **8** encomium **9** panegyric **procession: 6** exequy **7** cortege **service:**

7 requiem **9** obsequies *song:* **5** dirge, elegy **7** epicede **8** threnody **9** epicedium

funereal 4 back **5** bleak, grave **6** dismal, dreary, gloomy, solemn, somber **8** mournful **10** depressing, depressive, lugubrious, oppressive **13** disheartening

fungus 4 cepe, mold, rust, smut **5** ergot, morel, yeast **6** agaric, bolete, mildew **7** amanita, truffle **8** mushroom, polypore, puffball **9** earthstar, stinkhorn, toadstool **10** champignon **11** chanterelle *combining form:* **3** myc **4** myco **5** myces, mycet **6** mycete, myceto **7** mycetes *part:* **3** cap **4** gill, umbo **5** ascus, gleba, hypha, stipe, volva **7** annulus, cortina **8** basidium, conidium, mycelium

fungus disease 3 rot **4** mold, rust, scab, smut **5** ergot, tinea **6** blight, mildew, thrush **7** mycosis **8** lumpy jaw, ringworm **12** athlete's foot *suffix:* **4** oses (plural), osis

funk 4 odor, rage, reek **5** dread, panic, smell, stink **6** coward, craven, flinch, stench **7** chicken, dastard, quitter, shirker **8** poltroon **11** yellowbelly

funky 4 foul, rank **5** musty, stale **6** frowsy, smelly **7** noisome, panicky, reeking **8** stinking **10** malodorous

funnel 4 pipe **5** carry, widen **6** convey, narrow, siphon **7** conduct, traject **8** transmit

funny 3 odd **4** zany **5** antic, comic, droll, fishy, queer **6** sneaky **7** amusing, bizarre, comical, jocular, risible, strange **8** farcical, gelastic, humorous **9** facetious, fantastic, grotesque, laughable, ludicrous **10** ridiculous **11** underhanded

funnyman 3 wag, wit **5** comic, droll, joker **6** jester **8** comedian, humorist, jokester, quipster

fur 4 down, fell, flue, hide, lint, pelt, pile, skin **5** floss, fluff, stole **6** jacket, pelage, peltry *kind:* **3** fox **4** mink, seal **5** fitch, otter, sable **6** ermine, fisher, marten, nutria, tanuki **7** raccoon **10** chinchilla *lamb:* **6** galyak, mouton **7** caracul, karakul, krimmer **9** broadtail *medieval:* **4** vair **7** miniver

furbish 3 rub **4** buff **5** glaze, gloss, shine **6** glance, polish, revive **7** burnish **8** renovate

Furies 6 Alecto **7** Erinyes, Megaera **9** Eumenides, Tisiphone

furious 3 mad **4** wild **5** angry, dirty, hasty, irate, rabid, rough, upset **6** crazed, fierce, insane, maniac, raging, stormy **7** enraged, excited, extreme, fanatic, frantic, intense, violent **8** blustery, demented, feverish, frenetic, frenzied, furibund, incensed, maddened, provoked, terrible, vehement, vigorous, wrathful **9** desperate, energetic, excessive, exquisite, fanatical, impetuous, turbulent **10** bewildered, blustering, boister-

ous, corybantic, distracted, hysterical, infuriated, inordinate, irrational

furl 4 curl, fold, roll, wrap **5** cover **6** enfold **7** wrinkle

furnace 4 kiln, oven **5** forge, stove **6** heater **7** smelter **8** bloomery, tryworks **11** incinerator *part:* **4** port, vent **5** bocca **6** trompe, tuyere *tender:* **6** stoker

furnish 3 arm, rig **4** feed, gear, give, hand, lend **5** array, dower, endow, endue, equip, mount, yield **6** afford, clothe, fit out, outfit, supply **7** apparel, appoint, deliver, provide, turn out **8** accouter, dispense, hand over, transfer, turn over **10** contribute

furnishings 4 gear **5** decor **9** equipment, trappings

furniture 8 equipage, hardware **9** equipment **10** furnishing *style:* **4** Adam **6** Empire **8** Colonial, Sheraton **11** chinoiserie, Chippendale, Hepplewhite

furniture designer *American:* **5** Phyfe **7** Goddard, Haldane *British:* **6** Morris **7** Gibbons, Shearer **8** Sheraton **11** Chippendale, Hepplewhite *French:* **5** Marot **6** Boulle *Scottish:* **4** Adam

furor 3 ado, cry, fad **4** chic, coil, fury, mode, rage, stir, to-do **5** craze, mania, style, vogue, whirl **6** bustle, flurry, frenzy, pother, ruckus, rumpus, uproar **7** fashion, madness, shindig **8** foofaraw **9** commotion, whirlpool, whirlwind **10** dernier cri

furore 4 stir **5** craze **6** uproar **11** controversy

furrow 3 rut **4** fold, plow, ruck **5** plica, ridge, rivel, stria, sulci (plural) **6** cleave, course, crease, groove, rimple, striae (plural), sulcus, trench **7** channel, crinkle, wrinkle **11** corrugation

furrowed 6 rugose **7** sulcate **8** sulcated, wrinkled **10** corrugated

further 3 new **4** abet, also, else, help, more, then **5** added, again, fresh, serve **6** beyond **7** advance, besides, forward, promote **8** engender, generate, moreover **9** encourage, propagate **10** additional, in addition **12** additionally

furthermore 3 and, too, yea, yet **4** also **5** along **6** as well, withal **7** besides **8** likewise, moreover

furthermost 7 extreme **8** farthest, remotest

furthest 6 utmost **7** extreme, outmost **9** outermost, uttermost

furtive 3 sly **4** foxy, wary, wily **5** catty **6** artful, covert, crafty, feline, masked, secret, shifty, sneaky, stolen, tricky **7** catlike, cloaked, cunning, sub-rosa **8** cautious, guileful, hush-hush, scheming, stealthy **9** disguised, insidious **11** calculating, circumspect, clandestine **12** hugger-mugger

13 surreptitious, under-the-table *look:*
4 peek, peep
furuncle 4 boil 7 abscess
fury 3 ire, mad 4 rage 5 anger, wrath
6 frenzy 7 madness, passion 8 acerbity,
acrimony, afflatus, asperity, violence
9 vehemence 11 indignation
furze 4 whin 5 gorse *genus:* 4 Ulex
7 Genista
fuse 3 mix, run 4 flux, frit, meld, melt,
thaw, weld 5 blend, merge, smelt, unify,
unite 6 anneal, mingle, solder 7 compact,
liquefy 8 dissolve, intermix, liquesce 9 integrate 10 amalgamate, deliquesce, interblend 11 consolidate, incorporate
fusillade 4 hail 5 burst, salvo 6 shower,
volley 7 barrage 8 drumfire 9 broadside
11 bombardment
fusion 5 alloy, blend, union 6 merger
7 amalgam, mixture 8 compound 9 admixture, coalition, immixture, synthesis *combining form:* 3 zyg 4 zygo
fuss 3 ado, nag, row 4 cark, coil, crab, flap,
fret, kick, miff, stew, stir, to-do, wail, yaup
5 annoy, bleat, fight, gripe, haste, hurry,
speed, upset, whine, whirl, worry 6 bother,
bustle, carp at, flurry, hassle, hurrah, murmur, peck at, pother, putter, racket, repine,
ruckus, rumpus, shindy, squawk, yammer
7 agitate, dispute, fluster, henpeck, protest,
quarrel, shindig 8 complain 9 bickering,
commotion, complaint, objection, whirlpool,
whirlwind 11 controversy 12 perturbation
fussbudget 8 stickler 10 fuddy-duddy
12 precisionist 13 perfectionist

fussy 4 nice 5 exact, picky 6 dainty, lively,
ornate 7 careful, fidgety, finical, finicky, fretful, heedful 8 bustling, hustling 9 finicking,
irritable, querulous, squeamish 10 fastidious, meticulous, particular, pernickety, scrupulous 11 painstaking, persnickety, punctilious 13 conscientious
fustian 4 rant 7 bombast, pompous, useless 8 feckless, rhapsody, rhetoric
9 worthless 10 unpurposed 11 exaggerated, highfalutin, meaningless, purposeless
fusty 4 rank 5 close, dated, fetid, moldy,
musty, passé, stale 6 bygone, filthy, old hat,
putrid, rancid, sloppy, smelly 7 archaic, noisome, squalid, unkempt 8 outdated
10 antiquated, disheveled, malodorous
12 old-fashioned
futile 4 idle, vain 5 empty 6 hollow, otiose 7 useless 8 abortive, bootless, hopeless, nugatory 9 frivolous, fruitless, worthless 10 inadequate, unavailing 11 ineffective, ineffectual, inefficient 12 insufficient,
unprevailing, unproductive, unsuccessful
future 4 to-be 5 later 6 offing 7 by-and-
by 9 afterward, hereafter 10 subsequent
Futurism *founder:* 9 Marinetti *painter:*
5 Ballo, Carra 7 Russolo 8 Boccioni, Severini *sculptor:* 8 Boccioni
fuzz 3 nap 4 blur, down, flue, lint, pile
5 floss, fluff
fuzzy 3 dim 5 faint, vague 6 bleary, blurry,
frizzy 7 blurred, muddled, obscure, shadowy, unclear 8 confused 9 undefined
10 ill-defined, incoherent, indefinite, indistinct 12 inconclusive
fylfot 8 swastika

G

Gaal's father 4 Ebed

gab see **gabble**

gabbard 4 scow, ship 5 barge 7 lighter

gabber 6 magpie, prater 7 blabber 8 jabberer, prattler 9 bandar-log, blabmouth, chatterer 10 chatterbox

gabble 3 gab, jaw, yak 4 chat, talk 5 clack, drool, prate 6 drivel, gibber, gossip, jabber 7 blabber, blather, chatter, palaver, prattle, twaddle 9 yakety-yak

gabby 5 talky 6 chatty 9 garrulous, talkative 10 babblative, loquacious 11 loose-lipped 12 loose-tongued

gaberdine 4 coat, suit 5 cloth, cover, smock 7 garment

gable 4 wall 8 pediment *ornament:* 6 finial

Gabon *capital:* 10 Libreville *monetary unit:* 5 franc

gad 3 bat 4 band, roam, rope, rove 5 mooch, range, stray 6 ramble, wander 7 maunder, traipse 9 gallivant

Gad *brother:* 5 Asher *father:* 5 Jacob *mother:* 6 Zilpah *son:* 3 Eri 5 Ezbon, Haggi

gadfly 4 pest 6 bother, critic

gadget 4 tool 5 gizmo 6 device, dingus, doodad, hickey, jigger, widget 7 concern, dofunny, gimmick, utensil 9 apparatus, appliance, doohickey, rigamajig 11 contraption, thingamajig, thingumajig

Gadi's son 7 Menahem

gadwall 4 duck

Gaea 2 Ge *husband:* 6 Uranus *offspring:* 6 Giants, Titans, Typhon, Uranus 8 Erinyes 8 Cyclopes *parent:* 5 Chaos

Gaelic 4 Erse 5 Irish 6 Celtic 8 Scottish *god:* 3 Ler 5 Dagda *hero:* 5 Oisin 6 Ossian 11 Finn MacCool *king:* 9 Conchobar, Conchobor *language:* 4 Manx *poem:* 7 aisling *poet:* 4 bard, fili 6 Ossian *queen:* 4 Medb *soldier:* 4 kern 6 Fenian *spirit:* 7 banshee *tale:* 4 tain

gaff 3 fix 4 hoax, hook, spar, spur 5 abuse, fraud, trick 6 clamor, fleece, outcry, uproar 7 gimmick

gaffe 5 boner, break 7 blooper, faux pas 8 solecism 9 indecorum 11 impropriety

gag 3 jib, shy 4 balk, hoax, jape, jest, joke, keck, quip, ruse, wile 5 choke, crack, demur, heave, retch, sally, stick, trick 6 boggle, muzzle, strain 9 wisecrack, witticism

gage 6 pledge 8 security; (see also **gauge**)

Gaham *father:* 5 Nahor *mother:* 6 Reumah

Gaheris *brother:* 6 Gareth, Gawain *father:* 3 Lot *mother:* 8 Margawse, Morgause *uncle:* 6 Arthur *victim:* 8 Margawse, Morgause

gaiety 3 joy 4 glee 5 mirth, revel 7 jollity, revelry, whoopee 8 gladness, hilarity, radiance, reveling, vivacity 9 animation, festivity, geniality, happiness, merriment, revelment 10 liveliness 11 merrymaking

gain 3 get, net, win 4 earn, have, land, make, mend, reap 5 annex, clear, lucre, reach, score 6 attain, look up, obtain, perk up, pick up, profit, rack up, return, secure 7 achieve, acquire, bring in, clean up, improve, procure, realize 8 draw down, earnings, proceeds, windfall 9 knock down 10 accomplish

gainful 4 good, rich 6 paying 8 fruitful 9 lucrative 10 productive, profitable, satisfying, well-paying, worthwhile

gainly 8 graceful, pleasing

gainsay 4 deny 5 cross, fight 6 combat, impugn, negate, oppose, resist 7 dispute, subvert 8 disprove, negative, traverse 9 disaffirm, withstand 10 contradict, contravene, controvert

Gainsborough painting 7 Blue Boy

gait 3 run 4 lope, pace, rate, step, trot, walk 5 speed, strut 6 canter, gallop

gaiter 4 boot, shoe 8 overshoe

gala 3 gay 4 fair, fete 5 merry, party 6 festal, lively 7 festive 8 festival 9 festivity 11 celebration

Galahad *father:* 8 Lancelot 9 Launcelot *mother:* 6 Elaine *quest:* 9 Holy Grail

Galatea *father:* 6 Nereus *husband:* 9 Pygmalion *lover:* 4 Acis *mother:* 5 Doris

galaxy 6 nebula 8 Milky Way

Galba *predecessor:* 4 Nero *successor:* 4 Otho

gale 4 blow, gust, wind 5 blast, storm 6 squall 7 tempest 8 outburst 9 hurricane

Galen's forte 8 medicine

galilee 5 porch 6 chapel 7 portico

Galilee *town:* 4 Cana 7 Gergesa 8 Nazareth, Tiberias 9 Bethsaida, Capernaum

Galileo's birthplace 4 Pisa

gall 3 get, irk, rub, vex 4 face, fray, fret, rile, roil, wear 5 annoy, brass, chafe, cheek, chide, erode, grate, graze, harry, nerve, scurr, worry 6 abrade, bother, burn up, harass, ruffle, scrape 7 conceit, corrade, disturb, frazzle, inflame, provoke, scratch, torment 8 exercise, irritate 9 aggravate, arrogance, brashness, excoriate 10 confidence, effrontery *combining form:* 4 chol 5 chole, cholo

gallant 3 fop 4 beau, bold, buck, dude, game 5 blade, blood, brave, dandy, lover, manly, preux, Romeo, suave, swain, wooer 6 heroic, manful, suitor, urbane 7 amorist, courtly, coxcomb, Don Juan, stately 8 Casanova, gracious, lothario, paramour 9 dauntless, exquisite

gallantry 5 poise, valor 6 mettle, spirit 7 amenity, bravery, courage, heroism, prowess, suavity 8 courtesy, urbanity, valiance, valiancy 9 attention 10 resolution

gallery 5 porch 6 arcade, loggia, museum, piazza 7 balcony, passage, portico, veranda 8 audience, corridor 9 colonnade, promenade *ancient Greek:* 4 stoa

galley 4 boat, ship, tray 5 cuddy, proof 6 bireme 7 dromond, galliot, kitchen, trireme, unireme 9 cookhouse

Gallic 6 French

gallimaufry 4 hash, olio 6 jumble, medley 7 mélange, mixture 8 pastiche 9 potpourri 10 assortment, hodgepodge, miscellany, salmagundi

gallinaceous bird 3 hen 5 quail 6 grouse, turkey 7 chicken, hoatzin 8 curassow, megapode, pheasant 9 partridge

gallivant 3 bat, gad 4 roam, rove 5 mooch, range, stray 6 ramble, travel, wander 7 meander, traipse

gallows 5 frame 6 gibbet 7 hanging, potence *bird:* 7 villain 8 criminal

galore 7 aplenty, profuse 8 abundant 9 plentiful

galosh 4 boot, shoe 6 arctic 8 overshoe

Galsworthy work 7 Justice 14 The Forsyte Saga

galvanize 4 coat, move 5 pique, prime 6 arouse, excite 7 innerve, provoke, quicken 8 activate, energize, motivate, vitalize 9 innervate, stimulate

gam 3 leg, pod 5 visit

Gambia *capital:* 6 Banjul *monetary unit:* 6 dalasi

gambit 3 jig 4 move, play, ploy, ruse 5 trick 6 device 7 gimmick, whizzer 8 artifice, maneuver 9 stratagem

gamble 3 bet, lay, set 4 game, play, risk 5 put on, stake, wager 6 chance, hazard 7 venture 9 speculate

gambler 5 dicer, shark, sharp 6 bettor, player 7 sharper 8 gamester 10 speculator

gambling place 4 Reno 5 Vegas 6 casino 8 Las Vegas 10 Monte Carlo 12 Atlantic City

gambol 3 hop 4 lark, leap, romp 5 bound, caper, frisk, revel 6 cavort, frolic, spring 7 roister, rollick

Gambrinus' invention 4 beer

game 3 bet, fun, lay, set 4 bold, jest, joke, lark, play, prey 5 brave, chase, put on, sport, stake, trick, wager 6 gamble, quarry, spunky 7 contest, pastime, valiant, willing 8 fearless, intrepid, resolute, unafraid, valorous 9 amusement, dauntless, diversion, undaunted 10 courageous *ball:* 3 tut 4 golf, polo, pool 5 fives, rogue, rugby 6 hockey, pelota, soccer, squash, tennis 7 cricket, croquet, jai alai 8 baseball, football, handball, hardball, lacrosse, racquets, rounders, softball 9 billiards 10 basketball, volleyball 11 racquetball *Basque:* 6 pelota 7 jai alai *bird:* 5 quail 6 chukar, turkey 7 bustard 8 bobwhite, pheasant 9 partridge *board:* 5 chess, darts, salta 7 pachisi, reversi, squails 8 checkers 9 crokinole 10 backgammon *card:* 3 gin, loo, nap, pam, war 4 brag, faro, fish, skat, solo 5 monte, omber, ombre, pitch, poker, rummy, stuss, whist 6 Boston, bridge, casino, écarté, euchre, fan-tan, hearts, piquet 7 auction, bezique, canasta, cassino, coocan, muggins, old maid, primero, reversi, setback 8 baccarat, Canfield, conquian, cribbage, Michigan, napoleon, pinochle 9 blackjack, matrimony, Newmarket, solitaire, twenty-one, vingt-et-un 11 chemin de fer *child's:* 3 tag 5 potsy 8 leapfrog, peekaboo 9 hopscotch *confidence:* 4 scam 5 bunco, bunko, sting *court:* 5 roque 6 pelota, squash, tennis 7 jai alai 8 handball, racquets 9 badminton 10 basketball, volleyball *electric:* 7 pinball *English:* 5 kails, rugby 7 cricket, loggats, loggets 8 draughts *Irish:* 6 hurley 7 hurling *of chance:* 4 faro, keno 5 beano, bingo, boule, craps, lotto, rondo 6 fan-tan, hazard, policy, raffle 7 lottery, rondeau 8 crack-loo, roulette 9 crackaloo *parlor:* 5 jacks 8 charades *racket:* 5 bandy 6 squash, tennis 8 lacrosse, racquets 9 badminton 11 racquetball, table tennis *roulette-like:* 5 boule *rule maker:* 5 Hoyle *string:* 10 cat's cradle *table:* 4 pool 5 craps 7 mah-jong, snooker 8 dominoes, mah-jongg, roulette 9 bagatelle, billiards 11 table tennis *word:* 5 rebus 6 crambo, ghosts 7 anagram, hangman 8 acrostic, charades 9 crossword, logograph

game plan 6 design, scheme 7 project 8 strategy 9 blueprint

gamete 3 egg 4 ovum 5 sperm 8 oosphere

gamin 3 imp, tad 6 monkey, urchin

gamine 6 hoyden, tomboy

gaming cubes 4 dice

gammadion 8 swastika

gammon 3 ham 4 dupe, fool 5 bacon, feign 6 delude, humbug 7 deceive, pretend

gamut 4 note 5 range, scale 6 extent, series

gamy 4 olid, rank 5 fetid, funky 6 plucky, smelly, sordid, stinky, strong 7 noisome, reeking 10 malodorous

gander 4 fool, look 5 goose 6 glance 9 simpleton

Gandhi 6 Indira 7 Mahatma

ganef 5 thief 6 rascal

Ganesa, Ganesh *father:* 4 Siva 5 Shiva *head:* 8 elephant *mother:* 7 Parvati

gang 3 mob, set 4 band, crew, pack, team 5 group, horde 6 clique, outfit

gangling 4 bony 5 gaunt, lanky, rangy 6 skinny 7 spindly 9 spindling

ganglion 5 tumor 7 nucleus

gangly see **gangling**

gangrene 3 rot 5 decay 7 mortify 8 necrosis

gangster 4 goon, hood, thug 5 rough, thief, tough 6 bandit, gunman 7 mafioso, mobster 8 criminal 9 cutthroat *girl friend:* 4 moll

gangway 4 hall 5 aisle 7 passage 8 corridor

gannet 4 bird, ibis 5 solan

ganoid fish 3 gar 6 beluga, bowfin 8 sturgeon

Ganymede *abductor:* 4 Zeus 7 Jupiter *brother:* 4 Ilus *father:* 4 Tros *function:* 9 cupbearer

gaol 4 jail 6 prison

gap 3 col 4 hole, lull, pass, slit, slot 5 break, chasm, chink, cleft, clove, crack, gorge, gulch, pause 6 arroyo, breach, clough, cranny, hiatus, lacuna, ravine 7 caesura, crevice, fissure, interim, opening, orifice, rupture 8 aperture, cleavage, division, fracture, interval 10 separation 12 intermission, interruption 13 discontinuity

gape 3 eye, yaw 4 bore, gawk, gaze, look, ogle, peer, yawn 5 glare, gloat, stare 6 goggle 10 rubberneck

gaping 4 open 7 chasmal, yawning 9 cavernous

gar 4 fish, pike 8 billfish 10 needlefish

Garand 5 rifle

garb 4 clad 5 array, dress, getup, style 6 attire, clothe, outfit 7 apparel, garment, raiment 8 enclothe

garbage 4 junk, orts, slop 5 dregs, filth, offal, trash, waste 6 debris, kelter, litter, refuse, rubble, sewage 7 rubbish 8 riffraff *heap:* 6 midden

garble 4 sift, warp 5 belie, color, twist 6 jumble, mangle 7 becloud, distort, falsify, obscure, pervert 8 miscolor, misstate, mutilate 9 obfuscate 12 misrepresent

garçon 3 boy 6 waiter 7 servant

garden 3 hoe 4 Eden, farm, hall, park, plot, till, yard 5 grove, tract 8 rosarium 9 cultivate 11 commonplace *shelter:* 5 arbor 6 arbour

Garden City 7 Chicago

gardener 7 yardman 9 topiarist

garden house 6 alcove, gazebo, pagoda 9 belvedere

Garden State 9 New Jersey

garden tool 3 hoe 4 claw, fork, rake 5 mower, spade 6 pruner, scythe, sickle, trowel, weeder 8 clippers

Gareth *brother:* 6 Gawain 7 Gaheris *father:* 3 Lot *mother:* 8 Margawse, Morgause *slayer:* 8 Lancelot 9 Launcelot *uncle:* 6 Arthur *wife:* 6 Liones

Gargamelle's son 9 Gargantua

Gargantua *abbey:* 7 Theleme *author:* 8 Rabelais *father:* 12 Grandgousier *first word:* 5 drink *mother:* 10 Gargamelle *son:* 10 Pantagruel

gargantuan see **gigantic**

Garibaldi follower 8 redshirt

garish 4 loud 5 gaudy, showy 6 brazen, flashy, tawdry, tinsel 7 blatant, chintzy, glaring 12 meretricious

garland 3 ana, lei 4 band, posy 5 album, crown 6 anadem, wreath 7 chaplet, coronal, coronet, omnibus 8 analects 9 anthology 10 miscellany 11 florilegium

garlic 4 moly, ramp 5 clove 6 ramson

garment 4 cape, clad, coat, garb, gear, gown, robe, vest 5 array, cloak, dress, frock, habit, shirt, skirt, talar, tunic 6 attire, blouse, clothe 7 apparel, chemise, raiment 8 clothing, enclothe, vestment, wearable 10 habiliment *Afghan:* 6 postin 7 posteen 8 poshteen *African:* 6 kaross 7 dashiki *Arab:* 3 aba 4 haik *British:* 4 brat 10 mackintosh *Burmese:* 6 tamein *clergy's:* 3 alb 4 cope 7 cassock, soutane 8 vestment *close-fitting:* 6 girdle, tights 7 leotard *for sleeping:* 6 pajama 7 nightie 9 nightgown *Greek:* 5 tunic 6 chiton, peplos, tribon 7 chlamys 8 himation *Hindu:* 4 sari 5 saree *hooded:* 7 jellaba 8 djellaba *Japanese:* 6 kimono *lace:* 10 chemisette *Malay:* 6 sarong *men's:* 3 tie 4 vest 5 pants, shirt, socks 6 jacket, slacks 7 drawers 8 trousers *Muslim:* 4 izar *outer:* 4 cape, coat, robe, wrap 5 cloak, parka, shawl, smock, stole, wamus 6 capote, jacket, kimono, poncho, sarong, ulster, wammus 7 overall, paletot, pelisse, surtout, sweater, topcoat, zamarra **8** overcoat, pinafore, pullover, scapular **9** coveralls, gaberdine, polonaise *patchwork:* **5** cento **7** khirkah *Polynesian:* **5** pareu **8** lavelava *rain:* **6** poncho **7** oilskin, slicker *Roman:* **4** toga **5** stola, tunic *Scottish:* **4** jupe, kilt **7** sporran *sleeveless:* **3** aba **4** cape **6** mantle, tabard *trim:* **7** falbala *Turkish:* **6** dolman *women's:* **4** gown **5** dress, skirt **6** blouse, vestee **7** blouson, nightie, partlet **8** negligee, peignoir, pelerine

garner **4** cull, hive, reap **5** amass, glean, hoard, lay up, store, uplay **6** gather, pick up, roll up **7** extract, granary, harvest, store up **8** cumulate, ingather **9** stockpile **10** accumulate

garnet **5** jewel, stone **6** pyrope **8** essonite *black:* **8** melanite *red:* **9** almandite

garnish **4** deck, trim **5** adorn, prank **6** bedeck **7** dress up **8** beautify, decorate, ornament **9** embellish

garret **4** loft, room **5** attic, solar **6** sollar, soller **7** mansard **8** cockloft

garrison **4** fort, post **6** occupy **7** station **10** stronghold

garrote **4** kill **5** choke **7** execute **8** strangle, throttle **9** execution

garrulous see *gabby*

garter **4** band, belt **5** snake **7** elastic **9** supporter

gas **4** fuel, fume **5** steam, vapor **6** petrol **8** gasoline **9** petroleum *atmospheric:* **4** neon **5** argon, oxide, ozone, xenon **6** helium, oxygen **7** krypton, methane **8** hydrogen, nitrogen *combining form:* **3** aer **4** mano **5** pneum **6** pneumo **7** pneumat **8** pneumato *flammable:* **6** butane, ethane, ethyne **7** methane, propane, propene **8** ethylene *inert:* **4** neon **5** argon, radon, xenon **6** helium **7** krypton *intestinal:* **6** flatus *mine:* **8** firedamp **9** blackdamp, chokedamp *oxygen:* **5** ozone *toxic:* **5** sarin **6** arsine, ketene **7** mustard, stibine, yperite **8** phosphin

gash **3** cut **4** slit **5** carve, slash, slice, split, wound **6** incise, pierce

gasket **4** band, line, ring, seal **6** sealer

gasoline **4** fuel **6** petrol *rating:* **6** octane

gasp **4** blow, huff, pant, puff **5** heave

Gaspar *companion:* **8** Melchior **9** Balthazar *gift:* **12** frankincense

gassy **5** windy **8** inflated, vaporous

gastronome **7** epicure, gourmet **8** aesthete, gourmand **9** bon vivant

gastronomer, gastronomist see **gastronome**

gastropod **4** slug **5** cowry, murex, snail, whelk **6** cowrie, limpet, volute **7** abalone, mollusk **8** pteropod

gat **3** gun **6** pistol **7** channel, passage

gate **3** tap, way **4** cock, door, exit **5** hatch, valve **6** faucet, portal, spigot, wicket **7** hydrant, opening, petcock **8** stopcock **9** turnstile

gatefold **6** insert **7** foldout

Gates of Hercules **9** Gibraltar

gateway **4** arch, door **5** pylon, toran **6** portal, torana **8** entrance

gather **4** brew, cull, draw, heap, herd, loom, mass, meet, pick, pile, reap, take **5** amass, bunch, flock, glean, group, horde, infer, judge, pluck, raise, shirr, stack, think, troop **6** assume, deduce, deduct, derive, expect, garner, impend, muster, pick up, take in **7** believe, cluster, collect, extract, harvest, imagine, make out, round up, suppose, suspect **8** assemble, conclude, congress **9** aggregate, forthcome **10** accumulate, congregate, rendezvous, understand

gathering **4** bevy, crew, gang, mass, ruck **5** bunch, crowd, crush, flock, group, horde, party, press, swarm **6** klatch, muster **7** company, harvest, klatsch, meeting, reaping, reunion, turnout **8** assembly, cropping, junction **9** concourse, congeries **10** assemblage, collection, concursion, confluence, harvesting **11** aggregation **12** congregation *combining form:* **4** fest

Gath's giant **7** Goliath

gauche **5** crude, inept **6** clumsy, wooden **7** awkward, halting, unhappy **8** bumbling **9** ham-handed, maladroit

gaucho **6** cowboy **8** herdsman *weapon:* **4** bola **7** machete

Gaudeamus ___ **6** igitur

gaudy **4** loud **5** crude, feast, gross, showy **6** brazen, coarse, flashy, garish, tawdry, tinsel, vulgar **7** blatant, chintzy, glaring **8** festival **9** tasteless **12** meretricious, ostentatious

gauge **5** judge, meter, scale **7** measure **8** estimate, standard **9** benchmark, criterion, yardstick **10** touchstone

Gauguin's island home **6** Tahiti

Gaul **4** Celt **6** France **9** Frenchman

Gaulish **6** French *combining form:* **5** Gallo *god:* **4** Esus **7** Taranis *goddess:* **8** Belisama *priest:* **5** druid

gaunt **4** bony, lank, lean **5** lanky, spare **6** skinny, wasted **7** angular, scraggy, scrawny **8** rawboned, skeletal **9** emaciated **10** cadaverous

gauntlet **4** dare, test **5** glove **6** cestus, ordeal **9** challenge

Gautama **6** Buddha **10** Siddhartha *mother:* **4** Maya *son:* **6** Rahula *wife:* **9** Yasodhara

gauze **4** film, haze, leno, mist **5** cloth, crepe, lisse, tulle **6** fabric, tissue **7** bandage, chiffon **11** cheesecloth

gauzy **5** filmy, sheer **6** flimsy **7** tiffany **8** gossamer **10** diaphanous **11** transparent

gavel **6** hammer, mallet

gavial **7** reptile **9** crocodile

gavotte **5** dance

Gawain *brother:* **6** Gareth **7** Gaheris
father: **3** Lot *mother:* **8** Margawse, Morgause *slayer:* **8** Lancelot **9** Launcelot
uncle: **6** Arthur *victim:* **6** Uwayne **7** Lamerok **9** Pellinore

gawk **3** oaf **4** bore, gape, gaze, lout, lump, peer **5** glare, gloat, klutz, looby, stare

gawky **5** splay **6** clumsy, gauche **7** awkward, lumpish **8** ungainly **9** lumbering

gay **4** glad, keen, wild **5** alert, bonny, brash, brave, happy, jolly, merry, queer, riant, vivid **6** blithe, bright, colory, festal, frisky, jocund, jovial, lively, rakish, sporty **7** animate, festive, forward, gleeful, playful, pushful, raffish, uranian **8** animated, colorful, mirthful, rakehell, spirited, sportive **9** confident, homophile, presuming, sprightly, vivacious **10** blithesome, brassbound, frolicsome, homoerotic, homosexual

___ **Gay** **4** John **5** Enola

Gaza victor **7** Allenby

gaze **3** eye, see **4** bore, gape, gawk, leer, look, ogle, peer, pore, scan, view **5** glare, gloat, stare, watch **6** goggle, look at **7** observe **8** consider, look upon

gazebo **6** alcove, pagoda **8** pavilion **9** belvedere **11** garden house, summerhouse

gazelle **3** ahu, goa **4** admi, cora, dama, kudu, mohr, oryx **5** ariel, mhorr **6** dorcas **7** chikara, corinne **8** antelope

gazette **5** paper **6** record **8** courant, journal **9** newspaper

gazetteer **5** atlas, guide

Gazez's father **5** Caleb

Ge see **Gaea**

gear **3** arm, cam, cog, rig **5** dress, equip, goods, stuff **6** fit out, outfit, tackle, things **7** apparel, appoint, furnish, rigging, turn out **8** accouter, accoutre, cogwheel, materiel, property, tackling **9** apparatus, equipment, machinery **10** belongings **11** accessories, habiliments, possessions **13** accouterments, accoutrements, paraphernalia

Geats *king:* **7** Hygelac *prince:* **7** Beowulf

Geb *daughter:* **4** Isis **8** Nephthys *father:* **3** Shu *mother:* **6** Tefnut *sister:* **3** Nut *son:* **3** Set **6** Osiris *wife:* **3** Nut

gecko **6** lizard

Gedaliah *father:* **6** Ahikam **7** Pashhur **8** Jeduthun *slayer:* **7** Ishmael

Gehenna **3** pit **4** hell **5** abyss, hades, Sheol **6** Tophet **7** inferno **9** perdition **10** underworld **11** netherworld

geisha wear **6** kimono

gel **3** dry, set **4** clot, jell **5** jelly **6** gelate **7** congeal, jellify **9** coagulate

gelatin **4** agar **5** jelly **7** sericin

geld **3** fix **4** spay **5** alter, unsex **6** change, neuter **8** castrate, mutilate **9** sterilize **10** emasculate **11** desexualize

gelid **3** icy **4** cold, cool **5** chill, nippy **6** arctic, chilly, frosty **7** glacial **8** freezing

gem **3** jet **4** jade, onyx, opal, ruby, sard **5** agate, amber, beryl, coral, jewel, pearl, stone, topaz **6** amulet, garnet, jasper, scarab, sphene, spinel, zircon **7** bejewel, cat's-eye, citrine, diamond, emerald, enjewel, peridot **8** amethyst, diopside, fluorite, intaglio, obsidian, sapphire, sardonyx, tigereye **9** carnelian, danburite, moonstone, phenakite, scapolite, spodumene, turquoise **10** aquamarine, cordierite, tourmaline **11** alexandrite, chrysoberyl, chrysoprase, lapis lazuli, masterpiece *blue:* **6** zircon **8** sapphire **9** turquoise **10** aquamarine **11** lapis lazuli *carved:* **8** intaglio *changeable:* **9** chatoyant *cut:* **7** navette **8** baguette, cabochon, marquise **9** brilliant *face:* **5** facet *green:* **4** jade **7** emerald, peridot, smaragd **10** chrysolite **11** chrysoprase *red:* **4** ruby, sard **6** garnet, pyrope, spinel **9** carnelian *support:* **7** setting *weight:* **5** carat *yellow:* **5** amber, topaz **6** sphene **7** citrine

Gemariah *brother:* **6** Ahikam *father:* **7** Hilkiah, Shaphan

Gemini star **6** Castor, Pollux

gemmule **3** bud **8** antelope

gemsbok **4** oryx

Gem State **5** Idaho

gemütlich see **genial**

gendarme **7** soldier **9** policeman

gender **3** sex **4** kind, male, sort, type **5** class **6** female, neuter

genealogy **6** stemma **7** descent, history, lineage **8** pedigree **10** family tree

general **4** wide **5** broad, typic, usual **6** common, global, normal, public, vulgar **7** generic, natural, overall, regular, routine, typical **8** everyday, sweeping **9** all-around, inclusive, prevalent, universal **11** commonplace **12** run-of-the-mill **13** comprehensive *American:* **3** Lee **4** Pike, Wood **5** Clark, Grant, Meade, Scott, Smith, Stark, Worth **6** Custer, Kearny, Patton, Porter, Powell, Slocum, Spaatz, Taylor **7** Bradley, Fremont, Houston, Jackson, Lejeune, Ridgway, Sherman, Twining, Wallace, Wheeler **8** Burnside, Goethals, Marshall, Mitchell, Pershing, Sheridan, Stilwell **9** MacArthur, McClellan, Rosecrans, Schofield, Wilkinson **10** Eisenhower, Vandegrift, Wainwright **11** Schwarzkopf *American Revolutionary:* **4** Knox, Ward **5** Gates, Wayne **6** dekalb, Greene, Morgan, Putnam **8** Moultrie, Sullivan **10** Washington *Austrian:* **11** Wallenstein *British:* **4** Gage, Howe **5** Clive, Monck, Wolfe **6** Rupert **7** Amherst, Wingate **8** Burgoyne, Cromwell **10** Abercromby,

Cornwallis, Wellington **Carthaginian:**
8 Hamilcar, Hannibal 9 Hasdrubal **Chinese:** 3 Yen 4 Feng 5 Chang **combining form:** 3 cen, pan 4 caen, ceno, coen, pano 5 caeno, coeno **Confederate:** 3 Lee 4 Hill, Hood 5 Bragg, Ewell, Price, Smith 6 Morgan, Stuart 7 Forrest, Hampton, Jackson, Pickett 8 Johnston 9 Pemberton 10 Beauregard, Longstreet **French:** 4 Foch 6 Moreau, Petain 7 Lefebre, Weygand 8 deGaulle, Montcalm, Saint-Cyr 9 Frontenac 10 Rochambeau **German:** 4 Jodl 6 Kleist 10 Ludendorff **Greek:** 6 Nicias 9 Miltiades 10 Alcibiades 12 Themistocles **Japanese:** 4 Tojo 5 Koiso 6 Yasuda 8 Yamagata 9 Yamashita **Mexican:** 9 Santa Anna **Prussian:** 11 Scharnhorst **Roman:** 5 Sulla 6 Caesar, Fabius, Marius, Pompey, Scipio 7 Regulus, Ricimer 8 Agricola, Lucullus, Stilicho 9 Marcellus, Sertorius 10 Theodosius 11 Cincinnatus **Russian:** 7 Wrangel, Zhdanov 9 Yeremenko **Spanish:** 4 Alba, Alva 6 Franco **Swedish:** 7 Wrangel

general assembly 6 plenum
generalize 5 infer, widen 6 extend, induce, spread
generally 6 mainly, mostly 7 as a rule, chiefly, en masse, largely, overall, usually 8 all in all, commonly 9 primarily 10 altogether, by and large, by ordinary, frequently, on the whole, ordinarily 11 principally 13 predominantly
generate 4 bear, make, sire 5 beget, breed, cause, get up, hatch, spawn 6 create, father, induce, parent, whip up, work up 7 develop, produce, provoke 8 engender, multiply, muster up 9 originate, procreate, propagate, reproduce 10 bring about
generic 6 common 7 general 9 universal
generosity 7 charity, largess 8 largesse 10 liberality
generous 3 big 4 free, kind 5 ample, lofty, noble 6 kindly, lavish, plenty 7 copious, helpful, liberal, profuse 8 abundant, handsome 9 bounteous, bountiful, plenteous, plentiful, unselfish, unsparing 10 altruistic, benevolent, bighearted, charitable, chivalrous, freehanded, munificent, openhanded, thoughtful, ungrudging 11 considerate, kindhearted, magnanimous
genesis 4 dawn 5 alpha, birth, start 6 origin, outset, setout 7 dawning, opening 8 outstart 9 beginning 12 commencement
genetic 10 hereditary **material:** 3 DNA, RNA 7 cistron 9 chromatid 10 chromosome **term:** 8 synapsis 9 backcross
genial 4 warm 5 jolly, merry 6 benign, blithe, gentle, jocund, jovial, kindly 7 affable, amiable, cordial 8 amicable, cheerful,

friendly, gracious, sociable 9 congenial 10 neighborly
genie 4 jinn 5 afrit, jinni 6 afreet, spirit, yaksha
genitor 6 father, parent 7 creator
geniture 5 birth 8 nativity
genius 4 bent, bump, gift, head, turn 5 flair, knack 6 brains, talent, wizard 7 aptness, faculty 9 ingenuity, intellect 10 creativity 12 intelligence 13 inventiveness
Genoa's liberator 5 Doria
genre 4 kind, sort, type 5 class, style 7 species 8 category
gens 4 clan 5 group 6 family, people
Genseric's subjects 7 Vandals
genteel 4 nice, prig, prim 5 civil, noble 6 la-di-da, polite, prissy, stuffy, too-too, urbane 7 elegant, mincing, prudish, refined, stilted, stylish 8 affected, cultured, graceful, knightly, ladylike, mannerly, polished, precious, priggish, well-bred 9 courteous, distingué, Victorian 10 chivalrous, cultivated, tight-laced 11 fashionable, gentlemanly, pretentious, well-behaved 12 aristocratic, well-mannered 13 straightlaced
gentile 3 goy
gentility 5 elite 6 flower, gentry 7 aristoi, quality, society 8 breeding, optimacy 10 upper class, upper crust 11 aristocracy
gentle 4 calm, easy, kind, meek, mild, soft, tame 5 balmy, bland, faint, quiet, tamed 6 benign, genial, kindly, mellow, placid, serene, smooth, tender 7 affable, amiable, lenient 8 delicate, peaceful, pleasant, pleasing, soothing, tranquil 9 agreeable 11 softhearted, sympathetic, warmhearted 13 compassionate **creature:** 4 lamb
gentleman 6 aristo, fellow, mister 8 cavalier 9 blue blood, chevalier, patrician 10 aristocrat **English:** 6 milord **French:** 8 monsieur **Hindu:** 4 babu **Spanish:** 3 don 5 senor
gentleman friend 4 beau 5 swain
gentry 4 rank 5 elite 6 flower 7 aristoi, quality, society 8 optimacy 9 gentility 10 upper class, upper crust 11 aristocracy
genu 4 knee 5 joint
Genubath's father 5 Hadad
genuflect 5 kneel 6 kowtow
genuine 4 hard, real, true, very 5 plain, pucka, pukka 6 actual, dinkum, honest 7 factual, natural, sincere 8 absolute, bona fide, positive, trueborn 9 authentic, undoubted, unfeigned, veritable 10 heartwhole, sure-enough, unaffected
genus 4 kind, mode, sort, type 5 class, group, order 8 category
geode 6 cavity, nodule
geographer **American:** 10 Huntington **Flemish:** 8 Mercator **German:** 6 Ratzel **Greek:** 6 Strabo 7 Ptolemy

geologic *period:* **5** azoic **6** Eocene **7** Miocene, Permian **8** Cambrian, Cenozoic, Devonian, Jurassic, Mesozoic, Pliocene, Silurian, Triassic **9** Oligocene, Paleocene, Paleozoic **10** Cretaceous, Ordovician **13** Mississippian, Pennsylvanian *study:* **4** rock **5** earth **6** fossil

geometer **6** Euclid

geometric *coordinate:* **8** abscissa *curve:* **3** arc **6** spiral **7** cissoid, ellipse, evolute **8** parabola *solid:* **4** cone, cube **5** prism **7** pyramid **8** spheroid, spherule *surface:* **5** nappe, torus **6** toroid

geometric figure **4** cone, cube **5** prism, rhomb **6** circle, oblong, sphere, square **7** ellipse, hexagon, octagon, polygon, pyramid, rhombus **8** cylinder, heptagon, pentagon, rhomboid, spheroid, triangle **9** rectangle *combining form:* **5** hedra (plural) **6** hedron

geophagy **4** pica

Georgia *capital:* **7** Atlanta *college, university:* **4** Tift **5** Clark, Emory, Paine *founder:* **10** Oglethorpe *nickname:* **10** Peach State

Gera *father:* **4** Bela *grandfather:* **8** Benjamin *son:* **4** Ehud **6** Shimei

Geraint's wife **4** Enid

Gerda's husband **4** Frey

germ **3** bud, bug **4** seed **5** spark, spore, virus **6** embryo **7** microbe, nucleus **9** bacterium *cell:* **3** egg **4** ovum **5** sperm

German **4** Goth **6** Teuton *article:* **3** das, der, des, die *bomber:* **5** Gotha, Stuka *child:* **4** kind *coin:* **4** mark **5** taler **6** thaler **7** pfennig *empire:* **5** reich *head:* **4** kopf *highway:* **8** autobahn *leader:* **6** führer, kaiser *measles:* **7** rubella *mister:* **4** herr *no:* **4** nein *nobleman:* **6** Junker *pronoun:* **2** du, er, es **3** ich, sie, wir *rifle:* **6** Mauser *weight:* **3** lot **5** pfund, stein **8** vierling *woman:* **4** frau **8** fräulein

germane **5** ad rem **7** apropos, related **8** apposite, material, pointful, relevant **9** pertinent **10** applicable

Germany **11** Deutschland *capital:* **6** Berlin *monetary unit:* **4** mark; (see also **East Germany; West Germany**)

germinate **3** bud **6** evolve, sprout

Gershom, Gershon *father:* **4** Levi *son:* **5** Libni **6** Shimei

Gershwin **3** Ira **6** George *opera:* **12** Porgy and Bess

Gertrude *husband:* **8** Claudius *son:* **6** Hamlet

Gervaise's daughter **4** Nana

Geryon *dog:* **6** Orthus *father:* **8** Chrysaor *mother:* **10** Callirrhoe *slayer:* **4** herc **8** Hercules

Gesham's father **6** Jahdai

gest, geste **4** deed, feat **7** emprise, exploit, venture **9** adventure **10** enterprise

Gestapo chief **7** Himmler

gesticulate **6** motion **7** gesture

gesture **3** act, nod **4** flag, sign **5** token **6** motion, salute, signal **8** reminder **9** signalize **10** expression, indication *graceful:* **9** beau geste

get **3** bag, fix, win **4** beat, come, draw, earn, gain, gall, grow, have, land, move, rile, sire, sway, turn **5** annex, breed, catch, educe, evoke, learn, peeve, reach, ready, touch, upset **6** accept, affect, arrive, attain, become, bother, burn up, collar, elicit, extort, father, induce, make up, master, obtain, pick up, secure, show up, turn up **7** acquire, bring in, capture, chalk up, compass, disturb, extract, impress, nonplus, perturb, prehend, prepare, procure, realize, receive, win over **8** contract, convince, distress, draw down, irritate, memorize, persuade, sicken of, talk into **9** aggravate, argue into, influence, knock down, prevail on, procreate **10** exasperate, sicken with **11** bring around, prevail upon, progenerate **12** come down with

get away see **get out**

getaway **3** lam **4** slip **6** escape, flight **8** breakout, escaping **10** escapement

get back **6** recoup, regain **7** recover, recruit **8** retrieve **9** repossess

get by **4** fare **5** shift **6** manage

get off **2** go **4** exit, open, quit **5** begin, leave, start **6** depart, launch, retire **7** jump off, kick off, pull out **8** commence *prefix:* **2** de

get out **2** go **4** exit, kite, leak **5** break, issue, leave, scram, split **6** begone, decamp, depart, egress, escape **7** publish, skiddoo, take off **8** clear out, hightail **9** skedaddle

Gettysburg general **3** Lee **5** Meade

get up **4** rise **5** arise, breed, cause, hatch, mount, stand **6** induce, uprise **7** pile out, produce, roll out, turn out **8** engender, generate, muster up, occasion, upspring **12** rise and shine

getup **2** go **3** pep, rig **4** bang, push, snap, togs **5** dress, drive, guise, punch, vigor **6** outfit, setout **7** costume **8** vitality

get-up-and-go **3** pep **4** bang, push, snap **5** drive, punch, vigor **8** ambition, vitality **10** enterprise, initiative

gewgaw **3** toy **5** curio **6** bauble, trifle **7** bibelot, novelty, trinket, whatnot **8** gimcrack **9** objet d'art **10** knickknack

geyser **5** spurt **6** spring **11** Old Faithful

Ghana *capital:* **5** Accra *monetary unit:* **4** cedi

ghastly **3** wan **4** grim, pale **5** awful **6** grisly, horrid, shadow **7** hideous, macabre **8** dreadful, gruesome, horrible, nauseant, shocking, spectral, terrible **9** appalling,

deathlike, frightful, ghostlike, sickening
10 cadaverous, corpselike, disgustful, disgusting, horrifying, nauseating, terrifying
11 frightening

ghee 3 fat **6** butter

gherkin 6 pickle **8** cucumber

ghetto 4 slum

ghost 5 shade, spook **6** shadow, spirit, wraith **7** phantom, specter **8** phantasm **10** apparition **11** poltergeist

ghostlike see **ghostly**

ghostly 5 eerie, scary **6** spooky **7** shadowy **8** spectral **9** deathlike **10** cadaverous, corpselike

ghoul 4 ogre **5** fiend **7** monster

GI 7 fighter, soldier, warrior **9** man-at-arms **10** serviceman

giant 4 huge, Otus **5** gross, Gyges, Hymir, jumbo, titan, troll, whale **6** Cottus, Typhon **7** Aloadae (plural), Antaeus, Cyclops, mammoth, monster, titanic **8** behemoth, Briareus, colossal, colossus, gigantic, Orgoglio **9** cyclopean, Enceladus, Ephialtes, Gargantua, Herculean, leviathan, monstrous, polypheme **10** behemothic, gargantuan *armadillo:* **4** tatu **5** tatou *biblical:* **4** Anak **7** Goliath *cactus:* **7** saguaro *clam:* **8** tridacna *grass:* **5** otate *killer:* **4** Jack **5** David *one-eyed:* **5** Arges **7** Cyclops **10** Polyphemus *100-armed:* **9** Enceladus *100-eyed:* **5** Argus *perch:* **5** begti, bekti **6** cockup *rime-cold:* **4** Ymer, Ymir *sea god:* **5** Aegir

Giant author 5 Ferber (Edna)

gibber 5 prate **6** babble, drivel, gabble, jabber, yammer **7** blather, chatter, prattle

gibberish 5 Greek **6** babble, bunkum, drivel, gabble, jabber **7** blabber, blather, mummery, palaver, prattle, twaddle **8** claptrap, nonsense **10** double-talk, hocus-pocus, mumbo jumbo **11** abracadabra, jabberwocky **12** gobbledygook

gibbet 4 hang **5** noose, scrag **7** gallows, turn off **8** string up

gibbon 3 ape, lar **6** monkey **7** primate, siamang **10** anthropoid

gibbous 6 convex, humped **7** rounded, swollen **10** humpbacked

gibe 4 gird, jeer, jest, mock, quip **5** fleer, flout, gleek, scoff, sneer **6** quip at **7** scout at **8** ridicule

Gibraltar *colony of:* **12** Great Britain *conqueror:* **5** Tarik, Tariq *country:* **5** Spain *opposite:* **5** Ceuta

Giddalti *father:* **5** Heman *occupation:* **6** singer

giddy 5 dizzy, light, silly **6** swimmy, volage, yeasty **7** flighty, fribble **8** skittish, swimming **9** fribbling, frivolous **10** bird-witted, hoity-toity **11** empty-headed, harebrained, light-headed, vertiginous **13** rattlebrained

Gide 5 André

Gideon *father:* **5** Joash *servant:* **5** Purah *son:* **9** Abimelech

Gideoni's son 6 Abidan

gift 3 set, tip **4** alms, bent, boon, bump, head, turn **5** award, favor, flair, grant, knack **6** genius, legacy, reward, talent **7** aptness, cumshaw, faculty, handout, largess, present, subsidy **8** bestowal, donation, gratuity, offering **9** lagniappe **11** benefaction, benevolence **12** contribution, presentation

gig 3 jab, job **4** boat, fool, goad, prod **5** annoy, rotor, spear **6** chaise, harass **7** demerit, provoke

gigantic 3 big **4** huge, vast **5** giant, large **7** hulking, immense, mammoth **8** colossal, enormous **9** cyclopean, monstrous **10** gargantuan, prodigious, stupendous **11** elephantine

giggle 5 laugh, tehee **6** guffaw, hee-haw, teehee, titter **7** chortle, chuckle, snicker, snigger

Gilbert and Sullivan opera 8 Iolanthe, Patience **9** Ruddigore, The Mikado **11** H.M.S. Pinafore, Princess Ida, The Sorcerer, Trial by Jury **12** The Grand Duke **13** The Gondoliers

Gil Blas author 6 Lesage

gild 5 adorn, cover, tinge **7** overlay **8** brighten **9** embellish

Gilda's father 9 Rigoletto

Gilead *father:* **6** Machir *grandfather:* **8** Manasseh *son:* **8** Jephthah

Gilgamesh 4 epic *companion:* **6** Eabani, Engidu, Enkidu *home:* **5** Erech *mother:* **6** Ninsun *victim:* **7** Humbaba

gill 4 race **5** brook, creek **6** runnel, stream, wattle **7** rivulet *relating to:* **9** branchial

gilly flower 4 pink **9** clove pink

gilt 3 hog, pig, sow **4** gold **5** swine **6** gilded, golden

gimlet 4 tool **5** drink **6** pierce **7** gum tree **8** eucalypt **10** eucalyptus *ingredient:* **3** gin **9** lime juice

gimmick 4 ploy, ruse, wile **5** feint, gizmo, trick **6** gadget, gambit, jigger, widget **7** concern, whizzer **8** artifice, maneuver **9** stratagem

gimpy 4 lame **7** limping **8** crippled

gin 4 net **5** sloe, trap **5** catch, rummy, snare **6** liquor **7** springe **8** Hollands

Ginath's son 6 Tibni

ginger 3 fig, pep, vim **4** herb, stir **5** liven, spice, vigor **6** mettle, revive, spirit *cookie:* **4** snap

gingerly 4 safe, wary **5** chary **7** careful, guarded **8** cautious, discreet **11** calculating, circumspect, considerate

gingery 5 beany, fiery **6** spunky **7** peppery **8** spirited **10** mettlesome **11** high-hearted **12** high-spirited

gingham **5** cloth **6** fabric

gingiva **3** gum

ginseng **4** herb, root

Gioconda, La **8** Mona Lisa *composer:* **10** Ponchielli *painter:* **7** da Vinci (Leonardo)

giraffe **3** car **5** piano **8** ruminant **10** camelopard

girandole **6** mirror **7** earring, pendant **11** candelabrum

girasol **4** opal **8** fire opal **9** artichoke

gird **3** hem **4** band, belt, gibe, jeer, jest, ring, wrap **5** beset, brace, fleer, flout, ready, round, scoff, sneer, steel **6** circle, quip at **7** bolster, forearm, fortify, prepare, scout at, shore up, wreathe **8** begirdle, buttress, cincture, encircle, engirdle, surround **9** encompass, reinforce **10** encincture, strengthen

girdle **3** hem **4** band, bark, belt, ring, sash **5** beset, round **6** begird, cestus, circle, engird **8** ceinture, cincture, encircle, surround **9** encompass, waistband **10** encincture *combining form:* **3** zon **4** zono **6** pleura *of Aphrodite:* **6** cestus **7** caestus

girl Friday **9** secretary

girth **4** band, belt, bind, size **5** brace, cinch, strap **6** girdle **7** measure **8** cincture, encircle **10** dimensions **13** circumference

gist **4** core, meat, pith **5** sense, short **6** burden, matter, thrust, upshot **7** bearing **9** substance

gitano **5** gypsy

give **3** air, lot, pay **4** bend, cave, deal, fail, feed, find, hand, pose, sell, vend, vent **5** allot, allow, apply, award, break, grant, issue, offer, spend, throw, yield **6** accord, afford, assign, befall, bestow, betide, chance, confer, devote, direct, donate, expend, extend, fold up, happen, lay out, lot out, market, outlay, relent, render, strike, supply, tender, weaken **7** address, crumple, deliver, dish out, dole out, express, fall out, fork out, furnish, hand out, hold out, inflict, mete out, present, produce, proffer, provide, slacken **8** allocate, collapse, disburse, dispense, disperse, give away, hand over, shell out, transfer, turn over **9** admeasure, apportion, ventilate **10** buckle down, contribute, distribute

give away **4** tell **5** grant, mouth, spill **6** bestow, betray, devote, donate, reveal **7** blab out, divulge, hand out, present, unclose **8** disclose, discover

give back **4** echo **5** refund, retire, return **7** replace, restore, retreat **8** withdraw **9** reinstate

give in **5** yield **6** relent **7** indulge, succumb **9** surrender

give off **4** emit, flow, pour, vent, void **5** issue **7** release **8** throw off **9** discharge

give out **4** deal, dole, drop, emit, fail, mete, vent, wilt **5** issue **6** cave in, peg out, run out **7** release, succumb **8** collapse, throw off **9** break down

giver **5** donor **7** donator **8** bestower **9** conferrer, presenter

give up **4** cede, quit, sell **5** forgo, leave, waive, yield **6** forego, resign, vacate **7** abandon, despair, despond **8** abdicate, hand over **9** surrender **10** relinquish

gizmo see **gadget**

glabrous **4** bald **6** shaven, smooth **8** hairless **9** beardless **12** smooth-shaven

glacial **3** icy **4** cold **5** chill, gelid, nippy **6** arctic, chilly, frigid, frosty **8** freezing

glacier **3** ice **6** ice cap **8** ice sheet *Alaska:* **4** Muir, Taku **6** Bering *Antarctica:* **9** Beardmore *deposit:* **4** kame **5** esker **6** placer **7** moraine **8** diluvium *fissure:* **8** crevasse *fragment:* **4** berg **5** iceberg *hill:* **7** drumlin *Karakoram:* **5** Biafo **7** Baltoro *New Zealand:* **6** Tasman *pinnacle:* **5** serac

glad **4** fain **5** happy, jolly, merry **6** blithe, bright, cheery, genial, jocund, jovial, joyful, joyous **7** beaming, gleeful, pleased, radiant, tickled **8** cheerful, mirthful, pleasant, rejoiced **9** delighted, gratified **11** exhilarated **12** lighthearted

gladden **5** cheer, elate **6** arride, please **7** delight, gratify, happify, rejoice **8** pleasure

glade **5** grove, marsh **8** clearing

gladiator **7** battler, fighter **9** combatant *Roman:* **9** retiarius

gladly **4** fain, lief

gladness **3** joy **4** glee **5** bliss, cheer, mirth **7** jollity, joyance **9** happiness **10** joyfulness

gladstone **3** bag

glamorous **5** siren **8** alluring, charming, magnetic **9** seductive **10** attractive, bewitching, enchanting **11** captivating, fascinating

glamour **5** charm, magic **6** allure, appeal **8** charisma, witchery **9** magnetism **10** witchcraft **11** fascination

glance **3** rub **4** buff, kiss, peek, peep, skim, skip **5** brush, carom, flash, glaze, gleam, glime, glint, gloss, graze, shave, shine, touch **6** bounce, careen, polish, scrape **7** burnish, contact, furbish, glimmer, glimpse, glisten, glitter, shimmer, sparkle, twinkle **8** ricochet **9** coruscate

gland **5** gonad, liver, organ **6** thymus **7** adrenal, mammary, thyroid **8** exocrine, pancreas, prostate **9** endocrine, pituitary **11** parathyroid *secretion:* **7** hormone *sex:* **5** gonad *swelling:* **4** bubo

glare **4** bore, gape, gawk, gaze, glow,

peer **5** blaze, flame, flash, frown, gleam, gloat, lower, scowl, stare **6** dazzle, glower, goggle **7** glisten, glitter

glaring 4 loud, rank **5** gaudy, plain, vivid **6** brazen, flashy, garish, tawdry, tinsel **7** blatant, capital, chintzy **8** flagrant **9** egregious, obtrusive **10** noticeable **11** conspicuous, outstanding

Glasgow's patron saint 5 Mingo **9** Kentigern

glass 4 lens, pane **5** image, lense, prism **6** mirror **7** reflect **9** barometer, telescope *combining form:* **4** hyal, vitr **5** hyalo, vitro *container:* **3** jar **6** beaker, bottle *decorative:* **7** schmelz **8** schmelze *drinking:* **3** mug **5** stein **6** goblet, jigger, rummer, seidel **7** snifter, tumbler **8** schooner *gem:* **5** paste **6** strass *magnifying:* **5** loupe *milky:* **7** opaline *volcanic:* **7** perlite **8** obsidian

glasses 5 specs **6** shades **7** goggles **10** spectacles

glass-like 6 vitric **8** vitreous

glassmaker 6 blower **7** glazier, Tiffany

glassmaking *oven:* **4** lehr *tool:* **5** ponty **6** pontil **8** blowpipe

Glaucus *father:* **5** Minos **8** Sisyphus *mother:* **6** Merope **8** Pasiphae *son:* **11** Bellerophon

glaze 3 rub **4** buff, coat **5** glint, gloss, sheen, shine **6** enamel, glance, luster, polish **7** burnish, furbish

gleam 3 ray **4** beam, glow **5** flash, glint, sheen, shine **6** glance **7** glimmer, glisten, glitter, radiate, shimmer, sparkle, twinkle **8** radiance **11** coruscation, scintillate **13** scintillation

gleaming 5 shiny **6** glossy, sheeny **7** shining **8** lustrous, polished **9** burnished **10** glistening

glean 4 cull, reap **6** garner, gather, pick up **7** extract

glede 4 kite **6** osprey

glee 3 joy **5** mirth **6** gaiety, levity **7** delight, jollity **8** hilarity, pleasure **9** enjoyment, jocundity, joviality, merriment

gleeful 3 gay **4** boon **5** jolly, merry **6** blithe, jocund, jovial **8** mirthful **10** blithesome

glen 4 dale, vale **6** dingle, valley *deep:* **5** gorge **6** ravine *Scottish:* **5** heuch, heugh

glib 4 easy **5** slick **6** facile, fluent, smooth **7** voluble **8** eloquent, flippant, vocative, well-hung **9** talkative **10** articulate

glide 3 fly **4** flow, sail, skim, slip **5** creep, float, mouse, skate, skulk, slick, slide, slink, sneak, steal **7** gumshoe, slither **8** glissade, volplane **9** pussyfoot

glimmer 4 glow **5** flash, gleam, glint **6** glance **7** glisten, glitter, shimmer, sparkle,

twinkle **9** coruscate **11** coruscation **13** scintillation

glimpse 4 look, peek, peep **5** stime **6** glance

glint 5 flash, glaze, gleam, gloss, sheen, shine **6** glance, luster, polish **7** glimmer, glisten, glitter, shimmer, sparkle, twinkle **9** coruscate **11** coruscation **13** scintillation

glissade 4 skim, slip **5** glide, slick, slide **7** slither

glisten 5 flash, gleam, glint, shine **6** glance **7** glimmer, glitter, shimmer, sparkle, twinkle **9** coruscate **11** coruscation

glitter 5 flash, gleam, glint, shine **6** glance **7** glimmer, glisten, shimmer, spangle, sparkle, twinkle **9** bespangle, coruscate **11** coruscation **13** scintillation

glittering 5 gaudy, showy **7** shining **9** brilliant, clinquant, sparkling

gloaming 3 eve **4** dusk **7** evening **8** eventide, owl-light, twilight **9** nightfall

gloat 4 bore, gape, gawk, gaze, peer **5** exult, glare, stare **6** goggle

global 5 grand **6** cosmic **7** general, overall **8** all-round, catholic **9** inclusive, planetary, universal, worldwide

globe 3 orb **4** ball **5** earth, round, world **6** planet, sphere **7** rondure *half:* **10** hemisphere

globule 4 bead, drib, drip, drop **6** gobbet **7** driblet, droplet **8** spherule

gloom 3 dim **4** dusk, murk **5** bedim, blues, cloud, dumps, frown, lower, scowl **6** darken, glower **7** becloud, obscure, sadness **8** darkness, overcast **9** adumbrate, dejection **10** depression, melancholy, overshadow, the dismals **11** unhappiness **12** mournfulness

gloomy 3 dim, dun, sad **4** cold, dark, dour, drab, dull, glum, ugly **5** black, bleak, drear, dusky, morne, murky, muzzy, sulky, surly **6** dismal, dreary, morose, solemn, somber, sullen **7** crabbed, joyless, obscure, stygian, unhappy **8** dejected, desolate, downcast, funereal, mournful **9** cheerless, depressed, lightless, mirthless, oppressed, saturnine, tenebrous, woebegone **10** acheronian, acherontic, caliginous, depressant, depressing, depressive, despondent, lugubrious, melancholy, oppressive, tenebrific **11** dispiriting, pessimistic **12** disconsolate, discouraging

glorify 4 hymn, laud **5** bless, cry up, erect, exalt, extol, honor **6** praise, uprear **7** dignify, ennoble, magnify, sublime **8** eulogize **9** celebrate **10** aggrandize, panegyrize

glorious 5 grand, great, noble, proud **6** divine, groovy, superb **7** radiant, sublime **8** gorgeous, lustrous, majestic, splendid, stunning **9** beautiful, brilliant, effulgent, hunky-dory, marvelous, ravishing **11** magnificent, resplendent, splendorous

glory 4 fame, halo 5 exult, honor 6 praise, renown 7 acclaim, aureole, delight, triumph 8 eminence, jubilate, splendor 9 greatness 11 distinction 12 magnificence

gloss 4 buff 5 glaze, glint, sheen, shine 6 enamel, glance, luster, polish 7 burnish, furbish, varnish 8 annotate 9 sleekness, slickness

glossary 6 clavis 7 lexicon

gloss over 5 white 6 veneer, whiten 7 falsify, varnish 8 palliate 9 extenuate, sugarcoat, whitewash 12 misrepresent

glossy 5 shiny, sleek 6 sheeny, sleeky, smarmy 7 shining 8 gleaming, lustrous, polished 9 burnished 10 glistening *fabric:* 4 silk 5 satin *paint:* 6 enamel

glove 4 mitt 5 cover 6 mitten, sheath 8 gauntlet

glow 4 pink, rose 5 blare, blaze, bloom, blush, color, flame, flare, flush, glare, rouge, shine 6 mantle, pinken, redden 7 blossom, crimson, foxfire

glower 4 gaze 5 frown, gloom, scowl, stare

glowing 3 hot 5 fiery, flush, ruddy, shiny 6 ardent, fervid, florid, heated 7 blazing, burning, candent, fervent, flaming, flushed, radiant 8 dazzling, rubicund, sanguine 10 candescent, hot-blooded, passionate 11 full-blooded, impassioned 12 enthusiastic

gloze over see **gloss over**

Gluck opera 5 Orfeo 6 Armide 7 Alceste

glucose 5 sugar

glue 3 fix 4 join 5 epoxy, paste, stick 6 adhere, attach, cement 8 adhesive, mucilage

gluey 5 gooey, gummy 6 cloggy, sticky, stodgy 8 adhesive

glum 4 dour 5 moody, sulky, surly 6 gloomy, morose, silent, sullen 7 crabbed 8 taciturn 9 depressed, oppressed, saturnine

glut 4 clog, cloy, cram, fill, jade, pall, sate 5 feast, gorge, stuff 6 stodge 7 satiate, surfeit

glutinous 4 ropy 5 gluey, gummy 6 sticky 7 viscous

glutton 3 hog, pig 5 gulch 8 gourmand 9 chowhound

gluttonous 7 hoggish, piggish 8 edacious, ravening, ravenous 9 indulgent, rapacious, voracious 11 intemperate

gluttony 7 edacity 8 gulosity

G-man 3 fed

gnarl 4 bend, knot 5 snarl, twist 6 deform 7 contort, distort

gnash 4 bite 5 grind

gnat 3 fly 4 pest 6 insect

gnaw 3 eat 4 bite, chew 5 annoy, erode, harry, scour, tease, worry 6 harass, nibble, pester, plague 7 bedevil, consume, corrode, eat away, hagride 8 wear away

gnome 3 elf, saw 4 rule 5 axiom, dwarf, maxim, moral, troll 6 dictum, goblin, sprite, truism 7 brocard 8 aphorism, apothegm

gnostic 4 sage, wise 6 sophic 7 knowing 9 insighted, sagacious 10 discerning, insightful, perceptive 13 knowledgeable

go 3 act, die, fit, fly, hie, pep, run, set, try 4 bear, bout, exit, fare, flee, give, jibe, like, move, pass, quit, shot, wend, work 5 abide, agree, apply, brook, drive, enjoy, event, fit in, fling, leave, occur, range, recur, refer, siege, spell, stint, vigor, whirl 6 accord, become, belong, decamp, demise, depart, elapse, endure, energy, escape, expire, extend, get off, happen, pan out, pop off, push on, repair, resort, retire, thrive, travel 7 abscond, advance, come off, conform, crumble, decease, episode, get away, journey, potency, proceed, prosper, pull out, push off, succeed, success, succumb, take off 8 collapse, flourish, function, incident, occasion, pass away, run along, shove off, tolerate, vitality, withdraw 9 happening, hardihood 10 correspond, get-up-and-go, occurrence *against:* 5 fight 6 oppose *ahead:* 4 lead 7 precede, proceed 8 continue, progress *along:* 5 agree 6 concur *around:* 5 avoid 7 compass 10 circumvent *at:* 6 attack 8 approach *away:* 3 off 4 exit, quit, scat, shoo 5 leave, scram 6 depart, retire *back:* 6 recede, return, revert 7 regress, retreat *back on:* 6 betray, renege 7 abandon *back over:* 6 review 7 retrace *before:* 4 lead 7 precede 8 antedate *beyond:* 6 exceed 7 surpass *forward:* 7 advance, proceed 8 continue, progress *in:* 5 enter 7 ingress 9 penetrate *out:* 4 date, exit 5 leave 6 egress *Scottish:* 3 gae *through:* 3 cut 6 endure 7 undergo 9 penetrate 10 experience *together:* 3 fit 4 suit 5 agree, befit 6 become 9 agree with, harmonize *with:* 4 date, suit 5 befit 6 escort 9 accompany

goad 3 egg, sic 4 prod, spur 5 drive, egg on, impel, prick 6 exhort, prompt, propel 7 impetus, impulse 8 catalyst, stimulus 9 impulsion, incentive, stimulant

go-ahead 4 okay 9 clearance, gumptious 10 green light 11 up-and-coming 12 enterprising 13 authorization

goal 3 aim, end, use 4 duty, mark 6 object, target 7 purpose 8 ambition, function 9 objective, quaesitum

goat 3 kid, ram 5 billy, nanny, patsy 6 alpaca, angora, nubian 7 fall guy 8 cashmere 9 scapegoat *combining form:* 5 capri *female:* 3 doe 5 nanny *flesh:* 6 chevon *genus:* 5 Capra *Himalayan:* 4 tahr, thar

male: 4 buck 5 billy *wild:* 4 ibex
7 markhor
goat antelope 5 goral, serow 7 chamois
goatee 5 beard 7 Vandyke
goatfish 6 mullet
goatish 3 hot 4 lewd 7 caprine, hircine,
lustful, satyric 8 prurient 9 lickerish 10 lascivious, libidinous, passionate
12 concupiscent
goat-man deity 3 Pan
goat nut 6 jojoba
goatsfoot 8 goutweed
goatskin 9 chevrette
gob 3 wad 4 clod, hunk, lump, mass
5 chunk, mouth 6 nugget
gobbet 4 drip, drop 7 driblet, droplet,
globule
gobble 4 bolt, cram, gulp, slop, wolf
5 slosh 6 englut, guzzle 11 ingurgitate
gobbledygook see **gibberish**
go-between 5 agent, envoy 6 broker
8 attorney, emissary, mediator 9 middleman 10 arbitrator, interagent, interceder,
matchmaker, negotiator 11 intercessor
12 entrepreneur, intermediary, intermediate
13 intermediator
goblet 5 glass 6 vessel
goblin 3 elf, fay 4 bhut, bogy 5 bogie,
bogle, fairy, gnome, pooka 6 booger,
sprite 7 brownie 8 barghest, bogeyman
gobs 4 heap, wads 5 loads, reams, scads
6 oodles 8 slathers 10 quantities
god 4 idol 5 deity 7 creator 8 Almighty,
divinity, immortal *combining form:* 3 the
4 theo *false:* 4 baal *French:* 4 dieu *Latin:*
4 deus *Spanish:* 4 dios; (see specific
entries (as **Greek; Roman**) for names of
specific gods and goddesses)
God Bless America composer 6 Berlin
goddess 4 idol 5 deity 8 divinity, immortal
Latin: 3 dea; (see note at **god**)
godfather 3 don 4 capo 7 sponsor
God-fearing 5 pious 6 devout 8 reverent 9 religious
godforsaken 6 dismal 7 pitiful 8 desolate, pitiable, wretched 9 miserable,
neglected 11 unfortunate
Godiva's husband 7 Leofric
godless 6 wicked 7 impious, infidel
8 agnostic 9 atheistic 11 irreligious,
unreligious
godlike 6 deific, divine 8 deifical, immortal
godly 4 holy 5 pious 6 deific, devout,
divine 7 angelic, saintly 9 pietistic, prayerful, religious
go down 3 dip, sag, set 4 drop, fall, fold,
sink 5 droop, pitch, slump 6 cave in,
plunge, submit, topple, tumble 7 crumple,
decline, descend, founder, go under, succumb 8 collapse, keel over, submerge, submerse 9 surrender

God's acre 8 cemetery 9 graveyard
10 churchyard, necropolis 11 polyandrium
12 burial ground, memorial park, potter's
field 13 burying ground
godsend 4 boon, good 7 benefit 8 blessing 9 advantage 11 benediction
Goethe work 5 Faust 6 Egmont, Stella
7 Clavigo 10 Prometheus
goffer 5 crimp, flute, plait
go-getter 6 dynamo, peeler 7 hustler, rustler 8 live wire 11 self-starter
goggle 3 eye 4 bore, gape, gawk, gaze,
look, ogle, peer 5 glare, gloat, stare
goggles 5 specs 7 glasses 8 blinkers
10 spectacles
Gogol novel 9 Dead Souls 10 Taras
Bulba
Gog's land 5 Magog
goiter 6 struma 8 swelling
gola 4 cyma 7 granary 9 storeroom,
warehouse
Golconda see **gold mine**
gold 4 gilt 5 aurum, metal, money 6 riches,
wealth, yellow 7 bullion, element 8 treasure
bar: 5 ingot *combining form:* 4 auri, auro
5 chrys 6 chryso *fool's:* 6 pyrite *heraldic:*
2 or *Spanish:* 3 oro *symbol:* 2 Au
goldbrick 5 bum 4 idle, laze, lazy, loaf,
loll 6 dawdle, loiter, lounge 7 shirker,
slacker, slinker
Gold Bug author 3 Poe
gold cloth 4 lamé
gold-covered 4 gilt
golden 4 gilt, rich 5 blond, straw 6 blonde,
flaxen, gilded, liquid, mellow, yellow 7 aureate, aureous, honeyed 8 Hyblaean
golden-ager 5 elder 6 senior 7 ancient,
oldster 8 old-timer 13 senior citizen
golden apple 3 bel 6 tomato 7 hog plum
golden-apples guardian 5 Ithun
6 Ithunn
golden bough 9 mistletoe
golden-crowned accentor 8 ovenbird
goldeneye 4 duck 8 lacewing
9 merrywing
Golden Fleece seeker 5 Jason
8 Argonaut
Golden Hind captain 5 Drake
Golden Horde 6 Tatars 7 Mongols
golden horse 8 palomino
Golden State 10 California
golden wolf 6 chanco
goldfinch 8 graypate 12 yellowhammer
gold mine 7 bonanza 8 El Dorado, Golconda, treasury 13 treasure-house, treasure trove
golem 4 dolt 5 robot 7 machine 9 automaton, blockhead
golf *assistant:* 5 caddy 6 caddie *award:*
8 Ryder Cup 9 Curtis Cup, Walker Cup
club: 4 iron, wood 5 baffy, cleek, spoon,

wedge **6** driver, mashie, putter **7** brassie, niblick, pitcher **9** metal wood, sand wedge *club part:* **3** toe **4** face, grip, head, heel, neck, sole **5** hosel, shaft **6** socket *course:* **5** links *hazard:* **4** trap **6** bunker **8** sand trap *mound:* **3** tee *score:* **3** par **5** bogey, bogie, eagle **6** birdie **9** albatross *stroke:* **3** ace **4** chip, draw, fade, hook, putt **5** drive, pitch, shank, slice **6** sclaff *target:* **3** cup, par, pin **4** flag **5** green **7** fairway *term:* **3** lie **4** ball, club, fore, hole, loft **5** divot, rough, round, swing **6** course, hazard, marker, stance, stroke **8** approach, foursome, handicap **9** backswing, downswing, flagstick **10** Vardon grip

golfer **8** linksman *man:* **4** Ford (Doug), Kite (Tom) **5** Boros (Julius), Faldo (Nick), Floyd (Ray), Hagen (Walter), Hogan (Ben), Jones (Bobby), Irwin (Hale), Shute (Denny), Snead (Sam) **6** Casper (Billy), Miller (Johnny), Nelson (Byron), Ouimet (Francis), Palmer (Arnold), Player (Gary), Vardon (Harry), Watson (Tom) **7** Guldahl (Ralph), Sarazen (Gene), Stewart (Payne), Trevino (Lee), Woosnam (Ian) **8** Crenshaw (Ben), Nicklaus (Jack), Weiskopf (Tom), Rodriquez (Chi Chi) **10** Middlecoff (Cary) **11** Ballesteros (Seve) *woman:* **4** Berg (Patty), King (Betsy) **5** Lopez (Nancy), Rawls (Betsy), Stacy (Hollis), Suggs (Louise) **6** Alcott (Amy), Carner (Joanne), Daniel (Beth), Wright (Mickey) **7** Bradley (Pat), Sheehan (Patty) **8** Zaharias (Babe) **9** Whitworth (Kathy) **10** Stephenson (Jan)

Goliath **5** giant **10** Philistine *deathplace:* **4** Elah *home:* **4** Gath *slayer:* **5** David

Gomer *father:* **7** Diblaim *husband:* **5** Hosea

gonad **5** gland, ovary **6** testis

gondola **3** car **4** boat **5** chair

gone **4** away, dead, left, lost **6** absent, gravid, parous **7** defunct, extinct, lacking, missing, omitted, wanting **8** childing, departed, enceinte, pregnant, vanished

gonef see **ganef**

Goneril *father:* **4** Lear *husband:* **6** Albany *sister:* **5** Regan **8** Cordelia *victim:* **5** Regan

Gone with the Wind *author:* **8** Mitchell *character:* **6** Ashley **7** Melanie **11** Rhett Butler **13** Scarlett O'Hara *plantation:* **4** Tara

gonfalon **4** flag **6** banner, ensign **7** pendant, pennant **8** standard **9** banderole

goo **4** crud, gook, goop, guck, gunk, muck

goober **3** nut **6** peanut

good **3** apt, fit **4** able, boon, just, meet, nice, pure **5** brave, right, sound, whole **6** adroit, au fait, clever, cogent, common, decent, humane, intact, kindly, proper, seemly, toward, useful **7** benefic, benefit,

capable, fitting, gainful, godsend, healthy, helpful, welcome, welfare **8** adequate, all right, blessing, decorous, flawless, hygienic, innocent, interest, pleasant, pleasing, salutary, sensible, skillful, straight, unmarred, virtuous **9** advantage, agreeable, blameless, competent, congenial, exemplary, favorable, guiltless, healthful, incorrupt, justified, lilywhite, lucrative, qualified, righteous, tolerable, undamaged, untainted, well-being, wholesome, workmanly **10** acceptable, altruistic, beneficial, benevolent, charitable, gratifying, inculpable, profitable, propitious, prosperity, salubrious, sufficient, unblamable, unimpaired, worthwhile **11** appropriate, benediction, considerate, pleasurable, pleasureful, respectable, unblemished, uncorrupted, well-behaved, well-founded, workmanlike **12** advantageous, considerable, eleemosynary, humanitarian, remunerative, salutiferous, satisfactory, well-grounded **13** philanthropic *combining form:* **2** eu **5** agath **6** agatho *French:* **3** bon *German:* **3** gut *Spanish:* **5** bueno

good-bye **4** ta-ta **5** adieu, congé **6** so long **7** cheerio, parting **8** farewell, toodleoo **9** departing **11** leave-taking, valedictory *French:* **5** adieu *German:* **8** lebe wohl *Japanese:* **8** sayonara *Spanish:* **5** adios

Good Earth author **4** Buck

good-for-nothing **6** drafty, drossy, nogood, waster **7** fustian, inutile, nothing, rounder, useless, wastrel **8** feckless, unworthy **9** valueless, worthless **10** ne'er-do-well, profligate, scapegrace, unpurposed **11** meaningless, purposeless

good-humored see **good-natured**

good-looking **4** fair **6** comely, lovely, pretty **8** handsome **9** beauteous, beautiful **10** attractive

goodly **5** ample, large **6** comely, pretty **8** handsome **9** excellent **12** considerable

good-natured **4** easy, mild **6** genial, jovial **7** amiable, lenient **8** cheerful, obliging **9** gemütlich **10** altruistic, benevolent, charitable **11** complaisant

goodness **5** honor, merit **6** purity, virtue **7** honesty, probity **8** chastity, morality **9** integrity, rectitude, rightness **11** benevolence, uprightness **13** righteousness

goods **4** gear, line **5** stock, wares **7** effects **8** chattels, movables **9** vendibles **10** belongings **11** commodities, merchandise, possessions *smuggled:* **10** contraband *stolen:* **4** loot **5** booty **6** spoils *thrown overboard:* **5** lagan, ligan **6** jetsam

good-tasting **5** sapid, tasty **6** savory **8** tasteful **9** palatable, relishing, toothsome **10** appetizing, flavorsome

goodwill **5** amity, favor **6** comity **7** charity, rapport **8** alacrity, altruism, dispatch, kindness, sympathy **9** readiness, tolerance **10** expedition, friendship, generosity, kindliness **11** benevolence, helpfulness, promptitude **12** friendliness

goody **5** candy, treat **6** bonbon, dainty, morsel, tidbit, titbit **8** delicacy, kickshaw

goody-goody **4** prig **5** prude **6** Grundy **7** puritan **8** bluenose, comstock **9** Mrs. Grundy, nice Nelly

gooey **5** gluey, gummy, mushy, sappy, sobby, soupy **6** cloggy, drippy, slushy, sticky, stodgy **7** maudlin **8** adhesive **11** sentimental

goof **3** err **4** boob, dolt, mess **5** booby, botch, chump, dunce, gum up **6** bobble, bollix, bungle **7** blunder, fathead, louse up **8** dolthead, lunkhead

go off **4** blow **5** burst **7** explode **8** detonate

goofy **5** crazy, silly **6** stupid **7** foolish

gook **3** rot **4** crud, goop, gunk, muck **5** bilge, gumbo, hooey, trash **6** drivel

go on **3** act **4** bear, quit **5** carry **6** acquit, behave, demean, deport, hang on **7** carry on, comport, conduct, persist **8** continue **9** persevere

goon **3** sap **4** boob, dolt, dope, thug **7** hoodlum

gooney **9** albatross

goop **4** gook, gunk, muck **5** gumbo

goose **4** bird, dolt, poke **5** solan **9** simpleton *cry:* **4** honk, yang *genus:* **5** Anser *Hawaiian:* **4** nene *male:* **6** gander *relating to:* **8** anserine *snow:* **4** chen, wavy **5** wavey *wild:* **5** brant **7** graylag, greylag **8** barnacle, bernicle *young:* **7** gosling

goose egg **4** zero **5** aught, ought, zilch **6** cipher, naught, nought **7** nothing

gooseflesh **5** bumps **7** pimples

gopher **6** marmot, rodent **8** squirrel, tortoise

Gopher State **9** Minnesota

Gordian knot cutter **9** Alexander

Gordius' son **5** Midas

gore **4** stab, tush, tusk **5** blood, slime, wound **6** pierce

gorge **3** gap **4** cloy, fill, glut, jade, pall, sate **5** chasm, cleft, clove, flume, gulch, stuff **6** arroyo, clough, devour, gobble, guzzle, ravine, stodge **7** couloir, overeat, satiate, surfeit **11** overindulge *Arizona:* **11** Grand Canyon *China:* **7** Yangtze *Colorado:* **5** Royal

gorgeous **5** grand, plush, proud **6** lavish, lovely, pretty, superb **7** opulent, sublime **8** glorious, splendid **9** beautiful, luxurious, sumptuous **10** impressive **11** magnificent, resplendent, splendorous

Gorgon **6** Medusa, Stheno **7** Euryale *father:* **7** Phorcus, Phorcys *mother:* **4** Ceto

sentinel: **4** Enyo **5** Deino **6** Graeae, Graiae **8** Pephredo

gorilla **3** ape **6** monkey **7** primate **10** anthropoid

Gorki drama **14** The Lower Depths

gorse **5** furze **7** juniper

gory **6** bloody **7** imbrued **8** sanguine **10** sanguinary **11** ensanguined, sanguineous **12** bloodstained

gospel **5** truth **6** truism **8** doctrine, teaching

gossamer **3** web **5** filmy, gauzy, sheer **6** filmy **7** tiffany **10** diaphanous **11** transparent

gossip **3** cry **4** blab, buzz, chat, talk **5** clack, on-dit, prate, rumor, sieve, tabby **6** babble, claver, report, rumble, tattle **7** chatter, hearsay, prattle, rumorer **8** bigmouth, busybody, informer, quidnunc, telltale **9** carrytale, grapevine **10** circulator, mumblenews, newsmonger, talebearer **11** rumormonger, scandalizer, scuttlebutt

Gotham **7** New York

Gothic **4** rude, wild **5** crude **6** brutal, coarse, Hunnic, savage **7** Hunnish **8** barbaric **9** barbarian, barbarous **11** uncivilized

Gouda **6** cheese

gouge **3** con, dig **4** tool **5** cheat, exact, pinch, screw, wrest, wring **6** extort, wrench **7** squeeze, swindle **9** shake down **10** overcharge

goulash **4** stew **6** jumble, medley **8** mishmash

go under **4** fall, sink **6** go down, submit **7** founder, succumb **8** submerge, submerse **9** surrender

Gounod work **5** Faust **8** Ave Maria

gourd **4** pepo **5** fruit, melon **6** bottle, vessel **7** pumpkin **8** calabash, cucurbit *instrument:* **6** maraca

gourmand see **glutton; gourmet**

gourmet **7** epicure **9** bon vivant **10** gastronome **11** gastronomer **12** gastronomist

gout **4** blob, clot **5** spurt **6** splash **7** podagra **8** swelling

govern **3** run **4** head, lead, rule, sway **5** guide, reign, steer **6** direct, handle, manage, master, render **7** command, conduct, control, execute, oversee **8** carry out, dominate, overrule, regulate, shepherd **9** supervise **10** administer

governess **4** nana **5** nanny, nurse **6** duenna, nannie **8** mistress **9** nursemaid

government **4** rule **5** power **6** polity, regime **7** conduct, control, regency, regimen, tyranny **8** guidance, monarchy, republic **9** authority, autocracy, democracy, direction, hierarchy, oligarchy **10** management **11** aristocracy **12** dictatorship, organization *autocratic:* **7** czarism **9** despotism **10** absolutism **12** dictatorship *by a few:*

9 oligarchy *by eight:* **8** octarchy *by one:*
8 monarchy *by three:* **8** triarchy **11** triumvirate *by women:* **8** gynarchy *combining form:* **5** archy, cracy **6** ocracy *official:*
6 consul, syndic **8** diplomat **10** bureaucrat
relating to: **9** political *science:* **8** politics
without: **7** anarchy

government agency **2** VA **3** CIA, FAA,
FBI, FCC, FDA, FHA, GAO, GPO, HUD, ICC,
NBS, NRC, TVA **4** FEPC, NASA

governor **3** bey **4** head, lord **5** chief,
nabob, pilot, ruler **6** leader, rector, regent
7 captain, manager, viceroy **8** director, official **9** executive, regulator **10** commandant,
controller, magistrate *Chinese:* **6** tuchun *of a fort:* **7** alcaide **9** castellan, chatelain *Persian:* **6** satrap *Turkish:* **8** hospador

gown **4** robe, toga **5** dress, frock, habit,
tunic **6** banian, banyan, camise, clothe,
kimono, mantua **7** cassock, chemise, garment **8** peignoir *hospital:* **6** johnny

goy **7** gentile

grab **3** hog, nab **4** nail, take **5** catch, clasp,
grasp, seize **6** clutch, snatch, tackle
7 grapple

grabby **5** itchy **6** greedy **8** covetous,
desirous, grasping **10** prehensile
11 acquisitive

grace **4** ease **5** adorn, charm, favor,
mercy **6** lenity, polish, prayer, thanks, virtue **7** caritas, charity, dignify, dignity
8 blessing, clemency, easiness, elegance,
goodness, kindness, leniency, petition
9 embellish **10** indulgence, invocation, suppleness **11** benediction, forbearance
12 thanksgiving

graceful **4** airy, deft, easy **6** featly, gainly,
smooth, urbane **7** elegant, flowing, genteel,
refined **8** debonair, polished

graceless **4** wild **5** inept **6** vulgar **7** awkward, unhappy **8** barbaric **9** barbarian, barbarous, ill-chosen, tasteless **10** outlandish
11 unfortunate **12** infelicitous

Graces **6** Aglaia (brilliance), Charis, Thalia
(bloom) **8** Charites (plural) **10** Euphrosyne
(joy) *mother:* **5** Aegle

gracious **4** easy, kind, mild **5** preux
6 benign, clubby, genial, kindly **7** affable,
amiable, cordial, courtly, gallant, starchy,
stately **8** mannered, obliging, outgoing,
sociable **9** benignant, bonhomous, congenial, courteous

grackle **3** jaw **7** jackdaw **9** blackbird

gradation **4** step **5** range, shade **6** ablaut,
change, degree, nuance, series **8** position
9 variation **10** difference, divergence

grade **3** peg **4** lean, rank, rate, rung, sort,
step, tier, tilt **5** class, group, notch, order,
slant, slope, stage **6** assort, degree, estate,
league **7** arrange, caliber, incline, leaning,

quality **8** appraise, category, classify, evaluate, grouping

Grade A **3** top **4** fine **5** prime **7** capital
8 five-star, superior, top-notch **9** excellent,
first-rate, top-drawer **10** first-class

gradient **4** lean, ramp, tilt **5** slant, slope
7 incline, leaning **11** inclination *combining form:* **5** cline **6** clinal

gradine **4** seat, step **5** shelf **6** chisel

gradually **8** bit by bit **9** piecemeal **10** step
by step

graduate *female:* **6** alumna **7** alumnae
(plural) *male:* **6** alumni (plural) **7** alumnus

Graeae, Graiae **4** Enyo **5** Deino
8 Pephredo *father:* **7** Phorcus, Phorcys
mother: **4** Ceto *sisters:* **7** Gorgons

graft **4** join, mend **5** crime, scion, unite
6 attach, boodle, fasten, inarch **7** implant,
topwork

grail **3** cup **7** chalice, platter

grain **3** bit, jot, rye **4** corn, iota, meal, mite,
oats, rice **5** crumb, fiber, maize, speck,
trace, wheat **6** barley, cereal, tittle **7** granule, smidgen, sorghum, texture **8** molecule,
particle *bundle:* **4** bale **5** sheaf *chute:*
6 hopper *ear:* **5** spica, spike *elevator:*
4 silo *mixture:* **6** fodder *row:* **5** swath
7 windrow

grainy **6** coarse **8** granular

grammarian *Roman:* **7** Donatus

grammatical case **6** dative **8** ablative,
genitive, locative, vocative **9** objective
10 accusative, nominative, possessive,
subjective

grampus **5** whale **8** cetacean, scorpion
9 blackfish

Granada *building:* **8** Alhambra *citadel:*
8 Alcazaba *last Moorish king:* **7** Boabdil

granary **3** bin **4** gola, silo **10** repository,
storehouse

grand **4** epic, huge **5** gaudy, lofty, noble,
royal, showy **6** august, flashy, garish, lavish, lordly, ornate, superb **7** exalted, stately,
sublime **8** baronial, elevated, gorgeous,
imposing, magnific, majestic, princely, splendid, towering **9** luxurious, sumptuous
10 impressive, monumental, prodigious, stupendous, tremendous **11** magnificent
12 ostentatious

Grand Canyon *explorer:* **6** Powell
state: **7** Arizona

grande dame **6** matron **7** dowager
9 matriarch

grandee **5** pasha **6** bashaw **8** nobleman

grandeur **4** pomp **7** dignity, majesty
8 nobility, splendor, vastness **9** greatness,
largeness, loftiness, nobleness, sublimity
10 augustness **11** stateliness
12 magnificence

grand inquisitor *Spanish:*
10 Torquemada

grandiose 4 epic, vast 5 lofty, noble, royal, showy 6 august, cosmic, lordly 7 stately, utopian 8 imposing, majestic, princely 9 ambitious, visionary 11 magnificent, pretentious 12 ostentatious

grandmother *Russian:* 8 babushka *Scottish:* 6 gudame

grange 4 farm 5 lodge 9 farmhouse

granite 4 rock 6 aplite

Granite State 12 New Hampshire

grant 3 aid, own 4 alms, avow, cede, dole, gift, give 5 admit, allow, award, let on, own up, yield 6 accord, bestow, confer, donate, fess up, permit 7 charity, concede, confess, entitle, handout, present, subsidy 8 bequeath, donation 9 vouchsafe 10 assistance, relinquish, subvention 11 acknowledge, benefaction 12 contribution 13 appropriation

granular 5 rough, sandy 6 coarse, grainy

granule 4 pill, spot 5 grain 6 pellet 8 particle

grape 3 fox, uva 4 Bual 5 Gamay, Pinot 6 Arinto, Burger, Gentil, Merlot, muscat 7 Albillo, Aligote, Barbera, Catawba, Concord, Furmint, Niagara, sultana 8 Aleatico, Cabernet, Charbono, Delaware, Friularo, Grenache, Isabella, labrusca, malvasia, muscadel, Nebbiolo, Riesling, Semillon, Sylvaner, Thompson, Traminer, vinifera, Viognier 9 Chasselas, Lambrusco, Malvoisie, muscadine, Pinot Gris, Pinot Noir, Sauvignon, Trebbiano, zinfandel 10 Grignolino, muscadelle, Pinot Blanc, Verdicchio 11 Chenin Blanc, Mavrodaphne, Petite Sirah, scuppernong *dried:* 6 raisin *drink:* 4 wine *pulp:* 4 rape 6 pomace *residue:* 4 marc

grapefruit 6 pomelo

Grapes of Wrath *author:* 9 Steinbeck *family:* 4 Joad *people:* 5 Okies

grapevine 4 buzz, talk 5 on-dit, rumor 6 gossip, report, rumble 7 hearsay

graph 3 map 5 chart 6 sketch 7 diagram, outline 8 nomogram

graphic 5 clear, lucid, vivid 6 cogent, visual 7 precise, telling 8 clear-cut, definite, explicit, incisive, pictoric, striking 9 pictorial, realistic 10 compelling

graphite 4 lead 6 carbon 8 plumbago

grapnel 4 hook 6 anchor

grapple 3 nab 4 grab, grip, hold, take 5 catch, clamp, clasp, grasp, gripe, seize 6 bucket, clench, clinch, clutch, snatch, tenure, tussle 7 scuffle, wrestle

grasp 3 dig, see 4 grip, have, hent, hold, know, take 5 catch, clamp, clasp, gripe 6 accept, clench, clinch, clutch, fathom, follow, take in, tenure 7 cognize, compass, grapple 8 envisage, perceive 9 apprehend 10 appreciate, comprehend, understand

graspable 5 lucid 8 knowable 10 fathomable 12 intelligible 13 apprehensible

grasping 4 avid 5 itchy 6 grabby, greedy 8 covetous, desirous 9 extorting 10 prehensile 11 acquisitive

grass 3 pot, sod, tea 4 lawn, reed, turf, weed 6 moocah, redtop 7 herbage, panicum, pasture 8 cannabis, Mary Jane 9 cocksfoot, marijuana *African:* 6 imphee *annual:* 6 darnel 8 teosinte *Asian:* 7 vetiver, whangee *Australian:* 8 spinifex *beach:* 6 marram *cereal:* 3 oat, rye 4 milo, teff 5 kafir, maize, proso, wheat 6 kaffir, millet, sorgho 7 sorghum 8 feterita, triticum *clump:* 4 tuft 7 tussock *combining form:* 6 gramin 7 gramini *dried:* 3 hay *European:* 7 Bermuda, timothy *fiber:* 4 flax *fragrant:* 10 citronella *giant:* 5 otate *Mexican:* 7 zacaton *pasture:* 5 Bahia, grama *perennial:* 5 muhly 6 fescue, quitch, zoysia 7 esparto, galleta *prairie:* 8 bluestem *second growth:* 5 rowen *tropical:* 5 cogon 6 bamboo

grasshopper 4 grig 6 locust 7 katydid

grassland 3 lea 5 field 6 meadow 7 pasture, prairie *African:* 4 veld 5 veldt *flat:* 7 savanna 8 savannah *South American:* 5 pampa

grate 3 get, jar 4 bark, fray, gall, rasp, rile, skin 5 chafe, peeve, pique, scuff 6 abrade, burn up, nettle, scrape 7 provoke, scratch 8 irritate 9 aggravate

grateful 4 good 7 obliged, pleased, welcome 8 beholden, pleasant, renewing, solacing, thankful 9 agreeable, congenial, consoling, delicious, favorable, gratified

Gratiano *brother:* 9 Brabantio *friend:* 7 Antonio 8 Bassanio *niece:* 9 Desdemona *wife:* 7 Nerissa

gratify 4 baby, feed, sate 5 favor, feast, humor 6 arride, coddle, oblige, pamper, pander, please 7 appease, cater to, content, delight, gladden, happify, indulge, satisfy

grating 3 dry 4 grid, rasp 5 grill, harsh, rough 6 grille, hoarse 7 jarring, rasping, raucous 8 gridiron, strident 10 stridulent

gratis 4 free 8 costless 10 chargeless, gratuitous 13 complimentary

gratuitous 4 free 6 gratis, wanton 7 unasked, willing 8 baseless, costless 9 unfounded, voluntary 10 bottomless, chargeless, groundless, reasonless, ungrounded 11 uncalled-for, unwarranted 12 indefensible, supererogant 13 complimentary

gratuity 3 fee, tip 4 alms, gift, perk 5 bonus 6 reward 7 cumshaw, douceur, largess 8 donation, offering 9 baksheesh, lagniappe, pourboire 10 perquisite 11 benefaction 12 contribution

grave 3 pit, sad 4 dire, etch, fell, grim, tomb, ugly 5 awful, crypt, drive, fatal, heavy, major, pound, sober, staid, stamp, vault 6 burial, deadly, hammer, incise, sedate, severe, solemn, somber 7 austere, earnest, ghastly, impress, killing, ossuary, serious, weighty 8 catacomb, dreadful, grievous, horrible, terrible 9 dangerous, mausoleum, murderous, ponderous, saturnine, sepulcher, sepulture *marker:* 5 stela, stele 6 ledger 8 memorial, monument 9 footstone, headstone, tombstone 11 sarcophagus *mound:* 6 barrow 7 tumulus *robber:* 5 ghoul

gravel 4 dirt, grit, sand *ridge:* 5 esker

graven image 4 idol

graver 5 burin 8 sculptor

graveyard 8 boot hill, cemetery 8 God's acre 10 necropolis 11 polyandrium 12 burial ground, memorial park, potter's field 13 burying ground

gravid 6 parous 8 childing, enceinte, pregnant 9 expectant, expecting 10 parturient

gravity 6 weight 7 dignity 8 sobriety 9 heaviness, solemnity 10 importance, somberness 11 seriousness

gravy 5 juice, sauce 8 dressing, windfall *French:* 3 jus

gray 3 ash, old 4 aged, ashy, blah, drab, dull 5 ashen, bleak, color, hoary, slate, slaty, taupe 6 dismal, gloomy, leaden 7 elderly, grizzly, neutral 8 cinerous, gunmetal, overcast 9 colorless *brownish:* 7 fuscous *combining form:* 4 poli 5 glauc, polio 6 glauco

gray dawn 4 zinc

gray duck 7 gadwall, mallard, pintail

grayfish 7 pollack

gray matter 3 wit 4 head, mind, obex 5 brain 9 intellect

graze 3 dop, rub 4 feed, gall, harm, hurt, kiss, skim, skip, wear 5 brush, carom, chafe, erode, shave, wound 6 abrade, bruise, glance, injure, ruffle 7 contuse, corrade, pasture 8 ricochet

grease 3 fat, oil 4 lard, soil 5 smear 6 smooth 7 lanolin 9 lubricant, lubricate *combining form:* 4 sebi, sebo

greasy 4 oily 5 fatty, slick 6 slippy 7 pinguid 8 slippery, slithery, unctuous 10 lubricious, oleaginous

greasy spoon 4 café 5 diner 7 beanery, hashery 9 hash house, lunchroom 10 coffee shop

great 3 big, fat 4 bull, huge, vast 5 famed, grand, husky, large 6 famous, heroic 7 eminent, extreme, immense, notable, supreme, titanic 8 enormous, oversize, renowned 9 excellent, fantastic, important, prominent, wonderful 10 celebrated, celebrious, surpassing 11 illustrious, magnificent, superlative 13 distinguished *combining form:* 3 meg 4 mega 5 megal 6 megalo

Great Bear 9 Big Dipper, Ursa Major

Great Britain see **England**

Great Commoner, the 4 Pitt

Great Emancipator, the 7 Lincoln

greater 4 more, over 6 better, higher, larger 8 superior 9 overlying 11 superjacent

greatest 4 best, most 6 utmost 7 largest, noblest, supreme *amount:* 7 maximum

Great Expectations *author:* 7 Dickens *character:* 3 Pip 5 Biddy 7 Estella, Jaggers 8 Havisham, Magwitch

greathearted 3 big 5 brave, lofty, manly 6 heroic 7 gallant 8 fearless, generous 10 benevolent, chivalrous, courageous 11 considerate, magnanimous

Great Lake 4 Erie 5 Huron 7 Ontario 8 Michigan, Superior

Great Lake State 8 Michigan

grebe 4 bird, fowl 5 dabchick, didapper

Greece *capital:* 6 Athens *monetary unit:* 7 drachma

greed 7 avarice, avidity 8 cupidity, gluttony, rapacity, voracity 12 ravenousness

greedy 5 itchy 6 grabby 7 miserly, selfish 8 covetous, desirous, esurient, grasping 10 avaricious, gluttonous 11 acquisitive

Greek 6 babble, drivel, jabber 7 Achaean 8 Hellenic, nonsense 9 gibberish *alien resident:* 5 metic *assembly:* 5 agora, boule *coin:* 4 obol 5 hecte 6 lepton, stater *column:* 5 Doric, Ionic 10 Corinthian *contest:* 4 agon *counselor:* 6 Nestor *cup:* 5 kylix *dictator:* 7 Metaxas *dragon:* 9 Eurython *drink:* 4 ouzo *epic:* 5 Iliad 7 Odyssey *Fates:* 6 Clotho, Moirae 7 Atropos 8 Lachesis

god:

   chief: 4 Zeus *messenger:* 6 Hermes *of agriculture:* 6 Cronus *of death:* 8 Thanatos *of fire:* 10 Hephaestus *of healing:* 9 Asclepius *of love:* 4 Eros *of marriage:* 5 Hymen *of physicions:* 6 Hermes *of the sea:* 6 Triton 7 Oceanus 8 Poseidon *of the sun:* 6 Helios *of the underworld:* 5 Pluto *of the wind:* 5 Eurus, Notus 6 Aeolus, Boreas 8 Zephyrus *of war:* 4 Ares *of wine:* 8 Dionysus *of woods:* 3 Pan

goddess:

   of agriculture: 7 Demeter *of beauty:* 9 Aphrodite *of dawn:* 3 Eos *of discord:* 4 Eris *of flowers:* 7 Chloris *of harvests:* 4 Rhea *of hunting:* 7 Artemis *of justice:* 7 Astraea *of love:* 9 Aphrodite *of marriage:* 4 Hera *of night:* 3 Nyx *of peace:* 5 Irene *of retribution:* 7 Nemesis *of the earth:* 2 Ge 4 Gaea, Gaia *of the moon:* 6 Hecate, Hekate, Selena, Selene 7 Artemis, Astarte *of the seasons:* 5 Horae *of the underworld:* 6 Hecate, Hekate *of vengeance:* 7 Nemesis *of victory:* 4 Nike *of wisdom:* 6 Athena *of witchcraft:* 6 Hecate, Hekate *of womanhood:* 4 Hera *of youth:* 4 Hebe

hero: 4 Aias, Ajax 5 Jason 7 Theseus 8 Achilles, Argonaut, Heracles, Hercules, Odysseus 9 Achilleus *historian:* 8 Xenophon 9 Herodotus 10 Thucydides *lawgiver:* 5 Draco, Solon *leader:* 9 Agamemnon *letter:* 2 mu, nu, pi, xi 3 chi, eta, phi, psi, rho, tau 4 beta, iota, zeta 5 alpha, delta, gamma, kappa, omega, sigma, theta 6 lambda 7 epsilon, omicron, upsilon *magistrate:* 6 archon *marketplace:* 5 agora *measure:* 3 ona, pik 4 bema 5 cados, chous, digit, maris, pygon, xylon 6 acaena, bachel, barile, cotula, dichas, gramme, hemina, koilon, pechys, pelame, schene 7 amphora, cyathos, diaulos, hekteus, stadion, stadium, stremma 8 condylos, daktylos, dekapode, dolichos, medimnos, metretes, palaiste, plethron, spithame, stathmos 9 oxybaphon *porch:* 4 stoa *sandwich:* 4 gyro *shield:* 5 pelta *soldier:* 7 hoplite *theater:* 5 odeon, odeum *underworld:* 5 Hades *war cry:* 5 alala *warrior:* 4 Ajax 7 Ulysses 8 Achilles, Diomedes, Odysseus 9 Agamemnon, Palamedes *weight:* 3 mna, oka 4 mina 5 litra, livre 6 diobol, kantar, obolus, stater 7 chalcon, chalque, drachma 8 diobolon, talanton *wine:* 7 retsina, retzina

green 3 raw 5 alive, fresh, plaza, virid, young 6 callow, common, infant, square, unripe 7 celadon, emerald, untried, verdant 8 immature, juvenile, pistache, unversed, youthful 9 unfledged 10 unseasoned 11 unpracticed 13 inexperienced *bluish:* 8 glaucous *combining form:* 4 verd 5 chlor, verdo 6 chloro *grayish:* 5 olive *yellowish:* 7 luteous 10 chartreuse

greenbacks 4 cash, jack 5 bread, dough, money 6 wampum 7 scratch 8 currency 11 legal tender

green-eyed 7 envious, envying, jealous 9 invidious *monster:* 8 jealousy

greenfish 7 opaleye, pollack

greenfly 5 aphid

greengage 4 plum

greenhead 3 fly 5 scaup 7 mallard

greenheart 4 tree 7 bebeeru

greenhorn 4 hick, jake, rube, tyro 5 clown 6 novice, rustic 7 bumpkin, hayseed 9 hillbilly 10 clodhopper, provincial 12 backwoodsman

greenhouse 12 conservatory

Greenland *capital:* 7 Godthab 8 God-

thaab *discoverer:* 10 Eric the Red *native:* 3 Ita *settlement:* 4 Etah

green light 2 OK 7 go-ahead 9 clearance 13 authorization

Green Mansions *author:* 6 Hudson *character:* 4 Rima

green monkey 6 guenon

Green Mountain State 7 Vermont

greenness 5 youth 6 spring 7 puberty, rawness 8 verdancy, viridity 9 freshness, youthhood 10 callowness, juvenility, pubescence, springtide, springtime 11 adolescence 12 inexperience, youthfulness

green osier 7 dogwood

green plover 7 lapwing

green poppy 8 foxglove

greenroom 6 lounge

greenstone 7 diabase, diorite 8 nephrite

greet 3 cry 4 hail 6 accost, call to, salute 7 address, receive, welcome

greeting 3 ave, bow 4 hail 5 aloha, hello 6 salute 7 address, welcome 9 reception 10 salutation

gregarious 6 social 8 friendly, outgoing, sociable

gremlin 3 elf, imp 5 gnome 6 sprite

grenade 4 bomb 5 shell 7 missile 9 explosive

grenadier 4 fish 7 rattail, soldier

grenadine 4 pink, yarn 5 syrup 9 carnation

Grendel's slayer 7 Beowulf

Gretchen's lover 5 Faust

Grey's forte 7 Western

grid 5 grate 7 grating, network

griddle 3 pan 5 grill

griddle cake 7 pancake 8 flapjack

gridiron 5 field, grill 7 grating, network

grief 3 rue, woe 4 care 5 dolor, tears 6 regret, sorrow 7 anguish, chagrin, emotion, sadness, trouble 8 distress, hardship 9 bemoaning, bewailing, deploring, heartache, lamenting, suffering 10 affliction, heartbreak 11 lamentation

Grieg work 8 Peer Gynt

grievance 5 cross, rigor, trial, wrong 6 burden, injury 8 hardship 9 complaint, injustice 10 affliction 11 tribulation

grieve 3 cry, rue 4 bear, hurt, keen, moan, pain, wail, weep 5 mourn 6 bemoan, bewail, endure, injure, lament, sorrow, suffer 7 deplore 8 distress 9 constrain

grievous 3 sad 4 dire, fell, sore, ugly 5 grave, major, tough 6 bitter, taxing, woeful 7 exigent, galling, onerous, painful, serious, weighty 8 exacting 9 dangerous, demanding 10 afflictive, burdensome, calamitous, deplorable, lamentable, oppressive 11 distasteful, distressing, regrettable, unfortunate, unpalatable

grill 3 vex 4 cook, grid 5 broil, grate

7 afflict, griddle, torment 8 gridiron, question 11 third degree 12 cross-examine 13 interrogation

grilse 4 fish 6 salmon

grim 3 set 4 cold, dour, fell, firm, hard 5 angry, bleak, cruel, fixed, harsh, lurid, rigid, stern 6 dogged, fierce, grisly, mortal, savage, severe 7 adamant, austere, certain, ghastly, hideous, inhuman, macabre, ominous, wolfish 8 gruesome, horrible, inhumane, obdurate, resolute, ruthless, stubborn, terrible 9 barbarous, ferocious, loathsome, merciless, offensive, repugnant, repulsive, revolting, stringent, truculent 10 determined, forbidding, foreboding, horrifying, implacable, inevitable, inexorable, inflexible, ironfisted, off-putting, relentless, terrifying, unyielding, vindictive 11 unflinching, unforgiving

grimace 3 mop, mow, mug 4 face, moue 5 mouth, smirk, sneer 6 deform 7 contort, distort

grimalkin 3 cat, hag 6 feline

grime 4 dirt, foul, soil 5 dirty, sully 6 besoil, smirch, smooch, smudge, smutch 7 tarnish

grim reaper 5 death

grin 4 beam 5 fleer, risus, smile, smirk

grind 3 rut, vex 4 chew, grub, mill, moil, pace, plod, rote, slog, toil, work 5 crush, gnash, grate, labor, slave, sweat 6 crunch, drudge, groove, kibble 7 routine, travail 8 bullwork, drudgery, plugging 9 treadmill 10 donkeywork

grinder 4 hero 5 molar, stone, tooth 8 sandwich 9 submarine

grinding 5 harsh 6 severe 7 grating, wearing *stone:* 4 mano 6 muller, pestle

grip 4 hold, take, vice 5 clamp, clasp, grasp, seize 6 clench, clinch, clutch, duress, handle, tenure, valise 7 catch up, grapple 8 coercion, enthrall, handfast, handhold 9 fascinate, mesmerize, restraint, spellbind 10 constraint

gripe 4 beef, crab, fuss, hold, kick, yaup, yawp 5 bitch, bleat, brawl, clamp, clasp, croak, grasp 6 clench, clinch, clutch, grouch, grouse, murmur, mutter, squawk, take on, tenure, yammer 7 blow off, grapple, grumble 8 complain 9 bellyache

griper see **grumbler**

grippe 3 flu 7 disease 9 influenza

gripper 4 clip, hand, vice 5 clamp, clasp, tongs 6 pliers

gris-gris 5 charm, spell 6 amulet 8 talisman 11 incantation

grisly 4 grim 5 eerie, lurid, weird 6 horrid 7 ghastly, hideous, macabre, uncanny 8 gruesome, horrible, terrible 10 horrifying, terrifying

grist 3 lot 5 grain, stint 6 output 8 quantity

gristle 9 cartilage

grit 4 dirt, guts, sand, soil 5 earth, moxie, nerve, spunk 6 gravel 7 courage 8 backbone 9 fortitude

gritty 4 game 5 brave, dirty, sandy 6 plucky, soiled 8 resolute

groan 4 moan, rasp 5 creak, grate

grocery 5 store 11 supermarket *Spanish:* 6 bodega

grog 3 rum 5 booze, drink, hooch, juice 6 liquor, tipple 7 alcohol, spirits

groggy 4 logy, weak 5 dazed, foggy, tired 6 sleepy 7 muddled 8 sluggish

groin 4 fold 6 crotch, inguen *combining form:* 6 inguin 7 inguino

groom 4 comb, tidy 5 brush, clean, curry, ready, shave 6 neaten, polish, refine, toilet 7 prepare, servant 8 benedict 9 attendant 11 horsekeeper *Chinese:* 5 mafoo *Indian:* 4 syce

groove 3 rut 4 nurl, pace, rote, slot 5 canal, flute, glyph, grind, stria 6 fuller, furrow, gutter, hollow 7 chamfer, channel, routine

grope 3 pry 4 feel, poke, root, test 5 probe 6 fumble, handle, search 7 examine, explore, grabble 8 scrabble

grosbeak 4 bird 5 finch 8 haw finch

gross 3 all, big, fat, raw, sum 4 foul, mass, rank, rude 5 brute, crass, crude, heavy, obese, rough, stout, total, utter, whole 6 animal, carnal, coarse, damned, entire, fleshy, portly, smutty, vulgar 7 capital, extreme, glaring, obscene, perfect, porcine, sensual, uncouth, weighty 8 absolute, complete, entirety, flagrant, improper, material, outright, physical, sensible, sum total, tangible, totality 9 aggregate, corporeal, corpulent, downright, egregious, excessive, inelegant, loathsome, objective, offensive, out-and-out, repulsive, revolting, unrefined 10 exorbitant, immoderate

grotesque 5 antic, comic, droll, eerie, weird 6 rococo 7 baroque, bizarre, comical, extreme, uncanny 9 fantastic, ludicrous

grotto 4 cave, hole 5 crypt, vault 6 cavern *Capri:* 4 Blue

grouch 4 crab, sulk 5 crank, croak, grump, scold 6 griper, grouse, kicker, murmur, mutter 7 crabber, grouser, growler, grumble 8 grumbler, sorehead, sourpuss 10 bellyacher, complainer, crosspatch, malcontent 11 faultfinder

ground 3 bed, why 4 base, dirt, down, drop, fell, land, rest, root, seat, soil, stay, test 5 basis, cause, earth, floor, level, proof, trial 6 bottom, reason, whyfor 7 bedrock, dry land, flatten, footing, mow down, support, sustain 8 argument, basement, buttress, evidence **9** bring down, establish, knock down, predicate, testimony, throw down, wherefore **10** antecedent, foundation, substratum, terra firma *combining form:* **2** ge **3** geo, ped **4** pedo **5** chame **6** chamae

grounded 7 beached **8** stranded

groundhog 6 marmot **9** woodchuck

groundless 4 idle **5** false **8** baseless **9** unfounded **10** bottomless, gratuitous, ungrounded **11** uncalled-for, unwarranted

groundwork 3 bed **4** base, root **5** basis **6** bottom **7** bedrock, footing, support **8** basement **10** foundation, substratum **12** substruction, substructure, underpinning

group 3 lot, set **4** band, bevy, body, clot, club, crew, gang, mess, pool, push, ruck, sect, sort, team, tier **5** array, batch, bunch, chain, class, clump, covey, crowd, grade, horde, party, place, squad, suite, trust **6** adjust, assort, bundle, cartel, circle, clique, clutch, gather, huddle, league, muster, parcel, passel **7** arrange, battery, brigade, cluster, collect, combine, company, coterie, council, dispose, echelon, platoon, round up **8** assemble, assembly, category, classify, ensemble, organize **9** congeries, gathering, harmonize, syndicate **10** assemblage, categorize, collection *of angels:* **4** host *of ants:* **6** colony *of badgers:* **4** cete *of bears:* **6** sleuth *of bees:* **4** hive **5** grist, swarm *of birds:* **6** flight, volery *of boars:* **7** sounder *of cats:* **7** clowder, clutter *of cattle:* **5** drove *of chicks:* **5** brood **6** clutch *of clams:* **3** bed *of cranes:* **5** sedge, siege *of crows:* **6** murder *of ducks:* **5** brace *of eight:* **5** octet *of elephants:* **4** herd *of elks:* **4** gang *of fish:* **5** shoal **6** school *of five:* **5** quint **6** pentad **7** quinary, quintet *of four:* **6** tetrad **7** quartet *of foxes:* **5** leash, skulk *of geese:* **5** flock, skein **6** gaggle *of gnats:* **5** cloud, horde *of goats:* **4** trip **5** tribe *of goldfinches:* **5** charm *of gorillas:* **4** band *of greyhounds:* **5** leash *of grouse:* **5** covey *of hares:* **4** down, husk *of hawks:* **4** cast *of hounds:* **3** cry **4** mute, pack *of kangaroos:* **3** mob **5** troop *of kittens:* **6** kendle, kindle *of larks:* **10** exaltation *of leopards:* **4** leap *of lions:* **5** pride *of locusts:* **6** plague *of monkeys:* **5** troop *of mules:* **4** span *of nightingales:* **5** watch *of nine:* **5** nonet *of oysters:* **3** bed *of partridges:* **5** covey *of peacocks:* **6** muster *of pheasants:* **3** nye **4** nest, nide *of plovers:* **4** wing **12** congregation *of quail:* **4** bevy **5** covey *of seals:* **3** pod **5** patch *of seven:* **6** pleiad, septet *of sheep:* **5** drove, flock *of six:* **5** hexad **6** hexade, sextet *of swans:* **4** bevy *of swine:* **7** sounder *of teals:* **6** spring *of three:* **4** trio **5** triad **7** ternary, trinity, triplet *of toads:* **4** knot *of*

vipers: **4** nest *of whales:* **3** gam, pod *of wolves:* **4** pack *suffix:* **2** ad, et **3** ome **4** some

grouper 4 fish **8** rockfish **10** tripletail

grouse 5 croak, gripe, quail, scold **6** gorhen, grouch, murmur, mutter **7** gorcock, greyhen, grumble **8** complain, pheasant **9** blackcock, ptarmigan **10** whitebelly **12** capercaillie *extinct:* **8** heath hen *red:* **8** moorfowl *strut:* **3** lak

grouser see **grumbler**

grout 4 lees **5** dregs **6** cement, mortar **7** grounds, plaster **8** concrete

grove 3 bed **4** holt, wood **5** copse, hurst **7** boscage, coppice, orchard, thicket *suffix:* **3** eta (plural) **4** etum

grovel 4 fawn **5** cower, toady **6** cringe, kowtow, wallow **7** honey up, truckle **8** bootlick **9** brownnose **11** apple-polish

grow 3 age, get, run, wax **4** come, rear, rise, tend, turn **5** breed, nurse, raise, ripen, swell **6** become, expand, foster, mature, mellow, sprout, thrive **7** care for, develop, enlarge, gestate, nurture, produce **8** escalate, increase, maturate, mushroom **9** cultivate, propagate

growing 8 crescive, vegetive **10** vegetative

growl 3 grr **4** roll **5** snarl **6** mutter, rumble **7** grumble **8** complain **9** complaint

growler 3 can **4** crab, floe **5** crank, grump **6** griper, grouch **7** grouser, iceberg, pitcher **8** grumbler, sorehead, sourpuss **9** container **10** bellyacher

grow old 3 age **5** ripen **6** mature

growth 4 rise **5** swell, tumor **7** merisis **8** increase, progress, swelling **9** accretion, evolution, expansion, flowering, unfolding **10** evolvement **11** development, enlargement, progression *malignant:* **6** cancer *skin:* **3** wen **4** corn, mole, wart **6** bunion, keloid

grub 3 dig **4** beat, chow, comb, feed, food, hack, plod, poke, rake, root, slog, toil **5** grind, larva, scour, slave, spade, stump **6** burrow, drudge, forage, search, shovel, slavey, viands **7** edibles, grubber, nurture, ransack, rummage **8** excavate, finecomb, hireling, victuals **9** mercenary, provender

grubby 4 foul **5** black, dirty, grimy, nasty, soily **6** filthy, impure **7** squalid, unclean

grubstake 4 back **7** finance **8** bankroll

grudge 4 deny, envy **5** spite **6** injury, malice, refuse, spleen **7** despite, ill will **9** grievance, injustice, malignity **10** malignancy **11** malevolence **12** spitefulness

gruel 5 atole **8** porridge *Scottish:* **6** crowdy

gruesome see **grisly**

gruff 4 curt, dour, sour **5** bluff, blunt, husky, short, surly **6** abrupt, croaky, crusty,

fierce, hoarse, morose, snippy, sullen
7 bearish, boorish, brusque, crabbed
8 churlish, croaking, snippety 9 saturnine

grumble 4 beef, crab, fuss, kick, moan,
roll 5 bitch, brawl, croak, gripe, groan,
growl, scold, snarl, whine 6 grouch, grouse,
holler, murmur, mutter, repine, rumble,
squawk 8 complain 9 bellyache

grumbler 4 crab 6 grouch 7 grouser,
growler 8 sorehead 10 bellyacher, complainer, crosspatch, malcontent
11 faultfinder

grump 3 pet 4 crab, pout, sulk 5 crank
6 griper, grouch, kicker 7 growler 8 grumbler, sorehead, sourpuss 10 bellyacher

grumpy 5 moody, surly 6 crabby, cranky

guacharo 7 oilbird

Guam *capital:* 5 Agana *native:*
8 Chamorro

guanaco 5 llama 6 alpaca *kin:* 5 camel

guarantee, guaranty 3 vow 4 bail,
bond, oath, seal, word 5 token, vouch
6 assure, ensure, insure, pledge, surety
7 certify, earnest, promise, warrant 8 security, warranty 9 assurance 11 undertaking

guarantor 5 angel 6 backer, patron,
surety 7 sponsor 8 backer-up
11 underwriter

guard 4 fend, keep, mind, tend, ward
5 aegis, armor, cover, watch 6 attend, convoy, defend, escort, jailer, keeper, patrol,
picket, screen, secure, sentry, shield, warden, warder 7 bulwark, conduct, defense,
lookout, protect, turnkey 8 armament,
chaperon, security, sentinel, shepherd,
watchdog, watchman 9 accompany, patrolman, protector 10 protection

guarded 4 safe, wary 5 chary, privy
6 buried, covert, hidden 7 careful 8 cautious, discreet, gingerly, obscured,
shrouded, ulterior 9 concealed 11 calculating, circumspect, considerate

guardhouse 4 brig 6 prison

guardian 6 custos, keeper, parent, patron,
warden 7 sponsor 8 cerberus, claviger,
watchdog 9 custodian, protector

guardianship 4 care, ward 5 trust 7 custody, keeping, tuition 11 safekeeping

guava 4 inga, tree 5 fruit

gudgeon 3 pin 4 fish 5 pivot 6 socket

Gudrun *brother:* 6 Gunnar 7 Gunther
father: 5 Hetel *husband:* 4 Atli 5 Etzel
6 Sigurd 9 Siegfried

guerrilla 7 fighter, patriot, soldier 8 partisan 9 irregular 11 bushwhacker *Greek:*
6 klepht

guess 4 call, shot, stab 5 fancy, infer,
think 6 deduce, reason, reckon 7 predict,
presume, pretend, suppose, surmise 8 estimate 9 speculate 10 conjecture

guest 6 caller, lodger, patron, roomer
7 visitor

guff 3 jaw, lip 4 sass 5 hokum, hooey,
mouth, sauce, trash 6 bunkum 7 hogwash 8 back talk, claptrap, malarkey, nonsense 9 poppycock 10 balderdash

guffaw 5 laugh, tehee 6 giggle, hee-haw,
titter 7 chortle, chuckle, snicker, sniggle

guidance 7 auspice, conduct, control
9 direction 10 leadership, management

guide 3 see 4 airt, clue, dean, lead, show
5 airth, doyen, pilot, route, steer, teach,
usher 6 beacon, convoy, direct, escort,
leader, manage, manual, vector 7 conduct,
control, marshal 8 Baedeker, chaperon,
contrive, director, engineer, handbook,
maneuver, navigate, shepherd 9 accompany, conductor, lead pilot, vade mecum
10 bellwether, compendium 11 enchiridion

guidebook 6 manual 8 Baedeker, handbook 9 itinerary, vade mecum 10 compendium 11 enchiridion

guided missile 3 ABM 4 Hawk, ICBM,
IRBM, Nike, Thor, Zuni 5 Atlas, drone,
Snark, Titan 6 Bomarc, Falcon 7 Bullpup,
Polaris, Terrier 8 Redstone 9 Minuteman
10 Sidewinder

Guiderius *brother:* 9 Arviragus *father:*
9 Cymbeline

Guido's scale 2 fa, la, mi, re, ut 3 Ela, sol

guild 4 club 5 order, union 6 cartel,
league 7 society 8 sodality 10 fellowship,
fraternity 11 association, brotherhood

guile 4 wile 5 craft, fraud 6 deceit 7 cunning 9 duplicity 12 dissemblance

guileful 3 sly 4 deep, foxy, wily 6 artful,
astute, crafty, shifty, sneaky, tricky 7 cunning, devious 8 indirect, sneaking 9 insidious, underhand 11 duplicitous,
underhanded

guileless 5 naive 6 honest 7 artless, natural 8 unartful 9 ingenuous, unstudied,
untutored

guillemot 3 auk 5 murre

guillotine 6 behead 9 decollate
10 decapitate

guilt 3 sin 4 onus 5 blame, crime, fault,
shame 7 offense, remorse 11 culpability

guiltless 4 good, pure 5 clean 8 innocent,
unguilty, virtuous 9 blameless, crimeless,
exemplary, faultless, righteous 10 inculpable, unblamable

guilty 5 amiss 6 nocent, sinful, unholy,
wicked 7 ashamed 8 blamable, blameful,
culpable, indicted 9 impeached 10 answerable, censurable, blame-
worthy, responsible 12 incriminated

guinea fowl *genus:* 6 Numida *young:*
4 keet

guinea pig 4 cavy 6 rodent *genus:*
5 Cavia

Guinevere *husband:* 6 Arthur *lover:*
8 Lancelot 9 Launcelot
guise 3 hue, rig 4 face, mask, show
5 cloak, color, cover, dress, getup 6 facade,
outfit, setout 7 costume 8 coloring 9 semblance 10 appearance
guitar *part:* 3 nut, peg 4 fret, neck
5 brace 6 bridge, string 7 peghead
player: 7 plucker 8 strummer *small:*
3 uke 7 ukulele *soprano:* 5 tiple *tool:*
4 pick 8 plectrum
guitarist *American:* 9 Parkening *Australian:* 8 Williams *British:* 5 Bream *Italian:*
7 Ghiglia *Spanish:* 5 Yepes 6 Romero
7 Segovia
guitarlike instrument 3 uke 4 lute, vina
5 banjo, sitar 6 sancho 7 bandore, pandora, samisen, ukulele
gulch 3 gap 5 chasm, cleft, clove, gorge,
gully 6 arroyo, canyon, clough, ravine
gulf 3 arm, bay, pit 4 cave, cove, eddy,
well 5 abysm, abyss, bayou, bight, chasm,
firth, gulch, inlet, shaft 6 cavity, harbor, hollow, ravine, slough 8 crevasse *Adriatic
Sea:* 6 Venice *Aegean Sea:* 7 Saronic
8 Salonika *Africa:* 6 Guinea *Arabian Sea:*
4 Oman 7 Persian *Arctic Ocean:* 2 Ob
Australia: 9 Van Diemen 11 Carpentaria
Baltic Sea: 4 Riga 6 Danzig 7 Bothnia,
Finland *Bering Sea:* 6 Anadyr *Canada:*
13 Saint Lawrence *Caribbean Sea:* 8 Honduras 9 Venezuela *Central America:*
6 Panama 7 Fonseca *Djibouti:* 6 Tajura
8 Tadjoura *Europe:* 7 Bothnia, Gascony
8 Gascogne *Greece:* 7 Corinth, Lepanto
Indian Ocean: 4 Aden *Ionian Sea:*
7 Taranto *Iran:* 7 Arabian *Italy:* 5 Genoa
Mediterranean Sea: 5 Sidra, Tunis
8 Valencia 10 Khalij Surt 11 Syrtis Major
Mexico: 10 California *New Guinea:*
5 Papua 7 McCluer *New Zealand:* 7 Hauraki *North America:* 6 Alaska, Mexico
Northwest Territories: 7 Boothia
8 Amundsen 9 Queen Maud *Philippines:*
4 Asid 5 Davao, Leyte, Panay, Ragay *Red
Sea:* 4 Suez 5 Aqaba 11 Aelaniticus *Russia:* 8 Sakhalin *Solomon Sea:* 4 Huon,
Kula 5 Vella *South China Sea:* 4 Siam
6 Tonkin 8 Lingayen, Thailand *Tyrrhenion
Sea:* 7 Paestum *Yellow Sea:* 2 Bo, Po
6 Chihli
Gulf State 5 Texas 7 Alabama, Florida
9 Louisiana 11 Mississippi
gull 3 mew, sap 4 bird, dupe, fish, fool,
hoax 5 chump 6 befool, pigeon, sucker
7 chicane, fall guy, gudgeon, saphead
8 flimflam, hoodwink 9 bamboozle
11 hornswoggle *relating to:* 6 larine, laroid
gullet 3 maw 4 tube 6 dewlap, ravine,
throat 7 channel 9 esophagus

gullible 4 easy 5 naive 9 credulous
10 fleeceable 11 susceptible
Gulliver's Travels *author:* 5 Swift *land:*
6 Laputa 8 Lilliput 11 Brobdingnag *people:* 6 Yahoos
gully 5 gorge, gulch 6 arroyo, hollow,
ravine, valley 7 couloir
gulp 4 bolt, cram, glut, slop, swig, wolf
5 slosh, stuff, swill 6 devour, englut, gobble,
guzzle 7 swallow 11 ingurgitate
gum 4 chew, kino 5 botch, cheat, nyssa,
stick, tuart 6 bobble, bollix, bungle, chicle,
gluten, goof up, mucker, tupelo 7 bilsted,
exudate, gingiva, louse up 8 adhesive,
mucilage 9 sapodilla 10 eucalyptus *kind:*
6 acacia, Arabic, balata, bubble 7 chewing,
dextrin *resin:* 5 myrrh 7 gamboge
8 ammoniac, galbanum, scammony 9 asafetida 12 frankincense
gummy 5 gooey 6 cloggy, sticky, stodgy
7 viscous 8 adhesive
gumption 5 sense 6 wisdom 8 judgment,
sagacity 9 good sense 10 astuteness,
enterprise, horse sense, shrewdness
11 common sense
gums 3 ula 8 gingivae
gumshoe 3 cop, tec 4 dick, fuzz, heat,
lurk, slip 5 creep, shirk, skulk, slink, sneak,
snoop, steal 6 peeler, sleuth 7 officer
8 flatfoot, hawkshaw, Sherlock 9 detective,
policeman, pussyfoot 12 investigator
gun 3 gat, rod 5 rifle 6 cannon, heater,
mortar, musket, pistol, weapon 7 bazooka,
carbine, firearm 8 howitzer, revolver 9 derringer *antiaircraft:* 6 ack-ack, Bofors *British:* 4 sten *French:* 8 arquebus *German:*
5 Luger *mount:* 6 turret *part:* 3 pin 4 bolt,
bore, butt, lock 5 sight, stock 6 barrel,
breech, hammer, muzzle, safety 7 chamber,
trigger 8 cylinder, magazine 9 buttstock
gunfire 4 shot 5 salvo 6 ack-ack, strafe,
volley 7 barrage 9 fusillade
gung ho 4 keen 7 zealous 12 enthusiastic
Guni's father 8 Naphtali
gunk 3 goo 4 crud, gook, goop, muck
gunman 5 bravo 6 hit man 7 torpedo
8 assassin 9 cutthroat
Gunnar *brother-in-law:* 6 Sigurd *father:*
5 Hetel *sister:* 6 Gudrun *wife:* 8 Brynhild
gunnel 6 blenny 10 butterfish
gunner 7 shooter 8 marksman, rifleman
9 cannoneer 12 artilleryman
Gunther *sister:* 7 Gutrune 9 Kriemhild
slayer: 5 Hagen *uncle:* 5 Hagen *wife:*
8 Brunhild 9 Brynhilde 11 Brunnehilde
guppy 4 fish 6 minnow
gurgle 3 lap 4 wash 5 slosh, swash
6 bubble, burble
Gurkha knife 5 kukri
gurney 3 cot 9 stretcher
guru 5 guide 6 mentor 7 teacher

gush 4 flow, pour, roll, teem 5 flood, flush, issue, spout, spurt, surge 6 sluice, spring, stream 7 emanate

gusset 4 fold 5 armor, pleat 6 insert

gust 4 gale, puff, waft, wind 5 blast, burst, draft, sally, whiff 6 access, breeze, squall 7 bluster, flare-up 8 eruption, outburst

gusto 4 élan, zeal, zest 5 ardor, heart, taste 6 fervor, palate, relish, spirit 7 delight, passion 8 pleasure 9 enjoyment 10 enthusiasm 11 delectation

gut 4 draw 5 belly, bowel, clean, dress, inner 6 paunch 7 embowel, passage, stomach 8 interior, internal, intimate, visceral 9 visceral 10 disembowel, eviscerate, exenterate

Gutenberg *city:* 5 Mainz *invention:* 11 movable type *partner:* 4 Fust

gutless 6 coward, craven 7 chicken, unmanly 8 cowardly 9 spunkless 11 lily-livered, poltroonish 13 pusillanimous

guts 4 grit 5 moxie, nerve, pluck, spunk 6 mettle, spirit, tripes 7 courage, innards, insides, viscera 8 backbone, entrails, stuffing 9 fortitude, internals 10 resolution

gutsy 4 bold 5 brave, manly 6 manful, plucky, spunky 7 valiant 8 intrepid 9 unfearful 10 courageous

gutter 5 ditch, gully 6 furrow, groove, trench, trough 7 channel

guttural 4 deep 5 harsh, rough, velar 7 palatal, rasping, throaty

Guyana *capital:* 10 Georgetown *monetary unit:* 6 dollar

guzzle 4 bolt, cram, gulp, slop, soak, swig, wolf 5 booze, drink, slosh, swill 6 englut, gobble, imbibe, tank up, tipple 7 swizzle

Gwendolen's husband 7 Locrine

gymnast 7 acrobat, athlete, tumbler *American:* 5 Rigby (Cathy) 6 Retton (Mary Lou), Thomas (Kurt) *Romanian:* 8 Comaneci (Nadia) *Russian:* 3 Kim (Nelly) 6 Korbut (Olga)

gymnastics 5 sport 8 exercise, tumbling 9 athletics 10 acrobatics 12 calisthenics *apparatus:* 3 bar 4 beam, buck, ring, rope 5 horse *feat:* 3 kip 4 flip 5 vault 6 tumble 9 handstand, headstand 10 handspring, headspring, somersault

gyp 4 beat, bilk, fake, hoax, sell 5 cheat, cozen, fraud, phony, spoof 6 chisel, chouse, con man, diddle, humbug, rip off 7 defraud, diddler, sharper, swindle 8 swindler 9 defrauder, imposture, overreach, trickster 10 mountebank 11 flimflammer 12 double-dealer

gypsum 8 selenite 9 alabaster

gypsy 4 caló 5 caird, nomad 6 roamer, Romany 7 tzigane, zingana, zingano 8 Bohemian, wanderer *Spanish:* 6 gitano

gyrate 4 roll, spin, turn 5 twirl, whirl 6 circle, rotate 7 revolve 9 pirouette, whirligig

gyration 4 turn 5 round, wheel, whirl 7 circuit 8 rotation 10 revolution 11 circulation

gyre 4 ring, spin 5 twirl, whirl 6 rotate, spiral, vortex 7 revolve 10 revolution

gyro 8 sandwich 9 gyroscope

gyve 4 bond, iron 5 chain 6 fetter 7 shackle

H

H 4 high 5 aitch 7 hundred
habeus corpus 4 writ
habilimented 4 clad 7 clothed
habilitate 5 dress 6 clothe
habit 3 rut, set, use, way 4 bent, form, mode, rote, turn, wont 5 build, dress, style, trick, usage 6 clothe, custom, groove, manner, praxis 7 carcass, contour, fashion, habitus, outline, pattern, routine 8 behavior, physique, practice, tendency 9 addiction, framework 10 consuetude, convention, proclivity 11 disposition, inclination *riding:* 6 joseph 8 jodhpurs *wearer:* 3 nun 5 rider
habitant 5 liver 7 denizen, dweller, resider 8 occupant, resident 9 indweller
habitat 4 home, site 5 abode, haunt, range 6 locale 7 station 8 locality 9 territory 11 environment 12 surroundings *combining form:* 2 ec 3 eco, oec 4 oeco
habitation 3 pad 4 digs, flat, home, nest, nook, roof, seat 5 abode, astre, haunt, haven, house, place, roost 6 colony, hearth 7 housing, lodging 8 domicile, dwelling, fireside, lodgment, peopling, quarters, rooftree, tenement 9 apartment, homeplace, homestead, occupancy, residence, residency
habitual 6 addict, inborn, native, steady, wonted 7 chronic, regular, routine 8 accepted, addicted, constant, frequent 9 automatic, confirmed, continual, customary, ingrained 10 accustomed, inveterate, persistent 11 established, instinctive, involuntary
habituate 3 use 4 bear, wont 5 inure 6 addict, adjust, devote, endure, season, take to 7 support 8 accustom, devote to, tolerate 9 condition, confirm in 11 familiarize
habitué 3 fan 4 buff, user 5 hound, lover 6 addict, patron, votary 7 denizen, devotee, haunter 8 customer 10 frequenter
Hacaliah, Hachaliah *son:* 8 Nehemiah
hacienda 4 farm 5 ranch 6 estate 10 plantation
hack 3 cab, cut, hew, old, try 4 chip, chop, dull, fell, gash, grub, jade, mean, nick, poor, taxi, trim, turn 5 cabby, cough, frame, grind, horse, notch, petty, shape, slash, slave, stale, tired, trite, usual 6 cabbie, cliché, common, drudge, haggle, lackey, mangle, slavey 7 clichéd, grating, grubber, machine, outworn, plodder, potboil, servant, taxicab, trivial 8 déclassé, hireling, inferior, low grade, mediocre, ordinary, outmoded, timeworn, well-worn 9 cabdriver, mercenary, potboiler 10 second-rate, uninspired 11 commonplace
hackneyed 4 worn 5 stale, stock, tired, trite 6 cliché 7 archaic, clichéd, worn-out 8 bathetic, everyday, obsolete, outmoded, timeworn, well-worn 9 moth-eaten, out-of-date, quotidian 10 antiquated 11 commonplace
Hadad *father:* 5 Bedad 7 Ishmael *victim:* 6 Midian
Hadadezer *father:* 5 Rehob *kingdom:* 5 Zobah
hades 3 pit 4 hell 5 Sheol 6 Tophet 7 Abaddon, Avernus, Gehenna, inferno 8 Tartarus 9 barathrum, perdition 10 underworld 11 netherworld, Pandemonium *Babylonian:* 5 Aralu *god:* 3 Dis 5 Orcus, Pluto *guard:* 8 Cerberus *lake:* 7 Avernus *river:* 4 Styx 5 Lethe 7 Acheron, Cocytus 10 Phlegethon
hafnium *symbol:* 2 Hf
hag 3 hex 4 drab, trot 5 biddy, bruja, crone, harpy, lamia, shrew, vixen, witch 6 gorgon, virago 7 grandam 8 battle-ax, fishwife, harridan, slattern 9 sorceress 10 witchwoman 11 enchantress
Hagar's son 7 Ishmael
Hagen *father:* 8 Alberich *nephew:* 7 Gunther *slayer:* 9 Kriemhild *victim:* 9 Siegfried
haggard 3 wan 4 lank, lean, pale, worn 5 ashen, drawn, faded, gaunt, spare, tired 6 fagged, pallid, skinny 7 angular, pinched, scraggy, scrawny, wearied 8 careworn, fatigued, harrowed, worn-down 9 exhausted
Haggard novel 3 She
Haggi's father 3 Gad
Haggith *husband:* 5 David *son:* 8 Adonijah
haggle 4 deal, hack 5 cavil, slash, trade 6 barter, bicker, dicker, hackle, palter 7 bargain, chaffer, dispute, quibble, stickle, wrangle 8 huckster, squabble 10 horse-trade
hail 4 ahoy 5 greet, hallo, salvo, shout, storm 6 accost, call to, hallow, holler, kudize, praise, salute, shower, volley

7 acclaim, address, applaud, barrage, call out, commend **8** come from, drumfire **9** broadside, cannonade, fusillade, originate, recommend **10** salutation **11** bombardment

hair 3 ace, bit, jot **4** hint, mite, wool **5** pilus, trace **6** nicety, trifle **7** whisker **8** fraction, particle *animal:* **3** fur **4** mane, pelt **8** vibrissa **9** vibrissae (plural) *braid of:* **5** queue **7** pigtail *clip:* **8** barrette *coarse:* **7** bristle *combining form:* **3** pil **4** coma, pili, pilo **5** chaet, crini, thrix, trich **6** chaeta, chaeto, tricha, trichi, tricho, trichy **7** chaetae (plural), chaetes, chaetus, trichia **8** trichous *covering of:* **3** wig *facial:* **5** beard **6** goatee **8** mustache, whiskers **9** moustache, sideburns **11** muttonchops *fine:* **6** lanugo *front:* **4** bang *head of:* **9** chevelure *instrument:* **4** comb *knot of:* **3** bun **6** tangle *lock of:* **4** curl **5** tress **7** cowlick *loose roll:* **4** pouf **5** pouff **6** pouffe *matted:* **4** shag *ornament:* **7** topknot *preparation:* **6** pomade **12** brilliantine *relating to:* **8** hirsutal *root:* **6** fibril *set:* **4** perm *stiff:* **4** seta **5** setae (plural) *style:* **9** pompadour *tangled:* **7** elflock *tuft of:* **7** fetlock *unruly:* **3** mop **7** cowlick *without:* **4** bald

haircutter 6 barber **7** friseur

hairdo 4 perm **7** chignon **8** bouffant

hairdresser 6 barber **7** friseur **10** beautician **13** cosmetologist

hair-raising 4 eery **5** eerie **9** thrilling **10** terrifying

hairsplitter 8 quibbler

hairstyle 2 DA **4** Afro **7** beehive, crew cut, pageboy **8** bouffont, coiffure, ducktail, ponytail

hairy 5 bushy, crude, downy, furry, fuzzy, harsh, nappy, risky, rough **6** chancy, craggy, fleecy, fluffy, jagged, lanate, pilose, rugged, shaggy, tufted, uneven, wicked, woolly **7** bristly, hirsute, pileous, scraggy, unshorn, unsound, villous **8** asperous, perilous, scabrous, strigose, unsmooth **9** dangerous, hazardous, pubescent, tomentose, unhealthy, whiskered **10** jeopardous, unpleasant **11** frightening, treacherous *combining form:* **4** dasy, hebe

Haiti *capital:* **12** Port au Prince *export:* **6** coffee **7** bauxite *island:* **10** Hispaniola *location:* **10** West Indies *monetary unit:* **6** gourde *ruler:* **8** Duvalier

Hajji Baba creator 6 Morier

hake 5 gadid **7** codling, whiting *relative:* **3** cod

halcyon 4 calm **5** happy, quiet, still **6** golden, hushed, placid, serene, stilly **8** affluent **10** kingfisher, prosperous, untroubled

Halcyone *father:* **6** Aeolus *husband:* **4** Ceyx

hale 3 fit, tug **4** draw, pull, sane, well **5** husky, right, sound, stout **6** robust **7** healthy, summons **9** strapping, wholesome

Hale character 5 Nolan

haleness 6 health

half *prefix:* **3** sam **4** demi, hemi, semi

half-assed 7 lacking, wanting **9** defective, deficient **10** inadequate, incomplete, uncomplete

half-breed 4 mule **5** cross **6** hybrid **7** bastard, mestizo, mongrel, mulatto **8** mixblood

halfhearted 5 tepid **8** lukewarm

half-moon 7 scalare **8** demilune **9** blue perch

halfway 3 mid **6** almost, center, medial, median, middle **7** midmost, partial **8** amenably **9** partially **10** centermost, middlemost, more or less **11** equidistant

half-wit 4 dolt, fool, zany **5** ament, idiot, moron **6** cretin **7** natural **8** imbecile **9** blockhead, simpleton

half-witted 4 dull, slow **5** silly **7** foolish, moronic **8** backward, imbecile, retarded **9** senseless **12** feebleminded, simpleminded

hall 4 dorm **5** foyer, lobby, lycea (plural) **6** lyceum **7** couloir, passage **8** building, corridor **9** dormitory **10** auditorium, living room, passageway **12** entrance room *ancient Roman:* **5** oecus *exhibition:* **5** salon *Salvation Army:* **7** citadel

Halley's ___ 5 comet

Hallohesh's son 7 Shallum

hallow 5 bless **6** devote, revere **8** dedicate, sanctify, venerate **10** consecrate

hallucination 6 mirage, wraith **7** fantasy, phantom **8** delusion, illusion, phantasm **11** fata morgana, ignis fatuus

hallucinogen 3 LSD **9** mescaline **10** psilocybin **11** scopolamine

halo 4 aura **5** nimbi (plural) **6** gloria, nimbus **7** aureole **8** encircle, gloriole *combining form:* **7** stephan **8** stephano

halogen 6 iodine **7** bromine **8** astatine, chlorine, fluorine

halt 3 end **4** lame, limp, quit, stay, stop **5** cease, check, close, hitch, lapse, stall, waver **6** arrest, desist, dither, draw up, falter, finish, haul up, hobble, pull up, wind up, wrap up **7** bring up, fetch up, stagger, suspend, whiffle **8** complete, conclude, give over, hesitate, knock off, leave off, surcease, ultimate **9** determine, interrupt, terminate, vacillate **11** discontinue

ham 4 hock **5** emote, thigh **7** buttock, overact **8** overplay, strutter **13** exhibitionist

Ham *brother:* **4** Shem **7** Japheth *father:* **4** Noah *son:* **4** Cush, Phut **6** Canaan **7** Mizraim

Haman's father 10 Hammedatha

Hamilcar *conquest:* 5 Spain *home:* 8 Carthage *son:* 8 Hannibal *surname:* 5 Barca

hamlet 5 moray 7 grouper, village *Irish, Scottish:* 7 clachan

Hamlet *author:* 11 Shakespeare *beloved:* 7 Ophelia *castle:* 8 Elsinore *country:* 7 Denmark *friend:* 7 Horatio *mother:* 8 Gertrude *slayer:* 7 Laertes *uncle:* 8 Claudius *victim:* 7 Laertes 8 Claudius, Polonius

Hamlet, The *author:* 8 Faulkner *family:* 6 Snopes

Hammedatha's son 5 Haman

hammer 4 beat, cock, drub, form, maul, peen, pein, pelt, toil 5 drive, erect, gavel, grave, labor, pound, set up, shape, stamp, swage, thump 6 batter, mallet, pummel, sledge, thrash, wallop 7 belabor, build up, fashion, foliate, impress, malleus, planish, trippet 8 lambaste, malleate *type:* 3 air 4 claw 6 sledge 8 ball peen 9 pneumatic

hammerhead 3 bat 5 dunce, shark, stork 8 clodpate, numskull 9 hog sucker 10 thickskull

Hammoleketh's brother 6 Gilead

hamper 3 bar, rub, tie 4 balk, clog, curb, foil, snag 5 block, check, crimp, leash, limit, tie up 6 baffle, basket, cumber, fetter, hinder, hobble, hog-tie, hurdle, impede, lumber, retard, thwart 7 disrupt, inhibit, shackle, trammel 8 encumber, handicap, obstacle, obstruct, restrain, restrict 9 discomfit, embarrass, entrammel, frustrate

hamstring 6 hinder, impair, tendon 7 cripple, disable

Hamul's father 5 Perez 6 Pharez

Hamutal *father:* 8 Jeremiah *husband:* 6 Josiah *son:* 8 Jehoahaz, Zedekiah

Hanameel *cousin:* 8 Jeremiah *father:* 7 Shallum

Hanani *brother:* 8 Nehemiah *father:* 5 Heman, Immer *son:* 4 Jehu

Hananiah *father:* 4 Azur 5 Azzur, Bebai, Heman 7 Shashak 10 Zerubbabel *son:* 8 Jeshaiah, Pelatiah, Zedekiah

Hanan's father 4 Azel 6 Zaccur 7 Maachah, Shashak 8 Igdaliah

hand 3 aid 4 buck, feed, find, fist, furl, give, help, lift, pass, side 5 angle, facet, index, manus, phase, reach, skill, touch 6 aspect, assist, ductus, inning, pledge, relief, script, succor, supply, worker 7 ability, comfort, concern, conduct, deliver, dish out, laborer, provide, secours, support, workman 8 dispense, employee, interest, transfer, turn over 9 direction, operative, signature 10 assistance, penmanship, roustabout, workingman 11 calligraphy, chirography *clenched:* 4 fist *combining form:* 4 chir

5 cheir, chiro, palmi 6 cheiro, palmat 7 palmati *counting zero:* 8 baccarat *covering:* 5 glove 6 mitten *declarer's:* 7 laydown *down:* 8 bequeath *gestures:* 5 mudra *make:* 5 craft *on hip:* 6 akimbo *part:* 4 palm 5 thumb 6 finger *poker:* 5 flush 8 straight 9 full house *protector:* 5 glove 8 gauntlet

handbag 5 purse 8 reticule

handbill 5 flier, flyer 6 dodger, poster 7 affiche, leaflet, placard 8 circular

handbook 5 guide 6 manual 8 Baedeker 9 vade mecum 10 compendium 11 enchiridion *religious:* 9 catechism

handcuff 7 manacle 8 restrain *British:* 7 darbies (plural)

hand down 6 pass on 8 bequeath, transmit

Handel *aria:* 5 Largo *birthplace:* 5 Halle (Germany) *opera:* 4 Nero 5 Serse 6 Almira, Xerxes 7 Rodrigo 8 Berenice 9 Agrippina *oratorio:* 4 Saul 6 Esther, Joshua, Samson 7 Messiah 8 Jephthah

handicap 4 edge, load, odds 5 bulge, start 6 burden 8 drawback 9 advantage, allowance, detriment, head start 10 disability 11 encumbrance 12 disadvantage

handicraft 3 art 5 trade 6 métier 7 calling 8 vocation 10 profession

handkerchief 5 hanky 6 hankie 7 bandana 8 bandanna, mouchoir

handle 3 aim, ear, lay, paw, ply, run, try, use 4 ansa, bail, feel, grip, haft, knob, knop, name, play, take, test, wave, work 5 apply, guide, level, nomen, point, serve, shake, style, swing, title, touch, treat, wield 6 bestow, byname, byword, direct, employ, finger, govern, manage 7 act upon, conduct, control, exploit, moniker, operate, palpate, trade in, utilize 8 brandish, cognomen, deal with, dispense, dominate, doorknob, exercise, flourish, maneuver, nickname

handle-shaped 6 ansate

handling 4 care 6 charge 7 conduct, running 9 oversight 10 intendance, management 11 supervision

hand out 4 give 6 bestow, devote, donate 7 present 8 give away 10 administer

hand over 4 cede, feed, find, give 5 leave, waive, yield 6 commit, give up, resign, supply 7 abandon, commend, confide, consign, deliver, entrust, provide 8 dispense, relegate, transfer 9 deliver up, surrender 10 relinquish

handrail 8 banister

handsome 3 apt 4 chic, fair, free 5 noble, smart, sonsy 6 adroit, august, comely, lovely, modish, pretty, sonsie 7 dashing, liberal, sizable, stately, stylish 8 generous, majestic 9 beauteous,

beautiful, bounteous, bountiful, unsparing
10 attractive, munificent, openhanded
11 fashionable, good-looking

handspring 6 tumble *lateral:* 9 cartwheel

handwriting 6 ductus, script 8 longhand
10 manuscript, penmanship 11 calligraphy,
chirography *bad:* 10 cacography *study of:*
10 graphology

handy 4 deft 5 adept, utile 6 adroit,
clever, nearby, nimble, useful, wieldy
7 close-by 8 adjacent, skillful 9 adaptable,
dexterous, practical 10 beneficial, convenient, functional 11 practicable

handyman 6 jumper 8 factotum

hang 3 art, fix, jut, lop, pin, sag 4 hook,
idle, lean, loll, pend, rest 5 await, cling,
craft, drape, droop, float, hover, knack,
lynch, noose, pause, poise, scrag, skill,
sling, slope, stick, swing, trail, trick
6 adhere, attach, dangle, depend, gibbet,
impend, loiter, tack up, turn on 7 execute
back: 3 lag *loosely:* 3 sag 6 dangle

hangbird 6 oriole

hangdog 5 cowed 6 guilty 7 ashamed,
pitiful 8 dejected

hanger-on 5 leech 6 sponge, sucker
7 sponger 8 barnacle, follower, parasite
9 bystander, spectator, sycophant 10 freeloader 11 bloodsucker 12 lounge lizard

hanging 7 pendent, pensile 9 declivity,
pendulant, pendulous, suspended

Hanging Gardens 7 Babylon

hangings 5 arras 6 drapes 7 drapery
8 curtains, tapestry

hangout 4 dive 5 haunt, joint 6 resort
7 purlieu 9 honky-tonk 10 rendezvous
11 barrelhouse 12 watering hole

hang up 4 mire 5 delay, embog 6 detain,
retard 7 achieve, bog down, set back,
slacken 8 slow down 10 decelerate

hank 4 coil, loop, ring

hanker 3 yen 4 ache, long, lust, pine, sigh,
wish 5 covet, crave, yearn 6 desire, hunger, thirst

hanky-panky 5 fraud 7 chicane 8 trickery 9 chicanery, deception, fourberie
11 highbinding 13 double-dealing, sharp
practice

Hannah *husband:* 7 Elkanah *son:*
6 Samuel

Hannibal *defeat:* 4 Zama *father:* 8 Hamilcar *home:* 8 Carthage *surname:* 5 Barca
vanquisher: 6 Scipio *victory:* 6 Cannae

Hanniel's father 4 Ulla 5 Ephod

Hanoch's father 6 Midian, Reuben

hansa, hanse 5 guild 6 league
11 association

Hans Brinker author 5 Dodge

Hanseatic League City 6 Bremen,
Lubeck, Wismar 7 Cologne, Hamburg,
Rostock

Hansen's disease 7 leprosy

Hanun's father 6 Nahash

haphazard 5 about 6 anyhow, around,
chance, random 7 aimless, anywise,
unaimed 8 accident, at random, careless,
casually, randomly, slipshod 9 aimlessly,
desultory, hit-or-miss, irregular, unplanned
10 accidental, carelessly, designless 11 any
which way, unorganized 12 accidentally,
unconsidered, unsystematic 13 helter-
skelter

hapless 4 poor 6 woeful 7 unhappy,
unlucky 8 ill-fated, untoward, wretched
9 miserable 10 ill-starred 11 star-crossed,
unfortunate 12 infelicitous, misfortunate

happen 2 do, go 3 hit 4 bump, come, fall,
give, luck, meet, pass, rise 5 break, light,
occur 6 befall, betide, chance, drop in, tumble, turn up 7 come off, develop, fall out,
stumble, turn out 8 bechance 9 transpire
again: 5 recur *together:* 6 concur

happening 5 event, thing 7 episode
8 incident, occasion 10 occurrence
12 circumstance

happiness 3 joy 4 glee 5 bliss, cheer,
mirth 6 gaiety 7 content, delight, jollity
8 felicity, gladness, pleasure 9 beatitude,
enjoyment 11 delectation 12 satisfaction

happy 3 apt, fit, pat 4 glad, just, meet,
nice, well 5 lucky, right 6 casual, cogent,
joyful, joyous, proper, timely, upbeat 7 content, correct, fitting, pleased, telling
8 friendly, pleasant, suitable 9 befitting,
congenial, contented, effective, effectual,
efficient, favorable, fortunate, opportune,
satisfied, well-timed 10 accidental, convincing, felicitous, fortuitous, harmonious, incidental, propitious, prosperous, seasonable
11 appropriate, efficacious 12 lighthearted

happy-go-lucky 4 cool, easy 6 blithe,
casual 8 carefree, careless, cheerful, debonair, feckless, heedless, reckless 9 easygoing, lightsome 10 free-minded, insouciant,
nonchalant 11 unconcerned 12 devil-may-
care, light-hearted 13 lackadaisical

hara-kiri 7 seppuku, suicide 8 felo-de-se
10 self-murder 12 self-violence 13 self-
slaughter

Haran *brother:* 7 Abraham *daughter:*
5 Iscah 6 Milcah *father:* 5 Terah 6 Shimei
son: 3 Lot

harangue 4 rant, rave 5 mouth, orate
6 tirade 7 declaim, lecture, oration, soapbox 8 bloviate, diatribe, jeremiad, perorate
9 philippic 11 declamation

harass 3 irk, try, vex 4 bait, gnaw, pain,
raid, ride 5 annoy, chivy, devil, foray, harry,
hound, tease, worry 6 badger, heckle, hector, maraud, pester, plague, ratten, strain,
stress 7 bedevil, dragoon, exhaust, fatigue,

hagride, torment, trouble **8** bullyrag, distress **9** beleaguer

harasser 5 bully **6** hector **7** harrier **9** bulldozer **10** browbeater **11** intimidator

harassment 6 irking, vexing **8** vexation **9** annoyance, bothering, provoking **10** irritation **11** aggravation, disturbance, provocation **12** exasperation, perturbation

harbinger 4 omen, sign **6** herald, symbol **7** apostle, forerun, portent, presage **8** announce, foreshow, outrider **9** precursor **10** forerunner, indication **11** preindicate

harbor 3 arm, bay, hut **4** bunk, camp, cove, gulf, hide, live, port, roof, room **5** bight, board, cabin, cover, firth, guard, haven, house, inlet, lodge, nurse, put up, roost **6** asylum, bestow, billet, covert, encamp, foster, refuge, screen, shield, take in **7** chamber, cherish, conceal, contain, nurture, protect, quarter, retreat, seaport, secrete, shelter **8** domicile **9** anchorage, entertain, safeguard, sanctuary **11** accommodate *fee:* **7** keelage *Greece:* **5** Aulis *Guam:* **4** Apra *Hawaii:* **5** Pearl *Ireland:* **4** Cork *Long Island Sound:* **8** New Haven *Massachusetts:* **4** Lynn **9** Annisquam *New Jersey:* **9** Little Egg *Solomon:* **4** Viru *Washington:* **5** Grays

hard 3 bad, set **4** dark, deep, dour, dull, fast, firm, grim, iron, near, nigh **5** amiss, badly, bleak, close, crisp, cruel, fixed, harsh, heavy, horny, madly, rocky, rough, sharp, sober, solid, stark, tight, tough, vivid **6** actual, ardent, bitter, brazen, brutal, coarse, firmly, flinty, keenly, knotty, meanly, nearby, packed, rugged, severe, sorely, sticky, strict, strong, thorny, tiring, trying, unjust, uphill, wildly **7** angrily, arduous, austere, binding, briskly, callous, closely, compact, complex, cruelly, durable, factual, fixedly, genuine, glaring, harshly, hostile, intense, irksome, labored, largely, obscure, onerous, operous, petrous, precise, roughly, rowdily, serious, sharply, slavish, solidly, tightly, tiredly, toilful, violent, wearing **8** absolute, actively, bitterly, brutally, concrete, definite, dingdong, exacting, fiercely, forcibly, frugally, granitic, grievous, grinding, indurate, intently, involved, mightily, petrosal, pitiless, positive, profound, reliable, rigorous, savagely, scabrous, severely, shabbily, snappily, stormily, strident, strongly, tempered, terrible, toilsome, unfairly, urgently, wearying **9** alcoholic, arduously, austerely, awkwardly, bloodless, compacted, demanding, difficile, difficult, earnestly, effortful, fatiguing, furiously, inclement, indurated, insensate, intensely, intensive, intricate, laborious, massively, merciless, offensive, onerously, painfully, pointedly, practical, pragmatic, punishing,

realistic, resentful, resistant, searching, seriously, shameless, sprightly, straining, strenuous, stringent, unfeeling, unhandily, unsparing, viciously, violently, wearisome **10** adamantine, anesthetic, animatedly, bothersome, burdensome, compressed, cumbrously, exhausting, forbidding, forcefully, formidable, frenziedly, gruelingly, impassible, insensible, oppressive, perplexing, powerfully, rigorously, spiritedly, spirituous, sure-enough, thoroughly, toilsomely, unpleasant, unwieldily, unyielding, vigorously **11** assiduously, at close hand, complicated, difficultly, distressing, down-to-earth, exuberantly, ferociously, frantically, inequitable, insensitive, intemperate, intensively, intractable, laboriously, ponderously, rancorously, resentfully, searchingly, steadfastly, strenuously, troublesome, turbulently, unfantastic, unfavorable, unpalatable, unrelenting, unremitting, vivaciously **12** backbreaking, blood-and-guts, boisterously, burdensomely, concentrated, consolidated, cumbersomely, exhaustingly, exhaustively, incorrigible, intoxicating, matter-of-fact, meticulously, might and main, relentlessly, tumultuously *combining form:* **5** scler, stere **6** sclero, stereo *to please:* **7** finicky

hard-boiled 5 crude, rough, sober, stiff, tough **6** coarse **7** callous **8** obdurate, seasoned **9** heartless, practical, pragmatic, realistic, unfeeling **11** coldhearted, down-to-earth, unemotional, unfantastic, worldlywise **12** matter-of-fact, stonyhearted, unidealistic **13** sophisticated, unsympathetic

harden 3 dry, set **4** cake, firm **5** adapt, enure, inure, steel **6** adjust, anneal, callus, freeze, ossify, season, temper **7** calcify, callous, compact, conform, congeal, densify, lithify, petrify, stiffen, toughen **8** accustom, concrete, indurate, sclerose, solidify **9** acclimate, climatize, fossilize, habituate **10** strengthen

hardfisted 4 mean **5** close, tight, tough **6** stingy, strong **7** save-all **9** niggardly **11** tough-minded **13** penny-pinching

hardheaded 5 sober **6** mulish **7** willful **8** perverse, stubborn **9** obstinate, practical, pragmatic, realistic **10** self-willed **11** down-to-earth, intractable, unfantastic **12** matter-of-fact, pertinacious, unidealistic

hardhearted see **hard-boiled**

hardihood 3 pep **4** birr, grit, guts, sand, tuck **5** moxie, nerve, pluck, vigor **6** energy **7** potency **8** audacity, boldness, temerity **9** assurance, brashness, cockiness, fortitude, impudence, insolence, insolency **10** brazenness, disrespect, robustness

hardly ever 6 little, rarely, seldom **7** unoften **12** infrequently, unfrequently

hardness 5 rigor **8** adamancy, asperity,

obduracy, severity **9** callosity **10** difficulty, inclemency

hardscrabble **6** barren **8** marginal **9** infertile, unbearing, unfertile **12** impoverished, unproductive

hardship **4** toil **5** peril, rigor, trial **6** danger, hazard **7** travail **8** asperity, distress, drudgery **9** adversity, mischance, privation, suffering **10** affliction, difficulty, discomfort, misfortune **11** tribulation

Hard Times author **7** Dickens

hardy **4** bold **5** brave, tough **6** brazen, daring, robust, rugged, strong **8** resolute **9** audacious

Hardy *character:* **3** Sue **4** Alec, Clym, Jude, Tess **5** Angel **8** Arabella, Eustacia, Henchard *setting:* **6** Wessex

hare **3** wat **4** fool **6** rabbit **7** leporid *Belgian:* **8** leporide *combining form:* **3** lag **4** lago *female:* **3** doe *genus:* **5** Lepus *male:* **4** buck *young:* **7** leveret

harebrained **5** balmy, crazy, dizzy, giddy, loony, silly, wacky **6** absurd, insane **7** flighty, foolish **8** skittish **9** frivolous **11** empty-headed **12** preposterous

harefooted **4** fast **5** fleet, hasty, quick, rapid, swift **6** speedy **9** breakneck **10** expeditive **11** expeditious

harem **6** serail, zenana **8** seraglio *concubine:* **3** oda **4** odah **7** odalisk **9** odalisque *room:* **3** oda **4** odah

Hareph's father **5** Caleb

Harhaiah's son **6** Uzziel

hark **4** hear, heed, mind, note **6** attend, listen, notice

harlequin **4** zany **5** clown **6** mottle **7** buffoon

Harlequin *beloved:* **9** Columbine *rival:* **7** Pierrot

harm **3** mar, sap **4** hurt, ruin **5** abuse, spoil **6** damage, ill-use, impair, injure, injury, misuse, molest **7** blemish, marring, outrage, tarnish, vitiate **8** maltreat, mischief, mistreat, sabotage **9** incommode, mischance, prejudice, undermine **10** dilapidate, discommode, disservice, impairment, misfortune **11** banefulness, noxiousness

harmful **3** bad, ill **4** evil **5** risky, toxic **6** malign, nocent, unsafe **7** baleful, baneful, hurtful, malefic, nocuous, noisome, noxious **8** damaging **9** dangerous, hazardous, injurious, malignant, unhealthy **10** pernicious **11** deleterious, detrimental, mischievous, prejudicial, troublesome, unhealthful, unwholesome **12** insalubrious

harmless **4** safe **6** unhurt **8** innocent, nontoxic **9** innocuous, innoxious **11** inobnoxious, inoffensive, unoffending, unoffensive

Harmonia *daughter:* **3** Ino **5** Agave **6** Semele **7** Autonoe *father:* **4** Ares, Mars

husband: **6** Cadmus *mother:* **5** Venus **9** Aphrodite *son:* **9** Polydorus

harmonious **4** calm **5** sweet **6** amical, dulcet, irenic **7** chiming, chordal, musical, pacific, silvery, tuneful **8** amicable, blending, canorous, coactive, empathic, friendly, peaceful, pleasing, sonorous **9** accordant, agreeable, congenial, congruous, consonant, simpatico, symphonic **10** compatible, concinnate, concordant, empathetic, polyphonic, satisfying **11** cooperative, mellifluous, mellisonant, symmetrical, sympathetic **12** contrapuntal

harmonize **2** go **3** fit **4** jibe, tune **5** adapt, agree, blend, coapt, fit in, match, tally, unify, unite **6** accord, adjust, attune, concur, relate, square **7** arrange, concert, concord, conform **8** coincide, dovetail **9** cooperate, correlate, integrate, reconcile **10** coordinate, correspond, proportion, synthesize **11** accommodate, orchestrate **12** reconciliate

harmony **4** tune **5** chime, grace, peace, unity **6** accord, chorus, melody, unison **7** balance, concert, concord, dignity, empathy, kinship, oneness, rapport **8** affinity, diapason, elegance, sonority, symmetry **9** agreement, congruity, integrity, polyphony **10** accordance, coaptation, concinnity, conformity, consonance, musicality, proportion **11** concordance, concurrence, conformance, consistency, integration, tunefulness **12** articulation, togetherness *lack of:* **7** discord *of movement:* **8** eurythmy

Harnepher's father **6** Zophah

harness **4** gear, leaf, yoke **5** armor, hitch **6** couple, tackle **7** utilize **8** clothing **9** equipment *part:* **3** bit **5** girth, trace **6** collar **7** blinder, crupper **9** bellyband, breeching, checkrein **12** breast collar *ring:* **6** terret, territ

harp **4** lyre **9** harmonica *Irish:* **8** clarsach

harpsichord **7** cembalo **8** clavecin

harpsichordist *American:* **6** Fuller, Kipnis, Newman **7** Marlowe, Pinkham, Valenti **11** Kirkpatrick *English:* **7** Malcolm *German:* **7** Richter **9** Leonhardt *Italian:* **7** Sgrizzi *Polish:* **9** Landowska (Wanda)

harpy **4** leech, scold, shrew, vixen **6** amazon, ogress, virago **8** fishwife, swindler **9** termagant, Xanthippe

Harpy **5** Aello **7** Celaeno, Ocypete *father:* **7** Thaumas *mother:* **7** Electra *sister:* **4** Iris

harrier **3** dog **4** hawk **5** bully **6** hector, runner **8** harasser **9** bulldozer **10** browbeater **11** intimidator

harrow **3** try **4** bait, fret, rack **5** devil, tease, wring **6** badger, heckle, hector, martyr, needle, pester **7** afflict, agonize, bedevil, crucify, torment, torture **8** irritate **9** tantalize **10** excruciate

harry 3 irk 4 gnaw, raid, sack 5 annoy, foray, havoc, tease, upset, worry 6 attack, badger, harass, maraud, pester, plague, ravage, worrit 7 assault, bedevil, despoil, disturb, hagride, perturb, pillage, torment 8 desolate, irritate, spoliate, vexation 9 beleaguer, depredate

harsh 3 dry, raw 4 dour, grim, sour, tart 5 acerb, acrid, bleak, crude, cruel, gruff, loose, rough, rusty, sharp, stark, stern, tangy 6 biting, bitter, brassy, brutal, coarse, craggy, gruffy, hoarse, jagged, rugged, severe, shaggy, shrill, uneven 7 acerbic, austere, blaring, bristly, burning, grating, jarring, mordant, pungent, rasping, raucous, scraggy, squawky, squeaky, stubbly, uncomfy, unlevel 8 asperous, exacting, granular, grinding, jangling, piercing, rigorous, scabrous, scraggly, scraping, scratchy, strident, unsmooth 9 amaroidal, dissonant, inclement, stringent, unmusical 10 astringent, discordant, irritating, stridulent, stridulous

hart 4 stag 7 red deer *mate:* 4 hind

Hart, Moss *autobiography:* 6 Act One *collaborator:* 7 Kaufman

hartebeest 4 tora 5 bubal 6 lelwel 7 bubalis 8 antelope *family:* 7 Bovidae

Hartford *college:* 7 Trinity *economic activity:* 9 insurance

Harumaph's son 7 Jedaiah

Harum's son 7 Aharhel

haruspex 5 augur 7 prophet 8 foreseer 9 predictor 10 forecaster, foreteller, prophesier, soothsayer 11 Nostradamus

harvest 2 in 3 bin 4 crop, hide, reap 5 amass, cache, hoard, stash, yield 6 garner, gather 7 bearing, collect, reaping, store up, storing, vintage 8 assemble, cropping, fruitage, ingather, squirrel, stow away 9 garnering, gathering 10 accumulate *bug:* 4 mite 7 chigger *fly:* 6 cicada *former festival:* 6 Lammas

harvester *grain:* 6 header *of grapes:* 8 vintager

Harvey 5 pooka 6 rabbit *author:* 5 Chase

Hasadiah's father 10 Zerubbabel

hash 4 chop, mess, mull, muss, stew 5 botch, mince, mix-up 6 jumble, jungle, litter, medley, mess-up, muddle, review, tumble 7 clutter, mélange, mixture, rummage 8 botchery, consider, scramble, shambles 9 patchwork, talk about 10 assortment, hodgepodge, miscellany 11 gallimaufry

Hashabiah's father 6 Kemuel 8 Jeduthun

Hashabniah's son 7 Hattush

hashish 5 bhang, ganja 6 charas 8 cannabis, narcotic *plant:* 4 hemp

Hashubah's father 10 Zerubbabel

hasp 6 fasten 8 fastener

Hassenuah's son 8 Hodaviah

hassle 3 row, try 4 beef, miff, spar, to-do 5 argue, brawl, cavil, essay, fight, run-in, trial, whirl 6 argufy, bicker, clamor, hubbub, pother, tumult, uproar 7 attempt, dispute, quarrel, quibble, rhubarb, turmoil, wrangle 8 endeavor, squabble, striving, struggle 9 bickering, commotion 10 hurly-burly 11 altercation, controversy

hassock 4 gadi, pouf 5 gaddi 7 cushion, ottoman 9 footstool

haste 3 run 4 dash, pace, rush 5 drive, hurry, speed 6 barrel, bucket, bustle, flurry, hustle, rocket, rustle 7 beeline, hotfoot 8 celerity, dispatch, fastness, highball, rapidity, velocity 9 fleetness, quickness, swiftness 10 expedition, nimbleness, speediness 11 hurriedness, impetuosity 12 precipitance, precipitancy 13 impetuousness, impulsiveness, precipitation

hasten 3 fly, run 4 flit, rush 5 fleet, hurry, speed 6 barrel, hustle, step up, urge on 7 hotfoot, quicken, shake up, speed up, swiften 10 accelerate

hasty 4 fast, rash 5 agile, brash, brisk, eager, fleet, quick, rapid, swift 6 abrupt, brashy, madcap, nimble, speedy, sudden 7 cursory, hurried, rushing 8 headlong, reckless, slambang, slapdash 9 breakneck, hotheaded, impatient, impetuous, irritable, quickened 10 expeditive, harefooted, ill-advised, incautious, mad-brained 11 expeditious, precipitant, precipitate, precipitous, subitaneous, thoughtless

hat 5 derby, tuque 6 cloche, fedora, panama, topper 7 bicorne, chapeau, haircap, homburg, porkpie, stetson, tricorn 8 sombrero, tricorne 9 headpiece 11 chapeau bras *ancient Greek:* 7 petasus *brimless:* 7 pillbox *close-fitting:* 5 toque, tuque 6 toquet, turban *cone-shaped:* 3 fez *felt:* 5 derby 6 bowler, trilby *fur:* 5 busby *helmetlike:* 4 topi 5 topee *lightweight:* 6 panama *maker:* 8 milliner *military:* 5 shako 6 shacko *Muslim:* 6 turban 7 tarbush 8 tarboosh *Near East:* 3 fez *sheepskin:* 6 calpac, kalpak 7 calpack *soft:* 5 toque *straw:* 6 boater, panama, sailor 7 bangkok 8 sombrero *sun:* 5 terai *tall:* 9 stovepipe *wide-brimmed:* 9 sou'wester 11 southwester *woman's:* 4 coif 5 beret

hatch 4 door, line, make, sire 5 breed, brood, cause, cover, frame, get up, spawn 6 cook up, create, devise, father, induce, invent, make up, parent, stroke, vamp up, work up 7 concoct, dream up, produce, provoke 8 contrive, engender, generate, incubate, occasion 9 floodgate, formulate, originate, procreate 11 compartment

hatchet 8 dispatch, tomahawk

hatchet man 3 gun 6 critic, killer 7 torpedo 8 assassin 9 cutthroat 10 highbinder

hate 5 abhor, gripe, scorn, spite 6 animus, bother, detest, horror, loathe, rancor, resent 7 bugbear, contemn, despise, disdain, disgust, dislike, ill will, trouble 8 anathema, aversion, distaste, execrate, irritant, loathing, nuisance 9 animosity, antipathy, bête noire, deprecate, grievance, hostility, repulsion, revulsion 10 abhorrence, black beast, disapprove, repugnance 11 abomination, detestation

hateful 4 evil, foul, mean, vile 5 catty, nasty 6 bitchy, bitter, horrid, malign, odious, scurvy 7 vicious 8 accursed, annoying, damnable, infamous 9 abhorrent, execrable, malicious, obnoxious, repellent, repulsive, resentful 10 abominable, despicable, despiteful, detestable, ill-natured, malevolent 11 acrimonious, blasphemous, distasteful, distressing, opprobrious, uncongenial, unspeakable 12 contemptible 13 reprehensible

Hatfield vs. ___ 5 McCoy

Hathath's father 7 Othniel

hatred 5 odium, spite 6 animus, enmity, rancor 7 dislike 8 aversion, loathing 9 animosity, antipathy, hostility, repulsion, revulsion 10 abhorrence, repugnance 11 abomination, detestation, malevolence *combining form:* 3 mis 4 miso *of mankind:* 11 misanthropy *of marriage:* 8 misogamy *of women:* 8 misogyny

hats 9 millinery

Hattush's father 8 Shemaiah 10 Hashabniah

hauberk 5 armor 9 chain mail, habergeon

haughtiness 5 pride 6 morgue 7 disdain, hauteur 9 arrogance, insolence, superbity

haughty 5 aloof, lofty, proud 6 lordly, sniffy 7 distant 8 arrogant, cavalier, detached, insolent, parvenue, reserved, scornful, sniffish, superior, toplofty 9 egotistic 10 disdainful 11 indifferent, overbearing 12 contemptuous, supercilious

haul 2 go 3 lug, tow, tug 4 cart, come, drag, draw, lift, load, move, pull, take 5 boost, cargo, hoist, raise, shift 6 burden, lading, remove 7 elevate, freight, payload *with a tackle:* 5 bouse, bowse

haul up 4 stop 5 hoise, hoist *with a rope:* 5 trice

haunches 4 beam, rump, tail 7 hind end, hunkers, rear end 8 backside, buttocks 9 fundament, posterior

haunt 4 home, howf, site 5 ghost, howff, range, shade 6 affect, linger, molest, resort, shadow, spirit, wraith 7 habitat, hang out, phantom, purlieu, specter, trouble 8 frequent, locality, phantasm 10 apparition, hang around, rendezvous 12 watering hole

haunter 7 denizen, habitué 10 frequenter

hautbois 4 oboe

hauteur see **haughtiness**

haut monde 5 elite 6 gentry 7 quality, society, who's who 8 optimacy 9 blue blood 10 patriciate 11 aristocracy 13 carriage trade

have 3 buy, eat, fix, get, let, own, see, sop, use, win 4 bear, fool, gain, hire, hold, keep, know, land, lead, must, need, pass, show, take, undo, wear 5 admit, allow, annex, beget, bribe, carry, cheat, drink, enjoy, grasp, leave, smoke, trick 6 accept, buy off, convey, defeat, embody, fathom, obtain, outfox, outwit, permit, pick up, retain, square, suborn, suffer, take in 7 achieve, acquire, carry on, chalk up, cherish, cognize, compass, compose, contain, control, embrace, execute, exhibit, include, involve, outplay, perform, possess, procure, receive, subsume, support, sustain, undergo 8 comprise, dominate, engage in, exercise, manifest, outreach, outslick, outsmart 9 apprehend, bamboozle, encompass, out-jockey, overreach, partake of 10 appreciate, categorize, comprehend, experience

haven 4 port, roof 5 cover, house, roads 6 asylum, covert, harbor, refuge, riding, shield 7 chamber, retreat, shelter 9 anchorage, harborage, roadstead, sanctuary

haversack 3 bag 4 case 8 backpack

havoc 4 loss, ruin, sack 5 waste 6 ravage 7 despoil, destroy, pillage 8 calamity, desolate, lay waste, ravaging, spoliate 9 cataclysm, confusion, depredate, desecrate, devastate, pillaging, ruination, vandalism 10 despoiling 11 catastrophe, destruction, devastation

haw 4 tree, yard 5 berry, fruit, shrub

Hawaii *author:* 8 Michener *capital:* 8 Honolulu *discoverer:* 4 Cook *highest point:* 8 Mauna Kea *island:* 4 Maui, Oahu 5 Kauai, Lanai 6 Niihau 7 Molokai 9 Kahoolawe *nickname:* 10 Aloha State *state bird:* 4 nene *state flower:* 11 red hibiscus

Hawaiian *dance:* 4 hula *duck:* 5 koloa *feast:* 4 luau *god:* 2 Ku 4 Kane, Lono 5 Wakea 7 Kanaloa *goddess:* 4 Pele *goose:* 4 nene *instrument:* 3 uke 7 ukulele *lava:* 2 aa *neckwear:* 3 lei *nonnative:* 8 malihini *resident:* 8 kamaaina *thrush:* 4 omao

hawk 4 vend 5 buteo 6 monger, osprey, peddle 7 goshawk, haggard 8 caracara, huckster, roughleg 9 accipiter *Hawaiian:* 2 io *young:* 4 eyas

hawker 6 coster, monger, pedlar, pedler, vendor 7 packman, peddler 8 falconer, pitchman

hawk-eyed 7 lyncean 12 sharp-sighted

Hawkeye State 4 Iowa

Hawthorne *birthplace:* **5** Salem *novel:* **13** The Marble Faun

Haydn oratorio 10 The Seasons **11** The Creation

hay fever 10 pollenosis, pollinosis *cause:* **6** pollen **7** ragweed

haymaker 3 box **4** chop, cuff, poke, sock **5** clout, punch, smack **6** buffet

hayseed see **hick**

haywire 4 amok **5** amuck, crazy **8** confused **10** broken-down, out of order

hazard 3 bet **4** luck, risk **5** peril, wager **6** chance, danger, gamble, menace **7** fortune, imperil, venture **8** accident, endanger, jeopardy

hazardous 5 hairy, risky **6** chancy, wicked **7** unsound **8** aleatory **9** dangerous, unhealthy

haze 3 dim, fog **4** film, mist, murk, smog **5** befog, bloom, brume, cloud, dream, fog up, smoke, vapor **6** stupor, trance **7** becloud, obscure, reverie **8** overcast **9** mistiness, murkiness, overcloud, smokiness **10** bemusement, cloudiness, muddlement **11** muddledness **12** befuddlement

hazel 3 nut **6** muffin **7** filbert **8** noisette

Hazo *father:* **5** Nahor *mother:* **6** Milcah

hazy 3 dim **5** filmy, foggy, misty, murky, mushy, smoky, vague **6** cloudy, dreamy, vapory **7** bemused, blurred, clouded, nebular, obscure, tranced, unclear **8** nebulous, vaporous **9** stuporous, uncertain **10** indefinite, indistinct

head 2 go **3** aim, top, wit **4** arch, bent, bill, boss, bump, cape, cast, cock, flow, gift, john, make, mind, naze, neck, pate, poll, rise, stem, text, turn **5** arise, brain, caput, chief, crown, first, flair, front, issue, knack, level, motif, point, poise, privy, scalp, skull, start, theme, topic, train **6** climax, crisis, direct, genius, honcho, johnny, leader, master, matter, mazard, motive, noddle, noggin, noodle, scolex, sconce, set out, talent, toilet, zero in **7** address, aptness, cranium, emanate, faculty, incline, latrine, leading, premier, proceed, subject, surpass, take off **8** argument, brainpan, champion, coiffure, director, foreland, foremost, hierarch, lavatory, light out **9** capitulum, chieftain, decollate, dominator, originate, principal, strike out **10** decapitate, derive from, gray matter, guillotine, individual, promontory **11** convenience, water closet *area:* **5** crown **6** temple *back part:* **7** occiput *bone:* **5** skull **7** cranium **8** parietal *combining form:* **5** crani **6** cephal, cranio **7** cephalo **8** cephalic **9** cephalous *covering:* **3** cap, hat **8** kercheif *flower:* **6** arnica, button *monastery:* **4** dean **5** abbot **8** superior *nunnery:* **4** dame **6** abbess **8** superior *of hair:* **6** fleece *relating to:* **8** cephalic *shav-*

ing of: **7** tonsure *skin:* **5** scalp *tapeworm's:* **6** scolex *top:* **4** pate **5** crown

headache 6 megrim **7** problem **8** migraine **11** cephalalgia

headband 7 bandeau *ancient Greek:* **6** taenia **7** taeniae (plural)

headdress *bishop's:* **5** miter, mitre *medieval:* **5** barbe *military:* **5** busby, shako **6** helmet *nobleman's:* **7** coronet *prelate's:* **9** zucchetto *priest's:* **7** biretta *royal:* **5** crown, tiara **6** diadem *Spanish women's:* **8** mantilla *women's:* **6** bonnet; (see also **hat**)

headland 4 beak, bill, cape, naze, ness **5** point **10** promontory

headline 6 banner **7** feature **8** screamer

headlong 4 rash **5** hasty **6** abrupt, daring, rashly, sudden **7** hurried, rushing **8** gadarene, reckless **9** daredevil, foolhardy, impetuous **10** heedlessly, recklessly **11** precipitant, precipitate, precipitous, subitaneous

headmaster 9 principal

headshaker 7 skeptic, zetetic **9** pessimist **10** Pyrrhonian, Pyrrhonist

head-shaped 7 globose **8** capitate

head start 4 draw, edge, odds **5** bulge **7** vantage **8** handicap **9** advantage, allowance

headstone 6 ledger **8** monument **11** grave marker

headstrong 6 mulish **7** willful **8** stubborn **9** obstinate **10** refractory, self-willed **11** stiff-necked

heady 4 rash **5** cagey, giddy, smart **6** argute, astute, clever, shrewd **7** violent, willful **9** astucious, impetuous, sagacious **11** exhilarated, intoxicated **12** intoxicating

heal 4 cure, mend, scab **6** cement, remedy

healer *combining form:* **7** iatrist

healing 8 curative, remedial, sanative, sanatory **9** vulnerary, wholesome **11** restorative *combining form:* **5** iatro, iatry **7** iatrics *goddess of:* **3** Eir

health 7 stamina **8** euphoria, haleness, tonicity, vitality **9** soundness, well-being, wholeness

healthful 4 good **6** aiding **8** curative, hygienic, remedial, salutary, sanative **9** wholesome **10** beneficial, corrective, mitigative, profitable, salubrious **11** alleviative, restorative

healthy 3 fit **4** good, hale, iron, rosy, safe, sane, spry, well **5** agile, lusty, right, ruddy, sound, tough, whole **6** robust, rugged, strong, sturdy, vegete, viable **7** chipper, massive **8** blooming, hygienic, positive, rubicund, salutary, stalwart, thriving, vigorous **9** desirable, wholesome **10** beneficial, prosperous, salubrious, well-liking **11** flourishing, uninjurious *Scottish:* **5** gawsy **6** gawsie

heap 3 lot 4 bank, cock, cord, dump, fill, gobs, hill, load, lump, mass, much, pack, pile, rick, scad 5 amass, bunch, choke, clump, crate, drift, group, loads, mound, shock, stack, wreck 6 barrel, charge, gather, jalopy, junker, lumber, oodles 7 clunker, collect, deposit, jillion, million 8 assemble, cumulate, mountain, slathers, thousand, trillion 9 congeries, gathering, great deal, stockpile 10 accumulate, cumulation, quantities *combining form:* 5 cumul 6 cumuli, cumulo *combustible:* 4 pyre *of dead bodies:* 7 carnage

hearing 4 test 5 sound, trial 6 parley, tryout 7 earshot, meeting 8 audience, audition 9 interview 10 conference, discussion *combining form:* 4 acou 5 acouo, audio 6 acusia 7 acousia *distance:* 7 earshot

hearken 6 attend, listen

hearsay 3 cry 4 buzz, talk 5 on-dit, rumor 6 gossip, report, rumble 7 account 9 grapevine 11 scuttlebutt

heart 3 hub 4 core, guts, love, mood, pith, root, seat, soul, zest 5 ardor, bosom, focus, gusto, pluck, quick, spunk, taste 6 breast, center, mettle, palate, relish, spirit 7 courage 8 feelings, polestar 9 character 10 affections, compassion, conscience, enthusiasm, focal point *combining form:* 5 cardi 6 cardia, cardio 7 cardium *contraction:* 7 systole *dilation:* 8 diastole *part:* 6 atrium, septum 9 ventricle

heartache 3 rue, woe 4 care, pang 5 grief 6 regret, sorrow 7 anguish 10 affliction, cardialgia

heartbeat 5 pulse, throb 9 pulsation *irregular:* 8 arythmia

heartbreak 3 rue, woe 4 bale, care 5 agony, grief 6 regret, sorrow 7 anguish, torment 10 affliction

heartbreaking 4 dire 8 grievous 10 afflictive, calamitous, deplorable, lamentable 11 regrettable, unfortunate

heartburn 7 pyrosis 10 cardialgia

hearten 4 stir 5 cheer, nerve, rally, rouse, steel 6 arouse 7 animate, chirk up, enliven 8 energize, inspirit 9 encourage

heartfelt 4 deep, true 6 honest 7 earnest, genuine, sincere 8 bona fide, profound 9 unfeigned 11 whole-souled

heartleaf 6 ginger

heartless 5 cruel 7 callous 8 obdurate 9 unfeeling 10 hard-boiled 11 unemotional 13 unsympathetic

Heart of Dixie 7 Alabama

heartrending see **heartbreaking**

heartsease 5 pansy, viola 6 violet 9 smartweed

heart-shaped 7 cordate

heartsick 4 blue, down 8 cast down, dejected, downcast 9 depressed 10 dispirited 12 disconsolate

heartthrob 4 love 5 flame, honey, sweet 7 beloved, darling, passion 10 sweetheart

heartwood 7 duramen

hearty 4 deep, warm 5 ample 6 jovial, sailor 7 profuse, sincere 8 abundant, profound, vehement 9 approving, exuberant, flavorful, unfeigned 10 full-bodied, responsive 11 whole-souled 12 enthusiastic

heat 3 hot 4 cook, move, warm 6 excite, simmer, warmth 7 caloric, convect, furnace, hotness, inflame 8 pyrolyze *combining form:* 3 pyr 4 pyro 5 therm 6 calori, thermo, thermy 7 thermia *measuring device:* 11 colorimeter, thermometer *quantity:* 3 BTU

heated 3 hot, mad 4 warm, waxy 5 angry, fiery, irate, wroth 6 ardent, baking, fervid, fierce, hectic, ireful, steamy, wrathy 7 boiling, burning, fevered 8 broiling, feverish, scalding, sizzling, wrathful 9 indignant, scorching 11 acrimonious

heater 5 stove 7 furnace 8 radiator

heathbird 7 gray hen 9 blackcock 11 black grouse

heathen 5 pagan 6 ethnic 7 foreign, gentile, infidel, profane, strange 8 paganish, paganist 9 infidelic 10 unfamiliar

heat-producing 9 calorific

heave 3 gag 4 blow, cast, fire, gasp, huff, hurl, keck, pant, puff, rock, roll, toss 5 fling, labor, pitch, retch, sling, throw, vomit

heaven 3 God 4 Zion 5 bliss, glory 6 Canaan, utopia 7 arcadia, ecstasy, elysium, nirvana, rapture 8 empyrean, eternity, paradise, rhapsody 9 Cockaigne, hereafter, Shangri-la 10 afterworld, Civitas Dei, lubberland, wonderland 11 immortality, kingdom come 12 New Jerusalem, promised land 13 Abraham's bosom

heavenly 4 lush 5 yummy 6 divine, sacred 7 blessed, darling 8 adorable, empyreal, empyrean, luscious 9 ambrosial, celestial, delicious 10 delectable, delightful, enchanting 11 exceedingly, scrumptious

heavenly body see **celestial body**

heavy 3 big, fat 4 deep, drab, dull, gone, hard, loud, rich 5 acute, bulky, dopey, grave, gross, hefty, inert, obese, steep, stout, tough 6 clayey, cloggy, cloudy, clumsy, coarse, drowsy, fleshy, gravid, leaden, occult, orphic, parous, portly, secret, severe, sleepy, stupid, torpid 7 arduous, awkward, doleful, intense, labored, louring, massive, porcine, serious, unhandy, villain, weighty 8 abstruse, burdened, childing, comatose, cumbrous, enceinte, esoteric, grievous, hermetic, inactive, lowering, nubilous, overcast, pregnant, profound, sluggish, toilsome, unwieldy 9 corpulent, difficult, effortful, expectant, expecting, laborious, lethargic, lumbering, ponderous, recondite, strenuous **10** acroamatic, afflictive, burdensome, cumbersome, encumbered, formidable, lumbersome, oppressive, overweight, parturient, slumberous *combining form:* **4** bary, hadr **5** gravi, hadro

heavy-handed 5 inept **6** gauche, wooden **7** awkward, halting, unhappy **8** bumbling **9** maladroit, ponderous **10** uninspired

heavyhearted 3 sad **5** sorry **7** unhappy **8** mournful, saddened **10** dispirited, melancholy

heavyset 5 dumpy, thick **6** chunky, squdgy, stocky, stubby, stumpy **11** thick-bodied

heavyweight 3 VIP **4** lion **5** chief **6** big boy, leader **7** notable **8** big-timer

Hebe *father:* **4** Zeus **7** Jupiter *husband:* **8** Hercules *mother:* **4** Hera, Juno *successor:* **8** Ganymede

Heber *father:* **6** Beriah *grandfather:* **5** Asher *mother:* **4** Jael

hebetude 4 coma **5** sleep **6** stupor, torpor **7** languor, slumber **8** dullness, lethargy **9** torpidity

hebetudinous 5 dopey, heavy **6** stupid, torpid **8** comatose, sluggish **9** lethargic

Hebrew *bushel:* **4** epha **5** ephah *coin:* **4** beka, gera, mina, mite **5** bekah, gerah, maneh **6** lepton, shekel *festival:* **5** Pesah, Purim, Seder **6** Pesach, Succos, Sukkos **7** Hanukah, Sukkoth **8** Chanukah, Hanukkah, Hanukkah, Lag b'Omer, Passover, Shabuoth **9** Chanukhah, Chanukkah, Tishah-b'Ab, Yom Kippur **11** Rosh Hashana **12** Simhath Torah *God:* **2** El **5** Eloah, Yahwe **6** Adonai, Elohim, Yahweh **7** Jehovah *instrument:* **4** Asor **5** nabla, nebel *judge:* **6** Gideon *lawgiver:* **5** Moses *letter:* (see at **alphabet**) *measure:* **3** cor, hin, kab, log **4** bath, omer, seah, span **5** cubit, ephah, homer **6** finger **11** handbreadth *month:* **2** Ab **4** Adar, Elul, Iyar **5** Nisan, Sivan, Tebet **6** Kislev, Shebat, Tammuz, Tishri **9** Veadar (in leap year) **7** Heshvan *patriarch:* **3** Dan, Gad **4** Cain, Levi, Seth **5** Asher, David, Isaac, Jacob, Judah **6** Joseph, Reuben, Simeon **7** Abraham, Zebulun **8** Benjamin, Issachar, Naphtali *sacred city:* **5** Safad, Safed **6** Hebron **8** Tiberias **9** Jerusalem; (see also **Jewish**)

Hebron's father 6 Kohath

Hecate *father:* **6** Perses *mother:* **7** Asteria

heckle 3 nag **4** bait, faze, gibe, ride **5** chivy, hound, tease, worry **6** badger, harass, hector, molest, needle, plague, rattle **7** torment **8** bullyrag

hectic 3 red **6** fervid **7** burning, fevered,

flushed **8** feverish, habitual, restless **10** persistent

hector 3 cow **4** bait, ride **5** bully, chivy, hound **6** badger **7** dragoon, harrier, swagger **8** bludgeon, braggart, browbeat, bulldoze, bullyrag, harasser

Hector *brother:* **5** Paris **7** Helenus, Troilus **9** Deiphobus, Polydorus *father:* **5** Priam *mother:* **6** Hecuba *sister:* **6** Creusa **8** Polyxena **9** Cassandra *slayer:* **8** Achilles *victim:* **9** Patroclus *wife:* **10** Andromache

Hecuba *daughter:* **6** Creusa **8** Polyxena **9** Cassandra *father:* **5** Dymas *husband:* **5** Priam *son:* **5** Paris **6** Hector **7** Helenus, Troilus **9** Deiphobus, Polydorus *victim:* **11** Polymnestor

hedge 3 mew, pen **4** cage, coop, mure, trim **5** evade, fence, guard **6** corral, hinder, immure, weasel **7** enclose, protect, shuffle **8** encircle, restrict, roadside, sidestep

hedonist 4 rake **7** epicure, gourmet **8** gourmand, sybarite **9** bon vivant, debauchee, epicurean, libertine **10** voluptuary

heebie-jeebies 5 jumps **6** dither, shakes **7** jitters, shivers

heed 3 see **4** care, hark, mark, mind, note, obey **5** study, watch **6** attend, beware, debate, listen, notice, regard, remark **7** concern, hearing, hearken, observe, respect **8** audience, consider, interest **9** attention, awareness **10** cognizance, observance **11** application, carefulness, mindfulness

heedful 5 alert, exact, fussy **6** arrect **7** careful **8** punctual **9** advertent, attentive, intentive, observant, observing **10** meticulous, scrupulous, thoughtful **11** observative, painstaking, punctilious **12** conscionable **13** conscientious

heedless 8 uncaring **9** oblivious, unmindful, unrecking **10** unthinking **11** inadvertent, inattentive, unobservant **12** unreflective

heedlessness 6 apathy **8** lethargy **9** disregard, lassitude, unconcern **11** disinterest, insouciance **12** indifference

hee-haw 4 bray **5** laugh **6** giggle, guffaw, titter **7** chortle, chuckle, snicker

heel 3 run, tip **4** cant, hock, lean, list, rest, tilt **5** knave, rogue, slant, slope **6** rascal **7** balance, incline, lowlife, recline, remains, remanet, remnant, residue, villain **8** leavings, residual, residuum **9** miscreant, remainder, scoundrel **10** blackguard *bones:* **8** calcanea, calcanei

heft 4 lift **5** hoist, raise, weigh **6** weight **9** heaviness

hefty 3 big **5** beefy, burly, husky, large, major **6** mighty, rugged **7** massive, sizable **8** abundant, imposing, powerful

9 extensive, good-sized, plentiful, ponderous

Heidi *author:* **5** Spyri *setting:* **4** Alps

height 4 apex, rise **6** climax, summit, zenith **7** stature **8** altitude, highness, pinnacle, tallness **9** elevation, loftiness *combining form:* **3** acr, akr **4** acro, akro, hyps **5** hypsi, hypso

heighten 3 wax **4** lift, rise **5** boost, build, mount, raise, rouse **6** better, deepen, expand, extend **7** amplify, augment, elevate, enhance, enlarge, improve, magnify, sharpen, upsurge **8** compound, increase, multiply, redouble **9** aggravate, highlight, intensate, intensify **10** aggrandize

heinous 6 crying **8** shocking **9** desperate, execrable **10** abominable, outrageous

heinousness 8 atrocity, enormity

heir 3 son **5** heres **6** haeres **7** heredes (plural), heritor **8** haeredes (plural) **9** inheritor, successor *joint:* **8** parcener

Hel, Hela *father:* **4** Loki *hall:* **7** Niflhel **8** Niflheim *mother:* **9** Angerboda

Helah's husband 5 Ashur **6** Ashhur

Heleb's father 6 Baanah

Helek's father 6 Gilead

Helenus *brother:* **5** Paris **6** Hector **7** Troilus **9** Deiphobus, Polydorus *father:* **5** Priam *mother:* **6** Hecuba *sister:* **6** Creusa **8** Polyxena **9** Cassandra *wife:* **10** Andromache

helical 6 spiral

helicopter 7 chopper **10** whirlybird *armed:* **7** gunship

Helios 6 Apollo *daughter:* **5** Circe **8** Pasiphae *father:* **8** Hyperion *mother:* **5** Theia *sister:* **3** Eos **6** Aurora, Selene *son:* **8** Phaethon

heliotrope 10 bloodstone

Heli's daughter 4 Mary

helium *symbol:* **2** He

hell see **hades**

Hellen *father:* **9** Deucalion *mother:* **6** Pyrrha *son:* **5** Dorus **6** Aeolus, Xuthus

hellhole 8 dystopia

hellish 7 avernal, stygian **8** infernal, plutonic **9** cimmerian, plutonian **11** pandemoniac

helm 5 steer

helmet 3 cap **5** salet **6** barbut, casque, morion, salade, sallet **7** morrion **8** burgonet, headgear *medieval:* **5** armet **6** heaume, sallet **7** basinet *part:* **7** ventail **8** aventail *sun:* **4** topi **5** topee

Heloise *husband:* **7** Abelard *son:* **9** Astrolabe

Helon's son 5 Eliab

helotry 4 yoke **6** thrall **7** bondage, peonage, serfdom **9** servitude, thralldom, villenage **11** enslavement

help 3 aid, use **4** abet, ally, back, cure, hand, lift, mend **5** amend, avail, avoid, boost, do for, serve, stead **6** assist, better, fail in, profit, relief, remedy, second, succor, uphold **7** advance, ancilla, benefit, bestead, bolster, comfort, forward, further, improve, prevent, promote, relieve, secours, service, striker, support **8** befriend, benefact, champion, minister, mitigate, palliate **9** alleviate, assistant, attendant, extricate, meliorate **10** ameliorate, assistance, facilitate **11** cooperation *forward:* **7** further *hired:* **5** labor

helper 3 aid **6** deputy, server **7** ancilla, servant **8** employee **9** assistant, associate, attendant, auxiliary **10** apprentice, benefactor **11** subordinate

helpful 4 good **5** brave **6** aidant, aidful, aiding, toward, usable **7** benefic **8** favoring, salutary **9** assistive, effective, favorable, practical **10** beneficial, profitable, propitious **11** encouraging, serviceable **12** advantageous, constructive

helping 7 portion **8** friendly **9** auxiliary

helpless 4 weak **6** feeble, futile **7** forlorn **8** desolate, forsaken, impotent **9** abandoned **10** bewildered **11** unprotected

helter-skelter 6 anyhow, around, random **7** anywise, flighty, hotfoot, turmoil **8** at random, pellmell, randomly **9** haphazard, hit-or-miss **11** any which way, haphazardly, hurry-scurry, impetuously, precipitate

helve 4 haft **6** handle

Helvetian 5 Swiss

hem 3 pen, rim **4** brim, cage, edge, gird, ring, seam, shut **5** beset, bound, brink, fence, hedge, round, skirt, verge **6** begird, border, circle, corral, define, edging, fringe, girdle, immure, margin, stitch **7** close in, enclose, envelop, selvage, shorten **8** encircle, surround **9** encompass, perimeter, periphery *turned-back:* **4** cuff

Hemam's father 5 Lotan

Heman *father:* **4** Joel *grandfather:* **6** Samuel

hematite 3 ore **10** bloodstone **12** black diamond

Hemdam's father 6 Dishon

hemlock 4 herb, tree **6** conium

hemophiliac 7 bleeder

hemp 3 kef, kif **4** kaif, keef, kief **8** cannabis *fiber:* **5** oakum

hemplike 4 towy

hen *broody:* **6** sitter *coop:* **5** cavie *spayed:* **7** poulard **8** poularde *young:* **6** pullet

hence 2 so **4** away, ergo, thus **5** since **9** therefore, thereupon **11** accordingly **12** consequently

henceforth 9 from now on, hereafter

henceforward see **henceforth**

henchman 6 cohort, lackey, minion,

stooge **7** sectary **8** adherent, disciple, follower, partisan, retainer, sector **9** attendant, supporter

Hengist *brother:* **5** Horsa *kingdom:* **4** Kent *people:* **5** Jutes

Henley poem **8** Invictus

henpeck **3** nag **4** fuss **6** carp at

henpecked **8** uxorious

Henry II *adversary:* **6** Becket *son:* **7** Richard *surname:* **5** Anjou **11** Plantagenet *wife:* **7** Eleanor

Henry IV *surname:* **9** Lancaster *victim:* **7** Richard

Henry VIII *daughter:* **9** Elizabeth *son:* **6** Edward *surname:* **5** Tudor *victim:* **4** Anne **9** Catherine **10** Thomas More *wife:* **4** Anne, Jane **9** Catherine

Hen's father **9** Zephaniah

hepatic, hepatica **9** liverwort

Hephaestus **6** Vulcan *father:* **4** Zeus **7** Jupiter *mother:* **4** Hera, Juno *wife:* **6** Charis

Hepher's father **5** Ashur **6** Ashhur, Gilead

Hephzibah *husband:* **8** Hezekiah *son:* **8** Manasseh

Hera **4** Juno *father:* **6** Cronus, Saturn *husband:* **4** Zeus **7** Jupiter *messenger:* **4** Iris *mother:* **4** Rhea

Heracles, Hercules *beloved:* **4** Iole *brother:* **8** Iphicles *charioteer:* **6** Iolaus *father:* **4** Zeus **7** Jupiter *mother:* **7** Alcmene *son:* **6** Hyllus *victim:* **5** Hydra, Ladon **6** Geryon, Megara, Orthus **10** Nemean lion *wife:* **4** Hebe **6** Megara **8** Deianira

herald **4** hail, tout **5** crier, greet **6** signal **7** courier, forerun, precede, presage, trumpet **8** announce, ballyhoo, foreshow, outrider **9** announcer, harbinger, messenger, precursor, publicize, spokesman **10** forerunner, foreshadow **11** preindicate

heraldic *animal:* **7** gardant *border:* **4** orle *cross:* **6** fitchy, fleury, formée **7** fitchée **8** fourchée *design:* **5** giron, gyron **6** manche **7** saltier, saltire, sautoir **8** sautoire, tressour, tressure *term:* **4** ente, paty, pily **6** pattée **7** passant

heraldry **6** armory **9** pageantry *term:* **4** vert **6** moline, pommée, sejant **7** nombril, purpure, sejeant, statant

herb **4** forb, leek, mint, sage, wort **5** chive **6** allium, endive, garlic, pusley, pussly **7** campion, caraway, comfrey, gerbera, puccoon, pussley, spinach, spinage, tobacco **8** angelica, brassica, cilantro, costmary, deerweed, erigeron, gerardia, gromwell, hawkweed, marjoram, plantain, polygony, purslane, tithonia **9** buckwheat, clintonia, nemophila *African:* **7** freesia, tritoma *annual:* **4** dill, flax, okra **5** blite **6** crambe

7 bugseed, clarkia, clivers, sandbur, tampala, waxweed **8** euphrasy, sandburr, tidytips **9** bush basil **10** calliopsis *aquatic:* **6** elodea **7** nelumbo **8** hornwort *aromatic:* **5** basil, clary, thyme **6** catnip **7** catmint, chervil, monarda, oregano **8** origanum, woodruff *Asian:* **7** perilla, skirret **8** chickpea *biennial:* **11** blazing star *bitter:* **9** chamomile *bulb:* **5** onion *composite:* **8** knapweed **9** centaurea **10** bitterweed **11** bur marigold *cultivated:* **7** parsley *East Indian:* **8** pachouli, turmeric **9** patchouli, patchouly *Eurasian:* **6** mullen, squill **7** mullein *European:* **5** paris **6** axseed, betony **7** parsnip, salsify **8** earthnut, fleawort, lungwort, mandrake, oxtongue, rapeseed, samphire, snowdrop, wormwood **9** birthwort **13** Christmas rose *evergreen:* **5** galax *fragrant:* **6** cicely **7** pinesap **10** basil thyme **12** balm of Gilead *garlic:* **6** ramson *genus:* **7** solanum *Japanese:* **3** udo *leafless:* **9** broomrape *marjoram:* **6** origan *medicinal:* **6** borage, eringo, eryngo, hyssop **7** allheal, sanicle **8** blueball, camomile, centaury **9** chamomile *Mexican:* **4** chia **8** tuberose *mythical:* **4** moly *ornamental:* **8** dianthus *perennial:* **4** geum, sego **5** avens, camas, orpin, tansy **6** arnica, asarum, bennet, burnet, camass, fennel, henbit, lovage, madder, orpine, pyrola, yarrow **7** bistort, boneset, bugbane, chicory, cicoree, cudweed, dittany, dogbane, genseng, ginseng, jonquil, milfoil, pinweed, primula, quamash, redroot, rhubarb, shortia, succory, witloof **8** agrimony, boltonia, calamint, chiccory, dicentra, dropwort, eggplant, eremurus, feverfew, finochio, fireweed, gaywings, harebell, hepatica, honewort, licorice, mayapple, nutgrass, nutsedge, pokeroot, pokeweed, primrose, roseroot, sainfoin, selfheal, shinleaf, soapwort, stokesia, tarragon, toadflax, valerian **9** bloodwort, finocchio, squawroot *poisonous:* **6** conium **7** aconite, hemlock, henbane **8** veratrum *prickly:* **8** acanthus *purple:* **12** checkerbloom *Rocky mountain:* **10** bitterroot *salad:* **7** lettuce *seaside:* **8** saltwort *small-flowered:* **11** baby's breath *South African:* **12** Cape marigold *South American:* **3** oca *summer-blooming:* **11** bunchflower *tall:* **4** hemp *tropical:* **6** crinum **7** begonia, episcia, petunia **8** abelmosk, capsicum, cardamom, cardamon, cardamum *twining:* **8** lovevine *weedy:* **7** ragweed *wild garlic:* **4** moly *woody:* **8** bedstraw *yellow:* **9** celandine *yellow-rayed:* **9** calendula

herbicide **6** diquat, diuron **7** dalapon, monuron **8** picloram, simazine

Herculean **4** huge, vast **5** giant **7** immense, mammoth, titanic **8** colossal, enormous, gigantic **10** superhuman

Hercules see **Heracles**

herd 3 mob, run 4 lead 5 drive, drove, flock 6 gather 9 associate *sheep:* 6 hirsel

here and there 6 passim 7 at times 9 sometimes 11 irregularly

hereditary 9 ancestral

heredity unit 4 gene

heresy 5 error 6 schism 7 dissent, fallacy, impiety 9 defection, misbelief 10 dissidence, heterodoxy, infidelity, radicalism 11 revisionism, unorthodoxy 13 nonconformism, nonconformity

heretic 7 infidel, sectary 8 apostate, defector, recreant, recusant, renegade 9 dissenter, dissident, innovator 10 iconoclast, schismatic, separatist, unbeliever 11 misbeliever, revisionist, schismatist 12 deviationist 13 nonconformist

heretical 7 infidel 8 apostate 9 differing, dissident, heterodox, miscreant, sectarian 10 dissenting, dissentive, schismatic, unorthodox 11 disagreeing, dissentient, revisionist, unbelieving 12 misbelieving 13 nonconformist

heritage 6 legacy 9 patrimony, tradition 10 birthright

Hermes 7 Mercury *attribute:* 7 petasos, petasus, talaria 8 caduceus *father:* 4 Zeus 7 Jupiter *mother:* 4 Maia *winged cap:* 7 petasos, petasus *winged shoes:* 7 talaria

hermetic 4 deep 5 heavy 6 occult, secret 7 recluse, secluse 8 abstruse, airtight, profound, secluded 9 alchemist, recondite, seclusive 10 cloistered 11 sequestered

Hermia *beloved:* 8 Lysander *father:* 5 Egeus

Hermione *father:* 8 Menelaus *husband:* 7 Orestes, Pyrrhus 11 Neoptolemus *mother:* 5 Helen

hermit 7 eremite, recluse 8 solitary 9 anchorite

hermitage 8 hideaway 9 monastery

hernia 6 breach 7 rupture 10 protrusion *combining form:* 4 cele *of the bladder:* 9 cystocele *support:* 5 truss *type:* 6 cystic, hiatal 7 femoral 9 umbilical 10 incisional

hero 6 knight 7 demigod, paladin 8 champion 11 protagonist *American:* 6 Bunyan (Paul) 8 Superman *Babylonian:* 9 Gilgamesh *Celtic-French:* 7 Tristam, Tristan 8 Tristram *Crusades:* 7 Tancred 8 Tancredi *English:* 6 Arthur 7 Beowulf 9 Robin Hood *French:* 6 Roland 11 Charlemagne *German:* 5 Etzel 9 Siegfried *Greek:* 4 Ajax 5 Jason 7 Perseus, Ulysses 8 Achilles, Heracles, Hercules, Odysseus *Hebrew:* 5 David 6 Samson *Irish:* 9 Cuchullin 10 Cuchullain *Italian:* 7 Orlando *Roman:* 7 Romulus 8 Horatius

Scandinavian: 6 Sigurd *Scottish:* 5 Bruce (Robert) 6 Rob Roy *Spanish:* 3 Cid *Spartan:* 8 Leonidas *Trojan:* 6 Aeneas, Hector

Herod *daughter:* 6 Salome *father:* 7 Antipas 9 Antipater *kingdom:* 5 Judea 6 Judaea *mother:* 6 Cyprus *son:* 5 Herod (Antipas) 6 Joseph 7 Pheroas 9 Phasaelus

Herodias *daughter:* 6 Salome *father:* 11 Aristobulus *husband:* 5 Herod (Antipas)

heroic 4 bold, huge 5 brave 6 mighty 7 extreme, radical, valiant 8 colossal, enormous, fearless, gigantic, intrepid, unafraid, valorous 9 cyclopean, dauntless, Herculean, undaunted 10 courageous

heroin 4 skag 5 horse, smack 8 narcotic 11 diamorphine

heroism 5 valor 6 spirit 7 bravery, courage, prowess 8 boldness, chivalry, nobility, valiance, valiancy 9 gallantry 11 intrepidity 12 fearlessness, valorousness

Hero's love 7 Leander

herring 8 brisling *smoked:* 7 bloater *young:* 4 brit 5 britt

Herse *father:* 7 Cecrops *sister:* 8 Aglauros *son:* 8 Cephalus

Hersey *novel:* 7 The Wall 13 A Bell for Adano *town:* 5 Adano

Hesione *brother:* 5 Priam *father:* 8 Laomedon *husband:* 7 Telamon *rescuer:* 8 Heracles, Hercules *son:* 6 Teucer

hesitant 3 shy 5 chary, loath 6 afraid, averse, wobbly 7 halting, uneager 8 backward 9 faltering, tentative, uncertain, unwilling 10 indisposed, irresolute 11 disinclined, vacillating, vacillatory 12 wiggle-waggle

hesitate 4 balk, halt 5 delay, demur, pause, stall, stick, swing, waver 6 boggle, dawdle, dither, falter, mammer 7 scruple, stagger, stammer, stickle, stutter, whiffle 8 hang back 9 temporize 10 dillydally 12 shilly-shally, wiggle-waggle 13 procrastinate

Hesperia 5 Italy, Spain 9 butterfly

Hesperides 5 Aegle 8 Erytheia, Hesperis

Hesperus 5 Venus 11 evening star *father:* 8 Astraeus *mother:* 3 Eos

Hesse novel 6 Demian 11 Steppenwolf 12 Magister Ludi

Hestia 5 Vesta *father:* 6 Cronus, Saturn *mother:* 4 Rhea

heterodox 9 dissident, heretical, sectarian 10 schismatic 13 nonconformist

heterodoxy 6 heresy, schism 7 dissent 9 misbelief 10 dissidence 13 nonconformism, nonconformity

heterogeneous 5 mixed 6 motley, varied 8 assorted, chowchow 9 disparate 12 conglomerate

hew 3 cut 4 chop, fell 5 stick 6 adhere 7 conform, cut down

hex 3 hag 4 jinx 5 bruja, charm, lamia,

queer, spell, witch **6** hoodoo, voodoo, whammy **7** bewitch, enchant **9** ensorcell, sorceress **10** Indian sign, witchwoman **11** enchantment, enchantress

heyday 4 acme **5** prime **6** spring

Hezekiah *father:* **4** Ahaz **7** Neariah *mother:* **3** Abi *son:* **8** Manasseh *wife:* **9** Hephzibah

Hezion *grandson:* **8** Benhadad *son:* **8** Tabrimon **9** Tabrimmon

Hezron's father 5 Perez **6** Pharez, Reuben

hiatus 3 gap **5** break **6** breech, lacuna **7** interim **8** aperture, interval **12** interruption

Hiawatha *author:* **10** Longfellow *grandmother:* **7** Nokomis *mother:* **7** Wenonah *tribe:* **6** Ojibwa **7** Ojibway *wife:* **9** Minnehaha

Hibernia 4 Eire, Erin **7** Ireland

hick 4 jake, rube **5** yokel **6** rustic **7** bucolic, bumpkin, country, hayseed **8** cornball, ruralist, ruralite **10** clodhopper, provincial

hick town 4 burg **6** Podunk **7** mudhole **11** whistlestop

hidden 5 privy **6** buried, covert, secret **7** guarded, obscure **8** obscured, shrouded, ulterior **9** concealed **11** undisclosed *combining form:* **5** crypt, krypt **6** crypto, krypto

hide 3 fur **4** bury, coat, fell, flog, lash, life, lurk, mask, pelt, skin, veil, whip **5** cache, cloak, cover, inter, lodge, plant, shade, stash **6** entomb, harbor, jacket, lather, mantle, occult, screen, shield, shroud, stripe, thrash **7** conceal, cover up, curtain, leather, obscure, retreat, scourge, seclude, secrete, shelter, veiling **8** ensconce **10** flagellate *combining form:* **4** derm **5** derma **6** dermia, dermis **9** dermatous

hideaway 3 den **4** lair **6** refuge **8** secluded **9** concealed

hideous 4 ugly **5** lurid, nasty **6** grisly, horrid **7** ghastly, hateful, macabre **8** gruesome, horrible, shocking, terrible, uncomely **9** dismaying, frightful, loathsome, ludicrous, monstrous, offensive, repellent, repugnant, repulsive, revolting, unsightly **10** disgusting, horrifying, ill-favored, ill-looking, terrifying

hideout 3 den **4** lair **5** haven **6** covert, refuge **7** retreat, shelter **9** hermitage, sanctuary

hiding place 5 cache, cover **6** covert, refuge **7** retreat

hie 2 go **4** fare, pass, wend **6** hasten, push on, repair, travel **7** journey, proceed

hiemal 6 wintry

hierarch 4 boss, cock, head **5** chief **6** honcho, leader, master **7** headman **9** chieftain

hieratic 8 priestal, priestly **9** priestish **10** priestlike, sacerdotal **12** sacerdotical

high 3 big, gay **4** acme, dear, loud, olid, rank, rick, tall, thin **5** acute, doped, drunk, fetid, grand, grave, knoll, large, lofty, noble, sharp **6** aerial, argute, bright, costly, elated, florid, height, piping, putrid, raised, rancid, remote, richly, shrill, smelly, stoned, strong, treble, whiffy, zonked **7** ancient, drugged, eminent, extreme, intense, keyed up, reeking, serious, soaring, supreme, violent **8** abstruse, arrogant, cheerful, critical, edifying, elevated, eloquent, exciting, gigantic, hopped-up, long past, nidorous, piercing, powerful, stinking, towering, turned on, vehement, wrathful **9** ambitious, climactic, excellent, expensive, imperious, important, intensive, luxurious, prominent, spaced-out **10** boisterous, malodorous, pronounced, tripped out **11** anti-cyclone, extravagant, intoxicated *combining form:* **4** alti

high-and-mighty 5 proud **6** lordly **8** arrogant, cavalier, insolent, superior **9** imperious **10** disdainful **11** overbearing **12** supercilious

highball 3 fly, run **4** rush, whiz **5** hurry, speed **6** barrel, hustle **7** hotfoot

highbinding 6 fraud **7** chicane **8** trickery **9** chicanery, deception, fourberie **10** dishonesty, hanky-panky **11** skulduggery

highboy 5 chest **6** bureau

highbrow 7 Brahmin, egghead **8** cerebral **10** doubledome **12** intellectual

highest 3 top **5** chief **6** apical, astral, upmost **7** exalted, supreme, topmost **9** top-drawer, uppermost **10** top-ranking *point:* **4** acme, apex **5** crest **6** summit, zenith **8** pinnacle

highfalutin 4 rant **6** florid **7** aureate, bombast, flowery, fustian, pompous **8** rhapsody, rhetoric **9** bombastic **10** oratorical, rhetorical **11** declamatory, pretentious

high-handed 5 bossy **8** imperial **9** arbitrary, imperious, masterful **10** imperative, peremptory **11** domineering, magisterial, overbearing

high-hat 4 snub **5** potty **6** snobby, snooty **8** snobbish **12** aristocratic

high jinks 5 revel **7** fooling, revelry, wassail, whoopee, whoopla, whoop-up **9** horseplay, revelment, rowdiness, whoop-de-do **10** roughhouse, skylarking **12** roughhousing

highlight 6 stress **7** feature **9** emphasize

high-minded 5 moral, noble **8** elevated

high-muck-a-muck 3 VIP **5** nabob **6** big boy, bigwig **7** big shot, mugwump, notable

high-pitched 6 shrill **7** shrieky **8** agitated

high-principled 5 noble **6** worthy **8** sterling **9** estimable, honorable

high roller 7 gambler, spender, wastrel
8 prodigal, unthrift 10 profligate 11 scattergood, spendthrift, waste-thrift
high sign 3 nod, tip 4 wink 5 alarm 6 signal, tipoff 7 warning
high-sounding 3 big 4 arty 7 pompous
9 overblown 10 arty-crafty 11 pretentious
high-spirited 5 beany, brash, fiery, jolly,
merry 6 lively, spunky 7 gingery, peppery
8 mirthful 9 ebullient, exuberant, vivacious
10 mettlesome 12 effervescent,
lighthearted
high-strung 4 taut 5 jumpy, tense, tight
6 goosey, spooky 7 fidgety, jittery, nervous,
uptight 8 twittery 9 excitable, unrelaxed
hightail 4 kite 5 scram 6 begone,
decamp, get out 7 skiddoo, take off 8 clear
out 9 skedaddle
highway 4 path, pike, road 5 track
6 artery, avenue, street 8 turnpike 9 boulevard 12 thoroughfare *German:* 8 autobahn
Italian: 10 autostrada
Highwayman author 5 Noyes
hike 2 up 3 wax 4 jump, rise, rove, trek,
walk 5 boost, march, put up, raise, tramp,
tromp 6 jack up, ramble, stroll, trapes,
travel, wander 7 explore, journey, traipse,
upgrade 8 backpack, footslog, increase
9 walkabout 12 breakthrough
hilarious 5 funny, merry 8 humorous,
mirthful
hilarity 4 glee 5 cheer, mirth 6 gaiety
8 jocosity, laughter 9 merriment
12 cheerfulness
Hilkiah *father:* 4 Amzi 5 Hosah *son:*
7 Eliakim 8 Gemariah, Jeremiah
hill 3 kop 4 bank, bump, cock, heap, knob,
pile, rick 5 butte, drift, mound, ridge, shock,
slope, stack 6 cuesta, height 7 hummock,
incline 8 mountain 9 elevation, monadnock
African veld: 5 kopje *Charlestown:* 6 Bunker *craggy:* 3 tor *Cuba:* 7 San Juan *D.C.:*
7 Capitol *elongate:* 7 drumlin *high:*
5 mount *level-topped:* 4 mesa 5 butte *of
stratified drift:* 4 kame *rounded:* 5 swell
sand: 4 dune *small:* 5 knoll, kopje,
mound 6 koppie *surrounded by ice:*
7 nunatak
hillbilly 4 rube 5 yokel 6 rustic 7 bucolic,
bumpkin, hayseed 10 clodhopper
12 backwoodsman
hillock 5 knoll, mound *British:* 4 toft
hillside 5 slope *Scottish:* 4 brae
Himavat's daughter 4 Devi
hind 4 back, rear 5 after 6 retral, rustic
7 bailiff 9 posterior
hind end 4 beam, rear, rump, tail 7 hunkers 8 backside, buttocks, haunches
9 fundament, posterior
hinder 3 bar, dam, let 4 back, balk, clog,
curb, mire, rear 5 after, block, brake, check,

deter, embog 6 arrest, baffle, burden, cumber, fetter, hamper, hog-tie, impede, lumber,
retard, retral, thwart, tramel 7 inhibit, manacle, shackle, tramell, trammel 8 blockade,
handicap, obstruct, restrain 9 entrammel,
frustrate, hamstring, interrupt
10 overslaugh
hindmost 3 lag 4 back, last, rear 5 after,
final 6 latter, retral 7 closing 8 eventual,
terminal, ultimate 9 posterior 10 concluding
hindquarters 8 haunches
hindrance 4 clog 5 block 8 drawback,
obstacle 10 impediment
Hindu *age:* 4 yuga *ascetic:* 4 yogi *caste
(varna):* 5 Sudra 6 Vaisya 7 Brahman
9 Kshatriya *class:* 5 caste, varna *dancing
girl:* 8 devadesi *demon:* 4 Rahu 6 Ravana
essence: 5 atman *force:* 5 karma *garment:* 4 sari 5 saree *god:* 3 dev 4 deva
goddess: 4 devi *goddess of beauty:*
7 Lakshmi *goddess of destruction:* 4 Kali
god of fire: 4 Agni *god of love:* 4 Kama
god of the heavens: 7 Krishna *god of
war:* 6 Skanda 10 Karttikeya *god of wisdom:* 6 Ganesa, Ganesh *hell:* 6 Naraka
holy man: 5 sadhu 6 saddhu *leader:*
6 Gandhi *lowest caste:* 5 Sudra *lute:*
5 sitar *marriage:* 9 gandharva *nobleman:*
4 raja 5 rajah *precept:* 5 sutra, sutta
prince: 4 raja 5 rajah 8 maharaja 9 maharajah *queen:* 4 rani 5 ranee 8 maharani
9 maharanee *sacred thread:* 7 upavita *salvation:* 7 nirvana *scripture:* 12 Bhagavad
Gita *social group:* 5 caste, varna *teacher:*
4 guru *term of respect:* 5 sahib *twice-
born:* 6 Vaisya 7 Brahman 9 Kshatriya
hinge 4 pawl 5 joint, mount 12 turning
point *kind:* 4 butt 5 piano 10 hook-and-
eye
hint 3 beg, cue, key, tip 4 cast, clue, coax,
dash, fish, hair, lick, seek, sign, vein
5 angle, imply, plead, point, press, shade,
smack, smell, spice, taint, taste, tinge,
touch, trace, twang, whiff 6 advice, aiming,
breath, notion, shadow, smatch, strain,
streak, tipoff, trifle 7 connote, inkling,
pointer, presage, solicit, soupçon, suggest,
vestige, whisper 8 indicate, innuendo, intimate, overtone, particle, pointing, telltale,
tincture 9 adumbrate, direction, importune,
insinuate, prefigure, prompting, scintilla, suspicion, undertone 10 assistance, foreshadow, indication, intimation, sprinkling,
suggestion 11 adumbration, association,
connotation, forewarning, implication,
insinuation
hinterland 4 bush 6 sticks 8 backwash,
frontier, interior 9 backwater, backwoods,
up-country 10 background, wilderness
11 back-country
hip 4 coxa 6 haunch, huckle *bone:* 5 ilium,

pubis **6** pelvis **7** ischium *cattle:* **5** thurl
combining form: **5** ischi **6** ischio *disorder:* **8** sciatica
hippie **8** bohemian, longhair
Hippocratic ___ **4** oath
Hippodamia *father:* **8** Oenomaus *husband:* **6** Pelops **9** Pirithous **10** Peirithous *son:* **6** Atreus **8** Thyestes
Hippolytus *father:* **7** Theseus *mother:* **7** Antiope **9** Hippolyte *stepmother:* **7** Phaedra
Hippomenes'wife **8** Atalanta
Hirah's friend **5** Judah
hire **3** fee, let, pay **4** book, rent, wage **5** lease, put on, wages **6** employ, engage, salary, sublet, take on **7** charter, recruit
hireling **4** grub, hack **6** drudge, slavey **7** grubber **9** mercenary
hirsute **5** hairy **6** fleecy, pilose, shaggy, woolly **7** pileous **9** whiskered
Hispania **5** Spain **6** Iberia
hiss **3** boo **4** bird, buzz, fizz, hoot, pooh, sizz, whiz **5** bazoo, swish, whish, woosh **6** fizzle, sizzle, wheeze, whoosh **7** catcall, whisper, whistle **8** pooh-pooh, sibilate **9** raspberry
historian **8** annalist **10** chronicler *American:* **4** Webb **5** Adams, Beard, Foote **6** Durant, Malone, Miller, Muzzey, Nevins, Sarton, Sparks, Turner **7** Morison, Parkman, Ridpath, Woodson **8** Channing, Commager, Prescott, Robinson **11** Schlesinger *English:* **4** Bede, Stow, Ward **5** Acton, Grote, Wells **6** Camden, Gibbon, Namier, Stubbs **7** Hakluyt, Raleigh, Toynbee, Whewell **8** Geoffrey, Macaulay **9** Holinshed, Trevelyan *French:* **5** Renan, Taine **6** Guizot, Thiers, Volney **8** Hanotaux, Michelet *German:* **5** Ranke **7** Mommsen, Neibuhr **8** Spengler *Greek:* **8** Polybius, Xenophon **9** Dionysius, Herodotus **10** Thucydides *Italian:* **5** Croce **9** Salvemini *Jewish:* **8** Josephus *Roman:* **4** Livy **7** Sallust, Tacitus **9** Suetonius *Scottish:* **7** Carlyle **9** Robertson *Swiss:* **6** Müller *Welsh:* **7** Nennius
historical period **3** age, era **5** epoch **7** ancient **8** medieval
history **4** epic, saga, tale **5** diary, story **6** annals, memoir, report **7** account, journal, recital, version **8** relation **9** chronicle, narrative
histrionic **5** actor **6** staged **8** dramatic, theatral, thespian **10** theatrical **11** dramaturgic
hit **3** bop, rap, wow **4** bang, bash, bean, biff, blow, bump, bunt, butt, conk, cuff, ding, fill, fist, lick, luck, meet, slap, slog, slug, sock, swat, swot, wipe **5** clout, knock, light, occur, pound, skelp, smash, smite, swipe, whack **6** affect, attack, buffet, chance, hap-

pen, stress, strike, stroke, thwack, tumble **7** censure, stumble **8** bludgeon **9** collision, emphasize *baseball:* **5** homer, liner **6** double, single, triple **7** home run **9** line drive *golf ball:* **5** shank
hitch **4** jerk, lift, limp, yoke **5** thumb **6** couple, hobble **7** harness **8** stoppage **10** impediment **11** obstruction **12** entanglement
hitchhike **5** thumb
hither **4** here **6** nearer **11** to this place
hitherto **3** yet **4** here, once **5** as yet, prior, so far **6** before **7** earlier, thus far **8** formerly, previous **10** heretofore, previously
Hitler *follower:* **4** Nazi *title:* **6** Führer **7** Fuehrer *wife:* **5** Braun (Eva)
hit man **3** gun **5** bravo **7** torpedo **8** assassin, gangster **9** cutthroat **10** gunslinger
hit-or-miss **6** chance, random **7** aimless, unaimed **9** desultory, haphazard, irregular, unplanned **10** designless **12** unconsidered
hive **5** amass, lay up, uplay **6** apiary, garner, roll up **7** store up **8** cumulate **9** stockpile **10** accumulate
hoar **4** rime **5** frost
hoard **4** save **5** lay by, lay up, stash, stock, store, trove **6** garner **7** backlog, nest egg, reserve **8** squirrel, treasure **9** amassment, colluvies, inventory, reservoir, stockpile **10** accumulate, collection, cumulation **11** aggregation **12** accumulation
hoarder **5** miser
hoarfrost **4** rime
hoarse **3** dry **5** gruff, harsh, husky, rough, thick **6** croaky, rasped **7** grating, jarring, rasping, raucous, throaty **8** croaking, guttural, strident **10** discordant, stridulent, stridulous *Scottish:* **5** roupy **6** roupet
hoary **3** old **4** aged **5** stale, trite **6** ageold, remote **7** ancient, antique **8** Noachian, timeworn **9** canescent, hackneyed, venerable **12** antideluvian
hoax **3** gyp **4** dupe, fake, fool, gull, sell **5** fraud, phony, put-on, spoof, trick **6** befool, delude, humbug, take in **7** chicane, mislead **8** flimflam, hoodwink **9** bamboozle, imposture, mare's nest, victimize **11** hornswoggle
hob **4** nail **6** ferret, leader
Hobab *brother-in-law:* **5** Moses *father:* **5** Reuel
Hobbit creator **7** Tolkien
hobble **3** tie **4** clog, curb, halt, limp **5** hitch, leash **6** fetter, hamper, hog-tie, impede **7** cripple, trammel **8** obstruct **9** entrammel
hobby **7** pastime **9** avocation, diversion
hobgoblin **5** bogey **7** bugaboo
hobnail **4** stud
hobo **3** bum, vag **5** tramp **7** drifter, floater,

swagman, vagrant **8** derelict, vagabond **10** street arab

hock 4 knee, pawn **6** pledge **8** mortgage **9** hamstring **11** impignorate

hockey 6 shinny **7** shinney *arena:* **4** rink *cup:* **7** Stanley *implement:* **4** puck **5** stick *official:* **7** referee **8** linesman *player:* **3** Orr (Bobby) **4** Fuhr (Grant), Howe (Gordie), Hull (Bobby, Brett), wing **5** Bossy (Mike), Shore (Eddie) **6** center, Clarke (Bobby), Dryden (Ken), goalie, Harvey (Doug), Mikita (Stan), Morenz (Howie), Parent (Bernie), Potvin (Denis) **7** Bourque (Ray), forward, Gretzky (Wayne), Lafleur (Guy), Lemieux (Mario), Messier (Mark), Richard (Maurice) **8** Beliveau (Jean), Esposito (Phil, Tony), pointman, Trottier (Bryan) **10** defenseman, goalkeeper *stick:* **5** caman (Scottish, Irish), camog (Irish) **7** cammock (Scottish) *team:* **4** Jets **5** Blues, Kings **6** Bruins, Devils, Flames, Flyers, Oilers, Sabres, Sharks **7** Canucks, Rangers, Whalers **8** Capitals, Penguins, Red Wings **9** Canadiens, Islanders, Nordiques **10** Black Hawks, Maple Leafs, North Stars *term:* **3** box **4** cage, goal, puck, rink **5** bandy, bench, check, icing, stick **6** charge, crease, shinny **7** face-off, offside **8** blue line **9** back-check, body-check **10** center line, penalty box *variation of:* **9** broomball

hod 4 tray **6** trough **7** scuttle **11** coal scuttle

Hodaviah's father 8 Elioenai **9** Hassenuah

Hoder, Hoth *brother:* **6** Balder *slayer:* **4** Vali *victim:* **6** Balder

Hodesh's husband 9 Shaharaim

hodgepodge 4 hash **6** jumble, medley **7** mélange, mixture **8** eclectic, mishmash **9** patchwork, potpourri **10** hotchpotch, miscellany **11** gallimaufry

Hod's father 6 Zophah

hoe 4 till **9** cultivate

hog 3 pig, sow **4** boar **5** roach, swine **8** boshvark *family:* **6** Suidae *female:* **3** sow **4** gilt *genus:* **3** Sus *red:* **5** duroc *young:* **5** shoat, shote

hogback 5 chine, crest, ridge

Hoglah's father 10 Zelophehad

Hogni's victim 6 Sigurd

hogshead 3 keg, tun **4** butt, cask, pipe **6** barrel

hog-tie 4 clog, curb **5** leash **6** fetter, hamper, hobble **7** shackle, trammel **9** entrammel

hogwash 4 slop **5** bilge, hokum, hooey, swill **8** nonsense **9** poppycock

hoi polloi 3 mob **4** scum **5** dregs, trash **6** masses, rabble **8** populace, riffraff **9** multitude **11** proletariat

hoist 4 lift, rear, rise **5** boost, raise, winch **6** pick up, take up, uphold, uplift, uprear **7** derrick, elevate, upraise **8** windlass

hoity-toity 5 dizzy, giddy, silly **7** flighty, pompous **8** skittish **9** frivolous **11** harebrained, thoughtless **13** rattlebrained

hokum 4 bosh, jazz **5** hooey **8** flimflam, malarkey, nonsense **9** poppycock **11** foolishness

hold 3 fix, own **4** bear, deem, feel, grab, grip, halt, have, keep, last, stay, stop **5** apply, carry, clamp, clasp, cling, delay, enjoy, grasp, gripe, judge, limit, pause, poise, sense, think, value **6** accept, arrest, clench, clinch, clutch, credit, detain, esteem, harbor, prison, regard, retain, steady, tenure **7** believe, catch up, comport, contain, convene, convoke, custody, fermata, grapple, keep out, possess, reserve, support, sustain **8** conceive, consider, enthrall, keep back, maintain, preserve, purchase, restrict **9** fascinate, handclasp, mesmerize, spellbind *as precious:* **8** treasure *close:* **6** cuddle *dear:* **7** cherish *from proceeding:* **4** stay *in check:* **7** repress *in common:* **5** share *out:* **4** last **6** endure *together:* **4** bond **5** clamp **6** fasten *wrestling:* **8** headlock, scissors

hold back 3 bit **4** curb, deny, keep **5** check **6** bridle, detain, retain **7** abstain, inhibit, keep out, refrain, reserve **8** restrain **9** constrain

hold in 3 bit **4** curb **5** check **6** bridle **7** inhibit **8** restrain **9** constrain **10** keep silent

hold off 4 stay **5** defer, delay, rebut, remit, repel **6** rebuff, shelve **7** abstain, adjourn, repulse, suspend **8** hesitate, postpone, prorogue **9** withstand

hold up 4 halt, lift, stay **5** check, defer, delay, raise, remit, waive **6** put off **7** prevail, support, suspend, sustain **8** postpone, prorogue

hole 3 box, den, fix, gap, jam, pit **4** cave, cove, flaw, open, rent, rift, spot, vent, void **5** break, fault, niche **6** breach, burrow, cavity, corner, cranny, eyelet, hiatus, lacuna, outlet, pickle, pierce, plight, scrape, vacuum **7** dilemma, disrupt, fissure, opening, orifice, rupture, vacancy, vacuity **8** aperture **9** perforate **10** excavation, interstice **11** perforation

holiday 5 leave **6** May Day **7** festive, Flag Day **8** Arbor Day, carefree, vacation **9** Halloween **10** Father's Day, Mother's Day **12** All Saints' Day, Groundhog Day **13** St. Patrick's Day, Valentine's Day *Alaska:* **10** Seward's Day *British:* **9** Boxing Day *Canadian:* **11** Dominion Day, Victoria Day *Federal:* **8** Labor Day, New Year's **9** Christmas **11** Veterans Day **12** Armistice Day, Thanksgiving *Hawaii:* **8** Kuhio Day

13 Kamehameha Day *Jewish:* **8** Passover *Maryland:* **12** Defender's Day *Newfoundland:* **12** Discovery Day, St. George's Day **13** Orangemen's Day *Rhode Island:* **10** Victory Day *Texas:* **13** San Jacinto Day *Utah:* **10** Pioneer Day

holiness **5** piety **8** devotion, divinity, sanctity **12** consecration, spirituality

Holland see **Netherlands**

holler **3** cry **4** call, yell **5** gripe, shout **6** outcry **7** grumble **8** complain **9** complaint **10** vociferate

hollow **3** dip, sag **4** idle, sink, vain, void **5** basin, empty, false, notch, womby **6** cavity, dingle, otiose, ravine, sunken **7** channel, concave, echoing, sinkage, vacuity **8** complete, nugatory, resonant, sinkhole, sounding, thorough **9** cavernous, concavity, deceitful **10** depression, resounding, sepulchral *out:* **3** dig, gut **4** mine **5** gouge **8** excavate

holly **4** tree **5** shrub *genus:* **4** Ilex

holocaust **4** fire **7** inferno **9** sacrifice **11** destruction **13** conflagration

Holofernes' slayer **6** Judith

holy **3** god **5** pious **6** adored, devout, divine, sacred **7** angelic, awesome, blessed, revered, saintly **8** hallowed, priestly **9** glorified, pietistic, prayerful, religious, sanctuary, spiritual, unprofane, venerated, worshiped **10** reverenced, sanctified **11** consecrated, frightening *bread:* **7** eulogia **9** antidoron *combining form:* **4** hagi, hier **5** hagio, hiero *communion:* **9** eucharist *oil:* **6** chrism *person:* **5** saint **6** zaddik **8** zaddikim (plural) *Spirit:* **9** Paraclete *vessel:* **7** chalice **8** ciborium

holy place **6** shrine **7** sanctum **9** sanctuary **10** sanctorium

Holy Roman Emperor **4** Karl, Otto **5** Adolf, Franz, Henry, Louis **6** Albert, Arnulf, Conrad, Joseph, Lothar, Ludwig, Philip, Rudolf, Rupert, Wenzel **7** Charles, Francis, Leopold, Lothair **8** Heinrich **9** Ferdinand, Frederick, Friedrich, Sigismund **10** Maximilian

Holy Writ **4** Book **5** Bible **9** Scripture

homage **5** honor **7** respect, tribute **9** deference, obeisance, reverence

home **4** land, site, soil **5** abode, haunt, house, local, range **6** family, native **7** country, habitat, housing **8** domestic, domicile, dwelling, internal, locality, location, national **9** household, intestine, municipal, residence, residency **10** commoracy, fatherland, focal point, habitation, motherland **12** headquarters **13** mother country *country:* **7** cottage **8** bungalow

homely **3** dry **4** ugly **5** plain **6** direct, kindly, modest, simple **8** familiar, intimate, unpretty **10** unalluring, unhandsome **11** commonplace, inelaborate, unbeauteous, unbeautiful, unelaborate, ungarnished **12** unattractive, unornamented **13** plain-featured, unpretentious

Homer *epic* **5** Iliad **7** Odyssey

homesickness **9** nostalgia

homespun **6** folksy **9** practical **13** unpretentious

Home, Sweet Home *music:* **6** Bishop *words:* **5** Payne

homicidal **6** bloody **8** sanguine **9** murdering, murderous **10** sanguinary **11** sanguineous **12** bloodthirsty

homicide **5** blood **6** killer, murder, slayer **7** killing **8** foul play, murderer **9** manslayer **12** manslaughter

homilize **6** preach

homily **6** sermon **7** lecture **9** discourse **10** admonition

homogeneous **4** like, same **7** similar, uniform **10** comparable, compatible, consistent, equivalent *combining form:* **2** is **3** hol, iso **4** holo

Homo sapiens **3** man **5** flesh **7** mankind **8** humanity **9** humankind, mortality

homunculus **4** runt **5** dwarf, midge, pygmy **6** midget, peewee **7** manikin **8** Tom Thumb **11** hop-o'-my-thumb, lilliputian

honcho **4** boss, cock, head **5** chief **6** leader, master **7** headman **8** hierarch **9** chieftain

Honduras *capital:* **11** Tegucigalpa *monetary unit:* **7** lempira *neighbor:* **9** Guatemala, Nicaragua **10** El Salvador *product:* **6** coffee **7** bananas

hone **4** edge, whet **7** sharpen

honest **4** open, real, true **5** frank, plain, right **6** candid, humble, simple **7** genuine, sincere, upright **8** innocent, reliable, truthful **9** objective, reputable, unfeigned, veracious **10** forthright, heart-whole, legitimate, scrupulous, unaffected **11** undesigning **12** praiseworthy, undissembled **13** conscientious, dispassionate, unimpeachable

honesty **6** virtue **7** probity **8** goodness, justness **9** integrity, rectitude, sincerity **11** uprightness **12** incorruption, truthfulness

honey *combining form:* **4** meli, mell **5** melli *drink:* **4** mead

honey badger **5** ratel

honey bear **8** kinkajou

honeybee genus **4** Apis

honeyberry **5** genip

honey bread **5** carob

honey buzzard **4** hawk, kite, pern

honeydew **5** melon

honeyed **6** golden, liquid, mellow **8** Hyblaean **9** sweetened **11** mellifluent, mellifluous

honeysuckle **8** rewa-rewa **9** columbine **11** swamp azalea **13** pinxter flower

Hong Kong's capital 8 Victoria
honky-tonk 4 dive 5 joint 7 hangout
11 barrelhouse
honor 4 bays, fete, kudo 5 adorn, asset,
award, badge, erect, exalt, glory, kudos,
medal, mense 6 esteem, homage, praise,
regard, trophy, uprear 7 dignify, ennoble,
glorify, laurels, magnify, respect, sublime,
worship 8 accolade, approval, carry out,
devotion 9 adoration, adulation, deference,
integrity, obeisance, privilege, recognize,
reverence 10 admiration, aggrandize, blue
ribbon, compliment, decoration, reputation,
veneration 11 distinction, distinguish, recognition 12 incorruption
honorable 4 just, true 5 right 6 august,
worthy 7 ethical, upright 8 reverend, sterling 9 dignified 10 scrupulous, worshipful
11 illustrious 13 conscientious
hood 4 cowl, hide 5 cover 6 bonnet, helmet 7 bashlyk, blinder, capouch, capuche
8 covering *clergyman's:* 6 almuce
hoodlum 4 thug 7 mobster, ruffian 8 plug-
ugly 9 strong arm
hoodwink 4 dupe, fool, gull, hoax 5 blind,
trick 6 befool 7 chicane 8 flimflam 9 bamboozle 10 impose upon 11 hornswoggle
hooey 4 bosh, bunk 5 bilge 6 bunkum
7 baloney 8 claptrap, malarkey, nonsense
hoof 4 boot, foot, kick, pace, walk 5 eject,
troop 6 unguis, ungula 7 traipse, trample,
ungulae (plural) 8 ambulate, throw out *cloven:* 5 cloot
hoofer 6 dancer 7 danseur 8 coryphée,
danseuse, figurant 9 ballerina, figurante
hook 3 ear, nab, nim, nip 4 flag, gore, lift
5 catch, curve, hitch, pinch, steal 6 anchor,
fasten, pilfer, scythe, secure, sickle 7 cabbage, hamulus 8 crotchet *a fish:* 4 gaff,
snag *combining form:* 3 onc 4 onch, onci,
onco 5 oncho *for a watch:* 10 chatelaine
hooklike 7 falcate 8 unciform *part:*
5 uncus 7 hamulus
hookup 7 cahoots, circuit 8 alliance
10 connection 11 affiliation, association,
combination, conjunction, partnership
hooky 7 truancy 8 truantry
hooligan see **hoodlum**
hoop 4 band, ring 5 clasp 6 circle 7 circlet, enclose 8 surround 10 finger ring
Hoosier State 7 Indiana
hoot 3 boo, jot 4 bird, damn, hiss, iota,
jeer, whit 5 bazoo, ounce, scrap, shout,
whoop 7 catcall, modicum 8 particle, pooh-
pooh 9 raspberry
hop 3 run 4 ball, jump, leap, skip, tend,
trip 5 bound, dance, serve, vault 6 bounce,
hurdle, spring, wait on 7 rebound, saltate,
skitter 8 jump over
hope 4 look 5 await, faith, stock, trust
6 aspire, desire, expect 7 count on, prom-

ise 8 reliance 9 count upon 10 confidence
loss of: 7 despair
hopeful 4 easy, fond, rosy 5 happy,
sunny 6 bright, cheery, golden, hoping,
likely, secure, seeker, upbeat 7 assured,
budding, content, halcyon, roseate 8 aspirant, cheerful, cheering, sanguine 9 applicant, candidate, confident, expectant, promising, satisfied 10 auspicious, optimistic,
propitious 11 encouraging, rose-colored,
undisturbed, up-and-coming 12 advantageous, anticipative, Pollyannaish
hopeless 4 glum, vain 6 futile, gloomy,
morose 7 forlorn 8 downcast 9 desperate,
incurable, insanable, insoluble, uncurable
10 despairing, despondent, desponding,
impossible 11 immedicable, ineffectual,
irreparable 12 incorrigible, irredeemable,
irremediable 13 uncorrectable
hoper 8 optimist 9 Pollyanna
Hophni *brother:* 8 Phinehas *son:* 3 Eli
hopped-up 4 high 6 stoned, zonked
7 drugged
___ **Hopper** 5 Hedda
hopping 4 busy 5 fussy 6 lively
Horae 4 Dike 6 Eirene 7 Eunomia
Horam *kingdom:* 5 Gezer *slayer:*
6 Joshua
horde 4 push 5 crowd, crush, drove,
press, swarm 6 squash, throng 9 multitude
Hori's son 7 Shaphat
horizon 3 ken 4 goal, zone 5 limit, range,
reach 7 purview, skyline 8 prospect
horizontal 4 flat 7 general, overall
hormone 5 kinin 6 estrin 7 estriol,
estrone, gastrin, insulin, relaxin 8 autacoid,
estrogen, glucagon, kallidin, secretin
female: 8 estrogen *insect:* 7 ecdyson
8 ecdysone *pituitary:* 8 oxytocin *sex:*
6 prolan
horn 4 gore, toot 5 cornu, drink, glory,
power, pride 6 antler, claxon, klaxon, shofar, tootle 7 cuckold 10 cornucopia, projection *ancient Greek:* 5 rhyta (plural) 6 rhyton *animal:* 6 antler *combining form:*
4 cera 5 ceras, cerus, corne 6 corneo *signal:* 6 typhon
___ **Hornblower** 7 Horatio
horn in 4 fool 6 meddle 7 intrude,
obtrude 8 busybody 9 interfere, interlope
10 intertrude, monkey with, tamper with
hornlike 8 ceratoid, corneous
10 keratinous
horn-shaped 7 cornute 8 cornuted
hornswoggle 4 dupe, fool, gull, hoax
6 befool, pigeon 7 chicane 8 flimflam,
hoodwink 9 bamboozle
horny 4 hard 7 callous 8 keratoid
horrible 4 grim 5 awful, lurid, nasty
6 grisly 7 fearful, ghastly, hateful, hellish,
hideous 8 dreadful, gruesome, shocking,

terrible **9** abhorrent, appalling, frightful, loathsome, obnoxious, offensive, repellent, repugnant, repulsive, revolting **10** disgusting, terrifying

horrid see **horrible**

horrific 5 awful **7** fearful **8** dreadful, shocking, terrible **9** appalling, frightful **10** formidable

horrify 5 daunt, shake, shock **6** appall, dismay

horrifying 4 grim **5** lurid **6** grisly **7** ghastly, hideous **8** gruesome, terrible

horror 4 fear, hate, pain **5** alarm, dread, panic, shock, throe **6** dismay, fright, hatred, wrench **8** aversion, distress, loathing **9** repulsion, revulsion, trepidity **10** abhorrence, repugnance **11** abomination, detestation, trepidation

Horsa's brother 7 Hengist

hors d'oeuvre 4 whet **7** zakuska **9** antipasto, appetizer

horse 3 kid **4** buck, roam **5** act up, bronc, cut up, pacer, steed **6** bayard, bronco, brumby, equine, padnag **7** broncho, carry on, cavalry, palfrey, sawbuck, trestle, trotter **8** footrope, jackstay, palomino, skewbald, stallion, traveler *Asian:* **6** tarpan *Australian-bred:* **5** waler *battle:* **7** charger *breed:* **6** Morgan **7** Arabian, Belgian, Iceland **8** Shetland **9** Percheron **10** Lippizaner **12** Thoroughbred *collar:* **7** brecham, brechan *collar part:* **4** hame *combining form:* **4** hipp **5** hippo **6** hippus *covering:* **8** trapping *draft:* **10** clydesdale *extinct:* **8** eohippus *farm:* **6** dobbin *female:* **4** mare **5** filly *foot part:* **7** pastern *gait:* **4** trot **6** canter, gallop *gear:* **3** bit **4** rein **6** saddle **7** harness **9** checkrein *leg joint:* **7** fetlock *leg part:* **6** gaskin **7** gambrel *male:* **4** colt **8** stallion *mark:* **5** blaze *naturalized:* **7** mustang *nervous:* **5** shier, shyer *of the movies:* **6** Flicka, Silver **7** Trigger **8** Champion **11** Black Beauty *race:* **5** derby **6** mudder **8** Affirmed, Citation **9** Preakness **11** Seattle Slew, Secretariat **13** Belmont Stakes, Kentucky Derby *rump:* **7** crupper *saddle:* **9** Appaloosa *small:* **6** garron, jennet *spotted:* **5** Pinto **7** piebald *tan:* **8** palomino *thoroughbred:* **8** hotblood *war:* **8** destrier *wild:* **7** mustang

horseman 6 cowboy, knight **7** vaquero **8** cavalier **9** caballero, chevalier **10** equestrian

horsemanship 6 manege **10** equitation

horse opera 5 oater **7** western

horseplay 5 act up, cut up **7** carry on, fooling **8** clowning **9** high jinks, rowdiness **10** buffoonery, roughhouse, skylarking **12** roughhousing

horseshoer 6 smithy **10** blacksmith

horticulturist 7 Burbank

Horus *brother:* **6** Anubis *father:* **6** Osiris *mother:* **4** Isis *victim:* **4** Seth

hose 4 tube **5** water **8** stocking

Hosea's father 5 Beeri

Hoshaiah's son 7 Azariah **8** Jezaniah

Hoshea *father:* **3** Nun **4** Elah **7** Azaziah *victim:* **5** Pekah

hospice see **hostel**

hospitable 6 social **7** cordial **8** friendly **9** convivial **10** gregarious **11** cooperative

hospital 6 clinic **7** lazaret **9** infirmary *attendant:* **7** orderly *ship's:* **7** sickbay

host 4 army **5** cloud, crowd, emcee, flock **6** angels, legion, myriad, scores **7** compere **8** assemble **9** innkeeper, multitude

hostage 4 pawn **5** token **6** pledge, surety **7** earnest **8** guaranty, security **9** guarantee

hostel 3 inn **5** lodge **6** tavern, travel **7** auberge **9** roadhouse **11** caravansary, public house

hostile 3 dim, ill **4** dour, sour **5** enemy **6** bitter, fierce **7** adverse, opposed, warlike **8** contrary, inimical, militant, opposite, virulent **9** bellicose, rancorous, vitriolic **10** inimicable, pugnacious, unfriendly **11** belligerent, competitive, contentious, disaffected, unfavorable **12** antagonistic, disapproving **13** argumentative

hostility 6 animus, enmity, rancor **9** antipathy **10** antagonism

hot 5 eager, fiery, fresh, nifty, super **6** ardent, baking, banned, biting, groovy, heated, hectic, raging, stolen, sultry, torrid, tropic, unsafe, urgent **7** boiling, burning, febrile, fevered, goatish, lustful, peppery, pungent, satyric, summery, sweltry, violent, zealous **8** broiling, feverish, feverous, glorious, prurient, scalding, sizzling, tropical, vehement **9** lecherous, lickerish, marvelous, scorching **10** blistering, contraband, lascivious, libidinous, passionate, sweltering **11** radioactive **12** concupiscent

hot air 4 bosh **6** bunkum **7** blather, twaddle **8** flimflam, malarkey, nonsense **9** poppycock **10** double-talk

hot-blooded 5 fiery **6** ardent **7** blazing, burning, fervent, flaming **9** excitable **10** passionate **11** impassioned **12** highspirited

hotchpotch see **hodgepodge**

hot dog 5 frank **6** weenie, weiner, wiener, wienie **7** show-off **11** frankfurter, wienerwurst

hotel 3 inn, spa **5** lodge **6** boatel, tavern **7** auberge, hospice, pension **8** motor inn **9** roadhouse **11** caravansary, public house **12** lodging house, rooming house **13** boardinghouse *chain:* **5** Hyatt **6** Hilton **8** Marriott, Sheraton **9** Ramada Inn **10** Holiday Inn *inferior:* **7** fleabag

Hoth see **Hoder**

Hotham's father 5 Heber

hotheaded 4 rash 5 brash, fiery, hasty 6 madcap 8 reckless 9 impetuous

Hothir's father 5 Heman

hot spot 4 café 6 nitery 7 cabaret 8 nightery 9 nightclub 10 supper club 11 discotheque 12 watering hole 13 watering place

hot springs 7 thermae

hot-tempered 5 ratty, testy 6 cranky, tetchy, touchy 7 peppery 8 choleric 9 dyspeptic, irascible 10 passionate

hot water 3 box, fix, jam 4 hole 5 Dutch 6 corner, pickle 7 dilemma, trouble 8 quagmire 10 difficulty 11 predicament

___ **Houdini** 5 Harry

hound 3 dog, fan 4 bait, buff, ride, tyke 5 chivy, lover 6 addict, badger, bowwow, canine, heckle, hector, votary 7 devotee, dogfish, habitué 8 bullyrag 10 aficionado *Russian:* 6 borzoi

house 3 hut, ken 4 casa, clan, firm, folk, home, race, roof, shed 5 abode, board, dwell, folks, haven, hotel, lodge, put up, stock, tribe 6 bestow, biggin, billet, casino, encase, family, harbor, ménage, outfit, shield 7 château, company, concern, contain, cottage, enclose, kindred, lineage, mansion, quarter, saltbox, shelter, theater 8 audience, business, domicile, dwelling, messuage 9 caparison, entertain, residence, residency *clergyman's:* 5 manse 7 rectory 9 parsonage *country:* 5 manor 7 cottage 8 bungalow *dog:* 6 kennel *earth:* 5 adobe *Eskimo:* 5 igloo *lower:* 8 assembly *mean:* 5 hovel *of prostitution:* 4 crib 6 bagnio 7 brothel 8 bordello *religious:* 5 abbey 6 priory 7 convent, nunnery 9 monastery *room in a:* 7 chamber *rooming:* 5 lodge *Russian:* 5 dacha *small:* 5 shack *Spanish:* 4 casa *women's (Muslim):* 5 harem

housebreak 3 rob 4 tame 5 rifle 6 subdue 7 ransack 9 knock over 10 burglarize

household 4 home 5 folks 6 common, family, ménage 8 domestic, familiar *combining form:* 2 ec 3 eco, oec 4 oeco, oiko *gods (Roman):* 5 lares 7 penates

house of God see **house of worship**

house of prayer see **house of worship**

house of worship 5 abbey, stupa 6 bethel, chapel, church, pagoda, shrine, temple 7 chantry, minster, oratory 8 basilica 9 cathedral, sanctuary 10 tabernacle 11 conventicle *Aztec:* 6 teopan 8 teocalli *Jewish:* 7 synagog 9 synagogue *Muslim:* 6 masjid, mosque, musjid

housewife 5 hussy 8 hausfrau

housing 4 case 7 shelter 9 enclosure *rundown:* 4 slum

hovel 3 hut, sty 5 hutch, shack 6 burrow, pigpen, pigsty, shanty 10 tabernacle

hover 4 flit, hang 5 cower, dance, float, poise 7 flicker, flitter, flutter 9 hang about

howbeit 3 yet 4 when 5 still, while 6 much as, though, withal 7 whereas 8 after all, although 11 nonetheless, still and all 12 nevertheless

however 3 but, yet 4 only, save 5 still 6 except, though, withal 8 after all, although 9 per contra 11 nonetheless, still and all

howl 3 bay, cry, yip 4 bark, keen, riot, wail, weep, yell, yelp 5 quest 6 scream, squall, squawl, squeal 7 blubber, protest, ululate, whimper 9 caterwaul, complaint 11 oscillation 12 sidesplitter

hoyden 6 gamine, tomboy

Hreidmar's son 5 Regin 6 Fafnir, Reginn

Hrimfaxi's rider 4 Nott

H-shaped 5 zygal

hub 4 band, bell, nave, seat 5 focus, heart 6 barrel, center 8 polestar 9 master tap 10 focal point 11 nerve center

hubbub 3 din 4 stir, to-do 5 babel, whirl 6 clamor, hassle, jangle, pother, racket, rumpus, tumult, uproar 7 turmoil 8 brouhaha 9 commotion 10 hullabaloo, hurly-burly, tintamarre 11 disturbance, pandemonium

hubristic 4 vain 5 proud 7 haughty 8 arrogant, cavalier, insolent, superior 10 disdainful 11 overbearing 12 supercilious 13 high-and-mighty

Huckleberry Finn *author:* 5 Twain *character:* 3 Jim, Tom *river:* 11 Mississippi

huckster 4 hawk, vend 5 adman 6 dicker, haggle, hawker, higgle, monger, palter, peddle, vendor 7 bargain, chaffer, higgler, packman, peddler 8 outcrier

huddle 3 don 4 lump 5 bunch, chaos, crowd, get on, hunch, put on, snarl, throw, treat 6 advise, assume, ataxia, confab, confer, crouch, draw on, jumble, parley, powwow, slip on 7 clutter, consult, cover up, meeting 8 assemble, colloque, disarray, disorder 9 confusion 10 conference, discussion 11 confabulate, scrooch down

Hudson's ship 8 Half Moon

hue 4 cast, tint, tone 5 color, shade, shape, tinge 6 aspect, outcry 10 complexion

huff 4 blow, gasp, pant, rant, rile, roil, snap 5 annoy, grate, heave, peeve, pique, storm 6 nettle, put out 7 bluster, dudgeon, flounce, inflame, inflate, offense, provoke, umbrage 8 irritate 10 resentment

huffy 5 proud, waspy 6 touchy 7 fretful, haughty, peevish, pettish, waspish 8 arrogant, cavalier, insolent, petulant, snappish, superior 9 fractious, irritable, querulous 10 disdainful 11 overbearing 12 supercilious 13 high-and-mighty

hug 5 clasp, crowd, press 6 clutch, cuddle, enfold 7 cherish, embosom, embrace, squeeze 10 felicitate 12 congratulate

huge 4 vast 5 bulky, giant, grand, great, jumbo, large, lusty, massy, Titan 6 heroic, mighty, untold 7 Antaean, immense, mammoth, massive, monster, outsize, titanic, whaling 8 colossal, enormous, gigantic, oversize, pythonic, towering, whacking, whopping 9 cyclopean, extensive, gigantean, Herculean, leviathan, monstrous, planetary, unbounded, walloping 10 behemothic, dinosauric, gargantuan, mastodonic, monumental, prodigious, tremendous, unfathomed 11 Bunyanesque, elephantine, gigantesque, magnificent, mountainous

hugeness 8 enormity 9 immensity, magnitude

hugger-mugger 4 hash, hush, mash 6 covert, jumble, jungle, litter, muddle, secret, tumble 7 clutter, furtive, jumbled, rummage, secrecy, silence, sub-rosa 8 covertly, hush-hush, in camera, scramble, secretly 9 by stealth, confusion, furtively, privately 10 mumbo jumbo, secretness, stealthily, undercover 11 clandestine 13 clandestinely

Hugo, Victor *character:* 6 Javert 7 Cosette, Fantine, Valjean 9 Esmeralda, Quasimodo

Huguenot leader 5 Condé 6 Adrets, Mornay

Huguenots composer 9 Meyerbeer

Huldah's husband 7 Shallum

hulk 4 loom, ship

hull 3 pod 4 bark, case, peel, rind, skin 5 chaff, shell, shuck 6 casing 8 covering 9 cartridge 11 decorticate

hullabaloo 3 din 5 babel 6 clamor, hubbub, jangle, racket, tumult, uproar 8 ballyhoo 10 tintamarre 11 pandemonium

Hul's father 4 Aram

hum 4 buzz, moan, purr, sing, zing 5 drone 6 bumble, melody, murmur 7 vibrate

human 4 body, life, soul 5 being, party, wight 6 mortal, person 7 hominid, mankind 8 creature, hominine, hominoid 9 enigmatic, personage 10 anthropoid, ethnologic, individual 12 ethnological *being:* 6 mortal, person 7 primate *combining form:* 7 anthrop 8 anthropo *race:* 7 mankind

humane 4 good, kind, mild 6 gentle, kindly 8 merciful 10 altruistic, benevolent, charitable 11 kindhearted, soft-hearted 12 eleemosynary 13 compassionate, philanthropic

humanitarian 4 good 10 altruistic, benevolent, charitable 12 eleemosynary 13 philanthropic

humanity 3 man, men 5 flesh 6 people 7 mankind 9 mortality 10 compassion 11 benevolence, Homo sapiens

Humbaba's slayer 9 Gilgamesh

humble 3 low 4 base, mean, meek, sink 5 abase, abash, lower, lowly, quiet 6 bemean, debase, demean, modest, simple 7 chagrin, degrade, ignoble, lowborn, lowbred, mortify, subdued 8 baseborn, cast down, plebeian, resigned, unwashed 9 compliant, discomfit, embarrass, humiliate 10 submissive, unassuming, unennobled 11 acquiescent, unobtrusive 13 insignificant, unpretentious

humbug 3 gyp, rot 4 bosh, fake, hoax, sell, sham 5 bluff, faker, fraud, hokum, phony, spoof 6 betray, bunkum, cajole, delude, drivel, illude, juggle, piffle, take in 7 beguile, deceive, mislead 8 flimflam, impostor, malarkey, nonsense, quackery 9 hypocrite, imposture, pretender 10 balderdash

humdinger 5 dandy, doozy, nifty, peach 8 jim-dandy 11 crackerjack

humdrum 4 blah, dull 6 dreary, stodgy 7 prosaic 8 banausic, monotone, monotony, plodding, workaday 10 monotonous, pedestrian

humid 4 damp, dank 5 close, moist, mucky, muggy, soggy 6 clammy, sodden, sticky, stuffy, sultry 8 stifling, vaporous 10 oppressive, sweltering

humiliate 4 sink 5 abase, lower, shame 6 bemean, debase, demean, humble 7 chagrin, degrade, mortify 8 belittle, cast down, disgrace

humming 4 busy 5 brisk, fussy 6 lively 7 hopping, popping 8 bustling, hustling

hummingbird 5 sylph 6 sappho 7 vervain 9 thorntail, trochilus *genus:* 6 Sappho

humor 3 bee, wit 4 baby, mind, mood, tone, vein, whim 5 fancy, freak, spoil 6 banter, cocker, coddle, comedy, cosset, cotton, esprit, joking, levity, makeup, megrim, nature, pamper, strain, temper, vagary 7 boutade, caprice, cater to, conceit, gratify, gruntle, indulge, jesting, kidding 8 chaffing, chitchat, crotchet, drollery, jocosity, repartee 9 character, drollness, flippancy, funniness, jocundity, lightness, wittiness 10 comicality, complexion, jocularity, jocundness, pleasantry

humorist 3 Ade, wag, wit 4 card, Nash, Shaw, Ward, zany 5 Adams, Allen, clown, comic, cutup, droll, Dunne, joker, Twain, White 6 Browne, gagman, jester, kidder, Rogers, Runyon, Thorpe 7 buffoon, Burgess, Clemens, gagster, Hubbard, Marquis, punster, Thurber 8 Aleichem, banterer, Benchley, comedian, funnyman, jokester,

Perelman, quipster **9** jokesmith, prankster
11 merry-andrew *Canadian:* **7** Leacock
humorous 5 funny, witty **6** jocose **7** jocular, waggish, wagsome **9** facetious
humpback 5 whale **8** kyphosis
humpbacked 7 gibbous
Humperdinck opera 15 Hansel und
Gretel
humus 3 mor **4** mull, soil
hunch 3 gob, wad **4** arch, clod, lump,
push, rear **5** chunk, clump, crook, fudge,
shove, squat **6** crouch, curl up, huddle, jostle, nugget **11** scrooch down
Hunchback of Notre
Dame
9 Quasimodo *author:* **4** Hugo
hundred *combining form:* **4** hect **5** centi,
hecto **6** hecato **7** hecaton
hundredth *combining form:* **5** centi
Hungary *capital:* **8** Budapest *dog:* **4** puli
ethnic group: **6** Magyar *monetary unit:*
6 forint *national hero:* **5** Arpad *wine:*
5 tokay
hunger 3 yen **4** ache, long, lust, pine,
sigh **5** crave, yearn **6** famine, famish, hanker, thirst **7** craving
hungry 4 avid, poor **6** barren **7** starved
8 famished, ravenous, starving, underfed
hunk 3 gob, wad **4** clod, lump **5** chunk,
clump, piece **6** nugget
hunker down 5 squat
Hunnish 4 rude, wild **6** Gothic, savage
7 uncivil **9** barbarian, barbarous **11** uncivilized **12** uncultivated
hunt 3 dog, gun, run **4** hawk, kill, prey,
rout, seek **5** chase, drive, hound, quest,
shoot, snare, stalk, start, track **6** battue,
course, dig out, ferret, pursue, rabbit, safari,
shikar **7** capture, explore, rummage **9** cast
about, ferret out, search for, search out
birds: **4** fowl *illegally:* **5** poach
hunter 5 jager, yager **6** chaser, jaeger,
nimrod **7** stalker **8** chasseur, predator *biblical:* **6** Nimrod *cap:* **5** terai **7** montero
constellation: **5** Orion *cry:* **6** yoicks **7** tallyho *horn:* **5** bugle *mythological:* **5** Orion
7 Actaeon
hunting 5 chase **6** venery **7** angling, fishing, gunning, hawking **8** coursing, falconry
9 predatory **10** predacious *bird:* **6** falcon
call: **7** recheat *cry:* **7** tantivy *dog:* **4** alan
5 alant, hound **6** alaunt, basset, beagle,
borzoi, setter **7** pointer, spaniel *expedition:* **6** safari
huntress 5 Diana **7** Artemis **8** Atalanta
Hupham's father 8 Benjamin
Hur *grandson:* **8** Bezaleel *son:* **8** Rephaiah
hurdle 3 bar, hop, lop, rub **4** down, jump,
leap, lick, over, snag **5** bound, clear, throw,
vault **6** bounce, hamper, master, spring
7 barrier, conquer, saltate **8** mountain,

obstacle, overcome, overleap, surmount,
traverse **9** negotiate **10** impediment
11 obstruction
hurl 4 cast, fire, rush, toss **5** drive, fling,
heave, pitch, sling, throw, whirl **6** launch,
thrust **8** catapult *stones:* **8** lapidate
hurly-burly 4 to-do **5** melee, whirl
6 clamor, hassle, hubbub, pother, tumult,
uproar **7** turmoil **8** confused **9** commotion,
confusion
hurrah 4 coil, fire, fuss, romp, to-do, zeal
ardor, cheer, scold, spree, tease **6** fervor,
furore, harass, ruckus, rumpus, shindy,
uproar **7** dispute, fanfare, passion **8** argument, raillery **9** calenture, commotion
10 contention, enthusiasm **11** controversy
hurricane 5 storm **7** tornado, typhoon
8 williwaw **9** whirlwind **13** tropical storm
tropical: **7** typhoon
hurried 4 fast **5** hasty **6** abrupt, sudden
7 rushing **8** headlong **9** impetuous
10 tumultuous **11** precipitant, precipitate,
precipitous, subitaneous
hurry 3 fly, hie, jog, peg, run, zip **4** flit, pelt,
post, rock, rush, skin, trot, whiz **5** dig in,
fleet, haste, scoot, scour, skelp, skirr, skite,
smoke, speed, stave, whirl, whish, whisk,
whizz **6** barrel, breeze, bucket, bullet, bustle, hasten, hustle, rocket, rustle, step up,
tumult, whirry **7** beeline, hotfoot, quicken,
scutter, scuttle, shake up, skelter, swiften
8 celerity, dispatch, expedite, highball
9 bowl along, commotion, swiftness
10 accelerate, expedition, speediness
hurt 3 mar **4** ache, harm, pain, ruin
5 abuse, check, smart, spoil, wound,
wrong **6** damage, grieve, hamper, impair,
injure, injury, misuse, offend, suffer,
weaken **7** afflict, blemish, damaged, outrage, tarnish, vitiate, wounded **8** aggrieve,
distress, mischief, mistreat **9** constrain, detriment, prejudice, resentful, suffering
10 resentment
hurtful 4 evil, sore **6** aching **7** algetic,
harmful, nocuous, painful **8** damaging
9 injurious **10** afflictive **11** deleterious, detrimental, mischievous, prejudicial
12 prejudicious
hurtle 4 rush **5** crash, fling, shoot, throw
6 clater **8** catapult **9** collision
husband 3 man **4** lord, mate, save
6 manage, mister, spouse **7** consort,
hoarder **8** benedict, conserve, helpmate,
helpmeet **9** other half **10** bridegroom
husbandry 6 thrift **7** economy, farming
8 prudence **9** frugality **10** management,
providence **11** agriculture, thriftiness
12 conservation
hush 4 calm, lull **5** burke, quell, quiet,
shush, still, whist **6** shut up, silent, stifle,
stilly, whisht **7** mollify, secrecy, silence

8 choke off, suppress **9** cessation, noise-less, soundless, stillness **10** secretness **12** hugger-mugger **13** hugger-muggery, secretiveness

hush-hush 6 covert, secret **7** secrecy, silence, sub rosa **10** censorship, secret-ness, undercover **11** clandestine, suppres-sion **12** confidential, hugger-mugger **13** hole-and-corner, hugger-muggery, secre-tiveness, surreptitious, under-the-table

Hushim *father:* **3** Dan *husband:* **9** Shaharaim

husk 3 pod **4** case, peel, skin **5** bract, carob, hoose, shell, shuck, strip *combining form:* **4** lepo **7** siliqui

husky 3 big, fat **4** bull **5** beefy, burly, empty, great, gruff, hefty, large, stout **6** brawny, croaky, hoarse, mighty, robust, strong, sturdy **8** croaking, gigantic, muscu-lar, oversize, powerful, rattling, stalwart **9** Herculean, strapping, well-built **10** mem-branous **11** Bunyanesque

hustle 3 fly, rob, run **4** earn, move, push, rush, work **5** cheat, elbow, haste, hurry, press, shove, speed **6** gather, hasten **7** hotfoot, swindle **8** bulldoze, celerity, dis-patch, shoulder **9** swiftness

hustler 4 bawd, doer, drab, moll **5** whore **6** dynamo, harlot, hooker, hummer, peeler, vendor **8** call girl, go-getter, live wire, new broom **9** humdinger **10** powerhouse, prostitute **11** self-starter **12** streetwalker

hustling 4 busy **5** fussy **6** lively **7** hop-ping, humming, popping **9** energetic

hut 3 cot **4** camp, crib, room, shed **5** cabin, dacha, house, hovel, hutch, jacal, lodge, roost, shack **6** bestow, billet, cabana, cha-let, harbor, lean-to, shanty **7** cottage, edi-fice, quarter **8** building, domicile *American Indian:* **6** wikiup **7** wickiup, wickyup *Rus-sian:* **4** isba, izba *shepherd's:* **5** sheal, shiel **8** shealing, shieling

hutch 3 bin **4** cage **5** shack **6** locker, shanty

Huxley novel 11 Crome Yellow **13** Brave New World, Eyeless in Gaza

Hyacinthus *father:* **7** Amyclas *slayer:* **6** Apollo

hybrid 4 mule **5** cross **7** bastard, incross, mixture, mongrel **8** outcross **9** composite, crossbred, half blood, half-breed, loan-blend **10** crossbreed **11** combination

hybridize 5 cross **9** cross-mate **10** cross-breed, interbreed, intercross

Hydra *father:* **6** Typhon *mother:* **7** Echidna *slayer:* **8** Heracles, Hercules

hydrant 3 tap **4** cock, gate **5** valve **6** faucet, spigot **7** petcock **8** fireplug, stopcock

hydraulic device 3 ram **4** jack, lift, pump **5** brake, press **8** elevator

hydrocarbon 5 xylol **6** ethane, indene, xylene *liquid:* **6** octane **7** retinol, styrene **8** menthene *suffix:* **5** ylene

hydroid 5 polyp **6** medusa, obelia **9** jelly-fish, millepore

hydrometer scale 4 Brix **5** Baumé

hydrophobia 5 lyssa **6** rabies

hydroponics 11 aquiculture, tank farming

Hygeia 5 Salus *father:* **9** Asclepius **11** Aesculapius *goddess of:* **6** health

hygienic 4 good **7** healthy **8** salutary, sanitary **9** healthful, wholesome **10** salubrious

Hyllus' father 8 Heracles, Hercules

hymeneal 6 wedded **7** marital, married, nuptial, spousal **8** conjugal **9** connubial **11** matrimonial

hymn 3 lay **4** aria, laud, lied, sing, song **5** bless, carol, chant, cry up, ditty, extol, paean, trill, troll **6** choral, intone, praise, warble **7** chorale, descant, glorify, gradual, magnify **8** antiphon, canticle, doxology, eulogize **9** celebrate **10** panegyrize

hyperbole 8 coloring **12** embroidering, exaggeration **13** embellishment, overstatement

hyperbolic function 4 cosh, coth, csch, sech, sinh, tanh

hypercritical 7 carping **8** captious, cavil-ing **9** cavillous **10** censorious **12** faultfinding

Hyperion *daughter:* **3** Eos **6** Aurora, Selene *father:* **6** Uranus *mother:* **2** Ge **4** Gaea *son:* **6** Helios *wife:* **5** Theia

hypnotic 6 opiate, sleepy **8** mesmeric, somnific **9** somnolent, soporific **10** som-norific **11** somniferous

hypnotize 5 charm **6** trance **8** entrance **9** mesmerize, spellbind

hypocorism 6 byname, byword **8** nick-name **9** sobriquet

hypocrisy 4 cant, sham **6** humbug **7** pie-tism **8** glibness, quackery **9** casuistry **10** pharisaism, sanctimony, Tartuffery, Tar-tuffism **11** charlatanry, insincerity, religios-ity **12** pecksniffery, unctuousness

hypocrite 4 sham **5** actor, faker, fraud, phony, poser, quack **6** humbug, phoney, poseur **7** bluffer, pietist, Tartufe **8** deceiver, impostor, pharisee, Tartuffe **9** charlatan, lip server, pretender **10** dissembler **11** four-flusher, masquerader **12** dissimulator

hypocritical 4 glib, oily **5** bland, false **6** smooth **7** canting **8** affected, janiform, malafide, specious, unctuous **9** casuistic, insincere, pharisaic, pietistic, religiose **10** goody-goody, left-handed, moralistic **11** dissembling, double-faced **12** ambidex-trous, double-minded, mealymouthed, peck-

sniffian, smooth-spoken **13** double-dealing, doublehearted, double-tongued, sanctimonious, self-righteous, smooth-tongued
hypothesis 6 theory **8** supposal **11** supposition
hypothetical 5 ideal **7** assumed, reputed **8** abstract, doubtful, putative, supposed

11 conditional, conjectural, implication, problematic, suppositive, suppository **12** suppositious, transcendent **13** suppositional
Hypsipyle's father 5 Thoas
hyrax 4 cony **5** coney
hysterical fear 5 panic

I

Iago *general:* 7 Othello ***victim:* 6** Cassio, Emilia **7** Othello **9** Desdemona ***wife:* 6** Emilia
Iapetus *father:* 6 Uranus ***mother:* 2** Ge **4** Gaea ***son:* 5** Atlas **9** Menoetius **10** Epimetheus, Prometheus ***wife:* 7** Clymene
Iasion *brother:* 8 Dardanus ***father:* 4** Zeus **7** Jupiter ***lover:* 5** Ceres **7** Demeter ***mother:* 7** Electra ***son:* 6** Plutus
ibex 3 tur **4** tahr **8** wild goat ***family:* 7** Bovidae ***genus:* 5** Capra
Ibhar's father 5 David
ibis-headed god 5 Thoth
Ibneiah's father 7 Jeroham
Ibnijah's son 5 Reuel
Ibri's father 7 Jaaziah
Ibsen *character:* 3 Ase **4** Nora **5** Brand, Hedda **7** Solness **8** Peer Gynt ***country:* 6** Norway ***play:* 6** Ghosts **8** Peer Gynt **11** A Doll's House, Hedda Gabler, Little Eyolf, Rosmersholm, The Wild Duck
Icarius *brother:* 9 Tyndareus ***daughter:* 7** Erigone **8** Penelope ***mother:* 10** Gorgophone
Icarus'father 8 Daedalus
ice 4 rime, sish **5** chill, frost, glace **6** freeze ***area:* 4** rink ***combining form:* 6** glacio **8** crystall **9** crystallo ***floating:* 4** berg, floe ***glacial:* 5** serac ***hanging:* 6** icicle ***on rock:* 7** verglas ***pinnacle:* 5** serac
ice cream 7 spumone, spumoni, tortoni ***dish:* 4** soda **6** frappe, sundae
iced 5 glacé **6** glazed
ice field 7 glacier
ice game 6 hockey **7** curling
ice house 4 iglu **5** igloo
Iceland *capital:* 9 Reykjavik ***monetary unit:* 5** krona
Icelandic *epic:* 4 Edda ***hero:* 7** Grettir
Ichabod *father:* 8 Phinehas ***grandfather:* 3** Eli
Ichabod Crane's beloved 8 Caterina

icing 7 topping **8** frosting
icky 4 vile **5** nasty **6** sticky **7** noisome **8** horrible **9** loathsome, offensive, repellent, revolting, sickening **10** disgusting
icon 5 image
icy 4 cold **5** chill, gelid **6** arctic, chilly, frigid, frosty **7** glacial **8** chilling, freezing **11** emotionless, indifferent, unemotional
Idaho *capital:* 5 Boise ***nickname:* 8** Gem State ***state flower:* 7** syringa
Idas *brother:* 7 Lynceus ***father:* 8** Aphareus ***slayer:* 4** Zeus ***victim:* 6** Castor ***wife:* 8** Marpessa
Iddo *father:* 9 Zechariah ***grandson:* 9** Zechariah ***son:* 8** Ahinadab
idea 4 view, whim **5** fancy, guess, image **6** belief, notion, theory, vagary, whimsy **7** caprice, conceit, concept, fantasy, feeling, figment, inkling, opinion, subject, surmise, thought **8** judgment, reaction **9** sentiment, suspicion **10** assumption, brainstorm, conception, conclusion, conjecture, conviction, estimation, hypothesis, impression, perception, persuasion, reflection **11** inspiration
ideal 4 goal, very **5** jewel, model **6** mirror **7** classic, example, paragon, pattern, perfect, phoenix, typical, utopian **8** abstract, ensample, exemplar, flawless, nonesuch, notional, paradigm, standard **9** archetype, classical, exemplary, imaginary, nonpareil, visionary **10** archetypal, conceptual, ideational, prototypal **11** theoretical
idealist 7 dreamer, quixote, utopian **9** ideologue, visionary **13** castle-builder
idealistic 6 starry **7** utopian **8** poetical, quixotic, romantic **9** visionary **10** starryeyed **11** impractical, unrealistic
identical 3 one **4** like, same, self, very **5** alike, equal, exact **8** selfsame
identification *abbreviation:* 2 ID ***mark:* 5** brand, label
identify 3 tag **4** find, mark, name, spot

5 brand, place 6 finger, select 7 make out, pick out 8 diagnose, pinpoint 9 determine, establish, recognize

ideology 3 ism 4 view 5 credo, creed 7 outlook 10 philosophy

idiocy 5 folly 7 amentia, fatuity 9 stupidity

idiosyncratic 3 odd 5 queer, weird 6 proper 7 curious, erratic, oddball, strange 8 peculiar, singular 9 diacritic, eccentric 10 diagnostic, individual 11 distinctive

idiot 3 ass 4 fool, jerk, simp, zany 5 ament, dummy, dunce, moron, ninny, schmo 6 cretin, donkey, jester, motley, schmoe, stupid 7 dullard, half-wit, jackass, natural, tomfool 8 dullhead, dumbbell, imbecile, numskull 9 ignoramus, simpleton 10 nincompoop

idiotic 4 daft 6 stupid 7 foolish, moronic 9 senseless

idle 3 bum 4 laze, lazy, loaf, loll, rest, vain 5 amble, dally, drone, empty, inert, mooch, mosey, quiet, relax, sit by, tarry 6 asleep, dawdle, diddle, futile, hollow, linger, loiter, lounge, otiose, potter, repose, sleepy, stroll, unused, vacant 7 aimless, passive, saunter, sit back, useless 8 inactive, indolent, nugatory, slothful

idleness 4 laze 5 sloth 6 acedia, slouch 8 flânerie, laziness 9 indolence 12 slothfulness

idler 3 bum 4 slug 5 drone 6 loafer, slouch 8 dolittle, fainéant, slugabed, sluggard 9 do-nothing, lazybones

ldmon *daughter:* 7 Arachne *father:* 6 Apollo *mother:* 6 Cyrene

idol 3 god 4 hero, icon 5 image *Chinese:* 4 joss

idolatry 7 baalism, worship 9 adoration 11 idolization

idolize 5 adore 6 admire, dote on, revere 7 worship 8 dote upon, venerate

Idylls of the King *author:* 8 Tennyson *character:* 4 Enid 6 Arthur, Elaine, Gareth, Merlin, Vivien 7 Geraint, Lynette 8 Lancelot

iffy 5 dicey 6 chancy 7 erratic 8 doubtful 9 fluctuant, uncertain, whimsical 10 capricious 12 incalculable 13 unpredictable

Igal's father 6 Nathan 8 Shemaiah

Igdaliah's son 5 Hanan

igneous rock 4 lava 5 magma 6 basalt, gabbro, pumice, scoria 7 diabase, granite 8 obsidian, porphyry

ignis fatuus 6 mirage 8 delusion, illusion, phantasm 12 will-o'-the-wisp 13 hallucination

ignitable 8 burnable 9 flammable 11 combustible, inflammable

ignite 4 fire 5 light 6 excite, kindle 7 inflame 8 enkindle

ignited 3 lit 5 afire, fiery 6 ablaze, aflame, alight 7 blazing, burning, flaming, flaring, lighted

ignoble 3 low 4 base, mean, poor, vile 5 lowly, plain 6 abject, coarse, common, homely, humble, modest, scurvy, simple, sordid, vulgar 7 lowborn, peasant, popular, servile 8 baseborn, inferior, ordinary, plebeian, shameful, unwashed, wretched 10 despicable, inglorious, unennobled 11 disgraceful 12 dishonorable

ignominious 5 shady 6 shabby, shoddy 8 shameful 10 inglorious 11 disgraceful 12 dishonorable, disreputable 13 discreditable, unrespectable

ignominy 5 odium, scorn, shame 6 infamy 7 chagrin, despite, disdain, obloquy 8 contempt, disgrace, dishonor 9 discredit, disesteem, disrepute 10 opprobrium 13 mortification

ignoramus 4 dolt, fool 5 dummy, dunce, idiot, moron 6 nitwit, stupid 7 dullard 8 dullhead, dumbbell 9 simpleton

ignorance 7 naiveté, rawness 8 darkness 9 greenness, innocence, inscience, nescience 10 callowness, illiteracy, simpleness, simplicity 11 unawareness, uncouthness, witlessness

ignorant 3 raw 4 rude 5 crude, green, gross, naive 6 callow, simple, stupid 7 lowbrow, unaware, uncouth 8 backward, nescient, untaught 9 benighted, ingenuous, oblivious, unknowing, untutored, unwitting 10 illiterate, uncultured, uneducated, unfamiliar, uninformed, unlettered, unschooled 11 empty-headed, incognizant, know-nothing 12 inconversant, unacquainted, uninstructed

ignore 3 cut 4 fail, omit, snub 5 avoid, evade 6 forget, slight 7 blink at, neglect 8 discount, overlook, overpass 9 blink away, disregard

Igraine, Ygerne *husband:* 5 Uther 7 Gorlois *son:* 6 Arthur

iguana 6 lizard 7 tuatara

ilex 5 holly 7 holm oak

Iliad 4 epic *author:* 5 Homer *character:* 4 Ajax 5 Helen, Paris, Priam 6 Aeneas, Hector 8 Achilles, Diomedes, Odysseus 9 Agamemnon, Patroclus *city:* 4 Troy

Ilion, Ilium 4 Troy

ilk 4 kind, sort, type 5 breed, class 6 family, kidney, nature, stripe 7 variety

ill 3 bad 4 down, evil, rude, sick 5 amiss 6 malady, nocent 7 ailment, disease, harmful, hostile, hurtful, ill-bred, noxious, uncivil 8 damaging, disorder, feverish, feverous, impolite, inimical, nauseous, sickness, syndrome 9 affection, complaint, condition, infirmity, injurious

ill-adapted 5 inapt, unfit 6 unmeet

8 unfitted, unsuited **9** ill-suited **10** unsuitable **13** inappropriate

ill-advised 4 rash **5** brash, hasty **6** madcap, unwise **8** reckless **9** hotheaded, ill-judged, impolitic, imprudent **10** incautious, indiscreet, mad-brained **11** inadvisable, inexpedient, injudicious, thoughtless, unadvisable, unexpedient **13** inconsiderate

ill-boding 4 dire **7** baleful, baneful, fateful, ominous, unlucky **9** ill-omened **11** apocalyptic **12** inauspicious, unpropitious

ill-bred 4 rude **6** rugged **7** boorish, incivil, loutish, lowbred, uncivil **8** churlish, cloddish, impolite **9** unrefined **10** uncultured, ungracious, unpolished **11** disgracious, ill-mannered, impertinent, uncivilized **12** discourteous **13** disrespectful

ill-defined 3 dim **5** blear, faint, fuzzy, vague **6** bleary **7** shadowy, unclear **9** undefined **10** indistinct

illegal 3 hot **6** banned **7** illicit, lawless **8** criminal, nonlegal, outlawed, unlawful, wrongful **9** felonious, forbidden, irregular **10** actionable, contraband, prohibited, proscribed, unlicensed **11** interdicted, unwarranted **12** illegitimate, unauthorized *act:* **5** crime **6** felony *scheme:* **4** scam

illegible 5 faint **7** obscure, unclear **10** indistinct, unreadable

illegitimacy 8 bastardy **10** illegality **11** bar sinister, illicitness **12** unlawfulness

illegitimate 6 by-blow **7** bastard, bootleg, illegal, illicit, lawless, natural **8** baseborn, criminal, spurious, unlawful, wrongful

ill-fated 7 hapless, unhappy, unlucky **8** luckless, untoward **11** star-crossed, unfortunate **12** misfortunate

ill health 7 cachexy **8** cachexia

ill-humored 5 cross **6** cranky **7** peevish **8** choleric **9** dyspeptic **10** tempersome **11** bad-tempered, hot-tempered

illiberal 4 mean **5** petty, rigid, small **6** biased, little, narrow, paltry, stingy **7** bigoted, insular, partial **8** grudging, one-sided, partisan, rigorous **9** hidebound, jaundiced, parochial, stringent **10** brassbound, intolerant, prejudiced, provincial, unenlarged, ungenerous **11** opinionated, small-minded **12** narrow-minded, uncharitable

illicit 7 bootleg, illegal, lawless **8** criminal, unlawful, wrongful **12** illegitimate

illimitable 7 endless, eternal **8** infinite **9** boundless **10** perdurable **11** measureless, sempiternal **12** immeasurable, interminable

Illinois *capital:* **11** Springfield *college, university:* **5** Barat **6** De Paul **7** Wheaton **12** Northwestern *largest city:* **7** Chicago *nickname:* **11** Sucker State **12** Prairie State *state bird:* **8** cardinal *state flower:* **6** violet

illiterate 4 rude **8** ignorant, untaught **9** benighted, unlearned, untutored **10** analphabet, uncultured, uneducated, unlettered

ill-kempt 5 messy **6** sloppy, unneat, untidy **8** careless, slipshod, slovenly, uncombed **10** disheveled

ill-mannered 4 rude **7** incivil, uncivil **8** impolite **10** ungracious **11** disgracious, impertinent **12** discourteous **13** disrespectful

ill-natured 5 cross, nasty, surly **6** crabby **8** choleric **9** dyspeptic **10** tempersome **11** bad-tempered, hot-tempered

illness 6 malady **7** ailment, disease **8** cachexia, disorder, sickness, unhealth **9** infirmity **10** affliction **13** indisposition *mental:* **8** dementia

illogical 3 mad **5** false **6** absurd **7** invalid, unsound **8** specious **9** plausible, senseless, sophistic **10** fallacious, irrational, reasonless, unreasoned **11** meaningless, nonrational **12** unreasonable, unscientific

ill-starred 6 malign **7** baleful, bodeful, fateful, hapless, malefic, ominous, unhappy, unlucky **8** luckless, sinister, untoward **10** foreboding, portentous **11** star-crossed, unfavorable, unfortunate, unpromising **12** misfortunate, unpropitious

ill-suited 5 inapt, unfit **6** unmeet **8** unfitted **10** unsuitable **13** inappropriate

ill-tempered 4 sour **5** cross, huffy, surly **6** crabby, grumpy **7** crabbed, grouchy, peevish, waspish **8** choleric, petulant, shrewish, snappish, vixenish **9** dyspeptic, fractious, irritable, querulous

ill-timed 5 inept **8** improper, mistimed, unseemly, untimely **10** malapropos, unbecoming, unsuitable **11** inopportune, unbefitting **12** unseasonable **13** inappropriate

ill-treat 5 abuse, harry **6** harass, misuse, molest **7** outrage **8** aggrieve, maltreat, mistreat

illude 4 bilk **5** bluff, cheat, elude **6** betray, delude, humbug, juggle, take in **7** beguile, deceive, mislead **11** double-cross

illume 5 edify, light **6** uplift **7** improve, lighten **8** illumine **9** enlighten, irradiate

illuminate 4 fire **5** clear, edify, exalt, gloss, light **6** better, define, finish, ignite, kindle, mature, polish, refine, uplift **7** clarify, clear up, ennoble, explain, expound, express, improve, lighten, perfect **8** brighten, construe **9** dramatize, elucidate, enlighten, highlight, interpret, irradiate, spotlight

illuminati 7 clerisy **8** literati **13** intellectuals

illumination 8 lighting *unit of:* **3** lux **4** phot **5** lumen **6** candle **7** candela **10** footcandle

illumine see **illuminate**

illusion 5 dream **6** bubble, mirage **7** chimera, fantasy, rainbow, seeming **8** delusion, phantasm, phantasy **9** invention, pipe dream, semblance **10** appearance **11** ignis fatuus **12** will-o'-the-wisp **13** hallucination

illusionist 8 conjurer, magician **9** trickster

illusive 5 false **6** unreal **7** seeming **8** apparent

illusory 6 unreal **7** fictive, seeming **8** apparent, delusive, delusory, fanciful, illusive, semblant **9** deceptive, fantastic, fictional, imaginary, visionary **10** Barmecidal, chimerical, fictitious, misleading, ostensible

illustrate 4 mark, show **5** clear **6** embody, evince, expose, mirror, ostend, reveal, typify, vivify **7** clarify, clear up, display, enliven, exhibit, explain, expound, picture **8** disclose, discover, evidence, instance, manifest, proclaim **9** elucidate, epitomize, exemplify

illustration 4 case **6** sample **7** example, problem **8** ensample, instance, sampling, specimen

illustrative 7 graphic **8** pictoric **9** pictorial **12** iconographic

illustrator *American:* **5** Flagg **7** Burgess **8** Rockwell **9** Remington *English:* **6** Potter **7** Tenniel **9** Beardsley, du Maurier *French:* **4** Doré *German:* **5** Dürer

illustrious 5 famed, great, lofty, noted **6** famous, signal **7** eminent, exalted, notable, sublime **8** glorious, renowned, splendid, striking **9** prominent **10** celebrated, celebrious **11** conspicuous, outstanding, resplendent **13** distinguished

illustriousness 6 renown **8** eminence, prestige **10** prominence, prominency **11** distinction, preeminence

ill will 5 spite, venom **6** animus, grudge, malice, rancor, spleen **7** despite **9** hostility, malignity **10** malignancy **11** malevolence **12** spitefulness **13** maliciousness

Ilus *father:* **4** Tros *grandson:* **5** Priam *mother:* **10** Callirrhoe *son:* **8** Laomedon

image 4 copy, form, icon, idea, idol, limn **5** equal, fancy, glass, match, split, think **6** depict, double, effigy, mirror, notion, recept, render, ringer, vision **7** conceit, concept, fantasm, feature, imagine, picture, portray, realize, reflect, thought **8** conceive, describe, envisage, envision, likeness, phantasm, portrait **9** delineate, interpret, represent, semblance, visualize **10** conception, equivalent, impression, perception, simulacrum *Polynesian:* **4** tiki *Semitic:* **6** teraph **8** teraphim (plural)

imaginary 5 ideal **6** unreal **7** fancied, fictive, shadowy **8** abstract, chimeric, fanciful, illusory, imagined, notional, quixotic, spectral, visional **9** fantastic, fictional, figmental, visionary **10** chimerical, fictitious, phantasmal, phantasmic **11** imaginative **12** apparitional, hypothetical, suppositious **13** hallucinatory, unsubstantial

imagination 5 fancy **7** fantasy **8** phantasy **9** invention **10** creativity **11** inspiration **13** inventiveness, visualization

imagine 4 take **5** dream, fancy, guess, image, think **6** assume, expect, gather, vision **7** believe, feature, picture, realize, suppose, suspect **8** conceive, envisage, envision **9** fabricate, visualize **10** conjecture, understand

imbecile 3 ass **4** dolt, dull, fool, jerk, slow, zany **5** ament, idiot, moron, ninny **6** cretin, donkey **7** half-wit, jackass, moronic, natural, tomfool **8** backward, retarded **9** dimwitted, simpleton **10** half-witted, nincompoop, slow-witted **12** feebleminded, simpleminded

imbibe 3 sip **4** soak, swig, toss **5** booze, drink, quaff, sup up, swill **6** absorb, guzzle, insorb, sup off, tank up, tipple **7** inhaust, swallow, swizzle **8** liquor up **10** assimilate

imbricate 3 lap **4** ride **7** overlap, overlie, shingle **8** override

imbroglio 3 row **4** miff, spat **7** dispute, quarrel **8** squabble **9** bickering **10** falling-out **11** altercation, embroilment **12** disagreement

imbue 3 dye **4** soak **5** steep, tinge **6** infuse, invest, leaven **7** ingrain, suffuse **8** permeate, saturate **9** inoculate **10** impregnate

imitate 3 ape **4** copy, echo, mime, mock **5** mimic **6** parody **7** emulate, take off **8** travesty **9** burlesque, duplicate, replicate, reproduce **11** reduplicate *combining form:* **3** mim **4** mimo

imitation 4 copy, fake, mock, sham **5** dummy, false, phony **6** ersatz **7** forgery, replica **8** likeness, spurious **9** duplicate, semblance, simulated **10** artificial, simulacrum, simulation, substitute **11** counterfeit, counterpart **12** reproduction *suffix:* **3** een **4** ette

imitative 5 apish **6** echoic **7** parodic, slavish **9** emulative **12** onomatopoeic **13** onomatopoetic

Imlah's son 7 Micaiah

immaculate 4 pure **5** clean **6** chaste, decent, modest **7** cleanly, perfect **8** flawless, innocent, spotless, unsoiled **9** errorless, exquisite, faultless, stainless, taintless, undefiled, unsullied **10** impeccable **11** unblemished

immaterial 4 airy **6** aerial **7** foreign, ghostly, psychic, shadowy **8** bodiless, ethereal, heavenly, unbodied **9** asomatous, celestial, disbodied, spiritual, unearthly, unfleshly, unworldly **10** discarnate, extraneous, impalpable, inapposite, insensible, intangible, irrelative, irrelevant, subjective, unembodied, unmaterial, unphysical **11** disembodied, impertinent, incorporeal, nonmaterial, nonphysical **12** apparitional, imponderable, inapplicable, metaphysical, supernatural **13** insubstantial, unsubstantial

immature 3 raw **5** green, vealy, young **6** callow, infant, unripe **7** babyish, puerile **8** childish, juvenile, youthful **9** infantile, infantine, premature, unfledged **10** precocious **11** undeveloped

immaturity 6 nonage

immeasurable 7 endless **8** infinite **9** boundless, limitless, unbounded, unlimited **10** indefinite, unmeasured **11** illimitable, inestimable, measureless, uncountable **12** incalculable, unmeasurable, unreckonable

immediate 4 near, next, nigh **5** close **6** direct, nearby, urgent **7** instant, primary **9** first-hand, proximate **10** near-at-hand **11** hair-trigger **12** straightaway **13** instantaneous

immediately 3 now, PDQ **4** anon, away, soon, stat **6** at once, presto, pronto **7** shortly **8** directly, hereupon **9** forthwith, instanter, instantly, right away **11** straightway

immense 4 huge, vast **5** great, large **6** mighty **7** titanic **8** colossal, enormous, gigantic **9** monstrous **10** prodigious, tremendous

immensely 3 too **4** ever, over, very **6** overly, unduly **8** overfull, overmuch **9** extremely **11** exceedingly, excessively **12** inordinately

immensity 8 enormity, hugeness, vastness **9** magnitude **12** enormousness

immerse 3 dip **4** bury, busy, duck, dunk, sink, soak **5** bathe, douse, embed, souse **6** absorb, engage, occupy, plunge **7** asperse, baptize, engross, include **8** christen, saturate, sprinkle, submerge, submerse

immigrant 6 emigré *Israeli:* **6** halutz **7** chalutz **8** halutzim (plural) **9** chalutzim (plural) *Japanese:* **5** issei

imminent 5 loury **6** coming, likely, lowery **7** brewing, louring, nearing, ominous, pending **8** alarming, lowering, menacing, minatory, possible, probable, sinister, upcoming **9** gathering, impending, proximate **10** inevasible, inevitable **11** approaching, ineluctable, inescapable, overhanging, threatening, unavoidable, unescapable

immobile 3 set **5** fixed, inert, still **6** frozen, stable, static **8** immotile, immotive, stagnant, unmoving **9** immovable, steadfast, unmovable **10** motionless, stationary **11** irremovable

immobilize 6 disarm **7** cripple, disable **8** paralyze **9** prostrate **12** incapacitate

immoderate 5 dizzy, undue **7** extreme **8** towering **9** boundless, excessive, voracious **10** exorbitant, inordinate, untempered **11** extravagant, intemperate **12** unmeasurable, unreasonable, unrestrained **13** overindulgent

immoderation 6 excess **12** intemperance

immodest 4 bold, lewd **5** brash, gross **6** brazen **8** boastful, indecent, unchaste

immolate 4 kill **7** destroy **8** abnegate **9** sacrifice, victimize

immoral 3 bad **4** evil **5** dirty, loose, wrong **6** impure, sinful, wanton, wicked **7** corrupt, unclean, vicious **8** depraved, indecent, unchaste **9** dissolute, reprobate, uncleanly **10** iniquitous, licentious

immorality 4 vice **9** depravity **10** corruption, unchastity, wickedness

immortal 6 divine **7** abiding, endless, eternal, undying **8** enduring, timeless, unending **9** ceaseless, deathless, perpetual **11** amaranthine, everlasting, never-ending, sempiternal **12** imperishable

immotile 5 fixed **8** immobile, immotive **9** immovable, steadfast, unmovable **11** irremovable

immovable 3 pat, set **4** fast, firm **5** fixed, rigid, stuck **6** rooted, stable **7** adamant **8** constant, immobile, immotile, immotive, obdurate, unmoving **9** immutable, impassive, steadfast, unmovable **10** inflexible, invariable, stationary, unyielding

immunity 7 freedom **8** impunity **9** exemption

immunizer 7 vaccine **8** antibody

immure 3 hem, jug, pen **4** cage, coop, jail, mure, wall **5** fence, hedge **6** corral, intern **7** confine, enclose **8** bastille, cloister, imprison **9** constrain **11** incarcerate

immutable 4 firm **5** fixed **7** eternal **8** constant **9** immovable, unmovable **10** inflexible, invariable, unchanging **11** inalterable, unalterable **12** unchangeable, unmodifiable

Imnah *father:* **5** Asher *son:* **4** Kore

Imogen *father:* **9** Cymbeline *husband:* **9** Posthumus

imp 3 elf **4** brat, ouph, puck **5** cutup, demon, devil, gamin, gnome, pixie, scamp, troll **6** goblin, kobold, monkey, sprite, urchin **7** gremlin **9** hobgoblin

impact 3 hit, jar, rap **4** blow, bump, jolt, rock, slam, slap **5** brunt, clash, crash, crowd, pound, punch, quake, shake, shock, smash **6** bounce, buffet, jounce, quiver, strike, stroke, tremor, wallop **7** appulse, congest, impulse, meeting, smiting, tremble **9** collision, encounter **10** concussion, percussion

impair 3 mar, sap **4** harm, hurt **5** spoil **6** damage, debase, injure, lessen, weaken

7 blemish, cripple, tarnish, vitiate **8** enfeeble **9** prejudice, undermine

impaired 6 flawed, marred **7** damaged, spoiled **9** afflicted *prefix:* **3** dys

impale 4 spit, stab **5** lance, prick, punch, spear, spike **6** pierce, skewer, skiver **8** puncture, transfix **9** perforate **11** transpierce

impart 4 give, lend, tell **5** break, grant, share, yield **6** bestow, convey, pass on **8** disclose, transmit **11** communicate *knowledge:* **5** teach **6** inform **7** educate **8** instruct

impartial 4 even, fair, just **5** equal **7** neutral **8** unbiased **9** equitable, objective, uncolored **12** unprejudiced **13** disinterested, dispassionate

impasse 3 box, fix, jam **4** hole **6** corner, pickle, plight, pocket, scrape **7** dead end, dilemma **8** cul-de-sac, deadlock **9** stalemate **10** blind alley **11** predicament

impassioned 4 deep, warm **5** fiery, gushy, mushy **6** ardent, fervid, fierce, redhot, torrid **7** blazing, burning, fervent, flaming, furious, glowing, gushing, intense, maudlin, violent, zealous **8** eloquent, feverish, profound, romantic, vehement, whitehot **9** perfervid **10** hot-blooded, overheated, passionate **11** dithyrambic, sentimental **12** melodramatic **13** overemotional

impassive 3 dry **4** calm, cold, cool **5** stoic **6** bovine, placid, stolid, wooden **7** callous **8** composed, hardened, reserved, reticent, taciturn **9** apathetic, collected, heartless, inanimate, indurated **10** insensible, insentient, motionless, phlegmatic, spiritless **11** cold-blooded, coldhearted, emotionless, inexcitable, insensitive, passionless, unconcerned, unemotional, unexcitable, unflappable **12** inexpressive, matter-of-fact, unexpressive, unresponsive **13** dispassionate, imperturbable, unimpressible, unsusceptible

impassivity 6 apathy, phlegm **8** stoicism **9** stolidity **13** insensibility

impatient 3 hot **4** agog, avid, edgy, keen **5** eager, harsh, hasty, itchy **6** abrupt, ardent **7** anxious, athirst, chafing, fidgety, fretful, nervous, thirsty **8** appetent, headlong, restless **9** demanding, impetuous, irascible, irritable

impeach 3 tax **6** accuse, charge, indict **7** arraign, censure **9** criminate, inculpate **11** incriminate

impeccable 4 nice **5** clean, exact, right **7** correct, perfect, precise **8** absolute, accurate, flawless, unerring, unflawed **9** errorless, exquisite, faultless, feckless **10** immaculate, infallible **12** indefectible

impecunious 4 poor **5** needy **8** dirt poor, indigent **9** destitute, penniless, penurious

11 necessitous **12** impoverished, unprosperous

impecuniousness 4 need, want **6** penury **7** poverty **8** poorness **9** indigence, neediness, privation **11** destitution

impedance 4 clog **9** cumbrance, hindrance **10** impediment **11** encumbrance

impede 3 bar, bog, dam **4** clog, faze **5** block, brake, check, debar **6** hinder, hold up, rattle **8** obstruct **9** discomfit, embarrass

impediment 3 bar, rub **4** clog, snag **5** block, hitch **6** hamper, hurdle **8** obstacle **9** cumbrance, hindrance **10** difficulty **11** encumbrance, obstruction

impel 4 good, move, spur, urge **5** drive, force **6** compel, foment, incite, propel **7** actuate, inspire **8** mobilize, motivate **9** constrain, instigate, stimulate

impend 4 brew, hang, loom **6** gather, menace **8** approach, overhang **9** forthcome

impenetrable 4 firm, hard **5** dense, solid **6** arcane, mystic **8** numinous **9** mysterial, unguessed **10** cabalistic, impassable, impervious, mysterious, unknowable **11** impermeable, imperviable, inscrutable, substantial, ungraspable **12** incognizable, unfathomable

imperative 4 need, rule **5** acute, basic, bossy, guide, harsh, order, stern **6** crying, urgent **7** bidding, burning, claimed, clamant, command, crucial, exacted, exigent, instant **8** critical, demanded, imperial, ordering, pressing, required **9** clamorous, essential, imperious, insistent, mandatory, masterful, necessary, necessity **10** commanding, compulsory, high-handed, obligatory, peremptory **11** domineering, fundamental, importunate, magisterial, necessitous, overbearing **12** compulsatory, prerequisite

imperceptible 5 faint, vague **6** slight **7** obscure, trivial **8** fugitive **9** ephemeral, invisible, momentary **10** evanescent, impalpable, indistinct, insensible, intangible, unapparent **12** imponderable, unnoticeable, unobservable **13** inappreciable, inconspicuous, indiscernible, insignificant, unappreciable, undiscernible, unperceivable

imperceptive 7 cursory, shallow **8** slapdash **11** superficial, unobservant **12** impercipient, undiscerning, unperceiving, unperceptive

imperfect 4 sick **5** amiss **6** faulty, flawed, second **9** defective **10** defeasible, inadequate, incomplete, unfinished

imperfection 3 sin **4** flaw **5** fault **6** defect, foible **7** blemish, demerit, failing, frailty **8** weakness **10** deficiency **11** shortcoming

imperial 5 bossy, regal, royal **6** kingly **7** haughty **8** majestic **9** grandiose, imperious, masterful, sovereign **10** high-handed, imperative, peremptory **11** domineering, magisterial, overbearing

imperil 4 risk **6** hazard, menace **7** jeopard, venture **8** endanger, jeopardy, threaten **10** compromise, jeopardize

imperious 5 bossy **6** lordly, strict, urgent **7** haughty **8** absolute, arrogant, despotic, dominant, imperial, required **9** arbitrary, mandatory, masterful, stringent **10** commanding, compulsory, high-handed, imperative, obligatory, oppressive, peremptory, tyrannical **11** dictatorial, domineering, heavy-handed, magisterial, overbearing

impermanent 7 passing **8** fleeting, fugitive, unstable **9** ephemeral, fugacious, momentary, temporary, tentative, transient **10** evanescent, short-lived, transitory

impersonal 4 cold, fair **5** equal **7** neutral **8** abstract, detached, unbiased **9** colorless, equitable, impartial, objective, uncolored **10** poker-faced **11** cold-blooded, emotionless, unpassioned **12** matter-of-fact, unprejudiced **13** disinterested, dispassionate, unimpassioned

impersonator 4 mime **5** actor, mimic **6** mummer, player **7** actress, trouper **8** thespian **9** performer, playactor **13** impressionist

impertinence 4 sass **8** audacity, boldness **9** hardihood, impudence, insolence, insolency, unfitness **10** disrespect, incivility **11** irrelevance **12** insolentness

impertinent 4 bold, busy, nosy, pert, rude **5** brash, fresh, sassy, saucy **6** brazen, prying **7** foreign, ill-bred, uncivil **8** arrogant, impolite, impudent, insolent, meddling **9** audacious, intrusive, obtrusive, offensive, officious **10** extraneous, immaterial, inapposite, irrelative, irrelevant, meddlesome, procacious, ungracious **11** ill-mannered, inquisitive, interfering, uncalled-for **12** contumelious, discourteous, inapplicable, presumptuous **13** disrespectful

imperturbability 6 phlegm **7** ataraxy **8** calmness, coolness **9** composure, sangfroid **10** equanimity

imperturbable 4 calm, cool, smug **6** placid, serene **7** unmoved **8** composed, tranquil **9** collected, impassive, unruffled, untouched **10** complacent, nonchalant, phlegmatic, unaffected **11** unflappable **13** self-satisfied

impervious 5 tight **8** hardened **10** impassable **11** impermeable, imperviable **12** impenetrable, unpierceable

impetuous 3 hot **4** rash **5** eager, fiery, hasty **6** abrupt, ardent, fervid, sudden **7** furious, hurried, restive, rushing, violent **8** headlong, vehement **9** hotheaded, impulsive **10** passionate **11** impassioned, precipitant, precipitate, precipitous, spontaneous

impetus 4 good, spur **5** force **7** impulse **8** catalyst, momentum, stimulus **9** incentive, stimulant **10** incitation, incitement, motivation

impious 6 sinful, unholy, wicked **7** froward, godless, profane, ungodly, wayward **8** contrary, indevout, perverse, undevout **9** atheistic, unduteous, undutiful **10** irreverent, scandalous, unfaithful, unhallowed **11** disobedient, irreligious, wrongheaded **12** iconoclastic, sacrilegious

impish 4 arch, pert **5** elfin, fresh, giddy, saucy **6** casual, elfish, elvish **7** coltish, offhand, playful, puckish, roguish, waggish **8** flippant, pixieish, sportive **10** frolicsome **11** free and easy, mischievous

impishness 7 devilry, roguery, waggery **8** deviltry, mischief **9** devilment **11** roguishness, waggishness **12** sportiveness

implacable 4 grim **6** mortal **8** ruthless **9** merciless **10** inexorable, ironfisted, relentless, unyielding **11** unflinching, unrelenting **12** unappeasable

implant 4 root **5** embed, imbue, infix, inset **6** enroot, infuse, leaven **7** impress, ingrain, inspire, instill, pervade **8** permeate, saturate **9** inculcate, inoculate, insinuate, introduce, penetrate **10** impregnate, inseminate **11** impenetrate

implausible 4 thin, weak **5** fishy, thick **6** flimsy **7** dubious, suspect, tenuous **8** doubtful, puzzling **10** improbable, incredible **11** problematic **12** unconvincing

implement 4 tool **6** device, effect, gadget, invoke **7** enforce, execute, fulfill, perform, realize, utensil **8** complete **9** actualize, apparatus, appliance **10** accomplish, instrument, supplement **11** contraption, contrivance *cleaning:* **3** mop **5** broom, brush **6** vacuum **7** sweeper **10** whiskbroom *cutting:* **5** knife, mower, razor **6** scythe, shears, sickle **8** scissors *digging:* **5** spade **6** shovel *drawing:* **3** pen **6** eraser, pencil **7** compass **8** charcoal, template *eating:* **4** fork **5** knife, spoon *engraving:* **5** burin **6** graver *farm:* **4** disc, dish, plow **6** dibber, harrow, seeder, tiller **8** gangplow, reaphook *fireplace:* **5** tongs **7** andiron *fishing:* **3** rod **4** hook **7** harpoon, trident *garden:* **3** hoe **4** rake **6** trowel *grooming:* **4** comb **5** brush **8** tweezers **10** toothbrush *kind:* **3** die, saw **4** file **5** brace, clamp, drill, punch, tongs **6** chisel, hammer, pliers, reamer, sander, wrench **7** hacksaw, scraper **9** blowtorch **11** screwdriver *kitchen:* **3** pan, pot **4** mold **5** mixer **6** kettle, mortar, pestle **7** blender, skillet, spatula *logging:* **4** pevy **5** peavy, peevy **6** peavey **8** cant hook *measuring:* **4** gage, rule **5** gauge, ruler, scale **7** caliper, divider, trammel, T-square **10** micrometer, protractor

stone: 5 burin 6 colith 7 neolith
9 paleolith
implicate 4 mire 5 imply 6 affect, tangle
7 concern, embroil, implied, include, involve
8 implicit 11 incriminate
implication 4 hint 8 overtone 9 inference,
undertone 10 suggestion 11 association,
connotation
implicit 4 real 5 tacit 6 unsaid 7 genuine,
implied, virtual 8 absolute, complete,
inferred, unspoken 9 potential, practical,
unuttered 10 undeclared, understood
11 unexpressed, unqualified
implied 5 tacit 6 unsaid 8 implicit,
inferred, unspoken, wordless 9 unuttered
10 undeclared, understood
imploration 4 plea, suit 6 appeal, orison,
prayer 8 entreaty, petition 11 application,
imprecation 12 supplication
implore 3 ask, beg 4 coax, pray 5 crave,
plead 6 appeal 7 beseech, conjure,
entreat 9 importune 10 supplicate
imply 4 hint 5 point 7 connote, include,
suggest 8 indicate, intimate 9 insinuate
impolite 4 rude 5 crude, rough 7 ill-bred,
incivil, uncivil 10 ungracious, unmannerly,
unpolished 11 disgracious, ill-mannered,
uncourteous 12 discourteous
13 disrespectful
impolitic 5 brash 6 unwise 8 tactless
9 ill-judged, imprudent, maladroit, unpolitic,
untactful 10 ill-advised, indiscreet 11 inadvisable, inexpedient, injudicious, unadvisable, unexpedient 12 undiplomatic
import 4 mean, pith 5 count, sense, spell,
value, weigh, worth 6 convey, denote,
design, intend, intent, matter, moment,
object, stress, weight 7 add up to, concern,
connote, express, meaning, message, purport, purpose, signify 8 emphasis, indicate
9 magnitude, objective, substance
10 importance, intendment 11 acceptation,
consequence, weightiness 12 significance,
significancy
importance 4 mark, note, pith 5 value,
worth 6 import, moment, weight 7 account,
gravity 8 eminence, priority, salience, standing 9 magnitude, substance 10 notability,
prominence, reputation, worthiness 11 consequence, distinction, seriousness, weightiness 12 significance
important 3 big 5 grave, great, noted,
puffy, wiggy 6 famous, marked, potent,
stuffy, urgent, worthy 7 big-time, bloated,
crucial, eminent, fateful, notable, pompous,
salient, serious, telling, unusual, weighty
8 arrogant, eventful, material, powerful, top-
notch, valuable 9 effective, essential, first-
rate, front-page, memorable, momentous,
ponderous, prominent 10 first-class,
impressive, meaningful, noteworthy, notice-

able, pontifical, remarkable, worthwhile
11 conspicuous, distinctive, exceptional,
magisterial, outstanding, significant, substantial 12 considerable 13 consequential,
distinguished
importune 3 beg 4 pray, urge 5 annoy,
crave, plead, worry 6 appeal, invoke
7 beseech, entreat, implore, solicit, trouble
10 supplicate
impose 3 fob, set, use 4 lade, levy, wish
5 abuse, exact, foist, order, put on, visit,
wreak, wreck 6 assess, burden, charge,
compel, create, decree, demand, enjoin, fob
off, oblige, ordain, saddle 7 command, dictate, exploit, force on, inflict, intrude, lay
down, obtrude, palm off, presume, put upon,
require 8 encroach, generate, infringe, trespass 9 constrain, force upon
imposing 3 big 4 arty 5 grand, noble,
regal, royal 6 august, moving 7 stately
8 baronial, imperial, majestic, princely
9 grandiose, overblown 10 arty-crafty, commanding, impressive 11 magnificent, pretentious 12 high-sounding
imposition 3 tax 4 duty, fine, levy 6 burden 7 penalty 9 deception
impossible 6 absurd 8 cureless, hopeless 9 incurable, insanable, uncurable
10 infeasible, unfeasible, unworkable
11 immedicable, impractical, irreparable,
unthinkable 12 inexecutable, irrealizable,
irremediable, unacceptable, unattainable,
unobtainable, unrealizable, unreasonable
impost 3 tax 4 duty, levy 6 tariff, weight
7 tribute 10 assessment
imposter 4 fake 5 cheat, faker, fraud,
mimic, phony, quack 6 humbug 7 bluffer,
shammer, shyster 8 beguiler, deceiver, imi-
tator 9 charlatan, hypocrite, misleader, pretender, trickster 10 dissembler, mountebank 11 four-flusher, pettifogger
imposture 3 gyp 4 copy, fake, flam, hoax,
ploy, ruse, sell, sham, wile 5 cheat, feint,
fraud, phony, put-on, spoof, trick 6 deceit,
gambit, humbug 7 forgery, sleight, swindle
8 artifice, flimflam, maneuver, pretense
9 deception, falsehood, imitation, mare's
nest, stratagem 10 pretension 11 counterfeit, fabrication, make-believe
impotent 4 weak 5 frail 6 barren, effete,
feeble 7 sterile 8 boneless, crippled, disabled, helpless, infecund 9 enfeebled,
forceless, infertile, powerless, spineless
10 emasculate, inadequate, unfruitful
11 ineffective, ineffectual, slack-spined
12 invertebrate
impoverish 4 bust, draw, ruin 5 break,
drain, use up 6 beggar, fold up, pauper
7 deplete, exhaust 8 bankrupt, draw down
9 pauperize
impoverished 4 poor 5 needy 6 scanty

8 bankrupt, beggared, indigent 9 destitute, penurious 10 stone-broke 11 impecunious

impoverishment 4 need, want 6 penury 7 poverty 8 poorness 9 indigence, neediness, privation 11 destitution

impracticable 6 unwise 7 awkward, useless 8 unusable 9 imprudent 10 impossible, infeasible, unfeasible, unworkable

impractical 5 viewy 7 useless 8 quixotic, romantic, unusable 9 visionary 10 idealistic, impossible, infeasible, ivory-tower, starry-eyed, unfeasible, unworkable 11 theoretical, unrealistic

imprecation 4 oath, plea, suit 5 curse 6 appeal, orison, prayer 7 cursing, cussing, malison 8 anathema, entreaty, petition, swearing 9 blasphemy, profanity

impregnable 4 safe 6 secure 7 guarded 8 defended, shielded 9 protected 10 invincible, unbeatable 11 indomitable

impregnate 3 sop 4 soak 5 imbue, souse, steep 6 charge, drench, infuse, leaven, seethe, sodden 7 pervade 8 permeate, saturate, waterlog 9 fertilize, inoculate, penetrate, percolate, transfuse 10 inseminate

impresario 5 agent, Carte, Hurok (Sol) 7 manager 9 Diaghilev (Sergei) 10 D'Oyly Carte

impress 3 fix, get, set 4 etch, mark, move, seal, sway 5 brand, carry, drive, exert, force, grave, infix, pique, pound, print, stamp, touch 6 affect, effect, excite, hammer, strike, thrill 7 engrave, enthuse, implant, imprint, ingrain, inspire, provoke 8 inscribe 9 electrify, establish, galvanize, inculcate, influence, stimulate

impression 4 dent, dint, idea, mark, sign 5 image, print, shock, stamp, trace, track 6 hollow, impact, notion 7 conceit, concept, edition, impress, imprint, reissue, thought, vestige 8 printing, reaction

impressionable 7 plastic, sensile 8 sensible, sentient 9 sensitive 10 affectable, responsive, susceptive 11 impressible, susceptible 13 influenceable

impressionist *composer:* 5 Ravel 7 Debussy *mimic:* 6 Little (Rich) *painter:* 5 Degas, Manet, Monet 6 Renoir, Sisley 8 Pissarro; (see also **postimpressionist**)

impressive 5 grand, noble 6 august, lavish, moving, superb 7 notable 8 gorgeous, imposing, majestic, poignant, splendid, striking, touching 9 affecting, arresting, grandiose, luxurious, sumptuous

imprimatur 7 license 8 approval, sanction

imprint 4 etch, mark 5 press, stamp 7 engrave, impress 8 inscribe 10 impression

imprison 3 jug 4 cage, curb, jail 5 check,

limit 6 detain, immure, intern 7 confine, enclose 8 bastille, restrain, restrict 9 constrain 11 incarcerate 12 circumscribe

impromptu 7 offhand 9 extempore, makeshift, unstudied 10 improvised 11 extemporary, unrehearsed 13 autoschediasm, improvisation

improper 5 amiss, crude, fresh, inapt, inept, outré, rough, sassy, unapt, undue, unfit, wrong 6 gauche, unmeet 7 illicit, ungodly, unhappy 8 ill-timed, indecent, informal, tactless, uncomely, unseemly, untimely, untoward 9 incorrect, unfitting 10 inaccurate, inapposite, indecorous, indelicate, malapropos, malodorous, unbecoming, undecorous, unsuitable 11 impertinent, unbefitting 12 illegitimate, inadmissible, inapplicable, infelicitous, intempestive, unseasonable 13 inappropriate, unceremonious *prefix:* 3 mis

impropriety 5 boner, break, error, gaffe 7 blooper, faux pas 8 slangism, solecism 9 barbarism, indecorum, vulgarism 10 corruption, inelegance, unmeetness 12 unseemliness, untowardness 13 incorrectness

improve 4 edit, gain, help, mend 5 amend, edify, emend, rally, rub up 6 better, enrich, illume, look up, perk up, refine, reform, remedy, revise, revive, uplift 7 advance, augment, benefit, correct, develop, enhance, enlarge, perfect, recover, rectify, upgrade 8 illumine, increase, progress 9 cultivate, enlighten, intensify, irradiate, meliorate 10 ameliorate, convalesce, illuminate, recuperate, strengthen

improvident 6 lavish 7 profuse 8 careless, heedless, prodigal, reckless, unthrift, wasteful 9 imprudent, negligent, unthrifty 10 profligate, thriftless 11 extravagant, spendthrift 12 uneconomical

improvise 5 ad-lib 6 devise, invent 7 concoct 8 contrive 11 extemporize

improvised 7 offhand 9 extempore, impromptu, unstudied 11 extemporary, unrehearsed

imprudent 4 rash 6 unwary, unwise 7 foolish 8 reckless 10 ill-advised, incautious, indiscreet 11 inadvisable, inexpedient, injudicious, unadvisable, unexpedient 12 shortsighted

impudence 4 gall 8 audacity, boldness 9 arrogance, hardihood, insolence 9 insolency 10 disrespect, effrontery 11 presumption 12 impertinence, insolentness

impudent 4 bold, flip, pert, wise 5 brash, fresh, lippy, nervy, sassy, saucy, smart 6 arrant, brassy, brazen, cheeky 7 blatant, forward 8 flippant, insolent, overbold 9 audacious, barefaced, shameless, unabashed 10 procacious, unblushing

11 brazenfaced, impertinent, smart-alecky
12 contumelious **13** disrespectful

impugn **4** deny **5** cross, fight **6** assail, attack, negate, oppose, resist **7** gainsay **8** negative, traverse **9** disaffirm **10** contradict, contravene

impugnable **5** fishy, shady **7** suspect **8** doubtful **9** doubtable, equivocal, uncertain **10** borderline, suspicious **11** problematic

impulse **3** ate **4** goad, lust, push, spur, urge, whim **5** drive, force **6** impact, motive, thrust, whimsy **7** impetus, passion, whimsey **8** catalyst, excitant, stimulus **9** actuation, impulsion, incentive, stimulant **10** incitation, incitement, motivation **11** instigation

impulsive **5** hasty **6** abrupt, sudden **8** headlong, will-less **9** automatic, impetuous **10** unprompted **11** instinctive, involuntary, precipitate, spontaneous, unmeditated

impure **3** raw **4** foul, lewd, vile **5** black, crude, dirty, gross, mixed, nasty, soily **6** carnal, common, filthy, grubby, native, unholy **7** bastard, defiled, immoral, lustful, obscene, scarlet, sensual, squalid, unclean **8** immodest, indecent, polluted, profaned, prurient, unchaste, ungraded, unsorted **9** run-of-mine, uncleanly, unrefined **10** desecrated, indecorous, lascivious, unhallowed **11** adulterated

impute **3** lay **4** give, hint **5** refer **6** accuse, adduce, assign, charge, credit, impart, indict **7** ascribe **8** accredit, intimate **9** attribute

inability **9** inaptness, ineptness **10** inadequacy, inaptitude, incapacity, inefficacy, ineptitude **11** inadeptness **12** incapability, incompetence, inefficiency

inaccessible **3** far **6** closed, far-off, remote **7** distant, faraway **8** abstruse, esoteric **11** out-of-the-way, ungetatable, unreachable **12** unattainable, unobtainable

in accordance with **5** as per **10** pursuant to

inaccurate **5** false, wrong **6** faulty, untrue **7** inexact, unsound **8** specious **9** defective, erroneous, incorrect

inaction **5** drift **8** idleness, lethargy **9** indolence, inertness, slackness, torpidity **10** inactivity, quiescence **12** inactiveness, slothfulness

inactive **4** dead, idle, slow **5** inert, quiet, slack, still **6** asleep, latent, sleepy, static, supine, torpid **7** abeyant, dormant, jobless, passive **8** indolent, ossified, slothful, sluggish **9** do-nothing, lethargic, lymphatic, quiescent, sedentary, unworking **10** disengaged, motionless, unemployed, unoccupied

in addition **4** also, then **5** again **7** besides, further **8** moreover **12** additionally

inadequacy **4** lack **7** deficit, failure **8** shortage, underage **9** inability **10** deficiency, incapacity, inefficacy, scantiness **11** defalcation **12** incapability, incompetence **13** insufficience, insufficiency

inadequate **3** shy **4** weak **5** scant, short **6** meager, scanty, scarce, skimpy **7** failing, lacking, scrimpy, wanting **8** boneless, impotent **9** defective, deficient, forceless, spineless **10** emasculate, incomplete, uncomplete **11** ineffective, ineffectual, slackspined **12** insufficient

inadmissible **5** inapt, inept, unapt **8** illtimed, improper, unseemly, unwanted **9** unwelcome **10** ill-favored, malapropos, unbecoming **11** undesirable **12** unacceptable

inadvertent **8** careless, feckless, heedless, uncaring **9** negligent, undevised, unheeding, unplanned, unrecking, unthought **10** undesigned, unintended **13** unintentional

inadvisable **4** rash **6** unwise **7** foolish **8** careless **9** foolhardy, impolitic, imprudent, pointless **10** ill-advised, incautious, indiscreet, unsensible **11** harebrained, inexpedient, undesirable, unexpedient **13** inappropriate

inalterable **5** fixed **8** constant **9** immovable, immutable, steadfast, unmovable **10** inflexible, invariable **12** unchangeable, unmodifiable

inamorata **5** flame, honey, lover, woman **6** steady **7** beloved, sweetie **8** ladylove, mistress, paramour, truelove **10** girl friend, sweetheart

inamorato **4** beau **5** flame, lover **6** steady **7** beloved **8** truelove **9** boyfriend **10** sweetheart

inane **4** flat, idle, vain **5** blank, empty, silly, vapid **6** hollow, jejune, vacant **7** asinine, fatuous, foolish, idiotic, insipid, sapless, shallow, vacuous **8** mindless, trifling **9** driveling, frivolous, innocuous, pointless, senseless

inanimate **4** cold, dead, dull, late **5** inert **6** asleep **7** defunct, extinct **8** deceased, departed, lifeless **9** exanimate, insensate, senseless, unfeeling **10** insensible, insentient

inanity **5** folly **7** vacuity **8** insanity, unwisdom, vapidity **9** absurdity, craziness, dottiness, emptiness, frivolity, silliness **10** hollowness, triviality **11** foolishness, shallowness, witlessness **13** senselessness

inappreciable **6** meager, scanty, skimpy **7** scrimpy **10** impalpable, inadequate, insensible, intangible, unapparent **12** imponderable, insufficient, unobservable

inappropriate **5** inapt, inept, undue, unfit **6** clumsy, unmeet **8** ill-timed, improper, unfitted, unseemly, unsuited, untimely **9** ill-suited **10** ill-adapted, indecorous, malapropos, unbecoming, unsuitable **11** inconsonant, unbefitting **12** unseasonable

inapt 4 flat **5** banal, undue, unfit **6** clumsy, gauche, jejune, unmeet **7** awkward, inadept, insipid, unhandy **8** ill-timed, improper, inexpert, unfacile, unfitted, unsuited, untimely **9** ill-suited, maladroit, unfitting **10** amateurish, ill-adapted, inadequate, malapropos, unskillful, unsuitable

in arrears 6 behind **10** behindhand

inarticulate 4 dumb, mute **5** tacit **6** silent, unsaid **7** blurred, halting, implied, unvocal **8** implicit, inferred, mumbling, unspoken, wordless **9** faltering, stammered, unuttered, voiceless **10** hesitating, incoherent, indistinct, maundering, speechless, stammering, tongue-tied, undeclared **11** unexpressed

inasmuch as 2 as **3** for, now **5** since **7** because, whereas **8** as long as **11** considering

inattentive 3 lax **5** bored **6** ennuyé, remiss **8** careless, distrait, heedless **9** forgetful, negligent, unheeding, unmindful **10** abstracted, distracted, distraught, unnoticing, unthinking, unwatchful **11** inobservant, thoughtless, unobservant, unobserving

inaugural 5 first **7** initial, leading **8** foremost, headmost **9** induction **10** initiation **11** investiture **installation

inaugurate 4 open **5** begin, enter, set up, start **6** get off, induct, invest, launch **7** install, instate, jump off, kick off, usher in **8** commence, dedicate, initiate **9** institute, introduce, originate **10** consecrate

inauspicious 3 bad **4** dire, evil **7** adverse, baleful, baneful, fateful, ominous, unlucky **8** sinister **9** ill-boding, ill-omened **11** threatening **12** unpropitious

inborn 6 inbred, innate, native **7** connate, natural **8** inherent **9** essential, ingrained, inherited, intrinsic **10** congenital, connatural, deep-seated, hereditary, indigenous, indwelling, unacquired

inbred 6 inborn, innate **7** connate **8** inherent **9** ingrained, intrinsic **10** congenital, deep-seated, indwelling

Inca beverage: 5 chica **capital: 5** Cusco, Cuzco **conqueror: 7** Pizarro **god: 4** Inti **9** Viracocha **10** Pachacamac **half-breed: 5** Cholo **language: 8** Quechuan **priest: 3** umu **record: 5** quipu **ruler: 9** Atahualpa, Pachacuti **sacred object: 5** huaca **8** apacheta **socioeconomic unit: 5** ayllu

incalculable 4 iffy, vast **6** chancy, untold **7** erratic **8** enormous, infinite **9** boundless, countless, fluctuant, limitless, uncertain, whimsical **10** capricious, unmeasured, unnumbered **11** illimitable, inestimable,

innumerable, measureless, uncountable **12** immeasurable, unmeasurable

in camera 7 sub rosa **8** covertly, secretly **9** by stealth, furtively, privately **10** stealthily **12** hugger-mugger **13** clandestinely

incandescent 3 hot **5** lucid **6** ardent, bright, lucent **7** beaming, fulgent, glowing, lambent, radiant **8** luminous **9** brilliant, effulgent, refulgent

incantation 4 rune **5** chant, charm, magic, spell **7** sorcery **8** witchery, wizardry **9** conjuring, magicking **10** necromancy, witchcraft **11** bewitchment, conjuration, enchantment **Buddhist, Hindu: 6** mantra

incapable 5 inept, unfit **6** unable **8** inexpert, unexpert, unfitted **9** unskilled **10** ineligible, unequipped, unskillful **11** incompetent

incapacitate 6 disarm **7** cripple, disable **8** paralyze **9** disenable, prostrate **10** disqualify, immobilize

incapacity 9 inability **10** inadequacy, inefficacy **12** incapability, incompetence

incarcerate 3 jug **4** jail **6** immure, intern **7** confine, enclose **8** bastille, imprison **9** constrain

incarnadine 3 red **4** ruby **5** ruddy **6** redden, rubify, rubric, ruddle

incarnate 5 utter **6** embody **8** embodied, manifest **9** actualize, objectify, personify, personize **11** exteriorize, externalize, materialize, personalize, unspeakable **12** substantiate

incarnation 6 avatar **7** avatara **10** embodiment **Of Christ: 7** kenosis

incautious 4 bold, rash, wild **5** brash, hasty **6** madcap, unwary **7** unalert **8** carefree, careless, feckless, heedless, reckless **9** hotheaded, impetuous, impolitic, imprudent, negligent, uncareful, unguarded, unmindful **10** ill-advised, indiscreet, madbrained, neglectful, regardless, unvigilant, unwatchful **11** injudicious, thoughtless **13** inconsiderate, irresponsible

incendiary 5 torch **7** exciter, firebug **8** agitator, arsonist **10** pyromaniac **12** inflammatory

incense 3 ire, mad, oil **4** balm, burn **5** anger, aroma, scent, spice **6** arouse, enrage, homage, incite, madden **vessel: 6** censer **8** thurible

incentive 4 goad, spur **5** spark **6** motive **7** impetus, impulse **8** catalyst, stimulus **9** stimulant **10** incitation, incitement, inducement, motivation **11** provocation, stimulative **13** encouragement

inception 4 root, well **5** start **6** origin, source, whence **9** fountain **9** beginning **10** derivation, initiation, provenance, wellspring **11** provenience **12** commencement

inceptive 7 initial, nascent **9** beginning,

incipient **10** initiative, initiatory **12** introductory

incertitude 5 doubt **6** wonder **7** concern, dubiety **8** mistrust **9** dubiosity, suspicion **10** indecision, skepticism **11** uncertainty

incessant 6 steady **7** endless, eternal **8** constant, timeless **9** ceaseless, continual, perpetual, unceasing **10** continuous **11** everlasting, unremitting **12** interminable

inchoate 7 muddled **8** formless, unformed, unshaped **9** amorphous, expectant, incipient, potential, shapeless **10** contingent, disjointed, disordered, incoherent, incohesive, incomplete **11** imperfected, unconnected, unorganized **12** disconnected, uncontinuous **13** discontinuous

incident 4 akin **5** event **6** agnate, allied **7** cognate, connate, episode, kindred, related **8** accident, external, occasion **9** ancillary, attendant, attending, happening, satellite **10** affiliated, collateral, connatural, occurrence **11** concomitant, consanguine **12** accompanying, circumstance

incidental 3 odd **5** fluky **6** casual, chance **8** episodic **9** accessory **10** accidental, contingent, digressive, fortuitous **11** subordinate **12** nonessential

incidentally 6 obiter **8** by the bye, by the way, casually **9** in passing **12** accidentally, fortuitously

incipient 7 initial, nascent **8** inchoate **9** beginning, inceptive **10** commencing, initiative, initiatory **12** introductory

incise 3 cut **4** etch, gash, kerf, slit **5** grave, slash, slice **6** pierce **7** engrave

incisive 4 keen, tart **5** acerb, acute, crisp, sharp, terse **6** biting **7** acerbic, caustic, concise, cutting, ingoing, laconic, mordant **8** clear-cut, drilling, piercing, scathing, slashing, succinct **9** sarcastic, trenchant **11** penetrating

incite 3 egg, set **4** abet, goad, prod, spur, urge **5** raise, rouse, set on **6** arouse, compel, excite, exhort, foment, motive, set off, stir up, whip up **7** actuate, agitate, forward, further, inflame, promote, provoke, solicit, trigger **8** motivate **9** encourage, instigate, stimulate

incitement see **incentive**

inclement 3 raw **4** hard **5** harsh, rough **6** bitter, brutal, rugged, severe, stormy **8** rigorous **10** unmerciful **11** intemperate

inclination 3 bow, nod **4** bent, bias, lean, love, mind, tilt, will **5** fancy, grade, slant, slope, taste **6** ascent, desire, liking **7** descent, incline, leaning **8** affinity, appetite, fondness, gradient, penchant, pleasure, soft spot, tendency, velleity, weakness **9** affection **10** attachment, proclivity, propensity **11** disposition **12** predilection *rate of:* **8** gradient

incline 3 aim, lay, tip **4** bend, bias, cant, cast, hade, heel, lean, list, look, move, sway, tend, tilt, turn **5** drive, grade, impel, level, point, slant, slide, slope, train **6** affect, direct, induce, prompt, zero in **7** address, deflect, dispose, leaning **8** gradient, persuade **9** influence, prejudice *combining form:* **4** clin **5** clino

inclined 3 apt **4** fain, wont **5** given, prone, raked, ready **6** biased, graded, liable, likely, minded, sloped, tilted, tipped **7** dipping, leaning, oblique, pitched, sloping, tilting, willing **8** diagonal, disposed, pitching **9** declivate **11** declivitous, predisposed *way:* **4** ramp

include 4 have, hold **5** admit, bound, cover **6** embody, enfold, number, take in **7** confine, contain, embrace, enclose, involve, receive, subsume **8** comprise, encircle **9** encompass **10** comprehend

inclusive 6 global **7** general, overall **8** sweeping **9** all-around, enclosing **12** encompassing, encyclopedic **13** comprehensive

incognizant 7 unaware **8** ignorant **9** oblivious, unknowing, unwitting **10** unfamiliar, uninformed **12** inconversant, unacquainted, uninstructed

incoherent 5 loose **6** broken, raving **7** muddled **8** inchoate **9** illogical **10** discordant, disjointed, disordered, incohesive, maundering, tongue-tied **11** incongruous, inconsonant, nonadhesive, unconnected, unorganized **12** disconnected, inarticulate, incompatible, inconsequent, inconsistent, inharmonious, uncontinuous **13** discontinuous

incombustible 7 apyrous **12** nonflammable

income 4 gain, take **6** profit, return **7** annuity, comings, produce, revenue **8** interest, proceeds, receipts **9** emolument

incommode 3 irk, vex **5** annoy, block **6** bother, hinder, impede, molest, plague, put out **7** disturb, trouble **8** disquiet, obstruct, put about **9** disoblige **13** inconvenience

incommodious 5 cramp **7** awkward, cramped, squeezy **8** confined **12** discommoding, embarrassing, inconvenient

incommunicable 8 reserved, taciturn **9** ineffable, withdrawn **10** restrained, untellable **11** constrained, indefinable, inenarrable, unspeakable, unutterable **12** noncommittal **13** indescribable, inexpressible, undescribable, unexpressible

incomparable 7 supreme **8** peerless, towering, ultimate **9** matchless **10** preeminent, surpassing **11** unequalable, unmatchable **12** transcendent **13** unsurpassable

incompatible 7 adverse, counter **8** contrary, opposite **9** antipodal, dissonant, unmixable **10** antipodean, discordant, discrepant **11** conflicting, disagreeing, incongruent, incongruous, inconsonant, unadaptable **12** antagonistic, antipathetic, antithetical, disconsonant, inconsistent, inharmonious **13** contradictory, inconformable, unconformable, unsympathetic

incompetence 9 inability, unfitness **10** disability, inadequacy, incapacity, inefficacy **12** incapability **13** insufficiency

incompetent 5 inept, unfit **8** helpless, inexpert, unexpert, unfitted **9** incapable, unskilled **10** ineligible, unequipped, unskillful **11** inefficient, unqualified **12** disqualified, insufficient *legally:* **12** inadmissible

incomplete 4 part **5** bitty, short **6** broken **7** lacking, partial, scrappy, sketchy, wanting **8** immature **9** composite, defective, deficient **10** fractional, inadequate, incoherent, uncomplete, unfinished **11** fragmentary, imperfected **12** insufficient

incompliant 5 rigid, stiff **6** mulish **8** perverse, stubborn **9** impliable, obstinate, pigheaded, resistant, unbending **10** bullheaded, headstrong, inflexible, self-willed, unflexible, unyielding **11** immalleable, intractable **12** pertinacious

incomprehensible 7 cryptic, obscure, unclear **8** abstruse **9** enigmatic **10** fathomless, mysterious, mystifying, unknowable, unreadable **11** inscrutable, ungraspable **12** impenetrable, incognizable, unfathomable, unimaginable, unsearchable **13** imperceptible, inconceivable

inconceivable 4 thin, weak **6** flimsy **10** improbable, incredible, unknowable **11** implausible, incogitable, unthinkable **12** insupposable, unbelievable, unconvincing, unimaginable

in conclusion 6 lastly **7** finally

inconclusive 4 open **9** uncertain, undecided, unsettled **10** incomplete, indecisive, indefinite, unfinished **11** ineffective

incongruous 5 alien **6** absurd **7** bizarre, foreign **9** dissonant, fantastic, grotesque, unmixable **10** discordant, discrepant, extraneous **11** conflicting, inconsonant **12** disconsonant, incompatible, inconsistent, inharmonious

inconscient 4 lost **6** absent **7** bemused, faraway **8** distrait, mindless **10** abstracted **11** preoccupied **12** absentminded

inconsequential 5 petty, small **6** measly, paltry **7** trivial **8** picayune, trifling **10** irrelevant, picayunish

inconsiderable 4 puny **5** light, minor, petty, small **6** casual, little, meager, paltry, peanut, scanty, skimpy **7** scrimpy, trivial **8** picayune, trifling **9** small-beer **10** inadequate, negligible, shoestring **11** unimpor-

tant **12** inconsequent, insufficient, unconsidered **13** inappreciable, insignificant

inconsiderate 4 rash **5** brash, hasty, sharp, short **6** madcap, unkind **8** careless, heedless, reckless **9** hotheaded **10** illadvised, incautious, ungracious **11** precipitate, thoughtless

inconsistent 6 fickle **8** ticklish, unstable **9** dissonant, mercurial, uncertain, unmixable **10** capricious, changeable, discordant, discrepant, inconstant, lubricious **11** conflicting, incongruent, incongruous, inconsonant **12** disconsonant, incompatible, inharmonious **13** contradictory, inconformable

inconsolable 7 forlorn **8** dejected, desolate **9** heartsick **11** comfortless, heartbroken **12** disconsolate

inconspicuous 5 vague **7** obscure **10** indistinct, unemphatic **11** unobtrusive **12** unnoticeable

inconstant 5 false, light **6** fickle, shifty, untrue **7** elusive, erratic, mutable, protean, vagrant, variant, wayward **8** disloyal, slippery, ticklish, unstable, unsteady, variable, volatile, wavering **9** changeful, faithless, frivolous, mercurial, uncertain, unsettled **10** capricious, changeable, irresolute, lubricious, perfidious, traitorous, unreliable **11** chameleonic, light-minded, treacherous, vacillating **12** inconsistent, shilly-shally, undependable **13** temperamental

incontestable 4 sure **7** certain **8** positive **9** undoubted **10** undeniable **11** indubitable, irrefutable, unequivocal **12** indisputable

incontinent 4 fast, lewd **7** lustful, satyric **9** lecherous, libertine, salacious **10** lascivious, libidinous, licentious **12** unrestrained

incontrovertible 4 sure **7** certain **8** positive **10** inarguable, undeniable **11** indubitable, unequivocal **12** indisputable, undisputable **13** incontestable, uncontestable

inconvenience 3 try **4** fuss, stew **5** annoy, trial **6** bother, meddle, pother, put out **7** disturb, trouble **8** handicap, put about **9** aggravate, annoyance, disoblige, incommode, interfere **10** discomfort, discommode, discompose, exasperate **11** aggravation, awkwardness, intermeddle **12** disadvantage, discomfiture, exasperation **13** embarrassment

inconvenient 7 awkward, unhandy **8** annoying **10** bothersome, unsuitable **11** detrimental, inexpedient, inopportune, pestiferous, prejudicial, troublesome **12** discommoding, embarrassing, incommodious, unreasonable **13** discommodious

incorporate 3 mix **4** fuse, join **5** blend, merge, unite **6** absorb, embody, imbibe, insorb, mingle **7** combine, inhaust **9** integrate **10** assimilate

incorporeal 4 airy 8 bodiless 9 asomatous, spiritual 10 discarnate, immaterial, unembodied, unphysical 11 disembodied, nonmaterial, nonphysical 12 metaphysical 13 unsubstantial

incorrect 5 false, wrong 6 faulty, untrue 7 unsound 8 improper, specious 9 erroneous, imprecise 10 inaccurate, unbecoming *combining form:* 3 cac 4 caco *prefix:* 3 mis

increase 2 up 3 add, rev, wax 4 gain, grow, hike, jump, plus, push, rise, soup, teem 5 boost, build, mount, put up, raise, run up, swarm, swell 6 accrue, amount, beef up, dilate, expand, extend, gather, growth, jack up, markup 7 advance, amplify, augment, burgeon, distend, enhance, enlarge, inflate, magnify, prolong, pyramid, upgrade, upsurge 8 addition, compound, elongate, escalate, flourish, heighten, lengthen, manifold, multiply, protract, snowball 9 accession, accretion, aggravate, expansion, extension, increment, intensify, pullulate, reinforce 10 accelerate, accumulate, aggrandize, appreciate, strengthen 11 enlargement 12 augmentation, breakthrough 13 amplification *Scottish:* 3 eke *suddenly:* 4 zoom

increasing 8 crescent, crescive

incredible 4 thin, weak 5 thick 6 absurd, flimsy 8 unlikely 9 cockamamy, untenable 10 cockamamie, impossible, improbable, outlandish, ridiculous 11 implausible, incogitable, unthinkable 12 insupposable, preposterous, unbelievable, unconvincing, unimaginable 13 inconceivable

incredulity 7 unfaith 8 unbelief 9 disbelief

incredulous 4 wary 6 show-me 7 dubious 8 aporetic, doubting, hesitant 9 faithless, quizzical, skeptical, uncertain 10 suspicious 11 distrustful, distrusting, mistrustful, questioning, unbelieving, unconvinced, unsatisfied 12 disbelieving

increment 4 gain, rise 5 raise 6 growth 8 addition, increase 9 accession, accretion 11 enlargement 12 augmentation

incriminate 6 accuse, charge, indict 7 arraign, impeach, involve 9 implicate, inculpate

incrustation 4 rime, scab 5 scale 6 plaque, tartar

incubus 4 onus 5 demon 6 burden 9 nightmare 10 evil spirit

inculcate 5 infix, teach 6 impart, infuse 7 educate, implant, impress, instill 8 instruct 10 inseminate 11 communicate

inculpable 4 good, pure 5 clean 8 innocent, unguilty, virtuous 9 blameless, crimeless, exemplary, faultless, guiltless, righteous

incumbent 7 binding, leaning 8 occupant 9 overlying 12 superimposed

incur 3 get 6 induce 7 acquire, bring on 8 contract 9 encounter

incurable 8 cureless, hopeless 9 insanable 10 impossible 11 immedicable, irreparable 12 irremediable 13 irretrievable, uncorrectable, unrecoverable

incursion 4 raid 5 foray 6 attack, inroad 7 assault 8 invasion 9 irruption

incus 4 bone 5 anvil

indebted 7 obliged 8 beholden 9 dutybound, obligated 10 honor-bound

indebtedness 3 due 4 debt 7 arrears, failure 8 beholden 9 arrearage, liability 10 bankruptcy, insolvency, nonpayment, obligation 11 delinquency

indecent 4 foul, racy 5 dirty, gross, nasty 6 coarse, filthy, impure, risqué, smutty, vulgar 7 immoral, obscene, raunchy, ungodly 8 immodest, improper, off-color, unseemly, untoward 10 indecorous, indelicate, malodorous, ridiculous, scurrilous, unbecoming, undecorous 12 scatological

indecision 5 doubt 8 to-and-fro, wavering 9 hesitancy 10 hesitation 11 uncertainty, vacillation 12 irresolution, shilly-shally

indecisive 4 open 5 shaky, vague 7 dubious, halting, unclear, unfixed 8 doubtful, hesitant, wavering 9 equivocal, faltering, tentative, uncertain, undecided, unsettled 10 borderline, hesitating, indistinct, irresolute 11 problematic, vacillating

indecorous 4 rude 5 gross, loose, rough, unfit 6 coarse, vulgar 7 uncivil, ungodly 8 immodest, impolite, improper, indecent, shameful, unlawful, unseemly, untoward 9 incorrect, inelegant, irregular, offensive, tasteless, unfitting 10 indelicate, malodorous, ridiculous, unbecoming 11 ill-mannered, unbefitting, undignified 12 discourteous 13 inappropriate

indecorum 5 boner, break, gaffe 7 blooper, faux pas 8 solecism 10 inelegance, unmeetness 11 impropriety

indeed 3 nay, yea 4 even, well 5 truly 6 easily, really, verily 7 in truth 8 forsooth, honestly 9 assuredly, certainly 10 admittedly, positively, undeniably 11 doubtlessly, undoubtedly

indefatigable 6 dogged 7 patient 8 diligent, sedulous, stubborn, tireless, untiring, vigorous 9 assiduous, energetic, steadfast, strenuous, tenacious, weariless 10 determined, persistent, relentless, unflagging, unwavering, unwearying 11 painstaking, persevering, unfaltering, unflinching, unrelenting, unwearniable 13 inexhaustible

indefensible 9 untenable 10 inexpiable 11 inexcusable 12 unforgivable, unpardonable 13 unjustifiable

indefinable 5 vague 9 ineffable, uncertain 10 untellable 11 inenarrable, unspeakable, unutterable 13 indescribable, indeterminate, inexpressible, undescribable, unexpressible

indefinite 4 wide 5 broad, loose, vague 7 endless, general, inexact, obscure, unclear, unfixed 8 infinite 9 ambiguous, boundless, imprecise, limitless, unbounded, uncertain, undefined, unlimited 10 indistinct, inexplicit, unmeasured, unspecific 11 measureless 12 immeasurable, inconclusive 13 indeterminate *article:* 2 an *pronoun:* 3 all, any, few 4 each, many, most, none, some 6 anyone, nobody 7 anybody, several, someone 8 everyone, somebody 9 everybody

indehiscent fruit 3 nut 4 pepo 5 akene, berry, grain, grape, melon 6 achene, loment, samara, squash 7 pumpkin 8 cucumber 9 caryopsis 10 schizocarp

indelible 4 fast 5 fixed 7 lasting 8 enduring 9 permanent 10 inerasable, unerasable 12 ineffaceable, ineradicable, inexpungible, inextirpable, uneradicable 13 undestroyable

indelicate 3 raw 4 lewd, rude 5 crude, gross, rough 6 callow, coarse, wanton 7 uncouth, ungodly 8 impolite, improper, indecent, tactless, unseemly, untoward 9 unrefined 10 indecorous, malodorous, unbecoming

indemnify 3 pay 5 repay 7 requite 9 reimburse 10 compensate, recompense, remunerate

indemnity 6 amends 7 amnesty, redress 8 reprisal, security 9 exemption, quittance 10 protection, recompense, reparation 11 restitution 12 compensation

indentation 3 bay 4 dent, nick 5 notch, print, stamp 6 recess 7 impress, imprint

indenture 4 nick 5 notch 11 indentation

indentured 5 bound 8 articled 11 apprenticed

independent 4 free 6 closed 8 autarkic, separate 9 autarchic, sovereign 10 autonomous 11 self-reliant 12 self-centered 13 self-contained, self-sufficing, self-supported, self-sustained *combining form:* 4 self

indescribable 9 ineffable 10 untellable 11 indefinable, inenarrable, unspeakable, unutterable 13 inexpressible, unexpressible

indestructible 7 durable, lasting, undying 8 enduring, immortal 9 deathless, immutable, indelible, permanent, perpetual 10 changeless, inviolable, quenchless 11 unalterable 12 imperishable, ineradicable, inextirpable, irrefragable, unchangeable, unperishable, unquenchable 13 incorruptible, irrefrangible, undestroyable

indeterminate 5 vague 7 inexact, unfixed 9 uncertain, unlimited 10 indefinite, indistinct

index 4 list, mark, sign 5 table, token 7 catalog, indices (plural), indicia, symptom 8 evidence 9 catalogue

India *bread:* 7 chapati 8 chapatti *butter:* 3 ghi 4 ghee *capital:* 8 New Delhi *caste:* 5 Sudra 6 Vaisya 7 Brahman 9 Kshatriya *female dancer:* 8 bayadere *harem:* 6 zenana *lady:* 4 bibi 5 begum 8 memsahib *language:* 4 Urdu 5 Hindu, Tamil 6 Telugu 7 Bengali, Kannada, Marathi, Punjabi 8 Assamese, Gujarati, Kashmiri 9 Malayalam 10 Hindustani, Rajasthani *largest city:* 6 Bombay *monetary unit:* 5 rupee *nurse:* 4 amah, ayah *outcast:* 6 pariah *prime minister:* 5 Nehru 6 Gandhi *prince:* 4 raja, rana 5 rajah 8 maharaja 9 maharajah *princess:* 4 rani 5 begum, ranee *scholar:* 6 pandit, pundit *screen:* 6 purdah *seal, stamp:* 4 chop *soldier:* 4 peon 5 sepoy *teacher:* 4 guru *viceroy:* 5 nabob, nawab *weight unit:* 3 ser 4 cash, dhan, pank, pice, powe, rati, tank, tola 5 adpao, fanam, hubba, masha, maund, pally, pouah, ratti 6 dhurra, pagoda, pollam 7 chinnam, chittak

Indian, American *baby:* 7 papoose *ball game:* 8 lacrosse *carrier:* 7 travois *Central and South American:* 2 Ge 3 Ona 4 Cuna, Inca, Maya 5 Arara, Aztec, Carib, Olmec, Yagua 6 Arawak, Aymara, Jivaro, Omagua, Toltec, Yahgan 7 Chibcha, Quechua, Zapotec 8 Tarascan 10 Araucanian 11 Tupi-Guarani *drink:* 6 chicha *food:* 4 samp 5 maize 8 pemmican *game:* 6 chunky 7 chunkey *home:* 5 hogan, lodge, tepee 6 pueblo, teepee, wigwam 7 wickiup *leader:* 4 Popé 6 Wovoka 7 Cochise, Osceola, Pontiac, Sequoya 8 Geronimo, Hiawatha, Powhatan, Tecumseh 9 Massasoit 10 Crazy Horse 11 Cornplanter, Sitting Bull *money:* 5 sewan 6 wampum *North American:* 3 Oto, Sac, Ute 4 Cree, Crow, Hopi, Hupa, Iowa, Otoe, Pima, Pomo, Sauk, Taos, Yuma 5 Aleut, Caddo, Creek, Haida, Huron, Kansa, Kiowa, Maidu, Miami, Modoc, Omaha, Osage, Sioux 6 Apache, Cayuga, Dakota, Lenape, Mandan, Micmac, Mohawk, Munsee, Navaho, Navajo, Nootka, Ojibwa, Oneida, Paiute, Pawnee, Pueblo, Quapaw, Seneca, Siwash 7 Arapaho, Arikara, Bannock, Chilkat, Chinook, Choctaw, Dakotah, Klamath, Kutenai, Mohican, Naskapi, Natchez, Ojibway, Pontiac, Shawnee, Tlingit 8 Cherokee, Cheyenne, Chippewa, Comanche, Delaware, Illinois, Iroquois, Kickapoo, Kwakiutl, Nez Percé, Onondaga, Powhatan, Seminole, Shoshoni 9 Blackfoot,

Chickasaw, Menominee, Tsimshian, Tusca-
rora, Wampanoag, Winnebago 10 Assini-
boin, Chiricahua, Gros Ventre, Potawatomi
11 Massachuset, Narraganset *pipe:* 7 calumet *spirit:* 5 totem 7 kachina

Indiana *college, university:* 6 De Pauw,
Marion, Purdue 9 Ball State, Notre Dame
nickname: 12 Hoosier State *state bird:*
8 cardinal *state flower:* 5 peony

indicate 3 say 4 bode, hint, mark, mean,
read, show 5 argue, augur, imply, point,
prove 6 attest, denote, evince, import, record, reveal 7 bespeak, betoken, connote,
display, exhibit, express, presage, signify,
suggest, testify, witness 8 announce, disclose, evidence, intimate, manifest, register
9 designate 10 illustrate 11 demonstrate

indication 3 cue 4 clue, hint, mark, omen,
sign, type, wind 5 index, proof, token,
trace 6 notion, signal, symbol 7 gesture,
indicia, inkling, reading, symptom 8 evidence, reminder, telltale 9 testimony
10 expression, intimation, suggestion
11 significant 13 manifestation,
prefiguration

indicative 8 denotive, evincive, indicial,
symbolic 9 testatory 10 denotative, eviden-
tial, exhibitive, expressive, suggestive
11 designative, symptomatic
13 demonstrative

indicia 4 fact, mark, sign 5 index, token
7 symptom 8 evidence 9 criterion

indict 6 accuse, charge 7 arraign,
impeach 9 criminate, inculpate
11 incriminate

indifference 6 apathy 8 lethargy 9 aloofness, disregard, lassitude, unconcern
10 negligence 11 disinterest, insouciance
12 carelessness, heedlessness
13 unmindfulness

indifferent 3 icy 4 cold, cool, fair, mean,
numb, so-so 5 aloof, blasé, chill, equal,
stoic 6 casual, frigid, medium, remote
7 average, fairish, glacial, neutral, off-hand,
unmoved 8 by-the-way, careless, detached,
heedless, inferior, listless, mediocre, middling, moderate, passable, unbiased, uncaring 9 apathetic, equitable, impartial, impassive, incurious, negligent, objective,
uncurious, unmindful, withdrawn 10 impersonal, insensible, nonchalant, regardless,
unaffected, unsociable 11 unconcerned,
unemotional, unobserving 12 unimpressive,
uninterested, unprejudiced 13 disinterested,
dispassionate

indigence 4 lack, need, want 6 penury
7 poverty 9 neediness, privation
11 destitution

indigenous 6 inborn, innate, native 7 connote, endemic, natural 8 inherent 9 inher-

ited 10 aboriginal, congenital, connatural,
unacquired 13 autochthonous

indigent 4 poor 5 needy 6 beggar, pauper 8 dirt poor 9 destitute, penniless, penurious 11 impecunious, necessitous
12 impoverished

indigestion 9 dyspepsia

indignant 3 mad 5 angry, irate, wroth
6 heated, wrathy, wrothy 7 annoyed
8 incensed, wrathful, wrothful 9 irritated,
resentful

indignation 3 ire, mad 4 fury, rage
5 anger, wrath 10 resentment

indignity 3 cut 4 slap 5 wrong 6 injury,
insult, slight 7 affront, despite, outrage
9 contumely, grievance, injustice
13 disparagement

indigo 4 anil, blue

indigo bird 5 finch 7 bunting

indigo plant 4 anil

Indira Gandhi's father 5 Nehru

indirect 6 errant, shifty, sneaky 7 crooked,
devious, oblique, sinuous, vagrant, winding
8 circular, guileful, sneaking, tortuous, twisting 9 deceitful, dishonest, underhand, wandering 10 circuitous, collateral, meandering,
roundabout, serpentine 11 duplicitous,
underhanded

indiscreet 6 unwary, unwise 9 ill-judged,
impolitic, imprudent, untactful 10 ill-advised,
incautious 11 injudicious 13 inconsiderate

indiscretion 4 slip 5 folly 9 incaution
10 imprudence, unwariness

indiscriminate 4 spot, wide 5 broad,
mixed 6 motley, random, varied 7 aimless,
jumbled, mingled, shallow 8 assorted,
chowchow, confused, sweeping 9 desultory, extensive, haphazard, hit-or-miss,
unplanned, wholesale 10 designless, uncritical 11 promiscuous, purposeless, superficial 12 conglomerate, multifarious,
unconsidered

indispensable 5 basic, vital 6 needed
7 exigent, needful 8 cardinal 9 essential,
necessary, requisite 10 imperative
11 fundamental

indisposed 3 ill, low 4 mean, sick
5 loath 6 afraid, ailing, averse, offish,
poorly, sickly, unwell 7 hostile, underly, uneager 8 backward, hesitant, inimical, off-
color 9 reluctant, unwilling, unwishful
11 disinclined

indisposition 6 malady 7 ailment, dislike,
illness, malaise 8 aversion, bad books, disfavor, disorder, distaste, sickness,
unhealth 9 disliking, disrelish, infirmity
10 affliction, reluctance 11 displeasure

indisputable 4 real, sure, true 6 actual
7 certain, evident 8 positive, unfabled
9 veridical 10 undeniable 11 indubitable,

irrefutable, unequivocal **12** irrefragable **13** incontestable, uncontestable

indistinct 3 dim **4** hazy **5** faint, misty, vague **6** bleary, cloudy **7** blurred, inexact, obscure, shadowy, unclear **8** confused **9** uncertain, undefined **10** ill-defined, indefinite **12** undetermined **13** indeterminate

indistinguishable 4 same **5** equal **7** identic **9** duplicate, identical **10** equivalent, tantamount

indite 3 pen **5** write **6** scribe **7** compose, engross **8** inscribe

individual 3 one **4** body, lone, self, sole, soul, unit **5** being, human, party, stuff, thing **6** entity, matter, mortal, object, person, proper, single **7** several, special **8** creature, especial, existent, material, peculiar, personal, separate, singular, solitary, specific **9** diacritic, existence, personage, something, substance **10** diagnostic, individual, particular, respective **11** distinctive **13** idiosyncratic *combining form:* **4** idio

individualist 10 egocentric

individuality 4 self **5** seity, unity **6** makeup, nature, temper **7** ipseity, oneness, selfdom **8** identity, selfhood, selfness **9** character **10** complexion, difference, singleness, uniqueness, unlikeness **11** disposition, personality, singularity, temperament **12** independence, separateness, singularness

individualize 4 mark **7** qualify, specify **9** signalize **11** distinguish, singularize **12** characterize **13** particularize

Indochina country 4 Laos **5** Burma **7** Vietnam **8** Cambodia, Thailand

indoctrinate 5 teach, tutor **7** educate **8** instruct

indolence 4 laze **5** sloth **6** slouch **7** inertia, languor **8** idleness, laziness **10** inactivity **12** slothfulness, sluggishness

indolent 4 idle, lazy **5** drony **7** work-shy **8** fainéant, inactive, slothful, sluggish **9** easygoing, slowgoing

indomitable 4 wild **6** dogged, unruly **7** staunch **8** indocile, resolute, stubborn **9** fractious, steadfast **10** impassable, invincible, unbeatable **11** impregnable, insuperable, intractable **12** inexpugnable, invulnerable, pertinacious, recalcitrant, unassailable, undefeatable, ungovernable, unmanageable **13** unconquerable, undisciplined

Indonesia *capital:* **7** Jakarta **8** Djakarta *monetary unit:* **6** rupiah *president:* **7** Suharto

indubitable 4 flat, real, sure, true **7** assured, certain, evident, genuine **8** bona fide, positive **9** authentic, downright, undoubted, up-and-down, veritable **10** inarguable, sure-enough, undeniable **11** irrefu-

table **12** indisputable, irrefragable **13** incontestable, uncontestable

induce 3 get **4** abet, draw, lead, move, sway, urge **5** breed, cause, get up, hatch, impel, infer, tempt **6** arouse, draw in, draw on, effect, elicit, incite, prompt, work up **7** actuate, inspire, procure, produce, win over **8** activate, conclude, convince, engender, generate, motivate, muster up, occasion, oversway, persuade, talk into **9** argue into, encourage, influence, prevail on

inducement 4 bait, lure **6** motive **9** incentive **10** enticement **13** consideration

induct 4 lead **6** enroll, invest **7** conduct, install, instate **8** initiate **9** introduce

inductance unit 5 henry **6** henrys (plural) **7** henries (plural)

induction 8 entrance **9** accession, inaugural, inference **10** initiation **11** investiture **12** inauguration, installation, introduction

inductive 8 Baconian, epagogic **9** inducible, prefatial, prefatory, preludial, prelusive **11** a posteriori, prefatorial, preliminary, preparative, preparatory **12** introductory

indulge 3 pet **4** baby, bask, roll **5** favor, humor, revel, spoil **6** cocker, coddle, cosset, oblige, pamper, please, regale, wallow, welter **7** cater to, delight, gratify, rollick, satisfy **9** luxuriate **11** mollycoddle

indulgence 5 favor **6** liking, luxury **7** service **8** clemency, courtesy, fondness, kindness, lenience, leniency, mildness **9** benignity, tolerance **10** benignancy, benignness, gentleness, kindliness, toleration **11** forbearance **12** dispensation, mercifulness **13** gratification

indulgence seller 5 Tezel **6** Tetzel

indulgent 4 easy, kind, mild **6** benign, kindly **7** clement, lenient **8** excusing, merciful, tolerant **9** benignant, compliant, condoning, cosseting, forgiving, pampering, pardoning **10** charitable, forbearing, permissive

indurate 3 dry, set **4** cake **5** inure **6** harden **7** confirm, congeal **8** concrete, hardened, solidify, stubborn **9** unfeeling

industrialist 6 tycoon **7** magnate

industrious 4 busy, live **6** active **7** dynamic, operose, zealous **8** diligent, sedulous **9** assiduous

industry 4 work **5** labor, trade **7** traffic **8** business, commerce **9** diligence

inebriant 5 booze, drink **6** liquor **7** alcohol, spirits **9** aqua vitae **10** intoxicant

inebriate 3 sot **4** lush, soak **5** drunk, toper **6** bibber, boozer **7** tippler, tosspot **8** drunkard

inebriated 5 drunk, tight, tipsy **7** muddled **9** disguised, pixilated **11** intoxicated

inedible 7 baneful, insipid, noxious **9** poisonous, uneatable **10** inesculent

11 unwholesome 12 indigestible,
unappetizing

ineffable 4 holy 5 ideal, taboo 6 divine,
sacred 8 abstract, empyreal, empyrean,
ethereal, heavenly 9 celestial, spiritual
10 untellable 11 indefinable, inenarrable,
unspeakable, unutterable 12 transcendent
13 indescribable, inexpressible, undescribable, unexpressible

ineffaceable 9 indelible 10 inerasable,
unerasable 12 ineradicable, inexpungible,
inextirpable, uneradicable

ineffective 4 vain, weak 6 futile 7 useless 8 abortive, boneless, bootless, impotent, inferior 9 forceless, fruitless, incapable, spineless, worthless 10 emasculate,
inadequate, unavailing 11 incompetent, ineffectual, inefficient, slack-spined, unavailable 12 invertebrate, unproductive
13 inefficacious

ineffectiveness 9 inability 10 inadequacy, incapacity, inefficacy 12 incapability,
incompetence

ineffectual see **ineffective**

ineffectualness see **ineffectiveness**

inefficacious see **ineffective**

inefficacy see **ineffectiveness**

inefficient 5 inept 8 careless, inexpert,
slipshod, slovenly, unexpert, unfitted
9 incapable, unskilled, untrained 10 unprepared, unskillful 11 incompetent, ineffective,
ineffectual, unqualified 12 insufficient
13 inefficacious, unworkmanlike

inelaborate 5 plain 6 modest, simple
11 undecorated, ungarnished 12 unbeautified 13 unembellished, unembroidered,
unpretentious

inelastic 5 rigid, stiff 9 impliable, unbending 10 inflexible, unflexible, unyielding
11 immalleable, incompliant

inelegant 3 raw 4 rude 5 crass, crude,
gross, rough 6 coarse, vulgar 7 awkward,
uncouth 9 graceless, unrefined

ineligible 5 unfit 8 unfitted, unworthy
9 incapable 10 unequipped 11 incompetent, unqualified 12 disqualified

ineluctable 4 sure 5 fated 6 doomed
7 certain 9 necessary 10 ineludible, inevasible, inevitable, returnless, unevadable
11 ineluctable, inescapable, unavoidable,
unescapable

ineludible 7 certain 9 necessary 10 inevasible, inevitable, returnless, unevadable
11 ineluctable, unavoidable, unescapable

inept 4 dull 5 inapt, unapt, undue, unfit
6 clumsy, gauche, wooden 7 awkward,
foolish, halting, inadept, unhandy, unhappy
8 bumbling, bungling, ill-timed, improper,
inexpert, unexpert, unfacile, unseemly
9 graceless, ham-handed, ill-chosen, incapable, lumbering, maladroit, unskilled 10 inad-

equate, malapropos, unskillful, unsuitable
11 incompetent, inefficient, undexterous,
unfortunate

inequality 8 asperity, imparity, rugosity
9 disparity, roughness 10 cragginess, jag-
gedness, ruggedness, unevenness
12 irregularity, variableness
13 disproportion

inequitable 3 bad 5 undue, wrong
6 unfair, unjust 8 wrongful 9 arbitrary, inequable, unmerited 10 high-handed, oppressive, undeserved 11 unequitable,
unrighteous

inequity 5 wrong 9 injustice 10 unfairness, unjustness

inerasable 9 indelible 12 ineffaceable, ineradicable, inexpungible, inextirpable,
uneradicable

inert 4 dead, idle 5 quiet, still 6 asleep,
sleepy, stolid 7 neutral, passive 8 immobile, impotent, inactive, indolent, lifeless,
sluggish 9 apathetic, impassive, inanimate,
lethargic, powerless 10 motionless,
phlegmatic

inert gas 4 neon 5 argon, radon, xenon
6 helium 7 krypton 8 nitrogen, noble gas
13 carbon dioxide *suffix:* 2 on

inescapable see **inevitable**

inescapably see **inevitably**

inesculent 8 inedible 9 uneatable

in essence 6 au fond 7 morally 9 basically, virtually 11 essentially, practically
13 fundamentally

inessential see **unessential**

inestimable 6 costly 8 precious, valuable 9 priceless 10 invaluable, unmeasured 11 measureless, uncountable
12 immeasurable, incalculable, unmeasurable, unreckonable

inevitable 4 sure 5 fated 7 certain,
decided, settled 8 destined 9 necessary
10 ineludible, inevasible, inexorable, inflexible, returnless, unevadable 11 ineluctable,
inescapable, unavoidable, unescapable
12 foreordained, ineliminable
13 unpreventable

inevitably 8 perforce 10 helplessly, willy-
nilly 11 inescapably, unavoidably, whether
or no

inexcusable 8 blamable 9 untenable
10 censurable, inexpiable 11 blameworthy,
intolerable, unallowable 12 criticizable, indefensible, unforgivable, unpardonable
13 impermissible, reprehensible,
unjustifiable

inexhaustible 8 tireless, untiring 9 unfailing, weariless 10 unflagging, unwearying
11 unweariable 13 indefatigable

in existence 6 extant

inexorable 5 rigid 6 dogged, strict 7 adamant 8 immobile, obdurate, resolute

9 immovable, unbending 10 inflexible, relentless, unyielding 11 unrelenting 12 single-minded

inexpensive 3 low 5 cheap 6 frugal, undear 7 low-cost, popular 8 uncostly 9 low-priced 10 reasonable

inexperience 7 naiveté, rawness 8 verdancy 9 freshness, greenness, ignorance 10 callowness 13 unfamiliarity

inexperienced 3 row 5 fresh, green, inept, naive, young 6 callow 7 untried 8 ignorant, immature, inexpert, prentice, unversed 9 incapable, unskilled, untrained 10 amateurish, unfamiliar, unseasoned 11 unpracticed 12 unacquainted, unconversant

inexpert see **inexperienced**

inexplicable 3 odd 7 strange, uncanny 8 peculiar 9 ambiguous, enigmatic 10 mysterious, unsolvable 11 inscrutable, undefinable 12 unfathomable 13 indescribable, inexplainable, unaccountable, unexplainable

inexpressible 8 nameless 9 ineffable 10 untellable 11 indefinable, inenarrable, unspeakable, unutterable 13 indescribable

inexpressive 4 dull 5 blank, empty 6 vacant, wooden 7 deadpan

inexpugnable 5 fixed 6 stable 10 invincible, unbeatable 11 impregnable, indomitable, unopposable 12 invulnerable, irresistible, unassailable, undefeatable 13 unconquerable

inextricable 8 involved 9 insoluble, intricate, unsoluble 10 insolvable, unsolvable

infallible 4 sure 5 exact 7 certain, correct, perfect 8 flawless, inerrant, surefire, unerring 9 faultless, inerrable, unfailing 10 impeccable 11 indubitable 12 undeceivable

infamous 4 base, evil, vile 5 sorry 6 odious, rotten, scurvy 7 corrupt, hateful, heinous, vicious 8 ill-famed, perverse, shameful 9 abhorrent, atrocious, miscreant, nefarious, notorious, unhealthy 10 abominable, degenerate, despicable, detestable, flagitious, iniquitous, scandalous, villainous 11 disgraceful, ignominious, opprobrious 12 contemptible, disreputable

infamy 5 odium, shame 7 obloquy 8 disgrace, dishonor, ignominy 9 discredit, disesteem, disrepute, notoriety 10 opprobrium 13 notoriousness

infancy 6 nonage 8 babyhood, minority 9 childhood, juniority 10 immaturity, infanthood, juvenility

infant 4 babe, baby 5 child, green, minor, young 6 callow, unripe 7 neonate, newborn, toddler 8 bantling, immature, juvenile, nursling, youthful 9 unfledged **bed:** 4 crib 6 cradle 8 bassinet **food:** 3 pap 4 milk **room:** 7 nursery

infantile 7 babyish, puerile 8 childish, immature

infantryman 7 dogface 8 doughboy 11 foot soldier **Algerian:** 6 Zouave

infatuated 3 mad 5 dotty, silly 7 foolish 8 besotted, enamored, obsessed 9 bewitched 10 captivated, enraptured

infatuation 4 rage 5 ardor, craze, crush, folly 6 beguin 7 passion 8 devotion 9 obsession 11 fascination

in favor of 3 for, pro 4 with 10 impossible, unworkable 11 impractical 12 irrealizable, unattainable, unrealizable 13 impracticable

infect 5 taint 6 defile, infest, poison 7 pollute 11 contaminate

infection 6 plague, sepses (plural), sepsis 7 disease, illness **fungous:** 8 mycetoma **skin:** 6 herpes

infectious 5 toxic 6 taking 7 miasmic, noxious 8 catching, mephitic, virulent 9 pestilent, poisonous, vitiating 10 contagious, corrupting 11 sympathetic 12 communicable, pestilential 13 contaminating

infecund 6 barren, effete 7 sterile 8 impotent 9 infertile 10 unfruitful

infelicitous 5 inapt, inept, unapt 6 gauche 7 awkward, unhappy 9 defective, graceless, ill-chosen, imperfect, inapropos 10 deplorable, malapropos 11 regrettable, unfortunate 13 inappropriate

infer 4 draw, hint, make 5 glean, guess, judge, think 6 bestow, confer, deduce, deduct, derive, gather, induce, reason, reckon 7 collect, inflict, make out, surmise 8 conclude, construe

inference 5 guess 7 surmise 8 guessing, illation, judgment, sequitur 9 deduction, reckoning 10 assumption, conclusion, conjecture, derivation 11 presumption, supposition

inferior 3 bad, low 4 base, cull, fair, hack, mean, poor, punk, puny 5 cheap, lousy, lower, minor, petty, scrub, sorry, under 6 common, deputy, feeble, heeler, impure, junior, lesser, minion, nether, no-good, paltry, puisne, satrap, shoddy, sleazy, tawdry, tinpot, vassal 7 average, subject, unequal 8 adherent, declassé, disciple, follower, hanger-on, henchman, hireling, low-grade, mediocre, middling, ordinary, retainer, unworthy, wretched 9 attendant, auxiliary, no-account, satellite, secondary, subaltern, subjacent, sycophant, underling, valueless, worthless 10 inadequate, second-rate **prefix:** 3 sub 4 demi 5 infra

inferior one **suffix:** 3 een 4 ling 5 aster

infernal 6 Hadean 7 avernal, hellish, satanic, stygian 8 chthonic, damnable, demoniac, devilish, diabolic, fiendish, plutonic **9** chthonian, plutonian, Tartarean **10** diabolical, sulphurous

inferno 3 pit **4** fire, hell **5** abyss, hades, Sheol **6** blazes, Tophet **7** Gehenna **9** holocaust, perdition **11** netherworld

Inferno *division:* **5** canto *poet:* **5** Dante *verse form:* **9** terza rima

infertile 6 barren, effete **7** drained, sterile **8** depleted, impotent, infecund **9** exhausted, unbearing, unfertile **10** unfruitful **12** hardscrabble, impoverished, unproductive

infest 4 teem **5** annoy, beset, crawl, harry, haunt, swarm, worry **6** abound, harass, pester, plague **7** overrun **8** parasite **9** overswarm **10** overspread, parasitize

infidel 5 pagan **6** ethnic **7** gentile, heathen, profane, skeptic **9** infidelic **10** unbeliever

infidelity 7 falsity, perfidy, treason **9** falseness, treachery **10** disloyalty, fickleness **11** inconstancy **13** faithlessness

infiltrate 4 leak, seep, worm **5** foist **6** edge in, work in **9** insinuate

infinite 4 vast **7** endless, eternal, immense **9** boundless, countless, limitless, perpetual, unbounded, unlimited **10** indefinite, perdurable, unmeasured **11** everlasting, illimitable, measureless, sempiternal **12** immeasurable

infirm 4 lame, weak **5** anile, frail **6** ailing, feeble, flimsy, senile, weakly **7** fragile, unsound **8** decrepit **10** irresolute **11** debilitated, vacillating **13** unsubstantial

infirmity 3 ill **5** decay **6** foible, malady **7** ailment, disease, failing, frailty, illness, malaise **8** debility, disorder, sickness, syndrome, unhealth, weakness **9** affection, complaint, condition, weakening **10** affliction, feebleness, infirmness, sickliness, unwellness **11** decrepitude **12** debilitation, diseasedness, enfeeblement **13** indisposition, unhealthiness

infix 4 root **5** embed, lodge **6** insert **7** implant, impress, ingrain, instill **8** entrench **9** inculcate **10** inseminate

inflame 3 get **4** fire, gall, good, heat, rile, roil, stir **5** grate, light, rouse **6** arouse, burn up, enrage, excite, ignite, kindle, madden, put out, redden **7** incense, provoke **8** enkindle, irritate **9** aggravate, intensify **10** exasperate

inflammable 5 fiery **6** ardent **8** burnable **9** excitable, ignitable, irascible, irritable **11** combustible

inflammation 4 gout, sore **5** felon **6** quinsy **7** catarrh, coxitis, gonitis, rickets **8** adenitis, cystitis, neuritis, pleurisy, rachitis, swelling **9** arthritis, chilblain, gastritis, phlebitis **10** combustion **12** encephalitis **13** conflagration, poliomyelitis *ear:* **6** otitis

eye: **6** iritis **7** pinkeye **9** keratitis *horse:* **6** thrush **7** fistula, quittor **8** poll evil *intestines:* **7** ileitis **9** enteritis *suffix:* **4** itis

inflammatory 8 exciting, incitive **9** seditious **10** incendiary **11** instigative, provocative, seditionary **13** revolutionary

inflate 4 fill **5** bloat, elate, swell **6** dilate, expand, tumefy **7** amplify, distend

inflated 5 showy, tumid, windy, wordy **6** elated, prolix, turgid **7** aureate, bloated, diffuse, flowery, fustian, pompous, ranting, swollen, verbose **8** bladdery, dropsied **9** bombastic, distended, dropsical, flatulent, overblown, tumescent **10** rhetorical **11** exaggerated, pretentious, rhapsodical

inflection 4 bend, tone **5** curve **6** accent, timbre **8** tonality **9** accidence **10** intonation **11** enunciation **12** articulation **13** pronunciation

inflexible 3 set **4** grim, hard, iron **5** fixed, rigid, stiff, tough **6** dogged, strict **7** adamant, settled **8** constant, granitic, hard-line, immobile, ironclad, obdurate, rigorous, stubborn **9** immovable, immutable, impliable, inelastic, obstinate, rockbound, steadfast, unbending, unmovable **10** adamantine, brassbound, changeless, implacable, inexorable, invariable, invincible, relentless, rockribbed, unbendable, unchanging, unswayable, unyielding **11** unalterable, uncompliant, unrelenting **12** single-minded, unchangeable, unmodifiable **13** dyed-in-the-wool

inflict 4 deal, give **5** visit, wreak, wreck **6** expose, impose, strike **7** force on, subject

inflow 6 influx, inpour, inrush **9** influxion

influence 4 move, pull, sway **5** alter, bribe, carry, clout, force, impel, lobby, touch **6** affect, compel, credit, induce, modify, moment, strike, weight **7** command, control, impress, inspire, mastery **8** dominion, eminence, militate, persuade, prestige **9** authority, dominance

influenceable 8 suasible, swayable **9** acceptant, acceptive, receptive **10** responsive **11** persuadable, persuasible

influential 6 potent **8** powerful **9** effective, important

influx 6 inflow, inpour, inrush **7** illapse **8** increase **9** accession, inpouring **11** debouchment **12** augmentation

inform 3 rat **4** blab, clew, clue, fire, post, talk, tell, warn **5** endow, endue, exalt, imbue, peach, teach, train **6** advise, betray, fill in, infuse, leaven, notify, preach, snitch, squeak, squeal, tattle, turn in, wise up **7** animate, apprise, arrange, caution, educate, inspire **8** acquaint, forewarn, give away, instruct, permeate **9** advertise, enlighten **10** illuminate **11** familiarize

informal 6 breezy, casual, dégagé, simple **7** natural, private, relaxed, special, unfussy

8 familiar 9 easygoing, irregular 10 colloquial, unofficial

information 4 data (plural), fact, lore,
news, word 5 datum 6 advice, notice, wisdom 7 science, tidings 9 complaint, knowledge, speerings 11 instruction 12 intelligence *second hand:* 7 hearsay *suffix:*
3 ana 4 iana

information bureau *abbreviation:*
4 USIA, USIS

informative 8 edifying 9 educative
11 educational, elucidative, explanatory,
informatory, instructive 12 enlightening, illuminating 13 informational, instructional

informed 2 up 3 hip 4 wise 5 aware
6 au fait, posted, versed 7 abreast, knowing, versant 8 apprised, educated, familiar
9 au courant 10 acquainted, conversant,
cultivated 11 enlightened, intelligent

informer 3 rat, spy 4 fink 5 stool
6 canary, gossip, snitch 7 stoolie, tattler,
tipster 8 betrayer, busybody, squawker,
squealer, telltale 10 talebearer, tattletale
11 stool pigeon

infra 4 next 5 after, below, later, under
6 behind, within 7 beneath

infract 5 break 6 breach, offend 7 violate
8 infringe 10 contravene, transgress

infraction 3 sin 4 slip 5 crime, error,
lapse 6 breach 7 faux pas, offense 8 trespass 9 intrusion, violation 12 encroachment, infringement 13 contravention,
transgression

infrastructure 4 base, root 5 basis
6 bottom, ground 7 bedrock, footing
10 foundation, groundwork, substratum
12 substructure, underpinning

infrequent 3 few, odd 4 rare 5 scant,
stray 6 meager, scanty, scarce, seldom,
sparse 7 limited, unusual 8 isolated, sporadic, uncommon, unwonted 9 scattered,
spasmodic 10 occasional 11 exceptional

infringe 5 break 6 breach, defeat, impose,
invade, offend, refute 7 confute, infract,
intrude, obtrude, presume, violate
8 encroach, entrench, trespass 10 contravene, transgress

infuriate 3 ire, mad 5 anger 6 enrage,
madden 7 incense, steam up, umbrage

infuse 4 fill, fire 5 imbue, steep 6 inform,
invest, leaven 7 animate, diffuse, implant,
ingrain, inspire, instill, pervade, suffuse, suggest 8 intersow, permeate, saturate
9 inculcate, inoculate, insinuate, interfuse,
interlard, introduce 10 impregnate 11 intersperse 12 indoctrinate 13 intersprinkle

ingenious 3 sly 4 slim 5 acute, canny,
sharp, smart 6 adroit, clever, crafty 7 cunning 8 creative, original 9 demiurgic, deviceful, inventive 11 intelligent, originative,
resourceful 12 innovational

ingenuous 4 open 5 naive 6 simple,
unwary 7 artless, natural, unaware 8 innocent, unartful 9 childlike, guileless, unstudied 10 unaffected, unschooled
12 unartificial

Inge play 6 Picnic 7 Bus Stop

ingest 3 eat 4 meal, take 6 absorb,
devour, feed on, take in 7 consume,
swallow

inglorious 5 shady 6 shabby, shoddy
8 shameful 11 disgraceful, ignominious
12 dishonorable, disreputable 13 discreditable, unrespectable

ingot 3 bar, rod 4 slap 5 stick, strip
6 billet

ingrained 7 built-in, chronic 8 inherent
10 congenital, deep-rooted, deep-seated,
indwelling, inveterate

ingratiating 5 silky 6 silken 8 pleasing
9 adulatory 10 flattering, saccharine
11 deferential, sycophantic

ingredient 6 factor 7 element 9 component 11 constituent

ingress 3 way 4 adit, door, go in 5 enter,
entry 6 access, come in, entrée
8 entrance 9 admission, penetrate
10 admittance

ingurgitate 4 bolt, cram, gulp, slop, wolf
5 slosh, stuff, swill 6 devour, englut, gobble,
guzzle 7 swallow

inhabit 4 live 5 abide, dwell 6 occupy,
people, settle, tenant 8 populate

inhabitant 5 liver 6 inmate, native 7 citizen, denizen, dweller, resider 8 indigene,
resident 9 aborigine 10 autochthon *foreign:* 5 alien *indigenous:* 6 native
9 aborigine *suffix:* 3 ese, ite, ote

inhale 7 breathe, consume, respire
9 breathe in

inharmonious 6 atonal 7 jarring 9 cat-
and-dog, differing, dissonant, immusical,
unmusical 10 cacophonic, discordant
11 conflicting, conflictive, disagreeing, quarrelsome, uncongenial 12 antagonistic

inhere 3 lie 5 dwell, exist 6 belong,
reside 7 consist

inherent 4 born 5 basic 6 inborn, innate,
normal, built-in, connate, infixed, natural,
regular, typical 8 immanent, peculiar 9 elemental, essential, ingrained, intrinsic
10 congenital, deep-seated, elementary,
individual, indwelling, ingenerate

inherit 7 possess, receive, succeed

inheritance 6 devise, legacy 7 bequest
8 heritage 9 patrimony 10 birthright, entail-
ment 13 primogeniture

inherited 6 innate, native 7 connate, natural 10 congenital, connatural, indigenous

inheritor 4 heir 7 heretor, heritor, legatee
female: 7 heiress 8 heretrix, heritrix
10 heretrices (plural), heritrices (plural)

inhibit 3 ban 4 curb, ward 5 avert, check, taboo 6 bridle, enjoin, forbid, hinder, hold in, outlaw, reduce, retard 7 prevent, repress 8 diminish, hold back, hold down, prohibit, restrain, suppress, withhold 9 constrain

inhibited 4 cold 6 frigid 9 repressed 11 passionless 12 unresponsive

inhibition 3 ban, bar 6 hangup 9 restraint 10 impediment

inhuman 4 cold, fell 5 cruel 6 brutal, fierce, malign, savage 7 beastly, bestial, brutish, wolfish 8 devilish, fiendish, nonhuman 9 barbarous, ferocious, malicious, malignant, truculent 10 cannibalic, diabolical, impersonal, implacable, mechanical

inhumane 4 fell, grim 5 cruel 6 brutal, fierce, savage 7 wolfish 9 barbarous, ferocious, truculent

inhumation 6 burial 9 interment, sepulture 10 entombment

inhume 4 bury, tomb 5 inter, plant 6 entomb 7 lay away, put away 9 sepulcher, sepulture

inimical 3 ill 7 adverse, harmful, hostile 10 unfriendly 11 unfavorable

iniquitous 3 bad 4 evil 5 wrong 6 sinful, unjust, wicked 7 immoral, vicious 9 nefarious, reprobate

iniquity 3 sin 4 evil, tort 5 crime, wrong 9 diablerie, injustice 10 wickedness, wrongdoing

initial 5 basic, early, first, prime 6 letter, maiden 7 leading, nascent, opening, pioneer, primary 8 earliest, foremost, germinal, headmost, monogram, original 9 beginning, embryonic, incipient

initiate 4 open 5 admit, begin, enter, set up, start 6 enroll, get off, induct, invest, launch, take in, take up 7 install, kick off, usher in 8 commence 9 originate 10 inaugurate

initiation 7 baptism 9 admission, beginning, induction 10 admittance 11 origination 12 commencement, introduction

initiative 4 push 6 energy 8 ambition, aptitude, gumption 9 beginning 10 enterprise, get-up-and-go

injudicious 6 unwise 9 ill-judged, impolitic, imprudent 10 ill-advised, indiscreet 11 inexpedient

injunction 4 word 5 order 6 behest, charge 7 bidding, command, dictate, mandate 9 direction 11 prohibition

injure 3 mar 4 foul, harm, hurt, maim, pain 5 spoil, wound, wrong 6 batter, blight, bruise, damage, deface, deform, foul up, grieve, impair, mangle, offend, weaken 7 afflict, blemish, contort, cripple, disable, distort, louse up, tarnish, torment, torture, vitiate 8 aggrieve, disserve, distress, mal-treat, mutilate 9 bespatter, constrain, disfigure, prejudice 12 incapacitate

injurious 3 bad 4 evil 6 nocent 7 abusive, harmful, hurtful 8 damaging 9 offensive 10 defamatory 11 detrimental

injury 3 bad, ill 4 evil, harm, hurt, loss, pain, pang, ruin 5 agony, wound, wrong 6 damage, trauma 7 outrage 8 distress, mischief 9 detriment, grievance, injustice

injustice 4 harm, hurt, ruin, tort 5 crime, wrong 6 breach, damage, injury 7 outrage 8 inequity, mischief, trespass, villainy 9 grievance, violation 10 favoritism, partiality, unfairness, wrongdoing

ink 4 sign 9 autograph, signature, subscribe

inkling 3 cue 4 clue, hint, idea, wind 6 notion 8 telltale 10 intimation, suggestion

ink or rubber 5 India

inky 3 jet 4 ebon 5 black, ebony, jetty, raven, sable 9 cimmerian, pitch-dark 10 pitch-black 11 atramentous

Inland Empire 8 Illinois

inlet 3 arm, bay, cay, voe 4 cove, gulf 5 bayou, bight, creek, fiord, firth, fjord, sound 6 harbor, slough, strait 7 estuary *Admiralties:* 4 Kali *Adriatic Sea:* 5 Vlona, Vlorë *Aegean Sea:* 9 Saronicus 11 Saronic Gulf 12 Gulf of Aegina *Africa:* 6 Walvis 12 Gulf of Guinea *Alaska:* 4 Cook 5 Cross, Taiya 7 Glacier 8 Chilkoot *Aleutians:* 5 Holtz, Nazan *Angola:* 5 Bengo, Tiger 6 Tigres *Antarctica:* 3 Ice 7 McMurdo 8 Amundsen 10 Shackleton *Arabian Sea:* 4 Qamr 5 Kamar *Arctic Ocean:* 8 Gulf of Ob *Australia:* 4 King 6 Botany 9 Discovery 10 Broad Sound 13 Van Diemen Gulf *Baffin Bay:* 8 Melville *Baffin Island:* 9 Admiralty *Baltic Sea:* 4 Hano 6 Danzig 9 Pomerania 10 Gulf of Riga, Pomeranian *Barents Sea:* 4 Kola 7 Pechora *Beaufort Sea:* 7 Prudhoe 9 Mackenzie *Bering Sea:* 12 Gulf of Anadyr *Bismarck Sea:* 5 Kimbe *Brazil:* 9 Guanabara *Bristol Channel:* 10 Carmarthen *California:* 5 Morro 8 Monterey, San Diego 12 San Francisco *Canada:* 5 Fundy 9 Howe Sound *Cape Breton Island:* 4 Mira *Caribbean Sea:* 5 Limon 8 Chetumal, Honduras 9 Venezuela *Central America:* 7 Fonseca *Chile:* 5 Otway *China-Korea:* 8 Huang Hai, Hwang Hai 9 Yellow Sea *Crete:* 4 Suda 5 Canea *Denmark:* 3 Ise *Djibouti:* 6 Tajura 8 Tadjoura *East River:* 8 Flushing *Ecuador:* 5 Manta *Eire:* 4 Clew 7 Brandon *English Channel:* 3 Tor 5 Seine 8 Plymouth *Florida:* 8 Biscayne 10 Saint Lucie 11 Indian River *France-Spain:* 6 Biscay 13 Gulf of Gascony *Georgia:* 8 Altamaha *Greece:* 13 Gulf of Corinth, Gulf of Lepanto *Green-*

land: 6 Baffin *Gulf of Alaska:* 3 Icy 5 Woman 12 Resurrection *Gulf of Mexico:* 5 Tampa 6 Mobile 7 Aransas 8 Sarasota, Suwannee 9 Matagorda, Pensacola 10 San Antonio, Terrebonne 11 Atchafalaya, Mississippi, Ponce de Leon 12 Apalachicola 13 Corpus Christi *Gulf of St. Lawrence:* 5 Bonne, Gaspé *Hawaii:* 11 Pearl Harbor *Honshu:* 3 Ise 5 Osaka, Owari, Tokyo 6 Atsuta *Hudson Bay:* 7 Repulse *Hudson River:* 7 New York *Iceland:* 4 Axar, Eyja, Huna 5 Horna, Skaga, Vopna 8 Hunafloi *Indonesia:* 4 Bima 5 Saleh *Ionian Sea:* 7 Taranto *Irish Sea:* 4 Luce 7 Dundalk *Italy:* 11 Gulf of Genoa 14 Lagoon of Venice *Japan:* 4 Tosa *Java:* 4 Lada 5 Peper *Java Sea:* 7 Batavia 8 Djakarta *Kara Sea:* 6 Enisei 7 Yenisei *Labrador:* 8 Hamilton *Lake Erie:* 8 Put-in-Bay, Sandusky *Lake Huron:* 7 Saginaw, Thunder *Lake Michigan:* 5 Green 13 Grand Traverse *Lake Ontario:* 11 Irondequoit *Lake Superior:* 5 Huron 8 Keweenaw 9 Whitefish *Long Island:* 8 Rockaway *Long Island Sound:* 6 Oyster 5 New Haven *Madagascar:* 8 Antongil *Maine:* 5 Casco 7 Machias 9 Penobscot 12 Damariscotta *Maryland-Virginia:* 10 Chesapeake *Massachusetts:* 8 Buzzards, Plymouth 9 Annisquam *Massachusetts Bay:* 10 Lynn Harbor *Mediterranean Sea:* 8 Valencia 9 Famagusta 10 Khalij Surt 11 Gulf of Sidra, Gulf of Tunis, Syrtis Major *Mozambique:* 5 Memba, Pemba *Nantucket Sound:* 5 Lewis *New Brunswick:* 13 Passamaquoddy *Newfoundland:* 4 Hare 5 White 7 Fortune *New Guinea:* 3 Oro 5 Berau, Hansa 11 McCluer Gulf *New Jersey:* 5 Great 7 Raritan 8 Barnegat 9 Little Egg *New York:* 7 Jamaica *New Zealand:* 5 Hawke 6 Tasman *North Carolina:* 7 Roanoke 9 Albemarle *Northern Ireland:* 12 Belfast Lough *North Sea:* 4 Lyse 9 Hardanger *Northwest Territories:* 5 Wager 8 Bathurst, Franklin 9 Frobisher 12 Prince Albert *Norway:* 3 Tys 4 Bokn, Tana 5 Lakse, Sogne *Norwegian Sea:* 4 Nord, Salt, Stor, Vest 5 Ranen 8 Scoresby 9 Trondheim *Ontario:* 4 Owen *Oregon:* 4 Coos *Philippines:* 5 Baler, Pilar, Sogod 6 Butuan 9 Davao Gulf, Leyte Gulf, Panay Gulf *Puget Sound:* 4 Carr, Case *Quebec:* 6 Ungava *Red Sea:* 4 Foul *Rhode Island:* 12 Narragansett 13 Sakonnet River *Russia:* 5 Chaun 8 Sakhalin, White Sea 12 Sea of Okhotsk *Santo Cruz Islands:* 8 Basilisk *Sea of Japan:* 13 Peter the Great *Solomon Islands:* 4 Deep 8 Huon Gulf *South Africa:* 5 Table *South Carolina:* 4 Bull *South China Sea:* 4 Bias, Datu, Siam, Taya 5 Dasol, Subic, Subig 6 Brunei, Paluan 7 Camranh 8 Lingayen, Thailand *Spain:* 5 Cadiz *Spitsbergen:* 3 Ice 4 Bell 5 Kings *Strait of Gibraltar:* 7 Tangier *Sumatra:* 5 Bajur 10 Koninginne *Tasmania:* 5 Storm *Tyrrhenian Sea:* 6 Naples 7 Paestum 13 Gulf of Salerno *Wales:* 5 Burry *Washington:* 5 Dabob 6 Skagit 11 Grays Harbor

inmate 7 convict 8 occupant, prisoner 10 inhabitant

inmost part 4 core, pith 5 heart 6 center, depths, kernel, marrow 7 nucleus

inn 5 fonda, hotel, house, lodge, motel 6 hostel, posada, tavern 7 auberge, hospice 8 hostelry, wayhouse 9 roadhouse 11 caravansary, public house 13 boardinghouse *German:* 8 gasthaus *Turkish:* 6 imaret

innards 4 guts 6 tripes 7 viscera 8 entrails, stuffing

innate see **inherent**

inner 3 gut 5 close, focal 6 hidden, inside, inward, middle, secret 7 central, nuclear, private 8 familiar, interior, internal, personal, visceral 9 concealed, essential *combining form:* 3 ent 4 ento

innervate 4 move 5 pique, rouse 7 provoke, quicken 9 galvanize

Innisfail 4 Eire, Erin 7 Ireland

innkeeper 4 host 8 boniface, hosteler, publican

innocence 6 purity 7 naiveté 8 chastity 9 ignorance, silliness 10 simplicity 11 artlessness, sinlessness, unawareness

innocent 4 free, good, pure, void 5 clean, empty, legal, licit, naive, white 6 candid, chaste, devoid, lawful, simple 7 artless, natural, unaware 8 harmless, ignorant, unguilty, virtuous 9 blameless, childlike, crimeless, destitute, exemplary, faultless, guileless, guiltless, ingenuous, innocuous, permitted, righteous, stainless, unstained, unstudied, unsullied, untainted 10 inculpable, legitimate, tenderfoot, unaffected, unblamable, unschooled 11 inobnoxious, inoffensive, unoffending, unoffensive, white-handed 12 simpleminded, unartificial, unsuspecting

innocuous 4 flat 5 banal, bland 6 jejune, pallid 7 insipid, sapless 8 harmless 9 driveling 10 namby-pamby 11 inoffensive, unoffending, unoffensive 13 insignificant

innovation 6 change 7 novelty, wrinkle 11 vicissitude

innovative 3 new 5 novel 8 creative, original 9 demiurgic, deviceful, inventive

innovator 5 maker 7 builder 8 original, producer 9 architect, developer 10 originator

innuendo 4 clue, hint, slur 8 allusion 10 intimation 11 implication, insinuation

insect 367

innumerable 4 many 6 legion, myriad, untold 9 countless, uncounted 10 numberless

Ino *brother:* 9 Polydorus *father:* 6 Cadmus *grandfather:* 6 Agenor *husband:* 7 Athamas *mother:* 8 Harmonia *sister:* 5 Agave 6 Semele 7 Autonoe *son:* 8 Learchus, Palaemon 10 Melicertes

inobtrusive 5 quiet, tasty 7 subdued 8 tasteful 10 restrained

inoculate 5 admit, enter, imbue, steep 6 infuse, leaven 7 implant, suffuse

inoffensive 8 harmless 9 innocuous, peaceable

inopportune 8 ill-timed, mistimed, untimely

inordinate 5 dizzy, extra, undue 6 wanton 7 extreme, surplus 8 towering 9 excessive 10 disorderly, exorbitant, gratuitous, immoderate, irrational, untempered 11 extravagant, intemperate, superfluous, uncalled-for 12 unmeasurable, unreasonable, unrestrained 13 extraordinary

in passing 6 obiter 8 by the bye, by the way 12 incidentally

in perpetuum 4 ever 6 always 7 forever 8 evermore 9 eternally 11 forevermore

inquest 5 probe 6 search 7 delving, inquiry, probing 8 research 11 examination 13 investigation

inquietude 6 unrest 7 ailment, anxiety, ferment, turmoil 10 uneasiness 11 restiveness 12 restlessness 13 Sturm und Drang

inquire 3 ask 4 seek 5 query, study 6 search 7 examine 8 question 9 catechize 10 scrutinize 11 interrogate, investigate

inquiry 5 audit, check, probe, query, quest 7 delving, hearing, probing 8 question, research, scrutiny 11 catechizing, examination, questioning 13 investigation

inquisition 4 hunt 5 probe, quest 6 search 7 delving, inquiry, probing 8 grilling, research 11 examination 13 investigation

inquisitive 4 nosy 5 peery 6 prying, snoopy 7 curious 11 questioning

inquisitor *Spanish:* 10 Torquemada

in re 4 as to 5 about, as for 7 apropos 9 as regards, regarding 10 as respects, concerning, respecting

in respect to see in re

inroad 4 raid 5 foray 6 invade 7 overrun 8 invasion 9 incursion, irruption, overswarm 12 encroachment

ins and outs 5 ropes 6 quirks 7 details 8 minutiae, oddities 11 incidentals, particulars 13 peculiarities, ramifications

insane 3 mad, off 4 daft, nuts 5 crazy, daffy, dotty, loony, manic, nutsy, nutty, rocky, silly, wacky, wrong 6 absurd, crazed, cuckoo, maniac, screwy, teched 7 cracked, foolish, lunatic, strange, tetched, touched, unsound, witless 8 demented, deranged, fanciful, mindless 9 bedlamite, brainsick, eccentric, fantastic, imaginary, visionary 10 bewildered, disordered, distracted, distraught, irrational, reasonless, ridiculous, unbalanced 11 harebrained, impractical, unrealistic 12 crackbrained, preposterous, unreasonable

insane asylum 6 bedlam 8 loony bin, madhouse, nuthouse 9 funny farm 10 booby hatch, sanatorium, sanitarium

insanity 5 folly, mania 6 dotage, frenzy, lunacy 7 madness 8 delirium, delusion, dementia, hysteria, illusion 9 acromania, craziness, dottiness, silliness, unbalance 10 aberration, alienation 11 derangement, distraction, fatuousness, foolishness, psychopathy, witlessness 13 hallucination, senselessness

insatiable 6 crying, greedy, urgent 7 exigent 8 pressing, yearning 9 clamorous, demanding, voracious 10 quenchless 11 importunate 12 unappeasable, unquenchable

inscribe 4 book, etch, list 5 enter, print, write 6 enroll 7 catalog, engrave, engross, impress, imprint 8 enscroll

inscription 5 title 6 legend 7 epigram, epitaph, heading 8 epigraph 10 enrollment

inscrutable 6 arcane, mystic, secret 8 numinous 9 mysterial, unguessed 10 cabalistic, mysterious, unknowable 12 impenetrable, unfathomable

insect 3 bee, bug, fly 6 beetle *adult:* 5 imago *antenna:* 4 palp 6 feeler *butterfly:* (see **butterfly** entry) *combining form:* 5 entom 6 entomo *covering:* 6 chitin *immature:* 4 grub, pupa 5 larva, nymph 6 larvae (plural), maggot 8 wriggler 9 chrysalis 11 caterpillar *kind:* 3 ant 4 flea, moth, wasp 5 aphid, scale 6 bedbug, beefly, beetle, cicada, earwig, hornet, mantid, mantis, mayfly 7 ant lion, cricket, firefly, June bug, katydid, ladybug, termite 8 honeybee, horsefly, housefly, lacewing, mosquito, stinkbug 9 bumblebee, butterfly, damselfly, dragonfly 10 silverfish, springtail 11 grasshopper 12 walkingstick *luminous:* 7 firefly 8 glowworm *molt:* 7 ecdysis *moth:* 4 luna 6 sphinx 8 Cecropia 10 Polyphemus *multi-legged:* 8 diplopod 9 centipede, millepede, millipede *part:* 4 palp 5 cerci (plural) 6 cercus, labium, labrum, ocelli (plural), thorax 7 antenna, maxilla, ocellus 8 antennae (plural), mandible, maxillae (plural) 9 proboscis, spiracles 10 ovipositor 11 exoskeleton *pest:* 4 flea, lice (plural), mite 5 louse, midge, scale 7 blowfly, termite 8 horsefly, housefly, mealybug 9 cockroach, gypsy moth 10 boll

weevil, Hessian fly, silverfish *science:*
10 entomology *wingless:* **4** flea, lice (plural) **5** louse **8** firebrat **10** silverfish
11 bristletail

insecticide 3 DDT **5** mirex, naled
6 endrin, ronnel **7** lindane, phorate **8** carbaryl, dieldrin, rotenone **9** chlordane

insecure 4 weak **5** shaky **6** dickey, infirm, unsafe, unsure, wobbly **8** hesitant, rootless, unstable, wavering **9** fluctuant, unassured, uncertain **11** questioning, unconfident

inseminate 7 implant, instill **9** fertilize
10 impregnate

insensate 4 dull, hard **5** rocky, silly **6** simple **7** fatuous, foolish, witless **8** mindless **9** bloodless, brainless, nitwitted, unfeeling **10** anesthetic, unanimated **11** sheepheaded

insensibility 4 coma **6** apathy, phlegm, torpor **8** lethargy, stoicism **12** indifference

insensible 4 cold, dead, dull, hard, numb, rapt **5** blunt, rocky, stoic **6** asleep, intent, numbed, obtuse, stolid **7** brutish, callous **8** absorbed, benumbed, comatose, deadened, hardened, obdurate **9** apathetic, bloodless, engrossed, impassive, unfeeling **10** anesthetic, phlegmatic, unapparent **11** unconscious **12** anesthetized

insensitive 4 dead, dull, hard, numb **5** aloof, rocky **6** asleep, numbed **8** benumbed, deadened **9** bloodless, unfeeling **10** anesthetic, impossible **11** indifferent, unconcerned **12** anesthetized, unresponsive **13** insusceptible, unimpressible, unsusceptible

insert 5 admit, enter, infix, inlay, inlet, inset **6** fill in **7** implant, obtrude, throw in **9** interpose **11** intercalate, interpolate

in short 7 briefly, tersely **9** concisely **10** succinctly **11** laconically

inside 5 inner **6** closet, hushed, inward, within **7** private **8** interior **11** withindoors **12** confidential *combining form:* **3** end **4** endo

insidious 3 sly **4** deep, foxy, wily **6** artful, astute, crafty, subtle, tricky **7** cunning, gradual **8** guileful **9** deceitful **10** fraudulent **11** treacherous

insight 6 wisdom **8** sagacity, sageness, sapience **9** intuition **10** anschauung **11** discernment, penetration **13** intuitiveness, sagaciousness, understanding

insightful 4 sage, wise **6** sophic **7** gnostic, knowing **9** sagacious **10** discerning, perceptive **11** penetrating **13** knowledgeable

insignia 4 mark, sign **5** badge **6** emblem **8** brassard **10** decoration

insignificant 4 puny **5** dinky, light, minor, petty, small **6** casual, lesser, little, paltry **7** trivial **8** inferior, small-fry, trifling **9** pointless, secondary, senseless, small-beer,

small-time, unmeaning **10** shoestring **11** meaningless, minor-league, unimportant

insincere 5 false, lying **6** double, shifty, tricky **7** feigned **8** mala fide, slippery **9** deceitful, deceptive, dishonest **10** left-handed, mendacious, untruthful **11** double-faced **12** hypocritical

insinuate 4 hint, worm **5** foist, imply **6** allude, edge in, fill in, impugn, impute, insert, work in **7** ascribe, connote, implant, instill, suggest, throw in **9** introduce

insipid 3 dry **4** arid, dull, flat, mild, pale, soft, tame, thin, weak **5** banal, bland, dusty, plain, vapid **6** feeble, jejune, slight, swashy, watery **7** mundane, prosaic, sapless, subdued, tedious, tenuous **8** bromidic, lifeless, ordinary, unsavory, waterish, weariful **9** driveling, dryasdust, innocuous, pointless, savorless, tasteless, wearisome **10** flavorless, monotonous, namby-pamby, spiritless, wishy-washy **11** commonplace

insistent 4 dire **6** crying, dogged, urgent **7** burning, clamant **8** emphatic, forceful, pressing **9** assertive, clamorous, obtrusive **10** imperative, resounding **11** persevering

insolence 5 nerve **6** insult **8** audacity, boldness, contempt, rudeness **9** arrogance, hardihood, impudence **10** brazenness, disrespect, effrontery **11** haughtiness, presumption **12** impertinence

insolent 4 bold, pert, rude **5** lofty, proud, saucy **6** brazen **7** defiant, haughty, uncivil **8** arrogant, cavalier, impolite, impudent, superior **9** audacious **10** disdainful, imperative, peremptory, procacious, ungracious **11** dictatorial, impertinent, magisterial, overbearing **12** contumelious, discourteous, supercilious **13** high-and-mighty

insouciance 6 apathy **8** lethargy **9** disregard, lassitude, unconcern **11** disinterest **12** heedlessness, indifference, listlessness

insouciant 8 carefree, heedless **9** lightsome **10** free-minded **11** indifferent, unconcerned **12** happy-go-lucky, lighthearted

inspect 3 con, vet **4** view **5** check, study **6** notice, review, survey **7** canvass, check up, examine, observe **8** question **9** catechize, check over **10** scrutinize

inspiration 4 muse **6** animus, genius, vision **8** afflatus **9** brainwave, influence **10** brainstorm **13** enlightenment

inspire 3 get **4** fire, move, stir, sway **5** carry, elate, endow, endue, exalt, imbue, set up, touch **6** affect, excite, foment, incite, inhale, strike **7** animate, commove, enliven, impress, quicken **8** motivate, spirit up **9** breathe in, encourage, influence, stimulate **10** exhilarate

instability 9 shakiness **10** insecurity **11** inconstancy, unfixedness **12** unsteadiness **13** changeability, unsettledness

install 4 seat, vest 5 chair 6 induct, invest, settle 8 ensconce, enthrone, initiate 9 establish

instance 4 case, cite, item, name 5 proof 6 detail, ground, reason, sample 7 example, mention, request, specify 8 exponent, sampling, specimen 9 exemplify 10 illustrate, particular, suggestion 11 case history, instigation 12 illustration

instant 4 dire, time, wink 5 crack, flash, jiffy, point, shake, trice, while 6 minute, moment, second, urgent 7 current, exigent, present, twinkle 8 existent, juncture, occasion, pressing, todayish 9 immediate, insistent, twinkling 10 imperative, present-day

instantaneous 4 fast 5 quick, rapid 9 immediate, momentary 10 transitory 11 hair-trigger

instanter 3 now 4 away 5 right 6 at once 8 directly, first off 9 forthwith, right away 11 immediately

instantly 3 now 4 away 5 right 6 at once 8 directly, first off 9 forthwith, right away 10 pressingly

instead 4 else 6 in lieu, rather 11 alternately 13 alternatively

instigate 3 set 4 abet, fire, goad, hint, move, plan, plot, prod, spur, urge 5 impel, raise, set on 6 excite, foment, incite, scheme, stir up, whip up 7 provoke, suggest 8 motivate 9 stimulate

instill 5 imbue, infix 6 impart, infuse 7 implant 9 inculcate, introduce

instinctive 6 innate, normal 7 natural, regular, typical 8 inherent, visceral, will-less 9 automatic, intuitive, unlearned 10 congenital, unprompted, unreasoned 11 involuntary, spontaneous, unmeditated

institute 3 law 4 rule 5 begin, edict, found, set up, start 6 decree, launch, ordain 7 precept, usher in 8 decretum, initiate, organize 9 establish, introduce, ordinance, originate 10 inaugurate 12 organization

institution 4 rite 5 habit 6 custom 7 fixture 9 enactment 10 foundation 13 establishment *kind:* 6 school 7 academy, college 8 hospital 10 university

instruct 3 bid 4 lead, show, tell, warn 5 coach, drill, guide, order, pilot, steer, teach, train, tutor 6 assign, charge, define, direct, enjoin, inform, school 7 apprise, command, counsel, educate 8 acquaint, engineer 9 prescribe 10 discipline

instruction 6 advice, lesson 7 precept 8 teaching, training, tutelage 9 catechism, education, schooling 10 directions *place of:* 6 school 7 academe

instructive 8 didactic 10 moralistic, moralizing 11 educational

instrument 4 deed, gear, mean, tool 5 agent, means, organ 6 agency, device, medium, tackle 7 channel, utensil, vehicle 8 ministry 9 appliance, machinery 13 paraphernalia *aircraft:* 3 aba 5 radar, radio 7 compass 8 yawmeter 9 altimeter, gyroscope 10 altazimuth, tachometer 11 transponder *calculating:* 6 abacus 8 computer 9 slide rule *combining form:* 4 labe, stat 5 meter *graphic:* 6 camera 8 otoscope 9 telescope 10 binoculars, microscope 11 fluoroscope, stethoscope, stroboscope 12 bronchoscope, oscilloscope, spectrograph, spectroscope *measuring:* 5 clock, gauge, radar, scale, sonar 7 alidade, ammeter, balance, caliper, sextant, transit 8 quadrant 9 altimeter, astrolabe, barometer, bolometer, manometer, pedometer, sonometer, voltmeter 10 anemometer, fathometer, hydrometer, hygrometer, micrometer, radiometer, radiosonde, spirometer, tachometer, theodolite 11 chronometer, lie detector, range finder, seismograph, speedometer, thermometer 12 electroscope, galvanometer, oscillograph, oscilloscope 13 Geiger counter, potentiometer *medical:* 5 curet 6 lancet, plexor, trocar 7 curette, forceps, probang, specula (plural), tenacula (plural) 9 tenaculum *radiation-producing:* 5 laser, maser; (see also **implement; musical instrument; tool**)

instrumental 6 useful 7 helpful 9 conducive 11 serviceable

instrumentality 5 agent, force, means, might, organ, power 6 agency, energy, medium 7 channel, vehicle 8 ministry

insubordinate 5 rebel 6 unruly 7 riotous 8 factious, mutinous 9 seditious 10 headstrong, rebellious, refractory 11 disaffected, disobedient, dissentious, intractable, uncompliant, uncomplying 12 contumacious, recalcitrant, ungovernable

insubstantial 4 airy, puny, weak 5 frail 6 feeble, flimsy 7 fragile, tenuous, unsound 8 bodiless, decrepit 9 imaginary, unfleshly 10 intangible, unembodied 11 disembodied 12 apparitional

insufferable 7 painful 10 unbearable 11 distressing, intolerable

insufficiency 4 lack 7 failure, paucity, poverty 8 scarcity, shortage, underage 9 inability 10 inadequacy, scantiness, scarceness 11 defalcation

insufficient 3 shy 5 scant, short, unfit 6 scanty, scarce 7 failing, lacking, unequal, wanting 9 defective 10 inadequate, incomplete

insular 5 local 6 narrow 7 limited 8 confined, detached, islander, isolated, regional, secluded 9 illiberal, insulated, parochial, sectarian, sectional, small-town 10 prejudiced, provincial, restricted

insulate 6 cut off, enisle, island 7 isolate
8 close off 9 segregate, sequester

insult 4 gibe, gird, jeer, mock, rump, slap,
slur 5 abase, abuse, fleer, flout, scoff,
scorn, shame, sneer, taunt 6 debase,
deride, humble, offend, revile 7 affront,
degrade, despite, disdain, obloquy, offense,
outrage 8 contempt, disgrace, ignominy,
ridicule 9 contumely, humiliate, insolence
10 opprobrium 12 unpleasantry,
vituperation

insurance 8 guaranty, warranty 10 protection *agency:* 7 actuary 8 adjuster
11 underwriter *term:* 6 policy 7 annuity
8 coverage 9 bordereau 11 beneficiary

insure 5 cinch, guard 6 assure, shield
7 protect 9 safeguard 10 underwrite

insurgent 5 rebel 6 anarch 8 factious,
frondeur, mutineer, mutinous, revolter
9 anarchist, seditious 10 rebellious 12 contumacious 13 insubordinate

insurrection 6 mutiny, revolt 8 uprising
9 rebellion

insurrectionist 5 rebel 6 anarch 8 frondeur, mutineer, revolter 10 malcontent

insusceptible 6 immune 9 impassive,
unfeeling 10 insentient 12 unresponsive

intact 5 sound, whole 6 entire, maiden,
unhurt, virgin 7 perfect 8 complete, flawless, unbroken, unmarred, virginal
9 undamaged, uninjured, untouched
10 unimpaired

intangible 4 airy, rare, thin 5 vague 6 aerial, slight 8 aeriform, ethereal 10 immaterial, impalpable, unapparent 11 incorporeal

integer 5 digit 6 figure, number 7 chiffer,
numeral 11 whole number

integral 3 sum 4 full 5 whole 6 choate,
entire, entity, system 7 inbuilt, perfect
8 complete, inherent, totality 9 component,
composite 11 constituent

integrate 3 mix, sum 4 fuse, join, link,
tune 5 blend, merge, unify, unite, whole
6 attune, embody, entity, system 7 arrange,
combine, compact, conform, conjoin 8 coalesce, organize, totality 9 harmonize, reconcile 10 articulate, coordinate, proportion,
symphonize, synthesize 11 desegregate

integrity 5 honor 7 honesty, probity
9 constancy, soundness, wholeness
10 entireness, honestness, perfection
12 absoluteness, completeness, incorruption 13 honorableness

integument 4 coat 5 testa 7 coating,
cuticle 8 covering, envelope 10 investment
combining form: 4 derm, scyt 5 derma,
scyto 6 dermia, dermis 9 dermatous

intellect 3 wit 4 mind, nous 5 brain
6 genius, pundit, reason 7 egghead,
thinker 9 intuition, mentality 12 intelligence 13 comprehension, understanding

intellectual 5 brain 6 brainy, mental
7 Brahmin, egghead, psychic 8 highbrow,
longhair 9 reasoning 10 double-dome,
highbrowed, reflective

intelligence 3 wit 4 mind, news, word
5 brain, sense 6 acumen, advice, brains,
notice, reason, wisdom 7 tidings 8 judgment, learning, sagacity 9 knowledge, mentality, mother wit, speerings 10 brainpower,
shrewdness

intelligent 4 keen, wise 5 acute, alert,
aware, sharp, smart, sound 6 adroit, astute,
brainy, bright, clever, shrewd 7 cunning,
knowing, logical 8 rational, sensible 9 brilliant, ingenious, sagacious 10 reasonable
11 quick-witted, ready-witted 13 knowledgeable, perspicacious

intelligentsia 7 clerisy 8 literati, vanguard 10 avant-garde, illuminati

intelligible 5 clear, lucid, plain 8 luminous 10 conceptual 13 supersensible,
suprasensuous

intemperance 6 excess 10 debauchery
11 drunkenness 12 immoderation

intemperate 4 hard 5 harsh 6 bitter, brutal, rugged, severe 7 drunken, extreme, violent 8 bibulous, rigorous 9 bibacious, crap-
ulous, excessive, inclement 10 gluttonous,
immoderate, inordinate 12 unrestrained
13 overindulgent

intend 3 aim, try 4 mean, plan, plot
5 essay, spell 6 assign, denote, design,
import, scheme, strive 7 add up to, attempt,
connote, destine, express, propose, purpose, signify 8 endeavor 9 designate

intended 6 fiancé 7 engaged, fiancée
8 proposed 9 affianced, betrothed

intense 3 hot 4 deep, hard, keen 5 acute,
great, vivid 6 ardent, fervid, fierce, severe,
strong 7 extreme, fervent, furious, serious,
vicious, violent, zealous 8 enhanced, powerful, profound, stressed, terrible, vehement 9 assiduous, desperate, excessive,
exquisite 10 aggravated, emphasized,
heightened 11 accentuated
12 concentrated

intensify 4 rise 5 exalt, mount, rouse
6 accent, deepen, stress 7 enhance,
sharpen 8 heighten, increase, redouble
9 aggravate, emphasize 10 accentuate,
aggrandize 11 concentrate

intensity 5 depth 6 energy, fervor 7 passion 8 fervency, loudness

intensive 5 eager 7 zealous 10 exhaustive 12 concentrated *pronoun:* 6 itself,
myself 7 herself, himself 8 yourself 9 ourselves 10 themselves, yourselves

intent 3 aim, set 4 deep, plan, rapt, will
5 eager, fixed, sense 6 animus, design,
import 7 decided, earnest, engaged, meaning, minding, purport, purpose, riveted, set-

tled, wrapped **8** absorbed, conation, decisive, diligent, immersed, resolute, resolved, sedulous, volition, watching **9** engrossed, wrapped up **10** determined

intention **3** aim, end **4** goal, hope, plan, wish **6** animus, design, desire, object, scheme **7** meaning, purpose

intentional **5** meant **7** advised, studied, willful, willing, witting **8** designed, proposed, purposed, unforced **9** designful, voluntary **10** considered, deliberate **12** premeditated, unprescribed

intentionally **9** on purpose, purposely

inter **4** bury, tomb **5** plant **6** entomb, inhume **7** lay away, put away **9** sepulcher, sepulture

interact **4** join **5** merge, unite **7** combine **9** cooperate **11** collaborate

interbreed **5** cross **9** cross-mate, hybridize

intercede **6** step in **7** mediate **9** arbitrate, interpose, intervene

intercept **4** curb, grab, stop, take **5** block, catch, check, seize **6** cut off, hinder **9** forestall, interrupt

intercessor **6** broker **8** advocate, mediator **9** go-between, middleman **12** entrepreneur

interconnect **4** join **5** blend, unite **10** anastomose, inosculate

intercourse **5** truck **7** contact, dealing, traffic **8** business, commerce, converse **9** communion **10** connection **12** conversation **13** communication

intercross **9** decussate, hybridize

interdict **3** ban **4** veto **5** taboo **6** enjoin, forbid, outlaw **8** prohibit **9** proscribe

interest **4** care, good, lure, pull **5** claim, pique, share, snare, stake, tempt **6** appeal, arouse, behalf, excite, regard **7** attract, benefit, concern, passion, welfare **9** advantage, attention, curiosity, fascinate, tantalize, titillate, well-being **10** absorption, enthusiasm, excitement, prosperity

interested **4** rapt **6** caring **7** partial **8** partisan

interfere **3** bar **4** balk, foil, fool **5** block **6** baffle, butt in, hinder, horn in, impede, meddle, step in, tamper, thwart **7** intrude, mediate, trouble **8** busybody, obstruct **9** frustrate, incommode, intervene **10** discommode, monkey with, tamper with

interim **3** gap **5** break **6** acting, breach, hiatus, lacuna, pro tem, supply **8** meantime **9** temporary **10** pro tempore

interior **3** gut **5** belly, bosom, heart, inner **6** center, inland, inside, inward, within **8** visceral **9** viscerous

interject **6** fill in **7** throw in **9** introduce

interjection *agreement:* **6** righto **7** right on *attention-getter:* **3** hey **4** ahem, psst

5 heigh *calling pigs:* **5** sooey *cheer:* **3** rah **6** hooray, hurrah, hurray *contempt:* **3** poh **4** pooh **5** pshaw *disappointment:* **4** rats **6** shucks *disapproval:* **3** fie *disbelief:* **2** aw **3** huh *disgust:* **3** bah, pah, ugh **4** pugh, rats **5** faugh, nerts, yecch **6** phooey *dismay:* **2** oy **4** oh no *dismissal:* **3** git *farewell:* **4** by-by, ciao **6** bye-bye, so long *gratitude:* **8** gramercy *greeting:* **2** hi **4** ciao **5** aloha, hello *hesitation:* **2** er, um *in golf:* **4** fore *in hunting:* **6** yoicks *in marching:* **3** hup *joy:* **4** whee **6** hooray, hurrah, hurray, yippee **7** whoopee *mild apology:* **4** oops **5** woops **6** whoops *mild oath:* **3** gad, gor **4** darn, drat, egad, geez, gosh, heck, jeez **5** egads, golly, zooks **6** cracky, jiminy, zounds **7** begorra, begorry, gee whiz, jeepers, jimminy **8** gadzooks, gee whizz **13** gee whillikers, gee whillikins *of warning:* **8** gardyloo *O.K.:* **5** wilco *pain:* **2** ow **4** ouch, yipe **5** yipes *peace:* **6** shalom, sholom *regret:* **4** alas **5** alack **8** lackaday *relief:* **4** phew *request:* **7** prithee *silence:* **2** sh **3** shh *sneeze:* **5** achoo **6** atchoo **7** kerchoo *sorrow:* **4** alas **5** alack **8** lackaday *stop:* **4** whoa *surprise:* **2** ah, ho, lo, oh **3** aha, huh, oho, wow **4** gosh, oops, yipe **5** blimy, yipes, zowie **6** blimey *to a horse:* **4** whoa **6** giddap *toast:* **5** salud, skoal **6** cheers, prosit **7** l'chayim *triumph:* **3** aha, hah **6** eureka; (see also **exclamation**)

interlace **3** mix **5** braid, twine, weave **9** alternate, interlock **10** intertwine, interweave **11** intersperse

interlard **3** mix **6** mingle **7** diffuse

interlope **4** fool **6** butt in, horn in, meddle **7** intrude **8** busybody **9** interfere **10** monkey with, tamper with **11** intermeddle

interlude **4** lull, rest **5** break, idyll, pause, spell **7** episode, respite **8** breather, entr'-acte, interval, meantime **9** meanwhile

intermediary **3** mid **4** mean **5** agent, organ **6** agency, broker, center, medium, middle **7** central, channel, vehicle **8** mediator, ministry **9** go-between, middleman **10** interagent

intermediate **3** mid **4** fair, mean, so-so **6** broker, center, medium, middle, step in **7** average, between, central, fairish **8** middling **9** go-between, middleman **11** intervening **12** entrepreneur *combining form:* **3** mes **4** medi, meso **5** medio

intermediator **6** broker **9** go-between, middleman **12** entrepreneur

interment **6** burial **9** sepulture **10** inhumation

interminable **7** endless, eternal, lasting **8** constant, infinite, unending **9** boundless, ceaseless, continual, limitless, permanent, perpetual, unceasing, unlimited **10** continuous **11** everlasting

intermission 4 rest, stop **5** break, pause **6** recess **7** latency, respite **8** abeyance, abeyancy, doldrums, dormancy, interval **10** quiescence, quiescency, suspension **11** cold storage, parenthesis **12** interruption

intermit 4 stay **5** check, defer, delay **6** arrest, hold up, put off **7** hold off, suspend **8** hold over, postpone, prorogue **9** interrupt

intermittent 6 broken, cyclic, fitful, serial **7** checked, iterant **8** arrested, cyclical, metrical, periodic, rhythmic, seasonal, sporadic **9** alternate, iterative, recurrent, recurring, spasmodic **10** alternated, isochronal, occasional, periodical, rhythmical **11** interrupted, isochronous

intermix 6 mingle **8** comingle, immingle **9** commingle **11** intermingle

intermixture 5 blend **7** amalgam **12** amalgamation **13** miscegenation

intern 3 jug **4** jail **6** immure **7** confine, impound, trainee **8** bastille, imprison **9** constrain

internal 3 gut **4** home **5** inner **6** inward, native **7** private **8** domestic, inherent, interior, visceral **9** intrinsic, viscerous **10** subjective *prefix:* **5** intra

internal organs 4 guts **6** vitals **7** viscera **8** entrails

international organization 2 UN **3** FAO, IAM, ICJ, IFC, ILO, ITO, ITU, OAS, WHO, WMO **4** IAAF, IABA, IAEA, IARU, IATA, ICAO, IFIP, IMCO, NATO **5** ICFTU, SEATO **6** UNESCO, UNICEF

internuncio 5 envoy **6** bearer **7** carrier, courier **8** emissary **9** messenger

interpolate 3 add **5** admit, annex, enter **6** append, fill in, insert **7** throw in **8** superadd **9** introduce **11** intercalate

interpose 4 cast, push, toss **5** shove, throw **6** butt in, fill in, insert, meddle, step in, thrust **7** intrude, mediate, obtrude, throw in **8** moderate **9** arbitrate, insinuate, intercede, interfere, intervene, introduce, negotiate

interpret 4 limn **5** gloss, image **6** decode, depict, render **7** comment, explain, expound, picture, portray **8** annotate, construe, describe, spell out **9** delineate, exemplify, explicate, represent **10** commentate

interpretation 7 meaning, reading, version **8** exegesis **9** construal, rendering **11** explanation, translation

interpretive 8 exegetic **10** expository **11** explanatory, explicatory **12** expositional

interregnum 5 break **8** interval

interrogate 3 ask **4** quiz **5** grill, query **7** examine, inquire **8** question **9** catechize

interrupt 4 halt, stay, stop **5** break, check, cut in, defer, put in, stall **6** arrest, chip in **7** break in, chime in, disturb, suspend **8** postpone **9** intercept

interruption 3 gap **4** rent, rift **5** break, pause, split **6** breach, hiatus, lacuna **7** caesura, latency

intersect 4 meet **5** cross **8** crosscut, traverse **9** decussate **10** crisscross

intersection 8 crossing, junction **10** crossroads

intersperse 7 diffuse, scatter

interval 3 gap **4** lull **5** break, comma, pause, space **6** breach, hiatus, lacuna **7** caesura, interim, respite **9** pausation **11** parenthesis *music:* **4** rest

intervene 4 part **5** sever **6** divide, step in **7** mediate **8** separate **9** intercede, interpose

interweave 3 mix **4** fuse, join, link **5** blend **9** associate

intestinal fortitude 4 grit, guts, sand **5** nerve, pluck, spunk **6** mettle, spirit **7** courage **8** backbone **10** resolution

intestine 3 gut **4** tube **5** bowel, canal **6** inward, viscus **7** viscera (plural) *combining form:* **3** col **4** coli, colo **5** enter **6** entero *part:* **5** cecum, colon, ileum **6** rectum **7** jejunum **8** duodenum

in the same place 6 ibidem

intimacy 7 liberty **9** closeness **10** experience **11** familiarity **12** acquaintance

intimate 3 gut **4** cozy, fond, hint, next **5** amigo, close, crony, imply, inner, pally, privy, thick **6** attest, chummy, friend, impart, loving, notify, secret, sexual **7** bespeak, betoken, comrade, connote, devoted, nearest, suggest **8** announce, familiar, inherent, visceral **9** close-knit, companion, confidant, elemental, essential, ingrained, insinuate, intrinsic, viscerous **10** deep-seated, indwelling **11** cater-cousin **12** acquaintance, confidential

intimation 3 cue **4** clue, hint, wind **5** shade, tinge, trace **6** breath, shadow, strain, streak **7** inkling **8** telltale **10** suggestion

intimidate 3 awe, cow **4** bait, ride **5** abash, alarm, bully, chivy, daunt, deter, force, hound, scare **6** badger, coerce, compel, hector, oblige **7** bluster, buffalo, dragoon, overawe, terrify **8** bludgeon, browbeat, bulldoze, bullyrag, dispirit, disquiet, frighten **9** constrain, strong-arm, terrorize

intolerant 5 irate, upset **6** averse, narrow, stuffy **7** bigoted, waspish **8** dogmatic, obdurate, outraged, snappish, worked up **9** fractious, hidebound, illiberal, impatient, irritable **10** brassbound, disdainful, inflexible, prejudiced, unenlarged **11** small-minded, unindulgent **12** antipathetic, contemptuous, narrow-minded, unforbearing **13** unsympathetic

intonation 4 tone **5** chant **6** accent **10** recitation

in toto 3 all **4** just **5** quite, stick **6** wholly **7** exactly, utterly **10** altogether

intoxicant 5 booze, drink **6** liquor **7** alcohol, spirits **9** aqua vitae

intoxicated 3 cut, wet **4** high **5** blind, dopey, drunk, fried, loopy, soppy, stiff, tight, tipsy **6** elated, looped, rum-dum, sloppy, sodden, soshed, stewed, stoned, tanked, zonked **7** drunken, excited, maudlin, muddled, slopped, sozzled, unsober **8** cockeyed, polluted, squiffed, turned-on **9** inebrious **11** alcoholized, exhilarated

intoxication 7 elation **8** euphoria **11** drunkenness, inebriation

intractable 4 wild **6** mulish, unruly **7** willful **8** indocile, mutinous, obdurate, perverse, stubborn **9** fractious, obstinate **10** bullheaded, headstrong, refractory, self-willed, unyielding **11** unteachable **12** pertinacious, recalcitrant, ungovernable **13** undisciplined

intransigent 5 tough **7** willful **8** stubborn **9** obstinate, unpliable **10** self-willed, unyielding **12** pertinacious

intrepid 4 bold **5** brave, hardy **6** daring, heroic **7** gallant, valiant **8** fearless, resolute, unafraid, valorous **9** audacious, dauntless, undaunted **10** courageous

intricate 4 hard **5** fancy **6** daedal, knotty **7** arduous, complex, gordian **8** involved **9** Byzantine, difficult, elaborate **11** complicated **12** labyrinthine **13** sophisticated

intrigue 4 plot **5** amour, cabal, covin **6** affair, appeal, devise, excite, scheme **7** attract, beguile, collude, connive, liaison **8** cogitate, conspire, contrive, interest, practice **9** fascinate, machinate, scheme out **10** conspiracy **11** machination

intrinsic see **inherent**

intrinsically 5 per se **6** as such

introduce 4 lead, moot **5** admit, begin, enter, found, set up, usher **6** broach, fill in, insert, launch, unveil, work in **7** bring up, implant, install, instill, pioneer, precede, preface, present, throw in, usher in **8** acquaint, initiate, innovate, organize **9** establish, insinuate, institute, interject, interpose, originate

introduction 5 debut, proem **7** introit, preface, prelude **8** entrance, exordium, foreword, overture, preamble, prologue, protases (plural), protasis **9** prelusion **12** prolegomenon

introductory 7 initial, nascent **8** proemial **9** beginning, prefatial, prefatory, preludial, prelusive **11** prefatorial, preliminary, preparative

intrude 5 cut in **6** bother, butt in, horn in,

impose, invade, meddle, muscle, pester **7** disturb, presume **8** chisel in, encroach, entrench, infringe, trespass **9** interfere, interlope, interpose

intrusive 4 busy **7** curious **9** butting in, officious **10** meddlesome **11** impertinent **13** polypragmatic

in truth 6 indeed, really, verily **8** actually

intuition 7 insight **8** instinct **10** anschauung, sixth sense **11** second sight

inundate 5 drown, flood, swamp, whelm **6** deluge, engulf **8** overflow, submerge **9** overwhelm

inundation 4 pour **5** flood, spate **6** deluge **7** niagara, torrent **8** cataract, flooding, overflow **9** cataclysm

inure 3 use **4** wont **5** steel, train **6** harden, season **7** toughen **8** accustom **9** habituate **10** discipline **11** familiarize

inutile 6 draffy, drossy, no-good **7** nothing **8** unworthy **9** valueless, worthless

invade 4 loot, raid **5** foray **6** ravage **7** assault, overrun, pillage, plunder **8** encroach, entrench, infringe, permeate, trespass **9** overswarm **11** impenetrate

invalid 3 bad, mad **4** null, void **6** infirm, sickly **9** illogical, sophistic **10** fallacious, irrational, reasonless, unreasoned **11** nonrational, null and void **12** unreasonable

invalidate 4 undo **5** abate, annul, quash **6** offset **7** abolish, nullify **8** negative **9** discredit **10** circumduct, counteract, neutralize

invaluable 6 costly **8** precious **9** priceless **11** inestimable

invariable 4 same **5** fixed **6** steady **7** uniform **8** constant **9** continual, immovable, immutable, unfailing, unmovable, unvarying **10** consistent, inflexible, unchanging **11** inalterable, unalterable **12** unchangeable, unmodifiable

invariably 4 ever **6** always **7** forever **10** constantly **11** continually, perpetually

invasion 4 raid **5** foray **6** attack, inroad **9** incursion, intrusion, irruption, offensive **12** encroachment, entrenchment

invective 5 abuse **6** tirade **7** abusive, obloquy **8** diatribe, jeremiad, scurrile **9** contumely, damnatory, philippic, truculent **10** censorious, scurrility, scurrilous, vituperous **11** opprobrious, reproachful **12** billingsgate, condemnatory, contumelious, denunciatory, vituperation, vituperative, vituperatory

inveigh 4 kick, rail **6** except, object **7** protest **9** fulminate **11** expostulate, remonstrate

inveigle 4 bait, coax, lure, toll **5** decoy, snare, tempt **6** allure, cajole, entice, entrap, lead on, seduce **8** persuade

invent 4 coin, mint **5** frame **6** cook up,

create, design, devise, make up, patent, vamp up **7** concoct, dream up, fashion, hatch up, pioneer **8** conceive, contrive, discover, engineer, envision **9** fabricate, formulate, originate

invention 7 coinage, fiction **8** creation **10** brainchild, concoction, innovation **11** contrivance, origination

inventive 7 fertile, teeming **8** creative, fruitful, original **9** demiurgic, deviceful, ingenious **10** innovative, innovatory, productive

inventor 4 sire **5** maker **6** author, father **7** creator, founder **8** engineer, original **9** architect, generator, innovator, patriarch **10** discoverer, introducer, originator *air brake:* **12** Westinghouse *air conditioning:* **7** Carrier *automobile:* **7** Daimler *ballpoint pen:* **4** Loud *barbed wire:* **7** Glidden *barometer:* **10** Torricelli *bifocal lens:* **8** Franklin *camera:* **7** Eastman *cash register:* **5** Ritty *cotton gin:* **7** Whitney *cylinder lock:* **4** Yale *dirigible:* **8** Zeppelin *dynamite:* **5** Nobel *electric battery:* **5** Volta *electric fan:* **7** Wheeler *electric organ:* **7** Hammond *electric razor:* **6** Schick *electric stove:* **7** Hadaway *elevator:* **4** Otis *fountain pen:* **8** Waterman *friction match:* **6** Walker *gyrocompass:* **6** Sperry *helicopter:* **8** Sikorsky *hot-air baiioon:* **11** Montgolfier *incandescent lamp:* **6** Edison *induction motor:* **5** Tesla *lawn mower:* **5** Hills *Linotype:* **12** Mergenthaler *logarithm:* **6** Napier *machine gun:* **7** Gatling *microphone:* **8** Berliner *movable type:* **9** Gutenberg *parachute:* **9** Blanchard *pendulum clock:* **7** Huygens *phonograph:* **6** Edison *photography:* **6** Niepce, Talbot **8** Daguerre *piano:* **10** Cristofori *radio:* **7** Marconi *reaper:* **9** McCormick *revolver:* **4** Colt *rocket engine:* **7** Goddard *safety pin:* **4** Hunt *safety razor:* **8** Gillette *sewing machine:* **4** Howe *sleeping car:* **7** Pullman *spinning jenny:* **10** Hargreaves *steamboat:* **5** Fitch **6** Fulton, Miller, Rumsey **8** Jouffroy *steam engine:* **4** Watt *steam locomotive:* **7** Stephenson *stethoscope:* **7** Laennec *submarine:* **7** Holland *tank:* **7** Swinton *telegraph:* **5** Morse *telephone:* **4** Bell *telescope:* **10** Lippershey *television:* **5** Baird **6** Nipkow **8** Zworykin **10** Farnsworth *torpedo:* **9** Whitehead *vulcanized rubber:* **8** Goodyear *writing for the blind:* **7** Braille *zipper:* **6** Judson

inventory 3 sum **4** fund, list **5** hoard, stock, store, sum up, tally **6** digest, record, supply, survey **7** account, backlog, catalog, itemize, nest egg, reserve, specify, summary, summate **8** condense, nutshell, register, tabulate **9** checklist, enumerate, epitomize, reservoir, stockpile, summarize, synopsize

inverse 4 turn **6** change, revert **7** reverse **8** contrary, opposite **9** transpose **10** transplace *prefix:* **2** ob

inversion 4 turn **7** reverse, turning **8** reversal **9** about-face, turnabout, volteface **11** changeabout, reversement

invert 4 flip, turn **6** change **7** reverse, uranian, uranist **8** turn over **9** transpose **10** homosexual, transplace

invertebrate 4 weak **5** sissy **7** doormat, milksop **8** boneless, impotent, weakling **9** forceless, jellyfish, spineless **10** emasculate, inadequate, namby-pamby, pantywaist **11** ineffective, ineffectual, Milquetoast, mollycoddle, slack-spined *kind:* **4** worm **6** insect, sponge **7** mollusk **8** arachnid **12** coelenterate

invest 4 gird, veil, wrap **5** adorn, array, beset, dress, endow, endue, imbue, steep **6** clothe, confer, enfold, enwrap, induct, infuse, leaven, ordain, shroud **7** besiege, empower, enclose, envelop, ingrain, install, instate, suffuse

investigate 3 pry **4** poke, sift **5** probe, study **6** go into, search **7** dig into, examine, explore, inquire **8** look into, muckrake, prospect, research **9** delve into **10** scrutinize **11** inquire into

investigation 5 probe, quest **6** survey **7** delving, inquest, inquiry, probing **8** research, sounding **9** surveying **11** inquisition

investigator 4 dick **6** sleuth **7** gumshoe **8** hawkshaw, sherlock **9** detective

investiture 5 siege **8** blockage **9** inaugural, induction **10** initiation **12** inauguration, installation

inveterate 3 old, set **5** fixed, sworn **6** rooted **7** abiding, chronic, settled **8** deepdyed, enduring, habitual, hardened, lifelong **9** confirmed, hard-shell, ingrained, long-lived, perennial **10** continuing, deep-rooted, deepseated, entrenched, persistent, persisting **11** established

Invictus author 6 Henley

invidious 6 bitter, odious **7** envious, envying, hateful, jealous **8** libelous **9** abhorrent, green-eyed, injurious, malignant, maligning, obnoxious, repellent, repugnant, revulsive, vilifying **10** abominable, calumnious, defamatory, detestable, detracting, detractive, detractory, scandalous, slanderous

invigorate 4 stir, zest **5** brace, cheer, rally, renew, rouse **7** animate, enliven, fortify, refresh, restore **8** energize, vitalize **9** reinforce, stimulate **10** exhilarate, rejuvenate, strengthen

in vino ____ 7 veritas

inviolable 4 holy, pure **6** chaste, divine, sacred **7** blessed **8** hallowed **9** undefiled

10 sacrosanct 11 consecrated
13 incorruptible

Invisible Man, The *author:* 5 Wells

Invisible Man author 7 Ellison (Ralph)

invitation 4 call, lure 7 bidding, proffer,
request 8 entreaty, proposal, stimulus
9 incentive 10 attraction, suggestion
11 proposition

invite 3 ask, bid 4 call, lure 5 tempt
6 allure, call in, entice, summon 7 request,
solicit

invoice 3 tab 4 bill 5 score 7 account
9 reckoning, statement

invoke 3 beg 4 pray 5 crave, plead
6 appeal, effect 7 beseech, enforce,
entreat, implore 9 implement, importune
10 supplicate

involuntary 6 forced, reflex 8 will-less
9 automatic, impulsive, unwitting 10 compulsory, unintended, unprompted
11 instinctive, spontaneous, unmeditated
13 unintentional

involve 4 mire 6 embody, engage, entail,
take in, tangle 7 concern, contain, embrace,
embroil, include, subsume 8 comprise,
entangle 9 encompass, implicate 10 complicate, comprehend

involved 6 daedal, knotty 7 complex, gordian, muddled 8 affected, confused,
enmeshed 9 Byzantine, concerned, elaborate, entangled, intricate 10 implicated,
interested 11 complicated 12 labyrinthine

invulnerable 10 invincible, unbeatable
11 impregnable, indomitable

inward 5 entad, inner 6 inside, mental
8 interior, internal 9 innermore, intestine,
spiritual

inwards 4 guts 6 inside, tripes, within
7 innards, insides, viscera 8 entrails, interior 9 internals

Io *father:* 7 Inachus *guard:* 5 Argus *son:*
7 Epaphus

iodine source 4 kelp

Iolcus king 5 Aeson 6 Pelias

Iole *captor:* 8 Heracles, Hercules *father:*
7 Eurytus *husband:* 6 Hyllus

ion 6 ligand *kind:* 5 anion 6 cation
8 thermion *suffix:* 3 ium 5 onion

Ion *father:* 6 Apollo *mother:* 6 Creusa
stepfather: 6 Xuthus

Ionesco play 5 Chairs (The) 10 Rhinoceros (The) 11 Bald Soprano (The)

iota 3 bit, jot, ray 4 atom, mite, whit
5 crumb, grain, ounce, speck 6 tittle
7 smidgen 8 molecule, particle

IOU 4 debt *part:* 3 owe, you

Iowa *capital:* 9 Des Moines *college, university:* 3 Coe 5 Dordt, Drake, Loras *nickname:* 12 Hawkeye State *state bird:*
9 goldfinch *state flower:* 8 wild rose

Iphicles *brother:* 8 Heracles, Hercules
mother: 7 Alcmene *son:* 6 Iolaus

Iphigenia *brother:* 7 Orestes *father:*
9 Agamemnon *mother:* 12 Clytemnestra
sister: 7 Electra

Iphis' daughter 6 Evadne

Iran *capital:* 6 Tehran 7 Teheran *monetary unit:* 4 rial *oil center:* 6 Abadan

Iranian 7 Persian *language:* 5 Farsi
7 Kurdish, Persian *non-Persian people:*
5 Kurds *parliament:* 6 Majlis *sect:* 4 Shia
5 Sunni *sect member:* 6 Shiite 7 Sunnite
title: 4 shah

Iraq *capital:* 7 Baghdad *monetary unit:*
5 dinar

irascible 5 cross, huffy, irate, ratty, surly,
testy 6 cranky, ireful, snappy, tetchy,
touchy 7 bristly, peevish, peppery 8 choleric, petulant, snappish 9 fractious, impatient, irritable, querulous, temperish 10 passionate 11 belligerent, hot-tempered
12 cantankerous 13 quick-tempered

Ira's father 6 Ikkesh

irate 3 mad 4 waxy 5 angry, wroth 6 ireful, wrathy, wrothy 7 enraged, furious
8 choleric, incensed, provoked, wrathful

ire 3 mad 4 fury, rage 5 anger, wrath
6 enrage, madden, temper 7 incense,
steam up, umbrage 9 infuriate 10 exasperate 11 indignation 12 exasperation

Ireland see **Eire**

Irene 3 Pax *father:* 4 Zeus 7 Jupiter
mother: 6 Themis

irenic 4 calm 7 pacific 8 pacifist, peaceful
9 peaceable 10 nonviolent 12 conciliatory,
pacificatory

Iris *father:* 7 Thaumas *mother:* 7 Electra

Irish 4 Erse 6 Celtic, Gaelic *accent:*
6 brogue *battle cry:* 3 abu 4 aboo *cattle:*
5 Kerry *clan:* 4 sept *combining form:*
7 Hiberno *coronation stone:* 7 Lia Fail
cudgel: 9 shillalah 10 shillelagh *death
spirit:* 7 banshee *dirge:* 8 ullagone *dog:*
6 setter 7 terrier *elf:* 10 leprechaun *exclamation:* 3 aru 5 arrah *festival:* 4 feis *flag
color:* 5 green, white 6 orange *flower:*
8 shamrock *girl:* 4 lass 6 lassie 7 colleen
goblin: 5 pooka *god:* 3 Ler 5 Dagda
6 Aengus *goddess:* 4 Badb, Bodb 6 Brigit 8 Morrigan *harp:* 8 clarsach *hero:*
9 Cuchulain, Cuchullin 11 Chuchulainn *heroine:* 7 Deirdre *king:* 9 Brian Boru *lake:*
5 lough *language:* 6 Gaelic *legislature:*
4 Dail *militant force:* 3 IRA *nationalist:*
7 Parnell 8 O'Connell *nationalist society:*
8 Sinn Fein *noble:* 6 flaith *patron saint:*
7 Patrick *theater:* 5 Abbey *writing system:* 4 ogam 5 ogham; (see also **Gaelic;
Celtic**)

Irish moss 7 seaweed 9 carrageen

irk 3 try, vex 4 fret, gall, pain 5 anger,

annoy, peeve, pique, upset **6** abrade, bother, harass, nettle, ruffle, strain, stress **7** provoke, trouble **8** distress, exercise, irritate **10** exasperate

Irma ___ **7** La Douce

iron 4 hard **5** gyves, press **6** ferrum, fetter, strong **7** adamant, manacle, shackle **8** handcuff, obdurate **9** unbending **10** adamantine, brassbound, inexorable, inflexible, relentless, unyielding *combining form:* **5** ferri, ferro, sider **6** sidero *German:* **5** eisen *relating to:* **6** ferric **7** ferrous *symbol:* **2** Fe *wrought:* **5** mitis

ironbound 5 harsh, rough **6** craggy, jagged, rugged, uneven **7** scraggy **8** asperous, scabrous, unsmooth

Iron City 10 Pittsburgh

ironclad 5 fixed **8** constant **9** immovable, immutable **10** inflexible, invariable **11** inalterable, unalterable **12** unchangeable

ironhanded 5 rigid **6** strict **8** rigorist, rigorous **9** draconian, stringent **12** unpermissive

ironhearted 5 stony **7** callous **8** hardened, obdurate **9** heartless, unfeeling **10** hard-boiled **11** cold-blooded **13** unsympathetic

ironic 3 wry **6** biting **7** caustic, cutting, cynical, mordant, satiric **8** sardonic **9** sarcastic, trenchant

iron ore 8 goethite, hematite, limonite, siderite, taconite **9** magnetite

Iron Pants 6 Patton

irons 5 bonds, gyves **6** chains **7** fetters **8** manacles, shackles

Iroquois tribe 6 Cayuga, Mohawk, Oneida, Seneca **8** Onondaga

irradiate 5 edify **6** illume, uplift **7** improve **8** illumine **9** enlighten **10** illuminate

irrational 3 mad **5** crazy **6** absurd, insane **7** invalid **8** demented **9** illogical, senseless, sophistic **10** fallacious, reasonless, ridiculous, unreasoned **11** nonrational **12** unreasonable

irrefutable 4 sure **7** certain **8** positive **10** conclusive, inarguable **11** indubitable **12** indisputable **13** incontestable, uncontestable

irregular 3 odd **5** queer **6** fitful, off-key, patchy, random, spotty, uneven, unique **7** aimless, deviant, devious, erratic, strange, unaimed, unequal **8** aberrant, abnormal, atypical, informal, lopsided, partisan, peculiar, singular, sporadic, unstable, unsteady, variable **9** anomalous, desultory, divergent, eccentric, guerrilla, haphazard, hit-or-miss, spasmodic, unnatural, unregular, unsettled **10** asymmetric, changeable, designless, inconstant, off-balance, unbalanced, unofficial **11** exceptional, purposeless **12** over-

balanced, unconsidered, unsystematic *combining form:* **4** anom **5** anomo **6** anomal **7** anomali, anomalo

irregularity 7 anomaly **8** asperity, disorder **9** roughness **10** inequality, unevenness

irrelevant 7 foreign **9** unrelated **10** extraneous, immaterial, inapposite, irrelative **11** impertinent, inessential, unessential, unimportant **12** inapplicable **13** insignificant

irreligious 5 pagan **6** amoral, unholy **7** godless, impious, profane, ungodly, unmoral **8** indevout, undevout **11** blasphemous **12** sacrilegious

irreparable 8 cureless, hopeless **9** incurable, insanable, uncurable **10** impossible **11** immedicable **12** irredeemable, irremediable **13** irreclaimable, irrecoverable, irretrievable, uncorrectable, unrecoverable

irreproachable 4 good, pure **8** flawless, innocent, spotless, virtuous **9** blameless, errorless, exemplary, exquisite, faultless, guiltless, righteous **10** immaculate, impeccable, inculpable, unblamable

irresolute 6 fickle, unsure, wobbly **7** halting **8** doubtful, hesitant, unstable, wavering **9** faltering, tentative, uncertain, undecided **10** changeable, inconstant **11** fluctuating, vacillating, vacillatory **12** wigglewaggle

irresponsible 4 wild **8** carefree, careless, feckless, reckless **9** uncareful **10** incautious, unreliable **12** unanswerable, undependable **13** unaccountable, untrustworthy

irreverent 6 unholy **7** impious, profane, ungodly **10** unhallowed

irrevocable 4 firm **5** final **9** immutable **11** unalterable **12** irreversible, unchangeable, unmodifiable, unrepealable **13** nonreversible

irrigation ditch 5 flume **6** sluice **7** acequia

irritability 6 choler **9** petulance **11** fretfulness *abnormal:* **8** erethism

irritable 4 edgy **5** cross, huffy, raspy, techy, testy, waspy, whiny **6** cranky, ornery, snappy, tetchy, touchy, twitty **7** fretful, peevish, pettish, prickly, raspish, waspish **8** choleric, petulant, prickish, snappish **9** fractious, impatient, irascible, querulent, querulous, splenetic **12** cantankerous, disagreeable, querulential

irritant 4 pest **6** bother, pester, plague **8** nuisance **9** annoyance, besetment **10** botherment **11** botheration **12** exasperation

irritate 3 get, irk, rub, try, vex **4** fret, gall, goad, huff, rile, roil **5** anger, annoy, chafe, grate, peeve, pique, spite **6** abrade, badger, bother, burn up, harass, hector, madden, needle, nettle, offend, put out, ruffle **7** affront, inflame, provoke **8** acerbate

9 aggravate, stimulate **10** exacerbate, exasperate

irritated 5 irate, testy **7** fretful, peevish **8** choleric **9** impatient, irascible **11** hot-tempered

irritation 4 itch, rash, sore **5** uredo **9** annoyance **10** excitation

irrupt 4 spew **5** belch, eject, eruct, expel **7** intrude **8** disgorge

irruption 4 raid **5** foray **6** inroad **8** invasion **9** incursion

I.R.S. employee 4 acct **10** accountant

Iru's father 5 Caleb

Isaac *father:* **7** Abraham *mother:* **5** Sarah *son:* **4** Esau **5** Jacob *wife:* **7** Rebekah

isabella *brother:* **7** Claudio *husband:* **9** Vincentio

Isabella I *country:* **5** Spain *home:* **7** Castile *husband:* **9** Ferdinand

Isaiah's father 4 Amoz

Iscah *brother:* **3** Lot *father:* **5** Haran *sister:* **6** Milcah

Iseult, Isolde *beloved:* **7** Tristan *husband:* **4** Mark

Ishbak *father:* **7** Abraham *mother:* **7** Keturah

Ishbosheth's father 4 Saul

Ishi *father:* **6** Appaim *son:* **6** Zoheth

Ishmael 6 pariah **7** outcast **8** castaway, derelict, outsider **11** offscouring, untouchable *father:* **4** Azel **7** Abraham, Pashhur **9** Jehonanan, Nethaniah *mother:* **5** Hagar *son:* **5** Massa **6** Zebadiah

Ishmaiah's father 7 Obadiah

Ishpah's father 6 Beriah

Ishpan's father 7 Shashak

Ishtar *brother:* **7** Shamash *father:* **3** Anu, Sin *lover:* **6** Tammuz

Ishuah's father 5 Asher

Ishui's father 4 Saul **5** Asher

Isis *brother:* **6** Osiris *father:* **3** Geb *husband:* **6** Osiris *mother:* **3** Nut *son:* **4** Sept **5** Horus

Islam *adherent:* **6** Moslem, Muslim *founder:* **8** Mohammed, Muhammad *god:* **5** Allah *priest:* **4** imam *scriptures:* **5** Koran; (see also **Muslim**)

island 3 cay, key **4** holm, isle **5** atoll, islet **6** cut off, enisle, skerry **7** crannog, isolate **8** close off, insulate, separate **9** segregate, sequester *Admiralty group:* **5** Manus *Adriatic Sea:* **3** Vis **4** Brac, Cres, Hvar **5** Ciovo, Mljet, Solta **6** Lesina, Pharus *Aegean Sea:* **4** Scio **5** Chios, Khios, Samos, Thira **6** Ikaria, Lemnos, Lesbos, Limnos **7** Nikaria **8** Mitilini, Mytilene, Santorin **10** Sakis-Adasi, Susam-Adasi *Alaska:* **4** Adak, Atka, Attu, Kuiu **8** Wrangell *Aleutian group:* **3** Rat **4** Adak, Akun, Attu **5** Amlia, Kiska, Umnak **6** Kanaga, Tanaga, Unimak **8** Amchitka, Unalaska *American*

Samoa: **3** Ofu, Tau **4** Rose **6** Swains *Andaman Sea:* **4** Mali **5** Tavoy *Antarctica:* **5** Scott, Young *Apostle group:* **3** Oak **4** Long, Sand **5** Outer **8** Madeline, Michigan, Stockton *Arafura Sea:* **5** Dolak *Arctic Archipelago:* **6** Baffin **8** Victoria *Arctic Ocean:* **5** Senja *Australian:* **5** Cocos **8** Tasmania *Azores:* **4** Pico **5** Corvo, Faial *Bahamas:* **3** Cat, Rum **4** Long **5** Abaco, Exuma **6** Andros, Inagua **7** Acklins, Crooked **8** Watlings **9** Eleuthera, Mayaguana **11** San Salvador *Bahrain:* **5** Sitra **8** Muharraq *Balearic group:* **5** Ibiza **7** Majorca, Menorca, Minorca **8** Mallorca *Baltic Sea:* **4** Moon, Muhu **5** Faron, Mukhu, Rugen, Worms **6** Vormsi **7** Gotland **8** Bornholm, Gothland, Gottland *Barents Sea:* **4** Bear *Bay of Biscay:* **2** Re *Bay of Naples:* **5** Capri *Bay of Panama:* **4** Naos *Bering Sea:* **5** Medny **7** Nunivak **10** Big Diomede **13** Little Diomede *Bismarck Archipelago:* **5** Lihir **10** New Britain *Bristol Channel:* **5** Lundy *Buzzards Bay:* **9** Cuttyhunk *Canadian:* **5** Banks, Devon **6** Baffin **8** Bathurst, Melville, Somerset, Victoria **9** Anticosti, Ellesmere **10** Cape Breton **11** Axel Heiberg, Southampton **12** Newfoundland, Prince Edward *Canaries:* **6** Gomera **7** La Palma **8** Tenerife **9** Lanzarote *Cape Verde:* **4** Fogo, Maio, Mayo **5** Brava, Rombo *Caribbean Sea:* **4** Cuba **5** Aruba, Utila, Vache **6** Tobago **7** Antigua, Curaçao, Jamaica **8** Barbados, Dominica, Trinidad **10** Guadeloupe, Martinique, Puerto Rico; (see also **Virgin group**) *Carolines:* **5** Sorol **6** Ponape **9** Ascension *Chagos Archipelago:* **11** Diego Garcia *Channel group:* **4** Herm, Sark **5** Lihou, Sercq **6** Jersey **8** Guernsey *Chesapeake Bay:* **4** Deal, Kent **5** Smith, Watts *Chukchi Sea:* **6** Herald *Comoro group:* **7** Mayotte *Congo River:* **4** Bamu *Cook group:* **4** Atiu **5** Mauke *Croatia:* **3** Krk, Pag, Rab **5** Susak, Unije *Cyclades:* **3** Ios, Kea, Nio **4** Ceos, Keos, Milo **5** Delos, Melos, Milos, Naxos, Paros, Siros, Syros **6** Andros, Dhilos **7** Amorgos, Cythnos, Kithnos, Kythnos, Mykonos *Denmark:* **3** Als, Fyn, Mon **4** Aero, Fano, Moen, Mors **5** Alsen, Funen, Moers, Samso **8** Bornholm **13** Fanum Fortunae *D'Entrecasteaux group:* **8** Kaluwawa **9** Fergusson *Dodecanese group:* **3** Coo, Cos, Kos **4** Caso, Lero, Simi, Syme **5** Kasos, Leros, Lipso, Lisso, Patmo, Telos **6** Calino, Lipsos, Nisiro, Patmos **7** Calimno, Nisiros, Nisyros **8** Kalymnos *East River:* **5** Ward's **7** Welfare **9** Roosevelt *England's:* **7** Britian **9** Britannia **12** Great Britain *English Channel:* **5** Wight *Faeroes:* **4** Vago **5** Bordo, Sando *Fiji:* **4** Koro

5 Mango, Vatoa *Florida Keys:* 4 Long, Vaca, West 5 Largo 7 Big Pine 9 Matecumbe, Sugarloaf *Fox group:* 5 Umnak 6 Akutan, Unimak 8 Unalaska *French:* 7 Corsica 12 New Caledonia *French Polynesia:* 4 Rapa, Reao, Ua Pu 5 Ua Pau *Frisian group:* 3 Rom 4 Föhr, Sylt 5 Amrum, Juist, Mando, Texel 6 Borkum 7 Ameland 8 Langeoog, Pellworm, Vlieland 9 Helgoland, Norderney *Futunas:* 5 Alofi *Galápagos:* 5 Pinta 7 Chatham, Isabela 8 Abingdon 10 Albermarle *Georgia:* 5 Tybee *Germany:* 4 Fohr 7 Fehmarn 9 Helgoland 10 Heligoland *Greater Antilles:* 4 Cuba 7 Jamaica 10 Hispaniola, Puerto Rico *Greece:* 4 Milo, Rodi 5 Creta, Crete, Hydra, Idhra, Kriti, Rodos, Tenos, Tinos 6 Euboea, Evvoia, Hydrea, Rhodes, Rhodus 9 Negropont 10 Negroponte *Grenadines:* 5 Union *Gulf of Alaska:* 6 Kodiak *Gulf of Bothnia:* 5 Karlö *Gulf of Carpentaria:* 5 Maria 6 Groote 7 Eylandt *Gulf of Guinea:* 7 Sao Tomé 8 Principe, Sao Thomé 11 Saint Thomas *Gulf of Mexico:* 3 Cat 5 Lobos *Gulf of Panama:* 3 Rey *Gulf of St. Lawrence:* 5 Brion *Gulf of Thailand:* 3 Kut 5 Samui *Haiti:* 6 Gonave *Hawaii:* 4 Maui, Oahu 5 Kauai, Lanai 6 Niihau 7 Molokai 9 Kahoolawe *Hudson Bay:* 5 Coats *Indian Ocean:* 4 Mahé, Nias 5 Heard, Pemba 7 La Dique, Praslin, Réunion 8 Sri Lanka, Zanzibar 9 Mauritius 10 Madagascar *Indonesia:* 4 Bali, Biak, Java, Maja, Muna, Nias, Rhio, Riau, Roma, Roti, Savu, Sawu 5 Batam, Boano, Buton, Djawa, Japen, Lakor, Moena, Riouw, Rotti, Rupat, Sawoe, Solor, Sumba, Wetar, Wokam 6 Butung, Flores, Jappen, Lombok, Madura, Padang, Roepat, Romang, Soemba 7 Celebes, Madoera, Sumatra, Sumbawa 8 Boetoeng, Soembawa, Sulawesi 10 Bandanaira, Banda Neira, Sandalwood *Inner Hebrides:* 4 Coll, Eigg, Iona, Jura, Muck, Mull, Skye 5 Canna, Gigha, Islay, Tiree, Tyree *Ionian group:* 5 Corfu, Paxos, Zante 6 Cerigo, Ithaca, Leukas, Levkas 10 Santa Maura *Iran:* 5 Shahi *Ireland:* 4 Aran *Irish Sea:* 3 Man *Italy:* 4 Elba 6 Sicily 8 Sardinia *Japan:* 3 Iki, Uku 4 Naru, Yezo 5 Awaji, Fukae, Fukue, Hondo, Shodo 6 Honshu, Kyushu 7 Shikoku 8 Hokkaido 10 Shodoshima *Java Sea:* 4 Laut *Kiribati:* 6 Tarawa *Kuril group:* 4 Urup 5 Ketoi, Matua 6 Iturup 7 Etorofu, Matsuwa 8 Kunashir 9 Kunashiri *Lake Champlain:* 5 Grand *Lake Erie:* 9 North Bass, South Bass 10 Middle Bass *Lake Huron:* 8 Drummond 10 Manitoulin *Lake Michigan:* 3 Hog 4 High 6 Beaver *Lake Ontario:* 5 Wolfe *Lake Superior:* 4 Sand 6 Royale 7 Manitou *Lake Winni-*

peg: 5 Hecla *largest:* 9 Greenland *Leeward group:* 5 Nevis 7 Antigua, Barbuda, Redonda 8 Anguilla, Sombrero 10 Montserrat, Saint Kitts 13 St. Christopher *legendary:* 7 Cipango *Lesser Sundas:* 4 Alor 5 Ombai *Leti group:* 3 Moa 5 Lakor *Line group:* 5 Flint 6 Malden, Vostok 7 Fanning, Palmyra 8 Starbuck 9 Christmas *Long Island Sound:* 4 City, Hart 5 Goose, Harts *Loyalty group:* 3 Uea 4 Lifu, Maré, Uvea 5 Lifou *Malay Archipelago:* 5 Kisar, Larat, Timor 6 Borneo 9 New Guinea *Malaysia:* 6 Penang, Pinang 13 Prince of Wales *Malta:* 4 Gozo *Marianas:* 4 Maug, Rota 5 Pagan 6 Saipan *Marquesas group:* 4 Eiào, Ua Pu 6 Hatutu, Hiva Oa, Ua Huka 7 Tahuata 8 Fatu Hiva, Nuku Hiva *Marshall group:* 5 Wotho, Wotje 8 Eniwetok 9 Kwajalein *Massachusetts:* 9 Nantucket *Mediterranean Sea:* 4 Elba 5 Corfu, Crete, Malta 6 Cyprus, Euboea, Rhodes, Sicily 7 Corsica 8 Sardinia *Midway group:* 4 Sand 7 Eastern *Moluccas:* 4 Buru 5 Ambon, Ceram, Seram 6 Boeroe *Mozambique channel:* 10 Juan de Nova *Myanmar:* 5 Daung, Kadan, Lanbi *Narragansett Bay:* 5 Rhode 8 Prudence 9 Aquidneck, Conanicut *Netherlands:* 5 Texel 7 Ameland 8 Vlieland *Netherlands Antilles:* 7 Curaçao *New York:* 4 Fire, Long 9 Gardiners, Roosevelt *New York Bay:* 5 Ellis 6 Staten 7 Liberty 9 Governors, Manhattan *New Zealand:* 5 South, White 7 Chatham, Stewart 8 D'Urville *Niagara River:* 4 Goat *Nile River:* 4 Argo, Roda, Ruda 5 Rhoda 6 Rawdah 11 Elephantine *North Channel:* 3 Mew *Northern Cook group:* 7 Penrhyn 8 Manihiki 9 Tongareva *North Pacific:* 4 Wake *Northwest Territories:* 5 Banks, Bylot, Devon 8 Bathurst, Melville 9 Ellesmere 10 Cornwallis, Resolution 13 Prince of Wales *Norwegian:* 8 Jan Mayen *Norwegian Sea:* 5 Donna, Smola, Vikna *Nova Scotia:* 5 Sable 10 Cape Breton *off Alaska:* 4 Dall 5 Kayak *off Albania:* 5 Sazan 6 Saseno *off Australia:* 4 Dunk *off Belize:* 9 Ambergris *off Brazil:* 4 Apeu 5 Rocas *off British Columbia:* 4 King, Pitt 9 Vancouver *off Cape Cod:* 8 Muskeget 9 Nantucket *off Chile:* 5 Guafo, Mocha *off China:* 5 Ma-tsu 6 Hainan, Quemoy, Taiwan *off Crete:* 5 Dia *off Ecuador:* 4 Puna *off England:* 3 Man 5 Wight 6 Walney *off Florida:* 3 Dog 4 Pine 6 Amelia 7 Pelican, Sanibel 9 Anastasia *off France:* 2 If *off French Guiana:* 6 Devil's *off Georgia:* 10 Cumberland 11 Saint Simons *off Germany:* 4 Sylt *off Greenland:* 5 Disko *off Guinea:* 5 Tombo *off Hispaniolo:* 5 Beata *off Honduras:* 5 Tigre *off Iceland:* 7 Surtsey *off India:* 5 Sagar *off Ireland:* 4 Tory 5 Clare, Clear *off Kenya:* 4 Lamu *off Long Island:* 7 Fishers *off Louisiona:* 5 Marsh *off Maine:* 4 Deer, Orrs 5 Swans 8 Monhegan 11 Mount Desert *off Malay Peninsula:* 6 Phuket 9 Singapore *off Maryland:* 10 Assateague *off Massachusetts:* 4 Plum 7 Naushon *off Mexico:* 7 Cozumel *off Mississippi:* 4 Horn, Ship *off Mmozambique:* 3 Ibo *off New Brunswick:* 10 Campobello *off Newfoundland:* 4 Bell *off Nigeria:* 5 Lagos *off North Carolina:* 5 Bodie *off Norway:* 5 Bomlo, Froya, Hitra, Sotra, Stord, Vardo 8 Hitteren *off Panama:* 5 Coiba 6 Parida *off Poland:* 5 Wolin 6 Wollin *off Puerto Rico:* 4 Crab 7 Culebra, Vieques *off Rhode Island:* 5 Block *off Scotland:* 4 Bute 5 Arran *off South Carolina:* 5 North 6 Parris 10 Hilton Head *off Sri Lanka:* 5 Delft *off Staten Island:* 7 Hoffman *off Sumatra:* 2 We 3 Weh *off Sweden:* 5 Graso, Oland, Vaddo *off Syria:* 5 Arvad, Arwad, Rouad 6 Aradus *off Tanzania:* 5 Mafia, Pemba *off Tasmania:* 5 Bruni, Bruny *off Tunisia:* 5 Jerba 6 Djerba, Meninx *off Venezuela:* 5 Aruba 7 Bonaire 8 Buen Aire *off Virginia:* 5 Wreck *off Wales:* 5 Caldy 6 Caldey *Okinawa group:* 4 Kume *Orkneys:* 3 Hoy *Outer Hebrides:* 5 Barra, Scarp *Palmer Archipelago:* 6 Anvers 7 Antwerp, Brabant *Pearl Harbor:* 4 Ford *Persian Gulf:* 4 Qeys 5 Kharg, Khark *Philippines:* 4 Buad, Cebu, Fuga, Ilin, Poro, Sulu 5 Balut, Batan, Bohol, Coron, Daram, Leyte, Luzon, Panay, Samal, Samar, Sugbu, Talim, Ticao, Verde 6 Negros 7 Masbate, Mindoro, Palawan, Paragua 8 Limasawa, Mindanao 10 Corregidor *Phoenix group:* 4 Hull, Mary 6 Birnie, Canton 9 Enderbury *Puerto Rico:* 4 Mona *Quebec:* 4 Alma *Queen Charlotte group:* 7 Moresby *Red Sea:* 5 Tiran, Zugur, Zuqar *Russia:* 7 Wrangel *Ryukyu group:* 7 Okinawa *St. Lawrence River:* 4 Hare 5 Jesus 8 Montreal *San Francisco Bay:* 5 Angel *Santa Cruz:* 5 Anuda, Ndeni 6 Cherry *Sea of Japan:* 4 Sado 5 Rebun *Sea of Marmara:* 4 Avsa *second largest:* 9 New Guinea *Senegal:* 5 Gorée *Seychelles:* 4 Mahé 7 La Digue, Praslin *Shetland archipelago:* 4 Unst, Yell 5 Foula *Shumagin group:* 4 Unga *Sierra Leone:* 5 Tasso *Society group:* 5 Eimeo, Tahaa, Tahao, Taiti 6 Moorea, Tahiti 8 Otaheite *Solomon group:* 4 Buka, Gizo, Savo 7 Malaita 11 Guadalcanal 12 Bougainville *South Atlantic:* 5 Gough 6 Gough's 11 Saint Helena *South Korea:* 5 Cheju *South of Tokyo:* 3 Iwo 7 Iwo Jima, Naka Iwo *South Orkneys:* 10 Coronation *South Pacific:*

3 Hiu 4 Niue 5 Raoul 6 Savage, Sunday 7 Norfolk 8 Pitcairn *Spitsbergen archipelago:* 4 Edge *Strait of Hormuz:* 5 Qeshm, Qishm *Sulu Archipelago:* 4 Jolo 5 Lapac *Svalbard:* 4 Hope *Sverdrup:* 11 Axel Heiberg 12 Amund Ringnes *Swedish:* 3 Ven 4 Hven 5 Hveen, Orust *Tanzania:* 8 Zanzibar *Texas:* 5 Padre *Thames River:* 7 Sheppey *third largest:* 6 Borneo *Tierra del Fuego:* 5 Hoste *Tonga:* 3 Eua, Foa 4 Uiha 5 Haano *Treasury group:* 4 Mono *Truk group:* 3 Tol 4 Haru, Moen, Udot, Uman 5 Fefan *Tuamotu Archipelago:* 4 Anaa 5 Chain *Turkish:* 5 Imroz 6 Imbros *Tuvalu:* 7 Nanumea 9 Nukufetau *Tyrrhenian Sea:* 6 Ischia 11 Montecristo *Vanuatu:* 3 Api, Epi, Oba 4 Aoba, Gaua, Tana, Vate 5 Efate, Maewo, Tanna *Venezuelan:* 5 Patos 9 La Tortuga *Virgin group, American:* 9 Saint John 10 Saint Croix 11 Saint Thomas *Virgin group, British:* 5 Peter 6 Norman 7 Anegada, Tortola 11 Jost Van Dyke *volcanic:* 5 Tofua 7 Iwo Jima *Wales:* 8 Anglesea, Anglesey, Holyhead *Weddell Sea:* 4 Ross 6 Hearst *Western Samoa:* 5 Upolu 6 Savaii *West Indies:* 4 Mona, Saba, Salt 5 Nevis, Peter, Saona 6 Tobago, Tortue 7 Grenada, Tortuga 8 Trinidad 9 Santa Cruz 10 Concepción, Hispaniola, Montserrat, Saint Croix; (see also **Bahamas; Greater Antilles; Leeward group; Virgin group; Windward group**) *West of England:* 7 Ireland *West Pacific:* 5 Dyaul, Fauro, Ocean 6 Banaba, Marcus 7 Iwo Jima, Kita Iwo 9 Minami Iwo *Windward group:* 10 Martinique *with former penitentiary:* 8 Alcatraz

island group *Alaska:* 3 Rat 8 Aleutian, Pribilof 9 Andreanof, Catherine *Aleutians:* 4 Near *American Samoa:* 5 Manua *Arabian Sea:* 9 Laccadive *Arctic Archipelago:* 8 Sverdrup *Arctic Ocean:* 8 Svalbard 12 Novaya Zemlya *Bahamas:* 5 Berry, Exuma 6 Bimini *Banda Sea:* 5 Damar *Bangladesh:* 5 Hatia, Hatya *Bay of Bengal:* 7 Andaman, Nicobar *between England and France:* 7 Channel *Bismarck Archipelago:* 4 Feni 5 Tabar, Tanga *Bismarck Sea:* 4 Vitu *British:* 7 Bermuda *Caribbean Sea:* 4 Swan 5 Pearl 6 Cayman, Perlas, Pigeon 8 Pichones 10 Grenadines, West Indies *Carolines:* 3 Uap, Yap 4 Truk 5 Nomoi 7 Hogoleu *Central Pacific Ocean:* 4 Line 5 Samoa, Union 6 Danger, Midway 7 Phoenix, Tokelau 8 Manihiki 9 Polynesia 12 Northern Cook *Coral Sea:* 4 Huon *Cuba:* 8 Camaguey *East of Philippines:* 10 Micronesia *East Siberian Sea:* 4 Bear 5 Medvezhi *Ecuador:* 5 Colon 9 Galápagos *England:* 5 Farne *Fiji:* 3 Lau 7 Eastern *Formosa Strait:* 4 Hoko 6 Peng

hu **10** Pescadores *French:* **5** Salut
6 Safety **9** Kerguelen *French Polynesia:*
3 Low **6** Tubuai **7** Austral, Paumotu,
Société, Society, Tuamotu **9** Marquesas,
Touamotou *Germany:* **8** Halligen *Greece:*
6 Aegean, Ionian **8** Cyclades **10** Dodecanese **11** Dodecanesus *Hudson Bay:* **7** Belcher *Indian Ocean:* **7** Aldabra *Indonesia:*
4 Asia, Batu, Pagi, Sula **5** Babar, Batoe,
Pagai, Pageh, Penju, Spice, Wakde
6 Maluku *Ireland:* **4** Aran *Japan:* **5** Osumi
largest: **5** Malay **8** Malaysia *Lesser Antil-*
les: **8** Windward *Malay Archipelago:*
5 Sunda **6** Soenda *Mediterranean Sea:*
8 Baleares, Balearic *Moluccas:* **3** Kai, Kei,
Obi **4** Leti **5** Banda, Letti **8** Tanimbar
9 Timorlaut *New Caledonia:* **7** Loyalty
9 Loyalties *North of Australia:* **9** Melanesia
North of British Isles: **5** Faroe **7** Faeroes
North off Fiji: **5** Hoorn **6** Futuna *North of*
Madagascar: **7** Aldabra **8** Farquhar *North*
of New Caledonia: **5** Belep *North of New*
Guinea: **8** Bismarck **9** Admiralty
11 Admiralties *Northwest Territories:*
5 Parry *off Alaska:* **3** Fox *off Alaska Penin-*
sula: **8** Shumagin *off Cape Cod:* **9** Elizabeth *off eastern Asia:* **5** Kuril **6** Kurile *off*
England: **6** Scilly *off Florida:* **11** Dry Tortu-
gas *off Guinea:* **4** Los **4** Loos *off Hondu-*
ras: **5** Bahia *off Morocco:* **7** Madeira *off*
New Guinea: **3** Aru **4** Aroe *off Nicara-*
gua: **4** Corn *off northern Africa:*
6 Canary **8** Canaries *off northern Austra-*
lia: **7** Dampier *off Sicily:* **5** Egadi **8** Aega-
dian *Outer Hebrides:* **4** Uist *Pago Pago's:*
13 American Samoa *Papua New Guinea:*
5 Green *Persian Gulf:* **4** Tunb *Philip-*
pines: **4** Cuyo **5** Tapul **6** Lubang **7** Basilan, Bisayas, Visayan *Portuguese:*
6 Azores *Quebec:* **8** Magdalen **9** Madeleine *Ryukyus:* **5** Amami *St. Lawrence*
River: **8** Thousand *Sea of Japan:* **3** Oki
Sea of Marmara: **5** Kizil **7** Princes **11** Kizil
Adalar *South Atlantic Ocean:* **8** Falkland,
Malvinas *South China Sea:* **6** Hirata **7** Par-
acel, Spratly *South of New Zealand:*
8 Auckland *South Pacific:* **11** Austronesia
Sulu Sea: **7** Cagayan **9** Cagayanes
Tonga: **5** Vavau *Tyrrhenian Sea:* **5** Ponza
Venezuelan: **4** Aves, Bird **9** Los Roques
West Europe: **12** British Isles *West*
Indies: **6** Virgin **10** Guadeloupe *West of*
French Polynesia: **4** Cook *West of Scot-*
land: **7** Western **8** Hebrides *West Pacific*
Ocean: **4** Duff **5** Bonin, Mapia, Palau,
Pelew **7** Ladrone, Mariana, Solomon, Vanu-
atu **8** Marshall, Treasury **9** Ogasawara
10 Saint David
island nation *Atlantic Ocean:* **9** Cape
Verde *Indian Ocean:* **8** Malagasy, Mal-
gache, Sri Lanka **10** Madagascar, Sey-

chelles *Mediterranean Sea:* **6** Cyprus
Mozambique Channel: **6** Comoro
7 Comores *off southern China:* **6** Taiwan
south of Greenland: **7** Iceland *West*
Indies: **4** Cuba **7** Jamaica **8** Barbados
10 Saint Lucia *West Pacific Ocean:*
5 Nauru *Windward group:* **8** Dominica
island province 12 Prince Edward
island state 6 Hawaii
isle   see **island**
Ismene *brother:* **9** Polynices *father:*
7 Oedipus *mother:* **7** Jocasta *sister:*
8 Antigone *uncle:* **5** Creon
isochronous 8 periodic **9** alternate, recurrent, recurring **10** periodical **12** intermittent
isolate 5 alone, apart **6** cut off, detach,
enisle, island, remove **7** removed, seclude
8 block off, close off, detached, insulate, pinpoint, separate **9** segregate, sequester
13 unaccompanied
Isolde   see **Iseult**
Israel 4 Zion **5** Jacob **6** Canaan **9** Palestine *capital:* **9** Jerusalem *district:* **5** Haifa
7 Central, Tel Aviv **8** Northern, Southern
9 Jerusalem *legislature:* **7** Knesset *mone-*
tary unit: **6** shekel
Israelite   see **Hebrew; Jewish**
Issachar *father:* **5** Jacob *mother:* **4** Leah
issue 4 emit, flow, gush, pour, rise, seed,
stem, vent **5** arise, birth, brood, child, topic
6 effect, emerge, get out, put out, result, scions, sequel, source, spring **7** descent, edition, emanate, give off, give out, outcome,
problem, proceed, progeny, publish, release,
subject **8** bulletin, causatum, children, question, throw off **9** offspring, originate, posterity **10** derive from, distribute, end product
11 consequence, descendants, eventuality,
progeniture
Istanbul *ancient name:* **9** Byzantium *busi-*
ness section: **6** Galata *country:* **6** Turkey
foreign quarter: **4** Pera **7** Beyoglu *park:*
8 Seraglio *residential section:* **7** Uskudar
isthmus *Africa-Asia:* **4** Suez *Greece:*
7 Corinth *North America-South America:*
6 Panama
Italian *article:* **2** il, la **3** gli *automobile:*
4 Fiat *cathedral:* **5** duomo *condiment:*
6 tamara *dialect:* **6** Tuscan **8** Sicilian *dicta-*
tor: **9** Mussolini *family:* **4** Este **5** Cenci,
Savoy **6** Borgia, Medici, Orsini, Pepoli,
Sforza **7** Colonna, Gonzaga, Spinola **8** Visconti *fascist:* **10** Blackshirt *game:* **4** mora
5 bocce, bocci, morra **6** boccie *gentle-*
man: **3** ser **6** signor **7** signore *highway:*
10 autostrada *lady:* **5** donna **7** signora
9 signorina *magistrate:* **7** podesta *opera*
house: **7** La Scala *patriot:* **6** Cavour,
Rienzi, Rienzo **7** Mazzini **9** Garibaldi
reformer: **10** Savanarola *resort:* **4** Lido
5 Abano, Capri **7** Locarno **8** Sorrento

road: 6 strada *sausage:* 6 salami *soup:*
10 minestrone *square:* 6 piazza *street:*
3 via 5 corso *weight:* 5 libra, oncia
Italy *capital:* 4 Rome *monetary unit:* 4 lira
itch 4 ache, long, lust, pine, sigh, stew,
urge 5 crave, yearn 6 desire, hanker, hunger, seethe, thirst 7 craving, longing, passion 8 appetite, pruritus 9 eroticism, hankering, prurience, pruriency 10 aphrodisia,
appetition 11 lustfulness 13 concupiscence, lickerishness *combining form:*
4 psor 5 psoro
itching 8 pruritus 10 avaricious
itchy 5 jumpy 6 grabby, greedy 7 restive
8 covetous, desirous, grasping, prurient
10 prehensile 11 acquisitive
item 3 bit, too 4 also, more, well 5 along,
entry, point, scrap, thing, topic 6 detail,
matter 7 account, article, besides, element,
feature, product 8 clipping, likewise, moreover 9 commodity 10 particular
itemize 4 list 5 count, tally 6 number
7 catalog, specify 8 document, spell out
9 catalogue, enumerate, inventory 10 specialize 13 particularize
iterate 5 renew, resay 6 repeat 7 reprise
10 ingeminate
Ithaca king 8 Odysseus

Ithamar's father 5 Aaron
Ithiel's father 7 Jesaiah
Ithra *son:* 5 Amasa *wife:* 7 Abigail
Ithran's father 6 Dishon, Zophah
Ithream *father:* 5 David *mother:* 5 Eglah
Ithunn's husband 5 Brage, Bragi
itinerant 6 moving, roving 7 migrant,
nomadic, ranging, roaming, vagrant
8 ambulant, rambling, shifting, traveler, vagabond, wanderer 9 transient, unsettled,
wandering, wayfaring 10 ambulatory
11 perambulant, peripatetic
Ittai's father 5 Ribai
Ivanhoe *author:* 5 Scott *character:*
5 Isaac 6 Cedric, Rowena, Ulrica
7 Rebecca, Wilfred 9 Robin Hood
Ivory Coast 11 Cote d'Ivoire *capital:*
7 Abidjan *monetary unit:* 5 franc
ivory-tower 6 dreamy 8 escapist
11 impractical, unpractical, unrealistic
12 nonrealistic
Ixion *descendant:* 7 Centaur *father:*
8 Phlegyas
Izhar's father 6 Ashhur, Kohath
Izliah's father 6 Elpaal
Izrahiah's father 4 Uzzi
Izri's father 8 Jeduthun
Izziah's father 6 Parosh

J

jaal goat 4 ibex
Jaazaniah's father 4 Azur 5 Azzur
    7 Shaphan 8 Jeremiah
jab 3 dig, hit, jog 4 poke, prod, stab
    5 nudge, prick, punch 8 puncture
Jabal *brother:* 5 Jubal *father:* 6 Lamech
    mother: 4 Adah
jabber 3 gab, jaw, yak 4 chat 5 clack,
    Greek 6 babble, drivel, gabble, gibber
    7 blabber, chatter, palaver, prattle 8 non-
    sense 9 gibberish 11 jabberwocky
jabberer 6 gabber, gossip, magpie, prater
    7 blabber 8 prattler 9 bandar-log, blab-
    mouth, chatterer 10 chatterbox
    12 blabbermouth
Jabberwocky author 7 Carroll (Lewis)
Jabesh's son 7 Shallum
jabot 4 fall 5 frill 6 ruffle
jacamar 4 bird
jacare 6 caiman 9 crocodile
___ jacet 3 hic
Jachin's father 6 Simeon
jack 2 up 3 tar 4 card, flag, hike, jump, lift,
    salt 5 boost, color, knave, put up, raise
    6 banner, ensign, pennon, sailor, seaman
    7 mariner, pendant, pennant 8 bannerol,
    increase, standard, streamer 9 sailorman,
    tarpaulin
jackal god 5 Apuat 6 Anubis
jackanapes 3 ape 6 monkey 7 coxcomb
jackass 4 dolt, donk, fool, jerk 5 burro,
    idiot 6 donkey 8 imbecile 10 nincompoop
jackass deer 3 kob 8 antelope
jackdaw 4 bird 7 grackle 9 blackbird
jacket 3 fur 4 coat, Eton, fell, hide, pelt,
    skin 5 grego, parka, wamus 6 anorak,
    blazer, bolero, dolman, jerkin, reefer, wam-
    mus, wampus 7 cassock, doublet, peacoat,
    spencer 8 camisole 10 roundabout
    armored: 5 acton 7 hauberk 9 habergeon
    cowboy's: 8 chaqueta *Scottish:* 4 jupe
    sleeveless: 4 vest 6 bolero, jerkin
    9 waistcoat
jackhammer 5 drill 9 rock drill
jackknife 4 dive 6 barlow *game:*
    11 mumblety-peg
jackleg lawyer 7 shyster 11 pettifogger
jack-of-all-trades 6 tinker 8 handyman
Jack of clubs 3 pam
jack-o'-lantern 7 pumpkin

jackpot 4 pool 5 award, kitty 7 bonanza
    8 windfall 9 pot of gold
jackrabbit 4 hare
Jack's companion 4 Jill
jackstay 3 bar, rod 4 rope 5 horse 7 rig-
    ging, support
Jacob *brother:* 4 Esau *daughter:* 5 Dinah
    father: 5 Isaac *father-in-law:* 5 Laban
    mother: 7 Rebekah *new name:* 6 Israel
    son: 3 Dan, Gad 4 Levi 5 Asher, Judah
    6 Joseph, Reuben, Simeon 7 Zebulun
    8 Benjamin, Issachar, Naphtali *variant:*
    5 James *wife:* 4 Leah 6 Rachel
Jacob's rod 8 asphodel
jade 3 fag, gem 4 cloy, fill, glut, minx, pall,
    sate, slut, snip, tire, wear 5 drain, gorge,
    hussy, jewel, stone, tramp, weary, wench
    6 stodge, wanton 7 fatigue, jezebel, satiate,
    surfeit, trollop 8 malapert, saucebox, slat-
    tern, strumpet, wear down
jaded 4 full, worn 5 sated, tired, weary
    6 gorged 7 glutted, satiate, wearied, worn-
    out 8 fatigued, satiated, worn down
    9 surfeited
jaeger 4 bird, skua 6 hunter 8 huntsman,
    rifleman 9 boatswain
Jael *husband:* 5 Heber *victim:* 6 Sisera
jag 3 bum, dag, tab 4 barb, bolt, bust,
    soak, tear 5 binge, booze, drunk, notch,
    prick, souse, spell, spree 6 bender, thrill
    7 portion 8 quantity
jagged 5 erose, harsh, rough, sharp
    6 craggy, hackly, rugged, uneven
    7 scraggy, unlevel 8 asperous, scabrous,
    unsmooth
___ Jagger 4 Mick
Jaggers' ward 3 Pip
Jahaziah, Jahzeiah *father:* 6 Tikvah
Jahaziel's father 9 Zechariah
Jahzeel, Jahziel *father:* 8 Naphtali
jai alai 6 pelota *basket:* 5 cesta *court:*
    6 cancha 7 fronton
jail 3 can, jug, pen 4 coop, gaol, keep,
    poky, stir 6 cooler, immure, intern, lockup,
    prison 7 confine, freezer, slammer 8 bas-
    tille, hoosegow, imprison, rock pile, stock-
    ade 9 bridewell, constrain, guardroom
    11 incarcerate, reformatory 12 penitentiary
jailbird 3 con 5 loser 7 convict 8 prisoner
jailer 5 guard, screw 6 keeper, warden
    7 turnkey

Jair *father:* 5 Segub *grandfather:*
6 Hezron *son:* 7 Elhanan 8 Mordecai
Jakeh's son 4 Agur
jakes 5 privy 8 outhouse 9 backhouse
Jalam *father:* 4 Esau *mother:*
9 Oholibama
jalopy 3 car, dog 4 auto, heap 5 crate,
wreck 6 junker 7 clunker 10 automobile
jalousie 5 blind 6 window 7 shutter
jam 3 fix, ram 4 bear, bind, cram, push,
tamp 5 crowd, crush, jelly, press, stuff
6 plight, scrape, squash, squish, squush
7 dilemma, squeeze 8 bar-le-duc, conserve,
preserve 9 confiture, marmalade
11 predicament
Jamaica *capital:* 8 Kingston *monetary
unit:* 6 dollar
Jamaican *export:* 3 rum *hair style:*
10 dreadlocks *music:* 3 ska 6 reggae
nationalist: 6 Garvey
James *brother:* 4 John 5 Jesus, Joses
cousin: 5 Jesus *father:* 7 Zebedee
8 Alphaeus *mother:* 4 Mary 6 Salome
James novel 10 Confidence 11 Daisy
Miller, The American 12 The Europeans
13 The Bostonians, The Golden Bowl, The
Tragic Muse
Jamin's father 6 Simeon
Jammy and ____ 7 Kashmir
Jane Eyre *author:* 6 Brontë *lover:*
9 Rochester
jangle 3 din, jar 4 ring 5 babel, clash
6 clamor, hubbub, racket, tumult, uproar
7 discord 8 conflict, mismatch 9 disaccord 10 hullabaloo, tintamarre 11 pandemonium 12 disharmonize
jangling 5 harsh 7 grating 9 dissonant
10 discordant
janitor 6 porter 7 charman 9 caretaker,
custodian 10 doorkeeper
japan 7 varnish
Japan 5 Nihon 6 Nippon *capital:* 5 Tokyo
monetary unit: 3 yen
Japanese *aborigine:* 4 Ainu *apricot:*
3 ume *baron:* 6 daimio, daimyo *battle cry:*
6 banzai *Buddha:* 5 Amida, Amita *coin:*
2 bu 3 rin, sen, yen 4 oban 5 koban,
obang 6 kobang *court:* 5 dairi *dancing
girl:* 6 geisha *dish:* 5 kombu 7 tempura
8 sukiyaki, teriyaki *drink:* 4 sake, saki
emperor: 6 Mikado 8 Hirohito *festival:*
3 Bon *fish:* 3 ayu, tai 4 fugu *garment:*
5 haori 6 kimono *god:* 4 kami 5 Ebisu,
Hotei 7 Daikoku, Jurojin 8 Bishamon *goddess:* 6 Benten 9 Amaterasu *governor:*
6 shogun *grill:* 7 hibachi *instrument:*
4 koto 7 samisen *martial art:* 4 judo
6 karate 7 jujitsu, jujutsu *measure:* 2 bu,
go, jo, mo, ri, se, to 3 boo, cho, ken, rin,
sho, sun, tan 4 hiro, koku 5 shaku, tsubo
monastery: 4 tera *money:* 3 sen, yen *per-

simmon: 4 kaki *plum:* 6 loquat *poem:*
5 haiku, hokku, tanka 6 haikai *pottery:*
7 Satsuma *radish:* 6 daikon *religion:*
6 Shinto 8 Buddhism 9 Shintoism *rice
wine:* 4 sake, saki *robe:* 6 kimono *samurai
clan:* 5 Taira 8 Minamoto *servant:* 6 geisha *ship:* 4 maru *song:* 3 uta *suicide:*
7 seppuku 8 hara-kiri, hari-kari, kamikaze
sword: 5 catan 6 cattan, katana *theater:*
2 No 6 Kabuki *tidal wave:* 7 tsunami
tree: 4 kiri, kozo, sugi 5 akeki, kiaki
6 hinoki, keyaki *vehicle:* 7 ricksha 8 rickshaw *warrior:* 7 samurai *weight:* 2 mo
3 fun, kin, rin, shi 4 kwan, niyo 5 momme
8 hiyak-kin, hiyaku-me *wrestling:* 4 sumo
writing: 4 kana 8 hiragana, katakana
zither: 4 koto
Japanese-American 5 Issei, Kibei, Nisei
second generation: 6 Sansei
jape 3 gag 4 fool, jeer, jest, joke, mock,
quip 5 crack, taunt 7 waggery 8 drollery
9 wisecrack, witticism
Japheth *brother:* 3 Ham 4 Shem *father:*
4 Noah *son:* 5 Gomer, Javan, Madai,
Magog, Tiras, Tubal 7 Meshech
Japhia's father 5 David
jar 4 bump, ewer, jolt, olla, vase 5 clash,
crash, cruse, quake, shake, shock, smash,
upset 6 impact, jangle, jounce, tinaja,
tremor 7 discord, terrine, tremble, vibrate
8 conflict, gallipot, mismatch 9 collision,
container, disaccord, vibration 10 concussion 12 disharmonize *ancient:* 6 hydria,
krater 7 amphora 8 lecythus, lekythos, lek-
ythus *Egyptian:* 7 canopic *long-necked:*
6 goglet *Mexican:* 6 pinata *Philippine:*
5 banga
jardiniere 3 pot, urn 4 vase 5 stand
7 garnish 9 flowerpot
Jared *father:* 10 Mahalaleel *son:* 5 Enoch
jargon 4 cant 5 argot, idiom, lingo, slang
6 patois, patter, pidgin 7 chatter, dialect,
lexicon, palaver, twitter 8 language 9 gibberish 10 dictionary, vernacular, vocabulary 11 terminology *lawyer's:* 8 legalese
jarl 4 earl 5 chief, noble 8 nobleman
jarring 3 dry 5 harsh, rough 6 hoarse
7 grating, rasping, raucous 8 strident 9 dissonant 10 discordant, stridulent, stridulous
Jashub's father 4 Bani 8 Issachar
jasmine 4 vine 5 shrub 6 flower
7 perfume
Jason *father:* 5 Aeson *helper:* 5 Medea
lover: 6 Creusa, Glauce, Glauke *quest:*
12 Golden Fleece *ship:* 4 Argo *shipmate:*
8 Argonaut *teacher:* 6 Chiron 7 Cheiron
uncle: 6 Pelias *wife:* 5 Medea
jasper 6 morlop, quartz 10 chalcedony
jaundice 4 bias 7 disease, icterus 9 prejudice *combining form:* 5 icter 6 ictero —
Scottish: 7 gulsach

jaunt 4 perk, ride, trip 5 sally 6 junket, outing, ramble 7 journey, joyride 9 excursion
jaunty 4 airy 5 light, perky 7 perkish
8 debonair 9 sprightly 10 nonchalant
java 6 coffee
Java almond 7 talisay
Java cotton 5 kapok
Java jute 5 kenaf
Javanese *carriage:* 4 sado *civet:*
5 rasse *instrument:* 5 saron 6 bonang,
gender 7 gamelan *measure:* 4 paal
skunk: 6 teledu *tree:* 4 upas 7 gondang
village: 4 desa 5 dessa
Javan squirrel 8 jelerang
Java plum 5 jaman 6 jambul 7 jambool
javelin 5 lance, shaft, spear 6 weapon
7 assagai, assegai, harpoon
Javert's prey 7 Valjean
jaw 3 gab, wig, yak 4 chat, rail, rate, talk
5 baste, clack, prate, scold 6 babble,
berate, gabble 7 chatter, prattle, upbraid
9 yakety-yak 10 tongue-lash *relating to:*
7 gnathal, gnathic
jawbone 7 maxilla 8 mandible
jawbreaker 5 candy
jay 4 bird, hick, jake, rube 5 clown, dandy
6 rustic 7 bumpkin, hayseed 9 greenhorn
Jayhawker 6 Kansan, outlaw 9 guerrilla
State: 6 Kansas
jazz 4 guff, jive 5 bebop, swing 6 boogie
7 ragtime 8 malarkey, nonsense *up:*
7 enliven 10 popularize
jealous 5 green 7 envious, envying
8 doubting 9 demanding, green-eyed, invidious 10 possessive, possessory, suspicious 11 distrustful, mistrustful
Jecoliah's Son 6 Uzziah
Jediael's father 8 Benjamin
Jedidah *husband:* 4 Amon *son:* 6 Josiah
jeer 4 gibe, gird, jest, jibe, mock 5 fleer,
flout, scoff, sneer, taunt 6 deride, quip at
7 scout at 8 ridicule
Jeeves *creator:* 9 Wodehouse
employer: 7 Wooster (Bertie) *position:*
5 valet 6 butler
Jefferson *home:* 10 Monticello *state:*
8 Virginia
Jehiel *father:* 4 Elam 8 Hachmoni
11 Jehoshaphat *son:* 7 Obadiah
10 Shechaniah
Jehizkiah's father 7 Shallum
Jehoaddan's Son 7 Amaziah
Jehoahaz *brother:* 9 Jehoiakim *father:*
4 Jehu 6 Josiah 7 Jehoram *mother:*
7 Hamutal *son:* 5 Joash 7 Jehoash
Jehohanan *father:* 5 Bebai 6 Tobiah
8 Eliashib *son:* 7 Ishmael
Jehoiada *father:* 6 Paseah 7 Benaiah
son: 7 Benaiah *wife:* 9 Jehosheba
Jehoiakim *father:* 6 Josiah *mother:*
7 Zebidah *son:* 10 Jehoiachin

Jehoram *brother:* 7 Ahaziah *father:*
4 Ahab 11 Jehoshaphat *kingdom:* 5 Judah
slayer: 4 Jehu *wife:* 8 Athaliah
Jehoshaphat *father:* 3 Asa 6 Ahilud,
Nimshi, Paruah *father-in-law:* 4 Ahab *son:*
4 Jehu 7 Jehoram *wife:* 8 Athaliah
Jehosheba *father:* 7 Jehoram *husband:*
8 Jehoiada *sister:* 7 Ahaziah *son:* 5 Joash
Jehovah 3 God 5 Yahwe 6 Adonai, Elohim, Yahweh
Jehozabad's father 8 Obededom
Jehozadak see Jozadak
Jehu 6 driver *father:* 6 Hanani 11 Jehoshaphat *grandfather:* 6 Nimshi *son:* 8 Jehoahaz *victim:* 5 Joram 7 Jehoram
Jehudijah's husband 5 Mered
Jehush *father:* 4 Esau 5 Eshek 6 Bilhan,
Shimei 8 Rehoboam *mother:*
10 Oholibamah
jejune 4 dull, flat 5 banal, bland, inane,
trite, vapid 7 insipid, sapless, tenuous
9 innocuous 10 namby-pamby 12 milk-
and-water
Jekyll's alter ego 4 Hyde
jell 3 set 4 clot 6 gelate 7 congeal, pec-
tize, thicken 9 coagulate 10 gelatinize
jelly 3 gel, set 4 clot, pulp 5 aspic 6 gelate, pectin, spread 7 congeal, gelatin, pec-
tize, thicken 9 coagulate 10 gelatinize
jellyfish 3 sop 4 baby 5 sissy 6 medusa
7 acaleph, doormat, medusan, milksop
8 medusoid, weakling 10 pantywaist
11 Milquetoast, mollycoddle 12 invertebrate
Jemimah's father 3 Job
Jemuel's father 6 Simeon
jennet 3 ass 5 hinny, horse 6 donkey
jeopardize 4 risk 5 peril 6 expose, hazard, menace 7 imperil 8 endanger
10 compromise
jeopardy 4 risk 5 peril 6 danger, hazard,
menace 7 imperil 8 endanger, exposure
9 liability 10 compromise
Jephthah's father 6 Gilead
Jephunneh's son 5 Caleb
jeremiad 6 lament, tirade 8 diatribe,
harangue 9 complaint, philippic
Jeremiah *daughter:* 7 Hamutal *father:*
8 Hilkiath 10 Habaziniah *scribe:* 6 Baruch
son: 8 Jaazniah
Jericho's conqueror 6 Joshua
Jerimoth *daughter:* 8 Mahalath *father:*
5 David
Jerioth's husband 5 Caleb
jerk 3 ass, lug, tic 4 fool, snap, yank
5 idiot, lurch, ninny, throw, wrest, wring
6 twitch, wrench 7 flounce, jackass, tomfool 9 vellicate 10 nincompoop
jerked beef 7 charqui
jerkin 4 coat 6 jacket 9 gyrfalcon
jerky 4 meat 5 inane, wagon 7 charqui,
foolish, jolting 8 saccadic

Jeroboam *father:* 5 Joash, Nebat *foe:*
6 Abijam 8 Rehoboam *mother:* 6 Zeruah
son: 5 Nadab 9 Zechariah
Jerome's Bible 7 Vulgate
jersey 3 cow 5 shirt 6 tricot 7 sweater
8 pullover 10 undershirt
Jerusalem 4 Sion, Zion 5 Salem 8 Holy
City *hill:* 4 Sion, Zion 6 Moriah *market:*
4 souk *mosque:* 4 Omar *pool:* 6 Siloam
8 Bethesda
Jerusalem artichoke 5 tuber 7 girasol
8 girasole 9 sunflower
Jerusalem thorn 5 shrub 6 retama
7 catechu 9 horsebean
Jerusha *father:* 5 Zadok *husband:*
6 Uzziah *son:* 6 Jotham
Jeshaiah *father:* 7 Athalia 8 Hananiah,
Jeduthun, Rehabiah *son:* 6 Ithiel
Jeshua *father:* 7 Jozadek *son:* 4 Ezer
jess 5 strap
Jesse *daughter:* 7 Abigail, Zeruiah
father: 4 Obed *grandfather:* 4 Boaz *son:*
4 Ozem 5 David, Eliab, Elihu 6 Raddai
7 Shammah 8 Abinadab, Nethanel *young-
est son:* 5 David
Jessica *father:* 7 Shylock *husband:*
7 Lorenzo
jest 3 fun, gag, kid, rag, rib 4 butt, game,
gibe, gird, jape, joke, josh, mock, play,
quip, razz 5 chaff, crack, fleer, flout, scoff,
sneer, sport 6 banter, quip at 7 mockery,
scout at, waggery 8 derision, drollery, ridicule 9 pilgarlic, wisecrack, witticism
13 laughing stock
jester 3 wag, wit 4 fool 5 clown, comic,
droll, idiot, joker 6 motley 8 comedian, funnyman, humorist, jokester, quipster
Jesuit's founder 6 Loyola 8 Ignatius
jet 4 ebon, inky 5 black, ebony, plane,
raven, sable, sprit, spurt 6 engine, splurt,
squirt 8 airplane, fountain 9 pitch-dark
Jether *father:* 4 Ezra 6 Gideon, Zophah
son: 5 Amasa
Jethro *daughter:* 8 Zipporah *son-in-law:*
5 Moses
jetsam 7 flotsam 8 wreckage 9 driftwood
jettison 4 cast, dump, junk, shed 5 scrap
6 reject, slough 7 cashier, discard, dumping, junking 8 abdicate, disposal, riddance
9 scrapping, throw away 10 discarding
jetty 4 dock, ebon, inky, pier, quay, slip
5 berth, black, ebony, groin, levee, raven,
sable, wharf 9 pitch-dark 10 pitch-block
Jew 6 Essene, Semite 8 Judahite
9 Israelite
jewel 3 gem 5 adorn, begem, beset, bijou,
ideal, stone 7 paragon, phoenix 8 nonesuch, ornament 9 nonpareil; (see also **gem**)
jeweler 8 lapidary, lapidist *famous:*
7 Tiffany
jewelry 10 bijouterie *artificial:* 5 glass,

paste 6 strass 7 costume *piece:* 3 pin
4 ring 6 brooch 7 earring 8 bracelet, lava-
lier, necklace, tieclasp 9 lavaliere *set:*
6 parure
Jewish *bread:* 5 matzo 6 matzoh, mat-
zos 8 afikomen *ceremony:* 5 berit, brith
6 berith 10 bar mitzvah *combining form:*
5 Judeo 6 Judaeo *doctrine:* 6 Mishna
7 Mishnah *liturgy:* 6 maarib, maariv, min-
hah 7 minchah 9 shaharith *New Year:*
11 Rosh Hashana *organization:* 8 Hadassah 9 B'nai B'rith *pioneer:* 6 halutz 7 chalutz *prayer book:* 6 mahzor, siddur
7 machzor *sabbath:* 8 Saturday *scripture:*
6 Talmud *synagogue:* 4 shul 5 schul
teacher: 5 rabbi 6 Hillel; (see also **Hebrew**)
jezebel 4 jade, slut 5 hussy, tramp, trull,
wench 6 wanton 7 trollop 8 slattern,
strumpet
Jezebel *father:* 7 Ethbaal *home:* 5 Sidon
husband: 4 Ahab *slayer:* 4 Jehu *victim:*
6 Naboth
Jezer's father 8 Naphtali
Jezreel's father 5 Hosea
jib 3 gag, shy 4 balk, sail 5 demur, stick
jibe 2 go 5 agree, fit in, tally 6 accord,
square 7 conform 8 dovetail 9 harmonize
10 correspond
jiffy 5 crack, flash, hurry, shake, trice
6 minute, moment, second 7 instant
9 breathing 11 split second
jig 4 hook, play, ploy, ruse, wile 5 dance,
feint, trick 6 device, gambit 7 gimmick
jigger 3 cup 4 boat 5 gizmo, glass 6 dingus, doodad, gadget, widget 7 concern,
dofunny, gimmick, thingum 9 doohickey,
shot glass
jiggle 5 shake 9 oscillate
jigsaw 4 tool 6 puzzle
jihad 3 war 6 strife 7 crusade, holy war
8 campaign
jilt 6 reject 7 abandon, cast off, discard
jim-dandy 5 nifty 8 knockout
9 humdinger
jimmy 3 bar, pry 4 open 5 lever
7 crowbar
jingle 4 ring, song 5 chime, chink, clink,
verse 6 tinkle 7 chinkle
jinn 5 afrit, genie 6 afreet, spirit, yaksha
jinx 3 hex 5 charm, curse, spell 6 hoodoo,
voodoo, whammy 7 evil eye
jitters 5 jumps, panic 6 dither, nerves,
shakes 7 shivers, willies 9 whim-whams
13 heebie-jeebies
jittery 5 jumpy, nervy 6 goosey, spooky
7 fidgety, nervous 9 unrestful 10 high-
strung
jive 3 kid 4 jazz, talk 5 dance, music,
swing 6 jargon
Joab *brother:* 6 Asahel 7 Abishai *father:*

7 Seraiah, Zeruiah *slayer:* **7** Benaiah *uncle:* **5** David *victim:* **5** Abner, Amasa
Joah *father:* **5** Asaph **6** Joahaz, Zimmah **8** Obededon *son:* **4** Eden
Joanna's husband 5 Chuza
Joan of Arc *birthplace:* **7** Domremy *epithet:* **7** Pucelle **13** Maid of Orleans *victory:* **7** Orleans
Joan's husband 5 Darby
Joash *father:* **4** Ahab **7** Ahaziah **8** Jehoahaz *son:* **6** Gideon **7** Amaziah **8** Jeroboam *victim:* **9** Zechariah
job 4 dupe, duty, fool, gull, hoax, line, post, spot, task, work **5** berth, chare, chore, place, stint, trade **6** befool, billet, devoir, effort, office, pigeon **7** calling, chicane, posting, pursuit **8** business, flimflam, position, sinecure, taskwork, vocation **9** bamboozle, situation, victimize **10** assignment, connection, employment, engagement, occupation, profession **11** appointment
Job *daughter:* **6** Keziah **7** Jemimah *father:* **8** Issachar *friend:* **6** Bildad, Zophar **7** Eliphaz *home:* **2** Uz
Jobab's father 5 Zerah **6** Joktan **9** Shaharaim
jobber 6 trader **10** contractor, wholesaler
job-training program 4 CETA
Jocasta *daughter:* **6** Ismene **8** Antigone *husband:* **5** Laius **7** Oedipus *son:* **7** Oedipus **8** Eteocles **9** Polynices
Jochebed *brother:* **6** Kohath *father:* **4** Levi *husband:* **5** Amram
jockey 4 play **5** rider, trick **7** beguile, exploit, finesse **8** maneuver **10** manipulate *famous:* **5** Baeza (Braulio) **6** Arcaro (Eddie), Murphy (Isaac), Pincay (Laffit) **7** Cauthen (Steve), Cordero (Angel), Hartack (Bill), Longden (Johnny) **8** McHargue (Darrel), Turcotte (Ron) **9** Shoemaker (Willie)
jocular 3 gay **5** comic, jolly, merry, silly, witty **6** blithe, jocose, jovial **7** comical, playful **8** cheerful, humorous, sportive **9** facetious
jocularity 4 glee **5** mirth **7** jollity **8** hilarity **9** jocundity, joviality, merriment
jocund 3 gay **5** jolly, merry **6** blithe, jovial **7** festive, gleeful, playful **8** mirthful, sportive **10** blithesome **12** lighthearted
Joel *brother:* **6** Nathan *father:* **4** Nebo **5** Ladan **6** Samuel, Zichri **7** Azariah, Pedaiah, Pethuel *son:* **5** Heman
jog 3 dig, jab, run **4** lope, poke, prod, trot **5** nudge, punch, shake **6** remind
jogger 6 layboy, runner
joggle 5 dowel, joint, notch, shake **6** jostle
Johanan *father:* **6** Josiah, Kareah, Tobiah **8** Eliashib, Elioenai, Hakkatan *son:* **7** Azariah
john 2 WC **4** head **5** privy **6** toilet
7 latrine **8** lavatory **11** convenience, water closet
John *father:* **5** Accos, Simon **10** Mattathias *son:* **5** Peter **9** Eupolemus **10** Mattathias; (see also **John the Baptist; John the Evangelist**)
John *Irish:* **4** Sean
John Hancock 9 autograph, signature
Johnson's biographer 7 Boswell
John the Baptist *father:* **9** Zacharias *mother:* **9** Elisabeth
John the Evangelist *brother:* **5** James *father:* **7** Zebedee *mother:* **6** Salome
join 3 fay, mix, tie, wed **4** abut, ally, bind, bond, fuse, knot, line, link, mate, weld, yoke **5** affix, blend, march, marry, merge, piece, touch, unify, unite, verge **6** attach, border, butt on, couple, enlist, enroll, fasten, relate, sign up, splice **7** bracket, combine, connect **8** coagment, coalesce, compound, concrete, neighbor **9** associate, coadunate, conjugate, integrate
joint 3 ell, hip, tie **4** butt, crux, dive, knee, link, seam **5** ankle, elbow, hinge, scarf, union, wrist **6** common, mutual, public, shared, suture **7** hangout, knuckle, shiplap **8** abutment, communal, conjunct, coupling, junction, juncture, shoulder **9** honky-tonk **10** connection *combining form:* **5** arthr **6** arthro, condyl **7** condylo *disease:* **9** arthritis **10** rheumatism *prefix:* **2** co
join up 5 enter **6** enlist, enroll, muster, sign up
joist 4 beam, stud **6** timber **7** sleeper, support
joke 3 fun, gag, kid, pun, rag, rib, wit, yak **4** butt, dido, fool, game, jape, jest, josh, mock, play, quip, razz **5** antic, caper, crack, humor, jolly, prank, sally, sport **6** banter, jestee, parody **7** mockery, sarcasm, waggery **8** badinage, derision, drôlerie, drollery, repartee **9** burlesque, pilgarlic, wisecrack, witticism **10** caricature **11** monkeyshine **13** laughing stock *stale:* **8** chestnut
joker 3 wag, wit **4** card, zany **5** clown, comic, cutup, droll **6** gagman, jester **7** farceur **8** comedian, funnyman, humorist, quipster
Jokshan *father:* **7** Abraham *mother:* **7** Keturah *son:* **5** Dedan, Sheba
Joktan *brother:* **5** Peleg *father:* **4** Eber *son:* **4** Obal **5** Ophir
jollity 3 fun **4** glee, play, romp **5** cheer, mirth, revel, sport **6** frolic, gaiety, gambol **7** disport, revelry, rollick, whoopee **8** hilarity, reveling **9** festivity, jocundity, joviality, merriment, revelment **10** blitheness, jocularity **11** merrymaking
jolly 3 fun, gay, kid, rag, rib **4** glad, jest, josh, razz **5** chaff, merry **6** banter, blithe, jocund, jovial **7** festive, gleeful, jocular, play-

ful, roguish, waggish **8** mirthful, sportive **10** blithesome, frolicsome

Jolly Roger *flag:* **4** flag **6** ensign *user:* **6** pirate

jolt **3** jar, nip, tot **4** blow, bump, dram, drop, shot, slug **5** clash, crash, knock, shake, shock, snort **6** impact, jounce **7** snifter, startle **8** toothful **9** collision

Jonadab *cousin:* **5** Amnon *father:* **6** Rechab **7** Shimeah *uncle:* **5** David

Jonah **4** jinx **7** prophet *father:* **7** Amittai *son:* **5** Peter, Simon *swallower:* **5** whale

Jonathan *brother:* **7** Johanan *father:* **4** Jada, Saul **6** Joiada, Kareah, Uzziah **7** Absolom, Shimeah **8** Abiathar **10** Matthias *friend:* **5** David

Jones, John Paul *ship:* **15** Bonhomme Richard *victim:* **7** Serapis

jongleur **4** bard **6** singer **8** minstrel **10** troubadour

jonquil **8** daffodil **9** narcissus

Jonson play **6** The Fox **7** Epicene, Volpone

Joram *brother:* **7** Ahaziah *father:* **3** Toi **4** Ahab **11** Jehoshaphat *slayer:* **4** Jehu *son:* **7** Ahaziah

Jordan *capital:* **5** Amman *king:* **7** Hussein *monetary unit:* **5** dinar

jorum **3** cup, jug **4** bowl

Joseph *brother:* (see Jacob, son) *buyer:* **8** Potiphar *father:* **5** Asaph, Jacob **9** Zacharias **10** Mattathias *mother:* **6** Rachel *son:* **5** Jesus **7** Ephraim **8** Manasseh *wife:* **4** Mary **6** Asenath

Joseph's coat **6** coleus **7** tampala

josh **3** fun, guy, kid, rag, rib **4** jest, joke, razz **5** chaff, jolly, tease **6** banter

Joshua's father **3** Nun

Joshua tree **5** yucca

Josiah *father:* **4** Amon **9** Zephaniah *mother:* **7** Jedidah *son:* **8** Jehoahaz **9** Jehoiakim

joss **4** idol **5** image

Jo's sister **3** Amy, Meg **4** Beth

jostle **3** jar, jog **4** push **5** elbow, press, shove **6** hustle **8** bulldoze, shoulder

jot **3** bit **4** atom, iota, whit **5** grain, minim, speck **6** tittle **7** modicum, smidgen, smidgin **8** particle, smidgeon

jot down **4** note **5** write

Jotham *father:* **6** Gideon, Jahdai, Uzziah *mother:* **8** Jerushah

joule component **3** erg

jounce **3** jar, jog **4** bump, jolt **5** shock **6** impact, wallop **9** collision **10** concussion

journal **3** log **5** diary, organ, paper **6** record, review **7** gazette **8** magazine **9** newspaper **10** periodical

journalist **3** Bly (Nellie) **4** Will (George F.) **5** Baker (Russell) **6** Bierce (Ambrose), Ephron (Nora), Kennan (George), Murrow (Edward R.), Reston (James), Runyon (Damon), Shirer (William L.), Zenger (John Peter) **7** Cousins (Norman), Greeley (Horace), Gunther (John), Mencken (H. L.), Pearson (Drew), Tarbell (Ida), Trillin (Calvin) **8** Anderson (Jack), Atkinson (Brooks), Garrison (William Lloyd), Lippmann (Walter), Pulitzer (Joseph), Steffens (Lincoln), Thompson (Dorothy), Winchell (Walter) **9** Hohenberg (John), Watterson (Henry)

journey **2** go **3** hie **4** eyre, fare, pass, tour, trek, trip, wend **5** jaunt, sally **6** cruise, junket, push on, repair, safari, travel, voyage **7** odyssey, proceed, travels **8** progress **9** excursion **10** expedition, pilgrimage *route:* **9** itinerary

joust **4** tilt **5** fight **6** combat **10** tournament *arena:* **8** tiltyard

Jove see **Jupiter**

jovial see **jocular**

jowl **3** jaw **5** cheek **6** dewlap, wattle **8** mandible

joy **4** glee **5** bliss, mirth **6** gaiety **7** delight, ecstasy, elation, rapture **8** fruition, gladness, pleasure **9** enjoyment **11** delectation

Joyce, James *birthplace:* **6** Dublin *character:* **5** Bloom (Leopold), Bloom (Molly) **7** Dedalus (Stephen) *work:* **6** Exiles **7** Ulysses **9** Dubliners **13** Finnegans Wake

joyful see **joyous**

joyous **3** gay **4** glad **5** happy, merry **7** buoyant, festive, gleeful **8** ecstatic, mirthful **9** delighted, rapturous **12** lighthearted

Jozabad's father **6** Jeshua **7** Pashhur

Jozacar *mother:* **8** Shimeath *victim:* **5** Joash

Jozadak's son **6** Jeshua

Jubal *father:* **6** Lamech *mother:* **4** Adah

jubilant **6** elated **8** exultant, exulting **9** cock-a-hoop, triumphal **10** cock-a-whoop, triumphant

jubilate **5** exult, glory **7** delight, triumph

Judah *brother:* (see Jacob, son) *father:* **5** Jacob *king:* **3** Asa **4** Ahaz, Amon **5** Joash **6** Abijam, Josiah, Jotham, Uzziah **7** Ahaziah, Amaziah, Jehoram **8** Hezekiah, Jehoahaz, Manasseh, Rehoboam, Zedekiah **9** Jehoiakim **10** Jehoiachin **11** Jehoshaphat *mother:* **4** Leah *son:* **2** Er **4** Onan **6** Shelah

Judas **7** traitor *father:* **5** Simon **7** Chalphi **10** Mattathias *replacement:* **8** Matthias *suicide place:* **8** Aceldama, Akeldama

judge **3** put, ref, try, ump **4** call, draw, make, rule, test **5** check, court, infer **6** critic, decide, deduce, derive, gather, jurist, reckon, settle, umpire **7** arbiter, collect, justice, make out, referee **8** conclude, critique, doomster, estimate, mediator, sentence **9** arbitrate, criticize, determine **10** adjudicate, arbitrator, chancellor, magistrate, negotiator, reconciler **11** approximate, conciliator **12** intermediary *Athenian:* **6** dicast **7** heliast *bench:* **4** banc *chamber:* **6** camera *gown:* **4** robe, toga *in Hades:* **5** Minos **6** Aeacus **12** Rhadamanthys *mallet:* **5** gavel *Muslim:* **4** cadi **5** mufti

judgment 4 doom **5** award, sense, stock, taste **6** acumen, ruling, wisdom **7** insight, opinion, verdict **8** decision, estimate, gumption, illation, sagacity, sequitur **9** appraisal, criticism, deduction, good sense, inference **10** assessment, astuteness, conclusion, discretion, estimation, evaluation, horse sense, shrewdness **11** common sense, discernment **12** appraisement, perspicacity **13** determination, ratiocination

Judgment Day 8 doomsday

judicial 8 critical **10** judgmental *assembly:* **5** court *document:* **4** writ

judicious 4 fair, sage, sane, wise **7** prudent, sapient **8** rational, sensible **9** equitable, judgmatic, objective, sagacious **10** reasonable **13** dispassionate

Judith *father:* **5** Beeri *home:* **8** Bethulia *husband:* **4** Esau *victim:* **10** Holofernes

Judy's husband 5 Punch

jug 3 jar, pen **4** coop, ewer, jail, toby **5** gotch **6** cooler, immure, intern, lockup, prison, urceus **7** confine, pitcher **8** bastille, demijohn, imprison **9** constrain **11** incarcerate

jug band instrument 5 kazoo **6** bottle **7** washtub **9** stovepipe, washboard

Juggernaut's temple 4 Puri

juggle 5 bluff **6** betray, delude, humbug, illude, take in **7** beguile, deceive, mislead, shuffle

juice 3 sap **4** fuel, must, stum **5** cider, fluid **7** essence, vinegar **8** vitality **10** succulence **11** electricity *combining form:* **3** opo **4** chyl **5** chyli, chylo *fermented:* **4** wine **5** cider *Scottish:* **4** broo

juicy 4 racy **7** piquant **9** succulent

juju 4 luck, zemi **5** charm **6** amulet, fetish, mascot **7** periapt **8** talisman **10** phylactery

jujube 3 ber **4** gumdrop, lozenge

julep 5 drink

Julian's epithet 8 Apostate

Juliet *betrothed:* **5** Paris *father:* **7** Capulet *lover:* **5** Romeo

July 14 11 Bastille Day

jumble 3 mix, pie **4** hash, mess, olio **5** mix up, shake, snafu **6** foul up, litter, medley, mess up, muddle, muss up **7** clutter, confuse, derange, disturb, rummage, shuffle, snarl up **8** disorder, mishmash, pastiche, scramble **9** patchwork, potpourri **10** assortment, disarrange, miscellany, salmagundi **11** disorganize, gallimaufry

jumbo 4 huge **5** giant **6** mighty **7** mam-

moth **8** colossal, enormous, gigantic **9** cyclopean **10** prodigious **11** elephantine

jump 3 hop, lop **4** bolt, hike, jink, leap, loup **5** boost, bound, lunge, put up, raise, vault **6** bounce, hurdle, jack up, pounce, spring **7** saltate, startle **8** increase

jumper 5 dress, shirt, smock **6** blouse, jacket

jumping 7 saltant

jumping frog county 9 Calaveras

jump over 8 leapfrog

jumps 6 dither, shakes **7** jitters, shivers, willies **9** whim-whams **13** heebie-jeebies

jumpy see **jittery**

junction 4 seam **5** joint, union **6** suture **7** joining, meeting **8** coupling **9** concourse, gathering **10** concursion, confluence, connection

juncture 4 pass, seam **5** joint, pinch, point, union **6** crisis, moment, strait **7** instant, joining **8** coupling, exigency, zero hour **9** emergency **10** connection, crossroads **11** contingency **12** turning point

june bug 6 beetle

jungle 3 web **4** hash, knot, mash, maze, mesh **5** skein, snarl **6** jumble, litter, morass, muddle, tangle **7** clutter, mizmaze, rummage **8** mishmash, scramble **9** labyrinth

Jungle, The *author:* **8** Sinclair (Upton) *locale:* **7** Chicago

Jungle Books, The *author:* **7** Kipling *character:* **6** Mowgli *python:* **3** Kaa

juniper 4 cade, tree **5** cedar, larch, retem, savin

junk 4 boat, cast, dope, drug **5** offal, scrap, trash, waste **6** debris, kelter, litter, refuse, reject, slough **7** cashier, discard, garbage, rubbish, wash out **8** jettison, throw out **9** narcotics, throw away

junker 4 heap **5** crate, noble, wreck **6** jalopy **10** aristocrat

junket 4 trip, jaunt, sally **6** outing, picnic **9** excursion **10** roundabout

junkyard 4 dump

Juno *bird:* **7** peacock *epithet:* **6** Moneta; (see also **Hera**)

Junoesque 5 curvy **7** rounded **9** curvesome **10** curvaceous **11** curvilinear **13** well-developed

junta 5 group **7** council **9** committee **10** government

junto 5 cabal, group **7** coterie, faction

Jupiter 4 Jove, Zeus *angel:* **7** Zadkiel *cupbearer:* **8** Ganymede *daughter:* **5** Venus **7** Minerva *epithet:* **6** Fidius, Fulgur, Stator, Tonans **7** Pluvius *father:* **6** Saturn *lover:* **2** Io **6** Europa **8** Callisto *mother:* **3** Ops *satellite:* **2** Io **6** Europa **8** Callisto, Ganymede *son:* **5** Arcas **6** Castor, Pollux *temple:* **7** Capitol *wife:* **4** Juno

Jurgen *author:* **6** Cabell *trade:*
10 pawnbroker
juridical 5 legal **8** juristic
jurisdiction 3 law, see **4** sway **5** might,
power, range, reach, scope, venue
6 county, domain, parish, sphere **7** command, compass, control, diocese, mastery
8 dominion, province **9** authority, bailiwick,
territory **10** domination *suffix:* **3** dom
jurisprudence 3 law
jury 5 panel **9** committee *decision:*
7 verdict
just 3 all, apt, due, fit **4** even, fair, good,
meet, only, true **5** equal, happy, legal, quite,
right, sharp **6** as well, barely, cogent,
hardly, honest, in toto, merely, proper,
scarce, simply, square, wholly **7** condign,
exactly, fitting, merited, totally, upright,
utterly **8** all in all, deserved, faithful, rightful,
scarcely, squarely, suitable, unbiased
9 befitting, equitable, expressly, honorable,
impartial, justified, objective, precisely, requisite, uncolored, veracious, veridical
10 accurately, altogether, completely, felicitous, legitimate, scrupulous **11** appropriate,
undistorted, well-founded **12** unprejudiced,
well-grounded **13** conscientious, dispassionate, rhadamanthine
justice 3 law **5** court, judge **6** equity
7 honesty **8** evenness, fairness **10** magistrate **12** impartiality
justification 6 excuse, reason **7** account,

apology, defense **8** apologia **9** rationale
10 apologetic **11** explanation
justify 5 argue, claim **6** assert, defend,
excuse, uphold, verify **7** account, bear out,
confirm, contend, explain, support, warrant
8 maintain, validate **9** vindicate **11** corroborate, explain away, rationalize **12** authenticate, substantiate
justly 4 well **5** fitly **6** nicely **7** rightly
8 decently, properly **9** correctly, fittingly
10 decorously **11** befittingly
jut 4 hang, poke, pout **5** bulge, jetty,
pouch **6** beetle **7** project **8** bend over, lean
over, overhang, protrude, stand out, stick
out **9** outthrust **10** projection, protrusion
12 protuberance
jute 5 gunny **6** burlap **7** sacking *Indian:*
4 desi
Juvenal's forte 6 satire
juvenile 3 kid **5** child, green, young,
youth **6** callow, infant, moppet, unripe
8 immature, young one, youthful
9 unfledged, youngling, youngster
11 undeveloped
juvenility 5 youth **7** puberty **9** greenness,
youthhood **10** pubescence, springtide,
springtime **11** adolescence
12 youthfulness
juxtaposed 8 abutting, adjacent, touching **9** adjoining, bordering **10** approximal,
contiguous **12** conterminous

K

kabob 7 shaslik 8 shashlik 9 shashlick
kaddish 6 cantor, prayer
kady 3 hat 5 derby
Kafka, Franz *character:* 4 Olga 5 Samsa (Gregor) 6 Joseph (K.) *novel:* 7 Amerika 8 The Trial 9 The Castle
kaiser 5 ruler 7 emperor, monarch 9 sovereign
kaka 6 parrot
kakariki 6 lizard 8 parakeet
kakatoe 6 parrot 8 cockatoo
kale 4 cole 7 cabbage, collard 8 borecole, colewort
kaleidoscopic 7 diverse, various 8 colorful 10 variegated
Kali *aspect:* 5 Durga 7 Parvati *husband:* 4 Siva 5 Shiva
kalium 9 potassium
Kama *god of:* 4 love *mount:* 6 parrot 7 sparrow *wife:* 4 Rati
kambal 5 shawl 7 blanket
kamik 4 boot
kamikaze 7 suicide 8 airplane, suicidal
kampong 6 hamlet 7 village
Kampuchea see **Cambodia**
kangaroo 4 euro 6 leaper 7 bettong, wallaby 8 boongary, wallaroo 9 marsupial 10 macropodid *herd:* 3 mob *male:* 6 boomer *young:* 4 joey
kangaroo bear 5 koala
kangaroo rat 7 potoroo
kans 5 grass 6 glagah
Kansas *capital:* 6 Topeka *college:* 5 Tabor *fort:* 5 Riley *largest city:* 7 Wichita *nickname:* 14 Jayhawker State, Sunflower State *prison:* 11 Leavenworth
kaolin 4 clay
kapelle 5 choir 9 orchestra
kaput 6 ruined 7 done for 8 defeated, finished 9 destroyed
karakul 5 sheep
karakurt 6 spider 9 black wolf
Kareah's son 7 Johanan 8 Jonathan
karma 4 aura 5 force, power 6 spirit
kaross 3 rug 7 garment
kasha 4 mush 5 grain
katabasis 7 retreat 9 troparion
Katharina *father:* 8 Baptista *suitor:* 9 Petruchio
Katrina's suitor 9 Brom Bones 12 Ichabod Crane

katydid 6 insect 11 grasshopper
katzenjammer 6 clamor, nausea 8 hangover, headache
kava 3 awa 5 shrub 6 pepper
kayak 4 boat 5 canoe
kayo 8 knockout
Kazantzakis hero 5 Zorba
kea 6 parrot
Keats poem 5 Lamia 8 Endymion, Hyperion, Isabella, To Autumn 11 Ode to Psyche
kedge 6 anchor
keel 4 boat, drop, fall, ship 5 barge, pitch, ridge, slump, upset 6 carina, go down, plunge, topple, tumble 7 capsize 8 overturn 11 centerboard
keelbird 3 ani
keen 4 agog, avid, wail, yowl 5 acute, alert, eager, honed, nutty, sharp, smart 6 ardent, bewail, clever, fervid, gung ho, lively, shrewd 7 animate, anxious, athirst, fervent, thirsty, whetted, zealous 8 animated, appetent, spirited 9 impatient, perfervid, sensitive, sprightly, unblunted, vivacious 10 breathless, perceptive, razor-sharp 11 penetrating, penetrative, quick-witted, sharp-witted 12 enthusiastic, quick-sighted, sharp-sighted
keenness 3 wit 4 edge 6 acumen 9 sharpness 10 astuteness, shrewdness 11 discernment, penetration, percipience 12 incisiveness, perspicacity
keep 3 own, pen 4 curb, fend, have, hold, jail, mind, obey, save 5 carry, check, stock 6 bridle, comply, detain, direct, follow, hold in, living, lockup, manage, ordain, prison, retain 7 abstain, alimony, carry on, conduct, conform, control, forbear, inhibit, observe, operate, possess, refrain, reserve, support 8 conserve, hold back, hold down, maintain, preserve, restrain, withhold 9 celebrate, constrain, solemnize 10 livelihood, sustenance 11 commemorate, maintenance, subsistence
keep back 3 dam 4 deny, hold, save 6 detain, refuse, retain, retard 7 reserve 8 disallow, withhold
keeper 5 guard 6 custos, pastor, warden 7 curator 8 cerberus, claviger, guardian, watchdog 9 constable, custodian
keeping 4 care, ward 5 trust 6 charge,

saving **7** custody **9** salvation **10** caretaking **12** conservation, guardianship
keep on 7 persist **8** continue **9** persevere
keep out 3 bar **4** hold **5** debar **6** detain,
retain **7** reserve **8** hold back, withhold
keepsake 5 relic, token **6** trophy
7 memento **8** giftbook, memorial, reminder,
souvenir **11** remembrance
12 remembrancer
keep up 7 sustain **8** continue, maintain,
preserve
keeve 3 tub, vat **4** kier **5** basin
kef 4 hemp **7** languor, tobacco **10** dreami-
ness **12** tranquillity
keg 3 tun **4** butt, cask, pipe **6** barrel
7 barrico **8** hogshead
kegler 6 bowler
keister, keester 7 satchel **8** buttocks,
suitcase
keitloa 5 rhino
keloid 4 scar
kelp 3 ash **4** agar, alga **5** varec
7 seaweed
Kemuel *father:* **5** Nahor *mother:* **6** Milcah
son: **9** Hashabiah
ken 4 view **5** grasp, range, reach, scope,
sight **7** horizon, purview **10** perception
kenaf 4 hemp, jute **6** ambari **8** hibiscus
kench 3 bin **9** enclosure
Kenilworth author 5 Scott
kennel 3 den **4** pack **5** drain, house,
sewer **6** gutter **7** confine, shelter
9 enclosure
keno 4 game *similar to:* **5** beano, bingo,
lotto
Kentucky *capital:* **9** Frankfort *largest
city:* **10** Louisville *nickname:* **14** Bluegrass
State *state bird:* **8** cardinal *state flower:*
9 goldenrod
Kentucky bluegrass 3 poa
Kenya *capital:* **7** Nairobi *monetary unit:*
8 shilling
kepi 3 cap
kerchief 6 hankie **8** babushka, bandanna,
headrail, kaffiyeh *Scottish:* **5** curch
kerf 3 cut **4** slit **5** notch **6** groove
kermis 4 fair **8** carnival, festival
kernel 3 nub, nut **4** core, crux, gist, meat,
pith, seed **5** grain **6** matter, nubbin,
upshot **7** nucleus **9** substance *combining
form:* **4** cary, kary **5** caryo, karyo
Kerouac novel 6 Big Sur **9** On the Road
kestrel 4 bird, hawk **6** falcon, fanner
9 windhover
ketch 4 boat **8** sailboat
ketone 5 irone **7** acetone, camphor, mus-
cone **8** acridone, butanone, civetone
kettle 3 pot, vat **6** vessel **7** caldron, mar-
mite, pothole **8** cauldron, flambeau
kettledrum 5 naker, party **6** timbal, tymbal
Arabian: **6** atabal

Keturah's husband 7 Abraham
kevel 5 cleat, staff **6** cudgel, hammer, timber **7** bollard
key 3 cay **4** isle, reef, tone **5** islet, pitch,
vital **6** clavis, cotter, island, legend, opener,
samara, spline, ticket **7** central, digital
8 critical, passport, password, solution,
tonality **9** important **10** open sesame *combining form:* **5** clavi, clavo, cleid **6** cleido
notch: **4** ward
keyboard 6 manual **7** clavier **8** pedalier
10 claviature
key fruit 6 samara
key man 9 locksmith
keynote 4 tone **5** theme, tonic **7** feature
keynoter 6 orator **7** speaker
Keystone State 12 Pennsylvania
Keziah's father 3 Job
khaki 5 cloth, color **7** uniform
khamsin 4 wind
khan 5 chief, ruler **9** chieftain, sovereign
khedive 5 ruler **7** viceroy
Khomeini, e.g. 4 imam
Ki *brother, consort:* **2** An *mother:*
5 Nammu *son:* **5** Enlil
kiang 3 ass
kibble 4 meal **5** grain, grind
kibbutz 4 farm **7** commune **10** collective,
settlement
kibe 4 chap **5** crack **9** chilblain
kibitzer 5 prier, pryer, snoop **6** butt-in
7 meddler **8** busybody, observer, quidnunc **9** spectator **10** pragmatist,
rubberneck
kick 4 bang, boot, fuss, punt, wail
5 whine **6** except, murmur, object, repine,
thrill, wallop **7** grumble, protest **8** complain **11** expostulate, remonstrate
kicker 4 crab **5** crank **6** griper, grouch,
punter **7** growler **8** grumbler, sorehead,
sourpuss **10** complainer
kick off 4 open **5** begin, start **6** launch
8 commence, embark on, initiate **10** embark
upon, inaugurate
kick out 2 ax **4** drop, fire, sack **5** chase,
chuck, eject, evict **6** bounce **7** boot out,
cashier, dismiss, extrude **8** throw out
9 discharge
kickshaw 3 toy **5** goody, treat **6** bauble,
dainty, morsel, tidbit, titbit, trifle **8** delicacy
kid 4 bud, fun, guy, rag, rib **4** dupe, fool,
gull, hoax, jest, joke, josh, razz **5** child, jolly,
trick, youth **6** banter, befool, moppet
8 flimflam, hoodwink, juvenile, young one
9 bamboozle, youngling, youngster
kidnap 4 abduct, waylay **8** shanghai
10 spirit away
kidney 5 gland, organ *combining form:*
4 reni, reno **5** nephr **6** nephro **7** nephron,
nephros *Scottish:* **4** neer
kidney-shaped 8 reniform

kielbasa 7 sausage
kier 3 vat
kilderkin 3 keg 4 cask 6 barrel
kilim 3 mat, rug 6 carpet
kill 3 zap 4 bane, down, hang, slay, veto
5 croak, scrag, shoot 6 cut off, finish, lay
low, murder, poison, stifle 7 butcher,
destroy, execute, garrote, put away, take
off 8 carry off, dispatch, immolate, massacre, negative, strangle 9 non-placet, sacrifice, slaughter 10 annihilate 11 assassinate, exterminate
killer 6 gunman, hit man, slayer 7 torpedo
8 assassin, homicide, murderer *combining
form:* 4 cide 6 ctonus
killer whale 4 orca 7 grampus
killing 5 blood 6 murder 8 foul play, homicide 9 slaughter 12 manslaughter *combining form:* 5 cidal *of a race:* 8 genocide *of
bacteria:* 11 bactericide *of brother:*
10 fratricide *of father:* 9 parricide, patricide
of king: 8 regicide *of mother:* 9 matricide
of self: 7 suicide *of sister:* 10 sororicide
Kilmer poem 5 Trees
kiln 4 bake, burn, fire, oast, oven 7 furnace
kilt 5 skirt 7 filabeg, filibeg 8 fillebeg *fabric:* 5 plaid 6 tartan
kilter 4 trim 5 order, shape 6 fettle, repair
7 fitness 9 condition
kimono 4 gown, robe *sash:* 3 obi
kin 3 sib 4 clan, folk, race, sept 5 stock,
tribe 6 family 7 kindred, lineage, related
8 kinsfolk, relation, relative 9 cousinage
kind 3 ilk, way 4 good, mild, sort, type,
warm 5 breed, class, genre, genus, order
6 benign, gender, genial, gentle, humane,
kidney, nature, stripe, tender 7 affable, amiable, clement, cordial, feather, lenient, species, variety 8 merciful, obliging, tolerant
9 benignant, character 10 altruistic, benevolent, charitable, forbearing, propitious,
responsive 11 complaisant, considerate,
description, good-hearted, good-humored,
good-natured, openhearted, sympathetic,
warmhearted 12 eleemosynary, good-tempered, humanitarian 13 compassionate,
philanthropic
kindle 4 fire, move, stir, wake, whet 5 light,
rally, rouse, waken 6 arouse, awaken,
bestir, excite, foment, ignite, incite
7 inflame, provoke 9 challenge, instigate,
stimulate
kindliness 5 amity 6 comity 8 goodwill
10 friendship 11 benevolence
12 friendliness
kindly 4 well 6 benign 7 benefic
8 friendly, gracious 9 attentive, benignant,
heedfully 10 generously, neighborly
11 considerate, good-hearted 12 thoughtfully 13 considerately
kindness 5 favor 7 service 8 clemency,

courtesy, goodwill, sympathy 10 indulgence 11 benevolence 12 dispensation
kindred 3 sib 4 akin, clan, folk, race, sept
5 house, stock, tribe 6 agnate, allied, family 7 cognate, connate, lineage, related
8 incident 10 affiliated, connatural
11 consanguine
king 3 rex 4 czar, tsar 5 baron, mogul,
ruler 6 tycoon 7 magnate, monarch 9 sovereign *Albanian:* 3 Zog 7 William *Assyrian:* 6 Sargon 11 Sennacherib, Shalmaneser *Babylonian:* 6 Sargon 9 Hammurabi
10 Belshazzar *Belgian:* 6 Albert 7 Leopold 8 Baudouin *Bohemian:* 9 Wenceslas
10 Wenceslaus *Damascus:* 8 Benhadad
Danish: 4 Abel, Eric, Gorm, Hans, John,
Olaf 5 Sweyn 6 Canute, Harold, Magnus
8 Nicholas, Waldemar 9 Christian, Frederick 11 Christopher *Dutch:* 7 William *Egyptian:* 3 Tut 4 Pepi, Seti 5 Khufu, Menes,
Necho 6 Cheops, Ramses 7 Harmhab,
Osorkon, Psamtik, Ptolemy 8 Ikhnaton,
Thothmes, Thutmose 9 Amenhotep, Sesos-
tris 11 Tutankhamen *English:* 4 John
5 Henry, James 6 Alfred, Canute, Edmund,
Edward, Egbert, George, Harold 7 Charles,
Richard, Stephen, William 8 Ethelred
9 Athelstan, Ethelbald, Ethelbert *French:*
3 Odo, roi 4 John 5 Henry, Louis, Pepin,
Raoul 6 Philip, Robert, Rudolf 7 Charles,
Francis, Lothair 9 Hugh Capet 11 Charle-
magne *German:* 4 Karl 5 Louis 6 Lothar,
Ludwig 7 Charles, Lothair *Greek (modern):* 4 Paul 6 George 9 Alexander
11 Constantine *Hawaiian:* 10 Kamehameha
Hungarian: 6 Attila *Indian:* 4 raja 5 rajah
Irish: 9 Brain Boru *Italian:* 7 Humbert *Jor-
danian:* 5 Talal 7 Hussein 8 Abdullah
Judah: (see at *Judah*) *Judean:* 5 Herod
Lydian: 5 Gyges 7 Croesus 8 Alyattes
Norwegian: 4 Eric, Erik, Inge, Olaf
5 Sweyn 6 Haakon, Harald, Harold, Magnus, Sigurd, Sverre *Ostrogothic:* 9 Theodoric *Persian:* 5 Cyrus 6 Darius, Xerxes *Portuguese:* 4 John 5 Henry, Louis, Peter
6 Carlos, Edward, Manuel, Sancho
7 Alfonso 9 Ferdinand, Sebastian *Prussian:* 7 Wilhelm, William 9 Frederick, Friedrich *relating to:* 5 regal, royal *Saudi Arabian:* 4 Saud 6 Faisal 9 Abdul-Aziz
Scottish: 4 John 5 David, Edgar, James
6 Duncan 7 Macbeth, Malcolm, William
9 Alexander, Donalbane 10 David Bruce
11 Robert Bruce *Spanish:* 3 rey 5 Louis
6 Philip 7 Alfonso, Amadeus, Charles
9 Ferdinand *Spartan:* 8 Leonidas *Swedish:* 4 Eric, John 5 Oscar 6 Birger, Gustav,
Haakon, Magnus 7 Charles 8 Gustavus,
Waldemar 9 Frederick, Sigismund, Sten
Sture *Visigothic:* 6 Alaric
King Arthur *birthplace:* 8 Tintagel *chroni-*

cler: 8 Geoffrey **court site:** 7 Camelot
8 Caerleon **deathplace:** 6 Camlan **father:**
5 Uther **father-in-law:** 9 Laodogant, Leode-
gran 11 Leodegrance **foster father:**
5 Ector **jester:** 7 Dagonet **knight:** 3 Kay
4 Bors 5 Balan, Balin 6 Gareth, Gawain,
Modred 7 Galahad, Geraint, Lamerok,
Mordred, Tristan 8 Bedivere, Lancelot, Parsifal, Percival, Tristram 9 Percivale **lance:**
3 Ron **last abode:** 6 Avalon **last name:**
9 Pendragon **magician:** 6 Merlin **mother:**
6 Ygerne 7 Igraine **nephew:** 6 Gareth,
Modred 7 Mordred **queen:** 9 Guinevere
shield: 7 Pridwin **sister:** 7 Morgain
11 Morgan le Fay **slayer:** 6 Modred
7 Mordred **son:** 6 Modred 7 Mordred
steward: 3 Kay **sword:** 9 Excalibur **victim:** 6 Modred 7 Mordred **wife:**
9 Guinevere

king crab 7 limulus
kingdom 5 realm 6 domain, empire
7 demesne
kingfish 4 cero 7 croaker, whiting
8 mulloway
kingfisher 4 bird 6 alcedo, dacelo 7 halcyon 10 kookaburra
kingly 5 regal, royal 6 lordly, regnal
8 imperial, majestic, powerful, puissant
9 imperious, masterful, monarchal, sovereign 10 monarchial 11 monarchical
King Philip 9 Metacomet
Kingsley play 7 Dead End 10 Men in
White
Kingu **consort:** 6 Tiamat **slayer:** 6 Marduk
kink 4 bend, curl, turn, whim 5 cramp,
crick, quirk, snarl, twist 6 buckle, tangle
12 imperfection
kinky 3 odd 5 outré, ultra, weird 6 far-out
7 bizarre, crooked, deviant, strange,
twisted 10 outlandish
kiosk 5 booth 8 pavilion 9 newsstand
11 summerhouse
kip 3 bed 4 hide, pelt, skin 5 sleep
Kipling, Rudyard **trio:** 3 rag 4 bone
10 hank of hair **work:** 3 Kim, 6 L'Envoi
8 Gunga Din, Mandalay 10 Fuzzy Wuzzy
11 Recessional 13 Soldiers Three, The Jungle Book
kirsch 6 brandy
kirtle 4 coat, gown 5 dress, tunic
Kish **father:** 3 Ner 4 Abdi 5 Abiel, Jeiel
6 Jehiel **son:** 4 Saul
kismet 3 lot 4 doom, fate 5 moira, weird
7 destiny, portion 12 circumstance
kiss 4 buss, peck, skim 5 brush, graze,
shave, smack 6 glance, smooch 8 osculate
kisser 4 face 5 mouth
Kiss sculptor 5 Rodin
kit 3 bag, box, set 6 outfit 7 package
9 container 10 collection
kitchen 6 galley 7 cuisine 8 scullery **appli-**

ance: (see at **appliance**) **boss:** 4 chef; (see
also **cooking**)
kite 4 bird, hawk, sail 5 scram 6 begone,
decamp, get out 7 skiddoo, take off 8 clear
out, hightail 9 skedaddle
kith 7 friends, kindred 9 neighbors
kittenish 3 coy 6 elvish, frisky, impish
7 coltish, larkish, playful, roguish 8 prankish 10 frolicsome 11 mischievous
kitty 3 cat, pot 4 pool 6 feline, stakes
7 jackpot
kiwi 4 bird 5 fruit 7 apteryx
kleptomaniac 5 thief 10 shoplifter
klutz 3 oaf 4 gawk, lout, lump 5 looby
6 lubber, lummox 7 lobster, palooka
9 schlemiel
knack 3 set 4 bent, gift, hang, head, nose,
turn 5 skill, swing, trick 6 genius, talent
7 ability, aptness, command, know-how,
mastery 8 facility 9 dexterity, expertise,
expertism 10 expertness, mastership
knapsack 3 bag 4 case, pack 8 backpack, packsack, rucksack 9 haversack
knave 4 heel, jack 5 rogue, scamp 6 rascal, varlet 7 lowlife, villain 8 coistrel 9 miscreant, scoundrel 10 blackguard
knavery 5 fraud 8 mischief, trickery, villainy 9 rascality
knavish 5 lying 6 shifty 7 roguish
8 unhonest 9 deceitful, dishonest 10 mendacious, untruthful
knee 4 genu 5 joint **armor:** 6 poleyn
bend: 5 kneel 9 genuflect **bone:** 7 patella
kneeler 5 stool 7 cushion 8 prie-dieu
knell 4 bong, peal, ring, toll 5 chime
6 summon 7 warning
knickknack 3 toy 4 dido 5 curio, virtu
6 bauble, gadget, gewgaw, trifle 7 bibelot,
novelty, trinket, whatnot 8 gimcrack, souvenir 9 bric-a-brac, objet d'art 11 rattletraps
knife 3 cut, ulu 4 bolo, shiv, stab 5 blade,
bowie, corer, gouge, panga, slice, sword
6 barong, colter, coutel, cutter, dagger, kuttar, parang, sickle 7 cleaver, couteau,
machete, whittle 8 yataghan **case:**
6 sheath **maker:** 6 cutler 7 grinder **surgical:** 6 catlin 7 catling, scalpel 8 bistoury
knifelike 5 acute, sharp 8 piercing, shooting, stabbing
knight 3 dub, sir 5 eques 6 ritter 8 cavalier, chessman, horseman 9 caballero, chevalier **code:** 7 chivalry **competition:** 7 listing, tilting 8 jousting 10 tournament **flag:**
6 pennon 8 gonfalon, gonfanon **legendary:** 8 douzeper **servant:** 4 page 5 valet
6 squire **title:** 3 sir **wife:** 4 lady
knighthood 8 chivalry
knightly 5 brave, noble 7 gallant
10 chivalrous
Knight of the Round Table   see **King
Arthur**

Knight of the Rueful Countenance
10 Don Quixote

knit 4 bind, heal, join, mend, purl 5 plait, unite, weave 6 cement, stitch 7 conjoin, crochet, wrinkle 8 contract 10 intertwine

knitting 9 handiwork *material:* 4 yarn *stitch:* 3 rib 4 purl 6 garter 11 stockinette *tool:* 6 needle

knob 3 bun, bur, nub 4 bump, burr, dial, hill, lump, node, peak, umbo 5 bulge, gnarl, knoll, mound 6 button, finial, handle, nubble, pommel 7 hillock 12 protuberance *combining form:* 3 tyl 4 tylo 6 condyl 7 condylo

knobkerrie 3 bat 4 club, mace 5 billy 6 cudgel 7 war club 8 bludgeon 9 billy club, truncheon

knock 3 bob, hit, rap, tap 4 blow, bump, lick, skin, swat, tunk, wipe 5 blame, clout, pound, swipe, thump 7 censure, condemn 8 denounce 9 criticize, reprehend, reprobate 10 denunciate

knock down 3 get, win 4 drop, earn, fell, gain, make 5 floor, level 6 ground, lay low 7 acquire, bring in, flatten 8 bowl over

knocker 5 momus 6 carper, critic, Zoilus 7 caviler 9 aristarch 10 criticizer 11 faultfinder

knock off 4 do in, halt, quit, stop, take 5 cease 6 deduct, desist, finish, murder 7 execute, put away, take off, take out 8 discount, draw back, give over, leave off, subtract, surcease, take away 9 liquidate, substract 11 assassinate, discontinue

knockout 2 K.O. 4 kayo 5 dandy, peach 6 beauty, eyeful, looker, lovely 7 stunner 8 jim-dandy 9 humdinger 11 crackerjack

knock over 3 rob 4 down, drop, fell, loot 5 floor, rifle, upset, whelm 6 ground, lay low, topple 7 flatten, overset, plunder, ransack, stick up, tip over 8 bowl down, overcome, overturn 9 bring down, overpower, overthrow, overwhelm, prostrate

knoll 4 hill, knob 5 mound 7 hillock

knot 3 bow, tie, web 4 bond, bump, burr, link, loop, lump, maze, mesh, node, snag, yoke 5 bunch, gnarl, hitch, nexus, skein, snarl 6 jungle, morass, tangle 7 mizmaze 8 ligament, ligature, vinculum 9 labyrinth *in fiber:* 3 nep *kind:* 4 bend, loop, slip 5 hitch, honda 6 granny, splice, square 7 bowline

knotty 4 hard 5 rough, tough 6 daedal, rugged, sticky, uphill 7 complex, gordian, twisted 8 involved, terrible 9 Byzantine, difficult, effortful, elaborate, intricate 10 formidable 11 complicated 12 labyrinthine

knout 4 flog, lash, whip

know 3 see, wot 4 feel 5 grasp, savor, sever, taste 6 fathom, intuit, suffer 7 cognize, discern, realize, sustain, undergo 8 separate 9 apprehend, extricate, recognize 10 apperceive, appreciate, comprehend, difference, discrepate, experience, severalize, understand *Scottish:* 3 ken

knowable 5 lucid 8 luminous 9 graspable 10 cognizable, fathomable 11 cognoscible 12 intelligible 13 apprehensible

know-how 3 art 5 craft, knack, skill 7 ability, command, cunning, mastery 9 dexterity, expertise, expertism 10 adroitness, expertness, mastership

knowing 3 hep, hip 4 gash, sage, wise 5 alive, awake, aware, blasé, canny, quick, sharp, slick, smart 6 brainy, bright, clever, sophic 7 gnostic, witting, worldly 8 mondaine, sensible, sentient 9 brilliant, cognizant, conscious, insighted, observant, sagacious, world-wise 10 conversant, discerning, insightful, perceptive 11 intelligent, quick-witted, ready-witted, sharp-witted, worldly-wise 12 apprehensive, disenchanted, disentranced, nimble-witted, sophisticate 13 disillusioned, sophisticated *combining form:* 7 gnostic 9 gnostical

know-it-all 6 smarty 7 wise guy 8 wiseacre, wisehead 10 smart aleck 11 smartypants, wisecracker, wisenheimer

knowledge 4 data, lore, news 5 facts 6 wisdom 7 science 8 evidence, learning 9 cognition, education, erudition 10 cognizance 11 information, scholarship 12 intelligence 13 enlightenment *combining form:* 5 gnosy, sophy 6 gnosia, gnosis *from meditation:* 5 jnana *lack of:* 9 ignorance *mystical:* 6 gnosis *suffix:* 3 ics *systematized:* 7 science *universal:* 8 pansophy 9 pantology

knowledgeable 4 sage, wise 5 sharp, smart 6 brainy, bright, clever, sophic 7 gnostic, knowing 9 brilliant, insighted, sagacious 10 discerning, insightful, perceptive 11 intelligent, quick-witted, readywitted

know-nothing 4 dolt, dope, rude 5 dummy, dunce, idiot 6 dimwit 7 lackwit, pinhead, wantwit 8 ignorant, untaught 9 benighted, ignoramus, untutored 10 illiterate, uneducated, unlettered 11 emptyheaded

knuckle 5 joint *combining form:* 6 condyl 7 condylo

knucklehead 5 dunce 8 clodpate, numskull 10 thickskull

knuckle under 3 bow 4 cave 5 defer, yield 6 submit 7 succumb 10 capitulate

knurl 4 bead, knob, knot 5 ridge

K.O. 4 kayo 8 knockout

koan 7 paradox

kobold 5 gnome 6 goblin, spirit, sprite

Kohath *father:* 4 Levi *sister:* 8 Jochebed
 son: 5 Izhar
Kohinoor 7 diamond
kohlrabi 6 turnip 7 cabbage
kola 3 nut 7 extract
Kolaiah's son 4 Ahab
komatik 4 sled 6 sledge
kook 3 nut 5 crank 6 cuckoo 7 lunatic
 8 crackpot 9 ding-a-ling, harebrain, screwball 10 crackbrain
kopeck 4 coin *one hundred:* 5 ruble
Korah *father:* 4 Esau 7 Eliphaz *mother:*
 10 Oholibamah
Koran *chapter:* 4 sura *revealer of:*
 7 Gabriel *scholar:* 5 ulama, ulema
Korea see **North Korea; South Korea**
Korean *dynasty:* 2 Yi *national dish:*
 6 kimchi
kosher 3 fit 4 pure 5 clean 6 proper
 7 genuine 10 legitimate
Koussevitzky 5 Serge 6 Sergei
 9 conductor
kowtow 4 fawn 5 cower, toady 6 cringe,
 grovel 7 honey up, truckle 8 bootlick
 11 apple-polish
kraal 3 hut, pen 6 corral 8 manyatta
 9 enclosure

krater 6 vessel *ovoid:* 6 kelebe
Kriemhild *brother:* 7 Gunther *husband:*
 5 Etzel 6 Attila 9 Siegfried *slayer:* 10 Hil-
 debrand *victim:* 5 Hagen
kris 6 dagger
Krishna *avatar of:* 6 Vishnu *brother:*
 8 Balarama *father:* 8 Vasudeva *mother:*
 6 Devaki *uncle:* 5 Kansa *victim:* 5 Kansa
Krupp works site 5 Essen
krypton *symbol:* 2 Kr
kudize 4 hail 6 praise 7 acclaim, applaud,
 commend 9 recommend 10 compliment
kudo 7 bouquet, orchids 10 compliment
kudos 4 bays 5 award, badge, glory,
 honor 6 praise, renown 7 laurels 8 accolade, eminence, prestige 10 decoration,
 prominence, prominency 11 distinction
kudu 8 antelope
kukri 5 sword
kumquat 5 fruit *kin:* 6 orange
kusu 5 mouse
kuttar 6 dagger
kvass 4 beer
kylin 7 unicorn
kylix 3 cup 7 chalice
kyphosis 8 humpback 9 hunchback

L

Laadah *father:* 6 Shelah *grandfather:* 5 Judah

laager 4 camp, tent 6 encamp 7 bivouac

Laban *daughter:* 4 Leah 6 Rachel *father:* 7 Bethuel *grandfather:* 5 Nahor *sister:* 7 Rebekah

label 3 tag 4 band, mark 6 marker, ticket 8 classify *adhesive:* 7 sticker

labium 3 lip

labor 3 tug 4 moil, task, toil, work 5 drive, grind 6 strain, strive 7 slavery, travail 8 bullwork, drudgery, endeavor, slogging, struggle 10 birth pangs, childbirth, donkeywork 12 childbearing *group:* 3 AFL, CIO 5 ILGWU, union *leader:* 5 Hoffa, Lewis, Meany 6 Chavez 7 Gompers, Reuther 8 Randolph

laboratory *device:* 4 etna 5 flask 6 beaker, mortar, pestle, retort 7 pipette 8 crucible, test tube 12 Bunsen burner

laborer 3 man 4 hand, peon 5 hunky, navvy 6 bohunk, toiler, worker 7 workman 8 workhand 9 operative 10 roustabout, workingman *Mexican:* 7 bracero *Oriental:* 5 cooly 6 coolie

laborious 4 hard 5 heavy 6 uphill 7 arduous, labored, onerous, operose 8 toilsome 9 difficult, effortful, strenuous 10 burdensome

La Brea 4 pits 7 tar pits *fossil:* 10 sabertooth

labyrinth 3 web 4 knot, maze, mesh 5 skein, snarl 6 jungle, morass, tangle 7 mizmaze *builder:* 8 Daedalus *monster:* 8 Minotaur

labyrinthine 6 daedal, knotty 7 complex, gordian 8 involved, tortuous 9 Byzantine, elaborate, intricate 11 complicated

lace 3 net, tat, tie 4 beat, cord, lash, trim 5 adorn, braid, frill, liven, plait, twine 6 defeat, fabric, fasten, ribbon, string, thrash, thread 7 entwine, tatting 8 decorate, openwork 9 embroider 10 embroidery, intertwine, shoestring 11 needlepoint *edge:* 5 picot *ground:* 6 réseau *into:* 5 abuse 6 attack 7 condemn *kind:* 6 bobbin 7 Alençon, guipure, Maltese, Mechlin 8 Argentan, Brussels, Venetian 9 Chantilly 10 colberteen, colbertine 11 needlepoint 12 Valenciennes *make:* 3 tat *pattern:* 5 toilé

Lacedaemon 6 Sparta

lacerate 3 cut, rip 4 rend, tear 5 wound 6 mangle, pierce

lachrymose 3 sad 5 teary, weepy 7 tearful, weeping 8 mournful

lack 4 need, want 6 dearth, defect 7 absence, default, deficit, failure, require 8 shortage, underage 9 privation 10 deficiency, inadequacy, scantiness

lackadaisical 4 idle, lazy, limp 7 dieaway, languid, passive 8 fainéant, indolent, listless, romantic, slothful 9 enervated, incurious 10 languorous, spiritless

lacking 3 shy 4 away, gone, sans 5 minus, short 6 absent, devoid 7 missing, omitted, wanting, without 8 awanting 9 defective, deficient 10 inadequate, incomplete, uncomplete 12 insufficient

lackluster 3 dim, mat 4 dead, drab, dull, flat 5 blind, muted, prosy, rusty 6 leaden 7 prosaic 8 lifeless 9 colorless, tarnished

Laconian 7 Spartan *king:* 5 Lelex, Myles

laconic 4 curt 5 brief, pithy, short, terse 7 brusque, concise 8 succinct 11 compendiary, compendious 12 breviloquent

lacquer 5 gloss 6 finish 7 shellac, varnish

lacquered metalware 4 tole

lactate 4 salt 5 ester 7 secrete

lacteal 5 milky

lacuna 3 gap 5 break 6 breach, hiatus 7 interim 8 interval 12 interruption

lad 3 boy, son, tad 5 youth 6 shaver 9 shaveling, stripling *Scottish:* 6 callan 7 callant

ladder 3 run 5 scale 6 series *adjunct:* 4 rung 6 rundle

ladderlike 6 scalar 11 scalariform

lade 3 dip, tax 4 bail, clog, load, pack, ship, stow 5 ladle, scoop, weigh 6 burden, charge, cumber, saddle, weight 8 encumber

lading 4 haul, load 5 cargo 6 burden 7 freight, payload

ladle 3 dip 4 bail, lade 5 scoop, spoon 6 dipper

Ladon 6 dragon *father:* 7 Phorcus, Phorcys *mother:* 4 Ceto *slayer:* 8 Heracles, Hercules

lady *French:* 4 dame *Italian:* 5 donna 7 signora *Muslim:* 5 begum *Spanish:* 4 doña 6 senora

lady ___ 4 crab, fern, luck, palm 5 chair,

tulip **6** beetle, friend, killer **7** cracker **9** bountiful

ladybird 6 beetle **7** pintail

ladybug 6 beetle *Australian:* **7** vedalia

Lady Chatterley's Lover *author:* **8** Lawrence *character:* **6** Connie **7** Mellors **9** Constance

Lady of the Lake, The 5 Ellen, Nimue **6** Vivien *author:* **5** Scott

Lady Windermere's Fan author **5** Wilde

Laertes *father:* **8** Acrisius, Polonius *sister:* **7** Ophelia *son:* **7** Ulysses **8** Odysseus *wife:* **8** Anticlea

La Fontaine's forte 5 fable

lag 4 drag, last, poke, slow, stay, tire **5** dally, delay, final, tarry, trail **6** dawdle, deport, latest, latter, loiter, put off, retard **7** closing, slacken **8** eventual, hindmost, terminal, ultimate **10** concluding

lager 4 beer

laggard 4 slow **6** loafer, remiss **7** dawdler, unhasty **8** comatose, dawdling, delaying, dilatory, lingerer, loiterer, slowpoke, sluggish **9** apathetic, impassive, lazybones, leisurely, lethargic, loitering, slow coach, straggler, unhurried **10** deliberate, phlegmatic

La Gioconda *composer:* **10** Ponchielli *painter:* **7** da Vinci

lagniappe 3 tip **4** perk **7** cumshaw, largess, palm oil **8** gratuity **9** pourboire **10** perquisite

lagomorph 4 hare, pika **6** rabbit

lagoon 4 pond, pool **5** liman, sound **7** channel

____ **La Guardia 8** Fiorello

Lahmi *brother:* **7** Goliath *slayer:* **7** Elhanan

laic 6 layman

lair 3 den **4** cave **5** couch, haunt, lodge **6** burrow **7** hideout, retreat **8** hideaway

Laius *father:* **8** Labdacus *slayer, son:* **7** Oedipus *wife:* **7** Jocasta

lake 3 sea **4** loch, mere, pond, pool **5** lough **6** lagoon *Adriatic:* **6** Varano *Alberta:* **6** Louise *Algeria:* **5** Hodna *Alps:* **6** Annecy *Arizona-Nevada:* **4** Mead *Armenia:* **5** Sevan **6** Gokcha, Sevang **9** Lychnitis *Aswan's:* **6** Nasser *Australia:* **4** Eyre **5** Carey, Cowan, Frome, Wells **6** Barlee **7** Amadeus, Everard, Torrens **8** Gairdner *Austria:* **5** Atter, Traun **6** Kammer **8** Attersee **9** Kammersee *Bolivia:* **5** Poopo *Botswana:* **5** Ngami *British Columbia:* **4** Pitt **5** Atlin *California:* **4** Mono, Tule **5** Clear, Eagle, Honey *Cambodia:* **8** Tonle Sap *Canada:* **4** Dyke **8** Manitoba *central Africa:* **4** Kivu **5** Mweru **6** Albert *Central America:* **5** Guija *central Europe:*

5 Leman **6** Geneva, Lugano **7** Ceresio **8** Bodensee **9** Constance *central North America:* **5** Rainy *Chile:* **4** Laja **5** Ranco *China:* **6** Poyang **8** Dongting *Colorado:* **5** Grand *combining form:* **4** limn **5** limni, limno **6** limnia (plural) **7** limnion *Connecticut:* **6** Bantam **7** Gardner **8** Highland **10** Candlewood, Pocotopaug *Denmark:* **5** Esrum *east Africa:* **6** Rudolf **7** Turkana *east Asia:* **5** Hanka **6** Khanka **7** Xingkai **8** Hsingkai *east central Africa:* **8** Victoria **10** Tanganyika *east China:* **2** Ho **3** Tai **5** Dalai, Hulun *Ethiopia:* **4** Tana, Zwai **5** Abaya, Shala, Shamo, Tsana **8** Stefanie **9** Chew Bahir *Finland:* **5** Inari *Florida:* **5** Worth **10** Okeechobee *Germany:* **5** Ammer, Chiem **8** Ammersee, Chiemsee *Ghana:* **5** Volta *Great:* **4** Erie **5** Huron **7** Ontario **8** Michigan, Superior *Greece:* **5** Bolbe, Volvi *Guatemala:* **7** Atitlan *Honduras:* **5** Yojoa *Honshu:* **3** Omi **4** Biwa, Suwa, Yodo *Hungary:* **7** Balaton **10** Plattensee *Idaho:* **4** Waha **5** Grays **6** Priest **11** Coeur d'Alene, Pend Oreille *India:* **3** Dal **5** Wular **6** Chilka *Indonesia:* **4** Poso, Toba **5** Ranau *Iowa:* **5** Storm *Iran:* **5** Niriz, Shahi, Urmia **8** Matianus, Urumiyeh **9** Bakhtigan *Ireland:* **3** Gur, Ree **4** Conn, Derg, Mask **5** Allen, Arrow, Leane *Israel:* **12** Bahr Tabariya, Sea of Galilee *Israel-Jordan:* **7** Dead Sea *Italy:* **4** Como, Iseo, Nemi **5** Garda **6** Albano **7** Bolsena, Perugia **8** Maggiore **9** Trasimene *Japan:* **4** Imba **7** Imbanuma *Kazakh:* **7** Balqash **8** Balkhash *largest inland:* **10** Caspian Sea *Louisiana:* **4** Soda **5** Black, White **9** Catahoula **13** Pontchartrain *Maine:* **3** Big **6** Sebago **9** Moosehead *Mali:* **4** Debo *Manitoba:* **4** Gods **5** Cedar, Moose **8** Winnipeg *Mexico:* **7** Chapala *Michigan:* **4** Burt **5** Leech **6** Itasca **9** Mille Lacs **10** Minnetonka, of the Woods **11** Lac qui Parle *Minnesota-Wisconsin:* **5** Pepin *Mongolian:* **3** Har **5** Har Us, Khara **8** Khara Usu *Montana:* **8** Medicine *mountain:* **4** tarn *Myanmar:* **4** Inle *Nevada:* **4** Ruby **7** Pyramid *New Hampshire:* **4** Echo **5** Squam **7** Sunapee **13** Winnipesaukee *New Jersey:* **5** Union *New York:* **4** Long **5** Chazy, Keuka **6** Cayuga, George, Oneida, Otsego, Owasco, Placid, Seneca **7** Crooked, Saranac **8** Onondaga, Saratoga **10** Chautauqua **11** Canandaigua, Skaneateles *New Zealand:* **4** Ohau **5** Hawea, Taupo **6** Pukaki, Wanaka **8** Wakatipu *Nicaragua:* **7** Managua *North Africa:* **4** Chad *North America:* **9** Champlain *Northern Ireland:* **5** Neagh *Northwest Territories:* **4** Gras **5** Baker, Garry, Pelly **9** Great Bear **10** Great Slave *Norway:* **5** Mjosa *Nova*

Scotia: **7** Bras d'Or *Ontario:* **4** Rice, Seul
5 Trout *Oregon:* **5** Abert **6** Crater **7** Malheur, Wallowa *Paraguay:* **4** Ypoa *Peru:*
5 Junin **13** Chinchaycocha *Philippines:*
4 Bato, Taal **5** Lanao **6** Bombon *Poland:*
5 Mamry, Mauer *Quebec:* **5** Minto, Payne
Russia: **3** Seg **5** Chany, Ilmen, Lacha,
Onega **6** Ladoga **7** Rybinsk **10** Eltonskoye **11** Ladozhskoye *saline:* **5** chott,
shott *Saskatchewan:* **4** Cree **5** Ronge
Scotland: **3** Ard, Awe **4** Doon, Earn, Ness,
Oich, Shin, Sloy **5** Leven, Lochy, Maree,
Morar, Shiel **6** Lomond *Siberia:* **6** Baikal,
Baykal *South Africa:* **4** Kosi *South America:* **5** Merin, Mirim **8** Titicaca *South Carolina:* **11** Wateree Pond *South Dakota:*
5 Andes *southeast Africa:* **5** Nyasa
6 Nyassa *southern United States:* **5** Caddo
southwest Europe: **5** Ohrid **7** Okhrida
Sudan: **2** No *Sweden:* **5** Asnen, Roxen
6 Siljan, Vetter **7** Malaren, Vattern *Switzerland:* **3** Zug **4** Biel, Joux **5** Zuger **6** Bieler,
Bienne, Brienz, Sarnen, Sarner, Zurich
7 Lucerne, Lungern **8** Brienzer, Zuricher
9 Neuchatel, Zurichsee *Tadzhikistan:*
7 Karakul *Tanzania:* **5** Rukwa *Tibet:* **4** Namu **6** Nam Tso, Tengri *Turkey:* **2** Ak
3 Tuz, Van **4** Bafa, Nice **5** Iznik, Sugla
6 Nicaea *Uganda:* **5** Kyoga *Utah:* **6** Powell,
Sevier **9** Great Salt *volcanic:* **8** Ilopango
Wales: **4** Bala *Washington:* **4** Omak
5 Moses **6** Chelan **9** Wenatchee *western
China:* **4** Ai-pi **6** Ebinur *western United
States:* **4** Bear **5** Tahoe *Wisconsin:*
5 Green **9** Winnebago *Yellowstone
National Park:* **5** Heart, Lewis **8** Shoshone
Zaire: **5** Tumba *Zambia:* **9** Bangweolo,
Bangweulu
lake duck 7 mallard
lake herring 5 cisco
Lake poet 7 Southey **9** Coleridge
10 Wordsworth
lakes *central North America:* 5 Great
Connecticut: **4** Twin *Egypt:* **5** Balah
Maine: **8** Rangeley *New Hampshire:*
11 Connecticut *New York:* **6** Finger *Saskatchewan:* **5** Quill *Twin:* **8** Washinee
9 Washining *Wisconsin:* **4** Four
Lakmé *aria:* 8 Bell Song *composer:*
7 Delibes
Lakshmi *husband:* 6 Vishnu *son:*
4 Kama
lam 3 hit **4** beat, drub, pelt, slip **5** paste,
pound **6** batter, escape, flight, hammer,
pummel, thrash, wallop **7** getaway
8 breakout, escaping **10** escapement
La Mancha's knight 10 Don Quixote
lamb 4 cade, dupe, yean **5** sheep **6** cosset **8** yeanling *leg of:* **5** gigot
lambaste 3 pan **4** beat, drub, flay, lick,
pelt, slam, slap, trim, whip **5** paste, pound,

roast, scold, score, slash, smear **6** assail,
attack, berate, hammer, pummel, scathe,
scorch, thrash, wallop **7** blister, censure,
clobber, reprove, scarify, scourge, shellac,
smother **8** denounce, harangue, lash into,
squabash **9** castigate, criticize, excoriate
10 tongue-lash
lambent 6 bright, lucent **7** beaming, glowing, radiant **8** luminous, lustrous **9** brilliant,
effulgent, refulgent **12** incandescent
lamb of God 8 Agnus Dei
Lamb's pseudonym 4 Elia
lame 3 ill **4** halt, limp, sick, weak **6** feeble,
sickly **7** cripple, halting, hipshot, limping
8 crippled, disabled **13** incapacitated
lamebrain 4 dope **5** dunce, noddy, stupe
6 noodle **7** schnook **8** dumbhead
10 dunderhead
Lamech *daughter:* 6 Naamah *father:*
9 Methusael **10** Methuselah *son:* **4** Noah
5 Jabal, Jubal **9** Tubalcain *wife:* **4** Adah
6 Zillah
lament 3 cry, rue **4** keen, moan, pine, pity,
sigh, wail, weep **5** dirge, elegy, mourn
6 bemoan, bewail, grieve, plaint, regret,
repent, repine **7** deplore, despair, elegize
8 jeremiad **9** complaint
lamentable 3 sad **4** dire **6** rueful, woeful
7 doleful, pitiful **8** dolesome, dolorous,
grievous, mournful **9** plaintive, sorrowful
10 afflictive, calamitous, deplorable, lugubrious, melancholy **11** distressing, regrettable,
unfortunate **13** heartbreaking
Lamerok *father:* 9 Pellinore *lover:* **8** Margawse *slayer:* **6** Gawain
lamia 3 hag, hex **5** bruja, witch **9** sorceress **10** witchwoman **11** enchantress
Lamia *country:* 5 Libya *form:* **7** serpent
lover: **4** Zeus
lamina 5 blade, flake, layer, plate
lamp 3 eye, orb **4** davy **5** light, torch
6 ocular, oculus, peeper, winker **7** lantern
10 candelabra **11** candelabrum *floor:*
8 torchère *hanging:* **10** chandelier
lampblack 4 soot **6** carbon
Lampetia *father:* 6 Apollo, Helios *husband:* **9** Asclepius *mother:* **6** Neaera *sister:* **9** Phaethusa
lampoon 4 mock **5** squib **6** satire **7** pasquil **8** ridicule, satirize **10** pasquinade
lamprey 3 eel
lanai 5 porch **7** terrace, veranda
lanate 5 hairy **6** woolly
lance 3 cut **4** spit **5** blade, spear, spike
6 impale, pierce, skewer, skiver, weapon
7 javelin, transfix **11** transpierce
Lancelot, Launcelot *father:* 3 Ban
lover: **6** Elaine **9** Guinevere *son:* **7** Galahad *victim:* **6** Gawain
lancer *Prussian:* 4 Ulan **5** Uhlan
land 3 get, win **4** dirt, gain, have, home,

soil **5** acres, annex, catch, earth, light, manor, perch, roost, shore, terra, tract **6** alight, debark, estate, ground, obtain, pick up, quinta, secure, settle **7** acquire, acreage, country, procure, set down, sit down **8** plottage **9** disembark, touch down **10** terra firma **13** mother country *alluvial:* **5** delta *along a river:* **5** carse **7** bottoms *area:* **7** terrain, terrene *barren:* **5** waste **6** desert *combining form:* **3** geo **4** chor, gaea **5** choro *cultivated:* **4** farm **5** tilth **7** tillage *for grazing:* **3** lea, ley **5** range **6** meadow **7** pasture *high:* **4** hill, mesa **7** plateau **8** mountain *level:* **4** mesa **5** plain **7** plateau *low:* **4** vale **6** valley **9** intervale *measure:* **3** rod **4** acre **7** centare **8** centiare *open:* **5** field, plain *piece:* **3** lot **6** estate, parcel *reclaimed:* **6** polder *relating to:* **8** agrarian *sloping:* **6** cuesta *strip:* **7** isthmus *wet:* **3** bog, fen **4** moor **5** marsh, swamp **6** marish **7** maremma

land east of Eden 3 Nod
landing place of the Ark 6 Ararat
landmark 5 bound, cairn **9** milestone
Land of Cakes 8 Scotland
Land of Enchantment 9 New Mexico
Land of Lakes 8 Michigan
Land of Lincoln 8 Illinois
Land of Milk and Honey 6 Israel
land of Nod 5 sleep
Land of Opportunity 8 Arkansas
Land of Plenty 6 Goshen
Land of the Midnight Sun 6 Norway
Land of the Rising Sun 5 Japan
landowner 6 squire, yeoman *Anglo-Saxon:* **5** thane, thegn *Dutch:* **7** patroon *Scottish:* **5** laird
landscape 5 scene **7** picture, scenery **8** painting *gardener:* **9** topiarist
lane 3 way **4** path, road **5** aisle, alley, byway, track **6** street **7** loaning, pathway **8** footpath **10** passageway
Langobard see **Lombard**
lang syne 4 past, yore **8** foretime **9** yesterday **10** yesteryear
language 4 cant **5** argot, idiom, lingo, prose, slang **6** jargon, patois, speech, tongue **7** dialect, lexicon, palaver **10** dictionary, vernacular, vocabulary **11** terminology *ambiguous:* **6** jargon **8** newspeak **10** double-talk *ancient:* **5** Greek, Latin **6** Hebrew **8** Sanskrit *artificial:* **2** Ro **3** Ido **7** Volapük **9** Esperanto *classical:* **5** Greek, Latin *combining form:* **5** gloss, glott **6** glosso, glotto *expert:* **8** linguist *informal:* **5** lingo, slang *meaningless:* **9** gibberish *mixed:* **6** pidgin *pretentious:* **6** hot air **7** bombast **8** claptrap *regional:* **7** dialect *relating to:* **10** linguistic *Romance:* **6** French **7** Catalan, Italian, Spanish **8** Romanian, Rumanian **10** Portuguese *secret:* **4** cant, code

5 argot *structure:* **6** syntax **7** grammar *suffix:* **3** ese *written:* **5** prose
languid 4 limp, slow, weak **5** inert **6** supine, torpid **7** die-away **8** comatose, inactive, listless, slothful, sluggish **9** apathetic, enervated, impassive, lethargic **10** languorous, phlegmatic, spiritless **11** languishing **13** lackadaisical
languishing 4 limp **6** pining **7** die-away, languid, longing **8** fainéant, indolent, listless, weakened, yearning **9** enervated, enfeebled **10** languorous, spiritless **11** debilitated **13** lackadaisical
languor 3 kef, kif **4** coma **5** blues, dumps, ennui, sleep **6** stupor, tedium, torpor **7** fatigue, slumber **8** doldrums, dullness, hebetude, lethargy **9** lassitude, torpidity, weariness **10** depression, exhaustion
languorous 3 lax **4** limp, slow **5** loose, slack **7** die-away, laggard, languid, passive, relaxed **8** dilatory, fainéant, indolent, indulged, listless, pampered, slothful **9** enervated, leisurely **10** spiritless **11** languishing **13** lackadaisical
lank 4 bony, lean **5** gaunt, lanky, spare **6** gangly, skinny **7** angular, scraggy, scrawny **8** gangling, rawboned **10** attenuated, extenuated
lanyard 4 cord, line, rope
Laocoon *city:* **4** Troy *killer:* **7** serpent
Laodamia *father:* **7** Acastus *husband:* **11** Protesilaus
Laomedon *daughter:* **7** Hesione *father:* **4** Ilus *kingdom:* **4** Troy *mother:* **8** Eurydice *slayer:* **8** Heracles, Hercules *son:* **5** Priam **8** Tithonus
Laos *capital:* **9** Vientiane *monetary unit:* **3** kip
lap 3 lip, sip **4** lave, ride, wash **5** bathe, slosh, swash **6** bubble, burble, gurgle **7** overlie, shingle **8** override **9** imbricate
lapidary 6 cutter **7** jeweler **8** engraver, polisher
lapideous 5 stony
lapillus 4 lava **6** cinder
lapin 6 rabbit
Lapiths *foes:* **8** centaurs *king:* **5** Ixion
lappet 4 flap, fold, moth **5** lapel **6** infula
Lappidoth's wife 7 Deborah
Lapsang 3 tea
lapse 3 err, sin **4** bull, slip, trip, vice **5** boner, crime, error, fluff, slide **6** breach, bungle, foible, recede, return, revert **7** blooper, blunder, decline, descend, failing, frailty, mistake, offense, subside **8** trespass **9** backslide, decadence, recession, violation **10** apostatize, declension, degenerate, devolution, recidivate, regression, retrograde **11** backsliding, deteriorate **12** degeneration **13** deterioration, retrogression, transgression

Laputan 6 absurd 9 visionary

lar 3 god 6 gibbon, spirit

larboard 4 left, port

larcenist 4 prig 5 thief 6 nimmer, robber
7 burglar, filcher, stealer 8 pilferer
9 purloiner

larceny 4 lift 5 pinch, steal, theft 7 looting,
robbery 8 burglary, stealage, stealing, thievery, thieving 10 purloining *kind:* 5 grand,
petty

lard 3 fat 6 fatten, grease 10 shortening

larder 6 pantry

large 3 big, fat 4 bull, huge, vast 5 ample,
bulky, grand, great, hefty, husky, jumbo,
major 6 goodly 7 extreme, immense, mammoth, massive, outsize, sizable 8 colossal,
enormous, gigantic, oversize 9 excessive,
extensive, monstrous 10 exorbitant,
immoderate, inordinate, large-scale, monumental, prodigious, stupendous, tremendous, voluminous 11 extravagant *combining form:* 3 meg 4 macr, mega 5 macro,
megal 6 megalo

largess 3 tip 4 boon, gift, perk 5 favor
7 cumshaw, present 8 gratuity
9 lagniappe, pourboire 10 perquisite
11 benevolence

lariat 4 rope 5 lasso, noose, reata, riata
part: 5 honda, hondo *user:* 6 cowboy,
drover 10 cowpuncher

lark 4 bird, dido 5 antic, caper, prank,
shine, trick 6 frolic 7 rollick 8 carousal,
escapade 10 shenanigan, tomfoolery
11 monkeyshine

larrup 4 beat, drub, dust, flog, hide, lash,
lick, whip 5 mop up, whale 6 lather, stripe,
thrash 7 clobber, scourge, shellac 8 lambaste 9 overwhelm 10 flagellate

larva 3 bot 4 grub, worm 5 eruca 6 dobson, maggot 7 atrocha 8 cercaria, hornworm, mealworm 10 case bearer, helgramite 11 caterpillar 12 hellgrammite *amphibian:* 7 tadpole *crustacean:* 4 zoea
flatworm: 5 redia *free-swimming:* 7 planula *mollusk:* 7 veliger *moth:* 8 leafworm
tapeworm: 6 measle

larynx 8 voice box

lasagna 5 pasta 7 noodles

lascivious 3 hot 4 fast, lewd 5 gross
6 coarse, wanton 7 goatish, lustful,
obscene, satyric 8 prurient 9 lecherous, libertine, lickerish, salacious 10 libidinous,
licentious, passionate 11 incontinent
12 concupiscent

lash 3 jaw, wag 4 beat, bind, boil, bolt,
dash, flay, flog, hide, pour, race, rush, tear,
teem, wave, whip 5 baste, chase, fling,
scold, shoot, slash, whale 6 charge, drench,
lather, scathe, scorch, stripe, switch, thrash,
waggle, woggle 7 bawl out, blister, chew

out, scarify, scourge, tell off, upbraid 8 lambaste 9 castigate, excoriate 10 flagellate

lassitude 5 blues, dumps, ennui, sleep
6 apathy, stupor, tedium, torpor 7 fatigue,
languor, slumber 8 doldrums, dullness, hebetude, lethargy 9 disregard, impotence,
tiredness, torpidity, unconcern, weariness
10 depression, exhaustion, torpidness
11 disinterest, insouciance 12 heedlessness, indifference, listlessness

lasso see **lariat**

last 3 end, lag 5 abide, final 6 endure, latest, latter, utmost 7 closing, dernier,
extreme, perdure, persist 8 continue, eventual, furthest, hindmost, rearmost, remotest,
terminal, ultimate 9 outermost, umpteenth,
uttermost 10 bottommost, concluding
11 terminating *next to:* 6 penult
11 penultimate

last extremity 9 bitter end

lasting 3 old 6 stable 7 abiding, durable,
endless, eternal 8 enduring, lifelong 9 continual, diuturnal, incessant, indelible, perduring, perennial, permanent, unceasing
10 continuing, continuous, perdurable,
persisting

Last of the Goths 8 Roderick

Last of the Mohicans, The 5 Uncas
author: 6 Cooper *character:* 4 Cora
5 Alice, Magua, Uncas 11 Natty Bumppo
12 Chingachgook

Last of the Saxons 6 Harold

Last Supper, The *painter:* 7 da Vinci

Las Vegas district 5 Strip

latch 4 bolt 5 catch 6 fasten 8 fastener
British: 5 sneck

latchet 4 lace 5 strap, thong

late 3 new, old 4 cold, dead, once, past
5 tardy 6 asleep, bygone, former, modern,
recent, whilom 7 belated, defunct, extinct,
onetime, overdue, quondam 8 deceased,
departed, lifeless, sometime

Late George Apley, The *author:*
8 Marquand

latent 4 idle 5 inert 6 hidden, unripe
7 abeyant, dormant, lurking 8 immature,
inactive 9 concealed, potential, prepatent,
quiescent, unmatured *combining form:*
5 crypt, krypt 6 crypto, krypto

later 4 anon, next, soon 5 after, infra
6 behind 7 by and by, ensuing 8 latterly,
tomorrow 9 afterward, posterior 10 afterwhile, subsequent 12 postliminary, subsequently 13 subsequential

lateral 4 pass, side 8 sideways

laterally 8 crabwise, sideling, sidelong,
sideward, sideways, sidewise

latest 3 lag 4 last 5 final 6 latter, newest
7 closing 8 eventual, hindmost, rearmost,
terminal, ultimate 10 concluding

latex 5 paint 8 emulsion *product:* 6 balata, chicle, rubber

lath 4 slat 5 stave, stick, strip 8 forepole

lather 4 flap, flog, foam, hide, lash, moil, soap, stew, suds, whip 5 froth, spume, storm, yeast 6 bustle, clamor, dither, hassle, hubbub, pother, stripe, thrash, tumult 7 scourge, turmoil, whoopla 8 rowdydow 9 agitation, commotion, confusion

Latin 5 Roman 7 Italian 8 Hispanic *after:* 4 post *always:* 6 semper *and:* 2 et *before:* 4 ante, prae *book:* 5 liber *boy:* 4 puer *bronze:* 3 aes *brother:* 6 frater *but:* 3 sed *day:* 4 dies *dog:* 5 canis *foot:* 3 pes *force:* 3 vis *friend:* 6 amicus *god:* 4 deus *goddess:* 3 dea *grammarian:* 7 Donatus *hand:* 5 manus *is:* 3 est *law:* 3 ius, jus, lex *light:* 3 lux *peace:* 3 pax *pronoun:* 2 tu 3 ego, nos, vos *road:* 3 via 4 iter *see:* 4 vide *that is:* 5 id est *thing:* 3 res *this:* 3 hic, hoc 4 haec *thus:* 3 sic *war:* 6 bellum *wife:* 4 uxor *woman:* 6 femina *year:* 5 annus

Latin-American *country:* 4 Cuba, Peru 5 Chile 6 Brazil, Guyana, Mexico, Panama 7 Bolivia, Ecuador, Uruguay 8 Colombia, Honduras, Paraguay 9 Argentina, Costa Rica, Guatemala, Nicaragua 10 El Salvador *revolutionary:* 6 Castro (Fidel) 7 Bolivar (Simon), Guevara (Ché)

Latinus *daughter:* 7 Lavinia *father:* 6 Faunus 8 Odysseus *son-in-law:* 6 Aeneas *wife:* 5 Amata

latitude 4 play, room 5 scope, space 6 leeway, margin 7 freedom 9 elbowroom

latke 7 pancake 11 griddle cake

Latona 4 Leto *daughter:* 5 Diana 7 Artemis *father:* 5 Coeus *mother:* 6 Phoebe *son:* 6 Apollo

Latter-day Saint 6 Mormon

lattice 4 grid 5 grate 7 grating, trellis

Latvia *capital:* 4 Riga

Latvian 4 Lett *coin:* 7 santims *measure:* 4 stof 5 faden, kanne, stoff, stoof, vedro 6 kulmet, sagene, versta 8 krouchka

laud 4 hymn 5 adore, bless, cry up, extol 6 admire, praise, revere 7 flatter, glorify, magnify, worship 8 eulogize, venerate 9 celebrate, reverence 10 panegyrize

laudable 6 worthy 9 admirable, deserving, estimable, meritable, praisable 11 commendable, meritorious, thankworthy 12 praiseworthy

laugh 3 yuk 4 beam, crow, grin, ha-ha, roar 5 smile, smirk, snort, tehee, whoop 6 cackle, giggle, guffaw, hee-haw, simper, titter 7 chortle, chuckle, snicker, sniggle 10 cachinnate

laughable 4 rich 5 comic, droll, funny, witty 6 jocose 7 amusing, comical, jocular, mocking, risible 8 derisive, derisory, farcical, gelastic, humorous 9 diverting, facetious, ludicrous 10 ridiculous 12 entertaining

laughing 5 riant 8 derisive

laughingstock 4 butt, fool, jest, joke, mark, mock 5 sport 6 jestee, target 7 mockery 8 derision 9 pilgarlic

launch 4 cast, fire, hurl, open, toss 5 begin, fling, heave, pitch, set up, sling, start, throw 6 get off 7 jump off, kick off, usher in 8 commence, embark on, initiate 9 institute, introduce, originate 10 inaugurate

launching 7 lift-off, takeoff 8 blast-off

launder 4 wash 5 clean 7 cleanse

Laura's lover 8 Petrarch

laurels 4 bays 5 award, badge, honor, kudos 8 accolade 10 decoration 11 distinction

laurel tree nymph 6 Daphne

lava 2 aa 4 rock, slag 5 magma 6 latite, scoria 8 andesite, trachyte *cooled:* 8 pahoehoe *fragment:* 8 lapillus *stream:* 4 flow 6 coulee

lavalava 5 cloth, skirt

lavaliere 7 pendant 8 necklace

lavatory 2 WC 3 loo 4 head, john 5 basin, privy 6 johnny, toilet 7 latrine 8 bathroom, washroom 11 convenience, water closet

lave 3 lap, lip 4 pour, wash 5 bathe

Lavinia *father:* 7 Latinus *husband:* 6 Aeneas *mother:* 5 Amata

Lavinium's founder 6 Aeneas

lavish 4 free, lush 5 grand, spend, waste 7 opulent, profuse, riotous 8 gorgeous, prodigal, splendid, squander 9 exuberant, luxuriant, luxurious, profusive, sumptuous

law 3 act, lex 4 bill, code, doom, rule 5 axiom, canon, edict, nomos, Torah 6 assize, custom, decree, equity 7 command, dictate, justice, mandate, precept, statute, theorem 8 decretum, exigency 9 enactment, institute, necessity, ordinance, prescript, principle 10 principium, regulation 11 commandment, fundamental 12 constitution, prescription *body of:* 4 code 7 pandect 12 constitution *combining form:* 4 nomy *degree:* 3 LLB, LLD *expert:* 5 judge 6 jurist 7 justice *practitioner:* 6 lawyer 7 counsel 8 attorney *relating to:* 5 jural, legal 7 canonic 8 forensic, juristic 9 judiciary *violation of:* 3 sin 4 tort 5 crime, malum 6 felony

lawbreaker 5 felon 6 sinner 8 criminal, offender, scofflaw, violator 10 malefactor

lawcourt 3 bar 8 tribunal

lawful 3 due 5 legal, licit 7 condign 8 bona fide, innocent, rightful 9 allowable 10 legitimate

lawgiver 5 Moses, solon 10 legislator

lawlessness 4 riot 5 chaos 6 strife
7 anarchy, discord 8 conflict, variance
9 mobocracy 10 ochlocracy
lawman 7 marshal, officer, sheriff
9 policeman
Law of Moses 5 Torah 10 Pentateuch
Lawrence novel 8 Kangaroo 9 Aaron's
Rod 10 The Rainbow 11 Women in Love
13 Sons and Lovers
Lawrence of ____ 6 Arabia
lawrencium *symbol:* 2 Lr
lawsuit 4 case 5 cause 6 action
10 litigation
lawyer 6 jurist, legist 7 counsel, pleader
8 advocate, attorney 9 barrister, counselor,
solicitor 10 mouthpiece 12 jurisconsult,
jurisprudent 13 attorney-at-law *dishonest:*
7 shyster 11 pettifogger *fictional:* 10 Perry
Mason *French:* 6 avocat *Indian:* 5 vakil
6 vakeel
lawyers' patron saint 4 Ives
lax 4 ease, easy, open 5 loose, slack
6 loosen, remiss 7 ease off, lenient,
slacken 8 careless, derelict 9 forgetful,
negligent, oblivious, unmindful, untighten
10 behindhand, delinquent, neglectful,
regardless 12 disregardful
lay 3 aim, air, bet, fix, put, set 4 aria, cast,
cite, even, game, hymn, lied, play, song,
tune, turn 5 ditty, flush, level, offer, place,
plane, point, put on, refer, stake, stick, train,
wager 6 adduce, allege, assign, charge,
credit, direct, expose, gamble, impute, melody, settle, smooth, spread, strain, warble,
zero in 7 address, advance, ascribe, descant, flatten, incline, measure, melisma, melodia, present, profane, secular, subject,
uncover 8 accredit, diapason, smoothen,
temporal, unsacred 9 attribute, establish
lay aside 4 cast, save, shed 5 chuck,
ditch, put by, scrap 6 reject, slough 7 discard, neglect 8 jettison, salt away 9 throw
away
lay by 4 save 5 amass, hoard, store
7 deposit 8 salt away
lay down 3 set 4 cede 5 leave, waive,
yield 6 assign, decree, define, give up,
impose, ordain, resign 7 abandon, dictate
8 hand over 9 establish, prescribe, surrender 10 relinquish
lay eggs 5 spawn 8 oviposit
layer 3 hen, ply 4 coat, film, seam, tier
5 paver, sheet 6 folium, lamina, veneer
7 coating, provine, stratum 8 laminate,
membrane, sandwich, stratify *combining
form:* 5 cline, lamin, ptych 6 lamell, lamino,
ptycho, strati 7 lamelli *inner:* 6 lining *of
odds:* 6 bookie 9 bookmaker *of skin:*
6 dermis 9 epidermis *outer:* 4 skin
6 veneer
lay for 6 ambush, waylay 8 surprise

lay in see lay by
lay low 4 down, fell, hide, kill, slay 5 floor,
level, scrag 6 cut off, finish, ground
7 destroy, flatten, mow down, put away,
take off 8 bowl down, bowl over, dispatch
9 knock down, knock over, throw down
layman 4 laic 7 secular
lay off 4 halt, quit, stop 5 avoid, cease
7 dismiss, measure 9 disemploy
11 discontinue
lay open 4 bare, show 6 expose, reveal
7 uncover
lay out 3 pay 4 give, plan 5 spend
6 design, expend, map out, outlay, set out
7 arrange, fork out 8 disburse, shell out
lay waste 4 ruin 6 ravage 7 destroy
8 desolate 9 devastate
lazar 5 leper
Lazarus' sister 4 Mary 6 Martha
laze 3 bum 4 idle, lazy, loaf, loll 5 sloth
6 dawdle, loiter, lounge, slouch 7 goof off
8 idleness, laziness, malinger 9 goldbrick,
indolence
laziness 5 sloth 6 slouch 8 idleness
9 indolence
lazy 3 bum, lax 4 idle, loaf, loll 5 drony,
inert, slack 6 dawdle, loiter, lounge, remiss,
supine, torpid 7 goof off, languid, passive,
work-shy 8 comatose, fainéant, inactive,
indolent, listless, slothful, sluggish, trifling
9 easygoing, goldbrick, lethargic, negligent,
shiftless, slowgoing
Lazy Susan 4 tray 9 turntable
lea 6 fallow, meadow 7 pasture
8 unplowed 9 grassland
leach 4 suck 7 draw out 9 lixiviate, percolate 11 bloodsucker
lead 3 get, see 4 dean, head, move, show,
star 5 bring, doyen, guide, metal, pilot,
route, steer, usher 6 bullet, ceruse, direct,
escort, induce, leader 7 captain, conduct,
convert, plumbum, precede, preface, prevail 8 graphite, persuade, shepherd 9 introduce 10 bellwether *combining form:*
5 plumb 6 molybd, plumbo 7 molybdo
ore: 6 galena 8 galenite 9 anglesite, cerru-
site *oxide:* 6 sinter *sounding:* 7 plummet
symbol: 2 Pb
lead astray 4 undo 6 delude, entice,
seduce 7 corrupt, deceive, degrade, pervert
leaden 3 dun 4 drab, dull, flat, gray
5 heavy, inert 8 dragging, lifeless, sluggish
9 plumbeous
leader 4 boss, cock, dean, duce, head,
lead, lion, lord 5 chief, doyen, guide, pilot
6 bigwig, herald, honcho, master, rector
7 captain, foreman, general, headman, manager, notable 8 big-timer, big wheel, chairman, director, eminence, hierarch, luminary,
superior 9 chieftain, commander, conductor, dignitary, dominator, harbinger, pace-

maker, precursor, president, principal, straw boss **10** bellwether, chairwoman, forerunner, notability, pacesetter **11** chairperson

authoritarian: 10 Big Brother *combining form:* **4** arch *Cossack:* **6** ataman, hetman *German:* **6** führer **7** fuehrer *Japanese:* **6** shogun *military:* **7** admiral, general, warlord **9** commander **12** field marshal *Muslim:* **4** caid **5** calif **6** caliph, mollah, mullah *national:* **7** premier **9** president **12** chief of state *religious:* **4** pope **5** rabbi **6** bishop, priest **7** prelate **8** hierarch

leading 4 arch, head, main **5** chief, first, noted **6** famous **7** initial, popular, premier **8** champion, foremost, headmost **9** inaugural, notorious, principal, prominent, wellknown

lead on 3 toy **4** bait, fool, lure, toll **5** dally, decoy, flirt, tempt **6** allure, coquet, entice, entrap, seduce, trifle, wanton **8** inveigle **11** string along

leaf 4 foil, olla, page, scan **5** blade, bract, folio, frond, petal, scale, sepal **6** browse, spathe **7** dip into, run over **8** glance at **10** glance over, run through **11** flip through, riff through, skim through **12** thumb through **13** riffle through *aperture:* **5** stoma *axis:* **6** rachis *combining form:* **5** phyll **6** phylla (plural), phyllo **7** phyllum *edge:* **9** crenation *lily:* **3** pad *part:* **4** lobe, vein **5** blade, costa, stoma **7** petiole, stipule, tendril *pine:* **6** needle *scale:* **8** ramentum *vein:* **5** costa

leafage 7 foliage, umbrage, verdure

leaflet 5 pinna, sheet, tract **6** folder **8** circular, pamphlet

leafy 4 lush **5** green **7** foliate, foliose, folious **8** foliated, laminate

league 4 band, bond, club, loop, tier **5** class, grade, group, guild, order, union, unite, wheel **6** concur **7** circuit, combine, conjoin, society **8** alliance, category, coadjute, division, grouping, sodality **9** anschluss, coalition, cooperate **10** conference, federation, fellowship, fraternity, pigeonhole **11** association, brotherhood, confederacy **13** confederation

Leah *daughter:* **5** Dinah *father:* **5** Laban *husband:* **5** Jacob *sister:* **6** Rachel *son:* **4** Levi **5** Judah **6** Reuben, Simeon **7** Zebulun **8** Issachar

leak 3 out **4** drip, ooze, seep **5** bilge, break, crack **6** escape, get out **7** come out

leaky 6 porose, porous

lean 3 jut, tip **4** bend, bony, cant, hang, heel, lank, list, look, slim, tend, thin, tilt, turn, worn **5** curve, gaunt, grade, lanky, sheer, slant, slope, spare **6** beetle, divert, meager, skinny, slight, wasted **7** angular, deflect, haggard, incline, pinched, recline, scraggy, scrawny, slender, stringy, wizened **8** bend

over, gradient, overhang, rawboned, spareset **10** cadaverous

Leander's beloved 4 Hero

Leandre *beloved:* **7** Lucinde *father:* **7** Geronte

Leaning Tower site 4 Pisa

lean-to 3 hut **5** shack **7** shelter

leap 3 hop, lop **4** buck, jump, loup, over, rise, soar **5** arise, bound, caper, clear, mount, vault **6** ascend, bounce, gambol, hurdle, spring **7** saltate **8** capriole, surmount *ballet:* **4** jeté **9** entrechat *by a horse:* **7** gambade, gambado **9** ballotade

leaping light 3 arc

Lear *daughter:* **5** Regan **7** Goneril **8** Cordelia *servant:* **4** Kent

learn 3 con, get, see **4** find, hear **5** study **6** master, peruse, pick up, tumble **7** catch on, find out, realize, unearth **8** discover, memorize **9** ascertain, determine

learned 4 sage, wise **6** astute **7** bookish, erudite **8** abstruse, academic, cultured, educated, esoteric, pedantic, polymath **9** recondite, scholarly **10** cultivated, scholastic

learner 5 pupil **7** scholar, student, trainee **10** apprentice

learning 4 lore **6** wisdom **7** science **8** booklore, pedantry **9** education, erudition, knowledge **11** scholarship *man of:* **7** egghead, scholar, teacher **9** professor **12** intellectual

lease 3 let **4** hire, rent **7** charter **8** contract

leash 3 tie **4** bind, clog, cord, curb, rope **5** strap **6** fetter, hamper, hobble, hog-tie, tether **7** shackle, trammel **9** entrammel *hawk's:* **4** lune

leather 3 tan **4** hide, skin, whip **6** thrash *kind:* **3** kid, kip, oak **4** alum, bock, buff, calf, napa, ooze, roan **5** aluta, basil, crown, grain, japan, mocha, strap, suede, whang **6** castor, comber, latigo, levant, oxhide, patent, roller, saddle, skiver **7** buffalo, canepin, carding, chamois, hemlock, morocco, ostrich, peccary, rutland, saffian **8** capeskin, cheverel, cordovan, cordwain, shagreen *maker:* **6** tanner **7** tannery *piece:* **4** rand, welt **5** strap, thong, trank *prepare:* **3** sam, tan, taw **4** mull **5** curry, sammy *soft:* **5** aluta, mocha, suede **8** cabretta

Leatherneck 6 marine

Leatherstocking Tales, The *author:* **6** Cooper *title:* **10** The Prairie **11** The Pioneers **13** The Deerslayer, The Pathfinder

leave 2 go **3** let **4** cede, drop, exit, have, quit, will **5** allot, allow, scram, waive, yield **6** assent, assign, commit, decamp, depart, desert, devise, escape, get off, give up, legate, maroon, permit, resign, retire, strand, suffer, vacate **7** abandon, confide, consent, consign, entrust, forsake, get away, holiday, pull out **8** bequeath, emigrate, hand over, sanction, vacation, withdraw **9** allowance, apportion, surrender, terminate **10** permission, relinquish, sufferance **13** authorization

leaved **7** foliate, foliose, folious **8** foliated

leaven **5** imbue, steep, yeast **6** infuse, invest, temper, vivify **7** enliven, ingrain, qualify, quicken, suffuse **8** moderate **9** inoculate

leavening agent **5** yeast **12** baking powder

leave of absence **5** exeat **8** furlough

leave off **4** halt, quit, stop **5** cease **6** desist **8** give over, knock off, surcease **11** discontinue

leave out **4** omit, skip **5** elide **7** exclude

Leaves of Grass author **7** Whitman

leavings **4** heel, junk, lees, orts, rest **5** dregs, scrap **7** balance, remains, remanet, remnant, residue, rubbish **8** discards, portions, residual, residuum **9** fragments, remainder

Lebanon *capital:* **6** Beirut *monetary unit:* **5** pound

lecher **4** rake, roué **9** debauchee, libertine

lecherous **4** fast, lewd **7** goatish, lustful, satyric **9** libertine, salacious **10** lascivious, libidinous, licentious **11** incontinent

lectern **4** desk **5** stand

lecture **4** talk **5** scold, speak **6** preach, sermon, speech **7** address, oration, prelect **8** briefing **10** allocution

lecturer **6** docent, orator, reader **7** speaker, teacher **9** professor **10** praelector

Leda *daughter:* **5** Helen **12** Clytemnestra *father:* **8** Thestius *husband:* **6** Tyndareus *lover:* **4** swan, Zeus *son:* **6** Castor, Pollux

ledge **4** berm, lode, sill **5** berme, ridge, shelf

ledger **4** book **6** record **8** monument **9** footstone, headstone, tombstone **10** gravestone **11** grave marker

lee **5** haven **6** harbor **7** shelter

leech **4** worm **6** sponge, sucker **7** sponger **8** barnacle, hanger-on, parasite **10** freeloader **11** bloodsucker **12** lounge lizard

Leeds' river **4** Aire

leer **4** look, ogle **5** empty, fleer, smirk, sneer **6** glance **7** grimace

leery **4** wary **8** doubtful **10** suspicious **11** distrustful

lees **5** draff, dregs **6** dunder, refuse **7** deposit, grounds, vinasse **8** leavings, sediment **9** settlings **11** precipitate

leeward **8** downwind

leeway **4** play, room **5** scope, space **6** margin **8** latitude **9** elbowroom

left **4** port **8** larboard

left-handed **8** southpaw

left-hand page **5** verso

leftovers see **leavings**

leftward **4** levo **5** aport, laevo **8** levogyre **10** levogyrate *go:* **3** haw

leg **3** gam, run **4** gamb, limb, walk **5** gambe, shank **6** gammon **7** support **8** cabriole **9** appendage, drumstick *bone:* **4** shin **5** femur, tibia **6** fibula **7** patella *part:* **4** calf, crus, foot, knee, shin **5** ankle, thigh **6** cnemis

legacy **4** gift **6** devise **7** bequest **8** heritage **9** heritance, patrimony **10** birthright **11** inheritance

legal **5** licit **6** lawful **7** juridic **8** innocent **9** juridical **10** legitimate *matter:* **3** res **4** case, suit *order:* **4** writ **7** summons **8** subpoena *party:* **6** suitor **8** litigant **9** defendant, plaintiff *restraint:* **8** estoppel

legal aid group **4** ACLU

legal tender **4** cash **5** money **6** dollar **8** currency

legate **4** will **5** envoy, leave **6** deputy, devise **8** bequeath, delegate, emissary, governor **10** ambassador

legatee **4** heir **9** inheritor

legend **4** lore, myth, saga **5** fable, story **6** mythos, mythus **7** caption, fiction **8** folklore **9** mythology, tradition

legendary **6** fabled, mythic **7** fabular **8** fabulous, mythical **12** mythological

legerdemain **5** magic **8** trickery **9** conjuring

legging **5** chaps **6** puttee **7** gambade, gambado **11** spatterdash **12** antigropelos

leghorn **4** fowl **5** straw **7** chicken

legible **5** clear **8** distinct, readable

legion **4** army, host, many, rout **5** cloud, crowd, flock **6** scores, sundry **7** various **8** numerous, populous **9** multitude

legislate **5** enact

legislation **3** act, law **4** bill **7** statute

legislator **3** rep **5** solon **6** deputy **7** senator **8** lawgiver, lawmaker **9** statesman **10** politician **11** congressman

legislature **4** diet **5** house, junta **6** senate **7** council **8** assembly, congress **10** parliament *Communist:* **6** soviet **9** politburo, presidium *czarist Russian:* **4** duma *Danish:* **9** Folketing *Finnish:* **9** Eduskunta *German:* **9** Bundesrat, Bundestag *Iceland:* **7** Althing *Israel:* **7** Knesset *Norway:* **8** Storting *one-house:* **10** unicameral *Poland:* **4** Sejm *Spain:* **6** Cortes *Sweden:* **7** Riksdag *two-house:* **9** bicameral

legitimate **4** fair, just, true **5** legal, licit, sound, usual, valid **6** cogent, lawful, normal **7** natural, regular, typical **8** innocent, rightful **9** customary **10** recognized

leg of lamb **5** gigot

legume **3** pea, pod, soy **4** bean, guar,

seed, soya **5** pulse **6** lentil **7** soybean
9 bird's-foot, vegetable
leg up 5 boost
lei 6 wreath **7** garland **8** necklace
Leibnitz's invention 8 calculus
Leif Ericson *discovery:* **7** Vinland
father: **4** Eric
leisure 4 ease, rest, time **6** casual,
repose **10** relaxation **12** requiescence
leisurely 3 lax **4** easy, slow **5** slack
7 delayed, laggard, relaxed, restful,
unhasty **8** dilatory **9** slackened, unhurried
leitmotiv 5 theme **6** motive
lemma 5 bract, theme **7** premise, theorem
lemon 3 dud **4** bomb, bust, flop **5** fruit,
loser **7** failure
lemur 4 maki, vari **5** indri, locis, potto
6 aye-aye, colugo, macaco **7** half-ape, tarsier **9** babacoote
lend 4 give, loan **5** allow, grant **6** oblige
7 advance, furnish **11** accommodate
length 4 term **5** orbit, range, reach, realm,
scope **6** radius **7** compass, purview,
stretch, yardage **8** distance, panorama
lengthen 4 draw **6** expand, extend
7 draw out, prolong, spin out, stretch
8 elongate, increase, protract **10** prolongate
Scottish: **3** eke
lengthy 4 long **8** dragging, drawn-out,
elongate, extended, longsome, overlong
9 elongated, prolonged **10** protracted
leniency 5 mercy **8** clemency **9** tolerance **10** indulgence, toleration
11 forbearance
lenient 3 lax **4** easy, kind, mild, soft
5 balmy, bland, faint **6** benign, gentle,
kindly, smooth, tender **7** amiable, clement
8 excusing, humoring, merciful, obliging,
spoiling, tolerant **9** benignant, condoning,
forgiving, indulgent, indulging, pampering,
pardoning **10** charitable, forbearing
lenity 5 grace, mercy **7** caritas, charity
8 clemency **10** humaneness, tenderness
lens 5 glass **6** lentil **8** meniscus *kind:*
5 toric **6** convex **7** bifocal, concave
8 trifocal
lentigo 5 nevus **7** freckle
lentil 4 lens, seed **6** legume
Leofric's wife 6 Godiva
Leoncavallo opera 9 Pagliacci
leonine 8 lionlike
Leonora *alias:* **7** Fidelio *husband:*
9 Florestan
leopard 3 cat **7** panther
Leo star 7 Regulus
leper 6 pariah **7** Ishmael, outcast **8** castaway, derelict **10** Ishmaelite **11** untouchable
Leper King 7 Baldwin
Leper Priest 6 Damien
lepers' hospital 9 lazaretto
lepers' island 7 Molokai

lepidopter 4 moth **6** insect **9** butterfly
Leporello's master 11 Don Giovanni
leprechaun 3 elf **5** fairy **6** sprite *trade:*
8 cobbling
Lesage hero 7 Gil Blas
Lesbos poet 6 Sappho **7** Alcaeus
lesion 3 cut **4** flaw, sore **5** ulcer, wound
6 injury **10** impairment
Lesotho *capital:* **6** Maseru *monetary
unit:* **4** loti
lessen 4 clip, crop, ease, thin, wane
5 abate, close, drain, lower, taper **6** dilute,
minify, reduce, shrink, weaken **7** abridge,
assuage, curtail, dwindle, lighten, relieve
8 amputate, decrease, diminish, minimize,
mitigate, taper off, truncate **9** attenuate
lessening 5 letup **8** decrease, slowdown
9 abatement
lesser 3 low **5** dinky, lower, minor, small,
under **6** nether **8** inferior, small-fry **9** secondary, small-time, subjacent **11** minor-
league **13** insignificant
lesson 4 text **5** chide, moral, study
6 monish, rebuke **7** lecture, reading,
reprove, tick off **8** admonish, call down,
exercise, reproach **9** reprimand
11 instruction
lessor 6 bailor **8** landlady, landlord
let 4 have, hire, rent **5** allow, grant, lease,
leave **6** permit, suffer **7** approve, certify,
charter, concede, endorse, license
8 accredit, sanction **9** authorize
letdown 5 slump **7** decline **10** depression
let go 4 emit, fire, free **6** unhand **7** dismiss, release **9** discharge
lethal 5 fatal **6** deadly, mortal, poison
7 deathly **9** pestilent, poisonous
lethargic 4 dull, idle, slow **5** dopey, heavy,
inert **6** stolid, stupid, supine, torpid **7** dormant, laggard, languid, passive **8** comatose, dilatory, inactive, listless, sluggish
9 apathetic, impassive **10** languorous,
phlegmatic, slumberous, spiritless **12** hebetudinous **13** lackadaisical
lethargy 4 coma **5** sleep, sloth **6** apathy,
phlegm, stupor, torpor **7** inertia, languor,
slumber **8** dullness, hebetude, idleness,
laziness **9** disregard, inanition, indolence,
inertness, lassitude, torpidity, unconcern
10 inactivity, supineness, torpidness **11** disinterest, impassivity, insouciance,
passiveness
lethe 8 oblivion **13** forgetfulness
let in 5 admit
Leto see Latona
let off 5 spare **6** excuse, exempt
7 absolve, relieve **8** dispense **9** discharge
let on 3 own **4** avow, tell **5** admit, allow,
grant, own up, spill **6** betray, fess up,
reveal, unveil **7** concede, confess, divulge,
uncover **8** disclose, give away

letter 2 ar, ef, el, em, en, ex 3 bee, cee, cue, dee, ess, gee, jay, kay, pee, tee, vee, wye, zed, zee 4 line, mail, memo, note, rune 5 aitch, print, vowel 6 report, screed, symbol 7 epistle, message, missive 8 dispatch, inscribe 9 consonant *airmail:* 8 aerogram *Anglo-Saxon:* (see **Anglo-Saxon**) *Arabic:* (see **alphabet**) *Greek:* (see **alphabet**) *Hebrew:* (see **alphabet**) *kind:* 5 chain, roman 6 italic, uncial 8 Dear John *large:* 7 capital 9 majuscule, upper case *small:* 9 lower case, miniscule

lettuce 3 cos 4 Bibb, head 6 Boston 7 iceberg, romaine, Simpson 10 butterweed

let up 3 ebb 4 fall, wane 5 abate 6 relent 7 die away, die down, ease off, slacken

letup 5 break 7 respite 9 reduction

Levant, Levantine 7 eastern

levee 4 dike, dock, pier, quay, slip 5 berth, jetty, wharf 10 embankment

level 3 aim, lay, par 4 akin, cast, down, drop, even, fell, flat, like, raze, same, tier, true, turn 5 alike, equal, floor, flush, plane, point, train 6 direct, ground, smooth, zero in 7 address, aligned, flatten, incline, mow down, planate, regular, similar, uniform 8 parallel, smoothen 9 bring down

lever 3 bar, lam, pry 4 jack 5 helve, jimmy, peavy, prize 6 peavey 7 crowbar

leverage 5 power 9 influence

leveret 4 hare

Levi *father:* 5 Jacob *mother:* 4 Leah *son:* 6 Kohath, Merari 7 Gershon

leviathan 4 huge 5 giant, titan, whale 7 immense, mammoth, monster 8 behemoth, enormous, gigantic 9 cyclopean 10 gargantuan 11 elephantine

Leviathan author 6 Hobbes

levitate 4 lift, rise 5 float 7 suspend

levity 5 folly, humor 8 buoyancy 9 absurdity, flippancy, frivolity, lightness, silliness

levy 3 set, tax 4 duty 5 exact, lay on, place, put on, wrest, wring 6 assess, charge, impose, impost, tariff 10 assessment

lewd 4 base, fast 5 bawdy, gross 6 coarse 7 lustful, obscene, satyric, whorish 8 improper, indecent 9 lecherous, libertine, salacious 10 indelicate, lascivious, libidinous, licentious 11 incontinent

Lewis and Clark inter- preter 9 Sacagawea, Sacajawea

Lewis novel 7 Babbitt 9 Dodsworth 10 Arrowsmith, Main Street 11 Elmer Gantry

lexicographer 8 compiler *American:* 6 Porter 7 Webster 9 Worcester *English:* 4 Wyld 6 Fowler, Murray, Onions 7 Craigie, Johnson *French:* 6 Littré 8 Larousse

lexicon 4 cant 6 jargon 7 palaver 8 language, wordbook 9 word-hoard, wordstock 10 dictionary, vocabulary 11 onomasticon, terminology

liable 3 apt 4 open, tied 5 bound, given, prone 6 likely 7 exposed, subject 8 amenable, beatable, inclined, vincible 9 obnoxious, sensitive 10 answerable, assailable, attackable, chargeable, penetrable, vulnerable 11 accountable, conquerable, responsible, susceptible

liaison 4 bond 5 amour 6 affair 7 affaire 8 intrigue 12 relationship

liar 6 fibber 7 Ananias, fibster 8 fabulist, perjurer 9 falsifier 12 prevaricator *female:* 8 Sapphira

libation 5 drink 6 liquid 7 potable 8 beverage, potation

libel 6 defame, malign, vilify 7 asperse, calumny, slander, traduce 8 tear down, travesty 9 burlesque, denigrate 10 calumniate, caricature, scandalize

libelous 8 debasing 9 invidious, maligning, traducing, vilifying 10 backbiting, calumnious, defamatory, derogative, detracting, detractive, detractory, malevolent, pejorative, scandalous, slanderous

liberal 4 free, open, wide 5 ample, broad 6 lavish, plenty 7 copious, lenient, profuse, radical 8 abundant, advanced, generous, handsome, prodigal, tolerant 9 bounteous, bountiful, exuberant, indulgent, plenteous, plentiful, unsparing 10 benevolent, bighearted, charitable, forbearing, freehanded, munificent, openhanded

liberate 4 free 5 loose, remit 6 detach, loosen, unbind, unhook 7 manumit, release, unchain 8 untangle 9 discharge, unshackle 10 emancipate 12 disembarrass

liberator 7 messiah *of Argentina:* 9 San Martin *of Chile:* 8 O'Higgins *of Ecuador:* 5 Sucre *of Scotland:* 5 Bruce *of South America:* 7 Bolivar

Liberia *capital:* 8 Monrovia *monetary unit:* 6 dollar

Liberian *language:* 3 Kwa *native:* 3 Kru, Vai 4 Gola, Toma 5 Bassa, Grebo 6 Kruman

libertine 4 fast, lewd, rake, roué 7 lustful, satyric 9 debauchee, lecherous, salacious 10 lascivious, libidinous, licentious

liberty 5 leave 7 freedom, license 8 autonomy, delivery 10 liberation 12 emancipation, independence

libidinous 3 hot 4 fast, lewd 5 gross 6 coarse 7 goatish, lustful, obscene, satyric 8 prurient 9 lecherous, libertine, lickerish, salacious 10 lascivious, licentious, passionate 11 incontinent 12 concupiscent

Libni *father:* 5 Mahli 7 Gershon *grandfather:* 4 Levi

librarian 5 Dewey

library 7 archive 9 athenaeum 11 bibliotheca, reading room *desk:* 6 carrel

Libya *capital:* 7 Tripoli *chief export:* 3 oil *largest city:* 8 Benghazi *monetary unit:* 5 dinar *father:* 7 Epaphus *son:* 5 Belus 6 Agenor

license 3 let 5 allow, leave 6 enable, laxity, permit, suffer 7 certify, empower, freedom, liberty 8 accredit, passport, sanction, variance 9 authorize, looseness, slackness

licentious 3 lax 4 fast, lewd 5 loose, randy 6 amoral, animal, carnal 7 corrupt, fleshly, immoral, lustful, relaxed, satyric, sensual, unmoral 8 depraved, scabrous 9 abandoned, debauched, dissolute, lecherous, libertine, oversexed, reprobate, salacious 10 lascivious, libidinous, profligate 11 incontinent 12 unprincipled

lichen 4 moss 6 archil, litmus 7 oakmoss *genus:* 5 Usnea

licit 5 legal 6 lawful 8 approved, innocent, licensed 10 authorized, legitimate, sanctioned

lick 3 hit, lap, rap 4 beat, cast, dash, down, drub, flog, hint, swat, whip, wipe 5 knock, smack, smear, swipe, taste, throw, tinge, touch, trace, whiff 6 hurdle, master, thrash, tongue 7 clobber, conquer, shellac, smother 8 lambaste, overcome, surmount 9 overwhelm

lickerish see **libidinous**

lickety-split 4 fast 5 apace 7 flat out, hastily, quickly, rapidly, swiftly 8 speedily 9 posthaste 13 expeditiously

licorice 4 root 5 candy *pill:* 6 cachou

lid 3 cap, top 5 cover 8 covering *moss:* 9 operculum

lie 3 fib 4 flam, myth, rest, tale 5 dwell, exist, fable, libel, story 6 canard, delude, inhere, palter, repose, reside 7 beguile, consist, deceive, distort, falsify, falsity, forgery, lie down, mislead, perjure, perjury, recline, untruth 8 misguide, misstate, nontruth, untruism 9 falsehood, fish story, mendacity, misinform 10 dishonesty, distortion, equivocate, exaggerate, inaccuracy, inveracity, stretch out, taradiddle 11 fraudulence, misinstruct, prevaricate 12 misstatement, song and dance

Liebestraum composer 5 Liszt

lied 4 aria, hymn, song 5 ditty 7 descant

lie down 4 rest 6 repose 7 recline 10 stretch out

lief 4 fain 6 freely, gladly 9 willingly

liege 4 true 5 loyal 6 ardent, vassal 7 staunch 8 constant, faithful, resolute 9 steadfast

lien 5 claim 6 charge 8 interest, mortgage

lieu 5 place, stead

lieutenant 3 aid 4 aide, zany 7 officer 9 assistant, coadjutor 10 aide-de-camp, coadjutant

life 3 bio, man, vim 4 body, brio, dash, élan, soul, zing 5 being, blood, human, oomph, verve 6 energy, esprit, memoir, mortal, person, spirit 8 creature, vitality 9 animation, biography, existence, personage 13 autobiography *animal:* 5 fauna *animal and plant:* 5 biota *combining form:* 2 bi 3 bia, bio 4 bium, bius 5 biont 6 bioses (plural), biosis, biotic *plant:* 5 flora *relating to:* 5 vital 8 biologic 10 biological *science:* 7 biology

life jacket 7 Mae West

lifeless 4 cold, dead, drab, dull, flat, late 5 amort, inert, prosy 6 asleep, torpid 7 defunct, extinct, prosaic 8 deceased, departed 9 colorless, exanimate, inanimate 10 lackluster, lusterless

lifelike 6 verist 8 accurate, veristic 9 realistic

life of ____ 5 Riley 8 the party

Life with Father author 3 Day

lift 2 up 3 aid, nip 4 doff, hand, heft, help, hook, jack, rear, rise, soar 5 arise, exalt, filch, heave, hoist, mount, pinch, raise, shrug, steal, surge, swipe, theft, tower 6 ascend, aspire, assist, pick up, pilfer, recall, relief, repeal, revoke, rocket, snitch, succor, take up, uphold, uprear 7 comfort, elevate, larceny, magnify, purloin, rescind, reverse, secours, support, upraise 8 levitate, stealage, stealing, thievery

lift-off 6 launch 7 takeoff 9 launching

ligament 3 tie 4 band, bond, knot, link, yoke 5 nexus 8 ligature, vinculum

ligature see **ligament**

Ligeia author 3 Poe

light 3 gay, hit 4 airy, bump, dawn, deft, easy, fair, fast, fire, lamp, land, luck, meet, morn, neon, soft 5 blond, dizzy, flash, giddy, loose, minor, perch, petty, roost, royal, small, sunny, torch 6 aurora, beacon, bright, candle, casual, chance, facile, flimsy, fluffy, happen, ignite, illume, kindle, little, meager, settle, simple, slight, smooth, strobe, swimmy, tumble, wanton 7 downing, flighty, inflame, lantern, lighten, morning, set down, sit down, slender, stumble, sunrise, trivial, unheavy, whorish 8 cheerful, cockcrow, daybreak, daylight, enkindle, illumine, luminous, skittish, swimming, trifling, unchaste 9 frivolous, small-beer, touch down 10 bird-witted, chandelier, effortless, illuminate *combining form:* 4 luci, phos, phot 5 lumin, photo 6 lumini, lumino *measure:* 3 lux 4 phot 5 lumen 6 candle 7 candela *refractor:* 5 prism *relating to:* 6 photic *ring:* 4 halo 6 corona 7 aureola, aureole *science:* 6 optics 7 photics *source:* 3 sun 4 lamp

light-emitting *suffix:* 6 escent

lighten 4 dawn, ease, fade, thin 5 allay
6 bleach, dilute, illume 7 assuage, mollify,
relieve 8 brighten, illumine, mitigate 9 alleviate, attenuate, extenuate 10 illuminate

light-headed 5 dizzy, giddy 6 swimmy
7 flighty 8 swimming 9 frivolous 10 bird-
witted 11 vertiginous

lighthearted 3 gay 4 glad 5 happy, jolly,
merry 6 blithe, jocund, jovial, joyful, joyous,
lively 7 buoyant, festive, gleeful 8 carefree,
cheerful, mirthful, spirited, volatile 9 expansive, resilient, sprightly, vivacious 10 blithesome, free-minded, insouciant 12 effervescent, happy-go-lucky, high-spirited

lighthouse 5 guide, phare 6 beacon, pharos 7 warning 8 guidance 9 direction

lightless 3 dim 4 dark, dusk 5 dusky,
murky 6 gloomy 7 obscure 9 tenebrous
10 caliginous 11 unillumined

lightness 6 gaiety, levity 8 buoyancy,
vivacity 9 flippancy, frivolity 10 elasticity,
liveliness, resiliency, volatility 11 flightiness
12 cheerfulness 13 effervescence,
expansiveness

lightning bug 7 firefly

lignite 4 coal 9 brown coal

likable 6 genial 8 friendly, pleasant, pleasing 10 attractive

like 2 as 3 dig 4 akin, same, such, will,
wish 5 close, elect, enjoy, equal, match
6 admire, agnate, allied, choose, esteem,
please, prefer, regard, relish, select
7 approve, cognate, endorse, kindred,
related, respect, similar, uniform 8 parallel,
selfsame, suchlike 9 analogous, consonant,
identical 10 appreciate, comparable, comprehend, equivalent, resembling *combining
form:* 3 sym, syn 4 home 5 homeo,
homoe, homoi 6 homoeo, homoio *suffix:*
2 ar, ic, ly 3 ine, ish, oid 4 eous, ical 5 oidal

likelihood 6 chance 11 probability

likely 3 apt 4 rosy 5 given, prone 6 liable,
mortal 7 earthly, hopeful, roseate
8 inclined, possible, probable, probably
9 assumably, doubtless, promising 10 presumably, promiseful

liken 5 match 6 equate 7 compare, paragon 8 parallel 10 assimilate

likeness 4 copy, twin 5 image 6 effigy,
simile 7 analogy, picture, replica 8 affinity,
equality, identity, sameness 9 agreement,
facsimile, semblance 10 comparison, conformity, photograph, similarity, similitude,
uniformity 11 equivalence, parallelism,
resemblance

likewise 2 so 3 and, too 4 also, more
5 along 6 as well, withal 7 besides 8 moreover 9 similarly 11 furthermore

liking 4 lust, mind, will 5 fancy, gusto,
taste 8 affinity, appetite, fondness, pen-

chant, pleasure, soft spot, velleity, weakness 11 inclination 12 predilection *combining form:* 4 phil 5 phile 6 philic 7 philous

Lilith *husband:* 4 Adam *successor:* 3 Eve

lilliputian 3 wee 4 runt, tiny 5 dwarf,
midge, pygmy, teeny, weeny 6 midget, minute, peewee, teensy, teenty 7 manikin
8 Tom Thumb 10 diminutive, homunculus,
teeny-weeny 12 teensy-weensy

lilt 3 air 4 sing, song, tune 5 swing

lily 3 pad 4 aloe, ixia, sego 5 calla, tiger,
white, yucca 6 flower 7 leopard 8 mariposa *combining form:* 6 crinus

Lily ____ 4 Pons

lily of France 10 fleur-de-lis

lily-livered 6 coward, craven 7 chicken,
gutless, unmanly 8 cowardly 9 spunkless
11 poltroonish 12 poor-spirited
13 pusillanimous

lily-white 4 good, pure 8 innocent, virtuous 9 blameless, exemplary, guiltless, righteous 10 inculpable

lima 4 bean, seed 7 mollusk

liman 3 bay 6 lagoon 7 estuary

limb 3 arm, fin, leg 4 twig, wing 5 bough,
devil, rogue, scamp, shoot, spray, sprig
6 branch, member, rascal, switch 7 villain
8 mischief, scalawag 9 appendage

limber 5 agile, lithe, loose 6 pliant, supple
7 elastic, lissome, plastic, pliable, springy
8 flexible 9 lithesome, resilient

limbo 5 dance 6 prison 7 oblivion

lime 5 color, fruit, green 6 citrus

limen 9 threshold

limerick 4 poem 5 verse 8 fishhook
writer: 4 Lear

limestone 4 malm, tufa 5 chalk 6 marble,
oolite, oolith 7 coquina

lime tree 4 teil 6 linden

limit 3 bar, end, fix, rim, set 4 brim, curb,
edge, term 5 brink, check, pinch, quota,
verge 6 assign, border, curfew, define, hinder, lessen, margin, narrow 7 appoint,
extreme, mark out, measure 8 contract,
deadline, restrain, restrict 9 constrict,
demarcate, determine, extremity, prescribe

limitless 4 vast 8 infinite, termless
9 unbounded 10 indefinite, unmeasured
11 innumerable, undrainable 12 immeasurable, incalculable, unfathomable
13 inexhaustible

limn 4 draw 5 image 6 depict, render,
sketch 7 picture, portray 8 describe
9 delineate, interpret, represent

Limoges product 9 porcelain

limp 3 lax 4 halt, lame, wilt 5 hitch, loose,
slack 6 falter, flabby, floppy, hobble, muddle, sleazy, supple, toddle, totter, waddle,
wobble 7 die-away, flaccid, languid,
relaxed, shuffle, stagger, stumble 9 enervated 10 languorous, spiritless

limpid 4 pure 5 clear, lucid 10 see-through 11 translucent, transparent

limping 4 halt, lame 5 gimpy 8 lameness 12 claudication

Lincoln *assassin:* 5 Booth *biographer:* 7 Masters 8 Sandburg *debater:* 7 Douglas *law partner:* 7 Herndon *mother:* 5 Nancy *nickname:* 9 Honest Abe 12 Railsplitter *photographer:* 5 Brady *secretary of state:* 6 Seward *secretary of war:* 7 Stanton *wife:* 8 Mary Todd

line 3 job, pad, ray, row, way 4 abut, file, join, path, rank, road, rope, tier, work 5 align, array, goods, march, order, queue, range, route, touch, train, verge, wares 6 adjoin, border, butt on, column, course, policy, polity, series, string 7 arrange, calling, contour, echelon, marshal, passage, profile, program, pursuit 8 business, neighbor, ordinate, sequence 9 procedure, vendibles 10 employment, figuration, occupation, silhouette, succession *curved:* 3 arc *mathematical:* 6 vector *metrical:* 5 verse 6 verset 8 versicle

lineage 4 clan, folk, race 5 birth, blood, house, stock, tribe 6 family, origin, stirps 7 descent, kindred 8 ancestry, pedigree

lineal 6 direct 10 hereditary

lineament 7 contour, feature, outline, profile 10 figuration, silhouette

lineation see lineament

lined 5 ruled 7 lineate, striate, striped 8 lineated, streaked, wrinkled

linen 4 lawn 5 cloth, toile 6 byssus, damask, dowlas, fabric, forfar, napery, sheets 7 batiste, bedding, cambric, Holland, taffeta 8 cretonne, lingerie *fiber:* 3 tow 4 line *source:* 4 flax

liner 4 ship 6 insert, vessel

Linet, Lynette *brother:* 6 Liones *husband:* 6 Gareth

linger 3 lag 4 bide, drag, mope, poke, stay, wait 5 abide, amble, dally, delay, drift, mosey, tarry 6 bummel, dawdle, loiter, put off, remain, stroll 11 stick around

lingerie 6 undies 9 underwear

lingo 4 cant 5 argot, slang 6 jargon, patois, patter 7 dialect 10 vernacular

linguist 8 polyglot 11 philologist

linguistics 9 philology

liniment 3 oil 6 lotion 8 ablution, ointment

lining 6 facing, insert 8 wainscot *combining form:* 6 pleura

link 3 tie 4 bond, join, knot, yoke 5 nexus, unite 6 couple, relate 7 combine, conjoin, connect 8 catenate, vinculum 9 associate, conjugate

linksman 6 golfer

linnet 5 finch

lint 3 fur 4 down, flue, fuzz, pile 5 floss, fluff 7 charpie 9 ravelings

lion 3 cat, VIP 4 king, puma 5 chief 6 big boy, cougar, leader 7 notable 8 bigtimer, eminence, luminary 9 carnivore *group:* 5 pride *young:* 3 cub

lioness headed goddess 3 Mut 6 Sekhet

lionhearted 4 bold 5 brave 7 valiant 8 fearless, intrepid, unafraid, valorous 9 dauntless 10 courageous

lionlike 7 leonine

lion monkey 7 tamarin 8 leoncito, marmoset

Lion of Judah 13 Haile Selassie

lip 3 rim 4 brim, buss, edge, kiss, lave, peck, wash 5 bathe, smack 6 labium, labrum, margin, smooch 8 osculate *relating to:* 6 labial

lipid 3 fat, wax

lipped 7 labiate 9 bilabiate

lip server 8 pharisee, Tartuffe 9 hypocrite

liquefy 3 run 4 flux, fuse, melt, thaw, thin 6 soften 8 dissolve

liqueur 4 ouzo, raki 5 crème, noyau 6 kummel 7 cordial, curaçao, ratafia, rosolio, sloe gin 8 absinthe, anisette, prunelle 10 chartreuse, pousse-café

liquid 5 drink, fluid, sauce, water 6 golden, lotion, mellow, watery 7 honeyed 8 beverage, emulsion, Hyblaean 11 mellifluent, mellifluous *aromatic:* 7 eugenol 8 terpinol *container:* 3 cup, jug, mug 4 vial 5 glass 6 bottle, goblet 7 pitcher, tumbler *corrosive:* 5 oleum *flammable:* 3 gas, oil 5 ether, furan 6 butane, toluol 7 alcohol, dioxine, ligroin, toluene 8 furfuran, gasoline, ligroine, propenol, pyridine *measure:* 2 cc, ml, oz, pt, qt 3 cup, gal 4 pint 5 liter, ounce, quart 6 gallon *medicinal:* 8 liniment, ointment *oily:* 5 fusel 6 octane *resinous:* 6 tallol *scented:* 7 cologne, perfume *thick:* 5 sirup, syrup 8 molasses *volatile:* 6 hexane 7 naphtha, pentane 8 isoprene, phenetol

liquidate 3 pay 4 cool, do in, quit 5 clear, pay up, purge 6 murder, remove, settle, square 7 satisfy 8 amortize, clear off

liquor 4 grog 5 booze, drink 7 alcohol, potable, spirits 8 beverage, potation 9 aqua vitae, drinkable, firewater, inebriant, moonshine 10 intoxicant *add:* 4 lace 5 spike *homemade:* 9 moonshine 10 bathtub gin *inferior:* 5 hooch, smoke 6 rotgut *kind:* 3 gin, rum, rye 5 vodka 6 brandy, geneva, scotch 7 bourbon, whiskey 8 vermouth *malt:* 3 ale 4 beer 5 stout *measure:* 4 dram *Mexican:* 5 sotol 6 mescal 7 tequila *Oriental:* 4 sake, saki 6 arrack, samshu

liquor cabinet 10 cellarette

lissome 5 agile, lithe 6 limber, supple 8 flexible

list 3 tip 4 book, cant, file, heel, lean, menu, note, post, roll, tilt 5 count, index, slant, slope 6 agenda, detail, enroll, record, roster 7 catalog, incline, itemize, recline, specify, tick off 8 glossary, inscribe, numerate, register, roll call, schedule, tabulate 9 chronicle, enumerate, inventory 10 specialize 13 particularize

listen 4 hark, hear, heed, note 6 attend, harken 8 overhear 9 eavesdrop

listeners 8 audience

listless 4 dull, limp 6 drowsy, sleepy 7 die-away, languid 9 apathetic, enervated 10 languorous 11 languishing 13 lackadaisical

listlessness 6 apathy 8 doldrums, lethargy 9 disregard, lassitude, unconcern 11 disinterest, insouciance 12 indifference

litany 4 list 5 chant 6 ektene, prayer 7 synapte 8 rogation

literal 5 exact 7 precise 8 verbatim 11 word-for-word

literally 6 direct 8 verbatim 11 word for word

literary 7 bookish, erudite, learned 8 lettered, well-read

literary style *suffix:* 3 ese

literary work 4 book, opus, play, poem 5 cento, drama, essay, novel 10 short story

literature 4 kind 5 prose 6 poetry 7 fiction 10 nonfiction

lithe 4 lean, slim, thin 5 agile, spare 6 lissom, slight, supple, svelte 7 lissome, slender 8 graceful

lithium *symbol:* 2 Li

lithographer 4 Ives 7 Currier *French:* 5 Redon

Lithuanian 4 Balt 6 Baltic *capital:* 7 Vilnius *coin:* 6 centas

litigant 4 suer 6 suitor

litigation 4 case, suit 6 action 7 lawsuit

litter 3 bed 4 hash, junk 5 offal, trash, waste, young 6 basket, debris, jumble, jungle, muddle, refuse, tumble 7 garbage, rubbish, rummage, shuffle 8 mishmash, scramble 9 offspring, stretcher

little 3 set, wee 4 mean, puny, tiny 5 borne, light, minor, petty, short, small 6 bantam, casual, minute, monkey, narrow, paltry, petite, rarely, seldom 7 bigoted, limited, niggard, selfish, trivial, unoften 8 smallish 9 hidebound, illiberal, niggardly, secondary, small-beer 10 collateral, diminutive, fortuitous, hardly ever, incidental, provincial, shoestring, subsidiary 11 unimportant

little by little 8 inchmeal 9 gradually, piecemeal

Little Corporal 8 Napoleon

Little Dipper *constellation:* 9 Ursa Minor *star:* 5 North 7 Polaris

little finger or toe 7 minimus

Little Minister *author:* 6 Barrie *character:* 5 Gavin 6 Babbie 7 Dishart

little one *suffix:* 2 el, et, ey 2 ia (plural), ie 3 cle, ium, kin, ock, ula, ule, uli (plural) 4 ella, ette, illa, ling, ulae (plural), ulum, ulus 5 ellae (plural), illae (plural)

Little Women *author:* 6 Alcott *character:* 2 Jo 3 Amy, Meg 4 Beth *surname:* 5 March

liturgy 4 form, rite 7 service 8 ceremony 9 formality 10 ceremonial, observance

livable 4 cosy, snug 5 homey 6 viable 8 bearable, homelike 9 endurable

live 2 be, is 3 are 4 fare 5 abide, dwell, exist, green, vital 6 reside 7 breathe, dynamic, hang out, running, subsist, working

livelihood 3 art, fee, job, pay 4 keep, wage 5 bread, craft, trade 6 living, salary 7 alimony, stipend, support 9 emolument 10 handicraft, profession, sustenance 11 maintenance, subsistence

liveliness 4 brio, élan 5 verve 6 spirit 8 vibrance, vibrancy, vitality, vivacity

lively 3 gay 4 busy, fast, keen, pert, spry, yare 5 agile, alert, brisk, catty, fussy, jazzy, jolly, merry, peppy, zippy 6 active, blithe, bright, brisky, chirpy, frisky, jocund, nimble 7 animate, buoyant, chipper, dashing, driving, elastic, gleeful, hopping, humming, popping, rousing 8 animated, bustling, cheerful, chirping, chirrupy, hustling, mirthful, spirited, volatile 9 cock-a-hoop, energetic, expansive, hilarious, resilient, sprightly, vivacious

liven 5 cheer 6 vivify 7 animate, quicken

liver 4 foie 5 hepar 7 denizen 8 habitant, occupant, resident 9 indweller 10 inhabitant *combining form:* 5 hepat 6 hepato *disease:* 9 cirrhosis, hepatitis *lobster's:* 8 tomalley

liverwort 8 hepatica 9 bryophyte

livestock 6 cattle 7 animals

live wire 6 dynamo, peeler 7 hustler, rustler 8 go-getter 11 self-starter

livid 3 wan 4 ashy, pale 5 ashen, dusky, lurid, murky, waxen 6 doughy, gloomy, grisly, pallid, sultry 8 blanched 9 colorless

living 4 keep, salt 5 bread, vital 6 active, around, extant, zoetic 7 alimony, animate, dynamic, support 8 animated, existent 9 operative 10 livelihood, sustenance *combining form:* 3 ont 4 onto, vivi

living being 8 creature *combining form:* 2 zo 3 ont, zoa (plural), zoo 4 onto, zoon

living room 6 parlor 7 parlour 10 lebensraum

lizard 3 dab, eft, uma 4 adda, gila, newt, seps, uran 5 agama, anole, gecko, skink, teiid, tokay, varan, waral 6 dragon, goanna, iguana, moloch, worral, worrel 7 cheecha, monitor, reptile 8 basilisk, lacertid, slowworm, whiptail **9** alligator, blindworm, chameleon, crocodile **10** chuckwalla, salamander *combining form:* **4** saur **5** saura, sauro **6** sauria (plural) *genus:* **3** Uta **5** Agama **6** Ameiva, Anolis **7** Lacerta

llama 6 alpaca **7** guanaco

Lloyd's business 9 insurance

lo 4 hark, look

load 3 tax **4** bale, bear, care, cram, drag, duty, fill, glut, haul, lade, onus, pack, pile, task **5** cargo, carry, choke, drain, flood, gorge, laden, swamp, weigh **6** burden, charge, convey, cumber, debase, doctor, dope up, lading, parcel, saddle, weight **7** freight, surfeit **8** encumber, pressure, shipment **9** liability, millstone, transport

loaded 4 full **7** brimful **8** brimming **9** chock-full

loaf 3 bum **4** idle, laze, lazy **6** dawdle **9** goldbrick

loafer 3 bum **4** slug **5** idler **6** slouch **8** deadbeat, dolittle, fainéant, slugabed, sluggard **9** do-nothing, lazybones

loam 4 dirt, sand, silt, soil **7** topsoil *deposit:* **5** loess

loan 4 lend **5** prest **7** advance, imprest

loan shark 6 lender, usurer **7** Shylock **11** moneylender

loath 6 afraid, averse **7** uneager **8** hesitant **9** reluctant, unwilling **10** indisposed

loathe 4 hate **5** abhor, spurn **6** detest, refuse, reject **7** decline, despise **8** execrate **9** abominate, repudiate

loathsome 4 foul, ugly, vile **5** nasty **7** hateful, hideous **8** horrible **9** invidious, obnoxious, offensive, repellent, repugnant, repulsive, revolting **10** disgusting

lob 3 hit **4** shot, step, toss, vein **5** stair, throw

lobby 4 hall **5** foyer **8** anteroom **9** vestibule

lobe 4 flap **7** lobulus

lobo 4 wolf **10** timber wolf

lobster 10 crustacean *African:* **12** Cape crawfish *claw:* **5** chela **6** pincer *female:* **3** hen *male:* **4** cock *trap:* **3** pot **5** creel

local 6 native, insular, topical *combining form:* **3** top **4** topo

locale 4 area, site **5** place, scene, venue **6** region **8** district, vicinage, vicinity **11** mise-en-scène **12** neighborhood

locality 4 area, belt, home, seat, site, zone **5** field, haunt, range, tract **6** domain, region, sector, sphere **7** habitat, section **8** district, province, vicinage **9** bailiwick, territory **12** neighborhood

localize 8 pinpoint

locate 3 spy **4** espy, find, site, spot **5** place, trace **6** settle **7** situate, station, uncover **8** discover, pinpoint, position **9** establish

locating device 5 lidar, radar, sonar

location 4 area, site, spot **5** locus, place, point, scene, where **7** habitat

loch 3 bay **4** lake

lock 3 fix **4** bolt, curl, hank, tuft **5** click, latch, tress **6** bundle, fasten, secure **7** ringlet **8** fastener **9** fastening

Locke's tabula ___ 4 rasa

lockjaw 7 tetanus, trismus

Locksley Hall author 8 Tennyson

lockup 3 jug, pen **4** coop, jail **6** cooler, prison

loco 3 mad **5** crazy **6** insane

locomotive 5 cheer, dolly, train **6** engine **7** movable **8** moveable **9** camelback *small:* **5** dinky **6** dinkey *type:* **5** steam **6** diesel **8** electric

Locrine *daughter:* **7** Sabrina *father:* **4** Brut **6** Brutus *lover:* **9** Estrildis *wife:* **9** Gwendolen

locum tenens 3 sub **4** fill-in **7** stand-in **9** alternate, surrogate **10** substitute **11** pinch hitter, replacement, succedaneum

locust 5 carob **6** cicada, insect **11** grasshopper

locust bird 5 stork **7** grackle

locution 4 word **6** phrase **10** expression

lode 4 lead, vein **7** deposit

lodestar 5 guide **6** leader

lodestone 6 magnet **9** magnetite

lodge 3 cot, den, fix, hut, inn **4** camp, club, hold, lair, root, take **5** admit, board, cabin, couch, embed, hotel, house, infix, motel, put up, shack **6** accept, bestow, billet, burrow, harbor, hostel, shanty, tavern **7** auberge, contain, cottage, hospice, ingrain, quarter, receive **8** domicile, entrench, hostelry **9** entertain, roadhouse **11** accommodate, caravansary, public house

lodger 5 guest **6** renter, roomer, tenant

loess 4 loam **7** deposit

loft 3 bin **5** attic, raise **6** garret

loftiness 5 pride **6** height, morgue **7** disdain, hauteur, stature **9** arrogance, superbity

lofty 3 big **4** airy, epic, high, tall **5** grand, noble, proud **6** aerial, august, raised, superb **7** exalted, haughty, soaring, spiring, stately, sublime, topless, utopian **8** arrogant, cavalier, elevated, eloquent, generous, imposing, insolent, majestic, superior, towering **9** ambitious, grandiose, magnified, visionary **10** benevolent, chivalrous, disdainful **11** aggrandized, considerate, magnanimous, overbearing, pretentious, skyscraping **12** greathearted, supercilious

log 4 book, note, wood **5** diary, stick **6** record, timber **7** journal *mover:* **7** cantdog

logarithm inventor 6 Napier

loge 3 box **5** booth, stall **9** enclosure

logger 9 lumberman 10 lumberjack, wood-
cutter *legendary:* 10 Paul Bunyan
loggerhead 6 shrike, turtle
loggia 6 arcade 7 balcony, gallery
logic 6 reason 9 reasoning *specious:*
7 sophism 9 sophistry
logical 4 sane 5 clear, lucid, sound, valid
6 cogent, subtle 7 telling 8 analytic, sensible 10 compelling, convincing, reasonable
logjam 7 impasse 8 blockage, deadlock,
stoppage
logo 4 mark 5 brand 9 trademark
logogriph 6 puzzle 7 anagram
logroll 4 birl
logrolling contest 5 roleo
logy 4 dull, slow 5 dopey, heavy 6 drowsy,
groggy, torpid 8 listless, sluggish
Lohengrin *composer:* 6 Wagner *father:*
8 Parsifal, Parzival *wife:* 4 Elsa
loincloth *African:* 5 pagne *Hindu:* 5 dhoti,
dhuti 6 dhooti *Indian:* 5 lungi 6 lungyi
Loire, city on the 5 Blois, Tours
6 Nantes 7 Orléans
Lois *daughter:* 6 Eunice *grandson:*
7 Timothy
loiter 3 bum, lag 4 drag, idle, laze, lazy,
loaf, poke 5 dally, delay, tarry, trail 6 dawdle, diddle, lounge, put off
Loki *father:* 8 Farbauti *mother:* 3 Nal
6 Laufey *offspring:* 3 Hel 4 Hela 6 Fenris
7 Midgard *slayer:* 8 Heimdall *victim:*
6 Balder *wife:* 5 Sigyn 9 Angurboda
loll 3 bum 4 idle, laze, lazy 5 droop, slump,
tarry 6 dawdle, diddle, slouch
Lollards' leader 6 Wyclif
lombard 6 cannon
Lombard king 5 Cleph 6 Alboin, Audoin
7 Aistulf, Aripert, Authari 9 Liudprand
London *borough:* 5 Brent 6 Barnet, Bexley, Ealing, Harrow, Sutton 7 Barking,
Bromley, Chelsea, Croydon, Enfield, Hackney, Lambeth 8 Haringey, Havering, Houn-
slow, Lewisham 9 Greenwich, Islington,
Redbridge 10 Kensington 11 Westminster
cathedral: 7 St. Paul's *clock:* 6 Big Ben
district: 4 Soho 5 Acton 7 Chelsea, May-
fair *gallery:* 4 Tate *policeman:* 5 bobby
prison: 7 Newgate *river:* 6 Thames
square: 9 Leicester, Trafalgar *street:*
4 Bond 5 Fleet 6 Strand 7 Downing
9 Whitehall 10 Piccadilly *subway:* 4 tube
London novel 9 White Fang 10 Martin
Eden, The Sea Wolf 11 The Iron Heel
16 The Call of the Wild
lone 4 only, sole, solo 5 alone 6 single,
unique 8 deserted, forsaken, isolated,
secluded, separate, singular, solitary
lonely 4 lorn 5 alone 7 forlorn 8 deserted,
homesick, lonesome, solitary
loneness 8 solitude 9 isolation

loner 6 hermit 7 outcast, recluse 8 outsider, solitary
Lone Ranger, The *creator:* 7 Striker
(Fran) *helper:* 5 Tonto *horse:* 6 Silver
trademark: 4 mask 12 silver bullet
lonesome see **lonely**
Lone Star State 5 Texas
long 3 age, aim, yen 4 ache, aeon, itch,
lust, miss, pine, sigh, want 5 crave, dream,
wordy, yearn 6 aspire, hanker, hunger, prolix, thirst 7 diffuse, dog's age, lengthy, suspire, verbose 8 blue moon, coon's age,
dragging, drawn-out, eternity, extended
9 diffusive, extensive 10 protracted
long dozen 8 thirteen
long-drawn-out 7 lengthy 8 dragging
10 protracted
Longfellow poem 8 Christus, Hiawatha,
Hyperion, Kavanagh 10 Evangeline 11 My
Lost Youth 12 A Psalm of Life
long for 4 ache, pine, want 5 covet, crave,
yearn
longing 3 yen 4 wish 6 desire, thirst
7 craving 8 appetite
Long, Long Ago composer 5 Bayly
longshoreman 9 stevedore
long-suffering 7 patient 8 humility, meekness, patience 9 lowliness 11 forbearance,
patientness, resignation, subduedness
long suit 5 forte 6 medium, métier, oyster 8 eminency, strength 9 specialty
10 specialism
long-winded 5 wordy 6 prolix 7 diffuse,
lasting, lengthy, verbose 9 redundant
10 palaverous
loo 6 toilet
look 3 air, mug, see 4 cast, face, gape,
gawk, heed, hope, lean, leer, mien, mind,
note, ogle, peek, peep, peer, seem, show,
spot, tend, view 5 await, front, glare, gloat,
sight, slant, sound, stare, watch 6 appear,
aspect, attend, beware, divine, expect, eyeful, glance, glower, goggle, notice, regard,
squint, survey, visage 7 count on, display,
exhibit, express, glimpse, incline, observe,
seeming 8 forecast, foretell, indicate, manifest 9 count upon 10 appearance, expression, rubberneck 11 countenance,
physiognomy
look after 4 tend 6 attend 7 care for
look at 3 eye, see 4 ogle, view 6 behold
7 examine
look back 6 recall, review 7 reflect
8 remember 9 reminisce
look down 5 abhor, scorn, scout 7 contemn, despise, disdain, overtop 8 dominate,
outstare 9 tower over 10 tower above
looker 6 beauty, eyeful, lovely 8 knockout
looker-on 6 viewer 7 watcher, witness
8 beholder, by-sitter, observer 9 bystander,
spectator 10 eyewitness

look for 4 seek 5 await
looking glass 6 mirror
look into 5 study 7 examine, inspect
11 investigate
look out 4 mind 6 beware
lookout 4 ward 5 guard, scape, vigil, vista,
watch 6 affair, cupola, picket, sentry 7 concern, palaver 8 business, prospect, sentinel,
watchman 9 crow's nest, firetower, occasions, vigilance 10 observance, watchtower 9 widow's walk 11 observation,
observatory, perspective 12 surveillance
loom 4 brew, bulk, hulk, near, rear, show
5 tower 6 appear, come on, emerge,
gather, impend, make up, weaver
8 approach, stand out, threaten 9 forthcome *part:* 3 lam 4 caam 5 easer 6 hed-
dle 7 harness, shuttle, treadle, trundle
loon 3 nut 4 bird 5 grebe
loony 3 nut 5 batty, crazy, silly, wacky
6 absurd, dement, insane, madman,
maniac 7 foolish, lunatic, madling 9 bedlamite, non compos 10 Tom o' Bedlam
11 harebrained 12 preposterous
loony bin 6 asylum 8 madhouse, nuthouse 9 funny farm 10 booby hatch, crazy
house
loop 3 arc, eye 4 ansa, arch, bend, coil,
curl, gird, knot, ring 5 beset, curve, noose,
picot, wheel 6 begird, circle, girdle, league,
staple, wreath 7 circlet, circuit, compass
8 encircle, surround 9 encompass
13 circumference
looped 5 drunk 11 intoxicated
loophole 3 out 6 outlet 7 opening
loose 3 lax 4 bate, ease, easy, fast, fire,
free, limp, undo, vent 5 abate, clear, let up,
light, relax, shoot, slack, unbar, unfix, unpin,
untie 6 flabby, remiss, unbind, unbolt,
undone, unglue, unhook, unlace, unlash,
unlock, unsnap, wanton 7 ease off, flaccid,
manumit, relaxed, release, slacken, unchain,
unclasp, unhitch, unlatch, unleash, unscrew,
unstick, unstrap, whorish 8 detached, liberate, mitigate, reckless, separate, unbuckle,
unbutton, unchaste, unfasten 9 alleviate,
desultory, discharge, disengage, negligent,
take out on, unbandage, untighten 10 capricious, disjointed, emancipate, incoherent,
inconstant, unattached, unconfined, unfastened 11 disenthrall, extravagant, nonadhesive, unconnected 12 disconnected,
unrestrained
loose end 6 detail 8 fragment
loose-fitting 5 baggy 6 droopy
loose-lipped *see* **loquacious**
loosen 3 lax 4 ease, free 5 relax, slack,
untie 6 unbind 7 ease off, manumit,
release, slacken, unchain 8 liberate,
unbuckle, unfasten 9 discharge
10 emancipate

loosen up 5 relax 6 unbend, unwind
7 ease off
loot 3 rob 4 sack, swag 5 booty, dough,
lucre, money, prize, rifle, spoil 6 boodle
7 pillage, plunder, ransack, relieve, seizure,
stick up 9 knock over 10 plunderage
11 filthy lucre
looter 5 thief 6 reaver, riever 8 marauder,
pillager, ravisher
lop 3 cut 4 chop, clip, jump, leap, trim
5 bound, droop, slump, vault 6 bounce, hurdle, slouch, spring 7 pendent, saltate
8 truncate
lope 3 jog, run 4 gait, romp, skip, trip
6 spring, sprint 7 skitter
lopsided 6 uneven 7 crooked, difform,
unequal 8 top-heavy, unsteady 9 irregular
10 asymmetric, off-balance, unbalanced
13 unsymmetrical
loquacious 5 gabby, talky, wordy
6 chatty, prolix 7 verbose 9 jabbering, talkative 10 babblative 11 loose-lipped
12 loose-tongued, multiloquent
13 overtalkative
lord 2 Mr. 3 man, sir 4 boss, cock, earl,
peer 5 noble, put on, swank, swell 6 affect,
master, mister 7 husband, overawe, peacock, pretend, swagger 8 governor, nobleman, overbear 9 tyrannize *feudal:* 5 liege
8 seigneur, suzerain *Muslim:* 6 sayyid
Lord High Executioner 4 Koko
Lord Jim author 6 Conrad
lordly 5 grand, noble, proud 6 august,
puffed, uppity 7 haughty, swollen
8 affected, arrogant, cavalier, imposing,
insolent, magnific, majestic, princely, snobbish, superior 9 egotistic, grandiose 10 disdainful 11 dictatorial, magisterial, magnificent, overbearing 12 supercilious
13 authoritarian, high-and-mighty
Lord of the Flies author 7 Golding
Lord's Prayer 9 Our Father
11 Paternoster
lore 4 myth, saga, tale 5 fable 6 custom,
legend, mythos, wisdom 7 folkway, science 9 knowledge, mythology, tradition
11 information 12 old wives' tale,
superstition
Lorelei 5 siren 9 temptress 10 seductress 11 femme fatale *poet:* 5 Heine
river: 5 Rhine *victim:* 6 sailor 7 mariner
Lorenzo's beloved 7 Jessica
lorgnette 8 eyeglass 10 opera glass
Lorna Doone *author:* 9 Blackmore *hero:*
4 Ridd (John)
___-Lorraine 6 Alsace
lose 3 rid, rob 4 drop, fail, fall, miss, oust,
slip, tine, tyne 5 clear, shake, yield 6 divest,
give up, mislay 7 bereave, decline, deprive,
forfeit, regress, succumb 8 misplace, shake

off, throw off, unburden **9** sacrifice, surrender

lose feathers 4 molt

loser 3 dud **4** bomb, bust, flop **5** lemon **7** also-ran, convict, failure **8** jailbird

loss 4 leak, ruin **5** havoc, waste **6** damage, defeat, injury **7** failure, forfeit **8** decrease **9** confusion, mislaying, privation, ruination, sacrifice **10** divestment, forfeiture, misplacing **11** bereavement, deprivation, deprivement, destruction

lost 4 dead, gone **6** absent, astray, bygone, damned, doomed, hidden, musing, passed, ruined **7** bemused, defunct, extinct, faraway, lacking, mislaid, missing **8** absorbed, departed, distrait, vanished **9** condemned, daydreamy, graceless **10** abstracted **11** inconscient, irrevocable, preoccupied, unconscious, unconverted **12** absentminded, incorrigible, irredeemable, irreformable, unregenerate

Lost Horizon *author:* **6** Hilton *land:* **9** Shangri-La

lot 3 cut, ilk, set **4** bite, body, doom, fate, give, heap, kind, lump, mass, much, part, peck, plat, push, sort, type, yard **5** allow, array, batch, block, breed, bunch, clump, crowd, field, group, moira, patch, quota, share, slice, tract, weird **6** assign, barrel, bundle, circle, clutch, decree, kidney, kismet, parcel, stripe **7** cluster, destiny, feather, fortune, mete out, partage, portion, species **8** allocate, clearing, frontage **9** admeasure, aggregate, allowance, apportion, character, great deal

Lot *father:* **5** Haran *sister:* **5** Iscah **6** Milcah *son:* **4** Moab **5** Ammon *uncle:* **7** Abraham

Lotan's father 4 Seir

lothario 5 Romeo **7** amorist, Don Juan, gallant **8** Casanova, paramour

Loti, Pierre 5 Viaud

lotion 3 oil **4** balm **8** ablution, liniment, ointment

lottery 6 raffle **7** drawing **11** sweepstakes

lotus-eater 7 dreamer

loud 5 gaudy, harsh, noisy, showy **6** brassy, brazen, flashy, garish, hoarse, tawdry, tinsel, vulgar **7** blaring, blatant, booming, chintzy, glaring, pealing, raucous, ringing, roaring **8** piercing, resonant, sonorous, strident **9** deafening, obnoxious, obtrusive, offensive **10** bigmouthed, resounding, stentorian, stertorous, thunderous **11** ear-piercing, full-mouthed, fulminating, stentorious **12** ear-splitting

loudmouth 7 stentor **8** blowhard, braggart

loudspeaker 6 woofer **7** tweeter

Louise composer 11 Charpentier

Louisiana *capital:* **10** Baton Rouge *largest city:* **10** New Orleans *nickname:* **11** Creole State **12** Pelican State *state flower:* **8** magnolia *university:* **6** Tulane **9** Grambling

lounge 3 bar, bum, lie, pub, tap **4** idle, laze, lazy, loaf, sofa **5** dally, drift, slack **6** dawdle, loiter, saloon **7** barroom, buvette, lie down, recline, taproom

lounge lizard 3 fop **4** buck, dude **5** blood, dandy, leech **6** sponge, sucker **7** coxcomb, sponger **8** barnacle, hanger-on, macaroni, parasite **9** exquisite **10** freeloader **11** Beau Brummel, bloodsucker, petit-maître

Lourdes saint 10 Bernadette

louse 3 cur, dog, rat **4** snot, toad **5** aphid, skunk, snake **6** cootie, psylla, slater, wretch **7** stinker *egg:* **3** nit

louse up 4 mess, ruin **5** botch **6** bobble, bollix, bungle, mucker

lout 3 oaf **4** boor, dolt, gawk, hick, lump, mock, quiz, razz, rube, twit **5** churl, klutz, looby, rally, scout, taunt, yokel **6** deride, galoot, lubber, lummox, rustic **7** bumpkin, hayseed, lobster, palooka, peasant **8** ridicule, stinkard **10** clodhopper

Louvre masterpiece 8 Mona Lisa **11** Venus de Milo

lovable 4 dear **6** genial **7** winning, winsome **8** adorable, alluring, charming, engaging, fetching, pleasing **9** appealing, endearing, ravishing, seductive **10** attractive, bewitching, enchanting, entrancing **11** captivating, enthralling

love 3 pet **4** dear, like, lust, zeal **5** adore, amour, ardor, crush, Cupid, deify, exalt, fancy, honey, piety, prize, sweet, value **6** admire, affair, caress, cosset, cuddle, dandle, desire, enamor, fealty, fervor, fondle, liking, regard, revere **7** ardency, cherish, darling, emotion, idolize, loyalty, passion, romance, worship **8** devotion, fidelity, fondness, idolatry, treasure, venerate, yearning **9** adoration, affection, delight in, sentiment, sweetling **10** allegiance, appreciate, attachment, enthusiasm, honeybunch, sweetheart **11** amorousness, infatuation *combining form:* **5** phily **6** philia *French:* **5** amour *Italian:* **5** amore

love apple 6 tomato

lovebird 6 budgie, parrot **10** budgerigar

love feast 5 agape

love god 4 Amor, Eros, Kama **5** Bhaga, Cupid

love goddess 5 Athor, Freya, Venus **6** Hathor, Inanna, Ishtar **7** Astarte **9** Aphrodite, Ashtoreth

love letter 8 mash note **9** valentine **10** billet-doux

lovely 4 fair, rare **5** sweet **6** beauty, dainty, eyeful, looker, pretty **7** stunner **8** alluring, charming, delicate, engaging,

graceful, handsome, knockout **9** beauteous, beautiful, exquisite **10** attractive, bewitching, delectable, delightful, enchanting, entrancing **11** captivating, good-looking
love-potion 7 philter, philtre **11** aphrodisiac
lover 3 fan, man **4** beau, buff **5** flame, hound, leman, Romeo **6** addict, master, steady, votary **7** amorist, devotee, Don Juan, gallant, habitué **8** fancy man, lothario, mistress, paramour **9** boyfriend, inamorata, inamorato **10** aficionado, girl friend *of books:* **11** bibliophile
love song 5 canso **6** serena **8** serenade
love story 7 romance
love token 4 ring **6** amoret
loving 4 dear, fond, kind **6** ardent, erotic, tender **7** amatory, amorous, bound up, cordial, devoted, fervent **8** attached, enamored, faithful **9** attentive **10** benevolent, infatuated, passionate, solicitous **11** considerate, impassioned, warmhearted **12** affectionate *combining form:* **4** phil **5** phile, philo **6** philic **7** philous
low 3 bad, cut, moo, raw **4** base, blue, deep, down, flat, mean, neap, poor, rude, vile, weak **5** brief, broke, cheap, crass, crude, dizzy, faint, gross, needy, rough, short, under **6** abject, ailing, coarse, fallen, humble, lesser, nether, offish, poorly, scurvy, sickly, sordid, undear, unwell, vulgar, woeful **7** cut-rate, ignoble, nominal, popular, reduced, scrubby, scruffy, servile, slashed, uncouth, underly **8** atypical, baseborn, beggared, cast down, dejected, dirt poor, downcast, feverish, indigent, inferior, mediocre, moderate, off-color, plebeian, uncostly, unwashed, wretched **9** declining, depressed, destitute, inelegant, miserable, penurious, subjacent, subnormal, woebegone **10** despicable, economical, indisposed, marked down, reasonable, spiritless, subaverage, unennobled **11** crestfallen, downhearted
lowbred 7 boorish, loutish **8** churlish, cloddish, lubberly **9** unrefined **10** unpolished **11** uncivilized
low-cost 5 cheap **6** undear **7** popular **10** affordable, reasonable **11** inexpensive
low-down 4 base, mean, ugly, vile **6** scurvy **7** ignoble, servile **8** wretched **10** despicable
lowdown 4 dope **5** facts **11** information
lower 3 cut **4** clip, drop, fall, pare, peer, rail, sink **5** abase, abate, couch, decry, demit, droop, frown, gloom, scowl, shave, slash, stare, under **6** bemean, debase, demean, demote, humble, lesser, menace, nether, reduce **7** cut back, cut down, deflate, degrade, demerit, depress, descend, detrude, devalue, let down **8** cast

down, inferior, mark down, overcast, submerge, threaten, write off **9** devaluate, downgrade, humiliate, subjacent *combining form:* **4** bath, cato **5** batho *prefix:* **5** infra
Lower Depths author 5 Gorki, Gorky
lowest 5 least **6** bottom **7** deepest **9** undermost **10** bottommost, nethermost, rock-bottom
lowest point 5 nadir **6** trough *on earth:* **7** Dead Sea
low-grade 4 hack, mean, poor **6** common **8** declassé, inferior **10** second-rate **11** second-class **12** second-drawer
low-key 4 soft **5** sober **7** subdued **8** softened **9** toned down
lowland 4 flat, vale **6** valley **7** bottoms *Scottish:* **6** lallan **7** lalland
Lowlander 4 Scot **8** Scotsman
lowlife 4 heel, worm **5** knave, rogue **6** mucker, no-good, rascal, wretch **7** villain **8** wormling **9** miscreant, scoundrel **10** blackguard
lowly 4 base, mean, meek **6** humble, modest **7** ignoble, mundane, prosaic, servile, workday **8** baseborn, everyday, obeisant, plebeian, retiring, unwashed, workaday
low-pitched 4 bass
low-pressure 6 casual, degagé **7** relaxed, unfussy **8** informal **9** easygoing **10** unreserved **13** unconstrained
low-priced 5 cheap **6** undear **7** popular **8** uncostly **10** reasonable **11** inexpensive
low-spirited 4 blue, down **8** dejected, downcast **9** depressed, heartsore, woebegone
low tide 3 ebb **4** neap
loyal 4 firm, true **5** liege **6** ardent, trusty **7** devoted, staunch **8** constant, faithful, resolute **9** allegiant, steadfast
loyalist 4 Tory **7** patriot
loyalty 5 ardor, truth **6** fealty **8** adhesion, devotion, fidelity, trueness **9** adherence, constancy **10** allegiance, attachment **12** faithfulness
lozenge 4 pill **5** candy **6** tablet, troche **7** diamond, rhombus, tabella **8** pastille
LSD 4 acid *user:* **8** acidhead
lubricate 3 oil **6** grease **7** moisten
lubricious 4 lewd **5** slick **6** fickle, greasy, slippy, wanton **8** slippery, slithery, ticklish, unstable, variable, volatile **9** lecherous, salacious, uncertain **10** changeable, inconstant **13** temperamental
lucent 5 clear **6** bright **7** beaming, crystal, radiant, shining **8** clear-cut, luminous, pellucid **9** brilliant, unblurred **11** unambiguous
lucid 4 sane **5** clear, right **6** bright, normal **7** beaming, crystal, lambent, radiant **8** all there, clear-cut, knowable **9** brilliant, effulgent, graspable, refulgent, unblurred **10** fathomable **11** transparent, unambigu-

ous **12** compos mentis, incandescent, intelligible, transpicuous **13** apprehensible

lucidity 3 wit **4** mind **6** reason, sanity, senses **7** clarity **8** saneness **9** clearness, plainness, soundness **12** distinctness, explicitness

Lucifer 5 devil, fiend, Satan **6** diablo **7** Old Nick, serpent **8** Apollyon **9** Beelzebub **10** Old Scratch **13** Old Gooseberry

Lucinde *beloved:* **7** Leandre **9** Clitandre *father:* **7** Geronte **10** Sganarelle

luck 3 hap, hit, lot **4** bump, juju, meet, weal, zemi **5** break, charm, fluke, light **6** amulet, chance, fetish, happen, hazard, kismet, mascot, tumble **7** fortune, godsend, periapt, stumble **8** accident, fortuity, occasion, talisman, windfall **9** advantage **10** phylactery **11** opportunity **13** fortunateness *token:* **5** charm **6** amulet, clover, mascot **8** talisman **9** horseshoe

luckless 7 hapless, unhappy **8** ill-fated, untoward, wretched **9** miserable **10** ill-starred **11** star-crossed, unfortunate **12** misfortunate

lucky 4 well **5** happy **6** benign **9** favorable, fortunate **10** auspicious, beneficial, felicitous, profitable, propitious **12** advantageous, providential *Scottish:* **5** canny

lucrative 4 good **6** paying **7** gainful **10** productive, profitable, well-paying, worthwhile **11** moneymaking **12** advantageous

Lucrezia ___ 6 Borgia

ludicrous 5 antic, awful, comic, droll, funny, silly **6** absurd **7** bizarre, comical, foolish, risible **8** farcical, gelastic **9** fantastic, grotesque, laughable

Lud's town 6 London

lug 3 box, tow **4** bear, buck, drag, draw, haul, jerk, pack, pull, snap, tote, worm, yank **5** carry, ferry **6** convey, schlep, twitch **9** transport, vellicate

luggage 4 bags **7** baggage **9** suitcases

lugubrious 3 sad **4** dour, glum **5** black, bleak **6** dismal, dreary, gloomy, morose, rueful, somber, sullen, woeful **7** doleful, joyless **8** dolesome, mournful **9** cheerless, plaintive, saturnine, sorrowful **10** depressant, depressing, lamentable, melancholy, oppressing, oppressive **11** dispiriting

lukewarm 4 cool **5** tepid **8** hesitant **9** uncertain, undecided **10** indecisive, irresolute, irresolved, unresolved, wishy-washy **11** halfhearted, uncommitted

lull 3 ebb **4** balm, calm, hush, wane **5** abate, allay, comma, let up, pause, quiet, still **6** becalm, settle, soothe, temper **7** compose, die away, die down, ease off, qualify, slacken, subside **8** abeyance, interval, moderate **9** pausation **10** quiescence **11** tranquilize

lullaby 4 song **8** berceuse **10** cradlesong *Scottish:* **5** baloo, balow

lumber 3 tax **4** clog, lade, load, logs, plod, slog, wood **5** barge, clump, stump, weigh **6** burden, charge, saddle, timber, trudge

lumberjack see **logger**

Lumber State 5 Maine

luminance 10 brightness

luminary 3 big, sun, VIP **4** lion, name, star **5** light, nabob **6** leader **7** big name, notable **8** big-timer, eminence, somebody **9** celebrity **10** notability **12** leading light

luminous 5 clear, lucid **6** bright, lucent **7** beaming, crystal, fulgent, lambent, radiant, shining **8** clear-cut, knowable, pellucid **9** brilliant, effulgent, graspable, refulgent, unblurred **10** fathomable **11** translucent, transparent **12** incandescent

lummox 3 oaf **4** boor, gawk, lout **5** klutz, looby **7** lobster, palooka

lump 3 bit, gob, lot, oaf, wad **4** bear, blob, bulk, chip, clod, clot, gawk, heap, hunk, knot, lout, mass, much, peck, pile, welt **5** abide, batch, block, brook, bulge, bunch, chunk, crumb, hunch, klutz, looby, piece, scrap, stand, wedge **6** barrel, digest, endure, lubber, morsel, nugget **7** lobster, palooka, portion, stomach, swallow **8** swelling **12** protuberance

lumpy 3 raw **4** rude **5** crude, rough **8** clumpish, unformed **9** roughhewn, undressed

lunacy 5 folly, mania **7** fatuity, foolery, inanity, madness **8** delirium, insanity **9** absurdity, asininity, craziness, silliness, stupidity, unbalance **10** aberration, alienation, ineptitude, insaneness **11** derangement, distraction, foolishness, psychopathy, witlessness **13** senselessness

lunatic 3 mad, nut **4** kook, loon **5** crank, crazy, loony, raver, wacky **6** absurd, crazed, cuckoo, dement, insane, madman, maniac, psycho **7** cracked, foolish, madling, unsound **8** crackpot, demented, demonical, deranged, paranoid **9** bedlamite, ding-a-ling, energumen, fantastic, harebrain, neuropath, non compos, screwball **10** crackbrain, Tom o' Bedlam

lunch 4 meal, nosh **5** snack **6** tiffin

luncheonette, lunchroom 4 café **6** eatery **7** beanery **8** snack bar **9** cafeteria **10** coffee shop **11** eating house **12** sandwich shop

lune 5 leash

lung 5 organ **8** breather *combining form:* **5** pneum, pulmo **6** pneumo, pulmon **7** pulmoni, pulmono *disease:* **9** emphysema, pneumonia **12** tuberculosis

lunge 4 dive, stab **5** burst, drive, pitch **6** thrust

lunkhead 3 oaf 4 boob, dolt, goof
5 booby, chump, dunce
lupine 6 fierce 7 wolfish 10 bluebonnet
lurch 3 bob, yaw 4 bent, jerk, reel, rock,
roll, snap, swag, sway, tilt, toss, wave,
yank 5 swing, waver, weave, whirl
6 bumble, careen, falter, plunge, seesaw,
swerve, teeter, tilter, topple, totter, twitch,
wallow, wobble 7 blunder, leaning,
stagger, stumble 8 flounder, penchant,
tendency
lure 3 bag 4 bait, call, draw, fake, pull,
rope, toll, trap, wile 5 blind, catch, charm,
decoy, tempt, train, trick 6 ambush, appeal,
cajole, come-on, draw in, draw on, entice,
entrap, invite, lead on, seduce, suck-in
7 attract, beguile, bewitch, capture, con
game, enchant, ensnare, gimmick, wheedle
8 blandish, delusion, illusion, inveigle 9 captivate, fascinate, incentive, seduction, siren
song 10 attraction, camouflage, enticement, inducement, seducement, temptation
fishing: 3 fly 4 herl, worm 5 spoon 6 minnow 8 bucktail
lurid 3 wan 4 ashy, grim, pale 5 ashen,
livid, waxen 6 doughy, malign, sultry
7 baleful, ghastly, hideous, macabre,
malefic, tabloid 8 blanched, gruesome,
horrible, sinister, terrible 9 colorless
10 horrifying, maleficent, terrifying
11 sensational
lurk 4 hide, slip 5 creep, skulk, slide, slink,
sneak, steal 7 gumshoe 9 pussyfoot
luscious 4 rare, rich 5 sapid, tasty,
yummy 6 Capuan, choice, deluxe, florid,
ornate, rococo, savory 7 baroque, darling,
opulent, piquant, sensual 8 adorable, heavenly, palatial, sensuous 9 ambrosial, epicurean, exquisite, palatable 10 appetizing,
delectable, delightful, flamboyant, flavorsome 11 distinctive, scrumptious,
upholstered
lush 3 sot 4 rich 5 drunk, yummy 6 bibber, boozer, Capuan, deluxe 7 opulent, profuse, riotous, sensual 8 adorable, tippler
drunkard, heavenly, palatial, prodigal, sensuous 9 ambrosial, delicious, epicurean, exuberant, inebriate, luxuriant, luxurious, profusive, sumptuous 10 boozehound,
delectable, delightful, voluptuous
Lusitania 4 ship 5 liner 8 Portugal
lust 3 rut, yen 4 ache, heat, itch, long, pine,
urge, wish 5 crave, yearn 6 desire, fervor,
hanker, hunger, libido, thirst 7 craving, lechery, passion 8 appetite, coveting, cupidity,
priapism, salacity, satyrism, yearning 9 carnality, eroticism, lubricity, prurience, pruriency 10 aphrodisia, appetition, excitement,
satyriasis 11 nymphomania 13 concupiscence, lecherousness
luster 4 glow 5 glaze, gleam, glint, gloss,

sheen, shine 6 polish 8 radiance 9 after-
glow 10 brightness, brilliance, brilliancy,
effulgence, luminosity, refulgence 11 can-
descence, iridescence, opalescence
lusterless 3 dim, mat, wan 4 dead, drab,
dull, flat 5 blind, faded, muted, prosy
7 prosaic
lustful 3 hot 4 fast, lewd 5 rutty 7 burning, goatish, itching, ruttish, satyric 8 prurient 9 lecherous, libertine, lickerish, salacious 10 hot-blooded, lascivious, libidinous,
licentious, passionate 11 incontinent
12 concupiscent
lustrate 5 purge 6 purify 7 cleanse
lustration 9 catharsis, cleansing
lustrous 5 nitid, shiny 6 bright, gleamy,
glossy, sheeny 7 fulgent, lambent, radiant,
shining 8 gleaming, glinting, polished, splendid 9 brilliant, burnished, effulgent, refulgent, sparkling 10 glimmering, glistening
11 resplendent 12 incandescent
lusty 4 hale, huge, vast 5 hardy, vital
6 mighty, potent, robust, strong 7 dynamic,
healthy, immense, massive 8 enormous,
vigorous, whacking, whopping 9 energetic,
strenuous 10 full-bodied, prodigious, red-
blooded, tremendous
lusus 5 freak 7 monster 8 abortion
11 miscreation, monstrosity
lute 4 clay, ring, seal 6 cement 7 bandora,
bandore 10 chitarrone, instrument *Arabic:*
3 oud *Greco-Roman:* 7 pandura 8 pan-
doura *Oriental:* 3 tar *Russian:* 7 bandura
Spanish: 8 banduria *two-necked:*
7 theorbo
lutenist 4 Mace 6 Gallot, Mouton, Radolt
7 Bakfark, Dowland, Gautier, Perrine
8 Capirola, Gaultier
Lutetia 5 Paris
luxuriant 4 lush, posh, rank, rich 5 plush
6 Capuan, fecund, lavish 7 fertile, opulent,
profuse, riotous 8 fruitful, luscious, palatial,
prodigal, prolific 9 exuberant, sumptuous
luxuriate 4 bask, love, riot, roll 5 eat up,
enjoy, feast, revel 6 overdo, wallow, welter
7 indulge, rollick 11 overindulge
luxurious 4 lush, posh, rich 5 awful, fancy,
grand, plush, showy 6 Capuan, costly,
deluxe, lavish, palace, plushy 7 opulent,
sensual, stately 8 imposing, majestic,
palatial, splendid 9 elaborate, epicurean,
expensive, grandiose 10 impressive
11 extravagant, languishing, magnificent *situation:* 7 fat city 10 bed of roses, easy
street
luxury 5 frill 6 dainty 7 amenity, comfort
8 delicacy 10 redundancy 11 superfluity
12 extravagance 13 embellishment
Lycaon *daughter:* 8 Callisto *father:*
8 Pelasgus *mother:* 8 Meliboea
Lycidas author 6 Milton

Lycomedes *daughter:* 8 Deidamia *victim:* 7 Theseus

Lycus *brother:* 7 Nycteus *father:* 7 Pandion *slayer:* 6 Zethus 7 Amphion *wife:* 5 Dirce

Lydian *king:* 5 Gyges 7 Croesus 8 Alyattes *queen:* 7 Omphale

lye 7 caustic 8 lixivium

Lynceus *brother:* 4 Idas *father:* 8 Aphareus

lynch 4 hang 6 murder

Lynette see **Line**

lynx 3 cat 6 bobcat 7 caracal 9 catamount

Lyra star 4 Vega

lyre 4 harp 6 kissar 10 instrument

lyric 3 ode 4 odic, poem 5 melic 6 poetic 7 melodic, musical

lyric drama 5 opera

Lysander's beloved 6 Hermia

M

Maacah *father:* 5 Nahor 6 Talmai 7 Absalom *husband:* 5 David 6 Jehiel, Machir 8 Rehoboam *son:* 5 Hanan 6 Abijam, Achish 7 Absalom 10 Shephatiah

Maaseiah *father:* 6 Jotham 7 Shallum *son:* 7 Azariah 8 Zedekiah 9 Zephaniah

macabre 4 grim 5 lurid 6 deadly, grisly, horrid 7 deathly, ghastly, ghostly, hideous 8 gruesome, horrible, terrible 9 deathlike, ghostlike 10 horrifying, unpleasant

macaque 6 monkey, rhesus

macaroni 3 fop 4 buck, dude 5 dandy 7 coxcomb

Macbeth *character:* 4 Ross 5 Angus 6 Hecate, Lennox 7 Fleance *slayer:* 7 Macduff *successor:* 7 Malcolm *title:* 5 thane *victim:* 6 Banquo, Duncan

mace 3 bat, rod 4 beat, bilk, club 5 baton, billy, staff 6 cudgel, strike 8 bludgeon 9 billy club 10 knobkerrie, nightstick

Macedonia *capital:* 5 Pella 6 Skopje *king:* 6 Philip 9 Alexander *last king:* 7 Perseus

machete 4 bolo 5 knife 6 guitar

Machiavelli work 9 The Prince 11 The Mandrake

machinate 4 plot 6 devise, scheme, wangle 7 collude, connive, finagle 8 cogitate, conspire, contrive, engineer, intrigue, maneuver 9 scheme out

machine 3 car 4 auto 5 buggy, golem, motor, robot 6 device 7 autocar, fashion, vehicle 8 motorcar 9 automaton 10 automobile, conveyance 11 standardize *component:* 3 cam 4 belt, gear, seal 5 brake, chain, screw, shaft 6 clutch, spring 7 linkage 8 coupling *excavating:* 7 backhoe *humanlike:* 5 robot *laboratory:* 10 centrifuge

machine-gun 6 strafe

machine gun inventor 7 Gatling

machinery 4 gear, tool 5 agent, means, organ, works 6 agency, device, gadget, medium, outfit, tackle 7 channel, utensil, vehicle 8 matériel, tackling 9 apparatus, appliance, equipment, implement 10 instrument 11 contraption, contrivance

Machir's father 6 Ammiel 8 Manasseh

mackle 4 blur

macrocosm 5 world 6 cosmos, nature 8 creation, universe

McTeague author 6 Norris

mad 3 ire 4 daft, fury, rage, rash, sore, waxy, wild 5 anger, angry, crazy, irate, irked, loony, rabid, wacky, wrath, wroth 6 absurd, enrage, heated, insane, ireful 7 cracked, enraged, foolish, frantic, furious, incense, invalid, lunatic, steam up, umbrage 8 choleric, demented, deranged, frenetic, frenzied, offended, outraged, worked up, wrathful 9 affronted, delirious, fantastic, hilarious, illogical, infuriate, senseless, sophistic 10 corybantic, exasperate, fallacious, irrational, reasonless, unbalanced

Madagascar *capital:* 10 Tananarive 12 Antananarivo *export:* 5 sugar 6 cloves, coffee 7 vanilla *monetary unit:* 5 franc

Madame Bovary 4 Emma *author:* 8 Flaubert

Madame Butterfly *character:* 9 Cho-Cho-San, Cio-Cio-San, Pinkerton, Sharpless *composer:* 7 Puccini

madcap 4 rash 5 brash, hasty 8 reckless 9 hotheaded 10 ill-advised, incautious 11 thoughtless 13 inconsiderate

Mad Cavalier 6 Rupert

madden 3 ire 5 anger, craze 6 enrage,

frenzy **7** derange, incense, possess, shatter, steam up, umbrage, unhinge **8** distract **9** infuriate, unbalance

Madeira *capital:* **7** Funchal *export:* **4** wine **5** sugar **7** bananas

made-to-order **6** custom **10** customized **11** custom-built

madhouse **5** chaos **6** asylum, bedlam **8** loony bin **9** funny farm **10** booby hatch

madman **3** ass, nut **4** bawd, fool, jerk, loon **5** idiot, loony, ninny **6** dement, donkey, maniac, psycho **7** jackass, lunatic **8** imbecile **9** bedlamite, non compos **10** nincompoop, Tom o' Bedlam

madness **4** rage **6** lunacy, rabies **7** ecstasy **8** insanity **9** unbalance **10** aberration, alienation, enthusiasm **11** derangement, distraction, psychopathy

Madonna initials **3** BVM

Madras **9** Tamil Nadu *founder:* **3** Day (Francis)

Madrid museum **5** Prado

madrigal **4** glee, poem, song **8** part-song

madrigalist *Dutch:* **8** Arcadelt *English:* **4** Byrd **6** Morley, Wilbye **7** Tomkins, Weelkes *Flemish:* **8** Willaert *Italian:* **5** Festa **7** Landini **8** Marenzio **10** Monteverdi

maelstrom **4** eddy, fury **5** storm, whirl **6** vortex **7** turmoil **9** commotion, confusion, whirlpool

maestro see **conductor**

magazine **4** dump, Life, Time **5** cache, daily, depot, organ, store **6** annual, armory, digest, review, weekly **7** arsenal, gazette, journal, McCall's, monthly, Playboy, Redbook, TV Guide **8** biweekly **9** bimonthly, newspaper, quarterly, warehouse, Woman's Day **10** depository, lumber room, periodical, repository, semiweekly, storehouse **11** publication **12** Family Circle **13** Reader's Digest

maggot **4** grub, whim **5** fancy, freak, humor, larva **6** notion, vagary **7** boutade, caprice, conceit

Magi **6** Gaspar **8** Melchior **9** Balthazar *gift:* **4** gold **5** myrrh **12** frankincense

magian **6** mystic, witchy, wizard **7** charmer, warlock **8** conjurer, sorcerer, wizardly **9** enchanter, sorcerous **11** necromancer, necromantic **12** thaumaturgic

magic **5** charm, wicca **6** augury, mystic, witchy **7** alchemy, bewitch, conjury, devilry, gramary, sorcery **8** deviltry, divining, exorcism, gramarye, satanism, witchery, witching, wizardly, wizardry **9** conjuring, diablerie, diabolism, marvelous, occultism, sorcerous, sortilege, voodooism **10** mumbo jumbo, necromancy, prodigious, remarkable, stupendous, witchcraft **11** abracadabra, bewitchment, enchantment, incantation, leg-

erdemain, necromantic, soothsaying, thaumaturgy **12** thaumaturgic, unbelievable

magical **6** mystic, witchy **8** wizardly **9** sorcerous **10** bewitching **11** necromantic **12** thaumaturgic

Magic Flute composer **6** Mozart

magician **4** seer **5** brujo, witch **6** medium, shaman, voodoo, wizard **7** augurer, charmer, diviner, Houdini, prophet, warlock **8** conjurer, exorcist, satanist, sorcerer **9** archimage, diabolist, enchanter, exorciser, invocator, trickster, voodooist **10** soothsayer **11** illusionist, medicine man, necromancer, thaumaturge

magicking **7** sorcery **8** witchery, wizardry **9** conjuring **10** necromancy, witchcraft **11** bewitchment, enchantment, thaumaturgy

Magic Mountain, The *author:* **4** Mann *character:* **7** Castorp

magisterial **5** bossy, puffy, wiggy **6** lordly, stuffy **7** bloated, pompous **8** arrogant, dogmatic, insolent **9** dictative, imperious, important, masterful **10** disdainful, high-handed, imperative, peremptory, pontifical **11** doctrinaire, domineering, overbearing **12** supercilious **13** authoritarian, authoritative, self-important

Magister Ludi author **5** Hesse

magistrate **5** court, judge **7** bencher, justice **8** official *ancient Greek:* **5** ephor **6** archon *ancient Roman:* **5** edile **6** aedile, pretor **7** duumvir, praetor, questor **8** quaestor *Italian:* **7** podesta *Scottish:* **6** bailie *Venice (former):* **4** doge

Magna Carta *king:* **4** John *place signed:* **9** Runnymede

magnanimous **3** big **5** great, lofty, noble **7** liberal **8** generous, knightly, princely **9** forgiving, unselfish **10** altruistic, benevolent, chivalrous, highminded **11** nobleminded

magnate **4** czar, king, lion, name, peer **5** baron, mogul, nabob **6** biggie, big gun, fat cat, figure, prince, tycoon **8** big-timer, nobleman **9** personage, plutocrat

magnesium *symbol:* **2** Mg

magnet **8** terrella **9** lodestone

magnetic **7** drawing **8** alluring **9** appealing, arresting, seductive **10** attracting, attractive, bewitching, enchanting **11** captivating, charismatic, fascinating **12** irresistible *substance:* **4** iron **7** ferrite

magnetism **5** charm **6** allure, appeal, glamor **7** glamour **8** charisma, witchery **10** witchcraft **11** fascination

magnetize **4** draw, lure, take, wile **5** charm **6** allure **7** attract, bewitch, enchant **9** captivate, fascinate

magnification unit **8** diameter

magnificence 8 grandeur, splendor
13 sumptuousness
magnificent 5 grand, noble, proud
6 august, lordly, superb 7 opulent, stately,
sublime 8 glorious, gorgeous, imposing,
majestic, princely, splendid, standout 9 brilliant, grandiose, inspiring, luxurious, sumptuous 11 extravagant, outstanding, resplendent, splendorous, superlative
13 splendiferous
magnifier 4 lens *jeweler's:* 5 loupe
magnify 3 pad 4 hymn, laud, rise 5 add
to, bless, boost, color, cry up, erect, exalt,
extol, fudge, honor, mount, rouse, swell
6 beef up, deepen, dilate, expand, extend,
praise, uprear 7 amplify, augment, distend,
enhance, enlarge, ennoble, glorify, inflate,
sublime 8 eulogize, heighten, increase,
maximize, multiply, overdraw, overplay,
redouble 9 aggravate, celebrate, embellish,
embroider, intensate, intensify, overpaint,
overstate 10 aggrandize, exaggerate, overcharge, overstress, panegyrize
13 overemphasize
magnifying *combining form:* 4 micr
5 micro
magniloquent 7 aureate, flowery, swollen 8 sonorous 9 bombastic, overblown
10 euphuistic, rhetorical 11 declamatory
magnitude 4 pith, size, tune 5 order,
range 6 extent, import, matter, moment,
number, volume, weight 7 bigness, caliber,
measure, quality 8 enormity, hugeness,
loudness, quantity, vastness, vicinity
9 greatness, immensity, largeness
10 dimensions, importance, proportion
11 consequence, sizableness, weightiness
Magnolia State 11 Mississippi
magnum opus 7 classic 10 masterwork
11 chef d'oeuvre, masterpiece, tour de force
Magog's king 3 Gog
magpie 4 bird, crow 6 gabber, prater
7 blabber 8 jabberer, prattler 9 bandar-log,
blabmouth, chatterer 10 chatterbox, piping
crow 12 blabbermouth 13 miscellaneous
maguey 5 agave, fiber 7 cantala
magus 6 wizard 7 charmer, warlock
8 conjurer, sorcerer 9 enchanter
11 necromancer
Magyar 9 Hungarian
Mahalath *father:* 7 Ishmael 8 Jerimoth
husband: 4 Esau 8 Rehoboam
mah-jongg piece 4 tile
Mahli, Mahali *brother:* 5 Mushi *father:*
6 Merari
Mahlon *father:* 9 Elimelech *mother:*
5 Naomi *wife:* 4 Ruth
Mahol's son 5 Darda, Heman 6 Calcol
Maia *father:* 5 Atlas *mother:* 7 Pleione
sisters: 8 Pleiades *son:* 6 Hermes
7 Mercury

maid 3 gal 4 girl, lass, miss 5 biddy,
bonne, missy, wench 6 damsel, lassie, virgin 7 servant 8 charlady, domestic, factotum 9 charwoman, hired girl 10 au pair girl,
handmaiden *lady's:* 7 abigail
maiden 3 gal 4 burd, girl, lass, miss
5 first, fresh, missy, prime, wench 6 burdie,
damsel, intact, lassie, unused, virgin 7 dam-
osel, damozel, initial, pioneer, primary,
untaken, untried 8 earliest, original, virginal
10 old-maidish, spinsterly 11 husbandless,
spinsterish 12 undeflowered *combining
form:* 7 parthen 8 partheno *Muslim:*
5 houri *Norse mythological:* 6 valkyr 8 valkyrie, walkyrie
maidenhair tree 6 gingko, ginkgo
maidenhead 5 hymen 6 purity 9 freshness, virginity
maidenhood 9 virginity
maiden lady 7 old maid 8 spinster
10 spinstress
Maid of Astolat 6 Elaine
Maid of Orleans, The 4 Joan 7 Pucelle
author: 8 Schiller
___ **mail** 3 air 5 chain
maim 4 maul 5 break 6 batter, bung up,
mangle, mayhem 7 cripple, disable, dislimb
8 massacre, mutilate, paralyze 9 disfigure,
dismember, hamstring
main 3 big, sea 4 blue, deep, head, line,
star, very 5 brine, chief, drink, great, major,
ocean, sheer, vital 7 capital, high sea, leading, stellar 8 cardinal, foremost 9 essential,
paramount, principal 10 preeminent, prevailing 11 controlling, fundamental, outstanding, predominant
Maine *capital:* 7 Augusta *college:*
5 Bates, Colby 7 Bowdoin *highest point:*
10 Mt. Katahdin *largest town:* 8 Portland
motto: 6 dirigo 7 I direct *nickname:*
11 Lumber State 13 Pine Tree State
mainstay 3 key 4 prop 5 brace, staff
6 crutch, pillar, sinews 7 standby, support
8 backbone, buttress, upholder 9 supporter, sustainer
Main Street author 5 Lewis
maintain 4 aver, avow, save 5 argue,
claim, guard, right 6 affirm, assert, avouch,
back up, defend, insist, keep up, manage,
stress, uphold 7 care for, carry on, contend,
correct, declare, husband, justify, persist,
profess, protect, protest, rectify, support,
warrant 8 continue, preserve 9 cultivate,
emphasize, vindicate 10 provide for
maintenance 4 care, keep, salt 5 bread
6 living, upkeep 7 alimony, support 10 livelihood 11 subsistence 12 alimentation
worker: 7 janitor 9 custodian
maize 4 milo 10 Indian corn
majestic 5 grand, noble, regal, royal
6 august, kingly, lordly 7 courtly, stately

8 elevated, imperial, imposing, kinglike, magnific, princely 9 dignified, grandiose, monarchal, sovereign 10 monarchial 11 ceremonious, magnificent, monarchical
major 3 big 4 fell, main, star, ugly 5 chief, grave, hefty, large 6 better, higher, larger 7 capital, greater, serious, sizable, stellar 8 grievous, superior 9 dangerous, extensive, principal 10 large-scale, preeminent 11 outstanding, predominant 12 considerable
Major Barbara author 4 Shaw
majority 4 edge ·6 margin
make 3 act, eat, fit, fix, get, lay, net, run, set, tap, win 4 bear, brew, draw, earn, form, gain, head, mold, name, reap, sire 5 begin, build, catch, cause, clear, draft, enact, equal, erect, force, forge, frame, hatch, infer, judge, reach, ready, shape, spawn, start, write 6 attain, behave, coerce, compel, create, deduce, deduct, derive, draw on, draw up, effect, extend, father, finger, gather, intend, oblige, ordain, output, parent, secure, seduce, set out 7 achieve, acquire, appoint, bring in, clean up, collect, compose, concuss, count as, destine, fashion, harvest, perform, prepare, proceed, produce, serve as, shotgun, stretch, take off 8 assemble, break for, comprise, conclude, drag down, draw down, generate, initiate, light out, nominate, traverse 9 constrain, construct, designate, establish, fabricate, formulate, knock down, originate, procreate, strike out 10 bring about, constitute 11 manufacture, put together *amends:* 5 atone *a metallic sound:* 5 chink, clang *a mistake:* 3 err 4 goof *ashen:* 6 blanch *a statement:* 7 expound *a witty remark:* 4 jest *bare:* 5 strip 6 denude *believe:* 7 pretend *certain:* 6 assure 8 convince *cheerful:* 6 solace *coins:* 4 mint *different:* 6 change *fast:* 3 fix 4 gird 6 secure *hair curly:* 5 crimp 6 buckle *happy:* 5 bless 6 please 7 satisfy *holy:* 6 hallow *inoperative:* 5 annul *into a law:* 5 enact *known:* 3 air 6 expose, reveal, spread 7 declare, divulge, uncover 8 announce, disclose, proclaim *less severe:* 6 weaken 8 mitigate 9 attenuate *manifest:* 7 explain *melodious:* 6 attune *merry:* 5 cheer *numb:* 4 daze, stun *presentable:* 5 groom *quiet:* 4 calm 5 allay, quell 6 pacify 7 appease *ready beforehand:* 7 prepare *red:* 5 flush *rigid:* 5 brace 7 stiffen *sacred:* 8 sanctify *slick:* 3 oil 9 lubricate *small:* 8 belittle *smaller:* 8 compress *strong:* 7 fortify *suffix:* 2 en, fy 3 ify *suitable:* 5 adapt *supremely happy:* 7 beatify *unclean:* 4 soil *understandable:* 7 clarify *useful:* 7 utilize *use of:* 6 employ *vigorous:* 8 energize
make-believe 7 charade, feigned, fiction,

pageant 8 disguise, pretense 9 insincere, pretender 10 pretension
make off 2 go 3 fly, run 4 bolt, flee, quit, skip 5 leave, scoot, skirr 6 decamp, depart, escape, retire 7 abscond, run away, scamper 8 withdraw 9 skedaddle
make out 2 go 3 dig, see 4 draw, show 5 catch, grasp, infer, judge, prove, score 6 accept, arrive, deduce, deduct, derive, follow, gather, take in, thrive 7 collect, compass, discern, prosper, succeed 8 conclude, flourish, get along 9 apprehend, determine, establish, interpret 10 comprehend, understand 11 demonstrate
make over 4 cede, deed 5 alien 6 assign, convey, reform, remise 7 remodel 8 alienate, renovate, transfer 10 abalienate
makeshift 6 refuge, resort 7 stopgap 8 recourse, resource 9 expedient, temporary 10 expediency, substitute 11 provisional 13 rough-and-ready
make similar to *suffix:* 2 fy 3 ify
make up 3 fit, fix, get, mix, pay, sue, woo 4 fuse, meld, rise 5 atone, blend, court, frame, merge, ready, spark 6 decide, derise, gather, invent, mingle, offset, pursue, redeem, set off, settle 7 address, advance, arrange, balance, compile, compose, concoct, prepare, replace, reprint 8 approach, atone for, compound, comprise, contrive, intermix, outweigh 9 formulate, improvise, interfuse 10 compensate
makeup 3 lie 4 cast, face, form, mold, plan, vein 5 fiber, grain, humor, paint, setup, shape, stamp, style 6 design, nature, powder, stripe, temper 7 fiction 8 ordering, war paint 9 blackface, character, formation 10 complexion, maquillage 11 arrangement, composition, disposition, grease paint, personality, replacement, temperament 12 architecture, compensation, constitution, construction, organization *eye:* 4 kohl 7 mascara *facial:* 5 rouge 6 powder
maladroit 5 brash, inept 6 clumsy, gauche 7 awkward, halting, unhandy 8 bumbling, bungling, tactless 9 hamhanded, impolitic, lumbering, stumbling, unpolitic, unskilled, untactful 10 blundering, left-handed, ungraceful 11 floundering, heavy-handed 12 undiplomatic
malady 3 ill 7 ailment, disease, illness 8 disorder, sickness, syndrome 9 affection, complaint, condition, infirmity 10 affliction *suffix:* 4 itis
malaise 7 disease 8 debility 9 infirmity 10 feebleness, infirmness, sickliness 11 decrepitude 13 unhealthiness
Malaprop creator 8 Sheridan
malapropos 5 inapt, undue 8 ill-timed, improper, mistimed, unseemly, untimely 10 unsuitable 11 ill-seasoned, inopportune,

unbefitting **12** unseasonable, unseasonably **13** inappropriate, inopportunely

malaria **6** miasma **8** paludism *transmitter:* **8** mosquito

malarkey **4** guff **5** hooey **6** bunkum, bushwa **7** hogwash, twaddle **8** nonsense **9** poppycock **10** balderdash **12** blatherskite

Malawi *capital:* **8** Lilongwe *export:* **3** tea **7** tobacco *largest city:* **8** Blantyre *monetary unit:* **6** kwacha

Malaysia *capital:* **11** Kuala Lumpur *export:* **3** tin **6** rubber, timber **7** palm oil

Malchiel *father:* **6** Beriah *grandfather:* **5** Asher

Malchijah, Malchiah *father:* **5** Harim **6** Parosh, Rechab

Malchishua's father **4** Saul

malcontent **5** crank, rebel **6** anarch, griper, grouch, kicker, unruly **7** growler **8** factious, frondeur, grumbler, mutineer, mutinous, restless, revolter, sorehead **9** alienated, anarchist, estranged, insurgent, seditious **10** bellyacher, complainer, rebellious **11** disaffected, disgruntled, disobedient, faultfinder, ungratified **12** contumacious, dissatisfied, ungovernable

mal de _____ **3** mer

Maldives capital **4** Male

maldonite **9** black gold

male **3** tom **5** fella, manly **6** manful, virile **7** manlike **9** masculine, staminate *combining form:* **4** andr **5** andro *dark-haired:* **6** brunet

malediction **5** curse **7** malison **8** anathema

malefactor **5** felon, knave, rogue **6** rascal, sinner **8** criminal, evildoer, offender **9** miscreant, scoundrel, wrongdoer **10** blackguard, lawbreaker

malefic see **malicious**

malevolence **5** spite **6** grudge, malice, spleen **7** despite, ill will **9** hostility, malignity **10** abhorrence, antagonism **11** abomination, detestation **12** spitefulness **13** maliciousness

malevolent **4** evil **6** bitchy, malign, wicked **7** baleful, hateful, hurtful, vicious **8** sinister, spiteful **9** injurious, malicious, malignant **10** despiteful

malfunction **6** glitch

Mali *capital:* **6** Bamako *monetary unit:* **5** franc *product:* **4** fish **6** cotton **7** peanuts

malice **4** bane, bile, hate **5** spite, venom **6** animus, enmity, grudge, hatred, poison, spleen **7** despite, ill will, umbrage **8** meanness **9** animosity, antipathy **10** bitterness, resentment **11** hatefulness, malevolence **12** spitefulness **13** invidiousness

malicious **4** evil, mean **5** catty, green, nasty, petty **6** bitchy, wicked, witchy

7 baneful, hateful, heinous, jealous, spitish **8** spiteful, venomous, virulent **9** green-eyed, poisonous, poison-pen, rancorous **10** despiteful, malevolent

maliciousness see **malevolence**

malign **4** evil, slur, soil **5** decry, libel, smear, stain, sully, taint **6** befoul, defame, defile, revile, smirch, vilify, wicked **7** asperse, baleful, baneful, blacken, detract, hateful, hostile, noxious, pollute, slander, spatter, tarnish, traduce, vicious **8** backbite, besmirch, derogate, inimical, sinister, spiteful, tear down, virulent **9** bespatter, denigrate, disparage, injurious, rancorous **10** calumniate, depreciate, despiteful, maleficent, malevolent, pernicious, scandalize, villainize, vituperate **11** deleterious, detrimental, opprobriate **12** antagonistic, antipathetic

malignant **4** evil **6** wicked **7** baleful, hateful, vicious **8** devilish, fiendish, spiteful **9** injurious, rancorous **10** despiteful, diabolical, malevolent

malison **5** curse **8** anathema **11** commination, imprecation, malediction

mall **4** lane **5** alley **6** mallet **9** concourse, esplanade, promenade **10** passageway **11** median strip

malleable **6** pliant, supple **7** ductile, plastic

malleate **4** beat **5** pound **6** hammer

mallet **6** hammer, strike

Mallothi's father **5** Heman

Malluch's father **4** Bani **5** Harim

malodorous **4** foul, gamy, high, olid, rank, vile **5** fetid, fuggy, funky, fusty, musty, nasty, reeky, rough, stale **6** frowsy, putrid, rancid, rotten, smelly, stinky, strong, whiffy **7** decayed, noisome, noxious, reeking, spoiled, stenchy, tainted, ungodly **8** improper, indecent, mephitic, polluted, stinking, unseemly, untoward **9** offensive, poisonous, stenchful **10** decomposed, indelicate, nauseating, unbecoming **11** ill-smelling **12** pestilential

Malta *capital:* **8** Valletta *monetary unit:* **5** pound *product:* **8** textiles

Maltese Falcon, The *author:* **7** Hammett *detective:* **5** Spade (Sam)

maltreat **5** abuse **6** ill-use, misuse **7** outrage **8** disserve

mammal **3** ass **5** camel, daman, hippo, hyrax **6** alpaca, colugo, dassie **7** bearcat, primate **8** elephant **12** hippopotamus *African:* **5** okapi, zebra, zoril **7** zorilla, zorille, zorillo **8** aardvark, aardwolf *aquatic:* **5** yapok **6** desman, dugong, narwal, yapock **7** cowfish, manatee, narwhal, platypi (plural) **8** cetacean, narwhale, platypus, porpoise, sirenian **10** platypuses (plural) *arboreal:* **5** lemur **6** cuscus **7** opossum

8 kinkajou, lemuroid *Australian:* 5 coala, koala 8 kangaroo *burrowing:* 8 moldwarp, starnose, suricate *carnivorous:* 3 cat, dog, fox 4 bear, lion, mink, seal, wolf 5 genet, hyena, otter, panda, pekan, ratel, sable, tiger 6 badger, grison, marten, racoon, teledu, walrus 7 dasyure, genette, linsang, polecat, raccoon 8 carcajou, mongoose, mungoose *catlike:* 5 civet *doglike:* 6 jackal *extinct:* 6 quagga 8 mastodon, stegodon *feline:* 4 lion 5 tiger, tigon 6 tiglon 7 leopard, lioness, tigress *flying:* 3 bat *gnawing:* 3 rat 6 beaver, rodent 7 leporid 8 squirrel *goatlike:* 4 tahr 5 takin *harelike:* 5 hyrax 7 hyraces (plural), hyraxes (plural) 8 hyracoid *hoofed:* 2 ox 3 cow, pig 4 deer, goat, owse, oxen (plural) 5 camel, owsen (plural), sheep, tapir 6 alpaca, ovibos 7 peccary 8 ruminant, ungulate 12 hippopotamus *horned:* 4 goat *insect-eating:* 4 mole 5 shrew 6 tanrec, tenrec 8 hedgehog *long-necked:* 7 giraffe *marine:* 3 orc 4 orca 6 walrus 7 dolphin, grampus *marsupial:* 9 bandicoot *nocturnal:* 6 wombat *raccoon-like:* 8 cacomixl *ruminant:* 4 deer 5 llama, moose, sheep 6 vicuña 7 vicugna *small:* 4 pika 8 hedgehog, hedgepig *South American:* 7 guanaco *toothless:* 5 sloth 8 edentate, pangolin 9 armadillo *tropical:* 5 coati *unweaned:* 8 suckling *with flippers:* 8 pinniped *wolflike:* 5 hyena 6 hyaena

mammoth 4 huge 5 giant, whale 7 monster 8 colossal, enormous, gigantic 9 leviathan, monstrous 10 behemothic, gargantuan, mastodonic 11 elephantine

Mamre's brother 4 Aner 6 Eshcol

man 2 he, Mr. 3 boy, guy 4 body, buck, chap, cuss, gent, lord, soul 5 being, brace, flesh, lover, skate 6 fellow, galoot, mister, mortal, person, police, vassal 7 bruiser, fortify, husband, John Law, officer 8 bluecoat, creature, humanity, paramour 9 boyfriend, humankind, mortality, personage 10 individual 11 Homo sapiens *brass:* 5 Talos, Talus *castrated:* 6 eunuch *combining form:* 4 andr 5 andro, homin 6 homini *eccentric:* 6 codger, geezer *French:* 5 homme *Italian:* 4 uomo *Latin:* 3 vir 4 homo *Spanish:* 6 hombre *Yiddish:* 6 mensch *young:* 3 boy, lad 8 springal 9 springald, stripling

manage 2 do 3 run 4 fare, keep 5 get by, get on, guide, shift 6 afford, direct, effect, govern, handle, ordain 7 achieve, carry on, conduct, control, execute, husband, operate, steward, succeed 8 carry out, contrive, dominate, engineer, get along, work upon 9 cultivate, stagger on, supervise 10 accomplish, administer, adulterate, bring about 11 superintend 12 riding school, stagger along 13 muddle through

management 4 care 6 charge 7 conduct, running 8 handling, intrigue 9 oversight 10 conducting, intendance 11 supervising, supervision

manager 4 exec 6 gerent 7 handler, officer 8 director, official, producer 9 conductor, executive 10 impresario, supervisor 13 administrator *museum:* 7 curator *suffix:* 3 eer

Manahath's father 6 Shobal

Man and Superman author 4 Shaw

Manassas battle 7 Bull Run

Manasseh, Manasses *brother:* 7 Ephraim *father:* 6 Hashum, Joseph 8 Hezekiah 10 Pahathmoab *grandfather:* 5 Jacob *grandson:* 6 Gilead *mother:* 7 Asenath *son:* 6 Machir

man-at-arms 2 GI 7 fighter, soldier, warrior 10 serviceman 11 fighting man

mancipium 5 slave 7 bondman, chattel 8 bondsman 9 bondslave

Mandalay author 7 Kipling

mandarin 4 duck, tree 5 elder 6 orange 8 official 9 tangerine 10 bureaucrat

mandate 4 fiat, word 5 edict, order, ukase 6 behest, charge, decree 7 bidding, command, dictate 9 authority 10 imperative, injunction 13 authorization

mandatory 6 forced 7 binding, needful 8 required 9 de rigueur, essential, imperious, necessary, requisite 10 commanding, compelling, compulsory, imperative 11 involuntary 12 irremissible 13 indispensable

mandible 3 jaw

Manette's daughter 5 Lucie

maneuver 3 jig, ply 4 move, plan, play, plot, ploy, step 5 feint, swing, trick, wield 6 design, device, gambit, handle, jockey, scheme, tactic, wangle 7 beguile, exploit, finagle, finesse, gimmick, measure 8 artifice, demarche, dispense, engineer, exercise, intrigue, movement, navigate 9 machinate, procedure, stratagem 10 manipulate, proceeding, subterfuge 11 contrivance, machination 12 manipulation

maneuvering room 8 latitude

Man for All Seasons, A *author:* 4 Bolt *subject:* 4 More

manful see **manly**

manganese *ore:* 10 pyrolusite *symbol:* 2 Mn

manger 4 rack 6 cratch, trough

mangle 3 mar 4 hack, iron, maul 5 press 6 batter, damage, deface, deform, impair, injure, padder 7 butcher, contort, distort 9 disfigure

mangy 5 seedy 6 shabby, sleazy, tagrag 7 scruffy, squalid 8 decrepit, tattered 9 moth-eaten 10 down-at-heel

manhandle 4 maul 5 abuse 6 batter

7 rough up **8** maltreat, mistreat **10** knock about, roughhouse, slap around

Manhattan *purchaser:* **6** Minuit *school:* **9** Juilliard *university:* **8** Columbia

mania 4 rage **5** craze, fancy, thing **6** fetish, hangup **7** madness, passion **8** fixation, idée fixe, insanity **9** cacoëthes, fixed idea, obsession **10** compulsion, enthusiasm **11** fascination, infatuation

maniac 3 bug, mad, nut **4** loon, wild **5** bigot, crazy, fiend, freak, loony, rabid **6** crazed, dement, insane, madman, raging, zealot **7** berserk, cracked, fanatic, frantic, furious, lunatic, madling, ranting, unsound, violent **8** demented, deranged, frenetic, frenzied **9** bedlamite, delirious, non compos **10** enthusiast

manifest 4 mark, show, told, vent **5** clear, overt, plain, shown, utter, voice **6** appear, embody, evince, expose, ostend, patent **7** display, evident, evinced, exhibit, express, obvious **8** apparent, distinct, divulged, evidence, palpable, proclaim, revealed **9** disclosed, evidenced, incarnate, objectify, personify, personize, prominent **10** illustrate, indication, noticeable **11** demonstrate, exteriorize, externalize, materialize, personalize, unambiguous

manifestation 4 show **7** display **8** epiphany **10** revelation *combining form:* **5** phany

manifold 5 boost **6** beef up, expand **7** augment, diverse, enlarge, magnify **8** compound, increase, multiply, numerous **9** aggregate, multiform, multiplex **10** aggrandize, multiphase **11** diversiform, polymorphic **12** multifarious, multivarious

manikin 4 puny, runt **5** dwarf, midge, pygmy **6** midget, peewee **8** Tom Thumb **10** diminutive, homunculus

Manila *founder:* **7** Legaspi *victor:* **5** Dewey

manipulate 3 ply, rig, use **4** play **5** swing, wield **6** direct, doctor, handle, jockey, juggle, manage **7** beguile, conduct, control, exploit, finesse **8** dispense, engineer, maneuver **9** machinate **10** tamper with

Manitoba *capital:* **8** Winnipeg *university:* **7** Brandon **13** Saint Boniface

mankind 5 flesh, human **6** humans, people **8** humanity **9** mortality **11** homo sapiens

like 4 male **6** virile **8** hominoid, humanoid **9** masculine **10** anthropoid

manly 4 bold, male **5** brave **6** virile **7** gallant, valiant **8** fearless, intrepid, unafraid, valorous **9** dauntless, masculine, undaunted **10** courageous

man-made 9 synthetic **10** artificial, factitious *object:* **8** artefact, artifact

Mann character 7 Castorp **10** Felix Krull

manner 3 use, way **4** form, kind, mien, mode, sort, tone, turn, vein, wise, wont **5** habit, modus, mores, style, trick, usage **6** custom, method, system **7** bearing, fashion, p's and q's **7** quomodo **8** behavior, decorums, demeanor, habitude, practice, protocol **9** amenities, etiquette, technique **10** civilities, consuetude, deportment, elegancies **11** affectation, formalities, peculiarity, proprieties **12** affectedness, idiosyncrasy *combining form:* **4** wise *suffix:* **2** ic, ly **4** ical

mannered 6 cutesy **8** affected **9** conscious **13** self-conscious

mannerism 4 airs, lugs, pose **7** oddness **9** prettyism, queerness **10** preciosity **11** affectation, peculiarity, singularity **12** eccentricity, idiosyncrasy **13** artificiality

mannerless 4 rude **7** ill-bred, uncivil **8** impolite **11** disgracious **12** discourteous **13** disrespectful

mannerly 5 civil **6** polite **7** civilly, genteel **8** politely **9** courteous **10** respectful **12** respectfully

Manoah's son 6 Samson

Manon composer 8 Massenet

Manon Lescaut *author:* **7** Prevost *composer:* **7** Puccini

manor 4 land **5** acres, villa **6** castle, estate, quinta **7** château **12** landed estate

manservant 5 valet **6** butler

mansion 4 hall **5** house, villa **6** castle, estate **7** château

manslaughter 5 blood **6** murder **7** bump-off, killing **8** foul play, homicide

manslayer 6 killer **8** homicide, murderer

mantic 7 fatidic **8** Delphian, oracular **9** sibylline, vaticinal **11** prophetical

mantle 4 glow, pink, rose **5** blush, color, cover, flush, rouge **6** pinken, redden **7** crimson *combining form:* **7** chlamyd **8** chlamydo

Manto *father:* **8** Tiresias *husband:* **7** Rhacius *son:* **6** Mopsus

man-to-man 4 open **5** frank **6** candid **10** unreserved **11** openhearted, unconcealed, undisguised, unvarnished **12** undissembled

mantra 2 om **4** hymn **5** chant **6** prayer **11** incantation

manual 4 text **5** guide **6** primer **7** primary **8** Baedeker, handbook, hornbook, textbook **9** guidebook, vade mecum **10** compendium **11** abecedarium, enchiridion *religious:* **9** catechism *worker:* **7** laborer

manufactory 4 mill **5** plant, works

manufacture 4 form, make, mold **5** forge, frame, shape **6** create, invent **7** fashion, produce **8** creation **9** fabricate **10** production **11** put together

manumit 4 free 5 loose 6 loosen, unbind 7 release, set free, unchain 8 liberate 9 discharge, unshackle 10 emancipate

manure 4 dung 6 ordure 7 excreta 9 excrement 10 fertilizer

manuscript 4 hand *ancient:* 5 codex 7 codices (plural) *red part:* 6 rubric

Man Without a Country, The *author:* 4 Hale *character:* 5 Nolan

many 4 much 5 monie 6 divers, legion, myriad, sundry 7 copious, diverse, several, various 8 abundant, manifold, multiple, numerous, populous 9 abounding, bounteous, bountiful, countless, multitude, plentiful 10 multiplied, voluminous 12 multifarious, multiplicate, multitudinal 13 multitudinous *combining form:* 4 poly 5 multi, pluri

Maon's father 7 Shammai

map 4 plan, plat 5 chart, draft, graph 6 design, lay out, set out, sketch, survey 7 arrange, diagram, drawing, explore, outline, picture, tracing 9 cartogram, delineate *collection:* 5 atlas *line:* 6 isohel 7 contour, isobath, isogone, isogram, isogriv, isohyet, isotach 8 isarithm, isocheim, isochime, isogloss, isogonal, isogonic, isograph, isopleth, isotherm *maker:* 12 cartographer *making:* 11 cartography, chorography

map projection 5 Bonne, conic 6 Albers 8 gnomonic, Mercator 9 Mollweide, polyconic 10 sinusoidal 12 orthographic 13 stereographic

maquillage 4 face 5 paint 6 makeup 8 war paint

mar 4 flaw, harm, hurt, ruin, scar, warp 5 spoil, wreck 6 bruise, damage, deface, deform, impair, injure, injury 7 blemish, scratch, tarnish, vitiate 9 prejudice *the countryside:* 6 litter

marabou 4 silk 5 stork 12 adjutant bird

Marat *colleague:* 6 Danton *slayer:* 6 Corday

maraud 4 raid 5 foray, harry 6 harass

marauder 6 bandit, bummer, looter, pirate, raider, sacker 7 brigand, cateran, forager, ravager, spoiler, wrecker 8 pillager, ravisher 9 buccaneer, desperado, despoiler, plunderer, spoliator 10 depredator, freebooter

marble 3 mib, mig 4 immy, migg 5 aggie, rance 6 blotch, miggle, mottle, streak 7 cipolin, glassie, steelie

Marble Faun, The *author:* 9 Hawthorne *character:* 5 Hilda 6 Kenyon, Miriam 9 Donatello *setting:* 4 Rome

marblehearted 5 stony 7 callous 8 hardened, obdurate 9 heartless, unfeeling 10 hard-boiled 11 cold-blooded 13 unsympathetic

march 2 go 3 hem, rim 4 abut, jibe, join, line, move 5 agree, check, fit in, get on, skirt, sling, stalk, tally, touch, verge 6 accord, adjoin, border, butt on, course, extend, fringe, parade, square, stride, travel 7 advance, headway, ongoing, proceed 8 anabasis, boundary, dovetail, frontier, get along, neighbor, outlands, parallel, progress, traverse 9 periphery, provinces, territory 10 borderland, correspond 11 advancement

March *date:* 4 ides *sisters:* 2 Jo 3 Amy, Meg 4 Beth

March Hare creator 7 Carroll

March King 5 Sousa

Mardi Gras 8 carnival 10 Fat Tuesday *city:* 10 New Orleans

Marduk, Merodach *city:* 7 Babylon *consort:* 8 Zarpanit 9 Sarpanitu *father:* 2 Ea *victim:* 5 Kingu

mare 3 sea 5 horse 6 equine

Mareshah's son 6 Hebron

mare's nest 3 din 4 hoax, sell 5 babel, cheat, fraud, put on, spoof 6 clamor, hubbub, humbug, racket, uproar 7 swindle 8 flimflam 9 imposture 10 hullabaloo

margarine 4 oleo

margin 3 hem, rim 4 abut, brim, edge, join, line, play, room, side 5 bound, brink, frame, scope, shore, skirt, touch, verge 6 border, fringe, leeway 7 connect, minimum, outline, selvage 8 latitude, neighbor, surround, trimming 9 elbowroom, perimeter, periphery *of shortcoming:* 6 leeway

Marguerite's lover 5 Faust

Marianas *discoverer:* 8 Magellan *island:* 4 Rota 5 Pagan 6 Guguan, Saipan, Tinian 7 Agrihan, Aguijan

marijuana 3 boo, pot 4 hash, hemp, weed 5 grass, joint 6 moocah, reefer 7 hashish 8 cannabis

marina 4 dock 5 basin 8 boatyard 9 esplanade, promenade

marine 5 naval 6 dipsey, dipsie, gyrene 7 abyssal, aquatic, bathyal, benthic, deep-sea, fluvial, neritic, oceanic, pelagic 8 bathybic, nautical, seagoing, seamanly 9 bathysmal, seafaring, thalassic 10 fluviatile, lacustrine, oceangoing, seamanlike 12 hydrographic, navigational 13 oceanographic *crustacean:* 8 barnacle *deposit:* 5 coral *plant:* 4 alga, kelp 7 seaweed

mariner 3 gob, tar 4 jack, salt 6 rating, sailor, sea dog, seaman 7 jack-tar, old salt, swabbie 8 seafarer 9 sailorman, shellback, tarpaulin 10 bluejacket

marionette 6 puppet 10 bufflehead

marital 6 wedded 7 married, nuptial, spousal 8 conjugal, hymeneal 9 connubial

maritime 7 oceanic 8 nautical 9 thalassic 12 navigational

mark 3 aim, jot, map, sap, say, see, use

4 butt, cull, dupe, duty, fish, fool, goal, gull, heed, logo, look, note, pick, read, show, sign, type, view **5** bound, brand, chart, chump, elect, grade, index, label, limit, stamp, token, trait **6** assign, attend, behold, choose, denote, emblem, evince, lay off, lay out, notice, object, optate, opt for, ostend, pigeon, prefer, rating, record, regard, select, sucker, symbol, target, victim, virtue **7** bespeak, betoken, delimit, destine, discern, exhibit, fall guy, feature, gudgeon, indicia, initial, measure, observe, pick out, purpose, qualify, quality, scratch, signify, symptom **8** ambition, evidence, function, indicate, logotype, manifest, perceive, proclaim, property, register **9** affection, attention, attribute, character, demarcate, designate, determine, objective, quaesitum, signalize, single out **10** importance, indication **11** differentia, distinction, distinguish **12** characterize *a tree:* **5** blaze *by cutting:* **4** nick **5** notch **6** scribe *distinctive:* **7** indicia **8** indicium *identifying:* **6** signet *low-water:* **5** datum *musical notation:* **6** corona **7** fermata *of insertion:* **5** caret *of omission:* **8** ellipsis **10** apostrophe *over a vowel:* **5** breve **6** accent, macron *over n:* **5** tilde *punctuation:* **4** dash **5** colon, comma **6** hyphen, period **9** semicolon *skate:* **4** cusp *time:* **5** count *under a letter:* **7** cedilla *with welts:* **4** wale

Mark *cousin:* **8** Barnabas *mother:* **4** Mary

mark down 3 cut **4** clip, pare **5** decry, lower, shave, slash **6** reduce **7** cut back, devalue **8** write off **9** devaluate **10** depreciate, underprize, undervalue

marked 5 noted **6** signal **7** pointed, salient **8** striking **9** arresting, prominent **10** noticeable, remarkable **11** conspicuous, outstanding **12** considerable **13** distinguished *man:* **4** Cain

market 4 give, sell, shop, vend **5** cheap, store **6** outlet, retail, tryste **8** showroom **9** traffic in, wholesale **11** merchandise *kind:* **4** flea **5** money, stock

marketable 3 fit **4** good **5** sound **7** selling **8** vendible **9** wholesome **10** commercial

marketplace 5 agora, bazar **6** bazaar, rialto

marksman 4 shot **7** deadeye, shooter

marl 4 clay **5** earth **9** fertilize

marlin 9 spearfish

Marlowe play 8 Edward II **9** Dr. Faustus **11** Tamburlaine **13** The Jew of Malta

marmalade fruit 6 orange, quince

marmot 10 prairie dog

Marpessa *abductor:* **4** Idas *father:* **6** Evenus

Marquand character 4 Gray, Moto **5** Apley, Wayde **6** Pulham **7** Goodwin

Marquis *cat:* **9** Mehitabel *cockroach:* **5** Archy

marriage 5 match, union **6** bridal **7** nuptial, spousal, wedding, wedlock **8** espousal, monogamy, nuptials, polygamy, polygany **9** espousals, matrimony **11** conjugality **12** connubiality *combining form:* **4** gamy **6** gamous *notice:* **5** banns *outside a group:* **7** exogamy *second:* **6** bigamy, digamy *within a group:* **8** endogamy

marriageable 6 nubile

marriage broker 9 go-between **10** matchmaker *Jewish:* **8** shadchan

marriage portion 3 dot **5** dower, dowry

marrow 4 core, meat, pith, soul **5** heart, stuff **6** bottom, kernel **7** essence **9** substance **10** virtuality **12** essentiality, quintessence

marry 3 tie, wed **4** join, link, mate, wive, yoke **5** catch, hitch **6** couple, relate, splice, spouse **7** combine, conjoin, espouse, husband **9** associate, conjugate

Mars 6 planet *combining form:* **4** areo *moon:* **6** Deimos, Phobos *relating to:* **7** martian; (see also **Ares**)

Marseillaise composer 13 Rouget de Lisle

marsh 3 bog, fen **4** mire, ooze, quag **5** bayou, glade, swail, swale, swamp **6** maskeg, morass, muskeg, slough **7** baygall, wetland **8** moorland, quagmire **9** swampland *combining form:* **4** helo **6** paludi

marshal 5 array, guide, order, rally, space, usher **6** direct, escort, muster **7** arrange, dispose, officer **8** mobilize, organize, shepherd **9** methodize **10** distribute

marshland see **marsh**

marshlight 7 spunkie **11** ignis fatuus

Martha *brother:* **7** Lazarus *sister:* **4** Mary

martial 7 warlike **8** militant, military, spirited **9** bellicose, combative **10** aggressive, mettlesome, pugnacious **11** belligerent

Martial's forte 7 epigram

Martin Chuzzlewit author 7 Dickens

Martinique *capital:* **12** Fort-de-France *discoverer:* **8** Columbus

martyr 4 Paul, rack **5** Agnes, Alban, James, Peter, saint, wring **6** George, harrow, Justin **7** afflict, agonize, crucify, Cyprian, Stephen, torment, torture **8** Ignatius, Lawrence, Polycarp, sufferer **9** Joan of Arc, Sebastian **10** excruciate *Protestant:* **6** Ridley **7** Cranmer, Latimer

marvel 6 wonder **7** miracle, portent, prodigy, stunner **9** horehound, sensation **10** phenomenon **12** astonishment

marvelous 5 awing, nifty, super, swell **6** divine, dreamy, groovy, peachy **7** amazing, awesome, ripping **8** glorious, pleasant, striking, stunning, superior, terrific, wondrous **9** agreeable, enjoyable, excellent, hunky-dory, rewarding, wonderful **10** astounding, incredible, phenomenal, prodigious, satisfying, staggering, stupendous, surprising **11** astonishing, bewildering, confounding, exceptional, pleasurable, sensational, spectacular **12** awe-inspiring, supernatural, unimaginable **13** extraordinary, inconceivable

Marx, Karl *book:* **10** Das Kapital *collaborator:* **6** Engels

Marx brother **5** Chico, Harpo, Zeppo **7** Groucho

Mary *husband:* **6** Clopas, Joseph **8** Alphaeus *kinswoman:* **9** Elisabeth *son:* **4** Mark **5** James, Jesus, Joses

Maryland *academy, university:* **7** U.S. Naval **11** Towson State **12** Johns Hopkins *capital:* **9** Annapolis *largest city:* **9** Baltimore *nickname:* **12** Cockade State, Old Line State

mascot **4** juju, luck, zemi **5** charm **6** amulet, bat boy, fetish **7** periapt **8** talisman **10** phylactery

masculine **4** male **5** manly **6** manful, robust, virile **7** manlike **9** unwomanly *combining form:* **4** andr **5** andro

masculinity **8** machismo, virility **9** manliness

mash **4** mess, pulp **6** accost, bruise, jumble, jungle, litter, muddle, suitor, tumble **7** clutter, rummage **8** scramble **10** sweetheart **12** hugger-mugger

masher **4** wolf **5** flirt **6** chaser **7** Don Juan **8** Casanova **9** ladies' man, philander, womanizer **10** lady-killer **11** philanderer

mash note **10** billet-doux, love letter

mask **4** blur, face, pose, sham, show, veil **5** block, cloak, color, cover, front, guard, guise, put-on, visor **6** aspect, defend, domino, facade, fakery, flavor, screen, shield, veneer, visard, vizard **7** dress up, frisket, muffler, posture, pretext, protect, secrete, seeming, veiling **8** coloring, disguise, pretense **9** dissemble, doughface, false face, safeguard, semblance **10** appearance, camouflage, false front, simulation **11** affectation, dissembling, dissimulate **12** disguisement **13** dissimulation

masonry **9** brickwork, stonework *in a frame:* **7** nogging

masquerade **4** face, pose, show, veil **5** cloak, color, cover, front **6** facade, pass as **7** pass for, pass off, posture **8** disguise **10** camouflage **12** attitudinize

mass **3** lot, sum, wad **4** bank, body, bulk, clot, core, glob, heap, hill, lump, much, pack, peck, pile **5** clump, group, mound, shock, stack, total, whole **6** corpus, nugget, object, staple, volume **7** expanse, globule, pyramid, wadding **8** assemble, mountain **9** aggre-

gate, great deal, magnitude, stockpile, substance **10** generality **11** aggregation, proletariat **12** conglomerate *combining form:* **4** onco **5** oncho *confused:* **7** clutter **9** imbroglio *for departed:* **7** requiem *ice:* **4** calf, floe *indefinite:* **3** gob *jumbled:* **8** pell-mell, scramble *metal:* **5** ingot *muddy:* **6** sludge *of hair:* **3** mop *of individuals:* **5** crowd, horde, swarm **13** agglomeration *part:* **6** proper **8** ordinary *rock:* **4** dome *rounded:* **4** knob *suffix:* **3** ium, ome *swollen:* **4** cere *tight:* **4** knot

Massachusetts *capital:* **6** Boston *college, university:* **3** MIT **5** Clark, Curry, Smith, Tufts **6** Babson, Boston **7** Amherst, Harvard **8** Brandeis, Williams **9** Hampshire, Holy Cross, Merrimack, Radcliffe, Wellesley **11** Springfield **12** Mount Holyoke, Northeastern *highest point:* **10** Mt. Greylock *nickname:* **8** Bay State **9** Old Colony *state bird:* **9** chickadee

massacre **4** kill **6** mangle, murder, pogrom **8** butchery, decimate, genocide, mangling, mutilate **9** bloodbath, bloodshed, slaughter **10** annihilate, blood purge, decimation **11** exterminate, internecion

massage **3** rub **5** knead **7** rubdown

Massa's father **7** Ishmael

Massenet opera **5** Le Cid, Manon, Sapho, Thais **7** Werther

massive **4** huge, vast **5** bulky, giant, grand, heavy, hefty, hulky, jumbo, large, solid **6** mighty, mortal **7** compact, hulking, immense, mammoth, notable, weighty **8** colossal, cracking, cumbrous, enormous, gigantic, towering **9** fantastic, monstrous, ponderous **10** cumbersome, monumental, prodigious, stupendous, tremendous **11** elephantine, mountainous

master **3** get **4** best, boss, cock, down, guru, head, lick, rule, tame, whiz **5** adept, bwana, chief, crack, learn, lover, marse, ruler, sahib, swami, throw, tutor **6** artist, direct, domine, expert, genius, govern, honcho, hurdle, leader, pick up, ruling, savant, subdue, victor, wizard **7** artiste, captain, conquer, headman, maestro, overman, padrone, prevail, rabboni, regnant, skilled, subduer, triumph **8** defeater, dominant, dominate, employer, fancy man, governor, hierarch, overcome, overlord, overseer, paramour, regulate, skillful, superior, surmount, virtuoso **9** ascendant, authority, boyfriend, chieftain, conqueror, dominator, paramount, prevalent, principal, sovereign **10** proficient, subjugator, vanquisher **11** controlling, crackerjack, domesticate, domesticize, domiciliate, overbearing, predominant, predominate *combining form:* **4** arch

masterdom **8** dominion **9** ascendant, dominance, supremacy **10** ascendancy,

domination, prepotence, prepotency
11 preeminence, sovereignty
masterful **4** deft **5** adept, bossy, crack
6 adroit, expert **7** skilled, supreme **8** absolute, despotic, dogmatic, imperial, skillful,
vigorous **9** arbitrary, dexterous, dictative,
energetic, imperious **10** autocratic, high-handed, imperative, peremptory, preeminent, proficient, self-willed, tyrannical
11 crackerjack, dictatorial, doctrinaire, domineering, magisterial, overbearing, superlative **12** transcendent **13** authoritarian,
authoritative, high-and-mighty
masterly **5** adept, crack **6** expert
7 skilled, supreme **8** skillful **10** preeminent,
proficient **11** crackerjack, superlative
12 transcendent
Master of Ballantrae **6** Durrie *author:*
9 Stevenson
masterpiece **7** classic **9** objet d'art
10 magnum opus **11** chef d'oeuvre, tour de
force
mastery **4** sway **5** knack, might, power,
skill **7** ability, command, control, know-how **8** dominion **9** authority, expertise,
expertism **10** ascendancy, domination,
expertness **11** superiority **12** jurisdiction
masticate **4** chew, pulp **5** champ, chomp,
chump, crush, munch, smash **6** bruise,
crunch, squash **7** chumble, pulpify,
scrunch **8** macerate, ruminate **9** break
down
mastodonic see **mammoth**
mast support **4** bibb
mat **3** dim, rug **4** dead, dull, felt, flat, shag
5 blind, doily, muted **6** carpet **10** lackluster,
lusterless
matador **6** torero **8** toreador **11** bullfighter
adjunct: **6** muleta *move:* **4** pase **5** faena
8 veronica
Mata Hari **3** spy
match **3** con, pit, tie, vie **4** anti, bout,
game, like, meet, suit, twin **5** adapt, array,
equal, event, liken, rival, touch **6** amount,
double, equate, fellow, oppose **7** compare,
compeer, counter, opposer, paragon, play
off, stack up **8** analogue, approach, oppo-
nant, parallel **9** adversary, companion, correlate, duplicate, encounter, measure up,
oppugnant, partake of **10** antagonist,
assimilate, complement, coordinate,
engagement, equivalent, reciprocal, supplement **11** counterpart, countertype **12** correspond to **13** correspondent, harmonize
with *friction:* **5** fusee, fuzee **7** lucifer
8 locofoco
matchless **4** only **5** alone **6** unique
9 unequaled, unrivaled **10** inimitable
11 unparagoned **12** incomparable,
unparalleled
matchmaker see **marriage broker**

mate **3** pal, tie, wed **4** chum, pair, peer,
twin **5** amigo, breed, buddy, equal, hitch,
marry, parti, sosie **6** cohort, couple, double,
fellow, friend, helper, splice, spouse **7** compeer, consort, partner **8** alter ego, confrere,
familiar **9** associate, companion, confidant,
copartner, duplicate, procreate **10** complement, crossbreed, equivalent, reciprocal
11 cater-cousin, concomitant **12** acquaintance **13** accompaniment
maté **3** tea **5** holly **8** beverage
material **3** big **4** real, true **5** ad rem,
being, cloth, gross, stuff, tapis, thing, vital
6 actual, animal, bodily, carnal, entity, fabric,
matter, object **7** apropos, earthly, element,
fleshly, germane, sensual, weighty, worldly
8 apposite, cardinal, palpable, physical,
pointful, relevant, sensible, tangible **9** apparatus, component, corporeal, equipment,
essential, important, machinery, momentous, objective, pertinent, substance
10 applicable, individual, ingredient, meaningful, phenomenal **11** applicative, applicatory, appreciable, constituent, fundamental,
perceptible, significant, substantial **12** considerable **13** consequential *building:*
5 adobe, brick **7** plywood, shingle **8** concrete *cementing:* **7** plaster *combining
form:* **3** hyl **4** hylo *combustible:* **8** kindling
cushioning: **4** foam *glutinous:* **7** gelatin
hard: **7** carbide *hard covering:* **6** stucco
indecent: **4** smut *insulating:* **7** lagging
10 fiberglass *leftover:* **5** waste **7** rubbish
petrified: **8** gemstone
materialistic **6** carnal, earthy **7** earthly,
mundane, profane, secular, sensual, worldly
materialize **4** loom, rise, show **5** issue,
reify **6** appear, embody, emerge, entify,
show up, spring, typify **8** manifest **9** incarnate, objectify, personify, personize, take
shape **10** pragmatize **11** exteriorize,
hypostatize **12** substantiate
matériel **4** gear **6** outfit, tackle **8** tackling
9 apparatus, equipment, machinery
11 habiliments **13** accouterments, accoutrements, paraphernalia
maternal **6** mother **8** motherly
maternally related **5** enate
mathematician *American:* **6** Peirce, Veblen, Wiener *British:* **6** Stokes *Dutch:*
7 Huygens *English:* **6** Newton, Taylor, Tur-
ing, Wallis **7** Pearson, Russell **9** Whitehead
French: **5** Borel, Comte, Viète **6** Galois,
Pascal, Picard **7** Laplace, Vernier **8** Four-
nier, Painlevé, Poincaré **9** Descartes *German:* **5** Gauss, Wolff **6** Staudt **7** Riemann
11 Weierstrass *Greek:* **6** Euclid **10** Archimedes, Pythagoras *Italian:* **8** Volterra
10 Torricelli *Norwegian:* **7** Stormer *Russian:* **11** Lobachevsky *Scottish:* **4** Tait

6 Napier 8 Stirling *Swiss:* 5 Sturm
7 Steiner

mathematics *branch:* 7 algebra 8 calculus, geometry 10 arithmetic 12 trigonometry *proven statement in:* 7 theorem
____ **Mather** 6 Cotton 7 Richard
8 Increase

Matred *daughter:* 9 Mehetabel *father:* 7 Mezahab *son-in-law:* 5 Hadar

matriarch 4 dame 6 mother 7 dowager
10 grande dame 13 materfamilias

matrimonial 6 bridal, wedded 7 marital, married, nuptial, spousal 8 conjugal, hymeneal 9 connubial 11 epithalamic

matrimony 7 wedlock 8 marriage 11 conjugality 12 connubiality

matrix 3 die 6 cradle, gangue, strike
10 groundmass, truth table

matron 4 dame 7 dowager 10 grande dame, parlormaid

Mattaniah *father:* 4 Bani, Elam, Mica
5 Asaph, Heman, Zattu 6 Josiah
10 Pahathmoab *grandson:* 5 Hanan *son:* 6 Zaccur 8 Shemaiah

Mattatha *father:* 6 Nathan *grandfather:* 5 David

Mattathias *father:* 5 Simon 6 Ananos
7 Absalom, Boethus 10 Theophilus *son:* 8 Josephus

matter 3 pus 4 body, core, gist, head, mail, mean, meat, pith, text, to-do, tune 5 being, cause, count, motif, order, point, range, sense, stuff, theme, thing, topic, value, weigh, worry 6 affair, amount, burden, entity, extent, import, motive, object, source, upshot 7 concern, signify, subject 8 argument, business, material, vicinity 9 grievance, magnitude, substance, suppurate 10 individual 11 constituent, predicament 12 circumstance *added to book:* 8 addendum, appendix *coloring:* 3 dye 6 indigo 7 pigment 8 tinction 10 indigo blue *combining form:* 3 hyl 4 hylo *decayed organic:* 4 duff *diffused:* 5 vapor *in dispute:* 5 issue *inferior:* 5 trash *waste:* 5 dross 6 sewage 7 excreta *white:* 4 alba *worthless:* 4 slag 7 garbage

matter-of-fact 3 dry 4 cold 5 prose, prosy, sober, sound, stoic 6 earthy, stolid 7 prosaic, prosing 9 apathetic, impassive, objective, practical, pragmatic, realistic 10 hard-boiled, hardheaded, impersonal, phlegmatic, unaffected 11 cold-blooded, commonplace, down-to-earth, emotionless 12 unidealistic 13 unimpassioned, unsentimental

Matthew's father 8 Alphaeus

Mattithiah's father 4 Nebo 7 Shallum
8 Jeduthun

mattress 3 pad 4 sack *case:* 4 tick *fabric:* 7 ticking *straw:* 6 pallet

mature 3 age, due 4 grow, ripe, wane 5 adult, grown, olden, owing, ready, ripen, round 6 flower, grow up, mellow, season, unpaid 7 advance, blossom, decline, develop, grown-up, outgrow, overdue, payable, ripened 8 progress 9 developed, full-blown, full-grown *combining form:* 3 tel 4 tele, telo

maudlin 5 mushy, silly 6 addled, slushy, sticky 7 fuddled, mawkish, muddled 8 bathetic, confused, romantic 9 befuddled 11 sentimental, tear-jerking

Maugham character 4 Kear, Liza
5 Carey, Rosie, Sadie 7 Mildred 8 Craddock 10 Strickland

maul 3 paw, row 4 bang, bash, club, fray, lash, mace, whip 5 abuse, brawl, broil, flail, melee, pound, set-to 6 batter, beetle, buffet, fracas, hammer, injure, molest, sledge 7 rough up, ruction 8 dogfight, maltreat 9 manhandle 10 donnybrook

maunder 3 bat, gad 5 drift, mooch, range 6 ramble 9 gallivant

Mauritania *capital:* 10 Nouakchott *monetary unit:* 7 ouguiya

Mauritius *capital:* 9 Port Louis *export:* 5 sugar *monetary unit:* 5 rupee

Maurois biographee 4 Hugo, Sand
5 Byron, Dumas 6 Proust 7 Shelley
8 Disraeli

mauve 6 purple, violet

maven, mavin 5 adept 6 expert, master 8 virtuoso 9 authority 10 past master, proficient 12 professional

maverick 5 stray 8 bohemian, unmarked 9 unbranded 13 nonconformist

maw 4 crop 7 stomach 9 poppy seed

mawkish 4 flat 5 banal, mushy 6 slushy, sticky 7 cloying, maudlin 8 bathetic, romantic 9 sickening 10 lovey-dovey, nauseating 11 sentimental, tear-jerking

maxilla 3 jaw 4 bone

maxim 3 law 4 rule 5 axiom, gnome, large, moral, motto 6 dictum, saying, truism 7 brocard, precept, proverb, theorem 8 aphorism, apothegm 9 platitude, prescript 11 commonplace

maximal 3 top 6 utmost 7 highest, topmost 8 greatest

maximize 7 magnify 8 overplay 10 overstress 13 overemphasize

maximum 3 top 6 utmost 7 highest, largest, supreme, topmost 8 extremum, greatest

may 5 shrub 6 spirea 8 hawthorn

maybe 7 perhaps 8 possible, possibly 9 perchance 10 indecision 11 uncertainty

Mayflower *document:* 7 Compact *passengers:* 8 pilgrims

mayhem 4 maim 7 cripple, dislimb 8 mutilate 9 dismember

mayor 11 burgomaster *Chicago (former):*
5 Daley (Richard) *New York (former):* 9 La
Guardia *Spanish:* 7 alcayde
Mayor of Casterbridge, The *author:*
5 Hardy *character:* 8 Henchard
maze 3 web 4 knot, mesh 5 skein, snarl
6 jungle, morass, tangle 7 confuse 8 bewilder, mishmash 9 labyrinth 10 hodgepodge,
miscellany 11 gordian knot
MD 3 doc 6 doctor, medico 7 medical
8 sawbones 9 mediciner, physician
meadow 3 lea, ley 9 grassland *low-lying:*
5 haugh
meadow beauty 9 deer grass
meadow bird 8 bobolink
meadow chicken 8 sora rail
meadow hen 4 coot, rail 7 bittern
meadowlark 4 bird 5 acorn
meadow mushroom 6 agaric
meadow sorrel 4 dock
meager 4 bare, bony, lank, lean, mere,
poor, thin 5 gaunt, lanky, scant, short,
skimp, spare 6 lenten, scanty, scrimp,
shabby, skimpy, skinny, slight, sparse
7 angular, minimum, scraggy, scrawny,
scrimpy 8 exiguous, inferior, rawboned,
scrimpit 9 deficient, miserable 10 inadequate 12 insufficient
meal 3 eat 4 chow, fare, feed, grub, take
5 board, feast, lunch, salep, snack, table
6 brunch, devour, dinner, farina, feed on,
ingest, picnic, repast, spread, supper 7 consume, nooning 8 victuals 9 breakfast, collation, partake of, refection *army:* 4 mess
mealy 6 spotty, uneven 8 farinose 9 polli-
nose 11 farinaceous
mean 3 aim, low, mid, par, set, way
4 base, fair, hack, hint, mode, name, norm,
pile, plan, poor, sick, so-so, ugly, want,
wish 5 agent, borne, cheap, count, cruel,
imply, lousy, lowly, mingy, organ, pesky,
purse, rough, small, spell, tatty, tight, tough,
weigh 6 agency, ailing, attest, center, common, denote, design, desire, donsie, estate,
humble, import, intend, little, manner, matter, medial, medium, method, middle, narrow, offish, ornery, paltry, pocket, poorly,
rugged, scrimy, scummy, scurvy, shabby,
shoddy, sickly, sleazy, stingy, system,
trashy, unwell, wealth, wicked 7 add up to,
ashamed, average, betoken, capital, central,
channel, connote, express, fairish, fashion,
fortune, ignoble, limited, lowborn, miserly,
nest egg, niggard, pitiful, propose, purpose,
savings, scrimpy, signify, suggest, underly,
vehicle 8 baseborn, beggarly, count for,
déclassé, indicate, inferior, intimate, kindless, low-grade, mediocre, middling, ministry, moderate, off-color, ordinary, pitiable,
plebeian, rubbishy, unwashed 9 apparatus,
bastardly, designate, difficult, equipment,

low-minded, machinery, niggardly, penurious, troublous, vexatious 10 despicable,
despisable, formidable, indisposed, instrument, second-rate, unennobled 11 closefisted, contemplate, indifferent, ineffectual,
second-class, tightfisted, troublesome
12 contemptible, intermediary, intermediate,
narrow-fisted, second-drawer
meander 4 roam, rove, turn, wind 5 drift,
range, snake, stray, twist 6 ramble
7 traipse 8 vagabond 9 gallivant, labyrinth
meandering 5 snaky 7 sinuous, winding
8 flexuous, tortuous 10 convoluted, serpentine 11 anfractuous
meandrous see **meandering**
meaning 3 aim 4 hint, plan 5 drift, force,
point, sense, tenor, value 6 animus, design,
effect, import, intent, object, syntax
7 essence, message, purport, purpose
9 intention, substance 10 definition, denotation, intendment, intimation, suggestion
11 acceptation, connotation, implication, significant 12 significance, significancy 13 signification, understanding
meaningful 4 rich 6 facund 7 weighty
8 eloquent, material, pregnant 9 important,
momentous 10 expressive 11 sententious,
significant, substantial 12 considerable
13 consequential
meaningless 5 blank, empty 6 vacant
7 fustian 10 unpurposed 13 insignificant
meanings *diverse:* 8 polysemy *study of:*
9 semantics
means 5 funds, money 6 agency, assets
7 quomodo 8 finances 9 apparatus, equipment, resources 10 instrument
11 wherewithal
meantime 8 interval
measly 4 poor, puny 5 petty 6 paltry
7 trivial 8 blighted, inferior, niggling, picayune, piddling, trifling 10 picayunish
12 pettifogging
measure 4 beat, bill, deal, meed, move,
part, size, step, test, tune 5 bound, dance,
gauge, index, limit, meter, metre, quota,
rhyme, scale, share, shift, swing, weigh
6 amount, bounds, degree, effort, extent,
figure, govern, melody, ration, reckon,
resort, rhythm, size up, strain, survey
7 cadence, cadency, caliper, compute,
delimit, mark out, melodia, portion, project,
quantum, stopgap 8 calliper, estimate, indicate, maneuver, proposal, regulate,
resource, rhythmus, standard 9 allotment,
allowance, benchmark, calculate, calibrate,
criterion, demarcate, determine, expedient,
magnitude, makeshift, procedure, yardstick 10 delimitate, dimensions, indication,
moderation, proceeding, proportion, temperance, touchstone 11 denominator, proposition 13 apportionment *area:* 4 acre 7 hec-

tare **9** square rod **10** square foot, square inch, square mile, square yard **11** square meter *arrow weight:* **8** shilling *butter:* **4** span *capacity:* **4** gill, peck, pint **5** liter, minim, quart **6** bushel, gallon **8** fluidram **10** cubic meter, fluidounce, milliliter *cloth:* **3** ell *combining form:* **6** metric **8** metrical *depth:* **5** plumb, sound *electrical:* **7** coulomb *Hebrew:* (see at **Hebrew**) *horse height:* **4** hand *interstellar space:* **6** parsec *length:* **3** rod **4** foot, inch, mile, yard **5** cubit (ancient), meter **9** kilometer **10** centimeter *liquid:* **4** pint **5** pipet, quart **6** gallon **7** pipette *metrical foot:* **8** monopody *mixed drinks:* **6** jigger *of advantage:* **4** lead *of comparison:* **8** standard *out:* **5** batch *paper:* **4** ream *printer's:* **2** em, en **4** pica **5** point *radioactive decay:* **8** halflife *rotation:* **5** angle *silk size:* **8** drammage *Spanish dry:* **5** fanga **6** fanega *strength of solution:* **7** titrate *surface:* **3** are *thermodynamic:* **7** entropy **8** enthalpy *volume:* **9** cubic foot, cubic inch, cubic yard **10** cubic meter

Measure for Measure *character:* **6** Angelo, Juliet **7** Claudio, Mariana **8** Isabella **9** Vincentio *setting:* **6** Vienna

measurement **4** area **6** degree **8** capacity, quantity **9** dimension **11** mensuration *rain:* **8** udometry *weight:* **6** metage

measure up **3** tie **4** meet **5** equal, match, rival, touch

measuring *combining form:* **5** metry *device for liquid:* **7** venturi *rod:* **8** dipstick *stick:* **8** yardwand *tube:* **5** buret **7** burette

meat **4** core, food, gist, pith, pork, veal **5** flesh, jerky, sense, short, steak **6** burden, matter, thrust, upshot **7** charqui, edibles, nurture **8** victuals **9** foodstuff, provender, substance **10** provisions **11** comestibles *broiled:* **8** barbecue, grillade *broth:* **8** bouillon *cake:* **6** burger *cured:* **7** biltong *cut:* **3** rib **4** loin, rump **5** chuck, flank, plate, round, shank **7** brisket, sirloin **8** rib roast **9** club steak, short loin, short ribs **10** blade roast, flank steak, round steak, T-bone steak **11** arm pot roast **12** boneless neck, pinbone steak, sirloin steak **13** blade rib roast, crosscut shank *dealer:* **7** butcher *deer:* **7** venison *dried:* **5** jerky *fastening pin:* **6** skewer *holding rod:* **4** spit *juices:* **5** gravy *minced:* **7** rissole *packer:* **5** Swift **6** Armour *raw:* **6** gobbet *roasting shop:* **10** rotisserie *rounded mass of:* **9** croquette *seasoned:* **7** sausage **8** pastrami, pastromi *sheep:* **6** mutton *side:* **8** sowbelly *skewered:* **5** kabab, kabob, kebob *slice:* **6** cutlet, rasher *small portion:* **6** collop *tough part:* **7** gristle

meat-eating **11** carnivorous

meathead **3** oaf **4** gawk, lout, lump **5** klutz, looby **6** lubber **7** palooka

Mebd *husband:* **6** Ailill *victim:* **10** Cuchulainn

Mecca *country:* **11** Saudi Arabia *pilgrimage:* **4** hadj, hajj *port:* **5** Jidda *shrine:* **5** Caaba, Kaaba

mechanic **7** artisan **9** automatic, machinist **10** uninspired

mechanism **4** gear **5** ratch, slide, steer **6** cutoff, infeed, rachet **7** ratchet **8** rackwork, signaler **9** apparatus *bookbinder's:* **7** gripper *card game:* **7** holdout *clutch:* **8** throwout *dam:* **7** tripper *fastening:* **5** catch *firearm:* **7** ejector, gunlock *guiding:* **5** apron *part:* **7** trippet *printing:* **8** elevator *raising:* **4** lift *timepiece:* **7** setting

meddle **3** pry **4** fool, nose **5** snoop **6** butt in, dabble, horn in, invade, kibitz, monkey, putter, tamper, tinker **7** intrude, obtrude **8** busybody, trespass **9** interfere, interlope, intervene **10** mess around, monkey with, tamper with

meddlesome **4** busy **9** intrusive, obtrusive, officious **11** impertinent **13** polypragmatic

Medea *brother:* **8** Absyrtus *father:* **6** Aeëtes *husband:* **5** Jason **6** Aegeus *son:* **6** Medeus *victim:* **6** Creusa, Glauce, Glauke

medial **3** mid **4** fair, mean **6** center, middle **7** average, central, fairish, halfway, midmost **8** middling, moderate **10** centermost, middlemost **11** equidistant, indifferent **12** intermediary, intermediate

median see **medial**

mediate **6** convey, liaise, step in **9** intercede, interfere, interpose, intervene

mediator **5** judge **6** broker **7** arbiter **9** gobetween, middleman **10** interagent, interceder, peacemaker **11** intercessor

medical **3** doc **6** doctor **9** physician *instrument:* **11** cardiograph, stethoscope

medical treatment *combining form:* **5** iatry **6** iatric **7** iatrics **8** iatrical

medicament **4** cure **6** physic, remedy **9** pharmacon *inert:* **7** placebo

medication see **medicament**

medicinal **4** drug **8** biologic, salutary, sanative **12** pharmaceutic *extract:* **10** belladonna

medicine **4** cure **5** bromo **6** physic, remedy **7** anodyne, nostrum **8** busulfan, poultice **9** pharmacon **11** antipyretic, magical rite **12** magical power *ball:* **4** pill *bottle:* **4** vial *branch:* **7** surgery **8** posology **9** pathology **10** bariatrics, geriatrics, gynecology, obstetrics, pediatrics *cathartic:* **8** evacuant **9** purgative *combining form:* **5** iatro **8** pharmaco *quantity of:* **4** dose

6 dosage *shell:* **7** capsule *soothing:* **7** nervine **8** lenitive, sedative

medicine man　6 doctor, kahuna, shaman

medieval　*guild:* **5** Hanse *military unit:* **5** lance *study:* **5** logic **6** trivia (plural) **7** grammar, trivium **8** rhetoric

mediocre　3 bad **4** fair, hack, mean, poor, so-so **6** common **7** average, fairish **8** inferior, middling, moderate, ordinary, passable **10** bush-league **11** commonplace

meditate　4 muse, roll **6** intend, ponder **7** purpose, revolve **8** consider, mull over, ruminate, turn over **9** reflect on **10** deliberate **11** contemplate

meditator　4 yogi **5** yogin

Mediterranean　11 Mare Nostrum **12** Mare Internum *coastal region:* **7** Riviera *eastern shores:* **6** Levant *island:* (see at island) *vessel:* **5** setee **6** settee *wind:* **6** solano **7** mistral, sirocco

medium　3 par **4** fair, mean, so-so **5** agent, forte, organ, radio **6** agency, métier, milieu, normal, oyster, vulgar **7** ambient, average, channel, climate, fairish, neutral, popular, vehicle **8** ambience, eminency, long suit, middling, ministry, moderate, passable, standard **9** go-between, run-of-mine, tolerable **10** atmosphere, compromise, instrument, middle-rate, strong suit, television **11** clairvoyant, environment *nutrient:* **7** culture *of exchange:* **5** money *of radio transmission:* **3** air **7** airwave

medley　4 brew, olio **6** jumble **7** mélange **8** pastiche **9** pasticcio, patchwork, potpourri **10** assortment, hodgepodge, miscellany **11** gallimaufry

Medusa　6 Gorgon *father:* **7** Phorcus, Phorcys *mother:* **4** Ceto *offspring:* **7** Pegasus **8** Chrysaor *sister:* **6** Stheno **7** Euryale *slayer:* **7** Perseus

meed　3 due **4** part, plum **5** merit, prize, quota, share **6** amount, carrot, desert, ration, reward **7** guerdon, measure, portion, premium, quantum **8** dividend **9** allotment, allowance **12** recompensing, satisfaction **13** apportionment

meek　4 mild, tame, weak **5** lowly **6** gentle, humble, modest **7** lenient, patient **8** moderate, tolerant **10** forbearing, submissive, unassuming **13** long-suffering

meerschaum　4 pipe **6** gravel **9** sepiolite

meet　3 apt, fit, hit, sit, tie **4** bump, espy, face, fair, fill, find, good, join, just, luck, open, spot **5** brave, catch, clash, close, cross, equal, event, focus, front, greet, happy, hit on, light, match, right, rival, touch, unite **6** accost, answer, chance, descry, detect, engage, happen, oppose, proper, salute, settle, suffer, take on, tumble, turn up, tussle, useful **7** affront, collide, contest, convene, fitting, fulfill, grapple, hit upon, sat-

isfy, stumble, sustain, undergo, wrestle **8** approach, assemble, come upon, concours, conflict, confront, converge, cope with, suitable **9** concenter, conformed, encounter, equitable, impinge on, measure up, rencontre **10** applicable, congregate, convenient, experience, felicitous, provide for, reconciled **11** appropriate, competition *a bet:* **3** see *a need:* **7** suffice *athletic:* **8** gymkhana *by appointment:* **10** rendezvous

meeting　4 moot, talk **5** tryst **6** parley, powwow **7** contest, session **8** assembly, conclave, concours, conflict, congress, junction **9** concourse, encounter, gathering, rencontre **10** concursion, conference, confluence **11** competition **12** intersection *Anglo-Saxon:* **5** gemot **6** gemote *place:* **5** forum *spiritual:* **6** séance

Mefistofele composer　5 Boito

Megaera　see Erinyes

megaphone　7 address **8** bullhorn **10** mouthpiece

Megara　father:* **5 Creon *husband:* **8** Heracles, Hercules *king:* **5** Nisus

megillah　5 story **6** scroll **7** account

megrim　4 urge, whim **5** fancy, freak, humor, whiff **6** whimsy **7** boutade, caprice, conceit, impulse, vertigo **8** crotchet, migraine **9** dizziness

Mehetabel　*husband:* **5 Hadar *mother:* **6** Matred *son:* **7** Delaiah

Mehitabel　3 cat *creator:* **7** Marquis *friend:* **5** Archy

Mein Kampf author　6 Hitler

meiosis　7 litotes **12** cell division

Meistersinger　4 Folz **5** Sachs

melancholic　3 sad **6** triste **7** joyless **8** mournful **9** depressed, saddening **10** depressing

melancholy　3 sad **5** blues, dumps, ennui, gloom, sorry **6** dismal, dreary, gloomy, misery, rueful, somber, tedium, triste, woeful **7** boredom, despair, dismals, doleful, joyless, moanful, pensive, sadness, sighful, unhappy, wailful **8** dejected, dolesome, dolorous, funereal, mournful, saddened, sombrous **9** dejection, plaintive, saddening, sorrowful **10** afflicting, depressing, depression, disturbing, lachrymose, lamentable, lugubrious, perturbing, reflective, thoughtful **11** desperation, disquieting, unhappiness **12** discomposing, heavyhearted, mournfulness, wretchedness **13** miserableness

mélange　see medley

Melanippe's son　6 Aeolus

Melanippus　father:* **7 Theseus *slayer:* **10** Amphiaraus *victim:* **6** Tydeus

Melchior　companion:* **6 Gaspar **9** Balthazar *gift:* **4** gold

Melchizedek's kingdom 5 Salem
meld 3 mix **4** fuse **5** blend, merge **6** mingle **8** compound **9** interfuse **10** amalgamate, interblend **11** intermingle
Meleager beloved: 8 Atalanta **father: 6** Oeneus **mother: 7** Althaea **victim: 4** boar
Melech's father 5 Micah
melee 3 row **4** fray, hash, riot, stew **5** brawl, broil, brush, clash, fight **6** affray, fracas, jumble, ruckus **7** ruction, scuffle **8** dogfight, mishmash, pastiche, skirmish **9** potpourri, scrimmage **10** donnybrook, free-for-all, hodgepodge, miscellany
Melicertes father: 7 Athamas **mother: 3** Ino
meliorate 4 help **5** amend **6** better, soften **7** improve
Mélisande's lover 7 Pelleas
melisma 3 air, lay **4** song, tune **6** strain, warble **7** cadenza, descant, measure **8** diapason
mellifluous 5 sweet **6** dulcet, golden, liquid, smooth **7** honeyed, silvery **8** euphonic, Hyblaean, resonant **9** accordant **13** golden-tongued, silver-tongued
mellisonant 5 sweet **6** dulcet **7** tuneful **8** euphonic **10** euphonious
mellow 3 age **4** aged **5** ripen **6** genial, golden, grow up, liquid, mature **7** develop, honeyed, matured, ripened
melodic 5 sweet, tuned **6** dulcet **7** musical, songful, tuneful **8** canorous **10** euphonious
melodious 5 lyric, sweet, tuned **6** dulcet **7** musical, songful, tuneful **8** euphonic, soundful **9** cantabile
melody 3 air, lay **4** sing, song, tune **5** canto **6** lyrics, strain, warble **7** descant, measure **8** bel canto, diapason, vocalize **11** tunefulness
melon 4 pepo **5** gourd, mango **6** casaba, papaya **7** cassaba **8** honeydew **10** cantaloupe
Melpomene see **Muse**
melt 3 rin, run **4** bake, burn, cook, flux, fuse, thaw, warm **5** blend, broil, roast, sweat **6** scorch, soften, spleen **7** liquefy, liquify, swelter **8** dissolve, liquesce, perspire, unfreeze **9** disappear **10** deliquesce **down: 6** render **together: 4** fuse
Melville character: 3 Pip **4** Ahab, Toby **5** Bembo, Chase **6** Cereno, Jermin, Pierre **7** Fayaway, Ishmael **8** Bartleby, Queequeg, Starbuck **novel: 4** Omoo **5** Mardi, Typee **6** Pierre **7** Redburn **8** Moby Dick **11** White Jacket
member 3 cut **4** part **5** penis, piece **6** clause, moiety, parcel **7** portion, section, segment **8** division **architectural: 3** fan **7** cornice **armed forces: 5** cadet **6** airman, Marine, sailor **7** soldier **chivalry order:**

6 knight **combining form: 3** mer **4** crat, mere **5** ocrat **gang: 7** mobster **8** henchman **10** hatchet man **Girl Scout: 7** brownie, Cadette **household: 8** familiar **legislative: 7** senator **mendicant order: 5** friar **9** Dominican **middle class: 7** burgher **monastic order: 4** monk **5** friar **6** hermit **Parliament: 2** MP **political party: 4** Tory, Whig **7** Liberal **8** Democrat, Laborite **9** Communist, Socialist **10** Republican **12** Conservative **secret society: 7** DeMolay, tongman **8** Klansman, Ku Kluxer **senior male: 5** doyen **service club: 4** Lion **8** Kiwanian, Rotarian **structural: 4** arch **suffix: 2** ad, id **triangular: 5** gable
membrane 6 pleura **7** pleurae (plural) **bodily: 6** serosa **7** serosae (plural) **brain: 3** pia **combining form: 3** vel **5** chori, hymen **6** chorio, hymeno, mening, myring **7** meningi, meningo, myringo **diffusion through: 7** osmosis **dividing: 5** septa (plural) **6** septum **ear: 8** tympanum **enclosing: 8** indusium **thin: 6** lamina **7** lamella, laminae (plural) **8** lamellae (plural) **wing: 8** patagium
memento 5 relic, token, trace **6** shadow, trophy **7** vestige **8** keepsake, reminder, souvenir **11** remembrance **12** remembrancer
Memnon father: 8 Tithonus **mother: 3** Eos **6** Aurora **slayer: 8** Achilles
memoir 3 bio **4** life **6** record, report, thesis **8** anecdote, tractate, treatise **9** biography, discourse, monograph **10** monography **11** confessions, remembrance **12** disquisition, dissertation, recollection, reminiscence **13** autobiography
memoirist 7 Boswell **9** biographer
memorable 6 rubric **9** deathless, momentous, red-letter **10** impressive, noteworthy, remembered **11** significant **13** distinguished
memorandum 4 chit, note **5** diary **6** letter, minute, notice **7** epistle, message, missive, tickler **8** dispatch, notation, reminder **9** directive **12** announcement
memorial 4 note **5** relic, token, trace **6** record, trophy **7** relique **8** keepsake, monument, reminder, souvenir **10** dedicatory, enshrining **11** celebrative, remembrance **12** consecrative, remembrancer **13** commemoration, commemorative, commemoratory **mound: 4** carn **5** cairn
memorial park 8 cemetery, God's acre **9** graveyard **10** necropolis **11** polyandrium **12** burial ground, potter's field **13** burying ground
memorize 3 con, get **5** learn, study **8** remember
memory 4 mind **6** recall **8** mind's eye, souvenir **9** anamnesis, awareness, reten-

tion **10** cognizance, reflection **11** remembrance **12** recollection, reminiscence **13** concentration, consciousness, retentiveness, retrospection *assisting:* **8** mnemonic *combining form:* **4** mnem **5** mnemo **6** mnesia *loss:* **7** amnesia

menace 4 loom, risk **5** alarm, lower, peril, scare **6** danger, hazard, threat **7** imperil, jeopard, torment **8** endanger, frighten, jeopardy, threaten **10** jeopardize

ménage 5 folks, house **6** family **8** quarters **9** household **12** housekeeping

Menahem *father:* **4** Gadi *son:* **8** Pekahiah *victim:* **7** Shallum

mend 3 fix, sew **4** cure, darn, do up, gain, heal, vamp **5** patch, ready, renew **6** bushel, cobble, doctor, look up, perk up, reform, remedy, repair, revamp **7** correct, improve, patch up, rebuild, rectify, redress, restore, service **8** overhaul, renovate **9** condition, refurbish **10** ameliorate, convalesce, recuperate, rejuvenate **11** recondition, reconstruct

mendacious 5 false, lying, wrong **6** shifty **7** fibbing, knavish, roguish **8** unhonest **9** deceitful, dishonest, paltering **10** untruthful **12** equivocating **13** prevaricating

mendacity 7 dodging, fibbery, hedging **8** boggling, caviling, shifting **9** falsehood, quibbling **12** equivocation, sidestepping **13** truthlessness

mendelevium *symbol:* **2** Md

mendicancy 7 beggary, bumming, cadging **8** mooching, sponging **11** panhandling

mendicant 5 friar **6** beggar **7** begging

Mending Wall author 5 Frost

Menelaus *brother:* **9** Agamemnon *father:* **6** Atreus *kingdom:* **6** Sparta *mother:* **6** Aerope *wife:* **5** Helen

menial 5 lowly **6** humble **7** servile, slavish **8** obeisant **10** obsequious **11** subservient

Men in White author 8 Kingsley

Menlo Park inventor 6 Edison

menopause 11 climacteric **12** change of life

Menotti, Gian Carlo *character:* **5** Amahl *opera:* **9** The Consul, The Medium **12** The Telephone

men's store 12 haberdashery

mental 5 inner **6** genial **7** psychic **8** thinking **9** reasoning, spiritual **10** immaterial, telepathic **11** ideological, intelligent **12** intellective, intellectual **13** psychological *faculty:* **6** memory

mentality 3 wit **5** sense **6** brains **7** outlook **9** mother wit **10** brainpower **12** intelligence

mention 4 cite, name, note **5** quote, refer **6** advert, allude, detail **7** refer to, specify **8** instance **9** designate, reference **10** denominate

mentor 5 coach **7** teacher

Mentor's pupil 10 Telemachus

menu 4 card, diet **5** carte **7** regimen **10** bill of fare **11** carte du jour *item:* **4** soup **5** salad **6** entrée **7** dessert **9** appetizer

Mephibosheth *father:* **4** Saul **8** Jonathan *mother:* **6** Rizpah

Mephistophelian 7 satanic **8** devilish, diabolic

mephitic 4 olid **5** fetid, funky, musty **6** poison, smelly **7** noisome, noxious, reeking, stenchy **8** stinking, toxicant, venomous, virulent **9** poisonous **10** malodorous

Merab *father:* **4** Saul *husband:* **6** Adriel

Meraioth *father:* **6** Ahitub **8** Zerahiah *son:* **5** Zadok

Merari *brother:* **6** Kohath **7** Gershon *daughter:* **6** Judith *father:* **4** Levi *son:* **5** Mahli, Mushi

mercenary 4 grub, hack **5** venal **6** drudge, slavey **7** corrupt, grubber, soldier **8** hireling

merchandise 4 line, sell **5** cargo, goods, stock, trade, wares **6** deal in, job lot, market, retail **7** effects, staples, traffic **9** publicize, vendibles **11** commodities

merchandiser 9 tradesman **11** businessman

merchant 5 buyer **6** dealer, jobber, seller, trader, vender, vendor **7** peddler **8** purveyor, retailer **9** tradesman **10** specialist, trafficker, wholesaler **11** businessman, storekeeper *guild:* **5** hansa, hanse *Hindu:* **6** banian, banyan *League:* **9** Hanseatic *ship:* **5** oiler **6** argosy, coaler, galiot, packet, tanker **7** collier, galliot, steamer **8** Indiaman **9** freighter *wine:* **7** vintner

Merchant of Venice 7 Antonio *character:* **6** Portia **7** Jessica, Lorenzo, Nerissa, Shylock **8** Bassanio

merciful 4 easy, kind **6** benign, humane, kindly **7** clement, lenient, sparing **8** tolerant **9** condoning, forgiving, indulgent, pardoning **10** charitable, forbearing **11** softhearted **13** compassionate

merciless 4 grim **5** cruel, harsh **6** mortal, savage, wanton **9** cutthroat, ferocious, unpitying **10** gratuitous, implacable, ironfisted, unyielding **11** uncalled-for, unflinching, unrelenting **12** unappeasable

mercurial 6 adroit, clever, fickle, mobile **7** buoyant, cunning, elastic, movable **8** ticklish, unstable, variable, volatile **9** expansive, ingenious, resilient, sprightly **10** capricious, changeable, inconstant, lubricious **12** effervescent **13** temperamental

mercury 5 azoth 9 poison ivy 11 quicksilver *ore:* 8 cinnabar *symbol:* 2 Hg
Mercury 6 planet; (see also **Hermes**)
Mercutio *friend:* 5 Romeo *slayer:* 6 Tybalt
mercy 4 pity, ruth 5 grace 6 lenity 7 caritas, charity 8 clemency, goodwill, kindness, leniency 9 benignity, tolerance 10 compassion, generosity, kindliness 11 benevolence, forbearance 13 commiseration *petition for:* 5 kyrie 8 miserere
mere 3 fen 4 bare, lake, pool, pure, very 5 marsh 9 undiluted
Mered's father 5 Ezrah
merely 3 but 4 just, only 5 quite 6 simply, wholly
Meremoth's father 4 Bani 5 Uriah
meretricious 4 loud 5 gaudy 6 brazen, flashy, garish, tawdry, tinsel 7 blatant, chintzy, glaring 8 delusive, delusory 9 deceptive, insincere 10 misleading
merge 3 mix 4 fuse, join 5 blend, unify, unite 6 mingle 7 combine 8 coalesce, compound 9 commingle, interfuse 10 amalgamate, interblend 11 consolidate, intermingle
mergence see **merging**
merger 5 union 9 coalition 11 coadunation, combination, unification 12 amalgamation 13 consolidation
merging 5 union 9 coalition 11 coadunation, combination, unification 13 consolidation
meridian 4 acme, apex, peak 6 apogee, climax, comble, summit, zenith 8 pinnacle
merit 3 due 4 earn, rate 5 arete, award, lumps, repay, value, worth 6 reward, rights, virtue 7 caliber, deserts, deserve, entitle, justify, quality, requite, stature, warrant 9 deserving 10 excellence, excellency, perfection, recompense
meritable see **meritorious**
merited 3 due 4 just 5 right 7 condign 8 deserved, rightful, suitable 9 requisite 11 appropriate 13 rhadamanthine
meritorious 6 worthy 8 laudable 9 admirable, deserving, estimable, honorable, praisable 11 commendable, thankworthy 12 praiseworthy
merlin 6 falcon 10 pigeon hawk
mermaid 7 manatee 8 sirenian 11 sirenomelus
Merodach see **Marduk**
Merope *father:* 5 Atlas 8 Oenopion *husband:* 7 Polybus 8 Sisyphus 11 Cresphontes *lover:* 5 Orion *mother:* 7 Pleione *sisters:* 8 Pleiades *son:* 7 Aepytus, Glaucus
merriment 4 glee 5 mirth, revel 6 gaiety 7 jollity, revelry, whoopee 8 hilarity, reveling 9 festivity, jocundity, joviality 10 jocularity, jubilation 13 entertainment
merry 3 gay, mad 4 boon, gean, glad, high, wild 5 happy, jolly, riant, sharp 6 blithe, jocund, jovial, joyful, joyous, lively 7 festive, gleeful, intense 8 animated, cheerful, gleesome, laughing, mirthful 9 hilarious, sprightly, vivacious 10 blithesome 12 lighthearted 13 unconstrained
merry-andrew 4 zany 5 clown 7 buffoon 9 harlequin 10 mountebank
merrymaking 5 party, revel 6 gaiety 7 jollity, revelry, whoopee 8 pleasure 9 enjoyment, festivity, revelment 10 indulgence 12 conviviality
Merry Widow composer 5 Lehar
Merry Wives of Windsor, The *character:* 3 Nym 4 Ford, Page 5 Caius 6 Fenton, Pistol 7 Slender 8 Falstaff
mesa 5 bench 7 plateau 9 cartouche, tableland
mescal 5 agave 6 cactus, liquor, maguey
mesh 3 net, web 4 knot, maze, nett 5 skein, snarl 6 accord, engage, jungle, morass, tangle 7 mizmaze, netting, network 8 entangle 9 harmonize, interlock, labyrinth 10 coordinate
Mesha *father:* 9 Shaharaim *kingdom:* 4 Moab *mother:* 6 Hodesh
Meshech's father 7 Japheth
meshuggaas 4 guff 6 drivel 7 twaddle 8 claptrap, nonsense 9 poppycock 10 balderdash
Meshullam *father:* 4 Bani 5 Zadok 9 Berechiah, Besodeiah 10 Shephatiah, Zerubbabel 12 Meshillemith *son:* 5 Sallu 7 Hilkiah
Meshullemeth *husband:* 8 Manasseh *son:* 4 Amon
mesmeric 5 siren 7 drawing 8 alluring, charming 9 glamorous 10 attractive, bewitching, enchanting 11 captivating
mesmerize 4 grip, hold 7 catch up 8 enthrall, entrance 9 fascinate, hypnotize, spellbind
Mesopotamia *civilization:* 7 Assyria 9 Babylonia *river:* 6 Tigris 9 Euphrates
mess 4 hash, mull, play 5 botch, catch, gum up, mix up, snafu, wreck 6 bobble, bollix, bungle, dabble, doodle, fiddle, fright, goof up, jumble, muddle, potter, puddle, putter, tinker, trifle 7 bitch up, confuse, desight, eyesore, louse up 8 botchery, disarray, dishevel, disorder, shambles, wreckage 9 confusion 10 disarrange, hodgepodge, miscellany 11 monstrosity *up:* 5 touse 6 tousle, touzle, untidy
message 4 note, word 5 sense 6 import, letter, report 7 epistle, evangel, meaning, mission, purport 8 dispatch, telegram 9 directive, telegraph 10 communiqué,

intendment, memorandum **11** acceptation **12** significance **13** communication, signification

Messalina's husband 8 Claudius

mess around 4 fool, idle, wolf **5** flirt **6** butt in, dabble, dawdle, doodle, fiddle, horn in, meddle, potter, puddle, putter, tinker **7** intrude **8** busybody, womanize **9** associate, interfere, interlope, manhandle, philander **10** monkey with, tamper with

messenger 4 post **5** envoy **6** herald **7** apostle, courier **8** emissary **9** character, go-between **11** internuncio **12** intermediary *God's:* **5** angel *of the gods:* **6** Hermes **7** Mercury *Turkish:* **6** chiaus, chouse

Messiah composer 6 Handel

messy 5 dirty, grimy **6** botchy, sloppy, unneat, untidy **7** raunchy, unkempt **8** careless, ill-kempt, slapdash, slipshod, slovenly **10** disheveled, unthorough **12** unfastidious

Mestor *father:* **7** Perseus *mother:* **9** Andromeda

metal 4 gold **5** steel, sword **6** bronze *alloy:* (see alloy) *casting mold:* **5** ingot *corrosion:* **4** rust *design:* **7** chasing *dross:* **4** slag *drum:* **8** canister *fittings:* **5** brass *in mass:* **7** bullion *layer:* **7** plating *lump:* **6** nugget *piece:* **4** slug *refuse:* **6** scoria *sheath:* **5** armor *substance:* **5** alloy *surface scum:* **5** dross *thin:* **4** foil, leaf **5** plate *type:* **7** quadrat *worker:* **5** smith **10** blacksmith

metallic element 3 tin **4** gold, iron, lead, zinc **6** barium, cobalt, copper, nickel, radium, silver, sodium **7** arsenic, bismuth, lithium, mercury, uranium **8** aluminum, platinum, tungsten, vanadium **9** magnesium, manganese, potassium, strontium **10** molybdenum

metamere 6 somite **7** segment

metamorphic *rock:* **5** slate **6** gneiss, marble, schist **9** quartzite, soapstone

metamorphose 3 age **5** ripen **6** change, mature **7** commute, convert, develop **9** transform, translate, transmute **11** transfigure **12** transmogrify

metamorphosis 6 change **8** changing *combining form:* **3** ody

Metamorphosis author 5 Kafka

metanoia 7 rebirth **10** conversion

metaphor 5 trope **6** simile **7** analogy **8** allegory **10** comparison, similitude

metaphorical compound 7 kenning

metaphysical 8 bodiless, numinous, superior **9** unearthly, unfleshly **10** discarnate, immaterial, superhuman, suprahuman **12** supermundane, supernatural, supramundane, supranatural, transcendent **13** preternatural *poet:* **5** Donne **7** Crashaw, Herbert, Marvell

mete 4 deal, dole, give **5** allot **6** parcel **7** portion **8** allocate, dispense **9** apportion

meteor 8 fireball **12** shooting star *exploding:* **5** bolis **6** bolide *shower:* **5** Lyrid **6** Leonid, Taurid **7** Aquarid, Geminid, Orionid, Perseid **10** Quadrantid *suffix:* **2** id

meteorite 8 aerolite, aerolith **10** siderolite

meter 4 beat, scan **5** rhyme, swing **6** rhythm **7** cadence, cadency, measure, versify

metheglin 4 mead **8** beverage *ingredient:* **5** honey

method 3 way **4** form, line, mode, modi (plural), plan, wise **5** means, modus, order, style, track **6** course, design, manner, schema, scheme, system **7** fashion, formula, pattern, process, routine, technic, wrinkle **8** practice **9** procedure, technique **11** orderliness **13** modus operandi *careful:* **8** strategy *of employing troops:* **6** tactic *of procedure:* **2** MO **4** game

methodical 5 exact **7** careful, orderly, precise, regular **9** organized **10** scrupulous, systematic **12** systematized

Methuselah *father:* **5** Enoch *grandson:* **4** Noah *son:* **6** Lamech

Methushael *father:* **8** Mehujael *son:* **6** Lamech

meticulous 4 neat **5** exact, fussy, picky **6** strict **7** careful, finicky, heedful **8** punctual, thorough **10** pernickety **11** microscopic, painstaking **12** conscionable

métier 3 art **4** mode **5** craft, forte, trade **7** calling **8** business, eminency, long suit, vocation **10** handicraft, profession, strong suit

metrical foot 4 iamb **5** iambi (plural), paeon **6** cretic, dactyl, iambic, iambus **7** anapest, pyrrhic, spondee, triseme, trochee **8** bacchius, choriamb, spondaic, tribrach, trochaic

metric unit *area:* **7** centare, deciare, hectare *capacity:* **5** liter **9** decaliter, deciliter, kiloliter **10** centiliter, hectoliter, milliliter *length:* **5** meter **9** decameter, decimeter, kilometer **10** centimeter, hectometer, millimeter, myriameter *mass and weight:* **4** gram **7** quintal **8** decagram, decigram, kilogram **9** centigram, hectogram, metric ton, milligram *volume:* **5** stere **9** decastere, decistere

metropolis 4 city **7** capital **13** mother country

metropolitan 5 urban **6** urbane **10** archbishop

mettle 4 guts **5** heart, pluck, spunk **6** spirit, temper **7** cojones, courage **10** resolution **12** spiritedness **13** dauntlessness

mettlesome 4 edgy **5** beany, fiery **6** spunky **7** gingery, peppery **8** skittish, spirited **9** excitable, startlish **10** high-strung **11** high-hearted **12** high-spirited

mew 3 hem, pen **4** cage, coop, gull, molt, mure **5** fence **6** corral, immure, shut in **7** enclose **8** hideaway

mewl 4 meow **5** whine **7** whimper

Mexico *aborigine:* **4** Maya **5** Aztec *coin:* **7** centavo *conqueror:* **6** Cortes, Cortez *crop:* **5** sisal *emperor:* **10** Maximilian *estate:* **8** hacienda *ethnic group:* **6** Indian **7** Mestizo *export:* **6** coffee, cotton, sulfur **9** petroleum *food:* **4** masa, taco **5** chili, salsa **6** tamale **7** panocha, penuche, tostada **8** frijoles, tortilla **9** enchilada, guacamole **10** quesadilla *house:* **5** jacal *language:* **7** Spanish *liquor:* **7** tequila *monetary unit:* **4** peso *oil enterprise:* **5** PEMEX *revolutionist:* **5** Villa (Pancho) **6** Zapata **8** Carranza *stimulant:* **6** mescal

mezzanine 5 story **7** balcony **8** entresol

mezzo-soprano *American:* **5** Elias, Horne, Jones **6** Bumbry **7** Verrett **8** Troyanos, von Stade *Austrian:* **6** Ludwig *English:* **5** Baker *Italian:* **8** Cossotto

Miami *bowl:* **6** Orange *chief:* **12** Little Turtle *county:* **4** Dade *stadium:* **9** Joe Robbie *team:* **8** Dolphins

mib 5 agate **6** marble

mica 4 talc **7** biotite **8** silicate **9** muscovite

Mica *father:* **6** Zichri **12** Mephibosheth *grandfather:* **8** Jonathan

Micah *father:* **9** Meribbaal *son:* **5** Abdon

Micaiah *father:* **5** Imlah, Uriel **8** Gemariah *grandfather:* **7** Absalom *husband:* **8** Rehoboam *mother:* **5** Tamar *son:* **6** Abijah, Achbor

Michelangelo *painting:* **10** Holy Family **12** Last Judgment *statue:* **5** David, Moses, Pietà **7** Bacchus

Michener novel 6 Hawaii **8** Caravans, Sayonara **9** The Source **10** Centennial, Chesapeake **11** The Covenant, The Drifters **16** The Fires of Spring **18** The Bridges of Toko-ri

Michigan *capital:* **7** Lansing *college:* **4** Alma *highest point:* **9** Mt. Curwood *largest city:* **7** Detroit *nickname:* **9** Lake State **14** Wolverine State *state bird:* **5** robin *state flower:* **12** apple blossom

microfilm sheet 5 fiche

Micronesia *political division:* **4** Guam **5** Nauru **6** Tuvalu **8** Kiribati

microorganism 4 germ **5** virus **6** aerobe **7** bacilli (plural), microbe **8** bacillus, bacteria (plural), pathogen, protozoa (plural) **9** bacterium, protozoan

microphone 3 bug **4** mike *shield:* **4** gobo

microscope 7 magnify **9** magnifier **10** instrument *part:* **5** stage **6** mirror **8** eyepiece **9** objective

microscopic 4 tiny **5** small **6** minute

midday 4 noon, sext **8** noontide, noontime

middle 4 core, mean **5** waist **6** center, medial, median **7** central, halfway **8** interior **10** centermost **11** equidistant, intervening **12** intermediary, intermediate *combining form:* **3** mes **4** medi, meso **5** medio, mesio

Middle America country 4 Cuba **5** Haiti **6** Mexico, Panama **8** Honduras **9** Costa Rica, Guatemala, Nicaragua **10** El Salvador

Middle Atlantic State 7 New York **9** New Jersey **12** Pennsylvania

middlebrow 4 boob **7** Babbitt **10** philistine

middle class 11 bourgeoisie

middle-class 9 bourgeois

middle ear 5 incus **6** stapes **7** malleus *membrane:* **7** eardrum **8** tympanum

Middle East country 4 Iran, Iraq, Oman **5** Egypt, Qatar, Sudan, Syria, Yemen **6** Cyprus, Israel, Jordan, Kuwait, Turkey **7** Bahrain, Lebanon **11** Saudi Arabia

Middle Kingdom 5 China

middleman 6 broker **7** bailiff **8** mediator **9** go-between **10** interagent, interceder **11** intercessor **12** entrepreneur, intermediary, intermediate **13** intermediator

Middlemarch author 5 Eliot

middle-of-the-road 8 moderate **9** softshell

middling 4 fair, mean, poor, so-so **6** fairly, flitch, medium, rather **7** average, fairish **8** inferior, mediocre, moderate **10** moderately, second-rate **11** indifferent **12** intermediate

midge 3 fly **4** runt **5** dwarf, pygmy **6** peewee **7** manikin **8** mannikin, Tom Thumb **10** homunculus **11** lilliputian *larva:* **9** bloodworm

midget 3 wee **4** runt, tiny **5** dwarf, pygmy, teeny **6** peewee, punkie, teensy **7** manikin **8** dwarfish, mannikin, Tom Thumb **9** miniature **10** diminutive, homunculus **11** lhop-o'-my-thumb, illiputian

Midian *father:* **7** Abraham *mother:* **7** Keturah

mid-Victorian 4 fogy, prig **5** prude **6** fogram, fossil, square **7** puritan **8** bluenose, mossback **9** Mrs. Grundy **10** antiquated, fuddy-duddy, goody-goody **12** old-fashioned **13** stick-in-the-mud

midwife 10 accoucheur *Scottish:* **5** howdy **6** howdie

mien 3 air, set **4** look, port **6** aspect, manner **7** address, bearing, seeming **8** demeanor, presence **9** mannerism **10** appearance, deportment, expression **11** comportment

miff 3 fit **4** beef, spat **5** pique, run-in **7** dis-

pute, dudgeon, offense, quarrel, rhubarb,
umbrage **8** squabble **10** conniption, falling-
out, resentment **11** altercation
mig 6 marble
might 3 arm **4** beef, sway, thew **5** brawn,
force, means, power, sinew **6** energy, muscle **7** ability, command, control, mastery,
potency, strings **8** capacity, strength
9 authority, lustiness, resources, strong
arm **10** capability, competence, domination **12** forcefulness, jurisdiction, powerfulness, vigorousness **13** energeticness
mighty 4 high, huge, very **5** grand, great
6 august, heroic, hugely, moving, potent,
strong, wieldy **7** eminent, immense, massive, notable, violent **8** enormous, forceful,
forcible, gigantic, imposing, powerful, puissant, rattling, renowned, whacking, whopping **9** efficient, extremely, strenuous
10 impressive, monumental, prodigious, tremendous **11** efficacious, exceedingly, illustrious **12** surpassingly **13** extraordinary
combining form: **3** din **4** dein, dino
5 deino
Mignon composer 6 Thomas
mignonette 4 herb **6** reseda
migrant 5 mover, nomad **6** mobile
7 drifter **8** traveler, wanderer
migrate 4 move, roam, rove, trek **5** drift,
range, shift **6** wander **8** nomadize, transfer
migration 6 moving **8** diaspora, movement *of professionals:* **10** brain drain
migratory 5 nomad **6** errant, mobile, moving, roving **7** nomadic, ranging **9** wandering
Milan *family:* **6** Sforza **8** Visconti *opera
house:* **7** La Scala
Milcah *brother:* **3** Lot *father:* **5** Haran
10 Zelophehad *husband:* **5** Nahor *son:*
7 Bethuel
mild 4 calm, easy, meek, soft, tame
5 balmy, bland, faint **6** benign, choice,
dainty, docile, gentle, smooth **7** amiable,
clement, lenient, subdued **8** delicate, moderate, obeisant, obliging **9** benignant, exquisite, temperate **10** forbearing, submissive
mildew 4 mold **6** fungus, growth
___ **mile 7** statute **8** nautical
mileage recorder 8 odometer
milepost 5 event **6** marker **8** occasion
milestone 5 event **8** landmark, occasion
milieu 6 medium **7** ambient, climate, setting **8** ambience **10** atmosphere **11** environment, mise-en-scéne **12** surroundings
militant 5 pushy **7** fighter, martial, pushful,
pushing, scrappy, warlike **8** fighting
9 assertive, assertory, bellicose, combative,
truculent **10** aggressive, pugnacious
11 belligerent, contentious, quarrelsome
12 gladiatorial **13** self-assertive
military 5 troop **6** forces **7** martial, warlike **9** soldierly **10** jingoistic, servicemen

11 armed forces, soldierlike **12** chauvinistic,
warmongering *base:* **4** camp, fort, post
5 depot, field **6** billet **8** barracks, garrison,
quarters **10** encampment *officer:* **5** major
7 captain, colonel, general **9** brigadier
10 lieutenant *prisoner:* **3** POW *school:*
3 OCS, OTS **4** ROTC, USMA **9** West Point
sector: **10** combat zone **11** battlefront
store: **2** BX, PX **10** commissary *storehouse:* **5** depot, étape **6** armory **7** arsenal
supplies: **8** matériel, ordnance *unit:*
5 corps, squad, troop **7** company, platoon
8 division, regiment **9** battalion **11** battle
group *vehicle:* **4** jeep, tank **9** half-track
militate 4 tell **5** count, weigh
milk 4 draw, pump, rook, suck **5** bleed,
drain, educe, empty, evoke, exact, mulct,
nurse, stick, sweat, wring **6** elicit, evince,
extort, fleece, suckle **7** exhaust, exploit,
extract *coagulated:* **4** curd *combining
form:* **4** lact **5** lacti, lacto **6** galact **7** galacto *curdled:* **5** leben **7** clabber *fermented:* **5** kefir, kumys **6** kumiss, kumyss,
yogurt **7** koumiss, matzoon, yoghurt *liquid
part:* **4** whey *store:* **5** dairy *sugar:*
7 lactose
milk shake 6 frappe **7** frosted
milksop 4 baby **5** sissy **6** coward **7** doormat **8** weakling **9** jellyfish **10** effeminate,
namby-pamby, pantywaist **11** Milquetoast,
mollycoddle
milky 4 meek, mild, tame **5** white **6** chalky,
gentle **7** lacteal, lactean **8** timorous
Milky Way *combining form:* **6** galact
7 galacto
mill 4 beat, slug **5** dress, fight, plant, quern,
shape, works **6** finish, thrash **7** factory,
machine **11** manufactory
Miller, Arthur *play:* **9** All My Sons **10** The
Misfits **12** After the Fall *salesman:*
5 Loman (Willy)
mill fever 10 byssinosis
million *combining form:* **3** meg **4** mega
millionth *combining form:* **4** micr **5** micro
Mill on the Floss author 5 Eliot
millstone 3 tax **4** duty, load, onus, task
6 burden, charge, weight **9** buhrstone
10 affliction, deadweight
Milne bear 4 Pooh
Milquetoast, Caspar *creator:* **7** Webster; (see also **milksop**)
Miltiades' victory 8 Marathon
Milton work 5 Comus **7** Lycidas **8** L'Allegro **12** Areopagitica, Paradise Lost
mime 3 act **5** actor **6** act out, player
7 trouper **8** thespian **9** performer, playactor, represent **12** impersonator *famous:*
7 Marceau (Marcel)
mimic 2 do **3** act, ape **4** copy, mock,
play **5** actor, enact **6** hit off, mummer, parody, parrot, player **7** copycat, imitate, per-

form, take off, trouper **8** simulate, thespian, travesty **9** burlesque, imitation, pantomime, performer, personate, playactor **11** impersonate **12** impersonator

mimicry 4 echo, mock **5** apery **6** parody **9** imitation **10** caricature

mince 3 cut **4** chop, hash **5** cut up, strut **6** finick, sashay **7** finnick **8** moderate, restrain **9** euphemize

mincing 4 nice **5** fussy **6** dainty, la-di-da, too-too **7** finical, finicky, genteel, stilted **8** affected, delicate **9** squeamish **10** fastidious, particular, pernickety **11** persnickety

mind 3 eye, see, wit **4** care, espy, keep, look, mood, nous, obey, soul, tend, tone, vein, view, will, wish, wits **5** brain, fancy, humor, power, study, watch, weigh, worry **6** attend, behold, belief, beware, brains, comply, descry, desire, follow, govern, liking, memory, notice, ponder, psyche, reason, sanity, senses, spirit, strain, temper **7** care for, conform, discern, dislike, faculty, feeling, look out, observe, opinion, oversee, perpend, purpose **8** consider, function, lucidity, perceive, pleasure, remember, saneness, think out, villeity, watch out **9** intellect, intention, mentality, sentiment, soundness, supervise, think over **10** brainpower, conviction, discipline, excogitate, gray matter, persuasion **11** disposition, inclination, superintend, temperament **12** intelligence, recollection **13** consciousness *combining form:* **3** noo **5** menti, phren, psych **6** phreni, phreno, psycho

mindful 5 alert, alive, awake, aware **7** knowing **8** sensible, vigilant **9** attentive, au courant, cognizant, conscious, observant, observing, regardful **10** conversant **12** apprehensive **13** conscientious

mindless 3 mad **4** nuts **5** nutsy, silly **6** insane, maniac, simple, stupid **7** asinine, foolish, lunatic **9** nitwitted **10** unthinking **11** sheepheaded **13** unintelligent

mine 3 dig, pit, sap **4** lode, vein, well, work **5** delve, drill, scoop **6** burrow, quarry, spring **7** bonanza, extract **8** eldorado, excavate, Golconda, treasury **10** excavation, wellspring **13** treasure-house, treasure trove *coal:* **8** colliery *French:* **4** à moi **6** le mien

mine gas 9 blackdamp, chokedamp

miner 6 digger, pitman **7** collier

mineral 5 beryl, topaz, trona **6** augite, barite, garnet, iolite, pinite, rutile, sphene, spinel, sulfur, zircon **7** apatite, azurite, bornite, calcite, citrine, coesite, cyanite, jadeite, kernite, kunzite, olivine, zeolite **8** boracite, cinnabar, dolomite, epsomite, fayalite, feldspar, fluorite, hematite, lazulite, lazurite, siderite, sodalite, stibnite, triplite, wellsite **9** aragonite, celestite, cerussite, danburite, fosterite,

kaolinite, lawsonite, magnetite, malachite, muscovite, phenakite, scapolite, tridymite, turquoise, wulfenite **10** chalcedony, orthoclase, pyrrhotite, tourmaline **11** alexandrite, chrysoberyl, melanterite **12** brazilianite, chalcopyrite, tincalconite **13** rhodochrosite *combining form:* **3** ine, ite **4** lite, lith, lyte, xene **5** oryct **6** orycto *flaky:* **4** mica *greasy:* **4** talc **10** serpentine *hard:* **6** spinel **7** diamond **8** corundum *iridescent:* **4** opal *nonmetallic:* **5** boron **6** gypsum, halite **8** asbestos, graphite *shiny:* **4** gold **6** galena, pyrite, silver *soft:* **4** talc **6** gypsum **8** graphite *transparent:* **6** quartz

mineral water 7 seltzer

Minerva see Athena

mingle 3 mix **4** meld **5** merge **6** commix, make up **7** combine, concoct **8** intermix **9** socialize

mingy 4 mean **5** tight **6** stingy **7** scrimpy **8** ungiving **9** niggardly, penurious **11** closefisted

miniature 3 wee **4** copy, tiny **5** model, small, teeny, weeny **6** little, minute, teensy **8** portrait **9** itty-bitty **10** diminutive, small-scale, teeny-weeny **11** lilliputian **12** illumination

minify 5 dwarf **6** lessen, shrink **7** abridge, curtail **8** diminish

minim 3 jot **4** atom, iota **5** grain, speck **6** minute, smitch **7** modicum, smidgen **8** particle *music:* **8** half note, half rest

minimal 4 basic **6** lowest **8** littlest, smallest **9** slightest

minimize 5 decry, dwarf **6** reduce **7** run down **8** belittle, derogate, discount **9** disparage, dispraise **10** depreciate **11** detract from

minimum 3 dab, jot **4** hair, iota, whit **5** least, speck **6** lowest, margin **7** smidgen **8** particle, pittance, smallest

minion 4 idol, toad **6** yes-man **7** darling, spaniel **8** creature, favorite, truckler **9** sycophant, toadeater, underling **10** bootlicker **11** lickspittle, subordinate

minister 4 tend **5** agent, clerk, serve **6** cleric, curate, divine, parson **8** clerical, preacher, reverend **9** churchman, clergyman **10** ambassador **12** ecclesiastic *of state:* **10** chancellor

minister plenipotentiary 5 envoy

ministry 4 mean **5** agent, organ **6** agency, clergy, medium **7** channel, vehicle **10** instrument

Minnehaha's husband 8 Hiawatha

Minnesota *capital:* **6** St. Paul *nickname:* **11** Gopher State **14** North Star State *state bird:* **10** common loon

minor 4 fair **5** dinky, light, lower, petty, small, youth **6** casual, infant, lesser, little, medium, slight **7** average, trivial **8** inferior,

mediocre, piddling, small-fry, trifling
9 dependent, secondary, small-beer, small-time **10** bush-league, second-rate, shoestring **11** indifferent, unimportant **12** unnoticeable **13** insignificant

minority 6 nonage **7** infancy
10 immaturity

minor-league 5 dinky, small **6** lesser
8 small-fry **9** secondary, small-time
11 unimportant

Minos *daughter:* **7** Ariadne, Phaedra
father: **4** Zeus **7** Jupiter *kingdom:* **5** Crete
monster: **8** Minotaur *mother:* **6** Europa
son: **9** Androgeos *wife:* **8** Pasiphaë

Minotaur *father:* **4** bull *home:* **9** labyrinth
mother: **8** Pasiphaë *slayer:* **7** Theseus

minstrel 4 bard, wait **6** harper, singer
7 gleeman **8** jongleur **9** balladist **10** troubadour *end man:* **7** Mr. Bones, Mr. Tambo

mint 3 pot, wad **4** coin, pile **6** boodle, bundle, intact, packet, unused **7** fire-new, fortune, perfect, span-new **8** brand-new, lavender, original, spang-new, unmarred
9 blue curls, bugleweed, spearmint **10** peppermint **11** spanking-new **12** spick-and-span

Minuit's purchase 9 Manhattan

minus 4 less, sans **7** lacking, wanting, without **8** awanting, subtract **10** deficiency

minute 3 jot, wee **4** full, tiny **5** crack, flash, jiffy, light, petty, shake, small, teeny, weeny **6** little, moment, second, teensy, tittle **7** careful, instant, precise, trivial
8 detailed, itemized, thorough, trifling
9 breathing, clocklike, itty-bitty, small-beer
10 blow-by-blow, meticulous, particular, scrupulous, teeny-weeny **11** lilliputian, punctilious, split second, unimportant
13 infinitesimal, insignificant

minutes 6 record **7** summary

minutiae 5 ropes **6** trivia **7** details **9** small beer **10** ins and outs, triviality **11** particulars, small change **13** small potatoes

miracle 4 feat **6** marvel, wonder **7** portent, prodigy, stunner **9** sensation
10 phenomenon

miraculous 7 amazing, strange **8** superior **9** marvelous, unearthly, wonderful
10 astounding, prodigious, staggering, superhuman, suprahuman **11** astonishing, spectacular **12** supermundane, supernatural, supramundane, supranatural
13 preternatural

mirage 8 delusion, illusion, phantasm
11 fata morgana, ignis fatuus
13 hallucination

Miranda *father:* **8** Prospero *lover:*
9 Ferdinand

mire 3 bog, fen, mud **4** muck, ooze, quag, sink, soil, trap **5** cling, delay, embog, marsh, slush, stick, swamp **6** cleave, detain,

enmesh, entrap, hang up, morass, retard, slow up, tangle **7** baygall, bog down, embroil, ensnare, involve, set back, slacken
8 entangle, slow down **9** implicate

Miriam's brother 5 Aaron, Moses

mirror 5 glass, ideal, image, model
6 embody, typify **7** example, pattern, reflect **8** ensample, exemplar, paradigm, speculum, standard **9** archetype, beau ideal, body forth, epitomize, exemplify, personify, pier glass, reflector, represent, symbolize **10** illustrate **11** cheval glass, emblematize **12** looking glass *signaling:*
5 helio **10** heliograph, heliotrope

mirth 3 fun, joy **4** glee **5** cheer **6** gaiety, levity **7** jollity **8** gladness, hilarity **9** frivolity, happiness, jocundity, joviality, merriment, rejoicing **10** jocularity, joyfulness
12 cheerfulness

mirthful 3 gay **5** jolly, merry **6** blithe, jocund, jovial **7** festive **10** blithesome
12 lighthearted

miry 4 oozy **5** boggy, muddy

misadventure 4 bull, slip, woes **5** boner, error, lapse **6** howler, mishap **7** blunder, faux pas, tragedy **8** accident, calamity, casualty, disaster **9** cataclysm
11 catastrophe

misanthropic 7 cynical **8** reserved, solitary **9** reclusive **10** antisocial
11 standoffish

misappropriate 5 steal **8** embezzle

misbegotten 7 bastard, natural **8** baseborn, deformed, spurious **10** fatherless, unfathered **12** contemptible, illegitimate

misbehaving 3 bad **7** naughty

misbehavior 8 rudeness **10** misconduct, wrongdoing

miscalculate 3 err **8** discount, miscount, misgauge, overlook **9** disregard, overprize, overvalue **10** underprize, undervalue

miscarry 4 fail, flop **5** abort

miscellaneous 3 odd **4** many **5** mixed
6 divers, motley, sundry, varied **7** diverse, jumbled, mingled **8** assorted, chowchow, unsorted **9** different, disparate, divergent, scrambled **10** commingled, unassorted
12 conglomerate **13** heterogeneous

miscellany 3 ana **4** brew, hash, olio, posy, stew **5** album, melee, salad **6** jumble, medley, motley, muddle **7** garland, mélange, mixture, omnibus **8** analects, chowchow, mixed bag, pastiche, porridge
9 anthology, colluvies, congeries, pasticcio, patchwork, potpourri **10** assortment, cumulation, hodgepodge, hotchpotch, salmagundi **11** aggregation, combination, florilegium, gallimaufry, odds and ends, olla podrida, smorgasbord

mischance 6 mishap **7** tragedy **8** accident, casualty 9 adversity 10 misfortune 11 contretemps

mischief 3 ill 4 evil, harm, hurt, limb, ruin 5 devil, prank, rogue, scamp 6 damage, injury, rascal, strife 7 devilry, discord, dissent, outrage, roguery, trouble, villain, waggery 8 conflict, deviltry, division, hardship, scalawag, variance 9 devilment, diablerie, disaccord, skeezicks 10 contention, difference, difficulty, dissension 11 rapscallion, roguishness, waggishness 12 sportiveness

mischief-maker 3 imp 4 puck 5 devil, knave, rogue, scamp 6 rascal 7 villain 8 scalawag 9 prankster, trickster 11 rapscallion

mischievous 3 bad, ill, paw, sly 4 evil, foxy 5 antic, risky 6 artful, impish, irking, tricky, vexing, wicked 7 harmful, hurtful, irksome, larkish, naughty, playful, puckish, roguish, tricksy, waggish 8 annoying, damaging, prankish, sportive 9 bothering, injurious 10 bothersome, frolicsome, ill-behaved

mischievousness 4 evil, harm, hurt 6 injury 7 devilry, roguery, teasing, waggery 8 annoying, deviltry 9 devilment, diablerie, pestering

miscolor 4 warp 5 belie, twist 6 garble 7 distort, falsify, pervert 12 misrepresent

misconduct 10 wrongdoing 11 impropriety, malfeasance, misbehavior 12 malversation

miscreant 4 heel 5 knave, rogue 6 rascal, wretch 7 corrupt, heretic, infidel, lowlife, vicious, villain 8 depraved, infamous, perverse 9 heretical, nefarious, scoundrel, unhealthy 10 blackguard, degenerate, flagitious, unbeliever, villainous

miscue 4 miss, slip, trip 5 error, fluff, lapse 6 slipup 7 blooper, blunder, mistake

misdeed 3 sin 5 crime, wrong 7 offense 13 transgression

misdoubt 4 fear 5 dread 7 suspect 8 distrust 9 apprehend, suspicion

mise-en-scène 3 set 4 site 6 locale, medium, milieu 7 ambient, climate, setting 8 ambience, stage set 10 atmosphere 11 environment 12 stage setting, surroundings

miser 3 hog, pig 4 skin 5 chuff, hunks, nabal, piker, stiff 7 glutton, niggard, scrooge 8 muckworm, tightwad 9 skinflint 10 cheapskate

miserable 6 dolent, rueful, woeful 7 doleful, forlorn, piteous, pitiful, ruthful 8 dolorous, hopeless, shameful, wretched 9 afflicted, sorrowful, worthless 10 despairing, despondent, melancholy 12 contemptible 13 discreditable

Miserables, Les *author:* 4 Hugo *character:* 6 Javert 7 Cosette, Fantine, Valjean

miserly 4 mean 5 close, tight 6 abject, greedy, sordid, stingy 7 ignoble 8 covetous, grasping, stingily 9 penurious, scrimping 10 avaricious 11 closefisted, tightfisted 12 cheeseparing, parsimonious 13 penny-pinching

misery 3 woe 5 agony, dolor, grief 6 sorrow 7 anguish, passion, sadness, squalor 8 calamity, distress 9 adversity, dejection, privation, suffering 10 affliction, depression, desolation, melancholy 11 despondency, unhappiness 12 wretchedness

misfortune 3 woe 4 harm 5 cross, trial 7 tragedy, trouble 8 accident, calamity, casualty, disaster 9 adversity, cataclysm 10 affliction, visitation 11 catastrophe, contretemps, tribulation *Scottish:* 6 dirdum

misgiving 4 fear 5 doubt, qualm 7 anxiety, presage 8 distrust 9 prenotion, suspicion 11 premonition 12 apprehension, presentiment

misguided 5 wrong 9 erroneous 10 ill-advised

Mishael *brother:* 8 Elzaphan *cousin:* 5 Aaron *father:* 6 Uzziel

Misham's father 6 Elpaal

mishandle 5 abuse 7 pervert, rough up 10 knock about, prostitute, roughhouse, slap around

mishap 7 tragedy 8 accident, casualty 9 adversity 11 contretemps

mishmash 6 jumble, jungle, litter, medley, muddle, tumble 7 clutter, mélange, mixture, rummage 8 pastiche, scramble 9 pasticcio, patchwork, potpourri 10 hodgepodge, hotchpotch

misidentify 7 confuse 8 confound

misinterpret 3 err 7 misread

mislay 4 lose

mislead 3 lie 4 dupe, fool, lure 5 bluff, cheat, tempt 6 betray, delude, entice, illude, juggle, seduce, take in 7 beguile, deceive 8 hoodwink, inveigle 11 double-cross

misleading 5 false, wrong 8 delusive, delusory, specious 9 deceitful, deceiving, deceptive 10 fallacious, inaccurate 11 casuistical, sophistical

mismatch 3 jar 5 clash 6 jangle 7 discord 8 conflict 9 disaccord 12 disharmonize

misplace 4 lose

misrepresent 3 lie 4 gild, mask, warp 5 belie, cloak, color, dress, feign, gloss, twist, wrest 6 garble, palter, weasel, wrench 7 confuse, deceive, distort, falsify, pervert, varnish 8 disguise, simulate 9 dissemble, embellish, embroider 10 camouflage, equivocate 11 counterfeit, prevaricate

misrepresentation 3 fib, lie 4 tale 5 story 6 canard 7 falsity, untruth 8 untruism 9 falsehood

miss 3 err, gal 4 fail, girl, maid, omit 5 avoid, wench 6 damsel, escape, forget, ignore, lassie, maiden, slight 7 failure, neglect 8 discount, overlook 9 disregard

Missa Solemnis
  composer
9 Beethoven

misshape 4 warp, wind 6 deform 7 contort, distort, torture 9 deformity 10 distortion 12 malformation

missile 4 bolt, dart 5 arrow, shell, spear 6 bullet, rocket 10 cannonball, projectile *underwater:* 7 torpedo; (see also **guided missile**)

mission 4 goal, task 5 trade 6 errand 7 calling, embassy, purpose 8 business, legation, lifework, ministry, vocation

missionary 5 agent 7 apostle 8 emissary, promoter 10 colporteur, evangelist, revivalist 12 propagandist

Mississippi *capital:* 7 Jackson *highest point:* 9 Woodall Mt. *motto:* 14 By Valor and Arms *nickname:* 10 Bayou State 13 Magnolia State *state flower:* 8 magnolia *university:* 12 Jackson State

missive 4 memo, note 6 letter 7 epistle

Miss Julie author 10 Strindberg

Miss Lonelyhearts author 4 West

Miss-Nancyish 5 sissy 6 prissy 7 epicene, unmanly 9 pansified, sissified 10 effeminate

Missouri *capital:* 13 Jefferson City *college:* 5 Avila, Drury *nickname:* 11 Show Me State 12 Bullion State *state flower:* 9 hawthorne

misstate 4 warp 5 belie, color, twist 6 garble 7 distort, falsify, pervert

misstatement 3 fib, lie 4 tale 7 falsity, untruth 8 untruism 9 falsehood 10 taradiddle 13 prevarication

misstep 4 bull, slip 5 boner, error, fluff, lapse 6 slipup 7 blooper, blunder, faux pas

mist 3 dim, fog 4 blur, film, haze, murk 5 befog, brume, cloud, smaze 7 becloud, obscure 9 overcloud

mistake 3 err 4 bull, slip, trip 5 addle, boner, error, fluff, folly, lapse 6 boo-boo, bungle, jumble, lapsus, muddle, slight, slipup, tumble 7 blooper, blunder, confuse, neglect 8 confound, omission, omitting 9 confusion, slighting 10 inaccuracy, neglecting

mister 3 man, sir 4 lord 7 husband *French:* 8 monsieur *German:* 4 herr *Italian:* 6 signor *Spanish:* 5 senor

Mister Roberts author 6 Heggen

mistreat 5 abuse 6 ill-use 7 outrage

mistress 4 amie 5 lover, woman 6 harlot 7 bedmate, hetaira 8 dulcinea, ladylove, paramour 9 concubine, courtesan, inamorata, kept woman 10 chatelaine, girl friend

of Charles II: 4 Gwyn (Nell) 8 Villiers (Barbara) *of Edward III:* 7 Perrers (Alice) *of Henry II (England):* 8 Clifford (Rosamund) *of Henry II (France):* 9 de Poiters (Diane) *of Louis XV:* 9 Pompadour (Madame de)

mistrust 5 alarm, doubt, scare 6 appall, dismay, wonder 7 concern, dispute, dubiety, foresee, surmise, suspect 8 frighten, question 9 apprehend, challenge, dubiosity, suspicion 10 anticipate, foreboding, skepticism 11 incertitude, uncertainty, uncertitude 12 apprehension, presentiment

mistrustful 7 jealous 10 suspicious

misty 3 dim 4 hazy 5 foggy, mushy, vague 6 cloudy, vapory 7 obscure, unclear 8 confused, vaporous 10 indistinct

misunderstanding 7 quarrel 9 imbroglio 12 disagreement

misuse 5 abuse 7 outrage, pervert 8 illtreat, maltreat 10 prostitute *of a word:* 8 malaprop

mite 3 bit, jot 4 atom, iota 5 grain, minim, ounce, speck 6 acarid, minute, tittle 7 chigger, modicum, smidgen 8 molecule, particle, smidgeon *combining form:* 4 acar 5 acari, acaro *family:* 8 oribatid

mitigate 4 ease 5 abate, allay, relax, slake 6 lessen, soften, temper 7 assuage, lighten, mollify, relieve 8 palliate 9 alleviate, meliorate

mitigation 4 ease 6 relief 8 easement 10 moderation, palliation 11 alleviation

mitosis 12 cell division, karyokinesis *stage:* 8 anaphase, prophase 9 metaphase, telophase

mix 4 fuse, join, link, lump, meld, stir 5 blend, braid, merge, unite 6 blunge, fusion, jumble, make up, mingle, tangle, work in 7 amalgam, combine, concoct, confuse, conjoin 8 coalesce, comingle, compound, confound, immingle 9 associate, commingle, interflow, interfuse 10 amalgamate, crossbreed, inosculate, interblend 11 interfusion, intermingle, misidentify 12 amalgamation

mixable 8 miscible

mixed 6 impure, motley, varied 8 chowchow 9 irregular 11 promiscuous 12 conglomerate, multifarious 13 heterogeneous, miscellaneous

mixed bag 4 olio 5 salad 6 jumble, medley 8 pastiche 10 assortment, hodgepodge, miscellany 11 gallimaufry

mixed-blooded person 7 mestizo, mulatto 8 octoroon 9 half-breed

mixologist 6 barman 7 tapster 9 barkeeper, bartender

mixture 4 brew, hash, olio 5 alloy, blend 6 fusion, medley 7 amalgam, compost, farrago, mélange 8 compound, mishmash, solution 9 composite, potpourri 10 concoc-

tion, confection **11** interfusion
12 amalgamation

mix up 5 addle, dizzy **6** fuddle, jumble, muddle, tumble **7** confuse, derange, disrupt, fluster, misdeem, mistake **8** befuddle, bewilder, confound, disarray, disjoint, disorder, distract **9** distemper **10** disarrange, discompose **11** disorganize, misidentify

mix-up 4 hash, mess, mull, muss **5** blend, botch, melee **6** fusion, muddle, tangle **8** botchery, compound, shambles **9** composite, confusion **11** interfusion

mizmaze 3 web **4** knot, mesh **5** skein, snarl **6** jungle, morass, tangle **9** confusion, labyrinth **12** bewilderment

mks unit 3 lux, ohm **4** mole, volt, watt **5** farad, henry, hertz, joule, lumen, meter, metre, tesla, weber **6** ampere, kelvin, newton, pascal, second **7** candela, coulomb, siemens **8** kilogram

Mnemosyne 6 Memory *daughters:* **5** Muses *father:* **6** Uranus *lover:* **4** Zeus *mother:* **2** Ge **4** Gaea

Moabite *city:* **3** Kir *god:* **7** Chemosh *king:* **5** Eglon, Mesha

Moab's father 3 Lot

moan 4 weep **5** groan **6** bewail, grieve, lament **7** deplore **8** complain

mob 3 set **4** camp, clan, gang, herd, push, ring, riot, rout, scum **5** cabal, crowd, crush, dregs, horde, posse, press, swarm, trash **6** circle, clique, masses, rabble, throng **7** coterie, ingroup **8** canaille, riffraff, unwashed **9** camarilla **11** proletariat

mobile 5 fluid **6** liquid, moving **7** migrant, movable, protean **8** moveable, unstable, unsteady, variable, weathery **9** all-around, changeful, many-sided, mercurial, migrative, migratory, unsettled **10** capricious, changeable, inconstant **11** migrational

mobilize 5 drive, impel, rally **6** muster, propel, set off **7** actuate, marshal **8** activate, assemble, organize **9** circulate

Moby Dick 5 whale *author:* **8** Melville *character:* **3** Pip **6** Daggoo, Parsee **7** Ishmael **8** Queequeg, Starbuck, Tashtego *pursuer:* **4** Ahab *ship:* **6** Pequod

moccasin 3 pac **6** loafer **7** slipper **8** larrigan

mock 3 ape **4** butt, copy, defy, fake, gibe, jape, jeer, jest, joke, lout, quiz, razz, sham, twit **5** bogus, dummy, false, farce, feign, mimic, phony, quasi, rally, scout, sneer, sport, taunt **6** affect, assume, betray, delude, deride, ersatz, humbug, illude, jester, juggle, parody, pseudo **7** beguile, buffoon, deceive, imitate, mislead, sell out, take off **8** derision, ridicule, simulate, so-called, spurious, travesty **9** burlesque, disregard, imitation, pilgarlic, simulated **10** artificial,

caricature, fictitious, substitute **11** counterfeit, double-cross **13** laughingstock

mockery 4 butt, jest, joke, sham **5** farce, sport **6** japery, jester, parody, satire **7** takeoff **8** derision, ridicule, travesty **9** burlesque, imitation, pilgarlic **10** caricature **13** laughingstock

mocking 8 derisive, sardonic

mode 3 cry, fad, way **4** chic, rage, vein, wise **5** craze, state, style, vogue **6** custom, furore, manner, method, status, system **7** fashion, posture **9** condition, situation, technique **10** convention, dernier cri

model 4 copy, type, very **5** dummy, frame, gauge, ideal, shape **6** design, effigy, emblem, mirror, mockup, symbol **7** classic, epitome, example, fashion, imitate, manikin, paragon, pattern, perfect, replica, typical **8** ensample, exemplar, flawless, mannikin, nonesuch, paradigm, standard **9** archetype, beau ideal, blueprint, classical, criterion, exemplary, miniature, nonpareil **10** apotheosis, embodiment, prototypal, touchstone **11** commendable **12** indefectible, paradigmatic, prototypical, quintessence, reproduction *combining form:* **3** typ **4** typo *preliminary:* **8** maquette

moderate 3 ebb **4** calm, cool, even, fair, fall, mean, mild, slow, soft, so-so, wane **5** abate, bland, let up, small, sober **6** gentle, lessen, medium, paltry, reduce, relent, slight, soften, steady, subdue, temper **7** average, chasten, control, cushion, die away, die down, ease off, equable, fairish, lighten, qualify, relieve, slacken, subside, trivial **8** attemper, constant, decrease, diminish, discreet, mediocre, middling, piddling, restrain, trifling **9** alleviate, constrain, softshell, temperate, unextreme **10** abstemious, controlled, middle-road, reasonable, restrained **11** indifferent, unexcessive **12** conservative **13** unimpassioned

moderation 7 control, measure **9** restraint **10** abstinence, limitation, temperance **13** temperateness

moderator 5 judge **7** arbiter **8** chairman, examiner, governor, mediator **10** peacemaker **11** chairperson

modern 3 new **4** late **5** fresh, novel **6** latter, recent **7** current **8** neoteric, up-to-date **9** new-sprung, prevalent **10** coincident, concurrent, newfangled, present-day, prevailing **11** concomitant **12** contemporary, new-fashioned *combining form:* **2** ne **3** neo

modernize 5 renew **6** update **7** refresh, restore **8** renovate **9** refurbish **10** rejuvenate

modest 3 coy, dry, shy **4** meek, nice, prim, pure **5** clean, lowly, plain, timid **6** chaste, decent, demure, humble, prissy, proper, seemly, silent, simple, stuffy **7** bashful, prudish **8** decorous, discreet, moderate, priggish, reserved, reticent, retiring, spotless **9** diffident, stainless, temperate, unassured, undefiled, unsullied **10** immaculate, reasonable, unassuming, unboastful **11** inelaborate, puritanical, straitlaced, unassertive, unblemished, unelaborate, unpresuming, withdrawing **12** self-effacing, unornamented, unpretending **13** unembellished, unembroidered, unpretentious

Modest Proposal author 5 Swift

modesty 7 decency, pudency, reserve **8** chastity, humility, pudicity, timidity **10** diffidence

modicum 3 bit, jot **4** atom, iota, whit **5** grain, minim, ounce, scrap **7** soupçon **8** particle

modify 4 turn, vary **5** alter **6** change, mutate, temper **7** qualify **8** mitigate, moderate, restrain **9** refashion

modish 4 chic **5** smart, swank **6** with-it **7** dashing **9** exclusive **11** fashionable

Modred, Mordred *father:* **6** Arthur *mother:* **8** Margawse *slayer, victim:* **6** Arthur

modulate 4 sing **6** intone, temper **8** restrain

modus 3 way **4** wise **5** means **6** manner, method, system **7** fashion **9** technique

modus ___ 7 vivendi **8** operandi

mogul 4 czar, king, lord **5** baron, nabob, ruler **6** prince, tycoon **7** magnate

Mohammed see **Muhammad**

Mohawk chief 5 Brant **8** Hiawatha

Mohican chief 5 Uncas

moiety 3 cut **4** half, part **5** piece **6** member, parcel **7** element, portion, section, segment **8** division **9** component

moil 3 tug **4** grub, to-do, work **5** churn, drive, grind, labor, swirl **6** bustle, clamor, drudge, hubbub, lather, strain, strive, uproar **7** chaffer, ruction, slavery, travail, trouble, wrangle **8** drudgery, plugging, rowdydow, slogging **9** commotion, confusion **10** hurly-burly, turbulence

moira 3 lot **4** doom, fate **5** weird **6** kismet **7** destiny, portion **12** circumstance

moist 3 wet **4** damp, dank, dewy **5** gooey, humid, mushy, sappy, soggy, soupy **6** drippy, slushy, steamy, sticky, watery **7** dampish, maudlin, tearful, wettish

moisten 3 wet **6** dampen **8** humidify, saturate

moisture 5 vapor **11** tearfulness **13** precipitation *combining form:* **4** hygr **5** hygro

moistureless 3 dry **4** arid, sere **7** bonedry, parched, thirsty **8** droughty **9** unwatered **10** desiccated

molar 5 tooth **7** grinder *combining form:* **3** myl **4** mylo

molasses 7 treacle **8** theriaca **10** blackstrap

mold 3 die, hug, lot **4** cast, form, kind, make, soil, sort, type **5** adapt, build, class, erect, forge, frame, knead, shape, stamp **6** design, fungus, growth, nature **7** fashion, pattern **8** template **9** character, construct **11** description, put together *combining form:* **5** plasm, plast, plasy **6** plases (plural), plasia, plasis, plasma

moldable 6 pliant, supple **7** ductile, fictile, plastic, pliable **9** adaptable, malleable

molder 3 rot **4** turn **5** decay, spoil, taint, waste **7** crumble, putrefy **9** break down, decompose **11** deteriorate **12** disintegrate

molding 4 bead, cove, gula, list, reed, tore **5** angle, congé, ogive, talon, thumb **6** baston, nebulé, reglet **7** annulet, beading, cornice, reeding **8** cincture **9** baseboard *compound:* **4** beak, ogie **8** cymatium **9** cyma recta **10** serpentine **11** cyma reversa *edge:* **5** arris *flat:* **4** band, face **5** bevel, splay **6** fascia, fillet, listel, regula **7** chamfer *simple curve:* **4** roll **5** flute, ovolo, torus **6** scotia **8** astragal

moldy 5 dated, fusty, musty, passé **6** bygone, old hat, rococo **7** ancient, archaic **8** mildewed, outdated **9** crumbling, moth-eaten **10** antiquated **12** old-fashioned

mole 4 pier, quay **5** jetty, nevus **6** burrow, tunnel **9** birthmark **10** breakwater *combining form:* **5** talpi

molecule 3 bit, jot **4** atom, iota **5** minim, ounce, speck **7** modicum **8** fraction, fragment, particle

molest 3 vex **4** bait, raid **5** annoy, harry, tease **6** bother, harass, heckle, pester **7** disturb, torment, trouble **9** persecute

Moll Flanders author 5 Defoe

mollify 4 calm, ease **5** allay, relax **6** pacify, soften, soothe, temper **7** appease, assuage, lighten, placate, relieve, sweeten **8** mitigate **9** alleviate **10** ameliorate, conciliate, propitiate

mollusk 6 chiton *bivalve:* **4** clam **6** bankia, cockle, mussel, oyster, teredo **7** geoduck, scallop **8** shipworm *cephalopod:* **5** squid **7** octopus **8** argonaut, nautilus **10** cuttlefish *part:* **6** mantle, radula, siphon *tooth shell:* **9** dentalium *univalve:* **4** slug **5** conch, cowry, murex, snail, whelk **6** cowrie, limpet, triton **7** abalone **10** nudibranch, periwinkle

mollusk-like 8 limacine

Molly ___ 7 Maguire, Pitcher

mollycoddle 4 baby **5** humor, sissy, spoil **6** cocker, cosset, pamper **7** cater to, doormat, indulge, milksop, protect **8** weakling **9** jellyfish **10** goody-goody, pantywaist **11** Milquetoast **12** invertebrate

molt 4 cast, shed, slip 6 change, slough 7 discard, ecdysis 8 exuviate

molted covering 7 exuviae

molten 6 heated, melted 7 glowing

molten rock 4 lava 5 magma

molybdenum *symbol:* 2 Mo

moment 4 pith, time 5 crack, flash, jiffy, point, shake, while 6 import, minute, second, weight 7 instant 8 juncture, occasion 9 breathing, magnitude 10 importance 11 consequence, split second, weightiness 12 significance 13 consideration

momentary 5 brief, quick, short 8 fleeting, fugitive, volatile 9 ephemeral, fugacious, transient 10 evanescent, short-lived, transitory 11 impermanent

momentous 3 big 5 grave 7 epochal, fateful, serious, weighty 8 eventful, material 9 important 10 meaningful 11 significant, substantial 12 considerable 13 consequential

momentousness 4 pith 6 import, weight 9 magnitude 10 importance 11 consequence, weightiness 12 significance

momus 6 carper, critic, Zoilus 7 caviler, knocker 9 aristarch 10 criticizer 11 faultfinder, smellfungus

Monaco *casino:* 10 Monte Carlo *prince:* 6 Ranier *princess:* 5 Grace

monad 3 one 4 atom, unit 8 zoospore

Mona Lisa 10 La Gioconda *painter:* 7 da Vinci

monarch 4 czar, king, raja, tsar, tzar 5 queen, rajah, ruler 6 kaiser, prince 7 emperor 9 potentate, sovereign

monarchical 5 regal, royal 6 kingly 8 imperial, kinglike, majestic 9 sovereign

monarch's daughter 8 princess *Portuguese, Spanish:* 7 infanta

monarch's son 6 prince *French:* 7 dauphin *Portuguese, Spanish:* 7 infante

monastery 5 abbey 6 friary, priory 7 convent, nunnery *Buddhist:* 8 lamasery *Eastern Orthodox:* 5 laura *head:* 5 abbot, prior 7 hegumen

_____ Mondrian 4 Piet

monetary 6 fiscal, pocket 9 financial, pecuniary 10 numismatic

monetary rate 7 millage

monetary unit see at individual countries

money 4 bill, cash, coin, gelt, loot, pelf, swag 5 bread, chips, dough, funds, lucre, moola, rhino, rocks 6 boodle, change, dinero, mammon, mazuma, moolah, riches, specie, wampum, wealth 7 cabbage, capital, coinage, lettuce, needful, scratch, stipend 8 bankroll, currency, finances, treasure 9 resources 10 greenbacks 11 filthy lucre, legal tender

moneyed 4 rich 7 opulent, wealthy 8 affluent 10 well-heeled

moneygrubber 4 skin 5 chuff, miser, nabal, stiff 7 niggard, scrooge 8 muckworm 9 skinflint 10 cheapskate

moneymaking 6 paying 7 gainful 9 lucrative 10 profitable, well-paying, worthwhile 12 advantageous, remunerative

monger 4 hawk, rend 6 dealer, hawker, peddle, spread, trader, vendor 7 higgler, packman, peddler 8 huckster, outcrier

Mongol conqueror 9 Tamerlane 10 Kublai Khan 11 Genghis Khan, Tamburlaine

mongrel 3 cur 4 mule, mutt 5 cross 6 hybrid 7 bastard 9 crossbred, half blood, half-breed 10 crossbreed

monish 5 chide 6 rebuke 7 reprove, tick off 8 call down, reproach 9 reprimand

monition 6 caveat 7 caution, warning 11 forewarning

monitor 4 test 5 check, watch 7 adviser, observe 8 reminder 9 counselor *lizard:* 7 varanid

Monitor *designer:* 8 Ericsson *opponent:* 8 Virginia 9 Merrimack

monitory 7 warning 8 advisory 10 cautionary, cautioning, counseling 11 admonishing

monk 5 friar 7 brother 8 monastic 9 anchorite *Buddhist:* 4 lama 5 bonze *Eastern Orthodox:* 7 caloyer *Hindu:* 8 sannyasi *Roman Catholic:* 9 Dominican 10 Cistercian, Franciscan *room:* 4 cell *shaven crown:* 7 tonsure *title:* 3 dom, fra 5 padre

monkey 3 imp, sap 4 dupe, fool, gull, mark 5 cebid, gamin, small 6 bantam, butt in, ceboid, horn in, little, meddle, petite, simian, sucker, tamper, urchin, victim 7 fall guy 8 busybody, easy mark, smallish 9 interfere, interlope 10 tamper with 11 intermeddle *combining form:* 6 pithec 7 pitheco *New World:* 4 saki, titi 5 sajou 6 howler, spider, uakari, woolly 7 sapajou, tamarin 8 capuchin, marmoset, squirrel 11 douroucouli *Old World:* 4 douc, mona 5 Diana, drill, patas 6 grivet, guenon, langur, rhesus, vervet 7 colobus, hanuman, macaque 8 entellus, mandrill, mangabey, talapoin, wanderoo 9 proboscis 10 Barbary ape

monkeyshine 4 dido, lark 5 antic, caper, prank, trick 6 frolic 10 shenanigan, tomfoolery

monocratic 8 absolute, despotic 9 arbitrary, autarchic, tyrannous 10 autocratic, tyrannical

monogram 6 cipher, sketch 7 outline 8 initials

monograph 5 study 6 memoir, thesis

8 tractate, treatise **9** discourse **12** disquisition, dissertation

monopolize 3 hog **5** sew up **6** absorb, corner, manage **7** consume, control, engross

monopoly 5 trust **6** cartel, corner **7** control **9** ownership, syndicate **10** consortium **11** exclusivity

monotonous 4 blah, dull, poky, same **6** dreary, stodgy **7** humdrum, uniform **8** banausic, unvaried **10** pedestrian **11** repetitious

monotony 6 tedium **7** humdrum **8** flatness, sameness **10** uniformity

monster 4 huge, ogre **5** demon, devil, fiend, freak, giant, lusus, teras, whale **6** ogress **7** mammoth, titanic **8** abortion, behemoth, colossal, enormous, giantess, gigantic **9** hellhound, leviathan **10** behemothic, gargantuan **11** elephantine, miscreation *biblical:* **5** Rehab **8** Behemoth **9** Leviathan *combining form:* **4** pagi (plural) **5** pagus, terat **6** terato *female:* **6** Gorgon, Medusa, Scylla *fire-breathing:* **6** dragon, Typhon **7** Chimera **8** Chimaera *fowl-dragon:* **10** cockatrice *French:* **8** Tarasque *horse-fish:* **11** hippocampus *hundred-armed:* **9** Enceladus *hundred-eyed:* **5** Argus *hundred-handed:* **8** Briareus *lion-eagle:* **7** griffin *serpent-headed:* **6** gorgon *study of:* **10** teratology *three-bodied:* **6** Geryon *three-headed dog:* **8** Cerberus *two-headed dog:* **6** Orthos *water:* **6** kraken, nicker *winged dragon:* **6** wivern, wyvern *woman-bird:* **5** Harpy *woman-lion:* **6** Sphinx *woman-serpent:* **7** Echidna; (see also **dragon**)

____ monster 4 Gila

monstrosity 4 mess **5** freak, lusus, sight **6** fright **7** desight, eyesore **8** abortion **11** miscreation

monstrous 3 big **4** huge, rank, vast **5** awful, large **6** crying, mighty, mortal **7** glaring, heinous, immense, mammoth, massive, titanic **8** colossal, cracking, deformed, dreadful, enormous, gigantic, horrible, infamous, shocking, towering **9** atrocious, desperate, fantastic, malformed, unnatural **10** flagitious, gargantuan, impressive, monumental, outrageous, prodigious, scandalous, stupendous, tremendous **11** elephantine, magnificent

Montagues' enemies 8 Capulets

Montaigne's forte 5 essay

Montana *capital:* **6** Helena *highest point:* **11** Granite Peak *largest town:* **8** Billings *nickname:* **13** Mountain State, Treasure State *state flower:* **10** bitterroot

Monteverdi opera 5 Orfeo **7** Arianna

Montezuma *conqueror:* **6** Cortes, Cortez *people:* **6** Aztecs *revenge:* **8** diarrhea

month *combining form:* **4** meno *current:* **7** instant *following:* **7** proximo *Hindu:* **3** Pus **4** Asin, Jeth, Magh **5** Aghan, Chait, Sawan **6** Asargh, Bhadon, Kartik, Phagun **7** Baisakh *Jewish:* **2** Ab **4** Adar, Elul, Iyar **5** Nisan, Sivan, Tebet **6** Kislev, Shebat, Tammuz, Tishri **7** Heshvan *Muslim:* **4** Rabi **5** Rajab, Safar **6** Jumada, Sha 'ban **7** Ramadan, Shawwal **8** Muharram **9** Dhu'l-Hijja, Dhu'l-Oa'dah *preceding:* **6** ultimo

Montmartre church 10 Sacré Coeur

monument 5 relic, stela, stupa **6** ledger, record **7** chaitya, example, memento, tribute **8** archives, cenotaph, document, memorial **9** footstone, headstone, tombstone **10** gravestone **11** commemorate, grave marker, memorialize, testimonial *prehistoric:* **6** dolmen, menhir **8** cromlech, megalith

monumental 4 huge, vast **6** mighty, mortal **7** immense, mammoth, massive **8** cracking, enormous, gigantic, towering **9** fantastic, monstrous **10** prodigious, stupendous, tremendous **11** inestimable, mountainous **12** overwhelming

moocah 3 pot **5** grass **8** cannabis **9** marijuana

mooch 3 bat, beg **4** roam, rove **5** amble, cadge, drift, range, slink, sneak, steal, stray **6** ramble, sponge, wander **7** meander, saunter **8** straggle

mooching 7 beggary, bumming, cadging **9** mendicity **10** mendicancy **11** panhandling

mood 3 air **4** aura, feel, mind, tone, vein, whim **5** humor **6** aspect, spirit, strain, temper, timbre **7** caprice, emotion, feeling **8** ambiance, ambience **9** character, semblance **10** atmosphere **11** disposition, personality, temperament

moody 3 sad **4** glum **5** sulky **6** fickle, gloomy, grumpy **7** pensive **8** unstable **9** humorsome, mercurial, whimsical **10** capricious, inconstant **13** temperamental

moon 4 gape **5** dream **6** dawdle **9** satellite *combining form:* **5** selen **6** seleni, seleno *dark area:* **4** mare **5** maria (plural) *god:* **3** Sin **5** Nanna **6** Meztli *goddess:* **4** Luna **5** Diana, Tanit **6** Hecate, Hekate, Selena, Selene, Tanith **7** Artemis, Astarte

Moon and Sixpence author **7** Maugham

mooncalf 4 dolt, fool **5** idiot, ninny **6** doodle, madman **7** jackass, tomfool **8** imbecile

moonshine 4 bosh, jake **5** hokum **6** bunkum, humbug **7** bootleg, eyewash **8** homebrew, malarkey, nonsense **10** balderdash, bathtub gin, flapdoodle **11** mountain dew **12** blatherskite

Moonstone, The *author:* 7 Collins *detective:* 4 Cuff

moor 3 bog, fen 4 fell 5 berth, catch 6 anchor, Berber, fasten, Muslim, secure 8 Moroccan *fictional:* 7 Othello

moose 6 cervid *female:* 3 cow *male:* 4 bull *relative:* 3 elk 4 deer

moot 5 argue, plead 6 broach, debate 7 agitate, bring up, canvass, discept, discuss, dispute, dubious, suggest, suspect 8 arguable, disputed, doubtful 9 debatable, introduce, thrash out, uncertain, unsettled, ventilate 10 disputable, toss around 11 problematic 12 questionable 13 controversial

mooting 6 debate 8 forensic 9 dialectic 11 disputation 13 argumentation

mop 3 mug 4 swab, wipe 5 mouth 7 grimace, shellac, trounce

mope 4 ache, pout, sulk 5 ample, brood, drift, grump, mosey 6 bummel, dawdle, grieve, linger, stroll 7 despond, saunter

mopes 5 blues, dumps 7 dismals, sadness 8 dolefuls 10 depression, melancholy 11 unhappiness 12 mournfulness

mopey 3 low 4 blue, down 6 droopy 8 cast down, dejected, downcast 9 depressed 10 dispirited, spiritless

moppet 3 bud, kid, tot 4 chit, tyke 5 chick, child, youth 8 juvenile, young one 9 youngster

mop up 4 beat, drub, dust, lick, whip 6 absorb, garner 7 shellac, trounce 8 lambaste 9 overwhelm

moral 4 good, just, pure, rule 5 axiom, gnome, maxim, noble, right 6 chaste, decent, dictum, honest, proper, teachy, truism 7 brocard, ethical, preachy, upright 8 aphorism, apothegm, didactic, elevated, sermonic, virtuous 9 honorable, righteous 10 high-minded, principled, scrupulous 11 right-minded, sermonizing 13 conscientious

morale 4 mood 5 vigor 6 esprit, spirit 9 assurance 10 confidence 13 esprit de corps

moralistic 5 noble 7 ethical 8 didactic, virtuous 9 righteous 10 principled 11 right-minded

morality 5 ethic, mores 6 virtue 7 probity 8 goodness 9 rectitude, rightness 11 saintliness, uprightness 13 righteousness

moralize 6 preach 7 lecture 9 preachify, sermonize 11 pontificate

morals 5 mores 6 ethics 9 standards

morass 3 bog, fen, web 4 knot, maze, mesh, mire, quag 5 marsh, skein, snarl, swamp 6 jungle, tangle 7 mizmaze 8 quagmire

moratorium 3 ban 5 delay 8 suspense 10 suspension

morbid 4 dark, sick 5 moody 6 gloomy, grisly, morose, sickly, sullen 7 unsound 8 diseased, gruesome 9 saturnine, unhealthy 11 melancholic, unwholesome 12 pathological

mordacious see **mordant**

mordancy 7 acidity 8 acerbity, acridity, acrimony, asperity, pungency 10 causticity, trenchancy

mordant 4 keen 5 salty, sharp 6 biting 7 burning, caustic, pungent 8 incisive, scathing 9 sarcastic, trenchant

Mordecai *cousin:* 6 Esther *father:* 4 Jair *mother:* 6 Esther

more 3 new, too 4 also, else, plus 5 added, again, along, extra, fresh, older, other 6 as well, better, nearer, withal 7 another, besides, farther, further, greater 8 likewise, moreover 10 additional *combining form:* 4 pleo, plio 5 pleio

More book 6 Utopia

moreover 3 and, too, yet 4 also, then 6 as well, withal 7 besides, further 8 likewise 11 furthermore 12 additionally

mores 6 ethics, habits 7 customs, manners 8 decorums, folkways, morality 9 amenities, etiquette 10 civilities 11 proprieties

Morgana's brother 6 Arthur

morgue 5 pride 7 disdain, hauteur 8 mortuary 9 arrogance, loftiness, superbity 11 haughtiness

moribund 5 dying, going 6 fading 7 dormant 8 decaying, expiring 10 regressing 13 deteriorating

Mormon Church *administrative unit:* 4 ward 5 stake *founder:* 5 Smith *leader:* 5 Young *priest:* 5 elder

Mormon State 4 Utah

morn see **morning**

morne 4 cold 5 black, bleak 6 dismal, gloomy 8 desolate 9 cheerless 10 depressant, depressing, depressive

morning 4 dawn 5 light, sunup 6 aurora 7 dawning, sunrise 8 cockcrow, daybreak, daylight, forenoon *moisture:* 3 dew 8 dewdrops *song:* 6 aubade

Morocco *capital:* 5 Rabat *largest city:* 10 Casablanca *monetary unit:* 6 dirham

moron 4 fool, zany 5 ament, dummy, dunce, idiot 6 cretin, stupid 7 dullard, halfwit 8 dullhead, dumbbell, imbecile 9 ignoramus, simpleton

moronic 4 dull 6 simple, stupid 7 brutish 8 backward, imbecile, retarded 9 dim-witted 10 half-witted, slow-witted 12 feebleminded, simpleminded

morose 4 dour, glum, sick, sour, ugly 5 gruff, sulky, surly, testy 6 cranky, crusty, gloomy, morbid, sickly, sullen 7 crabbed,

unhappy 8 choleric **9** irascible, saturnine, splenetic **10** ill-humored

Morpheus *father:* **6** Hypnos *god of:* **5** sleep

Morse code *dash:* **3** dah *dot:* **3** dit

morsel 3 bit **4** bite, tapa **5** crumb, goody, mug-up, piece, scrap, snack, taste, treat **6** dainty, tidbit, titbit **8** delicacy, fragment, kickshaw, mouthful **11** bonne bouche

mortal 3 man **4** body, grim, weak **5** awful, being, fatal, frail, human, party **6** deadly, finite, lethal, person **7** deathly, earthly, extreme, fleshly, massive, tedious **8** creature, hominine, possible, probable, ruthless, temporal, towering **9** fantastic, merciless, monstrous, personage, pestilent **10** implacable, individual, ironfisted, monumental, prodigious, relentless, stupendous, tremendous, unyielding **11** conceivable, mortiferous, unflinching, unrelenting **12** overpowering, pestilential, unappeasable

mortality 5 flesh **7** mankind **8** fatality, humanity **9** humankind, lethality **10** deadliness

mortally 4 very **7** awfully, fatally, vitally **8** terribly **9** extremely, intensely **10** dreadfully, grievously **11** exceedingly

Morte d'Arthur author 6 Malory

mortgage 4 hock, pawn **6** pledge **10** obligation

mortician 8 embalmer **10** undertaker

mortiferous 5 fatal **6** deadly, lethal, mortal **7** deathly **9** pestilent **12** pestilential

mortified 5 stern **6** severe, shamed **7** ascetic, ashamed, austere **9** chagrined

mortuary 8 tumulary **10** sepulchral **11** funeral home

mosaic 5 inlay **7** chimera **8** terrazzo **9** composite, patchwork **12** tessellation *piece:* **6** smalto **7** tessera **8** tesserae (plural)

Moscow *citadel:* **7** Kremlin *resident:* **9** Muscovite

Moses *brother:* **5** Aaron *brother-in-law:* **5** Hobab *deathplace:* **4** Nebo *father-in-law:* **6** Jethro *sister:* **6** Miriam *son:* **7** Eliezer, Gershom *spy:* **5** Caleb *successor:* **6** Joshua *wife:* **8** Zipporah

mosey 4 mope **5** amble, drift **6** bummel, linger, ramble, stroll, wander **7** saunter

Moslem see **Muslim**

mosque 6 masjid *niche:* **6** mihrab *prayer caller:* **7** muezzin *pulpit:* **6** mimbar *turret:* **7** minaret

mosquito 5 culex **7** culicid **8** culicine *genus:* **5** Aëdes, Culex **9** Anopheles

moss 9 bryophyte *kind:* **8** sphagnum *part:* **4** seta **7** capsule, rhizoid *study of:* **8** bryology

mossback 4 fogy, hick **5** yokel **6** fogram, fossil, rustic, square **7** bumpkin, hayseed

9 hillbilly **10** clodhopper, fuddy-duddy, provincial **12** antediluvian, backwoodsman, mid-Victorian **13** stick-in-the-mud

most 3 too **4** best, much, nigh, very **5** about, chief, super **6** all but, better, nearly, utmost **7** greater, highest, largest, maximum **8** greatest, majority, mightily, mortally, well-nigh **9** eminently, extremely, principal **10** remarkably **11** exceedingly, practically **12** surpassingly **13** approximately

mostly 6 mainly **7** chiefly, largely, overall, usually **9** generally, primarily **11** principally **13** predominantly

mote 3 dot **4** hill **5** point, speck **6** barrow, height **7** tumulus **8** flyspeck, particle

moth 6 tineid **7** tineoid **8** bombycid *immature:* **5** larva **6** larvae (plural) **11** caterpillar *kind:* **4** luna **7** codling, tussock **8** Cecropia, silkworm **9** browntail *order:* **11** Lepidoptera

moth-eaten 4 worn **5** dated, dingy, faded, moldy, passé, seedy **6** bygone, old hat, patchy, rococo, shabby, tagrag **7** archaic, raggedy, run-down, unkempt **8** decrepit, outdated, outmoded, tattered **10** antiquated, down-at-heel, threadbare **11** dilapidated

mother 2 ma **3** dam, mom **4** mama, root **5** fount, mamma, mammy, mater, momma, mommy, mummy, nurse, serve **6** mammie, origin, source, wait on **7** care for, nurture, produce, rootage **9** prototype, rootstock **10** minister to, provenance, wellspring *combining form:* **4** matr **5** matri, matro

mother country 4 home, land, soil **8** homeland **10** fatherland

Mother Courage author 6 Brecht

Mother of Presidents 8 Virginia

Mother of the Gods 3 Ops **4** Rhea

motif 4 head, text **5** point, theme, topic **6** design, device, figure, matter **7** pattern, subject **8** argument **13** subject matter

motion 4 flag, move, sign, stir, sway **5** swing **6** signal **7** gesture **8** carriage, movement, proposal, stirring, wavering **9** agitation, signalize **10** suggestion **11** application, fluctuation, oscillation *combining form:* **3** cin, kin **4** cino, kine, kino, moto **5** cinet, kinet, phoro **6** cineto, kineto, praxia, praxis **7** cinesia, kinesia

motionless 5 fixed, inert, rigid, still **6** static **8** becalmed, immobile, immotile, immotive, stagnant, unmoving **9** immovable, sedentary, steadfast, unmovable **10** stationary, stock-still, stone-still

motion picture see **movie**

motivate 4 move **5** impel, pique, rouse **6** excite, incite, induce **7** innerve, inspire, provoke, quicken **9** galvanize, influence, innervate, stimulate

motivation 4 spur 5 drive 7 impetus,
impulse 8 catalyst, stimulus 9 incentive,
stimulant 10 incitation, incitement
11 instigation
motive 3 aim, end 4 good, head, spur,
text 5 cause, point, theme, topic 6 design,
device, figure, intent, matter, object, reason,
spring 7 impulse, pattern, purpose, subject 8 argument, stimulus 9 incentive,
intention 10 incitement, inducement
motley 4 fool 5 idiot, mixed, salad
6 jester, jumble, medley, varied 7 dappled,
diverse, mottled, piebald 8 assorted, chowchow, discolor, pastiche 9 colluvies, multihued 10 assortment, hodgepodge, miscellany, multicolor, variegated, versicolor
11 gallimaufry, promiscuous, varicolored
12 conglomerate, multicolored, multifarious,
parti-colored, versicolored 13 heterogeneous, miscellaneous *combining form:*
5 parti, party
motor 3 car 4 auto, ride, tool 5 buggy,
drive, pilot, wheel 6 engine 7 autocar,
machine 10 automobile
motorbike 5 moped
motorboat 7 cruiser, inboard 8 outboard,
runabout 12 cabin cruiser
motorcar 4 auto 5 buggy 10 automobile
motorcycle 7 chopper 8 minibike 9 trail
bike *adjunct:* 7 sidecar
motorist 6 driver 7 autoist 8 operator
12 automobilist
Motown 7 Detroit
mottle 4 spot 6 blotch, marble 7 splotch
motto 3 cry 5 adage, axiom, maxim
6 byword, saying, slogan, war cry 7 precept 8 aphorism 9 battle cry, catchword,
watchword 10 shibboleth 11 catchphrase,
rallying cry
moue 3 mow, mug 4 face, pout 5 mouth
7 grimace 8 mouthing
mound 4 bank, cock, heap, hill, hump,
mass, pile 5 cairn, drift, shock, stack 6 barrow, tumuli (plural) 7 bulwark, hillock, rampart, tumulus 8 mountain 9 elevation
10 embankment *Buddhist:* 5 stupa *burial,
Eastern Europe:* 6 kurgan *burial, Peruvian:* 5 huaca *of detritus:* 4 kame *of
sand:* 4 dune *of stones:* 5 cairn *Polynesian:* 3 ahu *Scottish:* 5 toman
mound-like 7 tumular
mount 2 up 3 alp, wax 4 back, hill, lift,
peak, pony, rise, show, soar, upgo 5 arise,
build, climb, frame, horse, put on, rouse,
scale, stage, steed, stuff 6 ascend, aspire,
deepen, expand, uprear 7 advance, augment, enhance, enlarge, magnify, produce,
support, upclimb, upsurge 8 bestride, escalade, escalate, heighten, increase, multiply,
redouble 9 aggravate, intensate, intensify
10 promontory

mountain 3 alp, lot 4 bank, dome, heap,
hill, hulk, lump, mass, mesa, much, peak,
peck, pile, slew 5 bluff, butte, drift, mound,
shock, stack 6 hurdle, sierra 8 obstacle
10 impediment 11 obstruction *Alaska:*
4 Bona 7 Foraker, Sanford 8 Wrangell
Alberta: 6 Castle 10 Eisenhower *Alps-
'highest:* 5 Blanc *Angola's highest:*
4 Moco *Antarctica:* 4 Mohl 7 Gardner
9 Elizabeth 12 Vinson Massif *Appalachians:* 10 Kittatinny *Argentina:* 9 Aconcagua
Australia: 4 Ziel 5 Bruce 6 Cradle 9 Kosciusko *beyond the:* 10 tramontane
11 transalpine *biblical:* 5 Horeb, Tabor
6 Hermon 8 Har Tavor *Black Hills:* 10 Har-
ney Peak *Bolivia:* 6 Sorata 8 Illimani *Borneo:* 8 Kinabalu, Kinabulu *California:*
5 Guyot 7 Palomar 8 Tuolumne 10 Buena
Vista, Sonora Peak, Stanislaus *China:*
4 Emei, Song *Colorado:* 9 Pikes Peak
13 Purgatory Peak *combining form:* 3 ore,
oro 4 oreo *Connecticut's highest:* 8 Fris-
sell *Costa Rica:* 6 Blanco 14 Chirripó
Grande *Cyprus' highest:* 7 Olympus, Troo-
dos *depression:* 3 col *Dominican Republic:* 6 Duarte 8 Trujillo *Egypt:* 4 Musa
5 Sinai *Fiji:* 8 Victoria 9 Tomaniivi *foot:*
8 piedmont *Gabon:* 8 Iboundji *Georgia:*
8 Springer 10 Oglethorpe *Germany:* 7 Zol-
lern 11 Fichtelberg *Greece:* 5 Ida 5 Athos,
Levka 7 Helicon 9 Parnassus, Psiloriti
10 Pendelikon, Pentelicus *Greenland:*
9 Gunnbjørn *Himalayas:* 10 Kula Kangri
India: 5 Japvo *Indonesia:* 4 Lawu
5 Kwoka, Lawoe, Raung 6 Raoeng *Israel:*
5 Meron 6 Carmel *Ivory Coast:* 5 Nimba
Japan: 4 Fuji 5 Iwate 7 Fujisan 8 Fuji-
yama 9 Iwate-yama 10 Fuji-no-Yama
Java: 5 Liman *Jordan:* 3 Hor 5 Harūn
Malaysia: 5 Ophir, Tahan 6 Ledang *Mediterranean entrance:* 5 Calpe 15 Rock of
Gibraltar *New York:* 4 Bear *North Ameri-
ca's highest:* 8 McKinley *Oman:* 4 Sham
Pakistan: 9 Tirich Mir *Papua New
Guinea:* 7 Wilhelm *Pennine Aips:* 4 Rosa
Philippines: 3 Apo, Iba 4 Labo 5 Silay
ridge: 4 spur 5 arête, crest 7 sawbuck
Romania: 11 Moldoveanul *South America:* 7 Roraima *South Dakota:* 10 Custer
Peak *Syria:* 4 Druz 5 Druze, Duruz *Tanzania:* 11 Kilimanjaro *Tasmania's highest:*
4 Ossa *Tennessee:* 7 Jumpoff, Lookout
11 Chimney Tops 13 Clingmans Dome
Togo: 4 Agou *Vermont:* 11 Glastenbury
Vietnam: 8 Ngoo Linh *West Africa:*
8 Cameroon *western hemisphere's highest:* 9 Aconcagua *world's highest:* 7 Ever-
est; (see also **peak**)
mountain chain *Asia:* 8 Tien Shan
Greece: 4 Oeta *Turkey:* 6 Taurus
mountain climbing *equipment:* 2 ax

3 axe, nut **5** piton **7** crampon **9** carabiner *maneuver:* **6** rappel **10** rappelling

mountain dew see **moonshine**

mountain formation 7 orogeny **9** orogenesy **10** orogenesis

mountain group *Czechoslovakia:* **5** Tatra **9** High Tatra *Germany:* **4** Harz *Idaho:* **10** Clearwater *New York:* **8** Catskill **10** Adirondack *Sinai:* **9** Gebel Musa *South Dakota-Wyoming:* **10** Black Hills *Utah:* **5** La Sal *Washington:* **7** Olympic *Zimbabwe:* **11** Matopo Hills **12** Matoppo Hills

mountainous 4 huge, vast **6** mighty **7** immense, mammoth, massive **8** enormous, gigantic **10** monumental, prodigious

mountain pass *Afghanistan-Pakistan:* **6** Khyber *Alps:* **5** Gries *California:* **4** Muir **6** Sonora *China-Myanmar:* **5** Namni *Colorado:* **3** Ute **5** Mosca, Muddy, Music, Raton *Europe:* **8** Moravian *Greece:* **5** Rupel *Hindu Kush Mts.:* **5** Dorah, Durah *Pakistan:* **5** Bolan, Gomal, Gumal *Sierra Nevada:* **4** Mono *Switzerland:* **5** Furka, Gemmi **7** Grimsel **8** Lötschen *Tunisia:* **4** Faïd *Ukrainian:* **5** Uzhok *Wyoming:* **5** Union

mountain range *Alaska:* **6** Brooks **7** Chugach **8** Wrangell *Alaska-Canada:* **10** Saint Elias *Algeria:* **3** Zab *Alps:* **8** Bavarian *ancient Edom:* **4** Seir *Antarctica:* **9** Ellsworth *Appalachian:* **4** Bald, Blue **5** Green **6** Unicoi **10** Great Smoky **12** Great Smokies *Arizona:* **8** Maricopa **10** Chiricahua *Australia:* **7** Darling **10** Macpherson *Brazil:* **5** Organ *California:* **4** Inyo **6** Nevada **7** Klamath **10** San Gabriel **13** San Bernardino *Canada:* **10** Laurentian *central Asia:* **9** Hindu Kush **11** Paropamisus *China:* **5** Helan *Colorado:* **7** San Juan *Czechoslovakia:* **11** East Beskids, West Beskids *England:* **12** Pennine Chain *Ethiopia:* **4** Gugu *Eurasia:* **8** Caucasus *Europe:* **4** Jura **8** Pyrenees *France:* **6** Vosges **8** Cévennes *Germany:* **4** Rhön **13** Thüringer Wald *Greece:* **6** Othris, Othrys, Pindus **7** Olympus **8** Taygetus *Hawaii:* **7** Waianae *Himalayas:* **8** Anapurna **9** Annapurna *Idaho:* **5** Lemhi **7** Wasatch *India:* **7** Vindhya **12** Eastern Ghats, Western Ghats *Indonesia:* **5** Maoke *Iran:* **6** Elburz *Iran-Turkmenistan:* **8** Kopet Dag *Ireland:* **7** Wicklow *Italy:* **9** Apennines *Kazakhstan-Russia:* **4** Ural *Kirghizia:* **4** Alai *McKinley's:* **6** Alaska *Massachusetts:* **6** Hoosac *Mexico:* **11** Sierra Madre *Minnesota:* **6** Mesabi *New Hampshire:* **12** Presidential *New Jersey:* **6** Ramapo *New Zealand:* **12** Southern Alps *North Carolina:* **5** Black *Northern Ireland:* **6** Mourne *Pakistan:*

8 Sulaiman *Papua New Guinea:* **6** Albert **11** Owen Stanley *Philippines:* **11** Sierra Madre *Rockies:* **11** Medicine Bow *Russia:* **8** Barguzin, Stanovoi *Scandinavia:* **5** Kölen **6** Kjølen *South Africa:* **9** Nieuwveld **10** Kwathlamba, Quathlamba **11** Drakensberg *South Asia:* **5** Ladak **6** Ladakh *Spain:* **6** Morena, Toledo **8** Maladeta **10** Cantabrian *United States:* **5** Uinta **7** Cascade **8** Gallatin, Ouachita *Venezuela:* **6** Mérida *Wales:* **8** Cambrian *Washington:* **6** Chelan *Wyoming:* **5** Teton **11** Sierra Madre *Yosemite National Park:* **9** Cathedral

mountains *Algeria:* **6** Hoggar **7** Ahaggar *Czechoslovakia:* **5** Tatra **9** High Tatra *England:* **8** Cumbrian *Idaho:* **10** Clearwater *New Hampshire:* **5** White *New York:* **8** Catskill **10** Adirondack *Pennsylvania:* **6** Pocono *study of:* **7** orology *Sudan:* **4** Nuba *Utah:* **5** La Sal *Washington:* **7** Olympic *western North America:* **11** Coast Ranges

mountain sickness 4 veta **7** soroche

Mountain State 7 Montana **12** West Virginia

mountain system *Asia:* **5** Altai **8** Himalaya **9** Himalayas *Europe:* **4** Alps **10** Carpathian *Iran:* **6** Zagros *North Africa:* **5** Atlas *North America:* **5** Rocky **7** Rockies **11** Appalachian **12** Appalachians *Scotland:* **9** Grampians **13** Grampian Hills *South America:* **5** Andes

mountebank 3 gyp **5** cheat, quack **6** con man **7** diddler, sharper **8** swindler **9** charlatan, defrauder, pretender, quackster **11** flimflammer, quacksalver **12** doubledealer, saltimbanque **13** confidence man

Mount St. Helens 7 volcano

mourn 3 rue **6** bemoan, bewail, grieve, lament, sorrow **7** protest

mournful 3 sad **4** dire **5** sorry **6** dismal, rueful, somber, triste, woeful **7** doleful, joyless, unhappy **8** dolesome, dolorous, funereal, grievous, saddened **9** plaintive, saddening, sorrowful **10** afflictive, calamitous, deplorable, depressing, dispirited, lamentable, lugubrious, melancholy **11** distressing, melancholic, regrettable, unfortunate **12** heavyhearted

mournfulness 5 blues, dumps, gloom **7** sadness **9** dejection **10** depression, melancholy, the dismals **11** unhappiness

Mourning Becomes Electra *author:* **6** O'Neill

mourning period *Jewish:* **5** shiva **6** shibah, shivah

mourning symbol 7 armband

mouse 3 pry **4** hunt, nose, poke, slip **5** creep, glide, slide, snoop, steal **6** shiner

7 explore, saunter 8 black eye, busybody *combining form:* 2 my 3 myo, mys

mouth 3 eat, gab, gob, mop, mow, yap 4 blow, brag, crow, face, guff, moue, puff, rail, rant, rave, sass, talk, tell, trap 5 boast, orate, prate, sauce, speak, spill, vaunt, voice 6 betray, mumble, palate, recite, reveal, tongue 7 blab out, declaim, divulge, grimace, soapbox, speaker, unclose 8 back talk, bloviate, disclose, discover, entrance, give away, harangue, perorate 9 gasconade, impudence, pronounce, spokesman 10 embouchure, volubility 11 rodomontade, spokeswoman 12 embouchement, spokesperson *combining form:* 3 ori, oro 4 stom 5 stoma, stome, stomi, stomo, stomy 6 stomat, stomia, stomum 7 stomata, stomate, stomato, stomous 9 stomatous

mouthing 3 mow, mug 4 face 7 grimace

mouthlike opening 5 stoma 7 stomata (plural)

mouthpiece 7 speaker 9 spokesman 11 spokeswoman 12 spokesperson

mouthward 4 orad

mouth-watering 5 sapid, tasty 6 savory, toothy 8 tasteful 9 aperitive, delicious, palatable, relishing 10 appetizing 11 goodtasting

mouthy 5 talky 9 bombastic, garrulous, talkative

movable 5 loose 6 mobile, motile, moving, roving 8 unstable, unsteady 10 changeable 11 unsteadfast

movables 5 goods 7 effects 8 chattels 10 belongings

move 2 go 3 act, hum 4 bear, blow, exit, goad, go on, lead, live, spur, step, stir, sway, turn, void 5 bring, budge, carry, drive, exist, get on, impel, leave, march, pique, rouse, shift, start, touch 6 acquit, affect, behave, convey, demean, depart, deport, excite, get off, incite, induce, kindle, motion, prompt, propel 7 actuate, advance, agitate, animate, breathe, comport, conduct, convert, disturb, get away, impress, innerve, inspire, measure, migrate, proceed, propose, provoke, pull out, replace, request, suggest, take off 8 activate, dislodge, displace, evacuate, get along, maneuver, mobilize, motivate, persuade, progress, relocate, resettle, stirring, supplant, transfer, transmit, withdraw 9 dislocate, galvanize, influence, innervate, instigate, stimulate, supersede, transport 10 proceeding

movement 3 act 4 deed, stir, time 5 tempo, trend 6 action, motion, rhythm 8 activity, dynamism, liveness, maneuver, stirring, tendency *away:* 6 exodus *combining form:* 3 cin, kin 4 cino, kine, kino 5 cinet, kinet 6 cineto, kineto 7 cinesia, kinesia *music:* 4 moto *reflex:* 5 taxis *stimulated:* 7 kinesis

movie 4 cine, film, show 5 flick 6 cinema 7 picture 9 photoplay 11 picture show 13 motion picture, moving picture *combining form:* 4 cine *cowboy:* 5 oater 7 western *short:* 4 clip 8 newsreel

movie director *American:* 3 Lee 4 Ford, Wise 5 Allen, Roach, Stone, Vidor, Wyler 6 Curtiz, Huston, Welles, Wilder 7 Coppola, Fleming, Kubrick, Nichols, Pollack, Stevens, Sturges 8 Minnelli, Scorsese 9 Hitchcock, Preminger, Spielberg, Sternberg *Austrian:* 4 Lang 8 Stroheim *French:* 4 Tati 5 Malle 6 Godard, Renoir 8 Truffaut *German:* 6 Herzog 10 Fassbinder 11 Riefenstahl *Italian:* 5 Leone 7 Fellini 8 Visconti 10 Bertolucci, Rossellini *Russian:* 10 Eisenstein *Swedish:* 7 Bergman 10 Zetterling

movie producer *American:* 5 Mayer, Roach 6 Kramer, Warner, Welles, Zanuck 7 De Mille, Goldwyn, Sennett 8 Griffith, Selznick *Austrian:* 9 Reinhardt *French:* 6 Renoir

moving 5 astir 6 mobile 7 emotive, rousing 8 arousing, exciting, gripping, pathetic, poignant, rallying, stirring, touching, unstable, unsteady 9 actuating, affecting, affective, awakening, emotional, provoking, transient 10 ambulatory, impressive 11 stimulating, unsteadfast

moving picture see **movie**

moving stairs 9 escalator

mow 3 cut, mop, mug 4 bank, clip, cock, crop, down, drop, face, fell, heap, hill, kill, moue, pile, rick, rout 5 drift, floor, level, mouth, shock, smash, stack 6 ground 7 grimace 8 bowl down, bowl over, mouthing 9 bring down, knock down, throw down

moxie 2 go 3 pep 4 birr, grit, guts, tuck 5 heart, nerve, pluck, spunk, vigor 6 energy, mettle, spirit 7 cojones, courage, potency 8 backbone 9 fortitude, hardihood 10 resolution 13 dauntlessness

Mozart *birthplace:* 8 Salzburg *cataloger:* 6 Köchel *deathplace:* 6 Vienna *opera:* 8 Idomeneo 10 Magic Flute 11 Don Giovanni 12 Cosi fan Tutte

MP's prey 4 AWOL 8 deserter

Mrs. Grundy 4 prig 5 prude 7 puritan 8 bluenose, comstock 9 nice Nelly 10 goody-goody

much 3 lot, oft 4 good, heap, long, lots, lump, many, mass, most, nigh, pack, peck, pile, scad, very 5 about, often 6 all but, almost, highly, hugely, nearly, plenty 7 greatly, notably 8 abundant, lashings, ofttimes, well-nigh 9 eminently, extremely, great deal, multitude 10 frequently, oftentimes, repeatedly *combining form:* 4 poly 5 multi

Much Ado About Nothing *character:*
4 Hero 7 Claudio, Don John 8 Beatrice, Benedick

much as 4 when 5 while 6 albeit, though 7 howbeit, whereas 8 although

muck 3 goo 4 crap, dirt, dung, gook, goop, grub, gunk, junk, mess, mire, murk, plod, slog, slum, soil, toil 5 dirty, filth, grime, grind, gumbo, muddy, offal, slave, slime, swill, trash, waste 6 debris, drudge, litter, manure, refuse, sludge, smirch, smooch, smudge, smutch 7 garbage, rubbish

muckamuck 3 VIP 5 nabob 6 bigwig 7 big shot, notable 8 somebody 9 dignitary 10 notability

mucker 3 cad, oaf 4 boor, punk, worm 5 botch, chuff, churl, clown, gum up, rough, rowdy, tough, yahoo 6 bobble, bollix, bungle, no-good, wretch 7 bitch up, blunder, grobian, louse up, lowlife, ruffian, toughie 8 bullyboy, wormling 9 roughneck 10 clodhopper

mucky 4 foul 5 black, dirty, dungy, humid, messy, muddy, muggy, murky, nasty, soggy 6 cloudy, filthy, grubby, sordid, sticky, sultry 7 clouded, squalid, unclean

mucous 5 slimy 6 viscid

mucronate 5 acute, piked, sharp 6 peaked 7 pointed 8 acicular 9 aciculate, acuminate, acuminous, cuspidate

mucus 9 secretion

mud 4 dirt, mire, ooze, rile, roil 5 dregs, slime 6 depths, sludge *combining form:* 3 pel 4 pelo

muddle 3 mix 4 blow, daze, hash, limp, mess, muck, mull, muss, rile, roil 5 addle, botch, mix up, muddy, ravel, snarl, waste 6 ataxia, drivel, foul up, fuddle, fumble, huddle, jumble, jungle, litter, mess up, mumble, murmur, muss up, mutter, tangle, tumble 7 clutter, confuse, fluster, fritter, perplex, rummage, shuffle, snarl up, stumble, stupefy, swallow 8 befuddle, bewilder, botchery, cast away, confound, disarray, disorder, distract, entangle, mishmash, scramble, shambles, squander, throw off, unsettle 9 confusion, throw away 10 complicate, disarrange, discompose, frivol away, trifle away 11 blunder away, disorganize

muddled 5 drunk, tight, tipsy, vague 6 cloudy 7 mixed-up 8 inchoate 9 disguised, pixilated 10 disjointed, disordered, incoherent, incohesive, inebriated 11 intoxicated, unconnected, unorganized 12 disconnected, uncontinuous 13 discontinuous

muddlehead 4 dolt 5 dunce, idiot, moron 6 dimwit 7 fathead 8 dumbbell 9 blockhead, simpleton 11 chowderhead

muddle through 2 do 4 fare 5 get by, get on, shift 6 manage 8 get along 9 stagger on 12 stagger along

muddy 3 dim, fog 4 base, blur, drab, dull, fade, foul, miry, oozy, pale, rile, roil, soil 5 befog, black, cloud, dirty, dungy, grime, murky, riley, roily, soily 6 cloudy, gloomy, sordid, turbid 7 becloud, begrime, bemired, confuse, squalid, subfusc, tarnish, unclean, unclear 8 confused 9 uncleanly

mudfish 6 bowfin

muezzin's faith 5 Islam

muff 4 blow, flub 5 botch, error, fluff 6 bobble, bollix, bungle, fumble, goof up 7 louse up

muffle 4 dull, mute, veil 5 shush 6 dampen, deaden, lessen, shroud, soften, stifle, subdue, wrap up 7 envelop, repress, silence, smother, squelch 8 bundle up, strangle, suppress, tone down 10 overspread

muffler 4 mask, veil 5 cloak, cover, guise, scarf 6 facade, veneer 8 disguise 10 masquerade 12 disguisement

muffler mangler 3 rut 7 pothole 9 chuckhole

mug 3 cup, mop, mow 4 boob, dolt, dope, face, fool, moue, phiz, punk, puss, thug, toby 5 dunce, grail, idiot, mouth, rough, rowdy, stein, stoup, tough 6 dimwit, mucker, seidel, visage 7 assault, chalice, grimace, ruffian, tankard 8 bullyboy, dumbbell, features, mouthing, numskull, plug-ugly, schooner 9 blockhead, ignoramus, roughneck 11 countenance

mugger 4 thug 9 assailant, assaulter

muggy 4 damp 5 humid, moist, mucky, soggy 6 moisty, sticky, sultry 7 dampish, wettish

Muhammad, Mohammed *adopted son:* 3 Ali *birthplace:* 5 Mecca *camel:* 5 Kaswa *daughter:* 6 Fatima *deathplace:* 6 Medina *deity:* 5 Allah *father:* 8 Abdallah, Abdullah *father-in-law:* 7 Abu Bakr *flight:* 6 hegira, hejira *follower:* 6 Moslem, Muslim *horse:* 5 Buraq 7 Alborak *religion:* 5 Islam *son:* 7 Ibrahim *son-in-law:* 3 Ali *successor:* 5 calif 6 caliph 7 Abu Bakr *tribe:* 7 Koreish *uncle:* 8 Abu Talib *wife:* 5 Aisha 6 Ayesha 7 Khadija

mulct 4 fine, milk, rook 5 bleed, cheat, stick, sweat 6 amerce, fleece 7 deceive, defraud, forfeit, penalty, swindle 8 penalize 10 amercement

mule 5 cross 6 hybrid 7 bastard, mongrel 9 crossbred, half blood, half-breed 10 crossbreed

muleheaded *see* **mulish**

mulish 5 balky 6 unruly 8 perverse, stubborn 9 obstinate, pigheaded 10 bullheaded, headstrong, inflexible, refractory, self-willed, unyielding 11 stiff-necked, wrongheaded

mull 4 hash, mess, muse, muss, numb,

poke, roll, stir **5** addle, blunt, botch, dally, delay, mix-up, tarry, think **6** ball up, bemuse, benumb, dawdle, deaden, fuddle, linger, loiter, mess-up, muddle, ponder, put off **7** confuse, crumble **8** befuddle, bewilder, botchery, cogitate, consider, distract, meditate, ruminate, shambles, throw off, turn over **9** pulverize **10** deliberate, dillydally **11** desensitize **13** procrastinate

mulligrubs **4** sulk **5** blues, dumps, gloom, mumps, pouts **6** grumps **7** sullens **9** dejection **10** depression, melancholy

multicolored **4** pied **6** motley **7** dappled **8** discolor **10** variegated, versicolor

multifarious **4** many **5** mixed **6** legion, motley, sundry, varied **7** diverse, various **8** assorted, chowchow, manifold, numerous, populous **10** voluminous **11** diversiform, promiscuous **12** conglomerate **13** heterogeneous, miscellaneous

multiform **7** diverse **8** manifold **11** diversiform **12** multifarious, multivarious

multiformity **7** variety **8** multeity **9** diversity **11** diverseness, variousness **12** multiplicity

multihued see **multicolored**

multilateral **9** many-sided

multiloquent **5** gabby, talky **6** chatty **9** garrulous, talkative **10** babblative, loquacious **11** loose-lipped **12** loose-tongued

multiplex see **multiform**

multiplicity **3** lot **4** mass, much, peck **6** barrel **7** variety **8** multeity **9** diversity, great deal **11** diverseness, variousness

multiply **3** wax **4** bear, rise **5** beget, boost, breed, build, mount **6** beef up, expand, extend, spread **7** amplify, augment, enlarge, magnify, produce, upsurge **8** generate, heighten, increase **9** procreate, propagate, reproduce **10** aggrandize

multitude **3** mob **4** army, host, many, rout **5** cloud, crowd, crush, drove, flock, horde, press, swarm **6** legion, oodles, public, scores, squash, throng **7** numbers

multitudinal see **multitudinous**

multitudinous **4** many **6** legion, myriad, sundry **7** various **8** manifold, numerous, populous **9** countless **10** innumerous, numberless, voluminous **11** innumerable **12** multifarious

multivocal **7** blatant **8** strident **9** clamorous, equivocal **10** boisterous, vociferant, vociferous **11** loudmouthed, openmouthed **12** obstreperous

mum **4** dumb, mute **5** still **6** silent **7** silence **8** wordless **10** speechless

mumble **4** chew **5** mouth, rumor **6** muddle, murmur, mutter **7** maunder, swallow, whisper **9** undertone **11** susurration

mumbo jumbo **7** mummery **9** gibberish **10** hocus pocus **11** abracadabra

mummer **4** mime **5** actor, mimic **6** player **7** trouper **8** thespian **9** performer, playactor **12** impersonator

mummery **6** acting **9** gibberish, hypocrisy **10** hocus pocus, mumbo jumbo **11** abracadabra

mummify **4** wilt **5** dry up, wizen **6** welter, wither **7** shrivel

mumpish **4** dour, ugly **5** sulky, surly **6** morose, sullen **9** saturnine

munch **3** eat **4** bite, chew **5** champ, chomp, chump **6** crunch **7** chumble, scrunch **8** ruminate **9** masticate

mundane **5** lowly **6** cosmic, earthy **7** earthly, prosaic, sensual, terrene, workday, worldly **8** banausic, everyday, telluric, workaday **9** sublunary, tellurian **11** commonplace, terrestrial, uncelestial **13** materialistic

municipal **4** city, home **5** urban **6** native **7** burghal **8** domestic, internal, national **9** intestine

munificent **4** free **6** lavish **7** liberal **8** generous, handsome **9** bounteous, bountiful, unsparing **10** freehanded, openhanded

munitions maker **5** Krupp

murder **4** cool, do in, hang, kill, slay **5** abate, blood, lynch, scrag **6** finish, mangle, rub out **7** abolish, blot out, destroy, execute, garrote, killing, put away, root out, smother **8** foul play, homicide, knock off, strangle, uncreate **9** eradicate, liquidate, slaughter **10** annihilate, asphyxiate, decapitate, extinguish, guillotine **11** assassinate, electrocute, exterminate **12** manslaughter **brother:** **10** fratricide **father:** **9** patricide **king:** **8** regicide **mother:** **9** matricide **parent:** **9** parricide **sister:** **10** sororicide

murderer **6** killer, slayer **7** butcher **8** assassin, homicide **9** manslayer **11** slaughterer

Murder in the Cathedral **author:** **5** Eliot **character:** **5** Henry **7** Beckett

murderous **6** brutal **9** ferocious **11** devastating **12** bloodthirsty

mure **3** pen **4** cage, wall **5** fence, hedge **6** shut in, thrust **7** close in, enclose, envelop, squeeze

murk **3** dim, fog **4** foul, haze, mist, soil **5** bedim, cloud, dirty, gloom, grime, muddy **6** besoil, darken, smirch, smudge **7** becloud, begrime, obscure, tarnish **8** darkness **9** obfuscate

murky **3** dim, dun **4** dark, drab, dull, dusk, foul **5** black, dirty, dusky, foggy, misty, muddy, nasty, roily **6** cloudy, filthy, gloomy, grubby, opaque, somber, sordid, turbid **7** obscure, squalid, subfusc, unclean **8** nubilous **9** ambiguous, equivocal, sibylline, tenebrous **10** caliginous

murmur **3** cry, hum **4** buzz, fuss, kick,

purr, talk, wail **5** croak, drone, rumor, scold, whine **6** fumble, gossip, grouch, grouse, muddle, mumble, mutter, repine, report, rumble **7** grumble, hearsay, swallow, whisper **8** complain **9** grapevine, grumbling, undertone **11** scuttlebutt, susurration

muscle 4 beef, thew **5** brawn, force, might, power, sinew **6** energy **7** potency **8** strength **9** necessity, strong arm *arm:* **6** biceps **7** triceps *back:* **9** trapezius *calf:* **6** soleus *chest:* **10** pectoralis *combining form:* **2** ei (plural) **3** eus, mya **6** muscul, myaria (plural) **7** musculo *jaw:* **8** masseter *kind:* **6** flexor, tensor **7** dilator, evertor, levator, rotator **8** abductor, adductor, extensor *loin:* **5** psoas *neck:* **8** platysma *shoulder:* **7** deltoid **10** deltoideus *study of:* **7** myology *thigh:* **8** gracilis **9** sartorius

muscle-bound 5 rigid, stiff **6** wooden **7** buckram, stilted **9** cardboard

muscular 4 ropy, wiry **5** beefy, burly, husky, stout **6** brawny, mighty, robust, sinewy, strong, sturdy, supple **7** fibrous, stringy, well-set **8** athletic, forceful, powerful, stalwart, vigorous, well-knit **9** Herculean, well-built

muse 4 bard, poet **5** study, think **6** ponder, trance **7** reflect, reverie **8** cogitate, meditate, mull over, ruminate, turn over **10** deliberate, excogitate **11** contemplate

Muse *father:* **4** Zeus **7** Jupiter *mother:* **9** Mnemosyne *of astronomy:* **6** Urania *of choral song:* **11** Terpsichore *of comedy:* **6** Thalia *of dancing:* **11** Terpsichore *of epic poetry:* **8** Calliope *of history:* **4** Clio *of love poetry:* **5** Erato *of lyric poetry:* **5** Erato *of music:* **7** Euterpe *of pastoral poetry:* **6** Thalia *of sacred poetry:* **8** Polymnia **10** Polyhymnia *of tragedy:* **9** Melpomene

museum 5 salon **7** exhibit, gallery **8** atheneum **10** collection, repository **11** pinacotheka

Mushi's father 6 Merari

mushroom 4 grow **5** burst, go off **6** blow up, expand, spread **7** explode **8** detonate *combining form:* **3** myc **4** myco **5** mycet **6** myceto *edible:* **5** morel **10** champignon **11** chanterelle *kind:* **6** agaric, bolete **7** inky cap, russula *part:* **3** cap **4** gill, ring **5** stipe, volva **6** pileus **7** annulus **8** mycelium *poisonous:* **7** amanita **8** death cup **9** toadstool

mushy 4 hazy, soft, weak **5** foggy, misty, pappy, pulpy, vague **6** cloudy, quaggy, spongy, sticky, vapory **7** blurred, maudlin, mawkish, pulpous, squashy, squishy, squushy **8** bathetic, effusive, romantic, sluggish, squelchy, vaporous **10** lovey-dovey **11** sentimental, tear-jerking

music *abbreviation:* **2** ff, mf, mp, pp, sf **3** sfz *bass staff lines:* **5** GBDFA *bass staff*

spaces: **4** ACEG *characteristic phrase:* **9** leitmotif, leitmotiv *chord:* **5** tonic **8** dominant **9** augmented **10** diminished *embellishment:* **3** run **4** turn **5** trill **7** cadenza, mordent, roulade **8** arpeggio, flourish **9** grace note *for eight:* **5** octet *for five:* **7** quintet *for four:* **7** quartet *for nine:* **5** nonet *for one:* **4** solo *for seven:* **6** septet *for six:* **6** sextet *for three:* **4** trio *for two:* **3** duo **4** duet *god:* **6** Apollo *hall:* **7** cabaret, theater *instrumental form:* **3** jig **4** jazz, reel **5** étude, fugue, gigue, march, polka, rondo, suite, swing, waltz **6** minuet, pavane, sonata **7** bourrée, gavotte, mazurka, prelude, ragtime, toccata **8** chaconne, concerto, courante, fantasia, galliard, nocturne, overture, rhapsody, ricercar, saraband, serenade, symphony, tone poem **9** allemande, polonaise **11** rock and roll *medley:* **4** olio *morning:* **6** aubade *Muse:* **7** Euterpe *night:* **8** nocturne, serenade *note:* **4** half **5** breve, minim, neume, whole **6** eighth **7** quarter **8** sixteenth *patron saint:* **7** Cecilia *period:* **6** Modern, Rococo **7** Baroque **8** Medieval, Romantic **9** Classical *reformer:* **5** Guido *symbol:* **3** bar, key **4** clef, flat, note, rest, slur, turn **5** sharp, staff **7** fermata, mordent **9** alla breve **10** accidental *treble staff lines:* **5** EGBDF *treble staff spaces:* **4** FACE *vocal form:* **3** air **4** aria, hymn, lied, mass, song **5** canon, chant, motet, opera, round **6** anthem, ballad **7** cantata, chanson, chorale **8** cavatina, madrigal, operetta, oratorio, serenade **9** cabaletta

musical 4 show **5** revue **6** turned **7** chiming, lyrical, melodic, songful, tuneful **8** blending, harmonic **9** consonant, melodious, symphonic **10** harmonious **11** symphonious

musical composition 4 aria, hymn, opus, solo **5** étude, fugue, motet, opera, psalm, rondo, suite **6** anthem, ballad, sonata, verset **7** cantata, chanson, chorale, prelude, requiem, toccata **8** concerto, madrigal, nocturne, operetta, oratorio, postlude, serenade, sonatina, symphony **9** bagatelle, cabaletta, interlude, toccatina **10** intermezzo

musical direction *accented:* **7** marcato **8** sforzato **9** sforzando *airy:* **7** sfogato *as written:* **3** sta *bold:* **6** audace *brisk:* **4** vivo **6** vivace **7** allegro, animato *connected:* **6** legato *detached:* **8** spiccato, staccato *dignified:* **8** maestoso *disconnected:* **8** staccato *dying away:* **7** calando *emotional:* **12** appassionato *emphatic:* **7** marcato *evenly:* **10** egualmente *excited:* **7** agitato **9** spiritoso *fast:* **4** vite, vivo **5** tosto **6** presto, veloce, vivace **7** allegro **10** tostamente *faster:* **7** stretto

11 accelerando *fluctuating tempo:*
6 rubato *forcefully:* 7 furioso *freely:* 9 ad
libitum *gay:* 7 giocoso *gentle:* 5 dolce
7 amabile, amoroso 9 affettuso *graceful:*
6 adagio 8 grazioso *half:* 5 mezzo *heavy:*
7 pesante *held firmly:* 6 tenuto *hurried:*
7 agitato *joyous:* 7 giocoso *less:* 4 meno
little: 4 poco *little by little:* 9 poco a poco
lively: 4 vite 6 vivace 7 allegro, animato,
giocoso 9 capriccio *loud:* 5 forte *louder:*
9 crescendo *lovingly:* 7 amabile, amoroso
majestic: 8 maestoso *moderate:*
7 andante 8 moderato *moderately loud:*
2 mf 10 mezzo forte *moderately soft:*
2 mp 10 mezzo piano *muted:* 5 sorda,
sordo *passionless:* 6 freddo *plaintive:*
7 dolente 8 doloroso *playful:* 7 giocoso
10 scherzando *plucked:* 9 pizzicato
quick: 4 vite, vivo 5 tosto 6 presto,
veloce, vivace 7 allegro 10 tostamente
quickening: 11 affrettando *repeat:* 2 DC
3 bis 6 da capo *sad:* 7 dolente 8 doloroso
separate: 6 divisi *showily:* 10 brilliante
silent: 5 tacet *singing:* 9 cantabile *sliding:* 9 glissando *slow:* 5 grave, largo,
tardo 6 adagio 7 andante 9 larghetto
slowing: 3 rit 6 ritard 10 ritardando
11 rallentando *smooth:* 5 dolce 6 legato
8 grazioso *soft:* 5 dolce, piano *softening:*
10 diminuendo 11 decrescendo *solemn:*
5 grave *sorrowful:* 7 dolente 8 doloroso
spirited: 4 vivo 6 audace, vivace 7 animato 9 spiritoso *stately:* 7 pomposo
8 maestoso *strong:* 5 forte *sustained:*
6 tenuto 9 sostenuto *sweet:* 5 dolce *tender:* 7 amabile, amoroso 10 affettuoso
together: 4 a due *tranquil:* 7 calmato *very
fast:* 11 prestissimo *very loud:* 2 ff 10 for-
tissimo *very soft:* 2 pp 10 pianissimo
musical drama 5 opera 8 operetta
9 singspiel
musical group 4 band, trio 5 choir,
combo 6 chorus 7 quartet 8 ensemble,
glee club, symphony 9 orchestra
musical instrument *African:* 5 mbira,
sansa, zanza 7 kalimba, marimba *ancient:*
4 lyre, rote 5 crwth, rotte, shawm 6 cither,
syrinx, trigon 7 cithara, mandola, pandura,
panpipe, serpent, sistrum, theorbo *Arabic:*
3 oud 6 atabal *bagpipe:* 7 musette,
pibroch *biblical:* 4 asor, harp, horn, pipe
5 flute 6 cymbal, sabeca, tabret 7 timbrel,
trumpet 8 psaltery *brass:* 4 horn, tuba
5 bugle 6 cornet 7 althorn, clarion, helicon,
saxhorn, trumpet 8 trombone 10 French
horn *Chinese:* 3 kin *Indian:* 4 vina
5 sarod, sitar, veena *Japanese:* 4 biwa,
koto 7 samisen *keyboard:* 5 organ, piano
6 spinet 7 celesta, cembalo, clavier 8 calliope, melodeon, virginal 9 accordion
10 clavichord, concertina, pianoforte

11 harpsichord *medieval:* 4 lute 5 naker,
rebab, rebec, shawm, tabor 6 citole 7 cow
horn, gittern, mandola, panpipe 8 cornetto,
doucaine, dulcimer, gemshorn, hornpipe,
Jew's harp, oliphant, recorder 9 mono-
chord, rommelpot 10 clavichord, hurdy-
gurdy *percussion:* 4 bell, drum 5 guiro,
piano 6 cymbal, maraca 7 marimba, timbrel, tympani 8 bass drum, castanet, triangle 9 snare drum, xylophone 10 kettledrum, tambourine, vibraphone *Persian:*
6 santir *pipe:* 6 syrinx 7 bagpipe, musette,
panpipe 9 cornemuse *reed:* 4 oboe 7 bassoon 8 clarinet 9 harmonica, saxophone
11 English horn *Renaissance:* 4 viol
5 regal, shawm 6 curtal, lirone, spinet
7 bagpipe, bandora, cittern, rackett, sackbut, serpent, theorbo, vihuela, violone
8 crumhorn, penorcon, recorder, virginal
9 angelique, cornamuse, orpharion, pandurina 10 bassanello, chitarrone, colascione
11 harpsichord *Russian:* 9 balalaika
stringed: 3 oud 4 asor, harp, lute, lyre,
vina, viol 5 banjo, cello, piano, rebec, sitar,
viola 6 fiddle, guitar, violin, zither 7 bandora, cittern, gittern, kantele, pandura, ukulele 8 autoharp, dulcimer, mandolin 10 contrabass, double bass 11 harpsichord,
violoncello *suffix:* 3 ina, ine *toy:* 5 kazoo
7 ocarina *two-necked:* 7 theorbo *woodwind:* 4 oboe 5 flute 7 bassoon, piccolo
9 flageolet, saxophone 11 English horn
musical interval 5 fifth, major, minor,
sixth, third 6 ditone, fourth, octave, second 7 perfect, seventh, tritone
musical syllable 2 do, fa, la, mi, re, si, ti,
ut 3 Ela, sol *Guido's:* 2 ut 3 Ela
musician 4 bard 5 piper 6 player 7 jazz-
man 8 minstrel, virtuoso 9 performer
muskeg 3 bog, fen 4 mire, quag 5 marsh,
swamp 6 slough 7 baygall
musket 5 fusil 6 dragon 7 dragoon
9 flintlock, matchlock 12 muzzleloader
medieval: 8 culverin
muskmelon 10 cantaloupe
Muslim, Moslem *ascetic:* 4 Sufi 5 fakir
7 dervish *Bible:* 5 Koran *body of schol-
ars:* 5 ulema *caller to prayer:* 7 muezzin
call to prayer: 4 adan, azan *cap:* 3 taj
creed: 6 Kelima 7 Kalimah *devil:* 5 Eblis
festival: 3 Eed 6 Bairam *garment:* 4 izar
5 ihram 6 chador *god:* 5 Allah *holy city:*
5 Mecca 6 Medina *holy war:* 5 jahad,
jehad, jihad *judge:* 4 cadi *lawyer:* 5 mufti
marriage: 4 mota, muta *mendicant:* 5 fakir
monastery: 5 ribat 7 khankah *month:* (see
at **month**) *month of fasting:* 7 Ramadan
mosque: 6 masjid *mystic:* 4 Sufi *nonbe-
liever:* 5 Kafir 6 Kaffir *nymph:* 5 houri *pilgrim:* 4 haji 5 hadji, hajji *pilgrimage:*
3 haj 4 hadj, hajj *priest:* 4 imam *prophet:*

8 Mohammed, Muhammad *religion:* 5 Islam *saint:* 3 pir 6 santon *saint's tomb:* 3 pir *shrine:* 5 Caaba, Kaaba 6 Kaabeh *student:* 5 softa *teacher:* 4 alim 5 mulla 6 mullah *temple:* 6 mosque *title:* 3 aga 4 agha, emir, said 5 calif, emeer, sayid 6 caliph *tradition:* 5 sunna 6 sunnah; (see also **mosque; Muhammad**)

muss 4 mess 5 botch, mix-up, upset 6 jumble, mess-up, muddle, rumple 7 disrupt, rummage, wrinkle 8 botchery, disarray, dishevel, disorder, shambles 10 disarrange 11 disorganize

mussel 5 naiad *genus:* 4 Unio 7 Mytilus 8 Anodonta *larva:* 9 blackhead

Mussolini, Benito 7 Fascist 8 dictator *title:* 4 Duce (Il)

mussy 5 messy 6 sloppy, sloven, unneat, untidy 7 unkempt 8 ill-kempt, slobbery, slovenly 10 disheveled

must 4 duty, have, need, want 5 ought 6 charge, devoir, should 9 committal, condition, essential, necessity, requisite 10 commitment, obligation, sine qua non 11 requirement 12 precondition, prerequisite

muster 4 call, roll 5 breed, cause, crowd, enter, get up, group, hatch, raise, rally 6 enlist, enroll, gather, induce, invoke, join up, number, roster, sample, sign on, sign up, summon, work up 7 collect, company, convene, develop, include, marshal, produce 8 assemble, assembly, comprise, congress, engender, generate, mobilize, occasion, organize 9 congeries, forgather, gathering, inventory 10 accumulate, assemblage, collection, congregate, rendezvous 11 aggregation, examination 12 accumulation, congregation

muster out 8 separate 9 discharge 10 demobilize

musty 4 dull, rank, sour 5 dirty, fetid, funky, moldy, stale, tired, trite 6 frowsy, old hat, smelly, whiffy 7 noisome, spoiled, squalid 8 shopworn, timeworn 10 antiquated, malodorous, threadbare

Mut *husband:* 4 Amen, Amon *son:* 5 Chons 6 Chonsu, Khonsu

mutable 5 fluid 6 fickle, mobile, shifty 7 protean 8 slippery, unstable, unsteady, variable, wavering, weathery 9 changeful, mercurial, uncertain, unsettled 10 capricious, changeable, inconstant 11 fluctuating, vacillating 12 inconsistent

mutate 4 turn, vary 5 alter 6 change, modify 7 commute 9 refashion, transform, transmute, transpose 11 transfigure 12 metamorphize, metamorphose, transmogrify

mutation 4 turn 6 change 7 novelty

9 variation 10 alteration, innovation 11 vicissitude 12 modification

mute 3 mum 4 dumb 6 dampen, deaden, muffle, reduce, silent, soften, stifle 8 silencer, wordless 9 voiceless 10 speechless 12 inarticulate, unarticulate

muted 3 dim, mat 4 dead, dull, flat 5 blind 6 silent 10 lackluster, lusterless, speechless

mutedly 6 weakly 7 faintly 9 sotto voce

mutilate 3 mar 4 geld, hurt, maim 5 alter, spoil, unsex 6 change, damage, deface, injure, mangle, mayhem, neuter 7 cripple, dislimb 8 castrate 9 disfigure, dismember, sterilize 11 desexualize

mutineer 5 rebel 6 anarch 8 frondeur, revolter 9 anarchist, insurgent 10 malcontent

mutinous 6 unruly 8 factious 9 insurgent, seditious, turbulent 10 rebellious 12 contumacious 13 insubordinate

mutiny 5 rebel 6 revolt 9 insurrect, rebellion 11 rise against 12 insurrection

mutt 3 cur, dog 4 boob, dolt, dope 5 dunce, idiot 6 dimwit 7 mongrel 8 dumbbell, numskull 9 blockhead, ignoramus

Mutt and ___ 4 Jeff

mutter 5 croak, growl, rumor, scold 6 fumble, grouch, grouse, muddle, mumble, murmur 7 grumble, swallow, whisper 9 undertone 11 susurration

muttonchops 9 burnsides, sideburns 10 sideboards 11 dundrearies 12 sidewhiskers

muttonhead 3 oaf 5 dunce, idiot 8 clodpate, numskull 9 blockhead 10 thickskull

mutual 5 joint 6 common, public, shared, united 7 related 8 communal, conjoint, conjunct 9 connected 10 associated, reciprocal, respective *prefix:* 2 co 5 inter

muzzle 3 gag, mug 4 face, nose, phiz 5 snout 6 nuzzle, visage 8 features, restrain 11 countenance

My Antonia author 6 Cather

My Last Duchess author 8 Browning

My Lost Youth author 10 Longfellow

myrmidon 8 follower, hireling, retainer 9 attendant, underling 11 subordinate

Myron's statue 10 Discobolus

Myrrha's son 6 Adonis

mysterious 6 arcane, mystic, occult, secret 7 cryptic, obscure, strange 8 abstruse, esoteric, numinous 9 ambiguous, enigmatic, equivocal, recondite, unguessed 10 cabalistic, unknowable 11 enigmatical, inscrutable, ungraspable 12 impenetrable, incognizable, inexplicable, unexaminable, unfathomable 13 unaccountable

mystery 5 poser 6 enigma, puzzle, riddle, secret 7 arcanum, problem, stumper 9 conundrum 10 closed book, perplexity,

puzzlement **13** Chinese puzzle, mystification *story:* **8** whodunit
mystic 4 seer **5** magic, vague **6** arcane, magian, occult, secret, witchy **7** magical, obscure **8** anagogic, esoteric, numinous, quixotic, telestic, wizardly **9** enigmatic, mysterial, sorcerous, unguessed **10** cabalistic, mysterious, unknowable **11** inscrutable, necromantic **12** impenetrable, thaumaturgic **13** unaccountable
mystical 4 deep, holy **6** covert, divine, orphic, sacred, secret **7** cryptic, furtive, sub-rosa **8** anagogic, hush-hush, orphical, profound, stealthy, telestic **9** spiritual **10** miraculous, symbolical **11** clandestine **12** hugger-mugger, supernatural, supranatural **13** hole-and-corner

mysticism 8 cabalism, quietism
mystify 6 puzzle **7** confuse, perplex **8** befuddle, bewilder **9** obfuscate
mystifying 4 dark **7** cryptic **8** Delphian **9** enigmatic
myth 4 lore, saga, tale **5** fable, story **6** legend **7** fiction, figment, parable **8** allegory, apologue, creation, folklore **9** invention, tradition **11** fabrication
mythical 6 unreal **7** created, fictive **8** fabulous, fanciful, invented **9** fantastic, fictional, imaginary, legendary, visionary **10** fictitious **12** mythological
mythological see **mythical**
mythologist 5 Tylor **6** Frazer **5** Mller **9** Euhemerus **10** Malinowski
mythology see **myth**

N

Naamah *brother:* **9** Tubalcain *father:* **6** Lamech *husband:* **7** Solomon *mother:* **6** Zillah *son:* **8** Rehoboam
Naaman *disease:* **7** leprosy *father:* **4** Bela *grandfather:* **8** Benjamin *healer:* **6** Elisha
Naam's father 5 Caleb
Naarah's husband 6 Ashhur
nab 3 nip **4** hook, nail, take **5** catch, pinch, run in, seize, steal **6** arrest, clutch, collar, detain, pickup, pull in, snatch **7** capture, grapple **9** apprehend
nabal 5 chuff, hunks, miser, stiff **7** niggard, scrooge **8** muckworm, tightwad **9** skinflint **12** moneygrubber
Nabal's wife 7 Abigail
nabob 6 biggie, bigwig, fat cat **7** notable **8** big chief, eminence **9** dignitary **10** notability
Nabokov novel 3 Ada **4** Pnin **6** Lolita, The Eye **7** Despair, The Gift **8** Mashenka, Pale Fire, The Event **10** The Defense, The Exploit
nacre 13 mother-of-pearl
nada 7 nullity, vacuity **8** nihility **11** nothingness **12** nonexistence
Nadab *brother:* **4** Kish **5** Abihu *father:* **5** Aaron, Jeiel **6** Gibeon **8** Jeroboam *mother:* **6** Maacah **8** Elisheba *slayer:* **6** Baasha
nadir 4 base, foot **6** bottom *opposite:* **6** zenith

nag 3 egg, irk, vex **4** bait, carp, fuss, goad, jade, prod, ride, urge **5** annoy, chivy, harry, hound, tease, worry **6** badger, bother, carp at, harass, heckle, hector, needle, peck at, pester, plague **7** henpeck, torment **8** harangue, irritate
Nahash's daughter 7 Abigail, Zeruiah
Nahath *father:* **5** Reuel *grandfather:* **7** Elkanah
Nahor *brother:* **5** Haran **7** Abraham *concubine:* **6** Reumah *father:* **5** Serug, Terah *grandson:* **7** Abraham *son:* **5** Terah **7** Bethuel *wife:* **6** Milcah
Nahshon *brother-in-law:* **5** Aaron *father:* **9** Amminadab *grandson:* **4** Boaz *sister:* **8** Elisheba *son:* **6** Salmon
naiad 5 nymph
naif 7 ingenue
nail 3 bag, get **4** brad, stud, tack, trap **5** catch, clone, spike, sprig **6** collar, secure, tacket, unguis, ungula **7** capture, prehend, ungulae (plural) **8** sparable *combining form:* **4** helo, onyx **5** onych, ungui **6** onycho **7** onychia **8** onychium
naive 4 easy **5** fresh **6** simple **7** artless, natural **8** gullible, innocent, original, unartful **9** ingenuous, unstudied **10** fleeceable, unaffected, unschooled **11** susceptible
naked 3 raw **4** bald, bare, mere, nude, open, pure **5** clear, sheer **6** meager, peeled, scanty, simple, unclad **7** denuded, evident, exposed, obvious, unarmed **8** buff-

bare, garbless, manifest, palpable, revealed, stripped **9** au naturel, colorless, destitute, disclosed, unclothed, uncolored, uncovered, undressed **10** discovered *combining form:* **4** gymn, nudi **5** gymno

Naked and the Dead author 6 Mailer

namby-pamby 3 sop **4** baby, flat **5** banal, bland, inane, sissy **6** jejune **7** doormat, insipid, milksop, sapless **8** weakling **9** driveling, innocuous, jellyfish **10** pantywaist, wishy-washy **11** Milquetoast, mollycoddle **12** milk-and-water **13** characterless

name 3 dub, nom, tab, tag, tap **4** call, cite, clan, make, race, term **5** alias, label, nomen, quote, state, style, title **6** byword, family, finger, handle, report, repute, rubric, ticket **7** appoint, baptize, declare, entitle, epithet, mention, moniker, notable, publish, specify **8** announce, christen, cognomen, identify, instance, luminary, monicker, nominate, somebody **9** advertise, celebrity, character, designate, incognito, pseudonym, recognize, sobriquet, stipulate **10** denominate, hypocorism, nom de plume, notability, reputation **11** appellation, appellative, designation *ancient Rome:* **7** agnomen **8** prenomen *assumed:* **5** alias **9** sobriquet *combining form:* **4** onym **7** onomato *family:* **8** cognomen *fictitious:* **9** pseudonym *giver:* **6** eponym

namely 5 to wit **8** scilicet **9** expressly, specially, videlicet **10** especially **12** particularly, specifically *abbreviation:* **3** viz

nana 5 nurse **9** nursemaid **11** nurserymaid

Nana *author:* **4** Zola *mother:* **8** Gervaise

Nanna *brother:* **6** Nergal, Ninazu *father:* **5** Enlil *husband:* **6** Balder *mother:* **6** Ninlil *son:* **3** Utu *wife:* **6** Ningal

nanny see nana

Naomi 4 Mara *daughter-in-law:* **4** Ruth **5** Orpah *husband:* **9** Elimelech *meaning:* **8** pleasant *son:* **6** Mahlon **7** Chilion

nap 3 nod **4** doze, rest **5** break, cover, let up, pause, relax, sleep, unlax **6** drowse, siesta, snooze **7** respite **10** forty winks

nape 6 scruff

Naphish's father 7 Ishmael

Naphtali *brother:* **3** Dan *father:* **5** Jacob *mother:* **6** Bilhah *son:* **4** Guni **5** Jezer **7** Jahzeel, Jahziel, Shallum

naphtha 7 solvent **9** petroleum

napkin 5 cloth, doily, towel **9** handcloth

napoleon 4 boot **6** pastry **8** card game **9** solitaire *bid:* **7** blucher **10** wellington

Napoleon *adversary:* **6** Nelson **7** Kutuzov **10** Wellington *birthplace:* **7** Ajaccio (Corsica) *brother:* **5** Louis **6** Jerome, Joseph, Lucien *brother-in-law:* **5** Murat *deathplace:* **8** St. Helena *defeat:* **7** Leipzig **8** Waterloo **9** Trafalgar *father:* **5** Carlo *island of exile:* **4** Elba **8** St. Helena *mar-*

shal: **3** Ney **5** Murat, Soult **6** Suchet *nickname:* **14** Little Corporal *sister:* **5** Maria **8** Carlotta, Carolina *victory:* **3** Ulm **4** Jena, Lodi **5** Ligny **6** Abukir, Arcole, Wagram **7** Bautzen, Dresden, Marengo **8** Borodino **10** Austerlitz *wife:* **9** Josephine **11** Marie Louise

narcissism 6 vanity **7** conceit **8** self-love, vainness **9** vainglory **10** self-esteem **11** amour propre, self-conceit **13** conceitedness

narcissistic 4 vain **7** stuck-up **8** conceity **9** conceited **12** vainglorious **13** self-conceited

Narcissus *father:* **9** Cephissus *mother:* **7** Liriope *rejected admirer:* **4** Echo

narcotic 3 hop **4** dope, drug, junk **5** opium **6** heroin, opiate **7** anodyne, cocaine, hashish **8** hasheesh, hypnotic, morphine, nepenthe, somnific **9** somnolent, soporific **10** somnorific **11** somniferous, soporifical *peddler:* **6** dealer, pusher

nark 3 rat **4** fink **5** peach, stool **6** canary, inform, snitch, squeak, squeal **7** tipster **8** betrayer, informer, squeaker, squealer **10** talebearer **11** stool pigeon

narrate 4 tell, yarn **5** state, story **6** detail, dilate, recite, relate, report **7** descant, recount **8** describe, rehearse **9** discourse

narrative 4 epic, myth, saga, tale, yarn **5** fable, story **6** legend, report **7** account, history, recital, version **8** anecdote **9** chronicle *medieval French:* **5** roman **7** romance *prose:* **5** novel **7** novella

narrow 3 set **4** mean **5** close, fixed, limit, small, taper, tense **6** lessen, little, meager, paltry, strait **7** bigoted, limited, precise **8** contract, decrease, definite, obdurate, straiten **9** confining, constrict, hidebound, illiberal **10** brassbound, constringe, inexorable, inflexible, intolerant, restricted

narrowly 6 barely **8** scarcely

narrow-minded 5 petty **7** bigoted, shallow **9** hidebound, illiberal **10** brassbound, intolerant, provincial, unenlarged

nasal 6 rhinal, twangy **9** nosepiece *combining form:* **4** rhin **5** rhino

nascency 5 birth **6** origin

nascent 7 initial **9** beginning, inceptive, incipient **10** initiative, initiatory **12** introductory

Naseby victor 7 Fairfax **8** Cromwell

nasicorn 10 rhinoceros

nasty 4 evil, foul, icky, mean, vile **5** black, cheap, dirty, gross, snide, soily **6** coarse, filthy, grubby, horrid, impure, malign, oafish, ribald, smutty, tawdry, vulgar, wicked **7** hateful, ill-bred, obscene, raunchy, spitish, squalid, unclean, vicious **8** improper, indecent, spiteful, unseemly **9** loathsome, malicious, malignant, offensive, repugnant,

repulsive, uncleanly, vexatious **10** disgusting, disturbing, indecorous, indelicate, malevolent
natant 8 swimming
Nathan *father:* **4** Bani **5** Attai, David *son:* **5** Zabad
national 4 home **5** civic, civil **6** public **7** citizen, subject **8** domestic, internal **9** intestine, municipal
National Basketball Association *Atlanta:* **5** Hawks *Boston:* **7** Celtics *Charlotte:* **7** Hornets *Chicago:* **5** Bulls *Cleveland:* **9** Cavaliers *Dallas:* **9** Mavericks *Denver:* **7** Nuggets *Detroit:* **7** Pistons *Golden State:* **8** Warriors *Houston:* **7** Rockets *Indiana:* **6** Pacers *Los Angeles:* **6** Lakers **8** Clippers *Miami:* **4** Heat *Milwaukee:* **5** Bucks *Minnesota:* **12** Timberwolves *New Jersey:* **4** Nets *New York:* **6** Knicks *Orlando:* **5** Magic *Phoenix:* **4** Suns *Portland:* **12** Trail Blazers *Sacramento:* **5** Kings *San Antonio:* **5** Spurs *Seattle:* **11** SuperSonics *Utah:* **4** Jazz *Washington:* **7** Bullets
National Football League *Atlanta:* **7** Falcons *Buffalo:* **5** Bills *Chicago:* **5** Bears *Cincinnati:* **7** Bengals *Cleveland:* **6** Browns *Dallas:* **7** Cowboys *Denver:* **7** Broncos *Detroit:* **5** Lions *Green Bay:* **7** Packers *Houston:* **6** Oilers *Indianapolis:* **5** Colts *Kansas City:* **6** Chiefs *Los Angeles:* **4** Rams **7** Raiders *Miami:* **8** Dolphins *Minnesota:* **7** Vikings *New England:* **8** Patriots *New Orleans:* **6** Saints *New York:* **4** Jets **6** Giants *Philadelphia:* **6** Eagles *Phoenix:* **9** Cardinals *Pittsburgh:* **8** Steelers *San Diego:* **8** Chargers *Seattle:* **8** Seahawks *Tampa Bay:* **4** Bucs *Washington:* **8** Redskins
national historical park *Alaska:* **5** Sitka *Idaho:* **8** Nez Percé *Kentucky-Tennessee:* **13** Cumberland Gap *Maryland-West Virginia:* **12** Harpers Ferry *Massachusetts:* **9** Minute Man *New York:* **8** Saratoga
National Hockey League *Boston:* **6** Bruins *Buffalo:* **6** Sabres *Calgary:* **6** Flames *Chicago:* **10** Black Hawks *Detroit:* **8** Red Wings *Edmonton:* **6** Oilers *Hartford:* **7** Whalers *Los Angeles:* **5** Kings *Minnesota:* **10** North Stars *Montreal:* **9** Canadiens *New Jersey:* **6** Devils *New York:* **7** Rangers **8** Islanders *Philadelphia:* **6** Flyers *Pittsburgh:* **8** Penguins *Quebec:* **9** Nordiques *St. Louis:* **5** Blues *San Jose:* **6** Sharks *Toronto:* **10** Maple Leafs *Vancouver:* **7** Canucks *Washington:* **8** Capitals *Winnipeg:* **4** Jets
nationalism 10 patriotism *excessive:* **8** jingoism **10** chauvinism
National League *Atlanta:* **6** Braves *Chi-*

cago: **4** Cubs *Cincinnati:* **4** Reds *Houston:* **6** Astros *Los Angeles:* **7** Dodgers *Montreal:* **5** Expos *New York:* **4** Mets *Philadelphia:* **8** Phillies *Pittsburgh:* **7** Pirates *St. Louis:* **9** Cardinals *San Diego:* **6** Padres *San Francisco:* **6** Giants
national military park *Alabama:* **13** Horseshoe Bend *Arkansas:* **8** Pea Ridge *Mississippi:* **9** Vicksburg *Pennsylvania:* **10** Gettysburg *South Carolina:* **13** Kings Mountain *Tennessee:* **6** Shiloh
national monument *Alabama:* **11** Russell Cave *Alaska:* **9** Aniakchak *Arizona:* **5** Tonto **6** Navajo **7** Saguaro, Wupatki **8** Tuzigoot **10** Chiricahua, Pipe Spring, Tumacacori **11** Hohokam Pima **12** Sunset Crater, Walnut Canyon *California:* **8** Cabrillo, Lava Beds **9** Muir Woods, Pinnacles **10** Joshua Tree **11** Death Valley *Colorado:* **10** Yucca House *Colorado-Utah:* **8** Dinosaur **9** Hovenweep *Florida:* **12** Fort Matanzas **13** Fort Jefferson *Georgia:* **8** Ocmulgee **11** Fort Pulaski **13** Fort Frederica *Iowa:* **12** Effigy Mounds *Louisiana:* **12** Poverty Point *Maryland:* **11** Fort McHenry *Minnesota:* **9** Pipestone **12** Grand Portage *Nebraska:* **9** Homestead **11** Scotts Bluff *New Mexico:* **5** Pecos **11** El Morro **9** Bandelier, El Malpais, Fort Union **10** Aztec Ruins, White Sands *New York:* **11** Fort Stanwix **13** Castle Clinton *South Carolina:* **10** Fort Sumter **13** Congaree Swamp *South Dakota:* **9** Jewel Cave *Utah:* **11** Cedar Breaks **13** Rainbow Bridge *Wyoming:* **11** Devils Tower, Fossil Butte
national park *Alaska:* **6** Denali, Katmai **9** Lake Clark **10** Glacier Bay **11** Kenai Fjords, Kobuk Valley *Angola:* **4** Iona, Mupa *Arizona:* **11** Grand Canyon *Arkansas:* **10** Hot Springs *Botswana:* **5** Chobe *California:* **7** Redwood, Sequoia **8** Yosemite **11** King's Canyon *Chad:* **5** Manda *Colombia:* **5** Uraba *Colorado:* **9** Mesa Verde **13** Rocky Mountain *eastern Africa:* **10** Mount Kenya *Florida:* **8** Biscayne **10** Everglades *Hawaii:* **9** Haleakala *India:* **5** Kanha *Japan:* **5** Nikko *Kentucky:* **11** Mammoth Cave *Kenya:* **4** Meru **5** Tsavo **10** Royal Tsavo *Lake Superior:* **10** Isle Royale *Maine:* **6** Acadia *Malaysia:* **8** Kinabalu *Minnesota:* **9** Voyageurs *Montana:* **7** Glacier *Nevada:* **10** Great Basin *Oregon:* **10** Crater Lake *Poland:* **5** Ojcow, Tatra *South Africa:* **6** Kruger *South Dakota:* **8** Badlands, Wind Cave *Sri Lanka:* **4** Yala *Sweden:* **5** Sarek *Tanzania:* **5** Ruaha **9** Serengeti *Texas:* **7** Big Bend *Utah:* **4** Zion **6** Arches **11** Bryce Canyon, Canyonlands, Capitol Reef *Virginia:* **10** Shenandoah *Washington:*

7 Olympic **12** Mount Rainier **13** North Cascades *Wyoming:* **10** Grand Teton *Wyoming-Idaho-Montana:* **11** Yellowstone *Zambia:* **5** Kafue *Zimbabwe:* **13** Rhodes Inyanga, Victoria Falls

native 3 raw **4** home, wild **5** crude, local **6** impure, inborn, innate, normal, simple **7** connate, endemic, indigen, natural **8** agrarian, agrestal, domestic, indigene, inherent, internal, national, ungraded, unsorted **9** inherited, intestine, municipal **10** aboriginal, congenital, connatural, indigenous, unacquired, unaffected *Acadian Louisiana:* **5** Cajun *China:* **3** Han **9** Celestial *India:* **5** sepoy *Japan:* **9** Nipponese *London:* **7** Cockney *New England:* **4** Yank **6** Yankee *New York:* **13** Knickerbocker *suffix:* **2** er **3** ese, ier, ite, ote, yer

Native Son author 6 Wright

Nativity 4 noel, Xmas, yule **5** birth **8** yuletide **9** Christmas

natty 4 jimp **5** doggy, jimpy, sassy, smart **6** dapper, spiffy, spruce, sprucy **7** bandbox, doggish **11** well-groomed

natural 4 easy, feeb, fool, open, wild, zany **5** ament, frank, idiot, moron, naive, plain, typic, usual, white **6** candid, common, cretin, folksy, inborn, innate, native, normal, rustic, simple **7** artless, bastard, connate, general, genuine, half-wit, regular, sincere, typical **8** agrarian, agrestal, baseborn, homespun, ignorant, imbecile, inherent, innocent, spurious, unartful **9** blackjack, childlike, guileless, impulsive, ingenuous, ingrained, inherited, prevalent, primitive, simpleton, unfeigned, unlabored, unstudied, untutored, unworldly **10** congenital, fatherless, indigenous, legitimate, provincial, unacquired, unaffected, unfathered, unschooled **11** commonplace, instinctive, misbegotten, spontaneous, undesigning

naturalist *American:* **4** Muir **5** Hyatt **7** Audubon, Verrill *English:* **3** Ray **5** White **6** Darwin **7** Wallace **10** Williamson *French:* **5** Fabre **7** Lamarck, Réaumur *Scottish:* **6** Wilson **10** Richardson

nature 3 ilk, way **4** kind, sort, type **5** being, humor, shape, world **6** cosmos, figure, kidney, kosmos, makeup, stripe, temper **7** anatomy, essence, texture, variety **8** creation, essentia, megacosm, universe **9** character, framework, macrocosm, normality **10** complexion **11** description, disposition, macrocosmos, personality, temperament **12** essentiality

naught 3 nil **4** zero **5** zilch **6** cipher, ruined **7** nothing **8** goose egg **11** nonexistent, nothingness **12** nonexistence

naughty 3 bad, paw **4** evil **5** rowdy **6** unruly, wicked **7** froward, wayward, willful **8** contrary, perverse **9** ruffianly **10** disorderly, headstrong, ill-behaved, indecorous, refractory **11** disobedient, intractable, misbehaving, mischievous **12** obstreperous, recalcitrant, ungovernable

nauseate 5 abhor, repel **6** loathe, reluct, revolt, sicken **7** disgust, repulse

nauseated 4 sick **6** queasy, queazy **7** carsick **9** squeamish

nauseating 4 foul, icky **5** nasty **7** noisome **9** loathsome, offensive, repugnant, repulsive, sickening

nauseous see **nauseated**

Nausicaa *father:* **8** Alcinous *mother:* **5** Arete

nautical 5 naval **6** marine **7** oceanic **8** maritime **12** navigational *instrument:* **3** aba **7** compass, pelorus, sextant

naval hero 5 Jones, Perry **8** Farragut, Lawrence

nave 3 hub

navel 6 middle **7** nombril **9** umbilicus **11** belly button *combining form:* **6** omphal **7** omphalo

navigate 4 move, sail, walk **5** pilot, steer

navigation 6 voyage **7** passage **8** piloting, seacraft, shipping

navigational system 5 loran **6** shoran **7** teleran

navigator 5 flyer, pilot **6** airman **7** copilot *Danish:* **6** Bering *Dutch:* **6** Tasman **7** Barents *English:* **4** Cook **5** Cabot, Drake **6** Hudson **7** Gilbert, Raleigh **9** Vancouver *French:* **7** Cartier **9** La Perouse *Italian:* **5** Cabot **8** Columbus, Vespucci **9** Verrazano *Norwegian:* **4** Eric **7** Ericson **8** Ericsson *Portuguese:* **4** Dias, Diaz **6** Cabral, da Gama **8** Magellan *Spanish:* **9** Fernandez

navy 5 fleet

Nazi 9 Hitlerite **10** brownshirt *admiral:* **6** Dönitz, Raeder **7** Doenitz *air force:* **9** Luftwaffe *armed forces:* **9** Wehrmacht *collaborator:* **5** Laval **8** Quisling *concentration camp:* **6** Belsen, Dachau **9** Auschwitz **10** Buchenwald, Nordhausen *field marshal:* **5** Model **6** Keitel, Paulus, Rommel **9** Rundstedt **10** Kesselring *greeting:* **4** Heil *leader:* **3** Ley **4** Hess, Röhm **5** Roehm **6** Führer, Göring, Hitler **7** Fuehrer, Goering, Himmler **8** Goebbels, Heydrich **9** Rosenberg *police:* **2** SS **7** Gestapo *propagandist:* **8** Goebbels *submarine:* **5** U-boat *surrender signer:* **4** Jodl **6** Keitel *symbol:* **6** fylfot **8** swastika *tactic:* **10** blitzkrieg *tank:* **6** panzer

NCO 3 cpl, sgt **8** corporal, sergeant

neap 4 tide

near 2 by **4** nigh **5** about, circa, close, round **6** almost, around, beside, narrow, stingy **7** close by, closely, close on **8** adjacent, approach, stingily **9** immediate, proximate, thriftily **10** intimately **11** approximate, at close hand, closefisted *combining form:* **5** juxta *prefix:* **2** ad, ep **3** eph, epi **4** peri, pros **5** plesi **6** plesio

nearby **4** nigh **5** about, aside, circa, close, handy, round **6** around, beside **7** closeby, close on, vicinal **8** adjacent **9** immediate, proximate **10** contiguous, convenient **11** neighboring

nearest **4** next **8** proximal

nearsighted **6** myopic

neat **3** net **4** deft, nice, prim, pure, snug, tidy, trig, trim **5** clean, clear, exact, kempt, plain **6** adroit, clever, dainty, dapper, spruce, sprucy **7** chipper, correct, finicky, orderly, precise, primsie, regular, unmixed **8** accurate, spotless, straight **9** ingenious, shipshape, undiluted **10** fastidious, gratifying, immaculate, methodical, systematic **11** uncluttered, well-groomed **12** spick-and-span **13** unadulterated

neb **3** ear, nib, tip **4** beak, bill, nose **6** pecker

Nebaioth *brother:* **5** Kedar *father:* **7** Ishmael

Nebraska *capital:* **7** Lincoln *college, university:* **4** Dana **5** Doane **9** Creighton *Indian:* **4** Otoe *largest city:* **5** Omaha *state flower:* **9** goldenrod

nebula **6** galaxy

nebulous **4** hazy **6** turbid **7** clouded **10** indistinct

necessary **5** vital **6** needed **7** certain **8** cardinal, inerrant, integral, unerring **9** essential, important, inerrable, mandatory, momentous, requisite **10** compelling, compulsory, imperative, ineludible, inevasible, inevitable, obligatory, unevadable **11** fundamental, ineluctable, inescapable, significant, unavoidable, unescapable **12** constraining, prerequisite **13** indispensable

necessitate **3** ask **4** take **5** crave **6** compel, demand **7** call for, require **9** constrain, force into

necessitous see **needy**

necessity **4** call, must, need **5** cause **6** duress **7** poverty **8** coercion, exigency, occasion **9** condition, essential, requisite **10** compulsion, constraint, obligation, sine qua non **11** needfulness, requirement **12** precondition, prerequisite **13** requisiteness

neck **3** pet **4** kiss **5** beard **6** behead, cervix, collet, fondle, smooch, strait **7** embrace **8** gorgerin **9** decollate **10** decapitate, guillotine *back of:* **4** nape **5** nucha **6** scruff *ornament:* **6** gorget, torque

necklace **4** band **5** chain **6** locket **7** rivière **8** carcanet

neckpiece **3** boa **5** scarf

necktie **5** ascot **6** cravat **10** four-in-hand *adjunct:* **6** tiepin **8** tie clasp

necrology **4** obit **8** obituary

necromancy **5** magic **7** sorcery **8** witchery, wizardry **9** conjuring, magicking **10** witchcraft **11** bewitchment, enchantment, thaumaturgy

necropolis **8** boneyard, boot hill, cemetery, God's acre **9** graveyard **12** burial ground

necropsy **7** autopsy **10** postmortem

need **3** use **4** call, duty, have, lack, long, must, pine, want, wish **5** claim, covet, crave, drive, exact, ought, yearn **6** charge, demand, desire, devoir, hanker, hunger, penury, thirst **7** deficit, poverty, require **8** exaction, exigency, occasion, poorness, shortage **9** committal, indigence, necessity, privation, requisite **10** commitment, compulsion, deficiency, dependence, obligation **11** destitution, requirement

neediness **4** want **6** penury **7** poverty **9** indigence, privation **11** destitution

needle **3** dun **5** annoy, tease, worry **6** harass, pester, plague **7** bedevil, hagride, obelisk, pricker, syringe *blunt:* **6** bodkin *case:* **4** etui *combining form:* **3** acu *hole:* **3** eye

needlefish **3** gar

needlelike **7** styloid **8** belonoid *part:* **7** acicula

needlepoint lace **7** alençon

needle-shaped **7** acerose, acerous, aciform

needlework **6** sewing **7** crochet, sampler, seaming, tatting **8** knitting **10** crocheting, embroidery

needy **4** poor **6** hard up **8** dirt poor, indigent, strapped **9** destitute, penniless, penurious **11** impecunious, necessitous **12** impoverished, unprosperous

ne'er-do-well **6** bad lot, no-good, waster **7** rounder, wastrel **9** shiftless **10** profligate, scapegrace **11** incompetent

nefarious **4** rank **5** gross **6** putrid, rotten **7** corrupt, glaring, heinous **8** flagrant, infamous, perverse **9** miscreant, monstrous **10** degenerate, detestable, outrageous, villainous

negate **4** deny, undo, void **5** abate, annul, cross, quash **6** impugn **7** abolish, gainsay, nullify, redress, vitiate **8** negative, traverse **9** cancel out, disaffirm, frustrate **10** annihilate, contradict, contravene, counteract, invalidate, neutralize **12** countercheck

negative **2** no **3** nix **4** deny, kill, veto **5** annul, cross, minus **6** impugn **7** adverse, gainsay, nullify, redress, refusal **8** abrogate, disprove, traverse **9** cancel out, disaffirm, frustrate, non-placet **10** contradict, contravene, counteract, invalidate, neutralize

11 detrimental, unfavorable *battery terminal:* **5** anode *ion:* **5** anion *Scottish:* **3** nae *sign:* **5** minus

neglect **4** fail, miss, omit, pass **5** elide, scant, scorn, shirk **6** forget, ignore, pass by, reject, slight **7** blink at, default, disdain, dismiss, failure **8** brush off, discount, omission, overleap, overlook, overpass, pass over, shrug off, slur over **9** blink away, disregard, oversight, pretermit, shrug away **10** brush aside, slough over

neglectful see **negligent**

negligee **4** gown **8** camisole **9** nightgown

negligent **3** lax **5** slack **6** remiss **7** offhand **8** careless, derelict, discinct, heedless, slipshod, slovenly **9** incurious, unheedful, unstudied **10** behindhand, delinquent, regardless, unthinking **11** inadvertent, inattentive, indifferent, thoughtless, unconcerned **12** disregardful **13** inconsiderate

negligible **4** slim **5** small **6** remote, slight **7** outside, slender **8** trifling

negotiate **4** leap, over **5** agree, clear, vault **6** adjust, handle, hurdle, manage, settle **7** arrange, bargain, compose, concert, conduct **8** complete, contract, covenant, overleap, surmount, transact **10** accomplish

Nehemiah's father **5** Azbuk **9** Hachaliah

Nehushta *father:* **8** Elnathan *husband:* **9** Jehoiakim *son:* **10** Jehoiachin

neigh **6** nicker, whinny **7** snicker, snigger

neighbor **4** abut, join, line **5** march, touch, verge **6** adjoin, border, butt on, corner **8** border on

neighborhood **4** area, tune **5** order, range **6** extent, matter **8** district, locality, vicinage, vicinity **9** magnitude, proximity

neighborly **6** social **7** cordial **8** amicable, friendly, gracious, sociable **10** gregarious, hospitable **11** cooperative

nematode **4** worm **7** eelworm **9** roundworm

Nemean predator **4** lion

neon **3** gas *symbol:* **2** Ne

neonate see **newborn**

neophyte see **newcomer**

Neoptolemus **7** Pyrrhus *father:* **8** Achilles *slayer:* **7** Orestes *victim:* **5** Priam *wife:* **8** Hermione

Nepal *capital:* **8** Katmandu **9** Kathmandu *forest land:* **5** Terai *monetary unit:* **5** rupee

nepenthe **6** opiate **7** anodyne **8** narcotic

Nepheg *brother:* **5** Korah **6** Zichri *father:* **5** David, Izhar

Nephele *daughter:* **5** Helle *husband:* **7** Athamas *son:* **7** Phrixos, Phrixus

Nephthys *brother, husband:* **3** Set **4** Seth

Neptune **6** planet *satellite:* **6** Nereid, Triton; (see also **Poseidon**)

Ner *father:* **5** Abiel, Jeiel *son:* **5** Abner

Nereides **6** Thetis **7** Galatea **10** Amphitrite *father:* **6** Nereus *mother:* **5** Doris

Nereus *daughters:* **8** Nereides *emblem:* **7** trident *father:* **6** Pontus *mother:* **2** Ge **4** Gaea *wife:* **5** Doris

Nergal *brother:* **5** Nanna **6** Ninazu *father:* **5** Enlil *mother:* **5** Ninlil

Neriah *father:* **8** Maaseiah *son:* **6** Baruch **7** Seraiah

Nerissa's husband **8** Gratiano

Nero *birthplace:* **4** Rome *mother:* **9** Agrippina *successor:* **5** Galba *victim:* **5** Lucan **6** Seneca **7** Octavia, Poppaea **9** Agrippina *wife:* **7** Octavia, Poppaea

Nero Wolfe creator **5** Stout (Rex)

nerve **4** face, gall, grit, guts, sand, vein **5** brass, cheek, cheer, crust, heart, moxie, spunk, steel **6** daring **7** animate, chirk up, hearten, sciatic, stamina **8** audacity, backbone, boldness, embolden, inspirit, strength, temerity **9** assurance, brashness, encourage, enhearten, fortitude, hardihood, hardiness **10** confidence, effrontery, strengthen **11** presumption *cell:* **6** neuron *cell group:* **7** ganglia (plural) **8** ganglion *combining form:* **4** neur **5** neura, neuro *cranial:* **4** vagi (plural) **5** optic, vagus **8** abducens *ending:* **8** receptor *lesion:* **8** neuritis

nerve center **3** hub **4** seat **5** focus, heart **8** polestar **10** focal point

nervous **4** edgy **5** jerky, jumpy, timid **6** feisty, goosey, spooky **7** fidgety, fretful, jittery, uptight, waspish **8** aflutter, agitated, critical, forcible, skittery, skittish, snappish, spirited, twittery, unsteady, volatile **9** difficult, excitable, irritable, querulous, unrestful **10** high-strung **12** apprehensive

nervy **4** bold, edgy, pert, wise **5** brash, fresh, jerky, jumpy, sassy, smart, tense **6** cheeky, goosey, spooky, uneasy **7** fidgety, forward, jittery, restive, twitchy, uptight **8** impudent, intrepid, twittery **9** excitable, unrestful **10** high-strung **11** smart-alecky

ness **4** cape **8** headland **10** promontory

Nessus' victim **8** Heracles, Hercules

nest **3** den **4** aery, home, lair, nidi (plural) **5** aerie, eyrie, nidus **6** nidify **7** hangout, shelter **8** smuggery **11** aggregation *eagle's:* **4** aery **5** aerie, eyrie *wasp's:* **8** vespiary

nest egg **5** hoard, stock, store **7** backlog, reserve **9** inventory, reservoir, stockpile

nestle **4** snug **5** house **6** burrow, cuddle, nuzzle **7** shelter, snuggle

Nestor *father:* **6** Neleus *kingdom:* **5** Pylos

net **4** gain, gist, make, mesh, pure **5** basic, catch, clear, seine, tulle, yield **6** maline **7** clean up, essence, malines *combining*

form: 5 dicty 6 dictyo *conical:* 5 trawl
fishing: 5 seine *hair:* 5 snood
Nethanel *brother:* 5 David *father:*
5 Jesse 7 Pashhur 8 Obededom *son:*
8 Shemaiah
Nethaniah's father 5 Asaph 6 Jehudi
7 Ishmael
nether 3 low 5 lower, under 6 lesser
8 inferior 9 subjacent
Netherlands *capital:* 9 Amsterdam *de
facto capital:* 8 The Hague *monetary
unit:* 6 florin, gulden 7 guilder *patron
saint:* 10 Willibrord *piano city:* 3 Ede
netherworld 3 pit 4 hell 5 abyss, hades,
Sheol 6 blazes 7 inferno 9 perdition
11 Pandemonium
netlike 9 reticular 10 reticulate
nettle 3 get, vex 4 huff, rile, roil 5 peeve,
pique, upset 6 incite, put out, stir up 7 agitate, disturb, perturb, provoke 8 irritate
10 discompose, exasperate
nettle rash 5 hives 9 urticaria
nettlesome 5 spiny 6 thorny 7 prickly
9 irritable 10 irritating
network 3 web 4 mesh 8 gridiron 9 reticulum *anatomical:* 4 rete 5 retia (plural)
neurotic 6 phobic 7 nervous 8 unstable
9 obsessive 10 compulsive
neuter 3 fix 4 geld 5 alter, unsex
6 change, worker 7 sexless 8 castrate,
mutilate 9 sterilize 11 desexualize
12 intransitive
neutral 4 calm, cool, easy 5 aloof 6 normal 7 hueless, relaxed 8 abstract, clinical,
composed, detached, middling, unbiased
9 collected, colorless, impartial 10 achromatic, impersonal, nonchalant, pokerfaced
11 indifferent, unpassioned 13 disinterested, dispassionate
neutralize 5 annul 6 defeat, negate, offset, subdue 7 balance, conquer, nullify,
redress 8 abrogate, negative, overcome,
override, overrule 9 cancel out, frustrate
10 compensate, counteract, invalidate
11 countervail 12 countercheck,
counterpoise
Nevada *capital:* 10 Carson City *largest
city:* 8 Las Vegas *nickname:* 11 Silver
State 14 Sagebrush State *state flower:*
9 sagebrush
névé 4 firn, snow
never-ending 7 endless, eternal 8 immortal 9 ceaseless 11 amaranthine, everlasting
never-failing 4 firm, sure 6 steady
7 abiding 8 enduring 9 steadfast 11 unfaltering, unqualified 12 wholehearted
13 unquestioning
nevertheless 3 but, yet 5 still 6 though,
withal 7 howbeit, however 8 after all
11 still and all
nevus 4 mole 9 birthmark

new 5 fresh, novel 6 afresh, lately, modern,
of late, recent 7 another, revived, strange
8 neoteric, pristine 9 first-hand, recreated,
refreshed, renovated 10 additional, unfamiliar 11 modernistic, regenerated 12 unaccustomed 13 reinvigorated *combining
form:* 2 ne 3 cen, neo, nov 4 caen, ceno,
novo 5 caeno *word:* 7 coinage, neology
9 neologism
newcomer 4 colt, tyro 6 novice, rookie
8 beginner, chechako, freshman, neophyte
9 immigrant, novitiate 10 apprentice,
tenderfoot
New Deal agency 3 CCC, NRA, TVA,
WPA
Newfoundland *capital:* 10 Saint Johns
discoverer: 5 Cabot (John) *part:*
8 Labrador
new gas 4 neon
New Hampshire *capital:* 7 Concord *college:* 9 Dartmouth 10 Keene State
12 Saint Anselms *highest point:* 12 Mt.
Washington *largest city:* 10 Manchester
motto: 13 Live Free or Die *nickname:*
12 Granite State *state bird:* 11 purple finch
state flower: 11 purple lilac
New Jersey *capital:* 7 Trenton *college,
university:* 4 Drew 6 Upsala 7 Rutgers
9 Princeton, Seton Hall 10 Bloomfield
11 Saint Peters *largest city:* 6 Newark
nickname: 11 Garden State *state bird:*
9 goldfinch *state flower:* 6 violet
New Mexico *capital:* 7 Santa Fe *largest
city:* 11 Albuquerque *state bird:* 10 roadrunner *state flower:* 5 yucca
news 4 dope, poop, word 5 rumor
6 advice, gossip, report, tattle 7 lowdown,
tidings 9 knowledge, speerings 11 information, scuttlebutt 12 announcement, intelligence *agency:* 2 AP 3 UPI 4 Tass
7 Reuters
newspaper 5 daily, organ 6 review
7 journal, tabloid 8 magazine 10 periodical
publisher: 6 Hearst
newt 3 eft 6 triton *green:* 5 ebbet
New Testament see at **Bible**
New York *academy, college, (university):* 3 RPI 4 Iona, Pace, SUNY 5 Keuka,
Kings, Nyack, Pratt, Siena, Utica 6 CW
Post, Elmira, Hunter, Ithaca, Marist, Queens,
Vassar 7 Adelphi, Colgate, Cornell, For-
dham, Hofstra, Niagara, St. Johns, Yeshiva
8 Brooklyn, Canisius, Columbia, Hamilton,
Hartwick, Skidmore, Syracuse 9 Juilliard,
Manhattan, St. Francis, St. Josephs, West
Point 10 Long Island 13 Sarah Lawrence,
St. Bonaventure *capital:* 6 Albany *motto:*
9 Excelsior 10 Ever Upward *nickname:*
11 Empire State *state flower:* 4 rose
New York City 6 Gotham *borough:*

5 Bronx 6 Queens 8 Brooklyn, Richmond 9 Manhattan

New Zealand *capital:* 10 Wellington *discoverer:* 6 Tasman *monetary unit:* 6 dollar *parrot:* 3 kea

next 4 then 5 after, below, infra, later, since 6 behind, coming, second 7 by and by, closest, ensuing 8 latterly 9 afterward, following, proximate 10 afterwhile, contiguous, succeeding

nexus 3 tie 4 bond, knot, link, yoke 8 ligament, ligature, vinculum 10 connection

Nez Percé chief 6 Joseph

niagara 5 flood, spate 6 deluge 7 torrent 8 cataract, flooding, overflow 9 cataclysm 10 inundation

nib 4 beak, bill 5 tooth 6 pecker 8 pen point

nibble 4 bite, gnaw, peck, pick

Nicanor's father 9 Patroclus

Nicaragua *capital:* 7 Managua *monetary unit:* 7 cordoba *neighbor:* 8 Honduras 9 Costa Rica

nice 4 fine, good, mild, neat, rare, sage, wise 5 exact, fussy, picky, right, rigid 6 benign, chaste, choosy, comely, dainty, decent, proper, queasy, seemly, strict, subtle 7 affable, careful, clement, correct, finical, finicky, fitting, precise, refined, welcome 8 accurate, becoming, clerkish, decorous, delicate, finespun, hairline, picksome, pleasant, pleasing, precieux, precious, rigorous, suitable, virtuous 9 agreeable, befitting, congenial, enjoyable, exquisite, favorable, finicking, judicious 10 attractive, conforming, delightful, discerning, fastidious, gratifying, meticulous, old-maidish, particular, pernickety, personable, scrupulous

niche 4 nook 5 place 6 cranny, crater, nestle, recess 7 byplace, secrete

Nicholas Nickleby author 7 Dickens

nick 4 deny, hack 5 cut in, notch, score, snipe 6 charge, record 9 indenture 11 indentation

nickname 3 tag 5 label, style 6 byword, handle 7 epithet, miscall, moniker 8 cognomen 9 sobriquet 10 hypocorism

Nicomede *conquest:* 10 Cappodocia *dramatist:* 9 Corneille *half-brother:* 6 Attale *stepmother:* 7 Arsinoë

nictate 3 bat 4 wink 5 blink 7 twinkle

nictitate see **nictate**

nifty 4 cool, keen, neat 5 adept, dandy, dilly, handy, peach, smart, super, swell 6 clever, corker, groovy, peachy 7 stylish 8 jim-dandy, knockout, splendid, terrific

Niger *capital:* 6 Niamey *export:* 7 uranium *monetary unit:* 5 franc

Nigeria *capital:* 5 Lagos *monetary unit:*

5 naira *people:* 3 Ibo 4 Igbo *product:* 3 tin 4 coal 5 cocoa 6 rubber

niggard 5 miser

niggardly 5 close, tight 6 scanty, stingy 7 miserly 9 penurious 11 closefisted, tight-fisted 12 cheeseparing, parsimonious 13 penny-pinching

niggling 5 petty 6 measly, paltry, peanut 8 picayune, piddling, trifling 10 picayunish

nigh 2 by 4 near 5 about, circa, close, round 6 all but, almost, around, beside, nearby, nearly 7 close on 8 approach 9 immediate, proximate 10 near-at-hand 11 approximate, at close hand, practically

night blindness 10 nyctalopia

nightfall 3 eve 4 dusk, even 6 sunset 7 evening, sundown 8 eventide, gloaming, owl-light, twilight

nighthawk 6 petrel 7 bullbat 10 goatsucker *Australian:* 8 morepork

nightingale 6 thrush

nightjar 5 potoo 10 goatsucker

nightly 9 nocturnal

nightmare 5 dream, fancy, worry 6 vision 7 fantasy, incubus 8 daydream, phantasm, phantasy, succubus 12 apprehension

nightshade 7 henbane 10 belladonna *weedy:* 11 bittersweet

nightstick 3 bat 4 club, mace 5 baton, billy 6 cudgel 8 bludgeon 9 billy club, truncheon

Nike *father:* 6 Pallas *mother:* 4 Styx

nil 4 zero 6 naught, nought 7 nothing 11 nonexistent

Nile 6 Al-Bahr *dam:* 6 Makwar 9 Aswan High 10 Gebel Aulia *explorer:* 5 Baker (Sir Samuel), Bruce (James), Grant (J. A.), Speke (J. H.) *queen:* 4 Cleo 9 Cleopatra *section:* 4 Abai, Abay 5 Abbai

nilgai 8 antelope, blue bull

nimble 3 yar 4 deft, spry, yare 5 agile, alert, brisk, catty, fleet, handy, light, quick, zippy 6 active, adroit, brisky, clever, limber, lively 8 vigilant, watchful 9 dexterous, lightsome, sprightly, wide-awake

nimble-witted 3 hep 4 wise 5 canny, quick, sharp, slick, smart 7 knowing

Nimrod 6 hunter *father:* 4 Cush

Ninazu *brother:* 5 Nanna 6 Nergal *father:* 5 Enlil *mother:* 6 Ninlil

nincompoop 3 ass 4 fool, jerk 5 idiot, ninny 6 donkey 7 jackass, tomfool 8 imbecile 9 simpleton

nine 12 baseball team *combining form:* 3 non 4 nona 5 ennea *goddesses:* 5 Muses *group:* 6 ennead *inches:* 4 span *instruments:* 5 nonet

nine day devotion 6 novena

Nine Worlds 3 Hel 6 Asgard 7 Alfheim,

Midgard **8** Niflheim, Vanaheim **10** Jotun-
nheim **12** Muspellsheim **13** Svartalfaheim
ninny *see* **nincompoop**
Ninsun's son 9 Gilgamesh
ninth *combining form:* **3** non **4** nona
Nintu *consort:* **4** Enki *son:* **6** Ninsar
Ninurta *father:* **5** Enlil *victim:* **3** Kur
Ninus *father:* **5** Belus *wife:* **9** Semiramis
Niobe *brother:* **6** Pelops *father:* **8** Tantalus *husband:* **7** Amphion *sister-in-law:*
5 Aedon
nip 3 bit, dig, hop, nab **4** balk, dart, dash,
dram, drop, hook, jolt, jump, lift, nail, peck,
shot, slug, soak, swig **5** blast, booze,
check, chill, clamp, drink, hurry, pinch,
sever, snort, steal, swill **6** arrest, blight,
guzzle, imbibe, snatch, tank up, thwart, tipple **7** cabbage, snifter, swizzle **8** compress,
cutpurse, liquor up, piquancy, toothful
9 frustrate **10** pickpocket
nipper 3 bud, kid **4** rack **5** chick, child
6 cunner, moppet **8** brakeman, juvenile,
young one **9** youngling, youngster
nipping 3 icy **4** cold, cool **5** chill, sharp
6 arctic, chilly, frosty **7** caustic, glacial, shivery **8** freezing
nipple 3 pap **4** teat **8** mammilla *combin-*
ing form: **4** mast **5** masto **6** papill
7 papillo
nipple-shaped 9 mammiform
Nippon 5 Japan
nippy *see* **nipping**
nirvana 4 Zion **5** bliss, dream **6** Canaan,
heaven **7** elysium **8** empyrean, oblivion,
paradise **10** Civitas Dei **12** New
Jerusalem
nisse 3 elf, fay **5** fairy, pixie **6** kobold,
sprite **7** brownie
Nisus *betrayer, daughter:* **6** Scylla
father: **7** Pandion
nitid 6 bright, glossy **8** lustrous
nitrogen 5 azote *combining form:* **2** az
3 azo
nitwit 4 dope, simp **5** cluck, dunce **7** pinhead **9** dumb bunny, dumb cluck, simpleton
nix 2 no **3** nay **4** kill, nope, veto **6** naught,
nought **7** nothing **8** negative
Njord, Njorth *daughter:* **5** Freya *son:*
4 Frey *wife:* **6** Skadhi, Skathi
no 3 nae, nay, nix **6** denial *combining*
form: **5** nulli
no-account *see* **no-good**
Noachian 3 old **4** aged **5** hoary **6** age-
old **7** ancient, antique **8** timeworn **9** venerable **12** antediluvian
Noah *father:* **6** Lamech **10** Zelophehad
grandson: **4** Aram **6** Canaan *great grand-*
son: **3** Hul *landing place:* **6** Ararat *son:*
3 Ham **6** Canaan **7** Japheth
Nobel Prize Winner
chemistry:

1902: **7** Fischer *1903:* **9** Arrhenius
1904: **6** Ramsay *1905:* **9** von Baeyer
1906: **7** Moissan *1907:* **7** Buchner
1908: **10** Rutherford *1909:* **7** Ostwald
1910: **7** Wallach *1911:* **5** Curie *1912:*
8 Grignard, Sabatier *1913:* **6** Werner
1914: **8** Richards *1915:* **11** Willstatter
1918: **5** Haber *1920:* **6** Nernst *1921:*
5 Soddy *1922:* **5** Aston *1923:* **5** Pregl
1925: **9** Zsigmondy *1926:* **8** Svedberg
1927: **7** Wieland *1928:* **7** Windaus
1929: **6** Harden *1930:* **7** Fischer *1931:*
5 Bosch **7** Bergius *1932:* **8** Langmuir
1934: **4** Urey *1935:* **11** Joliot-Curie
1936: **5** Debye *1937:* **6** Karrer
7 Haworth *1938:* **4** Kuhn *1939:* **7** Ruz-
icka **9** Butenandt *1943:* **6** Hevesy
1944: **4** Hahn *1945:* **8** Virtanen *1946:*
6 Sumner **7** Stanley **8** Northrup *1947:*
8 Robinson *1948:* **8** Tiselius *1949:*
7 Giauque *1950:* **5** Alder, Diels *1951:*
7 Seaborg **8** McMillan *1952:* **5** Synge
6 Martin *1953:* **10** Staudinger *1954:*
7 Pauling *1955:* **10** du Vigneaud *1956:*
7 Semenov **11** Hinshelwood *1957:*
4 Todd *1958:* **6** Sanger *1959:* **9** Heyrov-
sky *1960:* **5** Libby *1961:* **6** Calvin *1962:*
6 Perutz **7** Kendrew *1963:* **7** Ziegler
1964: **7** Hodgkin *1965:* **8** Woodward
1966: **8** Mulliken *1967:* **5** Eigen **6** Porter **7** Norrish *1968:* **7** Onsager *1969:*
6 Barton, Hassel *1970:* **6** Leloir *1971:*
8 Herzberg *1972:* **5** Moore, Stein
8 Anfinsen *1973:* **7** Fischer **9** Wilkinson
1974: **5** Flory *1975:* **6** Prelog **9** Corn-
forth *1976:* **8** Lipscomb *1977:* **9** Prigo-
gine *1978:* **8** Mitchell *1979:* **5** Brown
6 Wittig *1980:* **4** Berg **6** Sanger **7** Gilbert *1981:* **5** Fukui **8** Hoffmann *1982:*
4 Klug *1983:* **5** Taube *1984:* **10** Merri-
field *1985:* **5** Karle **8** Hauptman *1986:*
3 Lee **7** Polanyi **10** Herschbach *1987:*
4 Cram, Lehn **8** Pedersen *1988:*
5 Huber **6** Michel **11** Deisenhofer *1989:*
4 Cech **6** Altman *1990:* **5** Corey
economics:
1969: **6** Frisch **9** Tinbergen *1970:*
9 Samuelson *1971:* **7** Kuznets *1972:*
5 Arrow, Hicks *1973:* **8** Leontief *1974:*
5 Hayek **6** Myrdal *1975:* **8** Koopmans
11 Kantorovich *1976:* **8** Friedman *1977:*
5 Meade, Ohlin *1978:* **5** Simon *1979:*
5 Lewis **7** Schultz *1980:* **5** Klein *1981:*
5 Tobin *1982:* **7** Stigler *1983:* **6** Debreu
1984: **5** Stone *1985:* **10** Modigliani
1986: **8** Buchanan *1987:* **5** Solow
1988: **6** Allais *1989:* **8** Haavelmo *1990:*
6 Miller, Sharpe **9** Markowitz
literature:
1901: **9** Prudhomme *1902:* **7** Mommsen
1903: **8** Bjornson *1904:* **7** Mistral

9 Echegaray *1905:* 11 Sienkiewicz *1906:* 8 Carducci *1907:* 7 Kipling *1908:* 6 Eucken *1909:* 8 Lagerlof *1910:* 8 von Heyse *1911:* 11 Maeterlinck *1912:* 9 Hauptmann *1913:* 6 Tagore *1915:* 7 Rolland *1916:* 13 von Heidenstam *1917:* 9 Gjellerup 11 Pontoppidan *1919:* 9 Spitteler *1920:* 6 Hamsun *1921:* 6 France *1922:* 9 Benavente *1923:* 5 Yeats *1924:* 7 Reymont *1925:* 4 Shaw *1926:* 7 Deledda *1927:* 7 Bergson *1928:* 6 Undset *1929:* 4 Mann *1930:* 5 Lewis *1931:* 9 Karlfeldt *1932:* 10 Galsworthy *1933:* 5 Bunin *1934:* 10 Pirandello *1936:* 6 O'Neill *1937:* 12 Martin du Gard *1938:* 4 Buck *1939:* 9 Sillanpaa *1944:* 6 Jensen *1945:* 7 Mistral *1946:* 5 Hesse *1947:* 4 Gide *1948:* 5 Eliot *1949:* 8 Faulkner *1950:* 7 Russell *1951:* 10 Lagerkvist *1952:* 7 Mauriac *1953:* 9 Churchill *1954:* 9 Hemingway *1955:* 7 Laxness *1956:* 7 Jimenez *1957:* 5 Camus *1958:* 9 Pasternak *1959:* 9 Quasimodo *1960:* 5 Perse *1961:* 6 Andric *1962:* 9 Steinbeck *1963:* 7 Seferis *1964:* 6 Sartre *1965:* 9 Sholokhov *1966:* 5 Agnon, Sachs *1967:* 8 Asturias *1968:* 8 Kawabata *1969:* 7 Beckett *1970:* 12 Solzhenitsyn *1971:* 6 Neruda *1972:* 4 Böll *1973:* 5 White *1974:* 7 Johnson 9 Martinson *1975:* 7 Montale *1976:* 6 Bellow *1977:* 10 Aleixandre *1978:* 6 Singer *1979:* 6 Elytis *1980:* 6 Milosz *1981:* 7 Canetti *1982:* 13 Garcia Marquez *1983:* 7 Golding *1984:* 7 Siefert *1985:* 5 Simon *1986:* 7 Soyinka *1987:* 7 Brodsky *1988:* 7 Mahfouz *1989:* 4 Cela *1990:* 3 Paz

peace:

1901: 6 Dunant *1902:* 5 Gobat 8 Ducommun *1903:* 6 Cremer *1905:* 10 von Suttner *1906:* 9 Roosevelt *1907:* 6 Moneta 7 Renault *1908:* 5 Bajer 9 Arnoldson *1909:* 9 Beernaert *1911:* 5 Asser, Fried *1912:* 4 Root *1913:* 10 La Fontaine *1919:* 6 Wilson *1920:* 9 Bourgeois *1921:* 5 Lange 8 Branting *1922:* 9 Nansen *1925:* 5 Dawes 11 Chamberlain *1926:* 6 Briand 10 Stresemann *1927:* 6 Quidde 7 Buisson *1929:* 7 Kellogg *1930:* 9 Soderblom *1931:* 6 Addams, Butler *1933:* 6 Angell *1934:* 9 Henderson *1935:* 9 Ossietzky *1936:* 13 Saavedra Lamas *1937:* 5 Cecil *1945:* 4 Hull *1946:* 4 Mott 5 Balch *1949:* 3 Orr *1950:* 6 Bunche *1951:* 7 Jauhaux *1952:* 10 Schweitzer *1953:* 8 Marshall *1957:* 7 Pearson *1958:* 4 Pire *1959:* 9 Noel-Baker *1960:* 7 Luthuli *1961:* 12 Hammarskjold *1962:* 7 Pauling *1964:* 4 King *1968:* 6 Cassin *1970:* 7 Borlaug *1971:* 6 Brandt *1973:* 8 Le Duc Tho 9 Kissinger *1974:* 4 Sato 8 MacBride *1975:* 8 Sakharov *1976:* 8 Corrigan, Williams *1978:* 5 Begin, Sadat *1979:* 12 Mother Teresa *1980:* 8 Esquivel *1982:* 6 Myrdal 12 Garcia Robles *1983:* 6 Walesa *1984:* 4 Tutu *1986:* 6 Wiesel *1987:* 12 Arias Sanchez *1989:* 9 Dalai Lama *1990:* 9 Gorbachev

physics:

1901: 8 Roentgen *1902:* 6 Zeeman 7 Lorentz *1903:* 5 Curie 9 Becquerel *1904:* 6 Strutt *1905:* 6 Lenard *1906:* 7 Thomson *1907:* 9 Michelson *1908:* 8 Lippmann *1909:* 5 Braun 7 Marconi *1910:* 11 van der Waals *1911:* 4 Wien *1912:* 5 Dalen *1914:* 7 von Laue *1915:* 5 Bragg *1917:* 6 Barkla *1918:* 6 Planck *1919:* 5 Stark *1920:* 9 Guillaume *1921:* 8 Einstein *1922:* 4 Bohr *1923:* 8 Millikan *1924:* 8 Siegbahn *1925:* 5 Hertz 6 Franck *1926:* 6 Perrin *1927:* 6 Wilson 7 Compton *1928:* 10 Richardson *1929:* 7 Broglie *1930:* 5 Raman *1932:* 10 Heisenberg *1933:* 5 Dirac 11 Schrodinger *1935:* 8 Chadwick *1936:* 4 Hess 8 Anderson *1937:* 7 Thomson 8 Davisson *1938:* 5 Fermi *1939:* 8 Lawrence *1943:* 5 Stern *1944:* 4 Rabi *1945:* 5 Pauli *1946:* 8 Bridgman *1947:* 8 Appleton *1948:* 8 Blackett *1949:* 6 Yukawa *1950:* 6 Powell *1951:* 6 Walton 9 Cockcroft *1952:* 5 Bloch 7 Purcell *1953:* 7 Zernike *1954:* 4 Born 5 Bothe *1955:* 4 Lamb 5 Kusch *1956:* 7 Bardeen 8 Brattain, Shockley *1957:* 3 Lee 4 Yang *1958:* 4 Tamm 5 Frank 9 Cherenkov *1959:* 5 Segre 11 Chamberlain *1960:* 6 Glaser *1961:* 9 Mossbauer 10 Hofstadter *1962:* 6 Landau *1963:* 5 Mayer 9 Jensen, Wigner *1964:* 5 Basov 6 Townes 9 Prochorov *1965:* 7 Feynman 8 Tomonaga 9 Schwinger *1966:* 7 Kastler *1967:* 5 Bethe *1968:* 7 Alvarez *1969:* 8 Gell-Mann *1970:* 4 Neel 6 Alfven *1971:* 5 Gabor *1972:* 6 Cooper 7 Bardeen 10 Schrieffer *1973:* 5 Esaki 7 Giaever 9 Josephson *1974:* 4 Ryle 6 Hewish *1975:* 4 Bohr 9 Mottelson, Rainwater *1976:* 4 Ting 7 Richter *1977:* 4 Mott 8 Anderson, Van Vleck *1978:* 6 Wilson 7 Kapitsa, Penzias *1979:* 5 Salam 7 Glashow 8 Weinberg *1980:* 5 Fitch 6 Cronin *1981:* 8 Schaalow, Siegbahn 11 Bloembergen *1982:* 6 Wilson *1983:* 6 Fowler 13 Chandrasekhar *1984:* 6 Rubbia 11 van der Meere *1985:* 8 Klitzing *1986:* 5 Ruska 6 Binnig, Rohrer *1987:* 6 Muller 7 Bed-

norz *1988:* **8** Lederman, Schwartz
11 Steinberger *1989:* **4** Paul **6** Ramsey
7 Dehmelt *1990:* **6** Taylor **7** Kendall
8 Friedman
physiology or medicine:
 1901: **10** von Behring *1902:* **4** Ross
 1903: **6** Finsen *1904:* **6** Pavlov *1905:*
 4 Koch *1906:* **5** Golgi **11** Ramon y Cajal
 1907: **7** Laveran *1908:* **7** Ehrlich
 11 Metchnikoff *1909:* **6** Kocher *1910:*
 6 Kossel *1911:* **10** Gullstrand *1912:*
 6 Carrel *1913:* **6** Richet *1914:* **6** Barany
 1919: **6** Bordet *1920:* **5** Krogh *1922:*
 4 Hill **8** Meyerhof *1923:* **7** Banting, Mac-
 leod *1924:* **9** Einthoven *1926:* **7** Fibiger
 1927: **13** Wagner-Jauregg *1928:*
 7 Nicolle *1929:* **7** Eijkman, Hopkins
 1930: **11** Landsteiner *1931:* **7** Warburg
 1932: **6** Adrian **11** Sherrington *1933:*
 6 Morgan *1934:* **5** Minot **6** Murphy
 7 Whipple *1935:* **7** Spemann *1936:*
 4 Dale **5** Loewi *1937:* **12** Szent-Gyorgyi
 1938: **7** Heymans *1939:* **6** Domagk
 1943: **3** Dam **5** Doisy *1944:* **6** Gasser
 8 Erlanger *1945:* **5** Chain **6** Florey
 7 Fleming *1946:* **6** Muller *1947:* **4** Cori
 7 Houssay *1948:* **7** Mueller *1949:*
 4 Hess **5** Moniz *1950:* **5** Hench **7** Kendall **10** Reichstein *1951:* **7** Theiler
 1952: **7** Waksman *1953:* **5** Krebs **7** Lip-
 mann *1954:* **6** Enders, Weller **7** Robbins
 1955: **8** Theorell *1956:* **8** Cournand,
 Richards **9** Forssmann *1957:* **5** Bovet
 1958: **5** Tatum **6** Beadle **8** Lederberg
 1959: **5** Ochoa **8** Kornberg *1960:*
 6 Burnet **7** Medawar *1961:* **6** Bekesy
 1962: **5** Crick **6** Watson **7** Wilkins
 1963: **6** Eccles, Huxley **7** Hodgkin
 1964: **5** Bloch, Lynen *1965:* **5** Jacob,
 Monod **6** Lwolff *1966:* **4** Rous **7** Huggins *1967:* **4** Wald **6** Granit **8** Hartline
 1968: **6** Holley **7** Khorana **9** Nirenberg
 1969: **5** Luria **7** Hershey **8** Delbruck
 1970: **4** Katz **5** Euler **7** Axelrod *1971:*
 10 Sutherland *1972:* **6** Porter **7** Edelman
 1973: **6** Frisch, Lorenz **9** Tinbergen
 1974: **4** Duve **6** Claude, Palade *1975:*
 5 Temin **8** Dulbecco **9** Baltimore *1976:*
 8 Blumberg, Gajdusek *1977:* **5** Yalow
 7 Schally **9** Guillemin *1978:* **5** Arber,
 Smith **7** Nathans *1979:* **7** Cormack
 10 Hounsfield *1980:* **5** Snell **7** Dausset
 10 Benacerraf *1981:* **5** Hubel **6** Sperry,
 Wiesel *1982:* **4** Vane **9** Bergstrom
 10 Samuelsson *1983:* **10** McClintock
 1984: **5** Jerne **7** Koehler **8** Milstein
 1985: **5** Brown **9** Goldstein *1986:*
 5 Cohen **14** Levi-Montalcini *1987:*
 8 Tonegawa *1988:* **3** Black, Elion
 9 Hitchings *1989:* **6** Bishop, Varmus
 1990: **6** Murray, Thomas

Nobel's invention **8** dynamite
nobility **7** peerage, royalty **8** eminence,
 noblesse **11** aristocracy, superiority
noble **4** peer **5** grand, lofty, moral
 6 august, lordly, worthy **7** eminent, ethical,
 stately **8** baronial, elevated, heroical, high-
 born, highbred, imposing, magnific, majestic,
 princely, sterling, virtuous, wellborn **9** estimable, excellent, grandiose, honorable, righteous **10** high-minded, impressive, moralistic, principled **11** illustrious, magnificent,
 outstanding, right-minded **12** aristocratic
nobleman **4** duke, peer **5** baron **6** prince
 7 baronet **8** principe *British:* **4** earl **8** viscount *European:* **7** marquis **8** marquess
 French: **5** comte **7** vicomte *German:*
 4 Graf **8** burgrave, margrave **9** landgrave
 Indian: **6** sardar, sirdar **8** maharaja *Italian:* **8** marchese *Japanese (former):* **6** daimio, daimyo *Scandinavian:* **4** jarl *Spanish:* **7** hidalgo
noblewoman **4** lady **7** baronne, duchess,
 peeress **8** baroness, countess, princess
 European: **8** marquise *Italian:* **8** marchesa
nobody **4** none, zero **5** no man, no one,
 zilch **6** cipher **7** nothing, nullity, whiffet
 8 whipster **9** nonentity
nocturnal **5** night **7** nightly **10** night piece
nocuous **3** bad, ill **6** nocent **7** harmful,
 hurtful **8** damaging **9** injurious **11** deleterious, detrimental, mischievous
nodding **4** dozy **6** drowsy, sleepy,
 snoozy **8** slumbery **9** pendulous, somnolent, soporific **10** slumberous
noddle **4** bean, head, poll **6** noggin
 9 headpiece
noddy **4** dope, fool, jack, tern **5** dunce,
 stupe **6** fulmar, noodle **7** schnook **8** dumbhead **9** lamebrain, razorbill, simpleton
node **4** knob **5** point **11** predicament
 12 entanglement, protuberance
nog **3** ale, peg, pin **5** block
Nogah's father **5** David
noggin **4** bean, head, pate, poll **6** noddle,
 noodle
no-good **4** worm **6** bad lot, draffy, drossy,
 mucker, waster, wretch **7** inutile, lowlife,
 nothing, rounder, wastrel **8** unworthy,
 wormling **9** no-account, valueless, worthless **10** ne'er-do-well, profligate,
 scapegrace
Nohah's father **8** Benjamin
noise **3** din **4** blab, talk **5** babel, rumor,
 sound **6** clamor, gossip, hubbub, racket,
 ruckus, rumpus, tattle, uproar **7** ruction,
 sonance, stridor **8** resonant
 11 pandemonium
noiseless **4** hush **5** quiet, still, whist
 6 silent, stilly
noisemaker **4** horn **6** rattle **7** clapper
noisette **5** hazel

noisome 4 foul, rank, vile 5 dirty, fetid, funky, fusty, musty, nasty 6 filthy, horrid, putrid, rancid, sickly 7 harmful, noxious, squalid 8 nidorous, stinking 9 offensive, repulsive, revolting, sickening, unhealthy 10 disgusting, insalutary, malodorous, nauseating, unsalutary 11 destructive, distasteful, unhealthful 12 insalubrious

noisy 4 loud 7 blatant, clamant, rackety, squeaky 8 clattery, overloud, sonorous, strident 9 clamorous, turbulent 10 boisterous, clangorous, strepitous, tumultuous, uproarious, vociferous 12 obstreperous

nomad 6 roving *Arabic:* 6 beduin 7 bedouin

nomadic 6 roving 7 vagrant 8 vagabond 9 itinerant, itinerate, wandering, wayfaring 11 perambulant, peripatetic 13 perambulatory

nom de plume see **pen name**

nomen 4 name, noun 5 style, title 7 moniker 11 appellation, appellative, designation

nomenclature 4 list, name 7 catalog 9 designate 11 appellation, designation, terminology

nominal 5 rated 6 formal 7 alleged, seeming, titular 8 apparent, so-called, trifling 9 pretended, professed 10 ostensible 11 approximate 12 substantival 13 insignificant

nominate 3 tap 4 call, name 5 offer 6 tender 7 appoint, name off, present, proffer, propose, purpose

nonage 7 infancy 8 minority 10 immaturity

nonchalant 4 cool, easy, glad 5 light 6 casual, smooth 8 careless, cheerful, composed 9 collected, unruffled 10 effortless 11 unflappable 12 lighthearted 13 imperturbable

noncleric 4 laic 6 layman

nonclerical 3 lay

nonclerics 5 laity

noncommittal 7 neutral 8 reserved 10 restrained

nonconformist 5 rebel 6 hippie 7 beatnik, heretic, sectary 8 bohemian, maverick 9 dissenter, dissident, heretical, heterodox, sectarian 10 schismatic, separatist, unorthodox 11 misbeliever, schismatist

nonconformity 6 heresy, schism 7 dissent 9 misbelief 10 dissidence, heterodoxy 11 unorthodoxy 13 individualism

nonentity 4 zero 5 aught, zilch 6 cipher, nobody 7 nothing, nullity, sad sack, whiffet 8 small fry, unperson, whipster 9 obscurity, rushlight, small beer

nonesuch 5 ideal, jewel 7 paragon 9 matchless, nonpareil, unequaled, unrivaled

nonetheless 3 yet 5 still 6 though,

withal 7 howbeit, however 8 after all 11 still and all

nonexistence 4 nada 7 nullity, vacuity 8 nihility 11 nothingness

nonflammable 7 apyrous 13 incombustible

nonfunctional 7 useless 8 unusable 10 unworkable 11 impractical 13 impracticable, unserviceable

non-Hawaiian 5 haole

non-Jew 3 goy 5 goyim (plural) 7 gentile

nonmilitary 8 civilian

non-Muslim 6 giaour

no-nonsense 5 grave, sober, staid 6 sedate, solemn, somber 7 earnest, serious, weighty 10 sobersided

nonpareil see **nonesuch**

nonpartisan 4 fair, just 9 equitable, impartial, objective, uncolored 11 indifferent 12 unprejudiced 13 undistinctive

nonplus 4 balk, beat, faze 5 stick, stump, throw 6 baffle, boggle, flurry, muddle, puzzle, rattle, stymie, thwart 7 buffalo, confuse, dilemma, fluster, mystify, perplex, stagger 8 confound, overcome, paralyze, quandary 9 dumbfound, frustrate

nonprofessional 3 lay 4 laic, tyro 7 amateur, dabbler 9 smatterer 10 dilettante 11 abecedarian

nonrational 3 mad 7 invalid 9 illogical, sophistic 10 fallacious, reasonless, unreasoned 12 unreasonable

nonreligious 3 lay 7 godless, profane, secular 8 temporal

nonresistant 7 passive 8 resigned, yielding 10 submissive 11 acquiescent

nonsense 3 rot 4 blah, bosh, bull, bunk, crap, gook, guff, jazz, punk, tosh 5 bilge, drool, folly, fudge, Greek, hokum, hooey, trash 6 babble, blague, bunkum, bushwa, drivel, hot air, humbug, jabber, piffle 7 baloney, blather, eyewash, flubdub, foolery, fooling, hogwash, inanity, rubbish, trifles, twaddle 8 buncombe, claptrap, falderal, falderol, flimflam, malarkey, pishposh, slipslop, tommyrot, trumpery 9 gibberish, moonshine, poppycock 10 applesauce, balderdash, double-talk, flapdoodle, meshuggaas, tomfoolery 11 jabberwocky, whangdoodle, windbaggery 12 blatherskite, fiddle-faddle, fiddlesticks, flummadiddle 13 horsefeathers *British:* 10 codswallop

nonsensical 5 inane 6 absurd 7 foolish 9 unmeaning 12 preposterous

nonsuccess 6 defeat 7 failure

nonviolent 6 irenic 7 pacific 8 pacifist, peaceful 9 peaceable 12 pacificatory

noodle 4 bean, dope, head, poll 5 chump, dunce, ninny, noddy, stupe 6 noggin 7 schnook 8 dumbhead 9 blockhead, lamebrain, simpleton 10 dunderhead

nook 4 cove, hole 5 niche 6 alcove, corner, cranny, recess 7 byplace 9 cubbyhole
Noon Wine author 6 Porter
noose 3 tie 4 bond, hang 5 lasso, scrag, snare 6 entrap, gibbet, secure 7 turn off 8 string up
Nordhoff's partner 4 Hall
norm 3 par 4 mean, type 5 maxim, model 6 median 7 average, pattern
Norma *composer:* 7 Bellini *librettist:* 6 Romani
normal 4 mean, sane 5 lucid, right, typic, usual 6 common 7 average, general, natural, regular, typical 8 all there, ordinary, standard 9 customary, prevalent 11 commonplace 12 compos mentis
Normandy's capital 5 Rouen
Norns 5 fates, Skuld, Urdur 9 Verthandi
Norris novel 4 Blix 6 The Pit 8 McTeague 10 The Octopus
Norse *abode of the dead:* 8 Niflheim *alphabet:* 5 Runic *archer:* 4 Egil *bard:* 5 scald, skald *chieftain:* 4 jarl, Rolf 5 Rollo *demon:* 4 Mara, Surt 5 Surtr *dragon:* 6 Fafnir 8 Nithhogg *epic:* 4 Edda *explorer:* 4 Eric 7 Ericson 8 Ericsson *first man:* 3 Ask 4 Askr *first woman:* 5 Embla *giant:* 4 Egil, Wade, Wate, Ymer, Ymir 5 Aegir, Egill, Hymir, Jotun, Mimir 6 Fafnir, Jotunn *giantess:* 4 Egia, Norn, Nott *god:* 2 As, Ve 3 Asa, Ass 4 Surt, Vali, Vili 5 Aesir (plural), Surtr, Vanir (plural) 6 Hoenir, Vithar 7 Vitharr *blind:* 4 Hoth 5 Hoder, Hodur, Hothr *chief:* 4 Odin 5 Othin, Wodan, Woden, Wotan *guardian:* 7 Heimdal 8 Heimdall 9 Heimdallr *messenger:* 6 Hermod 7 Hermodr *of beauty:* 5 Baldr 6 Balder, Baldur *of evil:* 4 Loke, Loki *of fertility:* 4 Frey 5 Freyr *of justice:* 7 Forsete, Forseti *of light:* 3 Dag *of peace:* 5 Baldr 6 Balder, Baldur *of poetry:* 5 Brage, Bragi *of the hunt:* 3 Ull 4 Ullr *of the seas:* 5 Njord 6 Njoerd, Njorth 4 Hler 5 Aegir, Gymir *of the sky:* 4 Odin 5 Othin *of thunder:* 4 Thor 5 Donar *of war:* 3 Tiu, Tiw, Tyr, Zio, Ziu *wolf:* 6 Fenrir *goddess:* 3 dis 4 Saga 5 disir (plural) 7 Asynjur *of fate:* 3 Urd 4 Norn, Urth, Wyrd 5 Skuld 9 Verthandi *of healing:* 3 Eir *of love:* 5 Freya *of marriage:* 5 Frigg 6 Frigga *of night:* 4 Natt, Nott *of storms:* 3 Ran *of the earth:* 5 Joerd, Jorth *of the moon:* 5 Nanna *of the sea:* 3 Ran *of the sky:* 5 Frigg 6 Frigga *of the underworld:* 3 Hel 4 Hela *of youth:* 4 Idun 5 Ithun 6 Ithunn *gods' abode:* 6 Asgard *hall of heroes:* 8 Valhalla *king:* 4 Atli, Olaf *nobleman:* 4 jarl *patron saint:* 4 Olaf *poem:* 4 rune *poet:* 5 scald, skald *rainbow bridge:* 7 Bifrost *sea serpent:* 4 Wade, Wate 6 kraken

7 Midgard *smith:* 6 Völund *tale:* 4 saga *toast:* 5 skoal *watchdog:* 4 Garm 5 Garmr *world's destruction:* 8 Ragnarok *world tree:* 8 Ygdrasil 10 Yggdrasill
north *combining form:* 4 arct 5 arcto
North African *country:* 5 Egypt, Libya 7 Algeria, Morocco, Tunisia *fruit:* 3 fig 4 date *garment:* 4 haik *grass:* 4 alfa 7 esparto *jackal:* 4 dieb *language:* 6 Arabic, Berber *Muslim sect:* 6 Sanusi 7 Senussi *people:* 6 Berber, Hamite 7 bedouin *seaport:* 4 Oran, Sfax 6 Annaba 7 Tangier 10 Casablanca
North America *country:* 4 Cuba 5 Haiti 6 Canada, Mexico, Panama 7 Bahamas, Grenada, Jamaica 8 Dominica, Honduras 9 Costa Rica, Guatemala, Nicaragua 10 El Salvador, Saint Lucia 12 United States *ethnic group:* 5 Negro 6 Indian 7 Mestizo, Spanish *language:* 6 Creole, French 7 English, Nahuatl, Spanish
North Carolina *capital:* 7 Raleigh *college, university:* 4 Duke, Elon 8 Davidson 10 Wake Forest *largest city:* 9 Charlotte *nickname:* 12 Tar Heel State *state bird:* 8 cardinal *state flower:* 7 dogwood
North Dakota *capital:* 8 Bismarck *largest town:* 5 Fargo *nickname:* 10 Sioux State
northern 4 pike 6 boreal 11 hyperborean
northern limit of the world 5 Thule
North Korea *capital:* 9 Pyongyang *monetary unit:* 3 won
North Star State 9 Minnesota
Northwest Passage author 7 Roberts
Northwest Territories *capital:* 11 Yellowknife *district:* 8 Franklin, Keewatin 9 Mackenzie
north wind see at wind
Norway *capital:* 4 Oslo *inlet:* 5 fiord, fjord *monetary unit:* 5 krone *patron saint:* 4 Olaf *plateau region:* 5 fjeld
Norwegian *goblin:* 5 nisse *language:* 5 Norse 6 Bokmal 7 Bokmaal, Nynorsk, Riksmal 8 Landsmal, Riksmaal 9 Landsmaal
nose 3 pry 4 beak, bent, bump, gift, head, poke 5 aroma, flair, knack, prier, pryer, scent, smell, sniff, snift, snoop, snoot, snout, snuff 6 butt-in, genius, muzzle, nuzzle, pecker, talent 7 aptness, faculty, meddler, Paul Pry, smeller, sneezer 8 busybody, kibitzer, quidnunc, smell out 9 olfaction, proboscis, schnozzle *combining form:* 3 nas 4 nasi, naso 5 rhina, rhine 6 rhinus, rrhine *kind:* 3 pug 5 Roman 8 aquiline *lengthener:* 3 lie *opening:* 7 nostril
nosebleed 6 yarrow 9 epistaxis
nose-dive 3 dip 4 drop, fall, skid 6 plunge, tumble 7 plummet
nosegay 4 posy 7 bouquet
nosey see nosy

nosh 5 snack
Nostradamus 5 augur 6 auspex
7 prophet 8 foreseer, haruspex 9 predictor 10 forecaster, foreteller, prophesier
Nostromo author 6 Conrad
nostrum 6 elixir 7 cure-all, panacea
nosy 5 peery 6 prying, snoopy 7 curious
9 intrusive 11 inquisitive, inquisitory
not *prefix:* 2 an, il, im, in, ir, un 3 ant, dis,
non 4 anth, anti
notability 3 VIP 4 lion, name 5 celeb,
chief 6 leader 7 big name, big shot 8 bigtimer, eminence, luminary, somebody
9 celebrity, dignitary
notable 3 big, VIP 4 czar, king, lion, name,
star 5 baron, celeb, chief, famed, great,
light, mogul, nabob, nawob, power 6 big
boy, biggie, big gun, bigwig, famous, fat cat,
figure, leader, prince, rubric 7 big name, big
shot, eminent, magnate, mugwump, poohbah 8 big chief, big noise, bigtimer, big
wheel, eminence, great gun, luminary,
renowned, somebody, striking 9 big
cheese, celebrity, character, dignitary,
important, muckamuck, personage, prominent, red-letter 10 celebrated, celebrious,
noteworthy 11 conspicuous, heavyweight,
illustrious, personality 13 distinguished,
high-muck-a-muck
notarize 7 certify 8 validate
notch 3 cut, gap, peg 4 gash, mark, nick,
nock, rung, step 5 cleft, grade, score,
stage 6 degree, indent, record 7 scratch
8 incision, undercut 9 indenture 10 depression 11 indentation
note 3 cry, jot, see 4 call, chit, heed, mark,
memo, mood, odor, show, song, tone, view
5 motif, smell, sound, tenor 6 descry, letter,
regard, remark 7 comment, discern, element, epistle, jotting, missive, observe
8 annotate, eminence, indicate, perceive,
reminder 9 attention, knowledge 10 cognizance, commentary, memorandum, observance, reputation 11 distinction, distinguish,
information, observation 12 obiter dictum
notebook 3 log 5 diary 6 cahier 7 journal
noted 6 famous 7 eminent, leading, popular 9 prominent, well-known
noteworthy 6 patent, rubric 7 evident,
notable 8 manifest, nameable 9 memorable, prominent, red-letter 10 noticeable,
observable, remarkable 11 conspicuous,
exceptional, outstanding 12 considerable
13 extraordinary
nothing 3 nil, nix 4 zero 5 aught, nihil,
ought, zilch 6 cipher, draffy, drossy, naught,
nobody, no-good, nought, trifle 7 inutile,
nullity, whiffet 8 goose egg, unworthy,
whipster 9 bagatelle, no-account, nonentity,
valueless, worthless *French:* 4 rien *Ger-*

man: 6 nichts *Latin:* 5 nihil *Spanish:*
4 nada
nothingness 4 nada, void 5 death 6 vacuum 7 nullity, vacuity 8 nihility 9 emptiness 12 nonexistence
notice 2 ad 3 see 4 care, espy, heed,
mark, memo 5 favor, grasp, greet, refer,
sense, sight 6 advert, descry, regard,
remark, review 7 comment, concern, discern, observe, respect, thought 8 civility,
critique, perceive, reviewal 9 attention, criticism, directive, recognize 10 book review,
cognizance, evaluation, memorandum,
observance 11 acknowledge, distinguish,
information, observation 12 announcement
noticeable 6 marked, patent, signal 7 evident, obvious, pointed, salient 8 manifest,
striking 9 arresting, arrestive, prominent
10 noteworthy 11 conspicuous, eye-catching, outstanding, sensational, significant,
spectacular
notify 4 clew, clue, post, tell, warn
6 advise, fill in, inform, reveal, signal, wise
up 7 apprise, declare, divulge, publish
8 acquaint, announce, disclose, discover,
proclaim 9 broadcast 10 promulgate
notion 4 clue, hint, idea, term, whim
5 fancy, freak, humor, image 6 maggot,
phrase 7 boutade, caprice, conceit, concept, inkling, thought 8 crotchet, telltale
9 knowledge 10 impression, knickknack
12 apprehension 13 understanding
notional 5 ideal 6 unreal 7 fancied, shadowy 8 fanciful, imagined 9 crotchety, imaginary, visionary, whimsical 10 conceptual
11 theoretical
notorious 5 noted 6 famous 7 leading,
popular 8 ill-famed, infamous 9 prominent,
well-known
Nott's horse 8 Hrimfaxi
Notus 6 Auster *brother:* 5 Eurus
6 Boreas 8 Zephyrus *father:* 6 Aeolus
8 Astraeus *mother:* 3 Eos
noun 4 name 7 nominal 11 substantive
inflectional form: 4 case *suffix:* 2 et, ia,
ic 3 ent, ery, ier, ing, ion, ist 4 ence *verbal:* 6 gerund
nourish 4 rear 5 nurse, raise 6 foster, nursle, suckle 7 bring up, build up, nurture,
support 8 maintain 9 cultivate 10 breastfeed, provide for, strengthen
nourishment 3 pap 4 food, keep 6 living 7 aliment, pabulum, support 8 nutrient
10 sustenance 11 maintenance
nouveau riche 7 parvenu, upstart 8 roturier 9 arriviste
Nova Scotia *capital:* 7 Halifax *original
name:* 6 Acadia, Acadie
novel 3 new, odd 5 fresh 6 modern,
recent, unique 7 special, strange, unusual
8 neoteric, original, peculiar, singular,

uncommon 9 different, new-sprung 10 newfangled, unfamiliar 11 modernistic 12 new-fashioned

novelty 5 curio, sport 6 bauble, change, gewgaw, trifle 7 bibelot, newness, trinket, whatnot 8 gimcrack, mutation 9 objet d'art 10 innovation, knickknack

novice 3 cub 4 boot, colt, punk, tyro 6 greeny, rookie 7 amateur, learner, recruit, student, trainee 8 beginner, freshman, inexpert, neophyte, newcomer, prentice 9 fledgling, greenhorn, novitiate, postulant 10 apprentice, tenderfoot

Novum Organum author 5 Bacon

now 2 as 3 for 4 away 5 since, today 6 at once, hereat, seeing 7 anymore, because, present, whereas 8 as long as, directly, existing, first off, up-to-date 9 forthwith, instanter, instantly, presently, right away, sometimes 10 inasmuch as 11 considering, immediately, straightway

now and again 7 at times, betimes 9 sometimes

now and then see **now and again**

Nox, Nyx *brother:* 6 Erebus *daughter:* 3 Day 4 Eris 5 Light *father:* 5 Chaos *husband:* 6 Erebus *son:* 6 Charon, Hypnos 8 Thanatos

noxious 5 fetid 6 deadly, putrid, sickly 7 baneful, noisome 8 stinking 9 pestilent, unhealthy 10 insalutary, unsalutary 11 distasteful, pestiferous, unhealthful, unwholesome

nozzle 5 eject, spray 9 nose about

nuance 4 dash 5 shade, tinge, touch 6 nicety 7 soupçon 8 subtlety 9 gradation, suspicion 10 refinement, suggestion

nub 4 core, crux, gist, knob, lump, meat, pith 5 point, short 6 kernel, upshot 9 substance 12 protuberance

Nubian 8 Cushitic

nucha 4 nape

nuclear agency 3 AEC, NRC

nuclear particle 6 proton 7 neutron

nucleus 3 bud 4 core, germ, head, kern, ring, seed 5 focus, spark 6 embryo *material:* 8 karyotin

Nudd's son 6 Edeyrn

nude 3 raw 4 bald, bare 5 naked, stark 6 peeled, unclad 7 unrobed 8 buff-bare, stripped 9 au naturel, unattired, unclothed, uncovered, undressed 10 dishabille, starknaked 11 garmentless

nudge 3 dig, jab, jog, toe 4 near, poke, prod 5 punch 9 ease along

nugatory 4 idle, vain 5 empty 6 hollow, otiose 7 invalid 9 worthless

nugget 3 gob, wad 4 clod, hunk, lump 5 chunk, clump, hunch

nuisance 4 harm, pest 6 bother, injury, pester, plague 7 nudnick 8 irritant, pes-

terer 9 besetment 10 botherment 11 botheration 12 exasperation

null 3 bad, nil 4 knur, void, zero 5 annul, empty, knurl 7 destroy, expunge, invalid, useless 9 worthless 10 obliterate 11 ineffective, ineffectual, nonexistent 13 inefficacious, insignificant

nullify 4 undo 5 abate, annul, limit, quash 6 efface, negate, offset 7 abolish, confine, vitiate 8 abrogate, restrict 10 annihilate, compensate, counteract, invalidate, neutralize 11 countervail

nullity 4 nada, zero 5 zilch 6 cipher, nobody 7 nothing, vacuity, whiffet 8 whipster 9 annulment, nonentity 11 nothingness 12 nonexistence

numb 4 dead, dull, mull 5 aloof, blunt, chill, frost 6 asleep, casual, deaden, freeze, remote 8 comatose, deadened, detached 9 incurious, insensate, senseless, stupefied, uncurious, unfeeling 10 insensible, insentient 11 desensitize, indifferent, insensitive, unconcerned, unconscious 12 anesthetized, desensitized, uninterested

number 5 add up, count, digit, run to, sum to, tally, total 6 amount, cipher, come to, figure 7 chiffer, include, integer, numeral, numeric, ordinal, run into, several, sum into 8 cardinal, numerate, paginate 9 aggregate, enumerate *added to another:* 6 augend *combining form:* 7 arithmo *large indeterminate:* 7 zillion *resulting from division:* 8 quotient *resulting from multiplication:* 7 product *resulting from subtraction:* 10 difference *science:* 11 mathematics *whole:* 7 integer

number one 4 main 5 chief, major 6 Grade A 7 capital, stellar 8 dominant, five-star, foremost, superior 9 excellent, first-rate, front-rank, numero uno, topdrawer 10 blue-ribbon, first-class, preeminent 11 first-string, outstanding, predominant

numbness 6 stupor *combining form:* 4 narc 5 narco

numeral 5 digit 6 cipher, figure, number 7 chiffer, integer 11 whole number

numerate 4 list, tale, tell 5 count, tally 6 number 7 tick off

numerous 3 big 4 many 5 great, large 6 legion, sundry 7 several, umpteen, various 8 populous 9 plentiful 10 voluminous 12 multifarious, multitudinal 13 multitudinous

Numitor *brother:* 7 Amulius *daughter:* 9 Rea Silvia 10 Rhea Silvia *grandson:* 5 Remus 7 Romulus

numskull 4 dolt 5 dunce 8 bonehead, clodpate 9 blockhead, thickhead

numskulled 5 dense, thick 6 stupid 9 fat-

headed **10** beefheaded **11** blockheaded, thickheaded, thick-witted
nunnery 7 convent **10** sisterhood *head:* **8** superior
Nun's son 6 Joshua
nuptial 6 bridal, wedded **7** marital, married, spousal, wedding **8** conjugal, hymeneal **9** connubial, espousals **11** matrimonial
nurse 4 feed, nana, rear, suck **5** humor, nanny, serve **6** attend, foster, mother, pamper, suckle, wait on **7** advance, care for, cherish, educate, forward, further, indulge, nourish, nurture, promote **9** cultivate **10** minister to *children's:* **5** nanny **6** nannie *English:* **11** Nightingale *Indian:* **4** ayah *Oriental:* **3** ama **4** amah
nursemaid 4 nana **5** nanny **6** minder, nannie, sitter **9** governess **10** babysitter *Indian:* **4** ayah *Oriental:* **3** ama **4** amah
nursery 6 crèche **7** brooder
nurture 4 feed, food, grub, rear **5** nurse, raise, train **6** cradle, foster, nursle, school, uphold, viands **7** bolster, bring up, cherish, edibles, educate, nourish, support, sustain **8** tutelage, victuals **9** cultivate, provender **10** discipline, provisions, upbringing **11** comestibles
nut 2 en **3** bug **4** kook, loon **5** acorn, bigot, crank, fiend, freak, issue, loony, pecan, tryma **6** almond, cashew, cuckoo, dement, madman, maniac, zealot **7** fanatic, filbert, hickory, lunatic, madling, problem, trymata (plural) **8** crackpot, question **9** bedlamite, ding-a-ling, harebrain, macadamia, non compos, pistachio, screwball **10** crack-

brain, enthusiast, Tom o' Bedlam *combining form:* **4** cary, kary **5** caryo, karyo *European shrub:* **7** filbert *of a violin bow:* **4** frog, heel
Nut *consort:* **3** Geb, Keb *daughter:* **4** Isis **8** Nephthys *son:* **2** Ra **6** Osiris
nuthouse 6 asylum **8** loony bin **9** funny farm **10** booby hatch
Nutmeg State 11 Connecticut
nutria 5 coypu
nutriment 3 pap **4** food, keep **5** bread **6** living **7** pabulum, support **10** livelihood, sustenance **11** maintenance, subsistence
nutritious 9 healthful, wholesome **10** nourishing
nuts 3 mad **4** daft, wild **5** batty, crazy, wacky **6** insane, screwy **7** cracked **8** demented **10** unbalanced
nutshell 3 sum **5** sum up **6** digest **7** summate **8** condense **9** epitomize, inventory, summarize, synopsize
nutty see **nuts**
nuzzle 4 push, root, snug **5** nudge **6** burrow, cuddle, nestle, snudge, thrust **7** snoozle, snuggle
Nycteus *brother:* **5** Lycus *daughter:* **7** Antiope
nymph 5 deity, larva **6** maiden *changed into a bear:* **8** Callisto *changed into a laurel:* **6** Daphne *changed into a rock:* **4** Echo *mountain:* **5** oread *sea:* **6** Nereid **7** Calypso *water:* **5** naiad *wood:* **5** dryad
Nym's crony 8 Falstaff
Nyx see **Nox**

O

oaf 2 ox 3 dub 4 boob, bull, clod, dolt, gawk, goof, goon, hulk, lout, lump, slob 5 beast, booby, brute, chump, clown, dunce, klutz, looby 6 bohunk, galoot, lubber, lummox, slouch 7 bruiser, fathead, gorilla, lobster, lumpkin, palooka 8 bonehead, dolthead, lunkhead, meathead 9 blockhead, blunderer, simpleton

oak 4 tree, wood 9 broadleaf *African:* 7 turtosa *family:* 8 Fagaceae *fruit:* 5 acorn *genus:* 7 Quercus *kind:* 3 bur, pin, red 4 bear, cork, holm, ilex, live 5 black, holly, roble, white 6 barren, cerris, encina 7 durmast, English, moss-cup, valonia 9 blackjack *Mexican:* 8 chaparro *young:* 7 oakling 8 flittern

oar 3 row 4 pole, pull 5 rower, scull 6 paddle 7 paddler *part:* 4 loom, palm 5 blade, shaft 6 button, collar

oarsman 3 bow 5 rower 6 stroke 7 sculler *director:* 3 cox 8 coxswain

oasis 3 spa 4 wadi, wady 6 refuge, relief *ancient:* 4 Merv *Egypt:* 4 Siwa 5 Gafsa 6 Dakhla 7 Farafra 8 Ammonium *Libya:* 5 Mizda, Sebha 6 Sabhah 7 Gadames 8 Ghudamis *Niger:* 5 Bilma *Saudi Arabia:* 5 Hofuf, Taima 7 Al-Hufuf

oat 5 grain, grass 6 cereal *genus:* 5 Avena *Scottish:* 3 ait

oater 7 western 10 horse opera

oath 3 vow 4 cuss 5 curse, swear 6 pledge 8 cussword 9 expletive, profanity, swearword 11 affirmation *mild:* 3 gee 4 darn, drat, gosh 5 golly

oatmeal 6 burgoo 8 porridge *Scottish:* 8 drammock

Obadiah *father:* 4 Azel 6 Jehiel 8 Izrahiah, Shemaiah *son:* 8 Ishmaiah

obdurate 4 firm, hard 5 harsh, rigid, rough 6 dogged, mulish, rugged 7 adamant, callous 8 stubborn 9 heartless, immovable, unbending, unfeeling 10 brassbound, hard-boiled, inexorable, inflexible, relentless, unyielding 11 coldhearted, hardhearted, stiff-necked, unemotional 12 stonyhearted 13 unsympathetic

Obed *father:* 4 Boaz 6 Ephlal 8 Shemaiah *mother:* 4 Ruth *son:* 5 Jesse 7 Azariah

Obededom's father 8 Jeduthun

obedient 5 loyal 6 docile 7 duteous, dutiful, slavish 8 amenable, biddable, obeisant, yielding 9 compliant, sheeplike, tractable 10 law-abiding, submissive 11 acquiescent, subservient

obeisance 3 bow 5 congé, honor, kotow 6 curtsy, fealty, homage, kowtow, salaam 7 gesture, loyalty 9 deference, reverence 10 allegiance

Oberon *messenger:* 4 Puck *wife:* 7 Titania

Oberto composer 5 Verdi

obese 3 fat 5 gross, heavy, plump, pudgy, stout 6 fleshy, portly 7 porcine 9 corpulent 10 overweight 11 upholstered

obey 3 bow 4 heed, keep, mind 5 agree, defer, yield 6 accede, assent, comply, follow, regard, submit 7 conform, fulfill, observe, satisfy 8 carry out 9 acquiesce

obfuscate 3 dim 4 murk 5 befog, cloud, gloom 6 darken, shadow 7 becloud, confuse, obscure 8 overcast 9 adumbrate

obi 4 sash

obiter dictum 4 note 6 remark 7 comment 10 commentary 11 observation

obituary 9 necrology

object 3 aim, end, jib, use 4 balk, body, bulk, duty, goal, item, kick, mark, mass, rail, rant, rave, view 5 being, demur, frown, spurn, storm, stuff, thing 6 boggle, doodad, entity, except, gadget, matter, target, volume 7 article, dissent, protest, purpose, stickle 8 complain, disfavor, function, material 9 challenge, criticize, deprecate, disesteem, objective, substance 10 disapprove, discommend, individual

objection 5 demur 7 protest 8 demurral, demurrer, question 9 challenge, exception 10 difficulty 12 remonstrance 13 remonstration

objectionable 4 vile 5 unfit 8 unwanted 9 abhorrent, invidious, loathsome, obnoxious, offensive, repellent, repugnant, repulsive, revolting, unwelcome 10 censurable, ill-favored, unpleasant, unsuitable 11 distasteful, undesirable 12 disagreeable

objective 3 aim, end, use 4 duty, fair, goal, mark 5 gross, outer 6 object, target 7 outside, outward, purpose 8 ambition, external, function, material, physical, sensible, tangible, unbiased 9 corporeal, equitable, impartial, quaesitum, uncolored

10 impersonal, phenomenal **11** substantial **12** unprejudiced **13** dispassionate

objet d'art 5 curio, vertu (plural), virtu (plural) **6** bauble, gewgaw, trifle **7** bibelot, novelty, trinket, whatnot **8** gimcrack **10** knickknack

objurgate 4 damn **5** curse, decry **7** censure, reprove **8** execrate **9** castigate **12** anathematize

oblate 4 monk **5** offer

oblation 6 corban, korban **8** offering **9** sacrifice **12** presentation

obligated 5 bound **8** beholden, indebted

obligation 3 vow **4** call, debt, duty, must, need, oath, part **5** cause, ought, place **6** burden, charge, devoir, pledge **7** promise **8** business, contract, occasion **9** arrearage, committal, liability, necessity, restraint **10** commitment, compulsion, constraint **11** requirement **12** indebtedness

obligatory 7 binding **8** required **9** imperious, mandatory **10** compulsory, imperative

oblige 3 aid **4** help, make **5** avail, favor, force **6** assist, coerce, compel, please, profit **7** benefit, concuss, gratify, shotgun **9** constrain **10** contribute **11** accommodate

obliged 5 bound **8** beholden, grateful, indebted, thankful

obliging 4 easy, kind, mild **5** civil **7** amiable, lenient **11** complaisant, good-humored, good-natured **12** good-tempered

oblique 6 sloped, tilted, tipped **7** leaning, pitched, sloping, tilting **8** circular, inclined, indirect, pitching **9** inclining

obliterate 4 raze, x out **5** erase **6** cancel, delete, efface **7** blot out, expunge, wipe out **8** black out, cross out **10** annihilate

oblivion 5 lethe, limbo **6** pardon **7** amnesty, nirvana **13** forgetfulness, obliviousness

oblivious 7 unaware **8** absorbed, ignorant **9** forgetful, unknowing, unmindful, unwitting **10** unfamiliar, uninformed **11** incognizant, unconscious

oblong 4 oval **7** ellipse **9** elongated, rectangle **11** rectangular

obloquy 4 slam, slur **5** abuse, odium, shame **6** infamy **7** calumny, censure **8** disgrace, dishonor, ignominy **9** aspersion, contumely, discredit, disesteem, disrepute, invective, stricture **10** opprobrium, reflection, scurrility **12** billingsgate, vituperation

obnoxious 4 open, vile **5** prone **6** liable, odious **7** exposed, hateful, subject **9** abhorrent, invidious, offensive, repellent, repugnant, revulsive, sickening **10** disgusting

oboe 4 reed **7** hautboy **8** hautbois, woodwind *oriental:* **6** surnai, surnay

obscene 4 foul, lewd, rank, vile **5** bawdy, crude, dirty, gross, lurid, nasty **6** coarse, crusty, earthy, filthy, impure, ribald, risqué, smutty, sultry, vulgar **7** hideous, noisome, profane, raunchy **8** barnyard, horrible, indecent, scabrous **9** offensive, repellent, repugnant, salacious, sickening **10** disgusting, fescennine, lascivious, nauseating, scurrilous **11** foulmouthed, unprintable **12** pornographic, scatological

obscure 3 dim, far, fog, odd **4** blur, dark, dusk, fuzz, haze, hide, mask, mist, murk, veil **5** bedim, befog, belie, blear, blind, cloak, close, cloud, cover, dusky, faint, gloom, lowly, minor, murky, shade, shady, vague **6** bemask, bleary, cloudy, darken, dim out, far-off, gloomy, hidden, humble, mystic, opaque, remote, screen, secret, shadow, shroud **7** becloud, clouded, conceal, cryptic, devious, dislimn, distant, eclipse, falsify, removed, retired, shadowy, unclear, unfamed, unknown, unnoted **8** abstruse, Delphian, disguise, esoteric, lonesome, mystical, nameless, nubilous, overcast, puzzling, secluded, solitary **9** adumbrate, ambiguous, difficult, enigmatic, equivocal, illegible, lightless, obfuscate, overcloud, sibylline, tenebrous, uncertain, undefined, unheard-of **10** caliginous, camouflage, fuliginous, ill-defined, indecisive, indefinite, indistinct, mysterious, overshadow, umbrageous, unemphatic, unexplicit, unrenowned **11** double-edged, double-faced, inscrutable, out-of-the-way, sequestered, unimportant **12** inaccessible, inconclusive, inexplicable, misrepresent, uncelebrated, unfathomable, unnoticeable **13** inconspicuous, unilluminated

obsequies 5 rites **7** funeral

obsequious 6 menial **7** dutiful, fawning, servile, slavish **8** obedient, obeisant, toadying **9** parasitic **10** submissive **11** deferential, subservient, sycophantic

observance 4 heed, mark, note, rite **6** notice, regard, remark, ritual **7** liturgy, service **8** ceremony **9** attention, formality **10** ceremonial, cognizance **11** observation

observant 5 alert, awake, aware **6** arrect **7** heedful, mindful **8** watchful **9** advertent, attentive, regardful **10** thoughtful

observation 4 heed, mark, note **6** notice, regard, remark **7** comment **9** attention **10** cognizance, commentary **12** obiter dictum

observatory 5 tower **7** lookout, outlook **8** overlook *famous:* **4** Lick **6** Wilson, Yerkes **7** Palomar *instrument:* **9** telescope

observe 3 see **4** espy, keep, look, mark, mind, note, obey, twig, view **5** sight, study, watch **6** behold, comply, follow, notice, remark, revere **7** comment, conform, discern **8** perceive, venerate **9** celebrate, rev-

erence, solemnize **10** animadvert, commentate **11** commemorate

obsessed **4** held **5** beset, queer **6** dogged, hipped **7** gripped, haunted, plagued
8 harassed, overcome, troubled **9** bedev-
iled, bewitched, dominated, hagridden, possessed **12** prepossessed

obsession **5** craze, mania, thing **6** fetish,
hang-up **8** fixation **13** preoccupation

obsolete **3** old **4** dead **5** passé
6 démodé, old hat **7** worn-out **8** old-timey,
outmoded, time-worn **10** superseded
12 old-fashioned

obstacle **3** bar, dam, rub **4** bump, clog,
snag, wall **5** block, catch, crimp, hitch
6 hamper, hurdle **7** barrier **8** handicap,
hardship, mountain, traverse **9** hindrance
10 difficulty, impediment **11** Chinese wall,
encumbrance, obstruction, vicissitude

obstinate **4** deaf **5** balky, muley, stiff,
tough **6** dogged, mulish, unruly **7** crabbed,
staunch, willful **8** contrary, obdurate, perverse, renitent, resolute, stubborn, unpliant
9 pigheaded, resistant, steadfast, unbudg-
ing, unpliable **10** bullheaded, hardheaded,
headstrong, inexorable, inflexible, muleheaded, refractory, self-willed, unyielding
11 incompliant, intractable, opinionated,
stiff-necked, wrongheaded **12** closed-
minded, intransigent, pertinacious, pervica-
cious, recalcitrant

obstreperous **4** loud **5** noisy **6** unruly
7 blatant **8** strident **9** clamorous **10** boisterous, multivocal, vociferant, vociferous
11 disobedient, loudmouthed, openmouthed

obstruct **3** bar, dam, gag **4** clog, fill, plug,
stop **5** block, brake, choke, close **6** hinder,
impede, screen, shroud **7** congest, occlude,
shut off, shut out, stopper, trammel **8** block
out **10** bottleneck, overslaugh

obstruction **3** bar, dam, rub **4** snag
5 hitch **6** hamper, hurdle **8** mountain,
obstacle **9** hindrance **10** impediment

obtain **3** buy, eke, get, win **4** earn, gain,
have, reap **5** annex, reach **6** pick up,
secure **7** acquire, chalk up, procure
8 purchase

obtrude **5** cut in **6** butt in, horn in, impose
7 presume **8** chisel in, infringe

obtrusive **4** busy **5** pushy **7** forward
9 bumptious, officious **10** meddlesome
11 impertinent

obtuse **4** dull, mild **5** blunt, dense, thick
6 stupid

obverse **4** face, side **5** front
10 complement

obviate **4** ward **5** avert, deter **7** forfend,
prevent, rule out **8** preclude, stave off
9 forestall, interfere, interpose, intervene

obvious **5** clear, overt, plain **6** patent
7 blatant, evident, glaring **8** apparent, dis-

tinct, manifest, palpable **11** conspicuous,
unambiguous, unequivocal

oca **5** tuber **6** sorrel

___**O'Casey, dramatist** **4** Sean

occasion **3** use **4** call, need, shot, show,
time **5** basis, break, breed, cause, event,
hatch, right, thing, while **6** chance, demand,
excuse, ground, induce, look-in, moment,
reason, squeak, work up **7** episode, instant,
opening, produce, provoke, warrant
8 engender, generate, incident, milepost,
muster up **9** happening, milestone, necessity **10** antecedent, foundation, obligation,
occurrence **11** determinant, opportunity
12 circumstance **13** justification

occasional **3** few, odd **4** rare **6** casual,
random, scarce, seldom **8** sporadic, uncommon **10** incidental, infrequent, unfrequent

Occidental **7** Western **9** Westerner

occlude **4** clog, fill, plug, stop **5** block,
choke, close **7** congest, stopper **8** obstruct

occult **4** bury, deep, hide **5** cache, eerie,
heavy, magic, stash, weird **6** arcane, orphic,
screen, secret, voodoo **7** conceal, secrete
8 abstruse, ensconce, esoteric, hermetic,
mystical, profound **9** recondite, unearthly
10 acroamatic, cabalistic, mysterious
12 supernatural *ability:* **3** ESP *combining
form:* **5** crypt, krypt **6** crypto, krypto

occupant **5** liver **6** inmate, tenant **7** denizen, dweller, resider **8** habitant, resident
9 indweller **10** inhabitant *suffix:* **3** ite

occupation **3** job **4** line, work **5** trade
6 career, métier **7** calling, pursuit **8** business **9** occupancy, residence **10** employment, habitation, settlement

occupy **3** use **4** busy, fill, hold **5** seize
6 engage, people, tenant **7** engross,
immerse, inhabit **8** populate

occur **3** hap **4** pass **6** befall, betide,
chance, happen, strike **7** come off, develop,
fall out **9** transpire

occurrence **2** go **3** hap **4** pass **5** event,
state, thing **7** episode **8** exigency, incident,
juncture, occasion **9** adventure, condition,
emergency, happening, situation *extraordinary:* **7** miracle *unexpected:* **8** surprise
9 bombshell

ocean **3** sea **4** blue, deep, main **5** brine,
drink **6** Arctic, Indian **7** Pacific **8** Atlantic
9 Antarctic *movement:* **4** tide, wave

Oceania *country:* **4** Fiji **8** Kiribati **9** Australia **10** New Zealand **12** Western Samoa
ethnic group: **6** Fijian, Indian, Papuan,
Samoan **7** British **10** Melanesian, Polynesian **11** Micronesian *language:* **5** Hindi,
Maori **6** Fijian, Papuan, Pidgin, Samoan
7 English **10** Melanesian

oceanic **6** marine **7** pelagic **8** maritime
9 thalassic

Ocean State **11** Rhode Island

Oceanus *daughter:* 5 Doris 7 Oceanid 8 Eurynome *father:* 6 Uranus *mother:* 2 Ge 4 Gaea *sister:* 6 Tethys *son:* 6 Peneus 7 Alpheus *wife:* 6 Tethys

ocellus 3 eye 7 eyespot

ocelot 3 cat 7 wildcat

octave 4 cask, note 5 eight, scale 6 eighth

Octavia *brother:* 8 Augustus *grandson:* 8 Caligula *husband:* 4 Nero 6 Antony

octopus 7 mollusk 9 devilfish 10 cephalopod *arm:* 8 tentacle *genus:* 7 Polypus *kin:* 5 squid 10 cuttlefish

ocular 3 eye, orb 4 lamp 5 optic 6 oculus, peeper, visual, winker 7 optical, seeable, visible 8 viewable, visional

odd 4 lone, only, rare 5 extra, fluky, queer, rummy, weird 6 casual, chance, single, uneven 7 curious, erratic, oddball, strange, unusual 8 peculiar, singular, unpaired 9 eccentric, unmatched 13 idiosyncratic *combining form:* 5 azygo

oddball 4 case, quiz 5 queer, weird 6 oddity, weirdo, zombie 7 bizarre, curious, strange 8 original, peculiar 9 character, eccentric 10 outlandish 13 idiosyncratic

oddity 4 case, quiz 5 quirk 8 original 9 character, curiosity, eccentric 12 idiosyncrasy

odd job 5 chore

odds and ends 4 olio 5 melee 6 jumble, medley, motley, scraps 7 mélange, mixture 8 oddments, sundries 9 etceteras, leftovers, potpourri 10 assortment, hodgepodge, miscellany

ode 4 hymn, poem 5 lyric, psalm, verse

Oded's son 7 Azariah

Odets play 9 Golden Boy 10 Night Music 12 Awake and Sing, Paradise Lost 14 The Country Girl 15 Waiting for Lefty

odeum 4 hall 7 theater

Odin *brother:* 2 Ve 4 Vili *daughter-in-law:* 5 Nanna *father:* 3 Bor *hall:* 8 Valhalla *horse:* 8 Sleipnir *maiden:* 8 Valkyrie *mansion:* 9 Gladsheim *mother:* 6 Bestla *raven:* 5 Hugin, Munin *ring:* 8 Draupnir *ship:* 7 Naglfar 11 Skidbladnir *son:* 3 Tyr 4 Thor, Vali 6 Balder *spear:* 7 Gungnir *sword:* 4 Gram *throne:* 10 Hlidskjalf 11 Hlithskjalf *wife:* 4 Fria, Rind 5 Frigg 6 Frigga *wolf:* 4 Geri 5 Freki

odious 4 foul, vile 6 horrid 7 hateful 8 hateable 9 abhorrent, invidious 10 abominable, despicable, detestable

odium 4 blot, blur, hate, onus, slur, spot 5 brand, shame, stain 6 hatred, infamy, stigma 7 obloquy 8 black eye, disgrace, dishonor, ignominy 9 discredit, disesteem, disrepute 10 opprobrium 11 bar sinister

odontalgia 9 toothache

odor 4 funk 5 aroma, scent, smell *combin-*

ing form: 3 osm 4 osma, osmo *offensive:* 5 stink 6 stench

odorous 5 heady, sweet 6 smelly, strong 7 pungent, reeking, scented 8 aromatic, fragrant, redolent, smelling

Odysseus 7 Ulysses *dog:* 5 Argos *enchantress:* 5 Circe *father:* 7 Laertes *friend:* 6 Mentor *harasser:* 8 Poseidon *herb:* 4 moly *kingdom:* 6 Ithaca *mother:* 8 Anticlea *son:* 9 Telegonus 10 Telemachus *swineherd:* 7 Eumaeus *voyage:* 7 odyssey *wife:* 8 Penelope

Odyssey author 5 Homer

Oedipus *brother-in-law:* 5 Creon *daughter:* 6 Ismene 8 Antigone *father:* 5 Laius *foster father:* 7 Polybus *foster mother:* 8 Periboea *kingdom:* 6 Thebes *mother:* 7 Jocasta *son:* 8 Eteocles 9 Polynices 10 Polyneices *victim:* 5 Laius *wife:* 7 Jocasta

Oeneus *kingdom:* 7 Calydon *son:* 8 Meleager *wife:* 7 Althaea

Oenomaus *charioteer:* 8 Myrtilus *daughter:* 10 Hippodamia *kingdom:* 4 Pisa *slayer:* 6 Pelops

Oenone *husband:* 5 Paris *rival:* 5 Helen

oeuvre 4 work 6 corpus, output

of *French:* 2 de *German:* 3 aus, von

offal 4 junk 5 trash, waste 6 debris, litter, refuse, spilth 7 carrion, garbage, rubbish 9 sweepings *fish:* 5 gurry

off-balance 6 uneven 7 unequal 8 lopsided 9 irregular 10 asymmetric 13 unsymmetrical

off-center 9 eccentric

off-color 3 low 4 blue, mean, racy 5 broad, salty, shady, spicy 6 ailing, poorly, purple, risqué, sickly, unwell, wicked 7 underly 10 indisposed, suggestive

offend 3 sin, vex 4 gall, hurt, miff 5 break, pique, shock, sting, upset, wound 6 appall, breach, excite, insult, nettle 7 affront, disturb, horrify, infract, mortify, outrage, provoke, violate 8 aggrieve, distress, infringe, irritate, trespass 9 disoblige, displease

offender 5 felon 6 sinner 8 criminal, violator 10 lawbreaker, malefactor

offense 3 fit, pet, sin 4 huff, miff, tort 5 anger, crime, onset, pique, scene, tizzy 6 attack, catfit, delict, felony, insult, onfall 7 affront, assault, dudgeon, flare-up, misdeed, tantrum, umbrage 8 delictum, outburst 9 explosion, indignity, offensive, onslaught 10 aggression, assailment, conniption, resentment 11 displeasure, indignation, misdemeanor

offensive 3 bad 4 evil, foul, grim, icky, rank, vile 5 awful, lurid, nasty, onset 6 attack, grisly, horrid, odious, onfall 7 assault, beastly, fulsome, ghastly, hideous, noisome, obscene 8 dreadful, grue-

some, horrible, shocking, terrible, unsavory
9 abhorrent, appalling, atrocious, frightful,
loathsome, onslaught, repellent, repugnant,
repulsive, revolting, sickening **10** abominable, aggression, assailment, detestable, disgusting, nauseating, ungrateful, unpleasant
11 uncongenial, unpalatable, unwholesome
12 disagreeable, unappetizing
13 objectionable

offer **3** bid, lay, try **4** cite, give, pose, seek,
show **5** assay, essay **6** adduce, allege,
extend, strive, tender **7** advance, attempt,
display, exhibit, hold out, present, proffer,
propose **8** endeavor, proposal, struggle

offering **4** alms, gift **6** corban, korban, victim **7** charity, present **8** donation, oblation
9 sacrifice **11** benefaction, beneficence
12 contribution

offhand **6** casual **8** informal **9** extempore,
impromptu, unstudied **10** improvised
11 extemporary, unrehearsed

office **3** job **4** duty, post, role, spot
5 berth, place **6** billet **7** station **8** business,
function, position, province **9** situation
10 connection **11** appointment *head:*
4 boss **7** manager *machine:* **6** copier
9 stenotype **10** calculator, typewriter
seeker: **9** candidate **10** politician *suffix:*
2 cy **3** ate, dom, ure **4** ship *worker:*
5 clerk, steno **6** typist **9** secretary
10 bookkeeper **12** stenographer

officer **3** cop **4** exec **6** noncom, police
7 John Law, manager **8** official **9** executive
abbreviation: **2** Lt. **3** Adm., Col., Ens.,
Gen., Maj. **4** Capt., Cmdr. **5** Comdr., Lieut.
army: **5** major **7** captain, colonel, general
10 lieutenant *British:* **9** brigadier *court:*
7 bailiff *king's:* **11** chamberlain *law-
enforcement:* **3** cop **6** deputy, police
7 marshal, sheriff **9** constable, patrolman,
policeman *naval:* **4** mate **6** ensign **7** admiral, captain **9** commander, commodore
10 lieutenant *noncommissioned:* **5** sarge
8 corporal, sergeant *petty:* **5** bosun, chief
6 yeoman **7** teleman **9** boatswain *prison:*
5 guard **6** warden

official **4** exec **7** cleared, manager, officer
8 approved, endorsed **9** canonical, cathedral, certified, executive, ex officio
10 authorized, ex cathedra, sanctioned
13 administrator, authoritative *city or
town:* **5** mayor **6** alderman **9** selectman
10 councilman *diplomatic:* **5** envoy **6** consul **7** attaché **10** ambassador *govern-
mental:* **6** syndic *parish:* **6** beadle *sports:*
3 ref, ump **6** umpire **7** referee **8** linesman
university: **4** dean **6** bursar **7** provost
9 registrar **10** chancellor

officious **4** busy **9** intrusive, obtrusive
10 meddlesome **11** impertinent
13 polypragmatic

offing **6** future **7** by-and-by **9** aftertime,
afterward, hereafter **10** background

offscouring **5** filth, leper **6** pariah, refuse
7 Ishmael, outcast **8** castaway, derelict
10 Ishmaelite **11** untouchable

offset **4** stop **5** check **6** contra, make up,
redeem, set off **7** balance **8** atone for, outweigh **10** compensate **11** countervail

offshoot **5** scion **6** branch **7** spin-off **9** by-
product, outgrowth **10** derivative,
descendant

offspring **3** kid, son **4** seed **5** brood,
hatch, issue, scion, spawn, swarm, young
7 produce, product, progeny **8** children
9 posterity **10** descendant **11** progeniture
combining form: **3** gen, ped **4** geno, paed,
paid, pedo **5** paedo, paido, proli

Of Human Bondage
author
7 Maugham

Of Mice and Men *author:* **9** Steinbeck
character: **6** George, Lennie

ogee **3** ess **4** arch **5** curve **7** molding

Ogier the ___ **4** Dane

ogive **4** arch

ogle **3** eye **4** gape, gaze, leer, look
5 stare **6** goggle **10** rubberneck

ogre **5** beast, bogey, demon, giant
6 booger **7** bugbear, monster **8** bogeyman **9** boogeyman *Algonquian:* **7** windigo

ogress **5** harpy, scold, shrew, vixen
6 amazon, virago **8** fishwife **9** termagant,
Xanthippe

Ohio *capital:* **8** Columbus *college, university:* **5** Akron, Hiram, Miami **6** Dayton
7 Antioch, Denison, Oberlin **8** Defiance,
Ursuline **9** Kent State *largest city:* **9** Cleveland *nickname:* **12** Buckeye State *state
bird:* **8** cardinal

Oholibamah *father:* **4** Anah *husband:*
4 Esau

oil **3** fat, gas **4** balm, fuel, lube, oleo
5 oleum **6** anoint, grease **7** blarney,
incense, lanolin **8** flattery, soft soap **9** adulation, lubricant, lubricate, petroleum *combining form:* **3** ole **4** eleo, olei, oleo
5 elaeo, elaio *consecrated:* **6** chrism *fragrant:* **5** attar **6** neroli *fuel:* **3** gas **8** gasoline, kerosene, kerosine *relating to:* **5** oleic
ship: **6** tanker *well:* **6** gusher

Oil! author **8** Sinclair

oilbird **8** guacharo

oily **5** fatty, slick, soapy, suave **6** greasy,
smarmy, smooth **7** fulsome **8** unctious,
unctuous **10** oleaginous

ointment **4** balm, nard **5** cream, salve
6 cerate, chrism, lotion **7** unction, unguent
8 calamine, dressing, liniment **9** demulcent,
emollient **11** embrocation

OK, okay **3** aye, yea, yes **5** favor
6 agreed **7** approve, certify, endorse

8 accredit, all right, approval, blessing, sanction

Oklahoma *city:* **3** Ada **4** Enid **5** Tulsa *nickname:* **11** Sooner State *state flower:* **9** mistletoe *university:* **11** Oral Roberts

okra 4 soup **5** bendy, gumbo **8** hibiscus

old 4 aged, late, once, past **5** dated, hoary, passé, solid, stale **6** bygone, démodé, former, steady, versed, whilom **7** ancient, antique, archaic, elderly, lasting, onetime, overage, quondam, skilled, staying, veteran **8** enduring, lifelong, Noachian, outmoded, seasoned, sometime, timeworn **9** erstwhile, long-lived, perennial, perpetual, practical, practiced, primitive, venerable **10** antiquated, continuing, inveterate *Scottish:* **4** auld

old age 10 feebleness, senescence **11** decrepitude, elderliness, senectitude *combining form:* **6** geront, presby **7** geronto, presbyo *relating to:* **6** senile **8** gerontal, gerontic **9** geriatric

Old Bailey 5 court

Old Colony State 13 Massachusetts

Old Curiosity Shop author 7 Dickens

Old Dominion State 8 Virginia

Old English letter see **Anglo-Saxon,** *letter*

Old Faithful 6 geyser

old-fashioned 4 aged **5** dated, dowdy, drink, fusty, moldy, mossy, passé **6** bygone, crusty, démodé, old hat, quaint, rococo, stodgy **7** ancient, antique, archaic, belated, demoded, disused, fogyish, outworn, vintage **8** cocktail, obsolete, outdated, outmoded, unmodern **9** discarded, moss-grown, moth-eaten, out-of-date, Victorian **10** antiquated, fuddy-duddy, mossbacked

old hand 3 vet **7** veteran **9** longtimer

old hat 5 dated, stale, tired, trite **6** cliché, démodé **7** antique, archaic, clichéd, old-time, vintage **8** shopworn, timeworn, wellworn **9** hackneyed, out-of-date **10** antiquated, oldfangled, threadbare

Old Ironsides 12 Constitution *poet:* **6** Holmes

old liner 4 tory **5** right **7** diehard **8** rightist, standpat **11** bitter-ender, right-winger, standpatter **12** conservative

Old Line State 8 Maryland

old maid 7 fusspot **8** spinster

Old Line State 13 North Carolina

Old Rough and Ready 6 Taylor

Olds' car 3 Reo

Old Scratch 5 devil, fiend, Satan **7** Lucifer, Old Nick, serpent **8** Apollyon **9** Beelzebub

old-time 5 dated **6** bygone, old hat, versed **7** antique, archaic, skilled, veteran,

vintage **8** seasoned **9** practical, practiced **10** antiquated **11** experienced

old-timer 3 vet **5** elder **6** senior **7** ancient, old hand, oldster, veteran **10** golden-ager

old womanish 5 anile

Old World 6 Europe

oleaginous see **oily**

oleaster 5 olive **9** olive tree

olecranon 9 funny bone

oleo 9 margarine

oleoresin 10 turpentine

oleum 3 oil

olfaction 5 sense, smell **7** osmesis **8** smelling

olid 4 rank **5** fetid, funky **6** putrid, rancid, smelly **7** stenchy **8** mephitic, stinking **10** malodorous

olio 4 brew, hash, stew **6** medley **7** mélange, mixture **8** mishmash **9** potpourri **10** assortment, hodgepodge, miscellany **11** olla podrida

olive *genus:* **4** Olea *stuffing:* **7** pimento **8** pimiento

Oliver Twist *author:* **7** Dickens *character:* **5** Bates, Fagin, Nancy, Sikes **6** Bumble **7** Dawkins **12** Artful Dodger

olla podrida see **olio**

Ollie's pal 4 Stan

Olympian 3 god **5** lofty **7** athlete, exalted **8** majestic **10** competitor

Olympics 5 games **6** sports **9** athletics *place of origin:* **6** Athens *symbol:* **5** flame, torch

Oman *capital:* **6** Masqat, Muscat *monetary unit:* **4** rial

Omar 4 poet **7** Khayyém *country:* **6** Persia *father:* **7** Eliphaz *poem:* **8** Rubáiyát

omega 3 end **6** ending, letter *kin:* **3** zee

omelet 4 eggs *kind:* **7** foo yong, Spanish, western

omen 4 bode, sign **5** augur, token **6** augury, boding **7** auspice, betoken, portend, portent, presage, promise, warning **8** bodement, forebode, foreshow **9** foretoken **10** foreshadow, prognostic

ominous 4 dire, dour, evil, grim **6** dismal, malign **7** baleful, baneful, direful, doomful, fateful, hostile, malefic, unlucky **8** lowering, menacing, sinister **9** ill-boding, ill-omened **10** forbidding, maleficent, portentous, unfriendly **11** apocalyptic, threatening **12** inauspicious, inhospitable, unpropitious

omission 3 cut, gap **4** skip, slip **5** blank, break, chasm, error, lapse **6** hiatus, lacuna **8** eclipsis, ellipsis, overlook **9** exclusion *mark:* **5** caret **8** ellipsis **10** apostrophe

omit 3 cut **4** dele, drop, fail, skip **5** elide **6** cancel, delete, except, forget, ignore, slight **7** blink at, neglect **8** discount, leave out, overlook, overpass

Omni and Cobo 6 arenas

omnibus 3 ana 4 posy 5 album 7 garland, vehicle 8 analects 9 anthology 10 miscellany 11 florilegium *horse-drawn:* 10 shillibeer

omnipotent 3 god 5 deity 6 divine 7 godlike 8 almighty 9 unlimited 11 all-powerful

omnipresent 7 allover, endless 8 infinite, unending 9 boundless, limitless, universal 10 ubiquitous 12 immeasurable

omniscient 4 wise 7 learned 10 all-knowing

omnium-gatherum see olio

Omphale *domain:* 5 Lydia *slave:* 8 Heracles, Hercules

omphalos 5 navel 9 umbilicus 10 focal point

Omri's father 4 Imri 6 Becher 7 Michael

on 4 atop, over, upon, with 5 about, above, along, forth 7 forward

onager 5 kiang 8 catapult

Onan's father 5 Judah

once 3 odd 4 ever, late, past 5 at all 6 anyway, before, bygone, former, whilom 7 already, anywise, earlier, onetime, quondam 8 formerly, sometime *Scottish:* 4 anes 5 yince

once-over 6 glance, survey 10 inspection 11 examination

one 3 wed 4 join, link, lone, only, sole, unit 5 monad, unite 6 number, relate, single, unique, united 7 connect, numeral 8 coagment, coalesce, separate, singular, solitary 9 associate, coadunate, undivided 10 individual, particular *combining form:* 3 mon 4 heno, mono *French:* 2 un 3 une *German:* 3 ein 4 eine *prefix:* 3 uni *Scottish:* 2 ae 3 ane, yae *Spanish:* 2 un 3 uno

one and a half *combining form:* 6 sesqui

one-eyed giant 7 Cyclops 10 Polyphemus

one-handed god 3 Tiu, Tyr

one-horse town 4 burg 6 Podunk 7 mudhole 11 whistle-stop

one hundred 6 centum *years:* 7 century

O'Neill, Eugene *heroine:* 4 Anna, Nina *play:* 3 Ile 4 Gold 11 The Hairy Ape 12 Ah Wilderness, Anna Christie, Emperor Jones 13 Marco Millions 15 The Iceman Cometh 16 Strange Interlude, The Great God Brown

oneiric 6 dreamy 8 anagogic

oneness 5 unity 7 allness, unicity 8 entirety, identity, sameness, totality, uniquity 9 wholeness 10 entireness, singleness, uniqueness 11 singularity 12 completeness, selfsameness, singularness 13 identicalness, individuality

onerous 4 hard 5 heavy, hefty, tough 6 taxing, trying, unruly 7 arduous, driving, exigent, weighty 8 exacting, grievous, toil-some, unwieldy 9 demanding, difficult, laborious, ponderous 10 burdensome, cumbersome, oppressive 11 heavy-headed

oneself *combining form:* 3 aut 4 auto

one-sided 6 biased, unfair, unjust, warped 7 bigoted, colored, partial 8 lopsided, partisan, weighted 9 jaundiced 10 prejudiced

onetime 4 late, once, past 6 bygone, former, whilom 7 quondam 8 formerly 9 erstwhile

on hand 4 here 7 present

Onias' son 5 Simon

onion 4 bulb 5 cibol 7 shallot 8 eschalot *bulb:* 3 set *genus:* 6 Allium *kin:* 4 leek 6 garlic *kind:* 3 red 5 green 7 Bermuda, Danvers, Spanish *roll:* 5 bialy *young:* 8 scallion

only 3 but, one, yet 4 just, lone, mere, save, sole, solo 5 alone 6 except, merely, simply, single, solely, unique 7 however 8 entirely, peerless, separate, singular, solitary 9 matchless, unequaled, unmatched

onomasticon 7 lexicon 8 wordbook

onomatopoeic 5 mimic 6 echoic 7 mimetic, mimical 9 emulative, imitative 10 simulative

onomatopoetic see onomatopoeic

onrush see onslaught

onset 4 dawn 5 birth, start 6 attack, onfall, origin, outset, setout 7 assault, dawning, offense, opening 8 outstart 9 beginning, offensive, onslaught 10 aggression, assailment 12 commencement

onslaught 5 onset 6 attack, onfall, onrush 7 assault, offense 9 offensive 10 aggression, assailment

Ontario *capital:* 7 Toronto *university:* 4 York 5 Brock, Trent 8 McMaster

on the other hand 3 but 7 however

on the whole 7 en masse 8 all in all 9 generally 10 altogether, by and large

onto 4 atop

onus 3 tax 4 blot, blur, duty, load, slur, spot, task 5 blame, brand, fault, guilt, odium, stain 6 burden, charge, stigma, weight 8 black eye 9 millstone 10 deadweight

onward 4 alee, away 5 ahead, along, forth 7 forward

onyx 3 jet 4 inky 5 black, ebony, jetty, raven, sable 9 pitch-dark 10 chalcedony, pitchblack 11 atramentous

oodles 4 gobs, heap, slew 5 loads, scads 7 jillion 10 quantities

ooid 4 oval 5 ovate, ovoid 7 oviform

oolong 3 tea

oomph 3 vim 4 brio, dash, élan, gimp, life, push 5 drive, verve, vigor 6 esprit, pizazz,

spirit **7** pizzazz **8** strength, vitality
9 animation

ooze 3 mud **4** leak, seep, weep **5** bleed,
exude, marsh, slime, sweat **6** strain
7 secrete **8** transude

opah 4 fish **5** cravo

opal 3 gem **5** glass, jewel, stone **7** girasol,
hyalite **8** girasole **9** cacholong

opaque 4 dark, dull **5** dense, vague
6 cloudy, stupid **7** obscure, unclear
8 nubilous

OPEC nation 4 Iran, Iraq **5** Gabon, Libya,
Qatar **6** Kuwait **7** Algeria, Ecuador, Nigeria **9** Indonesia, Venezuela **11** Saudi Arabia

open 3 cut, tap **4** ajar, bare, free, gash,
hole, meet, undo, wide **5** agape, begin,
break, clear, cover, frank, naked, overt,
plain, prone, slash, start, swell, untie **6** billow, breach, broach, candid, dilate, expand,
expose, extend, fan out, gaping, get off,
launch, liable, mantle, patent, peeled, pierce,
public, reveal, spread, unbolt, unfold,
unlock, unseal, unshut, unstop, unveil,
unwrap, usable **7** convene, denuded, jump
off, kick off, outdoor, outside, release, rin-
gent, rupture, subject, unblock, unclose,
uncover, unlatch, without, yawning **8** commence, disclose, doubtful, embark on, initiate, outdoors, patulous, stripped, unbarred,
unbolted, unclench, unclosed, unclothe,
unlocked, unsealed **9** agreeable, ambiguous, available, dehiscent, dubitable, equivocal, obnoxious, operative, outspread, perforate, reachable, securable, sensitive,
uncertain, uncovered, undecided,
unimpeded, unsettled **10** accessible, attainable, embark upon, employable, inaugurate,
indecisive, obtainable, out-of-doors, outstretch, overspread, unfastened **11** practicable, problematic, susceptible, unconcealed, undisguised, unvarnished
12 undissembled, unobstructed, unrestricted *poetic:* **3** ope *slightly:* **4** ajar

open-air 7 outdoor, outside **8** alfresco
9 out-of-door **10** hypaethral

open-and-shut 5 clear, plain **6** patent
7 evident, obvious **8** apparent, distinct,
manifest

openhanded 4 free **5** clear, plain **6** patent **7** evident, liberal, obvious **8** apparent,
distinct, generous **9** bounteous, bountiful,
unsparing **10** bighearted, munificent

openhearted 4 kind, warm **5** frank, plain
6 candid

opening 2 os **3** gap, ora (plural) **4** dawn,
door, gate, hole, pass, pore, rift, rima, shot,
show, slit, slot, time, vent **5** birth, break,
chasm, chink, cleft, crack, debut, mouth,
onset, start, stoma **6** breach, chance, eyelet, lacuna, look-in, outlet, outset, setout,
squeak **7** crevice, dawning, fissure, orifice,

pinhole, ventage **8** aperture, crevasse,
débouché, occasion, outstart, overture
9 beginning **11** opportunity *bodily:* **4** pore
5 hilum, hilus **7** foramen, orifice, ostiole
8 fenestra *combining form:* **4** pora, pore,
pyle **5** stoma, stome, stomi, stomy, trema
6 stomia, stomum **7** stomata (plural), stomate, tremata (plural) *ship's:* **5** hatch
8 hatchway, porthole

openmouthed 5 agape **6** amazed, gaping **7** blatant **8** strident **9** clamorous
10 boisterous, multivocal, vociferant,
vociferous

open sesame 3 key **6** ticket **8** passport,
password

opera 7 musical *comic:* **5** buffa **6** bouffe
glasses: **9** lorgnette *kind:* **4** soap
5 comic, grand, horse, space *part:* **3** act
4 aria **5** scena *solo:* **4** aria *star:* **4** diva
10 prima donna *text:* **8** libretto (see also
individual titles and composers)

operate 2 go **3** act, cut, ply, run, use
4 keep, play, take, work **5** drive, pilot, react,
steer, wield **6** behave, direct, handle, manage, open up, ordain **7** carry on, conduct,
control, perform **8** function, maneuver
10 manipulate

operation 3 use **4** play **6** action **7** surgery **8** exercise, exertion, function **9** appliance, procedure **10** employment, exercising

operative 4 hand, live, open **5** agent,
alive **6** active, usable, worker **7** dynamic,
laborer, running, working, workman
8 mechanic, workhand **9** Pinkerton

operator 5 agent **6** doctor, driver **7** autoist, surgeon **8** motorist **9** conductor *suffix:* **3** ist **4** ster

operculum 3 lid **4** flap

operose 4 busy, hard **5** tough **6** severe
7 arduous **8** diligent, sedulous, toilsome
9 assiduous, difficult, effortful, laborious

Ophelia *beloved:* **6** Hamlet *brother:*
7 Laertes *father:* **8** Polonius

ophidian 5 snake **9** snakelike

Ophir's father 6 Joktan

opiate 4 dope, drug **6** deaden, sleepy
7 anodyne **8** hypnotic, narcotic, nepenthe,
somnific **9** soporific **10** somnorific

opine 4 deem, hold, view **5** judge, think
6 accept, regard **7** believe, suppose

opinion 3 eye **4** idea, mind, view **5** tenet,
think **6** belief, notion, theory **7** feeling,
thought **8** attitude, estimate, judgment,
reaction **9** sentiment **10** assumption, conclusion, conjecture, conviction, estimation,
impression, persuasion **11** speculation,
supposition *express an:* **4** vote **5** judge
9 criticize

opium 4 dope, drug **8** narcotic *derivative:* **6** heroin **7** codeine, meconin, narcein
8 laudanum, morphine, narceine **9** narco-

tine, paregoric *prepared:* **6** chandu
source: **5** poppy
opossum **9** marsupial *kin:* **8** kangaroo
oppidan **8** townsman
opponent **3** con, foe **4** anti **5** enemy,
match, rival **7** nemesis, opposer **9** adversary, assailant, combatant, oppugnant
10 antagonist, competitor **12** counteragent
opportune **3** fit **5** happy **6** timely **7** timeous **9** favorable, well-timed **10** auspicious,
felicitous, propitious, prosperous
11 appropriate
opportunity **4** hope, pass, room, shot,
show, time, turn **5** break, space, spell
6 chance, look-in, prayer, relief, squeak
7 opening **8** juncture, occasion
oppose **3** pit, vie **4** buck, duel, face
5 array, beard, fight, match, repel **6** combat,
differ, object, refute, repugn, resist **7** contest, counter, dispute, play off **8** confront,
contrast, traverse **9** withstand
10 contradict
opposite **2** to **4** foil **5** polar **6** contra, facing, unlike **7** antonym, counter, inverse,
obverse, opposed, reverse, unalike **8** antipode, antipole, contrary, contrast, converse,
separate **9** antipodal, diametric, different,
divergent, unrelated, unsimilar **10** antipodean, antithesis, antonymous, dissimilar
11 contrasting, counterpole, independent,
unconnected **12** antagonistic, antithetical,
counterpoint **13** contradictory *combining
form:* **7** enantio *French:* **8** en face de *prefix:* **2** ob **3** dis **5** retro **6** contra **7** counter
opposition **3** con **8** defiance **9** animosity,
hostility **10** antagonism, antithesis, resistance **11** contrariety
oppress **5** harry, wrong **6** burden, harass,
sadden, subdue **7** afflict, conquer, depress,
outrage, torment, torture, trouble
8 aggrieve, distress, overcome **9** overthrow, persecute, subjugate
oppressive **4** hard **5** black, bleak, harsh,
heavy, tough **6** dismal, gloomy, severe,
somber, taxing **7** exigent, onerous,
weighty **8** exacting, grievous **9** demanding **10** burdensome, depressing **11** dispiriting **12** discouraging **13** disheartening
oppressive force **4** onus, yoke **6** burden, weight **10** juggernaut
oppressor **6** despot, tyrant **8** dictator
9 strong man
opprobrious **7** abusive **8** ill-famed, infamous, scurrile **9** invective, notorious, truculent **10** scurrilous, vituperous **12** contumelious, vituperative, vituperatory
opprobrium **5** abuse, odium, scorn,
shame **6** infamy **7** obloquy **8** disgrace, dishonor, ignominy **9** discredit, disesteem, disrepute **10** scurrility **12** vituperation

oppugn **3** tug, war **5** fight **6** battle
7 contend
Ops **4** Rhea *consort:* **6** Cronus, Saturn
daughter: **5** Ceres **7** Demeter
opt **4** cull, mark, pick, take **5** elect
6 choose, decide, prefer, select **9** single out
optical **6** ocular, visual **8** visional *instrument:* **4** lens **5** glass, scope **7** transit
9 magnifier, optometer, periscope, telescope **10** microscope
optimist **5** hoper **7** dreamer **8** idealist,
micawber **9** Pollyanna **10** positivist
optimistic **4** fond, rosy **5** merry, sunny
6 bright, hoping, upbeat **7** assured, hopeful **8** cheerful, sanguine **9** confident
12 Pollyannaish
option **5** right **6** choice **8** election **9** privilege, selection **10** preference **11** alternative, prerogative
optional **4** free **8** elective **9** voluntary
11 alternative, facultative **13** discretionary
opulence **6** plenty, riches, wealth
9 affluence
opulent **4** lush, rich **5** plush, showy,
swank **6** Capuan, deluxe, lavish **7** elegant,
moneyed, profuse, wealthy **8** affluent, luscious, palatial, prodigal **9** exuberant, luxuriant, luxurious, profusive, sumptuous
opuntia **6** cactus
or **4** else, gold **6** golden, yellow
9 otherwise
oracle **4** sage, seer **6** medium, vision
8 prophecy **10** apocalypse, revelation *site:*
6 Claros, Delphi, Didyma, Dodona
9 Epidaurus
oracular **5** vatic **6** mantic **7** fatidic **8** Delphian **9** prophetic, sibylline, vaticinal
oral **4** told **5** vocal **6** sonant, spoken, verbal, voiced **7** related, uttered **8** narrated,
viva voce **9** recounted, unwritten
orange **5** color, fruit **6** citrus **8** jacinthe
brownish: **6** Titian *deep:* **11** bittersweet
genus: **6** Citrus *kin:* **9** tangerine **10** grapefruit *kind:* **4** sour **5** blood, chino, navel,
Osage, sweet **7** Seville **8** bergamot, mandarin, Valencia *seed:* **3** pip *skin:* **4** rind
orangutan **3** ape **4** mias **5** pongo
orate **4** rant, rave **5** mouth, speak, spiel
7 bombast, declaim, elocute, soapbox
8 blah-blah, bloviate, harangue, perorate
9 sermonize, speechify **11** rodomontade
oration **6** sermon, speech **7** address
9 discourse *funeral:* **6** eulogy
orator **7** demagog, speaker **9** demagogue
American: **4** Clay **5** Bryan, Henry **7** Calhoun, Douglas, Webster *British:* **5** Burke
8 Disraeli **9** Churchill, Gladstone *French:*
8 Mirabeau *Greek:* **5** Corax **8** Pericles
11 Demosthenes *Roman:* **6** Cicero
oratory **6** chapel **8** rhetoric **9** elocution,
eloquence **11** speechcraft

orb 3 eye 4 ball, lamp 5 globe, round 6 circle, ocular, oculus, peeper, sphere, winker

orbit 4 path 5 ambit, range, reach, scope, sweep, track 6 extent, radius *farthest point:* 5 apsis 6 apogee 8 aphelion *nearest point:* 5 apsis 7 perigee 10 pericenter, perihelion

orchard 5 copse 6 garden 8 arbustum 10 plantation

orchestra 4 band 5 combo, group 7 gamelan 8 ensemble, symphony 12 philharmonic *leader:* 9 conductor *section:* 5 brass 6 string 8 woodwind 10 percussion

orchestrate 5 blend, score, unify 7 arrange 9 harmonize, integrate 10 symphonize, synthesize

orchid 6 flower *kind:* 5 faham, vanda 7 calypso, pogonia 8 cattleya, oncidium 9 cymbidium 11 cypripedium *petal:* 3 lip 8 labellum *product:* 5 faham, salep *tuber:* 5 salep

Orcus see **Hades**

ordain 4 keep 5 order 6 decree, direct, impose, manage 7 carry on, command, conduct, dictate, lay down, operate 9 prescribe

ordeal 5 cross, trial 7 calvary 8 crucible 10 affliction, visitation 11 tribulation

order 3 bid, fix, ilk, row, set 4 case, club, fiat, gear, kind, line, plan, rank, rule, sort, tell, trim, tune, type, warn, word 5 align, array, breed, chain, edict, genus, grace, grade, guild, range, right, shape, train, union 6 adjust, behest, branch, charge, codify, decree, direct, enjoin, estate, extent, fettle, kidney, kilter, league, line up, matter, method, nature, police, repair, sequel, series, settle, status, stripe, system 7 aptness, arrange, arrayal, bidding, bracket, command, decorum, dictate, dispose, feather, fitness, mandate, marshal, pattern, probity, routine, society 8 approach, organize, regiment, regulate, sequence, sodality, tidiness, vicinity 9 allotment, amendment, arrayment, closeness, condition, following, integrity, magnitude, methodize, propriety, proration, proximity, rectitude, rightness, routinize 10 adjustment, allocation, correction, expediency, fellowship, fraternity, injunction, permission, pigeonhole, procession, properness, seemliness, streamline, succession, timeliness 11 alternation, arrangement, association, brotherhood, collocation, consecution, correctness, description, disposition, hierarchize, orderliness, progression, suitability, systematize *good:* 6 eutaxy *lack of:* 5 chaos 6 ataxia 7 anarchy, clutter 9 confusion 11 pandemonium *of business:* 6 agenda, docket *of preference:* 8 priority

orderly 4 aide, neat, snug, tidy, trig, trim 5 alike, exact 6 batman, formal 7 chipper, correct, precise, regular, uniform 8 accurate, methodic, picked up 9 shipshape 10 methodical, systematic 11 uncluttered, well-groomed 12 businesslike

ordinal 4 book 6 number *suffix:* 2 nd, st, th 3 eth

ordinance 3 law 4 fiat, rule 5 canon, edict 6 decree 7 precept, statute 8 decretum 9 prescript 10 capitulary, regulation

ordinary 4 so-so 5 banal, plain, trite, usual 6 common, normal 7 mundane, natural, prosaic, regular, routine 8 everyday, familiar, frequent, workaday 9 customary, plain Jane, quotidian 10 uneventful 11 commonplace 12 unnoteworthy

ordnance 4 guns 6 cannon 7 weapons 8 supplies 9 artillery 10 ammunition

ordure 9 excrement *combining form:* 4 copr, scat 5 copro, scato

ore 4 gold, rock 5 metal 6 copper, silver 7 mineral 8 platinum *analysis:* 5 assay *deposit:* 4 copr, vein *excavation:* 5 stope *iron:* 5 ocher 8 goethite, hematite, limonite *lead:* 6 galena *process:* 8 leaching, smelting *refuse:* 4 slag 5 dross, matte 6 scoria *smelted:* 6 speiss 7 regulus

oread 5 nymph

Oreb's slayer 6 Gideon

Oregon *capital:* 5 Salem *largest city:* 8 Portland *nickname:* 11 Beaver State, Sunset State 12 Webfoot State

Orel's river 3 Oka

Orestes *father:* 9 Agamemnon *friend:* 7 Pylades *mother:* 12 Clytemnestra *sister:* 7 Electra 9 Iphigenia *victim:* 9 Aegisthus 12 Clytemnestra *wife:* 8 Hermione

organ 5 agent, means 6 agency, medium, review 7 channel, journal, vehicle 8 magazine, ministry 9 newspaper 10 instrument, periodical *ancient:* 6 syrinx 9 hydraulus *barrel:* 10 hurdy-gurdy *bodily:* 3 ear, eye 4 lung, nose 5 gland, heart, liver 6 kidney, larynx, spleen, tongue, tonsil, viscus 9 intestine *combining form:* 6 viscer 7 visceri, viscero *mouth:* 9 harmonica *part:* 4 pipe, reed, stop 5 pedal, valve 6 blower 7 console, tremolo 8 keyboard, pedalier 9 wind chest *reed:* 8 melodeon 9 harmonium *stop:* 4 oboe, sext 5 gamba, quint, viola 6 dolcan, dulcet 7 bassoon, celesta, melodia, subbass, tertian 8 carillon, dulciana, gemshorn *tactile:* 6 feeler 8 tentacle

organ cactus 7 saguaro

organism 4 unit 5 being, biont, plant 6 animal *disease-producing:* 4 germ 5 virus 7 microbe 8 pathogen 9 bacterium *single-celled:* 5 monad 6 amoeba 9 protozoan *suffix:* 5 acean

organist *American:* 3 Fox 5 Biggs

6 Newman *Danish:* **9** Buxtehude *Dutch:*
9 Sweelinck *English:* **6** Wesley **7** Gibbons
French: **5** Widor **6** Franck **8** Messiaen
10 Schweitzer *German:* **4** Bach **6** Walcha
7 Richter *Italian:* **7** Germani **8** Gabrieli

organization **4** body, club, unit **5** group,
guild, setup **6** agency **11** arrangement,
association *college:* **4** frat **8** sorority
10 fraternity *criminal:* **4** gang **5** Mafia *fraternal:* (see **fraternal society**) *government:* (see **government agency**) *lack of:*
5 chaos *political:* **4** bloc **5** party **7** appa-
rat, machine

organize **4** form **5** array, found, order,
rally, set up, start **6** create, muster
7 arrange, dispose, marshal **8** mobilize
9 construct, establish, institute, integrate,
methodize, systemize **10** constitute, coordinate **11** put together

orgy **3** bat **4** romp, soak, tear **5** binge,
fling, party, revel, spree **6** ran-tan **7** blowoff, carouse, debauch, rampage, splurge,
wassail **8** carousal **9** bacchanal **10** saturnalia **11** bacchanalia

oriel **3** bay **6** window

orient **5** adapt, pearl, sheen **6** adjust, luster **8** acquaint **11** accommodate

Orient **4** Asia, East **7** Far East

Oriental **5** Asian **7** Asiatic, Chinese, Eastern **8** Japanese *chieftain:* **4** khan *coin:*
3 sen, yen *dish:* **5** pilaf *drink:* **3** tea
4 sake, tuba **6** arrack *inn:* **4** khan **5** serai
11 caravansary **12** caravanserai *litter:*
4 kago **5** dooly **6** doolie **9** palanquin *market:* **3** suq **4** souk **6** bazaar *nana:* **4** amah
prince: **4** raja *ruler:* **4** khan, raja, shah
5 calif, nawab, rajah **6** caliph, sultan
storm: **7** monsoon *taxi:* **7** ricksha **8** rickshaw **10** jinrikisha *title:* **4** raja **5** rajah
weight: **4** tael **5** catty, liang *worker:*
6 coolie

orifice see **opening**

oriflamme **4** flag **5** color **6** banner, pennon **7** pendant, pennant **8** bannerol, gonfalon, standard, streamer

origin **4** root, seed, well **5** birth, blood,
start **6** source, whence **7** descent, genesis,
lineage **8** ancestry, fountain, nascence, nascency, pedigree **9** beginning, inception,
maternity, parentage, paternity **10** derivation, extraction, provenance, wellspring
combining form: **4** geny *of a word:*
9 etymology

original **3** new **4** case, quiz **5** first, model,
novel, prime **6** maiden, mother, native, oddity, unique, zombie **7** initial, oddball, pattern,
pioneer, primary **8** creative, earliest, inventor **9** archetype, character, demiurgic, deviceful, eccentric, ingenious, innovator, inventive, precedent, precursor, primitive,
prototype, underived **10** archetypal, fore-

runner, innovative, innovatory, introducer
prefix: **4** arch **5** arche, archi

originate **4** coin, flow, make, open, rise,
sire, stem **5** arise, begin, birth, breed, hatch,
issue, set up, spawn, start **6** create, father,
launch, parent, spring **7** emanate, proceed,
produce, usher in **8** come from, commence,
generate, hail from, initiate, stem from
9 institute, introduce, procreate **10** derive
from, inaugurate, spring from

originator **4** sire **5** maker **6** author,
father **7** creator, founder **8** inventor
9 architect, generator, innovator, patriarch
10 introducer

oriole **4** bird **8** troupial *European:* **6** loriot
genus: **7** Icterus *golden:* **5** pirol **6** loriot
kind: **6** golden **7** orchard **8** Bullock's
9 Baltimore

Orion **6** hunter **13** constellation *beloved:*
3 Eos *belt:* **7** Ellwand *father:* **7** Hyrieus
8 Poseidon *slayer:* **5** Diana **7** Artemis
star: **5** Rigel **9** Bellatrix **10** Betelgeuse

orison **4** plea, suit **6** appeal, prayer
8 entreaty, petition **11** application, imploration, imprecation **12** supplication

Orithyia *lover:* **6** Boreas *son:* **5** Zetes
6 Calais

Orlando author **5** Woolf

Orlando Furioso author **7** Ariosto

Orleans heroine **9** Joan of Arc

orlop **4** deck

ornament **3** gem **4** deck, trim **5** adorn,
jewel, prank **6** bedeck, enrich, finial, tassel
7 dress up, garnish, jewelry, pendant, whatnot **8** beautify, decorate, filigree **9** embellish, embroider, lavaliere **10** lavalliere *architectural:* **7** crocket **10** ball-flower
Christmas tree: **4** bulb **5** angel **6** tinsel
lip: **6** labret *shoulder:* **7** epaulet

ornate **4** lush, rich **5** fancy, showy **6** florid,
frilly, gilded, rococo **7** aureate, baroque,
labored, opulent **8** luscious, overdone
9 elaborate, luxuriant, luxurious, sumptuous **10** flamboyant, overworked

ornery **4** mean **5** balky, nasty, waspy
6 cranky **7** bearish, froward, restive, waspish, wayward **8** cankered, contrary, perverse, stubborn, vinegary **9** crotchety
10 vinegarish **11** wrongheaded **12** cantankerous, cross-grained

ornithic **5** avian

ornithologist *American:* **7** Audubon, Bartram *English:* **5** Gould *Scottish:* **6** Wilson

ornithon **6** aviary

orotund **4** full, loud **5** round **7** aureate,
flowery, ringing, vibrant **8** plangent, resonant, sonorant, sonorous **9** bombastic, consonant **10** euphuistic, oratorical, resounding, rhetorical, stentorian **11** declamatory
12 magniloquent **13** grandiloquent

Orpah *husband:* 7 Chilion *sister-in-law:*
4 Ruth

orphan 4 lost, waif 5 alone, Annie
6 bereft 7 cast-off, ignored 8 forsaken,
slighted, solitary 9 abandoned, foundling,
neglected 10 parentless, unparented

Orpheus *father:* 6 Apollo 7 Oeagrus
home: 6 Thrace *instrument:* 4 lyre
mother: 8 Calliope *wife:* 8 Euridice

ort 3 bit 5 scrap 6 morsel 7 leaving, remnant 8 leftover

orthodox 4 good, tory 5 right, sound
6 proper, square 7 correct, die-hard, fogyish, oldline 8 accepted, admitted, approved,
official, received, standard, straight
9 canonical, customary 10 button-down,
recognized, sanctioned 11 reactionary, traditional 12 acknowledged, conservative,
conventional 13 authoritative

orthography 8 spelling

ortolan 4 sora 7 bunting 8 bobolink

Orwell novel 10 Animal Farm

oryx 7 gemsbok 8 antelope

os 4 bone 5 esker, mouth 7 orifice

oscillate 4 sway, vary 5 squeg, swing,
waver 7 vibrate 9 fluctuate, pendulate

osculate 3 lip 4 buss, kiss, peck 5 smack

osier 3 rod 6 willow 7 dogwood

Osiris *brother:* 3 Set 4 Seth *crown:*
4 atef *father:* 3 Geb, Keb, Seb *mother:*
3 Nut *scribe:* 4 Thoth *sister:* 4 Isis
slayer: 3 Set 4 Seth *son:* 5 Horus 6 Anubis *wife:* 4 Isis

osmium *symbol:* 2 Os

osmosis 4 flow 9 diffusion 10 absorption 12 assimilation

osprey 4 hawk 8 fish hawk

Ossa and ___ 6 Pelion

osseous 4 bony

ossicle 4 bone 5 incus 6 stapes
7 malleus

ossify 3 set 6 harden

ossuary 3 urn 4 tomb 5 vault

ostensible 7 alleged, seeming 8 apparent,
illusive, illusory, semblant, so-called, supposed 9 pretended, professed, purported

ostentation 4 show 7 display
9 showiness

ostentatious 4 loud 5 gaudy, showy,
swank 6 chichi 7 splashy 8 peacocky
10 flamboyant, peacockish 11 pretentious

ostiole 4 pore 5 mouth 7 orifice
8 aperture

ostracism 5 exile 9 expulsion 10 banishment, relegation 11 deportation
12 displacement

ostracize 3 cut 4 oust, snob, snub
5 exile, expel 6 banish, deport 7 cast out,
expulse 8 displace, throw out 9 blackball
10 expatriate 12 cold-shoulder

ostrich *female:* 3 hen *genus:* 8 Struthio
male: 4 cock

Ostrogoth king 9 Theodoric

otalgia 7 earache

Otello composer 5 Verdi 7 Rossini

o tempora! o ___! 5 mores

Othello *ensign:* 4 Iago *lieutenant:* 6 Cassio *victim, wife:* 9 Desdemona

other *combining form:* 3 all 4 allo
5 heter 6 hetero

others 4 rest 9 remainder *and:* 4 et al
6 et alii

Othniel *brother:* 5 Caleb *father:* 5 Kenaz
wife: 6 Achsah

Othni's father 8 Shemaiah

otic 5 aural 8 auditory 9 auricular

otiose 4 idle, lazy, vain 5 empty 6 futile,
hollow 7 surplus, useless 8 nugatory
11 inexcusable, purposeless, superfluous
13 supernumerary

Otis 7 bustard

Ottawa chief 7 Pontiac

otter *genus:* 5 Lutra 7 Enhydra

ottoman 4 seat 5 couch 9 footstool

Ottoman 4 Turk 7 Turkish *ruler:*
5 Osman 8 Suleiman

Otus 5 giant *brother:* 9 Ephialtes *father:*
6 Aloeus 8 Poseidon *mother:* 9 Iphimedia
slayer: 6 Apollo

ouch 2 ow 3 cry 5 bezel, jewel 6 brooch,
buckle 7 setting 8 bracelet, necklace
11 exclamation

ounce 3 cat 4 atom, doit, dram, drop
5 crumb, grain, minim, shred 6 weight
7 leopard, measure, smidgen 8 particle

ouph 3 elf

our *French:* 5 notre *German:* 5 unser *Italian:* 6 nostra

Our Town author 6 Wilder

oust 3 bar, rob 4 lose 5 eject, evict, expel
6 banish, deport, remove 7 bereave, cast
out, deprive, expulse, kick out 8 displace,
relegate 9 ostracize, transport 10 disinherit, dispossess

out 4 away, free, leak, show 5 break,
chase, chuck, douse, eject, evict, forth,
loose 6 absent, quench 7 dismiss, extrude,
showing 9 transpire 10 extinguish *of control:* 4 wild 7 chaotic *of gas:* 5 tired
9 exhausted *of line:* 4 awry, rude 5 askew,
fresh *of place:* 13 inappropriate *of sorts:*
5 cross 7 grouchy, peevish 9 irritable *of
the ordinary:* 3 odd 7 strange, unusual

outage 7 failure 8 blackout 12 interruption

out-and-out 5 gross, sheer, utter 7 perfect 8 absolute, complete, positive 10 consummate 13 thoroughgoing

outback 4 bush 10 wilderness

outboard 5 motor

outbreak 4 dawn, rash 5 burst, flare,

onset **6** plague, revolt **8** epidemic, eruption **9** beginning **12** commencement

outbreathe 6 exhale, expire

outburst 4 gale, gust, tiff **5** flare, sally, scene, storm **6** access, fantod, frenzy, tirade **7** flare-up, rapture, tantrum, torrent **8** eruption **9** explosion

outcast 4 hobo **5** exile, leper, tramp **6** pariah **7** Ishmael, vagrant **8** castaway, derelict, vagabond **9** reprobate **10** expatriate, Ishmaelite **11** offscouring, untouchable *Japanese:* **3** eta

outclass 4 best **5** excel **7** surpass

outcome 4 fate **5** event, issue **6** effect, result, sequel, upshot **8** causatum **9** aftermath **11** aftereffect, consequence

outcrop 4 rock **5** ledge **6** basset

outcry 4 yell **5** shout **6** clamor, tumult, upturn **7** ferment **8** upheaval **9** commotion

outdare 4 defy, face **5** beard, brave, front **7** venture **9** challenge

outdated see **out-of-date**

outdo 3 top **4** beat, best, down **5** excel, trump, worst **6** better, defeat, exceed **7** surpass, upstage **9** transcend

outdoor 7 open-air **8** alfresco **10** hypaethral

outer 5 ectad, ectal **6** remote **7** surface **8** exterior, external **9** extrinsic **10** extraneous **11** superficial

outermost 4 last **5** final **7** extreme **8** farthest, furthest, remotest

outfit 3 arm, kit, rig **4** band, firm, gear **5** corps, dress, equip, getup, guise, house, party, troop **6** tackle, troupe **7** appoint, company, concern, costume, furnish **8** accouter, accoutre, business, ensemble, materiel, tackling **9** apparatus, equipment, machinery **10** enterprise **11** habiliments **12** organization **13** accouterments, accoutrements, establishment, paraphernalia

outflow 4 flux **6** efflux **8** drainage, effluent

outfox see **outwit**

outgrowth 4 tuft **5** child, issue, shoot **6** branch, effect, member, result **7** process, product, spin-off **8** offshoot, swelling **9** byproduct, offspring, processus **10** derivative, descendant **11** aftereffect, consequence, enlargement, excrescence, excrescency

outhouse 5 jakes, privy **7** latrine

outing 4 trip **5** jaunt, sally **6** junket, picnic **9** excursion **10** roundabout

outland 5 rural **6** rustic **7** bucolic, country **8** agrestic, pastoral **10** campestral, provincial **11** countrified

outlandish 3 odd **4** back, wild **5** alien, kinky, queer, ultra, weird **6** remote, vulgar **7** bizarre, curious, extreme, foreign, strange, uncouth, unusual **8** barbaric, frontier, peculiar, singular **9** barbarian, barbarous, grace-

less, monstrous, tasteless, unsettled **10** unorthodox **11** extravagant

outlaw 3 ban **5** taboo **6** badman, bandit, enjoin, forbid, gunman **7** inhibit **8** criminal, prohibit, renegade **9** desperado, interdict

outlay 4 cost, give **5** spend **6** expend **7** expense **8** disburse **11** expenditure **12** disbursement

outlet 4 exit, hole, shop, vent **5** store **6** egress, escape **7** opening, orifice, release **8** aperture, showroom

outline 3 hem, map, rim **4** edge, form, limn, plan **5** bound, chart, draft, shape, skirt, trace **6** border, figure, fringe, margin, projet, sketch **7** contour, profile **8** skeleton, surround, syllabus **9** adumbrate **10** figuration, silhouette **11** skeletonize

outlive 7 survive

outlook 4 side, view **5** angle, scape, scene, sight, slant, vista **8** prospect **9** direction, viewpoint **10** standpoint **11** observatory, perspective, point of view

outlying 3 far **6** far-off, remote **7** distant, faraway, removed **8** far-flung

outmoded see **out-of-date**

out-of-date 3 old **5** dowdy, passé, tacky **6** démodé, frumpy, stodgy **7** antique, archaic, oldtime, vintage **8** frumpish **9** unstylish **10** antiquated **12** old-fashioned

out-of-the-way 5 aside **6** remote, secret **7** devious, obscure, removed, retired **8** lonesome

outpouring 4 flow, gush **8** effusion, outburst

output 4 crop, gain, take **5** yield **6** profit **7** harvest, produce, product **10** production

outrage 4 harm, hurt, rape, ruin **5** abuse, anger, force, spoil, wrong **6** defile, ill-use, injury, insult, misuse, offend, ravish **7** affront, oppress, violate **8** aggrieve, deflower, ill-treat, maltreat, mischief, mistreat

outrageous 5 awful, gross **6** crying, horrid, unholy, wicked **7** beastly, ghastly, obscene, ungodly **8** dreadful, flagrant, horrible, shocking, terrible **9** desperate **10** abominable, impossible **11** intolerable, unchristian, uncivilized **12** unreasonable

outré 5 kinky, ultra **7** bizarre, strange

outrigger 4 prao, prau, proa **5** canoe, prahu

outright 3 all **5** gross, total, utter, whole **6** entire **7** perfect **8** absolute, complete, positive **10** consummate **11** unmitigated **13** thoroughgoing

outrun 4 beat **6** exceed **7** surpass

outset 4 dawn **5** birth, start **7** dawning, opening **9** beginning **12** commencement

outshine see **outdo**

outside 3 bar, but, off, top **4** open, over, past, save, slim **5** after, alien, small

6 beyond, except, remove, saving, slight, utmost **7** foreign, maximal, maximum, open-air, slender, topmost **8** alfresco, exterior, external **9** apart from, excluding **10** hypaethral, negligible **11** exclusive of **prefix: 2** ec, ex **3** ect, exo **5** extra, extro

outsider 5 alien **7** inconnu **8** stranger **9** foreigner

outsmart see outwit

outspoken 4 free, open **5** bluff, blunt, frank, plain, round, vocal **6** candid, direct **8** explicit, strident **10** forthright, pointblank

outspread 4 open **6** expand, extend, unfold

outstanding 3 due **4** main, star **5** chief, major, noted **6** marked, mature, signal, superb, unpaid **7** capital, notable, overdue, payable, salient, stellar **8** dominant **9** arrestive, principal, prominent, unsettled **10** noticeable, preeminent, remarkable **11** conspicuous, magnificent, predominant, superlative

outstart 4 dawn **5** birth, onset **7** dawning, opening **9** beginning **12** commencement

outstrip 3 top **4** beat, best, lose, pass **5** excel **6** better, exceed **7** surpass **8** distance

outsweepings 4 junk **5** trash, waste **6** debris, litter, refuse **7** garbage, rubbish

outward 4 over **5** ectad, ectal, overt **7** visible **8** apparent, exterior, external **10** ostensible **11** superficial

outweigh 6 make up, offset, redeem, set off **7** balance **8** atone for, overbear **10** compensate **11** countervail, overbalance

outwit 3 fox **4** dupe, foil, gull, have, hoax, undo **5** trick **6** befool **8** hoodwink **9** bamboozle, frustrate, overreach

outworn see out-of-date

ouzel 4 bird **6** thrush **9** blackbird

oval 4 ooid **5** track **7** ellipse **8** elliptic **9** egg-shaped **11** ellipsoidal

ovation 6 homage, praise **8** applause

oven 4 kiln, lehr, oast **5** range, stove **6** calcar

over 2 by, on **3** mid, off, too **4** amid, anew, atop, away, done, leap, past, upon, with **5** about, above, again, aloft, clear, cross, due to, ended, extra, midst, round, vault **6** across, afresh, around, beyond, de novo, during, higher, hurdle, unduly **7** athwart, greater, outside, outward, owing to, through **8** exterior, external, finished, once more, superior, surmount **9** because of, extremely, immensely, negotiate **10** throughout **11** excessively, superjacent **12** inordinately, transversely *French:* **3** sur *German:* **4** über *prefix:* **2** ep **3** eph, epi, sur **5** extra, hyper, super, supra *Spanish:* **5** sobre

overabundance 6 excess **7** surfeit, sur-

plus **8** plethora **10** surplusage **11** superfluity

overact 3 ham, mug **4** rant **5** emote, spout

overage see overabundance

overall 6 global, mainly, mostly **7** chiefly, general, largely **8** sweeping **9** generally, inclusive, primarily **10** high and low, tar and wide **11** principally **13** comprehensive, predominantly

overalls 5 pants **8** trousers

over and above 6 beside, beyond **7** besides **8** as well as

over and over 3 oft **4** much **5** often **8** ofttimes **10** frequently, oftentimes, repeatedly

overbearing 5 bossy, proud **6** lordly, master **7** haughty, pompous, regnant **8** absolute, arrogant, cavalier, despotic, dominant, imperial, insolent, superior **9** ascendant, imperious, masterful, paramount, prevalent, sovereign **10** autocratic, disdainful, highhanded, imperative, peremptory, tyrannical **11** magisterial, predominant, predominate **12** preponderant, supercilious **13** high-and-mighty

overblown 3 big, fat **4** arty **5** gross, heavy, obese, stout, tumid, windy **6** fleshy, portly, turgid **7** aureate, flowery, porcine **8** dropsied, imposing, inflated, sonorous **9** bombastic, corpulent, dropsical, flatulent, tumescent **10** arty-crafty, euphuistic, oratorical, rhetorical **11** declamatory, exaggerated, pretentious **12** high-sounding, magniloquent **13** grandiloquent

overbold 6 arrant, brassy, brazen **7** blatant **8** impudent **9** barefaced, shameless, unabashed **10** unblushing **11** brazenfaced

overcast 3 cap, dim **4** dull, gray, hazy **5** cloud, cover, crown, dirty, heavy **6** cloudy, darken, shadow, sullen **7** becloud, blanket, louring, obscure **8** brooding, lowering, nubilous **9** adumbrate **10** oppressive

overcharge 3 gyp, pad **4** clip, skin, soak **5** gauge, stick **6** fleece **7** magnify **9** embellish

overcoat 6 capote, raglan, ulster **7** paletot, surtout **9** balmacaan, inverness **12** chesterfield

overcome 3 win **4** beat, best, down, lick **5** drown, throw, whelm **6** defeat, hurdle, master **7** conquer, outlive, prevail, triumph **8** surmount **9** prostrate *by grief:* **8** dejected, downcast **10** dispirited **12** disconsolate **13** broken-hearted

overconfident 5 brash, cocky **6** uppity **7** pushful **9** presuming **10** brassbound **12** presumptuous

overdo 7 exhaust, fatigue **10** exaggerate

overdue 4 late **5** lated, owing, tardy **6** mature, unpaid **7** belated, payable

9 unsettled **10** behindhand, unpunctual
11 outstanding

overemphasize 7 magnify
10 exaggerate

overflow 4 brim, pour, slop, teem
5 drown, flood, slosh, spate, spill, swamp,
whelm **6** deluge, engulf, excess **7** cascade,
niagara, surfeit, surplus, torrent **8** cataract,
flooding, inundate, plethora, spillage, submerge **9** cataclysm **10** inundation, surplusage **11** superfluity

overflowing 4 rife **5** alive, awash
7 replete, teeming **8** thronged
13 superabundant

overgrown 4 lush, rank **5** braky, copsy,
dense, thick **6** brushy, jungly **7** brambly
8 thickety **9** thicketed

overhang 3 jut **4** poke, pout **5** bulge,
jetty, pouch **6** beetle **7** project **8** protrude

overhaul 3 fix **4** do up, mend, take
5 catch, patch **6** doctor, repair, revamp
7 rebuild **8** renovate **11** recondition,
reconstruct

overhead 5 above, aloft **7** expense

overindulgence 6 excess **8** gluttony
12 immoderation, intemperance

overindulgent 9 excessive **10** immoderate, inordinate, untempered **11** intemperate **12** unrestrained

overkill 6 excess **7** surfeit, surplus
8 plethora **10** surplusage **11** superfluity

overlap 7 shingle **9** imbricate

overlay 3 cap **4** coat **5** cover, crown
6 veneer **7** blanket **8** covering

overload 4 glut **6** excess **7** surfeit

overlook 4 boss, fail, omit, skip **5** blank,
chasm **6** forget, ignore, slight, survey
7 blink at, condone, neglect **8** chaperon,
discount, dominate, omission **9** blink away,
chaperone, disregard, supervise **10** tower
above

overlord 5 chief, ruler **8** suzerain
9 chieftain

overpass 4 fail, omit **6** bridge, forget,
ignore **7** blink at, neglect **8** discount
9 blink away, disregard

overplay 6 accent **7** magnify, point up,
stretch **8** maximize **9** dramatize **10** accentuate, exaggerate **11** hyperbolize

overpower 4 rout **5** crush, drown,
whelm **6** defeat, master, reduce, subdue
7 conquer **8** bear down, vanquish **9** prostrate, subjugate

overreach 3 gyp **4** beat, bilk, undo
5 cheat, cozen **6** chouse, diddle, outfox,
outwit **7** defraud **8** flimflam, outslick, outsmart **11** outmaneuver

override 3 lap **4** veto **7** nullify, shingle
9 imbricate

overriding 7 central, pivotal, primary
8 cardinal **9** principal

overrule 4 sway, veto **5** reign **6** govern

overrun 4 beat, drub, lick, raid, trim, whip
5 beset, foray, smear, spill, swarm
6 exceed, infest, inroad, invade, thrash
7 outstep, surpass **8** lambaste

overseas 5 alien **6** abroad, exotic **7** foreign, strange **11** transmarine, ultramarine

oversee 3 run **4** boss **5** watch **6** survey
8 chaperon **9** chaperone, supervise
11 quarterback, superintend

overseer 4 boss, head **5** chief **7** foreman,
manager **8** chaperon **9** chaperone
10 supervisor

overshadow 3 dim **4** haze **5** cloud,
cover **6** darken **7** becloud, obscure
9 adumbrate

overshoe 4 boot **6** arctic, galosh, patten,
rubber

oversight 4 care, skip **5** aegis, blank,
chasm, check, error, guard **6** charge **7** conduct, control, custody, default, failure, keeping, mistake, neglect, running **8** handling,
omission, tutelage **10** ciceronage, intendance, management **11** chaperonage

overslaugh 3 bar, dam **5** block, brake
6 hinder, impede **8** obstruct

oversoon 5 early **7** betimes **8** previous,
untimely **9** premature **11** prematurely

overspread 3 cap **5** beset, cover, crown
6 infest **7** blanket

overstate 3 pad **5** color, fudge **7** magnify **9** embellish, embroider **10** exaggerate

overstep 6 exceed **7** surpass **8** infringe,
trespass **10** transgress

overstock 6 excess **7** surplus **9** remainder **10** surplusage

overstress 7 magnify **8** maximize
10 exaggerate

overswarm 4 raid **5** beset, foray **6** infest,
inroad, invade

overt 4 open **6** patent **7** obvious, outward,
visible **8** apparent, manifest

overtake 4 pass

over there 3 yon **6** yonder

overthrow 4 down, fell, oust, rout, ruin
5 purge, upset **6** defeat, depose, remove,
topple, tumble, unseat **7** beating, conquer,
debacle, destroy, licking, unhorse
8 dethrone, downcast, drubbing **9** liquidate,
trouncing **10** defeasance **11** shellacking
12 vanquishment

overtone 4 hint **8** harmonic **10** suggestion **11** association, connotation, implication

overture 3 bid **5** proem **6** tender
7 advance, preface, prelude **8** approach,
exordium, foreword, preamble, prologue,
proposal **9** prelusion **11** proposition
12 introduction, prolegomenon

overturn 3 tip **4** coup, down **5** upend,
upset **6** keel up, topple, tumble **7** capsize,

shake-up, unhorse **9** prostrate
10 revolution

overweening **5** brash **6** uppish, uppity
7 forward, pushful **8** arrogant **10** immoderate **12** presumptuous **13** self-assertive

overweight **3** fat **5** gross, heavy, obese,
stout **6** fleshy, portly **9** corpulent

overwhelm **4** beat, bury, drub, lick, ruin,
sink, trim, whip **5** crush, drown, flood, floor,
lower, smear, swamp, upset, wreck **6** deluge, engulf, thrash **7** destroy, disturb, shatter, shellac, smother **8** inundate, submerge **9** devastate, downgrade,
dumbfound, prostrate **10** demoralize
11 subordinate

overwhelmed **5** agape **6** aghast
7 stunned **13** thunderstruck

overword **6** burden **7** refrain

Ovid work **5** Fasti **7** Tristia **8** Heroides
13 Metamorphoses

oviform **4** ooid, oval **5** ovate **6** ooidal
9 egg-shaped

ovine **5** sheep **9** sheeplike

ovoid   see **oviform**

ovule **3** egg *fertilized:* **4** seed

ovum **3** egg **6** gamete **7** egg cell

owing **3** due **6** mature, unpaid **7** overdue,
payable **9** unsettled

owing to **4** over **7** through **9** because of

owl *Australian:* **7** boobook **8** morepork
cry: **4** hoot *kind:* **3** elf **4** barn, gray, lulu
5 eagle, gnome, madge, pygmy, snowy
6 barred, horned **7** saw-whet, screech
9 long-eared **10** short-eared **11** great
horned *resembling:* **8** strigine *snowy:*
7 harfang

Owl and Pussycat author **4** Lear

own **4** avow, have, hold **5** admit, allow,

enjoy, grant, let on **6** fess up, retain **7** concede, confess, possess **11** acknowledge

owner **4** lord **8** landlady, landlord **9** possessor **10** proprietor

ownership **4** hand **5** title **8** dominion,
property **10** possession **11** proprietary *perpetual:* **8** mortmain

ox **3** yak **4** anoa, buff, gaur, musk, zebu
5 bison, gayal, steer **6** bovine, ovibos
7 banteng, bantery, brahman, buffalo
Asian: **4** zebu *combining form:* **4** bovi
extinct: **4** urus **7** aurochs *family:* **7** Bovidae *relating to:* **6** bovine *Scottish:* **4** nowt,
owse *wild:* **4** anoa, gaur **7** banteng **8** sala-
dang, seladang

oxeye **5** daisy **6** flower

oxford **4** shoe **5** cloth, sheep

oxide *calcium:* **4** lime **9** quicklime *ferric:*
4 rust *sodium:* **4** soda

oxidize **4** rust

oxygen **3** air, gas **5** ozone **7** element *discoverer:* **9** Lavoisier *form:* **5** ozone *liquid:* **3** lox

oyster **5** forte **6** medium **7** bivalve, mollusk *bed:* **4** park **6** claire, cultch *combining
form:* **5** ostre **6** ostrei, ostreo *eggs:*
5 spawn *genus:* **6** Ostrea **11** Crassostrea
Long island: **9** bluepoint *product:* **5** pearl
shell: **4** test **5** shuck *young:* **4** spat

oysterbird **5** tirma **10** sanderling

oysterfish **6** tautog

oyster grass **4** kelp **10** sea lettuce

Oz *creator:* **4** Baum *inhabitant:*
8 Munchkin

Ozark State **8** Missouri

Ozem *brother:* **5** David *father:* **5** Jesse
9 Jerahmeel

Ozni's father **3** Gad

Ozymandias author **7** Shelley

P

pabulum 4 food 7 aliment 8 nutrient
9 nutriment 10 sustenance 11 nourishment
pace 3 rut 4 gait, hoof, rate, step, time,
walk 5 grind, speed, tempo, tread, troop
6 timing 7 example, fluency, forerun, precede, proceed, routine, traipse 8 ambulate,
antecede, celerity, rapidity, regulate, velocity 9 quickness, rapidness, swiftness,
treadmill
pachyderm 8 elephant
pacific 4 calm, meek, mild 6 gentle, irenic,
placid, serene 8 dovelike, peaceful, tranquil 9 appeasing, peaceable
Pacificator, Great 4 Clay
Pacific Ocean discoverer 6 Balboa
pacifist 4 dove 6 irenic 8 appeaser,
peaceful 9 peaceable 10 nonviolent, satya-
grahi 11 peacemonger
pacify 4 calm, ease, lull 5 allay, quiet, still
6 settle, soften, soothe, subdue, temper
7 appease, assuage, mollify, placate
pack 3 jam, lot, lug, mob, ram, wad 4 bear,
cram, fill, heap, load, lump, mass, much, pile,
stow, tamp, tote 5 carry, choke, crowd,
ferry, group, store, stuff, troop 6 barrel,
bestow, bundle, charge, convey, depart
7 compact 8 compress 9 container
pack animal 3 ass 4 mule 5 burro,
camel, horse, llama 6 donkey 7 jackass,
sumpter 13 beast of burden
packed 4 full 5 awash 7 brimful,
crowded, stuffed 8 brimming 9 chock-full
packet 3 pot, wad 4 boat, mint, pile
6 boodle, bundle, parcel 7 fortune
pact 4 bond 6 treaty 7 bargain, concord
8 alliance, covenant 9 agreement
pad 3 mat, wad 5 fudge, guard, quilt, stuff
6 muffle, shield, tablet, trudge 7 bolster,
cushion, magnify, stretch 8 overdraw
9 embellish, embroider, overpaint, overstate 10 exaggerate, overcharge
paddle 3 fin, oar, row 4 pull 5 spank
6 dabble, thrash 7 flipper
pagan 7 gentile, heathen, infidel, profane
8 idolator 9 infidelic 10 unbeliever *god:*
4 idol
page 4 book, call, leaf 5 folio, sheet
6 locate, summon 7 writing *left-hand:*
5 verso *reverse:* 5 verso *right-hand:*
5 recto

pageant 4 sham, show 7 charade 8 disguise, pretense 9 spectacle 10 exhibition
Pagiel's father 5 Ocran 6 Ochran
Pagliacci *character:* 5 Canio, Nedda,
Tonio 6 Silvio *composer:* 11 Leoncavallo
pagoda 2 ta 3 taa 6 alcove, gazebo, temple 9 belvedere 11 garden house, summerhouse
pail 6 bucket, piggin
pain 3 ail, irk, try 4 ache, care, hurt, pang
5 agony, cramp, grief, throe, upset, wound
6 effort, grieve, harass, harrow, injure,
stitch, stress, twinge 7 afflict, agonize,
anguish, crucify, provoke, torment, torture,
travail, trouble 8 aggrieve, convulse, distress, lacerate 9 suffering 10 affliction, discomfort, excruciate *abdominal:* 5 colic
back: 7 lumbago *combining form:* 3 alg
4 agra, algo, noci 5 agrae (plural), algia,
algic 6 odynia, odynic *ear:* 6 otalgy 7 otalgia *intensity unit:* 3 dol *muscular:*
7 myalgia
painful 3 raw 4 sore 5 acute, sharp
6 aching, bitter 7 algetic, galling, hurting,
irksome, racking 8 annoying, grievous,
piercing, shooting, stabbing, stinging, unsavory 9 agonizing, harrowing, torturous,
upsetting, vexatious 10 afflictive,
tormenting
painkiller 6 opiate 7 anodyne 8 morphine,
narcotic 9 analgesic 10 anesthetic
painstaking 5 exact, fussy 7 careful,
heedful 8 diligent, exacting, punctual
9 laborious 10 meticulous, scrupulous
11 punctilious
paint 4 coat, daub, face, limn 5 color,
japan, stain 6 depict, fresco, makeup
7 portray 9 delineate, represent
10 maquillage
painter 6 artist *American:* 4 West, Wood
5 Abbey, Henri, Hicks, Homer, Johns, Kroll,
Marin, Moses, Peale, Ryder, Shahn, Sloan,
Weber, Wyeth 6 Benton, Catlin, Copley,
Eakins, Hassam, Hopper, Leutze, Martin,
Rivers, Rothko, Stella, Stuart, Tanguy,
Thorpe, Warhol 7 Allston, Bellows, Cassatt,
La Farge, O'Keeffe, Parrish, Pollock, Sargent, Sheeler, Tiffany, Tworkov, Wiggins
8 Melchers, Rockwell, Sullivan, Trumbull,
Whistler 9 Feininger, Remington, Twacht-
man, Vanderlyn 10 Motherwell, Whit-

tredge **12** Lichtenstein *Austrian:*
9 Kokoschka *Belgian:* **6** Campin
8 Magritte *Canadian:* **4** Kane **6** Harris,
Watson **7** Jackson, Thomson **9** MacDonald
Chinese: **4** Wu Li **6** Ma Yüan **7** Wang
Wei **8** Yen Li-pen *Dutch:* **4** Hals, Lely,
Maas, Maes **5** Bosch, Steen **6** Potter **7** de
Hooch, de Witte, Hobbema, van Gogh, Ver-
meer **8** Mondrian, Ruisdael, Ruysdael, Ter-
borch **9** Rembrandt, Wouwerman **11** Ter-
brugghen *English:* **4** John, Lear **5** Bacon,
Blake, Brown, Lewis, Watts **6** Inness, Rom-
ney, Turner, Wilson **7** Hogarth, Kneller, Mil-
lais, Raeburn **8** Lawrence, Reynolds, Ros-
setti **9** Constable, Nicholson
12 Gainsborough *Flemish:* **4** Goes
6 Rubens, Weyden **7** Memling, Teniers,
Van Dyck, Van Eyck **8** Breughel, Brueghel
French: **4** Doré, Dufy **5** Corot, David,
Degas, Leger, Manet, Monet, Puvis, Redon,
Vouet **6** Braque, Breton, Claude, Clouet,
Gerome, Greuze, Ingres, Le Brun, Le Nain,
Millet, Renoir, Seurat, Sisley, Tanguy, Ver-
net **7** Bonheur, Bonnard, Cézanne, Chardin,
Courbet, Daumier, Duchamp, Gauguin,
Matisse, Morisot, Poussin, Rouault, Utrillo,
Watteau **8** Dubuffet, Pissarro, Rousseau,
Vlaminck, Vuillard **9** Delacroix, Fragonard,
Géricault, Laurencin **10** Meissonier **11** Le
Corbusier *German:* **5** Dürer, Ernst, Grosz,
Nolde **6** Muller **7** Cranach, Holbein, Loch-
ner, Schwind, Zoffany **8** Kirchner, Kollwitz
9 Grünewald, Kandinsky **10** Schongauer,
Wohlgemuth *Greek:* **6** Zeuxis **7** Apelles
10 Polygnotus *Irish:* **5** Yeats *Italian:*
4 Reni, Rosa, Tura **5** Campi, Lippi, Piero,
Sarto **6** Cosimo, Giotto, Romano, Sodoma,
Titian, Vasari **7** Bellini, Chirico, Cimabue, da
Vinci, Fiesole, Martini, Orcagna, Peruzzi,
Raphael, Tiepolo, Uccello, Zuccari **8** Del
Sarto, Fabriano, Giordano, Mantegna,
Masaccio, Montagna, Perugino, Pontormo,
Severini, Veronese, Vivarini **9** Carpaccio,
Correggio, Francesca **10** Caravaggio, Modi-
gliani, Signorelli, Tintoretto, Verrocchio, Zuc-
carelli **11** Ghirlandajo **12** Michelangelo, Par-
migianino *Japanese:* **5** Korin **6** Sesshu
Lithuanian: **7** Soutine *Mexican:* **6** Orozco,
Rivera, Tamayo **9** Siqueiros *Norwegian:*
5 Munch *Russian:* **7** Chagall, Roerich
9 Kandinsky *Scottish:* **6** Ramsay
7 Nasmyth, Raeburn *Spanish:* **4** Dali, Goya,
Gris, Miró, Sert **6** Ribera, Rincon, Tapies
7 El Greco, Herrera, Murillo, Picasso,
Zuloaga **8** Zurbaran **9** Velasquez, Velazquez *Swedish:* **4** Zorn **6** Roslin *Swiss:*
4 Klee, Witz
painting **3** oil **7** acrylic, picture **10** watercolor *circular:* **5** tondo *combining form:*
6 chromy *one-color:* **8** monotint **10** mono-
chrome *plaster:* **5** secco **6** fresco *style:*

6 cubism, Gothic, pop art, rococo
7 baroque, Bauhaus, dadaism, fauvism,
realism **8** Barbizon, futurism **9** Byzantine,
geometric, mannerism **10** avant-garde,
classicism, surrealism **11** romanticism
13 expressionism, impressionism *tech-*
nique: **3** oil **6** fresco, gouche, pastel
7 polymer, tempera **9** encaustic **10** watercolor *tool:* **5** brush, easel, knife, paint
6 canvas **7** palette *wall:* **5** mural
pair **3** duo, two **4** dyad, join, mate, span,
team, yoke **5** brace, match, unite **6** couple
7 doublet, twosome **8** geminate
Pakistan *capital:* **9** Islamabad *largest*
city: **7** Karachi *monetary unit:* **5** rupee
province: **4** Sind **6** Punjab **11** Baluchistan
pal **4** chum, mate **5** buddy, crony
6 comate, friend **7** comrade, partner
9 associate, companion **11** confederate
paladin see douzeper
Palal's father **4** Uzai
Palamedes *brother:* **6** Sforza **8** Achilles
father: **8** Nauplius *slayer:* **7** Corinda, Ulysses **8** Odysseus
palatable **5** sapid, tasty, yummy **6** savory,
toothy **8** luscious, pleasing, saporous,
savorous, tasteful, tempting **9** aperitive,
delicious, relishing, saporific, savorsome,
toothsome **10** appetizing, delightful,
flavorsome
palate **4** zest **5** gusto, heart, taste **6** relish
palatial **4** lush, rich **5** large, noble, plush
6 Capuan, deluxe, ornate **7** opulent,
stately **8** luscious, splendid **9** luxuriant, luxurious, sumptuous **10** impressive **11** magnificent, upholstered
palaver **3** gas, yak **4** blab, cant, chat, guff,
tack **5** clack **6** affair, babble, hot air, jargon,
parley **7** chatter, concern, lexicon, lookout,
prattle, seminar **8** business, colloquy, dialogue **10** colloquium, conference, discussion, rap session **12** conversation
palaverous **5** windy, wordy **6** prolix **7** diffuse, verbose **9** redundant **10** long-winded
pale **3** dim, wan **4** ashy, dull, fade, gray,
sick, weak **5** ashen, faint, fence, inane, livid,
lurid, muddy, pasty, stake, waxen, white
6 anemic, blanch, chalky, doughy, feeble,
jejune, pallid, picket, sallow, sickly, watery,
whiten **7** ghastly, insipid, tarnish, waxlike
8 blanched, encircle, waterish, whitened
9 bloodless, colorless, deathlike
paleness **6** pallor
palinode **5** unsay **6** abjure, recall, recant
7 retract **8** forswear, take back, withdraw
10 retraction **11** recantation
pall **4** bore, cloy, glut, jade, sate, tire
5 cloak, drape, ennui, gorge, weary **6** canopy, clothe, mantle, stodge **7** disgust, satiate, surfeit **8** covering **11** counterpane
palladium *symbol:* **2** Pd

Pallas *brother:* 6 Aegeus *father:* 7 Pandion *slayer:* 7 Theseus *wife:* 4 Styx; (see also **Athena**)

palliate 4 ease, hide, mask 5 cloak, cover, glass, gloze, salve 6 excuse, lessen, soften, temper, veneer, whiten 7 conceal, condone, cover up, lighten, qualify, varnish 8 disguise, mitigate, moderate, prettify 9 alleviate, dissemble, extenuate, glass over, gloze over, sugarcoat, whitewash

pallid 3 wan 4 ashy, dull 5 ashen, waxen 6 anemic, doughy, watery 8 blanched, waterish 9 bloodless, colorless

Pallu *father:* 6 Reuben *son:* 5 Eliab

pally 4 cozy 6 chummy 8 intimate

palm 3 tip 4 hide 5 bribe, merus, prize 6 thenar 7 conceal *beverage:* 4 nipa 5 assai *fiber:* 4 bass, bast 6 gomuti 7 bassine 8 piassava *fruit:* 4 date 7 coconut 11 coquilla nut *kind:* 3 fan, wax 4 coco, date, doom, hemp, nipa, sago 5 areca, assai, betel, datil, ivory, royal, tucum 6 gomuti, grigri, grugru, raffia, rattan 7 cabbage, feather, palmyra, talipot 8 carnauba, palmetto, piassava 12 Washingtonia *leaf:* 4 olla 5 frond *starch:* 4 sago *vine:* 6 rattan

palmer 7 pilgrim

Palmetto State 13 South Carolina

palm lily 2 ti

palm off 5 foist 7 deceive

Palmyra's queen 7 Zenobia

palooka 3 oaf 4 gawk, lout, lump 5 klutz 6 lubber, lummox

palpable 4 sure 5 clear, plain 6 patent 7 certain, evident, obvious, seeming, tactile 8 apparent, distinct, manifest, positive, striking, tangible 9 arresting 10 noticeable 11 perceptible, unequivocal

palpate 4 feel 5 touch 6 finger, handle

palpitate 4 beat 5 pulse, throb 6 quiver 7 flutter, pulsate 12 pitter-patter

palter 3 fib, lie 5 evade, fence 6 haggle, parley 7 bargain, chaffer, falsify 10 equivocate 11 prevaricate

Palti *father:* 5 Laish, Raphu *wife:* 6 Michal

Paltiel's father 5 Azzan

paltry 3 low, set 4 base, mean, poor, puny, vile 5 borne, cheap, petty, small, tatty, trash 6 common, little, measly, narrow, shabby, shoddy, sleazy, slight, trashy 7 limited, low-down, pitiful, rubbish, trivial 8 beggarly, inferior, picayune, piddling, rubbishy, trifling 9 worthless 10 despicable, picayunish 11 ineffectual, Mickey Mouse, unimportant 13 insignificant

Pamela author 10 Richardson

pamper 3 pet 4 baby 5 humor, spoil 6 caress, cocker, coddle, cosset, cuddle, dandle, fondle, regale, tickle 7 cater to, cherish, gratify, indulge 11 mollycoddle *Irish:* 6 cosher

pamphlet 5 tract 6 folder 7 booklet, leaflet 8 brochure 10 broadsheet

pan 3 rap 5 basin, blame, cut up, knock 6 attack 7 censure, condemn 8 denounce, ridicule 9 criticize, reprehend

Pan 5 Inuus 6 Faunus *father:* 6 Hermes *invention:* 6 syrinx *lower part:* 4 goat *mother:* 8 Penelope *pipe:* 6 syrinx *seat of worship:* 7 Arcadia *son:* 7 Silenus

panacea 4 cure 6 elixir, relief, remedy 7 cure-all, nostrum 10 catholicon

Panacea's father 9 Asclepius 11 Aesculapius

pancake 8 flapjack, slapjack *French:* 5 crepe *Jewish:* 5 latke 6 blintz 7 blintze *Russian:* 5 blini

Pandarus 6 archer 8 procuror *father:* 6 Lycaon *slayer:* 8 Diomedes

pandect 4 code 6 aperçu, digest, précis, sketch, survey 8 syllabus 10 compendium

pandemoniac 7 avernal, hellish, riotous, stygian 8 infernal, plutonic 9 cimmerian, plutonian

pandemonium 3 din 4 hell, sink 5 babel, Sodom 6 clamor, hubbub, jangle, racket, tumult, uproar 7 cesspit 8 cesspool, disorder 9 confusion 10 hullabaloo, tintamarre

pander 4 pimp 5 bully, cadet, cater 8 fancy man, procurer 9 procuress

Pandion *daughter:* 6 Procne 9 Philomela *son:* 6 Pallas

Pandora *creator:* 10 Hephaestus *husband:* 10 Epimetheus

pandurina 4 lute

panegyric 6 eulogy, praise 7 tribute 8 citation, encomium 9 laudation 10 salutation

panegyrical 9 laudative, laudatory, praiseful 10 eulogistic 11 encomiastic

panegyrize 4 hymn, laud 5 bless, cry up, extol 6 praise 7 glorify, magnify 8 eulogize 9 celebrate

panel 4 gore, jury 5 board, label 6 hurdle

pan-fry 5 sauté

pang 4 ache, pain, stab 5 agony, prick, spasm, throe 6 stitch, twinge 7 anguish, torment

Pangloss' pupil 7 Candide

panhandler 6 beggar

panic 4 fear, wild 5 alarm, dread, scare 6 dismay, frenzy, fright, horror, terror 8 cold feet, frighten, hysteria, stampede 11 trepidation 12 consternation

panoply 4 pomp, show 5 armor, array, shine 6 parade 7 display, fanfare

panorama 4 view 5 orbit, range, reach, scene, scope, sweep, vista 6 extent, radius 7 compass, purview 9 cyclorama

pan out 5 click 6 go over 7 come off, succeed

pant 3 aim 4 blow, gasp, gulp, huff, long,

puff, wind, wish **5** chuff, heave, throb, yearn **6** aspire, desire, hunger, thirst, wheeze **7** pulsate **9** palpitate

Pantagruel 5 giant *companion:* **7** Panurge *father:* **9** Gargantua *mother:* **7** Badebec

Pantaloon's daughter 9 Columbine

Panthea's husband 9 Abradatus

pantomime 6 ballet, dancer **7** charade **12** harlequinade

pantry 6 closet, larder **7** buttery

pants 5 jeans **6** slacks **7** drawers **8** britches, knickers, trousers

pantywaist 5 sissy **7** doormat, milksop

Panurge's companion 10 Pantagruel

Paolo's lover 9 Francesca

pap 4 food, mash, pulp, slop **5** paste, trash **7** aliment, garbage, rubbish **9** nutriment **10** sustenance **11** nourishment

papal 8 pontific **9** apostolic **10** pontifical *cape:* **5** fanon, orale *court:* **5** Curia *decree:* **8** decretal *envoy:* **6** nuncio **8** ablegate *letter:* **4** bull **10** encyclical

paper 4 card **5** essay, sheet, theme **6** letter, report **7** article, nominal **8** clerical, document **9** monograph, newspaper, wallpaper **10** memorandum **11** composition, publication **12** dissertation *arrangement:* **3** pad **6** tablet *coarse:* **9** newsprint *collection:* **4** file **7** dossier *combining form:* **6** papyro *copying:* **6** carbon *currency:* **5** scrip *measure:* **4** page, ream **5** quire, sheet *roll:* **6** scroll *scrap:* **4** chad *size:* **3** cap **5** demi, demy **5** atlas, crown, folio, legal, royal, sexto, sixmo **6** octavo, quarto **7** emperor **8** elephant, foolscap, imperial **10** typewriter *stiff:* **9** cardboard, wallboard **12** Bristol board *strong:* **5** kraft **6** manila *thin:* **4** bank **6** pelure, tissue **9** onionskin *transparent:* **8** glassine *writing:* **3** rag **6** vellum **9** parchment

paper folding *Japanese:* **7** origami

paphian 6 erotic, wanton

pappy 3 dad **4** soft **5** mushy **6** father, spongy **7** pulpous, squashy, squishy, squushy **8** squelchy, yielding **9** succulent

par 4 mean, norm **5** equal **6** median **7** average **8** equality, sameness, standard

parable 4 myth, tale **5** fable, story **8** allegory

parachute 7 bailout, skydive **8** paradrop *part:* **5** riser **6** canopy **7** harness, ripcord

paraclete 6 helper **8** advocate, consoler **9** comforter **10** Holy Spirit **11** intercessor

parade 4 brag, pomp, show **5** array, boast, flash, march, shine, strut **6** expose, flaunt, reveal **7** declare, display, disport, divulge, exhibit, fanfare, listing, marshal, panoply, publish, recital, show off, trot out **8** brandish, disclose, movement, proclaim **9** advertise, cavalcade, formation, pageantry, promenade **10** exhibition, masquerade

paradigm 5 ideal, model **6** mirror **7** example, pattern **8** ensample, exemplar, standard **9** archetype, beau ideal, prototype

paradise 4 Eden, Zion **5** bliss **6** Canaan, heaven, utopia **7** arcadia, elysium, nirvana **8** empyrean **9** Cockaigne, fairyland, Shangri-la **10** Civitas Dei, lubberland, wonderland **12** New Jerusalem, promised land

Paradise Lost author 6 Milton

paragon 3 gem **4** love, pick, tops **5** champ, cream, ideal, liken, match, model, peach, trump **6** beauty, equate, lovely **7** compare, epitome, pattern, phoenix **8** champion, exemplar, last word, nonesuch, parallel, ultimate **9** archetype, beau ideal, nonpareil **10** apotheosis, assimilate

Paraguay *capital:* **8** Asuncion *monetary unit:* **7** guarani

parallel 4 akin, even, like **5** align, alike, along, equal, liken, match **6** agnate, double, equate, line up **7** compare, similar, uniform **8** analogue **9** analogous, collimate, collocate, consonant, correlate, duplicate **10** assimilate, comparable, comparison, correspond, equivalent, similarity **11** counterpart, countertype, duplication, resemblance **13** correspondent, corresponding

parallelogram 5 rhomb **6** oblong, square **7** rhombus **8** rhomboid **9** rectangle

paralysis 5 palsy **9** impotence *combining form:* **5** lyses, lysis, plegy **6** plegia

paralyze 4 daze, maim, stun **5** close, daunt **6** appall, bemuse, benumb, deaden, disarm, dismay, weaken **7** astound, cripple, destroy, disable, horrify, nonplus, petrify, prevent, stupefy, unnerve **8** demolish, enfeeble, knock out, shut down **9** prostrate **11** flabbergast **12** incapacitate

paramount 5 above, chief **6** master **7** capital, regnant, supreme **8** cardinal, crowning, dominant, headmost, superior **9** sovereign, uppermost **10** commanding, preeminent

paramour 5 lover, Romeo **6** master **7** amorist, Don Juan, gallant **8** Casanova, fancy man, lothario, mistress **9** boyfriend, inamorata, inamorato **10** girl friend

parapet 4 wall **7** bastion, bulwark, rampart **10** battlement, breastwork *part:* **6** merlon

paraphernalia 4 gear **6** outfit, tackle **8** materiel, tackling **9** apparatus, equipment, machinery, materials, trappings **11** furnishings, habiliments **13** accouterments, accoutrements, appurtenances

paraphrase 6 reword **7** restate, version **9** rendering, summarize, translate **10** transcribe **11** restatement, translation

parasite 4 laze **5** idler, leech, toady

6 infest, sponge, sucker **7** sponger **8** barnacle, deadbeat, ectozoan, entozoan, hanger-on **9** dependent, sycophant **10** freeloader, smell-feast **11** bloodsucker
parasitic 7 fawning **8** cowering, cringing, sponging, toadying, toadyish **9** groveling, kowtowing, leechlike, truckling **11** bootlicking, freeloading, sycophantic
___ **paratus 6** semper
parboil 4 stew **5** sweat **6** seethe, simmer
Parcae 5 Fates *name:* **4** Nona **5** Morta **6** Decuma
parcel 3 box, cut, lot **4** body, clot, deal, mete, pack, part, plot, wrap **5** allot, array, batch, bunch, clump, group, piece, quota, share, tract **6** assign, bundle, clutch, divide, member, moiety, packet, ration **7** cluster, package, portion, prorate, section, segment **8** allocate, disburse, disperse, division, fragment **9** apportion **10** distribute
parch 3 dry **4** burn, sear **5** roast, toast **6** scorch **7** shrivel **9** dehydrate, desiccate, exsiccate
parchment 5 paper **6** vellum **8** document
pardon 4 free **5** remit, spare **6** accept, excuse **7** absolve, amnesty, condone, forgive, justify, release **8** liberate, reprieve, tolerate **9** acquittal, exculpate, indemnity, remission **10** absolution, indulgence **11** exculpation, exoneration, forgiveness, vindication
pardonable 6 venial **9** excusable
pare 3 cut **4** clip, crop, flay, peel, skin, trim **5** lower, prune, scalp, shave, shear, skive, slash, strip **6** reduce, remove **7** curtail, cut back, cut down, whittle **8** diminish
parent 4 make, sire **5** cause, hatch, spawn **6** author, create, father, mother, origin **7** forbear, produce **8** ancestor, begetter, forebear, generate **9** originate, procreate **10** forefather, progenitor
parenthetically 6 obiter **8** by the bye, by the way **9** in passing
parentless 6 orphan **8** orphaned
par excellence 4 fine **5** prime **6** famous **7** classic **8** champion, superior **9** classical, number one **10** first-class **12** preeminently
pariah 5 leper **7** Ishmael, outcast **8** castaway, déclassé, derelict **10** Ishmaelite **11** offscouring, untouchable *Japanese:* **3** eta
Paris *beloved:* **5** Helen *betrothed:* **6** Juliet *father:* **5** Priam *mother:* **6** Hecuba *slayer:* **11** Philoctetes *wife:* **6** Oenone
Paris *ancient name:* **7** Lutetia *avenue:* **13** Champs-Elysées *basilica:* **10** Sacré Coeur *cathedral:* **9** Notre Dame *city hall:* **12** Hôtel de Ville *college:* **8** Sorbonne *garden:* **9** Tuileries **10** Luxembourg *island:* **11** Île de la Cité *museum:* **4** Army **5** Cluny

6 Louvre *palace:* **6** Louvre **7** Bourbon *patron saint:* **9** Geneviève *racecourse:* **7** Auteuil *river:* **5** Seine *section:* **8** Left Bank **9** Right Bank **10** Montmartre **12** Latin Quarter *stock exchange:* **6** Bourse *subway:* **5** Metro *tower:* **6** Eiffel
Parisina *author:* **5** Byron *husband:* **3** Azo *lover:* **4** Hugo *slayer:* **3** Azo
parity 7 analogy **8** equality, likeness, nearness, sameness **9** closeness **10** adequation, similarity, similitude **11** equivalence
parka 6 anorak, jacket **8** pullover
park designer 4 Vaux **6** Paxton **7** Alphand, Olmsted
parlance 4 talk **5** idiom **6** phrase, speech **7** diction, wordage, wording **8** phrasing, verbiage **9** verbalism **11** phraseology
parley 3 bet, use **4** chat, talk **5** speak, treat **6** advise, confab, confer, huddle, powwow **7** consult, discuss, meeting, utilize **8** collogue, colloquy, converse, dialogue **9** discourse **10** conference, converse in, discussion, rap session **11** confabulate **12** conversation **13** confabulation
parliament see **legislature**
parlor 5 salon
parlous 4 very **5** hairy, risky **6** chancy, damned, mighty, wicked **7** greatly **8** critical **9** dangerous, extremely, hazardous **11** exceedingly, excessively
parochial 5 petty **6** narrow **7** bigoted, insular **9** sectarian, small-town **10** provincial
parody 3 ape, rib **4** mock **5** mimic, spoof **6** satire, send-up **7** imitate, takeoff **8** ridicule, spoofery, travesty **9** burlesque, imitation **10** caricature
paronomasia 3 pun **9** calembour
parous 6 gravid **8** childing, enceinte, pregnant **9** expectant, expecting
parrot 4 copy, echo **5** mimic, polly **6** repeat **7** chatter, imitate *kind:* **3** ara, kea **4** jako, kaka, lory **5** macaw **6** Amazon, budgie, kakapo **8** cockatoo, lorikeet, lovebird, parakeet **9** cockatiel, parrakeet **10** budgerigar
parrot fever 11 psittacosis
parrot fish 4 loro **5** lauia **6** scarid
parry 4 duck, fend, ward **5** avert, avoid, block, dodge, evade, fence, shirk **7** deflect, prevent **8** preclude, sidestep **9** forestall
Parsifal *composer:* **6** Wagner *magician:* **8** Klingsor *quest:* **5** grail *son:* **9** Lohengrin *temptress:* **6** Kundry
parsimonious 4 mean **5** cheap, close, tight **6** frugal, stingy **7** miserly **9** niggardly, penurious **11** closefisted, tightfisted **12** cheese-paring **13** penny-pinching
parson 5 clerk **6** cleric, divine, rector

8 clerical, minister, preacher, reverend
9 churchman, clergyman **12** ecclesiastic

parsonage **5** manse

parson bird **3** poe, tui **4** koko

part **3** bit, cut, lot **4** bite, chip, duty, meed, role, side, some, spot, unit **5** allot, chunk, organ, piece, place, quota, scrap, sever, share, slice **6** behalf, cleave, detach, detail, divide, member, moiety, office, ration, region, sector, sunder **7** break up, disjoin, dissect, element, measure, portion, quality, quantum, quarter, section, segment **8** dissever, district, disunite, division, fraction, fragment, function, separate **9** allotment, allowance, component *combining form:* **3** mer **4** mere, mero, mery, toma, tome, tomy **5** meric, meris, parti **6** merous

partake **5** share **6** accept **7** receive **11** participate

Parthenon *sculptor:* **7** Phidias *site:* **9** Acropolis

partial **6** biased, unfair, warped **7** colored, half-way **8** one-sided **9** jaundiced **10** fractional, incomplete, prejudiced **11** fragmentary, predilected, predisposed *prefix:* **4** demi, semi

partiality **4** bent, bias **7** leaning **8** penchant, tendency **9** inclining, prejudice **10** chauvinism **11** inclination **12** one-sidedness, predilection

participant **4** aide **5** actor **6** fellow, helper, sharer **7** sharing **8** confrere **9** colleague

participate **5** share **7** partake

particle **3** ace, bit, dot, jot, ray **4** atom, damn, doit, dram, drop, hoot, iota, mite, mote, snap, spot, whit **5** atomy, crumb, fleck, grain, minim, ounce, scrap, shred, speck, whoop **6** morsel, smidge, smitch, tittle **7** dribbet, granule, modicum, smidgen **8** fragment **9** scintilla *atomic:* **3** ion **5** anion **6** cation *combining form:* **5** plast *elementary:* **3** psi, tau **4** kaon, muon, pion **5** boson, meson **6** baryon, hadron, lambda, lepton, photon, proton **7** fermion, hyperon, neutron, nucleon, upsilon **8** electron, mesotron, neutrino, positron *hypothetical:* **5** gluon, quark **6** parton **8** graviton *suffix:* **2** id *virus:* **6** virion *with negative charge:* **8** electron *with positive charge:* **6** proton **8** positron

motley **7** piebald **8** skewbald **9** multihued **10** variegated

particular **3** one **4** full, item, lone, nice, only, sole **5** fussy, picky, point, thing **6** dainty, detail, minute, single, unique **7** careful, correct, element, finical, finicky, precise, several, special, unusual **8** accurate, detailed, distinct, especial, exacting, itemized, separate, solitary, specific, thorough **9** clocklike, finicking **10** blow-by-

blow, fastidious, individual, meticulous, pernickety, respective, scrupulous, speciality **11** appropriate, persnickety, punctilious

particularize **4** list **6** detail **7** itemize, specify **8** separate **9** enumerate, inventory, stipulate **11** specificate **13** individualize

parting **4** last **5** adieu, congé, final **7** good-bye **8** farewell **10** divergence, separation **11** leave-taking, valedictory

partisan **5** blind **6** backer, biased, cohort, warped **7** colored, devoted, devotee, diehard, fanatic, patriot, sectary **8** adherent, advocate, champion, disciple, follower, henchman, one-sided, sectator, stalwart, upholder **9** factional, guerrilla, irregular, jaundiced, satellite, sectarian, supporter *combining form:* **4** crat **5** ocrat

partition **4** deal, wall **6** divide, lot out, screen **7** divorce, dole out, portion, rupture, section, split-up **8** disburse, dispense, disperse, division **9** severance **10** detachment, distribute, measure out, separation

partner **4** ally, chum, mate, wife **5** buddy, crony **6** cohort, fellow **7** comrade, husband **8** confrere, sidekick **9** assistant, associate, bedfellow, colleague, companion **10** accomplice, consociate **11** confederate *prefix:* **2** co

partnership **4** firm **5** tie-up **6** hookup **7** cahoots, company **8** alliance **11** association, combination, conjunction **12** consociation, togetherness **13** participation

parturient **6** gravid, parous **8** childing, enceinte, pregnant **9** expecting

parturition **5** birth **7** bearing **8** delivery **10** childbirth **12** childbearing *combining form:* **4** toky

party **4** ball, band, bevy, bloc, body, crew, fete, orgy, ring, side **5** actor, being, bunch, cabal, corps, covey, group, human, revel, troop, union **6** fiesta, mortal, outfit, person, sharer, soiree, troupe **7** carouse, cluster, combine, company, debauch, faction, shindig **8** alliance, assembly, carousal, creature, litigant, wingding **9** bacchanal, coalition, gathering, personage **10** detachment, individual, saturnalia **11** bacchanalia, celebration, combination, participant

parvenu **7** upstart **8** roturier **9** arriviste **12** nouveau riche

Pasha or Baba **3** Ali

Pashhur *father:* **5** Immer **8** Malchiah *son:* **8** Gedaliah

Pasiphaë *daughter:* **7** Ariadne, Phaedra *husband:* **5** Minos *son:* **8** Minotaur

pass **2** go **3** die, end, hap, hie, jog, top **4** beat, buck, fare, give, hand, omit, pose, wend **5** cease, lapse, occur, outdo, reach, relay, spend, while **6** crisis, demise, depart, elapse, exceed, expire, forget, hand on, happen, ignore, perish, permit, push on, repair,

roll on, slight, slip by, strait, travel
7 approve, blink at, come off, decease,
develop, devolve, journey, neglect, proceed,
succumb **8** bequeath, exigency, fade away,
fork over, hand down, juncture, outmatch,
outshine, outstrip, overlook, peter out, transmit **9** blink away, disregard, emergency, terminate, transcend, transpire, while away
Afghanistan: **5** Murgh *Afghanistan-Paki-*
stan: **6** Khyber *Alaska:* **5** White *Alps:*
3 col **5** Cenis, Loibl **7** Brenner, Ljubelj, Simplon **9** St. Bernard *California:* **5** Cajon
China-India: **9** Karakoram *into law:*
5 enact *Pakistan:* **5** Kilik *Russian:* **12** Caspian Gates *Tennessee:* **10** Cumberland
Turkey: **13** Cilician Gates *Wyoming:*
5 South
passable **4** open **9** navigable, reachable,
tolerable, unblocked **10** accessible, attainable, negotiable, travelable
passably **4** so-so **6** enough, fairly, rather
9 averagely, tolerably **10** moderately
passage **3** way **4** exit, fare, hall, line, path,
road, text **5** route, shift **6** access, arcade,
avenue, course, egress, strait, trajet, travel,
tunnel, voyage **7** areaway, channel, couloir,
excerpt, hallway, journey, traject, transit
8 corridor, transfer, traverse **9** enactment,
quotation **10** transition, traversing
11 transmittal **12** transference, transmission **13** transmittance *air:* **7** windway
arched: **6** arcade *Atlantic-Pacific:*
9 Northwest *combining form:* **4** meat,
pora **5** meato *money:* **4** fare *roofed:*
6 arcade **9** breezeway *to water's edge:*
4 ghat
Passage to India author **7** Forster
pass away **2** go **3** die **4** drop **6** cash in,
demise, depart, elapse, expire, perish
7 decease, succumb
pass by **4** fail, omit **6** forget, ignore
7 neglect **8** overlook **9** disregard
passé **4** dead **5** dated **6** démodé, old hat
7 belated, demoded, disused, extinct, outworn **8** obsolete, outdated, outmoded
9 out-of-date **10** antiquated, superseded
12 old-fashioned **13** superannuated
passed master **5** maven, mavin **6** artist,
expert, wizard **7** artiste **8** virtuoso
9 authority
passel **4** body, clot **5** array, batch, bunch,
clump, group **6** bundle **7** battery, cluster
passenger **4** fare **8** traveler, wayfarer *hid-*
den: **8** stowaway *vessel:* **5** liner
7 steamer
passerine bird see *bird, songbird*
passing **5** death, sleep **6** demise **7** cursory, decease, elusory **8** fleeting, illusive,
illusory **9** ephemeral, fugacious, momentary, transient **10** evanescent, short-lived,
transitory

passion **3** ire **4** fire, fury, heat, itch, love,
lust, rage, urge, zeal **5** agony, amour,
anger, ardor, crush, dolor **6** béguin, desire,
fervor, hurrah, misery, temper **7** craving,
ecstasy, emotion, feeling, panting, rapture
8 appetite, devotion, distress, lyricism, outbreak, outburst **9** affection, calenture,
eagerness, eroticism, prurience, pruriency,
sentiment, suffering, transport **10** aphrodisia, appetition, dedication, enthusiasm,
heartthrob, sensuality **11** affectivity, amorousness, infatuation, lustfulness **12** sensu-
ousness **13** concupiscence, lickerishness
passionate **3** hot **5** fiery, testy **6** ardent,
fervid, steamy, sultry **7** amorous, blazing,
burning, excited, fervent, flaming, glowing,
goatish, lustful, peppery, satyric **8** headlong, prurient, vehement **9** impetuous, irascible, lickerish, quickened, steamed up
10 hot-blooded, lascivious, libidinous, stimulated **11** high-powered, hot-tempered, precipitate **12** concupiscent, high-pressure,
unrestrained **13** quick-tempered
passive **4** idle **5** inert, quiet, stoic
6 asleep, docile, latent, sleepy, stolid
7 bearing, patient **8** enduring, inactive,
resigned, yielding **9** apathetic, compliant,
lethargic, quiescent, tractable **10** nonviolent, phlegmatic, submissive **11** acquiescent, unresistant
pass on **3** die **6** convey, depart, expire,
impart **7** decease **8** transmit
11 communicate
pass out **5** faint, swoon
pass over **4** fail, omit, pass **6** forget,
ignore **7** neglect **8** overlook **9** disregard
Passover **5** Pasch *bread:* **4** azym
5 azyme, matzo **6** matzoh *meal:* **5** seder
past **2** by **3** ago, old **4** gone, late, once,
yore **5** above, after, prior **6** beyond,
bygone, former, gone-by, whilom **7** onetime, outside, present, quondam, without
8 anterior, foretime, lang syne, previous,
sometime **9** antiquity, erstwhile, foregoing,
precedent, preceding, yesterday **10** antecedent, yesteryear *combining form:* **6** preter
7 praeter *prefix:* **5** retro
pasta **5** dough, paste *kind:* **4** ziti **7** gnoc-
chi, lasagna, pastina, ravioli **8** alfabeto, lin-
guine, linguini, macaroni, rigatoni, tortelli
9 canneloni, quadrucci, spaghetti **10** malfat-
tini, tagliolini, tortellini, vermicelli **11** cappel-
letti, stricchetti **12** paglia e fieno
paste **4** beat, drub, glue **5** dough, pound,
stick, stuff **6** attach, batter, buffet, cement,
pummel, spread, thrash, wallop **7** belabor
8 adhesive, lambaste, material
Pasternak hero **7** Zhivago
pasticcio see **pastiche**
pastiche **6** medley **7** mélange **8** mishmash **9** potpourri **10** assortment, hodge-

podge, hotchpotch, miscellany
11 gallimaufry

pastime 4 game 5 hobby, sport 9 amusement, diversion 10 recreation
13 entertainment

past master see **passed master**

pastoral 5 rural 6 rustic 7 bucolic, country, idyllic, outland 8 agrarian, agrestic, innocent 10 campestral, out-country, provincial

pastor's assistant 6 curate

pastry 3 bun, pie 4 baba, cake, flan, tart 5 torte 6 cornet, Danish, éclair, gâteau, kolach, pirogi, strata, torten (plural) 7 baklava, beignet, bouchée, dariole, fritter, gâteaux (plural), kolacky, palmier, savarin, strudel, tartlet 8 napoleon, papillon, piroshki, turnover, vacherin 9 barquette, cream puff, gugelhupf, kugelhupf, madeleine, petit four, vol-au-vent 10 cheesecake 11 profiterole 12 millefeuille *kind:* 4 filo, puff 5 choux, flaky 6 phyllo *shell:* 7 timbale 8 meringue

pasty 5 gluey 6 chalky, pallid, sickly

patch 3 bit, fix 4 do up, mend 5 cover, scrap 6 doctor, emblem, repair, revamp

patchwork 4 hash, olio, stew 5 salad 6 jumble 8 mishmash 10 hodgepodge, hotchpotch, miscellany, salmagundi

patchy 6 spotty, uneven 9 irregular

pate 4 head, poll 5 brain, crown 6 noddle, noggin, noodle

patella 7 kneecap, kneepan

patent 4 open, rank 5 clear, gross, plain 7 evident, glaring, license, obvious 8 apparent, distinct, flagrant, manifest, palpable, unclosed 9 privilege, prominent

paternal 8 fatherly

path 3 way 4 fare, lane, line, road, walk 5 byway, route, track, trail 6 artery, avenue, course, street 7 highway, passage 9 boulevard 12 thoroughfare

pathetic 3 sad 4 poor 6 moving, rueful 7 piteous, pitiful 8 pitiable 9 affecting

Pathfinder *author:* 6 Cooper *hero:* 6 Bumppo (Natty)

pathogen 4 germ 5 virus 6 fungus 9 bacterium

pathological condition *suffix:* 2 ia

pathos 4 pity 9 poignance, poignancy

pathway 5 track, trail 6 course

patience 4 cool 9 composure, endurance, passivity, suffering, tolerance 10 equanimity, submission, sufferance, toleration 11 forbearance, longanimity, passiveness, resignation, self-control 13 long-suffering

patient 4 case, meek 6 patron 8 enduring 9 admitting, undaunted 11 susceptible 13 long-suffering *man:* 3 Job

patina 4 film 6 finish 7 surface 10 coloration

patio 5 court 7 terrace 9 courtyard

patois 4 cant 5 argot, lingo, slang 6 jargon 7 dialect 10 colloquial, vernacular

patriarch 4 sire 5 maker 6 author, father, gaffer 7 creator, founder 8 inventor 9 architect, generator, graybeard 10 originator *biblical:* 5 David, Isaac, Jacob 7 Abraham

patrician 6 aristo 9 blue blood, gentleman 10 aristocrat

patriciate 5 elite 6 flower, gentry 7 aristoi, quality 8 optimacy 9 blue blood, gentility 10 upper crust 11 aristocracy

patrimony 6 legacy 8 heritage 9 heritance 10 birthright 11 inheritance

patriot 8 loyalist, partisan 9 flag-waver, guerrilla, irregular 11 nationalist *overzealous:* 5 jingo 8 jingoist 10 chauvinist

Patroclus *friend:* 8 Achilles *slayer:* 6 Hector

patrol 5 scout, watch 7 protect

patrolman 3 cop 6 police 7 John Law, officer

patrol wagon 10 Black Maria

patron 5 angel 6 avowry, backer, client, surety 7 sponsor 8 backer-up, customer

patronage 5 aegis, trade 6 custom 7 backing, subsidy, traffic 8 auspices, business, cronyism 9 clientage, clientele 10 protection 11 benefaction, sponsorship 12 guardianship 13 pork-barreling

patronize 3 use 5 deign, favor 7 protect, support 8 frequent 10 condescend

patron saint *of beggars, cripples:* 5 Giles *of children:* 8 Nicholas *of England:* 6 George *of fishermen:* 5 Peter *of France:* 5 Denis *of Ireland:* 7 Patrick *of lawyers:* 4 Ives *of musicians:* 7 Cecilia *of Norway:* 4 Olaf *of physicians:* 4 Luke *of sailors:* 4 Elmo 8 Nicholas *of Scotland:* 6 Andrew *of shoemakers:* 7 Crispin *of Spain:* 5 James 8 Santiago *of Wales:* 5 David *of winegrowers:* 7 Vincent *of workers:* 6 Joseph

patsy 3 sap 4 dupe, fool, goat, gull, mark 5 chump 6 pigeon, sucker, victim 7 fall guy 9 scapegoat 11 whipping boy

patter 3 jaw, yak 4 cant, chat 5 argot, clack, lingo, prate, slang 6 babble, gabble, jargon, patois 7 chatter, dialect, prattle 9 yakety-yak 10 vernacular

pattern 4 plan 5 ideal, model, motif, order 6 design, device, figure, method, mirror, motive, system 7 example 8 ensample, exemplar, original, paradigm, standard, template 11 arrangement, orderliness

paucity 4 lack 6 dearth 7 fewness, poverty 8 scarcity 10 scarceness 13 insufficiency

Paulina's husband 7 Camillo 9 Antigonus

___ **Paulo** 3 São
Paul the Apostle *birthplace:* 6 Tarsus
companion: 5 Silas, Titus 7 Artemas, Timothy 8 Barnabas *original name:* 4 Saul
place of conversion: 8 Damascus *prosecutor:* 9 Tertullus *teacher:* 8 Gamaliel
tribe: 8 Benjamin
paunch 3 pod 4 draw 5 belly, bowel, tummy 6 venter 7 abdomen, embowel, stomach 8 potbelly 9 bay window
pauper 4 bust, ruin 5 break 6 beggar 7 almsman, have-not, lazarus 8 bankrupt, indigent 10 down-and-out, impoverish
pauperism 4 need, want 6 penury 7 beggary, poverty 9 indigence, neediness 11 destitution
pause 3 gap 4 halt, hush, lull, stop, wait 5 break, comma, lapse, letup 6 hiatus, recess 7 caesura, respite 8 interval 9 cessation, interlude 10 hesitation, suspension 12 intermission, interruption
pave 3 lay, tar 5 cover, floor 7 overlie, surface 8 blacktop
pavement 6 tarmac 7 macadam 8 concrete, flagging, sidewalk
paw 4 feel, foot, hand 5 touch 6 finger, handle 7 palpate
pawn 4 hock, tool 5 token 6 pledge, puppet, stooge 7 earnest, warrant 8 impledge
Pax see **Irene**
Pax 3 Dei 6 Romana 10 Brittanica
pay 3 fee 4 give, hire, quit, wage 5 clear, remit, spend, yield 6 defray, expend, lay out, outlay, pony up, render, return, salary, settle, square, tender 7 bring in, cough up, fork out, guerdon, requite, satisfy, stipend 8 clear off, disburse, pungle up, shell out 9 discharge, emolument, indemnify, liquidate, plunk down, reimburse 10 compensate, recompense, remunerate
payable 3 due 5 owing 6 mature, unpaid 7 overdue 9 unsettled 11 outstanding
payload 4 haul 5 cargo 6 burden, lading 7 freight
payment 3 fee, tax 4 duty 6 return 7 premium 12 compensation
payoff 3 fix 5 bribe 6 climax, profit, reward 8 decisive 11 retribution
PDQ 6 at once 8 directly, right off 9 forthwith, instanter, instantly, right away 11 immediately, straightway
pea 6 legume
peace 3 pax 4 calm, ease, rest 5 order, quiet 6 repose 7 concord, harmony 8 serenity 11 tranquility 12 tranquillity
peaceable 6 irenic 7 amiable, pacific 8 amicable, friendly, pacifist 10 neighborly, nonviolent 11 complaisant 12 pacificatory
peaceful 4 cool 6 irenic, placid, steady 7 equable, pacific 8 composed, constant, pacifist 9 collected, unruffled 10 nonviolent

peacemaker 8 appeaser, mediator, placater 10 arbitrator, negotiator 11 pacificator
peace officer 3 cop 6 police 7 John Law, officer 9 patrolman, policeman
peach 3 rat 4 blab 5 dandy, nifty 6 betray, inform, snitch, squeak, squeal 8 jim-dandy 9 freestone, humdinger, nectarine 10 clingstone 11 crackerjack
Peach State 7 Georgia
peachy 4 fine, nice 6 divine 8 glorious 9 excellent, hunky-dory, marvelous
peacockish 5 showy, swank 6 chichi 7 splashy 10 flamboyant 11 pretentious
peacock-like 8 pavonine
peak 3 alp, top 4 acme, apex, bill, roof 5 abate, crest, crown, mount, visor 6 apogee, lessen, rebate, recede, summit, vertex, zenith 7 dwindle 8 capsheaf, capstone, decrease, diminish, meridian, mountain, pinnacle, taper off *Adirondack:* 9 Whiteface *Africa's highest:* 4 Kibo *Alaska-Canada:* 12 Mt. Saint Elias *Andes:* 4 Ruiz 5 Torrá *Apennines:* 5 Amaro *Argentina:* 4 Azul 5 Negra, Payún *Bavaria:* 5 Arber *Berkshires:* 10 Mt. Greylock *Black Hills:* 10 Mt. Rushmore *Bolivia:* 5 Cuzco, Tahua, Ubina 6 Sajama *Borneo:* 4 Raja *California:* 6 Sonora 7 Palomar 8 Half Dome, Mt. Shasta 9 Excelsior *California's highest:* 9 Mt. Whitney *Canada:* 5 Keele *Canaries:* 5 Teide 8 Tenerife *Carpathian:* 4 Rysy *Catskill:* 5 Mt. Vly 8 Mt. Pisgah *Caucasus:* 5 Ushba 6 Elbrus *Chile:* 4 Mayo, Pili 5 Paine, Pular *Colombia:* 4 Tama 5 Neiva *Colorado:* 5 Pikes 9 Purgatory *combining form:* 3 acr, akr 4 acro, akro *Cuba:* 8 Turquino *Ecuador:* 10 Chimborazo *England:* 11 Scafell Pike *Ethiopia:* 4 Guna 5 Holla *France:* 5 Pilat *French Guiana:* 5 Amana *Georgia:* 16 Springer Mountain *Glacier National Park:* 8 Kootenai *Greece:* 6 Mt. Ossa 6 Pelion *Himalayas:* 3 Api 5 Kamet 7 Lhotse I 8 Lhotse II 10 Gasherbrum *Honshū:* 4 Yari 10 Yarigatake *Idaho:* 13 Mt. Pend Oreille *Iran:* 8 Damavand *Japan:* 4 Sobo 5 Oyama 7 Sobozan *Java:* 6 Slamet *Jordan:* 8 Mt. Gilead *Karakoram Range:* 10 Masherbrum *Karokoram Range's highest:* 7 Dapsang 12 Godwin Austen *Maine:* 10 Mt. Katahdin 10 Saddleback *Montana:* 8 Gallatin *Nevada:* 5 Mt. Ely *Newfoundland:* 9 Gros Morne *New Hampshire:* 11 Mt. Monadnock *New Zealand:* 5 Mt. Una 6 Mt. Cook 7 Aorangi 10 Mt. Aspiring *Oahu:* 5 Kaala *Oregon:* 6 Mt. Hood *Papua New Guinea:* 10 Mt. Victoria *Pennine Alps:* 10 Matterhorn, Mont Cervin *Philippines:* 4 High *Pyrenees:* 11 de Vignemale *Scotland:* 8 Ben Nevis *Spain:* 5 Yelmo 8 Mulhacén *Switzer-

land: **3** Dom **4** Dôle, Tödi **5** Eiger, Mönch **6** La Dôle, Rusein **7** Pilatus **8** Jungfrau *U.S.S.R.'s highest:* **9** Communism *Utah:* **5** Kings *Venezuela:* **7** Mt. Icutú *Vermont:* **8** Haystack, Stratton **10** Mt. Ascutney **11** Mt. Mansfield *Washington:* **9** Mt. Olympus, Mt. Rainier **13** Mt. Saint Helens *White Mts.:* **12** Mt. Washington *Wyoming:* **10** Grand Teton **11** Elk Mountain *Yukon:* **4** King **7** Mt. Logan

peaked 3 wan **4** pale, sick **5** acute, drawn, piked, sharp **6** sickly **7** pointed **8** acicular **9** aciculate, acuminate, acuminous, cuspidate

peal 4 bell, bong, ring, toll **5** chime, knell

peanut 4 mani, puny **5** petty, small **6** goober, measly, paltry **8** earthnut, picayune

pear 4 Bosc **5** Anjou, Hardy **6** Comice, Garber, Seckel **7** Kieffer, LeConte **8** Bartlett *cider:* **5** perry

Pearl Mosque site 4 Agra

Pearl of the Pacific 4 Guam

pearly 8 nacreous

pear-shaped 8 pyriform

peasant 4 boor, carl, hick, kern, peon, serf **5** churl, knave, yokel **6** rustic **7** bumpkin, hayseed, redneck, villein **9** hillbilly *Arab:* **6** fellah *Latin-American:* **9** campesino *Russian:* **5** mujik **6** moujik, muzhik, muzjik

peccary 7 tayassu **8** javelina

peck 3 lip, lot, nag **4** beak, buss, fuss, kiss, much **5** smack **6** carp at, smooch **7** henpeck **8** osculate **9** great deal

pecker 3 neb, nib **4** beak, bill, nose **5** snoot, snout **9** proboscis

peculate 8 embezzle

peculiar 3 odd **5** queer, weird **6** proper, unique **7** bizarre, curious, oddball, strange, unusual **8** singular **9** diacritic, eccentric **10** diagnostic, individual **11** distinctive

peculiarity 4 mark **5** savor, trait **7** feature, quality **8** property **9** affection, attribute, character

pecuniary 6 fiscal **8** monetary **9** financial

pedagogue 5 tutor **7** teacher **12** schoolmaster

Pedaiah *brother:* **9** Shealtiel *father:* **6** Parosh **7** Kolaiah *grandson:* **9** Jehoiakim *son:* **4** Joed, Joel

pedal digit 4 toe

pedantic 3 dry **4** arid, dull **5** booky **7** bookish, donnish, erudite, inkhorn, learned **8** academic, didactic **9** dryasdust, schoolish **10** scholastic **11** book-learned

peddle 4 hawk, push, sell, vend **5** shove **6** monger **8** huckster

peddler 6 hawker, monger, pusher, vendor **7** chapman, higgler, packman, roadman **8** huckster, mongerer, outcrier

9 cheap-jack, cheap-john, piepoudre **10** colporteur **12** costermonger

pedestal part 4 base, dado **6** plinth **7** surbase

pedestrian 4 blah, dull **5** banal, heavy, inane **6** dreary, jejune, stodgy **7** humdrum, prosaic **8** banausic, monotone, plodding, truistic **10** monotonous, wishy-washy **11** commonplace **13** unimaginative

pedigree 5 blood **6** origin, stemma **7** descent, lineage **8** ancestry, purebred **9** genealogy, pureblood **10** extraction, family tree

peduncle 4 stem

peek 6 glance **7** glimpse

peel 4 bark, pare, skin **5** flake, scale, strip **8** flake off **9** exfoliate **10** desquamate **11** decorticate, excorticate

peeled 4 bare, open **5** naked **7** denuded, exposed **8** stripped **9** uncovered

peep 3 pip, spy **4** chip, look, ogle, peer **5** cheep, chirp, stare, tweet **6** glance, peek in, squeak **7** chipper, chirrup, chitter, glimpse, look-see, peek out, tweedle, twitter **8** look-over, oeillade

peeping tom 5 snoop **6** peeper, voyeur **7** prowler, snooper

peer 3 eye, pry **4** bore, gape, gawk, gaze, lord **5** equal, glare, gloat, noble, snoop, stare **6** goggle, squint **9** associate *British:* **4** duke, earl **5** baron **7** marquis **8** viscount *highest:* **4** duke *lowest:* **5** baron

Peer Gynt *author:* **5** Ibsen *beloved:* **7** Solveig *composer:* **5** Grieg *mother:* **3** Ase

peerless 4 only **5** alone **6** unique **8** dominant **9** matchless, nonpareil, paramount, sovereign, unequaled, unmatched, unrivaled **11** unparagoned **12** unparalleled

peeve 3 get, irk **4** miff, rile, roil **5** pique **6** nettle, put out **7** disturb, provoke **8** irritate **9** aggravate **10** exasperate

peevish 5 huffy, waspy **7** carping, fretful, pettish, waspish **8** captious, caviling, critical, petulant, snappish **9** fractious, irritable

peewee 4 runt, tiny **5** dwarf, midge, pygmy **6** midget **7** manikin, minikin **8** dwarfish, Tom Thumb **9** miniature **10** diminutive, homunculus **11** lilliputian

Peewee or Della 5 Reese

peg 3 pin **4** plod, plug **5** dowel, prong, stake, throw **6** attach **8** identify

Pegasus 5 horse, steed *rider:* **11** Bellerophon

Pekah *father:* **8** Remaliah *slayer:* **6** Hoshea *victim:* **8** Pekahiah

Pekahiah *father:* **7** Menahem *slayer:* **5** Pekah

Pelatiah's father 4 Ishi **7** Benaiah **8** Hananiah

Peleg *father:* **4** Eber *son:* **3** Reu

Peleus *brother:* 7 Telamon *father:* 6 Aeacus *half brother:* 6 Phocus *son:* 8 Achilles *victim:* 8 Eurytion *wife:* 6 Thetis

pelf 5 money, rhino, stuff 7 needful

Pelias *country:* 6 Iolcus *father:* 8 Poseidon *half brother:* 5 Aeson *son:* 7 Acastus

Pelican State 9 Louisiana

Pelion and ____ 4 Ossa

Pelleas *beloved:* 9 Mélisande *brother, slayer:* 6 Golaud

Pelles *daughter:* 6 Elaine *grandson:* 7 Galahad

pellet 3 wad 4 ball, dung, shot 5 bolus 6 bullet

Pellinore *slayer:* 6 Gawain *son:* 5 Torre 6 Dornar 7 Lamerok 8 Percival 9 Agglovale

pell-mell 5 chaos, snarl 6 ataxia, huddle, muddle, rashly 7 clutter, hotfoot 8 disarray, disorder, headlong, stampede 9 confusion, hurriedly 10 carelessly, heedlessly 11 hurry-scurry, impetuously 12 indiscreetly 13 helter-skelter, incontinently

pellucid 5 clear, sheer 6 limpid, lucent 7 crystal 8 clear-cut, luminous 9 unblurred 10 see-through 11 crystalline, translucent

Pelops *father:* 8 Tantalus *son:* 6 Atreus 8 Pittheus, Thyestes *wife:* 10 Hippodamia

pelota see jai alai

pelt 3 fly, fur 4 beat, drub, fell, hide, rush, skin, whop 5 fleet, haste, hurry, pound, scoot 6 batter, hammer, jacket, pummel, thrash, wallop 7 beeline, belabor, hotfoot

pen 3 hem, mew 4 cage, coop, crib, jail, yard 5 fence, hedge 6 cooler, corral, kennel, prison, shut in, stylus 7 close in, enclose

penalize 4 fine 5 judge, mulct 6 amerce, punish 7 chasten, condemn, correct 8 chastise 9 castigate 10 discipline

penalty 4 fine, loss 5 mulct 7 forfeit 10 amercement

penance 3 rue 4 ruth 7 remorse 9 atonement, attrition, penitence, penitency 10 contrition, repentance 11 compunction

penchant 4 bent 7 leaning 8 tendency 9 inclining 10 proclivity, propensity 11 disposition, inclination 12 predilection

pendant 4 flag, jack 5 color 6 banner, ensign, pennon 7 pennant 8 bannerol, standard, streamer 9 correlate 10 complement

pendent 7 hanging, pensile 9 pendulant, pendulous, suspended, undecided, unsettled 12 undetermined

pending 6 during 9 undecided, unsettled 12 undetermined

____ Pendragon 5 Uther

pendulous 6 wobbly 7 hanging, pendent,

pensile 8 wavering 9 faltering, suspended, tentative 10 hesitating 11 vacillating

Penelope *father:* 7 Icarius *father-in-law:* 7 Laertes *husband:* 7 Ulysses 8 Odysseus *mother:* 8 Periboea *son:* 10 Telemachus *suitor:* 7 Agelaus

penetrable 6 porose, porous 8 pervious 9 permeable

penetrate 3 jab 4 bore, go in, stab 5 break, drill, drive, enter, knife, prick 6 charge, come in, insert, invade, pierce 7 ingress, pervade 8 encroach, permeate, puncture, saturate, trespass 9 insinuate, introduce, percolate, perforate, transfuse 10 impregnate

penetrating 4 keen 5 acute, crisp, sharp 6 astute, biting, shrewd 7 cutting, ingoing 8 clear-cut, incisive 9 trenchant 11 quickwitted, sharp-witted 12 quick-sighted, sharp-sighted

Peneus *daughter:* 6 Daphne *father:* 7 Oceanus *mother:* 6 Tethys

Peninnah's husband 7 Elkanah

peninsula 4 neck 10 chersonese *Alaska:* 5 Kenai 6 Seward *Australia:* 6 Tasman *Barents Sea:* 5 Kanin *British colony:* 9 Gibraltar *Canada:* 8 Labrador *Cape Cod:* 9 Race Point 12 Monomoy Point *Chile:* 5 Swett *Costa Rica:* 3 Osa *Denmark:* 7 Jutland *eastern United States:* 8 Delmarva *Estonia:* 5 Sorve *Florida:* 8 Pinellas 9 Canaveral *France:* 5 Giens *Greece:* 4 Acte 10 Chalcidice 11 Peloponnese 12 Peloponnesus *Guam:* 5 Orote *Hong Kong:* 7 Kowloon *Honshū:* 3 Izu 5 Miura *Massachusetts:* 7 Cape Ann, Cape Cod *Mexico:* 7 Yucatan 14 Baja California *Michigan:* 8 Keweenaw *Middle East:* 5 Sinai *New Guinea:* 4 Huon *New Jersey:* 9 Sandy Hook *New Zealand:* 5 Banks, Mahia *Northern Territory:* 4 Gove *Northwest Territories:* 4 Hall 7 Boothia 8 Melville *Ontario:* 5 Bruce *Persian Gulf:* 9 Ras Tanura 13 Ras at Tannurah *Quebec:* 5 Gaspé *Russia:* 4 Kola 5 Taman, Yamal 6 Kolski, Taimyr 9 Kamchatka *Scotland:* 7 Cantyre, Kintyre *South Australia:* 4 Eyre 5 Yorke 6 Yorkes *southeast Asia:* 5 Malay 9 Indochina 12 Farther India *southeastern Europe:* 6 Balkan *southwestern Asia:* 6 Arabia 7 Arabian *southwestern Europe:* 7 Iberian *Texas:* 9 Matagorda *Tierra del Fuego:* 5 Mitre *Turkey:* 8 Anatolia 9 Asia Minor *Ukraine:* 5 Kerch *Wales:* 5 Gower, Lleyn *Washington:* 7 Olympic *west Africa:* 11 Sierra Leone *Wisconsin:* 4 Door

Peninsular State 7 Florida

penis 7 phallus

penitence 3 rue 4 ruth 5 grief, qualm 6 regret, sorrow 7 anguish, penance, remorse, sadness, scruple **8** distress, humbling **10** contrition, debasement, repentance **11** compunction, degradation, humiliation, self-reproof **12** contriteness, self-reproach

penitent **5** sorry **8** contrite **9** regretful, repentant **10** apologetic, remorseful

penitentiary see **prison**

penman **5** clerk **6** author, scribe, writer **12** calligrapher **13** calligraphist

penmanship **4** hand **6** ductus, script **7** writing **11** calligraphy, chirography, handwriting

pen name **9** pseudonym **10** nom de plume *Addison (J.):* **4** Clio *Arouet (F.M.):* **8** Voltaire *Beyle (M.H.):* **8** Stendhal *Blair (E.):* **12** George Orwell *Brontë (A.):* **9** Acton Bell *Brontë (C.):* **10** Currer Bell *Brontë (E.):* **9** Ellis Bell *Clemens (S.):* **9** Mark Twain *Dickens (C.):* **3** Boz *Dodgson (C.L.):* **12** Lewis Carroll *Dupin (A.A.):* **10** George Sand *Evans (M.A.):* **11** George Eliot *Faust (F.):* **8** Max Brand *Franklin (B.):* **11** Poor Richard *Geisel (T.):* **7** Dr. Seuss *Glidd (F.):* **9** Luke Short *Lamb (C.):* **4** Elia *Munro (H.H.):* **4** Saki *Poquelin (J.B.):* **7** Molière *Porter (W.S.):* **6** O. Henry *Ramée (M.L.):* **5** Ouida *Russell (G.):* **2** AE *Thibault (J.):* **13** Anatole France *Viaud (L.M.J.):* **10** Pierre Loti

pennant **4** flag, jack **5** color **6** banner, ensign, pennon **7** pendant **8** standard, streamer **9** banderole

penniless **4** poor **5** broke **8** bankrupt **11** impecunious

pennilessness see **penury**

pennon **4** flag, jack **5** color **6** banner, ensign **8** bannerol, gonfalon, gonfanon **9** banderole, oriflamme

Pennsylvania *battlefield:* **10** Gettysburg *capital:* **10** Harrisburg *college, university:* **5** Gratz, Thiel **6** Drexel, Lehigh, Temple **7** La Salle **8** Alliance, Bryn Mawr, Bucknell **9** Dickinson, Lafayette, St. Joseph's, Villanova **10** Pittsburgh, Swarthmore *nickname:* **13** Keystone State *state bird:* **12** ruffed grouse *state flower:* **14** mountain laurel

penny pincher **5** miser, piker, stiff **7** niggard **8** tightwad **9** skinflint **10** cheapskate **11** cheeseparer **12** moneygrubber

penny-pinching **5** close, tight **6** stingy **7** miserly **9** niggardly, penurious **11** closefisted, tightfisted **12** cheeseparing, parsimonious

pensile **7** hanging, pendent **9** pendulant, pendulous, suspended

pensioner **7** retiree **8** retirant

pensive **3** sad **4** blue **6** musing **7** wistful **8** absorbed, saddened, thinking **9** pondering, withdrawn **10** abstracted, cogitative,

meditative, melancholy, reflecting, reflective, ruminating, ruminative, thoughtful **11** preoccupied, speculative **13** contemplative

Pentateuch **5** Torah **6** Exodus **7** Genesis, Numbers **9** Leviticus **11** Deuteronomy

Penthesilea *queen of:* **7** Amazons *slayer:* **8** Achilles

Pentheus *grandfather:* **6** Cadmus *king of:* **6** Thebes *mother:* **5** Agave

Penuel *father:* **3** Hur **7** Shashak *grandfather:* **5** Judah

penumbra **5** shade **6** shadow **7** umbrage

penurious **4** poor **5** close, needy, tight **6** stingy **7** miserly **8** beggared, dirt poor, indigent **9** destitute, niggardly **10** avaricious **11** closefisted, impecunious, necessitous, tightfisted **12** cheeseparing, impoverished, parsimonious **13** penny-pinching

penury **4** need, want **7** poverty **8** poorness **9** indigence, neediness, privation **11** destitution

peon **4** serf **5** slave **6** drudge, slavey, toiler **7** laborer, peasant **9** dray horse, workhorse **11** galley slave *Anglo-Saxon:* **4** esne

peonage **4** yoke **6** thrall **7** bondage, helotry, serfdom, slavery **9** servitude, thralldom, villenage **11** enslavement

people **3** kin, men **4** folk **5** plebs **6** occupy, plebes, public, tenant **7** inhabit, society **8** populace, populate **9** commonage, commoners, common men, community, plebeians **10** commonalty **11** inhabitants, rank and file, third estate *combining form:* **4** demo, ethn **5** ethno

pep **2** go **3** vim **4** dash, push **5** getup, punch, verve, vigor **6** energy, starch **7** potency **8** vitality **9** animation, hardihood **10** get-up-and-go, liveliness

pepo **5** gourd, melon **6** squash **7** pumpkin **8** cucumber

pepper **3** dot **5** chili, speck **7** cayenne, freckle, paprika, pimento, speckle, stipple **8** capsicum, pimiento, sprinkle **9** bespeckle

peppery **4** keen, racy **5** alert, cross, fiery, spicy, zesty **6** cranky, lively, snappy, spunky **7** gingery, piquant, pungent **8** choleric, poignant, spirited **9** irascible, temperish **10** mettlesome, passionate **11** highhearted, hot-tempered **12** high-spirited **13** quick-tempered

peppy **4** keen **5** alert **6** bright, lively **7** animate **8** animated, spirited **9** sprightly, vivacious

Pepys' journal **5** Diary

Pequod *cabin boy:* **3** Pip *captain:* **4** Ahab *harpooner:* **6** Daggoo **8** Queequeg, Tashtego *mate:* **8** Starbuck

per **2** by **3** via **4** with **7** by way of, through **8** by dint of **9** by means of

perambulate 4 walk **6** stroll **8** traverse **9** promenade

per capita 3 all **4** each **5** aside **6** apiece

perceive 3 see **4** espy, feel, know, mark, mind, note, take **5** grasp, seize, sense **6** behold, descry, detect, divine, notice **7** discern, observe, realize **8** identify **9** apprehend, recognize **10** comprehend, understand

perceptible 5 clear, lucid **6** signal **8** palpable, sensible, tangible **10** cognizable, detectable, noticeable, observable **11** appreciable, conspicuous, discernible, perspicuous **12** recognizable

perception 4 idea **5** image **6** acumen, notion **7** conceit, concept, insight, thought **9** cognition **10** impression

perceptive 4 keen, sage, wise **5** acute, aware, sharp **6** sophic **7** gnostic, knowing **9** insighted, sagacious, sensitive **10** discerning, insightful, prehensile, prehensive, responsive

perch 3 bar, set **4** land **5** light, roost **6** alight, settle **7** set down, sit down, station

perchance 5 maybe **7** perhaps **8** possibly

percipience 3 wit **6** acumen **8** keenness **10** astuteness, shrewdness **11** discernment, penetration **12** perspicacity

percolate 4 ooze, seep, sift **5** exude **6** charge, filter, strain **7** pervade **8** permeate, saturate, transude **9** penetrate, transfuse **10** impregnate **11** impenetrate

percussion 3 jar **4** bump, jolt **5** clash, crash, shock **6** impact **9** collision **10** concussion *instrument:* (see at **musical instrument**)

Perdita *father:* 7 Leontes *mother:* **8** Hermione

perdition 3 pit **4** hell **5** abyss, hades **7** Gehenna, inferno **9** barathrum, damnation **10** underworld **11** netherworld, Pandemonium

Père Goriot author 6 Balzac

peregrination 4 trek, trip **7** journey, travels **10** expedition

peremptory 5 bossy, fixed **7** certain, decided **8** absolute, decisive, imperial, positive **9** imperious, masterful, obstinate **10** high-handed, imperative **11** domineering, magisterial, overbearing

perennial 3 old **7** durable **8** enduring, lifelong **9** continual, long-lived, permanent, perpetual, unceasing **10** continuing, inveterate, perdurable **11** long-lasting

Perez *brother:* 5 Zerah *father:* **5** Judah *mother:* **5** Tamar

perfect 3 fit **4** full, pure, rank, very **5** exact, gross, ideal, model, right, round, sheer, sleek, slick, sound, utter, whole **6** choate, entire, expert, intact, needed, pol-
ish, proper, refine, simple, smooth **7** express, precise, unmixed **8** absolute, complete, finished, flawless, integral, masterly, outright, positive, required, suitable, unbroken, unflawed **9** downright, excellent, fleckless, masterful, requisite, unalloyed, undamaged, undiluted, uninjured **10** consummate, impeccable, unimpaired

perfection 5 arête, ideal, merit **6** virtue **7** paragon, quality **9** integrity, wholeness **10** entireness, excellence, excellency **12** completeness

perfidious 5 false, venal **6** untrue **7** unloyal **8** disloyal, recreant **9** alienated, deceitful, dishonest, estranged, faithless, mercenary **10** traitorous, unfaithful **11** treacherous

perfidiousness see perfidy

perfidy 6 deceit **7** falsity, sellout, treason **8** betrayal, foul play **9** falseness, treachery **10** disloyalty, infidelity **13** faithlessness

perforate 3 pit **4** bore **5** drill, drive, prick, probe, punch **6** pierce **8** puncture **9** penetrate

perform 2 do **3** act, end **4** play, take, work **5** enact, react **6** behave, effect, finish, wind up **7** achieve, execute, fulfill, operate, playact **8** bring off, complete, function **9** discourse, implement, personate **10** accomplish, perpetrate

peformance 3 act **4** deed, feat, show, work **5** stunt **6** acting, action **7** concert, exploit, matinee **8** behavior, efficacy **9** discharge, execution **10** efficiency **11** fulfillment **12** presentation

performer 4 doer, mime **5** actor, mimic **6** mummer, player, worker **7** actress, artiste, trouper **8** thespian **9** playactor **12** impersonator *suffix:* **3** ant, ent

perfume 4 balm **5** aroma, cense, scent, smell, spice **6** sachet **7** bouquet, incense, odorize **9** aromatize, fragrance, redolence *source:* **4** musk **5** attar, myrrh, orris **6** chypre **8** bergamot

perfumer 6 Chanel

perfunctory 4 cool **5** stock, usual **6** wooden **7** cursory, routine, unaware **8** careless, standard **9** automatic **10** impersonal, mechanical **11** indifferent, involuntary, superficial, unconcerned **12** uninterested

pergola 5 arbor, bower

perhaps 5 maybe **6** theory **7** suppose **8** feasibly, possibly **9** perchance **10** conjecture, imaginably **11** conceivably, speculation

periapt 4 juju, luck, zemi **5** charm **6** amulet, fetish, mascot **8** talisman **10** phylactery

Pericles *father:* 10 Xanthippus *mistress:* **7** Aspasia *mother:* **8** Agariste

peril 4 risk **6** danger, hazard, menace

7 jeopard **8** endanger, exposure, jeopardy, openness **9** liability **10** compromise, jeopardize, subjection **12** endangerment

perilous **5** hairy, risky, shaky **6** chancy, touchy, wicked **7** tottery, unsound **8** delicate, dreadful, ticklish, unstable, unsteady **9** dangerous, desperate, hazardous, unhealthy **10** jeopardous **11** treacherous

___ **Perilous** **5** Siege

perimeter **3** hem, rim **4** brim, edge **5** ambit, brink, skirt, verge **6** border, fringe, margin **7** circuit, compass **8** boundary **9** periphery **13** circumference

period **3** age, end, era **4** days, span, stop, term, time **5** close, epoch **6** ending, season **7** closing, closure **8** duration **9** cessation **10** conclusion, generation **11** termination

periodical **5** organ **6** review **7** journal **8** magazine **9** alternate, newspaper, recurrent, recurring **10** isochronal **11** isochronous **12** intermittent

Peri opera **5** Dafne **8** Euridice

peripatetic **6** roving **7** nomadic, vagrant **8** ambulant, vagabond **9** itinerant, itinerate, wandering, wayfaring **11** perambulant

periphery see **perimeter**

periphrasis see **pleonasm**

perish **3** die, end **4** pass **5** cease **6** demise, depart, expire, vanish **7** decease, decline, go under, succumb **8** collapse, pass away **9** disappear

perjure **3** lie **5** trick **6** delude **7** deceive, mislead **8** forswear **10** equivocate **11** prevaricate

perk **4** gain, mend **6** look up **7** freshen, improve, smarten **9** percolate **10** ameliorate, convalesce, perquisite, recuperate

permanent **5** fixed **6** stable **7** abiding, durable, lasting **8** constant, enduring **9** continual, diuturnal, perduring, perennial **10** invariable, perdurable **12** imperishable

permeable **6** porose, porous **8** passable, pervious **10** penetrable

permeate **4** fill, soak **5** imbue, steep **6** charge, drench, imbrue, infuse, invade **7** diffuse, ingrain, pervade, suffuse **8** saturate **9** interfuse, penetrate, percolate, transfuse **10** impregnate, infiltrate **11** impenetrate

permissible **7** allowed **8** approved, bearable, endorsed **9** allowable, permitted, tolerable, tolerated **10** acceptable, admissible, authorized, sanctioned **11** unforbidden **12** unprohibited

permission **5** leave **6** permit **7** consent, license **8** approval, sanction **9** allowance **10** acceptance, sufferance **11** approbation, endorsement **12** acquiescence **13** authorization

permit **3** let **4** have **5** admit, allow, grant, leave **6** suffer **7** consent **8** sanction, tolerate **9** allowance, authorize **10** permission, sufferance **13** authorization

permitted **5** licit

permutation **5** sport **6** change **7** novelty **10** alteration, innovation **11** vicissitude **12** modification

pernicious **3** bad **4** evil **5** fatal, swart, toxic **6** deadly, lethal, malign, mortal, wicked **7** baleful, baneful, harmful, hurtful, killing, malefic, miasmic, noxious, ruinous **8** malignant, sinister, venomous, virulent **9** malignant, miasmatic, pestilent, poisonous **10** maleficent **11** deleterious, destructive, detrimental, devastating

Pernod flavor **5** anise **8** licorice

perorate **4** rant, rave **5** mouth **7** declaim, soapbox **8** bloviate, harangue

perpend **4** mind **5** study, weigh **6** ponder **8** consider, think out **9** think over **10** excogitate **11** contemplate

perpendicular **5** plumb **7** stand-up, upright **8** straight, vertical **10** straight-up

perpetrate **2** do **4** pull **5** wreak **6** commit, effect **7** inflict, execute, perform

perpetual **7** endless, eternal **8** constant, unending **9** ceaseless, continual, incessant, perennial, unceasing **10** continuous **11** everlasting, unremitting **12** interminable

perpetuate **4** keep **6** secure **7** bolster, support, sustain **8** conserve, eternize, maintain, preserve **10** eternalize **11** immortalize

perplex **4** balk, pose **5** amaze, befog, ravel, snarl **6** baffle, bemuse, muddle, puzzle, tangle, thwart **7** astound, confuse, ensnarl, mystify, nonplus, perturb, stumble **8** astonish, bewilder, confound, entangle, surprise **10** complicate, discompose **11** intertangle

perquisite **3** tip **5** right **6** income **7** cumshaw, largess **8** appanage, gratuity **9** lagniappe, pourboire, privilege **10** birthright **11** prerogative

per se **5** alone **6** as such, solely **8** in itself

persecute **4** bait, rack, ride **5** harry, hound, worry, wrong **6** harass, heckle, molest **7** afflict, dragoon, oppress, outrage, torment, torture **8** aggrieve

Persephone **4** Kore **10** Proserpina *father:* **4** Zeus **7** Jupiter *husband:* **5** Hades, Pluto *mother:* **5** Ceres **7** Demeter

Perseus *father:* **4** Zeus **7** Jupiter *grandfather:* **8** Acrisius *mother:* **5** Danaë *victim:* **6** Medusa **8** Acrisius *wife:* **9** Andromeda

perseverance **8** tenacity **9** diligence, endurance **11** persistence **13** steadfastness

persevere see **persist**

persevering see **persistent**

Persian *fairy:* **4** peri *fire worshiper:*

5 Parsi **6** Parsee *governor:* **6** satrap *mystic:* **4** sufi *poet:* **4** Omar **5** Hafiz **8** Firdausi *prophet:* **9** Zoroaster *robe:* **6** caftan *sacred books:* **6** Avesta *sun-god:* **7** Mithras *title:* **4** shah *writing:* **9** cuneiform

persiflage 6 banter **8** backchat, badinage, raillery, repartee, snip-snap

persist 4 go on, last **5** abide **6** endure, hang on, linger, obtain **7** carry on, perdure, prevail **8** continue **9** persevere **12** carry through

persistence 3 run **6** course **8** duration **9** endurance **10** continuity **11** continuance **12** continuation *combining form:* **6** stasia, stasis

persistent 6 dogged **7** archaic **8** enduring **9** insistent, primitive, steadfast, tenacious, unevolved **10** determined, relentless, unshakable **11** perseverant, persevering, undeveloped, unremitting **13** perseverative

persnickety 4 nice **5** fussy, picky **6** choosy **7** finicky **8** clerkish **10** fastidious

person 3 guy, man, one **4** body, chap, coot, life, self, soul **5** being, human, stick **6** entity, fellow, galoot, mortal **8** creature, specimen **10** individual *admirable:* **6** mensch *ambitious:* **8** go-getter **10** up-and-comer *betrothed:* **6** fiancé **7** fiancée *clumsy:* **5** klutz **6** kludge *combining form:* **6** prosop **7** prosopo *contemptible:* **3** cad **4** heel **5** knave **6** varlet *distinguished:* **3** VIP **5** great *dressy:* **12** clotheshorse *eighty-year-old:* **12** octogenarian *energetic:* **10** ball of fire *guilty:* **7** culprit *meek:* **7** nebbish *ninety-year-old:* **12** nonagenarian *non-Jewish:* **3** goy **7** gentile *of mixed ancestry:* **5** métis **7** mestizo, mulatto **8** octoroon *one-hundred-year-old:* **11** centenarian *rude:* **4** boor *rural:* **4** hick *sixty-year-old:* **12** sexagenarian *virtuous:* **6** zaddik **7** tzaddik *wealthy:* **3** nob **5** nabob

personable 6 comely **7** shapely **8** charming, handsome **10** attractive **11** good-looking

personage 3 VIP **4** body, life, soul **5** being, chief, human, nabob **6** bigwig, mortal **7** big shot, notable **8** creature, eminence, somebody **9** dignitary **10** individual, notability **11** personality

personal 3 own **5** privy **7** private, special **8** peculiar **10** individual, particular *combining form:* **4** idio

personal effects 5 goods, stuff, traps **6** things, tricks **10** belongings **11** possessions

personality 3 ego, VIP **5** chief, humor, nabob, seity **6** makeup, nature, temper **7** big shot, ipseity, notable, selfdom **8** eminence, identity, selfhood, selfness, somebody **9** character, dignitary, personage

10 complexion, notability **11** disposition, singularity, temperament **13** individualism, individuality

personate 2 do **3** act **4** play **5** enact **6** embody, mirror, typify **7** perform, play-act **9** discourse, epitomize, exemplify, personify, represent **10** illustrate **11** emblematize

personify 6 embody, mirror, typify **8** manifest **9** body forth, epitomize, exemplify, incarnate, objectify, represent, symbolize **10** illustrate **11** emblematize, exteriorize, externalize, materialize, personalize, reincarnate **12** substantiate

perspective 5 scape, vista **7** lookout, outlook **8** prospect **9** viewpoint

perspicacious 4 keen **5** cagey, heady **6** argute, astute, shrewd **9** astucious, sagacious **10** perceptive **11** penetrating, sharp-witted **12** quick-sighted, sharp-sighted

perspicacity 3 wit **6** acumen **8** astucity, keenness **10** astuteness, shrewdness **11** discernment, penetration, percipience

perspicuity 7 clarity **8** lucidity **9** clearness, limpidity, plainness **12** explicitness

perspicuous 5 clear, lucid **6** lucent **7** crystal **8** clear-cut, luculent, luminous, pellucid **9** unblurred **11** unambiguous

perspiration 4 work **5** sweat **9** exudation *abnormal:* **8** hidrosis

perspire 5 sweat **7** swelter

persuadable 8 amenable, exorable, suasible, swayable **9** acceptant, acceptive, receptive

persuade 3 win **4** coax, draw, lead, move, sway **5** bring, touch **6** affect, assure, entice, induce, prompt, reason **7** convert, entreat, impress, satisfy, win over **8** convince, talk into **9** argue into, prevail on **11** bring around, prevail upon

persuasible see **persuadable**

persuasion 3 ilk, lot **4** bias, cast, cult, mind, mold, sect, sort, type, view **5** class, creed, faith, order **6** belief, church, nature **7** feeling, opinion **8** religion **9** character, communion, prejudice, sentiment **10** cajolement, connection, conviction, partiality **11** affiliation, description **12** denomination

Persuasion author 6 Austen

pert 4 arch, bold, keen, rude, wise **5** alert, fresh, nervy, sassy, saucy, smart **6** bantam, brazen, bright, cheeky, daring, lively **7** animate, forward **8** animated, impudent, spirited **9** audacious, sprightly, vivacious **11** smart-alecky **13** disrespectful

pertain 4 join, vest **5** apply **6** bear on, belong, relate **7** combine, concern, connect **8** bear upon **9** associate

pertaining to *suffix:* **2** al, an, ar, ic **3** ean, ese, ial, ile, ine, ist, ory **4** ical **5** ative, istic **6** itious **7** istical

pertinacious 6 dogged, mulish **7** willful **8** perverse, stubborn **9** obstinate, tenacious **10** bullheaded, headstrong, inflexible, refractory, self-willed, unshakable, unyielding

pertinent 3 apt, fit **5** ad rem **7** apropos, germane **8** apposite, material, pointful, relevant **10** applicable, pertaining **11** applicative, applicatory, appropriate

perturb 5 upset, worry **6** bother, dismay, flurry **7** agitate, disturb, fluster, trouble **8** disquiet, unsettle **10** discompose, disconcert

Peru *capital:* **4** Lima *conqueror:* **7** Pizarro *monetary unit:* **3** sol

peruse 4 read, scan **5** study **6** survey **7** examine

pervade 4 fill **5** bathe, imbue **6** charge **8** permeate, saturate **9** penetrate, percolate, transfuse **10** impregnate **11** impenetrate

perverse 5 balky **6** cranky, mulish, ornery, putrid, rotten **7** corrupt, froward, restive, vicious, wayward **8** contrary, depraved, stubborn **9** irritable, miscreant, nefarious, obstinate, unhealthy **10** degenerate, headstrong, refractory, self-willed, unyielding, villainous **11** stiff-necked, wrongheaded **12** cross-grained, pertinacious, unreasonable

pervert 4 ruin, skew, warp **5** abuse, belie, color, twist **6** debase, garble, misuse **7** corrupt, debauch, deprave, distort, falsify, outrage **8** ill-treat, maltreat, misapply, miscolor, misstate, mistreat **9** animalize, brutalize, misemploy, mishandle **10** bastardize, bestialize, demoralize, misimprove, prostitute **12** misrepresent

pervious 6 porose, porous **9** permeable **10** penetrable

pesky 4 mean, ugly **8** annoying **9** troublous, vexatious **10** bothersome **11** troublesome

pessimist 5 cynic **7** killjoy **9** Cassandra, defeatist, doomsayer, worrywart **10** fussbudget **11** crepehanger, misanthrope

pessimistic 6 gloomy **7** cynical **10** despairing

pest 4 bane **5** worry **6** bother, pester, plague, vermin **7** heckler, nudnick, trouble **8** badgerer, irritant, nuisance, vexation **9** annoyance, besetment, tormentor

pester 4 ride **5** annoy, devil, harry, tease, worry **6** badger, bother, harass, plague **7** bedevil, hagride, torment **8** irritant, nuisance **9** annoyance, beleaguer, besetment, tantalize **10** botherment **11** botheration

pesticide 7 biocide **9** fungicide, germicide, vermicide **11** bactericide, insecticide, microbicide, rodenticide

pestiferous 6 deadly **7** baneful, noxious **9** pestilent **10** pernicious **12** pestilential

pestilence 5 curse **6** plague **7** scourge

pestilential 5 fatal **6** deadly, lethal, mortal, vexing **7** baneful, deathly, noxious **9** pestilent **10** irritating, pernicious **11** mortiferous

pestle 4 mano **5** pilum **6** muller *vessel:* **6** mortar

pet 3 hug **4** dear, love, pout, sulk **5** grump, loved **6** caress, cosset, cuddle, dandle, fondle, stroke **7** beloved, cherish, darling, embrace, indulge **8** blue-eyed, favorite

petcock 3 tap **4** gate **5** valve **6** faucet, spigot **7** hydrant **8** stopcock

peter 4 fade, fail **5** abate, cease **6** lessen, rebate, recede **7** dwindle **8** decrease, diminish, taper off **9** drain away

Peter Pan *author:* **6** Barrie *character:* **4** John **5** Wendy **7** Michael **9** Tiger Lily **10** Tinker Bell *dog:* **4** Nana *pirate:* **4** Hook, Smee

Peter the Apostle *brother:* **6** Andrew *father:* **5** Jonah *original name:* **5** Simon

Peter the Great *father:* **6** Alexis *wife:* **7** Eudoxia **9** Catherine

Pethuel's son 4 Joel

petite 3 wee **5** dwarf, small **6** bantam, little, monkey **8** smallish **9** miniature **10** diminutive **11** lilliputian

petition 3 ask, beg, sue **4** plea, pray, suit **5** plead, sue to **6** appeal, orison, prayer, sue for **7** beseech, entreat, implore, request **8** entreaty **10** supplicate **11** application, imploration, imprecation **12** supplication

Petrarch's beloved 5 Laura

Petrified Forest author 8 Sherwood

petrify 4 daze, numb, stun **5** alarm **6** appall, bedaze, bemuse, benumb, dismay **7** horrify, startle, stupefy, terrify **8** frighten, paralyze

Petruchio's wife 9 Katharina, Katharine

pettifogger 6 lawyer **7** shyster **10** bush lawyer **13** jackleg lawyer

pettish see **petulant**

petty 4 base, mean, puny **5** light, minor, small **6** casual, little, measly, paltry, peanut **7** pimping, trivial, unvital **8** childish, niggling, peddling, picayune, piddling, piffling, trifling **9** frivolous, hair-drawn, small-beer **10** irrelevant, negligible, picayunish, shoestring, ungenerous **11** impertinent, Mickey Mouse, unimportant

petty officer 6 noncom, yeoman

petulant 5 cross, huffy, sulky, testy, waspy **7** fretful, grouchy, peevish, pettish, waspish **8** snappish **9** fractious, irascible, irritable, querulous

peyote 6 cactus, mescal *drug:* **9** mescaline

Phaedra *father:* **5** Minos *husband:*

7 Theseus *mother:* **8** Pasiphaë *sister:* **7** Ariadne *stepson:* **10** Hippolytus

Phaëthon's father 6 Helios **7** Phoebus

phantasm 5 dream, fancy, ghost, shade **6** mirage, shadow, spirit, vision **7** eidolon, fantasy, fiction, specter **8** daydream, delusion, illusion, revenant, spectrum **9** invention, nightmare **10** apparition **11** fabrication, ignis fatuus **13** hallucination

phantom 5 ghost, shade **6** shadow, spirit **7** eidolon, specter **8** phantasm, revenant, spectrum **10** apparition

Phanuel's daughter 4 Anna

pharaoh 3 Tut **4** Seti **6** Ahmose, Ramses **7** Harmhab **8** Ikhnaton, Thutmose **9** Amenhotep, Merneptah

pharisaism 4 cant **9** hypocrisy **10** sanctimony, Tartuffery, Tartuffism **12** pecksniffery

pharisee 8 Tartuffe **9** hypocrite, lip server **10** dissembler **12** dissimulator

pharmacist 8 druggist **10** apothecary *British:* **7** chemist

pharos 6 beacon **10** lighthouse

Pharsalus, battle of *vanquished:* **6** Pompey *victor:* **6** Caesar

phase 4 hand, look, side, view **5** angle, color, facet, state **6** aspect **7** posture **8** position **9** condition, semblance, situation, viewpoint **10** appearance, complexion

PhD exam 5 orals

pheasant 5 argus, monal **8** tragopan

Phebe's husband 7 Silvius

Phèdre author 6 Racine

phenomenal 4 rare **5** gross **6** unique **7** unusual **8** material, physical, sensible, singular, tangible, unwonted **9** corporeal, objective **10** remarkable **11** exceptional, substantial, unthinkable **13** extraordinary

phenomenon 4 fact **5** event **6** marvel, wonder **7** anomaly, miracle, paradox, portent, prodigy, reality, stunner **9** actuality, sensation **10** experience, uniqueness **11** peculiarity, singularity, unusualness

philander 4 wolf **5** chase, dally, flirt **6** chaser, masher, pursue, trifle **7** Don Juan **8** Casanova, womanize **9** ladies' man, womanizer **10** fool around, lady-killer, mess around, play around **11** philanderer

philanthropic 4 good **6** giving, humane **8** donating **10** altruistic, benevolent, bighearted, charitable, freehanded **11** civic-minded, freehearted, kindhearted, magnanimous, openhearted **12** contributing, eleemosynary, greathearted, humanitarian

philanthropist *American:* **6** Girard **7** Cornell **8** Carnegie **9** Rosenwald **11** Rockefeller *English:* **11** Wilberforce *Swedish:* **5** Nobel

Philemon's wife 6 Baucis

philharmonic 4 band **8** symphony **9** orchestra

Philip of Macedonia *father:* **7** Amyntas *son:* **9** Alexander

philippic 6 tirade **8** diatribe, harangue, jeremiad

Philippics author 6 Cicero

Philippines *capital:* **6** Manila *discoverer:* **8** Magellan *hero:* **5** Rizal *language:* **7** Spanish, Tagalog, Visayan **8** Filipino *liberator:* **9** MacArthur *monetary unit:* **4** peso *president:* **6** Marcos

Philippi victor 6 Antony **8** Octavian

Philip the Tetrarch *father:* **5** Herod *mother:* **9** Cleopatra

philistine 4 boob, boor, lout **5** clown **7** Babbitt **8** boeotian **9** barbarian, bourgeois, vulgarian **10** capitalist, middlebrow **11** materialist

Philistine *champion:* **7** Goliath *city:* **4** Gath, Gaza **5** Ekron **6** Ashdod **8** Ashkelon *foe:* **5** David **6** Samson *god:* **5** Dagon

Philoctetes *father:* **5** Poeas *victim:* **5** Paris

Philomela 11 nightingale *father:* **7** Pandion *ravisher:* **6** Tereus *sister:* **6** Procne

philosopher *American:* **5** Adler, James, Quine, Royce **6** Langer **7** Marcuse **9** Santayana *Arab:* **8** Avicenna *British:* **7** Russell **12** Wittgenstein *Chinese:* **6** Lao-tsu **7** Mencius, Tai Chen **9** Confucius *Danish:* **11** Kierkegaard *Dutch:* **7** Spinoza *English:* **4** Mill, More **5** Bacon, Locke, Moore, Occam **6** Hobbes, Ockham **7** Bentham, Russell, Spencer, Whewell **9** Whitehead *Finnish:* **11** Westermarck *French:* **5** Comte, Taine **6** Pascal, Sartre, Valery **7** Abelard **8** Maritain, Rousseau, Teilhard **9** Descartes **10** Saint-Simon, Schweitzer *German:* **4** Kant, Marx **5** Hegel, Wolff **6** Fichte, Herder **7** Jaspers, Leibniz **8** Leibnitz, Spengler **9** Heidegger, Nietzsche, Schelling **12** Schopenhauer **14** Albertus Magnus *Greek:* **4** Zeno **5** Plato, Timon **6** Thales **7** Gorgias, Proclus **8** Diogenes, Epicurus, Longinus, Socrates **9** Aristotle **10** Anaxagoras, Democritus, Empedocles, Heraclitus, Parmenides, Protagoras, Pythagoras, Xenocrates, Xenophanes **11** Anaximander **12** Theophrastus *Indian:* **13** Gautama Buddha *Irish:* **8** Berkeley *Italian:* **6** Ficino *Jewish:* **5** Buber, Philo *Roman:* **6** Seneca **8** Boethius, Plotinus **9** Lucretius *Scottish:* **4** Hume, Mill, Reid **7** Stewart *Spanish:* **6** Suarez **13** Ortega y Gasset *Swedish:* **10** Swedenborg

philosophers' stone 6 elixir

philosophical 4 calm **8** composed, rational **9** temperate

philosophy 3 tao **4** yoga **5** deism **7** dualism, inquiry, wholism **8** stoicism **10** empiricism, pragmatism **12** Cartesianism

Phineas *beloved:* 9 Andromeda *tormentors:* 7 Harpies *wife:* 9 Cleopatra

Phinehas *father:* 3 Eli 7 Eleazar *grandfather:* 5 Aaron

phlegm 6 apathy 7 ataraxy 8 calmness, coolness, stoicism 9 composure, sangfroid, stolidity, unconcern 10 equanimity 11 impassivity, nonchalance

phlegmatic 3 dry 4 calm, dull 5 aloof, stoic 6 stolid 8 sluggish 9 apathetic, impassive, incurious, lethargic 11 indifferent, unconcerned

Phlegyas *daughter:* 7 Coronis *father:* 4 Ares, Mars *son:* 5 Ixion

phobia see fear

Phobos 4 moon 9 satellite *brother:* 6 Deimos *father:* 4 Ares, Mars

Phocus *father:* 6 Aeacus 8 Ornytion *half brother:* 6 Peleus 7 Telamon *mother:* 8 Psamathe *slayer:* 6 Peleus 7 Telamon *wife:* 7 Antiope

Phoebe 5 Diana 7 Artemis *daughter:* 4 Leto *father:* 9 Leucippus *mother:* 2 Ge 4 Gaea

phoebus 3 sun 7 daystar

Phoebus see Apollo

Phoenician *city:* 4 Acre, Tyre 5 Sidon *colony:* 8 Carthage *god:* 4 Baal 6 Eshmun *goddess:* 6 Baltis 7 Astarte

Phoenix 4 bird *brother:* 5 Cilix *pupil:* 8 Achilles *sister:* 6 Europa

phony 4 fake, hoax, sham 5 bogus, cheat, faker, false, fraud, put-on, snide, spoof 6 humbug, pseudo 7 swindle 8 impostor, spurious 9 brummagen, charlatan, imposture, pinchbeck, pretender 11 counterfeit

photograph 3 mug, pic 4 film, snap 5 kodak, shoot 6 glossy 7 filmize, picture, tintype 8 cinemize, likeness, snapshot 9 snapshoot *three dimensional:* 8 hologram

photographer 8 camerist, photoist 9 cameraman 10 shutterbug 11 snapshooter *famous:* 4 Haas, Hine, Riis 5 Adams, Atget, Brady, Evans, Karsh, Lange, Weber, White 6 Brandt, Coburn, Newton, Porter, Siegel, Strand, Weston 7 Emerson, Jackson, Salomon, Siskind, Thomson 8 Cosindas, Kasebier, Steichen, Steinert 9 Feininger, Leibovitz, O'Sullivan, Rejlander, Rothstein, Stieglitz 10 Cunningham, Heartfield 11 Bourke-White

photographic 5 exact, vivid 7 graphic 8 accurate, detailed 9 pictorial 11 picturesque *solution:* 4 hypo 5 fixer, toner 7 reducer 9 developer

phrase 3 put 4 term, word 5 couch, idiom 6 byword, slogan 7 diction, express, styling, wordage, wording 8 locution, parlance, verbiage 9 catchword, formulate, verbalism, watchword 10 expression, shibboleth

Phrixus *father:* 7 Athamus *mother:* 7 Nephele *sister:* 5 Helle *wife:* 9 Chalciope

Phrontis *brother:* 5 Argus, Melas 9 Cytisorus *father:* 7 Phrixus *mother:* 9 Chalciope

Phrygian *god:* 3 Men 4 Atys 5 Attis *goddess:* 6 Cybele *king:* 5 Midas 7 Gordius

phthisis 2 TB 11 consumption, white plague 12 tuberculosis

phylactery 4 juju, luck, zemi 5 charm 6 amulet, fetish, mascot 7 periapt 8 talisman

physic 4 cure, heal 5 purge 6 remedy 7 relieve 8 medicant, medicine 9 cathartic, purgative 10 medicament, medication

physical 5 brute, gross, lusty 6 bodily, carnal 7 fleshly, natural, somatic 8 corporal, material, sensible, tangible, visceral 9 corporeal, elemental, objective 10 elementary, phenomenal 11 substantial

physician 2 MD 3 doc 5 medic 6 doctor, medico 7 medical, surgeon 9 mediciner 10 specialist 12 practitioner *American:* 4 Rush, Salk 5 Minot, Spock, Still 6 Jarvik, Murphy, Weller 7 Huggins, Robbins, Theiler 8 Richards 9 Sternberg *Arab:* 8 Avicenna *Austrian:* 6 Mesmer *Canadian:* 5 Osler *combining form:* 5 iatro 7 iatrist *English:* 4 Ross 6 Harvey, Jenner, Willis 8 Sydenham *French:* 5 Widal 7 Laveran 10 Schweitzer *German:* 7 Sylvius *Greek:* 5 Galen 11 Hippocrates *Italian:* 7 Galvani *slang:* 8 sawbones *South African:* 7 Barnard *Swiss:* 10 Paracelsus; (see also **Nobel Prize Winner,** *physiology or medicine;* **surgeon**)

physicist *American:* 4 Rabi, Ting 5 Fermi, Gibbs, Kusch, Mayer, Pauli, Pupin, Segre, Smyth, Stern 6 Teller, Townes, Wigner 7 Goddard, Purcell 8 Einstein, Gell-Mann, McMillan, Millikan, Mulliken, Shockley, Van Allen 9 Michelson, Schwinger 11 Oppenheimer *Austrian:* 4 Mach 7 Doppler 11 Schrodinger *British:* 6 Stokes 7 Tyndall 8 Thompson *Chinese:* 4 Yang *Danish:* 4 Bohr *Dutch:* 6 Zeeman 7 Huygens, Lorentz, Zernike 11 Van der Waals *English:* 4 Snow 5 Jeans, Joule 6 Dalton, Kelvin, Newton, Powell 7 Faraday, Hodgkin, Thomson 8 Rayleigh, Robinson 9 Wollaston 10 Richardson, Rutherford, Wheatstone *French:* 4 Neel 5 Arago, Binet 6 Ampere, Perrin 7 Coulomb, Kastler, Reaumur 8 Lippmann *German:* 3 Ohm 4 Laue, Wien 5 Hertz, Stark 6 Jensen, Lenard, Nernst, Planck 7 Meitner 8 Roentgen 9 Helmholtz, Kirchhoff, Mossbauer 10 Fahrenheit, Hofstadter *Indian:* 5 Raman *Irish:* 6 Walton *Italian:* 5 Rossi, Volta

7 Galileo, Galvani **10** Torricelli *Japanese:* **6** Yukawa **8** Tomonaga *Mexican:* **8** Vallarta *Russian:* **4** Tamm **6** Landau **9** Prokhorov *Scottish:* **4** Tait **6** Wilson **7** Maxwell *Swedish:* **7** Rydberg **8** Angstrom, Siegbahn *Swiss:* **6** Zwicky **7** Piccard; (see also **Nobel Prize Winner,** *physics*)

physiologist *English:* **8** Starling *German:* **5** Weber, Wundt **7** Schwann **9** Helmholtz *Italian:* **11** Spallanzani; (see also **Nobel Prize Winner,** *physiology or medicine*)

physique 4 body, form **5** build, frame, habit, shape **6** figure **7** anatomy, habitus **9** structure **12** constitution **13** configuration

pianist *American:* **4** Nero, Wild **5** Arrau, Davis, Janis, Tatum, Watts **6** Duchin, Joplin, Serkin, Waller **7** Cliburn, Istomin, Ohlsson, Perahia, Winston **8** Graffman, Grainger, Horowitz, Pennario **10** Johannesen, Rubinstein *Austrian:* **6** Czerny **8** Schnabel **9** Rosenthal *Bulgarian:* **11** Weissenberg *Cuban:* **5** Bolet *English:* **4** Hess **5** Katin, Ogdon **6** Curzon *Finnish:* **8** Palmgren *French:* **6** Cortot **7** Cziffra **9** Entremont **10** Saint-Saens *German:* **5** Bülow **6** Kempff **8** Schumann **9** Gieseking *Hungarian:* **5** Liszt **6** Vasary *Italian:* **6** Busoni **8** Clementi *Polish:* **6** Chopin **7** Hofmann **9** Landowska **10** Paderewski *Russian:* **6** Berman, Gilels **7** Richter **8** Pachmann **9** Ashkenazy, Prokofiev **10** Rubinstein **12** Rachmaninoff *Spanish:* **6** Iturbi **8** Granados **10** de Larrocha *Swiss:* **4** Anda

piano 5 grand **6** softly, spinet **7** quietly, upright *builder:* **5** Knabe, Stein, Zumpe **7** Baldwin **8** Steinway **9** Bechstein **10** Chickering, Cristofori, Silbermann *inventor:* **10** Cristofori *key:* **7** digital *pedal:* **6** damper **7** celeste

Piazza Tales author 8 Melville

picaroon 5 rogue, rover, thief **6** pirate, sea dog **7** brigand, corsair, sea wolf **8** sea rover **9** buccaneer, sea robber **10** freebooter

picayune see **piddling**

Piccini's rival 5 Gluck

pick 3 top **4** beak, best, cull, gaff, mark, take **5** elect, elite, pluck, pride, prime, prize **6** choice, choose, chosen, optate, opt for, prefer, select **8** plectrum, selected **9** exclusive, single out

picket 3 peg **4** pale, post, ward **5** guard, stake, watch **6** sentry, tether **7** lookout **8** palisade, sentinel, watchman

pick handle 5 helve

pickle 3 fix, jam **4** dill, spot **5** brine **6** capers, corner, plight, scrape **7** dilemma, gherkin, trouble **8** marinate **11** predicament

pickpocket 5 thief **8** cutpurse **11** purse cutter *slang:* **3** dip

pick up 3 get **4** cull, gain, land, lift, rear **5** annex, glean, hoist, learn, pinch, raise, renew, run in **6** arrest, detain, garner, gather, master, obtain, pull in, reopen, resume, uphold, uplift, uprear **7** acquire, compass, elevate, extract, procure, restart, upraise **8** continue **9** apprehend **10** recommence

pickup 5 truck **6** arrest **9** detention **10** arrestment, hitchhiker **11** arrestation, improvement **12** acceleration, apprehension

picky 4 nice **5** fussy **6** choosy, dainty **7** finical, finicky **9** finicking **10** fastidious, particular **11** persnickety

picnic 4 snap **5** cinch **6** breeze, outing *beach:* **8** clambake

picture 4 cine, copy, draw, film, idea, limn, show **5** flick, image, movie, photo, pinup, print **6** depict, render **7** drawing, portray, tableau **8** describe, painting, portrait **9** delineate, depiction, interpret, photoplay, portrayal, represent **10** simulacrum **11** delineation, description, portraiture, presentment **13** spitting image *stand:* **5** easel

picture show 4 cine, film **5** flick, movie **9** photoplay

piddling 4 puny **5** petty **6** measly, paltry **7** trivial **8** niggling, trifling **11** Mickey Mouse

pie 4 flan, tart **5** pasty **6** affair, pastry **7** cobbler **8** business, crustade, turnover

piece 3 cut **4** part **6** member, moiety, parcel **7** portion, section, segment **8** division, fraction, fragment

pièce de résistance 8 main dish **9** showpiece **11** centerpiece, chef d'oeuvre, masterpiece

piecemeal 7 gradual **8** bit by bit **9** gradually **10** step-by-step

pie chart 5 graph **11** circle graph

pier 4 dock, quay, slip **5** berth, jetty, levee, wharf **6** column, pillar **8** pilaster

pierce 3 cut **4** bore, gash, gore, slit, stab **5** slash, slice, spear **6** incise, riddle, skewer **8** transfix **9** penetrate, perforate **10** run through

piercing 4 high, keen, loud, thin **5** acute, sharp **6** argute, piping, shrill, treble **7** blaring, roaring **8** shooting, stabbing **9** knifelike **10** stentorian **12** earsplitting *tool:* **3** awl

piety 5 ardor **6** fealty, fervor **7** loyalty **8** devotion, fidelity, holiness, sanctity **9** godliness, reverence **10** allegiance, devoutness **12** faithfulness

piffle 4 bosh **5** hooey **6** bunkum **7** twaddle **8** malarkey, nonsense, pishposh **10** balderdash, flapdoodle **12** blatherskite

pig 3 hog **5** swine **6** farrow, porker **7** casting, glutton *breed:* **5** Duroc **8** Tamworth

9 Berkshire, Hampshire, Yorkshire **combining form: 3** hyo **7** choerus **female: 3** sow **4** gilt **feral: 9** razorback **litter: 6** farrow **male: 4** boar **6** barrow **meat: 3** ham **4** pork **5** bacon **7** sausage **8** chitlins **9** chitlings **12** chitterlings **wild: 7** peccary, warthog **8** babirusa **9** babirussa **young: 4** gilt **5** shoat **6** farrow, piglet

pigeon 3 sap **4** dupe, fool, gull, hoax, mark **5** chump, decoy **6** culver, sucker **7** fall guy, gudgeon **8** flimflam, hoodwink **9** bamboozle, victimize **11** hornswoggle **genus: 7** Columba **house: 4** cote, loft **kind: 4** barb, rock **5** homer **6** pouter, roller **7** carrier, crowned, dragoon, fantail, jacobin, tumbler **8** carneaux **relative: 4** dove **young: 5** squab

pigeonhole 4 slot, sort, tier **5** class, cubby, grade, group, niche **6** assort, league **7** catalog, cubicle **8** category, classify, grouping **9** cubbyhole **10** categorize

pigeon pea 3 dal **4** dhal, herb

piggish 6 greedy **7** selfish, swinish **10** gluttonous

pigheaded 6 mulish **7** willful **8** perverse, stubborn **9** obstinate **10** headstrong, self-willed, unyielding **11** intractable, stiff-necked

pigment 3 dye **5** color, paint, stain **8** colorant, dyestuff, tincture **black: 9** lampblack **blue: 4** cyan **5** azure, smalt **6** indigo **7** cyanine **8** cerulean **9** verdigris **11** ultramarine **brown: 5** sepia **umber: 6** bister, sienna **combining form: 5** chrom **6** chromo **dark: 7** melanin **green: 7** celadon **8** viridian **10** biliverdin **orange: 7** realgar **8** carotene **red: 4** lake **minium: 7** carmine, crimson, pimento, scarlet, sinopia **8** lycopene **9** bilirubin, vermilion **10** vermillion **toxic: 8** gossypol **yellow: 5** ocher, ochre **6** flavin, lutein **7** flavine, xanthin **8** luteolin, massicot

pigpen 3 sty **4** dump, mess

pigsty see pigpen

piker 3 bum, vag **5** miser, stiff **7** drifter, floater, niggard, vagrant **8** roadster, tightwad, vagabond **9** skinflint **10** cheapskate **11** cheeseparer **12** moneygrubber, penny pincher

pilaster 4 anta, pier **6** column, pillar

Pildash father: 5 Nahor **mother: 6** Milcah

pile 3 fur, lot, mow, pot, wad **4** bank, cock, down, fill, flue, fuzz, heap, hill, lint, load, lump, mass, mint, much, pack, peck, pyre, rick **5** choke, drift, floss, fluff, hoard, mound, shock, stack **6** barrel, barrow, boodle, bundle, charge, jumble, packet **7** edifice, fortune, haycock, hayrick, pyramid, tumulus, windrow **8** erection, haystack, mountain **9** aggregate, amassment, great deal, structure **10** assemblage, collection

11 aggregation, glomeration **12** accumulation

pileous 5 hairy **6** fleecy, pilose, woolly **7** hirsute **9** whiskered

pileup 5 crash, smash **7** crack-up, smashup **8** accident **9** collision

pilfer 3 rob **4** lift **5** filch, pinch, steal, swipe **6** finger, snitch, thieve **7** purloin **11** appropriate

pilferer 4 prig **5** thief **6** nimmer **7** filcher, stealer **8** larcener **9** larcenist

pilgarlic 4 butt **5** sport **6** jestee **8** baldhead **13** laughingstock

pilgrim 5 hadji, hajji **6** palmer **8** traveler, wanderer, wayfarer **famous: 5** Alden **6** Carver **8** Bradford, Brewster

pilgrimage 4 hadj, hajj, trip **7** journey

Pilgrims' interpreter 7 Squanto

Pilgrim's Progress 8 allegory **author: 6** Bunyan **hero: 9** Christian

pill 4 ball **5** bolus **6** pellet, pilule **7** capsule

pillage 3 nab **4** lift, loot, sack **5** filch, pinch, steal, swipe, usurp, waste **6** devour, maraud, pilfer, ravage, thieve **7** despoil, plunder, purloin **8** arrogate, desolate, spoliate **9** depredate, desecrate, devastate **10** confiscate **11** appropriate

pillager 6 looter, raider, sacker **7** forager, ravager, spoiler **8** marauder, ravisher **9** plunderer **10** freebooter

pillar 4 pier, post, prop **5** pylon, shaft, stela, stele **6** column, stelae (plural) **7** obelisk **8** backbone, mainstay, pedestal, pilaster **combining form: 4** cion, styl **5** ciono, style, stylo **6** stelic, stylar

Pillar of Hercules 5 Abila, Abyla, Calpe

pillow 3 pad **7** bolster, cushion

pilose see pileous

pilot 3 ace **4** auto, dean, lead, show, tool **5** doyen, drive, flier, guide, motor, route, steer, wheel **6** airman, direct, escort, flyboy, leader **7** aviator, birdman, conduct **8** aviatrix, helmsman, shepherd

pimp 6 pander **8** fancy man, procurer

pimple 3 dot, zit **4** boil, spot, stud **6** papule **7** abscess, pustule, speckle **8** furuncle, sprinkle **9** carbuncle

pin 3 fid, peg **4** clip **5** affix, dowel, stake, thole **6** broach, brooch, cotter, fasten, secure

pinch 3 nab, nip **4** lift **5** exact, filch, gouge, run in, screw, skimp, spare, steal, stint, swipe, theft, tweak, wrest, wring **7** larceny, squeeze **8** exigency, juncture, stealing, thievery, thieving, zero hour **9** apprehend, detention, emergency, shake down **10** arrestment, crossroads, purloining

pinchbeck 4 fake, sham **5** bogus, false, phony, snide **6** pseudo **8** spurious **9** brummagen **11** counterfeit

pinch hitter 3 sub **6** fill-in **7** stand-in

9 alternate, surrogate 10 substitute
11 locum tenens, replacement, succedaneum

Pindar *home:* 6 Thebes *poems:* 4 odes

pine 4 ache, fret, long, mope, sigh 5 brood, crave, dream, yearn 6 grieve, hanker, hunger, lament, repine, thirst 7 agonize

Pine Tree State 5 Maine

pinhead 4 fool, simp 5 dense, dunce 6 dimwit, nitwit, stupid 7 doltish, lackwit, wantwit

Pinkerton 6 shamus 9 detective, operative 10 private eye

pinnacle 3 top 4 acme, apex, peak 5 crest, crown 6 apogee, climax, summit, zenith 8 capsheaf, meridian 11 culmination *of a glacier:* 5 serac

pinniped 4 seal 6 walrus

Pinocchio author 7 Collodi 9 Lorenzini

pinochle *card:* 3 ace, ten 4 jack, king, nine 5 queen *term:* 4 meld 5 widow 7 auction *two-handed:* 7 goulash

pinpoint 4 spot 5 exact, place 6 finger 7 precise 8 diagnose, identify 9 recognize 11 determinate, distinguish 13 diagnosticate

pinto 4 pied 5 overo, paint 7 painted, piebald, tobiano 8 skewbald

pint-size 3 wee 4 tiny 5 teeny, weeny 6 midget, pocket, teensy 9 miniature 10 diminutive, pocket-size

pioneer 5 first, prime 6 maiden 7 initial, primary, settler 8 colonist, earliest, original *famous:* 5 Boone, Bowie, Clark, Lewis 6 Carson, Colter 7 Bridger, Chapman, Fremont, Whitman 8 Crockett

pious 4 holy 5 godly 6 devout 8 priestly 9 pietistic, prayerful, religious

pip 3 dot 4 blip, peep, root, seed, spot 5 image, speck

pipe 3 keg, tun 4 butt, cask 5 carry 6 barrel, convey, funnel, siphon 7 channel, conduct, conduit, traject 8 hogshead *ceremonial:* 7 calumet *combining form:* 3 aul 4 aulo 5 solen 6 siphon, soleno 7 siphono *part:* 4 bowl, stem

pipe down 5 dry up, quiet 6 dumb up, shut up

pipe dream 6 bubble 7 chimera, fantasy, rainbow 8 illusion, phantasy

pipeline 7 channel, conduit 8 supplier 10 connection

piquant 4 racy, tart 5 spicy, zesty 6 biting, snappy 7 peppery, pungent 8 poignant 9 sparkling 10 appetizing

pique 3 irk 4 huff, miff, move, rile, roil 5 annoy, peeve, plume, preen, pride, rouse, snuff 6 excite, irking, nettle, put out 7 dudgeon, innerve, offense, provoke, quicken, umbrage 8 irritate, motivate, vexation 9 aggravate, annoyance, galvanize, innervate, stimulate 10 exasperate, irritation, resentment

piranha 6 caribe

pirate 5 rover 6 looter, raider, robber, sea dog 7 brigand, corsair, sea wolf 8 marauder, picaroon, pillager, sea rover 9 buccaneer, plunderer, privateer, sea robber 10 freebooter *Celtic:* 5 Fomor 8 Fomorian *flag:* 10 Jolly Roger *French:* 7 Laffite, Lafitte *Scottish:* 4 Kidd

Pirithous' wife 10 Hippodamia

pirogue 5 canoe

pirouette 4 gyre, spin 5 twirl, whirl 6 gyrate 9 whirligig

piscator 6 angler 9 fisherman

pismire 3 ant

pistol 7 handgun 8 revolver 9 derringer *case:* 7 holster

pit 3 vie 4 hell, hole 5 abyss, chasm, hades, match 6 cavity, oppose 7 counter, Gehenna, inferno, play off 9 barathrum, perdition 10 underworld 11 netherworld, Pandemonium

Pit and the Pendulum author 3 Poe

pitch 3 dip, yaw 4 cant, cast, dive, drop, fall, fire, hurl, rock, roll, swag, tilt, tone, toss 5 burst, drive, fling, heave, lunge, lurch, sling, slump, spiel, throw 6 go down, launch, plunge, seesaw, tilter, topple, tumble, unseat 7 buck off, unhorse 8 keel over 12 song and dance

pitch-black see **pitch-dark**

pitch-dark 3 jet 4 ebon, inky 5 black, ebony, jetty, raven, sable 11 atramentous

pitched 6 sloped, tilted, tipped 7 leaning, oblique, sloping, tilting 8 inclined 9 inclining

pitcher 4 ewer, olla, toby 5 cruse 7 creamer *area:* 5 mound *handle:* 3 ear 4 ansa

pitch in 5 begin, set to, start 6 chip in, fall to, jump in, kick in 8 commence, jump into, start off 9 subscribe 10 buckle down, contribute 11 come through

piteous 4 poor 6 rueful, ruined 7 pitiful 8 pathetic, pitiable 12 commiserable

pitfall 4 lure, risk, trap 5 peril, snare 6 danger, hazard 7 springe 8 deadfall, trapfall 9 booby trap, mousetrap 12 entanglement

pith 3 nub 4 core, gist, meat, pulp, root, soul 5 focus, heart 6 center, import, kernel, marrow, matter, upshot, weight 7 essence, nucleus 9 magnitude, substance 10 importance 11 consequence, weightiness 12 essentiality, significance

Pithon's father 5 Micah

pithy 4 curt 5 brief, crisp, meaty, short, terse 6 compact, concise, marrowy 8 succinct 12 epigrammatic 13 short and sweet

pitiable see **pitiful**

pitiful 3 sad 4 poor 5 cheap, sorry 6 rueful, scummy, scurvy, shabby, woeful **7** forlorn, piteous **8** beggarly, pathetic, pitiable, wretched **9** miserable, sorrowful **10** despicable, despisable **12** commiserable, contemptible, heartrending

pitiless 5 cruel, stony **6** brutal, savage **8** inhumane, ruthless **9** barbarous, cutthroat, heartless, merciless, unfeeling, unpitying **10** relentless, unmerciful **11** coldhearted, hardhearted, ironhearted **12** stonyhearted **13** marblehearted

pittance 3 bit **4** mite **5** scrap, trace **6** trifle **7** dribble, driblet, smidgen

pity 3 rue **4** ache, ruth **5** mercy **7** feel for **8** clemency, sympathy **10** compassion **11** commiserate **13** commiseration

pivot 4 turn, veer, whip **5** avert, sheer, swing, wheel, whirl **6** divert, swivel **7** deflect

pivotal 3 key **5** vital **6** ruling **7** central, crucial **8** cardinal **9** essential **10** overriding

pixie 3 elf, fay **5** antic, devil, fairy, nisse, rogue, scamp **6** elvish, impish, rascal, sprite **7** brownie, coltish, playful, puckish **8** prankish, scalawag, slyboots **9** skeezicks

pixieish 5 antic **6** elvish, frisky, impish **7** playful, puckish **9** kittenish, pixilated **11** mischievous

pixilated 5 drunk **6** elvish, pranky, stoned **7** larkish, muddled, playful, puckish, roguish, waggish **9** disguised **10** frolicsome, inebriated **11** intoxicated

Pizarro *city founded:* **4** Lima *conquest:* **4** Peru *victims:* **5** Incas

placard 4 bill, post **6** poster **7** affiche **8** handbill

placate 4 calm **6** pacify, soothe **7** appease, assuage, comfort, mollify, sweeten **10** conciliate, propitiate **11** tranquilize

place 3 fix, job, lay, put, set **4** area, call, lieu, loci (plural), post, rank, site, spot, zone **5** berth, judge, locus, point, posit, state, stick, tract, where **6** billet, finger, office, reckon, region, settle, status **7** deposit, footing, install, situate, station **8** capacity, diagnose, district, estimate, identify, locality, location, pinpoint, position, standing, vicinity **9** character, establish, recognize *combining form:* **3** top **4** chor, loco, topo, topy **5** choro *of ease:* **10** bed of roses *of sin:* **5** Sodom *suffix:* **3** ary, ery, ory **4** aria (plural), oria (plural) **5** arium, orium

place-name 7 toponym

placid 4 calm, easy, mild **5** quiet, still **6** hushed, irenic, poised, serene, stilly **7** halcyon **8** composed, peaceful, tranquil **9** collected, easygoing, unruffled **10** unagitated, untroubled **12** self-composed **13** imperturbable, self-possessed

plague 3 vex **4** bane, fret, gnaw, pest,

rash **5** annoy, beset, curse, harry, hound, tease, worry **6** bother, harass, hassle, hector, pester **7** afflict, bedevil, disease, hagride, scourge, torment, trouble **8** epidemic, invasion, irritant, nuisance, outbreak **9** annoyance, beleaguer, besetment **10** affliction, black death, botherment, pestilence **11** botheration, infestation

plain 3 dry, lea **4** bald, bare, moor, neat, open, pure **5** campo, clear, frank, heath, llano, stark, usual, veldt **6** candid, homely, modest, pampas, patent, severe, simple, steppe, tundra **7** austere, evident, obvious, prairie, routine, savanna, Spartan, unmixed **8** apparent, discreet, distinct, everyday, homespun, manifest, ordinary, palpable, savannah, straight, uncomely, unpretty, workaday **9** inelegant, quotidian, unadorned, undiluted **10** unaffected, unalluring, unhandsome

plainclothesman 4 dick **6** sleuth **7** gumshoe **8** hawkshaw, Sherlock **9** detective **12** investigator

plain Jane 5 usual **7** routine **8** everyday, ordinary, workaday **9** quotidian **12** unremarkable

plainness 7 clarity **8** lucidity **9** clearness, limpidity

plainsong 5 chant **12** cantus firmus

plainspoken 4 open **6** candid, direct **10** forthright **11** undisguised, unvarnished

plaintive 3 sad **6** rueful, woeful **7** doleful, elegiac, piteous, pitiful **8** dolesome, dolorous, mournful **9** sorrowful **10** lamentable, lugubrious, melancholy

plait 4 fold **5** braid, weave **7** pigtail **10** intertwine

plan 3 aim, map, way **4** cast, mean, plot **5** chart, draft, frame, order **6** animus, budget, design, devise, intend, intent, lay out, map out, method, policy, projet, scheme, set out, sketch, system **7** arrange, concert, meaning, outline, pattern, program, project, propose, purpose, regimen, work out **8** conspire, contrive, engineer, organize, platform, schedule, strategy, think out **9** blueprint, calculate, figure out, formulate, intention **10** intendment

plane 3 jet, lay **4** even, flat **5** flush, level **6** smooth **7** flatten **8** aircraft, airliner, smoothen

plane surface 4 area

planet 4 Mars **5** Earth, Pluto, Venus **6** Saturn, Uranus **7** Jupiter, Mercury, Neptune *brightest:* **5** Venus *closest to sun:* **7** Mercury *farthest from sun:* **5** Pluto *largest:* **7** Jupiter *path:* **5** orbit *red:* **4** Mars *ringed:* **6** Saturn *satellite:* **4** moon *shadow:* **5** umbra *small:* **8** asteroid *smallest:* **7** Mercury

planetary 6 global 7 immense 8 colossal, enormous 9 universal, worldwide
plangent 5 round 6 rotund 7 orotund, ringing, vibrant 8 resonant, sonorant, sonorous 9 consonant 10 resounding
plank 4 slab 5 board 6 lumber, timber 7 deposit, support
plant 3 fix, pot, set, sow 4 bury, grow, hide, mill, root, seed, tomb 5 cache, cover, imbed, inter, place, put in, stash, works 6 entomb, inhume, occult, screen 7 conceal, factory, lay away, put away, secrete 8 colonize, populate 9 cultivate *African:* 4 aloe 6 acacia 8 stapelia *angiosperm:* 5 dicot 7 monocot *aquatic:* 4 reed 5 lotus, sedge 7 awlwort, cattail, fanwort, papyrus 8 duckweed, eelgrass, hornwort, pondweed 9 water lily 10 watercress 11 bladderwort 12 pickerelweed *Australian:* 6 mallee 7 banksia 8 blackboy 10 eucalyptus *body:* 4 stem 7 thallus *bract:* 5 glume 8 phyllary *bulbous:* 4 lily 5 camas, onion, tulip 7 jonquil 8 hyacinth 9 narcissus *cactus:* 5 nopal 6 cereus, mescal 7 opuntia, saguaro 11 prickly pear *carnivorous:* 6 sundew 10 butterwort 12 pitcher plant 13 Venus's-flytrap *cell layer:* 5 suber 7 phellem *climbing:* 3 ivy 4 vine 5 betel, liana, vetch 6 bryony, derris, smilax 7 creeper, jasmine 8 bignonia, fumitory, moonseed, scammony, wisteria 12 morning glory *coloring agent:* 8 carotene 11 chlorophyll, xanthophyll *combining form:* 4 phyt 5 chore, cocci (plural), oecia (plural), phyta (plural), phyte, phyto *cone-bearing:* 3 fir, yew 4 pine 5 cedar, cycad 6 gingko, ginkgo, spruce 7 conifer, cypress, redwood 10 arborvitae, gymnosperm *desert:* 4 aloe 5 agave 6 cactus, cholla 8 mesquite, ocotillo 9 paloverde 11 brittlebush, Welwitschia *disease:* 3 rot 4 gall, mold, rust, scab, smut, wilt 5 ergot 6 blight, mildew, mosaic 7 blister 8 clubroot 9 black spot 10 black heart *epiphyte:* 6 orchid 8 air plant 9 bromeliad 11 Spanish moss *evergreen:* 3 fir 4 pine 6 spruce 7 lycopod 8 boxberry, clubmoss 9 bearberry 11 wintergreen 12 partridge pea *extinct:* 8 calamite *fern:* 5 royal 6 Boston 7 bracken 8 polypody, staghorn 10 cliffbrake, maidenhair *flowerless:* 4 alga, fern, kelp, moss 5 algae (plural), fungi (plural) 6 fungus, lichen 7 seaweed 8 clubmoss 9 bryophyte, equisetum, horsetail, liverwort *fluid:* 3 gum, sap 4 milk 5 latex, resin *garden:* 4 iris, ixia, lily, pink, rose 5 aster, canna, daisy, oxlip, pansy, peony, phlox, stock, tulip 6 betony, cosmos, crocus, dahlia, lupine, malope, oxalis, salvia, violet, zinnia 7 anemone, begonia, bluecap, cowslip, fuchsia, gentian, jonquil, lobelia, petunia, statice, verbena 8 bluebell, cyclamen, daffodil, foxglove, gardenia, geranium, hyacinth, larkspur, marigold, primrose, sweet pea 9 amaryllis, campanula, carnation, cineraria, gladiolus, hollyhock, ligularia, narcissus, pimpernel, portulaca, saxifrage, sunflower 10 delphinium, marguerite, mignonette, nasturtium, snapdragon 11 forget-me-not 12 rhododendron, sweet william 13 bleeding heart, chrysanthemum *gland:* 7 nectary *grain:* 3 oat, rye 4 corn, rice 5 maize, wheat 6 barley, millet 9 buckwheat *hallucinogenic:* 4 hemp 6 mescal 8 cannabis 9 marihuana, marijuana *herb:* 4 balm, mint, sage 5 basil, calla, tansy, thyme 6 catnip, cicely, fennel 7 bitters, boneset, caraway, figwort, ginseng, parsley, saffron, vanilla 8 geranium, lavender, marjoram, rosemary, valerian 9 calendula, celandine, cineraria, coriander, horehound, portulaca, spearmint, spikenard 10 elecampane, pennyroyal *largest:* 7 sequoia *life:* 5 flora *marine:* 4 kelp 5 fucus 7 seaweed 10 sea lettuce *marsh:* 4 reed 5 carex, sedge 7 bogbean, bulrush, calamus, cattail 8 red maple, sphagnum 11 loosestrife *medicinal:* 4 aloe, sage 5 poppy, senna, tansy 6 catnip, fennel, garlic, ipecac, nettle 7 aconite, boneset, camphor, hemlock, henbane, juniper, lobelia, mustard, parsley 8 camomile, cinchona, licorice, pilewort, wormwood 9 asafetida, chamomile, dandelion, monkshood 10 peppermint 11 assafoetida *microscopic:* 4 mold 6 diatom 7 euglena 8 bacteria (plural) 9 bacterium *mushroom:* 5 morel 7 amanita 10 champignon 11 chanterelle *oldest:* 11 bristlecone *onion-like:* 4 leek 5 chive 7 shallot 8 scallion *opening:* 5 stoma 7 stomata (plural) *parasitic:* 6 dodder, fungus 9 mistletoe 10 beechdrops *part:* 3 bud, nut, sap 4 bark, bulb, cell, cone, corm, leaf, pome, root, seed, stem, wood 5 drupe, fruit, grain, spore, thorn, tuber, xylem 6 catkin, flower, nectar, phloem, raceme 7 rhizome 8 lenticel 9 cellulose, cotyledon 11 chlorophyll, chloroplast 13 inflorescence *pest:* 5 aphid, scale 6 chafer, thrips, weevil 7 cutworm 8 fruit fly, wireworm 9 gypsy moth 10 cankerworm, leafhopper, phylloxera 11 codling moth *poisonous:* 4 poke, upas 5 sumac 6 castor, croton, datura 7 amantia, cassava, cowbane, henbane, lobelia, tobacco 8 foxglove, larkspur, locoweed, mayapple, oleander, pokeweed 9 baneberry, monkshood 10 belladonna, jimsonweed, manchineel, nightshade *product:* 3 dye, tar 4 cork, drug, food, rope 5 fiber, paper, resin, rosin 6 lumber, rubber 7 alcohol, perfume, tobacco 10 turpentine *saprophytic:*

5 fungi (plural) **6** fungus **10** Indian pipe *shrub:* **3** box **5** broom, furze, lilac, sumac **6** azalea, datura, hyssop, privet, spirea **7** begonia, dogwood, spiraea **8** hawthorn, magnolia, oleander, plumbago, viburnum **9** forsythia *succulent:* **5** agave **6** cactus **10** bitterroot *suffix:* **2** ad **4** ales (plural) **5** aceae (plural), ineae (plural) *support:* **7** trellis *thorny:* **4** rose **5** briar **6** cactus, nettle, teasel, teazel, teazle **7** caltrop, thistle **8** cockspur **9** cocklebur *tissue:* **5** xylem **6** phloem **7** cambium, medulla **8** meristem *unit of structure:* **6** telome *wild flower:* **4** ramp **5** bluet, calla, daisy **6** adonis, lupine **7** arbutus, cowslip, gentian **8** fireweed, hepatica, toadflax, trillium **9** bloodroot, buttercup, campanula, columbine, dandelion, goldenrod *young:* **5** scion, shoot **6** sprout **7** cutting **8** seedling

plantlike 7 phytoid
plant louse 5 aphid
plaster 3 dab **4** coat, daub, sham **5** cover, gesso, salve, smear **6** bedaub, mortar, remedy, smudge, soothe, stucco
plastic 4 soft **5** vinyl **6** pliant, supple **7** ductile, organic, pliable **8** creative, flexible, moldable **9** adaptable, formative, malleable **10** sculptural
plat 3 lot, map **4** plan **5** chart, floor, tract **6** parcel **7** surface **8** platform
plate 4 base, coat, disc, dish, disk, tile **5** layer, paten, scute, slice **6** fascia, lamina, plaque **7** lamella, overlay
plateau 4 mesa **5** table **6** upland **9** altiplano, tableland *arid:* **4** puna *barren:* **5** field **6** paramo *dry:* **5** karoo **6** karroo
platform 3 map **4** bank, base, dais, deck, plan **5** forum, ledge, shelf, stage **6** design, podium, pulpit, scheme **7** balcony, pattern, rostrum **9** banquette **11** declaration *temporary:* **7** staging **8** scaffold *wooden:* **9** boardwalk
platinum *symbol:* **2** Pt
platitude 6 cliché, truism **7** bromide **8** banality, prosaism **10** prosaicism, shibboleth
Plato *father:* **7** Ariston *literary form:* **6** dialog **8** dialogue *school:* **7** Academy *work:* **3** Ion **4** Meno **5** Crito, Lysis **6** Laches, Phaedo **7** Apology, Gorgias **8** Phaedrus, Republic **9** Charmides, Symposium
platoon 3 lot, set **4** team, unit **5** array, batch, bunch, clump, group, squad **6** parcel **7** battery, cluster **8** division **9** formation
platter 6 salver **8** trencher
platypus 8 duckbill
plaudits 5 kudos **6** praise **7** acclaim **8** applause, encomium **11** acclamation, approbation

plausible 8 credible **10** believable, creditable
play 3 act, bet, fun, use **4** game, jest, joke, ploy, romp, room, take, wile **5** dally, drama, enact, feint, flirt, scope, serve, sport, stake, treat, trick, wager **6** cavort, comedy, device, fiddle, fidget, frolic, gambit, gamble, gambol, handle, jockey, leeway, margin, trifle **7** beguile, delight, disport, exploit, finesse, gimmick, perform, roister, rollick, twiddle **8** artifice, latitude, maneuver, pleasure, recreate **9** amusement, dalliance, discourse, diversion, elbowroom, enjoyment, pantomime, personate, stratagem **10** manipulate, recreation *kind:* **5** farce, opera **6** comedy **7** musical, tragedy **8** one-acter, operetta **9** melodrama, pantomime *part:* **3** act **5** exode, scene **8** epilogue, prologue
playact 2 do **7** perform **9** discourse, personate **11** impersonate
play down 4 mute **6** soften **9** soft-pedal **11** deemphasize
player 4 mime **5** actor, mimic **6** mummer **7** actress, trouper **8** thespian **9** performer **11** participant **12** impersonator
playful 3 gay **5** antic, jolly, merry, pixie **6** blithe, elvish, frisky, impish, jocund, joking, jovial, lively, pranky, wicked **7** coltish, dashing, gleeful, jocular, larking, larkish, puckish, roguish, waggish **8** gamesome, humorous, mirthful, pixieish, playsome, prankful, prankish, sportive **9** kittenish, pixilated, sprightly, whimsical **10** frolicsome, rollicking **11** mischievous **12** lighthearted
play off 3 pit, vie **5** match **6** oppose **7** counter
play on words 3 pun
play up 6 stress **7** feature **9** emphasize, italicize, underline **10** underscore
playwright 6 author, writer **9** dramatist **10** dramatizer, dramaturge
plaza 5 green **6** common, square **9** carrefour **11** marketplace
plea 4 suit **5** alibi **6** appeal, excuse, orison, prayer **7** apology, pretext, request **8** entreaty, overture, petition **11** application, imploration, imprecation **12** supplication *defendant's:* **4** nolo **6** guilty **9** not guilty
plead 3 beg, sue **4** pray **5** brace, crave **6** appeal **7** beseech, entreat, implore **9** importune **10** supplicate
pleasant 4 fair, fine, glad, good, nice **5** clear, sunny, sweet, tasty **6** cheery, genial, joyful, joyous, pretty **7** amiable, clarion, likable, welcome **8** amicable, charming, cheerful, cheering, engaging, gracious, grateful, likeable, pleasing, sunshine, sunshiny, tasteful **9** agreeable, appealing, cloudless, congenial, convivial, enjoyable, favorable, unclouded **10** delightful, gratify-

ing, undarkened *and unpleasant:*
11 bittersweet

pleasantry 3 fun **4** jest, joke **6** banter
10 jocularity

please 4 like, suit, will, wish **5** agree,
amuse, elate, elect, enjoy **6** arride, choose,
tickle **7** content, delight, gladden, gratify,
happify, indulge, satisfy **9** delectate, titillate

pleasing 4 good, nice **5** nifty **6** comely,
pretty, seemly **7** welcome, winning
8 charming, grateful, suitable **9** agreeable,
congenial, favorable, palatable **10** attractive, delectable, delightful, enchanting, gratifying **11** pleasurable **12** satisfactory

pleasingly plump 6 zaftig, zoftig

pleasurable see **pleasing**

pleasure 3 fun, joy **4** will **5** bliss, fancy,
mirth **6** arride, liking, relish **7** delight, gladden, gratify, happify, joyance **8** felicity, fruition, gladness, hedonism, velleity **9** amusement, delectate, diversion, enjoyment,
happiness, merriment

pleasuremonger 8 hedonist, sybarite

pleat 4 fold **5** crimp **6** crease **7** flounce

pleated 7 plicate

plebeian 3 low **4** base, mean **5** lowly
6 coarse, common, homely, humble, vulgar
7 ignoble, ill-bred, lowborn **8** baseborn,
everyday, ordinary, unwashed

plebeians see **populace**

plectrum 4 pick

pledge 3 row **4** bail, bond, gage, hock,
oath, pass, pawn, seal, word **5** drink,
swear, toast, token **6** engage, plight,
surety **7** earnest, hostage, promise, warrant **8** contract, covenant, guaranty, mortgage, security, warranty **9** assurance, certainty, guarantee, undertake **11** impignorate

pledget 3 wad **8** compress

Pleiades 4 Maia **6** Merope **7** Alcyone,
Celaeno, Electra, Sterope, Taygeta **8** Asterope *brightest star:* **7** Alcyone

plenteous see **plentiful**

plentiful 4 full, rich **5** ample **6** bumper,
galore, plenty **7** copious, fertile, fulsome,
liberal, opulent, profuse, teeming **8** abundant, affluent, bursting, fruitful, generous,
prolific, swarming, swimming **9** abounding,
bounteous, bountiful, plenteous, unstinted

plenty 3 lot **4** heap, much, pack, peck,
pile **5** ample **7** copious, liberal **8** abundant,
generous, mountain, opulence **9** abundance, bounteous, bountiful, great deal,
plenteous, plentiful **10** cornucopia

pleonasm 8 verbiage **9** tautology, verbality **10** periphrase, redundancy, roundabout
11 periphrasis **13** circumambages

plethora 4 glut **5** flood **6** deluge, excess
7 surfeit, surplus **8** fullness, overflow, overkill, overmuch, overplus **9** repletion **10** surplusage **11** superfluity **13** overabundance

plexus 4 rete **7** network

pliable see **pliant**

pliant 4 limp, soft **5** lithe **6** limber, supple
7 ductile, plastic, tensile, willowy **8** flexible,
moldable, workable, yielding **9** adaptable,
compliant, malleable, tractable **11** manipula-
ble **13** manipulatable

plica 4 fold, ruck **5** ridge, rivel **6** crease,
furrow, rimple **7** crinkle, wrinkle
11 corrugation

plight 3 box, fix, jam, vow **4** hole, spot,
word **5** swear **6** corner, engage, pickle,
pledge, scrape **7** betroth, dilemma, promise **8** covenant, quandary **9** betrothal
10 difficulty, engagement **11** predicament

plighted 7 engaged **8** intended **9** affianced, betrothed **10** contracted

plod 4 grub, slog, slop, toil **5** grind, slave,
tramp, tromp **6** drudge, stodge, trudge
7 trample **8** footslog, plunther

plot 4 plan **5** cabal, covin, tract **6** design,
devise, parcel, scheme **7** collude, compact,
connive, diagram, outline **8** cogitate, conspire, contrive, engineer, intrigue, practice,
scenario **9** collusion, conniving, machinate,
scheme out **10** complicity, connivance, conspiracy **11** machination

plover 4 bird **5** pewit, stilt **7** lapwing
8 dotterel, killdeer *relative:* **9** sandpiper,
turnstone

plow 3 dig **4** till, turn **5** break **6** furrow,
trench **8** turn over **9** cultivate *part:*
4 beam, frog **5** share **8** landside
9 moldboard

ploy 4 ruse, wile **5** feint, trick **6** device,
gambit **7** gimmick **8** artifice, maneuver
9 stratagem

pluck 3 tug **4** grit, guts, pick, pull **5** cheek,
heart, nerve, spunk **6** daring, mettle,
snatch, spirit, tweeze **7** bravery, cojones,
courage **8** gameness **10** resolution

plucky 4 bold, game **5** brave **6** spunky
7 doughty **8** fearless **9** dauntless, unfearing **10** courageous **11** undauntable

plug 3 tap **4** bung, clog, cork, fill, pack,
puff, push, stop, tout **5** block, blurb, boost,
choke, close, spile **7** congest, occlude, promote, puffing, stopper, stopple, tampion,
tompion, write-up **8** obstruct **9** advertise

plug-ugly 3 mug **4** thug **5** rowdy, tough,
yahoo **6** mucker **7** ruffian **8** bullyboy
9 roughneck

plum 5 prize **6** reward **7** guerdon, premium **8** dividend *dried:* **5** prune *kind:*
4 Agen **6** Damson, Duarte **7** bullace
8 Hortulan, Salicina **9** Green Gage, myroba-
lan *spiny:* **10** blackthorn

plumage 8 feathers *early:* **4** down

plumb 4 delve, probe, sound **6** fathom
7 explore, plummet **8** absolute, vertical
10 straight-up **13** perpendicular

plume 5 pique, preen, pride 7 feather
8 aigrette
plummet 3 dip 4 drop, fall, sink, skid
5 crash 6 plunge, tumble 7 decline,
descend 8 collapse, decrease, nose-dive
11 precipitate
plump 3 fat 5 buxom, podgy, pudgy,
round, stout, tubby 6 chubby, fleshy, portly,
rotund 8 roly-poly 10 roundabout
plunder 3 rob 4 loot, swag 5 booty, prize,
rifle, spoil 6 boodle 7 despoil, pillage, ransack, relieve, stick up 9 knock over
plunderage 4 loot, swag 5 booty, prize,
spoil 6 boodle
plunderer 6 looter, raider, sacker 7 forager, ravager 8 marauder, pillager, ravisher 9 despoiler 10 freebooter
plunge 3 dig, dip, ram, run 4 dive, drop,
fall, rush, sink, skid, stab 5 burst, douse,
drive, lunge, pitch, slump, stick 6 charge, go
down, thrust, topple, tumble 7 immerse,
plummet 8 keel over, nose-dive, submerge
plus 4 more, over 5 asset, boost, build
6 beef up, excess, expand 7 augment,
enlarge, magnify, overage, surplus 8 compound, increase 9 overstock 10 oversupply
plush 4 posh 6 Capuan, deluxe 7 opulent 8 luscious, palatial 9 luxuriant, luxurious, sumptuous 11 upholstered
Pluto 3 Dis 5 Hades *brother:* 4 Zeus
7 Jupiter, Neptune 8 Poseidon *father:*
6 Cronus, Saturn *mother:* 3 Ops 4 Rhea
wife: 10 Persephone, Proserpina
plutonic 6 Hadean 7 avernal, hellish, stygian 8 chthonic, infernal 9 chthonian, cimmerian, Tartarean 10 sulphurous
11 pandemoniac
plutonium *symbol:* 2 Pu
Plutus *father:* 6 Iasion *god of:* 6 riches,
wealth *mother:* 5 Ceres 7 Demeter
ply 4 bend, fold 5 exert, layer, swing,
throw, wield 6 handle, put out 7 belabor
8 dispense, exercise, maneuver 9 importune 10 manipulate
pneuma 4 soul 5 anima 6 animus, psyche, spirit 9 élan vital 10 vital force
pneumatic 4 airy 6 aerial 11 atmospheric
Pocahontas *father:* 8 Powhatan *husband:* 5 Rolfe
pock 3 pit 4 hole, spot 6 pimple 7 pustule
pocket 3 bag, nab, wee 4 hook, lift, sack,
tiny 5 filch, pinch, pouch, purse, steal,
swipe, weeny 6 accept, cavity 7 capsule,
conceal, dead end, impasse, swallow
8 abstract, bear with, cul-de-sac, dwarfish,
monetary, pint-size, tolerate, tough out
9 condensed, financial, itsy-bitsy, miniature,
pecuniary 10 blind alley, diminutive *billiards:* 4 pool
pocket money 6 change 9 petty cash
11 small change

pocket-size 4 tiny 6 midget, minute, peewee 8 dwarfish, pint-size 9 itsy-bitsy, miniature 10 diminutive
pod 3 bag, gam, sac 4 boll, case, hull,
husk, skin 5 shell, shuck 6 cocoon,
paunch, school 7 capsule, silique 8 potbelly, seedcase 9 bay window 11 corporation *combining form:* 7 siliqui *plant:*
3 pea 4 bean, okra 5 chili, gumbo 6 cassia, cowpea, legume, lentil, peanut, pepper
8 capsicum, mesquite, milkweed
9 lespedeza
pod-bearing tree 5 carob 6 locust
7 catalpa
podiatry 9 chiropody
Poe, Edgar Allan *detective:* 5 Dupin
poem: 6 Lenore 7 Israfel, To Helen, Ulalume 8 Eldorado, For Annie, The Raven
10 Annabel Lee *tale:* 6 Ligeia, Shadow
7 Morella, Silence 10 The Gold Bug
poem 3 ode 4 epic, epos, idyl, rime, rune,
song 5 ditty, elegy, epode, idyll, lyric,
rhyme, verse 6 ballad, epopee, jingle, ron-
del, sonnet 7 rondeau 8 limerick, madrigal
closing: 5 envoi, envoy *combining form:*
5 stich *division:* 4 foot, line 5 canto,
epode, stich, verse 6 stanza 7 refrain
8 epilogue, prologue *Japanese:* 5 haiku,
tanka *of eight lines:* 6 octave 7 triolet *of
four lines:* 8 quatrain *of fourteen lines:*
6 sonnet *of three lines:* 7 triplet *pastoral:*
7 eclogue, georgic *short:* 5 ditty 7 epigram
poet 4 bard, muse, scop 5 odist, skald
6 lyrist 7 elegist 8 idyllist, lyricist, satirist
9 balladist, sonneteer, sonnetist 10 Parnassian *American:* 3 Poe 4 Nash, Read, Tabb,
Tate 5 Auden, Benét, Crane, Field, Frost,
Guest, Moore, Plath, Pound, Riley, Wylie
6 Barlow, Bryant, Ciardi, Dunbar, Kilmer,
Lanier, Lowell, Millay, Ransom, Seeger,
Strand, Taylor, Warren, Wilbur 7 Emerson,
Jeffers, Lindsay, Markham, Merrill, Neme-
rov, Roethke, Shapiro, Stevens, Whitman
8 Cummings, Ginsberg, MacLeish, Robinson, Teasdale, Whittier, Williams 9 Dickinson, Santayana 10 Bradstreet, Longfellow
12 Wigglesworth *Anglo-Saxon:* 7 Caed-
mon, Cynwulf 8 Cynewulf *Arab:* 5 Jarir
Australian: 8 Paterson *Belgian:* 11 Maeterlinck *Canadian:* 5 Pratt 7 Roberts *Chinese:* 4 Li Po, Tu Fu *Danish:* 5 Evald,
Ewald *English:* 3 Gay 4 Gray, Owen,
Pope, Rowe, Tate, Wyat 5 Blake, Byron,
Donne, Eliot, Keats, Noyes, Wilde, Wyatt,
Young 6 Arnold, Brooke, Cowper, Dryden,
Graves, Milton, Savage, Sidney, Surrey,
Symons, Waller, Warton, Watson, Wotton
7 Chaucer, Herrick, Hopkins, Housman,
Layamon, Patmore, Quarles, Shelley, Skel-
ton, Southey, Spender, Spenser 8 Betje-
man, Browning, Langland, Lovelace, Mere-

dith, Rossetti, Suckling, Tennyson, Thompson 9 Coleridge, Swinburne 10 Wordsworth 11 Shakespeare *Finnish:* 8 Runeberg *French:* 5 Marot 6 Musset, Valery, Villon 7 Bourget, Chenier, Gautier, Rimbaud, Ronsard 8 Malherbe, Mallarmé, Verlaine 9 Lamartine 10 Baudelaire 11 Apollinaire *German:* 5 Heine, Rilke, Storm 6 Goethe, Uhland 7 Walther, Wolfram 8 Schiller 9 Klopstock *Greek:* 5 Arion, Homer 6 Erinna, Hesiod, Pindar, Sappho 7 Thespis 8 Anacreon 9 Simonides 10 Apollonius, Theocritus *Hindu:* 5 Naidu 6 Tagore 8 Kalidasa *Hungarian:* 6 Zrinyi *Irish:* 5 Moore, Synge, Wolfe, Yeats 8 Stephens *Italian:* 4 Rosa, Vida 5 Dante, Tasso 7 Ariosto, Manzoni, Montale 8 Leopardi, Petrarch 9 D'Annunzio, Marinetti, Ungaretti *medieval:* 8 minstrel, trouvère, trouveur 10 troubadour *nonsense:* 4 Lear *Norwegian:* 8 Björnson, Welhaven 9 Wergeland *Persian:* 4 Sadi 5 Attar, Hafiz 11 Omar Khayyam *Roman:* 4 Ovid 6 Horace, Vergil, Virgil 7 Juvenal, Statius 8 Catullus, Tibullus 9 Lucretius *Russian:* 7 Pushkin, Yesenin 9 Kheraskov, Pasternak *Scottish:* 4 Hogg, Muir 5 Burns, Scott 6 Ramsay 7 Thomson *Spanish:* 7 Jimenez *Swedish:* 5 Sachs 6 Tegner 8 Snoilsky 9 Karlfeldt *Swiss:* 9 Spitteler *Welsh:* 6 Thomas 7 Aneurin, Watkins

poetaster 6 rhymer, verser 7 bardlet 8 bardling, verseman 9 rhymester, versifier

poetic 5 lyric 6 bardic, dreamy 8 romantic

poetic contraction see at contraction

poet laureate 3 Pye 4 Rowe, Tate 6 Austin, Cibber, Dryden, Jonson 7 Bridges, Southey 8 Betjeman, Davenant, Day-Lewis, Shadwell, Tennyson 9 Masefield, Whitehead 10 Wordsworth

Pogo creator 9 Walt Kelly

poignancy 6 pathos

poignant 4 keen, racy 5 acute, sharp, spicy, zesty 6 moving, snappy, urgent 7 cutting, peppery, piquant, pungent 8 incisive, piercing, touching 9 affecting 10 impressive

point 3 aim, awn, bit, dot, jag, nib, tip 4 apex, barb, beak, bill, cape, cast, cusp, edge, head, hint, item, mite, mote, naze, site, snag, spot, tine, turn 5 brink, force, imply, level, locus, motif, place, prong, punch, refer, speck, spike, steer, theme, topic, trace, verge 6 allude, detail, direct, matter, moment, motive, tip-off, zero in 7 address, article, cogency, element, feature, instant, station, subject, suggest 8 argument, flyspeck, foreland, headland, indicate, juncture, location, particle, position, validity 9 birthmark, character, punctuate, situation, threshold, validness 10 particular, promontory 12 significance

Point Counter Point author 6 Huxley

pointed 5 acute, peaky, piked, sharp 6 marked, peaked, signal 7 salient 8 acicular, striking 9 aciculate, acuminate, acuminous, arresting, cuspidate, mucronate, prominent

pointer 3 dog, tip 4 dial, hint 5 arrow, steer 6 tip-off 9 indicator

pointillist 6 Seurat

point of view 5 angle 7 outlook 11 perspective

point out 8 indicate

poise 4 hang, tact 5 float, grace, hover 6 aplomb, stasis, steady 7 address, balance, ballast, dignity 8 calmness, elegance, serenity 9 assurance, diplomacy, equipoise, stability, stabilize 10 confidence 11 delicatesse, equilibrium, savoir faire, stabilitate, tactfulness, tranquility

poised 4 calm, easy 6 placid, serene 8 composed, tranquil 9 collected, easygoing, possessed 13 self-possessed

poison 4 bane, harm, loco, warp 5 stain, taint, toxic, toxin, venom, virus 6 debase, infect, toxine, toxoid 7 botulin, cacodyl, corrupt, debauch, deprave, destroy, envenom, pervert, vitiate 8 mephitic, toxicant, venenate, venomous, virulent 9 contagion 10 corruption, demoralize 13 contamination *arrow:* 4 inée 5 urare, urari 6 antiar, curara, curure 7 ouabain, woorali, woorari 8 antiarin *combining form:* 3 tox 4 toxi, toxo 5 toxic 6 toxico

poisoning *food:* 8 botulism *lead:* 8 plumbism

poisonous 5 fatal, toxic 6 deadly, lethal, mortal 7 baneful, miasmal, miasmic, nocuous, noxious, toxical 8 mephitic, toxicant, venenous, venomous, virulent 9 miasmatic, pestilent 10 nauseating, pernicious *alkaloid:* 8 nicotine 10 strychnine *element:* 7 arsenic

poke 3 box, dig, hit, jab, jog, jut, lag, pry 4 chop, cuff, dolt, dope, drag, nose, pout, prod, push, sock, stab, stir 5 bulge, chump, clout, dally, delay, dunce, idiot, moron, mouse, nudge, punch, rouse, shove, smack, snoop, spank, tarry, trail 6 arouse, awaken, beetle, buffet, cowboy, dawdle, dimwit, loiter, pierce, put off, putter, thrust 7 project 8 busybody

poker *bet total:* 3 pot *form:* 4 stud 8 baseball *hand:* 4 pair 5 flush 8 straight 9 full house 10 royal flush 13 straight flush *stake:* 4 ante *term:* 3 see 4 call, draw, open 5 raise *token:* 4 chip

poker-faced 5 grave, sober, staid 6 sedate, solemn, somber 7 earnest, neutral, serious

poky 4 blah, dull 6 dreary, stodgy 7 humdrum 8 banausic, monotone 10 monotonous

Poland *capital:* 6 Warsaw *labor leader:* 6 Walesa (Lech) *monetary unit:* 5 zloty

polar 8 opposite

pole 4 punt, spar 5 shaft, stick, stilt *Indian:* 5 totem *Scottish:* 5 caber

polecat 5 fitch, skunk 7 fitchet

polestar 3 hub 4 seat 5 focus, guide, heart 6 center 10 focal point 11 nerve center

policeman 3 cop 4 fuzz, heat 5 bobby 6 copper, peeler 7 gumshoe, John Law, officer, trooper 8 bluecoat, Dogberry, flatfoot, gendarme 9 constable, patrolman 12 peace officer *Italian:* 11 carabiniere *Parisian:* 4 flic 8 gendarme *Spanish:* 10 carabinero *Turkish:* 6 kavass 7 zaptiah, zaptieh

policy 3 wit 4 line 6 course, govern, wisdom 7 program 8 sagacity 9 procedure

polio vaccine developer 4 Salk 5 Sabin

polish 3 rub, wax 4 buff 5 glaze, glint, gloss, round, sheen, shine, sleek, slick 6 glance, luster, pumice, refine, smooth 7 brush up, burnish, culture, perfect, touch up 8 breeding, brighten 10 refinement

Polish *dumpling:* 7 pierogi *patriot:* 9 Kosciusko *pope:* 8 John Paul *sausage:* 8 kielbasa *soldier:* 7 Pulaski

polish off 5 eat up, shift, swill 6 devour, punish 7 consume, put away 8 dispatch

polite 5 civil 7 courtly, genteel 8 mannerly 9 attentive, courteous 10 thoughtful 11 considerate 12 well-mannered

politeness 8 chivalry, civility, courtesy

politic 4 wise 7 cunning, prudent, tactful 8 delicate, tactical 9 advisable, expedient, judicious 10 diplomatic 11 worldly-wise

political *association:* 4 bund *meeting:* 6 caucus *party:* 3 GOP 9 Communist, Socialist 10 Democratic, Republican *system:* 7 fascism 9 communism, democracy, socialism

politics *conservative:* 8 rightism *liberal:* 7 leftism

poll 4 clip, crop, head, nape 5 shear 6 noddle, noggin, noodle, survey 7 canvass

pollack, pollock 6 saithe 8 bluefish, coalfish

pollard 3 top 4 crop 8 truncate 10 detruncate

pollen-producing organ 6 stamen

pollex 5 thumb

polliwog 7 tadpole

polltaker 6 Gallup

pollute 4 foul, soil 5 dirty, taint 6 befoul, defile 7 corrupt, profane 11 contaminate

pollution 4 smog 8 impurity 10 defilement

Pollux 10 Polydeuces *brother:* 6 Castor *father:* 4 Zeus *mother:* 4 Leda *sister:* 5 Helen 12 Clytemnestra

Pollyanna 8 optimist 10 daydreamer *author:* 6 Porter

Pollyannaish 8 cheerful, sanguine 10 optimistic

Polonius *daughter:* 7 Ophelia *slayer:* 6 Hamlet *son:* 7 Laertes

poltergeist 5 ghost 6 spirit

poltroon 4 funk 6 coward, craven, funker 7 dastard, gutless, quitter, unmanly 8 cowardly 9 spunkless 11 lily-livered, yellowbelly

Polydorus *father:* 5 Priam 6 Cadmus *mother:* 6 Hecuba 8 Harmonia *slayer:* 8 Achilles 10 Polymestor 11 Polymnestor

polygon *eight-sided:* 7 octagon *five-sided:* 8 pentagon *four-sided:* 8 tetragon *nine-sided:* 7 nonagon *seven-sided:* 8 heptagon *six-sided:* 7 hexagon *ten-sided:* 7 decagon *three-sided:* 8 triangle *twelve-sided:* 9 dodecagon

Polyhymnia 4 Muse *invention:* 4 lyre

Polynesian 6 Maori 6 Samoan, Tongan 8 Hawaiian, Tahitian 9 Marquesan

Polynices *brother:* 8 Eteocles *father:* 7 Oedipus *mother:* 7 Jocasta *wife:* 5 Argia 6 Argeia

polyp 5 zooid 7 hydroid *freshwater:* 5 hydra

Polyphemus 7 cyclops *beloved:* 7 Galatea *father:* 8 Poseidon *victim:* 4 Acis

pome 4 pear 5 apple 6 quince 8 hawthorn

pommel 4 knob 6 finial

pomp 4 form, show 5 array, shine 6 parade, ritual 7 display, fanfare, liturgy, panoply 8 ceremony, splendor 9 formality

pompano 4 fish 6 permit 8 carangid 10 butterfish

Pompeii's volcano 8 Vesuvius

pom-pom 4 ball, tuft

pompous 4 vain 5 proud, puffy, wiggy 6 stuffy 7 aureate, bloated, flowery, stilted, stuck-up 8 arrogant, sonorous 9 bombastic, important, overblown 10 egocentric, euphuistic, hoity-toity, pontifical, rhetorical 11 declamatory, highfalutin, magisterial, pretentious

pond 4 mere 5 stank 6 lagoon, salina *combining form:* 4 limn 5 limni, limno

ponder 4 mind, mull, muse 5 brood, study, think, weigh 6 reason 7 perpend, reflect, revolve 8 appraise, cogitate, consider, evaluate, meditate, mull over, muse over, ruminate, think out, turn over 9 speculate, think over 10 deliberate, excogitate 11 contemplate

ponderous 4 dull 5 heavy, hefty, stiff, vapid 6 dreary, stodgy, stuffy, wooden 7 buckram, humdrum, massive, onerous,

stilted, weighty **8** plodding, unwieldy **10** burdensome, cumbersome, oppressive
poniard **6** dagger
Ponocrates' pupil **9** Gargantua
Ponte Vecchio *city:* **8** Florence *river:* **4** Arno
Pontiac's tribe **6** Ottawa
pontiff **4** pope **6** bishop
pontifical **5** puffy, wiggy **6** stuffy **7** bloated, pompous **8** arrogant, dogmatic **9** episcopal, important **11** magisterial
pony **4** crib, trot **5** horse **6** cayuse *breed:* **6** Exmoor **8** Shetland
Pooh creator **5** Milne
pooh-pooh **3** boo **4** bird, hiss, hoot, razz **5** bazoo **7** catcall, dismiss, kiss off **9** raspberry
pool **3** pot, pul **4** mere **5** chain, group, kitty, trust **6** cartel, lagoon, laguna, puddle **7** combine, jackpot **9** syndicate *player:* **7** Mosconi **13** Minnesota Fats
poor **3** bad, low **4** base, flat, hack, mean, punk **5** amiss, broke, cheap, needy, scant, skimp, spare, stony, tatty, wrong **6** common, crummy, humble, meager, paltry, rotten, rueful, scanty, scrimp, shoddy, skimpy, sleazy, sparse, trashy **7** piteous, pitiful, scrawny, scrimpy, squalid, trivial **8** bankrupt, beggared, beggarly, déclassé, exiguous, indigent, inferior, low-grade, pathetic, pitiable, rubbishy, strapped **9** deficient, destitute, insolvent, moneyless, penceless, penniless, penurious, unmoneyed **10** bankrupted, down-and-out, pauperized, secondrate, stone-broke **11** fortuneless, impecunious, indifferent, necessitous, second-class, unfavorable *combining form:* **3** mal
poorly **3** low **4** mean **6** ailing, offish, sickly, unwell **8** off-color **10** indisposed **11** undesirably **13** ineffectively
pop **3** dad, dot, gun, hit, try **4** dada, dart, ding, jump, papa, shot, slap, slog, sock, soda, stab, swat **5** break, catch, crack, daddy, drink, fling, shoot, smite, whack, whirl **6** attack, effort, father, strike **7** assault, attempt, explode, instant **8** backfire *in:* **3** see **4** call **5** visit **6** come by, drop by, look up, stop by **8** come over
pop artist **5** Blake **6** Warhol **7** Hockney, Indiana **9** Oldenburg, Wesselman
pope **3** Leo **4** John, Mark, Paul, Pius **5** Caius, Conon, Donus, Felix, Gaius, Lando, Linus, Peter, Soter, Urban **6** Adrian, Agatho, Fabian, Julius, Lucius, Martin, Sixtus, Victor **7** Anterus, Clement, Damasus, Gregory, Hadrian, Hyginus, Marinus, Paschal, Pontian, Romanus, Sergius, Stephen, Zosimus **8** Agapetus, Anicetus, Benedict, Boniface, Calixtus, Eugenius, Eusebius, Formosis, Gelasius, Hilarius, Honorius, Innocent, John Paul, Liberius, Nicholas, Pelagius,

Siricius, Theodore, Vigilius, Vitalian **9** Adeodatus, Alexander, Anacletus, Callistus, Celestine, Cornelius, Densdedit, Dionysius, Eutychian, Evaristus, Hormisdas, Marcellus, Miltiades, Severinus, Silverius, Silvester, Sisinnius, Sylvester, Symmachus, Valentine, Zacharias **10** Anastasius, Melchiades, Sabinianus, Simplicius, Zephyrinus **11** Christopher, Constantine, Eleutherius, Eutychianus, Marcellinus, Telesphorus
Pope poem **10** The Dunciad **12** An Essay on Man **16** The Rape of the Lock
Popeye *accessory:* **4** pipe *baby:* **8** Sweet Pea *energizer:* **7** spinach *friend:* **5** Wimpy **8** Olive Oyl *occupation:* **6** sailor *rival:* **5** Bluto
poplar **5** abele, alamo, aspen **9** tulip tree **10** cottonwood **12** balm of Gilead *North American:* **6** balsam
Poppaea's husband **4** Nero
poppycock **3** rot **4** bosh, guff **5** bilge, hokum **6** bunkum **8** malarkey, nonsense **10** balderdash **12** blatherskite, fiddle-faddle
populace **5** plebs **6** masses, people, plebes **9** commonage, commoners, common men, plebeians **10** commonalty **11** rank and file, third estate *combining form:* **3** dem **4** demo
popular **4** rife **5** cheap, noted **6** famous, public, ruling, vulgar **7** current, favored, general, leading, rampant, regnant **8** approved, favorite **9** notorious, preferred, prevalent, prominent, well-known, wellliked **10** democratic, prevailing, widespread
populate **6** occupy, people, tenant **7** inhabit
populous **7** crowded **8** numerous
Poratha's father **5** Haman
porcelain *Chinese:* **9** Lowestoft *English:* **3** Bow **5** Derby, Spode **6** Minton **7** Bristol, Chelsea **8** Caughley, Wedgwood *French:* **6** Sèvres **7** Limoges *German:* **7** Dresden, Meissen *ingredient:* **6** kaolin **8** petuntse *Italian:* **6** Doccia *Japanese:* **5** Imari
porch **5** lanai **7** galilee, passage, veranda **8** verandah
porcine see **portly**
porcupine **5** porky, prick **7** echidna **8** hedgehog
porgy **4** scup **6** sparid **7** margate, pinfish **8** menhaden
Porgy and Bess composer **8** Gershwin
Porgy author **7** Heyward
pork **3** ham, pig **5** bacon, swine **8** sowbelly *cut:* **3** ham **4** jowl, loin, side **7** fatback **8** forefoot, hind foot, spare rib **9** picnic ham **10** Boston butt
pork-barreling **9** patronage
pornographic **7** obscene
porous **5** leaky **6** leachy **8** pervious

9 permeable **10** cancellate, cancellous, penetrable **13** insubstantial

porridge 4 stew **5** brose, salad **6** crowdy, sowans, sowens **7** crowdie

port 3 air, set **4** goal, mien **5** cover, haven **6** asylum, covert, harbor, refuge, riding **7** address, bearing, retreat, shelter **8** demeanor, larboard, presence **9** anchorage, harborage, roadstead, sanctuary **10** deportment **11** comportment, destination

portable 5 handy **6** mobile, wieldy

portal 4 door, gate **5** entry **7** doorway **8** entrance, entryway **11** entranceway

portcullis 3 bar **4** shut **7** grating, lattice

portend 4 bode, omen **5** augur **7** betoken, predict, presage, promise, signify **8** forebode, forecast, foreshow, foretell, indicate, prophesy **9** adumbrate, foretoken **10** foreshadow, vaticinate

portent 4 omen, sign **6** augury, boding, marvel, wonder **7** miracle, presage, prodigy, stunner **8** bodement **9** foretoken, sensation

portentous 7 pompous, weighty **8** inflated **9** marvelous **10** prodigious

porter 5 carry, hamal **6** bearer, hamaul, hammal, redcap **7** carrier, drogher **9** transport **10** doorkeeper *airport:* **6** skycap

Portia *husband:* **6** Brutus **8** Bassanio *maid:* **7** Nerissa

portion 3 cut, lot **4** bite, doom, fate, meed, part **5** dower, endow, moira, piece, quota, share, slice, weird **6** divide, kismet, member, moiety, parcel **7** deal out, destiny, dole out, measure, mete out, partage, prorate, quantum, segment **8** dispense, division *largest:* **10** lion's share *unused:* **8** leftover

portly 3 fat **5** heavy, obese, stout **6** fleshy **7** weighty **8** imposing **9** corpulent, overblown **10** overweight

portmanteau 9 gladstone **12** traveling bag

portrait 4 bust **5** image **6** double, ringer, statue **7** picture **10** similitude, simulacrum

portray 4 limn **5** cameo, enact, image **6** depict, render **7** picture **8** describe **9** delineate, interpret, represent

portrayal 7 picture **9** depiction **11** delineation, description, presentment

Portugal 9 Lusitania *capital:* **6** Lisbon *coin:* **7** centavo *export:* **4** cork, wine **8** textiles *monetary unit:* **6** escudo *premier:* **7** Salazar

pose 3 ask, dog, put, sit **4** airs, fake, give, lugs, sham **5** befog, feign, offer, query, strut **6** baffle, extend, pass as, prefer, puzzle, stance, tender **7** confuse, hold out, pass for, pass off, peacock, perplex, present, pretend, profess, proffer, propone, purport, show off, stumble, suggest **8** attitude,

bewilder, carriage, confound, pretense, propound, question **9** mannerism **10** grandstand, masquerade, pretension **11** affectation, proposition **12** attitudinize

Poseidon 7 Neptune *brother:* **4** Zeus **5** Hades, Pluto **7** Jupiter *consort:* **4** Tyro **6** Medusa **7** Demeter *father:* **6** Cronus *mother:* **4** Rhea *offspring:* **7** Pegasus *son:* **5** Orion **6** Neleus, Pelias **7** Antaeus **10** Polyphemus *weapon:* **7** trident *wife:* **10** Amphitrite

posh 4 chic, tony **5** smart, swank **7** à la mode **9** exclusive **11** fashionable

posit 6 assume, thesis **7** premise, presume **9** apriorism **10** assumption, presuppose **11** presumption

position 3 job **4** rank, side, site, spot, view **5** angle, berth, color, locus, place, point, situs, slant, stand, state, where **6** belief, billet, cachet, locate, office, stance, status **7** dignity, emplace, footing, stature **8** attitude, capacity, judgment, prestige, standing **9** character, viewpoint **10** standpoint *troops:* **6** deploy

positive 4 firm, hard, rank, sure **5** clear, gross, sound, utter **6** actual **7** assured, certain, decided, express, factual, genuine, perfect **8** absolute, cocksure, complete, definite, emphatic, explicit, forceful, forcible, outright, specific **9** clockwise, confident, doubtless, downright, energetic, practical **10** consummate, inarguable, reasonable, sure-enough, undeniable **11** categorical, indubitable, irrefutable, right-handed, unambiguous, undoubtable, unequivocal, unmitigated **12** indisputable, irrebuttable, undisputable, unmistakable

possess 3 own **4** bear, have, hold, keep **5** carry, enjoy **6** retain

possessed 4 calm, easy **6** placid, serene **8** tranquil

possession 8 property **9** ownership **11** proprietary

possessive 7 jealous

possessive pronoun see at **pronoun**

possibility 2 if **9** potential **11** contingency

possible 6 latent, likely, mortal, viable **7** dormant, earthly **9** expedient, potential

possibly 5 maybe **7** perhaps **9** perchance

post 3 job, set **4** clew, clue, mail, spot, tell, warn **5** berth, place **6** advise, billet, fill in, inform, notify, office, wise up **7** apprise, placard, station **8** acquaint

poster 4 bill, sign **6** banner, notice **7** affiche, placard **8** handbill **9** billboard, broadside, signboard **12** announcement **13** advertisement

posterior 4 back, hind, rear, rump, seat, tail **5** after, later **6** behind, hinder, retral **7** ensuing, rear end, tail end **8** backside, buttocks, hindmost, rearward **10** subsequent **13** subsequential

posterity 4 seed **5** brood, issue **6** scions **7** progeny **8** children **9** offspring **11** descendants, progeniture

posthaste 4 fast **5** fleet, quick, rapid, swift **6** speedy **7** flat-out, fleetly, quickly, rapidly, swiftly **8** full tilt, speedily **9** breakneck **10** harefooted **11** expeditious **12** lickety-split

posimpressionist painter 6 Seurat **7** Cezanne, Gauguin, Van Gogh

postmortem 7 autopsy **8** necropsy

postpone 5 defer, delay **6** hold up, put off, shelve **7** hold off, lay over, suspend **8** hold over, prorogue, reprieve **9** carry over

postulate 4 aver, call **5** claim, exact **6** affirm, assert, assume, demand, thesis **7** premise, presume, require, solicit **9** apriorism, challenge **10** assumption, presuppose **11** presumption, requisition, supposition

posture 3 sit **4** mien, mode **5** state **6** manner, stance, status **7** bearing, pass for, pass off **8** attitude, carriage **9** condition, situation **10** deportment, masquerade **12** attitudinize

posy 3 ana **5** album, bloom **6** flower **7** blossom, bouquet, corsage, garland, nosegay, omnibus **8** analects **9** anthology **10** miscellany **11** florilegium

pot 3 bet, wad **4** ante, mint, olla, pile, weed **5** grass, kitty, stake, wager **6** boodle, bundle **7** fortune **8** cannabis **9** marihuana, marijuana, sideswipe *small:* **6** pipkin

potable 4 pure **5** clean, drink, fresh **6** liquor **8** beverage **9** drinkable

potassium 6 kalium *ore:* **6** sylvin **7** sylvine, sylvite

potato 3 yam **4** spud **5** praty, tater **6** murphy *bud:* **3** eye *cooked strips of:* **11** French fries

potbelly 5 stove **6** paunch **9** bay window

potency 3 pep **4** birr, tuck **5** force, might, power, sinew, vigor **6** energy, muscle, virtue **8** strength **9** hardihood, puissance **10** capability **13** effectiveness

potent 5 lusty **6** mighty, robust, strong, virile **8** forceful, forcible, powerful

potential 6 latent, likely **7** abeyant, dormant, lurking **8** possible, probable **9** plausible, prepatent, quiescent **10** imaginable **11** conceivable, possibility

pother 3 ado **4** cark, flap, fret, fuss, stew, stir, to-do **5** furor, whirl, worry **6** bustle, clamor, flurry, furore, hassle, hubbub, tumult, uproar **7** turmoil **9** agitation, annoyance, commotion, confusion, whirlpool, whirlwind **10** hurly-burly, turbulence

potion 7 philter, philtre

Potiphar's slave 6 Joseph

Potiphera *daughter:* **7** Asenath *son-in-law:* **6** Joseph

potpourri 4 hash **6** medley **7** mélange **8** mishmash, pastiche **9** patchwork **10** assortment, hodgepodge, miscellany, salmagundi

potshot 3 cut, dig **4** gibe, jeer **5** crack **6** insult **9** aspersion, criticism, sideswipe

potter 4 mess **6** doodle, fiddle, puddle **10** mess around *English:* **8** Wedgwood

Potter, Beatrix *creation:* **11** Peter Rabbit

potter's field 8 cemetery, God's acre **9** graveyard

pouch 3 bag, jut, sac **4** sack **5** bulge, burse **6** beetle, pocket **7** project, saccule **8** overhang, protrude, sacculus, stand out *bodily:* **5** bursa

pouf 5 quilt **9** comforter

poultice 7 plaster **8** compress, dressing **9** cataplasm

poultry 4 fowl *type:* **4** duck, swan **5** goose, quail **6** grouse, pigeon, turkey **7** chicken, ostrich, peacock **8** pheasant **9** partridge

pounce 5 swoop, talon **6** emboss, powder

pound 3 bat **4** bang, bash, beat, belt, biff, blow, drub, pelt, slam, sock **5** crack, drive, grave, smack, stamp **6** batter, buffet, hammer, pummel, thrash, wallop **7** belabor, impress **8** malleate

pound and sponge 5 cakes

pour 3 run **4** beat, emit, flow, gush, lash, rain, rill, roll, rush, teem, void **5** flood, issue, skink, spate, surge, swarm **6** decant, deluge, drench, sluice, spring, stream **7** cascade, give off, niagara, proceed, torrent **8** cataract, flooding, inundate, overflow *forth:* **7** effuse

pourboire 3 tip **7** cumshaw, largess **8** gratuity **9** lagniappe **10** perquisite

pout 3 pet **4** moue, sulk **5** bulge, grump **7** project **8** overhang, protrude

poverty 4 need, want **6** penury **7** beggary, borasca **8** poorness, scarcity **9** indigence, indigency, necessity, neediness, pauperism, privation, suffering **10** mendicancy, scarceness **11** destitution **13** destituteness, insufficiency, insufficiency, pennilessness *combining form:* **5** penia

poverty-stricken see **penurious**

POW camp *German:* **6** stalag

powder 4 bray, buck, dust, talc **5** crush **6** talcum **8** sprinkle **9** comminute, pulverize, triturate **10** besprinkle **12** contriturate *medicinal:* **7** lupulin

power 3 arm **4** dint, sway **5** force, might, right, sinew, steam, vigor **6** energy, muscle, talent, virtue, weight **7** ability, command, control, dynamis, faculty, mastery, potence, potency, voltage **8** aptitude, capacity, dominion, dynamism, function, imperium, prestige, strength **9** authority, direction, dominance, endowment, influence, masterdom, privilege, puissance, strong arm, supremacy **10** ascendancy, birthright, capability, competence, domination, management **11** prerogative, sovereignty, superiority **12** jurisdiction, potentiality **13** effectiveness *combining form:* **5** dynam **6** dynamo *in Hindu philosophy:* **4** maya *reduction:* **8** brownout *sacred:* **4** kami *unit of:* **4** watt

powerful 4 able **5** great **6** mighty, potent, strong, wieldy **7** capable, dynamic, weighty **8** almighty, dominant, forcible, puissant, vigorous **9** competent, effective, effectual, efficient, energetic, strenuous **10** convincing, invincible **11** efficacious, influential **13** authoritative

powerless 4 weak **5** inert, unfit **6** feeble, infirm, supine **7** passive **8** decrepit, impotent, inactive, nugatory **9** incapable **11** incompetent, ineffective

powwow 4 chat, talk **5** treat **6** advise, confab, confer, huddle, parley **7** consult, meeting **8** colleague **10** conference **11** confabulate

poyou 6 peludo **9** armadillo

practicable 4 open **5** handy, utile **6** useful **9** operative **10** functional

practical 5 handy, sober, utile **6** usable, useful, versed **7** old-time, skilled, veteran **8** banausic, implicit, seasoned, sensible **9** pragmatic, realistic **10** functional, hardboiled, hardheaded **11** down-to-earth, experienced, serviceable **12** businesslike

practically 4 most, much, nigh **5** about **6** all but, almost, nearly **8** as good as, as much as, well-nigh **9** in essence

practice 3 use, way **4** form, mode, plot, wont **5** cabal, covin, drill, habit, trick, usage **6** custom, follow, manner, method, pursue, repeat, scheme, system, usance **7** execute, fulfill, iterate, perform, process, utility **8** drilling, exercise, habitude, intrigue, rehearse **9** procedure **10** conspiracy, convenance, convention, proceeding *suffix:* **2** cy **3** ery, ics, ism

practitioner *combining form:* **4** path *suffix:* **5** ician

pragmatic 9 practical, realistic **10** hardboiled, hardheaded, unromantic **11** down-to-earth

pragmatist 7 realist

prairie antelope 9 pronghorn

prairie apple 9 breadroot

prairie berry 9 trompillo

prairie chicken 6 grouse

prairie hen 11 clapper rail

prairie potato 9 breadroot

prairie wolf 6 coyote

praise 4 hail, hymn, laud **5** bless, cry up, erect, exalt, extol, honor, psalm, roose **6** anthem, belaud, extoll, kudize, uprear **7** acclaim, adulate, applaud, commend, dignify, enhance, ennoble, flatter, glorify, hosanna, magnify, plaudit, puffery, resound, sublime **8** eulogize, heighten, proclaim, psalmody **9** celebrate, intensify, recommend **10** aggrandize, compliment, panegyrize *expression of:* **8** accolade

praiseworthy 7 palmary **8** laudable **9** admirable, deserving, estimable, meritable **11** commendable, meritorious

prance 4 step **5** strut, tread **6** curvet, foot it, hoof it, jaunce, sashay **8** cakewalk

prank 4 deck, lark, play, trim, whim **5** adorn, antic, caper, fancy, fix up, freak, spiff, sport, trick **6** bedeck, didoes, doll up, frolic, gambol, levity, shines, vagary, wheeze, whimsy **7** caprice, conceit, deck out, doll out, dress up, fooling, garnish, gussy up, rollick **8** beautify, decorate, escapade, ornament, spruce up **9** capriccio, embellish, frivolity, high jinks, horseplay, lightness, rowdiness, smarten up **10** roughhouse, shenanigan, skylarking, tomfoolery **11** monkeyshine *Scottish:* **6** shavie

prate 3 gab, jaw, yak **4** blab, blow, brag, chat, crow, puff, yack **5** boast, clack, drool, mouth, vaunt **6** babble, drivel, gabble, jabber, waffle, yabber **7** blabber, blather, chatter, palaver, twaddle, twattle **9** gasconade, yakety-yak **11** rodomontade

prater 6 magpie **9** bandar-log, blabmouth **10** chatterbox **12** blabbermouth

prattle see **prate**

prattler see **prater**

prawn 6 shrimp **8** crevette **13** Norway lobster

praxis 3 use **4** wont **5** habit, trick, usage **6** custom, manner **8** habitude **10** consuetude

Praxiteles statue 6 Hermes **8** The Satyr

pray 3 beg **5** brace, crave, daven, doven, plead **6** appeal **7** beseech, entreat, implore **8** meditate **10** supplicate

prayer 4 plea, suit **6** appeal, beggar, litany, orison, suitor **7** angelus, begging, complin, worship **8** blessing, compline, entreaty, petition, pleading **9** adoration, imploring, suppliant **10** beseeching, supplicant **11** application, imploration, imprecation, supplicator **12** supplication *beads:* **6** rosary *ending:* **4** amen *for the dead:* **7** requiem *Jewish:* **7** kaddish, kiddush **9** kaddishim (plural) *period:* **6** novena **7** triduum *shawl:* **6** tallis, tallit **7** tallith

prayer book 6 missal **8** breviary *Jewish:* **6** mahzor, siddur **7** machzor

prayerful 4 holy **5** godly, pious **6** devout

preach 7 address, lecture **8** advocate,

homilize, moralize **9** sermonize
10 evangelize

preacher 6 cleric, divine, parson **7** evangel **8** clerical, homilist, minister, reverend **9** churchman, clergyman **10** evangelist **12** ecclesiastic

preacher bird 5 vireo

preaching friar 9 Dominican

preamble 5 proem **8** exordium, foreword, overture, prologue **12** introduction, prolegomenon

precarious 4 iffy **5** risky **6** touchy, tricky **7** dubious **8** delicate, doubtful, insecure, ticklish, unstable **9** sensitive, uncertain

precaution 8 prudence **9** foresight, safeguard **10** providence **11** forethought

precede 4 lead, pace, rank **5** forgo, usher **6** forego, herald **7** forerun, outrank **8** announce, antedate **9** introduce

precedence 8 priority

precedent 4 past **5** prior **6** former **7** example **8** anterior **9** foregoing

preceding 4 past **5** prior **6** before, former **7** ahead of, prior to **8** anterior, hitherto **9** erstwhile **10** heretofore **11** in advance of *prefix:* **4** ante

precept 3 law **4** rule **5** axiom, canon, dogma, edict, tenet **6** behest, decree **7** bidding, statute **8** decretum, doctrine **9** ordinance, principle **10** injunction, regulation **11** fundamental

preceptive 8 didactic **9** mandatory

preceptor 5 tutor **7** teacher **9** principal **10** headmaster

precinct 6 domain, region, sector, sphere **7** quarter, section **8** district, dominion, province **9** bailiwick, territory

precious 3 pet **4** dear, nice, rare, rich **5** fussy, loved, picky, showy **6** artful, chichi, choice, choosy, costly, la-di-da **7** beloved, darling, finicky, genteel, studied **8** affected, blue-eyed, favorite, overnice, prizable, valuable **9** exquisite, priceless, prizeable, recherché **10** fair-haired, fastidious, invaluable, particular

precipitancy 4 rush **5** haste **9** hastiness **10** suddenness **11** hurriedness

precipitant 5 hasty **6** abrupt, sudden **7** hurried, rushing **8** headlong **9** impetuous

precipitate 4 lees **5** dregs, event, hasty, issue, sheer, steep **6** abrupt, effect, madcap, result, sequel, sudden, upshot **7** arduous, deposit, grounds, hurried, rushing **8** headlong, sediment **9** aftermath, breakneck, hotheaded, impatient, impetuous, impulsive, overhasty, settlings **10** headstrong, refractory, unexpected, unforeseen **11** aftereffect, consequence, subitaneous

precipitation 4 hail, lees, rain, rush, snow **5** dregs, haste, sleet **7** deposit, grounds

8 sediment **9** hastiness, settlings **11** hurriedness

precipitous 5 hasty, sheer, steep **6** abrupt, sudden **7** hurried, rushing **8** headlong

précis 6 aperçu, digest, sketch, survey **7** pandect, sylloge **8** syllabus **10** compendium

precise 4 nice, very **5** exact, fixed, right, rigid **6** narrow, prissy, proper, stuffy **7** correct, genteel, limited, missish, prudish **8** accurate, definite, priggish, rigorous, specific **9** clocklike, stringent **10** particular

preciseness see **precision**

precision 4 care, heed **6** timing **8** accuracy **9** exactness **10** definitude, exactitude **11** carefulness, correctness

preclude 4 quit, stop, ward **5** avert, cease, deter **7** forfend, obviate, rule out **8** stave off **9** forestall **11** discontinue

precondition 4 must **9** essential, necessity, requisite **10** sine qua non **11** requirement

precursor 6 herald **8** foregoer **9** harbinger, prototype **10** antecedent, forerunner

predate 7 forerun **8** antecede

predatory 9 rapacious, raptorial, vulturine, vulturous

predecessor 7 forbear **8** ancestor, forebear, foregoer **9** prototype **10** antecedent, forerunner

predestine see **preordain**

predetermine see **preordain**

predeterminism 8 fatalism

predicament 3 box, fix, jam **4** hole, pass, soup, spot **5** Dutch, pinch, rigor, state **6** corner, pickle, plight, scrape, strait **7** dilemma, impasse, posture, trouble **8** asperity, exigency, hardness, hardship, hot water, juncture, quagmire **9** condition, deep water, emergency, situation **10** difficulty

predicate 4 aver, avow, base, rest, stay **5** found **6** affirm, assert, avouch, depose, ground **7** declare, profess, protest **9** establish

predict 5 augur, guess, infer, judge **7** forbode, foresee, portend, suppose, surmise **8** conclude, forebode, forecast, forefeel, foreshow, foretell, prophesy, soothsay **9** adumbrate **10** conjecture, vaticinate **13** prognosticate

predictor 5 augur, weird **6** auspex **7** prophet **8** foreseer, haruspex **10** forecaster, foreteller, prophesier, soothsayer **11** Nostradamus

predilection 4 bent **7** leaning **8** penchant, tendency **9** inclining **10** proclivity, propensity

predispose 4 bend, bias, sway **6** strike **7** incline

predisposed 4 fain 5 prone, ready 7 willing 8 inclined

predisposition 4 bent 7 leaning 8 penchant, tendency 9 inclining 10 proclivity, propensity

predominant 4 main 5 chief, major 6 master 7 capital, general, primary 9 number one, paramount, principal, sovereign 11 outstanding, overbearing

predominate 4 rule 5 reign 6 master 7 regnant 9 ascendant, paramount, prevalent, sovereign 11 overbearing

preeminence 6 renown 7 primacy 8 dominion 9 masterdom, supremacy 10 ascendancy, domination 11 distinction, superiority

preeminent 4 main 5 chief, major 7 capital, stellar, supreme 8 dominant, towering, ultimate 9 number one, principal 10 surpassing 11 outstanding, unequalable, unmatchable 12 incomparable, transcendent *prefix:* 4 arch

preempt 4 take 5 annex, seize, usurp 6 assume 8 accroach, arrogate 9 sequester 10 commandeer, confiscate 11 appropriate, expropriate

preen 5 plume, pride, primp

preface 4 lead 5 proem, usher 6 prolog 8 exordium, foreword, overture, preamble, prologue 9 introduce 12 introduction

prefatory 8 proemial 9 inductive, preludial 12 introductory

prefer 3 put 4 cull, mark, pick, pose, take 5 elect 6 choose, optate, opt for, select

preference 6 choice, option 8 druthers, election 9 elevation, prelation, promotion, selection, upgrading 10 partiality

prefigure 4 hint 9 adumbrate 10 foreshadow

pregnancy 6 cyesis 9 fertility, gestation, gravidity

pregnant 4 rich 5 heavy 6 facund, gravid, parous 7 weighty 8 childing, eloquent, enceinte 9 expecting, momentous 10 expressive, meaningful, parturient 11 sententious

prehend 3 bag, get 4 nail, take 5 catch 6 collar, secure 7 capture

prehensile 6 grabby, greedy 8 covetous, desirous, grasping 11 acquisitive

preindicate 6 herald 7 forerun, presage 8 announce, foreshow 9 harbinger

prejudice 3 mar 4 bend, bias, harm, hurt, skew 5 angle, slant, spoil 6 damage, impair, injure, racism, sexism 7 bigotry, blemish, dispose, incline, leaning, tarnish, vitiate 9 influence 10 partiality 12 one-sidedness, partisanship

prejudicial 3 bad 4 evil 7 harmful, nocuous 8 damaging 9 injurious 11 deleterious, detrimental, mischievous

preknow 3 see 6 divine 7 foresee 8 forefeel 9 apprehend, visualize 10 anticipate

preliminary 5 basic 7 fitting 8 proemial, readying 9 elemental, inductive 11 fundamental 12 introductory

preliterate 9 primitive

prelude 5 proem 8 exordium, foreword, overture, prologue 12 introduction, prolegomenon

premature 5 early 8 oversoon, untimely 9 overearly

premeditated 7 advised, studied 8 designed, studious 10 considered, deliberate, thought-out

premier 4 arch, head 5 chief, first 7 leading 8 champion, foremost 9 principal

premise 5 posit 6 assume, thesis 9 apriorism, postulate 10 assumption 11 postulation, supposition

premium 4 agio, meed, plum 5 prize 6 carrot, reward 7 guerdon 8 buckshee, dividend, superior 11 exceptional

premonition 9 misgiving 10 foreboding 12 apprehension

preoccupied 4 deep, lost, rapt 6 absent, intent 7 bemused, engaged, faraway, wrapped 8 distrait, immersed 9 engrossed, forgetful, wrapped up 10 abstracted 11 inconscient 12 absentminded

preordain 4 fate 6 doom to 7 destine 9 determine 10 predestine 11 foredestine

preparation 7 fitness 8 training 9 readiness 11 compounding

preparatory 9 preludial, prelusive 11 prefatorial, preliminary

prepare 3 fit, fix, get 4 busk, gird, make 5 brace, dower, draft, endow, endue, equip, frame, prime, ready, steel, train 6 draw up, make up, outfit, supply 7 confect, dispose, fortify, furnish, provide 9 formulate 10 strengthen *for publication:* 4 edit 6 redact *leather:* 5 curry

prepared 3 set 5 ready

preponderance 8 dominion 9 ascendant, masterdom, supremacy 10 ascendancy, domination

preponderant 8 dominant, superior 9 paramount, sovereign 11 overbearing

preponderate 4 rule 5 reign 8 domineer

preposition 2 at, by, in, of, on, to, up 3 but, cum, ere, for, off, out, per, via 4 amid, down, from, into, like, onto, over, save, thru, till, unto, upon, with 5 about, above, after, along, among, anent, below, circa, since, tween, twixt, under, until 6 aboard, across, amidst, around, before, behind, beside, beyond, contra, except, gainst, inside, mongst, toward, versus, within 7 against, amongst, athwart, beneath, besides, between, betwixt, despite, outside, through, towards, without **10** throughout, underneath

prepossess **4** bias **5** imbue **6** absorb, engage, occupy **7** engross, immerse, involve **9** influence, prejudice, preoccupy

prepossessing **10** attractive

preposterous **4** wild **5** crazy, loony, silly, wacky **6** absurd, insane **7** foolish **9** fantastic **10** irrational **11** extravagant, harebrained **12** unreasonable

preposterousness **5** folly **8** insanity **9** absurdity

prerequisite **4** must **9** condition, essential, necessary, necessity **10** imperative, sine qua non **11** necessitous, requirement

prerogative **5** right **8** appanage, immunity **9** exemption, privilege **10** birthright, perquisite

presage **4** bode, omen **5** augur **6** augury, boding, herald **7** bespeak, betoken, forerun, portend, portent, predict, promise **8** announce, bodement, forebode, forecast, foreshow, foretell, indicate, prophesy, soothsay **9** adumbrate, foretoken, harbinger, misgiving, prenotion **10** foreboding, foreshadow, prognostic, vaticinate **12** apprehensive **13** prognosticate

presbyter **5** elder **6** priest

prescience **9** foresight

prescribe **3** fix, set **6** assign, choose, decide, decree, define, impose, ordain, select, settle **7** dictate, lay down, pick out **9** determine

prescript **3** law **4** rule **5** edict **6** decree **8** decretum **9** institute, ordinance **10** regulation

prescription **3** law **4** rule **5** edict **6** decree **8** decretum **9** institute, ordinance

presence **3** air **4** look, mien, port **6** aspect **7** address, bearing, seeming **8** demeanor

present **3** aim, lay, now **4** boon, cast, cite, gift, give, head, past, pose, show **5** favor, level, offer, point, today, train **6** adduce, allege, bestow, devote, direct, donate, extant, extend, modern, tender **7** address, advance, hand out, hold out, instant, largess, proffer **8** acquaint, nowadays, todayish, up-to-date **9** introduce **12** contemporary, newfashioned

presentable **3** fit **6** decent, proper **9** befitting **11** appropriate

presentiment see **premonition**

presently **3** now **4** anon, soon **5** today **7** by and by **8** nowadays

preservation **4** care, ward **5** guard **6** saving, shield **7** defense, keeping **9** safeguard **10** husbanding **11** conservancy, safekeeping

preserve **3** can, jam **4** save **6** keep up, pickle **7** sustain **8** maintain **9** confiture

preside **3** run **4** head, keep **5** chair **6** direct, handle, manage, ordain **7** carry on, conduct, control, operate, oversee

president *United States:* **4** Bush (George), Ford (Gerald R.), Polk (James K.), Taft (William H.) **5** Adams (John, John Quincy), Grant (Ulysses S.), Hayes (Rutherford B.), Nixon (Richard M.), Tyler (John) **6** Arthur (Chester A.), Carter (Jimmy), Hoover (Herbert), Monroe (James), Pierce (Franklin), Reagan (Ronald), Taylor (Zachary), Truman (Harry S.), Wilson (Woodrow) **7** Harding (Warren), Jackson (Andrew), Johnson (Andrew), Johnson (Lyndon), Kennedy (John F.), Lincoln (Abraham), Madison (James) **8** Buchanan (James), Coolidge (Calvin), Fillmore (Millard), Garfield (James), Harrison (Benjamin, William H.), McKinley (William), Van Buren (Martin) **9** Cleveland (Grover), Jefferson (Thomas), Roosevelt (Franklin D., Theodore) **10** Eisenhower (Dwight D.), Washington (George)

press **3** hug, jam, ram **4** bear, cram, iron, mass, move, pack, pile, push, rice, tamp **5** clasp, crowd, crush, drive, drove, elbow, force, horde, impel, shove, stuff **6** enfold, gather, goffer, hustle, jostle, propel, sadden, sinter, squash, squish, squush, throng, thrust **7** collect, embrace, gauffer, imprint, squeeze, squelch, squoosh **8** assemble, bulldoze, shoulder **9** constrain, multitude, weigh down **10** congregate

pressing **4** dire **5** acute **6** direct, urgent **7** clamant, crucial, exigent, instant **8** critical **9** clamorous, immediate, insistent **10** imperative **11** importunate

pressure **4** push, rush **5** drive, impel **6** strain, stress **7** tension **9** overpress *combining form:* **4** tono **5** piezo *instrument:* **9** barometer *unit:* **3** bar **5** barye

prestige **4** rank, sway **5** power, state **6** cachet, credit, renown, status, weight **7** dignity, stature **8** eminence, position, standing **9** authority, influence **10** prominence, prominency **11** consequence, distinction

prestigious **5** famed, great **7** eminent, notable **8** renowned **9** prominent **10** celebrated **13** distinguished

presto **4** fast **7** flat-out, hastily, quickly, rapidly **8** chop-chop, full tilt **9** posthaste **12** lickety-split **13** expeditiously

presumably **6** likely **9** doubtless

presume **4** guess, opine, posit, think **6** impose, reason **7** intrude, obtrude, suppose, surmise **8** infringe **9** postulate **10** conjecture

presuming see **presumptuous**

presumption **4** face, gall **5** brass, cheek, nerve, posit **6** thesis **9** apriorism, brashness, postulate **10** confidence, effrontery

presumptuous 4 smug 5 brash, lofty 6 uppish, uppity 7 forward, pushful, pushing 9 confident 10 brassbound, complacent 11 inexcusable, overweening, self-assured

presuppose 5 guess, infer, judge, posit, think 6 assume, deduce, expect, gather, reckon 7 believe, imagine, surmise, suspect 9 postulate

presupposition 5 guess, posit 6 belief, thesis 7 surmise 8 judgment 9 apriorism, inference, judgement, postulate 10 conjecture

pretend 3 act 4 fake, sham 5 bluff, feign, guess, put on, think 6 affect, assume, delude 7 beguile, deceive, mislead, profess, purport, suppose, surmise 8 simulate

pretender 4 fake 5 faker, fraud, phony 6 humbug 8 impostor

pretense 3 air 4 face, fake, mask, sham 5 claim, cloak, color, cover, fraud, guise, title 6 deceit, facade, humbug 7 charade, pageant 8 coloring, disguise 9 deception, imposture, mannerism 10 false front, masquerade 11 affectation, make-believe

pretension 5 claim, title 7 charade, pageant 8 disguise 11 make-believe 13 ambitiousness

pretentious 3 big 4 arty 5 lofty, put-on, showy, swank, tumid 6 chichi, la-di-da, tootoo, turgid 7 aureate, feigned, flowery, genteel, mincing, pompier, splashy, stilted, utopian 8 affected, imposing, inflated, peacocky 9 bombastic, grandiose, overblown, visionary 10 arty-crafty, euphuistic, flamboyant, peacockish, rhetorical 12 high-sounding, magniloquent *speech:* 7 bombast

preternatural 7 deviant 8 aberrant, abnormal, atypical, numinous, superior 9 anomalous, deviative, unearthly, untypical 10 miraculous, superhuman, suprahuman 11 heteroclite 12 supermundane, supramundane

pretext 4 mask 5 alibi, cloak, cover, front, guise 6 excuse 8 pretense

pretty 4 cute, fair, good, some 5 bonny, ducky 6 adroit, bonnie, clever, comely, fairly, incony, kind of, lovely, rather, seemly, sort of, wicked 7 cunning, darling, dollish 8 handsome, skillful, somewhat 9 beauteous, beautiful, moderately, more or less 11 good-looking

prevail 4 beat, rule 5 reign 6 affect, master 7 conquer, impress, triumph 8 dominate, domineer, overcome, override

prevailing see **prevalent**

prevalent 4 rife 5 usual 6 common, master, normal, ruling, wonted 7 general, natural, popular, rampant, regnant, regular, typical 8 dominant 9 ascendant, customary, paramount, sovereign 10 accustomed, widespread 11 commonplace

prevaricate 3 fib, lie 6 palter 7 falsify 12 misrepresent

prevarication 3 fib, lie 4 tale 5 lying, story 6 canard 7 falsity 9 falsehood

prevaricator 4 liar 6 fibber 7 Ananias, fibster 8 perjurer 9 falsifier 11 storyteller

prevent 3 bar, dam 4 balk, foil, ward 5 avert, block, check, debar, deter 6 arrest, baffle, forbid, hinder, impede, thwart 7 forfend, inhibit, obviate, rule out, shut out 8 obstruct, prohibit, stave off 9 forestall, frustrate, interdict, interrupt 10 anticipate *access:* 9 barricade

previous 4 fore, past 5 prior 6 before, former 7 earlier, forward 8 anterior, oversoon 9 foregoing, in advance, overearly 10 antecedent, beforehand

previously 4 once 6 before 7 already, earlier, priorly 8 formerly 9 erstwhile 10 heretofore

prey 4 game 5 chase 6 quarry, victim 8 casualty, underdog 9 bottom dog

Priam *daughter:* 6 Creusa 8 Polyxena 9 Cassandra *father:* 8 Laomedon *grandfather:* 4 Ilus *kingdom:* 4 Troy *slayer:* 7 Pyrrhus 11 Neoptolemus *son:* 5 Paris 6 Hector, Lycaon 7 Helenus, Troilus 9 Deiphobus, Polydorus *wife:* 6 Arisbe, Hecuba

Priapus *father:* 7 Bacchus 8 Dionysus *mother:* 5 Venus 9 Aphrodite

price 3 tab 4 cost, rate, toll 6 charge, tariff 7 expense

priceless 6 costly, valued 8 precious, valuable 9 cherished, treasured 10 invaluable

prick 3 cut, jab, sic 4 bore, goad, hole, prod, slit, spur, stab, urge 5 drill, egg on, enter, pique, punch, rowel, slash, sting, thorn 6 excite, exhort, prompt, propel 8 puncture 9 perforate, stimulate

prickly 5 burry, spiny 6 nettly, thorny, tingly, twitty 7 brambly, fretful, peevish, pettish, waspish 8 annoying, petulant, snappish 9 fractious, irritable 10 bothersome, nettlesome

pride 3 fat, top 4 best, brag, crow, face, pick 5 boast, cream, elite, pique, plume, preen, scorn, vaunt 6 choice, egoism, flower, morgue 7 bighead, conceit, dignity, disdain, egotism, hauteur 8 contempt, smugness, vainness 9 arrogance, cockiness, gasconade, insolence, loftiness, self-glory, self-trust, superbity, vainglory 10 felicitate, self-esteem, self-regard 11 amour propre, haughtiness, self-opinion, self-respect 12 congratulate, snobbishness 13 condescension, self-assurance

Pride and Prejudice author 6 Austen

prier 5 snoop 6 butt-in 7 meddler, Paul Pry 8 busybody, quidnunc 10 rubberneck

priest 9 clergyman 10 chancellor 11 chamberlain *ancient Roman:* 6 fecial, fetial, flamen 8 pontifex *Buddhist:* 4 lama *Celtic:* 5 druid *French:* 4 abbé, curé *Indian:* 6 shaman *military:* 5 padre 8 chaplain *Muslim:* 4 imam *of Bacchus:* 6 maenad 9 bacchante

priestly 8 hieratic 10 sacerdotal 12 sacerdotical

prig 5 prude, thief 6 Grundy, nimmer, stuffy, wowser 7 filcher, genteel, prudish, puritan, stealer 8 bluenose, comstock, larcener, pilferer 9 larcenist, Mrs. Grundy, nice Nelly, purloiner, Victorian 10 goody-goody, tight-laced 11 puritanical, straitlaced

priggish 4 smug 6 stuffy 7 genteel, prudish 9 Victorian 10 complacent, self-loving, tight-laced 11 puritanical, self-pleased, straitlaced 13 self-contented, self-esteeming, self-righteous, self-satisfied

prim 4 neat, nice, snug, tidy 5 rigid, stiff 6 formal, proper, stuffy, wooden 7 chipper, correct, genteel, missish, orderly, precise, prudish 8 decorous, straight 9 bluenosed, shipshape, Victorian 10 ceremonial, tight-laced 11 ceremonious, puritanical, straitlaced, uncluttered, well-groomed 12 conventional

prima facie 11 self-evident

primary 4 main 5 basal, basic, chief, first 6 bottom, direct 7 initial, pioneer, radical 8 earliest, original 9 firsthand, immediate, underived 10 underlying 11 fundamental 12 foundational, underivative *combining form:* 4 prot 5 proto *prefix:* 4 arch 5 archi

primate 3 ape, man 5 human 6 monkey 7 gorilla 10 anthropoid, chimpanzee, human being 11 Homo sapiens *nocturnal:* 7 tarsier *small:* 6 galago

prime 3 top 4 best, fine, morn, move, pick 5 cream, elite, first, sunup, youth 6 aurora, choice, excite, famous, spring 7 capital, initial, morning, provoke, quicken, sunrise 8 cockcrow, daybreak, earliest, motivate, original, superior 9 dayspring, excellent, first-rate, galvanize, stimulate, underived 10 first-class, juvenility, springtide 11 adolescence

primer 4 book 6 reader 8 hornbook

primeval 10 aboriginal; (see also primordial)

primitive 5 basic, early 7 archaic 8 original 9 barbarian, elemental, essential, underived, unevolved 10 elementary, persistent, substratal, underlying 11 fundamental, nonliterate, preliterate, uncivilized, undeveloped 12 uncultivated *combining form:* 4 pale 5 palae, paleo 6 archae, archeo,

palaeo, palaio 7 archaeo *prefix:* 4 arch 5 arche, archi

primogenitor 7 forbear 8 ancestor, forebear 9 ascendant 10 forefather

primordial 5 early, first 8 earliest, original 10 elementary 11 fundamental, undeveloped

primordium 6 anlage, origin 9 beginning

primp 5 fix up, slick, spiff 6 doll up 7 deck out, doll out, dress up, gussy up

prince *Anglo-Saxon:* 8 atheling *Arab:* 4 emir 5 emeer *Austrian:* 8 archduke *Ethiopian:* 3 ras *Indian:* 4 raja 5 rajah *Muslim:* 4 amir 5 ameer *of demons:* 9 Beelzebub *of Monaco:* 6 Ranier *of the church:* 8 cardinal *of Wales:* 7 Charles

Prince and the Pauper author 5 Twain

Prince Edward Island *capital:* 13 Charlottetown *discoverer:* 7 Cartier

Prince Igor composer 7 Borodin

princely 5 grand, noble, royal 6 august, lordly 8 baronial, imposing 9 grandiose 11 magnificent

princess *mythical:* 3 Ino *of Monaco:* 5 Grace

principal 4 arch, head, main, star 5 chief, first, major 7 capital, leading, premier, primary, stellar 8 champion, dominant, foremost 10 preeminent 11 outstanding, predominant *combining form:* 4 prot 5 proto *prefix:* 4 arch 5 archi

principium 3 law 5 axiom, basis 7 element, theorem 10 foundation 11 fundamental

principle 3 law 4 form, rule 5 axiom, basis, canon, tenet, usage 6 ground 7 precept, theorem 8 polestar 10 convention, foundation 11 fundamental

principled 5 moral, noble 7 ethical 8 virtuous 9 righteous 10 moralistic

print 4 type 5 litho, stamp, write 7 engrave, impress, publish, typeset 10 impression *style:* 5 roman 6 italic 7 cursive

printer *English:* 6 Caxton *Italian:* 6 Bodoni 8 Manutius (Aldus)

printers' mark see **proofreaders' mark**

printer's receptacle 7 hellbox

printing 7 edition, reissue 10 impression *measure:* 2 em, en 4 pica 5 agate 6 cicero *plate:* 6 stereo 7 linecut *process:* 4 roto 7 gravure *style:* 6 gothic

prior see **previous**

priority 5 order 8 ordering 9 supremacy 10 ascendancy, precedence

prison 3 pen 4 jail, keep 6 cooler, lockup 7 bastile, dungeon, slammer 8 bastille, stockade 11 reformatory 12 penitentiary *California:* 10 San Quentin *former:* 8 Alcatraz, Sing-Sing *New York:* 6 Attica 12 Rikers Island *Northern Ireland:* 4 Maze *resident:* 6 inmate 7 convict 8 jailbird

prissy 6 stuffy 7 epicene, finicky, genteel, missish, prudish, unmanly 9 pansified, sissified, squeamish, Victorian 10 effeminate, fastidious, tight-laced 11 puritanical, straitlaced 12 Miss-Nancyish

pristine 4 pure 8 earliest, original

privacy 7 secrecy 9 seclusion

private 6 closet, hidden, hushed, inside, secret 7 soldier 8 discreet, personal 9 concealed 10 closed-door 12 confidential

private detective see **detective**

privately 7 sub rosa 8 covertly, in camera, secretly 9 by stealth 10 stealthily

privation 4 lack, loss, need, want 6 dearth, defect, losing, misery, penury 7 absence, default, poverty 8 distress, poorness 9 indigence, mislaying, neediness, suffering 10 misplacing 11 deprivement, divestiture

privilege 4 boon 5 favor, right 8 appanage 9 allowance 10 birthright, concession, perquisite 11 prerogative *popegranted:* 6 indult

privy 2 WC 4 head, john 5 jakes 6 buried, covert, hidden, johnny, toilet 7 latrine 8 lavatory, obscured, outhouse, personal, shrouded, stealthy, ulterior 9 backhouse, concealed 11 convenience, water closet

prize 3 pry, top 4 best, loot, meed, pick, plum, swag 5 award, booty, cream, elite, jimmy, lever, spoil, value 6 boodle, carrot, choice, esteem, reward, trophy 7 cherish, guerdon, jackpot, plunder, premium 8 dividend, treasure 10 appreciate, plunderage 11 outstanding

prizefighting 8 pugilism 10 fisticuffs

pro 3 for, vet, wiz 4 whiz, with 5 adept, doyen 6 expert, master 9 authority, in favor of 10 master-hand

probable 6 likely 7 seeming 8 apparent, rational 10 reasonable

probe 3 ask 4 quiz, sift 5 query, quest, scout 6 go into 7 delving, dig into, examine, explore, feel out, inquest, inquire, inquiry 8 look into, research, sound out 9 catechize, delve into 11 inquire into, inquisition, interrogate, investigate, reconnoiter 13 investigation

probity 6 virtue 7 honesty 8 goodness 9 integrity, rectitude, rightness 11 uprightness

problem 3 nut 5 issue 6 enigma, puzzle 7 bugaboo, bugbear, dilemma, example, mystery

problematic 4 moot, open 7 dubious, suspect 8 arguable, doubtful, mootable 9 ambiguous, debatable, dubitable, uncertain, unsettled 10 disputable, indecisive, precarious 12 questionable

proboscis 4 beak, nose 5 snoot, snout 7 smeller

procedure 4 line, move, step 6 course, method, policy, polity 7 measure, program 8 demarche, maneuver

proceed 2 go 3 hie 4 fare, flow, head, move, pass, rise, stem, wend 5 arise, get on, issue, march, segue 6 push on, repair, spring, travel 7 advance, emanate, journey 8 get along, progress 9 originate 10 derive from

proceedings 8 goings-on *recorded:* 4 acta

proceeds 4 gain 5 lucre 6 profit, return 8 earnings

process 3 way 4 mode, wise 5 modus 6 manner, method, system 7 fashion, recycle, routine 9 operation, outgrowth, technique *combining form:* 4 typy *suffix:* 2 al, th 3 ing, ism, sis 4 ance, ence, esis, osis 7 ization

procession 5 order 6 parade, series 8 sequence 9 cavalcade 11 consecution *combining form:* 4 cade

proclaim 4 mark, show, vent 5 bruit, utter, voice 6 blazon, evince, herald, ostend 7 clarion, declare, exhibit, publish 8 announce, evidence, manifest, promulge 9 advertise, broadcast, ventilate 10 annunciate, bruit about, illustrate, promulgate 11 blaze abroad, demonstrate

proclivity see **penchant**

Procne *father:* 7 Pandion *husband:* 6 Tereus *sister:* 9 Philomela *son:* 4 Itys

procrastinate 3 lag 4 drag, poke, stay 5 dally, defer, delay, tarry 6 dawdle, linger, loiter, put off 7 prolong, suspend 8 postpone

procreate 4 bear, make, sire 5 beget, breed, hatch, spawn 6 father, mother, parent 7 produce 8 engender, generate, multiply 9 originate, propagate, reproduce

Procris' husband and slayer 8 Cephalus

Procrustean ___ 3 bed

proctor 9 supervise 10 supervisor

procure 3 get 4 draw, gain, have, land 5 annex 6 draw in, draw on, induce, obtain, pick up 7 acquire, compass, win over

prod 3 dig, jab, jog, sic 4 goad, poke, spur, urge 5 egg on, nudge, pique, prick, punch 6 excite, exhort 9 stimulate

prodigal 4 lush 6 lavish, waster 7 opulent, profuse, riotous, spender, wastrel 8 unthrift 9 exuberant, luxuriant, profusive 10 high roller, profligate, squanderer 11 scattergood, spendthrift, wastethrift

prodigious 4 huge, vast 6 mighty, mortal 7 amazing, immense, mammoth, massive 8 colossal, cracking, enormous, gigantic, towering 9 fantastic, marvelous, monstrous, wonderful 10 astounding, miraculous, monumental, staggering, stupendous, surprising

produce 4 bear, form, give, grow, make, show, sire 5 beget, breed, build, cause, erect, frame, get up, hatch, mount, put on, raise, spawn, stage, yield 6 create, draw on, effect, father, output, parent, secure, work up 7 deliver, fashion, outturn, turn out 8 engender, generate, multiply, muster up 9 construct, cultivate, fabricate, originate, procreate, propagate 10 bring about 11 manufacture, put together *combining form:* 3 fer, gen 4 gene 5 genic 6 genous 7 genetic

product 5 fruit, yield 6 effect, output, result 7 harvest, outcome, outturn, turnout 8 multiple, offshoot 9 handiwork, outgrowth 11 consequence *combining form:* 3 ade, ine, ite

production 5 fruit, yield 6 output 7 outturn, turnout *combining form:* 4 geny, gony 7 genesia, poiesis 8 fication

productive 4 rich 6 fecund 7 fertile 8 childing, fruitful, prolific, spawning 11 proliferant

proem see **prologue**

profane 3 lay 4 foul 5 dirty, nasty, pagan 6 coarse, ethnic, filthy, smutty, unholy, vulgar 7 earthly, gentile, heathen, impious, infidel, mundane, obscene, raunchy, secular, ungodly, worldly 8 indecent, temporal, unsacred 9 infidelic 10 irreverent, unhallowed 11 blasphemous, terrestrial 12 sacrilegious 13 irreverential

profanity 4 oath 5 curse 7 cursing, cussing 8 swearing 9 blasphemy 10 execration 11 imprecation

profess 4 aver, avow 6 affirm, assert, avouch, depose 7 declare, protest, purport 8 constate 9 predicate

profession 3 art, job 5 craft, trade 6 career, métier 7 calling 8 vocation 10 handicraft *suffix:* 4 ship

professional 3 pro 4 paid, whiz 5 adept 6 artist, expert, master 7 artiste 8 virtuoso 9 authority 10 past master, proficient

professor 3 don 7 teacher

proffer 4 give, pose 5 offer 6 extend, tender 7 hold out, present 8 proposal 10 invitation, suggestion 11 proposition

proficiency 5 march, skill 7 advance, headway, ongoing 8 anabasis, progress 9 adeptness

proficient 4 able, whiz 5 adept, crack 6 artist, expert, master 7 artiste, capable, drilled, skilled 8 finished, masterly, skillful, virtuoso 9 authority, competent, effective, effectual, efficient, exercised, masterful, practiced, qualified 10 checked-out, consummate, past master 11 crackerjack, experienced 12 accomplished, professional

profile 4 line 7 contour, outline 9 lineament, lineation 10 figuration, silhouette

profit 3 net 4 gain, take 5 avail, lucre, serve, yield 6 output, return 7 benefit, cleanup, killing, outturn, product, receipt, turnout, work for 8 cleaning, earnings, proceeds

profitable 6 paying 7 gainful 9 lucrative 10 well-paying, worthwhile 11 moneymaking 12 advantageous, remunerative

profligate 6 bad lot, no-good, waster 7 rounder, spender, wastrel 8 prodigal, unthrift, wasteful 9 abandoned, dissolute, reprobate 10 high roller, licentious, ne'er-do-well, scapegrace, squanderer 11 scattergood, spendthrift, wastethrift

profound 3 low 4 deep, hard, wise 5 heavy 6 occult, orphic, secret 7 abysmal, intense 8 abstruse, esoteric, hermetic 9 intensive

profoundness 5 abyss, depth 8 deepness 10 profundity

profundity see **profoundness**

profuse 4 lush 6 lavish 7 copious, liberal, opulent, riotous, teeming 8 abundant, generous, prodigal, swarming 9 abounding, bounteous, bountiful, excessive, exuberant, luxuriant 10 immoderate, munificent

profusive see **profuse**

progenitor 4 sire 8 ancestor, forebear 9 ascendant 10 forefather

progeny see **posterity**

prognosis 4 cast 5 weird 8 forecast, prophecy 9 prevision 10 prediction 11 foretelling

prognostic 4 omen, sign 6 augury, boding 7 portent, presage 8 bodement 9 foretoken

prognosticate see **predict**

program 4 bill, card, line, plan, sked 5 slate 6 agenda, course, docket, policy, polity 8 calendar, schedule 9 procedure, timetable 10 bill of fare *theater:* 8 playbill

progress 2 go 4 fare, grow, move 5 get on, march 6 course, growth 7 advance, headway, ongoing, passage, proceed, promote 8 anabasis, get along, upgrowth 9 evolution, flowering, unfolding 10 evolvement 11 advancement, development, proficiency *planned:* 7 telesis

progressing 5 afoot 8 under way

progression 3 row 5 chain, order, train 6 course, growth, sequel, series 7 advance 8 sequence, upgrowth 9 evolution, flowering, unfolding 10 evolvement, succession 11 alternation, consecution, development

progressive 4 wide 5 broad 7 liberal, radical 8 advanced, stepwise, tolerant

prohibit 3 ban, bar 5 taboo 6 enjoin, forbid, outlaw 7 inhibit 9 interdict

prohibited 5 taboo 6 banned 7 illegal, illicit 8 verboten 9 forbidden

project 3 jut, see 4 cast, feat, gest, plan, poke, pout 5 bulge, chart, image, pouch, thing, think 6 affair, beetle, design, devise, extend, intend, matter, scheme, vision 7 arrange, concern, diagram, dope out, emprise, exploit, feature, imagine, prolong, propose, purpose, venture 8 business, conceive, envisage, envision, game plan, lengthen, overhang, protrude, stand out, stick out, strategy 9 adventure, blueprint, delineate, visualize 10 enterprise 11 proposition, undertaking *trivial:* 10 boondoggle

projecting 7 salient

projection 3 jut 4 bump, hook, knob, spur 5 bulge, bunch, ledge, point, spine 8 eminence, forecast, salience, swelling 9 extension, outthrust 10 prominence, protrusion

projet 4 plan 5 draft

proletariat 3 mob 4 mass 6 rabble 7 workers 8 canaille, laborers

prolific 4 rich 6 fecund 7 fertile 8 breeding, childing, fruitful, spawning, swarming 9 abounding 10 generating, productive 11 propagating, reproducing 12 reproductive

prolix 5 windy, wordy 7 diffuse, irksome, tedious, verbose 8 tiresome 9 prolonged, redundant, wearisome 10 long-winded, palaverous, protracted

prolixity 9 verbalism, verbosity, windiness, wordiness 11 verboseness

prologue 5 proem 7 preface, prelude 8 exordium, foreword, overture, preamble 9 prelusion 12 introduction, prolegomenon

prolong 4 draw, last 6 endure, extend 7 draw out, persist, spin out, stretch 8 continue, elongate, lengthen, protract

prolonged 4 long 7 lengthy 8 dragging, drawn-out, longsome, overlong 10 protracted

promenade 4 deck, walk 5 dance 6 parade, stroll 7 balcony, gallery 9 boardwalk

Prometheus *brother:* 5 Atlas 9 Menoetius 10 Epimetheus *creation:* 3 man *father:* 7 Iapetus *gift to man:* 4 fire *mother:* 7 Clymene *rescuer:* 8 Heracles, Hercules

prominence 6 renown 8 eminence, prestige, salience 10 importance, projection 11 distinction *combining form:* 8 tubercul 9 tuberculo

prominent 5 famed, great, noted 6 famous, marked, signal 7 eminent, leading, notable, popular, salient 8 renowned, striking 9 arresting, arrestive, notorious, well-known 10 celebrated, celebrious, noticeable, remarkable 11 conspicuous,

illustrious, outstanding 13 distinguished *person:* 3 VIP 6 bigwig 7 grandee

promiscuous 5 mixed 6 motley, random, varied 7 aimless 8 assorted, chowchow 9 desultory, haphazard, hit-or-miss, irregular, unplanned 10 designless 11 purposeless

promise 3 vow 4 bode, oath, omen, pass, pawn, word 5 agree, augur, swear, token 6 accede, assent, assure, engage, ensure, insure, pledge, plight 7 bargain, betoken, compact, consent, earnest, portend, presage, warrant 8 contract, covenant, forebode, foreshow, security 9 assurance, foretoken, guarantee, undertake

promised land 4 Zion 6 Canaan, heaven, utopia 7 arcadia 8 paradise 9 cockaigne, fairyland, shangri-la 10 lubberland, wonderland

promising 4 rosy 6 likely 7 hopeful, roseate 11 encouraging, rose-colored

promissory note 3 IOU

promontory 4 beak, bill, cape, head, naze, peak 5 point 8 foreland, headland

promote 3 aid, cry 4 help, plug, puff, push 5 boost, serve 6 foster, impart, prefer 7 advance, build up, elevate, forward, further, upgrade 8 ballyhoo 9 advertise, encourage, publicize 10 press-agent

promoter 5 agent

promotion 7 advance, buildup, puffery 9 elevation, prelation, publicity, upgrading 10 preference, preferment 11 advancement, advertising 13 advertisement

prompt 3 apt, cue, get, sic 4 draw, fast, goad, prod, spur, urge 5 alert, egg on, prick, quick, rapid, ready, swift 6 exhort, induce, propel, speedy, timely 7 win over 8 convince, persuade, punctual, talk into

promulgate 4 toot 5 sound 7 declare, publish 8 announce, proclaim 9 advertise, broadcast 10 annunciate 11 disseminate

prone 3 apt 4 fain, flat, open 5 given, level, ready 6 liable, likely, minded, supine 7 exposed, subject, willing 8 disposed, inclined, resupine 9 decumbent, obnoxious, prostrate, reclining, recumbent, sensitive 11 predisposed, susceptible

prong 3 nib 4 fang, fork, stab, tine 5 point

pronghorn 6 cabree 8 antelope

pronoun *archaic:* 2 ye 3 thy 4 thou 5 thine *demonstrative:* 4 that, this 5 these, those *indefinite:* 3 all, any, few, one 4 both, each, none, some 5 no one, other 6 anyone, either, nobody 7 another, anybody, neither, nothing, someone 8 anything, somebody 9 everybody, something 10 everything *personal:* 2 he, it, my, we 3 her, him, his, its, our, she, you 4 hers, mine, ours, them, they, your 5 their, yours 6 theirs *possessive:* 2 my 3 her, his, its, our **4** hers, mine, ours, your **5** their, yours **6** theirs *reflexive:* **6** itself, myself **7** herself, himself, oneself, ourself **8** yourself **9** ourselves **10** themselves, yourselves *relative:* **3** who **4** that, what, whom **5** which, whose, whoso **6** whomso **7** whoever **8** whatever, whomever **9** whichever, whosoever **10** whatsoever, whomsoever **11** whichsoever

pronounce 3 say **5** speak, utter **6** recite **7** declare, phonate **9** enunciate **10** articulate

pronounced 7 assured, decided **8** clearcut, definite

pronouncement 9 statement **11** declaration, publication **12** proclamation, promulgation

pronto 4 fast **6** at once **7** quickly **8** promptly **9** posthaste **11** immediately

pronunciation 6 speech **9** utterance *distinctive:* **4** burr **5** drawl, twang **6** accent *study:* **8** orthoepy **9** phonetics

proof 4 test **6** galley **8** argument, evidence **9** testament, testimony **10** impression **11** attestation **12** confirmation

proofreaders' mark 3 cap, rom **4** dele, ital, stet **5** caret

prop 3 leg **4** stay **5** brace, carry, shore **6** bear up, buoy up, column, upbear, uphold **7** bolster, shore up, support, sustain **8** buttress **12** underpinning

propaganda 4 hype **8** agitprop **9** publicity

propagandist 7 apostle **9** missioner **10** colporteur, evangelist, missionary

propagate 4 bear, grow **5** beget, breed, raise, strew **6** spread **7** diffuse, produce, radiate **8** disperse, generate, multiply **9** circulate, cultivate, procreate, reproduce **10** distribute **11** disseminate

propel 4 goad, move, prod, push, spur, urge **5** drive, egg on, impel, power, prick, shove **6** exhort, prompt, thrust **7** actuate

propellant 4 fuel, spur **7** impetus, impulse **8** catalyst, stimulus **9** incentive, stimulant **10** incitation, motivation **11** provocative

propeller 3 fan, oar **5** screw **6** paddle

propensity see **penchant**

proper 3 apt, due, fit **4** able, good, just, meet, nice, prig, prim, true **5** exact, happy, right **6** au fait, comely, decent, prissy, stuffy, useful **7** capable, correct, desired, fitting, genteel, missish, precise, prudish **8** accurate, becoming, decorous, peculiar, priggish, rightful, rigorous, suitable **9** befitting, competent, diacritic, qualified **10** applicable, conforming, convenient, diagnostic, felicitous, individual **11** appropriate, comme il faut, distinctive, puritanical, straitlaced *combining form:* **4** orth **5** ortho

property 4 land, mark **5** trait, worth **6** estate, realty, riches, virtue, wealth **7** feature, fortune, quality **8** dominion **9** affection, attribute, character, ownership, resources, substance **10** possession, real estate *conveyor:* **7** alienor *private:* **8** peculium *recipient:* **7** alienee *seller:* **7** Realtor *transfer:* **8** alienate

prophecy 4 cast **5** weird **6** oracle, vision **8** forecast **9** prevision, prognosis **10** apocalypse, prediction, revelation **11** foretelling

prophesier 4 seer **5** augur **6** auspex **7** prophet **8** foreseer, haruspex **9** predictor **10** forecaster, foreteller **11** Nostradamus

prophesy 5 augur **7** portend, predict, presage **8** forecast, foretell, soothsay **9** adumbrate **10** vaticinate **13** prognosticate

prophet 4 seer **5** augur **6** auspex, oracle **7** seeress **8** foreseer, haruspex **9** predictor **10** forecaster, foreteller, prophesier, soothsayer **11** Nostradamus *Major:* **6** Daniel, Isaiah **7** Ezekiel **8** Jeremiah *Minor:* **4** Amos, Joel **5** Hosea, Jonah, Micah, Nahum **6** Haggai **7** Malachi, Obadiah **8** Habakkuk **9** Zechariah, Zephaniah

prophetess 4 Anna **5** Sibyl **6** Huldah, Miriam **7** Deborah, Noadiah **9** Cassandra

prophetic 5 vatic **6** mantic, mystic **7** fatidic, strange, vatical **8** Delphian, oracular **9** sibylline, vaticinal **10** mysterious, revelatory **11** apocalyptic, prophetical

propinquity 7 kinship **8** nearness **9** closeness, immediacy, proximity **10** contiguity

propitiate 5 adapt, atone **6** adjust, pacify **7** appease, assuage, conform, content, mediate, mollify, placate, satisfy, sweeten **9** intercede, reconcile **10** conciliate

propitiatory 7 lustral **9** expiative, expiatory, purgative

propitious 4 good, rosy **5** brave, white **6** benign, bright, dexter, timely, toward, useful **7** benefic, helpful, timeous **8** favoring **9** favorable, fortunate, opportune, welltimed **10** auspicious, beneficial, prosperous, seasonable **12** advantageous

proponent 6 backer **8** advocate, champion **9** expounder, supporter

proportion 4 rate, size, tune **5** ratio, scale **6** attune, degree, extent **7** balance, conform, harmony, measure, prorate **8** symmetry

proportional 5 equal **8** relative **9** dependent **10** contingent, reciprocal **11** correlative, symmetrical **12** commensurate **13** commensurable, corresponding

proposal 3 bid **4** idea, plan **6** motion, scheme **7** outline, proffer, project **10** invita-

tion, suggestion **11** proposition *final:*
9 ultimatum
propose 3 aim, ask, put **4** mean, plan,
pose **5** offer **6** design, intend, prefer, submit, tender **7** move for, present, purpose,
request, solicit, suggest **8** nominate, propound, theorize **11** contemplate
proposition 3 put **4** pose **5** lemma, offer
6 prefer, thesis **7** premise, proffer, propose,
suggest, theorem **8** proposal, propound
10 invitation, suggestion
propound 3 put **4** pose **6** prefer **7** propone, propose, suggest **11** proposition
proprietor 5 owner **6** holder **9** possessor
propriety 5 order **6** manner **7** aptness,
decency, decorum, dignity, fitness **8** meetness **9** etiquette, rightness **10** expediency,
properness, seemliness **11** correctness,
orderliness, suitability **12** appositeness, correctitude, decorousness, suitableness
propulsion 4 fuel, push **5** drive, power
prorate 5 allot, divvy, quota, share
6 divide, parcel, ration **7** portion
9 apportion
prorogate see **prorogue**
prorogue 4 rise, stay **5** defer, delay,
remit **6** hold up, put off, recess, shelve
7 adjourn, hold off **8** dissolve, hold over,
postpone **9** prorogate, terminate
prosaic 4 drab, dull, flat **5** lowly, prose,
prosy **6** actual, boring, common **7** factual,
irksome, literal, mundane, tedious, workday **8** everyday, lifeless, ordinary, workaday **9** colorless, practical **10** lackluster, lusterless, uneventful **11** commonplace
proscenium 5 stage **9** forestage
10 foreground
proscribe 3 ban **4** damn, doom **7** condemn **8** prohibit, sentence
proscription 3 ban **5** taboo **11** forbiddance, prohibition **12** interdiction
prosecute 3 sue **5** press **6** charge, indict
prosecutor 2 DA **6** lawyer **7** accuser
public: **6** fiscal
proselyte 7 convert, recruit **8** neophyte
prospect 4 mine, sift **5** probe, scape,
vista **6** go into **7** dig into, explore, lookout,
outlook **8** look into **9** candidate
prosper 3 dow **4** boom **5** score, yield
6 arrive, thrive **7** augment, make out, produce, succeed, turn out **8** flourish, increase
prosperity 4 boom, ease **6** growth, riches,
wealth **7** arrival, benefit, success, welfare
8 interest, thriving **9** abundance, advantage,
affluence, expansion, inflation, well-being
10 easy street **12** flying colors
Prospero *daughter:* **7** Miranda *servant:*
5 Ariel *slave:* **7** Caliban
prosperous 4 easy, rich, well **5** happy,
lucky, lusty, palmy **6** robust, strong, timely
7 booming, halcyon, opulent, roaring, thrifty,

timeous, wealthy, well-off **8** affluent, thriving, well-to-do **9** desirable, favorable, fortunate, opportune, well-fixed, well-timed
10 auspicious, convenient, felicitous, propitious, seasonable, successful, well-heeled
11 appropriate, comfortable, flourishing,
substantial
prostitute 4 bawd, doxy, drab, moll
5 abuse, madam, poule, quean, whore
6 callet, debase, harlot, hooker, misuse,
pickup, tomato, wanton **7** cocotte, corrupt,
cruiser, Cyprian, debauch, deprave, hustler,
joy girl, Paphian, vitiate **8** call girl, meretrix,
misapply, strumpet **9** cocodette, misemploy, mishandle, party girl **10** misimprove,
street girl **11** fille de joie, nightwalker
12 camp follower, streetwalker *reformed:*
8 Magdalen
prostitution 8 harlotry, whoredom
10 social evil **13** streetwalking *house of:*
7 brothel **8** bordello
prostrate 4 down, drop, fell, flat, poop
5 floor, level, prone, whelm **6** disarm,
ground, lay low, tucker **7** cripple, disable,
exhaust, frazzle, outtire, outwear, wear out
8 knock out, overcome, paralyze **9** decumbent, knock over, overpower, overwhelm,
reclining, recumbent, throw down
protagonist 4 hero, star **5** actor
6 leader **8** advocate, champion
9 spokesman
protean 5 fluid **6** mobile **7** mutable
8 unstable, unsteady, variable, weathery
9 changeful, unsettled **10** changeable
protect 4 fend, save **5** cover, guard
6 defend, harbor, screen, secure, shield
7 bulwark, shelter **8** conserve, preserve
9 safeguard
protected 4 safe **6** immune
protection 3 pad **4** ward **5** aegis, armor,
bribe, graft, guard **6** safety, shield
7 defense, squeeze **8** armament, security
9 extortion, safeguard, shakedown
protector 5 armor, guard **6** patron, shield
7 tutelar **8** guardian
protégé 4 ward **5** pupil **7** student
protein 4 zein **5** actin, opsin **6** avidin,
enzyme, fibrin, globin **7** albumin, elastin,
fibroin, histone, keratin, legumin, sericin
8 creatine, globulin, glutelin, prolamin, prota-
min, proteose, vitellin *complex:* **6** mucoid
derivative: **7** peptone *poisonous:* **5** abrin,
ricin *source:* **4** eggs, fish, meat, milk
6 cheese
pro tem 6 acting, supply **7** interim **9** ad
interim, temporary **10** pro tempore
protest 4 aver, avow, kick **5** demur, fight
6 affirm, avouch, combat, depose,
except, object, oppose, picket, resist
7 declare, profess **8** constate, demurral,
demurrer **9** challenge, objection

Protestant 5 Amish 6 Mormon, Quaker, Shaker 7 Baptist, Lollard, Pilgrim, Puritan 8 Anglican, Lutheran, Moravian 9 Adventist, Mennonite, Methodist, Unitarian 12 Episcopalian, Presbyterian *Bohemian:* 7 Hussite *dissenter:* 7 sectary *French:* 8 Huguenot *martyr:* (see at **martyr**)

prototypal see **prototypical**

prototype 5 model 8 ancestor, foregoer, original 9 archetype, precursor 10 antecedent, antecessor, forerunner, protoplast 11 predecessor

prototypical 5 ideal, model 7 classic 9 classical, exemplary 10 archetypal

protozoan 4 cell 5 ameba 6 amoeba 7 arcella, ciliate, stentor 10 flagellate, paramecium

protract see **prolong**

protrude 3 jut, pout 5 bulge, pouch 6 beetle 7 project 8 overhang, stand out, stick out

protrusion 3 jut, nub 4 bump, hump 5 bulge 8 eminence, swelling 9 outthrust 10 projection 12 protuberance

protuberance see **protrusion**

protuberate see **protrude**

proud 4 vain 5 huffy, lofty, noble, wiggy 6 lordly, stuffy, superb 7 bloated, haughty, pompous, stuck-up, sublime 8 arrogant, cavalier, glorious, gorgeous, insolent, misproud, orgulous, scornful, splendid, superior, toplofty 9 conceited, hubristic, imperious, important, masterful 10 disdainful, dismissive, high-handed 11 domineering, magnificent, overbearing, pretentious, resplendent, splendorous, toploftical 12 contemptuous, narcissistic, ostentatious, proudhearted, supercilious

prove 3 try 4 show, test 5 argue, check 6 attest, verify 7 bespeak, betoken, confirm, examine, make out 8 document, indicate 9 determine, establish 11 corroborate, demonstrate 12 substantiate

provenance 4 root, well 6 origin, source, whence 8 fountain 9 inception 10 derivation, wellspring 11 provenience

provender see **provisions**

provenience see **provenance**

proverb 3 saw 4 word 5 adage, axiom, maxim 6 byword, saying

provide 4 feed, give, hand 5 cater, endow, equip 6 afford, supply 7 deliver, furnish, support 8 dispense, hand over, maintain

provided 2 if 6 if only 8 equipped

providence 6 thrift 7 caution, economy 8 prudence 9 canniness, foresight, frugality, husbandry 10 discretion, precaution 11 forethought, thriftiness 12 discreetness

provident 5 canny, chary 6 frugal, saving, Scotch 7 sparing, thrifty 9 stewardly 10 economical, unwasteful

providential 4 kind, well 5 happy, lucky 6 kindly 9 benignant, fortunate

province 4 area, duty, role, walk, work 5 field 6 domain, office, sphere 7 calling, demesne, pursuit, terrain 8 business, district, dominion, function 9 bailiwick, champaign, territory 10 department *Greek:* 4 nome 8 nomarchy

provincial 4 hick, jake, rube 5 clown, local, rural 6 rustic 7 bigoted, bucolic, bumpkin, country, hayseed, insular, outland, peasant 8 agrestic, pastoral 9 hidebound, parochial, sectarian, small-town 10 campestral, out-country 11 countrified

provision 4 term 6 clause 7 proviso, strings 9 condition 11 reservation, stipulation

provisional 4 iffy 7 stopgap 9 dependent, makeshift, provisory, temporary, tentative 10 contingent 11 conditional 13 rough-and-ready

provisions 4 feed, food, grub 6 viands 7 edibles, nurture 8 supplies, victuals 9 provender 11 comestibles *dealer:* 8 chandler

proviso see **provision**

provocation 6 irking, vexing 8 vexation 9 annoyance, bothering, provoking 10 harassment

provocative 4 goad, push, spur 7 impetus, impulse 8 stimulus 9 incentive 10 incitation, incitement, motivation 11 challenging

provoke 3 bug, get, irk, vex 4 abet, fire, fret, gall, move, rile, roil, stir, wake, whet 5 anger, annoy, breed, cause, chafe, exalt, get up, grate, hatch, pique, prime, raise, rally, rouse, set on, upset, waken 6 abrade, arouse, awaken, bestir, bother, excite, foment, harass, incite, induce, inform, insult, kindle, madden, put out, ruffle, stir up, thrill, whip up 7 animate, build up, enthuse, incense, inflame, innerve, inspire, outrage, perturb, produce, quicken 8 engender, exercise, generate, irritate, motivate, muster up, occasion, titivate 9 aggravate, challenge, electrify, galvanize, innervate, instigate, stimulate, titillate

provost 4 head 6 keeper 7 marshal 8 director 13 administrator

prow 3 bow 4 beak, stem 5 front

prowess 5 skill, valor 7 address, heroism, sleight 8 deftness, valiance, valiancy 9 dexterity, gallantry, readiness 10 adroitness 12 valorousness 13 dexterousness

prowl 4 hunt, pace, roam 5 creep 6 wander

proximate 4 near, next, nigh, rude 5 close, rough 6 nearby 8 imminent 9 immediate, impending 10 near-at-hand

proximity 8 nearness, vicinity 9 adjacency, closeness, immediacy **10** contiguity **11** propinquity **12** togetherness

proxy **5** agent, power **6** deputy, factor **8** assignee, attorney **9** authority

prude **4** prig **6** Grundy **7** old fogy, old maid, Puritan **8** bluenose, comstock **9** Mrs. Grundy, nice Nelly **10** fuddy-duddy, fussbudget, goody-goody, spoilsport, wet blanket **12** stuffed shirt

prudence **3** wit **6** acumen, thrift, wisdom **7** caution, economy, insight **8** astucity, keenness, sagacity, sageness, sapience **9** canniness, chariness, foresight, frugality, husbandry **10** astuteness, discretion, expediency, precaution, providence, shrewdness **11** calculation, forethought, penetration, percipience, thriftiness **12** discreetness, perspicacity

prudent **4** sage, sane, wary, wise **5** canny, chary **7** politic, sapient **8** cautious, sensible, tactical **9** advisable, expedient, judicious

prudish **4** prim **5** stern **6** prissy, proper, severe, strict, stuffy **7** austere, genteel **8** priggish **9** Victorian **11** puritanical, straitlaced

prune **3** cut, lop **4** clip, crop, dolt, dope, pare, plum, thin, trim **5** brash, chump, dunce, fruit, idiot, moron, shave, shear, skive

prurience **4** itch, lust **6** desire **7** passion **9** eroticism **11** lustfulness **13** concupiscence

prurient **3** hot **4** lewd **5** bawdy **6** erotic **7** goatish, lustful, satyric, sensual **9** lickerish **10** lascivious, libidinous, passionate **12** concupiscent

pruritic **5** itchy

Prussian *aristocrat:* **6** Junker **12** Hohenzollern *prime minister:* **8** Bismarck *ruler:* **7** Wilhelm **9** Frederick

pry **4** lift, nose, open, peek, poke, rear, turn **5** hoist, jimmy, lever, mouse, prize, raise, snoop, twist **6** divide, pick up, take up, uphold, uplift, uprear **7** crowbar, disjoin, elevate, upraise **8** busybody, separate

psalm **3** ode **4** hymn, laud, poem, song **5** cry up, extol **6** praise **7** glorify, magnify **8** eulogize **9** celebrate *book:* **7** psalter *selection:* **6** hallel *word:* **5** selah

psalmist **4** poet **5** Asaph, David **6** cantor

pseudo **4** fake, mock, sham **5** bogus, false, phony, snide, wrong **8** spurious **9** brummagem, pinchbeck **11** counterfeit

pseudonym **5** alias **6** ananym, anonym **7** pen name **9** incognito, stage name **10** nom de plume **11** nom de guerre; (see also **pen name**)

psyche **4** mind, soul **5** anima **6** animus, pneuma, spirit **9** élan vital **10** vital force *part:* **2** id **3** ego **8** superego

Psyche's beloved **4** Eros **5** Cupid

psychiatrist **6** shrink *American:* **9** Menninger *Austrian:* **5** Adler *Swiss:* **4** Jung **9** Rorschach

psychic **6** mental **7** sensile **8** cerebral, sensible, sentient **9** sensitive, spiritual **10** responsive, susceptive, telepathic **11** impressible, susceptible **12** intellective, intellectual, supersensory **13** psychological *American:* **5** Cayce (Edgar) *power:* **3** ESP

psychoanalyst **5** Freud, Fromm **6** Horney

psychological **6** mental **7** psychic **8** cerebral **9** psychical **12** intellective, intellectual

psychologist **6** shrink *American:* **3** May **5** James **6** Rogers, Terman, Watson, Yerkes **7** Skinner **8** Brothers **9** Thorndike *English:* **4** Ward **8** Spearman, Tichener *German:* **5** Wundt **6** Muller, Stumpf **10** Wertheimer *Swiss:* **4** Jung **6** Piaget

psychopathy **6** lunacy **7** madness **8** insanity **9** unbalance **10** aberration, alienation, insaneness **11** derangement, distraction

psychotic **3** mad **5** crazy **6** insane **8** schizoid

ptarmigan **6** grouse

ptomaine **6** poison

pub **3** bar, inn **6** tavern **7** barroom, rummery, taproom **8** drinkery, groggery, grogshop

puberty **5** youth **6** spring **9** greenness, youthhood **10** juvenility, pubescence, springtide, springtime **11** adolescence *combining form:* **4** hebe

public **4** open **5** civic, civil, joint, state, suite, urban **6** common, mutual, people, shared, vulgar **7** general, popular, society **8** audience, communal, conjoint, conjunct, national, open-door **9** clientage, clientele, community, following, hangers-on, municipal, prevalent, universal **10** accessible, government, widespread **11** intermutual

publican **8** boniface, taverner **9** barkeeper, collector, innholder, innkeeper, saloonist **12** saloonkeeper, tax collector

publication **4** book **5** paper **7** journal **8** magazine, pamphlet **9** broadcast, newspaper **10** periodical **11** declaration *list:* **12** bibliography

public house **3** inn **5** hotel, lodge **6** hostel, tavern **7** auberge, hospice **8** hostelry **9** road-house **11** caravansary

publicity **4** hype, plug, puff **5** blurb **6** hoopla **7** buildup, puffery, réclame, write-up **8** ballyhoo, hard sell **9** promotion **11** advertising **12** announcement

publicize **3** cry **4** hype, plug, puff, push, tout **5** boost, bruit, extol **7** advance, build up, promote, trumpet **8** announce, headline, skywrite **9** advertise, broadcast **10** press-agent, promulgate **11** circularize **12** propagandize

publish 3 air **4** toot, vent **5** issue, print, utter **6** broach, get out, market, put out **7** declare, express, produce **8** announce, bring out, proclaim **9** advertise, broadcast, ventilate **10** annunciate, distribute, promulgate **11** blaze abroad, disseminate

publisher 6 editor **7** printer **10** journalist

Puccini, Giacomo *heroine:* **4** Mimi *opera:* **5** Edgar, Tosca **7** Le Villi **8** La Bohème, Turandot **12** Manon Lescaut, Suor Angelica

puck 3 elf, imp **4** disk **5** fairy **6** spirit, sprite **9** hobgoblin, prankster

pucker 4 fold **5** purse **6** cockle **7** wrinkle **8** contract

puckish 5 antic **6** impish, wicked **7** larkish, playful, roguish, waggish **8** prankish, sportive **11** mischievous

pudding 4 duff **6** burgoo **7** custard, dessert, tapioca *baked:* **10** brown Betty

pudgy 5 plump, round, squab, tubby **6** chubby, plumpy, rotund, squdgy, stumpy **8** plumpish, roly-poly **10** roundabout

pueblo 4 town **7** village **8** dwelling *ceremonial room:* **4** kiva

puerile 6 boyish **7** babyish **8** childish, immature

Puerto Rico *capital:* **7** San Juan *discoverer:* **8** Columbus

puff 3 cry **4** blow, brag, crow, drag, draw, gasp, huff, pant, plug, pouf, pull, push **5** blurb, boast, boost, heave, mouth, prate, quilt, vaunt **6** praise **7** build up, puffing, write-up **8** inhaling **9** advertise, comforter, gasconade, laudation, publicize

puffer 8 blowfish **9** globefish

puffery 7 buildup **9** promotion, publicity **11** advertising **12** press-agentry

puffin 4 bird **9** sea parrot **10** shearwater

puff up 5 bloat, swell **7** inflate

puffy 5 wiggy **6** stuffy **7** bloated, pompous **8** arrogant **9** important **10** pontifical **11** magisterial **13** self-important

pug 3 bun, dog **4** nose **5** boxer, track **9** footprint

pugilism 4 ring **6** boxing **10** fisticuffs **13** prizefighting

pugilist 5 boxer **7** fighter

pugnacious 5 pushy **7** defiant, pushing, scrappy, warlike **8** brawling, militant **9** bellicose, combative, truculent **10** rebellious **11** belligerent, contentious, quarrelsome

pugnacity 5 fight **6** attack **10** aggression **12** belligerence **13** combativeness

puisne 5 judge, later **6** junior **9** associate

puissance 4 sway **5** clout, force, might, power, sinew, vigor **6** energy, muscle, virtue **7** potency **8** strength **9** influence

puissant 6 mighty, potent, ruling, strong **8** forceful, forcible, powerful **10** commanding

pukka 4 real, true **5** right **7** genuine **8** bona fide **9** authentic, simon-pure

pule 3 cry **5** whine **7** whimper

Pulitzer Prize winner, fiction *1918:* **5** Poole *1919:* **10** Tarkington *1921:* **7** Wharton *1922:* **10** Tarkington *1923:* **6** Cather *1924:* **6** Wilson *1925:* **6** Ferber *1926:* **5** Lewis *1927:* **9** Bromfield *1928:* **6** Wilder *1929:* **8** Peterkin *1930:* **7** La Farge *1931:* **6** Barnes *1932:* **4** Buck *1933:* **9** Stribling *1934:* **6** Miller *1935:* **7** Johnson *1936:* **5** Davis *1937:* **8** Mitchell *1938:* **8** Marquand *1939:* **8** Rawlings *1940:* **9** Steinbeck *1942:* **7** Glasgow *1943:* **8** Sinclair *1944:* **6** Flavin *1945:* **6** Hersey *1947:* **6** Warren *1948:* **8** Michener *1949:* **7** Cozzens *1950:* **7** Guthrie *1951:* **7** Richter *1952:* **4** Wouk *1953:* **9** Hemingway *1955:* **8** Faulkner *1956:* **6** Kantor *1958:* **4** Agee *1959:* **6** Taylor *1960:* **5** Drury *1961:* **3** Lee *1962:* **7** O'Connor *1963:* **8** Faulkner *1965:* **4** Grau *1966:* **6** Porter *1967:* **7** Malamud *1968:* **6** Styron *1969:* **7** Momaday *1970:* **8** Stafford *1972:* **7** Stegner *1973:* **5** Welty *1975:* **6** Shaara *1976:* **6** Bellow *1978:* **9** McPherson *1979:* **7** Cheever *1980:* **6** Mailer *1981:* **5** Toole *1982:* **6** Updike *1983:* **6** Walker *1984:* **7** Kennedy *1985:* **5** Lurie *1986:* **8** McMurtry *1987:* **6** Taylor *1988:* **8** Morrison *1989:* **5** Tyler *1990:* **8** Hijuelos

pull 3 don, get, lug, oar, row, tow, tug, win **4** drag, draw, gain, haul, have, jerk, land, lure, puff, push, tear, yank **5** clout, drive, heave, impel, put on, shove **6** appeal, assume, commit, evulse, obtain, paddle, pick up, secure, strain, strike, take on, wrench **7** chalk up, extract, procure **9** influence, seduction **10** allurement, attraction, perpetrate, persuasion **12** drawing power

pull down 4 raze, ruin **5** wreck **7** destroy **8** decimate, demolish, destruct, tear down **9** dismantle **10** annihilate

pullet 3 hen

pulley 5 wheel **6** sheave *watch's:* **5** fusee, fuzee

pull in 3 bit, nab **4** curb **5** check, pinch, run in **6** arrest, bridle, detain, hold in, pick up **7** inhibit **8** hold back, hold down, restrain

pulling 8 traction *cable for:* **7** towline

Pullman 3 car **7** sleeper

pull out 4 exit, quit **5** leave, pluck **6** depart, get off, retire **7** retreat, take off **8** shove off, withdraw

pull through 7 recover, ride out, survive

pullulate 4 flow, teem **5** crawl, swarm **6** abound

pull up 4 halt, stop 6 draw up, haul up

pulp 4 mash, pith 5 crush 6 bruise, squash 7 bagasse, becrush

pulpit 4 ambo 7 lectern 8 ministry, platform *Muslim:* 6 minbar

pulsate 4 beat, drum, pump, roar 5 pound, throb, thrum 7 vibrate 9 fluctuate, oscillate, palpitate

pulse 4 beat 5 throb 6 rhythm *combining form:* 6 crotic 7 sphygmo *relating to:* 8 sphygmic

pulverize 4 beat, bray, buck, mill, mull, ruin 5 crush, flour, grate, grind, smash, wreck 6 abrade, crunch, powder, rub out 7 atomize, break up, crumble, destroy, shatter, smatter 8 decimate, demolish, destruct, dynamite, fragment, levigate, splinter, tear down 9 comminute, micronize, triturate 11 fragmentize 12 contriturate

puma 3 cat 6 cougar

pumice 5 glass, stone

pummel 4 beat, drub, pelt 5 pound 6 batter, buffet, hammer, thrash, wallop 7 belabor

pump 3 tap 4 draw 5 draft, drain 6 siphon 7 draw off, syringe

pumpernickel 3 rye 5 bread

pumpkin 4 pepo 5 fruit 6 cushaw, squash 12 jack-o'-lantern

pun 4 joke 9 calembour, equivoque 11 paronomasia

punch 3 box, dig, hit, jab, jog, pep 4 bang, bore, cuff, poke, prod, push, slap, snap, sock, stab 5 clout, drill, drive, force, getup, nudge, paste, point, prick, smack, vigor 6 buffet, starch, strike 7 cogency 8 puncture, uppercut, validity, vitality 9 perforate, validness 13 effectiveness

punch bowl 8 monteith

puncheon 4 tool 5 stamp

puncher 5 boxer 6 cowboy

Punch's wife 4 Judy

punctilious 4 nice 5 exact, fussy 6 formal 7 careful, heedful 8 punctual 9 observant 10 meticulous, scrupulous 11 painstaking

punctual 5 exact, fussy, quick, ready 6 prompt, timely 7 careful, heedful 10 meticulous

punctuate 4 mark 5 point 6 divide 8 separate

punctuation mark 4 dash 5 brace, colon, comma 6 hyphen, parens, period 7 bracket, virgule 8 diagonal, ellipsis 9 semicolon 10 apostrophe 11 parenthesis

puncture 3 jab 4 bore, hole, stab 5 drill, prick, punch, shoot 6 blow up, riddle 7 explode 8 disprove 9 discredit, perforate 11 perforation *surgical:* 8 centesis

pundit 4 sage 5 swami 6 critic 7 teacher

pungency 4 tang, zest 8 piquancy

pungent 3 hot 4 keen, racy, rich, salt 5 acute, salty, sharp, spicy, tangy, zesty 6 biting, bitter, snappy 7 cutting, peppery, piquant 8 exciting, incisive, poignant 9 trenchant 11 provocative, stimulating

punish 3 fix 4 fine, whip 5 mulct, shift, swill 6 amerce, avenge 7 chasten, consume, correct, put away, put down, reprove, revenge, scourge, torture 8 chastise, lambaste, penalize 9 castigate, criticize, polish off 10 discipline

punishment 3 rod 4 fine 5 mulct 7 penalty, reproof, revenge 8 punition 9 criticism 10 amercement, avengement, correction, discipline 11 castigation 12 chastisement *Scottish:* 6 dirdum

punitive 5 penal 8 punitory 9 punishing 11 castigating 12 correctional, disciplinary

punk 4 bosh, colt, hood, thug 5 rough, rowdy, tough, yahoo 6 bunkum, hot air, mucker, novice, rookie 7 baloney, hogwash, hoodlum, ruffian, toughie 8 beginner, bullyboy, claptrap, neophyte, newcomer, nonsense 9 fledgling, novitiate, roughneck 10 apprentice, balderdash

punt 4 boat, kick

puny 4 weak 5 frail, petty 6 feeble, infirm, measly, paltry, sickly, weakly 7 fragile, trivial, unsound 8 decrepit, niggling, picayune, piddling, trifling 10 picayunish

pupa 9 chrysalid, chrysalis

pupil 5 cadet, tutee 7 learner, scholar, student 8 disciple *French:* 5 élève

puppet 4 doll, dupe, pawn, tool 5 slave 6 stooge 7 cat's-paw

puppy 3 dog 5 whelp

Purcell opera 13 Dido and Aeneas

purchase 3 buy 4 take 6 obtain 7 acquire 11 acquisition

purchaser 4 user 5 buyer 6 client, emptor, patron, vendee 7 shopper 8 consumer, customer

pure 4 good, neat 5 clean, fresh, gross, plain, sheer, total, utter 6 chaste, decent, modest, simple 7 blasted, blessed, classic, genuine, perfect, plenary, sinless, unmixed 8 absolute, complete, infernal, innocent, spotless, straight, virtuous 9 authentic, blameless, exemplary, guiltless, inviolate, out-and-out, righteous, stainless, unalloyed, undefiled, undiluted, unsullied 10 confounded, immaculate, inculpable, unblamable, unblighted, unprofaned 11 unblemished, unmitigated, unqualified 13 unadulterated

purebred 8 pedigree 9 pedigreed 10 registered 11 full-blooded 12 thoroughbred

puree 4 soup 5 paste

purely 3 all 4 just 5 quite 6 in toto, wholly 7 exactly, totally, utterly 8 all in all 10 altogether

purfle 4 trim 6 border 8 decorate, ornament

purgation 9 catharsis, cleansing 10 lustration

purgative 5 jalap 7 lustral 9 cathartic, expiatory

purge 3 rid 4 oust 5 clear, debar, eject, erase, expel 6 purify, remove 7 absolve, cleanse, dismiss, exclude, expunge, shut out, wipe out 8 disabuse, lustrate, undelude 9 eliminate, expurgate, liquidate, undeceive 11 exterminate

purification 5 grace 7 rebirth 9 atonement, catharsis, cleansing, expiation, purgation, salvation 10 absolution, lustration, redemption 11 expurgation, forgiveness 12 regeneration *sacrament:* 7 baptism

purify 5 atone, clean, purge, remit 6 filter, refine 7 absolve, baptize, clarify, cleanse, expiate 8 depurate, lustrate 9 elutriate, expurgate

purist 7 diehard, Puritan 8 Atticist 9 precisian 10 classicist 11 bitter-ender 12 conservative, precisionist

puritan 4 prig 5 prude 6 Grundy 8 bluenose, comstock 9 Mrs. Grundy, nice Nelly

puritanical 4 prim 6 narrow, prissy, strict, stuffy 7 bigoted, genteel, prudish 8 priggish, rigorous 9 blue-nosed, hidebound, illiberal, victorian 10 intolerant, tight-laced 11 straitlaced 12 narrow-minded

purity 8 chastity 9 innocence

purl 4 eddy, knit 5 gurge, swirl, whirl, whorl 6 stitch, swoosh 9 whirlpool

purlieu 5 haunt 6 resort 7 hangout

purlieus 6 bounds, limits 7 compass, suburbs 8 boundary, confines, environs 9 outskirts, precincts

purloin 5 filch, pinch, steal, swipe 6 pilfer, rip off, snitch, thieve 7 cabbage 11 appropriate

purloiner 4 prig 5 thief 6 nimmer 7 filcher, stealer 8 larcener, pilferer 9 larcenist

purple 4 blue, plum, racy 5 broad, grape, lilac, mauve, regal, salty, shady, spicy 6 florid, maroon, murrey, risqué, turgid, violet, wicked 7 flowery, pompous, stilted 8 lavender, off-color 9 bombastic, highflown, overblown 10 oratorical, rhetorical, suggestive

Purple Heart 5 award, medal

purport 4 core, gist, meat, pith 5 drift, sense, tenor 6 burden, matter, thrust, upshot 7 meaning, message 9 substance 10 intendment 11 acceptation, connotation, implication 12 significance, significancy

purported 7 alleged, reputed, rumored 8 academic, so-called, supposed 9 pretended, professed, suspected 10 ostensi-

ble, postulated 11 presupposed, speculative

purpose 3 aim, use 4 duty, goal, mark, mean, plan 5 point 6 animus, decide, design, intend, intent, object, ponder, target 7 meaning, mission, resolve 8 ambition, conclude, consider, function, meditate, proposal 9 determine, direction, intention, objective 10 aspiration, intendment

purposeless 6 random 7 aimless, fustian, unaimed, useless 8 feckless 9 desultory, haphazard, hit-or-miss, irregular, senseless, unhelpful, unplanned, worthless 10 designless, unpurposed 11 meaningless, nonsensical, purportless 12 unprofitable

purposely 9 expressly 10 designedly, explicitly, prepensely 12 deliberately 13 intentionally

purr 3 hum 6 murmur

purse 3 bag, sum 4 knit 5 money, pouch, prize 6 pucker, wallet 7 handbag 9 clutch bag 10 pocketbook, prize money *Scottish:* 7 sporran

pursual 5 chase, quest 6 search 7 pursuit

pursue 3 woo 4 hunt, seek 5 chase, chivy, court, hound, spark, stalk, track, trail 6 badger, follow 7 address, oppress, persist 8 make up to 9 persecute, persevere

pursuit 3 job 4 hunt, line, work 5 chase, quest 6 racket, search 7 calling, seeking 8 business, reaching 9 following, obtaining 10 employment, occupation

pursy see portly

purvey 6 obtain, supply 7 provide

purview 3 ken 5 ambit, orbit, range, reach, scope, sweep 6 extent, radius 7 compass

pus 6 fester *combining form:* 2 py 3 pyo

push 3 dig, jam, lot, pep, ram, set 4 bang, bear, bump, butt, goad, move, plug, prod, snap, spur 5 boost, build, bunch, crowd, crush, drive, drove, elbow, force, getup, group, horde, hunch, impel, nudge, press, punch, shove, vigor 6 beef up, circle, expand, hustle, jostle, launch, peddle, propel, squash, squish, squush, starch, throng, thrust 8 ambition, bulldoze, compound, increase, oversell, pressure, shoulder, stimulus, vitality 9 advertise, incentive 10 aggrandize, enterprise, get-up-and-go, incitation, incitement, initiative

push around 4 bait, ride 5 bully, chivy, hound 6 badger, heckle, hector 8 bullyrag

pushful 5 brash 6 uppish, uppity 7 assured, forward, pushing 8 imposing, militant 9 assertive, assertory, confident, intrusive, obtruding, obtrusive, officious, presuming 10 aggressive 11 overweening 12 presumptuous 13 self-asserting, self-assertive

Pushkin *novel:* **12** Eugene Onegin *play:* **12** Boris Godunov

push off 2 go **4** exit, quit **5** leave **6** depart, get off **7** get away, pull out **8** withdraw

push on 2 go **3** hie **4** fare, pass, wend **6** repair, travel **7** journey, proceed

pushover 3 pie **4** snap **5** cinch, setup **6** breeze, picnic **8** duck soup, kid stuff **10** child's play

pushy see **pushful**

pusillanimous 6 coward, craven **7** chicken, gutless, unmanly **8** cowardly, poltroon **9** spunkless **11** lily-livered, poltroonish

puss 3 cat, kid, mug **4** face **5** child **6** kisser, kitten, moppet, nipper, visage **8** juvenile

pussyfoot 4 lurk, slip **5** creep, dodge, evade, glide, hedge, skulk, slide, slink, sneak, steal **6** weasel **7** gumshoe, shuffle **8** sidestep **10** equivocate, tergiverse **12** tergiversate

pustule 4 boil, wart **5** whelk **6** pimple **7** abscess **8** furuncle **9** carbuncle

put 3 air, fix, lay, set **4** call, give, levy, pose, turn, vent, word **5** couch, exact, focus, judge, place, rivet, state, stick **6** assess, fasten, fixate, impose, phrase, prefer, reckon, render, return, settle **7** express, propose, replace, restore, suggest **8** estimate, give back, propound **9** concenter

putative 7 reputed **8** supposed **11** conjectural, suppositive, suppository **12** hypothetical

put away 4 bury, do in, kill, slay **5** inter, plant, scrag, swill **6** cut off, entomb, finish, inhume, lay low, murder, punish **7** bump off, consume, destroy, dismiss, divorce, execute, reposit, take off, unmarry **8** carry off, dispatch, knock off **9** liquidate

put back 6 demote, return **7** replace, restore **8** give back **9** reinstate

put by 4 save **5** lay in, lay up **7** lay away **8** lay aside, salt away

put down 4 bump, bust **5** break, crush, quash, quell, shift, swill **6** demote, humble, punish, quench, squash, subdue **7** consume, declass, degrade, demerit, disrate, put away **8** disgrade, suppress **9** downgrade

put in 3 sow **4** seed **5** plant **6** insert

put off 5 delay, elude, repel **7** suspend **8** dissuade, postpone **9** frustrate **10** disconcert

put on 3 act, don, kid **4** fake, hire, pose, sham, show **5** bluff, feign, get on, mount, stage **6** affect, assume, draw on, employ, engage, slip on, strike, take on **7** mislead

put-on 3 act **4** face, fake, mask, sell, sham, show **5** cheat, cloak, cover, faked, guise, phony, posed, spoof **6** deceit, facade, parody **7** assumed, feigned **8** affected, disguise, mannered, spurious **9** deception, imposture **10** artificial, false front, masquerade

put out 3 ply, vex **4** gall, rile, roil **5** annoy, douse, exert, grate, issue, throw, wield **6** burn up, quench **7** inflame, publish, trouble **8** exercise, irritate **9** aggravate, disoblige, displease, incommode **10** discommode, dissatisfy, exasperate, extinguish **13** inconvenience

putrefy 3 rot **4** turn **5** decay, spoil, taint **6** molder **7** crumble **9** break down, decompose **12** disintegrate

putrid 3 bad **4** foul, high, olid **5** fetid **6** rancid, rotten, smelly, whiffy **7** corrupt, decayed, noisome, reeking, spoiled, vicious **8** depraved, nidorous, perverse **9** nefarious **10** malodorous *combining form:* **4** sapr **5** sapro

putter 4 club, mess **6** dawdle, doodle, fiddle, golfer, puddle, tinker **10** boondoggle

putting area 5 green

put together 4 form, join, make **5** build, erect, frame, shape, unite **7** fashion, produce **9** construct, fabricate

putty 3 mud **4** clay **6** cement

put up 3 can, hut **4** bunk, hike, jump, make, rear **5** board, boost, build, erect, forge, house, lodge, raise, set up, shape **6** bestow, billet, harbor, jack up, uprear **7** elevate, quarter **8** domicile, escalate, increase **9** construct *with:* **4** bear **5** stand **6** endure **8** tolerate

puzzle 3 why **4** foil, pose **5** addle, amaze, befog, poser, rebus, upset **6** baffle, enigma, fuddle, muddle, riddle **7** anagram, confuse, disturb, mystery, mystify, nonplus, perplex, problem, stumble **8** acrostic, befuddle, bewilder, confound, distract **9** conundrum, crossword, dumbfound, frustrate **10** closed book, disconcert, puzzlement **11** brainteaser *Chinese:* **7** tangram

puzzle out 5 break, solve **6** cipher, unfold **7** clear up, dope out, unravel **8** decipher, unriddle **9** figure out

Pygmalion *father:* **5** Belus *sister:* **4** Dido *statue, beloved:* **7** Galatea *victim:* **8** Sichaeus

pygmy 4 runt, tiny **5** dwarf, midge **6** midget, peewee **7** manikin, minikin **8** dwarfish, Tom Thumb **10** diminutive, homunculus, pocket-size **11** lilliputian

Pylades *companion:* **7** Orestes *father:* **9** Strophius *wife:* **7** Electra

pylon 4 post **5** tower **7** gateway

Pynchon novel 15 Gravity's Rainbow

pyramid 4 bank, heap, hill, mass, pile,

tomb **5** drift, mound, stack **7** windrow
builder: **5** Khufu **6** Cheops
Pyramus' beloved 6 Thisbe
pyre 4 heap, pile
pyromaniac 8 arsonist
pyrosis 9 heartburn
pyrotechnics 9 fireworks
Pyrrha's husband 9 Deucalion

Pyrrhonian 7 doubter, skeptic, zetetic
10 unbeliever
Pyrrhus *kingdom:* **6** Epirus *victory:*
7 Asculum; (see also **Neoptolemus**)
Pythias' friend 5 Damon
python 3 boa **5** snake
pyx 3 box **4** case **5** chest **6** coffer,
vessel

Q

Qatar's capital 4 Doha
Q.E.D. word 4 erat, quod
q.t., on the 8 in secret, secretly
qua 2 as **4** bird **5** heron
quack 3 cry **4** honk, sham **7** shammer
9 charlatan, pretender, quackster, simula-
tor **10** mountebank **12** saltimbanque *combining form:* **5** pseud **6** pseudo
quad see **quadrangle**
quadra 5 frame **6** border, fillet, listel, plinth
quadragenarian 8 fortyish
quadrangle 4 yard **5** court **6** figure,
square **9** courtyard, curtilage, enclosure
quadrant 6 fourth **10** instrument
quadratic 6 square **10** foursquare
quadriga 7 chariot
quadrille 5 dance, ombre **8** card game
quadrillion *combining form:* **4** peta
quadrillionth *combining form:* **5** femto
quadrivium subject 5 music **8** geometry **9** astronomy **10** arithmetic
quaestor 5 judge **8** official **9** paymaster,
treasurer **10** prosecutor
quaff 3 sip **4** toss **5** drink, sup up
6 imbibe, sup off **7** swallow
quagga 3 ass
quaggy 4 soft **5** boggy, mushy, pappy,
pulpy **6** spongy **7** squashy, squishy,
squushy **8** squelchy, yielding
quagmire 3 bog, box, fen, fix, jam **4** hole,
mire **5** marsh, swamp **6** corner, morass,
pickle, plight, scrape, slough **7** dilemma
9 marshland **11** predicament
quahog 4 clam **11** cherrystone
quail 4 bird **5** colin, cower, wince **6** blanch,
blench, cringe, flinch, recoil, shrink **7** mas-
sena, shudder, squinch, tremble **8** bobwhite
flock of: **4** bevy *young:* **7** cheeper
8 squealer
quaint 3 odd **5** droll, funny, queer
7 antique, archaic, curious, oddball, strange,

unusual **8** peculiar, singular **9** eccentric,
laughable, whimsical **10** antiquated
quake 3 jar **5** shake, shock, waver
6 dither, quaver, quiver, shiver, tremor
7 shudder, temblor, tremble, twitter, vibrate
8 trembler, tremblor **9** fluctuate
Quaker 6 Friend **9** broadbrim *city:*
12 Philadelphia *colonizer:* **4** Penn
founder: **3** Fox *poet:* **6** Barton **8** Whittier
state: **12** Pennsylvania
qualification 5 might **7** ability **8** adequacy, aptitude, capacity **10** capability,
competence
qualified 3 fit **4** able, good **5** fixed, tried
6 au fait, proper, proved, tested **7** capable,
limited, partial, quizzed, trained **8** definite,
eligible, examined, modified, reserved
9 competent **10** catechized, determined,
instructed, restricted **11** conditional,
disciplined
qualify 4 mark **6** assign, impute, soften
7 ascribe, certify, entitle, license, prepare
8 moderate **9** attribute, authorize
quality 4 fine, mark, rank **5** arete, class,
elite, grade, merit, place, prime, savor, state,
trait, value, worth **6** factor, flower, gentry,
Grade A, status, virtue **7** aristoi, caliber, element, feature, footing, society, station, stature **8** capacity, five-star, position, property,
standing, superior **9** affection, attribute,
blue blood, character, excellent, first-rate,
gentility, parameter, situation **10** blue-ribbon, excellence, first-class, patriciate, perfection, superbness *essential:* **8** suchness
suffix: **2** cy, ty **3** ice, ity **4** ance, ancy,
ence, ency, hood, ness, ship
qualm 5 demur, doubt **6** squeam, unease
7 scruple **8** mistrust **9** agitation, misgiving,
objection, suspicion **10** conscience, foreboding, impatience, insecurity, reluctance,
uneasiness **11** compunction, nervousness,

uncertainty **12** apprehension, perturbation, presentiment, remonstrance **13** unwillingness

qualmish 5 queer **6** queasy **9** nauseated

quandary 3 fix, jam **6** pickle, plight, scrape **7** dilemma **11** predicament

quantity 4 body, bulk, dose, unit **5** total **6** amount, budget, degree **9** aggregate *fixed:* **8** constant *small:* **3** bit, jot, ray **4** atom, dram, drop, iota, mite, whit **5** grain, scrap, shred, speck **7** modicum, smidgen

Quantrill's ___ 7 raiders

quantum 3 sum **4** body, bulk, meed, part **5** quota, share, total **6** amount, budget, ration **7** measure, portion **9** aggregate, allotment, allowance **13** apportionment *of radiant energy:* **6** photon *of vibrational energy:* **6** phonon *theory originator:* **6** Planck

quarantine 6 cut off **7** isolate **9** interdict, isolation

quarrel 3 row, war **4** beef, bolt, bump, dust, feud, fray, fuss, miff, spat, tiff, tile, vary **5** argue, arrow, brawl, broil, clash, fight, melee, run-in, scrap, set-to, words **6** affray, battle, bicker, chisel, differ, divide, dustup, fracas, hassle, ruckus, rumpus, squall, strife, thwart **7** bobbery, brabble, cast out, collide, contend, diamond, discord, dispute, dissent, fall out, rhubarb, ruction, scuffle, wrangle **8** catfight, conflict, squabble, to-and-fro, variance **9** altercate, bickering, brannigan, caterwaul, disaccord, imbroglio, scrimmage **10** contention, difference, difficulty, dissension, donnybrook, falling-out, free-for-all **11** altercation, battle royal, controversy, embroilment **12** disagreement

quarrelsome 6 brawly **7** adverse, counter, crabbed, hostile, scrappy, warlike **8** brawling, cankered, inimical, militant, ructious **9** bellicose, brawlsome, combative, irascible, irritable, rancorous, truculent **10** battlesome, pugnacious **11** belligerent, contentious **12** disputatious **13** argumentative

quarry 3 pit **4** game, mine, prey **5** chase, delve, pluck **6** victim **7** lozenge

quart 6 fourth *four:* **6** gallon *metric:* **5** liter, litre

quarter 3 hut **4** area, bunk, part **5** board, house, lodge, put up **6** barrio, billet, canton, fourth, harbor, sector **7** barrack, section **8** district, division, domicile, locality, precinct, quadrant **9** entertain **11** domiciliate *circle:* **8** quadrant *note:* **8** crotchet *pint:* **4** gill *ship's:* **6** fo'c'sle **10** forecastle *year, Scottish:* **5** raith

quarterback 4 boss **6** survey **7** oversee **9** supervise **10** footballer

quartet 4 four **6** tetrad **7** quatuor **8** foursome **10** quadruplet, quaternion

quartz 4 onyx, sard **5** agate, smoky **6** jasper, rubace **7** citrine, rubasse, sardius **8** amethyst, sardonyx, sunstone **9** cairngorm, carnelian **10** chalcedony

quash 4 undo, void **5** abate, annul, crush, quell **6** negate, quench, stifle, vacate **7** abolish, nullify, put down, repress, smother, squelch, vitiate **8** abrogate, dissolve, strangle, suppress **9** discharge

quasi 6 almost **7** seeming, virtual

Quasimodo 9 hunchback *creator:* **4** Hugo *occupation:* **10** bell ringer *residence:* **9** Notre Dame

quat 3 sty **4** beat, boil **6** squash **7** upstart

quaver 5 quake, shake, waver **6** dither, falter, shiver, tremor **7** shudder, tremble, twitter **8** hesitate **9** vacillate

quawk 5 heron **10** night heron

quay 4 dock, pier, slip **5** berth, jetty, levee, wharf

quean 4 bawd **5** wench, whore **6** harlot **7** hustler **8** meretrix **10** prostitute

queasy 4 open **5** fishy, queer, shady **6** qualmy **7** dubious **8** doubtful, qualmish **9** ambiguous, doubtable, nauseated, squeamish

Quebec *college, university:* **5** Laval, Lévis **6** McGill **9** Concordia *largest city:* **8** Montreal *peninsula:* **5** Gaspé *vehicle:* **7** caleche

queen 4 card **6** regina **7** goddess, monarch **8** chessman **9** sovereign *Austria-Hungary:* **12** Maria Theresa *Belgian:* **6** Astrid *Danish:* **8** Margaret, Margrete *Egyptian:* **9** Cleopatra **10** Hatshepsut *English:* **4** Anne, Mary **8** Victoria **9** Elizabeth *French and English:* **7** Eleanor *Netherlands:* **7** Beatrix, Juliana **10** Wilhelmina *of heaven:* **4** Mary, moon **7** Astarte *of Isles:* **6** Albion *of Ithaca:* **8** Penelope *of Navarre:* **8** Margaret *of Scots:* **4** Mary *of Sheba:* **6** Balkis *of the Adriatic:* **6** Venice *of the Antilles:* **4** Cuba *of the East:* **7** Zenobia *of the fairies:* **3** Mab **7** Titania *of the gods:* **4** Hera, Juno, Sati *of the Nile:* **9** Cleopatra *of the North:* **9** Edinburgh *of the underworld:* **3** Hel **4** Hela **10** Persephone, Proserpina *Spanish:* **8** Isabella *Swedish:* **9** Christina

Queen Anne's Lace 6 carrot

Queen of Spades *author:* **7** Pushkin *composer:* **11** Tchaikovsky

Queensland *capital:* **8** Brisbane *explorer:* **4** Cook

queer 4 droll, funny, weird **6** qualmy, queasy **7** bizarre, curious, dubious, oddball, strange, unusual **8** doubtful, obsessed, peculiar, qualmish, singular **9** eccentric, laughable, squeamish **10** outlandish

quell 5 crush, quash **6** quench, squash

7 conquer, put down 8 overcome, suppress, vanquish 9 subjugate 10 extinguish

Quemoy's neighbor 4 Amoy

quench 3 end, out 4 raze, ruin, sate 5 allay, crush, douse, quash, quell, slake, wreck 6 lessen, put out, reduce, squash 7 appease, assuage, content, destroy, gratify, lighten, put down, relieve, satiate, satisfy, shatter 8 decimate, decrease, demolish, destruct, diminish, mitigate, suppress 9 alleviate, terminate 10 extinguish

quenelle 8 meatball 9 forcemeat

quern 4 mill

querulous 5 huffy, waspy 6 crying 7 fretful, peevish, pettish, wailing, waspish, weeping 8 petulant, snappish 9 bemoaning, deploring, fractious, irritable, lamenting 10 blubbering, whimpering

query 3 ask 4 quiz 7 concern, dubiety, examine, inquire, inquiry 8 mistrust, question 9 catechize, dubiosity, dubitancy, suspicion 10 skepticism 11 interrogate, questioning, uncertainty, uncertitude 13 interrogation, interrogatory

quest 3 bay 4 howl, hunt, seek, wail 5 probe 6 search 7 delving, inquiry, probing, pursual, pursuit, seeking, ululate 8 pursuing, research 9 cast about, ferret out, pursuance, search for, search out 11 inquisition

question 3 ask, nut 4 poll, quiz 5 demur, doubt, issue, query 7 debrief, dispute, examine, inquire, inquiry, problem, protest, suspect 8 demurral, demurrer, mistrust 9 catechize, challenge, objection 10 difficulty, puzzle over 11 interrogate, wonder about 12 hesitate over, remonstrance 13 interrogation, interrogatory

questionable 4 moot 5 vague 6 unsure 7 dubious, obscure 8 arguable, doubtful, mootable, unlikely, untrusty 9 debatable, equivocal, refutable, trustless, uncertain 10 disputable, fly-by-night, improbable, unreliable 11 problematic 12 undependable

questioning 5 query 6 show-me 7 curious, inquiry 8 aporetic 9 inquiring, quizzical, skeptical 11 incredulous, inquisitive, unbelieving 12 disbelieving, disquisitive 13 interrogation, interrogatory, investigative

quetzal 4 bird, coin 6 trogon

queue 3 row 4 file, line, rank, tier 5 braid

quibble 4 carp 5 argue, cavil 6 argufy, bicker, hassle 7 chicane, dispute, wrangle 8 pettifog, squabble 9 criticize

quick 3 apt 4 able, core, deft, fast, keen, pith, root, wise 5 acute, agile, apace, brisk, canny, fleet, hasty, heart, rapid, ready, sharp, slick, smart, swift 6 abrupt, adroit, center, clever, nimble, prompt, speedy, sudden 7 capable, flat-out, hastily, knowing, rapidly, swiftly 8 speedily 9 breakneck,

competent, dexterous, effective, effectual, impetuous, posthaste 10 expeditive, harefooted 11 expeditious, intelligent, quick-witted, sharp-witted 12 lickety-split, nimblewitted 13 expeditiously *combining form:* 3 oxy 5 tachy

quick bread 6 muffin 7 biscuit

quicken 4 goad, move, spur, stir, wake 5 hurry, liven, pique, rouse, speed 6 arouse, awaken, excite, hasten, induce, step up, vivify 7 actuate, animate, enliven, innerve, provoke, shake up, swiften 8 activate, energize, motivate, vitalize 9 galvanize, innervate, stimulate 10 accelerate, exhilarate, invigorate, vivificate

quickness 4 gait, pace 5 speed 8 celerity, legerity, rapidity, velocity 9 rapidness, swiftness

quicksand 3 bog 4 mire, syrt 6 syrtis

quicksilver 7 mercury 9 mercurial

quick-tempered 5 cross, ratty 6 cranky 7 peppery 8 choleric 9 irascible 10 passionate

quick-witted 3 apt, hep 4 keen, wise 5 acute, alert, canny, ready, sharp, slick, smart, witty 6 brainy, bright, clever, prompt 7 knowing 8 humorous 9 brilliant, facetious 11 intelligent, penetrating, penetrative

quid 3 cut, wad 4 chew 5 pound 9 sovereign

quiddity 6 trifle 7 essence, quibble

quidnunc see **rumormonger**

quiescent 4 calm 5 quiet, still 6 hushed, latent, placid, stilly 7 abeyant, dormant, halcyon, lurking 10 untroubled

quiet 4 calm, hush, idle, lull, stop 5 abate, allay, inert, plain, shush, still, tasty, whist 6 asleep, becalm, homely, hushed, lessen, placid, settle, shut up, silent, simple, sleepy, soothe, stilly, subdue 7 compose, halcyon, hushful, passive, silence, subdued 8 choke off, decrease, inactive, tasteful 9 cessation, noiseless, soundless, stillness 10 restrained, untroubled 11 inobtrusive, termination, tranquilize, unobtrusive

quietus 5 death, sleep 6 demise 7 decease, passing, silence 8 curtains 10 inactivity

quill 3 pen 5 spine, spool 6 bobbin 7 feather 8 plectrum

quill pig 9 porcupine

quilt 4 pouf, puff 8 bedcover 9 bedspread, comforter, eiderdown 11 counterpane *design:* 8 trapunto

quink 5 brant, goose

quintessence 4 pith, soul 5 stuff 6 bottom, marrow 7 epitome 8 last word, ultimate 9 substance 12 essentiality

quintessential 4 pith, soul 5 ideal, model, stuff 6 bottom, marrow 7 classic, essence, typical **9** classical, exemplary, substance **10** archetypal, prototypal **12** prototypical

quintillion *combining form:* **3** exa

quintillionth *combining form:* **4** atto

quintuple 8 fivefold

quintuplets *famous:* **6** Dionne

quip 3 gag **4** gibe, gird, jape, jeer, jest, joke **5** crack, fleer, flout, sally, scoff, sneer **8** drollery **9** wisecrack, witticism

quipster 3 wag, wit **5** comic, droll, joker **6** jester **8** comedian, funnyman, humorist, jokester

quirk 4 bend, quip **5** crook **6** groove, retort **7** channel **9** mannerism **11** peculiarity

quirt 4 whip

quisling 7 traitor **8** turncoat

quit 3 act, pay **4** bear, drop, exit, halt, stop **5** carry, cease, chuck, clear, leave, pay up **6** behave, demean, depart, deport, desert, desist, get off, resign, retire, secede, settle, square **7** abandon, comport, conduct, forsake, get away, satisfy, take off **8** clear off, give over, knock off, leave off, renounce, surcease, withdraw **9** discharge, liquidate, surrender, terminate, throw over **10** relinquish **11** discontinue

quite 3 all, far **4** just, well **5** fully, in all **6** in toto, purely, rather, wholly **7** all told, exactly, totally, utterly **8** all in all, cleverly, entirely, somewhat **9** perfectly **10** altogether, completely, thoroughly

quittance 6 amends **7** redress **8** reprisal **9** indemnity **10** recompense, reparation **11** restitution **12** compensation

quitter 4 funk **6** coward, craven, funker **7** chicken **8** poltroon **11** yellowbelly

quiver 4 beat **5** flash, gleam, glint, pulse, quake, shake, throb **6** dither, glance, shiver, tremor **7** glimmer, glisten, glitter, pulsate, shimmer, shudder, sparkle, tremble, twinkle, twitter **9** palpitate

quiverleaf 5 aspen

quiver tree 4 aloe

Quixote see **Don Quixote**

quixotic 8 fanciful, illusory, romantic **9** fantastic, visionary **10** chimerical, idealistic **11** impractical

quiz 3 ask **4** lout, mock, razz, twit **5** query, rally, scout, taunt **6** deride, oddity, zombie **7** examine, inquire, oddball **8** original, question, ridicule **9** catechize, character, eccentric **11** interrogate

quizzical 6 show-me **7** curious, probing **8** aporetic **9** searching, skeptical **11** incredulous, inquisitive, questioning, unbelieving **12** disbelieving

quizzing glass 7 monocle

quodlibet 6 debate, medley **8** fantasia, question

quoin 5 angle, facet, wedge **6** corner **7** lozenge **8** keystone, voussoir

quoit 4 ring, rope **5** cover **6** circle

quoits 4 game *peg:* **3** hob

quondam 3 old **4** late, once, past **6** bygone, former, whilom **7** onetime **8** sometime **9** erstwhile

quorum 7 council **8** majority

quota 3 cut, lot **4** bite, meed, part **5** share, slice **6** divide, parcel, ration **7** measure, partage, portion, prorate, quantum **9** allotment, allowance, apportion

quotation 3 bid **5** offer, price **7** excerpt, passage

quotation mark *French:* **9** guillemet

quote 4 cite, list, mark **5** refer **6** adduce, notice, set off **7** excerpt

quotidian 5 daily, plain, usual **7** diurnal, routine **8** everyday, ordinary, workaday **9** circadian **12** unremarkable

Quo Vadis *author:* **11** Sienkiewicz *character:* **4** Nero **5** Lygia, Peter **8** Vinicius **9** Petronius

R

Ra *son:* 6 Khonsu *wife:* 3 Mut
Raamah *father:* 4 Cush *son:* 5 Dedan, Sheba
Rabbi Ben Ezra author 8 Browning
rabbit 4 cony 5 bunny, coney, lapin
  female: 3 doe *fictional:* 5 Fiver, Hazel, Mopsy, Peter 6 Flopsy, Harvey 7 Thumper 8 Crusader, Ricochet 9 Bugs Bunny 10 Cottontail 11 Easter Bunny
  food: 5 salad 6 carrot 7 lettuce
rabbitlike 8 leporine
rabble 3 mob 4 many, raff, rout, scum 5 dregs, scurf, trash 6 masses, people, polloi, public, ragtag 7 doggery 8 canaille, populace, riffraff, unwashed, varletry 9 hoi polloi, other half, tag and rag 10 commonalty, roughscuff 11 bourgeoisie, proletariat, rank and file
rabble-rouser 9 demagogue
Rabelais character 9 Gargantua 10 Pantagruel
rabid 3 mad 4 keen, wild 5 crazy, ultra 6 crazed, insane 7 extreme, fanatic, frantic, furious, radical, zealous 8 demented, deranged, frenetic, frenzied, obsessed, ultraist 9 delirious, extremist 10 corybantic 12 enthusiastic
rabies 5 lyssa 11 hydrophobia
raccoon 5 panda 10 cacomistle *relative:* 5 coati 10 coatimundi
race 4 boil, bolt, clan, dash, drag, folk, gill, lash, rush, tear, type 5 breed, brook, chase, creek, fling, house, shoot, speed, stock, tribe 6 career, charge, course, endure, family, nation, people, runnel, stream 7 culture, kindred, lineage, Negroid, rivulet, running, variety 8 marathon 9 Caucasian, Mongoloid *auto:* 5 rally 6 rallye 9 grand prix *combining form:* 3 gen 4 geno, phyl 5 ethno, phylo
racecourse 4 oval, turf 5 track *combining form:* 4 drom 5 drome, dromo
racehorse *champion:* 5 Kelso 6 Forego 7 Man O' War 8 Affirmed, Citation 9 Riva Ridge 10 War Admiral 11 Forward Pass, Seattle Slew, Secretariat 12 Native Dancer
Rachel *father:* 5 Laban *husband:* 5 Jacob *servant:* 6 Bilhah *sister:* 4 Leah *son:* 6 Joseph 8 Benjamin
rachis 4 back 5 spine 8 backbone 9 vertebrae

rachitic 5 shaky 6 wobbly 7 rackety, rickety 10 rattletrap
rachitis 7 rickets
___ Rachmaninoff 6 Sergei
racing enthusiast 8 railbird
rack 3 try 4 pain 5 frame, wring 6 harrow, martyr 7 afflict, agonize, crucify, oppress, sawbuck, torment, torture 8 distress, sawhorse 9 persecute 10 excruciate
racket 3 din 5 babel 6 clamor, hubbub, jangle, tumult, uproar 8 brouhaha 10 hullabaloo 11 pandemonium
rack up 3 win 4 gain 5 reach, score 6 attain 7 achieve, realize 10 accomplish
raconteur 11 storyteller
racy 4 blue 5 broad, fiery, salty, shady, spicy, zesty 6 purple, risqué, snappy, wicked 7 gingery, peppery, piquant, pungent 8 off-color, spirited 10 suggestive
Radames' beloved 4 Aïda
radar image 4 blip
Raddai *brother:* 5 David *father:* 5 Jesse
radiance 5 glory 8 splendor
radiant 4 glad 6 bright, cheery, lucent 7 beaming, fulgent, lambent 8 cheerful, luminous 9 brilliant, effulgent, refulgent 12 incandescent
radiate 4 beam, burn 5 gleam, shine, strew 6 spread 7 diffuse, diverge 8 disperse 9 circulate, eradicate, propagate
radiation unit 3 rem, rep 8 roentgen
radiator 6 cooler, heater 11 transmitter
radical 4 acyl, root 5 basal, basic, pinko, rabid, rebel, ultra, vital 6 bottom 7 extreme, fanatic, primary 8 advanced, agitator, cardinal, inherent, nihilist, reformer, tolerant, ultraist 9 anarchist, essential, extremist, insurgent, intrinsic 10 separatist, subversive, underlying 11 broad-minded, fundamental, out-and-outer, progressive, reactionary 12 foundational, revolutional, secessionist 13 revolutionary *combining form:* 2 yl 3 oyl 5 ylene *mathematical:* 4 surd
radicle 4 root 5 radix 9 hypocotyl
radio 8 wireless *frequency range:* 8 waveband
radioactive debris 7 fallout
radium *symbol:* 2 Ra
radius 5 ambit, orbit, range, reach, scope,

sweep **6** extent **7** compass, purview
9 extension
radix 4 base, root **6** etymon, source
radon 5 niton **6** thoron **7** actinon **symbol:**
2 Rn
raffish 4 fast, wild **6** sporty **8** rakehell
12 devil-may-care
raffle 4 game **6** refuse **7** lottery, rubbish,
serrate **8** riffraff
raft 3 lot, mat **4** slew **5** balsa, float
rafter 4 beam, bird **10** flycatcher
rag 3 fun, jaw, kid, rib **4** fool, jive, joke,
josh, rail, rant, razz **5** baste, jolly, scold,
tease **9** newspaper
ragamuffin 3 bum **4** hobo, waif **5** tramp
6 loafer, orphan **7** ragshag, vagrant, wastrel **8** vagabond **9** scarecrow
rage 3 cry, fad, ire, mad **4** boil, burn, chic,
fume, fury, mode, rant, whim **5** anger,
craze, fancy, freak, mania, style, upset,
vogue, wrath **6** blow up, frenzy, furore,
seethe, vagary **7** bristle, caprice, conceit,
fashion, flare up **8** acerbity, acrimony,
asperity, boil over, crotchet, hysteria **9** agitation **10** dernier cri **11** indignation
ragged 4 rent, torn **5** dingy, faded, seedy
6 frayed, shabby **7** patched, shreddy, worn-
out **8** battered, frazzled, tattered
10 threadbare **11** dilapidated
raging 4 wild **5** dirty, rough **6** stormy
7 furious **8** blustery **9** turbulent **10** blustering **11** tempestuous
rags 5 dress **6** attire, shreds, things
7 apparel, clothes, raiment, ribbons, tatters
8 clothing **10** attirement **11** habiliments,
odds and ends
ragtag see rabble
ragwort 7 senecio **10** butterweed
Rahab husband: 6 Salmon **son: 4** Boaz
raid 3 rob **4** loot, sack **5** foray, harry,
onset, rifle, waste **6** harass, inroad, invade,
maraud, pirate, ravage **7** assault, despoil,
overrun, plunder **8** invasion, picaroon, spoliate **9** devastate, incursion, irruption,
onslaught, overswarm
raider 6 looter, pirate, sacker **7** forager,
ravager, spoiler **8** marauder, picaroon, pillager, ravisher **9** plunderer **10** freebooter
11 bushwhacker
rail 3 jaw **4** rate **5** scold **6** berate, revile
7 bawl out, upbraid **8** banister **10** balustrade, tongue-lash, vituperate
rail bird 4 sora
railing 8 banister **10** balustrade **part:**
8 baluster
raillery 6 satire **10** lampoonery
13 satiricalness
railroad 5 frame **9** iron horse **car:**
5 coach, diner, stock **6** hopper **7** caboose,
gondola, Pullman **engine: 10** locomotive
station: 5 depot **underground: 6** subway

worker: 6 porter **7** fireman **8** brakeman,
engineer **9** conductor **10** dispatcher
11 gandy dancer
raiment 4 clad, duds, garb, togs **5** array,
dress **6** attire, clothe, things **7** apparel,
clothes, garment **8** clothing, enclothe
10 attirement **11** habiliments
rain 6 mizzle, shower **7** drizzle **8** downpour **combining form: 4** hyet **5** hyeto,
ombro, pluvi **6** pluvia, pluvio **fine: 6** serein
rainbow 3 arc **4** iris **5** gamut **7** fantasy
8 illusion, phantasy **9** pipe dream **bridge:**
7 Bifrost **chaser: 9** visionary **combining
form: 4** irid **5** irido **goddess: 4** Iris
rainbow fish 5 guppy, trout **6** wrasse
raincoat 3 mac **4** mack **6** poncho
7 slicker **10** mackintosh
rain gauge 8 udometer
rain leader 9 downspout
rain tree 9 monkeypod
raise 2 up **4** abet, ante, grow, hike, jack,
jump, lift, pump, rear **5** boost, breed, build,
erect, exalt, hoist, put up **6** foment, gather,
incite, jack up, muster, pick up, stir up, take
up, upbear, uphold, uplift, uprear, whip up
7 bring up, collect, elevate, enhance, inflate,
produce, provoke **8** addition, assemble,
congress, heighten, increase **9** accession,
accretion, construct, cultivate, forgather,
increment, instigate, propagate, resurrect
10 congregate, rendezvous **12** augmentation **nap: 5** tease **spirits: 5** elate
raisin 7 sultana
raison d' ___ 4 être
raja 4 king **5** chief, ruler **6** prince
9 dignitary
rake 3 cad **4** beat, comb, grub, roué, tool
5 angle, scour, slope **6** forage, rascal,
search **7** coxcomb, playboy, ransack, rummage **8** finecomb **9** implement, libertine
10 profligate **11** inclination
rakehell 4 fast, wild **6** rascal, sporty **7** raffish **8** rascally **9** dissolute, libertine
10 licentious, profligate **12** devil-may-care
rake's look 4 ogle
Rake's Progress engraver 7 Hogarth
rakish see rakehell
rally 4 fire, lout, mock, quiz, race, razz, stir,
twit, wake, whet **5** harry, renew, rouse,
scout, taunt, tease, waken, worry **6** arouse,
awaken, bestir, deride, harass, kindle, muster, perk up, pick up **7** brace up, enliven,
marshal, recover, refresh, restore **8** mobilize, organize, ridicule **9** challenge, come
round, tantalize **10** invigorate
rallying cry 5 motto **6** slogan
ram 5 Aries, crash, drive, sheep, stick,
stuff **6** plunge, strike, thrust **7** jam-pack,
warship
Rama's wife 4 Sita
ramble 3 gad **4** roam, rove, turn, walk

5 drift, range, stray 6 depart, sprawl, stroll, wander 7 digress, diverge, excurse, meander, saunter, traipse 8 divagate, straggle 9 gallivant

rambunctious 5 rowdy 6 unruly 7 raucous 8 rowdyish 9 termagant, turbulent 10 boisterous, rowdydowdy, tumultuous

ramification 6 branch 8 offshoot 9 branching, outgrowth 11 consequence

Ramona author 7 Jackson

ramose 8 branched

ramp 5 apron, climb, storm 6 easing

rampage 4 orgy 5 binge, fling, spree 6 uproar 7 splurge, turmoil

rampageous 4 wild 6 unruly 7 riotous

rampant 4 rank, rife 6 ruling 7 current, popular, regnant 9 excessive, prevalent 10 immoderate, inordinate, widespread

rampart 7 bastion, bulwark, parapet 10 breastwork

ramshackle 7 rickety 10 dissipated 11 dilapidated

ram's mate 3 ewe

ranch 8 estancia, hacienda **worker:** 6 cowboy, gaucho 7 cowgirl, cowhand, cowpoke 10 cowpuncher

rancid 4 high, olid 5 fetid 6 putrid, smelly, whiffy 7 noisome, reeking 8 nidorous 10 malodorous

rancor 6 animus, enmity 9 animosity, antipathy, hostility, virulence 10 antagonism, bitterness

rancorous 4 evil 6 bitter, malign, wicked 7 hateful, hostile, vicious 8 spiteful, virulent 9 malicious, malignant, vitriolic 10 despiteful, malevolent 12 antagonistic

Rand, Ayn *novel:* 6 Anthem 12 Fountainhead 13 Atlas Shrugged

random 4 spot 7 aimless, anywise, unaimed 8 slapdash 9 desultory, haphazard, hit-or-miss, irregular, unplanned 10 accidental, contingent, designless, fortuitous, incidental, objectless 11 any which way, haphazardly, promiscuous, purposeless

randy 4 lewd 7 lustful, satyric 9 lecherous, libertine 10 lascivious, libidinous, licentious 11 incontinent

range 3 ken, row, run 4 area, bias, home, line, roam, rove, site, sort, span, tune, vary 5 align, ambit, drift, field, gamut, haunt, orbit, order, reach, realm, scope, space, stray, sweep, width 6 assort, circle, differ, domain, extend, extent, length, line up, matter, radius, ramble, sphere, spread, wander 7 compass, dispose, earshot, expanse, eyeshot, habitat, horizon, meander, purview, stretch 8 confines, locality, panorama, province, straggle, vicinity 9 fluctuate, gallivant, magnitude, territory

range finder 9 telemeter 10 tachymeter

rangy 5 lanky 6 gangly 7 spindly 8 gangling

rank 3 row 4 file, foul, line, lush, olid, rate, sort, tier 5 class, dirty, fetid, funky, grade, gross, grown, humid, order, place, queue, state, utter 6 assort, cachet, coarse, estate, filthy, lavish, putrid, rancid, smelly, smutty, status, string, vulgar 7 arrange, capital, dignity, echelon, footing, glaring, noisome, obscene, peerage, perfect, precede, profuse, rampant, raunchy, reeking, station, stature 8 absolute, capacity, classify, complete, evaluate, flagrant, gentrice, indecent, outright, position, positive, prestige, standing, stinking 9 character, downright, egregious, exuberant, loathsome, luxuriant, overgrown, repulsive, situation 10 consummate, malodorous, noticeable 11 consequence, conspicuous, outstanding, unmitigated *honorary:* 8 brevetcy *suffix:* 2 cy

rank and file 5 plebs 6 people, plebes 8 populace 9 commonage, commoners, common men, plebeians 10 commonalty 11 third estate

rankle 3 irk, vex 5 annoy 6 bother, fester, harass, obsess, plague 7 torment 8 irritate 9 aggravate 10 exasperate

ransack 3 rob 4 beat, comb, grub, loot, rake 5 rifle, scour 6 forage, search 7 plunder, relieve, rummage, stick up 8 finecomb

Ran's husband 5 Aegir

ransom 3 buy 4 free 6 redeem, regain 7 recover, release 8 liberate, retrieve

rant 3 jaw, rag 4 huff, rage, rail, rate, rave 5 mouth, orate, scold 6 berate 7 bawl out, bluster, bombast, declaim, fustian, soapbox 8 bloviate, harangue, perorate, rhetoric 10 vituperate 11 rodomontade

ranula 4 cyst

rap 3 bob, hit, wig 4 chat, chin, lick, skin, swat, talk, tunk, wipe, yarn 5 blame, knock, prose, swipe 6 rebuke 7 censure, chiding, condemn, reproof 8 causerie, denounce, reproach 9 criticize, reprehend, reprimand, reprobate 10 admonition, conference, denunciate, discussion

rapacious 6 fierce 8 ravening, ravenous 9 predative, predatory, raptorial, vulturine, vulturish, vulturous 10 gluttonous 11 predatorial

rapacity 5 greed 6 demand 7 avarice, avidity 8 cupidity, exaction, voracity

rape 4 cole, ruin 5 spoil 6 defile, ravage, ravish 7 debauch, despoil, outrage, plunder, seizure, violate 9 violation 10 spoliation

Rape of the Lock *author:* 4 Pope *heroine:* 7 Belinda

Raphael *birthplace:* 6 Urbino (Italy) *subject:* 7 Madonna *teacher:* 8 Perugino

rapid 4 fast 5 agile, brisk, fleet, hasty, quick, swift 6 nimble, speedy 7 hurried

9 breakneck, quickened 10 expeditive
11 expeditious

rapidity 4 gait, pace 5 speed 8 celerity, velocity 9 quickness, swiftness

rapids 6 dalles 10 whitewater

rapine 7 pillage, plunder 10 spoliation

Rappaccini's Daughter 8 Beatrice
author: 9 Hawthorne

rapport 5 unity 7 concord, harmony

rapscallion see **rascal**

rap session 6 confab, parley 7 palaver
8 colloquy 10 colloquium, conference, discussion

rapt 4 deep 6 intent 7 engaged
8 absorbed, immersed 9 engrossed, wrapped up 11 preoccupied

raptorial see **rapacious**

rapture 6 heaven 7 ecstasy 8 rhapsody
9 transport 13 seventh heaven

rara ___ 4 avis

rare 3 few 4 fine, thin 6 choice, dainty, scarce, seldom, select, subtle, unique 7 elegant, subtile, tenuous, unusual 8 delicate, singular, sporadic, superior, uncommon, unwonted 9 attenuate, exquisite, recherché 10 attenuated, infrequent, occasional, unfrequent, unordinary 11 exceptional
13 extraordinary

rarefied 4 thin 6 subtle 7 subtile, tenuous 9 attenuate 10 attenuated

rarefy 4 thin 9 attenuate

rarely 5 extra 6 little, seldom 7 unoften
9 extremely, unusually 10 hardly ever

raring 4 agog, avid, keen 5 eager
6 ardent 7 anxious, athirst, thirsty 9 impatient 10 breathless

rarity 6 oddity 7 fewness 8 scarcity

rascal 5 devil, knave, rogue, scamp 7 lowlife, skellum, villain 8 mischief, scalawag
9 miscreant, scoundrel, skeezicks 10 blackguard 11 rapscallion *Irish:* 8 spalpeen

rash 5 hasty, silly 6 abrupt, daring, madcap, plague, sudden, unwary, unwise
7 foolish 8 careless, epidemic, headlong, heedless, outbreak, reckless 9 audacious, daredevil, foolhardy, hotheaded, impetuous, imprudent, impulsive, unadvised, venturous 10 ill-advised, incautious, incogitant, indiscreet, mad-brained, unthinking
11 adventurous, injudicious, precipitate, precipitous, temerarious, thoughtless, venturesome 12 unconsidered 13 adventuresome, inconsiderate

rasp 4 file 5 grate 6 scrape, wheeze
7 scratch

raspberry 3 boo 4 bird, hiss, hoot, pooh, razz 5 bazoo 7 catcall 8 pooh-pooh

raspy 3 dry 4 harsh, rough 5 hoarse, snappy 7 grating, jarring, peevish, pettish, raucous 8 petulant, prickish, snappish
9 irritable

rat 3 pad 4 fink, heel, scab 5 louse
6 defect, desert, inform, rodent, snitch, squeak, squeal 7 caitiff, stoolie 8 apostate, defector, informer, recreant, renegade, renounce, runagate, squealer, turncoat
9 bandicoot, repudiate, turnabout 10 apostatize, tergiverse 11 stool pigeon *female:*
3 doe

rate 3 tab 4 cost, earn, rail, rank 5 assay, class, grade, merit, price, scale, scold, set at, value 6 assess, berate, charge, degree, revile, survey, tariff 7 apprize, bawl out, chew out, deserve, upbraid, valuate
8 appraise, classify, estimate, evaluate, price tag 10 proportion, tongue-lash

rather 5 quite 6 enough, fairly, in lieu, kind of, pretty, sort of 7 instead 8 passably, somewhat 9 averagely, tolerably 10 moderately, more or less 11 alternately 12 considerably 13 alternatively

ratify 5 enact 7 approve, confirm, endorse, license 8 accredit, sanction, validate

rating 4 mark, rank 5 grade 6 rebuke
8 standing

ratio 5 scale 7 percent 8 quotient
10 proportion

ratiocination 8 judgment, sequitur 9 inference, reasoning 10 conclusion

ration 4 dole, meed, part 5 allot, quota, share 6 assign, divide, parcel 7 measure, mete out, prorate, quantum 8 allocate, division 9 allotment, allowance 10 assignment 13 apportionment

rational 4 calm, cool, sane 5 lucid, sober, sound 6 normal, stable 7 logical, prudent
8 sensible 9 judicious 10 consequent, reasonable 11 circumspect, intelligent, level-headed

rationale 6 reason 11 explanation
13 justification

rationalize 7 explain, justify 10 account for

rattle 3 gab, jaw, yak 4 chat, faze
5 abash, addle, clack, run on, upset 6 babble, gabble 7 chatter, clatter, confuse, disturb, perplex 8 bewilder, confound, distract 9 discomfit, embarrass

rattlebrained 5 dizzy, giddy, silly
7 flighty 8 skittish 9 frivolous 11 empty-headed

rattling 4 very 6 damned, mighty 7 parlous 8 snapping, spanking, whacking, whopping 9 extremely 11 exceedingly

ratty 5 cross, testy 6 cranky, shabby, tetchy, touchy 7 peppery, unkempt 8 choleric 9 irascible, temperish

raucous 3 dry 5 gruff, harsh, rough, rowdy 6 hoarse, unruly 7 brusque, grating, jarring, squawky 8 rowdyish, strident 9 termagant, turbulent 10 boisterous, disorderly,

rowdydowdy, stridulent, stridulous, tumultuous **11** rumbustious

raunchy 4 foul **5** dirty, messy, nasty
6 coarse, filthy, sloppy, smutty, unneat,
untidy, vulgar **7** obscene, unkempt **8** ill-
kempt, indecent, slipshod, slovenly
10 disheveled

ravage 3 rob **4** loot, raze, ruin, sack
5 crush, harry, havoc, spoil, strip, waste,
wreck **6** devast, devour, invade **7** despoil,
destroy, overrun, pillage, plunder, ransack,
scourge **8** deflower, demolish, desolate,
encroach, spoliate, trespass **9** depredate,
desecrate, devastate, overpower, overthrow, overwhelm

rave 4 rant **5** drool, mouth, orate
7 declaim, enthuse, soapbox **8** bloviate,
harangue, perorate, rhapsody
10 rhapsodize

ravel 5 snarl **6** muddle, tangle **7** perplex
8 entangle **10** complicate

ravelings 4 lint

Ravel work 6 Bolero

raven 3 jet **4** bird, ebon, inky, prey
5 black, ebony, jetty, sable **7** despoil, plunder **9** pitch-dark **10** pitch-black *combining
form:* **5** corax *relating to:* **7** corvine

Raven, The *author:* **3** Poe *refrain:*
9 Nevermore

ravenous 6 hungry **7** starved **8** edacious,
famished, starving **9** rapacious, voracious

ravine 3 cut, gap **4** gulf, pass **5** abyss,
chasm, cleft, clove, gorge, gulch, gully,
notch **6** arroyo, canyon, clough, coulee,
defile, gutter, nullah **7** crevice, fissure
8 barranca, barranco, crevasse *Mt. Washington's:* **9** Tuckerman

ravish 3 rob **4** rape **5** spoil **6** defile
7 despoil, outrage, pillage, violate
8 deflower, entrance, overcome **9** deflorate,
enrapture, transport

raw 4 nude, rude **5** crass, crude, fresh,
green, gross, naked, rough, young **6** callow,
coarse, impure, native, unclad, unhewn,
unripe, vulgar **7** uncouth, untried **8** buff-
bare, stripped, uncooked, unformed,
ungraded, unsorted, untaught, unversed
9 au naturel, inelegant, roughhewn, run-of-
mine, unclothed, undressed, unmatured,
unrefined, untutored **10** stark-naked, unfinished, unpolished, unseasoned **11** unfashioned, unpracticed **13** inexperienced

rawboned 4 bony, lank, lean **5** gaunt,
lanky, spare **6** skinny **7** angular, scraggy,
scrawny

ray 4 beam, beta **5** alpha, gamma, gleam,
light, manta, shaft, shine, shoot, skate,
trace **6** radius, streak **7** radiate, sawfish,
torpedo **8** particle **9** irradiate, radiation

raze 4 ruin, undo **5** wrack, wreck

6 unmake **7** destroy, unbuild, unframe
8 decimate, demolish

razor 3 cut **5** shave

razz 3 kid, rag, rib **4** fool, jest, joke, josh,
lout, mock, quiz, twit **5** jolly, rally, scout,
taunt **6** banter, deride, heckle **8** ridicule;
(see also **raspberry**)

re 4 as to **5** as for **7** apropos **9** as regards,
regarding **10** as respects, concerning,
respecting **13** with respect to

reach 2 go **3** get, ken, run, win **4** buck,
come, gain, hand, make, move, pass, show,
sway **5** ambit, get at, get in, orbit, range,
scope, score, sweep, touch **6** affect, arrive,
attain, extend, extent, rack up, radius, show
up, turn up **7** achieve, compass, contact,
horizon, purview, realize, stretch
8 approach **9** extension, influence
10 accomplish

react 6 behave **7** respond

____ **reaction 5** chain **7** nuclear
8 chemical

reactionary 4 fogy, tory **5** blimp, right
7 diehard, fogyish, old-line, radical **8** mossback, orthodox, rightist, royalist **11** bitter-
ender, right-winger, standpatter
12 conservative

reactionist see **reactionary**

reactivate 5 renew **6** revive **8** rekindle,
renovate, retrieve, revivify **9** resurrect
10 revitalize **11** resuscitate

read 3 say **4** mark, scan, show **5** proof
6 peruse, record **7** dictate **8** indicate, register *inability to:* **8** dyslexia

readable 7 legible

reader 6 lector, primer **8** bookworm
9 anthology

readily 4 well **6** easily, freely **7** lightly
12 effortlessly

readiness 4 ease **5** skill **7** address, fluency, prowess, sleight **8** alacrity, dispatch,
facility, goodwill **9** dexterity, eloquence
10 expedition, volubility **11** promptitude

reading 7 version **9** rendition

readjust 6 modify **7** reorder **8** reorient
9 rearrange, reshuffle **10** reorganize
11 reconstruct, reorientate

ready 3 apt, fit, fix, get, set **4** fain, gird,
live, make, prep **5** adept, brace, prime,
prone, psych, quick, steel **6** active, expert,
make up, minded, primed, prompt
7 dynamic, fortify, prepare, skilled, willing
8 adjusted, disposed, imminent, inclined,
masterly, prepared, skillful **9** qualified
10 proficient, strengthen **11** predisposed

real 4 true **5** being, pucka, pukka, sound,
valid **6** actual, honest **7** certain, genuine,
sincere **8** bona fide, existing **9** authentic,
necessary, undoubted, unfeigned, veridical
10 undeniable **12** indisputable

realism 6 verism **7** verismo

realistic 4 hard, sane 5 sober, sound
6 astute, earthy, shrewd 8 lifelike, rational,
sensible, veristic 9 practical, pragmatic
10 hard-boiled, hardheaded, reasonable,
unromantic 11 down-to-earth, nonaca-
demic, pragmatical, utilitarian 12 matter-of-
fact 13 unsentimental

reality 4 fact 5 truth

realize 3 win 4 gain 5 fancy, image,
reach, score, think 6 attain, rack up, vision
7 achieve, feature, imagine 8 conceive,
envisage, envision 10 accomplish

realm 5 orbit, range, scope, sweep
6 empire, extent, radius 7 compass, purview *suffix:* 3 dom

reanimation 7 rebirth, revival 10 renascence, resurgence 11 renaissance
12 risorgimento

reap 5 glean 6 garner, gather, thresh
7 harvest 8 ingather

rear 4 back, hind, lift, ramp, rump, seat, tail
5 after, breed, build, erect, fanny, hoist,
nurse, put up, raise, set up 6 behind, bottom, foster, hinder, pick up, retral, take up,
uphold, uplift 7 bring up, elevate, hind end,
nurture, upraise 8 backside, buttocks, hindmost 9 construct, posterior

rear end 4 rump, seat, tail 5 fanny
6 behind, bottom 8 backside, buttocks,
derriere

rearmost 4 last 5 final 6 latest, latter
7 closing 8 eventual, terminal, ultimate
10 concluding

rearrange see **readjust**

rearward 4 back 9 posterior

Rea Silvia, Rhea Silvia *father:* 7 Numitor *son:* 5 Remus 7 Romulus

reason 3 why, wit 4 mind, nous 5 cause,
infer, proof, think 6 ground, motive, sanity,
senses, spring, whyfor 7 account, reflect
8 argument, cogitate, logicize, lucidity, occasion, persuade, saneness 9 cerebrate, inference, intellect, rationale, soundness, speculate, wherefore 10 antecedent, deliberate
11 determinant, explanation 13 consideration, justification, ratiocination,
understanding

reasonable 3 low 5 cheap, sound
6 modest, undear 7 logical, low-cost, popular 8 discreet, moderate, rational, sensible,
uncostly 9 low-priced, temperate, unextreme 10 affordable, consequent, controlled, restrained 11 inexpensive, intelligent

reasoning 5 logic

reasonless 3 mad 4 daft 5 crazy
6 crazed, insane 7 cracked, invalid, lunatic
8 demented, deranged 9 bedlamite, illogical, sophistic 10 fallacious, irrational
11 nonrational

rebate 5 taper 6 lessen, reduce, refund
7 dwindle 8 decrease, diminish, discount,

taper off 9 abatement, deduction, drain
away, reduction 11 subtraction

Rebecca *beloved:* 7 Ivanhoe *father:*
5 Isaac

Rebekah *brother:* 5 Laban *father:*
7 Bethuel *husband:* 5 Isaac *nurse:* 7 Deborah *son:* 4 Esau 5 Jacob

rebel 6 anarch, mutiny, revolt, rise up
7 radical 8 attacker, debunker, frondeur,
mutineer, opponent, revolter, ultraist
9 adversary, anarchist, assailant, extremist,
insurgent, insurrect 10 antagonist, iconoclast, malcontent 11 rise against 13 revolutionary, revolutionist

rebellion 6 mutiny, revolt 8 sedition
10 revolution 12 insurrection

rebellious 8 mutinous 9 alienated,
estranged, insurgent 11 disaffected
13 insubordinate

rebirth 7 revival 8 metanoia 10 conversion, renascence, resurgence 11 reanimation, renaissance 12 resurrection,
risorgimento

rebound 7 recover 8 ricochet, snap back

rebuff 5 repel 6 reject 7 fend off, hold off,
keep off, repulse, ward off 8 stave off

rebuke 3 rap, wig 5 chide, scold, scorn
6 earful, lesson, monish 7 chiding, lecture,
reproof, reprove, tick off 8 admonish, call
down, reproach, scolding 9 reprimand, talk-
ing-to 10 admonition 12 admonishment,
dressing down 13 tongue-lashing

rebut 5 break, evert, repel 6 refute 7 confute, fend off, hold off, keep off, repulse,
ward off 8 confound, disprove, stave off
10 controvert, disconfirm

recalcitrant 4 wild 6 unruly 8 opposing,
stubborn, untoward 9 fractious, obstinate,
resisting 11 indomitable, intractable

recall 4 cite, lift, stir 5 educe, evoke,
renew, rouse, unsay, waken 6 abjure,
arouse, awaken, elicit, memory, remind,
repeal, retain, revive, revoke 7 bethink,
extract, rescind, restore, retract, reverse
8 forswear, palinode, remember, take back,
withdraw 9 anamnesis, dismantle, recollect,
reinstate, reminisce 10 retrospect 12 recollection, reminiscence

recant 5 unsay 6 abjure 7 retract 8 forswear, palinode, take back, withdraw

recap 4 tire 7 retread

recapitulate 5 sum up, unite 9 summarize

recapitulation 3 sum 5 sum-up 6 précis,
resumé 7 epitome, summary 9 summing-
up

recede 3 ebb 4 back 5 abate, close,
taper 6 depart, lessen, reduce, retire
7 dwindle, regress, retract, retreat
8 decrease, diminish, fall back, withdraw
9 drain away 10 retrograde, retrogress

receipts 6 income 7 revenue

receive 4 take 5 admit 6 take in
received 5 sound 8 accepted, orthodox
9 canonical 10 sanctioned 13 authoritative
receiver 5 donee, fence 9 treasurer
recent 3 new 4 late 5 fresh, novel 6 latest, modern 8 neoteric 9 new-sprung
10 newfangled 11 modernistic 12 newfashioned *combining form:* 2 ne 3 cen,
neo 4 caen, cene, ceno 5 caeno
receptacle 5 torus 6 cupule 8 placenta
9 container 10 repository *laundry:* 6 hamper *narrow:* 6 trough
receptive 4 open 8 amenable, friendly,
suasible, swayable 9 acceptant 10 accessible, open-minded, responsive 11 persuadable, persuasible, suggestible, sympathetic
recess 5 niche 6 alcove 7 adjourn 8 dissolve, prorogue 9 prorogate, terminate
Recessional author 7 Kipling
recessive 8 retiring 9 withdrawn
recherché 3 new 4 rare 5 fresh, novel
6 choice, dainty, exotic, select 7 elegant,
unusual 8 delicate, original, superior,
uncommon
recidivate 5 lapse 7 relapse 9 backslide
recipe 7 formula 12 prescription
reciprocal 4 mate, twin 5 match 6 double, fellow 9 companion, duplicate 10 coordinate *combining form:* 6 allelo *prefix:*
5 inter
reciprocate 5 repay 6 retort, return
7 requite 8 exchange, serve out 9 retaliate 10 compensate, recompense
11 interchange
recital 5 story 9 discourse, narration,
recountal 10 recounting 11 description
combining form: 3 log 5 logue
recite 4 tell 5 chant, count, state 6 number, relate, report 7 narrate, recount
8 describe, rehearse 9 enumerate
reckless 4 rash, wild 5 brash, hasty
6 daring, madcap 8 carefree 9 audacious,
daredevil, desperate, foolhardy, hotheaded,
uncareful, venturous 10 ill-advised, incautious, mad-brained 11 adventurous, temerarious, venturesome 13 adventuresome,
inconsiderate, irresponsible
reckon 3 add, put, sum 4 call, cast, deem,
foot, view 5 count, guess, judge, lot on,
place, total 6 bank on, cipher, figure, number, regard, rely on 7 account, build on,
compute, count on, lot upon, surmise, trust
in, trust to 8 bank upon, consider, depend
on, estimate, rely upon 9 calculate, enumerate 10 conjecture, depend upon
11 approximate, calculate on
reckoning 3 tab 4 bill 5 score 7 account,
invoice 8 figuring 9 ciphering, statement
10 arithmetic, estimation 11 calculation,
computation
reclaim 7 recover, restore 9 restitute

10 rejuvenate 11 recondition, reconstruct
12 rehabilitate
recline 3 lie, tip 4 cant, heel, lean, list, rest,
tilt 5 slant, slope 6 lounge, repose 7 lie
down 10 stretch out
reclining 4 flat 5 prone 9 decumbent,
prostrate, recumbent 10 procumbent
recluse 6 hermit 7 eremite 8 cenobite,
hermetic, secluded, solitary 9 anchorite,
seclusive 10 cloistered 11 sequestered
female: 7 ancress 9 anchoress
reclusive 8 eremitic, reserved, solitary
10 antisocial 11 standoffish
12 misanthropic
recognition 6 credit 9 awareness
10 cognizance *combining form:* 5 gnosy
6 gnosia, gnosis
recognize 4 know, note, spot 5 admit,
agree, place 6 finger, notice, recall, remark
7 observe 8 diagnose, identify, pinpoint,
remember 11 acknowledge, determinate,
distinguish
recoil 3 shy 4 balk, duck 5 dodge, quail,
quake, shake, start, stick, waver, wince
6 blanch, blench, falter, flinch, shrink,
swerve 7 shudder, squinch, stickle, tremble 8 hesitate, reel back
recollect 4 cite, stir 5 rally, rouse, waken
6 arouse, awaken, recall, remind, retain,
revive 7 bethink 8 remember 9 reminisce
10 retrospect
recollection 6 memory, recall 9 anamnesis 11 remembrance 12 reminiscence
recommence 5 renew 6 pick up, reopen,
resume, take up 7 restart 8 continue
recommend 4 hail, tout 6 advise, commit,
kudize, praise 7 acclaim, applaud, consign,
counsel, entrust 8 advocate 10 compliment
recommendation 6 advice 8 approval
9 character, reference 11 credentials,
endorsement, testimonial
recompense 3 pay 5 award, grant,
repay 6 accord, amends, offset, return,
reward 7 balance, redress, requite 8 reprisal 9 indemnify, indemnity, quittance, reimburse, retaliate, vouchsafe 10 compensate,
remunerate, reparation 11 reciprocate,
restitution
reconcile 3 fit 4 suit, tune 5 adapt
6 adjust, attune, square, tailor 7 conform
8 quadrate 9 harmonize, integrate 10 coordinate, proportion 11 accommodate
recondite 4 dark, deep, hard 5 heavy,
runic 6 mystic, occult, orphic, secret
7 cryptic, learned, obscure 8 abstruse, academic, anagogic, esoteric, hermetic, mystical, pedantic, profound 9 difficult, enigmatic, scholarly, sibylline 10 cabalistic
recondition 3 fix 4 do up, mend 5 patch
6 doctor, repair, revamp 7 rebuild, reclaim,

restore **8** overhaul **9** restitute **10** rejuvenate **12** rehabilitate

reconnoiter 5 probe, scout

reconsider 5 amend **6** review, revise **7** correct, draw off, rethink, re-treat, reweigh, sleep on **9** reexamine, think over **10** reevaluate

reconstruct 3 fix **4** do up, mend **5** patch **6** doctor, repair, retool, revamp **7** rebuild, reclaim, reorder, restore **8** overhaul, readjust, reorient **9** rearrange, reshuffle, restitute **10** rejuvenate, reorganize **12** rehabilitate

record 3 say **4** date, disc, mark, read, show **6** annals **7** archive, journal **8** archives, document, register **9** chronicle *combining form:* **4** gram **5** graph *of a meeting:* **7** minutes *of past events:* **7** history *of proceedings:* **4** acta *ship's:* **3** log **7** logbook

recorder 5 flute

record player 5 phono **9** turntable **10** phonograph

recount 4 tell **5** state **6** recite, relate, report **7** narrate **8** describe, rehearse

recoup 6 regain **7** get back, recruit **8** retrieve **9** repossess

recourse 5 shift **6** refuge, resort **7** stopgap **9** expedient, makeshift **10** expediency

recover 4 heal, mend **5** rally, renew, rewin **6** offset, perk up, redeem, regain, resume, retake, revive **7** balance, get back, improve, rebound, reclaim, recruit, refresh, restore **8** reoccupy, retrieve, snap back **9** come round, reacquire, recapture, repossess, restitute **10** bounce back, compensate, convalesce, recuperate, rejuvenate **12** rehabilitate

recreant 3 rat **5** false **6** coward, untrue **7** unloyal **8** apostate, defector, disloyal, renegade, turncoat **9** faithless, turnabout **10** perfidious, traitorous, unfaithful

recreate 4 play **5** amuse, renew, sport **6** divert **7** disport, refresh, restore **9** entertain

recreation 3 fun **4** ease, play **5** mirth, sport **6** frolic, repose **7** disport, leisure, rollick **9** amusement, diversion **13** entertainment

recrudesce 5 react, recur, renew **6** return, revert, revive **7** reoccur

recruit 4 hire, mend **5** raise, renew **6** enlist, muster, novice, recoup, regain, repair, rookie **7** draftee, get back, rebuild, recover, refresh, restore **8** beginner, enlistee, freshman, neophyte, newcomer, renovate, retrieve **9** fledgling, novitiate, repossess **10** apprentice, tenderfoot

rectifier 4 tube **5** diode **8** detector

rectify 4 mend **5** amend, emend, right **6** repair **7** correct, rebuild

rectitude 6 virtue **7** honesty, probity **8** goodness, justness, morality **9** rightness **11** uprightness **13** righteousness

rector 6 pastor **9** clergyman **10** headmaster

rectory 5 manse **9** parsonage

recumbent 4 flat **5** prone **9** prostrate, reclining

recuperate 4 gain, mend **6** look up, perk up **7** improve **10** convalesce

recur 6 repair, repeat, resort, return, revert **7** iterate **8** turn back **9** reiterate **10** recrudesce

recurrent see **recurring**

recurring 8 periodic **9** alternate **10** isochronal, periodical **11** isochronous **12** intermittent *combining form:* **6** ennial

red 4 laky, puce, ruby **5** gules, ocher, rouge, ruddy **6** bloody, cerise, florid, wanton **7** carmine, flushed, glowing, oxblood, radical, rubious, scarlet, stammel, vermeil **8** flagrant, sanguine **9** carnation *combining form:* **4** rhod **5** pyrrh, pyrro, rhodo **6** erythr, pyrrho **7** erythro

Red 6 commie **9** Bolshevik, Communist

redact 4 edit **5** frame **6** revise **7** compose

Red and the Black author 8 Stendhal

red ape 9 orangutan

red arsenic 7 realgar

red-backed parrot 7 grassie

red-backed sandpiper 6 dunlin **10** blackheart

Red Badge of Courage author: **5** Crane *hero:* **7** Fleming (Henry)

red-bellied snipe 9 dowitcher

red benjamin 9 birthroot

redbird 8 cardinal **13** summer tanager

redbird cactus 7 jewbush

red blindness 10 protanopia

red blood cell 11 erythrocyte

red-blooded 5 lusty, vital **7** dynamic **8** vigorous **9** energetic, strenuous

redbreast 4 knot **5** robin

red-breasted snipe 9 dowitcher

redbuck 6 impala

Redburn author 8 Melville

red carp 8 goldfish

red chalk 4 bole **6** ruddle

red cobalt 9 erythrite

red copper ore 7 cuprite

Red Cross founder: **6** Barton (Clara) *Knight:* **6** George

red currant 4 goya

redden 3 rud **4** glow, pink, rose, ruby **5** blush, color, flush, rouge, ruddy **6** mantle, pinken, rubify, rubric, ruddle **7** crimson **11** incarnadine

red dog 5 dhole, flour **8** card game

redecorate 9 refurbish

redeem 3 buy **4** free **5** loose **6** make up, offset, ransom, set off, unbind **7** balance, manumit, release, unchain **8** atone for, liberate, outweigh **10** compensate

redeemer 6 savior **7** messiah, saviour

redemption 6 ransom **7** release **9** atonement, expiation, salvation **11** deliverance

redeye 4 rudd **7** whiskey **8** rock bass, warmouth **10** copperhead

redfish 4 drum **6** salmon **11** channel bass

red grouper 5 negre

red grouse 8 moorbird, moorfowl, moor game

red hickory 6 pignut **9** mockernut

red hind 7 graysby **8** cabrilla

red-hot 2 up **5** fiery **6** ardent, fervid **7** abreast, blazing, boiling, burning, flaming, glowing **8** scalding, sizzling, up-to-date **9** au courant, scorching **10** blistering, passionate, sweltering **11** impassioned

red hot cattail 8 chenille

red Indian paint 9 bloodroot

red ink 7 deficit

red inkberry 8 pokeweed

red ironbark 5 mugga **8** eucalypt

red iron ore 8 hematite

red lauan 8 tanguile

red lead 6 minium

red lead ore 8 crocoite

red-legged crow 6 chough

red-legged plover 9 turnstone

red-letter 6 rubric **7** notable **8** nameable **9** memorable **10** noteworthy, observable

red-light district 5 levee, stews **10** tenderloin

red mite 7 chigger

red-neck 4 hick, rube **5** yokel **6** rustic **7** bumpkin, hayseed, peasant **9** hillbilly **10** provincial **12** backwoodsman

red-necked gazelle 5 addra

redo 5 renew **6** revamp **7** remodel, restyle **8** refinish, renovate **9** reproduce, restyling **10** redecorate, repetition

red ocher 4 bole

redolence 4 balm **5** aroma, scent, spice **7** bouquet, incense, perfume **9** fragrance

redolent 5 balmy, spicy, sweet **6** aromal, savory **7** perfumy **8** aromatic, fragrant, perfumed **9** ambrosial, remindful **11** reminiscent

redouble 4 rise **5** mount, rouse **6** deepen **7** enhance, magnify **8** heighten **9** intensify

redoubt 4 fort **7** citadel **8** fastness, fortress **9** stronghold

redoubtable 5 awful, famed, great **6** famous **7** eminent, fearful **8** dreadful, horrible, horrific, renowned, shocking, terrible **9** appalling, frightful, prominent **10** celebrated **11** illustrious **13** distinguished

redound 6 accrue **7** conduce **10** contribute

red pine 4 rimu **10** Douglas fir

Red Planet 4 Mars

redpoll 6 linnet

redraft 6 revamp, review, revise, rework **7** restyle, revisal, rewrite **8** rescript, revision, work over **9** recension

redrawer 6 winder

redress 5 annul, venge **6** amends, avenge, negate **7** revenge **8** negative, reprisal **9** balancing, cancel out, frustrate, indemnity, quittance, vengeance, vindicate **10** counteract, neutralize, offsetting, recompense, reparation **11** restitution, retaliation **12** compensation, countercheck

red roe 5 coral

redroot 7 alkanet, pigweed

red sable 8 kolinsky

red silk cotton 5 simal

red silver ore 9 proustite **11** pyrargyrite

red snapper 6 rasher

red sorrel 7 roselle

red squirrel 9 chickaree

red-stalk aster 6 cocash

reduce 3 cut **4** bate, clip, diet, pare, slow **5** abase, break, crush, lower, shave, slash, taper **6** debase, defeat, demote, humble, lessen, rebate, recede, subdue, weaken **7** conquer, cripple, curtail, cut back, cut down, declass, deflate, degrade, demerit, disable, disrate, dwindle **8** bear down, beat down, decrease, diminish, discount, disgrade, enfeeble, mark down, roll back, slim down, step down, taper off, unweight, vanquish **9** downgrade, drain away, humiliate, overpower, scale down, subjugate, undermine **10** depreciate, slenderize

reductio ad ____ 8 absurdum

reduction 6 rebate **7** cutback, cutdown **8** discount, markdown **9** abatement **11** downgrading *combining form:* **5** lyses (plural), lysis

redundancy 8 pleonasm, tumidity, verbiage **9** inflation, prolixity, tautology, turgidity **10** flatulence, periphrase, roundabout **11** periphrasis, superfluity

redundant 5 extra, spare, windy, wordy **6** prolix **7** diffuse, surplus, verbose **9** iterating **10** long-winded, palaverous **11** reiterating, repetitious, superfluous **13** supernumerary

red vitriol 9 bieberite, colcothar

redware 7 boccaro

red whelk 6 buckie

redwing 7 gadwall

redwing blackbird 6 maizer

redwood 5 rohun **7** amboyna, sequoia **8** mahogany **10** Scotch pine

reed 4 pipe **5** arrow

reedy 4 slim, thin **6** slight, stalky, twiggy **7** slender, squinny, tenuous **9** attenuate

reef 4 lode, vein **7** bioherm

reek 4 funk **5** smell, stink **6** stench

reeking 4 rank 5 fetid, funky, fusty
6 putrid, rancid, smelly 7 noisome
10 malodorous

reel 3 bob 4 spin, sway, swim, turn
5 lurch, swing, waver, weave, whirl
6 career, falter, teeter, topple, totter, wobble 7 stagger, stumble 8 titubate

reestablish 5 renew 6 recall, revive
7 restore 9 reinstate 11 reintroduce

reevaluate 6 review 7 rethink, re-treat,
reweigh 9 think over 10 reconsider

reeve 4 ruff 6 thread 8 official
10 magistrate

reexamine see **reevaluate**

refashion 4 turn, vary 5 alter 6 change,
modify

refection 4 feed, meal 6 repast

refectory 10 dining hall

refer 4 cite, name 5 apply, quote 6 advert,
advise, allude, assign, charge, credit, hand
in, impute, insert, submit 7 ascribe, bring
up, mention, specify 8 accredit, instance,
point out 9 attribute

referee 3 ump 5 judge 6 umpire
7 adjudge, arbiter 9 arbitrate 10 adjudicate, arbitrator

reference book 5 atlas 6 manual
7 almanac 10 dictionary 12 encyclopedia

reference guide 5 index

referendum 4 poll

refine 6 polish, smooth 7 improve, perfect

refined 4 nice 6 subtle, urbane 7 genteel
8 cultured, delicate, finespun, polished, précieux, well-bred 9 distingué 10 cultivated

refinement 5 couth, grace 6 finish, polish 7 culture, dignity, suavity 8 breeding,
civility, courtesy, elegance, urbanity
10 politeness 11 cultivation

reflect 4 echo 5 glass, image, study, think,
weigh 6 mirror, ponder, reason 7 sparkle
8 cogitate 9 cerebrate 10 deliberate

reflecting 7 pensive 8 lustrous 10 cogitative, meditative, ruminative, thoughtful
light: 8 relucent *suffix:* 6 escent

reflective 7 pensive 8 thinking 9 pondering 10 cogitative, meditative, ruminative,
thoughtful

reflux 6 ebbing 9 condenser, returning

reform 5 amend, emend 7 correct,
improve

Reformation leader 4 Knox 6 Calvin,
Luther 7 Zwingli

reformatory 3 pen 4 jail 6 cooler, lockup,
prison 7 borstal 8 stockade
12 penitentiary

refractory 6 mulish 8 perverse, stubborn
9 obstinate 10 bullheaded, headstrong,
self-willed, unyielding 11 intractable, stiff-
necked

refrain 4 curb, deny, halt, keep, stop

5 check 6 arrest, chorus 7 forbear, inhibit
8 hold back, withhold 9 interrupt

refresh 4 rest 5 amuse, renew 6 divert,
update, vivify 7 animate, enliven, quicken,
restore 8 recreate, renovate 9 modernize,
stimulate 10 rejuvenate

refresher 5 drink, tonic 6 bracer
9 stimulant

refrigerant 3 ice 5 freon 7 ammonia,
cooling 13 carbon dioxide

refrigerator 6 fridge, icebox 9 condenser

refuge 4 port 5 cover, haven, shift 6 asylum, covert, harbor, resort, shield 7 hideout,
retreat, shelter, stopgap 8 hideaway, immunity, recourse, resource 9 expedient, harborage, makeshift, sanctuary

refugee 2 DP 5 exile 6 emigré 7 evacuee 8 emigrant, fugitive 10 expatriate

refulgent 6 bright 7 beaming, radiant
8 luminous 9 brilliant

refund 5 repay 6 rebate 9 reimburse,
repayment

refurbish 5 renew 6 update 7 restore,
retouch 8 renovate 9 modernize
10 rejuvenate

refuse 3 jib 4 deny, dump, junk, nill
5 dreck, offal, spurn, swill, trash, waste
6 debris, kelter, litter, lumber, reject, scraps,
spilth 7 decline, dismiss, garbage, rubbish
8 disallow, dustheap, keep back, riffraff, turn
down, withhold 9 reprobate, repudiate,
sweepings 10 disapprove

refutation 8 disproof, elenchus

refute 5 break, evert, rebut 8 confound,
disprove 10 controvert, disconfirm

regain 6 recoup 7 get back, recover,
recruit 8 reassume, reoccupy, retrieve
9 repossess *possession:* 7 replevy
8 replevin

regal 6 august, kingly 7 queenly, stately,
sublime 8 glorious, imposing, kinglike,
majestic, princely, splendid 9 monarchal,
sovereign 10 monarchial 11 magnificent,
monarchical, resplendent

regale 5 feast 6 dinner, spread 7 banquet

regalia 5 cigar 6 finery 8 frippery 9 full
dress

Regan *father:* 4 Lear *husband:* 8 Cornwall *sister:* 7 Goneril 8 Cordelia

regard 4 care, deem, heed, mark, note,
rate, view 5 assay, favor, honor, value
6 admire, assess, esteem, homage, notice,
reckon, remark 7 account, concern, prizing,
respect, valuing 8 approval, consider, estimate, interest 9 attention, curiosity, deference 10 admiration, cherishing, cognizance,
estimation, observance, solicitude
11 approbation, carefulness, heedfulness,
observation 12 appreciation, satisfaction
13 consciousness, consideration *as perfect:* 8 idealize

regardful 6 arrect 7 duteous 9 advertent, attentive, intentive, observant, observing

regarding 4 as to, in re 5 about, anent 6 anenst 7 apropos 10 as respects 13 with respect to

regatta 4 race 6 fabric 7 liberty

regenerate 6 reform, revive 9 reproduce

regent 5 ruler 8 governor 9 professor

regicide's victim 4 king

regimen 4 rule 9 governing 10 government

region 4 area, belt, part, walk, zone 5 field, tract 6 domain, sector, sphere 7 demesne, terrain 8 province, vicinity 9 bailiwick, territory 12 neighborhood *elevated:* 8 highland

regional 5 local 9 localized 10 provincial

register 3 say 4 list, mark, read, roll, show 6 enroll, record 7 catalog 8 indicate

regnant 4 rife 6 master, ruling 7 current, popular 9 paramount, prevalent, sovereign 10 prevailing, widespread

regress 6 revert 9 throw back

regret 3 rue, woe 4 care 5 demur, grief, mourn, qualm 6 bemoan, bewail, grieve, lament, repent, sorrow 7 anguish, apology, deplore, scruple 9 deprecate, heartache, penitence 10 affliction, contrition, disapprove, heartbreak 11 compunction

regretful 5 sorry 8 contrite, penitent 9 repentant 10 apologetic 11 attritional, penitential

regrettable 4 dire 6 woeful 8 grievous 10 afflictive, calamitous 11 distressing, unfortunate 13 heartbreaking

regular 3 set 4 even 5 fixed, gross, typic, usual, utter 6 common, normal, steady 7 equable, general, natural, orderly, perfect, settled, typical, uniform 8 absolute, complete, constant, methodic, ordinary, outright, positive 9 clocklike, customary, downright, prevalent 10 consummate, methodical, systematic 11 commonplace, unmitigated 12 run-of-the-mill

regulate 3 fix 5 order 6 adjust, temper, tune up 7 arrange 8 organize 9 methodize 11 systematize

regulation 3 law 4 rule 5 canon, edict 6 curfew, decree 7 precept, statute 8 decretum 9 ordinance, prescript

regulator 8 governor

Rehabiah *father:* 7 Eliezer *grandfather:* 5 Moses

rehabilitate 7 reclaim, recover, restore 11 recondition

rehearse 5 drill, state 6 recite, relate, report 7 iterate, narrate, recount 8 describe, exercise, practice 10 run through

Rehoboam *father:* 7 Solomon *kingdom:* 5 Judah 6 Israel *mother:* 6 Naamah

reign 4 king, rule, sway 6 govern 7 prevail 8 dominate, domineer, overrule 11 predominate 12 preponderate

reimburse 3 pay 5 repay 7 balance, requite 9 indemnify 10 compensate, remunerate

rein 4 cool 7 collect, compose, control, repress, smother 8 restrain, suppress

reinforce 4 prop 5 super 6 pillar 7 augment, bolster, enlarge, fortify, sustain 8 buttress, energize, increase, multiply 10 invigorate, strengthen

reinstate 5 renew 6 recall, return, revive 7 put back, replace, restore 8 give back 11 reestablish

reintroduce 5 renew 6 recall, revive 7 restore 11 reestablish

reinvestment 8 plowback

reiterate 5 renew, resay 6 repeat 7 reprise

reject 4 cast, jilt, junk, shed 5 debar, scrap, spurn 6 rebuff, refuse, slough 7 cashier, decline, discard, dismiss, exclude, shut out 8 jettison, throw out, turn down 9 eliminate, reprobate, repudiate, throw away 10 disapprove

rejoice 3 joy 5 exult, glory 7 gladden

rejoin 5 reply 6 answer, come in, retort 7 respond

rejoinder 5 reply 6 answer, retort, return 7 respond 8 antiphon, response

rejuvenate 5 renew 7 reclaim, recover, refresh, restore 9 modernize, refurbish 11 recondition, reconstruct

Rekem's father 6 Hebron

rekindle 5 renew 6 revive 8 renovate, retrieve, revivify 9 resurrect 10 reactivate, revitalize 11 resuscitate

relate 4 join, link, tell, yoke 5 apply, unite 6 assign, bear on, couple, credit, depict, detail, impute, render, report 7 connect, divulge, express, itemize, pertain, recount 8 bear upon, describe, disclose 9 appertain, pronounce

related 4 akin 5 alike 6 agnate, allied 7 cognate, connate, germane, kindred 8 incident 9 analogous, identical, pertinent 10 connatural 11 consanguine *by marriage:* 7 affined

relating to *suffix:* 2 al, an, ar, ic 3 ean, ese, ial, ile, ine, ist, ory 4 ical 5 ative, istic 6 itious 7 istical

relation 3 kin 7 kinsman 9 kinswoman *on father's side:* 6 agnate *on mother's side:* 5 enate

relative 2 ma, pa 3 kin, mom, sib, sis, son 4 aunt, mama, nana, papa, sibb 5 madre, mamma, mammy, momma, niece, pappy, pater, poppa, uncle 6 agnate, cousin, father, mother, nephew, parent, sister 7 brother, cognate, kinsman, sibling 8 daughter, grandson 9 dependent, kins-

woman **10** contingent, grandchild
11 approximate, conditional, grandfather,
grandmother, grandparent
13 granddaughter

relatives 7 kinfolk **8** kinfolks

relax 4 ease, loll, rest **5** loose, slack **6** lollop, loosen, lounge, rest up, unbend,
unwind **7** ease off, slacken **8** loosen up
9 untighten

relaxation 4 ease, rest **6** repose **7** leisure **9** amusement **11** assuagement
12 requiescence

relaxed 4 mild, soft **5** loose, slack
6 breezy, casual, dégagé, gentle **7** lenient,
sinuous, unfussy **8** flexuous, informal
9 easygoing **10** unreserved **11** low-pressure

release 4 emit, free, vent **5** issue, loose,
unfix, yield **6** acquit, loosen, pardon, ransom, resign, unbind, uncage, uncoil **7** give
off, give out, manumit, unchain, unleash
8 liberate, throw off, unfetter, untether
9 discharge, exculpate, exonerate, surrender, take out on, unshackle **10** emancipate
conditional: **6** parole

relegate 5 exile, expel, refer **6** banish,
charge, commit, credit, deport **7** commend,
confide, consign, entrust, expulse
8 accredit, displace, hand over, turn over

relent 3 ebb **4** fall, wane **5** abate, let up
7 die away, die down, ease off, slacken,
subside **8** moderate

relentless 4 grim **5** cruel, rigid **6** dogged,
fierce, mortal, strict **7** adamant, inhuman
8 obdurate, rigorous **9** ferocious, stringent,
unbending **10** implacable, inexorable, inflexible, ironfisted, unyielding **11** unflinching
12 unappeasable

relevant 3 apt, fit **5** ad rem **6** allied,
proper **7** apropos, cognate, fitting, germane, weighty **8** apposite, material, pointful, suitable **9** allowable, important, pertinent **10** admissible, applicable
11 applicative, applicatory, appropriate

reliable 4 safe **5** sound, tried, valid
6 cogent, proven, secure, trusty **7** certain,
telling **8** accurate, apposite, attested, inerrant, unerring, verified **9** authentic, confirmed, validated **10** dependable **11** trustworthy **12** tried and true

reliance 4 hope **5** faith, stock, trust

relic 5 token, trace **6** shadow, trophy
7 memento, vestige **8** keepsake, memorial,
reminder, souvenir **11** remembrance

relict 5 widow **8** residual

relief 3 aid **4** ease, hand, help, lift **6** assist,
succor **7** comfort, secours, support
8 easement **9** allayment, softening
10 assistance, lightening, mitigation **11** alleviation, appeasement, assuagement

relieve 3 aid, rob, sub **4** ease, help, loot

5 allay, quiet, rifle, spare, spell **6** excuse,
exempt, fill in, lessen, let off, reduce, soften,
solace, soothe, subdue, supply, temper
7 absolve, appease, assuage, benefit, comfort, console, lighten, mollify, plunder, qualify, ransack, stick up, subvene **8** decrease,
diminish, dispense, mitigate, moderate, palliate, take over **9** alleviate, discharge

religion 4 cult, sect **5** creed, faith **6** belief,
church

religious 3 nun **4** holy, just, monk, true
5 godly, moral, noble, pious **6** devout,
priest, sister, votary **7** ethical, staunch,
upright, votress **8** faithful, monastic, votaress, votarist **9** pietistic, prayerful, steadfast
foot-washing ceremony: **6** maundy *offering:* **8** oblation *order member:* **5** friar
8 cenobite

relinquish 4 cast, cede, quit, shed
5 forgo, leave, waive, yield **6** desert, forego,
give up, resign **7** abandon, discard, forbear,
forsake, lay down, throw up **8** abdicate,
abnegate, hand over, lay aside, renounce
9 sacrifice, surrender

relish 4 like, tang, zest **5** enjoy, flair, gusto,
heart, sapor, savor, smack, taste **6** admire,
flavor, liking, loving, palate **7** leaning
8 enjoying, penchant, pleasure, sapidity
9 delight in, diversion, enjoyment, prejudice
10 appreciate, propensity **11** delectation

relucent 7 radiant, shining **10** reflecting

reluctant 3 shy **4** wary **5** chary, loath
6 afraid, averse **7** uneager **8** backward,
cautious **9** unwilling **10** indisposed
prophet: **5** Jonah

rely on 5 trust **7** count on **8** depend on

remain 4 bide, stay, wait **5** abide, tarry
6 linger **7** survive **11** stick around

remainder 6 excess **7** balance, residue,
surplus **8** leavings, leftover, residual,
residuum

remains 4 body, mort **5** stiff **6** corpse,
debris, fossil **7** balance, cadaver, carcass,
residue **8** leavings, residual, residuum

remark 3 see **4** heed, note **5** glass
6 notice, postil, saying **7** comment, discern,
mention, observe **8** exegesis, perceive,
scholium **9** assertion, attention, statement,
utterance **10** animadvert, annotation, cognizance, commentary, commentate, exposition **11** observation *in a play:* **5** aside
witty: **7** epigram

remarkable 4 rare **6** signal, unique
7 salient, strange, unusual, weighty **8** peculiar, singular, striking, uncommon,
unwonted **9** arresting, arrestive, important,
momentous, prominent **10** unordinary
11 conspicuous, exceptional, outstanding,
significant, uncustomary **13** extraordinary

_____ Remarque 5 Erich (Maria)

remedial 6 curing **7** healing **8** curative,

sanative, sanatory **9** vulnerary
11 restorative

remedy 4 cure, drug, heal **6** elixir, physic
7 cure-all, nostrum, panacea **8** antidote,
biologic, medicant, medicine, specific
9 medicinal, pharmacon **10** corrective,
medicament, medication **11** counterstep

remember 4 cite **5** educe, evoke **6** elicit,
recall, relive, retain **9** recollect
10 retrospect

remembrance 4 gift **5** favor, relic, token
6 memory, recall, trophy **7** memento, present **8** keepsake, memorial, souvenir
9 anamnesis **12** recollection

remind 3 jog **4** warn **5** alert **6** advise,
prompt **8** admonish

reminder 4 hint, memo, note, sign **5** relic,
token **6** notice, trophy **7** gesture,
memento, warning **8** keepsake, memorial,
souvenir **10** admonition, expression, indication, intimation, memorandum, suggestion

reminisce see **remember**

reminiscence 6 memory, recall **9** anamnesis **12** recollection

remise 4 cede, deed **5** alien **6** assign,
convey **8** alienate, make over, sign over,
transfer

remiss 3 lax **4** lazy **5** slack **8** careless,
derelict, fainéant, indolent, slothful **9** negligent **10** behindhand, delinquent, neglectful,
regardless **12** disregardful

remit 4 send, ship, stay **5** defer, delay,
route **6** excuse, hold up, pardon, put off,
shelve **7** address, condone, consign, forgive, forward, hold off **8** dispatch, postpone

remnant 4 heel, rest **7** balance, oddment,
residue **8** leavings, residual, residuum

remodel 6 revamp **11** reconstruct

remonstrance 5 demur **7** protest
8 demurral, demurrer, question **9** challenge,
objection

remonstrate 4 kick **5** fight **6** combat,
except, object, oppose, resist **7** protest
9 withstand

remonstration see **remonstrance**

remora 4 clog, drag **11** shark sucker,
sucking fish

remorse 3 rue **6** regret **7** penance **9** attrition, penitence, penitency **10** contrition,
repentance **11** compunction
12 contriteness

remorseful see **regretful**

remorsefulness see **remorse**

remote 3 far, off **4** back, slim **5** aloof,
small **6** casual, far-off, secret, slight **7** devious, distant, faraway, obscure, outside,
retired, slender **8** detached, far-flung, frontier, lonesome, off-lying, outlying **9** incurious, uncurious, unsettled, withdrawn
10 negligible, outlandish **11** indifferent, out-
of-the-way, unconcerned **12** uninterested

combining form: **3** tel **4** dist, pale, tele
5 disto, palea, paleo **6** palaeo, palaio

remotest 6 utmost **7** extreme, outmost
9 outermost, uttermost **11** furthermost

remove 4 doff, ship, skim **5** douse, erase,
purge, shift **6** efface, put off, unseat **7** blot
out, cast off, disturb, expunge, extract, take
off, take out **8** dislodge, displace, displant,
evacuate, take away, throw off, transfer,
withdraw **9** clear away, dislocate, eliminate,
eradicate, extirpate, liquidate **10** obliterate
11 exterminate *from office:* **6** depose
hair: **8** depilate *prefix:* **2** de

removed 3 far **5** alone, aloof, apart **6** far-
off, secret **7** devious, distant, faraway, isolate, obscure **8** detached, far-flung, isolated, lonesome, off-lying, outlying

remunerate 3 pay **5** award, grant, repay
6 accord **7** guerdon, requite **9** indemnify,
reimburse, vouchsafe **10** recompense

remunerative 6 paying **7** gainful **9** lucrative **10** profitable, well-paying, worthwhile
11 moneymaking **12** advantageous

Remus *brother:* **7** Romulus *father:*
4 Mars *mother:* **10** Rhea Silvia *slayer:*
7 Romulus

renaissance see **rebirth**

renal 7 nephric

rend 3 rip **4** rive, tear **5** split **6** cleave,
divide

render 3 put **4** limn, turn **5** image
6 depict, govern, return **7** execute, picture,
portray **8** carry out, describe **9** delineate,
interpret, represent, translate, transpose
10 administer **12** administrate *suffix:* **2** en

rendering 7 version **10** paraphrase
11 restatement, translation

rendezvous 4 date **5** haunt, raise, tryst
6 gather, muster, resort **7** collect, hangout,
purlieu **8** assemble, congress **9** forgather
10 congregate, engagement **11** appointment, assignation

rendition 7 reading, version **11** translation

renegade 3 rat **5** rebel **7** heretic **8** apostate, defector, deserter, forsaker, recreant,
turncoat **9** abandoner, insurgent, turnabout **10** iconoclast, schismatic
13 tergiversator

renege 5 welsh **6** cry off, resile **7** back off,
back out **8** back down **9** backpedal

renew 4 mend **5** fresh, resay **6** pick up,
recall, reform, reopen, repair, repeat,
resume, revise, revive, take up, update
7 correct, freshen, iterate, rebuild, rectify,
refresh, remodel, reprise, restart, restore
8 continue, make over, rekindle, retrieve,
revivify **9** modernize, refurbish, reinstate,
reiterate, resurrect **10** ingeminate, reactivate, recommence, rejuvenate, revitalize
11 reestablish, reintroduce

rennet 8 abomasum

renounce 3 rat 4 quit, turn 5 chuck, demit 6 defect, desert, resign 7 abandon, forsake 8 abdicate, disclaim 9 repudiate, throw over 10 apostatize, tergiverse

renovate 5 clean 6 revive 7 cleanse, refresh, restore 8 rekindle, retrieve, revivify 9 modernize, refurbish, resurrect 10 revitalize

renown 4 fame 5 éclat, kudos 6 repute 8 eminence, prestige 9 celebrity, notoriety 10 prominence, prominency, reputation 11 distinction, preeminence

renowned 5 famed, great 6 famous, lauded, signal 7 eminent, notable, praised 8 extolled 9 acclaimed, prominent 10 celebrated, celebrious 11 illustrious, outstanding 13 distinguished

rent 3 let 4 hire, rift, torn 5 break, lease, split 6 breach, schism, sublet 7 charter, fissure, mangled, rupture 8 fracture, sublease

rental 4 flat 5 rooms, suite 8 lodgings, tenement 9 apartment

renter 6 lessee

renunciation 6 denial 8 forgoing, yielding 9 eschewing, sacrifice, surrender 10 abjurement, forbearing, self-denial 11 forswearing

reopen 5 renew 6 pick up, resume, take up 7 restart 8 continue 10 recommence

reorder 6 retool 7 permute 8 readjust 9 rearrange, reshuffle 11 reconstruct 12 reconstitute

reorganization 7 shake-up 8 overturn, turnover

reorganize 6 retool 7 rebuild, refound 8 readjust, renovate, resettle 9 rearrange, reshuffle 10 regenerate 11 reconstruct, reestablish 12 reconstitute

reorient 6 retool 8 readjust 9 rearrange, reshuffle

repair 3 fix, hie, run 4 case, do up, fare, mend, pass, trim, turn, wend 5 apply, order, patch, recur, refer, shape 6 doctor, estate, fettle, kilter, push on, resort, revamp, travel 7 fitness, journey, proceed, rebuild, service 8 overhaul 11 recondition

reparation 6 amends, reward 7 redress 8 requital 9 atonement, indemnity, quittance 10 adjustment, recompense, settlement

repartee 3 wit 5 humor, irony 6 banter, retort, satire 7 riposte, sarcasm 8 backchat, badinage, comeback, response, snipsnap 9 rejoinder 10 back answer, persiflage

repast 4 feed, meal 9 refection

repay 5 award 6 accord, offset 7 balance, requite 9 indemnify, reimburse 10 compensate, recompense, remunerate

repeal 4 lift, void 6 recall, revoke 7 rescind, reverse 9 dismantle

repeat 4 copy, echo, harp, ring 5 chime, ditto, quote, recap, recur, renew, rerun, resay 6 parrot, recite, rehash, relate, retell, return 7 imitate, iterate, recount, restate 8 hash over, rehearse 9 duplicate, reiterate 12 recapitulate

repeater 7 firearm 10 recidivist

repeating 7 iterant

repel 4 buck 5 fight, rebut 6 combat, oppose, rebuff, reluct, resist, revolt, sicken 7 contest, disgust, dispute, fend off, hold off, keep off, ward off 8 nauseate, stave off

repellent 4 foul, vile 5 nasty 7 noisome 8 aversive, kindless, ungenial 9 invidious, loathsome, obnoxious, offensive, revolting, revulsive 10 disgusting 11 uncongenial

repent 3 rue 6 regret 7 deplore

repentance 3 rue 4 ruth 7 remorse 9 penitency 10 contrition 11 compunction 12 contriteness

repentant see **regretful**

repetition 4 copy 7 recital 8 iterance 9 rehearsal

rephrase 6 reword 7 restate

repine 4 fret, fuss, kick, wail 6 murmur 8 complain 10 discontent

replace 5 renew, shift 6 change, recoup, regain, return 7 put back, recover, restore 8 give back, retrieve, supplant, take back 9 reinstate, restitute, supersede

replacement 3 sub 6 fill-in 7 stand-in 9 alternate, surrogate 10 substitute 11 locum tenens, pinch hitter, succedaneum

replenish 5 refit, renew, stock 7 restore

replete 4 full, rife 5 alive, awash 6 jammed, loaded 7 brimful, crammed, crowded, stuffed, teeming 8 brimming, swarming, thronged 9 abounding, chockfull 11 overflowing

replica 4 copy 5 ditto 6 carbon 9 duplicate, facsimile 10 carbon copy

replicate 4 copy

reply 6 answer, come in, rejoin, retort, return 7 respond 8 response 9 rejoinder

report 3 cry 4 buzz, chat, dirt, fame, name, news, talk, word 5 brief, on-dit, rumor, state, story 6 advice, canard, gossip, impart, murmur, notice, recite, relate, review, rumble, speech, tattle 7 account, chatter, comment, hearsay, history, narrate, prating, recount, scandal, tidings, version 8 advisory, bulletin, chitchat, describe, rehearse 9 character, chronicle, grapevine, narrative, small talk, statement

reporter 7 newsman 10 journalist *inexperienced:* 3 cub

repose 3 lie 4 rest 7 leisure, lie down, recline, renewal 10 relaxation, stretch out 11 refreshment, restoration 12 requiescence

repository 5 depot, store 7 arsenal
8 magazine 10 storehouse
repossess see **regain**
reprehend 3 rap 4 rate, skin 5 blame,
chide, knock, scold 6 berate, rebuke 7 censure, condemn, upbraid 8 admonish,
denounce 9 criticize 10 denunciate
reprehensible 5 amiss 6 guilty, sinful,
unholy 8 blameful 11 blameworthy
13 demeritorious
represent 4 body, copy, limn, mean,
show 5 draft, image 6 denote, depict,
embody, mirror, relate, render, sketch, typify 7 display, exhibit, express, imitate, narrate, outline, picture, portray, realize, signify,
suggest 8 describe 9 body forth, delineate,
epitomize, exemplify, interpret, personate,
personify, symbolize 10 illustrate, substitute 11 emblematize, impersonate,
personalize
representation 6 symbol 7 picture
8 likeness 9 portrayal 11 portraiture
representative 4 case 5 agent, envoy,
ideal, model, typal, typic 6 deputy, sample
7 classic, example, typical 8 delegate, emissary, instance, monotype, sampling, specimen 9 catchpole, classical, exemplary
10 archetypal, prototypal 11 case history
12 illustrative, prototypical
repress 4 cool 5 shush 6 muffle 7 collect,
compose, control, smother, squelch
8 restrain
repression 4 curb 5 check 7 choking,
control, subdual 8 crushing, quashing,
quelling, stifling 9 clampdown, crackdown,
quenching, restraint, squashing
10 smothering
reprieve 7 respite
reprimand 3 rap, wig 5 chide 6 lesson,
monish, rebuke 7 chiding, tick off 8 admonish, call down 10 admonition
12 admonishment
reprisal 6 amends 7 redress, revenge
8 avenging, revanche 9 indemnity, quittance, vengeance 10 avengement, recompense 11 counterblow, retaliation,
retribution
reprise 5 renew, resay 7 iterate
9 reiterate
reproach 3 rap, wig 5 blame, chide,
taunt 6 lesson, monish, rebuke 7 censure,
chiding, upbraid 8 admonish, call down
9 discredit 10 admonition
12 admonishment
reprobate 3 bad, rap 4 evil, heel, skin
5 blame, knock, spurn, wrong 6 refuse,
reject, sinful, wicked 7 censure, condemn,
decline, dismiss, immoral, lowlife, vicious, villain 8 denounce, roperipe, turn down
9 abandoned, criticize, dissolute, miscreant,

scoundrel 10 blackguard, disapprove, iniquitous, licentious 12 unprincipled
reproduce 4 bear, copy 5 beget, breed
7 imitate 8 generate, multiply 9 duplicate,
procreate, propagate 11 reduplicate
reproduction see **replica**
reproductive cell 3 egg 4 ovum
5 sperm, spore 6 gamete 7 agamete
reproof 3 rap, wig 6 rebuke 7 chiding
8 scolding 10 admonition
12 admonishment
reprove 4 warn 5 blame, chide, scold
6 lesson, monish, punish, rebuke 7 censure, chasten, correct, counsel, tick off
8 admonish, call down, lambaste 9 criticize
reptile 5 snake 6 caiman, cayman, gavial,
lizard, turtle 7 tuatara 8 hatteria, tortoise
9 crocodile, sphenodon **combining form:**
6 herpet 7 herpeto **extinct:** 8 dinosaur
republic 5 state 6 nation **Africa:** 4 Chad,
Mali, Togo 5 Benin, Congo, Egypt, Gabon,
Ghana, Kenya, Niger, Sudan, Zaire
6 Angola, Gambia, Guinea, Malawi, Rwanda,
Uganda, Zambia 7 Algeria, Burundi, Comoros, Liberia, Namibia, Senegal, Somalia,
Tunisia 8 Botswana, Cameroon, Djibouti,
Tanzania 9 Cape Verde 10 Ivory Coast,
Madagascar, Mauritania, Mozambique
11 Sierra Leone 12 Guinea-Bissau **Asia:**
4 Iran, Iraq, Laos 5 China, India, Syria,
Yemen 6 Turkey 7 Vietnam 8 Maldives,
Mongolia, Pakistan, Sri Lanka 9 Indonesia,
Singapore 10 Bangladesh, North Korea,
South Korea 11 Philippines **Central America:** 4 Cuba 5 Haiti 6 Panama 7 Ecuador
8 Honduras 9 Costa Rica, Guatemala, Nicaragua **Europe:** 5 Italy 6 France, Greece,
Poland 7 Albania, Austria, Finland, Germany, Hungary, Iceland, Ireland, Romania,
Rumania 8 Bulgaria, Portugal 9 San Marino
Pacific: 5 Nauru 8 Kiribati **South America:** 4 Peru 5 Chile 6 Brazil, Guyana
7 Bolivia, Uruguay 8 Colombia, Paraguay
9 Argentina, Venezuela
Republican Party 3 GOP **mascot:**
8 elephant
Republic author 5 Plato
repudiate 4 deny 5 spurn 6 defect,
desert, disown, refuse, reject 7 abandon,
decline, disavow, discard, dismiss, forsake
8 disallow, disclaim, renounce, turn down
10 apostatize, disapprove, tergiverse
repugnance 4 hate 5 hatred, horror
8 aversion, loathing 11 abomination,
detestation
repugnant 4 foul, vile 5 alien, nasty
6 creepy, horrid 7 foreign, noisome 8 aversive, gruesome 9 abhorrent, extrinsic, invidious, loathsome, obnoxious, offensive,
repulsive, revolting, revulsive 10 disgusting
repulse 5 rebut 6 rebuff, reluct, revolt,

sicken **7** disgust, fend off, hold off, keep off, ward off **8** nauseate, stave off

repulsion see **repugnance**

repulsive see **repugnant**

reputation 4 fame, name **5** éclat **6** credit, renown, weight **8** prestige **9** authority, celebrity, character, influence, notoriety

reputed 8 putative, supposed **9** estimable **10** creditable **11** conjectural, respectable, suppositive **12** hypothetical, supposititious

request 3 ask, sue **4** pray **5** apply **6** appeal, desire, invite **7** solicit **8** entreaty, petition

Requiem for a Nun author 8 Faulkner

requin 5 shark **8** cub shark, man-eater

require 3 ask **4** call, lack, need, take, want **5** claim, crave, exact **6** demand **7** call for, solicit **11** necessitate

required 6 needed **9** mandatory **10** compulsory, obligatory **12** compulsatory

requirement 4 must, need, want **6** demand **9** condition, essential, necessity **10** sine qua non

requisite 3 due **4** just, must **5** right **6** needed **7** condign, merited, needful **8** deserved, rightful, suitable **9** condition, essential, necessity **10** sine qua non **11** appropriate **12** precondition

requisition 4 call **5** claim, exact **6** demand **7** solicit **9** challenge, postulate

requital 7 revenge **8** avenging, revanche **9** vengeance **10** avengement **11** counterblow, retaliation, retribution

requite 3 pay **5** repay **6** return **7** content, revenge, satisfy **9** indemnify, reimburse **10** compensate **11** reciprocate

reredos 6 screen **7** brazier **9** partition

rescind 4 lift **6** recall, repeal, revoke **7** reverse

rescue 4 free, save **6** ransom, redeem, regain **7** deliver, manumit, recover, release **8** conserve, liberate, preserve, retrieve **9** extricate **10** emancipate **11** disentangle **12** disembarrass

research 5 probe, quest **7** delving, inquest, inquiry, probing **11** inquisition **13** investigation

resect 6 cut out, excise **9** extirpate

resemblance 6 simile **7** analogy **8** affinity, likeness, parallel **9** alikeness **10** comparison, similarity, similitude

resemble 5 favor **8** look like, simulate

resembling *combining form:* **4** form **5** iform *suffix:* **2** ar **3** ful **4** eous, itic

resentful 4 sore **6** bitter, piqued, sullen **7** envious, jealous **9** grudgeful

resentment 4 huff, miff **5** pique, spite **6** animus, malice, rancor **7** dudgeon, ill will, offense, umbrage **9** animosity, antipathy, malignity **10** antagonism, malignancy

reservation 5 terms **7** proviso, strings

reserve 4 book, fund, hold, keep **5** hoard, stock, store **6** detain, engage, retain, supply **7** backlog, bespeak, keep out, nest egg **8** contract, hold back, keep back, withhold **9** inventory, preengage, stockpile

reserved 3 shy **5** aloof, close **6** formal, modest, offish, silent **7** bashful, distant, limited **8** eremitic, modified, reticent, solitary, taciturn **9** diffident, qualified, reclusive, withdrawn **10** antisocial, unsociable **11** ceremonious, close-lipped, constrained, standoffish, tight-lipped **12** closemouthed

reservoir 5 hoard, stock, store **7** backlog, nest egg **9** inventory, stockpile

reside 3 lie **4** live **5** dwell, exist **6** endure, inhere, occupy, people, tenant **7** consist, hang out, inhabit **8** continue, domicile

residence 4 home **5** abode, house **8** domicile, dwelling **9** occupancy **10** morancy, habitation, occupation, settlement **11** inhabitancy **12** inhabitation

resident 5 liver **7** denizen, dweller **8** habitant, occupant **9** indweller **10** inhabitant

residential area 5 exurb **6** suburb **7** exurbia **8** suburbia

resident of *suffix:* **2** er **3** ese, ier, ite, yer

residual 4 heel **7** balance, remains, remanet, remnant **8** leavings **9** remainder

residue 3 ash **4** heel **7** balance, remains, remanet, remnant **8** bone char, leavings **9** bone black, remainder **11** animal black *from honey:* **7** slumgum *metallic:* **4** slag *mineral:* **4** calx

resign 4 cede, drop, quit **5** demit, leave, waive, yield **6** give up, submit **7** abandon **8** abdicate, hand over, renounce **9** surrender, terminate **10** relinquish

resignation 7 modesty **8** meekness, patience **9** lowliness **10** compliance, conformity, humbleness **11** forbearance, longanimity, patientness **12** acquiescence

resigned 7 passive **8** yielding **10** submissive **11** acquiescent, unresistant, unresisting

resile 6 recede, recoil **7** rebound, retract, retreat

resilient 4 airy **6** bouncy, supple, whippy **7** buoyant, elastic, springy, stretch **8** flexible, stretchy, volatile **9** expansive

resin 4 balm **5** copal, damar, roset **6** dammar **7** acrylic, copaiba *aromatic:* **6** balsam, mastic **8** sandarac *fossil:* **8** retinite *fragrant:* **4** tolu **5** elemi **6** storax, styrax **7** ladanum **8** labdanum, olibanum *gum:* **4** kino **5** myrrh **7** benzoin **8** bdellium *medicinal:* **6** guaiac **8** guaiacum *of an insect:* **3** lac *synthetic:* **8** phenolic *used by bees:* **8** propolis

resist 4 balk, buck, defy, duel, foil, stem **5** check, fight, repel **6** assail, attack, baffle,

combat, hinder, impugn, oppose, thwart
7 assault, contest, counter, dispute, gainsay 8 obstruct, traverse 9 frustrate, withstand 10 contradict, contravene

resistance unit 3 ohm

resistor 8 rheostat

resolute 3 set 4 bent, fast, true 5 loyal 6 ardent, intent, steady 7 decided, settled, staunch 8 constant, decisive, faithful, stubborn 9 allegiant, obstinate, steadfast 10 determined 12 pertinacious

resolution 4 guts 5 heart, pluck, spunk 6 mettle, spirit 7 courage 8 analysis, decision, firmness 11 decidedness 13 dauntlessness, determination, purposiveness

resolve 3 fix, rid 4 rule, work 5 break, clear, purge 6 decide, dispel, figure, settle, unfold 7 analyze, clear up, dissect, unravel, work out 8 conclude, decipher, decision, disabuse, disperse, firmness, unriddle 9 anatomize, breakdown, decompose, determine, dissipate, puzzle out 11 decidedness 13 determination, purposiveness

resonant 3 fat 4 deep, full, loud, rich 5 noisy, round 6 mellow, rotund 7 beating, booming, orotund, pulsing, ringing 8 enhanced, plangent, powerful, profound, sonorous, sounding, strident 9 pulsating, thrilling, throbbing 10 clangorous, heightened, stentorian, thundering, thunderous 11 intensified 13 reverberating

resort 2 go 3 den, inn, spa, use 4 nest, turn 5 apply, haunt, haven, hotel, lodge, recur, refer, shift 6 affect, devote, direct, employ, harbor, refuge 7 address, hang out, purlieu, retreat, riviera, stopgap, utilize 8 frequent, recourse 9 expedient, makeshift 10 substitute *beach:* 4 lido

resound 4 echo, hymn, laud 5 bless, cry up, extol 6 praise 7 glorify, magnify 9 celebrate

resounding 5 round 6 rotund 7 orotund, reboant, vibrant 8 emphatic, forceful, plangent, sonorant, sonorous 9 assertive, consonant

resource 3 way 4 hope, mode, step 5 dodge, means, shift 6 device, lash-up, manner, method, refuge, relief, string, system 7 fashion, measure, stopgap 8 artifice, creation 9 expedient, invention, makeshift, stratagem, surrogate

resources 5 means, worth 6 assets, riches, wealth 7 capital, fortune 8 property 9 substance

respect 3 awe 4 fear 5 favor, honor 6 admire, devoir, esteem, regard, revere 7 account, worship 8 consider, venerate 9 adoration, reverence 10 admiration, estimation, veneration 13 consideration

respectable 4 done, good, nice 5 right 6 comely, decent, proper, worthy 7 correct,

reputed 8 adequate, all right, becoming, decorous 9 befitting 10 conforming, sufficient 11 appropriate 12 satisfactory 13 well-thought-of

respectful 5 civil 6 polite 7 duteous 8 gracious, obeisant, reverent 9 attentive, courteous 10 venerating 11 deferential, reverential

respecting 4 as to, in re 5 about 7 apropos 9 as regards

respire 7 breathe

respite 3 ten 4 blow, ease, lull 5 break, pause, spell 6 breath, recess 7 leisure 8 breather, reprieve 12 intermission

resplendent 5 proud 6 superb 7 blazing, flaming, glowing, sublime 8 glorious, gorgeous

respond 3 act 5 react, reply 6 answer, behave, come in, rejoin, retort, return 8 antiphon

response 5 reply 6 answer, retort, return 8 antiphon 9 rejoinder *involuntary:* 6 reflex 7 tropism

responsibility 4 duty, onus 6 burden, charge

responsible 6 liable 10 answerable, dependable 11 accountable

responsive 4 warm 6 tender 7 sensile 8 replying, sensible, sentient, suasible, swayable 9 acceptant, answering 11 impressible, kindhearted, persuadable, persuasible, softhearted, susceptible, sympathetic

rest 3 bed, lie, nap, nod, sit 4 base, calm, doze, ease, hang, heel, loaf, loll, lull, seat, stay 5 basis, count, found, hinge, let up, lie by, pause, peace, quiet, relax, sleep, spell, unlax 6 bottom, depend, ease up, excess, ground, lay off, lounge, repose, snooze, unbend 7 balance, breathe, ease off, footing, leisure, let down, lie down, recline, remains, remanet, remnant, seating, silence, slacken, slumber, surplus 8 interval, leavings, overplus, serenity, slack off, vacation 9 deferring, establish, placidity, predicate, remainder, stillness

restate 6 reword 8 rephrase 9 translate 10 paraphrase

restatement 7 version 9 rendering 10 paraphrase 11 translation

restaurant 4 café 5 diner 6 eatery 7 beanery, tearoom, teashop 8 teahouse 9 brasserie, cafeteria 10 coffee shop 11 coffeehouse *worker:* 4 chef, cook 6 busboy, waiter 7 maître d' 8 waitress 10 dishwasher, headwaiter 12 maître d' hôtel

____ **Restaurant** 6 Alice's

restful 6 placid 7 easeful, relaxed 8 tranquil

restitute 6 return 7 reclaim, recover,

replace **8** take back **10** rejuvenate **11** recondition, reconstruct **12** rehabilitate

restitution 6 amends **7** redress **8** reprisal **9** indemnity, quittance **10** recompense

restive 4 edgy **5** balky, nervy, tense **6** ornery, uneasy **7** fidgety, froward, uptight, wayward **8** contrary, perverse

restiveness 7 ferment, turmoil **8** disquiet **10** inquietude **11** disquietude

restless 5 itchy, jumpy **6** fitful, fretty, uneasy **7** fidgety, fretful, jittery, nervous, unquiet **8** agitated, fretsome, troubled **9** disturbed, perturbed, spasmodic, unsettled

restlessness see **restiveness**

restorative 5 tonic **6** curing **7** healing **8** remedial, roborant, sanatory **9** remedying, vulnerary, wholesome **10** astringent

restore 4 cure, heal, save, stir **5** amend, rally, renew, right, rouse **6** arouse, better, recall, recoup, redeem, reform, regain, remedy, repair, return, revise, revive, update **7** correct, get back, improve, put back, reclaim, recover, recruit, rectify, refresh, replace **8** give back, renovate, retrieve, revivify, take back **9** modernize, refurbish, reinstate **10** rejuvenate **11** recondition, reconstruct, reestablish, reintroduce **12** rehabilitate

restrain 3 bit, gag **4** cool, curb, keep, rein, stop **5** block, check, cramp, crimp, leash **6** arrest, bridle, coarct, halter, hamper, hinder, hold in, impede, muzzle, pull in, temper **7** collect, compose, control, forbear, harness, inhibit, prevent, repress, smother **8** hold back, hold down, moderate, modulate, obstruct, suppress, underact, withhold *trade:* **7** embargo

restrained 5 quiet, tasty **7** aseptic, subdued **8** discreet, moderate, retiring, tasteful **9** shrinking, temperate, unaffable, unextreme, withdrawn **10** controlled, reasonable

restraint 5 cramp **7** durance, embargo **8** pullback **11** confinement *legal:* **5** estop

restrict 3 bar, tie **4** bind **5** limit **6** shrink **7** confine, delimit **8** prelimit **10** delimitate **12** circumscribe *a will:* **6** entail

restriction 4 curb **5** brake, check, cramp, limit, stint **7** control **10** constraint **11** confinement

restyle 6 redraw, revamp, revise, rework **7** redraft, rewrite **8** work over

result 3 end **5** close, ensue, issue **6** answer, effect, finish, sequel, upshot **7** outcome, product **8** sequence, solution **9** aftermath **10** conclusion, production **11** aftereffect, consequence, eventuality, termination *incidental:* **7** spinoff *suffix:* **7** ization

resume 4 go on **5** renew **6** keep up, pick up, recoup, regain, reopen, retake, take up **7** carry on, reclaim, recover **8** continue, reoccupy, retrieve **10** recommence

resumé 5 sum-up **7** epitome, summary **9** summation, summing-up

resurgence 7 rebirth, revival **11** reanimation **12** risorgimento

resurrect 5 raise, renew **6** revive **8** rekindle, renovate, retrieve, revivify **10** reactivate, revitalize

resurrection 7 rebirth, revival **10** renascence **11** renaissance **12** reviviscence, risorgimento

resuscitate see **resurrect**

retail 4 sell **6** market **11** merchandise

retain 3 own **4** have, hold, keep **7** possess, reserve **8** continue, hold back, keep back, preserve, remember, withhold

retainer 3 fee **6** lackey, minion **7** servant **8** employee, follower **9** dependent

retaliate 5 repay **6** avenge, punish **7** requite, revenge **10** recompense **11** reciprocate

retaliation see **reprisal**

retaliatory *prefix:* **7** counter

retard 4 balk, clog, mire **5** delay, embog, stunt **6** baffle, detain, fetter, hamper, hang up, hinder, impede, lessen, reduce, slow up **7** bog down, inhibit, set back, slacken **8** decrease, restrain, slow down **10** decelerate

retarded 3 dim **4** dull, dumb, slow **6** opaque, simple, stupid **7** moronic **8** backward, imbecile **9** dim-witted **10** half-witted, slow-witted **11** exceptional

retch 3 gag **4** keck **5** heave, vomit

retention 6 memory **7** holding, keeping, storage

reticent see **reserved**

reticulate 6 meshed, netted **10** cancellate

retinue 4 band **5** suite, train **7** company, cortege **9** entourage, following

retire 2 go **3** bed **4** drop, exit, quit **5** leave, yield **6** depart, get off, recede, resign, turn in, vacate **7** abandon, dismiss, get away, pension, retreat, take off **8** fall back, give back, run along, withdraw **9** discharge, surrender, terminate **10** pension off, relinquish **12** superannuate

retired person 7 emerita **8** emeritus

retirement allowance 7 pension

retiring 3 shy **5** timid **6** demure, modest **7** aseptic, bashful, rabbity **8** backward, reserved **9** diffident, unaffable, unassured, withdrawn **10** restrained **11** unassertive

retool 7 reequip, reorder **8** readjust, reorient **9** rearrange, reshuffle **10** reorganize

retort 3 gag, mot **4** jape, jest, joke, quip, snap **5** crack, repay, reply, sally **6** answer, come in, rejoin, return **7** respond, revenge, riposte **8** antiphon, comeback, repartee, reprisal, response **9** rejoinder

retract 4 back 5 unsay 6 abjure, disown, recall, recant, recede, revoke 7 exclude, rescind, rule out, suspend, unswear 8 fall back, forswear, palinode, take back, withdraw

retral 4 back, hind, rear 5 after 6 hinder 8 backward, hindmost 9 posterior 10 retrograde

retread 4 tire 5 recap

retreat 2 go 3 den, fly 4 back, flee, port, quit 5 cover, haven, leave, quail 6 asylum, bow out, covert, decamp, depart, escape, harbor, recede, recoil, refuge, shrink, vacate 7 abandon, back out, pull out, shelter 8 back down, crawfish, evacuate, fall back, give back, hightail, withdraw 9 climb down, harborage, sanctuary *religious:* 5 asram 6 ashram

retrench 3 cut 4 omit 5 slash 6 delete, excise, lessen, reduce 7 abridge, curtail, cut back, shorten 9 economize

retribution 3 pay 6 return 7 revenge 8 avenging, reprisal, requital, revanche 9 vengeance 10 avengement, punishment, recompense 11 counterblow *goddess of:* 3 Ate 4 Fury 7 Nemesis

retrieve 5 renew 6 recall, recoup, regain, rescue, revive 7 get back, recover, recruit, salvage 8 rekindle, renovate, revivify 9 repossess, resurrect 10 reactivate, revitalize

retrograde 4 back, sink 5 lapse 6 invert, recede, retral, revert, worsen 7 decline, descend, inverse, relapse, retreat, reverse 8 backward, decadent, fall back, inverted, rearward 9 backslide 10 degenerate, disimprove 11 deteriorate 12 disintegrate, recapitulate

retrogress see **revert**

retrospect 4 cite 6 recall, remind, review, revive 7 bethink 8 remember, revision 9 reminisce 10 afterlight 13 reexamination

retrospective 6 review 8 backward 10 exhibition

return 3 lob, pay 4 gain, give 5 lucre, react, recur, renew, repay, reply, yield 6 advert, answer, bestow, come in, profit, rebate, regain, rejoin, render, retort, revert, rotate 7 bring in, put back, rebound, recover, reentry, reflect, replace, reprise, requite, respond, restore, revenue, reverse, revolve 8 antiphon, comeback, earnings, feedback, give back, proceeds, response, take back, turn back 9 reinstate, rejoinder, repayment, repercuss, restitute, retaliate, reversion 10 recompense, recrudesce, recurrence 11 reciprocate 12 reappearance, reoccurrence

Return of the Native *author:* 5 Hardy *character:* 4 Clym 8 Eustacia

Reuben *brother:* 6 Joseph *father:* 5 Jacob *mother:* 4 Leah *son:* 5 Carmi 6 Hanoch, Hezron, Phallu

Reuel *father:* 4 Esau 7 Ibnijah *mother:* 8 Basemath *son:* 5 Zerah 6 Mizzah, Nahath 7 Shammah 8 Eliasaph *son-in-law:* 5 Moses

revamp 5 patch, renew 6 redraw, repair, rework 7 rebuild, redraft, restyle, rewrite 8 make over, overhaul, renovate 11 recondition, reconstruct

reveal 3 bid, rat 4 avow, bare, blab, leak, open, show, talk, tell, vent 5 admit, break, let on, mouth, peach, spill 6 betray, expose, impart, squeak, unmask, unveil 7 bespeak, blab out, breathe, confess, declare, display, divulge, exhibit, give out, publish, unbosom, unclose, uncover, whisper 8 announce, decipher, disclose, discover, give away, unclothe 9 broadcast, uncurtain 11 acknowledge, communicate

revel 4 bask, hell, orgy, riot, roll 5 feast, gloat, spree 6 frolic, gaiety, wallow, welter 7 carouse, delight, indulge, jollity, roister, rollick, royster, wassail, whoopee, whoopla 8 carnival, festival 9 celebrate, festivity, high jinks, luxuriate, merriment, whoop-de-do 10 skylarking 11 merrymaking

revelation 4 tora 5 torah 6 oracle 8 epiphany, prophecy 9 discovery 10 apocalypse, disclosure 13 manifestation

reveler 8 bacchant, carouser 10 merrymaker

revelry 6 gaiety 7 jollity, wassail, whoopee, whoopla, whoop-up 8 carousal 9 festivity, high jinks, merriment, whoop-de-do 10 skylarking 11 merrymaking

revenant 5 ghost, shade 6 shadow, spirit, wraith 7 phantom, specter 8 phantasm 9 recurring 10 apparition

revenge 6 defend 7 justify, redress 8 reprisal, requital 9 vindicate 11 counterblow, retaliation, retribution

revenue 2 in 4 rent 5 gains, wages, yield 6 income, profit, return, salary 7 comings 8 earnings, interest, proceeds, receipts

reverberant 6 hollow 7 reboant 8 resonant

reverberate 4 echo, ring 5 repel 7 rebound, reflect, resound

revere 4 love 5 adore, enjoy, exalt, honor, prize, value 6 admire, esteem, hallow, regard 7 cherish, magnify, respect, worship 8 treasure, venerate 10 appreciate

revered 9 venerable

reverence 3 awe 4 fear 5 adore, dread, honor, piety 6 fealty, homage 7 loyalty, worship 8 devotion, venerate 9 deference, obeisance, solemnity *gesture of:* 3 bow 8 kneeling 11 genuflexion 12 genuflection

reverend 3 sri 4 holy 5 abbot, clerk

6 clergy, cleric, divine, parson, sacred **8** clerical, minister, preacher **9** churchman, clergyman, monsignor, venerable **11** patriarchal **12** ecclesiastic

reverent 6 devout **7** dutiful **10** respectful

reverie 4 muse **5** dream, study **6** musing, trance, vision **7** fantasy, thought **8** daydream, dreaming **10** absorption, brown study, meditation **11** abstraction, daydreaming

reversal 4 turn **5** check **6** change, switch **7** backset, setback, turning **8** backfire **9** about-face, inversion, turnabout, volte-face

reverse 4 lift, turn **5** annul, check, polar, shift, verso **6** change, contra, defeat, invert, recall, repeal, revoke **7** backset, capsize, counter, rescind, set back, subvert **8** antipode, antipole, backward, contrary, converse, disaster, exchange, opposite, overrule, overturn, transfer **9** about-face, antipodal, backwards, diametric, dismantle, overthrow, transpose, turnabout, volteface **10** antipodean, antithesis, misfortune, right-about, transplace *prefix:* **2** de, ob **3** dis, dys

reversion 4 turn **5** lapse **6** return **7** atavism, escheat, relapse **9** about-face, throwback, turnabout, volte-face **10** right-about **11** backsliding, changeabout

revert 4 turn **5** lapse, react, recur **6** change, return **7** decline, escheat, inverse, regress, relapse **8** turn back **9** backslide, throw back, transpose **10** degenerate, recrudesce, retrograde, retrogress, transplace

revetment 7 sodwork **9** barricade **10** embankment

review 4 edit, scan **5** audit, organ, recap, study **6** notice, parade, revise, survey **7** account, brushup, checkup, comment, journal, recense, redraft, rethink, re-treat, revisal, reweigh **8** analysis, critique, magazine, rescript, revision, scrutiny **9** checkover, criticism, criticize, recension, reexamine, think over **10** afterlight, inspection, periodical, reconsider, reevaluate, reflection, retrospect **11** examination **13** reexamination, retrospection, second thought

revile 4 hate, rail, rate **5** abuse, libel, scold **6** berate, defame, malign, vilify **7** asperse, bawl out, chew out, slander, traduce, upbraid **8** backbite, disgrace, execrate, reproach **9** blaspheme **10** calumniate, tongue-lash, vituperate

revise 4 edit **5** alter, amend, emend **6** change, polish, redact, redraw, reform, revamp, review, rework, update **7** correct, improve, perfect, recense, redraft, restyle, rewrite, upgrade **8** overhaul, rescript, work over **9** recension **10** blue-pencil, reorganize

revitalize see **revive**

revival 7 rebirth, renewal **8** wakening **10** renascence, resurgence **11** reanimation, renaissance, restoration **12** regeneration, rejuvenation, reproduction, resurrection, reviviscence, risorgimento **13** recrudescence, resuscitation

revive 4 wake **5** rally, renew, rouse **6** arouse, exhume, recall **7** bethink, enliven, freshen, quicken, refresh, respire, restore **8** activate, energize, reawaken, rekindle, remember, renovate, retrieve, revivify, vitalize **9** galvanize, reanimate, recollect, refreshen, reinstate, resurrect, stimulate **10** reactivate, recuperate, regenerate, rejuvenate, revitalize **11** reestablish, reintroduce, resuscitate **12** reinvigorate

revivify see **revive**

revoke 4 lift, void **5** adeem, annul, erase **6** abjure, cancel, recall, recant, remind, renege, repeal, expunge, nullify, rescind, retract, reverse **8** abrogate, forswear **10** invalidate **11** countermand

revolt 4 defy, riot **5** rebel, repel **6** mutiny, offend, oppose, reluct, resist, sicken, uprise, uproar **7** boycott, disgust, repulse **8** mutineer, nauseate, overturn, renounce, sedition, uprising **9** insurrect, overthrow, rebellion **11** rise against, turn against **12** insurrection

revolter 5 rebel **6** anarch **8** frondeur, mutineer **9** anarchist, insurgent **10** malcontent

revolting 4 foul, ugly, vile **5** nasty **6** horrid **7** hideous, noisome **8** shocking **9** loathsome, offensive, repellent, repugnant, repulsive **10** disgusting, nauseating

revolution 4 gyre, reel, riot, roll, spin, turn **5** cycle, round, twirl, wheel, whirl **6** change **7** circuit, shake-up **8** disorder, gyration, overturn, rotation, sedition, turnover, uprising **9** overthrow, pirouette, rebellion

revolutionary 5 rabid, rebel, ultra **7** extreme, fanatic, radical **8** mutineer, rotating, ultraist **9** extremist, insurgent **10** malcontent *American:* **4** Read **5** Shays *French:* **5** Marat **6** Mirabeau **11** Robespierre *Irish:* **4** Tone *Mexican:* **5** Villa **6** Zapata *Russian:* **5** Kirov **7** Trotsky **8** Kerensky **9** Kropotkin

revolutionist see **revolutionary**

revolutionize 5 alter **6** change, modify, recast, redraw, reform, revamp, revise **7** remodel, restyle **8** overturn **9** overthrow, refashion, transform **11** transfigure **12** metamorphose

revolve 4 birl, chaw, gyre, muse, roll, spin, turn **5** orbit, round, wheel, whirl **6** circle, gyrate, ponder, rotate **7** agitate, circuit **8** consider, gyration, meditate, mull over, rotation, ruminate, turn over revolver 3 gat, gun, rod 6 pistol 7 firearm, handgun

revulsion 4 hate 6 hatred, horror 8 aversion, loathing 9 repulsion 10 abhorrence, repugnance 11 abomination, detestation

reward 4 meed, plum 5 bonus, booty, crown, medal, prize 6 bounty, carrot, trophy 7 guerdon, premium 8 dividend, requital 10 compensate, honorarium, recompense, remunerate 12 compensation, remuneration

reword see restate

rework 6 redraw, revamp, revise 7 redraft, restyle, rewrite

rewrite see revise

Reynard the ___ 3 Fox

Rezon's father 6 Eliada

rhadamanthine 3 due 4 just 5 right 7 condign, merited 8 deserved, rightful, suitable 9 requisite 11 appropriate

Rhadamanthus 5 judge brother: 5 Minos father: 4 Zeus 7 Jupiter mother: 6 Europa

rhapsodic 8 ecstatic, effusive 9 emotional

Rhea 3 Ops daughter: 4 Hera, Juno 5 Ceres, Vesta 6 Hestia 7 Demeter father: 6 Uranus husband: 6 Cronus, Saturn mother: 2 Ge 4 Gaea son: 4 Zeus 5 Hades, Pluto 7 Jupiter, Neptune 8 Poseidon

rheostat 6 dimmer 8 resistor

rhesus 6 monkey 7 macaque

rhetoric 4 rant 6 speech 7 bombast, fustian, oratory 8 rhapsody 9 discourse, elocution, eloquence, verbosity 11 highfalutin, rodomontade, speechcraft 13 lexiphanicism term: 6 aporia, ecbole, simile 7 epandos, litotes 8 metaphor 10 apostrophe, digression 12 alliteration, onomatopoeia

rhetorical 4 glib 5 gassy, grand, showy, tumid, vocal, windy 6 florid, fluent, mouthy, ornate, purple, turgid 7 aureate, flowery, orotund, pompous, stilted, swollen 8 eloquent, forensic, imposing, inflated, overdone, sonorous, swelling 9 bombastic, grandiose, high-flown, overblown, tumescent 10 articulate, euphuistic, figurative, flamboyant, oratorical 11 declamatory, embellished, exaggerated, highfalutin, overwrought, pretentious 12 high-sounding, magniloquent, orchidaceous, ostentatious 13 grandiloquent

rhetorician 6 orator, writer 7 speaker Roman: 11 Quintillian

Rhine River city: 4 Bonn, Köln 5 Mainz 7 Cologne 8 Mannheim 9 Weisbaden 10 Dusseldorf golden ring: 9 Rheingold, Rhinegold nymph: 7 Lorelei tributary: 3 Aar, Ill 4 Aare, Lahn, Main, Ruhr, Waal

rhinoceros 5 badak 6 borele 7 keitloa, upeygan 8 nasicorn feature: 4 horn relative of: 5 tapir

rhizome 4 root, stem 5 shoot 6 branch

Rhode Island capital: 10 Providence college, university: 5 Brown 6 Bryant 10 Providence 11 Salve Regina founder: 8 Williams (Roger) nickname: 11 Little Rhody state flower: 6 violet

Rhodesia see Zimbabwe

rhombus 7 diamond, lozenge 13 parallelogram

Rhone River lake: 6 Geneva mountain: 4 Jura town: 4 Lyon 5 Arles 6 Geneva tributary: 5 Isère, Saône

rhubarb 3 row 4 beef 5 plant, run-in, set-to 7 dispute, quarrel, yawweed 8 pieplant 9 bickering 11 altercation, controversy

rhyme 4 beat, poem, rune, song 5 agree, check, meter, poesy, swing, verse 6 accord, cohere, poetry, rhythm 7 cadence, cadency, comport, conform, consist, consort, measure 8 dovetail, rhythmus 10 correspond

rhymer 4 bard, poet 5 rimer 7 bardlet 8 bardling, poetling, rimester, verseman 9 poetaster, poeticule, versifier 11 versemonger

rhymester see rhymer

rhythm 4 beat, lilt, time 5 meter, pulse, swing, tempo 6 accent 7 cadence, cadency, measure 8 movement, sequence

rhythmic 6 poetic 7 pulsing, regular 8 cadenced, measured, metrical 9 cadential, pulsating

rialto 4 mart 6 market 8 district, exchange

riant 3 gay 4 boon 5 jolly, merry 6 blithe, bright, jocund, jovial 7 festive, gleeful, smiling 8 cheerful, laughing, mirthful

riata 4 rope 5 lasso 6 lariat

rib 3 fun, kid, rag 4 band, bone, dike, fool, jest, joke, josh, purl, razz, stay, wale 5 chaff, costa, ridge, tease 6 banter, costae (plural), lierne combining form: 4 cost 5 costi, costo, pleur 6 pleuri, pleuro relating to: 6 costal 7 costate

ribald 3 devil, rogue, scamp 6 coarse, rascal, risqué, vulgar 7 obscene 8 indecent, mischief, scalawag, slyboots 9 skeezicks 10 irreverent 11 rapscallion

ribbon 3 bow 4 band, tape 5 braid, reins, shred, strip 6 cordon, fillet, stripe, tatter 7 bandeau, banding, binding 8 fragment, tressure 9 banderole combining form: 4 taen 5 taeni 6 taenio

rice 4 boro, paga, twig 5 arroz, bigas, canin, macan 6 branch 7 risotto boiled with meat: 5 pilaf, pilau combining form: 4 oryz 5 oryzi, oryzo cooked with meat: 7 risotto 9 jambalaya drink: 4 saki 7 pangasi field: 3 cut 4 padi 5 paddy, sawah husk: 5 lemma, shood, shude long-stemmed: 4 aman mountain: 5 smilo short-stemmed: 3 aus

rich 3 fat 4 dear, easy, high, lush, oofy, warm 5 ample, flush, heavy, meaty, plump, round, sweet, vivid 6 absurd, costly, creamy, daedal, facund, fecund, florid, fruity, hearty, mellow, monied, ornate, potent, rococo, sating, superb 7 amusing, baroque, cloying, copious, fertile, filling, moneyed, opulent, orotund, pinguid, wealthy, well-off 8 abundant, affluent, childing, eloquent, fruitful, well-to-do 9 abounding, bountiful, elaborate, laughable, luxuriant, oversweet, plentiful, satiating, sumptuous, well-fixed 10 expressive, flamboyant, meaningful, productive, prosperous, well-heeled 11 comfortable *person:* 5 Midas, nabob 7 Croesus 9 plutocrat

Richardson work 6 Pamela 8 Clarissa 15 Clarissa Harlowe

Richelieu's successor 7 Mazarin

riches 4 gold, pelf, weal 5 booty, lucre, worth 6 mammon, wealth 7 fortune 8 opulence, property, treasure 9 resources *demon of:* 6 Mammon

rick 3 mow 4 bank, cock, heap, hill, pile, ruck 5 drift, shock, stack

rickety 4 weak 5 shaky 6 feeble, senile, wobbly 7 unsound 8 rachitic, unstable, unsteady 10 ramshackle, rattletrap

ricochet 3 dap 4 skim, skip 5 bound, carom, graze 6 bounce, glance, recoil 7 rebound

rid 4 free, lose, quit, shed 5 clear, empty 6 remove, uproot 7 abolish, deliver, release, relieve 8 liberate, shake off, throw off, unburden 11 disencumber

riddle 3 pan, why 4 crux, sift 5 griph, rebus 6 enigma, pierce, puzzle, screen 7 griphus, mystery, perplex, problem 8 permeate, separate 9 conundrum, penetrate, perforate 10 puzzlement

ride 2 go 3 rib 4 auto, bait, last, lift, sail, spin, tour, trip, turn 5 chivy, coast, drift, drive, float, glide, hound, motor, tease 6 badger, banter, canter, gallop, harass, heckle, hector 7 journey, oppress, overlap, overlie, shingle, survive, torment, torture 8 bullyrag, carousel, ridicule 9 carrousel, excursion, imbricate, persecute

rider 6 clause, cowboy, jockey, knight 7 codicil 8 addendum, addition, appendix, horseman, reinsman 9 amendment 10 equestrian, supplement

ridge 3 rib, top 4 bank, brow, fold, hill, keel, reef, roll, ruck, seam, spur, wave 5 arris, chine, costa, crest, knurl, ledge, plica, quill, rivel, spine 6 crease, divide, furrow, rideau, rimple, saddle, summit 7 annulet, breaker, costula, crinkle, hogback, hummock, wrinkle 8 headland, shoulder 9 razorback 11 corrugation *gravelly:*

5 esker *on the skin:* 4 welt *sharp:* 7 hogback

ridicule 3 guy, pan 4 gibe, haze, jape, jeer, lout, mock, quiz, razz, ride, twit 5 chaff, flout, mimic, rally, roast, scoff, scout, sneer, squib, taunt 6 deride, satire 7 lampoon, mockery, pillory, sarcasm 8 derision, raillery, satirize, travesty 9 burlesque 10 caricature *god of:* 5 Momus *object of:* 4 butt 13 laughingstock

ridiculous 5 antic, comic, dotty, droll, funny, rough, silly 6 absurd, insane 7 amusing, bizarre, comical, foolish, mocking, risible, ungodly 8 derisive, derisory, farcical, gelastic, improper, indecent, unseemly 9 cockamamy, fantastic, grotesque, laughable, ludicrous 10 indecorous, irrational, outrageous, unbecoming 12 preposterous

riding *academy:* 6 manège *costume:* 5 habit *pants:* 8 jodhpurs *whip:* 4 crop 5 quirt

Rienzi composer 6 Wagner

rife 4 full, rank 5 alive, ariot 6 active, filled, strong 7 current, popular, rampant, regnant, replete, teeming 8 abundant, manifest, numerous, swarming, thronged 9 abounding, plentiful, prevalent 10 prevailing, widespread 11 overflowing

riff 4 scan, skim 6 browse

riffle 4 fret, scan, skim, wave 5 rapid, shoal 6 browse, cockle, dimple, ripple 7 dip into, run over, shuffle 8 glance at 10 glance over, run through 11 flip through, leaf through, skim through 12 thumb through

riffraff 3 mob 4 junk, mass, scum 5 dregs, offal, trash, waste 6 debris, kelter, litter, rabble, refuse, tagrag 7 garbage, rubbish 8 canaille, unwashed 11 proletariat

rifle 3 arm, gun, rob 4 loot 5 piece, steal, yager 6 furrow, groove, jaeger, weapon 7 carbine, despoil, firearm, pillage, plunder, ransack, relieve 9 chassepot *accessory:* 6 ramrod *kind:* 6 Garand, Mauser 7 Enfield 8 Browning 9 Remington 10 Winchester 11 Springfield *pin:* 4 tige

rift 3 gap 4 flaw, rent, rima, rime, rive 5 break, chasm, chink, cleft, crack, split 6 breach, cleave, divide, hiatus, schism 7 blemish, fissure, opening, rupture 8 crevasse, division, fracture, interval, rimation

rig 3 arm, fit, fix 4 gear, hoax, wind 5 dress, equip, getup, guise, trick 6 fit out, outfit, setout, tackle 7 appoint, arrange, costume, derrick, furnish, turn out 8 accouter, accoutre, carriage, equipage 9 apparatus, equipment

rigadoon 5 dance

rigamarole see **rigmarole**

rigging 3 net 4 duds, gear, togs 5 dress,

lines, ropes **6** attire, chains, tackle, things **7** apparel, clothes, raiment **8** clothing

right 3 apt, due, fit, ius, jus, now **4** away, bang, dead, done, fair, good, hale, jura (plural), just, nice, real, sane, tory, true, very, well **5** amend, amply, claim, clear, droit, emend, exact, fully, happy, legal, lucid, quite, sharp, sound, spang, title, whole **6** at once, comely, common, decent, dexter, direct, equity, highly, honest, lawful, normal, patent, proper, square, strict **7** condign, correct, diehard, exactly, fitting, fogyish, freedom, genuine, healthy, liberty, license, merited, notably, old-line, parlous, precise, rectify, redress, utterly **8** accurate, adequate, all there, appanage, becoming, bona fide, decorous, deserved, directly, easement, entirely, faithful, first off, interest, old liner, orthodox, properly, rigorous, smackdab, squarely, standpat, straight, suffrage, suitable, suitably, usufruct **9** authentic, authority, befitting, equitable, extremely, fittingly, forthwith, franchise, honorable, instanter, perfectly, precisely, privilege, propriety, requisite, simon-pure, tolerable, undoubted, veracious, veridical, veritable, wholesome **10** acceptable, acceptably, accurately, adequately, altogether, applicable, becomingly, completely, concession, felicitous, perquisite, properness, remarkably, scrupulous, straightly, sufficient, sure-enough, well-liking **11** appropriate, bitterender, comme il faut, correctness, exceedingly, immediately, indubitable, prerogative, reactionary, standpatter, undistorted **12** compos mentis, conservative **combining form: 4** orth, rect **5** dextr, ortho, recti **6** dextro **feudal: 4** soke **legal: 5** droit **8** usufruct **royal: 6** regale **7** regalia (plural)

right away 3 now **6** at once **8** directly, first off, straight **9** forthwith, instanter, instantly **11** immediately, straightway

righteous 4 good, holy, just, pure **5** godly, moral, noble, pious **6** devout, worthy **7** ethical, sinless, upright **8** innocent, virtuous **9** blameless, equitable, exemplary, guiltless **10** inculpable, moralistic, principled

righteousness 6 equity, virtue **7** justice, probity **8** goodness, holiness, justness, morality **9** rectitude **11** uprightness

rightful 3 apt, due, fit **4** fair, just, true **5** legal **6** honest, lawful, proper **7** condign, fitting, merited **8** deserved, suitable **9** befitting, equitable, impartial, requisite **10** applicable, legitimate **11** appropriate

right-handed 7 dextral **8** dextrous **9** clockwise, dexterous

right-hand page 5 recto

rightist 4 tory **7** diehard **8** old liner, standpat **11** bitter-ender, reactionary, right-winger, standpatter **12** conservative

right-minded 5 moral, noble **7** ethical **8** virtuous **10** moralistic, principled

Rights of Man author 5 Paine

rigid 3 set **4** firm, hard, taut **5** fixed, solid, stein, stiff, tough **6** formal, severe, strait, strict **7** adamant, austere, buckram, hardset **8** hard-line, ironclad, obdurate, rigorist, rigorous **9** draconian, immovable, impliable, inelastic, stringent, unbending **10** adamantine, inexorable, inflexible, ironhanded, motionless, relentless, unflexible, unyielding **11** immalleable

rigidity 5 frost **6** turgor **7** buckram **8** hardness, turgency **9** stiffness **muscular: 8** myotonia

rigmarole 6 ramble **8** nonsense **9** procedure **10** balderdash

Rigoletto composer: 5 Verdi **daughter: 5** Gilda

rigor 5 trial **7** cruelty **8** asperity, hardness, hardship, severity **9** austerity, harshness, roughness, sharpness, sternness **10** affliction, difficulty, exactitude, strictness, visitation **11** tribulation, vicissitude **13** inflexibility

rigorous 4 hard, nice **5** exact, harsh, right, rigid, rough, stern, stiff **6** bitter, brutal, proper, rugged, severe, strait, strict **7** ascetic, correct, drastic, onerous, precise **8** accurate, exacting **9** draconian, inclement, stringent **10** burdensome, inexorable, inflexible, ironhanded, oppressive

rile 3 mud, vex **4** roil **5** anger, annoy, grate, muddy, peeve, pique, upset **6** muddle, nettle, put out **7** agitate, disturb, inflame, provoke **8** irritate **9** aggravate

rim 3 hem, lip **4** bank, boss, brim, edge, ring **5** bezel, bezil, bound, brink, skirt, verge **6** border, flange, fringe, margin, shield **7** annulus, horizon, outline **8** boundary, surround **9** perimeter, periphery **of a basket: 4** hoop **of a cask: 5** chime, chine **of an insect's wing: 6** termen **of a spoked wheel: 6** felly **6** felloe **of a volcanic crater: 5** somma

rima 4 rift **5** chink, cleft, crack, split **7** fissure **8** aperture

rime 3 ice **4** cake, rift **5** chink, cleft, crack, crust, frost, split **7** encrust, fissure, incrust **10** incrustate **12** incrustation

Rimmon's son 6 Baanah, Rechab

rimple 4 fold, ruck **5** crimp, plica, ridge, rivel, screw **6** crease, furrow, ruck up, rumple **7** crimple, crinkle, crumple, scrunch, wrinkle **11** corrugation

Rinaldo beloved: 8 Angelica **cousin: 7** Orlando **father: 5** Aymon **horse: 6** Bayard **mother: 3** Aya **sister: 10** Bradamante **uncle: 11** Charlemagne

rind 4 bark, husk, peel, skin **5** crust **of roast pork: 9** crackling

ring 3 bee, eye, hem, mob, rim **4** bail, band,

bell, bloc, bong, camp, clan, cric, ding, dirl, echo, gird, gyre, hoop, loop, peal, toll **5** anlet, arena, bague, bezel, cabal, chime, clang, cycle, group, knell, knoll, party, rigol, round, sound **6** begird, boxing, circle, clique, collar, collet, dindle, famble, girdle, staple **7** annulus, clangor, combine, compass, coterie, faction, ferrule, grommet, ingroup, resound, vibrate **8** bracelet, cincture, encircle, pugilism, surround **9** camarilla, coalition, encompass **11** combination, reverberate *around sun or moon:* **5** broch **6** corona *combining form:* **3** gyr **4** cycl, gyro **5** cyclo *curtain:* **3** eye *for a compass:* **6** gimbal *for a lampshade:* **4** harp **7** gallery *harness:* **3** dee **6** button, larigo, terret, territ *heraldic:* **7** annulet *in a hinge:* **7** gudgeon *of chain:* **4** link **7** belcher *of color:* **8** stocking *of dots around a coin:* **8** graining *of leaves or flowers:* **6** wreath **7** garland *of light:* **4** halo **5** glory **6** corona, nimbus **7** aureole **8** halation *of Odin:* **8** draupnir *of rope or metal:* **4** hank **6** becket **7** garland, grommet, snotter, thimble *of two hoops:* **5** gemel **6** gemmel, gimmal *on a key, pocket watch or scissors handle:* **3** bow *on an archery target:* **4** sous **5** souse *relating to:* **7** annular *rubber, for a fruit jar:* **4** lute *used as a valve or diaphragm:* **5** wafer *used for securing a bird:* **6** vervel *used to enclose deer:* **7** tinchel *wedding:* **4** band

Ring and the Book author 8 Browning

ringed 8 annulate, circular **9** encircled **10** surrounded

ringer 4 fake, spit **5** image **6** double **7** picture **8** impostor, portrait **9** direct hit **10** simulacrum **13** spitting image

ringing 5 round **6** bright, fervid, jangle, rotund **7** clangor, orotund, vibrant **8** decisive, plangent, resonant, sonorant, sonorous **9** consonant **10** resounding

ringleader 4 boss **5** chief **6** honcho **10** instigator, mastermind

ringlet 4 curl, lock **5** tress **7** tendril

rinse 4 lave, wash **5** douse, swill **6** douche, sluice **7** cleanse *the mouth:* **6** gargle

riot 4 hell, howl **5** brawl, melee, revel, smash, spree **6** attack, bedlam, clamor, émeute, excess, frolic, jumble, scream, tumult, uproar **7** anarchy, carouse, debauch, dispute, misrule, quarrel, revelry, roister, wassail **8** carousal, disorder, uprising **9** anarchism, commotion, distemper, sensation **10** donnybrook **11** disturbance

riotous 4 loud, lush, wild **5** noisy **6** lavish, stormy, wanton **7** bacchic, opulent, profuse, roaring **8** bacchian, prodigal **9** exuberant, luxuriant, profusive **10** boisterous **11** saturnalian **12** unrestrained

rip 3 cut **4** rend, rent, rive, spit, tear **5** shred, slash, split **6** attack, cleave, sunder **7** sputter **8** lacerate, splutter

ripe 3 fit **4** aged, late **5** adult, grown, ready **6** mature, mellow, timely **7** grownup, matured, overdue **8** complete, finished **9** developed, full-blown, full-grown, perfected, virtuosic, well-timed **10** consummate, seasonable **11** full-fledged

ripen 3 age **4** grow **6** better, grow up, mature, mellow, season **7** develop, enhance, improve, perfect **8** heighten, maturate **9** intensify

ripening early 4 rath **5** rathe **8** rareripe

riposte 5 reply **6** retort, return, thrust **8** comeback, repartee **10** back answer **13** counterattack

ripping 4 fine **5** grand, nifty, super, swell **6** divine, peachy **7** capital **8** glorious, splendid, terrific **9** admirable, excellent, marvelous, wonderful **10** remarkable **11** sensational

ripple 3 cut, lap **4** curl, fret, riff, wave **5** acker **6** cockle, dimple, lipper, popple, riffle, rimple **7** crinkle, wrinkle

rip-roaring 5 noisy **6** lively **8** exciting **9** hilarious **10** boisterous, uproarious

ripsnorter 5 dandy **8** jim-dandy **9** humdinger **11** crackerjack

riptide 8 undertow

Rip Van Winkle *author:* **6** Irving *dog:* **4** Wolf

rise 2 up **3** wax **4** come, flow, grow, head, hike, lift, rear, soar, stem, well **5** awake, begin, boost, build, climb, get up, issue, mount, occur, raise, rebel, rouse, scale, sit up, stand, start, surge, swell, tower **6** ascend, ascent, aspire, awaken, befall, betide, chance, deepen, emerge, expand, growth, happen, recess, revolt, spring, thrive, uprear **7** adjourn, advance, augment, bristle, develop, elevate, emanate, enhance, enlarge, fall out, magnify, pile out, proceed, prosper, roll out, stand up, succeed, surface, turn out, upgrade, upstand, upsurge **8** addition, dissolve, eminence, heighten, increase, levitate, multiply, prorogue, redouble, upspring **9** accession, accretion, aggravate, ascension, increment, intensate, intensify, originate, prorogate, terminate, transpire **10** derive from *above:* **8** surmount *abruptly:* **9** skyrocket *again:* **7** resurge **9** resurrect *against:* **5** rebel **6** mutiny, revolt **9** insurrect *and fall:* **4** tide **5** heave **6** welter *and shine:* **5** get up **7** pile out, roll out, turn out *gradually:* **4** loom *swiftly:* **4** boil, boom **6** spring *up:* **4** fume, rear, well **5** rebel, swell, tower **6** ascend, revolt **9** insurrect

Rise of Silas Lapham author 7 Howells

riser 4 step

risible 5 comic, droll, funny 7 comical 8 farcical, gelastic 9 laughable, ludicrous 10 ridiculous

risk 4 dare, defy, face, luck, meet 5 beard, brave, peril, stake, wager 6 chance, danger, gamble, hazard, menace 7 fortune, imperil, jeopard, venture 8 accident, confront, endanger, exposure, jeopardy, openness 9 adventure, encounter, liability 10 compromise, jeopardize

risky 4 bold 5 hairy 6 chancy, daring, touchy, wicked 7 parlous, unsound 8 delicate, perilous, ticklish 9 dangerous, hazardous, sensitive, unhealthy 10 jeopardous, precarious 11 speculative, treacherous

risqué 3 raw 4 blue, foul, lewd, racy, sexy 5 broad, crude, dirty, gross, salty, shady, spicy 6 coarse, daring, earthy, purple, ribald, vulgar, wicked 7 naughty, obscene, raunchy 8 indecent, off-color, scabrous 9 audacious, inelegant, salacious, unrefined 10 indecorous, indelicate, suggestive

rite 4 cult, form 6 fetish, honors, office 7 liturgy, mystery, service 8 ceremony, hierurgy, occasion 9 formality, ordinance, procedure, sacrament, solemnity 10 ceremonial, initiation, observance 11 celebration, sacramental *aborigine:* 4 bora *American Indian:* 8 huskanaw 11 huskanawing *Buddhist:* 6 pansil *funeral:* 6 exequy 7 obsequy 8 exequies *Hindu:* 4 puja 5 pooja, sradh 6 poojah, sradha 7 sraddha *Jewish:* 4 bris 5 berit, briss, brith 6 berith 7 tashlik 8 tashlich 12 circumcision *Mayan:* 3 kex *of initiation or purification:* 7 baptism *of knighthood:* 8 accolade *of prophecy:* 6 augury *of recognition of merit:* 8 accolade; (see also **sacrament**)

ritual see **rite**

ritzy 6 modish 7 elegant, haughty 8 snobbish 9 expensive, luxurious 11 fashionable 12 ostentatious

rival 3 tie, try, vie 4 even, meet, peer, side 5 equal, fight, match, touch 6 amount, strive 7 attempt, compete, contend, contest, emulate, entrant, feuding 8 approach, emulator, opponent, rivalize, struggle 9 adversary, competing, contender, measure up, partake of 10 antagonist, competitor, contending, contestant 11 comparative, competition *prefix:* 3 ant 4 anth, anti

rivalry 6 strife 7 contest, warfare 8 conflict, jealousy, striving, tug-of-war 9 emulation 11 competition

rive 3 hew, rip 4 chop, plow, rend, tear 5 burst, sever, smash, split 6 cleave, divide, pierce, shiver, sunder, thrust 7 shatter 8 fracture, fragment, lacerate, separate, splinter, splitter 11 splinterize

river *Africa:* 4 Bomu 5 Congo, Mbomu, Zaire 6 Atbara 7 Aruwimi, Atbarah, Zambesi, Zambeze, Zambezi 9 Astaboras *Alabama:* 5 Coosa 6 Mobile 7 Conecuh, Perdido 9 Tombigbee 10 Tallapoosa *Alaska:* 5 Kobuk 6 Copper, Noatak, Tanana 7 Koyukuk, Susitna 9 Kuskokwim *Albania:* 4 Drin 5 Drini *Argentina:* 5 Negro 6 Parané 7 Matanza *arm:* 6 branch 9 tributary *Asia:* 4 Amur, Oxus 5 Indus 6 Jayhun 7 Oedanes 8 Amu Darya 9 Dyardanes 11 Brahmaputra *Australia:* 4 Daly 5 Roper, Yarra 6 Barwon, Culgoa, Dawson, DeGrey, Murray 7 Darling, Fitzroy, Lachlan 8 Victoria 10 Yarra Yarra *Austria:* 4 Enns *bank:* 5 levee *Belgium:* 5 Rupel, Senne, Weser 6 Dender, Dindar, Ourthe 8 Visurgis *Bolivia:* 4 Beni 5 Abuná 6 Mamoré *Borneo:* 5 Kajan *bottom:* 3 bed *Brazil:* 3 Ica 4 Pará, Paru 5 Negro, Xingu 6 Paraná 7 Madeira, Tapajós, Tapajoz *British Columbia:* 6 Skeena 10 Bella Coola *California:* 3 Eel, Pit 4 Kern, Yuba 6 Merced 7 Feather, Salinas, Trinity 8 Tuolumne 9 Mokelumne 10 Sacramento, Stanislaus *Cambodia:* 8 Tonle Sap *Canada:* 3 Bow 4 Back 5 Moose, Peace 6 Beaver, Fraser, Nelson, Ottawa 8 Gatineau, Saguenay 9 Athabasca, Great Fish, Mackenzie, Richelieu 11 Assiniboine *Carolinas:* 7 Catawba *central Africa:* 6 Ubangi *central Asia:* 6 Gandak 8 Syr Darya *central Canada:* 5 Slave *central Europe:* 4 Eger, Elbe, Labe, Ohře 5 Albis 6 Danube *central United States:* 3 Fox 5 Grand 6 Neosho, Platte, Wabash 8 Keya Paha, Missouri, Niobrara 9 Tennessee, Verdigris 10 Republican, Saint Croix 11 Mississippi *channel:* 6 alveus *Chile:* 3 Loa 5 Itata, Maule 6 Bio-Bio 8 Valdivia *China:* 2 Si, Xi, Zi 3 Bei, Hun, Wei 4 Dong 5 Baihe, Huang, Hwang, Tarim 6 Yellow 7 Kashgar, Yangtze *Colombia:* 4 Tomo 6 Atrato 9 Magdalena *Colorado:* 5 Yampa 8 Gunnison *combining form:* 5 fluvi, potam 6 fluvio, potamo *Connecticut:* 6 Thames 7 Niantic, Shepaug 9 Naugatuck 10 Farmington, Housatonic, Quinnipiac 11 Willimantic *crossing:* 4 ford *current:* 4 eddy 6 rapids *Czechoslovakia:* 3 Vág, Váh 4 Gran, Hron, Iser, Waag 5 Garam, Nitra 6 Jisera, Moldau, Neutra, Nyitra, Vltava *dam:* 4 weir *Denmark:* 4 Stor *dried bed:* 4 wadi 5 waddy *drowned:* 7 estuary *East Africa:* 4 Juba 5 Tsavo 6 Songwe *East Asia:* 4 Yalu 5 Amnok 7 Oryokko *eastern United States:* 7 Potomac *Ecuador:* 10 Esmeraldas *England:* 3 Esk, Exe, Nen, Ure 4 Aire, Avon, Eden, Nene, Ouse, Tees, Tyne, Wear 5 Swale, Trent 6 Mersey, Ribble, Thames *Ethiopia:* 3 Omo 4 Baro, Dawa *Europe:* 4 Oder 5 Saale 6 Danube, Ticino

Florida: 6 Indian 9 Kissimmee 10 Saint Johns 12 Apalachicola *France:* 3 Ain, Lot, Var 4 Aire, Aude, Cher, Eure, Gers, Loir, Oise, Orne, Saar, Tarn, Yser 5 Adour, Aisne, Drôme, Indre, Isère, Loire, Marne, Saare, Saône, Seine, Somme, Yonne 6 Allier, Ariège, Scarpe, Vienne 7 Durance, Garonne, La Riège 8 Charente, Dordogne *Georgia:* 6 Etowah, Oconee 8 Altamaha, Ocmulgee 13 Chattahoochee *Germany:* 3 Ems 4 Eder, Elbe, Isar, Main, Rems, Ruhr 5 Hunte, Lippe, Rhine, Spree, Werra, Weser 6 Neckar *Germany-Poland:* 4 Oder *Ghana:* 5 Volta *god:* 7 Alpheus, Inachus 8 Achelous *Greece:* 3 Iri 4 Arta 5 Lerna, Lerne 7 Alpheus, Eurotas 8 Achelous 9 Arakhthos *hazard:* 4 snag 6 rapids 7 Lorelei *Honduras:* 4 Ulúa 5 Aguán 6 Patuca *Iberian:* 5 Douro, Duero *Idaho:* 5 Lemhi *Illinois:* 8 Mackinaw *India:* 4 Sind 5 Sindh, Tapti 6 Chenab, Kaveri, Kistna 7 Cauvery, Krishna 8 Acesines, Godavari *Indian subcontinent:* 5 Ganga 6 Ganges *inlet:* 5 bayou 6 slough *Iran:* 3 Kor 4 Mand, Mund 5 Karun 8 Safid Rud, Sefid Rud *Ireland:* 3 Lee 4 Deel, Erne, Suir 5 Boyne, Clare, Foyle 6 Barrow, Liffey 7 Shannon *Italy:* 2 Po 4 Adda, Arno, Liri, Nera 5 Adige, Arnus, Etsch, Liris, Oglio, Padus, Piave, Tiber 6 Ollius, Rapido, Tevere, Trebia 7 Athesis, Rubicon, Secchia, Tiberis, Trebbia 8 Rubicone, Volturno *Kansas:* 6 Pawnee *Kazakhstan-Russia:* 4 Ural 5 Tobol 6 Irtysh *Kenya:* 4 Athi, Tana *Kubla Khan's:* 4 Alph *land:* 4 holm 5 carse, flats 7 bottoms *Latvia:* 2 Aa 5 Gauja *Latvia-Lithuania:* 7 Lielupe *Lebanon:* 6 Litani *Little Rock's:* 8 Arkansas *living in:* 9 rheophile *living on the bank of:* 8 riparian *longest:* 4 Nile *Louisiana:* 11 Atchafalaya *Maine:* 8 Kennebec 9 Aroostook, Penobscot *Malaysia:* 9 Trengganu 10 Terengganu *Maryland:* 8 Monocacy, Patapsco, Patuxent 9 Nanticoke *Massachusetts:* 7 Charles, Taunton 9 Westfield 8 Housatonic *Mexico:* 6 Pánuco, Sonora 7 Tabasco 8 Grijalva *Michigan:* 4 Cass 5 Flint, Huron 7 Detroit, Saginaw 8 Manistee, Muskegon 9 Cheboygan, Kalamazoo 10 Michigamme, Shiawassee *Mississippi:* 5 Pearl, Yazoo 10 Pascagoula *Moldova-Ukraine:* 8 Dneister *Missouri:* 5 Osage *Montgomery's:* 7 Alabama *mouth:* 4 lade 5 delta *Myanmar (Burma):* 4 Pegu 8 Chindwin, Irrawady *Nebraska:* 4 Loup 6 Nemaha, Platte 7 Elkhorn *Netherlands:* 4 Waal 5 Issel, Yssel 6 Ijssel 7 Vahalis *New England:* 4 Saco 6 Nashua 9 Merrimack 10 Blackstone 11 Connecticut 12 Androscoggin *New Jersey:* 6 Rahway 7 Passaic, Raritan 8 Tuck-ahoe *New York:* 4 East 5 Tioga 6 Hudson, Mohawk, Oneida, Oswego, Seneca 7 Chemung, Niagara 8 Chenango, Cohocton 9 Conhocton *New Zealand:* 7 Waikato *Nicaragua:* 4 Coco 7 Segovia *Nigeria:* 5 Benin *North Carolina:* 3 Haw, Tar 5 Neuse 6 Chowan 8 Alamance *northeast North America:* 13 Saint Lawrence *northeast United States:* 4 Ohio 6 Hoosic 7 Genesee, Hocking 8 Delaware, Mahoning 9 Allegheny 11 Monongahela, Susquehanna *Northern ireland:* 4 Bann 6 Mourne *North Korea:* 5 Daido 7 Taedong *northwest North America:* 5 Yukon *northwest United States:* 5 Snake 7 Klamath 11 Pend Oreille *Norway:* 4 Tana, Teno *nymph:* 4 nais 5 naiad *obstruction:* 4 snag *of fire:* 9 Phlegeton *of forgetfulness:* 5 Lethe *of ice:* 7 glacier *of woe:* 7 Acheron *Ohio:* 5 Miami 8 Cuyahoga, Sandusky 9 Muskingum 10 Tuscarawas *Oklahoma:* 8 Cimarron *Oregon:* 5 Rogue 6 Owyhee 7 Malheur 8 McKenzie 9 Clackamas, Deschutes 10 Willamette *Panama:* 5 Tuira 7 Chagres *Papua New Guinea:* 3 Fly 5 Sepik *Pennsylvania:* 6 Lehigh 10 Schuylkill *Peru:* 5 Rímac, Santa 7 Marañón 8 Apurímac, Huallaga, Urubamba *Philippines:* 4 Abra, Agno 5 Pasig 7 Cagayan 8 Cotabato, Mindanao, Pampanga *Poland:* 3 San 7 Vistula *Portugal:* 4 Sado 7 Mondego *relating to:* 7 fluvial, potamic 9 fluminose, fluminous *Rhode Island:* 7 Seekonk 8 Sakonnet 10 Providence *Romania:* 5 Arges *Russia:* 2 Ob, Om 3 Don, Oka, Ufa, Usa 4 Kama, Kara, Lena, Neva, Sura, Svir 5 Onega, Terek, Volga 6 Anadyr, Angara, Belaya, Kolima, Kolyma, Ussuri, Vyatka 7 Dnieper, Pechora, Yenisei, Yenisey 8 Barguzin, Kostroma, Voronezh, Vychegda *Russia-Ukraine:* 6 Donets *sacred:* 5 Ganga 6 Ganges *São Paulo's:* 5 Tietè *Scotland:* 3 Dee, Don, Esk, Tay 4 Doon, Nith, Spey, Tyne 5 Afton, Annan, Clyde, Forth, Tweed 6 Teviot 7 Deveron 8 Findhorn *Shanghi's:* 7 Huang-p'u, Hwang Pu *Sicily:* 5 Salso 6 Simeto *siren:* 7 Lorelei *South Africa:* 4 Vaal 6 Orange *South America:* 3 Apa 6 Amazon 8 Amazonas, Orellana, Paraguay 9 Pilcomayo *South Carolina:* 6 Saluda, Santee 7 Wateree 8 Congaree *South Dakota:* 3 Bad *southeast Africa:* 7 Limpopo 9 Crocodile *southeast Asia:* 6 Dza-chu, Mekong 8 Lan-ts'ang *southeast United States:* 6 Pee Dee 7 Noxubee, Washita 8 Escambia, Ouachita, Suwannee 10 Okanoxubee *southern United States:* 6 Sabine *South Korea:* 3 Kum *southwest Asia:* 6 Jordan 9 Euphrates *southwest United States:* 4 Gila, Zuni 5 Pecos 8 Col-

orado *Spain:* 4 Ebro 6 Aragon 12 Guadal-
quivir *Sweden:* 4 Göta 5 Kalix *Switzerland:* 3 Aar 4 Aare 5 Reuss *Syria:*
7 Orontes *Tbilisi's:* 4 Kura *Texas:*
5 Llano 6 Brazos, Nueces 7 San Saba,
Trinity 9 Guadalupe *Texas-Mexico:* 8 Rio
Bravo 9 Rio Grande *tidal:* 7 estuary *Tokyo's:* 6 Sumida *Turkey:* 6 Seihun, Seyhan
Ukrainian: 3 Bug 4 Alma *underworld:*
4 Styx 5 Lethe 7 Acheron, Cocytus
10 Phlegethon *Uruguay:* 5 Negro *Utah:*
5 Uinta, Weber 6 Jordan, Sevier *valley:*
6 strath *Venezuela:* 5 Apure, Caura
6 Caroní 7 Orinoco *Vermont:* 3 Mad
5 Onion, White 8 Winooski *Virginia:*
3 Dan 5 James 7 Rapidan 9 Nansemond
10 Appomattox, Shenandoah 12 Chicka-
hominy, Rappahannock *wailing:* 7 Cocytus
Wales: 4 Dyfi 5 Clwyd, Dovey, Teifi *Washington:* 6 Skagit, Yakima 9 Klickitat, Snohomish, Wenatchee *West Africa:* 5 Niger
6 Gambia 7 Senegal *West Asia:* 5 Dijla
6 Tigris 8 Hiddekel *western North America:* 8 Columbia, Flathead *western United
States:* 7 Laramie 11 Yellowstone *West
Virginia:* 7 Kanawha *Wisconsin:* 8 Kickapoo 9 Menominee *Wyoming:* 8 Shoshone
10 Gros Ventre 11 Medicine Bow
_____ **Rivera, Painter** 5 Diego
river duck 4 teal 6 wigeon 7 mallard, widgeon 9 greenwing
river horse 5 hippo 12 hippopotamus
riverine 7 potamic
rivet 3 fix 4 bolt, brad, stud 5 affix
6 attach, fasten 8 fastener
rivulet 3 run 4 burn, gill, race, rill 5 bache,
bayou, bourn, brook, creek 6 runlet, runnel,
stream 7 channel 9 streamlet
Rizpah *father:* 4 Aiah *lover:* 4 Saul *son:*
6 Armoni 12 Mephibosheth
roach 4 fish, rock, spot 6 braise
road 3 way 4 fare, lane, line, path 5 drive,
going, route, track 6 artery, avenue, career,
causey, course, street 7 highway, journey,
passage 8 causeway, chaussée, crossway,
highroad, pavement, speedway, turnpike
9 boulevard 12 thoroughfare *along a cliff:*
8 corniche *around a city:* 6 bypass 7 belt-
way *bend:* 7 hairpin *edge:* 4 berm
8 shoulder *French:* 6 chemin *in or to a
mine:* 4 bord 8 footrill *Irish:*
6 boreen 8 beallach *machine:* 4 harl
5 paver 6 grader 9 bulldozer *narrow (in
England):* 4 loke 5 drang, drong 8 drift-
way *of stones:* 7 telford *raised:* 5 agger
Roman: 3 via 4 iter *Scottish:* 4 brae
8 beallach *side:* 5 biway 6 branch 8 shunpike *Spanish:* 6 camino *surface:* 3 tar
6 bricks, gravel, stones 7 macadam 8 concrete, pavement *temporary:* 7 shoofly *zigzag:* 10 switchback

roadblock 7 barrier 8 blockade
9 barricade
road book 3 map 5 atlas 9 gazetteer,
itinerary
roadhouse 3 inn 5 hotel, lodge 6 hostel,
tavern 7 auberge, hospice 8 hostelry
11 caravansary
roadman 6 hawker, monger, vendor
7 drummer, higgler, packman, peddler
8 huckster, mongerer, salesman
9 canvasser
roadrunner 6 cuckoo 7 paisano
road rut 7 pothole 9 chuckhole
roam 3 bat, gad, run 4 rove, walk 5 drift,
prowl, range, stray 6 ramble, stroll, travel,
wander 7 meander 8 gadabout, straggle,
vagabond 9 gallivant
roamer 5 gipsy, gypsy, nomad, rover
6 gadder, walker 7 drifter, rambler 8 gadabout, stroller, traveler, vagabond, wanderer
9 meanderer 12 peregrinator, rolling stone
roar 3 cry, din 4 bawl, bell, boom, bray,
howl, rout, yell 5 laugh, shout 6 bellow,
clamor, outcry, scream, shriek 7 bluster,
rebound, ululate 9 repercuss 10 vociferate 11 reverberate *low:* 5 brool *of a boor:*
5 fream *of the surf:* 3 rut 4 rote
roast 4 bake, cook, flay, melt, razz, roti
5 broil, parch, score, slash 6 scathe,
scorch 7 blister, lambast, swelter, torrefy,
torrify 8 lambaste, lash into, ridicule 9 castigate, excoriate
rob 3 cop, mug 4 fake, flap, lift, loot, lose,
nick, oust, pelf, roll, sack, take 5 bribe,
cheat, filch, harry, heist, pinch, pluck, reave,
rifle, spoil, steal, touch 6 burgle, divest,
hijack, hold up, hustle, pilfer, pirate, ravage,
ravish, snatch, snitch, thieve 7 bereave,
defraud, deprive, despoil, pillage, plunder,
purloin, ransack, relieve, stick up, swindle
8 jackroll 9 knock over, strong-arm
10 burglarize
robber 4 yegg 5 crook, thief 6 bandit, cat-
man, pirate, rifler 7 brigand, footpad, heis-
ter, ladrone, raffles, reifier 8 hightoby,
hijacker, swindler 9 holdup man 10 cat burglar, highwayman, sandbagger, stickup
man 12 housebreaker *grave:* 5 ghoul
Irish: 8 woodkern *murderous (in India and
Burma):* 6 dacoit *of pedestrians:* 3 pad
7 footpad *on high seas:* 6 pirate
robbery 3 job 5 heist, theft 6 holdup,
piracy 7 larceny, stickup 8 banditry *Scottish:* 4 reif
robe 3 aba 4 mant, wrap 5 cloak, cover,
habit 6 caftan, clothe, mantle, revest
7 becloak, costume, garment, manteau
8 clothing, covering, dalmatic, vestment
ancient Greek tragedian's: 5 syrma *baptismal:* 7 chrisom *bishop's:* 6 chimer
7 chimere *coronation:* 8 colobium *Eastern*

Orthodox: **10** sticharion *Indian:* **4** jama **6** khalat, khilat *Jewish:* **6** kittel *knight's:* **6** cyclas *Latin:* **5** stola *loose:* **5** camis, camus **6** kimona *Mexican:* **5** manga *monarch's:* **7** pluvial *of Roman emperors:* **6** purple *of tartan:* **7** arisaid *Turkish:* **6** dolman *woman's:* **5** cymar, simar, symar

Robinson Crusoe author 5 Defoe

robot 5 golem **7** android, machine **8** automata (plural) **9** automaton

Rob Roy author 5 Scott

robust 4 hale, hard, iron, rude **5** hardy, lusty, sound, stout, wally **6** browny, hearty, potent, rugged, sinewy, strong **7** booming, healthy, roaring, thrifty, valiant **8** athletic, muscular, thriving, vigorous **9** strapping **10** boisterous, full-bodied, prospering, prosperous **11** flourishing **12** concentrated

robustious 6 rugged **7** boorish, ill-bred, loutish, lumpish **8** churlish, clownish, lubberly **9** unrefined **10** unpolished

rock 3 fly, zip **4** bill, crag, oner, reel, roll, rush, slip, sway, toss **5** boner, error, fluff, geode, heave, hurry, pitch, quake, shake, speed, swing **6** barrel, bullet, bungle, dollar, gangue, hustle, miscue, rocket, slipup, totter **7** agitate, blooper, blunder, boulder, breccia, concuss, hotfoot, misstep, tremble **8** astonish, convulse, undulate **9** oscillate *basaltic:* **5** wacke *cavity:* **3** vug **4** vugg, vugh *combining form:* **4** lite, lith, lyte, petr, saxi **5** clast, petri, petro, phyre *decomposed:* **6** gossan *fissile:* **5** shale *foliated:* **8** phyllite *formation:* **4** sial **5** nappe **6** pluton **7** rimrock, terrane **8** isocline, syncline *fragment:* **8** xenolith *fragmental:* **8** psephite *granular:* **6** norite *igneous:* **4** lava, sial, sima **6** basalt, dunite, gabbro, ophite, pumice **7** diabase, diorite, felsite, granite, greisen, picrite, sienite, syenite **8** eruptive, felstone, obsidian, porphyry, trachyte, traprock **9** tachylyte **10** travertine *layer:* **8** regolith **10** mantlerock *mass:* **5** scree **9** batholith *metamorphic:* **5** slate **6** gneiss, marble, schist **8** eclogite, ganister, mylonite **9** quartzite, soapstone *molten:* **4** lava *protruding:* **5** scaur *sedimentary:* **4** clay, coal **5** chalk, chert, coral, flint, shale **6** pelite **8** mudstone, psammite **9** limestone, sandstone, siltstone *silicate:* **8** hornfels *siliceous:* **9** buhrstone *soft:* **7** tripoli *suffix:* **3** ite *volcanic:* **4** tuff **5** trass **6** basalt, taxite, terras **8** pumicate, rhyolite, tephrite

rock badger 4 cony **5** coney, hyrax

rock bass 6 redeye **8** cabrilla

rock bottom 4 pith, root, soul **5** stuff **6** lowest, marrow **7** essence **8** cheapest **9** lowermost, substance, undermost **10** nethermost

rockbound 5 rigid **7** adamant **8** obdurate **9** unbending **10** inexorable, inflexible, unyielding **12** single-minded

rocker 6 cradle **7** shoofly

rocket 3 fly, zip **4** soar, whiz **5** arise, haste, hurry, mount, smoke, surge, tower, whish **6** ascend, bullet **7** missile, shoot up **8** firework, starship *engineer:* **8** Von Braun *landing:* **7** reentry **10** splashdown *launcher:* **7** bazooka *launching:* **7** liftoff **8** blastoff

rocketry father of: **7** Goddard

rockfish 5 reina, viuva **6** gopher, rasher, tambor **7** corsair, garrupa, grouper **8** bocaccio

___ **Rockne 5** Knute

rock-ribbed   see rockbound

rockweed 4 tang **5** fucus **7** seatang, seaweed

rocky 4 dull, hard, weak **5** dizzy, reefy, shaky, stony **6** stoney, tricky, wobbly **7** petrean **8** bouldery, obdurate, ticklish, unstable, unsteady **9** bloodless, difficult, insensate, rockbound, steadfast **11** insensitive

rocky hill 3 tor

rococo 4 arty **6** florid, ornate **7** baroque **8** luscious **9** fantastic **10** flamboyant

rod 3 bar, gad, guy **4** bolt, came, cane, good, pole, scob, slab, ward **5** ingot, lytta, osier, perch, power, spoke, staff, stick, strip **6** billet, broach, carbon, etalon, pistol, raddle, skewer, switch, toggle **7** baculus, crowbar, scepter, spindle **8** punition, revolver **9** authority **10** correction, discipline, oppression, punishment **11** castigation **12** chastisement *bundle of:* **6** fasces *combining form:* **5** rhabd **6** rhabdo *glassmaking:* **5** punty

rodent 3 rat **4** cavy, cony, degu, hard, mole, paca, pika, utia, vole **5** cavie, coney, coypu, gundi, hutia, jutia, lerot, mouse, zokor **6** agouti, agouty, beaver, biting, cururo, gerbil, gopher, jerboa, marmot, murine, nutria, rabbit **7** chincha, hamster, lemming, leveret, muskrat **8** abrocome, capibara, capybara, chipmunk, cricetid, dormouse, gerbille, leporide, pacarana, sewellel, squirrel, tuco tuco, viscacha, vizcacha, water rat **9** guinea pig, porcupine **10** chinchilla, field mouse, prairie dog, springhare **11** kangaroo rat, meadow mouse, pocket mouse **12** pocket gopher *aquatic:* **5** coypu **6** beaver, coypou, nutria **7** muskrat **8** musquash *burrowing:* **6** gerbil, gopher **7** hamster **8** gerbille, viscacha, vizcacha *Eurasian:* **6** suslik *family:* **5** murid **6** murine **7** Muridae, sciurid **9** Sciuridae **10** Cricetidae **12** Octodontidae *furry:* **10** chinchilla *genus:* **3** Mus **5** Lepus *relating to:* **8** rosorial *South American:* **4** mara

rodeo 7 contest, roundup **9** enclosure

10 exhibition 11 competition *animal:*
5 horse, steer 10 Brahma bull *event:*
10 calf roping 11 bulldogging 12 bronco
riding *performer:* 5 clown 6 cowboy

___ **Rodin** 7 Auguste

rodomontade 4 blow, brag, crow, puff,
rant 5 boast, mouth, prate, pride, vaunt
6 blower, braggy, vanity 7 bluster, boaster,
bombast, bragger, fustian, vaunter 8 blowhard, boastful, boasting, braggart, bragging,
puckfist, rhapsody, rhetoric, vaunting
9 gasconade, vainglory 11 braggadocio

Rodomonte *beloved:* 8 Doralice *slayer:*
8 Ruggiero

Rodrigo Diaz de Bivar 5 el Cid

rod-shaped 7 virgate 8 bacillar, rhab-
doid 9 bacillary, virgulate

roe 2 ra 3 ova, pea 4 deer, eggs, hart,
hind 5 coral, spawn 6 caviar 7 caviare

Roentgen's discovery 4 X ray

rogation 3 law 6 decree, litany, prayer
7 inquiry 8 petition, proposal
12 supplication

___ **Rogers** 3 Roy 4 Will

rogue 3 boy, guy, gyp, imp 4 heel, kite
5 cheat, crank, devil, gipsy, gypsy, hempy,
knave, scamp 6 beggar, canter, chiaus,
coquin, harlot, rascal 7 cheater, culprit,
erratic, lowlife, sharper, villain 8 mischief,
picaroon, scalawag, swindler 9 defrauder,
miscreant, scoundrel, skeezicks, trickster
10 blackguard, delinquent, mountebank
11 rapscallion *relating to:* 10 picaresque

roguery 5 fraud 7 devilry, waggery 8 deviltry, mischief, trickery 9 devilment, diablerie 11 waggishness 12 sportiveness

roguish 3 coy, sly 4 arch 5 antic, lying
6 impish, pranky, shifty, wicked 7 knavish,
larkish, playful 8 espiègle, prankful, prankish 11 mischievous

roil 3 mud, vex 4 foul, rile 5 annoy, dirty,
grate, muddy, peeve 6 befoul, burn up,
muddle, nettle 7 blunder, disturb, inflame,
pollute, provoke, turmoil 8 irritate 9 aggravate 10 exasperate 11 contaminate

roily 5 muddy, riley 6 turbid

roister 4 hell, riot 5 revel, spree 6 frolic
7 carouse, wassail

Roland 7 Orlando *beloved:* 4 Aude
betrayer: 4 Gano 7 Ganelon *friend:* 6 Oliver 7 Olivier *horn:* 7 Olivant *sword:* 8 Dur-
andal, Durendal *uncle:* 11 Charlemagne

role 3 bit 4 duty, face, look, part, show
5 guise 6 aspect, office 7 seeming 8 business, clothing, function, province 9 character, semblance 10 appearance

roll 3 bun, gad, rob 4 bask, bolt, bunn,
clew, coil, file, flow, furl, gush, gyre, list,
muse, pour, roam, rock, rota, rove, toss,
turn, wind, wrap 5 drape, drift, growl,
heave, pitch, range, revel, stray, surge, troll
6 bundle, circle, enwrap, goggle, grovel,
gyrate, muster, ponder, ramble, roster,
rotate, rumble, scroll, stream, swathe, wallow, wander, welter, whelve, wintle, wrap
up 7 biscuit, brioche, catalog, envelop,
grumble, indulge, revolve, rissole, rollick,
swaddle, trundle 8 enswathe, involute,
meditate, mull over, register, ruminate,
schedule, turn over *of coins:* 7 rouleau
sweet: 8 schnecke

roll about 6 wallow, welter

roll back 5 lower 6 reduce 7 repulse

roll call 4 list 6 roster 7 catalog 8 register, schedule

rolled 8 obvolute *backward:* 8 revolute
together: 9 convolute

roller 4 wave 5 finer, inker, winch
6 caster, fascia, rowlet 7 breaker, carrier
8 cylinder

rollick 4 bask, lark, play, roll, romp
5 caper, frisk, revel, sport 6 cavort, frolic,
gambol, wallow, welter 7 indulge
8 escapade

rollicking 3 gay 4 glad, wild 5 antic,
happy, merry 6 jovial, joyful, joyous, lively
7 playful 8 cheerful 9 hilarious, sprightly
10 frolicsome 12 lighthearted

rolling stock 4 cars 6 trucks 7 coaches,
engines 8 cabooses, Pullmans, sleepers,
trailers 11 locomotives

rolling stone 5 rover 6 roamer 7 drifter,
rambler 8 wanderer 9 meanderer

roll up 4 furl 10 accumulate

roly-poly see rotund

Roman 5 brave, Latin, papal 7 Italian
amphitheater: 9 Colosseum *assembly:*
5 forum 6 senate 7 comitia *building:*
5 Forum 6 Circus 8 basilica, Pantheon
comedy writer: 7 Plautus, Terence *conspirator:* 6 Brutus 7 Cassius 8 Catiline
date: 4 Ides 7 calends, kalends *emperors:* 4 Nero, Otho 5 Galba, Nerva, Titus,
Verus 6 Julian, Trajan 7 Hadrian, Maximus,
Severus 8 Augustus, Caligula, Claudius,
Commodus, Domitian, Tiberius, Valerian
9 Caracalla, Vespasian 10 Diocletian, Theodosius 11 Constantine, Valentinian
entrance hall: 5 atria (plural) 6 atrium
epic: 6 Aeneid *epigrammatist:* 7 Martial
family: 7 Gracchi *Fates:* 4 Nona 5 Morta
6 Decuma, Parcae *founder:* 5 Remus
7 Romulus *fountain:* 5 Trevi *garment:*
4 toga 5 palla, sagum, stola, stole, tunic
general: 5 Sulla, Titus 6 Antony, Marius,
Scipio 8 Agricola
god: 4 deus
  blind: 6 Plutus *chief:* 4 Jove 7 Jupiter
  messenger: 7 Mercury *of agriculture:*
  6 Saturn *of animals:* 6 Faunus *of
  death:* 4 Mors *of dreams:* 8 Morpheus
  of fire: 6 Vulcan *of gates and doors:*

5 Janus *of healing:* **11** Aesculapius *of heaven:* **6** Uranus *of households:* **5** Lares **7** Penates *of love:* **4** Amor **5** Cupid *of medicine:* **11** Aesculapius *of mirth:* **5** Comus *of regeneration:* **7** Priapus *of sleep:* **6** Somnus *of the sea:* **6** Pontus **7** Neptune, Proteus *of the sun:* **3** Sol **6** Apollo *of the underworld:* **3** Dis **5** Orcus, Pluto **8** Dispater *of the wind:* **5** Eurus, Notus **6** Aeolus, Aquilo, Auster, Boreas **8** Favonius, Zephyrus *of war:* **4** Mars **8** Quirinus *of wealth:* **6** Plutus *of wine:* **7** Bacchus *of woods:* **6** Faunus *two-faced:* **5** Janus

goddess: **3** dea
of agriculture: **5** Ceres *of beauty:* **5** Venus *of dawn:* **6** Aurora *of flowers:* **5** Flora *of handicrafts:* **7** Minerva *of harvests:* **3** Ops *of health:* **7** Minerva *of hope:* **4** Spes *of hunting:* **5** Diana *of justice:* **7** Astraea *of love:* **5** Venus *of marriage:* **4** Juno *of night:* **3** Nox *of peace:* **3** Pax *of springs:* **7** Juturna *of strife:* **9** Discordia *of the earth:* **6** Tellus *of the hearth:* **5** Vesta *of the moon:* **4** Luna *of the sea:* **10** Amphitrite *of the underworld:* **10** Proserpina *of victory:* **6** Vacuna *of war:* **7** Bellona *of wisdom:* **7** Minerva *of womanhood:* **4** Juno

greeting: **3** ave **helmet:** **5** galea **6** cassis **hero:** **6** Caesar **11** Cincinnatus **hill:** **7** Caelian, Viminal **8** Aventine, Palatine, Quirinal **9** Esquiline **10** Capitoline **historian:** **4** Livy **5** Nepos **king:** **7** Romulus, Servius, Tullius **12** Ancus Martius **13** Numa Pompilius **military formation:** **3** ala **6** alares (plural) **7** phalanx **military unit:** **6** cohort, legion **7** maniple **officer:** **9** centurion **official:** **5** augur, edile **6** aedile, censor, consul, lictor **7** praetor, prefect, tribune **8** irenarch, quaestor **people:** **5** Laeti **6** populi (plural) **7** populus, Sabines **8** plebeians **9** plebeians **10** patricians **philosopher:** **4** Cato **6** Seneca **physician:** **11** Aesculapius **port:** **5** Ostia **procurator:** **6** Pilate **racecourse:** **6** circus **road:** **4** iter **slave:** **9** Spartacus **statesman:** **4** Cato **5** Pliny **6** Caesar, Cicero, Seneca **7** Agrippa **8** Augustus, Maecenas **symbol of authority:** **6** fasces

roman à ___ **4** clef

romance **3** woo **4** gest, love, tale **5** amour, court, fable, fancy, feign, geste, novel, story **6** affair **7** fantasy, fiction **8** stardust **10** love affair

Romance language **6** French **7** Catalan, Italian, Spanish **8** Romanian, Rumanian **9** Provençal **10** Portuguese

Romania *capital:* **9** Bucharest **monetary unit:** **3** leu

romantic **4** wild **5** ideal, mushy **6** ardent, dreamy, exotic, gothic, poetic, slushy, sticky, unreal **7** maudlin, mawkish, strange **8** bathetic, fabulous, fanciful, invented, quixotic **9** fantastic, imaginary, visionary **10** idealistic, lovey-dovey **11** extravagant, sentimental

Romany **5** gipsy, gypsy

Romeo **7** amorist, Don Juan, gallant **8** Casanova, lothario, paramour *beloved:* **6** Juliet *enemy:* **6** Tybalt *father:* **8** Montague *friend:* **8** Mercutio

Rommel, Erwin *nickname:* **9** Desert Fox

romp **4** play, roil, rout **5** caper, frisk **6** cavort, frolic, gambol, hoyden **7** courant, gammock, rollick, runaway, skylark

Romulus *brother:* **5** Remus *father:* **4** Mars *mother:* **10** Rhea Silvia *victim:* **5** Remus

rondure **3** orb **4** ball **5** globe, round **6** circle, sphere

rood **5** cross **8** crucifix

roof **3** hip, top **4** apex, deck, dome, flat, peak **5** cover, crest, crown, haven, house **6** cupola, harbor, palate, shield, summit, vertex **7** chamber, mansard, shelter **8** covering, housetop **9** fastigium *automobile:* **8** fastback *false:* **7** cricket *material:* **3** tar, tin **4** tile **5** paper, slate, straw, terne **6** copper, gravel, thatch **8** shingles *of a cavern:* **4** dome *of the mouth:* **6** palate *part:* **3** hip **4** eave **7** cricket *peak:* **3** hip *structure:* **9** penthouse *type:* **5** gable **6** cupola **7** gambrel, mansard **9** butterfly **10** jerkinhead *vaulted:* **4** dome

roofer **5** tiler

rook **4** bird, crow, milk **5** bleed, cheat, mulct, raven, steal, stick, sweat **6** castle, fleece **7** defraud, swindle

rookery **5** roost **8** building

rookie **4** colt, tyro **6** novice **7** recruit, trainee **8** beginner, freshman, neophyte, newcomer **9** novitiate **10** apprentice, tenderfoot

room **3** den, hut **4** aula, cell, hall, play, rein, seat, sway **5** board, divan, house, lodge, place, put up, range, roost, salon, scope, space, study **6** billet, camera, harbor, leeway, margin, reside, studio **7** boudoir, cabinet, chamber, cubicle, expanse, gallery, lodging **8** domicile, latitude **9** apartment, clearance *ancient Roman:* **5** atria (plural) **6** oecus **7** fumaria **8** aedicule *eating:* **4** nook **7** cenacle, kitchen **9** refectory *food storage:* **6** larder, pantry *for paintings:* **7** gallery *for small meetings:* **7** seminar *in a monastery:* **4** cell **6** lavabo **8** locutory **9** refectory **11** calefactory *in a prison:* **4** cell **7** dungeon *in a tower:* **6** belfry *next to dining room:* **7** servery *on a ship:* **5** cabin **6** galley *public:* **7** theater *round:* **7** rotunda

room and board 7 lodging 8 lodgment
roomer 5 guest 6 lodger, tenant
7 boarder
roomy 4 wide 5 ample, broad, large,
spacy 7 spacial 8 spacious 9 capacious
10 commodious
Roosevelt, F.D. *birthplace:* 8 Hyde Park
dog: 4 Fala *message:* 12 fireside chat
mother: 4 Sara *predecessor:* 6 Hoover
program: 7 New Deal *successor:* 6 Truman *wife:* 7 Eleanor
roost 3 hut, sit 4 land, nest, room 5 board,
house, light, lodge, perch, put up 6 alight,
billet, garret, harbor, settle 7 dovecot, lodging, quarter, set down, sit down 8 domicile,
dovecote 9 touch down
rooster 4 cock 5 capon, gallo 8 game-
cock 11 chanticleer
root 3 dig, fix 4 base, bulb, core, grub,
moot, pith, soul, stem, well 5 basis, cheer,
embed, grout, heart, infix, lodge, plant,
quick, radix, shout, stuff, tuber 6 bottom,
center, etymon, ground, marrow, origin, rise
to, settle, source 7 applaud, bedrock,
essence, footing, ingrain, radical, support
8 entrench, fountain, radicate, wellhead
9 beginning, establish, inception, substance 10 derivation, foundation *aromatic:*
7 ginseng *combining form:* 4 rhiz 5 rhiza,
rhizo 6 rhizae (plural), rrhiza 7 rrhizae (plural) *edible:* 3 oca, oka, roi, yam 4 beet,
eddo 6 carrot, ginger, radish, turnip 7 parsnip 8 rutabaga, tuckahoe *fragrant:*
4 khus 5 orris 6 cuscus, kuskus 7 vetiver
8 khuskhus *main:* 7 taproot *medicinal:*
5 jalap 7 ginseng, zedoary *relating to:*
7 radical *starch:* 4 arum *tropical:* 4 taro
word: 6 etymon *yielding red dye:* 4 chay,
choy 5 chaya, choya 6 madder
rootlet 7 radicel, radicle, rhizoid
root out 4 grub, stub 6 evulse 7 abolish,
blot out, destroy, wipe out 8 demolish
9 eradicate, extirpate 10 annihilate, deraci-
nate, extinguish 11 exterminate
Roots author 5 Haley
rope 3 gad, guy, tie, toe 4 bind, cord,
hemp, line, stay 5 belay, bight, brace, cable,
chord, hoose, lasso, longe, riata, sheet,
widdy 6 becket, binder, fasten, halter, hawser, lariat, shroud, strand, string, tether
7 aweband, binding, bobstay, halyard, lash-
ing, marline, outhaul, painter, towline
8 backstay, buntline, downhaul, inveigle,
jackstay, lifeline, prolonge *loop:* 7 cringle
maker: 8 strander *mooring:* 6 hawser *of
flowers:* 3 lei *saving:* 8 lifeline *ship's:*
4 vang 6 parral, parrel, ratlin 7 laniard, lanyard, marline, marling, ratline, swifter
8 rattling
ropedancer 7 acrobat
rope off 6 cordon

ropes 8 minutiae 10 ins and outs, proce-
dures, techniques
ropy 4 wiry 6 sinewy 7 fibrous, stringy
8 muscular
roque 7 croquet
rorqual 5 whale 7 finback
Rosalind's beloved 7 Orlando
rosary 5 beads 7 chaplet, garland
8 beadroll
rose 4 glow, pink 5 blush, color, flush,
rouge 6 mantle, pinken, redden 7 crimson
10 erysipelas *Chinese:* 8 Cherokee *combining form:* 4 rhod 5 rhodo, roseo *cotton:* 7 cudweed *feature:* 5 thorn *kind:*
4 moss 5 Peace, Vogue 6 Circus, damask 7 Fashion, Granada, Iceberg, New
Dawn, Pascali, Tiffany 8 Rubaiyat 9 Flora-
dora, Montezuma, polyantha, Tropicana
10 Floribunda 11 grandiflora, Mount
Shasta 12 Crimson Glory, Paul's Scarlet,
Red Pinocchio 13 Golden Showers
14 Queen Elizabeth *wild:* 8 eglatere
roseate 3 red 4 pink 6 blushy, bright,
florid, likely 7 auroral, flushed, healthy,
hopeful 8 aurorean, blooming, blushful,
blushing, cheerful, rubicand 9 favorable,
promising 10 optimistic, promiseful
rose-colored see **roseate**
rosemary 4 mint 8 costmary 9 rosmarine
Rosenkavalier composer 7 Strauss
rose oil 5 attar
Rose Tattoo author 8 Williams
rosette 7 cockade 8 ornament
Rosh's father 8 Benjamin
Rosinante's master 7 Quixote (Don)
Rosmersholm author 5 Ibsen
____ **Rossetti** 5 Dante 9 Christina
12 Dante Gabriel *work:* 8 Sing-Song
11 Annus Domini, Seek and Find, Sister
Helen 12 Beata Beatrix 14 The House of
Life
Rossini opera 6 Otello 8 Tancredi
11 William Tell
Rostand hero 6 Cyrano
roster 4 list, roll, rota 5 slate 6 muster,
scroll 7 catalog 8 beadroll, register, roll call,
schedule 10 muster roll
rostrum 4 beak, dais 5 snout 6 pulpit
7 lectern, tribune 8 platform 9 proboscis
rosy see **roseate**
rot 3 ret 4 bosh, bull, crap, sink, turn,
warp 5 bilge, chaff, decay, hooey, spoil,
stain, taint, trash 6 banter, debase, fester,
molder, worsen 7 corrode, corrupt, crumble, debauch, decline, deprave, descend,
hogwash, pervert, putrefy, rubbish, vitiate
8 nonsense 9 animalize, break down,
decompose, poppycock 10 bestialize,
degenerate, demoralize, disimprove, retrograde 11 deteriorate 12 disintegrate
13 decomposition

rotary 6 circle 8 gyratory, spinning
rotate 4 gyre, pass, roll, spin, turn 5 pivot, twirl, wheel 6 circle, follow, gyrate 7 precess, relieve, revolve, succeed, trundle 8 exchange, rotiform, windmill 9 alternate 10 circumduct 11 interchange *a log:* 4 birl
rotation 4 gyre, turn 5 round, wheel, whirl 7 circuit, turning 8 gyration 10 revolution
rote 4 list, pace 5 grind, learn 6 course, custom, groove, memory, repeat, system 7 routine 8 practice 9 automatic, treadmill 10 memorizing, repetition 12 memorization
rotten 2 up 3 bad, bum 4 foul, poor, punk, sour 5 amiss, fetid, nasty, wrong 6 crappy, putrid 7 carrion, corrupt, decayed, spoiled, tainted, touched, unhappy, unsound, vicious 8 chiselly, depraved, perverse, unstable 9 nefarious, offensive, putrified, unhealthy 10 abominable, decomposed, degenerate, flagitious, putrescent, undermined, unpleasant, villainous 11 displeasing 12 disagreeable 13 disintegrated *combining form:* 4 sapr 5 sapro
rotter 3 cad, cur 7 bounder, shirker, slacker 9 yellow dog 10 blackguard
rotund 3 fat 5 beefy, buxom, dumpy, obese, plump, podgy, pudgy, round, squat, stout, thick, tubby 6 chubby, chunky, plumpy, spuddy, stocky, stubby 7 paunchy, ringing, vibrant 8 heavyset, plangent, plumpish, resonant, roly-poly, sonorant, sonorous, thickset 9 consonant, spherical 10 potbellied, resounding, roundabout
rouge 3 red 4 glow, pink, rose 5 blush, color, flush 6 mantle, pinken, redden 7 crimson
rough 3 bad, dry, raw 4 curt, firm, hard, punk, rude, wild 5 bluff, blunt, brief, brute, bumpy, crass, crude, draft, gross, gruff, hairy, harsh, heavy, raspy, rowdy, short, solid, tight, tough, uncut, yahoo 6 abrupt, broken, brushy, burred, choppy, coarse, craggy, crusty, hispid, hoarse, jagged, knotty, mucker, raging, rugged, severe, sketch, stormy, trying, uneven, unhewn, vulgar 7 arduous, boorish, brusque, cragged, furious, grating, jarring, operose, outline, rasping, raucous, ruffian, scraggy, toughie, tricksy, uncivil, uncouth, ungodly, unlevel, violent 8 asperous, block out, blustery, bullyboy, chalk out, churlish, impolite, improper, indecent, scabrous, skeleton, stormful, unformed, unseemly, unsmooth 9 adumbrate, difficult, imperfect, inclement, inelegant, ironbound, laborious, manhandle, mishandle, proximate, strenuous, turbulent, undressed, unrefined 10 blustering, boisterous, formidable, indecorous, indelicate, knock about, malodorous, ridiculous, slap around, stridulent, stridulous, tumultuous, unbecoming, undecorous, unfinished, ungra-

cious, unpolished 11 approximate, shortspoken, skeletonize, tempestuous, unfashioned 12 characterize, discourteous *combining form:* 6 trachy
roughhewn 4 rude 5 crude, plain, rough 8 unformed, unworked 9 undressed 10 unfinished, unpolished 11 unfashioned 12 uncultivated
roughhouse 7 fooling, rough up 9 high jinks, horseplay, manhandle, mishandle, rowdiness 10 knock about, skylarking, slap around
roughneck see **ruffian**
roughness 7 crudity 8 acrimony, asperity 10 inequality, unevenness 12 irregularity
rough out 5 draft 6 sketch 7 outline 8 block out, chalk out, skeleton 9 adumbrate 11 skeletonize 12 characterize
rough up 9 manhandle, mishandle 10 knock about, roughhouse, slap around
round 2 by 3 arc, bow, hem, orb 4 arch, back, ball, bend, bent, bold, fast, free, full, gird, gyre, most, near, nigh, over, rich, ring, tour, turn 5 about, again, ample, arced, bowed, brisk, crook, curve, cycle, globe, harsh, large, orbed, plain, plump, podgy, pudgy, sleek, slick, tubby, vocal, wheel, whirl 6 all but, almost, arched, around, begird, beside, chubby, circle, curved, girdle, mellow, nearby, nearly, plumpy, polish, refine, rotund, smooth, sphere 7 annular, arrondi, bulbous, circuit, compass, orotund, perfect, ringing, rondure, spheric, through, vibrant 8 arciform, as good as, backward, circular, complete, conglobe, encircle, ensphere, finished, globular, gyration, plangent, plumpish, resonant, roly-poly, rotation, sonorant, sonorous, surround, vigorous, well-nigh 9 consonant, curvation, curvature, encompass, in reverse, just about, orbicular, outspoken, spherical 10 conglobate, freespoken, resounding, revolution, throughout 11 circulation, curvilinear, cylindrical *combining form:* 5 globo, troch, ventr 6 trocho, ventri, ventro *prefix:* 4 peri
roundabout 4 tour 5 jaunt, plump, tubby 6 chubby, detour, junket, outing, plumpy, rotary, rotund 7 circuit, curving, oblique, winding 8 circular, indirect, pleonasm, plumpish, roly-poly, verbiage 9 excursion, runaround, tautology, verbality 10 circuitous, collateral, meandering, periphrase 11 periphrasis
rounded 4 bent 5 arced, bowed, curvy, round 6 arched, convex, curved, mellow 7 arrondi, gibbous 8 arciform, complete, sonorous 9 curvesome, Junoesque, perfected 10 curvaceous 11 approximate, curvilinear 13 well-developed
rounder 4 rake, roué 6 bad lot, no-good,

waster **7** wastrel **10** ne'er-do-well, profligate, scapegrace

roundly **4** most, well **5** about, à fond, fully, quite **6** all but, almost, nearly, wholly **7** bluntly, sharply, smartly, utterly **8** as good as, bitterly, candidly, entirely, promptly, wellnigh **9** just about, perfectly **10** altogether, completely, scathingly

round off **3** cap **5** crown **6** climax, top off **9** culminate, finish off

round robin **6** letter, series **7** protest **8** petition, sequence **10** tournament

round trip **4** tour **7** circuit **9** excursion

round up **5** group **6** gather **7** cluster, collect **8** assemble

rouse **4** call, move, rise, stir, wake, whet **5** alarm, awake, mount, pique, rally, waken **6** awaken, bestir, deepen, excite, foment, incite, kindle, revive, vivify **7** agitate, animate, disturb, enhance, enliven, innerve, magnify, provoke, quicken **8** heighten, motivate, redouble **9** aggravate, challenge, galvanize, innervate, instigate, intensate, intensify, stimulate

rousing **3** gay **4** keen **5** alert, brisk, peppy **6** bright, lively **7** animate, dashing **8** animated, exciting, spirited, stirring **9** inspiring, sprightly **10** exhilarant, eye-popping **11** stimulating, superlative **12** exhilarating, exhilarative, intoxicating

Rousseau work **5** Emile

roust **4** move, stir **5** pique, rouse **6** excite **7** innerve, provoke, quicken **8** motivate **9** galvanize, stimulate

roustabout **4** hand **6** worker **7** laborer, workman **8** deckhand, floorman, workhand **9** operative **10** workingman

rout **3** mob **4** army, bawl, beat, drub, dust, fuss, herd, host, lick, mass, roar, romp, root, whip **5** chase, cloud, crowd, dregs, drive, eject, expel, flock, trash **6** bellow, clamor, defeat, dig out, dispel, flight, hunt up, legion, number, rabble, scores, soiree, throng, wallop **7** beating, bluster, clobber, conquer, debacle, hunt out, licking, rummage, runaway, shellac, warming **8** cakewalk, drubbing, hunt down, lambaste, riffraff, stampede, walkaway, walkover **9** clean up on, hoi polloi, multitude, other half, overthrow, reception **10** defeasance, demoralize **11** proletariat

route **3** way **4** lead, line, path, road, send, ship, show **5** guide, pilot, remit, steer, track, trail **6** course, direct, divert, escort **7** address, channel, circuit, conduct, consign, forward, highway, journey, passage **8** dispatch, shepherd, transmit **9** direction, itinerary

routine **3** act, bit, rut **4** pace, rote **5** drill, grind, habit, plain, usual **6** course, groove, wonted **7** chronic, regular **8** accepted,

everyday, habitual, ordinary, standard, workaday **9** customary, plain Jane, quotidian, treadmill **10** accustomed **11** commonplace **12** unremarkable

rove **3** gad **4** move, roam **5** drift, prowl, range, stray **6** ramble, wander **7** meander, traipse **8** vagabond **9** gallivant

rover **3** gad **5** stray **6** gadder, pirate, roamer, sea dog **7** corsair, drifter, floater, rambler, sea wolf **8** gadabout, picaroon, runabout, traveler, wanderer **9** buccaneer, itinerant, meanderer, sea robber **10** freebooter **11** peripatetic **12** rolling stone

roving **6** errant, mobile **7** nomadic, roaming, vagrant **8** rambling, vagabond **9** itinerant, itinerate, wandering, wayfaring **10** discursive **11** perambulant, peripatetic

row **3** oar **4** beef, file, fray, fuss, line, list, pull, punt, rank, sail, scud, spat, tier, tiff **5** align, brawl, broil, chain, fight, melee, mouth, order, queue, run-in, scrap, scull, set-to, swath, train **6** affray, bicker, clamor, fracas, paddle, propel, sequel, series, string **7** brabble, dispute, echelon, quarrel, rhubarb, wrangle **8** argument, sequence, squabble **9** bickering, caterwaul, commotion **10** falling-out, succession **11** altercation, consecution, disturbance, progression

rowdy **4** punk, rude **5** rough, tough, yahoo **6** mucker, unruly, vulgar **7** hoodlum, raffish, raucous, ruffian, toughie **8** bullyboy, stubborn **9** roughneck, turbulent **10** boisterous, disorderly, tumultuous **11** rumbustious

Rowena *father:* **7** Hengist *guardian:* **6** Cedric *husband:* **7** Ivanhoe **9** Vortigern

Roxana *husband:* **9** Alexander *rival:* **7** Statira

royal **3** top **4** easy **5** grand, light, noble, prime, regal **6** august, facile, kingly, lordly, simple, smooth, superb **7** stately **8** baronial, champion, five-star, glorious, imperial, imposing, kinglike, majestic, princely, splendid, superior **9** classical, excellent, frontrank, grandiose, monarchal, number one, sovereign **10** effortless, monarchial **11** magnificent, monarchical

royalist **4** Tory **5** blimp, white **7** Bourbon, diehard **8** Cavalier **11** reactionary

rub **3** bar, irk, vex **4** buff, fret, gall, rasp, rile, snag, wear, wipe **5** annoy, chafe, crimp, erode, glaze, gloss, grate, graze, grind, peeve, scour, scrub, shine **6** abrade, bother, glance, hamper, hurdle, nettle, polish, ruffle, scrape, smooth, stroke **7** burnish, corrade, furbish, massage, provoke **8** irritate, obstacle, traverse **9** aggravate, excoriate, hindrance **10** difficulty, exasperate, impediment **11** obstruction

Rubaiyat author **11** Omar Khayyam

rubber **4** nose **5** snoop **6** butt-in, eraser

7 Paul Pry, trouble **8** busybody, quidnunc
9 whetstone **10** caoutchouc, misfortune
11 nosey Parker **12** intermeddler *basis:*
5 latex *hard:* **7** ebonite *synthetic:* **8** neoprene *tree:* **5** Hevea **7** manihot

Rubber City 5 Akron

rubberneck 3 eye **4** gape, gaze, look,
ogle **5** prier, pryer, snoop, stare **6** butt-in,
goggle **7** meddler, tourist, tripper **8** busybody, kibitzer, quidnunc, sight-see **9** buttinsky, sightseer **10** pragmatist
12 intermeddler

rubbish 3 pap, rot **4** bosh, crap, junk,
slop **5** bilge, dreck, dross, hooey, offal,
trash, waste, wrack **6** debris, kelter, litter,
pablum, refuse, rubble **7** garbage, hogwash **8** nonsense, tommyrot **9** poppycock,
sweepings **11** foolishness

rubbishy 4 base, mean, poor **5** cheap,
tatty **6** common, paltry, shoddy, sleazy,
trashy **9** worthless

rube 4 boor, hick **5** yahoo **6** rustic
7 bucolic, bumpkin, hayseed, redneck **9** hillbilly **10** clodhopper, provincial
12 backwoodsman

rubicund 3 red **5** flush, ruddy **6** florid
7 flushed, glowing **8** sanguine **11** fullblooded

rubidium *symbol:* **2** Rb

rub out 4 do in, kill, raze, ruin **5** smash,
wreck **6** finish, murder **7** bump off, destroy,
put away, shatter **8** decimate, demolish,
destruct, knock off **9** liquidate **10** annihilate, extinguish, obliterate **11** assassinate

rubric 3 rud **4** name, ruby **5** canon, class,
nomen, ruddy, style, title **6** redden, rubify,
ruddle **7** concept, notable **8** category, cognomen, nameable **9** memorable, red-letter
10 noteworthy, observable **11** appellation,
appellative, designation, incarnadine
12 compellation, denomination

ruck 3 mob **4** fold, heap, mass, pile
5 crimp, crowd, group, plica, ridge, rivel,
screw **6** crease, furrow, jumble, muster,
pucker, rimple, rumple **7** company, crimple,
crinkle, crumple, scrunch, wrinkle **9** congeries, gathering, multitude **10** assemblage,
collection, generality **11** aggregation,
corrugation

rucksack 4 pack **8** backpack

ruckus 3 row **4** coil, fuss, to-do **5** brawl,
broil, melee, scrap **6** fracas, furore, hassle,
rumpus, shindy, uproar **7** dispute, quarrel,
shindig, wrangle **8** squabble **9** bickering,
commotion, confusion **10** falling-out
11 altercation, controversy, disturbance

ruction see **ruckus**

ruddle see **redden**

ruddy 3 red **4** rosy, ruby **5** flush, vivid
6 blowsy, florid, lively, redden, rubify, rubric
7 bronzed, flushed, glowing **8** blooming,

rubicund, sanguine **11** full-blooded,
incarnadine

rude 3 ill, raw **4** curt, wild **5** bluff, crass,
crude, fresh, green, gross, gruff, harsh,
lumpy, rough, surly **6** abrupt, bitter, callow,
clumsy, coarse, crusty, Gothic, ribald, rugged, savage, simple, stormy, unhewn, vulgar **7** angular, boorish, brusque, crabbed,
Hunnish, ill-bred, incivil, inexact, loutish, natural, uncivil, uncouth **8** arrogant, barbaric,
churlish, clownish, ignorant, impolite, impudent, inexpert, insolent, inurbane, tactless,
unformed, unlicked, unsubtle, untaught,
unversed, unworked **9** barbarian, barbarous, benighted, dissonant, elemental,
imperfect, imprecise, incondite, inelegant,
intrusive, makeshift, primitive, proximate,
rough-hewn, truculent, turbulent, undressed,
unfleshed, unrefined, unwrought **10** cacophonic, discordant, illiterate, immoderate,
mannerless, meddlesome, uncultured, uneducated, unfinished, ungracious, unhandsome, unlettered, unmannered, unmannerly,
unpolished, unschooled **11** approximate,
cacophonous, disgracious, disharmonic,
empty-headed, ill-mannered, impertinent,
know-nothing, rudimentary, uncalled-for,
uncivilized, uncourteous, unfashioned,
unmitigated, unpracticed, unprocessed
12 discourteous, inharmonious, unconversant, uncultivated, unharmonious, uninstructed **13** disrespectful

rudiment 5 basic **6** anlage **7** element,
vestige **9** beginning, essential
11 fundamental

rudimentary 5 basal, basic **7** initial **8** simplest **9** beginning, elemental, vestigial
10 elementary **11** fundamental, undeveloped *prefix:* **3** pro

rue 3 woe **4** care, pity, ruth **5** dolor, grief,
mourn **6** bewail, grieve, lament, regret,
repent, sorrow **7** anguish, deplore, penance, remorse **8** sympathy **9** heartache,
penitence, penitency **10** affliction, compassion, contrition, heartbreak, repentance
11 compunction **12** contriteness

rueful 3 sad **4** poor **5** sorry **6** dolent,
woeful **7** doleful, piteous, pitiful, ruthful
8 contrite, dolesome, dolorous, hopeless,
mournful, pathetic, penitent, pitiable,
wretched **9** afflicted, depressed, miserable,
oppressed, plaintive, sorrowful **10** despairing, despondent, lamentable, lugubrious,
melancholy **11** weighed down

ruff 5 frill, perch **6** collar, fringe, pigeon, ruffle **9** sandpiper **11** pumpkinseed *female:*
5 reeve

ruffian 4 hood, punk, thug **5** bully, rough,
rowdy, tough, yahoo **6** brutal, coarse,
mucker **7** gorilla, hoodlum, toughie **8** bullyboy, hooligan **9** roughneck, strong arm

ruffle 3 bug, fan, irk, rub, vex 4 blow, fret, gall, wear, wind 5 annoy, chafe, erode, frill, graze, jabot, pleat, ruche 6 abrade, bother, gather, nettle, ripple, winnow 7 agitate, corrade, dispute, disturb, provoke, stiffen, trouble, wrinkle 8 dishevel, disorder, distract, drumbeat, exercise, furbelow, irritate, skirmish 10 disarrange, discompose

Rufus'father 5 Simon

rug 3 mat 4 wrap 5 cover 6 carpet, runner 7 blanket, laprobe 8 covering *kind:* 3 rag, rya 6 dhurry, hooked 7 braided, flokati, Persian 8 Aubusson, Oriental 10 Savonnerie

rugby *formation:* 5 scrum 9 scrummage *goal:* 7 dropped, penalty *period:* 4 half *player:* 6 center, hooker, winger 8 standoff 9 scrum half *scoring:* 3 try 4 goal 10 conversion *team:* 7 fifteen *term:* 4 heel 5 match 7 convert, dribble, hand off, knock on 9 fair catch *time-out:* 8 stoppage *version:* 5 union 6 league

rugged 3 dry 4 hard, rude, wild 5 burly, hardy, harsh, heavy, husky, rough, stern, tough 6 bitter, brawny, brutal, coarse, craggy, hoarse, jagged, knotty, robust, severe, strong, sturdy, uneven 7 arduous, austere, boorish, grating, ill-bred, jarring, loutish, lumpish, operose, rasping, raucous, scraggy, unlevel 8 asperous, churlish, clownish, lubberly, muscular, rigorous, scabrous, stalwart, unsmooth, vigorous 9 difficult, inclement, laborious, strenuous, unrefined, weathered 10 formidable, robustious, stridulent, stridulous, unpolished 11 intemperate

Ruggiero *guardian:* 7 Atlante *sister:* 7 Marfisa *slayer:* 11 Tisaphernes *wife:* 10 Bradamante

ruin 4 balk, bane, beat, bilk, bust, dash, do in, doom, draw, fall, foil, harm, hurt, loss, maim, raze, sack, undo 5 break, decay, drain, havoc, spoil, use up, waste, wrack, wreck 6 baffle, beggar, blight, damage, debase, deface, devour, fold up, impair, injury, mangle, pauper, ravage, reduce, thwart, unmake 7 atrophy, break up, corrupt, decline, deplete, despoil, destroy, exhaust, outrage, pillage, unbuild, undoing, unframe, vitiate, wipe out, wrecker 8 bankrupt, calamity, clean out, collapse, decimate, demolish, desolate, dishonor, downfall, draw down, mischief, mutilate, spoliate 9 confusion, crumbling, decadence, depredate, desecrate, destroyer, devastate, disfigure, disrepair, downgrade, frustrate, overthrow, pauperize 10 circumvent, declension, degeneracy, degenerate, devolution, dilapidate, disappoint, impoverish 11 destruction, devastation, dissolution 12 degeneration 13 deterioration

ruination 4 bane, loss 5 havoc 7 undoing 8 downfall 9 confusion, destroyer 11 destruction, devastation

ruinous 5 fatal 7 fateful 8 wrackful, wreckful 10 calamitous, disastrous, pernicious, shattering 11 cataclysmic, destructive 12 annihilative, catastrophic

rule 3 law 4 lead, sway 5 axiom, bylaw, canon, edict, gnome, guide, habit, infer, judge, maxim, moral, order, reign 6 assize, course, custom, decide, decree, deduce, dictum, direct, figure, gather, govern, manage, method, regime, settle, truism 7 brocard, command, control, decorum, precept, preside, prevail, regency, regimen, resolve, statute 8 aphorism, apothegm, conclude, decretum, doctrine, dominate, domineer, dominion, overrule 9 authority, determine, etiquette, influence, ordinance, principle, procedure, propriety 10 regulation 11 fundamental *absolute:* 8 autarchy *by a god:* 8 thearchy, theonomy *combining form:* 4 nomy 5 archy

rule out 3 bar 4 bate, ward 5 avert, debar, deter 6 except, forbid, refuse 7 exclude, forfend, obviate, prevent, scratch, suspend 8 count out, preclude, prohibit, stave off 9 eliminate, forestall

ruler 4 king, lord 5 queen 6 archon, dynast, gerent, prince, regent, satrap, sultan 7 emperor, monarch, viceroy 8 governor, hierarch, oligarch, pentarch, princess, theocrat 9 dominator, imperator, matriarch, patriarch, potentate, sovereign 12 straightedge *absolute:* 6 despot, tyrant 8 autocrat, dictator, omniarch, overlord *Arab:* 4 amir, emir 5 emeer, sheik 6 sharif, sheikh, sherif, sultan *Asian:* 4 khan *Byzantine Empire:* 6 exarch *combining form:* 4 arch *Egyptian:* 7 pharaoh *family:* 7 dynasty *Iranian:* 4 shah *one of four:* 8 tetrarch *one of seven:* 8 heptarch *one of three:* 7 triarch 8 triumvir *Persian:* 6 satrap *Russian:* 4 czar, tsar, tzar *Turkish:* 3 bey, dey

ruling 3 law 4 rife 5 chief, edict, ukase 6 decree 7 central, current, pivotal, popular, rampant, regnant, statute 8 cardinal, decision 9 directive, prevalent 10 overriding, prevailing, widespread 11 predominant

Rumania see **Romania**

rumble 3 cry 4 boom, buzz, clap, peal, roar, roll, talk 5 blast, burst, crack, crash, growl, ondit, rumor 6 gossip, murmur, report, uproar 7 hearsay, quarrel, resound, thunder 9 complaint, grapevine 11 disturbance, scuttlebutt

ruminant 3 cow, yak 4 deer, goat, tahr 5 bison, camel, goral, llama, okapi, serow, sheep, takin 6 alpaca, cattle, musk ox, vicuña 7 buffalo, chamois, chewing, giraffe, guanaco **8** antelope *stomach:* **5** rumen **6** omasum **8** abomasum **9** reticulum

ruminate　4 chew, mull, muse, roll **5** champ, chomp, chump, munch, think, weigh **6** crunch, ponder **7** chumble, reflect, revolve, scrunch **8** cogitate, consider, meditate, mull over, turn over **9** masticate **10** deliberate, excogitate **11** contemplate

ruminative　7 pensive **8** thinking **9** pondering **10** cogitative, meditative, reflecting, reflective, thoughtful **11** speculative **13** contemplative

rummage　4 beat, comb, fish, grub, hash, mash, poke, rake, rout, seek **5** mix up, scour **6** dig out, forage, hunt up, jumble, jungle, litter, mess up, muddle, search, spy out, tumble **7** clutter, disrupt, disturb, examine, hunt out, ransack **8** disarray, disorder, finecomb, hunt down, mishmash, scramble **9** ferret out, patchwork, potpourri, search out **10** collection, disarrange, discompose, hotchpotch, miscellany, scrutinize **11** disorganize

rummy　3 odd **4** lush **5** drunk, queer **6** boozer, lusher **7** bizarre, curious, guzzler, oddball, strange, swiller, tippler **8** drunkard, peculiar, singular **9** eccentric, inebriate **10** boozehound

rumor　4 blab, buzz, talk, word **5** on-dit, story **6** gossip, mumble, murmur, mutter, report, rumble, tattle **7** hearsay, tidings, whisper **9** grapevine, undertone **11** scuttlebutt, susurration

rumormonger　5 tabby **6** gossip **8** gossiper, quidnunc, telltale **9** carrytale **10** talebearer

rump　4 beam, hind, rear **5** fanny **6** behind, bottom **7** rear end **8** backside, buttocks, derriere, haunches **9** posterior *combining form:* **3** pyg **4** pyga, pygo **5** pygal, pygia

rumple　4 fold, muss **5** crimp, screw **6** tousle **7** crimple, crinkle, scrunch, wrinkle

rumpus　see ruckus

run　2 go **3** act, dig, fly, get, ram, set, use, wax **4** bolt, come, dart, dash, flee, flit, flow, flux, fuse, gill, grow, hare, herd, hunt, keep, line, make, melt, move, pour, race, rush, shin, sink, skip, stab, tear, thaw, trip, turn, vary, work **5** apply, blend, brook, chase, creek, drift, drive, fleet, haste, hurry, range, reach, recur, refer, scoot, skirr, speed, stick, swing, tenor, trend **6** become, bustle, career, course, direct, escape, extend, gallop, govern, handle, hustle, manage, ordain, plunge, repair, resort, runnel, scorch, scurry, sprint, stream, thrust **7** bearing, bootleg, carry on, conduct, current, hotfoot, liquefy, make off, operate, proceed, retreat, rivulet, scamper, scuttle, smuggle, stretch **8** dissolve, duration, function, highball, liquesce, tendency, traverse **9** direction, endurance,

skedaddle **10** continuity, contraband, deliquesce **11** continuance, persistence **12** continuation, prolongation

run across　4 meet **8** discover **9** encounter

runagate　3 rat, vag **4** hobo **5** tramp **7** drifter, floater, vagrant **8** apostate, defector, fugitive, recreant, renegade, roadster, turncoat, vagabond, wanderer **9** turnabout

run along　2 go **4** exit, quit **5** leave **6** depart, get off **7** pull out, take off **8** shove off

runaround　6 detour, escape **7** come off, elusion, evasion **8** escaping, eschewal, shunning **9** avoidance **10** roundabout

run away　4 bolt, flee **5** elope **6** desert, escape **7** abscond **8** stampede

runaway　8 decisive, deserter, fugitive

run down　3 hit **4** stop **5** decry, trace **6** pursue **7** downcry **8** belittle, derogate, diminish **9** disparage, dispraise **10** depreciate **11** detract from, opprobriate

run-down　5 dingy, seedy, tacky, tired **6** shabby, tagrag **8** decrepit, tattered, untended **9** exhausted, neglected **10** broken-down, down-at-heel, uncared-for **11** dilapidated

rune　4 poem, song **5** charm, ogham, poesy, rhyme, spell, verse **6** poetry **11** conjuration, incantation

rung　4 step **5** grade, notch, spoke, stage, stair, tread **6** degree, handle **10** crosspiece

run in　3 nab **4** bust **5** pinch, visit **6** arrest, come by, detain, drop by, look up, pick up, stop by **9** apprehend

run-in　3 row **4** tiff **5** brush, fight, set-to **6** hassle **7** dispute, quarrel, rhubarb **8** skirmish **9** bickering, encounter **10** falling-out, velitation **11** altercation

run into　4 meet **6** become **9** encounter

runnel　see rivulet

runner　3 rug **5** agent, blade, miler, racer **6** carpet, stolon **8** operator, sprinter **9** messenger

running　4 care, easy, live, race **5** alive **6** active, charge, fluent, linear, smooth **7** conduct, cursive, dynamic, flowing, working **8** handling, roadwork, together **9** operative, oversight **10** continuous, effortless, intendance, management **11** continually, functioning, night and day, supervision **12** continuously, successively **13** consecutively *combining form:* **4** drom **5** dromo **7** dromous

running mate　3 pal **4** chum **5** buddy, crony **7** comrade **9** associate, companion

run-of-the-mill　4 fair, mean **5** typic, usual **6** common, medium, normal **7** average, general, natural, regular, typical **8** mediocre, middling, moderate, ordinary, uncommon **9** prevalent **11** commonplace,

indifferent **12** intermediate
13 unexceptional
run on 3 gab, jaw, yak **4** chat, talk
5 clack **6** babble, gabble, rattle **7** chatter,
prattle **8** continue
run out 4 fail, flow, oust **5** exile, expel
6 banish, deport, elapse, expire **7** cast out,
give out **8** complete, displace **9** ostracize,
transport
run over 5 spill **6** exceed, repeat **7** examine **8** overbrim, overfill, overflow, rehearse
runt 5 dwarf, midge, pygmy **6** midget, peewee **7** manikin **8** Tom Thumb **10** homunculus **11** hop-o'-my-thumb, lilliputian
run through 2 go **4** scan **5** spend, use
up **6** browse, expend, finish, pierce **7** consume, dip into, examine, exhaust **8** glance
at, rehearse, transfix **10** glance over
runty 4 puny **5** small **7** stunted **8** dwarfish **10** diminutive, undersized
12 contemptible
run up 3 wax **4** rise **5** build, erect, mount
6 expand **7** augment, enlarge **8** increase,
multiply, snowball **9** construct
10 accumulate
runway 4 path **5** strip, track, trail
6 bridge **7** channel **8** airstrip, platform
rupture 4 hole, open, part, rend, rent, rift,
rive **5** break, burst, sever, split **6** breach,
cleave, divide, hernia, schism, sunder
7 blowout, break up, disjoin, disrupt, dissect, divorce, fissure, parting, split-up **8** disunion, disunite, division, fracture, separate
9 partition **10** detachment, separation
11 dissolution, divorcement *combining
form:* **7** rrhexes (plural), rrhexis
R.U.R. *author:* **5** Čapek (Karel) *character:*
5 robot
rural 6 rustic, simple **7** bucolic, country,
idyllic, natural, outland **8** agrestic, arcadian,
pastoral, villatic **10** campestral, out-country,
provincial **11** countrified
ruse 3 jig **4** hoax, ploy, wile **5** dodge, feint,
fraud, trick **6** deceit, gambit **7** gimmick
8 artifice, maneuver, trickery **9** stratagem
10 subterfuge
rush 3 fly, run **4** boil, bolt, dart, dash, flit,
flow, flux, lash, race, scud, tear, tide, whiz
5 break, chase, drift, fleet, fling, flood, haste,
hurry, onset, sally, scoot, shoot, spate,
speed, surge **6** attack, barrel, bustle,
career, charge, course, hasten, hurtle, irrupt,
plunge, stream **7** assault, cattail, current
8 stampede, vanquish **9** hastiness, overpower **11** hurriedness **12** precipitance, precipitancy **13** precipitation

rushing 5 hasty **6** abrupt, sudden **7** hurried **8** headlong **9** impetuous **11** precipitant, precipitate, precipitous, subitaneous
Russian *family:* **7** Romanov **9** Stroganov
monk: **8** Rasputin *peasant:* **5** kulak,
mujik **6** moujik, muzhik, muzjik *ruler:* (see
czar) *saint:* **15** Alexander Nevski *villa:*
5 dacha
rustic 3 jay, yap **4** hick, jake, rube, rude
5 churl, clown, plain, rough, rural, swain,
yokel **6** farmer, joskin, simple, sturdy, sylvan, woodsy **7** artless, bucolic, bumpkin,
country, granger, hayseed, hillman, hoosier,
outland, peasant, plowboy, plowman, redneck, uncouth **8** agrestic, mossback, pastoral **9** chawbacon, greenhorn, hillbilly
10 campestral, clodhopper, countryman,
exurbanite, husbandman, out-country, provincial **11** countrified, country jake, moun-
taineer **12** backwoodsman
rustle 5 haste, hurry, speed, steal, swish
6 forage, hustle, swoosh **7** crinkle **8** celerity, dispatch, susurrus **9** swiftness
10 expedition, speediness
rustler 5 thief **6** dynamo, peeler **7** hustler
8 go-getter, live wire **11** self-starter
Rustum's son and victim 6 Sohrab
rusty 3 dry **4** slow **5** harsh, hoary, inept,
rough **6** hoarse, rugged **7** grating, jarring,
rasping, raucous, restive **8** outmoded, strident **10** discolored
rut 4 heat, pace, rote **5** grind, track
6 estrus, furrow, groove **7** channel, routine
9 treadmill
rutabaga 5 swede **6** turnip
ruth 3 rue **4** pity **5** grief, mercy **6** regret,
sorrow **7** penance, remorse, sadness
8 distress, sympathy **9** attrition, penitence,
penitency **10** compassion, contrition, repentance **11** compunction
Ruth *husband:* **4** Boaz **6** Mahlon *mother-
in-law:* **5** Naomi *son:* **4** Obed
ruthenium *symbol:* **2** Ru
ruthful 6 dolent, rueful, tender, woeful
7 doleful, pitiful **8** dolorous, wretched
9 afflicted, miserable, sorrowful
ruthless 4 grim **5** cruel **6** mortal, savage
8 pitiless **9** ferocious, merciless, unsparing
10 implacable, ironfisted, relentless, unyielding **11** unflinching, unrelenting
12 unappeasable
ruttish 3 hot **5** rutty **7** goatish, lustful,
satyric **9** lickerish, salacious **10** lascivious,
libidinous **12** concupiscent
Rwanda *capital:* **6** Kigali *monetary unit:*
5 franc

S

Sabatini novel 11 Scaramouche 12 Captain Blood

sabbatical 4 rest 5 leave

saber 5 sword

sabertooth 3 cat 5 tiger

sable 3 jet 4 dark, ebon, inky 5 black, dusky, ebony, jetty, murky, raven 6 gloomy, mammal, somber 9 pitch-dark 10 pitch-black

sabot 4 clog, shoe

sabotage 5 block, wreck 6 damage, hamper, hinder, injury 7 break up, destroy, subvert 8 obstruct, wreckage, wrecking 9 frustrate, undermine 10 impairment, subversion 11 undermining 12 subversivism

Sabra *father:* 7 Ptolemy *husband, rescuer:* 8 St. George *son:* 3 Guy 5 David 9 Alexander

Sabrina *father:* 7 Locrine *mother:* 9 Estrildis

sac 4 cyst 5 pouch

Sacar *father:* 8 Obededom *son:* 5 Ahiam

saccharine 5 sweet 6 sugary, syrupy 7 candied, cloying, honeyed, sugared 9 disarming, oversweet 11 deferential, sugarcoated 12 ingratiating

sacerdotal 8 priestly 9 religious 10 priestlike 11 ministerial

sachem 4 boss 5 chief 6 leader

sachet 3 bag 6 powder 7 perfume

sack 2 ax 3 bag, bed 4 base, drop, fire, raid, ship, wine 5 expel, pouch, strip, waste 6 bounce, devour, forage, pocket, ravage 7 boot out, cashier, despoil, dismiss, kick out, pillage 8 desolate, spoliate 9 container, depredate, desecrate, devastate, terminate

sackbut 8 trombone

sacque 6 jacket

sacrament 4 rite, sign 6 symbol 7 baptism, penance 8 ceremony 9 eucharist, matrimony 10 holy orders 12 confirmation

sacrarium 6 chapel, shrine 7 oratory, piscina 8 sacristy 9 sanctuary

sacred 4 holy 5 godly 6 immune 7 angelic, blessed, guarded, saintly 8 defended, hallowed, numinous 9 cherished, inviolate, spiritual, unprofane 10 inviolable, sacrosanct, sanctified 11 consecrated, sacramental *combining form:* 4 hagi, hier, sacr 5 hagio, hiero, sacro *mon-*

key: 6 baboon, rhesus 7 hanuman *place:* 7 sanctum *weed:* 7 vervain

sacrifice 4 cede, drop, give, lose 5 forgo, yield 6 devote, donate, eschew, martyr, victim 7 forbear, forfeit, offer up 8 dedicate, hecatomb, immolate, oblation, offering

sacrilege 7 impiety, offense 9 blasphemy, violation 11 desecration, irreverence, profanation

sacrilegious 7 impious, profane, ungodly 10 irreverent 11 blasphemous, irreligious

sacristan 6 sexton

sacristy 6 vestry

sacrosanct 6 sacred 8 esteemed, regarded 9 inviolate, respected 10 inviolable

sad 4 blue, down 5 drear, dumpy, sorry 6 dismal, dreary, gloomy, morose, triste, woeful 7 doleful, dumpish, joyless, piteous, pitiful, unhappy 8 dejected, desolate, dolorous, downbeat, downcast, grieving, mournful, pathetic, pitiable, saddened, tristful 9 depressed, mirthless, sorrowful, woebegone 10 afflicting, depressing, dispirited, lamentable, melancholy 11 melancholic 12 heavyhearted

sadden 7 depress, oppress 9 weigh down

saddle 3 tax 4 lade, load, task 5 weigh 6 burden, charge, cumber, hamper, impede, impose, weight 7 aparejo, inflict 8 encumber, restrict *adjunct:* 7 stirrup *covering:* 7 mochila *part:* 6 cantle, pommel 8 tapadera, tapadero *strap:* 5 cinch, girth 6 latigo 7 harness

sadness 3 woe 4 funk 5 blues, dinge, downs, dumps, gloom, grief, mopes 6 misery, sorrow 7 anguish, dismals, megrims 8 doldrums, dolefuls, glumness, mourning 9 dejection, dysphoria, moodiness 10 blue devils, depression, desolation, melancholy 11 despondency, forlornness, melancholia, unhappiness 12 downcastness, hopelessness, listlessness, mournfulness 13 sorrowfulness

safari 4 hunt, trek, trip 7 caravan 10 expedition

safe 4 wary 5 chary 6 intact, secure, unhurt 7 careful, guarded, healthy 8 cautious, defended, discreet, gingerly, guarding, harmless, innocent, riskless, shielded, unharmed 9 innocuous, protected, sheltered, shielding, uninjured, unscathed, wholesome 10 inviolable, protecting, scatheless, sheltering 11 calculating, circumspect, considerate, impregnable, inoffensive, uninjurious 12 invulnerable, safeguarding, unassailable, unthreatened

safety 5 cover 7 defense, shelter 8 security 9 assurance 10 protection 13 inviolability

sag 3 dip 4 bend, drop, flag, flap, flop, sink, slip, swag, wilt 5 basin, droop, slide, slump 6 dangle, hollow, slouch 7 decline, drop off, falloff, sinkage, sinking 8 downturn, fall away, settling, sinkhole 9 concavity, downslide, downswing, downtrend 10 depression

saga 4 edda, epic, tale 5 story 6 legend 9 narrative

sagacious 4 sage, wise 5 cagey, heady, smart 6 argute, astute, clever, shrewd 7 gnostic, knowing, prudent, sapient 8 critical 9 astucious, far-seeing, insighted, judicious 10 discerning, insightful, perceptive 11 intelligent 13 knowledgeable, perspicacious

sagacity 5 grasp 6 wisdom 7 insight 8 prudence, sageness, sapience, wiseness 10 perception 11 discernment, penetration, sensitivity 13 comprehension, judiciousness, understanding

sagamore 5 chief 6 sachem

sage 4 mint, sane, wise 5 acute 6 expert, master, nestor, savant, sophic 7 gnostic, knowing, learned, probing, prudent, sapient, scholar, wise man 8 polymath, profound, sensible 9 insighted, judgmatic, judicious, sagacious 10 discerning, insightful, perceptive 11 penetrating, philosophic 13 knowledgeable *Hindu:* 5 rishi 6 pandit 7 mahatma

Sagebrush State 6 Nevada

sage cock 6 grouse

Sage of ___ *Chelsea:* 7 Carlyle *Concord:* 7 Emerson *Emporia:* 5 White *Ferney:* 8 Voltaire *Monticello:* 9 Jefferson *Pylos:* 6 Nestor

sagging 8 swayback

Sagittarius 6 archer 7 centaur 13 constellation

saguaro 6 cactus

saharan 3 dry 4 arid, sere 6 barren 8 deserted

sail 3 fly 4 boat, dart, flit, scud, skim, wing 5 fleet, float, mizen, shoot, skirr, sweep, yacht 6 cruise, mizzen 7 spencer 9 spinnaker *triangular:* 3 jib 5 genoa

sailboat 4 bark, yawl 5 ketch, skiff, sloop 8 skipjack

sailing vessel 4 bark, brig, saic 5 xebec 6 barque 7 frigate, galleon 8 schooner 10 barkentine, brigantine

sailor 3 tar 4 jack, salt 5 jacky 6 seaman, swabby 7 jack-tar, mariner, swabbie, yachter 8 seafarer, shipmate 9 tarpaulin, yachtsman 10 bluejacket *British:* 5 limey *fictional:* 6 Sinbad *patron saint:* 4 Elmo *song:* 6 chanty 7 chantey 9 barcarole

saint *biography:* 11 hagiography *list:* 9 hagiology; (see also **patron saint**)

Saint, the 12 Simon Templar *creator:* 9 Charteris (Leslie)

Saint Anthony's cross 3 tau

Saint Elmo's Fire 9 corposant

Saint Joan author 4 Shaw

Saint John's bread 5 carob

saintly 4 holy 5 godly, pious 6 devout, seraph, worthy 7 angelic, upright 8 seraphic, virtuous 9 righteous

Saint Paul's Church (London) *designer:* 4 Wren

Saint Peter's Basilica *architect:* 7 Bernini 12 Michelangelo *sculpture:* 5 Pietè

Saint Vitus' dance 6 chorea

sake 3 end 4 good 5 drink 7 purpose

salaam 3 bow 8 greeting

salacious 4 fast, lewd 7 lustful, satyric 9 lecherous, libertine 10 lascivious, libidinous, licentious 11 incontinent

salad 4 brew, hash, stew, toss 5 chef's 6 Caesar 7 mélange *item:* 3 egg 4 bean, cuke, herb 5 cress, fruit, olive, onion 6 carrot, celery, cheese, endive, pepper, potato, radish, tomato 7 anchovy, cabbage, crouton, lettuce, parsley, spinach 8 chick-pea, coleslaw, cucumber, garbanzo, mushroom, scallion 10 watercress 11 cauliflower

salamander 3 eft 4 newt 8 mudpuppy, waterdog *Mexican:* 7 axolotl

salient 6 marked, moving, signal 7 obvious, weighty 8 striking 9 arresting, arrestive, important, intrusive, obtrusive, pertinent, prominent 10 impressive, noticeable, pronounced, remarkable 11 conspicuous, outstanding, significant

saline 4 salt 5 briny, salty 8 brackish 10 saliferous

saliva 4 spit 5 water 6 slaver, sputum 7 spittle

salivate 5 drool 6 drivel, slaver 7 dribble, slabber, slobber

___ Salk 5 Jonas

sallow 3 wan 4 pale 6 willow, yellow

sally 3 gag 4 gust, jape, jest, joke, quip 5 burst, crack, jaunt 6 junket, outing 7 flare-up 8 drollery, eruption, outburst 9 excursion, explosion, wisecrack, witticism

salmagundi see **hodgepodge**

salmon 4 parr, pink 5 smolt 6 grilse 7 essling, geelbec, sockeye 9 brandling *female:* 4 raun *male:* 6 kipper *smoked:* 3 lox

Salmon *father:* 3 Hur 7 Nahshon *grand-father:* 5 Caleb *son:* 4 Boaz

Salmoneus *brother:* 7 Athamas 8 Sisyphus *daughter:* 4 Tyro *father:* 6 Aeolus *mother:* 7 Enarete

Salome *composer:* 7 Strauss *father:* 5 Herod *husband:* 6 Philip 7 Zebedee 11 Aristobulus *mother:* 8 Herodias *son:* 4 John 5 James

salon 4 hall, shop 5 suite 6 parlor 9 apartment, reception

saloon 3 bar 4 hall 6 tavern 7 barroom, cantina, gallery, taproom 8 drinkery

salt 3 tar 4 jack, keep, NaCl 5 brine, salty 6 sailor, saline, seaman 7 jack-tar, mariner 8 salinize 9 sailorman, tarpaulin 10 saliferous

salt away 4 save 5 lay by, lay in, lay up, put by 8 lay aside

saltpeter 5 niter, nitre

saltworks 6 salina 7 saltern

salty 4 blue, racy 5 briny, broad, shady, spicy 6 purple, risqué, saline, wicked 7 caustic, mordant 8 brackish, off-color, scathing 9 trenchant 10 mordacious, saliferous, suggestive

salubrious 4 good 7 bracing, healthy 8 hygienic, salutary 9 healthful, wholesome 11 stimulating 12 invigorating

Salus see **Hygeia**

Salu's son 5 Zimri

salutation 2 hi 4 hail 5 hello 7 Dear Sir 8 greeting *Arab:* 6 salaam *French:* 5 salut *German:* 4 heil *Hawaiian:* 5 aloha *Italian:* 4 ciao *Latin:* 3 ave *Spanish:* 4 hola

salute 4 hail, heil 5 greet 6 accost, call to 7 address 8 greeting

salvage 4 save 6 ransom, redeem, regain, rescue 7 deliver, reclaim, recover 8 retrieve

salvation 6 saving 7 keeping 9 preserval 11 conservancy, safekeeping 12 conservation, preservation, sustentation

Salvation Army founder 5 Booth

salve 3 aid 4 balm 5 cream 6 cerate, chrism, remedy 7 unction, unguent 8 ointment 9 emollient, lubricant

salver 4 tray

salvo 4 hail 5 burst, spray, storm 6 shower, volley 7 barrage, tribute 9 broadside, cannonade, discharge, fusillade 11 bombardment, testimonial 12 appreciation

samaritan 6 helper 8 welldoer 10 benefactor

same 4 idem, like, very 5 equal, exact 7 coequal, identic, similar 8 constant 9 duplicate, identical, unfailing, unvarying 10 comparable, consistent, equivalent, invariable, tantamount, unchanging

Samoa's capital 4 Apia 8 Pago Pago

samovar 3 urn

sampan 4 boat 5 skiff

sample 4 case, part, sign, unit 5 piece 7 element, example, portion, segment 8 fragment, instance, sampling, specimen 10 indication, individual 11 case history, constituent 12 illustration

Samson *betrayer:* 7 Delilah *birthplace:* 5 Zorah *deathplace:* 4 Gaza *father:* 6 Manoah *tribe:* 3 Dan

Samson Agonistes author 6 Milton

Samuel *father:* 7 Elkanah *grandson:* 5 Heman *mother:* 5 Hannah

samurai 7 soldier, warrior *code:* 7 bushido

sanctify 5 bless 6 hallow 10 consecrate

sanctimonious 5 false 7 canting 9 deceiving, pharisaic 11 pharisaical 12 hypocritical, pecksniffian 13 self-righteous

sanction 2 OK 4 fiat, okay 5 leave 6 permit, ratify 7 approve, certify, consent, endorse, license, support 8 accredit, approval 9 allowance, authorize 10 commission, permission, sufferance 11 approbation, endorsement 12 confirmation, ratification 13 authorization, encouragement

sanctity 8 holiness 9 godliness 11 saintliness, uprightness 13 righteousness

sanctuary 4 port 5 bamah, cover, haven, oasis 6 asylum, covert, harbor, refuge, shrine 7 retreat, sanctum, shelter 9 harborage, holy place

sanctum 6 shrine 9 holy place, sanctuary

sandal 4 zori 8 huarache, huaracho *winged:* 7 talaria (plural)

sandbar 4 reef, spit 7 tombolo

sand hill 4 dune

sandpiper 4 knot, ruff, stib 5 reeve, terek 6 dunlin, teeter

sandstone deposit 6 flysch

sandwich 3 BLT, sub 4 club 5 hoagy 6 hoagie 7 grinder 9 submarine *combining form:* 6 burger

sandy 6 beachy, gritty 7 arenose, arenous 8 sabulose, sabulous

sane 3 fit 4 good, hale, sage, well, wise 5 lucid, right, sober, sound 6 cogent, normal 7 healthy, logical, prudent, sapient 8 all there, balanced, oriented, rational, sensible 9 judgmatic, judicious, wholesome 10 compelling, convincing, reasonable, well-liking 11 levelheaded 12 compos mentis

San Francisco *hill:* 3 Nob 7 Russian *tower:* 4 Coit

sangfroid 6 phlegm 7 ataraxy 9 aloofness, composure, unconcern 10 equanimity 11 self-control 12 indifference

sanguinary 4 gory 6 bloody 7 imbrued 9 homicidal, murdering, murderous 12 bloodstained, bloodthirsty

sanguine 4 gory 5 flush, ruddy 6 bloody, florid, secure, upbeat 7 assured, flushed,

glowing, hopeful, imbrued **8** rubicund
9 confident, expectant, homicidal, murdering, murderous **10** optimistic, undoubtful
11 full-blooded, self-assured **12** bloodstained, bloodthirsty, Pollyannaish, undespairing **13** self-confident
sanitary 5 clean **8** hygienic **9** healthful
sanity 3 wit **4** mind **6** reason, senses
8 lucidity, saneness **9** soundness **12** intelligence **13** comprehension
Sanskrit 5 Indic **8** language *dialect:* **4** Pali
epic: **8** Ramayana *school:* **3** tol *Scripture:* **4** Veda
Santa Lucia composer 5 Denza
sap 4 dupe, fool, gull, mark, ruin **5** blunt, chump, drain, wreck **6** pigeon, sucker, weaken **7** cripple, deplete, destroy, disable, exhaust, fall guy, saphead, unbrace **8** enervate, enfeeble, knock out **9** attenuate, schlemiel, undermine **10** debilitate
Saph's slayer 8 Sibbecai
sapid 5 tasty **6** savory **8** saporous
9 aperitive, palatable, relishing, toothsome
10 appetizing, flavorsome
sapience see **sagacity**
sapient see **sagacious**
sapling 4 tree **5** youth
Sapphira *coconspirator, husband:*
7 Ananias
Sappho *forte:* **6** poetry *island:* **6** Lesbos
sappy 5 crazy, loony, mushy, silly, soupy
6 absurd, drippy, insane, slushy, sticky
7 foolish, maudlin, mawkish **8** bathetic
11 harebrained, sentimental
Saracen 4 Arab **6** Muslim *hero:*
9 Rodomonte
Sarah *husband:* **7** Abraham *maid:*
5 Hagar *son:* **5** Isaac
sarcasm 3 wit **4** gibe, jest **5** humor, irony, scorn **6** rancor, satire **7** mockery **8** acerbity, acrimony, mordancy, raillery, repartee, ridicule, sneering **9** invective, sharpness
10 causticity, lampooning **13** corrosiveness
writer: **7** ironist
sarcastic 3 dry **4** tart **5** acerb, sharp
6 biting, ironic **7** acerbic, caustic, cutting, cynical, jeering, mocking, mordant, pungent, satiric **8** incisive, sardonic, scathing, scornful, stinging **9** corrosive, trenchant
sarcophagus 4 tomb **6** coffin
sardine 4 sild **7** herring **8** pilchard
Sardinia's capital 8 Cagliari
sardonic 3 wry **6** ironic **7** caustic, cynical, jeering, mocking, satiric **8** derisive, scornful, sneering **9** corrosive, sarcastic, saturnine
10 disdainful **12** contemptuous
sarong 5 skirt **7** garment
Sarpedon *brother:* **5** Minos **12** Rhadamanthus *father:* **4** Zeus **7** Jupiter *mother:*
6 Europa **8** Laodamia
Sartre work 4 Kean **6** Nausea **7** The

Wall **8** The Flies **10** Baudelaire, Saint Genet
sash 4 belt **6** girdle **8** ceinture, cincture
9 waistband
sashay 4 perk **5** mince, strut **6** prance
7 flounce, swagger
Saskatchewan's capital 6 Regina
sass 4 guff **5** cheek, mouth, sauce **8** back talk, saucebox **9** insolence, sassiness
12 impertinence
sassafras 3 tea **6** saloop
sassy 4 bold, pert, wise **5** doggy, fresh, lippy, natty, nervy, smart **6** brazen, cheeky, dapper, spiffy, spruce, sprucy **7** bandbox, doggish, forward **8** impudent, malapert, sparkish **9** audacious, unabashed
11 smart-alecky, well-groomed
Satan 5 beast, demon, deuce, devil, fiend, viper **6** diablo **7** Lucifer, Old Nick, serpent, villain **8** Apollyon, devil-god, renegade, succubus **9** archfiend, Beelzebub **10** Old Scratch **13** Old Gooseberry
satanic 4 evil **6** wicked **7** demonic
8 demoniac, demonian, devilish, diabolic, fiendish **9** saturnine **10** serpentine, unhallowed **11** diabolonian
satanism 9 diabolism
satchel 3 bag **4** case **5** pouch **6** valise
sate 4 cloy, fill, glut, jade, pall **5** gorge, stuff **6** stodge **7** overeat, satiate, surfeit
8 overfill **9** overstuff
satellite 4 moon **6** cohort, minion **7** sectary, sputnik **8** adherent, disciple, favorite, follower, henchman, incident, partisan, sectator **9** ancillary, attendant, attending, supporter *of Jupiter:* **2** Io **6** Europa **8** Callisto, Ganymede *of Mars:* **6** Deimos, Phobos *of Neptune:* **6** Nereid, Triton *of Saturn:*
4 Rhea **5** Dione, Janus, Mimas, Titan
6 Phoebe, Tethys **7** Iapetus **8** Hyperion
9 Enceladus *of Uranus:* **5** Ariel **6** Oberon
7 Miranda, Titania, Umbriel
satiate see **sate**
satire 5 irony, spoof, squib **6** banter, parody **7** mockery, pasquil, takeoff **8** chaffing, raillery, ridicule, spoofery, travesty **10** causticity, lampoonery, pasquinade, persiflage
satiric 6 ironic **7** caustic, mocking **8** chaffing, farcical, ironical, spoofing **9** bantering, parodying **10** lampooning, ridiculing
satirist *English:* **5** Swift **7** Marston
French: **8** Rabelais, Voltaire *Greek:*
8 Menippus *Roman:* **6** Horace **7** Juvenal, Persius **9** Petronius
satirize 4 mock **5** spoof **6** parody **7** cartoon, censure, lampoon **8** ridicule
satisfaction 6 amends **8** pleasure
9 atonement **10** attainment **11** contentment, fulfillment, restitution **13** gratification
satisfactory 2 OK **4** fair, good, okay
5 solid, sound, valid **6** cogent, decent,

enough 8 adequate, all right, passable **9** competent, sufficing, tolerable **10** acceptable, convincing, sufficient **11** comfortable **13** unexceptional

satisfy 3 pay **4** fill, meet, quit, sate, suit **5** clear, humor, pay up, serve **6** answer, assure, induce, pacify, please, settle, square **7** appease, content, fulfill, gladden, gratify, indulge, placate, satiate, suffice, win over **8** clear off, convince, inveigle, persuade, pleasure **9** conform to **10** comply with

satrap 5 ruler **7** viceroy **8** governor, henchman **11** subordinate

saturate 3 sop, wet **4** soak, wash **5** bathe, imbue, madid, probe, souse, steep **6** charge, douche, drench, infuse, pierce, soaked, sodden, soused **7** instill, pervade, soaking, sopping, suffuse **8** drenched, dripping, permeate, waterlog **9** inoculate, penetrate, percolate, transfuse

Saturn see **Cronus**

saturnalia 4 orgy **5** party **7** debauch **9** bacchanal **11** bacchanalia

saturnine 4 dark, dour, glum, ugly **5** grave, staid, sulky, surly **6** gloomy, moping, morose, silent, solemn, somber, sullen **7** crabbed, serious **8** funereal, reserved, taciturn

satyric 4 lewd **5** horny, randy **7** goatish, lustful **8** prurient **9** lecherous, libertine, lickerish, salacious **10** lascivious, libidinous, licentious, passionate **12** concupiscent

sauce 4 guff, sass **5** mouth **6** relish **7** topping **8** back talk, pertness **9** condiment, impudence **kind:** **3** soy **4** hard, lear, mole **5** bercy, chili, curry, dashi, gravy, melba, pesto, salsa **6** catsup, chivry, Mornay, panada, Robert, tartar, tomato **7** catchup, chutnee, chutney, ketchup, marengo, Newburg, piquant, soubise, supreme, tartare, velouté **8** béchamel, duxelles, marinara, matelote, noisette, normande, normandy, poivrade, poulette, ravigote, remolade **9** bearnaise, lyonnaise, mariniere, remoulade **10** bordelaise, Provençale **11** hollandaise, vinaigrette

saucy see **sassy**

Saudi Arabia *capital:* **6** Riyadh *monetary unit:* **5** riyal

Saul *concubine:* **6** Rizpah *daughter:* **5** Merab **6** Michal *father:* **4** Kish *son:* **8** Jonathan *successor:* **5** David *uncle:* **3** Ner *wife:* **7** Ahinoam

saunter 4 mope, roam, rove, walk **5** amble, drift, mosey, tarry **6** bummel, linger, loiter, ramble, stroll, wander **7** meander **8** ambulate

sausage 5 wurst **6** banger, kishka, kishke, salami, Vienna, wiener **7** baloney, bologna, boloney, chorizo, saveloy **8** cerve-

lat, chaurice, drisheen, kielbasa, pemmican **9** bratwurst, frankfort, frankfurt, pepperoni, Thuringer **10** knackwurst, knockwurst, liverwurst, mortadella **11** frankforter, frankfurter

sausage-shaped 10 botuliform

savage 4 fell, grim, rude, wild **5** brute, cruel, feral, harsh, rabid, rough **6** bloody, brutal, fierce, Gothic, Hunnic, rugged **7** bestial, brutish, Hunnish, inhuman, untamed, vicious, wolfish **8** barbaric, inhumane, primeval, ravenous, unbroken **9** barbarian, barbarous, butcherly, ferocious, heartless, murderous, primitive, rapacious, truculent, unsubdued, voracious **10** implacable, relentless **11** coldhearted, uncivilized, unharnessed, unrelenting **12** bloodthirsty, uncontrolled, uncultivated, unsocialized

savanna 5 plain **9** grassland

savant 4 sage **7** scholar, wise man

save 3 bar, but, yet **4** bank, keep, only, Stow **5** cache, guard, hoard, lay by, lay in, lay up, put by, set by, skimp, spare **6** bating, defend, except, keep up, manage, rescue, saving, scrimp, shield, unless **7** barring, besides, collect, deliver, deposit, however, husband, lay away, protect, reclaim, reserve, salvage, store up, sustain, unchain **8** conserve, lay aside, maintain, preserve, salt away, squirrel **9** aside from, economize, excluding, safeguard, stash away, stockpile, unshackle **10** accumulate **11** exclusive of

saving 3 but **6** beside, except **7** barring, besides, sparing, thrifty **9** aside from, except for, excluding, preserval, provident, salvation, stewardly **10** economical, husbanding, unwasteful **11** conservancy, safekeeping **12** conservation, preservation, sustentation

savoir faire 4 tact **5** grace, poise, taste **6** aplomb **7** address, dignity, manners **8** elegance **9** blaséness, diplomacy **10** confidence, experience, refinement **11** delicatesse, tactfulness **13** self-assurance

savor 4 feel, know, mark, tong **5** sapor, scent, smack, smell, taste, tinge, trait **6** flavor, relish, virtue **7** feature, quality **8** property, sapidity **9** affection, attribute, character **10** experience

savory 5 balmy, sapid, spicy, sweet, tasty **6** aromal **7** flavory, gustful, perfumy **8** aromatic, fragrant, perfumed, pleasing, redolent, tempting **9** ambrosial, aperitive, palatable, relishing, toothsome **10** appetizing, flaversome

saw 3 hew **4** word **5** adage **6** byword, saying **7** proverb

___ **saw 3** bow, jig, pit, rip **4** band, buck, buzz, fret, hack, whip **5** chain, crown,

saber 6 coping, scroll **7** compass, keyhole **8** circular, crosscut

sawbuck 5 horse **7** trestle **9** workhorse

sawhorse see **sawbuck**

saw-toothed 7 serrate, serried **8** serrated **11** denticulate

Saxon serf: 4 esne **warrior: 5** thane

say 4 aver, avow, cite, give, mark, most, much, nigh, read, show, talk, tell **5** about, mouth, quote, speak, state, utter, voice **6** affirm, almost, assert, nearly, recite, record, remark, repeat **7** breathe, chime in, comment, declare, deliver, express, phonate, protest **8** announce, bring out, decision, indicate, proclaim, register, throw out **9** authority, enunciate, just about, pronounce **10** animadvert, articulate

saying 3 mot **4** word **5** adage, axiom, maxim **6** byword, dictum, truism **7** proverb

scab 5 crust **6** eschar **13** strikebreaker

scabbard 6 sheath

scabby 4 mean **5** scaly **7** blotchy **10** scurrilous

scabrous 5 downy, harsh, rough, scaly **6** craggy, jagged, knobby, knotty, rugged, scabby, scurfy, thorny, uneven **7** bristly, prickly, scraggy, unlevel **8** asperous, unsmooth

scads 3 lot **4** gobs, heap, much, slew, wads **5** loads, reams **6** oodles **7** jillion, million, umpteen, zillion **8** slathers, thousand, trillion **9** great deal, multitude **10** quantities

scaffold 5 stage **7** staging **8** platform

Scala, La city: 5 Milan **production: 5** opera

scalawag see **scamp**

scald 4 bard, boil, burn, poet **6** scorch

scale 4 peel, rate, skin, upgo **5** climb, flake, gauge, mount, ratio, scute, strip **6** ascend, degree, scutum, squama **7** chip off, measure **8** escalade, escalate, flake off, spall off **9** exfoliate **10** desquamate, proportion **11** decorticate, excorticate **auxiliary: 7** vernier **earthquake: 7** Richter **temperature: 6** Kelvin **7** Celsius **10** centigrade, Fahrenheit

scallion 4 leek **5** onion **7** shallot

scalp 4 skin **5** cheat **6** trophy

scalpel 5 knife **7** dissect

scamp 5 devil, joker, pixie, rogue **6** rascal, ribald **7** villain **8** mischief, scalawag, slyboots **9** prankster, skeezicks **11** rapscallion

scamper 3 fly, run **4** bolt, dash, flee, scud, shin, skip **5** scoot, shoot, skirr **6** scurry, sprint **7** dash off, make off, rush off, scuddle, scuttle, tear off, whip off, whiz off **8** hurry off, light out **9** hasten off, hurry away, skedaddle, speed away

scan 3 eye **4** view **5** audit **6** browse, review, survey **7** perusal, run over **8** analy-

sis, glance at, scrutiny **9** check-over **10** glance over, inspection, run through **11** examination, flip through, leaf through, observation, riff through, skim through **12** thumb through

scandal 4 tale **7** calumny **8** reproach **9** aspersion, discredit, disrepute **10** backbiting, defamation, detraction

scandalize 4 slur **5** libel, shock, smear **6** defame, malign **7** asperse, slander **9** denigrate **10** calumniate

scandalmonger 5 tabby **6** gossip **8** gossiper, quidnunc, telltale **9** backbiter, carrytale, muckraker **10** talebearer

scandalous 7 heinous **8** libelous, shocking **9** atrocious, desperate, maligning, monstrous, traducing, vilifying **10** backbiting, calumnious, defamatory, detracting, detractive, outrageous, slanderous

Scandinavia 6 Norway, Sweden **7** Denmark, Finland, Iceland

Scandinavian see **Norse**

scant 4 poor **5** chary, close, short, skimp, spare, stint, tight **6** meager, meagre, scarce, scrimp, skimpy, sparse **7** scrimpy, wanting **8** exiguous **9** deficient **10** inadequate **12** insufficient

scantiness 4 lack **6** dearth **7** deficit, failure, paucity, poverty **8** scarcity, shortage, sparsity, underage **10** deficiency, inadequacy, scarceness, sparseness **11** defalcation **13** insufficience, insufficiency

scanty see **scant**

scapegoat 4 mark **5** patsy **6** target, victim **7** fall guy **11** whipping boy

Scapin 5 rogue, valet **author: 7** Molière **employer: 7** Léandre

scar 3 cut, mar **4** flaw, scab **5** score **6** damage, deface, defect, keloid **7** blemish, blister, scratch **8** cicatrix, pockmark **9** cicatrize, disfigure **13** disfigurement **on a seed: 5** hilum

scarab 6 beetle

scaramouch see **scamp**

scarce 3 few, shy **4** just, rare **5** scant, short **6** barely, hardly, scanty, seldom **7** failing, wanting **8** sporadic, uncommon **9** curtailed, deficient, shortened, truncated **10** inadequate, infrequent, occasional **12** insufficient

scarceness see **scantiness**

scarcity see **scantiness**

scare 3 awe **5** alarm, panic, spook **6** freeze, fright **7** horrify, petrify, shake up, startle, terrify **8** affright, frighten, paralyze **9** terrorize

scarf 3 boa **5** ascot, fichu, nubia, plaid, shawl, stole **8** babushka, liripipe **Latin-American: 6** tapalo **long: 6** rebozo

Scarlet Letter, The author: 9 Hawthorne *character:* 5 Pearl, Roger 6 Arthur, Hester

Scarlet Pimpernel author 5 Orczy

Scarlett's home 4 Tara

scary 6 afraid, aghast, spooky 7 anxious, fearful 8 spookish 9 terrified 10 frightened

scat 4 flee, jazz 5 scoot, scram 7 singing

scathe 4 flay 5 slash 6 scorch 7 blister, scarify, scourge 8 lambaste, lash into 9 castigate, excoriate

scathing 5 salty 6 brutal 7 burning, caustic, mordant, searing 9 scorching, trenchant 10 mordacious, sulphurous

scatological 4 foul 5 dirty, nasty 6 coarse, filthy, smutty, vulgar 7 obscene, raunchy 8 indecent

scatter 3 sow 4 cast, part, shed 5 sever, straw, strew 6 dispel, divide, splash 7 bestrew, break up, disband, discard, disject, diverge, spatter 8 dispense, disperse, separate, splatter, sprinkle 9 broadcast, dissipate 10 besprinkle, distribute 11 disseminate

scatterbrained 5 dizzy, giddy, silly 7 flighty, foolish 9 frivolous

scavenge 5 clean 7 cleanse, collect, extract, salvage

scavenger 5 hyena 7 vulture

scenario 4 plot 6 script 7 outline 10 screenplay

scene 3 set 4 site, spot, view 5 arena, field, place, sight, vista 6 locale, milieu, sphere 7 compass, culture, outlook, setting, tableau 8 backdrop, hangings, locality, location, stage set 10 background 11 environment, mise-en-scène 12 stage setting

scenery 3 set 5 decor, props 7 setting 8 stage set 9 furniture 10 properties 11 furnishings, mise-en-scène 12 stage setting

scent 4 balm, nose, odor 5 aroma, smell, sniff, snuff, spice, whiff 7 bouquet, essence, incense, odorize, perfume 9 aromatize, fragrance, redolence

scepter 4 mace 5 baton, staff 11 sovereignty

schedule 4 list, roll, sked, time 5 chart, slate, table 6 agenda, docket, record, roster 7 catalog, program 8 calendar, register, roll call 9 catalogue, timetable

scheme 4 plan, plot 5 cabal, order 6 design, device, devise 7 collude, connive, project 8 cogitate, conspire, contrive, game plan, intrigue, ordering, practice, proposal, strategy 9 blueprint, expedient, machinate 10 conspiracy 11 arrangement, contrivance, machination

schism 4 rent, rift 5 break, chasm, cleft, split 6 breach, heresy 7 dissent, fissure, rupture 8 cleavage, division, fracture

10 dissidence, divergence, heterodoxy, separation 11 unorthodoxy 12 estrangement

schizoid 5 split

schlemiel 4 fool 7 bungler 10 ne'er-do-well

schlepp 3 lug 4 drag, haul, jerk

schmaltzy 5 showy 6 florid 11 sentimental

scholar 4 sage 5 pupil 6 savant 7 bookman, student, wise man 8 literati (plural), polymath 10 classicist *Hindu:* 6 pundit *Muslim:* 5 ulama, ulema

scholarly 7 erudite, learned, trained 8 educated, studious 10 scholastic 12 intellectual

scholarship 7 science 8 learning 9 education, erudition, knowledge 11 eruditeness, learnedness

scholastic 5 booky 6 versed 7 bookish, erudite, learned 8 academic, lettered, literary, pedantic 9 scholarly 10 conversant 11 book-learned, quodlibetic *life:* 8 academia

school 3 gam, pad 4 lead, show 5 guide, shoal, teach, train 6 direct, inform, manage 7 academy, advance, college, control, educate 8 instruct 9 cultivate 10 discipline *French:* 5 école, lycée *grounds:* 6 campus *Jewish:* 5 heder 7 yeshiva 8 yeshivah *judo:* 4 dojo *organization:* 3 PTA, PTO *religious:* 8 seminary *term:* 7 quarter 8 semester

schoolbook 4 text 6 primer, reader 7 speller

School for Scandal author 8 Sheridan

schooner 4 ship 5 stein, stoup 6 goblet, seidel 7 tumbler

science 4 lore 6 wisdom 8 learning 9 education, erudition, knowledge 11 information, scholarship *combining form:* 4 logy 5 logia, sophy *of agriculture:* 8 agronomy *of animals:* 7 zoology *of armorial bearings:* 8 heraldry *of criminal punishment:* 8 penology *of environment:* 7 ecology *of fermentation:* 8 zymology *of government:* 8 politics *of health:* 7 hygiene 9 hygienics *of heredity:* 8 genetics *of human behavior:* 10 psychology *of lawmaking:* 8 nomology *of measuring time:* 8 horology 10 chronology 11 chronometry *of motion:* 8 kinetics *of mountains:* 7 orology *of nutrition:* 8 sitology *of plants:* 6 botany *of projectiles:* 10 ballistics *of soils:* 8 agrology *of the earth:* 7 geology *of time:* 10 chronology 11 chronometry *of tumors:* 8 oncology *suffix:* 3 ics

scientific classification 8 taxonomy

sci-fi writer 5 Verne 6 Asimov 8 Bradbury, Heinlein, Sturgeon

scimitar 5 saber, sword

scintilla 3 jot 4 iota 5 trace 8 particle
scintillate 5 flash, gleam, glint 6 glance
7 glimmer, glisten, glitter, shimmer, sparkle,
twinkle 9 coruscate
scoff 3 boo 4 gibe, jeer, jest, mock, twit
5 fleer, flout, rally, scorn, sneer, taunt
6 deride, quip at 7 contemn, despise, disdain, scout at 8 pooh-pooh, ridicule
scold 3 jaw, rag, wig 4 chew, lash, rail,
rant, rate 5 baste, blame, brace, chide,
croak, grill, grunt, harpy, hound, shrew,
vixen 6 amazon, berate, grouch, grouse,
harass, murmur, mutter, ogress, rebuke,
revile, tongue, virago 7 bawl out, blister,
censure, chew out, grumble, reprove, tell off,
upbraid 8 admonish, denounce, execrate,
fishwife, lambaste, objurate, reproach
9 criticize, dress down, excoriate, reprehend, reprimand, reprobate, termagant,
Xanthippe 10 tongue-lash, vituperate
sconce 4 head, poll 5 cover 6 noggin,
noodle, screen 7 shelter 11 candlestick
scoop 3 dig, dip 4 bail, beat, grub, lade,
lift 5 gouge, ladle, spade 6 dig out, gather,
pick up, shovel 8 excavate 9 exclusive
scoot 3 fly, run, zip 4 bolt, dash, flee, rush,
shin, skip 5 fleet, hurry, scram, skirr 6 barrel, bustle, hasten, hustle, scurry, sprint
7 beeline, make off, scamper 8 highball
9 skedaddle
scope 4 area, play, room 5 ambit, orbit,
range, reach, sweep 6 extent, leeway, margin, radius 7 breadth, compass, purview
8 fullness, latitude, wideness 9 amplitude,
elbowroom, extension
Scopes trial lawyer 5 Bryan 6 Darrow
scorch 4 bake, burn, cook, flay, melt
5 broil, roast, slash 6 scathe, seethe, simmer 7 blister, scarify, scourge, swelter
8 lambaste, lash into 9 castigate, excoriate
score 3 cut, tab, win 4 bill, flay, gain, gash,
goal, line, mark, nick, slit 5 cleft, notch,
reach, slash, tally, total 6 arrive, attain, furrow, groove, grudge, rack up, record,
scathe, scorch, scotch, thrive 7 account,
achieve, invoice, make out, prosper, realize,
ream out, scarify, scourge, scratch, succeed 8 flourish, lambaste, lash into 9 castigate, excoriate, reckoning, serration, statement 10 accomplish
scorn 4 gibe, jeer, mock, pooh 5 abhor,
flout, scoff, scout, taunt 6 gibing 7 contemn, despise, despite, disdain, jeering,
mockery 8 contempt, derision, despisal,
flouting, look down, ridicule, scoffing, taunt-
ing 11 despisement 13 disparagement
Scorpius star 7 Antares
Scotch cocktail 6 Rob Roy
Scotland's capital 9 Edinburgh
Scott, Sir Walter *novel:* 6 Rob Roy
7 Ivanhoe, Waverly 8 The Abbot 9 Wood-

stock 10 Kenilworth 11 Redgauntlet, The
Talisman *poem:* 7 Marmion
Scottish *child:* 5 bairn *hero:* 5 Bruce
7 Wallace *hill:* 4 brae *outlaw:* 6 Rob Roy
patron saint: 6 Andrew *plaid:* 6 tartan
pudding: 6 haggis *spirit:* 5 kelpy 6 kelpie
scoundrel see **scamp**
scour 3 eat, fan, fly 4 beat, bite, comb,
find, flit, flux, gnaw, grub, rake, rout, seek
5 erode, fleet, hurry, range, rifle, scrub,
smoke, speed 6 bullet, forage, rocket,
search 7 beeline, corrode, eat away, look
for, ransack, rummage 8 finecomb, highball,
wear away 9 ferret out 13 fine-tooth comb
scourge 3 hit 4 flay, flog, hide, lash, sack,
whip, whop 5 curse, flail, knout, slash,
waste, whale 6 lather, plague, ravage,
scathe, scorch, stripe, thrash 7 blister,
despoil, pillage, scarify 8 desolate, lambaste, lash into, spoliate 9 castigate, depredate, desecrate, devastate, excoriate
10 flagellate, pestilence
Scourge of God 6 Attila
scouting group 3 BSA, GSA
scow 3 hoy 5 barge 6 garvey 7 lighter
scowl 5 frown, gloom, lower 6 glower
scrabble 6 scrawl 7 clamber, scratch
8 scramble, scribble, squiggle
scraggy 4 bony, lank, lean 5 gaunt, harsh,
lanky, rough, spare 6 jagged, rugged,
skinny, uneven 7 angular, dwarfed,
scrawny, scrubby, spindly, stunted, unlevel
8 asperous, gangling, rawboned, scabrous,
skeletal 9 spindling, undersize
scram 4 kite 6 begone, decamp, get out
7 skiddoo, take off 8 clear out, hightail
9 skedaddle
scramble 4 hash 6 jumble, jungle, litter,
muddle, ramble, scurry, sprawl, tumble
7 clamber, clutter, rummage, scuttle, shuffle 8 mishmash, scrabble, straggle
scrap 3 bit, end, jot, ort, row 4 cast, chip,
dump, fray, junk, shed, spat, tiff, whit
5 brawl, broil, crumb, fight, set-to, shred,
speck, waste, whoop 6 affray, bicker, fracas, reject, slough, smitch, tittle 7 bobbery,
brabble, cashier, cutting, discard, fall out,
quarrel, scuffle, wrangle 8 fragment, jettison, leftover, particle, squabble, throw out
9 caterwaul, scrappage, throw away
scrape 3 fix, jam, rub 4 hole, rasp, spot
5 chafe, get by, grate, graze, grind, pinch,
screw, scuff, shave, skimp, spare, stint
6 abrade, corner, pickle, plight, scrimp
7 dilemma, scratch, trouble 8 get along,
struggle 11 predicament
scrappy 6 brawly 7 warlike 8 brawling,
militant 9 bellicose, brawlsome, combative,
truculent 10 battlesome, pugnacious
11 belligerent, contentious, quarrelsome
scratch 4 claw, rake, rasp 5 grate, score

6 scotch, scrape, scrawl **8** scrabble, scribble, squiggle

scrawl 6 doodle **7** scratch **8** inscribe, scrabble, scribble, squiggle

scrawny 4 bony, lank, lean **5** gaunt, lanky, spare **6** skinny **7** angular, scraggy **8** rawboned

scream 3 cry, yip **4** howl, riot, roar, wail, yell, yowl **5** blare, shout **6** bellow, screak, shriek, shrill, squeak, squeal **7** grumble, protest, screech **8** complain **9** caterwaul

screech 4 hoot **6** pierce, screak, scream, shriek, shrill, squeal

screen 4 blip, bury, fend, hide, sift, sort **5** cache, cloak, close, cover, guard, shade, sieve, stash **6** censor, choose, defend, embosk, riddle, secure, select, shadow, shield, shroud **7** bulwark, conceal, cover up, extract, pick out, protect, seclude, secrete, shut off, shut out, sort out, umbrage, wall off **8** blindage, block out, disguise, ensconce, obstruct, separate **9** expurgate, filter out, inumbrate, safeguard, winnow out **10** bowdlerize, camouflage *Japanese:* **5** shoji

screw 5 crimp, exact, gouge, pinch, skimp, spare, stint, wrest, wring **6** extort, rimple, ruck up, rumple, scrape, scrimp, skinch, wrench **7** crimple, crinkle, crumple, scrunch, squeeze, wrinkle **8** thumbkin **9** shake down

screwy 3 mad **4** daft, nuts **5** wacky **6** insane **7** cracked, lunatic, unsound **10** unbalanced

scribble 5 write **6** scrawl, scribe **7** jot down, scratch **8** scrabble, squiggle

scribe 5 clerk, write **6** author, writer **7** copyist **9** secretary

scrimmage 4 fray **5** brawl, broil, brush, clash, fight, melee, set-to **6** affray, fracas, mellay **7** scuffle **8** skirmish **10** donnybrook, free-for-all

scrimp 4 save **5** stint **6** save up, scrape **9** economize

script 4 hand, text **10** penmanship **11** calligraphy, chirography, handwriting

scrivener 6 notary, scribe, writer **7** copyist

scrooge 5 miser **7** niggard **8** muckworm, tightwad **9** skinflint **10** cheapskate **12** moneygrubber

scrub 3 rub **4** buff, drop, wash **5** brush, scour **6** cancel, mallee, maquis, polish **7** call off, cleanse **8** inferior **9** chaparral, secondary, subaltern, underling **11** subordinate

scruff 4 nape, neck

scruffy 5 seedy, tacky **6** shabby, tagrag **7** run-down, scrubby **8** tattered **10** down-at-heel, threadbare

scrumptious 5 yummy **8** adorable, heavenly, luscious **9** ambrosial, delicious **10** delectable, delightful

scruple 3 bit, jot **4** atom, balk, fret, iota **5** demur, grain, qualm, scrap, shred, worry **7** modicum **8** particle, question **9** faltering, hesitancy **11** compunction

scrupulous 4 just, true **5** exact, fussy, right **6** honest, strict **7** careful, heedful, upright **8** critical, punctual **9** honorable **10** fair-minded, fastidious, meticulous, upstanding **11** painstaking, punctilious **12** conscionable **13** conscientious

scrutinize 3 eye **4** comb, scan **5** audit, probe, study, watch **6** peruse, survey **7** analyze, canvass, check up, dig into, dissect, examine, eyeball, inspect **8** consider, look over, pore over **9** check over **11** contemplate, perlustrate

scrutiny 3 eye **4** scan **5** audit, watch **6** look-in, review, survey **7** look-see **8** analysis, eagle eye, lookover **9** check-over **10** inspection **11** examination **12** surveillance **13** perlustration

scuba diver 7 frogman **8** aquanaut

scuff 6 scrape **7** scratch, shamble, shuffle

scuffle 3 row **4** cuff, fray **5** brawl, broil, fight, scrap, set-to **6** affray, fracas, shovel, tussle **7** bobbery, grapple, shamble, shuffle, wrestle

scull 3 oar, row **4** boat **6** propel

sculpt 5 carve **6** chisel

sculptor *American:* **4** Gabo, Taft **5** Pratt, Segal, Smith, Story **6** Aitkin, Calder, French, Powers, Zorach **7** Noguchi **8** Lachaise, Lipchitz, Nadelman, Nevelson **9** Mestrovic, Remington *Czech:* **6** Stursa *Danish:* **11** Thorvaldsen, Thorwaldsen *Dutch:* **6** Sluter *English:* **5** Moore, Watts **7** Epstein, Flaxman **8** Hepworth *French:* **3** Arp **4** Bloc **5** Rodin **6** Dubois, Houdon **7** Maillol, Pevsner **9** Bartholdi, Roubillac *Greek:* **5** Myron **7** Phidias **10** Polyclitus, Praxiteles **11** Polycleitus *Italian:* **5** Leoni, Salvi **6** Canova, Pisano, Robbia **7** Bernini, Cellini, da Vinci, Orcagna, Quercia **8** Ghiberti, Vittoria **9** Donatello, Sansovino **10** Verrocchio **12** Michelangelo *Rhodian:* **9** Polydorus *Rumanian:* **8** Brancusi *Russian:* **7** Zadkine *Swedish:* **6** Milles *Swiss:* **10** Giacometti

scum 3 cur, mob **5** dregs, dross, skunk, snake, trash **6** masses, rabble, refuse **7** stinker **8** canaille, riffraff, unwashed

scummy 3 low **4** base, mean, vile **5** cheap, sorry **6** scurvy, shabby **8** beggarly, pitiable **10** despicable, despisable **12** contemptible

scurrilous 4 foul **5** dirty, gross, nasty **6** coarse, filthy, smutty, vulgar **7** abusive, obscene, raunchy **8** indecent **9** insulting, invective, offending, offensive, outraging, truculent **10** outrageous, vituperous **11** opprobrious **12** blackguardly, contumelious, vituperative, vituperatory

scurry **3** fly, run **4** dart, dash, shin, tear **5** scoot, shoot **6** sprint **7** scamper, scuffle, scutter, scuttle, skelter

scurvy see **scummy**

scut **4** tail

scuttlebutt **4** buzz, talk **5** on-dit, rumor **6** gossip, report, rumble **7** hearsay **9** grapevine

Scylla **4** rock *father:* **5** Nisus *lover:* **5** Minos; (see also **Charybdis**)

scythe handle **5** snath **6** snathe

sea **4** blue, deep, main **5** brine, briny, drink, ocean *Antarctica:* **4** Ross **5** Davis **7** Weddell **8** Amundsen *Arctic:* **4** Kara **7** Chukchi **8** Beaufort, Karskoye **9** Chuckchee, Norwegian **11** Chukotskoye **12** East Siberian *Asia-Europe:* **5** Black *Asia Minor:* **7** Icarian *Atlantic:* **5** North **7** Weddell **9** Caribbean *Australia-Indonesia:* **7** Arafura *Balkan Peninsula-Italy:* **8** Adriatic *Bay of Bengal:* **7** Andaman *China-Korea:* **5** Huang, Hwang **6** Yellow *combining form:* **3** mer **4** mari **5** pelag **6** pelago **7** thalass **8** thalasso *Corsica-Italy:* **10** Tyrrhenian *Denmark-Norway:* **8** Skagerak **9** Skagerrak *Denmark-Sweden:* **8** Kattegat *England-Ireland:* **5** Irish *Fiji:* **4** Koro *France-Italy:* **8** Ligurian *Greece:* **5** Crete *Greece-Turkey:* **6** Ionian *Greece-Turkey:* **6** Aegean **8** Thracian *Honshu:* **6** Sagami *Indian Ocean:* **4** Savu, Sawu **5** Timor **7** Arabian *Indonesia:* **4** Bali **6** Flores *inland:* **3** Red **4** Aral **7** Caspian *Japan:* **3** Iyo, Suo **6** Inland *largest island:* **7** Caspian *Malay Archipelago:* **5** Banda *Mexico:* **6** Cortes *Netherlands:* **6** Wadden *North Atlantic:* **8** Sargasso *Northern Europe:* **6** Baltic, Ostsee **8** Suevicum **10** Baltiskoye *North Pacific:* **6** Bering *Novaya Zemlya-Svalbard:* **7** Barents *off Scotland:* **8** Hebrides *off Sweden:* **5** Aland *Pacific:* **4** Java **5** China, Coral **6** Maluku **7** Celebes, Eastern, Molucca, Solomon **9** East China, Moluksche **10** South China *Russia:* **5** White **7** Okhotsk *Russia-Ukraine:* **4** Azov **9** Azovskoye *South Pacific:* **4** Ross **6** Tasman **8** Amundsen *Turkey:* **7** Marmara **9** Propontis *West Pacific:* **5** Ceram, Japan **8** Bismarck **10** Philippine

sea anemone **7** actinia

seabird see **bird**, *aquatic*

sea channel **6** strait **7** euripus

sea cucumber **7** trepang **11** holothurian

sea dog see **sailor**

sea duck **5** eider, scaup **6** scoter **9** merganser

sea eagle **3** ern **4** erne **6** osprey

seafood dish **4** clam, crab, tuna **5** scrod **6** oyster, shrimp **7** lobster, scallop

seagoing **8** maritime, nautical

seal **5** sigil, stamp **6** cachet, signet **7** sticker *bearded:* **6** makluk *eared:* **5** otary *female:* **3** cow **5** matka *herd:* **3** pod **5** patch *male:* **8** seecatch *young:* **3** pup

sealant **4** lute **6** luting

sea lily **7** crinoid

seam **4** bond **5** joint, union **7** joining **8** coupling, junction, juncture **10** connection

seaman see **sailor**

sea monster **3** Orc *legendary:* **6** kraken

seamount *flat-topped:* **5** guyot

seamy **5** dirty, rough, seedy **6** sordid **12** disreputable

séance **7** meeting, session, sitting *holder:* **6** medium

seaport *Adriatic:* **5** Split **6** Spljet *Aegean:* **5** Vathy *Alaska:* **9** Anchorage *Albania:* **5** Vlona, Vlorë *Algeria:* **4** Bona, Oran **5** Arzew **6** Annaba **9** Arsenaria, Cherchell, Shershell *Angola:* **6** Lobito **7** Cabinda **8** Benguela **9** Mocamedes *Argentina:* **7** La Plata *Australia:* **4** Eden **5** Bowen **6** Brisbane, Wallaroo **10** Wollongong *Azores:* **5** Horta *Balearic:* **5** Ibiza *Baltic:* **5** Visby *Belgium:* **6** Ostend *Benin:* **6** Kotonu **7** Cotonou *Black Sea:* **6** Odessa *Bosnia and Herzegovina:* **4** Omis *Brazil:* **3** Rio **4** Para **5** Bahia, Belem, Natal **6** Recife, Santos **8** Salvador **10** Pernambuco **11** Pôrto Alegre, São Salvador **12** Rio de Janeiro *Bulgaria:* **5** Varna *Cameroon:* **5** Campo, Duala, Kampo, Kribi *Canaries:* **8** Arrecife *Celebes:* **7** Makasar **8** Macassar, Makassar *Chile:* **4** Lebu, Lota **5** Ancud, Arica **8** Coquimbo **10** Valparaiso *China:* **4** Amoy **6** Lushun, Xiamen *Colombia:* **6** Lorica **9** Cartagena *Corsica:* **5** Calvi *Costa Rica:* **10** Puntarenas *Crimean:* **10** Sevastopol *Croatia:* **4** Senj **5** Zadar **9** Dubrovnik *Cuba:* **5** Banes *Cyprus:* **7** Limasol **8** Limassol **9** Famagusta *Delaware:* **5** Lewes *Denmark:* **5** Arhus, Ronne, Vejle **6** Aarhus, Alborg **7** Aalborg **8** Elsinore *Djibouti:* **4** Obok **5** Obock **6** Tajura **8** Tadjoura *Ecuador:* **5** Manta **9** Guayaquil *Egypt:* **4** Said **8** Al Qusayr, Al Quseir, El Qoseir **10** Alexandria *Eire:* **6** Dingle, Tralee **10** Balbriggan *England:* **10** Portsmouth *Equatorial Guinea:* **4** Bata *Eritrea:* **4** Aseb *Estonia:* **5** Parnu **6** Pyarnu **7** Tallinn *Ethiopia:* **4** Zula *Finland:* **3** Abo **4** Kemi, Oulu, Pori, Vasa **5** Hango, Kotka, Rauma, Turku, Vaasa **8** Uleaborg **10** Bjorneborg *Florida:* **5** Miami, Tampa **9** Pensacola **12** Apalachicola, Jacksonville *France:* **4** Meze, Nice **5** Havre, Nizza **6** Calais, Cannes, Toulon **7** Dunkirk, Le Havre, Lorient **8** Bordeaux,

Boulogne 9 Cherbourg, Dunkerque, Marseille 10 Marseilles *French Polynesia:* 7 Papeete *Georgia:* 9 Brunswick *Georgia, Republic of:* 4 Poti *Germany:* 4 Kiel 5 Emden, Husum 6 Wismar 8 Cuxhaven 11 Bremerhaven 13 Wilhelmshaven *Ghana:* 4 Keta 6 Kwitta *Greece:* 4 Kimi, Kyme 5 Pylos, Syros, Volos 7 Piraeus 8 Peiraeus *Guatemala:* 7 San José 10 Livingston *Gulf of Aden:* 5 Alula *Haiti:* 5 Cayes 8 Aux Cayes *Honduras:* 8 Trujillo *India:* 3 Goa 4 Puri 5 Marud 6 Old Goa 9 Jagannath 10 Juggernaut *Ionian:* 5 Corfu *Iran:* 4 Jask 7 Bushehr, Bushire *Iraq:* 5 Basra *Israel:* 4 Acre, Akko, Elat, Yafa 5 Accho, Eilat, Elath, Haifa, Jaffa, Joppa 9 Ptolemais, Sycaminum *Italy:* 4 Bari 5 Anzio, Gaeta, Genoa, Pizzo, Trani 6 Naples, Pesaro, Venice 7 Leghorn, Rapallo, Salerno, Taranto, Trieste, Venedig 8 Sorrento 10 Senigallia *Ivory Coast:* 4 Tabu 5 Tabou *Jamaica:* 10 Montego Bay *Japan:* 5 Kochi, Rumoi, Ujina, Uraga 6 Sasebo 7 Fukuoka 8 Nagasaki, Yokohama *Java:* 5 Tegal, Tuban 8 Samarang, Semarang, Surabaja, Tjirebon *Jordan:* 5 Akaba, Aqaba, Elath 6 Aelana *Latvian:* 9 Ventspils *Lebanon:* 5 Saida 7 Tripoli *Libya:* 4 Homs 5 Khoms 6 Tobruk *Lithuanian:* 5 Memel 8 Klaipeda *Madagascar:* 8 Tamatave *Maine:* 7 Belfast 8 Portland *Malaysia:* 4 Miri, Weld 5 Pekan 6 Melaka, Pinang 7 Malacca 10 George Town *Massachusetts:* 9 Fall River *Mauritius:* 5 Louis *Mediterranean:* 4 Gaza, Oran, Said 5 Genoa, Haifa, Jaffa 6 Bayrut, Beirut 7 Algiers, Bizerte, Catania, Tripoli 8 Benghazi 9 Barcelona 10 Alexandria, Marseilles *Mexico:* 8 Acapulco, Veracruz *Minorca:* 5 Mahon *Moluccas:* 5 Ambon *Montenegro:* 5 Kotov *Morocco:* 3 Sla 4 Safi, Sale 5 Ceuta, Saffi 6 Agadir 7 Larache, Tangier 10 Casablanca *Mozambique:* 5 Beira, Pemba 6 Amelia, Xai Xai 11 Porto Amelia *New Hampshire:* 10 Portsmouth *New Zealand:* 8 Auckland *Nicaragua:* 5 Brito *Nigeria:* 8 Harcourt *Niger mouth:* 5 Bonny *North Korea:* 4 Yuki 5 Unggi *Norway:* 4 Bodo, Moss 5 Vadso 6 Tromso 9 Stavanger, Trondheim, Trondhjem 11 Fredrikstad *Oman:* 3 Sur 5 Sohar 6 Matrah *Pakistan:* 5 Pasni *Peru:* 3 Ilo 4 Eten 5 Paita, Pisco *Poland:* 6 Gdynia 7 Gdingen, Stettin 8 Szczecin *Portugal:* 4 Faro 5 Lagos 6 Oporto 7 Funchal 9 Lacobriga *Puerto Rico:* 5 Ponce *Russia:* 3 Kem 5 Anapa, Sochi 6 Vyborg 11 Kaliningrad, Vladivostok *Ryukyu:* 4 Naha, Nawa *Sakhalin Island:* 8 Korsakov *Saudi Arabia:* 4 Wejh 5 Jidda, Qatif, Yanbu, Yenbo 6 Juddah 7 Djeddah

Scotland: 3 Ayr 4 Oban 5 Alloa, Largs, Leven 6 Dundee *Sicily:* 5 Avola 7 Messina, Palermo 8 Syracuse *Slovenia:* 5 Kopar, Koper, Piran *Somalia:* 7 Berbera, Kismayu 9 Chisimaio *South Africa:* 6 Durban 8 Cape Town, Kaapstad *South Carolina:* 10 Charleston *South Korea:* 5 Mason, Mokpo 6 Inch'on, Jinsen 7 Masampo 8 Chemulpo *Spain:* 4 Adra, Noya, Vigo 5 Cadiz, Gadir, Gijon, Marin 6 Abdera 8 Alicante 9 Cartagena, Las Palmas *Sri Lanka:* 10 Batticaloa *Sumatra:* 6 Padang *Sweden:* 4 Umea 5 Gavle, Lulea, Malmo, Pitea, Ystad 8 Göteborg 10 Gothenburg *Tanzania:* 5 Lindi, Tanga *Thailand:* 4 Trat 8 Bang Phra *Tunisia:* 4 Sfax 5 Gabes 7 Bizerte, Safaqis *Turkey:* 4 Rize 5 Coruh, Sinop 6 Coroch *Ukrainian:* 7 Kherson *U.S. Virgin Islands:* 8 St. Thomas *Vanuatu:* 4 Vila *Vietnam:* 6 Da Nang 7 Tourane 8 Haiphong, Nha Trang *Virginia:* 10 Portsmouth *Yemen:* 5 Mocha, Mokha 7 Hodeida; (see also **seaport capital**)

seaport capital 4 Aden, Apia, Lomé, Suva 5 Accra, Adana, Alger, Dakar, Lagos 6 Banjul, Belize, Bissão, Bissau, Boston, Dublin, Eblana, Havana, Juneau, Kuwait, Lisbon, Maputo, Masqat, Muscat, Roseau 7 Algiers, Batavia, Colombo, Icosium, Jakarta, Moresby, San Juan 8 Al-Jazà'ir, Al-Kuwait, Bathurst, Castries, Djakarta, Freetown, Hamilton, Helsinki, Honolulu, Kingston, La Habana, Monrovia, Valletta 9 Annapolis, Mogadishu, Nukualofa, Porto-Novo, Reykjavik, Singapore 10 Bridgetown, Daressalem, Libreville, Mogadiscio, Paramaribo 11 Dar es Salaam, Port of Spain 12 Port-au-Prince

sear 3 dry 5 parch 6 burn up, scorch, sizzle 7 shrivel 9 cauterize, dehydrate, desiccate, exsiccate

search 4 beat, comb, grub, hunt, peer, rake, scan, seek 5 check, delve, frisk, quest, rifle, scour, study 6 ferret, forage, pry out 7 examine, hunting, inspect, manhunt, pursual, pursuit, ransack, rummage, run down, seeking 8 finecomb, look over, pursuing, scavenge, scout out, skirmish 9 cast about, ferret out, pursuance, scrimmage, shake down 10 scrutinize 11 scout around 13 fine-tooth comb *for gold:* 7 fossick

sea robber 5 rover 6 pirate 7 corsair 8 picaroon 9 buccaneer 10 freebooter

sea rover see **sea robber**

seasickness 8 mal de mer 9 naupathia

season 3 fit 4 fall, salt, term, time 5 spice, steel, train 6 autumn, harden, pepper, period, school, spring, summer, winter 7 prepare, toughen 8 marinade, marinate

9 acclimate, climatize **10** case harden, discipline **11** acclimatize

seasonable 3 apt **6** timely **7** apropos, timeous **8** relevant **9** favorable, opportune, pertinent, well-timed **10** auspicious, convenient, propitious, prosperous **11** appropriate

seasoning 4 herb, sage, salt **5** spice **6** fennel, garlic, pepper **7** cayenne, mustard, paprika **9** condiment

seat 3 bed, hub, put, sit **4** base, beam, rest **5** basis, focus, heart, place, usher **6** behind, bottom, center, settee **7** footing, fulcrum **8** backside, basement, buttocks, derriere, polestar **9** establish, fundament, posterior **10** focal point, foundation, groundwork **11** nerve center *church:* **3** pew *on a camel or elephant:* **6** howdah *upholstered:* **9** banquette

sea urchin 7 echinus **8** echinoid

seaweed 4 agar, alga, kelp **5** dulse **6** murlin **7** henware **9** carrageen **11** badderlocks *brown:* **6** fucoid **8** gulfweed, rockweed, sargasso *edible:* **4** ulva **7** redware *purple:* **9** carrageen, Irish moss

Sea Wolf, The *author:* **6** London *captain:* **10** Wolf Larsen *ship:* **5** Ghost

Sebastian *brother:* **6** Alonso *sister:* **5** Viola

secede 4 quit **5** leave **8** withdraw

seclude 4 hide **6** closet, immure, retire, screen **7** confine, enclose, isolate, shut off **8** cloister, separate, withdraw **9** sequester

seclusion 7 privacy **8** solitude **9** aloneness, isolation **10** detachment, retirement, separation, withdrawal **11** privateness **12** separateness

second 3 aid **4** abet, back, wink **5** flash, jiffy, trice **6** assist, minute, moment **7** endorse, instant, support **9** twinkling *combining form:* **4** deut **5** deuto **6** deuter **7** deutero

secondary 3 sub **5** dinky, minor, scrub, small, under **6** lesser **7** derived, subject **8** borrowed, derivate, inferior, small-fry **9** accessory, dependent, resultant, small-time, subaltern, tributary, underling **10** collateral, consequent, derivative, secondhand, subsequent **11** minor-league, subordinate, subservient *prefix:* **3** sub

second-class 4 hack, mean, poor **6** common **8** déclassé, inferior, low-grade

secondhand 4 used, worn **7** derived **8** borrowed

second-rate see **second-class**

second-string 3 sub **10** substitute

secrecy 4 hush **7** silence, stealth **8** hush-hush **10** censorship, covertness, subterfuge **11** concealment, furtiveness

secret 4 deep **5** heavy, sneak **6** covert, hidden, occult, orphic, remote **7** devious,

furtive, obscure, removed, retired, subrosa **8** abstruse, esoteric, hermetic, hush-hush, lonesome, mystical, profound, screened, stealthy, unavowed **9** concealed, recondite **10** acroamatic, classified, restricted, undeclared, undercover **11** clandestine, out-of-the-way, underhanded **12** confidential, hugger-mugger **13** surreptitious, under-the-table *combining form:* **5** crypt, krypt **6** crypto, krypto

secret agent 3 spy **8** emissary

secretaire 4 desk **10** escritoire

secretary 4 desk **5** clerk **6** scribe **10** amanuensis, escritoire *king's:* **10** chancellor

secrete 4 bury, hide **5** cache, cover, exude, plant, stash **6** screen **7** conceal, deposit **8** ensconce, withhold

secret society 3 KKK **4** Poro, tong **5** Mafia **7** camorra **10** Ku Klux Klan

sect 4 cult **5** creed, faith **6** church **8** religion **9** communion **10** connection, persuasion **12** denomination

sectarian 5 local **7** insular **8** splinter **9** dissident, heretical, heterodox, parochial, small-town **10** provincial, schismatic, unorthodox **13** nonconformist

sectary 5 bigot, rebel **6** cohort, hippie **7** beatnik, heretic, liberal, radical **8** adherent, bohemian, disciple, follower, henchman, maverick, partisan, sectator **9** dissenter, dissident, satellite, supporter, Young Turk **10** schismatic, separatist **11** misbeliever, schismatist **13** nonconformist, revolutionary

section 3 cut **4** area, belt, part, zone **5** field, piece, slice, split, tract **6** divide, member, moiety, parcel, region, sector, sphere **7** break up, portion, quarter, segment **8** district, division, locality, precinct, separate, vicinity **9** territory **11** subdivision *combining form:* **4** tome, tomy

sector 7 quarter, section **8** district, precinct

secular 3 lay **7** profane **8** temporal, unsacred **11** nonclerical **12** nonreligious

secure 3 bag, fix, get, set **4** bind, fast, fend, firm, gain, have, iron, land, lock, make, moor, nail, safe, sure, take **5** annex, catch, cause, chock, cinch, clamp, cover, fixed, guard, rivet, solid, sound, tight, tried **6** anchor, assure, cement, clinch, collar, defend, draw on, effect, ensure, fasten, insure, obtain, pick up, pinion, pledge, screen, shield, stable, strong, trusty **7** acquire, assured, bulwark, capture, chalk up, prehend, procure, produce, protect, settled, staunch, tie down **8** balanced, reliable, riskless, sanguine **9** confident, safeguard, tenacious **10** batten down, bring about, dependable, underwrite, undoubtful

11 established, self-assured, trustworthy **12** tried and true **13** self-confident

security 4 bail, bond, pawn, ward **5** aegis, armor, guard, token **6** pledge, safety, shield, surety **7** defense, earnest, warrant **8** armament, firmness, guaranty, safeness, strength, warranty **9** assurance, guarantee, safeguard, soundness, stability **10** protection, stableness, steadiness **13** certification

sedan 3 car **4** auto, limo **10** automobile

sedate 4 calm **5** grave, sober, staid **6** placid, proper, seemly, serene, solemn, somber **7** earnest, serious, weighty **8** composed, decorous, tranquil **9** collected, dignified, unruffled **10** no-nonsense, sobersided **13** dispassionate, imperturbable

sedative 4 balm **7** calmant **8** barbital, hyoscine, pacifier, quietive **9** calmative **10** depressant **11** barbiturate **12** sleeping pill, tranquilizer

sedentary 4 lazy **7** settled **8** inactive **10** stationary

sediment 4 lees, silt, slag **5** draff, dregs, dross **6** scoria **7** bottoms, deposit, grounds, heeltap **9** recrement, settlings **11** precipitate **13** precipitation *layer:* **5** varve

sedition 4 coup **6** action, mutiny, putsch, revolt, strike **7** protest, treason **8** uprising **9** coup d'etat, rebellion **10** alienation, revolution **12** disaffection, estrangement, insurrection

seditious 7 lawless, violent **8** disloyal, factious, mutinous **9** alienated, dissident, faithless, insurgent **10** perfidious, rebellious, traitorous **11** disaffected, treacherous

seduce 4 bait, coax, lure, rape, ruin, undo **5** decoy, tease, tempt, train **6** allure, betray, delude, entice, entrap, lead on, ravish **7** corrupt, debauch, deceive, degrade, enslave, mislead, pervert, violate **8** deflower, entrance, inveigle **9** overpower, overwhelm

seducer 7 Don Juan **8** lothario

seduction 4 call, draw, lure, pull, rape, ruin **6** appeal **9** siren song, violation **10** allurement, attraction, corruption, perversion, ravishment, seducement, temptation **11** deflowering

seductive 5 siren **7** drawing, vampish **8** alluring, magnetic **9** desirable **10** attracting, attractive, bewitching, enchanting **11** captivating, fascinating, provocative

seductress 5 siren **7** Lorelei **9** temptress **11** femme fatale

sedulous 4 busy **6** active **7** operose **8** diligent, hustling **9** assiduous **10** persistent **11** industrious, persevering, unremitting

see 4 call, date, espy, gape, gaze, have, hear, know, lead, look, mark, mind, note, peek, peep, peer, scan, show, take, twig, vide, view **5** catch, fancy, glare, grasp, guide, learn, pilot, pop in, probe, route, sight, stare, steer, study, think, visit, watch, weigh **6** accept, attend, behold, come by, descry, direct, divine, drop by, drop in, escort, follow, go with, look in, look up, notice, pierce, ponder, remark, step in, stop by, stop in, suffer, take in, tumble, vision **7** catch on, conduct, discern, examine, feature, find out, foresee, glimpse, imagine, inspect, look out, make out, observe, preknow, previse, realize, sustain, take out, undergo, unearth **8** appraise, come over, conceive, consider, discover, envisage, envision, forefeel, foreknow, perceive, shepherd, watch out **9** accompany, apprehend, ascertain, determine, penetrate, prevision, recognize, visualize **10** anticipate, comprehend, experience, scrutinize, understand **11** distinguish **12** discriminate

seed 3 bud, sow **4** core, germ **5** brood, image, issue, ovule, plant, put in, spark **6** embryo, kernel, notion, scions **7** conceit, concept, nucleus, progeny **8** children, rudiment **9** offspring, posterity **10** conception, impression **11** descendants, progeniture *aromatic:* **6** fennel *coating:* **5** testa **6** testae (plural) *combining form:* **3** gon **4** cocc, gono, spor **5** cocci, cocco, sperm, spori, sporo **6** sperma, spermi, spermo **7** spermae (plural), spermat **8** spermato *covering:* **4** aril *medicinal:* **7** ignatia *of a bean:* **7** haricot *of an herb:* **3** pea, soy **4** soya **7** soybean *of a vine:* **6** peanut *palm tree:* **6** jarina *poisonous:* **10** castor bean *prickly:* **6** bonduc *vessel:* **3** pod **5** fruit, pyxis **7** pyxides, pyxidia (plural), silicle, siliqua **8** pyxidium, sillique

seedcase 3 pod

seedy 5 dingy, faded, messy, tired **6** droopy, shabby, untidy, wilted **7** rundown, sagging, unkempt, wilting **8** decrepit, drooping, flagging, slovenly, tattered **9** neglected, overgrown **10** bedraggled, down-at-heel, threadbare

seek 3 dig, try **4** fish, hunt, nose, root **5** assay, delve, essay, mouse, offer, quest, sniff **6** strive **7** attempt, bird-dog **8** endeavor, smell out, struggle **9** cast about, ferret out, search for, search out, undertake

seem 4 hint, look **5** imply, sound **6** appear **7** suggest **8** intimate, resemble **9** insinuate

seeming *combining form:* **5** quasi

seemly 4 nice **5** right **6** decent, proper **7** correct **8** becoming, decorous, pleasing **9** befitting, congenial, congruous, consonant **10** compatible, conforming, consistent **11** comme il faut

seep 4 drip, flow, leak, ooze, weep
5 bleed, exude, sweat 6 strain 8 transude
seer 5 augur 6 auspex 7 prophet 8 foreseer, haruspex 9 predictor 10 forecaster,
foreteller 11 Nostradamus
seesaw 3 yaw 4 cant, lean, list, rock, roll,
swag, sway, tilt, toss 5 lurch, pitch 6 teeter, tilter 7 bascule, incline
seethe 3 sop 4 boil, burn, fret, fume, rage,
soak, stew, stir, teem 5 anger, churn, erupt,
souse, steam, steep, swarm 6 abound,
blow up, bubble, drench, simmer, sizzle,
sodden 7 bristle, ferment, flare up, parboil
8 boil over, overflow, saturate, waterlog
10 bubble over, impregnate
see-through 5 clear 6 limpid 8 pellucid
11 translucent, transparent
segment 3 cut 4 part 5 piece 6 divide,
member, moiety, parcel, set off 7 isolate,
portion, seclude, section 8 division, separate 10 categorize
sego 4 lily
segregate 6 choose, cut off, enisle, island,
select, single 7 isolate 8 close off, insulate,
separate 9 sequester 10 disconnect
segregation 9 apartheid, isolation, seclusion 10 jim crowism, separation, separatism 12 separateness 13 ghettoization
Segub's father 4 Hiel 6 Hezron
seidel 3 cup, mug 5 stein, stoup
seine 3 net 5 trawl
seismologist 7 Richter
seize 3 nab 4 grab, take 5 annex, catch,
grasp, usurp 6 abduct, arrest, clutch, kidnap, occupy, secure, snap at, snatch,
strike 7 afflict, capture, grapple, impound,
preempt 8 accroach, arrogate, carry off,
overtake, take over 9 apprehend, latch
onto, sequester, spirit off 10 commandeer,
confiscate, fasten onto, spirit away
11 appropriate, expropriate
seizure 3 fit 4 turn 5 spell, throe
6 access, attack, taking 9 breakdown
10 convulsion
seldom 3 few 4 rare 6 hardly, little, rarely,
scarce 7 unoften 8 scarcely, sporadic,
uncommon 10 hardly ever, infrequent,
occasional 11 irregularly 12 infrequently,
occasionally, sporadically
select 3 top 4 best, cull, fine, mark, pick,
rare, take 5 elect, elite 6 choice, choose,
chosen, culled, dainty, optate, opt for,
picked, prefer, single 7 elegant, favored
8 blue-chip, delicate, eclectic, screened,
superior 9 exclusive, exquisite, preferred,
recherché, single out, weeded out 11 win-
nowed out
selection 5 draft 6 acumen, choice,
option 7 culling, excerpt, insight, picking
8 choosing, drafting, election 10 preference 11 alternative, discernment

selective 5 fussy, picky 6 choosy
7 choosey, finicky 8 eclectic 10 particular,
scrupulous
Seled's father 5 Nadab
Selene 4 Luna 6 Hecate 7 Artemis
beloved: 8 Endymion *brother:* 6 Helios
father: 8 Hyperion *mother:* 4 Thea
selenium *symbol:* 2 Se
self 3 ego *combining form:* 3 aut 4 auto
self-acting 9 automatic
self-assertive 4 bold, sure 6 uppish,
uppity 7 forward, pushful, pushing 8 cocksure, militant 9 audacious, intrusive, obtrusive, officious, presuming 10 aggressive,
meddlesome 11 impertinent, overweening
12 presumptuous
self-assurance 6 aplomb 8 coolness
9 composure, sangfroid, self-trust 10 confidence, equanimity 13 collectedness
self-assured 4 smug 6 secure 8 sanguine 9 confident 10 undoubtful
self-complacent 4 smug 8 priggish
self-composed 4 calm, easy 6 placid,
poised, serene 8 tranquil 9 collected,
possessed
self-confidence 6 aplomb, hutzpa 7 chutzpa, hutzpah 8 chutzpah, sureness
9 assurance, cockiness, self-trust 12 san-
guineness 13 self-assurance
self-confident 5 cocky, janty 6 jaunty,
secure 7 assured, cockish 8 sanguine
10 undoubtful
self-conscious 4 prim 5 stiff 6 formal,
uneasy 7 anxious, flaunty, stilted
8 affected, mannered 9 ill at ease 10 artificial 12 ostentatious
self-control 4 will 7 balance, dignity,
reserve 9 stability, willpower 10 constraint,
discipline
self-defense 4 judo 6 aikido, karate
7 jujitsu, jujutsu
self-destruction 7 suicide 8 felo-de-se,
hara-kiri
self-discipline 4 will 9 willpower
self-effacing 3 shy 5 timid 6 modest
7 bashful, rabbity 8 backward, retiring 9 diffident, unassured 11 unassertive
self-esteem 5 pride 6 vanity 7 conceit
10 narcissism 11 amour propre
self-evident 5 clear, plain 7 obvious
8 manifest 10 prima facie 12 unmistakable
self-explanatory 5 clear, plain 7 evident,
obvious 8 manifest
self-governing 7 popular 10 autonomous, democratic
self-importance 5 pride 6 egoism
7 conceit, egotism 9 arrogance, pomposity,
vainglory
self-important 5 puffy, wiggy 6 stuffy
7 bloated, pompous 8 arrogant 10 pontifical 11 magisterial

self-indulgent 9 sybaritic 10 hedonistic, sybaritish 11 sybaritical

self-interest 6 egoism

selfish 6 stingy 7 hoggish, hoglike 8 egoistic 9 egotistic 10 egocentric 11 egomaniacal

self-love 6 vanity 7 conceit, narcism 8 vainness 9 vainglory 10 narcissism 11 amour propre 13 conceitedness

self-possessed 4 calm, easy 5 aloof 6 placid, poised, serene 8 composed, reserved, tranquil 9 collected, easygoing

self-proclaimed 9 soi-disant 10 self-styled

Self-Reliance author 7 Emerson

self-respect 5 pride 11 amour propre

self-righteous 7 canting 9 pharisaic 11 pharisaical 12 hypocritical, pecksniffian 13 sanctimonious

self-sacrificing 6 kindly 8 generous, selfless 9 unselfish 10 charitable 13 philanthropic

self-satisfied 4 smug 8 priggish 10 complacent

self-seeking 7 selfish 8 egoistic, selfhood 9 egotistic 10 egocentric 11 egomaniacal

self-service *combining form:* 5 teria

self-serving see **self-seeking**

self-starter 6 dynamo, peeler 7 hustler, rustler 8 go-getter, live wire

self-styled 5 quasi 7 would be 8 so-called 9 self-given, soi-disant

self-taught 12 autodidactic

sell 3 net 4 draw, hawk, mart, sale, vend 5 bring, fetch, trade, yield 6 barter, betray, deal in, market, peddle, retail, return 7 auction, bring in, command, realize, traffic 8 exchange

sell out 4 dump, move 5 cross 6 betray, delude, humbug, take in, unload 7 beguile, deceive, mislead 8 close out 9 four-flush, sacrifice 11 double-cross

semblance 3 air 4 aura, face, feel, look, mask, mood, pose, show, veil 5 front, guise 6 aspect, facade, simile, veneer 7 analogy, feeling, seeming, showing 8 affinity, disguise, likeness 9 alikeness 10 appearance, atmosphere, comparison, false front, masquerade, similarity, similitude, simulacrum 11 resemblance

Semele *father:* 6 Cadmus *mother:* 8 Harmonia *sister:* 3 Ino 5 Agave 7 Autonoe *son:* 7 Bacchus 8 Dionysus

semi 4 demi, half, hemi 6 partly 7 partial

seminar 8 colloquy 10 colloquium, conference

Seminole chief 7 Osceola

Semiramis *husband:* 5 Ninus *kingdom:* 7 Babylon

Semite 3 Jew 4 Arab 6 Hebrew 7 Maob-ite 8 Assyrian 9 Canaanite 10 Babylonian, Phoenician

Senapo *daughter:* 8 Clorinda *kingdom:* 8 Ethiopia

senate 7 council 8 assembly 11 legislature

senator 5 solon 8 lawmaker 10 legislator

send 4 mail, post, rush, ship 5 relay, remit, route 6 assign, commit, export, launch, thrill 7 address, advance, airmail, consign, enthuse, forward, mission, traject 8 allocate, delegate, dispatch, expedite, transmit 9 electrify *back:* 6 remand *forth:* 4 emit 7 emanate

senectitude see **senescence**

Senegal *capital:* 5 Dakar *monetary unit:* 5 franc

senescence 6 old age 8 caducity 11 elderliness, senectitude

senile 3 old 4 aged, weak 5 aging 6 doting, feeble 7 ancient, doddery 8 decrepit, doddered 9 doddering, enfeebled, senescent, shattered

senility 6 dotage 7 decline 8 caducity 10 senescence

senior 5 doyen, elder 6 better 7 ancient, doyenne, oldster 8 brass hat, higher-up, old-timer, superior 10 golden-ager

Sennacherib *father:* 6 Sargon *kingdom:* 7 Assyria *slayer, son:* 8 Sharezer 11 Adrammelech

sensation 4 bomb 5 sense 6 marvel, wonder 7 feeling, miracle, portent, prodigy, stunner 8 response 9 bombshell 10 impression, perception, phenomenon 11 sensibility, sensitivity 13 consciousness, sensitiveness *combining form:* 8 esthesio 9 aesthesio

sensational 3 hot 5 boffo, juicy, livid, lurid, smash 6 coarse, divine, groovy, marked, signal, sultry, vulgar 7 colored, piquant, pointed, pungent, rousing, salient, sensory, sensual, tabloid 8 crashing, glorious, slambang, smashing, stunning 9 arresting, hunky-dory, marvelous, prominent, sensatory, sensitive, sensorial, superfine 10 impressive, noticeable, remarkable 11 conspicuous, extravagant, outstanding

sense 3 wit 4 core, deem, feel, gist, hold, know, meat, pith 5 focus, short, smell, think 7 believe, feeling, meaning, message, nucleus, purport, realize 8 consider, gumption, judgment, perceive, prudence 9 awareness, foresight, mentality, mother wit, substance 10 anticipate, brainpower, cognizance, discretion, intendment 11 acceptation, discernment, penetration, recognition 12 appreciation, intelligence, significance, significancy 13 comprehension, consciousness, signification, understanding

Sense and Sensibility author 6 Austen
senseless 4 cold, dead, numb, surd
5 silly 6 asleep, numbed, simple, wooden
7 foolish, trivial, unaware, unwitty, witless
8 benumbed, comatose, deadened, mindless 9 brainless
senselessness 5 folly 7 inanity 8 insanity 9 absurdity, craziness, dottiness, silliness, stupidity 11 foolishness, witlessness
12 illogicality
sense organ 3 ear, eye 4 nose, skin
6 tongue
sensibility 5 heart, sense 7 emotion, feeling, insight 8 keenness 9 affection, sensation 11 discernment, penetration, sensitivity
sensible 4 good, sage, sane, wise 5 alive,
awake, aware, gross, smart, solid, sound
6 noting, patent, seeing 7 evident, knowing,
logical, obvious, prudent, sapient, sizable,
witting 8 concrete, imaginal, manifest,
material, palpable, physical, rational, sentient, tangible 9 au courant, cognizant, conscious, corporeal, judgmatic, judicious,
objective, observing, remarking, sensitive,
weighable 10 consequent, conversant,
detectable, observable, perceiving, percep-
tual, phenomenal, reasonable, responsive
sensitive 4 keen, open, sore 5 acute,
aware, prone, sharp, tense 6 liable, seeing,
touchy, tricky 7 exposed, feeling, knowing,
nervous, psychic, sensile, sensory, sensual,
subject 8 affected, delicate, disposed,
inclined, sensible, sentient, ticklish, unstable 9 cognizant, conscious, emotional,
impressed, irritable, obnoxious, sensatory,
sensorial 10 high-strung, influenced, insult-
able, perceiving, perceptive, precarious,
responsive, susceptive, umbrageous
11 emotionable, impressible, predisposed,
sensational, susceptible 13 understanding
sensitive plant 6 minosa *family:* 3 pea
sensual 4 lush 6 animal, carnal, earthy
7 fleshly, mundane, sensory, worldly 8 banausic, luscious, sensuous, temporal 9 epicurean, luxurious, sensatory, sensitive, sensorial 10 voluptuous 11 irreligious,
sensational, unspiritual 13 materialistic
sensuous 4 lush 6 carnal, fleshy
7 bacchic, fleshly, sensual 8 luscious
9 dionysiac, Dionysian, epicurean, luxurious,
sybaritic 10 hedonistic, voluptuous 12 sensualistic 13 self-indulgent
sentence 4 damn, doom, rule 5 blame,
judge 6 devote, ordain, punish 7 adjudge,
condemn 8 denounce, penalize 9 proscribe 10 adjudicate
sententious 4 rich 5 crisp, pithy, terse
6 facund 7 concise, piquant 8 eloquent,
pregnant 10 aphoristic, expressive, meaningful 11 significant
sentiment 3 eye 4 bias, mind, view
6 belief 7 emotion, feeling, leaning, opinion,
passion, posture 8 penchant, position, tendency 9 affection, inclining, sensation
10 conception, conviction, partiality, persuasion, propensity 11 affectivity, disposition,
inclination 12 emotionalism
sentimental 4 soft 5 gooey, gushy, inane,
moist, mushy, sappy, sobby, soupy, sweet,
vapid 6 dreamy, drippy, jejune, loving,
slushy, sobful, sticky, sugary, syrupy, tender 7 gushing, insipid, maudlin, mawkish
8 bathetic, effusive, romantic, schmalzy
9 misty-eyed, nostalgic, rosewater
10 lovey-dovey, moonstruck, namby-pamby,
passionate, saccharine, soft-boiled, sugar-
candy 11 tear-jerking 12 affectionate
13 demonstrative
sentimentalist 5 softy 6 softie
sentimentality 4 mush 7 schmalz
8 schmaltz
sentinel see **sentry**
sentry 4 ward 5 guard, watch 6 picket
7 lookout, outpost 8 sentinel, watchman
separate 3 one 4 comb, free, know, lone,
only, part, sift, sole, sort 5 apart, halve,
ravel, sever, split 6 cut off, detach, dispel,
divide, enisle, island, single, sunder, unglue,
unique, unjoin, unknit, unlink, winnow
7 break up, discern, disjoin, dislink, dispart,
dissect, diverse, divorce, isolate, quarter,
rupture, scatter, several, split up, unravel,
various 8 alienate, autarkic, close off,
detached, diffract, discrete, disjoint, disperse, dissever, dissolve, distinct, disunify,
disunite, estrange, insulate, peculiar, solitary, splinter, uncouple, unmingle, unsolder
9 autarchic, different, discharge, disengage,
disrelate, extricate, muster out, segregate,
sequester, sovereign, uncombine 10 autonomous, demobilize, difference, discrepate,
disengaged, disgregate, dissociate, particular, severalize 11 compartment, dichotomize, disassemble, discontinue, distinctive,
distinguish, independent 12 disaggregate,
disconnected, discriminate 13 differentiate
flax: 7 hatchel *into filaments:* 6 sleave
separation 6 schism 7 breakup, divorce,
parting, rupture, split-up 8 disunion, disunity, division, shedding 9 apartheid, dichotomy, dispersal, partition 10 detachment, dif-
fluence, diremption, dissection, separatism,
trichotomy 11 disjointure, disjunction, disre-
lation, dissolution, divorcement, segregation 12 dissociation 13 disconnection,
sequestration
separatism 9 apartheid 11 segregation
separatist 7 heretic, sectary 9 dissenter,
dissident 10 schismatic 11 misbeliever,
schismatist 13 nonconformist
sepia 3 ink 4 gray 5 brown
sepulcher 4 bury, tomb 5 grave, inter,

plant **6** burial, entomb, inhume **7** lay away, put away

sequel 3 end, row **5** chain, close, issue, order, train **6** effect, ending, finish, result, series, upshot **7** closing, outcome **8** causatum, epilogue, sequence **9** aftermath, finishing **10** succession **11** aftereffect, alternation, consecution, consequence, development, eventuality, progression, termination **12** continuation

sequence 3 row **5** chain, issue, order, train **6** effect, result, sequel, series, upshot **7** outcome **8** disposal, grouping, ordering **9** aftermath, cavalcade, placement **10** procession, succession **11** aftereffect, alternation, arrangement, consecution, disposition, eventuality, progression **12** distribution

sequential 6 serial **9** succedent **10** succeeding, successive **11** consecutive **12** successional

sequester 4 hide, take **5** annex, seize **6** attach, cut off, enisle, island **7** impound, isolate, preempt, seclude, secrete **8** accroach, arrogate, cloister, close off, insulate, separate **9** segregate **10** commandeer, confiscate, dispossess **11** appropriate, expropriate

seraglio 5 harem **6** bagnio **7** brothel, lupanar **8** bordello

Serah's father 5 Asher

Seraiah *brother:* **6** Baruch **7** Othniel *father:* **5** Asiel, Kenaz **7** Hilkiah **9** Tanhumeth *grandson:* **4** Jehu **6** Jeshua *son:* **4** Joab **7** Jozadak **9** Joshibiah

seraphic 4 pure **7** angelic, sublime

sere 3 dry **4** arid **5** parch **7** bone-dry, thirsty **8** droughty **9** unwatered, waterless **12** moistureless

Sered's father 7 Zebulun

serene 4 calm, easy **5** quiet, still **6** placid, poised **7** resting **8** composed, tranquil

serf 4 esne, peon **5** churl, helot, slave **6** thrall **7** villein *freeborn:* **7** colonus

series 3 row, run, set **4** tier **5** chain, group, scale, train **6** catena, column, parade, sequel, string **8** category, sequence **9** cavalcade, gradation **10** procession, succession **11** alternation, consecution, continuance, progression **12** continuation

serious 4 fell, grim, hard, ugly **5** grave, heavy, major, sober, staid, stern, tough **6** intent, sedate, severe, solemn, somber, steady **7** arduous, austere, earnest, intense, operose, pensive, unfunny, weighty **8** grievous, menacing, resolute, sobering **9** dangerous, difficult, humorless, important, laborious, strenuous, unamusing **10** determined, formidable, meditative, no-nonsense, poker-faced, purposeful, reflective, sobersided, thoughtful, unhumo-

rous **11** significant, steady-going, threatening **12** businesslike **13** contemplative

sermon 6 homily, preach, tirade **7** lecture **8** harangue **9** preaching **10** preachment **11** exhortation

sermonize 6 preach **7** descant, discuss, dissert **8** dilate on, homilize, moralize **9** discourse, expatiate, preachify **10** dilate upon, dissertate, evangelize

serpent 5 devil, fiend, Satan, snake **6** dipsas *combining form:* **4** ophi **5** ophio, ophis *fabled:* **8** basilisk *mythical:* **10** cockatrice *sound:* **4** hiss

serpentine 5 snaky **7** crooked, demonic, devious, satanic, sinuous, winding **8** demoniac, demonian, devilish, diabolic, fiendish, flexuous, tortuous **9** meandrous, snakelike **10** convoluted, meandering

serrated 6 scored **7** notched, serried, toothed **8** indented, saw-edged, sawtooth **10** saw-toothed **11** denticulate

Serug *father:* **3** Reu *son:* **5** Nahor

servant 4 maid **5** valet **6** butler, menial **7** famulus, footman **8** domestic, handmaid, houseboy, houseman, servitor **9** attendant **11** chamberlain, chambermaid *India:* **4** syce *kitchen:* **8** scullion

serve 3 act, fit, use **4** make, play, suit, take, work **5** avail, nurse, put in, spend, treat **6** foster, handle, mother, profit, wait on **7** advance, benefit, care for, forward, further, promote, satisfy, service, suffice, undergo, work for **8** deal with, function, minister **9** advantage, encourage, officiate **10** minister to

service 3 use **4** duty, rite **5** avail, cater, favor **6** action, combat, ritual **7** account, fitness, liturgy **8** ceremony, courtesy, fighting, kindness **9** advantage, formality, relevance **10** active duty, ceremonial, indulgence, observance, usefulness **12** dispensation **13** applicability

servile 3 low **4** base, mean, ugly, vile **6** abject, menial, scurvy, sordid **7** ignoble, passive, slavish, toadish **8** obedient, obeisant **9** groveling **10** despicable, obsequious, submissive **11** bootlicking, subservient, unresisting

servility 4 yoke **7** bondage, helotry, peonage, serfage, serfdom, slavery **9** servitude, thralldom **11** enslavement

serving 6 dollop **7** portion

sesame 3 til *grass:* **4** gama *seed:* **8** gingelly

session 6 assize **7** meeting, sitting *combining form:* **4** fest

set 3 aim, dry, fit, fix, gel, kit, lay, lot, put **4** firm, jell, park, sink **5** affix, array, batch, brood, bunch, crowd, fixed, group, place, put on, ready, rigid, scene, sited, stick **6** anchor, belong, circle, clique, gelate, go

down, harden, impose, placed, rooted,
secure, stated **7** arrange, certain, cluster,
congeal, decided, deposit, descend, dictate,
emplace, express, faction, install, jellify, lay
down, limited, located, prepare, scenery, situate, specify, station, valuate **8** appraise,
ensconce, estimate, evaluate, fastened,
grouping, prepared, resolute, resolved, situ-
ated, solidify, specific **9** confirmed, designate, establish, prescribe, specified, stipulate, tenacious, unbending **10** assortment,
determined, entrenched, gelatinize, inflexible, positioned, prescribed, stipulated,
unyielding **11** established, mise-en-scène *a
gem:* **6** collet *right:* **7** redress
set apart 7 isolate, seclude **8** dedicate
set aside 4 void **5** annul **8** overrule
set back 4 mire **5** delay, embog **6** detain,
hang up, retard, slow up
setback 5 check, rebuff
7 reverse **8** comedown, obstacle, reversal
9 hindrance **10** impediment, regression
set down 4 land **5** light, perch, roost
6 alight, record **9** establish, touch down
set fire to 4 burn **6** ignite **7** emblaze,
inflame
set free 7 manumit, unloose **8** liberate,
unloosen, untangle **10** emancipate
Seth *brother:* **4** Abel, Cain *father:* **4** Adam
mother: **3** Eve *son:* **4** Enos
set off 5 start **7** actuate, balance **8** activate, atone for, outweigh **9** circulate
10 compensate **11** countervail
12 counterpoise
set out 4 head, plan **5** start, state
6 design, intend **7** arrange, present, take
off **9** undertake
Set's victim 6 Osiris
setting 5 scene **7** scenery **11** mise-en-
scène *for a stone:* **4** ouch
settle 3 fix, lay, pay, put **4** calm, land, lull
5 allay, clear, light, pay up, perch, place,
quiet, roost, stick, still **6** alight, becalm,
clinch, decide, soothe, square, wind up
7 arrange, clean up, compose, concert,
install, resolve, satisfy, set down, sit down
8 clear off, colonize, conclude, ensconce
9 determine, discharge, establish, negotiate,
reconcile, touch down **11** tranquilize
settlement 7 quietus, village **8** decision
9 agreement **10** conclusion, habitation, resolution **13** determination *Israeli:* **6** moshav
settler 7 pioneer **8** colonist **9** colonizer
set-to 3 row **4** fray **5** brawl, broil, brush,
fight, run-in, scrap **6** affray, fracas, hassle
7 bobbery, dispute, quarrel, rhubarb, scuffle **8** skirmish **9** bickering, encounter
10 falling-out, velitation **11** altercation
set up 4 blow, open, rear **5** elate, erect,
found, put up, raise, stand, start, treat
6 create, excite, launch **7** build up, com-

move, inspire, start up, usher in **8** generate,
initiate, organize, spirit up **9** construct,
establish, hammer out, institute, introduce,
originate
seven *combining form:* **4** hept, sept
5 hepta, septi *group of:* **6** heptad
8 hebdomad
seventeenth century 8 seicento
sever 3 cut **4** chop, part **5** carve, slice,
split **6** cleave, divide, sunder **7** break up,
dissect, divorce **8** disjoint, separate
severe 3 raw **4** dear, dour, grim, hard,
sore **5** acute, bleak, grave, harsh, heavy,
rigid, sharp, smart, sober, stern, tough
6 bitter, brutal, crimpy, rugged, savage,
stormy, strict, wintry **7** arduous, ascetic,
austere, drastic, extreme, hostile, intense,
onerous, painful, serious, weighty **8** blustery, exacting, rigorous, toilsome **9** difficult,
effortful, inclement, laborious, mortified,
strenuous, stringent **10** astringent, blistering, blustering, forbidding, inflexible, iron-
willed, oppressive, unpleasant, unyielding
11 disciplined, heavy-handed, intemperate,
restrictive **12** disagreeable, inhospitable
sew 4 darn, mend, seam **5** baste **6** needle,
stitch, suture
sewing *aid:* **7** thimble *case:* **4** etui *kit:*
5 hussy **9** housewife
sewing-machine inventor 4 Howe
(Elias)
sexless 6 neuter **7** epicene
sex manual 9 Kama-sutra
sexton 9 custodian, sacristan
sexual *combining form:* **3** gam, gon
4 gamo, gono
sexual desire 4 eros
sexy 4 blue, racy **5** broad, salty, shady,
spicy **6** erotic, purple, risqué **8** off-color
10 suggestive
Sganarelle *brother:* **6** Ariste *daughter:*
7 Lucinde *ward:* **7** Leonore **8** Isabelle
wife: **7** Martine
Shaaph *father:* **5** Caleb **6** Jahdai
mother: **6** Maacah
shabby 4 bare, mean, poor **5** cheap,
dingy, dowdy, faded, mangy, ratty, seedy,
shady, sorry, tacky, tired **6** ruined, scummy,
scurvy, shoddy, sleazy, sordid, tagrag
7 outworn, rickety, ruinous, run-down,
scrubby, scruffy, squalid, worn-out,
wrecked **8** beggarly, decaying, decrepit,
desolate, dog-eared, pitiable, shameful, slipshod, tattered **9** abandoned, miserable,
moth-eaten, neglected, worm-eaten
10 bedraggled, broken-down, despicable,
despisable, disfigured, down-at-heel, inglorious, ramshackle, threadbare **11** dilapidated,
disgraceful, ignominious **12** contemptible,
deteriorated, dishonorable, disreputable

13 deteriorating, discreditable, unrespectable

shack 3 cot, hut **4** camp **5** cabin, hovel, lodge **6** shanty **7** cottage

shackle 3 tie **4** clog, curb, gyve, lash, rope **5** bilbo, bonds, chain, gyves, irons, leash, strap **6** anklet, chains, collar, fetter, hamper, hobble, hog-tie, pinion, secure **7** enchain, fetters, garrote, leg-iron, manacle, trammel **8** bracelet, handcuff **9** entrammel

shad 4 fish **7** clupeid, herring

shade 3 hue **4** cast, hint, tint, tone, veil **5** bogey, color, cover, ghost, spice, tinge, trace, umbra **6** awning, nuance, screen, shadow, spirit, streak **7** dimness, phantom, shelter, soupçon, specter, umbrage **8** darkness, penumbra, phantasm, tincture **9** blackness, gradation, intensity, inumbrate, obscurity, suspicion, variation **10** apparition, difference, saturation, suggestion **11** adumbration, distinction, obscuration

shadow 3 dim, dog, tag **4** haze, hint, tail **5** bedim, bedog, cloud, relic, shade, shady, smack, tinge, touch, trace, trail, umbra **6** breath, screen, shaded, spirit, wraith **7** becloud, eidolon, memento, obscure, phantom, predict, specter, suggest, umbrage, umbrous, vestige **8** forecast, foretell, overcast, penumbra, phantasm, revenant, shadowed, tincture **9** adumbrate, inumbrate, overcloud, prefigure, suspicion **10** apparition, intimation, suggestion, umbrageous **11** adumbration, prefigure *combining form:* **3** sci **4** scia, scio, skia

shadowy 3 dim **4** dark **5** faint, vague **7** ghostly **8** adumbral **10** indistinct

shady 4 blue, dark, racy **5** bosky, broad, dusky, fishy, salty, spicy **6** purple, risqué, shabby, shoddy, wicked **7** clouded, shadowy, suspect, umbrous **8** doubtful, off-color, screened, shadowed, shameful **9** equivocal, sheltered, uncertain, undecided **10** impugnable, indecisive, inglorious, suggestive, suspicious, umbrageous **11** disgraceful, ignominious **12** dishonorable, disreputable **13** discreditable

shaft 3 cut, jab, ray, rod **4** axle, barb, beam, dart, pole, stem **5** arrow, lance, shoot, spear **6** thrust **7** chimney, potshot **8** short end *of a vehicle:* **5** thill

shag 3 mat, nap, rug **5** chase, fetch **7** thicket **9** cormorant

shaggy 5 bushy, rough **7** thrummy, unkempt

shake 3 jar, jog, rid **4** deal, flit, jerk, jolt, lose, rock, roil, slip, whip **5** avoid, churn, clear, crack, daunt, elude, flash, jiffy, quail, quake, shock, trill, upset, waver, worry **6** appall, bother, bounce, dismay, dither, escape, jiggle, joggle, jostle, jounce, minute,

moment, outwit, quaver, quiver, rattle, ruffle, second, shimmy, shiver, stir up, tremor, wiggle **7** agitate, chatter, commove, concuss, disturb, flicker, flitter, flutter, horrify, instant, perturb, shudder, stagger, temblor, tremble, twitter, unnerve, vibrate **8** convulse, disorder, disquiet, throw off, tremblor, unburden, unsettle, unstring **9** breathing, fluctuate, oscillate, palpitate **10** discompose, earthquake **11** consternate, split second

shake down 5 frisk, gouge, pinch, screw, wrest, wring **6** extort, search, wrench **7** squeeze

Shakespeare, William *mother:* **9** Mary Arden *play:* **6** Hamlet, Henry V **7** Henry IV, Henry VI, Macbeth, Othello **8** King John, King Lear, Pericles **9** Cymbeline, Henry VIII, Richard II **10** Coriolanus, Richard III, The Tempest **11** As You Like It **12** Julius Caesar, Twelfth Night *theater:* **5** Globe *wife:* **12** Anne Hathaway

Shakespearean actor 4 Kean **5** Evans **7** Garrick, Gielgud, Olivier **8** Macready

shaky 4 weak **6** aquake, ashake, dickey, infirm, unsure, wobbly **7** aquiver, dubious, quaking, quivery, rackety, rickety, suspect, tottery, trembly, unclear, unsound **8** doubtful, insecure, rachitic, rootless, unstable, unsteady, wavering **9** fluctuant, quivering, tottering, trembling, tremorous, tremulous, uncertain, unsettled **10** indecisive, precarious, rattletrap **11** problematic, vacillating

shale 4 rock **5** slate

shallot 4 herb, tube **5** onion **8** eschalot

shallow 4 idle, vain **5** empty, petty, shoal **6** hollow, paltry **7** cursory, flighty, sketchy, surface, trivial **8** trifling **9** depthless **10** bird-witted, shallowish, uncritical **11** superficial

shallows 6 lagoon

Shallum *father:* **5** Shaul, Zadok **6** Jabesh, Josiah, Sismai, Tikvah **8** Colhozeh, Naphtali **9** Hallohesh *mother:* **6** Bilhah *nephew:* **8** Jeremiah *slayer:* **7** Menahem *son:* **6** Mibsam **7** Hilkiah **8** Maaseiah *victim:* **9** Zechariah

shalom 5 peace **8** farewell, greeting

sham 3 act, ape, lie **4** cant, copy, fake, hoax, mock, sell **5** bluff, bogus, cheat, dummy, false, farce, feign, phony, put on, snide, spoof **6** affect, assume, create, deceit, ersatz, facade, fakery, invent, pseudo **7** assumed, feigned, imitate, mislead, mockery, plaster, pretend **8** affected, flimflam, simulate, so-called, spurious, travesty **9** brummagem, burlesque, deception, hypocrisy, imitation, imposture, pinchbeck, simulated, synthetic **10** artificial, caricature, false front, fictitious, pharisaism, sanctimony, substitute, Tartuffery, Tartuffism **11** adulterated, counterfeit, make believe

12 pecksniffery *combining form:* **5** pseud
6 pseudo
Shamariah see **Shemariah**
Shama's father 6 Hotham
Shamash 6 sun-god *father:* **3** Sin *sister:*
6 Ishtar *wife:* **2** Ai **3** Aya
shamble see **shuffle**
shambles 4 mess **5** botch, mix-up
6 mess-up, muddle **8** botchery, wreckage
9 confusion
shame 5 abash, guilt, odium **6** infamy
7 chagrin, obloquy **8** disgrace, dishonor,
ignominy **9** discredit, disesteem, disrepute
10 opprobrium **11** self-reproof **12** self-
reproach **13** embarrassment, mortification
shameless 4 bold, lewd **6** arrant, brassy,
brazen, cheeky **7** blatant **8** immodest,
impudent, overbold **9** abandoned, audacious, bald-faced, barefaced, dissolute,
unabashed **10** high-handed, outrageous,
profligate, unblushing **11** brazenfaced, disgraceful **12** presumptuous
Shamgar's father 5 Anath
Shamir's father 5 Micah
Shammah *brother:* **5** David *father:*
4 Agee **5** Jesse, Reuel *grandfather:*
4 Esau **7** Ishmael *son:* **7** Jonadab
8 Jonathan
Shammai's father 4 Onam **5** Ezrah,
Rekem
Shammua *father:* **5** David, Galal **6** Bil-
gah, Zaccur *mother:* **9** Bathsheba *son:*
4 Abda
Shamsherai's father 7 Jeroham
shanghai 6 abduct, kidnap
Shangri-la 4 Zion **6** heaven, utopia
7 arcadia **8** paradise **9** Cockaigne, fairyland **10** lubberland, wonderland **12** promised land
shank 3 leg **4** shin, stem **5** stalk, tibia
shanty 3 cot, hut **4** camp **5** cabin, hovel,
lodge, shack **7** cottage
shape 3 fit **4** case, cast, form, look, make,
mold, plan, trim **5** build, forge, frame, order,
state, whack **6** aspect, devise, estate, fettle, figure, kilter, repair, tailor, work up
7 fashion, fitness **8** assemble **9** condition,
construct, fabricate, semblance **10** appearance **12** conformation **13** configuration
· *combining form:* **5** morph **6** morpho
shapeable 4 soft **6** pliant **7** ductile
shapeless 8 formless, inchoate,
unformed **9** amorphous, unshapely
shapely 4 trim **5** buxom **6** comely **7** regular, rounded **8** balanced, clean-cut
9 Junoesque **10** curvaceous, statuesque,
well-turned **11** clean-limbed, full-figured,
symmetrical **12** proportioned
Shaphan *grandson:* **8** Gedaliah *son:*
6 Ahikam **8** Gemariah **9** Jaazaniah

Shaphat *father:* **4** Hori **5** Adlai **8** Shemaiah *son:* **6** Elisha
Sharai's father 4 Bani
share 3 cut, lot **4** bite, meed, part **5** claim,
quota, slice, stake **6** assign, divide, parcel,
quotum, ration **7** deal out, dole out, give
out, measure, mete out, partage, partake,
portion, prorate, quantum, rake-off **8** dispense, interest, quotient **9** allotment, allowance, apportion **10** commission, experience, percentage, proportion
11 participate **13** apportionment
shared 5 joint **6** common, mutual, public
8 communal, conjoint, conjunct *prefix:* **2** co
Sharezer *father, victim:* **11** Sennacherib
shark 5 cheat **8** swindler *kind:* **4** blue,
gata, haye, mako, sand, tope **5** nurse, tiger,
whale, white **7** basking, dogfish, leopard
8 mackerel, maneater, thresher **9** porbea-
gle **10** great white, hammerhead *skin:*
8 shagreen
sharp 3 hep, sly **4** acid, cute, fast, high,
keen, sour, thin, tony, trig, wise **5** acrid,
acute, alert, blunt, canny, harsh, honed,
peaky, piked, quick, short, slick, smart,
swank, swish **6** adroit, argute, biting, bitter,
brainy, bright, clever, nimble, peaked, piping,
severe, shrewd, shrill, snappy, tonish,
treble **7** austere, caustic, dashing, exactly,
intense, knowing, odorous, pointed, prickly,
stylish, whetted **8** acicular, drilling, incisive,
original, piercing, shooting, stabbing, stinging, virulent **9** aciculate, acuminate, acuminous, agonizing, amaroidal, brilliant, cuspidate, ingenious, knifelike, precisely,
sensitive, unblunted, unethical, vitriolic
10 accurately, astringent, paralyzing, perceptive, ungracious **11** acrimonious, double-edged, intelligent, penetrating, penetrative, quick-witted, ready-witted, resourceful,
suffocating, thoughtless **12** excruciating,
nimble-witted, quick-sighted **13** inconsiderate, strong-scented, unceremonious *combining form:* **3** oxy **5** acuto ·
sharp-edged 8 cultrate
sharpen 4 edge, file, hone, whet **5** dress,
grind, strop **6** stroke
sharper 3 gyp **5** cheat **6** con man **7** diddler **8** swindler **9** defrauder, trickster
10 mountebank **12** double-dealer
sharpie see **sharper**
sharpness 4 edge **6** acumen **8** acrimony,
keenness **12** incisiveness
sharpshooter 8 marksman
sharp-sighted 4 keen **5** acute **7** lyncean **8** hawk-eyed, lynx-eyed **9** eagle-
eyed **11** penetrating, penetrative, quick-
witted
sharp-witted 3 hep **4** keen, wise
5 acute, canny, quick, slick, smart

6 shrewd 7 knowing 10 discerning
11 intelligent

Shashai's father 4 Bani

Shashak's father 6 Elpaal

shatter 4 dash, raze, rend, rive, ruin, snap
5 break, burst, clack, crack, crash, crush,
shoot, smash, split, wrack, wreck 6 bicker,
crunch, rattle, shiver 7 clatter, clitter,
destroy 8 decimate, demolish, destruct,
fragment, splinter, splitter 9 pulverize
10 annihilate 11 fragmentize, splinterize
12 disintegrate

shatterable 5 frail 7 fragile 8 delicate,
shattery 9 breakable, frangible
11 fracturable

Shaul's father 6 Simeon

shave 3 cut 4 clip, crop, kiss, pare, skim,
trim 5 brush, graze, lower, prune, shear,
shred, skive, slash 6 glance, reduce,
scrape, sliver 7 cut back, cut down, shingle,
tonsure, whittle 8 mark down

shaveling 3 boy, lad, son, tad 6 laddie
9 stripling

shaver 3 boy, lad 5 child, razor 6 barber
9 youngster

shawl 4 maud, wrap 5 cloak, manta
6 chadar, chador, sarape, serape 7 blanket,
tallith

shawm's descendant 4 oboe

Shawnee chief 8 Tecumseh 9 Cornstalk

Shaw play 6 Geneva 7 Candida 9 Pygmalion, Saint Joan 11 Misalliance 12 Major
Barbara

sheaf 6 bundle 7 cluster

Sheal's father 4 Bani

Shealtiel *father:* 4 Neri 8 Jeconiah *son:*
10 Zerubbabel

shear 3 cut, mow 4 barb, clip, crop, pare,
snip, trim 5 prune, shave, skive 6 barber
8 manicure

Shearjashub's father 6 Isaiah

shears 8 scissors

shearwater 4 bird 6 hagdon, haglet
7 skimmer

sheath 4 case, skin 5 cover 8 scabbard
combining form: 4 cole 5 coleo, theca

sheathe 4 case, clad, face, side, skin,
wrap 5 cover, panel 6 encase, jacket
7 envelop 8 surround

Sheba *father:* 6 Bichri *queen:* 6 Balkis

shebang 3 hut 6 affair 8 business

Sheber *father:* 5 Caleb *mother:*
6 Maacah

Shebuel *father:* 5 Heman 7 Gershom
grandfather: 5 Moses

Shecaniah *father:* 6 Jehiel 8 Jehaziel
son: 7 Hattush 8 Shemaiah *son-in-law:*
6 Tobiah

Shechem's father 5 Hamor 6 Gilead
8 Shemidah

shed 3 hut 4 abri, cast, doff, drop, junk,
molt, slip 5 scrap 6 divest, reject, slough
7 cashier, cast off, discard, ecdysis, take
off 8 exuviate, jettison, throw out 9 throw
away

Shedeur's son 6 Elizur

sheen 5 glaze, glint, gloss, shine 6 finish,
luster, polish 9 shininess

sheeny see shiny

sheep 5 dumba, ovine *Australian:* 7 jumbuck *breed:* 5 Tunis 6 Dorper, Dorset,
Merino, Navajo, No-Tail, Oxford, Panama,
Romney 7 Cheviot, Colbred, Karakul, Lincoln, Ryeland, Suffolk 8 Columbia, Cotswold, Polwarth 9 Hampshire, Leicester,
Montadale, Southdown 10 Corriedale,
Debouillet 11 Rambouillet *coat:* 4 wool
6 fleece *disease:* 3 gid 5 braxy 6 sturdy
female: 3 ewe *male:* 3 ram 6 wether
meat: 6 mutton *relating to:* 5 ovine *Scottish:* 9 blackface *skin:* 4 slat *sound:*
5 bleat *tender of:* 8 shepherd *wild:* 3 sha
5 urial 6 aoudad, argali, bharal, nahoor, oorial 7 bighorn, mouflon 8 moufflon *young:*
3 teg 4 hogg, lamb

sheepish 4 meek 5 timid 7 abashed,
bashful 9 diffident 11 embarrassed

sheepskin 4 roan 5 basil 6 mouton
7 diploma 9 parchment *prepare:* 3 taw

sheer 3 dip 4 airy, pure, skew, slue, thin,
turn, veer, whip 5 avert, filmy, gauzy, pivot,
steep, utter, wheel, whirl 6 abrupt, arrant,
divert, flimsy, simple, swerve 7 chiffon,
deflect, perfect, unmixed 8 absolute, complete, gossamer, outright 9 out-and-out,
unalloyed, undiluted 10 diaphanous, see
through 11 precipitate, precipitous, transparent, unmitigated

sheet 4 leaf, page, sail 5 cover, linen,
paper 9 newspaper *combining form:*
6 pallio

sheet ___ 3 ice 4 film 5 glass, metal,
music 6 anchor

Shehariah's father 7 Jeroham

Shelah *father:* 5 Judah 8 Arphaxad *son:*
4 Eber

Shelemiah *father:* 5 Cushi 6 Abdeel, Binnui 8 Hananiah *son:* 5 Jucal 6 Irijah
8 Hananiah

Sheleph's father 6 Joktan

Shelesh's father 5 Helem

shelf 4 bank, edge, reef, sill 5 ledge,
shoal 6 gradin, mantel 7 gradine
8 sandbank

shell 3 pod 4 boat, bomb, case, hull, husk,
rake, skin 5 blitz, conch, shuck 6 pepper
7 bombard, capsule, grenade, mollusk
9 cannonade, cartridge *combining form:*
5 conch 6 concho, ostrac 7 ostraca,
ostraco *defective:* 3 dud *explosive:*
4 bomb *layer:* 5 nacre *ornamental:*
5 cowry 6 cowrie *study:* 10 conchology

shellac 4 beat, drub, lick, rout, trim, whip
5 resin, smear 6 defeat, thrash 7 smother,
trounce 8 lambaste, vanquish
Shelley *elegy:* 7 Adonais *poem:* 7 Alas-
tor 8 Queen Mab, The Cloud 10 Ozymandias, To a Skylark
shellfish 4 clam, crab 5 conch, cowry,
prawn 6 cockle, limpet, mussel, oyster, triton 7 abalone, lobster, mollusk, scallop
8 barnacle 10 crustacean
shell out 3 pay 4 give 5 spend 6 expend,
outlay 8 disburse
shell-shaped 6 spiral 9 cochleate
Shelomi's son 6 Ahihud
Shelomith *father:* 5 Dibri, Izhar 8 Rehoboam 9 Josiphiah 10 Zerubbabel *mother:*
6 Maacah
shelter 3 den, hut, lee 4 abri, cote, fold,
hide, port, roof, shed, tent 5 arbor, benab,
bower, cloak, cover, haven, house, shack,
tower 6 asylum, burrow, covert, defend,
harbor, refuge, shield 7 chamber, defense,
foxhole, hideout, hospice, housing, lodging,
pergola, pillbox, protect, retreat 8 hideaway, security 9 dwellings, harborage, hermitage, hidey-hole, sanctuary 10 quarter-
age, retirement *for a car:* 6 garage *for
aircraft:* 6 hangar *for cows:* 4 barn, byre
toward: 4 alee
shelve 4 dish, drop, stay, tilt 5 defer,
delay, stock, waive 6 give up, hold up, put
off 7 hold off 8 hold over, postpone,
prorogue
Shem *brother:* 3 Ham 7 Japheth *father:*
4 Noah
Shemaiah *father:* 4 Joel 7 Delaiah
8 Adonikam, Nethanel, Obededom 9 Elizaphan, Shecaniah *son:* 5 Uriah 6 Urijah
7 Delaiah, Obadiah
Shemariah's father 4 Bani 5 Harim
8 Rehoboam
Shema's father 4 Joel 6 Hebron
Shemer's father 5 Mahli
Shemida's father 6 Gilead
Shemuel's father 4 Tola 7 Ammihud
shenanigan 4 game, lark, play, ploy, ruse,
wile 5 antic, caper, prank, stunt, trick
6 device, didoes, frolic, shines 7 fast one,
gimmick, whizzer 8 goings-on, maneuver
9 stratagem 10 tomfoolery 11 legerdemain, monkeyshine
Shenazzar's father 8 Jeconiah
10 Jehoiachin
Sheol see **hades**
Shephatiah *father:* 5 David 6 Maacah,
Mattan 11 Jehoshaphat *mother:* 6 Abital
shepherd 3 see 4 lead, show, tend
5 guide, pilot, route, steer, watch 6 direct,
escort, leader 7 conduct 8 guardian *dog:*
6 Collie *stick:* 4 kent 5 crook, staff
Shephi, Shepho *father:* 6 Shobal

Sheridan play 7 Pizarro 9 The Critic, The
Rivals
sheriff 6 lawman 7 marshal, officer *aide:*
6 deputy
Sherlock Holmes 6 sleuth 7 gumshoe
8 hawkshaw 9 detective 12 investigator
creator: 5 Doyle *sidekick:* 6 Watson
sherry 4 fino, wine 7 oloroso
11 amontillado
Sheshai's father 4 Anak
Sheshan's servant 5 Jarha
shibboleth 3 tag 6 byword, clich'e,
phrase, slogan, truism 7 bromide 8 banality, password, prosaism 9 catchword, platitude, watchword 10 prosaicism
11 catchphrase
shield 4 fend, roof, ward 5 aegis, armor,
cover, guard, haven, house 6 defend, harbor, screen, secure 7 buckler, bulwark, protect, shelter 8 defilade 9 safeguard
10 escutcheon *band:* 4 fess *bullfighter's:*
9 burladero *combining form:* 4 scut
5 aspid, scuti 6 aspido *large:* 5 pavis
6 pavise *light:* 5 targe *part:* 4 boss, umbo
7 bordure *Roman:* 6 scutum 7 clipeus,
testudo
shield-like 7 peltate, scutate 9 scutiform
shift 3 yaw 4 bend, bout, move, stir, tack,
time, tour, turn, vary 5 alter, budge, get by,
get on, spell, stint, trick 6 change, make do,
manage, remove, swerve 7 disturb, replace,
shuffle 8 get along, relocate, transfer
9 deviation, dislocate 10 alteration, changeover, conversion, deflection, transition
shiftless 4 lazy
shifty 5 cagey, lying, shady 6 crafty,
sneaky, tricky 7 cunning, devious, dodging,
elusive, evasive, furtive, knavish, mutable,
roguish 8 guileful, indirect, slippery, sneaking, unhonest, unstable, unsteady, variable
9 collusive, conniving, deceitful, dishonest,
insidious, shuffling, uncertain, underhand
10 changeable, fraudulent, inconstant, mendacious, untruthful 11 duplicitous, treacherous, underhanded 12 equivocating 13 pre-
varicative, prevaricatory
Shilem's father 8 Naphtali
Shilhi *daughter:* 6 Azubah *grandson:*
11 Jehoshaphat
shill 5 blind, decoy, stick 6 capper
shilling 3 bob
shilly-shally 4 halt 5 waver 6 dither, falter, wobbly 7 halting, stagger, whiffle
8 hesitate, to-and-fro, wavering 9 faltering,
hesitancy, vacillate, whiffling 10 hesitating,
hesitation, indecision 11 vacillating, vacillation, vacillatory 12 irresolution
Shilshah's father 7 Zophah
Shimea *brother:* 5 David *father:* 5 David,
Jesse *son:* 7 Jonadab 8 Jonathan
Shimeam's father 7 Mikloth

Shimei *brother:* **8** Conaniah, Cononiah
10 Zerubbabel *father:* **4** Bani, Gera, Kish
6 Hashum, Jahath **7** Gershon **8** Jeduthun
grandfather: **4** Levi
Shimeon's father 5 Harim
shimmer 5 flash, gleam, glint, spark
7 glimmer, glisten, glitter, spangle, sparkle,
twinkle **8** blinking, sparking **9** coruscate
11 coruscation, scintillate **13** scintillation
shimmy 5 dance, shake **7** chemise, vibrate
Shimrath's father 6 Shimei
Shimri's father 5 Hosah **8** Shemaiah
9 Elizaphan
Shimrith's son 9 Jehozabad
Shimron's father 8 Issachar
shin 3 run **4** dash **5** scoot, tibia **6** scurry,
sprint **7** scamper
shindig 4 ball, bash, coil, fête, gala, to-do
5 dance, party **6** affair, furore, ruckus, rumpus, shindy, uproar **7** shebang **8** foofaraw
9 commotion
shine 3 ray, rub **4** beam, buff, burn, glow,
pomp, show **5** array, flare, flash, glare,
glaze, gleam, glint, gloss, sheen **6** finish,
glance, luster, parade, polish **7** burnish, display, fanfare, furbish, glimmer, glisten, panoply, radiate, sparkle, twinkle **9** luminesce
10 incandesce
shiner 4 fish **8** black eye, cyprinid
Shinto gods 4 kami
shiny 6 glossy, sheeny **7** fulgent **8** gleaming, lustrous, polished **9** burnished
10 glistening
ship 4 boat, move, send **5** remit, route,
shift **6** direct, export, remove **7** address,
consign, disturb, forward, freight **8** dispatch, transfer, transmit *ancient:* **5** knorr
6 galley **7** galleon, trireme *attendant:*
7 steward *beam:* **7** carling, keelson *berth:*
4 dock, slip *boat:* **6** dinghy *body:* **4** hull
cabin: **9** stateroom *commercial:* **5** liner,
oiler **6** argosy, tanker, trader **9** freighter
crew member: **4** hand, mate **5** bosun
6 purser, sailor *deck:* **4** boat, main, poop
5 orlop **6** bridge **10** forecastle *fishing:*
6 lugger **7** trawler *fleet:* **6** armada *floor:*
4 deck *front:* **3** bow **4** prow, stem **8** cut-
water *hoister:* **4** boom **5** davit **7** capstan
kitchen: **6** galley *left side:* **4** port **8** larboard *merchant:* (see *commercial*) *mili-
tary:* **6** cutter, PT boat **7** carrier, cruiser
9 destroyer, submarine *officer:* **4** mate
5 bosun **6** purser **7** captain, steward *of the
desert:* **5** camel *part:* **3** bow **4** beam,
deck, helm, hold, hull, keel, mast, stem
5 bilge, hatch, stern **6** bridge, rudder
7 scupper *partition:* **7** bulwark **8** bulkhead
personnel: **4** crew *platform:* **9** crow's
nest, gangboard, gangplank *post:* **4** mast
7 bollard *prison:* **4** brig *projection:* **7** spon-
son *rear:* **5** stern *record:* **3** log *right side:*

9 starboard *room:* **4** brig **5** cabin **6** galley
rope: **4** line **7** halyard *sailing:* **4** brig,
dhow, prao, prau, proa, yawl **5** ketch,
prahu, sloop, xebec **6** chebec, lugger
7 caravel, galleon **8** bilander, schooner
spar: **6** bumkin *steerer:* **4** helm **6** tiller
storage area: **4** hold *submersible:* **9** submarine **11** bathyscaphe *to the rear of:*
3 aft **5** abaft **6** astern *valve:* **7** seacock
window: **4** port **8** porthole
Shiphi's father 5 Allon
Shiphtan's son 6 Kemuel
shipment 5 cargo **8** delivery
Ship of Fools author 6 Porter
ships *group of:* **4** navy **5** fleet, flota
6 armada **8** flotilla
shipshape 4 neat, snug, tidy, trig, trim
7 chipper, orderly **11** spic-and-span, uncluttered, well-groomed **12** spick-and-span
shire 5 horse **6** county **8** district
shirk 4 duck, lurk, shun, slip **5** creep,
dodge, fence, parry, skulk, slink, sneak,
steal **6** bypass, eschew **8** sidestep
shirker see **slacker**
shirt 4 sark **6** camisa, camise, jersey
7 garment **8** guernsey, pullover *armored:*
6 byrnie *hair:* **6** cilice *kind:* **3** tee **4** polo
5 dress, sport *Scottish:* **4** jupe
shirty 3 mad **4** waxy **5** angry, irate,
wroth **6** heated, ireful, wrathy **8** choleric,
wrathful
Shiva, Siva *consort:* **3** Uma **4** Devi, Kali
5 Durga, Gauri **6** Ambika, Chandi **7** Parvati **9** Haimavati *son:* **6** Ganesa, Skanda
7 Ganesha **10** Karttikeya
shiver 4 rive **5** burst, quake, shake,
smash **6** dither, quaver, quiver, tremor
7 shatter, shudder, tremble, twitter **8** fragment, splinter, splitter **11** splinterize
Shiza's son 5 Adina
shoal 3 bar **4** bank, hook, reef, spit **7** barrier, sandbar, shallow, tombolo **8** sandbank,
sand reef, seamount **9** coral reef **11** barrier
reef, superficial
Shobab *father:* **5** Caleb, David *mother:*
6 Azubah **9** Bathsheba
Shobal's father 3 Hur **4** Seir
Shobi's father 6 Nahash
shock 3 jar **4** bank, bump, cock, hill, jolt,
pile, rick **5** clash, crash, floor, mound,
quake, shake, smash, stack **6** appall,
impact, insult, offend, sicken, trauma,
tremor **7** astound, disgust, horrify, outrage,
pyramid, shake up, startle, temblor **8** astonish, knock out, nauseate, surprise, tremblor
9 collision, electrify, stockpile **10** concussion, earthquake, percussion, scandalize,
traumatism **11** prostration **12** stupefaction
shock absorber 6 spring **7** dashpot,
snubber
shocking 5 awful, lurid **6** crying, horrid

7 burning, direful, fearful, glaring, heinous 8 dreadful, horrible, horrific, shameful, terrible 9 appalling, atrocious, desperate, frightful, monstrous 10 formidable, outrageous, scandalous 11 disgraceful, unspeakable

shoddy 4 base, mean, poor 5 cheap, dingy, seedy, shady, tacky, tatty 6 common, paltry, shabby, sleazy, trashy 7 rundown, scruffy 8 rubbishy, shameful 9 makeshift, scambling 10 broken-down, down-at-heel, inglorious 11 dilapidated, disgraceful, ignominious 12 dishonorable, disreputable 13 discreditable

shoe 3 bal, pac 4 boot, clog, geta, mule, pump 5 gilly, plate, sabot, tegua, wedge 6 brogan, brogue, buskin, crakow, gaiter, galosh, gillie, loafer, oxford, patten, sandal 7 chopine, ghillie, slipper, sneaker 8 balmoral, moccasin, platform, plimsoll 9 brodequin, pampootie, spectator 10 clodhopper, espadrille *accessory:* 4 horn, tree 6 polish *armored:* 8 solleret *athlete's:* 7 sneaker *form:* 4 last, tree *kind:* 8 elevator, opentoed 10 high-heeled *part:* 3 tip, toe 4 arch, heel, lace, lift, sole, vamp 5 shank, upper 6 box toe, collar, foxing, insole, lining, throat, tongue 7 counter, outsole 8 backstay *protective:* 6 galosh, rubber *Roman:* 6 caliga, sandal *shiner:* 6 polish 9 bootblack *wooden:* 5 sabot 7 chopine

shoeless 6 unshod 8 barefoot

shoemaker 5 soler 7 cobbler, crispin *patron saint:* 7 Crispin *Scottish:* 6 souter

Shogun author 7 Clavell

Shoham's father 7 Jaaziah

Shomer *father:* 5 Heber *son:* 9 Jehozabad

shoo-in 9 sure thing

shoot 3 bud, fly, gun, ray 4 beam, bolt, dart, dash, fire, lash, race, raze, ruin, rush, sail, scud, skim, spew, tear 5 blast, chase, fling, float, loose, photo, shaft, skirr, snipe, spurt, wrack, wreck 6 branch, charge 7 destroy, explode, project 8 decimate, demolish, destruct, disprove, puncture 9 discharge, discredit 10 annihilate, photograph *combining form:* 5 blast, thall 6 blasto, thalli, thallo

shooting 5 acute, sharp 7 gunplay 8 piercing, stabbing 9 knifelike

shooting star 6 meteor 8 fireball

shoot up 4 soar 6 rocket 9 skyrocket

shop 4 hunt 5 store 6 market, outlet 8 boutique, emporium, showroom

shoplift 3 bag, cop 4 palm 5 pinch, steal, swipe 6 pilfer, rip off, snitch

shop owner 3 cit 8 merchant, retailer 10 proprietor

shopworn 5 stale, tired, trite 6 cliché 7 clichéd 8 overused 9 hackneyed 10 overworked 13 stereotypical

shore 4 bank, prop, stay 5 beach, brace, brink, carry, coast 6 bear up, column, rivage, strand, upbear, uphold 7 bolster, support, sustain 8 buttress, littoral, seacoast 9 coastland, coastline, riverbank, riverside, waterside 10 embankment, waterfront 11 underpinner 12 underpinning

shorebird see at bird

short 3 shy 4 core, curt, gist, meat, pith 5 aback, bluff, blunt, brief, crisp, dumpy, gruff, scant, sharp, skimp, spare, squat, stint, terse, thick 6 abrupt, amount, burden, chunky, crusty, low-set, meager, scanty, scarce, skimpy, snippy, sparse, stubby, sudden, thrust, upshot 7 asudden, brittle, brusque, compact, concise, crumbly, crunchy, curtate, failing, fragile, friable, lacking, laconic, needing, pointed, purport, scrimpy, slender, squatty, summary, unaware, wanting 8 abridged, abruptly, delicate, exiguous, lessened, snippety, succinct, suddenly, thickset, unawares 9 curtailed, decreased, decurtate, deficient, forthwith, irascible 10 diminished, inadequate, ungracious 11 abbreviated, compendiary, compendious 12 brevilbecause, insufficient, unexpectedly, unsufficient 13 inconsiderate, unceremonious *combining form:* 5 brevi 6 brachy

shortage 4 lack 5 pinch 6 dearth 7 deficit, failure 8 underage 10 deficiency, inadequacy, scantiness

shortcoming 3 sin 5 fault 7 demerit 10 deficiency 12 imperfection

shortcut 6 bypass, cutoff

shorten 3 bob, cut 4 clip, dock 5 elide, slash 6 lessen, reduce, shrink 7 abridge, bobtail, curtail, cut back, excerpt 8 compress, condense, contract, decrease, diminish, minimize, retrench, truncate 10 abbreviate

shorthand 11 stenography *method:* 5 Gregg 6 Pitman

shorthanded 7 wanting 11 undermanned 12 understaffed

shortly 4 anon, soon 6 pronto 7 briefly, by and by, in brief, quickly, tersely 8 directly 9 concisely, presently 10 succinctly 11 laconically

shortness 7 brevity

shortsighted 6 myopic

short-spoken 4 curt 5 bluff, blunt, brief, gruff 6 abrupt, crusty, snippy 7 brusque 8 snippety

short-tempered 5 testy 6 touchy 9 irascible

Shoshoni chief 8 Washakie 9 Pocatello

shot 2 go 3 nip, pop, try 4 dram, drop, jolt, show, slug, stab, time 5 break, carom, crack, fling, snort, whack, whirl 6 chance

7 snifter **8** occasion, toothful
11 opportunity

shoulder 4 edge, push, side **5** elbow,
press, shove **6** axilla, hustle, jostle **8** bulldoze *bone:* **7** scapula **8** clavicle *combining
form:* **2** om **3** omo *covering:* **6** tippet
8 scapular *muscle:* **7** deltoid *relating to:*
7 humeral **8** scapular

shoulder blade 7 scapula

shout 3 cry **4** bark, bawl, bray, call, howl,
roar, yell **5** blare, whoop **6** bellow, clamor,
holler, scream, shriek **7** exclaim
10 vociferate

shove 3 dig, jab, jam **4** cram, poke, prod,
push **5** drive, elbow, press **6** hustle, jostle,
peddle, propel, thrust **8** bulldoze, shoulder

shovel 3 dig **4** grub **5** scoop, scuff,
spade **6** dig out **7** scuffle, shamble, shuffle **8** excavate

shoveler 4 duck **9** broadbill

shovelhead 7 catfish

shove off 2 go **4** exit, quit **5** leave
6 depart, get off **7** pull out, take off **8** run
along

show 3 air, get, say, see **4** cine, come, fair,
film, lead, look, loom, mark, pomp, read
5 array, flash, flick, front, get in, guide,
mount, movie, offer, pilot, prove, revue,
sport, stage, steer, vaunt **6** appear, arrive,
blazon, chance, direct, emerge, escort,
evince, expose, flaunt, lay out, look-in,
ostend, parade, record, reveal, set out, submit, turn up, unveil **7** conduct, display, disport, divulge, exhibit, fanfare, make out,
panoply, picture, present, produce, proffer,
project, seeming, trot out **8** brandish, disclose, evidence, flourish, indicate, manifest,
occasion, proclaim, register, shepherd
9 determine, establish, photoplay, represent,
semblance, spectacle **10** appearance, exhibition, exposition, illustrate, simulacrum
11 demonstrate, materialize, opportunity,
performance **13** demonstration, motion picture, moving picture

Show Boat *author:* **6** Ferber *composer:*
4 Kern

showcase 7 exhibit, vitrine

shower 3 tub **4** hail, rain, wash **5** bathe,
burst, party, salvo, spray, storm **7** barrage,
shatter, spatter **8** downpour, rainfall
9 broadside, cannonade, fusillade **10** cloudburst **11** bombardment

showman 3 producer *famous:* **4** Cody
6 Barnum

Show Me State 8 Missouri

show off 4 brag **5** boast, flash **6** expose,
flaunt, parade **7** display, disport, exhibit,
swagger, trot out **8** brandish

showoff 6 hotdog **7** hotshot
13 exhibitionist

showpiece 3 gem **5** jewel, prize **11** chef
d'oeuvre, masterpiece

show up 3 get **4** come **5** get in, reach
6 arrive, debunk, expose, turn up, unmask
7 uncloak, undress **8** discover, unshroud
9 discredit **10** invalidate

showy 3 gay **4** arty, loud **5** gaudy, jazzy,
swank **6** chichi, flashy, garish, ornate,
sporty, tawdry **7** opulent, splashy **8** gorgeous, overdone, peacocky **9** luxurious,
sumptuous **10** flamboyant, peacockish
11 overwrought, pretentious, resplendent,
sensational **12** meretricious, orchidaceous,
ostentatious

shrapnel 8 fragment **10** projectile

shred 3 bit, dag, rag **4** iota **5** crumb,
grate, ounce, scrap, shave, speck **6** sliver
7 modicum, smidgen **8** fragment, particle

shrew 5 harpy, scold, vixen, witch **6** amazon, ogress, rodent, virago **8** fishwife, she-
devil, spitfire **9** termagant, Xanthippe

shrewd 3 sly **4** cagy, foxy, keen, tidy,
wise **5** acute, cagey, canny, heady, sharp,
slick, smart **6** argute, astute, clever, crafty,
polite, smooth **7** knowing, probing, prudent **8** piercing, sensible **9** astucious, ingenious, judicious, sagacious **10** farsighted
11 foresighted, intelligent, penetrating,
quick-witted **13** perspicacious

shriek 3 cry **4** yell **5** blare, shout
6 screak, scream, shrill, squawk, squeal
7 screech

shrill 4 high, keen, thin **5** acute, sharp
6 argute, piping, scream, shriek, squeal,
treble **7** screech **8** piercing, strident

shrimp 4 runt **5** prawn **10** crustacean
combining form: **5** caris

shrine 3 box **4** tomb **5** altar **6** temple
7 sanctum **9** holy place, reliquary, sanctuary **10** sanctorium *Buddhist:* **5** stupa
6 dagoba

shrink 3 shy **4** fail, funk, wane **5** cower,
demur, quail, slink, start, wince **6** blanch,
blench, boggle, cringe, crouch, flinch, huddle, recede, recoil, retire, weaken, wither
7 dwindle, retreat, scruple, squinch **8** compress, condense, contract, draw back, withdraw **9** constrict, fall short, shrivel up,
waste away **11** concentrate

shrinking 3 shy **5** timid **7** aseptic **8** retiring **9** unaffable, withdrawn **10** restrained
11 unexpansive

shrive 4 free **5** purge **6** pardon **7** confess

shrivel 4 wilt **5** dry up, parch, wizen
6 welter, wither

Shropshire Lad author 8 Houseman

shroud 3 lop **4** hide, veil, wrap **5** cloak,
close, cover, shade **6** enfold, enwrap,
invest, screen **7** enclose, envelop, shut off,
shut out **8** block out, cerement, obstruct
9 cerecloth

shrouded 5 privy 6 buried, covert, hidden 7 guarded 8 obscured, ulterior 9 concealed

shrub 3 lop 4 bush 5 elder, erica, hazel, plant, prune 6 cercis, muskit, privet 7 arboret, dyeweed, guayule 8 barberry, bluewood, boxthorn, inkberry, ironweed, rosebush 9 bearberry 10 bladdernut *Asian:* 4 bago 5 ramee, ramie 6 kerria 8 caragana, japonica 10 beauty bush *climbing:* 7 jasmine *combining form:* 5 thamn 6 thamno *desert:* 5 retem 6 alhagi 7 ephedra *dwarf:* 6 bonsai *East Indian:* 3 aal 4 sunn *European:* 4 cade 8 woodbind, woodbine *evergreen:* 3 box, kat, yew 4 ilex, khat, titi 5 furze, heath, holly, pyxie, savin, taxus, thuja, thuya, toyon, yapon 6 kalmia, laurel, myrtle, nandin, protea, sabine, savine, yaupon 7 boxwood, heather, jasmine, juniper, rosebay 8 lambkill, oleander, rosemary, tamarisk *flowering:* 5 lilac, ribes, tiara, wahoo 6 azalea, daphne, laurel, myrtle, spirea, wicopy 7 chamise, chamiso, fuchsia, mahonia, maybush, rhodora, spiraea, weigela 8 magnolia, mezereon, mezereum, nineback, oleander, oleaster, shadblow, shadbush, snowball, snowbell, snowbush, tornillo, viburnum, wistaria, wisteria *fragrant:* 4 mint, sage 5 thyme 8 rosemary 10 basil thyme *genus:* 4 Inga 7 Solanum 8 Euonymus *hardwood:* 6 cornel *Mexican:* 8 ocotillo *ornamental:* 6 privet 7 deutzia, jetbead, syringa, woodwax 9 bluebeard *pasture:* 8 cowberry *prickly:* 4 whin 5 briar, chico, furze, gorse 7 bramble, rhamnus 8 hawthorn, mesquite 9 buckthorn *South American:* 4 coca 7 rhatany *thicket:* 6 maquis 7 macchia 9 chaparral *tropical:* 4 kava 5 guava, henna 7 camelia, lantana 8 buddleia, camellia, gardenia 10 frangipani *West Indian:* 4 anil 7 acerola

shrug 6 jacket 7 gesture *off:* 5 evade 8 minimize

Shua *father:* 5 Heber *son-in-law:* 5 Judah

Shuah *father:* 7 Abraham *mother:* 7 Keturah

Shual's father 6 Zophah

shuck 3 pod 4 case, cast, hull, husk, junk, peel, shed, skin 5 chuck, ditch, scrap, shell, strip 6 reject, slough 7 discard 8 jettison 11 decorticate

shudder 5 quake, shake 6 dither, gyrate, quaver, quiver, shimmy, shiver, tremor 7 frisson, tremble, twitter

shuffle 4 hash, limp, mash 5 dodge, evade, hedge, scuff 6 jumble, jungle, litter, mess up, muddle, shovel, tumble, weasel 7 clutter, disrupt, disturb, rummage, shamble, stumble 8 disarray, disorder, mishmash, sidestep 9 dislocate, pussyfoot

10 disarrange, discompose, equivocate, tergiverse 11 disorganize 12 tergiversate

Shuham's father 3 Dan

shun 3 shy 4 duck, snub 5 avoid, elude, evade 6 double, escape, eschew, refuse, reject 7 decline, disdain

Shuni's father 3 Gad

shunt 4 move, turn 5 avert, shift 6 change, divert, switch 7 deflect, head off, shuttle 8 transfer 9 sidetrack

shush 4 hush 5 quiet, still 6 muffle, shut up 7 repress, silence, squelch 8 choke off, strangle, suppress

shut 4 lock, seal 5 close 6 fasten 7 confine 10 batten down *loudly:* 4 slam

Shute, Nevil *novel:* 7 Marazan 9 Pied Piper 10 On the Beach 11 So Disdained

Shuthelah's father 7 Ephraim

shut in 3 hem, pen 4 cage, coop, mure, wall 5 fence 6 immure 7 close in, confine, enclose, envelop 8 imprison

shut-in 7 invalid 12 convalescent

shut out 3 bar 5 close 6 screen, shroud 7 exclude 8 obstruct

shutter 5 blind 6 screen

shuttle 5 shunt 6 bobbin 9 alternate

shuttlecock 4 bird 6 birdie

shut up 3 gag 4 hush 5 dry up, quiet, shush, still 6 dumb up 7 dummy up, silence 8 choke off, pipe down 9 quiet down

shy 3 coy, gag, jib, pot 4 balk, bilk, duck, meek, shun, wary 5 avoid, chary, demur, elude, evade, loath, quail, scant, short, timid 6 afraid, averse, blench, boggle, demure, double, escape, eschew, modest, recoil, scanty, scarce, shrink 7 bashful, failing, fearful, lacking, nervous, potshot, rabbity, scruple, stickle, stumble, uneager, wanting 8 backward, cautious, hesitant, inturned, reserved, retiring, sheepish, skittish, timorous 9 conscious, deficient, diffident, introvert, reluctant, sideswipe, unassured, unwilling 10 backhanded, inadequate, indisposed, shamefaced, suspicious 11 circumspect, disinclined, introverted, unassertive 12 apprehensive, insufficient, introversive, self-effacing, unsufficient 13 self-conscious

Shylock 6 usurer 9 loan shark *daughter:* 7 Jessica

shyster 11 pettifogger

Siam see **Thailand**

Siamese coin see **coin,** *Thailand*

sib 3 kin 4 akin 6 sister 7 brother, kindred, related 8 relative

Sibbecai's victim 4 Saph

Sibelius composition 9 Finlandia

Siberian *antelope:* 5 saiga *dog:* 5 husky *gulf:* 2 Ob *native:* 5 Tatar, Yakut 6 Tar-

tar **9** Mongolian *plain:* **6** steppe *storm:*
5 buran *tent:* **4** yurt

sibilate 4 buzz, fizz, hiss, whiz **5** swish,
whisk **6** fizzle, sizzle, wheeze **7** whisper

sibling 6 sister **7** brother

sibyl 4 seer **7** prophet **10** prophetess
13 fortune-teller

sic 2 so **4** abet, goad, prod, spur, thus,
urge **5** egg on, favor, prick **6** exhort,
prompt, propel **7** agitate **8** catalyze,
inspirit **9** instigate

Sicilian *secret organization:* 5 Mafia *volcano:* **4** Etna

Sicily's capital 7 Palermo

sick 3 ill **4** down, mean, weak **5** amiss, fed
up, funny, lousy, peaky, rocky, tired, weary
6 ailing, faulty, flawed, laid up, morbid,
morose, peaked, rotten, unwell, wobbly
7 fevered **8** confined, diseased **9** defective,
disgusted, imperfect, tottering, unhealthy
10 disordered, indisposed **11** debilitated

sicken 5 repel, upset **6** reluct, revolt
7 derange, disgust, repulse, unhinge **8** disorder, nauseate, unsettle

sickle 5 blade, mower **8** crescent

sickly 3 ill, low **4** down, mean, puny,
weak **5** pecky **6** ailing, morbid, morose, offish, peaked, poorly, unwell **7** noisome, noxious, underly **8** diseased, off-color
9 unhealthy **10** indisposed, insalutary, unsalutary **11** unhealthful, unwholesome
12 insalubrious

sickness 3 ill **6** malady **7** ailment, disease, illness **8** disorder, syndrome,
unhealth **9** affection, complaint, condition,
infirmity **10** affliction, unwellness
12 diseasedness **13** indisposition,
unhealthiness

sic transit gloria ____ 5 mundi

side 4 clad, face, hand, part, skin **5** angle,
facet, flank, phase, slant, stand **6** aspect,
sector, stance **7** outlook, posture, sheathe
8 attitude, position **9** direction, viewpoint
10 standpoint **11** disposition *combining
form:* **5** later, pleur **6** lateri, latero, pleuri,
pleuro *sheltered:* **3** lee

sideboard 5 table **6** buffet **8** credence *for
wine:* **8** cellaret **10** cellarette

sideboards see **sideburns**

sideburns 9 burnsides **10** sideboards
11 dundrearies, muttonchops

side by side 8 together *combining form:*
3 par **4** para

sidekick 3 pal **7** partner **9** assistant,
companion

sidereal 6 astral, starry **7** stellar

side road 5 byway **8** bystreet, shunpike

sidestep 4 duck **5** avoid, burke, dodge,
evade, fence, hedge, parry, shirk, skirt
6 bypass, weasel **9** pussyfoot **10** circumvent, equivocate **12** tergiversate

sidetrack 5 shunt **6** divert, switch

sidewalk 6 paving **7** walkway **8** pavement **9** banquette

sidewhiskers see **sideburns**

side with 4 back **6** uphold **7** support
8 advocate, backstop, champion

sidle 4 ease, edge, slip **7** saunter

siege 4 bout **5** spell **6** attack **7** seizure
9 onslaught

Siegfried *mother:* 9 Sieglinde *slayer:*
5 Hagen *sword:* **7** Balmung *vulnerable
spot:* **4** back **8** shoulder *wife:* **9** Kriemhild

Sienkiewicz novel 8 Quo Vadis

sierra 4 fish **5** range

siesta 3 nap **5** sleep **6** catnap, dog nap,
snooze **10** forty winks

sieve 4 sift **5** clack, tabby **6** gossip,
screen **8** colander, gossiper, quidnunc,
strainer **10** talebearer

Sif's husband 4 Thor

sift 4 bolt, comb, cull, sort **5** probe, sieve
6 filter, go into, screen, winnow **7** dig into,
explore **8** filtrate, look into, prospect, separate **9** delve into **11** inquire into, investigate

sigh 3 sob **4** ache, blow, gasp, howl, long,
lust, moan, pant, pine, roar **5** crave, dream,
groan, sough, whine **6** exhale, hanker, hunger, murmur, thirst, wheeze **7** breathe,
respire, suspire, whisper, whistle

sight 3 aim, eye, spy **4** espy, look, mess,
view **5** scene **6** fright, seeing, vision **7** eyesore, outlook **11** monstrosity *combining
form:* **4** opsy **5** opsia, opsis *relating to:*
5 optic **6** ocular, visual **7** optical

sightseer 7 tourist **10** rubberneck

sign 3 cue, ink **4** flag, hint, mark, omen,
show **5** index, proof, token, trace **6** motion,
signal, symbol **7** earmark, endorse, exhibit,
gesture, indicia, initial, symptom, vestige,
warning **8** evidence, exponent, reminder
9 autograph, character, indicator, subscribe **10** expression, indication, suggestion **11** attestation **13** gesticulation, sym-
bolization *commercial:* **4** neon
directional: **5** arrow *of the zodiac:* (see
zodiac sign)

signal 3 cue **4** flag **5** alarm, alert, siren
6 beckon, famous, marked, motion, tocsin,
wigwag **7** eminent, gesture, salient **8** high
sign, movement, peculiar, renowned, striking **9** arresting, arrestive, prominent
10 individual, noticeable, remarkable
11 conspicuous, distinctive, illustrious, outstanding *distress:* **3** SOS **6** Mayday

signature 3 ink **4** name, sign **9** autograph, subscribe **11** John Hancock *flourish:* **6** paraph

signet 4 ring, seal **5** stamp

significance 4 pith **5** merit, sense
6 credit, import, moment, virtue, weight
7 meaning, message, purport **8** prestige

9 authority, influence, magnitude **10** excellence, importance, intendment, perfection **11** acceptation, consequence, weightiness

significant 3 big **4** rich **5** sound, valid **6** cogent, facund **7** telling, weighty **8** eloquent, forceful, material, powerful **9** important, momentous **10** compelling, convincing, expressive, meaningful **11** sententious, substantial **12** considerable **13** consequential

signification 4 gist **5** sense **6** import **7** essence, meaning, message, purport **8** implying **9** substance **10** intendment **11** acceptation, implication **12** construction **13** understanding

signify 4 bear, mean, show **5** carry, count, spell, weigh **6** convey, denote, import, intend, matter **7** add up to, bespeak, connote, express, purport

sign over 4 cede, deed **5** alien **6** assign, remise **8** alienate, make over, transfer **10** abalienate

sign up 4 join **5** enter **6** enlist, enroll, join up, muster

Sigurd *horse:* **5** Grani *slayer:* **5** Hogni *victim:* **6** Fafnir *wife:* **6** Gudrun

Sigyn's husband 4 Loki

silage 6 fodder

silence 3 gag **4** calm, dumb, hush, lull, mute **5** death, quash, quell, quiet, shush, sleep, still **6** dampen, deaden, demise, muffle, muzzle, shut up, squash **7** decease, passing, quietus, secrecy, squelch **8** choke off, curtains, hush-hush, quietude, suppress **9** quietness, stillness

silent 3 mum **4** dumb, hush, mute **5** close, muted, quiet, still, tacit, whist **6** curbed, stilly **7** checked, hushful **8** reserved, reticent, taciturn, unspoken, unvoiced, wordless **9** inhibited, noiseless, secretive, soundless, unuttered, voiceless **10** incoherent, restrained, speechless, tongue-tied, unsociable **11** close-lipped, shut-mouthed, tightlipped, unexpressed **12** close-mouthed, close-tongued, inarticulate, tight-mouthed

silhouette 4 line **6** shadow **7** contour, outline, profile **9** lineament, lineation **10** figuration **11** delineation

silicon *symbol:* **2** Si

silk 5 fiber, honan **7** foulard **8** sarcenet, sarsenet *fabric:* **4** gros **5** caffa, ninon, Pekin, satin, surah, tulle **6** cendal, mantua, pongee, samite, sendal, tussah **7** taffeta, tussore *factory:* **8** filature *hat:* **6** topper *maker:* **4** worm **7** thrower *raw:* **5** grège **6** greige *source:* **6** cocoon *waste:* **4** noil **5** floss *wild:* **6** tussah **7** tussore *yarn:* **4** tram

silkworm 3 eri **6** bombyx, tussah **7** tussore **8** bombycid

sill 5 bench, ledge, shelf **9** threshold

silliness 5 folly **7** inanity **8** insanity **9** absurdity, craziness, dottiness **11** foolishness, witlessness **12** illogicality **13** senselessness

silly 3 off **4** daft **5** crazy, daffy, dizzy, empty, funny, giddy, loony, sappy, wacky **6** absurd, insane, simple, unwise **7** asinine, fatuous, flighty, foolish, unwitty, vacuous, witless **8** ignorant **9** fantastic, nitwitted, senseless **10** bird-witted, irrational, weakheaded, weak-minded **11** empty-headed, harebrained, light-headed, sheep-headed **12** preposterous, unreasonable **13** rattlebrained, unintelligent

silt 4 scum, soil **5** dregs **7** deposit, residue **8** sediment

silver 4 coin **5** money, shiny **6** argent, dulcet **7** bullion, element **8** argentum, flatware, lustrous, sterling **9** argentine, tableware *relating to:* **5** lunar **8** argentic **9** argentine, argentous *symbol:* **2** Ag

silverfish 6 insect, tarpon

silver fox 5 caama

silversmith 6 Revere

silver-tongued 4 glib **7** voluble **8** eloquent

silvery 6 argent **7** frosted, shining **9** argentate, argentine, argentous, brilliant **10** glittering, shimmering

Silvia's beloved 9 Valentine

Simeon *father:* **5** Jacob *mother:* **4** Leah *son:* **4** Ohad **6** Nemuel

simian 3 ape **6** monkey **10** anthropoid

similar 4 akin, like **5** alike **6** agnate **7** uniform **8** parallel, suchlike **9** analogous, consonant **10** comparable, reciprocal **11** correlative **13** complementary, corresponding *combining form:* **3** hol, hom **4** holo, home, homo **5** homeo, homoe, homoi **6** homoeo, homoio

similarity 6 simile **7** analogy **8** affinity, likeness, parallel **9** alikeness, closeness, collation, semblance **10** comparison, similitude, synonymity **11** association, coincidence, correlation, resemblance

similarly 2 so **4** also **8** likewise

simile 7 analogy **8** affinity, likeness, metaphor **9** alikeness, semblance **10** comparison, similarity, similitude **11** resemblance *word:* **2** as **4** like

similitude 4 copy **6** double, simile **7** analogy, replica **8** affinity, likeness, metaphor **9** alikeness, semblance **10** comparison, similarity **11** resemblance

simmer 4 boil, stew, stir **5** churn **6** bubble, seethe **7** ferment, parboil, smolder

simmer down 4 cool **7** collect, compose, control, repress, smother, subside **8** restrain, suppress **9** quiet down, re-collect

Simon *brother:* **5** Jesus **6** Andrew

father: 5 Jonah **new name:** 5 Peter **son:** 5 Judas, Rufus 9 Alexander

Simon ___ 5 Magus 6 Legree 8 of Cyrene 9 the Zealot

Simon Maccabeus **father:** 10 Mattathias **nickname:** 6 Thassi **slayer:** 7 Ptolemy

simp 5 dunce 6 dimwit, nitwit 7 lackwit, pinhead, wantwit 13 featherweight

simper 5 smirk

simple 4 dull, dumb, dupe, easy, mere, pure, slow, soft 5 crass, dense, dopey, light, naive, plain, royal, sheer, silly, stark 6 doting, facile, modest, smooth, spoony, stupid 7 artless, asinine, fatuous, foolish, idiotic, moronic, natural, perfect, unmixed, unwitty, witless 8 absolute, backward, childish, discreet, gullible, ignorant, imbecile, mindless, retarded, trusting, unartful, untaught 9 brainless, childlike, credulous, dim-witted, ingenuous, nitwitted, senseless, unalloyed, unstudied 10 effortless, half-witted, illiterate, slow-witted, unaffected, uneducated, unschooled, weak-headed, weak-minded 11 fundamental, inelaborate, sheepheaded, undecorated, unelaborate, unmitigated, unqualified 12 feebleminded, unartificial, unbeautified, uncompounded, unornamented 13 inexperienced, unadulterated, unintelligent, unpretentious, untroublesome **combining form:** 3 apl 4 aplo, hapl 5 haplo

simpleminded 4 dull, slow 6 stupid 7 moronic 8 imbecile, retarded 9 dim-witted 10 half-witted, slow-witted

simpleton 4 dolt, fool, zany 5 ament, dummy, dunce, idiot, moron 6 cretin, stupid 7 bungler, dullard, half-wit, natural 8 dullhead, dumbbell, imbecile 9 ignoramus

simplify 6 reduce 7 abridge, clarify, clean up, cut down, shorten 8 boil down 10 disinvolve, streamline, unscramble 11 disentangle 13 straighten out

simply 3 but 4 just, only 6 merely

simulacrum 4 copy, face, show, spit 5 guise, image 6 double, ersatz, ringer 7 picture, seeming, showing 8 portrait 9 imitation, semblance 10 appearance 13 spitting image

simulate 3 act, ape 4 copy, fake, pose, sham 5 bluff, favor, feign, mimic, put on 6 affect, assume 7 imitate, play-act, pretend 8 resemble 11 counterfeit

simulated 4 fake, mock, sham 5 dummy, false, phony 6 ersatz 8 spurious 9 imitation 10 artificial, fictitious, substitute

simultaneous 6 coeval 8 agreeing 10 coetaneous, coexistent, coexisting, coinciding, concurrent, concurring, synchronal, synchronic 11 synchronous 12 contemporary

simultaneously 6 at once 8 together 12 coincidently, concurrently

sin 3 err 4 debt, evil, tort 5 crime, fault, wrong 6 offend 7 demerit 8 iniquity, trespass 9 diablerie 10 deficiency, transgress, wickedness, wrongdoing 11 shortcoming 12 imperfection **deadly:** 4 envy, lust 5 anger, pride, sloth 8 gluttony 12 covetousness

Sin 7 moon-god **daughter:** 6 Ishtar **son:** 7 Shamash **wife:** 6 Ningal

since 2 as 3 for 4 next 5 after, below 6 behind, seeing 7 because, whereas 8 as long as 9 following 10 inasmuch as 11 considering 12 subsequent to **Scottish:** 4 syne

sincere 4 dear, open, real, true 5 frank, meant, plain 6 actual, candid, devout, hearty, honest 7 genuine, serious 8 bona fide, faithful, heartful, truthful 9 authentic, heartfelt, unfeigned 10 aboveboard, forthright, heart-whole, unaffected 11 undesigning, whole-souled 12 frankhearted, undissembled, wholehearted 13 unpretentious

sincerity 6 candor 8 goodwill 9 bona fides, good faith 11 earnestness

sinecure 4 snap 5 cinch

sine qua non 4 must 9 condition, essential, necessity, requisite 11 requirement 12 precondition, prerequisite

sinew 5 force, might, power 6 energy, muscle, tendon 7 potency 8 strength

sinewy 4 ropy, wiry 5 tough 6 brawny, strong, sturdy 7 fibrous, stringy 8 athletic, muscular 9 tenacious

sinful 3 bad, low 4 base, evil, vile 5 amiss, wrong 6 guilty, unholy, wicked 7 immoral, peccant, vicious 8 blamable, blameful, culpable, damnable, shameful 9 reprobate 10 censurable, iniquitous 11 blameworthy, disgraceful 13 demeritorious, reprehensible

sing 3 hum 4 hymn, lilt, lull, tune 5 carol, chant, croon, yodel 6 intone, warble 7 confess, descant, lullaby 8 serenade, vocalize 10 cantillate

singe 4 burn, char 6 scorch

singer 4 alto, bass 5 tenor 6 cantor 7 crooner, soloist, songman, soprano 8 baritone, choirboy, songster, vocalist 9 balladeer, balladier, chorister **cabaret:** 11 chansonnier **female:** 9 chanteuse, chantres$_s$ 10 cantatrice **opera:** 4 diva 5 buffa, buffo **religious:** 6 cantor

singing **exercise:** 7 solfège **group:** 4 duet, trio 5 choir 6 chorus 7 quartet **voice:** 4 alto, bass 5 tenor 7 soprano 8 baritone 9 contralto 12 mezzo-soprano

single 3 hit, one 4 free, lone, only, open, sole 5 frank, plain, unwed 6 candid, maiden, screen, unique, virgin 7 base hit, special 8 celibate, distinct, especial, sepa-

rate, singular, solitary, specific, unshared
9 exclusive, unmarried **10** individual, particular, spouseless, unattached, unfettered
combining form: **3** apl, mon **4** aplo, hapl, mono **5** haplo *prefix:* **3** uni

single-minded 4 open **5** frank, plain, rigid **6** candid **7** adamant, bigoted, diehard **8** obdurate **9** unbending **10** brassbound, inexorable, inflexible, relentless, unyielding

single out 4 cull, mark, pick, take **5** elect **6** choose, optate, opt for, prefer, select

singular 3 odd **4** lone, only, rare, sole, solo **5** alone, queer, weird **6** unique **7** bizarre, certain, curious, oddball, strange, unusual **8** definite, discrete, peculiar, solitary, uncommon, unwonted **9** exclusive **10** individual, outlandish, particular, respective, unexampled, unordinary **11** exceptional **13** extraordinary

singularity 5 seity, unity **7** ipseity, oneness, selfdom **8** identity, selfhood, selfness **10** singleness **11** personality **13** individualism, individuality, particularity

singularize 4 mark **7** qualify **9** signalize **11** distinguish, individuate **12** characterize **13** individualize

sinister 4 dark, dire, evil **6** malign **7** baleful, doomful, fateful, malefic, ominous **8** lowering, menacing **9** ill-boding, illomened, malicious **10** maleficent, portentous **11** apocalyptic, threatening **12** inauspicious, unpropitious

sink 3 dip, pit, ram, rot, run, sag, set, sty **4** dive, pool, stab **5** abase, basin, demit, drive, droop, lower, slump, Sodom, stoop **6** bemean, debase, demean, go down, hollow, humble, plunge, thrust, worsen **7** cesspit, decline, degrade, depress, descend, founder, go under, let down, subside, torpedo **8** cast down, cesspool, hellhole, submerge, submerse **9** concavity, humiliate **10** degenerate, depression, disimprove, retrograde **11** deteriorate, pandemonium **12** Augean stable, disintegrate

sinker 4 drop **5** pitch **6** weight

sinkhole 3 dip, sag **5** basin **6** hollow **8** cesspool **9** concavity **10** depression

sinless 4 pure **5** innocent

Sinn ____ 4 Fein

sinuous 4 wavy **5** shaky **7** twisted, winding **8** flexuous, tortuous **9** meandrous **10** convoluted, meandering, serpentine **11** anfractuous, snake-shaped

sinus 6 cavity, hollow, recess

Sioux 6 Dakota *chief:* **8** Red Cloud **10** Crazy Horse **11** Sitting Bull

sip 4 toss **5** drink, quaff, sup up, taste **6** imbibe, sup off **7** swallow

siphon 3 tap **4** draw, pipe, pump **5** carry,

draft, drain **6** convoy, funnel **7** channel, conduct, draw off, traject **8** transmit

sir 4 lord **5** title **6** knight, mister **9** gentleman

sire 4 lord **5** beget, breed, hatch, maker, spawn **6** author, create, father, parent **7** creator, founder, produce **8** generate, inventor **9** architect, generator, originate, patriarch, procreate **10** originator **11** progenerate

siren 4 vamp **7** charmer, drawing, enticer, Lorelei **8** alluring, magnetic **9** seductive, temptress **10** attracting, attractive, bewitching, enchanting, seductress **11** captivating, fascinating, femme fatale

Siren 5 Ligea **8** Leucosia **10** Parthenope *German:* **7** Lorelei

siren song 4 bait, lure, trap **5** decoy, snare **6** come-on **10** allurement, enticement, seducement, temptation

sissy 4 baby **6** prissy **7** doormat, epicene, milksop, unmanly **8** weakling **9** jellyfish **10** effeminate, pantywaist **11** Milquetoast, mollycoddle

sister 3 nun **4** girl **7** sibling **8** relative

Sister Carrie author 7 Dreiser

sisterly 7 sororal

Sisyphus *brother:* 7 Athamas **9** Salmoneus *father:* **6** Aeolus *mother:* **7** Enarete *son:* **7** Glaucus

sit 4 meet, open, pose, rest, seat **5** brood, cover, perch, squat **6** settle **7** convene, install, posture **8** ensconce

Sita *abductor:* 6 Ravana *husband, rescuer:* **4** Rama

sit down 4 land **5** light, perch, roost **6** alight, settle **9** touch down

site 3 dig **4** home, spot **5** haunt, locus, place, point, range, scene, where **6** locale **7** habitat, station **8** locality, location, position

sit-in 7 protest

sitting 6 séance **7** session *prolonged:* **8** sederunt

Sitting Bull's tribe 5 Sioux

sitting duck 4 butt, mark **6** target

situate 3 put, set **4** site **5** place **6** locate **8** position

situation 3 job **4** mode, post, rank, site, spot **5** berth, locus, place, point, state, where **6** billet, office, status **7** bargain, footing, posture, station **8** location, position, standing **9** condition

situs 5 place

Siva see Shiva

six *combining form:* 3 hex, sex **4** hexa, sexi **5** sexti *group of:* **5** hexad **6** hexade, sestet, sextet **7** sestole, sextole **8** sestolet, sextette **9** sextuplet *on a die:* **4** sice *relating to:* **6** senary

sixfold 9 sextuplex

six-shooter 3 gun 6 pistol 8 revolver

sixth sense 3 ESP

sizable 3 big 4 good 5 hefty, large,
major 8 sensible 9 extensive 10 giant-
sized, large-scale 11 respectable
12 considerable

size 4 area, body, bulk, mass 5 width
6 extent, height, length, spread, volume
7 bigness, breadth, expanse, measure,
stretch 9 amplitude, dimension, extension,
greatness, largeness, magnitude 10 dimensions, proportion 11 measurement

sizzle 3 fry 4 buzz, fizz, hiss, sear, whiz
5 swish, whish 6 wheeze, whoosh
8 sibilate

sizzling 3 hot 5 fiery 6 baking, red-hot,
torrid 7 burning 8 broiling, scalding, white-
hot 9 scorching

skald 4 bard, poet

Skanda 6 war-god *brother:* 6 Ganesa
7 Ganesha *father:* 4 Siva 5 Shiva

skate 4 fish, skid 5 glide, slide 6 fellow
blade: 6 runner *kind:* 6 figure, hockey

skating site 3 ice 4 rink

skedaddle 3 fly, run 4 bolt, flee, kite,
skip 5 scoot, scram, screw, skirr, split
6 begone, cut out, decamp, get out 7 make
off, scamper, skiddoo, take off, vamoose
8 clear out, hightail

skeleton 5 bones, draft, frame 6 sketch
7 diagram, outline 9 framework *marine:*
5 coral, shell

skeptic 5 cynic 7 doubter, scoffer, zetetic
8 agnostic 10 headshaker, Pyrrhonian, Pyrrhonist, questioner, unbeliever
11 disbeliever

skeptical 6 show-me 7 cynical 8 aporetic,
doubtful, doubting 9 quizzical 10 dissenting, suspicious 11 incredulous, mistrustful,
questioning, unbelieving 12 disbelieving,
freethinking

skepticism 5 doubt, qualm 6 wonder
7 concern, dubiety 8 mistrust 9 dubiosity,
suspicion 11 incertitude, uncertainty

skerry 4 isle, reef

sketch 4 draw, line, plot 5 draft, trace
7 aperçu 6 depict, design, detail, lay out,
map out, précis, survey 7 develop, diagram,
outline, pandect, sylloge 8 block out, chalk
out, rough out, skeleton, syllabus 9 adumbrate, blueprint, delineate 10 compendium
11 skeletonize 12 characterize
13 diagrammatize

sketchy 5 rough 7 cursory, shallow
8 skeletal 9 depthless 11 superficial

skew 3 dip 4 bias, skid, slip, slue, veer
5 angle, sheer, slant, slide 6 swerve 8 train
off

skewer 3 rod 4 spit 5 lance, spear, spike
6 impale, skiver 8 transfix 9 brochette
11 transpierce

ski 5 glide, slide *lift:* 4 J-bar, T-bar 5 chair
7 gondola

skid 3 dip 4 drop, fall, skew, slue, veer
5 sheer, slide 6 plunge, tumble 7 plummet,
spinout 8 nose-dive

skid row 4 slum 6 bowery

skier *American:* 4 Kidd 5 Mahre *Austrian:* 6 Proell 7 Klammer, Schranz
expert: 6 kanone *French:* 5 Killy *Italian:*
6 Theoni *Swedish:* 8 Stenmark

skiff 4 boat 7 rowboat

skiing *area:* 3 run 5 slope *cross-coun-
try:* 7 touring *event:* 6 schuss, slalom
8 downhill 11 giant slalom *horse-drawn:*
9 skijoring *kind:* 6 Alpine, Nordic *position:*
7 vorlage *technique:* 6 wedeln 8 snowplow, traverse *turn:* 7 christy 8 christie

skill 3 art 5 craft, knack 7 ability, address,
command, cunning, know-how, mastery,
prowess, sleight 8 deftness 9 dexterity,
expertise, expertism, readiness 10 adroitness, expertness, mastership 13 dexterousness *combining form:* 6 techno, techny
suffix: 3 ics 4 ship

skillet 3 pan 6 frypan, spider 9 frying pan

skilful 4 deft, good 5 adept, crack
6 adroit, clever, daedal, expert, master,
pretty, wicked 7 learned, skilled, versant
8 masterly 9 masterful, workmanly 10 proficient, well-versed 11 crackerjack,
workmanlike

skim 3 dap, fly 4 dart, kiss, sail, scud,
skip 5 brush, carom, float, graze, shave,
shoot, skirr 6 glance 8 ricochet

skimpy 3 shy 4 poor 5 scant, short,
spare 6 meager, scanty, scarce, scrimp,
sparse 7 failing, scrimpy, wanting 8 exiguous 9 deficient 10 inadequate
12 insufficient

skim through 4 scan 6 browse 8 glance
at 10 glance over

skin 3 fur, gyp, pod, rap 4 clad, clip, face,
fell, hide, pare, peel, pelt, rind, side, soak
5 blame, cheat, cover, fleet, haste, hurry,
knock, miser, nabal, scale, stick, stiff, strip
6 barrel, bucket, bullet, con man, fleece,
hasten, hustle, sheath, slough 7 beeline,
censure, condemn, diddler, grifter, niggard,
scrooge, sharper, sheathe 8 denounce,
highball, swindler, tightwad 9 criticize,
defrauder, dermatous, excoriate, reprehend,
reprobate, sheathing 10 cheapskate, denunciate, overcharge 11 cheeseparer, decorticate, excorticate, flimflammer *animal:*
4 coat, hide, pelt 6 hackle, peltry *bird:*
7 pteryla *combining form:* 3 cut 4 cuti,
derm, scyt 5 derma, dermo, dermy, scyto
6 dermat, dermia, dermis 7 cutaneo, der-
mata (plural), dermato, epiderm 8 epidermo
depression: 6 dimple *disease:* 4 acne
5 hives, mange 6 eczema 10 dermatitis

dry: **5** scurf *fold:* **5** plica *layer:* **5** derma **6** corium, dermis **7** corneum, cuticle **9** epidermis *opening:* **4** pore *protuberance:* **4** mole, wart **6** pimple *rabbit:* **5** coney *retating to:* **6** dermal **9** cuticular, epidermal *seal:* **5** sculp *spot:* **7** freckle *tumor:* **3** wen

skinflint 5 chuff, miser, nabal **7** niggard **8** muckworm, tightwad **10** cheapskate **11** cheeseparer

skink 4 soup **6** lizard

skinny 4 bony, lank, lean **5** gaunt, lanky, spare, weedy **6** twiggy **7** angular, scraggy, scrawny **8** rawboned, skeletal **9** emaciated

Skin of Our Teeth author 6 Wilder

skip 3 dap, fly, hop, run **4** bolt, flee, jump, leap, lope, skim, trip **5** blank, bound, caper, carom, chasm, frisk, graze, scoot, skirr **6** bounce, cavort, curvet, gambol, glance, spring **7** make off, scamper, skitter **8** omission, overlook, ricochet **9** oversight, skedaddle **10** hippety-hop

skipjack 3 fop **4** fish **6** beetle **8** sailboat

skipper 6 leader **7** captain **9** commander

skirl 6 scream, shriek

skirmish 4 fray **5** brush, clash, melee, run-in, set-to **6** affray, ambush, attack, mellay **7** assault **9** encounter, scrimmage **10** velitation

skirr 3 fly, run **4** bolt, dart, flee, sail, scud, skim, skip **5** float, scoot, shoot **7** make off, scamper **9** skedaddle

skirt 3 hem, rim **4** brim, duck, edge, skip **5** avoid, bound, brink, burke, dodge, elude, evade, hedge, verge **6** border, bypass, define, detour, escape, fringe, ignore, margin **7** garment **8** sidestep, surround **9** perimeter, periphery **10** circumvent, equivocate *ballet:* **4** tutu *feature:* **3** hem **4** slit *long:* **4** maxi *Scottish:* **4** kilt *short:* **4** mini *style:* **5** A-line

skit 3 act **4** jibe **5** caper, taunt **6** parody, shtick, sketch **7** schtick **9** burlesque

skitter 3 hop **4** lope, skip, trip **6** spring

skittery see skitterish

skittish 4 edgy **5** dizzy, giddy **7** flighty, nervous, restive **8** agitable, unstable, volatile **9** alarmable, excitable, frivolous, startlish **10** capricious, unreliable

skivvies 9 underwear

skoal 5 drink, toast

skua 4 bird **6** jaeger

skulduggery 8 foul play, trickery

skulk 4 lurk, slip **5** creep, shirk, slink, sneak, steal **7** gumshoe **9** pussyfoot

skull 4 bone, head, mind **5** brain **7** cranium **8** brainpan **9** braincase *back of:* **7** occiput *bone:* **5** vomer **6** zygoma **7** ethmoid, frontal **8** parietal, sphenoid, temporal *jawless:* **9** calvarium *joint:* **6** suture *part:* **3** jaw **5** inion **6** basion

skullcap 5 calot **6** beanie, pileus

7 calotte **8** yarmulke **9** calvarium, zucchetto

skunk 3 cur, dog **4** beat, drub, lick, scum, snot, toad, whip **5** snake **6** thrash **7** polecat, shellac **8** conepate, lambaste **9** overwhelm *genus:* **8** Mephitis

sky 5 azure **6** heaven, welkin **7** heavens **8** empyrean **9** firmament *combining form:* **4** uran **5** urano *sky-blue:* **5** azure **8** cerulean **9** caerulean

sky chief 5 pilot

skylarking 5 revel **7** fooling, revelry, wassail, whoopee, whoopla, whoop-up **9** high jinks, horseplay, revelment, rowdiness, whoop-de-do **10** roughhouse **12** roughhousing

skylight 6 window

skyline 7 horizon

sky pilot 5 padre **6** cleric, divine, parson **8** chaplain, clerical, minister, preacher **9** churchman, clergyman **12** ecclesiastic

skyrocket 4 rise, soar **5** climb **7** shoot up **8** upspring

sky sighting 3 UFO

slab 3 bar, rod **4** tile **5** ingot, slice, stick, strip **6** billet

slabber 5 drool **6** drivel, slaver **7** dribble **8** salivate

slack 3 lax, off **4** down, ease, lazy, slow, soft, weak **5** inert, loose, relax **6** feeble, infirm, loosen, remiss, slow-up **7** ease off, laggard, passive, relaxed **8** careless, derelict, dilatory, fainéant, inactive, indolent, slothful, slowdown, sluggish, stagnant, unsteady **9** leisurely, lethargic, negligent, untighten

slacken 3 ebb, lax **4** ease, fall, mire, wane **5** abate, delay, embog, let up, loose, relax **6** detain, hang up, loosen, relent, retard, slow up **7** bog down, die away, die down, ease off, set back, subside **8** moderate, slow down **9** untighten **10** decelerate

slacker 5 idler **6** loafer **7** shirker, slinker **8** slugabed, sluggard **9** goldbrick

slag 4 lava **5** dross **6** cinder, debris, scoria

slake 5 allay **6** deaden, quench **7** crumble, hydrate, satisfy

slam 3 bat, dig, hit, jab, rap **4** bang, bash, beat, belt, blow, boom, clap, ding, drub, flay, mace, slug, slur, swat, wham **5** blast, burst, crack, crash, fling, knock, pound, slash, slate, smack, smash, swipe, whack **6** batter, cudgel, hammer, scathe, strike, thwack, wallop **7** clobber, obloquy, potshot, scourge **8** lambaste, lash into **9** aspersion, bastinado, castigate, stricture

slammer 3 jug, pen **4** jail **6** cooler, prison

slander 4 hurt, slur, tale **5** belie, libel, smear **6** assail, attack, damage, defame, injure, malign **7** asperse, calumny, scandal, traduce **8** muckrake, roorback, strumpet,

tear down 9 black wash, denigrate 10 backbiting, calumniate, defamation, detraction, muckraking 11 mud-slinging 12 back-stabbing, belittlement, deprecia- tion 13 disparagement

slang 4 cant 5 argot, lingo 6 jargon, pat- ois, patter 7 dialect 10 vernacular

slant 3 aim, tip 4 bank, bend, bias, cant, heel, lean, list, side, skew, tilt, veer, warp 5 angle, aside, bevel, color, focus, grade, point, slope, splay, train, twist 6 aslope, direct, orient, swerve 7 decline, descend, deviate, distort, diverge, incline, leaning, out- look, recline 8 gradient, sideways, side- wise 9 direction, influence, obliquely, preju- dice, viewpoint 10 standpoint 11 concentrate, inclination 12 predilection *combining form:* 4 clin 5 clino

slap 3 box, hit, pop, try 4 bash, blip, chop, cuff, drub, flay, poke, shot, slam, stab, swat, wham 5 clout, crack, fling, punch, score, slash, smack, spank, whack, whirl 6 buffet, insult, scathe, strike 7 affront, despite, scourge 8 haymaker, lambaste, lash into 9 castigate, contumely, indignity

slapdash 5 messy 6 botchy, random, sloppy, untidy 7 aimless 8 careless, slip- shod, slovenly 9 desultory, haphazard, hit- or-miss, irregular 10 designless, unthorough

slaphappy 7 foolish 8 carefree, reckless 10 punch-drunk

slash 3 cut 4 clip, flay, gash, hack, pare, slit 5 lower, shave, slice 6 hackle, haggle, incise, pierce, reduce, scathe, scorch 7 abridge, blister, curtail, cut back, cut down, scarify, scourge, shorten 8 lambaste, lash into, mark down, retrench 9 castigate, excoriate 10 abbreviate

slasher 5 knife, razor, sword 9 swords- man 12 swashbuckler

slat 4 lath 5 board, stave, strip 6 louver 7 airfoil 9 sheepskin

slate 4 gray, list, rock, tile 6 record, tablet, ticket 7 shingle 8 schedule 9 designate

slaughter 4 kill, maim, slay 6 mangle, mur- der 7 butcher, carnage, torture, wipe out 8 butchery, decimate, hecatomb, massacre, mutilate 9 bloodbath, bloodshed 10 annihi- late 11 destruction, exterminate 12 annihilation

slaughterhouse 8 abattoir

Slav 4 Pole, Serb, Sorb, Wend 5 Croat, Czech 6 Bulgar, Slovak 7 Russian, Ser- bian, Slovene 8 Bohemian, Croatian, Mora- vian 9 Bulgarian, Ruthenian, Ukrainian

slave 4 grub, help, peon, plod, serf, slog, toil 5 grind, helot 6 drudge, menial, thrall, toiler, vassal 7 bondman, chattel, servant 8 bondsman 9 dray horse, mancipium, workhorse *feudal:* 4 serf *harem:* 9 odal-

isque *liberated:* 8 freedman *Muslim:* 8 Mameluke *Spartan:* 5 helot

slave driver 6 tyrant 8 martinet, rawhi- der 10 taskmaster 11 Simon Legree

slaver 4 fawn, spit 5 cower, drool, toady, water 6 cringe, drivel, grovel, kowtow, saliva 7 dribble, honey up, slabber, slobber, spittle, truckle 8 bootlick, salivate

slavery 4 moil, toil, work, yoke 5 grind, labor 6 drudge, thrall 7 bondage, helotry, peonage, serfdom 8 bullwork, drudgery, plugging 9 servitude, thralldom, villenage 10 donkeywork

Slavic apostle 5 Cyril 9 Methodius

slavish 3 low 4 hard, tame 5 apish, heavy, rough 6 knotty, menial, rugged 7 operose, servile, subdued 8 obeisant, wretched 9 dif- ficult, emulative, imitative, laborious, miser- able, spineless, strenuous 10 formidable, obsequious, uninspired, unoriginal 11 subservient

slay 4 do in, down, kill 6 cut off, finish, lay low, murder 7 butcher, destroy, execute, put away 8 dispatch, knock off 9 liquidate, slaughter 11 assassinate

slayer 4 bane 6 killer 8 homicide, murderer

sleazy 3 low 4 mean, thin 5 cheap, dingy, seedy, tacky, tatty 6 cheesy, common, flabby, flimsy, floppy, paltry, shabby, shoddy, slight, trashy 7 flaccid, run-down, tenuous 9 gossamery 10 broken-down, down-at-heel 11 dilapidated 12 disreputable

sled 4 luge, pung 6 sleigh 7 coaster, tra- vois 8 toboggan *Russian:* 6 troika

sled dog 5 husky 8 malamute

sledge 6 hammer, sleigh *Eskimo:* 7 komatik

sleek 4 oily 5 round, slick 6 glassy, glossy, polish, refine, smarmy, smooth 7 perfect 8 lustrous, polished 10 glistening

sleep 3 nap 4 coma, doze, rest 5 death, relax, sopor 6 demise, repose, siesta, snooze, torpor 7 decease, languor, pass- ing, quietus, shut-eye, silence, slumber 8 dullness, hebetude, lethargy 9 lassitude, torpidity 10 defunction, torpidness 11 dis- solution, slumberland *bringer:* 7 sandman *combining form:* 4 hypn, narc 5 hypno, narco, somni *god:* 6 Hypnos, Hypnus, Somnus

sleeper 4 beam 7 Pullman, support 8 dor- meuse, long shot

sleeping 4 abed 7 dormant 8 comatose *disease:* 10 narcolepsy

sleeplessness 8 insomnia

sleepwalker 12 somnambulist

sleepy 4 dozy 5 dazed, dopey, inert, quiet 6 drowsy, opiate, snoozy, torpid 7 nodding, passive, poppied, yawning

8 comatose, hypnotic, inactive, listless, narcotic, oscitant, sleeping, sluggish, slumbery, somnific **9** heavy-eyed, lethargic, somnolent, soporific **10** nepenthean, slumbering, slumberous, somnorific **11** somniferous

sleigh 4 pung, sled **6** sledge

sleight 4 play, ploy, ruse, wile **5** skill, trick **6** device **7** address, gimmick, prowess **8** artifice, deftness, maneuver **9** dexterity, readiness, stratagem **10** adroitness **13** dexterousness

sleight of hand 5 magic, trick **9** dexterity **11** legerdemain

slender 4 lean, slim, thin, trim **5** lithe, reedy, scant, short, small **6** remote, scanty, scarce, skinny, slight, stalky, svelte, twiggy **7** outside, spindly, squinny, tenuous, wanting **8** slimmish **9** attenuate, deficient **10** inadequate, negligible **12** insufficient

sleuth 3 tec **4** dick **7** gumshoe **8** hawkshaw, Sherlock **9** detective **10** private eye **12** investigator

slice 3 cut, lot **4** bite, gash, part, slit **5** carve, quota, sever, share, slash, split **6** cleave, incise, pierce, sunder **7** dissect, partage, portion, segment **8** dissever **9** allotment, allowance

slick 4 oily, slip, wise **5** canny, fix up, glide, quick, round, sharp, sleek, slide, smart, soapy, spiff **6** doll up, glossy, greasy, polish, refine, slippy, smarmy, smooth **7** deck out, doll out, dress up, fulsome, gussy up, knowing, perfect, slither **8** glissade, slippery, slithery, spruce up, unctious, unctuous **10** lubricious, oleaginous **11** quick-witted, sharp-witted

slicker 4 dude **6** gypper **7** cheater, diddler, oilskin, sharper **8** raincoat, swindler **9** defrauder, trickster **11** flimflammer

slide 3 dip, sag **4** drop, fall, flow, lurk, move, skid, slip **5** chute, coast, crawl, creep, drift, glide, shift, shirk, skate, skulk, slick, slink, slump, sneak, spill, steal **6** stream, tumble **7** decline, drop off, fall off, slither **8** downturn, fall away, glissade **9** downswing, downtrend

slight 4 fail, omit, skip, slim, thin **5** flout, reedy, scoff, small **6** flimsy, forget, ignore, remote, sleazy, stalky, subtle, twiggy **7** blink at, contemn, despise, neglect, outside, slender, squinny, tenuous **8** delicate, discount, overlook, overpass, smallish **9** attenuate, blink away, disregard, gossamery, pint-sized **10** negligible

slim 4 thin **5** canny, lithe, reedy, small **6** adroit, clever, narrow, remote, skinny, slight, stalky, svelte, twiggy **7** cunning, lissome, outside, slender, squinny, tenuous **9** attenuate, dexterous, ingenious, lithesome **10** negligible

slim down 4 diet **6** reduce **10** slenderize

slime 3 mud **4** muck, ooze, scum, slum **6** sludge *combining form:* **3** myx **4** myxa, myxo

slimy 4 oozy, vile **7** viscous

sling 4 cast, fire, hang, hurl, sock, toss **5** fling, heave, march, pitch, stalk, throw **6** dangle, depend, launch, stride **7** suspend **8** catapult

slink 4 lurk **5** creep, shirk, skulk, slide, sneak, steal **6** weasel **7** gumshoe, sneaker **8** sneaksby **9** pussyfoot

slip 3 dip, lam, sag **4** bull, dock, drop, fall, lose, lurk, molt, pier, quay, shed, sink, skid, trip **5** berth, boner, crash, creep, erode, error, fluff, glide, jetty, lapse, levee, mouse, shake, shirk, skulk, slick, slide, slink, slump, sneak, steal, wharf **6** bungle, escape, flight, go down, slough, soften, topple **7** blooper, blunder, decline, drop off, fall off, faux pas, getaway, gumshoe, mistake, plummet, slither **8** breakout, downturn, escaping, exuviate, fall away, glissade, nose-dive, prolapse, throw off **9** downslide, downswing, downtrend, pussyfoot

slipper 4 mule, shoe **5** brake, romeo, scuff **6** juliet, sandal **8** babouche, pantofle

slippery 3 icy **4** eely, oily **5** slick **6** greasy, lubric, shifty **7** mutable **8** slithery, unstable, unsteady, variable **9** uncertain **10** changeable, inconstant, lubricious

slipshod 5 messy, tacky **6** botchy, faulty, shabby, shoddy, sloppy, tagrag, unneat, untidy **7** inexact, raunchy, scrubby, scruffy, unkempt **8** careless, fouled-up, ill-kempt, messed-up, slapdash, slovenly, tattered **9** botched-up, haphazard, imperfect, neglected, negligent, slaphappy **10** bedraggled, disheveled, down-at-heel, inaccurate

slipup 5 boner, error, fluff, lapse **6** bungle, miscue **7** blooper, blunder, mistake **9** oversight

slit 3 cut **4** gash, rent, tear **5** slash, slice **6** incise, pierce **7** opening **8** roulette

slither 4 lurk, slip **5** creep, glide, prowl, sidle, slick, slide, slink, snake, sneak, steal **8** glissade, undulate

slithery 5 slick **6** greasy, slippy **8** slippery **10** lubricious

sliver 5 carve, shave, shred, slice **6** haggle **8** splinter

slob 4 boor, clod **6** sloven

slobber 4 gush **5** drool **6** drivel, slaver **7** dribble, slabber **8** salivate

sloe 4 plum **10** blackthorn

slog 3 hit **4** ding, grub, plod, slop, sock, toil **5** catch, clout, grind, slave, smite, whack **6** drudge, stodge, strike, trudge **8** plunther

slogan 4 word **5** idiom, motto **6** byword, phrase **8** locution **9** catchword, watchword **10** expression, shibboleth **11** catchphrase

sloop **4** boat, dray **8** longboat, sailboat

slop **3** mud, pap **4** bolt, cram, food, gulp, plod, slog, toil, wolf **5** douse, plash, slosh, spill, squab, swash **6** englut, gobble, guzzle, pablum, splash, splosh, stodge, trudge **7** rubbish, spatter, splurge, spurtle **8** footslog, plunther, splatter **11** ingurgitate

slope **3** tip **4** bend, cant, heel, lean, list, rise, skew, swag, sway, tilt **5** grade, pitch, scarp, slant **6** ascent, escarp, glacis **7** descent, incline, leaning, recline, versant **8** gradient **9** acclivity, declivity, deviation, obliquity **10** deflection **11** inclination, obliqueness *combining form:* **5** cline **6** clinal

sloppy **4** poor, soft **5** drunk, gushy, messy **6** botchy, clumsy, unneat, untidy **7** awkward, gushing, muddled, unkempt **8** careless, effusive, ill-kempt, mediocre, slapdash, slipshod, slobbery, slovenly **9** disguised, pixilated **10** amateurish, disheveled, inebriated, slobbering, unthorough **11** intoxicated

slosh **3** bat, lap **4** bang, bash, belt, blow, bolt, cram, dash, gulp, gush, roar, rush, slam, slop, wash, wolf **5** churn, crack, douse, plash, pound, smack, swash, whirl **6** babble, bubble, burble, englut, gobble, gurgle, guzzle, ripple, splash, wallop **7** spatter, splurge, spurtle **8** splatter **9** bespatter **11** ingurgitate

slot **5** niche, notch, track, trail **6** groove, keyway **7** keyhole, opening, passage **10** pigeonhole

sloth **4** laze **6** acedia, apathy, idling, lazing, slouch **7** languor, loafing **8** idleness, laziness, lethargy **9** faineancy, heaviness, indolence, lassitude, torpidity **10** ergophobia **11** inattention, languidness **12** heedlessness, listlessness, slothfulness, sluggishness **13** shiftlessness *three-toed:* **2** ai *two-toed:* **4** unav

slothful **4** idle, lazy **5** drony **7** work-shy **8** faineant, indolent **9** easygoing, slowgoing

slouch **3** bum, hat, lop, oaf, sag **4** bend, gawk, laze, lean, loaf, loll, lout, lump, slug, wilt **5** droop, idler, klutz, looby, sloth, slump, stoop **6** loafer, lounge, lubber **7** saunter, shamble, shuffle, trollop **8** dolittle, faineant, idleness, laziness, meathead, slugabed, sluggard **9** do-nothing, indolence, lazybones **12** slothfulness, sluggishness

slough **3** arm, bay, bog, fen, mud **4** cast, cove, gulf, junk, mire, molt, shed, slip, sump **5** bayou, firth, inlet, marsh, scrap, swamp **6** harbor, morass, reject **7** cashier, discard **8** exuviate, jettison, quagmire, throw out **9** marshland, swampland, throw away

sloven **5** messy **6** sloppy, untidy **7** unkempt **8** careless, ill-kempt, slipshod, uncombed **10** disheveled

slow **3** low, off **4** down, dull, late, poky **5** brake, rusty, slack, tardy **6** leaden, retard, simple, steady, stupid **7** halting, laggard, lagging, limited, reduced, unhasty **8** backward, crawling, dawdling, delaying, dilatory, dragging, flagging, measured, plodding, retarded, sluggish, stagnant **9** dim-witted, leisurely, snaillike, unhasting, unhurried **10** deliberate, half-witted, snail-paced, straggling, unhurrying

slowpoke **5** snail **6** lagger **7** dawdler, laggard **8** lingerer, loiterer **9** slow coach, straggler

sludge **3** mud **4** mire, muck, ooze, slob **5** slime **8** sediment

slue **3** dip **4** skew, turn, veer **5** sheer **6** swerve **8** train off

sluff **7** discard

slug **3** bum, hit, nip, tot **4** belt, dram, drop, jolt, shot, slam **5** blast, idler, larva, smash, snail, snort **6** loafer, slouch, sloven, wallop **7** clobber, slacker, snifter **8** dolittle, faineant, toothful **9** do-nothing, lazybones *genus:* **5** Limax

sluggard **3** bum **5** idler **6** loafer, slouch **7** dawdler, laggard, lie-abed, shirker **8** dolittle, faineant, slowpoke, slugabed **9** do-nothing, goldbrick, lazybones, slow coach **10** sleepyhead

slugger **5** boxer **6** batter, hitter

sluggish **3** off **4** down, lazy, logy, slow **5** dopey, heavy, slack, stiff **6** draggy, leaden, stupid, torpid **7** costive, lumpish **8** comatose, dragging, slothful **9** apathetic, lethargic, stupified **10** slumberous **12** hebetudinous

sluice **4** flow, gush, pour, roll, soak, wash **5** douse, flush, surge **6** drench, stream

slum **4** dump **6** ghetto **7** skid row

slumber **4** coma, doze **5** sleep **6** drowse, stupor, torpor **7** lanquor **8** dullness, hebetude, lethargy **9** lassitude, torpidity

slumberous see **sleepy**

slump **3** dip, lop, sag **4** drop, fall, flag, loll, slip **5** droop, pitch, slide **6** cave in, go down, plunge, slouch, topple, tumble **7** decline, drop off, falloff, trollop **8** collapse, downturn, fall away, keel over **9** downslide, downswing, downtrend, recession **10** depression, stagnation

slur **4** blot, blur, lisp, onus, slam, spot **5** brand, odium, smear, stain **6** befoul, defame, insult, malign, slight, stigma **7** blacken, obloquy, traduce **8** black eye, tear down **9** aspersion, bespatter, denigrate, stricture **10** calumniate

slurp **4** suck **5** lap up, slosh, smack, swill **6** guzzle **8** wolf down

slush 3 mud **4** mire, muck, snow **5** grout
6 drivel

sly 4 deep, foxy, lurk, slim, wily **5** cagey,
canny, creep, shady, skulk, slick, slide, slink,
smart, sneak, steal **6** adroit, artful, astute,
clever, covert, crafty, shifty, smooth, subtle,
tricky **7** crooked, cunning, devious, furtive,
gumshoe, slanter, unfrank, vulpine **8** guileful, scheming, slippery, stealthy **9** design-
ing, dexterous, dishonest, ingenious, insidious, masterful, predatory, subdolous,
underhand **11** calculating, clandestine,
underhanded **12** disingenuous, unscrupulous **13** Machiavellian

slyboots see **scamp**

slyness 3 art **5** craft **7** cunning **8** artifice,
foxiness, wiliness **9** cageyness, canniness
10 artfulness, craftiness

smack 3 bat, bop, box, lip **4** bash, belt,
biff, blip, blow, buss, chop, cuff, dash, hint,
kiss, lick, peck, reek, slap, sock, tang
5 clout, crack, punch, sapor, savor, smash,
smell, spank, stink, taste, tinge, trace **6** buffet, flavor, relish, smooch **7** soupçon, suggest **8** osculate, resemble, sapidity, tincture **9** suspicion **10** sprinkling

small 3 off, set, wee **4** mean, puny, slim,
tiny **5** borne, dinky, light, minor, petty,
short **6** bantam, lesser, little, minute, monkey, narrow, paltry, petite, remote, slight
7 cramped, limited, outside, slender, trivial
8 picayune, piddling, pint-size, trifling **9** miniature, minuscule, secondary, two-by-four
10 diminutive, negligible, picayunish, undersized **11** ineffectual, minor-league, unimportant **12** inconsequent **13** insignificant
amount: see **particle** *combining form:*
4 lept, micr, mini, olig, parv **5** lepto, oligo,
parvi, parvo

small fry 4 kids **8** children

small-minded 4 mean **6** narrow **7** bigoted **9** hidebound, illiberal **10** brassbound,
intolerant, unenlarged

smallness *abnormal:* **6** nanism
8 dwarfism

small one *suffix:* **2** el, et, ey, ia (plural), ie
3 cle, ium, kin, ock, ula, ule, uli (plural)
4 ella, ette, illa, ling, ulae (plural), ulum, ulus
5 ellae (plural), illae (plural)

smallpox 7 variola

small talk 6 babblo, banter **7** chatter, prattle **8** babbling, badinage, chitchat, repartee,
trifling **9** bavardage, prattling

smalt 4 blue **5** glass

smarmy 4 oily **5** sleek, slick, soapy
6 glassy, glossy, sleeky **7** fulsome **8** polished, unctious, unctuous **10** oleaginous

smart 3 hep **4** ache, bite, bold, burn, chic,
hurt, pain, pert, trig, wise **5** alert, canny,
fresh, nervy, prick, quick, sassy, saucy,
sharp, slick, sting, swank, swish **6** brainy,
bright, cheeky, clever, dapper, modish,
shrewd, spruce, suffer, tingle, with-it
7 dashing, knowing, stylish **8** impudent
9 brilliant, exclusive, sprightly **11** fashionable, intelligent, quick-witted, ready-witted,
sharp-witted

smart aleck 7 show-off, wise guy **8** wiseacre **9** know-it-all **11** wisecracker, wisenheimer **12** grandstander **13** exhibitionist

smart-alecky 4 wise **5** fresh, nervy,
sassy **6** cheeky **8** impudent **9** bold-faced
10 procacious

smarten 5 fix up, primp, slick, spiff **6** doll
up, spruce **7** deck out, doll out, dress up,
gussy up **8** spruce up

smart set 3 ton **5** elite **6** bon ton **7** aristoi, society, who's who **10** blue bloods,
upper crust **11** aristocracy, Four Hundred

smash 3 hit, jar, wow **4** bang, bash, belt,
blow, boom, bump, clap, jolt, raze, rive, ruin,
slam, slug, sock, wham, whop **5** blast,
burst, clash, crack, crash, shock, whack,
wreck **6** impact, pileup, shiver, wallop
7 clobber, crack-up, debacle, destroy, shatter, smashup **8** collapse, decimate, demolish, destruct, fragment, knockout, splinter,
splitter, tear down **9** bastinado, breakdown,
collision, sensation, succès fou **10** annihilate, bell ringer, percussion **11** splinterize

smashup 5 crash, wreck **6** pileup
7 crack-up, debacle **8** collapse
9 breakdown

smattering 3 few **7** handful **10** sprinkling

smear 3 dab, rub, tar **4** beat, coat, daub,
drub, foil, lick, slur, soil, trim, whip **5** cover,
smarm, stain, sully, taint **6** bedaub, befoul,
defame, defile, malign, smirch, smudge,
spread, thrash **7** asperse, blacken, overlay,
plaster, repulse, shellac, slander, smother,
tarnish **8** besmirch, discolor, lambaste
9 bespatter, denigrate, frustrate **10** calumniate, overspread

smell 4 funk, hint, nose, odor, reek
5 aroma, scent, sense, smack, sniff, snuff,
stink, trace, whiff **6** detect, stench **7** soupçon **8** tincture **9** fragrance, redolence, suspicion **10** intimation, suggestion *combining
form:* **3** osm **4** osma, osmo

smell, sense of 9 olfaction, osphresis

smelly 4 olid, rank **5** fetid, funky, reeky
6 foetid, putrid, rancid, stinky **7** noisome,
reeking, stenchy **8** stinking **10** malodorous

smelt 4 flux, slag **6** reduce, refine, speise,
speiss, tomcod **7** scorify **8** sparling **9** sand
borer, sand lance, whitebait, sand lance

smidgen see **particle**

smile 4 beam, grin **6** simper

smirch see **smudge**

smirk 4 grin, leer **5** fleer, sneer **6** simper

smitch see **particle**

smite 3 bat, hit, try **4** belt, dash, ding, slog,

sock 5 catch, clout, whack 6 harrow, martyr, strike 7 afflict, agonize, clobber, crucify, torment, torture 10 excruciate

smithereens 6 pieces 9 fragments, particles

smitten 6 mashed, soft on 8 enamored, spoony on 10 spoony over

smoke 4 cure, floc, fume 8 fumigate 9 cigarette

smoking material 3 pot 4 hash 5 cigar, joint 6 reefer 7 hashish, tobacco 9 cigarette, cigarillo, marihuana, marijuana

smolder 4 boil, stir 5 burst, churn, erupt 6 bubble, seethe, simmer 7 explode, ferment 9 fulminate

smooch 3 lip 4 buss, foul, kiss, peck, soil 5 dirty, grime, smack 6 besoil, smirch, smudge, smutch 7 begrime, tarnish 8 osculate

smooth 3 lay 4 bald, easy, even, fair, flat, mild, soft 5 balmy, bland, faint, flush, level, light, plane, preen, round, royal, sleek, slick, suave 6 evenly, facile, flatly, fluent, gentle, glossy, polish, polite, refine, simple, sleeky, trowel, urbane, velure 7 courtly, cursive, flatten, flowing, jagless, lenient, perfect, planate, running 8 glabrate, glabrous, hairless, soothing, unbroken, waveless 9 agreeable, civilized, courteous, uniformly 10 effortless, rippleless, unwrinkled *combining form:* 3 lio 4 leio, liss 5 lisso

smoothen 3 lay 4 even 5 flush, level, plane 7 flatten

smooth-spoken 5 vocal 6 fluent 8 eloquent 10 articulate

smorgasbord 4 hash 6 jumble, medley 7 mélange 8 mishmash, pastiche 9 potpourri 10 hodgepodge, miscellany 11 gallimaufry

smother 4 beat, cool, cork, drub, lick, rein, trim, whip 5 choke, quash, quell, smear 6 hush up, muffle, quench, stifle, thrash 7 clobber, collect, compose, control, quackle, repress, shellac, squelch 8 lambaste, restrain, suppress 9 suffocate 10 asphyxiate

smudge 3 dab 4 daub, foul, soil 5 dirty, grime, smear, stain, sully, taint 6 bedaub, besoil, blotch, defile, smirch 7 begrime, besmear, plaster, splotch, tarnish 8 besmirch

smug 4 tidy 5 slick 6 spruce 8 priggish 10 complacent 11 self-pleased 13 self-contented, self-satisfied

smuggle 3 run 7 bootleg 10 contraband

smut 4 blot, soil 5 dirty, smear, stain, taint 6 defile 7 bestain 8 besmirch, discolor

smutty 4 foul 5 dirty, nasty 6 coarse, filthy, vulgar 7 obscene, raunchy 8 indecent 12 scatological

Smyrna 5 Izmir

snack 3 tea 4 bite, nosh, tapa 5 mug-up 6 morsel 9 collation 11 refreshment

snag 3 bar, rub 4 clog, curb, drag 5 brake, crimp 6 hamper, hold-up, hurdle 8 obstacle, traverse 10 impediment 11 obstruction

snail 8 escargot, ramshorn, slowpoke 9 band shell

snake 3 boa, cur, dog 4 scum, snot, toad 5 crawl, creep, prick, skunk, slide 6 python 7 serpent, slither 8 anaconda, ophidian, undulate *combining form:* 4 ophi 5 ophio, ophis *poisonous:* 3 asp 4 habu 5 adder, cobra, coral, krait, mamba, viper 6 elapid, taipan 7 rattler 8 cerastes, pit viper, ringhals 10 bushmaster, copperhead, fer-de-lance 11 cottonmouth 13 water moccasin *South African:* 5 aboma

snakebird 6 darter 7 anhinga

snake crane 7 cariama

snake-eater 7 markhor 8 mongoose 13 secretary bird

snakelike 7 anguine 8 ophidian

snakeroot 7 bugbane 10 wild ginger 11 blazing star

snakeweed 7 bistort 13 poison hemlock

snakewood 9 nux vomica 10 frangipani

snaky 7 sinuous, winding 8 flexuous, tortuous 9 meandrous 10 convoluted, meandering, serpentine 11 anfractuous

snap 3 bit, jot, lug, pep, pie 4 bang, bark, dram, drop, hoot, iota, jerk, push, yank 5 cinch, drive, getup, grain, lurch, punch, setup, vigor 6 breeze, picnic, starch, twitch 7 crackle, modicum 8 duck soup, fragment, kid stuff, particle, pushover, sinecure, vitality 9 soft touch, vellicate 10 child's play

snap back 7 rebound, recover

snape 5 taper

snappy 4 fast, racy, tony, trig 5 fleet, hasty, huffy, quick, rapid, raspy, ready, sharp, smart, spicy, swank, swift, swish, zesty 6 lively, prompt, speedy, twitty 7 dashing, peppery, piquant, pungent, raspish, stylish 8 animated, petulant, poignant, prickish 9 breakneck, fractious, irritable, vivacious 10 harefooted 11 expeditious

snare 4 bait, lure, trap 5 catch, decoy, tempt 6 come-on, enmesh, entrap, seduce, tangle 7 catch up, chicane, ensnarl, involve, springe, trammel 8 entangle 9 chicanery, deception, embrangle 10 allurement, enticement, entrapment, seducement, temptation 12 inveiglement

snarl 3 jam, web 4 bark, gnar, knot, maze, mesh, muck 5 chaos, gnarr, ravel, skein, swarm 6 ataxia, huddle, jungle, morass, muddle, tangle 7 clutter, mizmaze, perplex 8 disarray, disorder, entangle, mishmash 9 confusion, intricacy, labyrinth 10 complexity, complicate **11** intertangle **12** complication, entanglement **13** intricateness

snatch 3 nab **4** grab, jerk, nail, take, yank **5** catch, cotch, nip up, seize **6** clutch, whip up, wrench **7** grapple

sneak 3 cur, sly **4** heel, lurk, slip, toad, worm **5** crawl, creep, glide, knave, louse, prowl, shirk, skulk, skunk, slide, slink, steal **6** covert, secret, tiptoe, weasel **7** furtive, gumshoe, hangdog, reptile, slither, smuggle, sub-rosa **8** hush-hush, slyboots, stealthy **9** pussyfoot, scoundrel **10** blackguard, undercover **11** clandestine

sneaky 6 shifty **7** devious **8** guileful, indirect **9** underhand **11** duplicitous, underhanded

sneer 4 gibe, gird, grin, jest, pish **5** fleer, flout, scoff, smile, smirk **6** quip at **7** detract, scout at **8** belittle **9** disparage, underrate

snicker 5 laugh, tehee **6** giggle, guffaw, hee-haw, titter **7** chortle, chuckle

snide 4 fake, sham **5** bogus, false, phony **6** pseudo **7** corrupt, crooked **8** spurious **9** brummagem, dishonest, pinchbeck **11** counterfeit

sniff 4 nose **5** scent, smell

snifter 3 nip, tot **4** dram, drop, jolt, shot, slug **5** snort **8** toothful

snippety see **snippy**

snippy 4 curt **5** bluff, blunt, brief, gruff, short **6** abrupt, crusty **7** brusque

snit 3 fit **4** flap, fume, huff, stew **5** panic, pique, sweat, tizzy **6** dither, frenzy, swivet, taking **7** seizure **10** conniption

snitch 3 cop, nip, rat **4** beak, hook, lift, tell **5** filch, peach, pinch, steal, swipe **6** inform, squeal, tattle **7** purloin, tattler, tipster **8** betrayer, informer, squealer **11** stool pigeon

snob 5 toady **6** poseur **7** high-hat, parvenu, tinhorn, upstart **8** popinjay **9** sycophant

snobbish 5 aloof, potty, ritzy **6** remote, snooty, snotty, uppish, uppity **7** haughty, high-hat, pompous **9** high-flown **10** hoity-toity **11** patronizing, pretentious **12** supercilious **13** condescending

snook 5 cobia **6** robalo **12** sergeant fish

snoop 3 pry, spy **4** mess, nose, peek, peep, peer, poke **5** mouse, prier, pryer, stare **6** butt-in, meddle **7** intrude, meddler, Paul Pry **8** busybody, quidnunc **9** detective, inspector, interfere **10** rubberneck

snooper 3 spy **7** meddler **9** detective, inspector **12** investigator

snoopy 4 nosy **5** peery **6** prying **7** curious **11** inquisitive, inquisitory **13** inquisitorial

snoot see **snout**

snooty see **snobbish**

snooze 3 nap **5** dover **6** catnap, dog nap, siesta **10** forty winks

snort 3 nip, tot **4** dram, drop, jolt, shot, slug **7** snifter **8** toothful

snot 3 cur, dog, pig, rat, sod **4** puke, scum, toad **5** knave, louse, rogue, skunk, snake **6** wretch **7** high-hat, lowlife, reptile, stinker, villain **8** stinkard **9** scoundrel, stinkaroo

snout 4 beak, nose **6** pecker **7** smeller *combining form:* **6** rhynch **7** rhyncho **8** rhynchus

snow *combining form:* **4** chio **5** chion **6** chiono *glacial:* **4** firn, névé *melted:* **5** slush *pellet:* **7** graupel *ridge:* **8** sastruga, zastruga

snow apple 8 mushroom

snowball 3 wax **4** rise **5** build, mount, run up **6** expand **7** augment, upsurge **8** increase, multiply

snowberry 6 blolly

snowbird 9 fieldfare, ivory gull

Snow-Bound author 8 Whittier

snow eater 7 chinook

snow finch 9 brambling

snow goose 4 wavy **5** wavey

snow grouse 9 ptarmigan

snowlike 7 niveous

snowstorm 8 blizzard

snub 3 cut **5** spite, swank **6** slight **7** high-hat, put down **9** ostracize **12** cold-shoulder

snuff 4 kill, nose, odor **5** aroma, pinch, scent, smell, sniff **6** rappee **8** maccaboy

snug 4 cosy, cozy, easy, neat, soft, tidy, trig, trim **5** comfy, cushy **6** burrow, cuddle, nestle, nuzzle **7** chipper, croodle, easeful, orderly **9** shipshape **11** comfortable

snuggle 5 spoon **6** burrow, cuddle, curl up, huddle, nestle, nuzzle

so 3 sae **4** also, ergo, much, then, thus, very **5** hence **6** thusly **7** awfully, parlous **8** likewise **9** extremely, similarly, therefore, thereupon **11** accordingly, exceedingly **12** consequently

soak 3 wet **4** clip, lush, skin, swig **5** douse, drink, imbue, souse, steep **6** boozer, drench, fleece, infuse, seethe **7** guzzler, immerse, insteep, overwet **8** bedrench, drunkard, permeate, saturate, submerge **9** penetrate **10** impregnate, overcharge *flax:* **3** ret

soap 4 suds **7** flatter *hard:* **7** castile *ingredient:* **3** lye

soapbox 4 rant, rave **5** mouth, orate **7** declaim **8** bloviate, harangue, perorate

soaproot 8 sand lily

soapstone 8 steatite

soapwood 8 wild pear

soapwort 7 cowherd **11** bouncing Bet

soar 2 up **3** fly **4** lift, rise **5** arise, climb, mount, shoot **6** ascend, aspire, rocket, uprear **7** shoot up **9** skyrocket

sob 3 cry 4 blub, wail, weep 6 boohoo
7 blubber
sober 4 calm, cool, hard, soft 5 grave,
staid 6 low-key, placid, proper, sedate,
serene, solemn 7 earnest, serious, subdued, weighty 8 composed, decorous, forgoing, low-keyed, moderate, rational,
reserved, softened, tranquil 9 abstinent,
collected, continent, eschewing, inhibited,
practical, pragmatic, realistic, temperate,
toned down 10 abnegating, abstaining,
abstemious, controlled, forbearing, hard-
boiled, hardheaded, no-nonsense, reasonable, refraining, restrained 11 abstentious,
constrained, disciplined, down-to-earth
12 matter-of-fact, unidealistic 13 imperturbable, self-possessed, unimpassioned
sobriety 7 gravity 9 soberness 10 abstinence, continence, sedateness, temperance 11 seriousness
sobriquet 6 byname, byword 8 nickname
10 hypocorism
so-called 6 formal 7 alleged, nominal, titular 8 supposed 9 pretended, professed,
purported 10 ostensible
soccer *cup:* 5 World *official:* 7 referee
8 linesman *player:* 6 booter, goalie, kicker,
winger 7 forward, link man, striker,
sweeper 8 defender, fullback, halfback
10 goalkeeper *player of renown:* 4 Pele
term: 3 net 4 boot, chip, kick, trap 6 corner, header, tackle, volley 7 dribble, kickoff,
throw-in 8 back-heel, free kick, goal kick,
goal line 9 touchline 10 center spot, corner
flag, corner kick 11 dropped ball, halfway
line, penalty kick, penalty spot
sociable 5 close 6 genial 7 cordial
8 familiar, gracious, intimate 9 congenial,
convivial 10 gregarious 11 good-natured
social 6 genial 7 amusing, cordial
8 friendly, gracious, pleasant 9 convivial
10 gregarious, hospitable 11 pleasurable
12 entertaining 13 companionable *class:*
5 caste
Social Contract author 8 Rousseau
socialist *American:* 4 Debs (Eugene)
6 Ripley (George), Thomas (Norman)
English: 4 Webb (Sidney) 6 Morris (William) *French:* 7 Viviani (René) *German:*
4 Marx (Karl) 6 Engels (Friedrich) 9 Luxem-
burg (Rosa) 10 Liebknecht (Wilhelm)
socialize 3 mix 5 party 6 mingle
9 associate
social worker 4 Riis (Jacob), Wald (Lillian
D.) 6 Addams (Jane) 7 Alinsky (Saul D.),
Lathrop (Julia C.)
society 4 club 5 elite, guild, order, union
6 flower, gentry, league, masses, people,
public 7 aristoi, company, quality, who's
who 8 populace, sodality 9 community
10 fellowship, fraternity, patriciate, upper

class, upper crust 11 aristocracy, association, brotherhood 13 companionship *girl:*
3 deb 9 debutante *high:* 9 beau monde,
haut monde
Society Islands *capital:* 7 Papeete *discoverer:* 7 Queirós
sociologist *American:* 4 Ward 5 Balch,
Whyte 6 Du Bois, Summer 7 Johnson,
Riesman *English:* 7 Spencer *French:*
8 Durkheim *German:* 5 Weber *Italian:*
6 Pareto *Swedish:* 6 Myrdal
sock 3 bop, box, hit 4 bash, belt, blow,
chop, cuff, ding, slap, slog 5 clout, punch,
smack, smash, whack 6 argyle, buffet,
strike, thwack 8 stocking
socks 4 hose 7 hosiery
Socrates *birthplace:* 6 Athens *poison:*
7 hemlock *pupil:* 5 Plato *wife:* 8 Xantippe
sodality 4 club 5 guild, order, union
6 league 7 society 10 fellowship, fraternity 11 association, brotherhood
sodden 3 wet 4 soak 5 soppy, souse,
steep 6 drench, seethe, soaked, soused
7 soaking, sopping 8 drenched, dripping,
saturate, waterlog 9 saturated 11 wringing-wet
Sodi's son 7 Gaddiel
sodium 7 natrium *symbol:* 2 Na
Sodom and ___ 8 Gomorrah
sofa 5 couch, divan 7 ottoman
9 banquette
Sofia native 6 Bulgar 9 Bulgarian
soft 4 cozy, easy, mild, snug 5 balmy,
bland, comfy, cushy, downy, faint, mushy,
pappy, pulpy, silky, silly, sleek, sober,
wooly 6 doughy, flabby, fleshy, gentle, low-
key, pliant, quaggy, satiny, silken, simple,
smooth, spongy, spoony, tender, woolly
7 cottony, easeful, fatuous, foolish, lenient,
pillowy, pliable, pulpous, squashy, squishy,
subdued, velvety, witless 8 cushiony, formless, low-keyed, moderate, squelchy, woollike, workable, yielding 9 malleable, temperate, toned down 10 weak-headed, weak-
minded 11 comfortable 12 compressible
soft-cover 9 paperback
soft hail 7 graupel
softhearted 4 warm 6 tender 10 responsive 11 sympathetic 13 compassionate
soft palate 5 velum
soft-pedal 6 dampen, hush up, muffle,
subdue 7 conceal, cushion, silence 8 disguise, play down, suppress, tone down,
tune down 11 de-emphasize
soft-soap 3 con 4 coax 6 cajole 7 blarney, flatter, wheedle 8 blandish 9 sweet-
talk
Sohrab and Rustum author 6 Arnold
soil 3 mud, tar 4 daub, dirt, foul, home,
land, loam, mess, muck, murk 5 crock,
dirty, earth, glebe, grime, muddy, smear,

stain, sully, taint **6** bedaub, defile, ground, smirch, smooch, smudge, smutch **7** begrime, besmear, country, drabble, draggle, dry land, pedocal, pollute, regosol, tarnish **8** bedabble, besmirch, discolor, homeland, laterite, lithosol, pedalfer, planosol, rendzina, sierozem, solonets, solonetz **10** fatherland, motherland, terra firma **11** contaminate *aggregate:* **3** ped *clay:* **5** gault *combining form:* **2** ge **3** geo, ped **4** agro, pedo *dark:* **9** chernozem *deposit:* **5** loess **7** eluvium *infertile:* **6** podsol, podzol *layer:* **4** gley, sola (plural) **5** solum *prairie:* **8** brunizem *rich:* **6** hotbed *soft:* **4** mool *tropical:* **7** latosol

sojourn 4 stay, stop **5** abide, tarry, visit **6** linger **7** layover **8** stopover **9** tarriance

Sol 3 sun **7** daystar, phoebus *horse:* **4** Eous **5** Ethon **9** Erythreos; (see also **Helios**)

solace 5 cheer **6** buck up **7** comfort, console, upraise

solar disk 4 Aten

solarium 7 sunroom

solder 4 weld **5** braze

soldier 2 GI **4** swad **5** perdu **6** perdue **7** dogface, fighter, pandoor, pandour, pikeman, private, trooper, warrior **8** doughboy, fusileer, fusilier, partisan, rifleman **9** free lance, guerrilla, man-at-arms, mercenary **10** carabineer, serviceman **11** condottiere, fighting man, infantryman *ancient Greece:* **7** hoplite, peltast *British:* **5** Tommy **7** redcoat *cavalry:* **6** hussar **8** chasseur *Celtic:* **4** kern **5** kerne *Confederate:* **3** reb *French:* **5** poilu **6** Zouave *German:* **5** jerry *Greek:* **6** evzone **7** palikar *India:* **5** jawan, sowar **7** jemadar, jemidar *irregular:* **8** guerilla **9** guerrilla *Prussian:* **4** ulan **5** uhlan *Turkish:* **8** janizary **9** janissary

sole 3 one **4** lone, only **5** alone, unwed **6** bottom, single, unique **8** separate, singular, unshared **9** exclusive

solecism 5 boner, break, gaffe **7** blooper, faux pas **8** slangism **9** indecorum, vulgarism **11** impropriety

solemn 4 full **5** grand, grave, sober, staid **6** august, formal, sedate, somber **7** earnest, plenary, serious, stately, weighty **8** majestic **10** ceremonial, impressive, no-nonsense, sobersided **11** ceremonious, magnificent

solemnize 4 keep **5** honor **7** dignify, observe **8** venerate **9** celebrate **11** commemorate

solicit 3 ask, beg **4** call, drum, tout, turn **5** apply, claim, exact, refer **6** demand, desire, drum up, resort **7** beseech, bespeak, canvass, implore, request, require **9** challenge, postulate **11** requisition

solicitous 4 avid, keen **5** eager **6** ardent,

raring **7** anxious, athirst, thirsty **8** appetent **9** impatient

solicitude 4 care, heed **5** qualm, worry **6** regard, unease **7** anxiety, concern, scruple **8** disquiet **9** attention **10** uneasiness **11** compunction, concernment **12** presentiment, watchfulness **13** consideration

solid 4 firm, hard **5** sound **6** cogent, firmly, hardly, secure, square, stable **7** telling **9** compacted, unanimous **10** convincing

solidarity 5 union, unity **6** esprit, fixity **7** oneness **8** cohesion, firmness **9** integrity **10** singleness **12** cohesiveness, togetherness **13** esprit de corps, undividedness

solidify 3 dry, set **4** cake **6** harden **7** congeal **8** compress, concrete, contract, indurate

solitary 3 one **4** lone, lorn, only **5** alone, aloof **6** hermit, lonely, offish, single, unique **7** distant, recluse, uncouth **8** derelict, deserted, desolate, eremitic, forsaken, lonesome, reserved, separate, singular **9** abandoned, reclusive, withdrawn **10** antisocial, insociable, particular, unattended, unexampled, unsociable **11** standoffish **12** misanthropic, unrepeatable **13** companionless, unaccompanied

solitude 8 loneness **9** aloneness, isolation, seclusion **10** detachment, loneliness, quarantine, retirement, withdrawal **11** confinement **12** lonesomeness, separateness

solo 4 lone **5** alone

Solomon *brother:* **8** Adonijah *daughter:* **7** Taphath **8** Basemath *father:* **5** David *kingdom:* **6** Israel *mother:* **9** Bathsheba *son, successor:* **8** Rehoboam *victim:* **4** Joab **8** Adonijah

Solomon Islands' capital 7 Honiara

solution 6 answer, result *salt:* **6** saline

solve 3 fix **4** work **5** break **6** decide, settle, unfold **7** clear up, dope out, explain, unravel, work out **8** construe, decipher, unpuzzle, unriddle **9** determine, elucidate, enlighten, figure out, interpret, puzzle out

Somalia *capital:* **9** Mogadishu *monetary unit:* **8** shilling

somatic 6 bodily, carnal **7** fleshly **8** corporal, physical **9** corporeal

somber 3 dim **4** dark, dusk **5** black, bleak, dusky, grave, murky, staid **6** dismal, dreary, gloomy, sedate, solemn **7** earnest, obscure, serious, weighty **8** funereal **9** lightless, tenebrous **10** caliginous, depressing, depressive, no-nonsense, sobersided, tenebrific **11** dispiriting

somniferous see **sleepy**

somnolent see **sleepy**

Somnus *brother:* **4** Mors *god of:* **5** sleep *mother:* **3** Nox

song 3 air, cry, lay **4** aria, call, glee, hymn, lied, note **5** ditty, lyric, paean, piece, poesy,

rhyme, verse **6** ballad, melody, poetry
7 calypso, chanson, descant **8** alleluia,
cavatina *biblical:* **8** canticle *boat:* **9** barcarole **10** barcarolle *combining form:* **4** melo
French: **7** chanson *funeral:* **5** dirge *German:* **4** lied **6** lieder (plural) *lamentation:*
8 threnode, threnody *medieval:* **8** sirvente
morning: **6** aubade *of joy:* **5** paean *operatic:* **4** aria **8** cavatina **9** cabaletta *Portuguese:* **4** fado *sacred:* **5** psalm *sailor's:*
6 chanty **7** chantey, shantey *short:* **8** can-
zonet *wedding:* **8** hymeneal
song and dance **5** pitch, spiel
songbird see at bird
Song of Myself author **7** Whitman
Song of Solomon **9** Canticles
songwriter **8** composer, lyricist
Sonja ____ **5** Henie
Sonnambula composer **7** Bellini
sonnet *developer:* **8** Petrarch *part:*
5 octet **6** octave, sestet
Son of the Middle Border author
7 Garland
sonorous **5** noisy, round **6** rotund **7** aureate, flowery, orotund, rackety, ringing,
vibrant **8** clattery, noiseful, plangent, resonant, voiceful **9** bombastic, consonant,
overblown **10** euphuistic, oratorical,
resounding, rhetorical, uproarious
11 declamatory **12** magniloquent
13 grandiloquent
Sooner State **8** Oklahoma
soothe **3** pat **4** balm, calm, hush, lull
5 allay, salve, still **6** becalm, pacify, settle,
subdue **7** comfort, compose, console, massage, mollify, placate **11** tranquilize
soothsay **5** augur **7** portend, predict,
presage **8** forecast, foretell, prophesy
9 abumbrate **13** prognosticate
soothsayer **5** augur **6** auspex **7** prophet
8 foreseer, haruspex **9** predictor **10** forecaster, foreteller, prophesier *ancient
Roman:* **6** auspex **8** haruspex *blind:*
8 Tiresias; (see also *prophet*)
sop **3** buy, fix, wet **4** have, soak **5** bribe,
douse, drown, sissy, souse, steep **6** buy
off, deluge, drench, seethe, sodden, square
7 doormat, douceur **8** gratuity, saturate,
waterlog, weakling **10** namby-pamby, pantywaist, tamper with **11** Milquetoast,
mollycoddle
Sopater's father **7** Pyrrhus
sophic **4** sage, wise **7** gnostic, knowing
9 insighted, sagacious **10** discerning,
insightful, perceptive **13** knowledgeable
sophism see **sophistry**
sophisticate **6** debase **10** adulterate
11 disillusion
sophisticated **5** adult, blasé, bored,
couth, jaded, salty, suave **6** daedal, knotty,
mature, smooth, svelte, urbane **7** complex,

cynical, gordian, knowing, worldly
8 involved, mondaine, schooled, seasoned,
well-bred **9** Byzantine, elaborate, intricate,
practiced, skeptical, world-wise **10** world-
weary **11** experienced, worldly wise
12 cosmopolitan, disenchanted, disentranced, labyrinthine **13** disillusioned
sophistry **7** fallacy **8** delusion **9** ambiguity, casuistry, deception **12** equivocation,
speciousness, spuriousness
13 deceptiveness
Sophocles play **4** Ajax **7** Electra
8 Antigone **10** Oedipus Rex
Sophonisba *brother:* **8** Hannibal *father:*
9 Hasdrubal *husband:* **6** Syphax
soporiferous **6** opiate **8** hypnotic, narcotic, somnific **9** somnolent **10** somnorific
12 somnifacient
soporific **4** dozy **6** drowsy, opiate, sleepy,
snoozy **7** calming, nodding, numbing
8 hypnotic, narcotic, sedative, slumbery
9 deadening, somnolent **10** anesthetic,
quietening, slumberous **11** somniferous
12 somnifacient **13** tranquilizing
soprano *American:* **4** Pons **5** Costa,
Gluck, Moffo, Price, Sills **6** Arroyo, Battle,
Callas, Curtin, Donath, Farrar, Garden, Norman, Peters, Piazza, Resnik **7** Farrell, Kir-
sten, Stevens, Traubel **8** Ponselle *Australian:* **5** Melba **10** Sutherland *Austrian:*
7 Rysanek **9** Sembrich *Canadian:* **7** Stra-
tas *French:* **7** Crespin *German:* **6** Leider
7 Lehmann **11** Schwarzkopf *Italian:*
5 Freni, Grisi, Patti **6** Scotto **7** Tebaldi
10 Tetrazzini **11** Ricciarelli *Mexican:*
8 Cruz-Romo *Norwegian:* **8** Flagstad
Rumanian: **8** Cotrubas *Spanish:*
7 Caballe **8** Berganza **12** de los Angeles
Swedish: **4** Lind **7** Nilsson; (see also
mezzo-soprano)
sorcerer **4** mage **5** magus **6** wizard
7 charmer, warlock **8** conjurer, conjuror,
magician **9** enchanter, voodooist
11 necromancer
sorceress **3** hag, hex **5** bruja, Circe,
lamia, witch **10** witchwoman
sorcery **5** magic **8** diablery, witchery,
witching, wizardry **9** conjuring **10** necromancy, witchcraft **11** bewitchment,
enchantment, incantation, thaumaturgy *African:* **3** obe, obi **4** obia **5** obeah
sordid **3** low **4** base, foul, mean, vile
5 black, dirty, dowdy, nasty, seamy
6 blowsy, filthy, frowsy, grubby, impure,
scurvy, sodden **7** ignoble, low-down,
servile, squalid, unclean **8** slattern,
wretched **9** uncleanly **10** despicable,
slatternly
sore **5** angry, vexed **6** aching, bitter
7 algetic, chancre, hurtful, hurting, painful
9 rancorous, resentful **10** afflictive

sorehead 4 crab 6 griper, grouch
7 grouser, growler 8 grumbler, sourpuss
10 complainer, malcontent
sorrel 4 dock 7 roselle
sorrow 3 rue, sob, woe 4 care, moan
5 agony, dolor, grief, groan, mourn 6 grieve,
misery, regret 7 anguish, remorse, sadness 8 distress, grieving, mourning
9 dejection, heartache, suffering 10 affliction, depression, heartbreak, melancholy
11 lamentation, unhappiness 12 mournfulness, wretchedness
sorrowful 6 dolent, rueful, tragic, triste,
woeful 7 doleful, ruthful 8 dolesome, dolorous, mournful, tragical, tristful, wretched
9 afflicted, miserable, plaintive 10 lamentable, lugubrious, melancholy
sorry 3 bad, sad 4 mean, poor 5 cheap
6 cheesy, paltry, scummy, scurvy, shabby,
shoddy 7 scruffy, unhappy 8 beggarly,
contrite, mournful, penitent, pitiable, saddened, trifling, wretched 9 miserable,
regretful, repentant 10 apologetic, despicable, despisable, inadequate, melancholy,
remorseful 11 attritional, disgraceful, penitential 12 compunctious, contemptible,
heavyhearted
sort 3 ilk, lot, set 4 body, comb, cull, kind,
pick, sift, type 5 array, batch, class, group,
order, suite 6 choose, clutch, parcel, riddle,
screen, select, stripe, winnow 7 battery,
catalog, species, unravel, variety 8 classify,
separate 9 catalogue, character 10 categorize, pigeonhole
sortie 5 sally
sortilege 7 sorcery 8 witchery
10 divination
so-so 4 fair 6 enough, fairly, medium,
rather, subpar 7 average, fairish 8 mediocre, middling, moderate, passable, passably,
somewhat 9 averagely, tolerably 10 moderately 11 indifferent 12 run-of-the-mill
sot 4 lush 5 drunk 6 bibber, boozer 7 guzzler, tippler 8 drunkard 9 inebriate
10 boozehound
sotto voce 3 low 5 aside 6 softly,
weakly 7 faintly, mutedly, quietly 9 muf-
fledly, privately 11 mutteringly
souchong 3 tea
sough 4 sigh 7 suspire
soul 4 life, pith, anima, being, bosom,
heart, human, stuff, wight 6 animus, bottom, breast, marrow, mortal, person,
pneuma, psyche, spirit 7 essence 8 creature, noumenon, vitality 9 élan vital, personage, substance 10 conscience, individual,
virtuality, vital force 11 personality
12 essentiality, quintessence **combining
form:** 4 thym 5 psych, thymo 6 psycho
sound 3 fit 4 firm, hale, look, ping, sane,
seem, well 5 audio, exact, music, noise,

plumb, probe, right, sober, solid, valid,
whole 6 appear, cogent, fathom, intact,
secure, stable, unhurt 7 correct, declare,
earshot, feel out, healthy, hearing, logical,
perfect, precise, publish, sonance, sonancy,
telling 8 accepted, accurate, announce,
flawless, orthodox, proclaim, rational,
received, sensible, unbroken, unmarred
9 advertise, broadcast, canonical, errorless,
faultless, resonance, undamaged, uninjured,
vibration, wholesome 10 annunciate, consequent, convincing, impeccable, promulgate, reasonable, sanctioned, satisfying,
unimpaired 11 disseminate, intelligent, right-
minded, sober-minded, unblemished, well-
founded 12 satisfactory, well-grounded
13 authoritative, reverberation **combining
form:** 3 son 4 phon, soni, sono 5 audio,
audit, phone, phony 6 audito, phonia **high-
pitched:** 4 ping, ting **of a horn:** 7 tantara **of
disapproval:** 7 catcall **pleasant:**
7 euphony **quality:** 6 timbre **repeating:**
7 ratatat 8 rataplan **resounding:** 8 resonant **ringing in ears:** 8 tinnitus **rustling:**
8 froufrou **science:** 6 sonics 7 phonics
throaty: 8 guttural
Sound **Alaska:** 5 Cross **Antarctica:**
7 McMurdo **Australia:** 4 King 5 Broad
Bahamas: 5 Exuma **Canada:** 4 Howe
6 Nansen **Connecticut-New York:** 10 Long
Island **English Channel:** 8 Plymouth **Georgia:** 8 Altamaha **Greenland:** 5 Smith **Gulf
of Mexico:** 8 Suwannee 11 Mississippi
Massachusetts: 8 Vineyard 9 Nantucket
New England: 11 Block Island **North Carolina:** 4 Core 5 Bogue 7 Pamlico, Roanoke 9 Albemarle, Currituck **Northwest
Territories:** 4 Peel 8 Melville 9 Lancaster
12 Prince Albert **Norwegian Sea:**
8 Scoresby **Ontario:** 4 Owen **Scotland:**
3 Hoy 4 Jura, Mull 5 Inner **Spitsbergen:**
4 Bell **Washington:** 5 Puget
Sound and the Fury, The **author:**
8 Faulkner **character:** 5 Benjy, Caddy,
Jason 7 Quentin **family:** 7 Compson
soundness 3 wit 4 mind 6 health, reason, sanity, senses 8 lucidity, security,
strength 9 stability
sound off 7 speak up 8 speak out
soup **beet:** 6 borsch 7 borscht **bowl:**
6 tureen **clear:** 5 broth 8 bouillon, con-
sommé, julienne **cold:** 8 gazpacho
11 vichyssoise **curry:** 12 mulligatawny
okra: 5 gumbo **seafood:** 7 chowder
thick: 5 gumbo, puree 6 bisque, burgoo
vegetable: 10 minestrone
soupçon see **particle**
soupy 5 mushy, sobby 6 drippy, slushy,
sticky 7 maudlin, mawkish 11 sentimental,
tear-jerking
sour 3 bad, dry 4 acid, keen, tart 5 acerb,

acrid, sharp, tangy **6** acidic, bitter, rotten, turned **7** acerbic, acetose, unhappy **8** acescent, vinegary **9** acidulous, fermented

source 4 dawn, rise, root, well **5** cause, fount, onset, start **6** mother, origin, parent, rising, spring, whence **7** dawning, opening, rootage **8** fountain, starting, wellhead **9** beginning, inception, paternity, rootstock **10** antecedent, authorship, birthplace, derivation, provenance, wellspring **11** determinant, origination, provenience **12** fountainhead

sourness 7 acidity **8** acerbity **10** discontent

sourpuss 4 crab **5** crank **6** griper, grouch, kicker **7** grouser, killjoy **8** sorehead **10** complainer

south *combining form:* **3** not **4** noto **5** austr **6** austro *French:* **3** sud

South Africa *capital:* **8** Cape Town, Pretoria **12** Bloemfontein *colonizer:* **9** Pretorius *enclave:* **7** Lesotho *largest city:* **12** Johannesburg *monetary unit:* **4** rand *settlers:* **5** Boers

South America *country:* **4** Peru **5** Chile **6** Brazil, Guyana **7** Bolivia, Ecuador, Surinam, Uruguay **8** Colombia, Paraguay, Suriname **9** Argentina, Venezuela *ethnic group:* **5** Negro **6** Aymara, Creole, Indian **7** Mestizo, Mulatto, Quechua, Spanish **10** Amerindian, Portuguese *language:* **6** Aymara **7** Guarani, Quechua, Spanish **10** Portuguese

South Carolina *capital:* **8** Columbia *college, university:* **5** Coker **6** Furman **7** Clemson *nickname:* **13** Palmetto State *state flower:* **13** yellow jasmine

South Dakota *capital:* **6** Pierre *largest town:* **10** Sioux Falls *nickname:* **11** Coyote State **13** Sunshine State

southerly 7 austral

South Korea *capital:* **5** Seoul *monetary unit:* **3** won

South-West Africa 7 Namibia *capital:* **8** Windhoek

south wind see at **wind**

souvenir 5 relic, token **6** trophy **7** memento **8** keepsake, memorial, reminder **11** remembrance **12** remembrancer

sovereign 4 fine, free **5** regal, royal **6** kingly, master, regent **7** capital, guiding, highest, padshah, regnant **8** autarkic, champion, dominant, five-star, kinglike, loftiest, majestic, padishah, separate **9** ascendant, autarchic, classical, directing, excellent, monarchal, number one, paramount, prevalent **10** autonomous, blue-ribbon, commanding, first-class, monarchial **11** independent, monarchical, overbearing,

predominant, predominate **12** preponderant, self-governed

soviet 7 council **9** committee

sow 4 seed, toss **5** drill, fling, plant, put in, straw, strew **7** bestrew, disject, scatter **9** broadcast **11** disseminate *combining form:* **3** hyo **7** choerus

spa 5 baths, hydro, wells **6** resort, waters **7** springs **13** watering place *Czech:* **6** Bilina **8** Karlsbad *English:* **4** Bath **6** Buxton **9** Harrogate *German:* **3** Ems **5** Baden **6** Bad Ems **9** Kissingen

space 4 area, room **6** cavity, spread **7** breadth, expanse, stretch **8** distance, interval, universe **9** amplitude, expansion

spaced-out 4 high **5** doped **6** stoned, zonked **7** drugged **8** hopped-up, turned on

spacious 3 big **4** vast, wide **5** ample, great, large, roomy **7** immense **8** enormous, extended **9** boundless, expansive, extensive

spade 3 dig **4** grub **5** scoop **6** dig out, shovel **8** excavate

Spade, Sam 9 detective *creator:* **7** Hammett

Spain *ancient name:* **8** Hispania *capital:* **6** Madrid *former leader:* **6** Franco *monetary unit:* **6** peseta

spall 4 chip **5** flake **8** fragment

span 4 term, time **8** duration, interval

spangle 4 trim **5** adorn, flash, gleam **7** glimmer, glisten, glitter, shimmer, sparkle, twinkle **8** decorate, ornament **9** coruscate **11** scintillate

Spaniard 9 Castilian

Spanish *combining form:* **7** Hispano *hero:* **3** Cid **8** Palmerin *penal settlement:* **8** presidio *saint:* **7** Dominic **8** Ignatius *title:* **5** señor **6** señora **8** señorita *wine:* **4** sack

Spanish fly 9 cantharis

spank 3 box **4** blip, cuff, slap, sock **5** clout, punch, smack **6** buffet

spar 3 box **5** stall **7** dispute, wrangle **8** longeron *ship's:* **6** bumkin, sprite **7** boomkin, jibboom, spright, yardarm **8** bowsprit

spare 4 bony, lank, lean, poor, save **5** extra, gaunt, lanky, lay by, lay in, lay up, pinch, put by, scant, screw, short, skimp, stint **6** de trop, excess, excuse, exempt, let off, meager, scanty, scrape, scrimp, skimpy, skinny **7** absolve, angular, lay away, relieve, scraggy, scrawny, scrimpy, surplus **8** dispense, exiguous, lay aside, rawboned, salt away **9** discharge **11** superfluent, superfluous

sparing 4 wary **5** canny, chary, tight **6** frugal, saving, Scotch, stingy **7** thrifty **8** ungiving **9** provident, stewardly **10** economical, unwasteful **11** tightfisted **12** parsimonious

spark 3 bud, woo **4** beau, germ, seed **5** court, lover, swain, wooer **6** embryo, incite, suitor **7** gallant **8** activate

sparker 5 swain, wooer **6** suitor

sparkle 5 flash, gleam, glint **6** glance **7** glimmer, glisten, glitter, shimmer, twinkle **9** coruscate **11** coruscation, scintillate **13** scintillation

sparkling 6 lively **8** animated **9** brilliant **12** effervescent

sparling 5 smelt

sparse 4 poor, rare **5** scant, skimp **6** meager, scanty, scarce, scrimp, skimpy **7** scrimpy **8** exiguous, sporadic, uncommon **9** dispersed, scattered **10** infrequent, occasional

Sparta 10 Lacedaemon *country:* **7** Laconia *hero, king:* **8** Leonidas *opponent:* **6** Athens

Spartacus *author:* **4** Fast (Howard) *slayer:* **7** Crassus

spasm 3 fit **4** pang **5** burst, crick, throe *muscular:* **6** clonus

spasmodic 6 catchy, fitful, spotty **8** sporadic, spurtive **9** desultory

spat 3 row **4** beef, miff, tiff **5** fight, scrap **6** bicker, hassle **7** brabble, dispute, fall out, quarrel, wrangle **8** squabble **9** bickering, caterwaul **10** falling-out **11** altercation

spate 4 flow, flux, pour, rain, rush, tide **5** drift, flood, river, spurt **6** deluge, series, stream **7** current, torrent **8** cataract, flooding, overflow **9** cataclysm **10** inundation

spatter 3 few **4** slop, slur, spit, spot **5** douse, plash, slosh, smear, swash **6** befoul, bespot, defame, malign, smatch, sparge, splash, splosh **7** asperse, blacken, handful, splurge, spurtle, traduce **9** denigrate **10** scattering, smattering, sprinkling

spawn 4 make, sire **5** hatch **6** create, father, parent **7** produce **8** generate **9** originate, procreate

speak 4 talk, tell **5** blurt, drawl, mouth, orate, shout, spout, utter, voice **6** assert, convey, intone, mumble, murmur, mutter, parley **7** address, declaim, declare, descant, lecture, phonate, prelect, whisper **8** converse, dilate on, intonate, perorate, splutter, vocalize **9** discourse, expatiate, verbalize *confusedly:* **8** splutter *for:* **7** testify *hesitantly:* **7** stammer

speaker 9 spokesman **10** mouthpiece

spear 4 bore, pike, ream, spit **5** drill, gouge, lance, spike, stick **6** impale, pierce, skewer, skiver **7** fishgig, harpoon, leister, trident **8** transfix **9** penetrate **11** transpierce

special 4 rare **6** unique **7** express **8** peculiar, uncommon **9** earmarked

10 designated, particular **11** distinctive, exceptional

specialist *suffix:* **5** ician

specialize 4 list **7** itemize **9** enumerate, inventory **13** particularize

species 4 kind, sort, type **5** breed, class, order

specific 3 set **6** strict **7** express, limited **8** clean-cut, clear-cut, definite, especial, explicit, reserved **10** individual, particular **11** categorical, unambiguous

specify 3 fix, set **4** cite, list, name **5** limit **6** detail, settle **7** itemize, mention, pin down, precise **8** instance **9** condition, determine, enumerate, establish, inventory, stipulate **13** particularize

specimen 4 case, sort, type **6** sample **7** example, neotype, variety **8** instance, sampling **12** illustration *animal or plant:* **8** holotype *typical:* **8** topotype

specious 4 idle, vain **5** empty, false, wrong **6** hollow, untrue **7** seeming, unsound **8** apparent, nugatory **9** beguiling, colorable, erroneous, illogical, incorrect, plausible **10** inaccurate

speciousness 7 fallacy, sophism **8** delusion **9** casuistry, deception, sophistry **12** equivocation

speck 3 bit, dot, jot **4** atom, iota, mite, mote, tick **5** crumb, grain, point **6** pepper, smitch **7** freckle, stipple **8** molecule, particle, pinpoint, sprinkle

speckle 3 dot **4** spot, stud **5** flake, fleck **6** dapple, pepper, pimple **7** stipple **8** sprinkle

spectacle 4 show **7** display, pageant **10** exhibition **13** demonstration *combining form:* **4** cade

spectacular 5 stagy **7** amazing **8** dramatic, striking, wondrous **9** marvelous, thrilling, wonderful **10** astounding, eye-popping, histrionic, miraculous, prodigious, staggering, stupendous, theatrical **11** astonishing, sensational

spectator 4 seer **5** gazer **6** viewer **7** watcher, witness **8** beholder, observer, onlooker **9** bystander, perceiver **10** eyewitness

Spectator, The *author:* **6** Steele **7** Addison

specter 5 ghost, shade, umbra **6** shadow, spirit **7** eidolon, phantom **8** phantasm, revenant **10** apparition

spectral 6 ghosty, spooky **7** ghastly, ghostly, phantom, shadowy **9** deathlike, ghostlike, unearthly **10** cadaverous, corpselike, shadowlike **11** disembodied, phantomlike

spectrum 5 bogey, ghost, shade **6** spirit **7** eidolon **8** phantasm, revenant **10** apparition

speculate 5 study, think, weigh 6 reason, review 7 reflect 8 cogitate, theorize 9 cerebrate 10 deliberate, excogitate

speculation 6 review, theory 7 perhaps, suppose, thought 8 studying, weighing 9 brainwork 10 conjecture

speculative 5 pensy 6 closet, musing 7 curious, pensive 8 academic, thinking 9 inquiring 10 reflecting, ruminating, thoughtful 11 questioning, theoretical

Spedding biographee 5 Bacon

speech 4 talk 5 idiom, voice 6 debate, parley, tongue 7 address, dialect, lecture, monolog, oration, voicing 8 harangue, language, parlance, speaking, uttering 9 discourse, monologue, utterance 10 allocution, expressing, expression, vernacular, vocalizing 11 declamation 12 articulation, vocalization 13 verbalization

speechcraft 7 oratory 8 rhetoric 9 elocution

speechless 3 mum 4 dumb, mute 6 silent 7 aphonic

speed 3 aid, fly, rev, run, zip 4 clip, ease, gait, pace, race, rush, tear, whiz 5 chase, haste, hurry, tempo, woosh 6 barrel, bucket, burn up, career, course, goad on, hasten, hustle, rustle, smooth, spur on, step up, whoosh 7 quicken, swiften 8 alacrity, celerity, dispatch, expedite, fastness, highball, legerity, rapidity, velocity 9 fleetness, quickness, rapidness, swiftness 10 accelerate, cannonball, expedition, facilitate

speedy 4 fast 5 agile, brisk, fleet, hasty, quick, rapid, ready, swift 6 nimble, prompt, raking 8 hasteful 9 breakneck 10 harefooted 11 expeditious

spell 2 go 3 bit, fix, hex 4 bout, time, tour, turn 5 charm, shift, stint, throe, trick, while 6 access, attack, period, streak, voodoo 7 bewitch, enchant, relieve, seizure, stretch 9 ensorcell 11 conjuration, incantation

spellbind 4 grip, hold 5 charm 7 catch up 8 enthrall 9 fascinate, mesmerize

spelling 11 orthography *bad:* 10 cacography

spell out 7 explain, expound 8 construe 9 explicate, interpret

spend 3 pay 4 blow, drop, give, pass 5 use up, waste 6 lay out, outlay 7 consume, exhaust, fork out, hand out, splurge 8 disburse, shell out, squander 9 dissipate, throw away, while away 10 contribute, run through *wisely:* 7 husband

spender 6 waster 7 wastrel 8 prodigal, unthrift 10 high roller, profligate, squanderer 11 scattergood, wastethrift

spendthrift see **spender**

spent 5 all in 6 bleary, effete, used up 7 drained, far-gone, worn-out 8 depleted 9 exhausted, washed-out

spew 4 gush 5 belch, eject, eruct, erupt, expel, flood, vomit 6 irrupt, spit up 7 bring up, throw up, upchuck 8 disgorge

sphere 3 orb 4 ball, walk 5 field, globe, realm, round 6 circle, domain 7 demesne, rondure, terrain 8 conglobe, dominion, province 9 bailiwick, champaign, territory 10 conglobate 12 jurisdiction

spherical 5 round 6 global 7 globate, globose, globous 8 globated, globular 9 orbicular *combining form:* 5 globo

Sphinx *builder:* 6 Khafre *father:* 6 Typhon *head:* 3 man, ram 4 hawk 5 woman *mother:* 7 Echidna *query:* 6 riddle *site:* 4 Giza 6 Thebes

spice 4 balm, cast, dash, hint, lick 5 aroma, clove, scent, smack, smell, taste, tinge, touch, trace 6 ginger, nutmeg 7 bouquet, incense, perfume 8 cinnamon 9 fragrance, redolence

Spice Islands 8 Moluccas

spick-and-span 3 new 4 mint, neat, snug, tidy, trig, trim 5 clean, fresh 6 spruce 7 chipper, orderly 8 brand-new 9 shipshape 11 uncluttered, well-groomed

spicy 4 blue, racy 5 broad, fiery, salty, shady, sweet, zesty 6 aromal, purple, risqué, savory, snappy, wicked 7 gingery, peppery, perfumy, piquant, pungent, scented, zestful 8 aromatic, fragrant, off-color, perfumed, poignant, redolent, spirited 9 ambrosial 10 suggestive 12 high spirited 13 sophisticated

spider 6 frypan 7 araneid, skillet 8 arachnid 9 frying pan 10 black widow *combining form:* 6 arachn 7 arachno

spider monkey 7 sapajou

spiel 4 line 5 pitch 12 song and dance

spieler 6 gypper 7 cheater, diddler, grifter, sharper, slicker 8 swindler 9 defrauder 11 flimflammer 12 double-dealer

spigot 3 tap 4 cock, gate 5 valve 6 faucet 7 hydrant, petcock 8 stopcock

spike 5 lance, piton, spear 6 impale, skewer, skiver 8 transfix 11 transpierce

spile 4 bung 5 spout 8 forepole

spill 4 drip, drop, slop, tell 5 mouth, spray, squab 6 betray, reveal, splash 7 blab out, divulge, dribble, overrun, run over, spatter 8 disclose, discover, give away, overfill, overflow, well over

Spillane detective 11 Hammer, Mike

spin 4 gyre, reel, ride, swim, turn 5 dizzy, drive, giddy, mix up, swirl, twirl, wheel, whirl 6 gyrate, muddle, rotate 7 fluster, revolve, vibrate 9 oscillate, pendulate, pirouette, whirligig *a log:* 4 birl *out:* 4 draw 6 extend 7 prolong, stretch 8 elongate, lengthen, protract 10 prolongate

spinal column 6 rachis *curvature:* 7 lor-doma **8** lordosis *part:* **8** vertebra; (see also **spine**)

spindle 3 pin, rod **5** newel **6** rachis

spindly 5 lanky, rangy **6** gangly

spine 4 back **6** rachis **8** backbone **9** vertebrae

spineless 4 weak **8** impotent **9** weak-kneed **10** emasculate, inadequate, weak-willed **11** ineffective, ineffectual **12** invertebrate

spin-off 8 offshoot **9** by-product, outgrowth **10** derivative, descendant

___ **Spinoza 6** Baruch

spinster 7 old maid **10** maiden lady

spiny 6 thorny **7** prickly **8** echinate **10** nettlesome

spiral 4 coil, curl, wind **5** helix, twine, twist **7** entwine, helical, helices (plural), wreathe **8** gyroidal, volution **9** cochleate, corkscrew *combining form:* **3** gyr **4** gyro **5** helic **6** helico

spire 4 coil, curl **5** twist, whorl **6** sprout **7** steeple **8** pinnacle **9** germinate

spirit 3 pep, vim, zip **4** brio, dash, élan, gimp, grog, guts, life, mood, snap, soul, tone, zeal, zing **5** anima, ardor, drive, force, heart, might, moxie, oomph, pluck, power, shade, spunk, umbra, verve, vigor **6** animus, daimon, energy, esprit, fervor, ginger, mettle, morale, pneuma, psyche, shadow, starch, temper, timbre, wraith **7** cojones, courage, eidolon, passion, phantom, specter, spectre **8** phantasm, revenant, strength, vitality **9** animation, briskness, character, élan vital, substance **10** apparition, enthusiasm, get-up-and-go, liveliness, resolution, vital force **13** dauntlessness *away:* **6** abduct, kidnap, snatch *combining form:* **4** thym **5** psych, thymo **6** psycho, thymia **7** pneumat **8** pneumato *evil:* **5** afrit, demon **6** afreet **7** erlking, shaitan, sheitan *female:* **5** nymph **7** banshee, banshie, nymphet *good:* **7** eudemon **8** eudaemon *Hopi:* **7** kachina, katcina *Persian:* **4** peri

spirited 3 hot **4** avid, bold, game, keen **5** alert, beany, brave, eager, fiery, nervy, peppy, sharp **6** ardent, bright, gritty, lively, plucky, spunky **7** animate, chipper, fervent, gingery, peppery, valiant, zealous **8** animated, cheerful, fearless, intrepid, resolute **9** audacious, dauntless, sprightly, vivacious **10** courageous, mettlesome, passionate **11** high-hearted **12** enthusiastic

spirits 5 booze, drink **6** liquor, tipple **9** aqua vitae, firewater *low:* **5** blues **8** doldrums **10** blue devils, melancholy

spiritual 4 high **5** lofty **6** church, mental, sacred **7** saintly **8** bodiless, cerebral, churchly, elevated, mystical, numinous, platonic **9** unfleshly **10** discarnate, high-minded, immaterial, unphysical **11** disem-

bodied, incorporeal, nonmaterial, nonphysical **12** metaphysical, supernatural, supramundane

spiritualist 6 mystic

spit 5 lance, spear **6** impale, saliva, skewer, skiver, slaver, sputum **7** spatter, sputter **8** splutter, transfix **9** brochette **11** expectorate

spite 6 grudge, malice, rancor, spleen **7** ill will, revenge **9** vengeance **10** malignancy **11** malevolence **12** vengefulness **13** maliciousness

spiteful 4 evil **5** catty **6** malign, wicked **7** cattish, hostile, vicious **9** malicious, malignant, rancorous **10** malevolent, vindictive **12** antagonistic

Spitta biographee 4 Bach

spitting image 4 twin **6** double, ringer **7** picture **8** portrait **10** simulacrum

spittoon 8 cuspidor

splash 3 sop, wet **4** slop, soak **5** douse, drown, slosh, spray, swash, throw **6** dabble, drench, squirt **7** spatter, splurge, spurtle **8** sprinkle

splatter 4 slop **5** douse, plash, slosh, swash **6** splosh **7** splurge, spurtle

spleen see **spite**

splendor 4 pomp **5** adorn, glory, value, worth **6** beauty **8** grandeur **10** brilliancy, excellence **12** magnificence

splice 3 tie **4** join, mate **5** unite

splinter 4 rive **5** burst, smash, spail, spale **6** shiver **7** shatter **8** fragment

split 3 cut, rip **4** part, rend, rent, rift, rima, rime, rive, tear **5** break, carve, chasm, chink, cleft, crack, sever, slice **6** breach, cleave, cloven, divide, schism, sunder **7** break up, disjoin, dissect, divorce, fissate, fission, fissure, rupture **8** cleavage, dissever, fracture, rimation, separate **10** alienating, estranging **11** dichotomize *combining form:* **5** schiz **6** schizo **7** schisto

splotch 4 blob, blot, spot **5** fleck, stain **6** bespot, dapple, marble, motley, mottle **9** harlequin, variegate

splurge 4 orgy, slop **5** binge, douse, fling, plash, slosh, spree, swash **6** splash, splosh **7** rampage, spatter, spurtle **8** splatter **12** extravagance

spoil 3 mar, rot **4** baby, grab, harm, haul, hurt, loot, rape, ruin, sack, swag, take, turn **5** booty, decay, favor, force, humor, louse, prize, queer, snafu, taint, waste, wreck **6** boodle, cocker, coddle, cosset, damage, defile, impair, injure, molder, oblige, pamper, ravage, ravish **7** blemish, cater to, crumble, destroy, indulge, outrage, pillage, plunder, putrefy, tarnish, violate, vitiate **8** deflower, demolish, desolate, pickings, spoliate **9** break down, decompose, deflorate, depredate, desecrate, devastate **10** plunderage, spoliation **11** acquisition, mollycoddle

spoilsport 7 killjoy

spoke 3 bar, rod **5** chock, stake **8** baluster **11** obstruction

sponge 5 leech, mooch **7** moocher **8** parasite **10** freeloader *material:* **8** mesoglea *opening:* **6** oscula (plural), oscule **7** osculum, ostiole

sponger 5 leech **7** moocher **8** parasite **10** freeloader

spongy 4 soft **5** mushy, pappy, pulpy **6** quaggy **7** pulpous, squashy, squishy **8** squelchy, yielding

sponsor 5 angel **6** backer, patron, surety **8** advocate, backer-up, champion, Maecenas, mainstay, promoter, upholder **9** guarantor, preferrer, supporter **10** benefactor

sponsorship 5 aegis **7** backing **8** auspices **9** patronage

spontaneous 7 natural, offhand **8** unforced **9** automatic, extempore, impromptu, impulsive, unstudied **10** improvised, unprompted **11** instinctive, unmeditated **13** unconstrained

spontoon 3 bat **4** club, mace **5** baton, billy **6** cudgel **8** bludgeon **9** billy club, truncheon **10** nightstick

spoof 4 dupe, fake, fool, hoax, sell, sham **5** cheat, farce, phony, put-on, trick **6** befool, deceit, parody, send-up **7** chicane, takeoff **8** flimflam, hoodwink **9** bamboozle, deception, imposture **11** hornswoggle

spook 3 spy **5** agent, alarm, ghost, scare **6** fright **7** specter, startle, terrify **8** affright, frighten **9** terrorize **10** ghostwrite **13** undercover man

spooky 5 eerie, jumpy, nervy, weird **6** goosey **7** fidgety, jittery, nervous, ominous, uncanny **8** twittery **9** unearthly, unrestful **10** high-strung

spool 4 wind **6** bobbin, holder

spoon 3 pet, woo **4** neck **5** court, ladle, scoop **7** scraper

spoonbill 8 shoveler **9** ruddy duck **10** paddlefish

Spoon River Poet 7 Masters

spoony 5 silly **6** simple **7** fatuous, foolish, unwitty, witless **10** weak-headed, weakminded **11** sheepheaded *over/on:* **6** mashed **7** smitten **8** enamored

spoor 4 step **5** track, tract **7** vestige **8** footstep **9** footprint

sporadic 3 few **4** rare **6** catchy, fitful, scarce, seldom, single, spotty **8** separate, uncommon **9** desultory, irregular, spasmodic **10** infrequent, occasional, unfrequent

sport 3 fun **4** game, jest, joke, mock, play **6** frolic, racing, trifle **7** mockery, show off **9** diversion, high jinks, horseplay, pilgarlic **10** recreation *indoor:* **6** boxing, hockey,

squash **7** bowling **8** handball **9** wrestling **10** acrobatics, basketball, gymnastics **11** racquetball, table tennis *Olympic:* **4** judo **6** boxing, diving, hockey, rowing **7** archery, cycling, fencing, shot put **8** canoeing, football, high jump, long jump, marathon, shooting, swimming, yachting **9** decathlon, pole vault, water polo, wrestling **10** basketball, gymnastics, pentathlon, triple jump, volleyball **11** discus throw, hammer throw **12** javelin throw, steeplechase **13** weightlifting *water:* **6** diving, rowing **7** sailing, surfing **8** canoeing, swimming, yachting *winter:* **6** hockey, skiing **7** curling, lugeing, skating **8** biathlon, sledding **10** ski jumping **11** bobsledding, tobogganing

sporting house 6 bagnio **7** brothel **8** bordello, seraglio

sportive 5 antic **6** frisky, impish **7** larkish, playful, roguish, waggish **8** gamesome **10** frolicsome **11** mischievous

sportiveness 7 devilry, roguery, waggery **8** deviltry, mischief **9** devilment

spot 3 fix, jam, job, nip, see **4** drop, espy, find, iota, mite, onus, post, site, slug, whit **5** brand, catch, fleck, hit on, locus, place, point, speck **6** blotch, corner, dapple, descry, detect, dollop, finger, macula, mottle, office, pickle, pimple, plight, random, scrape, stigma, turn up **7** aimless, dilemma, freckle, hit upon, smidgen, spatter, speckle, splotch, station, unaimed **8** diagnose, flyspeck, identify, location, maculate, meet with, particle, pinpoint, position **9** bespatter, encounter, haphazard, hit-or-miss, irregular, recognize, situation, unplanned **10** connection, designless **11** determinate, distinguish, predicament *combining form:* **5** macul **6** maculi, maculo

spotless 4 pure **5** clean **6** chaste, decent, modest **7** cleanly **8** hygienic, sanitary, unsoiled **9** undefiled, unsullied **10** immaculate **11** unblemished

spotted eagle ray 6 obispo

spouse 4 mate, wife **5** hubby **7** consort, husband

spout 5 chute, falls, sault **6** nozzle **7** cascade **8** cataract **9** waterfall

sprain 4 pull, tear, turn **5** break, throw, twist **6** wrench **7** stretch **8** fracture **9** dislocate

sprawl 4 loll **5** drape, slump **6** extend, lounge, ramble, slouch, spread **7** stretch **8** scramble, straddle, straggle **11** spreadeagle

spray 3 fog **4** hose **7** aerosol **8** atomizer, fumigate, nebulize

spread 3 jam, lay, set, sow **4** deal, oleo, open, pâté, push **5** feast, jelly, noise, space, splay, strew, sweep **6** butter, dinner, expand, extend, fan out, pass on, peddle, regale, retail, unfold **7** banquet, breadth, diffuse, expanse, overrun, perfuse, pervade, radiate, scatter, slather, stretch, suffuse **8** bedcover, coverlet, dispense, disperse, distance, mushroom, permeate, transmit **9** amplitude, broadcast, circulate, diffusion, dissipate, expansion, extension, profusion, propagate **10** distribute, outstretch **11** communicate, counterpane, disseminate, enlargement *on:* **5** apply

spree 3 bat, jag **4** bust, hell, orgy, riot, tear **5** binge, fling, revel **6** bender, frolic, rantan **7** carouse, rampage, roister, splurge, wassail **8** carousal

sprig 4 brad, heir **5** dowel, scion **6** figure **7** pintail **9** ruddy duck

sprightly 3 gay **4** keen, yare **5** agile, alert, antic, brisk, perky, sharp, smart, zippy **6** active, breezy, brisky, clever, frisky, lively, nimble, volant **7** animate, coltish, playful, pungent **8** animated, spirited, sportive **9** vivacious **10** frolicsome, keen-witted, rollicking, unpedantic **11** quick-witted **13** scintillating

spring 3 hop, lop **4** bolt, come, flow, head, jump, leap, loom, lope, rise, root, skip, stem, trip, well **5** arise, begin, birth, bound, cause, fount, hatch, issue, start, vault, youth **6** appear, arrive, bounce, emerge, geyser, hurdle, motive, origin, reason, source, tittup, uncoil, updive, vernal **7** budtime, come out, emanate, impetus, proceed, puberty, rebound, saltate, skitter, startle **8** come from, commence, excitant, fountain, stimulus, wellhead **9** greenness, originate, stimulant, youthhood **10** derive from, incitement, juvenility **12** fountainhead, youthfulness *back:* **6** resile *combining form:* **4** cren **5** creno

springe 5 snare **7** pitfall **8** deadfall, trapfall **9** booby trap, mousetrap

springlike 6 vernal

springy 6 supple, whippy **7** elastic, stretch **8** flexible, stretchy **9** recoiling, resilient **10** rebounding

sprinkle 3 dot **4** dust, spot **5** shake, speck, strew **6** pepper, powder, sparge **7** asperse, drizzle, freckle, scatter, speckle, stipple **9** bespeckle

sprint 3 run **4** dash, shin **5** scoot **6** scurry **7** scamper

sprite 3 elf, fay **5** fairy, nisse, pixie **7** brownie *water:* **5** kelpy **6** kelpie

spritz 3 jet **5** spurt **6** squirt

sprout 3 bud **4** grow **5** scion, shoot **6** ratoon, sucker **8** offshoot **9** germinate *combining form:* **4** clad **5** blast, clado **6** blasto, blasty **7** blastic

spruce 4 trim **5** natty, sassy **6** dapper, spiffy **11** well-groomed *up:* **5** slick, spiff **6** doll up **7** deck out, gussy up

spry 4 yare **5** agile, brisk, quick, ready, sound, zippy **6** active, brisky, lively, nimble, prompt, robust, volant **7** healthy **8** vigorous **9** energetic

spud 6 potato **8** spade lug

spume 4 foam, suds **5** froth, yeast **6** lather

spunk 4 grit, guts, sand **5** heart, moxie, nerve, pluck **6** mettle, spirit **7** cojones, courage **8** backbone **9** fortitude **10** doggedness, resolution **13** dauntlessness

spunky 4 bold **5** beany, brave, fiery, gutsy **6** plucky **7** doughty, gingery, peppery **8** fearless, spirited **9** dauntless, unfearing **10** courageous, mettlesome **11** high-hearted, undauntable **12** high-spirited

spur 3 sic **4** goad, prod, stir, urge **5** egg on, favor, prick, rally, rouse, rowel **6** arouse, awaken, exhort, prompt, propel **7** impetus, impulse **8** catalyst, excitant, stimulus **9** actuation, incentive, instigate, stimulant **10** activation, incitation, incitement, motivation **11** countenance

spurious 4 fake, mock, sham **5** bogus, dummy, false, phony, put-on, snide **6** ersatz, pseudo, unreal **7** assumed, bastard, feigned, pretend **8** affected, baseborn **9** brummagem, imitation, pinchbeck, pretended, simulated, ungenuine **10** apocryphal, artificial, substitute **11** counterfeit, make-believe, misbegotten, unauthentic **12** illegitimate *combining form:* **4** noth **5** notho, pseud **6** pseudo

spurn 5 flout, scoff, scorn, scout, sneer **6** refuse, reject **7** conspue, contemn, decline, despise, disdain, dismiss **8** turn down **9** reprobate, repudiate **10** disapprove

spurt 3 jet **5** spout, surge **6** spritz, sprout, squirt

sputter 3 pop **4** fizz, hiss, rage, rant, rave, spit **6** gibber, jabber **7** bluster, crackle

spy 5 agent, scout, snoop, spook **6** beagle, sleuth **7** gumshoe **8** informer, saboteur **9** detective **12** investigator **13** undercover man *name:* **4** Boyd (Belle), Hari (Mata) **5** André (John)

Spy, The *author:* **6** Cooper

spying 9 espionage

squab 5 couch **6** pigeon **7** cushion

squabble see **spat**

squalid 3 low **4** base, foul, mean, ugly, vile **5** black, dingy, dirty, nasty, seedy, soily **6** filthy, frowzy, grubby, impure, scurvy, shabby, shoddy, sleazy, sloppy **7** ignoble, low-down, run-down, scrubby, unclean, unkempt **8** slipshod, slovenly, wretched **10** broken-down, despicable, disheveled, slatternly **11** dilapidated **12** disreputable

squall 3 caw, yap, yip 4 bark, bawl, beef, feud, howl, roar, wail, yaup, yawp, yell, yelp, yowl 5 brawl, croak, fight, shout 6 bellow, hassle, shriek, squeal 7 dispute, quarrel, screech 9 bickering 10 falling-out 11 altercation

squander 4 blow 5 waste 7 consume, fritter 8 fool away, unthrift 9 dissipate, overdoing, throw away 10 frivol away, lavishness, trifle away 11 prodigality, prodigalize 12 extravagance, extravagancy, wastefulness

squanderer see **spender**

square 3 fit, fix, pay, sop 4 bang, boxy, even, fair, fogy, have, jibe, just, quit, suit 5 adapt, agree, bribe, clear, equal, exact, fit in, green, pay up, plaza, right, sharp, spang 6 accord, adjust, buy off, common, fogram, fossil, settle, tailor 7 balance, boxlike, conform, exactly, satisfy 8 check out, clear off, coincide, dovetail, mossback, orthodox, quadrate, smack-dab, straight, unbiased 9 discharge, equitable, harmonize, impartial, liquidate, objective, precisely, quadratic, reconcile 10 accurately, button-down, correspond, fuddy-duddy 12 conventional 13 stick-in-the-mud

squash 3 jam 4 cram, mash, pepo, pulp 5 crush, gourd, press, quell 7 put down, squeeze, squelch, squidge 8 suppress 10 annihilate, extinguish *variety:* 5 acorn 6 cushaw, cymlin, Sibley, turban 7 cymling, dunkard, Hubbard, scallop 8 cymbling, pattypan, zucchini 9 butternut, cocozelle, crookneck 10 Marblehead

squat 5 dumpy, hunch, stoop, thick 6 chunky, crouch, hunker, stocky, stubby 8 heavyset, thickset 10 hunker down 11 thick-bodied

squawfish 4 chub 8 cyprinid

squawk 3 caw, yap, yip 4 beef, crab, fuss, yaup, yawp 5 bitch, bleat, gripe 6 yammer 7 protest 8 complain

squeak 3 rat 4 pipe, shot, show, talk, time 5 grate, peach 6 change, inform, look-in, scream, snitch 7 opening, screech 8 occasion 11 opportunity

squeal 3 rat, yip 4 howl, rasp, talk, yell, yowl 5 bitch, bleat, creak, grate, gripe, peach 6 inform, screak, scream, shriek, shrill, snitch, squawk 7 screech 8 complain

squealer 4 fink 6 canary, snitch 7 ratfink, tipster 8 betrayer, informer 10 talebearer 11 stool pigeon

squeamish 5 dizzy, fussy, queer, shaky, upset 6 dainty, qualmy, queasy 7 finical, finicky 8 nauseous 9 finicking, nauseated, unsettled 10 fastidious, particular, pernickety 11 persnickety, vertiginous

squeamishness 6 nausea

squeeze 3 hug, jam 4 bear, cram, push 5 clasp, crowd, crush, exact, gouge, juice, pinch, press, screw, wrest, wring 6 eke out, enfold, extort, squash, squish, squush, wrench 7 embrace, extract, scratch 8 compress, contract 9 shake down

squelch 5 shush 6 muffle, squash, squish, stifle 7 repress, squidge 8 strangle, suppress

squib 4 fire 6 filler 7 lampoon 8 scribble, shoot off 9 detonator

squid 7 calamar, mollusk 8 calamary 10 cephalopod *kin:* 7 octopus 10 cuttlefish

squiggle 4 worm 6 scrawl, writhe 7 scratch 8 scrabble, scribble

squinch 5 quail, start, wince 6 blanch, blench, recoil, shrink

squint 4 bent 5 trend 10 hagioscope, strabismus

squire 5 judge, lover 6 escort, lawyer 7 gallant 9 accompany

squirm 4 toss, worm 6 wiggle, writhe 7 agonize, wriggle

squirrel 5 hoard, stash *African:* 5 xerus *red:* 9 chickaree

squirrel-like 8 sciuroid

squirt 3 jet, pup 4 pour 5 puppy, sprat, spray, sprit, spurt, surge, twerp 6 splurt, spritz, stream 7 spatter

squish 3 jam 4 bear, push 5 crush, press 7 squeeze, squelch

squishy 4 soft 5 pulpy 6 quaggy, spongy 7 pulpous 8 squelchy

Sri Lanka *capital:* 7 Colombo *export:* 3 tea 6 rubber *former name:* 6 Ceylon *monetary unit:* 5 rupee

SRO 7 sellout

SS chief 7 Himmler

S-shaped 7 sigmoid 9 sigmoidal

stab 2 go 3 dig, pop, ram, run, try 4 dirk, poke, shot, sink, slap 5 crack, drive, fling, prick, prong, punch, spear, stick, whack, whirl 6 dagger, pierce, plunge, thrust 7 bayonet, poniard 8 puncture, stiletto

Stabat _____ 5 Mater

stabile 6 steady 9 sculpture 10 stationary

stabilize 3 fix, set 4 prop 5 poise 6 fixate, secure, settle, steady 7 balance, ballast, support, sustain

stable 3 set 4 even, fast, firm, safe, sure 5 fixed, solid, sound 6 poised, secure, steady, strong, sturdy 7 lasting, staunch, uniform 8 balanced, constant, enduring, resolute 9 diuturnal, perduring, permanent, steadfast, unvarying 10 perdurable, unchanging, unshakable

stack 4 bank, cock, heap, hill, load, mass, pile 5 drift, mound 7 pyramid

stadium 4 bowl 5 arena 6 garden 8 coliseum 9 gymnasium

staff 3 rod 4 club, prop, rung, wand

6 cudgel 7 support *bishop's:* 7 crosier, crozier *medical:* 8 caduceus

stage 4 give, open, play, rung, show, step 5 grade, level, mount, notch, phase, put on 6 degree, period 7 execute, perform, present, produce *direction:* 4 exit 5 enter 6 exeunt *scenery:* 8 backdrop *show:* 4 play 5 drama, revue 7 musical 9 burlesque 10 vaudeville *signal:* 3 cue *whisper:* 5 aside

stage set 5 scene 7 scenery, setting 11 mise-en-scène

stagger 4 halt, reel, sway 5 amaze, floor, lurch, shift, stump, swing, waver, weave, wheel 6 boggle, careen, dither, falter, puzzle, teeter, topple, totter, wobble 7 astound, nonplus, perplex, shatter, stumble, whiffle 8 astonish, bowl over, hesitate, paralyze, titubate 9 devastate, dumbfound, knock over, overpower, overwhelm, vacillate

stagnant 5 stale 6 static 8 immobile, unmoving 10 motionless, stationary

stagnate 6 stifle 7 trammel 8 stultify, vegetate

staid 4 cool, smug 5 grave, sober 6 formal, sedate, solemn, somber, stuffy 7 earnest, serious, starchy, weighty 8 composed, decorous, priggish

stain 3 dye, tar 4 blot, blur, daub, flaw, onus, slur, smut, soil, spot 5 brand, color, crock, odium, smear, sully, taint, tinge 6 bedaub, blotch, debase, defect, defile, embrue, imbrue, smirch, smudge, smutch, stigma 7 besmear, blemish, corrupt, debauch, deprave, pervert, pigment, tarnish 8 besmirch, black eye, colorant, discolor, dyestuff, tincture *combining form:* 5 macul 6 maculi, maculo

staircase *handrail:* 8 banister *outdoor:* 6 perron *post:* 5 newel 8 baluster

stake 3 bet, lay, pot, set 4 ante, back, game, play 5 claim, put on, share, wager 6 gamble 7 finance 8 bankroll, interest 10 capitalize

stale 4 rank 5 dusty, fetid, fusty, moldy, musty, tired, trite 6 cliché, smelly 7 clichéd, noisome, reeking, stenchy 8 shopworn, timeworn 9 hackneyed 10 malodorous 11 commonplace, stereotyped

stalemate 3 tie 4 draw 7 dogfall 8 deadlock, standoff

stalk 4 hunt, prey 5 chase, drive, march, sling, track 6 ambush, follow, pursue, stride, walk up 8 flush out *flower:* 8 peduncle *leaf:* 7 petiole

stall 4 halt 5 booth, brake, check, kiosk, stand 6 arrest, put off 7 hold off 11 compartment

stalwart 4 bold 5 brave, husky, stout, tough 6 brawny, sinewy, strong, sturdy 7 valiant 8 athletic, fearless, intrepid, mus-

cular, unafraid, valorous 9 dauntless, tenacious, undaunted 10 courageous

stamen *combining form:* 4 andr 5 andro 9 stemonous *part:* 6 anther 8 filament

stamina 9 endurance, tolerance 10 toleration

stammer 6 gibber, jabber 7 sputter, stutter 8 hesitate, splutter

stamp 3 ilk, lot 4 cast, etch, kind, mint, mold, seal, sort, type 5 clomp, clump, drive, grave, infix, pound, print, tromp 6 hammer, incuse, stripe 7 impress, imprint, sticker, trample 8 hallmark, inscribe 9 character 10 impression

stampede 4 bolt, dash, rout, rush, tear 5 chase, fling, shoot 6 charge 8 pell-mell

stamps 7 postage

stance 4 pose 5 color 7 posture 8 attitude, carriage, position, positure

stanch 4 stem, stop

stanchion 4 prop 5 brace 7 support

stand 4 bear, take 5 abide, booth, brook, kiosk, treat 6 endure, suffer 7 stomach, swallow 8 attitude, position, tolerate *artist's:* 5 easel *having three legs:* 6 tripod, trivet *ornamental:* 7 étagère *stiffly:* 7 bristle

standard 3 law, par 4 flag, jack, mean, norm, rule 5 axiom, color, gauge, ideal, model 6 assize, banner, belief, ensign, median, mirror, pennon 7 average, example, measure, pattern, pennant 8 bannerol, ensample, exemplar, paradigm, streamer 9 archetype, banderole, beau ideal, benchmark, criterion, principle, yardstick 10 touchstone 11 fundamental

stand-in 3 sub 6 second 9 alternate, assistant, surrogate 10 substitute 11 locum tenens, pinch hitter, replacement, succedaneum

standing 4 rank, term 5 place 6 cachet, status 7 dignity, footing, station, stature 8 capacity, position, prestige 9 character, situation 11 consequence

standoff see stalemate

standoffish 5 aloof 7 distant 8 eremitic, reserved, solitary 9 reclusive, withdrawn 10 antisocial, insociable, unsociable 12 misanthropic

stand out 3 jut 4 bulk, loom, poke, pout 5 bulge, pouch 6 beetle 7 project 8 overhang, protrude

standpatter 4 tory 7 diehard 8 old liner, rightist 11 bitter-ender, right-winger 12 conservative

standpoint 4 side 5 angle, slant 7 outlook 9 direction

standstill 4 halt, stop 5 check, pause 6 arrest 8 deadlock 9 cessation

Stanley Kowalski's wife 6 Stella

Stan's pal 5 Ollie

stanza 7 strophe *combining form:* 5 stich
of eight lines: 6 octave 8 octonary *of four
lines:* 6 ballad 8 quatrain *of six lines:*
6 sestet, sextet 7 sextain *of three lines:*
6 tercet 7 triplet 8 tristich *Persian:*
8 rubaiyat

star 4 main, nova 5 actor, chief, major,
novae (plural) 6 étoile 7 actress, capital
8 asterisk, dominant 9 principal 10 preeminent 11 outstanding, predominant *bright:*
4 Vega 5 Deneb, Rigel, Spica 6 Altair, Pollux, Sirius 7 Antares, Canopus, Capella,
Procyon 8 Arcturus 9 Aldebaran, Archer-
nar, Fomalhaut 10 Beta Crucis, Betelgeuse 11 Alpha Crucis 12 Beta Centauri
13 Alpha Centauri *combining form:* 4 astr
5 aster, astro 6 astero, sidero *five-
pointed:* 8 pentacle *giant:* 10 Betelgeuse
six-pointed: 8 hexagram *suffix:* 2 id

starch 2 go 3 pep 4 bang, push, snap
5 drive, getup, punch, vigor 6 amylum
7 stiffen 8 vitality *combining form:* 4 amyl
5 amylo

star-crossed 6 doomed 7 hapless,
unhappy, unlucky 8 ill-fated, luckless, untoward 10 ill-starred 11 unfortunate
12 misfortunate

Stardust composer 10 Carmichael

stare 3 eye 4 bore, gape, gawk, gaze,
look, ogle, peer 5 gloat 6 goggle 7 fish-
eye 10 rubberneck

stark 3 raw 4 bare, firm, nude, pure
5 bleak, clear, empty, naked, quite, rigid,
sheer, stout, utter 6 barren, robust, strict,
unclad, vacant, wholly 8 absolute, complete, desolate, stripped 9 au naturel, out-
and-out 10 absolutely

starry 6 astral 7 stellar 8 sidereal
9 stellular

Star-Spangled Banner writer 3 Key

start 4 bolt, dawn, draw, edge, jump, leap,
odds, open 5 alpha, arise, begin, bound,
bulge, crank, enter, found, onset, quail, set
up, wince 6 blanch, blench, bounce, create,
embark, flinch, get off, launch, outset, recoil,
setout, shrink, spring, take up, tee off
7 actuate, dawning, genesis, infancy, kickoff, opening, pioneer, proceed, squinch, trigger, vantage 8 activate, commence, drawback, embark on, handicap, initiate,
organize 9 advantage, allowance, beginning, establish, institute, originate 10 inaugurate 12 commencement

startle 3 awe 4 bolt, jolt, jump 5 alarm,
scare, shock, spook 8 affright, astonish,
frighten, surprise

starved 6 hungry 8 famished, ravenous,
underfed

stash 4 bury, hide 5 cache, hoard, plant
7 conceal, secrete 8 ensconce, squirrel

stasis 5 poise 7 balance 9 equipoise
11 equilibrium

state 3 air, put, say 4 aver, mode, rank,
tell, vent 5 opine, place, utter 6 affirm,
assert, cachet, define, recite, relate, report
7 declare, deliver, dignity, enounce, explain,
expound, express, footing, narrate, posture,
recount 8 attitude, bring out, capacity,
describe, position, prestige, set forth, standing 9 character, condition, elucidate, enunciate, interpret, situation, ventilate 11 body
politic *subdivison:* 6 county *suffix:* 2 cy,
th 3 ate, dom, ery, ion, ism, ity 4 ance,
ancy, ence, ency, hood, ment, ness, oses
(plural), osis, ship 5 ation 7 isation, ization

State abbreviation *Alabama:* 2 AL
3 Ala. *Alaska:* 2 AK 4 Alas. *Arizona:*
2 AZ 4 Ariz. *Arkansas:* 2 AR 3 Ark. *California:* 2 CA 3 Cal. 5 Calif. *Colorado:*
2 CO 3 Col. 4 Colo *Connecticut:* 2 CT
4 Conn. *Delaware:* 2 DE 3 Del. *Florida:*
2 FL 3 Fla. *Georgia:* 2 GA *Hawaii:* 2 Hi
Idaho: 2 ID 3 Ida. *Illinois:* 2 IL 3 Ill. *Indiana:* 2 IN 3 Ind. *Iowa:* 2 IA, Io. *Kansas:*
2 KS 3 Kan., Kas. 4 Kans. *Kentucky:*
2 KY 3 Ken. *Louisiana:* 2 LA *Maine:* 2 ME
Maryland: 2 MD *Massachusetts:* 2 MA
4 Mass. *Michigan:* 2 MI 4 Mich. *Minnesota:* 2 MN 4 Minn. *Mississippi:* 2 MS
4 Miss. *Missouri:* 2 MO *Montana:* 2 MT
4 Mont. *Nebraska:* 2 NE 3 Neb. 4 Nebr.
Nevada: 2 NV 3 Nev. *New Hampshire:*
2 NH *New Jersey:* 2 NJ *New Mexico:*
2 NM 4 N. Mex. *New York:* 2 NY *North
Carolina:* 2 NC 4 N. Car. *North Dakota:*
2 ND 4 N. Dak. *Ohio:* 2 OH *Oklahoma:*
2 OK 4 Okla. *Oregon:* 2 OR 3 Ore.
4 Oreg. *Pennsylvania:* 2 PA 4 Penn.
5 Penna. *Rhode island:* 2 RI *South Carolina:* 2 SC 4 S. Car. *South Dakota:* 2 SD
4 S. Dak. *Tennessee:* 2 TN 4 Tenn.
Texas: 2 TX 3 Tex. *Utah:* 2 UT *Vermont:* 2 VT 4 Verm. *Virginia:* 2 VA
4 Virg. *Washington:* 2 WA 4 Wash. *West
Virginia:* 2 WV 3 W. Va. *Wisconsin:*
2 WI 3 Wis. 4 Wisc. *Wyoming:* 2 WY
3 Wyo.

stately 5 grand, noble, preux, regal, royal
6 august, formal, kingly, lordly, solemn
7 courtly, gallant 8 gracious, imperial,
imposing, magnific, majestic, princely 9 dignified, grandiose 10 ceremonial 11 ceremonious, magnificent

statement 3 tab 4 bill, vent, word
5 score, voice 6 dictum 7 account, invoice,
recital 9 narrative, reckoning, testimony,
utterance 10 deposition, expression
11 description 12 vocalization 13 verbalization *introductory:* 7 preface 8 foreword,
prologue

stateroom 5 cabin

statesman 10 politician *American:* 3 Hay (John Milton) 4 Clay (Henry), Hull (Cordell), Otis (James), Root (Elihu) 5 Henry (Patrick), Lodge (Henry C.) 6 Morris (Gouverneur), Sumner (Charles) 7 Hancock (John), Kellogg (Frank B.), Lansing (Robert), Sherman, Stimson (Henry L.), Webster (Daniel) 8 Franklin, Hamilton, Pinckney, Randolph (E.J.), Rutledge (John), Trumbull 10 Stettinius (E. R.) *Australian:* 9 Wentworth *Austrian:* 6 Renner 7 Kaunitz 8 Dollfuss 10 Metternich 13 Schwarzenberg *Canadian:* 4 King 7 Laurier 8 Thompson 9 Macdonald, Mackenzie *Chinese:* 3 Yen 4 Kung, Wang, Yuan 9 Sun Yat-Sen *Dutch:* 6 de Witt 7 Grotius, Stikker *East German:* 8 Ulbricht *English:* 3 Fox 4 Eden, More, Peel, Pitt, Vane 5 Cecil, North 6 Morley, Sidney, Temple, Wolsey 7 Halifax, Reading, Russell, Stanley, Stewart, Warwick 8 Cromwell, Disraeli, Robinson, Villiers 9 Cavendish, Churchill, Gladstone, Salisbury, Strafford, Wellesley 10 Palmerston, Rockingham, Sunderland, Walsingham, Wellington 11 Chamberlain, Shaftesbury 12 Chesterfield *Finnish:* 9 Stahlberg *French:* 5 Sully 6 Guizot, Thiers, Turgot 7 Herriot, Mazarin, Schuman, Viviani 8 Hanotaux 9 Lafayette, Millerand, Richelieu 11 Clemenceau *German:* 5 Wirth 10 Stresemann *German-Danish:* 9 Struensee *Greek:* 6 Zaimes, Zaimis 8 Pericles 9 Aristides 11 Cleisthenes, Demosthenes 12 Themistocles *Israeli:* 5 Begin, Dayan *Italian:* 6 Cavour, Crispi 7 Orlando 11 Machiavelli *Japanese:* 5 genro, Kanoe 6 Kanoye *Norwegian:* 6 Nansen *Polish:* 7 Zaleski 9 Pilsudski 10 Paderewski *Prussian:* 5 Stein *Roman:* 4 Cato 6 Cicero, Pompey, Seneca 7 Agrippa 8 Gracchus, Maecenas 9 Symmachus *Russian:* 5 Witte 7 molotov 8 Potemkin 9 Vyshinsky *Scottish:* 4 Knox *South American:* 9 San Martin *Swiss:* 4 Ador 5 Welti

static 5 fixed, inert, rigid, stuck 6 stable, steady, sticky 7 stabile, stalled, stopped 8 constant, immobile, inactive, stagnant, unmoving 9 immovable 10 unchanging 13 unfluctuating

station 3 set 4 post, rank, site, spot 5 depot, locus, place, point, state, where 6 assign 7 appoint, footing 8 capacity, standing 9 character

stationary 5 fixed 6 static 8 immobile, stagnant, unmoving 9 immovable 10 motionless, stock-still

statue *base:* 6 plinth 8 pedestal *gigantic:* 8 Colossus *Greek:* 5 atlas 7 telamon 8 caryatid *religious:* 5 Pietà *small:* 8 figurine

statuesque 4 trim 7 shapely 10 well-turned 11 clean-limbed

stature   see **status**

status 4 rank 5 merit, place, worth 6 cachet, rating, renown 7 caliber, dignity, footing, posture, quality 8 capacity, eminence, position, prestige, standing 9 character, condition, situation 10 prominence 11 consequence, distinction

statute 3 act, law 4 rule 5 canon, edict 6 assize, decree 7 precept 8 decretum 9 enactment, ordinance 10 regulation

staunch 4 fast, firm, sure, true 5 liege, loyal 6 ardent, secure, stable, strong 8 constant, faithful, resolute 9 allegiant, steadfast

stave off 4 ward 5 avert, block, deter, parry, rebut, repel 6 rebuff 7 forfend, obviate, prevent, repulse, rule out, ward off 8 preclude 9 forestall

stay 3 lag 4 base, bide, halt, live, prop, rest, stop, wait 5 abide, brace, check, dally, defer, delay, dwell, found, remit, shore, tarry, visit 6 arrest, bottom, column, ground, linger, loiter, put off, remain, shelve 7 adjourn, sojourn, support, suspend 8 buttress, hold over, intermit, postpone, prorogue, stop over 9 establish, interrupt, predicate 10 dillydally, hang around 11 stick around

steadfast 4 firm, sure, true 5 fixed, liege, loyal, rigid 6 ardent 7 abiding, adamant, patient, staunch 8 constant, enduring, faithful, immobile, immotile, immotive, obdurate, resolute, stubborn 9 allegiant, immovable, unbending, unmovable 10 inexorable, inflexible, relentless, unwavering, unyielding 11 irremovable, unfaltering, unflinching, unqualified 12 never-failing, single-minded, wholehearted 13 unquestioning

steady 3 set 4 beau, even, fast, sure 5 fixed, flame, liege, lover, loyal, poise 6 ardent, stable, static 7 abiding, ballast, beloved, certain, durable, equable, stabile, staunch, uniform 8 constant, enduring, faithful, ladylove, reliable, resolute, truelove, unshaken 9 allegiant, boyfriend, inamorata, inamorato, stabilify, stabilize, unvarying 10 changeless, girl friend, sweetheart, unchanging, unswerving, unwavering 11 unfaltering 12 unchangeable, unflickering, wholehearted 13 unfluctuating

steak 4 club, cube 5 chuck, flank, round, T-bone 6 rib eye 7 sirloin 9 Delmonico, hamburger, Salisbury 10 tenderloin 11 porterhouse 13 chateaubriand

steal 3 cop, nab, nim, nip, rob 4 glom, grab, hook, kite, lift, loot, lurk, slip, take 5 annex, creep, filch, glide, grasp, heist, mooch, mouse, pinch, poach, prowl, rifle, seize, shirk, sidle, skulk, slide, slink, sneak, swipe, theft **6** burgle, collar, fleece, hijack, pilfer, pocket, rustle, smouch, snatch, snitch, thieve, tiptoe **7** bargain, gumshoe, larceny, pillage, plunder, purloin **8** shanghai, shoplift, thievery, thieving **9** pussyfoot **10** burglarize **11** appropriate *a vehicle:* **6** hijack **8** highjack

stealing 7 larceny *combining form:* **5** klept **6** klepto

stealthy 3 sly **4** wily **5** catty, quiet, sneak **6** covert, crafty, feline, secret, shifty, silent, slinky, sneaky **7** catlike, cunning, furtive, sub-rosa **8** hush-hush, skulking, slinking, sneaking **9** noiseless **10** pantherine, pantherish, undercover **11** clandestine **12** hugger-mugger **13** surreptitious

steam 5 force, might, power, sinew **6** energy, muscle **7** potency **8** strength **9** puissance *combining form:* **5** atmid **6** atmido

steam bath 5 sauna

steamboat structure 5 texas

steamer 4 boat, clam, ship

steam organ 8 calliope

steamship abbreviation 2 SS

steed 5 horse **7** charger

steel 4 gird **5** brace, cheer, nerve, rally, ready **6** buck up **7** animate, chirk up, fortify, hearten, prepare **8** embolden, inspirit **9** encourage, enhearten, reinforce **10** strengthen

steep 3 sop **4** high, soak **5** dizzy, imbue, lofty, sheer **6** abrupt, drench, infuse **7** arduous, extreme, suffuse **8** elevated, saturate **9** excessive **10** exorbitant, immoderate, impregnate, inordinate **11** precipitate, precipitous

steeple 5 spire **6** flèche

steer 3 see, tip **4** lead, show **5** guide, pilot, point, route **6** direct, escort, tip-off **7** channel, conduct **8** shepherd *a racing rowboat:* **3** cox **8** coxswain *a ship:* **4** conn, helm, luff **7** boxhaul

stein 3 cup, mug **5** stoup **6** goblet, seidel **7** tankard

Steinbeck novel 10 Cannery Row, East of Eden **12** Of Mice and Men, Tortilla Flat **13** Grapes of Wrath

Steinway product 5 piano

stellar 4 main **5** chief, major **6** astral, starry **7** capital, shining **8** dominant, gleaming, luminous, lustrous, sidereal, starlike **9** principal **10** preeminent **11** outstanding, predominant

stem 4 flow, head, rise, stop **5** arise, check, issue **6** arrest, spring, stanch **7** control, emanate, proceed **8** peduncle **9** originate **10** derive from *covering:* **5** ocrea *plant:* **4** halm **5** haulm *suffix:* **3** ome *underground:* **5** tuber **7** rhizoma, rhizome

stench 4 funk, reek **5** smell, stink

stenchful see **smelly**

stentorian 4 loud **5** rough **7** blaring, orotund, roaring **8** gravelly, piercing **9** clamorous **10** loud-voiced, vociferous **11** full-mouthed, loudmouthed **12** earsplitting **13** clarion-voiced

step 3 act **4** hoof, move, pace, rung, walk **5** dance, grade, notch, spoor, stage, stair, track, tract, tread, troop **6** action, degree, prance **7** measure, traipse **8** ambulate **9** footprint, procedure **10** proceeding *dance:* **3** pas *one of a series:* **6** gradin **7** gradine

step-by-step 7 gradual **9** piecemeal

stepmotherly 8 novercal

steppe 5 plain *Kazakhstan:* **6** Kirgiz **10** Betpak-Dala

Steppenwolf author 5 Hesse

stereotypical 4 hack **5** stale, trite **6** cliché, common **7** clichéd **8** bathetic, shopworn, timeworn **9** hackneyed **11** commonplace

sterile 3 dry **4** arid, bare, dead, flat **5** stale, vapid **6** barren, effete, fallow, jejune **7** insipid, worn-out **8** desolate, impotent, infecund **9** fruitless, infertile **10** uncreative, unfruitful, uninspired, unoriginal, unprolific **12** unproductive

sterilize 3 fix **4** geld, spay **5** alter, unsex **6** change, neuter **8** caponize, castrate, mutilate, sanitate, sanitize **10** emasculate, poulardize

sterilized 7 aseptic

sterling 4 pure, true **5** noble **6** worthy **9** estimable, honorable

stern 4 grim **5** sober, stony **6** flinty, severe, strict **7** ascetic, austere **9** mortified **10** astringent, implacable, inexorable, inflexible **11** unrelenting

Sterope *father:* **5** Atlas *mother:* **7** Pleione *sisters:* **8** Pleiades

Stevenson novel 9 Kidnapped

stew 4 boil, brew, cark, flap, fret, fume, fuss, hash, olio, olla, slum, snit **5** civet, daube, salmi, sweat, tizzy, worry **6** burgoo, dither, jumble, lather, medley, paella, pother, ragout, salmis, scouse, seethe, simmer, swivet, tumult **7** goulash, mélange, parboil, puchero, turmoil **8** mishmash, mulligan, pot-au-feu **9** agitation, Brunswick, cassoulet, commotion, confusion, pasticcio, potpourri **10** capilotade, hodgepodge, hotchpotch, miscellany, turbulence **11** olla podrida, ratatouille, slumgullion

steward 6 manage **7** manager

Stheno see **Gorgon**

stick 3 bar, dig, fix, gag, get, jib, lay, nod, put, ram, rod, run, set, shy **4** balk, beat, clip, glue, milk, pole, rook, sink, skin, slab, soak, stab **5** affix, baton, bleed, blind, cling, decoy, demur, drive, ingot, mulct, paste, place, shill, strip, stump, sweat **6** adhere, attach, billet, boggle, capper, cement, cleave, cohere, fasten, fleece, plunge, settle, strain, thrust **7** buffalo, nonplus, scruple, stumble **9** establish, shillaber **10** overcharge *combining form:* **5** rhabd **6** rhabdo

stick around 4 bide, stay, wait **5** abide, tarry **6** linger, remain

sticker 4 seal **5** stamp

stick-in-the-mud 4 fogy **6** fogram, fossil, square **8** mossback **10** fuddy-duddy

stick out 3 jut **4** bear, poke, pout, push, take **5** abide, brook, bulge, pouch, stand **6** beetle, endure, strike **7** project, protend, stomach, support **8** overhang, protrude, tolerate **9** outthrust **10** outstretch

stick up 3 rob **4** loot **5** rifle **7** plunder, ransack, relieve **9** knock over

sticky 4 hard **5** gluey, gooey, gummy, heavy, humid, muggy, mushy, rough, soggy, tacky **6** cloggy, knotty, resiny, rugged, slushy, stodgy, sultry, viscid **7** maudlin, mawkish, operose, viscous **8** adhesive, bathetic, resinous, romantic **9** difficult, laborious, strenuous **10** formidable **11** sentimental, tear-jerking

stiff 3 dry, set **4** arid, body, dull, hard, lush, mort, skin **5** drunk, miser, nabal, rigid, stark, steep, stock, tense, undue **6** boozer, corpse, mulish, wooden **7** buckram, cadaver, carcass, extreme, guzzler, muddled, niggard, scrooge, stilted, studied, swiller **8** drunkard, hardened, tightwad, towering **9** cardboard, disguised, excessive, impliable, inebriate, inelastic, obstinate, petrified, pixilated, resistant, skinflint, unbending **10** boozehound, bullheaded, cheapskate, exorbitant, hardheaded, immoderate, inebriated, inflexible, inordinate, mechanical, self-willed, unflexible, unyielding **11** extravagant, immalleable, incompliant, intoxicated, intractable **12** closed-minded, pertinacious

stiffen 6 harden, tauten **7** bolster, buckram, support, thicken **8** rigidify, solidify **9** constrict, formalize, stabilize **10** immobilize

stifle 4 mute **5** burke, choke **6** dampen, deaden, hush up, muffle **7** smother, trammel **8** stagnate, stultify, suppress **9** suffocate **10** asphyxiate

stigma 4 blot, blur, onus, slur, spot **5** brand, odium, shame, stain, taint **6** smudge, smutch **8** black eye, disgrace, dishonor, tainting **11** bar sinister **12** besmirchment

stigmatize 7 censure **8** denounce, identify **9** designate

still 3 too, yet **4** also, balm, calm, even, hush, lull, more **5** allay, along, quiet, shush, whist **6** as well, becalm, hushed, placid,

serene, settle, shut up, silent, though, withal **7** besides, compose, deathly, halcyon, howbeit, however, hushful, silence **8** after all, choke off, likewise, moreover, peaceful, quietude, stagnant, tranquil **9** deathlike, noiseless, quietness, soundless **10** motionless, untroubled **11** furthermore, nonetheless, tranquilize, unperturbed **12** additionally, nevertheless

stilt 4 bird, pole **8** longlegs

stilted 4 prim **6** formal, la-di-da, too-too, wooden **7** aureate, buckram, flowery, genteel **8** affected, decorous, sonorous **9** bombastic, cardboard **10** euphuistic

stilt-like bird 6 avocet

stimulant 4 goad, spur **7** caffein, impetus, impulse **8** caffeine, catalyst, excitant **9** incentive **10** incitation, incitement, motivation

stimulate 4 move **5** pique, rouse, set up **6** arouse, excite, vivify **7** commove, enliven, innerve, inspire, provoke, quicken **8** activate, dynamize, energize, motivate, spirit up, vitalize **9** galvanize, innervate **10** exhilarate

stimulus 4 goad, push, spur **5** boost, cause **6** motive, urging **7** impetus, impulse, piquing **8** catalyst, stressor **9** incentive **10** excitement, incitation, incitement, inducement, invitation, motivation, propellant **11** instigation, provocation, provocative **13** encouragement

sting 4 bite, burn **5** smart

stinging 8 aculeate

stingy 4 mean **5** close, scant, tight **6** frugal, narrow, scrimy **7** chinchy, costive, miserly, niggard, save-all, scrimpy, sparing, thrifty **8** pinching, ungiving **9** niggardly, penny-wise, penurious **10** economical, hardfisted, hardhanded, ironfisted, pinchpenny, ungenerous **11** closefisted, tightfisted **12** cheeseparing, parsimonious **13** narrowhearted, penny-pinching

stink 4 funk, reek **5** smell **6** stench **7** malodor **8** malaroma

stinker 3 cur, dog **4** scum, snot **5** skunk, snake

stinking see smelly

stinky see smelly

stint 2 go **3** job **4** bout, duty, task, time, tour, turn **5** chare, chore, cramp, pinch, scant, screw, share, shift, short, skimp, spare, spell, trick **6** amount, devoir, scrape, scrimp, skinch **8** quantity **9** allotment, stricture **10** assignment, limitation **11** restriction

stipend 3 fee, pay **4** hire, wage **5** award **6** salary **7** payment **9** emolument **13** consideration

stipple 3 dot **5** speck **6** pepper, streak **7** freckle, speckle **8** sprinkle **9** bespeckle

stipulate 5 state **6** detail **7** provide, specify **9** designate **13** particularize

stipulation 5 limit, terms 7 proviso, strings 9 provision

stir 3 ado, can, din, jug, mix, pen, set 4 abet, boil, fuss, jail, keep, moil, move, rout, wake, whet 5 awake, churn, drive, impel, raise, rally, rouse, roust, set on, waken, whirl 6 arouse, awaken, bubble, bustle, excite, flurry, foment, furore, hubbub, incite, kindle, motion, pother, seethe, simmer, tumult, whip up 7 actuate, agitate, ferment, inspire, provoke, quicken 8 activate, energize, movement, vitalize 9 agitation, challenge, commotion, galvanize, instigate, stimulate 11 disturbance, pandemonium

stirrup 6 stapes

stithy 5 anvil

stock 4 clan, folk, fund, have, hope, keep, race 5 carry, faith, hoard, house, tribe, trust 6 family, supply 7 backlog, furnish, kindred, lineage, nest egg, reserve 8 estimate, judgment, reliance 9 appraisal, inventory, reservoir 10 assessment, confidence, dependence, estimation, evaluation

stockade 3 can, jug 4 coop, jail 6 cooler, lockup, prison 8 hoosegow 9 calaboose, guardroom

stock exchange 6 bourse

stockings 4 hose 7 hosiery

stockpile 4 bank, heap, hill, hive, mass 5 amass, drift, hoard, lay up, mound, stack, store, uplay 6 garner, roll up 7 backlog, nest egg, pyramid, reserve, store up 8 cumulate, mountain 9 inventory, reservoir 10 accumulate

stocky 3 fat 5 bunty, cobby, dumpy, lumpy, plump, pudgy, short, squab, squat, thick 6 chuffy, chumpy, chunky, low-set, squdgy, stubby, stuggy, stumpy 7 lumpish 8 heavyset, thickset 9 corpulent 11 thickbodied

stodge 4 cloy, fill, flut, jade, pall, plod, sate, slog, slop, toil 5 gorge 6 trudge 7 filling, satiate, surfeit 8 footslog, plunther

stodgy 4 blah, dull 5 dowdy, dumpy, gluey, gooey, gummy, heavy, tacky 6 boring, claggy, clarty, cloggy, dreary, frumpy, sticky 7 humdrum, weighty 8 banausic, frumpish, outmoded, pedantic, plodding 9 hidebound, out-of-date, ponderous, unstylish 10 monotonous, pedestrian, unexciting

stoic 3 dry 5 aloof 7 patient, Spartan 8 detached, resigned 9 apathetic, impassive 10 phlegmatic 11 indifferent, indomitable, unconcerned

stoicism 4 grit, guts, sand 5 pluck 6 apathy 8 backbone 9 fortitude, stolidity 11 impassivity 13 insensibility *founder:* 4 Zeno

stoke 4 feed, poke, stir, tend 6 supply

Stoker, Bram *novel:* 7 Dracula

stolid 3 dry 4 dull, dumb, slow 5 blunt, dense, inert 6 bovine, obtuse, supine 7 passive 8 inactive, rocklike 9 apathetic, impassive 10 phlegmatic

stomach 3 gut 4 bear, craw, take 5 abide, belly, brook, stand, taste, tummy 6 digest, endure, paunch, venter 7 abdomen, swallow 8 appetite, tolerate 9 appetence *combining form:* 5 gastr 6 gaster, gastro, ventri, ventro 7 gastero, gastria *enzyme:* 6 pepsin, rennin *muscle:* 7 pylorus *ruminant:* 5 rumen 6 omasum 8 abomasum 9 reticulum *Scottish:* 4 kyte

stomachache 5 colic, gripe 6 misery 8 distress 12 collywobbles

stomp 5 tramp 7 trample

stone 3 gem 4 buhr, rock 5 lapis, logan, stane 6 pebble, testis 7 boulder, lapides (plural), surface 8 calculus *base:* 6 plinth *block of:* 8 monolith *combining form:* 4 lite, lith, lyte *cosmic:* 6 meteor 9 chondrite, meteorite *for grinding grains:* 6 metate *fruit:* 5 drupe *memorial:* 7 obelisk *monument:* 8 megalith *of a fruit:* 3 pit 6 pyrene *precious:* 6 ligure

____ **Stone** 7 Blarney, Rosetta

stonecrop 5 sedum

stoned 4 high 5 boozy, doped, drunk 6 canned, lushed, zonked 7 drugged, muddled 8 hopped-up, turned on, wiped out 9 disguised, pixilated, plastered, spaced-out 10 inebriated, tripped out 11 intoxicated

stonelike 7 lithoid

Stooge 3 Moe (Howard) 5 Curly (Howard), Larry (Fine)

stool pigeon 3 rat 4 fink, nark, pimp, sing 5 peach 6 canary, inform, snitch, squeak, squeal 7 tipster

stoop 3 dip 4 duck, sink, thaw 5 deign, favor, kneel, porch, relax 6 accord, crouch, oblige, unbend 7 concede, descend, portico 10 condescend 11 accommodate

stop 3 bar, can, dam, end, see 4 balk, call, clog, fill, halt, plug, quit, stay, stem, wall 5 block, brake, cease, check, choke, close, stall, tarry 6 arrest, cut off, desist, draw up, ending, haul up, hinder, kibosh, lay off, pull up, stanch 7 barrier, break up, bring up, closing, congest, disrupt, occlude, prevent, shut off, sojourn, suspend, turn off 8 blockade, knock off, leave off, obstruct, surcease 9 barricade, cessation, interrupt, roadblock, terminate 10 conclusion, desistance, standstill 11 discontinue, refrain from, termination *blood:* 6 stanch *up:* 4 cork, plug 7 occlude 8 obturate

stopgap 5 shift 6 refuge, resort 8 recourse, resource 9 expedient, makeshift 10 expediency, substitute 11 provisional

stopover 5 visit 7 sojourn 9 tarriance *for troops:* 5 étape

stoppage 6 strike *combining form:* 5 stasi 6 stases (plural), stasia, stasis *work:* 6 hartal, strike

stopper 4 clog, fill, plug 5 block, choke, close 7 congest, occlude 8 obstruct

store 3 bin 4 fund, hive, pack, shop, tank 5 amass, cache, depot, hoard, lay up, stash 6 bestow, bought, garner, market, outlet, roll up, shoppe, supply 7 arsenal, backlog, deposit, nest egg, reserve 8 cumulate, emporium, magazine, mothball, showroom, squirrel 9 inventory, reservoir, stockpile, warehouse 10 accumulate, depository, repository *candle:* 9 chandlery *in a silo:* 6 ensile 8 ensilage *shoe:* 7 bootery

storehouse 5 depot 7 arsenal, granary 8 magazine 10 depository, repository

storekeeper 8 merchant

storeroom 6 larder, pantry 7 buttery

storm 4 hail, to-do 5 beset, buran, burst, salvo 6 assail, attack, bustle, clamor, easter, fall on, hassle, hubbub, pother, strike, volley 7 aggress, assault, barrage, clatter, ruction, typhoon 8 drumfire, fall upon 9 broadside, cannonade, commotion, fusillade 10 hurly-burly 11 bombardment

storm trooper 10 brownshirt

stormy 4 foul, wild 5 dirty, dusty, murky, rough 6 raging 7 furious, howling, roaring 8 blustery 9 turbulent 10 blustering, riproaring 11 tempestuous, threatening

story 3 fib, lie 4 tale, yarn 5 conte, fable 6 canard, legend, report 7 account, falsity, fiction, märchen, untruth, version 8 allegory, anecdote, folktale 9 chronicle, fairy tale, falsehood, narration, narrative 11 description, fabrication 13 prevarication *involved:* 8 megillah *moral:* 7 parable *short:* 5 conte 8 anecdote

storyteller 4 liar 6 fibber 8 fabulist 9 raconteur

stoup 4 font 5 basin 6 flagon 7 tankard

stout 3 fat 4 bold, hard 5 brave, heavy, obese, tough 6 fleshy, heroic, portly, strong, sturdy 7 porcine, valiant, weighty 8 fearless, intrepid, resolute, stalwart, valorous 9 corpulent, steadfast, tenacious 10 courageous, invincible, overweight 11 indomitable, thick-bodied

Stout detective 5 Wolfe (Nero)

stouthearted 4 bold 5 brave 7 doughty, valiant 8 fearless, intrepid, unafraid 9 dauntless, undaunted 10 courageous

stove 4 kiln 5 range 8 potbelly

stow 4 pack 5 steeve 9 warehouse

stower 9 stevedore

Stowe work 4 Dred

strabismus 6 squint

straddle 6 ramble, sprawl, stride 8 bestride, scramble, sprangle 11 spread-eagle

straggle 4 roam, rove 5 drift, range, stray 6 ramble, wander 7 maunder, meander

straight 4 fair, good, neat, pure 5 plain, right 6 at once, direct, honest, linear, square 7 unmixed 8 directly, first off, orthodox 9 forthwith, instanter, right away, undiluted 10 aboveboard, button-down, forthright, unmodified 11 immediately 12 concentrated, conventional, plain dealing 13 unadulterated, undeviatingly, uninterrupted *combining form:* 4 orth, rect 5 ortho, recti

straightaway 3 now 6 at once 8 directly, first off 9 forthwith, instanter 11 immediately

straightedge 5 razor

straighten 5 align 6 unbend, uncurl *up:* 4 tidy

straightforward 5 frank 6 candid, direct, honest 7 precise 8 clearcut 9 outspoken 11 undeviating

strain 3 air, irk, lay, try, tug 4 hint, mind, moil, mood, ooze, pull, seep, toil, tone, tune, vein, work 5 drive, labor, shade, sweat, tinge, touch, trace 6 harass, melody, streak, stress, strive, warble 7 descant, measure, melisma, soupçon, tension, trouble 8 diapason, distress, pressure, transude 9 suspicion 10 suggestion

strait 4 bind, pass 5 pinch 6 crisis 7 squeeze 8 exigency, hardship, juncture 9 crossroad, emergency 10 difficulty, perplexity 11 contingency *Adriatic Sea-Ionian Sea:* 7 Otranto *Africa-Madagascar:* 10 Mozambique *Alaska:* 3 Icy *Alaska-Russia:* 6 Bering *Albania-Greece:* 5 Corfu *Asia-Europe:* 11 Dardanelles *Atlantic-Baffin Island:* 5 Davis *Atlantic-Gulf of Mexico:* 7 Florida *Atlantic-Mediterranean:* 9 Gibraltar *Atlantic-Nantucket Sound:* 8 Muskeget *Atlantic-North Sea:* 7 English *Atlantic-Pacific:* 5 Drake 8 Magellan *Atlantic-Saint Lawrence:* 5 Cabot *Baffin Island-Quebec:* 6 Hudson *Bering Sea-Sea of Okhotsk:* 5 Kuril 6 Kurile *Bismarck Sea-Solomon Sea:* 6 Vitiaz *Canada:* 3 Rae 5 Dease *East China Sea:* 5 Korea 8 Tsushima *East China-South China:* 6 Taiwan 7 Formosa *England-France:* 5 Dover *Flores Sea-Indian Ocean:* 4 Sape *Flores Sea-Savu Sea:* 4 Alor *Indian Ocean-Java Sea:* 5 Sunda *India-Sri Lanka:* 4 Palk *Indonesia:* 4 Alas, Alor, Bali 5 Tioro 6 Lombok 7 Dampier, Makasar 8 Makassar, Surabaja *Inner Hebrides:* 5 Tiree *Iran-Oman:* 6 Hormuz *Italy:* 7 Messina *Japan:* 4 Yura 5 Bungo, Kitan 7 Hayasui *Japan-Sakhalin Island:* 4 Soya *Lake Huron:* 10 Mississagi *Lake Huron-Lake Michigan:* 8 Mackinac *Malay Archipelago:* 5 Wetar *Malaysia-Singapore:* 6 Johore *Malay-Sumatra:* 7 Malacca *New Jersey-Staten Island:* 7 van Kull *New South Wales-Tasmania:* 4 Bass *New Zealand:* 4 Cook *Northwest Territories:* 6 Barrow 8 Franklin, Victoria 13 Prince of Wales *Nova Scotia:* 5 Canso *Pacific-San Francisco Bay:* 10 Golden Gate *Pacific-South China Sea:* 5 Luzon *Philippines:* 5 Bohol, Tanon 7 Iloilo 7 Basilan *Russia:* 4 Kara *Suvu Sea-Timor Sea:* 4 Roti *Sea of Azov-Black Sea:* 5 Kerch 7 Enikale *Sea of Japan:* 5 Tatar *Solomon Islands:* 12 Bougainville *South China Sea:* 7 Mindoro 9 Singapore *Turkey:* 8 Bosporus 9 Karadeniz *Vancouver-Washington:* 10 Juan de Fuca *Wales:* 5 Menai *Washington Sound:* 4 Haro

straitlaced 4 prig, prim 6 narrow, prissy, strict, stuffy 7 genteel, prudish 8 priggish, rigorous 9 hidebound, Victorian 10 intolerant 11 puritanical 12 narrow-minded

strand 4 bank 5 beach, coast, shore, wreck 6 pile up 8 cast away 9 shipwreck

strange 3 new, odd 5 alien, crazy, fishy, funny, kinky, kooky, nutty, outré, queer, weird 6 exotic, far-out, freaky, quaint 7 amazing, bizarre, curious, erratic, oddball, offbeat, uncanny, uncouth, unknown, unusual 8 aberrant, abnormal, atypical, peculiar, romantic, singular, wondrous 9 eccentric, fantastic, grotesque, marvelous, wonderful 10 astounding, miraculous, mysterious, off-the-wall, outlandish, stupendous, surprising, unfamiliar 11 astonishing, exceptional, spectacular 12 unaccustomed 13 idiosyncratic *combining form:* 3 xen 4 xeno

Strange Interlude author 6 O'Neill

stranger 4 unco 5 alien 7 inconnu, visitor 8 outcomer, outsider, wanderer 9 auslander, foreigner, immigrant, transient

strangle 5 burke, choke, shush 6 garote, muffle, quelch 7 garotte, garrote 8 suppress, throttle

strapping 6 robust

stratagem 4 play, plot, ploy, ruse, wile 5 feint, trick 6 device, gambit 8 artifice, intrigue, maneuver 10 conspiracy 11 machination

strategy 4 plan 6 design, scheme 7 project 8 game plan 9 blueprint

stratum 3 bed 5 layer

Strauss *opera:* 6 Salome 7 Elektra 13 Rosenkavalier *tone poem:* 7 Don Juan 10 Don Quixote

straw 3 sow 5 blond 6 flaxen, golden, thatch *braided:* 6 sennit *bundle:* 8 win-

dling *Japanese:* 4 toyo *mat:* 6 tatami *plaited:* 7 leghorn

stray 3 err, gad 4 roam, rove 5 range 6 depart, errant, ramble, random, wander 7 deviate, devious, digress, diverge, erratic, excurse, meander, runaway, traipse 8 divagate, sporadic 9 gallivant, wandering

streak 4 hint, spot, vein 5 fleck, shade, tinge, touch, trace 6 dapple, marble, mottle, strain, strake, stripe 7 striate 8 tincture 9 suspicion, variegate 10 intimation, suggestion *of color:* 5 vitta

streaked 8 brindled, grizzled

stream 3 run 4 burn, flow, flux, gill, gush, pour, race, roll, rush, tide 5 bourn, brook, creek, drift, flood, spate, surge 6 bourne, branch, rindle, runlet, runnel, sluice 7 current, rivulet 8 affluent *combining form:* 5 fluvi 6 fluvio *rapid:* 7 torrent *small:* 4 sike, syke *verbal:* 10 blue streak

streamer 4 flag, jack 5 color 6 banner, ensign, pennon 7 pendant, pennant 8 banderol, bannerol, standard

streamline 8 simplify

street 3 way 4 drag, path, road 5 drive, track 6 artery, avenue, ruelle 7 highway, roadway 9 boulevard 12 thoroughfare *border:* 7 curbing *material:* 6 cobble 7 asphalt 11 cobblestone *narrow:* 4 wynd *show:* 5 raree

streetcar 4 tram 7 trolley

Streetcar Named Desire, A *author:* 8 Williams *character:* 6 Stella 7 Blanche, Stanley

Street Scene author 4 Rice

strength 5 brawn, force, might, power, sense, sinew 6 burden, energy, muscle 7 potency, purport 8 firmness, security 9 soundness, stability, substance, toughness 10 stableness, steadiness, sturdiness

strengthen 4 beef, gird 5 brace, ready, sinew, steel 6 anneal, tone up 7 animate, chirk up, ensteel, fortify, hearten, prepare, support, toughen 8 embolden, energize, fortress, inspirit 9 encourage, enhearten, reinforce, undergird 10 invigorate

strenuous 4 hard, mean 5 lusty, tough, vital 6 uphill, wicked 7 dynamic, operose, toilful 8 toilsome, vigorous 9 difficult, effortful, energetic, Herculean, laborious

Strephon 8 shepherd *beloved:* 5 Chloe 6 Urania

stress 3 irk, try 4 pain 5 pinch 6 accent, burden, harass, import, play up, strain, weight 7 feature, tension, trouble 8 emphasis, pressure 9 emphasize, italicize, underline 10 importance, underscore 12 accentuation *in poetry:* 5 ictus

stretch 3 run 4 area, draw, time 5 fudge, range, reach, scope, space, spell, sweep, tract, while 6 extend, extent, length, limber, region, spread, supple, whippy **7** breadth, compass, draw out, elastic, expanse, magnify, prolong, purview, spin out, springy, tighten **8** distance, elongate, flexible, lengthen, protract **9** amplitude, dimension, embellish, embroider, expansion, overstate, resilient **10** exaggerate *on a frame:* **6** tenter *out:* **3** lie **4** rest **6** repose, sprawl

stretchable 7 elastic, tensile **8** tensible

stretched 4 taut

stretcher 5 dooly **6** dhooly, gurney, leader, litter **7** tail fly **8** tall tale

strew 3 sow **4** dust **5** cover **6** pepper, spread **7** diffuse, disject, radiate, scatter **8** disperse, sprinkle **9** broadcast, circulate, dissipate, propagate **10** distribute **11** disseminate

strict 4 dour, grim, just, true **5** harsh, right, rigid, tough **8** exacting, faithful, rigorous **9** draconian, unsparing, veracious, veridical **10** forbidding, hard-boiled, ironhanded, oppressive **11** undistorted **12** unpermissive

stricture 4 slam, slur **5** cramp, stint **7** obloquy **9** aspersion **10** limitation, reflection **11** restriction **12** ball and chain **13** animadversion

stride 5 march, sling, stalk **8** straddle

strident 4 loud **5** harsh **6** hoarse **7** blatant, dinsome, grating, jarring, rasping, raucous, squawky **9** clamorous **10** boisterous, stentorian, stertorous, vociferant, vociferous **11** loudmouthed **12** obstreperous

strife 4 fray **5** brawl, broil, fight **6** affray, combat, fracas **7** contest, discord, dispute, dissent, quarrel, rivalry, warfare, wrangle **8** argument, conflict, disunity, squabble, tug-of-war, variance **9** disaccord, emulation **10** contention, difference, dissension, dissidence **11** altercation, competition, controversy

strike 3 hit, pop, rap **4** bang, bash, beat, dash, deal, ding, give, kick, knap, mace, poke, rack, slam, slap, slog, slug, sock, swat, whap, whop **5** beset, carry, clout, crash, flick, knack, knock, occur, punch, smack, smite, storm, swipe, thump, whack **6** affect, assail, attack, cudgel, fall on, fillip, hammer, harrow, pummel, thrash **7** afflict, aggress, assault, deliver, impress, inflict, inspire, percuss, torment, torture **8** fall upon **9** detection, discovery, influence

striking 5 showy, vivid **6** cogent, marked, signal **7** salient, telling **8** forceful, powerful **9** arresting, arrestive, prominent **10** compelling, noticeable, remarkable **11** conspicuous, outstanding

Strindberg play 6 Easter **8** Comrades **9** Miss Julie, The Father **10** Master Olaf **12** Dance of Death, Gustavus Vasa, The Creditors

string 3 row **4** file, line, rank, tier **5** chain, order, queue, shift, train **6** refuge, resort, sequel, series **7** echelon, stopgap **8** recourse, resource, sequence **9** expedient, makeshift **10** substitude, succession *up:* **4** hang **5** noose, scrag **6** gibbet

string along 3 toy **4** fool **5** dally, flirt **6** coquet, lead on, trifle, wanton

stringent see **strict**

stringy 4 ropy, wiry **6** sinewy **7** fibrous **8** muscular

strip 3 bar, rod **4** band, bare, doff, flay, husk, peel, sack, skin, slab **5** ingot, scale, stick, waste **6** billet, denude, devest, divest, expose, fillet, flitch, ravage, ribbon **7** bandeau, banding, deprive, disrobe, pillage, take off, uncover, undress **8** bankrupt, denudate, desolate, spoliate, unclothe **9** depredate, desecrate, devastate, dismantle **11** decorticate, excorticate *leather:* **5** thong *of wood:* **4** lath, slat *skin:* **6** flench, flense

stripe 3 ilk **4** band, flog, hide, kind, lash, sort, type, whip **5** breed, order, whale **6** fillet, kidney, lather, ribbon, strake, streak, thrash **7** bandeau, banding, feather, scourge, species, variety **10** flagellate

stripling 3 boy, lad

stripper 6 peeler, teaser **9** ecdysiast

stripteaser see **stripper**

strive 3 try, tug, vie **4** cope, moil, seek, toil, work **5** assay, essay, labor, offer **6** resist, strain **7** attempt, travail **8** endeavor, struggle **9** undertake

stroke 3 hit, pet **4** hone, whet **6** caress, soothe **8** apoplexy **9** heartbeat

stroll 4 mope, muck, turn, walk **5** amble, drift, mosey, paseo **6** bummel, linger, ramble **7** saunter

stroller 4 pram **5** tramp **6** go-cart **7** vagrant

strong 4 fast, firm, hard, rich, sure **5** hardy, large, lusty, stout, tough **6** ardent, brawny, heroic, mighty, potent, robust, rugged, secure, sinewy, stable, sturdy, wieldy **7** durable, staunch, unmixed **8** enduring, forceful, muscular, powerful, stalwart, straight, vigorous **9** strapping, tenacious, undiluted **10** able-bodied, full-bodied, spirituous **12** concentrated

strong-arm 5 bully **6** bounce, hector **7** dragoon **8** bludgeon, browbeat, bulldoze, bullyrag **9** terrorize **10** intimidate

strongbox 6 coffer

stronghold 4 fort **7** citadel, redoubt **8** fastness, fortress

strong point 5 forte

strong suit 5 forte **6** medium, métier, oyster **8** eminency

strontium *symbol:* 2 Sr

strophe 6 stanza

structure 4 form, pile **5** build, frame **6** fabric, format, makeup, system **7** anatomy, complex, edifice, network **8** building, erection, skeleton **9** framework **10** morphology **11** arrangement, composition **12** construction *combining form:* **5** morph **6** morpho

struggle 3 try, vie **4** agon **5** assay, essay, offer, trial **6** hassle, strive, tussle **7** attempt, compete, grapple, scuffle **8** endeavor, flounder, striving **9** undertake **11** undertaking

strumpet 4 jade, slut **5** hussy, tramp, trull, wench **6** harlot, wanton **7** jezebel, trollop **8** slattern

strut 6 flaunt, parade, prance, sashay **7** flounce, peacock, swagger

stub 4 snag **5** fence, guard **6** strike **9** pulverize

stubborn 5 balky, rigid, stunt **6** dogged, mulish, ornery, wilful **7** adamant, bullish, wayward, willful **8** obdurate **9** obstinate, pigheaded, steadfast, unbending **10** bullheaded, headstrong, inexorable, inflexible, rebellious, refractory, relentless, unyielding **11** intractable **12** cantankerous, contumacious, single-minded

stubby 5 dumpy, puggy, squat **6** chumpy, chunky, squdgy, stocky, stuggy, stumpy **7** puggish **8** heavyset **11** thick-bodied

stuck-up 4 vain **8** conceity **9** conceited **12** narcissistic, vainglorious

stud 3 dot **4** male, nail, post, spot **5** cleat **6** button, pillar, pimple **7** speckle, upright **8** sprinkle

student 5 pupil **6** premed **7** protégé *college:* **13** undergraduate *combining form:* **3** log **5** logue *female:* **4** coed *first-year:* **8** freshman *fourth-year:* **6** senior *French:* **5** élève **8** étudiant *military:* **5** cadet *Muslim:* **5** softa *naval officer:* **5** middy **10** midshipman *of a guru:* **5** chela *placement:* **8** tracking *second-year:* **9** sophomore *third-year:* **6** junior *wandering:* **7** goliard

studio 4 shop **7** atelier, bottega **8** workroom, workshop

Studs Lonigan creator 7 Farrell

study 3 con, vet **4** heed, mind, muse, view **5** learn, weigh **6** debate, lesson, musing, ponder, survey, trance **7** analyze, canvass, check up, examine, inspect, reverie **8** consider, exercise, memorize, think out, weighing **9** attention, check over, pondering, think over **10** excogitate, meditation, rumination, scrutinize **11** abstraction, application, contemplate **12** deliberation **13** concentration, consideration, contemplation *combining form:* **5** sophy *group:* **7** seminar *hard:* **4** cram *suffix:* **3** ics

stuff 3 jam, ram **4** cram, pith, soul, tamp **5** being, crowd, gorge **6** entity, marrow, matter, object, things **7** essence, jam-pack **8** material, overcram, overfill **9** substance

10 individual, virtuality **12** essentiality, quintessence

stuffed shirt 4 prig, smug **5** Blimp, prude **7** diehard **10** fuddy-duddy **12** Colonel Blimp

stuffing 3 gut, tar **6** tripes **7** innards, insides, inwards, pudding, viscera **8** dressing, entrails **9** internals

stuffy 4 dull, prim **5** close, fuggy, heavy, humid, stivy, thick, wiggy **6** narrow, prissy, proper, shut-up, stodgy, sultry **7** airless, bloated, genteel, humdrum, pompous, prudish **8** arrogant, priggish, stagnant, stifling **9** hidebound, illiberal, important, Victorian **10** breathless, oppressive, pontifical, tight-laced **11** magisterial, puritanical, straitlaced, suffocating **12** narrow-minded **13** self-important

stultify 4 dull **5** check **6** deaden, impair, stifle, weaken **7** inhibit, nullify, repress, smother, trammel **8** enfeeble, restrain, stagnate, suppress **9** suffocate **10** constipate, discourage, invalidate

stumble 3 err, sin **4** slip, trip **5** demur, error **6** falter **7** blunder, scruple, stagger, stammer **8** hesitate

stump 3 get **4** beat, dare, defi, defy **5** barge, stick **6** cartel, lumber **7** buffalo, galumph, nonplus **8** defiance **9** challenge

stun 4 daze **5** amaze **6** bedaze, bemuse, benumb, dazzle **7** astound, nonplus, petrify, stupefy **8** bewilder, knock out, paralyze **11** flabbergast

stunt 4 curb, feat **5** check, dwarf, runty, trick **6** impair, runted **7** runtish, scrunty **8** hold back, suppress

stupefy 4 daze, dull, faze **5** addle, blunt **6** bedaze, bemuse, benumb, rattle **7** nonplus, petrify **8** hebetate, paralyze

stupendous 7 amazing, massive **8** cracking, towering, wondrous **9** fantastic, marvelous, monstrous, wonderful **10** astounding, miraculous, monumental, prodigious, staggering **11** astonishing, spectacular

stupid 4 dull, dumb, slow **5** brute, crass, dense, dopey, dummy, dunce, heavy, idiot, moron, silly, thick **6** dummel, goosey, oafish, simple, torpid **7** asinine, brutish, doltish, dullard, fatuous, foolish, idiotic, lumpish, pinhead **8** backward, blockish, comatose, dullhead, dumbbell, dummkopf, duncical, ignorant, retarded, sluggish **9** blear-eyed, fatheaded, half-assed, ignoramus, imbecilic, lethargic, lumbering, pinheaded, simpleton **10** beefheaded, beef-witted, half-witted, numskulled, slow-witted, slumberous **11** blockheaded, thickheaded, thick-witted **12** beetleheaded, hammerheaded, hebetudinous **13** chuckleheaded

stupor 4 coma **5** sleep **6** torpor **7** languor, slumber **8** dullness, hebetude, leth-

argy, narcosis **9** lassitude, torpidity
10 anesthesia **13** insensibility *combining
form:* **4** narc **5** narco
sturdy 5 sound, stout, tough **6** strong
7 healthy **8** stalwart **9** tenacious
11 substantial
sturgeon 6 beluga *roe:* **6** caviar **7** caviare
Sturm und Drang 6 unrest **7** ailment, ferment, turmoil **8** disquiet **10** inquietude
11 disquietude, restiveness **12** restlessness
St. Vitus' ___ 5 dance
sty 3 den, pen **4** dump, sink **5** Sodom
6 pigpen **7** cesspit, piggery **8** cesspool
stygian 7 avernal, hellish **8** infernal, plutonic **9** cimmerian, plutonian
11 pandemoniac
style 3 fad, way **4** chic, mode, rage, tone,
vein **5** craze, decor, thing, vogue **6** manner **7** fashion, wording **9** designate **10** dernier cri **11** appellation, appellative *hair:*
4 coif **8** coiffure *suffix:* **5** esque
stylish 2 in **3** mod, new **4** chic, posh, tony,
trig **5** doggy, natty, nifty, ritzy, sassy, sharp,
showy, sleek, slick, smart, swank, swell
6 chichi, classy, dapper, dressy, modern,
modish, new-day, rakish, snappy, snazzy,
spiffy, tonish, trendy, with-it **7** à la mode,
dashing, doggish, swagger **8** spiffing, up-to-
date **9** exclusive **10** newfangled **11** fashionable, modernistic, pretentious **12** new-
fashioned, ostentatious
Stymphalides' slayer 8 Heracles,
Hercules
styx 5 nymph, river **7** hateful *father:*
7 Oceanus *ferryman:* **6** Charon *location:*
5 Hades *mother:* **6** Tethys
Suah's father 6 Zophah
suave 5 bland, slick **6** genial, polite,
smooth, urbane **7** affable, cordial, courtly,
fulsome, politic, refined, tactful, worldly
8 cultured, gracious, polished, sociable, unctuous, well-bred **9** courteous, distingué
10 cultivated, diplomatic, soft-spoken
12 ingratiating **13** sophisticated
sub 5 under **6** fill-in **7** stand-in **9** alternate,
dependent, secondary **10** collateral
11 locum tenens, pinch hitter, replacement
subaltern 8 inferior **9** secondary,
underling
subdue 5 crush, quash, quell **6** defeat,
master, quench, reduce **7** conquer, put
down, squelch **8** bear down, beat down,
suppress, vanquish **9** overpower, subjugate
subdued 4 soft, tame **5** quiet, sober
6 low-key, mellow **7** neutral, serious **8** low-
keyed, softened, tasteful, tempered **9** mod-
erated, toned down **10** controlled,
restrained, submissive **11** inobtrusive,
unobtrusive
subjacent 3 low **5** lower, under **6** lesser,
nether **8** inferior

subject 3 apt **4** core, head, meat, open,
text **5** motif, point, prone, theme, topic,
under **6** expose, liable, likely, matter,
motive **7** citizen, exposed, lay open, problem, servile, slavish, uncover **8** argument,
material, notional, question **9** dependent,
leitmotif, leitmotiv, obnoxious, secondary,
sensitive, substance, tributary **10** collateral **11** subordinate, subservient,
susceptible
subjective 6 biased **10** prejudiced
subjugate see **subdue**
sublime 4 holy **5** erect, exalt, grand,
honor, ideal, lofty, noble, proud **6** august,
divine, sacred, superb **7** dignify, ennoble,
exalted, glorify, magnify **8** elevated,
glorious, gorgeous, majestic, splendid
9 spiritual **10** aggrandize **11** distinguish,
magnificent, resplendent, splendorous
12 transcendent **13** splendiferous
submerge 3 dip **4** duck, dunk, sink, soak
5 douse, drown, flood, souse, swamp,
whelm **6** deluge, drench, engulf, go down
7 founder, go under, immerse **8** inundate,
overflow, saturate
submerse see **submerge**
submissive 4 tame **6** menial **7** obeying,
servile, slavish, subdued, unerect
8 resigned, uxorious, yielding **9** complying
10 bowing down **11** acquiescent, conformable, subservient, unresistant, unresisting
12 nonresistant, nonresisting
submit 3 bow **4** cave, fall **5** bring, defer,
offer, refer, yield **6** go down, hand in, send
in, tender **7** deliver, go under, knuckle, present, proffer, provide, succumb, suggest
8 theorize **9** surrender **10** capitulate
11 buckle under **12** knuckle under
subordinate 5 minor, scrub, under
7 adjunct, subject **8** adjuvant, inferior, par-
ergal **9** accessory, auxiliary, dependent,
satellite, secondary, subaltern, tributary,
underling **10** collateral, subsidiary
suborn 6 incite, induce **9** instigate
sub rosa 8 covertly, in camera, secretly
9 by stealth, furtively, privately **10** stealthily **12** hugger-mugger **13** clandestinely
subscribe 3 ink, yes **4** sign **5** agree,
favor **6** accede, adhere, assent **7** approve,
consent, endorse **8** sanction **9** acquiesce,
autograph, signature **10** contribute
subsequent 4 next **5** after, later **6** serial
7 ensuing **9** following, posterior, resultant,
resulting, succedent **10** sequential, succeeding, successive **11** consecutive *prefix:* **4** post
subservient 4 mean **6** abject, menial
7 fawning, ignoble, servile, slavish **8** adjuvant, cowering, cringing, obeisant,
resigned **9** accessory, ancillary, auxiliary,

compliant, truckling **10** collateral, obsequious, submissive **11** acquiescent

subside 3 ebb **4** fall, lull, wane **5** abate, let up **7** die away, die down, ease off, slacken **8** moderate

subsidiary 5 minor **6** back-up **8** adjuvant **9** accessory, ancillary, tributary **10** collateral

subsidize 4 back, fund, help **5** endow **7** finance, promote

subsidy 4 gift **5** grant **6** reward **10** subvention **13** appropriation

subsist 2 be **4** live, move **7** breathe

subsistence 4 keep, salt **5** bread **6** living **7** alimony, support **10** sustenance **11** maintenance **12** alimentation

substance 3 nub **4** body, bulk, core, crux, gist, mass, meat, pith, soul **5** being, drift, focus, heart, point, sense, short, stuff, tenor, thing, worth **6** amount, bottom, burden, center, corpus, entity, import, kernel, marrow, matter, nubbin, object, riches, staple, thrust, upshot, wealth **7** essence, fortune, meaning, nucleus, purport **8** additive, material, property, strength, sum total **9** resources **10** individual, virtuality **12** essentiality, quintessence *combining form:* **3** hyl **4** hylo **5** phane, state *transparent:* **6** hyalin **7** hyaline

substantial 3 big **4** easy, snug, well **5** gross, solid **6** strong **7** weighty, well-off **8** material, physical, sensible, tangible, well-to-do **9** corporeal, important, momentous, objective, well-fixed **10** meaningful, phenomenal, prosperous, well-heeled **11** comfortable, significant **12** considerable

substantiate 3 try **4** test **5** prove **6** embody, verify **7** bear out, confirm, justify **8** manifest, validate **9** incarnate, objectify, personify, personize **11** corroborate, demonstrate, exteriorize, externalize, materialize, personalize **12** authenticate

substantive 4 firm, noun, real **5** solid **8** definite **9** essential

substitute 4 mock, sham, swap **5** dummy, false, locum, other, proxy, trade **6** back-up, change, deputy, double, ersatz, fill-in, refuge, resort, second, switch **7** another, replace, reserve, standby, stand-in, stopgap **8** exchange, recourse, resource, spurious, supplant **9** alternate, expedient, imitation, makeshift, simulated, surrogate **10** additional, artificial, expediency, suppletory, understudy **11** alternative, locum tenens, pinch hitter, replacement, succedaneum *combining form:* **5** pseud **6** pseudo *suffix:* **4** ette

substratum 4 base, core, meat, root, seat **5** basis, stuff **6** bottom, ground **7** bedrock, footing **10** foundation, groundwork **12** underpinning

substructure 4 base, seat **5** basis **6** bottom **10** foundation, groundwork

subsume 4 have **6** embody, take in **7** contain, embrace, include, involve **9** encompass **10** comprehend

subterfuge 5 cheat, fraud **6** dupery **7** chicane **8** trickery **9** chicanery, deception **10** dishonesty **11** highbinding **13** double-dealing

subterranean 4 cave **6** cavern, grotto **9** underfoot **10** underearth **11** underground

subtile 4 rare, thin **7** elusive, tenuous **8** rarefied

subtle 3 sly **4** deep, fine, foxy, nice, wily **6** artful, astute, crafty **7** cunning, logical, refined **8** analytic, delicate, finespun, guileful, hairline, skillful **9** dexterous, insidious **10** analytical

subtract 4 take **6** deduct **7** take off, take out **8** discount, draw back, knock off, take away

subtraction 6 rebate **8** discount **9** abatement *word:* **7** minuend **9** remainder

suburbs 7 fringes **8** environs, outskirt, purlieus

subversion 8 sabotage, wreckage, wrecking **10** destroying **11** demolishing, destruction, undermining

subvert 4 ruin **5** upset, wreck **6** debase **7** corrupt, deprave, destroy **8** demolish, overturn, sabotage **9** overthrow, undermine

subway *British:* **4** tube **11** underground *French:* **5** métro

succeed 2 go **4** boom **5** click, ensue, score **6** arrive, follow, go over, pan out, thrive, win out **7** catch on, come off, make out, prevail, prosper, triumph **8** flourish, get ahead, prove out **9** supervene **10** accomplish

success 3 hit **7** arrival, killing, triumph, victory **10** attainment, prosperity **11** achievement

successful 5 smash **7** notable **8** smashing, thriving **10** noteworthy, prosperous **11** flourishing

succession 3 row **5** chain, cycle, order, round, suite, train **6** course, sequel, series, string **8** sequence **11** consecution

succinct 4 curt **5** blunt, brief, short, terse **7** brusque, concise, laconic, summary **11** compendiary, compendious **12** breviloquent

succor 3 aid **4** hand, help, lift **6** assist, relief **7** comfort, secours, support **8** ministry **10** assistance, sustenance **11** maintenance, nourishment **12** ministration

succubus 5 demon, devil, fiend, Satan **9** archfiend

succulent 5 juicy, sappy

succumb 3 bow, die **4** cave, drop, fall, pass, wilt **5** defer, yield **6** cash in, cave in, demise, depart, expire, go down, peg out, perish, resign, submit **7** decease, give out, go under, knuckle **8** collapse, pass away **9** break down, surrender **10** capitulate **11** buckle under **12** knuckle under

such 4 akin, like, said, that **5** alike **7** similar **8** parallel **9** aforesaid, analogous **10** comparable, equivalent **13** corresponding

suck 3 lap, sip **4** draw **5** nurse **6** absorb, imbibe, inhale

sucker 3 gyp, sap **4** beat, bilk, dupe, fool, gull, mark **5** cheat, chump, cozen, leech **6** diddle, pigeon, sponge **7** defraud, fall guy, saphead, sponger **8** barnacle, hanger-on, parasite **9** schlemiel **10** freeloader

suckle 5 nurse **7** nourish **10** breast-feed

Sudan *capital:* **8** Khartoum *monetary unit:* **5** pound

sudden 4 fast **5** fleet, hasty, rapid, swift **6** abrupt **7** hurried, rushing **8** headlong **9** forthwith, impetuous, quickened **11** precipitant, precipitate, precipitous, subitaneous

suds 4 beer, foam, soap **5** froth, spume **6** lather

sue 3 woo **5** court, spark **6** appeal **7** address, implead **8** litigate, make up to, petition

suer 8 litigant

suet 3 fat **6** tallow *combining form:* **5** steat **6** steato

Suez Canal *builder:* **9** de Lesseps *city:* **8** Ismailia, Port Said

suffer 3 bow, let, see **4** bear, have, know, lump, take **5** abide, admit, allow, brook, leave, stand, yield **6** accept, endure, permit, submit **7** agonize, anguish, receive, stomach, sustain, swallow, undergo **8** tolerate **9** acquiesce **10** experience **11** countenance

sufferance 5 leave **6** permit **7** consent **8** sanction **10** permission **13** authorization

sufferer 6 victim *combining form:* **4** path

suffering 5 agony, dolor **6** misery **7** passion **8** distress **9** adversity **10** misfortune *combining form:* **5** pathy **6** pathic

suffice 2 do **5** serve **6** enough

sufficient 3 due **5** ample **6** common, decent, enough, plenty **8** adequacy, adequate, all right, pleasing **9** agreeable, competent, plenteous, plentiful, tolerable **10** acceptable, competence **11** comfortable **12** commensurate, satisfactory **13** commensurable, proportionate, unexceptional *poetic:* **4** enow

suffix *adjective:* **2** al, an, ar, er, ic, ly **3** ant, ary, ean, ent, ese, est, eth, fic, ful, ial, ian, ile, ine, ish, ist, oid, ory, ose, ous **4** able, eous, ible, ical, ious, less **5** ative, istic, oidal, ulent **6** escent, itious **7** istical *noun:* **2** ad,

al, cy, ee, er, et, il, on, or, th, ty **3** ade, ana, ant, ard, ata, ate, dom, een, eer, ery, ese, ice, ics, ier, ile, ine, ing, ion, ism, ist, ite, ity, ium, ive, ode, oma, ome, one, ote, sis **4** ance, ancy, ence, ency, esis, ette, etum, iana, itis, ling, ment, ness, osis, ship, ster, trix, tron **5** arian, arium, aster, ation, iasis, ician, onium, orium, tress **7** escence, isation, ization *verb:* **2** ed, en, fy, le **3** ate, ify, ing, ise, ize **4** lyse, lyze

suffocate 5 burke, choke, stive **6** stifle **7** quackle, smother **8** strangle **10** asphyxiate

suffrage 4 vote **5** voice **6** ballot **9** franchise

suffragist 4 Howe (Julia) **5** Stone (Lucy) **7** Anthony (Susan B.), Stanton (Elizabeth) **9** Pankhurst (Emmeline)

suffuse 5 imbue, steep **6** invest, leaven **7** ingrain **9** inoculate, interject, interpose, introduce

sugar 6 aldose, fucose, xylose **7** glucose, lactose, maltose, mannose, pentose, sorbose, sucrose, sweeten **8** fructose, furanose, levulose **10** saccharose *combining form:* **3** lyx **4** gluc, glyc, lyxo, sucr, thre **5** gluco, glyco, sucro, threo **7** sacchar **8** sacchari, saccharo *from palm sap:* **7** jaggery *Mexican:* **7** panocha, panoche *source:* **4** beet, cane, corn **5** maple *suffix:* **3** ose **5** ulose

sugarcane refuse 7 bagasse

sugarcoat 5 candy, honey, white **6** veneer, whiten **7** sweeten, varnish **8** palliate **9** extenuate, gloss over, gloze over, whitewash **10** blanch over, edulcorate

suggest 3 put **4** hint, pose **5** imply, point **6** prefer, submit **7** connote, propose **8** indicate, intimate, propound, theorize **9** adumbrate, insinuate

suggestion 3 cue **4** clue, hint, vein, wind **5** shade, smack, tinge, trace **6** advice, strain **7** inkling, proffer **8** allusion, innuendo, overtone, proposal, reminder, telltale **9** suspicion, undertone

suggestive 4 blue, racy, sexy **5** broad, salty, shady, spicy **6** erotic, purple, risqué, wicked **8** off-color **9** evocative

suicidal pilot 8 kamikaze

suicide 8 felo-de-se, hara-kiri **10** self-murder **13** self-slaughter *Japanese:* **7** seppuku

suit 2 do, go **3** fit **4** case, jibe, plea **5** adapt, agree, befit, cause, check, serve, tally **6** accord, action, adjust, appeal, asking, become, go with, orison, please, prayer, square, tailor **7** conform, enhance, flatter, lawsuit, request, satisfy, suffice **8** check out, entreaty, petition, quadrate **9** agree with, reconcile **10** go together, requesting, soliciting, tailor-make **11** accommodate, application, imploration, imprecation **12** solicitation, supplication **13** harmonize with *type:* **4** zoot **6** monkey, vested **9** paternity **10** pin-striped **11** class action

suitable 3 apt, due, fit **4** good, just, meet, nice **5** happy, right **6** proper, seemly, useful **7** condign, fitting, merited **8** deserved, eligible, rightful **9** requisite **10** convenient, felicitous **11** appropriate

suitcase 3 bag **4** grip **6** valise

suite 3 lot, row, set **4** body, flat, sort **5** array, batch, chain, group, rooms, train **6** clutch, parcel, rental, sequel, series, string **7** battery, lodging, retinue **8** chambers, sequence, tenement **9** apartment, entourage, following

suitor 4 beau **5** asker, lover, spark, swain, wooer **7** gallant, sparker **8** cavalier, paramour **9** boyfriend **10** petitioner

sulfur 9 brimstone *combining form:* **3** thi **4** thio

sulk 4 mope, pout **5** brood, frown, gloom, grump, scowl **6** glower

sulky 4 cart, dour, glum **5** huffy, moody, surly, testy **6** cranky, gloomy, morose, touchy **7** crabbed **9** irritable, querulous, saturnine **12** cantankerous

sullen 4 dour, glum, mean, sour, ugly **5** black, cross, moody, pouty, surly **6** crabby, gloomy, grumpy, morose **7** crabbed, cynical, fretful, hostile, mumpish, peevish, pouting **8** frowning, lowering, petulant, scowling **9** glowering, saturnine, tenebrose, tenebrous **10** ill-humored, malevolent, sourpussed, tenebrific **11** pessimistic

Sullivan's partner 7 Gilbert

sully 3 tar **4** soil **5** shame, smear, stain, taint **6** defile **7** besmear, pollute, tarnish **8** besmirch, discolor, disgrace

Sultan of Swat 8 Babe Ruth

sultry 3 hot **5** close, humid, livid, lurid, mucky, muggy, soggy, stivy **6** baking, redhot, sticky, stuffy, torrid **7** airless, burning, tabloid **8** broiling, sizzling, smothery, stifling **9** scorching **10** breathless, sweltering **11** sensational

sum 3 add, all, tot **4** bulk, mass, tote **5** gross, total, whole **6** amount, digest, entity, figure, resumé, system **7** epitome **8** condense, entirety, integral, nutshell, totality, totalize **9** aggregate, epitomize, integrate, inventory, synopsize *small:* **7** peanuts **8** pittance

Sumatra *country:* **9** Indonesia *highest peak:* **8** Kerintji *largest city:* **5** Medan *shrew:* **4** tana

Sumerian *city:* **2** Ur **4** Umma *dragon:* **3** Kur *god:* **2** An **3** Abu, Kur, Utu **4** Enki **5** Enlil, Lahar, Nanna, Nintu **6** Dumuzi, Nergal, Ninazu **7** Enkimdu *goddess:* **2** Ki **6** Ningal, Ninlil

summarize 5 brief, recap **6** digest, resumé **8** condense, nutshell **9** epitomize, inventory, synopsize **10** retrograde **12** recapitulate

summary 4 curt **5** brief, short, terse **6** aperçu, précis, resumé **7** compact, compend, concise, epitome, laconic, outline, roundup, rundown **8** drumhead, overview, scenario, succinct, synopses (plural), synopsis **9** compacted, inventory **11** compendiary, compendious **12** breviloquent

summerhouse 6 alcove, gazebo, pagoda **9** belvedere

summery 7 estival **8** aestival

summit 3 top **4** acme, apex, peak, roof **5** crest, crown **6** apogee, climax, vertex, zenith **8** capsheaf, capstone, meridian, pinnacle **9** fastigium **11** culmination *combining form:* **3** ace, acr, akr **4** acro, akro, apic **5** apici, apico

summon 3 bid **4** beck, call, cite **5** order **6** beckon, call in, enjoin, muster **7** command, conjure, convene, convoke, subpena **8** assemble, subpoena

sump 3 bog, fen **4** mire, quag **5** marsh, swamp **6** morass, slough **8** quagmire **9** swampland

sumptuous 4 lush, rich **5** grand, plush **6** Capuan, deluxe, lavish, superb **7** opulent **8** gorgeous, imposing, luscious, palatial, splendid **9** grandiose, luxuriant, luxurious **10** impressive **11** resplendent **12** aweinspiring

sun 3 orb, Sol **4** bask, star **7** daystar, phoebus **8** daylight, insolate, luminary, radiance **9** radiation **13** celestial body *combining form:* **4** heli **5** helio *disk:* **4** Aten *god:* **2** Ra **3** Lug, Sol, Tem, Utu **4** Amen, Atmu, Atum, Inti, Lleu, Llew, Lugh, Utug **5** Horus, Sunna, Surya **6** Apollo, Babbar, Helios, Marduk **7** Khepera, Ninurta, Phoebus, Shamash **8** Hyperion, Merodach

Sun Also Rises, The *author:* **9** Hemingway *character:* **6** Ashley (Brett), Barnes (Jake)

sunder 3 cut, rip **4** rend, rive **5** break, carve, sever, slice, split **6** cleave, divide **7** break up, disjoin, disrupt, dissect, divorce **8** disjoint, dissever, disunite, separate **11** dichotomize

sundew 7 drosera

sundial part 6 gnomon

sundries 7 notions **8** oddments **9** etceteras **11** odds and ends

sundry 4 many, some **6** divers, legion **7** diverse, several, various **8** manifold, numerous, populous **9** different **10** voluminous **12** multifarious, multitudinal **13** miscellaneous, multitudinous

sunfish 4 opah **8** bluegill

Sunflower State 6 Kansas

sun-god see at **sun**
Sun King 8 Louis XIV
sunny 4 fair, fine, warm 5 clear, happy
6 blithe, bright, cheery, chirpy, golden
7 clarion 8 cheerful, chirrupy, pleasant, rainless 9 brilliant, cloudless, lightsome,
unclouded 10 undarkened
sunrise 4 dawn, morn 5 light 6 aurora
7 dawning, morning 8 cockcrow, daybreak,
daylight *goddess:* 3 Eos 6 Aurora
sun-room 8 solarium
sunset 3 eve 4 dusk 7 evening 8 twilight
Sunset State 6 Oregon
Sunshine State 7 Florida 11 South
Dakota
sunspot portion 5 umbra 8 penumbra
sunup see **sunrise**
sup 3 eat 4 dine 5 drink, quaff 6 imbibe
7 swallow 8 mouthful
superannuate 6 retire 7 outdate, outmode 8 obsolete 9 antiquate, obsolesce
10 pension off
superb 4 best, fine, rich 5 grand, lofty,
noble, prime, proud, super 7 elegant,
exalted, optimal, optimum, opulent, rousing,
stately, sublime, supreme 8 crashing, elevated, glorious, gorgeous, imposing, majestic, slambang, splendid, standout 9 excellent, marvelous, wonderful 11 magnificent,
outstanding, resplendent, sensational,
splendorous, superlative 13 splendiferous
supercilious 5 proud 6 lordly, sniffy,
snifty, snippy, snuffy 7 haughty 8 arrogant,
cavalier, insolent, sneering, sniffish, snobbish, superior 10 disdainful 11 overbearing 13 high-and-mighty
superficial 5 hasty, shoal 6 casual, slight
7 cursory, general, shallow, sketchy, surface 8 skin-deep, smattery 9 depthless
10 uncritical
superfluity 5 frill, luxus 6 excess, luxury
7 amenity, surfeit, surplus, teeming 8 overflow, overkill, overmuch, overplus, plethora,
swarming 10 surplusage 11 overflowing,
prodigality 12 extravagance
13 overabundance
superfluous 4 over 5 extra, spare 6 de
trop, excess 7 surplus, unasked, useless
8 needless, unneeded, unwanted 9 excessive, redundant 10 gratuitous 11 dispensable, uncalled-for, unnecessary
12 nonessential
superhuman 6 divine 7 demigod,
uncanny 8 numinous 9 unearthly, unnatural 10 miraculous 13 extraordinary,
preternatural
superintend 4 boss 5 guide 6 direct,
manage, survey 7 control, oversee 8 chaperon, overlook 10 administer
11 quarterback
superintendence 4 care 6 charge

7 conduct, running 8 handling 9 authority,
direction, oversight 10 management,
presidence
superior 4 fine, head, lord, over, rare
5 above, dandy, elder, lofty, major, prime,
proud, upper 6 better, choice, dainty,
famous, higher, select, senior 7 capital, elegant, greater, haughty, premium, primary,
unusual 8 arrogant, brass hat, cavalier, delicate, dominant, five-star, higher-up, insolent,
numinous 9 excellent, exquisite, first-rate,
marvelous, overlying, recherché, unearthly
10 disdainful, first-class, miraculous, noteworthy, preeminent, preferable, remarkable,
suprahuman 11 exceptional, first-string,
heavyweight, overbearing, predominant
13 high-and-mighty, preternatural
superiority 6 better 7 victory 8 whip
hand 9 advantage, dominance, seniority,
supremacy, upper hand 10 ascendancy
superjacent 4 over 6 higher 7 greater
9 overlying
superlative 4 best 8 finished, peerless,
standout 10 consummate 11 magnificent,
outstanding 12 accomplished
superlative degree *suffix:* 3 est
Superman 9 Clark Kent *cartoonist:*
7 Shuster *girl friend:* 8 Lois Lane
supernatural 5 magic 6 divine
7 uncanny, unusual 8 heavenly, numinous
9 celestial, spiritual, unearthly 10 miraculous, paranormal, phenomenal 12 metaphysical 13 extraordinary
supernatural being 3 elf, god 5 angel,
deity, demon, fairy, gnome, nymph, troll
6 seraph, spirit 7 banshee, goddess
10 leprechaun *Muslim:* 4 jinn *Persian:*
4 peri
supernumerary 5 extra, spare 6 de trop,
excess 7 surplus
supersede 7 replace, succeed 8 displace,
outplace, set aside, supplant
supervene 5 ensue 6 follow 7 succeed
supervise 3 run 4 boss 5 guide, steer
6 direct, govern, manage, survey 7 conduct, control, monitor, oversee, proctor, referee 8 chaperon, overlook 10 administer
11 quarterback
supervision 4 care 6 charge 7 conduct,
running 8 handling 9 oversight 10 intendance, management
supervisor 7 foreman
supine 5 inert, prone, slack 6 abject
7 passive 8 inactive, indolent 11 indifferent
supper club 4 café 6 nitery 7 cabaret,
hot spot 8 nightery 9 night spot
supplant 4 oust 5 eject, expel, usurp
6 bounce, cut out 7 cast out, replace
8 crowd out, displace, force out, outplace
9 overthrow, supersede
supple 4 wiry 5 agile, lithe, withy 6 limber,

nimble, pliant, whippy **7** ductile, elastic, lissome, plastic, pliable, springy, stretch, willowy **8** flexible, graceful, moldable, stretchy **9** adaptable, lithesome, malleable, resilient

supplement 3 add, eke **5** rider **6** append **7** adjunct, codicil **8** addendum, addition, appendix **9** accessory **10** complement

suppliant 5 asker **6** beggar, prayer, suitor **9** solicitor **10** petitioner

supplicant see **suppliant**

supplicate 3 beg, sue **4** pray **5** crave, plead **6** appeal, invoke **7** beseech, entreat, implore, solicit **8** petition **9** importune

supplication 4 plea, suit **6** appeal, orison, prayer **8** entreaty, petition **11** application, imploration, imprecation

supplies 8 matériel **9** materials

supply 3 fit, man **4** feed, find, fund, give, hand, help **5** cache, equip, hoard, stock, store **6** outfit, purvey, succor **7** deliver, fulfill, furnish, provide, reserve, surplus **8** dispense, hand over, transfer, turn over **9** inventory, provision, reservoir, stockpile **12** accumulation

support 3 aid **4** back, base, bear, hand, help, keep, lift, prop, root, side, stay, take **5** abide, adopt, boost, brace, bread, brook, carry, favor, shore, strut, truss **6** anchor, assist, bear up, behalf, buoy up, column, crutch, defend, endure, girder, living, pillar, relief, second, succor, suffer, upbear, uphold, verify **7** alimony, applaud, approve, backing, bolster, bracing, comfort, confirm, embrace, endorse, espouse, footing, fortify, fulcrum, nourish, nurture, pull for, secours, shore up, stiffen, sustain, toehold **8** advocate, backstop, buttress, champion, foothold, mainstay, maintain, sanction, side with, underpin **9** encourage, reinforce, underprop **10** assistance, foundation, livelihood, provide for, strengthen, sustenance **11** corroborate, maintenance, subsistence, underpinner **12** alimentation, sustentation, underpinning

supporter 4 ally **6** cohort, patron **7** booster, sectary **8** adherent, advocate, champion, disciple, exponent, follower, henchman, partisan, sectator **9** expounder, proponent, satellite *combining form:* **4** crat **5** ocrat *suffix:* **3** ite

suppose 4 deem, take **5** allow, guess, infer, judge, opine, think **6** assume, expect, gather, reckon, repute, theory **7** believe, imagine, perhaps, presume, pretend, surmise, suspect **8** conclude, consider **10** conjecture, understand **11** speculation

supposition 5 posit **6** theory, thesis **7** premise, surmise **9** apriorism, postulate **10** assumption, conjecture, estimation,

hypothesis **11** postulation, presumption, speculation

supposititious 6 unreal **7** dubious, fictive, reputed **8** doubtful, fanciful, illusory, putative, spurious **9** fantastic, fictional, imaginary, pretended, simulated **10** chimerical, fictitious, fraudulent **11** conjectural **12** hypothetical, questionable

suppress 4 cool, curb, hide, kill, rein, stop **5** burke, check, choke, crush, drown, dwarf, quash, quell, shush, spike, stunt **6** arrest, censor, cut off, hush up, muffle, quench, retard, squash, stifle, subdue **7** abolish, collect, compose, conceal, control, destroy, prevent, put down, silence, smother, squelch, swallow **8** prohibit, restrain, slap down, strangle, withhold **9** overpower, overthrow **10** annihilate, extinguish

supra 5 above

supremacy 4 sway **5** power **7** control, mastery **8** dominion **9** ascendant, authority, dominance, masterdom **10** ascendancy, domination, mastership, prepotence, prepotency **11** preeminence, sovereignty, superiority **12** predominance, principality **13** preponderance, preponderancy, transcendence

supreme 4 last **5** alone, chief, final **6** master, superb, utmost **7** highest, maximum, perfect **8** absolute, crowning, foremost, peerless, towering, ultimate **9** excellent, marvelous, paramount, sovereign, unequaled, unmatched, unrivaled **10** preeminent, surpassing **11** unequalable, unmatchable, unsurpassed **12** incomparable, transcendent, unparalleled **13** unsurpassable

Supreme Being 3 God **5** Allah **7** creator, Jehovah **11** the Almighty

surcease 3 end **4** halt, quit, rest, stop **6** desist **7** refrain, suspend **8** give over, knock off, leave off, postpone **9** cessation **11** discontinue

sure 3 set **4** fast, firm, safe **5** cocky, fixed **6** indeed, secure, stable, steady, strong **7** abiding, certain, staunch **8** absolute, arrogant, cocksure, definite, enduring, inerrant, positive, reliable, surefire, unerring, unshaken **9** confident, convinced, inerrable, steadfast **10** convincing, dependable, infallible, undeniable, unshakable, unwavering **11** indubitable, trustworthy, unequivocal, unfaltering, unqualified **12** indisputable, never-failing, wholehearted **13** incontestable, uncontestable, unquestioning

sure thing 6 shoo-in, winner **9** certainty

surety 4 bail, bond **5** angel **6** backer, patron, pledge **7** sponsor **8** backer-up, guaranty, security, warranty **9** certainty, certitude, guarantee, guarantor **10** confidence, conviction

surface 3 top **4** face, pave, rise, skin

5 cover, facet **6** come up, facing, finish, patina, veneer **7** outside **8** covering, exterior **11** superficial

surfeit 4 cloy, fill, glut, jade, pall, sate **5** gorge, stall **6** excess, stodge **7** replete, satiate, satisfy, surplus **8** overfill, overflow, overkill, overmuch, overplus, plethora **10** surplusage **11** overindulge, superfluity **13** overabundance

surge 4 flow, gush, pour, rise, roll, rush, wave **5** swell **6** billow, sluice, stream **7** upswell

surgeon 8 sawbones *American:* **4** Mayo, Reed **6** Thorek **8** McDowell *British:* **6** Hunter *English:* **5** Paget **6** Lister *French:* **4** Paré *heart:* **7** Barnard *South African:* **7** Barnard *Swiss:* **6** Kocher

surgery 9 operation *instrument:* **5** clamp, curet, lance, probe **6** gorget, lancet, splint, stylet, trocar **7** forceps, scalpel

surgical removal 8 ablation *combining form:* **6** ectomy

surly 4 dour, glum, rude, ugly **5** cross, gruff, sulky **6** crusty, grumpy, morose, sullen **7** bearish, boorish, crabbed, haughty, waspish **8** churlish, snappish **9** fractious, irritable, saturnine **10** ungracious **11** ill-mannered **12** discourteous

surmise see suppose

surmount 3 cap, top **4** best, down, leap, lick, over **5** clear, crest, crown, excel, outdo, throw, vault **6** better, finish, hurdle, master, outtop **7** conquer, surpass **8** outstrip, outtower, overcome, overleap **9** negotiate, terminate, transcend

surpass 3 cap, cob, top **4** beat, best, pass, rank **5** excel, outdo, outgo, trump **6** better, exceed, outrun, outvie **7** eclipse, outpace, outrank, outstep **8** distance, outclass, outmatch, outpoint, outrange, outrival, outshine, outstrip, outweigh, overstep **9** transcend **10** outperform, overshadow **11** outdistance

surplice 5 cotta, ephod **8** vestment

surplus 5 extra, spare **6** de trop, excess **7** overage, reserve, surfeit **8** overflow, overkill, overmuch, plethora **9** overstock, remainder **10** oversupply **11** superfluent, superfluity, superfluous **13** overabundance, supernumerary

surprise 4 faze, grab, stun **5** amaze, catch, floor, grasp, seize **6** ambush, dismay, lay for, rattle, waylay, wonder **7** astound, capture, nonplus, stagger, startle, stupefy **8** astonish, bewilder, bowl over, confound, dry-gulch, overcome **9** amazement, bushwhack, discomfit, dumbfound, overpower **10** disconcert **11** flabbergast **12** astonishment

surrender 4 cede, fall **5** leave, waive, yield **6** commit, give in, give up, go down,

resign, submit **7** abandon, concede, consign, go under, succumb **8** dedition, hand over, yielding **9** relenting **10** capitulate, relinquish, submission, succumbing **11** appeasement **12** capitulation *sign:* **9** white flag

surreptitious see stealthy

surrogate 3 sub **6** deputy, fill-in, refuge, resort **7** stand-in, stopgap **8** recourse, resource **9** alternate, expedient, makeshift **10** expediency, substitute **11** alternative, locum tenens, pinch hitter, replacement, succedaneum

surround 3 hem, rim **4** edge, gird, loop, ring **5** beset, bound, limit, round, skirt, verge **6** begird, border, circle, engulf, fringe, girdle, margin **7** compass, confine, embosom, enclave, enclose, envelop, environ, outline **8** encircle **9** encompass **10** circumvent **12** circumscribe

surrounding 5 about **12** circumjacent *prefix:* **4** peri **6** circum

surroundings 6 medium, milieu **7** ambient, climate **8** ambience **10** atmosphere **11** environment, mise-en-scène

surveillance 3 eye, tab **4** tout **5** vigil, watch **7** lookout **8** eagle eye, scrutiny, stakeout **9** vigilance

survey 3 con, vet **4** boss, rate, scan, view **5** assay, audit, set at, study, value **6** aperçu, assess, digest, précis, review, search, sketch **7** canvass, check up, examine, inspect, oversee, pandect, preview, sylloge, valuate **8** analysis, appraise, chaperon, estimate, evaluate, overlook, scrutiny, syllabus **9** check over, supervise **10** compendium, inspection, scrutinize **11** examination, quarterback, superintend **13** perlustration

survive 4 last **6** endure, revive **7** carry on, outlast, outlive, outwear, persist, recover, ride out **8** continue, live down **11** come through, pull through

Surya 6 sun-god *son:* **4** Manu, Yama **5** Karna **6** Asvins **7** Sugriva *temple site:* **7** Konarak

susceptible 4 easy, open **5** naive, prone **6** liable **7** exposed, sensile, subject **8** disposed, gullible, inclined, sensible, sentient **9** obnoxious, receptive, sensitive **10** fleece-able, responsive, vulnerable **11** impressible, predisposed **12** nonresistant

Susi's son 5 Gaddi

suspect 4 open **5** doubt, guess, shaky, think **6** assume, expect, gather, unsure **7** believe, dubious, imagine, suppose, unclear **8** conceive, distrust, doubtful, misdoubt, mistrust **9** doubtable, uncertain **10** disbelieve, understand **11** problematic

suspend 3 bar **4** bate, hang, stay, stop **5** debar, defer, delay, hover, sling **6** dangle, depend, except, hold up, put off, shelve **7** adjourn, exclude, hold off, rule out **8** count out, intermit, postpone, prorogue **9** eliminate **11** discontinue

suspended 7 hanging, pendant, pensile **8** dangling, swinging **9** pendulant, pendulous

suspenders 6 braces **8** galluses

suspense 5 worry **6** unease **7** anxiety, concern, mystery **11** uncertainty **12** apprehension

suspension 4 stop **5** delay **7** latency **8** abeyance, abeyancy, doldrums, dormancy, stoppage **9** remission **10** moratorium, quiescence, quiescency **11** cold storage, withholding **12** intermission, interruption

suspicion 4 cast, hint **5** doubt, shade, smell, tinge, touch, trace, whiff **6** wonder **7** concern, dubiety **8** distrust, mistrust **9** dubiosity, misgiving **10** foreboding, intimation, skepticism, suggestion **11** incertitude, uncertainty, uncertitude

suspicious 4 wary **5** chary, leery, queer, shaky **6** unsure **7** careful, dubious, jealous, suspect **8** cautious, doubtful, watchful **9** doubtable, skeptical, uncertain **10** borderline **11** distrustful, mistrustful, problematic, unbelieving **12** questionable

suspire 4 sigh

sustain 4 bear, feed, prop, save **5** abide, brace, brook, carry, stand **6** bear up, buoy up, endure, foster, hold up, keep up, succor, suffer, upbear, uphold **7** bolster, confirm, nourish, nurture, prolong, receive, shore up, stomach, support, undergo **8** buttress, continue, preserve, tolerate **9** underprop, withstand **10** experience, strengthen

sustenance 3 pap **4** food, keep, meat, salt **5** bread **6** living, viands **7** aliment, alimony, pabulum, support **9** nutriment **10** livelihood **11** maintenance, nourishment, subsistence **12** alimentation

susurration 6 mumble, murmur, mutter, rustle **7** whisper **9** undertone

suture 4 line, seam **6** stitch

swab 3 mop **5** clean

swaddle 4 roll, wrap **5** drape **6** enwrap, swathe, wrap up **7** bandage, envelop **8** enswathe

swag 3 yaw **4** flag, loot, tilt, wilt **5** booty, droop, lurch, money, pitch, prize, spoil **6** boodle, seesaw, tilter **7** plunder **10** plunderage

swagger 4 brag, cock, lord **5** boast, strut, swank, swash, swell **7** bluster, peacock **8** flourish **11** pontificate, swashbuckle

swain 4 beau **5** lover, spark, wooer **6** suitor **7** admirer, sparker **9** boyfriend

swallow 3 sip **4** bear, bolt, down, gulp, take **5** abide, brook, drink, quaff, stand

6 absorb, accept, digest, endure, imbibe, ingest **7** believe, consume, stomach **8** bear with, tolerate **11** ingurgitate

swamp 3 bog, fen **4** mire, moss, muck, quag **5** drown, flood, glade, marsh, whelm **6** deluge, engulf, morass, muskeg, slough **7** baygall, bottoms **8** inundate, overcome, overflow, quagmire, submerge **9** marshland, overwhelm *Everglades:* **10** Big Cypress *Georgia:* **10** Okefenokee *North Carolina-Virginia:* **6** Dismal **11** Great Dismal

Swamp Fox 6 Marion

swan *female:* **3** pen *male:* **3** cob **4** cobb *young:* **6** cygnet

Swanhild *father:* **6** Sigurd *mother:* **6** Gudrun

swank 4 cock, lord, tony, trig **5** sharp, showy, swell, swish **6** chichi, classy, lively, snappy, tonish, trendy, with-it **7** peacock, splashy, stylish, swagger **8** peacocky **10** flamboyant, peacockish **11** pontificate, pretentious **12** orchidaceous, ostentatious

swap 5 trade, truck **6** barter, change, switch **7** bargain, traffic **8** exchange **10** substitute

swarm 4 flow, host, teem **5** crawl, crowd, flock, group, horde **6** abound, throng **7** overrun **9** multitude, pullulate **10** congregate

swarthy 4 dark **5** dusky **8** bistered **11** black-a-vised, dark-skinned

swash 3 lap **4** dash, slop **5** douse, plash, slosh **6** bubble, burble, gurgle, splash, splosh **7** bluster, spatter, splurge, spurtle, swagger **8** splatter

swat 3 bat, box, hit, rap **4** belt, blow, cuff, lick, slog, slug, sock **5** clout, knock, smack, smash, smite, swipe, whack **6** buffet, strike, wallop **7** clobber

swathe see **swaddle**

sway 3 get **4** bend, bias, move, rock, rule **5** carry, lurch, might, power, range, reach, reign, scope, sweep, swing, touch, waver, weave **6** affect, careen, direct, govern, manage, spread, strike, totter, waddle, wobble **7** command, dispose, expanse, impress, incline, inspire, mastery, stagger, stretch, strings **8** overrule **9** amplitude, authority, dominance, influence, oscillate, pendulate, vacillate **10** domination, predispose **11** fluctuation **12** jurisdiction

swear 3 vow **4** bind, cuss, damn, oath, rail, rant **5** abuse, curse **6** adjure, affirm, assert, attest, bedamn, depone, depose, pledge, plight, revile, vilify **7** declare, promise, testify **8** covenant, cussword, execrate **9** blaspheme, expletive, imprecate **10** asseverate, vituperate

swearword 4 cuss, oath **5** curse **9** expletive, obscenity **10** scurrility

sweat 4 emit, fume, milk, moil, ooze, rook, seep, snit, stew, toil, weep, work 5 bleed, exude, grind, labor, mulct, stick, tizzy 6 fleece, strain, swivet 7 excrete, slavery, travail 8 bullwork, drudgery, perspire, transude 10 donkeywork *combining form:* 4 hidr 5 hidro

sweater 8 cardigan, pullover, slipover

sweat out 2 go 4 bear, lump, take, wait 5 abide, brook, stand 6 endure 7 stomach 8 tolerate

sweaty 3 wet 6 clammy, sticky 7 labored 8 perspiry 10 perspiring

Sweden *capital:* 9 Stockholm *monetary unit:* 5 krona

Swedish Nightingale 4 Lind (Jenny)

sweep 3 fly 4 flit, sail, wing 5 ambit, broom, clean, clear, drive, fleet, orbit, range, reach, scope, surge 6 extent, radius 7 compass, purview 9 extension

sweeping 6 all-out 7 blanket, general, overall 8 whole-hog 9 all-around, extensive, inclusive, out-and-out, wholesale 12 all-embracing 13 comprehensive, thoroughgoing

sweepings 4 dust, junk 5 trash, waste 6 debris, litter, refuse 7 garbage, rubbish

sweet 5 candy, honey, spicy 6 aromal, dulcet, lovely, savory, sugary, syrupy 7 angelic, dessert, melodic, odorous, perfumy, scented, winning, winsome 8 aromatic, engaging, euphonic, fragrant, heavenly, loveling, luscious, perfumed, pleasant, pleasing, redolent 9 agreeable, ambrosial, beautiful, delicious 10 delectable, delightful *combining form:* 4 glyc 5 glyco

Sweet ___, song 7 Adeline

sweeten 5 candy, honey, sugar 6 pacify, refine, soften, solace 7 appease, assuage, lighten, mollify, placate, relieve 9 sugarcoat, sugar over 10 conciliate, propitiate

sweet potato 3 yam

sweet-talk 3 con 4 coax 6 banter, cajole 7 blarney, wheedle 8 blandish, soft-soap

swell 4 cock, grow, keen, lord, neat, pout, puff 5 bloat, bulge, dandy, nifty, pouch, super, surge, swank 6 billow, blow up, dilate, expand, groovy, tumefy 7 amplify, augment, balloon, distend, inflate, peacock, swagger, upsurge 8 increase, overblow, terrific 9 marvelous, wonderful *British:* 3 nob 4 toff

swelled head 5 pride 6 egoism 7 conceit, egotism 9 arrogance, vainglory 10 narcissism 11 amour propre 13 conceitedness

swelling 3 sty 4 bubo, gall, node 5 edema, tumid, tumor 6 bunion, growth 7 aureate, flowery, gibbous 8 tubercle 9 bombastic, carbuncle, chilblain, tumes-

cent 10 euphuistic, rhetorical 12 inflammation, magniloquent 13 grandiloquent

sweltering 3 hot 5 fiery 6 baking, sultry, torrid 7 burning 8 broiling, sizzling 9 scorching

swerve 3 dip, err 4 skew, slue, turn, veer 5 sheer, shift, stray, waver 6 depart, totter, wander 7 deflect, deviate, digress, diverge 8 train off

swift 4 fast 5 fleet, hasty, quick, rapid, ready 6 prompt, raking, snappy, speedy, sudden 7 flat-out, fleetly, quickly, rapidly 8 full tilt, headlong, promptly, speedily 9 breakneck 10 harefooted

___ Swift 3 Tom 8 Jonathan *character:* 8 Gulliver

swiftness 4 gait, pace 5 haste, hurry, speed 6 hustle, rustle 8 celerity, dispatch, rapidity, velocity 9 quickness, rapidness 10 expedition, speediness

swig 4 drag, pull 5 booze, draft, drink, swill 6 guzzle, imbibe, tipple 9 swizzle

swill 4 slop, swig, tope 5 booze, draft, drink, offal, rinse, slops, trash, waste 6 debris, guzzle, refuse, spilth, tank up, tipple 7 consume, garbage, hogwash, put away, put down, rubbish, swizzle 9 polish off

swim 4 reel, spin, turn 5 float, swoon, whirl 9 dizziness

swimmer 7 natator

swimming stroke 5 crawl 7 dolphin, trudgen 9 butterfly, dogpaddle

swindle 3 con, gyp 4 beat, bilk, dupe, fake, hoax, rook, scam, sell, sham, skin 5 bunco, cheat, cozen, fraud, phony, rogue 6 chouse, diddle, humbug 7 defraud 8 flimflam 9 imposture, victimize

swine see **hog**

swing 3 ply, wag 4 beat, hang, rock, roll, sway, turn, veer, wave, whip 5 avert, flail, knack, lurch, meter, pivot, rhyme, sheer, trick, weave, wheel, whirl, wield 6 careen, divert, handle, jiggle, rhythm, rotate, stroke, switch, waggle, wiggle, wigwag, wobble 7 cadence, cadency, deflect, measure, revolve, stagger, vibrate 8 brandish, dispense, maneuver, undulate 9 fluctuate, oscillate, pendulate 10 manipulate

swinish 5 brute, feral, gross 6 animal, brutal, coarse, ferine, greedy 7 beastly, bestial, boarish, brutish, porcine, sensual

swipe 3 cop, hit, nab, rap 4 blow, conk, hook, lick, lift, swat, wipe 5 draft, heist, knock, pinch, steal 6 pilfer, snatch, snitch, strike

swirl 4 eddy, purl, roil 5 curve, gurge, twist, whirl, whorl 6 swoosh, vortex 9 whirlpool 11 convolution

swish 2 in 4 buzz, fizz, flog, hiss, tony, whiz 5 smart, swank, whisk 6 classy, fizzle, sizzle, tonish, trendy, wheeze, whoosh, with-it **7** stylish **8** sibilate **9** exclusive

Swiss Family Robinson author
4 Wyss

switch 3 rod, wag **4** beat, flog, lash, swap, wand, wave, whip **5** shift, shunt, trade, whisk **6** change, strike, waggle, woggle **7** scourge **8** exchange **9** sidetrack **10** substitute

Switzerland *capital:* **4** Bern *largest city:* **6** Zurich *monetary unit:* **5** franc

swivel 4 turn **5** swing

swivet see **snit**

swizzle see **swig**

swollen 5 bulgy, tumid **6** turgid **7** aureate, bulbous, bulging, flowery, pompous **8** enlarged, inflated, varicose **9** bombastic, distended, tumescent **10** euphuistic, rhetorical **12** magniloquent **13** grandiloquent *combining form:* **4** phys **5** physo

swoon 4 coma, daze, fade **5** drown, faint **6** torpor **7** die away, pass out, rapture, syncope **8** black out

swoosh 4 eddy, gush, purl **5** gurge, swirl, whirl, whorl

sword 4 épée, foil, kris, pata **5** estoc, saber **6** barong, bilboa, creese, rapier, toledo **7** cutlass **8** claymore, falchion, scimitar, yataghan

sword of ___ 8 Damocles

sword-shaped 8 ensiform

sworn 6 avowed **7** devoted, settled **8** affirmed **9** confirmed, hard-shell **10** deep-rooted, deep-seated, entrenched, inveterate

sybarite 7 epicure **8** hedonist **10** voluptuary

sybaritic 6 carnal **7** sensual **8** sensuous **9** epicurean, luxurious **10** apolaustic, hedonistic, voluptuous **13** self-indulgent

sycophancy 7 calumny, scandal, slander **8** toadying **10** backbiting, defamation, detraction **12** backstabbing, belittlement, depreciation **13** disparagement

sycophant 5 toady **6** flunky, lackey, minion, stooge, yes-man **7** defamer, fawning **8** bootlick, cowering, cringing, groveler, lickspit, parasite, toadying, toadyish **9** easy rider, flatterer, groveling, kowtowing, parasitic, slanderer **10** bootlicker, self-seeker **11** bootlicking, lickspittle **13** apple-polisher

sycophantic 7 fawning, servile, slavish **8** cowering, cringing, toadying, toadyish **9** groveling, kowtowing, parasitic, truckling **10** defamatory, obsequious, slanderous **11** bootlicking

Sycorax's son 7 Caliban

syllable 3 bit, jot **4** atom, iota, whit **5** crumb, ounce, shred **7** modicum **8** particle *deletion:* **7** apocope *last:* **6** ultima *lengthening of:* **7** ectasis *next to last:*

6 penult *shortening:* **7** elision, systole *stressed:* **5** arsis

syllabus 6 aperçu, digest, précis, sketch, survey **7** epitome, outline, pandect, summary **8** abstract, headnote, synopsis **10** compendium

sylvan 5 bosky, woody **6** rustic, wooded *deity:* **3** Pan **4** Faun **5** dryad, satyr **6** Faunus **7** Silenus **8** Arethusa, Silvanus, Sylvanus

symbol 4 logo, mark, note, sign, type **5** badge, motif, stamp, token **6** design, device, emblem, figure, mascot **7** pattern **9** attribute, character **10** indication *chemical:* see individual element *Egyptian:* **4** ankh *musical:* **4** clef, flat, hold, note, rest, turn **5** presa, shake, sharp, trill **7** fermata, mordent, natural **8** arpeggio **9** crescendo **10** diminuendo **11** decrescendo

symbolic 10 emblematic **11** allegorical

symbolist poet 7 Rimbaud **8** Mallarmé, Verlaine

symbolize 6 embody, mirror, typify **7** express, signify **9** body forth, epitomize, exemplify, personify, represent **10** illustrate **11** emblematize

symmetrical 5 equal **7** regular **8** balanced **12** commensurate, proportional **13** commensurable

symmetry 5 order **7** balance, harmony **8** equality, evenness **9** agreement, congruity **10** conformity, proportion, regularity **11** arrangement

sympathetic 4 kind, warm **6** benign, humane, kindly, tender **8** amenable, favoring, friendly **9** agreeable, approving, benignant, congenial, congruous, consonant, favorable, receptive **10** compatible, consistent, responsive **11** kindhearted, softhearted, warmhearted **12** appreciating, well-disposed **13** compassionate, comprehending, understanding

sympathize 4 ache, pity **7** condole, feel for **10** appreciate, comprehend, understand **11** commiserate **13** compassionate

sympathy 3 rue **4** pity, ruth **5** heart **6** accord, warmth **7** empathy, harmony **8** affinity, kindness **9** agreement **10** benignancy, benignness, compassion, condolence, kindliness, tenderness **11** sensitivity **13** commiseration

symphonic 7 chiming, musical **8** blending, harmonic **9** consonant **10** harmonious

symphony 4 band **7** concord, harmony **9** orchestra **10** consonance **11** concert band **12** philharmonic

symptom 4 mark, note, sign **5** index, token **7** indicia **8** evidence **10** indication **11** significant

symptoms 8 syndrome

synagogue 8 assembly, building 9 community 12 congregation

synchronize 5 agree 6 concur 8 coincide

synchronous 6 coeval 8 existing 10 coetaneous, coexistent, coexisting, concurrent 11 concomitant 12 contemporary, simultaneous

syncope 4 coma 5 faint, swoon 8 blackout

syndicate 4 pool 5 chain, group, trust, union 6 cartel 7 combine 11 association, partnership 12 conglomerate, organization

syndrome 3 ill 6 malady 7 ailment, disease 8 disorder, sickness 9 affection, complaint, condition, infirmity 11 concurrence

synergic 8 coacting, coactive, conjoint

synod 4 body 7 council, meeting 8 assembly 10 convention, judicatory 11 convocation

synopsis 5 brief 7 epitome, summary 8 abstract, boildown, breviary, breviate 10 abridgment, conspectus 12 condensation

synopsize 3 sum 5 sum up 6 digest 7 summate 8 condense, nutshell 9 epitomize, inventory, summarize

synthesis 5 blend, union 11 combination 13 incorporation

synthesize 5 blend, unify 7 combine 9 harmonize, integrate

synthetic 7 man-made 10 artificial, fabricated

Syria *capital:* 8 Damascus *monetary unit:* 4 lira 5 pound

Syrinx 5 nymph 7 panpipe *pursuer:* 3 Pan

syrup 4 corn 5 maple 7 sorghum 8 molasses *almond-flavored:* 6 orgeat

syrupy 5 gooey, moist, mushy, sappy, sobby, sweet 6 drippy, dulcet, slushy, sticky 7 maudlin 11 sentimental

system 3 sum, way 4 code, mode, plan, wise 5 modus, order, setup, whole 6 entity, manner, method, scheme 7 complex, fashion, network, pattern, process, regimen 9 technique 10 regularity 11 arrangement, disposition, orderliness

systematic 7 logical, ordered, orderly, regular 8 arranged, methodic 9 organized 10 analytical, methodical 12 businesslike

systematize 5 array, order 6 adjust, codify 7 arrange, catalog, dispose, marshal 8 classify, organize, regiment 9 methodize

system of weights 4 troy 11 avoirdupois

T

tab 3 eye, tag 4 bill, cost, rate 5 check, price, score, watch 6 charge, tariff 7 account, invoice 8 eagle eye, price tag, scrutiny 9 reckoning, statement 12 surveillance

tabard 4 cape, coat 5 tunic 7 pendant

tabby 3 cat 6 feline, gossip 7 rumorer 8 gossiper, quidnunc, telltale 9 carrytale 10 newsmonger, talebearer 12 gossipmonger 13 scandalmonger

tabellion 6 scribe

tabernacle 6 church, temple 10 house of God 13 house of prayer

tabes 7 atrophy, wasting

Tabitha's Greek name 6 Dorcas

table 4 fare, list 5 bench, board, chart, stand 6 buffet, record, teapoy, upland 7 counter, plateau 8 mahogany 9 sideboard *ornament:* 7 epergne 11 centerpiece *spread:* 4 oleo 6 butter *wheeled:* 4 cart *writing:* 4 desk 9 secretary 10 escritoire

table game see at **game**

tableland 4 mesa 6 upland 7 plateau *Alabama-West Virginia:* 10 Cumberland *Arizona:* 5 Kanab 6 Kaibob *England:* 8 Dartmoor *India:* 5 Malwa; (see also **plateau**)

tablet 3 bar, pad 4 cake, disk, pill, slab 5 panel, slate 6 troche 7 lozenge *combining form:* 4 plac 5 pinac, pinak, placo 6 pinaco *ornamental:* 9 cartouche *stone:* 5 stela, stele *writing:* 3 pad 7 fanfold 8 triptych

tableware 4 cups 5 bowls, forks 6 dishes, knives, plates, silver, spoons 7 glasses, saucers

tabloid 5 livid, lurid, short 9 newspaper 11 sensational

taboo 3 ban 4 don't 6 enjoin, forbid, outlaw 7 inhibit 8 prohibit, sanction 9 interdict, restraint 10 inhibition, limitation, regulation 11 forbiddance, prohibition, reservation, restriction 12 interdiction, proscription

tabor 4 drum

taboret 5 stand, stool 7 cabinet

Tabrimmon *father:* 6 Hezion *son:* 8 Benhadad

tabula ___ 4 rasa

tabulation 5 chart, tally

tache 5 clasp 6 buckle

tacit 6 silent, unsaid 7 assumed, implied 8 hinted at, implicit, inferred, unspoken, unvoiced 9 alluded to, intimated, suggested, unuttered 10 undeclared, understood 11 unexpressed 12 inarticulate

taciturn 5 close 6 silent 7 laconic 8 reserved, reticent, wordless 10 silentious 11 close-lipped, tight-lipped 12 closemouthed

Tacitus work 7 Annales 8 Germania 9 Historiae

tack 3 pin, yaw 4 bend, brad, link, nail, turn 5 shift 6 double, swerve, zigzag 7 tangent 9 deviation 10 alteration, deflection, digression

tackle 3 rig 4 gear 5 throw 6 attack, burton, outfit, take on 7 lineman, rigging 8 matériel, set about 9 apparatus, equipment, machinery, undertake 10 footballer, plunge into 11 clothesline, habiliments 13 accouterments, paraphernalia

tacky 5 cheap, crude, dingy, dowdy, faded, gaudy, messy, seedy 6 blowsy, frowsy, frumpy, shabby, sloppy, sticky, stodgy, tagrag, untidy 7 run-down, unkempt 8 frumpish, outmoded, slovenly 9 incorrect, inelegant, out-of-date, tasteless, unstylish 10 broken-down, down-at-heel, threadbare, unbecoming, unsuitable 11 dilapidated

tact 5 poise, skill 6 acumen 7 finesse, suavity 8 civility, courtesy, deftness, urbanity 9 diplomacy, gallantry 10 adroitness, perception, politeness, smoothness 11 delicatesse, savoir faire, sensitivity

tactful 4 deft 5 suave 6 adroit, urbane 7 politic, skilled 8 delicate, discreet, polished, skillful 9 sensitive 10 diplomatic, perceptive

tactical 4 wise 7 politic, prudent 8 delicate 9 advisable, expedient 10 diplomatic, short-range

tactics 4 plan 6 method, system 9 maneuvers

tactile 8 palpable, tangible 9 touchable

taction 5 touch 7 contact 9 palpation

tad 3 bit, boy, lad, son 5 child 6 laddie 9 shaveling, stripling

tadpole 8 polliwog, pollywog

taffy 5 candy 8 flattery

tag 3 dog, end 4 flap, game, tail 5 bedog, label, trail 6 cliché, follow, shadow, ticket, truism **7** bromide **8** banality, prosaism **9** platitude **10** prosaicism, shibboleth

tagrag 5 dingy, faded, seedy, tacky **6** shabby **7** run-down **10** bedraggled, down-at-heel, threadbare **11** dilapidated

Tahan's father 7 Ephraim

Tahash's father 5 Nahor

Tahath's father 5 Bered **7** Eleadah

Tahiti *capital:* **7** Papeete *painter:* **7** Gauguin

tail 3 dog, end, eye, tag **4** butt, rear **5** bedog, cauda, hound, trail **6** pursue, shadow **7** hind end, rear end **8** backside, buttocks **9** posterior *relating to:* **6** caudal *short:* **4** scut

tailed 7 caudate

tailless 7 acaudal, anurous **8** ecaudate

tailor 3 fit, sew **4** suit **5** adapt, alter, style **6** adjust, sartor, square **7** conform, shape up **8** clothier, dovetail, quadrate, seamster **9** reconcile **11** accommodate *Hindu:* **5** darzi **6** durzee

taint 3 hue, rot, tar **4** blur, foul, harm, hurt, smut, soil, turn **5** brand, cloud, color, decay, dirty, smear, spoil, stain, sully **6** befoul, damage, defile, molder, smudge, smutch **7** besmear, blacken, crumble, pollute, putrefy, tarnish **8** besmirch, discolor **9** break down, decompose, discredit **10** stigmatize **11** contaminate

taipan 5 snake **8** merchant

Taiwan 7 Formosa *capital:* **6** Taipei

taj 3 cap

Taj Mahal 9 mausoleum *builder:* **9** Shah Jahan *site:* **4** Agra

take 3 bag, buy, cut, eat, get, gyp, nab, use, win **4** bear, beat, bilk, cull, down, draw, grab, grip, haul, pick **5** abide, admit, annex, brook, catch, charm, cheat, clasp, cozen, grasp, seize, share, stand, think, treat **6** accept, allure, assume, choose, clutch, collar, deduct, devour, endure, follow, gather, income, ingest, obtain, opt for, prefer, secure, select, snatch, strike, suffer **7** attract, believe, call for, capture, consume, defraud, enchant, grapple, imagine, receive, require, stomach, suppose, swallow **8** arrogate, contract, deal with, discount, flimflam, knock off, proceeds, purchase, receipts, subtract, tolerate **9** apprehend, captivate, fascinate, partake of, single out, substract **10** commandeer, comprehend, confiscate, sicken with, understand **11** appropriate **12** come down with *account of:* **6** notice *advantage of:* **5** abuse **7** exploit *after:* **6** follow **8** resemble *apart:* **7** analyze, dissect **9** dismantle *care:* **6** beware *care of:* **3** fix **4** tend **5** nurse **6** attend *exception:* **6** object *five:* **4** rest *from:* **7** deprive, detract **8** subtract *it easy:* **5** relax *on the:* **7** corrupt *part:* **4** join **5** share **11** partici-

pate *place:* **5** occur **6** happen *the cake:* **3** win *to:* **4** like *to task:* **5** scold **7** reprove *turns:* **9** alternate *unawares:* **8** surprise

take away 5 decry, wrest **6** deduct, remove **7** deprive, detract **8** belittle, derogate, diminish, discount, draw back, knock off, minimize, subtract, withdraw, write off **9** disparage, substract **10** depreciate **11** detract from

take back 5 unsay **6** abjure, recall, recant, return **7** replace, restore, retract **8** forswear, palinode, withdraw **9** repossess, restitute

take down 5 lower **6** reduce, tackle **8** dismount **9** dismantle, dismember **11** disassemble

take in 3 see **4** fool, have **5** admit, bluff, catch, grasp, trick **6** absorb, accept, betray, delude, embody, follow, illude **7** beguile, compass, contain, deceive, embrace, include, involve, receive, subsume **8** flimflam **9** apprehend, encompass, four-flush **10** assimilate, comprehend, understand **11** double cross

take off 2 go **3** ape **4** doff, down, exit, head, kill, kite, mock, quit, slay **5** douse, leave, mimic, scram **6** begone, decamp, deduct, depart, finish, get out, lay low, parody, remove, set out **7** destroy, get away, imitate, pull out, put away, skiddoo, vamoose **8** clear out, discount, dispatch, draw back, hightail, light out, subtract, withdraw **9** burlesque, skedaddle, strike out, substract

takeoff 4 jato, rato **6** launch, parody, send-up **7** lift-off **8** blast-off, travesty **9** burlesque **10** caricature *area:* **3** pad **6** runway

take on 3 add, don **4** face, hire, meet, pull **5** adopt, annex **6** append, assume, employ, engage, strike **7** embrace, espouse, subjoin **9** encounter

take out 4 date, vent **5** loose **6** deduct, remove **7** release, unleash **8** discount, draw back, knock off, subtract, withdraw **9** clear away, eliminate, substract

take over 5 seize, spell, usurp **7** relieve

take up 3 use **4** lift, open, rear **5** adopt, begin, enter, hoist, raise, renew, set to, start **6** assume, resume, tackle, uphold, uplift, uprear **7** elevate, embrace, espouse, kick off, restart, upraise **8** commence, continue, initiate **10** recommence

talc 4 mica **6** powder **7** agalite **8** steatite **9** soapstone

tale 3 fib, lie, sum **4** myth, saga, tote, yarn **5** fable, story, total, whole **6** canard, legend **7** calumny, falsity, fiction, scandal, slander, untruth **8** anecdote, entirety, sum total, totality, untruism **9** aggregate, falsehood, narration, narrative **10** backbiting, defamation, detraction **12** backstabbing, belittlement, depreciation **13** disparagement, prevarication *epic:* **4** saga *woeful:* **8** jeremiad

talebearer 4 fink **5** tabby **6** canary, gossip, snitch **7** rumorer, tattler, tipster **8** gossiper, informer, quidnunc, squealer **10** newsmonger **11** rumormonger, stool pigeon **13** scandalmonger

talent 4 bent, gift, nose **5** craft, flair, forte, money, skill **6** genius **7** aptness, faculty **9** endowment, expertise

Tale of Two Cities, A *author:* **7** Dickens *character:* **6** Carton (Sidney), Darnay (Charles) **7** Defarge, Manette (Alexander), Manette (Lucie)

Tales of a Traveller author 6 Irving

Tales of a Wayside Inn author **10** Longfellow

Tales of Hoffman composer **9** Offenbach

talipot 4 palm

talisman 4 juju, luck, zemi **5** charm, saffi **6** amulet, fetish, mascot, saphie **7** periapt **10** phylactery

Talisman, The *author:* **5** Scott

talk 3 gab, rap, yak **4** blab, buzz, chat, chin, sing, yarn **5** on-dit, prate, rumor, run on, speak, utter, voice **6** babble, dialog, gabble, gossip, parley, patter, powwow, report, speech, squeal, tattle **7** address, chatter, declaim, gabfest, hearsay, lecture, prattle **8** causerie, colloque, colloquy, converse, dialogue, harangue, perorate, vocalize **9** discourse, grapevine, hold forth, speechify, utterance, verbalize **10** allocution, discussion **11** scuttlebutt **12** conversation, deliberation **13** confabulation, verbalization *about:* **7** discuss *back:* **4** sass *combining form:* **3** log **4** logy **5** logia, logue *foolish:* **4** bunk **6** babble **7** chatter, palaver *indistinctly:* **6** mumble, mutter *over:* **7** discuss *slowly:* **5** drawl *small:* **8** chitchat *wildly:* **4** rant, rave

talkative 4 glib **5** gabby, vocal **6** chatty, fluent, mouthy **7** gossipy, voluble **9** garrulous **10** babblative, loquacious **11** looselipped **12** loose-tongued, multiloquent **13** multiloquious

tall 4 high **5** lanky, lofty, rangy **8** towering **11** skyscraping **12** altitudinous

tallow 3 fat **4** suet **6** grease *combining form:* **4** sebi, sebo **5** stear, steat **6** stearo, steato

tally 4 jibe **5** agree, count, fit in, match, score **6** accord, number, square **7** balance, catalog, conform, itemize **8** numerate **9** catalogue, enumerate, harmonize, inventory **10** correspond

Talmai *daughter:* **6** Maacah *father:* **4** Anak *grandson:* **7** Absalom

talon 4 claw

talus 5 ankle, scree, slope

tam 3 cap

Tamar *brother:* **7** Absalom *father:* **5** David **7** Absalom *father-in-law:* **5** Judah *half brother:* **5** Amnon *husband:* **2** Er *seducer:* **5** Amnon *son:* **5** Perez, Zerah

tamarisk 4 atle **5** athel, atlee

tambour 3 cup **4** bell, drum, wall **7** drummer

tambourine 4 dove, drum **7** timbrel

Tamburlaine the Great author 7 Marlowe

tame 4 meek, mild **6** docile, gentle, master, pliant **7** pliable, subdued, trained **8** amenable, biddable, broken in, domestic, obedient **9** tractable **10** submissive **11** domesticate, domesticize, domiciliate, housebroken **12** domesticated

Taming of the Shrew, The *character:* **6** Bianca **8** Baptista **9** Katharina, Petruchio

Tammany boss 5 Tweed

Tammuz' lover 6 Ishtar

tam-o'-shanter 3 cap

tamp 3 jam, mat, ram **4** cram, pack **5** pound, stuff

tampion 4 plug

tan 3 sun, taw **4** beat, ecru, flog, whip **5** beige, brown, toast **6** bronze, darken, thrash

tanager 4 bird, yeni

Tancred, Tancredi *beloved:* **8** Clorinda *father:* **3** Odo *mother:* **4** Emma *victim:* **8** Clorinda

tandem 4 pair **8** carriage

tang 3 nip **4** bite, odor, zest **5** aroma, sapor, savor, smack, taste **6** flavor, relish **8** piquancy, pungency, sapidity **9** spiciness

tangible 7 tactile **8** embodied, material, palpable, physical, sensible **9** corporeal, touchable **10** detectable, observable, phenomenal **11** appreciable, discernible, perceptible, substantial

tangle 3 mat, web **4** knot, maze, mesh, muck, trap **5** benet, catch, mix up, ravel, skein, snare, snarl **6** entrap, foul up, jungle, morass, muddle **7** catch up, embroil, ensnare, ensnarl, involve, mizmaze, perplex **9** implicate, labyrinth **10** complicate

Tanglewood Tales author 9 Hawthorne

tango 5 dance

tank 3 vat **5** basin **7** cistern, pachuca, vehicle **8** aquarium **9** container, reservoir *American:* **7** Sherman *German:* **6** panzer *part:* **6** turret

tankard 3 mug **5** stoup **6** flagon **9** blackjack

tanker 4 ship **5** oiler

Tannhäuser composer 6 Wagner

tantalize 4 bait, gnaw **5** annoy, harry,

taunt, tease, worry **6** harass, pester, plague **7** bedevil, hagride, torment **9** beleaguer, frustrate

Tantalus *daughter:* **5** Niobe *father:* **4** Zeus *son:* **6** Pelops

tantamount 4 same **5** alike, equal **8** selfsame **9** duplicate, identical **10** equivalent

tantara 5 blare **7** fanfare

tantivy 4 rush **6** gallop **8** headlong

tantrum 3 fit

Tanzania *capital:* **11** Dar es Salaam *monetary unit:* **8** shilingi

Taoism founder 6 Lao Tzu

tap 3 bar, bob, hit, pub, rap **4** cock, draw, name, pump, tunk **5** draft, drain, knock, nudge, thump, valve **6** faucet, finger, siphon, spigot, strike **7** appoint, barroom, draw off, hydrant, petcock **8** nominate, stopcock **9** designate

tape 4 band, belt, bind **5** strip **6** fillet, record, ribbon **7** bandage, measure *kind:* **5** inkle **6** ferret **7** masking **8** adhesive **9** measuring *machine:* **8** recorder

taper 4 wick **5** abate, close, spire **6** lessen, reduce **7** dwindle **8** decrease, diminish **9** drain away

tapering 5 conic, spiry **6** terete **7** conical, pointed **8** fusiform, subulate **9** acuminate

tapestry 5 arras, kilim **6** dossal **7** curtain, Gobelin, hanging *pattern:* **7** cartoon *tool:* **6** broché

tapeworm 6 taenia **8** parasite *body:* **8** strobila *combining form:* **4** taen **5** taeni **6** taenio *head:* **6** scolex

Taphath's father 7 Solomon

tapioca 7 cassava, pudding

Tappuah's father 6 Hebron

taproom 3 bar, pub **6** saloon, tavern

tapster 6 barman **7** barmaid **9** barkeeper, bartender **10** mixologist

tar 4 jack, pave, salt, soil **5** pitch, smear, stain, sully, taint **6** defile, sailor, seaman **7** asphalt, besmear, mariner **8** besmirch **9** sailorman

taradiddle 3 fib, lie **5** story **6** canard **7** falsity **9** falsehood **13** prevarication

tarantella 5 dance

tarantula 6 spider

Taras Bulba author 5 Gogol

tarboosh 3 fez, hat

tardy 3 lax **4** late, slow **7** belated, delayed, laggard, overdue **8** detained, dilatory **10** behindhand, delinquent, unpunctual

tare 4 seed **5** vetch **6** weight

target 3 aim **4** butt, goal, mark **6** object, victim **9** objective, quaesitum **11** sitting duck *center:* **8** bull's-eye *shooter's:* **10** clay pigeon

Tar Heel State 13 North Carolina

tariff 3 tab, tax **4** cost, duty, levy, rate **5** price **6** charge, impost **8** price tag **10** assessment

Tarkington, Booth *character:* **6** Penrod

tarn 4 lake, pool

tarnish 3 dim, mar, tar **4** dull, fade, foul, harm, hurt, pale, soil **5** dirty, grime, muddy, smear, spoil, sully, taint **6** besoil, damage, impair, injure, smirch, smudge, smutch **7** begrime, besmear, blemish **8** besmirch, discolor

taro 4 dalo, eddo, gabe, gabi **5** aroid, tania **6** yautia **7** dasheen, malanga *product:* **3** poi

tarpaulin 4 jack, salt **5** cover **6** sailor, seaman **7** mariner **9** sailorman

tarpon 4 fish **5** oxeye

tarry 3 lag **4** bide, drag, poke, stay, wait **5** abide, dally, delay, trail, visit **6** linger, loiter, put off, remain **8** stop over **11** stick around **13** procrastinate

Tarshish's father 6 Bilhan

tarsus 5 ankle

tart 3 dry, pie **4** acid, sour **5** acerb, sharp **6** pastry **7** acerbic, acetose, piquant, pungent **9** acidulous

Tartar 6 Mongol **7** Turkish **8** Mongolic **9** Mongolian

Tartuffe author 7 Molière

Tarzan *creator:* **9** Burroughs (Edgar Rice) *mate:* **4** Jane

task 3 job **4** duty, lade, load, toil, work **5** chare, chore, labor, stint, weigh **6** burden, charge, devoir, errand, lumber, saddle, weight **7** mission, project **8** encumber **10** assignment **11** undertaking

Tasmanian 4 wolf **5** devil

Tasmania's capital 6 Hobart

tassel 4 tuft **5** adorn **6** fringe **7** pendant **8** ornament

taste 3 eat, sip, try **4** dash, feel, hint, tang, zest **5** grace, gusto, heart, sapor, savor, smack, tinge, touch, whiff **6** degust, flavor, liking, palate, polish, relish, trifle **7** finesse, stomach **8** appetite, elegance, fondness, sapidity, soft spot, tincture, weakness **9** appetence **10** experience, partiality, refinement, sprinkling **11** inclination *combining form:* **6** geusia *kind:* **4** salt, sour **5** sweet **6** bitter *lacking:* (see **tasteless**) *organ:* **3** bud

tasteless 4 dull, flat, wild **5** bland, vapid **6** vulgar **7** insipid **8** barbaric, unsavory **9** barbarian, barbarous, graceless, inelegant, savorless, unrefined **10** flavorless, outlandish, unflavored, unpolished **11** ill-flavored, unpalatable **12** unappetizing **13** uninteresting

tasty 5 sapid **6** savory, toothy **9** palatable, relishing, toothsome **10** appetizing, flavorsome

Tate 7 Gallery

tatou 9 armadillo

tatter 3 rag, rip 4 tear 5 shred

tattered 5 dingy, seedy, tacky 6 frayed, ragged, shabby, tagrag 7 run-down, shreddy 8 frazzled 10 bedraggled, broken-down, threadbare 11 dilapidated

tattle 4 blab, buzz, talk 5 rumor 6 gossip, report 7 hearsay 9 grapevine 11 scuttlebutt

tattler see **talebearer**

tattletale see **talebearer**

tatty 4 base, mean, poor 5 cheap 6 common, paltry, shoddy, sleazy, trashy 8 rubbishy

taunt 4 gibe, lout, mock, razz, twit 5 scout, tease 6 deride 7 provoke 8 reproach, ridicule

taurine 6 bovine

Taurus 4 bull *star:* 9 Aldebaran

taut 5 close, tense, tight

tautology 8 pleonasm, verbiage 9 verbality 10 periphrase, redundancy, roundabout 11 periphrasis 13 circumambages

tavern 3 bar, inn, pub 5 hotel, lodge 6 bistro, hostel, saloon 7 auberge, barroom, hospice, taproom 8 alehouse, drinkery, hostelry 9 roadhouse 11 caravansary, public house 12 watering hole

taverner 8 boniface, publican 9 barkeeper, innholder, innkeeper, saloonist 12 saloonkeeper

taw 5 stake 6 marble

tawdry 4 loud 5 gaudy 6 brazen, flashy, garish, tinsel 7 blatant, chintzy, glaring 12 meretricious

tawny 3 tan 4 dark 5 brown 6 tanned *combining form:* 5 fusco, pyrrh, pyrro 6 pyrrho

tax 4 duty, lade, levy, load, onus, scot, toll 5 abuse, tithe 6 assess, burden, cumber, impost, saddle, strain, tariff, weight 7 tollage, tribute 8 encumber 10 assessment, deadweight *agency:* 3 IRS *feudal:* 7 scutage, tallage *kind:* 4 geld 5 sales, tithe 6 excise, income 7 chevage, prisage 8 property 9 surcharge *on salt:* 7 gabelle *rate:* 10 assessment

taxi 3 cab, car 4 hack

taxing 5 tough 6 trying 7 exigent, onerous, weighty 8 exacting, grievous 9 demanding 10 burdensome, oppressive

Taygeta *father:* 5 Atlas *mother:* 7 Pleione *sisters:* 8 Pleiades

tazza 3 cup 4 vase

Tchaikovsky, Peter *ballet:* 8 Swan Lake 10 Nutcracker *opera:* 12 Eugene Onegin 13 Queen of Spades

tea 5 drink, party 6 repast 8 beverage 9 marijuana, reception *black:* 5 bohea, oopak, pekoe 8 souchong *cake:* 6 cookie *genus:* 4 Thea *ingredient:* 8 caffeine

kind: 4 herb, Java 5 Assam, black, bohea, green, hyson, ledum, pekoe 6 Ceylon, congou, oolong 7 cambric 8 souchong 9 sassafras *of India:* 10 Darjeeling

teach 5 coach, train, tutor 6 impart, school 7 educate, instill 8 instruct 9 enlighten, inculcate 12 indoctrinate

teacher 4 guru, prof 5 coach, guide, tutor 6 docent, master, mentor, pedant 7 edifier, maestro, trainer 8 educator, magister 9 pedagogue, preceptor, professor 10 instructor 12 schoolmaster *Hindu:* 5 swami *Jewish:* 5 rabbi 7 rabboni *Muslim:* 3 pir 5 mulla 6 mollah, mullah *religious:* 8 mystagog 9 catechist

Tea for Two composer 7 Youmans

team 4 club, crew, gang, join, pair, side, yoke 5 group, squad, wagon 8 carriage *baseball:* 4 nine *basketball:* 4 five 7 quintet *football:* 6 eleven *kind:* 2 JV 6 jayvee 7 varsity *supporter:* 3 fan

tear 3 cut, rip, run 4 bolt, dash, gash, lash, race, rend, rift, rive, rush, slit 5 chase, fling, sever, shoot, shred, slash, speed, split 6 career, charge, cleave, course, incise, sunder, tatter 8 lacerate

tear down 4 raze, ruin, slur 5 smear, wrack, wreck 6 defame, malign 7 asperse, destroy, shatter, slander 8 demolish, destruct 9 denigrate 10 annihilate, calumniate, scandalize

tearful 3 sad 5 weepy 6 crying 7 bawling, sobbing, weeping 8 mourning 9 lamenting, sniveling 10 blubbering, lachrymose

tear-jerking 5 mushy 6 slushy, sticky 7 maudlin, mawkish 8 bathetic, romantic 11 sentimental

teary see **tearful**

tease 3 kid, rip 4 gnaw, josh, twit 5 annoy, chaff, harry, taunt, worry 6 harass, pester, plague 7 bedevil 8 ridicule 9 beleaguer

Tebah *father:* 5 Nahor *mother:* 6 Reumah

teched 4 daft 5 batty, crazy 6 crazed, insane 7 cracked, lunatic 8 demented, deranged 9 bedlamite

technicality 6 detail 8 loophole

technique 3 way 4 mode, wise 5 modus 6 manner, method, system 7 fashion *combining form:* 4 urgy

tectonic 10 structural

ted 5 strew 6 spread 7 scatter

tedious 3 dry 4 arid, dull 5 dusty 6 boring, tiring 7 insipid, irksome 8 boresome, bromidic, drudging, weariful 9 dryasdust, wearisome 13 uninteresting

tedium 4 yawn 5 ennui 7 boredom 8 doldrums, dullness, monotony

teem 4 flow 5 crawl, swarm 6 abound 9 pullulate

teeming 4 lush, rife 5 alive 6 aswarm

7 replete 8 swarming, thronged 9 abounding 11 overflowing

teen 5 youth 8 juvenile 9 youngster 10 adolescent

tee off 4 open 5 begin, drive, enter, start 6 take up 8 commence, initiate

teeter 5 lurch 6 falter, seesaw, topple, totter, wobble 7 stagger, stumble

teeth *false:* 8 dentures *grinding:* 7 bruxism *having:* 7 dentate *problem:* 5 decay 6 caries 8 overbite *relating to:* 6 dental; (see also **tooth**)

teg 3 doe 4 deer 5 sheep

tegua 8 moccasin

teju 6 lizard

telamon 5 atlas *counterpart:* 8 caryatid

Telamon *brother:* 6 Peleus *father:* 6 Aeacus *half-brother:* 6 Phocus *son:* 4 Ajax 6 Teucer

Telegonus *father:* 7 Ulysses 8 Odysseus *mother:* 5 Circe

telegraph 4 wire 5 cable 6 signal *code:* 5 Morse

Telemachus *Father:* 7 Ulysses 8 Odysseus *mother:* 8 Penelope

telephone 4 buzz, call, dial, ring 5 phone 6 ring up *inventor:* 4 Bell

Telephus *father:* 8 Heracles, Hercules *mother:* 4 Auge

telescope 5 glass 8 compress, condense, spyglass

television 2 TV 4 tube 5 video 8 boob tube *antenna:* 10 rabbit ears *award:* 4 Emmy *British:* 5 telly *frequency:* 3 UHF, VHF *interference:* 4 snow *network:* 3 ABC, BBC, CBS, NBC, NET, PBS *pioneer:* 5 Baird 8 Zworykin *program:* 4 news, show 5 rerun 6 series, sitcom 7 western 8 game show 9 broadcast, docudrama, soap opera *tube:* 4 kine 9 kinescope

tell 3 bid, say 4 clew, clue, post, tale, warn 5 mouth, order, spill, state, tally, utter 6 advise, betray, charge, direct, enjoin, fill in, inform, notify, number, relate, reveal, wise up 7 blab out, command, declare, divulge, narrate 8 bring out, disclose, discover, give away, instruct, numerate

teller 5 clerk 7 cashier, counter 8 informer, narrator

telling 5 solid, sound, valid 6 cogent 10 convincing, satisfying 12 satisfactory

tell off 3 jaw 4 rail 5 scold 6 berate, revile 7 bawl out, chew out, upbraid 8 call down 10 tongue-lash, vituperate

tell on 6 snitch, tattle

telltale 3 cue 4 clue, hint, wind 5 clack, tabby 6 gossip, notion 7 inkling 8 gossiper, quidnunc 9 carrytale 10 indication, intimation, newsmonger, suggestion, tale-

bearer 12 gossipmonger 13 scandalmonger

tellurian 6 earthy 7 earthly, mundane, terrene, worldly 9 sublunary 11 terrestrial, uncelestial

tellurium *symbol:* 2 Te

Tema's father 7 Ishmael

temblor 5 quake, shake, shock 6 quaker, tremor 10 earthquake

temerarious 4 rash 6 daring 8 heedless, reckless 9 audacious, daredevil, foolhardy, imprudent, venturous 10 incautious 11 adventurous, injudicious, venturesome 13 adventuresome

temerity 4 gall 5 nerve 6 daring 8 audacity, rashness 9 assurance, brashness, hardihood, hardiness 11 impetuosity 12 heedlessness, impertinence, recklessness 13 foolhardiness

temper 4 curb, mind, mood, tone, vein 5 humor 6 dilute, makeup, season, soften, spirit, strain, timbre 7 passion 8 moderate, modulate, restrain, tone down 10 complexion 11 personality 13 individualism, individuality

temperament 4 mood 5 humor 6 makeup, nature 9 character 10 complexion 11 disposition, personality

temperamental 5 moody 6 fickle 8 ticklish, unstable, variable, volatile 9 humorsome, mercurial, uncertain 10 capricious, changeable, inconstant

temperance 7 control, measure 8 sobriety 9 austerity 10 abstinence, continence, moderation 11 refrainment, self-control 12 moderateness *advocate of:* 6 Nation 7 Willard

temperate 4 calm, even 5 sober 6 modest, steady 8 discreet, moderate 9 abstinent, continent, regulated, unextreme 10 abstemious, controlled, reasonable, restrained 11 abstentious, unexcessive 12 conservative 13 unimpassioned

temperature 4 heat 5 fever 6 warmth 9 intensity

tempest 4 gale, rage, wind 5 storm 6 tumult, uproar 9 commotion, hurricane

Tempest, The *character:* 5 Ariel 7 Caliban, Miranda 8 Prospero 9 Ferdinand

tempestuous 4 wild 5 rough 6 raging, stormy 7 furious, violent 8 blustery 9 turbulent, unbridled 10 blustering, tumultuous

temple 4 fane 6 church 10 house of God, tabernacle 13 house of prayer *ancient:* 4 naos 5 speos 8 pantheon *Aztec:* 6 teopan 8 teocalli *Buddhist:* 2 ta 3 taa, wat *Eastern:* 6 pagoda *Greek:* 6 hieron 9 Parthenon *sanctuary:* 5 cella 6 adytum 10 penetralia

tempo 4 pace, rate, time 5 speed 6 rhythm *fast:* 6 presto 7 allegro *moder-*

ate: 7 andante **slow:** 5 grave, lento 6 adagio

temporal 3 lay 6 earthy 7 mundane, profane, secular, sensual, worldly 8 banausic, unsacred 13 materialistic

temporary 6 acting, pro tem, supply 7 interim 9 ad interim, transient 10 pro tempore

tempt 3 woo 4 bait, lure, risk, vamp 5 decoy, train 6 allure, entice, entrap, invite, lead on, seduce 7 solicit 8 inveigle 9 tantalize

temptation 4 bait, lure, trap 5 decoy, snare 6 come-on 10 allurement, enticement, seducement 12 inveiglement

temptress 4 vamp 5 siren 7 Delilah, Lorelei 10 seductress 11 femme fatale

ten *cents:* 4 dime *combining form:* 3 dec, dek 4 deca, deka 5 decem *dollars:* 7 sawbuck *mills:* 4 cent *thousand:* 6 myriad *years:* 6 decade

tenacious 3 set 4 fast, firm, true 5 fixed, stout, tight, tough 6 dogged, secure, strong, sturdy, viscid 7 viscose, viscous 8 resolute, stalwart, stubborn 9 obstinate, steadfast 10 bulldogged, persisting 11 bulldoggish, persevering 12 pertinacious

tenacity 8 firmness 10 resolution 11 persistence

tenant 6 holder, lessee, occupy, people, renter 7 boarder, dweller, inhabit 8 occupant, populate 9 collibert *feudal:* 4 leud 6 bordar, vassal 7 socager, sokeman *Indian:* 7 chakdar *Irish:* 7 cottier

tenantable 7 livable 9 habitable, lodgeable 10 occupiable 11 inhabitable

Ten Commandments 9 Decalogue

tend 4 care, lean, look, mind, till, work 5 dress, labor, nurse, serve, watch 7 care for, conduce, incline, redound 8 minister 10 contribute

tendency 3 run 4 bent, bias 5 drift, tenor, trend 7 current, leaning 8 penchant 9 inclining 10 proclivity, propensity 11 disposition, inclination 12 predilection *combining form:* 5 phily 6 philia *suffix:* 4 itis

tendentious 6 biased 7 colored, partial 8 one-sided, partisan 10 prejudiced

tender 4 fond, give, mild, pose, soft, sore, warm 5 offer 6 extend, gentle, humane, loving, submit 7 hold out, lenient, present, proffer, propose 8 yielding 9 forgiving 10 benevolent, charitable, responsive 11 considerate, kindhearted, softhearted, sympathetic, warmhearted 12 affectionate 13 commiserative, compassionate

tenderfoot 4 colt, tyro 6 novice, rookie 8 beginner, freshman, neophyte, newcomer 9 novitiate 10 apprentice

Tender Is the Night author 10 Fitzgerald

tendon 4 band, cord 5 sinew

tendril 4 curl 6 cirrus 7 ringlet

tenebrific 5 black, bleak 6 dismal, dreary, gloomy, somber 8 funereal 10 oppressive 11 dispiriting 13 disheartening

tenebrous 3 dim 4 dark, dusk 5 dusky, murky, vague 6 gloomy 7 obscure, unclear 9 ambiguous, equivocal, lightless, sibylline, uncertain 10 caliginous, unexplicit 13 unilluminated

tenement 4 flat 5 rooms, suite 6 rental 7 lodging 8 building 9 apartment

tenet 3 ism 5 canon, dogma 8 doctrine

tenfold 6 denary

Tennessee *capital:* 9 Nashville *college, university:* 5 Bryan 10 Vanderbilt *largest city:* 7 Memphis *nickname:* 14 Volunteer State *state flower:* 4 iris

tennis *award:* 8 Davis Cup *item:* 3 net 4 ball 6 racket 7 racquet *kind:* 5 table 7 doubles, singles 8 platform *score:* 4 love 5 deuce *serve:* 3 ace *shoe:* 7 sneaker *stroke:* 3 cut, lob 4 chop, drop 5 serve, slice 6 volley 8 backhand, forehand *term:* 3 let, set 5 court, fault 7 service 9 advantage, backcourt

tennis champ 4 Ashe (Arthur), Borg (Bjorn), Graf (Steffi), King (Billie Jean), Noah (Yannick), Wade (Virginia) 5 Budge (Don), Court (Margaret Smith), Evert (Chris), Laver (Rod), Lendl (Ivan), Perry (Fred), Seles (Monica), Vilas (Guillermo), Wills (Helen) 6 Agassi (André), Austin (Tracy), Becker (Boris), Edberg (Stephan), Fraser (Neale), Gibson (Althea), Kramer (Jack), Tilden (Bill) 7 Connors (Jimmy), Emerson (Roy), Lacoste (Rene), McEnroe (John), Nastase (Ilie) 8 Connolly (Maureen), Gonzalez (Pancho), Newcombe (John), Rosewall (Ken), Sabatini (Gabriela), Wilander (Mats) 11 Navratilova (Martina)

Tennyson poem 4 Maud 7 Ulysses 8 Tiresias 10 Enoch Arden, In Memoriam 12 Locksley Hall

tenor 3 run 4 body, mood, tone 5 drift, voice 6 singer 7 current, meaning, purport 8 tendency 9 substance *American:* 5 Lanza 6 Peerce, Tucker 8 Melchior 9 McCormack, McCracken *Canadian:* 7 Vickers *Czech:* 6 Slezak *German:* 10 Wunderlich *Italian:* 5 Gigli 6 Caruso 7 Corelli 8 Bergonzi 9 del Monaco, di Stefano, Pavarotti *Spanish:* 7 Domingo 8 Carreras *Swedish:* 5 Gedda 8 Bjorling 9 Bjoerling

tenpins 7 bowling

tense 4 edgy, taut 5 nervy, tight 6 uneasy 7 anxious, jittery, restive, uptight 8 strained *grammatical:* 4 past 6 future 7 perfect, present 8 preterit 9 preterite 10 pluperfect 11 progressive

tension 6 nerves, strain, stress, unease 7 anxiety 8 pressure, tautness 9 agitation 10 discomfort, uneasiness 11 nervousness, uptightness

tent 4 camp 5 bivvy, cover, lodge 6 canopy, encamp, laager, maroon 7 bivouac, shelter *Eskimo:* 5 tupik *kind:* 3 pup 4 bell, pawl, yort 5 Baker, tepee 6 teepee, wigwam 7 kibitka, marquee, wickiup 8 pavilion, umbrella *maker:* 4 Omar *material:* 6 canvas *part:* 3 fly, guy, peg 4 pole

tentacle 3 arm 6 feeler

tentative 4 test 5 trial 6 wobbly 7 halting 8 hesitant 9 faltering, makeshift, provisory, uncertain 10 irresolute 11 conditional, provisional, vacillating, vacillatory 12 provisionary

tenth 5 tithe *combining form:* 4 deci

tenuous 4 rare, slim, thin, weak 5 reedy 6 feeble, flimsy, slight, stalky, subtle, twiggy 7 slender, squinny, subtile 8 ethereal, rarefied 9 attenuate 10 attenuated 11 implausible 13 insubstantial, unsubstantial

tenure 4 grip, hold, term 5 clamp, clasp, grasp, gripe 6 clench, clinch, clutch, estate 7 grapple *feudal:* 7 burgage

tepid 4 mild, warm 7 warmish 8 lukewarm, milk-warm 9 temperate 11 halfhearted, indifferent

tequila source 6 mescal

Terah's son 5 Abram, Haran, Nahor 7 Abraham

teras 7 monster

terbium *symbol:* 2 Tb

Terentia's husband 6 Cicero

Tereus *son:* 4 Itys *wife:* 6 Procne

tergiversate 3 rat 4 turn 5 dodge, evade, hedge 6 defect, desert, weasel 7 shuffle 8 renounce, sidestep 9 pussyfoot, repudiate 10 apostatize, equivocate

term 3 dub 4 call, name, span, time, word 5 bound, hitch, spell 6 detail, period, tenure 7 article, baptize, stretch 8 christen, duration 9 designate 10 denominate, limitation, particular

termagant 5 harpy, rowdy, scold, shrew, vixen 6 amazon, ogress, unruly, virago 7 raucous 8 fishwife 5 rowdy 9 turbulent, Xanthippe 10 boisterous, disorderly, rowdydowdy, tumultuous 11 rumbustious

terminable 6 finite 7 endable, limited 9 limitable

terminal 3 end, lag 4 last 5 depot, final 6 latest, latter 7 closing, station 8 eventual, hindmost, ultimate 10 concluding *negative:* 7 cathode *positive:* 5 anode

terminate 2 ax 3 end 4 drop, fire, halt, quit, rise, sack, stop 5 close, leave 6 bounce, finish, recess, resign, wind up, wrap up 7 abolish, adjourn, boot out, cash-

ier, dismiss, kick out 8 complete, conclude, dissolve, prorogue, ultimate 9 determine, discharge, prorogate 10 extinguish 11 discontinue

terminology 4 cant 6 jargon 7 lexicon, palaver 8 language 10 dictionary, vocabulary

termite 3 ant

tern 4 trio 5 scray 8 schooner *genus:* 6 Sterna

ternary 6 triple 9 threefold

terpsichore see **Muse**

terrace 4 bank, dais, deck, roof, step 5 bench, porch 7 balcony, portico 8 platform

terra-cotta 4 clay 7 pottery

terra firma 4 dirt, land, soil 5 earth 6 ground 7 dry land

terrain 4 turf, walk 5 field 6 domain, sphere 7 demesne 8 dominion, province 9 bailiwick, champaign, territory 10 topography

terrapin 6 turtle

terrestrial 6 earthy 7 earthly, mundane, profane, prosaic, secular, terrene, worldly 8 telluric 9 earthlike, sublunary, tellurian 10 earthbound

terrible 3 bad 4 grim, hard 5 awful, heavy, tough 6 fierce, grisly, horrid, severe 7 arduous, fearful, furious, ghastly, hideous, intense, macabre, vicious, violent 8 dreadful, gruesome, horrible, horrific, shocking, toilsome, vehement 9 appalling, desperate, difficult, exquisite, frightful, laborious, strenuous 10 formidable, horrifying *combining form:* 3 din 4 dein, dino 5 deino

terrier 3 dog *kind:* 3 fox 4 blue, bull, Skye 5 cairn, Irish, Welsh 6 Boston 8 Airedale, Lakeland 9 Yorkshire

terrific 5 super, swell 6 superb 7 fearful 8 dreadful, glorious, horrible, horrific, shocking 9 appalling, frightful, marvelous, upsetting, wonderful 10 formidable 11 magnificent, sensational, terrorizing

terrify 3 awe 4 stun 5 alarm, scare 7 startle 8 affright, frighten 9 terrorize

terrifying 4 grim 6 grisly, horrid 7 ghastly, hideous, macabre 8 gruesome, horrible, terrible 10 horrifying

territory 4 area, belt, land, turf, walk, zone 5 field, tract 6 domain, region, sphere 7 demesne, terrain 8 dominion, province 9 bailiwick, champain

terror 4 fear 5 alarm, dread, panic 6 dismay, fright, horror 9 trepidity 11 fearfulness, trepidation 13 consternation

terrorist 4 thug 6 bomber 7 Jacobin 8 alarmist

terrorize 3 cow 5 alarm, bully, scare 6 fright, hector 7 dragoon 8 affright, bludg-

eon, browbeat, bulldoze, bullyrag, frighten **9** strong-arm **10** intimidate

terry 4 loop **6** fabric **8** toweling

terse 4 curt, taut **5** brief, crisp, pithy, short **7** compact, concise, laconic, summary **8** succinct **11** compendiary, compendious **12** breviloquent

tertiary 5 third

tessera 3 die **4** tile **6** tablet, ticket

test 3 try **4** exam, quiz **5** assay, check, essay, final, prove, trial, try on **6** sample, trying, try out, verify **7** confirm, examine, mid-term, proving **8** sounding, trial run **10** experiment **11** demonstrate, examination **12** experimental

testa 4 coat **5** shell **8** episperm **10** integument

testament 4 will **5** proof **7** witness **8** evidence **9** scripture, testimony **11** attestation, testimonial **12** confirmation

tester 5 frame **6** canopy, prover **7** assayer

testifier 7 witness **8** deponent **9** proselyte

testify 5 argue, swear **6** attest, depone, depose **7** bespeak, betoken, point to, witness **8** announce, indicate

testimonial 5 proof, salvo, token **6** salute **7** tribute, witness **8** evidence, memorial, monument **9** character, reference, testament **10** indication **11** attestation, credentials **12** appreciation, confirmation

testimony 5 proof **7** witness **8** evidence **10** indication **11** affirmation, attestation **12** confirmation **13** documentation

testy 5 cross, ratty **6** cranky, tetchy, touchy **7** grouchy **8** choleric **9** irascible, irritable, temperish **10** ill-humored **12** cantankerous **13** quick-tempered

tetanus 7 lockjaw, trismus

tetchy see **testy**

tête-à-tête 4 chat, coze, talk **7** vis-à-vis **8** causerie **10** discussion **12** conversation

tether 3 tie **4** bind, rope **5** cable, chain, scope **6** fasten

Tethys *daughters:* **9** Oceanides *father:* **6** Uranus *husband:* **7** Oceanus *mother:* **2** Ge **4** Gaea **5** Terra

tetrad 4 four **7** quartet, quatuor **8** foursome **9** quartetto **10** quaternion

Teucer *father:* **7** Telamon **9** Scamander *stepbrother:* **4** Ajax

Teutonic 6 German **8** Germanic *language:* **5** Dutch **6** Danish, German, Gothic **7** English, Flemish, Frisian, Swedish **9** Afrikaans, Norwegian

Texas *capital:* **6** Austin *college, university:* **3** SMU **4** Rice **5** Lamar, Wiley **6** Baylor *largest city:* **7** Houston *nickname:* **13** Lone Star State *state flower:* **10** bluebonnet

text 4 head **5** motif, point, theme, topic

6 matter, motive **7** subject **8** argument **13** subject matter

textbook 6 manual, primer

textile 6 fabric *dealer:* **6** mercer *machine:* **8** calender *shop:* **7** mercery *treat:* **9** mercerize

texture 3 web **5** being, fiber **6** fabric, nature **7** essence

Thackeray novel 9 Pendennis **10** Vanity Fair **11** Henry Esmond

Thailand 4 Siam *capital:* **7** Bangkok *language:* **3** Lao *monetary unit:* **4** baht **5** tical *temple:* **3** wat

Thaïs 7 hetaera **9** courtesan *author:* **6** France (Anatole) *composer:* **8** Massenet

thalassic 6 marine **7** oceanic **8** maritime

Thalia see **Graces; Muse**

thallium *symbol:* **2** Tl

Thanatopsis author 6 Bryant

Thanatos 5 death *brother:* **6** Hypnos *mother:* **3** Nyx

thankful 7 obliged **8** grateful **12** appreciative

thanks 2 ta **5** grace **8** blessing **9** gratitude **11** benediction **12** appreciation, thanksgiving

Thanksgiving 5 feast **7** holiday *first celebrant:* **6** Indian **7** Pilgrim *food:* **6** turkey

thatch 4 roof **5** cover

that is 2 i.e. *Latin:* **5** id est

Thaumas *daughter:* **4** Iris **5** Aello, Harpy **7** Celaeno, Ocypete *daughters:* **7** Harpies *father:* **6** Pontus *mother:* **2** Ge **4** Gaea *wife:* **7** Electra

thaumaturgic 5 magic **6** magian, mystic, witchy **7** magical **8** wizardly **9** sorcerous **11** necromantic

thaumaturgy 5 magic **7** sorcery **8** witchery, wizardry **9** conjuring **10** necromancy, witchcraft **11** bewitchment, enchantment, incantation

thaw 3 run **4** flux, fuse, melt **7** liquefy **8** dissolve, liquesce **10** deliquesce

the 7 article *French:* **2** la, le **3** les *German:* **3** das, der, die *Italian:* **2** il, la *Spanish:* **2** el, la **3** las, los

Thea *daughter:* **6** Selene *father:* **6** Uranus *husband:* **8** Hyperion *mother:* **2** Ge **4** Gaea

theater 4 hall **5** drama, house, odeum, stage **6** boards **9** playhouse **10** footlights *award:* **4** Tony *entrance:* **5** foyer, lobby *Greek:* **5** odeum *movie:* **6** cinema *outdoor:* **7** drive-in *part:* **3** box, pit **4** loge **5** skene, stage, wings **7** balcony, parodos, parquet **10** proscenium

theatrical 5 stagy **6** staged **8** affected, dramatic, mannered, thespian **10** artificial, histrionic **11** dramaturgic, exaggerated **12** melodramatic *agent:* **6** Morris *device:* **4** prop *group:* **6** troupe

Theban Eagle 6 Pindar
Thebes *founder:* 6 Cadmus *king:*
5 Laius 7 Oedipus *queen:* 7 Jocasta
theft 4 lift 5 pinch, steal 6 piracy 7 larceny, robbery, robbing, swiping 8 burglary,
filching, stealage, stealing, thievery, thieving 9 pilferage, pilfering 10 purloining *combining form:* 5 klept 6 klepto
The Golden 3 Ass 4 Bowl 5 Bough
6 Fleece, Legend
theme 4 head, text 5 essay, motif, paper,
point, topic 6 matter, motive, thesis 7 article, subject 8 argument 11 composition
13 subject matter
Themis *father:* 6 Uranus *goddess of:*
3 law 7 justice *husband:* 4 Zeus 7 Jupiter
mother: 2 Ge 4 Gaea
then 2 so 4 also, anon, ergo, thus, when
5 again, hence 7 besides, further 9 therefore, thereupon 10 in addition 11 accordingly 12 additionally, consequently
thence 4 away 7 thereof 9 therefrom
theologian *American:* 7 Edwards, Nie-
buhr, Tillich, Walther *Dutch:* 6 Jansen
English: 4 Bede 5 Pusey, Watts 6 Alcuin,
Wesley 8 Langston, Pelagius, Wycliffe
French: 6 Calvin 7 William 8 Sabatier *German:* 6 Rahner 7 Eckhart 9 Niemoller
14 Albertus Magnus *Greek:* 9 Zygomalas
Italian: 7 Aquinas, Socinus *Scottish:*
10 Duns Scotus *Spanish:* 6 Suarez 7 Vitoria 8 Servetus *Swedish:* 9 Soderblom
Swiss: 5 Barth, Vinet
Theologica 5 Summa
theological *school:* 8 seminary *virtue:*
4 hope 5 faith 7 charity
theorbo 4 lute 8 archlute
theorem 3 law 4 rule 5 axiom 9 principle 10 principium 11 fundamental
theoretical 5 ideal 8 abstract, academic,
notional, unproved 11 conjectural, speculative 12 hypothetical, transcendent 13 problematical, suppositional
theorize 6 submit 7 suggest 9 postulate
theory 7 perhaps, premise, suppose, surmise 8 supposal 10 conjecture, hypothesis 11 speculation, supposition *astronomical:* 7 big bang *combining form:* 4 logy
5 logia, ology *suffix:* 3 ism
therapy 9 treatment *combining form:*
5 pathy 6 pathic
therefore 2 so 4 ergo, then, thus
5 hence 11 accordingly 12 consequently
therefrom 6 thence
thereupon 4 then 6 at once
therm 7 calorie
thermal 3 hot 4 warm *unit:* 3 Btu
6 degree 7 calorie
thermometer 9 indicator *kind:* 7 Celsius,
Reaumur 10 centigrade, Fahrenheit
Thersander's father 9 Polynices

Thersites' slayer 8 Achilles
The Saint 12 Simon Templar
the same 4 idem 5 ditto 8 likewise
9 identical
thesaurus 7 lexicon 10 dictionary *editor:*
5 Roget
Theseus *father:* 6 Aegeus *mother:*
6 Aethra *slayer:* 9 Lycomedes *son:*
10 Hippolytus *victim:* 6 Sciron 8 Minotaur
10 Procrustes *wife:* 7 Phaedra
thesis 5 essay, point, posit 6 belief, memoir 7 premise 8 tractate, treatise 9 apriorism, discourse, monograph, postulate
10 contention, exposition, monography
11 postulation, proposition, supposition
12 disquisition, dissertation
thespian 4 mime 5 actor, mimic 6 mummer, player 7 trouper 8 dramatic, theatral,
theatric 9 performer, playactor 10 histrionic, theatrical 11 dramaturgic
12 impersonator
Thespis' forte 5 drama 7 tragedy
Thessalian hero 5 Jason 8 Achilles
the Terrible 4 Ivan
"The Thinker" sculptor 5 Rodin
Thetis 6 Nereid *father:* 6 Nereus *husband:* 6 Peleus *mother:* 5 Doris *son:*
8 Achilles
theurgist 8 magician
thew 4 beef 5 brawn, might, power,
sinew 6 muscle 8 strength
thick 3 fat 4 dull, dumb, wide 5 broad,
bulky, burly, close, dense, dumpy, husky,
obese, squat 6 chummy, chunky, flimsy,
obtuse, stocky, stupid 7 compact,
crammed, crowded, doltish, massive, viscous 8 blockish, duncical, familiar, heavyset, intimate 10 numskulled *combining
form:* 4 dasy, hadr 5 hadro, pachy
thicket 4 bosk, bush, wood 5 clump,
copse, grove 6 bosket, tangle 7 boscage,
coppice, spinney 9 brushwood, chaparral
Scottish: 4 rone
thickness 5 layer 7 density 9 callosity
thief 3 dip, nip 4 prig 5 ganef 6 bandit,
lifter, looter, nimmer, pirate, robber
7 booster, burglar, filcher, stealer
8 hijacker, larcener, pilferer 9 larcenist, purloiner 10 cat burglar, pickpocket, shoplifter
12 housebreaker
thieve 3 nip 4 hook, lift 5 filch, pinch,
steal, swipe 6 pilfer, snitch 7 purloin
thievery see **theft**
thievish 9 larcenous
thigh 3 ham 5 flank 6 gammon *bone:*
5 femur *combining form:* 3 mer 4 mero
5 cruro, merus 6 femoro *relating to:*
6 crural
thimble 3 cup 5 cover
thin 3 cut 4 fine, high, lank, lean, puny,
rare, slim, weak 5 acute, gaunt, lanky,

reedy, sharp, spare, wispy **6** argute, dilute, flimsy, meager, piping, rarefy, shrill, skinny, slight, sparse, stalky, treble, twiggy, watery, weaken **7** scrawny, slender, squinny, subtile, tenuous **8** piercing, rarefied, rawboned, skeletal, twiglike, wiredraw **9** attenuate, extenuate **10** attenuated **11** implausible, watered-down **12** unconvincing **13** unsubstantial *combining form:* **4** lept **5** lepto

thing 2 go **3** act, cry, fad **4** deed, item, mode, rage **5** being, craze, doing, event, mania, point, stuff, style, vogue **6** action, affair, detail, entity, fetish, furore, matter, object **7** article, concern, element, episode, fashion **8** business, existent, fixation, incident, material, occasion **9** existence, happening, obsession, substance **10** dernier cri, individual, occurrence, phenomenon *additional:* **5** bonus *in law:* **3** res *insignificant:* **6** trifle *rare:* **4** oner *single:* **4** unit *suffix:* **2** ia (plural) **3** ant, ory **4** oria (plural) **5** orium *to do:* **3** job **5** chore *unusual:* **5** freak **6** oddity *worthless:* **4** junk **5** waste

thingamajig 5 gizmo **6** dingus, doodad, gadget, jigger **7** dofunny **9** doohickey **10** thingumbob

things 4 duds, togs **5** dress, goods, stuff, traps **6** attire, tricks **7** apparel, clothes, effects, plunder, raiment **8** chattels, clothing, movables **10** attirement, belongings, habiliment, possession *for sale:* **11** merchandise

think 4 deem, feel, mull, muse **5** brood, fancy, guess, study, weigh **6** assume, expect, gather, ideate, ponder, reason **7** believe, imagine, perpend, presume, realize, reflect, suppose, surmise, suspect **8** cogitate, conceive, consider, envisage, envision, logicize, meditate, ruminate **9** cerebrate, speculate, visualize **10** conjecture, deliberate, excogitate, logicalize **11** contemplate, rationalize *out:* **4** plan *piece:* **7** article

third 8 tertiary *combining form:* **4** trit **5** trito *power:* **4** cube

third degree 5 grill **8** grilling **13** interrogation

third estate 5 plebs **6** people, plebes **8** populace **9** commonage, commoners, plebeians **10** commonalty **11** rank and file

Third Man, The *author:* **6** Greene

thirst 3 yen **4** ache, itch, long, lust, pine **5** crave, yearn **6** hanker, hunger

thirsty 3 dry **4** agog, arid, avid, keen, sere **5** eager **6** ardent **7** anxious, athirst, bone-dry, parched, droughty **9** impatient, unwatered, waterless **12** moistureless

this and that 8 oddments, sundries **9** etceteras **11** odds and ends

Thisbe's lover 7 Pyramus

This Side of Paradise author 10 Fitzgerald

thistle 4 weed **7** caltrop *Russian:* **10** tumbleweed

thistlebird 9 goldfinch

thither 3 yon **5** there **6** yonder

thole 3 peg, pin

___ Thomas, Welsh author 5 Dylan

Thomas à ___ 6 Becket, Kempis

Thomas' Greek name 7 Didymus

Thompson 5 Sadie **7** Dorothy, Francis

thong 4 lace, lash, rein **5** romal, strap, strip **7** amentum, babiche, latchet **8** whiplash

Thor 5 Donar *father:* **4** Odin *god of:* **7** thunder *hammer:* **8** Mjollnir *mother:* **5** Jordh, Jorth

thorax 5 chest

Thoreau, Henry David *friend:* **7** Emerson *work:* **6** Walden

thorium *symbol:* **2** Th

thorn 5 briar, brier, spine **7** acantha, spinule **9** annoyance **10** irritation *combining form:* **4** spin **5** spini, spino **6** acanth **7** acantho, spinoso **8** acanthus

thorny 5 sharp, spiny **6** tricky **7** prickly, spinate **9** difficult, vexatious **10** nettlesome **11** troublesome

thorough 4 full **6** minute **8** complete, detailed, itemized, whole-hog **9** clocklike **10** blow-by-blow, exhaustive

thoroughbred 5 horse **8** pedigree, purebred **9** pedigreed, pureblood **11** full-blooded

thoroughfare 3 way **4** drag, path, road **5** track **6** artery, avenue, street **7** highway **9** boulevard

thoroughgoing 4 rank **5** gross, utter **8** absolute, complete, outright, whole-hog **9** out-and-out **10** consummate, exhaustive **11** straight-out, unmitigated

though 3 yet **5** still, while **6** albeit **7** however, whereas **8** after all **11** nonetheless **12** nevertheless

thought 4 idea, mind **5** image **6** musing, notion **7** concept, opinion **9** brainwork, pondering **10** cogitation, conception, meditation, reflection, rumination **11** cerebration, speculation **12** deliberation, intellection **13** contemplation *combining form:* **3** log **4** logo

thoughtful 6 polite **7** careful, gallant, heedful, logical, mindful, pensive, serious **8** gracious, rational, studious, thinking **9** attentive, courteous, pondering, regardful **10** cogitative, meditative, reflecting, reflective, ruminative, solicitous **11** considerate **12** intellectual **13** contemplative

thoughtless 4 rash, rude **5** brash, hasty

6 madcap 7 selfish 8 careless, feckless, heedless, impolite, reckless, uncaring 9 hotheaded, unheeding, unrecking 10 illadvised, incautious, mad-brained, ungracious, unthinking 11 inadvertent 12 discourteous, irreflective, unreflective 13 inconsiderate

thousand *combining form:* 4 kilo *dollars:* 5 grand *years:* 10 millennium

thousandth 10 millesimal *combining form:* 5 milli

thrall 4 yoke 7 bondage, helotry, peonage, serfdom, slavery 9 servitude, villenage 11 enslavement

thrash 4 beat, drub, flog, hide, lash, lick, maul, pelt, whip 5 paste, pound, smear, whale 6 batter, buffet, larrup, pummel, stripe, wallop 7 belabor, scourge, shellac 8 lambaste 10 flagellate

thrash out 4 moot 5 argue 6 debate 7 agitate, canvass, discept, discuss, dispute 10 kick around, toss around

thread 4 line, vein, yard 5 fiber, reeve, weave 6 strand, stream, string 8 filament *ball of:* 4 clew, clue *combining form:* 3 mit, nem 4 fili, mito, nema, neme, nemo 5 nemat 6 nemata (plural), nemato *dental:* 5 floss *holder:* 6 bobbin *kind:* 4 silk, yarn 5 floss, lisle, watap 6 cotton, lingel 8 surgical *loose:* 8 raveling 9 ravelling *surgical:* 5 seton 6 catgut, suture

threadbare 4 hack, worn 5 dingy, faded, seedy, stale, tacky, tired, trite 6 cliché, frayed, ragged, shabby, tagrag 7 clichéd, run-down, worn-out 8 bathetic, shopworn, tattered, timeworn, well-worn 10 down-atheel 11 commonplace, dilapidated

threadlike 6 filose

threads 8 clothing

threat 6 duress, menace 7 warning

threaten 3 cow 4 warn 5 augur 6 menace 7 caution, portend, presage 8 browbeat, bulldoze, forebode, forewarn 10 intimidate

three 4 trey 5 crowd *combining form:* 3 ter, tri *group of:* (see **threesome**)

threefold 6 thrice, triple

Three Musketeers 5 Athos 6 Aramis 7 Porthos *author:* 5 Dumas

Threepenny Opera, The *author:* 6 Brecht *music:* 5 Weill

threescore 5 sixty

Three Sisters, The 4 Olga 5 Irina, Masha *author:* 7 Chekhov

Three Soldiers author 9 Dos Passos

threesome 4 trio 5 triad, trine 6 triple, triune, troika 7 trinity 11 triumvirate

three-wheeler 8 tricycle

threnody 5 dirge, elegy

thresh 4 beat, flog, whip 5 flail 6 strike

threshold 3 eve 4 edge, gate 5 brink, limen, point, verge

thrice 9 threefold *a day:* 3 t.i.d. 8 ter in die

thrift 7 economy 8 prudence 9 frugality, husbandry 11 economizing

thriftiness see thrift

thrifty 5 canny, chary 6 frugal, robust, saving 7 booming, roaring, sparing 8 thriving 9 provident, stewardly 10 conserving, economical, preserving, prospering, prosperous, unwasteful 11 flourishing

thrill 4 bang, boot, kick, send 6 excite, wallop 7 enthuse 9 electrify, galvanize 10 excitement 11 titillation

thriller 6 gothic 7 chiller, mystery, shocker 9 dime novel 13 penny dreadful

thrive 2 go 4 boom, grow 5 score 6 arrive 7 develop, make out, prosper, succeed 8 flourish

throat 3 maw 4 gula, tube 6 groove, gullet 7 channel, weasand, weazand *combining form:* 3 der 4 dero 6 bronch 7 broncho *inflammation:* 5 croup 6 angina, quinsy 10 laryngitis *relating to:* 8 guttural *upper:* 4 gula *warmer:* 5 scarf

throb 4 ache, beat 5 pulse 7 pulsate 9 palpitate

throe 3 fit 4 ache, pain, pang 5 spell 6 access, attack, stitch, twinge 7 seizure 10 convulsion

thrombus 4 clot

throne 4 apse, seat 5 chair, gaddi, power 8 cathedra 11 sovereignty

throng 4 host, pack, push 5 bunch, crowd, crush, drove, flock, group, horde, press 6 squash 9 multitude

throttle 5 choke 7 garrote 8 strangle 11 accelerator

through 2 by 3 per, via 4 done, over, past, with 5 about, due to, ended, round 6 around, direct 7 by way of, done for, owing to 8 by dint of, complete, finished, straight, washed-up 9 because of, by means of, completed, concluded 10 by virtue of, terminated, throughout 13 uninterrupted *prefix:* 2 di 3 dia, per

throughout 3 mid 4 amid, over 5 about, midst, round 6 around, during 7 all over, overall 10 everyplace, everywhere, far and near, far and wide, high and low *combining form:* 3 hol 4 holo

Through the Looking Glass *author:* 7 Carroll *character:* 5 Alice

throw 3 peg, put 4 cast, fire, hurl, toss 5 fling, heave, pitch, sling 6 launch, propel, unseat 7 buck off, project, unhorse *in the towel:* 4 quit 6 give up

throw away 4 blow, cast, junk, shed 5 scrap, waste 6 reject, slough 7 cashier, consume, discard, fritter 8 jettison, squander

throw back 6 reject, revert 7 regress
10 retrogress

throwback 7 atavism 9 reversion

throw down 4 fell 5 level 6 lay low
8 bowl over 9 knock over, overthrow, prostrate *the gauntlet:* 4 defy 9 challenge

throw off 3 rid 4 emit, lose, shed, slip,
vent 5 addle, eject, expel, issue, mix up,
shake 6 ball up 7 confuse, fluster, give out,
release 8 befuddle, bewilder, distract,
unburden *the track:* 6 derail 7 confuse,
mislead

throw out 4 cast, junk, shed 5 addle,
chuck, eject, evict, mix up, scrap 6 ball up,
reject, slough 7 cashier, confuse, discard,
dismiss, extrude, fluster 8 befuddle, bewilder, distract, jettison

throw up 4 barf 5 heave, vomit
7 upchuck 8 disgorge 10 jerry-build

thrush 4 bird 5 robin, veery 8 bluebird
European: 5 mavis, ouzel 6 mistle
9 blackbird, mistletoe 11 nightingale

thrust 3 dig, jab, ram, run 4 core, gist,
meat, pith, push, sink, stab 5 drive, sense,
short, shove, stick 6 burden, plunge, propel, upshot 7 intrude, purport, riposte
9 substance

thug 3 mug 4 goon, hood, punk 5 bully,
rough, rowdy, tough, yahoo 6 gunman,
mucker 7 hoodlum, mobster, ruffian
8 gangster, hooligan, plug-ugly 9 cutthroat,
roughneck, strong arm 10 hatchet man

thulium *symbol:* 2 Tm

thumb 5 digit, hitch 6 pollex 8 pollices
(plural) 9 hitchhike

thumb through 4 scan 6 browse 7 dip
into, run over 8 glance at 10 glance over

thunder 4 bang, roar 6 rumble 8 rum-
bling 11 fulmination *combining form:*
5 bront 6 bronto, ceraun 7 cerauno,
kerauno

thunderbolt 9 lightning

thunderclap see thunder

thunder lizard 10 brontosaur

thunderstruck 5 agape 6 aghast
7 shocked, stunned 8 dismayed 9 stag-
gered 10 bewildered, confounded
11 dumbfounded, overwhelmed

Thurber character 11 Walter Mitty

thurify 5 cense

thus 2 so 3 sic 4 ergo, then 5 hence
9 therefore, thereupon, thus and so
11 accordingly 12 consequently *French:*
5 ainsi

Thus Spoke Zarathustra *author:*
9 Nietzsche

thwack 3 bop 4 biff, blow, sock, whop
5 crack, pound, smack, whack

thwart 4 balk, beat, bilk, curb, dash, foil,
ruin 6 arrest, baffle, scotch, stymie 8 traverse 9 checkmate, crosswise, frustrate

10 circumvent, disappoint, transverse
11 transversal

Thyestes *brother:* 6 Atreus *daughter:*
7 Pelopia *father:* 6 Pelops *mother:* 10 Hippodamia *son:* 9 Aegisthus

Tiamat *husband:* 4 Apsu *slayer:*
6 Marduk

tiara 5 crown 6 diadem 9 headdress

Tibetan *animal:* 3 yak 5 manul *coin:*
5 tanga *gazelle:* 3 goa *monk:* 4 lama *people:* 6 Bhotia, Sherpa

Tibet's capital 5 Lhasa

tibia 8 shinbone

Tibni's father 6 Ginath

tic 5 spasm 6 twitch 9 twitching

tick 6 credit, insect 8 arachnid, parasite
11 bloodsucker *combining form:* 4 acar
5 acari, acaro

ticker 4 bomb 5 clock, heart, watch

ticket 3 key, tag 4 vote 5 label, slate
6 ballot 8 passport, password 10 open
sesame 12 carte d'entrée *seller:* 7 cashier,
scalper

tickle 4 stir 5 amuse, tease, touch
6 arouse, excite, please, tingle 7 delight,
gratify, provoke 9 stimulate, titillate

ticklish 5 risky, rocky 6 fickle, touchy,
tricky 8 delicate, unstable, variable, volatile
9 mercurial, sensitive, uncertain 10 capricious, changeable, inconstant, precarious

tick off 4 list 5 chide 6 monish, rebuke
7 reprove 8 admonish, call down, numerate,
reproach 9 enumerate, reprimand

tidal flood 4 bore 5 eagre

tidbit 5 goody, treat 6 dainty, morsel
8 delicacy, kickshaw 11 bonne bouche

tide 4 flow, flux, rush 5 drift, flood, spate,
surge 6 stream 7 current, holiday *lowest:*
4 neap *type:* 3 ebb, low 4 high, neap
5 flood 6 spring

tidings 4 news, word 6 advice 7 message 9 speerings 11 information
12 intelligence

tidy 4 neat, snug, trig, trim 7 chipper,
orderly 9 shipshape 11 uncluttered, well-
groomed 12 spick-and-span

tie 3 rod, wed 4 band, bind, bond, cord,
draw, gird, join, knot, lash, link, mate, moor,
rope, yoke 5 ascot, cinch, equal, jabot,
leash, marry, match, nexus 6 attach, cravat,
fasten, fetter, hamper, hobble, secure,
splice 7 connect, dogfall, shackle, trammel,
truss up 8 deadlock, fastener, ligament, ligature, standoff, vinculum 9 entrammel, fastening, stalemate 10 attachment, four-in-
hand

tier 3 row 4 file, line, rank 5 class, grade,
group, queue, story 6 league, string 7 echelon 8 category, grouping

tiff 3 row 4 spat 5 run-in, scrap 6 bicker
7 brabble, dispute, fall out, quarrel, rhubarb,

wrangle **8** squabble **9** bickering, caterwaul **10** falling-out **11** a!tercation
tiffany 5 gauze **11** cheesecloth
tiger 3 cat **6** feline **9** carnivore *young:*
3 cub
tight 3 set **4** fast, firm, hard, snug, taut,
trim **5** cheap, close, dense, drunk, fixed,
tense, thick **6** firmly, secure, stingy **7** compact, crowded, drunken, fixedly, miserly, solidly **9** niggardly, penurious, tenacious
10 contracted, inebriated **11** closefisted,
constricted, intoxicated, steadfastly
12 cheeseparing, parsimonious
13 pennypinching
tightfisted   see **stingy**
tight-lipped 5 close **6** silent **8** reserved,
reticent, taciturn **12** closemouthed, close-
tongued
tightwad 4 skin **5** miser, nabal, stiff **7** niggard, scrooge **9** skinflint **10** cheapskate
11 cheeseparer
Tikvah's son 7 Shallum **8** Jahaziah
tile 3 hat **5** brick, guard, plate, slate
6 domino, tegula **7** abacula, tessera *roof-*
ing: **7** pantile
till 2 to **3** sow **4** plow, tend, turn, up to,
work **5** until **6** before, harrow **7** prior to
9 cultivate **11** in advance of
tillable 6 arable **10** cultivable
12 cultivatable
tillage 4 farm, land **5** crops **11** cultivation
tiller 4 helm **6** farmer, rudder **7** steerer
Tilon's father 6 Shimon
tilt 3 tip, yaw **4** cant, cock, heel, lean, list,
swag **5** grade, lurch, pitch, slant, slope
6 seesaw **7** incline, leaning, recline **8** gradient **11** inclination
timbal 4 drum **10** kettledrum
timber 3 log **4** balk, beam, tree, wood
5 board, joist, plank, trees, weald, woods
6 forest, girder, lumber, rafter **8** woodland
decay: **4** dote, doze *joint:* **4** coak *mine:*
5 stull *Philippine:* **5** lauan *ship's:* **3** rib
4 bibb, keel, mast, skeg **7** stemson
8 sternson *supporting:* **4** stud **6** purlin,
putlog, rafter **8** puncheon *uncut:* **8** stump-
age *wolf:* **4** lobo
timbre 4 mood, tone **6** spirit, temper
timbrel 4 drum **10** tambourine
time 2 go **3** age, bit, day, era **4** book, bout,
date, hour, pace, plan, shot, show, span,
term, tour, turn **5** break, clock, epoch, set
up, shift, space, spell, stint, tempo, trick,
while **6** chance, look-in, moment, period,
season, squeak **7** instant, opening, program, stretch **8** duration, occasion, schedule **11** opportunity *ahead of:* **5** early *com-*
bining form: **5** chron, semic **6** chrono
8 chronous *gone by:* **4** past **9** yesterday
long: **3** age, eon, era **4** aeon *of day:*
4 dawn, dusk, noon **5** night **6** sunset

7 evening, morning, sunrise **8** daybreak,
twilight **9** afternoon *olden:* **4** yore **10** yesteryear *period:* **3** age, day, eon, era
4 aeon, hour, week, year **5** epoch, month
6 decade, minute, moment, second **7** century, instant **9** fortnight **10** millennium *pres-*
ent: **3** now *relating to:* **8** temporal *short:*
5 jiffy **6** moment, second **7** instant *suffix:*
2 ad *to come:* **6** future **8** tomorrow
waste: **4** loaf **5** dally **6** loiter
time and again 3 oft **5** often **8** ofttimes
10 frequently, oftentimes, repeatedly
11 over and over
timeless 7 ageless, endless, eternal
8 dateless, unending **9** ceaseless, continual, perpetual, unceasing **10** intemporal
11 everlasting, unremitting **12** interminable
timely 3 fit **4** meet, soon **5** early **6** likely,
prompt, proper **7** betimes, fitting, timeous
8 punctual, suitable **9** favorable, opportune,
promising, well-timed **10** auspicious, propitious, prosperous, seasonable, seasonably
11 appropriate
Time Machine, The *author:* **5** Wells
Time magazine founder 4 Luce
6 Hadden
Time of Your Life, The *author:*
7 Saroyan
timepiece 5 clock, watch **7** horloge, sundial **8** horologe **9** clepsydra **11** chronograph, chronometer, chronoscope
timetable 4 card, plan, sked **6** agenda,
docket **7** program **8** calendar, schedule
timeworn 3 old **4** aged, hack **5** hoary,
stale, trite **6** age-old **8** Noachian **9** hackneyed, venerable **12** antediluvian
time zone, U.S. 7 central, eastern,
Pacific **8** mountain
timid 3 coy, shy **4** mild, wary **5** chary,
mousy, pavid **6** afraid, demure, gentle,
modest, yellow **7** bashful, chicken, fearful,
halting, nervous, panicky, rabbity **9** diffident, faltering, milk-toast, mouselike, shrinking, tentative, unassured, uncertain
10 irresolute **11** unassertive, vacillating,
vacillatory **12** apprehensive, fainthearted
Timna *brother:* **5** Lotan *father:* **4** Seir
son: **6** Amalek
Timon's servant 7 Flavius
timorous 5 timid **7** fearful **8** quailing,
undaring **9** quivering, recoiling, shivering,
shrinking, trembling **10** shuddering
Timothy's associate 4 Paul
tin 3 box, can **5** metal **7** element, stan-
num **9** container *combining form:* **5** stann
6 stanni, stanno *mining region:* **8** stannary
relating to: **7** stannic **8** stannous *sheet:*
6 latten *symbol:* **2** Sn
tincture 3 dye **4** cast, hint, tint **5** color,
shade, stain, tinge, touch, trace **6** streak

8 colorant, dyestuff **10** complexion, intimation, suggestion

tinder 4 punk **8** kindling

tine 5 point, prong, spike **6** branch

tinge 3 dye, hue **4** cast, hint, tint, tone **5** color, shade, tinct, touch, trace **6** strain **8** tincture **10** complexion, intimation, sprinkling, suggestion

tinker 3 fix **4** mend, mess **6** doodle, fiddle, mender, potter, puddle, putter, repair **9** repairman **10** mess around

tinkle 3 gab, gas, jaw, yak **4** chat, ting **5** chink, clack, clink, plink **6** babble, jangle, jingle, rattle, tingle **7** chatter, prattle

tinny 4 thin **5** cheap, harsh **8** metallic

Tin Pan Alley acronym 5 ASCAP

tinsel 4 loud **5** gaudy **6** brazen, flashy, garish, tawdry **7** blatant, chintzy, glaring **8** ornament **9** clinquant **12** meretricious

tint 3 dye, hue **4** cast, tone, wash **5** color, shade, tinge, touch **7** touch up **8** tincture **10** coloration, complexion **12** pigmentation

tiny 3 wee **5** bitsy, dwarf, minim, pygmy, small, teeny, weeny **6** midget, minute, peewee, pocket, teensy, teenty, weensy **7** minikin **8** dwarfish, pint-size **9** itsy-bitsy, itty-bitty, miniature, minuscule **10** diminutive, minuscular, pocket-size, teeny-weeny **11** lilliputian, microscopic **12** teensy-weensy **13** infinitesimal

tip 3 cap, cue, top **4** apex, cant, clue, cusp, heel, hint, lean, list, peak, perk, tilt **5** point, slant, slope, steer, upset **6** advice, topple **7** cumshaw, incline, largess, overset, pointer, recline **8** forecast, gratuity, overturn, turn over **9** baksheesh, knock over, logniappe, overthrow, pourboire **10** perquisite, prediction **11** information *combining form:* **3** acr, akr **4** acro, akro, apic **5** apici, apico

tip-off 4 hint **5** point, steer **7** pointer, warning **8** giveaway, jump ball **10** indication

Tippecanoe and ___ too 5 Tyler

tippet 4 band, barb, cape **5** scarf

tipple 3 bib, sip **4** grog, soak, swig **5** booze, drink, swill **6** guzzle, imbibe, liquor, spirit, tank up **7** swizzle **8** liquor up **9** aqua vitae, firewater

tippler 3 sot **4** lush, soak **5** drunk, toper **6** bibber, boozer **7** tosspot **8** drunkard **9** inebriate

tipstaff 7 bailiff

tipster 4 fink, nark **6** canary, snitch **7** tattler **8** betrayer, informer, squealer **10** talebearer **11** stool pigeon

tipsy 5 drunk, tight **7** drunken **8** unsteady **10** inebriated **11** intoxicated

tiptoe 5 creep, steal **7** gumshoe **9** pussyfoot

tirade 4 rant **5** abuse **6** screed **7** censure **8** berating, diatribe, harangue, jere-

miad **9** invective, philippic **10** revilement **11** rodomontade **12** condemnation, denunciation, vituperation **13** tongue-lashing

tire 3 sap **4** bore, hoop, jade, pall, poop, wear **5** drain, ennui, weary, wheel **6** tucker, weaken **7** exhaust, fatigue, wear out **8** enervate, enfeeble, wear down **10** debilitate *airless:* **4** flat **7** blowout *kind:* **4** bias, snow **6** radial **7** retread **9** whitewall

tiredness 7 fatigue **8** collapse **9** lassitude, weariness **10** exhaustion **11** prostration

tireless 4 busy **6** active **8** untiring **9** weariless **10** unflagging, unwearying **11** unweariable **12** enthusiastic **13** indefatigable, inexhaustible

Tiresias 4 seer **10** soothsayer

tiresome 4 dull, hard **6** boring, jading, tiring **7** irksome, onerous, tedious **8** boresome, drudging **9** difficult, wearisome **10** burdensome, oppressive

Tirhanah *father:* **5** Caleb *mother:* **6** Maacah *uncle:* **9** Jerahmeel

Tiriac of tennis 3 Ion

tiring see **tiresome**

Tirol, Tyrol *capital:* **9** Innsbruck *country:* **7** Austria *mountains:* **4** Alps

Tirzah's father 10 Zelophehad

Tisiphone see **Erinyes**

tissue 3 web **4** mesh **5** fiber, gauze, paper **6** fabric *anatomical:* **4** tela **5** fiber **6** diploe **8** ganglion **10** epithelium *combining form:* **4** hist **5** histi, histo, hypho **6** histio *connective:* **6** stroma, tendon **9** cartilage *kind:* **3** fat **5** nerve **6** muscle **7** nervous **8** muscular **10** connective, epithelial *layer:* **6** dermis **7** stratum *plant:* **4** bast, wood **5** xylem **6** phloem

Titan *father:* **6** Uranus *female:* **4** Rhea **6** Tethys, Themis *male:* **6** Cronus **7** Iapetus, Oceanus *mother:* **2** Ge **4** Gaea

Titan, The *author:* **7** Dreiser

Titania's husband 6 Oberon

titanic 4 huge **5** great **6** mighty **8** colossal, enormous, gigantic **9** cyclopean, Herculean, monstrous **10** gargantuan, tremendous

titanium *symbol:* **2** Ti

tithe 3 tax **5** tenth

Tithonus *beloved by:* **3** Eos *father:* **8** Laomedon

title 3 dub, due **4** call, deed, dibs, name, term **5** claim, merit, nomen **7** baptize, caption, heading **8** christen, cognomen, pretense **9** designate **10** denominate, pretension **11** appellation, appellative, designation **12** championship, compellation, denomination *Dutch:* **7** mynheer *ecclesiastic:* **8** reverend *feminine:* **2** Ms. **3** Mrs. **4** dame, lady, ma'am, miss **5** madam **6** milady, missus **8** mistress *French:*

6 madame 8 monsieur 12 mademoiselle *German:* 4 Frau, Herr 8 Fraulein *holder:* 5 noble 8 champion *Indian:* 3 sri 4 raja, shri 5 sahib 7 bahadur *Islamic:* 6 sayyid 9 ayatollah *Italian:* 5 donna 6 signor 7 signora 9 signorina *monk's:* 3 fra 7 brother *of nobility:* 3 sir 4 Duke, Earl, King, Lord, sire 5 Baron, Count, Queen 6 Prince 7 Baronet, Marquis 8 Archduke, Princess, Viscount *Oriental:* 4 khan *Persian:* 5 mirza

titmouse 4 bird 6 tomtit, verdin 7 bushtit 9 chickadee

titter 5 laugh, tehee 6 giggle, guffaw, heehaw 7 chortle, chuckle, snicker

tittle 3 bit, jot 4 atom, iota, mite 5 minim, speck 6 smitch 7 smidgen 8 particle

titular 6 formal 7 nominal 8 so-called

Tityus *father:* 4 Zeus *slayer:* 6 Apollo

Tiu see **Tyr**

tizzy 4 fume, snit, stew 5 sweat 6 dither, swivet

T-man 5 agent 8 revenuer

TNT 8 dynamite 9 explosive

to 2 at 3 ere, for 4 ante, till 5 until 6 before, toward, up till 7 against, ahead of, prior to 8 opposite, touching 9 preceding 11 in advance of *be sure:* 6 indeed 9 certainly *prefix:* 2 ac, ad, af, ag, al, ap, as, at *Scottish:* 3 tae *wit:* 3 viz 6 namely 8 scilicet

toad 4 agua, hyla, scum 6 anuran, peeper 7 crapaud, stinker 8 lickspit, truckler 9 amphibian, sycophant 10 batrachian, bootlicker, footlicker 11 lickspittle *combining form:* 7 batrach 8 batracho 9 batrachus *genus:* 4 Bufo

toady 4 fawn 5 cower, kotow 6 cringe, flunky, grovel, kowtow 7 honey up, truckle 8 bootlick, lickspit, truckler 9 brownnose, sycophant 10 bootlicker, footlicker 11 apple-polish, lickspittle

To Althea from ___ 6 Prison *author:* 8 Lovelace

toast 5 bread, brown, drink, skoal 6 cheers, pledge, prosit, salute 7 wassail *Jewish:* 7 lehayim 8 lechayim *kind:* 5 melba 6 French 8 zwieback

toastmaster 2 MC 5 emcee

To a Waterfowl author 6 Bryant

tobacco 4 leaf, weed *cask:* 8 hogshead *chewing:* 4 chaw, quid *Cuban:* 4 capa *ingredient:* 3 tar 8 nicotine *juice:* 6 ambeer *kind:* 4 shag 5 bogie, snuff 6 bright, burley 7 caporal, perique, Turkish 9 broadleaf, mundungus *pipe:* 4 heel 6 dottle *rolled:* 5 cigar *Turkish:* 7 latakia

Tobacco Road author 8 Caldwell

to be *Latin:* 4 esse

Tobias *father:* 5 Tobit *son:* 8 Hyrcanus

toboggan 4 sled 7 coaster

toby 3 cup, mug 5 cigar

tocsin 3 SOS 4 sign 5 alarm, alert 6 alarum, signal

today 3 now 7 present 8 nowadays 9 presently

toddle 4 walk 6 stroll 7 saunter

toddy 3 sap 5 drink

to-do 4 coil, fuss 5 whirl 6 clamor, furore, hassle, hubbub, hurrah, pother, ruckus, rumpus, shindy, tumult, uproar 7 turmoil 9 commotion 10 hurly-burly

toe 3 tip 5 digit, touch *big:* 6 hallux *combining form:* 6 dactyl, digiti 7 dactylo, dactyly 8 dactylia 9 dactylism, dactylous *little:* 7 minimus

toehold 7 footing

toffee 5 candy

toga 4 gown, rope, wrap 5 tunic

together 6 at once, joined, united 7 jointly 8 mutually 10 conjointly 11 concertedly 12 coincidently, collectively, concurrently *prefix:* 2 co 3 col, com, con, cor, sym, syn

togetherness 5 union 7 cahoots 8 alliance, cohesion 10 connection, solidarity 11 affiliation, association, combination, conjunction, partnership

Togo *capital:* 4 Lome *monetary unit:* 5 franc

tog out 5 fix up, slick, spiff 6 doll up 7 dress up, gussy up 8 spruce up 9 smarten up

togs 4 duds 5 dress 6 attire, things 7 apparel, clothes, raiment 8 clothing 10 attirement, habiliment

To Have and to Hold author 8 Johnston

To His Coy Mistress author 7 Marvell

toil 3 net, tug 4 grub, plod, slog, slop, work 5 drive, grind, labor, slave, sweat 6 drudge, stodge, strain, strive, trudge 7 travail 8 bullwork, drudgery, footslog, plunther, slogging

toiler 4 peon 5 slave 6 drudge, slavey 9 dray horse, workhorse 11 galley slave

toilet 4 head, john 5 dress, privy 6 johnny 7 latrine 8 bathroom, lavatory 11 convenience, water closet *British:* 3 loo

toilsome 4 hard 6 uphill 7 arduous, labored, operose 9 difficult, effortful, laborious, strenuous

Toi's son 5 Joram 7 Hadoram, Jehoram

Tokay 4 wine

token 4 mark, pawn, sign 5 index, relic 6 pledge, trophy 7 earnest, gesture, indicia, memento, minimal, symptom, warrant 8 evidence, keepsake, memorial, reminder, security, souvenir 9 indicator 10 expression, indication 11 remembrance 12 remembrancer

Tokyo *formerly:* **3** Edo
Tola's father 4 Puah **8** Issachar
tolerable 2 OK **4** fair **6** common, decent
7 livable **8** adequate, all right, bearable
9 endurable **10** acceptable, sufferable, sufficient **11** presentable, respectable, supportable, sustainable **12** satisfactory
tolerably 4 so-so **6** enough, fairly, pretty,
rather **8** passably **9** averagely
10 moderately
tolerance 7 stamina **8** clemency, lenience,
leniency, patience **9** endurance **10** indulgence, resistance, steadiness, sufferance
11 forbearance **13** steadfastness
tolerant 4 easy **5** broad **7** clement,
lenient, liberal **9** condoning, forgiving, indulgent **10** charitable, forbearing, open-
minded, permissive **11** broad-minded, progressive, sympathetic **13** understanding
tolerate 4 bear, take **5** abide, allow, brook,
stand **6** accept, endure, permit, suffer
7 condone, stomach, swallow **8** bear with,
tough out **11** countenance
Tolkien creature 3 Ent **6** Hobbit
toll 3 tax **4** bait, bell, bong, cost, lure, peal,
ring **5** chime, decoy, knell, price, tempt
6 allure, charge, entice, entrap, lead on,
seduce **7** expense, lockage **8** inveigle
tollbooth 11 customhouse
Tolstoy novel 11 War and Peace
12 Anna Karenina
tomato 5 fruit **9** love apple
tomb 4 bury **5** grave, inter, plant **6** burial,
inhume **7** lay away, put away **8** mausolea
(plural) **9** mausoleum, sepulcher, sepulture
11 ensepulcher *ancient Egyptian:* **7** mas-
taba **8** mastabah *circular:* **6** tholoi (plural),
tholos *empty:* **8** cenotaph
tomboy 6 gamine, hoyden
Tom Brown's School Days *author:*
6 Hughes
tombstone 6 ledger **8** memorial, monument **11** grave marker *inscription:* **3** RIP
8 hic jacet
tome 4 book **6** volume
tomfool 3 ass **4** fool, jerk **5** crazy, idiot,
loony, ninny, silly **6** absurd, donkey, insane
7 foolish, jackass **8** imbecile **9** fantastic
10 nincompoop **11** harebrained
12 preposterous
tomfoolery 4 dido, lark **5** antic, caper,
prank, shine, trick **6** frolic **7** hogwash, rubbish, twaddle **8** claptrap, malarkey, nonsense **9** poppycock **10** balderdash, shenanigan **11** monkeyshine **12** blatherskite
Tom Jones author 8 Fielding
tommyrot 4 bash, bull, crap **5** bilge,
hooey, trash **7** hogwash, rubbish
8 nonsense
Tom o'Bedlam 3 nut **4** loon **5** loony

6 dement, madman, maniac **7** lunatic,
madling **9** bedlamite, non compos
tomorrow 6 future, mañana
Tom Sawyer *author:* **5** Twain *character:* **5** Becky **8** Huck Finn, Injun Joe **9** Aunt
Polly **10** Muff Potter
Tom Thumb 4 runt **5** dwarf, midge,
pygmy **6** midget, peewee **7** manikin
10 homunculus **11** lilliputian
ton 3 fad **4** chic, rage **5** craze, style,
vogue **6** furore **7** fashion
tone 3 hue **4** cast, mode, mood, tint, vein
5 color, humor, pitch, shade, style, tinge
6 accent, manner, spirit, strain, temper, timbre **7** fashion **10** inflection *combining
form:* **4** phon **5** phono
toned down 4 mute, soft **5** sober **6** low-
key, mellow **7** subdued **8** low-keyed,
softened
tongue 4 lick **6** glossa, lingua, speech
7 dialect **8** language **10** vernacular *click
of:* **3** tch *combining form:* **4** glot **5** gloss,
lingu **6** glossa, glosso, lingua, lingui, linguo
7 glossia
tongue-lash 3 wig **4** lash, rail **5** scold
6 berate **7** bawl out, chew out, tell off,
upbraid
tonguelike part 7 languet
tonic 5 sharp **7** bracing **8** renewing, roborant **9** animating **10** astringent, quickening,
refreshing, vitalizing **11** restorative, stimulating, stimulative **12** exhilarating, exhilarative, invigorating **13** strengthening *extract:*
4 cola **9** berberine
tonsorialist 6 barber
tony 2 in **4** chic **5** swank, swish **6** modish **7** a la mode, stylish **9** exclusive
11 fashionable
too 4 also, ever, more, over, very **5** along
6 as well, highly, overly, unduly, withal
7 awfully, besides, greatly, notably **8** likewise, moreover, overfull, overmuch
9 extremely, immensely **10** remarkably,
strikingly **11** exceedingly, excessively, furthermore **12** additionally, exorbitantly,
immoderately, inordinately, unmeasurably
13 exceptionally
tool 3 awl, zax **4** pawn **5** drive **6** puppet,
rimmer, stooge **7** cat's-paw, hayfork,
machine, rounder, utensil **8** picklock
9 implement, mechanism **10** instrument
axlike: **3** adz *barrel making:* **5** croze
6 crozer *boring:* **5** auger, drill *carving:*
6 veiner *cleaving:* **4** froe *cobbler's:* **3** awl
cutting: **2** ax **3** adz, axe, saw **4** adze
5 knife **6** shears **8** billhook *digging:*
4 pick **7** mattock *engraving:* **5** burin
7 scauper *farm:* **6** seeder *filing:* **4** rasp
7 riffler *garden:* **3** hoe **4** rake **5** spade
6 trowel, weeder *grasping:* **6** pincer
7 tweezer **8** tweezers *prehistoric:* **5** flint

6 eolith *pruning:* **6** shears **8** secateur *rubbing:* **9** burnisher *scooping:* **6** router *toothed:* **3** saw **7** ripper *woodworking:* **3** saw **5** bevel, plane **6** chisel, hammer

toot **3** bat, jag **4** bust, tear **5** binge, drunk, sound, spree **6** bender **7** blowoff, carouse

tooth **5** molar **7** incisor **8** bicuspid, premolar *combining form:* **4** dent, odon, odus **5** denti, dento, odont **6** odonta, odonto, odonty **7** dentate, odontes, odontia *cuspid:* **6** canine **8** dogtooth, eyetooth *cutting:* **10** carnassial *decay:* **6** caries *doctor:* **7** dentist *pointed:* **4** fang **6** canine, cuspid *small:* **8** denticle *surface:* **5** mensa

toothless **8** edentate

toothsome **5** sapid, tasty **6** savory **8** pleasant, pleasing, tasteful **9** agreeable, delicious, palatable, relishing **10** appetizing, attractive **11** good-tasting

top **3** cap, tip **4** acme, apex, beat, best, clip, crop, cusp, dock, face, fine, head, peak, pick, roof **5** cream, crest, crown, elite, excel, outdo, point, pride, prime, prize **6** apical, better, choice, climax, exceed, height, summit, utmost, vertex **7** capital, highest, maximal, maximum, outside, pollard, surface, surpass **8** five-star, loftiest, outshine, outstrip, pinnacle, superior, surmount **9** excellent, fastigium, first-rate, transcend, uppermost **10** first-class **11** culmination, first-string *combining form:* **3** acr, akr **4** acro, akro

tope **3** nip **4** soak **5** booze, drink, shark **6** guzzle, imbibe, tank up, tipple **7** swizzle **8** liquor up

toper **3** sot **4** lush, soak **5** drunk **6** bibber, boozer **7** tippler, tosspot **8** drunkard **9** inebriate

Tophet **4** hell **5** hades, Sheol **6** blazes **7** Gehenna, inferno **9** barathrum, perdition **10** underworld **11** Pandemonium

topic **4** head, text **5** issue, motif, point, theme **6** matter, motive **7** subject **8** argument **11** proposition **13** subject matter

top-notch **4** fine **5** prime **7** capital **8** fivestar, superior **9** excellent, first-rate **10** firstclass **11** first-string

top off **3** cap **5** crown **6** climax **8** round off **9** culminate, finish off

topography **7** terrain

topple **4** drop, fall **5** lurch, pitch, slump, upset **6** falter, go down, plunge, teeter, totter, tumble, wobble **7** overset, stagger, stumble, tip over, unhorse **8** keel over, overturn, turn over **9** knock over, overthrow

topsy-turvy **8** cockeyed, inverted, unhinged **10** disjointed, disordered, downside-up, upside-down **11** disarranged

toque **3** cap, hat

tor **4** hill, peak **5** mound **8** pinnacle

torch **7** firebug **8** arsonist, flambeau **10** incendiary

toreador **6** torero **7** matador **11** bullfighter

torment **3** try **4** bait, hurt, pain, rack **5** smite, wring **6** harass, harrow, heckle, molest, plague **7** afflict, agonize, crucify, torture, trouble **8** distress **9** persecute **10** excruciate

torn **4** rent **7** mangled **9** lacerated

tornado **7** cyclone, twister **9** whirlwind

toro **4** bull

torpedo **3** gun **4** mine **6** gunman, hit man **8** assassin **9** cutthroat, explosive **10** gunslinger, hatchet man, projectile, triggerman

torpid **5** dopey **8** comatose, sluggish **9** lethargic **10** slumberous **12** hebetudinous

torpor **4** coma **5** sleep **6** stupor **7** languor **8** dullness, hebetude, lethargy **9** lassitude, passivity, stolidity **10** stagnation **12** listlessness

torque **5** chain, twist **6** collar

torrent **5** flood, spate **6** deluge **7** niagara **8** cataract, flooding, overflow **9** cataclysm **10** inundation, outpouring

torrid **3** hot **5** fiery **6** ardent, fervid, heated, red-hot, sultry **7** blazing, burning, flaming **8** broiling, scalding, sizzling, whitehot **9** scorching **10** hot-blooded, passionate, sweltering **11** impassioned

tort **3** sin **4** evil **5** crime, wrong **8** iniquity **9** diablerie **10** wrongdoing

tortilla **4** cake, taco

Tortilla Flat author **9** Steinbeck

tortoise **6** turtle **8** terrapin **9** chelonian *freshwater:* **4** emyd *shell:* **8** carapace

tortuous **5** snaky **7** sinuous, winding **8** flexuous, involute, involved **9** meandrous **10** convoluted, meandering, serpentine **11** anfractuous, vermiculate

torture **3** try **4** hurt, maim, rack, warp **5** smite, wring **6** deform, harrow, mangle **7** afflict, agonize, contort, crucify, distort, oppress, torment **8** misshape, mutilate **10** excruciate

tory **5** right **7** diehard, fogyish, old-line **8** loyalist, old liner, orthodox, rightist, standpat **11** bitter-ender, reactionary, right-winger, standpatter **12** conservative

Tosca *character:* **5** Mario **7** Scarpia *composer:* **7** Puccini

___ Toscanini **6** Arturo

tosh **5** bilge, hooey **6** bunkum **7** eyewash **8** malarkey, nonsense, pishposh

toss **4** cast, fire, flip, hurl, rock, roll **5** bandy, drink, fling, heave, pitch, quaff, sling, throw **6** imbibe, launch, seesaw, squirm, writhe **7** agonize

tosspot see **tippler**

tot 3 add, nip, sum 4 cast, dram, drop, foot, jolt, shot, slug 5 child, snort, total 6 figure 7 snifter, summate, toddler

totable 8 portable

total 3 add, all, sum 4 body, bulk, cast, come, foot, full, tale 5 add up, equal, gross, run to, smash, sum to, utter, whole, wreck, yield 6 all-out, amount, budget, entire, figure, number 7 crack up, destroy, full-out, overall, perfect, plenary, quantum, run into, stack up, sum into, summate 8 absolute, complete, comprise, demolish, entirety, outright, positive, quantity, result in 9 aggregate, consist of, full-blown, full-scale, inclusive, out-and-out, unlimited 10 consummate, unreserved 11 unmitigated 13 comprehensive, thoroughgoing *combining form:* **3** hol **4** holo

totalitarian 6 all-out 7 full-out 8 absolute 9 full-blown, full-scale, unlimited 11 dictatorial 13 authoritarian

totality 3 all, sum 4 tale 5 gross, whole 6 entity, system 7 allness, oneness 8 entirety, integral 9 aggregate, integrate, wholeness 10 entireness 12 completeness

totalize 3 add, sum, tot 6 figure 7 summate

tote 3 add, lug 4 bear, buck, cart, haul, pack 5 carry, ferry 6 convey, figure 7 summate 9 transport

totem 4 clan, pole 6 emblem

To the Lighthouse author 5 Woolf

totter 4 reel 5 lurch, wheel 6 falter, topple, wobble 7 stagger, stammer 8 titubate

touch 3 dab, pat, paw, rub 4 abut, dash, feel, hand, hint, join, line, meet, move, palm, stir, sway 5 brush, carry, graze, march, probe, shade, smack, thumb, tinge, verge 6 adjoin, affect, amount, arouse, border, butt on, caress, excite, finger, fondle, handle, streak, strike, stroke 7 contact, feeling, impress, inspire, palpate, quicken, taction, toy with, verge on 9 influence, palpation, stimulate, tactility *combining form:* **6** thigmo

touchable 7 tactile 8 palpable, tangible

touch down 4 land 5 light, perch, roost 6 alight, settle 9 six points

touching 2 to 4 as to, in re 5 about, anent, as for 6 moving, tender 7 against, apropos, meeting, piteous, pitiful 8 abutting, adjacent, pitiable, poignant, stirring 9 adjoining, affecting, as regards, bordering, impinging 10 approximal, as respects, concerning, contiguous, impressive, juxtaposed, responsive 11 overlapping, sympathetic, tear-jerking 12 conterminous 13 compassionate

touchstone 4 test 5 check, gauge, proof, scale, trial 7 measure 8 standard 9 barometer, benchmark, criterion, yardstick 13 demonstration

touch up 4 do up 5 fix up 6 polish 7 brush up, improve, perfect

touchy 5 cross, dicey, miffy, ratty, risky, testy 6 cranky, tetchy, tricky, unsafe 7 harmful 8 choleric, delicate, ticklish, volatile 9 hazardous, irascible, sensitive, temperish 10 precarious 11 thin-skinned 13 oversensitive, quick-tempered, temperamental, unpredictable

tough 3 bad, fit, mug 4 goon, hard, hood, punk, taut, thug 5 bully, fixed, hardy, harsh, lusty, rigid, rough, rowdy, stiff, stout, teuch, teugh, yahoo 6 accept, anneal, flinty, ghetto, mucker, mulish, narrow, robust, rugged, severe, strict, strong, sturdy, taxing, trying, unsafe, uphill, viscid 7 arduous, drastic, exigent, healthy, hoodlum, labored, onerous, ruffian, steeled, toilful, viscose, viscous, weighty 8 bullyboy, exacting, grievous, hardcase, hardened, hard-line, hooligan, obdurate, plug-ugly, rigorous, seasoned, stalwart, stubborn, toilsome, vigorous 9 arbitrary, confirmed, dangerous, demanding, difficult, effortful, hard-shell, immutable, inner city, laborious, obstinate, pigheaded, resistant, roughneck, strenuous, tenacious 10 bullheaded, burdensome, disorderly, hard-bitten, hard-boiled, hardfisted, hardhanded, hardheaded, headstrong, inflexible, oppressive, refractory, self-willed, unyielding 11 conditioned, intractable, procrustean, unalterable, unbreakable 12 pertinacious, withstanding

toughen 6 anneal, harden, season 7 develop 9 acclimate, climatize 10 strengthen 11 acclimatize

toughie 4 punk 5 heavy, rough, rowdy, yahoo 6 mucker 7 ruffian 8 bullyboy 9 roughneck

toupee 3 wig 6 peruke, wiglet 7 periwig, wiggery

tour 4 bout, time, trip, turn 5 round, shift, spell, stint, trick 6 travel, troupe 7 circuit 9 round trip 10 roundabout

tour de force 4 deed, feat 7 classic, exploit 10 magnum opus, masterwork 11 achievement, chef d'oeuvre, masterpiece

tour guide 8 cicerone

tourist 7 tripper, visitor 8 traveler 9 sightseer, traveller 10 day-tripper, rubberneck 12 excursionist

tournament 4 tilt 5 joust 7 tourney

tousle 4 mess, muss 6 rumple 8 dishevel, disorder

tout 4 laud, plug 5 vigil, watch 6 herald, praise 7 acclaim, lookout, promote, trumpet 8 ballyhoo, proclaim 9 publicize, vigilance

tow 3 lug, tug 4 drag, draw, haul, pull

toward **6** contra, facing **7** against, apropos, benefic, helpful, vis-à-vis **8** favoring, fronting **9** favorable, regarding **10** beneficial, propitious *prefix:* **2** ac, ad, af, ag, al, ap, as, at, il, im, in, ir **4** pros *suffix:* **2** ad

towel word **3** his **4** hers

tower **5** spire **7** overtop **8** dominate, look down, overlook *Babylonian:* **8** ziggurat *on a mosque:* **7** minaret *small:* **6** turret

towering **4** airy, high, tall **5** dizzy, lofty, undue **6** aerial **7** extreme, massive, soaring, spiring, supreme **8** ultimate **10** exorbitant, immoderate, inordinate, monumental, preeminent, prodigious, stupendous, surpassing, tremendous **11** extravagant, skyscraping **12** altitudinous, overpowering, overwhelming, transcendent

towhee **5** finch

to wit **3** viz **6** namely **8** scilicet **9** videlicet

town **4** burg **6** podunk **7** borough, village *medieval:* **5** bourg

town and ___ **4** gown **7** country

townsman **3** cit **6** townee **7** burgher, citizen, oppidan

town square *Italian:* **6** piazza

toxic **6** poison **8** mephitic, venomous, virulent **9** poisonous

toxin **5** venin, venom **6** poison

toy **3** pet **4** fool, play **5** curio, dally, flirt, sport, tease **6** bauble, caress, coquet, cosset, cuddle, dandle, frolic, gewgaw, lead on, popgun, trifle, wanton **7** bibelot, disport, dreidel, novelty, trinket, whatnot **8** gimcrack, pinwheel **9** plaything **10** fiddle with, knickknack **11** string along

trace **4** hint, mark **5** relic, shade, smell, tinge, track, trail, tread, whiff **6** nuance, shadow, strain, streak **7** memento, soupçon, vestige **9** suspicion **10** intimation

trachea **8** windpipe

track **3** dog, way **4** drag, find, mark, path, road, sign, step, tail, walk **5** chase, cover, print, spoor, trace, trail, tread **6** artery, avenue, follow, pursue, shadow, street, travel **7** footway, highway, imprint, monitor, pathway, vestige **8** footpath, footstep, hunt down, pass over, smell out, traverse **9** footprint *combining form:* **4** ichn **5** ichno

track-and-field event **4** dash, race **7** shot put **8** footrace, high jump, long jump **9** broad jump, decathlon, pole vault, relay race **10** heptathlon, pentathlon, triple jump **11** discus throw **12** steeplechase

tract **3** lot **4** area, belt, plat, plot, zone **6** parcel, region **7** portion, terrain **9** territory

tractable **6** docile, pliant **7** pliable, subdued **8** amenable, biddable, flexible, obedient **10** manageable

tractate **6** memoir, thesis **8** treatise **9** discourse, monograph **10** monography **12** disquisition, dissertation

trade **3** art **4** deal, sell, swap, work **5** craft, truck **6** barter, change, custom, market, métier, peddle, switch **7** bargain, calling, pursuit, traffic **8** business, commerce, exchange, industry, merchant, vocation **9** patronage **10** employment, handicraft, occupation, profession, substitute **11** merchandise *illicit:* **11** black market *suffix:* **3** ery

trademark **4** logo **5** brand **8** logotype

trade route **7** sea-lane

tradition **4** lore, myth **6** custom, legacy, legend, mythos **8** folklore, heritage **9** mythology **10** convention

traditional **3** old **4** oral **5** fixed, usual **6** common, spoken, verbal **7** popular **8** habitual, orthodox **9** ancestral, customary, unwritten **10** immemorial **11** established, word-of-mouth **12** acknowledged, conventional, tralatitious

traditionalist **6** purist **9** precisian **12** precisionist

traditionalistic **4** tory **5** right **7** die-hard, fogyish, old-line **8** orthodox **11** reactionary **12** conservative

traduce **5** libel **6** betray, defame, malign, vilify **7** asperse, slander, violate **8** disgrace **9** denigrate **10** calumniate, scandalize

Trafalgar commander **6** Nelson

traffic **4** push, swap **5** fence, trade, truck **6** barter, custom, deal in, travel **7** bargain, bootleg **8** business, commerce, dealings, exchange, industry **9** communion, patronage **11** black-market, intercourse

trafficker **6** dealer, trader

tragedy **3** lot **4** blow, woes **5** curse, shock **6** mishap **8** calamity, disaster **9** adversity, cataclysm, mischance **10** misfortune **11** catastrophe, contretemps **12** misadventure

trail **3** dog, lag, tag **4** drag, flag, halt, path, plod, poke, tail **5** bedog, chase, chivy, dally, delay, tarry, trace, track **6** dawdle, falter, follow, linger, loiter, pursue, shadow, trudge **7** draggle, footway, gumshoe, pathway, traipse **8** footpath, footwalk **10** bridle path *emigrant:* **6** Oregon *Florida:* **7** Tamiami *Georgia-Maine:* **11** Appalachian *Indian:* **5** Great

trailer truck **4** semi

train **3** aim, lay, row, run **4** bait, cast, head, line, lure, tier, toll, turn **5** chain, coach, decoy, level, order, point, scale, shape, suite, teach, tempt **6** allure, course, direct, entice, harden, lead on, school, season, seduce, sequel, series, thread, zero in **7** develop, educate, incline, retinue **8** accustom, instruct, inveigle, sequence **9** cultivate, entourage, following, gradation, habituate

10 discipline, succession **11** alternation, consecution, progression

training 7 tuition **8** teaching, tutelage **9** education, schooling **11** instruction
horses: **6** manege

train off 3 dip **4** skew, slue, veer **5** sheer **6** swerve

traipse 3 gad **4** dowd, drab, drag, hoof, pace, roam, rove, slut, step, walk **5** dowdy, drift, mooch, range, trail, tread, troop **6** foot it, ramble, wander **7** draggle, meander **8** ambulate, slattern **9** gallivant **11** draggletail

trait 4 mark **5** point, savor **6** virtue **7** feature, quality **8** property **9** affection, attribute, birthmark, character **11** denominator

traitor 5 Judas **6** Arnold **8** betrayer, quisling, renegade, renegado, traditor, turncoat

traitorous 5 false **6** untrue **7** unloyal **8** apostate, disloyal, mutinous, recreant, renegade **9** alienated, estranged, faithless, seditious **10** perfidious, rebellious, unfaithful **11** disaffected, treacherous, unpatriotic

traject 4 pipe **5** carry **6** convey, funnel, siphon **7** channel, conduct **8** transmit

tram 3 car **7** trolley **9** streetcar

trammel 3 tie **4** bind, clog, curb **5** leash, limit **6** enmesh, fetter, hamper, hobble, hogtie, stifle **7** confine, enchain, ensnarl, manacle, shackle **8** entangle, handcuff, stagnate, stultify **9** embrangle, entrammel **12** circumscribe

tramontane 7 foreign **10** outlandish **11** transalpine

tramp 3 vag **4** hike, hobo, jade, plod, thud, walk **5** march, stamp, stomp **6** ramble, stodge, stroll, trudge **7** drifter, floater, saunter, traipse, vagrant **8** derelict, footslog, vagabond **9** walkabout **10** street arab

trample 5 pound, stamp, stomp, tromp **7** tread on **8** override

trance 4 muse **5** study **6** ravish **7** reverie **8** enravish, hypnosis **9** enrapture, transport **10** brown study

tranquil 4 calm, easy **5** quiet, still **6** irenic, placid, poised, serene, stable, steady **7** pacific, restful **8** composed, peaceful **9** collected, easygoing **13** self-possessed

tranquilize 4 balm, calm, hush, lull **5** quiet, still **6** becalm, sedate, settle, soothe, subdue **7** compose

tranquilizer 6 downer, opiate **8** diazepam, pacifier, sedative **10** depressant

transaction 4 bond, pact **7** bargain, compact, dealing **8** contract, covenant **9** agreement **10** convention

transcend 3 top **4** beat, best **5** excel, outdo **6** better, exceed **7** surpass **8** outshine, outstrip

transcendent 5 ideal **7** perfect, supreme **8** abstract, towering **10** consummate, preeminent, surpassing **11** theoretical, unequalable, unmatchable **12** hypothetical, incomparable **13** unsurpassable

Transcendentalist 7 Emerson, Thoreau

transcribe 4 copy **5** write **6** record **9** translate **13** transliterate

transfer 4 cede, deed, feed, find, give, hand, move, ship **5** alien, carry, shift **6** assign, change, convey, remise, remove, supply **7** convert, deliver, devolve, disturb, provide **8** alienate, dispense, hand over, make over, relocate, sign over, turn over **9** carry over, dislocate **10** abalienate

transfix 4 spit **5** lance, spear, spike **6** impale, skewer, skiver

transform 5 alter **6** change, mutate **7** commute, convert **8** denature **12** metamorphize, metamorphose

transformation 5 shift **10** alteration, changeover, conversion

transfuse 6 charge **7** pervade **8** permeate, saturate **9** penetrate, percolate **10** impregnate **11** impenetrate

transgress 3 sin **5** break **6** breach, offend **7** infract, violate **8** infringe, overstep, trespass **10** contravene

transient 7 passing **8** fleeting, flitting, fugitive, temporal, unstable, volatile **9** ephemeral, fugacious, momentary, temporary **10** evanescent, short-lived, transitory **11** impermanent **12** momentaneous **13** insubstantial

transit 5 shift **6** travel **7** passage **8** carriage, carrying **9** transport **10** alteration, conveyance **12** transporting

transition 5 shift **6** change, growth **7** passage **8** progress **9** evolution **10** alteration, conversion **11** development **13** metamorphosis

transitory see **transient**

translate 3 put **4** turn **6** change, render, reword **7** commute, convert, restate **8** rephrase **9** interpret **10** paraphrase **12** metamorphose

translation 7 version **9** rendering **10** paraphrase **11** restatement

translucent 5 clear, lucid **6** limpid **7** crystal, obvious **8** apparent, clear-cut, luminous, pellucid **9** unblurred **10** see-through *combining form:* **4** hyal **5** hyalo

transmarine 7 oversea **8** overseas

transmission 7 gearbox *combining form:* **8** phoreses (plural), phoresis

transmit 4 pipe, send, ship **5** break, carry, radio, route **6** convey, funnel, hand on, impart, pass on, siphon **7** address, channel, conduct, consign, forward, instill, traject **8** bequeath, dispatch, hand down

transmogrify see **transform**

transmute see **transform**

transoceanic message 9 cablegram

transparent 5 clear, filmy, gauzy, lucid, plain, sheer 6 flimsy, limpid, lucent 7 crystal, tiffany 8 clear-cut, gossamer, luminous, pellucid 9 tralucent, unblurred 10 diaphanous, see-through, translucid 11 crystalline, translucent *combining form:* 4 hyal 5 hyalo 7 diaphan 8 diaphano

transpire 3 hap, out 4 leak 5 occur 6 befall, betide, chance, happen 7 develop

transport 3 lug, wow 4 bear, buck, move, oust, pack, send, slay, tote 5 ardor, carry, exile, expel, ferry, truck 6 banish, convey, deport, excite, fervor, heaven, ravish, stir up, thrill, trance, uplift 7 agitate, cast out, delight, ecstasy, elevate, expulse, inflame, passion, provoke, quicken, rapture, transit, vehicle 8 carriage, carrying, displace, enravish, entrance, relegate, rhapsody 9 carry away, enrapture, happiness, stimulate 10 conveyance, enthusiasm, imparadise

transportation 6 moving 7 hauling, transit, vehicle 8 carriage, carrying 10 conveyance

transpose 4 turn 6 change, invert, render, revert 7 commute, convert, inverse, reverse 12 metamorphose

transubstantiate see **transform**

transude 4 ooze, seep, weep 5 bleed, sweat 6 strain

Transvaal *capital:* 8 Pretoria *natives:* 7 Bushmen 10 Hottentots *resource:* 4 gold

transversal 4 bent 6 thwart 8 crossing 9 crosswise 12 intersecting

transverse 5 cross 6 across, thwart 7 crossed, oblique 8 crossing, diagonal 9 crosswise

trap 3 net 4 bait, lure, plot, ploy, ruse, snag, tree, wile 5 benet, catch, decoy, feint, snare 6 ambush, come-on, gambit, tangle 7 catch up, ensnare 8 artifice, birdlime, entangle, intrigue, maneuver 9 ambuscade, stratagem 10 allurement, conspiracy, enticement, seducement, temptation 11 machination 12 inveiglement *an animal:* 8 deadfall

trappings 4 gear 5 dress 10 decoration 13 embellishment

Trappist 4 monk *writer:* 6 Merton (Thomas)

trash 3 mob, rot 4 bosh, crap, junk, plod, scum, slog, slop, toil 5 bilge, dregs, hokum, offal, waste, wreck 6 bunkum, debris, kelter, litter, masses, rabble, refuse, shlock, stodge, trudge 7 garbage, rubbish 8 canaille, claptrap, doggerel, dustheap, footslog, leavings, malarkey, nonsense, plunther, riffraff, unwashed 9 sweepings, vandalize 11 proletariat

trash can 7 dustbin

trashy 4 base, mean, poor 5 cheap, tatty 6 common, cruddy, paltry, shoddy, sleazy 8 rubbishy 9 third-rate

trauma 4 blow 5 shock, upset 6 stress 8 collapse 11 disturbance

travail 4 moil, task, toil, work 5 grind, labor, pains 6 drudge 7 slavery 8 bullwork, drudgery, plugging, struggle 10 birth pangs, childbirth 11 parturition 12 childbearing, contractions

travel 2 go 3 hie 4 fare, pass, roam, tour, trek, wend 5 cover, cross, jaunt, track 6 move on, push on, repair, voyage 7 explore, journey, passage, proceed, process, traffic, transit 8 pass over

travelable 8 passable 9 navigable 10 negotiable

traveling library 10 bookmobile

traverse 3 bar, rub 4 buck, deny, duel, snag, walk 5 cover, cross, fight, repel 6 combat, hamper, hurdle, impugn, negate, oppose, patrol, resist, thwart, travel 7 contest, dispute, gainsay 8 crossing, negative, obstacle, pass over 9 crosswise, disaffirm, withstand 10 contradict, contravene, crisscross, impediment 11 obstruction, perambulate

travesty 3 ape 4 mock, sham 5 farce, mimic 6 parody 7 imitate, mimicry, mockery, take off 8 ridicule 9 burlesque 10 caricature, distortion 12 exaggeration *satanic:* 9 Black Mass

Traviata, La *character:* 7 Alfredo, Germont 8 Violetta *composer:* 5 Verdi

trawl 3 net 4 fish 5 troll 7 setline

tray 6 salver, server 7 platter 8 teaboard *revolving:* 9 lazy Susan

treacherous 5 false, hairy, Punic, risky 6 chancy, tricky, untrue, wicked 7 unloyal, unsound 8 disloyal, perilous, recreant, ticklish 9 betraying, dangerous, deceptive, faithless, hazardous, unhealthy 10 jeopardous, misleading, perfidious, precarious, traitorous, unfaithful 12 falsehearted

treachery 7 perfidy, sellout, treason 9 falseness 10 disloyalty, infidelity 11 double cross 13 double dealing, faithlessness

treacle 5 syrup 6 remedy 8 molasses

tread 4 hoof, pace, step, walk 5 dance, march, stamp, stomp, trace, track, tramp, tromp, troop 6 foot it, hoof it, prance, stride 7 traipse, trample 8 ambulate

treadle 5 lever, pedal

treadmill 3 rut 4 pace, rote 5 grind 6 groove 7 routine

treason 6 deceit 7 perfidy 8 betrayal, sedition 9 duplicity, treachery 10 disloyalty, misprision 13 deceitfulness, faithlessness, seditiousness

treasure 4 find, plum, save 5 catch, guard, pearl, prize, trove, value 6 esteem, revere 7 apprize, cherish, idolize, worship 8 con-

serve, preserve, venerate **9** reverence
10 appreciate
Treasure Island *author:* **9** Stevenson
narrator: **10** Jim Hawkins
treasurer 6 bursar, purser **11** chamberlain
Treasure State 7 Montana
treasure trove 4 find, mine **7** bonanza
8 eldorado, Golconda, gold mine
treasury 4 mine **5** chest **6** coffer,
museum **7** bonanza, gallery **8** archives,
eldorado, Golconda, gold mine, war chest
9 exchequer **10** depositary, depository,
repository, storehouse *state:* **4** fisc
treat 3 use **5** goody, nurse, serve
6 advise, confab, confer, dainty, doctor, do
with, handle, huddle, manage, morsel, parley, physic, powwow, regard, tidbit, titbit
7 care for, consult **8** collogue, deal with,
delicacy, kickshaw, medicate, medicine
10 minister to **11** bonne bouche, confabulate *animals:* **3** vet *leather:* **3** tan, taw
6 shammy, shamoy **7** chamois, tanning
treatise 4 book **6** memoir, thesis **7** writing **8** argument, tractate **9** discourse,
monograph **10** discussion, exposition, monography **12** disquisition, dissertation *combining form:* **3** log **4** logy **5** logia, logue *suffix:* **3** ics
treatment 4 care **7** therapy *combining
form:* **6** praxes (plural), praxis
treaty 4 pact **6** accord **7** charter, compact,
concord **8** contract, covenant **9** agreement,
concordat **10** convention
treble 4 high, thin **5** acute, sharp **6** argute,
piping, shrill **8** piercing
tree *African:* **4** akee, cola, shea **5** limba,
sassy **6** baobab **7** avodire, bubinga
8 sasswood **9** berberine *Asian:* **4** dhak,
upas **6** banyan, kamala *Australian:* **7** blue
gum **8** lacewood, quandong **9** casuarina
branch: **5** bough *Brazilian:* **3** apa **7** arar-
iba, seringa, wallaba *Chinese:* **4** tung
5 yulan **6** gingko, ginkgo, litchi **7** kumquat
citrus: **4** lime, lemon **6** orange **8** bergamot **10** calamondin *combining form:*
3 dry **4** dryo **5** dendr **6** dendra (plural),
dendro **7** dendron *coniferous:* **3** fir, yew
4 pine **5** alder, cedar, larch **6** spruce
7 cypress, hemlock, juniper, redwood,
sequoia *dwarf:* **8** arbuscle **10** chinquapin
East Indian: **4** neem, poon, teak, toon
6 banyan, deodar, durian, durion
7 amboina, amboyna, cajaput, cajeput, cajuput, champac, champak, deodara **11** chaul-
moogra *elm:* **4** wych *Ethiopian:* **5** cusso,
kusso **6** kousso *Eurasian:* **5** abele, rowan
6 medlar *European:* **5** osier **8** bourtree,
caprifig *European oak:* **7** murmast *evergreen:* **3** fir, yew **4** atle, pine, titi **5** athel,
bunya, carob, cedar, piñon, taxus, thuja,
thuya **6** arbute, cullay, dahoon, jarrah,

loquat, mallee, pinyon, sapota **7** arbutus,
camphor, conifer, inkwood, juniper, lentisk,
madrona, madrone, madrono, peebeen, quil-
lai, redwood, sequoia **8** eucalypt, loblolly,
longleaf, tamarisk **9** balsam fir **12** balm of
Gilead *evergreen oak:* **6** encina *fig:*
5 pipal **6** peepul *flowering:* **5** sumac
6 acacia, sumach **7** dogwood **8** sourwood
hardwood: **3** oak **5** beech, birch, ebony,
maple **6** cherry, copalm, cornel, walnut
7 bilsted, hickory, shittah **8** chestnut,
mahogany **9** primavera *Japanese:* **4** kaki
7 zelkova *linden:* **8** basswood *mulberry:*
8 sycamine *North African:* **5** babul **7** bab-
bool *nut-bearing:* **4** cola, kola **5** hazel,
pecan, piñon **6** almond, cashew **7** buckeye,
filbert, hickory **9** pistachio *oak:* **5** roble
8 bluejack *oil-yielding:* **3** ebo **4** eboe,
tung **7** cajaput, cajeput, cajuput *ornamental:* **3** box **5** holly **6** gingko, ginkgo,
mimosa, myrtle, redbud **8** laburnum, magnolia **9** poinciana **12** rhododendron *palm:*
4 coco, nipa **5** ratan **6** cohune, gomuti, grugru, pinang, raffia, raphia, rattan **7** babassu,
coquito, talipot **8** carnauba, ladypalm *Peruvian:* **8** cinchona *Philippine:* **4** dita, pili
6 bataan, molave **7** tindalo **10** calamondin
resinous: **10** candlewood *shade:* **3** elm,
oak **5** maple **6** linden **8** sycamore **10** chi-
naberry *softwood:* **5** alamo **6** tupelo
8 black gum, corkwood; (see also *coniferous*) *South American:* **3** apa **4** ombu
7 wallaba **8** oiticica **9** Brazil nut *swamp:*
11 bald cypress *tropical:* **4** akee, ohia,
sago, teak **5** areca, assai, balsa, cacao,
ceiba, genip, lehua, mahoe, mamey, mamie
6 acajou, balata, baobab, bustic, citrus,
degame, degami, fustic, kabiki, mammee,
mammey, padauk, padouk, santol, souari
7 arnotto, bebeeri, genipap, logwood, maja-
gua, mameyes, palmyra, quassia, soursop
8 allspice, barbasco, cocobola, cocobolo,
jelutong, mahogany, mangrove, milkwood,
palmetto, porkwood, rosewood, simaruba,
soapbark, sweetsop, tamarind **9** candlenut,
cherimoya, jacaranda **10** breadfruit, manchineel **11** candleberry, coconut palm
trunk: **4** bole *willow:* **5** osier, sauch,
saugh **6** poplar *young:* **7** sapling
trefoil 4 leaf **6** clover
trek 4 trip **7** journey, travels **10** expedition
trellis 6 screen **7** lattice
tremble 3 jar **5** quake, shake **6** dither,
quaver, quiver, shiver, tremor **7** shudder,
twitter, vibrate *Scottish:* **4** dirl
tremblor see **temblor**
tremendous 4 huge, vast **5** awful
6 mighty, mortal **7** fearful, immense, massive, titanic **8** colossal, cracking, dreadful,
enormous, gigantic, horrible, shocking, terrible, terrific, towering **9** appalling, fantastic,

frightful, monstrous **10** formidable, monumental, prodigious, stupendous

tremolo 7 vibrato

tremor 3 jar **5** quake, shake, shock **6** dither, quaver, quiver, shiver **7** shudder, temblor, tremble, twitter, vibrate **8** tremblor **10** earthquake *muscular:* **8** dystaxia *Scottish:* **6** dindle

tremulous 5 aspen, quaky, shaky **6** aguish, aquake, ashake **7** aquiver, ashiver, quaking, quivery, shaking, shivery **9** quivering, shivering, trembling, tremorous, tremulant, vibrating **11** palpitating

trench 4 sink **5** ditch, drain, drill, fosse, gully, verge **6** border, furrow, trough **8** approach *Caribbean:* **6** Cayman *combining form:* **5** bothr **6** bothro

trenchant 5 acrid, crisp, salty **6** biting **7** caustic, cutting, ingoing, mordant, probing, satiric **8** clear-cut, incisive, piercing, sardonic, scathing **9** sarcastic **10** mordacious, razor-sharp **11** penetrating

trencher 4 tray **7** platter

trend 3 fad, run **4** flow, mode, rage, wind **5** craze, drift, style, swing, tenor, vogue **6** furore **7** current, fashion **8** movement, tendency **9** direction **10** dernier cri

trendy 2 in **3** hep, hip **4** tony **5** faddy **6** modish, tonish, with-it **7** a la mode, faddish, stylish **11** fashionable, ultramodern

Trent's Last Case author 7 Bentley

trepidation 4 fear **5** alarm, dread, panic **6** dismay, fright, horror, terror **13** consternation

trepidity 4 fear **5** alarm, dread, panic **6** dismay, fright, horror, terror **13** consternation

trespass 3 err, sin **5** lapse, poach **6** breach, invade, offend **7** intrude **8** encroach, entrench, infringe, invasion **9** interlope, intrusion, obtrusion, violation **10** infraction, transgress **11** intermeddle **12** encroachment, infringement **13** contravention, transgression

tress 4 curl, hair, lock **5** braid, plait

trestle 4 buck **5** horse **7** sawbuck **8** sawhorse **9** workhorse

tret 9 allowance

triad 4 trio **5** trine **6** triple, triune, troika **7** trinity **9** threesome **11** triumvirate

trial 3 try, woe **4** care, test **5** agony, cross, essay, grief, rigor, worry **6** hassle, misery, ordeal, sorrow **7** anguish, attempt, calvary, trouble **8** crucible, distress, endeavor, hardship, striving, struggle **9** adversity, suffering **10** affliction, difficulty, experiment, heartbreak, misfortune, visitation **11** tribulation **12** experimental

trial balloon 6 feeler

trial run 4 test **10** experiment

triangle type 5 right **6** obtuse **7** scalene **9** isosceles **11** equilateral

triangular 6 cuneal **7** cuneate, hastate *combining form:* **6** trigon **7** trigono

tribal unit 7 phratry

tribe 4 clan, folk, race **5** house, stock **6** family **7** kindred, lineage *combining form:* **4** phyl **5** phylo

tribulation 5 cross, trial **6** ordeal **7** calvary **8** crucible, wronging **10** affliction, oppression, visitation **11** persecution

tribunal 3 bar **5** court **8** lawcourt

tributary 3 sub **5** minor, under **7** subject **8** influent **9** dependent, satellite, secondary **10** collateral **11** subordinate

tribute 5 salvo **6** eulogy **8** citation, encomium **9** panegyric **10** salutation **11** recognition, testimonial **12** appreciation *feudal:* **6** heriot

trice 4 wink **5** shake **6** moment, second **7** instant **9** twinkling **11** split second

trick 3 jig **4** bout, dupe, feat, fool, gull, hang, hoax, lark, play, ploy, ruse, sham, tour, turn, wile **5** antic, blind, bluff, caper, craft, cully, curve, dodge, feint, fraud, knack, prank, shaky, shift, slick, spell, stall, stint, stunt **6** chouse, device, didoes, frolic, gambit, outwit, praxis, scheme, shines, touchy **7** boutade, chicane, dodgery, finagle, gimmick, sleight **8** artifice, escapade, flimflam, hoodwink, maneuver, outtrump, skin game, unstable **9** bamboozle, deception, defective, diversion, stratagem, victimize **10** expediency, red herring, shenanigan, tomfoolery, unreliable **11** contrivance, hornswoggle, monkeyshine **12** undependable **13** practical joke, untrustworthy *Scottish:* **6** shavie

trickery 5 cheat, fraud **7** chicane, knavery **8** hokypoky **9** chicanery, deception, fourberie **10** hanky-panky **11** double-cross, highbinding **13** double-dealing, sharp practice

trickle 4 drib, drip, drop, weep **5** trill **7** distill, dribble

trickster 5 cheat **6** con man **7** cheater, diddler, grifter, sharper **8** conjurer, magician, swindler **9** defrauder **11** flimflammer, illusionist **12** double-dealer

tricksy 5 rough, tight **6** trying **7** arduous **8** prankish

tricky 3 sly **4** foxy, wily **5** rocky **6** artful, astute, crafty, quirky, shifty, touchy **7** cunning **8** delicate, delusive, delusory, gimmicky, guileful, ticklish, unstable **9** deceitful, deceptive, difficult, dishonest, insidious, sensitive **10** misleading, precarious **12** undependable

trident 5 spear **7** scepter

tried 6 proved, secure, tested, trusty **7** staunch **8** approved, faithful, reliable

9 certified, steadfast **10** dependable **11** trustworthy

tried and true 6 secure, trusty **8** reliable **10** dependable **11** trustworthy

trifle 3 toy **4** fico, fool, mash, muck, play **5** curio, dally, flirt, use up, waste **6** bauble, burn up, coquet, fiddle, fidget, gewgaw, lead on, misuse, mucker, wanton **7** bibelot, consume, fribble, fritter, novelty, trinket, twiddle, whatnot **8** fool away, gimcrack, kickshaw, play with, squander **9** dissipate, objet d'art, philander, throw away **10** frivol away, knickknack, mess around, potter away **11** prodigalize, string along

trifolium 6 clover **8** shamrock

trig 4 chic, neat, prim, snug, tidy, trim **5** sharp, smart, swank **6** classy, modish, snappy **7** chipper, dashing, orderly, stylish **9** shipshape **11** fashionable, spic-and-span, uncluttered, well-groomed **12** spick-and-span

triggerman 3 gun **5** bravo **6** gunman, hit man **7** torpedo **8** assassin **9** cutthroat **10** gunslinger, hatchet man

trigonometric function see at **function**

trill 4 drib, drip, drop, weep **5** shake **7** distill, dribble, trickle

trillion *combining form:* **4** tera, treg **5** trega

trillionth *combining form:* **4** pico

trim 3 cut, fit **4** beat, clip, crop, deck, drub, lick, neat, pare, snug, tidy, trig, whip **5** adorn, order, prank, prune, shape, shave, shear, skive **6** barber, bedeck, dapper, fettle, kilter, repair, ricrac, spruce, sprucy, thrash **7** chipper, dress up, fitness, garnish, orderly, shapely, shellac **8** beautify, cleancut, decorate, lambaste, manicure, ornament, rickrack, shapeful **9** condition, embellish, shipshape **10** statuesque, well-turned **11** clean-limbed, spic-and-span, streamlined, uncluttered, well-groomed **12** spick-and-span *a tree:* **5** prune **7** pollard

trine see **triad**

Trinidad and Tobago *capital:* **11** Port of Spain *monetary unit:* **6** dollar

trinity see **triad**

trinket 5 curio **6** bauble, gewgaw, tinsel, trifle **7** bibelot, novelty, whatnot **8** frippery, gimcrack, kickshaw, nicknack **9** plaything **10** knickknack

trinkets 10 bijouterie

trio *of goddesses:* **5** Fates **6** Furies, Graces; (see also **triad**)

trip 3 hop, run **4** bull, lope, skip, slip, tour, trek **5** boner, error, fluff, lapse **6** bungle, spring **7** blooper, blunder, journey, mistake, skitter, stumble, travels **10** expedition

tripes 4 guts **7** innards, insides, inwards, viscera **8** entrails, stuffing **9** internals

triple 4 trio **5** triad, trine **6** treble, triune, troika **7** trinity **9** threesome **11** triumvirate

Triple Crown winner 1919: 9 Sir Barton **1930: 10** Gallant Fox **1935: 5** Omaha **1937: 10** War Admiral **1941: 9** Whirlaway **1943: 10** Count Fleet **1946: 7** Assault **1948: 8** Citation **1973: 11** Secretariat **1977: 11** Seattle Slew **1978: 8** Affirmed

tripped out 4 high **5** doped **6** stoned, zonked **7** drugged **8** hopped-up, turned on, wiped out **9** spaced-out

Triptolemus *father:* **6** Celeus *gift to man:* **5** grain *mother:* **9** Metaneira

Tristan, Tristram *beloved:* **6** Iseult, Isolde

triste 3 sad **7** joyless **8** mournful **9** saddening **10** depressing, melancholy **11** melancholic

Tristram Shandy author 6 Sterne

trite 3 set **4** dull, flat, hack **5** banal, chain, corny, musty, stale, stock, tired, vapid **6** cliché, common, jejune, old hat, used-up **7** clichéd, drained, prosaic, worn-out **8** bathetic, bromidic, mildewed, ordinary, shopworn, timeworn, well-worn **9** hackneyed **10** threadbare **11** commonplace, stereotyped **13** platitudinous, stereotypical

triton 3 eft **4** newt **10** salamander

Triton 6 merman *attribute:* **5** conch *father:* **7** Neptune **8** Poseidon *mother:* **10** Amphitrite

triturate 4 bray, buck **5** crush, grind **6** powder **9** comminute, pulverize

triumph 3 joy, win **4** beat, best, gain **5** exult, glory **6** master **7** conquer, delight, prevail, prosper, succeed, victory **8** conquest, jubilate, overcome, reveling, surmount **9** exultance, festivity, jubilance **10** ascendancy, exultation, jubilation **11** surmounting, vanquishing **12** vanquishment

triumphal see **triumphant**

triumphant 8 exultant, exulting, jubilant **9** rejoicing

triumvirate see **triad**

Triumvirate, First *member:* **6** Caesar, Pompey **7** Crassus

Triumvirate, Second *member:* **6** Antony **7** Lepidus **8** Octavius

triune see **triad**

trivet 4 rack **5** stand **6** tripod

trivia 8 minutiae **9** small beer **11** small change **13** small potatoes

trivial 4 puny **5** light, minor, petty **6** casual, little, measly, paltry, slight **7** shallow **8** captious, picayune, trifling **9** fribbling, frivolous, small-beer **10** negligible, picayunish, shoestring **11** Mickey Mouse, superficial, unimportant **13** insignificant

troche 6 tablet **7** lozenge **8** pastille

troglodyte 7 caveman **11** cave dweller

troika 8 carriage; (see also **triad**)

Troilus *beloved:* 8 Cressida *father:*
5 Priam *mother:* 6 Hecuba *slayer:*
8 Achilles
Troilus and ___ 8 Cressida, Criseyde
Trojan *horse builder:* 5 Epeus *king:*
5 Priam *priest:* 7 Laocoon *soothsayer:*
7 Helenus 9 Cassandra *warrior:* 5 Paris
6 Aeneas, Agenor, Hector 9 Euphorbus
Trojan Horse builder 5 Epeus 6 Epeius
troll 4 fish, lure, roll, sing 5 angle, dwarf,
giant
trolley 3 car 4 cart, tram 8 carriage
9 streetcar
Trollope, Anthony *novel:* 11 Ayala's
Angel, Phineas Finn 12 Phineas Redux
13 The Claverings
trombone 4 wind 5 brass 7 sackbut
tromp 4 beat, drub, hike, pelt, slog
5 pound, stamp, stomp, tramp 6 batter, buffet, pummel, thrash, trudge 7 belabor, trample 8 lambaste
troop 4 army, band, hoof, host, pace, step,
walk 5 corps, tread 6 foot it, forces, legion,
outfit 7 company, traipse 8 ambulate,
assembly, military, soldiers 9 gathering,
multitude 10 collection, combatants, servicemen 11 armed forces
trope 5 irony 6 simile 8 metaphor, metonymy 10 synecdoche
Trophonius *brother:* 8 Agamedes *temple
site:* 6 Delphi
trophy 5 relic, token 7 memento 8 keepsake, memorial, reminder, souvenir
11 remembrance 12 remembrancer
tropical 3 hot 4 warm 6 jungly, sultry, torrid 10 equatorial
tropical cyclone see **typhoon**
tropical storm see **typhoon**
Tropic of Cancer author 6 Miller
Tros' son 4 Ilus 8 Ganymede
trot 3 jog 4 crib, gait, lope, pony
11 translation
troth 8 espousal 10 engagement
trot out 4 show 5 flash 6 expose, flaunt,
parade 7 display, disport, exhibit, show off
8 brandish
Trotsky, Leon *associate:* 5 Lenin
troubadour 4 bard, poet 6 rhymer 8 jongleur, minstrel, musician 9 balladist,
rhymester
trouble 3 ado, ail, irk, try, vex 4 care, cark,
fret, fuss, pain 5 annoy, Dutch, harry,
haunt, pains, rowel, trial, upset, while,
worry 6 bother, bustle, effort, flurry, harass,
kiaugh, pester, plague, pother, put out,
strain, stress 7 afflict, agitate, disturb,
intrude, perturb, torment 8 disquiet, distress, exertion, hardship, hot water, impose
on, irritate, mischief, put about, vexation
9 disoblige, incommode 10 difficulty, discommode, discompose, disconcert, impose

upon 11 bedevilment, elbow grease, predicament 13 inconvenience
troublemaker 6 heller 7 hellion, inciter
8 agitator, inflamer 10 instigator
troublesome 4 mean, ugly 5 pesky
6 vexing, wicked 7 painful 8 alarming,
annoying 9 upsetting, vexatious 10 bothersome, disturbing 11 disquieting
troublous 4 mean, ugly 5 pesky
6 stormy, wicked 9 turbulent, vexatious
trough 3 hod 4 bowl, tank 5 basin, drain
6 manger, vessel 7 channel 9 container
combining form: 5 bothr 6 bothro
trounce 4 beat, drub, rout, trim, whip
5 whomp 6 thrash, wallop 7 clobber, shellac 9 overwhelm
troupe 4 band 5 corps, party 6 outfit
7 company
trouper 4 mime 5 actor, mimic 6 mummer,
player 7 artiste 8 thespian 9 performer,
playactor 11 entertainer 12 impersonator
trousers 5 pants 6 slacks 8 britches *tartan:* 5 trews
trout *kind:* 3 sea 4 char, lake 5 brook,
brown, river 7 rainbow 8 speckled
9 steelhead
Trovatore, Il *character:* 7 Azucena, Leonora, Manrico 11 Count di Luna *composer:* 5 Verdi
trove 5 hoard 9 amassment, colluvies
10 collection, cumulation 11 aggregation
12 accumulation 13 agglomeration
Troy 5 Ilium *epic of:* 5 Iliad *excavator:*
10 Schliemann *founder:* 4 Ilus *modern
site:* 9 Hissarlik; (see also **Trojan**)
truant 4 idle 7 shirker 8 shirking
13 irresponsible
truce 4 lull 5 letup, pause, peace
6 accord 7 respite 9 armistice, cease-fire
truck 3 van 4 swap 5 lorry, trade 6 barter,
handle, peddle, retail 7 bargain, traffic
8 commerce, dealings, exchange *military:*
6 camion
truckers' communicators 3 CBs
truckle 3 tag 4 fawn, tail 5 cower, toady,
trail 6 cringe, follow, grovel, kowtow
7 honey up, succumb 8 bootlick 11 apple-
polish
truckler 4 toad 5 toady 7 spaniel 8 lickspit 9 sycophant, toadeater 10 bootlicker,
footlicker 11 lickspittle
truculent 4 fell, grim 5 cruel, harsh, rough,
sharp 6 cowing, fierce, savage, severe
7 abusive, inhuman, scrappy, warlike, wolfish 8 bullying, inhumane, militant, scathing,
scurrile 9 barbarous, bellicose, combative,
ferocious, invective, trenchant, vitriolic
10 pugnacious, scurrilous, terrifying, vituperous 11 belligerent, browbeating, contentious, frightening, opprobrious, quarrelsome,

terrorizing **12** contumelious, gladiatorial, intimidating, vituperative, vituperatory

trudge 4 plod, slog, slop, toil, trek **6** stodge **8** footslog, plunther

true 4 just, real, very **5** liege, loyal, right, sooth, valid **6** actual, ardent, honest, kosher, strict, trusty **7** factual, genuine, precise, staunch, unfaked, upright **8** accurate, bona fide, constant, faithful, resolute, rightful, unfabled **9** allegiant, authentic, honorable, steadfast, trustable, undoubted, unfeigned, veracious, veridical, veritable **10** creditable, dependable, legitimate, sureenough, undeniable **11** appropriate, indubitable, trustworthy, undesigning, undistorted **12** indisputable, undissembled **13** authoritative *combining form:* **2** eu **4** orth **5** ortho

true-blue 5 loyal **8** faithful **10** unswerving

truism 4 rule **5** axiom, gnome, maxim, moral **6** cliché, dictum, gospel, verity **7** brocard, bromide **8** aphorism, apothegm, veracity **9** platitude **10** shibboleth **11** commonplace

Truk Island 3 Tol **4** Moen, Udot, Uman **5** Fefan **6** Dublon

truly 3 yea **4** even, very, well **6** easily, indeed, really, surely, verily **7** de facto **8** actually **9** genuinely, veritably **10** absolutely, positively **11** confidently, doubtlessly, undoubtedly

Truman, Harry S *birthplace:* **5** Lamar (Missouri) *predecessor:* **3** FDR *successor:* **3** DDE

trump 3 cap, top **4** beat, best, pass, ruff **5** excel, outdo **6** better **7** manille, surpass **8** clincher, outstrip, spadille

trumpery 4 base, mean, poor **5** bilge, cheap, hokum **6** bunkum, bushwa, cheesy, common, paltry, shoddy, trashy **7** twaddle **8** claptrap, flimflam, malarkey, nonsense, rubbishy **10** double-talk

trumpet 4 horn, tout **6** herald **8** ballyhoo *call:* **6** sennet *ram's horn:* **6** shofar

trumpeter 4 Hirt **5** André, Davis **6** Alpert, Voisin **7** Schwarz **9** Armstrong, Gillespie

truncate 3 lop, top **4** crop **5** shear **6** cut off **7** abridge, pollard **10** abbreviate

truncheon 3 bat **4** club, mace **5** billy **6** cudgel **8** bludgeon **9** billy club **10** knobkerrie, nightstick

trundle 3 bed, tub **4** bowl, cart, haul, push, roll **5** churn, wheel **6** lumber

trunk 3 box **4** body, case, stem **5** chest, torso **7** channel, circuit, luggage *elephant:* **9** proboscis *tree:* **4** bole

truss 3 tie **4** bind, pack **5** brace **7** support **9** supporter **10** strengthen

trust 4 care, hope, pool, rely, ward **5** chain, faith, group, lot on, stock **6** assume, bank on, belief, cartel, charge, commit, credit, rely on **7** build on, combine, confide, consign, count on, custody, keeping, presume **8** bank upon, credence, depend on, reckon on, reliance, rely upon, sureness **9** assurance, certainty, certitude, syndicate **10** confidence, conviction, dependence, depend upon **11** calculate on, safekeeping **12** conglomerate, guardianship, positiveness *Scottish:* **6** lippen

trustworthy 4 true **5** exact, tried, valid **6** honest, secure **7** upright **8** accurate, credible, faithful, reliable **9** authentic, realistic, veracious **10** convincing, dependable, scrupulous **12** tried and true **13** authoritative

trusty 4 firm **5** sound, tried **6** secure, stable **7** convict, turnkey **8** credible, faithful, reliable **9** authentic **10** convincing, dependable **11** predictable, responsible **12** tried and true

truth 5 axiom, maxim, sooth **6** candor, gospel, verity **7** lowdown, reality, veritas **8** veracity **9** precision, rightness **11** genuineness **12** authenticity, veridicality **13** veraciousness, veritableness *goddess:* **4** Maat *serum:* **11** scopolamine

truthful 4 real **5** frank **6** candid, honest **7** factual, sincere, veridic **8** accurate **9** realistic, veracious, veridical

truthfulness 5 truth **6** verity **8** veracity **12** veridicality **13** veraciousness

try 2 go **3** aim, irk, pop, vex **4** pain, rack, seek, shot, slap, stab, test **5** annoy, assay, check, crack, essay, exert, fling, offer, prove, trial, whack, whirl, wring **6** aspire, bother, harass, harrow, hassle, martyr, strain, stress, strive **7** afflict, agonize, attempt, crucify, test out, torment, torture, trouble **8** distress, endeavor, striving, struggle **9** undertake **10** excruciate, experiment

trying 5 rough, tight, tough **6** sticky, taxing, tricky, vexing **7** arduous, exigent, irksome, onerous, tricksy, weighty **8** annoying, exacting **9** demanding, strenuous **10** bothersome, burdensome, irritating, oppressive **11** troublesome

try out 8 audition

tryst 4 date **7** meeting **10** engagement, rendezvous **11** appointment, assignation

tsetse fly 8 glossina

tsunami 9 tidal wave

tub 3 vat **4** bath, wash **5** keeve **6** shower **8** dumpling **10** butterball

tuba 7 helicon

Tubalcain *father:* **6** Lamech *mother:* **6** Zillah

Tubal's father 7 Japheth

tubby 5 plump, podgy, pudgy **6** chubby, plumpy, rotund **8** plumpish, roly-poly **10** roundabout

tube 2 TV **4** duct, hose, pipe **5** buret,

pipet **6** siphon, subway, tunnel, vessel **7** burette, conduit, cuvette, pipette, syringe **8** pipe-line *anatomical:* **3** vas **4** duct, vasa (plural) **7** salpinx **9** salpinges (plural) *combining form:* **5** solen **6** siphon, soleno, syring **7** siphoni, siphono, syringo

tuber 4 bulb, corm, stem **6** potato **7** rhizome

tuberculosis 2 TB **8** phthisis **11** consumption, white plague

tuck 2 go **3** pep **4** birr, chow, eats, feed, food, grub, meat **5** bread, moxie, scoff, vigor **6** energy, viands **7** potency **9** hardihood, provender

tucker 4 poop, wilt **5** gruel **7** exhaust, frazzle, tire out, wear out **8** knock out **9** prostrate

tuft 5 clump, mound **7** cluster *combining form:* **4** loph **5** lophi, lopho **6** lophio *of feathers:* **7** panache *of hair:* **4** tate *ornamental:* **6** pompon *vascular:* **6** glomus

tufted 8 floccose

tug 3 lug, tow, war **4** drag, draw, haul, moil, pull, toil, work **5** drive, fight, labor **6** battle, oppugn, strain, strive **7** contend

tug-of-war 6 strife **7** contest, rivalry, warfare **8** conflict, striving **9** emulation **11** competition

tuition 8 teaching, training, tutelage **9** education, schooling **11** instruction

tumble 3 dip, hit **4** bump, down, drop, fall, fell, hash, hear, luck, mash, meet, skid, trip **5** floor, learn, level, light, mix up, pitch, snafu, upset **6** chance, foul up, go down, happen, jumble, litter, mess up, muddle, muss up, plunge, topple **7** catch on, clutter, confuse, descend, disturb, find out, flatten, overset, plummet, rummage, shuffle, snarl up, unearth, unhorse **8** bowl down, bowl over, come down, disarray, discover, disorder, keel over, mishmash, nose-dive, overturn, scramble, unsettle **9** ascertain, bring down, determine, knock down, knock over, overthrow **10** disarrange, discompose

tumbler 5 glass **11** cartwheeler

tumbrel 4 cart **5** wagon **7** vehicle **8** dumpcart

tumescent 6 turgid **7** aureate, bloated, bulging, flowery, swollen **8** dropsied, inflated, swelling **9** bombastic, dropsical, flatulent, overblown **10** euphuistic, rhetorical **12** magniloquent **13** grandiloquent

tumid see tumescent

tummy 3 gut **5** belly **6** paunch, venter **7** abdomen, stomach

tumor 3 wen **4** cyst **5** myoma **6** emerod, glioma, lipoma, myxoma **7** desmoid, emeroid, myeloma, neuroma, osteoma, sarcoma **8** blastoma, hepatoma, lymphoma, neoplasm, teratoma **9** carcinoma *benign:* **7** fibroid, fibroma *combining form:* **3** oma

4 cele, myom, onco **5** myomo, omato (plural), oncho **6** gangli **7** ganglio *hard:* **8** scirrhus *soft:* **5** gumma

tumult 3 din **4** flap, stew, to-do **5** babel, noise, whirl **6** clamor, dither, hassle, hubbub, jangle, lather, outcry, pother, racket, uproar, upturn **7** ferment, turmoil **8** disorder, paroxysm, seething, upheaval **9** agitation, commotion, confusion, maelstrom **10** convulsion, hullabaloo, hurly burly, turbulence **11** disturbance, pandemonium **12** unsettlement

tumultuous 5 rowdy **6** unruly **7** raucous **8** rowdyish **9** termagant, turbulent **10** boisterous, disorderly, rowdydowdy **11** rumbustious

tumulus 4 hill **5** mound **6** barrow **7** hillock

tun 3 keg, vat **4** butt, cask, pipe **6** barrel **8** hogshead

tune 3 air, fix, lay **4** dial, sing, sync **5** carol, chant, chime, order, range, synch **6** accord, adjust, chorus, extent, matter, melody, strain, warble **7** concert, concord, conform, descant, harmony, measure, melisma, melodia **8** diapason, regulate, vicinity, vocalize **9** agreement, harmonize, integrate, magnitude, reconcile **10** consonance, coordinate, proportion **11** accommodate, composition, concordance **12** neighborhood, reconciliate

tuneful 5 sweet, tuned **6** dulcet **7** lyrical, melodic, musical, songful **8** euphonic **9** melodious **10** euphonious **11** mellisonant

tungsten 7 wolfram

tunic 5 gipon, jupon **6** caftan, kaftan, kirtle *Greek:* **6** chiton

tunicate 4 salp **5** salpa **6** salpid **8** ascidian, doliolid **9** sea squirt

Tunisia *monetary unit:* 5 dinar *ruins:* **8** Carthage

tunnel 4 tube **6** burrow **7** conduit **8** crawlway *Alps:* **7** Simplon *France:* **4** Rove *Hudson river:* **7** Holland, Lincoln *Nevada:* **5** Sutro *railroad:* **6** Hoosac **7** Cascade

tunny 4 tuna **7** bluefin

Turandot *character:* 3 Liu **5** Calaf *composer:* **7** Puccini *suitor:* **5** Calaf

turban 6 pugree **7** pugaree, puggree **8** bandanna, puggaree **9** headdress

turbid 4 dark **5** dense, mucky, muddy, murky, riley, roily, smoky, thick **6** cloudy, opaque **7** clouded, obscure

turbulence 3 din **4** flap, stew **5** babel, fight **6** dither, fracas, lather, pother, tumult, uproar **7** turmoil **9** agitation, commotion, confusion **10** unruliness **11** pandemonium

turbulent 4 fast, wild **5** roily, rough, rowdy **6** raging, stormy, unruly **7** boiling, furious, howling, moiling, raucous, riotous, roaring, ruffled **8** agitated, blustery, brawling, mutinous, rowdyish, stormful, swirling **9** clamorous, convulsed, stirred up, termagant **10** blustering, boisterous, disorderly, rip-roaring, roisterous, roughhouse, rowdydowdy, tumultuous **11** rumbustious, tempestuous, uninhibited **12** rambunctious **13** tempest-tossed

turf 3 sod **4** area **5** divot, track **6** region, sphere, swarth **7** terrain **9** racetrack, territory

turgid *see* **tumescent**

turkey *disease:* **9** blackhead *female:* **3** hen *head growth:* **5** snood **7** dewbill *male:* **3** tom **7** gobbler *throat pouch:* **6** wattle *young:* **5** poult

Turkey *capital:* **6** Ankara *largest city:* **8** Istanbul *monetary unit:* **4** lira **5** pound

turkey buzzard 4 aura

Turkey in the ___ 5 Straw

Turkish *empire:* **7** Ottoman *governor:* **4** vali *inn:* **6** imaret *music:* **9** janissary *palace:* **5** serai *province:* **7** vilayet *soldier:* **5** nizam **8** janizary **9** janissary *sultan:* **5** Ahmet, Selim **7** Bajazet, Ilderim *sword:* **8** yataghan *title:* **3** aga, bey **4** agha **5** pasha **6** vizier

turmeric 4 herb **5** spice **8** curcumin **9** bloodroot

turmoil 4 flap, moil, riot, stew, to-do **5** whirl **6** clamor, dither, hassle, hubbub, lather, pother, strife, tumult, unease, unrest, uproar **7** anxiety, ferment, garboil **8** disorder, disquiet, distress, upheaval **9** agitation, commotion, confusion **10** disruption, hurly burly, inquietude, turbulence, uneasiness **11** anxiousness, disquietude, jitteriness, nervousness, restiveness **12** restlessness **13** Sturm und Drang

turn 3 aim, yaw, zag, zig **4** bend, bias, bout, cast, eddy, grow, gyre, plow, reel, roll, sour, spin, swim, tack, tour, vary, veer, whip, wind **5** alter, angle, avert, curve, orbit, pivot, point, refer, round, sheer, shunt, spell, stint, swing, swirl, train, twirl, twist, upset, weave, whirl **6** become, change, circle, defect, desert, detour, direct, divert, gyrate, hang on, invert, modify, mutate, obvert, plow up, render, repair, resort, revert, rotate, sicken, sprain, switch, swivel, wrench, zero in, zigzag **7** circuit, convert, deflect, derange, deviate, digress, diverge, flexure, hinge on, inverse, passade, reflect, reverse, revolve **8** disorder, flection, gyration, mutation, renounce, reversal, rotation, unsettle **9** about-face, deviation, oscillate, pirouette, rechannel, refashion, repudiate, reversion, sidetrack, translate, transpose, variation, volte-face **10** alteration, apostatize, change into, circumduct, deflection, double back, revolution, right-about, tergiverse, transplace **11** changeabout, reversement **12** modification, tergiversate *combining*

form: **4** trop **5** trope, tropy **6** tropic **7** trophic, tropism, tropous *to stone:* **8** lapidify

turnabout 3 rat **6** coward **7** quitter, reverse **8** apostate, defector, recreant, renegade, reversal, runagate **9** about-face, reversion, volte-face **10** backslider, rightabout **11** changeabout, reversement **13** tergiversator

turn aside or away 4 skew, veer, ward **5** avert, shunt **6** divert **7** deflect, shuttle

turn back 5 react, recur, repel **6** return, revert **10** recrudesce

turncoat 3 rat, spy **7** quisler, traitor **8** apostate, betrayer, defector, deserter, quisling, recreant, renegade, runagate **9** straggler, turnabout **13** tergiversator

turn down 4 veto **5** spurn **6** refuse, reject **7** decline, dismiss **9** reprobate, repudiate **10** disapprove

turned on 4 high **5** doped **6** stoned, zonked **7** drugged **8** hopped-up **9** spacedout **10** tripped out

turn in 3 bed **5** rat on **6** betray, retire **7** deliver, produce **8** hand over, inform on

turning point 4 crux **5** pivot **6** climax, crisis **8** landmark

turnip 5 swede **8** rutabaga *Scottish:* **4** neep

turnip-shaped 8 napiform

turn left 3 haw

Turn of the Screw, The *author:* **5** James *character:* **5** Flora, Miles **10** Peter Quint *composer:* **7** Britten

turn over 4 feed, find, give, hand, muse, plow, roll **5** break, upset **6** assign, commit, give up, plow up, ponder, supply, topple **7** commend, confide, consign, deliver, entrust, furnish, overset, provide, revolve **8** delegate, meditate, ruminate, transfer **9** overthrow **10** deliberate, relinquish

turnpike 4 road **7** highway, tollway **8** toll road

turn right 3 gee

turn up 3 get **4** come, espy, find, show, spot **5** catch, get in, hit on, pop in, reach **6** appear, arrive, descry, detect, louden, roll in, show up **7** hit upon, uncover, unearth **8** meet with **9** encounter, track down **11** materialize

Turnus *beloved:* **7** Lavinia *slayer:* **6** Aeneas

turpentine 7 galipot, solvent, thinner *ingredient:* **6** pinene *tree:* **4** pine **9** terebinth

turret 5 tower **8** bartizan

turtle 8 terrapin, tortoise **9** chelonian *edible part:* **7** calipee **8** calipash *sea:* **6** ridley **8** hawkbill *shell:* **8** carapace *shell part:* **8** plastron

Tuscany *city:* **4** Pisa **8** Florence *river:* **4** Arno *tower:* **4** Pisa *wine:* **7** chianti

tusk 4 fang 5 ivory, tooth

tussle 4 spar 5 scrap 6 hassle 7 grapple, scuffle, wrestle 8 skirmish

tutelage see **tuition**

tutor 5 coach, teach 6 docent, mentor 7 teacher 9 pedagogue 10 instructor

Tut's tomb discoverer 6 Carter

TV see **television**

twaddle 3 jaw, yak 4 bosh, chat 5 clack, drool, prate, run on 6 babble, dither, drivel, gabble, hot air 7 blabber, blather, chatter, prattle 8 claptrap, malarkey, nonsense, tommyrot, wish-wash 9 poppycock 10 balderdash

Twain biographer 5 Paine

tweak 3 jog 4 jerk, pull 5 pinch 6 snatch, twitch

Twelfth Night character 5 Maria, Viola 6 Olivia 8 Malvolio 9 Sebastian, Toby Belch

twelve *combining form:* 5 dodec 6 dodeca

twenty *combining form:* 4 icos 5 icosa, icosi

twerp 4 brat, fool, jerk 5 sprat 6 squirt 7 upstart

twibil 2 ax 3 axe 8 battle-ax 9 battle-axe

twice 3 bis 5 twofold *combining form:* 2 di 3 bis *prefix:* 2 bi 3 dis

twice a day 3 b.i.d. 8 bis in die

twice a year 8 biannual

Twice-Told Tales author 9 Hawthorne

twig 5 shoot, sprig 6 branch *bundle of:* 5 fagot 6 faggot

twiggy 4 slim, thin 5 reedy 6 slight, stalky 7 slender, squinny, tenuous 9 attenuate

twilight 3 end, eve 4 dusk 5 gloom 6 sunset 8 gloaming, glooming, owl light 9 attenuate, nightfall

Twilight of the Gods 8 Ragnarok

twill 5 cloth, serge, weave 6 fabric 9 gabardine 11 herringbone

twin 4 dual, like, mate 5 match 6 bifold, binary, double, fellow, paired 7 matched, similar, twofold 8 matching 9 companion, duplicate, identical 10 coordinate, reciprocal *combining form:* 5 didym 6 didymo

Twin Cities 6 St. Paul 11 Minneapolis

twine 4 coil, curl, wind 5 twist 6 enmesh, spiral, tangle 7 entwine, wreathe 8 entangle 9 corkscrew 10 interweave

twinge 4 ache, pain, pang 5 throe 6 stitch

twinkle 3 bat 4 wink 5 blink, flash, gleam, glint, light, shake, shine, trice 6 minute, moment, second 7 flicker, glimmer, glisten, glitter, instant, light up, nictate, shimmer, sparkle 8 coruscate, nictitate, twinkling 10 illuminate 11 coruscation, scintillate, split second 13 scintillation

twin stars 6 Castor, Pollux

twirl 4 gyre, spin 5 whirl 6 gyrate 9 pirouette, whirligig

twist 3 wry 4 coil, curl, slub, turn, warp, wind, wisp 5 belie, color, gnarl, pivot, quirk, thraw, twine, wring 6 garble, intort, spiral, sprain, squirm, torque, widdle, wrench, writhe 7 contort, distort, entwine, falsify, intwine, pervert, wreathe, wriggle 8 miscolor, misstate, squiggle 9 corkscrew 12 misrepresent *combining form:* 4 spir 5 spiri, spiro

twisted 3 wry 4 awry 5 askew 6 knurly, thrawn, warped 7 tortile

twister 7 cyclone, tornado 9 whirlwind

twit 4 jive, josh, lout, mock, quiz, razz 5 blame, chide, rally, scout, taunt, tease 6 deride 7 censure, reprove 8 reproach, ridicule 9 reprehend

twitch 3 lug, nip 4 jerk, snap, yank 5 grasp, lurch, pinch, pluck, tweak 6 clutch, snatch 9 vellicate

twitter 3 gab, jaw 4 chat, chip, peep 5 cheep, chirp, quake, run on, shake, tweet 6 babble, cackle, dither, quaver, quiver, rattle, shiver, tremor 7 chatter, chipper, chirrup, chitter, prattle, shudder, tremble, tweedle

twittery 5 jumpy, nervy 6 goosey, spooky 7 fidgety, jittery, nervous 9 flustered 10 high-strung

two 3 duo 4 duet, pair 5 twain 6 couple *combining form:* 2 dy 3 bis, duo, dyo *divide into:* 4 fork 6 bisect 9 bifurcate *prefix:* 2 bi 3 twi

twofold 4 dual, twin 5 binal, duple 6 binary, double, duplex, dyadic, paired 9 dualistic *combining form:* 2 di 4 dipl 5 diphy, diplo 6 diphyo

Two Gentlemen of Verona *character:* 5 Julia 6 Silvia, Thurio 7 Proteus 9 Valentine

two-horned 10 bicornuate

twosome 3 duo 4 dyad, pair 5 brace 6 couple 7 doublet

two-time 5 bluff 6 delude, humbug, illude, juggle, take in 7 beguile, deceive, mislead 11 double-cross

two-wheeler 4 bike 5 cycle 7 bicycle 10 velocipede

two-winged 9 dipterous

Two Years Before the Mast author 4 Dana

Tybalt *cousin:* 6 Juliet *family:* 7 Capulet *slayer:* 5 Romeo *victim:* 8 Mercutio

Tyche *goddess of:* 7 fortune

tycoon 4 czar, king 5 baron, mogul, nabob 6 prince 7 magnate

tyke 3 dog 5 child, hound 6 canine 7 mongrel

tympanum 7 eardrum 9 middle ear

Tyndareus *kingdom:* **6** Sparta *wife:*
4 Leda

type **3** cut, ilk, lot, way **4** cast, form, kind,
mold, sort **5** breed, class, genre, order,
print, serif, stamp **6** kidney, nature, stripe
7 feather, species, variety **8** category
9 character **10** persuasion **11** description
bar: **4** slug *combining form:* **5** morph
6 morpho *jumbled:* **2** pi **3** pie *measure:*
2 em, en **4** pica **5** point *set:* **7** compose
setter: **10** compositor *size:* **4** pica
5 agate, pearl *stroke:* **5** serif *style:*
5 roman **6** Gothic, italic **7** Fraktur **8** boldface, sanserif **9** lightface, sans serif *tray:*
6 galley

Typee *author:* **8** Melville *character:*
4 Toby

typewriter *part:* **3** key **6** platen, spacer
type size: **4** pica **5** elite

Typhon **3** Set **7** monster **8** Typhoeus *offspring:* **6** Sphinx **7** Chimera **8** Cerberus,
Chimaera *wife:* **7** Echidna

typhoon **9** hurricane **13** tropical storm

typical **5** ideal, model, usual **6** common,
normal, old hat **7** classic, general, natural,
regular **9** classical, exemplary, prevalent
11 commonplace

typical of *suffix:* **2** ic, ly **3** ish, ist **4** ical
5 istic **7** istical

typify **6** embody, mirror **9** body forth, epitomize, exemplify, personify, represent, symbolize **10** illustrate **11** emblematize

typo **5** error **8** misprint

typographer **7** printer **10** compositor

Tyr **3** Tiu *brother:* **4** Thor *father:* **4** Odin
god of: **3** war *mother:* **5** Jordh, Jorth

tyrannical **5** harsh **6** brutal **8** absolute,
despotic **9** arbitrary, autarchic, roughshod
10 autocratic, monocratic, oppressive

tyrannize **5** crush **7** dictate, oppress,
shackle, trample **8** dominate, domineer,
overlord **9** despotize, terrorize

tyrannous **6** lordly **8** absolute, despotic
9 arbitrary, autarchic, fascistic **10** autocratic, monocratic **12** totalitarian

tyranny **7** fascism **8** totality **9** autocracy,
despotism, terrorism **10** absolutism, domination, oppression **12** dictatorship

tyrant **4** duce **6** despot **8** autocrat, dictator **9** oppressor, strong man **12** totalitarian

Tyrian _____ **6** purple

tyro **4** colt **6** novice, rookie **7** amateur,
dabbler **8** beginner, freshman, neophyte,
newcomer **9** novitiate, smatterer
10 apprentice, dilettante, tenderfoot, uninitiate **11** abecedarian

Tyrol see **Tirol**

Tzar see **czar**

U

übermensch **7** overman **8** superman

ubiquitous **7** allover **9** universal **10** everywhere **11** omnipresent

Uel's father **4** Bani

Uganda *capital:* **7** Kampala *monetary unit:* **8** shilling

ugly **3** bad, low **4** base, dour, fell, foul, glum, mean, ugly, vile **5** awful, cross, grave, major, pesky, plain, sulky, surly, toady **6** cranky, gloomy, homely, morose, sordid, sullen, wicked **7** bizarre, crabbed, hideous, ignoble, low-down, serious, servile, vicious **8** grievous, gruesome, uncomely, unlovely, wretched **9** dangerous, grotesque, repelling, repugnant, repulsive, saturnine, troublous, unsightly, vexatious **10** despicable, ill-favored, ill-looking, uninviting, unpleasing **11** ill-tempered, threatening, troublesome, unbeautiful **12** unattractive

Ugly Duckling author **8** Andersen

ugni blanc **4** wine **9** Trebbiano

ukase **5** edict, order **6** decree, ruling **7** command **9** directive **12** proclamation

Ukraine *capital:* **4** Kiev *folk dance:* **5** gopak *soldier:* **7** cossack

Ulalume author **3** Poe

Ulam's father **5** Eshek

ulcer **4** sore *kind:* **6** peptic **8** duodenal *mouth:* **10** canker sore

uliginous **3** wet **4** damp, oozy **5** moist, muddy **6** swampy

ulna **5** cubit **7** cubitus, forearm

Ulrica **5** sibyl, sybil, witch

Ulster hero **4** Emer, Medb **5** Cu Roi, Etain, Noisi **6** Ailill, Fergus **7** Cathbad, Conaire, Da Derga, Deirdre **8** MacDatho **9** Conchobar, Cuchullin, Finnabair **10** Cuchulainn

ulterior **4** dark **5** later, privy **6** buried, covert, future, hidden, latent **7** cryptic, further, guarded, obscure, remoter, thither **8** obscured, shrouded **9** ambiguous, concealed, enigmatic, equivocal **10** subsequent, succeeding **11** undisclosed

ultimate **3** end, lag **4** dire, last **5** basic, close, final, grand, lofty **6** finish, latest, latter, utmost, wind up, wrap up **7** closing, epitome, exalted, extreme, maximum, sublime, supreme **8** absolute, complete, conclude, earliest, empyreal, empyrean, eventual, farthest, hindmost, last word, original, terminal, towering **9** determine, elemental, terminate **10** apotheosis, concluding, consummate, preeminent, surpassing **11** categorical, fundamental, unequalable, unmatchable **12** incomparable, quintessence, transcendent **13** unsurpassable

ultimatum **5** order **6** demand, threat

ultra **5** kinky, outré, rabid **6** beyond, farout **7** extreme, fanatic, forward, radical **9** excessive, extremist, fanatical **10** outlandish **11** extravagant

ultraconservative **4** tory **5** blimp, white **7** Bourbon, diehard **8** royalist **9** right-wing **11** reactionary, reactionist **13** reactionarist

ultraist **5** rabid **7** extreme, fanatic, radical **9** extremist

ultramarine **7** new blue, oversea **8** overseas **10** French blue **11** lapis lazuli, transmarine

ululate **3** bay **4** hoot, howl, wail, yelp **5** quest **6** bewail, lament **7** screech

Ulysses *author:* **5** Joyce *character:* **5** Bloom, Molly **6** Boylan **7** Dedalus (Stephen); (see also **Odysseus**)

umber **5** brown, shade **6** darken, shadow **8** grayling **9** hammerkop

umbilicus **4** core **5** heart, hilum, navel *combining form:* **6** omphal **7** omphalo

umbra **4** fish **5** ghost, shade **6** shadow **7** eidolon, phantom **8** darkness, phantasm, revenant **10** apparition

umbrage **3** ire **4** fury, huff, miff, rage **5** anger, doubt, pique, shade, trace, umbra, wrath **6** enrage, irking, madden, offend, screen, shadow **7** dudgeon, foliage, incense, leafage, offense, pretext, steam up, verdure **8** nettling, vexation **9** annoyance, infuriate, provoking, semblance, suspicion **10** irritation, resentment **11** displeasure **12** exasperation

umbrageous **5** shady **6** shaded, shadow **7** shadowy **8** shadowed **9** resentful **11** belligerent

umbrella **5** guard, shade **6** brolly, pileus, screen **7** parasol, shelter **10** protection **11** bumbershoot *large:* **4** gamp

umbrous **5** shady **6** shaded, shadow **7** shadowy **8** shadowed

umph see **oomph**

umpire **5** judge **7** adjudge, arbiter, ref-

eree **9** arbitrate **10** adjudicate, arbitrator
call: 3 out **4** balk, ball, safe **6** strike
unabashed 6 arrant, brassy, brazen
7 blatant **8** impudent, overbold **9** barefaced, shameless **10** unblushing
11 brazenfaced
unabbreviated see **unabridged**
unable 8 helpless, impotent **9** incapable
11 incompetent, inefficient, unqualified
13 incapacitated
unabridged 5 uncut, whole **6** entire,
intact **8** complete, undocked **11** uncondensed, whole-length **13** unabbreviated
unacceptable 4 poor **7** boorish **8** below
par, unwanted **9** unwelcome **10** ill-favored,
unpleasing, unsuitable **11** undesirable
12 inadmissible **13** below standard, exceptionable, objectionable
unaccompanied 4 bare, sole **5** alone,
apart **6** single **7** isolate, removed
8 detached, isolated
unaccomplished 7 jackleg **8** dabbling,
ungifted **9** unskilled **10** amateurish, dilettante, incomplete, unfinished **12** dilettantish, dilettantist
unaccountable 6 arcane, mystic
7 strange **8** numinous **9** mysterial,
unguessed **10** cabalistic, mysterious,
unknowable **11** inscrutable **12** impenetrable, inexplicable, unfathomable **13** inexplainable, irresponsible, unexplainable
unaccustomed 3 new **6** unused
7 strange **8** uncommon **10** unfamiliar
unacquainted 7 strange, unaware,
unusual **8** ignorant **9** oblivious, unknowing,
unwitting **10** unfamiliar, uninformed
11 incognizant **12** inconversant, uninstructed **13** inexperienced
unacquired 6 inborn, innate, native **7** connate, natural **9** inherited **10** congenital,
connatural, indigenous
unadorned 3 dry **4** bald, bare **5** naked,
plain, stark **6** rustic, simple **7** austere
11 undecorated, unelaborate, ungarnished
12 unbeautified, unornamented **13** unembellished, unembroidered, unpretentious
unadulterated 4 neat, pure **5** plain,
sheer **6** honest, simple **7** genuine, perfect,
sincere, unmixed **8** absolute, straight
9 unalloyed, undiluted **11** unmitigated,
unqualified
unadvisable see **inadvisable**
unaffable 7 aseptic **8** retiring **9** shrinking,
withdrawn **10** restrained **11** unexpansive
unaffected 4 easy, real **5** naive, plain
6 rustic, simple **7** artless, natural, sincere
9 ingenuous, unstudied, untouched, untutored **10** unschooled **12** unartificial,
uninfluenced
unafraid 4 bold, cool, sure **5** brave
7 assured, defiant, valiant **8** composed,

fearless, intrepid, valorous **9** audacious,
confident, dauntless, undaunted **10** courageous **13** imperturbable
unaimed 6 random **7** aimless **9** desultory,
haphazard, hit-or-miss, unplanned
10 designless **11** purposeless
12 unconsidered
unalike 7 distant, diverse, unequal, various **9** different, disparate, divergent, unsimilar **10** dissimilar
unalloyed 4 deep, pure **5** sheer, solid
6 simple, virgin **7** genuine, perfect,
unmixed **8** absolute **9** undiluted **11** unmitigated, unqualified **13** unadulterated
unalluring 5 plain **6** homely **8** uncomely,
unpretty **10** unhandsome **11** unbeauteous,
unbeautiful **12** unattractive
unalterable see **inalterable**
unambiguous 5 clear, lucid, plain **6** patent **7** crystal, evident, express, obvious
8 apparent, clean-cut, clear-cut, definite, distinct, explicit, luminous, manifest, palpable,
pellucid, specific **9** unblurred **10** definitive
11 categorical, translucent, transparent
12 transpicuous
unanimated 4 cold, dead, dull, flat
5 vapid **6** asleep **7** insipid
unanimous 5 solid **6** agreed, united
8 agreeing, univocal **10** concordant, concurrent, harmonious **11** consentient
13 consentaneous
unappeasable 4 grim **6** mortal **8** ruthless **9** insatiate, merciless, unsatiate
10 implacable, insatiable, ironfisted, quenchless, relentless, unyielding **11** unflinching,
unrelenting **12** unquenchable
13 unsatisfiable
unappetizing 4 flat **7** insipid **8** unsavory
9 savorless, tasteless **10** flavorless **11** distasteful, ill-flavored, unpalatable **12** unattractive **13** uninteresting
unappreciative 9 thankless **10** ungrateful, unthankful
unapproachable 5 aloof **6** offish **7** distant, stately **8** reserved **9** unbending, withdrawn **10** insociable, unsociable **11** standoffish, ungetatable, unreachable **12** inaccessible, unattainable
unarm see **disarm**
unarmed 4 bare **5** inerm **8** unbarbed
11 defenseless *combining form:* **5** anopl
6 anoplo
unartful 5 naive **6** simple **7** artless, natural **9** ingenuous, unstudied **10** unaffected,
unschooled **12** unartificial
unarticulate see **inarticulate**
unasked 5 unbid **6** wanton **8** arrogant,
impudent, unbidden, unsought, unwanted
9 uninvited, unwelcome, voluntary **10** gratuitous **11** overbearing, spontaneous,

uncalled-for, unrequested **12** presumptuous, supererogant, unacceptable

unassailable 5 stout, tough **6** secure, strong, sturdy **8** stalwart **9** tenacious **10** invincible, unbeatable **11** impregnable, indomitable **12** inexpugnable, invulnerable, undefeatable **13** inconquerable, unconquerable

unassertive 3 shy **4** meek **5** timid **6** modest **7** bashful, rabbity **8** backward, retiring **9** diffident, unassured **12** self-effacing

unassuming 3 shy **4** meek **5** lowly **6** humble, modest, simple **7** natural **8** retiring

unassured 3 shy **5** timid **6** modest, unsafe, unsure **7** bashful, rabbity **8** backward, insecure, retiring **9** diffident **10** unreliable **11** unassertive, unconfident **12** self-effacing, undependable **13** untrustworthy

unattached 4 free **5** loose **6** single **9** unmarried

unattractive 4 rude, ugly **5** plain **6** homely **8** frumpish, uncomely, unpretty **9** unlikable **10** unalluring, ungracious, unhandsome, unlikeable **11** unbeauteous, unbeautiful

unauthentic 7 bastard **8** spurious **9** ungenuine **10** apocryphal

unavailing 4 vain **6** futile **7** useless **8** abortive, bootless, gainless **9** fruitless **11** ineffective, ineffectual **12** unproductive

unavoidable 7 certain **9** necessary **10** ineludible, inevasible, inevitable, returnless, unevadable **11** ineluctable, inescapable, unescapable

unavoidably 8 perforce **10** helplessly, inevitably, willy-nilly **11** inescapably, whether or no

unaware 5 aback, short **6** sudden **7** unready **8** ignorant, suddenly **9** oblivious, unknowing, unwitting **10** unfamiliar, uninformed, unprepared **11** incognizant **12** inconversant, unacquainted, unexpectedly, uninstructed

unawares 5 aback, short **8** suddenly **12** unexpectedly

unbalance 5 craze **6** frenzy, lunacy, madden **7** derange, madness, unhinge **8** distract, insanity **10** aberration, alienation, insaneness **11** derangement, distraction, instability, psychopathy

unbalanced 3 mad **4** daft **5** batty, wacky **6** crazed, insane, uneven **7** unequal, unsound **8** demented, deranged, lopsided **9** irregular **10** asymmetric **13** unsymmetrical

unbeautiful 4 ugly **5** plain **6** homely **7** hideous **8** uncomely, unpretty **9** unsightly **10** ill-favored, ill-looking, unalluring, unhandsome **12** unattractive

unbecoming 4 rude **5** inapt, inept, rough, undue **6** clumsy, gauche, indign, unmeet **7** awkward, beneath, ungodly **8** improper, indecent, uncomely, unseemly, untimely, untoward, unworthy **9** incorrect, inelegant, maladroit **10** indecorous, indelicate, malapropos, malodorous, undecorous, unsuitable **11** disgraceful, unbefitting **12** unattractive, unseasonable **13** inappropriate

unbefitting see **unbecoming**

unbelievable 4 thin, weak **5** thick **6** flimsy **8** fabulous **9** fantastic **10** improbable, incredible **11** implausible, incogitable, unthinkable **12** insupposable, unconvincing, unimaginable **13** inconceivable, unsubstantial

unbeliever 5 pagan **6** giaour **7** atheist, doubter, heretic, infidel, scoffer, skeptic, zetetic **8** agnostic **10** headshaker, Pyrrhonian, Pyrrhonist **11** free-thinker

unbelieving 6 show-me **8** aporetic, doubting **9** quizzical, skeptical **11** distrusting, incredulous, questioning **12** disbelieving

unbending 5 aloof, rigid, stern, stiff **6** offish **7** distant **8** obdurate, reserved, resolute **9** impliable, inelastic, withdrawn **10** brassbound, inexorable, inflexible, insociable, relentless, unflexible, unsociable, unswayable, unyielding **11** immalleable, incompliant, standoffish **12** single-minded

unbiased 4 fair, just **5** aloof, equal **8** detached, tolerant **9** equitable, impartial, objective, uncolored **12** uninterested, unprejudiced **13** dispassionate

unbidden 7 unasked **8** unsought **9** uninvited **11** unrequested

unbind 4 free, undo **5** loose, unfix, untie **6** detach, loosen, ungird **7** absolve, deliver, manumit, release, unchain, unloose **8** dissolve, liberate, unfasten, unloosen, unswathe **9** discharge, disengage, unshackle **10** emancipate

unblamable 4 good, pure **8** innocent, virtuous **9** exemplary, guiltless, righteous **10** inculpable

unblemished 4 pure **5** clean, sound, whole **6** chaste, decent, intact, modest, unhurt **7** perfect **8** flawless, spotless, unmarred **9** stainless, undamaged, undefiled, uninjured, unsullied **10** immaculate, unimpaired

unblock 3 ope **4** open, undo **6** unshut, unstop **7** unclose

unblunted 4 keen **5** honed, sharp **7** whetted **10** razor-sharp

unblurred 5 clear, lucid **7** crystal **8** clear-cut, luminous, pellucid **11** translucent, transparent, unambiguous **12** transpicuous

unbolt 4 open **5** unbar, unpin **6** loosen, unlock **8** unfasten

unbosom 4 open, tell 6 betray, reveal, unveil 7 divulge, unclose, uncover 8 disclose, discover 9 uncurtain

unbound 4 free 5 loose 10 unconfined, unfastened

unbounded 4 huge, open 7 endless 8 infinite 9 boundless, limitless, unchecked, unlimited 10 indefinite, unmeasured 11 measureless 12 immeasurable, uncontrolled, unrestrained

unbridled 4 free 5 loose 7 violent 9 dissolute, unchecked 10 licentious, ungoverned 11 uninhibited 12 uncontrolled, unrestrained

unbroken 3 one 5 solid, sound, whole 6 entire, intact, single, unhurt 7 perfect, untamed 8 straight, unmarred, unplowed 9 continual, undamaged, undivided, uninjured, unsubdued 10 continuous, unimpaired 13 uninterrupted

unburden 3 rid 4 ease, lose 5 clear, empty 6 unload 7 relieve 8 shake off, throw off 9 discharge 11 disencumber

uncalled-for 4 rude 5 silly 6 absurd, wanton 7 foolish, incivil, unasked, uncivil 8 baseless, impolite, needless, unneeded 9 intrusive, officious, unfounded, unneedful 10 bottomless, gratuitous, groundless, ungracious, ungrounded, unrequired 11 disgracious, ill-mannered, impertinent, inessential, unessential, unnecessary, unwarranted 12 discourteous, preposterous, supererogant 13 disrespectful

uncanny 4 eery 5 eerie, scary, weird 6 creepy, spooky 7 ghostly, strange 9 unearthly, unnatural 10 mysterious, superhuman 11 supernormal, supranormal 12 supernatural 13 superordinary

uncared-for 7 run-down 8 untended 9 neglected

uncareful 4 wild 8 feckless, reckless 10 incautious 13 irresponsible

uncaring 8 feckless, heedless 9 oblivious, unheeding, unrecking 10 unthinking 11 inadvertent, thoughtless 12 irreflective, unreflective

unceasing 7 endless, eternal 8 constant, unending 9 ceaseless, continual, incessant, perpetual 10 continuous 11 everlasting, unremitting 12 interminable 13 uninterrupted

unceremonious 4 curt 5 bluff, blunt, sharp, short 6 abrupt 8 familiar, informal 9 irregular 10 ungracious, unofficial 11 thoughtless 13 inconsiderate

uncertain 4 asea, dark, hazy, iffy, moot, open 5 fluky, vague 6 chancy, fickle, fitful, queasy, shifty, unsure, wobbly 7 dubious, erratic, halting, mutable, obscure, protean, suspect, unclear 8 aleatory, arguable, doubtful, flickery, hesitant, insecure, moota-

ble, slippery, ticklish, unstable, unsteady, variable, volatile 9 ambiguous, debatable, equivocal, faltering, fluctuant, mercurial, sibylline, tenebrous, tentative, undecided, unsettled, whimsical 10 borderline, capricious, changeable, disputable, inconstant, indecisive, indefinite, irresolute, lubricious, precarious, unexplicit 11 problematic, vacillating, vacillatory 12 incalculable, questionable, undependable, unexpectable, wigglewaggle 13 indeterminate, problematical, temperamental, unforeseeable, unpredictable, untrustworthy

uncertainty 5 doubt, maybe, query, worry 6 bother, gamble, wonder 7 anxiety, concern, dubiety, reserve, trouble 8 disfaith, disquiet, distress, distrust, mistrust, suspense 9 agitation, dubiosity, dubitancy, suspicion 10 hesitation, skepticism, uneasiness 12 doubtfulness, perturbation

unchain 4 free 5 loose 6 loosen, unbind 7 manumit, release 8 liberate 9 discharge, unshackle 10 emancipate

unchangeable 4 fast 5 fixed 7 eternal 8 constant 9 immovable, immutable, unmovable 10 inflexible, invariable 11 inalterable, unalterable 12 unmodifiable

unchanging 4 even, same 6 stable, static, steady 7 equable, eternal, forever, settled, stabile, uniform 8 constant 9 immutable, steadfast, unfailing, unvarying 10 consistent, invariable, stationary 13 unfluctuating

unchaste 4 easy, fast, lewd 5 bawdy, dirty, light, loose 6 coarse, impure, wanton 7 haggard, immoral, obscene, scarlet, unclean 9 uncleanly

unchecked 4 free 5 loose 7 rampant 9 unbounded, unbridled 11 uninhibited

uncivil 4 rude, wild 5 crass, crude, rough 6 brutal, coarse, crusty, Gothic, rugged, savage 7 Hunnish, ill-bred, incivil 8 barbaric, clownish, impolite 9 barbarian, barbarous 10 indecorous, ungracious, unsuitable 11 disgracious, ill-mannered, impertinent, uncivilized, uncourteous 12 discourteous, uncultivated 13 disrespectful

uncivilized 4 rude, wild 6 brutal, Gothic, Hunnic, rugged, savage, unholy, wicked 7 boorish, Hunnish, ill-bred, loutish, lowbred, ungodly 8 barbaric, churlish, cloddish 9 barbarian, barbarous, unrefined 10 outrageous, uncultured, unmannerly, unpolished 12 uncultivated 13 unenlightened

unclad see **unclothed**

uncle *Dutch:* 3 oom *Scottish:* 3 eme *Spanish:* 3 tio

unclean 4 foul, tref, vile 5 black, dirty, nasty, soily 6 common, filthy, grubby, impure 7 defiled, immoral, obscene, squalid 8 polluted, profaned, unchaste 10 desecrated 11 unwholesome

unclear 3 dim 4 hazy, open 6 bleary, blurry, opaque, unsure 7 dubious, obscure, shadowy, suspect 8 doubtful, nebulose, nebulous 9 ambiguous, equivocal, tenebrous, uncertain, undefined, unsettled 10 ill-defined, indistinct, unexplicit 11 problematic

Uncle Remus creator 6 Harris

Uncle Tom's Cabin *author:* 5 Stowe *character:* 5 Eliza, Topsy 6 Legree (Simon) 9 Little Eva

Uncle Vanya author 7 Chekhov

uncloak 6 debunk, expose, show up, unmask 7 undress 8 discover, unshroud

unclothe 5 strip 6 denude, devest, divest, expose, reveal, unveil 7 display, disrobe, uncloak, uncover, undress 8 disclose 10 dishabille

unclothed 3 raw 4 nude 5 naked 6 unclad 8 buff-bare, stripped 9 au naturel, undressed 10 stark-naked

unclouded 4 fair, fine, open 5 clear, sunny 7 clarion 8 pleasant, rainless, sunshiny 10 undarkened

uncluttered 4 neat, snug, tidy, trig, trim 7 chipper, orderly 9 shipshape 11 spic-and-span, well-groomed 12 spick-and-span

uncolored 4 fair, just 5 equal 8 unbiased 9 equitable, impartial, objective 12 unprejudiced 13 dispassionate

uncombed 5 messy 6 sloppy, unneat, untidy 7 unkempt 8 ill-kempt, slipshod, slovenly 10 disheveled 12 unfastidious

uncombine 4 free, part 5 loose, sever 6 divide, sunder 7 disjoin 8 disjoint, dissever, disunite, separate 11 dichotomize

uncomely 4 ugly 5 inapt, inept, plain, undue 6 homely 7 hideous 8 improper, indecent, unpretty, untimely 9 unsightly 10 ill-favored, ill-looking, malapropos, unalluring, unbecoming, unhandsome, unsuitable 11 unbeauteous, unbeautiful, unbefitting 12 unattractive 13 inappropriate

uncomfortable 4 sick 5 harsh 6 queasy, uneasy 7 prickly 8 easeless, scratchy 11 distressing 13 disconcerting

uncommon 3 few, odd 4 rare 5 novel 6 choice, scarce, seldom, unique 7 special, strange, unusual 8 esoteric, especial, singular, sporadic, unwonted 10 infrequent, occasional, remarkable, unfrequent, unordinary 11 exceptional, unthinkable 12 unaccustomed, unimaginable 13 extraordinary

uncommunicative 4 dumb 5 aloof, close 6 offish, silent 7 distant, private 8 reserved, reticent, taciturn 9 unbending, withdrawn 10 insociable, unsociable 11 close-lipped, standoffish, tight-lipped 12 closemouthed, close-tongued, tight-mouthed

uncompassionate 5 stony 7 callous 8 obdurate 9 heartless, unfeeling 10 hard-boiled 11 coldhearted, hardhearted, unemotional 12 stony-hearted 13 unsympathetic

uncompliant 5 rigid 8 obdurate 9 untending 10 brassbound, inexorable, inflexible, unswayable, unyielding 12 single-minded

uncomplicated 5 basic, plain 6 honest, simple 10 elementary

uncomplimentary 9 slighting 10 derogatory, detracting, pejorative 11 disparaging, dyslogistic 12 depreciative, depreciatory

uncomprehensible see **incomprehensible**

uncompromising 4 firm 5 rigid, stern, tough 6 strict 7 extreme 8 hard-line, obdurate 9 unbending 10 brassbound, determined, inexorable, inflexible, relentless, unyielding 11 uncompliant 12 intransigent, single-minded

unconcealed 4 bare, open 5 frank, overt, plain 6 candid 8 apparent 11 openhearted, undisguised, unvarnished 12 undissembled 13 undissembling

unconcern 4 cool 6 apathy 8 coolness, lethargy 9 disregard, lassitude 11 disinterest, insouciance, nonchalance 12 heedlessness, indifference, listlessness 13 unmindfulness

unconcerned 4 cool 5 aloof 6 casual, remote 8 composed, detached 9 apathetic, collected, incurious, lethargic, uncurious, unmindful, withdrawn 10 nonchalant 11 indifferent 12 uninterested 13 disinterested

unconditional 4 free 5 frank, utter 6 simple 8 absolute, explicit, termless 10 unreserved

unconfined 3 lax 4 free 5 loose 9 boundless, limitless, unlimited 12 unrestrained

uncongenial 8 aversive, kindless 9 repellent, repugnant, unlikable 10 discordant, unpleasing 11 displeasing, inconsonant 12 antipathetic, inharmonious, unattractive, unharmonious 13 unsympathetic

unconnected 5 gappy 7 muddled 8 detached, inchoate, rambling, separate 10 disjointed, disordered, incoherent, incohesive 11 unorganized 12 uncontinuous 13 discontinuous

unconquerable 6 secure 9 resistant 10 impassable, invincible, unbeatable 11 impregnable, indomitable, insuperable 12 inexpugnable, invulnerable, unassailable, undefeatable

unconscionable 5 undue 6 unholy, wicked 7 extreme, ungodly 8 towering 9 barbarous, excessive 10 exorbitant, immoderate, inordinate, outrageous 11 extravagant, unchristian, uncivilized, unwarranted 12 unmeasurable, unprincipled, unreasonable, unscrupulous **13** unjustifiable, unwarrantable

unconscious 3 out **4** cold **5** brute **6** asleep, blotto, torpid **7** out cold, stunned, unaware **8** comatose, ignorant, mindless **10** insensible

unconsciousness 4 coma **5** faint **6** torpor, trance

unconsidered 4 puny, rash **5** brash, hasty, petty, small **6** paltry, random **7** aimless, trivial **8** picayune, reckless, trifling **9** desultory, haphazard, hit-or-miss, hotheaded, unadvised, unplanned **10** designless, ill-advised, incautious, objectless **11** promiscuous, thoughtless **12** inconsequent

unconsolable see **inconsolable**

unconstrained 4 easy, free **6** casual, dégagé, simple **7** natural, relaxed, unfussy **8** familiar, informal, outgoing **9** easygoing, expansive **10** unreserved **11** low-pressure **13** demonstrative

unconstraint 4 ease **7** abandon, freedom, naiveté **10** simplicity **11** naturalness, spontaneity **13** impulsiveness, ingenuousness

uncontrollable 4 wild **6** unruly **8** indocile **9** fractious **11** indomitable, intractable **12** recalcitrant, unmanageable **13** insuppressive, irrepressible, uncontainable, undisciplined

uncontrolled 4 free, wild **5** loose **9** irregular, unbounded, unmanaged **10** hysterical, licentious, ungoverned **11** unregulated **12** unrestrained

unconventional 3 odd **5** loose, outré, queer **6** casual **7** devious, offbeat, strange, unusual **8** Bohemian, informal **10** unorthodox **13** unceremonious

unconversant 3 raw **5** green, young **6** callow **7** untried **8** unversed **9** unfleshed **10** unseasoned **11** unpracticed **13** inexperienced

unconvincing 4 thin, weak **5** fishy, thick **6** flimsy **10** improbable, incredible **11** implausible **12** unbelievable **13** inconceivable, unsubstantial

uncooked 3 raw

uncork 6 unplug **7** release

uncorrectable 8 cureless, hopeless **9** incurable, insanable, uncurable **10** impossible **11** immedicable, irreparable **12** irremediable **13** unrecoverable

uncorrupted 4 pure **5** naive **6** virgin **8** innocent, pristine **9** unspoiled

uncouple 3 cut **5** loose, unfix **6** detach **8** abstract, unfasten **9** disengage **10** disconnect, dissociate **12** disassociate

uncourteous 4 rude **7** uncivil **8** impolite **10** ungracious **11** disgracious, ill-mannered, impertinent, uncalled-for **13** disrespectful

uncouth 3 odd, raw **4** lorn, rude **5** crass,

crude, gross, queer, rough, rummy **6** coarse, quaint, vulgar **7** awkward, bizarre, boorish, curious, erratic, ill-bred, loutish, oddball, strange, uncivil **8** backwood, derelict, deserted, desolate, forsaken, impolite, solitary, ungainly **9** abandoned, eccentric, inelegant, unrefined **10** uncultured, unpolished **11** disgracious, ill-mannered, impertinent, uncalled-for **12** discourteous, uncultivated **13** disrespectful *person:* **3** oaf **4** boor, lout **5** yokel **6** bumkin, rustic **7** bumpkin

uncover 4 bare, open, tell **5** strip **6** betray, denude, detect, divest, expose, remove, reveal, unmask, unveil **7** display, divulge, lay open, subject, unbosom, unclose, undrape, unearth **8** disclose, unclothe **9** uncurtain

uncovered 4 bare, open **5** naked **6** peeled **7** denuded, exposed **8** stripped, unmasked

uncritical 6 casual **7** cursory, inexact, offhand, shallow, sketchy **8** careless, slipshod **9** depthless, imprecise **10** inaccurate **11** perfunctory, superficial

uncrown 6 depose, unmake **8** dethrone, discrown, displace **9** disthrone **11** disenthrone

unction 3 oil **4** balm **5** cream, salve **6** cerate, chrism **7** suavity **8** ointment

unctuous 3 fat **4** oily **5** fatty, slick, soapy, suave **6** greasy, smarmy **7** fulsome **10** oleaginous

uncultivated 3 raw **4** arid, rude, wild **5** crass, crude, feral, gross, rough **6** coarse, desert, fallow, Gothic, incult, native, savage, sloven **7** deserty, Hunnish, natural, uncivil **8** agrarian, agrestal, barbaric **9** barbarian, barbarous, inelegant **11** uncivilized

uncultured 3 raw **4** rude **5** crass, crude, gross, rough **6** coarse, incult, vulgar **7** artless, boorish, ill-bred, loutish, lowbred, uncouth **8** churlish, cloddish **9** unrefined **10** unpolished **11** clodhopping, uncivilized

uncurbed 9 audacious **10** ungoverned, unhampered **11** uninhibited, untrammeled **12** uncontrolled, unrestrained

uncustomary 4 rare **6** unique **7** unusual **8** singular, uncommon, unwonted **10** unordinary **11** exceptional, unthinkable **13** extraordinary

uncut 5 whole **6** entire **8** complete, undocked **10** full-length, unabridged **11** uncondensed, whole-length **13** unabbreviated

undamaged 5 sound, whole **6** intact, unhurt **8** flawless, unbroken, unmarred **9** uninjured **10** unimpaired **11** unblemished

undaring 5 timid **8** timorous

undarkened 4 fair, fine **5** clear, sunny

7 clarion 8 pleasant, rainless, sunshiny
9 cloudless, unclouded

undaunted 4 bold 5 brave 7 Spartan, valiant 8 fearless, intrepid, valorous 9 audacious, confident 10 courageous
11 unconquered

undeceive 5 purge 8 disabuse, undelude 11 disillusion

undecided 4 moot, open 6 unsure
7 dubious, pendent, pending, unclear
8 doubtful, wavering 9 equivocal, uncertain, unsettled 10 borderline, indecisive
12 undetermined

undecipherable 9 illegible 10 unreadable

undecisive see **indecisive**

undeclared 5 tacit 6 secret, unsaid
7 implied 8 implicit, inferred, unspoken, wordless 9 unuttered 10 understood
11 unexpressed

undecorated 5 plain 6 homely, simple
9 unadorned 11 inelaborate, ungarnished
12 unbeautified, unornamented 13 unembellished, unembroidered

undefiled 4 pure 5 clean 6 chaste, decent, intact, modest, virgin 8 innocent, spotless, virtuous 9 stainless, unsullied
10 immaculate 11 unblemished

undefined 3 dim 5 faint, vague 6 bleary
7 obscure, shadowy, unclear 10 indistinct
12 undetermined

undemonstrated 7 untried 8 unproved, untested 11 unpracticed

undemonstrative 3 icy 4 calm, cold, cool 5 aloof, chill 6 frigid 7 aseptic, distant, glacial, laconic 8 reserved, retiring 9 shrinking, unaffable, withdrawn 10 restrained, unsociable 11 emotionless, indifferent, standoffish, unemotional, unexpansive
12 uninterested

undeniable 4 real, true 6 actual 7 certain 8 positive, unfabled 9 veridical
10 inarguable 11 indubitable, unequivocal
12 indisputable, undisputable 13 incontestable, uncontestable

undependable 5 trick 6 casual, tricky, unsafe, unsure 7 dubious, erratic
8 untrusty 9 trustless, unassured 10 fly-by-night, unreliable 12 questionable 13 irresponsible, untrustworthy

under 3 low, sub 5 below, lower, neath
6 lesser, nether 7 beneath, subject 8 inferior 9 dependent, secondary, subjacent, tributary 10 collateral, underneath 11 subordinate *prefix:* 3 hyp, sub 4 hypo

underage 4 lack 7 deficit, failure 8 shortage 10 deficiency, inadequacy, scantiness
11 defalcation 13 insufficience, insufficiency

undercarriage 5 frame 6 struts 8 supports 9 framework 11 landing gear

undercover 6 covert, secret 7 furtive, sub rosa 8 hush-hush 11 clandestine 12 hug-

ger-mugger 13 hole-and-corner, surreptitious, under-the-table *person:* 3 spy
4 mole 5 agent, spook 9 detective
10 counterspy 12 counteragent

undercroft 5 crypt, vault 7 chamber
8 catacomb

underdeveloped 7 dwarfed, stunted
8 backward 10 behindhand
13 unprogressive

underdog 4 prey 5 loser 6 victim 8 casualty 9 dark horse

underdone 4 rare

underestimate 8 disprize, minimize
9 underrate 10 undervalue

undergarment 3 bra 4 slip 5 teddy
6 bodice, briefs, cilise, corset, girdle, shorts, skivvy, undies 7 chemise, dessous, drawers, panties, step-ins 8 flimsies, knickers, lingerie, pretties, skivvies 9 brassiere, petticoat, underwear 10 foundation

undergo 3 bow, see 4 bear, have, know, pass 5 abide, carry, defer, serve, yield
6 endure, submit, suffer 7 sustain 8 tolerate 10 experience

undergoer *suffix:* 2 ee

undergraduate 4 coed 6 junior, senior
7 student 8 freshman 9 sophomore

underground 5 train 6 hidden, secret, subway 7 beneath, illegal, off-beat 8 hypogeal, hypogean 9 underfoot 10 undercover, underearth 11 disapproved 12 subterranean 13 surreptitious
14 counterculture

underhand 3 sly 4 mean, wily 5 shady
6 crafty, secret, shifty, sneaky, tricky, unfair 7 crooked, cunning, devious, furtive, hangdog, oblique, stealth 8 guileful, indirect, sinister, sneaking 9 deceitful, dishonest, insidious 10 circuitous, fraudulent
11 duplicitous

underhanded 3 sly 4 mean 5 shady
6 secret, shifty, sneaky, unfair 7 devious
8 guileful, indirect, sneaking, unfairly
9 deceitful 10 circuitous, fraudulent
11 clandestine, duplicitous, shorthanded, undermanned 12 understaffed

underived 5 prime 7 primary 8 original
9 primitive

underlease 6 sublet 8 sublease, underlet

underlet 6 sublet 8 sublease
10 underlease

underlie 4 bear 7 subtend, support

underline 4 mark 6 legend, play up, stress 7 caption, feature 9 emphasize, italicize 10 underscore

underling 5 scrub 6 menial, minion 8 inferior 9 secondary, subaltern 11 subordinate 12 poor relation

underlying 5 basal, basic, vital 6 bottom, covert 7 crucial, needful, obscure, primary, radical 8 cardinal, critical, implicit 9 elemental, essential, necessary, primitive **10** elementary, substratal **11** fundamental **12** foundational **13** indispensable

Under Milk Wood author 6 Thomas

undermine 3 sap **4** cave, foil, ruin **5** blunt, drain, erode, wreck **6** impair, thwart, weaken **7** cripple, disable, founder, subvert, unbrace **8** enfeeble, sabotage, supplant **9** attenuate, frustrate **10** debilitate, demoralize **12** unstrengthen

undermost 6 bottom, lowest **9** lowermost **10** bottommost, nethermost, rock-bottom

underneath 4 sole **5** below **6** bottom, secret **9** underside **10** undercover **12** undersurface **13** surreptitious *prefix:* **5** intra

underpin 4 base, prop, root, seat, stay **5** brace, shore **7** justify, support **8** buttress, maintain **12** substantiate

underpinning 4 base, prop, root, seat, stay **5** basis, brace, shore **6** column, ground **7** bedrock, footing, seating, support **8** buttress **10** foundation, groundwork, substratum **12** substruction, substructure **13** underpropping

underpowered 4 slow, weak **6** anemic **8** sluggish

underprivileged 4 poor **5** needy **7** hapless, unlucky **8** deprived, ill-fated **9** depressed **10** ill-starred **11** handicapped, unfortunate **12** impoverished **13** disadvantaged

underprize 5 decry, lower **7** devalue **9** devaluate, write down **10** depreciate, devalorize, undervalue

underprop 4 stay **5** brace, shore **6** buoy up, uphold **7** bolster, support, sustain **8** buttress

underpropping 4 prop, stay **5** brace, shore **6** column **7** support **8** buttress

underrate 5 decry, lower **7** devalue **8** discount, mark down, write off **9** devaluate, write down **10** depreciate, devalorize, undervalue **13** underestimate

underscore 6 play up, stress **7** feature **9** emphasize, italicize, underline

undersexed 4 cold **6** frigid **9** inhibited **11** passionless **12** unresponsive

underside 4 sole **6** bottom **10** underneath **12** undersurface *combining form:* **6** infero

undersized 4 puny **5** dwarf, runty, scrub, small **6** little **7** scrubby, stunted

understand 3 con, dig, get, ken, see **4** have, know, sabe, take, twig **5** catch, fancy, grasp, guess, infer, savvy, seize, sense, think **6** accept, assume, deduce, expect, fathom, figure, follow, gather, reason, take in **7** believe, cognize, discern, imagine, presume, realize, suppose, surmise, suspect **8** conceive, conclude, consider, perceive **9** apprehend, interpret, penetrate **10** appreciate, comprehend, conjecture

understandable 3 lay **5** clear, lucid, plain **6** simple **7** popular **8** clear-cut, exoteric, knowable, luminous **9** graspable, unblurred **10** fathomable **11** unambiguous **12** intelligible **13** apprehensible

understanding 3 ken, wit **4** deal, idea **5** grasp, sense **6** accord, humane, import, kindly, notion, reason, treaty **7** compact, concept, empathy, entente, insight, knowing, meaning, message, purport **8** attitude, contract, daylight, judgment, sympathy **9** agreement, awareness, diagnosis, intellect, intuition, knowledge, tolerance **10** acceptance, intendment **11** acceptation, discernment, intelligent, penetration, sympathetic **12** apprehension, intelligence, significance, significancy **13** comprehension, signification

understatement 7 litotes

understood 5 clear, lucid, tacit **6** unsaid **7** implied **8** implicit, inferred, unspoken, wordless **9** unuttered **10** undeclared **11** unexpressed

understudy 6 double **7** stand-in **10** substitute **11** replacement

undertake 2 do, go **3** try **4** dare, pass, seek **5** assay, begin, essay, offer, start **6** accept, assume, engage, incept, pledge, strive, take on, take up **7** attempt, certify, emprise, execute, perform, promise, warrant **8** commence, contract, covenant, endeavor, struggle

undertaker 8 embalmer **9** mortician **12** entrepreneur

undertaking 3 job, try **4** task **5** essay, trial **6** cautio, charge, effort, hassle, scheme, voyage **7** attempt, calling, emprise, emprize, project, venture **8** covenant, endeavor, striving, struggle **9** adventure **10** enterprise **11** proposition

under-the-table 6 covert, secret **7** furtive, sub-rosa **8** stealthy **10** undercover **11** clandestine **13** surreptitious

undertone 4 hint **5** aside, rumor **6** mumble, murmur, mutter **7** inkling, subtone, whisper **8** overtone **10** suggestion **11** association, connotation, implication, susurration

undertow 4 eddy **6** vortex **7** current, riptide, sea puss **8** seapoose, sea purse

undervalue see **underrate**

underwater 9 submarine **10** subaquatic, subaqueous *breathing apparatus:* **5** scuba *captain:* **4** Nemo *chamber:* **7** caisson *device:* **8** paravane *missile:* **7** torpedo *sound detector:* **5** sonar

underwear see **undergarment**

underwood 5 frith 7 boscage, coppice
10 underbrush 11 undergrowth

underworld 4 hell 5 abyss, hades, Orcus,
Sheol 6 Erebus, Tophet 7 Gehenna,
inferno, xibalba 8 gangland 9 barathrum
11 netherworld, Pandemonium *boatman:*
6 Charon *deity:* 3 Dis 4 Bran 5 Pluto
6 Osiris 8 Dispater *goddess:* 6 Hecate
10 Persephone *organization:* 5 Mafia *relating to:* 8 chthonic *watchdog:* 8 Cerberus

underwrite 4 back, sign 6 assure, insure,
pay for 7 endorse, finance, sponsor, support 9 subscribe

undesigning 4 real, true 6 honest, simple 7 artless, genuine, sincere
9 unfeigned 10 heart-whole
12 undissembled

undesirable 8 unwanted 9 unwelcome
10 ill-favored 12 inadmissible, unacceptable 13 exceptionable, objectionable

undesired 8 unsought, unwanted,
unwished 9 unwelcome 10 quenchless

undestroyable see **indestructible**

undetermined 3 dim 5 faint, unset,
vague 6 bleary 7 dubious, obscure, pendent, pending, shadowy, unclear 8 aoristic,
doubtful 9 equivocal, undecided, undefined,
unsettled 10 ill-defined, indistinct

undeveloped 5 crude 6 latent 7 archaic
8 backward, immature, juvenile 9 primitive,
unevolved 10 behindhand, persistent
13 unprogressive

undiluted 4 mere, neat, pure 5 plain,
sheer 6 simple 7 perfect, unmixed 8 absolute, straight 9 unalloyed 11 unmitigated,
unqualified 13 unadulterated

undiplomatic 5 brash 8 tactless 9 impolitic, maladroit, unpolitic, untactful

undisciplined 4 wild 6 unruly, wanton
8 untoward 9 fractious, untrained
11 intractable 12 recalcitrant, ungovernable, unmanageable

undisclosed 6 hidden, sealed, secret
8 ulterior 12 confidential

undisguised 4 bald, open 5 frank, overt,
plain 6 candid 9 barefaced 11 openhearted, unconcealed, unvarnished
12 undissembled 13 undissembling

undissembled 4 open, real, true 5 frank,
plain 6 candid, honest 7 genuine, sincere
9 unfeigned 10 heart-whole 11 openhearted, unconcealed, undesigning, undisguised, unvarnished

undistinguished 5 gross 6 common
8 mediocre, noteless 9 unnotable
12 unnoteworthy

undistorted 4 just, true 5 clear, right
6 strict 8 faithful 9 veracious, veridical

undivided 3 one 5 fixed, total, whole
6 entire, intact 8 complete, unbroken

10 continuous, unswerving 12 concentrated, undistracted

undo 3 ope 4 have, open, raze, ruin
5 abate, annul, loose, quash, unfix, untie,
wrack, wreck 6 defeat, diddle, negate, outfox, outwit, seduce, unbind, unmake,
unshut, unsnap, unstop 7 abolish, debauch,
destroy, nullify, unblock, unbuild, unclose,
unframe, unloose, unravel, vitiate 8 abrogate, decimate, demolish, outreach, outslick,
outsmart, unfasten, unloosen 9 disengage,
outjockey, overreach 10 annihilate, invalidate, outgeneral 11 outmaneuver

undoing 4 bane, ruin 8 downfall
9 destroyer, overthrow, ruination
11 destruction

undoubtedly 4 well 5 truly 6 easily,
indeed, really, surely 7 frankly 11 doubtlessly, indubitably

undoubtful 6 secure 7 assured 8 sanguine 9 confident 11 self-assured 13 self-confident

undress see **unclothe**

undressed 3 raw 4 nude, rude 5 crude,
naked, rough 6 unclad, unhewn 8 buffbare, stripped, unformed, unworked 9 au
naturel, roughhewn, unclothed 10 starknaked, unfinished, unpolished
11 unfashioned

undue 5 dizzy, inapt, inept, unapt
7 extreme 8 ill-timed, improper, towering,
untimely 9 excessive, unfitting 10 exorbitant, immoderate, inordinate, unsuitable
11 extravagant, unwarranted 12 unreasonable, unseasonable 13 inappropriate, unjustifiable, unwarrantable

undulant fever 11 brucellosis

undulate 4 roll, swag, sway, wave
5 snake, swing 6 ripple 7 slidder, slither
9 fluctuate

unduly 3 too 4 ever, over 6 overly 8 overfull, overmuch 9 extremely, immensely
11 excessively 12 inordinately

undutiful 7 impious

undying 7 ageless, endless, eternal
8 immortal, unending 9 continual, deathless, unceasing 10 continuing, persistent
12 imperishable, interminable, unquenchable

uneager 3 shy 5 loath 6 afraid, averse
8 backward, hesitant 9 reluctant, unwilling
10 indisposed 11 disinclined

unearth 3 dig, see 4 hear, show 5 delve,
learn 6 exhume, expose, reveal, tumble
7 catch on, exhibit, find out, uncover 8 disclose, discover 9 ascertain, determine

unearthly 4 eery 5 balmy, crazy, eerie,
loony, silly, wacky, weird 6 absurd, insane,
spooky 7 awesome, foolish, uncanny,
ungodly 8 numinous, superior, terrific
9 appalling, fantastic 10 miraculous, mysterious, outlandish, superhuman, suprahu-

man **12** preposterous, supermundane, supernatural, supranatural **13** preternatural

unease 4 care **5** worry **6** unrest **7** anxiety, concern, tension, trouble **8** disquiet **9** abashment, confusion **10** discomfort, discontent, solicitude **11** concernment, displeasure, disquietude, uptightness **12** apprehension, discomfiture, discomposure **13** disconcertion, embarrassment

uneasiness see **unease**

uneasy 4 edgy **5** nervy, shaky, tense **6** unsure **7** anxious, awkward, careful, fidgety, restive, suspect, unquiet, uptight, worried **8** agitated, doubtful, restless **9** ambiguous, concerned, difficult, disturbed, doubtable, perturbed, uncertain, unrestful, unsettled **10** borderline, disquieted, precarious, solicitous, unpeaceful, untranquil **13** uncomfortable

uneducated 4 rude **6** simple **8** ignorant, untaught **9** benighted, untutored **10** illiterate, unlettered, unschooled **11** emptyheaded, know-nothing **12** uninstructed

unembellished 3 dry **5** plain **6** simple **7** austere, prosaic **9** unadorned **11** undecorated, unelaborate, ungarnished **12** unbeautified, unornamented **13** unembroidered, unpretentious

unembroidered see **unembellished**

unemotional 3 dry, icy **4** cold, cool **5** chill, stoic, stony **6** frigid **7** callous, glacial, stoical **8** obdurate **9** heartless, impassive, unfeeling **10** hard-boiled, phlegmatic **11** coldhearted, hardhearted, indifferent **12** stonyhearted **13** dispassionate, unsympathetic

unemployed 4 free, idle **5** fired **6** otiose, unused **7** jobless, laid off **8** inactive, workless **9** unengaged **10** unoccupied

unending 7 eternal, undying **8** constant, immortal, timeless **9** ceaseless, continual, perpetual **10** continuous **11** amaranthine, everlasting, unremitting **12** interminable **13** uninterrupted

unenlightened 7 heathen **8** backward, ignorant **9** benighted **13** unprogressive

unenthusiastic 4 cold, cool **8** lukewarm **9** apathetic, unexcited **10** spiritless **11** perfunctory **12** uninterested

unequal 5 impar **6** uneven, unfair, unjust, unlike **7** distant, diverse, unalike, various **8** inferior, lopsided, variable **9** different, disparate, divergent, irregular, unsimilar **10** asymmetric, dissimilar, off-balance **11** fluctuating **12** overbalanced **13** unsymmetrical *combining form:* **4** anis **5** aniso

unequalable 7 supreme **8** towering, ultimate **10** preeminent, surpassing **11** unmatchable **12** incomparable, transcendant **13** unsurpassable

unequaled 4 only **5** alone **6** unique

7 supreme **8** nonesuch, peerless **9** matchless, unmatched, unrivaled **10** surpassing **11** unparagoned **12** unparalleled **13** unprecedented

unequipped 5 unfit **8** unfitted **9** incapable **10** ineligible, unprepared **11** incompetent, unqualified **12** disqualified

unequivocal 5 clear, plain **6** direct, patent **7** certain, decided, evident, obvious **8** apparent, definite, distinct, explicit, manifest, palpable, positive **10** undeniable **11** categorical, indubitable **12** indisputable, undisputable **13** incontestable, uncontestable

unerasable see **inerasable**

unerring 4 dead, sure, true **5** exact **7** certain, correct, precise **8** accurate, reliable **9** unfailing **10** dependable, infallible **11** trustworthy

unescapable see **inevitable**

unessential 8 needless, unneeded **9** extrinsic, unneedful **10** unrequired **11** dispensable, uncalled-for, unimportant, unnecessary **13** insubstantial

unethical 5 venal, wrong **6** amoral **7** corrupt, immoral **9** mercenary **10** praetorian **12** unprincipled, unscrupulous

unevadable see **inevitable**

uneven 3 odd **4** wavy **5** bumpy, erose, harsh, jaggy, rough **6** craggy, jagged, patchy, rugged, spotty, unfair, unjust, unlike **7** scraggy, streaky, unequal, unlevel, varying **8** asperous, lopsided, scabrous, scraggly, scratchy, unsmooth **9** anomalous, differing, disparate, irregular **10** asymmetric, discrepant, ill-matched, off-balance, unbalanced **11** fluctuating **12** inconsistent, overbalanced **13** unsymmetrical

unevenness 4 bump, wave **7** anomaly **8** asperity, imparity **9** disparity, roughness **10** inequality **12** irregularity **13** disproportion

uneventful 6 common **7** prosaic **8** ordinary **11** commonplace **12** unnoteworthy **13** unexceptional

unexampled 4 lone, only, sole, solo **5** alone **6** unique **8** singular, solitary **12** unrepeatable

unexceptional 5 usual **6** common, decent **7** prosaic, regular **8** adequate, all right, ordinary **9** tolerable **10** acceptable, sufficient, uneventful **11** commonplace **12** satisfactory, unnoteworthy **13** unimpeachable

unexcited 4 calm **5** level, stoic **7** stoical **8** tranquil

unexciting 4 dead, dull, tame **6** boring **7** prosaic **13** uninteresting

unexpectedly 5 aback, short **6** sudden **7** unaware **8** abruptly, suddenly, unawares **10** unawaredly **12** accidentally

unexpended 6 saving 7 reserve, surplus
8 left over 9 remaining
unexperienced see **inexperienced**
unexpired 5 alive, valid 8 left over
9 operative, remaining
unexplicit 4 hazy 5 vague 7 obscure,
unclear 8 nebulous, nubilous 9 ambiguous,
equivocal, tenebrous, uncertain
10 indistinct
unexpressed 5 tacit 6 silent, unsaid
7 implied 8 implicit, inferred, unspoken,
wordless 9 unuttered, voiceless 10 undeclared, understood
unfadable 4 fast 7 sunfast 9 colorfast
unfaded 5 fresh 6 bright
unfailing 4 same, sure 6 deadly 7 certain 8 constant, reliable, surefire, unerring
9 unvarying 10 consistent, infallible, invariable, unchanging, unflagging
13 inexhaustible
unfair 4 foul, hard 5 wrong 6 biased,
shabby, uneven, unjust 7 devious, unequal
8 wrongful 9 dishonest, inequable, unethical 11 inequitable, underhanded, unequitable, unrighteous 12 dishonorable
unfairness 5 wrong 8 inequity 9 injustice 10 unjustness
unfaithful 5 false 6 untrue 7 infidel, traitor, unloyal 8 disloyal, recreant, turncoat
9 faithless 10 adulterous, inaccurate, perfidious, traitorous 11 treacherous
13 untrustworthy
unfaltering 4 firm, sure, true 5 brave
6 steady 7 abiding 8 enduring, unerring
9 steadfast 11 unqualified 12 never-failing,
wholehearted 13 unquestioning
unfamiliar 3 new 6 exotic 7 curious, foreign, strange, unaware, unknown 8 ignorant, peculiar 9 oblivious, unknowing, unwitting 10 remarkable, uninformed 11 incognizant 12 inconversant, unaccustomed,
unacquainted, uninstructed
unfamiliarity 9 ignorance, innocence,
inscience, nescience 11 unawareness
13 unknowingness
unfashionable 5 dated, passé
6 démodé 8 outmoded 9 out-of-date
unfasten 4 free, open, undo 5 loose,
unbar, unfix, unpin, untie 6 detach, loosen,
unbind, unlace, unlock, unsnap 7 unhitch,
unloose 8 unanchor, unloosen, untether
9 disengage
unfathomable 7 abysmal 8 profound
9 plumbless, soundless 10 bottomless,
fathomless, mysterious, unknowable
11 inscrutable, ungraspable 12 impenetrable, incognizable
unfavorable 3 bad, ill 4 evil, foul, poor
6 averse, unfair, unkind 7 adverse, awkward, froward, hostile, unhappy 8 backward, contrary, inimical, negative, sinister,
unkindly 11 detrimental *prefix:* 3 dys
unfavorably 4 awry 5 amiss, badly,
wrong 6 afield, astray
unfearful 4 bold 5 brave 7 valiant 8 fearless, intrepid, valorous 9 audacious, dauntless, undaunted 10 courageous
unfeasible 10 impossible, infeasible,
unworkable 11 impractical 12 irrealizable,
unattainable, unrealizable 13 impracticable
unfeeling 4 cold, dead, dull, hard, numb
5 crass, cruel, harsh, stern, stony, surly,
tough 6 asleep, brutal, leaden, marble,
numbed, severe, stolid, unkind 7 callous
8 benumbed, churlish, deadened, exacting,
hardened, obdurate, pitiless, ruthless
9 apathetic, bloodless, crotchety, heartless,
inanimate, indurated, insensate, merciless,
senseless, unamiable, uncordial 10 hard-
boiled, insensible, insentient 11 cold-
blooded, coldhearted, hardhearted, insensitive, ironhearted, unemotional 12 anesthetized, cantankerous, curmudgeonly, rough-
hearted, stonyhearted 13 marblehearted,
unsusceptible, unsympathetic
unfeigned 4 open, real, true 6 hearty,
honest 7 genuine, natural, sincere 9 heartfelt 11 undesigning 12 undissembled,
wholehearted
unfertile see **infertile**
unfinished 3 raw 4 rude 5 crude, rough
6 unhewn 7 jackleg, sketchy 8 dabbling,
unformed, ungifted, unworked 9 imperfect,
roughhewn, undressed, unskilled 10 amateurish, dilettante, incomplete, unpolished
11 unfashioned 12 dilettantish, dilettantist
Unfinished Symphony composer
8 Schubert
unfit 3 bad 4 sick 5 inapt, inept, wrong
6 faulty, unmeet 7 awkward, unhandy
8 bungling, disabled, improper, inexpert,
unsuited 9 ill-suited, incapable, maladroit
10 blundering, discordant, ill-adapted, ineligible, unbecoming, unequipped, unskillful,
unsuitable 11 handicapped, heavyhanded,
incompetent, incongruous, inefficient,
maladjusted, uncongenial, unqualified
12 disqualified, incompatible, infelicitous,
inharmonious, unproficient 13 inappropriate,
incapacitated *Jewish law:* 4 tref 6 trefah
7 terefah
unfitting 5 inapt, inept, unapt 8 improper,
unseemly 10 malapropos, unbecoming,
unsuitable 13 inappropriate
unfix 4 undo 5 loose 6 detach, loosen,
unbind 7 unloose 8 abstract, dissolve,
uncouple, unfasten, unloosen, unsettle
9 disengage 10 disconnect, dissociate
12 disassociate
unflagging 6 steady 8 constant, tireless,
untiring 9 weariless 10 unwearying

11 unweariable **13** indefatigable, inexhaustible

unflappable 4 cool, easy **7** relaxed **8** composed **9** collected, unruffled **10** nonchalant **13** imperturbable

unflawed 7 perfect **8** absolute, flawless **9** fleckless **10** impeccable **11** note-perfect **12** indefectible

unfledged 5 green, young **6** callow, infant, unripe **8** immature, juvenile, youthful **11** undeveloped, unfeathered

unflexible see **inflexible**

unflinching 4 firm, grim **5** level **6** mortal **7** staunch **8** resolute, ruthless **9** merciless, steadfast **10** implacable, ironfisted, relentless, unwavering, unyielding **11** unrelenting **12** unappeasable

unfluctuating 4 even **6** stable, steady **7** equable, stabile, uniform **8** constant **9** unvarying **10** unchanging

unfold 4 open, show **5** break, burst, solve **6** deploy, evince, evolve, expand, expose, extend, fan out, flower, reveal, spread, unfurl, unroll, untuck, unwrap **7** blossom, clear up, develop, display, divulge, dope out, exhibit, explain, release, resolve, unravel **8** decipher, disclose, dissolve, evidence, manifest, unriddle **9** elaborate, explicate, figure out, outspread, puzzle out **10** outstretch **11** demonstrate

unforbearing 9 impatient **10** intolerant **11** unindulgent

unforced 4 easy **7** natural, willful, willing, witting **9** voluntary **10** deliberate **11** intentional **12** unprescribed

unforeseen 6 sudden **10** accidental, unexpected

unforgivable 9 untenable **10** inexpiable **11** inexcusable **12** indefensible, unpardonable **13** unjustifiable

unformed 4 rude **5** crude, rough **6** callow, unhewn **8** formless, inchoate, unshaped, unworked **9** amorphous, roughhewn, shapeless, uncreated, undressed **10** unfinished, unpolished **11** undeveloped, unfashioned

unfortunate 3 bad, ill, sad **4** dire, poor **5** inept **6** woeful, wretch **7** awkward, hapless, malefic, unhappy, unlucky **8** grievous, ill-fated, luckless, untoward, wretched **9** graceless, ill-chosen, miserable **10** afflictive, calamitous, deplorable, ill-starred, lamentable **11** distressing, regrettable, starcrossed **12** inauspicious, infelicitous, misfortunate, unsuccessful **13** heartbreaking

unfounded 4 idle, vain **8** baseless **9** deceptive, dishonest **10** bottomless, chimerical, gratuitous, groundless, mendacious, misleading, ungrounded, untruthful **11** uncalled-for, unwarranted

unfrequented 5 empty **6** lonely **8** isolated, solitary

unfriendly 3 ill **4** cold, cool, foul **5** chill **6** bitter, chilly, fierce, frosty, remote **7** hostile **8** inimical, unsocial **10** inimicable

unfruitful 6 barren, effete, wasted **7** sterile, useless **8** impotent, infecund **9** infertile **12** unproductive, unprofitable

unfurl 4 open **6** spread, unfold, unroll, unwind **7** develop

unfurnished 4 bare **6** vacant

unfussy 6 casual, common, dégagé **7** relaxed **8** informal **9** easygoing **10** unreserved **11** low-pressure **13** unconstrained

ungainly 5 gawky, lanky, splay **6** clumsy **7** awkward, boorish, lumpish, uncouth **8** clownish, lubberly, unlicked, unwieldy **9** lumbering, maladroit **10** blundering **11** elephantine, splathering

ungarnished 3 dry **5** plain **6** modest, simple **9** unadorned **11** inelaborate, unelaborate **12** unornamented **13** unembellished, unembroidered

ungenerous 4 mean, puny **5** close, harsh, nasty, petty, small, tight **6** paltry, peanut, shabby, stingy **7** miserly **8** grudging, picayune, trifling, ungiving **9** niggardly, penurious **12** inconsequent, parsimonious **13** pennypinching

ungenuine 7 bastard **8** spurious **10** apocryphal **11** unauthentic

ungiving 4 mean **5** close, tight **6** stingy **7** miserly, save-all **9** niggardly, penurious **11** tightfisted **12** parsimonious

ungodly see **unholy**

ungovernable 4 wild **6** unruly **7** froward **8** untoward **9** fractious, unbridled **10** disorderly, headstrong, rebellious **11** intractable **12** recalcitrant, unmanageable **13** irrepressible, undisciplined

ungoverned 8 uncurbed **9** audacious **10** unhampered **11** uninhibited, untrammeled **12** unrestrained

ungraceful 5 lanky **6** clumsy **7** angular, awkward, halting **8** untoward **9** inelegant

ungracious 4 hard, rude **5** gruff, sharp, short **7** uncivil **8** churlish, impolite, snappish **9** offensive **10** unmannerly, unpleasant **11** disgracious, ill-mannered, impertinent, thoughtless, uncalled-for, uncourteous **12** discourteous, unattractive **13** disrespectful, inconsiderate, unceremonious

ungraded 3 raw **5** crude **6** impure, native **8** unsorted **9** run-of-mine, unrefined

ungraspable 10 unknowable **12** impenetrable, incognizable, unfathomable

ungrateful 4 foul **7** hideous **8** horrible **9** loathsome, offensive, repellent, repugnant, repulsive, revolting, thankless **10** disgusting, unthankful **13** unappreciated

ungratified 9 uncontent 10 discontent, malcontent 11 disgruntled, uncontented, unsatisfied 12 discontented, dissatisfied, malcontented

ungrounded 8 baseless 9 unfounded 10 bottomless, gratuitous, groundless, uninformed 11 uncalled-for, unwarranted 12 uninstructed

unguarded 6 unwary 7 unalert 8 careless 9 imprudent 10 incautious, unvigilant, unwatchful 11 defenseless, thoughtless, unprotected

unguent 4 balm 5 cream, salve 6 cerate, ceroma, chrism 7 unction 8 ointment 9 lubricant

ungulate 3 hog, pig 4 deer 5 horse, tapir 6 hoofed 8 amblypod, elephant 10 rhinoceros

unhallowed 6 impure, unholy 7 demonic, impious, profane, satanic, ungodly 8 demoniac, demonian, devilish, diabolic, fiendish 10 desecrated, irreverent, serpentine 11 diabolonian 13 irreverential

unhampered 4 free 5 loose 6 direct 8 uncurbed 9 audacious, expedited 10 ungoverned 11 expeditious, uninhibited, untrammeled 12 unrestrained

unhandsome 4 mean, rude 5 plain 6 homely 7 ill-bred, uncivil 8 impolite, uncomely, unpretty 10 unalluring, unbecoming, ungracious 11 disgracious, ill-mannered, impertinent, unbeauteous, unbeautiful 12 discourteous, unattractive 13 disrespectful

unhandy 5 inapt, inept, unapt 6 clumsy, gauche, wooden 7 awkward, halting, inadept, unhappy 8 bumbling, cumbrous, inexpert, unfacile, unwieldy 9 ham-handed, maladroit, ponderous 10 cumbersome, unskillful 11 undexterous 12 inconvenient, unproficient

unhappiness 3 woe 5 blues, dolor, dumps, gloom, grief, worry 6 misery, mishap, sorrow, unrest 7 dismals, ill-luck, sadness 9 dejection 10 depression, melancholy 12 mournfulness, wretchedness

unhappy 3 bad, sad 4 evil, sour 5 black, bleak, inept, sorry 6 clumsy, dismal, dreary, gauche, gloomy, rotten, wooden 7 awkward, halting, joyless, unhandy, unlucky 8 bumbling, chiselly, dejected, ill-fated, luckless, mournful, saddened, untoward, wretched 9 cheerless, graceless, ill-chosen, maladroit, woebegone 10 depressant, ill-starred, melancholy, oppressive, unpleasant 11 dispiriting, displeasing, heavy-handed, melancholic, star-crossed, unfortunate 12 disagreeable, heavyhearted, inauspicious, infelicitous, misfortunate

unharmed 4 safe 6 unhurt 9 unscathed 10 scatheless

unharness 6 disarm, divest, ungear 7 outspan, unhitch, unhorse, unstrap 8 untackle

unhealthiness 7 disease, illness, malaise 8 debility, disorder, sickness 9 infirmity 10 affliction, feebleness, infirmness, sickliness 11 decrepitude 12 diseasedness 13 indisposition

unhealthy 3 bad, ill 4 sick 5 hairy, risky 6 chancy, infirm, putrid, queasy, rotten, sickly, unhale, wicked 7 corrupt, noisome, noxious, unsound, vicious 8 depraved, diseased, perilous, perverse 9 dangerous, hazardous, nefarious 10 degenerate, flagitious, insalutary, jeopardous, unsalutary, villainous 11 treacherous, unwholesome 12 insalubrious

unheard-of 3 new 7 obscure, strange, unfamed, unknown, unnoted 8 nameless 10 unrenowned 12 uncelebrated 13 extraordinary, unprecedented

unheeding 4 deaf 8 careless, feckless, heedless, ignoring, uncaring 9 unrecking 10 unnoticing, unthinking, unwatchful 11 inadvertent, inattentive, inobservant, insensitive, thoughtless, unobservant, unobserving 12 disregarding, irreflective, unperceiving, unreflective

unhesitating 4 free 5 ready 8 haltless 9 immediate 10 forthright 12 wholehearted

unhinge 4 turn 5 craze, upset 6 bother, flurry, frenzy, madden, sicken, untune 7 agitate, derange, disturb, fluster, perturb 8 disorder, disquiet, distract, unsettle 9 unbalance 10 discompose

unholy 5 amiss, rough 6 guilty, impure, sinful, wicked 7 corrupt, impious, profane, raucous, ungodly 8 blamable, blameful, culpable, dreadful, fiendish, god-awful, improper, indecent, shocking, unseemly, untoward 9 atheistic, atrocious, barbarous, frightful, malicious, unearthly 10 censurable, indecorous, indelicate, irreverent, malodorous, outrageous, scandalous, unbecoming, undecorous, unhallowed 11 blameworthy, unbelieving, unchristian, uncivilized 13 demeritorious, irreverential, reprehensible

unhorse 5 pitch, throw 6 topple, tumble, unseat 7 buck off, overset 8 dislodge, dismount, overturn, unsaddle 9 overthrow

unhurried 4 easy, slow 7 laggard, unhasty 8 dilatory 9 leisurely 10 deliberate

unhurt 4 safe 5 sound, whole 6 entire, intact 7 perfect 8 unbroken, unharmed, unmarred 9 undamaged, uninjured 10 unimpaired

unicity 7 oneness 8 uniquity 10 singleness, uniqueness

unicorn *antelope:* 5 takin *Chinese:* 5 kilin, kylin 6 chi-lin *fish:* 7 narwhal

unidealistic 4 hard 5 sober 9 practical,

pragmatic, realistic **10** hard-boiled, hard-headed **11** down-to-earth, unfantastic **12** matter-of-fact

unification 5 union **6** hookup, merger **7** joining, linkage, melding, merging **8** alliance, coupling, mergence **9** coalition **10** connection **11** affiliation, coadunation, combination **12** interlocking **13** consolidation

uniform 4 akin, even, like, suit **5** alike, blues, dress, equal, khaki, level **6** agnate, livery, outfit, stable, steady, whites **7** equable, ordered, orderly, regular, similar, stabile **8** constant, parallel **9** analogous, consonant, unvarying **10** comparable, compatible, consistent, invariable, monotonous, unchanging **11** homogeneous **13** corresponding, unfluctuating *combining form:* **2** is **3** iso

uniformity 7 oneness **8** equality, evenness, monotony, sameness

uniformly 6 always, evenly, flatly, smooth **8** smoothly

unify 3 tie **4** bind **5** blend, merge, order, unite **6** cement **7** arrange, compact **8** coalesce, organize **9** harmonize, integrate **10** articulate, centralize, symphonize, synthesize **11** concatenate, concentrate, consolidate, orchestrate, systematize

unilluminated 3 dim **4** dark, dusk **5** dusky, murky **6** gloomy **7** obscure **9** lightless, tenebrous **10** caliginous

unimaginable 4 rare **6** unique **7** unusual **8** singular, uncommon, unwonted **10** incredible, unknowable, unordinary **11** exceptional, incogitable, unthinkable **12** insupposable, unbelievable **13** extraordinary, inconceivable

unimaginative 4 dull **7** limited, literal, prosaic **10** pedestrian

unimpaired 4 free **5** fresh, sound, whole **6** entire, intact, unhurt **7** perfect **8** unbroken, unmarred **9** undamaged, uninjured

unimpassioned 4 calm, cold **5** sober, stoic **6** placid, steady, stolid **8** moderate, tranquil **9** impassive, temperate **10** impersonal, phlegmatic **11** cold-blooded, emotionless **12** matter-of-fact

unimpeachable 6 common, decent **8** adequate, all right **9** blameless, faultless, tolerable **10** acceptable, sufficient **12** satisfactory **13** unexceptional

unimportant 5 light, minor, petty, small **6** casual, little, paltry **7** trivial **9** small-beer **10** negligible, shoestring **13** insignificant

unindifferent 6 biased **7** colored, partial **8** one-sided, partisan **9** jaundiced, unneutral **10** prejudiced **11** tendentious **12** prepossessed

uninformed 7 unaware **8** ignorant **9** oblivious, unknowing, unwitting **10** unfa-

miliar **11** incognizant **12** inconversant, unacquainted, uninstructed

uninhabited 4 wild **5** empty **6** desert, vacant **8** deserted, desolate

uninhibited 3 lax **4** free, open **5** loose **8** uncurbed **9** audacious **10** boisterous, ungoverned, unhampered **11** untrammeled **12** unrestrained

uninitiate 4 tyro **7** amateur, dabbler **9** smatterer **10** dilettante **11** abecedarian

uninjured 5 sound, whole **6** entire, intact, unhurt **7** perfect **8** unbroken, unmarred **9** undamaged **10** unimpaired

uninspired 4 dull **6** stodgy **7** sterile **9** ponderous **10** uncreative, unoriginal **11** elephantine, heavy-footed, heavy-handed, noncreative, uninventive **13** unoriginative

uninstructed 4 rude **7** unaware **8** ignorant, untaught **9** benighted, oblivious, unknowing, untutored, unwitting **10** illiterate, uneducated, unfamiliar, uninformed, unlettered **11** empty-headed, incognizant, know-nothing **12** inconversant, unacquainted

unintelligent 4 dumb **5** brute **6** obtuse, simple, stupid, unwise **7** asinine, fatuous, foolish, vacuous, witless **8** ignorant, mindless **9** brainless, insensate, senseless **10** irrational, weak-headed, weak-minded

unintended *see* **unintentional**

unintentional 6 chance, random **9** causeless, haphazard, undevised, unplanned, unthought, unwitting **10** accidental, undesigned, unexpected, unforeseen, unpurposed, unthinking **11** inadvertent, purposeless, unlooked-for **13** unanticipated

uninterested 5 aloof **6** casual, remote **8** detached **9** incurious, uncurious, withdrawn **11** indifferent, unconcerned

uninteresting 3 dry **4** arid, drab, dull, flat **5** dusty, stale **6** boring, jejune, prolix, stupid **7** humdrum, insipid, tedious **8** bromidic, tiresome, weariful **9** colorless, dryasdust, wearisome **10** unexciting

uninterrupted 6 direct **7** endless, eternal, through **8** constant, straight, unending **9** ceaseless, continual, incessant, perpetual, unceasing **10** continuous **11** everlasting, unremitting **12** interminable

uninvited 7 unasked **8** unbidden, unsought **11** unrequested

union 4 bloc, club, seam **5** alloy, group, guild, hansa, hanse, joint, order **6** enosis, fusion, league, merger **7** amalgam, joining, melding, merging, society **8** alliance, congress, coupling, junction, juncture, marriage, mergence, sodality, together **9** anschluss, coalition **10** connection, federation, fellowship **11** association, brotherhood, coadunation, coalescence, combination, confeder-

acy, unification **13** confederation, consolidation *combining form:* **3** zyg **4** gamy,
zygo **6** gamous *labor:* **3** AFL, CIO, UAW
5 ILGWU *of two gametes:* **7** zygoses (plural), zygosis
Union Of Soviet Socialist Republics
see **U.S.S.R.**
unique 3 odd, one **4** lone, only, rare, sole,
solo **5** alone, queer **6** single **7** special,
strange, unusual **8** peculiar, peerless, separate, singular, solitary, uncommon,
unwonted **9** matchless, unequaled,
unmatched, unrivaled **10** particular, unexampled, unordinary **11** exceptional, unparagoned **12** unparalleled, unrepeatable
13 extraordinary
uniqueness 4 mark, note **6** import,
moment, oddity **7** oneness, unicity
10 notability, quaintness, singleness
11 curiousness, peculiarity, singularity,
strangeness, unusualness **12** memorability,
significance
____-Unis 5 Etats
unit 3 one **4** item **5** digit, group, monad,
whole **6** entity **7** element, measure **10** individual *administrative:* **6** agency, bureau
8 district *boy scout:* **5** troop *educational:*
6 course *military:* (see at **military**) *of acceleration:* **3** gal *of action:* **7** episode *of
advertising space:* **4** line **6** column **7** mil-
line *of a fire department:* **9** battalion *of an
element:* **4** atom **8** molecule *of angular
measure:* **6** radian **7** centrad *of area:*
4 acre **6** morgen **7** hectare *of astronomical distance:* **6** parsec **9** light-year *of
brightness:* **5** stilb **7** lambert *of capacity:*
2 cc, ml **4** gill, peck, pint **5** liter, litre, minim,
ounce, quart **6** bushel, firkin, gallon **8** fluidram *of computer information:* **3** bit *of
conductance:* **3** mho **7** siemens *of distance:* **4** mile **5** meter **7** furlong *of electricity:* **3** amp **4** volt, watt **6** ampere
7 coulomb *of electromotive force:* **4** volt *of
energy:* **3** erg **5** joule **7** quantum **8** watt-
hour *of explosive force:* **7** megaton *of
fineness:* **5** carat, karat *of fluidity:* **3** rhe *of
force:* **4** dyne **6** newton **7** poundal *of frequency:* **5** hertz **7** fresnel *of grain:*
5 sheaf **6** thrave *of heat:* **3** BTU **5** therm
7 calorie *of illumination:* **3** lux **4** phot *of
inductance:* **5** gauss, henry *of length:*
3 mil **4** foot, inch, yard **5** fermi, meter
6 micron *of loudness:* **4** phon, sone
7 decibel *of lumber:* **9** board foot *of magnetic flux:* **5** weber **7** maxwell *of magnetic
induction:* **5** tesla *of magnetic intensity:*
5 gamma **7** oersted *of magnetomotive
force:* **7** gilbert *of pressure:* **3** bar **4** torr
5 barye **10** atmosphere *of radiation:*
3 rad **8** roentgen *of radioactivity:* **5** curie
of resistance: **3** ohm *of solar radiation:*

7 langley *of sound absorption:* **5** sabin *of
speech:* **4** word **6** toneme **7** phoneme
8 morpheme, syllable *of speed:* **3** CPS,
MPH, RPM **4** knot *of temperature:*
6 degree, kelvin *of time:* **3** day **4** beat, bell,
hour, week **5** month **6** minute, season, second **8** svedberg *of viscosity:* **5** poise *of
weight:* **3** ton **4** dram, gram, tael **5** carat,
grain, ounce, pound, stein, tonne **6** drachm,
kantar **7** gigaton, kiloton, millier, quintal,
scruple *ancient Roman:* **5** libra *Asian:*
5 Picul, tical **6** cattie, miskal *British:*
3 tod *Chinese:* **5** liang *Hebrew:* **5** gerah
Indian: **3** ser **4** tola *Muslim:* **4** rotl
Russian: **4** pood *Turkish:* **3** oka,
oke *of work:* **3** erg **5** ergon,
joule *social:* **4** clan **5** tribe **6** family
7 chapter
unite 3 add, mix, sew, tie, wed **4** ally, band,
bind, bond, fuse, join, knit, link, weld
5 blend, graft, marry, merge, unify
6 adhere, adjoin, attach, cement, concur,
couple, gather, league, mingle, relate, solder, splice **7** combine, conjoin, connect
8 assemble, coadjute, coalesce, compound,
copulate, federate **9** affiliate, aggregate,
associate, commingle, cooperate **10** amalgamate, federalize **11** concentrate, confederate, incorporate **12** conglutinate
United Arab Emirates 5 Ajman, Dubai
7 Sharjah **8** Abu Dhabi, Fujairah
United Kingdom *capital:* **6** London *monetary unit:* **5** pound *part:* **5** Wales
7 England **8** Scotland
unities, dramatic 4 time **5** place
6 action
unity 5 union **7** concord, harmony, oneness, rapport **8** identity, sodality, soleness,
uniquity **9** agreement, communion, congruity **10** singleness, solidarity, uniformity,
uniqueness **11** conformance, conjunction,
singularity **12** selfsameness, singularness
13 individuality
universal 3 all **5** broad, total, whole
6 common, cosmic, entire, global **7** allover,
general, generic **8** catholic, ecumenic,
sweeping **9** extensive, planetary, unlimited,
worldwide **10** ecumenical, ubiquitous
11 omnipresent **12** all-embracing, all-inclusive, all-pervading, cosmopolitan *combining
form:* **3** omn **4** omni
universe 3 all **5** world **6** cosmos, nature,
system **8** creation, megacosm **9** macrocosm **11** macrocosmos *combining form:*
4 cosm **5** cosmo
unjust 4 hard **5** cruel, wrong **6** unfair,
wicked **7** unequal **8** improper, wrongful
9 dishonest, inequable **10** iniquitous
11 inequitable, unequitable, unrighteous
unjustifiable 5 undue **7** invalid **9** untena-

ble **10** inexpiable **11** inexcusable, unwarranted

unkempt 5 messy **6** frowsy, frowzy, shaggy, sloppy, unneat, untidy **7** ruffled, tousled **8** draggled, ill-kempt, scraggly, slipshod, slovenly, strubbly, uncombed **10** disarrayed, disheveled **12** unfastidious

unkind 3 bad, ill **4** mean, vile **5** cruel, harsh, rough, stern **6** severe **8** ungenial **9** inclement **10** ungenerous, ungracious **11** unfavorable

unknit 4 undo **5** ravel, relax, untie **7** unravel

unknowable 6 arcane, mystic **8** mystical, numinous **9** enigmatic, mysterial, unguessed **10** cabalistic, mysterious **11** inscrutable, ungraspable **12** impenetrable, incognizable, unexaminable, unfathomable, unimaginable **13** inconceivable

unknowing 7 unaware **8** ignorant **9** oblivious, unwitting **10** unfamiliar, uninformed **11** incognizant **12** inconversant, unacquainted, uninstructed

unknown 6 nobody, secret **7** obscure, strange, unfamed, unnoted **8** nameless **9** anonymous, incognito, unheard-of **10** unfamiliar, unrenowned **12** uncelebrated *Scottish:* **6** unkent

unlawful 7 bootleg, illegal, illicit, lawless **8** criminal, improper, wrongful **9** irregular, nefarious **10** contraband, flagitious, iniquitous **11** black-market, intolerable **12** illegitimate **13** exceptionable, objectionable

unlearned 7 natural **8** ignorant, untaught **9** inerudite, unbookish, untutored **10** illiterate, uneducated, unstudious **11** instinctive, unscholarly

unleash 4 free, vent **5** loose **7** release

unless 3 but **4** save **6** except, saving **7** without **9** excepting

unlettered see **uneducated**

unlike 7 distant, diverse, unequal, various **9** different, disparate, divergent, unsimilar **10** dissimilar

unlikely 5 unfit **7** dubious **8** doubtful **10** improbable, unsuitable **11** unpromising **12** questionable, unattractive

unlikeness 8 alterity, contrast **9** otherness **10** difference, divergence, divergency **11** discrepancy, distinction **12** disagreement, dissemblance **13** dissimilarity, dissimilitude, inconsistence

unlimited 4 vast **5** total **6** all-out **7** endless, full-out **8** infinite **9** boundless, fullblown, full-scale, unbounded, undefined, universal **10** indefinite, unconfined, unmeasured **11** measureless, untrammeled **12** immeasurable, totalitarian, unrestricted **13** indeterminate

unload 4 drop, dump, land **5** empty, unbox **6** debark, remove, unlade, unpack,

unship, unstow **7** deliver, lighten, off-load, relieve, uncrate **8** jettison **9** disburden, discharge, disembark, liquidate, stevedore **11** disencumber

unloose, unloosen 4 undo **5** unfix **6** unbind **7** unrivet **8** unfasten **9** disengage

unloyal see **disloyal**

unlucky 3 bad, ill **4** dire **7** baleful, baneful, direful, doomful, fateful, hapless, ominous, unhappy **8** ill-fated, tragical, untoward **9** illboding, ill-omened **10** calamitous, disastrous, ill-starred **11** apocalyptic, cataclysmic, star-crossed, unfortunate **12** catastrophic, misfortunate

unman 4 undo **5** abase, crush, drain, unfit **7** degrade, deplete, exhaust, unnerve **8** castrate, enervate, paralyze, unstring **9** prostrate **10** disqualify, emasculate, impoverish

unmanageable 4 wild **6** unruly **7** restive **8** indocile **9** fractious **10** disorderly **11** indomitable, intractable **12** recalcitrant, ungovernable **13** undisciplined

unmanly 5 sissy **6** coward, craven, prissy **7** chicken, epicene, gutless **8** childish, cowardly, poltroon **9** pansified, sissified, spunkless **10** effeminate **11** lily-livered **12** Miss-Nancyish, poor-spirited **13** pusillanimous

unmannered 4 open, rude **5** frank, plain **6** candid **7** boorish, ill-bred, uncivil **8** impolite, man-to-man **10** ungracious, unmannerly **11** disgracious, openhearted, undisguised, unvarnished **12** discourteous, undissembled **13** disrespectful

unmarred 5 sound, whole **6** entire, intact, unhurt **7** perfect **8** pristine, unbroken

unmarried 4 lone, sole **5** unwed **6** single **10** spouseless

unmask 6 debunk, expose, reveal, show up, unveil **7** uncloak, undress **8** disclose, discover, unshroud

unmatchable 7 supreme **8** towering, ultimate **10** preeminent, surpassing **11** unequalable **12** incomparable, transcendent **13** unsurpassable

unmatched 3 odd **4** only **5** alone **6** unique **8** peerless, unpaired **9** matchless, unequaled, unrivaled **11** unparagoned **12** unparalleled

unmerciful 5 cruel **8** pitiless, ruthless **9** merciless, unpitying **10** relentless

unmethodical 7 cursory, erratic **9** desultory

unmindful 7 unaware **8** careless, heedless **9** forgetful, negligent, oblivious, unwitting **10** neglectful **11** inattentive

unmistakable 4 flat, open **5** clear, frank, plain **6** patent **7** evident, express **8** apparent, distinct, manifest, palpable, univocal

unmitigated 4 mere, pure, rank **5** gross,

sheer, utter **6** arrant, damned, simple
7 perfect, unmixed **8** absolute, clearcut,
complete, outright **9** out-and-out, unalloyed,
undiluted **10** unmodified **11** straight-out,
unqualified **13** thoroughgoing,
unadulterated

unmixed 4 deep, mere, neat, pure **5** plain,
sheer, utter **6** simple **7** perfect, sincere
8 absolute, straight **9** unalloyed, undiluted
11 unmitigated, unqualified
13 unadulterated

unmodern 3 old **5** dated, passé
7 antique, archaic, old-time, vintage **9** out-
of-date **10** antiquated, oldfangled **12** old-
fashioned

unmodifiable 5 fixed **8** constant,
straight **9** immovable, immutable, unmovable **10** inflexible, invariable **11** inalterable,
unalterable **12** unchangeable

unmovable see **immovable**

unmoved 4 calm, cool, firm **5** stony
6 serene **7** adamant **8** obdurate, stubborn,
unshaken **9** apathetic, impassive

unmoving 5 inert **6** static **8** immobile,
stagnant **10** stationary

unnamed 8 nameless **9** anonymous
10 innominate **12** undesignated

unnatural 6 off-key **7** deviant, uncanny
8 abnormal **9** anomalous, divergent, irregular, unregular **10** superhuman **11** supernormal, supranormal **13** superordinary

unneat 5 messy **6** sloppy, untidy
7 unkempt **8** careless, ill-kempt, slipshod,
slovenly, uncombed **12** unfastidious

unnecessary 6 excess, lavish **7** profuse,
surplus **8** needless, prodigal **9** redundant
10 gratuitous, unrequired **11** inessential,
superfluous, uncalled-for, unessential

unneeded see **unnecessary**

unnerve 3 sap **5** unman, upset
6 weaken **7** agitate, perturb **8** bewilder,
castrate, confound, distract, enervate,
enfeeble, unstring **9** undermine
10 emasculate

unneutral 6 biased, warped **7** colored,
partial **8** one-sided, partisan **9** jaundiced
10 prejudiced **11** tendentious
12 prepossessed

unnoted 7 obscure, unfamed, unknown
8 nameless **9** unheard-of **10** unobserved,
unremarked, unrenowned **12** uncelebrated,
unconsidered

unobservant 9 unheeding **10** unnoticing,
unwatchful **11** inattentive **12** unperceiving

unobserving see **unobservant**

unobstructed 4 open **5** clear **8** unclosed

unobtrusive 5 quiet, tasty **7** subdued
8 tasteful **10** restrained

unoccupied 4 free, idle **5** empty
10 unemployed

unofficial 8 informal **9** irregular
13 unceremonious

unorganized 7 muddled **8** inchoate
10 disjointed, disordered, incoherent, incohesive **11** unconnected **12** disconnected,
uncontinuous **13** discontinuous

unoriginal 3 dry **4** arid, dull **5** staid **6** barren, stodgy, stuffy **7** prosaic, sterile,
unfired **10** uncreative, uninspired **11** noncreative, uninventive

unornamented 3 dry **5** plain **6** simple
9 unadorned **11** inelaborate, unelaborate,
ungarnished **12** unbeautified **13** unembellished, unembroidered

unorthodox 9 dissident, heretical, sectarian **10** schismatic **13** nonconformist

unorthodoxy 6 heresy, schism **7** dissent
9 disbelief **10** dissidence **13** nonconformism, nonconformity

unpaid 3 due **5** owing **6** mature **7** overdue, payable **8** freewill, wageless **9** unsettled, voluntary, volunteer **10** gratuitous
11 outstanding **13** uncompensated, unrecompensed, unremunerated

unpalatable 4 flat, thin, weak **5** washy
6 bitter, watery **7** galling, insipid, painful
8 grievous, nauseous, unsavory **9** loathsome, savorless, sickening, tasteless
10 afflictive, flavorless **11** distasteful, ill-flavored **12** unappetizing

unparalleled 5 alone **6** unique **8** peerless **9** matchless, unequaled, unmatched,
unrivaled

unperceiving see **unobservant**

unpermissive 5 rigid **6** strict **8** rigorist,
rigorous **9** draconian, stringent
10 ironhanded

unphysical 8 bodiless **9** asomatous
10 discarnate, immaterial, unembodied
11 disembodied, incorporeal, nonmaterial

unpierceable 10 impervious **11** impregnable **12** impenetrable

unpitying 9 merciless **10** unmerciful

unplanned 6 random **7** aimless, unaimed
9 desultory, haphazard, hit-or-miss, undevised, unthought **10** designless, undesigned,
unintended, unpurposed **11** inadvertent,
purposeless **12** unconsidered
13 unintentional

unpleasant 3 bad **4** sour **5** seamy **6** rotten **7** unhappy **11** displeasing, distasteful
12 disagreeable *combining form:* **3** cac
4 caco

unpliable 6 mulish **8** perverse, stubborn
9 obstinate, pigheaded **10** bullheaded,
headstrong, self-willed **12** pertinacious

unplug 3 ope **4** open **6** uncork
7 unblock **10** disconnect

unpolished 4 rude **5** crude, rough
6 unhewn **7** boorish, ill-bred, incivil, loutish,
lowbred, uncivil **8** churlish, cloddish, impo-

lite, unformed, unworked **9** roughhewn, undressed, unrefined **10** uncultured, unfinished, ungracious **11** clodhopping, disgracious, ill-mannered, uncivilized, unfashioned **12** discourteous **13** disrespectful

unpracticed 3 raw **5** fresh, green **6** callow **7** untried **8** untested, unversed **13** inexperienced

unpredictable 4 iffy **6** chancy **7** erratic **9** fluctuant, uncertain, whimsical **10** capricious

unprejudiced 4 fair, just **5** equal **8** unbiased **9** equitable, impartial, objective, uncolored **13** dispassionate

unpressed 7 wrinkly

unpretentious 5 plain **6** modest, simple **10** unaffected **11** inelaborate, unelaborate, ungarnished **12** unbeautified **13** unembellished

unpretty 5 plain **6** homely **8** uncomely **10** unalluring, unhandsome **11** unbeauteous, unbeautiful **12** unattractive

unprincipled 5 venal **7** corrupt, crooked **9** abandoned, dishonest, dissolute, mercenary, reprobate, unethical **10** licentious, praetorian, profligate **12** unscrupulous

unproductive 4 vain **6** barren, futile **7** useless **8** impotent, infecund **9** fruitless, infertile, unbearing, unfertile **10** unavailing **11** ineffectual, unavailable **12** hardscrabble

unprofitable 4 idle, vain **7** useless

unprogressive 8 backward, ignorant **9** benighted **10** behindhand **11** undeveloped **13** unenlightened

unpropitious 4 dire **7** adverse, baleful, baneful, counter, fateful, ominous, unlucky **9** ill-boding, ill-omened **11** threatening **12** antagonistic

unprosperous 3 low **4** poor **5** broke, needy **8** indigent **9** destitute, penurious **11** fortuneless, impecunious **12** impoverished

unprotected 6 unsafe **8** helpless, insecure **9** unguarded **10** undefended, unshielded **11** defenseless, unsheltered

unproved 7 untried **8** untested

unpunctual 4 late **5** lated, tardy **7** belated, overdue **10** behindhand

unqualified 4 firm, pure, rank, sure **5** clear, gross, sheer, unfit, utter **6** entire, simple, steady **7** abiding, blasted, blessed, express, perfect, unmixed **8** absolute, complete, enduring, explicit, infernal, unfitted **9** incapable, out-and-out, steadfast, unalloyed, undiluted, unlimited, unskilled **10** confounded, ineligible, unequipped, unreserved, unsuitable **11** incompetent, unfaltering, unmitigated **12** never-failing, wholehearted **13** unadulterated, unconditional

unquenchable 9 insatiate, unsatiate **10** insatiable

unquestionable 4 flat, real, true, very **7** certain, genuine **8** bona fide, positive **9** authentic, downright, undoubted, up-and-down **10** sure-enough **11** established, well-founded **12** well-grounded

unquestioning 4 firm, sure **5** fixed **6** steady **7** abiding **8** enduring, unshaken **9** steadfast **10** unshakable **12** never-failing

unravel 5 break, solve **6** unfold, unknit **7** dope out, resolve, unsnarl **8** decipher, dissolve, unriddle, untangle **9** extricate, figure out, puzzle out **11** disentangle

unreadable 9 illegible

unreal 7 fictive **8** chimeric, fanciful, illusory **9** fantastic, fictional, imaginary **10** chimerical, fictitious **12** suppositious *combining form:* **5** pseud **6** pseudo

unrealistic 8 fanciful **10** ivory-tower **11** impractical, unpractical **12** ivory-towered **13** ivory-towerish

unreasonable 3 mad **5** loose, undue **7** invalid **8** improper, overmuch, unlawful, wrongful **9** arbitrary, excessive, illogical, sophistic **10** fallacious, immoderate, inordinate, irrational, peremptory, reasonless, unrightful **11** incongruous, nonrational, unwarranted

unreasoned 3 mad **7** invalid **9** illogical, sophistic **10** fallacious, irrational, reasonless **11** nonrational

unrecompensed 6 unpaid **13** uncompensated

unrefined 3 raw **4** rude **5** crass, crude, gross, rough **6** coarse, impure, native, vulgar **7** boorish, ill-bred, loutish, lowbred, natural, uncouth **8** churlish, cloddish, ungraded, unsorted **9** inelegant, roughcast, roughhewn, run-of-mine, undressed **10** uncultured, unpolished **11** clodhopping, uncivilized, unprocessed

unreflective 8 careless, feckless, heedless, uncaring **9** unheeding **10** unthinking **11** inadvertent, thoughtless

unrehearsed 7 offhand **9** extempore, impromptu, unstudied **10** improvised **11** extemporary

unrelated 8 discrete, separate **9** disjoined

unrelenting 4 grim **6** mortal **8** ruthless **9** merciless **10** implacable, ironfisted, unyielding **11** unflinching **12** unappeasable

unreliable 5 false, slick **6** fickle, shifty, tricky, unsafe, unsure, untrue **7** dubious, inexact **8** slippery, untrusty **9** faithless, trustless, unassured **10** fly-by-night, inaccurate, inconstant, perfidious, unfaithful **11** vacillating **12** falsehearted **13** untrustworthy

unreligious 7 godless

unremarkable 5 plain, usual **7** routine **8** everyday, ordinary, workaday **9** plain Jane, quotidian

unremitting 7 endless 8 constant, unending 9 ceaseless, continual, perpetual, unceasing 12 interminable 13 uninterrupted

unremorseful 7 unsorry 10 impenitent, regretless, uncontrite

unremunerated 6 unpaid

unrenowned 7 obscure, unfamed, unknown, unnoted 8 nameless 9 unheard-of 12 uncelebrated

unrepentant 7 unsorry 10 impenitent, regretless, uncontrite 11 remorseless

unrepresentative 7 deviant 8 aberrant, abnormal, atypical 9 anomalous, untypical 11 heteroclite

unrequested 7 unasked 8 unbidden, unsought 9 uninvited

unrequired 8 needless, unneeded 9 omissible, unneedful 11 dispensable, inessential, uncalled-for, unessential, unnecessary 12 nonessential

unreserved 4 open 5 frank, plain 6 breezy, candid, casual, dégagé 7 relaxed, unfussy 8 informal, outgoing, outright 9 easygoing, expansive 11 low-pressure, openhearted, unconcealed, undisguised, unvarnished 12 undissembled 13 demonstrative, unconstrained

unresolved 8 hesitant, wavering 9 faltering, uncertain 10 hesitating, indecisive, irresolute, undecisive 11 vacillating 12 shilly-shally

unrespectable 5 shady 6 shabby, shoddy 8 shameful 10 inglorious 11 disgraceful, ignominious

unresponsive 4 cold 6 frigid 9 inhibited 10 insentient, undersexed 11 insensitive, passionless 13 insusceptible, unimpressible, unsusceptible

unresponsiveness 6 apathy, phlegm 8 stoicism 9 stolidity 11 impassivity 13 insensibility

unrest 5 chaos 6 tumult 7 ailment, anarchy, ferment, turmoil, unquiet 8 disorder, disquiet, upheaval 9 agitation, commotion, confusion 10 convulsion, inquietude, turbulence 11 disquietude, restiveness 13 Sturm und Drang

unrestrained 4 free, open 5 bluff, blunt, frank, loose 6 brusque, rampant 8 outgoing, reinless, uncurbed 9 audacious, excessive, expansive 10 forthright, immoderate, inordinate, ungoverned, unhampered, untempered 11 intemperate, plainspoken, uninhibited, untrammeled 13 demonstrative, overindulgent

unrestraint 4 ease 7 abandon 11 naturalness, spontaneity 13 impulsiveness

unrestricted 4 free, open 6 public 10 accessible

unrighteous 6 unfair, unjust 9 inequable 11 inequitable, unequitable

unripe 5 green, young 6 callow, infant 8 immature, juvenile, youthful 9 unfledged

unrivaled 4 only 5 alone 6 unique 8 peerless 9 matchless, unmatched 11 unparagoned 12 unparalleled

unrobe see **unclothe**

unroll 6 extend, uncoil, unfurl, unwind 7 open out

unromantic 4 cool, hard 5 sober 9 practical, pragmatic, realistic 10 hard-boiled, hardheaded 11 down-to-earth 12 matter-of-fact 13 unsentimental

unruffled 4 calm, cool 6 serene 8 composed, tranquil 9 collected 10 nonchalant 11 unflappable 13 imperturbable

unruly 4 hard, wild 5 rowdy, tough 7 froward, naughty, raffish, raucous, wayward 8 contrary, indocile, perverse, rowdyish, untoward 9 fractious, obstinate, ruffianly, termagant, turbulent 10 boisterous, disorderly, rampageous, rebellious, rowdy-dowdy, tumultuous 11 disobedient, indomitable, intractable, rumbustious 12 contumacious, incorrigible, obstreperous, rambunctious, recalcitrant, ungovernable, unmanageable 13 insubordinate, undisciplined

unsacred 3 lay 7 profane, secular 8 temporal

unsafe 5 risky, shaky 6 chancy 7 erratic, tottery, unsound 8 insecure, perilous, unstable 9 dangerous, hazardous, unassured, uncertain 10 jeopardous, unreliable 12 undependable 13 untrustworthy

unsaid 5 tacit 7 implied 8 implicit, inferred, nonvocal, unspoken, wordless 9 unuttered 10 undeclared, understood 11 unexpressed

unsalutary 7 noisome, noxious 9 unhealthy 11 unhealthful, unwholesome 12 insalubrious

unsatisfactory 3 bad, bum 4 poor, punk 5 amiss, wrong 6 rotten

unsatisfiable 9 insatiate 10 quenchless

unsavory 4 flat 7 insipid 9 tasteless 10 flavorless 11 distasteful, ill-flavored, unpalatable 12 unappetizing

unsay 6 abjure, recall, recant 7 retract 8 forswear, palinode, take back, withdraw

unscathed 4 safe 8 unharmed

unscented 8 odorless

unschooled 5 naive 6 simple 7 artless, natural 8 ignorant, untaught 9 benighted, ingenuous, unstudied, untutored 10 illiterate, unaffected, uneducated, unlettered 11 emptyheaded, know-nothing 12 unartificial, uninstructed

unscramble 5 untie 7 untwine 8 untangle 9 extricate 10 disembroil, disentwine, unentangle **11** disencumber, disentangle **12** disembarrass

unscrupulous 5 shady, venal **6** crafty **7** corrupt, crooked **8** improper, scheming, sinister, unseemly, wrongful **9** deceitful, dishonest, mercenary, underhand, unethical **10** praetorian **12** questionable, unprincipled

unseasonable 5 inapt, inept, unapt, undue **8** ill-timed, improper, mistimed, untimely **10** malapropos, unbecoming **11** inopportune, unfortunate **12** inauspicious, inconvenient, infelicitous **13** inappropriate

unseasoned 3 raw **5** fresh, green, young **6** callow **7** untried **8** unversed **9** unfleshed **11** unpracticed **13** inexperienced

unseat 5 pitch, throw **6** depose, remove **7** buck off, unhorse **8** dethrone

unseemliness 9 indecorum **10** inelegance **11** impropriety

unseemly 5 crude, inapt, inept, rough, rowdy, unapt **6** coarse **7** raffish, ungodly **8** ill-timed, improper, indecent, untoward **9** inelegant, ruffianly, unrefined **10** indecorous, indelicate, malapropos, malodorous, unbecoming, undecorous, unsuitable **11** unbefitting **13** inappropriate

unseen 9 invisible

unsentimental see **unromantic**

unserviceable 7 useless **11** impractical **12** unfunctional **13** nonfunctional

unsettle 4 turn **5** upset **6** bother, flurry, jumble, sicken **7** agitate, derange, disturb, fluster, perturb, rummage, trouble, unhinge **8** disarray, disorder, disquiet **9** incommode **10** disarrange, discommode, discompose **11** disorganize

unsettled 3 due **4** back, open **5** fluid **6** mature, mobile, queasy, remote, uneasy, unpaid **7** clouded, dubious, mutable, overdue, payable, pendent, pending, protean, unclear, unquiet **8** doubtful, frontier, restless, unstable, unsteady, variable, weathery **9** changeful, dubitable, uncertain, undecided, unrestful **10** changeable, indecisive, unpeaceful, untranquil **11** outstanding, problematic **12** undetermined

unsex 3 fix **4** geld **5** alter **6** change, neuter **8** castrate, mutilate **9** sterilize **11** desexualize

unshackle 4 free **5** loose **6** loosen, unbind **7** manumit, release, unchain **8** liberate **9** discharge **10** emancipate

unshakable 4 firm, sure **5** fixed **6** steady **7** abiding **9** steadfast **10** unwavering **11** unfaltering **12** never-failing **13** unquestioning

unshaped 8 formless, inchoate, unformed **9** amorphous

unshared 4 sole **6** single **9** exclusive

unship 6 unlade, unload, unstow **7** offload **9** disburden, discharge

unshod 8 barefoot, shoeless **10** unsandaled

unshroud 6 debunk, expose, show up, unmask **7** uncloak, undress **8** discover

unshut 3 ope **4** open, undo **6** unstop **7** unblock, unclose

unsightly 4 drab, dull, ugly **7** hideous **8** uncomely **9** ill-shaped, unshapely **10** ill-favored, ill-looking, lackluster, unesthetic **11** unbeautiful

unsimilar 6 unlike **7** distant, diverse, unalike, unequal, various **9** different, disparate, divergent

unskilled 5 green, inept **7** amateur, jackleg **10** amateurish **12** dilettantish, dilettantist **13** unworkmanlike

unskillful 5 inapt, inept, unapt **6** clumsy, gauche **7** awkward, inadept, unhandy, unready **8** inexpert, unexpert, unfacile, unfitted **9** butcherly, incapable **11** incompetent, inefficient, undexterous, unqualified **12** unproficient **13** unworkmanlike

unsleeping 5 alert **7** wakeful **8** openeyed, vigilant, watchful **9** wide-awake

unsmooth 5 harsh, rough **6** craggy, jagged, ruffly, rugged, uneven **7** scraggy, unlevel **8** asperous, scabrous

unsnarl see **untangle**

unsociable 3 shy **4** cool **5** aloof, timid **6** offish, remote, shut-in **7** distant, prickly **8** brooding, reserved, solitary, standoff **9** diffident, exclusive, secretive, sensitive, unbending, withdrawn **11** indifferent, standoffish **12** inaccessible

unsoiled 5 clean **7** cleanly **8** spotless **9** taintless, unsullied **10** immaculate

unsophisticated 5 crude, green, naive **6** callow, simple **7** artless, genuine, natural, uncouth **9** ingenuous, untutored, unworldly **10** unaffected, unschooled **12** unartificial

unsorted 3 raw **5** crude, mixed **6** impure, motley, native, varied **8** ungraded **9** unrefined **11** promiscuous **12** multifarious **13** heterogeneous, miscellaneous

unsought 7 unasked **8** unbidden, unwanted, unwished **9** undesired, uninvited, unwelcome **11** unrequested

unsound 3 mad **4** daft, weak **5** batty, false, frail, hairy, risky, wrong **6** chancy, crazed, faulty, flawed, flimsy, infirm, insane, untrue, weakly, wicked **7** cracked, damaged, fragile, lunatic **8** decrepit, demented, deranged, perilous, specious **9** dangerous, erroneous, hazardous, imperfect, incorrect, unhealthy **10** inaccurate, jeopardous, unbalanced **11** treacherous **13** insubstantial, unsubstantial *mentally:* **6** insane

unsparing 4 free **6** severe **7** liberal

8 generous, handsome **9** bounteous, bountiful **10** freehanded, munificent, openhanded

unspeakable 6 odious **7** hateful **9** atrocious, loathsome, obnoxious, offensive, repellent, repugnant, repulsive, revolting **10** disgusting, outrageous **11** distasteful **13** inexpressible, unexpressible

unspoiled 6 intact, virgin **8** pristine, untapped, virginal **9** undefiled, untouched

unspoken 4 mute **5** tacit **6** hinted, silent, unsaid **7** implied **8** implicit, inferred, unstated, unvoiced, wordless **9** intimated, suggested, unuttered **10** undeclared, understood **11** unexpressed

unstable 4 weak **5** fluid, rocky, shaky **6** dickey, fickle, mobile, moving, shifty, tricky, unsure, wobbly **7** buoyant, dubious, elastic, protean, suspect **8** doubtful, freakish, insecure, rootless, slippery, ticklish, volatile, wavering, weathery **9** ambiguous, changeful, fluctuant, mercurial, resilient, uncertain, unsettled **10** borderline, capricious, inconstant, lubricious, precarious **11** vacillating **12** effervescent **13** temperamental

unsteady 5 fluid, rocky, tippy **6** jiggly, mobile, moving, shifty, wobbly **7** movable, mutable, protean, rickety, tottery **8** slippery, staggery, tittuppy, variable, weathery **9** changeful, uncertain, unsettled **10** changeable, inconstant *British:* **5** wonky

unsteel 5 unarm **6** disarm **7** win over

unstop 3 ope **4** open, undo **6** uncork, unplug, unshut **7** unblock, unclose

unstow 6 unlade, unload, unship **7** offload **9** disburden, discharge

unstrengthen 3 sap **5** blunt **6** weaken **7** cripple, disable, unbrace **8** enfeeble **9** attenuate, undermine **10** debilitate

unstudied 5 naive **6** simple **7** artless, natural, offhand **8** unversed **9** extempore, impromptu, ingenuous, unlearned, untutored **10** improvised, unaffected, unschooled **11** extemporary, spontaneous, unrehearsed **12** unartificial

unstylish 5 dowdy, tacky **6** démodé, frumpy, stodgy **8** frumpish, outmoded **9** out-of-date

unsubstantial 4 thin, weak **5** frail, shaky **6** feeble, flimsy, infirm, weakly **7** fragile, tenuous, unsound **8** bodiless, decrepit, insecure **9** spiritual **10** immaterial, improbable, incredible, unembodied, unphysical **11** implausible, incorporeal, nonmaterial, nonphysical **12** metaphysical, unbelievable, unconvincing, undependable **13** inconceivable

unsuccess 4 bomb, flop **6** defeat **7** failure, reverse, setback

unsuitable 5 inapt, inept, undue, unfit

6 unmeet **7** unhappy **8** ill-timed, improper, unfitted, untimely **9** ill-suited **10** ill-adapted, unbecoming **11** unbefitting **13** inappropriate

unsuited 5 inapt, unfit **6** unmeet **8** unfitted **10** ill-adapted, inadequate **12** inadmissible, unacceptable **13** disappointing, inappropriate, objectionable

unsullied 4 pure **5** clean **6** chaste, decent, modest **7** cleanly **8** spotless, unsoiled **9** stainless, taintless, undefiled **10** immaculate **11** unblemished

unsure 4 open, weak **5** shaky **6** dickey, wobbly **7** dubious, unclear **8** doubtful, insecure, rootless, unstable, untrusty, wavering **9** fluctuant, trustless, unassured, uncertain, undecided **10** borderline, indecisive, suspicious, unreliable **11** problematic, unconfident, vacillating **12** questionable, undependable **13** untrustworthy

unsurpassable 7 supreme **8** towering, ultimate **10** preeminent **12** transcendent

unsusceptible 9 impassive **10** insentient **11** insensitive **12** unresponsive

unsuspecting 6 unwary **9** credulous

unsuspicious see **unsuspecting**

unswayable 5 rigid **8** obdurate **10** inflexible, relentless, unyielding **11** uncompliant **12** single-minded

unswerving see **unfaltering**

unsymmetrical 6 uneven **7** unequal **8** lopsided **9** irregular **10** off-balance **12** overbalanced

unsympathetic 4 cold, cool **6** frigid **7** callous **8** aversive, kindless, lukewarm, obdurate, ungenial **9** heartless, repellent, repugnant, unfeeling, unlikable **10** dislikable, hard-boiled, unpleasant, unpleasing **11** coldhearted, displeasing, halfhearted, hardhearted, indifferent, uncongenial, unemotional **12** stonyhearted **13** disinterested

untactful 5 brash **9** impolitic, maladroit, unpolitic **12** undiplomatic

untamed 4 wild **5** feral **9** unsubdued

untangle 7 unsnarl, untwine, untwist **9** discumber, extricate **10** disembroil, disentwine, unscramble **11** disencumber **12** disembarrass

untapped 6 virgin **8** virginal **9** unspoiled, untouched

untaught 8 ignorant **9** benighted, untutored **10** illiterate, uneducated, unlettered, unschooled **11** empty-headed, know-nothing **12** uninstructed

untempered 9 excessive **10** immoderate, inordinate **12** unrestrained **13** overindulgent

untended 7 run-down **9** neglected **10** uncared-for

Unter den ____ 6 Linden

untested 7 untried 8 unproved
11 unpracticed
unthankful 9 thankless 10 ungrateful
unthinkable 4 rare 6 unique 7 unusual
8 singular, uncommon, unwonted
10 incredible, unordinary 11 exceptional
13 extraordinary
unthinking 8 careless, feckless, heedless,
uncaring 9 unheeding 11 inadvertent,
thoughtless 12 irreflective, unreflective
unthorough 5 messy 6 botchy, sloppy,
untidy 8 careless, slapdash, slipshod,
slovenly
unthought 9 undevised, unplanned
10 undesigned, unintended, unpurposed
11 inadvertent 13 unintentional
unthrift 5 waste 6 lavish, waster
7 spender, wastrel 8 prodigal, squander
9 overdoing 10 high roller, lavishness, profligate, squanderer 11 improvident, prodigality, scattergood 12 extravagance, extravagancy, wastefulness
unthrifty 6 lavish 8 prodigal, wasteful
10 thriftless 11 extravagant, improvident
untidy 5 messy 6 botchy, sloppy, unneat
7 unkempt 8 careless, ill-kempt, slapdash,
slipshod, slovenly, uncombed 10 disheveled, unthorough 12 unfastidious
untie 6 loosen, unknot, unlace, unlash
8 unstring 9 extricate 10 disembroil, disentwine, unentangle, unscramble 11 disencumber, disentangle 12 disembarrass
untighten 3 lax 4 ease 5 loose, relax,
slack 6 loosen 7 ease off, slacken
until 2 to 4 till, up to 5 since 6 before
7 prior to 11 in advance of
untimely 4 soon 5 early, inapt, unapt,
undue 8 ill-timed, improper, mistimed, oversoon, previous 9 overearly, premature
10 malapropos, unsuitable 11 ill-seasoned,
inopportune 12 intempestive, unseasonable 13 inappropriate
untiring 8 tireless 9 weariless 10 unflagging, unwearying 11 unweariable 13 indefatigable, inexhaustible
untold 4 huge, vast 6 mighty 7 immense,
mammoth, titanic 8 enormous, gigantic
9 countless, monstrous, uncounted, unrelated 10 innumerous, numberless, prodigious, unnumbered 11 innumerable,
uncountable 12 unnumberable
untouchable 5 leper 6 pariah 7 Ishmael,
outcast 8 castaway, déclassé, derelict, out-
caste, outsider 10 Ishmaelite
11 offscouring
untouched 4 pure 5 sound, whole
6 entire, intact, virgin 7 perfect 8 flawless,
pristine, unmarred, untapped, virginal
9 undamaged, unspoiled 11 unblemished
untoward 4 wild 5 rough 6 unruly 7 hapless, ungodly, unhappy, unlucky 8 ill-fated,

improper, indecent, indocile, luckless,
unseemly 9 fractious 10 ill-starred, indecorous, indelicate, unbecoming, undecorous
11 intractable, star-crossed, unfortunate
12 misfortunate, recalcitrant, ungovernable,
unmanageable 13 undisciplined
untrained see **unskilled**
untrammeled 8 uncurbed 9 audacious
10 ungoverned, unhampered 11 uninhibited 12 unrestrained
untried 3 raw 5 fresh, green 6 callow,
unripe 8 immature, unproved, untested,
unversed 9 half-baked 10 unseasoned
11 unpracticed 12 unconversant
13 inexperienced
untroubled 4 calm 5 quiet, still 6 hushed,
placid, stilly 7 halcyon
untroublesome 4 easy 5 light, royal
6 facile, simple, smooth 10 effortless
untrue 5 false, wrong 7 inexact, unloyal,
unsound 8 disloyal, forsworn, perjured, recreant, specious 9 erroneous, faithless,
imprecise, incorrect, unprecise 10 inaccurate, perfidious, traitorous, unfaithful
11 treacherous **combining form:** 5 pseud
6 pseudo
untruism 3 fib, lie 4 tale 5 story
6 canard 7 bouncer 9 falsehood
13 prevarication
untrustworthy 6 unsafe, unsure 7 dubious 9 unassured 10 fly-by-night, unreliable 12 questionable, undependable
untruth 3 fib, lie 4 tale 5 error, story
6 canard 7 fallacy, falsity 9 falsehood,
falseness 13 erroneousness, prevarication
untruthful 5 false, lying, wrong 6 shifty
7 knavish, roguish 8 delusive, delusory,
unhonest 9 deceitful, deceptive, dishonest,
incorrect 10 inaccurate, mendacious,
misleading
untruthfulness 7 fibbery 9 falsehood,
mendacity 10 unveracity
untune 5 upset 6 bother, flurry 7 agitate,
disturb, fluster, perturb, unhinge 8 disquiet
10 discompose
untutored see **unschooled**
untwine see **untangle**
untwist see **untangle**
untypical see **unusual**
unusable 7 useless 11 impractical
12 unfunctional 13 nonfunctional
unused 4 idle 6 vacant
unusual 3 odd 4 rare 6 freaky, quaint,
unique 7 bizarre, curious, deviant, oddball,
strange 8 aberrant, abnormal, freakish,
peculiar, singular, uncommon, unwonted
9 anomalous, eccentric, untypical 10 outlandish, unordinary 11 exceptional, unthinkable 12 unimaginable 13 extraordinary
combining form: 4 anom 5 anomo

unusually 5 extra 6 rarely 8 uncommon
9 extremely 10 uncommonly
unutterable 5 awful 7 awesome 8 wondrous 9 marvelous, wonderful 10 incredible, prodigious 13 inexpressible,
unexpressible
unuttered see **unspoken**
unvaried 5 alike 7 uniform
10 monotonous
unvarnished see **undisguised**
unvarying see **unchanging**
unveil see **uncover**
unversed 3 raw 5 fresh, green 6 callow
7 untried 9 unfleshed 10 unseasoned
11 unpracticed 12 unconversant
13 inexperienced
unvigilant 6 unwary 7 unalert
9 unguarded 10 incautious, unwatchful
unvital 5 petty 6 paltry, peanut 7 trivial
8 piddling, trifling 12 inconsequent
unvoiced see **unspoken**
unwanted see **unwelcome**
unwarranted 5 undue 8 baseless
9 unfounded 10 bottomless, gratuitous,
groundless, ungrounded 11 uncalled-for
12 unreasonable 13 unjustifiable
unwary 4 rash 5 brash, hasty 7 unalert
8 reckless 9 credulous, hotheaded, unadvised, unguarded 10 ill-advised, incautious,
unvigilant 11 thoughtless 12 unsuspecting,
unsuspicious 13 inconsiderate
unwashed 3 low, mob 4 base, mean,
scum 5 dregs, lowly, trash 6 humble,
masses, rabble 7 ignoble, lowborn 8 baseborn, canaille, plebeian, riffraff 10 unennobled 11 proletariat
unwasteful 5 canny, chary 6 frugal, saving 7 sparing, thrifty 9 provident, stewardly 10 economical
unwatchful 7 unalert 9 unguarded,
unheeding 10 incautious, unnoticing, unvigilant 11 inattentive, inobservant, unobservant, unobserving 12 unperceiving
unwatered 3 dry 4 arid, sere 7 bone-dry,
thirsty 8 droughty 9 waterless
12 moistureless
unwavering see **unfaltering**
unwearying 6 steady 8 constant, tireless,
untiring 9 unceasing, weariless 10 unflagging 12 interminable 13 indefatigable,
inexhaustible
unwed see **unmarried**
unwelcome 7 unasked 8 unsought,
unwanted, unwished 9 obnoxious, repellent, undesired 10 ill-favored, unpleasant,
unpleasing 11 distasteful, undesirable
12 inadmissible, unacceptable 13 exceptionable, objectionable
unwell 3 ill, low 4 mean, sick 5 frail, rocky,
shaky 6 ailing, feeble, infirm, offish, poorly,
queasy, sickly, weakly, wobbly 7 underly

8 off-color, qualmish 9 squeamish
10 indisposed
unwholesome 4 foul 6 sickly 7 baneful,
harmful, hideous, hurtful, noxious, obscene
8 horrible 9 injurious, offensive, repellent,
repulsive, unhealthy 10 disgusting, insalutary, pernicious, unsalutary 11 deleterious,
detrimental, unhealthful 12 insalubrious
unwieldy 5 bulky, heavy 6 clumsy 7 awkward, massive, onerous, unhandy 8 cumbrous 9 lumbering, ponderous 10 burdensome, cumbersome 11 encumbering
12 inconvenient, unmanageable
unwilling 4 loth 5 loath 6 afraid, averse
7 uneager 8 backward, hesitant 9 reluctant 10 indisposed 11 disinclined
unwind 5 relax, unlax 6 unbend, unreel,
unroll 7 ease off 8 loosen up
unwise 5 inane, inept, naive 7 fatuous,
foolish, unsound, witless 8 childish, immature 9 ill-judged, impolitic, imprudent, misguided, senseless 10 ill-advised, indiscreet
11 impractical, injudicious, thoughtless,
undesirable, unfortunate 13 inappropriate,
unintelligent
unwished see **unwelcome**
unwishful 4 loth 5 loath 6 afraid, averse
7 uneager 8 backward, hesitant 9 reluctant 10 indisposed 11 disinclined
unwitting 7 unaware 8 ignorant 9 forgetful, oblivious, unknowing, unmindful
10 unfamiliar, uninformed 11 incognizant
12 inconversant, unacquainted, uninstructed
unwitty 5 silly 6 simple 7 asinine, fatuous,
foolish, witless 8 mindless 9 brainless
10 weak-headed, weak-minded
unwonted 4 rare 6 unique 7 unusual
8 singular, uncommon 10 unordinary
11 exceptional, unthinkable 12 unimaginable 13 extraordinary
unworkable 7 useless 10 impossible,
infeasible, unfeasible 11 impractical
12 unfunctional 13 nonfunctional
unworked 4 rude 5 crude, rough
6 unhewn 8 unformed 9 roughhewn,
undressed 10 unfinished, unpolished
11 unfashioned
unworkmanlike 5 inept 8 inexpert, unexpert 9 incapable, unskilled 10 unskillful
11 incompetent, inefficient
unworldly 5 naive 6 astral, dreamy, simple 7 artless, natural 9 daydreamy, ingenuous, unstudied, untutored, visionary
10 unaffected, unschooled 11 daydreaming 12 unartificial
unworthy 6 drossy, no-good 7 inutile,
nothing 9 no-account, valueless, worthless
unwrap see **uncover**
unwrinkled 6 smooth
unwritten 4 oral 6 spoken, verbal 11 traditional, word-of-mouth

unwrought see **unworked**

unyielding 4 firm, grim, hard 5 fixed, rigid, stern, stiff, tough 6 mortal, mulish 8 hardcore, hard-line, obdurate, ruthless, stubborn 9 impliable, inelastic, merciless, obstinate, pigheaded 10 bullheaded, headstrong, implacable, inexorable, inflexible, ironfisted, refractory, relentless, selfwilled, unflexible, unswayable 11 immalleable, incompliant, intractable, uncompliant, unflinching, unrelenting 12 pertinacious, single-minded, unappeasable

unyoke 5 untie 6 unbind, unlink 7 disjoin, outspan, unhitch

up 4 hike, jump, lift, rise, soar 5 arise, boost, mount, raise 6 ascend, aspire, au fait, red-hot, uprear, versed 7 abreast, versant 8 familiar, increase, informed 9 au courant 10 acquainted, conversant, down-to-date 12 contemporary *prefix:* 2 an 3 ana, sur

up-and-coming 4 keen 5 alert, eager, ready 7 go-ahead 9 gumptious 12 enterprising

upbear 4 prop 5 brace, carry 7 bolster, shore up, support, sustain 8 buttress

upbeat 4 fond 8 sanguine 10 optimistic 12 Pollyannaish

upbraid 4 lash, rate 5 scold 6 berate, revile 7 bawl out, chew out 8 bless out 10 tongue-lash, vituperate

upchuck 4 barf, spew 5 vomit 6 spit up 7 bring up, throw up 8 disgorge

upcoming 7 nearing 8 foreseen 11 approaching, prospective

up-country 4 bush 6 sticks 8 backland, backwash, frontier 9 backwater, backwoods, boondocks 10 hinterland

update 5 renew 7 refresh, restore 8 renovate 9 modernize, refurbish 10 rejuvenate

Updike novel 10 Rabbit, Run, The Centaur, Bech is Back 11 Rabbit Redux 12 Rabbit at Rest, Rabbit is Rich

upend 4 beat, drub, lick, trim, whip 6 wallop 7 clobber, shellac, trounce 9 overwhelm

upgrade 3 wax 4 hike, rise 5 boost 6 prefer 7 advance, elevate, promote 8 increase 12 breakthrough

upgrowth 8 progress 9 evolution, flowering, unfolding 10 evolvement 11 development, progression

upheaval 6 change, clamor, outcry, tumult, upturn 7 ferment, heaving 8 churning, disaster, stirring 9 cataclysm, commotion 10 alteration, convulsion 11 catastrophe

uphill 4 hard, rugged 7 arduous, labored, operose 8 toilsome 9 difficult, effortful, laborious, strenuous

uphold 3 aid 4 back, help, lift, prop, rear 5 brace, carry, hoist, raise 6 assist, bear up,

buoy up, defend, pick up, take up, upbear, uplift, uprear 7 bolster, elevate, justify, shore up, support, sustain, upraise 8 advocate, backstop, buttress, champion, maintain, side with 9 underprop, vindicate

upland 5 table 7 plateau

uplift 4 rear 5 edify, hoist, raise 6 illume, pick up, take up, uphold, uprear 7 elevate, improve, upraise 8 illumine 9 enlighten, irradiate 10 illuminate

upon 4 atop *prefix:* 2 ep 3 eph, epi

upper class 5 elite 6 flower, gentry 7 quality, society, who's who 9 blue blood, gentility 11 aristocracy

upper crust see **upper class**

upper hand 6 better 7 victory 9 advantage 11 superiority

uppermost 3 top 6 apical 7 highest 8 loftiest

uppity 5 brash 7 forward, pushful, pushing 9 presuming 11 overweening 12 presumptuous 13 self-asserting, self-assertive

upraise 4 lift, rear 5 cheer, hoist 6 buck up, pick up, solace, take up, uphold, uplift, uprear 7 comfort, console, elevate

uprear 4 lift, rise, soar 5 arise, build, erect, exalt, hoist, honor, mount, put up, raise 6 ascend, aspire, pick up, take up, uphold, uplift 7 dignify, elevate, ennoble, glorify, magnify, sublime, upraise 9 construct 10 aggrandize 11 distinguish

upright 4 fair, good, just, pure, true 5 erect, moral, noble 6 arrect, honest, raised 7 ethical, stand-up 8 elevated, virtuous 9 blameless, equitable, exemplary, honorable, impartial, righteous 10 high-minded, principled, scrupulous, straight-up, upstanding 13 conscientious *combining form:* 4 orth 5 ortho

uprightness 6 virtue 7 honesty, probity 8 morality, nobility 9 integrity, rectitude 12 reputability

uprising 6 revolt 9 rebellion 10 revolution 12 insurrection

uproar 3 din 4 coil, to-do 5 babel, brawl, broil, chaos, furor, melee, whirl 6 clamor, fracas, furore, hassle, hubbub, jangle, pother, racket, ruckus, rumpus, shindy, tumult 7 shindig, turmoil 8 brouhaha, disorder, foofaraw 9 commotion, confusion 10 hullabaloo, hurly-burly, tintamarre, turbulence 11 pandemonium

uproarious 5 noisy 7 rackety 8 clattery, noiseful, sonorous 10 clangorous

uproot 4 move 5 abate, shift 6 uptear 7 abolish, blot out, destroy, replace, subvert, wipe out 8 demolish, displace, overturn, supplant, uncreate 9 eradicate, extirpate, overthrow, supersede 10 annihilate, transplant 11 exterminate

upset 3 ail 4 bend, cark, turn 5 curve, lay

up, mix up, unman, worry **6** bother, flurry, invert, jumble, muddle, sicken, suffer, topple, tumble **7** afflict, agitate, derange, disturb, fluster, invalid, perturb, reverse, rummage, tip over, trouble, unhinge, unnerve **8** bewilder, confound, disarray, disorder, disquiet, distract, distress, overturn, turn over, unsettle **9** indispose, knock over, overthrow **10** debilitate, disarrange, discompose **12** incapacitate

upshot 4 core, gist, meat, pith **5** event, issue, sense, short **6** burden, climax, effect, ending, finish, result, sequel, thrust **7** outcome, purport **9** aftermath, substance **10** completion, conclusion **11** aftereffect, consequence, culmination, eventuality, termination

upside-down 5 snafu **7** chaotic, haywire, jumbled, mixed-up **8** confused, fouled-up, inverted, reversed **10** downside-up, topsy-turvy **13** helter-skelter

upspring 4 flow, head, rise **5** arise, get up, issue **6** uprise **7** emanate, proceed, stand up **9** originate **10** derive from

upstanding see **upright**

upstart 3 cad **4** boor, lout, slob **5** comer, rowdy **6** mucker **7** bounder, parvenu **8** outsider, roturier **9** arriviste, roughneck, vulgarian **11** guttersnipe **12** nouveau riche **13** social climber

upsurge 3 wax **4** rise **5** build, mount **6** expand **7** augment, enlarge **8** heighten, increase, multiply

uptight 4 edgy **5** nervy, tense **6** uneasy **7** restive

uptightness 6 unease **7** tension

up till 2 to **5** until **6** before **7** prior to **11** in advance of

up to 9 4 till **5** until **6** before **11** in advance of

up-to-date 6 modern, modish, red-hot, timely **7** abreast, a la mode, dashing, fitting, stylish **8** advanced, suitable **9** au courant, expedient, opportune **10** convenient **12** contemporary

Urania see **Muse**

Uranus *mother, wife:* **2** Ge **4** Gaea *offspring:* **6** Titans **8** Cyclopes *overthrower, son:* **6** Cronus

urban 4 city, town **5** civic **6** public **7** burghal, oppidan, popular, village **9** inner city, municipal **12** metropolitan

urbane 5 bland, civil, suave **6** poised, smooth **7** affable, genteel, refined **8** balanced, cultured, gracious, obliging, polished, well-bred **9** civilized, courteous, distingué **10** cultivated **12** cosmopolitan, metropolitan

urbanize 6 citify

urchin 3 imp **4** brat **5** child, gamin, scamp, whelp **7** dickens, mudlark **8** bratling

10 ragamuffin, street arab **11** guttersnipe, hobbledehoy *combining form:* **6** echino

Urdur, Urth see **Norn**

urge 3 egg, sic **4** coax, goad, itch, lust, prod, push, rush, sick, spur **5** drive, egg on, hurry, impel, press, prick, set on, shove, tar on, tarre **6** cajole, compel, desire, exhort, hustle, incite, motive, needle, prompt, propel, spring **7** craving, impulse, passion, provoke, solicit, wheedle **8** appetite, blandish, pressure **9** constrain, encourage, incentive **10** appetition **12** high-pressure

urgency 8 entreaty, exigence, instancy, pressure **10** insistence **11** importunity

urgent 6 crying **7** burning, clamant, driving, instant **8** pressing **9** clamorous, demanding, impelling, insistent **10** imperative **11** importunate

Uriah, Urijah *father:* **8** Shemaiah *slayer:* **9** Jehoiakim *son:* **8** Meremoth *wife:* **9** Bathsheba

Uriel 9 archangel *father:* **6** Kohath *grandson:* **6** Abijah

Uris, Leon *novel:* **6** Exodus **9** Battle Cry **13** The Angry Hills

Uri's son 5 Geber **7** Bezalel

urn 4 vase **5** samovar *Greek:* **7** amphora

Ursa Major 9 Great Bear

Ursa Minor 10 Little Bear *star:* **7** Polaris

Ur's son 7 Eliphal

Uruguay *capital:* **10** Montevideo *monetary unit:* **4** peso

usable 4 open **9** operative **10** accessible, functional

usage 3 way **4** form, lead, wont **5** habit, trick **6** choice, custom, manner, praxis **7** guiding, process **8** ceremony, guidance, habitude, practice **9** formality, procedure **10** convenance, convention, preference, proceeding *combining form:* **4** nomo

use 3 ply, run, way **4** duty, goal, mark, need, play, take, talk, wont, work **5** apply, avail, habit, inure, serve, speak, treat, trick, value, wield, worth **6** bestow, custom, demand, employ, govern, handle, manage, manner, object, parley, praxis, profit, target **7** account, benefit, control, exploit, fitness, operate, purpose, service, utility, utilize **8** accustom, ceremony, deal with, efficacy, exercise, exertion, function, habitude, impose on, occasion, practice, regulate **9** advantage, appliance, formality, habituate, objective, operation, relevance **10** converse in, employment, exercising, impose upon, manipulate **11** application, familiarize **12** adaptability, availability **13** applicability

used 8 shopworn **10** secondhand

used up 5 all in, spent **6** bleary, effete **7** drained, far-gone, worn-out **8** depleted **9** exhausted, washed-out

useful 3 fit **4** good, meet **5** brave, handy,

utile **6** proper, toward **7** benefic, helpful **8** favoring, suitable **9** favorable, practical **10** beneficial, convenient, functional, propitious **11** appropriate, practicable, serviceable **12** advantageous

usefulness 7 account, service, utility **9** advantage, relevance **13** applicability

useless 4 vain **6** futile **7** fustian, inutile **8** abortive, unusable **10** unavailing, unpurposed, unworkable **11** impractical, ineffective, ineffectual, unavailable **12** unfunctional, unproductive **13** impracticable, nonfunctional, unserviceable

user 6 addict **7** pothead **8** utilizer *suffix:* **4** ster

use up 3 eat **4** draw **5** drain, spend **6** devour, expend, finish **7** consume, deplete, exhaust **8** bankrupt, draw down **10** impoverish, run through

usher 4 lead **7** precede, preface **9** introduce

usher in 5 set up **6** launch **8** initiate **9** institute, introduce, originate **10** inaugurate

U.S.S.R *capital:* **6** Moscow *leader:* **6** Stalin (Joseph) **7** Kosygin (Aleksei) **8** Andropov (Yuri), Brezhnev (Leonid), Podgorny (Nikolai) **9** Chernenko (Konstantin), Gorbachev (Mikhail) **10** Khrushchev (Nikita) *monetary unit:* **5** ruble *republic:* **5** Uzbek **6** Kazakh, Kirgiz, Latvia, Russia **7** Armenia, Estonia, Georgia, Tadzhik, Turkmen, Ukraine **8** Moldavia **9** Lithuania **10** Azerbaijan, Belorussia

usual 4 rife **5** plain, typic **6** common, normal, wonted **7** chronic, current, general, natural, regular, routine, typical **8** accepted, everyday, familiar, ordinary, workaday **9** customary, plain Jane, prevalent, quotidian **10** accustomed, prevailing **11** commonplace **12** unremarkable

usually 7 as a rule **8** commonly, wontedly **9** sometimes **10** by ordinary, frequently, now and then, ordinarily **11** customarily, now and again **12** consistently, once and again

usurer 7 Shylock **9** loan shark

usurp 6 assume, cutout **7** preempt **8** accroach, arrogate, displace, supplant **10** commandeer **11** appropriate

Utah *capital:* **12** Salt Lake City *college, university:* **10** Weber State **12** Brigham Young *neighbor:* **5** Idaho **6** Nevada **7** Arizona, Wyoming **8** Colorado *nickname:* **11** Mormon State **12** Beehive State *state flower:* **8** sego lily

utensil 4 fork, tool **5** knife, spoon **8** coquille, teaspoon **9** implement **10** instrument *cooking:* see at **kitchen**

uterus 4 womb

Uther Pendragon *son:* **6** Arthur *wife:* **6** Ygerne **7** Igraine

utile 5 handy **6** useful **9** practical **10** functional **11** practicable, serviceable

utilitarian 4 hard **7** practic **9** practical, pragmatic, realistic **10** unromantic **11** down-to-earth, pragmatical **12** matter-of-fact, unidealistic *philosopher:* **4** Mill **7** Bentham

utility 3 use **7** account, fitness, service **9** advantage, relevance **10** usefulness

utilize 3 use **5** apply **6** bestow, employ, handle **7** advance, exploit, forward, further, promote **8** exercise

utmost 3 top **7** extreme, maximal, maximum, outside **8** damnedest, darndest, farthest, furthest, remotest **9** damnedest, darnedest

utopia 4 Zion **6** heaven **7** arcadia **8** paradise **9** Cockaigne, dreamland, fairyland, Shangri-la **10** dreamworld, lubberland, never-never, wonderland **12** promised land

Utopia author 4 More

utopian 5 ideal, lofty **6** edenic **7** dreamer **8** abstract, arcadian, idealist **9** ambitious, grandiose, ideologue, visionary **10** idealistic, impossible, millennial, unfeasible **11** pretentious **12** otherworldly **13** castle-builder, impracticable

Uttar Pradesh *capital:* **7** Lucknow *country:* **5** India

utter 3 say **4** blue, dang, darn, durn, pure, rank, talk, tell **5** black, blank, gross, sheer, speak, stark, state, total, voice **6** arrant, blamed, dashed, deuced **7** blasted, blessed, chime in, declare, deliver, doggone, flat-out, goldarn, perfect, regular **8** absolute, all-fired, blighted, blinding, bring out, complete, crashing, infernal, outright, positive, throw-out, vocalize **9** dad-blamed, dad-burned, downright, out-and-out, verbalize **10** blithering, confounded, consummate, dad-blasted, double-dyed **11** come out with, straight-out, unmitigated, unqualified **13** blankety-blank, thoroughgoing

utterance 4 talk, vent, word **5** parol, voice **6** speech **8** speaking, vocalism **9** discourse, statement **10** expression **12** articulation, vocalization **13** verbalization

utterly 3 all **4** just, well **5** à fond, fully, plumb, quite **6** in toto, purely, wholly **7** exactly, totally **8** all in all, entirely **9** perfectly **10** altogether, completely, thoroughly

uttermost 7 extreme **8** farthest, furthest, remotest

Utu 6 sun-god *father:* **5** Nanna *mother:* **6** Ningal

Uzai's son 5 Palal

Uzal's father 6 Joktan
Uzbek capital 8 Tashkent
Uzzah *father:* 6 Shimei 8 Abinadab *son:*
6 Shimea
Uzzi *father:* 4 Bani 5 Bukki 6 Michri *son:*
4 Elah 8 Zerahiah

Uzziah *father:* 5 Harim, Shaul 7 Amaziah
son: 6 Jotham 8 Jonathan
Uzziel *brother:* 5 Amram, Izhar *father:*
6 Kohath 8 Harhaiah, Jeduthun *grandfa-*
ther: 4 Levi *son:* 6 Sithri 7 Mishael
8 Elzaphan 9 Elizaphan

V

vacancy 4 void 6 vacuum 7 vacuity
8 voidness 9 blankness, emptiness 11 vacuousness 12 desertedness
vacant 4 bare, idle, void 5 blank, clear,
empty, inane, stark, unlet 6 unused
7 deadpan, untaken, vacuous, witless
8 unfilled 10 tenantless, unoccupied
11 emptyheaded, thoughtless 12 inexpressive, unexpressive
vacate 4 quit, void 5 annul, clear, empty,
leave, quash 6 give up, repeal, revoke
7 abandon, rescind, retract, reverse 8 abrogate, dissolve, part from, part with 9 discharge 10 relinquish
vacation 4 rest, trip 5 break, leave
6 recess 7 holiday, respite, time off 8 furlough 12 intermission *resort:* 3 spa
vacationer 7 tourist, tripper
vaccination 4 shot 7 booster 9 injection
11 inoculation
vaccine 4 shot 5 serum *inventor:*
6 Jenner
vacillate 3 wag 4 halt, swag, sway
5 dally, waver 6 dawdle, dither, falter, seesaw, teeter, waggle, wigwag, wobble
7 stagger, swither, whiffle 8 hesitate
9 alternate 12 fiddle-faddle, shilly-shally,
teeter-totter, wiggle-waggle
vacillating 4 weak 5 shaky, timid
6 dickey, fickle, unsure, wobbly 7 erratic,
halting, unfixed 8 dallying, dawdling, doubtful, doubting, hesitant, insecure, rootless,
shifting, stalling, unstable, unsteady, volatile,
wavering 9 demurring, eccentric, faltering,
fluctuant, mercurial, pendulous, tentative,
uncertain, unsettled, weak-kneed, whiffling
10 changeable, hesitating, inconstant, indecisive, irresolute, undecisive, unresolved
11 fluctuating, oscillating 12 double-
minded, shilly-shally, wiggle-waggle
13 dillydallying
vacillation 5 doubt 8 dallying, demurral,
stalling, to-and-fro, wavering 9 hesitancy

10 hesitation, indecision 12 irresolution,
shilly-shally 13 dillydallying
vacuity 4 hole, nada, void 6 cavity, hollow 7 inanity, nullity, vacancy 8 bareness,
dullness, nihility, voidness 9 blankness,
bleakness, emptiness, inaneness, stupidity
10 barrenness, hollowness 11 nothingness,
vacuousness 12 desolateness,
nonexistence
vacuous 4 bare, dull, void 5 blank, clear,
empty, inane, silly, stark 6 stupid, vacant
7 foolish, shallow 11 empty-headed,
superficial
vacuousness 7 vacancy, vacuity 8 voidness 9 blankness, emptiness
vacuum 4 void 5 space 9 emptiness
vacuum tube 5 diode 6 triode 7 pentode,
tetrode *casing:* 4 bulb *suffix:* 4 tron
vade mecum 5 guide 6 manual 8 Baedeker, handbook 9 guidebook 10 compendium 11 enchiridion
vadimonium 4 bond 6 pledge 8 contract,
security
____ **Vadis** 3 Quo
vagabond 3 bum 4 hobo, roam, rove
5 drift, gypsy, piker, range, rogue, rover,
stiff, stray, tramp 6 beggar, boomer, canter,
picaro, ramble, roamer, roving, wander
7 drifter, floater, gangrel, meander, migrant,
nomadic, swagger, swagman, traipse,
tramper, vagrant 8 bohemian, clochard,
derelict, picaroon, roadster, runabout, runagate, straggle, traveler, wanderer 9 itinerant, itinerate, straggler, transient, wandering, wayfaring 10 street arab
11 perambulant, peripatetic, Weary Willie
13 parambulatory
vagarious 5 kinky 7 erratic 8 freakish,
whimsied 9 arbitrary, whimsical 10 capricious 12 unreasonable
vagary 3 bee 4 kink, whim 5 dream,
fancy, freak, humor, quirk 6 megrim 7 bou-

tade, caprice, conceit, fantasy 8 crotchet, day-dream

vagrancy 6 roving 7 hoboism, roaming 8 nomadism, rambling 9 itinerary, wandering 10 itinerancy

vagrant see **vagabond**

vague 3 dim 4 hazy 5 blear, faint, foggy, misty, muddy, mushy 6 bleary, blurry, cloudy, dreamy, opaque, vapory 7 bleared, obscure, shadowy, unclear, unplain 8 nebulous, vaporous 9 ambiguous, dreamlike, equivocal, tenebrous, uncertain 10 ill-defined, indefinite, indistinct, unexplicit 12 undetermined 13 indeterminate, unsubstantial

vain 4 idle, puny, void 5 empty, pensy, petty, proud 6 futile, hollow, otiose, paltry 7 foppish, haughty, stuck-up, trivial, useless 8 abortive, arrogant, boastful, bootless, conceity, dandyish, delusive, delusory, egoistic, nugatory, trifling 9 conceited, fruitless, valueless, worthless 10 egocentric, misleading, profitless, unavailing 11 coxcombical, ineffective, ineffectual, unavailable 12 narcissistic, self-exalting, unproductive, unprofitable, vainglorious 13 inefficacious, self-conceited, self-important, swollen-headed

vainglorious 7 stuck-up 8 boastful, bragging, conceity, insolent, vaunting 9 conceited 10 disdainful 12 narcissistic, supercilious 13 self-conceited

vainglory 5 pride 6 egoism 7 bombast, conceit, egotism 8 parading 9 arrogance, flaunting, self-glory, self-pride 10 exhibition 11 haughtiness, self-opinion 12 boastfulness

vainness see **vanity**

valance 5 drape 7 curtain, drapery

vale 4 dale, glen 5 combe 6 valley 8 farewell

valediction 7 good-bye 8 farewell

valedictory 7 good-bye, parting 8 farewell 9 departing

valentine 4 card 7 beloved 10 sweetheart

Valentine *beloved:* 6 Silvia *sister:* 8 Margaret *slayer:* 5 Faust *twin brother:* 5 Orson *wife:* 9 Clerimond

valet 3 man 4 goad 7 servant 10 manservant

Vali *father:* 4 Odin *guardian of:* 7 justice *mother:* 4 Rind 5 Rindr *victim:* 5 Hoder

valiance see **valor**

valiant see **valorous**

valid 4 just, true 5 legal, licit, solid, sound 6 cogent, lawful, potent, strong 7 telling 8 attested, decisive, verified 9 confirmed, effective, effectual 10 acceptable, conclusive, convincing, definitive, determined, persuasive, satisfying 11 established 12 corroborated, demonstrated, satisfactory 13 determinative, substantiated

validate 5 prove 6 ratify, verify 7 approve, bear out, confirm, endorse, justify, probate 8 legalize, sanction 11 corroborate, rubber-stamp 12 authenticate, substantiate

validity 5 force, point, punch 7 cogency, gravity, potency 8 efficacy 9 soundness 13 effectiveness

validness see **validity**

valise 3 bag 4 grip 7 luggage 8 gripsack, suitcase

Valjean's pursuer 6 Javert

Valkyrie 6 maiden 8 Brynhild

valley 4 dale, dell, glen, vale 5 basin, combe, gorge, gully, swale 6 canyon, dingle, hollow, ravine, rincon 10 depression *Africa-Asia:* 4 Rift 9 Great Rift *Alps:* 11 Grindelwald *ancient Greece:* 5 Nemea *arid:* 6 bolson *California:* 4 Napa 5 Death, Squaw 8 Imperial, Yosemite 11 San Fernando *Dead Sea area:* 6 Arabah *Dominican Republic:* 5 Cibao *Egypt:* 6 Kharga *Eire:* 5 Avoca *England:* 5 Doone *Greece:* 5 Tembi, Tempe *India:* 4 Kulu 5 dhoon *Israel:* 4 Elah *Lebanon:* 4 Bika *moon:* 5 rille *New York:* 6 Sleepy 12 Sleepy Hollow *Pennsylvania:* 7 Nittany *Scotland:* 7 Glen Roy *steep:* 6 ravine *Switzerland:* 5 Hasli *Virginia:* 10 Shenandoah *volcanic:* 5 atrio *Washington:* 11 Grand Coulee

vallum 4 wall 7 rampart

Valmiki's epic 8 Ramayana

valor 4 guts, sand 6 mettle, spirit 7 bravery, courage, heroism, prowess 8 backbone, tenacity, valiance, valiancy 9 fortitude, gallantry 10 resolution

valorous 4 bold 5 brave 7 doughty, valiant 8 fearless, intrepid 9 audacious, dauntless, undaunted 10 courageous

valuable 4 dear 6 costly, prized, worthy 7 admired 8 esteemed, precious, property 9 expensive, priceless, respected, treasured 11 appreciated

valuate 4 rate 5 assay, set at 6 assess, survey 8 appraise, estimate

valuation 4 cost 5 price, worth 6 charge, rating 7 account, opinion 8 estimate, judgment 9 appraisal 10 assessment, estimation 12 appraisement

value 4 cost, rate 5 assay, gauge, merit, price, prize, set at, worth 6 assess, charge, esteem, figure, reckon, revere, survey, virtue 7 account, apprize, caliber, care for, cherish, compute, expense, quality, stature 8 appraise, estimate, treasure, venerate 9 appraisal, reverence 10 appreciate, assessment *Scottish:* 4 feck

valueless 6 draffy, drossy, no-good 7 inutile, nothing 8 unworthy 9 worthless

valve 3 tap 4 cock, gate 6 faucet, poppet,

spigot **7** hydrant, petcock, shutoff **8** stopcock *cardiac:* **6** mitral **8** bicuspid

vamoose 4 kite, scat **5** scram **6** begone,
decamp, get out **7** skiddoo, take off **8** clear
out, hightail **9** skedaddle

vamp 3 fix **4** do up, mend **5** fix up, flirt,
frame, patch, siren **6** cook up, devise,
invent, make up, repair **7** brush up,
charmer, concoct, dream up, enticer, furbish, hatch up, rebuild, touch up **8** contrive,
coquette, overhaul **9** formulate, inveigler,
refurbish, temptress **10** gold digger, seductress **11** enchantress, femme fatale, recondition, reconstruct

vampire 3 bat **7** Dracula **9** Nosferatu
11 bloodsucker

van 3 car **4** head, lead **5** truck, wagon
6 leader **7** vehicle

vandal 4 lout **6** looter, ruiner **7** defacer,
hoodlum, ravager, ruffian, spoiler, wrecker
8 hooligan, pillager, ruinator **9** despoiler,
destroyer, plunderer, spoliator **10** devasta-
tor, iconoclast

vandalize 3 mar **5** trash, wreck **6** deface,
rip off, tear up **7** destroy

Vandal king 8 Genseric

Vandyke 5 beard

vane 3 arm **9** indicator **11** weathercock

vanguard 9 forefront

Vaniah's father 4 Bani

vanilla 7 extract

vanish 3 die **4** fade, melt **5** clear **8** dissolve, evanesce, melt away **9** disappear,
evaporate **13** dematerialize

vanity 6 egoism **7** conceit **8** self-love
9 vainglory

Vanity Fair author 9 Thackeray

vanquish 4 beat **5** crush **6** defeat, humble, reduce, subdue **7** conquer, subvert,
trample **8** bear down, beat down, overturn,
surmount **9** overpower, subjugate

vanquisher 5 champ **6** master, victor,
winner **7** subduer **8** champion, defeater
9 conqueror **10** subjugator

vanquishment 4 rout **6** defeat **7** beating,
debacle, licking, mastery, subdual **8** drubbing **9** overthrow, trouncing **10** defeasance **11** shellacking, subjugation

vantage 4 draw, edge, odds **5** bulge,
start **8** deadwood, handicap **9** allowance,
head start

vapid 4 dull, flat, weak **5** inane **6** jejune
7 insipid, sapless **9** driveling, innocuous,
milk-toast, tasteless **10** flavorless, namby-
pamby, wishy-washy **13** unimaginative,
uninteresting

vapor 3 fog, gas **4** haze, mist, smog
5 brume, cloud, smoke, steam **6** breath,
nimbus *combining form:* **3** atm **4** atmo,
mano **5** atmid **6** atmido **7** pneumat

8 pneumato *condensed:* **3** dew *frozen:*
4 rime **5** frost *noxious:* **6** miasma

vaporize 4 boil **9** evaporate

vaporous 4 airy, hazy **5** foggy, gassy,
misty, mushy, vague, wispy **6** aerial, cloudy,
unreal **7** gaseous **8** ethereal, illusory
13 unsubstantial

vaquero 6 cowboy **8** herdsman

varia 10 miscellany

variable 5 fluid **6** fickle, fitful, mobile,
shifty **7** mutable, protean, unequal **8** slippery, ticklish, unstable, unsteady, volatile,
weathery **9** changeful, irregular, mercurial,
spasmodic, uncertain, unequable, unsettled,
ununiform **10** capricious, changeable,
inconstant **13** temperamental

variance 6 change, strife **7** discord, dissent **8** conflict, disunity, division, severing
9 deviation, disaccord, sundering, variation
10 contention, difference, dissension, dissidence, separation **11** fluctuation

variation 4 turn **5** shift **6** change **8** mutation, variance **9** disparity **10** alteration,
deflection, difference, divergence **11** discrepancy **12** modification **13** dissimilarity

varicolored see **variegated**

varicose 7 cirsoid, dilated, swollen

varied 5 mixed **6** motley **8** assorted,
chowchow **11** promiscuous **12** conglomerate, multifarious **13** heterogeneous,
miscellaneous

variegated 4 pied **5** pinto **6** calico, motley, mottle **7** checked, dappled, flecked,
freaked, marbled, mottled, piebald, spotted
8 discolor, skewbald, speckled, stippled,
streaked **9** checkered, multihued, spat-
tered **10** multicolor, parti-color, polychrome,
versicolor **11** varicolored **12** multicolored,
parti-colored, versicolored **13** polychromatic

variety 3 ilk **4** kind, rank, sort, type
5 grade **6** medley, nature, stripe **7** species **8** multeity **9** character, diversity, variation **10** assortment, miscellany **11** description, diverseness, variousness
12 multiformity, multiplicity
13 heterogeneity

various 4 many, some **6** divers, legion,
sundry, unlike, varied **7** certain, distant,
diverse, several, unalike, unequal, variant,
varying **8** assorted, changing, discrete, distinct, numerous, peculiar, populous, separate **9** different, disparate, divergent, unsimilar **10** dissimilar, individual, omnigenous,
voluminous **11** distinctive **12** multifarious,
multitudinal **13** heterogeneous, miscellaneous, multitudinous

varlet 5 knave **6** rascal **9** scoundrel

varmint 6 animal, rascal **7** critter

varnish 4 coat **5** glaze, japan, white
6 veneer, whiten **7** shellac **8** palliate
9 extenuate, gloss over, gloze over, sugar-

coat, whitewash **10** blanch over **compo-nent:** 5 resin

vary 3 run 4 part, turn 5 alter, range 6 change, depart, differ, divide, extend, modify, mutate 7 deviate, digress, discord, dissent, diverge, qualify 8 disagree, modu-late, separate 9 disaccord, refashion

vase 3 jar, urn 4 ewer 6 crater, krater, vessel 7 amphora, potiche 8 boughpot

Vashni's father 6 Samuel

Vashti's husband 6 Xerxes 9 Ahasuerus

vassal 4 esne, leud, serf 5 helot, liege, slave 6 tenant, varlet 7 bondman, feodary, homager, peasant, servant, subject 8 liege-man 9 dependent, underling 11 beneficiary, subordinate **high-ranking:** 7 vavasor 8 vavasour **office:** 5 feoff

vast 3 big 4 huge, wide 5 ample, broad, giant, large 6 cosmic 7 immense, titanic 8 colossal, enormous, far-flung, gigantic, spacious, whopping 9 capacious, expan-sive 10 monumental, tremendous, wide-spread 12 astronomical

vastness 8 enormity, hugeness 9 immen-sity, magnitude 12 enormousness

vat 3 tub, tun 4 back, beck, cask, kier, tank 5 keeve, kieve 6 barrel, vessel 7 cis-tern 8 cauldron **cheese:** 7 chessel

vatic 6 mantic 7 fatidic 8 Delphian, oracu-lar 9 prophetic, sibylline 11 apocalyptic, prophetical

Vatican **chapel:** 7 Sistine **church:** 11 Saint Peter's **ruler:** 4 Pope **site:** 4 Rome

vaticinal see **vatic**

vaticinate 4 call 5 augur 7 portend, pre-dict, presage 8 forecast, foretell, prophesy 9 adumbrate 13 prognosticate

vaudeville 4 song 5 revue 7 variety 9 burlesque 13 entertainment

vaudevillian 5 actor, comic 6 dancer, singer 7 acrobat 9 performer 11 entertainer

vault 3 hop, lop, pit 4 arch, cave, dome, jump, leap, over, rise, room, soar, tomb 5 bound, clear, crypt, mount 6 ascend, bounce, cavern, cellar, hurdle, spring, upleap 7 saltate 8 catacomb, overjump, overleap, surmount, upspring 9 negotiate 10 undercroft

vaulting 7 emulous 8 aspiring 9 ambi-tious 12 enthusiastic 13 opportunistic

vaunt 4 blow, brag, crow, puff 5 boast, mouth, prate 6 expose, flaunt, parade 7 display, exhibit, show off 8 brandish 9 gasconade 11 rodomontade

Ve **brother:** 4 Odin, Vili **victim:** 4 Ymir

veal 4 calf **cutlet:** 9 schnitzel **roasted:** 10 fricandeau **shank:** 8 osso buco

vector 7 carrier

Vedic **god:** 4 Agni, Soma, Vayu 5 Aditi, Bhaga, Dyaus, Indra, Mitra, Rudra 6 Aditya, Varuna 7 Savitar **goddess:** 4 Usas 5 Ushas **hymn:** 6 mantra **language:** 8 San-skrit **writing:** 7 Samhita

veer 3 dip, yaw 4 skew, slue, turn, whip 5 avert, pivot, sheer, shift, twist, wheel, whirl 6 depart, divert, swerve 7 bear off, deflect, deviate, digress, diverge 8 angle off, train off 9 volte-face

vega 5 plain 6 meadow

vegetable 3 pea, soy, yam 4 bean, beet, corn, kale, leek, okra, soya, taro, wort 5 chive, cress, green, onion, plant 6 carrot, celery, cowpea, endive, garlic, lentil, peanut, pepper, potato, radish, sorrel, squash, tomato, turnip 7 cabbage, chayote, dullard, lettuce, mustard, parsley, parsnip, pumpkin, rhubarb, salsify, shallot, soybean, spinach 8 broccoli, collards, cucumber, eggplant, kohlrabi, lima bean, rutabaga, scallion 9 artichoke, asparagus, muskmelon 10 watermelon 11 cauliflower, horseradish, sweet potato **dish:** 5 salad **mold:** 5 humus **oyster:** 7 salsify **pear:** 7 chayote **seller:** 6 grocer 7 grocery 12 costermonger **sponge:** 5 luffa **spread:** 4 oleo 9 margarine

vegetarian 9 herbivore

vegetate 4 idle, laze 8 languish, stagnate 9 hibernate

vegetation 5 flora 6 growth, plants 7 ver-dure 8 greenery **floating:** 4 sudd 8 pleuston

vehement 3 hot 4 wild 5 rabid 6 ardent, fervid, fierce, hearty, heated, lively, potent 7 fervent, frantic, furious, intense, vicious, violent, zealous 8 emphatic, forceful, pow-erful, terrible 9 delirious, desperate, ener-getic, exquisite, perfervid 10 passionate, pronounced 11 impassioned 12 concentrated

vehicle 3 bus, car, van 4 auto, tool 5 agent, buggy, means, organ, sedan, wagon 6 agency, medium, vector 7 carrier, channel 8 ministry 9 implement, transport 10 automobile, conveyance, instrument **baby's:** 4 pram 6 carriage, stroller **child's:** 4 bike 5 trike 7 bicycle, scooter 8 tricycle **combining form:** 6 mobile **farm:** 4 wain 7 tractor **horse-drawn:** 4 cart, dray 5 buggy, lorry, sulky, wagon 6 han-som, landau 8 carriage **military:** 4 jeep, tank **one-wheeled:** 8 unicycle **passenger:** 3 bus, cab, car 4 auto, taxi 7 ricksha **pub-lic:** 3 bus 4 tram 5 train 6 subway 7 omnibus, trolley **Roman:** 7 chariot **win-ter:** 4 sled 6 sleigh 8 snowplow

veil 4 hide, mask, wrap 5 cloak, color, cover, front, guise 6 enfold, enwrap, facade, invest, mantle, screen, shroud 7 blanket, conceal, cover up, curtain, enclose, envelop, secrete **8** calyptra, coloring, disguise, enshroud **10** camouflage, false front, overspread, spread over *Muslim:* **7** yashmak *netting:* **6** maline **7** malines

vein 3 way **4** hint, line, lode, mind, mode, mood, seam, tone, tube, vena **5** humor, shade, style, tenor, tinge, touch, trace **6** fettle, manner, nature, spirit, strain, streak, temper, vessel **7** channel, fashion **8** tincture **9** character, suspicion **10** complexion, suggestion **11** disposition, temperament *combining form:* **3** ven **4** veni, veno **5** phleb **6** phlebo *deposit:* **3** ore *fluid:* **5** blood *leaf:* **3** rib *leg:* **7** saphena *neck:* **7** jugular *small:* **6** venule *varicose:* **5** varix

velar 7 palatal

veldt 5 plain **6** meadow **9** grassland

velitation 5 brush, run-in, set-to **8** skirmish **9** encounter

velleity 4 mind, will, wish **5** fancy **6** liking **8** pleasure, volition **11** inclination

vellicate 3 jig, lug, nip **4** jerk, snap, yank **5** lurch, pinch **6** fidget, jiggle, twitch

velocipede 4 bike **5** cycle **7** bicycle **10** two-wheeler

velocity 3 bat **4** gait, pace **5** haste, hurry, speed **7** headway, impetus **8** celerity, dispatch, momentum, rapidity **9** quickness, rapidness, swiftness **10** expedition

velum 4 veil **8** membrane

velvet 5 cloth **6** fabric, profit **8** winnings *on:* **4** rich, safe **7** wealthy

velvety 4 soft **5** plush, silky, sleek, slick **6** glossy, plushy, satiny, silken, smooth **7** cottony **10** velutinous

venal 4 hack, paid **6** sordid **7** buyable, corrupt, crooked, ignoble, vicious **8** bribable, hireling, infamous **9** mercenary, nefarious, unethical **10** flagitious, iniquitous, praetorian **11** corruptible, purchasable **12** unprincipled, unscrupulous

vend 4 give, hawk, sell, toot **5** sound **6** blazon, market, monger, peddle **7** declare, publish **8** announce, huckster, proclaim **9** advertise, broadcast **10** promulgate

vendee 5 buyer **6** emptor **9** purchaser

vendetta 4 feud **9** blood feud

vendible 7 salable **8** sellable **10** marketable

vendibles 5 goods, wares **11** commodities, merchandise

vendor 6 duffer, hawker, seller **7** higgler, packman, peddler, roadman **8** huckster, merchant, outcrier, salesman **9** cheap-jack, cheap-john

vendue 5 sale **7** auction

veneer 4 face, mask, show, veil **5** cover, front, gloss, white **6** facade, whiten **7** coating, varnish **8** disguise, palliate **9** extenu-

ate, gloss over, gloze over, sugarcoat, whitewash **10** blanch over, false front

venerable 3 old **4** aged **5** hoary **6** ageold, sacred **7** ancient, antique, elderly, honored, revered, stately **8** imposing, Noachian, reverend, timeworn **9** admirable, dignified, estimable, honorable **10** reverenced, worshipful **11** patriarchal, reverential **12** antediluvian

venerate 5 adore, honor **6** revere **7** idolize, worship **9** reverence

veneration 3 awe **5** dulia, honor **6** esteem, homage **7** respect, worship **9** reverence

venery 4 game **5** chase **7** hunting

venesection 10 phlebotomy **12** bloodletting

Venetian *boat:* **7** gondola *boatman:* **9** gondolier *canal:* **3** rii (plural), rio *ruler:* **4** doge *street:* **5** canal

Venezuela *capital:* **7** Caracas *monetary unit:* **7** bolivar

Venezuelan *herdsman:* **7** llanero *liberator:* **7** Bolivar *people:* **5** Carib **6** Timote

venge 9 redress **9** vindicate

vengeance 6 return **7** revenge **8** avenging, reprisal, requital, revanche **9** repayment **10** avengement **11** counterblow, retaliation, retribution

vengeful 7 hostile **8** inimical, wreakful **9** rancorous **10** vindictive **12** antagonistic

venial 5 minor **7** trivial **8** harmless, trifling **9** allowable, excusable, tolerable **10** forgivable, pardonable, remittable **13** insignificant

Venice of the East 7 Bangkok

Venice of the North 9 Stockholm

Veni, Creator ___ 8 Spiritus

venireman 5 juror

venison 4 deer

veni, vidi, ___ 4 vici

venom 4 bane **5** virus **6** poison, rancor **7** ill will, vitriol **9** contagion, malignity, virulence

venomous 5 toxic **6** deadly, malign, poison **7** baleful, malefic **8** mephitic, toxicant, viperish, viperous, virulent **9** malignant, poisonous, viperlike **10** maleficent, malevolent

vent 3 air, put **4** emit, give, hole, slit, slot **5** issue, loose, state, utter, voice **6** assert, outlet **7** cast out, declare, exhaust, express, give off, give out, opening, orifice, release, unleash **8** aperture, throw off **9** discharge, statement, take out on, utterance **10** expression **12** articulation, vocalization **13** verbalization

venter 3 gut **5** belly **6** paunch **7** abdomen, stomach

ventilate 3 air, put **4** give, moot **5** state **6** broach, debate, go into, take up, talk of **7** bring up, discuss, express, publish **8** rap about, talk over **9** advertise, broadcast, introduce, thresh out **10** deliberate

ventral area 7 abdomen *combining form:* **5** gastr **6** gaster, gastri, gastro **7** gastero

ventricle 7 chamber *combining form:* **4** cele, coel **5** coele

ventriloquist *companion:* **5** dummy *famous:* **6** Bergen

venture 3 bet, try **4** dare, defy, face, feat, gest, risk **5** beard, brave, crack, fling, front, peril, stake, wager **6** banter, chance, expose, gamble, hazard **7** attempt, emprise, exploit, imperil, jeopard, lay open, operate, outdare, outface, play for **8** endanger, jeopardy **9** adventure, challenge, speculate **10** enterprise, jeopardize **11** speculation, undertaking

venturesome 4 bold, rash **5** brave, stout **6** daring, sturdy **8** overbold, reckless, stalwart **9** audacious, daredevil, foolhardy **11** adventurous, temerarious

venturous see **venturesome**

venue 4 side, site **5** place **6** ground, locale

Venus 6 planet, Vesper **8** Hesperus; (see also **Aphrodite**)

Venus de ___ 4 Milo

veracious 4 just, true **5** right, valid **6** direct, strict **8** accurate, faithful, truthful **9** veridical **11** true-tongued, undeceitful, undeceptive, undistorted, unvarnished **12** truth-telling **13** truth-speaking

veracity 4 fact **5** truth **6** gospel, truism, verity **7** honesty **8** accuracy **9** actuality, exactness, frankness **11** correctness, factualness **12** truthfulness, veridicality

veranda 5 lanai, porch **6** piazza **7** balcony, gallery, portico

verb *auxiliary:* **2** am, be, do, is **3** are, can, did, had, has, may, was **4** have, must, were, will **5** could, might, shall, would **6** should *form:* **6** active, gerund **7** passive **10** infinitive, participle *kind:* **10** transitive **12** intransitive *linking:* **6** copula *mood:* **8** optative **10** imperative, indicative **11** subjunctive *suffix:* (see at **suffix**) *tense:* **4** past **6** aorist, future **7** perfect, present **9** predicate **10** pluperfect

verbal 4 oral **6** spoken **7** literal **8** verbatim **9** unwritten **11** traditional, word-forword, word-of-mouth

verbalism 6 phrase **7** diction, styling, wordage, wording **8** parlance, phrasing, verbiage **9** prolixity, verbosity, windiness, wordiness **10** prolixness **11** phraseology, verboseness

verbalization 4 talk **6** speech **8** speaking **9** discourse, utterance

verbalize 3 air, say **4** give, talk, vent, word **5** speak, state, utter, voice **7** express **8** vocalize **9** ventilate

verbatim 5 close, exact **6** direct, strict, verbal **7** exactly, literal, precise **8** directly, faithful **9** literally, literatim, precisely **10** accurately **11** word-for-word

verbiage 6 phrase **7** diction, wordage, wording **8** parlance, phrasing, pleonasm **9** floridity, tautology, verbalism, verbality, verbosity **10** floridness, periphrase, redundancy, roundabout **11** periphrasis, phraseology

verbose 5 windy, wordy **6** prolix **7** diffuse, flowery **9** redundant **10** long-winded, palaverous, pleonastic **11** tautologous **12** magniloquent, periphrastic **13** grandiloquent

verboseness see **verbosity**

verbosity 7 bombast **8** verbiage **9** prolixity, verbalism, windiness, wordiness **10** prolixness, redundancy **11** verboseness

verboten 5 taboo **6** banned **8** outlawed **9** forbidden **10** disallowed, prohibited, unlicensed **11** disapproved **12** unauthorized, unsanctioned

verdant 3 raw **5** green **6** grassy

verdict 6 ruling **7** finding, opinion **8** decision, judgment

Verdi opera 4 Aida **6** Ernani, Oberto, Otello **7** Nabucco **8** Don Carlo, Falstaff **9** Rigoletto **10** La Traviata **11** Il Trovatore

verdure 5 green **7** foliage, leafage, umbrage **8** greenery **10** vegetation

verge 3 hem, lip, rim **4** abut, brim, edge, join, lean, line **5** bound, brink, march, point, skirt, touch **6** adjoin, border, butt on, fringe, margin, tend to, trench **7** incline, outline, selvage, touch on **8** approach, neighbor, surround **9** threshold, touch upon **10** border line, tend toward **11** butt against, communicate

Vergil *epic:* **6** Aeneid *poems:* **8** Bucolics, Georgics

veridical see **veracious**

verification 5 proof **12** confirmation

verify 3 try **4** test **5** prove **6** settle **7** bear out, confirm, justify **8** document, validate **9** establish **11** corroborate, demonstrate **12** authenticate, substantiate

verily 3 yea **4** even **5** truly **6** indeed

verisimility 5 color **12** plausibility

veritable 4 real, true, very **6** actual **7** factual, genuine **8** bona fide, undenied **9** authentic, undoubted, unrefuted **10** sureenough **11** indubitable

verity 5 truth **6** gospel, truism **8** veracity **12** truthfulness, veridicality **13** veraciousness

vermeil 4 ruby

vermiform 8 wormlike

vermilion 3 red

vermin 4 lice, mice, rats **5** fleas **7** bedbugs

verminous 6 filthy 7 noxious 9 offensive

Vermont *capital:* 10 Montpelier *college, university:* 7 Norwich 10 Middlebury, St. Michaels *state bird:* 12 hermit thrush *state flower:* 9 red clover

vernacular 4 cant 5 argot, idiom, lingo, slang 6 jargon, patois, patter, speech, tongue, vulgar 7 dialect, vulgate 8 language 10 colloquial 12 mother tongue

vernacularism 8 slangism, solecism 9 barbarism, vulgarism 10 corruption 11 impropriety

vernal 6 spring 10 springlike

Verne, Jules *character:* 4 Fogg (Phileas), Nemo 12 Passepartout *submarine:* 8 Nautilus

versant 2 up 6 au fait 7 abreast 8 familiar, informed 9 au courant 10 acquainted

versatile 4 able 5 handy 6 adroit, facile, gifted, mobile 7 elastic, plastic, pliable, skilled 8 flexible, skillful, talented 9 adaptable, all-around, dexterous, many-sided 10 conversant 11 well-rounded

verse 3 lay, ode 4 epic, poem, rune, song 5 lyric, poesy, rhyme, stich 6 ballad, jingle, poetry, sonnet, stanza 11 familiarize *analysis:* 8 scansion *four-line:* 8 quatrain *six-line:* 6 sestet *three-line:* 6 tercet *two-line:* 7 couplet *writer:* 4 poet; (see also **poem**)

versed 2 up 3 old, vet 5 adept 6 au fait 7 abreast, old-time, skilled, versant, veteran 8 familiar, informed, seasoned 9 au courant, competent, practical, practiced 10 acquainted, conversant 11 experienced

verseman 4 bard, poet 6 rhymer 9 poetaster, rhymester, versifier 12 balladmonger

versicolor see **variegated**

versifier see **verseman**

version 4 tale 5 story 6 report 7 account, history, reading 9 chronicle, narrative, rendering, rendition, rewording 10 paraphrase 11 restatement, translation 12 condensation 13 clarification, restipulation

versus 3 con 6 contra 7 against, vis-à-vis 11 over against

vertebra 4 bone *combining form:* 7 spondyl 8 spondyli (plural), spondylo 9 spondylus *kind:* 6 dorsal, lumbar, sacral 8 cervical, thoracic

vertebrae 4 back 5 spine 6 rachis 8 backbone 12 spinal column

vertebrate 6 animal *characteristic:* 5 spine 7 cranium *kind:* 4 bird, fish, frog 5 shark 6 mammal 7 lamprey, reptile

vertex 3 cap, top 4 apex, peak, roof 5 crest, crown 6 apogee, summit, tip-top, zenith 9 fastigium

Verthandi see **Norn**

vertical 5 erect, plumb, sheer, steep 7 upright 9 up-and-down 10 straight-up

13 perpendicular *combining form:* 4 orth 5 ortho

vertiginous 5 dizzy, giddy, light 6 rotary, swimmy 8 swimming 11 light-headed

vertigo 6 megrim 9 dizziness

verve 3 pep, vim, zip 4 brio, dash, élan, fire, life, zest, zing 5 gusto, oomph 6 bounce, esprit, spirit, spring 8 buoyancy, vivacity 9 animation 10 elasticity, liveliness, resiliency

very 2 so 3 too 4 bare, mere, most, much, real, same, true 5 ideal, model, pesky, quite, super, truly 6 damned, highly, hugely, mighty, really 7 awfully, de facto, genuine, greatly, notably, parlous, precise, vitally 8 actually, bona fide, mightily, mortally, rattling, selfsame, snapping, spanking, terribly, whacking, whopping 9 authentic, eminently, extremely, genuinely, identical, tellingly, undoubted, veritable, veritably 10 dreadfully, insatiably, remarkably, strikingly, sureenough, thoroughly 11 exceedingly, indubitable 12 surpassingly 13 exceptionally *French:* 4 très *German:* 4 sehr *Scottish:* 3 gey

vesicle 3 sac 4 cyst 6 cavity 7 bladder, blister

Vesper 5 Venus 8 Hesperus 11 evening star

vespers 6 prayer 7 service 8 evensong

____ **Vespucci** 7 Amerigo

vessel 3 ama, can, cup, jar, pan, pot, pyx, tub, urn 4 boat, bowl, drum, ewer, pail, ship, tank, tube, vase, vein 5 canal, craft, cruse, laver 6 artery, barrel, bottle, bucket, firkin, flagon, kettle, krater, pottle, situla 7 cresset, pitcher 8 crucible 10 receptacle *combining form:* 3 vas 4 ange, angi, vasi, vaso 5 angia (plural), angio 6 angium, arteri, vascul 7 arterio, vasculo *drinking:* 3 cup, mug 4 toby 5 cylix, flask, glass, gourd, kylix, stein, stoup 6 goblet, seidel 7 tankard, tumbler *Indian:* 4 lota 5 lotah *sailing:* (see at **ship**) *Scottish:* 3 cog 6 cootie, quaich, quaigh 7 yetling

vest 4 coat 6 belong, invest, jacket, weskit 7 empower, pertain 9 appertain, authorize, waistcoat

Vesta see **Hestia**

vestal 3 nun 4 pure 6 chaste, virgin 8 virginal

vestibule 4 hall 5 entry, foyer, lobby 6 portal 7 narthex, portico 8 anteroom, entryway 11 antechamber 12 entrance hall

vestige 3 rag, tag 4 path, step 5 relic, scrap, spoor, trace, track, tract, trail 6 shadow 7 memento, remains, remnant 8 footstep 9 footprint, remainder

vestment 3 alb 4 cope, garb, gown, pall, robe 5 amice, cotta, dress, fanon, orale, stole, tunic 6 rochet, sakkos 7 cassock, garment, maniple, pallium, tunicle **8** chasuble, cincture, dalmatic, parament, surplice **9** phelonion *ancient Hebrew:* **5** ephod

vestry 4 room **6** closet **8** sacristy

vesture 5 cover **6** clothe **7** apparel, costume, envelop, garment **8** clothing

Vesuvius 7 volcano

vetch 4 tare *bitter:* **3** ers **5** ervil

veteran 4 wise **6** expert, master, versed **7** old hand, old-time, skilled, worldly **8** old-timer, seasoned **9** longtimer, practical, practiced **10** past master **11** experienced **13** sophisticated

veto 3 nix **4** deny, kill **6** defeat, forbid, refuse, reject **7** decline **8** disallow, negative, prohibit **9** blackball, non-placet

vex 3 bug, ire, irk **4** chaw, fret, gall **5** anger, annoy, chafe, tease **6** abrade, bother, plague **7** provoke, torment **8** exercise **9** embarrass, infuriate

vexation 6 irking **9** annoyance, bothering, provoking **10** harassment, irritation **11** aggravation, bedevilment, provocation

vexatious 4 mean, ugly **5** pesky **6** wicked **9** troublous **11** troublesome

via 2 by **3** per **4** over, road, with **5** along **7** by way of, passage, through **8** by dint of **9** by means of **10** by virtue of

viable 6 doable **8** feasible, possible, workable **11** practicable

viaduct 6 bridge

vial 5 ampul, flask, glass, phial **6** ampule, beaker, bottle, vessel **7** ampoule **8** test tube

viands 4 eats, fare, feed, food, grub **7** edibles, nurture **8** victuals **9** provender **10** provisions **11** comestibles

viator 8 traveler, wayfarer

vibrant 5 alive, round, vital **6** rotund **7** orotund, ringing **8** plangent, resonant, sonorant, sonorous **9** consonant **10** resounding

vibrate 3 jar **4** rock **5** quake, shake, trill, twang **6** shiver, tremor **7** shudder, tremble

vibration 4 vibe **5** quake, shake, trill **6** quaver, quiver, tremor **7** flutter, shaking **8** fremitus **9** trembling **11** oscillation *Scottish:* **6** dindle

vicar 6 priest **8** minister **9** clergyman

Vicar of Wakefield *author:* **9** Goldsmith *character:* **8** Primrose

vice 3 ill, sin **4** evil, flaw **5** fault, wrong **6** defect, foible **7** blemish, failing, frailty **9** depravity, indecency **10** corruption, debasement, debauchery, immorality, perversion, unchastity, wickedness **11** shortcoming

vice-president 4 veep **9** executive *American:* **4** Burr, Bush, Ford, King **5** Adams, Agnew, Dawes, Gerry, Nixon, Tyler **6** Arthur, Colfax, Curtis, Dallas, Garner, Hamlin, Hobart, Morton, Quayle, Truman,

Wilson **7** Barkley, Calhoun, Clinton, Johnson, Mondale, Sherman, Wallace, Wheeler **8** Coolidge, Fillmore, Humphrey, Marshall, Tompkins, Van Buren **9** Fairbanks, Hendricks, Jefferson, Roosevelt, Stevenson **11** Rockefeller **12** Breckinridge

viceroy 5 nabob, ruler **6** exarch, satrap **7** khedive **8** governor **9** butterfly

vice versa 10 contrawise, conversely **12** contrariwise

vicinage 4 area **8** district, locality, vicinity **12** neighborhood

vicinity 4 area **5** range **6** extent, matter, region **8** district, locality, nearness, vicinage **9** magnitude, proximity **12** neighborhood

vicious 4 evil, mean, wild **5** feral, wrong **6** fierce, malign, putrid, rotten, savage, sinful, wicked **7** brutish, corrupt, furious, hateful, immoral, intense, violent **8** depraved, infamous, perverse, spiteful, terrible, vehement **9** desperate, malicious, malignant, miscreant, nefarious, rancorous, reprobate **10** degenerate, despiteful, flagitious, iniquitous, malevolent, villainous **12** blood-thirsty

vicissitude 5 rigor, trial **6** change **7** novelty, variety **8** asperity, hardness, hardship, mutation, reversal **9** adversity, diversity, mischance **10** affliction, difficulty, innovation, misfortune **11** permutation, progression, tribulation, ups and downs

victim 4 butt, dupe, fool, gull, mark, prey **5** chump **6** pigeon, quarry, sucker **7** fall guy, gudgeon **8** casualty, offering, underdog **9** bottom dog, sacrifice

victimize 4 dupe, fool, gull, hoax **5** trick **6** pigeon **8** flimflam, hoodwink, immolate **9** bamboozle, sacrifice **11** hornswoggle

victor 3 top **5** champ, first **6** master, winner **7** subduer **8** champion, defeater **9** conquerer **10** subjugator, vanquisher

Victoria, Queen *family:* **7** Hanover *father:* **6** Edward *husband:* **6** Albert *son:* **6** Edward

Victorian 4 prig, prim **6** prissy, stuffy **10** old-maidish, tight-laced **11** puritanical, straitlaced **12** old-fashioned

victory 3 win **6** better **7** command, control, mastery, success, triumph **8** conquest, dominion, walkaway, walkover, whip hand **9** advantage, supremacy, upper hand **11** subjugation, superiority *costly:* **7** Pyrrhic *easy:* **8** cakewalk, walkaway *monument:* **4** arch **13** Arc de Triomphe *reward:* **6** spoils *sign:* **3** vee *symbol:* **4** flag **6** laurel, wreath

Victory author 6 Conrad

victuals 4 chow, eats, feed, food, grub **6** viands **7** edibles **9** provender **10** provisions **11** comestibles

____ Vidal 4 Gore

videlicet 3 viz 5 to wit 6 namely 8 scilicet

vie 3 pit 5 match, rival 6 oppose, outvie 7 compete, contend, contest, counter, play off 9 challenge

Viennese *city hall:* 7 Rathaus *family:* 8 Hapsburg *palace:* 7 Hofburg *park:* 6 Prater

Vientiane's land 4 Laos

Vietnam *Capital:* 5 Hanoi *monetary unit:* 4 dong

Vietnamese New Year 3 Tet

view 3 aim, con, eye, see, vet 4 deem, espy, goal, look, mark, mind, plan, scan 5 audit, scene, sight, study, vista 6 behold, belief, descry, design, look at, notice, notion, object, regard, review, survey 7 canvass, check up, discern, examine, feeling, inspect, observe, opinion, outlook, picture, scenery 8 analysis, consider, gaze upon, look upon, panorama, perceive, prospect, scrutiny 9 check over, objective, sentiment 10 conviction, inspection, persuasion, scrutinize 11 contemplate, distinguish, examination, perlustrate 13 perlustration

viewable 6 ocular, visual 7 seeable, visible

viewer 7 watcher, witness 8 beholder, bysitter, looker-on, observer, onlooker 9 bystander, spectator 10 eyewitness

viewing instrument 5 glass, scope 7 glasses 9 telescope 10 binoculars, microscope *combining form:* 5 scope

viewpoint 3 eye 4 side 5 angle, slant, stand 7 outlook, posture 8 attitude, position 9 direction 10 estimation, standpoint 11 perspective

vigil 4 tout 5 watch 7 lookout 12 surveillance, watch and ward

vigilance see **vigil**

vigilant 4 agog, avid, keen 5 acute, alert, awake, aware, eager, sharp 7 anxious, wakeful 8 open-eyed, watchful 9 attentive, sharp-eyed, wide-awake 10 unsleeping

vignette 5 scene 6 sketch 7 picture 8 ornament

vigor 3 pep, vim, zip 4 bang, beef, birr, dash, fire, push, snap, tuck, zing 5 drive, force, getup, might, moxie, oomph, power, punch, steam 6 bounce, energy, muscle, spirit, starch 7 ability, potency 8 dynamism, strength, virility, vitality 9 hardihood, lustiness, manliness, puissance, soundness 10 capability, enterprise, get-up-and-go 11 healthiness

vigorous 5 brisk, hardy, husky, lusty, proud, stout, tough, vital 6 hearty, lively, potent, robust, sinewy, strong, sturdy 7 dashing, driving, dynamic, healthy, zealous 8 athletic, bouncing, muscular, powerful, slashing, spirited 9 energetic, exuberant, masterful, strenuous 10 mettlesome,

red-blooded, survigrous 11 hard-driving, hard-hitting 13 rough-and-ready

Viking see **Norse**

vile 3 low 4 base, evil, foul, mean, ugly 5 gross, nasty 6 coarse, horrid, sordid, vulgar 7 debased, ignoble, low-down, noisome, obscene, servile, squalid 8 depraved, wretched 9 abhorrent, corrupted, debauched, loathsome, offensive, perverted, repugnant, repulsive, revolting 10 despicable, disgusting 12 contemptible

Vili *brother:* 2 Ve 4 Odin *victim:* 4 Ymir

vilify 5 abuse, libel 6 assail, attack, berate, defame, malign, misuse 7 asperse, outrage, slander, traduce 8 denounce, mistreat, tear down 9 denigrate 10 calumniate, villainize

villa 5 manor 6 castle, estate 7 chateau, mansion

village 4 burg, town 5 bourg, thorp 6 hamlet 7 townlet *African:* 4 dorp, stad 5 kraal *Indian:* 6 bustee, pueblo *Japanese:* 4 mura *Jewish:* 6 shtetl *Malay:* 7 campong, kampong *Russian:* 3 mir

Village Blacksmith author 10 Longfellow

villain 4 heel 5 devil, heavy, knave, rogue, scamp 6 meanie, rascal, sinner 7 lowlife 8 criminal, evildoer, mischief, offender, roperipe, scalawag 9 miscreant, reprobate, scoundrel, skeezicks 10 blackguard, malefactor 11 rapscallion *classic:* 4 Iago

villainous 6 putrid, rotten 7 corrupt, debased, heinous, vicious 8 contrary, infamous, perverse 9 abandoned, atrocious, dissolute, miscreant, nefarious, offensive, perverted 10 degenerate, detestable, flagitious, outrageous, profligate 13 objectionable

villainy 5 crime 9 depravity

villein 7 peasant 8 villager

villenage 4 yoke 6 thrall 7 bondage, helotry, peonage, serfdom, slavery 9 servitude, thralldom 11 enslavement

vim 4 brio, dash, élan, kick, life, push, zing 5 oomph, verve 6 esprit, pepper, spirit 9 animation

vinaigrette 3 box 4 cart 5 sauce, wagon 6 bottle

vinculum 3 tie 4 bond, knot, link, yoke 5 nexus 8 ligament, ligature

vindicable 6 venial 7 tenable 9 excusable 10 condonable, defensible 11 inoffensive, justifiable, warrantable

vindicate 4 free 5 argue, claim, clear, guard, prove, venge 6 acquit, assert, avenge, defend, refute, second, shield, uphold 7 absolve, bear out, confute, contend, justify, protect, redress, revenge, support, warrant 8 advocate, disprove, maintain, plead for **9** exculpate, exonerate **10** disculpate **11** rationalize

vindictive 5 nasty **6** malign **8** punitive, spiteful, vengeful, wreakful **9** malicious, malignant, merciless **10** implacable, relentless, revengeful **11** unrelenting

vine 3 hop, ivy, pea **4** gogo, soma **5** betel, buaze, guaco, kudzu, liana, liane, luffa, maile **6** cowage, cowpea, loofah, maypop **7** chayote, climber, copihue, creeper, cupseed **8** catbrier, clematis **10** chile-bells **11** bittersweet *combining form:* **4** viti *East Indian:* **6** pikake

vinegar 3 vim **6** acetum **8** sourness *combining form:* **4** acet **5** aceto *relating to:* **6** acetic *steep in:* **6** pickle

vinegarish 4 sour **5** waspy **6** bitter, cranky, ornery **7** bearish, waspish **8** cankered **9** crotchety, irascible **12** cantankerous, cross-grained

Vinegar Joe 8 Stilwell

vinegary 4 sour **6** acetic **7** acetose, acetous

vineyard 7 grapery *French:* **3** cru

Vinland discoverer 7 Ericson **8** Ericsson

vintage 3 old **4** crop, wine **5** dated, passé **6** démodé **7** antique, archaic, classic, harvest **8** outdated, outmoded **9** classical **10** antiquated **12** old-fashioned

Viola *brother:* **9** Sebastian *husband:* **6** Orsino

Viola da ____ 5 gamba

violate 3 err, sin **4** rape **5** break, force, spoil **6** breach, defile, offend, ravish **7** infract, outrage **8** deflower, infringe, overpass, trespass **9** deflorate, disregard, trample on **10** contravene, transgress **11** trample upon

violation 5 break, crime, wrong **6** breach **7** offense **8** defacing, trespass **9** blasphemy, sacrilege **10** defacement, illegality, infraction **11** desecration, misdemeanor, profanation **12** encroachment, infringement **13** contravention, transgression

violence 4 fury, riot **5** clash, force **6** attack, duress, frenzy, tumult, uproar **7** assault, rampage **8** coercion, foul play, savagery, struggle **9** onslaught **10** compulsion, constraint

violent 5 acute, harsh, rough **6** fierce, mighty, potent, strong **7** cutting, extreme, furious, intense, vicious **8** forceful, forcible, piercing, powerful, terrible, vehement **9** desperate, exquisite, splitting **10** immoderate, inordinate **11** destructive **12** concentrated

violently 4 hard **5** madly **6** wildly **8** fiercely, stormily **9** furiously, ruinously **10** frenziedly **11** combatively, frantically, turbulently **12** tumultuously **13** destructively

violet 5 mauve **6** flower, purple

violin 6 fiddle **10** instrument *kind:* **4** bass **5** Amati, cello, Strad **7** quinton **10** double bass, Guarnerius, Stradivari **12** Stradivarius *part:* **3** bow, nut, peg, rib **4** neck **5** belly **6** bridge, corner, pegbox, saddle, scroll, string **8** chin rest, purfling **11** fingerboard *precursor:* **5** gigue, rabab, rebec **6** vielle

violinist *American:* **5** Elman, Fodor, Rabin, Ricci, Stern **6** Midori, Powell, Rosand **7** Heifetz, Menuhin, Szigeti **8** Kreisler, Milstein, Spalding, Zukofsky **9** Zimbalist *Belgian:* **5** Ysaye **8** Grumiaux *Canadian:* **6** Staryk *Czech:* **3** Suk *French:* **12** Francescatti *German:* **9** Hindemith *Hungarian:* **6** Tatrai **7** Joachim *Israeli:* **7** Perlman **8** Zukerman *Italian:* **6** Viotti **7** Corelli, Vivaldi **8** Paganini **9** Geminiani *Romanian:* **6** Enesco *Russian:* **8** Oistrakh

violin maker 4 Salo **5** Amati **7** Maggini **8** Guarneri **10** Stradivari

VIP 4 lion **6** biggie, bigwig, fat cat, leader **7** big shot, notable, someone **8** big wheel, luminary, somebody **9** big cheese

viper 3 asp **5** adder, snake **10** bushmaster, copperhead, fer-de-lance **11** rattlesnake

virago 5 harpy, scold, shrew, vixen **6** amazon, ogress **8** fishwife **9** termagant, Xanthippe

Virgil see **Vergil**

virgin 3 new **4** pure **5** fresh, unwed **6** intact, maiden, single, vestal **8** celibate, innocent, primeval, pristine, unmarred, untapped **9** abstinent, unmarried, unspoiled, unsullied, untouched **10** spouseless **12** undeflowered *combining form:* **7** parthen **8** partheno

virginal 4 pure **6** intact, maiden **8** untapped **9** unspoiled, untouched **12** undeflowered

Virgin Goddess 5 Diana **7** Artemis

Virginia *capital:* **8** Richmond *college, institute, university:* **7** Hampton **8** Richmond **11** Old Dominion **13** Randolph Macon **14** William and Mary *nickname:* **11** Old Dominion *state bird:* **8** cardinal

Virginian, The *author:* **6** Wister *character:* **7** Trampas

Virgin Islands of the U.S. 6 St. John **7** St. Croix **8** St. Thomas

virginity 6 purity **8** chastity **10** chasteness, maidenhead, maidenhood

Virgin Queen 10 Elizabeth I

Virgo star 5 Spica

viridity 5 youth **9** freshness, greenness, innocence

virile 4 male **5** manly **6** manful, potent, robust **7** driving, manlike, mannish **8** decisive, forceful **9** energetic, masculine

virose 5 fetid **6** poison **9** poisonous

virtual 5 basic 8 implicit 9 essential, practical 11 fundamental 12 constructive

virtuality 4 pith, soul 5 stuff 6 bottom, marrow 7 essence 9 substance 12 essentiality, quintessence

virtually 6 almost, nearly 7 morally 8 actually 9 basically, in essence 10 absolutely 11 essentially, practically 13 fundamentally

virtue 4 dint, mark 5 arête, merit, piety, trait, value, vigor, worth 7 caliber, feature, potency, probity, quality, stature 8 efficacy, goodness, morality, property 9 affection, attribute, character, puissance, rectitude, rightness 10 excellence, excellency, perfection 11 uprightness 13 effectiveness, effectualness, righteousness *cardinal:* 4 hope 5 faith 7 charity, justice 8 prudence 9 fortitude 10 temperance

virtuosic 4 ripe 6 expert 8 finished 9 masterful, perfected 10 consummate 12 accomplished

virtuoso 4 whiz 6 artist, expert, master, musico, wizard 7 artiste, dabster 8 musician 9 authority 10 past master 12 professional

virtuous 4 good, pure 5 moral, noble 6 worthy 7 ethical, sinless 8 innocent, spotless 9 blameless, effective, effectual, efficient, exemplary, faultless, guiltless, righteous, unsullied, untainted 10 inculpable, moralistic, principled, unblamable 11 efficacious, right-minded, untarnished

virulent 5 sharp, toxic 6 biting, bitter, malign, poison 7 cutting, hateful, hostile 8 mephitic, scathing, spiteful, stabbing, toxicant, venomous 9 malignant, poisonous, rancorous, vitriolic 10 unfriendly 12 antagonistic

virus 4 bane, germ 5 venom 6 poison 9 contagion, infection

vis 5 force, might, power

visage 3 mug 4 cast, face, look, phiz 6 kisser 8 features 10 expression 11 countenance

vis-à-vis 6 contra, facing, toward, versus 7 against 8 fronting, opposite 9 tête-à-tête 10 coordinate 11 counterpart, over against

viscera 4 guts 7 innards, insides, inwards 8 entrails, stuffing 9 internals *combining form:* 9 splanchno

visceral 3 gut 5 inner 8 interior, internal, intimate 9 intuitive 11 instinctive, instinctual

viscid see **viscous**

viscount 4 peer 7 sheriff 8 nobleman

viscous 4 ropy, sizy 5 gummy, slimy, stiff, thick, tough 6 sticky 9 glutinous, semifluid, tenacious

vise 4 grip, tool 5 clamp

Vishnu 4 Hare, Hari *avatar:* 4 Rama 5 Kurma 6 Buddha, Matsya, Vamena, Var-

aha 7 Krishna 9 Narasinha *consort:* 3 Sri 4 Shri 7 Lakshmi *home:* 4 Meru

visible 4 seen 6 ocular, visual 7 seeable 8 apparent, viewable

Visigoth *conquest:* 4 Rome *king:* 6 Alaric

vision 3 eye 4 muse 5 dream, fancy, image, sight, think 6 beauty, oracle, seeing 7 fantasy, feature, imagine, realize 8 conceive, daydream, envisage, eyesight, phantasm, phantasy, presence, prophecy 9 nightmare, visualize 10 apocalypse, apparition, phenomenon, revelation *combining form:* 4 opsy, opto 5 opsia, opsis 6 optico *deceptive:* 6 mirage *defect:* (see at *eye*) *in bright light:* 8 photopia *in dim light:* 8 scotopia *relating to:* 5 optic 6 visual 7 optical *without:* 5 blind

visionary 5 ideal, lofty, noble 6 astral, dreamy, musing 7 dreamer, exalted, radical, utopian 8 idealist 9 ambitious, daydreamy, grandiose, ideologue, unworldly 10 abstracted, idealistic 11 daydreaming, impractical, pretentious 12 otherworldly 13 castle-builder, introspective

visionless 4 dark 5 blind 7 eyeless 9 sightless 10 stone-blind

Vision of Sir Launfal, The *author* 6 Lowell

visit 3 gam, see 4 call, chat, chin, pain, stay, talk, yarn 5 pop in, run in, tarry, wreak, wreck 6 avenge, bother, come by, drop by, drop in, impose, look in, look up, punish, reside, step in, stop by, stop in 7 afflict, force on, inflict, sojourn, trouble 8 colloque, come over, converse, frequent, stopover 9 force upon, tarriance *often:* 8 frequent

visitation 4 call 5 cross, trial 6 ordeal 7 calvary 8 calamity, crucible, disaster 9 mischance 10 affliction 11 catastrophe, tribulation

visitor 5 guest 6 caller 7 company, invitee

vison 4 mink

visor 4 bill, mask, peak 6 domino, vizard 8 eyeshade 9 doughface, false face

vista 4 view 5 range, scape, scene, scope, sight 6 survey 7 lookout, outlook 8 panorama, prospect 11 perspective

visual 5 optic 6 ocular 7 optical, seeable, visible 8 viewable, visional 11 discernible, perceivable, perceptible

visualize 3 see 4 view 5 fancy, image, think 6 call up, divine 7 feature, foresee, imagine, picture, preknow, previse, realize 8 conceive, envisage, envision, forefeel, foreknow 9 apprehend, conjure up, objectify, prevision 10 anticipate

vital 5 alive, lusty 6 living, needed, zoetic 7 animate, dynamic, needful 8 animated, cardinal, integral, required, vigorous 9 breathing, energetic, essential, requisite, strenuous 10 red-blooded 11 fundamental **12** constitutive, prerequisite **13** indispensable

vital force 4 soul **5** anima **6** animus, pneuma, psyche, spirit **9** élan vital

vitality *see* **vigor**

vitalize 5 liven, pep up **6** actify, excite, vivify **7** animate, enliven, provoke, quicken **8** activate, activize, dynamize, energize **9** galvanize, stimulate **10** invigorate, strengthen

vitally 4 very **6** hugely **7** notably, parlous **9** extremely **10** remarkably, strikingly **11** exceedingly **12** surpassingly **13** exceptionally

vitals *see* **viscera**

vitamin 6 biotin, niacin **7** choline, folacin **8** carotene, inositol, thiamine **9** cobalamin, folic acid, pyridoxal **10** calciferol, pyridoxine, riboflavin, tocopherol **12** ascorbic acid, bioflavonoid, meso-inositol

Vito Nuova, La *author:* **5** Dante

vitellus 4 yolk

vitiate 3 mar **4** harm, hurt, soil, undo **5** abate, annul, quash, spoil, sully, taint **6** damage, debase, defile, impair, injure, negate **7** abolish, blemish, corrupt, debased, debauch, deprave, nullify, pervert, tarnish **8** abrogate, depraved **9** brutalize, corrupted, debauched, perverted, prejudice **10** annihilate, bastardize, bestialize, demoralize, invalidate

vitreous 6 glassy

vitriol 7 sulfate **9** virulence

vitriolic 6 bitter **7** hostile **8** virulent **9** rancorous **12** antagonistic

vituperate 4 lash, rail, rate **5** abuse, curse, scold **6** bark at, berate, malign, revile, yell at **7** asperse, bawl out, chew out, condemn, growl at, upbraid **8** lambaste **10** tongue-lash

vituperation 5 abuse, blame **7** censure, obloquy **8** scolding **9** contumely, invective **10** revilement, scurrility **12** billingsgate **13** tongue-lashing

vituperative 6 severe **7** abusive, railing **8** critical, scolding, scurrile **9** invective, truculent **10** censorious, scurrilous **11** opprobrious **12** contumelious

vivacious 3 gay **4** cant, keen **5** alert, brash, canty, zesty **6** breezy, lively **7** animate, playful, vibrant **8** animated, spirited, sportive **9** ebullient, exuberant, sprightly **10** frolicsome **12** effervescent, high-spirited

vivacity *see* **verve**

Vivaldi, Antonio *epithet:* **12** il prete rosso, the red priest

_____ **vivant 3** bon

vivarium 3 zoo

vivid 3 gay **4** keen, rich **5** acute, alive, brave, sharp **6** bright, colory, lively, living **7** graphic, intense **8** animated, colorful, dramatic, eloquent, spirited, vigorous **9** pictorial **10** expressive, meaningful, theatrical **11** dramaturgic, picturesque **12** photographic

vivify 5 liven, renew **6** excite, revive **7** animate, enliven, quicken, refresh, restore **9** galvanize

vixen 3 fox, nag **5** harpy, scold, shrew **6** amazon, ogress, virago **8** fishwife **9** termagant, Xanthippe

viz 5 to wit **6** namely **8** scilicet **9** videlicet

vizard 4 mask **5** visor **6** domino **9** doughface, false face

vocabulary 4 cant **5** words **6** jargon **7** lexicon, palaver **8** language **9** word-hoard, word-stock **10** dictionary **11** phraseology, terminology

vocal 4 oral **6** fluent, sonant, spoken, voiced **7** uttered, voicing **8** eloquent **9** expressed, intonated, outspoken **10** articulate, expressing, expressive, free-spoken

vocalic 5 vowel **6** vowely **9** vowellike

vocalist 6 singer **8** songster **9** performer **11** entertainer

vocalization 5 mouth, voice **6** speech **7** diction, voicing **8** mouthing, sounding, speaking, uttering **9** utterance **11** enunciation **12** articulation **13** verbalization

vocalize 4 sing, talk, tune **5** chant, speak, utter, voice **6** convey, impart, let out **7** express **9** enunciate, pronounce, verbalize **11** communicate

vocal organ 6 larynx *bird:* **6** syrinx

vocation 3 art, job **4** work **5** craft, trade **6** métier **7** calling, mission **8** lifework **10** handicraft, occupation, profession

vocative 4 case **6** fluent **7** voluble **9** garrulous

vociferate 3 cry **4** call, yell **5** hallo, hollo, shout **6** holler

vociferous 4 loud **5** noisy **6** shrill **7** blatant, dinsome **8** strident **9** clamorous **10** boisterous, multivocal **11** distracting, loudmouthed, openmouthed **12** obstreperous

vogue 3 cry, fad **4** chic, mode, rage **5** craze, style, trend **6** bon ton, furore **7** fashion **10** dernier cri **11** stylishness

voice 3 put, say **4** talk, tell, vent **5** say-so, sound, speak, utter **6** phrase, speech **7** present, recount **8** vocalize **9** enunciate, formulate, pronounce, statement, utterance, verbalize **10** articulate, expression *combining form:* **4** phon **5** phone, phono, phony **6** phonia *female:* **4** alto **5** mezzo **7** soprano **9** contralto *high:* **5** tenor **7** soprano **8** falsetto *in grammar:* **6** active **7** passive *Latin:* **3** vox *male:* **4** bass **5** tenor **8** baritone *quality:* **5** pitch **6** timbre *quiet:* **7** whisper *relating to:* **5** vocal **8** phonetic *without:* **4** dumb, mute

voice box 6 larynx
voiced 4 oral 5 vocal 6 sonant, spoken
10 articulate
voiceless 3 mum 4 dumb, mute 6 silent
10 speechless 12 inarticulate, unarticulate
void 3 bad, gap 4 bare, emit, flow, hole,
null, pour 5 abyss, annul, clear, drain, eject,
empty, quash, scant, short 6 bereft, cavity,
devoid, hollow, remove, vacant, vacate, vacuum 7 denuded, deplete, give off, invalid,
negated, vacuity, vacuous 8 abrogate,
deprived, dissolve, evacuate, innocent,
throw out 9 destitute, discharge, eliminate
10 disembogue
voiture 3 car 8 carriage
volage 5 dizzy, giddy 7 flighty 9 frivolous
10 bird-witted 11 empty-headed, harebrained 13 rattlebrained
volant 4 spry, yare 5 agile, brisk, catty,
zippy 6 active, lively, nimble 9 sprightly
volary 6 aviary 8 birdcage
volatile 4 airy, edgy 6 bouncy, fickle,
lively 7 buoyant, elastic, flighty, protean
8 agitable, fleeting, flippant, fugitive, skittery,
skittish, ticklish, unstable, variable 9 alarmable, ephemeral, excitable, expansive,
explosive, frivolous, fugacious, mercurial,
momentary, resilient, startlish, transient
10 capricious, changeable, evanescent,
inconstant, lubricious, short-lived, transitory 11 impermanent, light-minded
12 effervescent 13 temperamental
volatility 6 levity 9 animation, flippancy, frivolity, lightness 11 flightiness, inconstancy,
instability, variability 13 changeability, mer-
curialness, sprightliness
volcanic *crater:* 4 maar *explosion:*
8 eruption *glass:* 8 obsidian *matter:*
3 ash 4 lava, tufa, tuff 5 magma, trass
6 scoria *mound:* 4 cone 7 hornito *passage:* 6 throat 7 conduit *vent:* 8 fuma-
role 9 solfatara
volcano 8 mountain *Alaska:* 11 Mount
Katmai *Andes:* 5 Omate 12 Huaina Putina
Antarctica: 11 Mount Erebus *Azores:*
4 Alto *California:* 10 Lassen Peak *Canaries:* 5 Teide 8 Tenerife *Colombia:* 5 Huila,
Pasto 6 Purace 7 Galeras *Costa Rica:*
4 Poás 5 Barba, Irazú *Ecuador:* 8 Coto-
paxi *extinct:* 5 Iriga 8 Mauna Kea 9 Mount
Popa 10 Mount Kenya *Guatemala:*
4 Agua 5 Fuego 7 Atitlán *Hawaii:*
8 Mauna Loa *Honshū:* 4 Nasu 5 Asama,
Azuma 8 Nasudake 9 Asamayama *Iceland:* 5 Askja, Hekla *Indonesia:* 7 Tam-
bora 9 Gunung Awu 10 Peak of Bali
11 Gunung Agung *island:* 8 Krakatau, Kra-
katoa *Italy:* 8 Vesuvius 9 Stromboli
Japan: 3 Aso 5 Unzen 6 Asosan *Java:*
4 Gede 5 Bromo, Gedeh, Kelud, Salak
Madeira: 5 Ruivo *Martinique:* 10 Mount

Pelee *Mexico:* 6 Colima 7 Orizaba 9 Pari-
cutin 12 Popocatepetl *New Zealand:*
7 Ruapehu 9 Ngauruhoe *Philippines:*
4 Taal 10 Mount Mayon 13 Mount Pina-
tubo *Saint Vincent:* 9 Soufrière *Sicily:*
4 Etna 5 Aetna *Solomons:* 5 Balbi *South
America:* 5 Lanin, Maipo *Sumatra:*
5 Dempo
___ **volente** 3 Deo
volition 4 will 6 choice, desire, option
8 election 9 selection 10 preference
volley 4 hail, shot 5 burst, round, salvo,
storm 6 shower 7 barrage 8 drumfire
volplane 5 glide
Volpone 3 fox *author:* 6 Jonson *servant:*
5 Mosca
Volsung *grandson:* 6 Sigurd 9 Siegfried
great-grandfather: 4 Odin *son:* 7 Sigmund
Voltaire *drama:* 5 Zaïre 6 Alzire, Brutus,
Mèrope, Oedipe 7 Mahomet 8 Tancrède
novel: 5 Zadig 7 Candide *real name:*
6 Arouet (François Marie)
volte-face 4 turn, veer, whip 5 avert,
pivot, sheer, wheel, whirl 6 divert 7 deflect,
reverse 8 reversal 9 about-face, face
about, reversion, turnabout 10 right-about
11 changeabout, reversement
voluble 4 glib 6 fickle, fluent 8 vocative
9 talkative 13 silver-tongued
volume 4 body, book, bulk, mass, size,
tome 6 amount, object 7 content 8 capacity, loudness, quantity
voluminous 4 full, many 6 legion, sundry
7 several, various 8 numerous 12 multifarious, multitudinal 13 multitudinous
Volumnia's son 10 Coriolanus
Völund 5 smith 7 Wayland *brother:*
4 Egil 5 Egill
voluntary 4 free 5 opted 6 chosen
7 elected, willful, willing, witting 8 elective,
optional, unforced 10 autonomous, deliberate, volitional 11 independent, intentional
12 unprescribed
volunteer 5 offer 6 enlist *hospital:*
12 candy striper
Volunteer State 9 Tennessee
voluptuous 4 lush 6 wanton 7 sensual
8 luscious, sensuous 9 abandoned, dissolute, epicurean, excessive, indulgent, luxurious 10 dissipated 12 sensualistic
volute 6 scroll, spiral
volution 5 twist, whorl
vomit 3 gag 4 barf, spew 5 eject, expel,
retch 6 spit up 7 bring up, throw up,
upchuck 8 disgorge 11 regurgitate
vomiting 6 emesis
Von Flotow opera 6 Martha
Von Stroheim film 5 Greed 13 Blind
Husbands, Grand Illusion
voodoo 3 hex 4 jinx, mage 5 charm,
magus, obeah, spell, witch 6 whammy, wiz-

ard 7 bewitch, enchant, warlock 8 conjurer, magician, sorcerer 9 enchanter, ensorcell 10 Indian sign 11 necromancer

voodooist 4 mage 5 magus 6 wizard 7 charmer, warlock 8 conjurer, magician, sorcerer 9 enchanter 11 necromancer

Vophsi's son 5 Nahbi

voracious 4 avid 6 greedy, hungry, sating 7 gorging 8 covetous, edacious, grasping, ravening, ravenous 9 devouring, rapacious, satiating 10 gluttonous, insatiable, surfeiting 11 acquisitive

vorago 5 abyss, chasm

vortex 4 eddy, gyre 5 spout, whirl 6 spiral 9 maelstrom, whirlpool

votary 3 fan 4 buff 5 freak, hound, lover 6 addict, zealot 7 admirer, amateur, devotee, fancier, habitué 8 disciple 10 aficionado

vote 4 poll 5 elect 6 ballot, choice, choose, decide, ratify, ticket 7 opinion 8 election, suffrage 9 franchise *affirmative:* 3 aye, nod, yea, yes 6 placet *kind:* 5 proxy, straw, voice 6 secret 7 write-in 10 plebiscite, referendum *negative:* 2 no 3 nay *right to:* 8 suffrage 9 franchise

voter 7 chooser, elector *kind:* 8 absentee

vouch 5 prove 6 assure, attest, uphold, verify 7 certify, confirm, support, witness 9 guarantee 11 corroborate 12 substantiate

voucher 4 chit 5 proof 7 receipt 9 affidavit 10 credential 11 certificate

vouchsafe 4 give 5 award, deign, favor, grant, stoop 6 accord, oblige 7 concede 10 condescend 11 accommodate

vow 4 oath, swan 5 swear 6 assert, pledge, plight, prayer 7 declare, promise 8 covenant

vowel 5 vocal 6 letter *kind:* 4 long

5 glide, schwa, short 9 diphthong *omission:* 7 aphesis 11 contraction *variation:* 6 ablaut, umlaut

vowely 5 vocal 7 vocalic

voyage 4 tour, trip 6 cruise, travel 7 journey 9 excursion 10 expedition, pilgrimage

voyeur 6 peeper 10 peeping Tom

Vronski's lover 12 Anna Karenina

Vulcan see **Hephaestus**

vulgar 3 low, raw 4 base, rude, vile, wild 5 crass, crude, dirty, gross, nasty, rough 6 coarse, public, ribald, smutty, spoken 7 general, obscene, popular, profane, uncouth 8 barbaric, barnyard, improper, indecent, unseemly 9 barbarian, barbarous, graceless, idiomatic, incorrect, inelegant, loathsome, offensive, repulsive, revolting, tasteless, unrefined 10 colloquial, indecorous, indelicate, outlandish, ungraceful, unpolished, vernacular 12 scatological

vulgarism 8 slangism, solecism 9 barbarism 10 corruption 11 impropriety 13 vernacularism, vernacularity

vulgate 6 patois 10 colloquial, vernacular

Vulgate translator 6 Jerome

vulnerability 8 exposure, openness, weakness 9 liability 11 vincibility

vulnerable 4 open, weak 6 liable 7 exposed

vulnerary 6 curing 7 healing 8 curative, remedial, sanative, sanatory 9 remedying, wholesome 11 restorative

vulpine 3 sly 4 foxy, wily 6 artful, astute, crafty, tricky 7 cunning 8 guileful 9 insidious

vulture 4 hook, lift 5 filch, pinch, steal, swipe 6 condor, snitch 7 buzzard 8 aasvogel 11 lammergeier *food:* 7 carrion

vulturine 9 predative, predatory, rapacious, raptorial 10 predacious 11 predatorial

W

wacky 3 mad 4 nuts 5 crazy, loony, silly 6 absurd, crazed, insane 7 cracked, foolish, lunatic 8 demented, deranged 11 harebrained 12 preposterous

wad 3 gob, pot 4 bomb, clod, hunk, lump, mint, pile 5 chunk, clump, hunch 6 boodle, bundle, nugget, packet 7 fortune

waddy 3 peg 4 club 5 stick 6 cowboy 7 rustler

wade 4 ford, plod *into:* 6 attack

wadi 3 bed 4 wash 5 gully 6 ravine

wafer 4 cake, disk 7 cracker

waft 4 gust, puff, wave 5 drift, float, whiff

wag 3 wit 4 beat, card, lash, wave, zany 5 clown, comic, cutup, droll, joker, shake 6 jester, kidder, madcap, switch, twitch, waggle, wiggle, wigwag, woggle 7 farceur, show-off 8 comedian, funnyman, humorist, jokester, quipster 9 oscillate, prankster 11 wisecracker

wage 3 fee, pay 4 hire, take 6 income, return, reward, salary 7 stipend 8 earnings, receipts 9 emolument 10 recompense 12 compensation, remuneration

wager 3 bet, lay, pot, set 4 ante, game, play, risk 5 put on, stake 6 chance, gamble, hazard, impone 7 venture 9 adventure

waggery 3 gag 4 jape, jest, joke, quip 5 crack 7 devilry, roguery 8 deviltry, drollery, mischief 9 devilment, wisecrack, witticism 10 impishness 11 roguishness, waggishness 12 sportiveness

waggish 4 arch, pert 5 antic, comic, droll, funny, saucy, witty 6 impish, jocose 7 comical, jocular, playful, puckish, roguish 8 humorous, prankish, sportive 9 facetious, laughable, ludicrous 10 frolicsome 11 mischievous

waggle 4 beat, lash, sway, wave 6 switch, waddle, wobble

Wagner, Richard *birthplace:* 7 Leipzig *deathplace:* 6 Venice *father-in-law:* 5 Liszt *opera:* 6 Rienzi 8 Parsifal 9 Lohengrin, Siegfried 10 Die Walküre, Tannhäuser 12 Das Rheingold *recurring theme:* 9 leitmotif, leitmotiv *wife:* 5 Minna 6 Cosima

wagon 3 car, van 4 cart, dray, wain 5 gilly 6 telega 7 fourgon, vehicle

wah 5 panda

wahoo 4 fish 5 shrub 8 basswood, mackerel 11 burning bush

waif 5 stray 7 vagrant 8 wanderer 9 foundling

wail 3 bay, cry, sob 4 bawl, blub, fuss, howl, keen, kick, weep, yowl 5 quest, whine 6 boohoo, murmur, repine, squall 7 blubber, ululate 8 complain

wailful 6 rueful, woeful 7 doleful 8 dolesome, mournful 9 plaintive, sorrowful 10 lamentable, lugubrious, melancholy

wain 5 wagon

waistband 4 belt, sash 6 girdle 8 ceinture, cincture

waistcoat 4 vest 6 jerkin

wait 4 bide, stay 5 abide, nurse, serve, tarry 6 expect, linger, mother, remain 7 care for, foresee 10 anticipate, minister to 11 stick around

waiter 6 garçon 7 servant 9 attendant

Waiting for ___ 5 Godot, Lefty

waive 4 cede, stay 5 allow, defer, delay, grant, leave, yield 6 give up, hold up, put off, resign, shelve 7 abandon, concede, hold off, suspend 8 hand over, hold over, postpone 9 surrender 10 relinquish

wake 4 stir, whet 5 arise, get up, rally, renew, rouse 6 arouse, bestir, kindle 7 freshen, roll out 9 challenge

wakeful 5 alert 8 restless, vigilant, watchful 9 sleepless

waken see **wake**

Walden author 7 Thoreau

wale 3 rib 4 weal, welt 5 ridge, wheal, whelk

Wales 5 Cymru *capital:* 7 Cardiff *language:* 6 Cymric *Latin name:* 7 Cambria *patron saint:* 5 David

walk 3 leg, run 4 foot, hike, hoof, pace, plod, race, reel, slog, step, turn 5 amble, field, march, mince, strut, stump, tramp, tread, troop 6 airing, domain, foot it, lumber, parade, ramble, sphere, stride, stroll, strunt, toddle, trudge 7 alameda, demesne, saunter, stretch, terrain, traipse 8 ambulate, dominion, province, traverse 9 bailiwick, champaign, promenade, territory 11 base on balls, perambulate 12 deambulation

walkaway 4 romp, rout

walking shorts 8 Bermudas

walking stick 4 cane 5 staff 6 kebbie
8 ashplant
walk out 5 leave 6 strike
walkway 4 path 7 catwalk 9 promenade
ancient Greek: 4 stoa
wall 3 bar, hem 4 cage, coop, stop
5 block, fence, hedge 6 corral, immure
7 barrier, close in, enclose, envelop 8 blockade 9 barricade, roadblock *hanging:* 8 tapestry *protective:* 7 parapet *top of:*
6 coping
wallaba tree 3 apa
wallaby 8 kangaroo
wallet 8 billfold 10 pocketbook *items:*
5 bills
wallop 3 bat, bop, jar 4 bang, bash, beat,
belt, blow, boot, bump, drub, jolt, kick, lick,
pelt, slam, slug, trim, whip, whop 5 baste,
blast, clash, crash, paste, pound, shock,
smack, smash 6 buffet, impact, pummel,
thrash, thrill, thwack 7 belabor, shellac,
trounce 8 lambaste 9 collision
10 percussion
walloping 4 huge 5 giant 7 immense,
mammoth, monster 8 colossal, enormous,
gigantic 10 gargantuan, prodigious
wallow 4 bask, roll 5 enjoy, lurch, revel
6 welter 7 blunder, indulge, rollick, stumble 8 flounder 9 delight in, luxuriate
____ **Walpole, writer** 6 Horace
walrus 6 mammal *relative:* 4 seal *tooth:*
4 tusk
____ **Walton, writer** 5 Izaak
waltz 3 zip 6 breeze
Waltz King 7 Strauss
Wampanoag chief 9 Massasoit, Metacomet 10 King Philip
wampum 5 beads, money, sewan 6 shells
wan 4 ashy, pale, weak, worn 5 ashen,
livid, waxen 6 anemic, doughy, pallid,
sickly 7 haggard 8 blanched, bleached,
boneless, impotent 9 bloodless, colorless,
forceless, spineless, washed-out 10 cadaverous, emasculate 11 ineffective, ineffectual, slack-spined 12 invertebrate
wand 3 rod 4 pole, tube 5 baton, staff
combining form: 5 rhabd 6 rhabdo
wander 3 bat, bum, err, gad 4 roam, roll,
rove 5 amble, drift, gypsy, mooch, range,
stray, tramp 6 depart, gander, ramble,
stroll 7 deviate, digress, diverge, excurse,
maunder, meander, saunter, traipse 8 divagate, straggle, vagabond 9 gallivant
wanderer 5 nomad, rover 6 errant,
roamer 7 drifter, pilgrim, rambler, tzigane,
vagrant 9 meanderer 12 rolling stone
wane 3 ebb 4 fail, fall 5 abate, let up
6 relent, shrink, weaken 7 decline, die
away, die down, dwindle, ease off, slacken,
subside 8 moderate 9 fall short, waste
away

wangle 7 finagle 8 engineer, maneuver,
outflank 9 machinate, overreach 10 outgeneral 11 outmaneuver
want 4 lack, must, need, wish 5 covet,
crave, ought 6 dearth, defect, demand,
desire, penury, should 7 absence, default,
poverty, require 8 exigency, poorness
9 indigence, necessity, neediness, privation
10 desiderate, inadequacy, meagerness,
scantiness, skimpiness 11 destitution,
requirement 12 exiguousness
13 insufficiency
wanting 3 shy 4 away, gone, sans
5 minus, scant, short 6 absent, scanty,
scarce 7 failing, lacking, missing, omitted,
without 9 defective, deficient 10 inadequate, incomplete, uncomplete 12 insufficient, unsufficient
wanton 3 lax, toy 4 doxy, easy, fast, fool,
jade, slut 5 cruel, dally, flirt, hussy, light,
loose, slack, tramp, trull, wench 6 coquet,
harlot, lead on, trifle 7 baggage, cyprian,
jezebel, trollop, unasked, wayward, whorish 8 contrary, perverse, slattern, spiteful,
strumpet, unchaste 9 malicious 10 gratuitous, malevolent, prostitute 11 string along,
uncalled-for 12 supererogant
wapiti 3 elk 4 deer, stag
war 3 tug 4 feud 5 fight 6 battle, combat,
oppugn, strife 7 contend, crusade 8 struggle *German:* 5 krieg 10 blitzkrieg *god:*
3 Tyr 4 Ares, Mars, Odin 5 Wodan, Woden
goddess: 4 Enyo 5 Anath 6 Inanna, Ishtar 7 Bellona *Latin:* 6 bellum *Muslim:*
5 jehad, jihad *relating to:* 7 martial
War and Peace *author:* 7 Tolstoy *composer:* 9 Prokofiev
warble 3 air, lay 4 sing, tune 6 melody,
strain 7 descant, measure, melisma, melodia 8 diapason
warbler 7 kinglet 8 songster 9 blackpoll
11 gnatcatcher *European:* 10 chiffchaff
war club 3 bat 4 mace 5 baton 6 cudgel
8 bludgeon 9 truncheon 10 knobkerrie
war cry 5 motto 6 slogan *Greek:* 5 alala
ward 4 balk, care, fend, foil, halt, stay, turn
5 aegis, armor, avert, block, check, deter,
guard, parry, rebut, repel, trust, watch
6 divert, picket, rebuff, sentry, shield, stymie, thwart 7 custody, defense, deflect,
fend off, forfend, hold off, keeping, keep off,
lookout, obviate, prevent, repulse, rule out
8 armament, preclude, security, sentinel,
stave off, watchman 9 forestall, frustrate,
interrupt, safeguard 10 protection 11 safekeeping 12 guardianship
warden 6 custos, jailer, keeper, ranger
8 cerberus, claviger, guardian, watchdog
9 custodian
wardrobe 4 room 5 trunk 6 closet
12 clothespress

ware 4 shun 5 avoid, awake, aware, cloth, goods 7 fabrics, knowing, pottery 8 sensible 9 cognizant, conscious

warehouse 4 pack, stow 5 étape, guard, store 6 bestow 7 protect, shelter, storage 8 entrepôt 11 accommodate *oriental:* 6 godown

wares 4 line 5 goods 9 vendibles 11 commodities, merchandise

warfare 6 strife 7 contest, rivalry 8 conflict, striving 9 emulation 11 competition *combining form:* 5 machy

warhorse 7 charger, courser

warlike 7 hawkish, martial, warring 8 battling, fighting, militant, military, ructious 9 bellicose, combative, truculent 10 contending, pugnacious 11 belligerent, contentious, quarrelsome 12 gladiatorial

warlock 4 mage 5 magus 6 wizard 7 charmer 8 conjurer, magician, sorcerer 9 enchanter, voodooist 11 necromancer

warm 4 heat 5 tepid 6 ardent 7 affable, cordial, fervent, sincere, zealous 8 gracious 9 heartfelt 10 passionate, responsive 11 kindhearted, softhearted, sympathetic 12 enthusiastic, wholehearted 13 compassionate *air:* 7 thermal

warmed-over 5 stale, tired, trite 6 old hat 7 clichéd 8 shopworn, timeworn, well-worn 9 hackneyed, twice-told

warmhearted 4 kind, warm 6 benign, kindly, tender 8 outgoing 9 benignant 10 responsive 11 sympathetic 13 compassionate

warn 3 bid, tip 4 clew, clue, post, tell 5 alert, guide, order 6 advise, beacon, charge, direct, enjoin, fill in, inform, monish, notify, wise up 7 apprise, caution, command, counsel 8 acquaint, instruct

warning 3 tip 4 hint 6 advice, caveat 7 caution, counsel, sematic 8 guidance, monition, monitory 10 admonition, admonitory, cautionary, cautioning, monitorial, suggestion 11 admonishing, commonition *legal:* 6 caveat

War of the Worlds author 5 Wells

warp 4 bend, kink, wind 5 color, twist, wrest 6 debase, deform, garble, wrench 7 confuse, contort, corrupt, debauch, deprave, distort, pervert, torture, vitiate 8 miscolor, misshape 9 brutalize 10 bastardize, bestialize, demoralize 12 misrepresent

warrant 4 back, pawn, word 5 argue, basis, claim, state, token 6 affirm, assert, assure, defend, ensure, insure, pledge, secure 7 call for, certify, contend, earnest, justify, require, sponsor 8 guaranty, maintain, mittimus, security 9 assurance, guarantee, stipulate, vindicate 10 foundation

warranty 4 bail, bond 6 surety 8 guaranty, security 9 guarantee

warrior 2 GI 4 hero, swad 7 fighter, soldier 9 man-at-arms 10 serviceman 11 fighting man *female:* 6 Amazon *Japanese:* 7 samurai

Warsaw *castle:* 5 Zamek *river:* 7 Vistula

warship see **ship,** *military*

wart 6 lesion 7 verruca

wary 4 safe 5 canny, chary, leery 6 frugal, saving, scotch 7 careful, guarded, sceptic, skeptic, sparing, thrifty 8 cautious, discreet, doubting, gingerly, vigilant, watchful 9 provident, stewardly 10 suspicious, unwasteful 11 calculating, circumspect, considerate, distrustful

wash 3 lap, lip, tub 4 lave, ride, suds 5 bathe, clean, drift, float, slosh, swash 6 bubble, burble, gurgle, shower, sluice 7 launder, shampoo

washed-out 5 all in, spent 6 bleary, effete, used up 7 drained, far-gone, worn-out 8 depleted 9 exhausted

washed-up 4 done 7 done for, through 8 finished

washing 4 bath 6 lavage 8 ablution *ceremonial:* 6 lavabo

Washington *capital:* 7 Olympia *largest city:* 7 Seattle *nickname:* 12 Chinook State 14 Evergreen State *state bird:* 9 goldfinch *state flower:* 12 rhododendron

Washington, D.C. designer 7 L'Enfant

Washington's home 11 Mount Vernon

Washington Square author 5 James

wash out 4 cast, fail, flop, junk, shed 5 elute, scrap 6 reject, slough 7 cashier, discard, flummox 8 jettison 9 throw away

wasp 6 hornet, vespid

waspish 5 huffy, sharp 6 cranky, ornery 7 bearish, crabbed, fretful, peevish, pettish 8 cankered, contrary, perverse, petulant, snappish, spiteful 9 crotchety, fractious, impatient, irritable, malicious, querulous 10 vinegarish 12 cantankerous, cross-grained

waspy see **waspish**

wassail 3 bat 4 bust, hell, riot, soak, tear 5 binge, revel, spree 6 bender, frolic, rantan 7 carouse, revelry, roister, whoopee, whoopla, whoop-up 8 carousal 9 high jinks, revelment 10 skylarking

waste 4 blow, fail, junk, sack, wane, wild 5 offal, trash 6 barren, debris, desert, devour, drivel, kelter, litter, ravage, refuse, sewage, shrink, trifle, weaken 7 badland, consume, despoil, dwindle, fritter, garbage, pillage, rubbish, sullage 8 cast away, desolate, emaciate, fool away, misspend, riot away, spoilage, spoliate, squander, unthrift, wild land, wildness 9 depredate, desecrate, devastate, dissipate, fall short, overdoing, sweepings, throw away **10** frivol away, lavishness, muddle away, potter away, trifle away, wilderness **11** blunder away, dribble away, prodigality, prodigalize **12** extravagance, extravagancy *allowance:* **4** tret *from a mine:* **7** mullock *time:* **5** dally **6** dawdle, footle, piddle

waste away **4** fail, wane **5** dwine **7** atrophy, decline

wasted **4** worn **5** gaunt **6** meager **7** wizened **8** skeletal, withered **9** emaciated, shriveled **10** cadaverous

wasteful **6** lavish **8** prodigal **10** thriftless **11** extravagant, improvident

wastefulness **8** squander, unthrift **9** overdoing **10** lavishness **11** prodigality **12** extravagance, extravagancy

wasteland **4** wild **6** barren, desert **8** wildness **10** wilderness

Waste Land author **5** Eliot

waster **5** idler **6** loafer, no-good **7** lounger, rounder, spender, wastrel **8** prodigal, unthrift **9** fritterer **10** dissipater, high roller, ne'er-do-well, profligate, scapegrace, squanderer **11** scattergood, spendthrift

wastrel **3** rip **4** rake, roué **5** idler, knave, rogue, scamp **6** lecher, loafer, no-good, rascal **7** lounger, rounder, spender **8** prodigal, scalawag, unthrift **9** fritterer, libertine, scoundrel **10** blackguard, black sheep, dissipater, high roller, ne'er-do-well, profligate, scapegrace, squanderer **11** rapscallion, scattergood, spendthrift

watch **3** eye, see, spy, tab **4** look, mind, scan, tend, tout, ward **5** guard, vigil **6** attend, follow, picket, sentry **7** care for, examine, eyeball, inspect, lookout, monitor, surveil **8** eagle eye, scrutiny, sentinel, watchman **9** timepiece, vigilance **10** scrutinize **11** chronograph, chronometer **12** surveillance *chain:* **3** fob *maker:* **10** horologist

watchdog **6** custos, keeper, warden **8** cerberus, claviger, guardian **9** custodian

watcher **6** viewer **7** guarder, lookout, witness **8** beholder, by-sitter, guardian, looker-on, observer, onlooker **9** bystander, spectator **10** eyewitness *combining form:* **6** scopus

watchfire **6** beacon

watchful **4** wary **5** alert, chary, quick, ready **6** prompt **7** wakeful **8** cautious, open-eyed, vigilant **9** wide-awake **10** unsleeping **11** circumspect *Scottish:* **5** tenty **6** tentie

watchman **4** ward **5** guard **6** picket, sentry **7** lookout **8** sentinel

watch out **4** mind **6** beware **7** look out

watchtower **7** lookout **10** lighthouse

watchword **6** slogan **10** shibboleth **11** catchphrase, countersign

water **5** fluid **6** dilute, liquid **7** moisten

8 irrigate, moisture, snowmelt *body:* **3** bay, sea **4** gulf, lake, pool **5** ocean **6** lagoon, strait **9** reservoir *combining form:* **4** aqua, aqui, aquo, hydr **5** hydat, hydro **6** hydato, limnia (plural) **7** limnion *French:* **3** eau *goddess:* **4** Nina **7** Anahita, Anaitis *Latin:* **4** aqua *Spanish:* **4** agua

water buffalo **4** arna **7** carabao *female:* **5** arnee

water clock **9** clepsydra

water closet **2** WC **4** head, john **5** privy **6** johnny, toilet **7** latrine **8** lavatory **11** convenience *British:* **3** loo

watercourse **4** duct **5** canal **6** course **7** channel, conduit **8** aqueduct, headrace, tailrace

water cow **7** manatee

water eagle **6** osprey

watered-down **4** thin, weak **5** washy **6** dilute, watery **7** diluted **8** waterish

water elephant **12** hippopotamus

waterfall **4** eddy **5** chute, falls, sault, shoot, spout, surge **6** rapids, riffle, vortex **7** cascade **8** cataract **9** whirlpool *California:* **8** Yosemite *Canada:* **5** Grand *Canada-U.S.:* **7** Niagara *former Nile:* **5** Ripon *Kentucky:* **5** Great **10** Cumberland *Niagara:* **8** American, Canadian **9** Horseshoe *Oregon:* **9** Multnomah *Snake river:* **4** Twin **8** Shoshone *world's highest:* **5** Angel *Yellowstone:* **5** Tower *Zambezi:* **8** Victoria

waterfinder **6** dowser

water hole *desert:* **5** oasis

water horse **6** kelpie **11** hippocampus

watering hole **3** bar, pub **4** café **5** haunt, oasis **6** lounge, nitery, resort, saloon, tavern **7** barroom, cabaret, hangout, hot spot, purlieu **8** drinkery, nightery **9** nightclub, nightspot **10** rendezvous, supper club **11** discotheque

water jar **4** ewer, lota, olla **5** banga, lotah **6** hydria, kalpis

waterless **3** dry **4** arid, sere **7** bone-dry, thirsty **8** droughty **9** unwatered **12** moistureless *combining form:* **6** anhydr **7** anhydro

waterlog **3** sap **4** soak **5** souse, steep **6** drench, sodden **7** insteep **8** saturate

water nymph **4** lily **5** naiad **6** Nereid **7** Oceanid **9** dragonfly *female:* **5** nixie

water oscillation **6** seiche

water pipe **5** hooka **6** hookah **8** narghile, nargileh

water plant **7** aquatic **10** hydrophyte

water rat **4** vole **6** rodent **7** muskrat

water spirit **6** undine

waterspout **6** funnel **10** cloudburst

water sprite see **water nymph**

water tank **7** cistern

waterwheel **5** noria **6** sakieh

watery 4 pale, thin, weak 5 banal, bland, vapid, washy 6 anemic, dilute, jejune, pallid, sluicy 7 diluted, insipid, sapless 9 bloodless 10 namby-pamby, wishy-washy

wattle 3 rod 4 pole 10 interweave

wattle and ___ 4 daub

wave 3 wag 4 beat, flap, lash 6 marcel, ripple, switch, waggle, woggle 7 flutter, ripplet 8 brandish, undulate *combining form:* 3 cym, kym 4 cymo, kymo *large:* 7 tsunami

waver 4 halt, trim 5 hedge, shift 6 dither, falter, palter, seesaw, teeter 7 flicker, stagger, whiffle 8 hesitate 9 vacillate 12 shilly-shally, wiggle-waggle

wavering 4 weak 5 shaky 6 dickey, unsure, wobbly 7 halting 8 insecure, rootless, to-and-fro, unstable 9 faltering, fluctuant, hesitancy, vacillant, whiffling 10 hesitating, hesitation, indecision 11 vacillating, vacillation, vacillatory 12 irresolution, shilly-shally, wiggle-waggle

Waverly author 5 Scott

wavy pattern 5 moiré

wax 3 get, run 4 come, grow, hike, rise, turn 5 boost, build, lipid, mount 6 become, expand 7 augment, enlarge, upgrade, upsurge 8 heighten, increase, multiply, paraffin, simonize *combining form:* 3 cer 4 cero

waxen 3 wan 4 ashy, pale 5 ashen, livid 6 doughy, pallid 8 blanched 9 colorless

waxlike 9 ceraceous

way 3 ilk 4 adit, door, kind, lane, mode, path, road, sort, type, wise, wont 5 alley, breed, class, entry, habit, modus, order, route, style, track, usage 6 access, artery, avenue, course, custom, entrée, manner, method, praxis, street, system 7 fashion, ingress, species, variety 8 distance, entrance, habitude, practice 9 admission, boulevard, technique 10 admittance, consuetude 12 thoroughfare *combining form:* 3 ode

wayfaring 6 roving 7 nomadic, vagrant 8 vagabond 9 itinerant, itinerate, wandering 11 perambulant, peripatetic 13 perambulatory

waylay 6 ambush 8 surprise

Way of All Flesh author 6 Butler

Way of the World author 8 Congreve

way or sea ___ 5 farer

wayward 5 balky 6 fickle, ornery 7 erratic, froward, restive 8 contrary, freakish, perverse, unstable, variable, whimsied 9 arbitrary, vagarious, whimsical 10 capricious, inconstant 11 wrongheaded 12 cross-grained

we *French:* 4 nous *German:* 3 wir *Italian:* 3 noi *Spanish:* 8 nosotros

weak 3 wan 4 puny, thin 5 faint, frail,

shaky, washy 6 dickey, dilute, feeble, flimsy, infirm, sickly, unsure, watery, wobbly 7 diluted, fragile, rickety, sapless, spindly, unsound 8 boneless, decrepit, impotent, insecure, rootless, thewless, unstable, wavering 9 enfeebled, fluctuant, forceless, powerless, spineless, uncertain 10 emasculate, improbable, impuissant, inadequate, incredible, irresolute, unreliable 11 debilitated, implausible, ineffective, ineffectual, slack-spined, vacillating, watered-down 12 invertebrate, unbelievable, unconvincing, undependable 13 insubstantial, unsubstantial *combining form:* 4 lept 5 lepto 6 asthen 7 astheno

weaken 3 cut, sap 4 fade, fail, flag, thin, wane 5 blunt, unman 6 damage, dilute, impair, infirm, injure, lessen, reduce, shrink, soften 7 cripple, decline, disable, dwindle, unbrace, unnerve 8 enervate, enfeeble, languish, minimize, paralyze 9 attenuate, fall short, undermine, waste away 10 debilitate, emasculate 11 deteriorate 12 incapacitate, unstrengthen

weak-kneed 5 timid 6 wobbly 8 wavering 9 faltering, uncertain, whiffling 10 irresolute 11 vacillating 12 double-minded, wiggle-waggle

weakling 3 sop 4 baby, butt, drip, mark 5 sissy 6 misfit, sucker 7 doormat, milksop, sad sack 8 mama's boy, pushover 9 jellyfish 10 mother's boy, namby-pamby, pantywaist, sissy-pants 11 Milquetoast, mollycoddle 12 invertebrate 13 sissy-britches

weakness 5 taste 6 foible, liking 7 frailty 8 adynamia, appetite, fondness, soft spot 12 Achilles' heel

weal 4 wale, welt 5 ridge, wheal, whelk 6 stripe 7 welfare 9 well-being

weald 5 woods 6 forest, timber 8 woodland 10 timberland

wealth 4 mean, pelf 5 goods, worth 6 assets, estate, mammon, riches 7 capital, fortune 8 golconda, holdings, nabobism, opulence, property 9 resources, substance 11 possessions *combining form:* 4 plut 5 pluto

Wealth of Nations author 5 Smith

wealthy 4 rich 7 moneyed, opulent 8 affluent

wean 5 alien, spean 8 alienate, disunify, disunite, estrange 9 disaffect

weapon 3 gun 4 bola, bolo, club, dart, dirk, épée, foil, mace, nuke, pike 5 arrow, knife, lance, rifle, saber, sabre, sling, spear, sword 6 dagger, magnum, musket, pistol, poleax, rapier 7 bazooka, carbine, firearm, halberd, halbert, javelin, machete, missile, poleaxe, shotgun, trident 8 battle-ax, catapult, crossbow, petronel, revolver, spontoon, tomahawk **9** battle-axe, blackjack, boomerang, derringer **11** blunderbuss **13** brass knuckles

weapons 7 arsenal

wear 3 rub **4** fray, gall, jade, tire **5** chafe, drain, erode, graze, grind, weary **6** abrade, ruffle, tatter **7** corrode, fatigue, frazzle

wear away 3 eat **4** bite, gnaw **5** erode, scour **6** abrade **7** corrode

wear down 4 jade, tire **5** drain, weary **6** weaken **7** exhaust, fatigue

weariness 5 ennui **7** fatigue **9** lassitude, tiredness **10** exhaustion

wearisome see **tiresome**

wear out 3 fag **4** poop **6** tucker **7** exhaust, frazzle, outtire **8** knock out, overstay, overtoil **9** prostrate

weary 4 bore, jade, pall, sick, tire, worn **5** drain, fed up, jaded, tired **6** tucker, weaken **7** fatigue **8** enfeeble, fatigued, footsore, footworn, overtire, overwork, wear down, worn down **9** disgusted **10** debilitate

weasand 5 gullet, throat **8** windpipe

weasel 5 dodge, evade, hedge, slink, sneak, stoat **6** ermine, ferret **7** shuffle, sneaker **8** sidestep, sneaksby **9** pussyfoot **10** equivocate, tergiverse **12** tergiversate *Scottish:* **8** whittret

weather 5 clime **7** climate *combining form:* **6** meteor **7** meteoro

weathercock 4 vane

weave 4 reed, spin, sway **5** braid, lurch, swing, twill **6** careen, damask, pleach, raddle, tissue, wattle, wobble **7** stagger, texture

Weaver of Raveloe 6 Marner (Silas)

web 3 net **4** knot, maze, mesh **5** fiber, skein, snare, snarl, toils **6** cobweb, fabric, jungle, meshes, morass, tangle **7** ensnare, mizmaze, network, texture **8** entangle **9** labyrinth **10** enmeshment, entrapment **11** embroilment, ensnarement, involvement **12** entanglement *combining form:* **5** hypho *of a feather:* **5** vexil **8** vexillum

Weber opera 6 Oberon **9** Euryanthe **13** Der Freischütz

____ **Webster 4** Noah **6** Daniel

wed 3 tie **4** join, link, mate, yoke **5** catch, marry, unite **6** marrow, relate, splice **7** combine, conjoin, connect, espouse **9** associate

wedded 7 marital, married, nuptial, spousal **8** conjugal, hymeneal **9** connubial **11** matrimonial

wedding 6 bridal **7** spousal **8** espousal, marriage, nuptials

wedding anniversary *fifteenth:* **7** crystal *fifth:* **6** wooden *fiftieth:* **6** golden *first:* **5** paper *seventy-fifth:* **7** diamond *tenth:* **3** tin *twentieth:* **5** china *twenty-fifth:* **6** silver

wedge-shaped 7 cuneate, sphenic

wedlock 8 marriage **9** matrimony **11** conjugality **12** connubiality

wee 4 tiny **5** teeny **6** minute, teensy, weensy **7** teentsy **9** miniature **10** diminutive, teeny-weeny **11** lilliputian **12** teensyweensy

weed 4 dock, tare **5** chess **6** darnel, dodder, lupine, nettle, sorrel, teasel **7** burdock, burseed, hemlock, mullein, solanum, thistle, tobacco **8** amaranth, charlock, gromwell, purslane, toadflax **9** cocklebur, dandelion, glasswort, goldenrod, horsetail, knotgrass, marijuana, poison ivy, poison oak, stickseed **10** cinquefoil *European:* **6** spurry **7** spurrey **8** pingrass *killer:* **8** paraquat **9** herbicide *Western:* **4** loco

week 8 hebdomad *two weeks:* **9** fortnight

weep 3 cry, sob **4** blub, drib, drip, drop, moan, ooze, seep, wail **5** bleed, exude, greet, sweat, trill **6** bemoan, bewail, boohoo, grieve, lament, strain **7** blubber, deplore, distill, dribble, trickle **8** transude

weepy 5 teary **7** maudlin, tearful **10** lachrymose

weevil 4 boll **7** billbug **8** curculio *tropical:* **7** zyzzyva

weft 3 web **4** pick, woof, yarn **6** fabric, thread

weigh 3 tax **4** lade, load, mind, rate, tare **5** count, study **6** burden, charge, cumber, lumber, ponder, saddle, weight **7** balance, perpend **8** appraise, consider, encumber, evaluate, militate, think out **9** think over **10** excogitate **11** contemplate

weigh down 5 press **6** sadden **7** depress, oppress

weight 3 tax **4** duty, lade, load, onus, pith, task **6** burden, charge, credit, cumber, debase, import, lumber, moment, saddle **7** potency **8** efficacy, encumber, prestige **9** authority, influence, magnitude, millstone **10** adulterate, importance **11** consequence **12** forcefulness, forcibleness, powerfulness, significance *allowance:* **4** tare, tret **7** scalage *apothecary:* **4** dram **5** grain, pound **7** scruple *Asian:* **6** cattie *combining form:* **3** bar **4** baro *gem:* **5** carat *measure of:* **3** ton **4** dram, gram **5** grain, ounce, pound **7** long ton, scruple **8** kilogram, short ton **9** metric ton *system:* **3** net **4** troy **6** metric **10** apothecary **11** avoirdupois

weightiness 4 pith **6** import, moment, weight **9** magnitude **10** importance **11** consequence **12** significance

weight lift 5 press **6** snatch **12** clean and jerk

weighty 3 big, fat **5** grave, gross, heavy, hefty, obese, sober, staid, stout, tough **6** fleshy, portly, sedate, severe, solemn, somber, taxing **7** earnest, exigent, massive, onerous, porcine, serious **8** cumbrous, exacting, grievous, material **9** corpulent, demanding, important, momentous, ponderous **10** burdensome, cumbersome, meaningful, no-nonsense, oppressive, overweight, sobersided **11** significant, substantial **12** considerable **13** consequential

weir 3 dam **9** fishgarth

weird 3 lot, odd **4** cast, doom, eery, fate **5** awful, eerie, moira, queer **6** creepy, kismet, spooky **7** bizarre, curious, destiny, eldrich, fearful, oddball, portion, strange, uncanny, uncouth **8** dreadful, eldritch, forecast, haunting, horrific, peculiar, prophecy, singular, supernal **9** eccentric, prevision, prognosis, unearthly, unnatural **10** mysterious, outlandish, prediction **11** foretelling, inscrutable **12** awe-inspiring, circumstance, supernatural **13** preternatural

welcome 4 hail **5** greet **6** genial **7** cordial **8** pleasant, pleasing **9** agreeable, congenial, favorable **10** contenting, gratifying, satisfying **11** pleasurable, pleasureful, sympathetic

weld 5 unite **6** solder **11** consolidate

welfare 4 good **7** benefit, fortune, success **8** interest **9** advantage, happiness, well-being **10** prosperity

welkin 3 sky **7** heavens **9** firmament

well 3 far, fit **4** easy, hale, sane **5** amply, clear, fitly, fully, happy, lucky, quite, right, sound, truly **6** aright, freely, indeed, justly, kindly, likely, nicely, origin, rather, really, source, wholly **7** happily, healthy, lightly, perhaps, readily, rightly, roundly, utterly **8** decently, entirely, facilely, fountain, possibly, probably, properly, smoothly, somewhat, suitably **9** correctly, favorably, fittingly, fortunate, inception, perfectly, tolerably, wholesome **10** acceptably, adequately, altogether, becomingly, completely, decorously, generously, pleasantly, prosperous, provenance, swimmingly, thoroughly **11** approvingly, befittingly, comfortable, doubtlessly, fortunately, provenience, substantial **12** considerably, effortlessly, fountainhead, prosperously, providential, satisfyingly, successfully **13** appropriately, significantly **combining form: 2** eu

well-being 4 ease, good **7** benefit, welfare **8** euphoria, interest, thriving **9** abundance, advantage **10** easy street, prosperity

well-bred 6 urbane **7** genteel, refined **8** cultured, polished **9** distingué **10** cultivated

well-developed 5 curvy **7** rounded **9** curvesome, Junoesque **10** curvaceous **11** curvilinear

well-disposed 8 friendly **9** receptive **11** sympathetic

Welles movie 7 Macbeth, Othello **11** Citizen Kane, Touch of Evil

well-favored 4 fair **6** comely, lovely, pretty **8** handsome **9** beauteous, beautiful **10** attractive **11** good-looking

well-fixed see **well-to-do**

well-founded 4 good, just **5** meaty, pithy, sound, valid **6** cogent **7** telling **8** rational, reasoned **9** justified **10** reasonable **11** fundamental, substantial

well-groomed 4 neat, snug, tidy, trig, trim **5** doggy, natty, sassy **6** dapper, spiffy, spruce, sprucy **7** chipper, doggish, orderly **8** sparkish **9** shipshape **11** spic-and-span, uncluttered **12** spick-and-span

wellhead see **wellspring**

well-heeled see **well-to-do**

Wellington *horse:* **10** Copenhagen *victory:* **7** Vitoria **8** Talavera, Waterloo **9** Salamanca

well-known 5 noted **6** famous **7** leading, popular **9** important, notorious, prominent **11** conspicuous, outstanding

well-liked 7 favored, popular **8** favorite **9** preferred

well-mannered 5 civil **6** polite **7** genteel **9** courteous

well-nigh 4 most, much, nigh **5** about **6** all but, almost, nearly **8** as good as, as much as **11** essentially, practically

well-off see **well-to-do**

well-paying 7 gainful **9** lucrative **10** profitable, worthwhile **11** moneymaking **12** advantageous, remunerative

well-proportioned see **well-turned**

wellspring 4 root **6** origin, source **8** fountain **9** inception **10** provenance **11** provenience **12** fountainhead

well-thought-of 7 reputed **9** estimable, reputable **10** creditable **11** respectable

well-timed 7 timeous **9** favorable, opportune **10** auspicious, propitious, prosperous, seasonable

well-to-do 4 easy, rich **7** wealthy **8** affluent **10** prosperous **11** comfortable, substantial

well-turned 4 trim **7** shapely **8** shapeful **10** statuesque **11** clean-limbed

well-worn 5 stale, tired, trite **9** hackneyed **10** threadbare **11** commonplace, stereotyped

welsh 6 cry off, renege, resile **7** back off, back out **8** back down **9** backpedal, backwater **10** declare off **11** crawfish out

Welsh see **Cymric**

welt 4 wale, weal **5** ridge, wheal, whelk

welter 4 bask, roll, wilt **5** dry up, mummy, revel, wizen **6** wallow, wither **7** indulge, mummify, rollick, shrivel **9** luxuriate

___ Welty, writer 6 Eudora
wen 4 cyst 6 growth 11 excrescence
wench 3 gal 4 girl, jade, lass, maid, miss 5 hussy, missy, tramp, trull 6 damsel, lassie, maiden, wanton 7 jezebel, servant, trollop 8 slattern, strumpet
wend 2 go 3 hie 4 fare, pass 6 push on, repair, travel 7 journey, proceed
werewolf 11 lycanthrope
Werther's beloved 5 Lotte
Wesleyan 9 Methodist
West 8 Occident
West African *baboon:* 5 drill 8 mandrill *city:* 5 Accra, Dakar, Lagos *country:* 4 Togo 5 Benin, Gabon, Ghana 6 Gambia, Guinea 7 Liberia, Nigeria, Senegal 8 Cameroon 10 Ivory Coast 11 Sierra Leone *fetish:* 4 juju *native:* 3 Ibo 5 Hausa 7 Ashanti
western 5 oater 9 shoot-em-up 10 horse opera
Western organization 3 OAS 4 NATO
Western Samoa *capital:* 4 Apia *monetary unit:* 4 tala
West Germany *capital:* 4 Bonn
West Indies *boat:* 7 drogher *country:* 4 Cuba 5 Haiti 7 Grenada, Jamaica 8 Dominica 10 Saint Lucia 13 Bahama Islands *language:* 6 Creole, French 7 English, Spanish
West Point *father of:* 6 Thayer *freshman:* 5 plebe *student:* 5 cadet
West Virginia *capital:* 10 Charleston *nickname:* 13 Mountain State *state bird:* 8 cardinal *state flower:* 12 rhododendron
west wind see at **wind**
wet 3 dew, sop 4 damp, dank, lave, soak, wash 5 bedew, douse, drown, drunk, madid, moist, rainy, rinse, soggy, soppy, souse, water 6 dampen, deluge, drench, drippy, soaked, sodden, soused, sweaty, vapory 7 moisten, slopped, soaking, sopping 8 drenched, dripping, humidify, irrigate, saturate 9 saturated 10 inebriated 11 intoxicated *combining form:* 4 hygr 5 hygro
wet blanket 7 killjoy 10 spoilsport
wether 4 goat 5 sheep
wetland 3 bog, fen 5 marsh, swamp
whack 2 go 3 bat, hit, pop, try 4 bash, blow, ding, shot, slap, slog, sock, stab, whop 5 catch, crack, fling, smack, smash, whirl 6 strike, thwack, wallop 7 stagger
whale 4 flog, hide, lash, whip 5 giant 6 stripe, thrash 7 mammoth, monster, scourge 8 behemoth 9 leviathan 10 flagellate *arctic:* 7 bowhead *combining form:* 3 cet 4 ceto *group:* 3 pod *killer:* 4 orca *kind:* 3 sei 4 blue 5 right, sperm 6 baleen, beluga, killer 7 narwhal, rorqual 8 cachalot

tale: 8 Moby Dick *toothed:* 9 blackfish *young:* 4 calf
whalebone 6 baleen
wham 4 bang, boom, clap, slam 5 blast, burst, crack, crash, smash
whammy 3 hex 4 jinx 6 hoodoo, voodoo 10 Indian sign
wharf 4 dock, pier, quay, slip 5 berth, jetty, levee
Wharton novel 10 Ethan Frome 12 House of Mirth
whatnot 5 curio 6 bauble, gewgaw, trifle 7 bibelot, novelty, trinket 8 gimcrack 9 objet d'art 10 knickknack
wheal 4 wale, welt 5 whelk 6 strake, streak, stripe
wheat 5 durum, emmer, spelt, trigo 6 speltz 7 einkorn *beard:* 3 awn *beat:* 6 thresh *chaff:* 4 bran *crushed:* 6 bulgur *disease:* 4 rust, smut
wheedle 3 con 4 coax 6 cajole 7 blarney 8 blandish, soft-soap 9 sweet-talk
wheel 5 auto, gyre, loop, reel, tire, tool, turn, veer, whip 5 avert, cycle, dolly, drive, motor, pilot, pivot, round, sheer, whirl 6 circle, divert, league, totter 7 circuit, deflect, stagger 8 gyration, rotation, titubate 9 volte-face 10 charioteer, conference, revolution 11 association, circulation *combining form:* 5 troch 6 trocho *part:* 3 hub, rim 5 spoke *rim:* 5 felly 6 felloe *spoke:* 6 radius *toothed:* 3 cog 4 gear
wheel-like 8 rotiform
wheelman 6 driver 7 cyclist 8 helmsman
wheel-shaped 5 round 7 trochal 8 circular
wheeze 4 buzz, fizz, hiss, lark 5 antic, caper, prank, swish, trick 6 didoes, fizzle, frolic, shines, sizzle, whoosh 7 whisper 8 sibilate 10 shenanigan 11 monkeyshine
whelk 4 wale, weal, welt 5 wheal
whelm 5 drown, flood, swamp 6 deluge, engulf 8 inundate, overcome, overflow, submerge 9 knock over, overpower, overwhelm, prostrate
whelp 3 boy, cub, pup 4 girl 5 child, puppy
when 4 anon 5 again, while 6 albeit, much as, though 7 howbeit, whereas 8 although
where 4 site, spot 5 locus, place, point 7 station, whither 8 location, position 9 situation
whereas 2 as 3 for, now 4 when 5 since, while 6 albeit, much as, seeing, though 7 because, howbeit 8 although, as long as 10 inasmuch as 11 considering
wherefore 3 why 5 proof 6 ground, reason, whyfor 8 argument
wherewithal 5 means, money 9 resources
wherry 4 boat 5 barge 7 rowboat
whet 4 edge, hone, stir, wake 5 rally,

rouse, waken **6** arouse, awaken, bestir, kindle **7** sharpen, zakuska **9** antipasto, appetizer, challenge **11** hors d'oeuvre

whiff 4 dash, hint **5** shade, smack, tinge, trace **6** breath, trifle **7** soupçon **8** tincture

whiffet 4 zero **5** zilch **6** cipher, nobody **7** nothing, nullity **8** whipster **9** nonentity

whiffle 4 halt **5** waver **6** dither, falter **7** stagger **8** hesitate **9** vacillate **12** shilly-shally, wiggle-waggle

while 2 as **3** bit **4** pass, time, when **5** fleet, pains, space, spell, spend **6** albeit, effort, moment, much as, though **7** beguile, howbeit, instant, stretch, trouble, whereas **8** although, exertion, occasion

whim 3 bee **4** idea **5** dream, fancy, freak, humor **6** megrim, vagary, vision **7** boutade, caprice, conceit, fantasy, thought **8** crotchet **11** disposition, inclination

whimper 3 cry **4** mewl, pule **5** whine

whimsical 4 iffy **6** chancy **7** erratic, wayward **8** freakish, whimsied **9** arbitrary, fluctuant, uncertain, vagarious **10** capricious **12** incalculable **13** unpredictable

whimsy 4 idea **5** dream, fancy, freak, humor **6** megrim, vagary, vision **7** boutade, caprice, conceit, fantasy, thought **8** crotchet **9** capriccio **11** disposition, inclination

whine 4 fuss, kick, pule, wail **6** murmur, repine, snivel, yammer **7** whimper **8** complain

whinny 5 neigh **6** nicker **7** whicker

whiny 5 raspy, waspy **6** snappy, twitty **7** peevish, raspish, waspish **8** snappish **9** irritable, querulous

whip 3 set **4** abet, beat, cane, drub, dust, flog, hide, lash, lick, rout, trim, turn, veer **5** avert, blast, curry, mop up, pivot, quirt, raise, set on, sheer, upend, whale, wheel, whirl, whisk, whomp **6** cudgel, defeat, divert, foment, incite, lather, stir up, stripe, subdue, switch, thrash, wallop **7** curbash, deflect, kurbash, overrun, provoke, rawhide, scourge, shellac, trounce **8** bludgeon, courbash, kourbash, lambaste, overcome, vanquish **9** bastinado, instigate, overwhelm **10** flagellate **13** cat-o'-nine-tails **braided: 10** blacksnake **combining form: 6** mastig, mastix **7** mastigo **riding: 4** crop

whippersnapper see **whiffet**

whipping boy 4 goat **5** patsy **7** fall guy **9** scapegoat

whippy 6 supple **7** elastic, springy, stretch **8** flexible, stretchy **9** resilient

whir 3 fly **4** buzz **5** chirr **6** chirre **7** revolve, vibrate

whirl 2 go **3** ado, pop, try **4** eddy, flit, fuss, gyre, moil, reel, shot, slap, spin, stab, stir, swim, turn, veer, whip, whiz **5** avert, crack, fleet, fling, gurge, hurry, pivot, round, sheer,

speed, stave, storm, twirl, whack, wheel, whish, whisk **6** barrel, bullet, bustle, divert, flurry, furore, gyrate, hassle, hubbub, pother, swoosh, vortex **7** circuit, clatter, deflect, ruction, stagger, whoopla **8** gyration, rotation, rowdydow **9** commotion, maelstrom, pirouette **10** hurly-burly, revolution **11** circulation

whirligig 4 gyre, spin **6** beetle, gyrate **8** carousel **9** carrousel, pirouette **12** merry-go-round

whirlpool 3 ado **4** eddy, fuss, purl, stir **5** gurge, whorl **6** bustle, flurry, furore, pother, swoosh, vortex **8** vortices (plural) **9** maelstrom, whirlwind **combining form: 4** dino

whirlwind 2 oe **3** ado **4** fuss, stir **6** bustle, flurry, furore, pother, whirly **7** tornado **9** dust devil, hurricane, rainspout, sand spout **10** sand column, waterspout

whish 3 fly **4** buzz, fizz, flit, hiss, whiz **5** fleet, hurry, speed, stave, whirl **6** bullet, fizzle, sizzle, wheeze **7** whisper **8** sibilate

whisk 3 fly, zip **4** beat, flit, whip, whiz **5** hurry, speed **6** barrel, bullet

whisker 3 ace **4** hair **11** hairbreadth

whiskered 5 hairy **6** fleecy, pilose, woolly **7** barbate, bearded, hirsute, pileous

whiskers 5 beard **6** beaver

whiskey 3 rye **5** hooch, usque **6** hootch, Scotch **7** bourbon **8** usquabae, usquebae **with beer chaser: 11** boilermaker

whisper 4 buzz, dash, fizz, hint, hiss, whiz **5** rumor, shade, swish, tinge, touch, trace, whiff **6** breath, fizzle, mumble, murmur, mutter, rustle, sizzle, wheeze, whoosh **7** breathe, confide **8** sibilate **9** suspicion, undertone **11** susurration

whist 4 game, hush **5** quiet, still **6** silent, stilly **7** hushful **9** noiseless, soundless **card hand: 10** Yarborough

whistle 4 pipe **5** flute **6** signal

whit 3 bit, jot **4** atom, damn, hoot, iota **5** shred, whoop **7** modicum **8** particle

white 5 hoary, milky **6** albino, benign, blanch, bleach, blench, bright, dexter **7** decolor **8** palliate **9** canescent, extenuate, favorable, fortunate, gloss over, gloze over, sugarcoat **10** auspicious, blanch over, decolorize, propitious **combining form: 3** alb **4** albo, cali, calo, leuc, leuk **5** callo, leuco, leuko **egg's: 5** glair **6** glaire **7** albumen

white cliffs of ___ 5 Dover

White Fang author 6 London

White House designer: 5 Hoban **first occupant: 5** Adams

white lightning 7 bootleg **9** moonshine **10** bathtub gin **11** mountain dew

whiten 3 dim **4** dull, fade, pale **5** frost **6** blanch, bleach, blench, silver, veneer

7 decolor, grizzle, lighten, varnish **8** etiolate, palliate **9** extenuate, gloss over, gloze over, sugarcoat **10** blanch over, decolorize

white plague 2 TB **8** phthisis **11** consumption **12** tuberculosis

whitewash 6 veneer **7** varnish **8** palliate **9** extenuate, gloss over, gloze over, sugarcoat **10** blanch over

whither 5 where **7** whereto **9** whereunto **11** whereabouts

whiting 4 fish, hake

Whitsunday 9 Pentecost

whittle 3 cut **4** pare **5** carve, shape

whiz 3 fly, zip **4** buzz, fizz, flit, hiss, zoom **5** adept, hurry, speed, swish, whirl, whish, whisk **6** bullet, expert, fizzle, master, sizzle, wheeze, whoosh, wizard **7** whisper **8** sibilate, virtuoso **10** past master **12** professional

whole 3 all, fit, sum **4** full, hale, sane **5** fixed, gross, right, sound, total **6** choate, entire, entity, intact, system, unhurt, unrent **7** gestalt, perfect, plenary **8** complete, entirety, flawless, integral, outright, sum total, totality, unbroken, unmarred **9** aggregate, exclusive, integrate, undamaged, undivided, uninjured, untouched **10** unimpaired, unswerving **11** unblemished **12** concentrated, undistracted *combining form:* **3** hol, pan **4** holo, pano, toti **7** integri

wholehearted 4 sure **6** ardent, hearty, steady **7** abiding, earnest, fervent, genuine, serious, sincere **8** bona fide, enduring **9** authentic, heartfelt, steadfast, unfeigned **10** passionate, unwavering **11** impassioned, unfaltering, unqualified **13** unquestioning

whole-hog 8 complete, thorough **9** fulldress **10** exhaustive **13** thoroughgoing

wholeness 5 vigor **6** health **7** allness, oneness **8** entirety, haleness, totality **9** integrity, soundness **10** entireness, heartiness, perfection, robustness **11** healthiness **12** completeness

whole note 9 semibreve

whole number 5 digit **6** cipher, figure **7** chiffer, integer, numeral

wholesome 3 fit **4** good, hale, safe, sane, well **5** right, sound **6** curing **7** healing, healthy **8** curative, hygienic, remedial, salutary, sanative, sanatory **9** healthful, remedying, vulnerary **10** salubrious, well-liking **11** restorative

wholly 3 all **4** just, well **5** fully, quite **6** in toto, purely **7** exactly, roundly, totally, utterly **8** all in all, entirely **9** perfectly **10** altogether, completely, thoroughly *combining form:* **4** toti

whomp 4 beat, drub, whip **5** smear **6** thrash, wallop **7** shellac, trounce **8** lambaste

whoopee 3 fun **5** revel **6** gaiety **7** jollity, revelry, wassail **8** reveling **9** festivity, high jinks, merriment, revelment **10** skylarking **11** merrymaking

whoopla 4 to-do **5** revel, whirl **6** clamor, hassle, pother, tumult, uproar **7** revelry, turmoil, wassail **9** commotion, high jinks, revelment **10** hurly-burly, skylarking

whop 3 bat, bop **4** bash, beat, biff, blow, drub, sock **5** baste, pound, smack, whack **6** batter, buffet, hammer, pummel, thwack, wallop **7** belabor **8** lambaste

whopping 4 huge, much, very **6** damned, highly, hugely, mighty **7** awfully, immense **8** colossal, enormous, gigantic **10** gargantuan, prodigious **11** exceedingly

whorl 4 eddy, purl **5** gurge, swirl **6** swoosh **9** whirlpool *combining form:* **7** spondyl **8** spondylo

why 5 proof **6** enigma, ground, puzzle, reason, riddle **7** mystery **8** argument **9** conundrum, wherefore **10** puzzlement **13** Chinese puzzle, mystification

wicked 3 bad **4** blue, evil, mean, racy, ugly **5** antic, broad, hairy, pesky, risky, salty, shady, spicy, wrong **6** adroit, au fait, chancy, clever, cursed, impish, malign, pranky, purple, risqué, sinful, unholy **7** hateful, heinous, immoral, larkish, playful, roguish, ungodly, unsound, vicious **8** fiendish, off-color, perilous, prankful, prankish, spiteful **9** barbarous, dangerous, hazardous, malicious, malignant, rancorous, reprobate, troublous, unhealthy, vexatious **10** despiteful, iniquitous, jeopardous, malevolent, outrageous, suggestive **11** mischievous, treacherous, troublesome, unchristian, uncivilized

wickedness 3 sin **4** debt, evil, vice **5** wrong **9** depravity **10** corruption, immorality

wicker 3 rod **4** twig **5** osier, withe

wicket 4 arch, door, gate, hoop **6** window

wickiup 3 hut **5** lodge, tepee **7** shelter

wide 5 ample, broad, roomy **6** scopic, sweepy **7** liberal, radical **8** advanced, extended, scopious, spacious, tolerant **9** capacious, expansive, extensive **10** commodious **11** broad-minded, progressive *combining form:* **4** eury, lati

widen 4 ream **6** dilate **7** broaden **9** breadthen

wideness 5 scope **7** breadth **8** fullness **9** amplitude

widespread 4 rife **6** ruling **7** current, popular, rampant, regnant **9** prevalent **10** prevailing

widget 5 gizmo **6** gadget, jigger **7** gimmick

width 5 ambit, orbit, range, scope **6** circle,

length, radius **7** breadth, compass **8** panorama **9** extension

wield 3 ply **5** exert, swing, throw **6** handle, put out **7** conduct, control **8** dispense, exercise, maneuver **10** manipulate *the gavel:* **7** preside

wieldy 6 mighty, strong **8** powerful

wiener 3 dog **5** frank **6** hot dog **11** frankfurter, wienerwurst

wife 3 Mrs. **4** mate **5** bride **6** matron, missis, missus, spouse **7** consort, dowager **8** helpmate, helpmeet **9** other half *Latin:* **4** uxor *of a rajah:* **4** rani **5** ranee

wifely 7 uxorial

wig 3 jaw, rap **4** rail, rate **5** scold **6** berate, peruke, rebuke, revile, toupee **7** bawl out, chiding, reproof, upbraid **8** reproach **9** reprimand **10** admonition, tongue-lash **12** admonishment

wiggle 4 worm **6** squirm, writhe **8** squiggle *Scottish:* **5** hotch

wight 5 being, human **6** mortal, person **8** creature **9** personage **10** human being, individual

wigwam 3 hut **5** lodge, tepee

wild 3 mad **4** fast **5** crazy, dirty, feral, rabid, rough, waste **6** barren, brutal, desert, ferine, Gothic, raging, rakish, savage, stormy, unruly, vulgar **7** badland, frantic, furious, Hunnish, natural, raffish, uncivil, untamed, vicious **8** agrarian, agrestal, barbaric, blustery, carefree, feckless, frenetic, frenzied, rakehell, reckless, stormful, untoward **9** barbarian, barbarous, delirious, fantastic, fractious, graceless, tasteless, turbulent, uncareful, unsubdued, wasteland **10** blustering, corybantic, incautious, outlandish, wilderness **11** extravagant, intractable, tempestuous, uncivilized **12** devil-may-care, preposterous, recalcitrant, uncultivated, ungovernable, unmanageable **13** irresponsible, undisciplined *combining form:* **5** agrio

wild ass 5 kiang **6** onager

Wild Duck author 5 Ibsen

wildebeest 3 gnu

wilderness 5 waste **6** barren, desert **7** badland **9** backlands, wasteland **10** hinterland **11** backcountry

Wilder play 7 Our Town

wild-eyed 6 raving **7** radical **9** visionary

wild ox 4 anoa

wile 4 draw, ploy, ruse **5** charm, feint, guile, trick **6** allure, deceit, device, gambit **7** attract, beguile, bewitch, chicane, cunning, enchant, gimmick **8** artifice, maneuver, trickery **9** captivate, chicanery, fascinate, magnetize, stratagem **13** dissimulation

wiliness 3 art **5** craft **7** cunning, slyness **8** artifice, foxiness **9** cageyness, canniness **10** artfulness, craftiness

will 4 like, mind, wish **5** elect, fancy, leave **6** choose, devise, legate, liking, please **8** bequeath, pleasure, velleity, volition **9** testament **10** discipline **11** inclination, self-command, self-control, self-mastery **13** determination, self-restraint *addition:* **7** codicil *maker:* **8** testator **9** testatrix *without:* **9** intestate

willful 6 dogged, mulish, unruly **7** decided **8** factious, perverse, resolved, stubborn, unforced **9** obstinate, pigheaded, purposive, voluntary **10** deliberate, determined, headstrong **11** intentional, intractable, stiffnecked, wrongheaded **12** contumacious, pertinacious, unprescribed

Williams play 10 Camino Real **13** The Rose Tattoo

William Tell composer 7 Rossini

willies 5 jumps **6** creeps, dither, shakes **7** jitters, shivers **9** whim-whams **13** heebie-jeebies

willing 3 apt **4** fair, game, open **5** prone, ready **6** minded, prompt **7** forward, witting **8** disposed, inclined, unforced **9** agreeable, compliant, favorable, voluntary **10** deliberate **11** intentional, predisposed **12** unprescribed

willow 5 osier, salix **6** sallow *flower cluster:* **6** catkin *kind:* **5** crack, pussy, white **6** basket **7** weeping

willowy 4 tall **5** lithe **6** pliant **7** slender **8** graceful

wilt 3 sag **4** drop, flag, swag **5** droop, dry up, mummy, wizen **6** cave in, peg out, welter, wither **7** give out, mummify, shrivel, succumb **8** collapse **9** break down

wily 3 sly **4** deep, foxy **6** artful, astute, clever, crafty, shrewd, tricky **7** cunning, knowing **8** guileful **9** insidious, sagacious

wimble 4 bore **5** auger, brace, scoop **6** gimlet

Wimbledon's game 6 tennis

wimple 4 veil, wrap **6** ripple

win 3 get **4** beat, earn, gain, have, make, take **5** annex, reach, score, yield **6** attain, defeat, obtain, pick up, rack up, secure **7** achieve, acquire, bring in, chalk up, conquer, procure, produce, realize, triumph, victory **8** conquest, drag down, draw down, overcome **9** knock down **10** accomplish *over:* **6** disarm, induce **8** convince, persuade, talk into **9** prevail on

wince 5 cower, quail, start **6** blanch, blench, cringe, flinch, recoil, shrink **7** squinch

wind 3 fan, nil **4** bend, blow, clue, coil, curl, gale, gird, gust, hint, reel, warp, wrap **5** curve, spool, twine, twist, weave **6** breath, breeze, circle, deform, enlace, girdle, naught, notion, nought, ruffle, spiral, winnow, zephyr **7** contort, distort, enclose, entwine, envelop, inkling, meander, monsoon, nothing, torture, wreathe **8** easterly, encircle, misshape, surround, westerly **9** corkscrew **10** indication, intimation, suggestion *cold:* **4** bise, bora **6** sansar, sarsar **7** mistral, pampero, wulliwa **8** williwaw, willywaw *combining form:* **4** anem **5** anemo, venti, vento *east:* **5** Eurus *gentle:* **6** breeze, zephyr **7** cat's-paw *hot:* **6** samiel, shamal, simoom, solano **7** sirocco *instrument:* **3** sax **4** horn, oboe, tuba, vane **5** flute **7** bassoon, trumpet **8** trombone **10** anemometer **11** weather vane *into:* **8** aweather *measure of speed:* **4** knot *Mediterranean:* **7** etesian **8** levanter *north:* **6** Boreas *scale:* **8** Beaufort *south:* **5** Notus **6** Auster *southwest:* **8** libeccio *stormy:* **4** gale **7** cyclone, tornado, twister **9** hurricane **11** northeaster *warm:* **4** föhn **5** foehn **7** chinook *west:* **6** zephyr **8** Zephyrus

winding 5 snaky **6** spiral **7** bending, coiling, crooked, curving, devious, sinuous **8** flexuous, indirect, tortuous, twisting **9** meandrous **10** circuitous, convoluted, meandering, roundabout, serpentine **11** anfractuous

window 3 bay, eye **4** pane **5** oriel **6** dormer **7** fenster, lucarne, luthern, opening **8** aperture, casement, jalousie *cover:* **5** blind **7** curtain, shutter *French:* **7** fenêtre *over a door:* **7** transom **8** fanlight *part:* **4** came, pane, sash, sill **5** frame *projecting:* **3** bay **5** oriel *relating to:* **9** fenestral *roof's:* **6** dormer **8** skylight *Scottish:* **7** winnock *ship's:* **4** port **8** porthole *ticket:* **7** guichet

windpipe 6 throat **7** trachea *combining form:* **6** bronch, trache **7** bronchi, broncho, tracheo **8** bronchio

windrow 4 bank, heap, hill, mass, pile **5** drift, mound, stack **6** furrow **7** pyramid **8** mountain

wind up 3 end **4** halt **5** close **6** finish, settle, wrap up **7** clean up **8** complete, conclude **9** determine, terminate

windup 3 end **5** close **6** ending, finale, finish **10** conclusion

windy 4 airy **5** blowy, brisk, fresh, gusty, tumid, wordy **6** breezy, drafty, prolix, turgid **7** diffuse, verbose **8** blustery, dropsied, inflated **9** dropsical, flatulent, overblown, redundant **10** palaverous

wine 4 vino **5** drink, juice **8** beverage *aromatized:* **8** vermouth **9** hippocras, Quinquina *beverage:* **5** clary, mulse, negus, punch **6** bishop **8** sangaree **9** hippocras *bottle:* **6** fiasco, magnum **8** decanter, jeroboam *cabinet:* **8** cellaret *cask:* **3** tun, vat **4** butt, pipe **8** puncheon *cellar:* **6** bodega *combining form:* **2** en **3** eno, oen **4** oeno

discoverer: **4** Noah *disorder:* **5** casse *distillate:* **6** brandy, cognac *dry:* **3** sec **4** brut *film:* **8** beeswing *flavor:* **4** mull *fortified:* **4** port **6** Malaga, sherry **7** Madeira, marsala *fragrance:* **7** bouquet *golden:* **4** Bual **7** Amoroso, Madeira, Moscato, Oloroso, Sercial **8** Bucellas, Moscatel, muscatel *lover:* **9** oenophile **11** oenophilist *maker:* **7** vintner **8** vigneron **13** viticulturist *merchant:* **7** vintner *pitcher:* **4** olpe **5** olpae (plural) **8** oenochoe *red:* **4** port, tent **5** Gamay, Macon, Marco, Medoc, Rioja **6** Aleyor, Barolo, Beaune, claret, Volnay **7** Almissa, Barbera, Chianti, Falerno, Inferno, Margaux **8** Aleatico, Alicante, Ambonnay, Bordeaux, Gragnano, Julienas, Nebbiolo, Sassella **9** Adlesberg, Hermitage, Lambrusco, Pinot Noir, St. Emilion, zinfandel **10** Barbaresco, Beaujolais, Roussillon, Sangiovese, Valtellina, Verdicchio **11** Affenthaler, Mavrodaphne, Petite Sirah **12** Valpolicella *relating to:* **5** vinic **6** vinous *residue:* **4** marc *rice:* **4** sake *richness:* **4** body *sediment:* **4** lees **5** dregs *shop:* **6** bistro, bodega *sparkling:* **4** sekt **8** cold duck, mousseux, Spumante **9** champagne, Lambrusco *specialist:* **9** enologist **10** oenologist *spiced:* **9** hippocras *steward:* **9** sommelier *study of:* **7** enology **8** oenology *sweet:* **4** Bual, port, tent **5** Almus, Tokay **6** Albana, canary, d'Yquem, Malaga, muscat **7** Almissa, bastard, Catawba, Madeira, malmsey, marsala, Moscato, Oloroso, Orvieto, Vouvray **8** Aleatico, Alicante, Malvasia, Moscatel, muscadel, muscatel, sauterne **9** Sauternes **11** Mavrodaphne, scuppernong *sweeten:* **4** mull *unfermented:* **4** must *vessel:* **3** ama **5** amula **7** chalice *white:* **4** hock, sock **5** Almus, Rhine, Soave **6** Alella, Barsac, Gentil, Graves, Saumur, Valmur **7** Banyuls, Catawba, Chablis, Chacoli, Conthey, Dezaley, Falerno, Moselle, Orvieto, Vouvray **8** Aiglerie, Amarante, Bordeaux, Frascati, Riesling, Semillon, Sylvaner, Traminer, Vaudesir, vermouth **9** champagne, Hermitage, Meursault, Neuchatel, Sansevero, Teneriffe, Zeltinger **10** Hochheimer, Montrachet **11** Chenin Blanc, Niersteiner, Rudesheimer, scuppernong **12** Geisenheimer **13** liebfraumilch *year:* **7** vintage

wing 3 ala, arm, ell, fly **4** flit, limb, sail **5** annex, block, bulge, fleet, pinna, sweep **9** expansion, extension **10** projection, protrusion **12** prolongation, protuberance *combining form:* **3** ali **4** pter **5** ptera, ptero **6** pterus, pteryg **7** pterous, pterygo *relating to:* **4** alar **5** alary **6** pteric

winged 5 alate **7** pennate *horse:* **7** Pegasus

wingless 7 apteral **8** apterous

winglike 4 alar 7 aliform *part:* 3 ala 4 alae (plural)

wink 3 bat 5 blink, shake, trice 6 minute, moment, second 7 instant, nictate, twinkle 9 nictitate, twinkling 11 split second

winner 6 victor 8 champion 9 conqueror

Winnie-the-Pooh *author:* 5 Milne *character:* 3 Roo 5 Kanga 6 Piglet, Tigger

winning 5 sweet 6 dulcet, profit 8 conquest, engaging

winnow 3 fan 4 blow, comb, sift, sort, wind 6 delete, remove, ruffle 8 separate

winsome 5 sweet 6 dulcet 7 lovable, winning 8 adorable, cheerful, engaging, lovesome

winter 6 season *French:* 5 hiver *Spanish:* 8 invierno

Winter's Tale character 7 Camillo, Leontes, Perdita 8 Florizel, Hermione 9 Polixenes

wintry 3 icy 4 cold 5 hoary, snowy 6 frigid, hiemal, stormy 8 hibernal, storming

wipe 3 mop 4 x out 5 abate, annul, erase, towel 6 cancel, delete, efface 7 abolish, blot out, expunge 8 black out, decimate, massacre 9 eradicate, extirpate, slaughter 10 annihilate, extinguish, obliterate 11 exterminate

wire 3 rod 4 cord, line 5 cable 6 thread 7 message 8 telegram 9 telegraph *measure:* 3 mil 5 gauge

wireless 5 radio

wiry 4 lean, ropy 6 sinewy 7 fibrous, stringy 8 muscular

Wisconsin *capital:* 7 Madison *college, university:* 5 Ripon 9 Marquette *largest city:* 9 Milwaukee *nickname:* 11 Badger State *state bird:* 5 robin *state flower:* 6 violet

wisdom 4 lore 5 sense 7 insight, science 8 gumption, judgment, sagacity, sageness, saneness, sapience 9 good sense, knowledge 10 horse sense, shrewdness 11 common sense, information 12 perspicacity 13 judiciousness, sagaciousness *combining form:* 5 sophy

wise 3 hep, hip, way 4 bold, clew, clue, flip, keen, mode, pert, post, sage, sane, tell, warn, wily 5 acute, alert, aware, brash, cagey, canny, cocky, fresh, lippy, modus, nervy, quick, sassy, saucy, sharp, slick, smart 6 advise, artful, astute, bright, cheeky, crafty, fill in, inform, manner, method, notify, shrewd, smooth, sophic, system, tricky 7 apprise, cunning, fashion, forward, gnostic, knowing, politic, prudent, sapient 8 acquaint, arrogant, discreet, flippant, impudent, insolent, sensible, slippery, tactical 9 advisable, bold-faced, expedient, insighted, intuitive, judgmatic, judicious, provident, sagacious 10 cogitative, discern-

ing, insightful, perceptive, procacious, reflective, thoughtful 11 foresighted, impertinent, intelligent, quick-witted, sharp-witted, smart-alecky 12 nimble-witted 13 contemplative, knowledgeable, perspicacious *person:* 4 sage 6 savant 7 scholar

wiseacre see **wise guy**

wisecrack 3 gag 4 jape, jest, joke, quip 5 sally 7 waggery 9 witticism

wise guy 6 smarty 9 know-it-all 10 smart aleck 11 smarty-pants

Wise Men see **Magi**

wish 4 hope, like, long, want, will 5 covet, crave, elect, fancy, foist, yearn 6 desire, expect, impose, please 7 longing 10 desiderate

wishbone 7 furcula 8 furculum

wishful 5 eager 7 longing 8 desirous

wishy-washy 4 weak 5 banal, bland, vapid 6 jejune, watery 7 insipid, languid, sapless 8 listless, waterish 9 enervated, savorless 10 flavorless, namby-pamby, pantywaist, spiritless 13 characterless

wisp 5 strip 6 streak 7 handful 8 fragment

wispy 5 frail 8 nebulous

wisteria 4 fuji, vine

Wister novel 12 The Virginian

wistful 3 sad 7 pensive 10 meditative, melancholy

wit 3 ESP, wag 4 head, mind 5 brain, comic, droll, grasp, humor, joker, sense 6 acumen, brains, esprit, jester, reason, sanity, satire, senses, wisdom 7 balance, insight, punster, sensing 8 astucity, comedian, funnyman, humorist, jokester, keenness, lucidity, prudence, quipster, repartee, sagacity, sageness, saneness, sapience, wordplay 9 alertness, awareness, mentality, smartness, soundness 10 astuteness, brainpower, brilliance, cleverness, divination, gray matter, perception, shrewdness 11 discernment, penetration, percipience, rationality 12 apprehension, clairvoyance, intelligence, perspicacity 13 comprehension, sagaciousness, understanding

witch 3 hag, hex 4 drab, trot 5 biddy, bruja, charm, crone, lamia, spell 6 beldam, voodoo 7 enchant 8 magician, sorcerer 9 ensorcell, sorceress 11 enchantress *companion:* 3 cat *group:* 5 coven *male:* 6 wizard 7 warlock *meeting:* 6 sabbat *Scottish:* 6 cummer *vehicle:* 5 broom

witchcraft 5 charm, magic 6 allure, appeal, voodoo 7 glamour, hexerei, sorcery 8 charisma, witchery, wizardry 9 conjuring, magnetism 10 black magic, necromancy 11 enchantment, fascination, incantation, thaumaturgy

witch hazel 8 hornbeam 11 tobaccowood, winterbloom *lotion:* 9 hamamelin

witchy 5 magic 6 magian, mystic 7 magical 8 wizardly 9 sorcerous 11 necromantic 12 thaumaturgic

with 2 by, on 3 for, per, pro, via 4 over, upon 5 about 7 by way of, through 8 by dint of 9 by means of, in favor of 10 by virtue of *French:* 4 avec *German:* 3 mit *Italian:* 3 con *Latin:* 3 cum *prefix:* 2 co 3 col, com, con, cor, sym, syn

withal 3 too, yea, yet 4 also, more 5 still 6 as well, though 7 besides, howbeit, however 8 after all, moreover 9 per contra 11 furthermore, nonetheless 12 additionally, nevertheless

withdraw 2 go 4 exit, quit 5 leave, quail, unsay 6 abjure, depart, get off, recall, recant, recede, recoil, remove, retire, secede, shrink 7 get away, retract, retreat, take off, take out 8 fall back, forswear, give back, palinode, run along, take away, take back

withdrawal 4 exit 6 egress, exodus 7 exiting, pullout, retreat 8 offgoing 9 departure, egression 10 setting-out *from reality:* 6 autism

withdrawn 4 cool 5 aloof 6 casual, offish, remote 7 aseptic, distant 8 detached, reserved, retiring, solitary 9 incurious, shrinking, unaffable, uncurious 10 restrained, unsociable 11 indifferent, standoffish, unconcerned, unexpansive 12 uninterested *from reality:* 8 autistic

wither 3 age, dry 4 wane, wilt 5 dry up, mummy, wizen 6 shrink, welter 7 decline, mummify, shrivel

withered 4 sere 8 shrunken

withhold 3 bit 4 curb, deny, keep 5 check 6 bridle, detain, refuse, retain 7 abstain, forbear, inhibit, keep out, refrain, reserve 8 disallow, keep back, restrain 9 constrain

within 4 into 5 among 6 inside 7 indoors, inwards 8 interior *combining form:* 3 end, ent 4 endo, ento *prefix:* 2 il, im, in, ir 5 infra, inter, intra, intro

with-it 2 in 4 tony 5 swank, swish 6 modish, tonish, trendy 7 à la mode, stylish 11 fashionable

without 4 open, past, sans 5 after, minus 6 beyond 7 lacking, open air, outside, wanting 8 awanting, outdoors 10 out-of-doors *combining form:* 4 lipo *Latin:* 4 sine *suffix:* 4 less

with respect to 2 re 4 as to 5 as for 7 apropos 8 touching 9 as regards, regarding 10 concerning

withstand 4 bear, buck, duel 5 abide, fight, repel 6 combat, endure, oppose, resist, suffer 7 contest, dispute 8 tolerate, traverse

withy 4 twig 5 osier 6 branch, willow

witless 4 daft 5 crazy, silly 6 crazed, insane, simple, stupid 7 asinine, cracked, unwitty 8 demented, deranged, mindless 9 bedlamite, brainless, nitwitted, senseless 10 reasonless, weak-headed, weak-minded

witlessness 5 folly 7 inanity 8 insanity 9 absurdity, craziness, dottiness, silliness 11 foolishness 13 senselessness

witness 3 see 4 view 5 argue, proof, vouch 6 attest, viewer 7 bespeak, betoken, certify, testify, watcher 8 announce, beholder, by-sitter, evidence, indicate, looker-on, observer, onlooker 9 bystander, spectator, testament, testimony 11 attestation, testimonial 12 confirmation

witticism 3 gag, pun 4 jape, jest, joke, quip 5 crack 7 waggery 8 drollery 9 wisecrack

wittiness 5 humor 6 comedy 8 drollery 9 drollness, funniness

witting 4 ware 5 alive, awake, aware 7 knowing, willful, willing 8 sensible, sentient, unforced 9 cognizant, conscious, voluntary 10 deliberate 11 intentional

witty 5 funny 6 clever, jocose 7 amusing, jocular, probing, risible 8 humorous, piercing 9 diverting, facetious, sparkling 10 ridiculous 11 penetrating 12 entertaining 13 scintillating

witty saying 3 mot 4 quip 7 epigram 8 facetiae (plural)

wiz 6 artist, expert, master 8 virtuoso 9 authority 10 past master

wizard 4 mage, sage, whiz 5 magus 6 artist, expert, master 7 warlock 8 conjurer, magician, sorcerer, virtuoso 9 archimage, authority, enchanter 10 past master, proficient 11 necromancer

wizardly 5 magic 6 magian, mystic, witchy 7 magical 9 sorcerous 11 necromantic 12 thaumaturgic

Wizard of Menlo Park 6 Edison

Wizard of Oz *author:* 4 Baum *character:* 7 Dorothy 9 Scarecrow 10 Tin Woodman 12 Cowardly Lion *dog:* 4 Toto

wizardry 5 magic 7 sorcery 8 witchery 9 conjuring, magicking 10 necromancy, witchcraft 11 bewitchment, enchantment, incantation

wizen 3 dry 4 wilt 5 dry up, mummy 6 welter, wither 7 mummify, shrivel

wobble 4 sway 5 lurch, quake, shake, swing, waver, weave 6 careen, dither, falter, quaver, quiver, shimmy, shiver, teeter, topple, totter 7 shudder, stagger, stumble

wobbly 4 weak 5 shaky 6 dickey, unsure 7 halting, rackety, rickety, shaking 8 hesitant, insecure, rachitic, rootless, unstable, unsteady, wavering 9 faltering, fluctuant, tentative, uncertain 10 irresolute, rattletrap 11 vacillating, vacillatory 12 wiggle-waggle

Wodehouse character 6 Jeeves, Psmith 7 Wooster 8 Mulliner

Woden see **Odin**

woe 3 rue 4 care 5 grief 6 misery, regret, sorrow 7 anguish, sadness, trouble 9 bemoaning, bewailing, deploring, heartache 10 affliction, heartbreak 11 lamentation, unhappiness 12 wretchedness

woebegone 3 low 4 blue, down, worn 5 black, bleak 6 dismal, dreary, gloomy, shabby 8 dejected, downcast, funereal 9 depressed 10 depressing, dispirited, lugubrious, melancholy, oppressive, tenebrific 11 crestfallen, dilapidated, dispiriting, downhearted 12 disconsolate

woeful 3 sad 4 dire 5 grave, wrung 6 dismal, dolent, paltry, racked, rueful 7 crushed 8 dejected, dolesome, dolorous, downcast, grievous, harrowed, mournful, overcome, stricken, tortured, wretched 9 afflicted, depressed, heartsick, miserable, plaintive, sorrowful 10 afflictive, calamitous, deplorable, dispirited, lamentable, lugubrious, melancholy 11 distressing, downhearted, low-spirited, regrettable, unfortunate 12 disconsolate, inconsolable 13 heartbreaking, unprecedented

wold 5 plain

wolf 4 bolt, cram, grub, gulp, lobo, roué, slop 6 canine, chaser, coyote, englut, gobble, guzzle, lecher, masher 7 amorist, Don Juan, rounder 8 Casanova, lothario, womanize 9 ladies' man, libertine, philander, womanizer 10 fool around, lady-killer, mess around, play around, profligate 11 ingurgitate, philanderer *combining form:* 3 lyc 4 lyco *genus:* 5 Canis *group:* 4 pack *young:* 5 whelp

wolfish 4 fell, grim 5 cruel 6 fierce, lupine, savage 7 inhuman 8 inhumane 9 barbarous, ferocious, truculent

wolverine 8 carcajou *European:* 7 glutton *genus:* 4 Gulo

Wolverine State 8 Michigan

woman 4 dame, lady 5 madam 6 female, matron 8 mistress *attractive:* 5 belle 6 beauty, eyeful, looker 7 stunner 8 knockout *Australian:* 4 bint *combining form:* 3 gyn 4 gyne, gyno, gyny 5 gynec, gyneo 6 gynaec, gynaeo, gyneco, gynous 7 gynaeco *courageous:* 7 heroine *dignified:* 6 matron 7 dowager 10 grande dame *dowdy:* 5 frump *Dutch:* 4 vrow 5 vrouw *English:* 6 milady *first, biblical:* 3 Eve *first, mythological:* 7 Pandora *French:* 5 femme *German:* 4 frau 8 fräulein *Hawaiian:* 6 wahine *Indian:* 5 squaw *intellectual:* 12 bluestocking *Italian:* 5 donna 7 signora *lewd:* 5 hussy 6 harlot, wanton 7 trollop *little:* 3 Mrs. 4 wife *old:* 3 hag 4 dame 5 crone 6 beldam, carlin, gammer, granny

pregnant: 7 gravida *resembling:* 8 gynecoid *royal:* 5 queen 8 princess *sailor:* 4 Wave *scheming:* 7 jezebel *servant:* 4 maid *slovenly:* 8 slattern *soldier:* 3 Wac *Spanish:* 4 doña 6 senora *strong:* 6 amazon, virago *unmarried:* 4 miss 6 maiden 8 spinster *young:* 4 girl, lass 6 lassie, maiden

womanize 4 wolf 9 philander 10 fool around, mess around, play around

womanizer 4 wolf 6 chaser, masher 7 Don Juan 8 Casanova 9 ladies' man, philander 10 lady-killer 11 philanderer

womb 6 uterus *combining form:* 4 metr, uter 5 metra, metro, utero 6 hyster, metria (plural) 7 hystero, metrium

wombat 9 marsupial

women *hatred of:* 8 misogyny *organization of:* 3 DAR, NOW 7 sorosis 8 sorority

Women in Love author 8 Lawrence

wonder 3 awe 5 amaze, doubt 6 marvel 7 concern, dubiety, miracle, portent, prodigy, stunner 9 mistrust 9 amazement, dubiosity, marveling, sensation, suspicion 10 admiration, phenomenon, skepticism 11 incertitude, uncertainty, uncertitude 12 astonishment, bewilderment

wonderful 5 great, super, swell 6 divine, groovy, peachy 7 amazing, strange 8 glorious, terrific, wondrous 9 marvelous 10 astounding, miraculous, staggering, stupendous, surprising 11 astonishing, sensational

wondrous 7 amazing, strange 9 marvelous, wonderful 10 astounding, miraculous, stupendous, surprising 11 astonishing, spectacular

wont 3 apt, use, way 5 habit, inure, trick, usage 6 custom, manner 8 accustom, habitude, practice 9 habituate 10 consuetude 11 familiarize

wonted 5 usual 7 chronic, routine 8 accepted, habitual 9 customary 10 accustomed

woo 3 sue 5 court, spark 6 pursue 7 address 8 make up to 10 sweetheart

wood 5 weald 6 forest, lumber, timber 10 timberland *combining form:* 3 hyl, xyl 4 hylo, lign, xylo 5 ligni, ligno, xylon, xylum *decayed:* 4 punk *eater:* 7 termite *for burning:* 5 fagot 6 tinder 8 kindling *golf:* 5 spoon 6 driver 7 brassie *hard:* 3 elm, eng, oak 4 ebon, poon, rata, teak 5 beach, birch, ebony, maple 6 cherry, walnut 8 chestnut, mahogany, sycamore *imperfection:* 4 knot 5 gnarl *kind:* 5 xylem 6 phloem *made of:* 5 treen *pattern in:* 5 grain 6 figure *product:* 3 tar 5 paper 10 turpentine *soft:* 4 pine

wood alcohol 6 methyl 8 methanol

woodchuck 6 marmot 9 groundhog

wood coal 7 lignite
wooded 5 bosky 6 sylvan 8 sylvatic
wooden 4 dull 5 inept, stiff, treen
6 clumsy, gauche 7 buckram, halting,
stilted, unhandy 8 bumbling 9 cardboard,
ham-handed, maladroit 11 heavy-handed,
muscle-bound
woodland 5 weald, woods 6 forest,
timber
wood nymph 5 dryad
woodpecker 7 flicker, piculet, wryneck
9 sapsucker *genus:* 5 Picus *kind:*
5 downy, green, hairy 8 imperial, pileated
9 redheaded 11 ivory-billed *relating to:*
6 picine 8 piciform
woodsman 6 logger, ranger 7 bushman
8 forester 11 bushwhacker
wood sorrel 3 oca 6 oxalis
woodsy 6 rustic, sylvan
woodwind 4 oboe 5 flute 7 bassoon
8 clarinet 9 saxophone 10 instrument
woodworker 9 carpenter
12 cabinetmaker
woody 6 xyloid 8 ligneous; (see also
wooded)
Woody Allen film 5 Alice, Zelig
7 Bananas, Sleeper 9 Annie Hall, Interiors,
Manhattan, Radio Days, September
12 Love and Death
wooer 4 beau 5 spark, swain 6 suitor
7 sparker
woof 4 weft, yarn 5 weave 6 fabric,
thread 7 texture
wool 3 fur 4 coat, hair 6 fleece *coarse:*
3 abb *combining form:* 3 lan 4 erio, lani,
lano *cut:* 5 shear *fabric:* 4 felt 5 baize,
crepe, serge, tweed 6 covert, kersey,
mohair, poplin, shoddy, velour 7 duvetyn,
flannel, worsted 8 cashmere, chenille
9 gabardine 10 broadcloth *fat:* 7 lanolin
kind: 4 hogg 6 angora, hogget, virgin *low-
quality:* 5 mungo 6 shoddy *matted:*
7 daglock, taglock *musk-ox:* 6 qiviut *process:* 7 carding 8 skirting *source:* 4 goat,
lamb 5 camel, llama, sheep
woolly 5 hairy 6 fleecy, lanate, lanose,
pilose 7 hirsute, lanated, pileous
9 whiskered
woozy 4 sick, weak 5 dizzy 6 blurry
8 nauseous
word 3 cry, put, say, vow 4 buzz, news,
oath, talk, tell, term 5 order, rumor, state
6 advice, behest, charge, convey, gossip,
pledge, plight, report, rumble, saying 7 bidding, command, dictate, express, hearsay,
mandate, message, promise, tidings, voca-
ble, warrant 8 locution 9 assurance, directive, formulate, guarantee, speerings, statement, utterance 10 commitment,
expression, injunction 11 countersign, declaration, information, scuttlebutt

12 announcement, intelligence 13 communication, pronouncement *combining form:*
3 log 4 logo, onym 7 onomato *connective:* 11 conjunction *group:* 6 clause,
phrase 8 sentence *misused:* 8 malaprop
11 malapropism *naming:* 4 noun *new:*
7 coinage 9 neologism *of action:* 4 verb *of
honor:* 4 oath 7 promise *origin:* 9 etymology *part:* 8 syllable *root:* 6 etymon *scrambled:* 7 anagram *shortened:* 11 contraction 12 abbreviation *square:* 10 palindrome
with opposite meaning: 7 antonym *with
same meaning:* 7 synonym *with some
pronunciation:* 7 homonym 9 homophone
with some spelling: 7 homonym
9 homograph
wordbook 7 lexicon 8 libretto 9 thesaurus 10 dictionary
word for word 8 verbatim
wordiness 8 verbiage 9 prolixity, verbalism, verbosity, windiness 10 prolixness
11 verboseness
word-of-mouth 4 oral 6 spoken, verbal
9 unwritten
wordy 4 glib 5 tumid, windy 6 prolix, turgid 7 diffuse, verbose, voluble 8 inflated
9 bombastic, flatulent, garrulous, redundant,
talkative 10 long-winded, loquacious, palaverous, rhetorical
work 2 go 3 act, fix, job, run, tug, use
4 duty, line, moil, opus, take, tend, till, toil
5 chore, craft, dress, drive, grind, labor,
react, solve, sweat, trade 6 behave,
drudge, effort, handle, métier, racket, strain,
strive 7 calling, operate, perform, pursuit,
resolve, slavery, travail, trouble 8 bullwork,
business, drudgery, exertion, function, plugging, slogging, striving, vocation 9 cultivate 10 employment, handicraft, occupation, profession *combining form:* 3 erg
4 ergo *together:* 9 cooperate 11 collaborate *unit:* 3 erg 5 joule
workaday 4 dull 5 lowly, plain, usual
7 mundane, prosaic, routine 8 everyday,
ordinary 9 quotidian 11 commonplace
worker 4 doer, hand 6 toiler, wallah 7 artisan, laborer 8 employee, mechanic, operator 9 craftsman, operative 10 roustabout
combining form: 5 ergat 6 ergato *fellow:*
7 comrade, partner 9 colleague *group:*
4 crew, gang 5 shift, staff, union *hard:*
5 slave 6 beaver, drudge *itinerant:*
6 boomer 7 migrant *slow:* 7 plodder
unskilled: 4 peon 7 jackleg, laborer
working 4 busy, live 5 alive 6 active
7 dynamic, engaged, running 8 employed,
occupied 9 operative 11 functioning *not:*
5 kaput 6 broken
workless 4 idle 7 jobless 10 unemployed
workman see **worker**

work out 3 fix 5 solve, train 7 resolve 8 exercise

workout 8 exercise, practice

work over 4 redo 6 beat up, redraw, rehash, revamp, revise, rework 7 redraft, restyle, rewrite 9 manhandle

workroom 3 lab 4 shop 6 studio 7 atelier 10 laboratory

works 4 mill 5 plant 7 factory

Works and Days author 6 Hesiod

world 5 earth, globe 6 cosmos, kosmos, nature, planet 8 creation, megacosm, universe 9 macrocosm 11 macrocosmos *combining form:* 4 cosm 5 cosmo

worldly 5 blasé 6 earthy 7 earthly, knowing, mundane, sensual, terrene 8 banausic, mondaine, telluric, temporal 9 sublunary, tellurian 11 terrestrial 12 disenchanted, sophisticate 13 disillusioned, materialistic, sophisticated

World War I *battle:* 5 Marne, Somme, Ypres 6 Verdun 7 Jutland, Lemberg 10 Tannenberg *battle line:* 9 Siegfried *hero:* 4 York 7 Pershing 12 Rickenbacker *treaty:* 10 Versailles

World War II *admiral:* 6 Halsey, Nimitz *alliance:* 4 Axis 6 Allies *battle:* 5 Anzio, Bulge 6 Bataan, Midway, Tarawa, Warsaw 7 Iwo Jima, Okinawa 8 Normandy 10 Stalingrad *general:* 6 Patton, Rommel 7 Bradley 10 Eisenhower, Montgomery *hero:* 6 Murphy *journalist:* 4 Pyle *vehicle:* 4 jeep *weapon:* 5 A-bomb 6 rocket

worldwide 6 cosmic, global 8 catholic 9 planetary, universal 10 ecumenical 12 cosmopolitan *combining form:* 5 globo

worm 3 eel, loa, lug 4 grub, nema 5 borer, fluke, leech 6 edge in, maggot, mucker, no-good, squirm, wiggle, work in, wretch, writhe 7 carbora, distome, lowlife, serpent, triclad, wriggle 8 helminth, nematode, squiggle 9 insinuate, planarium, trematode 10 infiltrate *combining form:* 5 nemat, vermi 6 nemato, scolec, scolex 7 scoleco 8 helminth 9 helmintho *marine:* 3 lug 4 naid 6 nereis, palolo 7 annelid, tubifex 11 chaetognath *parasitic:* 5 fluke, leech 7 ascarid, ascaris, cestode, filaria 8 strongyl, trichina *relating to:* 7 vermian *resembling:* 11 helminthoid

worm-eaten 6 pitted 7 decayed, worn-out 10 antiquated

worn 5 drawn, erose, jaded, tired, weary 6 eroded 7 haggard, pinched, wearied 8 careworn, fatigued

worn-out 4 sere 5 all in, spent, stale, tired, trite 6 bleary, effete, used up 7 clichéd, drained, far-gone 8 depleted 9 exhausted, hackneyed, washed out 10 threadbare 11 stereotyped

worried 8 distrait, harassed, troubled

9 tormented 10 distracted, distraught, distressed

worry 3 ail, dun, nag, tew, try, vex 4 care, cark, fret, fuss, gnaw, stew, test 5 annoy, beset, harry, tease, trial, upset 6 bother, harass, needle, pester, plague, pother, unease 7 afflict, anguish, anxiety, bedevil, disturb, hagride, oppress, torment, torture, trouble 8 aggrieve, distress 9 beleaguer, tantalize 10 solicitude, uneasiness 11 concernment, disquietude *without:* 8 carefree

worrywart 7 fusspot 9 Cassandra, pessimist 11 crepehanger

worse 4 less 6 poorer 8 inferior

worsen 3 rot 4 sink 6 debase 7 decline, degrade, descend 10 degenerate, retrograde 11 deteriorate

worship 4 love 5 adore 6 dote on, revere 7 idolize, lionize, liturgy 8 dote upon, idolatry, venerate 9 adoration, affection, reverence 10 veneration 11 idolization *combining form:* 5 latry *object of:* 3 god 4 icon, idol *place of:* 5 altar 6 church, mosque, shrine, temple 9 cathedral, synagogue

worshiper 6 votary 7 devotee 8 disciple *combining form:* 5 later

worst 4 beat, best, down 5 least, outdo 6 defeat, lowest

worsted 4 yarn 5 serge 6 fabric, poplin 9 gabardine

wort 4 herb 5 plant

worth 4 mark, note 5 merit, price, value 6 moment, riches, wealth 7 account, caliber, fortune, quality, stature 8 property 9 resources, substance, valuation

worthless 4 mean 5 junky, sorry 6 draffy, drossy, no-good, trashy 7 fustian, inutile, nothing, useless 8 feckless, unworthy 9 cheapjack, incapable, valueless 11 incompetent, meaningless, purposeless, unqualified 12 contemptible

worthwhile 4 good 6 paying 7 gainful 9 lucrative 10 profitable, well-paying 11 moneymaking 12 advantageous, remunerative

worthy 4 good 5 noble 6 divine 8 laudable, pleasing, precious, sterling 9 admirable, deserving, desirable, estimable, honorable, meritable, praisable, priceless 10 invaluable, satisfying 11 commendable, meritorious

Wotan see **Odin**

Wouk novel 14 The Caine Mutiny

wound 3 cut 4 blow, harm, hurt 6 damage, injure, injury, lesion, trauma 8 lacerate 10 laceration *combining form:* 7 traumat 8 traumato *discharge:* 3 pus *sign:* 4 scab, scar 5 blood 7 blister

wow 3 hit 4 bang 5 smash 7 success 9 succès fou 10 bell ringer 11 exclamation

Wozzeck composer 4 Berg

wrack 4 kelp, raze, ruin, undo 5 wreck 6 unmake 7 destroy, seaweed, unbuild, unframe 8 decimate, demolish

wraith 5 ghost, shade, spook 6 shadow, spirit 7 phantom, specter 8 phantasm 10 apparition

wrangle 3 row 4 spat, tiff 5 argue, fight, scrap 6 argufy, bicker, fracas, hassle 7 brabble, dispute, fall out, quarrel, quibble 8 squabble 9 bickering, caterwaul 11 altercation

wrangler 6 cowboy 9 disputant

wrap 4 mask, roll, veil 5 cloak, drape, paper, shawl 6 enfold, invest, muffle, shroud, swathe 7 blanket, enclose, envelop, muffler, swaddle 8 bundle up, enshroud, enswathe, wax paper 10 camouflage

wrapped up 4 deep, rapt 6 intent 7 engaged 8 absorbed, immersed 9 engrossed 11 preoccupied

wrapper 4 gown 5 cover, shawl 6 jacket

wrap up see **wind up**

wrath 3 ire 4 fury, rage 5 anger 8 acerbity, acrimony, asperity 10 resentment 11 indignation

wrathful 3 mad 4 waxy 5 angry, irate, wroth 6 heated, ireful, wrothy

wreak 5 exact, visit, wreck 6 impose 7 force on, inflict 9 force upon

wreath 3 lei 4 bays 5 crown, torse 6 anadem, laurel 7 chaplet, coronal, coronet, garland

wreathe 4 coil, curl, wind 5 twine, twist 6 spiral 7 contort, entwine 9 corkscrew

wreck 3 dog 4 do in, heap, hulk, raze, ruin, undo 5 beach, crash, crate, smash, total, visit, wrack, wreak 6 damage, impose, jalopy, junker, pileup, ravage, strand, unmake 7 clunker, crack-up, debacle, despoil, destroy, disable, force on, inflict, plunder, smashup, subvert, unbuild, unframe 8 bankrupt, cast away, collapse, decimate, demolish, sabotage 9 breakdown, force upon, undermine, vandalize

wreckage 6 jetsam 7 flotsam 8 sabotage 9 driftwood 10 subversion 11 undermining

wrench 3 wry 4 pull, tool, turn, warp 5 exact, force, gouge, pinch, screw, twist, wrest, wring 6 coerce, compel, extort, garble, sprain 7 distort, pervert, squeeze 9 constrain, shake down 12 misrepresent *kind:* 6 monkey 7 ratchet

wrest 3 wry 4 warp 5 exact, gouge, pinch, screw, twist, wring 6 extort, garble, wrench 7 confuse, distort, extract, pervert, squeeze 9 shake down 12 misrepresent

wrestle 4 moil, toil 5 essay, exert, fight, labor 6 strain, strive, tussle 7 contend, grapple, scuffle, stretch, travail 8 endeavor, struggle

wrestling *hold:* 4 lock 6 nelson 8 headlock, scissors *kind:* 4 sumo *term:* 3 pin 4 fall 5 throw 8 takedown

wretch 3 cur, dog 4 scum, snot, toad, worm 5 devil, knave, rogue, skunk, snake 6 mucker, no-good, rascal, rotter 7 caitiff, lowlife, stinker, villain 8 scalawag, stinkard, wormling 9 scoundrel, stinkaroo 10 blackguard, ne'er-do-well 11 rapscallion

wretched 3 low 4 base, mean, vile 6 abject, dismal, dolent, paltry, rueful, scurvy, sordid, woeful 7 doleful, forlorn, ignoble, piteous, pitiful, ruthful, servile 8 dolorous, hopeless, pitiable 9 afflicted, miserable, sorrowful 10 despairing, despicable, despondent, melancholy

wretchedness 3 woe 6 misery 11 unhappiness

wriggle 4 worm 6 squirm, writhe 8 squiggle

wring 3 wry 4 rack 5 exact, gouge, pinch, screw, wrest 6 extort, harrow, martyr, wrench 7 afflict, agonize, torment, torture 10 excruciate *the neck:* 5 scrag

wringing-wet 5 soppy 6 soaked, sodden, soused 7 soaking, sopping 8 drenched, dripping 9 saturated

wrinkle 4 fold, line, ruck, ruga, seam 5 crimp, plica, ridge, rivel, screw 6 crease, furrow, method, rimple, ruck up, rumple 7 crimple, crinkle, crumple, novelty, scrunch, shrivel 9 crow's foot 10 innovation 11 corrugation

wrinkled 5 lined 6 rugate, rugose, rugous, rumply 8 rugulose

wrist 5 joint 6 carpus *bone:* 6 carpal, hamate, lunate 8 capitate, pisiform 9 navicular 10 triangular 11 multangular *combining form:* 4 carp 5 carpo

writ 5 breve, brief, order, tales 6 capias, elegit, venire 7 mandate, precipe, summons, warrant 8 document, mandamus, mittimus, praecipe, replevin, subpoena 10 certiorari, distringas, injunction 12 habeas corpus

write 3 ink, jot, pen 4 draw, note, sign 5 chalk, draft 6 author, indite, pencil, scrawl, scribe 7 compose, dot down, engross, scratch 8 inscribe, scribble 10 correspond

write down 4 note 6 record

write off 5 decry, lower 6 cancel 7 devalue, downcry, run down 8 belittle, derogate, discount, mark down, minimize 9 devaluate, disparage, downgrade, underrate 10 depreciate, undervalue 11 detract from

writer 4 poet 6 penman, scribe 7 penster

8 composer, novelist *bad:* 4 hack *combining form:* 7 grapher; (see also **author**)

writhe 4 bend, curl, toss, worm 5 twist 6 squirm, wiggle 7 agonize, contort, distort, wriggle 8 squiggle

writing 4 book, hand 5 essay, paper, print, prose, words 6 letter, script 7 epistle 8 document, longhand 9 allograph, signature 10 literature, manuscript, penmanship 11 calligraphy, composition, inscription, publication *character:* 6 letter 9 cuneiform 10 hieroglyph *combining form:* 4 gram 6 grapho, graphy 7 graphia *for the blind:* 7 braille *instrument:* 3 pen 5 chalk, quill 6 pencil, stylus *kind:* 5 prose, verse 6 poetry *sacred:* 5 Bible, Koran 6 Talmud, Tantra 9 scripture *secret:* 4 code *surface:* 5 board, paper, slate 6 scroll 9 parchment

wrong 3 bad, ill, off, sin 4 awry, debt, evil, harm, hurt, poor, tort 5 abuse, amiss, badly, crime, false, inapt, unfit 6 afield, astray, injure, injury, offend, rotten, sinful, untrue, wicked 7 immoral, oppress, outrage, vicious 8 aggrieve, ill-treat, improper, inequity, iniquity, maltreat, mistaken, mistreat 9 diablerie, erroneous, grievance, incorrect, injustice, misguided, persecute, reprobate, unfitting 10 inaccurate, iniquitous, unfairness, unjustness, unsuitable, wickedness

11 unfavorably 12 infelicitous 13 inappropriate *prefix:* 3 mis

wrongdoer 5 felon 6 sinner 8 criminal, offender 9 miscreant 10 malefactor

wrongdoing 3 sin 4 evil, tort 5 crime 7 misdeed, offense 8 iniquity 9 diablerie, violation 10 misconduct 11 malefaction, misbehavior

wrongful 7 illegal, illicit, lawless 8 criminal, unlawful 12 illegitimate

wrongheaded 5 balky 6 mulish, ornery 7 froward, restive, wayward 8 contrary, perverse, stubborn 9 obstinate 10 self-willed 11 stiff-necked 12 cross-grained, pertinacious

wrought 4 made 6 formed, shaped, worked 7 created 8 finished, hammered 9 fashioned, processed 10 ornamented 12 manufactured *up:* 7 excited, stirred

wry 4 bent 5 twist, wrest, wring 6 ironic, wrench 7 cynical, twisted 8 sardonic

wryneck 10 woodpecker

Wuthering Heights *author:* 6 Brontë *character:* 7 Hindley 9 Catherine 10 Heathcliff

Wycliffite 7 Lollard

Wyoming *capital:* 8 Cheyenne *nickname:* 13 Equality State *state bird:* 10 meadowlark

X

x 3 chi, ten 4 kiss, mark 5 annul, cross, erase, error, times, wrong 6 cancel, delete, efface 7 blot out, expunge, mistake, wipe out 8 abscissa, black out 9 signature 10 obliterate

Xanadu *country:* 5 China *river:* 4 Alph

xanthic 6 yellow 9 yellowish

Xanthippe 3 nag 5 harpy, scold, shrew, vixen 6 nagger, ogress, virago 8 fishwife 9 termagant *husband:* 8 Socrates

xanthous 6 yellow

xebec 4 boat, ship 6 vessel 10 pirate ship

xenium 4 gift 7 present

xenon *symbol:* 2 Xe

Xenophon work 8 Anabasis 9 Cyropedia, Hellenica

Xeres 4 wine 5 Jerez 6 sherry

xerophyte 6 cactus

xerosis 7 dryness

Xerxes *defeat:* 7 Salamis *father:* 6 Darius *kingdom:* 6 Persia *mother:* 6 Atossa *wife:* 6 Esther

Xmas 4 Noel, yule 8 Nativity, yuletide 9 Christmas

X ray *discoverer:* 8 Roentgen *science:* 9 radiology 13 roentgenology

xurel 4 scad 6 saurel

xyloid 5 woody 8 ligneous

xylophone 5 saron, vibes 7 gambang, gamelan, marimba 8 gamelang, gigelira, sticcado 10 vibraphone

xystus 4 stoa, walk 5 porch 7 portico, terrace

Y

yacht 4 boat, race, sail, ship 5 craft
6 cruise, sonder 8 keelboat
yahoo 4 lout, punk 5 brute, clown, rough,
rowdy, tough 6 mucker, savage 7 bumpkin, ruffian, toughie 8 bullyboy 9 roughneck
Yahweh 3 God 6 Jahvah 7 Jehovah
yak 2 ox 3 gab, jaw 4 blab, chat 5 clack,
laugh, prate 6 babble, gabble, jabber, sar-
lak, sarlyk, yammer 7 blabber, buffalo, chatter, palaver, prattle
yakety-yak 3 gab, jaw 4 blab, chat
5 clack, prate 6 babble, gabble, jabber
7 blabber, chatter, palaver, prattle
Yale 3 Eli 4 lock 10 university
Yalta participant 6 Stalin 9 Churchill,
Roosevelt
yam 3 ube, ubi 5 tugui 6 igname, potato
7 boniata 11 sweet potato
yammer 3 cry, gab, jaw, yak 4 chat, crab,
fuss, yaup, yawp, yell 5 bleat, clack, gripe,
whine, yearn 6 babble, clamor, gabble,
squawk 7 chatter, grumble, prattle 8 complain 9 bellyache, yakety-yak
yank 3 lug, tug 4 grab, jerk, pull, snap,
tear 5 hoick, lurch 6 clutch, evulse, snatch,
twitch 7 extract 9 vellicate
yap 4 bark, hick, jake, yelp 5 clown, mouth,
scold 6 bowwow, rustic 7 bumpkin, chatter, hayseed 9 hillbilly 10 clodhopper, provincial 12 backwoodsman
yard 4 lawn, quad, spar 5 court, garth,
patio, stick 9 curtilage, enclosure 10 play-
ground, quadrangle *enclosed:* 5 garth,
patio *five and one-half:* 3 rod *part of:*
4 foot, nail *shelter:* 6 gazebo *sixteenth
of:* 4 nail *two hundred and twenty:*
7 furlong
yardstick 5 gauge 7 measure 8 standard 9 benchmark, criterion 10 touchstone
yare 4 spry 5 agile, brisk, catty, ready
6 active, brisky, lively, nimble, volant
9 sprightly
yarn 3 rap 4 chat, chin, garn, tale, talk
5 fiber, floss, grain, prose, story, visit 6 caddis, cotton, crewel, strand, thread 7 caddice, genappe, schappe 8 anecdote, causerie, colloque, converse 9 narration, narrative
ball of: 4 clew, clue *coil:* 5 skein 6 skeane
cotton: 10 candlewick *for fastening a
sail:* 6 roband, robbin *woolen:* 6 crewel,
worset 7 worsted 8 shetland

yate 8 eucalypt
yaw 4 bend, gape, swag, tack, tilt, turn,
veer, yawn 5 lurch, pitch, shift 6 double,
seesaw, swerve, tilter 7 deviate 9 deviation 10 deflection
yawn 4 gape 5 ennui 6 tedium 7 boredom 8 doldrums
yawning 5 bored 6 gaping 7 chasmal
8 oscitant 9 cavernous
yawp 3 bay, caw, cry 4 bawl, crab, fuss,
gape 5 bleat, gripe 6 squall, squark,
squawk, yammer 8 complain
yea 2 ay, OK 3 aye, nay, too, yes, yet
4 also, even, more, okay 5 along, truly
6 agreed, assent, as well, indeed, really, verily 7 besides 8 all right, likewise, moreover,
positive 11 affirmative 12 additionally
yeanling 3 kid 4 lamb 7 newborn
year *academic:* 7 session *combining
form:* 6 ennial *division:* 5 month 6 season 9 trimester *kind:* 4 leap 5 lunar, solar
6 fiscal 8 calendar, sidereal, tropical
12 astronomical *Latin:* 5 annus *Scottish:*
7 towmond, towmont
yearbook 5 annal 6 annual 7 almanac,
annuary
yearling 4 colt
Yearling *author:* 8 Rawlings *character:*
4 Jody
yearly 6 annual 8 annually
yearn 3 yen 4 ache, burn, long, lust, pant,
pine, sigh, wish 5 covet, crave, dream
6 desire, grieve, hanker, hunger, thirst,
yammer
yearning 4 wish 5 eager 6 desire, hanker 7 craving, wistful 8 homesick, lovesick
years *eight:* 9 octennial *five:* 7 lustrum
12 quinquennial, quinquennium *four:*
11 quadrennial, quadrennium *one hundred:* 7 century 9 centenary 10 centennial
one thousand: 10 millennium *ten:* 6 decade 9 decennary, decenniad, decennial,
decennium *three:* 9 triennial, triennium
yeast 3 bee 4 barm, foam, suds 5 froth,
spume 6 lather, leaven 7 ferment
yeasty 5 dizzy, giddy, light 6 frothy
7 flighty 8 restless 9 exuberant, fribbling,
frivolous 11 light-headed
Yeats *beloved:* 9 Maud Gonne *birthplace:* 6 Dublin *play:* 7 Deirdre 9 Purga-

tory **12** The Herne's Egg *poem:* **9** Byzantium **11** Lapis Lazuli

yegg 5 thief **6** robber **7** burglar **8** criminal **11** safecracker

yell 3 cry, yip **4** call, howl, roar, wail, weep, yowl **5** cheer, hallo, hollo, shout, whoop **6** bellow, bemoan, bewail, clamor, holler, lament, outcry, scream, shriek, squall, squeal, yammer **7** deplore, roaring **10** vociferate

yellow 4 mean **5** amber, blake, favel, lemon, ochre **6** coward, craven, flavid, flaxen, golden, sallow **7** gutless, mustard, saffron, unmanly, xanthic **8** cowardly, xanthous **9** jaundiced, spunkless **11** lily-livered **12** dishonorable **13** pusillanimous *brownish:* **3** dun **5** aloma, amber, straw **6** manila *combining form:* **4** flav **5** chrys, flavo, luteo, xanth **6** chryso, xantho *dye:* **5** morin **6** orlean **7** annatto **9** morindone *greenish:* **5** olive **6** acacia **10** chartreuse

yellowbelly 3 rat **4** funk **6** coward, craven, funker **7** chicken, dastard, quitter **8** poltroon

yellow dog 3 cad, cur **6** rotter **7** bounder

yellowhammer 5 ammer, finch, skite **6** gladdy **7** bunting, flicker, yeldrin **8** yoldring

yellowish brown 4 gold **7** mustard **9** butternut **12** butterscotch

Yellowstone attraction 4 bear **6** geyser **11** Old Faithful

yelp 3 cry, yap, yip **4** bark **5** boast, shout **6** outcry, squeal **8** complain

Yemen *capital:* **4** San'a *monetary unit:* **4** rial **5** dinar, riyal

Yemen, People's Democratic Republic of *capital:* **4** Aden *monetary unit:* **5** dinar

yen 4 ache, long, lust, pine, sigh, urge **5** crave, yearn **6** desire, hanker, hunger, thirst **7** craving, longing

yeoman 5 churl, clerk **6** farmer **7** freeman **8** retainer **9** assistant, attendant, beefeater, landowner **10** freeholder **11** subordinate

yeomanly 5 brave, loyal **6** sturdy **8** faithful **9** laborious **11** hardworking

yes 2 OK **3** aye, yea, yeh, yep, yup **4** okay, yeah **5** agree **6** accede, agreed, assent, gladly **7** consent, exactly **8** all right **9** acquiesce, assuredly, certainly, precisely, subscribe, willingly **11** affirmation, affirmatively, undoubtedly *French:* **3** oui *German:* **2** ja *Italian:* **2** si *Russian:* **2** da *Spanish:* **2** si

yes-man 5 dummy, toady **6** minion, stooge **7** spaniel **8** bootlick, groveler, truckler **9** sycophant **10** bootlicker

yesterday 4 past, yore **8** foretime *French:* **4** hier

yesteryear 4 past, yore **8** foretime

yet 3 but, too **4** also, even, more, only, save **5** along, so far, still **6** as well, except, though, withal **7** besides, earlier, finally, further, howbeit, however, someday, thus far **8** after all, hitherto, likewise, moreover, sometime, somewhen **10** eventually, ultimately **11** furthermore, nonetheless, still and all **12** additionally, nevertheless

Yevtushenko poem 7 Babi Yar

Ygerne see **Igraine**

yield 3 bow, net, pay **4** bear, bend, cave, cede, cess, crop, emit, fail, fold, give, obey, quit, vent **5** admit, agree, allow, award, break, bring, defer, eject, grant, leave, offer, repay, waive **6** accede, accord, afford, bounty, buckle, comply, fold up, give up, impart, output, profit, relent, render, resign, return, reward, soften, submit, supply, tender **7** abandon, bring in, concede, consent, crumple, deliver, furnish, harvest, hold out, indulge, knuckle, outturn, produce, product, proffer, provide, revenue, succumb, truckle, turnout **8** collapse, hand over **9** acquiesce, discharge, surrender **10** capitulate, production, recompense, relinquish **11** buckle under **12** knuckle under

yielding 4 meek, soft, waxy **5** mushy, pappy, pulpy **6** feeble, flabby, limber, pliant, quaggy, spongy, supple **7** bearing, flaccid, flexile, passive, squashy, squishy, squushy **8** flexible, resigned, squelchy **9** tractable **10** manageable, submissive **11** acquiescent, unresistant, unresisting **12** nonresistant, nonresisting *combining form:* **6** ferous

yin and ____ 4 yang

yip 4 howl, yell, yelp, yowl **6** scream, squeal

yoke 3 tie, wed **4** bail, bond, join, knot, link, pair, span, team **5** bangy, hitch, marry, nexus, unite **6** banghy, couple, inspan, tackle **7** bondage, combine, conjoin, connect, harness, helotry, oppress, peonage, serfage, serfdom, slavery **8** ligament, ligature, vinculum **9** associate, conjugate, servility, servitude, thralldom **10** oppression **11** enslavement *combining form:* **3** zyg **4** zygo *part:* **5** oxbow

yokel 3 oaf **4** boor, clod, hick, jake, rube **6** rustic **7** bucolic, bumpkin, hayseed **8** Abderite **9** chawbacon, hillbilly **10** clodhopper **12** backwoodsman

yolk 6 center, yellow **7** essence *combining form:* **6** lecith, vitell **7** lecitho, vitello *egg:* **8** vitellus

yon see **yonder**

yonder 5 there **7** farther, further, thither

yore 4 past **8** foretime **10** yesteryear

you 2 ye **3** one **4** thee, thou *French:* **2** te, tu **4** vous *German:* **2** du **3** sie

young 3 fry, new, raw **4** baby, rude, tyro, weak **5** brood, fresh, green **6** callow,

infant, junior, litter, unripe **7** untried **8** childish, immature, juvenile, unformed, unversed, youthful **9** unfledged, unfleshed **10** unfinished, unseasoned **11** unpracticed **13** inexperienced *animal:* **3** cub, fry, pup **4** calf, colt, fawn, foal, joey, lamb **5** puppy *bird:* **5** chick *hare:* **7** leveret *sheep, goat:* **6** yeelin **8** yeanling
younger 6 junior
youngling see **youngster**
Young Lions author 4 Shaw
youngster 3 boy, cub, kid, lad, tad, tot **4** girl, lass, tike **5** chick, child **6** moppet, shaver, urchin **8** juvenile *suffix:* **4** ling
youth 5 prime **6** spring **7** puberty **8** juvenile, teenager **9** fledgling, stripling **10** adolescent, callowness, immaturity, juvenility, pubescence, springtide, springtime **11** adolescence **12** inexperience *ancient Greek:*

7 ephebos, ephebus *goddess of:* **4** Hebe *mythological:* **6** Adonis, Apollo, Icarus **8** Ganymede *time of:* **9** salad days; (see also **youngster**)
youthful 5 fresh, green, young **6** boyish, callow, infant, junior, maiden, unripe, virgin **7** puerile **8** immature, juvenile, virginal **9** beardless, unfledged
yowl 3 cry, yip **4** bawl, howl, wail, yell, yelp **6** scream, squall, squeal
yucca 5 palma **9** bear grass
Yugoslavia *capital:* **8** Belgrade *monetary unit:* **5** dinar *president:* **4** Broz, Tito *republic:* **6** Serbia **7** Croatia **8** Slovenia **9** Macedonia **10** Montenegro
Yukon *capital:* **10** Whitehorse *region:* **8** Klondike *town:* **6** Dawson
yule 4 Noel, Xmas **8** Nativity, yuletide **9** Christmas **13** Christmastide

Z

Zabbai *father:* **5** Bebai *son:* **6** Baruch
Zabud's father 6 Nathan
Zaccur *father:* **4** Imri **5** Asaph **7** Jaaziah **9** Mattaniah *son:* **5** Hanan
Zacharias *father:* **9** Barachias *son:* **4** John **6** Joseph *wife:* **9** Elisabeth
Zadoke *daughter:* **7** Jerusha *father:* **5** Baana, Immer **6** Ahitub **8** Meraioth *grandson:* **6** Jotham *son:* **7** Ahimaaz, Shallum
Zaire *capital:* **8** Kinshasa *former name:* **5** Congo **12** Belgian Congo
zakuska 4 whet **9** antipasto, appetizer **11** hors d'oeuvre
Zalmunna's slayer 6 Gideon
Zambia *capital:* **6** Lusaka *monetary unit:* **6** kwacha
zampogna 7 bagpipe, panpipe
zany 3 wag **4** card, fool **5** ament, clown, comic, crazy, cutup, dotty, idiot, joker, moron, nutty **6** cretin **7** buffoon, farceur, half-wit, pranker **8** clowning, clownish, comedian, funnyman, humorist, imbecile, jokester **9** harlequin, prankster, simpleton, trickster
Zauberflöte composer 6 Mozart
zeal 4 fire, zest **5** ardor, gusto **6** desire, energy, fervor, hurrah, spirit **7** avidity, passion, urgency **8** devotion, keenness **9** calenture, eagerness, intensity, readiness, sin-

cerity, vehemence **10** enthusiasm, fanaticism, fierceness **11** earnestness, seriousness
zealot 3 bug, nut **5** bigot, fiend, freak **6** maniac, votary **7** devotee, fanatic, sectary **8** adherent, disciple, follower, partisan **10** enthusiast
zealous 4 avid, keen, warm **5** afire, eager, fired, nutty, rabid **6** ardent, fervid, gung ho, hearty **7** devoted, earnest, fanatic, fervent **8** frenetic, obsessed, wild-eyed **9** dedicated, possessed **12** enthusiastic
Zebadiah *father:* **6** Asahel **7** Jeroham **11** Meshelemiah *uncle:* **4** Joab
Zebah's slayer 6 Gideon
Zebedee *son:* **4** John **5** James *wife:* **6** Salome
zebra 4 duaw *extinct:* **6** quagga *resembling:* **7** zebrine, zebroid
Zebulun *brother:* **4** Levi **5** Judah **6** Simeon *father:* **5** Jacob *mother:* **4** Leah *son:* **4** Elon **5** Sered **7** Jahleel
zecchino 6 sequin
Zechariah *daughter:* **3** Abi **6** Abijah *father:* **4** Elam, Iddo **5** Bebai, Hosah **7** Isshiah **8** Jehoiada, Jeroboam, Jonathan **9** Berechiah **11** Jeberechiah, Jehoshaphat, Meshelemiah *grandson:* **8** Hezekiah *slayer:* **7** Jehoram, Shallum *son:* **4** Iddo **8** Jahaziel

Zedekiah *brother:* 8 Jehoahaz *father:* 6 Josiah 8 Hananiah, Jeconiah, Maaseiah 9 Chenaanah *mother:* 7 Hamutal

Zeeb's slayer 6 Gideon

zenana 5 harem, harim 8 seraglio

zenith 4 acme, apex, peak 6 apogee, climax, height, summit, vertex 8 capstone, meridian, pinnacle 11 culmination *opposite:* 5 nadir

Zenobia *husband:* 9 Odenathus *kingdom:* 7 Palmyra

Zeno follower 5 stoic

Zephaniah *father:* 8 Maaseiah *son:* 6 Josiah

Zephi, Zepho *father:* 7 Eliphaz *grandfather:* 4 Esau

Zephon's father 3 Gad

Zephyrus 4 wind 6 breeze 8 west wind *father:* 6 Aeolus 8 Astraeus *mother:* 3 Eos 6 Aurora *wife:* 4 Iris

zeppelin 5 blimp 7 airship 9 dirigible

Zerah *brother:* 5 Perez *father:* 5 Judah, Reuel 6 Simeon *grandfather:* 4 Esau *mother:* 5 Tamar

Zerbino *beloved:* 8 Isabella *friend:* 7 Orlando *sister:* 7 Ginevra *slayer:* 11 Mandricardo

Zeresh's husband 5 Haman

zero 2 oh 3 aim, lay, nil, nul 4 cast, head, nowt, turn, void 5 aught, blank, empty, level, ought, point, train, zilch 6 cipher, direct, naught, nobody, nought 7 address, nothing, nullity, scratch, whiffet 8 goose egg, whipster 9 nonentity

Zeruah *husband:* 5 Nebat *son:* 8 Jeroboam

Zerubbabel *daughter:* 9 Shelomith *father:* 7 Pedaiah *grandfather:* 10 Jehoiachin *son:* 4 Ohel

Zeruiah *brother:* 5 David *sister:* 7 Abigail *son:* 4 Joab 6 Asahel 7 Abishai

zest 4 edge, élan, tang, zeal 5 ardor, gusto, heart, taste 6 fervor, flavor, palate, relish 7 delight, ecstasy, elation, passion 8 piquancy, pleasure 9 eagerness, enjoyment 10 enthusiasm 11 delectation 12 satisfaction

zesty 4 racy 5 spicy 6 breezy, hearty, snappy 7 peppery, piquant, pungent 8 poignant

Zetes *brother:* 6 Calais *father:* 6 Boreas *mother:* 8 Orithyia *slayer:* 8 Heracles, Hercules

zetetic 6 seeker 7 doubter, skeptic 10 headshaker, pyrrhonian, pyrrhonist, unbeliever

Zethus *brother:* 7 Amphion *father:* 4 Zeus 7 Jupiter *mother:* 7 Antiope

Zeus 7 Jupiter *father:* 6 Hades 8 Poseidon *daughter:* 3 Ate 4 Hebe, Kore 5 Helen, Irene 6 Athena 7 Artemis, Astraea 9 Aphrodite 10 Persephone, Proserpina 12 Clytemnestra *father:* 6 Cronus *lover:* 2 Io 4 Leda, Leto, Maia 5 Danae, Dione, Metis 6 Aegina, Europa, Latona, Semele, Themis 7 Alcmene, Antiope, Demeter 8 Callisto, Eurynome *messenger:* 4 Iris *mother:* 4 Rhea *nurse:* 8 Cynosura *oracle:* 6 Dodona *shield:* 5 aegis *sister:* 4 Hera, Juno 6 Hestia *son:* 4 Ares 5 Arcas, Argus, Minos 6 Aeacus, Apollo, Hermes, Zethus 7 Amphion, Perseus 8 Dionysus, Heracles, Hercules, Sarpedon, Tantalus *tree:* 3 oak *wife:* 4 Hera, Juno 5 Metis 6 Themis

Zibiah *husband:* 7 Ahaziah *son:* 7 Jehoash

Zichri *father:* 5 Asaph 6 Shimei 7 Jeroham, Shashak *son:* 4 Joel 7 Amasiah, Eliezer 10 Elishaphat *victim:* 8 Maaseiah

zigzag 4 tack, turn 5 angle, crank, weave 7 chevron 8 flexuose, flexuous

zilch 4 zero 5 aught, ought 6 cipher, naught, nobody, nought 7 nothing, nullity, whiffet 8 goose egg, whipster 9 nonentity

Zillah *husband:* 6 Lamech *son:* 9 Tubalcain

Zilpah's son 3 Gad 5 Asher

zimarra 5 cloak 7 cassock, soutane

Zimbabwe *capital:* 6 Harare *former name:* 8 Rhodesia

Zimran *father:* 7 Abraham *mother:* 7 Keturah

Zimri *father:* 5 Zerah *grandfather:* 5 Judah *victim:* 4 Elah

zinc *impure oxide:* 5 tutty *ingot:* 7 spelter *ore:* 6 blende 10 sphalerite *symbol:* 2 Zn

zing 3 pep, vim, zip 4 brio, dash, élan, life, snap 5 ardor, force, oomph, verve, vigor 6 energy, esprit, spirit 9 animation, eagerness 10 enthusiasm

zingel 5 perch

Zion 5 bliss 6 canaan, heaven, Israel, utopia 7 arcadia, elysium, nirvana 8 empyrean, paradise 9 cockaigne, fairyland, Shangri-la 10 Civitas Dei, wonderland 12 New Jerusalem, promised land 13 Abraham's bosom

Zionist *American:* 5 Szold *English:* 8 Zangwill *German:* 6 Nordau *Israeli:* 5 Buber 8 Weizmann

zip 3 fly, pep, vim 4 dash, rush, snap, whiz, zing 5 force, hurry, speed, waltz, whisk 6 breeze, bustle, energy, hasten, hustle

zipper 8 fastener

Zipporah *father:* 5 Reuel 6 Jethro *husband:* 5 Moses *son:* 7 Eliezer, Gershom

Zippor's son 5 Balak

zippy 4 keen, spry, yare 5 agile, alert, brisk, catty, ready 6 active, brisky, lively, nimble, snappy 7 dynamic, intense 8 forceful 9 sprightly